The
WORLD *of* WOMEN
in Classical Music

Dr. Anne K. Gray

WORDWORLD
La Jolla, California

WordWorld
P.O. Box 90309
San Diego, CA 92169
(800) 354-5348

Distribution: Seven Locks Press
                  3100 W. Warner Avenue #8
                  Santa Ana, CA 92704
                  (800) 354-5348
                  sevenlocks@aol.com
                  www.sevenlockspublishing.com

Cover design by Kira Fulks ©2007 www.kirafulks.com

Individual Sales. This book is available through most bookstores or can be ordered directly from WordWorld at the above address.

Quantity Sales. Special discounts are available on quantity purchases by corporations, associations, and others. For details, contact the "Special Sales Department" at the publisher's above address.

Printed in the United States of America

Library of Congress Cataloging-in-Publication Data
is available from the publisher
978-1-59975-320-1 EAN

Dedication

To my husband, Charlie
My son, Adrian
and all the women
—past and present—
in these pages . . .

OTHER BOOKS BY ANNE K. GRAY

The Wonderful World of San Diego
First and Second Editions

Where Have You Been All Your Life?

How To Hang Onto Your Husband!

The Popular Guide to Classical Music

Table of Contents

Acknowledgements

Like all books of this dimension, there are always invaluable people whose input helps the author get the daunting task accomplishedñeven *if it takes close to eleven years*, which this did!

Delving into the treasure trove of the Art and Music Department of the San Diego Public Library, my initial thanks go to former Head Librarian **Gene Fischer** who, with his assistants **Christina, Marilyn, Brenda** and **Jackie**, fed me information for seven years until his retirement in 2001; likewise **Nancy Assaf**, Head Librarian, Scripps Ranch branch, and her staff—especially "Sweet" Sue Fox.

In the ranks, much appreciation goes to **Joan Follis** (euphonium), who marched through the West Point Band for women bios, ditto **Mark Weaver** with the Coast Guard, and various Army and Navy personnel in the Pentagon. **Betsy Melvin**, Vermont Pen Woman/photographer, who connected me with her friend **Elsa Hilger** (1904–2005), first female cellist in the Philadelphia Orchestra, who was still performing at age niney-seven! **Dennis McIntire**, lexicographer for *Baker's Biographical Dictionary of Musicians* and other tomes, kept me tuned in on maestros switching musical podia, and the passings of those who left us for the Heavenly Concert Hall. *In high places* were **Sarah Billinghurst**, Assistant General Manager, Metropolitan Opera, and her kind assistants, Claire Avery and Siu Li; **Ian Campbell**, General Director, and **Marianne Flettner**, Assistant Manager, San Diego Opera; **Robert Rund**, former editor, *Musical America*; and Lynn Wall, Subscription VIP of that fantastic fount of classical music personnel. Special mention of helpful **Doris O'Connell**, righthand woman to Chairman of Lincoln Center (1994–2002), **Beverly Sills**.

Further personal contacts were with *American authors* whose well-researched books helped nail in the pitons to access the bottomless chasm of information: **Christine Ammer, Jane Bowers, Larae Brittain, Marcia Citron, Karin Pendle, Julie Anne Sadie, Rhian Samuel, Cecilia Dunoyer, Jan Bell Groh, Karen Shaffer, Pam Blevins, Victoria Sirota, Judith Tick, Heidi van Gunden, Victoria Bond, Katherine Hoover, Libby Larsen, Shulamit Ran, Hilary Tann, Joan Tower, Judith Zaimont, Ellen Zwilich** and a multitude of others. *European composers* included **Tera de Marez Oyens** (Holland, 1932–96), **Baroness Jacqueline Fontyn** (Belgium), **Annette Degenhardt** and **Violeta Dinescu** (Germany), **Nicola LeFanu** (England) and **Jane O'Leary** (Ireland). **Letiticia Armijo** (Mexico) introduced me to other Latin American composers. Subsequent Spanish translation credits go to Roxana Vincent, Penelope James, Anne Válades, and the distinguished nonagenarian, Anita Figueredo, MD.

Conductor and *Musician* contacts included **Gisèle Ben-Dor** and **JoAnn Falletta, Susan Slaughter**, (Principal Trumpet, St. Louis Symphony), and **Marie Speziale** who polished my knowledge of brass players. *Harpists* **Alice Chalifoux** (1908–), **Lucile Lawrence** (1907–2004), **Joann Turovsky** and my dear friend **Mary Coppa** (1929–2006) who located **Edna Phillips**, the first woman harpist of the Philadelphia Orchestra for me. **Richard Newhouse**, husband of violin Master Teacher **Dorothy DeLay** (1917–2002), *Violinists* **Pamela Frank, Zina Schiff, Eileen Wingard, Maria Newman**; **Cynthia Phelps** (viola); *Cellists* **Dorothy Lawson, Sharon Robinson**, *Pianists* **Anne-Marie McDermott, Olga Kern**; **Jennifer Paul** (harpsichord). *Flutists* **Carol Wincenc, Eugenia Zukerman, Sarah Tuck**; **Heather Buchman** (trombone) and **Mary Ann Craig** (tuba), were among the many who gave me enlightening interviews.

For valuable orchestra histories I consulted friendly *Archivists* **JoAnne Barry** (Philadelphia Orchestra), **Orrin Howard**, **Steve LaCoste** (Los Angeles Philharmonic), **Steven W. Johnson** (LA Opera), **Richard Wandel** (New York Philharmonic), **Frank Villella** (Chicago Symphony), **Nick Hansinger** (Atlanta Symphony), **Judith Johnson** (Lincoln Center), **Carol Jacobs** (Cleveland Orchestra) and **Suzanne Flandreau** (Black Research Center, Columbia College, Chicago). Other cooperators were *Music Publishers* **Judith Ilicka** (Theodore Presser), **Chris McGlumphy** (G. Schirmer) and **Steve Swartz** (Boosey & Hawkes).

Appreciation also to the many *Agents* all over the world—especially **Del Rosenfield** (New York), **Betsy Crittenden** (CAMI), **Lee Lamont** (ICM), **Karin Wylach** (Germany), **Beatrice Vesper** (Switzerland)—who responded to requests for bios/photos, as I discovered yet another star to add to the Performers' firmament. A warm hug to **Alice Straschil** who kept me updated on her cousin, Agent Nelly Walter (1901–2001).

Noted Helpful Fingers: **Evelyn Wilson**, Brit typing whiz, who left the state to be with her grandchildren far too early in the manuscript . . . **Rachel Huber** and **Andrea Forshaw,*** for more secretarial duties, and **Dana Sendziol**, who flew from her Illinois college graduation (1994), to spend the summer organizing my chaotic files. *Andrea later shone as a proofreader.

But above all, *a Most Special Kudo* must go to **Bruce Johnson**, Supervisor of Art and Music (2001–06) at the San Diego Public Library, who always found the information I sought, no matter how elusive, and who has been my lifesaver, guru and champion since he came on board, to the entry of the final word!

To my new colleagues, **Paul Bryant** of Birmingham Press, my Rock through the rocky rapids of final completion; **Kira Fulks** who designed the wonderful cover, **Jackie Zucker** who created other cover choices—and **Jim Riordan**, President of Seven Locks Press, who let the world in with his knowledge of marketing and distribution.

Appreciation goes to "Layout Lady" **Heather Buchman** who brought her experience to months of work on the *gargantuan* task of 1072 pages of manuscript. Her expertise helped to see this project to completion and its global destiny!

Lastly (or firstly), my younger son, **Adrian**, who, as in my previous book, *The Popular Guide to Classical Music*, once again came through with *an utterly enormous amount* of technical computer help and the *scanning of all those photographs*! Couldn't have accomplished this feat without him!

Finally, my husband **Charlie** who, after forty years together, was still able to surprise me with his editorial prowess, taking charge of the monstrous Orchestra Survey, helping research Women in Military Bands, and all that Brass, stringing the Harpists together, and managing the masterful job of creating The INDEX . . . He truly deserves to blow his own flugelhorn for processing reams of information into cohesive text, and (gasp!) editing and *re-editing* and **re-editing** the Final Version of 1072 pages of manuscript! (It should be mentioned that in the process, he proved that one *can* progress from computer *surly* to— *almost*— computer *friendly*. Or, in other words, one *can* teach a median-aged spouse new tricks!)

[A final mixed blessing thank-you to our older son, Charles, for his singular role of too frequently kidnapping his father away from the computer for twenty-five mile bicycle rides to keep him fit and trim.]

My heartfelt gratitude to you ALL!

TGIF—(Thank God It's Finished!)

Enjoy and be amazed at what we "gals" can achieve against unreal odds~~~~

Anne K. Gray

Christmas, 2006

Introduction

The Eras

Since Eve piped a tune on a hollow reed, women have been *performing* music. From earliest recorded history women have been *writing* music. Between the two disciplines it is logical to assume that women also *conducted* music and wrote historical references about it.

All through the ages, creative women have made valuable contributions to the esoteric world of music. As civilizations, cultures and social mores changed, much information on these ladies became buried during—there is no other way to phrase it—*centuries of male domination*. As women *re*-establish more equal roles in modern society, much research is being done in the sphere of feminine musicology with most enlightening results.

Discoveries of important women in music range from as far back as Mesopotamia and the Princess-Priestess **Enheduanna** (*c* 2500 BC)—believed to be the first woman to leave written records—to the egalitarian societies of ancient Egypt and Greece, especially Sparta and Lesbos where the great lyric poet **Sappho** penned immortal odes around the turn of the 6th century, to the cloisters of the Dark and Middle Ages when the visionary **Hildegard of Bingen** (1098–1179), wrote literature, poetry, history, music and texts on medieval medicine. The 1990s witnessed a remarkable surge of recognition and popularity of this original "Superwoman," resulting in the flowering of von Bingen societies, books, theses, dissertations, CDs of her chants, and worldwide celebrations of the nine hundredth year of her birth, 1998.

In the next major societal era, the emergence of the **renaissance**, with its doctrine of freedom of expression, ironically marked the beginning of the decline of women's voices, figuratively and literally. Craftsmens' Guilds now barred women. (In 1321, there had been eight women in the thirty-seven member Paris Musicians' Guild). The Catholic Church, via the 1563 Council of Trent, forbade women to sing religious polyphonic music. While this edict was directed at nuns, there is ample evidence that many convents continued clandestine chorusing.

Despite these barriers, several names managed to make their mark in musical history during this period. Even the ill-fated **Anne Boleyn** (*c* 1507–36) composed a hymn in the Tower of London before losing her head. In Italy, then composed of city-states, the Duke of Ferrara established the first *concerto delle donne* (women's musical ensemble) in 1580, the success of which had the courts of Mantua, Florence and Venice vying with each other to also hire the finest female singers and musicians. Prominent women of the time were **Maddalena Casulana** (*c*1540–90) and **Francesca Caccini** (1587–1640), whose work crossed the bridge into the **Baroque Period**. Caccini was followed by **Barbara Strozzi** (1619–64), **Antonia Bembo** (1643–1715), and **Elisabeth Claude Jacquet de la Guerre** (1666–1729), the latter important enough to have France's Louis XIV strike a medal in her honor after her death.

During the following **Classical Period**, when Gluck, Haydn, Mozart and a young Beethoven held sway, respected women composers emanating from the nobility or well-connected musical families numbered **Princess Anna Amalia** (1723–87), youngest sister of Frederick the Great, her niece **Anna Amalia**, Duchess of Saxe-Weimar (1739–1807), **Maddalena di Lombardini Sirmen** (1735–1818), **Marianne von Martinez** (1744–1812), and the blind prodigy **Maria Theresia von Paradis** (1759–1824), godchild of the Empress Maria Theresa, among significant others.

In the Golden Age of Music, the **Romantic Period**, more women forged their names on the roster of composition. In Germany, **Louise Reichardt** (1779–1826), **Fanny Mendelssohn Hensel** (1805–47), sister of Felix, and **Clara Wieck Schumann** (1819–96), wife of Robert, were well known. In Poland, the music of **Marie Szymanowska** (1789–1831) was the inspiration for young Frédéric Chopin, while France produced **Louise Dumont Farrenc** (1804–75), **Pauline Viardot Garcia** (1821–1910) and **Cécile Chaminade** (1857–1944) who lived through WWII. England's contribution, **Ethel Smyth** (1858–1944), whose *Mass in C* was favorably compared to that of Beethoven, hobnobbed with musical giants like Liszt, Brahms and Dvořák.

Women in America also came out of the parlor to enter conservatories and write orchestral music. One of the most celebrated of her day was **Amy Marcy Cheney Beach** (1867–1944), whose *Piano Concerto* and *Gaelic Symphony* defied the listener to determine the gender of their composer. Bridging the centuries, there emerged what is known as the *Second* New England School with Beach as their leader—the first (school) having originated in the 18th century with early American male composers.

The 20th century brought modern trends into music, especially after WWI. The 1920s saw the blooming of *avant-garde* styles on both sides of the Atlantic taking such forms as *aleatory* or *atonal* music, *serialism* and experiments with twelve tone scales. Music notation, too, literally went off the charts, some doing away with the familiar staff. In Europe, **Lili Boulanger** (1893–1918) and **Germaine Tailleferre** (1892–1983) enhanced the palette of French Impressionism, while across the English Channel **Elisabeth Lutyens** (1906–83) and **Elizabeth Maconchy** (1907–94) were pushing through the tonal "envelope." Women explored these new fields and then threw themselves into the next phase: multimedia, electronic and computer music, with Americans like **Wendy Carlos** and **Pauline Oliveros** coming into prominence. After the '70s the pendulum began swinging back to what has come to be called *neo-romanticism*, which reverts to more structured versions of tonality, harmony, and meter, yet still utilizes freer forms. This is reflected in the music of women composers of the 1980s and '90s and on into the new millennium. On this wave came such firsts as Pulitzer Prize winners **Ellen Zwilich**, **Shulamit Ran** and **Melinda Wagner**.

Meanwhile, behind the former "Iron Curtain" forged by the communist regimes of Eastern Europe after WWII, many creative women were able to take advantage of the equality status of education, especially in music. Some, like **Violeta Dinescu** and **Adriana Hölsky**, escaped to the West, while others like the Russians **Sofia Gubaidulina** and **Elena Firsova** had to wait for history to roll over and rust away the barriers before their work was known to the rest of the world. In Red China, women survived hard labor camps, practicing and writing music secretly. In a niche of their own, a nucleus of African-American women composers triumphed over the double bias of skin color and gender. Pioneer **Florence Price Smith** (1888–1953), whose music is enjoying a vital rebirth, blazed the trail for her followers.

By the close of the 20th century there were more opportunities for women in composition, as a younger generation emerged, led by such talents as **Augusta Read Thomas**, **Melinda Wagner** and **Dalit Warshaw**.

Conductors

Women on the podium have had—and continue to have—a different set of challenges. From the time nuns directed their cloistered choirs, women conductors have been shunted either into choral directing or onto the podia of their own gender. Women's orchestras proliferated from the turn of the century until World War II, to accommodate the slew of female musicians pouring out of conservatories only to find positions in established all-male symphony orchestras closed to them. Some women conductors established their own aggregations, such as **Gena Branscombe** (1881–1977) with her Branscombe Chorale, **Antonia Brico** (1902–89), the Brico Symphony, and **Frédérique Petrides** (1908–83) with her Orchestrette Classique. In Europe, pioneer spirits **Ethel Leginska** (1886–1970) and **Ethel Smyth** left their homes in England to study on the Continent where they received more recognition. Leginska went on to guest conduct major orchestras on both sides of the Atlantic, while Smyth gained directorial respect by virtue of conducting her major compositions. France's **Nadia Boulanger** (1887–1979), besides being the most honored teacher to a generation of composers, guest conducted the Boston Symphony, Philadelphia Orchestra, National Symphony and New York Philharmonic.

Today, several maestras have reached prominence in America: **JoAnn Falletta**, music director of the Buffalo (New York) Philharmonic, guest conducts all over the world; **Victoria Bond** completed eight seasons with the Roanoke Symphony in 1995, and three with Opera Roanoke; **Karen Keltner** has been associate conductor of San Diego Opera since 1982, and has also led New York City Opera and other orchestras; **Kate Tamarkin** was associate conductor of the Dallas Symphony; **Barbara Yahr** assisted Lorin Maazel at Pittsburgh; **Marin Alsop**'s talented baton directed the Colorado Orchestra, 1993–2003, going on to the Bournemouth (UK) and Baltimore Symphonies; and **Gisèle Ben-Dor**, director of Boston's Pro-Arte, Israel Chamber and Santa Barbara Symphony (1994–2005), has ably led the New York Philharmonic on several occasions.

In England, names like **Jane Glover**, **Anne Manson**, **Sian Edwards**, **Odaline de la Martinez**, and the late **Iona Brown** are well-known. Australian **Simone Young** enjoys a fantastic career ranging from her native land to the Paris Opera. In Israel, **Dalia Atlas** has been called the "First Lady of the Baton." Middle Europe, Germany, and France still hold to ancient prejudices, therefore the ratio of female orchestral musicians versus men is minuscule, and women conductors still have to create their own groups like the Amadeus Orchestra of Polish **Agnieszka Duczmal**.

Performers

As to **performers**, women vocalists had the easier task, having been accepted for their talents early in history in convents, courts and as courtesans. By the first part of the 18th century they were gradually replacing countertenors and *castrati*—men who had traditionally sung female roles since the inception of opera. It took another hundred years for prima donnas to become the pampered stars of society.

Instrumentalists had, and in many cases still have, far harder barriers to surmount. First there was the original connotation as to which instruments were considered "ladylike." This confined women mainly to the keyboard: harpsichord, clavichord, and then the newly invented piano which, as it became a household instrument, was a considered a "must" to complete a young lady's education. Public performance was not encouraged, although young girl prodigies were accepted. A few women, notably **Clara Wieck Schumann**,

Teresa Carreño, and Americans Julie Rivè-King and Olga Samaroff, were among the pioneers of international keyboard virtuosity. Fanny Mendelssohn, an excellent pianist, was confined by her family only to *private* performance.

Organists received early sanction and even (underpaid) employment as more churches acquired organs, while several major orchestras let down the portcullis of prejudice when it came to the harp. "Lady violinists" had a much tougher breakthrough because holding this instrument under a dainty chin was not considered complimentary to the feminine facial configuration. It was not until 1875 that Czech-born Wilma Normann-Neruda (1838–1911) and French-born American Camilla Urso (1842–1902) achieved recognition equal to the foremost male violinists of their time, such as Scandinavian Ole Bull, Frenchman Henri Vieuxtemps and Hungarian Joseph Joachim. In Urso's footsteps came American-born Maud Powell (1868–1920) and other stalwarts to turn the page into the 20th century. In the hiatus between the two world wars, Viennese emigrée Erica Morini (1904–95) and Polish refugee, prodigy Ida Haendel stand out in the 1930s and '40s—the latter still active in her career. It has taken until the late '80s and '90s, with the influx of many Asian prodigies, Midori, Akiko Suwanai, Anne Akiko Meyers, Chee-Yun, Tamaki Kawakubo, and Sara Chang—plus Caucasians Leila Josefowitz and Hilary Hahn—for the ratio of female soloists to start equaling their brother artists.

The cello, a *really* ungracefully-positioned instrument, was not (literally) embraced by women until the late 19th century. From Boston, home base of America's principal cello teachers, Lettie Launder, Laura Webster, Georgia Pray Lasselle and Lucy Campbell made names for themselves, as did Swiss Elsa Rügger—although none achieved the international stature of Urso and Powell. Englishwoman May Mukle (1880–1936) and Portuguese-born Guilhermina Suggia (1885–1950) were well-known in Europe. The all-too-brief star of Jacqueline DuPré (1945–87) stands out with Sharon Robinson, Wendy Warner, Allison Eldredge, Nancy Green, Shauna Rolston and Alisa Weilerstein among soloists in today's cello sphere.

In the woodwind family, as documented in ancient Sumerian, Egyptian and Greek drawings and writings, women were playing flute-like instruments. The early Christian edicts forbidding women to sing in churches also extended to the playing of instruments, which left the legacy to courtesans, female troubadours (*trobairitz*), and peasants. Renaissance enlightenment reclothed with respectability flutes, virginals (early harpsichords), viols, lutes and the like, for ladies of the aristocracy. The esteemed Italian singer-composer Tarquinia Molza (1542–1617) organized her own women's orchestra. The orphan conservatories of 16th century Venice trained all-girl ensembles. Yet in the 19th century, lady flutists were still considered a novelty. Despite this, in France a Madame Rousseau and Mademoiselle Lorenzine Meyer rose to prominence around 1830, and Venetian Maria Bianchini was praised by renowned Austrian critic Eduard Hanslick in 1880.

Brass instrumentalists appeared as ladies' orchestras proliferated. American cornetist Anna Berger was said to have "electrified" audiences at the London Promenade Concerts where, in 1889, she played fifty nights in succession. Unique, even for men, was the saxophone on which, in 1909, virtuoso Elise Hall became the first amateur ever to play with the Boston Symphony.

Women had long been told they were not strong enough to play heavy instruments, thus double bassists, tubists and percussionists emerged only with the growth of women's ensembles and orchestras at the turn of the 20th century. In these could be found musicians playing other instruments regarded as "too difficult" for ladies: oboes, clarinets, bassoons, trombones, etc. Today, there are prominent women soloists on most instruments, albeit piano and violin are still in the majority. The orchestral ratio of men to women is still barely five to one, but in this country in the last two decades the union-required "blind audition"—behind a curtain (*when it is adhered to*)—is making opportunities for qualified women professionals somewhat fairer. This cannot yet be said for Europe.

In Academics and Out in the Business World

The field of **Musicology**, long the eminent domain of men, now has a firm entrenchment of women, especially in the academe. Writers and teachers are enjoying productive careers in universities and conservatories, contributing greatly to our knowledge of women in music.

Women in the Business of Music, the fifth enlightening section of this book, once again proves women rising to the top in what they do best—NURTURING! Thus, these ladies are experiencing unprecedented success as agents, orchestra and opera company managers, running recording and publishing companies, plus myriad other positions involved in dealing with *people*.

Not to be forgotten are the women **philanthropists** who have given generously of their own and/or their husbands' wealth, helping to found orchestras, underwrite the building of concert halls, creating outdoor venues and, in general, helping to sustain fine music.

For those keeping their fingers on the pulse of feminism in general, and the vast field of classical music in particular, as this Introduction indicates, we are now ready to delve into this intriguing world, a world which is being uncovered, rediscovered and brought to the forefront where it belongs: The WORLD of *WOMEN in Classical Music*!

Postscripts

1. Gentle readers are asked to keep in mind that ONE person cannot possibly cover, *uncover* or *discover every woman* involved in classical music . . . thus I offer apologies to anyone missing herein and ask that you enjoy the glimpses into the lives of those gone before us, and the many who came into my life over the last decade to be part of this landmark book!

2. In the course of the eleven years it has taken to complete this book, I have "gone around the world" five times (via phone, fax , e-mail, etc.,) in the effort to keep up with the living. There is obviously a limit to this gargantuan exercise and the author asks that you take for granted that composers will keep composing, conductors continue leading orchestras, singers keep singing, instrumentalists keep playing, musicologists continue teaching and writing, and women in the *business* of music will either remain in their positions, or move on . . .

Therefore, in order for me to get this unique tome out into the world, I must now enter "***The End.***"

CHAPTER ONE
In Ancient Times

ANCIENT
Enheduanna (*c* 2500 BC)
Megolastrata of Sparta
Telesilla of Argos
Corinna of Búotia
Praxilla of Sicyon
Sappho of Lesbos (6th Century)

DARK AGES
Clotilde (*c* 474–546)
Kassia (*c* 810–*before* 867)
Pope Joan (853–855)
Adelheid of Landau
Mechtilde of Magdebourg (1212–82)
Hroswitha (10th Century)
Herrad of Landsberg (?–1195)
Hildegard of Bingen (1098–1179)
Eleanor of Aquitaine (1122–1204)

RENAISSANCE
Raffaella Aleotti (*c* 1574–*c* 1646)
Vittoria Aleotti (*c* 1573–after 1620),
Beatrice d'Este (1475–97)
Isabella d'Este (1474–1539)
Lucrezia Borgia (1480–1519)
Tarquinia Molza (1542–1617)
Maddalena Casulana (*c* 1544–*c* 1590)
Francesca Caccini (1587–*c* 1645)

Women have been creating music since the dawn of time. Apart from rock paintings depicting female musicians, some of the earliest artifacts unearthed in Palestine date back to the Iron Age (*c* 1000 BC–100 AD), and consist of numerous terra cotta clay figurines of women holding disk-shaped hand drums. Archeological evidence also links women to playing other types of drums and percussion instruments. Of these figurines, females outnumber males. Those holding lyres and flutes have been traced to the 13th century BC.

In primitive societies women were responsible for fertility, childbirth and other rites which involved making music. Cradles of civilization sprang up in China, the Nile Delta of Egypt, the Indus Valley at the foot of the Himalayas, and in Mesopotamia (present-day Iraq) between the Tigris and Euphrates Rivers, where cuneiform stone tablets of hymn cycles written by Enheduanna (born *c* 2500 BC) daughter of King Saragon of Ur and High Priestess of the Moon Goddess Nanna, have been unearthed.

The Kingdoms of Egypt

Perhaps the most continuously important status of women was found in Egypt which, from 4000 BC until the Muslims conquered it in the 7th century AD, had a highly cultured standard of living. Of their five major deities, three were female. Music was an integral part in secular and religious life. Priestesses from the nobility, and women who served in religious rites, were proficient in musicianship and singing ability. The framework of Egyptian history up to the conquest of Alexander the Great is generally divided into *kingdoms*, each under several dynasties. Records of the Old Kingdom (*c* 2755–2255 BC) show women musicians with harps and percussion, as well as singers and dancers. The Middle Kingdom (2134–1668 BC) had women playing oboe and flute. By the time of the New Kingdom (1570–1070 BC) they had graduated to every known instrument except the trumpet. Women of all classes were permitted to be entertainers. In the secular world, women assumed equal roles with men as singers, dancers and instrumentalists.

The Middle East and the Orient

The importance of women in music also emerges in the cultures of Sumeria—which included Assyria, Chaldea and Babylonia—as well as Greece, Crete, Rome, China, Arabia, East India, the Saracens and the Jews.

An empress of China (*c* 2500 BC) is credited with creating a tonal system for her musicians. The cultural lifestyle of Babylonia during this era allowed women to learn to read. There are even records of a women's college. Convents of women were part of the temples. They created elegant music under the direction of high priestesses. There are references to Queen Shu-bad of Ur who played the harp.

Another great society existed in Crete. This small Mediterranean island, southeast of Greece, flourished for over a thousand years during the Bronze Age (3000–1200 BC) under a non-militaristic matriarchy. Priestesses predominated, as did their music. Frescoes picture men and choirboys dressed as women, since women were considered close to divine.

Religion, in the sense of some form of worship of an unknown Higher Power, has always been intertwined with music. Myths and legends abound with stories of and references to goddesses of the arts.

The Aryan Migration

Between 2000 and 1000 BC, Aryans, progenitors of the Greek civilization, began migrating and absorbing civilizations. They traced their ancestry to Helen, Goddess of the Moon, and retained the common bond of their language.

The Greeks: Myth and Magic

The core of Greek belief was that music represented the flow of the universal life force. In the 5th century BC, the philosopher **Pythagoras** and his musician-poet wife, **Theano**, wrote of the stars and planets being moved through eternity via music. Music was the most important power of cultural influence until about 400 BC, when Greek drama caught the public's imagination, influencing their lifestyle. Basically, music was composed for work, recreation and religious rites, which included magic. A most important instrument was the *kithara*, a square, shallow box with two thick, armlike extensions connected by a crossbar with from five to eleven thick gut strings that were plucked with a plectrum (pick). Since women were at the center of these activities, it is logical to assume that they composed much, if not most, of the music, songs and dances. Both Homeric poems, the *Iliad* and the *Odyssey*, evince the protective spirit of Woman. Besides being respected as priestesses, there were exclusive women's cults with secret ceremonies forbidden to men, although only fragments of their hymns and songs have been preserved. A few names have survived: **Megolastrata** of Sparta, **Telesilla** of Argos, **Corinna** of Bœotia—teacher of Pindar—**Praxilla** of Sicyon, known for her drinking songs, **Erinna**, **Nissis**, **Anyte**, and the most noted, **Sappho** of Lesbos, whose fame still endures after twenty centuries.

Sappho

Sappho

The Archaic Age (*c* 550–400 BC) produced several lyric poetesses, the most noted of whom was Sappho of Mitylene, the chief city of Lesbos. In the prosperous, cultural climate of 7th century BC, Lesbos, an island near Turkey, held women in high regard, socially and politically. They were well-educated, free to travel and own property. There was even a women's college for study of the arts. In such a milieu the independently wealthy and talented Sappho was able to realize her full potential. She was admired throughout Greece as a lute player, singer, poet and composer. Instruments associated with her are the *barbiton*, similar to the kithara, the *chelys* (lyre) and *pectis*, a harplike instrument. While her poetry includes references to sexual activities between women, Sappho is reputed to have been married and have had a daughter.

Brief Rays of Sunshine

With the many wars fought to gain land, male warriors became symbols of glory and reverence and men began to take over reins of ritual held by women. A short resurgence of goddess religions occurred after Alexander's conquest of the ancient world in the 4th century BC. After the death of Alexander the Great (323 BC), during the Hellenistic Period of Ancient Greece women achieved some degree of social, economic and educational reform. Aristotle advocated that women should learn reading, writing, music and gymnastics. This enabled even respectable women to have concert careers for which they received a salary. Polgnata, daughter of Socrates, was included in this group. There were all-female choirs. The Hetairai were the highest class of "companions." Like geishas, they were beautiful, intelligent and educated. However, since their purpose was to entertain men, these ladies could never attain respectability.

The Creeping Blight

The hiatus of tolerance was not to last. Around 500 BC, like a blight moving slowly across the world, once again Greek women came under subjugation. Controlled and restricted in their activities, the main conduit of expressing their opinions was in the form of ritual *laments*, a type of public mourning which allowed them to infuse the lyrics of their chants with social and political issues. These also became part of the choruses in dramas whereby playwrights began to express their views. Laments reached such a passionate pitch that eventually men felt threatened and banned these emotional outbursts. Ironically, for the Greeks, a parallel to the Eve story was Zeus' creation of Pandora who opened her box and let evil into the world. But a contrary version of the myth portrays her as a beautiful Earth Mother whose box was filled with nature's bounty!

As women became excluded from rituals, male priests subverted religion into pseudo-sorcery. Men dominated women by virtue of their superior physical strength. In China, foot-binding insured that women could not stray. The tenets of Confucius would not even permit the clothing of a man and woman be hung next to each other. Similar domination in India was in the form of the Aryans' creation of the caste system which outlawed any mingling with the darker native race.

The Jewish Legacy

Wherever Jews were scattered, or exiled, or conquered, they remained amazingly cohesive, bound by the Torah, God's Laws. A patriarchal religion, tradition dictated men's and women's roles. Marriages were arranged by the parents. Men tilled the soil, raised crops, cattle and sheep. Wives kept house and raised children. They cooked, baked, spun fabric, made clothes, served their husbands and sons, and ate after the men had finished. They received no formal education, were denied inheritance if there were male heirs, and were segregated in the synagogues lest they be a distraction. First and foremost they were breeders. A man could have more than one wife at a time . . . he was even obligated to marry his brother's widow and adopt her children! Sons were brought into the world with great rejoicing, but unlike the pagans, girls were not drowned or exposed to the elements to die—a variation of which is still rampant in 21st century China, while India eliminates girl fetuses more sophisticatedly via ultrasound and abortion—leaving a whole generation of young men with a shortage of marriageable women.

Compassion and modesty were two essential qualities of the ideal Jewish wife—hygienic laws dictating isolation and freedom from work during menses and after childbirth were for women's *protection*, to give their vulnerable immune system a chance to rest and recuperate—an entirely different concept from the Gentile "unclean" connotation of these events. Also, sex was to be enjoyed—*within marriage*. Maybe love bloomed, as in *Fiddler on the Roof*—but wives were still a man's *possession*.

Jesus and Early Christianity

In *Eunuchs for the Kingdom of God*, German theologian Uta Ranke-Heinemann exposed the incredible denigration of women in the history of the Catholic Church. An example: "Jesus was a friend of women, the first and practically the last friend women had in the Church." He treated women with respect and equality. Contrary to popular belief, Mary Magdalene[1] was not a woman of the streets, but a close disciple, as were others who had leadership roles in the earliest Christian churches. Records of these were expunged by the 3rd century. Jesus countered accepted polygamy and concubinage with, "Whoever divorces his wife and marries another woman commits adultery!" Catholic theologians such as Pope Clement I (88–97), Augustine (396–430) and Jerome (420) re-instilled the subjugation of women. Much of early Christianity grew out of pagan rituals in which women still played an important part. There were girl choirs up to the 4th century. By the 5th century, however, fierce debates raged as to Mary's—and women's—status. In fact, Christianity owes much of its early survival to women's support. It was they who established organizations (convents) which kept the cause alive a good century before monasteries came into existence.

The Bachelor and the Women

Paul (originally Saul) of Tarsus (*c* 5–*c* 65 AD) never married, but set himself up as an authority on women. Born in Greece and raised a Jew, around age thirty-five he experienced a call to Christianity and thereafter preached, travelled and wrote. His epistles to the Colossians, Corinthians, Ephesians, Galatians, Hebrews, Philippians, Romans, Thessalonians, and other eager ears and souls seeking to know more of the new religion, exhorted teachings that denigrated women, although he acknowledged female preachers in the early years of his evangelism.

Spreading the Word

Jesus aimed his preaching at the Jews. Paul and other apostles spread Christianity to the Romans and Greeks—henceforth known as Gentiles—and as far west as France (Gaul), Germany and England.

With the conversion of the Emperor Constantine in 312 AD, Christianity became "legitimate," but all aspects of it were dominated by men, with women excluded from anything religious. Liturgical music was preserved in thousands of manuscripts copied by monks, but women had no access to these. Because of its association with prostitutes, instrumental performance was forbidden to unmarried girls, as was the singing of liturgical music—this from an edict of Paul. There was music in theatrical performances, but churchmen called these the "Theater of the Devil." Dancers, admired by the public, were not permitted to enter churches. Chastity was "in."

The Veil Descends

By 325 AD Christianity had become the official religion of the Holy Roman Empire and with it the patriarchal concept ingrained in our social conscience to this day. God was referred to only in the masculine gender. The Holy Ghost, formerly a feminine spirit, had a sex change. Back in the 2nd century the foundation of anti-feminism was

---

1. Several books, notably Dan Brown's *The Da Vinci Code*, and films like Mel Gibson's *The Passion of the Christ* (2005) and Martin Scorsese's *The Last Temptation of Christ* (1988) suggest that Magdalene was the wife of Jesus and bore him a child. This follows the custom that Jewish men, by age twenty has entered into (a usually arranged) marriage.

devastatingly laid by Clement of Alexandria (150?–200?) in the declaration, *"Every woman ought to be filled with shame at the thought that she is a woman!"* He fed the growing emphasis on celibacy and virginity with the statement that "marriage and fornication were not the same, but that the difference was so fine that it resolved itself into a mere legal fiction . . ." Giving birth—once considered the holy participation of the mystery of creation—was now considered "unclean." Sexual intercourse, even in marriage, became a "sin." Saint John Chrysostom (354?–407), a church father, clinched that belief with, "Woman is a necessary evil, a natural temptation, a desirable calamity, a domestic peril, a deadly fascination, and a painted ill."

Therefore, although the Roman Empire and other civilizations decayed from within or fell to the Barbarians, and the Dark Ages would bury previous cultures for centuries, women began to carry a new legacy within their genes: a built-in inferiority complex—a lot of which lingers insidiously in the psyche of at least the older generations to this day.

OUT OF THE DARKNESS

Women Regain A Little Limelight

The only gleams of light in the Dark Ages were the flickering candles of Roman Catholic missionaries who set out to bring civilization—on *their* terms—back to Northern Europe. In Germany, strong women of Teutonic tribes sought the protection of the Church, on *their* terms, founding monasteries forbidden to men, on land *they* owned and were not about to transfer to their husbands. Marriage was also on *their* terms. Foremost among these was **Clotilde** (*c* 474–545) who married Barbarian King Clovis (*c* 466–511) in 492 or 493, on condition that he and his subjects convert. They founded the Merovingian dynasty, brought Christianity to the Franks, who in the next three centuries took over most of Europe and produced Charlemagne, crowned Emperor of the Holy Roman Empire in 800 AD. Another princess, **Radegund** (520/5–587), was married to Clotaire II (*d* 629), King of France, Thuringia and parts of Italy and Spain. She left her husband to his six other wives—even though he wanted her back—talked the bishops into consecrating her a deaconess and set up a religious center in Poitiers where women were taught to read, write and learn church music, which by this time had reached the polished form of the Gregorian plainchant, named after Pope Gregory I (*c* 540–604) credited with organizing the myriad of extant chants. Women once again regained their own "room" to make music.

The Men Take Over—Almost . . .

Until 800 AD, Christians were still fighting Barbarians from the North and Saracens from Spain in the South. For centuries, the only centers of formal learning and music were monasteries and convents. As the hierarchy of the church was established—popes, cardinals, bishops, priests, clerics, monks—nuns were relegated to the bottom of the order. Still, many noblewomen entered convents to avoid marriage (read *bondage*) and motherhood (read *breeder*). Until the 13th century, priests were allowed to marry, while women in religious orders were expected to live up to an unrealistic ideal of virginity and psyche-suppression. In their cloisters, however, women had more freedom than their married sisters, especially to circumvent, unofficially, St. Paul's injunction "to keep silent in the churches." In fact, all nuns were required to have enough musical education to sing the liturgy. The abbesses, prioresses and cantrixes (female singers) in charge of these communities also needed knowledge of Latin. Manuscripts exist from English and French abbeys describing convent life ranging from stark to luxurious, depending on the founding, funding, class and education of their members. One of the largest and wealthiest establishments was Las Huelgos near Burgos in northern Spain. Founded in 1160 by Alfonso VIII of Castile, most of its nuns came from noble families, even bringing servants and furnishings to the convents they entered. The famous *Las Huelgos Codex*, discovered in 1904 and traced to the 14th century, contains 136 polyphonic chants for two, three and four voices—the very form of singing forbidden to women by Paul and subsequent popes.

The Byzantine Empire

Meanwhile, by the 5th century, another empire, the Byzantine, evolved from the eastern part of the Roman Empire. Lasting over a thousand years until 1453, it established continuous restraints on women. They were segregated in church and in court. While they were permitted to perform at *symposia*—court banquets which included female musicians, singers and dancers—these celebrations were condemned by the church.

Another reason for the apparent dearth of women composers during these centuries was the high regard for anonymity—which applied to men as well. Nevertheless, a few names have drifted down to us: **Theodosia**, abbess of a convent near Constantinople wrote canons in the 9th century, as did **Thekla** in the same period at a similar location. The most prominent woman composer of Byzantine music was **Kassia**, whose music is still found in Eastern Orthodox hymnals.

Kassia, the "Fallen" Woman

Daughter of a high court official, **Kassia** (*c* 810–before 867), born in or near Constantinople, was beautiful and well-educated. Part of the "bride show" for the Emperor Theodophilos, as he walked between the two rows of lovely virgins, he tested their intellect. To Kassia he observed that women had been the cause of much evil—referring to Eve. Kassia responded with the fact that women had also been the cause of much good—referring to the Virgin Mary. This display of quick wit was evidently too much for the Emperor's ego, and he chose a more modest maiden. Kassia was mortified. She retired to a convent and wrote bitter poetry about the fate of women. Her music however, took the more traditional form of the *sticheron*, a verse chant still used in morning and evening services. She left 261 secular verses, and twenty-four chants, with twenty-six more credited to her. Her most famous composition, *The Fallen Woman*, is thought to be about Mary Magdalene or autobiographical. Apparently Theodophilos regretted passing over Kassia, and attempted to meet her again. Although she avoided this, in her heart she apparently returned his love and branded herself a fallen woman. This romantic tragedy, plus her poetry and music, continues to be popular in arrangements by Greek composers.

Pope Joan

The 9th century marked the ending of one civilization with the collapse of the Roman Empire. Europe, still one country, half of whose population had been eviscerated by plague, famine, civil wars and barbarian invasions, had a complete breakdown of law and order before the onset of feudalism would recreate some sort of social and economic structure. Women had no legal rights, could be beaten by their husbands—rape was a mere technicality—and education, an impossible dream, was considered unnatural and dangerous.

It was during these violent times that an item of unique and subsequently altered history happened, which after 300 years is resurfacing into a controversy as to whether this example of female ingenuity really existed! The startling revelation resurfaced in 2005, that from 853–855 *a woman disguised as a man sat on the throne of St. Peter and reigned as Pope.* Unearthed in the guise of a 1996 historical "novel," *Pope Joan*, by Donna Woolfolk Cross, it tells of a young girl who managed to learn to read and write and take her dead brother's place in a *schola* (seminary) and subsequently within an order of monks in Frankland (the origin of Germany). Her knowledge and skill in medicine brought her to Rome and Pope Leo's entourage. After his death, she was elected Pope John Anglicas in 853. The Pope's gender was only discovered when, two years later during a procession, she had a miscarriage, hemorrhaged and died. (Keep in mind that apart from hands and face, people did not bathe in those days!) All these were reasonably well-known facts until 300 years ago when church scribes finalized the writing out of this succession—via falsifying dates—to eradicate this highly embarrassing event. Gradually, some written reports are emerging, but one of the main items of evidence that this is *not* fiction is the existence in Rome to this day of a wooden chair known as the *sella stercoraria* ("dung seat") because of a hole cut into the middle like a toilet. Since Joan's discovery, as part of the nominating ceremony, subsequent papal candidates until the 16th century were made to sit upon the *sella* for an examination of their genitals.

Pioneers of Poetry and Plainchant

By the 14th century, church control of women was stronger than ever. Nuns' access to the more advanced polyphonic (many-voiced) form of music was blocked by their male counterparts. Thus, there is no known early polyphonic music written by women. Female images, however, continued as allegorical personification of the arts, just as the Muses had been to the Greeks. Women were the inspiration of men, who assumed the role of the seekers. Of the nine Muses, Terpsichore was of choral songs and dance, and St. Cecilia was the patroness of music. Women, no doubt, continued to be active in music in the late Middle Ages (13th century) but, as in the Byzantine custom of anonymity, they did not put names on their work because decorum and their social position forbade it. This is the only logical explanation for the huge gap in women composers before the 1500s. Also, before the era of printing, many manuscripts were lost.

From Antiquity to the end of the Byzantine Empire women were considered inferior and tainted by the symbolic evil of Pandora/Eve. An interesting concept has been put forward that Eve was actually doing Adam a favor by opening his eyes to knowledge via the "apple," but to espouse such a radical theory would twist theology to the "core." (And where would it leave the snake?)

Controlled by a patriarchal society, the women who did "make a name" for themselves were of the aristocracy and well educated. Convents provided cultural havens for those in the upper classes who did not marry, as well as opportunities for singing and composition of sacred music.

Noted Nuns

Adelheid of Landau and **St. Mechthilde of Magdebourg** were among the nuns who wrote sacred music and whose names have survived extinction. The latter gained fame with her book *The Flowing Light of the Godhead*. Persecuted during her life, she was old and blind when she came to the monastery of Helfta, and was taken in by the nuns who enabled her to complete the work's final (seventh) chapter at eighty-six. Her original Low German version was translated into Latin, enabling Dante to read it and adapt the imagery of light into his *Paradiso*. Heinrich of Nördlingen so loved the work he translated it into High German and sent it to Margaret in the Dominican convent of Medingen and Christina Ebner, her sister, Abbess of the convent of Engenthal.

Also gaining early fame was **Hroswitha**, a 10th century canoness from the German convent at Gandersheim, recognized as a center of intellectual and religious activity. It was one of many founded under the sponsorship of the Saxon dukes. A canoness could leave the convent for outside visits, thus giving Hroswitha the chance to view the world beyond the abbey, and the knowledge to create her epic poem recounting the rule of Otto I, "the Great," the German Holy Roman Emperor who gave her her own court, knights for protection, the right to coin money and attend the meetings of his Diet. Just as centuries later **Clara Schumann** would feel the need to denigrate her compositions because she was a woman, apologizing for her "arrogance" and noting in her diary that "women were not supposed to compose," so Hroswitha cloaked her talent and waived the recognition she attained by claiming to be a vessel of God's grace and demurring that her creations "exceed the grasp of my woman's mind."

In Alsace, **Herrad of Landsberg**, Abbess of Hohenburg from 1167 to 1185, wrote *Hortus deliciarum* (Garden of Delights) to instruct the sixty nuns under her care. The work is a masterful gathering, in one volume, of most of the knowledge up to her time. Interspersed among the excerpts of various authors were many original poems set to music by Herrad herself. After having been preserved for centuries at her own monastery, about the time of the French Revolution it passed into the municipal library of Strasbourg. There, the miniatures were copied by Engelhardt in 1818. The text was recopied and published by Straub and Keller (1879–1899). Tragically, the original of this beautifully written and illustrated masterpiece was destroyed in a fire during the siege of 1870 in the Franco-Prussian War. Fortunately, we still have some example of the artistic and literary value of Herrad's work.

The most famous nun of all, a "Renaissance woman" three centuries before the renaissance, was **Hildegard of Bingen**.

Hildegard von Bingen: *"The Sibyl of the Rhine"*

This legendary woman was born in 1098, the tenth child of an aristocratic family and, as per a contract[2] with the church, was given at the age of eight by her parents, Hildebert and Mechtild as a "tithe" to God. To the concern of her family, very early in life the child had been describing experiences and visions of a white light which filled her with heavenly joy. The "cloister" Hildegard was relegated to was actually a hut adjoining the Benedictine monastery of St. Disibode, where she was placed in the care of Jutta of Spanheim, a nun of noble family.

The regimen was harsh: Eight daily rituals of prayer and chanting, beginning at two in the morning, plus work, lessons, silence, fasting and only two meals a day at 3:00 A.M. and 3:00 P.M. (Jutta was permitted only one meal.) After the shock of being torn from the people she loved and, for the times, an opulent lifestyle, in the course of several months, the child began to thrive. She took the veil in her teens, by which time other young women had joined them. Sister Jutta was made magistra (administrator) of the group.

Going Public

When Jutta died in 1136, Hildegard, at age thirty-eight, became *magistra*. Four years later she had the strongest vision yet. She saw tongues of flames descending from the heavens and settling on her, commanding that she reveal her experiences. The concept of breaking decades of silence and "going public," and the fact that she was "only a woman," created such a conflict that Hildegard, prone to migraines, became sick to the point of depression. After much soul searching, however, she came to the theological conclusion that it was God's will to have such a "weak vessel" carry His message. Thus far, only her confessor, the monk Volmar, knew of her visions. Convinced of their veracity, he had passed the information on to his superiors. The word got to Bishop Henry of Mainz who deemed the visions to be divinely inspired and ordered a written record. Always decrying the fact that she had not received an adequate education—Jutta's Latin having been just enough for the church service—Hildegard dictated her work to the supportive Volmar. It took ten years to finish her first book, *Scivias*, (Know the Ways), which contained twenty-six visions, theological philosophy, and a morality play, *Ordo virtutum* (Drama of the Virtues), the earliest of its kind by more than a century. Dealing with the battle of the soul between the Virtues and the Devil, who only speaks and does not sing, the work is comprised of eighty-two songs and a mystical language. (At its "premiere," probably to celebrate the opening of Hildegard's new abbey, Volmar played the Devil.)

Changing the Course of History

Word of the nun's works and visions began to spread. One of her most influential admirers was Abbot Bernard of Clairvaux—later to become a saint. Through him, Hildegard's accomplishments reached the ears of Pope

---

2. Every tenth child of nobility was automatically tithed to the church, which gained great income from the dowries of these future brides of Christ.

Eugenius III (1145–53). With the papal seal of approval, *Scivias* was circulated and Hildegard made pilgrimages to other monasteries and convents, often aghast at the violations against the Word of God she witnessed, even to fornication between monks and nuns. She lectured, she reviled, she was fearless. There was much correspondence with popes, kings, emperors and other notables who sought her advice. She became known as "The Sibyl (prophetess, oracle) of the Rhine." Also attributed to her were visions concerning the Crusades, which the Pope conveniently interpreted as God's continuing approval for reclaiming the Holy Land.

The crusades actually began in 1095 and continued until 1270. The Ottoman sultans of Turkey, beginning in the eleventh century, had overrun Syria, Palestine, part of the Byzantine Christian Empire (Greece, Armenia). By the twelfth century, Europe had begun an era of dramatic growth of population and commerce. These military campaigns provided the Church with a cause as well as opportunities for land-hungry nobles, knightly missions, commercial expansion for merchants, and release from fiefdom for serfs and peasants—all of which marked the break-up of feudalism.

Nobles and knights made pilgrimages to Hildegard for her blessing and guidance before setting forth on a Crusade, many with wives accompanying them, on a quest that would change European history forever.

Intrigue and Expansion

By 1147, so many women wanted to enter Hildegard's order that she asked permission of Abbot Kuno to found a new convent at St. Rupertsberg on the grounds of a ruined monastery above the Rhine at Bingen. Permission was denied—her celebrity was pouring money into Disibodenberg's coffers and the Abbot had no wish to lose his source of cash. Hildegard called the abbot an unprintable name and made dire predictions as to what would happen to him if he thwarted God's will. He still refused to let her go. Then, as in many times of stress, she fell extremely ill. The length and severity of her condition frightened Kuno into relenting, and Hildegard made a miraculously rapid recovery.

By 1150, fifty nuns and their dowries were at the new location. The Abbess's design specifications for the new building even included piped in water! Not only did she get away from Kuno, but Hildegard was now directly under the (self-serving) Archbishop Henry of Mainz and had the protection of King Frederick I (c 1122–90). Known as Frederick Barbarossa (Red Beard), he was to become one of the fiercest of warriors, conquering much of the Roman Empire, defying the Church by dethroning popes and establishing his anti-popes. In the end, as the abbess had envisioned at his coronation, he reinstated Pope Alexander III (1151–81) and humbled himself to get back into the good graces of the Church. Meanwhile, Hildegard used her new freedom to educate the nuns both at Bingen and eight miles away across the Rhine at Eibingen, where in 1165, after overcoming more opposition, she founded another convent, commuting regularly by boat between the two, a remarkable feat for one of such advanced years.

Besides Volmar, Hildegard's other secretary was her special protégé, Richardis (or Rikkarda), the daughter of the Marchioness von Stade who had contributed substantially to the new convent. There was, however, an unconcealed rivalry between these two strong women. The Marchioness felt that not only was Hildegard usurping her mother role, but was using her daughter's excellent Latin for her own purposes to the detriment of any promotion for the young woman. To this end, the Marchioness made a new endowment to set her daughter up as head of her own abbey. Besides not wanting to lose the von Stade money, Hildegard warned that the girl was frail, and the responsibility would be too much for her. True to her predictions, within two years Richardis was dead, a sad loss for the Abbess.

A Woman for All Reasons

In her writings, after *Scivias*, Hildegard brought out *Liber Viae Moratorium* (the Book of Life's Rewards) and *De Operation Dei* (The Book of God's Works). She even created a mystical language she called *Lingua Agnate* (ignored or unknown tongue), some of which can be found in her hymns and poems. Between 1150–60, in the field of natural history, science and medicine, she wrote *Physical and Cause et cure*. These collections of natural remedies are still used as source books on medieval medicine. She can be credited as a pioneer of holistic medicine. Her ideas included the four principles of good health: a balanced diet, exercise, rest and a moral lifestyle. Hildegard propounded that the elements of heat, cold, moisture and dryness must be in balance in the body as an organized system of energies. Most unique of all was her understanding of obstetrics and gynecology at a time when physicians (all male) would not even accept women patients other than the most high born.

Above All—the Music!

The Quadrivium represented the highest form of education available, and that only to men of the upper class. Its four subjects were astronomy, geometry, mathematics and music. Since women were considered incapable of thinking in abstract forms, Hildegard had received no formal musical training, yet she composed over sixty works. She felt that music was a symbol of the original link between God and man, and that living a virtuous life was the path to regain the harmony of the Garden of Eden. Her music style, like her lifestyle, was original. Unlike the structured plainchant, she used a larger range of tones, soaring melodies, and allowed the music to flow with the words. Some of the most beautiful songs and lyrical poems of the Middle Ages radiated from her spiritual genius. It is believed that she also wrote other poems of such a passionate nature that—against her wishes—her superiors felt it their responsibility to destroy them. She compiled all her works into a liturgical cycle, *Symphonia armonia celestium revelationum* (Symphony of the Harmony of Heavenly Revelations). The only other medieval composer who attempted such a large project was the French theologian-philosopher, Peter Abelard (1079–1142?). They never met, and neither did Hildegard know of Hroswitha or Herrad, her two prominent predecessors in her own country.

Defying the Church!

At the age of eighty—a phenomenal longevity for the times—Hildegard was placed under a Church interdict prohibiting all holy rituals and sacraments within her convent. This, because she had buried the body of a young knight who had been excommunicated. The punishment was like a mortal wound to her soul, but she refused to exhume the body. She blessed the grave, eradicated its whereabouts, and made the arduous journey in person to plead for the sentence to be lifted, giving evidence that the youth had confessed and been anointed. In line with her philosophy of the power of music, she warned that the force of the Devil would be unleashed upon those who had silenced her nuns' singing. The worst agony for her was the thought of being denied Last Rites—the anointing before death that allows the soul to enter heaven. After months of correspondence, the interdict was removed in March 1179. Hildegard died in peace on September 17.

Elusive Sainthood

Already considered a saint during her lifetime by most of Europe, during their respective terms Popes Gregory IX (1227–41), Innocent IV (1243–54), Clement V (1305–14) and John XXII (1316–34) attempted, without success, to make Hildegard's canonization official. (Red tape is, apparently, not a modern innovation.)

Hildegard's name began appearing in the 16th century in the Roman Martyrology, which designated her feast day as September 17. Pope John Paul II (1978–2005) considered her a saint. In the early 1990s, her feast day was also placed on the Episcopalian calendar.

Other Facets of Hildegard

The International Society of Hildegard von Bingen Studies was founded by Professor Bruce Hozeski of Ball State University (Indiana) English department in 1984 for the purpose of researching everything about the Abbess. Besides translations of the first two books of her visions, he has worked on all her correspondence. The Society's second president, Audrey Davidson of Western Michigan University, published the morality play *Ordo Virtutum*. Third president (1992–), composer **Pozzi Escot**, has lectured internationally on von Bingen, and published a series of articles on her scientific and other writings, as well as her music. The society sponsors a twice yearly newsletter, *Quadlibet,* and an annual International Congress on Medieval Studies in May at Western Michigan University in Kalamazoo. Of its 500-plus membership the majority are medieval scholars. They celebrated their twenty-fifth anniversary in 2006.

Musicologist/pianist/composer **Nancy Fierro** of Los Angeles' Mount St. Mary's College also lectures on Hildegard internationally, and has recorded a unique monograph of her music.

In April 1995, Britain's *Women in Music*, founded in 1987, sponsored an International Conference on Hildegard von Bingen in Winchester.

Popular pilgrimages continue to the Abbey at St. Rupertsberg in Germany. In 1998, the 900th anniversary of Hildegard's birth was celebrated with festivals throughout Germany, as well as other parts of the world where scholars of this unique woman abound.

Believe It Or Not

Hildegard's presence was felt strongly by musicologist Reverend **Victoria Sirota** during the service of her ordination to the priesthood, September 17, 1994. It was not until months later she learned that the date was the Abbess's Feast Day.

Joan Ohanneson, author of *Scarlet Music*, a biographical novel on the life of Hildegard, based on doctoral dissertations and other research, avers that in the course of the ten years it took to complete this work, she was visited by Hildegard many times, and literally "prodded" by her in 1997 into the momentum to finish the project. In the process, many clairvoyants sought out the author to tell of their experiences with the abbess.

It was February 1995 when I began writing the insert on Hildegard for this book. I was playing a CD of her chants. It was at that moment Zaida, a "visionary" lady of my acquaintance, walked into my office. With very little knowledge of classical music, and *none* of Hildegard, she immediately told me that she saw "a woman in a white robe kneeling in the corner of the room, weeping." She further elaborated that the abbot had burned some of the nun's poems because they were too passionate. (This was confirmed in *Scarlet Music*.) She also named Voldemar as Hildegard's confessor. (*Zaida had absolutely no prior knowledge of any of this! A Panamanian, not fluent in English, she was not even acquainted with the word, "confessor"!*)

I have since been informed from other sources that all the women "on the other side" have been waiting to have their stories told . . . and for this book to come out into the world.

Take it or leave it. Trust me, I am *not* weird . . . but I still get chills recalling this experience!

Hildegard called herself "a feather on the breath of God." In reality she was a pioneer, the mother of modern feminism, (re)asserting the powerful role of women as lifegivers and nurturers of "man"kind. Her example proved that, even in a male-regimented era, the remarkable capability of women in intellectual areas—in *her* case, to the accompaniment of her own divinely inspired music[3]—is a powerful force of enlightenment.

---

3. Renewed popularity of the medieval chant has brought with it a resurgence of interest in Hildegard's music, now available on numerous CDs.

Her prophecies included forewarnings of the Reformation—the schism between the Catholicism and Protestantism, brought on by Martin Luther's Edicts in 1517—of Earth's ecological perils, the promotion of holistic healing, and the restoration of the feminine face of God present in the Hebrew Bible and the New Testament.

> "Underneath all the texts, all the sacred psalms and canticles, these . . . sounds and silences, terrifying, mysterious, whirling . . . must somehow be felt in the pulse, ebb and flow of the music that sings in me. My . . . song must float like a feather on the breath of God."
> —Hildegard von Bingen

MEANWHILE—IN THE SECULAR WORLD

In the 12th and 13th centuries, the center of music in the secular world emanated from France, spreading from there to the rest of Europe. In the lower classes, beyond the control of the Church, folk music owes its survival to strolling minstrels—many of them women known as *jougleresses. Carmina Burana*, dated 1280, a collection of over 200 poems in English, French and German dialect, was discovered in the Benedictine monastery at Beuron. Some of the poetry is quite bawdy and profane, with subjects covering drinking, wenching, religious satire, dancing, roving and love. In 1937, Carl Orff (1895–1982) set several of these poems to music in cantata form in twenty-five movements for soloists and boys choir. It is often performed with dancers. (This music reached an even wider audience when used in the 1976 film, *The Omen*).

In the upper classes, lyric male poet-musicians—troubadours or trouvères—also sang in the vernacular. Their main subject was courtly love. The objects of their adoration, usually married, were placed upon idealistic and unrealistic pedestals. Responses to this illusion have survived in the form of songs written by *trobairitz*, Provençal lady poet-composers and singers, expressing themes of love, capitulation and abandonment. **Beatriz, Countess of Dia** (twelfth century) left the only example of both melody and poetic text for this unique feminine perspective. Wife of Guilhèm de Poitiers, she lived in southern France in a period favorable for economic independence of aristocratic women, even to being able to inherit property. They often ruled their family estates while their husbands were away fighting in the Crusades.

Eleanor of Aquitaine

The first nobleman troubadour is believed to be William IX (1071–1127), Count of Poitiers, Duke of Aquitaine and grandfather of the most powerful woman of her time, Eleanor of Aquitaine (1122–1204), whose duchy was larger than the whole of France. Married at fifteen to Louis VII, she bore him two daughters, accompanied him on the Second Crusade, divorced him on their return (1152) and married the younger Henry Plantagenet of Anjou, who two years later became Henry II of England. Their four sons included Richard the Lion-Hearted and John, whose abuses of power caused the nobles to draw up and force him to sign the Magna Carta (1215), the first document to grant civil rights and liberties, and regularize the judicial system. Besides collaborating on affairs of state, Eleanor brought with her the literature, art and music she had learned in the East. She also invited Celtic singers to her court. After the death of Henry in 1189, and until Richard's return from the Third Crusade in 1194, Eleanor ruled as Regent, foiling John's plot to displace his brother.

Eleanor arranged for her granddaughter, **Blanche of Castile** (1188–1202), to marry the future Louis VIII of France. Blanche in turn became the most powerful woman in Europe when she acted as Regent for her twelve-year-old son, after her husband's death. In his turn, when Louis IX went on a Crusade in 1248, he left his sixty-year-old mother to rule the country.

One of the most important ladies in Eleanor's court was **Marie de France**, who wrote masterful adaptations of folklore and legends in the form of lays (or lais)—defined as usually consisting of a dozen unequal stanzas sung to different tunes. Mistress of entertainment, Marie is thought to be the daughter of Geoffrey Plantagenet (1151–1212), sometime Bishop of York (England) and Tours (France), who, although illegitimate, was the most faithful of Henry II's sons.

Female entertainers of the time were courtesans who lived in the courts and, like the wives of their masters, sang and played instruments such as the harp, *vielle* (an early violin), *psaltery* (zither family), *guiterne* (early lute) and *citole* (dulcimer). Like the nuns, these women performed and composed monophonic (single melody line) music on an equal basis with men. As composition advanced to multi-voiced polyphony, men had the advantage of education and musical training in universities and church schools. Deprived of these privileges, women fell behind technically. At the same time increasing social strictures dictated that their legal rights and personal freedom become more and more curtailed.

INTO THE RENAISSANCE

The period from 1450 to 1600, designated the *renaissance*, witnessed the *rebirth* of the arts and humanities, especially classical Greek and Roman literature. Centered in Italy, which had prospered from the trade opened between East and West by the Crusaders, came the products, music and culture of Middle Eastern countries. Enriched by the crusades, nobility transformed grim castle walls with sumptuous tapestries, covered floors with Oriental carpets and set their tables with gold plates and engraved goblets. Artists, weavers and craftsmen were put to work. Paintings appeared on walls, sculptures in halls. Artistic themes were taken from the Bible, Greek myths and Roman legends.

The Press is Mightier Than the Quill

In 1450, the invention by Joseph Gutenberg of the printing press revolutionized all the arts. The art of paper-making, begun in the second century in China, spread to Europe by the thirteenth and fourteenth, and paper was in plentiful supply by the fifteenth. The rise of a literate middle class increased the demand for books, and the impact on music was significant since more could be printed in one month than in an entire year of painstaking hand copying.

Education—Implementing the Gender Bias

The emphasis was on liberal arts. Boys were taught Greek, Latin, rhetoric, mathematics, astronomy, music theory and physical education. The aristocracy and wealthy upper class might permit their daughters a similar course of studies, but the principal aim for this would be to make a better match. Needlework, drawing, playing music and singing were considered female pastimes. Modesty and obedience, piety and chastity were the ideals. Marriage, children and running a household were the desired goals. Girls wed in their early teens, often to men at least a decade older. Only high-born Roman Catholic females still had the choice of entering convents. Even there, a dowry was expected. These nuns usually made good use of their education within the cloister.

While girl prodigies were accepted, much musical talent was buried once women became wives. Ladies' accomplishments were permitted exhibition only in the private sphere. In the latter half of the 16th century a handful of women rose above these strictures.

The Singing Nuns

The Council of Trent, held in northern Italy (1545–63), was the nineteenth ecumenical council of the Roman Catholic church. It spanned the papal reigns of Paul III, Julius III, Marcellus II, Paul IV and Pius IV. Addressing the challenge of the Protestant Reformation, it set the dogmas of the Counter-Reformation. One of its decrees was:

"They [nuns] shall abstain from singing either in the choir or elsewhere . . . the figured chant (polyphony)." Strict limitations were placed on outsiders. Only a nun could teach music to other nuns, and the organ was the only permitted instrument. Yet convents in Milan, Mantua, Bologna and the renowned San Vito in Ferrara under composer/organist Sister **Raffaella Aleotti** (*c* 1570–after 1646) featured sacred plays, instruments and choirs that attracted large audiences who brought in alms. In 1593, Aleotti's was the first collection of polyphonic motets by a woman. These concerts were curtailed when further edicts forbade outsiders to enter convent grounds. Her younger sister, **Vittoria Aleotti** (*c* 1573–after 1620), who entered San Vito at fourteen, was known for her *Madrigals*, published in 1593. Their father was Ferrara court architect Giovanni Battista Aleotti.

Women of Independent Means

In the secular world, following the example of **Eleanor of Aquitaine**, noblewomen patronized the arts. Two of the greatest renaissance patrons were the sisters **Beatrice** (1475–97) and **Isabella d'Este** (1474–1539) from the court of Ferrara. Music, poetry, dance and all forms of entertainment flourished under their aegis. Both were composers and instrumentalists who understood polyphony and participated actively in the music they sponsored. Married at fourteen, Beatrice brought her culture to the court of her husband, the Duke of Milan. Despite her death in childbirth at twenty-two, she is remembered as a major patron. Her sister, Isabella, married the Duke of Mantua and lived to be sixty-five. A skilled performer and critic, she was able to hire the finest musicians. In her forty-nine years as Marchesa over the city and territory of Mantua, Isabella used her authority to raise musical tastes in her considerable sphere of influence.

At the same time, **Lucrezia Borgia** (1480–1519), illegitimate daughter of the Spanish Cardinal Rodrigo Borgia who became Pope Alexander VI (1492–1503), was being used as a pawn through three marriages, the last to Alfonso d'Este. Her court, musicians, clothes and jewels were in constant rivalry with Isabella's. Contrary to the evil picture painted of her by biographers, Lucrezia was also a great patron of music who in later years retired to a Franciscan convent.

Royal ladies throughout Europe followed the Italian example. Some, like **Anne Boleyn** and her daughter **Queen Elizabeth I**, and **Lucrezia Tuonabuoni**, wife of Pietro de' Medici, also composed music. Upon their marriages, noblewomen infused their musical and cultural heritage into the courts of their husbands. **Eleanor** of **Aragon** brought the fifteenth century *Mellon Chansonnier* (songbook) when she wed Matthias Corvinius, King of Hungary, in 1476. **Margaret** of **Austria** transported a chanson album from the ducal library of Savoy to the Netherlands in 1507. She was also a composer, poet and an instrumentalist, as were **Marie** of **Burgundy** and **Anne** of **Brittany**.

Margaret Stuart (1424–45), eldest daughter of James I of Scotland, himself a good poet, was sent to France to marry the young dauphin, Louis, at Tours in 1436. Her failure to bear an heir was blamed on two causes: The negative philosophy that has dogged women throughout recorded history, namely that the creative process has pathological consequences for women, particularly insanity; and tight lacing, eating sour apples and drinking vinegar. The latter conditions were part of an interesting means of self-preservation practiced by medieval women who could, by their eating habits, exert some measure of control over fathers or husbands, even to the point of avoiding unwanted marriages or preventing pregnancy. When Margaret died at twenty-one, the doctors pronounced the cause as pneumonia brought on by her writing. Or, as Erasmus of Rotterdam put it in his treatise, *The Abbott and the Learned Woman*, "books destroy women's brains."

Women of Dependent Means

As the renaissance progressed, besides the need for secular entertainment, courts had chapels which necessitated choirs, organists, orchestras and the composition of sacred music. Women's voices became prized. The taboo against their playing instruments disintegrated. Courts vied with each other to hire the finest performers. Very well paid, and with fringe benefits such as being set up in sumptuous living quarters, these talented women were composers, too.

TARQUINIA MOLZA (1542–1617). Duke Alfonso II of Ferrara was the first to establish a *concerto delle donne* (ensemble of women) in 1580. His "star" was Tarquinia Molza, an accomplished singer and instrumentalist who composed for voice, lute, viol and harp. She directed an all-women court orchestra and formed a trio with talented singers **Laura Perperara** and **Lucrezia Bendidi**. Molza's brilliant career ended in 1589 when the Duchess Margherita discovered her love affair with composer Jacques de Wert. She retired in disgrace to her mother's estate. Meanwhile, other women were making a names for themselves.

MADDALENA CASULANA, born *c* 1544 near Siena (Italy), may have been the first woman to consider herself a professional composer. She was definitely the first to have her music printed when she published her three books containing some sixty-six madrigals. Some of her four-voice compositions also appeared in anthologies with masters like **Orlando di Lasso** (1532–94). It was the latter who, as music director of the court of Bavaria, arranged a performance of one of her operas for the wedding of Duke William.

Independent of any particular court, Casulana would dedicate her works to prominent persons to secure patrons. One such was wealthy Venetian merchant and amateur performer Antonio Molino who, at age seventy, took theory lessons from her and wrote madrigals dedicated to her. Another patron was Isabella de Medici, with whom Maddalena shared early feminist views in a letter mentioning "the vain error of men . . . who cannot conceive that a woman could equal them in intellect or ability."

Casulana is documented performing as a singer and teacher in upper class houses in Venice in the 1560s. After 1570, she added Mezari to her name and it is assumed that she married. There is a ten year hiatus in her career. She was heard from again in 1583. Her last madrigal appeared in 1586. Her music, with its use of dissonances, is considered masterful and modern for the time. She died *c* 1590 in Vicenza.

Another respected woman composer of the time was **Caterina Willaert**, who wrote operas and may have been the niece of Flemish composer Adrian Willaert (1490–1562).

Francesca Caccini

FRANCESCA CACCINI, born September 18, 1587, in Florence, was the eldest daughter of singer Lucia Caccini and Giulio Caccini (1546–1618), a member of the *Camerata*[4] and composer of the "new music" marking the beginning of the baroque era. Francesca had a professional head start by virtue of her father's connection with the Medici Court. She also belonged to a unique musical family. Giulio, his first wife Lucia, his second Margherita, daughters Francesca and Settimia, also a composer, and son Pompeo entertained at various courts. Between travels, Francesca received a superior literary and musical education and became a virtuoso singer, lutenist and harpsichordist—all vital requirements for feminine recognition. Records show that she sang at the wedding of Henry IV of France to Maria de Medici (1600). In 1607, Caccini married Giovanni Battista Signorini, also employed by the Medicis. They had one daughter, Margherita, born 1622, who in her teens began to perform with her mother. The same year, Francesca officially entered court service, becoming the highest paid composer at the Court of Tuscany under three Grand Dukes, Ferdinando I, Cosimo II and Ferdinando II. In 1615, Francesca played the role of the gypsy in her own *Ballo delle zingare*. 1616 saw her traveling from Florence to Rome with Cardinal Medici and his entourage. Her virtuosity was praised everywhere she appeared. **Claudio Monteverdi** (1567–1643), the most prominent Italian composer of the time, considered her "a marvel," both as an instrumentalist and singer. She was also valued as a composer. From 1618–23, she taught singers at the music school she founded. During this time she set to music *La Fiera*, a play by Michelangelo Buonarroti the Younger, grandnephew of the sculptor/artist, whose plot shocked the court because it portrayed women in pregnancy and labor.

---

4. The *Camerata*—literally an informal gathering in a chamber, from the Latin root for vaulted roof or arch—consisted of a group of Florentine poets and musicians who met from 1580 on, and from whose discussions *dramma per musica* or *opera* developed.

For over twenty years she composed and performed secular songs, madrigals, canzonettas and dramatic entertainment. In 1624, Caccini sang for Pope Urban VIII. Her *La Liberazione di Ruggiero*, produced in Florence in 1625 for the visit of Prince Wladislaw Sigismund of Poland, is believed to be the first Italian opera written by a woman. An allegory contrasting the power of virtuous women versus temptresses, it was also the first opera based on Ariosto's *Orlando Furioso*, and was the first Italian opera seen outside Italy when it was performed in Warsaw in 1682.

Signorini died in 1626. Francesca left the Medicis the following year to marry the wealthy Tomaso Raffaelli. This marriage gave her considerable social standing. She was widowed again three years later, now the mother of a son, Tomaso, born in 1628. Her husband's will made her executrix of a large estate and gave her shares in a silk exporting business. Quarantined in Lucca for three years because of the plague, her name once again appears on the Medici Court payroll, 1633–37. Since she did not need the money, it must be assumed that she enjoyed using her talents. Sadly, her life ended with cancer of the mouth. She died in Florence between 1640 and 1645.

Francesca Caccini insured the preservation of her work by publishing, in 1618, *Il primo libro delle musiche*, one of the largest and most well organized collections of early monophonic music, both secular and sacred. There is much evidence of the universal respect she commanded as a performer, teacher and composer.

Open-Ended Eras

Eras do not end on a specific date. The renaissance fulfilled its promise as an age of enlightenment, and is generally said to have ended in Italy in the 1580s, but actually continued into the 17th century in northern Europe where it had a later start. Both sexes benefitted by the trove of new knowledge and discovery, but for the majority of women it was through a filtered system—via the superior education of their fathers and husbands. Whatever their accomplishments, women were considered adjuncts to men—their *masters*. As usual, and as documented, there are always exceptions. In music history, several women composers also made their mark in the next period, the baroque.

CHAPTER TWO

The Baroque Period (1600–1750)

BAROQUE (1600–1750)

Barbara Strozzi (1619–c 1664)
Isabella Leonarda (1620–1704)
Elisabeth Claude Jacquet de la Guerre (c 1665–1729)
Antonia Bembo (c 1670–c 1725)
Nannette Streicher (1769–1833)

CLASSICAL (1750–1830)

Princess Anna Amalia (1723–87)
Duchess Anna Amalia (1739–1807)
Marianne von Martinez (1744–1812)
Corona Schröter (1751–1802)
Anna Maria Mozart (1751–1829)
Maria Theresia von Paradis (1759–1824)
Constanze Mozart (1762–1842)

The term *baroque* originally referred to a style in the visual arts characterized by the ornate architecture of Austria and Germany during the 17th and 18th centuries. It was later applied to the period of music history beginning about 1600 and lasting until the deaths of Bach and Handel in 1750. Although the emphasis was still on vocal music, especially *opera* and *oratorio*, instrumental accompaniment became more intricate and interesting. Glorious stringed instruments were being created in Cremona by Amati, Guarneri and Stradivari. Chamber works, keyboard music and instrumental forms like the *concerto* were coming into their own. Several women left their mark on the evolving style of music during this period.

Barbara Strozzi

BARBARA STROZZI was born in Venice in 1619, the daughter of poet/librettist/dramatist Giulio Strozzi (1583–1652) and his long-time housekeeper Isabella Garzoni. Brought up in a rarefied musical atmosphere, from 1629–36 the girl studied with the leading composer of Venice, Francesco Cavalli (1602–76), a pupil of Monteverdi. In 1635, her father founded the *Academia degli Unisoni* as a showplace for his daughter's outstandingly lovely voice. Her public career consisted of publishing her own compositions beginning in 1644 with her first volume of madrigals for two to five voices, based on texts written by her father. 1651 saw the publication of several cantatas, ariettas and duets. After the death of her father, who left little money, Strozzi's works were dedicated to members of the nobility in efforts, not always successful, to secure patronage. Among the names appearing on her manuscripts were Ferdinand II of Austria, Eleanora of Mantua, Anne of Austria, Vittoria della Rovere, Grand Duchess of Tuscany and the Doge of Venice.

While enjoying all the benefits of belonging to a musical family, Strozzi was never exposed to the public other than in her father's academy whose audience was comprised of leading men of arts and letters. She received a lifetime of recognition for the eight volumes of music published between 1644 and 1664, which made her one of the most prolific composers of secular vocal chamber music of the early baroque. She died in Venice c 1664.

The Nuns Will Not Be Silenced!

Despite the injunctions of the Council of Trent, over half of women's music came from convents. Nuns wrote masses and other parts of the liturgy: motets, psalms, etc., some with violin and organ accompaniment. The 17th century was also marked as an era of "living female saints," nuns living in a chain of convents in Spain, France and Italy. Through them the deification of the Virgin Mary and Mary Magdalene, and the concept of *intercession*—praying to the Virgin to intercede with God on one's behalf—came into being. The music created by these women mirrored the rapturous meditational states attained by these mystics.

The most prolific, devout, cloistered composer was Isabella Leonarda with over two hundred works in twenty volumes to her credit.

ISABELLA LEONARDA was born in Novara, Italy, September 6, 1620, into a family of high church and government officials. Her father was Count Gianantonio Leonardi, a doctor of law. She entered the Convent of St. Ursula of Novara at sixteen and remained there for the rest of her life. From 1635–41, she studied with Gaspare Casati (1610–41) the chapel master. Her first compositions were two motets for two voices which appeared in Casati's Third Book of Sacred Motets in 1642. Leonarda's most prolific period was 1665–1700. All her vocal music contains parts for tenor and bass. She became Mother Superior of the convent in 1686 and *Madre vicaria* in 1693, the year she published a set of trio sonatas at age seventy-three. Finally, she was made *consigliera* (counselor). In 1696, her harmonically advanced Sonata for Solo Violin and *continuo* (accompaniment) established her as the first Italian woman to compose in the new baroque instrumental styles.

Leonarda was the exception to the means of women attaining musical recognition in that she did not perform. Like Hildegard of Bingen, Isabella's works, mostly sacred vocal music, including masses, were dedicated to the Virgin Mary. She died February 25, 1704, in Novara.

Those Remarkable Venetian Orphanages

Set up to care for orphaned or abandoned girls were four institutions which provided an excellent education for those who showed musical talent. As such, these establishments could be called the first conservatories. They even gave their graduates a third option of *teaching*, versus marriage, or the convent. By the early 17th century each *ospedale* had its own girl choir and orchestra. Their performances were heard by visitors from all over Europe. The main teacher at the *Ospedale della Pietà* was *il prete rosso* (the red-haired priest) **Antonio Vivaldi** (1678–1741), one of Italy's greatest composers. It was he who defined the concerto form with his fantastic output of 500 concerti, 230 of them for violin, including the famous set, *The Four Seasons*. He also wrote sacred music and operas.

These conservatories lasted until the invasion of Napoleon's armies in 1806, which wreaked havoc all over Europe. They served the purpose of creating a repertoire of choral music written especially for their choirs, as well as an acceptance that was to become a demand for women's voices.

From Italy to France

During the baroque era, with the exception of wealthy middle class merchants in German cities like Leipzig, Frankfurt and Hamburg, the courts of Europe still dictated the social culture. Foremost was the court of the "Sun King," Louis XIV of France. His extravagant palace at Versailles outside Paris was being imitated all over Europe, architecturally and socially. Dance and ballet, already popular with Louis XIII, developed forms like the *minuet, gigue, gaillard, courant,* etc., and were polished by an Italian turned Frenchman, Jean-Baptiste Lully (1632–87), who became the king's composer and set the style of French music that was imitated for decades, even after his death.

French Women: Basking Under the Sun King

The most musically influential women in France were the wives and mistresses of the aristocracy, especially those of the Bourbon kings. They sang and played "feminine" instruments: harpsichord, harp, lute and later in the century, piano. All of them held *salons*—concerts—in their apartments, in palaces, or their stately homes. These included Anne of Austria, mother of Louis XIV, the king's mistresses Mesdames de Montespan and de Maintenon, his daughter-in-law, the Duchesse de Maine, and in her turn, Louis XV's mistress, Madame de Pompadour. Marie-Antoinette, wife of Louis XIV, herself musically proficient, organized private concerts and was patroness to the "father of the modern opera," **Christoph Willibald Gluck** (1714–87), and the Belgian master, **André Grétry** (1741–1813).

Daughters of noble families reveled in the status of taking lessons with famous composers like **François Couperin** (1668–1733), whose own daughter, Marguerite-Antoinette (1705–78), was accomplished enough to succeed her father. She was the first woman to become the royal chamber harpsichordist. His other daughter, Marie-Cécile (1690–1742), was a nun and organist at the royal abbey at Maubuisson.

Talented far above all these women, a child prodigy arrived on the scene around 1676.

Elisabeth de la Guerre

ELISABETH CLAUDE JACQUET de la GUERRE is recorded as being baptized March 17, 1665, in Paris. Like Caccini and Strozzi, she had the advantage of being the daughter of a famous musician, Claude Jacquet, an instrument-maker, organist and harpsichordist to the court of Louis XIV. Her talent soon manifested, and the king himself undertook her education under the supervision of his mistress Madame de Montespan. The 1677 *Mercure galant* referred to her as "the child wonder who sang the most difficult pieces at sight, and who could also accompany and compose little pieces in all keys." By 1678 the same French journal called her the Marvel of France.

When the French Court moved to the new palace at Versailles in 1683, Elisabeth remained in Paris and the following year married organist Marin de la Guerre. In 1704, after his death and that of her only son, also a musical prodigy, Jacquet de la Guerre filled her life with composing and giving harpsichord recitals in her home, which great musicians and other literati eagerly attended.

In 1685, she composed her first major work, a *pastorale*, which was performed at the French court. This was followed in 1687 by her first volume of harpsichord pieces, and a ballet in 1691. In 1694, her opera *Céphale et Procris* was performed in Paris. (This was successfully revived in 1989). In 1708, she published her first book of cantatas to great critical acclaim. She retired from public performance in 1717. Her *Te Deum* was sung in 1721 to celebrate the recovery from smallpox of eleven-year-old Prince Louis XV. Many of her manuscripts, written in her own hand, have survived. More of her music was published after the turn of the century, including a volume of harpsichord pieces, a set of solo violin sonatas and two books of cantatas on biblical themes unique in that three are about women: *Esther, Judith,* and *Susannah and the Elders.*

As a creative artist, Jacquet de la Guerre was fortunate to have belonged to a court over-flowing with culture: the music of Couperin, ballets of Lully, and dramas of Molière. The court recognized her genius as well and was able to showcase her artistry in the new tradition of the *salon*.

When Elisabeth died at the age of sixty-three in 1729, the king struck a commemorative medal in her honor and Evrard Titon du Tillet wrote: "One can say that never had a person of her sex had such talents as she for the composition of music, and for the admirable manner in which she performed it at the harpsichord and on the organ."

The Mystery Woman

As public as was Jacquet de la Guerre's career, so private was that of a Venetian woman who came to Paris under shrouded circumstances, made the city her home and contributed a treasury of compositions which are preserved to this day in the Paris National Library.

ANTONIA BEMBO, born *c* 1670 in Venice, was the only child of Dr. Giacomo Padovani and Diana Daresco Meglini. She studied with Francesco Cavalli in 1654. A marriage to nobleman Lorenzo Bembo, in 1659, produced Andrea, Giacomo and Diana, after which begins the mystery. Around 1676 Antonia left Venice for Paris with "someone." Having sung for Louis XIV many years before, she arrived at the court in distress—abandoned. The king took her under his protection, gave her a pension and installed her in a convent, although she never became a nun. Her compositions date from 1697 to 1707 and are dedicated to the royal family. They include sacred and secular vocal works, a collection of forty-one chamber pieces with Italian, French and Latin texts, and an opera. Most of the arias and cantatas are for very high soprano and *continuo*. Her style progressed from the Italian to the French influence of her adopted country. Her last known work is a musical setting of seven psalms from the French translation of artist/musician Elisabeth-Sophie Chéron (1648–1711). Fragments of Bembo's biography have been gleaned from prefaces and dedications in her six volumes of manuscripts. Documents discovered in Venice, in 1992, corroborate their autobiographical authenticity.

She lived to see the establishment of the *Concert spirituel* in 1725, which offered the opportunity to hear contemporary music and virtuosos of all nationalities. Until the Revolution (1789), the rich concert life of Paris was mainly enjoyed by the social elite. After 1790 entertainment of the masses began to develop.

Money is the Route of Opportunity

In the main, like their public or private performances, women's attempts at composition were mostly undertaken before the bonds of marriage and motherhood enfolded them. Royalty had wet-nurses and servants to ease the mother's lot, and it is in those ranks we find two notable composers as we enter the Classical Period. But first, mention should be made of a unique woman in a singular profession.

The Soft-Loud Revolutionizes the Musical Scene

The piano made its appearance in 1709, invented by harpsichord maker Bartolomeo Cristofori (1655–1731), music curator for the Medici family. He called it a *gravicembalo col piano e forte*—"a keyboard instrument with soft and loud." Beginning in 1725, German builders took over. One of the most important improvements came from **Johann Andreas Stein** (1728–92) who invented an *escapement*—making the hammer action capable of playing repetitive notes. This was the foundation of the "Viennese" piano praised by Mozart. Stein's son Matthaus (1776–1842) and daughter Nannette (1769–1833) were in the business with him.

A Woman Builds Pianos!

In 1794, two years after her father's death, **Nannette Stein** married pianist Johann Andreas (coincidence!) **Streicher** who went into the business when she and her brother moved it to Vienna. In 1802, Matthaus left the partnership to establish a rival company, André Stein, which was then carried on by *his* son, Carl Andreas (1797–1863) who was also a pianist and composer. Nannette's son, Johann Baptiste (1796–1871), took complete control after his parents' deaths which occurred within four months of each other. He invented the action of the hammer striking from above, and was also on friendly terms with Beethoven. In 1857, his son Emil (1836–1916) became a partner, but the business was dissolved on his retirement because Emil's son, Theodor (1874–1940), pursued a composing career which, however, enjoyed only a few early successes.

Pianos, Pianos, Everywhere!

By the middle 1800s there were piano factories all over Europe. Bechstein, Blüthner, and Steinweg—later translated into the English Steinway—from Germany, Bösendorfer in Austria, Érard and Pleyel in France, Broadwood in England—the latter building, in 1817, a six octave instrument able to do justice to Beethoven's forceful style. (All these manufacturers are still in business!) Interest in the harpsichord declined because the piano could be heard above the now larger orchestras. In the 1820s, John Hawkins of Philadelphia replaced the wooden frame with one of cast iron, permitting more tension and thicker strings, which gave the instrument a fuller, more brilliant sound.

The Piano Girl

Since the keyboard had always been considered a feminine instrument, there was a piano in almost every home of the burgeoning middle class, which put more publishers and composers to work churning out pieces for amateurs, while a succession of professional lady pianists literally set the stage of a new career for women. (See Pianists.)

THE CLASSICAL PERIOD (1750–1830)

The dates 1750–1830 are rough delineators marking an artistic period following the baroque era and preceding the Romantic. Not to be confused with the generic term *classical music*, the Classical *Period* loosened the strictures of baroque forms with expanded rhythm patterns, broader dynamics (loudness/softness) and richer harmonies and orchestration. Its "stars" were **Christoph Willibald Gluck** (1714–1787) who introduced opera to Germany; **Franz Joseph Haydn** (1732–1809) who became known as the "Father of the Symphony, Sonata and the String Quartet"; **Wolfgang Amadeus Mozart** (1756–91), the complete genius; and **Ludwig van Beethoven** (1770–1827) the master who bridged the musical style into the Romantic Golden Age.

In the women's sphere the importance of convents was declining. Socially, the courts began losing their influence as the French Revolution of 1789 snapped the first link in the chain of European monarchies. Toward the end of the era, public paid concerts would garner large audiences of the *nouveau riche* middle class. Several women reached prominence during this period—two of German royalty—only to become buried in the dust of centuries because their music did not get into the repertoire of male performing groups.

An Abused Child

In 18th century Germany, Lutheran girls learned to sing and play hymns mainly to become good Christian mothers. In the royal court of Prussia, the fourteen children of the militaristic King Frederick William I (1688–1740) had to sneak their artistic education. While he made his country the third ranking military power in Europe, he hated music and was a cruel father, sometimes dragging his daughters across a room by their hair. Fortunately, the palace was large enough for their mother, Queen Sophia Dorothea of Hannover (1666–1726), to secretly arrange music lessons. Not only did this provide an escape from the children's unhappiness, but three of them turned out to be quite talented: Princess Wilhelmina, who would marry the Margrave of Brandenburg; Frederick (1712–86) who became "the Great," and was not only a prolific writer, but a fine flutist and composer whose music is still heard today; and taught by her brother, Princess **ANNA AMALIA**, who became proficient in violin, flute and harpsichord.

An Affair to Forget

Born in Berlin, November 9, 1723, Anna Amalia's life changed when at seventeen her father died and her brother ascended the throne. Frederick immediately imported musicians, writers and philosophers, including **Voltaire** (1694–1778), intent on making his court, *Sans Souci*, as cultured and sumptuous as that of Louis XIV. A new world opened for the young princess. Unfortunately, she fell in love with someone beneath her station. Her brother slapped the young man into solitary confinement for ten years, and cloistered Anna Amalia in her own castle in Berlin with the title, Abbess of Quedlinburg.

A Late Start and a New Beginning

The princess concentrated on music for the rest of her life, beginning studies in theory, counterpoint and composition at age thirty-five. She had an organ built and took lessons with Johann Philip Kirnberger, a pupil of Bach. She wrote her main compositions past the age of forty in a style similar to that of her contemporary, Bach's third son, Carl Philipp Emanuel (1714–88). Besides being an important patron whose *soirees* included musicians from all over Germany, Anna Amalia collected old manuscripts. Her most important contribution to music was founding her library, the Amalien-Bibliothek. Housed in Berlin, it contains some 3,000 books and her priceless collection of six hundred volumes including manuscripts by **Palestrina**, **Bach**, **Handel**, **Telemann**, and **C.P.E. Bach**. The catalogue was continued by **Johann Friedrich Reichardt** (1752–1814), father of Louise, and **Carl Friedrich Zelter** (1758–1832) teacher of Fanny and Felix Mendelssohn, and collaborator with the latter in the revival of Bach's music. Anna Amalia died September 30, 1787, in Berlin.

ANNA AMALIA Duchess of Saxe-Weimar, was born October 24, 1739, near Weimar, to Karl I of Brunswick and the Duchess Philippine Charlotte, sister of Frederick the Great and Princess Anna Amalia. The child was named after her aunt, and received a thorough musical education during her childhood. Married at seventeen to the eighteen-year-old Duke Ernst August Konstantin of Saxe-Weimar, by nineteen she was a widow with two infant sons. For seventeen years (1758–75), until her eldest son Karl August took over, Anna Amalia ruled the Duchy as Regent. She and her children studied composition.

The Dramatist and the Duchess— Forging the Cultural Future of Germany

While her aunt was preserving the past, Duchess Anna Amalia looked to the future, patronizing young writers, poets, dramatists and musicians. With the twenty-four-year-old poet-dramatist-novelist-social scientist **Johann Wolfgang von Goethe** (1749–1832) as her cultural advisor and minister of state, Johann Ernst Bach, nephew of J.S. as chapelmaster, plus many musical productions, her court came to be called the *Müsenhof* (Court of the Muses). The culturally elite flocked to Weimar. In 1776, Anna Amalia composed her greatest success, the music to Goethe's libretto, *Erwin and Elmire*, which was performed in May of that year. She also wrote folk-like songs and *divertimenti* (light, recreational music).

Goethe arranged for the Duchess to tour Italy during 1788–90, where she acquired some 2,000 books which repose in the beautiful library that bears her name in Weimar.[5] With Goethe, a man considered the personification of German literature, by her side, Anna Amalia truly influenced Germany's entry into the Romantic era. She died in Weimar, April 10, 1807.

Marianne Martínez

MARIANNE von MARTÍNEZ, born May 4, 1744, in Vienna, was descended from a minor noble Spanish family. Her father had been sent to Vienna as assistant to the papal *nuncio*, which gave him a privileged position in aristocratic circles. The apartment building on the Michaelplatz housed an assortment of tenants, which in reverse to the penthouse concept, but in keeping with the climbing stair principle, dictated that people were poorer the higher up they lived. The Dowager Princess Esterhazy was on the first floor. The Martínez family shared the third floor with the imperial court poet and opera librettist **Pietro Metastasio** (1698–1782). (His seventy-two libretti were set to music over eight hundred times by composers of the 18th and 19th centuries.) In the attic rooms, rented to poorest tenants, was a young man dismissed from the security of the Vienna Boys' Choir in 1750 when puberty claimed his clear, boy soprano voice. His name was **Franz Joseph Haydn**.

---

5. A September 2004 fire, caused by faulty wiring, destroyed and/or damaged some 30,000 irreplaceable volumes.

As a child, Marianne appeared as a singer and pianist at court, and performed in the salons of the aristocracy. Metastasio recognized the child's talent, and by the time she was ten arranged for her to study with the great Italian singing teacher and composer **Nicola Porpora** (1686–1768). She took harpsichord lessons with Haydn. She also studied composition, and counterpoint, and by the 1760s was writing large church works, symphonic masses, oratorios—two with libretti by Metastasio—cantatas, motets and choral litanies.

When Emperor Joseph II ascended the throne, he brought back the old rule against women singing in church, after which Martínez wrote no more masses. She composed much piano music. **Mozart** wrote his Piano Concerto in D major for her. Her fame spread to Italy where she was admitted to the Accademia Filarmonica of Bologna in 1773, having written a *Miserere* and a psalm as her entrance qualifications. She was the first woman granted admission.

Marianne and her sister Antonia looked after the aging Metastasio. When he died in 1782, he left his large estate to the two sisters. This freed them from the need to marry. Their new home became a center for musical soirées. Haydn and Mozart were frequent guests. In 1796, Marianne opened a singing school in the house, which produced many fine female singers. Both Martínez' and Haydn's last public appearance was to hear Salieri conduct Haydn's oratorio *The Creation*, on March 27, 1808. (The seventy-six-year-old Haydn was carried in a chair). Marianne died within two days of Antonia, on December 13, 1812.

One of the few women to write for full orchestra, Martínez produced the largest body of music by a woman during the Classical Period. Her compositions and the well-trained singers of her school greatly contributed to Vienna's own golden age. Meanwhile, back in Weimar . . .

Corona Schröter

Born January 14, 1751, in Guben, Germany, multi-talented **CORONA SCHRÖTER** was given her first music lessons by her father, oboist Johann Friedrich Schröter. Around 1763, the family moved to Leipzig where she studied with **Johann Adam Hiller** (1728–1804), originator of the *singspiel* (sing play). She appeared in his Grand Concerts and became a favorite prodigy. After a successful tour of Europe, in 1776 **Goethe**, who had met her earlier, procured for her the position of chamber musician at the Weimar court of the Duchess Anna Amalia. Schröter also began making a name for herself as an actress, playing the lead in many of Goethe's dramas. She composed the music for his *singspiel Die Fischerin*, including a folklike setting for his poem *Der Erlkönig*, which would be immortalized later by Schubert's more dramatic accompaniment. After leaving the court in 1788, the court theater having been replaced by a professional company in 1783, Schröter sang in private salons. She also taught singing and concentrated on her other talents of poetry, drawing and painting. During these years she developed a warm friendship with Germany's other renowned poet, writer, dramatist, philosopher and historian, **Friedrich von Schiller** (1759–1805), setting some of his poetry to music. These have been lost, but two collections of *lieder* were published in 1786 and 1794 respectively. In 1801, Corona went to Ilmenau with her lifelong companion Wilhelmine Probst, hoping to alleviate a respiratory disease, but she died the following year, August 23, 1802.

While Schröter gained renown in Weimar, a child prodigy was making her mark in Vienna.

MARIA ANNA (Nannerl) MOZART was born July 31, 1751, in Salzburg to Leopold and Anna Mozart. Her mother, Anna Pertl, was the granddaughter of a court musician on *her* mother's side. With five years head start on her brother Wolfgang, "Nannerl" established her own talent and received her father Leopold's attention with music lessons and encouragement. An excellent pianist and skilled improvisor, for a while she shared the limelight with the boy genius, touring in Western Europe and Vienna. By 1769, however, she was considered too old to be exhibited as a prodigy and was relegated to stay home, to be comforted by her mother. In 1784, she married Johann Baptist von Berchtold zu Sonnenburg. Of their three children only the eldest son survived childhood. Her husband, fifteen years her senior, died in 1801, after which she did some teaching and could have developed her gifts as a composer had the times permitted.[6] In 1770, she sent one of her songs to her brother who, it is documented, exclaimed that he had forgotten how well she composed! Her mother died in Paris, July 4, 1778, on a concert trip with Wolfgang. She was fifty-seven. Unfortunately for posterity, none of Nannerl's compositions survive and she too, would be forgotten but for her illustrious name. She died in Salzburg October 29, 1829.

Dark Victory

Daughter of the Imperial Secretary to the court of Maria Theresa, **MARIA THERESIA von PARADIS** was thought to have been the Empress' goddaughter. Born May 15, 1759, on December 9, 1762, the three-year-old suddenly became blind. Even the efforts of Dr. Anton Mesmer (1734–1850), the physician who discovered the power of hypnosis (*mesmerism*), could not help the child. Already showing great musical talent, the Empress herself undertook the guidance of Maria Theresia's musical education. Her teachers included **Antonio Salieri** (1750–1825), who composed his only organ concerto for her. (Contrary to Hollywood, he did *not* murder Mozart.) In 1770, the prodigy accompanied herself on the organ while singing the soprano part of **Pergolesi's** *Stabat Mater*. The Empress reigned from 1740 until her death in 1775 when she was succeeded by her son, Joseph II, who cancelled von Paradis' pension. It was restored by his successor, Leopold II. In the course of singing and playing the piano in salons and concert halls, the blind pianist met **Mozart** in 1775. Ten years later he wrote his *Piano Concerto No. 18 in B flat* (K456) for her.

The Grand Tour

The years 1783–1808 were spent in extensive touring throughout Europe with her mother and librettist Johann Riedinger, who devised a wooden pegboard using different shapes for note values which enabled the blind woman to compose. Fantastically, she memorized over sixty piano concertos and was heard in such cities as London, Paris, Switzerland, Berlin, Brussels, Amsterdam, Prague, and Hamburg, where she met **C.P.E. Bach**, and her home base, Vienna. In London, in 1784, she played for George III and accompanied the Prince of Wales on the cello. In Paris she performed fourteen concerts, including a series at the *Concerts Spirituels*, which lasted from 1725–90 and became the center of concert life in the capital. Maria Theresia also assisted Valentin Haüy in establishing the first school for the blind. She was in Prague in 1797 for the premiere of her opera *Rinaldo und Alcina*, yet another version of *Orlando Furioso*, the subject of Francesca Caccini's opera 200 years earlier. In 1808, after the death of her father, von Paradis founded and headed the Institute for Music Education in Vienna, specializing in singing and piano for both sighted and blind girls.

A Great Contribution and Another Mystery

Paradis' lifetime spanned those of Mozart, Salieri, Haydn, Beethoven and Schubert. Her works included cantatas, songs, piano pieces, two operas, an operetta, a melodrama, two piano concerti, a piano trio, sixteen piano sonatas and two piano fantasies. Much of this music has been lost. Remaining are a sonata for piano and violin, a piano toccata, various vocal compositions and a *Sicilienne* attributed to her, but more likely by violinist Samuel Dushkin (1891–1976). Highly valued and respected as a singer, pianist, composer, teacher, and for her work with the blind, Paradis died February 1, 1824 in Vienna and, like Mozart, was buried in St. Mark's Cemetery in an unknown gravesite.

---

6. While the 18th century was known as the Age of Enlightenment, women were branded as inferior and considered "a mere appendage to the human race." Protestants were worse than Catholics. They threw out all images of Madonna and Child, not wanting to depict the Son of God under the power of a woman!

The Classical Period gave way to the Romantic Period, a time of greater freedom for emotion and feeling to find their way into all the arts, but not necessarily a time of greater freedom for women. At a snails' pace, and with a few stalwart souls of superior talent pioneering the way, better educational opportunities grudgingly opened to the "weaker sex," permitting more outlets for creativity.

It may be appropriate to note one of these "pioneers" was no less than the widow of Wolfgang Amadeus Mozart (1756–91). Having suffered poverty and imminent bankruptcy for most of her married life, **Constanze Mozart** (1762–1842) showed considerable enterprise in arranging concerts of her late husband's work. She was finally able to get money out of publishers by selling his manuscripts—during his lifetime, his music was the property of the emperor—and she helped write the first proper biography of the genius. This laid the foundation of worldwide appreciation and ultimate universal success of his music, both of which had eluded him throughout his brief life.

CHAPTER THREE
The Romantic Period (1830–1920)

Louise Benda Reichardt (1779–1826)
Emilie Zumsteeg (1796–1857)
Anette von Droste-Hülshoff (1797–1848)
Maria Szymanowska (1789–1831)
Louise Dumont Farrenc (1804–75)
Fanny Mendelssohn Hensel (1805–47)
Johanna Kinkel (1810–58)
Alma Mahler (1879–1964)

Josephine Lang (1815–80)
Clara Wieck Schumann (1819–96)
Pauline Garcia-Viardot (1821–1910)
Augusta Holmès (1847–1903)
Agathe Backer-Grøndahl (1847–1907)
Adolpha Luise LeBeau (1850–1927)
Cécile Chaminade (1857–1944)

Breaking the Ties That Bind

The Romantic Period, its dates open-ended, is named after medieval *romances*—stories and poetry idolizing heroic figures, written in the language of the country rather than scholarly Latin. The beginning of the era traces its roots to the French Revolution (1789) when the lower classes actually managed to overthrow the Bourbon monarchy. Using 1920 to mark the end of the Romantic Period is generally accepted because the next "revolution," World War I (1914–18), forever changed the map and make-up of Europe. While the baroque and classical eras were objective and followed structured form, *romanticism* meant personal expression not only in music, but painting, sculpture, architecture and all the arts. Rather than *sonata* or *symphony*, composers often gave works, such as *suites* or *tone poems*, specific titles to convey their emotions. Music and art now told stories.

Expanding Musical Horizons

Railroads and steamships eased travel and touring for composers and artists to such far-flung places as America, Australia and Africa. Tchaikovsky was heard in Carnegie Hall. Jenny Lind wowed gold diggers in California. **Conservatories** were now established in most of the major cities of Europe: Paris (1795), Milan (1807), Prague (1811), Brussels (1813), Vienna (1817), Berlin (1822), London (1823), Leipzig (1843, founded by **Felix Mendelssohn**), Munich (1846), Cologne (1850), Dresden (1856), Bern (1857), St. Petersburg (1865), Moscow (1866), Naples (1872) and Frankfurt (1878). The arts having been put "in limbo" during the Civil War, America, especially in Boston and New York, was doing its best to shed the mantle of being considered an artistic backwater. The first American conservatory was at Oberlin (Ohio, 1865), followed by the New England, Boston, Cincinnati—all in 1867—and Peabody (Baltimore, 1868). Several New York schools failed until the 1885 founding, by Jeannette Thurber, of the National Conservatory of Music in America with backers such as Andrew Carnegie and Theodore Thomas. **Antonín Dvořák** was its director, 1892–95.

A Woman's Place is . . .

For women, the biggest impact of the era was the rise of the middle class. No self-respecting home was without a piano, and amateur lady musicians blossomed profusely on family trees. Composers were in demand and publishing houses poured "schmaltzy" music out for Clara Schumann emulators. On the professional scene, paying audiences flocked to theaters, opera houses and concert halls. Actresses, prima donnas, ballerinas and the few women who made it to the top as instrumental virtuosi—mainly pianists—were pampered and idolized.

Mostly, however, women were still kept in "their place" by fathers and husbands, laboring at home and in child-birth. Public display, let alone the publishing of any music they might have written, was considered bad taste by an upper middle class which had replaced the aristocracy in dictating the mores of society. Women in a position to seek an education found many doors closed. Although it was in conservatory charters to admit girls, there were few joint classes. The sexes were segregated or taught on separate days. It was assumed that females were studying to become teachers or performers. Not until the 1870s were women given the opportunity to study composition, orchestration or even violin. Inevitably, as had happened before, a nucleus of women rose above these strictures and achieved renown as close to equal status as the social consciousness of the times, and their own self-image, permitted.

An Early Freelancer

Born April 11, 1779, in Berlin, to composer Friedrich Reichardt (1752–1814), chapel master to the court of Frederick the Great, and **Juliane Benda** (Reichardt) (1752–83), singer, pianist and composer, **LOUISE REICHARDT** was motherless by age four and educated by her father. Among the notable figures who frequented their home were the Grimm brothers of fairy tale fame. In 1800, four of Louise's songs appeared in one of her father's anthologies.

Ghost Conductor

In 1809, she moved to Hamburg, supporting herself by teaching and composing. In 1817, she organized and conducted women's choruses for concerts in Lübeck and Hamburg. For a woman to conduct large mixed choruses in public was unheard of, so although she prepared and rehearsed the singers for the Hamburg Music Festival where Handel's *Messiah* and the Mozart *Requiem* were given before audiences numbering 6,000, it was a male director who got the glory.

Reichardt typified the Romantic spirit in that, without the benefit of a performing career, she struck out on her own and was not dependent upon patrons or royalty. Between 1819–20, she established a singers' studio, teaching and conducting, translating Latin texts into German and championing Handel's oratorios. She also supported herself by writing *lieder* (songs) in the style of Schubert. Hers, however, have simpler, folkstyle accompaniments in keeping with the Romantic tradition of communion with nature, religious overtones and sentimentality.

Reichardt is credited with composing over ninety songs and choruses, both sacred and secular, which appeared in many anthologies and were popular throughout the 19th century.

Jinxed in Love

In her personal life, Louise was engaged to the poet Friedrich Eschen who died suddenly before the wedding. A few years later this tragedy was repeated with her fiancé, painter Franz Gareis. From then on she devoted herself to her students, later turning to religion and writing two books of sacred songs. Although she never conducted in public, as a teacher, composer and conductor, Reichardt had a profound influence on the musical life of Hamburg. She died there on November 17, 1826.

Other Song Composers

Since song writing did not require knowledge of orchestration, the *lieder* form was deemed appropriate for ladies to attempt, and several women composing in that genre appeared on the scene. Sixty songs are credited to **EMILIE ZUMSTEEG**, daughter of composer Johann Rudolf Zumsteeg who himself wrote about two hundred songs. Born December 9, 1796, in Stuttgart, the youngest of seven children, Emilie was only seven when her father died. Her mother opened a music shop where the child helped. Talented as an alto, she concertized, accompanying herself on the piano. She came in contact with the leading artists and *literati* of the day and occupied a prominent position in the musical life of Stuttgart. She died in that city August 1, 1857.

Born January 14, 1797, in Westphalia into a musical family, **ANNETTE von DROSTE-HÜLSHOFF** received the usual piano and singing lessons, but made her reputation as both a poet and composer. Her folk-like songs were set to her own poems as well as those of her contemporaries and friends, **Goethe**, **Brentano** and **Byron**. Although she considered her compositions her more important achievement, von Droste-Hülshoff is recognized as one of the leading German Romantic poets. She died in Meersburg, May 24, 1848.

The Forerunner of Frédéric Chopin

One of the innovators of the nocturne, etude and elegant style of salon music was a Polish woman who had the courage of her convictions when it came to preserving her career, even at the cost of her marriage.

On Her Own With the Famed at Her Feet

MARIA SZYMANOWSKA (née Wolowska) was born December 14, 1789, in Warsaw, during turbulent times in the history of her country. Napoleon was slicing up Poland for Russia, Prussia and Austria. (He created the Duchy of Warsaw to appease the natives.) Under these repressive circumstances, the middle-class Jewish Wolowskas became baptized Christians. Maria showed her musical talents early and was given the advantage of the best teachers, including Antoni Lisowski and Tomasz Gremm. She made her performing debut in Warsaw and Paris in 1810, the same year she married Josef Szymanowski, a wealthy landowner. They had three children, but because her husband refused to let her continue her professional career, she managed to make two revolutionary moves: she left his bed and board in 1820, and got away with taking the children. (The marriage was later dissolved.)

Szymanowska supported herself concertizing, teaching and composing. She toured Germany, France, Italy, England, Poland, Austria, Belgium, Holland and Russia. Her legendary beauty and brilliant playing (she may have been the first virtuosa pianist playing from memory) drew large audiences and commanded high ticket prices. One of Germany's (and Literature's) greatest romantic poets, novelists, playwrights and philosophers, **Johann Wolfgang von Goethe** (1749–1832) fell in love with her. She became the inspiration for several of his poems. Renowned composers **Johann Nepomuk Hummel** (1778–1837) and the Irish **John Field** (1782–1837), another forerunner of Chopin, wrote pieces for her. **Luigi Cherubini** (1762–1842), director of the Paris Conservatory, dedicated his *Fantasia in C major* to her. Most importantly, "The Poet of the Piano," young **Frédéric Chopin** (1810–49), heard her in concert and was profoundly influenced by her brilliant style and forms of concert etude, mazurka, and nocturne.

A Royal Post . . . A Haven . . . A Tragic Ending

Szymanowska returned to Russia, where in 1828 she was appointed court pianist to the Tsarina. Her *salon* became the center of cultural life in St. Petersburg, giving refuge to Polish emigrés and other patriots whose lives were in danger. Her musical autograph album is filled with short pieces of music by visitors like **Beethoven**, **Robert** and **Clara Schumann**, **Chopin**, **Liszt**, **Field**, **Rossini**, **Meyerbeer** and **Mozart's** son, **Franz Xavier**.

Her compositions number over a hundred, many of them virtuoso piano works: études, nocturnes, waltzes, all in the elegant salon genre. She was one of the first composers to use folk melodies and patriotic dances such as the polonaise and mazurka. Critics praised the fact that she represented the essence of Romanticism in her compositions and in her playing. **Robert Schumann** gave her his usual back-handed compliment, describing her études as having been "written by the feminine Field . . . [with] the most remarkable qualities *for a woman composer* . . . (author's italics).

Szymanowska's rich, full life was cut short when she fell victim to a cholera epidemic, July 25, 1831, in St. Petersburg.

Resurrected and Rediscovered

A successful triple career distinguishes the next composer, whose work has been rediscovered performed and recorded thanks to the efforts of contemporary women's musical organizations.

LOUISE DUMONT FARRENC, sister of sculptor laureate Auguste Dumont, was descended from a long line of royal artists, including several women painters. Born May 31, 1804, in Paris, she showed great talent in art and music at a very early age. By fifteen, she had developed into a pianist of professional caliber, and showed great promise in her composition studies with **Anton Reicha** (1770–1836) at the Paris Conservatory, who thirteen years later would have Pauline Garcia Viardot as his student.

Marriage, Motherhood and Heartbreak

In 1821 Dumont married Aristide Farrenc, an amateur musician and scholar. In 1825, while her husband was establishing his music publishing business, Louise, with interruptions for concert tours, finished her Conservatory studies and wrote her earliest piano pieces, two sets of variations. 1826 saw the birth of her only child, Victorine Louise, who would become her mother's best student, winning the first prize for piano in 1844 at the conservatory. Her death at the age of thirty-three, in 1859, cut short a great career and extinguished her mother's creative urge.

Praise and Precedents

Meanwhile, 1825–39 was a period of prolific composition during which Farrenc wrote most of her piano works. They were published by her husband as well as major companies in Bonn and London. **Schumann** extolled her compositions in his respected magazine, *Neue Zeitschrift für Musik*. **Hector Berlioz** (1803–69), who had written the definitive book on the subject, praised her orchestrations. Paris critic Maurice Bourges' 1840 article in *Revue et Gazette Musicale* lauded Farrenc's thirty etudes. Written in every major and minor key, these became required study for all piano students at the Paris Conservatory.

At the invitation of its director, composer **Daniel François Auber** (1782–1871), 1842 marked the beginning of a distinguished thirty-year teaching career at the conservatory—the only woman to hold such a post for so long. Between 1841–47, Farrenc wrote three symphonies which were performed in Paris, Brussels, Geneva and Copenhagen. Most of her chamber and piano music was written between 1844–1862. In 1861, she was the first person to win the *Prix Chartier de L'Institut de France* for her chamber music. She won it again in 1869. Subsequent winners were **César Franck** (1822–90), **Édouard Lalo** (1823–92) and **Gabriel Fauré** (1845–1924).

The Final Chapter of Success

In 1861, Farrenc joined her husband in his lifelong research which culminated in a twenty-three volume anthology of harpsichord and piano music, *Le trésor des pianistes* (The Pianists' Treasury), encompassing 300 years of repertoire. In the years from 1865, after the death of Aristide, to 1874, a year before her own passing on September 15, 1875, she completed this monumental work. (*The Introduction on Baroque Ornamentation* was published separately in 1895). This established Louise Dumont Farrenc as a significant scholar, adding to her importance as a composer, teacher and performer.

Rooted in Classical traditions, her harmonies followed major Romantic forms rather than the popular light salon style. Her *Nonetto* (Op 38, 1849) was performed so frequently that the publicity prompted the conservatory to raise the composer's salary to the level of the male professors(!) Living during the full bloom of French

Romantic music, with **Franck**, **Bizet**, **Saint-Saëns**, **Chaminade**, **Dukas**, and **Fauré** as her contemporaries, Louise Dumont Farrenc enjoyed the success and esteem for which women composer-musicologists are still striving a century later.

Another Case of a Brother's Shadow

Moses Mendelssohn (1729–86) was a revered philosopher known as the "German Socrates." His most important contribution was translating from the Hebrew the first five books of the Old Testament, the Psalms and other sections of the Bible into German. His least important contribution was his attitude toward women. His granddaughter was no doubt aware that he had told *his* fiancée (in 1762), "a girl who has read her eyes red, deserves to be laughed at." His opinions were transmitted to his son Abraham, who told his daughter Fanny, "for you it [music] will always be an ornament; [it] can never . . . become the foundation of your existence." **Felix Mendelssohn** (1809–47), who had the greatest respect for his sister's compositions, even depending on her to critique his, was a victim of the same social brainwashing, as in this quote from a letter: "Fanny, as I know her, neither wishes to be a composer, nor has she the vocation for it—for that she is too much a woman." Being a *woman* meant being a wife and mother. That was the goal. Those were the limits, and Fanny for the most part lived dutifully within them. But two of the most important other people in her life, her mother and her husband, supported and encouraged her creative talent, and would not let it wither away.

A Most Unusual Inheritance

Fanny Mendelssohn

Born November 14, 1805, in Hamburg, **FANNY MENDELSSOHN HENSEL** inherited her musical talent through the unique women on her mother's side of the family. The most prominent was her great-aunt Sara Itzig Levy (1763–1854), a gifted harpsichordist and student of **Wilhelm Friedmann Bach** (1710–84), oldest son of J.S. She had performed at the Berlin *Singakademie* under its founder **Carl Friedrich Fasch** (1736–1800). After her marriage, she became a patron of Bach's third son, **Carl Philipp Emanuel** (1714–88), hosting soirées which championed the music of his illustrious family. Sara owned many valuable manuscripts which she left to **Carl Friedrich Zelter** (1758–1832), successor to Fasch at the Singakademie, and who later became the Mendelssohn children's teacher. Fanny's mother, Lea Salomon (1777–1842), received a practically unheard of education for a girl of her time: besides music, she could read French, English and Greek. Her piano teacher was **Johann Philipp Kirnberger** (1721–83), a pupil of the great Bach himself. It was Lea who saw to it that her oldest daughter received as good a musical education as her gifted first son Felix. Rebecca and Paul, the two younger siblings, apparently did not show any precocious musical aptitude.

A Thorough Education

While the family lived in Paris, the children studied with Marie Bigot, whose playing had been praised by **Haydn** and **Beethoven**. When they returned to Berlin their teacher was Ludwig Berger, who had studied with two other great composers, **Muzio Clementi** (1752–1832) and **John Field** (1782–1837). Composition and theory were with **Zelter**, who steeped Fanny and Felix in **Mozart** and **Beethoven**, one reason why their own compositions spanned from baroque and classical forms, cantatas, oratorios, chorales, preludes and fugues, to the styles of their own period, romantic *lieder*, songs without words—their own invention—and Felix's symphonies and concerti. They also studied languages and drawing.

Private Exposure

Although her father could not help but be proud of his daughter's accomplishments—at thirteen Fanny memorized all twenty-four Bach preludes from *The Well-Tempered Clavier* for his birthday—Abraham, a banker and practical man, consistently stressed that the girl's most important role was to be a housewife. When she was fifteen she met court artist Wilhelm Hensel, her husband-to-be, but Lea made sure that there would be no rushing into marriage. She wanted Fanny to have time to develop her obvious talents as a pianist and composer.

In 1816, the Mendelssohns converted to Christianity, adding the name Bartholdy, which Lea's brother had adopted at his conversion some years before. This was a political rather than religious step, since there has always been prejudice against Jews. The children never really acknowledged the added name or the faith, although both Fanny and Felix married Protestants.

In 1822, the family began a tradition of Sunday concerts in their home which throughout her life would expose Fanny to important men of culture such as **Goethe**, who wrote poems for her to set to music, the writer/poet **Heinrich Heine**, the scientist **Alexander von Humboldt**—she attended his lectures on physical geography—the philosopher **Georg Wilhelm Friedrich Hegel**, **Niccolò Paganini**, the incredible violinist Fanny described as looking like an "insane murderer," and many others. In later years, the soirées became larger and more elaborate with performances of chamber music and cantatas featuring choirs. Once **Franz Liszt** (1811–86) and eight princesses were in the audience.

These *Sontagsmusik* recitals were Fanny's stage, and when he was home, Felix's. She only performed once in public—to good reviews—playing her brother's G minor Concerto at a charity concert in 1838. Felix freely admitted that his sister's piano technique was superior to his, as were her songs. In fact, he gave up composing *lieder* and concentrated on larger symphonic works. Beyond spurring each other on, there was little rivalry between these two, rather a spiritual bond of musical consciousness. They critiqued each other's music and Fanny accepted her brother's, and father's, objections to her playing in public, or publishing her music. Yet her music *was* published—but under her brother's name. On one of his ten trips to England, Queen Victoria praised one of his songs as her favorite, and Felix was honest enough to admit it was Fanny's. This double standard ran strong for most of Fanny's life. Her diaries and letters do not, on the surface, show frustration with her lot, but it is obvious that Felix's approval was vital to her. Her voluminous correspondence with family and friends provides an important window to the times, being full of prominent names of historical significance.

Just a Housewife

In 1825, Abraham bought a mansion on Leipzigerstrasse with such a huge garden that each daughter, after her marriage, would have a house on either side within the grounds, strengthening the bonds of this close-knit family. Fanny married in 1829, and the following year had her only child, Felix Ludwig Sebastian, named after all her favorite composers. Despite the almost spiritual tie between brother and sister, neither attended each other's wedding. Fanny even had to compose her own wedding prelude the night before, because although she had asked him, Felix could not get inspired to do so. The marriage was supremely happy. After the birth of the baby, Felix actually expected her to stop composing, but fortunately Fanny had a husband who knew she needed her music to survive. Mendelssohn, who had his pick of adoring women, did not marry until 1837. His wife, Cécile, was the parallel of Wilhelm. Both had calm personalities and adored their spouses.

A long-delayed trip to Italy was finally made by the Hensels in 1839. This was something that Fanny had dreamed of since she was a child. The experience was a turning point for her. In Rome, among other famous musicians, she met the young French composer, **Charles Gounod** (1818–93). They had a great influence on each other. Gounod was unfamiliar with German music. Fanny played for him, by memory, hours of Bach, Beethoven, her brother's and some of her own pieces. He could not get enough. His *Ave Maria* "superimposed" on Bach's *C Major Prelude* was one result. The music Fanny wrote to Goethe's *Faust* may have been the inspiration for Gounod's most famous opera of the same name. The Frenchman's esteem and urging were major catalysts in finally, at age forty, slipping out of the yoke Felix and her father, who had died just after her birthday in 1835, had placed upon her.

At Last—Public Exposure!

With publishers vying for the honor, Fanny surprised her brother with a letter asking for his blessing to release some of her music. After a long silence he finally replied that he hoped she would not be sorry to expose herself to the public, and (reluctantly) approved. Two volumes of songs and piano works—*Lieder ohne Worte* (Songs Without Words)—a form she invented and for which Felix got the credit, hit the presses under the name Hensel. Favorable reviews included Robert Schumann's *Neue Zeitschrift für Musik* with the same backhanded compliment he had given Maria Szymanowska, "the composition(s) betray absolutely no trace of the female hand."

The Suddenness For Them All!

In the first few months of 1847 Fanny experienced several severe nosebleeds. On May 14, while she was conducting a rehearsal of her brother's secular cantata, *Walpurgisnacht*, she suddenly felt her hands go numb. Someone replaced her at the piano, and she went to a room offstage to soak her hands in warm vinegar. She called through the open door how lovely it sounded. These were her last words. She was found unconscious by her younger brother, Paul. Four hours later she was dead. (Both Lea and Abraham died within a few hours of feeling ill.) According to his doctor, when Felix heard the news he let out such a scream that a blood vessel burst in his head. From then on he was plagued with severe headaches. He composed one more quartet and a song, "Gone is the Light of Day," before he joined his beloved sister, November 4, of the same year. In his last letter to Fanny, he had said they would be together by her next birthday, November 14.

Rebecca took over the upbringing of Sebastian. Although Wilhelm lived fifteen more years, the light had gone out of *his* life. He painted no more. On November 24, 1861, he was fatally injured while saving a child from being run over.

Time to See the Light?

Had Fanny not come from wealth, she might have been forced into the public sphere. With more support and recognition, she might have attempted major works. Of her over 500 compositions: lieder, part songs, piano works, sonatas, string quartets, cantatas, an oratorio and an overture, only about 10 percent have been published. The rest lurk in libraries in Berlin, Washington and private collections. Perhaps these institutions will one day permit all of her work to see daylight so that the rest of the world may enjoy them. Several CDs featuring her works are now available. It is time to put this great composer in the forefront, where she belongs.

Credit for much of the information on Fanny Hensel comes from the diligently researched PhD dissertion of Reverend Dr. Victoria Sirota, with permission. (See Musicologists.)

The Time is Ripening

Germany was a central destination on the superhighway of Romanticism's Golden Age. German opera came into its own with **Carl Maria von Weber's** *Der Freischütz* in 1821, and by 1842 transcended all prior parameters with the mammoth productions and new, unheard-of, "unplayable," *avant-garde* music of **Richard Wagner** (1813–83). Reigning supreme in the realm of symphonic music was **Johannes Brahms** (1833–97), Clara Schumann's closest friend and admirer. This cultural climate with its nationalistic emphasis, the evolving opportunities for education, as well as the women who had already forged the way, were all conducive factors to producing more composers of the feminine gender.

Another Abused Wife

Daughter of Anna Maria Mockel and Joseph Mockel, a lecturer at the French lycée in Bonn, **JOHANNA KINKEL** came into the world July 8, 1810, in Beethoven's birthplace. She studied piano and composition with Franz Anton Ries, Beethoven's first teacher. Later, she wrote of him, "Besides holding Beethoven as a musical god and Rossini as the antichrist, Ries taught hopelessly old fashioned piano and composition lessons."

In 1829, she took over the direction of the musical group formed by Reis' students and friends. In 1830, she began composing lieder, duets and stage works for amateurs. Throughout her life she was to divide her time between composing, conducting, and writing poetry, political articles and art criticism. In 1831, she became acquainted with the Cologne book and music dealer, Paul Matthieux. They married, but were separated within six months, during which Johanna came close to a nervous breakdown. Her husband firmly believed that "tension and quarrelling strengthened the nerves" and that "a peaceful life is for weaklings." He was planning to make even stricter rules in the treatment of his wife, when the doctor told Johanna's parents that she might die if she returned to this man. It took two years before the divorce was settled in 1839.

By 1836 Johanna, realizing that she was not progressing in her field, decided to go to Berlin for more serious music study. Her parents, afraid for her reputation, were completely against this venture. This was to be Johanna's continual conflict, to have her talent crying for expression while the social mindset dictated that her destiny was to be a housewife and a mother. Even as a child, she had rebelled against the obligatory sewing lessons; she would much rather have learned music notation. Despite the opposition, Johanna set out on her journey, stopping in Frankfurt where she was introduced to **Felix Mendelssohn**, who became a permanent admirer of her work. In Berlin she studied composition with Karl Böhmer and piano with Wilhelm Taubert. In order to finance this she again resorted—reluctantly—to piano teaching. She gradually gained entrance into the upper class salons and made friends with important women like **Fanny Mendelssohn Hensel** and singer/composer **Bettina Brentano** (1785–1859), a friend of Beethoven and one of the leading figures in the world of politics and the arts.

Kinkel gained popularity in Berlin writing comic opera. She also produced romantic songs using her own texts as well as poems by Goethe, Heine and other famous poets. These lieder came to the attention of **Robert Schumann** and received favorable reviews in his *Neue Zeitschrift für Musik* and other important newspapers. As a pianist, her repertoire spanned from the baroque to Mendelssohn and Chopin. About the latter she wrote a unique and prophetic essay in which she analyzed his use of chromatic scales and wide intervals: "[Chopin] knocks on the mysterious closed door of quartertones which will some day be as [familiar] to us as the minor second, and as the interval of the third was to our predecessors."

Out of the Fire into Another Marriage

In 1839, Johanna returned to Bonn in order to finalize her divorce from Matthieux. While the endless legal suit and hostility of the authorities had induced depression and thoughts of suicide, she still managed to participate in her music circle, compose a religious work for choir and orchestra, conduct Mozart's *Requiem* and continue her teaching and essay writing. Fanny Hensel was now her role model.

In 1840, she met the theologian and amateur poet Gottfried Kinkel. They developed a spiritual and passionate relationship. This love affair with a Catholic, emancipated, divorced—therefore *immoral*—woman, curtailed Kinkel's prospects for a higher position, and demoted him to assistant preacher. Johanna and Gottfried became members of a group of poets who promoted the patriotic poetry of the Rhine region. Johanna wrote a series of piano songs to their texts. In 1843, after Johanna became a Protestant to please Gottfried, they were married. He now pursued his non-paying career as an art-historian, leaving all financial responsibilities on his wife. Fortunately her songs were always in demand by publishers, and her prestige as a piano teacher brought her the children of the snobbish Bonn officials. Again she wrote of her inner conflict, that she had to use her valuable time earning money rather than improving her knowledge of music. To add to her burdens, in the first six years of marriage

Johanna had four children, each a difficult birth. With all his æstheticism Gottfried still expected order and cleanliness in his home, and gave little consideration to his wife's frustration with household chores versus lack of cultural stimulation.

No Freedom in Exile

At this point in history, the shock waves of the French Revolution set off a series of uprisings in Germany which, although suppressed, eventually culminated in a liberal constitution and a united country. By 1848 this "revolution" reached the Rhineland. Gottfried Kinkel gained prominence as a political leader, but following a demonstration in 1849 was imprisoned. Her husband having been the founder of the *New Bonn Newspaper*, "the last press of freedom in the Rhine country," placed Johanna in a critical position. Her contributions to this radical publication, plus the hate-mongering of the town women, forced her to flee to Cologne and her parents' house, continuing to teach and compose. She compared her situation to the days of witches being burned at the stake. Her faith in Gottfried was broken. Even while incarcerated, he had become somewhat of a hero to the ladies. In her deepening depression, Johanna once again spoke of divorce and suicide. After her husband's release from Spandau prison, the family went into exile in London where Gottfried became a lecturer on art and history while Johanna worked as a music teacher. During these years her letters were full of her unbearable workload and the fact that her husband rarely had time for his family, but catered to exiled Democrats—among them a very pretty woman—who made themselves at home in their house. Johanna was expected to be hospitable and serve all these people. Of course she no longer found time for composing. Another cause of marital dissension was Gottfried's favoring his sons and withholding education from his daughters. In a two-volume autobiographical novel, *Hans Ibeles in London—a Family Portrait from the Exile's Life*, Johanna wrote critically of the one-sided male perspective on women's rights.

In London, on November 15, 1858, she "fell" out of her bedroom window. According to Gottfried, "from an attack of heart pains." One of the poets proclaimed that Johanna, "the composer of courageous songs, had been killed on the battleground of exile." The truth was that she had lost the hopeless war against an egocentric husband who was no longer the kind, philosophic person she had married. In the final sentences of her novel, Johanna had prophetically written, "It seemed to her that she lay deep in the earth and heard her children running over the grass of the mounded grave, laughing and dancing."

The death of Johanna Kinkel snuffed out the flame of one of the most productive composers of the German Romantic era while shedding a much-needed spotlight on the social injustice and the [still] many unsolved problems of the roles of women.

A More Liberated Lifestyle

In contrast to the confined life of her contemporary, Fanny Mendelssohn Hensel, **JOSEPHINE LANG**, born March 14, 1815, in Munich, to her opera singer mother and court musician father, was to gain much attention in the public sphere. Her childhood studies consisted of singing and piano. At fifteen, she met **Felix Mendelssohn** who was so greatly impressed by her songs and her voice that he gave her lessons in fugue, counterpoint and theory. By the age of eighteen, Josephine was a professional singer at the Munich court. The following year, **Robert Schumann** gave a favorable review of her song, *Das Traumbild* (The Dream Picture) in his *Neue Zeitschrift für Musik*—although with his usual deprecation: "for a woman." 1837–43 saw one of Lang's most productive periods of composition.

The Marriage-Mother-Widowhood-Always-a-Mother-Cycle

In 1842, after a two year love affair during which she set forty-one of his poems to music, she married Christian Köstlin, a poet and law professor at the University of Tübingen. Their home was a meeting place for poets. She used the works of Schiller, Goethe, Heine and Byron as lyrics for her songs. Between 1843 and 1856, the year of her husband's death, Lang gave birth to six children in the course of which, understandably, her musical output declined. As a widow, she plunged back into composition and, with the help of **Ferdinand Hiller** (1811–1885), the composer/conductor who replaced his friend Mendelssohn at the Leipzig Gewandhaus Orchestra, many of Lang's songs and piano pieces were published. It was at this time that her *lieder* progressed from the style of Schumann and Mendelssohn to those of Brahms. She also taught voice and piano to survive the many problems of her brood: the eldest, a victim of paranoia, was sent to an asylum where he died in a fire; the second son was permanently handicapped and died in 1873; her third son, Eugene, suffered from a nervous fever and lived at home until his death in 1880.

A Songbook of the Soul

1868-80 brought public recognition. With over 150 songs to her credit, Lang became one of the most published of Romantic composers, receiving not only many favorable newspaper reviews, but encouragement from other composers like **Mendelssohn, Robert** and **Clara Schumann, Stephen Heller** (1813–88) and **Hiller**. She revealed that her songs were her diary. Most of them deal with love and nature, and are written in a bright personal style that has the advantage of the composer's vocal and technical knowledge as a singer.

After Lang's death December 2, 1880, her surviving son, Heinrich (1846–1907), published an 1881 biography of his mother in Leipzig, while her daughter Maria Fellinger, who lived until 1925, became a close friend of Brahms and introduced her mother's songs to him. In 1882, the major music publishing company Breitkopf and Härtel brought out a collection of forty previously unpublished songs.

About As Far As a Woman Then Could Go

Towering above her female contemporary performers—though her compositions had to wait a century to begin receiving proper recognition—is a child prodigy who caused as much excitement in her time as Mozart's little fingers did in his.

A Case of Reverse Discrimination

Clara Schumann

CLARA SCHUMANN's mother was Marianne Tromlitz, a gifted singer and pianist, her father, Friedrich Wieck (1785–1873), a teacher, amateur pianist and owner of a piano company in Leipzig. After Clara arrived September 13, 1819, three boys were subsequently born, in 1821, '23, '24. Four months after the last birth, Marianne sought a divorce from her domineering husband. By Saxon law, children were the property of their father. Babies were allowed to stay with their mothers, as was Clara for the few months until her fifth birthday. Perhaps this turbulent domestic scene may have been the cause of the child not speaking a single word until she was four years old! Wieck began educating his daughter as soon as she returned to him. By age six, Clara was receiving formal lessons in piano, violin, singing, theory, harmony, counterpoint and composition, and being molded by Wieck into a superb musician. Although her general education was sparse, she studied English and French in preparation for future trips to those countries. Despite his violent temper and the grueling practice regimen, the obedient child thrived. Meanwhile, in a reversal from the gender norm, her brothers' education was all but neglected.

The Prodigy

In 1828 her father remarried, and the Wieck home became a center for musicians, writers and publishers before whom the nine-year-old performed. Clara's first public appearance was in October of that year at one of Europe's major concert halls, the Leipzig Gewandhaus. 1828 also marked the publication of her Opus 1, *Four Polonaises*.

Acclaimed throughout Europe as a gifted child, the girl spent the next decade concertizing, composing and basking in the admiration of such luminaries as **Goethe, Mendelssohn, Chopin, Paganini** and **Liszt**. Her work was published by major houses: Haslinger, Diabelli and Plechetti in Vienna, and Breitkopf and Härtel in Leipzig.

In the course of 1828, father and daughter met **Robert Schumann** in the home of friends. The handsome eighteen-year-old was taken with Clara and most impressed with her playing. Diaries and letters preserve evidence of the instant attraction between the two despite the nine year age difference. Given her background and training, Clara was mature far beyond her age. Robert began studying with Wieck, moving into their home as a boarder for a while in 1830. In the next five years Robert was establishing himself as a composer—his pianistic career thwarted because he had crippled a finger with an "exercising device." In 1834 he founded a respected weekly music journal, *Der Neue Zeitschrift für Musik*, with Friedrich Wieck initially as one of the co-editors.

In 1838, in an effort to separate Clara from Robert, Wieck took her on a second Viennese tour. This time the Royal Family bestowed their highest musical award upon the eighteen-year-old, *Königliche und Kaiserliche Kammer Virtuosin* (Royal and Imperial Chamber Virtuoso)—an amazing honor for one so young, a woman, a foreigner and a non-Catholic! A further honor was Franz Grillparzer, Austria's leading poet, writing *Clara Wieck and Beethoven*, immortalizing her performance of the master's *Appassionata Sonata*.

The World's Most Tumultuous Betrothal

Although he was well aware of Herr Wieck's temperament, having witnessed incidents of what today is called *child abuse*—such as Friedrich wrenching one of his sons off the piano stool and flinging him on the floor—nevertheless, in 1837, Schumann dared to ask for his daughter's hand in marriage. Considering that Clara was the focal point of her father's existence, that up to this point he was in complete control of her life, arranging concerts, travelling with her, consorting with the famous, collecting her earnings, even writing or dictating her diary, it was not surprising that Wieck was not ready to give his claim to fame to an impoverished composer with doubtful prospects. Under the circumstances, probably no man would have been acceptable. His actions and reactions to the proposal brought out the full violence and possessiveness of his nature. He sent Clara to Paris—alone for the first time—hoping she would fail. Instead, she stayed with friends, gave piano lessons to sustain herself, arranged her own concerts and was, as usual, a great success.

Wildly jealous that she could exist without him, Wieck threatened to disinherit her and keep all her money if she did not give up Robert. Clara loved her father, but this was too much. The young couple was forced to resort to the courts. Robert sent his fiancée the money to come back to Leipzig where she found herself locked out of her own home. For a while she went to live in Berlin with her mother who had remarried. Meanwhile, Wieck went berserk. He opened Clara's locked box and copied excerpts of Schumann's letters using these as "evidence" that the man was a drunkard and a mediocre composer who would not be able to support his daughter. He also claimed (with some truth) that Clara was not fit to be a housewife since she had only been trained as a concert artist. He wrote raving letters to the musical community, managers, critics, etc., calling his daughter an ungrateful girl who would ruin any piano she played! His main fear was that after marriage she would give up her career like the other famous women pianists of her time, **Léopoldine Blahetka** (1811–87), **Anna de Belleville** (1808–80), and **Marie Pleyel** (1811–75). While Clara had no thought of giving up either her career or her fiancé, she was torn with anguish at the humiliation her father was bringing on himself and, by confiscating her money and leaving her without a dowry, bringing shame on her. It was a court battle in which today's media would have gloried. After a bitter year, the betrothed won their case and were married September 12, 1840, the day before the bride's twenty-first birthday.

C is for - Composition - Confinement - Career - Compromise . . .

Like all marriages combining two careers, the Schumanns' relationship had its challenges. Given the social mores of the time, Robert was a remarkably progressive (read "permissive") husband. He did not expect his wife to give up her concertizing—indeed, most of the time it was *her* earnings that were their main income. As a newlywed, Clara at first experienced some real happiness. The pair played music together, composed a set of songs, *The Springtime of Love*, under both their names, which confounded the critics who could not figure out who had written which—exposing as a sham the prevailing theory that women's compositions were inferior to men's! They also kept a joint—and revealing—marriage diary which duly recorded the puncturing of the bliss bubble. Robert had to have silence when he composed. This meant that Clara could not practice or work on her own compositions. There is a frantic entry, "*There is not even one little hour in the day for myself!*" Nevertheless, March 31, 1841, six months after her wedding and three months into her first pregnancy, she played her first concert as Clara Schumann, at the Gewandhaus. Her worries about getting rusty or being forgotten were erased by the thunderous ovation.

C is also for Children

19th century women did not appear in public once their expectant condition was showing. If Clara had observed this convention her career would truly have been at an end. In the course of her fourteen year marriage, Clara was pregnant ten times, miscarried twice, and gave birth to eight children: Marie, 1841, Elise, 1843, Julie, 1845, Emil, 1846, (who died at sixteen months), Ludwig, 1848, Ferdinand, 1849, Eugenie, 1851 and Felix, 1854. (With the patter of all those little feet, one wonders how she kept the house quiet in order for her husband to compose anything!) Sometimes she performed within a week of giving birth!

Over the years the children were left under various forms of care, including wetnurses and Robert's brother, Carl, while Robert, as decorum demanded, accompanied his wife on her tours. Even this became an increasing source of conflict, as Schumann felt he was losing time from composing. During a four month Russian tour in January 1844, he was sick and depressed the whole time while his wife thrived on getting up at three in the morning to be on the road by four to travel by sleigh in the frigid Russian winter to their next destination. On their return to Leipzig, Robert sold his magazine—his main link with the outside world.

D is for Düsseldorf, Directing and Depression

Concentrating on composing, working day and night, left him drained and depressed. In August he suffered his first breakdown. In December, the Schumanns moved to Dresden for the recuperative effects of a slower pace of life. It was anything but that for Clara, who in their five year stay there gave birth to four children. With fewer concerts during this period, she had to teach piano to supplement their income. She did, however, compose some of her best works, including her most played piece, the *Piano Trio in G minor*, Opus 17, for violin, cello and piano, which was highly praised by her husband and Felix Mendelssohn.

In 1849, a rebellion broke out in the city and Clara had to hide her ailing husband to avoid his being dragged into the rebel forces. In September 1850, they moved to Düsseldorf where Robert, although not adequate to the task, took the job of conductor for the Düsseldorf Orchestra and Chorus. Clara ended up attending rehearsals, acting as accompanist, directing the chorus and instructing the musicians on the interpretation of her husband's music. The latter, torn between appreciation and wounded masculine pride, verbally lashed out at the fingers that supported him.

Enter the Third of the Three Bs

At this point a ray of sunshine swept into their household. On September 30, 1853, a twenty-year-old stranger with long blond ringlets knocked at their door and asked if he could play some of his compositions. It was the right door. The unknown composer found a home and an appreciative audience. Robert wrote his first critical essay in ten years, praising the young man's style, and helping him get published. From then on **Johannes Brahms** was part of Clara's life, helping her cope with Robert's suicide attempt—he was pulled out of the river by fishermen—and his two year confinement in an asylum. He died there in 1856, in his wife's arms.

Motherhood Never Lets Up

After Robert's death, Clara settled in Berlin, and then Baden-Baden. But she was not finished with tragedy. In 1873 her father died, and later, two of her children. Julie married an Italian count and succumbed to tuberculosis at twenty-seven, while expecting her third child. At twenty-two, Ludwig had to be committed to a mental institution where he died at fifty-one. Ferdinand returned from the Franco-Prussian War addicted to morphine, which had been given to him to alleviate the pain from his rheumatism. In and out of hospitals seeking a cure, he died at forty-one leaving his widow and six children for his mother to support. Felix, born after his father's death, inherited Robert's looks and talent, but his mother asked him to use a pen name when he wanted to publish his poems in case they were "not good enough" to bear the Schumann name! Very hurt, he was not given time to prove himself. The tuberculosis he contracted as a teenager killed him at twenty-four. Marie, Elise and Eugenie fared better, becoming piano teachers. Marie never married, but stayed with her mother as her assistant. Elise married at thirty-four and had four children. Eugenie also never married, and after living with her mother and Marie for twenty years, emigrated to England where, besides teaching piano, she had a successful career as a performer and wrote *Robert Schumann: A Portrait of My Father* and *Memoirs*, about her own life in the Schumann family.

A New Career at Sixty

Despite increasing pain from neuralgia and rheumatism, as well as encroaching deafness, at fifty-nine (1879) Madame Schumann became the principal piano teacher at the Hoch Conservatory in Frankfurt. There she remained until age seventy-two (1893). Competition—by audition—was keen to get into her classes. In 1888, her fiftieth anniversary as a performer was celebrated throughout the music world. In all, this phenomenal woman gave 1,300 performances, including nineteen tours to England, and set the record with seventy-four recitals at the Gewandhaus where her closest fellow performer was Mendelssohn with forty-seven concerts. Clara's last public appearance was in Frankfurt, 1891, performing Brahms' *Variations on a Theme by Haydn*. She "retired," teaching in her home for the rest of her long life. After suffering a stroke in March 1896, she died May 20, while listening to her grandson, Ferdinand, play Robert's F sharp Major *Romance for Piano*.

To the credit of her father and her upbringing, Clara Wieck Schumann always thought of herself as a performer first, and in this category had no complex about being a woman. She was accepted on an equal footing with her male contemporaries. As a mother, she did her best under the circumstances. Fortunately, middle class families usually were able to afford one or two servants due to the low wages paid. As the older children grew up they took care of the younger. While not happy at the constant separations, the family understood that mother was an artist. The older ones knew that basically she was the main breadwinner during their father's lifetime and the *only* means of their support after his death.

Secret Lovers? The Grand Finale

The extent of intimacy between Clara and Brahms has always been a mystery. They took a vacation together in Switzerland after Robert's death, then went separate ways, keeping in touch with letters and visits. Fourteen years older than Johannes, the thought of more childbearing, or of having to "serve" another husband, may have been vital factors in Clara's decision to remain single. Her widowhood lasted forty years. Brahms never married and died eleven months after Clara. While many of their letters were preserved, no one will ever know how many were burned. Clara's later diaries—willed to her daughter, Marie—were lost or also burned.

Recognition—Renewed and Revitalized

As a composer Clara was programmed into the social attitude. Never satisfied with her creations, she accused herself in her diary of "arrogance" in presuming that *she* would be the one to break the barrier which dictated that a woman is not supposed to compose! Yet her compositions have withstood both her own denigrating opinion and almost a century of neglect, and are now coming into their own. Available on numerous CDs, and gaining recognition in performance, are her *Piano Concerto in A minor*, Op. 7 (1835–36), *Piano Trio in G minor*, Op. 17 (1846), complete piano music, and *lieder* whose romantic themes feature a delicate balance between lyrics and accompaniment.

After her husband's death, she composed no more, devoting herself instead to editing Robert's music as well as performing it. She is therefore responsible for Schumann's secure niche in the Romantic Composers' Hall of Fame.

But it is Clara Schumann who should head the list in a Women Composers Hall of Fame: Artist, Composer, Wife, Mother, Tragedy and Triumph—she did it all!

Clara's Contemporaries and Followers

PAULINE GARCIA-VIARDOT (1821–1910) is known primarily for her career as a foremost mezzo of her time, but she was also a talented composer. She wrote transcriptions of Chopin mazurkas which were performed by Chopin himself (1848), and over 100 songs, most with complex accompaniments showing her own virtuosic piano skill. With writer **Georges Sand**, mistress of Chopin, Viardot collected and transcribed French folksongs. (The heroine of Sand's novel, *Consuelo*, was inspired by Pauline.) Three of her four operettas had libretti by **Ivan Turgenev** (1818–83), the Russian author/poet who was also her lover—her husband and manager, **Louis Viardot**, whom she married in 1840, was twenty-one years her senior. (Between 1841–57 she bore him three daughters and a son, all with musical careers.) Turgenev lived with the family in a *ménage à trois* from 1871 until his death. Viardot helped create the music for roles written specifically for her. Her fourth operetta, *Le dernier Sorcier* (The Last Wizard), was conducted by Brahms at Weimar. Her opera *Cendrillon* (Cinderella, 1904) saw a revival in Newport, Rhode Island, 1971, and in the UK, 1972 and 1981. (See Immortal Divas of the Past.)

Augusta Holmes

AUGUSTA HOLMÈS was born December 16, 1847, in Paris, the only daughter of an Irish officer who had settled in France and a mother of mixed Scottish and Irish origins. Her parents were in close contact with many leading artistic personalities of the time, with their home in Versailles a meeting place of leading musicians, artists and writers. The writer Alfred de Vigny (1797–1863), Augusta's godfather, was rumored to have been her real father. Early in childhood she showed an aptitude for music as well as poetry and painting. Her mother discouraged her musical talents, but died when Augusta was only eleven. She had her first lessons with Henry Lambert, organist of Versailles Cathedral. Later came instrumentation lessons from **Hyacinthe Klosé** (1808–80), who taught at the Paris Conservatory. In 1875, she was accepted into the elite group of pupils of **César Franck** (1822–90). She heard *Das Rheingold* in 1869, making her a fan of Wagner. His music and that of Franck were the dominant influences in her works. Based on classical or mythological subjects, she used a variety of styles from folk to neoclassicism. One of her early pieces was the symphonic poem *Hymn to Apollo* (1872), which followed the French vocal tradition. Her large orchestral works feature soloists and chorus. Dramatic symphonies and symphonic poems include *Orlando furioso* (1877), *Lutèce* (1878), *Irlande* (1882), *Pologne* (1883) and *Andromède* (1901). She enjoyed success with choral works, especially *Les Argonautes* (1881), programmed for the *Concerts Populaires*, part of the Parisian musical scene from 1861–84. *Ludus pro patria* (1888) and the *Ode triomphale* were written for the Paris Exposition of 1889, celebrating the centennial of the French Revolution. Of her four operas, *La montagne noire* was produced by the Paris Opera, February 5, 1895, but not well received. She also wrote over 130 songs.

Having refused a proposal from no less than **Camille Saint-Saëns**, Augusta never married, but was involved with the poet Catulle Mendes (1841–1909) by whom she reputedly had three children. Her ancestry revealed itself in her passionate temperament and Irish patriotism. She converted to Roman Catholicism shortly before her death in Paris, January 28, 1903. Ironically, she is remembered more for her beauty and vibrant personality which dominated the literary and musical salons, than for her music.

A Happy Housewife

AGATHE BACKER-GRØNDAHL was born December 1, 1847, in Holmestrand, Norway. For an interesting change we find a woman who managed to combine a happy home life with a successful career. In fact she surprised young George Bernard Shaw, in his then role of music critic, by assuring him that her musical fulfillment came from being a wife and mother! Her childhood years were spent in a cultured family. She began piano early, and after Norwegian schooling went to the Berlin Music Academy (1865–67), studying with **Theodor Kullak** (1818–82). From 1871–72 she studied with famed conductor **Hans von Bülow** (1830–94) in Florence, and with **Franz Liszt** (1811–86) in Weimar. She had a successful performance career until her marriage in 1875 to Olaus Andreas Grøndahl. The birth of her three sons interrupted her concert career for eight years. She started touring again in 1883, playing regularly in Stockholm, and appearing in 1889 in Paris and in 1889 and 1890 in London with great success. Bernard Shaw, also music critic under the name Corno di Bassetto, liked her playing enormously, and ranked her among the greatest pianists of her time. From 1889 onwards, Agathe dedicated herself more and more to composing, interrupting once more her concert career. When she started giving concerts again, from 1898 to 1901, she played mostly her own pieces. She went on composing until her death in Oslo in 1907, aged sixty. Her well-crafted lyrical songs—almost 200 of them—apparently influenced her husband to become a choral conductor. Her output also includes piano music in a similar genre to **Cécile Chaminade** (1857–1944). Rather than following the folksong trend of her fellow Scandinavians, her style reflects the Romantic influence of Schubert, Mendelssohn and Chopin. Agathe died June 4, 1907, in Christiania (now Oslo).

A Tale of Success and Frustration

Distinguished from other women composers by her large output of orchestral works, **LUISE ADOLPHA Le BEAU** was also a pianist and music critic. Her family support system was utterly unique in that her parents devoted themselves and their resources completely to their daughter's career, which in several instances involved moving out of town when critics or politics made it necessary.

Shortly after Luise's birth on April 25, 1850, in Rastatt, Germany, came the first move to Karlsruhe where the child showed an early interest in music and composed her first piece at age eight. Wilhelm Le Beau, a general in the Baden army and an amateur conductor and singer, arranged for his daughter to study piano, voice and composition. He himself taught her geometry and other subjects not considered suitable for girls, which caused disapproval among the locals. Luise's debut at eighteen featured Mendelssohn's Piano Concerto in G minor with the Baden Court Orchestra under Hermann Levi. This was followed by a tour that included Heidelberg and Basel, Switzerland. In 1873, at the urging of Levi, Luise went to the famous spa of Baden-Baden to study with **Clara Schumann** who was summering there. The great conductor **Hans von Bülow**, also vacationing there, evaluated her pianistic and compositional skills, and was impressed enough to give her letters of recommendation to study with Josef Rheinberger (1839–1901), a prominent composer-pedagogue in Munich. In 1874, after her father retired and Luise completed a Dutch concert tour, the family made their first "career" move to Munich. Reviewing her *Violin Sonata*, op. 10, Rheinberger made an exception to his rule of not teaching women. They were not admitted into his Königliche Musikschule (Royal Music School), so he taught her privately.

Between recitals—which included playing for Kaiser Wilhelm I—and establishing a school for piano and theory for "Daughters of Educated Station," Le Beau's eleven years in Munich produced some of her best works: a cantata, *Ruth*, choral music, lieder, a viola suite, two cello pieces, and for piano, a trio, quartet and fantasy with orchestra. She and others who played her works on the Continent received rave reviews, although critics invariably remarked on the "manliness" of Le Beau's style. One gave her the big daddy of backhanded compliments: "If many men did not write truly bad music, I would praise her by saying: she composes like a man!" The overall critical reaction was one of respect for the energy, power, technical skill and pleasing tone of her work.

In May 1882, her *Four Pieces for Cello with Piano Accompaniment* won first place in an international competition—a great surprise for the judges when a woman's name was revealed from the sealed envelope! In 1883, Luise met **Liszt** in Weimar, who thought highly of her work, as did **Brahms** and the major music critic **Eduard Hanslick**, whom she met while on tour in Vienna the following year. Her *Piano Quartet* was an unprecedented success at the Leipzig Gewandhaus.

Since 1864, when King Ludwig II established the volatile Wagner at the Bavarian Court in Munich, there had been a "war" between proponents of his new music and Brahmsian conservatives, among whom was Rheinberger. Because she refused to take sides, Le Beau's relationship deteriorated with her teacher. Gradually she found herself in a no-win situation. Despite her acclaim, she was still considered an outsider by a city which doted on its other famous inhabitants. Once again, the family decided to move.

The mayor of Baden-Baden discouraged their settling in his town because of competition with local musicians. Wiesbaden was more receptive, and after arriving in October 1885, Luise was much in demand for performing and teaching. By 1886, however, new theater managers who controlled concert scheduling deprived her of any chance to perform. From 1890–93 the Le Beaus lived in Berlin, but embittered at the musical community as a whole, Luise refused many offers of performing contracts and an opportunity to teach at a conservatory—although without the title "professor" since this, too, was reserved for men only. She was also asked to send one of her compositions to Chicago for the milestone Women's Exposition of 1893. Nevertheless, her music was being played as far away as Turkey and Australia, and her biography was appearing in newspapers and encyclopedias.

Her "isolation" was spent completing her folktale opera *Hadumoth*, for which her parents rented a printing press. It took them a whole year to produce the vocal and orchestral parts. After many disillusioning rejections, the family moved back to Baden-Baden in September 1893, where the opera and most of Le Beau's other works were performed many times to favorable reviews in the western part of Germany.

In 1896 Luise's beloved, generous parents both died, leaving her devastated. Their emotional and financial support had enabled her to fulfill her talent, and given her the option of not having to marry and subjugate herself to the wishes of a husband—as did Clara Schumann, Alma Mahler and so many other women composers whose careers ended or were eroded by marriage. Her parents' support also maintained for Le Beau the vital respectability and credibility as a lady. (Her mother usually accompanied her on her tours.)

Alone, she continued writing music critiques, performing selectively and doing some composing. Her friends sponsored a seventy-fifth birthday concert of her works in 1925.

Luise Adolpha Le Beau lived in socially changing times. The Industrial Revolution hit Germany between the 1870s and 1880s. A growing need was emerging for women in factories and other professions. They needed the training and education that had been denied them—and the lack of which prevented them from passing the qualification examinations to enter universities. The Association for the Education of Women, founded in Leipzig, 1865, and the Society for Promoting the Employment of Women, Berlin, 1866, had for decades been challenging the separate educational systems for boys and girls. By the efforts of these organizations, women were finally admitted to German universities by 1910, and got the vote in 1918. Still the ancient prejudices were never far from the surface: such as the "temptations" facing men once women were allowed into their sacrosanct milieux. (Naturally, men would continue to be held blameless in the face of such "seduction.") Moreover, critics lashed out defensively, claiming that the inclusion of women would cause institutions to be "watered down" and "feminized" and inevitably deteriorate.

Despite the frustration of having to put up with the adjective "manly" in praise of her work, Le Beau definitely experienced success. She died in 1927, in Baden-Baden, born just three-quarters of a century too soon.

A French Legend

Cécile Chaminade

One of the most prolific (400 works), successful and long-lived women composers, **CÉCILE CHAMINADE** was born in Paris, August 8, 1857, into an upper middle class family, the third of six children. (Two died.) Both her parents were amateur musicians. Her mother was her first piano teacher. Cécile started composing at age eight. No less personage than **Hector Berlioz** (1803–69) recommended that she enter the Paris Conservatory, but her father's strict views on what was proper for young ladies prohibited this. Instead, he gave her the best of both worlds by arranging private study with professors from the faculty: piano with **Félix Le Couppey** (1811–87), counterpoint and harmony with **Augustin Savard** (1841–81), violin with **Martin Marsick** (1848–1924) and composition with **Benjamin Godard** (1849–95)—all prominent men in the French music world. At eighteen she made her public debut as a pianist, and for most of her life successfully maintained dual careers of composing and performing mostly her own compositions. She concertized throughout Europe, with annual visits to England, and made the long journey to America from October to December, 1908, covering twelve cities and going as far west as Minneapolis. She was so popular in the U.S. that several Chaminade Clubs were founded by women. Other outlets for her music were the many piano rolls she recorded with the Aeolian Music Company in London (1913–14).

Published by the most famous companies in Europe, including Durand in France, Schott in Germany, and Hutchings and Romer in London, Chaminade's music also crossed the Atlantic via the Anglo-Canadian Music Publishing Association in Toronto. Her compositions were well received: *Suite d'orchestre* (1881), a one-act opera *La Sévillane* (1882), a symphony, *Les Amazones* (1884–88), *Carillhoë*, a ballet (1888) and the very successful *Concertstück for Piano and Orchestra* with which she made her American debut, conducting the Philadelphia Orchestra. These compositions, plus the popular *Concertino for Flute and Orchestra* (1902) were the extent of her orchestral works. The rest of her enormous output comprises 135 songs and a body of elegant, lyrical piano pieces. All are classic examples of true "salon music" reflecting *La Belle Époque*, the era of opulence and gaiety that was Paris before World War I.

Her Name Was Never Forgotten

In her youth, Chaminade was part of the rising tide of French musical nationalism which included the venerated Romantic giants **César Franck** (1822–90), **Camille Saint-Saëns** (1835–1921), and **Emmanuel Chabrier** (1841–94), as well as the champions of Wagner, **Henri Duparc** (1848–1943), and **Vincent D'Indy** (1851–1931). It was a time when audiences flocked to the *Concerts Populaires* featuring orchestras numbering 100 musicians directed by **Jules Pasdeloup** (1819–87), and the *Concerts du Châtelet* with conductor **Eduard Colonne** (1838–1910). (*Concerts Colonne*, renamed in honor of their originator, are still on the Paris scene.) Contemporary French composers were well represented in these programs. As the century progressed, there was a piano in practically every home, creating a voracious demand for music. One result was that publishers churned out compositions of lesser quality, giving the term "salon music" an inferior connotation. Unfortunately, this was the main cause for the trivializing of Chaminade's works. This, plus the trend toward "modernism" in the 1920s, the advent of jazz and phonograph records, caused a decline of the popularity of salon music.

In her personal life, Cécile had a close relationship with her family, especially her mother. After the death of her father, Hippolyte, in 1887, finances became straitened, causing her to abandon composing in larger forms in order to gain income from short pieces. She engaged in a platonic marriage in 1901 with a friend, Louis-Mathieu Carbonel, a Marseilles music publisher twenty years her senior, commenting that an artistic woman needs to marry a man who appreciates her talent(!) [Author's heartfelt exclamation mark] Nevertheless, she was accused of "wasting her time nursing a sick man" when her husband lingered with a lung disease from 1903 until his death in 1907.

Chaminade continued to enjoy great respect during her long lifetime. She received many awards, including the Jubilee Medal from Queen Victoria (1897), the Chefekat from the Sultan of Turkey (1901), and was the first woman composer to be made a *Chevalière de la Legion d'Honneur*, one of France's highest decorations. During World War II, she lived in neutral Monte Carlo. Her strict vegetarian diet is blamed for decalcification of her bones. Her left foot had to be amputated in 1938. She refused a wheelchair and was incapacitated the rest of her life. She died April 13, 1944, a year before the end of the war.

Once remembered only for her light melodies, such as *The Flatterer* and *Scarf Dance*, which still find their way into every piano album, compact discs are now available with most of her piano pieces and several of her orchestral works.

Always a Bride

It may seem strange to include a woman who lived eighty-four years and only wrote fourteen songs. By her marriages to illustrious men and an active love-life between, **ALMA MAHLER (WERFEL)**, born August 31, 1879, in Vienna, has secured a place in most anthologies of women in music, so far be it for me to leave her out!

Her father, Emil Schindler, was a portrait painter, associated with artistic notables in a pre-World War I Vienna where the transition from romantic to modern started gently with **Anton Bruckner** (1826–96) and **Gustav Mahler** (1860–1911) and jarred into harshness by the Twelve-Tone Trio: **Arnold Schoenberg** (1874–1951), **Alban Berg** (1885–1935) and **Anton Webern** (1883–1945).

Marriage to Mahler

By 1900, twenty-one and beautiful, Alma was studying composition with **Alexander Zemlinsky** (1871–1942), the composer-conductor who lost out on his proposal of marriage when he introduced his student to Gustav Mahler, nineteen years her senior. Her father, whom Alma adored, had died in 1892. Perhaps this may have been part of the reason she was attracted to Gustav. They married in March 1902, with his proviso that Alma give up composing. She agreed and became a copyist for him. Of the two daughters from this marriage, one died young and the other, Anna, became a sculptor. In 1910, a crisis in the marriage caused Gustav to consult Sigmund Freud, after which he did an about face and begged his wife to take up composition again. With his help the resulting *Five Lieder* was published.

Mahler died the following year and Alma began an intense relationship with the painter Oscar Kokoschka, again playing a subordinate role to her man's career. After she broke up with him, she married prominent architect **Walter Gropius** (1883–1969) in 1915, and for the third time had the satisfaction of fulfilling what she termed her destiny to inspire great men. In 1919, Gropius founded *Bauhaus*, the school of architecture that combined fine art with functional design. Their daughter, Manon, died in 1935. It was Gropius who, in 1963, co-designed one of New York's landmark skyscrapers: the Pan-Am Building. (Purchased by Metropolitan Life Insurance in 1980, it is now known as the Metlife Building.)

While her husband was away at war, Alma met the poet Franz Werfel, whom she married in 1929 after divorcing Gropius. This was her only happy relationship. Because he was Jewish they had to flee Vienna in 1938. They were among the illustrious Jews smuggled out of Marseilles by "righteous gentile" Varian Fry,[7] and ended up in Los Angeles where Alma led the côterie of other musical refugees like **Arnold Schoenberg**, conductor **Bruno Walter** and writer **Thomas Mann**. Werfel died in 1945, after which his widow moved to New York. Her autobiographical books on her life with Mahler (1940) and her other relationships with men, *And the Bridge is Love*, published in 1959, but written much earlier, were considered very indiscreet for the time.

Besides the early songs, two other sets were published, *Four Lieder* (1915) contains "Ansturm" (Assault), considered the earliest work by a woman dealing with sexual desire. The second set of *Five Lieder* (1924) follows the pattern of passion declaimed with bold chromatic harmony. It is rumored that other manuscripts were lost in the bombing of Vienna during World War II. Alma Mahler died in New York, December 11, 1964, a modern woman before her time, who went through men the way men have for centuries discarded women. Two of her enduring legacies are the 1924 publication of Mahler's letters and a reproduction of the unfinished manuscript of his 10th Symphony.

End of an Era

The end of the Romantic Period dovetailed into the Modern roughly after the first decade of the 20th century when both peasants and the middle class rattled their chains against the remaining monarchies and aristocracy—chains that were smashed by the advent of World War I. World War II completed the loss of social innocence. This was irrevocably reflected in modern music, whose experimentation probed ever widening strata until it made the quantum leap into computer technology emerging in the late 1960s.

---

7. A Righteous Gentile is a non-Jew who risked his or her life to save Jews from Nazi persecution. Varian Fry (1907–67) was one of these when he left New York City in 1940 and established an "office" of the "American Relief Center." His assignment was to save prominent artists, musicians, writers, scientists, professors and political figures whose works had marked them as enemies of the Third Reich. With ample funds, but no training, Fry relied on his air of authority, poker face and sartorial elegance, and performed miracles under the noses of the Gestapo. He smuggled over 2,000 Jews out of France, including painter **Marc Chagall**, harpsichordist **Wanda Landowska**, political scientist **Hannah Arendt**, writer **Lion Feuchtwanger**, and **Franz Werfel**, author of *The Song of Bernadette*, and his wife **Alma Mahler Werfel**. Expelled from France in 1941, Fry tried to alert America to the grim situation in Europe. As editor of *The New Republic*, on December 21, 1942 he wrote *The Massacre of the Jews*, predicting the Holocaust to come. Fry's death at his home in Connecticut, at age fifty-nine, went almost unnoticed. Shortly before, the French government had awarded him the *Croix de Chevalier de la Legion d'Honneur*. Otherwise, his heroism was not recognized until 1991, when the U.S. Holocaust Memorial Council posthumously awarded him the Eisenhower Liberation Medal. In 1994, he was also honored by Yad Vashem as a "Righteous Among the Nations" for his rescue activities—the only American so honored. The Varian Fry Foundation was formed in 1997, under the auspices of the International Rescue Committee.

British (United Kingdom) Composers

ENGLAND

Maude Valérie White (1855–1937)
Dame Ethel Smyth (1858–1944)
Liza Lehmann (1862–1918)
Rebecca Clarke (1886–1979)
Elisabeth Lutyens (1906–1983)
Elizabeth Maconchy (1907–94)
Imogen Holst (1907–84)
Minna Keal (1909–99)
Phyllis Tate (1911–87)
Ruth Gipps (1921–99)
Janet Beat
Diana Burrell
Tansy Davies
Evelyn Ficarra
Alison Gould
Dierdre Gribbin
Nicola Lefanu
Odaline de la Martinez

Katharine Norman
Vivienne Olive
Alwynne Pritchard
Rebecca Saunders
Errollyn Wallen
SCOTLAND
Sally Beamish
Thea Musgrave
Judith Weir
WALES
Morfydd Owen (1891–1918)
Grace Williams (1906–77)
Dilys Elwyn-Edwards (1918–)
Hilary Tann
IRELAND
Eibhlis Farrell
Jane O'Leary

ENGLAND

Until Ethel Smyth forged her way into the public eye, there had been no known British women composers since **Anne Boleyn** and **Elizabeth I**. In fact, there had been a long, dry spell in British music between the Elizabethan **Henry Purcell** (1659–95) and Victorian **Sir Edward Elgar** (1857–1934), who did not achieve public recognition until 1897. That era, however, produced several genteel ladies who composed parlor music and dainty ballads. One of the most well known in this genre was Maude White.

Composer/writer, **MAUDE VALÉRIE WHITE** was born June 23, 1855, in Dieppe, France, of English parents who had returned to Europe from a stay in Chile. The family moved back to England before Maude was a year old. She began piano as a child and continued lessons wherever she was, which included studies in Heidelberg and Paris. In 1876, at the age of twenty-one, she persuaded her mother, who was firmly opposed to women taking up public careers, to allow her to study further. She went to the Royal Academy of Music, where she studied composition for the next three years, attempted to learn the violin, but had to give it up because of severe muscular pains in her arms. During her years at the Academy she published many songs with English, German and French lyrics, some under the name M. White to pacify her mother's fear of public exposure. These began to be performed by three cousins who were professional singers.

A First Relinquished

In 1879, she was the first woman to win the Mendelssohn Scholarship,[8] but in 1881, devastated by her mother's death, she gave up the scholarship to stay the next ten months in Chile with her elder sister to be near family. Here she learned to play the guitar and collected many Chilean folk tunes which she arranged for piano duet. On her return to England in 1882, these were published as *Eight South American Airs*. The winter of 1883 was spent in Vienna completing her musical education with **Robert Fuchs** (1847–1927), one of whose pupils was **Gustav Mahler**. Fuchs tried to persuade her to progress from vocal music, but like so many women of her time, White did not feel capable of writing instrumental or orchestral music, although she did compose a piece for cello and piano, *Naissance d'Amour*, and several piano pieces in the 1880s and '90s. Her output from 1883 included four songs from Alfred Tennyson's *In Memoriam*, which she performed for the great poet himself. One of her bestsellers was a setting of Byron's *So we'll go no more a roving*. A visit to Sweden in the summer of 1884 resulted in several settings of Swedish and Norwegian lyrics. During the last decade of the century, Maude was at the height of her success, with her songs being performed throughout Britain and Europe by the best-known singers of the day, and her music included in concert series. She also started organizing public concerts of her own works.

Mixed Blessings

For much of her life, White suffered from bad health and journeyed all over Europe searching for suitable climates. As a result she became a proficient linguist, translating many of her song texts as well as some books. From 1901, at forty-six, she divided her time between Sicily and England, or travelled, staying with friends and composing wherever she was. Most of her 200 songs fell into the category of the Victorian drawing-room ballad, but her sometimes intricate accompaniments followed the style of Robert Schumann. After a trip to southern Russia in 1912, she wrote *Trois chansons tziganes* (Three Gypsy Songs), a setting of three poems of Leo Tolstoy in French translation. During World War I, she organized concerts for war charities and wrote two patriotic ballads. In her later years she lived in England, authoring two volumes of her memoirs, *Friends and Memories* (1914) and *My Indian Summer* (1932). She continued to organize concerts of her music, working with **Roger Quilter** (1877–1953) and his protegé, singer Mark Raphael. Well-recognized and successful, Maud White died in London, at eighty-two, November 2, 1937.

Ethel Smyth

Composer and writer **DAME ETHEL SMYTH**, born in London, April 23, 1858, was one of the most original figures in British music history. She attained international recognition as an opera composer at a time when women, other than performers, were still considered amateur musicians, and there were certainly no major British women composers.

Hers was a prosperous military family. She was first exposed to music at twelve through her governess, who had studied at the Leipzig Conservatory. Determined to avoid the strictures of Victorian society, Ethel, who had no interest in being a performer, wanted to become a serious composer. At seventeen, she was pounding Wagner operas on the piano, and taught herself orchestration from a borrowed copy of Berlioz' *Treatise on Instrumentation*. At nineteen, after much arguing with her parents, she got permission to study at the Leipzig Conservatory, but after one year there was bored with the formal training and began private studies with the Austrian composer **Heinrich von Herzogenberg** (1843–1900). Through him she was introduced to **Brahms**, **Clara Schumann**, **Grieg**, **Dvořák**, **Tchaikovsky** and violinist **Joseph Joachim**, all of whom accepted her as a promising composer.

---

8. The Mendelssohn Scholarship was, interestingly, a fund founded in England in 1848 to further music study. Its first recipient was Sir Arthur Sullivan, of Gilbert and Sullivan fame, in 1856. By 1890, it was restricted to composers. An equivalent grant was not established in Mendelssohn's native Germany until 1878.

She returned to England in 1890 and made her debut with *Serenade*, a four-movement work for orchestra, which premiered at the Crystal Palace in London. Her overture, *Antony and Cleopatra*, followed six months later. Their success inspired her to compose the *Mass in D* (1891), which she performed for Queen Victoria, playing the piano and singing as many parts as she could. Joseph Barnby and the Royal Choral Society performed the Mass in 1893 at the Royal Albert Hall. The music was so powerful and well executed that the critics had to resort to the adjective "unfeminine" when they compared it to the choral works of Bach, Brahms, and Beethoven's *Missa Solemnis*. The German conductor, Hermann Levi, urged her to write an opera.

No Phantom at the Opera

London's musical elite were not being receptive to English opera. Like many other English composers before World War I, Smyth was forced to write her operas in German and gain first performances on the Continent. In 1898, at age forty, she debuted in Weimar with *Fantasio* (1894). Her second opera, *Der Wald* (The Wood), was staged in Berlin, April 1902. After the premiere, the conductor was taken ill, so the composer took over and got her first opportunity to lead an orchestra. The opera was produced at Covent Garden three months later. The following year, on March 11, *Der Wald* made history as the first opera by a woman composer to be staged at New York's Metropolitan. The ovation was said to have lasted ten minutes. Her third and best known opera, and considered her finest work, *The Wreckers*, received its first two performances in Leipzig and Prague in 1906. In subject matter and mood, *The Wreckers* anticipates Benjamin Britten's most successful opera, *Peter Grimes*,[9] written in 1945, a year after Smyth's death. Both operas use a powerful chorus and a hymn being sung offstage accompanying the soloists onstage. The orchestral portrayal of the sea is heard in Smyth's prelude to the second act, *The Cliffs of Cornwall*, while Britten wrote the *Four Sea Interludes*, which are often played apart from his opera.

Sir Thomas Beecham (1879–1961), famous for declaring "There are no women composers, there never have been, and possibly never will be," reversed his opinion, calling *The Wreckers* one of the (then) few English operas with "real musical merit and vitality." The English premiere was May 28, 1908, in a concert version, and was staged June 22, 1909, at His Majesty's Theatre with Beecham conducting. He also included the opera in his debut season at Covent Garden a year later.

Sufffering Suffragettes!

From 1910–12, Smyth interrupted her career to join the suffragist movement, helping Emmeline Pankhurst, founder in 1903 of the Women's Social and Political Union (WSPU), to fight for women's right to vote. Ethel's *March of the Women* became their anthem. She even spent three weeks in prison when a group of suffragettes was arrested after a stone throwing rampage. (The female vote was granted in 1918.)

It is a known fact that Ethel Smyth preferred the company of women. She had announced early in her career, "No marriage, no ties, I must be free!" But there *was* one man in her life, Henry Brewster, her librettist and the only man she ever loved. Utterly distraught when he died in 1913, she went to Egypt. There she composed one of her most overtly feminist works, *The Boatswain's Mate*, a lively comic opera in the style of Gilbert and Sullivan. She used *March of the Women* in the overture to add to its popular appeal. She now began to hear ringing in her ears, and by the end of World War I realized that she was going deaf. Despite this, she composed two more operas, *Fête Galante* (1922), which she called a "dance-dream" and later arranged as a ballet, and *Entente Cordiale* (1925). In 1927, she wrote a *Concerto for Violin, Horn and Orchestra*, and in 1930 her last work, *The Prison*, a memorial to Brewster, for orchestra and voice, based on his text.

---

9. Britten claimed he had not heard of Smyth's opera, yet the manuscript was found in his library after his death.

Royal and Public Recognition

In 1922, Smyth was named Dame Commander of the British Empire—the female equivalent of being knighted. Her increasing deafness led to a new career. She wrote ten mostly biographical books, full of wit, illuminating portraits of notables of her day, including Queen Victoria. Outspoken in her opinions, she dubbed Schoenberg and his twelve-tone followers "impotent wrigglers." Her friend, author Virginia Woolf, thought Ethel's writings represented "the soul of the [18]90s."

As a feminist, Smyth was the first to openly expound upon "the difficulties in a world arranged by man for man's convenience [which] beset a woman who leaves the traditional path to compete for bread and butter, honors and emoluments." She overcame all these obstacles and, with her speeches, articles and books, was influential in getting men, and society in general, to regard women in music with greater respect. Her friend, conductor **Sir Henry Wood** (1869–1944), was the first to allow women musicians into his orchestra. Gradually other maestros followed suit. Ethel Smyth fulfilled her dream, and is ranked with her British musical male peers **Sir Arthur Sullivan** (1842–1900), **Sir Hubert Parry** (1840–1900), **Sir Charles Villiers Stanford** (1852–1924) and **Sir Edward Elgar**. She died May 9, 1944, in Woking, Surrey, outside London. After the usual hiatus of almost half a century, a good deal of her music is finding its way onto compact discs, including the *Mass*, and a two-CD set of *The Wreckers*, with the famous Huddersfield Choral Society conducted by **Odaline de la Martinez**.

Composer/soprano **LIZA LEHMANN** was the daughter of Amelia, known as "A.L.," a teacher, composer and arranger of songs, and Rudolf Lehmann, a German painter. Born July 11, 1862, in London, Liza spent the first five years of her life in Italy, thus Italian was her first language. The family returned to London, but continued to spend every winter in France, Italy or Germany. Her first musical memories were of the soirées her parents held in their house. Her first singing lessons were from her mother. Later, she attended classes taught by the most famous singer of the time, **Jenny Lind** (1820–87). She also learned piano, and when the family was abroad, studied composition in Rome and Wiesbaden (Germany). She wanted to write music from an early age, but felt that women were not taken seriously as composers. Coming from a family of artists and musicians there were no objections to her taking up a musical career and she was encouraged by her mother to become a professional singer. Although her voice lacked the strength for opera, her wide vocal range provided a successful career as a recitalist, and she appeared in concert, at private parties and festivals all over Britain. Her repertoire combined old English music by composers such as Henry Purcell and Thomas Arne, with her own songs. Her *Album of Twelve German Songs* came out in 1889. Three years later, two of her instrumental works were published, a *Romance* for piano and a *Romance* for violin and piano.

Marriage and No Regrets

In 1894, at the age of thirty-two, she married Herbert Bedford, a student at the Guildhall School of Music, who had become a partner in a London company, and also composed. Her marriage enabled Liza to retire from her singing career and concentrate on composing. The couple lived in Pinner, outside London, near her friend Maude White. The two encouraged each other's work. Her greatest success as a composer came in 1896 with the song cycle *In a Persian Garden*, a setting for four voices and piano of Edward Fitzgerald's translation of the *Rubáiyát of Omar Khayyam*. She followed this, and White's example, with a cycle of Tennyson's *In Memoriam* for voice and piano.

Bedford's business was affected by the Boer War (1899–1902), and the family, which now included two sons, moved to Wimbledon. At this time Lehmann produced two large works, *Endymion*, a setting of John Keats' poem, for soprano and orchestra, and *Young Lochinvar*, for baritone, chorus and orchestra, from the Walter Scott tale. In 1900, she wrote *The Daisy-Chain*, a song cycle for four voices and piano, using children's poetry by Robert Louis Stevenson and others. This was followed in 1902 with *More Daisies*. The same year she wrote the incidental music for Ludwig Fulda's production, *The Twin Sister*. In 1904, she became the first woman commissioned to write a musical comedy when she was asked to compose the music for *Sergeant Brue*. A big success, it ran in London for nine months and toured the provinces. Two years later, she wrote her light opera *The Vicar of Wakefield*, with a libretto by Laurence Housman after the Oliver Goldsmith novel. William S. Gilbert came to the first night and was so impressed that he suggested they work together. (One wonders why she never took him up on the offer?)

Not to be Taken Seriously

Lehmann was a prolific composer and the sales of her music helped the family finances. She became increasingly frustrated, however, by the success of only what she regarded as her lightweight music. This included the witty *Nonsense Songs* (1908), settings of lyrics by Lewis Carroll from *Alice in Wonderland*, *Four Cautionary Tales and a Moral* from French-born British poet-historian Hilaire Belloc's humorous verse for children, and her most famous children's songs, *Daddy's Sweetheart* and *There are Fairies at the Bottom of the Garden*. Her serious work included *The Golden Threshold, an Indian Song-Garland* (1906), the cantata *Leaves from Ossian* (1909), the songs *Magdalen at Michael's Gate* and *When I am dead my dearest*. *Four Shakespearean Part-Songs* came out in 1911 from major British music publisher Ivor Novello. They were well received, but her opera, *Everyman*, was a failure, perhaps because the audience was not expecting such a solemn work. In 1909, she made the first of two American tours, encountering enthusiastic receptions. These travels inspired the song cycles *Prairie Pictures* (1911) and *Cowboy Ballads* (1912).

By her fifties, as a successful and popular composer, she had become an important role model for other women. She was the first president of the Society of Women Musicians, formed in 1911, and a few years later accepted a professorship at the Guildhall School of Music. After World War I broke out in 1914, her son Rudolph joined the army, but died of pneumonia while in training. Devastated by his death, she fell ill herself, dying on September 19, 1918, at fifty-six, shortly after completing her memoirs, *The Life of Liza Lehmann*.

Rebecca Clarke

REBECCA CLARKE was born August 27, 1886, in Harrow, outside London, to a German mother and an abusive American father, who had been sent to England to work for Eastman Kodak. An amateur cellist who loved to play chamber music, he literally forced his wife take up the viola and Rebecca to begin violin at eight. In 1902, she entered the RAM to study violin, but left after two years when her harmony teacher, Percy Miles, continually harassed the eighteen-year-old to marry him. Her father later bequeathed her a Stradivarius, the sale of which enabled her to institute the **May Mukle**[10] Prize at the RAM. Meanwhile, she transferred to the RCM in 1907, whose faculty boasted the most celebrated pedagogues of the era. She became the first female composition student of **Sir Charles Villiers Stanford**, teacher of **Ralph Vaughan Williams** (1872–1958); studied counterpoint with composer-conductor **Sir Frederick Bridge** (1844–1924); and viola with the foremost proponent of that instrument, **Lionel Tertis** (1876–1975).

Penniless into the Pit

In 1910 her father, who disapproved of Rebecca's professional ambitions, threw her out of the house, penniless. She became a professional violist, and in 1912, at the invitation of **Sir Henry Wood** (1869–1944), joined the Queen's Hall Light Orchestra, becoming the first woman in a professional orchestra in London. As a chamber musician, over the years she played with such renowned soloists as cellist **Pablo Casals** (1876–1976), violinists **Jacques Thibaud** (1880–1953) and **Jascha Heifetz** (1901–87), and pianists **Artur Schnabel** (1882–1951), **Arthur Rubinstein** (1887–1982), and **Dame Myra Hess** (1890–1965), one of England's most prominent pianists and a friend from academy days. She became a member of a women's string quartet with **Adila and Jelly d'Aranyi**, and

---

10. May Mukle, celebrated cellist who toured with violinist Maud Powell in America.

cellist **Guilhermina Suggia**, and founded an all-female piano quartet, the English Ensemble, with Marjorie Haywood, **May Mukle** and Kathleen Long, touring throughout England.

In 1916, Clarke came to the U.S. and established herself as a violist and composer. In 1918, her *Morpheus* for viola and piano was premiered at Carnegie Hall under the pseudonym, Anthony Trent. The following year she submitted her *Sonata for Viola and Piano* in the anonymous competition at the Berkshire Music Festival (Tanglewood). It tied for first place with **Ernest Bloch's** (1880–1959) *Suite for Viola and Piano*. The jurors were (naturally) surprised to discover the top prize contender was a woman. The deciding vote—*not* in Clarke's favor—was cast by the competition's wealthy and influential founder, **Elizabeth Sprague Coolidge**. Three years later, the 1921 Berkshire Festival second prize again went to Clarke, for her *Piano Trio* for violin, cello and piano. Perhaps to make up for her previous prejudiced vote, Mrs. Coolidge commissioned *Rhapsody* for cello and piano, premiered in 1923 at Tanglewood by **May Mukle** and **Myra Hess**. In 1924, Clarke wrote *Midsummer Moon* for violin and piano dedicated to, and first performed by, Adila d'Aranyi. She also composed many songs during the 1920s, all displaying a strong lyrical talent.

1923 brought Clarke back to England. The next two decades saw European performance tours with her English Ensemble. In 1929, she wrote the entries on *viola*, and *Ernest Bloch*, in her friend, W.W. Cobbett's 'Cyclopedic Survey of Chamber Music. From 1923 until her marriage, she continued using the pseudonym Anthony Trent, composing over twenty instrumental and chamber works. Not until a 1976 interview, at age ninety, did she admit that her works received more attention as a male composer.

WWII—the Changer of Destinies

During the 1930s she wrote no music, later admitting that an affair she was having with a married man took all her energies away from composing. At the outbreak of World War II in 1939, she was in the U.S. and unable to return to England. She worked as a governess in Connecticut and began composing again. After a chance meeting in 1944, at age fifty-eight, she married Scottish composer/pianist James Friskin (1886–1967), who was teaching at Juilliard—their paths had first crossed in 1916 at the RCM. After her marriage she settled in New York, and although she composed and performed very little, still pursued an active musical and social life, occasionally lecturing and broadcasting on music. In August 1942, she was the only woman composer among the prestigious attendees at the ISCM in San Francisco, where her *Prelude, Allegro and Pastorale* for clarinet and viola was critically acclaimed. In 1945, she became a lecturer at the Chautauqua (New York) Institute and hosted a weekly radio program on chamber music. Her works enjoyed a rebirth around her ninetieth birthday. She was working on her autobiography when she died in New York at ninety-three, October 13, 1979.

In her early compositions, Clarke used English folk tunes and followed the Romantic heritage of Elgar and Smyth, but by the '20s and '30s she was influenced by her acquaintance with Ravel and Bloch. The attention accorded Dame Ethel helped pave the way for Rebecca Clarke who, after the Victorians, stood alone in her generation, and in her country, until the emergence of the modernists **Elisabeth Lutyens** (1906–83) and **Elizabeth Maconchy** (1907–94) two decades later.

An English Avant-Gardist—Ahead of Her Time

Elisabeth Lutyens

ELISABETH LUTYENS was born July 26, 1906, in London, to the distinguished architect Sir Edwin Lutyens and Lady Emily Lytton. With groundwork laid by Smyth and Clarke, she was able to follow her interest in music without opposition. She studied violin and piano and began composing at an early age, encouraged by her aunt, Constance Lytton, a militant suffragette. Impressed by the music of Debussy and Ravel, which was just beginning to filter across the English Channel, Elisabeth persuaded her parents to let her go to Paris. She studied at the

École Normale (1922–23), while living with **Marcelle de Manziarly** (1899–1989), a young composer and student accompanist of **Nadia Boulanger**. For the next three years Elisabeth traveled with her mother and sister, studying theosophy[11] in Europe, India and Australia. Returning to London, she attended the RCM (1926–30), where she studied composition with **Harold Darke** (1888–1976) rather than Vaughan Williams or John Ireland, whom she called "cowpat" composers—presumably because she considered them "mired" in tradition.

In 1931, anxious to get her music performed, she suggested to violinist **Anne Macnaghten** and conductor **Iris Lemare** to organize concerts for *her* work and that of other unknown British composers. These *Macnaghten-Lemare Concerts* became an important showcase for new music in the '30s, at which Britten, Rawsthorne, Maconchy and others first came to public notice.

In 1933, Elisabeth married singer Ian Glennie, giving birth to her first child in 1934, and twins in 1936, all the while continuing her composing. In 1938, she met BBC programmer Edward Clark, nineteen years her senior, who had been a student of Schoenberg and was an influential force in contemporary music. They traveled to Poland together in 1939 to hear her second string quartet played at the ISCM Festival. On their return she left her husband to move in with Clark. In 1941 she had a child with him. They married the next year after Glennie finally gave her a divorce.

Becoming an Outcast

In the 1930s and '40s, while claiming that she knew very little of Schoenberg, Lutyens developed her own twelve–tone technique from studying the independent part-writing of the string fantasias of Elizabethan composer **Henry Purcell** (1659–95). Her first work in this genre was *Three Pieces for Orchestra* (1939) and *Chamber Concerto No. 1* (1940). For decades this serial style isolated her from her English contemporaries, who were not ready to accept atonal music. In the '40s, Clark was never able to hold a steady job, but Elisabeth found a source of income writing nearly 200 scores for radio and documentary films in a more popular style, although she considered this commercial work artistically insignificant and seriously hindering her development.

In the next decade, she began drinking heavily and had a nervous breakdown. Separated from Clark, she wrote *String Quartet No. 6* (1952), a motet, a series called *Music for Orchestra* (1953–55), and a cantata based on Chaucer's *De Amore* (1957). During the '50s, she began teaching. Her students included composers **Alison Bauld** and **Richard Rodney Bennett** (*b* 1936).

By the '60s, Lutyens finally came into her own as the winds of change were felt in music. Her *Quincunx*, a piece for wordless soprano, baritone and orchestra, met with success in 1962. This was followed by other vocal works, *Suddenly It's Evening* (1966), *Essence of Our Happiness* (1968), *Requiescat* (1971), in memoriam to Stravinsky, and three operas: *The Numbered* (1965–7), *Time Off? Not a Ghost of a Chance!* (1967–68) and *Isis and Osiris* (1969–70). A City of London award in 1969 provided the money to establish Olivan Press, her own publishing company. The same year brought the honor of Commander of the British Empire (CBE). Despite crippling arthritis in later years, she continued to compose to the end of her life, April 14, 1983, in London, and left behind a prolific body of work.

Elizabeth Maconchy

An English composer of Irish descent, **ELIZABETH MACONCHY** was born March 19, 1907 in Broxbourne, Hertfordshire. After the end of World War I the family returned to Ireland, where she had lessons in harmony, counterpoint, and piano. The household did not even own a radio or a record player, and the only music she heard was what she composed on the piano. At fifteen, she attended her first concert when the Hallé Philharmonic played in Dublin. After her father died in 1922, her mother moved the family back to London where Elizabeth entered

---

11. Theosophy - a religious philosophy founded on the mystical premise that God must be experienced directly via meditation, intuition and revelation. Based in India, it swept through Europe and America in the late 19th century and continues to have devout followers. Its principles are found in major Asian religions.

the RCM (1923–29), studying composition with British greats **Charles Wood** (1866–1926) and **Ralph Vaughan Williams**, who recognized her talents. She formed a lifelong friendship with her classmate, Welsh composer **Grace Williams**, with whom she explored modern composers.

It was still a time when publishers refused to accept serious works by women. In spite of winning many prizes and scholarships, Maconchy was denied the prestigious Mendelssohn Scholarship. She did win the Octavia Travelling Scholarship in 1929, which took her to Prague where she studied with Karel Jirák (1891–1972). Her first major work, *Concertino* for piano and orchestra, was played by the Prague Philharmonic in 1930, and well received. Her orchestral suite, *The Land*, was put on that summer by Sir Henry Wood at the London Proms, receiving good press notices. The same year she married Irish scholar William LeFanu, who would become Librarian of the Royal College of Surgeons (1937–68). The Proms triumph launched her professional career. Her songs and chamber works were heard on the BBC, at the *Macnaghten-Lemare Concerts* and in recitals.

A Splendid Isolation

In 1932, she contracted tuberculosis, the disease which killed her father, and was forced to move out of London's mainstream to Kent. She isolated herself in a hut at the far end of her garden and continued composing. The need to conserve her strength turned Maconchy's attention to chamber music. The thirteen string quartets written from 1933 to 1984 form the core of her output. The first was played in 1933 at one of the Macnaghten concerts in London; the second premiered at the Paris ISCM Festival in 1937; the third at a BBC contemporary music concert in 1938. Concerts of her chamber music were given in Cracow and Warsaw in 1939, just before the outbreak of WWII.

War and Peace

During the war she was mainly occupied raising vegetables, chickens and her daughters Anna, born 1939, and **Nicola** in 1947, the latter following in her mother's footsteps, becoming a prominent British composer. After the war, commissions poured in from all over the world. Like Vaughan Williams, whose example had an enduring influence on her, Maconchy was a tireless worker for her fellow musicians as the first chairwoman of the Composers' Guild (1959–60), as president of the Society for the Promotion of New Music (SPNM), and in many other capacities. She received the Cobbett Medal for her services to chamber music, was awarded the CBE in the 1977 New Year's Honours List and was made a Dame of the British Empire (DBE) in 1987.

Besides her many chamber works, in the '70s and '80s Maconchy turned to vocal and choral music with her largest work, *Héloïse and Abelard*, a cantata based on the tragedy of the twelfth century lovers. She also wrote children's operas. Early critics thought her work too modern—there are parallels between her music and that of Bartók, whom she discovered in her student days. She died, much respected, November 11, 1994 in London. Like Elisabeth Lutyens, the passing years have proved only that Elizabeth Maconchy was ahead of her time.

The Elizabeth Maconchy Composition Fellowship was initiated in 1996, administered by the Contemporary Music Centre, and is awarded every three years. The Fellowship enables a composer from the Republic of Ireland to complete a PhD in composition at the University of York in England, where the music department is headed by **Nicola LeFanu**, the composer's younger daughter. Funding of £24,000 (Irish) over the three-year period is provided by the Arts Council/An Chomhairle Ealaíon.

A Prodigious Daughter

Composer, conductor, writer on music and administrator, **IMOGEN HOLST**, born April 12, 1907, in Richmond, Surrey, began to compose as a child. From 1921–25, she attended St. Paul's Girls School, where her father, **Gustav Holst** (1874–1934), one of the leading British composers of the early 20th century, was music

Imogene Holst

director. She studied piano, but also loved ballet and dance, and at sixteen joined the English Folk Dance Society. In 1926, she entered the RCM where she studied composition with George Dyson and Gordon Jacob. Several of her chamber works were performed at informal student concerts. In 1928, she won the Cobbett Prize for her *Phantasy String Quartet*. The following year she won the Arthur Sullivan prize for composition, and her overture *Persephone* was conducted by the prominent **Sir Malcolm Sargent** (1895–1967) at the Patrons' Fund Concerts. She was a member of the Society of Women Musicians, who put on a performance of her prize-winning string quartet in the summer of 1930. That year she won an Octavia Travelling Scholarship, which she used for study in Austria, Germany, Holland and Hungary. In Vienna, she met **Grace Williams** who was there on the same scholarship. She returned to London in 1931, where her *Quintet for Oboe and Strings* and *Suite for Viola* were performed at the early *Macnaghten-Lemare Concerts*. During the 1930s, she worked as a freelance musician and teacher. Well known for folk song arrangements, such as *A Book of Tunes for the Pipes* (1932) and *Four Somerset Folk Songs* (1934) collected by Cecil Sharp, Holst published a wide variety of teaching pieces for choirs, string players and pianists, but her serious compositions remained underestimated and largely unknown until the 1980s. When her father died in 1934, she wrote her first book about him, *Gustav Holst: A Biography* (1938). In the early years of the war she worked for CEMA (Council for the Encouragement of Music and the Arts), the forerunner of the Arts Council of Great Britain, and travelled throughout Southwest England encouraging music in rural communities. From 1942 until 1951, she lived and worked in the artistic community at Dartington in Devon, where she established a thriving music department and wrote her second biography, *The Music of Gustav Holst* (1951). She stressed the importance of music-making, including composition, for everyone regardless of experience or ability.

The Write Hand of Britten

Imogen met **Benjamin Britten** and **Peter Pears**, and orchestrated Britten's *Rejoice in the Lamb* for the 1952 Aldeburgh Festival, in Suffolk, founded by Britten in 1947. For twelve years, 1952–64, Holst was his music assistant there. During this time she wrote several books: *The Story of Music* (1958), *Henry Purcell* (1961), *Tune* (1962), and *An ABC of Music* (1963). She also continued composing and the 1950s saw her song collection, *Singing for Pleasure*, published in collaboration with the National Federation of Women's Institutes (1957). She directed the Purcell Singers, 1953–67. From 1964, she concentrated on writing about, editing, and promoting the work of her father, meanwhile bringing out her *String Trio* (1962), *The Fall of the Leaf* (solo cello, 1964), and a cantata, *The Sun's Journey* (1965). Her later works included the intense, three-movement *String Quintet* (1982) and her last completed piece, *Homage to William Morris* (1984) for double bass and bass voice. She died March 9, 1984, in Aldeburgh.

Minna Keal

MINNA KEAL was born March 22, 1909, in London, of Byelorussian-Jewish parents who settled in London and ran a Hebrew publishing and bookselling business in Petticoat Lane— the famed street of outdoor markets. As a child, Minna had piano lessons and was happily exposed to endless recordings of violin and operatic virtuosi. Her father died in 1926, and two years later, at eighteen, she entered the RAM where she studied piano with Thomas Knott and composition with **William Alwyn** (1905–85), winning the Elizabeth Stokes Bursary for composition in her second year. Several of her chamber works were performed at the Academy and public concerts, including *Fantasie in C minor* for violin and piano, *Ballade in F minor* for viola and piano, and *Three Summer Sketches* for piano. In 1929, aged twenty, she gave up her musical studies to help her mother with the family business. She married in the early 1930s and had a son. Although she stopped composing, she continued to play the piano, and her early works were occasionally heard.

In the late '30s, she set up a committee to help Jewish children escape from Nazi Germany. When her marriage broke up during the Second World War, she moved to Slough (Berkshire) to work in an aircraft factory. There she met her second husband, Bill Keal, although they would not to marry until 1959. In 1963, the Keals moved to Chesham (Buckinghamshire), where Minna worked in the fur trade. At fifty-four, she resumed her piano studies, this time at the Guildhall School of Music. Six years later, at age sixty, having qualified as a piano teacher, she retired from work and began taking a few pupils.

The Later and Better

Keal met composer Justin Connolly in the 1970s, who suggested she start writing again. Besides a few piano pieces, her first work was *String Quartet* (1978), followed by *Wind Quintet* (1980). With Connolly's encouragement, she started work on her *Symphony* which took five years to complete. Surprising audiences with its grit and power, the first complete live performance was at a Promenade Concert at the Royal Albert Hall, London, September 4, 1989, six months after her eightieth birthday. Her next work, *Cantillation for Violin and Orchestra*, was premiered December 5, 1991, by the European Women's Orchestra conducted by **Odaline de la Martinez**, with soloist Ann Hooley. Her *Cello Concerto*, commissioned by the Aldeburgh Foundation with financial assistance from the Eastern Arts Board, received its premiere August 26, 1994. Subsequent performances were on March 13, 1996, in Glasgow, with the BBC Scottish Symphony Orchestra under Martyn Brabbins, and October 12, 1996, at the Barbican Centre with the London Sinfonia conducted by Richard Hickox—all with cellist Alexander Baillie. This was released on CD in 1997. A cello version of her *Ballade in F* was performed by the same artist, May 17, 1995, at London's Wigmore Hall. *Duettino for Flute and Clarinet* was heard at the Windsor Arts Festival, September 27, 1996, the same year a CD of her works, containing the *String Quartet*, *Wind Quintet*, *Cantillation* and her *Symphony*, was released. A string quartet featuring two cellos was one of her last compositions.

I last spoke to Minna in the spring of 1997. Her youthful voice and attitude belied her eighty-seven years. She died two years later, November 14, 1999. In the words of Nicola LeFanu, "She was a remarkable person."

PHYLLIS TATE, born April 6, 1911, in Gerrards Cross (Buckinghamshire), began composing foxtrots on her ukulele as a teenager. From 1928 to 1932, she attended the RAM where she studied composition, conducting, timpani and piano. Her early works include an operetta, *The Policemen's Serenade*, songs, a string quartet, a violin sonata, a cello concerto and a symphony. Her first published work, *Cradle Song*, for tenor and piano, was performed at the Academy, and the *Macnaghten-Lemare Concerts* by the Bournemouth Municipal Orchestra, as well as at concerts organized by Hubert Foss of Oxford University Press (OUP). She also wrote and arranged commercial light music, often using the pseudonyms Max Morelle or Janos. In 1935, she married music publisher and clarinetist Alan Frank. Their first child was born in 1940.

Tate destroyed almost all her pre-war music. The first work she acknowledged was her brilliant *Saxophone Concerto* (1944), a BBC commission. In 1947, she came to public attention when her *Sonata for Clarinet and Cello* was performed at a London Contemporary Music Centre concert, and her *Nocturne for Four Voices* was broadcast on the BBC. These works showed her propensity for unusual instrumental combinations. After some years of illness, she finished her *String Quartet in F major* just before the birth of her second child in 1952. Next came *The Lady of Shalott* (1956), a setting of the Tennyson poem, for tenor, viola, two pianos, celesta and nine percussion instruments, followed by vocal chamber music and several large-scale choral works: *A Secular Requiem* (1967), *St. Martha and the Dragon* (1976), and her acclaimed opera, a musical thriller, *The Lodger* (1960), based on the Jack the Ripper legend. Later works included *Explorations Around a Troubadour Song* (1973) for piano, *The Rainbow and the Cuckoo* (1974) for oboe and string trio, *Sonatina pastorale* (1974) for harmonica and harpsichord and *Prelude-Aria-Interlude-Finale* (1981) for clarinet and piano. In later life, she also wrote music for young people, including several operettas. Her compositions were geared to her belief that music should be accessible, entertain and give pleasure.

From the mid-1950s, Tate lived in Hampstead, North London, and became involved with local music clubs and choral societies such as the Composers' Guild of Great Britain and the Performing Rights Society. She died at her home, May 29, 1987.

Ruth Gipps

RUTH GIPPS was born in Bexhill-on-Sea, Sussex, February 20, 1921. Her parents, Bryan Gipps and Swiss pianist Hélène Johner, had met at the Frankfurt Conservatory. From age four, Ruth studied piano with her mother, then headmistress at the Bexhill School of Music. The child gave her first public piano concert at eight, and continued to perform throughout her teenage years. In 1937, she entered the RCM where she continued piano, studied oboe with **Leon Goossens** (1897–1988), and composition with **Ralph Vaughan Williams**. Her early compositions were performed there, including the symphonic poem *Knight in Armour* (1940), the string quartet *Sabrina* (1940), and piano quartet *Brocade* (1941). Her quintet for oboe, clarinet and string trio was premiered at Wigmore Hall in July 1941. The clarinetist for this performance was Robert Baker, whom she married in 1942, at the height of WWII, while he was home on leave from the RAF. She wrote the first of her five symphonies in 1942 and took the second oboe position with the City of Birmingham Orchestra. *Rhapsody* for clarinet and string quartet (1942) was composed for her husband, a violin concerto, op. 24 (1943) for her brother, and a piano concerto, op. 34 (1948) for her mother. The director of the CBSO, **George Weldon** (1906–63), supportively included many of her works in his repertoire. He premiered her Symphony No. 1 in 1945, with Gipps on English horn, and featured her as soloist for the Glazunov Piano Concerto No. 1 in the second half of the concert.

Opportunities Denied and Given

Ruth's son, Lance, was born in 1947. The following year she received her PhD in composition from Durham University. Her meager finances were helped by her concertizing, writing program notes, and composing incidental music for the BBC. Although Weldon taught her how to conduct, and made her the chorus master of the City of Birmingham Choir, the time had not yet come for women to direct in public. When Weldon was forced to leave the CBSO in 1951, the idea that this competent woman would be an ideal replacement was not even considered. Like many excellent female directors before her, she was permitted to conduct rehearsals only. When she interviewed for the conductorship of the BBC Midlands Orchestra, she was told that there was no way men would accept direction from a woman. To add to her problems, in 1954, at thirty-three, an old hand injury began bothering her, eliminating piano performance. Determined to conduct, she founded the London Repertoire Orchestra in 1955, taking no pay, and remaining with it until 1986. She made an American tour in 1959, on an English Speaking Union/Ford Foundation funding. In 1961, thanks to a small inheritance received by her husband which he donated to her, she formed the Chanticleer Orchestra. Made up of professionals, the orchestra gave opportunities to young soloists who went on to greatness, like violinist/conductor **Iona Brown** and cellist **Julian Lloyd Webber** (brother of Andrew of *Phantom of the Opera* fame). They programmed new music of British composers such as **William Alwyn** (1905–85), **Arthur Bliss** (1891–1975) and **Malcolm Arnold** (1921–2006)—the last two were later knighted. Forming her own orchestra enabled Gipps to establish a conducting career, as well as perform her own music—now neglected by the BBC and the rest of the musical establishment. Yet, often after she premiered her works, they were performed by other orchestras.

A Time for Reparation

Gipps' distinguished teaching career included Trinity College (1959–66), RCM (1966–76), and Kingston Polytechnic (1979). In 1967, she became chairman of the Composers' Guild of Great Britain and was instrumental in establishing the vital British Music Information Centre in London. In 1981, she was made a Member of the British Empire (MBE) for her services to music. For her sixtieth birthday, her dedicated orchestra members and soloists treated her to the vacation of a lifetime in India and Nepal. From 1982, she lived in Eastbourne, Sussex, conducted choral societies, played the organ in local churches, and continued to compose. Her œuvre contains five symphonies, six concertos, and many choral and woodwind works such as *A Weldon Suite* (1991) for four clarinets, *Cool Running Water* (1991) for bass flute and piano, and *Pan and Apollo* (1992) for two oboes, English horn and harp. Her style has been described as accessible without needing a great number of hearings. She died February 23, 1999. All that remains, is for Gipps' music, like that of her colleagues all over the world, to attain further well-deserved recognition and performance.

The Contemporary Generation

While her parents wanted her to join the family engineering business, **JANET BEAT**, born December 17, 1937, in Streetly, Staffordshire, started composing secretly. Apart from piano and French horn lessons, she received no formal musical education until her studies at Birmingham University (1956–68), earning a BM (1960) and MM (1968). In 1963 she went to Italy, researching early opera, at the same time absorbing contemporary music at the Venice Biennale. Before taking up a full-time teaching post at the Royal Scottish Academy of Music and Drama in Glasgow, in 1972, she was a freelance orchestral horn player, which gave her good experience for composing.

On the UpBeat

One of the women pioneers in electronic music composition in Great Britain, Beat's earliest works date from the late 1950s. She established the electronic music and recording studios at the Academy. From 1991, she short-ened her teaching schedule to allow more time for composing. In 1992, she became Visiting Composer at the Meistersinger-Konservatorium in Nuremberg.

Conscious of sounds, Beat finds infinite variety in nature's music—birds, wind, water. Yet, as a child, when taken around the family's factories in the West Midlands, the man-made metallic noises of industry and the work-place also imbued her with a fascination for "things technical." Feeling a close parallel between the assembling of components in an electronic circuit and the combination of harmonic and melodic components, her compositions feature interaction between live performers and electronic or computer generated music, with the influences of Bartók, Stockhausen and, via her Asian travels, the music of Japan, Tibet, India and Indonesia. Her works have been recorded and performed at world music festivals, with several premieres on the BBC and commercial radio. In 1992, *Mandala* was selected to be included in the first CD issue of audio magazine "Unknown Public." Beat also writes music for film and television, including the BBC-TV video *As she opened her eyes . . .* , in which she per-formed. She was the featured composer at *Tage für neue Musik* in Nuremberg (1992), and at Contempofest in Queensland, Australia. In 1993, her music was performed during the womens' conference, *Music Alaska*, and in the Sonic Arts Network series at London's South Bank Centre. 1995 saw the premiere of *Joie de Vivre*, commis-sioned by the Royal Society of Arts, Music and Drama (RSAMD) for the *Academy Now!* series. Other titles include *Le Tombeau de Claude* (1973); *Fêtes pour Claude* (homages to Debussy, 1992); *Apsara Music 1*; *Arabesque*; *Aztec Myth*; *Fireworks in Steel*; *Cross Currents and Reflections*; *Puspawarna*; *Echoes from Bali*; *A Vision of the Unseen Nos. 1 and 2*; *A Springtime Pillow Book*; and *Scherzo notturno*. 1999 saw the completed String Quartet begun in 1992. Her Vincent Sonata was performed by violinist Valerie Rubin in Nuremberg, and *Dynamism : Scherzo-Toccata* for two pianos, eight hands, both received their premieres December 2000, the latter at South Bank Centre by the London Piano Quartet for whom it was written. The work was also performed in May 2002 by Piano 40. *Hunting Horns are Memories* was heard June 2002.

Besides radio and television appearances, Janet Beat has published scholarly editions of baroque music. She is a founding member of the Scottish Society of Composers, the Scottish Electro-Acoustic Music Association and the contemporary music ensemble, Soundstrata (1989).

Now an honorary research fellow, in 1996 she joined the faculty of Glasgow University to lecture in music technology and composition. 1998 saw a sixtieth birthday concert at St. John's Smith Square, London, and a whole program devoted to a retrospective of her electronic works broadcast by Portuguese Radio.

DIANA BURRELL was born in Norwich, October 25, 1948, where her schoolteacher father was assistant organist at the famed cathedral. She started composing in high school, but concentrated on performance at Cambridge. After receiving her BA (1971), she taught at Sutton High School for Girls in Surrey for four years, composing music for school plays and an opera. Her next few years were as a freelance violist, playing for the City of London Sinfonia, Sadler's Wells Ballet and the London Festival Ballet. During this time she married a freelance singer and had two children.

Her first work to attract attention was *Missa Sancte Endeliente* (1980) for five soloists, chorus and orchestra, written for Cornwall's St. Endellion Festival with conductor **Richard Hickox**. Next came the BBC broadcast of *Io Evoe!* (1984), combining ancient Gallic and native American ritual chants. Beginning in 1985, with commissions from leading orchestras and artists, she cut down her performing career to concentrate on composition. *Arched Forms with Bells* (1990) for organ, was for the BBC Promenade Concerts, and *Resurrection* (1993) for the Bournemouth Sinfonietta, plus music for dance and television. Writing to celebrate primitiveness and energy, Burell views her work as "architectural shapes on paper" communicating directly with the audience in clear, bold musical language, all of which is heard in *Landscape* for orchestra, for the 1988 Piccadilly Festival, where birdcalls, scrap metal and steel pans are used to help create a primeval urban landscape. A dramatic example of Burrell's mystical qualities, *Barrow* (1991) for chamber ensemble, evolved from a dream of a primitive ritual at this 55 AD ancient burial mound, and features haunting drumming.

Appointed composer-in-association to the City of London Sinfonia in 1994, *Enchaînements*, her first piece for them, was premiered that December. Next came a song cycle *Dunkelhvide Måne-stråler*, set to poems by the Danish writer Tove Ditlevsen, premiered in the orchestra's twenty-fifth anniversary season, October 1996. The 1994 "Living Composers" project of the Eastern Orchestral Board featured Burrell's music performed by the Orchestra of St. John's Smith Square, Bournemouth Sinfonia, English Sinfonia and others. Other 1994 premieres included the *Viola Concerto* at the Norfolk and Norwich Festival; *Tachograph* for baritone and piano for South Bank Centre; a carol, *Christo Paremus Cantica* (for King's College Cambridge) and the string quartet *Gulls and Angels*—juxtaposing the screeching of gulls against the sonorous harmony of angels—by the Sorrel Quartet in Germany. September 1996 saw the premiere of her *Clarinet Concerto* by the Northern Sinfonia at the Abbey Festival. The world premiere of *Benedicam Dominum* for choir and organ, at Westminster Cathedral, came in November, and in December her *Viola Concerto* played by the Brunel Ensemble at Bristol. In 1997, the BBC Symphony gave a world premiere of *Symphonies of Flocks, Herds and Shoals* at Royal Festival Hall, and her opera *The Albatross* was produced at Trinity College of Music. Involved in educational projects, Burrell also writes for young players, including a Flute Concerto for the London Schools Symphony Orchestra, which was premiered in the Barbican Centre, January 1998, by flutist William Bennett. October of that year saw the premiere of the string quartet, *Earth*, by the New Zealand String Quartet in Hamilton. 1999 brought *Double Image* for flute, clarinet, violin, cello and piano and *Ritual Sentences*, for violin, viola and cello, commissioned by the Enesco Trio, premiered at Wigmore Hall, London. Sharp Edge, the new music ensemble of the Royal Philharmonic, commissioned *Athletes*, for two-part chorus and mixed ensemble, first performed May 2000 at the Albert Hall, Nottingham. The same year produced *Black Starlight, bright Cinnamon Earth* for piano and strings. *Gold* (brass ensemble and piano), a joint commission from Huddersfield Festival and Thames Valley University, was premiered November 2001 by the Royal Northern Brass Ensemble and Philip Mead. The same year she wrote *Lucid* for double wind quintet and *Festival* for organist David Titterington.

Tansy Davies

Born May 29, 1973, in Bristol, **TANSY DAVIES** was playing French horn and piano by age eleven and electric guitar at fourteen. Her introduction to music was via the radio, and her interest in anything unusual or experimental led her to contemporary classical music. She received her BA with honors (1994), went on to Guildhall, studying composition with Simon Bainbridge, earning her MM with distinction (1998), and PhD (2001) at Royal Holloway with Simon Holt.

Competition successes include the Gregynog Young Composer of Wales Award 1995; BBC/Lloyds Bank Young Composers' Workshop (1996); Brunel/Maggini String Quartet Competition (1998); and the Oxford and Cambridge Musical Club Centenary Composition Prize in 2000.

Interested in using scientific principles to create musical form, her works have been performed by the Brunel Ensemble, a commission at the Hoxton/Almeida Festival; Duke Quartet; Quintessence, who recorded her wind quintet on CD; Composers Ensemble; BBC Philharmonic, and London Sinfonietta. Performances at festivals include Spitalfields and Isleworth (1998), Hoxton and Huddersfield (1999). *Small Black Stone*, a commission from Music Past and Present, and *Picking Raspberries at Eagles Nest Lake*, a Bath Festival commission, were premiered in the spring of 2000, with other works featured at the State of the Nation, Brighton, and Hoxton music festivals. 2001–02 commissions were for the London Sinfonietta, Composers Ensemble, and a solo violin piece for Simon Blendis.

Evelyn Ficarra

EVELYN FICARRA was born in California in 1962, but moved to Britain in 1975. She studied composition with Jonathan Harvey and Peter Wiegold, earning her MA from the University of Sussex (1986). Her interests focus on cross-arts work and electro-acoustic media. She studied at the National Film and Television School and, besides concert works, has written music for dance, theater, film and radio.

Commissions and support have come from the Arts Council of England, London Arts Board and Sonic Arts Network, with awards from the Ralph Vaughan Williams Trust (1993), through which she spent six months at the International Electronic Music Studio (EMS) in Stockholm creating a solo tape piece, *Source of Uncertainty*, which later became a finalist in the 1993 Prix Noroit. The Hinrichsen Foundation Award came in 1996. Her works have been performed at the Bourges and Luigi Russolo competitions. At the turn of the 21st century she wrote *Search*, for Lucy Bailey's music theater group, *The Gogmagogs*, *Borrowing Intimacy*, a collaboration with composer John Sweeney and choreographer Sarah Fahie, and *last june - 4:30 A.M.*, a sound/image collaboration with film maker Suse Bohse, which was included in the "State of the Nation" event at the South Bank Centre, April 2000. A solo CD of her electro-acoustic works, *Frantic Mid-Atlantic*, has been released on the Sargasso label.

DIERDRE GRIBBIN, born in Belfast May 24, 1967, started flute and piano at age seven, but did not begin composing until she was twenty-one. Going to Ulster Orchestra concerts with her aunt, plus traditional Irish music, were influences on her choice of career. Although she did not study art formally, her painting is also an inspiration for compositions.

She received the Holst Foundation award for composition, earned a BM from Queen's University (Belfast) and a PhD from Royal Holloway in 2000. She became a Fulbright Fellow based in New York the same year, and a Trinity College Cambridge Visiting Arts Fellow in 2001.

2001 also marked the launching of her own ensemble, Gribbin Music.

Nicola Lefanu

One of England's foremost contemporary composers, **NICOLA LEFANU**, born April 28, 1947, in Essex, is the daughter of composer **Dame Elizabeth Maconchy** and William LeFanu, a noted British medical historian and descendant of Victorian writer Sheridan LeFanu. Brought up with music and literature, she lived in an ideal environment for a budding composer. She learned piano and cello, wrote and produced school plays, composed music, and soon realized this as a natural gift. In 1968, she received her BA from St. Hilda's College, Oxford, meanwhile taking private composition lessons with **Egon Wellesz**, **Thea Musgrave** and **Maxwell Davies** in England, and Goffredo Petrassi in Italy, followed by postgraduate work at the RCM (1968–69). In 1973, she won the prestigious Mendelssohn Scholarship and the Harkness Award, which took her to America (1973–74) where she studied with Earl Kim and Seymour Shifrin and wrote a cycle of fifteen songs, *The Same Day Dawns*, using translations of Tamil, Chinese and Japanese (angst) poetry.

Passing the Notes

Besides composition, LeFanu has enjoyed a rewarding teaching career, first at Francis Holland School (1969–72), then as headmistress of the St. Paul's School for Girls (1975–77), following in the hallowed footsteps of Gustav Holst and his daughter, Imogen. During a six month leave of absence in 1976, she directed composers' seminars and workshops in Australia, where she met composer David Lumsdaine, whom she married in 1979. Their son, Peter, was born in England in 1982. (He is, according to his mother, "a keen and quite accomplished all-round musician." He entered Cambridge in 2001 to study Mathematics.) From 1977–94, she taught at King's College, University of London, then moved to York University as head of the music department (1994–2001) where she still teaches. In 1995, she was awarded an honorary DMA from Durham University and appointed a fellow of the Royal College of Music.

Le Fanu's large *œuvre* ranges from unaccompanied pieces, music for orchestra, chamber groups, several operas and many vocal works. Her first major orchestral work, *The Hidden Landscape*, was performed at a London Prom concert in 1973 by the BBC Symphony Orchestra under Norman Del Mar (1919–94). Her operas include *Dawnpath* (1977); a chamber opera, *The Old Woman of Beare* (1981) for soprano and thirteen instruments, one of her most successful works; *The Story of Mary O'Neill*, a radio opera (1986); *The Green Children* (1990), set in the twelfth century dealing with two green children who come from another world; and *Blood Wedding* (1992) from the play by Federico Garcia Lorca. Her fifth opera, *The Wildman*, was commissioned and premiered by the Aldeburgh Foundation, June 1995, then toured England and Scotland. Sextet (*a wild garden*), written in 1996, was premiered in London and Dublin by the Concorde Ensemble, April 1997. The same month her *String Quartet No. 2* was commissioned to be the test piece in the International String Quartet Competition. May saw the premiere of *On the wind—a lament* at the Cork (Ireland) International Choral Festival. A 1999 commission, *Duo Concertante* for solo violin and viola and orchestra, was premiered by the Northern Sinfonia, March 2000. *Miniature and Canon* was written for Chamber Music 2000, a project of the Schubert Ensemble, begun in 1998 to commission new chamber works for children and adults at all levels of musical ability. The orchestral work *Catena*, for eleven solo strings, was premiered January 2001, at London's South Bank by Opus 20. This and three other string works are on a 2004 Naxos CD. Other 2004 premieres include *Amores* for solo horn and strings, and a chamber opera, *Light Passing*.

One of the founders of the group Women in Music (1987), LeFanu's article, "Master Musicians: an Impregnable Taboo?" was a pioneering study of the reception of British women composers, focusing on the neglect of their music. (How much have things changed?)

ODALINE DE LA MARTINEZ, based in London, has a thriving dual career, composing and conducting. (See Conductors.)

Katharine Norman

KATHARINE NORMAN is the only woman heading a major electronic music studio in the United Kingdom. Born in Essex, May 11, 1960, to amateur musician parents, she began piano at ten and oboe at sixteen. After a background of Bach, Beethoven, etc., her unusual mother, who started learning trumpet at age sixty, heard the music of Stockhausen on the radio in 1974, and bought a record of *Kontakte*, because she liked it. It was this piece of music which influenced Katharine to be a composer and study electroacoustic music, although the latter did not happen until she went to Princeton in 1989. After her BM with honors (1982) and MM (1985) from Bristol University, in 1989 she won a Fulbright and in 1990 a Wingate Scholarship, which she used to study computer music and composition with Paul Lansky at Princeton, where she completed her PhD in Composition (1993).

Norman has taught at Bristol University, Dartington College of Arts, Sussex University, Guildhall School of Music and, from 1994–97, was Lecturer in Composition at Sheffield University where she set up and directed their sound studio (SUSS). Since 1998, she has lectured at Goldsmiths College, University of London, where she is director of the Stanley Glasser Electronic Music Studios, and presents seminars about her work for BBC Radio Training Courses.

One of few British women working in this area as an established composer, besides instrumental music, Norman combines instruments or voices with tape and electronics, and uses recorded "real world" sounds, designated as a "radiophonic soundscape." Her major titles include *In her own time*, tape (London CD, 1992); *Trilling Wire*, for clarinet and tape, which received honorable mention in the 1994 Russolo International Composition Competition; *Hard Cash (and small dreams of change)*, picked by the American Composers' Forum for their CD, "Sonic Circuits V"; *Icarus*, for voices and tape, selected for the 1995 ISCM World Music Days; and *memory places*, for small ensemble, which reached the finals of the Alea III International Composition Competition. *Transparent things* (piano solo), was a Holst Award commission (1995). She entered the millennium with *Helpful Instructions for Circus Performers* (percussion, 2000) and *Insomnia* (percussion, oboe and tape, 2001).

Norman's computer and radiophonic work is broadcast and performed particularly in Germany, America and Canada. Her CDs feature instrumental and computer music, such as that on the Metier label with pianist Philip Mead. *London* (NMC), music for tape, and clarinet and tape, was voted "critics choice" by *The Wire*. *Leonardo's Lists*, was written for Bristol-based multimedia ensemble Elektrodome, *Fuga Interna (II - Sequence)* for Jane O'Leary's Dublin ensemble, Concorde, and *(Fuga Interna III)*, a solo percussion work, for members of the Composers' Ensemble. Her CD ROM commission from Sonic Arts Network was featured at "The State of the Nation" April 2000.

A past director of Sonic Arts Network, Norman was artistic director of their fifteenth birthday South Bank festival, *PLUGGED!* She was also a board member of the International Computer Music Association, editing the ICMA newsletter, *Array*. She writes on aesthetic issues in electroacoustic/computer music. A book on the subject, *Sounding Art*, was published by Ashgate Press in February 2004.

Katharine is married to Jonathan Dore, a commissioning editor for publishing.

Alwynne Pritchard

ALWYNNE PRITCHARD was born in Glasgow in 1968. Encouraged by her composer father, Gwyn Pritchard, she began writing music as a teenager. She studied composition with Robert Saxton at Guildhall, and later with Justin Connolly and Michael Finnissy at the RAM where she was awarded many prizes for her work, including a joint PRS (Performing Rights Society) award at the Southampton New Music Week. A Licentiate of the Royal Academy of Ballet (RAB, 1992), she earned her MM (1998), plus an associate degree. While completing her PhD at the University of Bristol, her dissertation being a commentary on her own work, she was appointed artist-in-residence at the Kulturhuset, Bergen (Norway), European City of Culture for the year 2000.

Prtichard's music has been performed by the Arditti String Quartet, Bournemouth Sinfonietta, Ian Brown, Nicolas Hodges, John Kenny, London Sinfonietta, Lontano, Uroboros Ensemble, and at festivals in Bath, Brighton, Chard, Glasgow (Music Nova) and Huddersfield, as well as venues throughout Europe and Scandinavia, with broadcasts on the BBC and abroad. She wrote a work for the Schubert Ensemble Chamber Music 2000 project, a piece for solo guitar for the Bath International Guitar Festival and *Invisible Cities*, for pianist Ian Pace, released on a CD of piano music by Alwynne Pritchard and other British composers. Also a teacher, she presents and reviews for BBC Radios 3 and 4. Her music has been distinguished for its "strong spare language and restrained eloquence."

REBECCA SAUNDERS was born in London December 19, 1967, to musical parents. Following her early training as a violinist, she studied music at Edinburgh University. A Fraser Scholarship from there, and awards from the German Academic Exchange Service, sent her to study composition with Wolfgang Rihm at the Musikhochschule in Karlsruhe (1991–94), where between 1992 and 1995 many of Saunders' works were performed in association with the New Composers' Society. She received her PhD in Composition, studying with Nigel Osborne on an Edinburgh University Premier Scholarship (1994–97). A Busoni bursary in 1995 from the

Academy of Arts in Berlin, and the Ernst von Siemens Foundation scholarship (1996), enabled Saunders to work for several months in New York and Brussels.

Saunders' works have been performed in numerous concert series and festivals, including those in Illingen (1992, 1994), Darmstadt (1993, 1998), Heidelberg (1993, 1994), Stuttgart (1994), Edinburgh (1994, 1995), Aarhus (Holland) (1994, 1995), Bludenz (1995), Graz (Austria) (1995, 1997), Witten (1996, 1998), Forbach (1997) and Middelburg (1998), all in Germany. In July 1997, her orchestral work *G and E on A* was premiered by Germany's Hesse Radio Symphony in the New Music Forum series. By 1999, her music had been heard in Helsinki, Oslo, Huddersfield (England), the Berlin Biennale and London's "State of the Nation." Her chamber work *Into the Blue* was selected for performance at the ISCM World Music Days (1999). *Molly's Song* was performed in Brussels by the ensemble Q-02 and *Duo 3* by Ars Music (2000), the year which also marked her composer-in-residency at the Darmstadt Summer School, and the release of a portrait CD by MusikFabrik. A double concerto for trumpet, percussion and orchestra was commissioned by West German Radio in 2001. Saunders' music has been broadcast throughout Europe. She makes her home in Berlin.

ERROLLYN WALLEN born in Belize, has made her name in the UK. (See Women of Color.)

SCOTLAND

SALLY BEAMISH, born August 26, 1956, in London, started writing music at an early age. She studied viola at the Royal Northern College of Music, and composition with Anthony Gilbert and Sir Lennox Berkeley. For a decade her career centered on viola, mainly as a member of the Raphael Ensemble with whom she made recordings of string sextets. But she always considered herself a composer, and honed her skills playing with contemporary music groups such as the London Sinfonietta and Lontano,[12] where she became acquainted with prominent composers and gained insights into their working methods.

Beginning a Scottish Heritage

A 1989 Arts Council Composer's Bursary prompted a move to Scotland, where she and her husband, cellist Robert Irvine, founded the Chamber Group of Scotland with co-director James MacMillan. She was composer-in-residence with the Scottish Chamber Orchestra, and assistant to **Sir Peter Maxwell Davies** (*b* 1934) on the SCO composers' course in Hoy (1994–95). Commissions began arriving from the London Philharmonic, Royal Scottish National Orchestra, Philharmonia of London and Birmingham Contemporary Music Group, for whom she wrote *A Book of Seasons*—a "picture book" for daughter Stephanie. *Tuscan Lullaby* was written to celebrate son Laurie's arrival. 1993 saw her first symphony, premiered by the Iceland Symphony, and a new octet for the Gaudier Ensemble at the Cheltenham Festival. *Concerto Grosso* for the BT Scottish Ensemble opened their autumn season. In September, she received the prestigious Paul Hamlyn Foundation Award for outstanding achievement in composition, and was one of four composers invited to write music for four BBC television documentaries. "The Loch" was shown in Autumn 1993. A quintet for the Schubert Ensemble premiered in 1994, and has since received numerous performances. *Walking Back*, for the Academy of St. Martin-in-the-Fields' thirty-fifth anniversary, was broadcast live from the Royal Festival Hall in October. The premiere of her Violin Concerto for Anthony Marwood and the BBC Scottish Symphony took place, January 1995. Her Viola Concerto premiered at the 1995 London Proms with Philip Dukes and the London Mozart Players, conducted by Mathias Bamert. That year her work was performed in Antwerp, Prague, Vienna, Tokyo and New York. The concerto form is a continuing source of inspiration. Her first two were followed by ones for cello, performed by Robert Cohen and the Academy of St Martin-in-the-Fields, and saxophone with John Harle and the St. Magnus Festival, as well as Swedish Chamber Orchestras. Her first major CD on the

---

12. Contemporary Music Ensemble founded in the early '70s, and led by Odaline de la Martinez.

Swedish label BIS (1999), features three concerti. The second CD (2000) has the saxophone concerto and *The Imagined Sound of Sun on Stone*. Both are recorded by the Swedish Chamber Orchestra with Ola Rudner, and have received excellent reviews. Further discs are scheduled on BIS over the next decade. Beamish has worked for BBC Radio Manchester and Radio Scotland as a presenter of music programs, and made appearances on BBC TV, STV and Channel 4, discussing her work. She has written several film and television scores, and helped set up the Irvine Wilson Company, specializing in music for film. An excerpt from her oboe concerto, performed by Douglas Boyd with the BBC Scottish Symphony under Martyn Brabbins, was featured on BBC TV's Autumn 1994 series of *Soundbites*, presented by percussionist **Evelyn Glennie**. Her second Symphony was premiered by the Royal Scottish National Orchestra. Her compositions also encompass non-professional performers and theater, in the form of a children's nativity musical, works for amateur strings and full orchestra, and a series commissioned by Children's Classic Concerts, featuring the different sections of the orchestra.

Beamish was one of the first artists to be awarded a Lottery grant of £25,000 by Creative Scotland/Scottish Arts Council, which went towards her oratorio for the BBC Proms, premiered by the BBC Symphony Orchestra and Chorus with **Sir Andrew Davies**. The work, *Knotgrass Elegy*, underlines her concern for the environment and her interest in jazz, with a major part for saxophonist Tommy Smith. The words were commissioned from Scottish poet Donald Goodbrand Saunders.

2001 compositions included *October Serenade* (organ), *Opus California* (string quartet), *Bugs*, a blues for strings and jazz kit and *Variations for Bass Trombone*. With Swedish composer Karin Rehnqvist, Beamish shares a joint composer-in-residence with the Swedish and Scottish Chamber Orchestras, an innovative appointment which offers each composer four major commissions over four years, to be performed by both orchestras. She collaborated with Scottish writer Janice Galloway on a full-length opera based on the life of Mary Shelley, creator of *Frankenstein*, commissioned by the Brighton Festival and Scottish Opera, premiered in 2002. Other premieres include concertos for percussionist **Evelyn Glennie**, violist Tabea Zimmerman, flutist Sharon Bezaly, and famed trumpeter **Håkan Hardenberger** (2003), commissioned by the Scottish National Youth Orchestra.

Sally and her husband live in a remote farmhouse in Stirlingshire, with their two sons, Laurie, born 1989, Thomas, 1991, and daughter Stephanie Rose who arrived October 1995.

Judith Weir

Born May 11, 1954 in Cambridge, **JUDITH WEIR**'s Scottish origin influences her distinctive music. She studied composition with **John Tavener** (*b* 1944) in London, and played oboe and percussion in the National Youth Orchestra of Great Britain. After a semester at Massachusetts Institute of Technology (MIT) working on computer music with Barry Vercoe, she entered King's College, Cambridge (1973–76) for further composition study. Her student work, *Where the Shining Trumpets Blow*, was performed by the Philharmonia Orchestra of London (1974). A 1975 Koussevitzky Fellowship from the Boston Symphony won her a summer at Tanglewood with Gunther Schuller, where she wrote the wind quintet *Out of the Air*, her first published work.

She'll Take the Highlands

After her 1976 graduation from Cambridge, Weir was composer-in-residence for the Southern Arts Board until 1979. She taught at Glasgow University (1979–82), and while there wrote vocal pieces based on Scottish poems. She returned to Trinity College, Cambridge, for two years on a creative arts fellowship, composing *Sketches from a Bagpiper's Album* (1984), *Serbian Cabaret*, based on folk songs, a children's opera, *Black Spider*, and *The Consolations of Scholarship* (1985) in the style of early Chinese Yuan dramas. 1988–91 saw her back in Glasgow as the Guinness composer-in-residence at the Royal Scottish Academy of Music and Drama. Several of her early works grew directly out of her interest in Scottish culture, such as *Black Birdsong* (1977), a setting for baritone and four instruments of two traditional poems. *King Harald's Saga* (1979) reflects her interest in medieval history and literature, *Grand Opera in Three Acts* for solo soprano tells the story of an unsuccessful Norwegian invasion of England in 1066. *Missa del Cid* for unaccompanied choir and speaker, combining a bloodthirsty medieval Spanish epic poem with the liturgy of the Mass, was composed for the 1988 BBC *Sounds on Film* series. She collaborated with choreographer Ian Spink, and the dance company Second Stride, on *Heaven Ablaze in his Breast* (1989), based on E.T.A. Hoffmann's story "The Sandman," and wrote incidental music for the theater, including Peter Shaffer's *The Gift of the Gorgon* (1992) and Caryl Churchill's *The Skriker* (1993).

Into the Majors

Weir attained international recognition with *A Night at the Chinese Opera* (1986–87), in three acts for eleven singers and orchestra, with her own libretto, commissioned by the BBC for the Kent Opera. Other opera commissions, *The Vanishing Bridegroom* (1990) and *Blond Eckbert* from ENO, premiered in London, April 1994, and Santa Fe (New Mexico) in July. Reworking music of earlier composers, she re-composed *Scipio's Dream* (1991) from Mozart for BBC television, and *Combattimento II* (1992), after Monteverdi. Her BSO commission, *Music, Untangled*, was for the 100th anniversary of Tanglewood (1991). *Heroic Strokes of the Bow* (*Heroische Bogenstriche*, 1992), inspired by a Paul Klee painting, was a Westdeutsche Sinfonia commission. 1995 saw *Forest*, premiered by Simon Rattle and the CBSO; *Moon and Star*, for the BBC Proms, premiered at the Albert Hall with the BBC Symphony Orchestra and Singers; *Our Revels Now Are Ended* and *Sleep Sound Ida Mornin'* for two violins, performed at Boston's New England Conservatory. 1996 premieres were *Horse d'œrvres*, songs with texts about horses, and *Waltraute's Narration*, an ensemble arrangement from Wagner's *Götterdämmerung*, Act I. 1997 brought a piano concerto.

From 1995–98, Weir was the CBSO's Composer in Association, and for six seasons, 1995–2000, she was the artistic director of the Spitalfields Festival in London's East End, famed for its programs combining early and contemporary music. She is the holder of a Critics' Circle Award (1994), a CBE (1995), and the Lincoln Center's Stoeger Prize (1997). In 1999, she held the Hambro Visiting Professorship in Opera Studies at Oxford University.

By the turn of the century, she wrote an extended series of chamber works for strings and piano, including a piano quartet, *Arise! arise! you slumbering sleepers* (2000), for her longtime collaborators the Schubert Ensemble, and several works combining instrumental groups and voices. She devised a long series of workshop pieces for amateur musicians, including three symphonies for performers in the Birmingham suburb of Sheldon, and three more for the Alveley Village Band in Shropshire.

We are shadows, a cantata combining Taoist philosophy and Scottish gravestone inscriptions, was premiered March 2000 by Sir Simon Rattle and the CBSO and choruses. That month also saw the first performance of *woman.life.song*, a fifty-minute song cycle commissioned by soprano **Jessye Norman**, which she sang in Carnegie Hall and then at the Proms in Summer 2000. Autumn 2000 marked the collaboration with storyteller Vaya Naidu, tabla player Sarvar Sabri and the Birmingham Contemporary Music Group (BCMG), to create *Future Perfect*, an evening of storytelling and music, which toured throughout England and India.

Weir taught at Princeton February to May 2001.

WALES

Morfydd Owen

MORFYDD OWEN, composer, mezzo-soprano, and pianist, was born October 1, 1891, in Treforest, South Wales. Demonstrating a precocious musical talent inherited from gifted parents—her father led a children's choir, and founded a church—she was given piano lessons as a child and, imbued early in life with a profound religious faith, started writing hymn tunes. At sixteen, she began private lessons in composition and piano from Welsh composer **David Evans** (1843–1913), and while at school her popular hymn tune, *Morfydd*, was published in 1909. At eighteen, she entered University College in Cardiff as the first holder of the Caradog

Scholarship. Better known as a pianist than a singer at this point, she had played the Grieg Concerto in one of her concerts. Many of her compositions were performed in student recitals including, *Romance* for violin and piano, keyboard, choral pieces and the part-song, *My Luve's Like a Red, Red Rose*. Her song writing began drawing attention. Before graduation in 1912, she wrote what is considered the most emotionally charged of her songs, *To Our Lady of Sorrows*. Her final exam consisted of composing an *Ave Maria* for mezzo-soprano, chorus and orchestra. Adding an accompaniment to her father's setting of verses by Eliot Crawshay-Williams, M.P. so impressed the Member of Parliament, who was also secretary to Prime Minister David Lloyd-George, that he invited her to London for further study. Although single girls still needed a chaperone, her parents overcame their qualms in order not to stand in the way of their daughter's music. She moved to the capital, September 1912, to study at the RAM, where she added voice training, winning many prizes. In 1913, she made her first appearance in a student concert at Bechstein Hall, singing four of her own songs. Many of her works were heard at the Academy, including *Nocturne in D flat* and her cantata, *Pro Patria*, for soprano, baritone, chorus and orchestra, performed at a December 1915 concert.

Led Into Folkways

Morfydd's Welsh circle of friends in London organized private concerts in their homes at which she performed. These artistic friendships, frowned upon by her chapel-going supporters, included the "risqué" novelist, D. H. Lawrence, American poet Ezra Pound and several Russian émigrés. This led to her interest in Russian folk songs, but WWI (1914–18) cancelled plans to study in St. Petersburg. Instead, she began collaborating with ethnomusicologist Ruth Lewis, a leading member of the Welsh Folk Song Society, transcribing and writing accompaniments for collections. Their volume of *Folk Songs Collected in Flintshire and the Vale of Clwyd* was published in 1914. After Owen's death, Lewis used more of her friend's music in her *Second Collection of Welsh Folk Songs* (1934).

The Unfairness of Fate

Appointed sub-professor in sight-singing and transposition at the Royal Academy, Morfydd's singing career also progressed from a soloist in Verdi's *Requiem* in Wales, to engagements at the Pump Room in Bath, (Kent, England), to Oxford, to WWI fundraisers, to her professional debut at London's prestigious Aeolian Hall, January 1917. The month before, however, she had met Ernest Jones, twelve years her senior, who would make a name for himself as the biographer of Sigmund Freud. After only two months' acquaintance, they were married February 6, 1917, much to the consternation of her friends. He was taken by her beauty, but what did she see in him? Stability and security? She had had a stream of proposals, and at twenty-five was considered a little old to be still unmarried. She remained at the RAM until that summer, but running her husband's home in London and their Jacobean cottage in the country kept her so busy that her composing output was greatly diminished, from 150 compositions before 1916 to only a dozen thereafter. Her singing career also declined as Jones' avant-garde leanings—psychoanalysis was still regarded with great distrust—were not well accepted by the London Welsh upper crust. For her part, Morfydd's photographs as Mrs. Jones testify that she was not happy. The following summer, on holiday in Wales, she suddenly developed acute appendicitis, and died on September 7, 1918, three weeks before her twenty-seventh birthday. The exact cause of her death—whether or not it was from the operation—is still shrouded in mystery.

Many of Owen's compositions, orchestral, choral, chamber, piano and vocal, are imaginatively infused with folk song themes. Edited by her husband and composer Frederick Corder (1852–1932), a four volume memorial edition of her work, illustrating the distinctive quality of her style, was published in 1923.

Interest in Morfydd's music has never waned in her native country, and Welsh emigrants brought it across the Atlantic to Canada where it enjoys great popularity in the Welsh community. In 1998, **Dr. Keith Davies Jones'** orchestration of the *Prelude in F* was premiered by the Winnipeg Chamber Ensemble. In 1999, the St. David's Society (an international society devoted to the perpetuation of the Welsh language, customs and traditions), which has played and sung many of Owen's compositions over the years, organized a Festival of her music in Winnipeg, giving the North American premieres of many of her songs and piano pieces. Music historian **Rhian Davies** lectured on the composer's life and, with Dr. Jones, sang the world premiere of *Yr Arglwydd ar fy Nhaith* (The Lord on my Journey). In September 1999, Davies lectured on Owen at the National Gymanfa Ganu (Festival of Wales Singfest) in Minneapolis. In 2000, mezzo **Heulwen Jones** won the Welsh National Gymanfa Ganu Association Eisteddfod in Ottawa with a performance which included *Suo Gân* (Lullaby). *Threnody for String Orchestra* received a 2000 performance in Winchester, Virginia, conducted by Larry Strachan. *Gweddi Y Pechadur* (The Sinner's Prayer) is one of the few pieces on recording. It is considered one of the most stunning and soul-searching solos ever written by a Welsh composer, and remains the work that Morfydd Owen is most remembered by in Wales. In December 2001, her *Ave Maria* was premiered in the Welsh capital by the Cardiff University Choral and Orchestral Union, directed by Dr. Timothy Taylor.

Rhian Davies wrote her University of Wales (Bangor) 1999 PhD dissertation: *A Beautiful and Refined Talent: Morfydd Owen (1891–1918)*, which followed her 1994 book, *Never so Pure a Sight, Morfydd Owen (1891–1918): A Life in Pictures*. A fuller biography was published in the 21st century.

"It was the unanimous verdict of her generation that Morfydd Owen was the most supremely gifted and diversely talented musician Wales had yet produced."[13]

Grace Williams

Born February 19, 1906, in Barry, South Wales, both of **GRACE WILLIAMS**' parents were schoolteachers who loved music. Her father was conductor of the Romilly Boys Choir for whom, as a young girl, Grace was accompanist. She wrote music while still at school and claimed her earliest inspiration was attending a performance of *Morfa Rhuddlan* by Morfydd Owen. In 1923, she won the Morfydd Owen Musical Scholarship to University College, Cardiff (BM, 1926), where one of her teachers was David Evans who had taught Owen. Next came the RCM, studying composition with major British composers **Ralph Vaughan Williams** and **Gordon Jacob** (1895–1984). Her fellow students there included **Dorothy Gow** (1893–1982), **Imogen Holst** and **Elizabeth Maconchy**, women composers who maintained contact with each other throughout their illustrious careers. In 1930, Williams went to Vienna under an Octavia Travelling Scholarship to study with avant-gardist **Egon Wellesz** (1885–1974). After her return to London, she taught for several years at Camden School for Girls and at Southlands College of Education. During the 1930s she enjoyed the friendship of **Bengamin Britten**, who was instrumental in her working for the Strand Film Company in 1936. However, she declined an invitation to act as his assistant, a position later occupied by Imogen Holst.

Home to Green Valleys

In 1946, Williams returned to Wales, worked on educational programs for the BBC and gradually made her name as a freelance composer. Most of her major works were written on commissions from the BBC, the Royal National Eisteddfod, and festivals at Llandaff, Cardiff and Swansea. She wrote mainly for orchestra, two symphonies (the first of which she withdrew and the second she was revising when she died); three concertos; choral works with orchestra; a one-act opera and a mass. She claimed to have no talent for chamber music. Her most well-known work is the *Fantasia on Welsh Nursery Tunes* (1940). Other significant compositions are *Sinfonia Concertante* for piano and orchestra (1941), and *Sea Sketches* (1947) for string orchestra.

After WWII, she was drawn back to London, but the stress of teaching and composing demanded too much of her health. Home to Barry in 1947, she lived in an apartment in her parents' home and freelanced, writing

---

13. Quoted from *Never So Pure a Sight* with permission.

scripts for the BBC and incidental music for radio, television and film. The creative years between 1955–61 yielded the beautiful *Penillion* (Verses) *for Orchestra*, written for the National Youth Orchestra of Wales (1955), her Second Symphony (1957), a Concerto for her favorite instrument, the trumpet (1963) and *Carillons* (1965) for oboe and orchestra.

She set to music *Four Medieval Welsh Poems* (1962) for contralto, harp and harpsichord, and *Two Ninth Century Welsh Poems* (1965) for baritone and harp. Her only opera, *The Parlour*, was written at age sixty in 1966, from her own libretto, adapted from the Guy de Maupassant short story, *En famille*. *Ballads for Orchestra* (1968) "swaggers" with jousting knights. A major achievement of her later years is the *Missa cambrensis* (1971), a large-scale setting of the mass written for the Llandaff Festival. Her last work was *Two Choruses* (1975) for chorus, harp and two horns, based on works by Rudyard Kipling and Thomas Beddoes. She died in Barry, February 10, 1977, just nine days before her seventy-first birthday.

Although Williams wrote mostly orchestral works, making use of the octatonic scale, she is one of the most "Welsh" of composers because of the influence of the rhythms of Welsh poetry in her music, especially in *Penillion*.

Dilys Elwyn-Edwards

DILYS (née Roberts) **ELWYN-EDWARDS** was born August 19, 1918 in Dolgellau, Wales. After graduating with a BM from University College, Cardiff, she studied composition with Herbert Howells at the RCM. She taught at various schools and later became a piano tutor at the Normal College and the University College of North Wales. After teaching over a decade at Bangor, she retired in 1990. She devoted herself to small-scale vocal music, producing part-songs and anthems, including settings of Psalms xxiii, and cxxi (1985), and a number of songs and song cycles for voice and piano to both English and Welsh texts. *In Faëry* (1959), *Caneuon y Tri Aderyn* (Songs of the Three Birds, 1962), and *Hwiangerddi* (Lullabies, 1986) are in the British 20th century art-song tradition.

A telephone interview in 2001 confirmed that she was still living in Caernarvon, Wales, and still composing, having recently completed two song settings of poet Walter De LaMare's "Music" and "Epitaph" to be published by Gwynn. Welsh soprano **Charlotte Church**, at thirteen, recorded three of Elwyn-Edwards' songs, *The Curlew*, *The Owls* and *There is Longing in the Sea* on her first spectacular CD, *Voice of An Angel* (1999). All three are settings of Welsh poet Robert Williams-Parry (1884–1956). Dilys admitted, "enjoying the CD royalty income—especially from America."

Elwyn-Edwards is one of the best-loved composers of Wales, having contributed some of the most popular and most enduring items to the repertoire of the Welsh Art Song.

Author's Notes:

Much firsthand knowledge and inside information for *The Welsh Contingent* was kindly supplied by Keith Davies Jones, MD, president of the St. David's Society of Winnipeg, an organization founded around the beginning of the 20th century for the purpose of celebrating the language, history, culture and heritage of Wales, with membership open to everyone. Their magazine, *Welsh Music*, has featured a number of articles written by Dr. Jones on these three Welsh composers, as well as **Hilary Tann**. (See Contemporary American Composers.) Dr. Jones heads the Radiation Oncology department at the University of Manitoba (Canada). His wife, Gwyneth, a native Trinidadian, has a PhD in radio-immuno chemistry/immunology/cancer research, and is also a tax accountant. Their daughter, Heulwen, is well on her way to a successful singing career.

An *Eisteddfod* is a competitive annual festival in which awards are given for the most worthy efforts in everything from pottery to poetry, as well as singers, instrumentalists, composers, etc. Many well-known musicians have begun their careers on the eisteddfod stage. The 2001 Eisteddfod, August 4–12, in Denbigh, Vale of Clwyd, North

Wales, although held in a large tent, had enough rain for the "usual sea of mud." But this year history was made as, for the first time, the chair, or Archdruid, was won by a woman poet, Mererid Hopwood—Bardic poetry having until now been an all-male preserve. Also, young soprano Fflur Wyn, won a top vocal award.

IRELAND

EIBHLIS FARRELL, born July 27, 1953, in Rostrevor, County Down, Northern Ireland, comes from a creative family. Her sister, Kathleen O'Farrell, is a prizewinning playwright, novelist and composer. Her brother, Liam, is a doctor, medical journalist and fiction writer. In contrast to the strife that divided Northern Ireland during her childhood, Eibhlis grew up in the Mourne Mountains, an area noted for its great natural beauty and known since early Celtic times as a place of healing and learning. As a child, she had piano lessons at the local convent school, and played the Irish fiddle. She began writing music at school and knew she wanted to compose. She received her BM from Queen's University, Belfast, although there was no formal composition teaching, then went to Bristol University, earning an MM in composition. Returning to Ireland in 1983, she became deputy principal and head of musicianship at the College of Music, Dublin Institute of Technology. In November 1996, she became acting head of the college. Despite many administrative responsibilities, she remains faithful to her creative gift. In 1988, she took a two year leave of absence for a fellowship at Rutgers University in New Jersey, where she studied with **Charles Wuorinen** (*b* 1938), and received her PhD in composition in 1991.

Tintinnabulation

Farrell's influences come from the rich tradition of Irish music, and her thorough training in plainchant from an early age at school and church. Her local church houses an eighth century bell from nearby ancient monastic ruins, and her childhood memories are of the wonderful, elemental tones of the bell rung during services. *Changeringing*—the art of ringing a series of unrepeated changes on a set of tuned bells—was also a feature of local sounds. She says, "I've always had bells in my head!" Her output includes orchestral, vocal, chamber and theater music, with performances and broadcasts in Ireland, Britain, USA, France, Italy and Belgium. Commissions have come from Radio Telefis Eirean, the Arts Council of Ireland and Cork International Choral Festival. The International Congress of Women in Music, Alaska, commissioned *The Lovesong of Elias and Isabella Cairel* (1992), a chamber concerto for mezzo-soprano, oboe, viola and glockenspiel. For the Italian Lir Ensemble, she wrote *The Silken Bed* (1993) for cello, violin, harpsichord and mezzo-soprano. She represented Ireland at the 1993 International Composers' Rostra in Paris, and appeared in **Patricia Chiti**'s series *Donne in Musica* on Italian television (1994). The premiere of *The Rose*, for soprano and piano, was heard in Pisa the same year. Her commissions for a cantata, *The Táin*, based on the mythological Irish epic equivalent to the Ring cycle in Gaelic literature, *Arioso* for saxophone, *Skyshapes*, and *Penelope weaving* for solo viola, were heard at the March 1996 Women in Music Conference at the University of Indiana in Pennsylvania. In October, *Windfalls* for soprano, Irish harp, bodhrán (frame drum), violin, flute and clarinet was aired in Riga, Latvia. *A Centenary Mass*, for the Redemptorist order of priests at the Clonard Monastery in Belfast, was a major 1997 commission. *O Star Illumined by the Sun*, for chamber orchestra, was a 1998 commission from Adapt, the Limerick Women's Refuge. Her two settings of Hildegard von Bingen's *O Ruber Sanguinis* and *Caritas Abundat*, have been published by the Hildegard Publishing Company.

Farrell has composed for the president of Ireland. Her music is included on CDs of Irish music. She is a Fellow of the Royal Society of Arts and, in April 1996, was elected to Aosdána, the academy of creative artists, sponsored by the Irish Government Arts Council. This prestigious organization is predicated on the ancient Celtic concept that, based on their contributions, creative artists hold a special place in society. After **Jane O'Leary**, Eibhlis Farrell is only the second woman so honored. In 2000, she was guest composer for the Anna Livia International Opera Festival in Dublin, and Tufts University/New England Conservatory International Composers' Conference in Talloires, France. 2001 performances included *Mólaigían Tiarna* (Malta), *The Silken Bed* (Turin), *Maria, Dolce Maria* for two sopranos and organ, text adapted from **Francesca Caccini**, and *Morning Star* for soprano, saxophone and organ, both in Venice.

Farrell's academic status as of 2001 was deputy principal in the Conservatory of Music and Drama at the Dublin Institute of Technology.

JANE O'LEARY was born to an artist mother and architect father, October 13, 1946, in Hartford, Connecticut. She started piano at five, later adding organ and harpsichord to her keyboard mastery. After graduating *summa cum laude* with a BA in music performance from Vassar in 1968, she earned a PhD in composition from Princeton, where she studied with **Milton Babbitt** (*b* 1916).

Adopting O' the Green

Jane O'Leary

Jane married a fellow Princeton student, Patrick O'Leary, from Waterford, Ireland. They moved to Galway in 1972. Jane has adopted her new country completely, right down to speaking with a brogue. In 1976, she gave birth to their son, Owen, and founded the chamber group **Concorde**, which has been the leading showcase for contemporary music in Ireland for over twenty-five years, and is a vital forum for her own music. She also initiated a two year music theory course, after which students are eligible to sit the diploma examinations at the Royal Irish Academy of Music. Her first international recognition as a composer came in 1978, when she was awarded the W. K. Rose Fellowship in Creative Arts from Vassar. In 1981, she became one of the founders of *Music for Galway*, which promotes concerts, recitals, workshops and master classes. The same year, she was appointed to Aosdána, Ireland's government-sponsored academy of creative artists—and was its only woman composer member until **Eibhlis Farrell's** appointment in 1996. This honor came with a yearly grant to concentrate full time on composition. In 1983, daughter Catriona was born.

Honors and Images

Since 1986, O'Leary has been on the executive board of the International League of Women Composers (now International Alliance) and the board of directors of the National Concert Hall, where she was reappointed for another five years (1992–96). In 1989, she was appointed chairman of the Contemporary Music Centre, Dublin. From 1990–94, she was a member of the Department of Foreign Affairs, Cultural Relations Committee, chaired by Professor Brendan Kenelly, whose poems *Three Voices: Lightning, Peace, Grass, Filled Wine Cup, Begin*, and *Poem from a Three Year Old*, she set to music. Despite all this activity, plus the demands of being a wife and mother, Jane has never let up on composing. Her major works include: *from the flatirons* (1984–85), named after visiting that mountain range in Colorado, *the petals fall* (1986–87), *A Silver Thread* (1988), *Summer Stillness* (1986–89), *Is It Summer?* (1988), *sky revelation* (1988–89), *Mirror Imaginings* (1988–91), *To Listen and to Trust* (1990) and *A Woman's Beauty*, from a poem of Yeats (1991).

A major work, *Islands of Discovery* (1991), is a five part orchestral piece. According to the composer: "The musical shape of this work arose from a contemplation of emotions relating to search and discovery, and by the celebration of the 500th anniversary of Christopher Columbus' epic first voyage across the Atlantic when he linked Europe to a number of 'unknown' islands off the American coast." It was awarded a Special Commendation from Vienna Modern Masters Awards (1992). *Silenzio della terra*, for flute and percussion (1993), was issued on a 1995

CD sampler, "Contemporary Music from Ireland," by the Contemporary Music Centre (CMC) in Dublin, resulting in many international broadcasts. The composer was invited to Brest (France) for a performance of this work by the French ensemble, *Sillages*, as part of a promotion of Irish art in France, *"L'imaginaire Irlandais."* Also written in 1993 was the piano solo *From the Crest of a Green Wave*, published by the CMC, a commission by the GPA Dublin International Piano Competition and performed as a test piece at the 1994 competition. The same year brought *Duo* for violin and cello. *Settings of Stein* for recorders and drums (speaker and dance optional), premiered March 1995. January 1996 marked the first performance of *Duo for Alto Flute and Guitar*, written for Dublin guitarist John Feeley and Australian flutist Laura Chislett. *Mystic Play of Shadows*, a string quartet movement, was premiered in June by the Radio Telefis Eireann (RTE) Vanbrugh String Quartet at the West Cork Chamber Festival. In 1996, *Concorde* performed in Venice and Romania. A CD of *Concorde* performances was released in 1997. The same year marked the January premiere, in the National Concert Hall, of *Dream Songs*, a major choral work commissioned for the Dublin Secondary Girls' Schools Choir, made up of 500 girls.

Her music has been widely performed in Ireland and abroad, including international festivals in Atlanta, Heidelberg, Utrecht, Bilbao (Spain), and Fairbanks, Alaska. In 1992, she was a guest composer with the contemporary ensemble Voices of Change, in Dallas. In 1994, she won the prestigious Marten Toonder Award[14] for her work as a composer. *Concorde* took part in the thirteenth Gegenwelten Festival in Heidelberg, October 1999 and their November 9 concert included music by **Nicola LeFanu**, her husband, David Lumsdaine and her mother, **Elizabeth Maconchy**.

O'Leary was invited as guest composer for three performances of her music at the 1999 ISCM World Music Days in Romania, which featured *A Silver Thread* for violin and percussion, *Duo for Violin and Cello* and her major orchestral work *Islands of Discovery*, all played by Romanian performers. Also in November, *From Sea-Grey Shores* for orchestra was performed at five venues in Ireland. *Into the Blue* premiered at Kennedy Center in May 2000, during an Irish Festival.

Celtic Connections, on Capstone, is a *Concorde* CD featuring music by **Nicola LeFanu**, **Hilary Tann** and O'Leary. Her quartet, *Mystic Play of Shadows*, is on a 2001 CD published in Italy with the Paul Klee Quartet of Venice. This work, performed in Limerick by the Vanbrugh Quartet, was broadcast live throughout Europe by the European Broadcasting Union, December 2000.

In September 2000, Jane O'Leary was appointed composer-in-residence at the Royal Irish Academy of Music in Dublin. This is the first such post at the Academy.

November 2005, *Concorde* presented music for voice and instruments from the 20th and 21st centuries in the Autumn Concert Series at the National Gallery of Ireland.

Unlike others who knew early in life what they wanted to be, O'Leary's composing career has been, according to her, " . . . something which evolved in Ireland over a long period of time." She has broken free of twelve-tone, calculated construction, and now writes "by instinct," letting the wild spaciousness of her adopted country flow into her music in long, melodic lines, with particular attention to beauty of sound and fluid textures.

(Although the Republic of Ireland, home of Jane O'Leary, is an independent country and *not* part of the UK, it is included here because of geographic location.)

---

14. Marten Toonder (1912–2005), a Dutch writer and legendary cartoonist of WWII, chose to make his home in Ireland. He made a major donation to the government for an annual award to be given by the Arts Council to an Irish artist, rotating each year among writers, visual artists and composers. He married the late Dutch composer **Tera de Marez Oyens**, in May 1996.

Outsourced Brits

Several British composers have established careers in other countries, or have made equal marks in dual careers:

ALISON GOULD - renaissance lutenist and composer. (See Guitarists.)

THEA MUSGRAVE was born May 27, 1928, near Edinburgh. She has lived in the U.S. for over thirty years. (See American Contemporary Composers.)

VIVIENNE OLIVE, born in London, resides, and has made a name for herself, in Germany. (See International Musicologists.)

HILARY TANN, born 1947, Ferndale, Wales, settled in America, but writes on Welsh themes. (See American Contemporary Composers.)

Composers from English-Speaking Countries

AUSTRALIA
Margaret Sutherland (1897–1984)
Peggy Glanville Hicks (1912–90)
Dulcie Holland (1913–2000)
Miriam Hyde (1913–2005)
Ros Bandt
Alison Bauld
Betty Beath
Anne Elizabeth Boyd
Ann Carr-Boyd
Margaret Brandman
Mary Finsterer
Jennifer Fowler
Helen Gifford
Moya Henderson
Sarah Hopkins
Elena Kats-Chernin
Liza Lim
Mary Mageau
Cathie Travers

NEW ZEALAND
Annea Lockwood
Gillian Whitehead

CANADA
Sophie-Carmen Eckhardt-Gramatté (1899–1974)
Violet Archer (1913–2000)
Jean Coulthard (1908–2000)
Barbara Pentland (1912–2000)
Micheline Coulombe Saint-Marcoux (1938–85)
Diane Chouinard
Vivian Fung
Alice Ho
Melissa Hui
Hope Lee
Alexina Louie
Ramona Luengen
Svetlana Maksimovic
Kelly-Marie Murphy
Juliet Palmer
Deirdre J. Piper
Elizabeth Raum
Anita Sleeman

SOUTH AFRICA
Priaulx Rainier (1903–86)
Jeanne Zaidel-Rudolph

By the 19th century, after over a hundred years of colonization, the British Empire covered 25 percent of the world's area and population. As a generation of white settlers was born overseas and able to govern themselves, "Dominions" were formed, the first being Canada in 1867, followed by Australia (1900), New Zealand (1907) and South Africa (1910). Still part of the British Commonwealth they answered to the government in London regarding foreign policy, and were conscripted to fight in WWI. Gradually complete independence was attained by most countries, many of whom sent men to serve in WWII of their own volition. Today, there exists a free association of forty-nine former British colonies in the "Commonwealth of Nations." Most retain English as a common language, albeit in differing accents and forms of pronunciation. Australia and New Zealand still feature a miniature version of the British Union Jack in the upper left hand corner of their flags, and profess some allegiance to British royalty.

In the history of composers from these major English-speaking countries, tradition and opportunities continue to draw many to study in London at the Royal Academy (RAM) or the Royal College of Music (RCM), as well as at music centers on the Continent. More contemporary composers, however, are proving that to be accepted, they no longer have to write music in the European tradition, but rather give voice to the multi-cultural legacies existing within their own borders.

AUSTRALIA

In Melbourne in the late 19th and early 20th centuries there was a viable cultural atmosphere, enhanced by the influence of the Melbourne University Conservatorium, foundation of many a career, after which many women traveled to England and Europe to further their studies. Strong female networks and organizations supported semi-professional concerts. *Professional* performances of compositions by women were rare.

While some were, and are, able to earn a living as teachers or musicians, it was almost impossible for a woman to depend on royalties from her compositions. The demands of family and social mores limited creativity in sheer terms of time. Despite domestic demands, two world wars limiting travel, and other obstacles, women still composed. From correspondence and other memorabilia in the collection of the Percy Grainger Museum,[15] the value and significance of the contributions of these earlier composers and musicians served to prepare the path for future generations of Australian women in music.

MARGARET SUTHERLAND was born November 20, 1897 in Adelaide, into a musical family. Her father was a writer and amateur pianist, and other relatives included musicians, artists, scientists and academics. In 1914, she was awarded a scholarship to study piano with Edward Goll, and composition with Fritz Hart. She studied both at Marshall Hall, now the Melba Conservatorium, and later at the Melbourne University Conservatorium. At nineteen, she was invited by Henri Verbrugghen, director of the New South Wales State Conservatorium, to appear as soloist with the NSW State Orchestra in public concerts under his direction. She gave recitals, taught theory and piano during World War I and, up to 1923, wrote a number of short teaching pieces for piano. She left Australia in 1923 for further study in composition, orchestration and conducting in Vienna and London, where for a time she was a pupil of **Sir Arnold Bax** (1883–1953), who became a valued friend and musical mentor. During this period she produced her first published works, including the Violin Sonata, praised by Bax. She returned to Melbourne in 1925.

After a fallow period, 1925–1935, for the next thirty-five years she was active as a composer, chamber music performer and teacher, contributing greatly to the cultural development of Australia. She also helped to build a complex used for major international arts attractions, on the banks of the Yarra River. A champion of Australian composers, for many years her own works gained little attention. During the 1960s, however, with the rapid growth of performances, recordings, publication and commissioning of Australian compositions, Sutherland's considerable services gained official recognition. In 1969, she was awarded an honorary DM from the University of Melbourne, and in 1970 received an OBE. Failing eyesight precluded further composition in the final decade of her life.

Her music combines elements of romanticism and modern dissonance, with lyrical qualities in her many songs. The most well-known works are the string quartet *Discussion* (1954), a violin concerto (1954), *Haunted Hills* (1954), a musical evocation of the Dandenong Ranges near Melbourne, and the *Concerto grosso* (1955). Her one-act chamber opera, *The Young Kabbarli*, premiered at the Festival of Contemporary Opera and Music in Hobart (Tasmania,1965). Sutherland died August 12, 1984, in Melbourne.

---

15. The Percy Grainger Museum at the University of Melbourne was designated in 1938 by Australia's most celebrated early 20th century composer who lived from 1882 to 1961. The institution is dedicated to the preservation of musical manuscripts, photos, letters, etc., to provide inspiration for present and future composers.

Peggy Glanville-Hicks

PEGGY GLANVILLE-HICKS, born December 29, 1912 in Melbourne, was at the Conservatorium from 1929 to 1931, the year she won a scholarship to the RCM in London. For the next five years she studied with England's musical elite: composition with **Ralph Vaughan Williams** (1872–1958), piano with Australian born **Arthur Benjamin** (1893–1960), and conducting with **Constant Lambert** (1905–51) and **Malcolm Sargent** (1895–1967). Her first big success came in 1938, when **Sir Adrian Boult** (1889–1983) conducted her *Choral Suite* at the London ISCM Festival. In 1936, another scholarship permitted study in Vienna with **Egon Wellesz** (1895–74), and Paris with **Nadia Boulanger**.

In 1940, Glanville-Hicks moved to New York, remaining there twenty years and becoming an American citizen in 1948. She served as director of the Composers' Forum, organized contemporary music concerts, and was a respected music critic for the *New York Herald-Tribune*. Besides composing major works, she received two Guggenheim Fellowships (1956–57), as well as Fulbright (1957–58) and Rockefeller (1961) grants, which enabled her to follow her interest in North African and Eastern music. Her travels took her to Morocco, Greece and Italy.

Her compositions include ballets, operas, concertos for flute and piano, chamber works, vocal music and film scores. *Letters from Morocco*, for tenor and orchestra, was premiered by **Leopold Stokowski**. *Transposed Heads*, with libretto by Thomas Mann, was the first opera commission awarded to a woman. Produced in 1954 by Kentucky Opera and the Louisville Symphony, it was recorded and performed again in 1958 in New York. Set in India, the music incorporates Hindu melodies and rhythms and is representative of the composer's style in which, like most non-Western music, harmony plays a minor role. In subsequent compositions, she continued to seek methods of uniting heard and seen elements. American composer Virgil Thomson (1896–1989) said of her that she created her own idiom from the elements of Greek, Indian and North African music.

In 1961, Glanville-Hicks moved to Greece, producing another full-length opera, *Nausicaa* (1961). It was broadcast in the U.S. *Sappho*, for San Francisco Opera (1963), also drew on Greek material. In 1975, she returned to her homeland and set up a highly successful Asian Music Studies program at the Australian Music Centre. She died June 25, 1990, in Sydney.

Dulcie Holland

Born January 5, 1913, in Sydney, **DULCIE HOLLAND** trained at the New South Wales State Conservatorium, where she studied piano with Frank Hutchens, cello with Gladstone Bell, and composition with Alfred Hill. After graduating with a Teacher's Diploma (1933), she taught piano and continued further study with the composer Roy Agnew. Traveling to London, she attended the RCM with the Blumenthal Scholarship for Composition and studied with **John Ireland** (1879–1962). She was awarded the Cobbett Prize for Chamber Composition in 1938. The outbreak of World War II, September 3, 1939, prompted a return to Sydney and freelance composition.

Holland had a distinguished career as a pianist, organist, composer, choir director and broadcaster. With commissions from Balmain Teachers College, Commonwealth Department of the Interior, Shell Oil Company, North Sydney Council, Barbara Stackpole and the Ravenswood Choir, her works also include a myriad of educational piano solos. She was the author of numerous publications, which made her name synonymous with piano methods and music theory. As an examiner for the Australian Music Education Board (1967–84), she was known to generations of piano pupils. Innumerable honors spanned her career: The Australasian Performing Rights Association (APRA) ABC Award (1933, 1944, 1951, 1955), General Motors Theatre Award (1963), and Henry Lawson Award (1965). In 1977, Holland was awarded the Order of Australia, and in 1993 received an honorary music doctorate from Macquarie University.

In 1940, Dulcie married Dr Alan R. Bellhouse (1914–1980), a musician and mathematics teacher. They had two children. Her creative powers, as well as performing her own pieces, continued well into her eighties. The

Cello Sonata dates from 1993. One of her last works was a piano suite depicting hope, courage and wisdom as parts of the process of grieving. Up to her death, May 21, 2000, she was still composing—with the aid of a magnifying glass. She has been called a first rate miniaturist. Her archive, comprised of seven folio boxes, is housed at the National Library of Australia.

Miriam Hyde

Born January 15, 1913, in Adelaide, **MIRIAM HYDE** took piano lessons first with her mother and subsequently with William Silver at the Elder Conservatorium, Adelaide, also studying composition. After earning the University's diploma, and winning the South Australian prize for the LAB (1928), she earned her BM (1931) and won the Elder Scholarship to the RCM (1932–35). In London, her professors included **Arthur Benjamin** for piano, and **Gordon Jacob** (1895–1984) for composition. She won three composition prizes and was soloist in performances of her two piano concertos with the London Symphony, London Philharmonic and the BBC Orchestra. She also made broadcasts on short wave radio to countries of the British Empire, including Australia. In 1935, she added the (Associate) ARCM and (Licentiate) LRAM to her diplomas.

Returning to Adelaide in South Australia's Centenary year, 1936, she wrote much of the orchestral incidental music for the pageant *Heritage*, produced in the Tivoli theatre. Of this music, her *Fantasia on Waltzing Matilda*, an overture to one of the scenes, is well known in her various arrangements as an independent piece. Also in that year, her *Adelaide Overture* was premiered by celebrated British conductor **Malcolm Sargent**. Hyde moved to Sydney and taught for several years at the Kambala School, while continuing as a composer, recitalist, teacher, examiner, lecturer and writer of many articles for music journals. During World War II, when her husband, Marcus Edwards, was a prisoner of war in Germany, she returned to Adelaide, wrote her dramatic *Piano Sonata in G minor* and taught piano and other courses at the Conservatorium.

Her works written between 1934–82 feature numerous piano pieces, from Preliminary to Diploma standards, two piano concertos, much chamber music, three organ pieces, sonatas for viola, clarinet and flute, four overtures—*Happy Occasion Overture* was performed in the inaugural concert of the Australian Youth Orchestra in Sydney Town Hall (1957)—and other orchestral works. Her fifty-plus songs, several set to her over 500 poems, include *Elfin Fantasy, Winter Willow Music, Sunrise by the Sea*, etc., and won many prizes.

For many years, beginning in1976, she was a tutor in "workshops," an innovation to benefit teachers and students in remote country areas of New South Wales. She performed concertos with most major Australian orchestras and with conductors of eminence, including Sir Malcolm Sargent, Constant Lambert, Georg Schneevoigt, Sir Bernard Heinze, Dr. Edgar Bainton, Joseph Post and Geoffrey Simon, with whom, in 1975, she recorded both her concertos with the ABC's Western Australia Symphony Orchestra. In 1971, Hyde gave a recital of her own works at Australia House, London, and in 1973 three recitals in Jakarta, Indonesia. *Valley of Rocks* became her best known piano solo after the 1988 Sydney International Piano Competition, in which it was the favorite choice among the seven Australian works submitted.

In 1977, she was awarded membership of the Order of Australia and received an OBE in 1981. The title "International Woman of the Year for Service to Music" (1991–92), was bestowed by the International Biographical Centre, Cambridge. She was made an honorary fellow of music in 1995. Other awards were honorary life member of the Fellowship of Australian Composers, Patron of the Music Teachers' Associations of New South Wales and South Australia, plus the Blue Mountains Eisteddfod, Australian Musicians' Academy and the Victoria Music Teachers' Association. Honored by the Strathfield Symphony during an Australian Composers' Seminar, April 1996, in Hobart, she played the solo part of her *Fantasy Romantic*—her first performance of this since 1963.

Miriam's eightieth birthday celebrations in 1993 were marked by tribute concerts of her works, and recitals with the composer as soloist in Adelaide, Perth, Sydney and Ingham (Queensland). Her Sydney recital comprised her two favorites, the monumental sonatas of Liszt (B minor) and Brahms (F minor). Later in that year, she played her *Concerto No. 2* with the Sydney Symphony at Goossens Hall.

In the '90s, the octogenarian recorded two CDs of her own piano works for the National Anthology (CSM No. 16) and Southern Cross (No. 1027). In 1996, the ABC produced a CD of her two concertos and the orchestral work *Village Fair*. Her *Clarinet Sonata* is included in a Tall Poppies label release. The Macquarie Trio recorded her *Fantasy Trio* for the ABC. Her 1992 piano piece, *The Vision of Mary MacKillop*, about a nun (1842–1909) destined to become Australia's first saint is in the Jade series. A great tribute to the composer was the Walsingham Classics CD, by Australian pianist and Paris Conservatory diplomate James Muir, with the Sydney Chamber Players, featuring works that Muir had rescued from deteriorating manuscripts.

Hyde's autobiography, *Complete Accord*, combining her domestic and professional roles, was published in Sydney in 1991, and Film Australia made a documentary on her life in 1996. Macquarie University bestowed an honorary doctorate upon her. In 2002, Miriam received the Award for Long-Term Contribution to the Advancement of Australian Music at the APRA/Australian Music Centre Classical Awards. Miriam's nintieth birthday celebrations in 2003 included a concert of her works presented at Eugeue Goossens Hall in Sydney. She left us January 11, 2005, four days before her ninety-fourth birthday.

Carrying the Australian Torch into the 21st Century

ROS BANDT, born August 18, 1951, is a sound artist, composer, researcher and scholar. Her BM is from Sydney, and PhD in musicology from Monash is in performance practice of repetitive music. In 1976, she studied performance in Switzerland and America. After returning to Australia, she mounted her first public interactive sound installation, the "Coathanger Environment Exhibition." Since 1977, she has pioneered interactive sound installations, sound sculptures, creating sound playgrounds, spatial music systems and sound installations worldwide. In 1981, she built Australia's first permanent sound playground, and designed the SSIP (1986), an eight track interactive listening environment.

In addition to her original compositions and sound sculptures, she has worked for TV, radio, film, and visual artists and dancers. She records and tours with the early music group La Romanesca. Her music uses tape, computer sampling, environmental sound recordings, ceramic gongs and wind chimes, as well as conventional instruments. Representative pieces are: *Aqua Musica* (1989) for Rollins thongaphone, whirlies, trombones, choir, environmental water recordings and live performance; *Gulf Song* (1991) for ceramic gongs, voice and tape; *Secluded Ponds* (1992) for the Back to Back Zithers; and *Night on the Indian Ocean* (1993) for Flagong and tape.

Bandt's original works are recorded on New Albion Records USA, Move Records, Melbourne, and EMI/ABC, Sydney. Her book on Sound Sculpture was published by Fine Arts Press, Gordon Breach Group, April 2001. In 2004 she continued the Australian/International public connections in her position as a senior research fellow at the Australian Music Centre, University of Melbourne, steering a large analytical study of sound design practice, plus curating sound performances, exhibitions and events.

ALISON BAULD, born May 7, 1944, in Sydney, showed early promise as a pianist, but studied drama at the National Institute of Dramatic Arts (1961–62) and worked briefly as an actress before entering Sydney University to read English and Music (BM, 1968). In 1969, she was awarded a two-year Moss Traveling Scholarship to London, where she studied with **Elisabeth Lutyens** and Hans Keller. She earned her PhD from York University in Northern England (1974), becoming a lecturer on theater history there. The following year she received a Gulbenkian Dance Award for composition. From 1975–78, she was music director of the Laban Centre at Goldsmiths College, London, after which she returned to Australia to become composer-in-residence at the New South Wales Conservatorium in Sydney. She fulfilled numerous commissions, and in 1980 received a bursary from the Arts Council of Great Britain.

Her knowledge of theater runs through many of her works, especially in her studies of Shakespearean heroines: *Banquo's Buried Cry*, *Cock-a-Doodle-Doo* and *The Witches' Song*. She favors writing for the voice, often setting her own texts, producing works with dramatic content such as her ballad opera *Nell*, first staged at the Donmar

Warehouse as part of the 1988 London International Opera Festival. Her works have also been performed and broadcast at the London, Aldeburgh, York and Edinburgh Festivals. She devoted the early 1990s to preparing a series of original keyboard tutors, *Play Your Way*, which use newly composed material.

At the turn of the century, Bauld completed three volumes of *Play Your Way*, in which she explores the credo that "mistakes" can be used to stimulate musicianship, and that learning to use errors creatively is an important part of acquiring keyboard and compositional techniques.

She has written a novel, *Mozart's Sister*, based on the life of Nannerl Mozart, which has been proposed for a series of broadcasts on ABC radio. Her music was the subject of a master's thesis by Marcia Gronewold (Mills College, California), and an article examining her songs, by Joyce Andrews, was published in 2003 in the American National Association of Teachers' *Journal of Singing*.

Alison is married, has two grown children, and lives in London, composing, writing and teaching American students who come abroad to study.

Betty Beath

BETTY BEATH, the eldest of five girls, born November 19, 1932, in Bundaberg, Queensland, was a gifted child pianist who began musical training at three. With her father away for years fighting in World War II, her mother was the dominant figure in her life. By the time Betty was seventeen, she had won many Eisteddfod competitions and had twice been a finalist in the ABC Concerto Competition. She won a Queensland University Music Scholarship to the Sydney Conservatorium, but graduated from the Queensland Conservatorium, specializing in piano and voice.

In 1974, she was awarded a South East Asian Fellowship by the Australia Council jointly with writer/illustrator David Cox—whom she married in 1976—which allowed them to carry out research on the cultures of Bali and Java. Her compositions show the influence of this experience. As Beath-Cox Art Enterprises, the couple have co-produced many projects unique in bridging the cultures.

In her long career of dual roles of composer, pianist and educator at the Queensland Conservatorium (1969–97) and St. Margaret's Girls' School, Brisbane (1967–95), Beath has produced much work in the fields of art song, chamber music and music drama, which has been broadcast and performed in recitals and theater presentations in Australia, the U.S., UK, Europe, Mexico and Indonesia. Her works for children have been performed extensively throughout Australia.

In 1984, she represented women composers of Australia at the Third International Congress on Women in Music in Mexico City, and was elected to the Executive Board of the International League of Women Composers, a position she held through 1994, developing a platform for performance and broadcasting of womens' music. In 1987, she was resident composer at North Adams State College, Massachusetts, where her commissioned vocal works, including *Points in a Journey*, were performed in recital.

Highlights of her career include the performance of *Songs from the Beasts' Choir* at Carnegie Recital Hall and the Symphony Space, both in New York, and the performance by the Tasmanian Symphony of the love poem *Asmaradana*, for the Music for Australia program during the Trade and Cultural Mission in Jakarta, "Australia Today Indonesia 94." Her work has been recorded by the ABC, Grevillea, Jade CDs and Vienna Modern Masters, and published by Allans Publishing, Melbourne, J. Albert & Son Pty Ltd, ASMUSE, Five Line Publishing, London, Addison Wesley, Boolarong Publications, and McGraw Hill-Australia.

Other compositions include the operas *The Strange Adventures of Marco Polo* (1973) and *Balyet* (1990); and vocal works, *In this Garden* (1973), *Indonesian Triptych* (1977), *Poems from the Chinese* (1979), *Three Psalms* (1981), *Ninya* (1985), *Points in a Journey* (1987), *Contrast for Piano* (1990), and *River Songs* (1991), nominated for the 1991 APRA Music Award in the category Contemporary Classical Composition of the Year. *Encounters, a musical dialogue in five movements* was a 1995 commission by violinist Mary Nemet and cellist Gary Williams. *From a Quiet Place*, for viola, piano, and singing bowls, was premiered in recital at the ABC studios in Brisbane, August 22, 1999.

Beath's orchestral suite *Dreams and Visions*, on Vienna Modern Masters' *Music from Six Continents*, was nominated in the Best Classical Release of 1998 category by ABC Classic FM Recoding Awards. She turned the century with *Woman'song, Allegro Vivace for Strings* (2000), and *Night Songs* (2000), two pieces for solo alto recorder, published by The Keys Press, released on JAD's "American Dream" CD. *Lament for Kosovo* and *Adagio for Strings* (2000) were recorded by the Moravian Philharmonic Orchestra, Toshiyuki Shimada conducting, and released by Vienna Modern Masters on Music From Six Continents, 2001 Series. The latter work was premiered by the Portland (Maine) Symphony Orchestra, October 2001, under the same conductor. Other 2001 compositions include *From a Bridge of Dreams*, flute and piano; *Heart Song*, voice, alto recorder and cello; *Chorale*, organ; *Let's Dance*, tenor recorder and guitar; *Preludes 1 & 2*, piano. *A Garland for St.Francis* (2002), for voice and instrumental ensemble, was commissioned by Larry Rachleff for a 2003 performance at the Shepherd School of Music, Rice University, Houston, Texas. Two piano pieces *Merindu Bali . . . Bali Yearning*[16] and *Key Connections* were written for KEYS, the National Piano Competition 2003 for Australian Works.

ANNE (ELIZABETH) **BOYD** was born April 10, 1946, in Sydney. Her father died when she was three and a half, and her mother, unable to support the family of three children, sent Anne to live with her aunt at Maneroo, an isolated sheep station in remote central Queensland. Schooling for Anne and her cousins was by correspondence, overseen by her aunt. When she was five, her sister sent her a recorder and a teach-yourself book for Christmas, which is just what she did, composing her first pieces using drawings and symbols that to her represented music. Living in the Australian bush imbued her with independence and nurtured her creativity. Listening to the radio was her only link to the outside world.

At age eleven, she returned to Sydney to live with her mother and begin formal education. Shortly after she arrived her mother died, a tragedy that would strongly affect her for life. Now an orphan, the isolation with which she had learned to cope in the bush country extended to an isolation in her own world without the love, understanding and encouragement of parents. She was boarded with friends of her sister so she could continue in school. The family put together a small fund for her education, including one year of private piano lessons with a Hungarian woman who introduced her to Bartók and Bach. In high school Anne began to play the school-owned flute, but had to give up piano lessons because there was not enough money. She found that playing the flute and writing music helped compensate for her personal loss. She won a Commonwealth Scholarship to the University of Sydney, where a great influence was Peter Sculthorpe's composition and ethnomusicology classes which introduced her to a wide spectrum of non-Western music.

Her music was performed and enthusiastically received throughout the 1960s. *Exegesis No.1* for four flutes and two piccolos, was written in 1964. The following year, her *Trio* (oboe, clarinet and bassoon) was performed in Melbourne. In 1965, she wrote *The Creation* (five recorders and percussion). *The Fall of Icarus* (flute, cello, clarinet and piano) was heard at the Adelaide Festival of the Arts (1966). Her early compositions were influenced by the music and philosophy of **John Cage**, Asian music—particularly Japanese—and medieval music. *Shineberg* was a thirty-minute documentary for the ABC. She was commissioned by Ballet Australia to write *the Stairway*. In 1968, *Alma Redemptoris*, for two choirs and two pianos, was premiered at the Adelaide Festival. She was active in the Vietnam Moratorium movement and was commissioned by the Vietnam Arts Festival in Sydney to compose the work *Tu Dai Oan*. In 1969, she received the first Commonwealth Overseas Grant for composition, with which she earned her PhD (1972) at York University (England). She studied with **Bernard Rands**, and under his guidance wrote what she considers her most important piece of music, *The Voice of the Phoenix*, scored for orchestra, amplified solo piano, guitar, harp, harpsichord, ten percussion players, augmented woodwinds and an electronic musical instrument designed for live performance. 1971 brought *The Metamorphosos*

---

16. This piece was commissioned by Javanese pianist Ananda Sukarlan, and included in a series of memorial concerts he performed, consisting of new piano works dedicated to the memory of the victims of the Bali nightclub bombings—the tragedy which occurred October 12, 2002.

of a Solitary Female Phoenix. The Rose Garden, written at York, was an hour long experiment in music theater to a text by the English poet Robin Hamilton.

Boyd was appointed lecturer at the University of Sussex (1972–77) until a Special Purpose Grant from the Music Board of the Australia Council enabled her to return home. In 1978, she was commissioned to write for the Sydney University Musical Society Centenary Festival and composed her first major choral work, an oratorio on a text by Korean-born writer Don'o Kim, *The Death of Captain Cook*, for soprano, tenor and baritone soloists, three small choirs, large SATB chorus and full orchestra. Ahead of Disney, her children's opera in two acts, *The Little Mermaid* (1978), is a brilliantly atmospheric adaption of Hans Christian Anderson's well-known story set to music with strong Asian rhythmic and melodic influences. *My Name is Tian*, for soprano, flute, viola, harp and percussion, was commissioned by the Seymour Group and the Music Board of the Australian Council. Her choral symphony *Coal River*, scored for orchestra, brass band, a hundred voice choir and soloists, was commissioned by the Newcastle City Council (England) for the golden jubilee of the Civic Theatre. Her 1999–2000 output includes: *The Burning Babe*, soprano solo, women's or boys' voices *a capella*; *Kakan*, alto flute, marimba, piano; *Wind Across Bamboo*, woodwind quintet; *A Song of Rain*, SSA choir, solo voice, wind maker; and *Beside Bamboos*, solo violin.

Appointed head of the music department at the University of Hong Kong in 1981, Boyd holds the rare distinction of a foreigner being admitted to the Hong Kong Composers' Guild and of lecturing on her own work at the Shanghai Conservatory. Her daughter, Helen-Louise Freda, was born in Hong Kong in 1983. *A Rain Song* is dedicated to the baby. In 1991, Boyd became professor of music at the University of Sydney. *At the Rising of the Sun*, for orchestra, was commissioned by the Kuringgai Symphony Orchestra for performance in Sydney, May 2001.

One of Boyd's most meaningful contributions is being a leading proponent of the concept that, with Australia's multi-cultural traditions, acceptable music no longer has to be written in the European tradition.

Margaret Brandman

MARGARET BRANDMAN, educator and author of the innovative *Playing Made Easy* Music Education Method, was born in Sydney, September 19, 1951, into a musical family where, from age four, she learned accordion and piano. Guitar and clarinet came in her teens. At the Sydney Conservatorium High School she studied piano, clarinet, harmony and composition, graduating one of the top three students in the State (1969). A scholarship brought her to the University of Sydney for a BM in composition with major Australian composer **Peter Sculthorpe**. She also acquired her piano teacher diploma, teacher of musical arts and associate performer degrees.

Brandman's over thirty-five year career encompasses pedagogy, performance and music journalism. She has written a complete range of music education materials, including the high school text *Accent on Music*, whose first edition sold out in eight months, *The Contemporary Piano Method*, *The Contemporary Aural Course*, numerous theory texts, and a video demonstrating her unique teaching method. Her works have pioneered new and enduring methods of teaching music. New examination syllabuses now include Brandman materials on improvisation, more efficient reading skills, chord and harmonic understanding and keyboard topography. Her *Playing Made Easy* methods of teaching have been refined, streamlined and applied to piano, keyboards, recorder, theory and ear-training.

Her concert works for piano, instrumental combinations and orchestra, with titles like *Undulations* (string orchestra), *Sonorities* (piano), *Saxophone Quartet* and *Churinga* (keyboards), have been heard internationally in concert and on radio in live and recorded performances.

Turn of the century projects include *Pictorial Patterns for Keyboard Scales and Chords*, a piano album, *Twelve Timely Pieces*, and a work for Mandolin Orchestra. She has embarked on a series of easy piano arrangements of current chart hits for the Four Hot Hits series, published by Music Sales. Her works and education materials are distributed worldwide.

Ann Carr-Boyd

ANN CARR-BOYD, born into a musical family, July 13, 1938, in Sydney, took piano lessons at seven from her father, a teacher, composer and musician who wrote down her early pieces. She was the first music graduate at Sydney University (1960). Her master's thesis (1963) was "The First Hundred Years of Music in Australia (1788–1888)." She won a Sydney Moss Scholarship, and chose to go to London's RCM for keyboard and harpsichord study. Her *String Quartet* and *Symphony in Three Movements* were performed there. She composed a chamber work, *Theme and Variations*, which was premiered in London at the New Music Concerts in 1965.

She met and married Peter Murray Carr-Boyd in England, where two of their three daughters were born. In 1967, they decided to return to Australia to raise their family. She taught at the University of Sydney from 1967–73. In l974, she wrote *Trois Leçons* for harpsichord, solo voice and chimes, a commission from harpsichordist Robert Goode, premiered at the Music Viva Festival in Geelong, Victoria. Her symphony (1964) and two string quartets were followed by *Three Songs of Love* and *The Boomerang Chocolate Cake*, a humorous song for soprano and harpsichord.

Her output includes a large body of chamber and keyboard works, and pieces commissioned by educational organizations. A distinctive feature of her work is a number of pieces for mandolins in small and large groups, commissioned by the Sydney Mandolins. Her music style includes elements from twelve-note serialism to ragtime, as well as unusual combinations of instruments. She is also well known as a writer and broadcaster. A flute work for Jane Rutter, commissioned by Ars Musica Australis, was performed with the Sydney Youth Orchestra in 2003.

Complementing her work as a composer, Ann Carr-Boyd continues her pioneering work in documenting the history of European music in Australia. She has contributed to many publications, including *The New Grove Dictionary of Music and Musicians* (1980) and *The Australian Dictionary of Biography*. She has also initiated and presented many radio programs on Australian music and musicians.

Born August 25, 1962, in Canberra, **MARY FINSTERER** studied jazz improvisation and music education at the NSW State Conservatorium of Music before moving to Melbourne University in 1984, from which she earned her BA (1987), receiving the Ormond Exhibition Award and Honors in Composition. She completed an MM at Melbourne and postgraduate studies at the Royal Conservatory of The Hague (Netherlands). She also attended courses in music editing, composing and filmscore writing at the Australian Film and Television School. Her composition teachers included **Gillian Whitehead**, Martin Wesley-Smith, Peter Tahourdin, Barry Conyngham, Brenton Broadstock and **Louis Andriessen**. In her senior undergraduate year she was appointed student-composer-in-residence at the National Music Camp, for which she composed the chamber orchestral work *Piece for 29*. Chosen for the National Composers Orchestral School, she wrote *Atlas* for the Tasmanian Symphony (1988). It was played by the Melbourne and Queensland Symphonies (1989), the latter performed her *Continuum* the same year. In 1988, she was commissioned by the Elision Ensemble and the Australia Council to write *Cyme*. On receiving the Dorian Le Gallienne Award, she wrote the opera *Madame He*. She was composer/performer of original music for the Great Hawthorn Town Hall Centenary show, and wrote synthesized music for several Melbourne-based cabaret/comedy acts.

In 1990, she formed the company "Top Billings," composing and performing music for shows in theater and cabaret venues in Melbourne. She wrote musical scores/soundtracks for independent film makers. In September 1991, *Madame He* was selected for the ISCM World Music Days and performed in Switzerland. The following October, *Ruisselant* was premiered by Le Nouvel Ensemble Moderne, and was one of the three winners in Forum 91. Other works include *Nextwave Fanfare, Omaggio alla Pietà, Tract, Scat, Catch, Ceres da Linqua* (1994) for chamber orchestra, *Scimmia* (1994) for string orchestra, *Cor* (1994) for orchestra, and *Nyx* (1996) for chamber orchestra solo flute, bass clarinet and piano, composed for the Het Trio and the Pittsburgh New Music Ensemble. *Ascension and Descend* was premiered November 7, 2001, by the Sydney Symphony under Scottish composer James McMillan and recorded for New Music Australia.

Finsterer was composer-in-residence with the Sydney Symphony Orchestra (1992–94) when she received an Australia Council Fellowship, which allowed her to travel to Amsterdam, September 1993, to continue composition studies with prominent Dutch composer/pedagogue **Louis Andriessen**. Her music has represented Australia at the Contemporary World Music Days in Austria 1991, Germany 1995, England 1998 and Romania 1999; at such events as the Holland Festival, Pittsburgh Music Lives, Adelaide, Sydney, Nextwave and Sydney Spring Festivals, and IRCAM (France); and performed by Pittsburgh New Music Ensemble, New Modern Set of Montreal, and prestigious orchestras of Australia, Europe, Canada and America.

JENNIFER FOWLER was born April 14, 1939, in Bunbury, Western Australia. She started piano at nine, and by eighteen was at the University of Western Australia, Perth, where she won several composition prizes and was awarded the University's Convocation Award. While still a student, she had pieces performed in the Festival of Perth and broadcast by the ABC. She graduated in 1960, one of the first students at that university to gain an arts degree specializing in music.

In 1968, she attended the University of Utrecht's Electronic Music Studio on a Dutch Government Scholarship. She moved to London in 1969, and taught for several years at Wykeham Secondary School. Her first big success came in 1970, when one of her Utrecht works, *Hours of the Day* (1968) for four sopranos, two oboes and two clarinets, won a prize from the Akademie der Künste in Berlin. The following year, she was a joint winner of a Radcliffe award for her string quintet *Revelation* (1970–71). Other works include a humorous piece, *Chimes, Fractured*, for double woodwind, organ, bagpipes and percussion, featuring distinct theme strands interacting and literally fracturing one another. In *Reeds, reflections . . .* (1990), instruments are set in haunting waves of motion. *Veni Sancte Spiritus - Veni Creator* is a choral work for twelve solo singers based on a medieval plainsong.

In 1971, Fowler married British computer designer Bruce Patterson. They have two children. The 1970s produced several important works, including the complex orchestral work *Chant with Garlands* (1974), which uses elements from Australian Aboriginal musical culture. *Voice of the Shades* (1977) is a lyrical work for soprano, oboe or clarinet and violin.

Several of Fowler's works continue to use elements of Aboriginal music, such as *When David Heard* (1982) for choir and piano, and *We Call to You, Brother* (1988) for flute, English horn, cello, percussion and two trombones. Her setting of the Magnificat, *Tell Out my Soul* for soprano, cello and piano, written in 1980 and revised in 1984, has text expressing a particularly feminine kind of joy. The expression of woman's experience is more explicit in her BBC commission of 1989, *And Ever Shall Be* for mezzo-soprano, oboe, clarinet, trombone, string trio and percussion, which sets four traditional songs dealing with various significant moments in a woman's life. Her *Lament for Mr. Henry Purcell* (1995), for alto flute, viola, and harp, received its American premiere at the 9th Annual Concert of Chamber Music by Women, June 20, 1999, at the National Museum of Women in the Arts, Washington, DC. A commission from The Song Company of Sydney of a cycle of nine songs, *Eat and Be Eaten*, was premiered in Sydney, June 2001. The subject is food: all its myths, metaphors, and significance. The cycle has been performed several times and broadcast by the ABC. The work won the 2001 Paul Lowin Prize for a Song Cycle, by being given a High Commendation. (These awards are Australia's richest composition prizes.) A new version of *Echoes from an Antique Land* was performed as part of the ControCanto series in Rome (2002) and Dublin, May 2003, given by the Concorde Contemporary Music Ensemble. It was adopted as a set-work for final year secondary school music students in Western Australia for the years 2000–03. *Spiral*, a commission from COMA South, premiered March 2002 in Southampton (UK), as part of the celebration for International Women's Day. *Hymn for Saint Brigid* (SATB choir, *a cappella*), was chosen for performance in the 700th anniversary celebrations of St. Brigid in Rome, October, 2002. *Magnificat* and *Nunc Dimittis* were part of the "Magnificat Project," a Women in Music Commissioning Fund award winner. A commission from APSARA ensemble, *Apsaras Flying* (three recorders, cello, harpsichord) was premiered in the new concert hall in Bruges, May 2003.

Fowler's work, with which she wants to stimulate the imagination into taking a step forward, has been performed at such international festivals as the ISCM World Music Days; Gaudeamus Music Week, Holland;

Huddersfield Festival of Contemporary Music; Sydney Proms; International Sydney Spring Festival; "Ring of Fire" Festival, London; the Festival of Perth and Women in Music festivals in London, Atlanta, Alaska, Melbourne, Sydney and Canberra. Her music, broadcast by radio stations all over the world, is available from the British Music Information Centre in London, or the Australian Music Centre, Sydney.

HELEN GIFFORD, born in Melbourne, September 5, 1935, studied at the University there with Dorian Le Gallienne (1915–1963) who, upon Helen's 1958 graduation, convinced her to become a composer. *Phantasma* (1964) for string orchestra was chosen by the Australian jury for submission to the ISCM Festival in Copenhagen that year. After winning the Le Gallienne Award for composition, she produced her String Quartet, performed at the 1966 Adelaide Festival. Touring in Europe in 1962, she became influenced by the contemporary idioms of **Witold Lutoslawski** and the Polish school. Travels in India, 1967, and Indonesia, 1971, brought the influence of Asian music into her work.

She was composer-in-residence for the Melbourne Theater Company in 1970, and Australian Opera in 1974. She has written commissions for the Melbourne Chorale, Astra Chamber Music Society, Australian Broadcasting Commission, and the Australian Percussion Ensemble. She was chairman of the Composers' Guild of Australia 1976–78, and in 1980 was appointed to the Australia Council's Artists in the Schools program. In 1994, she received a commission from the Alpha Centauri Ensemble for *A Plaint for Lost Worlds*, a trio for piccolo, clarinet and piano.

In 1996, Gifford was awarded Doctor of Letters by Monash University. In 1999, ABC Classic FM commissioned the piano piece *As Foretold to Khayyám*, for Michael Kieran Harvey. The same year she completed a fifty-minute work for choir and instruments, *Choral Scenes: The Western Front, World War I*, commissioned by Astra, which was a setting of verse from that time, in English, French and German. Astra also performed her choral work, *Catharsis* (2001).

Born in Quirindi, New South Wales, August 2, 1941, **MOYA HENDERSON** spent nine years as a nun at the Sacré-Cœur Convent in Melbourne before leaving the order in 1969 to study music at the University of Queensland. After graduation in 1972, she was appointed Resident Composer to the Australian Opera. At the end of the year, she was awarded a Scholarship from the Music Board of the Australian Council for the Arts, which enabled her to travel to Germany to study theater with Maurice Kagel and music with **Karlheinz Stockhausen** (*b* 1928) in Cologne. She returned to Australia in 1976 and settled in Sydney. Her works focus on cultural myths, encompassing aboriginal people, women, landscape and conservation. They include: *Sacred Site* (1983) for organ and tape; *Celebration 40,000* (1987) piano concerto; *Currawong: A Symphony of Bird Sounds* (1988); *Waking Up the Flies* (1990) piano trio; and *Wild Card* (1991) for soprano, cello and piano. Two works in 1995 were *G'day Africa II* for piano, clarinet, viola and cello, a commission from Perihelion, and *G'day Africa III* for piano, clarinet, viola and cello. In 1996, she wrote *In Paradisum* for SATB choir, dedicated "In loving memory of my brothers Michael and Peter." Besides numerous residencies and awards, including the OAM (1996), she has had commissions for Musica Viva, the Seymour Group, Sydney Opera Trust and Perihelion. She was appointed Macgeorge Fellow with the University of Melbourne's music department for the first quarter of 1995.

Henderson is the inventor of the Alemba percussion instruments. She has written a number of imaginative and striking works, especially for the radio medium, which have been broadcast in Germany and in "The Listening Room" on the ABC, Classic FM. One piece with considerable impact is *Meditations and Distractions on the Theme of the Singing Nun*. She is also the inventor of the Tosca Bells, and developed the "noose" for stringed instruments, which enables the composer to write "natural" harmonics on virtually every note within the range of the string orchestra. The first work to make use of this invention was *The Dreaming*, composed to a commission from Musica Viva for the Australian Chamber Orchestra. Her opera, *Lindy* (1997), based on the Azaria Chamberlain case, received its premiere by Opera Australia at the Sydney Opera House, October 2002.

Born in Lower Hutt, New Zealand, August 13, 1958, **SARAH HOPKINS** came to Australia with her family in 1964. She attended the NSW Conservatorium High School and the Victorian College of the Arts, graduating in

1979. As a cellist, she has toured throughout Australia, Britain, Europe and the U.S. She has been musician-in-residence at GIAE, Gippsland, Victoria, (1978) and CIT Caulfield, Victoria (1979); composer-in-residence at Arts Victoria Music '81; composer-performer-in-residence at the Darwin Theater Group (1984); Artist in Schools (1985–86); Sky Song Project, Darwin (1987–88); and performer-in-residence, Exploration San Francisco (1988).

Her solo, ensemble and choral music is of a holistic nature, drawing upon the natural beauty of the cello, voice, handbells, wind chimes and whirly instruments—plastic tubes of various lengths and diameters which make harmonic overtones when spiraled overhead—as used in *Whirlies* (1983) and *Deep Whirly Duo* (1984). Her ensemble music uses these instruments as well as poetry, theater, dance and film. Her unique style of cello playing embraces new and ancient sounds, including musical bird calls, deep earthy drones, didjeridu bowing and bowed harmonics. Vocally, she specializes in harmonic overtone singing, which she often uses in combination with her cello. In 1995, she received a commission from St. Margaret's Anglican Girls School for *Return to Joy* for treble or mixed voice *a cappella* choir.

Living in Brisbane, Hopkins tours nationally and internationally, performing her music, running workshops in Harmonic Singing and Holistic Music, and working as an artist-in-residence. She has represented Australia at cultural relations performance tours to the Philippines, Thailand, Malaysia, Korea and Germany; and played for over 50,000 people at the opening ceremony of the Fourth World Athletics Championships in Stuttgart. Her acclaimed choral work, *Past Life Melodies*, was performed in the Sydney Opera House by an 800 voice choir, and her *Sky Song* music, co-composed with Alan Lamb, was featured on Australia's Olympics 2000 bid CD.

Elena Kats-Chernin

ELENA KATS-CHERNIN was born on November 4, 1957, in Tashkent in the Uzbek region of what was then the USSR. Her studies, begun at Yaroslav Music School, continued at age fourteen at the Gnessin Musical College in Moscow. She emigrated to Australia with her family in 1975, where she studied composition under Richard Toop at the NSW Conservatorium. She played her own piano concerto as her graduation piece (1979). Further studies were in Germany at the Hochschule für Musik in Hanover. She remained in Europe for over a decade, during which time she wrote several ballets and incidental music for the State theaters in Berlin, Vienna, Hamburg and Bochum. She collaborated as a performer with the German choreographer Reinhild Hoffman in experimental theater productions in Tokyo, Lisbon and Karlsruhe (Germany).

After frequent visits for performances of her work, Kats-Chernin returned to Australia in 1994, settling in Sydney. In addition to her solo and chamber works are the piano concerto and a violin concerto (1990). In 1995, she was commissioned by Sydney Alpha Ensemble for *Cadences, Deviations and Scarlatti* for fourteen instruments; and the Adelaide Festival of the Arts for *ProMotion* for clarinet, percussion, guitar, piano, cello and bass, for the 1996 *Bang on a Can Allstars*. *Clocks* (1993), premiered by Ensemble Modern, has had numerous performances throughout the world. Its first movement forms the basis of a short film by Kirsten Winter, which won second prize at the 1995 Montreal Film Festival. In 1995, Kats-Chernin composed the soundtrack for the Swedish silent move *Körkarlen*. Also commissioned by ZDF/Arte was her score for Pabst's 1928 silent film *Abwege*. Her second collaboration with Kirsten Winter, the ten minute film *Smash*, won first prize for Best Use of Sound at the Ottawa International Film Festival, 1998.

Her CD, on the ABC Classics label with the Alpha Ensemble, contains *Clocks* and *Cadences, Deviations and Scarlatti*, which won the Sounds Australian Award (1996). Her operas *Iphis* and *Matricide* have received successful premiere seasons. Among many concert pieces, *Zoom and Zip* for seventeen strings, premiered by the Australian Chamber Orchestra, has found its way in the repertoire of many ensembles. The orchestral works *Stairs*, *Transfer*, and *Retonica*, have been performed by Australian orchestras, including the Sydney Symphony.

March 2001 saw the largest ever retrospective of an Australian composer's works when the Musica Nova Festival in Helsinki presented twelve works by Elena Kats-Chernin over five concerts. The festival was a great success, with several works being picked up by European and American orchestras for future performances. Elena, who was delighted with the festival, took the opportunity to reassess and revise some of the programmed works. *Vitalia's Steps*, an innovative work for toy pianos, percussion and piano, premiered in New York at the end of March, with soloists Emanuel Ax, **Evelyn Glennie** and Margaret Leng Tan.

Elena resides in Germany and in Paddington, New South Wales.

LIZA LIM, born 1966, in Perth, studied composition at Victoria College of the Arts (BM, 1986), and MM from the University of Melbourne (1996). She was Lecturer in composition there in 1991, having taught other courses since 1989. With commissions from the Elision Ensemble, Ensemble intercontemporain, Michael Vyner Trust, Milano Musica, Radio Bremen, Rantos Collegium, Seymour Group, Cologne West German Radio and a joint commission from the Australian and BBC symphonies, her works have been performed in international festivals, such as the Brisbane Biennial, Gaudeamus, Melbourne International, Musica del Nostro Tempo, Milano Musica, Pro Musica Nova, Pittsburgh Music Lives, Sendai Asian Music, New Music Days—Zurich and Vienna Modern.

In 1992, she received an Australia Council composer fellowship, enabling her to complete *The Oresteia*, a memory theater (opera) in seven parts based on Aeschylus' drama, produced in 1993 by Treason of Images. She has also composed for the Melbourne and BBC Symphony Orchestras and participated in projects with installation artist Domenico de Clario and musicians of the Elision Ensemble. With de Clario, she wrote *Bar-do'-thos-grol - The Tibetan book of the dead* (1994) for voices, clarinets, saxophones, viola and cello. For the ABC she wrote *Cathedral* (1994) for orchestra, and for Frankfurt's Ensemble Moderne, *Street of Crocodiles* (1995). Many of her titles convey her Asian ancestry, like *Garden of Earthly Desire*, *Hell*, *Koto*, *Li Shang Yin*, and *Voodoo Child*. Her compositions represented Australia at the ISCM World Music Days in Hong Kong (1988), Zurich (1991), and Seoul (1997). In 1998, she was a guest lecturer at the Darmstadt (Germany) Ferienkurse für neue Musik (Summer courses for new music). Portrait Concerts of Lim's music have been presented by Radio Bremen (1996), Ensemble for New Music, Zurich (1997, 2000), UC San Diego, California, (Search Events 2000), Cornell University, New York, and West German Radio (2000). Her numerous awards include the Young Australian Creative Artist Fellowship (1996) and a major Australia Council Fellowship in 2000.

Jué Lìng Jié (Moon Spirit Feasting) was produced at the 2000 Adelaide Festival. Return seasons of this opera were produced for the 2001 Melbourne Festival, and in 2002 at the Agora Festival in Paris, Hebbel Theatre, Berlin, and Saitama Arts Centre, Japan. Other 21st century productions are *Machine for Contacting the Dead* (1999–2000), premiered February 2001 by the Ensemble intercontemporain on the occasion of an exhibition of Chinese archaeological artifacts at the Cité de la Musique, Paris, and *The Tree of Life* (2001), commissioned by the SWR-Sinfonie Orchester for Donaueschinger Musiktage, Germany, October 2001. 2001–2002 commissions included *Xi* (Double Happiness) for six voices and *qin* from The Song Company, and *Ecstatic Architecture* from the Los Angeles Philharmonic. She was the winner of the 2002 APRA-Australian Music Centre Classical Music Award for Best Composition.

Born September 4, 1934, in Milwaukee, Wisconsin, **MARY MAGEAU** studied composition at DePaul University, Chicago (BM with honors), and the University of Michigan, Ann Arbor, where she was awarded an MM. In 1970, Mary participated in the Composer Fellowship Program at Tanglewood. She taught in Minnesota and Wisconsin before moving to Australia in 1974, where she married architect Kenneth White, became a permanent resident of Queensland with Australian/American citizenship, and was prominent in lobbying for opportunities for women composers.

Throughout the '70s and '80s, she composed for chamber and solo instruments, chorus, and orchestra, and in 1985 wrote a children's opera, *The Rabbit Who Knew Too Much*. Her major work, composed for the Queensland Symphony, is the *Triple Concerto* (1990) for violin, cello, piano and orchestra. In 1994, she was commissioned by Audrey Green for *Riding the Ghan* for harpsichord. 1995 brought a piano concerto, *The Furies*, a commission from the University of Southern Queensland for their pianist-in-residence, and 1996 *Shades of Brass* for horns, trumpets and trombones, as a school music resource.

During 1987 Mary experienced a spiritual awakening, which led her into an intensive study and practice of meditation. Since 1995, she has regularly led meditation groups, and promotes widespread participation in global meditations. From 1998–2000, she worked as a consultant for the Australian educational publisher Knowledge Books and Software, researching and writing the materials for a set of three videos and accompanying study guides. Entitled *Women's Work - Composers & Painters of the 18th to the 20th Centuries*, her video program, designed for use in high school art/music elective studies, has become an important resource for the Australian educational curriculum.

Following several years as a rock musician, **CATHIE TRAVERS**, born September 25, 1959, studied at the University of Western Australia, receiving her BM with performance prizes both as a soloist and chamber musician. From 1985–86, she continued piano studies in England and America. By 1987, her concert pianist career became secondary to her new passion for electronic and new music. She developed an impressive reputation as both a performer and composer, with exposure in Australia, Canada, America and Japan. Since her return to Australia, she has been a member of the new-music groups Alea, Nova Ensemble, West Australian Symphony Orchestra (WASO), 20th century Music Ensemble and Magnetic Pig—all in Perth. Her commissions have come from those groups, as well as the Australia Chamber Orchestra, Chrissie Parrot Dance Company, the ABC, Hitchiker Films and the Perth Jazz Society. Beginning in 1987, using computers, she has done music score typesetting for orchestras, film companies and music theater. By 1994, she developed solo repertoire for a MIDI instrument setup for interactive performance with technology she learned at the IRCAM in Paris.

As a multi-keyboardist, performing predominantly Australian new art-music, Travers has performed with other artists at national arts festivals in Sydney, Melbourne, Adelaide, Hobart and Perth for ABC radio programs and numerous West Australia arts events. Her career as an accordionist began in 1992. Since 1997, after she finally *took lessons* on the instrument, she has written a number of works which combine accordion and electronics. Last heard, she was on the lookout for more buttons to push, in wild and weird combinations.

Her compositions include *Obsession* (1990) for percussion, piano, soprano, alto, and baritone saxophones, plus synthesizers; *Paleyaga* (1991) for flute or saxophone, keyboard, percussion, Mac computer and synthesizers; and *Paleyagan tales* (1993) for orchestra. Much of 2000 and 2001 was devoted to a collaboration with SiN on a multi-part cyber-electronic opera titled *Utopia Dissolve*, which consists of segments for live performance, and some segments for the Web. *PhanTom DATA*, a recent orchestral work, was premiered at the Perth Concert Hall, June 2000, by the West Australian Symphony Orchestra, conducted by Vladimir Verbitsky. *ALyx-er*, for piano, was premiered by Michael Kieran-Harvey on the millennium New Year's Eve TV extravaganza involving sixty participating international broadcasters.

NEW ZEALAND

ANNEA LOCKWOOD was born July 29, 1939 in Christchurch. (See American Contemporary Composers.)

Gillian Whitehead

Composer and teacher **GILLIAN KARAWE WHITEHEAD**, who is one eighth Maori, was born into a musical family on April 23, 1941, in Wangarei. During her childhood, she absorbed the natural world of sea, hills and trees about her, especially its Maori associations. She began composing as a child, always attracted to themes with literary associations. After attending the University of Auckland (1959–62), where she worked under Ronald Tremain, and Victoria University, Wellington (BM, 1964), she studied composition with **Peter Sculthorpe** at the University of Sydney (MM, 1966). **Peter Maxwell Davies'** lectures on analysis and composition in Adelaide (1966) stimulated her to continue studying with him in England the following year, where she went on to establish a career as a freelance composer. During 1968–70, with a New Zealand Arts Council grant, she was able to compose in Italy and Portugal. She was composer-in-residence at Northern Arts, Newcastle-upon-Tyne (UK, 1978–80), before joining the staff at the

Sydney Conservatorium in 1981. She later became head of composition there, taking leave every second year to concentrate on her own work. In 1995, she retired from the conservatorium after fifteen years to give her undivided attention to composing and writing.

As a first-year student, she wanted to compose music that was Debussyan in harmony, Webernian in orchestration and Dufay-like in structure. In her forty-year career she has adhered to those aims to a certain extent. A series of works on Maori themes, *Pakkuru* (1967) and *Whakatau-ki* (1970), describing the seasonal cycle in vivid imagery, was succeeded by string and piano compositions. In 1978 came the success of her first chamber opera, *Tristan and Iseult* (1975). With the poet Fleur Adcock, she wrote a number of larger-scale vocal works: *Inner Harbor* (1979); *Hotspur* (1980), a north country dramatic saga for soprano and chamber ensemble; the opera *The King of the Other Country* (1984); and *Out of this nettle danger*, a monodrama sung by Glenese Blake at a Karlheinz Company concert, May 2002, at the Music Theatre, University of Auckland. *Nga Haerenga* (The Journeys) are stories about mythical and legendary journeys. A world premiere performance was recorded by ABC Classic FM in Eugene Goosens Hall, ABC Centre, Ultimo, June 2001. Whitehead makes intermittent use of her own version of the "magic square," a number grid projecting pitches and rhythms often used as a pre-compositional device by Maxwell Davies. She feels music is a totality of form, rhythm and melody. Her works can glow with color, warmth, and the influence of natural sounds, "of birds, the sound of wind from nothing, the sound of rain and the great sense of space and the changing light."

With homes in Dunedin (NZ) and Sydney, and with a strong allegiance to both countries, Gillian Whitehead is shared and claimed by both her native New Zealand and by Australia.

CANADA

Those Gone Before

A cosmopolitan import, **SOPHIE-CARMEN ECKHARDT-GRAMATTÉ** was born in Moscow, January 6, 1899. She studied piano with her mother, a pupil of Nicholas Rubinstein, and at the Paris Conservatory, where she also took violin with **Guillaume Rémy** (1856–1947) and chamber music with **Vincent d'Indy** (1851–1931). At eleven, she made a double debut on violin and piano, and by 1919 was performing concertos on both instruments. Moving to Berlin, she studied violin with **Bronislaw Huberman** (1882–1947), and in the 1920s toured with Swiss pianist **Edwin Fischer** (1886–1960) as a two-piano team. In 1920, she married the painter Walter Gramatté, and in 1929, after his death, embarked on an American tour, playing her own works with **Leopold Stokowski** (1882–1977) and the Philadelphia Orchestra, and **Frederick Stock** (1872–1942) and the Chicago Symphony.

In 1934 she settled in Germany, where she married art historian Ferdinand Eckhardt. From 1936–42, she studied with Max Trapp at the Prussian Academy in Berlin, turning almost exclusively to composition. The couple moved to Winnipeg 1954, where she had many commissions and continued an active musical life, becoming a Canadian citizen in 1958. In 1970, she received both an honorary music doctorate from the University of Brandon and the title of professor from the minister of education in Vienna. In 1974, she was the first Canadian composer to receive the Diplôme d'Honneur, and shortly before her tragic death in a traffic accident in Stuttgart on December 2, 1974, the CBC produced a two-hour documentary of her life.

Eckhardt-Gramatté's works number three piano concertos, two violin concertos, two symphonies, suites for piano and violin, plus numerous pieces for other instruments. Her style was aggressive, but closer to late romanticism than 20th century. Her use of dissonance was logical, but never reaching the atonality of the Viennese School of Schoenberg, Berg and Webern.

The Doyennes of Canada

A trio of women dominated the Canadian music scene in the middle of the 20th century. They were born within five years of each other and uncannily all died at the turning of the millennium in the year 2000.

Violet Archer

VIOLET ARCHER was born April 24, 1913 in Montreal, while her parents were in Canada looking for a new home. Her two brothers, aged five and six, had been left with their grandparents in their native Italy. Cesare Balestreri found a job as a chef, and sent his wife Beatrice, with baby Violet, to fetch their sons. They arrived in Italy a few weeks before WWI started, August 1914, and were "stuck" until July 1919 before the whole family could return to Canada. In honor of their new citizenship, their name was changed, in 1940, from Balestreri, meaning *crossbow*, to Archer.

Careering Through Her Education

Violet studied piano, organ and composition at McGill University in Montreal (BM 1936), going on to further composition studies in the U.S. at Yale (BM 1948, MM 1949), where her teachers included **Béla Bartók** and **Paul Hindemith**. Meanwhile, she played percussion in the Montreal Women's Symphony Orchestra, 1940–47, taught piano and theory, and worked as an accompanist. She was also a percussionist in the New Haven (Connecticut) Symphony (1947–49). Her *Scherzo sinfonico* was performed by the Montreal Symphony in 1940, and when her *Britannia: a Joyful Overture* (1941) was selected by celebrated British conductor **Sir Adrian Boult** for broadcast by the BBC in 1942, and relayed to the troops in Europe, her career as a composer was launched.

Her choral/orchestral work, *The Bell*, won the Woods-Chandler prize at Yale (1949). She taught summer school at the University of Alberta (1948–49), and traveled to Europe in 1950, performing her music in England. She was composer-in-residence at North Texas State College (1950–53), simultaneously studying musicology with Otto Kinkeldey. She taught at Cornell (1952), and the University of Oklahoma (1953–61). In 1962, she moved to the University of Alberta where, after fifteen years, she retired as professor emeritus (1978), continuing part time as lecturer and composition teacher to young people. She was also an active organizer for Canada Music Week in Edmonton, and a competition adjudicator. One of Canada's most prolific composers, she wrote more than 250 works for stage, orchestra, piano, organ, choir, electronic media and film scores.

A Cavalcade of Honors

In 1971, Archer was awarded a honorary music doctorate by McGill. 1986 brought a Doctorate from the University of Windsor, and in 1989 an LLD came from the University of Calgary. Her many distinctions include the Creative and Performance Award of Edmonton (1972), induction into Edmonton's Cultural Hall of Fame (1987), membership to the Order of Canada (1983) and the Canadian Music Council's Composer of the Year award (1984). Her donation of $50,000 to the University of Calgary, doubly matched by the Province of Alberta, resulted in the creation of a fund to maintain and improve their library, named after her at a formal ceremony in November 1987.

Although she taught the twelve-note technique to her students in the U.S., she did not use it in her own music, but rather explored new sonorities using parallelism and folk tunes. Her open-minded approach to new sounds included the use of electronic music. In her words, it was her continuing project "to expose young musicians to contemporary music suitable at their level, so that when they grow up they will not feel estranged from 20th century music."

After her decision to move from Edmonton to Ottawa, the University of Alberta Department of Music produced a farewell concert of her works, April 25, 1998, in her honor. Much loved and respected, Violet died in Ottawa, February 21, 2000.

Jean Coulthard

JEAN COULTHARD, born in Vancouver, February 10, 1908, first studied piano with her mother. On a scholarship from the Vancouver Woman's Musical Club, she attended the RCM in London (1928–30), where she studied with one of England's greatest composers, **Ralph Vaughan Williams**. Back in Vancouver, she became head of the music departments at St. Anthony's College (1934–36) and the Queen's Hall School (1936–37), then went on to the positions of lecturer in composition (1947–57) and senior instructor (1957–73) at the University of British Columbia. Her early compositions were for voice and piano. She turned to orchestral composition in 1939, and from 1945 to 1950 to larger forms and more diverse instrumentation. She took her compositions for criticism to the 20th century giants—Schoenberg, Bartók, Milhaud and Copland. 1944–45 was spent studying with Bernard Wagenaar (1894–1971) at Juilliard. In 1955, she was in Paris on a Royal Society of Canada Scholarship, where she began work on her opera *The Return of the Native*, completed in 1979.

During the 1960s, Coulthard wrote increasingly complex works for ensemble, including four symphonies, concertos, sonatas for almost all instruments, hundreds of keyboard, choral, and vocal works, and also produced significant teaching materials. In recognition of her achievements, several doctoral theses have been written on her life and work. Her honors include being made an Officer of the Order of Canada (1978), and named Composer of the Year (1984) by PRO Canada. In June 1994, she was inducted into the Order of British Columbia. In February 1998, the musical community of Vancouver celebrated her ninetieth birthday with a week-long festival of concerts, lectures and radio broadcasts devoted to her music. She continued writing, finishing a sonata for unaccompanied cello just months before her sudden death, March 9, 2000.

Barbara Pentland

BARBARA PENTLAND, composer, pianist and teacher, was born in Winnipeg, January 2, 1912. She began piano studies at Rupert's Land Girls School at age nine and attempted composition. A heart disorder curtailed her activities, and her parents considered her desire to compose too exciting for a delicate child. After boarding school in Montreal, Barbara went to finishing school in Paris where, beginning in 1929, she attended formal composition classes with Cécile Gauthiez, a pupil of famous French composer **Vincent d'Indy** (1851–1931). Returning to Canada in 1930, Barbara continued piano and organ studies, and was active as a performer until 1936 when she won a fellowship to Juilliard, where she studied 16th century counterpoint and the new music of the day, including the works of Hindemith and Stravinsky. Back in Canada, from 1939 to 1942 she was at the University of Manitoba, taught privately and composed incidental music, ballet music, piano pieces and a violin concerto. During the summers of 1941–42, she studied at the Berkshire Music Center (Tanglewood) with **Aaron Copland** (1900–90).

In 1942 she moved to Toronto, teaching composition and theory at the Toronto College of Music, continuing composing and establishing herself as a radical. In her visits to the MacDowell Colony, 1947–48, **Dika Newlin**, a disciple of Arnold Schoenberg, interested Pentland in the twelve-tone principles. In 1949, Pentland relocated to Vancouver to teach at the University of British Columbia until 1963. Her works during this time show the Schoenberg technique. A decade later, she maintained that she treated twelve-tone serialism as a governing principle rather than a straitjacket. Her *String Quartet No. 2* was chosen to represent Canada at the 1956 ISCM festival in Stockholm. In 1999, Vancouver New Music's "Countdown to the End of the 20th Century" performed her *Symphony for Ten Parts* for chamber ensemble.

The catalogue of Pentland's works shows close to 100 instrumental pieces spanning sixty years, and touches on all standard media and genres. Her list of piano solo works is the most extensive of Canadians of her generation. In 1989, she was named a Member of the Order of Canada. She passed away February 5, 2000.

It is significant that within a matter of *weeks* these three women pioneers of Canadian composition were gone! In their wake follow the next generations—all talented, well trained and innovative, taking advantage of the technology of the new age as their music forges a path in the 21st century.

MICHELINE COULOMBE SAINT-MARCOUX, born in Notre-Dame-de-la-Doré, Québec, August 9, 1938, began harmony and piano studies with François Brassard, continuing in Montréal at the Institut Cardinal-Léger with Yvonne Hubert, and the École Vincent-d'Indy with Claude Champagne.

In 1965, she spent the summer session in France at the Académie Internationale d'été de Nice. In 1967, the Conservatoire de musique du Québec awarded her a Premier prize in composition for *Modulaire*, a work for large orchestra and *ondes Martenot*,[17] and the Académie de musique du Québec awarded her its Prix d'Europe. In 1968, she worked with composers at ORTF in Paris. In 1969, she took part in international festivals and founded, with five other composers, the *Groupe international de musique électro-acoustique de Paris* (GIMEP), which performed in Europe, South America and Canada between 1969 and 1973. Returning to Québec in 1971, in addition to teaching at the Montréal Conservatory, Saite-Marcoux became involved with the Québecois and Canadian musical world while maintaining her contacts with Europe, composing for small ensembles and Canadian orchestras. Her sadly premature death from a brain tumor occurred February 2, 1985.

The Next Generation

DIANE CHOUINARD was born in Montreal in 1950. She studied Spanish at Harvard, and piano, theory and harmony at the Royal Conservatory of Music in Toronto. In 1982, she returned to her city of birth, continuing her musical training with Mihran Essegulian at the University of Montreal, receiving BM and MM degrees in composition, including electroacoustic music.

Her diverse styles have been commissioned by musicians and playwrights, and performed in concerts, plays and radio broadcasts throughout Canada, North and South America and France. Her music is inspired by world events and the environment. One tone poem is *Les Eaux Chantantes de Mestemek*, regarding Beluga whales. A second, *Le Crépuscule de Kwimu*, inspired by the song of the loons, was chosen at a competition organized by the Association of Canadian Women Composers and performed by the Composers' Orchestra at the Glenn Gould Studio in Toronto.

Inspired by her French-Canadian heritage, Chouinard has written several works for vocal ensembles based on Quebec folk themes. Three of her vocal adaptations were chosen by ATMA Records for the CD *Serenades* (1994). Her incidental music for the play *El Señor de las Luces* was performed in Santiago in 1992 and throughout Chile by 1997.

Living in Vancouver since 1998, she has been a member of the ACWC (Association of Canadian Women Composers) since 1993 and a member of their administrative board beginning in 1995.

Diane married Serge Theriault, in 1970. They have three children, Jean-François, Melanie and Justin.

VIVIAN FUNG, born in Canada in 1975, studied composition in Edmonton with **Violet Archer** and piano with Ernesto Lejano. She went to Juilliard for composition with **David Diamond** and Robert Beaser, and piano with **György Sándor**, earning her BM and MM, and was awarded the Peter Mennin Prize for outstanding achievement and leadership in music. She completed her DMA, May 2002, at Juilliard, with a full tuition scholarship and grant from the Canada Council.

Commissions have come from orchestras and music organizations in Canada, America and abroad, including *Concertino Notturno* (San José Chamber Orchestra, 2001), *Night Songs* (Pittsburgh New Music Ensemble, 1999), *Blaze* (Seattle Symphony/Canada Council grant, 1998), *Scherzo for Piano Trio* (Music Teachers' Association of California, 1998), *Lustra Variations* (Millennium Chamber Music Society, 1996) and *Flares* (Gerard Schwarz and the New York Chamber Symphony, 1995), the latter winning the Stephan Albert Award from the American Music Center, and receiving its Canadian premiere with the Edmonton Symphony. Following *Night Songs*, which won a Student Composer Award from BMI, Fung received a second BMI Composer Award for *Love Songs in Chinese*.

---

17. An "other-worldly" electronic instrument played by manipulating sound waves. (See Unique Instruments.)

Fung's works have been performed in Moscow, Bowdoin Music Festival, Maine, Canada's Banff Centre, and Schola Cantorum, Paris, among other venues. She completed several residencies at the MacDowell, Yaddo, and Banff arts colonies, and was composer-in-residence with the Billings Symphony (1999–2000). She completed a residency as an associate artist at the Atlantic Center for the Arts, where she worked with Richard Danielpour and completed *Pizzicato* for the American String Quartet. She is a member of the Canadian League of Composers, the MacDowell Colony Executive Fellows Committee, an associate composer with the Canadian Music Centre, and attended the Film Scoring Program at the summer 2001 Aspen Music Festival. Her string quartet, funded in part by the Composer Assistance Program of the American Music Center, was premiered by the Avalon String Quartet, January 2004, at the Columbus (Ohio) Chamber Music Society. *Songs of Childhood* was performed at the North/South Consonance series in New York, *Kecak!* for *a cappella* mixed choir was premiered by the Pacific Mozart Ensemble in San Francisco, both Spring, 2004. A new work for traditional Chinese instruments for Music From China, a New York-based ensemble; and a new work for the Castro-Balbi/Lin duo came in 2005. Funding from the Meet the Composer Music Alive! program enabled a composer-in-residence for the San Jose Chamber Orchestra during the 2004–05 season, which included writing a new work and participating in outreach activities.

Fung is on the Literature and Materials of Music faculty at Juilliard, a member of SOCAN (Society of Composers, Authors, and Music Publishers of Canada), and an associate composer of the Canadian Music Centre.

Alice Ho

ALICE HO, a freelance composer/pianist dedicated to new music, was born in Hong Kong and emigrated to Canada in 1982, making her home in Toronto. Her composition degrees are from Indiana University (BM) and University of Toronto (MM). She has received awards from the Du Maurier Arts Ltd., Canadian Composers Competition, Martin Hunter Artists Award (2000), MACRO International Composition Competition (1999), Percussive Arts Society Composers Competition, and the International League of Women Composers Competition. Her music has been featured at new music festivals, including Made In Canada, Vancouver International, Winnipeg, ISCM World Music Days 2000 in Luxembourg, Asian Music Week 2000 in Yokohama, and Musicarama International Contemporary Music Festival in Hong Kong. The CBC Vancouver Orchestra, Winnipeg Symphony, Windsor Symphony, Hamilton Philharmonic, Canadian Chamber Ensemble, Le Nouvel Ensemble Moderne and Toronto New Music Ensemble have performed her works.

Ho has written a double concerto for violist **Rivka Golani** and bassist Joel Quarrington, a percussion concerto for Canadian percussionist Beverley Johnston, a piano concerto for the Scarborough Philharmonic Orchestra, a cello concerto for the Hong Kong Sinfonietta, a violin concerto for the Brandon Chamber Players, and a film/music project for the new music group, Continuum. In 2001, she wrote her opera *The Imp of the Perverse*, with librettist Michael O'Brien and Tapestry New Opera Works.

Born April 21, 1966, in Hong Kong, **MELISSA HUI** was raised in Vancouver. She received her BM from the University of British Columbia, MFA from the California Institute of the Arts, and MM and DMA from Yale. She taught at Mannes College of Music (New York), Wilfrid Laurier University (Ontario, Canada), and became an assistant professor of composition and theory at Stanford (Palo Alto, California). During the summer of 1995, she served as composer-in-residence at the Marlboro Festival in Vermont. She has received awards and grants from the Vancouver New Music Society (1989), Winnipeg Symphony Orchestra Composers Competition (1992), Taiwan Symphony (1993), a Guggenheim fellowship (1997), Fromm Foundation commission (2000), plus grants from the Canada Council, Meet the Composer, and ASCAP. Her CDs on Centredisc, UMMUS and CRI include *Speaking in Tongues*, *San Rocco*, and *Solstice*.

In 1992, her trumpet concerto *Two Sides to the Wind* was chosen to represent Canada at the International Rostrum of Composers in Paris. In 1996, as Composer of the Season, the Saskatoon (Saskatchewan) Symphony premiered her commission *Inner Voices*. Her chamber music has been performed by the San Francisco Contemporary Music Players and the Canadian Chamber Ensemble in Kitchener, Ontario, Société de Musique

Contemporaine du Québec in Montréal, Opus 415—the Bay Area New Music Marathon in San Francisco—the IJsbreker in Amsterdam, Esprit Orchestra (Toronto), Nevada Symphony, and chamber ensembles throughout Europe and Asia. Her chamber work *Solstice* was selected for performance at the 1996 International Gaudeamus Music Week.

Commissions have come from ASCAP, the CBC, Nouvel Ensemble Moderne (Montréal), Vancouver New Music Society, Hammerhead Consort (Edmonton), New Music Concerts (Toronto), Pittsburgh New Music Ensemble, NUMUS (Kitchener, Ontario), and the orchestras of Vancouver, Winnipeg, National Arts Centre and Oregon.

Hui has been an assistant professor of music at Stanford University since 1994.

HOPE LEE, born on January 14, 1953, in Taiwan, began piano studies at age four. She moved to Canada in 1967 and was naturalized in 1974. She studied piano and theory while intending to pursue a career in medicine. In 1974, she switched to music with undergraduate and graduate work at McGill University (1974–81) on piano, composition, and electronic music. She also attended the Stätliche Hochschule für Musik in Freiburg (1981–83), while participating in music courses and festivals in Darmstadt, Hong Kong, and the Center for Computer Research in Music and Acoustics (CCRMA) at Stanford.

Between 1987–90 at Berkeley, she developed studies on Chinese traditional music and poetry, plus the ideology, philosophy and notation of ch'in (Chinese seven-string zither) music, as well as computer music, all of which is integrated into her style. Her numerous works have been presented at international festivals from Tokyo to Hong Kong to Salzburg. Lee attended the First International Women Composers' Conference in Berlin (1982), and was composer-in-residence at the Künstlerhaus Bosweil (Switzerland, 1985). Her complex, atonal music exploits conventional instruments in unusual combinations. Works include *entends, entends le passé qui marche . . .* (piano and tape), NOHR (brass sextet), *Voices in Time* (chamber ensemble), *In a Mirror of Light* (ensemble and tape) and three Onomatopœiae: *Chan Chan*, *Jia Yuan* and *Tiáo Tiáo*. *Tangram*, for harpsichord, bass clarinet and tape, the latter performed by the works' commissioners, Annelie de Man and Harry Sparnaay in 1999 in Holland, Dublin and Sarajevo. *Fei Yang* (string quartet and accordion), received its premiere in 2001.

In 1980, she married composer David Eagle. They moved to Calgary in 1990. In 1999, Lee was invited to teach composition at the University of Calgary.

ALEXINA LOUIE was born in Vancouver, July 30, 1949, to second-generation Canadians of Chinese descent. She received her BM from the University of British Columbia in 1970, where she studied piano and composition while supporting herself playing cocktail piano music. She attended UCSD (San Diego) on a Regents Fellowship and studied composition with **Pauline Oliveros**, receiving her MM in 1974. She taught piano, theory, and electronic music at Pasadena City College (1974–80), and concurrently at Los Angeles City College (1976–80). During that time she continued her studies of Oriental music, particularly the Chinese tradition and the structural elements of Indonesian gamelan ensembles. Since settling in Toronto in 1980, the main focus of her career has been composing, but she continued to teach theory and composition at York University and the University of Western Ontario. Her style acknowledges traditional structures of her favorite composers, Bach, Mozart and Mahler, combined with contemporary language.

With commissions from the CBC and the Canada Council, she has been sought after for symphonic and chamber works, many of which have received performances in Canada and abroad. *The Ringing Earth* was commissioned for the opening of Expo '86 in Vancouver, the same year the Canadian Music Council named her Composer of the Year. In 1990, she received the first SOCAN concert music award as the most performed composer of the year, an honor repeated in 1992. Following the Chalmers Award (1994), she received a Canada Council "A" Grant (1995), and in 1996 was appointed composer-in-residence with the Canadian Opera. The following year, she attained an honorary doctorate from the University of Calgary, and the CBC released a disc featuring Steven Dann's performance of *Winter Music*, a chamber concerto for viola and eleven performers commissioned by the Vancouver New Music Society. This was nominated for a Juno award for Best Classical Composition in 1998. 1999 brought the Jules Léger Prize for New Chamber Music for *Nightfall* (14 strings) written for I Musici de Montréal; a CBC CD of some of her larger works performed by the National Arts Centre Orchestra; and the National Ballet of Canada premiered *one hundred words for snow* during the "Inspired by Gould" conference. The CBC recording received two Juno nominations in 2000, with Best Classical Composition awarded the title track, *Shattered Night, Shivering Stars*. In October 2001 *Music For A Thousand Autumns* was performed before Canada's governor general at a concert in Dresden, and in November, Louie received the Order of Ontario, the province's most prestigious honor.

Alexina is married to composer/conductor Alex Pauk.

RAMONA LUENGEN was born in Vancouver in 1960. She received both her BM (1983) and MM (1986) from the University of British Columbia, where she studied piano and composition. In 1996, she completed her doctor of music in composition from the University of Toronto. While composing extensively in the choral genre, she has also written *Cello Suite* (1991) for cello solo, *Theme and Variables for Woodwind Quintet* (1991), and several piano solo pieces. In 1993, she was invited as one of three international composers to the World Symposium on Choral Music held in Vancouver.

Her works have been commissioned and recorded by the CBC Radio Orchestra and Canada's major choirs, such as the Vancouver Cantata Singers, Arioso Women's Choir (Edmonton), Winnipeg Singers, University of Toronto Women's Chorus, the 1992, 1994 and 2000 National Youth Choirs of Canada, Chanticleer, and the Bitterfelder Kantorei (Germany), with performances in North America, Europe, Australia, New Zealand and Japan.

Besides the CBC, Luengen's music has been broadcast all over Europe.

SVETLANA MAKSIMOVIC, composer and musicologist, was born in 1948 in Yugoslavia. After attending the Music Conservatory, she completed her master's in composition in 1977 at the Belgrade University of the Arts. From 1972–80, she took courses in Byzantine-Slavic Orthodox and Russian Orthodox singing of the 13th to 17th centuries. She became professor of music at the conservatory, teaching harmony, counterpoint and composition, and published scientific papers on Serbian Orthodox singing of the 14th and 15th centuries. Having earned her reputation as a composer in her homeland, she moved to Canada in 1993 continuing writing and teaching. Her first Canadian commission came October 1997, for the orchestral work *Light Approaching*, which premiered March 1998. Her internationally performed works include compositions for voice, solo instruments, a sonata and a set of variations for two pianos, a string quartet, and music for orchestra.

Kelly-Marie Murphy

KELLY-MARIE MURPHY was born in Sardinia (Italy), but grew up on armed forces bases all across Canada. She began her studies in composition at the University of Calgary and later received a PhD in composition from the University of Leeds, England. She has won first prizes in the New Works Calgary Composers Competition (1992), Bradford Young Composers Competition for Electro-acoustic Music in Dance (1993), People's Choice Award at the CBC Young Composers Competition (1994), and earned a place in the top ten recommended works at the International Rostrum of Composers (Paris, 1996) for her first orchestral piece, *From the Drum Comes a Thundering Beat* . . . . In April 1998, she was awarded first and second prizes in the Maryland Composers Competition at Loyola College, and in November was recommended for a music award from the American Academy of Arts and Letters. *Utterances* won third place in the Alexander Zemlinsky Prize for Composition (1999); *Departures and Deviations* came in first in the International Horn Society's Composer's Competition (2001).

Murphy has completed short residencies at the Snowbird Institute for the Arts, Utah; Tapestry Music Theatre/Canadian Opera Company, Toronto; rESOund Festival of Contemporary Music, Edmonton; Strings of the Future International String Quartet Festival, Ottawa; Encounters/Soundstreams, Toronto; and the Banff Centre for the Arts. Her music has been performed in England, Poland, Spain, Japan and North America. She has written for Canada's leading performers, including the Winnipeg, Toronto and Edmonton Symphony Orchestras, plus cellist **Shauna Rolston**, violist **Rivka Golani**, and the Gryphon Trio.

Since 1994, Murphy has been living in Washington, DC, working as a freelance composer.

JULIET PALMER was born in 1967, in New Zealand, where she pursued undergraduate and graduate studies prior to attending Princeton (PhD, 1999). Her teachers included Louis Andriessen and Brian Ferneyhough. A resident of Toronto, she has received commissions from Continuum, Eve Egoyan, New Zealand String Quartet, Piano Circus, Mercer Union Gallery, and Aukland Philharmonia Orchestra. Palmer's music has been featured at New York's Bang On A Can Festival, Royaumont's Voix Nouvelles (France), SoundCulture (Japan), the Huddersfield and Bath Festivals (UK), Ars Electronica (Austria), Tot En Met XXII (Amsterdam), Toronto's Water Sources 2, the New Zealand Festival and the Adelaide Festival.

Her sound installations have been presented by New Zealand's Artspace Gallery and Toronto's Mercer Union. Performers of her music include Les Percussions de Strasbourg (France); Piano Circus (UK); California EAR Unit, Marimolin and the Bang on a Can All-Stars (USA); Tapestry New Opera Works, Eve Egoyan, Arraymusic and Continuum (Canada); Veni Ensemble (Slovakia); Ensemble för Ny Musik (Göteborg, Sweden); 175 East, the New Zealand String Quartet and Auckland Philharmonia. Danny Tunick and Kathy Supové premiered *mindmeat* for percussion and piano with poetry by Dennis Lee, November 2003. 2004 included commissions from Toronto's Ergo Ensemble, the Gryphon Trio, the Windsor Symphony Orchestra and Los Angeles violinist Mark Menzies.

DEIRDRE J. PIPER, born and educated in England, studied organ and cello at the RCM, and University of Manchester (BM, PhD Historical Musicology). She taught at the University of Manchester and Huddersfield Polytechnic School of Music before moving to Ottawa, where she is associate professor of music and supervisor of Performance and Practical Studies at Carleton University. Her areas of teaching are composition, theory, analysis, counterpoint, orchestration, and issues of concert music since the second World War.

Piper is organist and director of choirs at St. Matthias Anglican Church (Ottawa), performs as an ensemble pianist, and is co-founder and vocal accompanist with soprano Gloria Jean Nagy in *Due Cantabile*, performing art songs from baroque to Broadway, to contemporary Canadian, both religious and secular. A member of the Canadian League of Composers, she has produced works for various solo, chamber and choral media, and has had many performances and broadcasts of her concert music.

She is a member of the Royal Canadian College of Organists, and has been president of the National Capital Suzuki School of Music and Espace Musique Concert Society.

Oboist/composer **ELIZABETH RAUM**, born January 13, 1945 in Berlin, New Hampshire, earned a BM in oboe performance from Eastman (1966). She was active as an oboist in Boston, and from 1968 as principal oboe in the Atlantic Symphony Orchestra in Halifax (Nova Scotia) for seven years before moving west to Regina (Saskatchewan) in 1975 with her husband and three children, earning her MM in composition from the University there in 1985, and playing principal oboe in the Regina Symphony.

Her works have been heard in North America and Europe, and broadcast on the CBC. Her three operas, *The Garden of Alice*, *The Final Bid*, and *Eos: The Dream of Nicholas Flood Davin*, have been recorded by the CBC. She produced Canada's first classical video with originally written music, titled *Evolution: A Theme With Variations*, which premiered on the CBC in 1986. Her music for the documentary *Saskatchewan River* was named best musical score at the Saskatchewan Film and Video Showcase (1992), and the following year she received the same honor for the documentary *Like Mother, Like Daughter*, which included her violin concerto, *Faces of Woman*, written for her daughter, violinist Erika Raum. Other film collaborations include *Prelude to Parting*, *The Green Man Ballet*, winner of the Can Pro '94 Gold Award, and *Symphony of Youth*, winner of the Can Pro '95 Gold Award, a 1993 commission from the City of Regina. Other commissions have been from the CBC, Canada Council and Saskatchewan Arts Board. She has served on juries for the Canada Council, the Saskatchewan Arts Board, the Manitoba Arts Council, the CBC, and the Canadian Music Centre.

Her music is published by Editions Bim (Switzerland), Virgo and Warwick (UK), Southern, Alry and the Tuba/Euphonium Press (U.S.). She is also in demand as a speaker on composition and has given lectures at conferences for SOCAN, Orchestras Canada, Scotia Festival of Music, Saskatchewan Federation of Music Teachers, Saskatchewan Music Festival Association and the Alliance for Canadian New Music Projects.

Raum's CDs include the Regina Symphony Orchestra recording of her *Prairie Alphabet Musical Parade*, inspired by the popular children's book *A Prairie Alphabet*, and her tuba concerto, *The Legend of Heimdall*, recorded by the Orchestra of the Capella of St. Petersburg, Russia, with John Griffiths, soloist, and conducted by her husband, trombonist Richard Raum, (CMC, 2002).

ANITA SLEEMAN (née Andrés), born December 12, 1930, in San Jose, California, began piano lessons at age three, adding trumpet and horn during her school years. Her first composition was a processional march for band, played at her community college graduation. After marriage and six children, she returned to school at University of British Columbia, studying with **Jean Coulthard** and Cortland Huttberg, (BM, 1971, MM, 1974). At the University of Southern California, she studied composition with Frederick Lesemann, composition and orchestration with James Hopkins, contemporary conducting and composition with Earle Brown, and master classes with Charles Wuorinen, receiving her PhD in 1982.

In February 1997, the Galiano Trio (flute, clarinet, bassoon), assisted by dancers and projection graphics, presented a concert of Sleeman's works as part of the "Little Chamber Series That Could" season. In September of that year, she represented Canada at the *Donna in Musica* festival in Fiuggi, Italy. In 1999, her piece *Picasso Gallery II* was chosen for performance at the IAWM Festival in London. The composer attended the event via a travel grant from the Canada Arts Council. Her *Capriccio for Trombone, Violin and Orchestra* was premiered by the Windsor (Ontario) Symphony, January 2000, with Dale Sorenson, trombone, Lillian Scheirich, violin, **Susan Haig** conducting. Her *Cryptic Variation*, commissioned by Vancouver Community College in commemoration of its twenty-fifth anniversary, was premiered by the college's wind ensemble, March 2000. In January 2002, her string quartet *Cantigas* was premiered in Ottawa by the Arthur Leblanc Quartet, at the "Then, Now and Beyond" series sponsored jointly by ACWC and Ottawa Chamber Music Society. The performance was repeated August 6th at the Ottawa Chamber Music Festival.

The music of French modernists Messiaen, Varèse, Stravinsky, Koechlin and Ligeti have been important to the development of Sleeman's eclectic style, which is also influenced by her Spanish and Russian ethnic background and her interest in jazz. She composes for most media, but favors instrumental writing, especially woodwinds. A member of the Association of Canadian Women Composers and IAWM, she conducts the Ambleside Orchestra of West Vancouver, and plays horn in wind ensembles.

SOUTH AFRICA

Priaulx Rainier

Of English-Huguenot origin, **PRIAULX RAINIER** was born February 3, 1903, in Natal, South Africa. Early musical experiences came from Western classical music played by her two older sisters, one of whom, Nella, gave her her first piano lessons. Violin lessons started at seven. After an early childhood in Zululand, the family moved to Cape Town when she was ten. Priaulx became a violin student at the South African College of Music in 1913. In 1920, at seventeen, she won a University of South Africa Overseas Scholarship to study the violin at the RAM. Here she produced a string quartet movement in 5/8 time, which ended on a discord. In 1925, after leaving the Academy, Rainier taught at Badminton School and also worked as a violinist, sometimes playing in cinemas as an accompaniment for silent films.

In the mid-1930s, Rainier had a serious car accident which damaged her shoulder. While recuperating, she wrote a duo for violin and piano which was performed at Wigmore Hall by her violinist friend, Orrea Pernel, with pianist **Harriet Cohen**. Impressed by the music she produced, some friends anonymously gave her a small sum of money so that she could concentrate on composing. In 1937, she went to Paris to study with **Nadia Boulanger** for three months, the only composition teaching she ever received. That year she wrote *Three Greek Epigrams*, to words from Anyte of Tegea, followed in 1939 by her string quartet. In 1943, Rainier became a professor of composition at the RAM (1943–61), gaining a reputation as an excellent teacher, although the job left her with little time for composition. She became friendly with William Glock, later to become BBC controller of music, with **Michael Tippett**, and through him with **Benjamin Britten** and his partner, singer **Peter Pears**, who was to commission several works from her. Tippett requested a piece for the Morley College orchestra, and she produced the powerfully rhythmic *Sinfonia da Camera* for string orchestra. In the late 1940s, Rainier met **Igor Stravinsky** whose love of dynamic rhythms so closely matched her own. Her music from this period included two songs for voice and guitar, *Dance of the Rain* and *Ubunzima*, as well as the popular *Barbaric Dance Suite* for piano.

In 1952, the Worshipful Company of Musicians awarded her the John Clementi Collard Fellowship. Thirty years later she became the first woman to be elected to the livery of this ancient guild. The fellowship enabled her to give up some of her teaching and spend more time on composition. In 1953, her *Cycle for Declamation*, a passionate setting of John Donne's *Devotions*, was commissioned and premiered by Peter Pears. In 1956, he sang the first performance of her deeply moving *Requiem* for solo tenor and unaccompanied chorus. After her retirement in 1961, she received many commissions, including *Vision and Prayer* and the *Concertante* for two winds and orchestra, both funded by the Arts Council of Great Britain. The BBC commissioned *Ploërmel*, the cello concerto *Acquora lunac*, written for the Cheltenham Festival, and *Due canti a finale* for **Yehudi Menuhin**. Although she always denied using explicit references to African music, many critics have seen links in the all-important rhythmic patterns and use of space in her music. In June 1982, she received an honorary music doctorate from the University of Cape Town.

Rainier continued to compose into the 1980s. Her last works included *Grand Duo* (1980–82) for cello and piano, which has received many performances, and *Wildlife* (1984) for violin and orchestra. She died October 10, 1986, in Besse-en-Chandesse, France.

JEANNE ZAIDEL-RUDOLPH was born into a very musical family on July 9, 1948, in Pretoria, South Africa. Her father was a superb tenor, and her mother a fine pianist. Her brother was also very musical. She began piano at age five, with her aunt, Goldie Zaidel, and started on the recorder at six, the age she began composing. In 1966, she entered the University of Pretoria, where she obtained her BM and MM degrees *cum laude* (1971). She also entered graded piano examinations at the University of South Africa, winning honors in every one. Her postgraduate study began in 1973 at the RCM (London), with classes in piano, composition

Jeanne Zaidel-Rudolph

and electronic music. The following year she was accepted at the Hochschule für Musik (Hamburg), to study with **György Ligeti** (*b* 1923). In 1975, she returned to South Africa and was appointed lecturer in the music department of the University of the Witwatersrand, Johannesburg, teaching composition, harmony, counterpoint and piano. By the 21st century she was creating new courses and academic development, especially in digital music technology.

In 1976 Jeanne married Michael Rudolph, a professor of dentistry, and began PhD research. She received this degree in 1979 from Pretoria University, becoming the first South African woman to obtain a doctorate in composition. With multi-role female ability, she also gave birth to her first three children, Natalie (1977), Sara (1979) and Tamar (1981). Devorah (Nisi) arrived in 1989.

Besides being an active lecturer, with such seminars as "Transcultural Influences of African Music on Western Art Music," in 1981 Zaidel-Rudolph founded the New Music Network, a society for the promotion of 20th century music. In subsequent years, she has performed, presented papers, and attended festivals on Women in Music in New York, Rome and Israel. Her music reflects some of the indigenous African musical styles, as in the ballet *The River People*, which tells the story of a mythical tribe and uses almost hypnotic rhythms combined with the Western influence of electronic music. Judaism is also present in many of her works. *At the End of the Rainbow*, for full orchestra, refers to the biblical story of the flood. *Masada*, for bassoon and string quartet, embodies the courage of the 1,000 Jewish men, women and children who, after a two-year siege on this mountain top (71–73 AD), chose to die by their own hand rather than be slaughtered by the invading Romans. She also composed a score for the movie *African Dream*. Her recordings on the EMI label include religious Jewish music she composed and arranged for two live concerts. A 1994 Claremont CD, *Music of the Spheres*, contains six compositions reflecting her fascination with mankind's religious instinct. Included on the disc are *Masada*, the *Sefirot Symphony*, for wind, brass, percussion and harp, and *At the End of the Rainbow*.

In 1995, Zaidel-Rudolph was invited to serve on the South African Anthem Committee and rewrote a full orchestral version, which has been accepted as the new official South African National Anthem. In 1996, she was asked to compose part of the *Human Rights Oratorio* which was presented as South Africa's gift to the Olympic Games in Atlanta, Georgia (USA). Written for full orchestra, choir and soloists, this has been released on CD. During the 1996–97 season, her works were conducted by **Tania León** with the Johannesburg Symphony. She was commissioned to compose a song in honor of President Nelson Mandela, which was premiered at his Doctoral Award Ceremony in Cape Town in 1997. Titled *He Walked to Freedom*, it was later released on EMI. Also in 1997, she was nominated as a finalist in the South African Woman of the Year Award.

1999 saw the premiere of her two-piano work *The Juggler and the King*, commissions for an *African Song Cycle* for soprano Hilary Friedland, music for a multi-media opera on the Centenary of the Anglo-Boer War, all the while teaching full time at the University. On the home front were the happy occasions of the marriage of her eldest daughter, Natalie, July 28. In 2000, she was chosen "The Best of the Best" composer by Canary Burton's WOMR Radio Station in Cape Cod, Massachusetts.

On April 12, 2001, Natalie presented the family with its first grandson, Aharon David. Shortly thereafter, Jeanne embarked on a concert tour to Los Angeles, Las Vegas and Chicago with her all-male Sydenham Choir, made up of college students, professional men ranging from lawyers to doctors and computer scientists, to her resident cantor. Upon her return, she was asked to become head of the music department, a position entailing administration of a staff of fifteen, managing student affairs of eighty undergraduates and twenty-six postgraduates working on their masters or doctorates, plus producing her own academic papers on analysis for conferences, as well as teaching and composing! She was made a professor soon after this promotion. Even with the challenge of the department's relocation to a larger facility, which included moving fifty-four pianos, seventeen offices and lecture theaters, she managed to complete two commissioned works, *a 5 6 7 8* for piano, for the University of South Africa (UNISA)—the country's largest—and *Ebony and Ivory* for harpsichord for the International Music Competition in South Africa.

March 2002 brought a whirlwind tour of Miami, where she lectured at the University, Boca Raton (Florida) and Atlanta, where the Sydenham Choir and her small orchestra gave three acclaimed productions of *CELEBRATION 2*, a Jewish musical for which Zaidel-Rudolph composed original songs and arranged the music. An updated version of this was performed in March 2003, at London's Royal Festival Hall to an audience of almost 3,000 whose response was overwhelming, as was the reception of the encore of *He Walked to Freedom*.

April 2003 saw a field trip to a remote area in the Eastern Cape to research, record and video a group of African Nqgoko (Xhosa) women who sing in multi-phonics—"overtone" Tibetan monklike singing. Discovered by a German monk, they are considered a national treasure. Commissioned by the International Classical Music Festival to compose a thirty-minute work using this unique music in a multicultural choral composition, transcribing the rhythmic and melodic material into Western notation was daunting, but *LIFECYCLE* premiered November 5 at UNISA to great acclaim from a predominantly African audience, including several State leaders. This was followed a week later with a gala performance in Cape Town at the Baxter Theatre.

July found the composer on her annual U.S. tour, this time with *CELEBRATION 2*. In Houston, where she had been asked to write a special song in memory of Ilan Ramon, the Israeli astronaut who had lost his life in the space shuttle Columbia, his widow, Rona Ramon, was in the audience. It was a very moving experience for all present. Then to Boston performing at Berklee College Auditorium, and Great Neck (Long Island) New York, and a triumphant finale in Toronto at the Ford Centre. In August, Zaidel-Rudolph presented a paper at a conference on

"Gender and Sexuality" at Pretoria University, its title, "Pride, Prejudice and Power," about being a woman composer in South Africa. It was published in the *IAWM Journal* in 2004.

2004 also saw a commission from SAMRO (South African Music Rights Organisation) for a set of piano pieces for the American pianist, David Arden. (With two grand pianos in our home, Arden, who runs a highly successful music school in San Francisco, once "housesat" for us early in his career . . . small world!)

On the home front, Devorah became bat mitzvah (confirmed) at age twelve in 2002. Sara works in real estate in New York. Tamar came home from the beaches of Malibu, California, and spent 2003 teaching Nutrition at both the Torah Academy Primary and High School. And Natalie did it again! On June 14, she gave birth to Ashira, the first granddaughter in the family.

Reward for a dedicated career came to Jeanne Zaidel-Rudolph October 31, 2004, in a ceremony at the Union Buildings in Pretoria, when President Thabo Mbeki presented her with the Order of Ikhamanga. These National Orders are the highest awards the country bestows. She was one of thirty South Africans so honored, "who excel in the fields of arts, culture, literature, music, journalism and sport."

"The president placed an Ikhamanga (strelitzia) medal around my neck and handed me the beautiful gold scroll. It was an honour, a privilege and a humbling experience to be part of South African history at this time. I was extremely moved by the citations and awards for people who had come from such deprived and disadvantaged beginnings, and the courage and determination that had brought them so far. It is in this spirit that I will try to help young talented music students at [my] University who cannot afford to study further."

The wording on the gold scroll reads, "For her outstanding contribution as a composer, pianist and teacher in the development of music in South Africa and internationally."

Thus is the life of a woman composer—or that of so many women in any field—comprised of the challenging juggling of home, family and career!

[But we do it . . . .]

Western European Composers

FRANCE
Cécile Chaminade (1857–1944)
Germaine Tailleferre (1892–1983)
Lili Boulanger (1893–1918)
Marcelle De Manziarly (1899–1990)
Claude Arrieu (1903–90)
Yvonne Desportes (1907–95)
Ida Gotkovsky
Betsy Jolas
Édith Canat de Chizy
Graciane Finzi

BELGIUM
Yolande Uyttenhove (1925–2000)
Jacqueline Fontyn

THE NETHERLANDS
Elisabeth Kuyper (1877–1953)
Tera De Marez Oyens (1932–96)

GERMANY
Barbara Heller
Adriana Hölszky
Babette Koblenz
Ruth Schonthal (1924–2006)
Ruth Zechlin

ITALY
Sonia Bo
Elisabetta Olga Laura Brusa
Patricia Chiti
Biancamaria Furgeri
Ada Gentile
Patrizia Montanaro
Teresa Procaccini
Irma Ravinale
Roberta Silvestrini

SPAIN
Teresa Catalán
Consuelo Diez
Marìa Escribano
Iluminada Perez Frutos
Concha Jerez
Mercedes Zavala

NORWAY
Agathe Backer-Grøndahl (1847–1907)

SWEDEN
Elfrida Andrée (1841–1929)

FINLAND
Kaija Saariaho

The European Continent, being "on site," felt the winds of change blow stronger with the advent of World War I than provincial, "isolated" America. Women in the European music world were achieving a fair amount of respect from their male peers. While a mini-multitude of ladies got their name in print for one or two pieces of "parlor music," a select few persevered their way above the crowd, producing serious music and exploring, along with their male counterparts, the new frontiers of serial, aleatory, acoustical and electronic music. Time, audiences and financial considerations will inevitably dictate which works will survive. (It would also help if more women's music were programmed into the orchestral repertoire and aired on classical music radio stations . . .)

FRANCE

CÉCILE CHAMINADE (1857–1944) remains one of France's most popular composers known for her melodic salon music. (See Romantic Period.)

Germaine Tailleferre

GERMAINE TAILLEFERRE, born April 19, 1892 in Parc-St-Maur, near Paris, entered the Paris Conservatory in 1904, despite her father's opposition, and her equal talent in art. As a piano prodigy with an amazing memory, she won numerous prizes. In 1913, she met fellow composers **Georges Auric** (1899–1983), **Arthur Honegger** (1892–1955) and **Darius Milhaud** (1892–1974) in Georges Caussade's counterpoint class. By 1917, iconoclastic composer **Erik Satie** (1866–1925) was so impressed with her two-piano piece, *Jeux de plein air*, that he christened her his "musical daughter," and it was he who first brought her to prominence as one of his group of *Nouveaux Jeunes*. She became the only female member of *Les Six*[18]—so dubbed by music critic Henri Collet—followers of Satie and the equally unconventional poet-novelist-film maker, **Jean Cocteau** (1889–1963). Her career was also assisted by the Princesse Edmond de Polignac, who liked her ballet *Le marchand d'oiseaux* (1923) enough to commission a piano concerto (1923–24), which proved quite successful. Her talents fitted in perfectly with the trend of neo-classicism, set by Russian emigré composer **Igor Stravinsky** (1882–1971) during his years in Paris. But she was also influenced by major French composers **Gabriel Fauré** (1845–1924) and **Maurice Ravel** (1875–1937), her orchestration teacher, with whom she remained in close contact throughout the 1920s.

Les Six Minus Cinq - an Uneven Equation

Tailleferre never regained the acclaim she enjoyed through her association with *Les Six* after they disbanded in the early '20s. Two unhappy marriages (to caricaturist Ralph Barton in 1926, and lawyer Jean Lageat in 1931) stressed her creative energies, plus continual financial problems forced her to compose mostly to commission, resulting in many uneven and quickly written works. In addition, her natural modesty and an unjustified sense of artistic insecurity prevented her from promoting herself properly. She considered herself a craftsman who wrote cheerful music as a release from the problems of her private life. Her concertos of the 1930s were successful, as was her dramatic *Cantate de Narcisse* (1938). Other compositions include a string quartet (1918), violin sonata (1921), *Sicilienne* for piano (1928), chamber music, songs, operas, ballets and film music. After a non-productive period in America (1942–46), she produced the excellent Second Violin Concerto (1947–48) and turned her attention towards opera. She gave successful concert tours with baritone Bernard Lefort, for whom she wrote the *Concerto des vaines paroles* (1954), and in 1957 experimented briefly with serial techniques in her *Clarinet Sonata*. Although she continued to write prolifically and teach until the end of her life, Tailleferre resorted increasingly to self-borrowing and familiar formulae, as seen her quick completion of the *Piano Trio* in 1978 which she had begun in 1916. Meeting conductor Désiré Dondeyne in 1969 sparked a new interest in composing for wind band. Germaine was devoted to children and their music, which accounts for the spontaneity and charm characterizing her best works. She died in Paris, November 7, 1983.

Juliette Marie Olga (**LILI**) **BOULANGER** was born in Paris, August 21, 1893, into a prominent musical family. Her Russian mother, Raissa, was a singer. Her father, Ernest, taught cello at the Paris Conservatory, and married his student despite a forty year age difference. Her sister **Nadia** (1887–1979) became one of the most famous composition teachers of the 20th century.

At the age of two, Lili suffered a severe case of bronchial pneumonia which for the rest of her short life left her susceptible to many illnesses, especially the debilitation of what is

Lili Boulanger

18. Les Six included Georges Auric, Louis Durey, Paul Honegger, Darius Milhaud, Francis Poulenc and Tailleferre.

now known as Crohn's disease. Counteracting this affliction was growing up in the stimulating company of her father's Conservatory colleagues, such as **Jules Massenet** (1842–1912) and **Gabriel Fauré**, and being part of the new impressionism of **Claude Debussy** (1862–1918) and **Maurice Ravel**, as well as savoring the new horizons forged by **Igor Stravinsky**. Her father's death when she was only seven was a great shock, but her mother continued cultivating their musical circle. Both in the Paris apartment and the Boulanger country home at Gargenville, names like violinist **Eugène Ysaÿe** (1858–1931) and Dutch conductor **Willem Mengelberg** (1871–1951) would be among the illustrious on the guest list.

At age five, Lili started auditing the organ, piano and composition classes her eleven-year-old sister was taking at the conservatory. At eight, she made her first public performance as a violinist. 1904 saw her debut as a pianist, as well as her sister's graduation from the conservatory.

A Pioneer for the Prix de Rome

By 1905 ill health was forcing Lili to be sent to various spas in Germany and Switzerland. She continued her music studies at home and also read Greek classics and French poets. In 1909, she began composing, arranging psalms for soloist and orchestra. She also added proficiency on the harp and cello to her instrument mastery. Formal lessons in harmony, counterpoint and composition continued, 1909–11. At seventeen, an awareness of the likelihood of an early death spurred Lili to concentrate her energies on composition. The next two years were spent studying for the Prix de Rome. Amongst her rivals was **Marcel Dupré** (1886–1971), who was to become one of the world's greatest organists. Despite stiff competition, Lili won for her cantata, *Faust et Hélène*, making her the first woman to ever win the *Prix de Rome*, the Paris Conservatory's highest recognition, dating back to 1803. (Nadia had won second place in 1908. Other former winners include Berlioz, Bizet, Massenet, Debussy and her own father in 1835.)

As part of the prize, the young composer took up residence at the Villa de Medici in Rome, although bouts of illness forced her to spend much time in bed. Her mother stayed nearby. The four year Prix term was cut short with the outbreak of World War I. Lili returned to Paris, and between 1914–16 joined the war effort founding an organization to write to Conservatoire musicians in the army. She signed a contract with one of Europe's top publishing companies, Ricordi. The next two years produced seven more works, the last two dictated from her sickbed. Her final composition reflected the Catholicism which marked a strong influence in the latter part of her brief span: *Pié Jesu* for voice, string quartet, harp and organ.

A Short Time Capsule

After all the years of suffering and bouts of depression, Lili died at twenty-four on March 15, 1918, leaving behind a remarkable ten year output of close to fifty works, including many songs, choral works with orchestra, two symphonic poems, piano pieces, and an uncompleted opera, *Princess Maleine*, from a story by Belgian mystic poet and dramatist Maurice Maeterlinck (1862–1949). Demonstrating great skill and imagination, her style reflects the transitions that were taking place: Romanticism interlaced with impressionist techniques and hints of the modernism to come. Many of her works were published posthumously. Despite the war, the Paris press gave considerable space to her passing. Her obituary was prominent on the front page of *Le temps*. The U.S. journal, *The Musician*, honored her with two columns. Her works were featured in memorial concerts throughout Europe. In New York, maestro **Walter Damrosch** (1862–1950), director of the New York Symphony Society—forerunner of the Philharmonic—programmed several of her works as a tribute. During one of her American trips, Nadia had established the Lili Boulanger Memorial Fund in Boston. In 1965, Les Amis de Lili Boulanger was founded in Paris with the same goal, to promote her works and give scholarships to young composers. Officially recognized by the French government in 1977, its committee included such royalty as Queen Elisabeth of Belgium and the Prince and Princess of Monaco, plus renowned music names like Lord Yehudi Menuhin, Olivier Messiaen, Darius Milhaud, Igor Stravinsky and its first president, Igor Markevitch, who was also responsible for the first recording of Lili's works. Half a century later, The Women's Philharmonic of San Francisco included her *D'Un Soir Triste* (On a Sad Evening) and *D'un Matin de Printemps* (Spring Morning) in their 1992 CD, **JoAnn Falletta**, conducting. *Clairières dans le ciel* (Clearings in the Sky, a song cycle), *Les sirènes* (Sirens), *Renouveau* (Renewal), *Hymne au soleil* (Hymn to the Sun), *Pour les funérailles d'un soldat* (For the Burial of a Soldier) and *Soir sur la plaine* (Evening on the Plain) came out on a 1994 Hyperion CD, James Wood conducting the New London Chamber Choir.

Between the supportive atmosphere of her upbringing and education, the wealth of style progression and the example of (almost) unfettered feminism in the role model of her beloved sister, Lili lived in the best of musical milieux. It must be left to the imagination what this woman would have accomplished had her time not been so brief.

MARCELLE DE MANZIARLY was born in Kharkov, Russia, October 13, 1899, of Russian and American parentage. She started composing at age twelve and was one of Nadia Boulanger's first composition pupils in Paris, remaining her lifelong friend. Later, she studied conducting with Felix Weingartner in Basel (1930–31) and piano with Isabelle Vengerova in New York (1943). Boulanger promoted Manziarly's music in Paris, conducting the *Triptyque pour une madone de Lorenzo d'Alessandro* (1934) in her first appearance on the podium in the French capital. Boulanger also introduced Marcelle to Princesse Edmond de Polignac, who commissioned several works.

Considered a French composer, Manziarly's career was divided between France and America. She taught privately in both countries, and appeared as a pianist and conductor in New York. Her works in the 1920s, including *Impressions de mer* for piano (1922), reveal Debussy's influence, with strains of Stravinsky's neo-classicism. *Sonate pour Nôtre-Dame de Paris* for orchestra (1945), is a set of variations inspired by the Liberation of Paris after World War II. In the '60s, serialism and atonality crept into her style. A visit to India stimulated an interest in Hindu rhythms and scales. She wrote for the stage, orchestra, chamber, piano and vocal music and a piano concerto. Most of Manziarly's works from the 1950s onwards were published by the composer. She died in Ojai, California, May 21, 1989.

Born November 30, 1903, in Paris, **CLAUDE ARRIEU** studied at the Paris Conservatory with **Paul Dukas** (1865–1935), earning a *premier prix* in composition there in 1932. She also studied piano with **Marguerite Long**. A prolific composer, she followed the Parisian neo-classic style, her musical forms following in the direct line of composers descending from **Emmanuel Chabrier** 1841–1894). Interested in new trends, she experimented with electronic music, but never used it in her concert works. Her career also included teaching and radio, where from 1946 she was a producer and assistant head of sound effects. Her compositions include several comic operas, successful theater scores, concertos for violin and piano, and chamber works. Her radio score *Frédéric Général* won a Prix Italia in 1949. Arrieu died March 7, 1990 in Paris.

YVONNE DESPORTES, daughter of French composer Emil Desportes, was born July 18, 1907, in Coburg, France. She studied with the brothers Jean and Noël Gallon, and **Paul Dukas** at the Paris Conservatoire, where she won first prizes in harmony (1927), counterpoint and fugue (1930), composition and piano accompaniment (1930), and the prestigious Prix de Rome (1932), residing in the Italian capital, 1933–37. In 1943, she returned to the Conservatoire to teach solfège, and in 1959 was appointed to teach counterpoint and fugue. She also taught piano accompaniment at the Lycée La Fontaine.

A prolific composer and well-known pedagogue, she authored many theoretical and practical works on music education. Her style is vivid, bright, humorous and descriptive. Although she composed in all genres, the greater part of her output is instrumental, much of it chamber music with wind and percussion instruments. Her works include a ballet, *Trifaldin* (1934), a violin concerto (1955), two concertos for percussion (1957), three symphonies (1958, 1964, 1969), a Requiem (1950), and works for chorus and orchestra. She died in Paris in 1995.

IDA GOTKOVSKY was born August 26, 1933, in Calais, and grew up in a family of musicians with her father, Jacques, and sister, Nell, both noted violinists. Beginning as a student at the Paris Conservatory—where one of her teachers was **Nadia Boulanger**—through the years of a distinguished career she won innumerable prizes, including the Prix Lily Boulanger, Prix Blumenthal, Premier Prix du Référendum Pasdeloup, Prix International de Divonnes les Bains, Grand Prix Musical de la Ville de Paris, three prizes from the Institut de France, Médaille de la Ville de Paris, SACEM and the Golden Rose (U.S.), among others.

Her compositions, most of which were commissioned, include symphonic works, chamber music, instrumental, vocal and lyric pieces, and have been performed in Europe, America, Russia, Japan, Asia and Australia. Her major works are concertos for clarinet, two volins, cello, saxophone, trombone and trumpet. There are also three symphonies; one ballet, *Rien ne va plus*; and an opera, *La Rêve de Makar* (1964), which won first prize, Ville de Paris (1966).

Betsy Jolas

Born in Paris, August 5, 1926, of intellectual American parents, **BETSY JOLAS** grew up in a cultured circle. She studied piano, and able to sight read at an early age, accompanied her family and at school recitals. Her mother, Marie, was a fine musician and translator, her journalist/poet father, Eugène, founded the international literary review, *Transition*. Their home was the meeting place for such artistic elite as Ernest Hemingway, James Joyce, Sylvia Beach, Edgard Varèse and Henri Matisse.

At the beginning of World War II in 1939, the family moved to New York where she was educated at the Lycée Français and the Dalcroze School of Music. At fifteen, her experience as a chorister, as well as piano and organ accompanist with the famed Norman Dessoff choir, was to be an important influence in developing her career and establishing her abiding interest in renaissance music. At Bennington College (BA, 1946), she studied harmony with Paul Boepple, organ with Carl Weinrich, and piano with Helen Schnabel. While a student, she composed her first important piece of music, an oratorio for chorus and orchestra, which was performed by student music groups and local talent.

Following graduation, WWII having ended the year before, she returned to Europe. At the Paris Conservatory, she studied composition with **Darius Milhaud** (1892–1974), counterpoint with Simone Plé-Caussade, and analysis and aesthetics with avant-gardist **Olivier Messiaen** (1908–92). From 1971–74, she often substituted for Messiaen, teaching his composition classes when he was on tour. In 1975, she was appointed professor of Advanced Musical Analysis at the Conservatoire National Supérieur de Musique (Paris Conservatory).

Marriage, Family and Career - the Usual Juggling Act

Jolas married Gabriel Illouz, a French physician, in 1949, and had two sons and one daughter. Although at times family commitments slowed down her creative endeavors, she continued studying and composing. From 1955–65, she was the editor of *Écouter Aujourd'hui*, (Listen Today), the periodical of the French Radio-Television Network. This gave her the opportunity to meet many important French musicians, including conductor/composer **Pierre Boulez** (*b* 1925), who greatly influenced her music. Boulez showcased modernists Karlheinz Stockhausen, Luciano Berio, *et al*, in his Domaine Musical concerts. After offering technical suggestions, he premiered Jolas' *Quatuor II*. The composition was recorded, launching her career as a serious composer. Within ten years, she attained status as one of the finest contemporary composers in France. She received the Copley Foundation Award (Chicago, 1954), and the prize for French-speaking composers (1961). She held various temporary appointments in American universities, and was composer-in-residence at Tanglewood (1976–77). *D'un opéra de poupée en sept musiques*, premiered at IRCAM (1984), combined conventional wind instruments with electric keyboards, guitar and electro-acoustical devices.

Her many awards and distinctions include prizes from the American Academy of Arts (1973), a Koussevitzky Foundation Award, French Grand Prix National de la Musique (1974), Grand Prix de la Ville de Paris (1981), and Prix International Maurice Ravel (1992). She was elected a member of the Institute of the American Academy and Institute of Arts and Letters (1983), named personality of the year by SACEM, Paris (1993) and elected to the Academy of Arts and Sciences in 1995.

Jolas wrote many vocal works mixing timbres and sonorities in her exploration of the relationships between words and music. Her enormous output includes chamber music, opera and orchestral works. In 1994, she was the Fromm visiting professor of music at Harvard for the winter semester. In the spring of 1995, Opéra de Lyons presented the world premiere performances of her opera *Schliemann*, about the life of the eccentric archeologist who discovered the ruins of Troy. She continued active into the new century. Her concerto, *Oh, Night, Oh! . . . . .* for piano and chorus premiered September 2001 at the Strasbourg Festival, and October at the Normandy Festival. The soloist was her long time friend Jay Gottlieb.

October 26, 2001, found her at Yale lecturing on her famous parents and their influential literary magazine, *Transition*, which in the course of its eleven-year history (1927–38) featured the work of noted writers/ poets James Joyce, Samuel Beckett, Gertrude Stein, Hart Crane, Archibald MacLeish, William Carlos Williams and Erskine Caldwell, as well as translations of works by leading European writers such as Franz Kafka. (A month before, Yale had hosted an international conference, attended by speakers from universities all over the world, and sponsored by the Whitney Humanities Center and the Beinecke Rare Book and Manuscript Library, with the journal as its focus. All issues of *Transition* were on view at the library.)

Speaking of her parents' accomplishments, Betsy revealed that Maria Jolas founded a bilingual school in France, and was considered one of the finest literary translators of her time. She was also a political activist, supporting the French Resistance during World War II and serving on the Paris American Committee to Stop War during the Vietnam War. Her father, by virtue of trilingual upbringing, advocated a "revolution of the word," and experimented with multilingual poetry. A collection of Jolas papers at the Beinecke Library at Yale includes drafts of Eugene Jolas' autobiography, *Man from Babel*, published 2001 by Yale University Press.

The Next Generation

ÉDITH CANAT de CHIZY was born March 26, 1950, in Lyon, but has lived in Paris since 1970. Growing up in a music-loving environment, she began violin studies at seven. Her training as a violinist is evident in her compositions, which are generally dominated by stringed instruments. She studied at the Conservatoire National Supérieur de Musique de Paris where, between the years 1978–83, she received six Premiers Prix in harmony, fugue, counterpoint, analysis, orchestration and composition. She was led to and encouraged in composition by her professor Maurice Ohana.

Her awards include the Tribune Internationale des Compositeurs for the orchestral work *Yell* (1990); composition prizes Hervé Dugardin and Georges Enesco (1987, '91); Paul-Louis Weiller composition prize from the Académie des Beaux-Arts (1992); created Chevalier des Arts et des Lettres (1994); and named to the Victoires de la Musique (2000) for the release of her CD *Exultet-Siloël-Moïra*.

Of her thirty-four works, seventeen are for orchestra, nine for soloist with orchestra, and eight of vocal music. Some of the titles are: *Yell* for orchestra (1985); *Canciones del Alma* for twelve solo voices, and *Siloël* for twelve strings (both 1992); *Tombeau de Gilles de Rais* for choir and orchestra (1993); *Exultet* concerto for violin (1995); and *Moïra* concerto for cello (1998).

Since 1986, Canat de Chizy has been the director of the Music Academy in the fifteenth district of Paris, a position she says provides a human element in her life to the otherwise solitary existence of a composer. She is married to François Porcile, a film maker and musicologist.

Graciane Finzi

GRACIANE FINZI was born into music July 10, 1945, in Casablanca (Morocco). Her father and mother were teachers at Casablanca's Music Academy and coached their daughter until she attained the qualifications to enter the Paris Conservatory at age ten. She studied piano with Joseph Benvenuti, earning four first prizes: Harmony (1962), Counterpoint (1964), Fugue (1964), and Composition (1969). From 1975–79, she was director of the Festival de la Défense (Paris).

Her list of honors includes the Grand Prix de la Promotion Symphonique de la SACEM (the French equivalent of ASCAP), from whom she also received the Prix Georges Enesco and the 2001 Grand Prix for her entire oeuvre. The Society of Authors, Composers and Dramatic Art awarded her the Prix SACD for her two act opera, *Pauvre assassin* (1997), based on the play by Pavel Kohout.

Finzi's catalogue comprises over sixty works, vocal and orchestral, most of them commissions from the French Ministry of Culture, Radio France, contemporary music festivals, etc. *La tombée du jour* (Dusk), three melodies for baritone and orchestra, based on the beginning of Robert Schumann's madness, received its first performance by Belgian baritone **José van Dam** (1998). *Concerto for Cello and Orchestra* was commissioned by Gary Hoffman; *Concerto for Piano and Orchestra* was premiered by Jean-Claude Pennetier. *Brume de sable* (Sand Mist—impressions of the Moroccan desert), for percussion and orchestra, was written in 1999. *Je me souviens* (I Remember, 2000), for baritone, soprano and piano, is a memoriam to World War I. *Espressivo* for harpsichord, played by Elisabeth Chojnacka, was released in 2001 on an Opus CD.

Her works, employing extratonal harmonic and chromatic sequences, use orchestral instruments and voices, uniting them in juxtaposed groups, while taking into account their individual dynamics and bio-rhythm. They have been performed all over the world: Paris, New York, London, Manchester, Rome, Moscow, Helsinki, Vancouver, Nuremberg, Mainz, Bremen, Cologne, Banff, Calgary, Rio de Janeiro and Buenos Aires, by leading soloists and orchestras.

A professor at the Paris Conservatory since 1979, and vice president of the International Society of Composers (ISCM) since 1992, Graciane is married to Gilbert Lévy, a drama teacher/theater producer who added music to his career, collaborating with his wife and writing libretti to her operas. Their son, Luigi, born May 20, 1971, is a viola player, and daughter, Mélanie Thiebaut, born September 28, 1964, is a conductor.

BELGIUM

Born July 25, 1925, in Leuze-en-Hainaut, Belgium, **YOLANDE UYTTENHOVE** studied piano, harmony, counterpoint, fugue and music history at the Royal Conservatory of Brussels. As a pianist, she won prizes in every competition she entered. Her 1983 recording of Fauré's *Sonata for Violin and Piano*, with violinist Fernand Léonard, was considered in France to be the best recording of Fauré's work. She won a Gold Medal in the international composition competition at Lutèce, Paris (1984) for her *Sonata per Violin and Piano*, op. 95. She was a licentiate of London's Royal Academy of Music, an officer of the Order of Léopold II, honorary director of the Academy of Music of Braine-l'Alleud, and for many years president of the Union des Compositeurs Belges (Belgian Composers Union). She wrote more than 200 works for orchestra, chamber music, voice, and instrumental, and lectured on women in music. She concertized widely in Europe and the U.S., and made recordings with her husband, René de Macq and son Thierry, both flutists, and her younger son, Renaud, a pianist. Chosen "Belgian Composer for the Year 2000," the concert of her works on October 25, 2000, at the Royal Conservatory in Brussels to celebrate the occasion sadly became a memorial concert with her untimely death on February 2, 2000.

Jacqueline Fontyn

JACQUELINE FONTYN was born December 27, 1930, in Antwerp. The youngest of three girls, she would hear her sisters practice, then go to the piano and pick out their tunes with one finger. For her fifth birthday, her parents presented her with piano lessons. She learned to read notes before she could read the alphabet. Her teacher, a seventy-year-old Russian, Ignace Bolotine, had been a pupil of **Alexander Ziloti** (1863–1945) who had been a pupil of **Franz Liszt** (1811–86). As a child during WWII, with Belgium under the Nazis, her saddest experience was the death of her beloved piano teacher in 1942, on the day the Gestapo came to arrest him.

A Pupil of Franz Liszt?

By the time she was fourteen, Jacqueline knew she wanted to be composer. Her mother died when she was only sixteen, but her father supported her efforts until his own passing eight years later. From 1942–49, she continued her piano studies with Marcel Maas (1897–1950) who had been a student of Arthur Degreef, who had also been a student of Liszt. Thus, Fontyn feels she can consider herself a third-generation student of the greatest pianist of the 19th century! In the course of the next seven years, Maas introduced her to the music of Ravel, Debussy, Hindemith and Bartók. She took theory and composition with Belgian composer **Marcel Quinet** (1915–86), who suggested she go to Paris in 1954, where **Max Deutsch** (1892–1982), the Austrian-born French composer who had studied with Schoenberg, introduced her to serial techniques. She then went to Vienna for conducting lessons with the famed **Hans Swarowski** (1899–1975), and back home in 1956 to the Music Chapel of Queen Elisabeth of Belgium, where she graduated in composition (1959). Winning the coveted Prix de Rome the same year is what she considers her "first and last scholastic diploma."

Marriage and a Successful Career

In 1961, she received the Oscar Espla Prize for *Psalmus Tertius*, and the same year married prominent Belgian organist, pedagogue and composer **Camille Schmit** (1908–76), then a professor at the Liège Conservatory, and later director of the French section of the Brussels Conservatory (1966–73). Her composing blossomed under his influence and encouragement. They had two children, Pierre, in 1963, and Ariane, 1967. Her son presented her with three granddaughters, Manon born 1992, Fanni 1994 and Lea, 1998.

In 1964, Fontyn was awarded the prestigious Queen Elisabeth of Belgium Prize for Composition. Her own teaching career spanned almost thirty years as professor of counterpoint at the conservatories of Antwerp (1963–70) and Brussels (1969–71), adding composition to her curriculum at the latter from 1971 until she retired in 1990. During this time, her violin concerto, *Reveries & Turbulence*, was commissioned for performance in 1976 at the Queen Elisabeth of Belgium International Competition. She won the Arthur Honegger Prize (1987) for *Quatre Sites*, and a coveted Koussevitzky Foundation grant in 1989 for *Rivages Solitaires* (Solitary Shores)—a renaming of her violin concerto. Fontyn has guest lectured in Washington, DC, New York, Cairo, Seoul, Taipei, Los Angeles, Tel Aviv, Krakow (Poland), Stuttgart, Paris, Baltimore, Oakland, Wellington (New Zealand), Budapest, Singapore, China and Utrecht (Holland), among many other places.

Recognition and a Noble Title

Since 1991, Fontyn has devoted herself entirely to composition. Early works were in the neoclassical idiom, notably the *Piano Trio* (1956), a tribute to her teacher Marcel Quinet. *Capriccio* for piano (1954) was her first attempt at serialism. Thereafter, until 1969, her style became atonal, as in her *Ballade* (1963). In 1969, with *Filigrane*, she abandoned the bar line in favor of free rhythm, and after 1979, with *Ephémères*, moved away from serial technique towards the modal and aleatory. Her music has been called "modern impressionism." More than half of her output is written for large ensembles. Later works include *Meglio Tardi* (1995) for flute, bass clarinet, and piano; *Vent D'est* (1995) for classical accordion and strings, a commission of the Ministry of Culture of the French community of Belgium, premiered May 1996 in Antwerp by Daniel Gruselle; and *I fiamminghi* conducted by Rudolph Werthem. *Sul cuor della terra* was premiered April 1996, in New York by a Juilliard ensemble conducted by Joel Sachs. *La Fenêtre Ouverte*, for traverso, viola da gamba, and harpsichord, commissioned by the Conservatoire du XIVe arrondissement (14th District Conservatory) of Paris, was premiered there April 1997. The same month saw the Winterthur Festival premiere of *L'anneau de Jade* for orchestra, a commission of the Association of Swiss Musicians. In 1998, she wrote *Ich Kannte Meine Seele Nicht* for six mixed voices, followed by *Goeie Hoop* (Good Hope) for orchestra, dedicated to the people of South Africa, and *Aube* for flute guitar and piano.

2000 brought *Es ist ein Ozean*, a double concerto for flute, harpsichord and strings, commissioned by the Bachfest Leipzig, and *Au Fil des Siècles* a commission from L'Orchester des Staatstheaters Kassel, premiered there November 2001. *Ein Kleiner Winternachtstraum* (A Little Winter Night's Dream) came in 2002, as did *Virus Alert*, a teen chamber opera featuring saxophone, percussion and synthesizer, and *Poissonerie 2* for percussion and piano. A recital at the 2003 International Viola Congress (Kronberg, Germany) featured her *Fougères*. The International Festival of Flemish Music at St. Petersburg featured her organ works (2002, 2004), and *Battements d'ailes* (Beating Wings), for string orchestra. Another 2004 piece was *Tree of Life* for percussion quartet, a prestigious second commission from the Koussevitzky Foundation. *Capricorne* for percussion and chamber orchestra received a Luxembourg premiere, January 2005, while *Iris* for flute, violin and alto, premiered in Switzerland. *Hamadryades* was first heard in Tokyo in May. *Seagulls* for contralto, viola and piano was premiered in Germany in October. One of her pieces was part of the final testing in the 2005 International Piano Festival. 2005–06 saw the release on CD of many of her works.

Fontyn is a member of the *Académie Royale des sciences, des lettres et des beaux-arts*. In 1994, she was given the title of Baroness by the King of Belgium in recognition of her artistic merits which, in her own words, she feels, " . . . is for me a recognition of a life of hard work, and of the profession of composer." She travels to many performances of her work and maintains a steady flow of composing. Her seventy-fifth birthday in 2003 was honored with a public celebration. Regarding the status of women composers, she told me, "I'm against *apartheid*!! Also in music!"

(The author was a guest in Jacqueline's charming house in 1995. The baroness was a most gracious hostess.)

THE NETHERLANDS (HOLLAND)

ELISABETH KUYPER was born in Amsterdam, September 13, 1877. She studied with Daniël de Lange and Frans Coenen, receiving her piano teaching certificate in 1895, then with **Max Bruch** (1838–1920) at the Berlin Hochschule für Musik, where from 1908–1920 she taught theory and composition. Not only was she the first woman to teach there, she was also the first woman to win the Mendelssohn State Prize for Composition (1905). Her works for orchestra include *Ballade* (1903), *Serenade* (1905) and a violin concerto (1908). Other compositions number a violin sonata (1901), a piano trio (1910), six lieder (1922) and *American Lovesong* (1944) for chorus. A proponent for women composers, she founded four women's symphony orchestras, Berlin (1910), The Hague (1922), London (1922–23) and the American Women's Symphony Orchestra in New York (1924–25). Although these were basically vehicles for her conducting career, the orchestras were all well received but short-lived because of inadequate finances. In 1925, she left the U.S. to settle in Switzerland, where she died in Viganello, February 26, 1953.

Tera Marez Oyens

TERA de MAREZ OYENS was born Tera Wansink, August 5, 1932, in Velsen, Holland. With supportive parents, she began piano at age four and violin at eight. Like **Jacqueline Fontyn**, she was able to write musical notes before she could write words. (The two women were good friends). During World War II, the Wansinks sheltered a Jewish boy and girl from the Nazis. After the war, the family moved to Hengelo where her father became director of the Social Academy. Even in high school Tera devoted all her time to music. She had to walk hours to get to her piano lessons, but commented, "I didn't mind, because the lessons allowed me to forget the destruction, the hunger and the fear. For me, reality has always been piano and violin playing, and composition." At sixteen, after being prepared by her teacher, Gerrit de Marez Oyens, Tera secretly sat for the admittance examination, then surprised her parents with her acceptance to the Amsterdam Conservatory. They gave her permission to quit high school and dedicate herself completely to music.

Finally . . . Only Music!

Tera used her time at the conservatory to the fullest extent: "I worked at [there] . . . like a fanatic. It was wonderful to finally be able to do what I really wanted to." Besides her piano major, she studied harpsichord, violin and conducting. She also learned to play the recorder and viola da gamba. Her mastery of different instruments was invaluable to her composing, as was the continuous stimulation of harmony lessons with Jan Felderhof. At age twenty, she received her diploma as a practicing musician. After graduation, she took private composition lessons from Hans Henkemans, who taught her instrumentation. When her work veered towards the modern, their ways parted, but she stayed loyal to Henkermans' principle of transparency of score.

The "Eighth Wonder of the World"

Three days after graduation from the Amsterdam Conservatory, Tera married her former piano teacher, de Marez Oyens. Their marriage was built around music, with organized musicales in their home on a regular basis. Even with four children, Tera never neglected her composing. Her gift of concentration permitted her to work while the children crawled around her. The family enlarged when, after the death of her sister, she took on the upbringing of three more children. The outside world marvelled at this combination of motherhood and composer. The *Phillips Courier* (1968) headlined, "Mother of Seven Children Composes Electronic Music!" intimating this to be one of the wonders of the world. Her compositions for children, including operas, drew much attention. In the early 1960s, she was the only known female composer in Holland.

What's in a Name . . . A New Career . . . and Belief System

When the twenty-year marriage ended in divorce, despite her ex's demur, Tera kept the name. "Just imagine if J.S. Bach, on his fortieth birthday, would have to change his name to Johann Schmidt! My career began at twenty as *de Marez Oyens*. I already had over 200 compositions under that name!"

In 1977, Oyens was honored by an invitation to teach contemporary music at the prestigious Zwolle Conservatory. Her duties soon expanded to teaching composition—a position never previously held by a woman in Holland.

In her younger years, the Protestant religion played a large role in Tera's life. Earlier works, such as *Partita for Organ* (1958) and *Motet Over Psalm 69* (1957), were created from religious involvement. The *Liedboek voor de Kerken* (Church Hymn Book) includes thirteen of her hymns. In the '70s, she broke with the Christian faith and followed the Eastern philosophy of Sufi, which taught her to appreciate other religions. Then, like her father, she became an agnostic—all of which profoundly influenced her music.

Besides composing, she also conducted. On September 6, 1975, she was the first woman to conduct the Overjissels Philharmonic Orchestra. When someone beforehand asked if she felt able to handle directing men, she retorted, "If you are ruled by a woman (referring to then Queen Juliana), why wouldn't a woman be able to conduct?" She went on to conduct her own works throughout the world.

True Happiness—Cut Short

Married for thirteen idyllic years to dissident political scientist/writer Menachem Arnoni, the death in 1985 of her second husband brought to an abrupt end a fruitful era in Tera's life. Arnoni's texts had been the source of inspiration for many of her compositions, including the choral work *From Death to Birth* (1975), and *Three Hymns* (1979). Arnoni, who had survived Auschwitz concentration camp, also wrote the libretto for her most ambitious work, a two-hour oratorio *The Odyssey of Mr. Goodevil,* for full symphony orchestra, two choirs, four soloists and two narrators. The work describes the atrocities of the war as seen from the unique perspective of a concentration camp inmate whose existence teetered on the continuous borderline between life and death. *Charon's Gift*

(1981) for piano and tape, celebrated the recuperation from her husband's suicide attempt. He was apparently driven to this after a visit to Poland intensified his war memories. Tera wrote the epilogue to his collection of essays, *The Right to be Pessimistic*, which was published posthumously. An unfulfilled plan was a book about her years with Arnoni.

Rebirth and Renown

In 1987, Oyens gave up her position at the Zwolle Conservatory to devote more time to composition. The same year, she finished the imposing work, *Symphonia Testimonial*, for choir, orchestra and band, commissioned by AVRO, a Dutch television network. Also on commission, *Symmetrical Memories for Cello and Orchestra* became the required work for the 1988 International Music Competition at Scheveningen. Her larger works include *Litany of the Victims of War* (1985) for orchestra, *Structures and Dance* (1985) for violin and orchestra, *Symmetrical Memories* (1988) for cello and orchestra, and *Confrontations* (1990) for piano and orchestra. Besides teaching an annual summer seminar in Vienna for many years, she was constantly requested to conduct improvisation workshops all over the world, including Alaska, Korea and Brazil. She also lectured in many countries on electronic music, the teaching of music, and the role of women in music. She was a co-founder of the *Stichting Vrouw en Muziek* (Foundation for Women in Music), active in Holland since 1985, and sat on many other boards, including the International League (now Alliance) of Women Composers. Her philosophy was that women composers should not lament their lot, reminding them, "It's not easy for men, either." Her output of orchestral, choral, electronic works and chamber music for diverse instruments set an exceptional performance record.

Command Performances

In August 1995, after her Vienna seminar,[19] she went on to Prague for a concert of her works at the Norstiz Palace—scene of performances by Mozart. In October, in Rotterdam, the orchestral work *UNISON*, commemorating the fiftieth anniversary of the United Nations, was performed by the Rotterdam Philharmonic and attended by Queen Beatrix and ministers of state. December found her in the U.S., lecturing and performing in New York, Chicago, Boston and other cities.

In January 1996, knowing her time was limited, Oyens completed *The Narrow Path* for soprano, flute and two guitars, *Muraroa*, for saxophone, accordion and double bass, and the *Prague Castel Symphony*, dedicated to Olga Havlová, wife of Czech President Václav Havel, which premiered in Prague in 1997. Her final composition, *Towards an unknown goal . . .* was dedicated "To Jane O'Leary and her remarkable ensemble Concorde," based on poetry Tera wrote while in Cleveland. An aura of loneliness pervades this work, similar to the verses of Japanese poet Basho (1643–94) on his wanderings through *his* country. O'Leary edited the draft in close cooperation with the composer.

On May 23, 1996, after having been introduced to him by O'Leary the year before, Tera married the celebrated Dutch writer/cartoonist Marten Toonder. Stricken by a recurring cancer, she left Ireland to return to her home in Hilversum where, surrounded by her family, my friend Tera de Marez Oyens Arnoni Toonder peacefully left this world August 29, 1996, at the height of her fame and newfound happiness.

GERMANY

BARBARA HELLER was born in 1936 in Ludwigshafen on the Rhine. From 1958–62, she worked at the Staatliche Hochschule für Music und Theater in Mannheim as pianist, piano teacher and composer. After postgraduate composition studies in Mannheim, Munich and Siena, she moved to Darmstadt. One of the founders of

---

19. Where, after over a year of faxing friendship, we met in person!

the International Arbeitkreis Women and Music (1978), she furthered the cause of women's music through lectures, concerts and radio broadcasts. She has prepared numerous scores for publication, particularly the piano music of Fanny Mendelssohn-Hensel. From 1986–93, she was on the board of the Institute for New Music in Darmstadt. Her compositions range from piano, chamber and film music to experimental and tape techniques and sound installations.

ADRIANA HÖLSZKY was born an ethnic German in Bucharest, Rumania, June 30, 1953, to Austrian-German parents, both scientists. She began piano studies at the Bucharest music school in 1959 and composition with Stefan Niculescu. Piano continued at the conservatory (1972–75). When the family moved to Germany in 1976, she added electronic music to her composition studies. She attended the summer academy at the Salzburg Mozarteum (1977, 1978) and the Accademia Chigiana in Siena (1980). She was the pianist for the Lipatti Trio (1977–1980) and taught at the Stuttgart Musikhochschule (1980–1989). Her many compositional prizes include the Gaudeamus (1981), German record critics' prize (1988–89), GEDOK, Mannheim (1985, '89) and the Women Composers' prize in Heidelberg (1990). She taught at the Darmstadt summer master classes and sat on many international juries. Her works include much chamber music for solo instrument, instrumental ensemble, and solo voice. Her opera, *Bremer Freiheit* (1987), follows the plot line of a female *Bluebeard, Die Wände* (The Walls) a joint commission between Stuttgart and Vienna State Opera, had a successful premiere, May 1995. *Tragœdia - the invisible area*, written in 1997, was performed at the 2003 Gegenwelternfest, a celebration of women composers. One of the most performed women composers in Germany, Hölszky has received recognition throughout Europe.

BABETTE KOBLENZ was the 1997 winner of the Heidelberg Künstlerinnen Preis, an honor bestowed annually upon an outstanding woman composer. Born August 22, 1956, in Hamburg, she studied composition with György Ligeti at the Musikhochschule there. Her work focuses on the development of new styles of music theater, opera, and modern vocal techniques. She concertizes singing her own songs. 1984 marked the premiere of her opera *Hexenskat* at the Saar State Theater in Saarbrücken. Other works include *Alla Testa* for actors, vocalists and instrumental ensemble, and *Ikarus* (1990) presented at the second Munich Biennale. She participates in the summer festivals for new music in Darmstadt. After living in Spain and Italy, whose influences are apparent in her work, Koblenz returned to Hamburg. Her honors include grants from the Jürgen-Ponto Foundation, the Hamburg Bach stipend and the Schreyahn Stipend of Lower Saxony. She won the Rome Prize in 1988. 1995 brought *The Children of Bjelaja Zerkow*, her collaboration in a documentary about the shooting of ninety Jewish children in this Ukranian village in August 1941. Her composition *Search* was featured at the 1997 Munich Biennale, another composition was used in a "Portrait Concert," May 2001.

RUTH SCHÖNTHAL born June 27, 1924, in Hamburg, is the youngest student ever accepted by the Stern Conservatory in Berlin. In 1938, the family was forced to flee when Hitler began his persecution of the Jews. The Schönthals lived in Stockholm until 1941, by which time that neutral city had become a hotbed of spies during World War II. Their escape involved three months of a *film noir* journey via the Trans-Siberian Railway to its terminal in Vladivostok, a voyage across the Sea of Japan, a stop near Los Angeles where no one was permitted to step ashore and, after an earthquake at sea, arrival in Mexico. An excellent pianist, Ruth got a scholarship to Yale and remained in the U.S. (See 20th Century American Composers.)

Ruth Zechlin

RUTH ZECHLIN, considered one of the most important composers in the country, was born June 22, 1926, at Gross Hartmannsdorf, Saxony, and studied composition and organ at the Leipzig Hochschule (1934–39). From 1950, she taught at the Hans Eisler Hochschule, in what was then East Berlin, becoming a full professor in 1984—the first woman in Germany to be so appointed! In 1970, she was made a member of the East Germany Academy of the arts where she was responsible for the master's degree curriculum in composition. In 1990, she became vice president of the Berlin Arts Academy and a member of the German Music Council. 1997 brought her chamber opera, *Die Reise* (The Journey), based on the work of Heiner Müller.

As a performer, Zechlin specialized in early English keyboard music as well as Bach, who influenced her many chamber, vocal, dramatic and orchestral compositions. She evolved from the free tonality in the '60s to balanced formal structures in the '90s. She was winner/honorée of the 1996 Heidelberg Competition. (See Rothwitha Sperber.) By 2000, her output numbered over 260 compositions.

ITALY

Sonia Bo

Born March 27, 1960, in Lecco, **SONIA BO** began piano at age ten, and after classical studies took composition lessons, choral music and choral conducting at the Milan Conservatory, graduating in 1985. She continued postgraduate studies at the Academia di Santa Cecilia in Rome. Winner of national and international awards, including the Fondazione Guido d'Arezzo International Competition (1985) for *Frammenti da Jacopone* for female choir, the G. Savagnone (Rome, 1986) and the Alpe Adria Giovani (Trieste, 1988), her compositions have been performed in various concert centers and broadcast in and outside Europe. *Da una lettura di Husserl* for orchestra (1984) was an acoustical sensation. This was followed by a string quartet (1985), *Come un'allegoria* for soprano, clarinet, cello and piano (1986), two *Bagatelles* for flute and guitar (1988), and *Polittico*, five songs for chamber ensemble (1992). Her international competition winnings include first prize, Gaudeamus (Amsterdam, 1990) for *Déjà*, violin, bass clarinet and piano; second prize, C. Togni (Brescia) for *Aske - II*, string quartet; and third prize, Contilli (Messina, 1995) for *The Waves*, concertante for violin and orchestra. In 1997, Bo was selected by the reading committee of Ensemble intercontemporain and received a commission for *Maree: quaderno primo*, a work for small orchestra. Other commissions have come from the Arturo Toscanini Foundation, Teatro Comunale (Bologna) and the Gaudeamus Foundation. Her connection with IRCAM in Paris has produced much use of computer technology in her work, combining this with voice and orchestral instruments.

Bo's works, which encompass pieces for violin, piano, saxophone, organ, orchestra, voice and voice with small ensembles, have been performed in major theaters and concert halls at numerous festivals and exhibitions by such aggregations as Teatro alla Scala, Cantelli, Verdi and Angelicum Orchestras, at venues in Milan, Rome, Florence, Genoa, Catania, Progetto Dionysos Musica 2000, in collaboration with La Fenice, Venice, Turin, and Como—all in Italy; Festival Focus at Juilliard (New York); Almeida Theatre (London); Niewe muziek, Middelburg and Muziek-centrum Vredenburg, Utrecht, The Netherlands; Europhonia (Zagreb); Musica Nova (Sofia); Altes Schlachthaus (Bern); as well as Chicago and Mexico City; and have been broadcast and recorded by RAI, Radio France and Dutch Radio, among others, and published by Ricordi, Curci, Rugginenti and Edi-Pan. 21st century titles include *L'arbitro, il marlo, il vaporetto cha va a Ischia*, flute solo, *Umbram* for organ, *Per Alda*, piano (all in 2000), *Filastrocche del cavallo parlante*, for narrator, female choir and instruments, a Verdi Orchestra commission, and *Come un allegoria II* for soprano and percussion, premiered in New York, 2001.

Bo has taught at the Conservatorio di Ferrara (1984–85), Conservatorio di Verona (1985–86), Conservatorio di Pesaro (1986-89), Conservatorio di Piacenza (1989–90, 1996–97) and Milan Conservatory from 1997 to the present. She is married to composer/pianist Giuseppe Colardo.

ELISABETTA Olga Laura **BRUSA**, born in Milan April 3, 1954, started piano lessons (which she didn't like) at age five, and composition (which she loved) at nineteen. Unguided, her passion for composing came naturally. Her parents were understanding and encouraging during her years at the Milan Conservatory, where she received a diploma in composition (1980), studying with Bruno Bettinelli and Azio Corghi. Her studies also included courses at Dartington Hall (London) with Sir Peter Maxwell Davies and Hans Keller. In 1982, she won first prize in the Washington International Competition for Composition for *String Quartet*, and at the Contemporary Music Forum of Washington, DC, with her *Belsize String Quartet*. In 1983, she was awarded a Fromm Foundation Fellowship and Fulbright travel bursary for study at Tanglewood with Hans Werner Henze and Gunther Schuller.

During 1988–90, she received MacDowell Colony Fellowships for artistic residencies to work on her First Symphony and other compositions.

In 1997, she married a conservatory classmate, conductor Gilberto Serembe who, since the death of Hans Keller, has provided her with both moral and musical encouragement. Since 1985, she has been a member of the composition faculty at the Milan Conservatory. Brusa's compositions have been performed in Italy, America, England, Russia, Canada, Austria, Switzerland, Czechoslovakia, Albania, and Korea by orchestras including the BBC Philharmonic, London Chamber Symphony, CBC Vancouver, Virtuosi of Toronto, New England Philharmonic of Boston, Contemporary Music Forum of Washington, DC, The Women's Philharmonic of San Francisco and the Frauen Kammerorchester of Vienna. She has also been a featured composer in the "Donne in Musica" Festivals in Italy.

Elisabetta's love of all the arts, painting, sculpture, architecture and literature, is channeled into a deeper understanding of the art of composition.

PATRICIA CHITI - Composer/Singer/Author/Producer - *Donne in Musica* (See European Musicologists.)

BIANCAMARIA FURGERI, born October 6, 1935, in Rovigo, began her piano studies at age seven, composition at sixteen, and organ at eighteen. Her conservatory diplomas are from Milan (Piano, 1956), Venice (Choral Music, 1958), and Padua (Organ, 1959, Composition 1962). Since her first award in 1964, at the Magadino (Switzerland) International Competition for her *Sonata for Organ*, she has continued in her chosen field of creating rather than performing music, winning competitions in Italy, Germany (GEDOK), Switzerland (International Competition for Women Composers), and Poland (Wieniawski International Competition). Her compositions include a *Mass*, *Tre Episodi* (string quartet), *Levia* (string orchestra), *Antifonie* (piano and orchestra) and *Duplum*, (violin and piano). Other works are *Cantico a Mathilda*, for two voices and string orchestra (1991); *Piccola Cantata*, for soprano, tenor, baritone, flute, double string quartet, and harpsichord (1999); *and Quasi una Fantasia*, for piano (2000).

Married since 1963 to economist Cosimo Oliva, their son, Guido, a nuclear engineer, has given them two grandchildren.

Ada Gentile

Born July 26, 1947, in Avezzano, **ADA GENTILE** earned piano and composition diplomas at the Santa Cecilia Conservatory (1974), completing composition studies with Goffredo Petrassi at the Accademia di Santa Cecilia (1975–76). A winner of international competitions, Gaudeamus, Amsterdam (1982) and ISCM (Budapest, 1986, Essen, 1995), her works have been performed throughout Europe, North America, Australia, China, Korea and Japan, at such venues as the Centre Georges Pompidou, Paris; Carnegie Hall, New York; Madrid's Teatro Real; Art Institute, Chicago; Le Fenice, Venice; Accademia Filarmonica Romana, and Milan's *Musica nel nostro tempo*. Her music, characterized as "sonic impressionism," can be heard on Beat Records (Rome).

She participates in major contemporary music festivals in Salzburg, Budapest, Warsaw, Alicante (Spain), Huddersfield (England), Aarhus (Netherlands), Prague, Würzburg, Heidelberg, Zagreb, Kassel (Germany), Bacau, Paris, Vienna, Madrid, Lisbon and Montreal. Her commissions come from the RAI (Italian television) in Rome, Naples and Milan, from the French Ministry of Culture, and the Accademia Nazionale di Santa Cecilia. In 1988, she was given an award for "cultural merit" by the Polish Ministry of Culture.

In 1978, Gentile founded and has been artistic director of "Nuovi Spazi Musicali" (New Musical Spaces)—an annual event in Rome broadcast by RAI, for whom she also presents other contemporary music festivals. From 1986–88, she was artistic director of the Goffreddo Petrassi Chamber Orchestra. In 1993, she was a member of the organizing committee of the Venice Biennial. In October 1992, she prepared "New Instrumental Techniques in Contemporary Music," a series for their third program. The same year she was commissioned by Hans Werner Henze for a chamber opera, performed at the Munich Biennial in 1994. The work is a free reconstruction of Francesca Caccini's *Liberazione di Ruggiero dall'isola di Alcina*, based on Ludovico Ariosto's famous poem, *Orlando furioso.* Since 1995 she has been an advisor for the Nuova Cansonanza Festival in Rome, and from 1996–99 was art director of the lyric theater Ventidio Basso in Ascoli Piceno. In 1997, she sat on the jury of the International Competition of Composition in Trieste. She is on the faculty of the Santa Cecilia Academy.

1995 world premieres included a saxophone quartet at the Salzburg Mozarteum; *Adagio* and *Adagio Primo*, for string orchestra, commissioned by the New Music in Old Krakow Festival, performed by *Capella Cracoviensis* in Rome, Bari (Italy), Paris and New York; *Concerto per voce femminile e orchestra* at a sacred music festival; and *Zapping*, for flute, violin, clarinet and viola, at the Pontino Festival. 1996 brought a concert in Bergamo featuring *Adagio*, and other works played in Seoul and Brazil. In May, Gentile was the only Italian composer invited to the NEMO (New European Music Overseas) Festival in Chicago, where three of her works were performed. While there, she lectured at the Universities of Chicago and Northwestern. Later in the year there were concerts in Germany and an invitation for a "Composer Portrait" in Vienna. Other premieres were concertos for voice and orchestra, and clarinet and orchestra, plus *Musica per scena* in Rome by the Kiev Orchestra, *Pervioloncellosolo*, performed by Madeleine Shapiro in New York, *Scaglie de mare*, a harp solo with Cristina Bianchi in Genoa's Teatro Carlo Felice, *Shading*, for guitar and orchestra, and a CD with *Criptografia*, for viola and orchestra. 1998 brought *Slowly for a summer* (flute and continuo) and *A gift for you* (clarinet). *Adagio per un'estate* for flute and strings, commissioned by the Vivaldi Festival, was premiered in July at the Venetian church of Santa Maria della Pieta, where Antonio Vivaldi (1678–1741) was the priest for more then twenty-five years.

The new century brought *The Potter and the Clay* (flute and continuo), *As fiumana* (quartet with narrator), *Quartet III*, and a *Mass for Peace* with full orchestra. *Improvviso* for string orchestra, premiered on June 21, 2001 in Trier (Germany) by the State Orchestra conducted by Istvan Denes. *Come fiumana*, for string quartet and voice, was a commission from Torino to celebrate the anniversary of the death of the famous Italian painter Pellizza da Volpedo. Premiered in his native town, Volpedo, it was broadcast and recorded December 30, 2000 in Rome, in front of an audience of 4,000. The final work commissioned by Vatican City for the Great Jubilee of 2000, *Cantata Per La Pace* (Cantata for Peace), for large orchestra, choir and narrator, is a twenty-five minute piece containing a *Kyrie*, *Credo* and *Sanctus*. Repeat performances were in Brasilia (November 2001), St. Petersburg (February 2002), Ascoli Piceno, Italy, (March 2002), and Bejing, (April 2002). That year's music was performed all over the world: New York, Marseilles, Vienna, Madrid, Salzburg, Russia, Uzbekistan, Rabat (Morocco), Tehran (Iran) and Brazil.

March 2002 she was invited by the Chamber Music Society of Lincoln Center for the performance of her *Momento Veloci* for flute and harp, with flutist Tara Helen O'Connor and harpist Deborah Hoffmann—part of the concert series *Double Exposure* conducted by Bruce Adolphe. On March 18, she lectured at Juilliard. Later that year, a series of fifteen concerts was played by the Orchestra of the Santa Cecilia Academy in Rome. April 2003 found her lecturing at Wayne State University (Detroit, Michigan), along with a concert of her works.

2005 was a busy year with travels to Hong Kong, Shanghai, Beijing, Seoul, New York, Amsterdam and Algiers. In China, she lectured at Academy of Performing Arts (Hong Kong) and at the Shanghai Central Conservatory. Radio 4 of Hong Kong broadcast an extensive interview, aired in October, a month dedicated to Italian music. The Seoul Philharmonic and Metropolitan Choir performed her *Cantata per la pace* at the Sejong Center Theater, in front of 3,000 listeners including the Italian ambassador. Broadcast on Radio Netherland, the Dutch Zephyr Quartet played *Quartetto III* at the Concertgebouw, Amsterdam. New York's Hunter College saw a chamber concert by I Cameristi del Conservatorio Santa Cecilia of *Improviso* for strings, together with works by Respighi, Nino Rota and Franco Mannino, in a concert dedicated to Italian music of today. In May, the Orchestra Sinfonica Abruzzese premiered her latest work, *Monodia*, in Rome and in the San Marco Church (Venice). With the support of the Italian Embassy, she organized two concerts for the Algerian Ministry of Culture, with five teachers of Santa Cecilia Conservatory teaching master classes to the musicians of the National Algerian Symphony, after which the orchestra played two separate programs which were evaluated by Gentile. The whole endeavor was a great success. *Perviolinosolo* was written for American violinist Mark Menzies to play at Ada's Twenty-sixth Nuovi Spazi

Musicali Festival (Rome), October, 2005. Her concert schedule for late 2006 and early 2007 already covers St. Petersburg, Istanbul—where she was "Honored Composer from Italy,"—Madrid, Rome, Beograd, Copenhagen, Los Angeles and San Diego. In 2007 she became director of the famous Santa Cecilia Conservatory, selected over six male candidates.

Ada has been happily married to Franco Mastroviti since 1972. A retired director of the Ministry of Employment, he is now (like *my* husband) his wife's secretary, translator, press agent and general manager.

(My son, Adrian, a violinist who makes annual trips to Italy, had the pleasure of meeting Ada and her husband at one of her concerts in 2004. We had our warm meeting in Rome, October 2006.)

PATRIZIA MONTANARO was born in Bologna on January 1, 1956. After hearing her first piano recital, she began piano studies at age six and decided to become a musician. She received her Diploma in Piano from the Martini Conservatory in Bologna (1978), and Diploma in Composition from the Rossini Conservatory (1992). She began studying composition to better understand the music for her piano performances. Now her love of composition outweighs her desire to perform. Her compositions have won prizes in international competitions including GEDOK (Mannheim). Her works include *di spessori e dissolvenze* (oboe, bassoon and piano, 1996); *su echi della memoria* (mezzo, baritone and five instruments, set to verses of Hildegard von Bingen, 1997); *Concerto* (piano and string orchestra, 1998); and *come vento sul monte* (bass flute, 2001).

TERESA PROCACCINI, born March 23, 1934, in Cerignola, Foggia, received her diploma in piano from the Foggia Conservatory (1952), and in organ and composition (1958), studying with Virgilio Mortari. Advanced studies covered film music at the Rome Conservatory, and composition at Chigiana. Her prizes include the Viotti Competition (1956), Casella Prize (1970), and the International String Quartet Competition, San Francisco (1981). She taught organ and composition at the Foggia Conservatory and was their director (1972–73). In 1979, she became a lecturer in composition at the Rome Conservatory. Her large output includes chamber and orchestral works, many for young performers.

IRMA RAVINALE, born in Naples, October 1, 1937, began piano at seven. Her studies at the Rome Conservatory included piano, choral music, conducting and band instrumentation. She received her diploma in composition there, 1957, studying with Goffredo Petrassi. In 1966, she was appointed chair of composition at the Rome Conservatory, the first woman to hold this position. Her courses have trained many well-known Italian musicians. From 1982–89, she was director of the Naples Conservatory, after which she returned to the Rome Conservatory as emeritus director. She is an honorary academic of the Angelica Costantiniana Academy for Arts, Letters and Science, a member of the International Honor committee of the Fondazione Adkins Chiti: Donne in Musica, and holds the title Comendatore, Italy's highest honor.

Her prizes are from the Teatro Communale of Florence for young composers (1969), the Italian Radio RAI Prize for her one-act opera *The Portrait of Dorian Gray* (1975), and first prize in the International Competition in Trieste (1976) for her symphonic music. Other important works include *Sinfonia Concertante for Guitar and Orchestra* (1972); *Spleen* (baritone and orchestra, 1976); *Les Adieux* (violin and orchestra, 1983); *Poem for Oscar Romero* (baritone, mixed choir and orchestra, 1990); and *Quel che resta del giorno* (string orchestra, 1997).

ROBERTA SILVESTRINI was born in Milan, January 3, 1964, to parents who loved music. She began piano at six and also had a good singing voice. She attended the Rossini Conservatory in Pisaro, Martini Conservatory in Bologna, the Academies of Santa Cecilia in Rome and Chigiana in Siena, amassing diplomas in Composition (1989), Orchestral Conducting (1992), Band Instrumentation (1986), Music Education (1989), Choral Music and Choir Direction (1987), Composition, with Franco Donatoni (Chigiana, 1991), and again with him at Santa Cecilia (1993), as well as Film Music with Ennio Morricone (1991). Her awards include a 1991 S.I.A.E. Scholarship from Chigiana, Finalist at the Premio 900 Musicale Europeo

Roberta Silvestrini

(Naples, 1987), Premio V. Bucchi Prize, Velluti Competition (Venice), and the Piano Competition in Senigallia.

In collaboration with international soloists, theater associations and national and foreign groups, her works are performed in major concerts halls and at renowned festivals. Her scores are published, recorded on CDs, and broadcast by RAI and other radio stations.

Silvestrini is also conductor of the San Giovanni Battista Choir of Senigallia since 1997, and manager of *Musica Antica E Contemporanea* music association of Senigallia and of the *Musica Nuova Festival*, a summer program of contemporary music.

Roberta is married to Dr. Lorenzo Brunelli, and on the faculty of the Pergolesi di Fermo State Music Conservatory at Ascoli Piceno.

SPAIN

Teresa Catalan

TERESA CATALÁN was born in Pamplona, April 12, 1951. She studied at the Pamplona Conservatory and the Pablo de Sarasate Conservatory, receiving degrees in piano and composition. Her teachers included Fernando Remacha, Juan Eraso, Luis Morondo and Luis Taberna. Further composition studies were in Chigiana (Italy) with Franco Donatoni. Her master's degrees in esthetics and music creation are from the University of Valencia. As a composer, she pursued studies aimed at perfecting her style, including the sociology of music as taught by Ramon Barce, and techniques of contemporary composition with Augustin Gonzalez Acilu.

Catalán is a founding member of the Pamplona Composers Group, with whom she has created a large body of work. Her articles and dissertations on her many compositions form a part of the curricula of many Spanish conservatories. Her music is regularly programmed at festivals throughout the world, including Germany, Italy, France, Holland, Rumania, Russia, Argentina, Cuba and the U.S.

Her CDs include *Las Mujeres Y La Musica* (Women and Music) from the "RNE, RTV Musica" television series (1990), *Hommage*, recorded by Hungarian Radio of Budapest (1996), the collection *Ars Incognita* (1997), and *Estol del Master II*, released in 2000 by the University of Valencia.

Teresa's husband is in the Civil Service. They have three grown children, Cecilia, born 1974, Carlos, 1977 and Irene, 1978.

CONSUELO DIEZ, born in Madrid, August 16, 1958, was singing before she could talk. With her mother's consistent support, she began piano at nine and continued until 1984, when she received degrees in Piano and Composition from the Royal Superior Conservatory of Music of Madrid, followed by Theory in 1988. Her undergraduate degree is in Art History from Madrid's Complutense University (1980). Encouragement in composition from her teacher, Luis Rodríguez Sainz, brought her to America where she earned her MM (1987) and DMA (2001) at the Hartt School of Music, University of Hartford (Connecticut).

Meanwhile, Diez was gathering honors like the Norman Bayles Award (U.S., 1987), Panorama of Young Composers (Spain, 1988), Young Creators Prize (Spain, 1989), and the City of Heidelberg Prize (Germany, 1996). She was selected for the European Art Biennale, Bologna (Italy, 1988), Rostrum of Composers (electro-acoustic music, UNESCO, 1992) and the ISCM (1994, 1998, 2000).

Besides her mother, who passed away in August 2000, Consuelo's husband, Antonio Martín-Carrillo, an aeronautical and space engineer, and a good poet, have helped in her career. Her son, Antonio Martín-Carrillo Díez III, born August 21, 1996, already likes contemporary music because he is used to it. He has been going to concerts with his parents since he was one year old, and is learning the piano.

MARÍA ESCRIBANO was born January 24, 1954 in Madrid. With her parents' encouragement, she began piano at nine, and by fifteen was committed to a career in composition. At the Royal Conservatory of Music in Madrid, her studies included five years of solfége, four years of harmony, three years of counterpoint and fugue, and three years of composition. This was followed by composition master classes in Spain, Germany, and in the

U.S. at Carnegie Mellon (Pittsburgh). A grant from the Juan March Foundation enabled her to go to France for a year to write a work for the Roy Hart Theatre.

She has written much orchestral, chamber and piano music , including *Ven, Ven, Quien Quiera Que Seas*, which was played at the Basilica Santa Maria Sopra Minerva in Rome by the Madrid Symphony with the Royal Capilla Choir directed by Ignacio Yepes. *El Mago, Travesia De Luz* for orchestra, two pianos and narrator, premiered November 2001 at the Teatro Principal de Mallorca, with the Baleares orchestra and the composer participating. Her *Concierto Cuentro* and *Chinese Zodiac Suite* are on CD. Escribano's works have been heard at many festivals throughout Europe. In summer 2001, at the Piano Aux Pyrénées à Barèges Festival (France), she led a conference about her music in relation to creating music, and a workshop for piano improvisation.

María has three grown children, Raul Méndez, born 1973, Elías Azquinezer, 1981, and Iris Azquinezer, 1983. She considers "the highest level of artistry is making an art of one's life."

ILUMINADA PEREZ FRUTOS was born in Gerona. She began her piano and guitar studies at age eight under the tutelage of Aurora Chacon and Enrique Molina. At eleven, she represented the town of Estremadura at the Union Europea de Radiodifusion, and at thirteen in the program "Musiquisimo" on Spanish television. She completed her piano studies with Karine Guenbandobar, and guitar with Molina, Dean of the Conservatorio Superior de Musica de Badajoz, where she earned degrees in classical guitar, melody, theory, composition, diplomas in piano transposition and accompaniment, and a teaching certificate in accounting and business science. Later in her career, she perfected her piano and guitar technique, took conducting at the Pablo Casals School in Seville with Juan Luis Perez, and Haydn, Mozart, Beethoven and Chopin Analysis Studies. She received fellowships to the Escorial for conducting with Pedro Halffter and composition with the renowned masters Cristobal Hilffter, Tomas Marco, José Maria Sanches Verdu and Mauricio Sotelo.

Frutos' many compositions, including *Evocación* for piano, and the trio *Donde habite el Silencio* for violin, cello and piano, have been heard throughout Spain and Italy. Her string quartet was a commission from the Fondazione Donne in Musica. Her guitar piece, *Tanidos de Silencio*, was premiered by Fernando Bermejo. A CD has been released featuring her works with those of Salvatore Sciarrino and Ennio Morrone.

Perez Frutos is also a professor of music under the Education Council of Spain.

CONCHA JEREZ was born in Las Palmas de Gran Canaria in 1941. She earned her degree in piano in the conservatory, and licenciate at the School of Political Science, both in Madrid. Beginning in 1976, she focused her work on avant-garde music performance. Since the end of the '80s, she has composed works for Radio France, ORF, RAI (Italy), YLE, ABC (Australia), RNE and WDR of Cologne (Germany). Her works, which include forty-six "installations"(intermediate studies), and eighteen expositions, have received many performances, some of which were with composer and intermediate artist Jose Iges, with whom she also has collaborated since 1989, bringing out eighteen audio and visual "Space"and "Action" compositions.

Her titles include, *Fuera de Formato* (1983), *Taidehalli* (1985), *Schloss Solitude, Plane und Projekte* (1986), *Balcon 2* (1988), *Antics* (1989), *Do(K)s* (1993), *La Nevera* (1993), and *Atlantica* (1998). They have been heard in Spain, Germany, France, Italy, Denmark, Switzerland and Finland. Her publications include fifteen personal catalogues, and a CD-ROM.

Jerez' works are in the archives of the Modern Kunst Museum of Norrköping (Sweden), Stattsgallerie de Stuttgart, Museum Wiesbaden (Germany), and in Spain at Museo Vosstell de Malpartida, Museo de Bellas Artes de Alava, Museo de Bellas Artes de Santander, Museo Jovellanos and Museo de Vallafamees among others, as well as in private collections at the Fundaciao Caixa de Pensiones de Barcelona, Metronom, Brigitte March de Stuttgart and Schuppenhauer de Colonia.

She has been an associate professor of the School of Fine Arts of the University of Salamanca since 1991.

MERCEDES ZAVALA, born in Madrid, 1963, is a composer, pianist, and professor of harmony at the Madrid Conservatory. (See International Musicologists.)

NORWAY

AGATHE BACKER-GRØNDAHL (1847–1907) (See Romantic Period.)

SWEDEN

ELFRIDA ANDRÉE (1841–1929) wrote more than 100 works for organ. (See Organists.)

FINLAND

Kaija Saariaho

KAIJA SAARIAHO was born October 14, 1952, in Helsinki. After completing her composition studies at the Sibelius Academy in 1981, she went to Freiburg (Germany) to study at the Hochschule für Musik with Brian Ferneyhough and Klaus Huber. From there, she attended a computer music course at IRCAM in Paris, where she has lived and worked since 1982. 1988–89 was spent at UCSD, San Diego, California.

Interested in enlarging the potential of traditional instruments, she utilizes electronic technology such as computer analysis to produce harmonies out of sound spectra. Her works include *Verblendungen* (1984) for orchestra and tape, *Lichtbogen* (1986) for nine instruments and electronics, *Jardin Secret I* (1984), *Jardin Secret II* (1986) for harpsichord and tape, *Io* (1987) for ensemble, tape and electronics, *Nymphea* (1987) for string quartet and electronics, written for the Kronos Quartet on a commission from Lincoln Center, a radiophonic work, *Stilleben* (1988), plus the orchestral pieces *Du Cristal* (1990) and . . . *à la fumée* (1990), a commission from the Los Angeles Philharmonic, the Helsinki Festival and Finnish Radio. Her interest in other art forms created her ballet in seven scenes, *Maa* (1991). Other commissions are *Amers* (1992) for cello, ensemble and electronics, *Près* (1992) for cello and electronics, both from the Barbican Centre, London, and IRCAM, *Solar* (1993), for ensemble and electronic keyboards, from the City of Antwerp, and *Trois Riviéres* (1994) for percussion quartet and electronics, from the Strasbourg Festival.

In 1995, her violin concerto *Graal Théâtre* for **Gidon Kremer** was played by him with the Rotterdam Philharmonic, Orchestre National de France and BBC Symphony. In 1996, *Château de l'âme* for soprano, eight female voices and orchestra was premiered in Salzburg by the Philharmonic Orchestra under **Esa-Pekka Salonen** with **Dawn Upshaw**. The soprano part was composed specifically for Upshaw, who was also the source of inspiration for *Lonh*, for soprano and electronics, with texts by twelfth century Provençal troubadour Jaufré Rudel, premiered at the Vienna Modern Festival. *Lonh* was awarded the Nordic Music Prize in 2000. A major work for chorus and orchestra, *Oltra mar*, was premiered by the New York Philharmonic, November 11, 1999, as part of their millennium series of commissions. As a follow up to *Lonh*, her opera, *L'amour de loin* (Love from Afar), with libretto by Lebanese French resident Amin Maalouf, is based on the life of Rudel, whose poetry of courtly love set women to be worshipped from afar. Written for, and premiered at the Salzburg Festival, August 15, 2000, with Dawn Upshaw as Clémence, the idealized heroine, it received its second performance at the Théâtre du Châtelet in Paris, November 2001. The modern music, with infused electronic elements, reflects two geographical settings: the poet in Europe and the countess in Asia Minor. The two meet at the end, but their love remains on a lofty plane as the poet dies from an illness contracted on the voyage to his beloved. *L'amour de loin* was brought to the U.S. by Santa Fe Opera in the summer of 2002. In 2003, Robert Spano and the Chicago Symphony premiered her song cycle, *Five Reflections*, with soprano **Heidi Grant Murphy** and baritone Brett Polegato at the Ravinia Summer Festival. Spano also introduced her song cycle *Château de l'âme* (Castle of the Soul), with the New York Philharmonic.

Saariaho receives an artist's salary for her compositional work from the Finnish Government. She was awarded the Kranichstein Prize at the new music summer courses in Darmstadt (1986), Prix Italia (1988) for *Stilleben*, and in 1989 the Prix ars Electronica for *Stilleben* and *Io*. 2001 brought the Rolf Schock Prize (Sweden) and Kaske Prize (Germany). In 2003, she won the University of Louisville (Kentucky) $200,000 Grawemeyer Award for *L'Amour du loin*.

Her music is available on the Finlandia, Ondine, Wergo, Neuma and BIS record labels. Her CD, *Prisma*, came out in 2003 via her non-profit website *Petals*, which produces recordings and other projects not in the commercial mainstream. Of Scandinavian contemporary composers, Saariaho is among those who have received most recognition. As in the works of Sibelius, the stark beauty of her native country comes through in her music—in which one can see the *Aurora Borealis*, feel glistening ice crystals and catch the fragrance of fir trees in the snow.

Kaija has lived in Paris for over two decades. Her husband, Jean-Baptiste Barrière, is production editor at IRCAM. They have two children, Alex, born 1989 and Alisa, 1994, a concert pianist.

Central and East European Composers

CROATIA
Olja Jelaska
Dora Pejačević

YUGOSLAVIA
Ljubica Marić(1909–2003)
Natasha Bogojevich
Katarina Miljković
Ivana Stefanović

POLAND
Tekla Badarzewska-Baranowska (1834–61)
Irena Wieniawska (Mr. Poldowski) (1879–1932)
Grażyna Bacewicz (1909–1969)
Joanna Bruzdowicz
Barbara Jazwinski
Hanna Kulenty
Bernadetta Matuszczak
Krystna Moszumańska-Nazar
Marta Ptaszyńska
Elżbieta Sikora
Anna Zawadzka
Lidia Zielińska

ROMANIA
Myriam Marbe (1931–97)
Violeta Dinescu
Irina Ogadescu
Doina Rotaru
Cornelia Tăutu
Marina (Marta) Vlad
Diana Voda-Nuteanu
Mihaela Vosganian

CZECH REPUBLIC
Sláva Vorlová (1894–1973)
Vítězslava Kaprálová (1915–1940)
Jana Obrovská (1930–1987)
Elena Petrová (1929–2002)
Sylvie Bodorová
Marta Jiráčková
Ivana Loudová

RUSSIA
Valerija Besedina
Elena Firsova
Sofia Asgatovna Gubaidulina
Svetlana Lavrova
Sofia Levkovskaja
Olga Magidenko
Olga Petrova
Irina Tsesljukevitch
Galina Ivanovna Ustvols'kaya
Tatyana Voronova

SLOVAKIA
Petra Bachratá
Ol'ga Danášová
Viera Janárčeková
Ol'ga Kroupová
Lucia Papanetzová
Ľubica Salamon-Čekovská
Iris Szeghy
Larisa Vrhunc

UKRAINE
Lara Levina (1906–76)
Svitlana Azarova
Lesia Dychko
Julia Gomeloskaya
Hanna Havrylets
Iryna Kyvrylina
Victoria Poleva
Aljona Tomljonova
Karmella Tsepkolenko
Ludmilla Yurina
Alla Zagaykevich

TURKMENISTAN
Iraida Yusupova

AZERBAIJAN
Franghiz Ali-Zadeh

Concrete Walls and Iron Curtains

On June 12, 1987, standing at the base of the Brandenburg Gate, the voice of **Ronald Reagan** could be heard in both West and East Berlin when he demanded, "Mr. Gorbachev! Tear down this wall!" The American president's speech that day is considered to have initiated the beginning of the end of the Cold War and the fall of communism. From November 9–11, 1989, the people of a free Berlin tore down that wall.

Depending upon their age, women composers in Eastern Europe either remember life before the communist regime, or were born into it and able to take advantage of free schooling and equal opportunities. Since the fall of the Iron Curtain in 1990, they have had to adapt to a more democratic lifestyle with certain elements to their disadvantage, mainly the lack of state subsidies for the arts. Again, depending on the country, there were degrees of transition, especially economically. East Germany was able to be swiftly reunited with its western counterpart through efficient negotiations from July to October 1990, because not only was wealthy West Germany able to foot the bills involved in such a momentous planned event of history, but despite a forty-four year separation—since the end of World War II in 1945—each sector had retained their common sociological foundation of race and language. Poland, with its strong independent traditions, also made the switch to democracy fairly smoothly, beginning via elections of the unions for striking workers in 1989. In 1999 it became part of NATO[20] and in 2004 joined the European Union (EU). Czechoslovakia split peacefully into the Czech Republic and Slovakia, January 1, 1993. (Poland, the Czech Republic, Slovakia and Hungary are now considered *Central* Europe.) Yugoslavia, which had been formed in 1915 after WWI, by the union of Serbs, Croats and Slovenes, after WWII, under Tito, covered six republics: Serbia, Croatia, Bosnia-Herzegovina, Macedonia, Slovenia and Montenegro. Although a communist, Tito made it clear that he was not a Russian puppet. After his death in 1980, the union unraveled over the next ten years and in 1991 became the independent republics of Slovenia, Macedonia, and Croatia. Bosnia-Herzegovina became a federation, while Serbia and Montenegro, under Slobodan Milošević,[21] became the Federal Republic of Yugoslavia. In 2000, a popular uprising caused the dictator to step down. In 2003, the Republic was renamed Serbia and Montenegro, and Yugoslavia ceased to exist.

Cold War Meltdown

The USSR came unglued thanks to the policies of **Mikhail Gorbachev** in the late 1980s. They were *glasnost* (openness) and *perestroika* (restructuring of the Soviet political and economic systems). Although he was not permitted to reap the glory of his accomplishments, the decade beginning in 1991 marked the dissolution of the major power communist union into independent republics of Moldavia, Ukraine, Belorussia, Armenia, Azerbaijan, Kazakhstan, Russia, Uzbekistan, and the Baltic countries of Latvia, Lithuania and Estonia. As the 21st century progressed, the Russian people gradually acquired the mindset for free enterprise after two generations of having been "spoonfed" communist doctrine and dependence on a dictatorial government. Today, computer technology draws the world into a "global village." Information flies across borders in nanoseconds making national secrets almost impossible to keep from the public. Despite all this turmoil, the inner core of culture continues to bond those in the arts. Many women left their homelands in the quest for recognition. Here follows some of the background to the contemporary scene.

---

20. North Atlantic Treaty Organization, created in 1948 of former Allied Countries to counteract Communist powers.
21. As of 2006, Milošević was still defending himself at the UN International Criminal Tribunal in The Hague, Netherlands, in a trial that began in 2002. He was found dead in his cell from a heart attack, March 11.

CROATIA

OLJA JELASKA, born in Split, on the Adriatic Coast, attended music schools graduating from the Zagreb Music Academy in musical theory (1992) and composition (1994). In 1993, she won the Rector's Award and the Croatian Musical Institute Award in 1994. She specialized in courses for composition in Bialystok (Poland, 1995) and Darmstadt (Germany, 1996). Among other venues, her compositions have been performed at the Music Biennale in Zagreb and at the International Music Festival in Opatija.

DORA PEJAČEVIĆ, the first female composer in Croatia, was born in Budapest, September 10, 1885. The daughter of Croatian Count Teodor Pejačević and Hungarian Baroness Lilla Vay de Vaya, Dora inherited her musical talent from her mother and wrote her first composition at age twelve. She studied at the Croatian Music Institute in Zagreb, then briefly in Dresden with Percy Sherwood and in Munich with Swiss composer Walter Courvoisier (1875–1931). For the most part, however, she was self-taught and developed her musical talents through contact with other artists. Her home was at Nasice (near Osijek) where she worked, but she also traveled to Budapest, Munich, Prague and Vienna. After her marriage to Ottomar von Lumbe in 1921, she lived mainly in Munich where she died, March 5, 1923.

Her best known works are a Symphony op.41 (1918) and Piano Concerto op.33 (1913). In late Romantic style, they are infused with Impressionist harmonies and lush orchestral colors, showing the influence of Tchaikovsky, Schumann, Grieg and Brahms.

Pejačević introduced the orchestral song into Croatian music. Among her vocal works, her greatest achievement is the *Drei Gesänge* (Three Songs, op.53) for voice and piano. Her late piano miniatures, lyrical and meditative, include *Two Nocturnes* op.50, and *Humoreske und Caprice* op.54. In the *Phantasie concertante* op.48 for piano and orchestra and in the Piano Sonata in A, op.57, she followed the Lisztian concept of the single movement sonatafantasy.

Almost all of her fifty-seven known compositions, including lieder, violin sonatas and piano trios, survive as a single collection in the Croatian Music Institute in Zagreb.

The Former YUGOSLAVIA
(Slovenia, Bosnia-Herzegovina, Serbia, Montenegro, etc.)

Ljubica Maric

Serbian composer **LJUBICA MARIĆ,** born March 18, 1909, showed early talent, studying with noted Yugoslav composer and pedagogue **Josip Slavenski** (1896–1955) at the Belgrade School of Music, and in 1929 was the first woman composer to graduate from this Conservatory. She continued her studies at the Prague Conservatory with the renowned **Josef Suk** (1874–1935), and after graduation learned the concept of quarter-tone music with its European innovator, **Alois Haba** (1893–1973). She also studied conducting with two of the world's leading maestros, **Nikolai Malko** (1883–1961), and in Strasbourg with **Hermann Scherchen** (1891–1966).

Marić returned to Belgrade as a professor at the Stanković School (1938–45), teaching theory at the Academy of Music until 1967. Her cantata *Songs of Space* (1956), a performance of which Shostakovich proclaimed as one of his "loveliest memories of Yugoslavia," ushered in the most productive decade of her creativity. Her style progressed from expressionism to a personal classicism. Her next work, *Passacaglia* (1958) for symphony orchestra, beautifully mirrored her affinity for baroque music. Fascinated by the poetics of national origins, she found a boundless source of inspiration in Serbian folk music and in the Byzantine musical heritage. The *Byzantine Concerto* (1959) for piano and orchestra is a complex musical vision of the Serbian Middle Ages. 1961 brought *The Threshold of a Dream*, linked by the same loyalty to the word of the poet as her cantata, *Chants of Darkness* (1984).

Her work encouraged many of her country's composers to turn to the roots of their musical heritage, thus initiating a very productive branch of Serbian music. Marić held a prominent place in the history of Serbian contemporary music, enjoying prestige into her nineties until her death in Belgrade, September 17, 2003.

Natasha Bogojevich

NATASHA BOGOJEVICH, born January 1, 1966, in Valjevo, studied music in Belgrade, beginning in primary school. She received her BM in Piano and Composition from the University of Belgrade (1991), with further courses in chamber, electronic, computer and film music.

In 1988, she won of the Association of Composers of Serbia award for *Shall I Sprinkle You with Leaves?* Her *Circulus Vitiosus, opus Alchymicum*, for symphony orchestra, was honored with the October Prize of the City of Belgrade in 1991. At UNESCO's Rostrum of Composers in Paris, her composition *Formes Differentes de Sonneries de la Rose + Croix*, won third prize and was placed on the "top ten" list recommended for broadcasting and performing all around the world. Her commissions include European Festival of Experimental Music, France, for *Full Moon Circle of Ground*; Concert for World Peace, Tokyo, 1993, for *L'incertezza del poeta*; Youth Music Forum, Ukraine (1993, '95); Tokyo String Quartet (1997); Women Composers in the Avant-garde, Middelburg (Xenakis Ensemble, 1998); and Festival Nieuwe Muzeik, Amsterdam, 1999 (Fransis B. Quartet).

Besides performing contemporary music all over Europe, she has written works for theater, television and ballet. Other important compositions include *A Journey Through Grammar*, *Fleeting A*, *La nostalgia dell' infinito*, *La-da-nja* (Pastoral), *The Dream of Orpheus* and *Sonority of Dynamical Heart*.

Bogojevich was music editor for the magazine *Beorama*, and collaborated in Belgrade Television Culture and Arts programs between 1984–1990. She was an assistant professor at the Belgrade Faculty of Music, composition and orchestration department until 1995 when, after the birth of daughter Maria, February 8, she moved to the Chicago area where she runs a successful piano studio, and since 2004 teaches at De Paul University.

A major production in 2001 was the birth of her son, Dushan Stefan, March 2.

2005 marked a new venture, writing for movies with *Where It Gets You* by Bad Penny Films. She also composed music for the play *The Birds*, by Aristophanes, staged in March by the Tuta Theatre Company of Chicago. Her miniature, dramatic Oratorio, for soprano, flute, violin, viola and cello, was premiered by the New York Miniaturist Ensemble, August 31, and called "brilliant!"

Between the university position, over fifty private students and two children to raise—now by herself—the challenge is to find composition time! When I last spoke to Natasha, she had an opera waiting to be born . . .

KATARINA MILJKOVIĆ, born in 1959, in Leskovac, studied composition at the Belgrade Faculty of Music with Enrico Josif and Vlastimir Trajkovic, graduating in 1984. She earned her MM in Composition in 1990, and after a year with Radio Belgrade became assistant at the department of musical theory at the Faculty of Music.

Since 1978, she has been a active participant in the musical life of Belgrade, Novi Sad, Zagreb and Ljubljana. Her works have been performed at the Zagreb Biennial of Contemporary Music, Belgrade Music Festival, Budapest Festival of New Music, World Festival of Chamber Music (Zagreb), Rostrum of Yugoslav Music Festival and Music in Serbia Festival. Her honors include the Josip Slavenski Award (1985) for *Swifts, Sequence for Symphony Orchestra*. In 1986, her *Rondo - Sequence No. 3* was awarded the Students' October Prize of the City of Belgrade. This piece also won a prize in 1990 at an international composers competition in Miami, Florida.

IVANA STEFANOVIĆ, born September 14, 1948, studied violin and composition with Enrico Josif at the Music Academy in Belgrade. From 1979–81, she took advanced training in Paris, first at IRCAM, and later worked with composer and conductor, Gilbert Amy. Her compositions, mostly designed for varied and unconventional ensembles, have been performed internationally at festivals and competitions. Much of her research is related to sound sources—electronic, "concrète," environmental, and traditional instruments. Since 1976, she has been associated with Radio Belgrade as an editor and program writer, becoming head of music production on their first program in 1990. She founded and edited the Sound Workshop in 1985, and through this became a member of the Ars Acoustica steering committee of the European Broadcasting Union. During the last decade, she taught a course on stage music at the Belgrade Faculty of Music.

Her works include *Hommage à François Villon*, for voice and early instruments (1978), *Fragment of a Possible Order*, two pianos, harpsichord, organ, cello, accordion (1979), *Whereto with the Bird on the Palm of the Hand*, percussion, tape (1980), *Interpretation of a Dream*, flute, two speakers, tape (1984), *Lingua/Phonia/Patria*, experimental radiophonic work (1989), *When Cometh No Succour*, traditional and ancient instruments, strings, percussion (1989), *Psalm*, mezzo, mixed voices (1990), *Isidora* (ballet), tape (1992), *The Metropolis of Silence (Ancient Ras)*, radiophonic poem, (1992), *Lacrimosa*, tape (1993), *Tree of Life*, strings (1997).

POLAND

TEKLA BĄDARZEWSKA-BARANOWSKA (1834–61), a composer of salon music, at age seventeen won an almost immortal claim to fame for having written *Modlitwas dziewicy*, known popularly as *The Maiden's Prayer*. Published in Poland (1856), and as a supplement to the Paris *Revue et gazette musicale* (1859) under the title *La prière d'une vierge*, the piece was pounced upon by more than eighty publishers throughout Europe, America and Australia, metamorphosizing into arrangements for piano solo, duet and other instruments. As a salon piece of no real outstanding originality, its success was an unequaled phenomenon. While she wrote thirty-four more piano pieces in the salon style, none matched the success of this simple composition.

IRENA REGINA WIENIAWSKA, youngest daughter of Polish violinist Henryk Wieniawski (1835–80) and his Irish wife, Isobel Hampton, published her music under the name, **Mr. Poldowski**. She was born in Brussels, March 18, 1879, a year before her father died penniless in Moscow. At age twelve she entered the Brussels Conservatory, where she studied piano and composition with François Gevaert (1828–1908). In London her teacher was Percy Pitt (1870–1932), music advisor to the BBC and music director of Covent Garden and British National Opera companies.

In 1901, she married baronet Sir Aubrey Edward Henry Dean Paul, thus becoming a titled British citizen. Her husband was an amateur musician and baritone, who not only gave his wife freedom to study and write, but also paid for many of her publications and performances, as well as participating in her concerts, singing her songs under the pseudonym, Edward Ramsey.

A son, Aubrey, was born in 1902, after which Irena studied in Paris with André Gédalge (1856–1926). After the child's tragic death in 1904, and following the birth of Brian in 1905, she returned to Paris to study with Vincent d'Indy (1851–1931) at the Schola Cantorum. A daughter, Brenda, was born in 1907.

"Mr." Poldowski is best remembered for French songs written in impressionist style to twenty-one poems of the Frenchman Paul Verlaine. Her oeuvre of over thirty songs, an operetta, *Laughter*, works for orchestra, a woodwind suite, eleven piano solos, and two violin and piano pieces includes: *Caledonian Market* (1923), a suite of eight pieces for piano; *Berceuse de l'enfant mourant* and *Tango* (both 1923) for violin and piano; two symphonic sketches, *Tenements*, and *Nocturnes*, premiered at the Proms in 1912 by Sir Henry Wood, her orchestral champion. At the 1919 Proms, she was soloist in her *Pat Malone's Wake*, for piano and orchestra. Despite the support of Wood, and good reviews, most of her large scale compositions went unplayed.

During the 1920s, Wieniawska's works were performed regularly in Belgium, Holland, London, Paris and New York, although her musical language did not go down well with more conservative critics.

Five years before her death, with conditions in the musical world offering little remuneration, Lady Dean Paul canvassed and directed work for a London window-cleaning firm in which a friend, the Marchioness of Garisbrooke, also had an interest. Irena was known to have said the humor in the situation made it endurable. It is believed she was living apart from her husband, and her music royalties were assigned to creditors when, after a long illness, she died of bronchitis, January 28, 1932.

Between 1915–1935 Chester Music Company published her songs, which are still available, but most of her symphonic music was destroyed during World War II.

Grazyna Bacewicz

One of the most honored composers of her country, **GRAZYNA BACEWICZ**, born February 5, 1909, in Lodz, came from a musical family and was already performing recitals by age seven. At eleven she entered the private Lodz Conservatory, continuing her violin and piano training. She graduated in 1932 from the Warsaw Conservatory, after studying violin with Józef Jarzebski (1878–1955), piano with Józef Turczyeski (1884–1953) and composition with one of her country's most prominent composers, **Kazimierz Sikorski** (1895–1986). Another major influence was her meeting **Karol Szymanowski** (1882–1937) at the conservatory. At his urging, she joined the illustrious throng of students of **Nadia Boulanger** in Paris, at the same time taking violin there with **André Touret**. After concertizing as a violinist in Spain, she returned to Warsaw, but in 1934 went back to Paris for further studies with Boulanger, as well as the brilliant Hungarian violinist/pedagogue **Carl Flesch** (1873–1944). In 1935, at the first Wieniawski International Violin Competition, she received honorable mention to **David Oistrakh**'s second place, and **Ginette Neveu**'s first place. (Neveu and Oistrakh went on to major international careers.)

Home again in 1936, Bacewicz played principal violin for two years in the Polish Radio Orchestra. The same year she married Dr. Andrzej Biernacki, who later became a professor at the Medical Academy and secretary to the Polish Academy of Science. Besides being an accomplished pianist, and a notable interpreter of her own *2nd Piano Sonata*, she was also a successful writer of short stories, novels and autobiographical material. Along with her orchestra tenure, Bacewicz concertized on the Continent, getting back to her country just two months before the outbreak of World War II, September 3, 1939.

A Personal Torch of Liberty

During the hardship and horror of the German occupation, the Biernacki home was a refuge to war victims. Bacewicz' secret concerts kept Polish culture alive and helped raise money for relief funds. In 1942, daughter Alina was born, which helped Grazyna avoid being deported to Germany after being part of the August 1944 uprising by the Polish resistance forces—quelled by the Germans via putting Warsaw to the torch.

After this, like most Poles, the family went through a period of homelessness and did not get back to the capital until the war ended in May 1945. Bacewicz renewed her concert career, playing Szymanowski's *Violin Concerto #1* in Paris in 1946. Her compositional craft also flourished with her first major success, *Concerto for String Orchestra* (1950), for which she won the Polish National Prize. The American premiere in Washington, DC (1952), established her as an important composer. Among other numerous awards was top prize in the 1949 Chopin Competition for Composers, for her *Piano Concerto*; first prize in the 1951 International Composers Competition in Liège (Belgium) for *String Quartet No. 4*; first prize at the 1960 UNESCO International Rostrum of Composers in Paris for *Music for Strings, Trumpets and Percussion*—one of her most frequently heard works in Europe—; and the gold medal in the Queen Elisabeth International Music Competition (Brussels, 1965) for her *Violin Concerto No. 7*.

In 1932, Bacewicz' style started out as neoclassical, with some incorporation of folk tunes. In the war years, she began veering away from classical structure, gradually developing distinctive innovations. She managed to stay clear of the cultural influences of the Stalin era, and in the '60s flirted fleetingly with serialism and the twelve-tone scale. By 1953, she began to withdraw from performing and devoted herself to composition. Her prodigious output includes six symphonies (the first two are lost), seven string quartets, a concerto for string orchestra, five violin sonatas, seven violin concertos, a concerto for orchestra, a viola concerto, a cello concerto, a piano quintet plus other keyboard and vocal music, and her last great work, a ballet, *The Desire* (1969).

Grazyna Bacewicz made an indelible mark on 20th century music. Even her earliest works are still being performed all over the world. She maintained her individuality versus the inroads of *avant-garde* in the 1950s. She won the State Award for artistic accomplishment, 1950, 1952. After serving many years as their vice chairman, in 1960 she received the Award of the Polish Composers Union. From 1966, she taught at the State School of Music, which regained its original name, the Warsaw Conservatory, in the 1980s.

In January 1969, a case of influenza turned into pneumonia, which was misdiagnosed. Given incorrect medication, she suffered a heart attack. Her unexpected death, January 17, 1969, in Warsaw, plunged her country into mourning for one of its greatest artists. Two streets and eight schools have been named after her. Her statue stands in front of Philharmonic Hall in the city of Bydgoszcz.

As her renowned peer and countryman **Witold Lutoslawski** (1913–94) wrote in the Foreword of the 1984 definitive book, *Grazyna Bacewicz: Her Life and Works*, by **Judith Rosen** (See Musicologists.):

> She was born with an incredible wealth of musical talent, which she succeeded to bring to full flourish through an almost fanatic zeal and unwavering faith in her mission. The intensity of her activities was so great that she managed, in such a cruelly shortened life, to give birth to such treasures that any composer of her stature with a considerably longer life span could only envy.

Bacewicz carried the torch for the Polish women composers who followed.

JOANNA BRUZDOWICZ was born May 19, 1943, in Warsaw to musical parents. Her father was an architect, linguist and cellist, her mother, an accomplished pianist. Early piano studies inspired composing by age twelve. She received her master's in piano and composition in 1966 from the Chopin Academy of the Warsaw Conservatory, with **Kazimierz Sikorski** as her principal composition teacher. She began a public career as a pianist, concertizing throughout central Europe. Via a French government scholarship in 1968, she studied composition in Paris with **Nadia Boulanger**, as well as **Olivier Messiaen** and **Pierre Schaeffer** (1910–95), the latter the inventor of *music concrète*—an avant-garde method of incorporating natural sounds such as taped birdsongs or street noises into compositions. Her doctoral thesis "Mathematics and Logic in Contemporary Music" was written at the Sorbonne.

Bruzdowicz has been active in the promotion of contemporary music as founder of Jeunesses (Youth) Musicales of Poland, founder/president of the Chopin and Szymanovska Society of Belgium, and vice president of the International Federation of Chopin Societies. She was a member of the Groupe de Rechèrches Musicales of the ORTF, often heard on Radio France, the RTBF (Radio-Television) in Belgium, and the former West German Radio. She lectures internationally on contemporary, electronic and acoustic music and has taught composition courses at Aix-en-Provence (France), Canada's University of Montreal, and in the U.S. at MIT, UCLA and Yale.

Of her four operas, *Tides and Waves* was written under the patronage of UNESCO for the 1992 Olympic Games in Barcelona. It is based on a story and libretto by Horst-Jürgen Tittel, whom she married in 1975. Together they have written a number of television scripts using her music. Her orchestral works include a Piano Concerto (1974), Symphony (1975), Violin Concerto (1975), Double Bass Concerto (1982), *Four Seasons' Greetings* (1989), and *The Cry of the Phoenix* (1994), for cello and symphony. She has also written for piano and organ, as well as electronic and electroacoustic pieces.

Bruzdowicz was the only Polish composer and the only woman selected to the final round of twelve composers invited to create a new hymn for the Vatican (a French composer won). Her *Stabat Mater* (1993) was written and performed for the unveiling, in a restored theater, of Jan Styka's monumental (93 by 178 feet) painting of the *Crucifixion* at Forest Lawn Memorial in Glendale, California, originally commissioned by Ignacy Jan Paderewski at the turn of the century. In attendance, among the over 1,000 guests, were representatives of the City and County of Los Angeles, and the Polish government. Life size portraits of Paderewski and Styka are also at this location.

In 2001, Bruzdowicz received the highest distinction from the Polish government, the Order of Polonia Restituta, for her contribution to Polish culture. As part of her passion for promoting Polish music, she produced hours of programs devoted to this subject for radio stations in France, Germany, Belgium, Italy, Spain and the U.S.

December 7, 2003, saw her delivery of the annual Ignacy Jan Paderewski lecture at USC commemorating the legacy of the noted composer/musician/statesman. The occasion also marked the West Coast premieres of her String Quartet No. 2, *Cantus Aeternus*, for reciting actor and string quartet, and *Song of Hope and Love* for cello and piano, dedicated to Holocaust victims.

Joanna lives near Brussels with her husband and their two sons.

BARBARA JAZWINSKI, daughter of scientist parents, was exposed to music from birth with chamber concerts in her home, in which she later participated. In Poland's liberal music education program, if a child showed talent, he or she was admitted to special courses at the elementary school level. Thus Barbara began her formal training at age seven, which went on through high school—all free. Next came composition and theory at the Warsaw Academy of Music (now renamed the Fryderyk Chopin Academy), where her principal teacher was modernist Andrzej Dobrowolski (1921–90). The Polish "brand" of communism permitted travel to Western Europe, provided one had the means, which enabled her to visit England, France and Italy and have a familiarity with the music world denied many of her Iron Curtain colleagues.

In 1970, she married an American who had been living in Warsaw for eight years. They have two sons, Michael and Peter. After completing the third year of study at the academy, they moved to the U.S. where she earned her MA in composition and piano from Stanford and her PhD in composition from City University of New York (CUNY,1984). Her famous teachers included electronic composers **Mario Davidovsky** (*b* 1934), **György Ligeti** (*b* 1923) and **John Chowning** (*b* 1934). Among her awards are the 1981 Prince Pierre of Monaco Musical Competition for her *Sextet*, first prize in the Nicola De Lorenzo Composition Contest for *Music for the Chamber Orchestra*, and a *special prize* awarded by the Polish Composers' Alliance in the *First Competition for Improvised Music*, Gdansk, Poland.

Jazwinski is the recipient of numerous commissions, grants and fellowships, including commissions from NYU New Music Ensemble, Louisiana Sinfonetta, Chamber Music Center at the Composers' Conferences at Wellesley College, an artist fellowship from the Louisiana State Arts Council, grants from the Presser, Newcomb and Metzner Foundations, Meet the Composer (New York), and fellowships to composers conferences at Johnson, Vermont, and Wellesley, Massachusetts. Active as a performer, conductor, and promoter of contemporary music, she has been music director of *Spectri Sonori*, the award-winning chamber music concert series which also sponsors the annual International Composition Contest. Her compositions *Stryga* and *Sequenze Concertanti* are recorded on CD by the Polish Radio and TV Orchestra of Kracow and by the Koszalin Philharmonic on Vienna Modern Masters. 1995 brought *Phantasy on Jazz* (clarinet solo with symphony orchestra) and Quintet for flute, B♭clarinet, bassoon, trumpet and piano. The same year, she entered her position in the theory and composition program at the Newcomb College Music Department of Tulane University, New Orleans. By 2003, she had been made head of the music department and occupied the chair of Virginia Beer professor of music composition and theory.

Her music is heard worldwide, presented at well-known concert series and festivals, including the League of Composers-ISCM, the Koszalin Philharmonic, Polish Music Festival in Montreal, Laboratory of Contemporary Music in Siedlce, Poland, New Music Festival, Edmonton Composers' Concert Society, NYU New Music Ensemble, Sixth International Festival of Contemporary Music "Laboratorium," Washington Square Contemporary Music Series, Fanfare Festival, and Gegenwelten Festival (Mannheim-Heidelberg).

Hanna Kulenty

Born March 18, 1961, in Bialystok, **HANNA KULENTY** began her music education as a pianist at the Grazyna Bacewicz Elementary Music School in Warsaw. She studied composition from 1980–86 with **Wlodzimierz Kotoński** (*b* 1925) at the Chopin Academy and post-graduate work from 1986–88 at The Hague Royal Conservatory with **Louis Andriessen** (*b* 1939), one of the sons of the renowned family of Dutch composers. She participated in International Courses for Young Composers organized by the Polish Section of ISCM, and International

Summer Courses of New Music in Darmstadt (Germany). She has been the recipient of numerous commissions and scholarships, including the Composers Competition of the Warsaw Branch of the Polish Composers Union, Deutscher Akademischer Austauschdienst (DAAD) in the Berlin Arts Program (1990–91) and from the Dutch government.

Her earlier music, known for its patterns of emotional "arcs," has an orchestral style that has been compared to her countryman **Krzyzstof Penderecki** (*b* 1933), and Greek-born French composer **Iannis Xenakis** (1922–2001). In 1985, her composition for symphony orchestra, *Ad Unum*, won second prize at the European Composers' Competition in Amsterdam, and when performed at the Warsaw Autumn Festival it received a review from music critic Jan Weber in which he said to Kulenty's male colleges, "Gentlemen, hear and tremble."

Since *Ad Unum*, her orchestral works include three Symphonies, No.1 (1986), No. 2 (1987) and No.3 (1998); Piano Concerto No.1 and 2 (1990, 1991); Violin Concerto No.1 and 2 (1992, 1995); a Flute Concerto (2001), and Trumpet Concerto (2002), which won the Unesco Picasso-Miro Medal at the International Rostrum of Composers in 2003.

Her turn towards minimalism, attributed to studying with Andriessen, she calls her "European trance music." Examples of this style are: *A Fourth Circle* for violin and piano (1994), *A Fifth Circle* for alto flute, and *A Sixth Circle* for trumpet and piano (1995). The *Fourth Circle* was premiered at the New Music Festival, Musikhost, in Odense, Denmark, 1994, where the main theme of the festival was "Three Polish Women: Bacewicz, Moszumanska-Nazar, and Kulenty."

Other works include: *Sinequan Forte A* for amplified cello and symphony orchestra; *Sinequan Forte B* for amplified cello and chamber orchestra; *A Cradle Song* for violin, cello and piano; *Lysanxia* for gamelan ensemble and tape; *A Third Circle* for piano solo; and *Sierra* for violin and cello, commissioned by the 1996 Munich Biennale. It was here that Hamburg Opera premiered her *Mother of Black-Winged Dreams*, a chamber opera exploring the complex subject matter of "multiple personality syndrome," touching upon issues of suffering, child abuse and gender relations. With the scenario penned by Canadian Paul Goodman, a Dutch resident, the work is structured as one huge arc of increasing tension, spanning the duration of the piece. 1996 also produced *Blattinus*, for saxophone quartet. *Certus*, for chamber orchestra, *Waiting for . . .* (piano solo and voice) and *Elfen*, ballet music for chamber orchestra, were written in 1997. The following year brought *Part One* of her third symphony, *Stretto* (flute, clarinet, cello and guitar), and *Rapidus*, for saxophone quartet. *Harmonium*, a solo for that instrument, and *MM-blues* (two pianos and percussion) came in 1999. 2000 marked *Decimo*, for choir, six voices, *Drive Blues*, for piano, and the completion of *Symphony No. 3*, while the *Flute Concerto No. 1*, for flute and chamber orchestra, and *Asjaawaa*, for mezzo soprano, flute, harp, piano and electronics were finished in 2001.

Her newest compositional technique, the polyphony of time dimensions, emphasizes the circularity of time and the simultaneity of time-events occurring on different temporal planes. The technique supplants the polyphony of arches used until about 1993–94, and the European trance music used until 2001. It is used in her opera, *Hoffmanniana*, completed in 2003.

Her music is featured at festivals in Poland, Denmark, England, Germany and Holland. 2000–01 found her as composer-in-residence of the Gelders Orchestra in the Netherlands. In 2001, she was a lecturer at the Seventh International Courses for Young Composers in Apeldoor, Holland, organized by the Gaudeamus Foundation. In the following years she has continued her European lectures, receiving grants from Fonds voor de Scheppende Toonkunst, Holland.

Since 1992, Kulenty has divided her residences between Holland and her native country. She married Martin Majoor, typographer and graphic artist in 1996. They have two children, Piotr born July 31, 1997, and Kaja, October 3, 1998.

BERNADETTA MATUSZCZAK, born March 10, 1937, in Toruń, studied music theory and piano at the State Higher School of Music in Poznań, composition at the Chopin Academy of Music in Warsaw, then enriched her education with **Nadia Boulanger** in Paris. She was a winner of the Young Polish Composers' Competition (1965), and many others including the famous Jeunesses Musicales (1967). Like other composers of this era, her music graduated from the aleatory experimentation of the '60s and '70s to more harmonic forms in the next decades.

A religious Catholic, she was greatly affected by the horrors of WWII she saw in her childhood—people being arrested and killed. Her philosophical outlook became "Death is the only inevitability of life which is otherwise filled with free choices." This infiltrated compositions such as *Elegy about a Polish Boy*, *Apocalypsis* and the chamber opera *Juliet and Romeo*. Among her settings to music of several literary classics, she turned to the historical novel *Quo Vadis* by Henryk Sienkiewicz, portraying the martyrdom of Christians in Nero's Rome. In the form of a music drama, this commission from the Warsaw Chamber Opera was premiered 1996.

Not widely known outside Poland, her work is mainly for the stage, oratorios, songs with orchestra, and music for children. In 1997, she ended her active career and moved back to her home town of Toruń. Self-effacing and modest, Matuszczak never promoted her works, which has sadly resulted in their neglect.

KRYSTYNA MOSZUMAŃSKA-NAZAR (*b* 1924). (See International Musicologists.)

Marta Ptaszynska

MARTA PTASZYŃSKA, born July 29, 1943 in Warsaw, is considered the most prominent contemporary woman composer of Poland, although she lives in America. As a child, she played the piano as soon as she could reach the keys, and was composing melodies at age four before she could write music. She reaped the benefits of the Communist regime with its emphasis on education and excellence. Her talent was rewarded through, as she puts it, "endless exams and winning competitions," affording the opportunity for a thorough and *free* musical education which in the course of seventeen years earned her three masters degrees at the Warsaw Academy (Chopin Academy of Music) in composition, percussion, and music theory. Her mentor was her country's most renowned composer **Witold Lutoslawski**. After graduation, a French government grant enabled Marta to become part of the illustrious entourage of **Nadia Boulanger**, and while in Paris she also studied with **Olivier Messiaen** (1908–92) at ORTF, the electronic music center. The Kosciuszko Foundation[22] provided the means to study at the Cleveland Institute of Music (1972–74), where she earned an artist diploma in percussion. She taught at Bennington College (Vermont), Indiana University (Pennsylvania), the College Conservatory of Cincinnati, and was composer-in-residence at UC-Berkeley and Santa Barbara (California), and Northwestern University near Chicago. In 1998, she joined the faculty of the University of Chicago where she is a tenured professor in music and the humanities. In 2005 she received an endowed chair making her the Helen B. and Frank L. Sulzberger Professor in Composition.

Polishing the Polish Tradition

Since its 1955 inception, the Festival of Contemporary Music has given Polish composers an advantage over other former Iron Curtain nations, in that Poland was exposed to new trends and visiting composers. This can be heard in Ptaszyńska's music and that of her famous friends and fellow countrymen, **Wojciech Kilar** (*b* 1932), **Krysztof Penderecki** (*b* 1933) and **Henryk Gorecki** (*b* 1933).

In November 1995, Ptaszyńska was honored with the Officer Cross of Merit, presented by the Polish government from President Lech Walesa,[23] for her cultural activities in the U.S., including her assistance in arranging the Festival of Polish Arts at the New York Public Library of the Performing Arts in Lincoln Center. In 1997, she received the Alfred Jurzykowski Award in New York for overall creative achievements, and in 2000, an award from the Polish government for outstanding contributions to Polish culture. She was also honored with a medal from the Union of Polish Composers.

---

22. The Kosciuszko Foundation has been promoting educational and cultural exchanges and relations between America and Poland since 1925.

23. Lech Walesa, electrician, union organizer, won heretofore unheard-of freedoms during the '70s from the controlling Communist Party, aided by the example of Karol Cardinal Wojtyla, a strong advocate of human rights. The Cardinal became Pope John Paul II in 1978. Walesa won the Nobel Peace Prize in 1983.

A Somber Remembrance and Children in the Spotlight

Ptaszyńska's *Holocaust Memorial Cantata* gained worldwide recognition during the fiftieth anniversary celebrations of the liberation of Auschwitz, the infamous concentration camp located in Poland. The piece was played at international festivals during 1993, under the baton of **Lord Yehudi Menuhin** at the Schleswig-Holstein Festival, and in January 1994 at the MIDEM Women in Music Conference in Cannes (France). In 1999, Warsaw National Opera premiered her children's opera *Mr. Marimba*, based on her own fairy tale *The Enchanted Song*, with libretto by eminent Polish writer Agnieszka Osiecka. The plot centers on two children searching the world for a crystal music box whose tune enables them to understand the speech of all animals. The production, with children in the chorus and in leading roles, plus audience participation, interweaves folksongs of Europe, Asia, Africa and Latin America, presenting an overall theme of "Unite Our World." As of 2005 there have been 112 sold-out performances in Warsaw. (The composer journeys to Poland each summer, participating in festivals and seminars.)

In 1974, her *Spectri sonori* was premiered by the Cleveland Orchestra. The same year, *Siderals* won a prize at the Percussive Arts Society competition, and *Classical Variations* won in 1976. *La novella d'iverno* placed second in the 1986 UNESCO International Rostrum of Composers in Paris, and *Marimba Concerto* written for Keiko Abe, renowned Japanese marimbist, was honored in the 1987 International Composers Competition in New York. The Cincinnati Symphony premiered her *Fanfare for Peace* as part of their 100th anniversary (1995) celebration. *Liquid Light*, for mezzo soprano, piano and percussion, was written for singer-conductor-composer **Patricia Adkins Chiti** (see Musicologists), whom Ptaszyńska accompanied in a recital of her music, May 1995, in Italy. This received its American debut the next month at the Polish National Alliance concert in Chicago, honoring Polish women composers. Its Polish premiere was at the Warsaw Autumn Festival of Contemporary Music, September 1996. In December, her composition *Silver Echoes of Distant Bells* was premiered at the seventieth anniversary of the Kosciuszko Foundation. July 1996 saw the presentation of *Concerto Grosso* for two violins and chamber orchestra, dedicated to Lord Yehudi Menuhin for his eightieth birthday celebration. *Letter to the Sun*, to the poetry of her daughter Julia Rafalski, was written the same year for narrator and percussion quartet. She also wrote a *Percussion Concerto* for **Evelyn Glennie**. Her commission *Scherzo di Fantasia*, for euphonium and orchestra, premiered at the 1997 International Women's Brass Conference in June. Next came the premiere of her saxophone concerto, *Charlie's Dream*, at the European Month of Culture Festival in Ljubljana, Slovenia (formerly Yugoslavia). A Chicago Symphony commission for the orchestral work *Inverted Mountain* was premiered March 2001, receiving eight performances. In December 2001, her music was featured in a *Donne in Musica* program in Rome. Her piano piece, *Pianophonia*, a commission from the Chicago Symphony for their contemporary music series MusicNOW, was premiered in their fifth season opener, February 16, 2005. Written for the World Congress of Violists, *ELEGIA Papa Giovanni Paolo* (Elegy for Pope John Paul II), who died April 2, 2005, was premiered in Reykjavik, Iceland, June 4, 2005. In October Ptaszyńska gave an acclaimed lecture on Polish statesman/composer/pianist **Jan Paderewski** (1860–1941) at the Thornton School of Music (USC) in conjunction with a concert of her music. She has also written for Poland's foremost contralto, **Ewa Podleś.**

On May 17, 2006, the American Academy of Arts and Letters in New York honored Marta with the Benjamin H. Danks Award for creative music achievements. Given to an exceptional composer of large works—symphonic, opera, oratorio, candidates are nominated by the 250 members of academy.

Multi-faceted Marta

Marta maintains a triple professional career as composer, percussionist and master teacher. With her interest in the younger generation of musicians, she serves as a juror at international competitions such as that in Geneva, Composers Contest of ASCAP, New York, and the Penderecki Contests for Performance of Contemporary Music in Kracow. She has performed as soloist and chamber player promoting contemporary music. She describes her composing style as "a connection of new sounds with tradition."

A resident of the U.S. since 1972, she lived in Pennsylvania with her husband Andrew Rafalski, from 1974 until 2000, when the family moved to Chicago. Daughter Julia, born 1981, was completing her masters in visual arts at the University College of London in 2006.

ELŻBIETA SIKORA was born in Lwów, October 20, 1944. She completed studies in sound engineering at the State Higher School of Music in Warsaw. From 1968–70, she studied electroacoustic music under Pierre Schaeffer and François Bayle at the Paris Groupe de Rechèrches Musicales. After her return to Warsaw, she took up composition studies with Tadeusz Baird and Zbigniew Rudziński. During her studies, together with Krzysztof Knittel and Wojciech Michniewski, in 1973 she formed the KEW composers' group, with which she toured in Poland, Sweden, Austria and West Germany. Since 1981, she has lived in Paris where she studied computer music at IRCAM (Institut de Recherché et Coordination Acoustique/Musique) and composition with **Betsy Jolas**. A recipient of grants from the French government, the city of Mannheim and the Kosciuszko Foundation, she worked under **John Chowning** for several months at the Center for Computer Research for Music and Acoustics (CCRMA), at Stanford. She is a professor at the conservatory in Angoulême, France, where she teaches electroacoustic music.

Her awards include winner of the Young Composers' Circle of the Polish Composers' Union Prize (1978), for *According to Pascal*; Weber Competition (Dresden, 1978, second prize) for her chamber opera *Ariadna*; Electroacoustic Music Competition (Bourges,1979–80), for *The Waste Land* and *Letters to M.*; and first prize in the GEDOK Competition (Mannheim, 1981), for *Guernica, hommage à Pablo Picasso*. The next decade brought the Prix de la Partition Pédagogique for *Chant'Europe*, and the Prix Stéphane Chaperlier- Clergue-Gabriel-Marie (both from SACEM, 1994), and the SACD Prix Nouveau Talent Musique (1996) in Paris for her opera *L'Arrache-coeur*. In 1997, Sikora was honored with one of her country's highest awards, Poland's Cavalier Cross of Merit. In 2000, she received a Prix Magistère from the Bourges Festival of Electroacoustic Music, and the Heidelberger Künstlerinnen-Preis. 2003 brought a special mention from the Académie du Disque Lyrique in Paris for a Le Chant du Monde recording. The same year she lectured and her music was again represented at the Gegenwelten Festival in Heidelberg.

Sikora's works, covering chamber, orchestral, choral, vocal, instrumental and electroacoustic, have been performed in Europe and America, at such venues as the Avignon Festival, Festival de Paris, Dresdner Musikfestspiele, "Fylkingen" in Stockholm and GMEB in Bourges, as well as at the "Warsaw Autumn" Contemporary Music Festival. She received a prestigious commission to write a cantata for the 100th anniversary of her home city of Gdańsk.

ANNA ZAWADZKA (married name Golosz) was born in Krakow, December 1, 1955. She graduated from the city's Music Academy, where she studied composition and theory with **Krystyna Moszumańska-Nazar**, and experimental music with Józef Patkowski. She collaborated with the Experimental Music Studio of Polish Radio in Warsaw, and continued studies at the Folkwanghochschule für Music, Theater und Tanz in Essen-Warden (Germany). Her compositions are primarily instrumental chamber music and electroacoustic works. She teaches composition and music theory at the Krakow Music Academy and Krakow Academy of Theater.

LIDIA ZIELIŃSKA was born in Poznań, October 9, 1953. After graduating from that city's State Higher School of Music in composition (1979), she was a violinist in the Poznań Philharmonic Orchestra and the **Agnieszka Duczmal** Chamber Orchestra. She also worked with the Eighth Day Theater in visual art, drama and experimental film, composing theater and film music. From 1978–87, she received prizes in Poland, Yugoslavia, Germany, Switzerland and France for her musical and multimedia pieces. She was artistic director of the "Poznań Music Spring" festival (1982–92), and composer-in-residence at the Electronic Music Studio in Stockholm (1995–96). A guest lecturer at summer courses throughout Europe and professor of composition at the Poznań Academy of Music, she has been on the board of the Polish Society for Contemporary Music, the Poznań branch of the Polish Composers' Union, "Warsaw Autumn" festival repertoire committee, and secretary of the Coordination Committee for Creative and Visual Art Circles.

Zielinska is president of the "House of World Rhythms" foundation and co-founder of the "Brevis" music editions and "Monochord" quarterly.

ROMANIA

MYRIAM MARBE, born April 9, 1931, in Bucharest, began piano with her mother Angela, and graduated from the Music Conservatory of Bucharest. From 1953–54, she was music editor at the Cinema Studio, then took a post as professor of composition at the conservatory (1954–88). She received many awards, including six first prizes from the Composers' Union of Romania, GEDOK in Mannheim (1961, 1966, 1970), Bernier Prize of the Académie des Beaux Arts, Paris (1972), and the Heidelberg Künstlerinnen prize (1977). Her early works reflect an avant-garde style, as in *Ritual for the Thirst of the Earth*, featuring musical sounds intermixed with words. Her Requiem *Fra Angelico - Chagall - Voronet*, draws on Latin, Byzantine, Hebrew and Romanian traditions. *Passages in the Wind* (1994) reflects the simpler, purified style seen in her later compositions. Other vocal works include *Time Rediscovered* and *Jocus Secundus*. Her orchestral works include a viola concerto and saxophone concerto, plus a large output of chamber pieces. She wrote articles for the periodical, *Muzica*, and an essay on the role of women in Romanian folklore, published by the Fifth International Congress on Women in Music. She died December 25, 1997. In 2000 a two-CD set of concert excerpts was released during a celebration of her work at the Nuremberg-Augsberg Academy of Music. Her Requiem received a 2003 performance in the Meistersinger Hall in Nuremberg.

Violeta Dinescu

VIOLETA DINESCU was born in Bucharest on July 13, 1953. As a girl in Romania, she thrived on what was the main *positive* aspect of the communist regime, that men and women were treated fairly equally. During studies at the George Enescu School and the Bucharest Conservatory (1973–78), there were sometimes more women than men in her classes. Her composition mentor, **Myriam Marbe**, encouraged her creativity and became a lifelong friend. An early work, *Anna Perenna* (1978), named after the Roman goddess of spring, a mythological symbol of reincarnation, follows experimental principles. The same year, she began teaching harmony, theory and counterpoint at the Enescu School (1978–82).

In 1982, she travelled to Germany to receive the GEDOK Composition Prize. She decided to stay. She had nothing but the few clothes she had brought with her. She recalls this as "a very dangerous way to force one's destiny . . . I lived in great tension . . . survival was my main activity." Though not personally subjected to gender bias, she joined women's organizations to support the cause of women in music.

As she established a reputation for her innovative style, Dinescu was invited to join the faculty of the Hochschule für Kirchenmusik (Church Music) in Heidelberg (1986–91), was an instructor of harmony and counterpoint at the Hochschule für Musik in Frankfurt (1989–91), and professor of theory, harmony and counterpoint at the Academy of Church Music in Bayreuth (1990–94), meanwhile guest lecturing internationally, including the U.S. and South Africa. Since 1996, she has been a composition professor at the Carl von Ossietzky University of Oldenburg (Germany).

Dinescu has won over fifty prizes from her native land (four Romanian Composers Union awards, 1975, '76, '80, '83), as well as Hungary, Poland, and Austria; Italy (third prize at the G.B. Viotti International Music and Dance Competition, 1983); Germany (second prize at the 1982 GEDOK), Carl Maria von Weber Preis for her opera *Hunger und Durst* (1985); the USA (first prize at the International Competition for Composers, Utah, 1983); and from Colombia (South America), South Africa, England and Canada. Many of these awards were won "anonymously," in that the competition judges did not know the gender of the entrant. Her compositions include orchestral and vocal pieces, chamber music and chamber ensembles, four operas and a children's opera, ballet and experimental music, and one film score, TABU, based on the 1931 silent film directed by F. W. Murnau (1888–1931). Her airy textures and feeling for subtle shifts of instrumental color are distinctive features of her flowing style, which includes an interweaving of her native Romanian folk music into an avant-garde approach, sometimes with long solo passages for voices alternating without interruption.

Her ballet, *Effi Briest*, premiered July 1998 at the Magdeburg Theater, Germany. Her 1999 premieres include: *Jardins Perdus*, a trio for flute, harp, piano; *Rondel*, for two recorders and piano, performed at the Expan 99 Festival in Spital, Austria; *Weil ich singen werde* for two choirs and ensemble of ancient instruments in May, at Heidelberg; *In Memoriam Myriam Marbe* for the Heidelberger Madrigal choir; and *Der 35 Mai*, (The 35th of May), a children's opera at Stuttgart Opera. In March 1999, she received the Composition Prize at the NYU International New Music Consortium (INMC). The same year, she conducted a workshop at the IGNM New Music Festival in Kärntnen, Austria. 2000 brought the premiere of *Tabar*, for percussion and large orchestra, a commission of the Mannheim Music Academy. 2001 premieres in Germany featured *Requiem for a 60th Birthday* for voices and ensemble; *Bekenntnis für Augustinius* (Recognition of Augustinius) for voice, violin, cello, saxophone and organ (May, in Mannheim); *Wenn Ich Die Wahrheit Sage* (When I Say the Truth—from a biblical text), for voice, horn, trumpet, trombone and organ, at the Munich Festival; and *Anthem for Zither Orchestra* at the Zither Festival, also in Munich. August saw the Bayreuth premiere of *Cronica Trovada Dos Indios* (text by Cecilia Meireles) for baritone and piano, and November featured workshops and concerts of her compositions at the *Weingartener Tage Für Neue Musik* (New Music Days). 2002 premieres included *Ichthys*, variations for flute, cello and piano, in Bamberg; three Songs based on poems by Brasilian Hilda Hilst in Bayreuth; *Et Veniens Veni* (voice with percussion and viola); *Laus Trinitati* (voice with percussion) both based on texts by Hildegard von Bingen; *Lullaby* (voice with percussion and viola), in Kassel; and her opera *Erendira* (text: Gabriel Garcia Marquez), at the State Theater of Oldenburg. She was represented at the Heidelberg Spring Festival in 2002 with *Flugspiele* for youth orchestra, and in 2003 with a Festival Fanfare for brass quintet with the Bamberger Symphony. Other 2003 world premieres were *Ismail Si Tirnavitu* (electric guitar and guitar) in Leipzig, and *Wie Tau Auf Dem Bergen Zions*, an Oratorio for choir and orchestra at Osnabrück, which was broadcast and recorded. Other CDs of her music were released this year. She organized a Composers Colloqium in 2005.

Ranked as one of the foremost women composers of Europe, Violeta is married to Romanian mathematician, Nicolae Manolache.

IRINA ODAGESCU was born in 1937 in Bucharest. With a love of music, she began piano at eight. She studied at Bucharest Music University (1957–63) and became a professor there. She has been secretary of the Composers and Musicologists Union of Romania since 1990, and was still in her position in 2006! Her composition awards include the Composers and Musicologists Union of Romania Prize (1978, 1979, 1981, 1986, 1998); silver medal for *Ballad* (female chorus) at the International Polyphonic Music Competition in Ibague (Colombia, 1981); medal and diploma from the International Composition Competition "Viotti-Valsesia," for *Sonata* for violin and piano (Vercelli, Italy, 1982); and the IGNM award at World Music Days in Graz (Austria, 1982) for choir poem *De doi*. 1990 she founded the 'Asociatia Nationala Corala din Romania' (The National Choral Association of Romania) with composer Dan Buciu. She was their vice president until 1998. In 1997, she received the Great Trophy awarded by the "Peace of Religions" Association for the choral poem, *Our Father*.

Irina is married to Teodor Tutuianu, professor of polyphony at Bucharest Music University.

DOINA ROTARU was born September 14, 1951, in Bucharest, to a musical mother who had studied at the Iasi University of Music. Doina started piano at five. Her studies at the University of Music, Bucharest, were 1970–1975. She earned her PhD in 1998.

She has been a composer and member in SACEM since 1985, member of the Romanian Association of Composers since 1977, and professor of composition at the Bucharest University of Music since 1990. Her awards include the Romanian academy prize 1986, and the Romanian Union of Composers prizes in 1981, '86, '89, '90, '92, '94, '97. Her works, besides chamber music and three string quartets, include three symphonies (1986, 1989, 2001), the second a first prize winner at the GEDOK Mannheim International Competition for Women Composers (1994). The third, *Spirit of the Elements*, a Tokyo Suntory Hall commission, premiered September

2001, with the Tokyo Philharmonic. Her four flute concertos are *Spiralis II* (1993), *Magic Circles*, a Radio France commission first performed in Paris, April 1995, *Florilegium*, premiered in The Hague, November 1996, with the French and Dutch Flute Orchestras, soloist Pierre-Yves Artaud, and *Wings of Light*, commissioned by the French Ministry of Culture and premiered by the French Flute Orchestra, Luxembourg, October 2000. Other works are a *Saxophone Concerto* (1993), *Cello Concerto* (1998), and *Percussion Concerto*, premiered in Taipei, Taiwan, January 2001.

CD releases are titled *The Magic Flutes, Spiralis II, Dor,* and *Magic Circles* and *Florilegium*, both by Romanian Radio Broadcasting. *Over Time*, for shakuhachi (a traditional bamboo flute), and bass flute, *Metamorphosis* (bass clarinet), *Troite* (trio), *Masks* (clarinet and cello), *Noesis* (four percussionists) are on an MPS English label. Her Flute Concerto No 1, Symphony No.2, and Saxophone Concerto are also recorded.

Doina married Mihai Rotaru, an engineer, June 22, 1974. Their daughter, Diana, born September 24, 1981, followed in her mother's footsteps to become a student at the Bucharest University of Music, where she studied composition, and graduated in 2005.

CORNELIA TĂUTU was born in Odorhei, Harghita County, March 10, 1938, inheriting her love of music from her mother who played the violin. Her childhood piano lessons were followed with studies in music theory, conducting and composition at the Ciprian Porumbescu Conservatory in Bucharest (1960–67), and postgraduate work at Long Island University (New York, 1971–72). Concurrently, she was a researcher at Bucharest's Ethnological and Dialectological Research Institute (1965–75). Her many awards include prizes for her music from the Association of Romanian Filmakers (ACIN, 1975, 1988), Romanian Film Festival for Youth, (Costinesti, 1977, 1984) and the Romanian Academy (1987). Her compositions spanning 1965–96 include concertinos, sonatas, divertimenti, chamber and piano music, vocal, choral, film and theater works.

Cornelia has a daughter, Gabriela Wulkan, born August 6, 1956, who is a counselor at the Emigration Department in Waren, Germany.

MARINA (Marta) **VLAD** was born March 8, 1949, in Bucharest. From early childhood, she was fascinated by her mother's piano playing, and would press the keys and listen to each sound. She started piano at four and violin at seven. Graduating in composition from Bucharest National University of Music (1973), with a prize for her cantata *Resonance*, she became a university assistant (1973–1991), and professor since 1991. She has been a member of the Union of Composers and Musicologists of Romania since 1981.

Her many compositions, recorded by Romanian Radio, began in 1978 with sonatas for violin and piano, works for string orchestra, string quartets and piano music in the '80s, adding woodwinds in the '90s and culminating in a series of "Still Lifes": *Still Life I for Oboe Solo*, 1996; *Still Life II for Clarinet Solo*, 1997; *Still Life III for Piano Solo*, 1997; *Still Life IV for Violin Solo*, 1998; *Still Life V for Viola Solo*, 1999; *Still Life VI for Cello Solo*, 2000; *Still Life VII for Flute Solo*, 2000; and *Still Life VIII for Bassoon*, 2001. Her music scores are printed by the Musical Publishing House, Bucharest.

Marina married composer Vlad Ulpiu on September 15, 1973. He is also a professor at the Bucharest National University of Music. Their son, Roman, born October 11, 1982, is a graduate of the George Enescu Lyceum of Music in Bucharest and composes and performs popular music.

Diana Voda-Nuteanu

DIANA VODA-NUTEANU was born December 1, 1967, to an engineer father and homemaker mother. Diana demonstrated an excellent singing voice by age three. By five, she was heard by a music school board and admitted at that tender age to begin learning music theory. Serious piano studies began at age seven. Her degrees are from the Music University in Bucharest: composition (1986–1990) and a masters (1991). She received several student awards between 1987–99. Like many of her colleagues, she began teaching at the same institution. Her subject is harmony. She earned her PhD in musicology in 2001. Her major compositions from 1987–2003 are *Sonatina* for piano, Quintet for wind instruments, *Hai-ku* for flute, *Exorcism* (wind quintet and mezzo soprano), *Hai-ku* for solo violin, *Dance* (three percussion instruments), *Old mint street* (large chamber ensemble), *Fleurs du champ* (Pan flute, C flute, G flute), and *Fibers* (Pan flute, three bassoons).

In 1999, she married Dr. Liviu Nuteanu, a neurosurgeon and specialist in bio-energy. Their lovely daughter, Doina, was born March 29, 2003.

MIHAELA Stănculescu **VOSGANIAN** was born May 7, 1961, in Ploiesti. With a music teacher mother, she began piano at five. Graduating from the Music University of Bucharest in 1985 with a degree in composition, she taught piano for the next five years at the Ploiesti Music School. Beginning in 1990, she became a lecturer in counterpoint at Bucharest Music University, at the same time getting her PhD in musicology with the dissertation *Polyphonic Typologies in the Romanian Creations of the Second Half of the 20th Century* (2000). Her awards number the G. Dima Composition Prize (1984, '85), Union of Romanian Composers Prize (1986), International New Music Consortium Award (1998), and Santa Cecilia Alba Adriatica Composition Prize (1999). She is president of ARFA (Romanian Association of Women in Art), a member of Union of Romanian Composers, International League of Women in Music (now IAWM), and is in the directory of the International Society of Contemporary Music, Romanian section. She has been an active participant at the International Composers' Workshop, Amsterdam, the British Association for Central and Eastern Europe in London and Huddersfield, *Ateneo De Musica y Danza*, Málaga, Spain (2001), a guest lecturer at the International Festival of Women Composers, Indiana University of Pennsylvania (1996, '98), and the Symposia and Festivals of *Donne in Musica*, Fiuggi, Italy (1997, '98, '99, 2001), the Eleventh IAWM Congress (London, 1999), and *Romanian Music Days* (Women's Contemporary Music, Bucharest 2001).

Vosganian's numerous compositions include music for solo instruments: *Evolutiv*, for double bass, premiered in Bucharest (1986), Sonata, for solo clarinet, premiered in Chisinou (1994), and *Sax-Suggestions*, for soprano saxophone, baryton (horn) and two alto mouthpieces (2001). Of her chamber music, *Reverberations* for trombone, percussion and live electronics, premiered during International Week of Contemporary Music, Bucharest (1997), and *Intro, Fugato and Synthesis* for organ premiered in London (1999). *Symphony I*, for three cadential groups of instruments and string orchestra, was premiered by the Ploiesti Philharmonic (1988), *Symphony II*, for organ, percussion and string orchestra, premiered in 1995, and *Saxophone Symphony-Concerto* (1998). *Essences*, concerti for flute(s) and orchestra (2000), were both premiered by the Bucharest National Radio Orchestra. Her choral works feature *De-a v-ati ascunselea*, a poem for mixed chorus, premiered in Bucharest (1995) and *Credo*, for mixed chorus, also premiered in the capital (1999). Other performances and commissions have been for concerts and festivals in Romania, Poland, England, Germany, Italy, Spain, Switzerland and America. Several CDs of her music have been recorded in Romania.

Vosganian is the founder of INTE-ART, a contemporary music and dance group with whom she tours throughout Europe (U.S., 1998; Italy, 2001; Switzerland, 2002), performing her music. In 2003, she was the director of the Thirteenth International Week of New Music.

In 1987, Mihaela married Varujan Vosganian, an economist and president of the Union of Armenians in Romania. Their daughter, Armine, was born May 22, 1992.

CZECH REPUBLIC

Slava Vorlova

SLÁVA VORLOVÁ was born March 15, 1894, in Náchod. Her father, Rudolf, founded the town band and her mother was her first piano teacher. Following the popular trend of the day, the family played four-hand arrangements of Beethoven, Schubert, Brahms and Dvořák symphonies. Sláva studied singing for a short time under Rosa Papier in Vienna, but lost her voice due to illness. Returning to her home town, which was evolving into a center of modern trends in art and music, she fell under the spell of Debussy and Ravel, whose influence became a common thread in her style. In 1916, her composition classes with Czech impressionist **Vítězslav**

Novák (1870–1949), and piano lessons with Francophile Václav Stepán, brought the music of **Milhaud**, **Honegger** and the early **Stravinsky** into her life. She passed the state examinations in 1918, but after marrying manufacturer Rudolf Vorel in 1919, discontinued composing until 1932. Up to the onset of WWII, she and her husband held informal musical evenings attended by well-known musicians such as cellist Milos Sádlo, pianist Frantisek Maxian and the Ondricek Quartet, which premiered her String Quartet Op. 1 (1933). The success of this work encouraged her, after the war, to continue her studies in piano and composition when the Prague Conservatory reopened in 1945.

During World War II, her music contributed to the morale of the resistance movement, especially the cantatas *Malicka zeime* (The Small Country, 1941) and a work for women's chorus *Bílá oblaka* (White Clouds), containing overtones of the national anthem. At the same time, her chamber works were gaining recognition in Europe. After the war, she graduated from Jaroslav Řidký's class at the Prague Conservatory (1948), having written *Symphony JM* Op.18, dedicated to Czech statesman-hero **Jan Masaryk** (1886–1948).

Encased Within the Iron Curtain

When the communist regime took power in the 1950s, Vorlová's artistic opportunities and social position were stifled. To avoid the frustration imposed by doctrinal mass culture, she turned to folk music and historical themes, as in the operas *Zlaté ptáče* (The Golden Bird, 1950), *Rozimarynka* (1953) and *Náchodska kasace* (Náchod Cassation, 1955). In an effort to earn money, she wrote songs and other compositions in jazz style, under the pseudonym Mira Cord, but these were never performed.

Sláva Vorlová was the first modern Czech composer to employ the trumpet and bass clarinet as solo instruments in concertos. During the '60s, she also wrote concertos for oboe, clarinet, cello, and a double concerto for trumpet and harp. Her later works used modernistic techniques without sacrificing melody. For *Bhukhar* (Feverish Birds, 1965), she devised her own numerological method for serial music, which produced some of her best works.

On her sixty-fifth birthday in 1959, she was given a decoration "For Outstanding Merit" by the Czech government for her remarkable and varied output. By age seventy-five, she had written exactly seventy-five works. She died August 24, 1973, in Prague.

A Precious Legacy

Vitezslava Kapralova

Encouraged by her father, composer Václav Kaprál, **VÍTĚZSLAVA KAPRÁLOVÁ**, born January 24, 1915, in Brno, began composing at age nine. At the Brno Conservatory (1930–35), and later at the Prague Conservatory, her composition and conducting teachers were the most prominent Czechs in the field: composers **Vilém Petrzelka** (1889–1967), a pupil of **Janáček**, **Václav Chalalbala** (1899–1962), **Vitezslav Novák** (1870–1949) and international maestro **Václav Talich** (1883–1961). Novák was at the time responsible for honing many outstanding young composers of Czech, Slovak, Yugoslav, Polish and Moravian music. He was the ideal teacher to nurture Kaprálová's budding talent that blossomed in her graduation project, a piano concerto, which she conducted. A French government scholarship brought her to Paris in 1937, where she immersed herself in the progressive cultural and political currents. She was one of the favorite pupils of **Charles Münch** (1891–1968), who later became conductor of the Boston Symphony, **Bohuslav Martinů** (1890–1959), a composer who, with **Leoš Janáček** and **Bedřich Smetana**, is considered the embodiment of Bohemian music, and briefly with **Nadia Boulanger**. Kaprálová was more than a student to Martinů. Several of their works show their influence on each other, e.g. Martinů's *Madrigaly*, and Kaprálová's *Koleda milostna*, (Love Carol); Martinů's *Tre ricercari* and Kaprálová's *Partita Op. 20*.

Kaprálová's output in Paris shows a mastery of contemporary music, tinged with a unique wistfulness. Major compositions of this period are *Six Variations on the Chimes of St. Étienne-du-Mont* for piano, *Partita* for piano and strings, the unfinished *Concertino* and orchestral *Suita rustica*, considered her best work.

In 1938, she conducted the BBC Symphony in her *Military Sinfonietta* with great success at the ISCM Festival in London. At the end of that year, she visited her home in Moravia, but the threat of World War II caused her to return to Paris in January 1939. She married Jirí Mucha, son of artist Alfons Mucha. During the evacuation of Paris, she fell ill, succumbing to miliary tuberculosis June 16, 1940, in Montpellier. Like Lili Boulanger, the promising career of Vítezslava Kaprálová was cut short by her death at twenty-five, by which age her music had already attained recognition for its originality and range of expression.

In 1946, the Czech Academy of Arts and Sciences awarded her membership *in memorium*, and in 1981 appraised her work as a distinctive and progressive moment in the development of Czech music. The Kápralová Society was founded in 1997, in Prague, to promote interest in her life and work. In 1998, the society was moved to Ontario, Canada, by its founding director Karla Hartl. The organization continues to promote interest in Kaprálová as well as other women in music.

Another Untoward Abbreviation

Born into an artistic family on September 13, 1930, in Prague, **JANA OBROVSKÁ** had a significant musical career which was also cut short. From 1949–55, she attended the Prague Conservatory, studying piano with Berta Kabelácová, theory with Jaroslav Řidký (1897–1956), and composition with **Emil Hlobil** (1901–87). Her graduation composition, *Piano Concerto No. 1*, was much acclaimed. She worked as an editor for the Supraphon music publishing house in Prague. Married to guitarist Milan Zelenka, her pieces for that instrument display an ethereal quality. *Passacaglia-Toccata* won at the International Guitar Competition in Paris in 1972, and her *Hommage à Béla Bartók* became the compulsory piece for the 1975 competition and found a place in the repertoire of European guitarists. Her output includes three piano concertos (1955, 1960, 1973), *Concertino meditativo* for guitar and strings (1971), *Concerto for Two Guitars* (1977), a *Concertino* for violin, viola, double bass and strings (1981), and chamber and vocal music also featuring the guitar, most of which enjoyed international success. She died April 4, 1987, in Prague.

Living Through Changing History

Sylvie Bodorova

SYLVIE BODOROVÁ, born December 31, 1954, in České Budějovice, grew up in a medical family environment, which provided a financially secure background for developing her musical gifts. She entered the Bratislava Conservatory in 1972, for piano and composition, then continued composition studies at the Janáček Academy in Brno (1974–79) under Ctirad Kohoutek, and at the Prague Academy of Musical Arts. Further work was with Franco Donatoni at the composition course at Siena, Italy (1981), and from 1987 with Ton de Leeuw in Amsterdam which completed her training. She taught briefly at the Brno Janáček Academy. 1994–96 were spent in America as composer-in-residence at the Cincinnati College Conservatory, although since 1982 she has lived in Prague, where she married Jiri Stilec in 1984.

Devoting herself exclusively to composing, she has won many prizes within the Czech Republic. In the 1980s, her compositions were often drawn from gypsy music. Beginning in the mid-'90s, her study of the work of J.S. Bach is reflected in her *Concerto dei fiori* for violin and orchestra, premiered at the 1997 Prague Spring Festival, and her transcriptions of Bach's *Prelude in c minor*, and *Toccata and Fugue in d minor* in arrangements for leading Czech soloists. She is also influenced by the European avant-garde, the Polish "school" and her own Hungarian roots which give her a strong sense of rhythm. But attempting to apply the principles of New Music conflicted with her natural musical instincts and aesthetic feelings. The results of re-thinking her approach are in *Passion Plays* for viola and orchestra (1982), *Pontem Video, Struggle with the Angel*, and the string quartet *Dignitas Homini*. All of which met with deserved recognition.

Her 1998 *Terezín Ghetto Requiem*, for baritone and string quartet, was written for the Warwick Festival in Great Britain and subsequently performed at Wigmore Hall (London), Norwich and Leicester. In Germany, it was performed in Munich and at the Deutsche Oper (Berlin) as part of the tenth anniversary celebrations of the fall of the Berlin Wall, November 8,1999. The work was heard also in Prague in 1998 and two years later at the Prague Spring Festival. It has now successfully entered the international string quartet repertoire. By 2000 it had come to America.

Sylvie Bodorová is a member of the eminent group of four Czech composers, Quattro, with Otmar Macha, Zdeněk Lukáš and Luboš Fišer (1935–99). She also chairs the committee of the foundation of the Czech performing rights society, OSA.

MARTA JIRÁČKOVÁ, born March 22, 1932, in Kladno, spent her childhood in an art-loving family. She studied composition (1952–58) at the Prague Conservatory with **Emil Hlobil**, and from 1962–64 modern harmony and composition with **Alois Hába** (1893–1973), whose teaching, together with her friendship with **Sláva Vorlová**, proved significant to her development as a composer. Her postgraduate study was at the Janáček Academy of Performing Arts in Brno with Ctirad Kohoutek and Alois Piňos (1976–78).

Marta was married in 1964 to conductor Václáv Jiráček, by whom she was greatly influenced and with whom she had two daughters. Her husband died in a tragic accident. She worked for more than thirty years as a music editor for Czechoslovak Radio in Prague, which provided great enrichment of musical knowledge, and encouraged her to write electroacoustic music. Most of this is for film, television and radio.

Her works number more than forty compositions covering, with the exception of concertos, virtually all other musical genres. Her interest in the use of the human voice as a musical instrument is heard in compositions such as her cycle of choruses, *Eight Wonders of the World* (1976), *Three Songs Without Lyrics* and the ballet, *Loď bláznů* (The Ship of Fools, 1991), which won a Czech Music Fund Prize.

As a mother of two daughters, Marta creatively considers the role of women. This is a central theme in the electroacoustic ballet variation *Five Times A Woman* (1992), and other pieces. Her first symphony, *Nanda Devi*, portrays the tragic fate of a young mountaineer Nanda Devi Unsoeld, who died while ascending the Himalayan mountain of the same name.[24] Her musical style, based on 20th century music linked with European musical tradition, reflects her efforts to write comprehensive music as illustrated by her Second Symphony, *Silbo*.

Jiráčková also wrote significant works in the field of educational music, as her song cycle *A Fairy-Tale Train* and the collection of piano studies, *The World of Children*, performed at educational concerts. As a reaction to the political regime which overshadowed so much of her lifetime, her artistic credo has been to protest against inhumanity whenever it occurs and write music to help restore the purity of the human spirit.

Born March 8, 1941, in Chlumec nad Cidlinou, **IVANA LOUDOVÁ** studied composition at the Prague Conservatory and the Academy of Music and Dramatic Arts, with two of the outstanding representatives of modern Czech music, **Miloslav Kabeláč** (1908–79)—she was his class assistant from 1968 to 1972—and **Emil Hlobil**. A scholarship enabled graduate study in Paris under **Olivier Messiaen** and **André Jolivet** (1905–74), and at the experimental studio Centre Bourdan attached to ORTF. In 1973, she married Miloš Haase. They have one son.

Her contemporary compositional techniques are heard in the varied genre of her works—orchestral, chamber and vocal—eliciting exciting new sounds from winds in *Magic Concerto, Luminous Voice, Per tromba, Quintetto giubiloso, The Sleeping Countryside, Hymnos*, and three concertos with solo percussion. She also writes for film, stage, and children. Her inspiration runs the gamut from Italian renaissance—*Meeting with Love, Italian Triptych*—to modern Czech poetry.

---

24. Nanda Devi's American mountaineer and wilderness explorer father, Willi Unsoeld (1926–79), had named his daughter after the mountain, said to be the highest peak in India and home of the Goddess Nanda. He lost his life two years later in an avalanche on a winter expedition up Mt. Rainier in Washington state.

Recipient of numerous awards, Loudová won a prize for her *Rhapsody in Black* (GEDOK competition, Mannheim, 1967), three prizes in the Guido d'Arezzo competition for *Sonetto per voci blanche* (1978), *Italian Triptych* (1980), *Occhi lucenti e belli* (1984), and awards at the Jihlava and Jirkov competitions in Moscow (1978) and Olomouc, Czechoslovakia (1983). Two radio plays have received awards, and her *Lieder auf der Flucht* won first prize in the women composers' competition at Unna (1987). Since 1992, she has been teaching composition at the Academy of Music and Dramatic Arts in Prague, and in 1996 founded "Studio N" for the further development of contemporary music. She also won two prizes at the Mannheim international competition for women composers in 1994, first prize at the Bratislava chamber music competition in 1996 and the Wolfgang Zippel prize in 1997.

ELENA PETROVÁ, born November 9, 1929, in Modrý Kameň, did not follow a direct path to success as a composer. Gifted in playing the piano, and fluency in foreign languages, she studied aesthetics and musicology at Charles University, Prague, where she subsequently devoted a life career teaching music theory. Further courses were in her native Slovakia, studying piano with Karel Hoffmeister at the College of Arts and Music, and composition under Jan Kapr at the Janáček Academy of Music in Brno.

Her main creative focus was vocal and dramatic music, for which she wrote her own texts and scenarios. Her works include an opera, *Kdyby se slunce nevrátilo* (Suppose the Sun Did Not Return), several ballets, a symphony and other orchestral music. She won many prizes in her own country and abroad. She died in 2002.

Historical Haunting of Czech Music

One of the most insidious deceptions of Hitler propaganda was perpetrated in the small city of Terezín, northwest of Prague. Originally built in 1780 by the Emperor Joseph II and named for his mother, Maria Teresia, it is known in German as Theresienstadt.

In World War II the world was hoodwinked into believing that this "camp" was a place built for the "protection" of Jews brought from all countries of Europe. Noted leaders, writers, artists and musicians were sent there for "safekeeping." A film was made showing "idyllic" conditions there. The *one visit* by a Red Cross representative found a row of shops filled with food and goods—that the residents had never seen before and would never see again! Several inmates were dressed and rehearsed for the occasion. The favorable report fooled the world for years! In reality, Terezín was a way station to the death chambers of the other concentration camps. The final toll from there was 97,297 dead, among whom were 15,000 children. Only 132 children are known to have survived!

Why Terezín will continue to haunt generations to come is that the enormous number of musicians sent there was enough to fill two large symphony orchestras, plus many chamber groups. To keep up the sham, Nazi authorities permitted a wide range of cultural activities, including an active schedule of musical performances—an almost daily soul-sustaining diversion. Despite the conditions, distinguished artists continued creating, but in the end the death list of Terezín residents sent to Auschwitz contains some of the foremost Czech composers' names of the first part of the 20th century. Among them was **Erwin Schulhoff** (1894–1942), who fled to Russia, but was murdered. Camp victims were **Viktor Ullmann** (1898–1944), director of all musical activities there, **Pavel Haas** (1899–1944), **Hans Krása** (1899–1944), and the youngest, **Gideon Klein** (1919–45), who was mistakenly shot in the turmoil of the Liberation.

The most famous work to come out of Terezín was Hans Krása's *Brundibar* (the Bumble Bee), a children's operetta which received an astounding fifty-four performances for both inmates and jailers. This, and other compositions were resurrected in the '90s and are now being played throughout Europe and America.[25] The discoveries of manuscripts, writings and art from all the camps continues to this day. (See Bibliography: *Music at Terezín: 1941–1945*.)

---

25. English born, Canadian violinist/composer **Ruth Fazal** wrote her *Terezin Oratorio* based on poems by captive children. Premiered in Toronto, November 2003, it has been performed in Prague, Vienna, Bratislava, Israel (May 2005, during the sixtieth anniversary of the Holocaust) and at Terezín itself. A U.S. tour is planned 2006–07.

RUSSIA

VALERIJA BESEDINA was born August 29,1964 in Lvov (Ukraine). Her father was a former navy officer and her mother a teacher of world culture at Moscow Pedagogical University. Valerija began piano at age five. From 1971–81, she attended the Lvov special children's music school named after pianist Krushelniskaja. 1981–83 found her in the composition class of professor Tihon Hrennikov in the Central Special Musical School attached to the Tchaikovsky Conservatory in Moscow. From 1983–89, she studied at the conservatory. In 1985, she won the All Russia Competition for Young Composers.

Her compositions include the ballets *Goja*, *VIJ* (after Gogol), *Sulamith*, (1997), and *The fire virgin*, a rock opera-ballet (1998); two children's musicals (1991, 2001); two concertos, for cello and orchestra and trumpet and orchestra; radio and film music, plus compositions for other instruments.

Valerija is married to bassist Maxim Palej, a competition winner and performer at Ekaterinburg's opera and ballet theater. Their son, Svjatoslav, was born April 30, 1992. He enjoys music and theater. In 2002, he won the regional competition for young narrators.

ELENA FIRSOVA was born March 21, 1950, in Leningrad (St. Petersburg) into a family of physicists. She began composing at twelve. Four years later she entered music college, and in 1970 the Moscow Conservatory, where for the next five years she studied composition and analysis. Twenty compositions from her student days are still in her repertoire.

Her music was first heard outside the Soviet Union in 1979, when her *Sonata for solo clarinet* was performed in Cologne, and her *Petrarca's Sonnets* in Paris and Venice. The following year *Petrarca's Sonnets* was heard in England, performed by the London Sinfonietta, which led to a commission by the BBC for *Earthly Life*, premiered by the Nash Ensemble in November 1986.

Within the next few years, as changes occurred internationally and personally, and as soon as travel barriers were removed, Elena and her husband, composer Dmitry Smirnov, left Moscow, arriving in London in April 1991 with their two young children.[26] They survived financially by writing music on commission—Firsova completing six works in 1991 alone—and by means of short-term residency invitations from Cambridge University and Dartington College of Arts. In January 1993, they began a long-term connection with the music department at the University of Keele. In 1998 they became British subjects. Her *Nostalgia* for orchestra was first performed at the Festival of Women's Music in Hamburg in 1992, *Crucifixion* for Cello and Bayan was heard in Dresden in 1994, and her chamber operas, *The Nightingale*, *Forest Walks*, and *Before the Thunderstorm* were given their premieres by the Nash Ensemble who, together with the BBC, have been stalwart champions of her music.

From the beginning of her career, Firsova's compositions have, like short stories, developed in a single unbroken span, many not more than fifteen minutes. Her larger-scale works, for violin, cello, flute and piano, are mostly in *concertante* forms. Apart from one opera, *Feast in Plague Time*, her works for vocal, choral, instrument, chamber, and solo instrument with orchestra, avoid the dramatic and programmatic. Her now considerable output features, vocal, choral, piano, orchestral and chamber music. She has also written for stage, screen, and some music for television in collaboration with her husband.

SOFIA Asgatovna **GUBAIDULINA** was born in Chistopol, in the Tatar Republic, October 24, 1931. A Russian composer of unique individuality, she is descended from a Tatar father and a Russian-Jewish mother. (Her grandfather was a *mullah*—a religious teacher.) Her sources of inspiration are similarly diverse, extending from mystical Eastern elements to the Catholic and Russian Orthodox. She studied piano and composition at the Kazan Conservatory (1949–54), and composition with Nikolai Peyko, assistant of Shostakovich. Her post-graduate work

---

26. One of their daughters, Alissa Firsova, born July 24, 1986 in Moscow, is an up and coming pianist who has already played at Buckingham Palace (2000). She studied with Tatiana Kantorovich (1994–99) and Steven Kovacevich before going on to the Purcell School of Music. On February 10, 2001, she played the world premiere of *String of Destiny* (4th Piano Sonata) by her father, at St. Albans Music Club. By 2003, several of her compositions had been performed.

Sofia Gubaidulina

was under Vissarion Shebalin at the Moscow Conservatory (1954–63). After completing her education, she worked primarily as a freelance composer in Moscow, including writing for films, and was briefly a staff member at the Moscow Experimental Electronic Studio (1969–70).

In 1975, together with Viktor Suslin and Vyacheslav Artyomov, she founded the Astreya Ensemble, which specialized in improvising on rare Russian, Caucasian, Central Asian and East Asian folk and ritual instruments. These hitherto unknown sounds, timbres and ways of experiencing musical time had a profound influence on her creativity. Since the early 1980s, her works have been performed widely in western countries. With Edison Denisov (*b* 1929), Alfred Schnittke (*b* 1934), and Valentin Silvestrov (*b* 1937), she is seen to be one of the leading representatives of New Music in the former Soviet Union.

Between 1990–92, festivals of her music took place in Russia, Japan, Italy and Germany. In 1992, she moved to Germany, living near Hamburg, and is a member of the Akademie der Künste in Berlin, and the Freie Akademie der Künste.

Gubaidulina made her first visit to North America in 1987 as guest of Louisville's "Sound Celebration." She returned as featured composer of many festivals, including Boston's "Making Music Together" (1988), Vancouver's "New Music" (1991) and Tanglewood (1997). Other acclaimed performances include the retrospective concert by Continuum (New York, 1989) and world premieres of the commissioned works *Pro et Contra* (Louisville Orchestra, 1989), *String Quartet No. 4* (Kronos Quartet, Carnegie Hall, 1994), *Dancer on a Tightrope* with Robert Mann and Ursula Oppens (Washington, DC, 1994), *Alleluia* for orchestra and chorus by the American Symphony in Avery Fisher Hall, and *Figures of Time* for orchestra by the City of Birmingham Symphony. In 1995, her *Concerto for Bassoon and Low Strings* was played by the Chamber Music Society of Lincoln Center, *Music for Flute, Strings and Percussion* by the Orchestre National de France in Paris, *Stimmen Verstummen . . .* (Stilled Voices), Symphony in 12 Movements, by the Tanglewood Music Center Orchestra, and *Concerto for Two Orchestras* for Symphony and Jazz Band with the Berkeley Symphony under **Kent Nagano**. 1997 brought the Viola Concerto, commissioned by Yuri Bashmet, with the Chicago Symphony, also conducted by Kent Nagano. On April 29, 1999, *Two Paths* (*Dedication to Mary and Martha*), commissioned by Tomoko Masur, a former violist and wife of maestro **Kurt Masur**, with viola solos performed by **Cynthia Phelps** and **Rebecca Young**, was premiered by the New York Philharmonic. Simultaneously, Japan's NHK Symphony Orchestra, with soloist Kazue Sawai under the baton of Charles Dutoit, toured the U.S. with the American premiere of *In the Shadow of the Tree*, for koto, bass koto, zheng—a twenty-one stringed lap harp whose origin dates back 2,400 years—and orchestra. The new millennium brought *Johannes-Passion* (in Russian), for soprano, tenor, baritone, bass, two choruses, orchestra (2000) and *Risonanza* for three trumpets, four trombones, organ and six strings (2001).

Among her numerous awards are the Rome International Composers Competition (1974), Prix de Monaco (1987), Koussevitzky International Record Award for her violin concerto *Offertorium* (1989) and her symphony, *Stimmen verstummen . . .* (1994), *Premio Franco Abbiato* (1991), Künstlerinnenpries (Woman Composers Prize, Heidelberg, 1991), Russian State Prize (1992), Kulturpreis des Kreises Pinneberg (1997), Praemium Imperiale (Japan, 1998), Sonning Prize (Denmark, 1999), Preis der Stiftung Bibel und Kultur (1999), Stockholm Concert Hall Foundation's Honorary Medal in Gold (2000), Germany's Order of Merit (2000), and the Goethe Medal of the City of Weimar (2001).

Gubaidulina's music is published in North America by G. Schirmer, Inc., and is well represented on CD with major releases on the DG, Chandos, Philips, Sony Classical, BIS, and Berlin Classics labels, with such artists as **Gidon Kremer**,[27] violin, with the Boston Symphony, and cellist **Yo-Yo Ma**.

---

27. Gidon Kremer (*b* 1947), brilliant Latvian violinist, contributes to modern music in his presentation of new works of Soviet composers, especially those of Schnittke and Gubaidulina.

SVETLANA LAVROVA was born July 19, 1980 in Leningrad (St. Petersburg). Her father is a musician, and her mother, a fashion decorator and amateur musician. Svetlana began piano at age five and later, organ. Following the St. Petersburg Conservatory's Lyceum, she attended the conservatory (1988–94), with post-graduate work (1995–98). She then took a one-year course at the Royal Koninklijk Conservatory in Holland in The Hague. Her compositions include *Concerto-pyramis* (1993) for string quartet and orchestra, an opera, *In Expectation of Rainbows* (2001), a *Trio-concerto* for harp, piano, percussion and orchestra (2001), *Terrible Fairytale* for orchestra (2002), and *Communal Requiem* (2002), with texts by D. Charms and Eliot. Her husband is also a musician. Their daughter, Voynova Zlata, was born in 1997.

SOFIA LEVKOVSKAJA was born November 25, 1965, in Leningrad (St. Petersburg). Encouraged by her father, she began piano at age three. She studied piano at children's musical school, choir conducting in college, and composition at the Leningrad Conservatory, finishing postgraduate work in 1993, the same year she received a prize from the American Acoustic Society. Her works include *Concerto for Orchestra* (1993), ballet, *Africa* (1999), Concerto for Choir, *Alleluia* (2001), *Formula of Spring* (2002), plus film and electronic music. Her husband is also a composer, writing songs and music for theater. Their son, Lev, was born in 1998.

OLGA MAGIDENKO, born in Moscow, May 9, 1954, graduated from the Moscow Conservatory with distinction as a pianist, and in 1979 with distinction as a composer, having studied with the famed **Aram Khachaturian** (1903–78). She was a member of the Union of USSR Composers. In 1989, she spent a five month residency at Stetson University (Deland, Florida). In 1994, she was artist-in-residence for the Stipendium Arno Schmidt in Germany. She now lives in Heidelberg. Her major works include *Trio Two Esse* (clarinet, viola, cello), Trio Op. 15 (clarinet, viola, piano), Symphony No. 3 *Pianto*, (string orchestra), Nonet Op. 30, and *Einsiedler* (string quartet and soprano). She was the winner of the Gegenwelten (Heidelberg) Women Composers Prize in 2002.

OLGA PETROVA was born in Leningrad in 1956. Both her parents were musicians and exposed her to classical music, starting her on piano at age five. She attended the Special Music School of the Leningrad Conservatory, graduating from the conservatory in 1979, having won the All-Russian Competition of Young Composers in 1978. Starting in 1978 with a chamber cantata, she has composed a ballet, two operas, three symphonies, a concerto for clarinet and chamber orchestra, and a musical, *The Stork Caliph*, for the St. Petersburg Musical Comedy Theater (1998). Married since 1981, her son, Peter, was born the same year and her daughter, Manana, in 1982.

IRINA TSESLJUKEVITCH was born in Belorussia on February 25, 1955, to a doctor mother and engineer father. With music always in the home, Irina began piano at seven and flute at twelve. She attended the Special Children's music school attached to the Leningrad Conservatory (1967–74) and entered the conservatory in 1974, remaining through postgraduate studies until 1982. Her awards are from the Young Composers Competition (Leningrad, 1976), and the All-Russian Competition of Young Composers (1980). Her works include music for movies and theater, chamber music, a ballet, *The Ugly Duckling*, plus the operas *The End of Casanova* (1987), *Let's Travel Along the Limpopo* (1988), and *The History of the Dwarf Jakov and Princess Mimi* (1998). Her husband, Jurij, whom she married in 1984, works at the Hermitage Museum. Her daughters are Anne, born in 1976, and Sofia, 1985.

Galina Ustvolskaya

GALINA Ivanovna USTVOLS'KAYA was born on June 17, 1919, in Petrograd—the name of St. Petersburg before it became Leningrad upon the death of Lenin in 1924. She studied at the college attached to the Leningrad Conservatory (1937–39) and then with the great **Dmitri Shostakovich** (1906–77) at the conservatory itself (1937–47), where they maintained a close, and closely guarded, relationship until 1956 with his unexpected marriage to Margarita Kainova. After an interruption for military hospital service during World War II, Ustvols'kaya was appointed to teach composition at the college in 1947. She remained until 1975. Shostakovich so admired her work he sent some of his own unfinished works to her for comment. He incorporated quotations from her Trio for clarinet, violin and piano (1949) into his Fifth String Quartet and into his *Michelangelo Suite* no. 9.

Her catalogue runs to twenty-one works, including five symphonies, six piano sonatas, and a number of chamber works, ranging from her Piano Concerto (1946) to her Symphony No. 5 (1990). She concentrated on writing for instruments, although some of her symphonies include voice, and are composed for unusual combinations of soloists, while maintaining that these are *not* chamber works. Her music, while not religious in a liturgical sense, is infused with a religious spirit, invoking Gregorian plainsong, Russian Orthodox chant and the mourning ritual of folk traditions.

Despite her modernism and dissonant music, Ustvol'skaya needed to survive and was forced to come to an arrangement with the State, writing charming pieces in the best socialist/realist tradition, including songs and movie music.

Galina strongly felt that, "no distinction should be made between the music of men and women. If there are festivals of music by women, should there not also be festivals of music by men?" Critics have commented on the masculinity in many of her scores: "Few men, let alone women, have written music this violent." Coincidentally, she dislikes having her music performed by women.

TATYANA VORONOVA was born in Leningrad January 12, 1932, and began piano at age four. Her grandfather was the cantor of the synagogue in Riga (Latvia), her mother is a philologist, and her father, an engineer. A graduate of the Special Children's school of the St. Petersburg Conservatory, she graduated from the conservatory proper in 1957 with degrees in piano and composition, and began teaching chamber ensemble. She was named an Official of Culture of the Russian Federation. Her works include a concerto for piano and orchestra, a chamber cantata, a piano sonata, six vocal series, two string quartets, two sonatas for violin and piano, a sonata for two violins, and three sonatas for flute and violin. Divorced, her ex-husband, Rane Laul, is a composer and professor at the St. Petersburg Conservatory. They have a daughter, Maria.

SLOVAKIA

PETRA BACHRATÁ was born in 1975, in Krupina. Between 1992 and 2000 she studied medicine at the Comenius University in Bratislava, and composition at the Academy of Performing Arts in Bratislava. In 1997, she took composition courses at IRCAM, Paris, with Brian Ferneyhough and Ivana Loudová.

She participated in the International Composition and Interpretation Project "Music Without Borders in the Heart of Europe" (1999, 2000), and in 2001 won the Ján Levoslav Bella Prize for her chamber work *Ontogenesis*. Since 2000, she has been a doctor at the Faculty Hospital in Bratislava.

O'GA DANÁŠOVÁ, born July 16, 1961, in Hnúšťa, studied composition, conducting and piano at the Music Academy (1977–82), and composition at the Academy of Music and Drama (1982–89), both in Bratislava. After working as an editor at the music publisher OPUS, she became a teacher at the Private Slavic Secondary School (Bratislava), conducting both a children's choir and chamber choir. In 1998, she began postgraduate studies at the Pedagogical Faculty of Comenius University in classical harmony and arrangements. She writes chamber and folk music adaptations for schools.

VIERA JANÁRČEKOVÁ, born September 23, 1941, in Svit, studied piano at the State Conservatory in Bratislava (1956–61) and piano and harpsichord at the Academy of Music and Drama in Prague (1962–67). For the next fourteen years she was a teacher, concert soloist, recording and radio artist. She moved to Germany in 1972, residing near Kassel, and since 1981 has been a freelance composer of orchestral, chamber and choral works, plus music for radio.

As both composer and painter, she has evolved from the traditional to the experimental with commissions and radio presentations evincing recognition of her works which include *Orie*, (recorder quartet) *Janik*, *Heftige Landschaft mit dreizehn Bäumen* (string orchestra), Piano Concerto (1991), *Hymnos an Vater Lärm* (mezzo and percussion), and Christmas music for voice, violin and viola (1995). Two radio plays have received awards, and her *Lieder auf der Flucht* won first prize in the women composers' competition at Unna in 1987. She also won two prizes at the Mannheim international competition for women composers in 1994, first prize at the Bratislava chamber music competition in 1996 and the Wolfgang Zippel Prize in 1997.

OĽGA KROUPOVÁ was born 1966 in Bratislava. She earned a composition degree from the conservatory there (1988), and was then employed by the scores archive of the Slovak Music Fund. She continued studies in composition at the Bratislava Academy of Music and Drama, and the Liszt Academy in Budapest (1991–94), where she studied electronic composing and served an internship in the Hungarian Radio electronic studio. Between 1994–96, she completed postgraduate studies in composing at the Hochschule für Musik in Detmold, Germany, where she has lived since 1996, working as a freelance composer specializing in electroacoustic chamber works.

LUCIA PAPANETZOVÁ, born 1978, in Lučenec, completed her studies in sacred music, choir conducting and organ at the Ján Levoslav Bella Conservatory in Banská Bystrica (1997). Her first encounter with composing came as part of her studies of church music. She completed her composing degree at the Academy of Music and Drama in Bratislava (2003). She composes choral works for chamber orchestra, and in 2003 won the Ján Levoslav Bella Prize for *Passacaglia*.

ĽUBICA SALAMON-ČEKOVSKÁ was born March 16, 1974 in Humenné. She completed degrees in Musicology (1998) and Composition (2000) at the Academy of Music and Drama, Bratislava. Following summer classes for young composers in Poland with **Krzysztof Penderecki** (*b*1933), she completed postgraduate studies at the RAM, London, with Paul Patterson (*b*1947). She is a teaching assistant at the Academy of Music and Drama, composing choral chamber works.

IRIS SZEGHY, born May 5, 1956 in Prešov, studied composition and piano at the Košice Conservatory (1971–76). Continuing studies were at the Academy of Music and Drama, Bratislava, graduating in composition 1981. Following a short teaching career, she returned to AMD earning a PhD in composition (1989).

She won fellowships that took her to Budapest (1989), Warsaw (1991), and Stuttgart, where she was composer-in-residence at the Akademie Schloss Solitude. Other visiting composer residencies were at the University of California, San Diego (1994), Steim Studio (Amsterdam, 1995), Hamburg Opera (1995), and one year at the Künstlerhäuser Worpswede (Germany, 1999). In 2001, she received a composer's commission from the Helvetia Foundation in Zurich, which included a two-month stay at the Künstlerhaus Boswil (Switzerland).

Since 1990, Szeghy has been a freelance composer, writing numerous pieces for orchestra, chamber orchestra and choir, and as of this writing is working on an opera.

In 2002, she had a wonderful excuse for not being present for the performance of one of her pieces at the "Warsaw Autumn" festival. She wrote, "I am getting married on September 19, and on the day of the concert I shall be on my honeymoon."

LARISA VRHUNC, born in 1967 in Ljubljana, studied music education (1985–90) and composition (1989–93) at the city's Music Academy, then composition and orchestration at the Geneva Conservatory (1994–96). She completed her composition studies at the Conservatoire National Supérieur in Lyon (France, 1999). She has participated in compositional courses given by **Sofia Gubaidulina**, Brian Ferneyhough, Maurice Jarrell, Klaus Huber, Helmut Lachenmann, Hanspeter Kyburz and Pascal Dusapin, plus training in computer music at IRCAM in Paris.

Her works for chamber orchestra, solo instruments, and chorus have been performed at numerous concerts and festivals in Slovenia and abroad, and recorded for Slovene Radio and television. She has won many prizes at these festivals, including the European Women Composers' Contest in Nijmegen (Holland).

Vrhunc is a professor of music analysis and instrumentation at the Department of Musicology of the University of Ljubljana.

UKRAINE

LARA LEVINA was born February 5, 1906 in Simferopol (Crimea). She graduated with a gold medal from the Odessa Conservatory, and in 1932 from the Moscow Conservatory, where she studied piano with Felix Blumenfeld (1863–1931) and composition with Nikolai Miaskovsky (1881–1950) and Reinhold Glière (1875–1956).

In her youth in Odessa, she was overwhelmed by the music of Rachmaninoff, Scriabin and Prokofiev, as well as Beethoven and Schumann, whose influence can be heard in her works. Her style was melodic, lyrical and personal as evidenced in her vocal music (more than 200 romances) and vocal miniatures for children. Her heroic and passionate spirit of the 1930s was extended to light music in the late 1940s, although children's music was always a central motif. A spirit of patriotism pervaded her tragic monologues of the war years, and in the severe and mournful romances based on African poetry that comprised her output during the 1960s. Simple melodies and delicate harmonies are stamped with her individuality of fine detail, supple modulation and varied texture. Besides vocal music, there are two piano concertos and chamber music for solo instruments and combinations with piano.

Levina died June 27, 1976 in Moscow.

SVITLANA AZAROVA, born January 9, 1976, in Izmail (Odessa region), graduated from Izmail Pedagogical Institute (1996), and as a composer in 2000 from Odessa State A.V. Nezhdanova Conservatory (now Musical Academy). She attended International summer master-courses in the Czech Republic (1996, 1997), held by composers such as Marek Kopelent (*b* 1932), Paul Méfano (*b* 1937), Jean-Ives Busser, and Zygmunt Krauze (*b* 1938).

She has participated in the festivals "On the Threshold of the 21th Century" (Nizhnij Novgorod, Russia, 1999), "Informal Meeting of European Composers" (Baku, Azerbaijan, 2000; Krakow, Poland, 2001), "International Forum of Young Composers" (Kiev, Ukraine, 2001), International Festival of Modern Art "Two Days and Two Nights of New Music"

Svitlana Azarova

(Odessa, Ukraine, 2001–02), and Creative Youth Forum (Kiev, 2002).

Her works, written in various genres, including chamber, solo instruments, instruments with piano, and a symphonic poem for large symphony orchestra, have been performed in Russia, Italy, Poland, Lithuania and Ukraine.

Azarova is a member of the Association New Music (Ukraine Section of ISCM) and Ukrainian Composers' Union.

LESIA DYCHKO, born October 24, 1939, in Kiev, graduated from the Kiev M.V. Lysenko Secondary Musical School in theory (1959) and from Kiev State Tchaikovsky Conservatoire (now National Musical Academy of Ukraine) in composition (1964). She finished her postgraduate studies in Moscow (1971). She also attended lectures on art studies at Kiev Artistic Institute (1968–1972), and theater history at Kiev Theatre Art Institute (1966–1969).

From 1972–94 she lectured in music history at Kiev Pedagogical Institute and Kiev Artistic Institute (now Arts Academy). Since 1965, she has been in the Studio of the Honoured Ukrainian State Bandura Players Choir, and has been a docent at the National Musical Academy

Lesia Dychko

of Ukraine in composition and music theory since 1994. In 1989, she lectured about contemporary Ukrainian choral music in Canada.

She is a member of the Ukrainian Musical Fund (1973–), Coordinating Council of the All-Ukrainian Musicians' Union, Organizing Committees of the festivals "Kiev-Music-Fest," "Premieres of the Season," and the Choral Festival "Zolotoverkhyi Kiev." She has been on the jury of the World Choral Competition for Contemporary Music (Debrezen, Hungary), the Choral M.Leontovych Competition, and head of the jury of the Choral Forum of Ukrainian Christian Youth (Kiev, Ukraine, 1999). A member of the Ukrainian State T.G. Shevchenko Prize Committee and Committee of Ministry of Culture and Arts of Ukraine, Dychko collaborated with Kiev Patriarchy organizing the Centennial Patriarch Mstyslav concerts and "Spiritual Youth Week" concerts.

She has written three ballets, choral works, a symphony and vocal symphony, chamber music, four cycles of sacred music for organ and soloists, vocal cycles for voice and chamber orchestra, music to films and animated films, and forty-five songs. With her preferred genre of choral music, she continues the Ukrainian tradition of religious music, her style uniting features of Ukrainian folk and church choral singing. Her works are performed at choral festivals, competitions and concerts in America, Canada, France, Great Britain, Germany, the Netherlands, Belgium, Denmark, Spain, Italy, Hungary, Bulgaria, Poland, Russia and Ukraine.

Dychko's honors include first prize at the All-Union Young Composers' Competition (Moscow, 1962, 1969), Ukrainian Republic Komsomol M.Ostrovsky Prize (1970), Patriotic Song Competition (Kiev, Ukraine, 1997 - first prize), Arts of Ukraine (1982), People's Artist of Ukraine (1995), Ukrainian State T.G. Shevchenko Prize (1989), Ukrainian Orthodox St. Volodymyr Order (third degree, 1998) and the Order of Princess Olga (1999).

She has been a member of Ukrainian Composers' Union and its board since 1968, and was its secretary 1994.

Julia Gomeloskaya

JULIA GOMELOSKAYA, born March 11, 1964, in Ukraine, graduated as a pianist from Simferopol Musical College of Ukraine (1983) and as a composer from Odessa State A. Nezhdanova Conservatory (1990). In 1995, she was awarded a fellowship by the Guildhall School of Music and Drama (London), earned an MM in composition with distinction from City University (London), and a 1997 PhD in Composition at the University of Sussex (England).

Her compositions since 1987 include works for small orchestra, a symphony, a violin concerto, string quartets, solo instruments and piano, and chamber cantatas.

Hanna Havrylets

HANNA HAVRYLETS, born April 11, 1958, in Vydyniv, Ukraine, graduated as a composer from the L'vov State M.Lysenko Conservatory (now Musical Academy) in 1982. She completed her postgraduate studies at the Kiev State P.I. Tchaikovsky Conservatory (now National Musical Academy of Ukraine) where, since 1992, she has lectured in composition.

Her output includes symphonic, chamber instrumental, vocal with instrumental and choral music. Her works have been performed in Ukraine, Russia, Poland, Canada, Slovakia, Slovenia, USA, Switzerland, France and Germany.

Havrylets, a Laureate of the International Ivanna and Mar'jan Kots' Composers' Competition (Kiev, 1995), was awarded the Ukrainian National T. Shevchenko Prize (1999), and won the Grand Prix of the All-Ukrainian Composers' Competition "Spiritual Psalms of the Third Millennium" during the Zolotoverkhyj Kiev Choir Fest (2001).

She has been a member of the Ukrainian Composers' Union since 1985, and deputy head of the Kiev Branch of the Ukrainian Composers' Union since 1999.

IRYNA KYVRYLINA, born March 25, 1953 in Dresden (Germany), graduated from Kiev Musical College in Theory, and Kiev State P.I. Tchaikovsky Conservatoire (National Musical Academy of Ukraine) in musical history and composition. Until 1982, she was a teacher at Kiev Music School and Children's Schedryk Chorus. Since 1982, she has been a freelance composer.

Her output includes chamber, choral, theater and children's music, Ukrainian folklore arrangements and over 2,000 popular songs. Her works have been performed in the USA, Canada, Austria, England, the Germany, the Netherlands, Poland, France, Switzerland and Sweden, and recorded by Ukrainian State Radio and TV.

Her songs have won many theater and popular music competitions, and at music festivals such as the International Puppet Show Competition (1988), International Children's Festival (1993–1997), and All-Ukrainian Radio Festival (1998–2001).

Kyvrylina's honors include the Ukrainian Republican Komsomol M.Ostrovsky Prize (1988), Arts of Ukraine (1999), and winner of the Ukrainian President's Prize (1999).

She has been a member of Ukrainian Composers' Union since 1980.

Victoria Poleva

VICTORIA POLEVA was born September 11, 1962, in Kiev. She graduated from the Kiev State P.I. Tchaikovsky Conservatory (National Music Academy of Ukraine) in 1989 as a composer, and completed postgraduate studies in 1995. She has been a lecturer there since 1990.

Although her works are primarily for voice, including *Simeon's Song* (2002), for soprano, mixed chorus and symphony, she also writes for chamber orchestra, solo instruments, string quartet and quintet. Her compositions have been performed at the International Youth Music Forums (Kiev, 1992–95, 1998); Kiev-Music-Fest (1992–2002); Musical Premieres of the Season (Kiev, 1994–2000); the International Festival "Contrasts" (Kiev, 2001–02); and "Two Days and Two Nights of New Music" (Odessa, 1998, 2000, 2002).

Poleva won the L. Revutsky Prize of the Ministry of Culture and Arts of Ukraine (1995) and the first prize in the "Third Millennium Psalms" competition (2001).

Aljona Tomljonova

ALJONA TOMLJONOVA, born March 26, 1963, in Odessa, graduated from the Odessa Stoliarsky Special Music School in music theory (1981), and from Odessa State A.V. Nezhdanova Musical Academy in composition (1986). Since 1994, she has taught composition at Odessa Children's Music School, and in 2000 was artistic director of the Ukrainian Children's Composer's Festival, "Orpheus."

Her compositions include a chamber opera, string quartets, a violin concerto, two violin sonatas, a symphonic poem, and two symphonies written in 1998 and 2001.

Her compositions have been performed at the Austrian-Ukrainian Musical Dialogue-Symposium (Odessa, 1994); Kiev-Music-Fest (1994, 1998–2002); First International Festival of Audio-Visual Actions "Prima Vista" (Odessa, 1998); Two Days and Two Nights of New Music (Odessa, 1999–2002); and the International Forum of Composers and Musicologists "Past and Future" (Odessa, 1999, 2000).

Karmella Tsepkolenko

KARMELLA TSEPKOLENKO was born February 20, 1955, in Odessa, where she studied piano and composition at the Stoliarsky Special Music School (1962–73). At Odessa State Conservatory (1973–79), her composition studies continued with O. Krasotov, and piano with L. Ginzburg. Next came the Moscow Pedagogical Institute under G. Tsypin (1986–89; PhD 1990), and composers' master courses in Germany (Darmstadt, 1992, 1994, Bayreuth, 1993). Since 1980, she has been composition professor at the Odessa State A.V. Nezhdanova Conservatory, acquiring the title *docent* in 1999. She has been a member of Ukrainian Composers' Union since 1982, and is one of its founders (1996). She is also president of the Board of the Association of New Music—the Ukrainian section of the ISCM—which organizes festivals, conferences, master classes, recordings, music publications, CDs, etc., to disseminate information on New Music from Ukraine to further international collaboration.

For her achievements, Tsepkolenko has received awards at Soviet All-Union composers' competitions in Russia (1978), Armenia, Germany (1983) and France (1990, 1993). Composer residencies have included the *Heinrich Boell Foundation* (1995); *Cultural Links Program* (New York, 1996); DAAD and *Brahmshaus Foundation* (Germany, 1996), *Künstlerhof Schreyahn* (1998), *Worpswede Künstlerhäser* and *Die Höege Stipendium* (Holland, 2002, 2003). Grants for her cultural projects have come from the *International Renaissance Foundation* (Ukraine), *Kultur Kontakt* (Austria), *Pro Helvetia* (Switzerland), and *Ernst von Siemens Stiftung* (Germany).

She is co-founder and has been artistic director of the Odessa annual international festival *Two Days and Two Nights of New Music* (1995–2001), the Odessa festival series *Wandering Music Academy* (1997, '98), and other global cultural events. Her works have been performed at the International Piano Forum for New Music (Heilbronn, Germany, 1996), where she appeared as composer and pianist, and *Contrast* in Ukraine, featuring her chamber opera, *Zwischen Zwei Feuern* (Between Two Fires), based on Herman Hesse's *Steppenwolf.* 1997 and 1998 found her at the Vienna Modern Festival, *Summergarden* (New York, 2000). ISCM *World Music Days* brought her to Bucharest (Romania,1999), and Yokohama (Japan, 2001). She was on the jury of the Eleventh International Competition for Women Composers (GEDOK, Mannheim, 1997), and led the contemporary music workshop at the international pianists master class in Biel (Switzerland, 2001). Her works were featured in the 2001 Berlin Biennale.

Tsepkolenko's output of over eighty works, dating from 1979, includes three operas, three symphonies, a piano concerto, vocal and chamber pieces and electronic music. Some of her works have been commissioned by the Culture Ministry of France, and premiered at such venues as the Dresden Center for Contemporary Music (October 2003), SPAZIOMUSICA (Cagliari Sassari, Italy; November 2003), and in Paris (January 2004). Besides published scores, her music is on over a dozen CDs recorded from broadcasts in Ukraine, Germany, Denmark, France and other countries.

She initiated the foundation of the *Music Information Center* and the online magazine *Musica Ukrainica* (2000); is project manager of the Ukranian-English CD ROM *New Music of Ukraine composers, works, performers: multimedia database* (Odessa, 2000), and a multimedia database of Ukranian women composers (Odessa, 2002), as well as being in charge of the *Contemporary Composers of Ukraine* edition of the Ukrainian-English Handbook (Odessa, 2002).

Karmella is married to Alexander Pereplitsa, PhD, with whom she published the monograph *Artistic Games* (1990), covering new artistic educational methods, which can be viewed on *Musica Ukrainica*. Alexander is a graduate of the Odessa Musical College and Conservatory. A coordinator of culture programs at Odessa Regional Department of the International Renaissance Foundation (1990–94) and, since 1999, head of the Public Institute of Regional Development, Culture and Education, he is a director of the Association of New Music.

Their son, Alexander, born November 6, 1983, also graduated from the Stolyarsky Special Music School (2001), and went on to the Odessa State Conservatory. He has participated in international piano competitions and other musical events, and concertized in Europe and Ukraine.

Of life in present day Ukraine, Karmella speaks of the economic challenges and universal struggle for artists to survive. To quote her upbeat philosophy: "I feel that music can help each person find themselves. For this reason, I have dedicated my life to creating music which takes people to new horizons."

LUDMILLA YURINA, president of Women in Music Ukraine, was born January 16, 1962, in Uzin', Kiev region. She graduated from Kiev's R.M. Glière Music College as a pianist (1981) and from the National Music Academy of Ukraine as a composer (1990), where later she completed postgraduate studies (1998). In Germany, she attended master classes in Rheinsberg and Dresden, and residencies in "Künstlerhof Schreyahn" (1998), the Experimental Electronic Music Studio of "Südwestrundfunk" (Southwest Radio, Freiburg, 1999), and the Baden-Württemberg Ministry of Research, Science and Art (Baden-Baden, 2001).

During 1990–92, she was the music director of the theater studios "Kolo" and "ARS" (Kiev). Since 1993, she has been a member and a coordinator of the organizing committee of the "International Youth Music Forum" in Kiev, and in 1997 was artistic director of the Ukrainian Contemporary Art Festival, also in Kiev. Since 1995, she has been associate professor of composition and orchestration at the National Music Academy of Ukraine.

Yurina's works include voice, piano, solo instruments, a concerto for trombone and orchestra, and film music. They can be heard on the CD *Two Days and Two Nights of New Music: Festivals 1998–2000*.

ALLA ZAGAYKEVICH, born in Khmelnytsky (Ukraine) December 17, 1966, graduated from the National Music Academy of Ukraine in composition and orchestration (1990), with postgraduate studies in music theory and composition (1993–94). In 1995–96, she attended composition courses at IRCAM (Paris). From 1986–99, she was a member of the folklore ensemble "Drevo" of the academy, researching Ukrainian folk songs.

Since 1998, she has been a professor at the National Music Academy of Ukraine, where she founded the Electronic Music Studio.

Alla Zagaykevich.

Her oeuvre of symphonic and chamber music, chamber music theater, and electroacoustic music has been performed at international festivals for contemporary music.

TURKMENISTAN

IRAIDA YUSUPOVA, born February 20, 1962, in Ashgabat, graduated from Moscow State Conservatory as a composer in 1987. She is a member of the Composers' Union of Russia, Filmmakers' Union of Russia, Association of Contemporary Music (ACM), and the Theremin Center since 1994.

She has participated at music festivals including Alternative, Moscow Autumn, Moscow Forum, and the international festivals of Gidon Kremer in Lockenhouse (Austria), Bach-2000, White Nights' Stars (St. Petersburg), Ghent-Moscow-Ghent (Belgium), Klang och Rubel (Sweden), and Delphi's Games—2002 (St. Petersburg).

Iraida Yusupova

She writes for symphony orchestra, chamber symphony, solo instruments and piano.

AZERBAIJAN

FRANGHIZ ALI-ZADEH, born May 28, 1947, in Baku, studied piano with Ulfan Khalilov and composition with **Kara Karayev** (1918–82), a pupil of **Shostakovich**, at the Baku Conservatory, from which she graduated as a pianist in 1970, and composer in 1972. She assisted Karayev during her postgraduate studies (1973–76). In 1976, she started teaching musicology at the conservatory, and in 1990 became a professor of contemporary music and the history of orchestral styles.

In 1976, she introduced her piano sonata, *In Memoriam Alban Berg* (1970), to a western audience at the Pesaro (Italy) music festival. Thereafter, her music was played at festivals

Franghiz Ali-Zadeh

throughout Europe. Numerous performances, broadcasts and CDs have made her name known as far as Mexico, America and Australia. In 1980, she won the Azerbaijani Composers' Union prize. In 1988, she became a member of the Friends of Arnold Schoenberg Institute in Los Angeles. In 1990, she was accorded the title of "outstanding artist" by the Azerbaijan SSR. By November 2000, her honorary title was "People's Artist of the Republic of Azerbaijan."

In 1989, she completed her doctoral thesis, *Orchestration in Works by Azerbaijani Composers*. From 1993–96, she conducted the choir of the opera house in Mersin, Turkey, and taught piano and music theory for two years at the Mersin Conservatory before returning to Baku, December 1998. In August 1999, she was the first woman composer-in-residence to be invited to the International Festival of Music Lucerne. During 1999–2000, she received a fellowship from the DAAD (German Academic Exchange Service) to work in Berlin. She was also honored with a composer portrait concert from the Berlin broadcasting station SFB and a workshop/concert at the Hans Eisler Musikhochschule. In February 2000, a composer portrait concert with the Ensemble Continuum took place in New York. In April of the same year, the Seattle Chamber Players invited her to that city for concerts, workshops and interviews. Autumn 2000 found her a guest at the Künstlerhaus of Schloss (Castle) Wiepersdorf in Brandenburg.

Ali-Zadeh participated in Yo-Yo Ma's *Silk Road Project* with her composition, *Dervish*. In 2002, she received a stipend to work in the artist's colony of Schreyahn in Lower Saxony.

Two concerts with her works were performed at the inaugural festivities for the restored Baku Philharmonic in May 2003, under the baton of **Mstislav Rostropovich** and Rauf Abdulayev. The program featured the percussion concerto *Silk Road*, the cello concerto *Mersiye*, and the large scale oratorio *Journey to Immortality*. In August of that year she participated at the Young Artists Festival in Bayreuth, directing a workshop centered around *Mirage* for chamber ensemble. Meanwhile, she was appointed composer-in-residence with the Beethovenhalle Orchestra in Bonn, Autumn 2003. November 28 marked the world premiere of *Sehnsucht* (Sadness), concerto for soprano, cello and orchestra, commissioned by the Beethovenhalle. The Kronos Quartet of San Francisco produced a CD devoted exclusively to her music, featuring her as piano soloist.

Most of Ali-Zadeh's music is based on her own national heritage, using semi-oriental Tatar and Asian traditions, combined with the avant-garde innovations of composers like Polish **Witold Lutoslawski**, Americans **John Cage** (1912–92) and **Geroge Crumb** (*b* 1929) and the Second Viennese School of **Arnold Schoenberg** (1874–1951), whose music she often features in her piano performances. In her own words: "I am working on a combination of West European compositional techniques and Eastern monodic. Imitating the timbres of Azerbaijani folk instruments by means of European instruments has always particularly interested me."

Her works include a piano concerto, a symphony, choral, stage and instrumental compositions. Her harp duo *Deyishme*[28] is a commission from the Istanbul Foundation for Culture and Arts. The work received its world premiere with harp duo "Noon Star" (Sirin Pancaroglu and Tine Rehling), June 29, 2001, at the Istanbul Music Festival.

Married to the filmmaker Jahangir Zeynally, Franghiz, as of this writing, was living in Berlin.

The Silk Road

For 2,000 years, the so-called Silk Road, a network of trade routes connecting East Asia to the Mediterranean Sea, was the main conduit for the exchange of products and culture between Europe and Asia. Religions also found new territories as Buddhism spread from India to China, Korea, and Japan; Islam from the Middle East to Turkey and Southeast Asia; and forms of Christianity to the Far East. As silk, spices, gunpowder, paper, printing methods, the magnetic compass, ceramics and lacquerware flowed West, glassware, gold and silver metalwork flowed East. From 500 BC–1500 AD theories in math and science, and developments in art and music were exchanged, permanently enriching each end of the road.

Cellist **Yo-Yo Ma** founded the Silk Road Project in 1998 to explore classical music worldwide and support collaborations between composers and musicians from all ethnicities, thus having a magnet to draw together the peoples of Asia, Europe and North America. Underwritten by the Aga Khan Trust, concerts began in June–July 2001 at the famed Smithsonian Folklife Festival, an annual summer event in Washington, DC, in August at Schleswig-Holstein (Germany), and was heard in major Japanese cities in October. 2002–03 spread the project further into Europe and America. Spring 2003 brought performances in Central Asia: Kazakhstan, Tajikistan and the Kyrgz Republic. The calendar for 2004–05–06 onwards continues global coverage.

With Ma as artistic director and driving force, assembling masters of classical music throughout Eurasia, commissioning works and mounting performances around the world, the success of the Silk Road project is assured as the new trans-highway of culture.

---

28. *Deyishme* means argument, excited discussion of opinions, a verbal exchange of blows. According to the composer there is a similarity in sound between the harp and the *saz*, an Azerbaijani plucked instrument of nine to eleven strings, played with a plectrum and tuned in pure, non-tempered fourths and fifths. Its silvery sound is the favorite instrument of the Aschugs—poet-singer-dancers—who participate in outdoor contests executing dance steps, moving in a circle and raising and lowering the saz in time with the music. Their theme derives from the Turkish *asig—being in love*, which in turn can refer to love of beauty, a woman, nature, poetry or one's homeland, etc. She says, "In my *Deyishme* I wanted to reproduce this festive atmosphere of a musical contest—between two harps."

CHAPTER FIVE
PART C

Other International Composers

Three countries whose names, coincidentally, all begin with "I," do not fall into either Western or Eastern Europe, but have their own representation in women composers.

ICELAND

Karolina Eiriksdottir

KARÓLÍNA EIRÍKSDÓTTIR, born January 10, 1951, in Reykjavík, majored in piano at the Reykjavik College of Music and took composition with Thorkell Sigurbjörnsson, continuing her studies at the University of Michigan with George Wilson and William Albright, where she earned two masters degrees: composition, and music history and musicology. Since 1979, she has been active in her country's music as a composer and teacher—theory and composition— at the Reykjavik College of Music. She was chairman of the board of the Iceland Music Information Centre (1983–88), where her manuscripts are housed, and on the board of the Society of Icelandic Composers (1988–91), and again (1995–98). 2003 found her continuing on the board of the Icelandic Academy of the Arts.

Her works are heard throughout the world. The orchestral piece *Sónans* was performed at the opening of Scandinavia Today in Washington, DC (1980). In 1985, *Sinfonietta* was commissioned by Icelandic Television for the Icelandic Symphony Orchestra, and in 1988 the opera *Någon har jag sett* (I have seen someone) was performed in Reykjavik, London and Sweden. Other works include *In Vultu Solis* (1980) for violin, *Trio* (1986), *Rhapsody* (1986) for piano, *Five Pieces for Chamber Orchestra* (1986), *Land Possessed by Poems* (1987) and *Someone I Have Seen*, performed in Greifswald, Germany, among other venues. 1990s commissions and premieres are *Three Paragraphs* (1993) for orchestra, at the Stockholm New Music festival, a clarinet concerto (1996), by the Aalborg Symphony Orchestra in Denmark, a cello solo at the Skálholt Summer Festival (1997), and performances by the BBC Scottish Symphony (Glasgow), Arditti String Quartet (London), Icelandic Sinfonietta at Kennedy Center, Nordic Music Days, Kuhmo Festival (Finland), Dark Music Days (Iceland) and electroacoustic festivals in Sweden and Iceland.

Many of her compositions have been recorded by the Iceland Symphony and Iceland State Broadcasting Service. *Portrait* is a seventy-three minute CD collection, ranging from her solo violin piece, *In Vultu Solis*, to the orchestral *Sinfonietta*. A second CD, entitled *Spil*, was released in 1999, containing *Flautuspil* (Flute Reel) for solo flute, *Skýin* (Clouds) for solo cello, *Hvaðan kemur lognið?* (Whence this calm?) for solo guitar, *Spil* (Jouissance) for two flutes, *Heimkynni við sjó* (Living by the Sea), a song cycle for soprano and piano. Other works include *Saxophone Quartet*, commissioned by Nomus and the Stockholm Saxophone Quartet, the chamber opera *Maður lifandi* (Man Alive), staged in 1999 in Reykjavíík, and *Toccata* for orchestra, performed October 1999 at Berlin Philharmonie Hall by the Nordic Orchestra at the inauguration of the Nordic Embassies. In 2001, her Guitar Concerto was premiered in Santa Fé, Argentina, the same year she was composer in residence at the Skálholt Summer Festival in Iceland which featured the premiere of her *Aðiðka gott til æru* (Prizing Virtue). In 2002 Höfuðstafir (Main Staves), written for the Caput group, was premiered at Reykjavík City Theatre. Gradus ad Profundum for Þórir Jóhannsson, double bass, came February 26, in Salurinn. Christmas Song was commissioned by the Icelandic State Broadcasting Service as "Radio Christmas Song of the Year." It was broadcast in Europe from Reykjavík's Hallgrímur Church, December 2002. Sólin er runnin upp (The Sun Has Ascended - to his text), for soprano and piano, celebrated the seventieth birthday of poet Hannes Pétursson in 2003. Strenglag (String Tune) saw its first performance at Iceland's National Art Gallery, October 2005, with Gudrun Hrund Hardardóttir, viola, and daughter Tinna Thorsteinsdóttir, piano.

Karólína is married to Thorsteinn Hannesson, a PhD chemist. Tinna was born March 24, 1974. Her piano diploma is from the Hochschule für Musik in Detmold-Münster, Germany. In 2001 she won a Fulbright to the New England Conservatory, where she received a graduate diploma in piano performance in 2003. Her career has taken off with solo recitals in Iceland, Germany, China and Dark Music Days Festival in Reykjavík, February 2006. April took her to the American West Coast, playing with an Icelandic new music group. June found her in Norway at the International Bergen Festival.

INDIA

Born in New Delhi in 1960, **PRITI PAINTAL** was influenced by a variety of music during her childhood. Her grandfather had a love for Western classical music, her uncle encouraged classical Indian music, and Priti grew up in the era of fusion and rock music. Playing piano from an early age, she became more interested in composition than performance. After her 1980 BA in anthropology from Delhi University, she earned a master's in ethnomusicology, studying tribal and folk music of Himalayan villages. During this time her orchestral piece, *Anubhav*, was performed by the Delhi Symphony, and a piano composition broadcast on All India Radio. After studying at York University and the Royal Northern College of Music in Britain, she received her master's in composition in 1985.

Paintal developed her own style based on both classical and folk music from India, Africa and the West. Her chamber opera, *Survival Song* (1988), commissioned by the Royal Opera House, is set in South Africa. This same year she founded ShivaNova, a band combining the diverse sounds of Asian, African and Western instruments to craft a unique global sound. Integrating components of Asian, jazz, classical, club dance and ambient styles by using the sitar, sarod, saxophone, percussion and piano/keyboards, they have produced the well-received albums *Polygamy* and *Urban Mantras*. She has composed many works for the group, including *Evening Rhythms* (1988) and *Euro-Asian Quintet* (1989). By 2003, ShivaNova was on its third CD, *7th Heaven*.

1992 saw the creation of her full length opera *Biko*, another commission from the Royal Opera House. The opera tells the story of the South African hero Steve Biko, and features spoken text and singing, rather than an elaborate operatic style. In later works, she used more improvisation with ShivaNova, bringing other musicians in for specific pieces. *Polygamy* (1993) has three instruments entirely improvising, while the others play from a written score. Her 1995 opera, *Gulliver*, was written for the Maidstone schools in Kent (England) where she resides.

Having become a mother, Priti envisions handing down her musical skills to her daughter, but says, "It's up to her to make up her mind and decide if she wants to follow in my footsteps."

ISRAEL

Verdina Shlonsky (1905–90)
Yardina Alotin (1930–94)
Hilat Ben Kennaz
Noa Blass
Tsippi Fleischer
Rachel Galinne

Nurit Jugend
Hagar Kadima
Betty Olivero
Sara Shoham
Elena Sokolovsky

VERDINA SHLONSKY, born in Kremenshug, Ukraine, January 19 or 22, 1905—sources differ—studied at the Berlin Hochschule für Musik and took piano with world-famous artists **Egon Petri** (1882–1962) and **Artur Schnabel** (1882–1951). Next came composition in Paris (1930–32) with **Nadia Boulanger**, **Max Deutsch** (1892–1982), and the avant-garde **Edgard Varèse** (1883–1965), who profoundly influenced the direction of new music. She moved to Israel (then Palestine) in 1929, working as a concert pianist and theater composer, teaching many years at the Tel-Aviv Academy of Music.

In 1931, her *Poème hébraïque*, for voice and piano, won first prize in a French government competition for women composers. In 1948, her String Quartet won the Bartók Prize. She wrote many piano works, including two concerti (1942, 1968) and educational pieces, as well as song cycles. Her compositions include a symphony (1935), *Praise*, a cantata for mixed voices (1948), *Divertimento* for woodwind quintet (1954), two sonatas for violin and piano (1951, 1955), *Psalms* for *a cappella* choir (1956), *Introduction and Scherzo* for piano (1964), *Reflexion symphonique* (1966), a violin concerto (1967), *Concertino* (1970), and *Euphony* (1980) for chamber orchestra. Besides her many art songs to texts by French and German poets, considered most noteworthy are the songs to texts by her brother, Israeli poet, journalist and "national treasure" **Abraham Shlonsky** (1900–73). Shlonsky's last work was *Oreah* (1984), for voice and piano. Her musical style developed from traditional to Romantic, and then to the twelve-note system which prevailed in her later works. She died in Tel-Aviv, February 20, 1990.

YARDENA ALOTIN was born in Tel Aviv, October 19, 1930, attended Tel Aviv Music Teachers' College (1948–50), and the Israel Academy of Music (1950–52), where she studied with the foremost pedagogues of the time, **Alexander Uriah Boskovich** (1907–64) theory, **Mordecai Seter** (1916–94) harmony and counterpoint, **Paul Ben-Haim** (1897–1984) orchestration, **Ilona Vincze-Kraus**, piano, and composition privately with Oedeon [Ödön] Partos (1907–77). Her style is based on baroque and classical forms, with rich lyric melodic lines and dramatic developments via changing meters and rhythms, which were evident right from her first work, *Yefei Nof*, for mixed choir. It won the Nissimov Prize and was premiered by the Rinat Choir in Tel Aviv, of which she was a member, as well as at the Paris International Festival, 1956. *Al Golah Dvuyah*, for mezzo-soprano and orchestra, was written in 1958. Biblical canticles appear in her *Cantata* for choir *a cappella* (1958), performed at the Perugia (Italy) Religious Music Festival, 1960, and in her frequently played *Sonatas for Violin and Piano* (1960), and for cello solo (1976), both on IMI CD, written while she was composer-in-residence at Bar-Ilan University. She also used polyphonic techniques, as in the *Lament* for string trio (1960), and Piano Trio (1979). *Shir Hag* (Festive Song) for unaccompanied mixed choir, was commissioned by the Tel Aviv Foundation for Culture and Art on the Seventy-fifth anniversary of that city in 1984. She is best known for her flute piece *Yefei Nof*, published by the Israeli Music Institute (1978), commissioned by **James Galway** and performed many times by him as an encore piece.

A piano soloist and teacher, Alotin also wrote children's and educational music. She died in New York, October 4, 1994.

Today's Israeli Music Scene

Hilat Ben Kannaz

HILAT BEN-KENNAZ was born in Israel on February 25, 1970, adding to the long heritage of musicians dating back to the beginning of the 20th century, when her mother's grandparents came to Israel from Russia and established the first musical instruments store, "Havivi Depot," in the new and developing town of Tel Aviv. They taught the love of music to their son (Mosa Havivi) and two daughters. One of them, Raaya, Hilat's grandmother, formed the Havivi Trio (cello, violin, piano), who played numerous concerts in Tel Aviv through the 1930s. Later, Mosa became a cellist with the British and New York Philharmonic Orchestras. He established one of New York's leading stringed instruments shop. Her grandmother stayed in Tel Aviv and became her first piano teacher when she was five. Both relatives were the mentors and professional inspiration in her musical upbringing.

In 1992, Ben-Kennaz completed the Levinsky Seminar, studying music education. She then joined the Tel Aviv University Academy of Music, where she received her BM and master's in composition (2001) under the guidance of Leon Schidlowsky. In 1999, the "Musica Nova" ensemble played *Acceptation*, her first publicly performed work. It was played again in 2000 at the founding concert of the Israeli Women Composers Forum. One of her new pieces was selected to represent the IWCF in a festival in Korea.

Hilat is married to business executive, Eran Ben-Kennaz. Their daughter, Danielle, born March 19, 1999, showed musical inclinations even before birth.

NOA BLASS, born in Israel, December 19, 1937, was brought up by classical music loving parents who encouraged her piano lessons at eight. At this young age she knew that music would become her lifelong profession. She continued with piano at the conservatory and the Israeli Academy of Music. At thirty, she studied flute for seven years, viola one year, composition for ten years, and taught herself percussion. In 1996, she received an honorary PhD from the university in Montreal where she taught for six years.

Blass specializes in three fields of music: composition, music education and yoga with music. She has written seventeen books on these subjects. Her compositions include some thirty songs for voice and piano, plus compositions for gongs, Tibetan cymbals, vibraphone, bells and chimes with voice, as well as works for viola, violin and cello. In 1988, her *7 Egyptian Hymns*, for voice and piano, was chosen to represent Israel in the country's fortieth anniversary in Jerusalem. The same composition, plus *Turning Point*, were featured in April 1990 at an NYU sponsored concert of modern Israeli music in Carnegie Hall's Merkin Recital Hall, with the composer at the piano. *Circles* for gongs and chimes was selected by Israeli Radio for broadcast in Lubljana (Yugoslavia, 1996). In 1997, she participated in a festival of Israeli Music in Virzburg (Germany), where she played a concert with gongs and Tibetan singing bowls, including *7 Ancient Egyptian Hymns*. In her homeland, she performs in many modern music concerts and on Jerusalem radio.

Besides musical education for children, over the last quarter century Blass has developed seven Special Education music methods, focusing on the severely mentally handicapped. These include classical works, jazz and songs, and are in constant use by music therapists treating some 5,000 people in institutions throughout Israel. Following through on her teaching of yoga through vibrations of gongs and bells, which she has covered in fifteen years of seminars in Israel, France, Canada, Germany and England, in 2000 the composer was invited to demonstrate her gong methods for UNESCO in Paris.

Noa married in 1956. Her very supportive husband is a consultant to large firms on pension policies. They have a daughter, Sari, born 1958, who uses her business degrees in banking. Son Uri, born 1967, is a mathematician.

Tsippi Fleischer

Leading the way for the next generation of Israeli women composers is **TSIPPI FLEISCHER**, born May 20, 1946, in Haifa, who graduated from the Tel-Aviv Teachers' College for Music (1967) with degrees in Middle Eastern subjects, a BM in Music from the Rubin Academy, Jerusalem (1969), and a BA in Arabic Language and Literature, Tel-Aviv University (1973). She followed this with an M.Mus. Ed from New York University (1975). Her PhD in musicology was earned exactly twenty years later from Bar-Ilan University, Israel (1995), with a dissertation on Cherubini's *Medea*, an opera admired by Beethoven, in which she compares this mythical figure to Gluck's *Alcestis* and Beethoven's *Leonora*.

A dedicated pedagogue, Fleischer teaches theory at Tel-Aviv and Bar-Ilan Universities and at the Hebrew Union College, Jerusalem. After two decades of composing music for films, theater and television, in 1977 she began to write for the concert hall. Using her knowledge of the indigenous cultures of her homeland, added to the firm foundation of experience of Western culture, her music combines Eastern and Western elements. For her first stage work, the symphonic poem *A Girl Named Limonad* (1977), she corresponded under a pseudonym with the Lebanese Christian poet Shawqi Abi-Shaqra. When she finally revealed her identity as an Israeli woman, he almost severed connections, but continued writing to her through an Italian monk. One of her most popular works, *Girl-Butterfly-Girl* (1977), a song cycle for high voice and ensemble, is based on Syrian and Lebanese poems and can be performed in Hebrew or Arabic. The London premiere, June 1992, was followed by performances in Paris and Amsterdam. *Lamentations* (1985), for soprano, women's chorus, two harps and percussion, has been played in Germany and America. *Oratorio 1492–1992*, commemorating the 500th anniversary of the expulsion of the Jews from Spain, and based on texts by medieval Hebrew sages, premiered in Israel, February 1992.

Perhaps the only Israeli woman to venture into Arab territories in Israel and Egypt, Fleischer has been recognized as the first truly authentic pioneer in the exploration of the cultural duality—Jewish and Arab—of her country. Her music forges a bond between the two cultures, combining historical Western style with the singular qualities of Middle Eastern sounds. By setting Arabic poetry into the language of contemporary music, she has achieved an original union of two diverse societies. For *Gown of Night* (1988), she traveled to the Negev desert to hear the voices of Bedouin children. *In the Mountains of Armenia* (1988), for children's chorus, represented Israel in the 1989 UNESCO International Rostrum for Composers in Paris. She constantly seeks new territories—literally and figuratively. *Daniel in the Lions' Den* (1995), sung in the Coptic language, is inspired by limestone biblical art in the Coptic Museum in Cairo. (The Copts are the original Egyptian Christians). *Daniel* premiered in September 1996 in the Jordan Valley on Lake Kenneret (the Sea of Galilee). A video production followed, with filming in Egypt and Israel. *Girl-Butterfly-Girl* was digitally recorded in Rome, February 1996, featuring **Patricia Adkins-Chiti** singing in Arabic.

Fleischer took a sabbatical in 1997 to write two new books on the Theory and History of Hebrew Songs. With her unique knowledge, she lectures internationally on topics such as the Middle East as a cultural realm, and the roles and rights of women under Islam, Judaism and Christianity. She is considered one of the leading researchers of the Hebrew song style in music and history, publishing books in this field—which is also linked to her status as an educator.

A major project, *The Suite of Four Multimedias in Ancient Semitic Languages*, comprised of *Daniel in the Lions' Den*, sung in Coptic, *The Goddess Anath*, sung in Ugaritic, *Appeal to the Stars*, sung in Acadian (Old Babylonian) and *The Judgment of Solomon*, in Biblical Hebrew, is on CD. The Warsaw Philharmonic recorded her first symphony, *Salt Crystals*, April 1996, which was one of the works selected for ISCM World Music Days-1999, and performed in Bucharest and Cluj, Romania. Symphonies No. 2, "The Train," commissioned by OPUS ONE and recorded by the Polish National Symphony in April 1999, in Katowice, Poland, and No. 3 "Regarding Beauty," were produced by the Moravian Philharmonic in Olomouc, (Czech Republic), June 2000. Symphony No. 4 "A Moving Shadow," for two soloists on exotic folklore instruments and string orchestra, was produced in Prague, October 2001, by the Czech Philharmonic.

Besides becoming active in the Israeli Women Composers' Forum, 2000 marked the recording of her second, third and fourth, symphonies on Vienna Modern Masters. Her fifth symphony, inspired by sounds of Israeli rock, came in 2001. Her second chamber opera, *Cain and Abel*, was produced in October 2002 for the opening of 2002–03 season in the Tel Aviv Museum, with the CD out in 2003. Other 21st century CDs, on the U.S. label OPUS ONE, are *Israel at 50—A Celebration with Music of Tsippi Fleischer*, and *Ethnic Silhouettes*, covering her '90s works that incorporate ancient, ethnic and contemporary sources.

Tsippi is married to Aron Dolgopolsky, a professor of linguistics at Haifa University, who emigrated from Moscow in 1976. They met when he began lecturing in Israel while she was studying for her MA in Semitic Linguistics. Their son, Jacob, born 1982, now known as Yaakov Dolgo, is a poet, dramatist and actor, involved in advanced modern techniques and concepts of theater.

Rachel Galinne

RACHEL GALINNE was born February 7, 1949, in Stockholm, where her parents met at the Royal Institute of Technology and married in 1946—part of the wave of Jewish refugees who emigrated to Sweden after World War II. Of Polish origin, her parents grew up in the "stetls"—Jewish communities within cities, or entire villages populated mainly by Jews—as portrayed in the musical, *Fiddler on the Roof*. Her childhood was filled with their singing cantorial and secular Jewish songs, melodies remembered from before the war. At age five, Rachel heard the Mozart piano variations of the children's song *A vous dirais-je maman* (also known as *Twinkle, Twinkle, Little Star*). This sparked the child's interest in musical composition. She wanted to be able to write such variations! She took piano with, among others, Gottfried Boon, a pupil of the great **Artur Schnabel**. Her subjects at Stockholm University were Musicology, Film Science and Education, but she graduated from Uppsala University (1974), where she earned her BA in Semitic languages, Hebraistic line. The following year she moved to Israel, where she completed her first and second degree in composition at the Rubin Academy of Music (1984), and Tel Aviv University (1988) as a student of Leon Schidlowsky,[29] with whom she enjoyed sharing his acquaintance with contemporary European trends and his knowledge of the German musical culture. In 1980, Galinne participated in a composition course in France led by **Witold Lutoslawski** (1913–94) and **Henri Dutilleux** (*b* 1916). 1984 found her at the Darmstadt Seminar of Contemporary Music.

Most of Galinne's works have been published by the Israel Music Institute. These include two symphonies, four other orchestral compositions, vocal music, chamber works and pieces for solo instruments. Her music has been performed by the Swedish Radio Symphony Orchestra, Swedish Radio Choir, Israel Philharmonic, Jerusalem Symphony Orchestra, Brooklyn Philharmonic, Maros Ensembel (Sweden) Ensemble Echo (Berlin, 2000) and Musica Nova (Israel).

In 1990, Galinne's work *Islossning* (Breaking the Bonds of Ice) represented Israel at the Rostrum Competition in Paris. In 1993, she was honored with the Israeli Prime Minister's Award for Composers, the year *Cycles for Orchestra* received a special commendation from the Fourth Annual Vienna Modern Masters Orchestral Recording Awards. Her choral work *Uneginotai Nenagen* (And We Shall Sing My Songs of Praise) received the Israeli ACUM award in 1994, and in 1996 her First Symphony was one of three pieces selected to be performed by the Israel Philharmonic at the final concert of the Sixtieth Anniversary Jubilee Contest. The same year, *Cycles*, which had premiered in Sweden in 1992, was given its Israeli premiere by the Israel Philharmonic. In 1999, the first CD of works by Galinne was released by the Israeli Music Center.

Able to devote herself exclusively to composition, in 1999 she worked on the computer version of the score of her Second Symphony. In 2000, she wrote her string quartet, *Amitai in memoriam*, in memory of her friends' seventeen-year-old son who died in an accident in 1990, and *Disconsonance* was performed by the Echo Ensemble in Berlin. In 2001, her song cycle *Schwarze Gesaenge*, with text by Else Lasker-Schueler, was performed in Mainz (Germany), within the framework of the "Week of Jewish Music" that took place there. A concert dedicated solely to her chamber works was held in Mainz, November 2003, sponsored by the Annie Eisler-Lehman Foundation. The program included two world premieres of vocal chamber music, as well as earlier works. March 2004 saw all-Galinne concerts in Tel Aviv and Haifa, which included the Israeli premieres of two new string quartets.

Nurit Jugend

NURIT JUGEND was born March 23, 1972, in Haifa. She wanted to play the violin at age five, but her parents took her to a music teacher who decided that it would be a waste of time. At nine, when the family was living in Boston for two years, she brought a violin home from school. She started to study the violin seriously at twelve, but was told it was too late for a career. Nevertheless, she joined the Haifa Youth Symphony and became principal second violin. Another rejection was at the Wizo high school music department, but she persevered, finally got in, finishing with honors. Her real musical education began at the Rubin Academy, where she studied under Ari Ben-Shabetai, earning a BA in Music Theory and Composition (1993–97). Next came the Hochschule de Künste (School of Arts) in Berlin, with Walter Zimmermann and Frederic Rzewski (1997–98). 1999 found her in Northern California, embarking on the four year program for her DMA at Stanford, under Jonathan Berger, Jonathan Harvey and Brian Ferneyhough.

---

29. Leon Schidlowsky (*b* 1931, Santiago, Chile) studied at the National Conservatory and Darmstadt, Germany. Returning to Chile, he founded an avant-garde group. He emigrated to Israel in 1969, and was appointed to the faculty of the Rubin Academy. In Israel, with its relatively traditional musical climate, he has been characterized as a "revolutionary" composer.

As of 2003, Jugend's more than dozen published works have been performed in France, Israel, U.S., Italy, Luxembourg, Germany, Yugoslavia and Austria, and were part of the Luxembourg ISCM World Music Festival 2000, Belgrade Festival for Contemporary Music, Tel-Aviv 2000 Biennale Festival for Contemporary Music and many radio broadcasts. Artists performing her music include the Amber Trio, Sirius Group, 21st Century Contemporary Players of Israel and the Haifa Symphony. Her awards include special mention in the Arturo Toscanini Foundation Competition for her symphony *Parody*; first prize in composition at the Klon Competition for Composers, where she played *Gustav Klimt-Impressions* from her piano trio, and *A Thought . . .* , from *4 Miniatures for Piano Solo*; and first prize at the Liebersohn Composition Competition for Orchestral Works for her *The Voice Of Silence*.

Hagar Kadima

HAGAR KADIMA, founder of the Israeli Women Composers' Forum, was born in Haifa, May 1957, to music loving parents. Her father, born in Vienna and a living encyclopedia of music, could still sing arias from operas he had heard fifty years before in Naples. A piano student of Naomi Meiron, Hagar was writing little pieces in early childhood and became a composition student of Professor Abel Ehrlich at the Rubin Academy of Music. She received her BA, *cum laude*, in Music and Philosophy from Tel Aviv University (1981). She was a teaching assistant while earning her MA (1983) at UC Santa Barbara, studying with Edward Applebaum, **Emma Lou Diemer**, and Peter R. Fricker. She became a Visiting Lecturer there while earning her PhD (1988) in Composition. A summer at Aspen, 1985, included mentors **Luciano Berio** (1925–2003), Earl Brawn, **Joseph Druckman** and Bernard Rands.

Published by the Israeli Music Institute (IMI), her chamber and orchestral music has been performed and broadcast in Israel, U.S., Germany, Romania, Austria, Poland and Belgium. Summer 1996, she was a guest artist at Mishkenot Sh'ananim in Jerusalem. *Not a Lament*, for mezzo soprano solo, written in memory of the late Prime Minister Yitzhak Rabin, was premiered in Germany, September 1996. Other titles are: *The Wonders* (female choir), Concerto for String Quartet and Orchestra, *A Friend and I* (children's choir) for the National Council of Culture and Art, 1994, and *Sounds* (five vocalists).

Among her honors are the Sherill Corwin Award (1984), annual ACUM Prizes, and winning the 1987 Rostrum (European Radio) Competition. She represented Israel in the international *In Aspekte* Salzburg Festival (1990), the ISCM festival in Warsaw (1992), and Ireland (1995) as part of an Ireland-Israel cultural exchange.

In 1990, she joined the music faculty at Levinsky College, Tel Aviv, where she teaches solfeggio, harmony and composition. She is chairperson of the Israeli Women Composers' Forum, which she helped found in 2000.

Timing, for women's choir with text by poetess Sh. Shifra, was performed November 2002 in Jerusalem, and March 2003 and January 2004 in Tel-Aviv by the Hemiola Women's Choir, Rachel Kochavi-Laventer, conductor. *A Dubious Closing Gesture* (violin, cello, piano) was heard February 2003 at Henry Crown Hall, Jerusalem, and March 2003 at the Tel-Aviv Museum of Art. *Seven Women* (mezzo soprano, three alto recorders, oud) premiered January 1, 2004, at Bialik House, Tel Aviv, with mezzo Hadas Gur, Naomi Rogel, Alon Shav, Tamar Lalo on recorders and Bashir Mansoor on the oud (a Middle Eastern lute) with text by Sh. Shifra.

Hagar married Yuval Greenzweig in1981. Their three sons are: Sivaan, born 1986, and twins Tomer and Meitar, born 1997.

BETTY OLIVERO, born May 16, 1954, in Tel-Aviv, studied at the Samuel Rubin Academy of Music, and Tel-Aviv University, with Ilona Vincze-Kraus for piano and Yizhak Sadai and Leon Schidlowsky for composition (1972–78). She went to the U.S. for further study, graduating from the Yale School of Music (1981), where her composition teachers were **Jacob Druckman** and **Gilbert Amy**. In 1982, she was awarded a Leonard Bernstein Scholarship to the Berkshire Music Center in Tanglewood, where she studied with Luciano Berio, continuing her training and collaboration with him in Italy through 1986. Her music, with its massive orchestration and rhythmic complexities, is inspired from the rich variety of the Jewish heritage which she blends with contemporary composition techniques. It has been performed by the Chicago Symphony, New York, Israel, Munich and Royal Stockholm Philharmonics, Berlin Radio and Cologne Radio Symphony Orchestras and the London Sinfonietta, among others, and has been played in festivals such as the ICSM World Music Days in Stockholm, Munich Biennale, Horizons Festival in New York, Aspen Festival, Colorado, Gaudeamus Music Week, Amsterdam, and the Israel Festival, Jerusalem. In 2000, she also became active in the Israeli Women Composers' Forum.

SARA SHOHAM was born in Tel-Aviv. After playing the piano by ear at the age of two and a half, she had her first teacher at six and a half. Classical music was the only kind of music heard on the family radio. She received her BA from the Rubin Academy of Tel-Aviv University. With further studies in Israel and abroad, she pursued her particular interest in vocal music. She has composed for numerous choral and instrumental ensembles for radio and television. She won the Levin Kipnis Prize for Art Composition, the Public Council Prize, in collaboration with the music department of the Israel Broadcasting Authority, and was awarded grants for creative writing by the Public Council for Arts and Culture, Tel Aviv Arts and Culture Foundation, and prizes from the Minister of Science and Culture, among others. Her . . . *And they shall not learn war any more* (Isaiah 13:4) received an award from the Czech Ministry of Culture. *Enfants! faîtes attention aux baobabs!* (Antoine de Saint-Exupéry) won a prize in the prestigious Florilège International Competition for Choral Music in Tours (France); *Loquimini Veritatem!* (Biblical verses), earned a prize at the Spoor International Choir Composition Contest (Belgium).

Most of Shoham's works are for leading choirs in Israel and abroad. During 2000, she trained Israeli and Palestinian teachers of music and drama as part of a special collaborative project through MECA (the Middle East Children's Association). She was the recipient of the 2002 Prime Minister's Prize for Composition.

(Y)ELENA SOKOLOVSKY was born in Moscow in 1967, and has lived in Israel since 1995. She studied at the Moscow Conservatory with Edison Denisov (1989–94), the Jerusalem Conservatory (1994) with Mark Kopitman, and in the Hans Eisler Conservatory (Germany, 1994), with Hans-Paul Dietrich.

Her compositions include orchestral, piano and works for voice and ballet. Her three short symphonies were written in 1994 and 1998. Some of her instrumentation includes the modern keyboard. They have been performed in Yugoslavia, Germany, Russia and Israel. Her music has been performed at the Israel Women Composers Forum.

The Vanguard

In Summer 2000, a group of women musicians established the Israel Women Composers' Forum (IWCF) with a goal of providing a showcase for their work. One third (60) of Israeli concert music composers are women, but barely 5 percent of their music is broadcast, recorded or receives public performances. Unlike Europe or the U.S., until 2000 there were no women on any composition faculty of universities or colleges in Israel. Since its inception in 1936, the Israel Philharmonic Orchestra has performed many musical works written by Israeli male composers, but only four written by women. Israeli-born, American resident **Shulamit Ran** served as composer-in-residence of the Chicago Symphony Orchestra (1990–97), a prestigious assignment so far unheard of in any Israeli's three major and eight regional orchestras.

The IWCF, founded by Dr. Hagar Kadima, was established to call attention to the absence of women on the contemporary music scene. Their first concert/show of dance and music, "Patches," September 3, 2000, featuring music by Nurit Jugend, Hilat Ben-Knaz, Hadas Goldschmidt, Hagar Kadima and Yelena Sokolowsky, received a standing ovation from the audience and music critics. Organized only five months before, the Forum received offers from festivals and ensembles in Israel and abroad. Among their goals are to produce concerts, record CDs, and build a data base of all concert music written by Israeli women composers, to be available to performers and teachers. Other plans are to build coalitions with women from all fields of visual and performing arts. The Forum was endowed with the sponsorship of the Institute of Music Education at the Levinsky College of Education.

The second successful concert, March 4, 2001, now part of the College Concert Series of the Institute, wove together contemporary Israeli works and classical European pieces. Represented were: Betty Olivero, Sara Feigin,

Hagar Kadima, Miriam Shatal, Tsippi Fleischer, Noa Blass, Yardena Alotin, plus Alma Mahler and **Fanny Mendelssohn**. March 2002 brought "Women-Sounds-Women," a theater and concert/show at the Jaffa Music Center, with works by Verdina Shlonsky, Aviya Kopelman, Irena Svetova, Sara Feigin, Sigal Goldsobel, Merav Cohen-Hadar, plus Rebekka Wedell (England) and **Clara Schumann**. In July 2002, at Harishonim House, Givataim, a workshop with the New Vocal Ensemble was presented with rehearsal and recording of works by Merav Cohen-Hadar, Michelle Catalove and Yakira Levi. October 2002, at the Tel Aviv Museum of Art, "Women and Sounds" featured a vocal concert as part of the International Festival for New Music, "Tempo Fugit," with music by Sara Shoham, Dina Smorgonskaia, Hagar Kadima, Michelle Catalove, Yakira Levi, plus **Hildegard von Bingen**. December 2002, saw a children's choir concert at the Levinsky Auditorium (Tel Aviv), with works by Aviya Kopelman, Sara Shoham, Irena Svetova, Bat-Zion Goldberg and Hadas Goldschmidt. May 2003 brought "The Return of Leonarda," a theatrical concert for string quartet and electronics at the Enav Culture Center (Tel Aviv), presenting works by **Isabella Leonarda** from the Italian baroque and contemporary Israelis: Dikla Baniel, Nurit Jugend, Irena Svetova and Kiki Keren-Huss.

Latin American Composers

MEXICO
Graciela Agudelo
Leticia Armijo
Georgina Derbez
Maria Granillo
Claudia Herrerias
Ana Lara
Alejandra Odgers
Gabriela Ortíz
Marta Garcia Renart
Marcela Rodriguez
Gloria Tapía (Mendoza)
Veronica Tapía
Mariana Villanueva

ARGENTINA
Alicia Terzian

URUGUAY
Beatriz Lockart
Graciela Paraskevaídis

Irma Urteaga

VENEZUELA
Diana Arismendi
Josefina Punceles de Benedetti
Adina Izarra

MEXICO

Women south of the border are coming into their own as patriarchal traditions are giving way to the inroads of feminism in the latter part of the 20th century, and the strides forward—in some nations—of the 21st.

Graciela Agudelo

GRACIELA AGUDELO was born December 7, 1945, in Mexico City. Her mother was a pianist, and father, a poet. Her grandparents also loved the arts, and the child grew up in an atmosphere of creativity and imagination. She studied piano at the National School of Music of the University of Mexico (UNAM), and composition with Hector Quintanar and Mario Lavista in the music composition workshop of the National Institute of Fine Arts (INBA).

Founder of the Sociedad Mexicana de Musica Nueva (Mexican Society of New Music), from 1990–92 Agudelo was associate producer of the radio program "Hacia una Nueva Musica" (Towards a New Music) broadcast for Radio UNAM. In 1992, she won a scholarship to study at the International Music Institute in Darmstadt (Germany). The following year, she was appointed Artistic Creator of the Sistema Nacional de Creadores de Arte. In 1998, she was awarded first prize in Short Stories, "Espacio 22," Mexico. Her literary and journalism contributions are published in such periodicals as: *Plural*, *Pauta*, *El Huevo*, *Le Magazine*, *La Gaceta*, etc. She was director of *Armonía*, a magazine of ENM/UNAM, and founder of the children's magazine *Letras de Cambio*. She has written over thirty short stories and many articles on music.

Agudelo's works have been commissioned by soloists, music groups, as well as Mexican and international cultural institutions. They have been performed in the U.S., Europe, South America, Japan, Israel and the former Soviet Union. Author of the *Metodo GAM de Iniciación Musical para Niños* (GAM Method Musical Introduction for Children, 1998), and *El Hombre y la Musica* (Man and Music, 1993), in 1996 she founded the ONIX Nuevo

Ensemble de Mexico, a chamber group devoted to promoting world music. 2000 found her chairman of the Consejo Mexicano de la Musica (Mexican Council of Music) and principal at the Escuela de Iniciación a la Musica y la Danza del Centro Cultural Ollin Yoliztli. By 2005, as president, she collaborates with UNESCO and helps the development of young composers.

In 2001, she was invited by the International Council of Music (CIM/UNESCO) to join their Executive Committee. She is a member of the Committee of Honor of the General Council of Music of Barcelona, as well as a member of the Fundación Musicae of Spain. In 2002, she was awarded the Xochipilli Prize (Comuarte/INBA) as an outstanding creator in the field of Music in Mexico. A highlight of 2002 was Agudelo's coordination of a Pan American Forum and Symposium in Mexico to promote education, composition and the identity of Latin American music.

Widowed since 1992, her husband, Rubén Montaño, was an accountant with a strong bass-baritone voice who, in his youth, was soloist of the University of Mexico choir, premiering Bach's *St. Matthew's Passion* and other great choral works in his country. Their two daughters are Ileana, born 1967, an artist who lives in Mexico City and has given Graciela her first grandson, Iñaki Blasco Montaño, born June 5, 2000, who loves Mozart; and Leticia, born 1970, a baroque cellist, who studied at the National Conservatory in Mexico, then went to Amsterdam in 1999 to specialize in baroque cello performance. She moved to Barcelona in 2001 to join an orchestra.

Aguedelo's pieces for children, the piano suites *Aventuras* and *Juegos*, and *El Carnaval de los Niños*, (Children's Carnival) as well as poems and stories, are dedicated to her grandson to whom she began giving music lessons when he was four. March 2006 saw the release of a CD, *Aventuras*.

Leticia Armijo

LETICIA ARMIJO was born May 24, 1961. Her maternal grandfather, Gonzalo Torres, was a violinist in the Mariachi Vargas de Tecalitlán, Jalisco. Her father, Segio, played the guitar and accordion with her mother, Leticia Torres, singing together in a duo of traditional Mexican music. Leticia began guitar and accordion at four, violin at fourteen at the National Music Conservatory of the Institute of Fine Arts, and since sixteen has been part of Mexican traditional music groups.

She graduated with honors from the Escuela Nacional de Música de la Universidad Nacional Autónoma de México (UNAM) in composition, received her MM, and then a PhD at the Universidad Autónoma de Madrid, with the thesis: "Mexican Women Composers in the Second Half of the 20th Century: The works of Gloria Tapía, Lilia Vázquez and Maria Granillo." She is a professor at UNAM, belonging to the first generation of composers in electroacoustic music, where she has promoted seminars in electroacoustic music, computer assisted music, and music in the arts. She belongs to the Promotion of Mexican Concert Music and the Spanish Association of Cultural Heritage, promoting women's rights in Mexican musical and artistic life, encouraging their works for performance in the orchestral repertory and in publishing. She is director of the collective Women in Music, an organization belonging to the International Women in Music and Art and the International Spanish-American Women in Music and Art, with representation in UNESCO.

In addition to her performance career, she has composed for the theater and radio, and lectured on women composers in Vienna, Madrid and Mexico City. Since 1997 she has organized three international meetings on Women in Music, seven on Women in the Arts, and five on Latin American Women in the Arts.

Her compositions include: *Apasionado* for solo violin; *A tus recuerdos*, Theme and Variations for orchestra, world premiere by the Orquesta Sinfónica Nacional conducted by Enrique Diemecke, and performed by the Orquesta Sinfónica de Cuba; a String Quartet *A pesar de todo; Ayer su silencio hoy su voz*, original music for a play; and *Villancicos de navidad*, for orchestra, premiered by the Orquesta de Cámara del Nuevo Mundo in the Blas Galindo Hall, conducted by Johannes Bruno Ullrich. They have been performed in Mexico, France, Japan, Austria, Spain, Lisbon and the U.S. She and her music have been featured at the Festival Internacional Cervantino, Festival Cultural de Sinaloa, Primer Festival de Canto Nuevo, organized for channel 13 television, and the Segundo Encuentro de la Composición en México.

GEORGINA DERBEZ was born September 2, 1968, in Mexico City. Her mother, a ballerina, also played piano and recorder. Her psychiatrist father was a lover of classical music, with a huge collection of LPs. Georgina was taken to many concerts, and began piano at seven. Improvising came naturally to her, and she was soon composing little piano pieces which she played at recitals. Her teachers included Lea Levine and **Marta Garcia Renart**, followed by Ana Maria Tradatti at the Escuela Superior de Musica. A blossoming piano career was sadly cut short by acute tendonitis, so her focus returned to composition. This transition was greatly helped by studies with Arturo Marquez, and at the Escuela Superior de Musica (1994). Enrichment courses were with Robert Sierra (1994), Franco Donatoni (1996), Thierry Pecou (1997), as well as Theo Loevendie, Javier Alvarez, Herbert Vázquez, Mario Lavista, Carlos Schachter and **Ana Lara**, with whom she explored analysis of 20th century music. 1998–99 brought a fellowship from the National Culture and Arts Foundation to compose a string quartet and a percussion piece based on the *Cancionero del Duque de Calabria* (Spain, 1556), which was premiered by Ay Luna que Reluzes! during the International New Music Forum, with the renowned *Tambuco* percussion ensemble.

Derbez' workshops and courses range from the music of Bela Bartók, with Elliot Antokolletz at the 2000 Bartók Congress at the University of Texas (Austin), to *Composition Encounter* in Málaga and Madrid with Cristobal Halffter and Mauricio Sotelo (July 2000). May 2001 found her at Northeastern University in Illinois lecturing on Mexican composers, a course she repeated in Spain in July of that year.

Her music, reflecting influences of Debussy, Bartók, Messiaen and Ligeti as well as the Spanish renaissance, has been performed at major universities and festivals in Mexico and the U.S. Her *Nocturno*, for bassoon, clarinet and piano, was played by the Trio Neos at Vassar College (New York, 1998) and recorded on *Music of Women Composers of the Americas* (Quindecim Records, 2000). The Arditti String Quartet performance/recording of her String Quartet No. 1 (October 1999), was published by Hildegard Music. Other CDs include *Canciones de Luna* (Songs of the Moon) (Euram Records, 1999) with mezzo Encarnación Vázquez and pianist Alberto Cruzprieto. Pianist Ana Cervantes performed the U.S. premiere of *Cuatro Piezas en Seis Sonidos* in March 2001 during the Clausura concert of the *Muchas Voces/Many Voices* group residency at the Instituto Cultural de México of Washington, DC, with subsequent performances in New York, Wisconsin, San Antonio and Albuquerque.

Now on the composition faculty of the Superior School of Music of the National Center for the Arts in Mexico City, after her December 2000 graduation concert, Georgina received a commission from the National Symphony of Mexico, which premiered October 2001.

Maria Granillo

MARIA GRANILLO was born January 30, 1962, in Torreón Coahuila, Mexico. Her father is an engineer and mother, a painter. They exposed Maria to all kinds of music in her childhood. She studied guitar from age nine to fifteen, and piano from fifteen to twenty-five. She has a BM in Composition from Universidad Nacional Autónoma de México (UNAM), a Graduate Diploma (1990) from the Guildhall School of Music and Drama (London), MM from the University of York (England), and DMA (2003) from the University of British Columbia (Canada).

After teaching Music Education for Children at the Artene Institute, she became a professor of composition at UNAM since 1993, where she was head of the department from 1994–96. In 1997, the Cultural Domecq Institute and the Austrian Embassy in México awarded her the Mozart Medal, and in 1998 she was nominated for Best Original Music for the film *Luces de la Noche* by the Mexican Academy of Sciences and Cinematographic Arts.

Granillo's compositions include: *Dos Danzas para un Principio* (1991) for mixed choir, brass quintet and percussion, a selected work in the 1996 ISCM World Music Days in Denmark; *Marinas* (1994) for mixed choir, which won second place in Mexico's National Competition for Choral Music in 1998; *Trance* (1999) for flute, clarinet, trumpet, trombone, piano, harp, string quintet, timpani and vibraphone; *Contratiempos* (2001), a commission from the National Symphonic Orchestra of México; Concerto (2002) for recorder, flutes and string orchestra; *Glimpse* (2003) for chamber orchestra; *Misterios* (2003) for mixed choir; and *Breathing Music* (2005) for orchestra.

Maria has a daughter, Valentina Sandoval, born December 12, 1994.

CLAUDIA HERRERIAS was born November 4, 1962, in Mexico City. Her father, a graphic designer and painter, listened to classical music while he worked, so Claudia has enjoyed music since childhood. She took guitar lessons as a child, playing popular music, studied piano in school, but never considered music as a profession until at eighteen, while on holiday in Quebec, she met some jazz musicians who changed her mind.

She attended the Universidad Nacional Autónoma de México (UNAM), studying both piano and bassoon, before moving to Germany. She lived in Nuremberg and attended the conservatory there, studying composition with British musicologist **Vivienne Olive**. After graduation (1996), she earned her MM in Composition from the University of Glasgow, Scotland (2004).

Her compositions, which have been performed in Germany, Madrid, Havana, Veracruz and Mexico City, include: *Voghú* (1990) for three recorders and marimba; *Tortillas con Salsa* (1991) for chamber ensemble; *3 guitarras 3* (1992); *Preludio a lo impredecible* (1992) for piano; *Las chimeneas que observo a través de mi ventana* (1993) for oboe; *Tres en do* (1994) for percussion ensemble; *Siete* (1995) for chamber ensemble; *Otro Uno* (2003) for piano; *Nocturno* (2004) for chamber ensemble; *El barco* (2004) for orchestra.

Ana Lara

ANA LARA was born November 30, 1959, in Mexico City, the eighth of nine children. Although her parents were not into arts, most of their children had cultural careers, with the eldest brother a writer, two philosopher sisters and another a painter. Ana loved music ever since she could remember and started learning piano when, on a whim, her father decided to buy one when she was twelve. It was love at first sight and, she says, "From then on, I have lived in, on and for the music."

She studied composition at the National Conservatory of Music with Daniel Catán and Mario Lavista, participating in workshops of Humberto Hernandez Medrano and Carlos Chavez. She also studied with Federico Ibarra at CENIDIM. Her postgraduate studies were with Zbigniew Rudzinski and Wlodzimierz Kotónski at the Warsaw Academy of Music on a Mexican-Polish study grant.

In 1998, she founded the International Festival Música y Escena and has since served as its artistic director. This festival won the annual Award of the Mexican Union of Critics of Theater and Music (2001).

She has lectured at the Darmstadt Summer Courses in Germany, in the U.S. at Princeton, Rutgers and CUNY, Stony Brook, and in Canada at McGill and Montreal Universities. In 1989, she founded the Mexican Society of New Music, serving as president for two years, and was a member of the board of ISCM (1990–93). Since 1990, she has been producer of the radio program, "Hacia una nueva musica" at University Radio (UNAM).

She was composer-in-residence at the National Symphony of Mexico (1993–94), has won successive grants from the Mexican Ministry of Culture for young composers (1994–97, 1998–2001), the U.S./Canada/Mexico Creative Artists' Residency Program Grant (1997), and the Bellagio Artistic Residency (2000). The same year she was a Latin Grammy nominee for producer of Best Classical Album. In 2001, she won the annual Award of the Mexican Union of Critics of Theater and Music.

Alejandra Odgers

Lara's compositions, ranging from solo to orchestral works, chamber music, choral and vocal, plus stage and dance, have been performed in Mexico, Europe, North, Central and South America.

She received her master's degree in ethnomusicology from the University of Maryland in 2004.

ALEJANDRA ODGERS was born November 26, 1967, in Mexico City. Although her parents were not musical—her father is a mathematician and mother a physician—she was introduced to music in school, where she played percussion instruments. She began piano studies at twelve and oboe at seventeen. At the Universidad Nacional Autónoma de México (UNAM), she graduated with a performance degree in oboe (1997), in composition (2000), then earned MM and PhD degrees in composition from the University of Montreal. In addition to teaching at UNAM, she has been a director of special projects there and musicians' manager of the Mexico Philharmonic.

Her compositions include: *Discusión* for viola and piano (1995–98); *Trajín* for orchestra (1999) (revised 2003) which received honorable mention in the composition competition SIMFONICA (1999); *Nitiicasi* for bass flute, flute, and electroacoustic sounds (2000); *Auka* for orchestra (2001); *Drok Newodhow* for chamber orchestra (2003); *Yoania* for orchestra (2004); Concerto for bass clarinet and orchestra (2005); and *Icnocuícatl* for orchestra and choir (2004), which represented Mexico in the International Rostrum of Composers (2005).

Odgers' love of classical music also includes traditional Mexican music and folk dances. Within her family's love of the arts are sisters, Olga, a sociologist and dancer, and Elena, a painter.

Alejandra was married to conductor César Amora for seven years.

Born December 20, 1964, in Mexico City, **GABRIELA ORTÍZ** studied piano with José Kahan at the Escuela Vida y Movimiento (1985–87), analysis and composition with Mario Lavista at the National Conservatory of Music (1985–90), and under Federico Ibarra for her Licentiate in Composition at the National School of Music, University of Mexico (1987–90). She continued her studies at the Guildhall School of Music and Drama in London (1990–91), taking a postgraduate course in composition with Robert Saxton. She attended City University, London (1992–94), where she earned her PhD, and where I met her. In 1992, she participated at the International Course for Professional Choreographers and Composers, directed by Robert Coham, and in a course directed by Jonathan Harvey at the Dartington (England) Summer School for Electroacoustic Music.

Ortiz' works include *Danza* and *Patios Serenos*, for piano; *Divertimento* for solo clarinet; *Huitziti* for baroque flute; *Cuarteto 1* for string quartet; *Apariciónes* for wind quintet and string quintet; *Elegia* and *En Pares*, *Patios*, for orchestra, plus *Concerto for Percussion and Orchestra*. Her electroacoustic music compositions include *Magni Sin* for steel drum and tape; *Five Micro Etudes* for solo tape; and *Things like that Happen* for cello and tape. Multimedia works include *Hacia ia Deriva*, music written for Mandinga Dance Company; *Music for sculptures*, in collaboration with sculptor Elena Osterwalder; and *Eve and all the rest*, for the London Contemporary Dance Theatre.

MARTA GARCIA RENART was born in 1942 in Mexico City. She began studying music at age six, and received a scholarship from the Curtis Institute of Music in Philadelphia in 1959, where she studied with **Rudolf Serkin**. She graduated in 1964, the same year she won a scholarship to study for three years at the Mannes College of Music in New York with Carlos Schachter. In 1994, she received a grant from the government of the state of Queretaro. She is a founding member of Trío Mavros, which in 1999 won the National Chamber Music Competition. 2001 brought a grant to further the Trío with tours and records. Pursuing a busy career as a concert pianist, teacher and composer, Renart is at the same time the proud mother of Mara, Cora and Marco, whom she describes as "young people in full personal development." She also makes it clear that she plays with the same enthusiasm in Carnegie Hall (1964) as in the smallest of communities. An album of two CDs containing her most significant works was released in 2001, containing excerpts from *Cincos Miniaturas* with Andrea Lieberherr, flute, and **Virginia Eskin**, piano.

Marcela Rodriguez

MARCELA RODRÍGUEZ was born in 1951 in Mexico City. She studied composition with Maria Antonieta Lozano and Leo Brower. Her output includes three string quartets, symphonic pieces, five concertos—cello, guitar, percussion and two for flute—songs and works for solo instruments, many of them commissioned by festivals and institutions. Her opera *La Sunamita* (on CD) premiered at the Festival of Mexico City, 1991. Concerto for Recorders and Orchestra (Ofunam CD) was performed by the American Composers Orchestra at Carnegie Hall (1994), San Antonio Orchestra with Dennis Russell Davies (1996), and Simon Bolivar Orchestra (Venezuela, 1997), among others. Her guitar, cello and percussion concertos were played at the Festival Cervantino 1996, 1997 and 1998, by Sinfónica Nacional de Mexico and Orquestra sinfónica de Jalapa. Her *La Fábula de las Regiones* for string orchestra (on CD) has been performed in such far-flung places as Moldavia, Greece, Spain, Venezuela as well as her native Mexico. Also enjoying international success are her songs with text by Sor Juana Ines de la Cruz, titled *FUNESTA* (CD), and eight arias for soprano or tenor and harpsichord, *adúltera, enemiga*, text by Juan Ruiz de Alarcón. March 1998 marked the premiere of *Cantata del Tequila* for mixed choir and chamber orchestra, commissioned by the Festival del Centro Histórico de Mexico.

Rodríguez has been writing for theater and dance since 1979, working with major Mexican producers. She was a member of Sistema Nacional de Creadores (Composer Scholarships) 1994–2000. Besides more chamber music and theater pieces, 2001–02 saw the creation of two chamber operas, *Seneca* and *Sor Juana Inés de la Cruz* with libretti written expressly for her. In March 2001, pianist Ana Cervantes performed the U.S. premiere of *Como el Agua en el Agua* (Rodríguez' first work for solo piano) at the Mexican Cultural Institute of Washington, DC, with the composer in attendance. The world premiere of *El fuego* was performed at the *XXIX Festival Internacional Cervantino* in October of 2001 with the U.S. premiere, March 2002. *Flor robada #2: Arabesco* was composed during that same Spring of 2001 and received its world premiere with Cervantes in Washington, DC, November 2002.

GLORIA TAPÍA (MENDOZA) was born in Michoacán, Mexico, April 16, 1927. Although neither of her parents were musical, her grandmother, who studied singing, was a contributing influence to Gloria's love of music, and saw that she began piano at age eight.

She studied Philosophy at the Iberoamerican University where she met Rafael Vizcaino Treviño (1927–81), a Psychology major, who also loved music. After their marriage in October 1951, they both studied composition at the National Conservatory of Music in Mexico City, where they were living. Rafael became both a teacher—at UNAM and the conservatory—and a composer.

Gloria has been associated with the Ministry of Education since 1965. She was chairman of the National Program of Promotion of Music (1965–87); founder/chairman of the National Music Teachers' Competition (1979–86); professor at the Higher School of Music of the National Institute of Beauty Arts (1968–79); professor of music at the Latin American Institute of Communication and Education (1979–83); and professor at the National Conservatory of Music since 1983. She is also a founder/member of the League of Concert Music Composers of Mexico (1973)—she was their president four times—and in 1985 was chairman of the National Corrido Mexicano Contests.

Tapía's compositions include three symphonies, a piano concerto, clarinet concerto, five sonatas, twenty-five songs, twenty-three chamber music "Recreativas," and pieces for organ, guitar, wind instruments and symphonic band. Her music has been performed throughout Mexico, and in Norway, Austria, Japan, Peru, Venezuela and America. Her works have been the subject of four theses at UNAM, including that of **Leticia Armijo**.

Her Juvenile Suite in four movements, *Children's Hospital of Mexico* (1993), received the Ixtliton Award from the National Institute of Pediatrics on its fiftieth anniversary. She earned the Rafael Ramirez Teaching Medal from the Ministry of Education of the Government of Mexico for her thirty years of teaching, and the Goddess Xochipilli Award for Composers from the International Association of Women in the Arts.

Of Gloria's seven children, six are living, ranging in age from thirty-two to fifty-two. Ana Maria is a lawyer, Rebeca and Ignacio are mathematicians working in computers, Luis is a real estate administrator, Cecilia a journalist, and Gloria (Jr.) a biomedical researcher.

VERONICA TAPÍA, born January 12, 1961, in Puebla, Mexico, was led to music by her mother who sang and played guitar. Veronica began guitar and piano at age eleven, and flute at twenty. She earned her composition degree from the Universidad Nacional Autónoma de México (UNAM) in 1989, an MM from the University of York (England), 1999, and PhD from the University of Calgary (Canada), 2006. In addition to teaching positions from primary to university in Mexico, she also taught composition at the University of Calgary (2002–05).

Veronica Tapia

Her compositions include a suite for cello and piano (1984); *Tres en el alba* (wind quintet, 1993), which placed in the Xalitic National Composing Competition in Jalapa; *Veracruz* (mixed choir), won second prize in the 1995 National Sor Juana Inés de la Cruz Competition; *Biggidibella* (mezzo, soprano sax, clarinet and percussion, 1997), a third place winner in the R. Murray Schafer International Composers Competition in Poland; *The Lord's Prayer* (male choir or mixed choir, 1998), presented at the University of York, England); *Waking Dreams* (soprano and piano, 1998); *Errree* (children's or female choir, 2002); *Nuestro Amor* (tenor and piano, 2002); *Trio* (violin, cello and piano, 2003); *Three Orchestral Scenes* (orchestra, 2004); *Ladano*, bass clarinet and tape, 2004); and *Polarity* (percussion, 2005).

Veronica has a daughter Andrea, born May 19, 1991; and a son Manuel, April 14, 1995.

MARIANA VILLANUEVA was born in Mexico City in 1964. With her father the director of the "Casa del Lago," from the time she was seven she was exposed to the artistic realms of poetry, dance, theater and music. At a very young age, she received her first composition classes under the tutelage of Maria Antonieta Lozano. Later, she studied melody, harmony, counterpoint and piano with various other teachers and joined the group of Ollin Yoliztli, working with maestro Mario Lavista in analysis and composition. She entered the National Conservatory of Music as a member of his composition workshop. In 1985, she worked with the pilot workshop organized by CENIDIM, which included renowned Mexican pedagogues Daniel Catán, Julio Estrada, Federico Iarra and Mario Lavista. In 1988, she went to Pittsburgh to study at Carnegie Mellon University, where she obtained her teaching certificate and master's degree. Her principal teachers there were Leonardo Balada, Lukas Foss and Reza Vali in composition, and Robert Page in choir and choral arrangements.

In 1995, she participated in the International Course for professional choreographers and composers held each summer in England. Since 1987, her music has been programmed regularly in Mexico in venues dedicated to contemporary music such as the International Forum of New Music, Composers of the '50s–'60s, Cervantine Festival, etc. In the U.S., her work has been presented in New York, Indiana, New Mexico and Pittsburgh. In Europe, in Spain, Sweden and Switzerland. She has received awards from Carnegie Mellon and the National and State Fund for Culture and Arts (FONCA), the Fideicomiso MEXICO/USA and, in 1999, a Guggenheim grant.

Her U.S. commissions have been for the Carnegie Mellon Trio through violinist Andres Cardenes, from David Stock for the Pittsburgh New Music Ensemble, and in Mexico from the National Fund for Music and Bellas Artes, from Luis Gumberto Ramos and Victor Flores. In addition to composing for soloists, chamber groups and orchestra, Villanueva has written music for theater and collaborated with the Ballet of Space Theatre. By 2003 she had received her doctorate in history at the Universidad Autonóma Metropolitana.

ARGENTINA

Composer, musicologist, conductor **ALICIA TERZIAN**, born July 1, 1938, in Córdoba, is of Armenian descent. She studied composition with **Alberto Ginastera** (1916–83) at the Conservatorio Nacional de Música in Buenos Aires, from which she graduated in 1958, winning the Gold Medal in 1959. She researched sacred Armenian musicology of the 4th to 12th centuries with Father Leoncio Daian in Venice and pursued private conducting studies with Mariano Drago. Her many awards for composition include the Municipal Prize (1964), National Fund of the Arts Prize (1979, 1982), and National Grand Prize for Music (1982). She has been decorated as a Knight of the Order of the Academic Palms by the French government (1987), received the St. Dahag and St. Mesrob medals from His Holiness the Catholic Pope of all Armenians Vazken I (1988) and the Mozart Medal from the International Council of Music (1995). Commissions have come from the Gulbenkian Foundation of Lisbon, London Ices Festival, Festival of Zagreb, Aspekte Salzburg Festival, Banco Mayo Foundation, Grenoble Orchestra, Radio France, Dutch pianist Marcel

Alicia Terzian

Worms, Argentine organist Adelma Gómez, Ensemble Contemporánea of Denmark, Dutch bass clarinetist Harry Sparnaay and the Simón Bolívar Orchestra of Venezuela, among many others.

In 1968, she organized the Encuentros Internacionales de Música Contemporánea Foundation, whose members, since 1979, are the representatives of the International Society for Contemporary Music in Argentina. Through this institution she organized concerts, seminars, radio and television programs, the Argentine Tribune of Composers, and editions of compact discs. As conductor of GRUPO ENCUENTROS (created in 1978), they have participated in over twenty-five international tours on four continents with more than 200 concerts, and presented new works, specifically avant-garde, written by Argentine and Latin American composers. As of 2004 their CDs are: *American Roots, The Vanguards in Argentina, Tangos and something more*, and *Encounters . . . with the tango in France*.

Terzian's compositions include orchestral and chamber music. Her Violin Concerto (1955), now on CD with Rafael Gustily and the Symphonic Orchestra of Zurich under Daniel Schweitzer, features brilliant technical display of the solo instrument. Its elegiac slow movement is based on an Armenian folk song. Other early works are *Danza Criolla* (1954) and *Tres Madrigales para coro femenino* (1958). *Cuaderno de imágenes* (1964) incorporates unusual striking effects on the organ. *Caren criatennuralis* (1971) contains a horn soliloquy in a framework of grotesque sonorities, while *Voces* (1979) dramatically uses verbal sounds and musical tones. Later works are *Yagua-Ya Yuca* for mezzo, flute, clarinet, piano, violin, cello and tape (1992), *Les yeux fertiles* (piano, 1998), *Tango Blues* (piano, 1999), *Le viol des anges* (1999), *Percusionista Ofrenda a Bach* (organ, 2000), and *À côté des rêves* (2001) for piano, violin and clarinet, plus a ballet. Her works are performed and broadcast worldwide.

Terzian has chaired the departments of composition, orchestration, counterpoint, history and esthetics of music at the National Conservatory of Music, Municipal Conservatory and School of Fine Arts of the University of La Plata and the Higher Institute of Art of the Teatro Colón of Buenos Aires. She has given numerous seminars at more than 3,000 major conservatories and universities of Europe, the Far East and the three Americas, as well as on European and American radio.

A member of the National Academy of Bellas Artes of Chile and artistic director of the Foundation for International Meetings of Contemporary Music, she is a frequent jurist on international instrumental and composition contests. As director of the Society for the Promotion of New Music in North and South America, as well as executive secretary of the Latin American and Caribbean divisions of the International Music Council of UNESCO, she helped create the National Councils of Music of UNESCO in Mexico, Guatemala, El Salvador, the Dominican Republic, Ecuador, Colombia, Venezuela, Bolivia, Uruguay, and revitalized the Councils of Cuba, Chile and Costa Rica. With this nucleus of Latin American countries, in March 2000 she organized a meeting in Cuba with the goal of promoting a major musical event involving all the countries of the continent.

As artistic director of the Encuentros Foundation, over the past thirty years, she has arranged the presentation of Argentine composers performing their works in the International Tribunal of Composers (UNESCO, Paris) and the annual festivals of World Music Days organized by the SIMC.

In October 2003, in Montevideo (Uruguay), Terzian was voted as a new honorary member of the International Music Council of UNESCO as part of the thirtieth General Assembly. Thus, she joins a roster of illustrious names such as Aram Katchaturian, Alberto Ginastera, Yehudi Menuhin, Isaac Stern, Claudio Abbado, Jorge Boulez, Mstislav Rostropovich, Joan Sutherland, Seiji Ozawa, Ravi Shankar, Dmitri Shostakovich, Witold Lutoslawski and José Carreras.

URUGUAY

BEATRIZ LOCKHART was born in the capital, Montevideo, January 17, 1944. Although her parents were not musical, there was a piano in their house which she began playing at age six. She studied at the National Conservatory of Music, graduating in composition.

She was professor of harmony and counterpoint at the Juan José Landaeta School of Music in Caracas, Venezuela, from 1979–87. In 1988, she returned to Montevideo and became professor of harmony at the conservatory, now named Escuela Universitaria de Música.

Her compositions include *Masia Muju* for flute and orchestra, *Homenaje a Astor Piazzolla* for solo piano, and *Pieza Montevideana No.2* for double bass and orchestra.

She is married to Antonio Mastrogiovanni, also a composer. Their daughter, Mariana, born 1980, is a violist.

GRACIELA PARASKEVAÍDIS, born April 1, 1940, in Buenos Aires, Argentina, studied composition with Roberto García Morillo at the Conservatorio Nacional de Música in Buenos Aires. From 1965–66, on a scholarship from the Centro Latinoamericano de Altos Estudios Musicales (CLAEM), she took courses with Gerardo Gandini and Iannis Xenakis at the Instituto Torcuato Di Tella, also in Buenos Aires. She completed her composition studies with Wolfgang Fortner at the Musikhochschule Freiburg/Breisgau (Germany, 1971), on a grant from the Deutscher Akademischer Austauschdienst (DAAD). She also attended Darmstadt in 1972.

A composer of chamber, choral, vocal, and piano works that have been performed and received awards in the Americas, Asia and Europe, she taught at the Universidad Nacional in Montevideo, Uruguay (1985–92), as well as privately, and has given lectures, seminars and workshops in Argentina, Austria, Brazil, Chile, Colombia, Germany, Greece, Sweden, Switzerland, the UK and Uruguay.

In 1984, she served a guest residency at the Berliner Künstlerprogramm of DAAD and attended the First Symposium of Artists and Intellectuals of Greek Origin (1985), by invitation of the Greek government. In 1994, she received the Goethe Medal from the Goethe Institute, Munich. She was an organizer for the permanent collective of the Cursos Latino Americanos de Música Contemporánea (CLAMC) from 1975–89, is a member of the Núcleo Música Nueva de Montevideo and the Sociedad Uruguaya de Música Contemporánea, and a former member of the Núcleo Música Nueva de Buenos Aires and the Sociedad Argentina de Música Contemporánea. In 2004, she co-founded, with Max Nyffeler, the website latinoamérica música and serves as its co-editor.

Specializing in 20th century Latin-American music since 1975, her essays have been published in the journals *Pauta* (Mexico) and *MusikTexte* (Germany). Her books include *La obra sinfónica de Eduardo Fabini* (1992) and *Luis Campodónico, compositor* (1999). She served as co-editor of *World New Music Magazine* (1990–99), the ISCM yearbook, and has contributed to the dictionary *Komponisten der Gegenwart* since 1992.

Graciela has lived in Uruguay since 1975 and holds both Argentinean and Uruguayan citizenship.

IRMA URTEAGA was born March 7, 1929, in San Nicolás, Buenos Aires. Her father was not musical, but her mother, a painter, played the piano and sang. When Irma was five, she admired a cousin who played piano, and at six, after frequent appeals, was given piano lessons.

She received her degrees in piano and composition from the National Conservatory of Music, and studied choral and orchestral conducting at the Institute of the Teatro Colón. Between 1974–78, she was co-director of the opera studio there, serving as pianist, singer coach and répétiteur. She also held a similar position at Opera Ecuador in Quito, from 1986–88. A professor of piano at the National Conservatory from 1973–86, she was on the Board of the Argentinian Association of Composers (1973–2002), as vice secretary from (1973–80) and vice president (1995–2002). She continues her collaboration with them. In 2004, the National Conservatory created the Argentine Forum of Women Composers where she became vice president.

Her compositions are mainly vocal in a neo-romantic style, while occasionally using avant-garde techniques, as in her chamber opera *La Maldolida* (1987; revised 2002). They include: *Ambitos* (1970) for orchestra; *Existenciales* (1974), three works for mezzo and piano; *Turbulencias* (1979) for violin and piano; *Sueños de Yerma* (1986) for mezzo soprano, flute, clarinet, violin, cello and piano; *World of Existence* (1990) for mezzo and orchestra; *Los alumbramientos* (The Enlightened Ones, 1992) a cantata for women's and children's chorus with string orchestra; *Cánticos para soñar* (1993), four pieces for soprano and piano; Concerto for Marimba and orchestra (1995); *Time for Memories* (1996) for clarinet, cello and piano; a ballet *Shining Light* (2001), which incorporated *Los Alumbramientos; Tangoforte* (2003) for violin, cornet and piano; and *Green, Green Sea* (2004) for soprano, baritone, and six percussionists. Works for piano include a Sonata (1968), *Escaléncicas* (Scales, 1992), *Variations on a theme by Beatriz Sosnik* (1997), *Ayer del Buen Ayer* (2001), revised for two pianos (2004).

In the course of her career, she has won the Gold Medal for Composition (1971); the National Conservatory Luis Gianneo Award (1974); City of Buenos Aires Award (1974, '76, '77); National Foundation of the Arts Award (1976, '80, '88); Society of Argentine Authors and Composers (1990); and the San Telmo Award of La Scala (2005).

Irma was married in 1953, divorced in 1966, and widowed in 1980. She has no children and never remarried.

VENEZUELA

A native of Caracas, **DIANA ARISMENDI** was born in 1962, to a mother who played Debussy for her as a baby, which led to piano lessons when she was able to reach the keyboard. At seventeen, she made the difficult decision to give up her piano career for composition, immersing herself in contemporary music trends, including electronic and atonal. In the 1980s, she went to Paris to study at L'École Normale de Musique, receiving her diploma in 1984, and the Diplôme Supérieur de Composition in 1986. She completed her masters in Composition and Latin American Music, and DMA (1994) at the Catholic University of America (Washington, DC).

Her output includes orchestral, choral, vocal, electronic, opera and chamber music. Her music has been performed by important soloists and orchestras in major concert halls of Venezuela, at the International Festival of Electronic Music, (Bourges, France), Women in Music Chard Festival (England), New Music Forum (Mexico City) and Kennedy Center, as well as Canada, Germany, Belgium, Spain, Luxembourg, Iceland, Mexico, Ecuador, Colombia, Cuba and El Salvador. Her opera, *The Cat and the Swallow: a Love Story*, premiered in Spain (1993), and Venezuela (1996). Her first CD, *Ficciones*, came in 1995. A second, devoted to her music, has also been released. Orchestral pieces dedicated to the memory of her brother, who died in 1994, was a 1996–97 project. Part of the Latin American Music Festival of Caracas since 1992, she has been their executive director since 1996.

Arismendi is a professor at the Simón Bolívar University, where she is coordinator of the Music Master's Degree Program. She has also been an academic advisor of the National Youth Orchestra.

JOSEFINA PUNCELES De BENEDETTI was born in New Haven, Connecticut, September 17, 1953, studied piano in London and Caracas, receiving a degree in choral conducting from the Instituto Universitario de Estudios Musicales (1991) and in composition from the Juan José Landaeta Conservatory (1994), both in Caracas. Her compositions include: *Canción de Cuna* for soprano and piano; *Palabreo* for mixed choir; *Guatopo* for mixed choir; *Requiem por un siglo* for mixed choir; and *Macuro* for orchestra, choir, ballet and narrator. Her works have been performed in Venezuela, Ecuador, Cuba, France and the U.S. Since 1995, she has been president-manager of the Orquesta Filarmónica Nacional in Caracas. She is also the secretary of the Venezuelan Music Council of UNESCO, where her work is oriented to the promotion of Venezuelan composers, and organizing contemporary Venezuelan orchestra and chamber music concerts.

Adina Izarra

ADINA IZARRA, born August 27, 1959, in Caracas, studied piano and composition at the Music Conservatory of Juan José Landaeta under the tutorship of Alfredo del Mónaco, graduating in 1977. She went to England for her BA (1983) and her PhD (1988) from York University, where she studied with Richard Orton and Vic Hoyland. Returning to Caracas, Izarra founded the group NOVA MUSICA for the performance of mixed electronic compositions. Her works have won many national prizes in Venezuela and are featured in international festivals. She writes incidental music for a leading Venezuelan theater company, and since 1988 has taught at the Simón Bolívar University in Caracas. In 1994, she participated in a festival of the American Composers Orchestra at Carnegie Hall. From 1999–2001, she was member of the executive committee of the International Society for Contemporary Music (ISCM).

Asian Composers

CANADA
Alice Ho
Melissa Hui
Alexina Louie

CHINA
Joan Huang
Jing Jing Luo Haven
Chen Yi
Li Yiding

JAPAN
Nagako Konishi
Karen Tanaka

KOREA
Unsuk Chin
Jee Young Kim
Hyo-Shin Na
Younghi Pagh-Paan

MACAU
Bun-Ching Lam

MALAYSIA
Su Lian Tan

TAIWAN
Shih-Hui Chen

Making a name for themselves in all fields of music are women born in Asian countries. The following are representative of those recognized in the field of composition. Some have remained in their own countries, while others have settled in America and Europe, adding oriental flavor to the variegated melting pot that is late 20th and early 21st century music.

SHIH-HUI CHEN, born in Taipei, Taiwan, came to the U.S. in 1982 and received her DMA in composition from Boston University. Her works have been performed by the Cleveland Chamber Symphony, Aspen Music Festival, Voices of Change in Dallas, Empyrean Ensemble in California, and at festivals in Taiwan, Korea, Japan, Germany, Rome and Amsterdam. She has received grants from the Fromm Foundation, NEA, Meet the Composer, Tanglewood, Massachusetts Cultural Council, ASCAP (1995 to present), the Mary Ingraham Bunting Institute of Radcliffe College, American Academy in Rome (1999), the Guggenheim Foundation (2000) and Barlow Commission (2001).

Her filmscore for the documentary, *Once Removed*, by film maker Julie Mallozzi, was premiered at the Museum of Fine Arts in Boston. To educate children about new music, she wrote *Little Dragonflies*, a set of children's piano pieces based on Taiwanese folk melodies and an orchestral piece, *Moments*, premiered by the Philadelphia and Cleveland Orchestras for their educational programs. She was composer-in-residence at the Boston University Tanglewood Institute (2000), is the music advisor to the Foundation for Chinese Performing Arts, and assistant professor of composition at the Shepherd School of Music, Rice University (Houston, Texas).

UNSUK CHIN was born in 1961, Seoul, Korea. Lessons in piano and music theory came at a very early age. Her studies at the National University of Seoul included piano and composition with Sukhi Kang, who introduced her to musical modernism. She appeared as pianist at the Pan Music Festivals, and in 1984 her work *Gestalten* (Figures) was selected for the ISCM World Music Days in Canada and for the UNESCO "Rostrum for Composers." In 1985, she moved to Europe when she received the DAAD stipend for study in Germany, and took composition lessons with **György Ligeti** (*b* 1923) in Hamburg until 1988. Since then, she has lived in Berlin, composing and working in the electronic studio of the Technical University. Her compositions have been performed at numerous festivals throughout Europe and the Far East, with commissions from the Paris Ensemble intercontemporain, Gaudeamus Foundation, Tokyo Metropolitan Symphony and the Inventionen Festival in Berlin. She sees a distinct compositional divide between acoustic and electronic scores and does not integrate their musical strands.

Her works include *Trörinnen* (from Euripides' play *The Trojan Women*), a setting for three female soloists, women's chorus and orchestra. The orchestral work *santika Ekatala* won first prize in a competition celebrating the fiftieth anniversary of the Tokyo government (1993). The title is taken from Sanskrit and means *harmony to ward off evil consequences*, a reference to the Buddhist-Shamanistic tradition of a ritual to summon good prospects at the start of any important undertaking. *Akrostichon-Wortspiel* (Acrostic-Wordplay), written in 1991 for soprano and eleven instruments—some with microtonal tunings—is a fantastical cycle of seven wordless studies, demonstrating the composer's meticulous ear for imaginative textures and vivid instrumental colors. Other scores include a chamber piece for the Ensemble intercontemporain. *Fantaisie mécanique*, premiered in Paris in 1994.

She was the 2004 Grawemeyer Award winner for Music Composition for her Concerto for Violin and Orchestra. Unsuk Chin is the third woman to win this prize since it was instituted in 1985. The other winners are **Joan Tower** (1990) for her orchestral *Silver Ladders*, and **Kaija Saariaho** (2002) for her opera *l'amour de loin*.

ALICE HO (See Canadian Composers.)

Joan Huang

JOAN HUANG was born in Shanghai, December 27, 1957, where she received her early music education from her parents, both musicians. When the Cultural Revolution of Mao Tse Tung (Zedong) broke out in 1966, her parents burned most of their musical scores, books and records in fear of the Red Guards who frequently stormed homes in search of evidence to persecute the "elitist" and the "bourgeois." Joan's teenage years were lived in a montage of the misery of these times. Schooling was disrupted. The curriculum was dictated by Chairman Mao's doctrines. In high school, Joan secretly wrote songs and asked some of her classmates to sing them. Not allowed to go to college—college was only for the youth of the working class—she was exiled to hard labor with other "children of the bourgeois." In Joan's case, this was on a farm for three years to accept "re-education" and excavate waterways and ditches from morning until night. One positive aspect was that during this time Joan was exposed to the authentic Chinese traditional music of the local farmers. She taught herself theory by studying her mother's old music homework, which she had managed to hide in her meager luggage. After six months, when it came to light that she had musical ability, her workday was limited to mornings and her afternoons were spent assigned to an ensemble, writing songs in praise of Chairman Mao and the Revolution. In the evenings, while the rest of the ensemble led the singing, Joan accompanied them on her violin, which she had managed to bring from Shanghai.

With music her only outlet, after she fed the pigs she would sometimes stay in the sty playing "politically acceptable revolutionary songs" just to be able to practice! At other times she and her friends, some of whom had smuggled in some politically unacceptable Paganini etudes, would walk twenty minutes to the ocean to play where they could not be heard. In 1978, the more moderate Deng Xiaoping came to power, and the tumultuous revolution that had shackled ten precious years of culture, in the course of which many artists had been killed or committed suicide, finally came to an end with the reopening of the Shanghai Conservatory of Music. Out of 1,600 vying to get in, after grueling examinations, Huang was among the top 1 percent who qualified to enter. She obtained both BA and MA degrees from the conservatory after an equally grueling eight years, during which the specter of expulsion hovered over anyone who was late for class or sick.

In 1986, Joan came to the U.S. via an advertisement about music studies at UCLA. Five years later (1991) she received her PhD, after studying with **Elaine Barkin** and American composer **William Kraft**—whom she married November 30, 1991. The same year she was the only finalist for an assistant professorship in composition at UC Irvine.

Huang has embarked upon creating a fusion of Chinese traditional musical language with Western contemporary compositional techniques. Her awards include two from Phi Beta Kappa for international students, and two Aspen Music Festival Scholarships. In 1991, she was a visiting composer in the Contemporary Music Concert Series by the National Repertory Orchestra at Keystone, Colorado, where her chamber piece *Yellow Land* (flute, clarinet, percussion, piano, violin, cello) received a lauded performance by the Aspen Contemporary Music Ensemble. In 1992, pianist **Gloria Cheng** commissioned a work for her concert at Weill Recital Hall in Carnegie Hall, February 1993. The piece, *Pipa Journey*, received critical acclaim on both coasts. (A pipa is a Chinese lute-like instrument.) In 1993, Huang's string quartet, *Yang-guan Songs*, premiered by the Ying Quartet, was well-received during the Tanglewood Contemporary Music Week.

She was one of seven guest composers attending the New Music Festival, "New Directions in Asian-American Music," held at UC Santa Barbara where her *Two Poems from Ancient China* was premiered. In 1994, *The Legend of Chang-e* (violin and marimba) won first prize in Marimolin's[30] Seventh Annual Composition Contest. The same year the L.A. Philharmonic commissioned *Tu-fia Dance*, and Pittsburgh New Music Ensemble, *Meng-long*, which won the Alea III International Composition Prize (1995), and was subsequently heard in Boston and Pittsburgh. 1995 also saw performances of *Yellow Land* in Chicago, Iowa City and Austin. In 1996, Piano Sphere commissioned *Reflection after a Rainbow*, and premiered it in Los Angeles. Ekko performed *The Legend of Chang-e* in Washington, DC, and *Gallerie Chinoise Post-'89* was aired at the International Double Reeds Convention in Orlando, Florida. The Women's Philharmonic performed *The Myth of the Leifeng Pagoda*, a concerto for violin and chamber orchestra (1996, '97) in San Francisco, and *Settings for Twelve Chinese Symbols* received its premiere by the Southwest Chamber Music Society in Los Angeles. *Yellow Land* is featured on an Innocent Eyes & Lenses CD, titled *Sounds Like 1996: Music by Asian American Artists*. In March 1996, Huang was part of a Composers Forum at USC. May 1997 marked another performance of *The Myth of Leifeng Pagoda*, by the Cleveland Chamber Symphony, with soloist Sharan Leventhal. The Boston Artist Ensemble commissioned and premiered her piano trio *Remembering South River Land* (February 2000). The same piece was performed in October 2000, when Huang was invited by the American Composers' Orchestra to participate in the Pacific Rim Music Festival in New York. It was heard again March 2002, with members of the New West Symphony during the New Music Festival (Ventura, California), and July 2002, by the Triplehelix Piano Trio in Boston. *The Ambuscade* (Piano and Percussion) was performed at USC, February 2002.

After an absence of seven years, Huang returned to Shanghai in 1993. In 1994, she acted as interpreter when her husband guest conducted the Shanghai Philharmonic. She visited her family again in 1995. With each successive tour she finds the political climate more liberal, the economy slowly veering toward capitalism, with emphasis on science and technology, while culture and the arts are withering from lack of government subsidies. (Dare we say, much like America?)

Since March 1997, Joan has been a regular columnist with the bimonthly Chinese professional magazine *The Music Lovers* in Shanghai.

2001 marked the beginning of a major project commissioned by Chinese-American cellist Frank Su Huang (a friend, but no relation) of sixteen pieces based on Chinese music treasures, such as regional operas, folk songs, children's folk nursery rhymes, street vendors' tunes, etc. Combining avant-garde compositional techniques with very authentic sounds of various Chinese traditional instruments, the main purpose is to rescue these characteristic tunes and bring them to life in 21st century modern China. The cello is the only Western instrument used. Recorded with local musicians on the Shanghai Audio-Video Publisher label, the CD entitled *We Are Huang* was released January 2004.

---

30. Marimolin consists of the successful duo, begun in 1986, of Nancy Zeltsman, marimba, and Sharan Leventhal, violin. Recipients of many grants, their commissions are prized. They reprised Huang's *The Legend of Chang-e* in Germany, 1996.

Joan's *Four Madrigals of Li Bai* (a Chinese poet) was commissioned and performed by the Pacific Symphony at the Trade Winds from China Festival (Costa Mesa, California), March 2004.

MELISSA HUI - (See Canadian Composers.)

Korean-born composer **JEE YOUNG KIM** studied composition at Yonsei University in Seoul (BM), Indiana University (MM), and Yale (DMA, 2001). Her music, harmonizing the unique cultural aspects from Eastern and Western traditions, has won awards from ASCAP, IAWM, NACUSA, Meet the Composer, Aspen and Norfolk Chamber Music Festivals, and has been performed by chamber orchestras and ensembles in the U.S., Europe and Asia as well as the Seattle Symphony, Su-Won Philharmonic Orchestra (Korea), De ereprijs in the Netherlands, ISCM International Summer Course for Young Composers (Poland), Four Plus Percussion Group (Korea), American Composers Forum, and Silk Road Ensemble—a 2001 commission for *Tryst*—led by world-famous cellist, **Yo-Yo Ma**.

NAGAKO KONISHI, born September 16, 1945, in Agematsu, Nagano, Japan, received an advanced degree from Tokyo National University of Fine Arts (1971), where she studied with Tomojiró Ikenouchi, Makoto Moroi and Akio Yashiro. From 1976–78, as a graduate student at UC Berkeley, she continued composition studies with American composer **Andrew Imbrie** (*b* 1921). She was chairperson of the Federation of Women Composers in Japan, 1981–94. Her works, such as *Misty Poem* for alto flute and harp (1982), are written for both Japanese and Western instruments in a style reflecting the importance of resonance. Others include *Transience I* (1979), *Transience II* (1982) and *Transience III* (1984), *Path of the Wind* (1986), *Away the White* (1989), *Serenade* (1990), *Sinful Petals* (1991), *Death Valley* (1992), *Bright Steps* (1993), *Inner Eyes* (1993), *Romanze-IV* (1994), *Ode for the Eleven* (1995).

Bun-Ching Lam

Composer, pianist and conductor **BUN-CHING LAM**, born in Macau, June 26, 1954, began studying piano at age seven and gave her first public solo recital at fifteen. In 1973, she was an exchange student at the University of Redlands, California. In 1976, she received a BA in piano performance from the Chinese University of Hong Kong. Lam accepted a scholarship from UCSD (San Diego), where she studied composition with Bernard Rands, Robert Erickson, Roger Reynolds and **Pauline Oliveros**, receiving a PhD in 1981. She continued her association with the latter, and in 1995 was elected a Board member of the Pauline Oliveros Foundation. In 1981, Lam joined the faculty of the Cornish College of the Arts (Seattle), teaching composition, theory and piano until 1986. In 1983, she performed with avant-garde composer **John Cage** (1912–92), recording *Atlas Eclipticalis* with Winter Music. The same year she presented a concert of her own music. In 1984, she received a commission from Miles Anderson for *Three Easy Pieces*.

A winner of the Prix de Rome in 1991, Lam has also been awarded first prizes at the Aspen Music Festival, Northwest Composers' Symposium, Hong Kong Conservatory Art Songs Competition, and the highest honor at the Shanghai Music Competition—the first international composers' contest to take place in China. She is also a recipient of grants and fellowships from the New York Foundation for the Arts, NEA, Meet the Composers' Composer/Choreographers Project (1989, 1992), American Composers' Orchestra, Meet the Composer/Reader's Digest Commissioning Program, Kings County Arts Commission and Seattle Arts Commission. Her works have been performed at music festivals such as the "Pacific Sounding" (Japan), Aspeckte (Austria), ISCM World Music Days (Hong Kong), New Music America (Los Angeles), Sound Shape III Festival (San Diego), the First Contemporary Chinese Composers' Festival (Hong Kong) and the 24 Hours Communications (Belgium).

Lam conducted the Macau Sinfonietta in a program which included the premiere of *Saudades de Macau*, commissioned by the Macau Cultural Institute. Among her other commissioned works are *The Child God*, a puppet opera with Chinese Shadow Figures for Bang on a Can Festival (New York), *Impetus* for the Hong Kong Chinese Orchestra, and *Klang* for Swiss percussionist Fritz Hauser. In October 1994, *Sudden Thunder* had its world premiere at Carnegie Hall as part of the American Composers Orchestra program, and was again performed by The Women's Philharmonic in San Francisco. Her twenty-minute score, *Like Water*, premiered as a concert work by the San Francisco Contemporary Music Players, March 1995, was composed for a dance by choreographer June Watanabe and performed in May at Theater Artaud. *Last Spring*, for pianist **Ursula Oppens** and the Arditti Quartet, premiered at the 1996 Twelfth Tokyo Summer Festival. Lam spent March and April of 1996 as artist-in-residence at the Rockefeller Foundation's Bellagio Center in Italy, where she worked on *Bigorio*, a film score. In May of that year, her *Last Love Songs* for baritone and piano was premiered at Weill Recital Hall of Carnegie Hall. Her use of Chinese instruments like the xun, di, pipa and zheng give her compositions a unique sound.

In 1997, she was a visiting professor in composition at Yale and Bennington College, Vermont. During the 2000–01 season, she was composer-in-residence with the New Jersey Symphony Orchestra. In 2002, she spoke in the Distinguished Alumni Lecture series at Chung Chi College, Hong Kong, celebrating their fiftieth anniversary. She was the recipient of a Guggenheim Fellowship, the Rome Prize, and received first prizes at the Aspen Music Festival, Northwest Composers' Symposium and Shanghai Music Competition. Her chamber opera, *Wenji - Eighteen Songs of the Nomad Flute*, premiered at the Asia Society in New York and the Hong Kong Arts Festival.

Lam now lives and works in New York.

ALEXINA LOUIE (See Canadian Composers.)

JING JING LUO HAVEN was born Beijing, October 26, 1953. Her father was a famous Chinese opera composer, her mother, an opera singer. Piano lessons began for the child at age four. As a teenager, Jing Jing entered nurses training at the military hospital in Hunan, but drawn to music she studied composition and piano performance at the Shanghai Conservatory (BA 1980). She came to the U.S. to study composition, piano and organ performance at the New England Conservatory (MM 1987). Next came SUNY Stony Brook, for composition and electronic music with **Daria Semegen** (PhD 1993).

Her numerous awards for composition, both in China and U.S., include six consecutive ASCAP awards. Although the majority of her commissions and awards are for chamber music, she also writes orchestral, vocal, choral, and electronic music. In April 1999, The Women's Philharmonic premiered *The Slough*, for chamber orchestra.

Divorced, she lives with her two children, Sarah born July 16, 1991, in Beijing, while Luo was there as a Fulbright Scholar, and Jonah, born May 23, 1995, in Ashland (Oregon), about whom Jing Jing proudly proclaims, "Jonah can run for president when he grows up, because he was born in the USA."

Luo Haven was assistant professor at the China Conservatory (1980–83), teaching assistant at New England (1982–87), and Stony Brook (1987–90). Since 1993, she has been adjunct professor at Ashland University, and guest composer/lecturer at Oberlin (Ohio). In addition to teaching and composing, she is piano accompanist for the Ashland Theater Department, and organist at St. Timothy Lutheran Church.

In 2001, she received a Rockefeller Foundation Grant for the summer residency program at Bellagio, Italy, where beside beautiful Lake Como she could compose in heavenly tranquility. 2002–03 found her as composer-in-residence with the Nazareth College Chamber Quartet in Rochester, New York.

San Francisco-based composer **HYO-SHIN NA**, born in Seoul, Korea, October 28, 1959, began piano lessons at six and composing at ten. Her BA is from Ewha University (Korea, 1982), MM from Manhattan School of Music (1985) and DMA from University of Colorado, Boulder (1988). She is the youngest person ever to receive the Korean National Composers Prize (1994).

Her music, for both western and traditional Korean instruments, has been performed at festivals in Korea, Malaysia, Japan, Israel, Germany, throughout the U.S., and by the San Francisco Contemporary Music Players, Earplay, and Stanford String Quartet. In 1999, the Kronos Quartet commissioned *Song of the Beggars*, which was performed in Europe, Canary Islands, Canada, U.S., and heard on NPR, German and Belgian Radio. Her music for solo piano has been played by her husband, Thomas Schultz, in San Francisco, New York and Kyoto, and by Yuji Takahashi at the Pacific Music Festival in Sapporo (Japan). Yuji and Aki Takahashi have performed her music for two pianos in Tokyo.

Na has received commissioning awards from the Fromm Foundation for the San Francisco Contemporary Music Players, the National Cultural Center of Korea for the Seoul Contemporary Music Festival, and ASCAP Standard Awards (1998 through 2001). She has lectured in Korea and America on the relationship between her work and traditional Korean music. In summer 1999, she was composer-in-residence at the National Center for Korean Traditional Performing Arts in Seoul. In 2000, she received an Asian American Arts Foundation Fellowship and was a Djerassi Foundation Resident Artist.

On February 3, 2001, the Contemporary Music Ensemble Korea, performing at the Asian Arts Museum, San Francisco, premiered two of her works which explored relationships between Korean and Western-based instruments, *Blue Yellow River* for kayagum (Korean zither), cello, and double bass, and *Chung-Ji-Hyang*.

She is the author of *Conversations with Kayageum Master Byung-ki Hwang* (Pulpit Press), and has released two CDs of her music, *Blue Yellow River* (Top Arts Inc.) and *Music for piano and strings* (Seoul Records, Inc).

Younghi Pagh-Paan

South Korean composer **YOUNGHI PAGH-PAAN**, born on November 30, 1945, in Cheongju, is the daughter of a bridge builder. She learned to play the piano as a child, and put her first composition to paper at twelve. She studied music theory and composition at the Seoul National University (1965–72), and at the Academy of Music in Freiburg (1974–79) via a scholarship. Her teachers there were Klaus Huber, composition, Brian Ferneyhough, analysis, Peter Förtig, music theory, and Edith Picht-Axenfeld, piano. By 1978, she had won the jury prize at the Fifth International Composers' Seminar in Switzerland for *Man-Nam* (clarinet and string trio), and in 1979, Korea's Nan-Pa music prize and first prize at the UNESCO International Rostrum of Composers in Paris for the same piece. Since 1979, she has lived as a freelance composer in Bremen, Germany, and Panicale, Italy. In the 1980s, she received German endowments from the Strobel Foundation and Baden-Würtemberg. She was a guest composition professor at the Academy of Music, Graz (Austria) since 1991 and, beginning in 1992, at the Academy of Music in Karlsruhe (Germany). Since 1994, she filled the same position at the Hochschule für Künste at Bremen.

Although Pagh-Paan's early works were mostly instrumental, her later compositions show more vocal writing. She combines constructive principles of avant-garde with traditions and aesthetics of her East Asian origins. Strongly influenced by Shamanism, she wrote *Aa-ga 1*, for cello solo, which has principles of *p'ansori*, an opera with one voice accompanied only by one drum. There are only five p'ansories extant from ancient times. It is a form that is seeing a revival. Her works for orchestra include *Sori* (1980), *Nim* (1987) and *Hong* (1993). *Hang-Sang* (1995) for two clarinets, and *Noch* (1996) for soprano and viola, are heard at contemporary music festivals across Europe.

In 1995, Pagh-Paan received the top female composer prize at the Heidelberg Gegenwelten Festival.

Her father, who died at a young age, wrote poems and played the Korean bamboo flute. His daughter has followed in his artistic footsteps, building *her* bridge between East and West. She lives in Holland with her Dutch husband.

SU LIAN TAN, born in Malaysia, is assistant professor in composition, voice, and flute at Middlebury College, Vermont. She received her musical training at Princeton (James Randall, Steven Mackey, and Scott Burnham), Juilliard (**Vincent Persichetti**, **Milton Babbitt**, and **Bernard Rands**) and Bennington (Lou Calabro and **Vivian Fine**).

As a flutist, at age fourteen she was recording for radio and television, and at seventeen became both a fellow and licentiate of Trinity College, London. She worked with Jacob Glick at Bennington in chamber music, had private studies with Claude Monteux, and master classes with renowned flutist **Jean-Pierre Rampal** (1922–2000). She has been a soloist with orchestras in the U.S. and abroad, including an eleven performance tour with the Vermont Symphony in her own work, *Autumn Lute Song*. She appeared at the SEAMUS National Conference as a soloist, and performs regularly with the Middlebury Chamber Soloists both as flutist and singer.

As a composer, Tan won an ASCAP award, Meet the Composer grant, Irving Berlin Scholarship, Naumburg Fellowship, residency fellowships at the Yaddo and McDowell colonies, and was composer-in-residence at the Composer's Forum of the East, and at the Warebrook Festival. She was a finalist in the Kucyna International Competition, the International Composer's Competition (NEM), and her *Two Scenes* won the composition competition of the IWBC.

Her works have been performed by the Seattle Symphony, Da Capo Chamber Players, Middlebury Chamber Soloists, Vermont Symphony, The Core, Mosaic, Cassatt Quartet, Chicago Ensemble, Perpetuum Mobile Ensemble, ALEA III, Amici Musici and Meridian Arts Ensemble, who performed *Moo Shoo Rap Wrap*, a commissioned work, on their tours in America and the Netherlands.

Karen Tanaka

KAREN TANAKA, born in 1961 in Tokyo, began her musical education with piano lessons when she was four. She quickly developed a passion for composition, receiving formal tuition by age ten. During her four years' study at the Toho Gakuen School of Music, she won several major composition awards including prizes at the Viotti and Trieste competitions in Italy and the Japan Symphony Foundation Award. Her first international success came with her orchestral work, *Prisms*, which was premiered by the Toho Philharmonic in Tokyo (1984), and two years later played at the ISCM World Music Days in Budapest. This work has subsequently been performed widely in Europe and recorded on the Swedish BIS label. Fascinated by the effects of light through a prism, she set out to demonstrate these various phenomena in sound using the different instrumental colors of the orchestra. This process of gradual transfiguration through circular transformation appears in the construction of her other work from this period, the trio *Tristesse* (Sadness, 1983), inspired by Edgar Allan Poe's *The Raven*. *Tristesse* personifies poignant sadness for the inevitability of death.

While the simplicity and delicacy of language remained in later compositions, the move to Paris in 1986 brought out a new voice. A French government scholarship enabled studies with Tristan Murail. She also worked at IRCAM. Extremely interested in science and technology, at the beginning of 1992 Tanaka returned to IRCAM for an extended period of study after which the use of the computer became an integral part of her compositional process.

Residency in Europe opened up access to new audiences for her music, which over the next four years was performed in the Netherlands, Spain, Britain, France, Italy, Germany, Norway, Sweden and Poland—where she was featured in an ISCM/Polish Television film on international composers. Her first work composed in Paris, *Anamorphose* (1986), a piano concerto, won the Gaudeamus Prize at the International Music Week in Amsterdam in 1987. The word, taken from the technology of optics, means a distorted figuration, which she transposed into musical terms by distortions of timbres and structure.

Constantly seeking new material, Tanaka went to the Banff Centre (Alberta, Canada) in 1988 to take part in the Advanced Musical Studies Course. Lessons with Italian modernist **Luciano Berio** (1925–2003) inspired the glass hard sounds demanded of the pianist in *Crystalline* (1988). Other exquisitely crafted works include *Lilas* (cello, 1988), *Jardin des herbes* (1989) for harpsichordist Frances-Marie Uitti, and *Hommage en cristal* (1991) for piano and strings, commissioned by the Norwegian Ultima Festival, premiered in Oslo in autumn 1991. A major work, *Initium*, was an orchestral commission for the Tokyo Symphony. *Polarization*, for two percussionists, was commissioned by Radio France. *Wave Mechanics* for twenty instrumentalists and *Wave Mechanics II* (violin solo and electronics), were performed in Japan (1994). *Metallic Crystal* (solo percussionist and electronics) premiered at IRCAM in 1995. Other works in 1995–96 were *Echo Canyon*, performed in Nagoya and London, *Crystalline II*, piano solo commissioned by the city of Yokohama, and *Invisible Curve*, premiered in the same city. *The Song of Songs*, *Metal Strings* and *Celestial Harmonics* (1997), all received first performances in Japan. 1998 brought *Festival Presences* for Radio France and a chamber orchestra piece for the Bergen (Norway) Festival.

Other late '90s works such as *The Song of Songs*, *Night Bird* and *Metal Strings*, use the latest technology and reflect different aspects of contemporary culture. Tanaka's love of nature and concern for the environment is heard in *Frozen Horizon* (written for BIT20 in Norway), and the tape piece, *Questions of Nature* and *Water and Stone*, commissioned by Radio France and premiered in Paris in 2000.

2000 also produced a second string quartet, *At the Grave of Beethoven*, written for the Brodsky Quartet; two solo piano works, *Techno Etudes*, written for Tomoko Mukaiyama, and *Crystalline III* for Eve Egoyan; an orchestral piece, *Departure*, for the BBC Symphony; *Guardian Angel*, commissioned by New York's Music From Japan for their Twenty-fifth Anniversary Gala at Carnegie Hall; and two commissions, one from Japan's NHK Symphony Orchestra and the second from the Michael Vyner Trust, premiered at Tokyo's Suntory Hall in a concert conducted by Esa Pekka Salonen. Many of her works are on CD.

Based in Paris, Tanaka visits Japan regularly where she is co-artistic director of the Yatsugatake Kogen Music Festival, previously directed by famed Japanese composer **Toru Takemitsu** (1930–96).

Chen Yi

CHEN YI (her family name is Chen) has become one of the foremost contemporary Chinese composers. Born into a musical family in Guangzhou, April 4, 1953—both her parents were physicians—she began violin and piano at age three. The so-called "Cultural Revolution" of the 1960s made it safer to practice her violin with a mute attached. Later, she was sent to a forced labor camp in the countryside, but managed to smuggle in her instrument and practice behind bushes away from the others. The positive side of this experience was that Yi learned much of folk music and her people. After two years she was allowed to return home. At seventeen, she became concertmaster and composer with the Beijing Opera Troupe and began her eight year research into Chinese traditional music and Western and Chinese theory. When the school system was restored in 1977, she managed, amid fierce competition, to get into the Beijing Conservatory, where she studied composition and conducting. In 1983, she composed the first Chinese viola concerto (*Xian Shi*). In 1986, in honor of her becoming the first Chinese woman to receive a master of arts degree in composition, the Chinese Musicians Association, the conservatory, Radio Beijing, CCTV and the Central Philharmonic of China, gave a joint concert of her orchestral pieces, subsequently releasing a collection of her works by the China Record Company.

1986 was also the year Chen Yi was permitted to come to the U.S. for further studies. By 1989, her chamber music was featured in "Sound and Silence," a series of ten films on contemporary music produced by ISCM, Adamov Films and Polish TV, and broadcast on the European TV network. In 1993, she obtained her DMA, with distinction, from Columbia, and received an appointment through Meet the Composer residencies program for a three-year term at The Women's Philharmonic, the *a capella* choral group Chanticleer and the Aptos Creative Arts Program—all in San Francisco. Her many honors include a 1994 NEA composer fellowship, the 1994 Lili Boulanger Award, and awards from the Fromm and Ford Foundations, New York Society of Composers and Artists, and Meet the Composer/Reader's Digest Consortium Commissioning program. Chen also serves as Composer Advisor with the American Composers Orchestra in New York and is a member of ASCAP.

Worldwide commissions and performances range from the Los Angeles Philharmonic, England's Hallé Orchestra, Kammerphilharmonie of Holland, Iceland Symphony, Hong Kong Chinese Orchestra and Kronos Quartet, to the San Francisco Contemporary Music Players and many others. Her œuvre, encompassing orchestral works, chamber, vocal and instrumental music, bear lyrical titles like *Sparkle*, *Tang Poems*, *Chinese Myths Cantata*, *The Linear*, *Shuo*, *The Tide*, *Antiphony*, *Song in Winter*, *Duo Ye*, *Sprout* and *The Points*. She has also written *A Set of Chinese Folk Songs*, *Overture* and *Overture No. 2*, concertos for piano, cello, clarinet and other major forms. The 1995–96 season saw premieres of *Chinese Myths Cantata* for Choir and Orchestra, by The Women's Philharmonic under **JoAnn Falletta**; *Singin' in the Dark* with Chanticleer and the San Francisco Symphony; *Sakura, Arirang*, an arrangement of Japanese and Korean Folk Songs performed by Chanticleer on their Asian tour, and *Romance of Hsiao and Ch'in* for Two Violins and String Orchestra, first conducted in Gstaad, Switzerland, by the dedicatee, **Lord Yehudi Menuhin**, at the Festival bearing his name. He also conducted the American premiere, August 11, 1996, at the first Lincoln Center Festival. 1997 premieres included *Fiddle Suite* for Chinese fiddles and string quartet with the Kronos Quartet in New York, *Sound of the Five*, for cello and string quartet with Mimi

Hwang and the Ying Quartet, *QI* with the San Francisco Contemporary Music Players and *Golden Flute* with **James Galway** and the Wichita Symphony under Zuohuang Chen, and a new clarinet concerto.

In 1996, she joined the composition faculty at the Peabody Conservatory. After winning the CalArts Alpert Award in 1997, she came to the attention of the faculty at the University of Missouri at Kansas City, and in 1998 left Peabody to become the Lorena Searcey Cravens/Millsap/Missouri endowed professor of composition—one of three endowed chairs in the music department. The others are for cello and piano. In 2002, she was awarded the Elise Stoeger Award from the Chamber Music Society of Lincoln Center; an honorary doctorate from Lawrence University (Appleton, Wisconsin); and the Friendship Ambassador Award, Edgar Snow Fund of Kansas City, Missouri. In 2002, she was profiled in the documentary film *Chen Yi in America* (*A Cantonese in New York*). She was the Karel Husa visiting professor at Ithaca College, 2002–03. In March 2004, her cello concerto, commissioned by the Pacific Symphony, was premiered by Yo-Yo Ma at the Trade Winds from China Festival (Costa Mesa, California).

As an ethnomusicologist in Chinese music, Chen Yi is a frequent guest lecturer throughout the U.S. and China. She was the recipient of the prestigious Charles Ives Living Award from the American Academy of Arts & Letters (2001–2004).

Her husband since 1983, Long Zhou, a graduate from the Central Conservatory in Beijing (1983) and PhD from Columbia (1993), is a composer of orchestral, chamber and vocal works. Teaching at the same university as his wife, he is the visiting professor of composition at UMKC Conservatory, and co-senior-composer-in-residence of the Chamber Music Conference and Composers Forum of the East at Bennington College, Vermont.

A Daughter's Legacy

When Chen Yi's *Symphony No. 2* was premiered in San Francisco by The Women's Philharmonic, these thoughts of the composer appeared in print:

> I hear the tragic motif in my symphony again and again, and can't stop a tear from running down my cheek. That motif has been haunting me since I first learned my dear father had a heart attack. It is the main element in the symphony, written in memory of my father, Chen Er-nan, a medical doctor who devoted his whole life to the people of his homeland. He led me into the realm of music when I was only three, and helped me understand the sincerity and simplicity of Mozart, in which the weeping tear hid behind a smiling face. The love of music helped me survive the dark period, when the political tragedy of the Cultural Revolution overtook China. I tried hard then to continue my musical studies, practicing violin at home with the mute attached, because classical music was forbidden. I even took my violin with me into the countryside, where I was sent to work for two years, twelve hours a day, climbing to the top of mountains, carrying on my back hundred-pound loads of rocks and mud for building irrigation walls. I played simple songs to farmers, between excerpts from the standard repertory. I tried to educate the poor children in the village. I started thinking about civilization, the value of individual lives and the importance of education in society. The more I touched the ground, the more I learned from the common people who have carried on China's rich culture for thousands of years.

> As my *Symphony No. 2* fills the concert hall, I remember when the school system was restored in 1977. I enrolled in the Beijing Central Conservatory and eagerly studied composition and Chinese traditional music for eight years. I gave a whole evening's concert of my orchestral works in 1986. A collection of my orchestra works was released by the China Record Company.

As my symphony ends, an audience of a thousand, filling the hall, stands up, shouting and clapping for me so long and so loud, I can't remember later how I was called to run up on stage and received so many flowers and a certificate from the California State Senate.

My dear father, do you know how much I want you to hear my symphony? I wish you could see me working in this new society, where education is improving through music and a new culture is growing up. Here is my second symphony. It is for you—it contains the experiences of waking up to reality, introspection and longing. Its heavy atmosphere is interrupted by sharp percussive sounds, symbolizing the sparkle of sudden epiphanies. The end, with soft, lingering gestures on percussion and sliding harmonics on strings, carries a mysterious dream toward the future.

Li Yiding

LI YIDING a native of Beijing, was born into the family of a Chinese literature professor. Her BA in composition is from Shenyang Conservatory of Music (1982). Since that year she was a composer for China Central Television (CCTV) and the China Teleplay Production Center (CTPC), both in Beijing. In 1986, she traveled to Pakistan on assignment for a TV play. 1999 found her in London for the Eleventh International Congress on Women in Music. She is a member of the Chinese Musicians' Association, Council of the Chinese Audio-Visual of Film and TV Exchange Society, Chinese Music Copyright Association, Chinese TV Music Research Society, and co-founder of the Chinese Association of Women Composers. In 2000, she visited America for an International Alliance for Women in Music board meeting, and became the liaison with China for the IAWM. She was elected to their board of directors in 2001.

Her symphonic poem, *The Romance of the Three Kingdoms*, was performed in 1998 by the Orchestra of Shenyang Conservatory. The piano suite, *Pakistan Sketch*, was first performed in 1999 in London by Sara Torquati. *Zhaxi Island Rhapsody*, for clarinet and piano, was performed by the American Price Duo (Deon Price, piano and her son, Dr. Berkeley A. Price, clarinet), and *Guge Kingdom Ruins*, for cello and piano, by Friedrich Gauwerky of Germany, both in Beijing, 2001. Li completed the String Quartet *Tibet Langda* the same year. Some of her some articles and tapes have been published. By 2004, she had composed music for more than twelve films and seventy teleplays, sixteen of them award winners, and published nearly 100 songs.

Li Yiding is married to television and film actor Wang Dong.

She brings her own unique message to the world:

In recent years, Beijing [formerly Peking] has changed greatly, with many good concert halls and theaters, ideal places for musical performances. A new national theater, costing hundreds of millions of yuan was completed in 2003 in the center of the city, near TianAnMen Square. Imported from the U.S., we have the greatest pipe organ in China, in the concert hall in Sun Yat-sen Park.

It is reasonable to hope, that [in the future] we can create conditions to hold an IAWM event of major proportions in Beijing. China is a country with a long history and culture. Chinese music has deep historical origins. China is a great country with many talents in music.

Let us try hard, striving for increased exchange and flow of ideas!

Let the world understand China better and China the world!

Let us work hard to raise the levels of the world's women musicians!

On July 13, 2001, Beijing was elected host city for the XXIX Olympiad in 2008 . . . with the evaluation that "a Beijing games would leave a unique legacy to China and to sports. The commission was confident that Beijing could organize an excellent games."

CHAPTER SIX

The Second New England School

Clara Kathleen Rogers (1844–1931)
Helen Hopekirk (1856–1945)
Margaret Ruthven Lang (1867–1972)
Amy Beach (1867–1944)
Mabel Daniels (1878–1971)

The nucleus of music in colonial America was Boston. **William Billings** (1746–1800) is considered the "Father of New England Music," and early American composers, most of whom wrote church music and songs, have been grouped into what is known as the New England School. Not until three quarters of a century later did another group of American composers emerge, and by virtue of being born or settling in the same geographical location, were dubbed the Second New England School. Led by **John Knowles Paine** (1839–1906), Harvard's first professor of music and the first to hold such a position in the country, and **George Whitefield Chadwick** (1854–1931), director of the New England Conservatory, the group included **Arthur Foote** (1853–1937), **Edward MacDowell** (1860–1908), **Frederick Shepherd Converse** (1871–1940), **John Alden Carpenter** (1876–1951) and five prominent women. Part of the school, yet standing alone as the American forerunner of modern music, was **Charles Ives** (1854–1954), the only member educated exclusively in America.

Amongst them they amassed a repository of symphonies, orchestral works, organ music, oratorios, chamber and choral works, songs, piano pieces, etc., forming a foundation for American music, although all but Ives had engaged in periods of study in Europe. MacDowell, Converse, and Carpenter were pupils of Paine. Margaret Ruthven Lang and Mabel Daniels studied with Chadwick.

The Women of the Second New England School

These ladies had much in common: each came from well-to-do families, each was encouraged in her aspirations and each studied in Europe with leading pedagogues of the day. Those who married had the support of their husbands to continue their career. Most importantly, each was successful, respected and ran into very little gender bias.

CLARA KATHLEEN BARNETT ROGERS, born January 14, 1844, in Cheltenham, England, was the granddaughter of cellist Robert Lindley and daughter of composer John Barnett. She received musical instruction from her parents before entering the Leipzig Conservatory at age twelve,[31] where she studied harmony with Paperitz and E.F. Richter, singing with Hermann Goetz and composition with Louis Plaidy and **Ignaz Moscheles** (1794–1870), a friend of Beethoven and student of **Antonio Salieri** (1750–1825). The youngest student the conservatory had ever accepted, she graduated in 1860 deciding to concentrate on singing as a career. After further lessons in Berlin and Milan, she made her debut in Turin under the name **Clara Doria**. She spent several years as an opera singer in Italy before returning to London in 1866 to continue her concert career. In 1871, she went on a U.S. tour with the Parepa-Rosa Opera Company. The following year she settled in

---

31. Like many prodigies, Clara's mother put her child's career before her marriage, and lived with her daughter in Europe.

America, first in New York, then Boston, where she performed and taught singing. In 1878, she married Boston lawyer Henry Munroe Rogers, after which she retired from performing in public but continued to teach. She became involved in local music clubs and founded a Bach club in 1883. She also gave weekly musicales at her house to which flocked Boston musicians and composers.

Meanwhile, Rogers continued to compose. Her first set of *Six Songs* was published in 1882. These were followed by several piano pieces, including a *Scherzo* (1883), and a *Romanza* (1895). She also authored several books on singing, including *The Philosophy of Singing* (1893).

In 1902, Rogers accepted George Chadwick's offer of a post as professor of singing at the New England Conservatory. She was unimpressed by the ultra-modern music of the 1920s, which she found monotonous. Her own music, much of which remained in manuscript, always retained the harmonies and structures of the romanticism of her youth. Her output includes two string quartets, sonatas for violin and cello, piano works and some 100 songs. She died in Boston at eighty-seven March 8, 1931.

HELEN HOPEKIRK was born May 20, 1856, in Edinburgh, Scotland. A composer, pianist and teacher, her earliest musical studies were with Professor G. Lichtenstein and the Scottish composer, Sir Alexander Mackenzie (1847–1935). At age twenty, she went to Leipzig, studying at the conservatory for two years, with **Carl Reinecke** (1824–1910), Salomon Jadassohn (composition), E.F. Richter (counterpoint) and piano with Louis Maas (1852–89) a student of Franz Liszt. She formed lifelong friendships with fellow students **Karl Muck**[32] (1859–1940), who went on to become conductor of the Boston Symphony (1906–08, 1912–17), and **George Chadwick**, "co-father" of the Second New England School. Helen made her debut as a pianist with the prestigious Leipzig Gewandhaus Orchestra in November 1878, and at the Crystal Palace (London) Concerts in 1879, after which she toured England and Scotland. By this time she was already composing. Her earliest surviving work, the song *Sigh, My Lute*, was published *circa* 1880 in London.

In 1882, Hopekirk married Scottish painter, music critic and businessman William A. Wilson, who became her concert manager. She made her American debut in 1883 with the Boston Symphony Orchestra, and following three highly successful years touring the U.S., felt the need for more training. In 1887 she went to Vienna, studying piano for two years with **Theodor Leschetizky** (1830–1915), a pupil of **Carl Czerny**, and composition with Karel Navrátil.

In 1890, she embarked on her second American tour, playing her own *Sonata in E minor* for violin and piano at a concert in Boston, March 1891. From this time on, composing played an increasingly important part of her professional life. Two years were spent in Paris for further composition study with Richard Mandl, at the end of which she wrote a *Concertstück* (Concert Piece) for piano and orchestra. Its premiere in Edinburgh in 1894 by the Scottish Orchestra was conducted by Georg Henschel (1850–1934). That same year saw the publication of her *Five Songs* to words by Robert Burns and Heinrich Heine.

Joining the Crowd at the Conservatory

After her husband's severe injury in a traffic accident, Hopekirk, like Rogers, accepted Chadwick's offer of a teaching post at the New England Conservatory in 1897. The couple settled in Boston and eventually became American citizens. Involved in the musical life of the city, she gave regular recitals including her own works. In 1900, the Boston Symphony Orchestra performed her *Piano Concerto in D major*. The following year, she resigned from the conservatory and concentrated on private teaching, establishing a work pattern whereby she practiced the piano and composed in the morning and gave piano lessons in the afternoon.

---

32. Muck, a friend of Kaiser Wilhelm, allowed himself to be interned in his Boston home for the remainder of WWI. He returned to his native Germany in 1919.

Hopekirk's music is characterized by her Celtic heritage. She frequently returned to Scotland, embracing the folk music she had heard as a child and in later visits to the Highlands. In 1905, she edited and arranged a collection of *Seventy Scottish Songs*, which became very popular. Her use of traditional Scottish rhythmic and harmonic material is evident in *Iona Memories*, four pieces for piano published in 1909. Around this time she became an ardent suffragette. In 1919, she and Wilson enjoyed a year in Edinburgh. In February 1920, she gave a concert in Glasgow where she played her Concerto and selections from *Serenata*, a classical suite of piano pieces. After the death of her husband in 1926, Hopekirk continued to perform and compose. She gave a farewell concert of her own works April 1939, at age eighty-two, six years before her death, November 19, 1945, in Cambridge, Massachusetts.

MARGARET RUTHVEN LANG was born November 27, 1867, in Boston. Her father, Benjamin Johnson Lang, was an important figure in the city's musical life at the end of the 19th century, having studied in Europe and worked as organist and conductor with many of Boston's important musical institutions such as the Handel and Haydn Society. Margaret's mother was an amateur singer. Benjamin took his daughter's ambitions seriously, giving her piano lessons and providing a fine musical education. She started writing music at an early age, producing a movement of a piano quintet when she was twelve. She took violin lessons with Louis Schmidt, continuing with Franz Drechsler and Ludwig Abel (1834–95) in Munich (1886–87), where she also studied counterpoint and fugue with Victor Gluth. On her return to Boston, she worked on orchestration with George Chadwick, but her father continued to be her main teacher and mentor.

Another Feminine First

Lang's first works to be performed publicly were five songs which received favorable reviews. Her song *Ojalá* was performed at a concert of representative American works[33] at the Paris Exposition of 1889, and Washington, 1890, which established her reputation. In 1893, the Boston Symphony Orchestra gave the premiere of her *Dramatic Overture*—the first time a major American orchestra played a work by a woman composer. That same year her overture, *Witchis*, received three performances at the World Columbian Exposition in Chicago.

Some of her compositions draw on Scottish and Irish folk elements, such as *Six Scotch Songs* and *An Irish Mother's Lullaby*. Others, like *The Jumbles*, contain humor. *Day is Gone* and the *Nonsense Rhymes* are witty miniatures. She adapted her music to the texts she was setting. Other titles include *Three Songs of the East* (1892) and *Four Songs* (1892). In 1895, *Sappho's Prayer to Aphrodite* for contralto and orchestra was performed in New York and, in 1896, *Armida* for soprano and orchestra was played by the Boston Symphony. Unfortunately, most of her orchestral works were not published and have not survived, apparently Lang destroyed them. She continued to compose after her father's death in 1909, although while he was alive she depended on his approval before offering a piece for publication. Her later works include *Wind* (1913), *The Heavenly Noel* (1916), and *Elegy* (1917). Her last work appeared in 1919. She remained interested in new music, and continued to attend concerts of the Boston Symphony Orchestra. She died in her native Boston, May 30, 1972, at 104.

Amy Beach

AMY MARCY CHENEY BEACH was America's first major woman symphonic composer. Born September 5, 1867, in Henniker, New Hampshire, she was the only child of Clara Marcy, a pianist and singer, and Charles Cheney, a paper manufacturer and also very musical. Her ancestry designated her a Daughter of the American Revolution (DAR). At four, Amy was already composing little waltzes and at six began piano lessons with her mother. From 1881–82, she studied harmony—the only formal theory lessons she would ever receive. (She taught herself orchestration from reading the book by Hector Berlioz). In 1883, at sixteen, she made her debut with the Boston Symphony performing the Moscheles Piano Concerto in G

---

33. American Composers' Concerts was a movement of the 1880s–'90s showcasing U.S. music.

minor. In March 1885, she appeared with the same orchestra playing the Chopin *Concerto in F minor* under the baton of the famed **Arthur Nikisch** (1855–1922) who would lead the BSO until 1893 before resuming his international career.

The Marriage Shelter

In December 1885, Amy married Dr. Henry Harris Aubrey Beach, a wealthy Boston surgeon twenty-four years her senior, who numbered Chief Justice Oliver Wendell Homes amongst his friends. During her marriage, most of her concertizing was confined to the Boston and New England area with weekly salons at their house—for which the rich and famous vied to be on the guest list. (The good doctor did not wish his wife to be exposed to criticism.) Fortunately, he respected her composing. The *Mass in E flat* was begun in 1889, and premiered in 1892 by Boston's prestigious Handel and Haydn Society. She was the first woman to compose a work of such scope. (England's Ethel Smyth wrote her *Mass in D* in 1891. Its premiere was 1893.) On the same program, Amy performed the piano part in Beethoven's Choral Fantasy. At the 1893 Columbian Exposition in Chicago, for the May opening of the Woman's Building, Beach's commission, *Festival Jubilate*, was sung by 300 voices and an orchestra under **Theodore Thomas** (1835–1905), first conductor of the Chicago Symphony. Amy returned to this World's Fair in July when the Woman's Musical Congress presented works by fifteen women. She performed her *Romance* with **Maud Powell**, the piece having been dedicated to the virtuoso violinist.

In July 1895, Amy's father, only fifty, died of blood poisoning following an operation. In October, her grandmother died, leaving her mother all alone in New Hampshire. Mrs. Cheney was immediately welcomed into the Beach home on Commonwealth Avenue in Boston. Now, between her mother and the servants, Amy had no housekeeping duties and could concentrate fully on composition. The following years saw the publication of compositions ranging from numerous songs, piano pieces, chamber music, a violin sonata, church music—anthems, cantatas, a motet, a *Te Deum*—and the great *Gaelic* Symphony, the first full symphony ever written by a woman. The premiere was October 30, 1896, with the Boston Symphony under **Emil Paur** (1855–1932), the Austrian maestro who had succeeded his fellow countryman, Nikisch. The critics were ecstatic. The work was considered the most successful symphony by *any* composer in her generation, and was subsequently performed in New York and Chicago. Her post-Brahmsian style was typical of the late Romantics, with broad melodies, complex harmonies, altered chords and intricate theme development. (It is now on CD). She was later influenced by Debussy and **Arthur Foote** (1853–1937), one of the foremost composers of the New England School. The *Brooklyn Eagle* critic commented, "We may pride ourselves on being the only nation that has a [woman] composer of symphonies . . . we may yet hear more admirable works from her pen."

On Her Own for the First Time

After her husband's death at sixty-six, June 28, 1910, caused by falling down a flight of stairs during a housecall on April 25 (those were the days!), Amy was free to travel. Her mother, who had been a dominant force in her professional life, once again began to make big plans for her daughter's career to expose her to the world from which the doctor had sheltered her. Amy depended on her and when Mrs. Cheney died suddenly February 18, 1911, she would have been overwhelmed had she not "found religion" in the intervening months between the two bereavements. With the loss of both her mother and husband within a short time of each other, she could appreciate how they helped further her career. For the first time in her life, she had to take charge of her own management, finances, etc.

Her *Piano Concerto in C# minor*, premiered 1900, was dedicated to **Teresa Carreño** the Caracas-born opera singer-pianist-composer, considered the leading female performer of her day, who brought the work before European audiences. With her name already known in Europe, between 1911–14 Beach toured in Hamburg,

Leipzig, Berlin, Rome and other cities, playing her concerto and her own sophisticated and technically challeng-ing piano pieces to critical acclaim and appreciative audiences. She was fêted wherever she appeared.

The political tensions building up in Europe had little effect on wealthy Americans living abroad. Not until she was on one of the last boats to America before the outbreak of World War I, did Mrs. H.H.A. Beach, as she signed her manuscripts, realize her narrow escape. She settled in New York, making further concert tours, composing and spending summers at her retreat in Cape Cod and the MacDowell Artists' Colony in Peterborough, New Hampshire, founded by her friend Marian MacDowell in honor of her late husband, composer Edward MacDowell (1860–1908). Commissions were pouring in and Amy Beach clubs sprang up all over the country. She played many concerts to benefit American Pen Women branches throughout New England. Her fame was at its height, with an all-Beach program at Carnegie Hall, her symphony played by the Philadelphia Orchestra to rave reviews, and a trip to California for the 1915 Pan American Exposition in San Diego where a day was named in her honor. She also performed in Los Angeles and San Francisco to great acclaim. Heading homeward, she concertized in Salt Lake City and Chicago among other cities in the Midwest. She toured Europe again, 1926–27, returning in November for the Pen Women Convention in New York, she also attended concerts by such immortals as **Béla Bartók**, **Percy Grainger** and **Sergei Rachmaninoff**. She later toured the south.

In 1932, at age sixty-five, Beach composed an opera, *Cabildo*. Her Piano Trio was written at seventy. In 1933, she received a medal at the Chicago International Exposition. In 1940, in New York 's Town Hall, she was hon-ored at a dinner attended by 200 musicians, composers and friends.

The Composer Happens to be a Woman

Beach was not a feminist and never felt limited because she was a woman. She was not affected by the fact that it took until the turn of the century for conservatories to permit women to study *composition* versus only instru-mental performance. Nevertheless, she continuously encouraged other women composers. Her marriage placed her in a privileged position in Boston society, with no financial worries. She had no children. Her only conflict was allotting time spent composing or concertizing. Celebrated as the foremost woman composer of her era, Amy Beach was the first American woman to succeed writing in large scale musical forms. She was active up to the last month of her life. Six weeks after her death of a heart ailment, December 27, 1944, in New York City, the Handel and Haydn Society honored her with a fifty-second anniversary performance of her *Mass*. On October 5, 1945, her ashes were laid beside those of her husband in Boston.

Interest in her music began to wane in her last years, but after a hiatus of nearly half a century, her work is receiving renewed recognition. May 1995 saw a highly successful Beach concert performed in Alice Tully Hall, Lincoln Center, with a pre-concert lecture by co-producer and Beach authority, musicologist **Adrienne Fried Block**. Besides songs and piano works, the program concluded with the first professional performance of her one act opera, *Cabildo*.

The product of over ten years of research[34] by **Adrienne Fried Block**, *Amy Beach, Passionate Victorian: The Life and Work of an American Composer, 1867–1944*, was published in 1998 by Oxford University Press, New York.

MABEL WHEELER DANIELS was born into a musical family, November 27, 1877, in Swampscott, Massachusetts. One of her grandfathers was a choir director and the other an organist and member of the Handel and Haydn Society. Both her parents sang with the Society, and her father was its president from 1899–1908. She began piano lessons as a child, and wrote her first piano piece, *Fairy Charm Waltz*, at ten. In college, her fine soprano voice got her into the Radcliffe Glee Club, where she was given leading roles in their operetta presenta-tions. She wrote two operettas for them and became their director. After graduating *magna cum laude* in 1900, she studied with **George Chadwick**, with whom she developed a close friendship, at the New England Conservatory.

---

34. Been there, done that . . . AG

In 1903, she went to Germany to work with Ludwig Thuille, becoming the first woman to be admitted into a score reading class at the Munich Royal Conservatory. (They had only recently permitted women into counterpoint).

An American Girl in Munich

After two years and winning a medal, Mabel returned home and joined the mixed chorus of the Cecilia Society to learn more of orchestration and scores. During that time she wrote of her experiences in Germany in a popular book published in 1905, *An American Girl in Munich: Impressions of a Music Student*, giving glimpses of the Spartan conditions under which students—male and female—lived and studied in Europe. In 1908, the Boston Pops under Gustav Strube, performed Daniels' first work for orchestra, *In the Greenwood*. She returned to Radcliffe in 1911 as director of the Glee Club, remaining until 1913. From 1913–18, she was head of the music department at Simmons College (Boston), after which she retired from teaching and, with the financial support of her family, devoted herself to composing.

The Endless Summers

In 1913, Marian MacDowell, widow of Edward, asked Daniels to conduct her cantata, *The Desolate City*, for baritone solo, chorus and orchestra, at the MacDowell Colony Summer Festival. Marian was so impressed, she asked Mabel to return the following summer as a resident artist. She in fact returned there for twenty-four summers, meeting with fellow female composers, and writing many inspired pieces, including her most popular work, the prelude *Deep Forest* for chamber orchestra. This was first performed in 1931 by Georges Barrère and the Little Symphony of New York, and later revised for full orchestra and premiered in 1940 by the Women's Symphony Orchestra of Boston.

Ninety Years in Boston—A Three Time Winner

Daniels lived her whole life in Boston. She was a member of the advisory committee on music for the Boston public schools, served as a trustee of Radcliffe, and was an active member of the Society of American Women Composers. Many of her sacred works got their first hearing at her own place of worship, Boston's Arlington Street Church. For the fiftieth anniversary of Radcliffe (1929), she wrote *Exultate Deo* for mixed chorus and orchestra. This was subsequently performed by the Boston Symphony under **Serge Koussevitzky** (1874–1951), BSO conductor from 1924–49, and became one of her best known choral works. In 1954, for Radcliffe's seventy-fifth anniversary, she wrote her last large choral work, *A Psalm of Praise* for mixed chorus, three trumpets, percussion and strings. Two years later it was performed by the Boston Symphony, making Daniels the first woman to have three different works played by that orchestra—the other two were *Exultate Deo* (1932) and *Deep Forest* (1937). Daniels' style was rooted in the romanticism of the Second New England School, although she introduced modern idioms in her later works such as one her most important compositions, *The Song of Jael*[35] (1937), a cantata for soprano solo, mixed chorus and orchestra based on the poem *Sisera* by her close friend, American poet Edwin Arlington Robinson. Daniels' last piece was *Piper Play On!* (1961), a choral work from a Greek text.

The Magic Female Formula

Unmarried, Daniels felt her sex was handicapped by the amount of time-consuming obligations, both domestic and social, expected of wives. She pointed to four requisites—besides talent—indispensable to women: a strong constitution, perseverance, ingenuity and, above all, courage. She died, much respected, March 10, 1971, in Cambridge, Massachusetts.

---

35. Jael was the Jewess who slew the tyrant Sisera and became a heroine.

CHAPTER SEVEN

Pen Women in Music

Carrie Jacobs Bond (1862–1946)
Amy Beach (1867–1944)
Mary Carr Moore (1873–1957)
Mary Carlisle Howe (1882–1964)
Beth Joerger-Jenson (?–1991)
Elinor Remick Warren (1900–91)
Dorothy Dushkin (1903–92)
Radie Britain (1903–94)
Harriet Bolz (1909–95)
Julia Smith (1911–89)
Roslyn Pettibone (1912–93)
Vera N. Preobrajenska (?)
Marion Morrey Richter (1900–96)
Minuetta Kessler (1914–2002)
Nancy Faxon (1914–2005)
Arwin Sexauer (1921–92)
Jeanne Singer (1924–2000)
Nancy Reed (1924–2000)
Sarah Bennett
Louise Canepa
Frances Chadwick

Nancy Deussen
Sheila Firestone
Genevieve Fritter Bieber
Beverly Glazier
Lucille Greenfield
Joanne Hammil
Jane Hart
Marguerite Havey
Winifred Hyson
Elizabeth Lauer
Bette Miller
Elizabeth Nicols
Linda Ostrander
Julie Rivers
Eugénie Rocherolle
Dorothy Ross
Gail Smith
Marjorie Tayloe
Marilyn Thies
Wang An-Ming
Harriet Woodcock

Celebrating its Centennial in 1997, the National League of American Pen Women (NLAPW) was founded June 26, 1897, a time when women were barred from the National Press Club in the nation's capital. Three professionals, **Marion Longfellow O'Donohue**, a poet and reporter for the *Boston Transcript*, *Boston Herald* and *Washington Post*, and niece of Henry Wadsworth Longfellow, **Margaret Sullivan Burke**, the first woman to be admitted into the Press Gallery[36] of the Houses of Congress as an accredited telegraphic correspondent, and **Anna Sanborne Hamilton**, social editor of the *Washington Post* and special proofreader for the U.S. government, met with fourteen other ladies to found the League of American Pen Women. With twenty charter members, the league's original aim was to create a forum for women journalists, authors and illustrators "to promote . . . action . . . on libel law, copyright laws, plagiarism and for inspiration and mutual aid." When a music category was added in 1916, among its first prestigious members was **Amy Beach**, leading a line of prolific women composers such as **Mary Howe**, **Carrie Jacobs Bond**, **Elinor Remick Warren**, **Radie Britain** and **Julia Smith**, who were followed by contemporaries, **Jeanne Singer**, **Eugénie Rocherolle**, and others. Their first convention was held April 1921, with President and Mrs. Warren G. Harding, herself a member, in the receiving line. Subsequent first lady members include Edith Bolling Wilson, Grace Coolidge, Eleanor Roosevelt, Rosalynn Carter, Barbara Bush, Hillary Rodham Clinton and Laura Bush. Over the decades branches have sprung

---

36. The Press Gallery was established in 1877 from which women were also originally prohibited.

up in cities large and small—the first on the West Coast was 1915 in Los Angeles. Membership now numbers around 4,000, with over 1,000 artists and eighty in music.

Major Music Leaguers

Carrie Jacobs Bond

The name of **CARRIE JACOBS BOND** has become immortalized on the basis of two romantic songs. Born in Janesville, Wisconsin, August 11, 1862, with no formal musical training other than local teachers, she showed an amazing talent for improvising songs to her own words. At eighteen, she married E. J. Smith, with whom she had a son. They separated in 1887. Two years later she married Frank Lewis Bond. Her first songs, *Is My Dolly Dead?* and *Mother's Cradle Song*, came out in 1894. After her husband died in 1895, she had difficulty getting more of her songs into print, so she formed her own publishing company, Carrie Jacobs-Bond & Son. To help make her name known, influential friends arranged for her to perform for President Teddy Roosevelt at the White House. Designing her own sheet music covers, she published 175 songs, of which two were successful beyond her wildest dreams. *I Love you Truly* (1901) sold over one million copies and became a wedding standard. [At the End of] *A Perfect Day* (1910) sold eight million copies and five million records. Carrie moved her publishing company eight times in Chicago to accommodate its growth, and in 1920 moved the company to Hollywood, California. She also published her autobiography, *The Roads of Melody* (1928), and a book of her poetry and philosophical commentary, *The End of the Road* (1940). Her last song, *Because of the Light*, was copyrighted in 1944 when she was eighty-two. She died in Hollywood on December 28, 1946.

One of the most important and world-famous Pen Women in music was **AMY MARCY CHENEY BEACH**, America's first major woman symphonic composer. Born September 5, 1867, in Henniker, New Hampshire, she lived until 1944, experiencing an illustrious career and a rewarding life. (See Second New England School.)

Mary Carr Moore

MARY CARR MOORE, born in Memphis, Tennessee, August 6, 1873, moved with her family to California in 1885. She was one of three women who composed operas in California during the early 1900s, the others being Elsie Maxwell, of San Francisco, and Abbie Gerrish Jones, of Sacramento. Mary studied voice and composition in San Francisco, and by 1889 was teaching and composing. Her first operetta was *The Oracle*, in which she sang the leading role in a San Francisco production in 1894. After this she gave up singing and devoted the rest of her life to teaching and composition. She taught in Lemoore (California), Seattle, San Francisco, and in Los Angeles at the Olga Steeb Piano School (1926–43). Concurrently, she was a professor of theory and composition at Chapman College (1928–47). A promoter of American music, she organized an American Music Center in Seattle in 1909 and worked for the Federal Music Projects in Los Angeles, 1936–42, promoting performances by local composers.

A Mother-Daughter Team

Two of her operas, *Narcissa* (1909–11) and *The Flaming Arrow* (1919–20), used American themes and Native American materials. *Narcissa* was performed in Seattle (1912), San Francisco (1925), and Los Angeles (1945), all staged and conducted by the composer. Ahead of her time, the libretto was by her mother, Sarah Pratt Moore, and dealt with the shameful ways Europeans had treated American Indians. It was based on the 1847 massacre of missionaries Marcus and Narcissa Whitman in the Oregon Territory. The originality lies in that it presents the drama through a woman's eyes.

To celebrate the 150th anniversary of the founding of Los Angeles, Carr Moore wrote *Los Rubios*, premiered in 1931. It was followed by her two-act *David Rizzio* (1927–28), first performed at the Los Angeles Shrine Auditorium (1932). This was also about a strong woman, Mary, Queen of Scots. Two other operas, *The Leper* (1912) and *Legende provençale* (1929–35), were unperformed. Through her own efforts, mixed groups of amateurs and professionals performed her operas and operettas, but she felt that *Narcissa, David Rizzio*, and *Los Rubios* too difficult for amateurs. Her other works included sixty-five songs, fifteen choral works, chamber and solo, and piano works. Her suite, *Four Love Songs* for voice, strings, and piano, won an award from the NLAPW in 1932. Carr Moore died in Inglewood, California, January 9, 1957.

MARY Carlisle HOWE, a most prominent Pen Woman, was a friend of Amy Beach. Born April 4, 1882, in Richmond, Virginia, she grew up in Washington, DC, where her father, Calderon Carlisle, was an international lawyer. She was given a private education and excelled at the piano. As per the European tradition, public performance in her prominent and wealthy circle was still frowned upon, so Mary played only at private social gatherings.

In 1900, Howe was accepted at the Peabody Conservatory in Baltimore, and commuted from Washington for piano studies. After her father died in 1901, she traveled to Europe with her mother, playing in private recitals there, and studying piano briefly in Dresden (1904). During the Taft and Teddy Roosevelt administrations, Mary was a frequent guest at the White House as well as a chamber player at the Friday Morning Music Club, with whom she continued her association until 1940.

In 1912, she married her brother Mandeville's law partner, Walter Howe, and devoted the next few years to her children, Bruce, born 1912, Calderon, 1916, and a daughter, Mary, 1918. When they were old enough, she formed a madrigal group with them which she named "The Four Howes." They performed benefit concerts for clubs in which she was involved.

Going Public as a Duo-Piano Team

Howe had become acquainted with pianist **Anne Hull** at Peabody. Beginning in 1912, they began their long-standing series of duo piano recitals. In 1920 they started concertizing with symphony orchestras, including Baltimore, Cleveland and the touring Russian Symphony. Also in 1920, Mary began to concentrate more on composing, returning to the conservatory for further study. In 1924, she and Hull made their New York debut at the Aeolian (later Town) Hall, to enthusiastic reviews.

During this decade she met **Amy Beach**. Together they gave the Washington premiere of Beach's *Suite for Two Pianos* at a 1925 benefit for the MacDowell Colony. Sponsored by Beach in 1927, Howe became a fellow at the Colony, spending nearly every summer there for the next twenty years. At this time she also met music patron **Elizabeth Sprague Coolidge**, and helped establish the first Coolidge Festival in Washington, October 28, 1925. She also organized the Washington Chamber Music Society which became the present day Friends of Music of the Library of Congress.

The *Chain Gang Song* was Howe's first public success as a composer. Its premiere at the 1925 Worcester Festival featured 275 voices and the New York Symphony directed by Albert Stoessel (1894–1943). One critic wrote, "a powerful piece of writing with no trace of femininity . . . " As usual, critics' highest praise for a woman's work alluded to its masculinity—or absence of femininity. Her miniature tone poem, *Sand*, played by the Philadelphia Orchestra in 1934, was hailed by its conductor **Leopold Stokowski** as a new use of staccato.

In 1930, Howe helped raise $40,000 to establish the National Symphony of Washington, DC, which she and her husband continued to support for the next eighteen years. The orchestra regularly performed her works, including *Castellana* for two pianos and orchestra, a brilliant piece based on Spanish folk tunes. *Spring Pastoral* was featured on their 1936–37 tour, along with *Sand* and *Stars*. Although Anne Hull moved to New York, the duo-piano recitals continued. Besides Howe's music, they played her transcriptions of Bach. Her arrangement of the chorale *Sheep May Safely Graze* is a standard in two-piano literature.

In 1933, during a year spent in France, Howe studied with **Nadia Boulanger**. Throughout the '30s, besides orchestral compositions, she wrote chamber, choral and vocal music. Seven volumes of her songs were published in 1959. She was one of the first members of the Society of American Women Composers, founded in 1924, of which Amy Beach was president. They regularly played Howe's music. Conductor **Antonia Brico** performed *Sand* with the National Symphony in 1940 and the symphonic poem *What Price Glory* the following year.

A Celebrated Sunset

Howe's last two orchestral works, *Paean* and *Potomac*, were completed at the outbreak of World War II. Busy with Red Cross work, she still found time to compose *Prophecy, 1792* (1943), for the Army Music School Choir, who sang it at the National Gallery.

The composer continued to be active through the 1950s. In 1952 an all-Howe program was played by the National Symphony under Howard Mitchell (1911–88). After the death of her husband in 1954, Mary went to Vienna for a concert of her music played by the Vienna Symphony. The program, which included *Sand*, *Stars*, and *Rock*, received unheard of plaudits for a foreigner, and a woman, at that! A standing ovation also greeted her at Constitution Hall, February 1956, at another National Symphony concert of her works. *The Interlude Between Two Pieces* for flute and piano, *Violin Sonata in D*, and choral works and songs were featured at her eightieth birthday, which was attended by some 200 guests at the Mayflower Hotel in the capital.

Among her last tributes was an honorary doctorate from George Washington University. Of her style, Howe professed no allegiance with any school. "I write what I want to write . . . dissonance, if I want to use [it] . . . feeling, if I want to express [it]." Her views on women composers might have been written today: "[They] should be played more than they are . . . I'm not a feminist . . . but I think I would have gotten along faster if I'd been a man." In later life she wrote: "The crux [is] that one should never stop—but close in with the work itself, without thought of performance . . . or age, 'or any other creature.'"

In 1959, her autobiography, *Jottings*, was privately printed. The same year, Galaxy Music Publishers brought out a seven-volume edition of her songs. Mary Howe died September 14, 1964 in Washington, DC.

BETH JOERGER-JENSON, who died in 1991 at the age of 100, was a Pen Woman from 1950, during which time she sold seventy songs to children's magazines.

ELINOR REMICK WARREN, a most prolific composer, was born in Los Angeles in 1900, and worked actively until her death in 1991. Although she lived on the West Coast most of her life, she gained an international reputation with her major orchestral works. (See Contemporary American Composers.)

DOROTHY DUSHKIN (1903–92) produced an extensive body of works for chamber music, orchestra that included two piano concertos, and choral works. Her oeuvre is within the Sophia Smith Collection at Smith College, and at the Music Library of Kinhaven Music School, Weston, Vermont, which she and her husband David founded in 1952.

RADIE BRITAIN was born March 17, 1903, in Silverton (near Amarillo), Texas. Her affluent father, ranch owner Edgar Charles Britain, arranged for his daughter to have the best musical training. After graduating in piano from the American Conservatory in Chicago (BM, 1924), Radie went to Europe, studying with famed pianist **Leopold Godowsky** (1870–1938), composition and theory with **Albert Noelte** (1885–1946) and organ with the renowned **Marcel Dupré** (1896–1971). Her debut as an American composer in Munich with a concert of her songs was well received. Returning to America in 1926, she studied further at the Chicago Conservatory. She also spent two seasons at the MacDowell Colony, where she composed her successful *Southern Symphony*, and the symphonic poem *Light*, dedicated to Thomas Edison, which won the First National Prize of the Boston's Women's Symphony. From 1930–34, she taught harmony and composition at the Girvin Institute of Music, Chicago, and from 1934–39 was on the faculty of the Chicago Conservatory.

From Cactus to Outer Space

Her first orchestral composition, *Symphonic Intermezzo* (1927), received its world premiere by the Women's Symphony of Chicago under the baton of **Ethel Leginska**. *Heroic Poem*, commemorating Lindbergh's first transatlantic flight to Paris in 1927, was premiered by **Howard Hanson** and the Rochester Symphony in 1932. With her unusual first name, he did not find out until two years later that Radie was a woman. Written in 1929, the piece was also performed by the Chicago Women's Symphony, conducted by **Ebba Sundstrom**, won the Hollywood Bowl International Prize and, in 1945, established Britain as the first woman to receive the Juilliard Publication Award. Over fifty of Britain's 150 compositions received national or international awards. They have been played on world tours by the United States Air Force Band, Chicago, Los Angeles, Atlanta and Moscow Symphonies and other famous orchestras. Her compositions were performed as part of the Federal Music Project, created to keep music alive during the Depression. She won the 1956 "Award of Merit" from the NLAPW. Her twenty-four articles as editor of *The Pen Woman* were published as *Composer's Corner* in 1978. She treasured the honorary doctorate from the Musical Arts Conservatory of Amarillo (Texas), and was the recipient of ten ASCAP awards. She wrote an opera, *Carillon* (1952), to a text by Rupert Hughes (1872–1956), George Washington biographer and author of *Music Lovers 'Cyclopedia*.

Britain's lyrical, atmospheric style is inspired by American scenery, especially that of the southwest and her native Texas, with such titles as *Canyon, Drouth, Red Clay, Paint Horse and Saddle, Cowboy Rhapsody* and *Cactus Rhapsody*.

Love in Three Guises

In 1930 she married Leslie Moeher. Their daughter was christened Lerae, a combination of each of her parents' first names. Lerae later wrote the lyrics to some of her mother's songs, which were put into the book *Lakalani*, named after a Hula goddess, and published while she was teaching at what is now Brigham Young University of Hawaii. Her daughter also saw to it that all her mother's manuscripts, tapes, scrapbooks and papers were safely reposited at the Universities of Texas and Indiana, and the Fleischer Gallery of Philadelphia. Her research into Hawaiian culture culminated in her mother's preservation of authentic Polynesian chants and dances in piano form. The pair collaborated on a piano book, *Pianorama 'O Hawai'i.*

In the early '30s, Radie met sculptor Edgardo Simone, whom she married in 1939 after divorcing Moeher. Her unpublished book *Bravo!* details this meeting of destiny when, at a concert featuring her *Light* and *Prison* (*Lament*), performed in Chicago, a voice shouted "Bravo!" "Bravo!" above the applause after each composition. (*Prison* was later performed at the White House in 1936, making Britain the second American woman composer, after Amy Beach, to be so honored.) Between world travels, the Simones settled in San Diego, moving to Hollywood two years later where Radie taught piano and composition privately. Their never-a-dull-moment match came to an untimely end when Edgardo died of a stroke in 1949. (It is interesting to note that Radie's father's name was Edgar.)

In 1959, the composer married a gentle, supportive husband, aviation pioneer Ted Morton, who had been influential in opening several Midwest airports and had trained many pilots during WWII at his Morton Air Academy. Their hideaway in Palm Desert, California, proved conducive to creativity.[37] *Cosmic Mist Symphony* (1962), Britain's foray into impressionism, is dedicated to Morton. It won the First National Prize of the NLAPW, and two years later was selected for the symposium sponsored by the Rockefeller Foundation and performed by the Houston Symphony. Britain was very interested in the concept of the universe, and with the advent of space probes dedicated her *Translunar Cycle*, celebrating the first landing on the moon in 1969, to the National Aeronautics and Space Administration (NASA). In 1981, she wrote *Ode to NASA* for brass quintet.

---

37. The composer was very much attuned with her concept of the spirit of the universe. She wrote: "I'm a very spiritual person. I believe the energy and rhythm of life is around and through us. I am able to block out all things of this world and meditate. The music flows through me and I just write as fast as I can. I will hear a melody, those voices coming from an external sphere, realizing there is a power greater than me coming through."

In 1990, Radie received a letter from Queen Elizabeth II commending the composer for her remarkable achievements. After a long illness, Radie died May 23, 1994, in Palm Desert.

A writer as well as a musician, Britain wrote her autobiography, *Ridin' Herd on Writing Symphonies*, in 1992. It was published posthumously by Scarecrow Press (1996). Her own words best describe her aspirations: "I wish to feel in American music the conquest of the pioneer . . . the beauty of a sunset, the nobility of the Rockies, the wonder of the Grand Canyon, the serenity of the hidden violet and the purity of the wildflower."

HARRIET BOLZ (1909–95) won first prize from the National Federation of Music Clubs for her piano piece, *Floret—A Mood Caprice*. Many NLAPW awards followed, the last one in 1987 for *The Kaleidoscope* which sold over 400 copies. She weaned audiences to new music with her pre-concert lectures and wrote for many organizations. Her music was programmed into several American Woman Composer concerts. In 1984, *Polychrome Patterns* was heard at the prestigious Wolf Trap Farm for the Performing Arts near Washington, DC. Her professional correspondence is in the Library of Congress as part of the Arsis Press Archives.

Composer, pianist and writer on music, **JULIA SMITH** was born January 25, 1911, in Denton, Texas, and was given piano lessons by her mother who had studied voice and piano. Julia graduated from North Texas State University in 1930 at nineteen. She studied piano, and subsequently composition with Rubin Goldmark on a fellowship at the Juilliard Graduate School (1929–32). She completed her MA (1933) and PhD (1952) from New York University, where **Marion Bauer** was among her teachers. In 1933, she became the pianist for conductor **Frédérique Petrides'** newly-formed all-woman Orchestrette Classique. The Orchestrette gave several premieres of Smith's early works, such as the *Little Suite Based on American Folk Tunes*, first performed in the Aeolian Hall in New York (1936), *Episodic Suite* (1937), and *Hellenic Suite*, from Greek folklore (1941). She often used folk idioms from the music of both the Native Americans and the white settlers in the Southwest. A prolific composer, she wrote many orchestral works and six operas, as well as chamber and vocal music.

In 1938, she married Oscar Vielehr, a friend of Petrides, a supportive husband who copied her music and encouraged her composition and performance. In February 1939, Smith had her first big success when her opera *Cynthia Parker* was premiered at the North Texas State College in a performance partly sponsored by Juilliard. In 1939, the Juilliard Orchestra gave the first performance of her *Piano Concerto*, a three-movement work using folk and jazz idioms. She continued to compose and perform while taking on a number of teaching positions over the next few years, working at Juilliard (1940–42), New Britain (Connecticut) State Teachers' College (1944–46), as well as founding a music education department at Hartt College of Music in Hartford, Connecticut (1941–46).

Smith was the first woman guest conductor of the Dallas Symphony, when she directed her *Episodic Suite*, scored for large orchestra, March 17 and 18, 1940. The same year, she—and eighteen men, including Aaron Copland—received commissions from CBS to write a work based on an American folk tune. Hers, *Liza Jane*, a short orchestral piece, was performed at a 1946 Carnegie Hall Pops concert by the New York Philharmonic. Another opera, *The Stranger of Manzano*, was premiered in Dallas (1946). Her children's opera, *The Gooseherd and the Goblin*, was commissioned by Hartt College (1947). *Folkways Symphony* (1949) makes extensive use of Western-American hoedown and fiddle tunes. She wrote three more operas, *Cockcrow* (1953), *The Shepherdess and the Chimney Sweep* (1963), and *Daisy*, about Juliette (Daisy was her nickname) Gordon Lowe, founder of the Girl Scouts of America, for the sixtieth anniversary of that organization. A patriotic large-scale choral orchestral work, *Our Heritage*, was commissioned by the Texas Boys Choir and performed in 1957.

As a writer, Smith added to the literature with her book *Aaron Copland: His Work and Contribution to American Music* (New York, 1955). A strong supporter of other women composers, in the late 1960s she organized a chamber-music concert of works by five women composers from all over the U.S.: Elizabeth Gould, Mabel Daniels, Louise Talma, Elinor Remick Warren and herself. At the request of the National Federation of Music Clubs, in which she was very active, she edited and published a sixty-page *Directory of American Women Composers* in 1970—the first recognized such source—and in the process learned that no woman had ever received a grant. Thereupon, she went to the president of the NEA in Washington, DC, and within three years eighteen women were named as grantees. Smith herself was the recipient of several commissions and awards, among them two Ford Foundation recording grants and three Meet the Composer grants. She was named first chairman of American Women Composers, forerunner of other women's music organizations.

Remembered for her great contributions to music, Julia Smith died in New York, April 27, 1989.

ROSLYN PETTIBONE, born in Cleveland, Ohio, May 18, 1912, was an important part of the Cleveland musical community. She married cellist/music teacher John Raish. Both taught music at the prestigious Hawkins School. They had two children, David, 1947, and Jocelyn, born 1951. Many summers were spent in rural Mexico taping and transcribing folk music. Roslyn was president of the Cleveland Composers Guild until her health gave way. She wrote orchestral, chamber, and choral works which won many Pen Women and other awards. Several of her compositions were played by the Cleveland Chamber Orchestra. One of her compositions was performed at Kennedy Center. At age fifty-nine, her husband was tragically killed in an auto accident in 1972. In 1974, she married Milton Pettibone, who died less than two years later. Still active in the music community, Roslyn passed away in November 1993.

VERA N. PREOBRAJENSKA, PhD, (dates unknown) studied with eminent composers **Darius Milhaud**, **Roger Sessions**, **Ernst von Dohnanyi** and **Dmitri Shostakovich**. Her output numbers vocal, choral, orchestral and chamber works, ballet and opera. Her scores are in the International Contemporary Music Library, Paris, and the National Library in Ljubljana, Yugoslavia (Serbia).

MARION MORREY RICHTER, PhD, born October 2, 1900, was a pianist, musicologist and lecturer. She was a graduate of Ohio State (BA), Juilliard, Columbia (MA and PhD, Education), and member of Delta Omicron sorority. A well-known composer and performer, she acted as department chairman of American music for the National Federation of Music Clubs (NFMC) for many years, as well as president of their New York chapter for two four–year terms, 1976–84.

She wrote choral, vocal, instrumental and piano music and a full length opera. Her works have been widely heard and published. As a pianist, her "Americana" program introduced audiences both here and abroad to the range and quality of American piano composition. She was heard on WNYC broadcasts from 1961–80, presenting noted artists, composers, premieres, ensembles etc. She also reached people via her workshops for teachers and youth: "Concerts with Commentary," "Aspects of Americana," "Russian and Soviet Music," and "Contemporary Music." She toured all over the U.S., England, Mexico and the Orient. Most notable was her Bicentennial Around the World American Music Tour of twenty-four concerts in the fall of 1975 at age seventy-five!

Besides being on the music faculties of Columbia and Juilliard for many years, Richter gave music study courses at Japan House in New York City. She received honors for her *Timberjack Overture* in the American Bandmasters Concert, and among her citations for American Music is one from the U.S. 8th Army of Korea.

Richter embarked on another international concert tour in her eighties, and celebrated her ninetieth birthday at the 1991 NLAPW Composers Concert at Lincoln Center, playing the piano part of her *Sonata for Trio* for violin, cello and piano. She died January 6, 1996, in Millbrook (upstate New York) at age ninety-six, leaving an immortal legacy at Cornell University via the Marion Morrey Richter American Music Composition Award for eligible students between ages eighteen to twenty-six.

Minuetta Kesler

MINUETTA KESSLER was born September 5, 1914, in Russia, because her mother was homesick. The child was two years old before Luba Lubinsky braved the dangers of crossing the Atlantic in WWI to return to Calgary, Alberta, Canada, where she and her husband had emigrated previously. True to her mother's dream, beautiful, curly blonde Minuetta became a child prodigy, composing and performing her own piano pieces by age five, and being compared to a young Mozart. Given a scholarship, she entered New York's Juilliard School of Music at age fifteen. Upon graduation in 1934, and following postgraduate work, 1936, she concertized at New York's Town Hall and Carnegie Hall as well as with the Boston Civic Symphony and the

Boston Pops, conducted by the famed Arthur Fiedler. The *New York Times* called her, "A rare phenomenon among the younger pianists of today."

She composed hundreds of pieces, her most famous being the *Alberta Concerto* for piano and orchestra, which she performed all over Canada and the U.S. She received the Gold Key to the City of Calgary in 1948. In addition to piano music for teaching, she wrote for solo instruments and instrumental ensemble, and was twice selected for Canadian ASCAP awards. Her *New York Suite* for small ensemble, *Spanish Rhapsody* and *String Quartet No.1*, commissioned by the MTNA for their 1981 convention, all received NLAPW awards.

Kessler settled in Belmont, Massachusetts in 1953, was a major figure on the Boston music scene, and named Woman of the Year by the Boston Chapter of the music fraternity, Sigma Alpha Iota. In 1990, she received honorary membership in the New England Piano Teachers Association. Until 1998, when her memory began to fail, she taught piano in her spacious home. Her last composition was a 302-page opera, *The Doukhabors* (The Spirit Wrestlers), about a Russian religious sect who had emigrated to Canada in 1898 to escape the domination of the Russian Orthodox Church. The work has been described as *Romeo and Juliet* as Tolstoy would have written it. Boston Pen Woman soprano Leslie Holmes arranged to have excerpts performed in Minuetta's home, May 20, 2001.

Minuetta had a fascination with scientists and married two of them. Her marriage to Dr. Ernest Borek, a Columbia University microbiologist, with whom she had son Ronald in 1943, ended in divorce due to career conflict. In 1952, she became happily married to Dr. Myer M. Kessler, an MIT physicist, who died in 1997. Their daughter, Jean, was born in 1954. Ron became a journalist and bestselling author. Each of her offspring presented her with two grandchildren.

Much esteemed by generations of students and colleagues, Minuetta died in her home, November 30, 2002.

NANCY PLUMMER FAXON, born November 19, 1914, in Jackson, Mississippi, had a prodigious collection of commissioned choral orchestral works to her credit, spanning over half a century. By 1938, she was a soloist with Chicago's Sorrentino Touring Opera Company. From 1940–41, she sang with the Chicago Opera Chorus, going on to become a choir director, church organist and teacher of voice, piano and theory. With degrees from Millsaps College, Jackson (BS Music; Pre-Med, 1936), Chicago Musical College (MM, Piano, 1938; MM Voice, 1941), and composition studies there with Max Wald (1938–41), she received many honors and awards, including first prize, National Composer's Clinic, for *Rhapsody for Orchestra with Piano* (1941), and being listed in the first edition of *Who's Who of American Women* (1958). In the 1980s, concerts of her compositions were performed at Boston University, Trinity and Old South Churches in Boston, Brookline Library Music Association, and the Boston Alumni chapter of Mu Phi Epsilon, the international music fraternity from whom she received the Orah Ashley Lamke Distinguished Alumni Award (1986), and who established the annual Nancy Plummer Faxon Scholarship from the proceeds of performances. Nancy's works list is at the Wellesley (Massachusetts) College Library, in Boston Area Music Libraries, and *The Boston Composers Project, A Bibliography of Contemporary Music*, published by MIT Press.

Besides Pen Women, Faxon's affiliations encompassed membership in the DAR, United Daughters of the Confederacy, Women's Guild of Boston University, Brookline Chamber Music Society (past president) and Brookline Library Music Association (board member).

She married George Faxon December 27, 1941. They moved to the Boston area in 1946 after World War II. A renowned church organist/choirmaster, who culminated his distinguished career at Boston's Trinity Church (1954–80), George was also professor of organ at Boston University. Nancy wrote *God Is . . .* for organ and cello, in memory of his passing in 1992. Of their three children, Emily, (*b* 1945), became a professional violinist, and produced the only two grandchildren, Tenaya (*b* 1973) and Christopher (*b* 1976); Nancy "Penni" (*b* 1947), who retired from her administrative career at the University of Massachusetts (Amherst), December 2003; and son Walter (*b* 1952), who lived at home, caring and acting as historian for his ninety-year-old still "with it" mother until her death, February 1, 2005.

ARWIN SEXAUER, PhD, was born August 18, 1921. She was a Dame Commander of New Zealand, Order of Astra, a recipient of President Reagan's Medal of Merit, and a member of ASCAP with twenty-two popular panel awards. Several of her compositions are in the repertoire of the U.S. Army, Navy and Air Force bands. Her literary and music works are recognized worldwide. She died in Vermont, June 1992.

Jeanne Singer

Composer/pianist **JEANNE SINGER**, born August 4, 1924, in New York, began composing at age five, having already learned notation and harmony from her mother. She attended the all-women Barnard College, but had to go to the affiliated mens' Columbia University to take theory classes where she was forced to compose the serial music she despised in order to "get an A." She graduated *cum laude* in 1944. In 1945, she married Richard George Singer, whom she supported through medical school. Their son, Richard, was born in 1945 (*d* 9–19–2002). The same year, she embarked upon fifteen years of piano study and a lifelong friendship with the great **Nadia Reisenberg** (1904–83). There being very little music for duo piano, Jeanne wrote a "signature piece" which was an instant hit.

For over thirty years, Singer performed as soloist with chamber ensembles and on radio and television. Her 1980 series, *Turn the Tables*, broadcast nationally, featured music composed by American women. She founded the Long Island Trio in 1969, and in 1986 the Musinger Players, a vocal-chamber ensemble, for whom she remained director and pianist until 1998.

Her compositions won numerous national and international honors from the Composers Guild, Composers and Songwriters International, National Federation of Music Clubs, and NLAPW for whom, as national music chairman, she organized annual Composers Concerts at Lincoln Center for eleven years. From 1978 on, she received a Meet the Composer Grant for performances of her works. Her 1996–97 ASCAP Award was her 19th consecutive winning of this honor.

Honoring a Hero

Besides much chamber and piano music, Singer used the creations of modern women poets for her extensive output of contemporary songs. In 1992, to celebrate the eightieth birthday of Raoul Wallenberg (1912–1947), the Swedish diplomat who risked his life saving over 100,000 Budapest Jews in World War II, she set to music *To Be Brave Is All*, from a poem by Madeleine Mason. A second memorialization of Wallenberg was *Avenue of the Righteous*, based on a work of fellow Pen Woman poet, **Anne Marx**. The title refers to a row of trees on the grounds of the museum of Yad Vashem, outside Jerusalem, dedicated to the Righteous Gentiles—Christians who saved Jews from the Holocaust. Each tree bears the name of such a hero. Both pieces, originally written for voice, violin and piano, were orchestrated by Singer and released along with twenty-three of her art songs, first on a Cambria CD (1991) titled *To Stir a Dream - American Poets in Song*, and re-released in 1999 by MMC Recordings as *Tribute to Raoul Wallenberg - Movements I and II*. A third CD is a collection of her works under the title *Of Times Past*, featuring the Slovak Radio Symphony Orchestra and Moravian Philharmonic, which she traveled to Eastern Europe to record.

Gone to the Cats

Jeanne Singer was also known as Madame Siamese. For four decades, the bloodlines of Grand Champions from her SINGA cattery were in demand all over the world. In November 1998, Jeanne married fellow cat breeder, and tenor soloist in many of her works, Austin Miskell. They had met twenty years earlier when he came to New York to purchase one of her kittens. Retired, he had been professor of voice and director of the opera department at the National University in Bogota, Colombia, where he promoted many of Singer's works in the course of the years.

In the Right Place at the Right Time

In April 1996, on a book-signing trip, I was flying from Boston to New York with a date to meet Jeanne at LaGuardia. When she failed to show, I called her home. A heavy smoker, she was gasping for breath and seemed disoriented when she answered the phone. I had to call three police departments in different parts of Long Island before I could get an ambulance sent to her house. (She never remembered how she got to the hospital.) Later that day, I was gratified to learn that my actions had indeed saved her life! Three years later, in October 1999, Jeanne suffered a stroke which necessitated giving up her home. After a protracted illness lasting several months, one of Pen Women's most prolific composers passed away, June 20, 2000, in Long Island, New York.

From manuscripts provided by Florence Hechtel, the American Music Center in Manhattan, American Heritage Center in Laramie, Wyoming, the Long Island Composers Archive at Long Island University, and co-sponsored by the New York State Council on the Arts, the Professor Edgar H. Lehrman Memorial Foundation, the Port Washington Memorial Library and the Aviva Players, a group devoted to presenting music by women composers with whom Jeanne had often performed, a memorial concert featuring her music was celebrated June 10, 2001 at the Shelter Rock Library in Manhasset, Long Island.

NANCY BINNS REED was born in Palo Alto, California, December 11, 1924, into a musical family. As a child, she taught herself trumpet and joined school bands. She began composing early, and in her teen years wrote a camp song, *Oh Happy Day*, which became an international hit. She did some ranching and even rounded up cattle. Her marriage to Ogden C. Reed, a civilian working for the U.S. Army, afforded her the experiences of living eleven years in Japan, Okinawa and Korea, as well as four years in Heidelberg, getting to know most of Europe. Although she continued composing, *and* painting *and* writing, her husband and four children were her top priority during the years of their upbringing. The family returned to Washington, DC, in 1974, and settled in Virginia. She wrote the musical *Tocqueville!* in 1976 and *Ali Baba* in 1977. Her style expanded to include ragtime, rock, chamber music, marches—which she had begun writing in Germany—opera and works for symphony orchestras. Her titles include *Frank Rowley's Rally*, a concert band piece which was performed by the Richmond Pops in 1990; *Vive Leche!* (*The Breasts of Patrona*), a musical play which ran for a month in 1992 in Providence, Rhode Island, and later in Georgetown; and *David, David, Jesse's Son*, a contemporary opera that premiered during the Northern Virginia Community College SpringFest 1993, and was described by the *Washington Post* as "powerful."

Reed's home-based studio was equipped with electronic keyboard and computer, on which she created her music. Recognition came in the shape of the National Award in 1992 for *American Polyphonic Theory*, and an ASCAP award each year (1977–99). She won numerous Pen Women awards, including two Biennial Competition prizes for *The Hounds of Hell*, an electro-acoustic piece from her *Blue Opera*, and *Saxophone Quartet for a Rainy Afternoon*, both in 1994, a fitting tribute to her seventieth birthday.

A half hour video on the composer was aired on local television, April 1995, featuring her music, paintings and sculpture. Active almost to the end, Binns Reed, a self-confessed unable-to-quit smoker, died of lung cancer, February 26, 2000.

Her marches have been played by the U.S. Army Band at the Pentagon for over thirty years, and her music performed at Kennedy Center.

Other Pen Women Who Have Made Their Mark in Music

SARAH SALLY ISABEL BENNETT, whose lyrics have been recorded by the orchestras of Glenn Miller, Guy Lombardo and Sammy Kaye, was raised in Philadelphia in a musical family. She studied piano in her youth, becoming a musician, composer, radio and television personality. She attended the University of Pennsylvania. After working as a model and legal secretary, she became a writer, talk-show hostess, and disc jockey at WBGS radio and WLWA-TV in Atlanta. She married Paul Bennett, a sales manager for Dow Chemical, November 1947.

When the company transferred him to Ohio, Sally became one of Cleveland's first ladies. As a member of the Cleveland Yachting Club, she wrote, produced, and directed ten annual regatta shows. In the twenty-three years Sally and Paul lived in Cleveland, she was a founding member of the Cleveland Indians Basebelles, president of the Cleveland Branch of Pen Women, on the board of the Cleveland Symphony and president of the Cleveland Women's Symphony Orchestra. Socially, she hob-nobbed with the Duchess of Windsor who, like Sally, worked for the humane treatment of animals. Since Grace Kelly and Sally had known one another in Philadelphia, she got to visit the Princess in Monaco and presented her with a "Woman of the Year of the National League of American Pen Women" certificate. During the Eisenhower administration, Sally became a founding board member of Washington's Kennedy Center of the Performing Arts and was also with "Ike" at the opening of the St. Lawrence Seaway. Another jewel in Sally's social crown was being aboard the yacht *Britannia*, with Queen Elizabeth II and Prince Philip.

From 1935–50, radios played swing tunes on *Your Hit Parade*. The show moved to TV from 1950–59. One of Bennett's major contributions to culture was founding, in 1966, the Big Band Hall of Fame. All famous big bands were automatically installed therein. The youngest inductee was Harry Connick, Jr., at age twenty-four. In 1966, Sally also initiated the Composers' Showcase, featuring new compositions written in big band style. After ten years of Composer's Showcase Balls, the Big Band Hall of Fame Museum was dedicated May 12, 1975, in Cleveland— its founder and president, Sally Bennett.

1972 brought her first book, *Sugar & Spice*, subtitled *A Collection of All American Poems and Song Lyrics*, via her own Knockemstiff Publishing Company. Other claims to fame included being the first Met Opera female supernumerary portraying a male role (April 1965, the monk in *Tosca*). She appeared in Philadelphia, New York, Atlanta, Cleveland—wherever she happened to live—when the Met came on tour. She was an extra in the Jack Lemmon film *Fortune Cookie* (1966), and *Traces of Red* (1992) with James Belushi.

The Bennetts retired to Palm Beach, Florida, in 1979, bringing the Composers' Showcase Ball and other Big Band activities with them. Their fourteenth ball in February 1997, with music by the Glenn Miller Orchestra, was highlighted with Sally's receiving the "Music of Your Life Award" for her *Magic Moments*. After years of diligent negotiations and fund raising, the Big Band Hall of Fame Museum was opened at the Palm Beach Community College in West Palm Beach on March 22, 1999.

In 2001, the biography of this flamboyant lady, *Magic Moments*, was brought out by Richard Grudens of Celebrity Profiles Publishing.

LOUISE CANEPA, a native of Monterey, California, wrote the area theme song, "Old Monterey." She won NLAPW and other awards for her lyric writing at the 1978 American Song Festival. In 1992, she received the NLAPW First National Prize for her art song, "Bella Mia Piccina." Her opera, *Sicilians of Monterey*, the romantic story of her own parents, premiered in the area in 1995 and met with great success. The following year, it was produced by the Italian American Heritage Foundation in San Jose (California) and aired on local public television. In April 1999, the Napa Valley Branch presented her three part tone poem for piano, *Mount St. John*, dedicated to Margaret Mondavi of the famous winery in the region. An all-Canepa program was presented in May 2000, featuring art songs and works for piano and cello. Her musical comedy, *Over the Bridge*, was a highlight at the 2002 Pen Women Biennial in San Francisco. A CD entitled *Napa Valley Serenity*, featuring charming songs, melodic piano pieces and works for string orchestra, was released the same year.

FRANCES R. CHADWICK was adopted at birth, March 6, 1951, and raised in Wichita, Kansas. Her adoptive father was a violinist in a symphony orchestra and her daily alarm clock was his walking by her door to the music room to start morning practice. At four, she was composing at the piano, improvising, adapting, experimenting, and coming back the next day to take "the melody of the week" through another series of variations. A few years later as her father stood sightreading over her shoulder, playing the melody line of the piece she was practicing, came an epiphany: even though he was playing a different instrument, music is a universal language.

Formal piano lessons began at five, violin at eight, weekly performances singing alto in the youth girls' choir at church, and flute at eleven. Unfortunately, her piano teacher chastised her severely for improvising and embellishing. She stopped composing until she took up folk guitar at thirteen.

She attended three semesters at Dirkson School of Fine Arts at Wichita State in the early 1970s, and subsequently earned a BS in Music Theory and Composition at East Texas State (Commerce, 1992). (The University has since merged with Texas A&M.) A summer course in ancient music at the RCM in London (1994), was followed in 1996 with an MM in composition at Southern Methodist University in Dallas. She also sang with the Women's Chorus of Dallas, a professional SSA choir (1997–2000).

She was the first composition major at ETSU in ten years to be offered a senior recital to showcase her undergraduate work. In her senior year she composed a chamber opera, *The Lost Silk Hat* (1993), which earned her acceptance into NLAPW. Her master's thesis was a recital of the compositions she had completed during her two years at SMU. The main composition, *Five Mothers of Israel*, based on five women of the Hebrew Bible, is set for choir with soloists, various instruments and piano.

To Chadwick, "Music is a verb, something to be done, a lifestyle, my life's blood. Having sung for forty-five years I also think in harmony." She also says, "For me, English is a second language. I could read and write music before I could read and write English." In kindergarten she told the teacher that the alphabet was A through G, and just keep repeating that as many times as you need.

Married since 1984 to Steve Chadwick, PhD, an electronic engineer who teaches computer science, he handles her performance sound equipment and maintains her synthesizer studio in top operating condition.

NANCY Bloomer **DEUSSEN**, born February 1, 1931, heard classical music throughout her childhood. Both her parents played piano, and her father, Horace Van Norman, a professional musician before going in the record business, encouraged his daughter's composing, teaching her notation and starting her on piano at age six. She also studied flute and recorders. Her mother, Julia Thomas Van Norman, also a first class pianist and musician, maintained a personal friendship with George Gershwin (1898–1937) during the last ten years of his life.[38]

With absolute pitch, Nancy began composing at fourteen. It was her major at the Manhattan School of Music. She also holds a BM in music education from the USC School of Music, with graduate studies at USC, UCLA and San Jose State University—all in California. Her composition teachers were Vittorio Giannini (1903–66), Lukas Foss (*b* 1922) and, at USC, Ingolf Dahl (1912–70).

Since age eighteen, she has performed as a classical pianist, primarily her own compositions, and as a jazz/cocktail pianist. She taught at Mission College and the University of Santa Clara (California), and "retired" to teach private composition classes as well as being an Early Music conductor and teacher.

Deussen's first period of composing was from 1945–65, a time when, as she says, "It was very difficult to get any performances (especially orchestral) because of discrimination against women composers. Most people didn't know we even existed!" She spent the next twenty years raising her three children, Christopher Webster, born December 8, 1953, Jennifer De Guzman, May 24, 1963, and Elizabeth McComb, May 10, 1965. As a single parent, she had her own piano technician (tuning) business (1972–87), returning to composition in 1985.

Her works, inspired by nature with an ecological message, include: *Woodwind Quintet*, first prize Mu Phi Epsilon International Composition Competition (1985); *Trio for Violin, Clarinet and Piano*, first prize at the Britten-on-the-Bay National Competition (1996); *Reflections on the Hudson*, for orchestra, winner of the Bay Area Composers Symposium Competition sponsored by the Marin Symphony (1996); *Concerto for Clarinet and Small Orchestra*, first prize Mu Phi Epsilon (1999); and *Woodwind Quintet # 2*, first prize Marmor Chamber Music Competition (Stanford University, 2002). *Flowers by the Sea* and *Sacred Places of the Earth* were for the De Anza Chorale and Women's Chorus; and *Tribute to the Ancients* (brass quintet) was commissioned by Sempervirens to

---

38. Confirmed in *The Memory of All That*, a Gershwin biography by Joan Peyser. (See Bibliography.)

celebrate their centennial and their work of saving the California Redwoods. Her music is on a CD titled *Reflections on the Hudson*.

Nancy's husband, Gary Deussen, is also a piano technician, who tunes and rebuilds pianos. Of her children, Christopher inherited his mother's perfect pitch, runs a limousine service and plays jazz piano gigs on the side. Jennifer sings in choruses and has two sons, Mac, born 1996 and Aidan, 1999. Elizabeth has Gabriela, born 1990, and Daniela, 1993. A singer/songwriter, she brought out her first CD, *Ebb and Flow*, in 2004.

SHEILA FIRESTONE, born in the Bronx, New York, December 20, 1941, began piano lessons at age ten. During junior high school, she spent one year the Brooklyn Academy of Music. Her parents had no musical training and did not view Sheila as having a serious commitment. Undisciplined in practicing, she soon abandoned her childhood dreams of being a pianist and settled into the realities of marriage and motherhood and the joy of teaching children via her education degree (Florida Atlantic University, Boca Raton, 1972), MS in special education (Florida International University, Miami, 1973), plus independent gifted education studies. A full time teacher of the gifted, she was a Florida Exceptional Teacher of the Year finalist in 1989, received the Very Special Arts Honor Award, Dade County, 1990, and Teacher of Note from Young Patronesses of the Opera, 2002.

With no musical plans, at age forty-five, in 1988, Sheila began a remarkable journey with mentor Joseph Dillon Ford, a Harvard degree musicologist, and a violinist friend, Bill Winnick, who helped her write down her melodies via solfeggio.

After retiring from her teaching career in 1998, and moving to Boca Raton, she studied composition and theory privately with Dr. Thomas McKinley, a professor at Lynn University Conservatory. Piece by piece, thought by thought, she learned to appreciate the rare, the unexpected, the melodious and the beauty of chromaticism.

In 2003, Firestone was awarded first place for *Trio-Introduction and Dance* in the instrumental division of the Florida Pen Women State Association Music Awards, and second place in the piano music category for the first movement of her *Sonatina No. 1*, a piece that has since been developed as a three movement work. She premiered a song, *On This Day*, at FAU (2002), the same year she released several CDs, including neo-classical/post modern works, *Piano Favorites #1*, a meditation album, *Peaceful Journeys*, and an interactive curriculum with songs called *Sing and Think*—dawn to dusk activities for young children. Sigma Alpha Iota, the National Music Sorority at the University of Miami, of which she is the patroness chapter president, performed a complete concert of her works, including *Sonata No.1 in A minor*, *The Peace Patch* (a dance suite for children), *Let Me Hear You, Oh Lord*, (solo vocal), *Chaconne in A Minor* (piano), a string quartet setting from *The Peace Patch*, and *Psalm 1* for string quartet for their vespers concert (1997). A Miami Youth Symphony premiered two pieces: *Because I Love*, and a setting of *Psalm 117*.

Married since 1961, her husband Bruce, a retired English professor, began a new career in video film editing and has created several CD, DVD projects making use of some of his wife's music for backgrounds. In his DVD for Alyn Hospital (Israel), a facility which changes the lives of handicapped children, the background music uses the song, *The Special Child*, Sheila donated to their cause. It was featured at Special Arts Festivals in the state of Florida.

Their grown children are Wayne, born 1964, an attorney and youth coordinator for Hillel programs, and Evan, born 1967, a real estate mortgage broker.

The output of violinist, pianist and composer **GENEVIEVE** Devisson **FRITTER BIEBER** covers orchestral, instrumental ensemble, and solo works for instrument and voice. While serving as music director of the Montgomery (Maryland) Ballet Company, she composed six full-length ballets for children.

Born December 13, 1916, in Clarksburg, West Virginia, into a musical family, her childhood was spent hearing the great Irish voice of one grandfather and the renowned country fiddling of the other. Her first violin came when she was eight. Self-taught, she was also an accomplished pianist. During the Depression, her sister Thelma, nine years her senior, contributed her meager paycheck for violin lessons and even postponed her marriage so that Genevieve could finish Judson College in Marion, Alabama, (BM, 1937). She won Juilliard scholarships two consecutive summers at Chatauqua, New York. Placing first in a young artists' competition enabled her to solo with the Birmingham Symphony, with whom she subsequently played from 1939–40—a time when there were only half a dozen women in the orchestra, all violins. During this period, she was Supervisor of Music in two Alabama public school systems. An early song, *Monotone*, won a first prize National Federation of Music Clubs award, and was published by the prestigious G. Schirmer.

Genevieve married Eldon Fritter in 1940. Daughter Jeanie, assistant director of the National Cathedral Choral Society since 1986, arrived in 1941. Three years later, the family moved to Cleveland where she taught violin at the Quinn School of Music and became known as a soloist and chamber musician. She was also a member of the music fraternity, Mu Phi Epsilon. With a supportive husband looking after the baby, she was able to study violin with Mihail Stolarezsky at the Cincinnati Conservatory. As in her childhood, Genevieve was always spared household chores to preserve her fingers. Daughter Priscilla, who became an accomplished flutist, was born in 1946. A move to the Washington area in 1953 resulted in both mother and younger daughter playing in the National Ballet Orchestra, where Fritter was concert mistress (1965–70), as well as playing in the newly-built (1971) Kennedy Center and its Opera House Orchestra where Priscilla joined her mother the following year. Genevieve spent twenty years in the orchestra until her retirement in 1992. Priscilla graduated to principal flute (1979) until *her* retirement in 1994. (She continues to play there, part time.)

Eldon Fritter passed away in 1975. Charles "Ted" Bieber, who had known Genevieve since third grade, was widowed in 1990. The two married in 1991. Her daughters have each presented her with two grandchildren: Jeanie's Faisal (1973), and May (1978), and Priscilla's Adam (1984) and Julia (1990). All are musical.

BEVERLY GLAZIER, born of parents who emigrated from Russia, is the daughter of a cantor and a mother also possessed of a lovely voice. After getting a BS in education from the University of Syracuse (New York), Beverly studied for music degrees there and at Wayne State (Ohio). One of her composition teachers was Howard Boatwright, a protegé of Paul Hindemith. A member of the ASCAP Serious Music category, she has served on the board of directors for the Syracuse Symphony and sung with the Early Music Ensemble of Syracuse. Her choral works include much Jewish liturgical music, some of which has been performed in Israel. She was an award winner in the Temple Sinai Composers Contest in Sharon, Massachusetts, two years in a row with *Akdamut*, a non-verbal hallelujah for piano, and *A New Song Unto the Lord* for choir and piano. Besides voice, she also writes pieces for flute, cello and piano which have been heard at the Society for Music, Civic Morning Musicals (played by the Syracuse Symphony) and Pen Women Concerts at Lincoln Center.

Woman of Vision, for which she wrote words and music, is dedicated to her mother, Frances Kaplan, and her daughters Sharon and Marilyn, who respectively turned to the East (Israel) and the West (America), in their lifestyle choices. As the text suggests, the process of *becoming*, rather than the end result, can be the greatest influence on one's path. *Maduah Yehudi?* (Why a Jew?) challenges the biblical concept of the "chosen people." The music demands to know why Jews have been subjected to such misery and persecution of pogroms and the Holocaust. These compositions have earned ASCAP performance points. *Screaming Eagle* and *In Freedom Rejoice* were written in 1976 and sung by the multi-voice Central New York Bicentennial Festival Chorus (which included the composer). The pieces received many performances throughout that year.

One of Glazier's significant contributions is an anti-smoking musical for children, *Professor Schnitzelcreen and His Self-Esteem Machine*, co-written with Pen Woman Ida Mescon of Syracuse. Many of its songs are appropriate to all ages, such as the western ballad *Smoking Fools*, and *Welcome to the Spider's Web*. This presentation is offered to all schools via the New York State Board of Education.

A poignant work was dedicated to her husband for their forty-fifth anniversary. Titled *Currents*, it represents the elements of a long, enduring relationship, "the tides, the crashing waves, the smooth, placid waters, the ripples and rivulets . . . the whirlpools . . . the currents that make up the moods and depth . . . of a marriage."

Also giving voice to the perennial challenge faced by many women, and composers in particular, Glazier observes: "Words as well as music have longed for expression since I became aware of sound. They flow together for me and find expression now here and now there, fanned by experiences erratically spaced with the flow between higher priorities of family . . . who have always come first."

LUCILLE GREENFIELD was born in New York City, February 24, 1929. Her father played violin, and at five she was playing the pieces her brother was learning on the piano, after which she received her own lessons. She studied at Greenwich House and Manhattan School of Music with famed avant-gardist, Vladimir Ussechevsky (1911–90). Her compositions include music for chamber orchestra and voice with piano. She has also written music for plays, such as *Catch a Falling Star* and *Rachel*, the latter performed in Nashville (2003). The first movement of her *War Symphony* (1990) is dedicated to victims of the Holocaust. As a pianist, she has done much concertizing in and around Manhattan.

JOANNE HAMMIL, born in Brooklyn, October 31, 1947, was guided by her own natural love of music. She began piano at six, took violin lessons later, and taught herself guitar. She always loved to sing. After majoring in music at Smith College, where she earned her BA in 1969, she taught vocal and general music from elementary through high school in Massachusetts and New York for the next five years, during which she spent a year in Paris studying piano and dance. She switched to giving piano lessons at home when her children, Adam, born November 11, 1976, and Lisa, born December 14, 1978, were very young. (Adam is also a musician.)

From writing songs for her own children, she progressed to directing children's choirs, and expanding to intergenerational choruses—advertised for ages ten through one hundred and ten. She is now well-known around the country for her concerts and workshops for music teachers, families, musicians and communities—several with folk singer Pete Seeger. She served as president of the Children's Music Network for many years.

Her numerous CDs include her original songs for children, "Pizza Boogie," "The World's Gonna Listen!" and for adults, "Joanne Hammil's Rounds & Partner Songs Volumes I & II" and "Don't Give Me a Label." Her songs have been published by McGraw-Hill, Heinemann, Silver-Burdett-Ginn, Child Care Information Exchange, etc., and have been performed and recorded by many artists and labels, including *Music For Little People*. One of her songs is featured in the 2002 *Teaching Tolerance* CD & Songbook, a collection of twenty-five great songs for children, which includes songs by Louis Armstrong, Woody Guthrie, Malvina Reynolds, and Rodgers and Hammerstein.

Among Hammil's passions is writing *rounds*. These have become standards in books and harmony circles. Two CDs containing fifty-four of them were released in 2003. In June 2003, she sang several of her rounds on the radio show, "Prairie Home Companion."

JANE SMITH HART, composer and pianist, adapted American spirituals and wrote a collection of children's folk songs, *Singing Bee*, which *Parents' Choice Magazine* selected in 1990 as a "great contribution to children's lives." New York Women Composers' catalogue lists three pages of her works.

MARGUERITE HAVEY, a graduate of Juilliard (1933), and associate of the American Guild of Organists, composed for chorus, solo vocal, instrumental pieces for piano, organ, cello and clarinet, and men's chorus—a body of work dating from 1945 to 1985. She was choir director and organist for the Church of the Epiphany in New York City for eighteen years (1939–57), and in the music department of the Brearley School (1958–1976). Born in New York City, December 16, 1910, she retired to Vermont in 1979 and, from a kit, built a Schober two-manual electronic organ which was still in use as of 2000. In May 2002, she moved to Equinox Terrace, a retirement home in her same village, Manchester Centre, where I spoke to her in 2004 in her ninety-fourth year.

WINIFRED HYSON, composer of piano, voice and piano, choral works and chamber music, was born February 21, 1925, in Schenectady, New York. She began piano at eight, going on to voice and flute at fourteen. Her maternal grandmother was a pianist and a fine musician. Her father played violin, her mother, piano, and her younger brother, clarinet. Family chamber concerts and classical music were always part of home life. After her BA, *magna cum laude* in physics from Radcliffe College (Phi Beta Kappa), she studied music theory and composition at the American University. Piano study was with Evelyn Swarthout Hayes, and Roy Hamlin Johnson.

Hyson's many awards include first place in the 2000 NLAPW Biennial Composition Contest with other winnings 1990, '92, '98; first place, vocal category, 2000 Composers Guild Composition Contest (other awards 1995, '99); as well as a 1999 Fellowship Grant from the Arts Council of Montgomery County (Maryland, 1999). In 1994, she was elected to ACME (Distinguished Artists, Composers, Musicologists and Educators) by Mu Phi Epsilon, with whom she has won five competitions since 1983. She has also received grants from Meet the Composer, Inc. Her compositions have been performed by National Capital Area Composers Consortium Concert Series, Charles Ives Center for American Music, Southeastern Composers League Forum, Cantate Chamber Singers, Alexandria Choral Society, Music of Washington Composers, MusicALASKAWomen FESTIVAL (1993), Mostly Women Composers Festival (1995), Canadian Chamber Ensemble, plus numerous Pen Women events. In 2000, her work "Eleanor Roosevelt" was presented at the NLAPW Biennial. Her musical, *LADIES FIRST: Songs, Rhymes and Times of the Presidents' Wives*, was presented as part of the Citywide Celebration/Jacqueline Kennedy's Washington. *Somewhere in the Wild*, for soprano, flute, viola and piano, commissioned by the Maryland State Music Teachers Association premiered at the association's 2002 convention, and awarded top prize in the 2003 Mu Phi Epsilon Original Composition Contest. *Love and Beyond*, a work for soprano, flute and koto, was performed as part of the Asian Song Festival on May 12, 2003 at Kennedy Center.

Wells of Salt, Knives of Song was performed October and November 2004 in the Mansion at Strathmore in Rockville, Maryland, which also saw the performances of *Rokudan: Variations for Clarinet and Koto*, April 2005, *Love and Beyond* for soprano, flute and koto, November 2005, and March 2006. *Wells of Salt, Knives of Song* received another hearing October 2005 at the Dennis and Phillip Ratner Museum in Bethesda, as part of the NLAPW Maryland State Conference. During 2003–05, the chamber group EcoVoce performed her *Somewhere in the Wild* and *Tales Undersea*. Her work was featured at the Pen Women Bienniale in Denver in 2006.

Winifred married Charles D. Hyson in 1946. An economist who served in U.S. Foreign Service, he passed away March 8, 2004. Their three offspring are: David Hyson (*b* 1950), a graphic designer, Pamela Hyson Martin (*b* 1952), pianist, teacher and chamber music coach, and Christopher Hyson, MD (*b* 1955). Hyson holds a Lifetime Master Teacher Certificate in Piano from the Music Teachers National Association (MTNA).

ELIZABETH LAUER, born in Boston, December 2, 1932, began singing "with my mother, words and music, at about fifteen months; at three, I listened to the songs in my head; at four, I started singing counterpoint to the songs in my head." She started piano at nine, and percussion in college and graduate school. She attended Bennington College (BA, 1953), Columbia University (MA, 1955), and the Staatliche Hochschule für Musik, Hamburg (1955–57) on a Fulbright Scholarship. Returning home, she worked at Columbia Records, starting as a typist and five months later as assistant, for over five years, to the legendary Goddard Lieberson (1911–77), president of Columbia from 1955–66 and 1973–75.

She was composer-in-residence for Bennington Chamber Music (1982); has won many Pen Women awards since 1984; was Percussive Arts Society first prize winner (1992); and has commissions from the Fisher Piano Competition (2001) and Connecticut State Music Teachers Association (CMSTA, 2002).

In addition to her many published works is an all-Lauer CD (I Virtuosi label), *Joyce Sings* (2001), *Two Shakespearean Settings* for *a cappela* chorus (2004)—both on Capstone—the latter published by Arsis.

Symbiosissimi, a collection of six harpsichord pieces, is a 2006 commission by Courtenay Caublé.

BETTE MILLER, PhD, pianist and composer, was born in Boston to a father who demanded rigorous piano practice. She studied with conductor/pedagogue **Fiora Contino**, a student of **Arturo Toscanini**, and graduated from the University of Massachusetts with degrees in piano performance and social science, also attending the Hartt School of Music and Eastman, before getting her MM from the University of Miami and PhD from Boston U. She has concertized throughout the Southeast U.S., became a professor of education at USIU, San Diego, California, and enjoyed a long career in social sciences as a contract administrator for the County of San Diego.

Upon her retirement, she became an associate of the Sisters of Social Service in San Diego, composing, performing and producing the 1999 CD, *Classic Inspirations*, a selection from which was chosen as first place winner at the NLAPW 2000 Biennial. She has also performed her own compositions for the American Association of University Women, PEO, and the Ecumenical Council, among many other organizations. She co-produced La Jolla Branch's *Arts in Concert*, a presentation which brought together the unities of art, literature and music—the core of Pen Woman philosophy.

ELIZABETH NICHOLS, a brilliant, creative musician, has contributed significantly to music education and preservation of Native American songs. She studied with Carl Orff (1895–1982), and taught in South Africa, and at Ball State University. She performed in numerous ensembles and orchestras, and was awarded a special certificate for her work in the Colorado Springs schools. She has written several books for beginning musicians.

Following an injury to her hand, Liz gave up playing the silver flute to play Indian flute. Several masters have presented her with hand-carved flutes, and at least one Indian tribe asked her to play at Indian pow wows in Colorado.

She plays recorder in a renaissance consort, and has given lessons and musical instruments to students who could not otherwise afford them.

Now living in Topeka, Kansas, she collaborated with **Marilyn Thies** on the background music for a promotional video. She was a soloist at the 2006 Denver NLAPW Bienniale.

LINDA Woodaman **OSTRANDER** has had a dual career in music and higher education. Born February 17, 1937, in New York City, she began studying piano at age six. Her father, a trumpeter with big bands, led her to both jazz and classical music. She also played trumpet. Her degrees include a BM (Oberlin, 1958), MA (Smith College, 1960), DMA (Boston U., 1972), all in Music Composition, plus a PhD in Cultural Studies (Union Institute, 1994). A Bunting Institute Scholar and Harvard Fellow, she has received NEA awards and Pen Women first prizes in 1985, '86, '88, '92. She was chosen for the Boston Composers' Project, Leaders for the '80s Program, and the American Council on Education for leadership training, and was 1985 MTNA Massachusetts Composer of the Year.

Ostrander has been Dean at several colleges and, in conjunction with her husband, continues her Professorship at Lesley University and Cambridge (Massachusetts) College, teaching arts and humanities, and education.

Her compositions cover voice, piano, ensemble and orchestra. Works written before 1994 are catalogued and housed at the Wellesley College Library. Her four children's musicals have been featured on NPR and broadcast in France, Belgium, Australia and Canada. She has been a pianist for Woman Song International, and accompanies her husband, storyteller Edmund Ostrander, in their performances of music and tales for audiences of all ages.

Julie Rivers

Eugénie Rocherolle

Linda met Edmund at Oberlin. They married in 1957. Their daughters, Melinda (*b* 1960), and Elisa Beth (*b* 1966) are both musicians. Melinda plays flute, and has three children. "Lisa" has her own band in New York.

JULIE RIVERS has won many NLAPW Music Competitions. She met composer/pianist **Eugénie Rocherolle** through Pen Women, which resulted in the successful 1995 CD *Spinning Gold*, in which she performs Eugénie's works. This was followed by *Tidings of Joy*, Rocherolle's arrangements of Christmas music, and *Romancing the Piano*—all on Rocherolle's label, Aureus.

Julie subsequently founded her own Earth Star Recordings, bringing out *One Starry Night* and its sequel *The Kiss of the Sun* (1999); *Christmastide* (2000), with Rivers' arrangements and solos; and *As Far As the Heart Can See* (2003), featuring her own compositions. (See Pianists.)

Modern Romantic **EUGÉNIE** (Ricau) **ROCHEROLLE**, a most prolific composer of tuneful music, whom I have dubbed "the Cécile Chaminade of the modern era," has been a Pen Woman in the Connecticut Pioneer Branch since 1979, tracing her roots as a Daughter of the American Revolution. (See Contemporary American Composers.)

DOROTHY STRUBHAR ROSS was born June 5, 1922, in Illinois, showing musical talent at an early age. By fourteen, two of her original operettas had been given major school productions and other works were widely performed in the area. Three summers in her teens were spent at Interlochen. She attended Eastman on a composition scholarship, graduating in 1944 with a BM and becoming a member of the prestigious music fraternity Sigma Alpha Iota.

After joining her family, who had moved to Miami, she worked as a scriptwriter at radio station WQAM, later becoming music director at CBS affiliate WGBS. In 1948, she married Bill Ross who became a weather announcer for NBC in Miami. They had two daughters, Kathleen and Ellen and a son Thomas. Dorothy was on the faculty of the Miami Conservatory (1949–69), a music critic for *The Week* magazine and the *Miami Herald*, and librarian/arranger for the Greater Miami Philharmonic Society. She served on the piano faculty at Miami-Dade Community College 1969–89.

Through a Library of Congress course, she qualified as a certified Braillist—music Braille is derived from literary Braille—and was for many years deeply involved in teaching and working with the blind. She also sang and played piano in nursing homes, recalling this a joyous time working with gifted and responsive people.

It was Hurricane Andrew which blew her out of town to Knoxville, Tennessee, to live near daughter Kathleen and her first grandson, and later a second. The storm destroyed her home in Miami except for—miraculously—her music scores and her box of photographs, which sustained only a little damage at the edges without marring any faces! The only way she could identify her house was via the three legs of her grand piano sticking up out of the rubble. In 1998, she retired to a small mountaintop home in North Carolina she had owned since 1975.

Written in a neo-romantic style, Ross' compositions cover sacred, secular, chamber, orchestral, piano and choral. With most of her pieces having been written for a specific person or occasion, her oeuvre contains a full Mass, *Capriccio for Piano and Orchestra*, as well as organ and brass works.

GAIL Esther **SMITH**, music chairman of the 1996 and 2000 NLAPW Biennials in Washington, DC, is a pianist in the sacred music field, as well as a concert and recording artist. She has given workshops and concerts throughout the U.S., Germany and Japan, and seminars on the effect of music on emotions, health and well-being. Her musical lecture recitals are unique in that she portrays the wife of a composer, like Anna Magdalena Bach, Marian MacDowell, etc., an effective way to reach her audience with music history. In addition to her many piano instruction books, and the important *The Complete Book of Improvisation, Fills and Chord Progressions*, she has written *The Life and Music of Edward MacDowell* and *The Life and Music of Amy Beach*, joining the revival of interest in the latter's music. Her "trademark" compositions are *palindromes*, piano solos that can be played backwards as well as forwards and sound the same.

MARJORIE TAYLOE, harpist, organist, composer and producer of shows, has given close to 2000 concerts, and is known to 1,500 couples as the "Wedding Harpist." She played on the soundtrack for Prince, in the film *Purple Rain*, and has entertained for Michael and Lisa Jackson. For three years she was one of the directors of the Hollywood Bowl Easter Sunrise Service, and continued to assist there for many years. For thirteen years every Monday evening, she performed on the great Kimball pipe organ for a Los Angeles radio station, filling the airwaves with "Music Until Midnight." Already accomplished on viola and organ, she decided to master the harp. Like the early minstrels, she has traveled extensively with her harp to Canada, Paraguay, England, Wales, Scotland and Ireland, across the channel to Holland, Paris, Salzburg and Denmark. In Wales, she fell in love with the unique triple stringed harp and found a new challenge to master. She also developed an interest in handbells and discovered the Thurlstone Bell Orchestra of Yorkshire, for whom she served as manager on their two western tours of the U.S.

Marjorie Tayloe

Married to Dr. Ralph Tayloe, a retired Los Angeles teacher and college administrator, for fifteen years Marjorie was director, arranger and teacher of their five children who sang and played harp and handbells professionally, touring as the Tayloe Family. They appeared on TV shows such as the *Bob Hope Special, Donny and Marie*, plus many commercials. The Welsh BBC came to her house to film her fabulous harp collection, which is in the

Guinness Book of World Records as the largest *private* collection of harps in the world! She also made the Guinness Book for having the largest gathering of twins, triplets (fifty-three sets) and quads (four sets), June 10, 1982, the eighteenth birthday party for her own set of triplets, two identical girls, Sarah Lee and Susan Marie and a boy, John Daniel, born in 1964. The party was written up in many papers all over the world. Marjorie's other children are Mary Ellen (*b* 1962) and David Chester (*b* 1963).

Tayloe has produced nine books and many recordings, and had a syndicated television show, *The Language of Music*. She helps promising young musicians find scholarships, and in case there is a moment to spare, she teaches and coaches harp, voice, organ and elocution in her Musical Arts Academy, which she moved from Hollywood to Solvang when her husband relocated in 1992, and where she has been director of the famous Solvang Nativity Pageant since 1995. Fall 1997 saw another Marjorie Tayloe tour of Germany, Austria, Denmark and England. She was president, and a member for thirty-five years, of Greater Los Angeles Branch of Pen Women—the first on the West Coast, established 1915. This multi-talented lady has played for four presidents: Eisenhower, Nixon, Carter and Reagan; Queen Elizabeth II at Cardiff Castle (Wales, 1960), and Holyrood Castle (Scotland, 1967). In 2000, she was listed among *Entertainers of the Century*, and in 2003 received the *Mother of the Year* Award from the state of California.

MARILYN THIES began piano and harmony at age four, studying with her mother, a violinist and pianist who could play by ear—a practice considered just this side of evil in those days. By ten, she had performed her first Mozart piano concerto. At twelve she studied at the Kansas City Conservatory, and after playing for Karl Friedberg was invited to Juilliard, but chose instead French, classical studies and journalism. She won the Baird Prize in Classical Studies/Latin from University of Missouri (1955), and earned her BA in French from UC Boulder, where she won the Prix d'Excellence (1958). After a summer at the Sorbonne, studying education, ancient history, French and Latin, she taught these languages in public school, along with English as a second language. Musically, during high school and college she was a professional accompanist, and in later years played in a duo-piano team.

In her thirties she returned to composition, and won third place at the NLAPW 1990 Convention for *Chagrin d'Amour* for soprano and piano. She was Pen Women National Music chair (1990–92); Kansas Composer of the Year (1992); and Kansas Commissioned Composer (1998).

Her compositions are for piano, piano with voice and instruments, and SATB choir. *Pour Sylvie* (flute, and piano) was presented at the Terrace Theater, Kennedy Center (1988). *Velvet Shoes* (double quartet) was performed at the Kansas Governor's Mansion (1992), by SATB choir in Master Teacher Summer Concert at Kansas State (1999), and Washburn University Fall Concert (2002). *Sweetgrass Summer's Day* (piano, four hands), commissioned by Kansas Master Teachers Association, was played at their 2000 Convention. 2002 brought *A Song for Christmas Night*, a CD of her music.

She produced a program for preschoolers in the Kansas School system on tone training used in "kindermusic," working with elementary school children on writing and improvising, following which program the children appear and perform at Kansas State in a symposium for teachers of music.

Married in 1960, her retired husband is interested in philanthropy and mentoring. Their children include a daughter born in 1961, a son born 1970, and son John (1964–94), whose music and humor are kept alive in memory, and a scholarship in his name for music students.

In 1992, Thies compiled a Composers Catalogue for the League, which provided part of the foundation for this section. In 2004, she again helped the author by compiling an updated list of music members.

WANG AN-MING was born November 7, 1926, in Shanghai, and began piano at eight. She came to America in 1938 with her parents, but returned to earn her bachelor's degree in education (1947) from Central China University. Her father (Economics BA, Yale), (MA, Princeton), a banker, established the Bank of China on Wall Street (NYC), in 1936. Her mother studied music (BA, Wellesley). Returning to the U.S. in 1948, Wang attended Wesleyan Conservatory (BM, 1950) and Columbia (MA, 1951).

Among her major works are: *Lan Ying* (opera in three acts), premiered 1996 at Kennedy Center, and won third place Pen Women Music Award; *Kapalua* for flute and piano, won first place in 2001; *Concerto for Piano and Orchestra*, premiered 2002 and received Maryland State Arts Council Award.

She married William K. Mak, an importer-exporter (now deceased) in 1951. Their children are Elise, born 1953, and Darrell, 1964, both married and working in their (non-musical) careers.

HARRIET FAY WOODCOCK, a third generation violinist, award-winning poet, non-fiction and children's author, has written and produced a dozen musicals including *A Cruise for Cherie*, *The Song of Sidney Lanier*, *Egmont and Ark*, about the founding of Georgia by James Oglethorpe, and *They Call Me Gainesville*. Her 1976 march, *Rise Up to the Flag*, has been performed by the President's Own Marine Band. She also wrote the prize-winning state song for Georgia Pen Women, *Look to the Future* (1990). Born in Gainesville over seventy years ago, she still lives on the same street! Her musical about Georgia poet Byron Reece (1917–58), *A Man of Soul and Soil*, was premiered in 2002. She was national music chair (1997–99) and was state music chair 1995–2003.

Not all composers can have their music played by major orchestras or well-known soloists. Many of these women, and not just Pen Women, wrote for schools, houses of worship or community events—venues which make up the fabric or our communities, a fabric very much a part of the grand tapestry of great music.

CHAPTER EIGHT

Women of Color—Triumph and Tragedy

Nora Douglas Holt (1885–1974)
Florence (Smith) Price (1888–1953)
Avril Coleridge-Taylor (1903–98)
Undine Smith Moore (1905–89)
Zenobia Powell Perry (1908–2004)
Evelyn (LaRue) Pittman (1910–92)
Margaret Bonds (1913–72)
Julia Amanda Perry (1924–79)
Betty Jackson King (1928–94)

Eleanor Alberga
Lettie Beckon Alston
Regina A. Harris Baiocchi
Valerie Capers
Tania Justina León
Lena Johnson McLin
Dorothy Rudd Moore
Nkeiru Okoye
Patrice Rushen
Errollyn Wallen

As if being a woman were not challenging enough to make a name for oneself as a composer, being black posed a double-edged sword for the first two-thirds of the 20th century, especially in the (then) bias-ridden American South.

NORA DOUGLAS HOLT was born in Kansas City, and graduated from Western University at Quindaro, Kansas. She continued her studies at Chicago Musical College. In 1918, she became the first black person in the U.S. to receive a master's degree in music. Her thesis composition was an orchestral work, *Rhapsody on Negro Themes*. The following year, she co-founded the National Association of Negro Musicians. She went abroad for twelve years, singing at exclusive night clubs and private parties in Paris, Monte Carlo, London, Rome, Tokyo and Shanghai. On her return to America, she settled in New York City where she became music critic for the *Amsterdam News* (1943–1956) and producer/director of radio station WLIB's "Concert Showcase" (1953–1964). She also composed some 200 works, including orchestral music, chamber music and songs. When she departed for Europe, she placed all manuscripts in storage, but on her return discovered that they had been stolen. *Negro Dance*, in syncopated ragtime style, was the only piece that survived, since it had been published in her short-lived journal, *Music and Poetry* (1921).

Florence Price

Less than a quarter century after Abraham Lincoln's Emancipation Proclamation **FLORENCE (Smith) PRICE** was born April 9, 1888, in Little Rock, Arkansas. Her father was the first black dentist to have an office on Main Street. Her mother was of black and white ancestry and came from a wealthy, land-owning family. She gave her young daughter piano lessons. Later the child studied violin and organ, and was already composing and performing her first pieces at four. Her first published work came at age eleven.

These were remarkable achievements considering the milieu of black prejudice. By 1906, lawmakers had managed to establish all-white primary elections, white schools, restaurants— even gas station toilets were segregated. Despite this, Florence graduated from high school at fourteen and was valedictorian of her class. Wanting to avoid any unpleasantness, her mother wrote Mexico as her birthplace on the application form for the New England Conservatory, even though the school had already accepted two black students. (Although barred from many white institutions, blacks were being admitted to

Oberlin, Boston, New England and Cincinnati Conservatories and the Chicago Musical College. Famed African-American composer **William Grant Still** (1895–1978), who had attended the same elementary school as Florence, entered the NEC a few years after her.) Florence majored in piano and organ and studied composition with the scions of the New England School, **George Chadwick** and **Frank Converse**. While still a student, she wrote a string quartet and a symphony.

At nineteen, she returned to Arkansas, teaching in the primary and secondary grades. Later, she took over the music department at Shorter College in Rome, Georgia. In 1912, she married Thomas Price, a lawyer. Their son, Tommy, died as an infant. Daughters Florence and Edith arrived in 1917 and 1921. Although highly respected in their community, the Prices nevertheless moved to Chicago in 1927 to escape Southern race riots.

Using the opportunity for further study, Florence took language and liberal arts courses at various universities in the area, including the American Conservatory. Her compositions began to be published. In 1932, she won the then handsome sum of $500 in the Wanamaker Foundation Awards for her *Symphony in E minor*. $250 was won by **Margaret Bonds**, who had been one of her composition students. Margaret's mother, Estella, was an important person in Chicago's black cultural circles. Through her, Florence met foremost black poet **Langston Hughes**. Mrs. Bonds also gave the Prices a home when they first arrived in town.

In 1933, the winning symphony was performed by **Frederick Stock** and the Chicago Symphony at the Chicago World's Fair "Century of Progress" Exposition. Price became the first black woman and the second black composer to have a work played by a major orchestra. In 1934, Margaret Bonds was soloist, with the composer conducting a performance of her *Piano Concerto in F minor*. In 1935, Price had the satisfaction of returning to Little Rock for a concert of her music, which most of the town turned out to hear.

November 1940 found Eleanor Roosevelt in the Detroit audience when Florence played her second piano concerto, and the Michigan WPA orchestra performed her third symphony. The first lady congratulated the composer on the contribution she was making to music.

Price was widowed in 1942. She continued teaching and composing. Modest and deeply religious, her style, rooted in traditional harmony and classical forms, is original in its infusion of the rich heritage of Afro-American rhythms. Arrangements of spirituals, art songs, piano and organ music, teaching pieces and band music comprise a teeming repertoire which also includes three piano concertos, one violin concerto, concert overtures, *Abraham Lincoln Walks At Midnight* for chorus and orchestra, and a string quartet, *Suite of Negro Dances*, commissioned by British conductor **Sir John Barbirolli** (1899–1970). *Two Traditional Spirituals* (1949) were dedicated to black contralto **Marian Anderson**, who had made Price's earlier *Songs to a Dark Virgin* (text by Langston Hughes) into what one critic called, "one of the greatest immediate successes ever won by an American song." G. Schirmer published this in 1941. One of Price's most famous songs is, "My Soul's Been Anchored in de Lord."

Her music was played all over the world. She was preparing for a trip to Europe when she became ill and died June 3, 1953. In 1974, daughter Florence Price Robinson donated her mother's papers to the Special Collections Department, University of Arkansas Libraries in Fayetteville. Consisting of correspondence of mother and daughter, diary fragments, programs, photographs and musical scores arranged according to keyboard, voice, string, and symphonic works, they were collated by researchers Mary Dengler Hudgins and **Barbara Garvey Jackson**. They were made available to the public in 1975. In October 1989, the Price papers were reprocessed by Norma Ortiz-Karp, with instrumental parts of the *Symphony in E minor* prepared by the North Arkansas Symphony Orchestra, incorporated into the collection. Price's piano music is on CDs featuring such artists as pianists **Virginia Eskin** and **Althea Waites**. In 2000, The Women's Philharmonic released a CD of her orchestral works on the Koch label, entitled *Florence Price*.

AVRIL COLERIDGE-TAYLOR, born Gwendolen, in London, March 8, 1903, was the daughter of **Samuel Coleridge-Taylor** (1875–1912), a well-known English composer of African descent. (His father was a doctor from Sierra Leone, his mother was white English). Avril, who studied at the Guildhall School of Music and Trinity

College, was a pianist, conductor and composer. She made her conducting debut at the Royal Albert Hall in 1933, and was the first woman to conduct the Band of the Royal Marines, as well as the London Symphony Orchestra, BBC Symphony and other orchestras and ensembles. Her more than ninety compositions include orchestral works, songs, keyboard and chamber works. In 1957, she composed the *Ceremonial March* to celebrate Ghana's independence. In her biography of her father, *The Heritage of Samuel Coleridge-Taylor*, she admits that while traveling in South Africa in the 1950s, she felt a little guilty for staying in accommodations meant for whites. (*Her* mother was also a white Englishwoman.) Married to Englishman Harold Dashwood, they had a son Nigel. Avril died in Seaford, England, December 21, 1998 at ninety-five.

Undine Moore

Born August 25, 1905 in Jarratt, Virginia, American composer, choral conductor and educator **UNDINE SMITH MOORE** began piano lessons at age seven with Lillian Allen Darden. She received the first scholarship ever given by Juilliard for music study at Fisk University (Nashville, Tennessee), where she completed her BA, and diploma in music, 1926. While there, she was a piano and organ student of Alice M. Grass. In 1931, she earned an MA and professional diploma at Teachers College of Columbia University, New York, studying theory and composition with Howard Murphy. She also attended the Manhattan School of Music and Eastman in Rochester, (upstate) New York.

Married in 1938 to Dr. James Moore, their daughter, Mary Hardie, was born in 1941. James died in 1963.

Moore taught in Goldsboro, North Carolina, then Virginia State College, Petersburg (1927–71), where she co-founded and co-directed the Black Music Center (1969–72). She lectured extensively as a visiting professor, gave workshops and toured the U.S. and West Africa, receiving many awards, including a Certificate of Appreciation from Mayor John Lindsay of New York City (1972).

The composer's style drew on her African-American heritage. Writing in a variety of forms, her compositional techniques ranged from conventional (tonal), including the European art song tradition, to the atonal and twelve-tone. *Before I'd Be a Slave* was composed for choreographer Barbara Hollis and the Modern Dance Group. Moore is best known for choral compositions and arrangements of spirituals. Like Price, she set one of Langston Hughes' poems to music, *Mother to Son* (1955), for alto solo and mixed chorus. *Lord, We Give Thanks To Thee* (1971) was written for the 100th anniversary of the Fisk (University) Jubilee Singers. *Scenes from the Life of a Martyr* (to the Memory of Martin Luther King, Jr.), an oratorio for narrator, chorus and orchestra, was nominated for a 1982 Pulitzer Prize. Her later works include *Soweto* for violin, cello and piano (1987), in memory of the 1976 massacre in South Africa. Her forty-five years at Virginia State College (1927–72) contributed to the education of many celebrated musicians. She continued lecturing and giving workshops after her retirement, and served on the board of directors of the Richmond Symphony Orchestra, 1983–87. Her over 100 works composed between 1925–87 cover choral, solo voice and piano, and instruments without voice. She died February 6, 1989, in Petersburg, Virginia.

Zenobia Perry

American pianist, teacher and composer **ZENOBIA POWELL PERRY** was born October 3, 1908, in Boley, Oklahoma. Her father, Calvin, was a physician, and her mother, Birdie Lee Thompson, came from Creek Indian and black heritage. She was a special student in piano at Eastman at age fourteen, studying with R. Nathaniel Dett. She received her BS degree from Tuskegee Institute, Alabama (1938), and her MA from the University of Northern Colorado (1945). Further composition studies were with **Darius Milhaud** at the University of Wyoming. She taught at Arkansas Agricultural, Mechanical and Normal College (1946–55), and Central State University at Wilberforce, Ohio (1955–82).

In April 1986, she was guest composer at the Dana New Music Festival at Youngstown State University, Ohio, where several of her compositions were conducted by Jo Ann Lanier whose doctoral dissertation at the American Conservatory of Music in Chicago, Illinois, was "The Concert Songs of Zenobia Powell Perry." She was honored in 1987 by the Ohioan Library Association with a special citation for her distinguished service to Ohio in the field of music. Her opera, *Tawawa House*, was premiered at Central State University the same year. Some of her works were included on the programs of the 1987 "Symposium in Celebration of Black American Women in Music" at Cal State, Northridge, and her *Four Mynyms for Three Players* was performed at the Smithsonian Institute, Washington, DC (1988). In 1989, *Ships That Pass in the Night*, for winds, percussion and narrator, was premiered at West Virginia University. Besides the opera, songs, and chamber works, Powell composed a mass, and pieces for band and orchestra. Her style incorporates contrapuntal, tonal, mild dissonance, with some jazz and folk influence.

In August 2003, Mu Phi Epsilon honored Perry at their Bicentennial Convention in Cincinnati, and further ninety-fifth birthday celebrations included an October concert tour, showcasing her music, in Cleveland, Columbus, Dayton, Cincinnati, Yellow Springs, Xenia, and Wilberforce. The performers included her daughter, soprano Janis-Rozena Peri, and the Price Duo (Deon Nielsen Price, piano, and Berkeley Price, clarinet).

She died in Xenia, Ohio, January 17, 2004. (Biographer Jeannie Pool completed her PhD dissertation on Perry, May 2002. See Musicologists.)

American educator, choral director, author and composer, **EVELYN (LaRue) PITTMAN** was born in McAlester, Oklahoma, January 6, 1910. After her father's death, the family relocated to Oklahoma City. She completed high school at Highland Park, Detroit, where she had moved to live with her older brother. Active in the school's musical organization, she became the first black to sing in their well-known choir. In 1929, she enrolled at the all-black Spelman College in Atlanta, where she studied with Kemper Harreld, renowned black violinist and head of the music departments at Spelman and Morehouse Colleges. Pittman composed her first music at Spelman. Following graduation in 1933, she entered Langston University in Langston, Oklahoma, to complete requirements for teaching certification. She began her teaching career in Oklahoma City at Wheatly Junior High School, where she organized and trained a thirty-piece orchestra and a forty-voice chorus, and presented an operetta. *Rich Heritage*, a collection of songs about black leaders, was published in 1944.

In 1948, Pittman moved to New York City to attend Juilliard, studying composition with Robert Ward. While there, she wrote music for a stage work, *Again the River*, with story narration by Helen Schuyler. When white universities lifted racial bars in the South and bordering states, she entered the University of Oklahoma (Norman) for composition classes with Harrison Kerr, dean of the College of Fine Arts. Here she began her all-black folk opera, *Cousin Esther*, originally entitled *Esther and Cousin Mordecai*, after the Biblical story. She wrote the libretto and music, orchestrated and produced the opera. The first scene of the work became her MM thesis (1954).

In 1956, Pittman was invited to study with **Nadia Boulanger** in France. *Cousin Esther* was performed during her stay in Paris at the International Theater. After her return to America, excerpts from the opera were presented at Carnegie Recital Hall, Manhattan's Colonial Park, the American Church, and for UNESCO (April 1957). In 1958, Pittman moved to White Plains, New York, where she joined the music faculty at Woodlands High School in nearby Hartsdale. Her high school chorus sang at the World's Fair in New York in 1965, and had the distinction of being one of the few high school groups to perform with Duke Ellington's band. She also developed and trained the Bethel Baptist Church Choir in Westchester County.

The opera, *Freedom Child*, about Martin Luther King Jr., was part of a program on the life of King, presented by her students in 1970. The Woodlands Touring Choir performed this music drama in the Northern and Southeastern states and on a tour of the Scandinavian Countries of Norway, Sweden and Denmark, 1971 and 1972. The Woodlands ensemble and an Oklahoma cast have since performed the work in several other states, and countries including England, Scotland, Italy, Liberia and Ghana.

Pittman's other compositions include *Rich Heritage*, a collection of songs and stories about eminent blacks, published in two editions (1944, 1968), and arrangements of choral works and spirituals, showing the influence of black church music. She died in Oklahoma City, December 15, 1992.

Margaret Bonds

MARGARET BONDS, born in Chicago, March 3, 1913, took lessons from her mother Estella, a church organist and excellent musician. Their home was a meeting place for eminent blacks such as sculptor Richmond Barthe, poet Langston Hughes, soprano Abbie Mitchell, and popular composer Will Marion Cook. In high school, Margaret studied piano and composition with **Florence Price**. She helped establish the junior division of the National Association of Negro Musicians, which promotes black music and black musicians. She earned money as an accompanist in night clubs and shows. She also copied music for black composers. In the midst of the Depression, Bonds was one of the small minority of black students at Northwestern University, and by age twenty-one had both her bachelor's and master's degrees. During this time, Florence Price and her two children lived with the Bonds family while she was having trouble with her second marriage.

In 1939, Bonds left Chicago for New York where several of her popular songs were published. In 1940, she married Lawrence Richardson. They named their only daughter, Djane, born 1946, after pianist Djane Lavoie-Herz (1888–1982), with whom Margaret studied at Juilliard. Her composition teacher was **Roy Harris** (1898–1979).

From the 1940s to the 1960s, Bonds appeared as soloist with several orchestras, including the New York Symphony, Chicago Symphony and Chicago Woman's Symphony with whom, in 1934, she performed Price's piano *Concerto in D minor*, **Ebba Sundstrom** conducting. She formed the Margaret Bonds Chamber Society in 1956 to present black musicians in works of black composers. She was also music director and pianist for numerous theatrical productions.

Among her honors was a Wanamaker Award, a Roy Harris Fellowship and several ASCAP awards. Her compositions show the influence of jazz and blues and include original melodies in spiritual style. An excellent pianist, her pieces are often technically difficult. Of her more than 200 works, including orchestral, piano and choral music, art and popular songs, the best known is *The Negro Speaks of Rivers*, a setting of Langston Hughes' first published poem.

In 1967, Bonds moved to Los Angeles and devoted the rest of her life teaching music to children at the Los Angeles Inner City Cultural Center and Repertory Theater. On May 21,1972, in a tribute to black composers, the Los Angeles Philharmonic under **Zubin Mehta** performed excerpts from *Credo* for chorus and orchestra—the only known performance with orchestra—just one month after her death, April 26, 1972.

Margaret Bonds is best remembered for her arrangements of spirituals, some of which are full-fledged compositions in their own right. They can be heard on recordings by **Kathleen Battle**, **Jessye Norman** and **Leontyne Price**.

Julia Perry

Born March 25, 1924, in Lexington, Kentucky, **JULIA AMANDA PERRY** grew up in Akron, Ohio, studying piano, violin and voice. Her physician father was a pianist, her two older sisters studied violin, and Mother made sure everyone practiced. Julia knew early that she wanted to be a composer. After graduation from Akron High School, she attended Westminster Choir College, Princeton, New Jersey (BM, MM 1948), adding conducting and composition to her other studies. Her master's thesis was *Chicago*, a secular cantata based on poems by **Carl Sandburg**, scored for baritone, narrator, mixed chorus and orchestra. She moved to New York and studied at Juilliard. Her cantata, *Ruth*, was performed at the Riverside Church, April 1950.

In 1954, the Columbia Opera Workshop produced her one-act opera *The Cask of Amontillado*, based on the Edgar Allan Poe story.

Awarded a Guggenheim fellowship, she went to Europe in 1952, studied with **Nadia Boulanger**, winning the Boulanger Grand Prix Fontainebleu for her viola sonata. *Stabat Mater*, for solo voice and string orchestra, made her famous. It was performed, with the composer as soloist, in Italy, Germany and Austria. A second Guggenheim (1954) provided a return to Europe, this time to Italy for study at the Accademia Chigiana in Siena with Luigi

Dallapiccola (1904–75), with whom she had worked at Tanglewood in 1951. In 1957, Perry organized and conducted a series of successful concerts in Europe under the sponsorship of the U.S. Information Service. She returned to America in 1959, giving up singing to devote herself to composition and teaching until illness forced her into early retirement.

Perry taught at Florida A&M University (Tallahassee, 1967), and was visiting music consultant at the Atlanta Colleges Center (1969). In 1964, she won the American Academy and National Institute of Arts and Letters Award, and in 1969 made honorable mention in the ASCAP Awards to women composers for symphonic and concert music.

Her early works are infused with black musical idioms. Beginning in the 1950s, Perry turned from vocal music to instrumental compositions such as *Requiem for Orchestra* (1959), also called *Homage to Vivaldi*, based on themes by that composer. In 1962 at the MacDowell Colony, she composed her second and third symphonies and *Dance for Chamber Orchestra*. She wrote her own libretto to an opera-ballet based on Oscar Wilde's fable, *The Selfish Giant* (1964). *The Symplegades*, a three act opera about the 17th century Salem witchcraft trials, took over a decade to write and was completed in 1974. By 1971, she had written twelve symphonies, a violin concerto, two piano concertos, four operas, cantatas, choral pieces, songs and numerous instrumental chamber and solo works.

That year she suffered a paralytic stroke and was hospitalized for several years. She taught herself to write with her left hand and returned to composing. 1977 produced *Bicentennial Reflections* for tenor solo and six instruments, and 1978, *Suite for Brass and Percussion*. Her music reflects wide cultural interests; its style is neo-classical with dissonant harmonies combined with intense lyricism. In her late works, like *Soul Symphony* (1972), she returned to using African folk idioms. Her *Prelude for Piano* has been recorded by Leonarda. She had plans to arrange it for string orchestra.

Julia Perry died April 29, 1979, in Akron. Only fifty-four of her approximately 108 works survive.

Betty King

BETTY JACKSON KING began music training in Chicago with her mother, Gertrude Jackson Taylor, and sang in the Jacksonian Trio with her mother and sister, Catherine. She completed her BM in piano and MM in composition at Chicago Musical College of Roosevelt University, also studying at Peabody and Westminster Choir College.

King taught at the University of Chicago Laboratory School and Dillard University (New Orleans). From 1979–84, she was president of the National Association of Negro Musicians. She was active as a choir director in Chicago, and after moving to New Jersey, at Riverside Church in New York. Her Biblical opera *Saul of Tarsus*, the subject of her master's thesis, was widely performed after its premiere in 1952 by Chicago's Imperial Opera Company. She wrote many choral works, art songs, arrangements of spirituals, and two other operas, *My Servant Job* and *Simon of Cyrene*. The libretti for these operas were written by her father, the Reverend Frederick D. Jackson, always her staunch supporter. King's style is marked by an extended harmonic language, concentrated chord clusters, and simultaneous layers of sound.

Her delicate piano solo, *Spring Intermezzo* from *Four Seasonal Sketches*, has been recorded on Leonarda and Kathleen Battle recorded King's arrangements of spirituals on Deutsche Gramophone at her 1990 Carnegie Hall Concert of Spirituals. Other CDs which feature her works are *Watch and Pray* (Koch) and *Let It Shine* (1994).

Married to Vincent King, they had one daughter, Rochelle. Betty relocated to New Jersey in 1969 when the Reverend Dr. William Faulkner encouraged her move from New Orleans, thus integrating the Wildwood Public School teaching staff with her position at Wildwood High School, where she received the Teaching Recognition Award from then Governor Thomas Kean.

Jackson King died in Wildwood, New Jersey, June 1, 1994.

On the Contemporary Scene

Born September 30, 1949, in Kingston, Jamaica, **ELEANOR ALBERGA** went to England in 1970 on an RAM scholarship for piano and voice study. She was a member of the internationally known Jamaican Folk Singers, performing three years with an authentic African dance company.

Her music reflects her classical training and the diversity of her dance and folk song background. Regarded as one of the most innovative composers on the contemporary music scene, her music for London Contemporary Dance Theatre resulted in commissions for concert music including solo works, chamber music, orchestral pieces and electronic scores. Her works have been performed at the Royal Albert Hall, throughout the UK and abroad, by such aggregations as the Women's Festival Orchestra, London Chamber Symphony, European Women's Orchestra, Bournemouth Sinfonietta, London Philharmonic and Royal Philharmonic Orchestras.

In 1990, Alberga was the first composer to be commissioned for the inaugural Festival of Women in Music, and in 1991 was invited to participate in the prestigious Composer-to-Composer Festival in Colorado. She has been a featured composer at the Vale of Glamorgan Festival in Wales. Her music for the film *Escape from Kampala*, was nominated for a BAFTA award (1991). Other commissions include works for the London Mozart Players and Smith String Quartet. A second quartet was premiered by the latter in 1994. The same year, the London Philharmonic Orchestra gave the first performance of *Snow White*, a commission from the Dahl Foundation, with its Australian premiere performed by the Adelaide Symphony Orchestra in 1995. She also received two choral commissions from the Birmingham Bach Choir. *Mythologies* was premiered in June 2000 with Leonard Slatkin conducting, as was *Dancing with Shadows* for Lontano, and *Glinting, Glancing Shards* for the Delta Saxophone Quartet. A violin concerto, commissioned by the Scottish Chamber Orchestra, was premiered with her husband Thomas Bowes as soloist in November 2001.

Lettie Alston

LETTIE BECKON ALSTON (*b*1953) is a composer/pianist, and was one of four finalists in Detroit Symphony Orchestra's Unisys African-American Composers Forum Competition in 1993. She received her DMA in Composition at the University of Michigan, where her teachers included Leslie Bassett, **William Bolcom**, Eugene Kurtz, and George Wilson. Alston is an associate professor at Oakland University (Michigan) and a former faculty member of Eastern Michigan University. She composes in a variety of styles. Her works include *The Eleventh Hour* for orchestra, *Moods* for solo piano, and *Three Spiritual Settings* for men's chorus. Her solo violin piece, *Pulsations*, is on the Leonarda label. Her music reflects her expertise in clarinet, guitar, piano and keyboards. She is one of a few black women to embrace the composition of electronic music.

REGINA HARRIS BAIOCCHI, the third of seven siblings, was born in Chicago, July 16, 1956. A composer of works for orchestra, chorus, voice, chamber groups, and solo instruments, she attended Roosevelt University, earning a BA in Composition (1978), going on to study at the Illinois Institute of Technology's Institute of Design (1984–86), and NYU, where she earned a public relations certificate. From 1979–86, she taught mathematics and social studies at the high school level, was a writer and quality control analyst, then public relations director at the Catholic Theological Union College (1989–94). In 1995, she earned an MM from DePaul University (Chicago).

Of her works, her *Orchestral Suite* was one of four finalist compositions in the 1992 Detroit Symphony Orchestra Unisys African-American Composers Forum competition. *Etude No. 2*, subtitled "Equipoise by Intersection," is the second of *Two Piano Etudes* combining serial techniques. Her more than sixty works include instrumental, solo voice, chorus, stage and chamber opera.

She also has a career in public relations, and is an author of short stories and poetry under her pen name, Ginann. She married Gregory Baiocchi in 1975.

VALERIE CAPERS, born May 24,1935, was trained as a classical pianist, but encouraged to play jazz by her late brother, saxophonist Bobby Capers, and her father, jazz pianist Alvin Capers. She has appeared at the Newport and Kool Jazz Festivals and on radio and television. Blind since the age of six, her early schooling was at the New York Institute for the Education of the Blind, where she received an education her parents could not have afforded if she had been sighted. Capers earned her BM and MM at Juilliard (their first blind student), and taught at Hunter College and Manhattan School of Music (1968–75) where she started the jazz department. She was at the Bronx Community College Department of Music and Art from 1971, where she rose to full professor and chair of the department in 1987. She retired in 1995, becoming artist-in-residence.

Her works include a Christmas cantata; a choral and instrumental work, *In Praise of Freedom*, based on the March on Washington speech of Dr. Martin Luther King, Jr.; and an "operatorio" on the life of **Sojourner Truth** (1797–1883), the former New York slave, preacher, abolitionist and suffragette. *Portraits in Jazz* consist of twelve piano solo teaching pieces, each dedicated to a particular musician. Of these, *Cool-Trane* has a melodic line akin to that played on the saxophone by John Coltrane, and *Billie's Song* is a ballad dedicated to Billie Holiday.

Tania Leon

Composer/conductor/professor **TANIA** Justina **LEÓN** was born in Havana, Cuba, May 14, 1943, of French, Spanish, African, Chinese and Cuban descent. She studied piano from age four, and earned degrees from the Alfredo Peyrellade Conservatory, Havana (BM, 1963), (MMus Ed, 1964). She moved to New York in 1967, where she met choreographer Arthur Mitchell who was forming the Dance Theatre of Harlem. She became the company's musical director (1969–80), founding the music department, music school and orchestra. At Mitchell's request, she started writing music for the company, producing her ballet *Tones* (1970), *The Beloved* (1972), *Dougla* (1974), in collaboration with Geoffrey Holder—danced by several companies, particularly in Europe—and *Spiritual Suite* (1976), premiered with the great **Marian Anderson** as narrator. In 1992, León traveled with the DTOH to Johannesburg, South Africa, where they became the first multi-racial arts group to perform and teach in that country.

In the 1970s, she studied composition at NYU with **Ursula Mamlok**. In 1977, at the invitation of American composer **Lukas Foss**, León founded the Brooklyn Philharmonic Community Concert Series. As part of the 1978 Tanglewood Conducting Program, she coached with both **Leonard Bernstein** and **Seiji Ozawa**. She has also guest conducted for the Alvin Ailey Dance Theater, Radio City Music Hall and many leading orchestras in America and abroad, as well as being music director for *The Wiz* (1978) and several other Broadway shows.

León began teaching at Brooklyn College in 1985, where she was made music director of the resident orchestra (1991), professor of music (1994), and in 2000 was named Tow Distinguished Professor. She was visiting professor of composition at Yale (1993), visiting lecturer at Harvard (1994) and gave master classes at the Hamburg Musikschule (1995). Appointed Revson Composer Fellow by the New York Philharmonic in 1993, she subsequently held a four-year position as new music advisor to Kurt Masur and the orchestra. She is Latin American music advisor to the American Composers Orchestra, where she co-founded the award winning *Sonidos de las Americas* festival.

Her compositions show the influence of Cuban rhythms and American idioms like gospel and jazz. Her works are characterized by dense textures and colorful orchestration. *Carabali*, for orchestra, was premiered by the Cincinnati Symphony to celebrate their 1994 centennial. Her first opera, *Scourge of Hyacinths*, won the BMW Prize for Best Composition at the 1994 Munich Biennale for New Music Theater—she wrote the libretto and conducted the premiere in 1996. Other performances were in Switzerland, France, Austria in 1999, and in March 2001 during the Festival Centro Historico, in Mexico City. Other commissions include a work for the men's vocal ensemble, Chanticleer; a song cycle in collaboration with poet Rita Dove for the chamber ensemble, Continuum; *Para Viola y Orquesta*, premiered by a consortium of four American orchestras; and *Hechizoe* (Spells), for the Ensemble Modern of Berlin and premiered March 1995.

Indigena, a 1994 CRI CD, features León's chamber music; Louisville Orchestra's First Edition Records brought out *Bailarín* with David Starobin on guitar (1998), and *Bata* and *Carabali*. Other CDs that include her works are: *Salsa Nueva* (SOMM), *Percussion* (Castigo), *A City Called Heaven* (aca), and *Visiones Panamericanas* (Urtext).

Horizons was written for the NDR Symphony in Hamburg, premiered July 1999. The same year brought *Ivo Ivo, Sequitur, At the Fountain of Mpindelela*, part of the National Musical Arts program "Africa Spirit Ascending," and *May the Road Be Free*, at Lincoln Center. 2000 saw *Alegre* at the American Composers Forum (New Band Horizons), *De Memorias* (Mexico City Woodwind Quintet at the Mexico/U.S. Fund for Culture), *Caracol* (Manchester Music Festival), *Turning* (Musical Arts, Franklin and Marshall College), *Fanfarria* (Library of Congress, Copland Centennial Celebration) and *Canto* (Mutable Music). 2001 commissions were from the Los Angeles Master Chorale for *Rezos* (SATB choir, text by Jamaica Kincaid), and *Desde . . .* from the American Composer's Orchestra/ Koussevitzky Music Foundation. 2002 featured more ballet, choral compositions, a work for violin and orchestra premiered at the Bologna Festival (Italy), and the commission project work for violin and electronics, Mari Kimura, soloist, at the 2002 ISCM World Music Days in Hong Kong. In 2003, she wrote *Mística* for pianist **Ursula Oppens**. 2004 brought *Hebras d'Luz*, for solo electric viola; *La Tina*, piano; and *Azulejos*, for mixed ensemble. For 2005 were *Tumbao*, piano, and *Samarkand*, narrator, chorus, children's chorus, and mixed ensemble.

León has received awards for her work from the New York State Council on the Arts, the ASCAP Morton Gould Award for Innovative Programming, CINTAS, NEA Meet the Composer, and the American Academy of Arts and Letters. She was recipient of a MacArthur Foundation Residency at Yaddo Music Camp, and a Rockefeller Foundation residency at the Bellagio Festival in Italy. 1998 brought the New York Governor's Lifetime Achievement Award and the Fromm Residency at the American Academy in Rome. In 1999, she was a speaker at the World Economic Forum in Davos, Switzerland. In 2004, she was part of the "Portraits of Latino Achievement" exhibition at the Smithsonian Center for Latino Initiatives.

Her publications include *Africana*, Encyclopedia of the African and African American Experience (Basic Civitas Books, 1999), *Musik und Mythos*, "Polyrhythmia in the Music of Cuba" (Fischer Taschenbuch Verlag, Germany, 1999), *Americanos, Latino Life in the United States* (Little, Brown, 1999), *Oral History American Music* (Yale School of Music and Library, 2001), *Review*, Latin American Literature and Arts, vol. 63, Fall 2001, and *Women and Music in America since 1900* (Greenwood Publications Group, 2003).

A board member of the Academy of American Poets, American Composers Orchestra and Meet the Composer, León was the U.S. Representative for the U.S.-Mexico Fund for Culture (1994–95). Her numerous television appearances include Profiles, *Women of Hope; Latinas Abriendo Camino; The Sensual Nature of Sound; CBS Sunday Morning* with the late Charles Kuralt; and GEMS TV *Mujeres Protagonistes*.

Her composer residencies have been at such prestigious institutions as the Cleveland Institute, Bellagio (Italy), American Academy of Rome, Hamburg Musikschule, Berlin Biennial Music Festival, Carnegie Mellon, Harvard, California State University and many others. In 1999, Tania Léon was the recipient of an honorary doctorate from Colgate University, and from Oberlin in 2002.

Lena Mclin

Born September 5, 1929, in Atlanta, Georgia, American choral conductor, educator, pianist and composer **LENA Johnson McLIN**'s family was very musical. During her childhood, she lived for several years in the Chicago home of her uncle, Thomas A. Dorsey, called the "Father of Gospel Music." She was cared for by her grandmother, who told her about life under slavery and sang slave songs. These were important influences on McLin's musical style. She completed a degree in piano at Spelman College, Atlanta (BM, 1951), despite surgery on a bone tumor in her right hand, then won a scholarship to the American Conservatory in Chicago to study theory and composition. Graduate work was at Roosevelt University in voice, theory, composition and electronic music. She taught music for many years in the Chicago public secondary schools, composing rock music for high school groups, and organized and directed the pilot music program at Kenwood Academy High School (1970–1991). She also conducted choral workshops in many states.

Founder and pastor of the Holy Vessel Christian Center in Chicago, McLin's religious and secular choral works show the influence of her early gospel background. Her style incorporates traditional black idioms and

20th century blues, gospel, jazz and rock. One of her most notable pieces is *The Torch Has Been Passed*, for *a capella* chorus, based on President Kennedy's text for world peace. Her cantata, *Free at Last* (1964), in memory of Martin Luther King Jr., was performed both in Carnegie Hall and Italy, where it was recorded. She has also written cantatas, masses, anthems, operas, songs, arrangements of spirituals, piano, orchestral and electronic music. Her piano solo *A Summer Day* is an example of her improvisational style.

Composer, singer and poet, **DOROTHY RUDD MOORE**'s interest in music began at an early age. Born June 4, 1940, in New Castle, Delaware, she is the oldest of six siblings. Her mother, a singer, was her first piano teacher. At ten, she had formal instruction at the Wilmington School of Music. She also sang and performed in church and school choirs. She studied composition with Mark Fax at Howard University (Washington, DC), while majoring in music theory with minors in voice and piano (BA, *magna cum laude*, 1963). After graduation, she received a Lucy Moten fellowship for study with **Nadia Boulanger** at the American Conservatory at Fontainebleau, Paris (1963), and with Chou Wen-Chung in New York (1965). Moore taught theory and piano at the Harlem School of the Arts, 1965–66 (founded in 1965 by concert singer **Dorothy Maynor**), at NYU (1969) and Bronx Community College (1971). She also published poetry, some of which she set to music.

In 1964, she met and married cellist, conductor, composer **Kermit Moore**, who performed many of her compositions, including *Baroque Suite*, for unaccompanied cello—her wedding present to him. *From the Dark Tower*, for mezzo-soprano, cello and piano, premiered in 1970. A chamber version, first heard 1972, was recorded in 1978 with Kermit Moore, cello, Hilda Harris, mezzo and Wayne Sanders, piano. Kermit premiered *Dirge and Deliverance*, a cello sonata, in Alice Tully Hall, 1972, recorded on the Performance label in 1978. He also conducted *In Celebration* for chorus, soloists, and orchestra, and *Transcension* for chamber orchestra. Her works, characterized by dramatic intensity, include *Dream and Variations*, for piano; *Moods* for viola and cello; *Piano Trio No. 1*, *Flowers of Darkness*, for tenor and piano; and *Weary Blues*, based on a poem of noted black poet Langston Hughes (1902–67).

In 1968, with Steve Chambers, Benjamin Patterson, and Carman Moore, Dorothy and Kermit founded the Society of Black Composers. Mayor John Lindsay named a Composers Recognition Week in their honor, May 1969, with a concert in City Hall. In a 1975 concert of her own compositions in Carnegie Recital Hall, Moore gave the New York premiere of *Songs from the Rubáiyat*. In 1980, she returned to the Wilmington School of Music to give a voice recital of her *Sonnets on Love, Rosebuds*, and *Death*, for soprano, violin and piano. One of her largest works, an opera, *Frederick Douglass*, for which she wrote the music and libretto, was performed by Opera Ebony at CUNY's Aaron Davis Hall (1985). *Modes*, for String Quartet, was recorded in 1991 on the Opus One label by the Meaux String Quartet of Oberlin Conservatory. Leonarda released a 1993 CD featuring *Three Pieces for Violin and Piano*. *Dream and Variations*, and the New York premiere of *Night Fantasy* for clarinet and piano, were heard in concert at the Greenwich House Music School in May 1995. 1997 brought Rudd Moore's second opera, based on the theme of Phaedra. She has received commissions from Meet the Composer, American Music Center, and the New York State Council on the Arts. Rudd Moore resides in New York City, where she teaches voice, sightsinging and ear training.

Nkeiru Okoye

NKEIRU OKOYE, born July 18, 1972, of Nigerian and American heritage, grew up in New York. Her mother had a small organ, for which Nkeiru showed such an interest it was replaced with a piano and music lessons starting at eight. She began writing music at thirteen. Her degrees are a BM in composition (Oberlin, 1993), MA in music composition and theory (Rutgers, 1996), and PhD in music composition and theory (Rutgers, 2001). She received an ASCAP Grant for Young Composers in 1995, and a UNISYS African American Composer Residency as the protégé composer with the Detroit Symphony in 1997. She was composer-in-residence at the Washington Academy of Music (New Jersey, 1998–99), and adjunct professor of music at Bloomfield College, New Jersey (1999–2000). Also in 1999, she received the Yvar Mikhashoff Trust for New Music Grant.

In addition to her composing, she was on the faculty of Norfolk State University as guest lecturer, film composer, and concert producer, before joining Morgan State (Baltimore) early in 2002. Among her over thirty works are *The Genesis* for orchestra (1995); *Ruth*, an orchestral choreopoem (1998); *Spanish Songs from Personal Memoirs* (1999); *The Creation*, for speaker and orchestra (2000); *Expressions of Freedom*, electronic media (2001); and *Voices Crying Out*, for orchestra (2002). Premieres have featured Virginia, Richmond and Detroit Symphonies, among others.

PATRICE RUSHEN, born in 1954, in Los Angeles, attended USC where she received training as a classical and jazz pianist. She is also a singer, songwriter, and arranger and producer for television and film. (See Film Composers.)

Errollyn Wallen

ERROLLYN WALLEN was born April 10, 1958, in Belize, Central America. At age two, she and her sister were brought to Britain and raised by an aunt and uncle who gave them music and dancing lessons. At thirteen, Errollyn decided to be a ballet dancer, but was told that would be impossible because she was black. Nevertheless, her aunt and uncle enrolled her in Hollington Park School for Girls, where there were weekly ballet classes. Teacher Mary Pearse took an immediate interest in the girl, encouraging her to also work for the Associated Board exams in piano. She introduced her to Bach, who became Errollyn's greatest musical inspiration for his range of expression, effortless technique, phrasing and humanity. At sixteen, she attended a masterclass with Guildhall School of Music teacher and concert pianist Edith Vogel, with whom she later studied.

Wallen also spent time in New York, taking courses at the Dance Theater of Harlem before returning to England and Goldsmiths' College, London University. After graduation, she continued music studies at King's College with **Nicola LeFanu**, receiving an MM in1983. Next, she joined Pulse, an alternative cabaret band, composing songs and performing with them until 1985. She worked as a performer/composer in pop, jazz and classical music, and as a freelance keyboardist until meeting Steve Parr in 1986. They created Wallen Parr, a recording studio and music production company in North London. She wrote music for corporate videos, film and television, as well as classical concert music, such as her *Second String Quartet* (1988). In 1990, she formed *Ensemble X*, who regularly perform her music. In 1993, her first opera, *Four Figures with Harlequin*, was premiered as part of the Royal Opera House "Garden Venture." *In Our Lifetime* (1990), celebrating Nelson Mandela's release from prison, was choreographed by Christopher Bruce and retitled *Waiting*, for London Contemporary Dance Theatre. It was premiered at the Nottingham Theatre Royal, October 1993, and received its London premiere at Sadler's Wells Theatre in November of the same year. *The Concerto for Percussion and Orchestra*, commissioned by the BBC and Lloyd's Bank, was given its televised world premiere by the finalist of the 1994 Young Musician of the Year, Colin Currie, at the Barbican Music Centre in April. Throughout 1995–96, Wallen continued to compose for BBC television and radio, interviewing and broadcasting her own and others' music. A notable BBC television production was her documentary on African-English composer **Samuel Coleridge-Taylor** (1875–1912). She was also commissioned to write the score of the film *Just Be My Honey*. *Music for Alien Tribes* was a collaboration with drummer/bassist/DJ Gerald Simpson, which they performed at the *Nottingham Now* Festival, November 1996. 1997 commissions included *Nijinska*, a music theater piece with libretto by Kate Westbrook, for Sphinx Theatre, and *Chrome* for the National Youth Brass Band, an amalgamation of over seventy players. In 1999, she was appointed research associate of Middlesex University's Rescen to investigate artistic process. She contributed to *Art, Not Chance*, published June 2001, a book of artists' diaries commissioned by the Gulbenkian Foundation, and received an honorary M.PhD, from King's College, Cambridge.

Commissions have come from the Birmingham Contemporary Music Group, Royal Ballet, BBC Channel 4, Granada Television, Cripplegate Foundation, Union Dance, Royal College of Organists, Women's Playhouse Trust, Continuum Ensemble, British Flute Society, COMA, Broomhill Opera, Faber Music, plus many theaters and festivals, including Bath International Guitar (UK) and *Other Minds* (San Francisco), an annual international avant-garde music festival whose founding director, Charles Amirkhanian, invites a large proportion of women composers as guests.

With her music played by the BBC Symphony (1998 Proms), Royal Scottish National Orchestra and National Youth Orchestra of Great Britain, amongst others, Wallen's international reputation increased with concerts in Europe, America, Africa, Australia and worldwide televised performances. 1999 brought a James and Jeanne Newman fellowship from the Djerassi Foundation (California) and the 1999/2000 Norton Stevens fellowship from the MacDowell Artists' Colony in New Hampshire. She was a featured composer and performer in the 1999 Huddersfield International Contemporary Music Festival and Composer of the Month (May) at the 2000 Chard Festival (UK). 2001 marked over seventy public performances of her work, a highlight of which was *X-panded*, a concert of her music at London's South Bank, featuring such titles as *Hunger, Horseplay, The Girl in My Alphabet, Are You Worried About The Rising Cost of Funerals?, Louis' Loops, Greenwich Variations and Dervish*, and *Tiger* at St. Paul's Cathedral. (*The Girl in My Alphabet* is a 2002 CD release).

She presented her work at the New York Public Library for the Performing Arts as part of "UK in NY," a festival of British music (October 2001). The Edinburgh Festival, August 2001, saw the newly formed Errollyn Wallen Company perform *Jordan Town*. Based around her songs, it is a collaboration with filmmakers, the Honey Brothers and Royal Ballet choreographer/dancer Tom Sapsford. Her new solo show, *Words Without Music With Words*, premiered December 2001. 2002 included a work for the Brodsky Quartet, a composition for solo percussion, two operas and other commissions. Another 2002 project was a trip to South America, at the invitation of the British Council, to collaborate with Venezuelan musicians in concerts of her music. In 2003 her *When the Wet Wind Sings*, for forty voices, was sung by the Tallis Singers at the Old Royal Naval Chapel in Greenwich. *Another America: Earth*, a commission from the Royal Opera House and Nitro, was premiered in November. *All the Blues I See*, for flute and string quartet, received its first performance March 4, 2004, with Emily Beynon, principal flutist of the Concertgebouw Orchestra, and the Brodsky Quartet in a BBC broadcast.

Errollyn continues her performance career with her band and as a soloist at festivals, concert halls, cathedrals and clubs. Moving seamlessly from blues to Bach to gospel to modern styles, her songs are as vital to her creative development as her classical works. She is the personification of the motto of her *Ensemble X*: "*We don't break down barriers in music . . . we don't see any!*"

Continental Europe has not been as prone to the "color bar" prevalent in U.S. history. This gave many black artists opportunities across the Atlantic earlier in the century. In the 21st century, the winds of change now blow much warmer for "equal opportunity" in America.

An erudite source on a select number of American Black Composers is the 2002 book *From Spirituals to Symphonies* by Helen Walker-Hill. (See Musicologists and Bibliography.)

20th Century American Composers

Catherine Urner (1891–1977)
Louise Lincoln Kerr (1892–1977)
Marion Bauer (1882–1955)
Elinor Remick Warren (1900–1991)
Ruth Crawford Seeger (1901–1953)
Radie Britain (1903–1994)
Miriam Gideon (1906–1996)
Louise Talma (1906–1996)
Dana Suesse (1909–1987)
Vivian Fine (1913–2000)

Netty Simons (1913–1994)
Dika Newlin (1923–2006)
Jean Eichelberger Ivey (1923–) retired
Ruth Schonthal (1924–2006)
Jeanne Singer (1924–2000)
Cathy Berberian (1925–1983)
Claire Polin (1926–1995)
Lucia Dlugoszewski (1929?-2000)
Sylvia Glickman (1932–2006)

History and customs eased into the 20th century without much noticeable ruffling of tradition. Women still wore long skirts and became their husbands' property as soon as the gold ring graced their fingers. In the music world they proliferated at the piano and fiddled their way into violin performance, showing their male counterparts that "delicate fingers" could equal or outmatch masculine dexterity. They gradually graduated to other instruments—mostly strings and woodwinds—brass and percussion were still ramparts which would require further scaling before girls could blow their own trumpets and beat the drums quickly. In composition, conservatories were relaxing the rules of segregation of classes, allowing women to take orchestration, thus enabling them to attempt larger scale compositions.

The catalyst was World War I (1914–18). Women suddenly found jobs hitherto unavailable to them, orchestras needed musicians, and enough women composers had forged the way in the last century to inspire their modern sisters to drive the wedge further into the male-dominated domain. Skirts and hair got shorter, demands for equality got louder. New freedoms swept through feminine ranks, and the end of the war could not turn back the clock. Women got the vote in 1918. Barred from yet another male bastion, the symphony orchestra, they formed their own ensembles, produced competent conductors of their own sex and proved in general—and in music—that they were not inferior beings.

Composers born into the new century inherited the progress made and enlarged upon it with experimentation like *aleatory* music, in which the elements are determined by the performer rather than the composer; *serialism*, based on a succession of notes, rhythms and other elements which are repeated over and over throughout the work; *atonality*, where the definite key (tonal center) is avoided; and *graphic notation*, where the standard staff is replaced by drawn indications of how the work should be performed. In the early '60s, coinciding with early computers and synthesizers, further experimentation took place in the form of *electronic music*. The last decade of the 20th century, however, influenced by economics, *i.e.* audience receptiveness, the cost of mounting performances and other factors, saw the pendulum swinging back to tonal music falling under an elastic definition of *neo-romantic*. As can be seen in the following, women were just as influenced as their male counterparts by these trends.

Making Their Mark in the 20th Century

Catherine Urner

The career of **CATHERINE MURPHY URNER** involves a tale of two cities: Paris, and Oakland, California. Born March 23, 1891, in Mitchell, Ohio, her music studies were in piano, voice, and composition at Goucher College, Peabody Conservatory, and Ohio's Miami University, from which she graduated in 1912. Postgraduate work was at UC Berkeley (1914–16), where she composed *Aranyani of the Jasmine Vine*, based on scenes by Maude Meagher, for the Spring 1916 University Women masque *The Partheneia*. The music won the George Ladd Prix de Paris for 1920, enabling her to go to Paris to study voice with Andrée Otémar, and advanced composition and orchestration with **Charles Koechlin** (1867–1950), a prolific composer, writer and music lecturer, and student of **Gabriel Fauré**. She returned to the U.S. in 1921 and was appointed director of vocal music at Mills College (Oakland, California), a position she held until 1924 when she left to pursue full time careers as composer and concert singer.

Urner began concertizing in the U.S., Italy, and France, where premieres of her works took place under the auspices of the Salle Pleyel and the Société Musicale Indépendante, founded in 1909 by Koechlin, Florent Schmitt (1870–1958) and **Maurice Ravel** (1875–1937) to advance contemporary music. She became recognized as an accomplished singer of ancient and classic songs, French Impressionist chansons and, one of her main interests, American Indian tribal melodies. Her programs featuring this music were given in native American costume and performed on authentic Indian instruments.

Urner composed in all areas of music, and collaborated with Koechlin on his symphonic poems *The Bride of a God*, *Sur les flôts lointains*, and the *Trois sonatines* for organ. Koechlin described her as a true artist with special gifts in composition, and proclaimed that she had an intelligence more profound and more European than any other American musician he had known.

Katherine arranged for Koechlin to come to the U.S. in 1928, to teach a summer course at Berkeley and at her studio in Oakland. After his receiving the Hollywood Bowl Prize in 1929, he persuaded her to return with him to France, where she lived in a *ménage à trois* with him and his wife Suzanne until 1933. On her return to America, at the height of the Depression, she taught harmony from a text by Koechlin, which she had translated from the French, at UCLA extension courses at the Scripps Campus in San Diego. In 1937, she again arranged for Koechlin to come to the U.S., this time to San Diego where he gave classes in the studio of **Charles Rollin Shatto**, a composer, pianist and organist whom Catherine married in October 1937. Born in 1908, he was seventeen years her junior. They lived happily in La Jolla, collaborating on many projects and concertizing throughout Southern California. Charles was also civic organist at San Diego's Spreckels Organ Pavilion, on the world's largest outdoor organ.

On April 30, 1942, with Charles driving and Catherine in the back seat, the car was in a rollover accident and burst into flames. Shatto tried desperately to get his wife out, but was unable to. The grieving widower was in the hospital for eighteen months receiving numerous skin grafts on his arms and hands until he was able to play again. After his recovery, he moved to San Francisco in 1957 where he taught and played organ at the French Catholic Church, Notre Dame de Victoire, until his death in 1983. In 1945, it was **Darius Milhaud** (1892–1974), who had been teaching at Mills College (1940–47), who wrote Koechlin of Catherine's passing. He orchestrated her *Esquisses normandes*, a four movement suite for chamber orchestra, to honor her. Forty-five years later, on April 20, 1990, it received its American premiere with The Women's Philharmonic, **JoAnn Falletta** conducting.

The music of Charles Shatto, Catherine Urner, plus many compositions sent her by Koechlin, are in the L. Eugene Miller Foundation, housed at the music library at UC, Berkeley. A biography (Ashgate Press, 2003) of this dynamic woman has been written by her niece, **Barbara Urner Johnson**, after many years of research on both sides of the Atlantic. (See Bibliography.)

American composer, violist and patroness of the arts, **LOUISE LINCOLN KERR** was born April 24, 1892, in Cleveland, Ohio, daughter of John C. Lincoln, an engineer and real-estate tycoon who founded Lincoln Electric of Cleveland and invented the arc welder. Her mother, Myrtle, taught her six-year-old to play the piano, violin came at seven, and later the viola. In 1910, Louise entered New York's elite Barnard College, the "girls" adjunct to Columbia, where she studied music composition—at a time when women were not generally allowed degrees in composition—with two prominent Columbia professors, Cornelius Rubnor and David Gregory Mason. She continued her violin study with Christiaan Timmer. In 1913, Louise left Barnard to accept an offer to play in the Cleveland Symphony, the first woman violinist ever to join that orchestra as well as one of its youngest members. Love arrived and she married Peter Kerr, moved to the East Coast and raised a family of eight children. There, she worked for the Aeolian Company on Duo Arts Records in the sound booth helping conductors correct mistakes, and meeting such music elite as George Gershwin, Serge Prokofiev and pianist Alfred Cortot. She also numbered renowned conductor Dimitri Mitropoulos amongst her friends.

The Kerrs moved to Arizona in 1936 for the health of one of their children. Their home in Phoenix became a focal point for chamber music concerts and cultural activities. Peter died in 1939. Louise performed in the Pasadena Symphony in California (1942–45). As a founding member of the Phoenix Symphony (1947), she was their principal violist for many years. She was also a member of string quartets in Flagstaff and Phoenix. By 1959 Louise had finished building a home and music studio in Scottsdale, working towards founding an artists' colony on her property, although cattle drives were still run through the center of town at that time. She invited the Juilliard and Budapest String Quartets and other notable players to perform there.

As a composer, Kerr wrote over one hundred works, including symphonic tone poems, chamber music, a violin concerto, numerous piano pieces, duets for piano and other instruments, string quartets and trios, ballets, vocal and incidental music. Her native American inspired symphonic work *Enchanted Mesa* was premiered in 1950. In 1957, her ballet *Naked Came I* was performed at ASU. Another ballet, *Tableau Vivant*, was performed for the dedication of John Waddell's sculpture group *Dance* (1974) in front of Phoenix Symphony Hall. The symphonic work *Arizona Profiles* was commissioned for the opening of the Scottsdale Center for the Arts and performed for its dedication in 1968. Kerr received a gold medal for distinguished contribution to the arts from the National Society of Arts and Letters and was given an honorary doctorate from ASU shortly before her death, although unable to go in person to receive the award. She died December 10, 1977, in Cottonwood, at her ranch, now the home of artist John Waddell.

As a violist and violinist with several symphony orchestras, Kerr had a rich background upon which to draw for her many string works. With college training in composition and music theory, she added to these qualifications the colorful flavors of the Southwest and a love of French Impressionism. The result is a treasure of charming miniatures as yet to be discovered by the string world. Her oeuvre includes five viola and piano duets; twenty-one violin and piano duets; two violin and viola duets; two cello and piano duets; movements for string quartets; piano quartets and quintets; a trio for clarinet, cello and piano; chamber works for string orchestra; *Sonata in A Major for Violin and Piano* and a complete violin concerto.

Kerr described her composing goals in a newspaper interview at age eighty. "We need some new exciting music, and yet not things that are difficult to listen to. There are people with new ideas, and in the future we will have different rules to break, but we have to do that intelligently."

As of this writing there have been no published editions of her music. Louise Lincoln Kerr is in need of recognition. To that end, conductor/educator **Carolyn Broe** wrote her 2001 doctoral dissertation on Kerr, whom she discovered when she entered ASU as a doctoral student. Perhaps that, and this book will succeed in directing the eluded spotlight on one of the finest Southwest Impressionists and women composers in our country.

A major American composer, **MARION EUGÉNIE BAUER**, born August 15, 1882, in Walla Walla, Washington, was the youngest of seven children born to parents of French descent. Her mother, Julia Heyman, was a gifted linguist who spoke six languages fluently and became a teacher of French, German, Spanish, and Italian, first in her home and later at Whitman College. Her father, Jacques, born in France, was an enthusiastic amateur musician who, upon settling in America, joined the Army band of the Ninth Infantry. After his discharge in Walla Walla in 1860, he opened a general store supplying miners on their way to Washington and Idaho. When he died in 1890, the family moved to Portland, Oregon, where Julia taught in the public schools. Marion had her first piano lessons from her eldest sister Emilie Frances who, in 1896, moved to New York where she later became a well known music critic. After leaving school at sixteen, Marion joined her sister in New York, started to write songs and continued her piano and harmony studies with Emilie and other teachers.

Boulanger's First American!

In 1906, Marion went to France to stay with violinist Raoul Pugno and his family, whom she had met and taught English when they were in the United States the previous year. Pugno gave her piano lessons and introduced her to **Nadia** and **Lili Boulanger**, then in their teens. Bauer gave the sisters English lessons in exchange for harmony lessons from Nadia, becoming the very first of Boulanger's many American pupils. She also studied orchestration with **Pierre Monteux** (1875–1964), destined to become a world-famous conductor. After one year in Paris she returned to New York, lived with Emilie, taught theory and piano privately, as well as continuing her own studies, and had some of her impressionistic songs published and performed. Her first published song, *Light*, was introduced by internationally celebrated soprano **Ernestine Schumann-Heink**, who at the time often appeared in concerts presented by **Adella Prentiss Hughes**. (See The Unforgotten.)

In 1910, Bauer made her second trip to Europe and studied counterpoint and form for a year in Berlin, where her experiences included hearing the earliest avant-garde compositions of Schoenberg and running up against prejudice against American composers in general and women in particular. She continued to write songs, and on her return to New York arranged a seven year contract with the publisher Arthur Schmidt. Now she began to write piano pieces and chamber music as well as songs, producing works such as *Up the Ocklawaha* (1913), for violin and piano, commissioned by and dedicated to her friend, pioneer woman violinist **Maud Powell**. Many summers were spent at the MacDowell Colony where she met several other women composers, including Amy Beach, Mabel Daniels, Mary Howe, Miriam Gideon and Ruth Crawford. The ambience and surroundings provided the inspiration for one of her best-known piano works, the suite *From New Hampshire Woods* (1923).

On her third trip to Europe, Bauer returned to Paris in the spring of 1923 where she spent nearly three years taking lessons in fugue with **André Gédalge** (1856–1926), teacher of Ravel, Enesco, Milhaud, Honegger, etc., and making important contacts with French musicians and composers. During this time she wrote several chamber works, including *Fantasia Quasi una Sonata*, op. 18, for violin and piano and a String Quartet, op. 20. She returned to the United States when Emilie became seriously ill.

After Emilie's death, Marion took over her sister's job as New York music critic for the Chicago journal *Musical Leader*, a position she held until her death. As a critic, journal contributor, and author of several books on music, she commanded great respect in musical circles. Another facet of her career was teaching music history and composition at New York University (1926–51) and Juilliard (1940–44), while lecturing widely, including summer sessions at Mills College, Carnegie Institute of Technology, and the Cincinnati College Conservatory of Music.

Bauer's music showed the influence of the years spent in France, remaining basically tonal and impressionistic, although she succumbed to modern trends and became increasingly dissonant in her later compositions. She sometimes used elements of music from other cultures in works such as *Indian Pipes* (1927) for orchestra and *A Lament on African Themes* (1928) for chamber orchestra. In 1921, she was the only woman founder of the American Music Guild and the only woman on the executive board of the American Composers Alliance, founded by Aaron Copland in 1937. She was also a member of the Society of American Women Composers, one of the forerunners of today's International Alliance of Women in Music (IAWM).

A Proponent for Modern Music

Always supportive of American music in general and contemporary music in particular, in 1926 she joined the boards of the League of Composers and the Society for the Publication of American Music. She expounded upon the vicious cycle of publishers not publishing modern teaching pieces because teachers didn't buy them, and therefore not teaching modern music because publishers did not publish it. So she continued to write teaching pieces, including the *Symphonic Suite for Strings* (1940), and *American Youth Concerto* (1943) for piano and orchestra, as well as composing more choral, chamber and orchestral works. In support of her interest in modern music, she wrote the book *Twentieth Century Music* in 1933. In the 1947–48 season, with the playing of *Sun Splendor*, an orchestrated version of her original piano piece, she enjoyed the distinction of being one of the few women whose works were performed by the New York Philharmonic, conducted by **Leopold Stokowski** (1882–1977). In 1951, a concert of her music was given at Town Hall in New York with first performances of her Trio Sonata No. 2, for flute, cello and piano, and *Moods for Dance Interpretation* op. 46 for dancer and piano. The same year she retired from her teaching post at NYU, and four years later, a few days before her sixty-eighth birthday, August 9, 1955, Marion died at South Hadley, Massachusetts.

Elinor Warren

ELINOR REMICK WARREN was one of the first women on the West Coast to make her name known as an orchestral composer. Los Angeles industrialist James B. Warren and his musical wife celebrated the new century with the birth of Elinor, February 23, 1900. The child lived in a cultured atmosphere. Her father had a fine tenor voice which her mother accompanied on the piano. In 1918, while still in high school, she wrote *A Song of June*, sent it to G. Schirmer who published it the following year. In 1919, Elinor entered Mills College in Oakland, but left after one year to go to New York where she studied accompanying and art songs with one of the greatest accompanists of his time, Frank LaForge, and composition with composer-organist Clarence Dickinson. She become an accompanist, and toured with great opera singers like **Lucrezia Bori** (1887–1960), **Richard Crooks** (1900–72) and **Lawrence Tibbett** (1896–1960). Elinor also performed at the Hollywood Bowl in 1923, and with the Los Angeles Philharmonic in 1926. In 1925, she married a Los Angeles physician, with whom she had a son, James, in 1928. Unhappy, they were divorced a year later. In 1932 she met Z. Wayne Griffin, who had studied singing for a career as a tenor, but ended up in radio and film production in San Francisco. Not until he had an opportunity to return to Los Angeles, to produce the *Burns and Allen Show*, were they able to be married. The ceremony took place December 12, 1936. Their son Zachary Wayne, Jr. was born in 1938, and daughter Elayne came in 1940. Meanwhile, Elinor had her own successful music appreciation weekly radio program (1938–39), playing the music of composers she discussed. As her growing family took precedence over her work, Warren still wrote each day in her house near Hancock Park. Though she often gathered her three children, and later her grandchildren, around the piano to sing, Warren's composition room was off limits when she was at work.

Wife-Mother-Composer—A Nation is Intrigued

Warren's first large work, *The Harp Weaver*, for women's chorus, baritone soloist and full orchestra, set to an Edna St. Vincent Millay poem, was premiered at Carnegie Hall in 1936. In 1940, the Los Angeles Philharmonic, under English conductor Albert Coates (1882–1953), premiered her choral symphony, *The Legend of King Arthur*. Broadcast nationwide, the country was intrigued that a beautiful young wife and mother was writing music serious enough to be played by a major orchestra under an internationally famous director. The work was a huge success, and excerpts were programmed at the Hollywood Bowl with famed British maestro **Sir John Barbirolli**, the San Francisco Symphony under **Pierre Monteux**, and broadcast with the NBC Symphony among others. In 1971, it was presented by **Roger Wagner** at the Dorothy Chandler Pavilion in Los Angeles. Half a century later it was recorded on a Cambria CD by producer Lance Bowling, a great admirer of Warren.

Her extensive repertoire of choral and vocal music, including many lovely songs, was performed in concert and on radio by many noted opera singers, among them **Lucrezia Bori**, Richard Crooks, Lawrence Tibbett, **Rose Bampton**, **Bidú Sayão**, **Gladys Swarthout**, **Dorothy Maynor**, **Eleanor Steber**, **Kirsten Flagstad**, **Helen Traubel**, **Rise Stevens**, **Regina Resnik**, **Eileen Farrell**, **Jeannette MacDonald** and Nelson Eddy. She also wrote chamber and piano pieces, and orchestral impressionistic works like *The Fountain* and *The Crystal Lake* (1946).

In 1953 the *Los Angeles Times* named Warren "Woman of the Year," and in 1954 she was presented with an honorary doctorate from Occidental College. She received an ASCAP award each year from 1959, "for significant contribution to the cultural growth and enrichment of our nation's musical heritage."

The Forty-Year Dream

In 1959, established, successful, and almost sixty years of age, Elinor realized a childhood dream and went to Paris for three months to study with **Nadia Boulanger**. They became great friends. Boulanger helped augment the American's neo-impressionist style and gift of melody. Returning to the U.S., Warren wrote *Abram in Egypt* for chorus, orchestra and baritone soloist. In 1966, **Roger Wagner** (1918–1992), who had premiered many of her works with the Los Angeles Master Chorale, commissioned a Requiem which took three years to complete.

In 1967, the Griffins were among the exclusive 500 guests invited by Prince Rainier and Princess Grace of Monaco for the surprise eightieth birthday party of Nadia Boulanger. Her gift was a portfolio of works written by all her now prominent students. Elinor wrote a song for her. Wayne knew Grace Kelly from Hollywood days, and he and Elinor were invited to the palace for tea the next day. Also in the 1960s, two of their children married and gave them grandchildren.

Continuing to compose and perform in the '70s and '80s, 1976 brought a fellowship from the NEA. 1978 saw a revision of *The Singing Earth*, for soprano and orchestra, based on Carl Sandburg poems. In 1987 Cambria released a CD of art songs sung by Elinor's friend Marie Gibson, accompanied by the composer—still a marvelous pianist at age eighty-seven! The recording—her first in over thirty years—was made in her music room seated on her mother's piano chair at the Steinway the composer had bought many years ago out of her own professional earnings.

Departure of the Soul-Mate

In September 1981, after a twenty year valiant struggle with Parkinson's disease, Wayne Griffin died at home surrounded by his family. Despite two distinct careers, theirs had been an idyllic union, a real love match. Elinor's last years alone were hard to bear, but her lifelong career proved to be her sustenance.

Although she was financially secure, Warren was a lifelong hard worker, creating and revising constantly, as well as continuing a regular piano practice regimen. Even though her music was performed internationally, she lived and worked most of her life in Los Angeles. She also accumulated an extensive collection of art songs, which amounted to over 1,400 when bequeathed to baritone **Thomas Hampson** after her death, April 27, 1991, at age ninety-one. (She retained her delicate beauty and slim figure all her life.)

Like Amy Beach, Elinor Remick Warren felt that there was "no gender in music." In a newspaper interview she once said, "If I hadn't married and had a family, I would naturally have had much more time to devote to music, but certainly I'm a far richer, happier person for having taken the path I did."

In her last fifteen years, however, she took great interest in reviving the work of women composers, a trend which continues with ever-gaining momentum.

In 1996, her family founded the Elinor Remick Warren Society to perpetuate her musical legacy of the romantic idiom in serious music through the contribution of scholarships, and performances and recordings of the solo and choral vocal repertoire of the 19th and 20th centuries. The society assisted with the March 2000 Warren Centenary Celebration in Washington, presenting to the Library of Congress the Elinor Remick Warren Collection of manuscripts and memorabilia from the composer's seventy-five-year career. The weekend included a symposium on the composer's life and work, a recital of her songs and piano works at the LOC with Thomas Hampson, soprano **Christine Goerke**, mezzo **Margaret Lattimore**, tenor Stanford Olsen and pianist Craig Rutenberg, plus a striking performance at Washington National Cathedral, where the Cathedral Choral Society, led by J. Riley Lewis, with Hampson as soloist, performed *The Legend of King Arthur*.

Ruth Crawford Seeger

Composer and folk music specialist **RUTH CRAWFORD** (Seeger) was born July 3, 1901, in East Liverpool, Ohio. She studied piano (1925–27) with **Djane Lavoie-Herz**, a disciple of the great Russian mystical pianist/composer **Alexander Scriabin** (1872–1915), and through her came into contact with modernists **Henry Cowell** (1897–1965), **Edgard Varèse** (1883–1965) and the mystic **Dane Rudhyar** (1895–1985), also a follower of Scriabin. She was exposed to the music of England's **Ralph Vaughan Williams** (1872–1958), and the modern Parisian contingent, **Igor Stravinsky** (1882–1971), **Darius Milhaud** (1892–1974) and **Paul Hindemith** (1895–1963). By 1926, Ruth had met the leading Chicago poet **Carl Sandburg**, assimilated his philosophy, and contributed folksong arrangements to his landmark anthology, *The American Songbag*.

In 1926, Henry Cowell put her on the board of his New Music Society and published several of her works in the "New Music Quarterly." She was a board member of the Pro Musica Society and in 1928 a founder member of the Chicago Chapter of the International Society for Contemporary Music (ISCM). The first professional performance of her music, her second piano prelude, was given in New York, November 1925. In 1927, her Violin Sonata was played at a League of Composers concert of music by six "Young Americans" (including **Aaron Copland** and **Marc Blitzstein**). Three of her piano preludes were included in a recital, May 6, 1928, in the Copland-Sessions series in New York.

In 1929, she met **Marion Bauer** at the MacDowell Colony in New Hampshire. After being introduced by Cowell, Crawford settled in New York to study dissonant counterpoint with the composer/musicologist **Charles Seeger** (1886–1979), who, until reviewing her *Five Preludes* for piano (1924–25), and *Suite for Small Orchestra* (1926), felt women composers were a waste of time. She helped him revise *Tradition and Experiment in New Music* and a *Manual on Dissonant Counterpoint*. His ideas were crucial to the development of her second style period (1930–33), which produced her *String Quartet, 1931*, incorporating serialism, tone clusters and diverse metrical patterns.

A Gender Milestone

In 1930 Crawford became the first woman—one of only five in the next fifteen years—to win a Guggenheim fellowship in composition. This enabled her to go to Europe, where in Berlin she met avant-gardists **Alban Berg** and **Egon Wellesz**; in Paris, **Maurice Ravel**; and Budapest, **Béla Bartók**. She returned to New York in late 1931, moved in with Seeger and married him October 1932, after his first wife consented to a divorce. Her music was being performed at the New School for Social Research, which had Seeger and Cowell on the faculty. Her *Three Songs* for voice, oboe, percussion and strings represented the U.S. at the 1933 ISCM Festival in Amsterdam.

Little Folks and Old Folk Songs

Despite his new wife's talents, Seeger had the traditional patriarchal ideas about a woman's "place." Their first child, Michael, was born in 1933, Margaret (Peggy), 1935, Barbara, 1937 and Penelope (Penny) in 1943. In case that did not keep Ruth busy enough, Charles' first three children also lived with them. In 1936 they moved to Washington, DC. Seeger was appointed to the music division of the Resettlement Agency, part of the New Deal. Crawford began working with John and Alan Lomax at the Archive of American Folk Song at the Library of Congress. The Seegers were one of other important "families" in the folk music revival of the late 1930s and '40s.

Stepson **Pete Seeger** became a leading folk singer, and Mike and Peggy were also professional musicians. Crawford's only original composition during this period was *Rissolty Rossolty*, an "American Fantasia for Orchestra" based on folk tunes, commissioned by CBS for its radio series, American School of the Air.

With the publication of *Our Singing Country* (1941), she became well known for her transcriptions. She also developed folk music programs for progressive private schools in the Washington area. Compiled from 1941–46, her classic *American Folksongs for Children* (1948), was followed by *Animal Folksongs for Children* (1950) and *American Folk Songs for Christmas* (1953). The *Suite for Wind Quintet* (1952) marked a return to composition, winning first prize at the DC chapter of the National Association of American Composers and Conductors.

Crawford's original music falls into two style periods: Her Chicago compositions (1924–29) filled with dissonance, and her New York period (1930–33) which established her as an innovative and experimental composer. However, her flawless folksong transcriptions, faithful to both the sound and the spirit of the original field recordings, have marked her place in musical history.

In the summer of 1953, as she was returning to composition, she was diagnosed with cancer. She died November 18, 1953, in Chevy Chase, Maryland, the day she was supposed to appear at a children's folk festival in Washington. Her music has come to be recognized as twenty years ahead of its time.

RADIE BRITAIN, born Texas, 1903, died, Palm Desert, 1994. (See Pen Women in Music.)

MIRIAM GIDEON was born October 23, 1906, in Greeley, Colorado, into an intellectual Jewish family— both parents were teachers—yet had no opportunity to hear music until at nine she began piano with a cousin. Radio did not yet exist, and there were few recordings and even fewer live performances out West. A move to New York brought summers spent in Boston with Uncle Henry Gideon, organist, choral and music director of Temple Israel who, when Miriam was fourteen, prevailed upon her parents to let her stay with him so that he could nurture his niece's talents. This exposure to the choir, synagogue services and the organ had a permanent influence in her works.

After graduating at nineteen with a BA from the College of Liberal Arts in Boston, she decided to become a composer rather than a pianist. Courses at NYU brought her in contact with **Marion Bauer**, Nadia Boulanger's first American student. She also studied composition with Russian composer Lazare Saminsky (1882–1959), music director of New York's Temple Emanu-El, who allowed her to develop her individuality, then guided her to the eminent **Roger Sessions** (1896–1985) with whom she studied for eight years. In 1939, although there was already danger for Jews, she went to Europe for further study, but had to return in September when WWII broke out.

From 1944–54 Gideon taught at Brooklyn College, where she met and married English professor Frederic Ewen—their happy forty year union ended with his death in 1989. In 1946, twenty years after her BA, she earned a master's in musicology from Columbia. She also taught at City College (1947–55, 1971–76), where she was made professor emeritus; the Manhattan School of Music (1967) and the Jewish Theological Seminary (1955–), who awarded her a doctorate of Sacred Music in Composition in 1970 when she was sixty-four.

Personal Premieres

In 1971, she became the first woman to be commissioned to compose a Jewish service. *Sacred Service* was first performed by the Temple in Cleveland, Ohio. In 1974, another service, *Shirat Miriam L'shabbat* for cantor, chorus and organ was commissioned and performed at the Park Avenue Synagogue. In 1975, she became the second woman elected to the American Academy and Institute of Arts and Letters. Despite these "milestones," she did not want to be stereotyped as either "Jewish" or "woman." Her vast output, combining a freely atonal style with Jewish musical traditions, includes *The Hound of Heaven* (1945), *How Goodly Are Thy Tents* (1947), *Adon Olam* (1954), *Three Masques* (1958), *The Resounding Lyre* (1979), incorporating one of her husband's poems, *Woman of Valor* (1982) and *Steeds of Darkness* (1986). Her song cycles often mixed poetry of different centuries and different languages within each setting. She also composed for orchestra, dramatic works, chamber music with and without voice, works for keyboard, solo voice and chorus. In her time she was the most recorded woman composer, but she felt that women were doing their work an injustice by featuring concerts of only women's music. Although she withdrew many of her early pieces, as a composer she helped pave the way for the acceptance of women in the field. Her works have been performed all over the world.

After a long bout of illness, she died in her home, June 18, 1996. For the last half century of her life Miriam Gideon lived in the same building on Central Park West in Manhattan as her contemporary, **Louise Talma**, who shared her birth year and passed away eight weeks after her long time friend.

Louise Talma

LOUISE TALMA was born on October 31, 1906, in Arcachon, France, of American parents. Her father, Frederick, a pianist, died when she was an infant, and her mother, Alma Cecile Garrigue, an operatic singer, gave up her own musical career and turned to teaching to direct her daughter's musical education, starting the child on piano at age five. The family returned to the U.S. in 1914, and after graduating from high school Louise studied theory and composition from 1922–30 at the Institute of Musical Art in New York, which later became the Juilliard School of Music. During the summers (1926–39), she studied at the American Conservatory at Fontainebleau, perfecting her piano technique with the eminent French pianist **Isidore Philipp** (1863–1958)—whose pupils included humanitarian Albert Schweitzer—and took harmony, counterpoint, composition and organ with the great **Nadia Boulanger**. With a BM (NYU, 1931) and MA (Columbia, 1933), her first teaching position was at the Manhattan School of Music (1926–28), her second at Hunter College (1928–78) where, upon reaching the mandatory retirement age after *fifty years*, she stayed on without pay!

A Change of Direction and a First

Talma originally intended to become a pianist. It was Boulanger who convinced her that she had a gift for composition and was the most important influence in her development as a composer, introducing her to the works of Igor Stravinsky, whose neoclassic style was incorporated in her early music. She became the first American to teach at Fontainebleau, joining their faculty in 1936. Meanwhile, her teaching income from Hunter College was the sole source of support for herself and her mother, whose health worsened in late 1930s. A devoted daughter, it was not until her mother died in 1943 that Louise became a fellow at the MacDowell Colony and began composing again.

Many of her works of the '40s and '50s are vocal, but in 1945 she completed her Piano Sonata No. 1 and her big success, the orchestral *Toccata*, which was performed by the Baltimore Symphony and won the Juilliard Publication Award (1946). She also continued to write for her own instrument, the piano, including *Alleluia in Form of Toccata* (1945), which incorporated elements of jazz and Americana. Playwright Thornton Wilder, whom she met at the MacDowell Colony, was so impressed by her music he asked her to write an opera with him. With his libretto, based on his play *Life in the Sun*, she spent five years on the work culminating in 1958 with *The Alcestiad*. This was premiered in 1962 for eight performances at Frankfurt-am-Main, in German. It was the first time a work of an American woman had been produced by a major European opera house. It has never been performed in the original English.

In the 1950s, Talma became interested in twelve-tone music—a development Nadia Boulanger regarded as "musical heresy." Nonetheless, she continued to write music in all genres through the '70s and '80s. Her later instrumental works include *Lament* for cello and piano (1980), *The Ambient Air* for flute, violin, cello and piano (1983), *Kaleidoscopic Variations* (1984) for piano, and *Full Circle* for orchestra with prominent piano part, first performed by the Prism Orchestra a few days before her eightieth birthday in 1986.

Talma was the first woman to win two Guggenheim Fellowships (1946, 1947), a Senior Fulbright Research Grant (1955–56) for *The Alcestiad*, the first woman to win the Sibelius Medal for Composition from the Harriet

Cohen International Awards (London, 1963), and the first woman composer elected to the American Institute of Arts and Letters (1974).

In later years, she spent each August at the Yaddo Music Camp near Saratoga, in upstate New York. It was here she passed away peacefully in her sleep, the night of August 12, 1996.

(Author's Note: I had been trying to telephone her that weekend and may have been the second person to know . . .)

(Nadine) **DANA SUESSE** (pronounced Sweese) was born December 3, 1909, Kansas City, Missouri, into a lively era in music and entertainment. When she grew too tall for ballet, she started piano lessons, debuting in Drexel Hall, Kansas City, June 29, 1919. A year of organ studies with Hans Fell resulted in a recital on December 17, 1922. He also taught her orchestration. In 1926, Dana and her mother traveled to New York to advance her studies with the great **Alexander Siloti** (1863–1945)—at that time one of the four surviving pupils of Franz Liszt—and Rubin Goldmark, a former teacher of George Gershwin.

She began experimenting with the jazz idiom. Her composition *Syncopated Love Song* bridged the gap between classical and this new form. Written in 1928, it was popularized when **Nathaniel Shilkret** (1895–1982), music director of the Victor Talking Company, recorded it in 1929. Leo Robin created a lyric, and it became the hit song "Have You Forgotten." Subsequently teamed with lyricist Edward Heyman, she wrote two more hits, "Ho Hum" and "My Silent Love."

A Carnegie Hall Premiere and the Bright Lights of Broadway

Prominent orchestra leader **Paul Whiteman** (1890–1967), who had introduced Gershwin's *Rhapsody In Blue*, was planning another "Experiment In Modern Music," and his arranger, **Ferde Grofé** (composer of the *Grand Canyon Suite*), accepted Suesse's *Concerto In Three Rhythms*. She premiered it at Carnegie Hall on November 4, 1932.

Broadway beckoned, and beginning with **Billy Rose**'s first Broadway show, *Sweet And Low* (1930), Dana contributed to all of the great showman's spectacular revues, including *Casa Mañana*, the *Aquacade* and *Diamond Horseshoe* revues. She also contributed songs to the *Ziegfeld Follies*—"The Night is Young and You're So Beautiful" (1934)—*Earl Carroll Vanities* (1935), *The Red Cat* (1935), and the score to the film *Sweet Surrender* (Universal, 1935). Her hit song "You Oughta Be In Pictures" (lyrics by Edward Heyman) came from a long-forgotten film short called *New York Town* (Columbia, 1934). Incidental music was also written for numerous plays, including *The Seven Year Itch* (1955) starring Marilyn Monroe, produced by her first husband, H. Courtney Burr.

Meanwhile, Suesse's concertos and other classical works were featured at that super cinema, Radio City Music Hall, Carnegie Hall, Madison Square Garden and the Metropolitan Opera House. Maestros including **Robert Russell Bennett**, **Frederick Fennell**, **Arthur Fiedler**, **Eugene Goossens**, **Ferde Grofé**, **Nathaniel Shilkret**, **Alexander Smallens**, **Alfred Wallenstein** and **Meredith Willson** performed her works in concert halls and on radio throughout the U.S. She was the only American composer other than George Gershwin to be invited to perform on the now legendary General Motors Symphony concert series of nationwide broadcasts.

Despite her success in music, Dana continued to aspire to be more than a composer, writing scripts for many plays, with and without music. She also wanted to be a lyricist as well as a playwright, but her attempts in the latter field never achieved success. One comedy, *It Takes Two*, written with Virginia Faulkner, ran a short time to miserable reviews in New York (February 1947), but this did not prevent Dana from enjoying half of the $50,000 paid out for film rights.

Awakening in Paris

At this time she took the opportunity to fulfill a lifelong dream. She moved to Paris for three years to study with **Nadia Boulanger**, re-learning orchestration and composing canons, string quartets, rondos, etc. On her return, Dana was fascinated with the new progressive jazz sounds created by such pianists as Cy Coleman, **Marian McPartland** and Billy Taylor. **Frederick Fennell** (1914-2004), conductor of the Eastman School of Music, heard about her *Concerto in Rhythm* (later called *Jazz Concerto in D Major for Combo and Orchestra*), requested she play it for him on the piano, then insisted that he be the first to conduct it.

Before an appreciative audience of 2000, Suesse played the solo part as Fennell conducted the Rochester Civic Orchestra on Saturday night, March 31, 1956. The *Rochester Times-Union* said: "This is melodic music, full of surging pulse and vitality, fashioned as a work of art . . . "

After Dana's mother and stepfather died, she became disenchanted with Manhattan and the post-War music business. In April 1970, she moved to New London, Connecticut, where she met her next husband, C. Edwin Delinks. In 1974, after three years of marriage, they decided to invest their own money in an all-Suesse symphony concert at Carnegie Hall. Dana engaged Frederick Fennell and attended to the million details. The concert was given on December 11, 1974, with Cy Coleman as soloist with the American Symphony Orchestra. The *New York Times* reported, " . . . The highlight of the evening came when Miss Suesse herself joined the orchestra to play 'The Blues,' which is the second movement of the *Concerto* she performed with Paul Whiteman at her debut forty-two years ago." A year later the prestigious Newport (Rhode Island) Music Festival presented four of her works in a concert series devoted to women.

She Took Manhattan

In 1975, the couple moved to Frederiksted, St. Croix, in the Virgin Islands. After a number of health crises, Ed died in a Miami hospital on July 7, 1981. Dana, who still read the *New York Times* daily, decided she'd had enough of white beaches and turquoise seas and returned to Manhattan in 1982, renting two adjoining apartments at the Gramercy Park Hotel. A revival of interest in American music made her popular again for interviews and songwriters' concerts.

Dana had a few distinct musical favorites. She loved Debussy's only completed opera, *Pelléas et Mélisande*. She saw it twice in Paris—once with Boulanger—and at least twice in America. She even wrote a piece called *Afternoon of a Black Faun* in emulation. The music she would select to take with her "to a desert island" was Bach's *Passacaglia and Fugue in C Minor*. Just before her death from a stroke, October 16, 1987, she was putting the finishing touches to her new musical *Mr. Sycamore*, which had been optioned for off-Broadway. She was also looking for a New York theater for a straight play, *Nemesis*.

In her own words, "I don't want any personal fame, I just want the works to speak for themselves." The time has come for deserved recognition of both.

(Most of this material was taken from information sent by musicologist Peter Mintun, who has devoted his career to music of the '30s and '40s. A special protégé of the composer, Suesse gave him her scrapbooks, recordings and sold him—"for a song"—her Steinway piano.) (See also *TIME*, February 5, 1996.)

Vivian Fine

VIVIAN FINE, born September 28, 1913, in Chicago, had her mother as her first piano teacher. At age five she entered the Chicago Musical College on a scholarship. By eleven her piano teacher was **Djane Lavoie-Herz**. From twelve to seventeen, she studied with one of the first female composers of atonal music, **Ruth Crawford**, who introduced her young pupil to other *avant-garde* composers **Dane Rudhyar** (1895–1985), a French-born emigré who assumed a Hindu name and pioneered the study of Asian musical concepts, and **Henry Cowell** (1897–1965), teacher of John Cage and George Gershwin.

The first public performance of her solo for oboe was at sixteen. In 1932, she went to New York alone—a daring feat in those days! She became the only female member of the Young Composers Group organized by **Aaron Copland** (1900–90), and earned a living accompanying modern dance, gaining a reputation for being able to play complicated contemporary music. She also wrote ballets for legendary choreographers Doris Humphrey, Charles Weidman, Hanya Holm and Jose Limón. At the same time, she studied harmony and composition privately with American composer **Roger Sessions**, who was then teaching at Princeton.

She married sculptor Ben Karp in 1935, and had two daughters, Peggy born 1942, and Nina, 1948. In 1937, Fine helped found the American Composers' Alliance. She began a prestigious composition and piano teaching career in the 1940s at NYU, SUNY (Potsdam) and Juilliard. 1964 marked the start of her tenure at Bennington College (Vermont) which lasted until 1987.

Fine's earliest works were dissonant and contrapuntal, developing later into a more expressive range, such as the 1960 ballet, *Alcestis*, written for Martha Graham; *Meeting for Equal Rights, 1866* (1976) for chorus and orchestra, a thoroughly researched piece based on an actual event and utilizing the speeches of Susan B. Anthony, Elizabeth Cady Stanton, Frederick Douglass and suffragettes who, having been successful in their abolition campaigns, now demanded the womens' vote; *Missa Brevis* (1972) a major composition for four cellos and taped voice; and the popular opera *The Women in the Garden* (1978), presented in San Francisco. Commissions produced *Drama for Orchestra* (San Francisco Symphony, 1980), *Poetic Fires* (Koussevitzky Foundation, 1984), *Ode to Purcell* (Elizabeth Sprague Coolidge Foundation, 1984), and *Emily's Images* (1987).

She composed *The Triple Goddess* (1988) for concert band, the same year her seventy-fifth birthday was celebrated with The Women's Philharmonic's commission of *After the Tradition*, reflecting her Jewish roots. Subsequent works include *Madrigali Spirituali*, for trumpet and string quartet, *Discourse of Goatherds*, for bass trombone, *Asphodel*, for voice and chamber ensemble (all written in 1989), *Portal* (1990), for violin and piano, commissioned and performed by **Pamela Frank** at Alice Tully Hall in Lincoln Center, and *Canciones y Danzas* (1991), for flute, guitar and cello. A chamber opera with film, *Uliana Rooney*, centered around a fictitious composite woman composer, premiered in 1994—this a commission from the Lila Acheson Wallace[39] Fund. Several of her works are on a CD released by Composers' Recordings, Inc., (CRI).

Fine's honors include an NEA grant (1977), and an award from the American Institute of Arts and Letters (1979) plus election to membership in this prestigious organization the following year—only the third woman composer to receive this honor. (**Louise Talma** and **Miriam Gideon** were the first and second, respectively.)

In 1996, the octogenarian composer told me that after seventy years of composition, she was taking a sabbatical. On March 20, 2000, with her eighty-nine-year-old sister Adelaide at the wheel, a car accident tragically took the lives of both women. Vivian is survived by her daughters and two granddaughters, Keli and Dora.

The Music of Vivian Fine, by Dr. Heidi Von Gunden, professor of composition and theory at the University of Illinois (Champaign-Urbana), was published in 2000 by Scarecrow Press.

Netty Simons

NETTY SIMONS, born in New York City, October 26, 1913, began music studies with her older sister, a student of **Walter Damrosch** (1862–1950). Her interest in composition brought her to NYU where her teachers were **Percy Grainger** (1882–1961) and **Marion Bauer**. She accepted a one-year scholarship to study piano at Juilliard with **Alexander Siloti** (1863–1945), a pupil of Franz Lizst, and then returned to NYU studying the next three years with **Stefan Wolpe** (1902–72). Concurrently, she composed, performed and presented music broadcasts on New York radio station WHN, and taught at the Third Street School. She married in 1936, raised two children, and thirty years later returned to radio (1965) where she wrote and produced broadcasts of new music for WNYC, and the University of Michigan's WUOM.

Her early compositions were mostly chamber works: *Duo for Violin and Cello* (1939), *String Quartet* (1950), *Quartet for Flute and Strings* (1951), *Piano Work* (1952), *Night Sounds* (1953), and *Set of Poems for Children* (1949) for winds, strings, and narrator. She then turned from traditional styles to aleatory and graphic notation. These

---

39. Founder, with her husband, of *Reader's Digest.*

works include *Design Groups I* (1966) for percussion, *Design Groups II* (1968), a duo for high-and-low pitched instruments, *Silver Thaw* (1969) for one to eight players, and *The Great Stream Silent Moves* (1974) for piano, harp and percussion. Many of her pieces may be performed as theater pieces, employing dancers and actors as well as, or instead of, musicians. After her death on April 1, 1994, in New York, her music was donated to the New York Public Library in Lincoln Center.

DIKA NEWLIN, musicologist and composer, was born November 22, 1923, in Portland, Oregon, but raised in Michigan after her English professor father moved to Michigan State College. She began piano at six, and at eight wrote *Cradle Song*, which was performed by the Cincinnati Symphony in 1935. While a student at Michigan State, she heard of **Arnold Schoenberg** (1874–1951) who had fled Nazi Germany and was teaching at UCLA, so she went there for her master's (1941). In 1945, she set a precedent, earning Columbia University's first doctorate in musicology. Her dissertation, *Bruckner, Mahler, Schoenberg* (1947, revised 1978) became a standard reference work on these composers. In 1957, she won the Mahler medal from the Bruckner Society. While in New York she also studied composition with **Arthur Farwell** (1872–1952) and **Roger Sessions**, and piano with two of its greatest interpreters, **Rudolf Serkin** (1903–91) and **Artur Schnabel** (1882–1951).

A True Disciple of Schoenberg

Newlin returned to Los Angeles in the summers of 1949 and 1950 to work with Schoenberg, who died the following year. Making the decision to write his biography, she was able to get a Fulbright grant and spent 1951 and 1952 in Austria doing research. While there, she performed in Vienna and Paris, and was the soloist in her piano trio at the 1952 ISCM Festival in Salzburg. On her return she taught at Western Maryland College (1945–49), Syracuse University (1949–51), Drew University (1952–65) and North Texas State (1963–75). After a two-year sabbatical devoted to writing and composition, she joined the faculty at Virginia Commonwealth University, Richmond (1978–2003), where she developed a new doctoral program in music. She edited and translated many writings by and about Schoenberg. Her biography, *Schoenberg Remembered: Diaries and Recollections, 1938–1976*, was published in 1980.

An excellent pianist, most of Newlin's important works are for that instrument. *Sinfonia for piano* (1947), was followed in 1948 by her Piano Trio, a twelve-tone piece structured à la Schoenberg. Her *Chamber Symphony*, for twelve solo instruments, was premiered in America (1960) after first being played in Darmstadt (Germany, 1949). Other works include the operas *Feathertop* (one act, 1942), *The Scarlet Letter* (three acts, 1945), and *Smile Right to the Bone*; plus songs, piano and chamber works including Piano Quintet (1941), Violin Sonata (1942), Piano Trio (1951), a piano concerto and a symphony for chorus and orchestra, *The Eumenides* (1941). Her later music employed the newer developments of electronic and computer music, mixed-media and experimental music-theater. In 1994, a documentary entitled "Dika: Murder City," featuring her performing her song *Murder City* and other pieces, was shown as a music video at the Cinevue International Film Festival in Washington, D.C. A 2004 CD, "Ageless Icon," featured her punk rock songs.

She passed away July 22, 2006.

Jean Ivey

JEAN EICHELBERGER IVEY, born July 3, 1923, in Washington, DC, studied piano and organ, and began composing at an early age. She graduated from Trinity College (BA, 1944), Peabody (MM, 1946, Piano), Eastman School of Music (MM, 1956, Composition) and the University of Toronto (DMA, 1972, Composition). Among her early works are *Little Symphony* (1948), *Theme and Variations* (1952), *Scherzo* (1953), *Festive Symphony* (1955), and *Pianoforte* (1957). These influenced by Bartók and Ravel, she explored the sounds, textures and colors of electronic music of the 1960s. Her first tape work, made at Brandeis University Electronic Studio, was *Pinball* (1965), a collage of clicks, rattles, bells and other sounds from a pinball machine, a piece later used in the film, *Montage V: How to Play Pinball*.

An Important Contribution

As coordinator of the composition department of Peabody Conservatory (the music school of Johns Hopkins University), Ivey founded the Peabody Electronic Music Studio in 1967. Here she composed *Cortège—for Charles Kent* (1969), *Tribute: Martin Luther King* (1969) and *Continuous Form*, this in combination with visual images put together by Wayne Sourbeer, and used in the breaks between television programs. She often wrote her own texts to her vocal works, as in her monodrama *Testament of Eve* (1976), *Prospero* (1978), and her opera *The Birthmark* (1980–82).

A professional pianist, Ivey toured the U.S., Mexico and Europe in programs which included her own compositions. Her awards number a Guggenheim fellowship, two fellowships from the NEA—where she served as a panelist—residencies at the MacDowell Colony and Yaddo (the music camp at Saratoga Springs, New York), a grant from the Martha Baird Rockefeller Fund, American Music Center, many ASCAP awards, the Distinguished Achievement Citation of the National League of American Pen Women, the Peabody Distinguished Alumni Award, the Peabody Director's Recognition Award, and a 1992 Artists' Fellowship from the New York Foundation for the Arts. Author of numerous music articles, she was the subject of many interviews and articles, and the WRC-TV documentary, *A Woman is . . . a Composer.*

Happy Seventieth Birthday!

Her seventieth birthday was celebrated in the music world with many premieres, including: *Forms in Motion* (3 movement orchestral work, Peabody Symphony); *A Carol of Animals* (Concordia College); *Ariel in Flight* (violin and tape, Columbia, NY, and Goucher College, Baltimore); *Aldébaran* (viola and tape—part of the twenty-fifth anniversary of the Peabody Electronic Studio); *Suite for Cello and Piano* (a College Music Society program); *Sonata da Chiesa* (solo harp, Fifth World Harp Conference, Copenhagen); *Triton's Horn* (tenor saxophone and piano, Friday Morning Music Club, Washington, DC); *Skaniadargo* (piano and tape, Catholic University, Washington, DC); *My Heart Is Like a Singing Bird* (women's chorus, flute choir to a text by Christina Rossetti); *Flying Colors* (fanfare for brass, 1994, premiered at Shippensburg U., Pennsylvania); and *Notes Toward Time* (mezzo, flute, alto flute and harp, Baltimore Chamber Music Society).

A CD of Ivey's orchestral works (*Testament of Eve, Tribute: Martin Luther King,* etc.) was released in 1996. The thirtieth anniversary of Jean's founding of the Computer Studio was celebrated by the conservatory in 1997, with Jean as guest of honor. She retired in 1998 due to ill health.

Ruth Schontal

RUTH SCHÖNTHAL was born June 27, 1924, in Hamburg of Viennese parents. She composed her first piece at five becoming, at that tender age, the youngest student ever accepted by the Stern Conservatory in Berlin. In 1938 the family fled from Hitler and moved to Stockholm, where Ruth attended the Royal Academy of Music (1938–41). Her *Sonatina* for piano was published in 1940. In the first years of World War II, as the Nazis overran Europe and headed for the Scandinavian countries, Sweden would remain neutral, but was a hotbed of spies. Another exodus became necessary in 1941, just three months before Ruth's graduation. Traveling the "safe" route across Russia, they stopped in Moscow where, upon playing her *Sonatina* at the conservatory, Ruth was offered, at the government's expense, a choice of studying with two of the country's greatest composers, **Dmitri Shostakovich** (1906–75), or **Serge Prokofiev** (1891–1953). It was a difficult decision, but her father declined the tempting honor and the family continued on their nightmarish three month journey via the Trans-Siberian Railway to its terminal in Vladivostok. From there they took a ship across the Sea of Japan, past Korea and Hawaii to Los Angeles where, because of immigration regulations, no one was permitted to step ashore. After a harrowing earthquake at sea, the Schönthals finally arrived in Mexico in June.

As an impressionable teenager, Ruth absorbed the exotic new atmosphere, rushing at seventeen into marriage, motherhood—a son Benjamin—and divorce. Fortunately, her career did not suffer. Besides winning first prize in piano at the National Conservatory, she studied with renowned Mexican composer **Manuel Ponce** (1882–1948) who introduced her to some of the world's most celebrated artists, including guitarist **Andrés Segovia** (1893–1987) and violinist **Henryk Szeryng** (1918–88).

She came to the attention of German composer **Paul Hindemith** (1895–1963) during his Mexican concert tour. Impressed with her music, he arranged for a two-year scholarship to study with him at Yale. She received her BA in 1950. A meeting with graduate art student Paul Seckel led to a happy marriage the same year. Little Benjamin was sent for from Ruth's parents in Mexico City, and the new family settled in New York. Paul obtained a teaching position at City College, while Ruth helped support the family playing piano in nightclubs as she had done in Mexico under the name "Carmelita." After the birth of Bernhard Alexander in 1953, Ruth embarked upon a piano teaching career. A third son, Alfred Paul, arrived in 1958.

With new focus on electronic and experimental music, Schonthal considered the traditional was "dead." Encouragement of American composer **Paul Creston** (1906–85) inspired the award-winning *String Quartet No. 1*; *Totengesänge* (*Songs of Death*) with her own texts; *Sonata Breve* and *Sonatensatz*; *Variations in Search of a Theme*; *Four Epiphanies*; *By The Roadside*, a short song cycle with words by Walt Whitman; *Bird Calls*, and *Miniatures*, all expressed a unique blend of European tradition and contemporary techniques. In 1979, she was a finalist in the Kennedy-Friedheim Award for *In Homage Of . . .*, a set of twenty-four short piano preludes displaying her piano mastery and in 1980 was again a finalist in the New York Opera competition with *The Courtship of Camilla*. *Fragments from a Woman's Diary* was written in 1982. 1983 marked the first of annual journeys to her homeland. Reflecting deep distress over the havoc wrought by Hitler, her *Nachklänge* (Reverberations) for timbred piano, was chosen to be performed in the "Education for Peace Through Music" programs in the German schools and played frequently in concerts.

Other titles in her variety of styles include: *Operatic Cradle Song* (1987), based on Garcia Lorca's *Blood Wedding*; *Canticles of Hieronymus*, honoring the fourth century monk, St. Jerome, who wrote the Vulgate (Catholic Bible); and an anti-war cantata, *The Young Dead Soldiers*, whose American premiere at SUNY was attended by an audience of two thousand. A spate of commissions produced the two act opera *Princess Maleen*, plus many chamber works for traditional instruments. Modern innovations of prepared piano, synthesizer, electric guitar and taped sounds include: *Toccata and Arietta*, *Sonata in 2 Movements*, *The Temptation of St. Anthony* (organ) and *Six Times Solitude* (soprano and piano). *Collage* (1990), for soprano, vibraphone, glockenspiel, synthesizer, etc., is dedicated to artist Hannah Hoch (1889–1978), one of the German founders of Dadaism and a friend of the Schönthals in the Berlin years.

In the prolific 1990s came *Self-Portrait of the Artist as an Older Woman*, *Evening Music*, *Night Fantasy with Ocean Waves*, *A Bird Flew Over Jerusalem*, *Homage a Garcia Lorca*, *Soundtrack for a Dark Street*, *Improvisation for Solo Violin*, *Improvisation for Solo Clarinet*, *Ingrid's Songs* (a song cycle for mezzo and piano dedicated to Dr. Ingrid Olbricht), *Improvisation in 3 Interconnected Sections* (violin), *Variations on a Jewish Liturgical Theme*, *Trompetengesänge*, based on a poem by the composer, *The Bells of Sarajevo*, and *Sonata No. 5* (cello and piano). 1994 brought the world premiere of *Abendruhe mit süssem Traum* (Evening Calm with Sweet Dream), *The Wall-Before and After*—referring to the Berlin Wall—and in 1995, *Meditations and Celebrations*, sixty-five preludes, interludes and postludes for church services.

Her major works are on CDs, including: *Fiestas y Danzas* (Leonarda), *The Canticles of Hieronymus*, *Gestures*, *Self-Portrait of the Artist as an Older Woman* (Cambria), and *Fragments From a Woman's Diary* (Cambria)—the last two emphasizing life from a woman's point of view.

Recipient of many ASCAP awards and Meet the Composer grants, in 1981 Schönthal was awarded the Certificate of Merit for Outstanding Service to Music from the Alumni Association of the Yale School of Music. A master teacher, she has served on the board of the IAWM and on the faculties of the Westchester Conservatory, Adelphi University and NYU. Her students have won national and international prizes.

Seventieth Birthday Honors

In April 1994, celebration of her seventieth birthday began with concerts in New York. In October, the composer was honored with the annual *Heidelberger Künstlerinnen Preis* (International Women Artists Prize). The same year, the book *Ruth Schonthal: Ein kompositorische Werdegang im Exil* (A Compositional Development in Exile), was published from the two-volume PhD dissertation (in German) by Dr. Martina Helmig of the Freie University of Berlin. The work took eight years to complete, with an English translation by Vanessa Agnew (1996).

Honored as the featured composer at the March 1995 International Festival of Contemporary Music at Heidelberg, Schönthal's annual visit to Germany also included concertizing, performances and broadcasts of her music in Hamburg, Lübeck and Freiburg. In November, a concert was given in her honor in Berlin. June 6th and 23, 1996, marked two world premieres: the Second String Quartet (1995 version), and the *Heidelberger Fanfare and Variations* for piano. The same year she composed *Early Songs*, from the works of German lyric poet Rainer Maria Rilke (1875–1926), and was honored by NYU with their library ordering her complete works. Her *Piano Pentatonics* was published in three volumes by Carl Fischer. In May 1997, she played her *Reverberations* at NYU, which honored her with a Certificate of Excellence in recognition for her renowned accomplishments as a composer and pedagogue. The same year saw her as performer in several recitals of her works. Her opera *Jocasta*, based on the Œdipus tragedy, was staged by the Voice and Vision Theatre Company in Spring, 1998. Her first CD, featuring *The Bells of Sarajevo*, was released the same year. This has been followed by numerous releases on Cambria.

In 1999, Berlin's Akademie der Künst (Academy of the Arts) purchased all manuscripts, music originals and archives spanning her life and career. (Her music is published in Germany by Furore in Kassel.) Coinciding with her seventy-fifth birthday and the opening of the Schönthal Archives in June, the Akademie presented concerts and radio broadcasts of her music, and produced a CD of her piano compositions which was voted best in all categories by the German magazine *Piano News* (September/October 1999). NYU also honored her seventy-fifth birthday with a concert devoted to her music, November 22, 1999. A video documentary, featuring the 150th anniversary of the Stern Conservatory (Hochschule für Musik) and honoring Ruth Schönthal, their youngest student ever, was filmed, November 2000, in Berlin. Introductory remarks were provided by musicologist **Nancy B. Reich**.

On July 20, 2000, the Manchester Music Festival, which gave the commission, premiered her *Piccolo Concerto for Flute, Bassoon & Harpsichord* with famed harpsichordist **Alexander Kipnis**. Her String Quartet #3, *Holocaust in Memoriam* (1997) and *Bird over Jerusalem* for flute, tape and prepared piano, with the Eastman Chamber Players, is now included in the Collection of American Jewish Music by the Milkin Foundation, a recording project released in 2001. In August 2003, Ruth attended "Songs of the Americas," an all professional festival in La Paz, Bolivia. Featured was her *Wilderness Cycle* which received an outstanding ovation. An October visit to Vienna for an interview at the Holocaust Museum completed an eventful year.

Illness dogged her in the next two years, but she rallied in 2006, spending time transcribing earlier works into her computer, and writing a piano piece, *Adagio Harmonioso*. Her son Bernhard, who had moved into the house a few years previously, told me that his mother was enjoying life right up until her last day. She passed away July 10, 2006.

Composer/pianist **JEANNE SINGER** (1924–2000) left an immortal legacy with her composition *To Be Brave is All*, dedicated to Raoul Wallenberg the Swedish diplomat who risked his life saving thousands of Hungarian Jews. (See Pen Women.)

CATHY BERBERIAN, singer/composer, was born on July 4, 1925, in Attleboro, Massachusetts. She studied mime, singing, dancing and composition at NYU and Columbia, then went to the Verdi Conservatory in Milan to study voice with Giorgina del Vigo, gaining attention when she performed John Cage's ultrasurrealist *Fontana Mix*, featuring a fantastic variety of sound effects. This, in turn, attracted other avant-garde composers to write for her incredible three-octave range voice with which she could evoke squeals, grunts, clucks, screeches and other animal noises, as well as sub-and superhuman sounds. She was married to the Italian avant-garde composer **Luciano Berio** (1925–2003) from 1950–66, which influenced many of his compositions utilizing her unique vocal skills. She continued to perform his music after their divorce in 1968. Her best known original composition is *Stripsody* (1966), written for her own voice and containing labial and laryngeal sounds. It uses comic strips as a cultural discourse, and includes material based on Charles Schulz's cartoon, "Peanuts." Her other works for solo voice are *Awake and ReadJoyce* and *Anathema con VarieAzioni* (both 1972), and a piano piece *Morsicat(h)y* (1971). She died in Rome on March 6, 1983, shortly after an appearance on Italian television singing the *Internationale*, commemorating the centennial of the death of Karl Marx.

CLAIRE POLIN, composer, musicologist and flutist, was born in Philadelphia, January 1, 1926. The youngest of ten children of a Turkish father and Franco-Russian mother, she began piano at age six, and wrote her first symphony at ten, even though she had no knowledge of scoring. She studied flute with **William Kincaid** (1895–1967), Philadelphia Orchestra principal flute, and, after his death published a five-volume flute method series based on his notes. She studied composition with **Vincent Persichetti** (1915–87) at the Philadelphia Conservatory, earning an MM (1950) and DMA (1955), with **Peter Mennin** at Juilliard, and **Roger Sessions** and **Lukas Foss** at Tanglewood. She joined the faculty of Rutgers in New Jersey in 1962, teaching art history and composition until her retirement in 1991. She died of cancer at her home in Merion, Pennsylvania, December 6, 1995.

In the 1960s, Polin was the model of the feminist composer, keeping house, raising two sons, teaching, performing and composing. She led a lifelong fight against the term "woman composer," with statements such as: "Inequality in music? I meet it every day, but I continue writing and performing." "I don't sign a man's name to my music; that wouldn't settle anything." In 1968, she won a fellowship for a year's study in Wales. The same year she was named a MacDowell Colony fellow. Her later compositions reflected her experience with early Welsh music and folklore, the music of biblical and medieval times, and Russian folk music. Her output includes solo works for flute, three symphonies, and a large catalogue of chamber music and songs.

As near as one can make out with various age discrepancies, **LUCIA DLUGOSZEWSKI** was born in Detroit, Michigan, June 16, 1929, of immigrant Polish parents. She started composing at three, and studied piano at the Detroit Conservatory from age six. Her father, *Czeslav*, a self-made man, took his savings for a car and instead bought his daughter a piano. When he could spare the money, he bought one concert ticket so that his daughter could go in while he waited outside to take her home. She enrolled as a pre-med student at Wayne State University (1949–52), and graduated in physics and chemistry, all the while continuing her piano and composition studies at the conservatory.

Abandoning plans to become a doctor, Lucia moved to New York and attended Mannes College of Music studying analysis with Austrian theorist **Felix Salzer** (1904–86), and composition with avant-garde **Edgard Varèse** (1883–1965). She continued her piano studies with Bach specialist and avant-garde proponent **Grete Sultan** (1906–2005). For this we have the year 1948, and her student's age as nineteen. A dancer-choreographer named Erick Hawkins, who had studied with the great George Balanchine, occupied the studio next door. Grete introduced the pair. Although Lucia was married to sculptor Ralph Dorazio, the meeting with Erick hit her, in her own words, "like a firestorm." She divorced Ralph in 1954—they remained friends—and married Hawkins in 1962. Dorazio became a set designer for the dance company. Meanwhile, the passionate love match which, amazingly, they managed to keep a secret for over fifty years, was sundered by Erick's death, November 1994, at eighty-five.

The Erick Hawkins Dance Company lived on in his name, with Dlugoszewski as composer-in-residence, and from 1996 as artistic director, writing, choreographing, and accompanying many dance productions at New York's Joyce Theater and other venues. In 1999, she made her formal debut as a choreographer.

Searching for new sonic horizons, she refrained from using synthesizers or other electronic equipment to generate sounds, instead utilizing traditional instruments in unconventional ways. In 1951, she built her unique *timbre piano*, a conventional piano with the strings sounded by various beaters, picks and bows. She also invented more than one hundred percussion instruments, including elegant ladder harps and various rattles made by Dorazio. (These mysteriously disappeared after her death.) She used her inventions in many compositions, including a theater score *Desire Trapped by the Tail* (voice and timbre piano, 1952), *Archaic Timbre Piano Music* (1954–57), *Skylark Cicada* (violin and timbre piano,1964), *Velocity Shells* (timbre piano, trumpet and percussion, 1970) and *Duende Newfallen*[40] (bass trombone and timbre piano, 1982–83).

Regarded by many as one of America's most prominent avant-garde composers, Dlugoszewski was the first woman to win the Koussevitzky International Recording Award (1977) for *Fire Fragile Flight* (1974), and was also the recipient of grants from the NEA, NARAS, and a Tompkins Award for poetry. Her opera, *The Heidi Songs* (1970), with libretto by poet John Ashbery, used experimental contemporary idioms. From 1960, she taught at the Foundation for Modern Dance, NYU, and the New School for Social Research. Her first major commission was from the New York Philharmonic for *Abyss and Caress* (1975), premiered by avant-garde composer/conductor **Pierre Boulez**. At this time she began work on pieces for large ensembles: *Strange Tenderness of Naked Leaping* (1977) and *Wilderness Elegant Tilt* (1981).

For the next decade there was little time for composition, as Lucia cared for her ailing mother until her death in 1988. Returning to music, Dlugoszewski began to use "otherness"[41] or "strangeness" as a compositional tool. In the early 1990s, she produced a series of chamber works for flute, clarinet, trumpet, trombone, violin and bass, including *Radical Otherness Concert* (1991) and *Radical Suchness Concert*[42] (1991), plus a piece exploring subtlety, *Radical Narrowness Concert* (1992). Her daring, yet tender creation, *Radical Quidditas For An Unborn Baby* (1991) is for a large ensemble of traditional percussion instruments, plus her own innovations, all played by one performer. *Disparate Stairway Radical Otherness* (1994) was a commission from ballet star **Mikhail Baryshnikov**. 1995 brought *Depth Duende Radical Otherness* and 1996, *Multiple Symphony for 7 Instruments Suchness Concert* for flute piccolo, clarinet, bass clarinet, B flat trumpet, bass trombone and percussion, performed at the Danny Kaye Playhouse, Hunter College. 1997 commissions included *Wilderness Elegant Tilt* for the Lincoln Chamber Society and *Radical Quidditas Dew Tear Duende* for the American Composers Orchestra.

Lucia had not been heard from for several days when opening night, April 11, 2000, of the Erick Hawkins production at the 91st Street Playhouse sponsored by the 92nd Street Y Harkness Dance Center arrived, but Lucia did not. Someone was sent to her apartment. It was the sad duty of playhouse director Joan Finkelstein to announce that the evening's choreographer, pianist and composer had died. The performance, conducted by Joel Thome, was dedicated to Lucia. The performers took no bows. The audience held their applause. Memories flowed in the silence.

Both Hawkins and Dlugoszewski died intestate, and while most of Erick's material has ended up in the New York Public Library and Library of Congress, the State of New York owns Lucia's properties, which as of this writing are being sought by the Hawkins Foundation. We can only hope that all rights will be regained so that the combined talents of this couple can continue to live in future performances . . .

Renata Celichowska, former dancer with the Erick Hawkins Dance Company, now director of the 92nd Street Y Harkness Dance Center and author of *The Erick Hawkins Modern Dance Technique* (2000), shared these memories with the author:

> I remember the first time I danced to Lucia's music during a performance of *Black Lake* in the Erick Hawkins Modern Dance Company. The extraordinary intricate time measures and unique sounds and instruments she used blended into what at first seemed a cacophony of barnyard animals. As I moved

---

40. *Duende* (Spanish) is used in flamenco art meaning a tragic sense of life.

41. *Otherness* or *strangeness* is the shattering of ordinary reality.

42. *Suchness*, from the Zen *tathata*, refers to one's bedrock sense of being. James Joyce called this quidditas.

within the sound, it magically transformed into a dancing partner—a Chinese gong . . . the sound of ripping paper . . . it all made sense in connection with Erick's choreography.

Erick and Lucia transformed the way in which I see dance and hear music. Both disciplines are equal partners that have the ability to dance and sing together in a way that heightens the immediate experience of each.

SYLVIA GLICKMAN (1932–2006) was a composer, pianist, musicologist, author, editor and president of Hildegard Publishing. (See Women in the Business of Music.)

Contemporary American Women Composers

Beth Anderson
Laurie Anderson
Elinor Armer
Elizabeth Bell
Natasha Bogojevich
Victoria Bond
Wendy Carlos
Andrea Clearfield
Emma Lou Diemer
Lori Dobbins
Deborah Dratell
Pozzi Escot
Tania Gabrielle French
Barbara Harbach
Sorrel Hays
Jennifer Higdon
Katherine Hoover

Laura Kaminsky
Barbara Kolb
Joan LaBarbara
Libby Larsen
Annea Lockwood
Ursula Mamlok
Meredith Monk
Erica Muhl
Thea Musgrave
Maria Newman
Pauline Oliveros
Marta Ptaszynska
Shulamit Ran
Marga Richter
Eugénie Rocherolle
Daria Semegen
Alex Shapiro

Alice Shields
Sheila Silver
Laurie Speigel
Hilary Tann
Augusta Read Thomas
Joan Tower
Ludmila Ulehla
Mary Jeanne Van Appledorn
Nancy Van de Vate
Melinda Wagner
Gwyneth Walker
Joelle Wallach
Dalit Hadass Warshaw
Chen Yi
Judith Lang Zaimont
Ellen Taaffe Zwilich

Beth Anderson

BETH ANDERSON was born January 3, 1950 in Lexington, Kentucky, into a music-loving, supportive family. She studied piano and began composing as a child, attended the University of Kentucky for two years and graduated from UC Davis, where she studied with **John Cage**, her idol since high school days. She received master's degrees in piano performance and composition from Mills College (Oakland, California), studying with **Terry Riley** (*b* 1935). After graduation, she became known in the San Francisco area for radical new music techniques in voice, instrumental and tape collage compositions. In 1975, Anderson moved to New York. Her music began to receive European performances, notably her quartet *The Eighth Ancestor*, which was chosen by the ISCM and performed at the Royal Conservatory in Brussels, Belgium.

Having been a dance accompanist is reflected in some of her music. She has also taught university courses and published many articles. She describes herself as an *avant-garde romantic* composer. The Cagian influence lasted from 1966 to 1979, after which she began to compose in tonal-modal elements—pieces she refers to as "cut-ups"—but non-modernist.

Since 1985, she has been composing *swales* for various instrumental combinations. The composer herself coined the word *swale* as a musical term. The dictionary definition is "a meadow or marsh where a lot of wild things grow together." This aptly describes Anderson's collage-like style. Her catalogue of compositions includes an opera, *Queen Christina*, an oratorio, *Joan*, numerous works for solo instruments and tape, scores for two off Broadway shows, film music, and pieces for various instrumental, vocal and dance ensembles with such colorful titles as *Valid For Life*, *The Praying Mantis and the Bluebird*, *Preparation For The Dominant: Outrunning the Inevitable* and *Peachy Keen-O*. *Belgian Tango* (1993) and *Minnesota Swale* (1995) have been recorded by Opus One. In May 1995, *Trio: Dream in "d"* for violin, cello and piano, and *Network* for piano solo was released on an Italian label. In April 1997, a full evening of her work was performed on the North River Concert Series at Greenwich House, followed in October on the Interpretations series at Merkin Hall. Her *August Swale* was a featured work at the Ninth Annual IAWM Concert of Chamber Music by Women, June 20, 1999, in Washington, DC. The Soho Baroque Opera commissioned an operetta on the book and lyrics of Royce Dendler. Titled *Qoheleth*, for contralto, tenor, harpsichord, percussion and string quartet, it was premiered in 2001. In October of that year at the Flanders Festival (Belgium), the premiere of her *Three Swales* received such accolades as, "an-over-the-top exuberant set of flamboyant pieces in the post Dvořák vein, played . . . with collective virtuosity and much adored by the audience." "Beautiful music with a vengeance!"

2002 saw more European performances with the octet version of *Revel* in April at the Royal Conservatory in Ghent (Belgium), and *Kentucky Swale* with the Orchestra Sinfonica di San Remo (Italy) in July. In the U.S., the University of Kentucky Symphony honored their local composer by playing the same composition to Anderson's hometown audience in Lexington.

In May 2003, her work was celebrated at a women's music festival at Cal State, Sacramento, with *September Swale* for solo piano, with Kathleen Foster Poe. In October, The International Choir Contest of Flanders performed *Precious Memories* and *In the Company of Women*. November brought "Swales and Angels," a concert of Anderson's compositions, performed in Carnegie Hall's Weill Recital Hall featuring the Rubio String Quartet of Belgium, Jessica Marsten, soprano, Joseph Kubera, piano/celesta, Andrew Bolotowsky, flute, Andre Taratiles, harp, David Rozenblatt, percussion, and Darren Campbell, string bass. The program consisted of *January*, *March*, *Pennyroyal*, *Rosemary*—all Swales for string quartet; *New Mexico Swale* for flute, percussion and strings; *Piano Concerto* with strings and percussion, and *The Angel* for soprano, harp, celesta and strings, based on a Hans Christian Anderson tale. It was an extravaganza tribute to the composer. A New World CD, *Swales and Angels*, with most of this music was released in 2004. Her flute solo, *Comment*, was premiered at the "Women's Work" series at Greenwich House Arts, February 2004, as were selections from her cycle *Cat Songs*, which include *Lazy Pussy*, words by Palmer Cox (1840–1924), inspired by Eartha Kitt; *Kilkenny Cats*, Edward Penfield (1866–1925); *Tyger Tyger*, from the famous poem by William Blake (1757–1827); *Hey Diddle Diddle*, from the traditional nursery rhyme with the music emanating from the composer's experience playing improvisational piano for modern dance at the Alvin Ailey American Dance Center; *She Sites A Bird*, a transparent and dramatic Emily Dickinson (1830–1886) poem; and *The Widow and Her Cat*, based on the treatise by Jonathan Swift (1667–1745), of a cat transforming itself from a gentle creature into a fierce beast. Also on the program were works by **Ruth Schönthal**, **Joelle Wallach** and **Jacqueline Fonteyn**. In June, the Chamber Orchestra Kremlin performed *Three Swales* on a concert series premiering contemporary American works in Moscow. Two premieres in 2005 were her renditions of *Killdeer and Chicory*—a reminiscence of her family's farm in Kentucky—at the Roaratorio Festival in Geneva, where she also played pieces from her CD *Peachy Keen-O* (Pogus); and *Jasmine Swale*, a commission of the Jade String Trio, performed at St. Joseph's College, Patchogue, Long Island, NY.

Beth Anderson is active in promoting success for future generations of female composers, serving as treasurer for *New York Women Composers, Inc.*, a not-for-profit corporation of women who support their not-so-recognized sister composers. She also teaches piano at New York's Greenwich House Music School. One of her greatest contributions is—in her later works—helping erase the image that all modern classical music consists of dissonance and noise.

LAURIE ANDERSON, born June 5, 1947, in Chicago, Illinois, received her musical training as a violinist. After moving to New York, she studied at Barnard College (BA, Art History, 1969), followed by an MFA in Sculpture from Columbia in 1972. She became a teacher of art history at City College (CUNY), as well as writing art criticism, exhibiting sound-object sculpture, graphic collages and illustrating books. Her first performance piece was *Automotive* (1972), an outdoor concert for car horns. In 1973 she debuted *The Life and Times of Josef Stalin*, a twelve–hour audio-visual interpretation of his biography. By 1974 she was making her own instruments, notably modifying the violin, culminating in 1977 with the tape-bow violin, consisting of a violin with a tape playback head mounted on the bridge and a bow with pre-recorded lengths of audio tape instead of hair—the performer draws the bow across the head, controlling the speed, intensity, and direction of the playback.

In 1983, she premiered her *United States* at the Brooklyn Academy of Music. Listed as an opera, it was in effect a compilation of everything she had produced up to that date and lasted seven hours—performed over a two-night period. She continued with her performance tours of Europe, and after having her song *O Superman* place number two on the British pop charts, she signed a contract with Warner Brothers and released two recordings, *Science* and *Mister Heartbreak*, which won her a progressive-rock audience. Her popularity as an American performance artist was at its peak in 1986, when she toured internationally with a pop band, appeared in an American Express commercial, and directed *Home of the Brave*, a feature film of one of her performances. By 1992 she returned to a more intimate style, appearing alone or with a few backing musicians. She has continued to enrich her musical and visual resources with the evolving technology, and with each new performance adds different and more advanced computer graphics.

Her *Songs and Stories from Moby Dick* is a late 20th century multi-media opera based on the 19th century classic. It translates, via unique staging, her favorite parts of the book into an electronic universe of images and audioscapes. It was also her debut as a director, for the first time other actors are on stage with her. The work premiered at UCLA Performing Arts, October 20, 1999.

Following the 9/11 attack, she and her band have toured Europe and the Far East with *Happiness*. Her tour schedule through 2005 also includes *Songs for Amelia Earhart*, with venues in the UK, Italy, Austria, Sweden, Belgium, Quebec, and the U.S.

ELINOR ARMER maintains that the most important influences in her composing life were early training, parental encouragement, and the Women's Movement of the 1970s and '80s. Born in Oakland, California, October 6, 1940, she grew up in Davis. Piano began at eight, and within a year she had conquered four-part dictation. Her cultured and creative parents supported her musical education, her choice of career, and applauded her successes. Mills College brought piano with Alexander Liberman, and composition with **Darius Milhaud** and Leon Kirchner. Graduate studies at UC Berkeley included theory, composition and analysis, culminating with an MA in composition from California State University, San Francisco (1972).

After graduation, Armer taught piano and theory, at the same time concertizing and composing. Family and societal expectations prevented full pursuit of a composing career. It was in her forties, upon involvement in the Women's Movement, that her career gained momentum. During the 1980s, she received Fellowships to the MacDowell Colony, Charles Ives Center for American Music, and Yaddo (NY). She has received eight Meet the Composer grants since 1986, and yearly ASCAP Awards from 1979.

Besides composing, she has continued her private teaching, was an instructor in piano, theory and composition at the San Francisco Conservatory preparatory department (1969–75), and has been professor of musicianship, harmony, counterpoint, orchestration and composition at the San Francisco Conservatory since 1976, during which time she was the chair of the composition department (1985–96).

Her speaking and guest composer positions include the University of Oregon, Music From the Pacific Rim Festival (Santa Cruz, California), Third International Harp Congress (Tacoma, Washington), and in Georgia, La Grange College, and the Decatur Music Festival.

In 2000, the San Francisco Conservatory celebrated her sixtieth birthday with a concert of her music, and awarded her the George Sarlo Award for Excellence in Teaching (2003).

Armer is the adoptive mother of son Kellon, born September 14, 1992, and daughter Hope, born March 30, 1995, who, at seventeen months, made the journey by herself from Addis Abbaba, Ethiopia, via Frankfurt, to Oakland. While raising her children is keeping Elinor active, her composing continues apace with a 2005 Piano Concerto for soloist Lois Brandwynne.

Elizabeth Bell

ELIZABETH BELL, born December 1, 1928 in Cincinnati, Ohio, studied piano throughout her childhood and teens, and was taken to children's concerts where she learned to love classical music. She majored in music at Wellesley College, graduating as a Wellesley Scholar, after which came a degree in composition from Juilliard. She put aside her career for marriage and raising a family, then resumed composing in the late 1960s, writing for orchestra, chamber groups, solo instruments, and voice, with commissions from numerous musicians and performing groups, as well as the New York State Council for the Arts. She has received many grants from Meet the Composer, plus prizes in the Farmington (Utah) Composition Competition and the Delius Contest, among others. Her works have been recorded on the CRS, Classic Masters, Vienna Modern Masters and North/South Records labels, the latter featuring *Variations and Interludes* with pianist Max Lifchitz, released in 1998. *Soliloquy for Solo Cello*, with John Littrell, was part of the Fourth Festival of Women Composers at Indiana University of Pennsylvania (1996). In May 1998, Elena Ivaniva played Bell's *Night Music* in Moscow. June saw *Andromeda* for piano, string orchestra and percussion receive its world premiere in Lvov, Ukraine, with Ocsana Rapita as soloist. Later that month, *Second Sonata for Piano* was performed by pianist Anna Stoytcheva in Sofia, Bulgaria.

In December 1999, Master Musicians Collective (MMC) released *The Music of Elizabeth Bell*, featuring her piano concerto *Andromeda* and *Symphony #1*, performed by the Seattle Symphony, **Gerard Schwarz** conducting; plus her *String Quartet* with the Moyzes Quartet, and *Perne in a Gyre* for clarinet and piano with string trio by the Slovak Chamber Players.

In May 1998, a retrospective concert of Bell's music at Greenwich House Music School included *Loss-Songs* for soprano and piano, *Duovarios, Millennieum, Soliloquy for Solo Cello*, and the sonata for violin and piano *Les Neiges d'Antan*. *Spectra*, which won the grand prize at the 1996 Utah Composers' Competition, was performed by Gerard Schwarz and the New York Chamber Orchestra, March 2000. The same month, *Perne in a Gyre* was heard at the American Composers' Alliance program in New York.

Bell is one of the founders and officers of New York Women Composers, as well as a member of BMI and the American Composers Alliance. She and supportive husband, Robert Friou, have four children and two grandchildren. Her oldest son, Stephen David Drake, is a cellist in the Nashville Symphony.

Celebrating Elizabeth's seventy-fifth birthday in 2003 were two retrospective concerts: at Christ and St. Steven's Church, NYC; and the inaugural concert of the twenty-fourth season of North/South Consonance, featuring the North/South String Quartet performing chamber works written between 1957–91.

NATASHA BOGOJEVICH, born January 1, 1966, in the former Yugoslavia, is making a name for herself in the Chicago area. (See Chapter 5 Part B.)

Victoria Bond

VICTORIA BOND, born May 6, 1945, in Los Angeles into a family of musicians, began improvising at the piano as soon as she was able to reach the keyboard. Her mother, **Jane Courtland** (see **Welton**, Women in Business), then a concert pianist, recognized and encouraged her daughter's talents, teaching her basic theory and harmony and helping to notate her improvisations. Victoria began formal training at the Mannes School of Music, studying theory, harmony, piano and chamber music. Further piano studies were with the distinguished **Nadia Reisenberg** (1904–83), becoming her youngest pupil. She often performed in concert with her mother or accompanied her father, whose dual careers included physician and opera singer.

Moving to California, she studied composition at USC with Swedish-born composer **Ingolf Dahl** (1912–70). During this time, a concert of her music was given at the Los Angeles Natural History Museum and broadcast over radio station KFAC (now KMZT). While in Los Angeles, she studied with **Paul Glass** (*b* 1937), becoming his protégée and assisting with the orchestration and arranging of film scores at Universal and Metromedia studios. Her graduate studies were at Juilliard with celebrated composers **Roger Sessions**

(1896–1985) and **Vincent Persichetti** (1915–85), and conductors **Jean Morel** (1903–75), **Sixten Ehrling** (1918–2005) and **Herbert von Karajan** (1908–89).

Another Pioneer

Like Marin Alsop, Victoria Bond is credited with a series of firsts. She was the first woman awarded a doctorate in Conducting at Juilliard; the first woman appointed Exxon/Arts Endowment Conductor with a major orchestra, the Pittsburgh Symphony—working with **André Previn**; and the first woman to receive a conducting grant from the National Institute for Music Theater to work at the New York City Opera.

In 1977, she was commissioned by the Pennsylvania Ballet to create a full-length work with choreographer Lynne Taylor-Corbett. Entitled *Equinox*, it became the centerpiece in that company's repertory, performed extensively throughout America. The two women collaborated on three other commissioned ballets: *Other Selves* (Jacob's Pillow Dance Festival, Lenox, Massachusetts, 1979), *Sandburg Suite* (performed at the historic White Barn Theater, Connecticut, 1980), and *Great Galloping Gottschalk* (American Ballet Theater, 1981).

During a residency at Fairmont College, West Virginia, another commission, *Tarot*, for chorus and percussion orchestra, was presented in a week of concerts devoted to Bond's music. Her song cycles *From An Antique Land* and *Peter Quince at the Clavier* were premiered at the 92nd Street Y in Manhattan. On July 4, 1986, she conducted the Houston Symphony as part of the state's Sesquicentennial celebration and premiered her fanfare-overture, *Ringing*, commissioned for the occasion.

Her next appointment was music director of the Empire State Youth Orchestra. During her tenure the orchestra, together with the Empire State Institute for the Performing Arts, commissioned her to write two works for young audiences: *The Frog Prince*,[43] (1984) and *What's the Point of Counterpoint* (1985), both written for TV personality Bob McGrath who recorded and toured both throughout America.

Woman of Virginia

Bond became music director of the Roanoke Symphony Orchestra in 1986 and artistic director of Opera Roanoke in 1989. More commissions included *Everyone is Good for Something*, a music theater work from Louisville's STAGE ONE. Its success prompted the company to commission a second work entitled *Gulliver*, based on Jonathan Swift's 1726 classic satire, *Gulliver's Travels*, which was given a 1988 workshop performance in Louisville and became the basis for Bond's opera, *Travels*, premiered with Opera Roanoke, May 1995.

A Fulfilling Duality

The composer's love for Irish author James Joyce's *Ulysses* was the impetus to write a forty-five-minute monodrama, *Molly ManyBloom*, using the text of the *Molly Bloom* portion of James Joyce's *Ulysses* for soprano and string quartet. Commissioned and premiered by L'Ensemble in Albany, New York, 1990, it was brought to New York City and performed as the final work in "Bloomsday" at Symphony Space, and broadcast over radio station WNYC. A 1993 Women's Philharmonic commission produced *Urban Bird*, a concerto for alto saxophone and orchestra. The composer conducted the premiere in San Francisco with **Cynthia Sikes** as soloist, and performed it the following year with the Roanoke Symphony. 1997 saw an Ann Arbor, Michigan, premiere. A 1994 Audubon Quartet commission resulted in a string quartet, *Dreams of Flying*. The joint commission, *Thinking Like a Mountain*, an orchestral work written for the opening of Virginia's Explore Park, an environmental theme park, is based on an essay by noted environmentalist Aldo Leopold, and has been performed by the Billings (Montana)

---

43. The composer was narrator at a performance in Philadelphia, March 1996.

Symphony, Elgin (Illinois) Symphony, Erie Philharmonic (1995), and Shanghai Symphony of China, where it was recorded in September 1994, with Bond as guest conductor. A Blue Ridge Public Television documentary based on the work gave it national exposure. It is recorded on the Protone label. A CD of her chamber works was released in 1996. Her Piano Concerto, *Black Light*, was premiered in Czechoslovakia in 1997 with Kirk Trevor conducting the Martinů Philharmonic, Paul Barnes soloist. Her First Symphony (1997) is a work each of whose four movements can be performed as individual compositions.

Profiled in the *New York Times* and the *Wall Street Journal*, Victoria Bond was voted Virginia's Woman of the Year (1990, 1991) and awarded an honorary doctorate from Washington and Lee University (1993). After eight acclaimed seasons, Bond left Roanoke in June 1995 to devote more time to composition, recording and guest conducting internationally.

In 1997, she was appointed artistic advisor and principal guest conductor of China's Wuhan Symphony Orchestra. She conducted *La Bohème* in the 1998 season with Opera Carolina in Charlotte, returning in 1999 for *Madama Butterfly*. April 1999 marked the inauguration of her "Cutting Edge Concerts," a chamber series at the Greenwich House Music School in New York, devoted to performing the works of living composers. As artistic director for the Harrisburg Opera in Pennsylvania, in 1999 she conducted *Faust* and *The Abduction from the Seraglio*, and *La traviata*, May 2000.

Her own second opera, *Mrs. Satan*, with librettist Hilary Bell, is based on a real figure in American history, Victoria Woodhull, the first woman to run for president at a time when women did not even have the vote! She was also the first woman stockbroker—it was she who guided Cornelius Vanderbilt into his successes—and the first woman to run a newspaper. (Her weekly brought out the first publication of Karl Marx' *Communist Manifesto* in the U.S.) She ran against Ulysses Grant in 1873. Vilified by the press, political cartoonist Thomas dubbed her "Mrs. Satan," which gave Bond the title for her opera. A workshop version was produced in New York by the Center for Contemporary Opera, April 27, 2000. May 2001 brought performances of excerpts by New York City Opera as part of their series "Showcasing American Composers" with Bond conducting the NYCO Orchestra and soloists. May 2001 also found Bond directing Harrisburg Opera's production of *Marriage of Figaro*. In June, *Molly ManyBloom* was part of the thirtieth *Bloomsday on Broadway* event. A performance in September 2002, in the "Festival of Women's Voices," was described as "stunning"!

2002 was a busy year. In June, a grant from Brahmshaus enabled Bond to live three weeks at the residence in Baden-Baden (Germany) where Johannes Brahms spent many a creative summer. She used the time to begin her second piano concerto, *Ancient Keys*, commissioned by the Indianapolis Chamber Orchestra and pianist Paul Barnes. This was premiered November 4 and recorded by the Slovak Radio Orchestra on November 22 in Bratislava (Slovakia). July found Victoria as composer-in-residence at the Chamber Music Conference and Composers' Forum of the East in Bennington, Vermont, where the commissioned *Elevator Music* was premiered. Other performances included the completed *Mrs. Satan*, performed in concert August 29 at the John Drew Theater, East Hampton, New York, with full cast and chorus, conducted by the composer. In October, Bond conducted *The Barber of Seville* with Harrisburg Opera.

2003 saw a reading of *Molly ManyBloom* with Met soprano Carol Meyer and the Clearstone Quartet. June brought the release of *Yes* on the Albany label, featuring *Molly ManyBloom*, and *A Modest Proposal*, to the text of the Jonathan Swift essay, performed by tenor Paul Sperry and the Cleveland Chamber Symphony conducted by Bond. Other airings were *Power Play*, commissioned by the contemporary music ensemble Sequitur; *My Grandfather's Balalaika*, an Elements String Quartet commission; *Breath*, for flute and guitar; and her string quartet, *Dreams of Flying*, performed at the Music Festival of the Hamptons (NY).

May 14, Bond conducted a concert with **Ray Charles** (1931–2004) and the Dallas Symphony Orchestra. In June, she was invited to teach at the Conductor's Institute in South Carolina. Summer activities concluded with an August performance of *Molly ManyBloom* at East Hampton's John Drew Theater.

In 2004, Cutting Edge Concerts continued their popular momentum. May featured the Center for Contemporary Opera's workshop presentation of *A More Perfect Union,* an imaginative dance opera about the Constitution, with music by Bond and a satirical libretto by Isaiah Sheffer.

The 2005 season of Cutting Edge Concerts, moderated and hosted by Bond, included her music and a number of other composers. Also appearing was the Duo Gelland from Sweden, performing works by Swedish composers Carl-Axel Hall, Kerstin Jeppsson, Erik Forare. In April, Renée Jolles, violin, and Susan Jolles, harp, premiered her *Sacred Sisters,* commissioned by The American Society for Jewish Music, and performed at the Center for Jewish History in NYC. Another premiere was *Binary,* for two pianos, a commission from Pianofest at East Hampton, where she was composer-in-residence. During May and June, she conducted Chamber Opera Chicago in Menotti's *The Medium* and *The Telephone,* with a return engagement in 2006 for *The Consul.*

Commissions for 2007 include a triple concerto for the Aurea Trio and the Gettysburg Chamber Orchestra, based on a Civil War theme; and *Pater Patriae,* for narrator and wind ensemble, a collaboration with historian Dr. Myles Lee, using the words of George Washington. This musical portrait, inspired by Aaron Copland's *Lincoln Portrait,* will premiere at Mount Vernon.

(Author's note: On July 13, 2003, I attended the nintieth birthday celebration in Los Angeles of Victoria's mother, **Jane Welton,** retired president of Protone Records. It was lovely to see both ladies again, the last occasion having been the 1993 premiere of *Urban Bird* in San Francisco. Jane died May 24, 2005.)

WENDY CARLOS, born Walter, November 14, 1939, in Pawtucket, Rhode Island, worked with Ron Nelson at Brown University (BA, 1962), then studied composition with electronic pioneers **Otto Luening** (1900–96), **Vladimir Ussachevsky** (1911–90), and **Jack Beeson** (1921–76) at Columbia (MA, 1965). The collaboration with another pioneer electronic experimenter, **Robert Moog** (1934–2005), began in 1964 when Carlos, helping modify and perfect the Moog synthesizer, developed a method of creating electronic versions of orchestral sounds. History was made with the sale of over a million albums of the 1968 LP recording *Switched On Bach,* which established the synthesizer as a musical instrument and won three Grammys.

In 1971, at the age of thirty-two, after realizing that he was a woman trapped in a man's body, Walter underwent a highly publicized surgical procedure and become Wendy.

Carlos' virtuosity and creativity as an arranger is heard in all her compositions. Examples are *Timesteps* (1970); the film score of Stanley Kubrick's *A Clockwork Orange,* which introduced *vocorders* for synthesized singing, long before space movies featured synthetic voices; and for the same director, the horror music for his classic, *The Shining* (1980); as well as the merging of orchestral and synthesizer sounds achieved for the Disney sci-fi film, *TRON* (1982).

With advanced technology, she has not only produced near perfect replicas of instrumental voices, but worked with digital synthesis discovering early the limitless possibilities of programming synthesizer codes into a computer. Her first excursions into this realm were *Cosmological Impressions* and *Digital Moonscapes* (1984), which introduced the "LSI Philharmonic," a digital replica of orchestral timbres. In 1987 came eight more pieces on a disk entitled *Beauty in the Beast,* which combined old world cultures with new ideas. As a sequel to her bestseller, in 1992 she used the latest computer technology in the CD boxed set, *Switched-on Bach 2000.* Later works include *Tales of Heaven and Hell,* a musical dramatic work, and the score for the British anti-war film *Woundings.* A remastering of most of her back catalogue on East Side Digital, including a boxed set of her pioneering Bach & Baroque albums, were released in 1999. Besides her roles as lecturer and computer engineering consultant, Wendy is a dedicated astronomer who has followed eclipses around the world resulting in breathtaking photographs.

ANDREA CLEARFIELD was born in Philadelphia on August 29, 1960, to a pianist mother and clarinetist father. By age six she was studying piano. Her BA with piano concentration is from Muhlenberg College (1982), her MM in piano performance from Philadelphia College of the Performing Arts (1984), and her DMA in Composition from Temple University (2000). Her dissertation, *Women of Valor,* is an hour long oratorio for soprano, mezzo, narrator and orchestra, based on women in the Old Testament from Sarah to Esther, as seen from the perspective of ten contemporary women poets. Premiered April 16, 2000, by the Los Angeles Jewish Symphony, directed by **Noreen Green**, portions of the work were broadcast on NPR's "All Things Considered." Since then, it has seen many performances both with orchestra and chamber ensemble. In March 2004, Green programmed excerpts in a concert of women composers entitled "Kolot Hanasheem" (Voices of Women).

Since 1986, Clearfield has been an Associate on the Piano Faculty at the Sarasota (Florida) Music Festival. The same year, she joined the Music Faculty of her alma mater, now known as The University of the Arts, and became founder/host/producer of the SALON Performance Series, bringing together musicians and audiences in her home in a contemporary version of the 19th century musical salon. The series, which features classical, contemporary, jazz, and electronic music, has become so popular that in its seventeenth year, 2004, Clearfield had to find a larger venue. Another outlet for the composer's talents has been as pianist in the Relâche Ensemble for Contemporary Music since 2001.

Clearfield was the 1996 winner of the IAWM "Search for New Music," the Nancy Van De Vate Prize for Orchestral Music and, in 1998, received an Award from the American Composers Forum for Outstanding Achievement. The continuing successes of her sxity-plus compositions include works for instrumental and vocal soloists, chamber ensembles, chorus, orchestra and dance. Recorded in Oslo, Norway, *Songs of the Wolf* for horn and piano, was released on Crystal Records (1996), with hornist **Frøydis Ree Wekre** (see Brass) and the composer at the keyboard. A 2004 Norwegian CD featured *Into The Falcon's Eye*, a trio for two horns and piano with Clearfield, Wekre and Lisa Ford, principal horn of the Göteborg Orchestra of Sweden and a former pupil of Wekre. Another 2004 premiere was the cantata, *The Long Bright*, for soprano, girls' chorus and orchestra, commissioned by David Wolman, and based on ten of his poems in memory of his wife, Anni Baker, and her five-year battle with breast cancer. Baker, a former opera and Broadway singer, was a strong supporter of the arts in the Philadelphia area. The cantata featured Hila Plitmann, soprano, the Temple University Music Preparatory Children's Choir and Orchestra and was premiered at the new Kimmel Center, home of the Philadelphia Orchestra. Oboist Andrea Gullickson commissioned and soloed in *Unremembered Wings*, for oboe and piano, also a 2004 release on Crystal Records. Commissioned by the Philadelphia Classical Symphony, an April 2005 premiere was a marimba concerto for Angela Zator Nelson, a member of the Philadelphia Orchestra.

EMMA LOU DIEMER, born November 24, 1927, in Kansas City, Missouri, was a child prodigy who by age thirteen had written several piano concertos. Her BM (1949), and MM (1950), are from Yale, where she studied composition with **Paul Hindemith** (1895–1963). A Fulbright Scholarship took her to the Royal Conservatory in Brussels (1952–53) and the Berkshire Music Center at Tanglewood (1954–1955) under **Ernst Toch** (1887–1964) and **Roger Sessions**. 1960 marked her PhD from Eastman where one of her teachers was **Howard Hanson** (1896–1981), and one of her classmates, **Mary Jeanne van Appledorn**, who became a lifelong friend.

Diemer was composer-in-residence in Arlington, Virginia (1959–61), and composer-consultant to the Baltimore public schools (1964–65) before serving as professor of theory and composition at the University of Maryland (1965–70), and the University of California, Santa Barbara (1971–91). She was composer-in-residence (1990–92) with the Santa Barbara Symphony, which has premiered several of her works including, in 1996, the *Santa Barbara Overture*, conducted by the orchestra's music director (1994–2006) **Gisèle Ben-Dor**, and recorded by the London Symphony under Llewellyn Jones on the Master Musicians Collective (MMC) label. Of her over 100 works, both choral and instrumental, several use twelve-note serial technique. Catching the fever of electronic music in the early 1970s, one of her most avant-garde piano compositions, *Homage to Cowell, Cage, Crumb and Czerny* (1981), features note clusters and on-the-strings playing. By the '90s, her works veered toward the neo-classical and neo-romantic using free tonality.

In July 1995, her *Concerto in One Movement for Piano* was recorded by the Czech Radio National Symphony. This work made the finals in the 1992 Friedheim Awards in Orchestral Music and was performed at Kennedy

Center by the National Symphony Orchestra. *Concerto in One Movement for Marimba* (1991), was commissioned by The Women's Philharmonic and premiered in 1991. *Fantasy for Piano*, a 1994 commission by Karen Scoville of Los Angeles, was premiered by her at Merkin Hall in New York. *Kyrie* (mixed chorus, piano four-hands, and organ), was commissioned and premiered in 1993; *Catchaturian Toccata*, for flute and piano, premiered in 1995. In January 1996, her organ concerto, *Alaska*, received its first performance by the Arctic Chamber Orchestra at the University of Alaska-Fairbanks, with the composer as featured soloist. She was guest composer at the California State University (Stanislaus) Hildegard Festival of Women in the Arts, March 1999, and at the Lawrence University Festival of Contemporary Piano Music the same year. At the Berlin (Germany) Botanical Gardens, October 2000, mezzo-soprano Suzanne Summerville, accompanied by pianist Raminta Lampsatis, introduced *Frisch Gesungen*. Diemer's *Mass* (*Kyrie, Gloria, Credo, Sanctus* and *Agnus Dei*) for choir, two pianos and percussion, was premiered by the Ojai (California) Camerata under William Wagner in November 2000 at the Ojai First Presbyterian Church.

Duo, for cello and piano, was presented at the Indiana University of Pennsylvania Festival of Women Composers, March 2001, with Ellen Grolman Schlegel and Joan Dixon Broyles. The May 2001 "Mostly Tchaikovsky" concerts at the Berlin Botanical Gardens, opened with Diemer's *Homage to Tchaikovsky*, an original commission from the Santa Barbara Symphony. Other 21st century commissions include *Concerto in One Movement*, for organ and orchestra, recorded by **Marilyn Mason** and the Czech National Symphony (Albany Records, 2004); *Chumash Dance Celebration* for the Santa Barbara Symphony's 2004 Young Peoples Concerts; and *Songs for the Earth*, a San Francisco Choral Society commission, premiered 2005. Besides composing, Diemer is a keyboard performer on piano, organ, harpsichord and synthesizer. Although piano is her principal instrument, she has been a church organist since age thirteen, and written many hymns and much church music. Among her awards are those from the Ford Foundation, National Federation of Music Clubs, NEA, AGO and ASCAP. Her recordings include *Fantasy*, Leanne Rees, piano; *Suite of Homages*, Halle State Philharmonic Orchestra, Rudolph Werthen, conductor (Contemporary Record Society); and *Variations on "Rendez à Dieu"* and *Variations on "Abide with Me,"* Joan Dixon Broyles, organ (RBW Record Co.).

Emma Lou is convinced that a composer needs to be a practicing musician and in constant need of challenge in order to write a variety of music for all levels of performers. Therefore, to stimulate appreciation of the arts, she writes for both amateur and professional.

LORI DOBBINS, born May 10, 1958, in Aberdeen, Maryland, grew up in California, took piano lessons and sang in choirs during her childhood, but did not begin serious music studies until her college years at San Jose State University where she received her BA. Her MFA from the California Institute of the Arts came in 1982, studying composition with **Mel Powell** (*b* 1923), who was the most significant influence on her work, introducing her to contemporary classical music and jazz idioms. Her PhD is from UC Berkeley, where her teachers included **Gunther Schuller** (*b* 1925), known for his revival of ragtime, and Andrew Imbrie (*b* 1921).

Her fellowships and honors include the Lili Boulanger Award from the National Women Composers Resource Center, 1992; the Goddard Lieberson Fellowship from the American Academy and Institute of Arts and Letters, 1989; ASCAP Special Award for Composition, 1988–97; first (1989) and second (1988) prizes in the International League of Women Composers Composition Contest; grants from Meet the Composer, 1990, 1992, 1993; and several awards from UC Berkeley for her work in composition. She was in residence at the Atlantic Center for the Arts in 1995, and the MacDowell Colony in the summers of 1995 and 1996, and the fall of 2000. In 1996, she was a fellow at the August Composers Conference in Wellesley, Massachusetts, where her Violin Concerto was premiered.

With commissions from the Koussevitzky Foundation in the Library of Congress (1988), the St. Paul Chamber Orchestra (1989), the Fromm Foundation (1991), and Pro Arte Chamber Orchestra of Boston (1996), her works have been played by the St. Paul Chamber Orchestra, Collage, New Music Consort, and San Francisco Contemporary Music Players, among others. Her composition for chamber orchestra, *Fire and Ice*, was released on the Vienna Modern Masters label. *Fantasy* for solo violin was composed in 1992, *All for One* for percussion solo, in 1994. *All Souls* for soprano and string quartet received its premiere at Lafayette College with the New Music Consort, Susan Narucki, soloist. *Percussion Quartet* was performed by the New Jersey Percussion Ensemble at the Piccolo Spoleto Festival in Charleston, South Carolina, May 1995. In 2004, the New England Conservatory Percussion Ensemble premiered her Percussion Quintet.

Dobbins' music has been described as "an intelligent exploration of a commanding musical palette."

DEBORAH DRATTELL was born in Brooklyn, New York, December 27, 1956. She began violin at seven in a public school string program for the gifted. She started composing at eighteen, while continuing violin at Brooklyn College, from which she graduated in 1976. Her PhD is from the University of Chicago, where she studied composition with **Ralph Shapey** (1921–2002). She was associate professor of composition and theory at Tulane University (1981–90), as well as music director of the First Monday Contemporary Chamber Ensemble and the *Vivace* Festival in New Orleans. Other positions include artistic director of the Bryant Park Young Performers Concert Series, New York Historical Society Series, Minerva World Premiere Chamber Music Series, director of the Chamber Music Society of Lincoln Center's Young Performers Series, and composer-in-residence of the Denver Symphony. While there, she wrote *Sorrow is Not for Melancholy* for string orchestra, the orchestral suite *Lilith*, a Meet the Composer commission premiered by the New York Philharmonic, *Fire Dances* commissioned by clarinetist David Shifrin, *The Fire Within*, a flute concerto for Ransom Wilson and *Syzygy*, for the New Orleans Symphony—all on a '95 Delos CD with the Seattle Symphony under Gerard Schwarz.

Other compositions are a saxophone concerto for **Cynthia Sikes**, a double violin concerto for **Gil Shaham** and his wife, **Adele Anthony**, works for flutist **Eugenia Zukerman** and the Chamber Music Society of Lincoln Center, as well as the Essex, Brentano and Chester String Quartets.

A New Voice in Opera

From 1998–2001, Drattell was composer-in-residence at New York City Opera, where she inaugurated the annual Showcasing American Composers. In August 1999, Glimmerglass Opera (upstate New York) premiered *The Festival of Regrets*, with **Lauren Flanigan**, one of three one-act operas under the title *Central Park*. Reviewers called it the strongest of the three with its "klezmer-favored score" and "heart-on-sleeve wisecracks" by librettist **Wendy Wasserstein** (1950–2006) recipient of a Guggenheim Fellowship, Pulitzer Prize and New York Drama Critics' Circle, Tony and Emmy Awards. Other collaborations with Lauren Flanigan include *Letters Home*, based on Sylvia Plath's poetry, *Eishes Chayll*, from an ode to a Jewish woman which comprises the last twenty-two verses of Proverbs, and *The Lost Lover*, premiered in 2000 by the New York Chamber Symphony with Gerard Schwarz, an early champion of the composer.

Her first full-length opera, *Lilith*, with libretto by David Cohen, after being heard in concert form at Glimmerglass (1998), was stage produced at NYCO (2001). Dealing with the biblical figure of Adam's first wife, before Eve, it played to sold-out houses. *Marina*, with libretto by Annie Finch, was a 2003 American Opera Projects premiere at the Off Broadway D.R.2 Theater. The first work of a trilogy, *Three Mothers*, is based on the life of Marina Tsvetaeva (1892–1941), a feminist Russian poet, exiled in the 1920s and '30s for her political views. Returning to the Soviet Union, she was ostracized by the literary community and committed suicide. *Nicholas and Alexandra*, with libretto by Nicholas Von Hoffman, was a commission from Los Angeles Opera that premiered in September 2003, with Rodney Gilfry, Nancy Gustafson, and **Plácido Domingo** as Rasputin, conducted by Mstislav Rostropovich. A documentary was made of the process of this creation. The opera *Alma Mahler* (2004), focuses on her life after the death of her husband Gustav in 1911, and her three year liaison with Austrian avant-garde artist/author Oskar Kokoschka (1886–1980). A comic character opera, *Best Friends*, a modern satire on New York society and the arts, another collaboration with the late Wendy Wasserstein, was scheduled for a summer 2005 premiere at the Intiman Theater in Seattle.

Drattell's honors include commissions from the Fromm Foundation, Concert Artists Guild and the New Orleans Symphony; first prize from the International Women's Brass Conference; fellowships from Vermont Composers, and Leonard Bernstein in Composition at Tanglewood; plus grants from the NEA, Meet the Composer, American Music Center, Louisiana Arts Council and several ASCAP Awards.

Deborah was married, December 1988, to gastroenterologist Dr. Yacov Stollman. Their four children are Gabrielle, born September 28, 1989, Isaac, August 27, 1991, Leila, March 17, 1994 and Este, April 29, 1996. The family lives in an old Victorian house in Brooklyn.

Pozzi Escot

American composer, theorist, author and professor, of French (Huguenot) and Moroccan-Jewish descent, **POZZI ESCOT** was born October 1, 1933, in Lima, Peru, the fifth of six children of French scientist-diplomat, Dr. M. Pozzi-Escot. The family moved to Europe, but returned to Lima during WWII. Pozzi studied mathematics at San Marcos University, and composition under Belgian-born composer André Sas at his Music Academy in Lima (1949–53). Her composition, *Little Symphony* (1953), was performed by the Peruvian National Symphony. In 1956, at the age of twenty-three, she was named Laureate Composer of Peru. She emigrated to America in 1953 and became a U.S. citizen in 1963. She attended Juilliard (BS 1956; MS 1957) studying with **William Bergsma** (1921–94) and **Vincent Persichetti**, then went to Germany for composition with Philipp Jarnach at the Hamburg Hochschule für Musik. Her four years there (1957–61) were affected by the recent events of World War II. *Trilogy for the Six Million: Lamentus, Cristhos*, and *Visione* (1962–64) was written as a tribute to the six million martyrs of the concentration camps, Treblinka, Dachau, Mauthausen, Buchenwald, Auschwitz and Bergen-Belsen. She lectured in Europe, then returned to teach theory and composition at the New England Conservatory (1964–67, 1980–81). She continues on the faculty of their graduate program.

In 1963, Escot was one of two honored by the Composers' Forum of New York. Her orchestral work *Sands* (1965), first performed by the New York Philharmonic in 1975, commanded considerable attention. Scored for seventeen violins, nine basses, five saxophones, electric guitar, and four bass drums, it was written on a commission from the government of Venezuela for the 400th anniversary of the city of Caracas, and premiered by the National Symphony of Venezuela, May 1966. In 1974, Escot was chosen as one of ten American composers to appear on the National Television of Belgrade, Yugoslavia. *Cristhos*, from *Trilogy*, was used as the basis of the film *Razapeti*, which won first prize and was presented at the Prix Italia International Festival of Florence the same year. In 1975, with a Marshall Plan fellowship, she was named one of the five most remarkable women composers of the 20th century, and her Fifth Symphony was performed by the New York Philharmonic under the direction of **Sarah Caldwell** (the other composers were **Grazyna Bacewicz**, **Ruth Crawford**, **Thea Musgrave** and **Lili Boulanger**).

Escot has written mainly for orchestra (six symphonies), chamber ensembles and piano. Her rigorous pre-compositional mathematical planning, sometimes computer-assisted, results in highly structured forms. As a commentator on contemporary music, she contributes to theory journals and, in 1980, co-founded and became editor-in-chief of *Sonus: Journal of Investigation into Global Musical Possibilities*. With husband/composer Robert Cogan, she wrote *Sonic Design: The Nature of Sound and Music* (1976), which proposed analytic concepts and principles applicable to the understanding of music from cultures and historical periods. This was translated into Japanese in 2003 by Professor Takashi Koto.

In 1991, Escot became president of the International Society of Hildegard von Bingen Studies. Other honors include MacDowell Colony and Radcliffe Institute fellowships; Ford Foundation grant; Carnegie-Mellon University Composers Forum; First International Avant-Garde Festivals of Madrid and Rio de Janeiro; inauguration of IRCAM in Paris; guest conductor at Tanglewood; guest lecturer on Non-Linearity in Germany; keynote speaker at the Music and Gender Conference 1991, King's College, London; and Guest Composer and Lecturer at the Gubbio International Festival and Societa Italiana di Analisi Musica. An Outstanding Educator of America, during the spring of 1999 she was composer-in-residence at Rice University (Texas) and Grinnell College (Iowa).

Escot's writings include numerous articles on Hildegard von Bingen, including "Hildegard's Christianity: An Assimilation of Pagan and Ancient Classical Traditions" and "The Mathematical Mean as Symbol of Hildegard's Universal Thought." The literature on the renowned abbess was further enriched by the 1999 publication of her book, *Oh How Wondrous: Hildegard von Bingen, Ten Essays: Mathematical Models in Music*. Her other 1999 book, *The Poetics of Simple Mathematics in Music*, discusses the underlying mathematical patterns of music from medieval to modern. From May to August 2000, she was in France working with the publishers of the French translation. The same year she was selected for a commission by OTIO (The Gathering/Unification of the Native American Tribes Foundation, Utah) for her Sixth Symphony. On June 6, 2001, she was the keynote speaker for Cube Contemporary Music Ensemble's Eightieth Birthday Tribute to American composer **Ralph Shapey**. He died the following year. Escot's Violin Concerto (2002–2003) was composed in his memory.

A much sought-after lecturer, Escot has been heard at Columbia, Princeton, Harvard, Berkeley, Stanford, as well as the universities of Chicago, Illinois, London, Edinburgh, Nice, Eichstatt, Augsburg, Helsinki, Hamburg, Leuven, Sorbonne, Darmstadt, Dublin Institute of Technology, SIdAM-Milan, IRCAM-Paris, Beijing, Shanghai, Hanyang (China), and Yonsie, Kunitachi and Hiroshima (Japan), which included a concert of her music. 1992, '96 and 2000 found her, with husband Robert Cogan, directing the Talloires International Composers' Conference at the Tufts University European Center in France near the Swiss border. Two major performances in 2000 were her *Jubilation* string quartet at Carnegie Recital Hall in March, and in May, *Visione*, for contrabass, the last of her chamber trilogy, in Tokyo. This piece was also released on CD. In February 2003, she was a speaker at the Library of Congress as part of its fortieth anniversary celebration. March 2004 saw her a headline composer for the University of New Mexico's (Albuquerque) Symposium, and in April she was NYU's First Performance lecturer. The same year selected works were featured at New Music Festivals in Almaty, Kazakhstan and Quito, Ecuador. 2005 brought her participation in the celebration of Milton Babbitt's ninetieth birthday; world premieres of her *Clarinet Concerto*, at Jordan Hall, Boston, commissioned by soloist Michael Norsworthy, and *Aria III* by the New York modern chamber group, Second International Unit; a February residency at Bates College as the Woodrow Wilson Visiting Fellow; Plenary Speaker at the University of Montreal in March; and giving the Convocation Address at Carnegie Mellon University in October. February 2006, had the Second International Unit playing her work in Chicago under the auspices of the Cube Ensemble of the University there; April saw a performance of *Virelai*—a medieval title—at Carnegie Recital Hall, another Second International Unit commission.

Pozzi Escot figures prominently at major contemporary European music events. She has established an important position as a music theorist and is the principal exponent of the relationship between music and mathematics.

Tania French

TANIA GABRIELLE FRENCH was born May 6, 1963, in Alexandria, Virginia, into an artistic family. She and her younger sisters wrote and performed music together—her first musical work came at age four. Her parents formed a children's choir, which included their four girls, and performed in such places as the Kennedy Center and Wolf Trap Farm Park. Deciding against a music conservatory and the competitive atmosphere there, French attended Amherst College for composition and conducting studies. She worked with two Pulitzer Prize-winning composers, Lewis Spratlan at Amherst and Bernard Rands at Aspen. During her senior year, in 1985, she received five commissions for compositions. In 1986, French moved to London, continuing to amass commissions. There she met violinist Clayton Haslop, whom she married October 29, 1989. She has written several works for him, including a concerto.

Amongst instrumentalists and artists who have featured her music are the Angeles String Quartet, and cellists Bion Tsang, Jeffrey Solow, Ronald Leonard, and Alexander Baillie. 1996 saw the world premiere of *Four Illuminations* for oboe and piano trio, commissioned by Allan Vogel, principal oboe of the Los Angeles Chamber Orchestra. Its New York premiere was by the St. Luke's Chamber Ensemble, and was performed in

2002 at Sweden's Bastad Music Festival. This piece and four other works were recorded on Centaur by members of Los Angeles Chamber Orchestra and Los Angeles Piano Trio. Her tone poem, *Inner Voyage*, was performed in an all-woman composers concert by the Marina Del Rey-Westchester Symphony under Frank Fetta, March 1997, with this author as pre-concert lecturer.

Continental Flavors, a Townhall CD by the Haslop/Sanders Duo, features French's *Harbors of Light* and *Three Landscapes* for violin and guitar. The Guitar Foundation of *America's Soundboard Magazine* called these "haunting, evocative, strongly romantic with an impressionistic flavor." Her orchestral *Galactic Voyage*, a semi-finalist in the BBC Master-prize Competition, was performed in the 1999 Plymouth Music Series, an American Composers Forum Orchestra Reading Project in Minneapolis.

The 1999–2000 season brought premieres of *Glissonance* for orchestra, and *Chelsea by the Sea* for violin, cello, and guitar. For their debut concert, January 2001 at the Colburn School in Los Angeles, the New Hollywood String Quartet, of which French's husband is a founding member, commissioned her second string quartet. May 2002 brought a top honors award at the Oregon Bach Festival's "Waging Peace through Singing" for her work, *In Paradisum*, an English translation from the Fauré *Requiem* for mixed chorus and strings. This was a commission from the San Francisco Solano Church in memory of those who lost their lives on September 11, 2001. Her String Quartet No. 2, *Communications*, was taken on tour in North America and Europe by the prestigious Artis Quartet, who gave the European premiere at the Musikverein in Vienna, December 5, 2002. (It was later recorded during a performance by the New Hollywood String Quartet.) *In Paradisum* received a world premiere, May 2003, in the Holy Cross Church, Oberpfaffenhofen, Germany. *Ancient Echoes* for flute, violin, viola, and cello, was performed the same year in Düsseldorf. *Silhouettes at Sunrise* for violin, cello and piano, was featured at the Hildegard Festival, Cal State, Stanislaus, March 2003. A suite based on themes from the film *Vertigo*, featuring the New Hollywood String Quartet, was premiered at the Orange County Performing Arts Center, February 2004.

Of French's subtle style, which taps into spiritual roots, the composer says, "It is inspired from nature and is an expression of the unseen." She also posits that there *can* be differences between male and female composers because it is a more natural process for women to be receptive to these unseen feelings. Several of her works are published by Frank E. Warren Music Service. Her music has been heard on radio broadcasts around the globe.

June 24, 2002, brought the arrival of Tania and Clayton's adorable daughter, Clara, named in honor of Clara Schumann and pianist Clara Haskil.

BARBARA HARBACH is a Renaissance woman living in the new millennium. Born on Valentine's Day, 1946, in Lock Haven, Pennsylvania, she knew she wanted to be a musician from age three. Trained early on keyboard instruments, she is recognized as an outstanding organist and harpsichordist. After growing up near Pennsylvania State University, where she completed an accelerated undergraduate program, she went to Yale to study with organist Charles Krigbaum. She also met her husband to be, Thomas F. George. In 1970, she earned her MMA and got married, after which came study in Germany with Helmut Walcha at the Musikhochschule in Frankfurt. She received her degree in performance in 1971, despite the two factors against her: "First I was an American, and second I was a *woman*. There is a German attitude that women were not supposed to play organs." After her return to the U.S., she earned a DMA in 1981 at Eastman.

"There Are No Women Composers . . . "

Early in the course of her performance tours, Harbach overheard a university musicologist comment that "there have never been any women composers and if there were any, they wouldn't be any good." Challenged, she began gathering evidence to refute this outrageous claim. The result was her book, *Woman Composers for the Harpsichord* (Theodore Presser, 1986). This was followed by a recording, *Music for Solo Harpsichord by 18th Century Women Composers* (Kingdom CD, 1989). Meanwhile, she lectured and was a professor at Nazareth College (New York, 1974–85), Coordinator of Keyboard Studies at SUNY, Buffalo (1985–91) and professor of music at Washington State University, (1991–97).

Penwoman, Performer, Pedagogue, Presser of Print and Platters!

Harbach's research and performance of women's music continued, culminating in 1990 with the co-founding of Vivace Press with Jonathan Yordy. The company focuses on the publication of classical keyboard music by women composers from the 16th century to the present. Of great importance is their journal, *Women of Note Quarterly*, containing reviews of women's music and scholarly profiles of composers, both historical and contemporary. Two recent additions, *Women of Note* cards, feature quotes by women composers, and the production of compact disks under the Hester Park label, as a medium for the exposure of music by under-represented composers, primarily women. The CD label name was inspired by the English composer Maria Hester Park (1760–1813), one of the first women she researched.

The first title from Hester Park was *Sonatas by Elizabeth*, with Harbach as harpsichordist, playing six sonatas by Elisabetta de Gambarini (1731–65) and six sonatas by Elizabeth Hardin (*c* 1770), both English. The second, *Close Your Eyes*, contains songs by jazz and popular women composers. Other releases include *Classical Prodigies*, with keyboard music of Mozart at age eight, and Elizabeth Weichsell Billington, eleven, written in the same period by these (then) child composers. *Summer-shimmer* features music for organ by **Maddalena Lombardini Sirmen**, **Clara Schumann**, **Fanny Mendelssohn**, **Ethel Smyth**, Jeanne Demessieux, **Mary Jeanne van Appledorn**, **Libby Larsen** and Harbach herself, as composer and soloist.

Knowledge Breeds Audiences

The driving force behind these projects is the credo that accessibility is as important as musical appeal to the audience. Harbach's enthusiasm for teaching follows the same theme: "I like to challenge and stimulate students, I like to—although some people think it's a dirty word—entertain them! Making classical music alive for all . . . creates knowledgeable consumers to attend orchestral concerts, recitals and operas."

Barbara's husband was made chancellor of the University of Wisconsin, July 1996. In May 1997, she moved her businesses and career to Wisconsin, joining the faculty at the University's Oshkosh campus as associate professor of mathematics and computing. A scholar, musician, educator and advocate, Barbara Harbach is truly "a woman of note."

SORREL HAYS, born Doris, August 6, 1941, in Memphis, Tennessee, moved to Chattanooga when she was five. The following year, she began studying piano with a woman whom she credits with helping her develop the rhythmic precision that has played an important part in her career. At thirteen, she continued with Harold Cadek, dean of the Cadek Conservatory, and started to earn money accompanying a boys' choir, as well as getting solo and chamber performing jobs. She received her BM from the University of Chattanooga (1963). Fluent in German, and encouraged by her teachers, she went to Munich in 1963 on a McClellan Foundation grant to study at the Hochschule für Musik. Here she earned a piano diploma in 1966. On her return, she obtained her MM from the University of Wisconsin (1968), where her teachers included world-famous pianist **Paul Badura-Skoda** (*b* 1927). After teaching at Cornell College in Iowa, she moved to New York where, while working as a clerk at ASCAP, she wrote short pieces of electronic music and developed recording studio techniques on her own time using the facilities of the Electronic Music Studio at Queens College. These were later published by Peer-Southern.

She began her international career as composer/pianist in 1971 when she won first prize in the Gaudeamus Competition for Interpreters of Contemporary Music in Rotterdam, and toured Europe and America as a performer and advocate of new music. She was invited to celebrate the sixtieth birthday of **John Cage** (1912–92) by performing his *Concerto for Prepared Piano and Orchestra* with the Orchestra at The Hague. She gave a performance of her own music at the Gaudeamus Composers Week in Holland in 1972, with *Hands and Lights* for piano strings and photocell activated flashlights beamed across the interior of the piano.

From ASCAP Clerk to ASCAP Composer

In the 1970s Hays produced the largest piece among her multi-media works, the sculpture-music-dance *Sensivents*, which was well received in the 1976 Lincoln Center Festival. Working over a period of six years, she presented four versions of this. 1976 saw the premiere of *Sunday Nights* for piano. In 1977, she received a $4,000 NEA grant which she used to compose the ballet music, *Uni Suite*. This began a new series of her compositions, scored for solo instruments, string quartets, chamber groups, orchestra, and chorus with such titles as *Sunday Mornings*, *Saturday Evenings*, *Southern Voices* and *Tunings*. The latter, scored for string quartet, violin duo, or chamber combinations, includes a hymn tune written by her grandfather when she was ten years old. *Tunings* received its European premiere at the Frau und Musik Festival in Bonn and Cologne, (then West Germany), November 1980. It was also performed in the first concert of women's music at the Library of Congress.

Giving Women the Air

As assistant chair of the International League of Women Composers (ILWC, 1976–85), Hays produced its radio series, "Expressions" (1980–88), broadcast on 200 American stations, showcasing the work of over 100 women composers. She also directed a series of women's concerts "Meet the Woman Composer" at the New School in New York (1976) with co-director **Beth Anderson**.

Hays' lobbying with ASCAP accomplished the placement of the first woman to sit on their Standard Awards panel, with a resultant rise of the number of women recipients of the awards. She reminisces, "The achievements of 1976–86 were hard-won, and some have been lost again." She made similar successful lobbying efforts with the Rockefeller Foundation, Pulitzer and other male bastions. Her involvement in the feminist and peace movements in the mid-1970s became central to her work as a composer during the 1980s. Many mixed-media compositions, such as the radio drama commissions from Radio Cologne, enabled her to create substantial works in this genre. Her opera, *The Glass Woman* (1989–93), a most ambitious three-hour work, is based on the life of an eccentric Arkansas antiques collector. Another work dedicated to influential women is *90's, A Calendar Bracelet* (1990), a cycle of pieces for midi grand piano and tone generator. *The Clearing Way* for contralto and orchestra is based on Native American rituals for the passing of the spirit of the dead, and cleansing of the dwelling of the departed. Other works include the 1998 two-act opera *Mapping Venus*, with principal text by Gertrude Stein, based on the text-sound Hörspiel, *Dream in Her Mind*, which premiered at West German Radio Cologne in 1995. *Dream in Her Mind* uses an imaginary meeting of Gertrude Stein, Hildegard von Bingen, Simone de Beauvoir, Jessamyn West and others on the planet Venus to explore the landscapes of personal consciousness. The opera features six singers, eleven actors, electronic instrumental sounds, and sound effects incorporating actual radio signals from the planet. Made possible by an NEA grant, *In the Grasses* (1995) is a children's opera in which the boy and girl grow small and have adventures in the "everybodydom" of the grasses. *The Tower* was composed and performed in a *son et lumière* (sound and light) spectacle on the River Rhine at Cologne in 1995 to celebrate the leasing—for ninety-nine years—of its oldest tower, the Baientürm, by the German Feminist Archives. At the July 1996 Copenhagen, Cultural Capital of Europe, Festival, she performed her *Take a Back Country Road* on an interconnected system of a Casio saxophone and midi keyboard with tone generator. The Copenhagen Festival also featured Lyd Lab, a city sound laboratory where Hays lectured and performed her electro-acoustic music. Music representing different cities featured Hays' *The Hub, Metropolis Atlanta*, installed at the site of the Little Mermaid in Copenhagen harbor. Outside Copenhagen, the Rothskilde Media Museum, replete with listening chairs, beamed *Dream in Her Mind*, which became a film video project in 1997. She played another in this series of *Traveling Pieces* March 1997, in Merkin Hall, New York.

Hays has been on the faculties and a guest lecturer at numerous universities in the U.S., and in 1998 was consulting designer and director of the new graduate program in electronic music at Yildiz University, Istanbul. She worked with Turkish composer Ilhan Mimaroglu, and was presented by the Istanbul Yapi Kredi Festival in October 1998 in a concert of her electro-acoustic and piano keyboard music, as well as works by Mimaroglu and Cowell.

A Compact With Cowell

Early in her career, Hays began performing the piano music of **Henry Cowell** (1897–1965) because its distinctly rebellious nature appealed to her. Her own piano style is in the tradition of Cowell and Charles Ives (1874–1954), juxtaposing bombastic tone clusters with serene hymn-like passages. She is now recognized as a specialist in Cowell's music as performer, lecturer and writer. In 1978, she gave the premiere of his *Concerto for Piano and Orchestra*. In January 1997, Townhall Records reissued her landmark recording "Sorrel Doris Hays Plays Henry Cowell" to commemorate Cowell's 100th birthday. Performances of his and her music were presented at Merkin Hall, March 13,1997, for the Henry Cowell's Musical Worlds Festival, and at the Berkeley (California) Cowell and His Legacy Festival, where she premiered *Rocker Parts* for two pianos commissioned by the Festivals. In 1998, she was awarded a New York Foundation for the Arts Fellowship. In 2001, Townhall Records brought out a CD, *Adoration of the Clash*, with music of Cowell, Hays, and **Vivian Fine**.

Queen Bee-ing, The Bee Opera was commissioned by Medicine Show Theater and premiered with twelve performances October–November 2003, with support of the Cary Trust, the American Music Center, the NY State Council on the Arts, and Phaedrus Foundation. The composer was invited to bring her Bee Opera Ensemble to Latvia, April 2005, to perform the work in collaboration with Fortius/Balta Singers of Riga. In March 2004, Sorrel collaborated with Norwegian American soprano Kristin Norderval in "Debushing America," with live electronics and vocals, Hays on synthesizer and electronic saxophone, in concert at the Flea Theater, Roulette Series of Newest Music (New York City).

JENNIFER HIGDON was born in Brooklyn, December 31, 1962, of artistic parents. As early as five she felt the "power of music," as she puts it, but did not do anything about it until age fifteen when she saw a flute in a pawn shop, started teaching herself and eventually followed through with a BM in Flute Performance from Bowling Green (Ohio) State College (1986), an Artists Diploma in composition from Curtis (1988), and an MA and PhD in composition from the University of Philadelphia (1994).

Active as a flutist, conductor and composer, she was named a 1999 Pew Fellow in the Arts and appointed composer-in-residence at the American Composers Forum's Continental Harmony Project. She has also served in this capacity with the Norfolk Chamber Music Festival, Summit Institute, Walden School, and Prism Saxophone Quartet. Other awards have come from the Guggenheim Foundation, American Academy of Arts & Letters, Lee Ettelson Prize from Composers, Inc., International League of Women Composers, University of Delaware New Music Competition, Louisville Orchestra, Cincinnati Symphony's Young Composers Competition and ASCAP. In addition, she has received grants from the NEA, Meet the Composer, and Pennsylvania Council on the Arts. Her work *Shine* was named Best Contemporary Piece of 1996 by *USA Today* in their year-end classical picks.

Higdon's commissions include works for the Philadelphia Orchestra (a Centennial commission), Minnesota Orchestra, Orchestra of St. Luke's, American Composers Orchestra, Oregon Symphony, The Women's Philharmonic, National Flute Association for flutist **Carol Wincenc**, Verdehr Trio, DaVinci String Quartet, Van Cliburn Piano Competition, a work for left hand for Gary Graffman, and music for the all-women Lark String Quartet. Her works have had performances at the White House, Weill, Merkin, Alice Tully, and Carnegie Recital Halls, by such performers as Jeffrey Khaner, Marc-Andre Hamelin, Cassatt and Pacifica String Quartets, and Prism Sax Quartet, American Composers Orchestra, Louisville Orchestra, New England Philharmonic, and Oregon, Cincinnati and Knoxville Symphonies.

She was composer-in-residence at the Yerba Buena Art Center 1999–2000. 2001 brought performances of *Fanfare* by the Minnesota Orchestra and Orchestra of St. Luke's, and a 2002 commission of *Concerto for Orchestra* by the Philadelphia Orchestra under Wolfgang Sawallisch. The Sparx flute and harp duo premiered *Furioso* at the 2004 American Harp Society Conference in Philadelphia. At **Marin Alsop**'s Cabrillo Festival in Santa Cruz, California (August 2004), Higdon was composer-in-residence and her *Concerto for Orchestra* and *blue cathedral* were featured. The Brooklyn Philharmonic, under Michael Christie, commissioned *Dooryard Bloom*, for baritone, on the Walt Whitman text, for their fiftieth anniversary.

Higdon's works have been recorded on over two dozen CDs, on the CRI, Crystal, Centaur, Edition de la Rue Margot, and the Flute Choir Label. 2000 releases included *Deep In The Night* and *Sing, Sing* by the New York Concert Singers, Judith Clurman conducting (New World), plus *My True Love's Hair*, *Imagine*, *A Quiet Moment*, *Voices*, and *wissahickon poeTrees*, on separate discs. *Autumn Reflection* was recorded by Philadelphia Orchestra principal flutist, Jeffrey Khaner. Telarc released *blue cathedral* (2003) and *City Scape* and *Concerto for Orchestra* (2004), both recorded by the Atlanta Symphony under Robert Spano. As a flutist, Higdon is recorded on the Access and I Virtuosi labels, and as a conductor on CRI. She founded Lawdon Press to make her music more accessible.

Jennifer joined the faculty at Curtis in 1994, after having served as a visiting professor in Composition at Bard College.

Katherine Hoover

Born into a non-musical environment December 2, 1937, in Elkins, West Virginia, **KATHERINE HOOVER** and her family moved to Philadelphia when she was two. She began studying piano when she was five and flute in school at ten. Her high school music education was mediocre, so she studied theory and piano on her own, and arranged music for singing groups and shows which she helped to write and direct. Encouraged by her family to pursue academics, she enrolled in a program at the University of Rochester, New York, combining music with other subjects, but transferred to Eastman in her junior year. Studying with Joseph Mariano, she received the prized Performance Certificate in Flute and her bachelor's in music theory in 1959.

From 1959–61, Katherine studied with **William Kincaid**, principal flute of the Philadelphia Orchestra (1921–60), after which she taught flute in the preparatory department at Juilliard until 1967. Composing did not become a serious part of her life until several years after graduation. In 1965 her *Duet For Two Violins* received its first performance. Teaching flute and theory at the Manhattan School of Music (1969–84), she earned a master's in music theory there in 1973, the same year her *Three Carols* were published by Carl Fischer. She wrote a wind quintet *Homage to Bartók*, a *Divertimento* for flute and string trio (1975) and a *Trio for violin, cello and piano* which reached the semi-finals in the first Kennedy Friedheim Competition (1978). In 1979 Hoover was awarded an NEA Composers Fellowship. The years 1978–81 were also spent originating and organizing four Festivals of Women's Music in New York City.

In 1981, she received a commission from the Episcopal Diocese of New York which resulted in her *Psalm 23* being performed by a chorus of 400 voices with orchestra at the Cathedral of St. John the Divine. During the early 1980s, commissions for chamber works produced the *Lyric Trio*, *Qwindtet*, *From the Testament of François Villon* and *Summer Night* for flute, horn and strings which she recorded with the Bournemouth Sinfonietta in England in 1986.

Based on a true story, her *Eleni: A Greek Tragedy* for full orchestra, was given its premiere in February 1987 by the Harrisburg Symphony, the first of many performances by different orchestras throughout the country. Her *Clarinet Concerto*, written for jazz virtuoso Eddie Daniels, premiered in September of the same year with the Santa Fe Symphony. In May 1989, the New Jersey Chamber Music Society premiered her *Quintet (Da Pacem)* for piano and string quartet at Alice Tully Hall in Lincoln Center. In 1989, The Women's Philharmonic commissioned and performed *Two Sketches*. *Kokopell* for solo flute, based on a Hopi Indian legend, won the National Flute Association's 1991 Newly Published Music Competition, an honor that had been awarded to her *Medieval Suite* in 1987. The Vinland Duo premiered *Sonata for Oboe and Piano* in Carnegie's Weill Recital Hall in April 1991, and in

May, her *Double Concerto*, commissioned and previously performed by the Southeastern Kansas Orchestra was played by the Bach Orchestra of Baltimore.

Hoover's works have been published by Theodore Presser, Carl Fischer and Papagena Press, recorded on Koch, Delos, Parnassus, Gaspard, Albany and Centaur, as well as performed by numerous orchestras and chamber groups here and abroad. In celebration of her fiftieth birthday, Robert Sherman's "Listening Room" on New York's classical music radio station, WQXR, was dedicated to performances of her works. She has been interviewed on public radio and television. In the January 1997 edition of *Classical Pulse*, critic Leslie Gerber picked Hoover's quintet *Da Pacem* as one of the five best recordings of 1996.

Adding a new dimension to her career, Hoover began studies in 1989 at the Conductor's Institute. In January 1994, she conducted the premiere of her *Night Skies* for full orchestra, with the Harrisburg Symphony. Her *Lyric Trio* was named a winner in the 1994 National Flute Association Competition—her fourth such award. The same year, she was one of four composers to receive a $7,500 Academy Award in Music from the American Academy of Arts and Letters. In October 1995, her *Dances and Variations* for flute and harp was premiered at Kennedy Center, and a video about the commissioning, rehearsal and premiere of this work was released on PBS, September 1996. Also in 1995, a CD was recorded by the Bratislava Radio Orchestra of her *Night Skies, Eleni,* and *Canyon Echoes.* In Spring of 1996, Hoover was composer-in-residence at Indiana University of Pennsylvania for the Fourth Annual Festival of Women Composers, where an entire evening of her compositions was performed.

Hoover's tone poem for cello and orchestra, *Stitch-te Naku*—the Native American creation legend about the Spider Grandmother who wove the world in her web—was premiered in October 1996 by **Sharon Robinson** with Orchestra Sonoma, conducted by **Nan Washburn**. Robinson was again soloist in 2000 in performances of this work by the Long Beach Symphony and The Women's Philharmonic. At the Grand Canyon Festival, September 1999, the composer introduced her *Canyon Shadows* for flute, Native flute and percussion.

Night Skies, a 1998 Parnassus CD of Hoover's orchestral works includes *Eleni: A Greek Tragedy,* and *Two Sketches,* recorded in Bratislava by Joel Eric Suben, and *Double Concerto* for two violins and string orchestra recorded by the Wisconsin Philomusica under Vartan Manoogian. Her 1999 *String Quartet* was written for, and has been performed numerous times by, the Colorado Quartet. Her two dozen CDs include 2005 releases of *Medieval Suite* with flutist Alexa Still on Koch, and *Clarinet Concerto,* Robert Spring, soloist, on Summit.

2001 saw many performances of her compositions, including *Mariposas* and *Celebration* for multiple flutes premiered at the National Flute Convention in Dallas. Her *Double Concerto* was performed in Carnegie Hall, December 28, with **Pamela Frank** and her husband Andre Simonescu, with the Orchestra of the New York Festival of Strings conducted by Jaime Laredo. Two pieces for women's voices, *Prayer in Time of War* and *Peace is the Way* were written shortly after the U.S. invasion of Iraq. They reflect the fact that war is a human failure. They were premiered by the New York Treble Singers, December 2003. 2002 brought *Requiem: A Service of Remembrance 1865/2001,* poetry by Walt Whitman, a musical statement about the events of 9/11. In March 2004, Sharon Robinson and Joseph Kalichstein premiered her cello piece *El Andalus,* a Robinson commission from the Tucson Friends of Music. The Colorado String Quartet toured with her Second String Quartet in 2006.

Katherine married guidance counselor Richard Goodwin in May 1985. Her son, Norman, has presented her with Linda, born 1994, and John, 2001.

Innovative **LAURA KAMINSKY** was born in New York, September 28, 1956, attended Oberlin and received her MA in composition from the City College of New York (1980). Her works have been commissioned by many organizations, including the New York State Council on the Arts and the 92nd Street Y, where she was associate director for Education in the Humanities, 1984–88. She received a fellowship from the Tuch Foundation (1978–80), and was awarded grants from Meet the Composer annually from 1983. She has been a featured composer at numerous festivals and conferences throughout the U.S. and abroad, including Soundfest at Cape Cod, Skopje International Festival of Contemporary Music, Macedonia, The Women's Philharmonic National

Conference (New York), Stony Brook Women in Music Festival, Bar Harbor Music Festival, Walt Whitman Centennial Celebration (NY), University of Puerto Rico and Festival of North American Music in Madrid.

In 1980, she co-founded Musicians Accord, an ensemble dedicated to 20th and now 21st century chamber music. The group, in residence at City College, records on the Mode, CRI and North/South labels. The ensemble's *Mosaic: Chamber Music of Henry Cowell*, with the Colorado Quartet, was selected as one of the best recordings of 1999 by *Gramophone*. From 1988–92, she was artistic director of Town Hall, New York, where she developed "The New Tradition," an award winning annual concert series of jazz, ethnic, experimental and chamber music, and "Century of Change," a ten year-long music festival.

From 1992–93, Kaminsky was a visiting lecturer at the National Academy of Music in Winneba, Ghana, where she produced concerts for the U.S. and Swiss Embassies as well as television and radio concerts for the Ghana Broadcasting Corporation. She spent the middle '90s as director of music and theater programs at the New School in New York, where she produced "Ladyfingers: The Women Pianists and Composers Marathon" and "Oboe Blow-Out, New York." From 1996–97, she was director of the European Mozart Academy, an international postgraduate chamber music institute based in Poland. In this capacity she presented concerts and festivals throughout Central Europe, including Bulgaria, Croatia, Czech and Slovak Republics, Hungary, Macedonia, Poland, Rumania, as well as a two-week festival in Venice. Since 1999, she was chair of the music department at the Cornish College of the Arts, Seattle, and in 2004 became director of the Conservatory of Music at SUNY, Purchase.

Her compositions include chamber music with such challenging titles as *Proverbs of Hell* for soprano, marimba and piano, *Triftmusik* (piano), *13 Ways of Looking at a Blackbird* (chorus and flute, 1977), *And Trouble Came: an African AIDS Diary* for narrator, viola, cello and piano (1993), *Two Songs of Emily Dickinson* (soprano and flute, 1980), *There is a Season* (chorus, clarinet, cello, percussion and piano, 1992), *Future Conditional* (piano, 1996), and a string quartet, *Transformations*, commissioned by the Colorado Quartet and the Serage Foundation (1999–2000). 2001 brought her string quartet *Transformations II*; 2002 *Danza Piccola* for solo piano; 2003 a piano quartet; and 2004 another string quartet, *Transformations III*.

Barbara Kolb

BARBARA KOLB was born February 10, 1939, in Hartford, Connecticut. Her early musical training was influenced by her father, Harold Judson Kolb, a self-taught musician. A pianist, organist and composer of popular music, he was the director of music on WTIC radio station in Hartford, and also conducted semi-professional bands. During her childhood, Barbara often sang on the radio and made recordings. She studied clarinet and composition at Hartt College of Music (1957–61, BM *cum laude*; MM, 1965). In 1964, she studied composition at Tanglewood with **Gunther Schuller** (*b* 1925) and **Lukas Foss** (*b* 1922). She earned a Fulbright Scholarship for music study in Vienna, then returned to Tanglewood in 1968, the same year getting her first fellowship to the MacDowell Colony.

Another Historic First

Barbara Kolb made musical history becoming the first American woman to win the Prix de Rome in composition, where she then resided (1969–1971), becoming a trustee of the American Academy in Rome (1972–75). Her many commissions in the 1970s were from the Koussevitzky Foundation, New York State Council on the Arts, Washington Performing Arts Society, Music Teachers' National Association, and the Fromm Foundation (1970, 1980). She was also awarded grants from the Institute of Arts and Letters (1973), and the NEA (1974, 1979, 1981).

Trobar Clus, a Fromm Foundation commission, premiered at Tanglewood (1970). *Solitaire* (1971) was the first of a series featuring pre-recorded sounds with various instruments. Her works have been performed by the New York Philharmonic with **Pierre Boulez**, and the Boston Symphony led by **Seiji Ozawa**, who took them on tour to Japan, March 1978. From 1979 to 1982, Kolb was artistic director of contemporary music at the Third Street Music School Settlement, presenting the *Music New to New York* concert series. In 1982, she created a tape collage score for the film *Cantico*, based on the life of St. Francis of Assisi. The following year, *Cavatina* for solo violin was written for Pina Carmirelli. During 1983–84, Kolb spent nine months in Paris at IRCAM with a commission for *Millefoglie* for chamber ensemble and computer tape. This won the prestigious Kennedy Center Friedheim Award.

From 1984–85, Kolb was a visiting professor at Eastman. In 1986, she completed, under the auspices of the Library of Congress, a music theory instruction program for the blind and physically handicapped. The same year, *Umbrian Colors* for violin and guitar was premiered at the Marlboro Festival. *Yet That Things Go Round*, a Fromm Foundation/NY Chamber Symphony commission, received its world premiere in 1987 with **Gerard Schwarz**. '90s premieres and commissions were *The Enchanted Loom* (Atlanta Symphony, 1990, **Robert Shaw**), *Soundings, Voyants*, for solo piano and chamber orchestra (Radio France, Paris, February 1991), *Cloudspin* for organ and brass quintet (Musart Society of the Cleveland Museum of Art, October 1991), *Monticello Trio* (piano trio, Charlottesville, Virginia, October 1992), *All in Good Time* (New York Philharmonic's 150th anniversary, February 1994, with **Leonard Slatkin**), and *Turnabout* (1994) for flute and piano (flutist Renée Krimsier, Merkin Hall, March 1994).

Kolb resided in Vienna for several years before returning to the "Big Apple" to write chamber works such as *New York Moonglow*, scored for a mixed sextet of saxophones, trumpet, strings and percussion; and *Sidebars*, a duet for bassoon and piano. *Virgin Mother Creatrix*, an *a cappella* choral work inspired by the mysticism of **Hildegard of Bingen**, premiered in March 1998 at the International Festival of Women Composers at Indiana University of Pennsylvania, where Kolb was the featured composer.

JOAN LaBARBARA, composer, vocal performer and sound artist, explores the human voice as a multi-faceted instrument. Born June 8, 1947, in Philadelphia, she started piano lessons at four, sang in church choirs and in a folk group in high school. Voice lessons began at fifteen. She delved into vocal experimentation in 1969 when she moved to New York, attending Syracuse University for three years where she studied voice with **Helen Boatwright**. In her senior year, she switched to NYU, graduating with a BS in Music Education (1970). Two summers at Tanglewood brought her under the influence of renowned voice pedagogue **Phyllis Curtin** (*b* 1922). She also studied privately with Marian Szekeley-Freschl at Juilliard.

Going far beyond traditional boundaries, La Barbara has created works for multiple voices, chamber ensembles, music theater, orchestra and interactive technology. A pioneer in the field of contemporary classical music and sound art, and one of the most unique vocal virtuosas of our time, she has developed a unique vocabulary of experimental and extended vocal techniques, including *multiphonics*—the simultaneous sounding of two or more pitches—circular singing, ululation and glottal clicks that have become her "signature." She gives worldwide workshops on her techniques and composition. She has been on the faculty of Hochschule der Künste, Berlin, California Institute of the Arts (1981–86), served as vice president of the American Music Center until 1993, and was co-artistic director of the New Music America Festival in Los Angeles (1985). In addition to composing and concertizing, she has been a contributing editor for Schwann/Opus, and has contributed to *Musical America* magazine, the *Grove Dictionary of Music and Musicians*, and newspapers here and in Europe. Since 1989, she has produced and co-hosted a weekly radio program, "Other Voices, Other Sounds," focusing on late 20th century contemporary classical music and sound art. She was artistic director of the Carnegie Hall series "When Morty met John," celebrating the music of **John Cage** and **Morton Feldman**, February 2001, April 2002 and October 2003. She is artistic director and host of "Insights" for the American Music Center, and co-producer of EMF @ Chelsea Art Museum, June 2003, May 2004 and, for 2004–05, celebrating the tenth anniversary of the Electronic Music Foundation.

LaBarbara's many commissions include a chamber ensemble piece, *Awakenings, In the Dreamtime*, a sonic self-portrait; *Klangbild Köln*, a sound painting of Cologne—both commissions from the West Deutscher Rundfunk-Köln; *in the shadow and act of the haunting place*, for voice and chamber ensemble, premiered by the San Francisco Contemporary Chamber Players; *Calligraphy II/Shadows* for voice and Chinese instruments for Nai-Ni Chen Dance Company (1996); and *73 Poems*, an edition of prints, book and CD with visual/text artist Kenneth

Goldsmith. She has produced several recordings of her own work, served as producer on recordings of music by John Cage and Morton Feldman, and premiered landmark compositions written for her by noted American composers, including Cage, Feldman, **Philip Glass**, **Mel Powell**, and **Morton Subotnick**, whom she married December 18, 1979. They have a son, Jacob, born September 2, 1984.

Her works have been choreographed by John Alleyne for Ballet British Columbia, Martha Curtis, Catherine Kerr and Merce Cunningham ("Events"). In 1991, she composed a filmscore for *Anima*, for voices, middle-eastern drums, handheld percussion, cello, gamelan, keyboard synthesizers, computer and electronics. Other film work includes scoring and performing the angel voice for the feature film, *Date with an Angel*, and a setting for voice with electronics for Steve Finkin's animation of the signing alphabet for Children's Television Workshop/Sesame Street, to assist hearing children in communicating with the deaf. This has been broadcast worldwide since 1977. She has also written additional music for films by Richard Blau, Monica Gazzo, Amy Kravitz, Marijn Maris, Elyse Rosenberg and Steven Subotnick. Other recording projects released on CD are: "John Cage at Summerstage with Joan La Barbara, William Winant and Leonard Stein" (New Albion, 1995); Cage's final concert performance July 23, 1992 in Central Park, New York; and "Only: Music for Voice and Instruments by Morton Feldman" (New Albion, 1996).

Awards and fellowships include NEA, Meet the Composer, ASCAP, ISCM International Jury Award, plus numerous commissions for concert, theater and radio works in America and Europe. Concertizing worldwide, LaBarbara has appeared with many orchestras, including the Los Angeles Philharmonic, San Francisco Symphony, New York Philharmonic, The Women's Philharmonic, and such events as Festival d'Automne à Paris, LA Festival, American Music Theatre Festival and at Morton Feldman Retrospective at the Lincoln Center Festival (Summer, 1996). 1996 also brought three all-LaBarbara concerts, which included works written for her, at Merkin Hall, New York, and Bucknell University, Pennsylvania. In 1997, she performed in the premiere of Morton Subotnick's opera, *Intimate Immensity*, based on the dramatic changes wrought by the communications revolution and its effect on people. Her music from *Shaman Song* was used as the filmscore for *Buffalo & Maine*, shown at the Tribeca Film Festival, May 2004. On April 7, 2004, she received a Guggenheim Fellowship in music composition, to be used for an opera about Virginia Woolf.

Libby Larsen

LIBBY LARSEN was born December 24, 1950 in Wilmington, Delaware, but raised around the lakes of Minnesota which instilled a love of water, wind and sky in the imaginative child. She grew up with an interesting combination of the music of Broadway, boogie and Gregorian chants. She sang the latter from ages six to eleven when the Ecumenical Council expunged them from the Catholic Service. She loved singing, started piano when she could barely reach the keys, and was also fascinated with dancing and ballet. At school Libby sang in choirs and began composing songs and choral pieces. In 1971, she received her BM in theory from the University of Minnesota, then went to work as a secretary in an insurance company. She used her coffee breaks to write music, and after six months realized that this was the true direction of her life. Back at the U of M, she earned an MM (1975) and a PhD (1978). Meanwhile, in 1973 Larsen cofounded, with composer Stephen Paulus, the Minnesota Composers Forum (now the American Composers Forum), an organization set up to support composers in the creation and performance of their music. She married attorney James Reece in 1975. Their daughter, Wynne, born May 28, 1986, as of 2006 was in the pre-med program at the University of Minnesota.

From 1983–87 Larsen was composer-in-residence with the Minnesota Orchestra under **Sir Neville Marriner** (*b* 1924), which premiered her *Deep Summer Music* (1982) and *Symphony: Water Music*, inspired by her love of the lakes (1985). Works in this decade also include *Pinions* (1981), performed by the St. Paul Chamber Orchestra, and *Overture: Parachute Dancing* (1983), based on a renaissance court dance where participants danced along walls and then jumped off opening their silk umbrellas. Following another of her interests—strong women—the American frontier is the backdrop in *The Settling Years* (1987) based on pioneer texts. *Songs from Letters* (1989) contain excerpts from Calamity Jane's diary to her daughter Janey. *Ghosts of an Old Ceremony* (1991) was written in collaboration with choreographer Brenda Way for orchestra and dancers, with narration from journals of pioneer women. Also showcasing women is a 1988 song cycle set in collaboration with the late soprano **Arleen Augér**, featuring six of Elizabeth Barrett Browning's *Sonnets from the Portuguese*, whose theme was mature love. The opera *Mrs. Dalloway* is based on **Bonnie Grice**'s libretto of the novel by Virginia Woolf. *Mary Cassatt* for mezzo soprano and orchestra uses slides of the artist's paintings. *ME (Brenda Ueland)*, is a song cycle for soprano and piano based on the life of the writer of the same name.

Popular music is another source of inspiration, as in *Collage: Boogie* (1988), *Trumpet Concerto: Since Armstrong* (1991), homage to Louis Armstrong, premiered by the Minnesota Orchestra, and *Marimba Concerto: after Hampton* (1992), honoring Lionel Hampton, one of the greatest exponents of the instrument—the latter a commission from a consortium of twelve American orchestras. 1995 featured premieres of *Short Symphony* by the Air Force Band, and *Ring of Fire* with the Charlotte (NC) Symphony, inspired by T.S. Eliot's poem *Little Giddings*.

Larsen's compositions draw on a variety of modern styles with imaginative titles. *Coming Forth Into Day* (1986), on the theme of war and peace, integrates the writings of Jihan Sadat, widow of assassinated Egyptian president Anwar Sadat. Madame Sadat narrated the premiere. One of Larsen's greatest successes is her seventh opera, *Frankenstein, the Modern Prometheus*, commissioned by Minnesota Opera and selected as one of the eight best classical music events of 1990 by *USA Today*. Making use of her earlier *What the Monster Saw* (1987), the monster's viewpoint is presented via large video screens. The work is scored for amplified chamber ensemble with three keyboards. The set consists of ropes and ladders extending into the theater, innovatively involving the audience in the action. In 1992 **Eugenia Zukerman** premiered *The Atmosphere as a Fluid System*, a bravura piece for flute. In 1993 Larsen organized and became artistic director of the Hot Notes Series (sponsored by the Schubert Club of St. Paul), which focuses on the interaction of performer and synthesized sounds.

A much commissioned composer, her catalogue of over 220 works encompass orchestra, dance, opera, choral, theater, chamber and solo repertoire, are performed in the U.S. and Europe under prominent conductors, and have been recorded on over fifty CDs. Her ballet, *Slang*, was staged August 1995 at New York's Joyce Theater—the "Lincoln Center" of the dance—and recorded as part of an all-Larsen clarinet repertoire release with soloist Caroline Hartwig. The 1996–97 season brought several choral works: *So Blessedly It Sprung* (SATB, viola, harp); and *Billy the Kid* (SATB) with the King's Singers, for which she went to London for rehearsals. In September 1996, Larsen was guest composer at Indiana University for performances of *Seven Ghosts* and her Third Symphony. October 18 marked a performance at New York's 92nd Street Y of *Sonnets from the Portuguese*. In November, she gave a keynote address in Dallas for the National Association of Schools of Music, and July 1997 another keynote address before the American Council of Lutheran Churches. December 1996 brought an honorary degree from the University of Nebraska. 1997 saw premieres in Baltimore, and later that spring in Birmingham (England), Kansas and Missouri. Two new anthems (SATB a capella) were written for the ordinations of two ministers. In November 1998, Opera Omaha gave the highly successful world premiere of *Eric Hermannson's Soul*, a two-act chamber opera based on a 1900 short story of the same name by Willa Cather.

In December, the Minnesota Orchestra premiered Symphony No. 4, the *String Symphony*. Other 1998 works included an SATB, brass choir and percussion piece for the AGO National Convention with the Colorado Symphony Chorus and Denver Brass, plus a new composition for the Air Force female group, *Singing Sergeants*. The Colorado Symphony premiered Symphony No. 5, the *Solo Symphony*, October 1999. A 2000 commission, *Still Life with Violin* by the Bravo! Vail (Colorado) Valley Festival, was premiered by **Pamela Frank** and the Rochester Symphony, July 26, 2000. A new song cycle, *Love After 1950*, was commissioned by and premiered by mezzo-soprano **Susanne Mentzer** at the Ravinia (Illinois) Festival, August 7, 2000. Koch International Classics released *Libby Larsen*, with Benita Valente, soprano, and the Scottish Chamber Orchestra, featuring *String Symphony*, *Songs From Letters*, and *Songs of Light and Love*. 2001–2003 saw a slew of new compositions, including the operas *Barnum's Bird* (libretto, Bridget Carpenter), co-commissioned and premiered at the

Library of Congress, and *Dreaming Blue*, co-commissioned by the 2002 Olympic Arts Festival and the City of Salt Lake, and premiered there in February. Choral works include *The Ballerina and the Clown* (text by Sally Gall), *Eine Kleine Snailmusik*, premiered by the Toronto Children's Chorus, *The Apple's Song* (baritone, piano), and *Hell's Belles* for mezzo and handbell choir, whose movements name Tallulah Bankhead, Billie Jean King and Gertrude Stein, premiered by **Frederica von Stade** who also sang the September 2002 premiere of *Raspberry Island Dreaming* with the St. Paul Chamber Orchestra under **Andreas Delfs**. *Try Me, Good King: Last Words of The Wives of Henry VIII* (Katherine of Aragon, Anne Boleyn, Jane Seymour, Anne of Cleves, Katherine Howard, Katherine Parr), a twenty-five minute song cycle for soprano and piano, was commissioned by the Marilyn Horne Foundation and performed in Alice Tully Hall. *Patterns for Orchestra, Fanfare: Sizzle* (Joann Falletta and the Buffalo Philharmonic), was followed by *A Brandenburg for the New Millennium* (trumpet, marimba, electric guitar, amplified harpsichord, string orchestra), and *Notes Slipped under the Door* (soprano, flute, orchestra) with flutist Eugenia Zukerman. Other 21st century titles from this amazingly prolific composer are *Brazen Overture* (brass quintet); *How to Songs* (children's chorus); *Lord, Before this Fleeting Season* (choral - SATB, a cappella); *A Lover's Journey* (six-voice male *a cappella* group, text: James Joyce, Shakespeare and other poets); *Mephisto Rag* (solo piano); *Psalm 121* (anthem, adapted by Larsen); *De Toda La Eternidad* (soprano, piano, text: Sister Juana Inez de la Cruz); *Dreams and Imaginations* (orchestra); *Licorice Stick* (clarinet, piano); *May Sky* (choral, SATB, a cappella, text: Japanese poets); *On a Day of Bells* (organ); *Patterns for Orchestra* (orchestra) and *Strut* (concert band). 2005 brought the premiere of *Saxophone Concerto* with Eugene Rousseau at the Iowa World Saxophone Congress. November 2006 marked the first production at Sonoma (California) City Opera of *Every Man Jack* with Rodney Gilfry as Jack London and Jennifer Lane as his wife, Charmian. Other opera commissions include *Picnic*, an adaptation of the 1955 play by William Inge, scheduled for North Carolina Opera (Greensboro, 2008).

A crusader for contemporary music and musicians—especially women—Larsen has served on the NEA Music Panel and on directorial boards including the American Symphony Orchestra League. Among her numerous awards are composer fellowships from the NEA and, as a producer, a Grammy Award for her CD, *The Art of Arleen Augér* (1994). She also received the Eugene McDermott Award in the Arts from the Massachusetts Institute of Technology

The millennium year brought a Lifetime Achievement Award from the Academy of Arts and Letters. Having served as composer-in-residence of the Minnesota Orchestra and Charlotte Symphony, 2000 marked her appointment to that position for the Colorado Symphony Orchestra. In 2003 she was named Harissios Papamarkou Chair in Education and Technology in the John W. Kluge Center of the Library of Congress. Her one-year appointment provided a unique opportunity to bring artists and educational organizations together to put projects in motion to bring American music to the public. Her new book, *The Concert Hall That Fell Asleep and Woke Up as a Car Radio*, came in 2007.

Writing on the cultural effects of music/electricity/sound and transportation, Libby says, "Music exists in an infinity of sound. I think of all music as existing in the substance of the air itself. It is the composer's task to order and make sense of sound, in time and space, to communicate something about being alive through music."

Annea Lockwood

ANNEA LOCKWOOD, born July 29, 1939, in Christchurch, New Zealand, challenges the line between sound and noise, adapting what she terms environmental applications of taped sounds. After attending Canterbury University, New Zealand (BM 1961), she studied piano and composition at the RCM, London (diplomas 1963), summer courses in Germany, Darmstadt (1961–62), the Stätliche Hochschule für Musik in Cologne, the Electronic Music Centre, Bilthoven (1963–64) and in London at the Putney Electronic Music Studio (1970). From 1969–72, she studied psycho-acoustics at Southampton University Institute of Sound and Vibration Research. She taught at Hunter College Electronic Music Center (part of City University of New York, or CUNY, since 1973). In 1982, she joined the faculty of Vassar College where she taught composition, theory and electronic music, and served as chair of the music department. She has performed and given lectures on her works throughout Europe, New Zealand and Australia. Her honors include Arts Council awards (1970, 1972, 1973), Gulbenkian Foundation grants (1972, 1973), a Creative Artists Public Service grant (1977), an NEA fellowship (1979–80), and an honorary doctorate from Clark University, Massachusetts. In 1999, she was resident-fellow at the Rockefeller Foundation's Bellagio Study and Conference Center in Italy.

Lockwood's early compositions are atonal and include environmental sounds, improvisation and *musique concrète*. *Tiger Balm* (1970) contains a purring cat, heartbeats, a tiger and other effects. Her work as an instrument builder began with *Glass Concert* (1966) for two performers and glass objects that serve as both scenery and instruments. Later, she increasingly turned her attention to electro-acoustic pieces that include taped environmental sounds. From 1970, she composed mainly electronic and performance pieces. She also began to explore documentary forms, mixed media and environmental sound. The River Archive was begun in the mid-'60s, and culminated in an installation work for which she is best known, *A Sound Map of the Hudson River* (1982), commissioned by the Hudson River Museum, Yonkers, New York, and shown in England, New Zealand, Germany and at New York's Whitney Museum in their retrospective, "The American Century: 1950–2000." In *World Rhythms* (1975), the strokes on a single gong are not in response to the natural sounds played back from ten tape tracks, but created by the bio-rhythm generated from the activity itself. These works demonstrate the holistic and meditation techniques Lockwood learned from studying non-Western music and in her activities in avant-garde theater.

In 1987, Lockwood turned again to instrumental and vocal composition, producing works for various chamber ensembles. By the 1990s her works were performed throughout the U.S. In 1995, *Monkey Trips*, created in collaboration with the California E.A.R. Unit, was performed at the Walker Art Center in Los Angeles. *Thousand Year Dreaming* (1991), for multiple didjeridoos, conches, frame drums, wind and percussion, including slides of the cave paintings at Lascaux, France, was presented in the Bang-on-a-Can Marathon at Lincoln Center. *The Angle of Repose* was included in the Second Smokefree Women Composers Festival in Wellington, New Zealand. Lockwood was also the Rosekrans artist-in-residence at Mills College (Oakland), in 1995. *Ear-Walking Woman* (1996), composed for pianist Lois Svard, uses sounds created inside the piano with rocks, bubble-wrap, bowl-gongs, and other implements. *Duende* (1997), for voice and tape, was composed collaboratively with baritone Thomas Buckner. *Floating World* (1999) weaves together recordings made by friends from places spiritually important to them. It premiered at the 2000 Santa Fe Electroacoustic Music Festival.

Ursula Mamlok

URSULA MAMLOK, born in Berlin, February 1, 1928, studied piano and composition as a child. As part of a family escaping Hitler, they lived in Ecuador for one year before emigrating to New York in 1941. Ursula became a U.S. citizen in 1945. She went to the Mannes College of Music (1942–46) where she was a pupil of the illustrious maestro **George Szell** (1897–70), who encouraged her to attend rehearsals when he guest conducted the New York Philharmonic and the Met. (She sometimes met Alma Mahler on these occasions.) Her BM, 1957 and MM, 1958, are from the Manhattan School of Music under **Vittorio Giannini** (1903–66). She also studied privately with American composers **Roger Sessions** (1896–1985) and **Ralph Shapey** (1921–2002). From 1967–76, she was on the faculties of NYU, and Kingsborough Community College (1972–75). She began her long tenure at the Manhattan School in 1974, and in 2003 was honored as a composer and teacher, receiving a medal and the title professor emeritas upon her retirement.

Mamlok has written much chamber and piano music, including deftly constructed and challenging teaching pieces. In 1987, a retrospective concert held at Merkin Hall, New York, presented music composed between 1956 and 1986. One of her most popular compositions, *Der Andreas Garten* (1989), with text by her husband Gerard Mamlok, for mezzo, flutes and harp, is set in a garden on the San Andreas earthquake fault which runs through California. Her orchestral work *Constellations*, commissioned by the San Francisco Symphony, was performed five times in 1994 under the baton of **Herbert Blomstedt**. A solo organ piece, *Festive Sounds*, was commissioned by the AGO and performed at their national convention in New York City, July 1996. Also in 1996, the Lincoln Center Chamber Music Society premiered *Girasol* (Sunflower), for flute, clarinet, violin, viola, cello and piano.

Her CDs feature *Rhapsody* (clarinet, violin and piano), *Designs* (violin and piano), *From My Garden* (violin solo), Sonata (violin and piano) and *Panta Rhei* (violin, cello and piano) with the Francesco Trio of San Francisco. In 1998, the Cassatt Quartet gave the first performances of her *String Quartet No. 2*, which they recorded in 2002 for a compilation CD on CRI, including *Constellations* with Gerard Schwartz and the Seattle Symphony, *Polarities* and *Girasol* by the Parnassus Ensemble, and *Der Andreas Garten* by the Jubal Trio.

In February 2000 the composer went to Germany for lectures and concerts of her music in Cologne and Berlin. The latter was broadcast nationally in June. April featured a concert of her *Second String Quartet* in San Francisco. The same work was played in New York, May 2001. In October 2004, her compositions *Inward Journey* and *In High Spirits* were played at the twenty-fifth anniversary of the Women's Composer Archive in Berlin.

Ursula Mamlok has been the recipient of many honors, including NEA grants (1974, 1981), acting as the U.S. representative at the International Rostrum of Composers (1984), a Broadcast Music Inc. (BMI) Commendation of Excellence (1987), the Walter Hinrichsen Award of the American Academy of Arts and Letters (1989), Fromm Foundation Award (1994) and a Guggenheim Foundation Fellowship (1995). Published since 1971 by the prestigious firm of C.F. Peters, her music continued its trajectory in the 21st century.

MEREDITH MONK was born November 20, 1943, in Lima (Peru) while her mother, a pop and show singer, was on tour. She grew up in New York and Connecticut where her early musical training included piano, voice and Dalcroze Eurythmics. In 1964 she received a BA in performing arts from Sarah Lawrence College. She became a member of the "downtown" avant-garde, and an innovator and creator of music-theater, in which music, film, dance, acting and text are combined to create the flow produced in conventional opera by music alone. Her first piece, *Juice: A Theater Cantata in 3 Installments*, was premiered at New York's Guggenheim Museum in 1969. *Quarry* (1976) is one of her most highly developed works in this genre. In 1978 she founded the Meredith Monk Vocal Ensemble, a chamber group, which performs with her internationally. Also an accomplished film maker, *Ellis Island* appeared in 1981, followed by *Book of Days*, her first feature-length film, which she conceived, wrote and directed in 1988. Her 1991 opera *Atlas*, commissioned by the Houston Grand Opera, is made up of nonsense syllables voicing the emotions of the characters. Other works include *Three Heavens and Hells* (1992); *Custom Made* (1993); *Volcano Songs #1* (1994); *American Archaeology #1: Roosevelt Island* (1994); *Nightfall*, and *Denkai and Krikiki Chants* (1995). *The Politics of Quiet*, a "non-verbal oratorio," was given its world premiere July 17, 1996, at the Copenhagen Cultural Capital of Europe Festival. Another 1996 commission was *Celebration*, a non-denominational service for the Union Theological Seminary, containing religious music set to eighth century Indian, Buddhist, Hasidic, Sufi, Chinese, Osage (Native American), Afghanistan and Ethiopian texts, plus a Christian prayer by Hildegard. *Steppe Music* for soprano was commissioned for the January 1997 Henry Cowell Festival in Berkeley (California). Her science fiction chamber opera, *Magic Frequencies*, premiered in Munich, October 1998.

Added to her many recordings are two 1995 CDs: *Key*, a montage of dream-narratives and dream-like songs begun in 1967; and *Monk and the Abbess* featuring seven of her works—including the choral piece *Nightfall*, with chants of **Hildegard von Bingen**. *Volcano Songs* is a 1997 CD on ECM New Music Series, with the composer as soloist accompanied by the Meredith Monk Vocal Ensemble. An *a capella* vocal composition for ten voices, keyboard, bowed psaltery, viola and French horn was premiered by the Western Wind Ensemble at Merkin Hall that year.

Spanning over three decades, Monk's career encompasses composing, singing, dancing, film making, choreography and directing. Acclaimed by audiences and critics as a major creative force in the performing arts, she has received numerous awards including two Guggenheim Fellowships, a Brandeis Creative Arts Award, two Obie awards (*Vessel*, 1972, and *Quarry*, 1976), first prize in the music-theater category at the 1975 Venice Biennale (for *Education of the Girlchild*), the 1986 National Music Theater Award, sixteen ASCAP Awards for Musical Composition, the 1992 Dance Magazine Award, the highly remunerative MacArthur Prize (1995), and the

Samuel H. Scripps Award (1996). She has also been made an honorary Doctor of Arts by Bard College, the University of the Arts and Juilliard. She was the only woman composer represented in the June 1996 festival, *An Afternoon of American Visionaries*, featuring compositions played by the San Francisco Symphony under **Michael Tilson Thomas**.

A singular honor was the May through September 1996 exhibit *Meredith Monk: Archeology of an Artist*, with manuscripts, tapes, costumes, photographs, etc., at the New York Public Library of Performing Arts at Lincoln Center.

In 1999 she was honored by *Chamber Music Magazine* (for *The Tale*, 1973) on their Century List, described as the "100 Reasons to Play This Century's Music."

In 2001, Monk created *mercy*, with Ann Hamilton. A dramatic musical theater piece, it was uncannily prescient of the September 11 terrorist attack on the World Trade Center Towers. Its message is an offering of hope, of uplifted hearts and a meditation on the concept of mercy. After its Ohio premiere in October 2002, performances were in Los Angeles, Minneapolis, Chicago and Miami. Meredith continues her unique performances in the New York area. The following year, her sixtieth birthday was celebrated in musical circles.

Erica Muhl

ERICA MUHL was born in Los Angeles, California, October 26, 1959. With her mother Barbara, an author, and her father Edward Muhl, vice president in charge of production at Universal Studios until his retirement in 1973, she grew up among the elite of the literary and film worlds. Instead of choosing either of these paths, she knew early in her life that she wanted to be a composer. She started piano at ten and was writing songs by her early teens. After graduating from high school at a precocious sixteen, she met **Marcelle de Manziarly** (1899–1989), a close associate of **Nadia Boulanger**, who invited her to Paris to study with the distinguished legend. Boulanger, then eighty-nine, was loved and respected by generations of her world-famous students who included Aaron Copland, Roy Harris and Leonard Bernstein. Her American Conservatory, headquartered in winter in her palatial apartment on the Rue Ballu, and in summer at the Palais de Fontainebleau, introduced high standards of musicianship and an international orientation for her students. For Muhl it was a significantly influential experience, shaping her musical development for many years to come.

On her return from France, she earned her BM at Cal State, Northridge (1982). A Rotary Foundation Scholarship enabled her to return to Europe for graduate diplomas from the Accademia di Santa Cecilia in Rome, and the Accademia Chigiana in Siena, where she studied with **Franco Donatoni** (*b* 1927), and private study in conducting with **Fritz Zweig** (1893–1984), former principal conductor of the Deutsche Oper, Berlin, Prague Opera, and a pupil of Schoenberg, and with Walter Cataldi-Tassoni, conductor/stage director for Rome Opera, and a pupil of Pietro Mascagni.

In 1989, she married Mark Borchetta, a Los Angeles-based film maker. In 1991, she completed a DMA at USC, where she studied with American composer James Hopkins. Through master classes and symposia, she has worked with composers **William Kraft**, **John Harbison**, **Samuel Adler**, and Cambodian-American **Chinary Ung**. Dr. Muhl never severed her connection with USC's Thornton School of Music. After completion of her doctorate, she became an assistant professor of composition (1990), received her tenure as associate professor in 1996 and full professorship in the fall of 2003.

A Role Model

Muhl has found teaching the fulfillment of being a role model for the many women in her classes. One of her own role models is **Joan Tower**, whom she met at USC. She worked with her at the 1998 Deer Valley Festival and Institute, Park City, Utah, where her string quartet *Trucco* was performed. This has also been played in festivals in the U.S., Europe, Mexico, South America, as well as on tour internationally with the Cuarteto Latinoamericano. At the Charles Ives Center for American Music, *Trucco* won first prize for Excellence in the Arts (Los Angeles Arts

Council) in 1991, part of the winning submission to the American Academy of Arts and Letters with her *Variations for Piano.*

In Triple Roles

For many years Muhl was assistant conductor, coach and accompanist for Los Angeles Opera Theater and Seattle Opera Association, and composer-in-residence at Minnesota Opera's New Music Theater Ensemble. Performances and broadcasts of her work have been with Italy's Orchestra della RAI, The Women's Philharmonic, Charles Ives Center for American Music, Arditti Quartet, France's Ensemble intercontemporain, National Public Radio (NPR), Canadian Broadcasting Corporation (CBC), Radio-Televisione Italiana and the Cuarteto Latinoamericano, the latter bringing great popularity to her *Trucco* string quartet. *Trucco* was performed in June 1995 by Mexico's Cuarteto Carlos Chavez at the Palacio de Bellas Artes in Mexico City, and broadcast on Mexican network television.

She has received grants and awards from the NEA, Opera America, Meet the Composer, Rotary International and ASCAP Awards 1992–1996. Besides guest lecturing at universities, she has given pre-concert talks for the Los Angeles Philharmonic and LA Opera, authored articles on computer assisted instruction, and translated French and Italian text for other composers.

In 1993, Muhl was honored with a first prize for Excellence in the Arts from the City of Los Angeles, and received the prestigious commissioning prize from The Women's Philharmonic of San Francisco. That commission resulted in her mystically impressionistic work *What is the sound of an angel's voice . . .*, which was premiered in 1994 to great acclaim and nominated for the Pulitzer Prize in music. One of her most successful piano pieces, *The Lost Mariner*, underwent major revisions and became *Variations for Piano*, which has been played throughout the U.S. A world premiere of *Truccorchéstra*, the orchestral version of her string quartet, was performed by Venezuela's Orquesta Filarmònica Nacional at the Ninth International Festival of New Music in Caracas, November 19, 1995. *Variations for Orchestra*, commissioned by New England's Colonial Symphony on the occasion of their forty-fifth anniversary, was premiered on May 10, 1996.

In May 1999, Muhl was presented an Academy Award in Music by the American Academy of Arts and Letters in New York, which included a cash prize and a recording grant. The CD of her chamber works (partially funded by the grant) include *Trucco,* for string quartet; *Variations,* for piano; *Pulse/Shiver/Stomp,* for percussion ensemble and piano; and *Tremor,* for marimba. Her second string quartet was written for Cuarteto Latinoamericano, the quartet-in-residence at Carnegie Mellon, and *Trio,* for cello, percussion and piano, for Alvaro Bitran, their cellist, who premiered it at the 2001 International Forum for New Music in Mexico City.

October 25, 2002 brought the West Coast premiere of the orchestral version of *Consolation,*[44] written for the families of those lost on 9/11/01, with the USC Thornton Chamber Symphony under the baton of the composer. This chamber ensemble work was an original commission from the Cleveland Chamber Symphony who recorded it as part of an all-Muhl CD titled *RANGE OF LIGHT, Selected Chamber Works by Erica Muhl*, released on Albany in June 2004.

Her 2003 commission from the Orchestra of St. Luke's in New York resulted in a March 2004 premiere of *. . . to a thin edge* for violin, cello and piano, performed by their Chamber Ensemble. June 2004 saw the premiere of *While Millions Join the Theme* for soprano with piano accompaniment, at Songfest in Malibu (California). The American Guild of Organists' 2003 commission became *Fleet for organ and percussion*, and was performed at their July 2004 National Convention in Los Angeles. In the composer's words, "It goes like a bat out of hell!"

As a full professor, at the University of Southern California (USC) Flora L. Thornton School of Music, Erica's greatest 21st century production, with a little help from her husband, was the birth of son Ryan Michael, born April 26, 2001!

---

44. The occasion also marked the meeting of composer and author who share an October 26 birthday.

Thea Musgrave

THEA MUSGRAVE was born May 27, 1928, near Edinburgh. At nineteen she entered the University there to study medicine, but switched to music, graduating with a bachelor's degree in 1950, after which she went to the Paris Conservatoire for four years and became part of the illustrious stream of students of the immortal pedagogue **Nadia Boulanger** (1887–1979). In 1959, she came to the U.S. on a scholarship to the Berkshire Music Center (Tanglewood). There she studied with **Aaron Copland** (1900–90), met **Milton Babbitt** (*b* 1916) a serialist and early experimenter with electronic synthesizer music, and became acquainted with the music of **Charles Ives** (1874–1954). From 1958–65 she was an extra-mural lecturer at London University. In 1970, she returned to America as visiting professor of composition at University of California, Santa Barbara, a position which confirmed her increasing involvement with the musical life of the U.S., where she has resided since 1972. In 1971, she married violist Peter Mark who, in 1975, became artistic director and conductor of the Virginia Opera Association in Norfolk.

A Philadelphia First

In 1976, in a performance of her *Concerto for Orchestra*, Musgrave became the first woman to conduct the Philadelphia Orchestra. In 1977, she made her New York debut conducting her chamber opera *The Voice of Ariadne*, with New York City Opera, which also produced her *Mary, Queen of Scots* in 1981, for which she wrote both music and libretto. Since then, she has conducted her own compositions with major orchestras on both sides of the Atlantic. Utilizing 20th century techniques, including serialism and chromaticism, her unique contribution has been what she calls "dramatic abstract," in which instruments take on character roles and players sometimes walk about the stage from one section of the orchestra to another, playing with each in turn, as in her Horn Concerto (1971) and in her Viola Concerto (1973), written for Peter Mark. *A Christmas Carol*, from Dickens, an opera using traditional British carols, was premiered in Virginia (1977–78), as was *Harriet, the Woman Called Moses* (1985), which incorporates spirituals and African-American folk music and is based on the life of Harriet Tubman, the escaped 19th century slave who helped others to freedom via the "Underground Railroad"—a series of safe houses for runaways. *Rainbow* (1990), with synthesizer, was commissioned for the opening of Glasgow's new concert hall. *Wild Winter*, a set of lamentations in English, French, German, Italian, Spanish and Russian, for voices and viols, using texts about war, was commissioned for the 1993 Litchfield (England) Festival. Three works were premiered at the 1994 Cheltenham (England) Festival: *Autumn Sonata*, a bass clarinet concerto; a choral work, *On the Underground, Set No. 1: On gratitude, love & madness*; and *Journey through a Japanese Landscape*, inspired by haiku, for marimba and wind orchestra, with piano, harp and percussion, with **Evelyn Glennie** who was also the soloist in the American premiere, February 29, 1996, at the New England Conservatory. Continuing with her settings of poems from the book by the same title, Musgrave's *On the Underground Set No. 2: The Strange and the Exotic* was performed in 1994, and in November 1995 a performance of her final collection, *On the Underground Set No. 3: A Medieval Summer.*

1995 was a banner year. Her opera *Simón Bolívar*, written in both Spanish and English, using traditional Spanish and Latin-American music, commemorates the hero who, in the early 19th century, liberated Venezuela, Colombia, Ecuador, Peru and Bolivia from the Spanish. Featured character is Manuela Saenz de Thorne, who left her husband to spend her life with the great South American. It was premiered by Peter Mark in Norfolk in January. April saw a performance of the opera in German at the Regensburg Stadt Bühner. Excerpts were played at the BBC Proms in August. *Helios*, her oboe concerto, was heard at the Orkney Summer Festival, played by the Scottish Chamber Orchestra under Nicholas Daniel, with Nicholas Kraemer, soloist. *The Voice of Ariadne* received its German premiere in November. In June 1996, the BBC Scottish Symphony gave the world premiere of *Songs for a Winter's Evening*, based the poems of Robert Frost, followed by the premiere of her flute trio, *Circe*, in August at the National Flute Convention in New York. *Threnody* for clarinet and piano, commissioned by Victoria Soames, received its first performance in June 1997, as did *Canta Canta* for clarinet and ensemble, also written for Soames and the Muhfield Ensemble. The same artist is heard on the 1997 Cala CD of Musgrave's music with the composer conducting the BBC Scottish Orchestra, containing *The Seasons, Clarinet Concerto* and *Autumn Sonata*. In March, her ballet *Beauty and the Beast* was produced in Rouen, France. In April, she performed some of her chamber music in San Francisco. Honored as a distinguished professor at Queens College, Musgrave gave her acceptance lecture there, May 1, on "The Three Faces of Women: Queen, Slave and Mistress," based on her three operas, *Mary, Queen of Scots, Harriet, The Woman Called Moses* and *Simon Bolívar*.

In February 1998 her orchestral work, *Phoenix Rising*, was premiered by the BBC Symphony Orchestra at Royal Festival Hall, with the U.S. premiere, November 1999, by the Boston Symphony. January 23, 1999, The Women's Philharmonic premiered excerpts from *Three Women—Queen, Slave, Mistress. Celebration Day*, for chorus and orchestra, was premiered in December. *Lamenting with Ariadne*, commissioned by the Birmingham Contemporary Music Group, premiered January 2000. *Echoes of Time Past* (2002) was written as a companion piece to Messiaen's *Quartet for the End of Time*.

October 2003, New Orleans Opera premiered *Pontalba: A Louisiana Legacy* to celebrate the 200th anniversary of the Louisiana Purchase. In the historical women theme of her previous works, this opera is based on Christina Vella's 1997 book, *Intimate Enemies*, the story of Baroness Micaela Almonester de Pontalba, the philanthropist responsible for the spectacular architecture of New Orleans' Jackson Square.

Among other honors, Thea Musgrave has won the Koussevitsky Foundation Award (1974) and two Guggenheim Fellowships (1975, 1982), in recognition of the esteem with which her work is regarded in America.

Born January 18, 1962 in Beverly Hills into one of the most respected musical families in Hollywood, **MARIA NEWMAN** is the youngest daughter of nine-time Academy Award winning film composer **Alfred Newman** (1900–70). After growing up in a musical environment, she received her formal training at Eastman, then earned her MM from Yale. Her works have been performed at major music festivals including the Martes Musicales Festivals in Guadalajara, Mexico; Banff Centre for the Arts, Alberta, Canada; and New Music Festival for the Society of Composers in Memphis, Tennessee and Albuquerque, New Mexico. The International Viola Congress featured *Quemadmodum* for two violas and two pianos (1995) and *Duet for Trumpet and Viola* (1996). Her many commissions include the San Luis Obispo Symphony, Santa Monica Symphony—in honor of their fiftieth anniversary—Heller Foundation, Icicle Creek Music Center and the Viklarbo Chamber Ensemble, which she founded in 1987, and was ensemble-in-residence at USC (1991–95). She has been their composer-in-residence since 1994. Other commissions are from the Mary Pickford Foundation, Turner Classic Movies, Timeline Films, and the Library of Moving Images to compose original scores for numerous vintage silent films. Among them are *Daddy Longlegs* (1918) with Mary Pickford, (Alfred Newman wrote the music for the 1955 Fred Astaire-Leslie Caron version); *Tom Sawyer* (1917) with Mary's brother Jack Pickford, who was always in his sister's shadow; *Lovelight* with Frances Marion, a pioneer woman in the industry; and *Mr. Wu* (1927) with Lon Chaney, Sr., known as *The Man of a 1000 Faces*. These are enjoying performances at various film festivals.

Newman was composer-in-residence with the St. Matthew's Chamber Orchestra (1993–94), Central Washington University (1995), and the Los Angeles Mozart Orchestra, under **Lucinda Carver** (1995–96 season). She fills this position year-round for the Icicle Creek (Summer) Music Center in Leavenworth, Washington. An acclaimed international violin and viola soloist, she made the world premiere recording (Varèse Sarabande) of Miklos Rozsa's Viola Concerto with the Nuremberg Symphony (1991), and gave the American premiere of his 1928 *Violin Concerto* in Los Angeles (1993).

The birth of her first child, in 1996, was followed in close succession by three June premieres: *The Ninth Hour of Divine Office*, a sonata for tuba and piano commissioned by James Self, tubist with the Hollywood Bowl Orchestra, Los Angeles Opera Orchestra, Pasadena Symphony and number one tuba player in studio orchestras, for the International Brass Festival; *Kestrel and Leonardo*, three songs on poems by Susan Musgrave, by Viklarbo; and *Precipice Garden*, five songs on poems by retired Oregon Symphony Conductor **James DePreist**, for harp, soprano and clarinet, commissioned and premiered by harpist **JoAnn Turovsky** for the July 1996 World Harp Congress in Tacoma, Washington, with Emily Bernstein, clarinet, and Anne Marie Ketchum, soprano. An Icicle Creek commission, *Le petit duel*, premiered in August. The *Te Deum*, written for the twenty-fifth anniversary of the Yakima (Washington) Symphony Chorus, and *Concerto Grosso* for string orchestra, for the San Luis Obispo Symphony, premiered in March before the blessed event. 1997 brought premieres and commissions from the Cal-Tech Womens Glee Club, on poems of women writers; *Quartet for Oboe and Strings*, commissioned by Pacific Serenades; *Blesdian*, performed in a concert of works by women composers with the Marina Del Rey-Westchester Symphony (this author was pre-concert lecturer); and *One Song from Eden* for string quartet and soprano. 1997 also brought CDs: *Requiem for the Innocents*; *Te Deum* and *Nissuin*, Jewish wedding ceremonial music taken from the Song of Solomon; *Seven Blessings*, performed by Viklarbo; and *Chilmark*, from the work written for the tricentennial of this town in Martha's Vineyard. The CD soundtrack of her 1996 film score for *Bao*—an Asian father and son saga—features the composer performing on piano, violin and viola, and her husband on brass, percussion and electronic instruments. *The Birthday of the Infanta* with the Kairos String Quartet and *Sonatas for Brass: Sacred and Secular* were released in 2000, and an all orchestral work commissioned by the University of Kansas in 2001. February of that year, she was acting concertmaster in a tribute to her father's music by the Los Angeles Jewish Orchestra under the direction of both **Noreen Green** and popular music icon/singer/ songwriter, cousin Randy Newman.

Maria's honors include annual ASCAP Awards dating from 1994, two Composers Guild Awards (1994), and the sole female prize winner in the 1994 MTNA Shepherd Composer of the Year Award, 2002 Debut Award from the Young Musicians Foundation and many others. She is featured as a soloist on the Varèse Sarabande and Raptoria CAAM labels, which include performances by Randy Newman, and actor **Charlton Heston**. She also plays in film studio orchestras. Her own publishing business, Raptoria Camm, makes her music easily accessible, with the result that much of her work is enjoying multiple performances.

Her 2002 violin concerto with string orchestra, *Lux Eterna*, was performed in Budapest, Prague, Vienna and other European cities in 2004 by the Santa Monica Symphony under Allen Gross. The 2003 Cortes Festival (Wenatchee, Washington) honored Newman with a week of concerts of her orchestral and chamber works. Summer 2004 found her as composer-in-residence of Songfest at the Icicle Creek Music Center and Brevard Music Festival in North Carolina.

One of Maria's favorite compositional outlets is creating liturgical works for the Palisades Presbyterian Church where, besides composer-in-residence, she is director of the orchestral and choral choirs. But her major productions have been Martha Jeannette, born May 5, 1996, Isabella, November 12, 1998, and Samuel, April 3, 2000.

PAULINE OLIVEROS is credited as the innovator of meditative music. She is the founder of a meditation concept called "Deep Listening," which explores unusual acoustic environments and phenomena. Born May 30, 1932 in Houston, Texas, she learned music from her mother and grandmother, then studied violin, accordion and horn. She continued accordion at the University of Houston (1949–52) and received her BA in composition from San Francisco State College (1960). She became director of the pioneer Mills College Tape Music Center in Oakland, California (1966–67), developing and performing her early electronic music and theater pieces. From 1967 to 1981 she was a professor of music at UCSD, and director of its Center for Music Experiment (1976–79). In 1973, she received a Guggenheim Fellowship for composition. In 1985, she joined the faculty of the Theater School for New Dance in Amsterdam. The same year, she founded and became president of the Pauline Oliveros Foundation, Inc., a center for artists and audiences to explore new relationships and technologies.

Oliveros has received annual ASCAP awards (1982–1994), NEA composer's fellowships (1984, 1988, 1990), and a Foundation for Contemporary Performance grant (1994). In 1996, she was composer-in-rresidence at Northwestern and Alfred Universities, and the Darius Milhaud professor of composition at Mills College. She has authored *Pauline's Proverbs* (1976), *Initiation Dream* (1982), *Software for People* (1984) and *The Roots of the Moment* (1996). Recordings with the Deep Listening Band include *The Ready Made Boomerang* (1989), *Deep Listening*

(1989), *Crone Music* (1989), *Troglodyte's Delight* (1990) and *Pauline Oliveros and American Voices 1994*, recorded in a stone chapel in Pomfret, Connecticut.

Sound and the Environment

Her compositions range from music for acoustic instruments to mixed-media pieces with electronic and live sounds, films, texts, theatrical events and dance. Her works frequently involve audience participation via sonic meditations, characterized by drone effects, which foster a sense of communion. Her innovative titles include *Aeolian Partitions*, a 1968 theater piece for flute, clarinet, violin, cello and piano; *Double Basses at 20 Paces*, for two basses, their seconds, referee and tape; *Meditation on the Points of the Compass* for chorus, 1970; *To Valerie Solanas and Marilyn Monroe in Recognition of Their Desperation*, ensemble or orchestra, 1970; and *Njinga the Queen King*, a music theater work presented at the Next Wave Festival at the Brooklyn Academy of Music, December 1993. It was performed again at Lincoln Center, August 1995, and at the Folger Shakespeare Elizabethan Theater in Washington, DC, February 1996.

Her film, *The Sensual Nature of Sound*, was aired on the Public Broadcasting channel (PBS), Spring 1996. *Ghostdance*, with American and Mexican dancers, was staged at Lincoln Center, August 1996. *Echoes from the Moon* sent sounds to the moon via radio from the Klangturm (Sound Tower) at a cultural event marking the opening of federal buildings at Saint Pölten, Austria.

A highlight of her life was the 1983 celebration in Houston, Texas, of Pauline Oliveros Day and Thirty-Year Retrospective. She was also honored with a retrospective at the Kennedy Center in Washington, DC, 1985, and received an honorary DMA from the University of Maryland, 1986. In 1999, she was honored at the annual conference of the Society for Electro-Acoustic Music in the United States (SEAMUS) with the society's Lifetime Achievement Award.

Exploring the potential of meditation, ritual, and myth, Pauline Oliveros has extended the boundaries of her art with her unique approach to sound and non-sound worlds. Her *Deep Listening* continues to gather devotees from all over the world. A global celebration of the fiftieth anniversary of her work was held in 2000 with the commission and performance of *Lunar Opera: Deep Listening For Tunes*, at Lincoln Center.

Polish-American composer **MARTA PTASZYNSKA**, University of Chicago professor, has resided in the U.S. over thirty years. (See Central and East European Composers.)

Shulamit Ran

SHULAMIT RAN, born October 21, 1949, in Tel-Aviv, Israel, started composing before she ever touched a piano. She would hear melodies with every poem she read. When she began piano lessons at age eight, the teacher wrote the melodies down and sent them to the radio station where they were sung by a children's choir—a thrilling experience for the gifted child. She began composition lessons with prominent Israeli composers **Alexander Uriah Boskovich** (1907–64) and **Paul Ben-Haim** (1897–1984). When **Nadia Reisenberg** came to Jerusalem to teach master classes, the renowned pianist arranged for the talented fourteen-year-old to receive a full scholarship to the Mannes College of Music in New York, where she studied piano with Reisenberg and composition with **Norman Dello Joio** (*b* 1913). After graduating, she continued piano with the renowned **Dorothy Taubman**. Shortly after her arrival in the U.S., Shulamit auditioned with **Leonard Bernstein** for his Young People's Concerts, playing her own composition, *Capriccio* for piano and orchestra, and was chosen to play with the New York Philharmonic on the televised series in 1963.

Between 1968–73, Ran toured America and Europe and premiered her *Concert Piece for Piano and Orchestra* with the Israel Philharmonic under **Zubin Mehta**. During 1972–73 she was also artist-in-residence at St. Mary's University, Halifax, Nova Scotia (Canada). A Vox recording of her 1969 *O the Chimneys*, a setting of Nelly Sachs' poems about the Holocaust, prompted **Ralph Shapey**, with whom she later studied composition, to invite Ran to join the faculty of the University of Chicago, October 1973. She was made an associate professor of composition in 1978 and full professor in 1986. She holds the William H. Colvin chair at the department of music. The spring semester of 1987 was spent as visiting professor at Princeton University. Commissions poured in: Chamber Music America for *String Quartet No. 1* (1984); American Composers Orchestra for *Concerto for Orchestra* (1986); and from the Eastman School of Music, *Amichai Songs* for faculty member mezzo-soprano **Jan DeGaetani** (1933–89), who had a unique career as an exponent of ultra-modern music.

After the success of her *Concerto for Orchestra*, conducted by him in 1988, music director **Daniel Barenboim** named Ran to succeed **John Corigliano**, becoming the second composer-in-residence for the Chicago Symphony. Her numerous awards, fellowships and commissions include those from the NEA (1975, '84, '88), Guggenheim Foundation (1977, '90), Fromm Foundation (1974), Da Capo Chamber Players, Chamber Music Society of Lincoln Center (1987), and honorary doctorates from Mount Holyoke College (1988), Spertus Institute, Chicago (1995), Beloit College (1996) and the new School of Social Research, New York (1997). *Hyperbolae*, for piano, won the competition for a set piece for all the participants in the second Arthur Rubinstein International Piano Competition in Israel (1977). *East Wind*, for solo flute, was commissioned by the National Flute Association for its 1988 Young Artists Competition. *Inscriptions*, for solo violin, was commissioned and premiered by Samuel Magad, co-concertmaster of the Chicago Symphony, June 1991. In 1989, she received an award from the American Academy and Institute for Arts and Letters. *Chicago Skyline*, commissioned by WFMT in celebration of the station's fortieth anniversary, premiered in December 1991, with **Pierre Boulez** conducting the Chicago Symphony.

Since the 1985 cultural exchange accord between Russia and the U.S., a landmark was established with Ran's second string quartet, *Vistas*, the first American commission given to a Soviet chamber ensemble, the Taneyev Quartet of Leningrad (St. Petersburg), courtesy of C. Geraldine Freund, a Chicago patron of the arts. Ran's *Symphony*, commissioned by the Philadelphia Orchestra, made her the second woman in history to win the Pulitzer Prize in Music (1991), and the Kennedy Center Friedheim Award (1992). Fourteen of Ran's works were released through 1996 on CDs by Bridge, CRI, Erato, Koch International Classics and Vox. Her music is published by Theodore Presser, Carl Fischer and the Israeli Music Institute.

The Cleveland Orchestra, under **Christoph Von Dohnanyi**, included Ran's *Concert Piece for Piano and Orchestra* on two American tours (1991, 1993), culminating in a Carnegie Hall performance with pianist Alan Feinberg. 1993 produced *Legends*, honoring the centennials of both the Chicago Symphony and the University of Chicago, with Daniel Barenboim conducting its premiere. *Invocation*, written in honor of the seventy-fifth anniversary of the Los Angeles Philharmonic, received its first performance in February 1995. *Yearning*, for violin and string orchestra, was premiered August 1995, with violinist Edna Michell at the Gstaad Music Festival, Switzerland, **Lord Yehudi Menuhin** (1916–99) conducting, and first performed in the U.S. at Lincoln Center's Avery Fisher Hall, August 11, 1996.

In 1996, although on a one year sabbatical from her post as composer-in-residence, at the request of Maestro Barenboim, Ran returned to the Chicago Symphony in the fall for her sixth season with the orchestra. In the interim, the composer served as artistic director for the First through Third International Biennale of Contemporary Music at the Tel Aviv Museum (1996–2000). In May 1996, *Legends* was played by the Jerusalem Orchestra as part of the Israel Festival, and broadcast live in sixteen European countries.

As the fifth Brena and Lee Freeman, Sr.'s composer-in-residence of the Chicago Lyric Opera, 1994–97, Ran's major project was *Between Two Worlds*, (*The Dybbuk*),[45] an opera composed on a libretto by Charles Kondek. The Jewish play by S. Ansky (1863–1920), on which Ran's opera is based, had the first of its over one thousand performances in 1914, when actor-director Konstantin Stanislavsky brought a Russian version to the Moscow Art Studio Theater. Ansky died November 8, missing the December 8 Warsaw premiere. The play crossed the ocean to New York in 1922 with Maurice Schwartz, and in 1925 was at Manhattan's Neighborhood Playhouse. Its long Broadway run at the 4th Street Theater began in 1954 with Theodore Bikel, Ludwig Donath, Jack Guilford and

---

45. A dybbuk according to Jewish folklore is the spirit of a dead person who enters and possesses the body of a living person.

Carol Lawrence, then surfaced on television (1960, 1961) with the same cast, as the Play of the Week directed by Sidney Lumet. Translations exist in Yiddish, Hebrew, English, Russian, Siberian, Ukranian, Bulgarian, French, Swedish and Japanese. Ran's opera version had a rousing Chicago Lyric Opera premiere, June 20, 1997. Its European premiere was in a series of seven performances at the Bielefeld Opera in Germany, in a German translation, beginning May 1999.

Vessels of Courage and Hope was commissioned by the Baltimore Symphony, in commemoration of the fiftieth anniversary of the State of Israel, and of the voyage of the SS *President Warfield* ("*Exodus 1947*"). It was premiered May 1998, Stephen Sanderling conducting. The same year, Ran received a commission from the Koussevitzky Foundation for a work composed for the San Francisco Contemporary Players, and the National Flute Association for a flute concerto for their 2000 convention. Titled *Voices*, for flute, amplified alto flute, piccolo, and orchestra, it was premiered August 17, with Patricia Spencer, flutist, Ransom Wilson, conductor. 2001 also saw many new CD releases of her music, including a commemorative Chicago Symphony Centennial set containing seventeen of her works. 2003 brought a June premiere of her Violin Concerto at Carnegie Hall, with soloist Ittai Shapiro, and the Orchestra of St. Luke's, Charles Hazlewood, conductor.

One of the highlights of 2004 was the bar mitzvah of son David, for which his mother wrote two songs. 2005 saw the premiere of a Koussetvizky Foundation commission, *Under the Sun's Gaze* (Concerto da Camara III), performed by the San Francisco Contemporary Music Players led by David Milnes.

In 1986, Shulamit married Dr. Abraham Lotan, a head and neck, ear, nose and throat surgeon. They are parents of two sons, David, born September 20, 1991, and Yaron, June 28, 1993.

MARGA RICHTER was born into a musical family, October 21, 1926, in Reedsburg, Wisconsin. Her mother was singer Inez Chandler and her grandfather, composer-conductor Richard Richter. Marga was already studying piano and composing small pieces at age three. In 1945, upon acceptance to Juilliard, her family moved to New York. With teachers like renowned pianist **Rosalyn Tureck** (1914–2003), herself a former Juilliard student, and American composers **Vincent Persichetti** and **William Bergsma** (*b* 1921), she earned her BM in composition, followed by an MM in 1951.

Marga Richter

In 1953, Marga married Alan Skelly, later chairman of the philosophy department of C.W. Post College on Long Island. With the births of Michael (1955) and Maureen (1957), the years until 1971 were focused on parenting. (She now has four grandchildren, born 1987, '89, '91 and '92.) Her music came to national attention with the MGM recording of her *Sonata for Piano; Concerto for Piano and Violas, Cellos and Basses*, which she performed with the Oklahoma Symphony in 1976; *Lament* for string orchestra; *Aria and Toccata* for viola and string orchestra; *Transmutation* for voice and piano; and *Two Chinese Songs* for voice and piano. From 1971–73 Richter taught at Nassau Community College on Long Island. In 1972, she founded, with Herbert Deutsch, the Long Island Composers' Alliance. She is also one of the founders of the League of Women Composers, now part of the IAWM. 1975 brought an exclusive contract with prominent music publisher Carl Fischer. She has received grants from the NEA, Martha Baird Rockefeller Fund, ASCAP and the National Federation of Music Clubs.

Her music, in a variety of genres, has had worldwide performances. *Blackberry Vines and Winter Fruit* was recorded by the London Philharmonic Orchestra (Leonarda, 1989). Other works are concertos for full orchestra, string orchestra, strings and piano, solo piano, harpsichord, woodwind, brass and vocal music. Her ballet, *Abyss* (1964), has been performed by the Joffrey, Harkness and Boston ballet companies. The paintings of Georgia O'Keeffe were the inspiration for the series: *Landscapes of the Mind*, I (Concerto No. 2, for piano and orchestra), II (violin and piano), III (violin, cello and piano)—all published in the '70s. *Qhanri* (Snow Mountain), Tibetan variations for cello and piano, premiered in 1991 with David Wells, cello, and the composer at the piano. This work, and *Requiem* for solo piano have also been recorded on Leonarda. *Into My Heart*, a choral composition dedicated to her husband, based on seven poems connected with his life and death, was performed by Georgia State in 1991.

The same year came *Quantum Quirks of a Quick Quaint Quark*, a five-minute amusing orchestral piece, played by the Long Island Philharmonic, April 1992, **Marin Alsop** conducting. It was recorded by Gerard Schwarz and the Czech Radio Orchestra. The Triple Concerto for Viola, Piano and Cello, *beside the still waters*, premiered July 1993 at the Eastern Music Festival, Greensboro, North Carolina. A one-act chamber opera, *Riders to the Sea*, commissioned by Opera Millennium Minnesota (1995–96) and premiered in 1997, features ethnic instruments: an Irish harp and drum, penny whistles, guitar, string quintet, bass accordion and four voices—two sopranos, mezzo/contralto and tenor. *Spectral Chimes/Shrouded Hills* was released on MMC in 1998, George McKinley conducting. December 19, 1999, *Seacliff Variations* was presented by the New Artists Piano Quartet, at Symphony Center, in Sarasota, Florida. 2000 brought more performances of the opera plus another *Triple Concerto*, this time for piano, violin and cello. The same year saw CD releases of *Variations and Interlude on Themes from Monteverdi and Bach* with Joel Sabin and the Kadowice (Poland) Radio Symphony, and *Out of Shadows and Solitude*, with Gerard Schwarz and the Seattle Symphony.

Marga continues to be active in the Long Island Composers' Alliance, while her compositions are performed in various U.S. venues, including Victoria Bond's *Cutting Edge Concerts*. Richter's style has been termed " . . . a blend of realism and transcendentalism, unconventional but not eccentric, dissonant without being offensive, complex yet uncomplicated . . . " The composer says, "I've never followed a prescribed theory of composition. My music is intensely personal, belonging to no school or movement, yet . . . belonging in the musical mainstream."

EUGÉNIE (Ricau) **ROCHEROLLE** is a most prolific composer, whom I have dubbed "the Cécile Chaminade (1857–1944) of the modern era." A long time Pen Woman in the Connecticut Pioneer Branch, Eugénie traces her roots as a Daughter of the American Revolution (DAR). Born August 24, 1936, in New Orleans, she grew up with both the classics and popular music, from operas to Broadway shows. Her mother, a pianist, exposed the child to Beethoven, Chopin, Debussy and Gershwin. Her father sang arias and ballads in his fine bass baritone. Added to this was the ambiance of her hometown with its blues, gospel and jazz. Eugénie started piano in fourth grade, but found learning to read music a chore, wanting only to play by ear. Fortunately, she resumed lessons in ninth grade, and at the end of the school year won first place in a piano competition. During that summer she began to experiment with some original themes and composed her first serious work, *Fantasia*, which she played on local radio and TV. She entered Sophie Newcomb College of Tulane University (New Orleans) as a piano major, but graduated with a composition degree, having spent an inspirational junior year in Paris studying with the great **Nadia Boulanger**, who had a long line of American composers on her list of students.

A Shipboard Romance!

In 1960, Eugénie married Didier Rocherolle, whom she met on board ship returning from France in 1957. French-born, Didier grew up with his family in New York, where his father ran the U.S. division of the family's famed toiletries company, Roger & Gallet, Paris. After the birth of their first two children, Valérie and Laurent, Eugénie began experimenting with choral music, a field in which she has great success. To this she added writing for concert band. *America, My Home*, for the 1976 bicentennial and *The New Colossus* in 1986, commemorating the 100 year anniversary of the Statue of Liberty, combined chorus and band. The arrival of her third and fourth children, Damien and Justin, inspired yet another extremely successful genre, piano repertoire for students. (As of 2005, her grandchildren numbered seven, ranging in age from Nina, eighteen to Emma, six.)

Composer, lyricist, pianist and teacher, Rocherolle writes at the piano. "I am inspired by the whole creative process, the feel of the keys, the sounds, the variety of touch and tone of the acoustic keyboard." She uses many key changes, lilting melodies, warm, rich harmonies and lively, sometimes jazzy, rhythms. From her first book, *Six Moods for Piano* (1978), to the many that have followed, her delightfully lyrical and wide range of piano music, many for two pianos, has been published by Kjos and Belwin, the latter owned by Warner Brothers Publications with whom she became associated in 1999. A member of ASCAP, Rocherolle is active in the National Federation of Music Clubs, Music Teachers Association and is listed in the *International Encyclopedia of Women Composers*, *Baker's Biographical Dictionary of 20th Century Classical Musicians* as well as several editions of *Who's Who*. In 1995, she was honored by her alma mater, Tulane University, with their Outstanding Alumna Award. She received ASCAP Awards in 2001–02 and 2003–04.

In 2001, she presented selections from several of her piano collections on the Warner Brothers Publishers Showcase at the MTNA National Convention in Washington, DC. Her WB Summer and Fall workshop tours included Indiana, Colorado, New Mexico, New Jersey and Connecticut. For the 2003 MTNA Convention in Salt Lake City, she was the guest composer for the panel session, "The Anatomy of An Ideal Teaching Piece," and then presented a master class at École de Musique Vincent d'Indy (Montreal) in September. Following the March 2004 MTNA Annual Convention in Kansas City, she was the composer/clinician at Hollins University, Roanoke, Virginia, and at the 2004 Pen Woman Biennial, first place winner in the piano category for *Prelude: Red*.

Echoes of Candlelight and Crinolines

Her multitude of piano works include *Bayou Reflections*, *Sonatina No.1* and *Sonata No.2*, collections such as *Just for Friends*, containing gems like *Dreamscape*, *Quiet Nights*, *Cantico Iberico*, *Rapsodie des Pyrénées*, *The Way We Danced*, *Blues Concerto* (all for 2 pianos), *Romancing in Style* (piano solo), *Parisian Promenade*, *Adagio for the Left Hand* and *Souvenirs de Château*, which paints sound pictures of scenes from the family's medieval French castle, the Château de la Rocherolle. *Touch of Blue* and *A Touch of Romance* came out in 2000. An anthem for Our Lady of Fatima church choir and a piano trio for the Wilton Arts Council program were part of the celebration of that Connecticut town's 2002 Bicentennial. For 2004, her piano solo collections included *Mementos*, *Seven Sketches* and *Trois Preludes*, *Five Scenes*; and for two pianos, *Melody Times Two*, music of Irving Berlin and Frank Loesser, plus her arrangement of *April in Paris*. Her 1995 CD *Spinning Gold* is a lovely tapestry of her works played to perfection by talented pianist **Julie Rivers.** (See Pianists.) The same talented duo brought out *Tidings of Joy*, traditional Christmas music arranged by Rocherolle, and a 1998 release, *Romancing the Piano*, all on the Aureus Recordings label.

Long a resident of Connecticut, Eugénie has been honored with the Women in the Arts Award of Stamford, for her works, including the 2003 *Adieu La Jeunesse* by the Schubert Club Solo Singers. Since 2005 she has been published by Hal Leonard, the world's largest print music company, which offers her more artistic freedom. They have published a collection of her solo arrangements of the music of Jerome Kern entitled *Jerome Kern Classics*, and released a duet collection entitled *Christmas Time is Here*. July 23, 2005, marked the premiere of a commission from the Musical Arts Society of New Orleans: *Jambalaya—A Portrait of New Orleans* for two pianos, eight hands. April 2006 brought a dazzling duo piano concert with Julie Rivers at the Pen Women Biennial in Denver.

In an era of musical experimentation sometimes bordering on just plain *noise*, Rocherolle's harmonies unabashedly recreate the wonderful world of *salon music*, reminiscent of **Cécile Chaminade**, with a progressive soupçon of French modernist **Francis Poulenc**, blended with her own unique contemporary innovations. Eugénie Rocherolle is truly a modern Romantic composer.

DARIA SEMEGEN's schoolteacher parents fled the Russians in the Ukraine. Traveling through Eastern European countries to reach the West, they sometimes had to hide by lying precariously on the roof of the train. They managed to get to Munich. Their daughter was born June 27, 1946, in Bamberg, then West Germany, and occupied by the Allies in the aftermath of WWII. Daria came to America as a refugee, Valentine's Day, 1951. By age seven she was already studying piano and composing. Educated at Eastman (BM 1968), and on a Fulbright scholarship (1969) at the Warsaw Conservatory with **Witold Lutoslawski** (1913–1994), she went on to win a fellowship to Yale where she earned her MM in 1971. From 1971–75 she taught at the Columbia-Princeton Electronic Music Center, collaborating with electronic music pioneers **Vladimir Ussachevsky** (1911–90) and **Otto Luening** (1900–96) in preparation of their works for performance and recording on CRI. In 1974, she joined the composition faculty of SUNY, Stony Brook, as associate director of the Electronic Music Studio, becoming director in 1988.

Since 1974, she served on many award judging panels including those of the NEA, Meet the Composer, New York Foundation for the Arts, MacDowell Colony, SEAMUS, BMI, as well as being on the board of governors of the American Composers Alliance.

Semegen's works have been cited in numerous books, articles, and dissertations as "textbooks for electronic music composition." An article in *Perspectives of New Music*, 1996, Vol. 32, No.1, pp 219–222, entitled "COMPLEXITY: Points to Ponder" details exactly this composer's perspective:

> The transforming experience of composing electronic music, with its extraordinary array of sonic resources, influenced her instrumental composition. She believes that while electronic music has evolved as technology's enabled extension of instrumental music, it is a more flexible medium in which the composer can work as a painter or sculptor in creating a work. In turn, the athletic and expressive capabilities of live instrumental music performance can be a role model for electronic music composition in terms of musical gestures, richness of nuance and expressive complexity. Semegen favors refined editing techniques, both analog and digital, as an essential tool enabling her to produce a highly personalized sonic library of "sound sculpture" consisting of textures of varying densities and complexities, and unusual sound successions. She developed partially indeterminate multi-track recording techniques to generate new and unexpected "hybrid" sound combinations. Using both analog and digital technology, she devised a parallel formats method of archiving analog electronic compositions, specifically the body of work by pioneer Blent Abel.

Winner of many honors, including six NEA grants, two BMI awards, the ISCM International Electronic Music Competition prize, MacDowell Colony and Yaddo fellowships, and a National Academy of Recording Arts and Sciences (NARAS) award, in October 1994 Semegen was honored with the Distinguished Alumni Achievement Award from the Eastman School of Music, and in 1987 was the first woman to be awarded the McKim Commission from the Library of Congress. In the course of almost a decade, 1990–99, Semegen was commissions coordinator for the World Premieres Concert Series presented by the Stony Brook Contemporary Chamber Players, and helped establish the World Premieres Concert as a annual New York City event. Her works are recorded on New World Records, CRI, Opus One, Finnadar and Columbia/Odyssey.

Alex Shapiro

ALEX SHAPIRO was born in New York City, January 11, 1962. Early composition studies were at Mannes College of Music (1977) and Aspen (1978, 1979). A composition student of Craig Shuler and Bruce Adolphe at Juilliard (1979–1980), she also studied at the Manhattan School of Music (1980–1983) with **Ursula Mamlok** and **John Corigliano**. An accomplished pianist as well as composer, Alex was a student of New York recitalist Marshall Kreisler (1973–1980).

Shapiro moved to Los Angeles in 1983, beginning a career composing scores for films, television and documentary projects. In 1996, she returned her focus to concert music and is now steadily commissioned to compose new pieces for musicians and ensembles, many of whom have previously performed her work. Her scores are published by Activist Music Publishing, and can be found in many libraries and universities across North America. Her award-winning chamber works are heard in concerts in the U.S. and abroad, and have been recorded on the Cambria and Innova labels. She is the recipient of honors and grants from the American Music Center, American Composers Forum, Mu Phi Epsilon and ASCAP, as well as fellowships from the MacDowell Colony and California Arts Council.

An active participant in the Southern California music community, Shapiro is vice president of the board of directors of the American Composers Forum of Los Angeles, chairperson of ACFLA's Advisory Council, and moderator of the organization's popular bimonthly Composers' Salon series in Hollywood. She has also served as an officer of NACUSA, the College Music Society, and Society of Composers and Lyricists.

Steeped in computer technology, in her professional digital recording studio Shapiro enjoys control over her career from publishing her scores to programming her own award-winning website. She has also used those technologies in a more personal pursuit, in 1999 meeting a software developer named Charles Richardson via a dating website. They were married October 4, 2003. They reside on the Pacific coast in Malibu, as well as on a sailboat in Santa Barbara, where Alex's love of the ocean inspires much of her music.

A catalogue of over forty works includes *Trio for Clarinet, Violin and Piano*, recorded in 1999 by Berkeley Price, clarinet, Nancy Roth, violin and **Deon Nielsen Price**, piano, on Cambria's "Clariphonia: Music of the 20th Century on Clarinet," and *Sonata for Piano*, featured on Teresa McCollough's Innova CD, "New American Piano Music," released in 2000. The new millennium also brought a string quintet for two violins, two violas and cello, commissioned by Gerry Aster and J. Christopher Kennedy for Pacific Serenades, which premiered March 2003 in Los Angeles. *At the Abyss*, a three movement work for piano, marimba, vibraphone and metal percussion, commissioned and premiered by pianist Teresa McCollough, April 2003, in San Francisco, won the 2003 Best Original Composition Award from Mu Phi Epsilon, the international music fraternity, and released on Innova's "Music for Hammer and Sticks" (2005). *Journey* and *Desert Waves*, for five-string electric violin, performed by Sabrina Berger, were featured on **Victoria Bond**'s Cutting Edge series (April 2004). Two other 2005 CDs featuring Shapiro's works are "Above and Beyond" (Los Angeles Flute Quartet), with *Bioplasm*; and "Coast to Coast" with New York Philharmonic principal tubist Alan Baer playing *Music for Two Big Instruments*, with pianist Bradley Haag.

Alice Shields

Native New Yorker **ALICE SHIELDS**, born February 18, 1943, is a composer, poet and opera singer, performing traditional and modern roles at New York City Opera, Opera Society of Washington, DC, Clarion Opera Society (Italy), and Wolf Trap Opera. With a PhD in composition (Columbia, 1975), she became associate director of the Columbia-Princeton Electronic Music Center, a position she held until 1982. She was one of the first women to work extensively in the electro-acoustic medium and, in 1985, became technical instructor at the center, serving as personal technician and collaborator with pioneer electronic composer **Vladimir Ussachevsky** on electronic music for film and opera. Her *Apocalypse*, an electronic opera utilizing texts in English, classical Greek, Gaelic and Sanskrit, for live and recorded singers and choreographed in the style of Hindu Bharata Natyam dance-drama, was released on CRI Records (1993), and contains taped portions of the work created with both MIDI and analog electronic music technology. A 1994 CD, *Organ Screaming* and *The Dawn Wind*, contains two scenes from this opera sung by the composer.

Based on her own encounter in an 18th century Rhode Island farmhouse with an apparition purported to be the ghost of Jonathan Kramer, who died in 1780, she premiered her *Mass for the Dead: An Awesome Coup de Theatre*, in 1993 at the American Chamber Opera. True to the thread of multiculturalism which runs through her works, the *Mass* contains Gregorian chants, an aria inspired by Monteverdi's *Orfeo*, and original melodies for live and electronically modified voices, using her techniques to create an eerie supernatural atmosphere. Also in 1993, she produced a concert of American Computer Music for the Akademie der Künste in Berlin where her *Shivatanz* for mezzo-soprano and tape, choreographed in Bharata Natyam style, was premiered with the composer as soloist.

1996 produced *It's Haunted Here*, a digital multimedia work, and in 1999, *Komachi at Sekidera*, for soprano, alto flute and koto, and *Vegetable Karma*, a computer piece written for the International Festival of Electroacoustic Music while composer-in-residence at Brooklyn College. *Rani tero* (2000), a chamber work for singer, violins and tambura was her first contribution to the millennium.

For the decade 1985–95, Shields studied Bharata Natyam (Indian classical dance) and began performing in traditional dance pieces. She also studied North Indian (Hindustani) raga singing and the South Indian music for Bharata Nataym. While not presenting herself as a singer of Hindustani music, she has used the techniques and ragas in her own music in *Dust* (2001), for modern dance, which toured India in 2002; *Kirtannam* (2002), for flute and oboe, *Azure* (2003), for flute, violin, viola and cello, and *From Saundarya Lahari: The Ocean of Beauty* (2004) for flute, viola and harp.

Shenandoah (2002), computer music for modern dance, which is also in concert version, and *The Mud Oratorio* (2003), commissioned by Dance Alloy and Frostburg State University, were followed by *Mioritza - Requiem for Rachel Corrie* (2004), for trombone and computer music on tape, a commission by **Monique Buzzarte**; *Kyrielle* (2004/2005), for violin and tape, a commission by Airi Yoshioka; and *The Flowers of Srebrenica* (2006) for trombone and tape.

From 1994–96 Shields was director of development at Columbia's Computer Music Center, and in 1996 adjunct assistant professor at NYU's psychology department, where she taught Psychology of Music, with emphasis on how music communicates meaning. She has also lectured on nonverbal communication in sound for the Santa Fe Opera, the CUNY Center for Developmental Neuroscience, and the International Society for Research on Emotion.

SHEILA SILVER, born October 3, 1946, in Seattle, Washington, began piano studies at age five. Upon graduation from UC Berkeley (1968), she was awarded the George Ladd Prix de Paris for two years' study of composition in the French capital, as well as Stuttgart (Germany) where her mentors were Erhard Karkoschka and **György Ligeti** (*b* 1921). She returned to the U.S. to earn her doctorate at Brandeis University (1976) under the mentorship of Arthur Berger, Harold Shapero and Seymour Shifrin.

Recipient of numerous awards, prizes and residencies, including the Prix de Rome, a Koussevitsky Fellowship for Tanglewood, a composer award from the American Academy and Institute of Arts and Letters, an NEA Fellowship and two-time winner of the ISCM national composers competition, in 1991 she had a Camargo Foundation residency at Cassis (France). During the summer of 1995, she was a resident at Rockefeller's Bellagio (Italy) Study and Conference Center where, funded by the NEA, she composed *From Darkness Emerging* for harp and string quartet, written for **Heidi Lehwalder** and the Muir String Quartet, which premiered in October at Boston, Providence, Rhode Island, Kennedy Center and Seattle. In 1996 came *Etudes for String Quartet*, commissioned and premiered by the Ying String Quartet at Eastman, March 1997, and funded by Eastman, Stanford (University) Lively Arts, San Francisco Performances, and the Universities of Illinois and Kansas. She also completed a piano concerto for Russian virtuoso Alexander Paley, commissioned by a Barlow Foundation consortium of the Illinois, Richmond and Annapolis Symphonies and the American Composers Orchestra, who gave the premiere April 1997, in Carnegie Hall. It was recorded by Paley and the Lithuanian State Symphony in February 2001, and released in the fall.

Sources for Silver's melodically rich music include classical Greek, Roman and Indian mythology, American jazz, Jewish chant, and transcultural elements of the East, like Buddhist chanting, worked into Western-style textures. Her allegorical opera, *The Thief of Love*, for which she also wrote the libretto, is based on an 18th century Bengali tale. In 1992, her piece for strings, *To the Spirit Unconquered*, was commissioned by Chamber Music America for the Guild Trio. This poignant work was inspired by the Holocaust and written as a tribute to the ability of the human spirit to survive. Other compositions include *Three Preludes for Orchestra*, *Dance of Wild Angels*, *Sonata for Cello and Piano*, *Dance Converging*, *Six Preludes Pour Piano*, *Canto*, *Chariessa* and *Transcending*, *Three Songs for Michael Dash*, *in memoriam* (1995).

Besides her concert music, she scored the film *Alligator Eyes* (1991), written, produced and directed by her husband, John Feldman, and for *Dead Funny* (1995) with the title song, *Playing with Knives*—both of which have been released on video. A 1997 score for *Jacob's Secret* includes original concert music as well as the film's underscore as star Martin Landau plays a retired concert pianist. An all-Silver CD, *To the Spirit Unconquered*, was released March 1996, featuring the title piece, and *Six Preludes for Piano*, *Dance Converging* and *Dynamis* for solo horn. *To the Spirit Unconquered*, based on Primo Levi's writings on the Holocaust, was heard at the U.S. Memorial Holocaust Museum in Washington, DC, March 26, 2000, and on the series "Music and the Jewish Spirit" at New York's 92nd

Street Y, May 2, 2000. Her three act comic opera, *The Thief of Love*, was featured in New York City Opera's "Showcasing American Composers" series, May 2000, at Lincoln Center, and received its fully staged premiere performance on March 9, 2001 by the Opera Ensemble and Orchestra of Stony Brook.

Silver lives outside New York City with her film writer/director husband and their son Victor, born June 23, 1998. She is professor of music at SUNY, Stony Brook. In 1997, she was appointed Charles and Andrea Bronfman distinguished visiting professor of Judaic Studies at the College of William and Mary in Williamsburg, Virginia. Also an amateur artist, her paintings can be seen on the covers of several of her recordings.

LAURIE SPIEGEL was born September 20, 1945, in Chicago, Illinois. After completing her social sciences degree (Shimer College AB, 1967), which included a special studies program at Oxford University (philosophy, literature, 1966–67), she pursued private studies in classic guitar, theory and counterpoint in London (1967–68), followed by compositional studies with Jacob Druckman (1928–96) at Juilliard (1969–1972), and Brooklyn College, CUNY (1973–75), resulting in an MA in Composition (1975).

Her compositions draw on a variety of musical roots and instrumental backgrounds, encompassing mandolin, banjo, folk and classic guitar, renaissance and baroque lute. She is best known, however, for her work in electronic media, with which she has been involved since the late 1960s. After several years of instrumental, analog electronic and tape composition, she decided her music needed the greater power of computers. She began work at Bell Telephone Laboratories, where she wrote interactive software for both music and image compositions (1973–79, 1984), working with Emmanuel Ghent, Kenneth Knowlton and Max Mathews.

Spiegel taught composition and electronic and computer music at Aspen (1971–73), Bucks County (Pennsylvania) Community College (1981–85), Cooper Union for the Advancement of Science and Art in New York (1980–82), and New York University, where she founded the computer music studio (1982–83). She has also done extensive work in various visual arts. In 1976, she was an artist-in-residence in video at the WNET Experimental Television Laboratory (PBS Channel 13, NY), where she produced computer animated "visual music" as well as composing soundtrack music for other video artists and series music for WNET's weekly experimental video art series "VTR." Subsequent to her early work at Bell Labs, she designed and wrote software for more accessible personal computer music systems, including the early Alpha Syntauri for Apple II computer (1979–81), the McLeyvier music system (1981–85), and her widely used computer program, "Music Mouse—An Intelligent Instrument," for Macintosh, Amiga, and Atari personal computers (1985). Although Spiegel has specialized in interactive process composition and logic-based instruments, her musical works can nevertheless be characterized as Romantic, some having roots in folk music.

Spiegel in Space

The composer often explores relationships between music and other media, as in *Voyages* (1978), for sound with computer-generated video images, and *A Living Painting* (1979), for video images alone, which explore the musical structuring of abstract time-based visual art. Her 1977 computer realization of Kepler's *Harmony of the Planets* was sent into space as the opening cut of the Voyager Spacecraft's golden record, "Sounds of Earth."

Her best known recordings include "The Expanding Universe" (Philo Records, 1980), and her CD "Unseen Worlds" (Aesthetic Engineering, 1994). Spiegel has received fellowships, grants, and awards from CAPS, ASCAP, Meet the Composer, the Institute for Studies in American Music, where she did research in pre-Civil-War American music, and the New York Foundation for the Arts Fellowship in Composition. She freelances as a composer for film, video, dance, concert, and other media, publishes her own computer software under the business name "Aesthetic Engineering," and is a consultant in computer music, digital audio, and other areas of information technology.

HILARY TANN, born November 2, 1947, in Ferndale, Wales, wrote her first piece of music at age six. She earned her BM in 1968 from the University of Wales in Cardiff. Impressed with visiting Schoenberg lecturer Ben

Hilary Tann

Boretz from Princeton, she decided to study there, and came to America in 1972 as a visiting fellow, receiving her MM in 1975 and PhD in 1981. Working her way upriver, she substituted for Joan Tower's 1977 sabbatical leave at Bard College at Annandale-on-the-Hudson, then stayed until 1980 when she paddled even further north to become chair of the performing arts department at Union College, Schenectady, New York. At the same time she served on the executive board of the International League of Women Composers (now the IAWM) and was the editor of its *Journal* from 1982–88. After co-editing, in 1989, a volume of *Perspectives of New Music* about Japanese music, she took a sabbatical to go to Japan in 1990, and taught at Kansai University, as well as studying the *shakuhachi* (bamboo flute). She also wrote a series of articles, "Tradition and Renewal in the Music of Japan," and an orchestral work *From Afar*, incorporating Japanese influences, which was premiered in November 1996 by the Knoxville Symphony under Kirk Trevor.

Tann's music often reflects the lovely countryside of her youth, or is inspired by world events such as *The Open Field*, subtitled *In memoriam, Tiananmen Square, June 1989*. *Adirondack Light* was commissioned by the Glens Falls (NY) Symphony for the 1992 Centennial of Adirondack Park in scenic upstate New York—near the Hudson River, of course. In September 1994, she was present at the premiere of *With the Heather and Small Birds* at the Cardiff Festival, played by the European Women's Orchestra conducted by **Odaline de la Martinez**. On the same trip, Tann was the featured composer at the Presteigne Festival where her *Cresset Stone*[46] for solo violin (recorded by the Irish contemporary ensemble, Concorde) was premiered, along with performances of *Water's Edge* and *Of Erthe and Air*. A June 28, 1995 premiere at the Criccieth (Wales) Festival, commissioned in part by the Welsh Council of Arts, featured *From the Song of Amergin*, part of Robert Graves' *The White Goddess*. Three lines:

> *I am the a wind; on a deep lake*
> *I am a tear; the Sun lets fall,*
> *I am a hawk; above the cliff,*

caught the composer's imagination to translate into a trio for flute, viola and harp. It was recorded by the ensemble Gemini in Manchester.

In recognition of the quality of her work, Tann was awarded a prestigious Meet The Composer/ *Reader's Digest* Fund commission for a consortium of orchestras: the Santa Fe, Knoxville, Augusta and University of South Carolina Symphonies, The Women's Philharmonic and Columbus Pro Musica. A violin concerto, *Here, the Cliffs*, was written for and premiered by **Corine Cook**, October 17, 1997, with the North Carolina Symphony led by Gerhard Zimmerman, a consortium commission. The piece has received many performances.

Her first setting in the Welsh language was commissioned by the Madog Center for Welsh Studies in Rio Grande, Ohio, a piece for soprano and mezzo entitled *The Moor*, from a poem by R.S. Thomas. *Cân Merch i'w Mam* (A Girl's Song to her Mother), poetry by Menna Elfyn, premiered at St. George's Anglican Church, Winnipeg (Canada), July 30, 1999, by Mari Morgan (mezzo soprano) and Sherry Bonness (oboe). The anthem, *Psalm 104* (*Praise, My Soul*), for chorus, organ and two trumpets, was premiered in Minneapolis, September 4, at the North American Welsh Choir's Sixty-ninth Gymanfa Ganu (Singing Festival). It uses the verses of George Herbert and a Welsh hymn tune and may be sung in Welsh or English. Tann was one of the composers invited to contribute to Mary Wiegold's compilation, *The Composers Song Book*. Her song, *Mother and Son*, was aired at the Almeida Theatre Company Festival in London. A solo oboe piece written for Melinda Maxwell is included on "Celtic Connections" (Capstone Records) a CD of British women composers, released July 20, 1999, with pieces by **Jane O'Leary** (founder of Concorde) and **Nicola LeFanu**.

2000 performances of Tann's music include the premieres of two more concertos: *In the First, Spinning Place* for alto saxophone and orchestra, commissioned and premiered at the North American Saxophone Alliance,

---

46. A medieval method of lighting was a hollowed out stone filled with oil, with a lighted wick. Tann was fascinated by the concept of the flame fading, leaving the warm stone . . . There is a cresset stone in Brecon Cathedral in South Wales near the composer's place of birth.

performed by Debra Richtmeyer (U. of Arizona Symphony); and *Anecdote*, a soliloquy for cello and orchestra premiered by Ovidiu Marinescu and the Newark (Delaware) Symphony. *The Walls of Morlais Castle* for oboe, viola and cello, was premiered by the Ovid Ensemble at the Presteigne Festival, and *Water's Edge* for piano duet at the Vale of Glamorgan Festival—both in Wales. *From Afar*, a major work for triple-wind orchestra, based on the composer's recollections of the ancient music of Japan, was performed by the BBC National Orchestra of Wales. 2001 saw Tann as composer-in-residence with the Louisville Symphony. Her premieres that year included *Fanfare for a River* (Knoxville, Tennessee), *The Open Field* (Louisville, Kentucky), her *Violin Concerto* (Monterey, California), and *The Grey Tide and the Green*, premiered at St. David's Hall, Cardiff, with the Royal Liverpool Philharmonic under Owain Arwel Hughes, July 25, at the Final Night of the Welsh "Proms"—a Royal Liverpool Philharmonic Orchestra commission. (Having one's music performed on the last night is a singular honor!)

May 2002 brought "The Power of Nature: Music of Hilary Tann," a concert at the University of Wisconsin, River Falls. *From Afar* was selected for the opening concert of the April 2003 International Festival of Women in Music Today, in Seoul, Korea, conducted by **Apo Hsu**. In 2004–05 several of Tann's works were recorded on four CDs, including *Lullaby* for solo cello, two songs for voice and oboe, a string orchestra piece and a solo organ work. A 2005 CD, commissioned and recorded by the Meininger Trio,[47] includes *Llef* (cello/ flute), based on a hymn tune of the same name, translated "a cry from the heart," *Windhover* (solo flute), *The Cresset Stone* (solo cello version), and the new flute/cello/piano trio, *The Gardens of Anna Maria Luisa De Medici*,[48] which premiered May 2004, in Bad Waldsee (Germany) at the Bodensee Festival.

Keith Davies Jones, MD, president of St. David's Society of Winnipeg and a choir singer himself, wrote of a rehearsal that Hilary conducted at which he was present, "Hilary radiates a creative energy and tension. Her music is just like she is . . . know one, and you will know the other. Feminine, beautiful, sensuous, a little exotic, about an equal mix of tranquillity and incandescence . . . "

Hilary's close interest in Japan—and wearing a shirt with Japanese imprint—one Sunday led to a closer meeting with church organist, David Bullard, who is also an apple farmer. August 15, 2002 was their happy wedding day. A 1770 house in upstate New York, used by the British in the Revolutionary War and now a National Historic site, is their home.

Following in the footsteps of her countrywomen, **Grace Williams** and **Morfydd Owen**, strongly nationalistic Wales has reason to be proud of this composer leading her country's music into the 21st century and into the rest of the world.

Augusta Thomas

AUGUSTA READ THOMAS born April 24, 1964, in Glen Cove, New York, grew up in a large family, the tenth of ten children (she has a twin brother), and was nurtured in an environment where love for the arts, passion for education, respect for creativity, and an appreciation of codes of discipline were an integral part of her upbringing. She has been composing since childhood. Her education included Northwestern University (BM, 1987), where she studied with Alan Stout, Yale University (MM, 1988) under Jacob Druckman, and the Royal Academy of Music, London, where she received an advanced course diploma in music composition. Seven years after her graduation she was elected an associate, an RAM honorary degree. She was also awarded fellowships from the Bunting Institute of Radcliffe College, Tanglewood Music Center, Aspen Music Festival, and the Fontainebleau School of Music (Paris). Between 1991–94, she was a

47. Additional funds were provided by the International Festival of Lake Constance, also known as the Bodensee Festival, which traditionally moves from town to town in the bordering countries of Germany, Austria and Switzerland.

48. In 2003, flutist Christiane Meininger asked the composer to write a trio about the last of the Medicis, the remarkable Anna Maria Luisa (1667–1743) who left Italy for twenty-six years while married to Johann Wilhelm of Saxony. Each of the composition's three movements reveals Anna's love of cultivated nature. The first is inspired from her desire to see something beautiful, even in her bedchamber, where she kept bowls of tulips. The second reflects the park-like grounds of Schloss (Castle) Benrath, her German home. The third takes us to the Villa La Quiete near Florence, whose formal garden Anna created to console herself after the death in 1723 of her father, Grand Duke Cosimo III.

junior fellow at Harvard, going on to the Eastman composition faculty 1994–2001. Since 2000 she has been on the board of directors of the American Music Center (AMC), a national service and information center for new American music. In 2005, she became their chair, a three-year volunteer term. She is on the faculty of Tanglewood Music Center, and was the Wyatt professor of music at Northwestern University until 2006.

A 1989 Guggenheim Fellowship permitted full time composing. Her works have been premiered by such orchestras as Philadelphia, New York Philharmonic, Cleveland Chamber, Dallas, Seattle, Memphis, Louisville, Boston and Moscow with a roster of world-famous conductors including Mstislav Rostropovich, Pierre Boulez, Seiji Ozawa, Hans Vonk, Gerard Schwarz, **JoAnn Falletta**, **Gisèle Ben-Dor** and Lawrence Leighton Smith. Her lyric, atmospheric style encompasses works for chorus, solo instruments, chamber music and chamber orchestra, orchestra with soloist, and large orchestra. The triple concerto *Nights' Midsummer Blaze* (1989), for flute, viola, and harp, was the winner of the ASCAP Nissim Prize. *Ancient Chimes* (1993) for orchestra, was commissioned by Mstislav Rostropovich for a tour throughout Russia with the National Symphony. Her chamber-opera *Ligeia*, based on a story by Edgar Allan Poe, with librettist Leslie Dunton-Downer, was premiered at the 1994 Evian (France) Festival, winning the International Orpheus Prize and received its American premiere in July 1995 at Aspen. October saw the Russian premiere with Rostropovich and the Moscow Opera. *Manifesto*, a fanfare for the National Symphony, was commissioned to commemorate the twenty-fifth anniversary of the Kennedy Center. The same month brought the Eastman Philharmonia commission *Conquering the Fury of Oblivion* (text by Leslie Dunton-Downer, narrated by Almeta Whitis), a theatrical oratorio honoring the seventy-fifth anniversary of the nineteenth amendment and to celebrate women's rights in America. *Trilogy* for cello, piano and percussion and *Incantations* for solo violin were performed in November.

1996 performances were the piano concerto *Five Haiku*, with Sara Wolfensohn and the New York Chamber Symphony under Gerard Schwarz in January; *Angel Musings* in February, by the Society for New Music in Syracuse; and in May, *On This Occasion*, for soprano, cello, harp, commissioned and premiered by the Harvard Society of Fellows. The double concerto *Eclipse Musings* for flute, guitar, and chamber orchestra received its first performance in August at the National Flute Convention in New York (released on Albany Records, October 1999, with **Liona Boyd** and Nicholas Goluses), and . . . *words of the sea* . . . for orchestra, was commissioned and premiered by the Chicago Symphony in December. 1997 began with *Spirit Musings* for solo violin in January at Northwestern University. *Chanson*, for cello and orchestra, also commissioned by Rostropovich, received a Boston Symphony premiere, April 1997, with Seiji Ozawa and Rostropovich as soloist. The same month featured *Love Songs* for twelve male voices for the vocal ensemble, Chanticleer, in San Francisco.

Trombone Concerto received a 1997 premiere by the Brevard (North Carolina) Music Center Orchestra. 1998 premieres were: *Concerto for Flute and Chamber Orchestra*, by the Chamber Orchestra of the South Bay (San Francisco), *Concerto for Saxophone Quartet* by the American Composers Orchestra (New York) and *Overture* by the Rochester Philharmonic. *Ritual Incantations*, a concerto for cellist David Finckel, premiered during the Aspen Music Festival's Fiftieth Anniversary season, July 1999. *For Emily* (choral), was sung by the Dale Warland Singers, December 4, 1999, Hugh Wolf conducting.

Read Thomas turned the century with several commissions: *Ceremonial*, introduced by the Chicago Symphony under **Daniel Barenboim**, January 6, 2000; *To the Wild Sky* (text by Tennyson), for chorus and orchestra, presented by the Washington Choral Arts Society February 25 at Kennedy Center; and the Santa Fe Chamber Music Festival premiered *Invocations*, with the Miami String Quartet, March 19. The Berlin Philharmonic Orchestra gave the first performance of *Aurora: Concerto for Piano and Orchestra*, with Barenboim as pianist and conductor, June 10.

Augusta Read Thomas succeeded **Shulamit Ran** as Mead composer-in-residence with the Chicago Symphony in the fall of 1997, the only fully-endowed composer-in-residence position for a major American orchestra. She was composer-in-residence at SummerFest La Jolla, August 2000. She is also the recipient of many of music's most distinguished awards, including the Ernst von Siemens Music Prize 2000, and an award from the American

Academy of Arts and Letters (2001) for lifetime achievement in music and as a composer who has arrived at his or her own voice.

2002 commissions brought *Canticle Weaving* for trombone and orchestra, for principal trombone Ralph Sauer, premiered by the Los Angeles Philharmonic under Esa-Pekka Salonen; *Trainwork* for Chicago Symphony's Ravinia Festival; *Light the First Light of Evening*, by the London Sinfonietta in honor of Oliver Knussen's fiftieth birthday (June 2002); *Chanting to Paradise* for soprano, chorus and orchestra, by the Norddeutscher Rundfunk (North German Radio), Christoph Eschenbach conducting (November), which received its American premiere with the Philadelphia Orchestra and Eschenbach, January 2003; *In My Sky at Twilight* for soprano and ensemble, premiered by Christine Brandes, Pierre Boulez, and musicians of the Chicago Symphony (December); *Sun Threads* for string quartet performed by the Avalon String Quartet; *Two New Etudes*, for piano, from the American Pianists Association for James Giles; *Four Basho Settings* for England's Farnham Youth Choir; *To the Rain* for Youth Pro Musica and the Greater Boston Youth Chorus.

2003–04 premieres gave us *Tangle* for the Chicago Symphony, conducted by David Robertson; *Galaxy Dances* (Ballet for Orchestra) commissioned by the National Symphony Orchestra, Mstislav Rostropovich conducting; *Bubble: Rainbow (spirit level)*, written for soprano Lucy Shelton and Ensemble Sospeso in honor of Elliott Carter's Ninety-fifth Birthday; and *Silver Chants the Litanies* for horn and wind ensemble, in homage to Lucian Berio, commissioned by the Meadows Wind Ensemble of Southern Methodist University. The London Sinfonietta, Oliver Knussen conducting, presented the European premiere of *In My Sky at Twilight* with soprano Claire Booth, January 2004, released on CD in November.

Read Thomas was distinguished guest composer of the Winnipeg Symphony's 2004 Centara Corporation New Music Festival. Her works were performed as part of a residency with the Lutoslawski Philharmonic in Wroclow (Warsaw), Poland. Her music is recorded on Teldec, CRI, Albany, BIS, GM Recordings, Gasparo, Centaur, Louisville Orchestra, Four–TAY and Open Loop. After many years with publisher Theodore Presser, her music is now published exclusively by G. Schirmer, Inc.

On May 21, 2005, the San Diego Symphony, under their new conductor Jahja Ling, who conducted several of Thomas' works in Cleveland, gave the world premiere of *Credences of Summer*, a three-movement work with the poetic titles "Trace the Gold Sun about the Whitened Sky," "Pure Rhetoric of a Language Without Words," and "A Mountain Luminous Halfway in Bloom." It was also the occasion for author and composer to happily meet!

Forthcoming commissions are for the Orchestra of Paris, Christoph Eschenbach, for the opening of the renovated Salle Pleyel (2007); a violin concerto to celebrate Pierre Boulez's birthday concert (2007), also in Paris; and *Astral Canticle* for a Chicago Symphony premiere (2006).

2006 brought the conclusion of her ten, what she calls, "fantastic years" as composer-in-residence with the Chicago Symphony. She also resigned from her secure, tenured, endowed-chair at Northwestern. As she told me just before this book went into print, "I will be unemployed soon, which is a bit daunting, but the chance to compose full time with no distractions is worth the risk."

Augusta and Pulitzer Prize winning British composer Bernard Rands, whom she met at concerts, were married September 5, 1994.

Joan Tower

JOAN TOWER was born in New Rochelle, New York, September 6, 1938. Her father, a geologist, was the musical parent, playing violin and singing. His work took the family to South America in 1947, where they lived in Bolivia, Peru and Chile. Joan had started piano lessons at six, and in the course of the years managed to find music teachers wherever she lived. The family returned to America when she was sixteen, and from 1958–61 she attended Bennington College (Vermont) where she majored in music and started composing, although her main focus was still the piano. After graduating with a BA, she moved to New York and spent the next six years teaching piano at the Greenwich House Music School, while working on her master's in theory and music history at Columbia University. Studies with electronic music pioneer

Otto Luening, serial composer **Ralph Shapey** and French modernist **Darius Milhaud** culminated in 1978 with a DMA in composition.

In 1969, Tower founded the Da Capo Chamber Players (flute, clarinet, violin, cello, piano), specializing in contemporary music, and remained their pianist for fifteen years until 1984. They showcased her *Platinum Spirals* (solo violin, 1976), *Hexachords* (solo flute), *Wings* (solo clarinet, 1981), *Petroushskates* (1980)—reflecting Stravinsky's *Petrushka* with images of ice-skating—and *Amazon I* (1976). In 1973 the group won the prestigious Naumburg Award for Chamber Music.

The Piece That Changed Her Life

In 1979, the American Composers Orchestra asked Tower to write her first orchestral work, *Sequoia*. It was the piece which brought her into the limelight. Dennis Davies premiered it with the American Composers Orchestra and Zubin Mehta performed it with the New York Philharmonic at Avery Fisher Hall for the televised United Nations Day celebration. Leonard Slatkin took it all over the world, and on a U.S. tour with the St. Louis Symphony. It has been performed by major orchestras in the U.S. and Europe. A choreographed version by the Royal Winnipeg Ballet toured throughout Canada, Europe and Russia.

Clarinetist **Richard Stoltzman** commissioned her *Fantasy for Clarinet and Piano* (1983). In 1984 her cello concerto was recorded by **Lynn Harrell** and the St. Louis Symphony. 1987–93 produced five *Fanfare(s) for the Uncommon Woman*, for brass and percussion, dedicated to "adventurous women who take risks"—the first, a tribute to Aaron Copland, composer of *Fanfare for the Common Man*, the third for the 100th anniversary of Carnegie Hall.

Her chamber works, 1976–77, were inspired by gem imagery, in memory of her father: *Platinum Spirals*, *Black Topaz* and *Red Garnet Waltz*. These were followed by *Snow Dreams* (1983), commissioned for flutist **Carol Wincenc** and guitarist **Sharon Isbin**, *Fantasy . . . Harbor Lights* (1983), *Clocks* (1985) for Isbin, and *Island Prelude* (1989), which draws on the tropical environment of her childhood.

The Big Prize and a Prolificacy of Premieres

From 1985–88, Tower was composer-in-residence at the St. Louis Symphony as part of the Meet the Composer Orchestra Residency program. *Silver Ladders* (1986), commissioned by them, won the prestigious $150,000 Grawemeyer Award for Music Composition in 1990. The next decade brought a ballet, *Stepping Stones* (1993), *Night Fields* (string quartet, 1994), *Like a . . . an Engine*, and *Très Lent* (*In Memoriam: Olivier Messiaen*). She conducted her *Celebration*, October 1993, at the International Women's Forum in Washington, DC. In January 1994, Leonard Slatkin led the New York Philharmonic in the premiere of *Concerto for Orchestra*, commissioned by the Philharmonic and St. Louis and Chicago Symphonies. 1995 began with the January premiere of *Duets*, commissioned by the Los Angeles Chamber Orchestra, featuring duets by pairs of cellos, flutes and horns, followed by a trio of fast duets by violins, clarinets, oboes and percussion and tympani. This composition marked a return to large orchestral music after several years of chamber, solo, and stage works. The Lincoln Center Chamber Players premiered her clarinet quintet *Turning Points*. 1996 featured *Ascent*, her first organ piece for the International Organ Society. 1997 was the significant d'Note Recordings' release of four solo concerti with the Louisville Orchestra, featuring **Ursula Oppens** in the Piano Concerto, **Carol Wincenc** in the Flute Concerto, **Elmar Oliveira** in the Violin Concerto, and **David Shifrin** in the Clarinet Concerto—the latter reprised with the Long Beach Philharmonic under **JoAnn Falletta**. The Louisville Orchestra was conducted by Joseph Silverstein for the Violin and Piano concerti, and Spanish maestro Max Bragado-Darman for the Flute and Clarinet. The same year she wrote *Rainwaves* for the Verdehr Trio. *Tambor*, for the Pittsburgh Symphony, premiered May 7, 1998, with Mariss Jansons conducting. Also in 1998, she was the recipient of the Delaware Symphony's Alfred I. Dupont Award for Distinguished American Composers and Conductors, and was inducted into the membership of the American

Academy of Arts and Letters. *Big Sky*, piano trio, was written in 2000, while composer-in-residence at SummerFest La Jolla, and premiered by David Finkel, cello, **Wu Han**, piano, and **Chee-Yun**, violin. *Fascinating Ribbons* (2002), her foray into the world of band music, was a consortium commission of thirty-four bands, and premiered at the annual conference of college band directors.

The composer can be heard as a performer on New Worlds Records' *Très Lent*, for cello and piano, written for André Emellanoff. The Colorado Symphony, conducted by **Marin Alsop**, recorded *Fanfares Nos. 1–5*, *Duets*, and *Concerto for Orchestra* on Koch.

Eight summers were spent as composer-in-residence at the Norfolk Chamber Music Festival at Yale as well as ongoing composer-in-residence with the Muir Quartet in Park City Utah, and the Tanglewood Contemporary Music Festival. She has served as composer-in-residence for the Orchestra of St. Luke's since 1999. With the St. Luke's players, she established and runs the series "Second Helpings," which introduces the works of living composers in a three part series. 2003 brought the forty-fourth annual Composer's Award from the Lancaster (Pennsylvania) Symphony Orchestra.

Her second String Quartet, *In Memory* (2001), a commission by the Tokyo Quartet, has been performed by them around the world, and the Emerson Quartet performed her third string quartet, *Incandescent* (2004), on three continents and at the Aspen Festival where she was a visiting composer. The quartet took the same work to Tanglewood in July.

2004 continued to be a year of singular events. In January, Carnegie Hall's Making Music series featured a retrospective of her work. The event showcased numerous artists who perform her music, including the Tokyo String Quartet, pianists Melvin Chen and Ursula Oppens, violist Paul Neubauer, oboist Richard Woodhams (principal oboe, Philadelphia Orchestra) and the New England Conservatory Percussion Ensemble. The concert was recorded for Naxos. In March, she attended the premiere of *For Daniel*, written for the Kalichstein-Laredo-Robinson Trio, at the Tucson Winter Festival. Tower played the piano part with members of the Muir Quartet at the Deer Valley Festival, Utah. Her composition *Tambor* was played by the Pittsburgh Symphony at the ASOL convention in June, conducted by Pascal Tortelier. Her Flute Concerto was performed at the Flute Convention in Nashville in August. In the Fall, she was inducted in the Academy of Arts and Sciences at Harvard University.

Tower emerged the leading candidate out of numerous American composers, receiving the commission to write a piece for the Ford Made in America Project,[49] a unique consortium of sixty-five small budget orchestras—representing the fifty states—with music expertise provided by the American Symphony Orchestra League and Meet the Composer.[50] The piece, *Purple Rhapsody*, for viola and orchestra, for Paul Neubauer,[51] premiered November 5, 2005, with JoAnn Falletta and the Omaha Symphony, and was played by eight more orchestras during the 2006–07 seasons. Other commissions included a work for the American Brass Quintet to celebrate Juilliard's 200th anniversary (founded as the Institute of Musical Art in 1905), and *Chamber Dance* for the Orpheus Chamber Orchestra, premiered at Carnegie Hall, May 6, 2006.

The Asher Edelman professor of music at Bard College (upstate New York) since 1972, Joan Tower is one of today's most dynamic composers. She can also add conductor to her list of accomplishments, having conducted some twenty concerts of her works in various states during 2005–07.

Joan is married to William Litfin, her companion of thirty-five years.

---

49. The Made in America Project was started by Robert Rosoff, executive director of the Glens Falls Symphony (New York), and subsequently grew under the sponsorship of the Ford Motor Company.

50. Meet the Composer, Inc., founded in 1974, now a national organization, has revolutionized the environment for U.S. composers, enabling them to make a living writing music through establishing standards of payment, commissioning, opening doors to residencies in cultural institutions and universities, plus audience interaction programs.

51. Neubauer joined the New York Philharmonic in 1984 at age twenty-one, the youngest principal string player in the orchestra's history. Married to **Kerry McDermott** (violinist in the McDermott Trio), he retired from the orchestra in 1990 to pursue a solo career.

LUDMILA ULEHLA, born May 20, 1923 in Flushing, New York, began writing music at age five while learning to play piano and violin under her Czech parents' tutelage. She went on to study composition with **Vittorio Giannini** (1903–66), flute with Arthur Lora, and theory pedagogy with Howard Murphy at the Manhattan School of Music, where she earned a BM, 1946 and MM, 1947. She was on the composition faculty at Manhattan School, 1947–2002, and chair of the composition department, 1972–89. She is now professor emeritus. She also taught classes (1968–91) at the Hoff-Barthelson Music School, Scarsdale, New York, was chairperson for the American Society of University Composers (1972–73), program chair for the National Association for American Composers and Conductors (1967–74), and received awards and grants from ASCAP and Meet The Composer.

In an output spanning over fifty years, Ulehla's compositions include much chamber music, violin sonatas, divertimenti, etc.; piano music, including children's pieces; choral and solo vocal works, some based on Shakespeare's sonnets and poems of Elizabeth Barrett Browning; as well as orchestral and band music, including a piano concerto (1947).

Her chamber opera, *Sybil of the American Revolution*, was premiered (1993). *Symphony in Search of Sources* (1990), was performed in the Ukraine, April 1996, by the Lvov Philharmonic. On June 9, 1996, *Three Fun Pieces* was part of the program at the National Museum for Women in Music in Washington, DC. *Visions* (1998), for Chamber Quintet, was commissioned by the Stony Brook Chamber Players.

1999 premieres were *Undersea Fantasy* for orchestra by the Manhattan School of Music, David Gilbert conductor; *Vivo* for Youth Orchestra, commissioned by the New Jersey Youth Symphony, premiered at Alice Tully Hall, Adrian Bryttan conductor; and *Memorial for the People of Turkey*, inspired by their great earthquake in August of that year, for trumpet, tenor sax, electric guitar and drums, premiered by the Other Quartet at the Manhattan School of Music, and the Knitting Factory, NYC.

Her publications, printed by Advance Music in Germany, include *Sonata for Improvisation* for clarinet, soprano saxophone, and piano, and a new edition (1995) of her book, *Contemporary Harmony*.

While Ulehla's music is definitely contemporary, classical tradition and Slavic influences are part of her style. Having removed herself from anything electronic, the composer is considered neo-romantic.

MARY JEANNE van APPLEDORN, born October 2, 1927, in Holland, Michigan, received a BM in piano (1948), MM in theory (1950) and PhD (1966) from Eastman, where she studied composition with celebrated American composer **Alan Hovhaness** (1911–2000), and wrote her dissertation on Debussy's *Pélleas et Mélisande*. Her post-doctoral studies were at MIT (1982). She made her piano debut at the Weill Recital Hall, Carnegie Hall, New York, in March 1956.

Her numerous works, covering orchestra, band, vocal, choral and chamber music, have won honors and awards and many have been recorded. Among her commissions are: *West Texas Suite* (1975), *Carillion Suite* for the World Carillon Federation (1980), *Lux Legend of Santa Lucia* for band (1982), Concerto for Trumpet, International Trumpet Guild (1985), New York City Ballet Fortieth Anniversary Festival (1988), *Set of Seven* (1988), *Concerto for Trumpet and Band* (1992), *Terrestrial Music*, Double Concerto for Violin and Piano (1992), *A Liszt Fantasie* (1992), *Reeds Afire*, clarinet and bassoon (1994), *Les hommes vidés* (1994) based on T.S. Eliot's *The Hollow Men*, *Ayre for Strings* (1994), and *Cycles of Moons and Tides* for symphonic band (1995). Her 1995 recordings include *Atmospheres for 12 Trombones* and *Rhapsody for Trumpet and Harp*, plus other commissions from the Texas Composers Guild, Women Band Directors National Association and the National Intercollegiate Bands.

In 1971, van Appledorn was selected as one of the three most outstanding Texas women composers. Two years later she was inducted into the Hall of Fame of Texas Women Composers. Between 1980–2000, she received twenty-one ASCAP Awards. She was one of three American composers whose works were chosen for performance in the International Concert Band Competition, July 10, 1994, at Le Havre, France. In May 1995, she was featured artist for the Meet the Composer series at the Bloomingdale House of Music in New York City, the same month *Duos* for viola and cello received a New York premiere. Also in 1995, *Terrestrial Music* was the featured work performed by the New York Inoue Chamber Ensemble with the Oberlin Conservatory String Orchestra for the Third

International Peace Concert Tour in Japan, Hawaii and Seattle. Her *Trio Italiano* for trumpet, horn and trombone received an award in the 1996 International Trumpet Guild's brass trio composition competition. The same year her *Passages for Trombone and Piano* was performed in Austria, and received an award in the British Trombone Association Competition.

MELIORA: Fanfare for Orchestra was commissioned by The Women's Philharmonic and premiered May 26, 2000 in San Francisco. Her *Rhapsody for Violin and Orchestra*, performed by Charles Rex, associate concertmaster of the New York Philharmonic, with the Polish Radio National Symphony, was released on Opus One CD. *Gestures* for clarinet quartet was featured at the International Clarinet Conference, July 2000.

As of this writing, van Appledorn continues as the Paul Whitfield Horn professor of theory and composition at the school of music, Texas Tech University (Lubbock), where she began her teaching career in 1950.

Nancy Van de Vate

NANCY VAN DE VATE, born December 30, 1930, in Plainfield, New Jersey, began her musical studies at Eastman on piano and viola, and graduated from Wellesley in 1952. She married Dwight Van de Vate the same year, and in 1955 moved to Mississippi with her husband and baby. While continuing piano, she also studied composition and graduated from the University of Mississippi (MM, 1958). The family relocated to Florida in 1963, where she continued composition studies at Florida State (DMA, 1968). During the '60s and '70s she taught at various American educational institutions, including Memphis State and Hawaii Loa College; composed mainly chamber music and songs; and engaged in post-doctoral work in electronic music at Dartmouth and the University of New Hampshire (1972). One of the pioneers in championing women's music, in 1975 she founded the International League of Women Composers which merged with the IAWM in 1995.

After divorcing her first husband in 1976, she married Clyde Smith in 1979. From 1982–85 they lived in Indonesia and traveled widely. In 1985 they became residents of Vienna. She began working closely with the Polish composers **Witold Lutoslawski** (1913–94) and **Krzysztof Penderecki** (*b* 1933). Their influence, plus her visits to Indonesia and Hawaii, are reflected in her later music. Her large-scale works feature clusters, aleatory passages, lyric solos and background ostinatos within a carefully devised formal structure.

An Important Recording Company is Born

In 1990, she and her husband founded Vienna Modern Masters, of which she is vice-president and artistic director. Devoted to the production of CDs of contemporary classical music, the company has issued most of Van de Vate's significant works, from the *Adagio* (1957) and chamber works of the '70s, to recent orchestral pieces. They also seek out little-known works by a wide variety of composers from all over the world through their International Orchestral Recording Award Competitions, begun in 1994. The first five competitions were annual, but now the award is given every two years. The first prize is the recording of an orchestral work and its release on CD at no charge to the winning composer. This has resulted in a number of significant releases of chamber and solo works. Obtaining live performances of contemporary orchestral music is notoriously difficult, and by setting up the company she has ensured that this music, as well as her own, reaches a wide public. By 2004 the catalogue numbered well over a hundred.

Van de Vate is the recipient of many honors and awards in recognition of the caliber and variety of her over 130 works, which range from serious to witty to experimental. (Among her original tonal sounds is having the violin played below the bridge in *Suite for Solo Violin*.) *Journeys* (1981–84) and *Chernobyl* (1987) utilize *sound mass* technique—a concept transcending the boundaries between sound and noise. The latter was written, according to the composer, "to express universal feelings about the event—the explosion at the Russian nuclear reactor—and its meaning for all peoples . . . " In 1989, she wrote *Katyn* for large orchestra and chorus. It is dedicated to the Polish officers imprisoned in the Ukraine in 1939, and later murdered in the Katyn forest by Stalin's secret police.

In the 1990s she composed a Viola Concerto (1990), *Adagio and Rondo* for violin and string orchestra (1994), and *Concerto No. 2 for Violin and Orchestra* (1994). She has turned increasingly to vocal music, with works such as *How Fares the Night?* for violin, women's chorus and orchestra, plus opera and musical theater. Her English-language chamber opera, *In the Shadow of the Glen*, after the play by J. M. Synge, was completed in 1994 and premiered at the Longy School of Music, Cambridge, MA, in March 1999. Her German-language opera *Nemo: Jenseits von Vulkania* was completed in 1995. Another opera, *All Quiet on the Western Front*, after the Erich Maria Remarque anti-war novel, was completed in English in 1998 and German in 1999. The English-language chamber opera, *The Death of the Hired Man*, after the Robert Frost poem, was premiered at the University of Mississippi in November 1999. The turn of the century brought another premiere at the Kunstverein Wien (Vienna). On the same program, *Eine Nacht im Royal Ontario Museum*, with mezzo soprano Sulie Girardi, was heard for the first time. The Portland (Maine) Symphony gave the first performance of *A Peacock Southeast Flew: Concerto for Pipa and Orchestra* with Gao Hong pipa soloist, and Toshiyuki Shimada conducting. In Europe, *Music for Viola, Percussion and Piano* was performed in Krakow, Poland, and the Moravian Philharmonic, Jiri Mikula, conductor, performed *Gema Jawa* and *Adagio for Orchestra* at Philharmonic Hall, Olomouc, Czech Republic. *Dark Nebulae* was performed by Niederosterreichisches (Lower Austria) Tonkunstler Orchester, with Carlos Kalmar, at the Grosser Saal Musikverein, Vienna, and again at the Festspielhaus, St. Polten, Austria, both in January 2000.

In 1989, 1993, and 1997 Van de Vate was a nominee for the Ianamori Foundation's quadrennial Kyoto Prize in Music, at fifty million yen this is the world's largest music award.

Melinda Wagner

MELINDA WAGNER, born February 5, 1957, in Philadelphia, was already proficient on piano at age six, but hated to read music and would pick up everything by ear. She overcame her aversion and received her BA from Hamilton College (1979), MA from the University of Chicago (1981) and PhD from the University of Pennsylvania.

While at Tanglewood in the summer of 1978, she met a fellow student named James Saporito whom she did not see again for nine years. Meanwhile, she was a lecturer at Swarthmore College (1987), after which she joined the faculty at Syracuse University as an assistant professor. In 1988, aware that Saporito was at Eastman nearby, she sent him a "Hi! Remember me?" note. They met at spring break, got engaged two weeks later and were married August 20, 1989. Their son, Benjamin, was born April 7, 1993, daughter Olivia arrived June 1, 1998. A freelance percussionist and drummer, James is in demand in classical, Broadway and film spheres.

A 1988 Guggenheim Award enabled Wagner to concentrate on composing. She had already written the song cycle *Circles, Stones and Passage* (1981), *Tremor Cordis* (viola and piano, 1984) and the orchestral *Passages* (1985). *Sextet* for flute, clarinet, violin, viola, cello and piano was premiered by the Syracuse Society for New Music (1990) and released on Opus One (1995). *Sleep Awake*, for mezzo, clarinet and piano, debuted September 1993 at the Danny Kaye Playhouse of Hunter College, where Wagner was engaged as an assistant professor. *Tuesday Music* received its first performance with the Aeolian Chamber Players in 1994. *Falling Angels* was premiered by the Chicago Symphony with **Daniel Barenboim** in 1993, with a repeat performance in January 1996. *Thinking About the Moon*, for flute, clarinet, violin, cello and piano, was performed April 1996, by the Stonybrook Contemporary Chamber Players, and *Psalm* for clarinet, cello, percussion and piano was featured at Concordia College for the New York State Teachers Annual Conference in October, and again in April 1997, by the all-women Cassatt String Quartet. A flute concerto for Paul Dunkel, their associate conductor, was part of the 1998 celebration of the fifteenth anniversary of the Westchester Philharmonic. Two days after the premiere, she gave birth to Olivia. Three weeks before its May 23, 1999 performance by the National Women's Symphony, Wagner learned she won the Pulitzer Prize for her *Concerto for Flute, Strings and Percussion*, becoming the fifty-eighth American composer and the third woman (after **Ellen Zwilich** and **Shulamit Ran**) to win the honor. Three of her teachers, George Crumb, Richard Waernick, and Shulamit Ran, all Pulitzer winners, applauded the choice. Said Crumb, "Her music was always very elegantly made. I felt in recent years she was really developing a personal idiom."

Melinda Wagner is part of the next generation of composers whose style explores new frontiers yet still keeps the sensibilities of the audience in mind.

Gwyneth Walker

A rarity among composers of either sex, **GWYNETH WALKER** supports herself entirely by her writings, which include over 100 commissioned works for orchestra, band, chorus, and chamber ensembles. Born March 22, 1947, in Connecticut, she now makes her home on a dairy farm in Braintree, Vermont. She began composing at age two, and developed an interest in folk music and rock and roll before beginning formal music studies. She graduated from Brown University (BA, 1968) and from Hartt School of Music (MM 1970, DMA 1976), where her principal composition teacher was Arnold Franchetti. After a fourteen year career as a teacher of theory and composition at Oberlin and Hartt, she left in 1982 to pursue composition full-time.

In 1988, she helped found the Consortium of Vermont Composers, of which she later became director. In 1993, the Vermont Teachers Association selected her as "Vermont Composer of the Year." As winner of a national Call-for-Scores Competition sponsored by the Florida West Coast Symphony, her overture, *Open the Door*, opened the '94–'95 Sarasota season.

Commissions for '95–'96 included a Tuba Concerto, *Chanties and Ballads*, for Mark Nelson and the Millikin-Decatur (Illinois) Symphony; *An American Concerto*, for violinist **Susan Pickett** and the Walla Walla (Washington) Symphony; a set of *American River Songs* for chamber orchestra and chorus for the Assabet Valley (Massachusetts) Mastersingers; a third *String Quartet* for the Quapaw Quartet of the Arkansas Symphony; and a cello concerto, *North Country Concerto*, for Frances Rowell and the Pennsylvania Sinfonia. Her concerti are usually intended for performance by players within the orchestra, rather than an imported soloist.

Walker's move to Vermont initiated a grass roots approach, writing for performers of all skills from community and school groups to professional orchestras and concert soloists. Her works are programmed on regular concerts as well as pops and young audiences events. In her concern for accessibility, she has brought familiar aspects of life to the concert platform. In *Three Songs in Celebration of the Family Farm*, the chorus imitates the sound of farm machinery and cows, and the conductor uses milking gestures. She has staged performances at such non-traditional sites as a dairy barn, and even linked compositions with athletics, as in *Holding the Towel*, a comic song cycle for Super Bowl Sunday 1992 and, most notably, in *Match Point*, where the tennis player Billie Jean King performed as guest soloist at Lincoln Center, bouncing tennis balls on percussion instruments and performing a mimed rally with the conductor who conducted with a tennis racquet.

Walker's music is marked by a contagious energy and lyric intensity with fresh, contemporary sounds. In *Braintree Quintet*, *Fanfare for the Family Farm*, and *An Adventure at Grannie's*, she fuses a theatrical temperament with her distinctive musical vitality and humor.

Commissions for 1997 were a Trumpet Concerto, *A Concerto of Hymns and Spirituals*, jointly commissioned by the Farmington Valley (Connecticut) Symphony, and the Carson City (Nevada) Chamber Orchestra, and *Bicycle Waltz* for the Amherst Ballet Company and Springfield (Massachusetts) Symphony Orchestra. The same year, the Vermont Symphony premiered *About Leaves*. An October 1999 premiere was *Symphony of Grace*, a joint commission for five orchestras: The Women's Philharmonic, Brevard Symphony (Florida), Holyoke (Massachusetts) Civic Orchestra, Susquehanna (Maryland) Symphony and Carson City (Nevada) Symphony.

Major 21st century works are: *Concerto for Bassoon and Strings* (2000), for Janet Polk and the Vermont Symphony; *Rejoice!* (2001), Christmas Music for Chorus and Orchestra, commissioned by Luther College, Decorah, Iowa; *Come Life, Shaker Life!* (2001), a thirty-minute work for Chorus, Children's Chorus and Orchestra, with dance, based on Shaker songs, commissioned by the Sonoma Valley (California) Chorale; *A Vision of Hills* (2002), a piano trio jointly commissioned by Trio Tulsa of Oklahoma, and the Bartholdy Ensemble of Montpelier, Vermont; *Symphonic Dances* (2003) to celebrate the twentieth season of the Carson City Symphony; and *Woodwind Quintet* (2005), for the Equinox Chamber Players to perform in the schools throughout St. Louis.

The composer accepts commissions within a given year for one or two orchestral works, a chamber work, a choral work and perhaps one not categorized work. To celebrate the year 2000, she undertook the Millennium Fest Commission from Sarasota and Bradenton, Florida, featuring the Sarasota Pops Orchestra, Combined Community Chorus, School Chorus and Brass Ensemble.

Projects which incorporate some elements of theatricality within a musical context are of special enjoyment to her. For example, *Letters to the World*, a piano quartet, incorporates readings from the poetry of Emily Dickinson. *Acquaintance With Nature*, for chorus, clarinet, piano and narrator, weaves music around the writings of Henry David Thoreau. *The Magic Oboe*, an oboe concerto, transforms the conductor into a magician and the oboe soloist into the magician's assistant for performing magic tricks on stage, with orchestral accompaniment. *Climbing to Heaven*, a thirty-minute staged work based on writings of Thomas Merton, combines readings, chamber music and a cast of actors portraying fourth century monks.

The composer says, "I believe in engaging the audience in as many ways as I can to enhance enjoyment of the music."

Commissioned years in advance, Walker's calendar is filling up to 2007.

JOELLE WALLACH, born in New York, June 29, 1946, spent part of her childhood in Morocco, until she returned to attend Juilliard Preparatory School where she studied piano, voice, theory, bassoon and violin. Her composition degrees are from Sarah Lawrence College (1967), Columbia (MA, 1969), and the very first doctorate in composition granted by the Manhattan School of Music (1984), where she was a student of American composer **John Corigliano** (*b* 1938). She has served as composer-in-residence with many regional orchestras, was a teaching fellow at the Manhattan School of Music, assistant professor of music at Fordham University, has performed as a singer and pianist, and done improvisational work for dance companies. Since 1990, she has been a pre-concert lecturer at the New York Philharmonic, presenting a broad range of musical repertoire from the familiar to the modern to the rarely heard. In 1980, her choral work *On the Beach at Night Alone* won first prize in the Inter-American Music Award, followed by many firsts in international composition competitions. Her published works include orchestral, vocal and choral, solo instrumentals, chamber and stage. A chamber opera, *The King's Twelve Moons*, was given sixteen performances in New York City. The New York Choral Society commissioned her secular oratorio *Toward a Time of Renewal* for its thirty-fifth anniversary season (Carnegie Hall, 1994). The New York Philharmonic Ensembles premiered her octet *From the Forest of Chimneys*, written to celebrate their tenth anniversary. Her ballet, *Glancing Below* (1994), was commissioned by the Carlisle Project and taken into the repertory of the Hartford Ballet. It received its New York City premiere, June 1995, and was the Juilliard Dance Theater's showcase production in February 1999. Her *String Quartet 1995* was the American Composers Alliance nominee for the 1997 Pulitzer Prize in music. Other premieres included *Loveletter, Postmark San Jose* (1999), by the San Jose Chamber Orchestra, Barbara Day Turner conducting; *Orison of Saint Theresa* (2000) for chorus and string orchestra, performed at St. Peter's Church in New York City; *A Revisitation of Myth* (2000) for viola, piano and medium voice, performed at Rutgers University; and *Incantation*, an *a cappella* choral work which the Collegiate Choir of Illinois Wesleyan University commissioned for their national tour. *From the Almanac of Last Things*, was a commission from Paul Sperry for New York's The Joy of Singing's Millennial Concert in Spring 2001. Her recordings include *The Tiger's Tail, Mourning Madrigals, Organal Voices*, and *Three 20th Century String Quartets: three historical premieres*, which included *String Quartet 1986* with the Philadelphia Quartet, *String Quartet 1995*, La Musica Festival, and *String Quartet 1999* with the Muir Quartet, released by Capstone in Spring 2001. *Firefighter's Prayer* (tenor solo with chamber or jazz ensemble, also arranged for chorus and piano, or chorus and strings) was composed in response to the events of 9/11/01, and premiered September 11, 2002 on Cape Cod. *Hope Remains* (2002), for chorus, with chamber ensemble, is also in response to 9/11.

Wallach has been featured in Victoria Bond's Cutting Edge concert series.

Dalit Warshaw

One of the younger generation of composers, **DALIT HADASS WARSHAW** was born August 6, 1974 in New York City, of an Israeli mother and an American father. She started piano studies at three and a half with her mother, Ruti Hadass Warshaw, a pupil of **Nadia Reisenberg**. As a freshman at Columbia, Dalit was already taking doctoral seminars. Her senior year there— she graduated with a double degree in music and literature—overlapped with her Juilliard courses where she won the Gretchaninoff Prize in 1995. The same year, she won the prestigious Charles Ives Scholarship from the American Academy of Arts, enabling her to achieve an MM in Composition and a secondary major in Piano. With a William Hearst Scholarship and C.V. Starr Doctoral Fellowship, she received her DMA from Juilliard, May 2003, where she had been on the faculty since 1996 teaching instrumentation and advanced orchestration. From September 2003–May 2004, she was a visiting professor of composition at Middlebury College (Vermont).

A fine pianist, Warshaw has performed publicly since she was eight. She composes at the keyboard as she has done since she was a little girl, thinking first about the message she wants to get across, which may be as much philosophical as musical. Her scores have been evaluated by her mentors, including composers **David del Tredici**, **Victoria Bond**, **Samuel Adler**, **Milton Babbitt**, and the late **Jacob Druckman**. Also since she was eight, her orchestral works have been played by major orchestras, among them the New York and Israel Philharmonics, both conducted by **Zubin Mehta**, as well as the Boston, Cleveland, Denver, Houston, Colorado, Albany, Knoxville, Roanoke, and Haifa Symphonies. As both soloist and chamber musician, besides the U.S., Dalit has been heard in France, Israel and other countries. She played the theremin in the London Philharmonic recording of Miklos Rozsa's filmscore *Spellbound*, and in the 1999 world premiere of David Del Tredici's *Dracula*. Nadia Reisenberg and her sister **Clara Rockmore** were part of her life since childhood, when she already showed an aptitude for the theremin. Since Clara's death, Dalit inherited the first theremin built by Robert Moog (of synthesizer fame), to have been approved by Rockmore, as well as the original model constructed by Leon Theremin for Rockmore in the 1930s.

Among her many compositions, Warshaw's *Maid of Domremy*, from a commission by the Empire State Youth Orchestra for their fifteenth anniversary, was premiered March 1995. *Rose of Sharon* was performed at the New York Festival of Song at the 92nd Street Y Center, May 1996, as part of the world premiere of *American Love Songs*, commissioned by the Festival. Her works include solo instrumental, vocal, chamber ensemble, and orchestral. *Rhapsody* for clarinet and piano was written in 1998; her string quartet, *Nota Bene*, and her orchestral piece *Fata Morgana*, presented as part of her Doctoral thesis, were written in 2000. *Kidush Halevana* (Hebrew for Prayer for the Moon) for soprano and piano, was composed while on a Fulbright Scholarship to Israel (2001–02). *Camille's Dance*, named for the mistress of the sculptor, Rodin, premiered by the Grand Rapids Symphony May 2002, was also performed by the American Composers Orchestra.

In 1984, she was the youngest person to win the BMI Award for Student Composers for her orchestral piece *Fun Suite*, written at age eight. She has since won four ASCAP grants for Young Composers, the Aaron Copland International Competition, the Cincinnati Symphony Young Composers Competition, a Fromm Music Foundation Grant from Harvard, and residencies at both Yaddo and MacDowell.

21st century commissions and premieres include *Al ha-Shminit: Interludes on a Bygone Mode*, a chamber suite for twelve instruments written for Joel Sachs and the New Juilliard Ensemble (November 2003), and *Tehinnot*, a song cycle for "Pierrot" ensemble written for soprano Re'ut Ben Zeev and the Bowdoin International Music Festival (July 2004).

In September 2004, she became a full-time faculty member of the composition/music theory department at the Boston Conservatory. She also teaches piano and composition privately.

Dalit Warshaw has made the challenging transition from child prodigy to mature artist, to excel in a rewarding career as composer, pianist and educator.

CHEN YI, in the U.S. from China since 1986, has made important contributions to the American musical scene. (See Asian Composers.)

Judith Zaimont

JUDITH LANG ZAIMONT, born November 8, 1945, in Memphis, Tennessee, was raised in New York in a musical family. She began playing piano at five, starting at the Juilliard Preparatory School when she was eleven. After receiving her diploma from the Long Island Institute of Music (1966), she toured the country playing duo-piano recitals with her sister Doris. (See **Kosloff.**) Her BA (Queens College, NY, 1966) was followed by formal composition study with **Hugo Weisgall** (1912–97), **Jack Beeson** (1921–76) and noted pioneer electronic experimentalist **Otto Luening** (1900–96) at Columbia, earning a master's in 1968. A Debussy scholarship made possible orchestration study in Paris (1971–72) with **André Jolivet** (1905–74).

She joined the faculty of Peabody Conservatory, and was named "Teacher of the Year" in 1985. She was a resident at the MacDowell Colony, taught at Hunter College (1980–88), served as chairman of the music department, Adelphi University, New Jersey (1989–91) and, from 1991 to 2005 was a professor of composition at the University of Minnesota School of Music.

Also a writer, Zaimont is editor-in-chief of a landmark book series of three volumes, *The Musical Woman: An International Perspective*, which covers the worldwide contribution of women to music, and for which she has received several awards, a grant from NEH, and the 1993 first prize in the Pauline Alderman International Competition for Scholarship on Women in Music. She has contributed to *Women Composers: The Lost Tradition Found* (1988), and the text *Making Music Your Own* (Silver/Burdett/Ginn 1995).

Zaimont's music is tonal, neo-romantic and reveals a rhythmic affinity with French composers Debussy, Ravel, Messiaen and Francophile Stravinsky. Her impressive catalogue of over a hundred works includes many prize-winners. *Chrome—Northern Lights* won first prize in the National Competition for Chamber Orchestra in honor of the 1976 Statue of Liberty Centennial. Other prestigious awards are Guggenheim and Maryland State Arts Council Fellowships, Woodrow Wilson Foundation, Presser Foundation, Delius and Gottschalk Competitions, a National First Prize for Orchestra Music, and grants from the NEA and Minnesota Composers Forum. Her orchestral works have been programmed by orchestras throughout the U.S. Her chamber opera, *Goldilocks and the Three Bears*, written in collaboration with her sister, was given at Lincoln Center and by the Eugene (Oregon) and Connecticut Opera companies. Her chamber works have been performed by many artists and ensembles at Carnegie Hall, Merkin Hall, Lincoln Center, the National Gallery, J. Paul Getty Museum and other major venues on three continents.

A Real Prizewinner

Zaimont's Symphony No.1, originally commissioned and premiered by the Central Wisconsin Symphony in 1994, won first prize in the 1995 International McCollin Competition for Composers. Not given more than twice a decade—it was won in 1938 by **Béla Bartók**—this prestigious award brought with it $5,000 and premiere performances during subscription concerts of the Philadelphia Orchestra under the baton of **Zdeněk Mácal** which, during January 1996, honored the 175th anniversary season of the Musical Fund Society of Philadelphia, administrator of the competition. Other commissions have been from the Gregg Smith Singers, Dale Garland Singers, Baltimore, Harrisburg and Jacksonville Symphonies, Connecticut Opera, Baltimore Dance Theatre, Pro Arte Chamber, and the American Guild of Organists (AGO).

Beginning in 1995, under a grant from the Aaron Copland Foundation, Arabesque Records released a series of CDs of her instrumental music including *Neon Rhythm: Chamber Music of Judith Lang Zaimont* (1996), *ZONES* (1997) for strings, and *reSOUNDings—Orchestral Music of Judith Lang Zaimont* (2000). Other recordings are on Northeastern, Centaur and **Leonarda** labels. She was profiled in *Women of Note Quarterly* (November 1995), and in 1996 by *Fanfare* magazine. Her composition *Doubles*, for oboe and piano from *Neon Rhythm*, was chosen for the

"Century List" in the June 1999 issue of *Chamber Music Magazine*. Her *Symphony No.2 for Symphonic Strings* was premiered in March 1999. 2000 commissions included *Spirals* for string trio, *Jupiter's Moons* (piano), and *Tanya, Three Poems for Solo Cello*. In 2001, *Impronta Digitale* (Fingerprint) was selected and played by Stanislav Ioudenitch and **Olga Kern**, co-gold medal winners of the eleventh Van Cliburn International Competition. It was also performed in recital by five of the twelve semi-finalists in the solo piano round of the competition: Italy's Maurizio Baglini, Japan's Masaru Okada, China's Wang Xiaohan, as well as the two gold medalists. Recognized as an honored composer, Zaimont was awarded $2,500 as one of the two prize winners in the inaugural American Composers Invitational program sponsored by the Van Cliburn Foundation. The presentation, on the stage of Bass Hall in Forth Worth, Texas, was accompanied by a kiss from Van Cliburn himself.

In 2002, she was featured composer for the National Federation of Music Clubs and the National Conference on Women Composers (October, Mississippi). 2003 was a banner year with being elected *Commissioned Composer* at both the International San Antonio Piano Competition and Music Teachers Association of California. She was profiled on a two-part Minnesota Public Radio program celebrating women composers. (Her works form title music for this three-year series on women in music, broadcast nationally.) Magazine interviews include *Clavier*, April 2003, and *Chamber Music*, January 2004. The same month Zaimont appeared in a one-hour profile on Texas Public Radio. She also received recording grants from American Music Center and the Ditson Fund of Columbia University. A performance of the *Sonata for Piano Solo* was featured at the National Museum of Women in the Arts in Washington, DC, as part of the annual IAWM Feature Concert, June 1, 2003. The soloist was Joanne Polk, who is the pianist for the 2003 Albany Records release of Zaimont's solo piano works.

A major event was Zaimont's winning the 2003 *Aaron Copland* Award, a much coveted opportunity to reside alone for three weeks to two months at Copland House, the composer's restored Hudson River Valley home (from 1960 until his death in 1990), an hour north of New York City. The focus is on creativity free from the distractions of daily life, housekeeping and other professional responsibilities.

Long term appointments include election to the national board of the College Music Society, 2003–2005, and a second term on the IAWM Advisory Board, 2004–2007.

Zaimont holds a 2005 Bush Foundation Artist Fellowship. The same year, she retired after three decades of teaching in higher education. (Peabody Conservatory, CUNY, Adelphi University, University of Minnesota.)

Judy has been married to Gary Zaimont since 1967. They have a son, Michael, born 1981. Beginning in fall 2005, she and Gary will live in the greater Phoenix area.

Ellen Zwilich

ELLEN Taaffe ZWILICH, born April 30, 1939, in Miami, Florida, began piano lessons when she was five and later studied violin and trumpet. By age ten she had begun to write down the sounds she heard in her head, and in her teens was not only proficient on piano, trumpet and violin, but conducted, arranged and composed for her school band and orchestra. She went to Florida State University (Tallahassee, BM, 1960, MM, 1962, in Composition). In 1964, she moved to New York to study violin with the celebrated **Ivan Galamian** (1903–81) and acquired valuable musical training as a freelancer. From 1965–72, she played in the American Symphony Orchestra under **Leopold Stokowski** (1882–1977). During this period she married Joseph Zwilich, a violinist in the Metropolitan Opera Orchestra. In 1974 she was awarded the Elizabeth Sprague Coolidge Chamber Music Prize. She received a gold medal at the Twenty-sixth Annual International Composition Competition in Vercelli, Italy (1975). This was also the year she made history by becoming the first woman to receive a doctorate in composition from Juilliard. Her major teachers there were foremost modern American composers **Roger Sessions** and **Elliott Carter**. In 1979, when her husband tragically died of a heart attack, she wrote *Chamber Symphony* in his memory. 1982 saw the premiere of her *Symphony No.1* by the American Composers Orchestra, led by Gunther Schuller, and *Passages* for soprano, flute, clarinet, violin, viola, cello, piano and percussion. The orchestral version was premiered by the St. Paul Chamber Orchestra,

Gerard Schwarz conducting, November 17, 1983. The same year, Zwilich again made history by being the first woman to win a Pulitzer Prize in music composition for her *Symphony No. 1*.

Commissions Galore

Commissions came pouring in: *Celebration* for orchestra (Indianapolis Symphony), the *Double Quartet for Strings* (Chamber Music Society of Lincoln Center), *Concerto for Trumpet and 5 players* (Pittsburgh New Music Ensemble), *Symphony No. 2* the "Cello" (San Francisco Symphony), *Concerto Grosso* (Washington Handel Festival Orchestra, commemorating the Handel Tricentennial, 1985), and *Concerto for Piano and Orchestra* (American Symphony Orchestra League, Carnegie Hall and the Detroit Symphony). *Images for Two Pianos and Orchestra* premiered at the opening of the National Museum of Women in the Arts by the National Symphony, Washington, DC.

In 1986, Zwilich received the Arturo Toscanini Music Critics Award for the New World recording of her *Symphony No.1*, and *Prologue and Variations for String Orchestra*. More commissions included *Trio for Violin, Cello and Piano* (Kalichstein-Laredo-Robinson Trio), *Tanzspiel*, a ballet in four scenes (New York City Ballet) and *Symbolon* by the New York Philharmonic, who gave the world premiere in [then] Leningrad (St. Petersburg) under **Zubin Mehta**, June 1988. The same year marked performances of the *Piano Trio* in San Francisco, Los Angeles, Chicago, New York and Washington, and *Praeludium for Organ*, premiered by James Christie at the AGO annual meeting in Boston. A 1989 highlight was *Concerto for Trombone and Orchestra*, commissioned by the Chicago Symphony, **Sir Georg Solti** conducting, with soloist Jay Friedman. Chicago also commissioned the *Concerto for Bass Trombone, Strings, Timpani and Cymbals*, premiered by Charles Vernon under **Daniel Barenboim**. The Cleveland Orchestra commissioned *Concerto for Oboe and Orchestra* (1990) with soloist John Mack and conductor **Christoph von Dohnanyi**. Subsequent commissions were *Quintet for Clarinet and String Quartet* (1990); *Concerto for Flute* (1989), premiered by flutist **Doriot Anthony Dwyer**, the Boston Symphony with **Seiji Ozawa**; *Concerto for Violin and Cello* (1991), **Jaime Laredo**, violin, **Sharon Robinson**, cello, **Lawrence Leighton Smith** conducting the Louisville Symphony, later released on the Louisville label; and *Immigrant Voices for Chorus, Brass, Strings and Timpani* (1991). *Concerto for Bassoon* (1992) had a May 1993 premiere by **Nancy Goeres**, with **Lorin Maazel** and the Pittsburgh Symphony. *Symphony No. 3* saw a February 1993 premiere under **Jahja Ling** as part of the celebration of the 150th anniversary of the New York Philharmonic. *Concerto for Horn and Strings* (1993), *Romance for Violin and Chamber Orchestra* (1993), and *American Concerto for Trumpet and Orchestra* (1994) were all prolific outpourings at the beginning of the decade.

February 1996 marked the premiere of her *Triple Concerto* for violin, cello, and piano, commissioned by the New Jersey Symphony and Minnesota Orchestra, again featuring the Kalichstein-Laredo-Robinson Trio, **Zdeněk Mácal** conducting the Minnesota Orchestra. *Peanuts Gallery*, based on Charles Schulz's cartoon characters, a commission from Carnegie Hall for the conductorless Orpheus Chamber Orchestra, premiered March 1997. The composer enjoyed some unique notoriety when, in the cartoon strip, Lucy asks Schroeder what he is playing on his piano, and he answers, "The music of Ellen Zwilich." Her *Concerto for Violin and Orchestra*, written for and performed by **Pamela Frank**, premiered March 26, 1998, with the Orchestra of St. Luke's, conducted by **Hugh Wolff** at Carnegie Hall, which was also the site of String Quartet #2 with the Emerson String Quartet. Frank subsequently recorded the concerto with Michael Stern and the Saarbrucken Radio Symphony, released on Naxos in 2005.

Commissioned by a consortium of twenty-seven American orchestras in twenty-five states, since its premiere[52] September 2000, with pianist Jeffrey Biegel[53] and Jesus Lopez-Cobos leading the Cincinnati Symphony, *Millennium*

---

52. After the premiere, Zwilich was given the Key to the City by the Mayor of Cincinnati.
53. Biegel commissioned, raised the funds, and provided the title for the piece. He played it with the American Symphony Orchestra, April 2005. He also collaborates with **Alicia Zizzo**, performing her Gershwin discoveries. (See Musicologists.)

Fantasy for Piano and Orchestra continues to be heard at many venues in the course of the 21st century. Symphony No.4, *The Gardens*, was a commission by Michigan State University alumni Jack and Dottie Withrow in 2000 to commemorate the beauty of MSU campus and gardens. A film, *The Making of the 4th Symphony of Ellen Zwilich*, which captured the creative process used by Zwilich, was produced by MSU's WKAR-TV and aired on PBS in 2001. 2002 brought a premiere of her Clarinet Concerto featuring David Shifrin and the Buffalo Philharmonic conducted by **JoAnn Falletta**. 2004 featured *Episodes* for violin and piano, first performed by Itzhak Perlman, violin, and Rohan de Silva, piano, February 21, which they took on tour during 2004–05, and *Rituals* for five percussionists and orchestra, commissioned by the IRIS Orchestra with Michael Stern and the Nexus Ensemble. The *Concerto for Violin and Cello*, again with Jaime Laredo and Sharon Robinson, was part of the St. Louis Symphony's programming in February 2004. *Symphony No. 3* was played by Charles Dutoit and the Philadelphia Orchestra in August 2004, and by Peter Leonard and the Norddeutsche Philharmonie in April 2005. Her *Horn Concerto* was played by the New York Philharmonic, April 2006, and String Quartet No. 2 performed by the Penderecki Quartet in Madrid in May.

Honors Heaped Upon Honors!

Ellen Taaffe Zwilich knew she wanted to become a composer since elementary school. By the time she was twenty-two, her works were already being performed publicly. As a violinist, she has played under such famous conductors as **Leopold Stokowski**, **Karl Boehm** and **Ernst Ansermet**. **Pierre Boulez** premiered her *Symposium for Orchestra* in the 1970s. In 1990 she was composer-in-residence both at the American Academy in Rome and the Santa Fe Chamber Music Festival. Other honors include the Alfred I. Dupont Award, her election to the Florida Artists Hall of Fame, and to the American Academy of Arts and Letters, plus the distinction of being named, in 1995, to the first composer's chair in the history of Carnegie Hall, a position she held until 1999. One of her initial projects there was creating the important video archive of composers. In 1996, she was made an honorary music member of the 108-year-old (in 2005) National League of American Pen Women, and in 1999 was named *Musical America's* composer of the year, really great recognition. In August 2004, she was composer-in-residence at the Saratoga Chamber Music Festival (New York), where her commissioned *Quartet for Oboe, Violin, Viola and Cello* was premiered by Richard Woodhams, principal oboe of the Philadelphia Orchestra, and members of the Festival. In Spring 2004, conductor of the Key West Symphony, **Sebrina Maria Alfonso**, directed some of Zwilich's work in Havana. Another great honor later that year was being elected to the American Academy of Arts and Sciences. On Valentine's Day, 2006, the California Ear Unit premiered *Luvn Blm* at Disney Hall in Los Angeles.

The composer's sizable discography was added to with the 2002 Koch Classics CD of her Piano Concerto, Double Concerto and Triple Concerto with the Kalichstein-Laredo-Robinson Trio and the Florida State University Orchestra under Michael Stern. The First Edition Recording (distributed by harmonia mundi) of the Chamber Symphony, Double Concerto, and Symphony No. 2 (Cello Symphony) was reissued in 2004.

Ellen Zwilich has taught master classes at Juilliard, and has been the Francis Eppes professor of music at her alma mater, Florida State University, since 1999. After thirty-five years as a musician, she returned to FSU saying, "I believe if we don't educate young minds, we've lost everything."

Her music has graduated from the dissonant modernism of thirty years ago to the attractive, tonal post modernism of today. In 1990, *Baker's Biographical Dictionary of Musicians* (eighth edition) stated: "There are not many composers in the modern world who possess the lucky combination of writing music of substance . . . at the same time exercising an immediate appeal to mixed audiences. Zwilich offers this happy combination of purely technical excellence and a distinct power of communication."

Into the Future

An appropriate end note to this chapter is this quote from a composer who experienced the experimentation of the '70s early in her career and now, besides participating in the overall maturing of trends, embraces the advantages of exploring the limitless frontiers opened by new technology:

The beginning of the 21st century is an exciting and inclusive time for composers. Economically, the advent of home computers brought a newfound power in our ability to self publish, and we are no longer at the mercy of publishing and recording companies to get our work heard around the world. Musically, the broad reach of the Internet and cable television has infused our formerly Eurocentric culture with a vast array of music from every part of the globe. Many of today's finest composers use these influences to create a new breed of cross-pollinated music, with an often glorious result. I can't think of a more wonderful time in which to live and work on this planet as a music maker.

—Alex Shapiro

CHAPTER TEN

Women Behind the Silver Screen

Mary Alwyn

Marilyn Bergman

Betty Comden

Linda Danly

Anne Dudley

Dorothy Fields

Sylvia Fine

Cynthia Millar

Hélène Muddiman

Rachel Portman

Dory Previn

Shirley Walker

Debbie Wiseman

Composing music for the movies is still not a major role for women, although more female names are appearing in the music credits each year. Early "pioneers" in the field include **Ann Ronell**, who scored *The Story of G.I. Joe*, with Robert Mitchum (1945), but shared credits with two men. She also scored *One Touch of Venus* (1948), based on the Kurt Weill musical, starring Ava Gardner, and *Love Happy* (1949) with the Marx Brothers. **Elizabeth Firestone**, daughter of tire magnate Harvey S. Firestone, was actually the first woman to score a complete film, *Once More, My Darling* (1949) starring Ann Blyth, directed by Joan Harrison, who later directed many of the Alfred Hitchcock television episodes. Firestone also scored *That Man from Tangier* (1953). British composer **Elisabeth Lutyens** composed the music for several films, including the sci-fi *World Without End* (1956), and *Dr. Terror's House of Horrors* (1964).

In the last two decades, **Carole King** scored *Murphy's Romance* (1985), starring James Garner and Sally Field, **Anne Dudley** wrote for *The Crying Game* (1992), British composer **Jocelyn Pook** did the score for Stanley Kubrick's *Eyes Wide Shut* (1999), with Tom Cruise and Nicole Kidman, and others like **Jill Fraser**, **Laura Karpman**, **Nan Schwartz Mishkin** and **Angela Morely** have scored both film and television shows. Several other women have had, and are having, quite successful careers in movie music.

MARY ALWYN, née Doreen Carwithen, was born in 1922, in Haddenham, England. Her mother, a music teacher, taught her piano and violin beginning at four, continuing with piano until her daughter entered the RAM as the Buckinghamshire County Scholar in 1941. She also had cello lessons with Peers Coetmore and, while still at school, played the cello with a string quartet as well as in local orchestras. The family did not have a record player, so she was dependent on the radio for her knowledge of orchestral music. As it was wartime, this was limited to concerts on the BBC Home Service, which she followed on scores, providing a vital help in her future career. Her awareness of music-making was also enhanced by playing piano duos with her sister Barbara, who had followed her to the RAM, in competitions, festivals, concerts, and wartime entertainments for the troops.

In 1947, J. Arthur Rank started an apprenticeship program for composers to specialize in the study of film music. Carwithen was the first RAM student to be selected, and subsequently wrote scores for over thirty films, including *Harvest from the Wilderness* (1948), *Boys in Brown* (1950), *Mantrap* (1952), *Man in Hiding* (1953), *East Anglian Holiday* (1954), and *Break in the Circle* (1955). Her documentaries included *Teeth of the Wind*, a study of locusts, and the official film of the coronation—*Elizabeth is Queen* (1953). Among her feature films are two in which music takes the place of dialogue: *On the Twelfth Day* and *The Stranger Left No Card*, which received the Cannes Festival award for best short fictional film. It was then shown at the Edinburgh Festival. The same year, her overture ODTAA (One Damn Thing After Another), was the first new score chosen by the London

Philharmonic Orchestra Music Advisory committee. This premiered at Covent Garden, March 1947, conducted by Sir Adrian Boult. Its great success was followed by many performances and broadcasts. 1952 marked the premieres of the overture *Bishop Rock*, which opened the City of Birmingham Orchestra's Promenade Concerts, and Concerto for Piano and Strings at the Henry Wood Promenade Concerts, making Carwithen the only woman composer to be represented that season.

In spite of the initial success of these works, publishers were not interested in a "woman composer." Scores and parts were gradually returned, rarely getting a hearing. Her two string quartets remain unknown, although winning the principal awards for Chamber Music: the A.J. Clements Prize (1948) and the Cobbett Award (1952).

In 1961, Doreen Carwithen became amanuensis and literary secretary to William Alwyn, her composition professor at the RAM, whom she later married and became known as Mary Alwyn (Mary was her middle name). After his death in 1985, she established the William Alwyn Archive of music, poetry and art, and formed the William Alwyn Foundation to promote his music. To this end she instigated and supervised recordings, edited his unpublished works and wrote liner and program notes. She continued to oversee Alwyn research projects and help students from all over the world with doctoral studies of Alwyn's life and music. This enlarged her teaching career, which began as substitute professor of composition at the RAM, and music lecturer at Furzedown Teacher Training College.

She began to draft a third quartet. There was even talk of a symphony—though, as ever, her own work took second place to her promotion of her husband's. In 1997, Chandos released two CDs of Mary's music. The book *The Best Years of British Film Music, 1936–1958* (The Boydell Press, 2002), includes a 1997 interview with Alwyn. Hopes for a second phase to her career were dashed in 1999 when a severe stroke left her paralyzed down one side. After a period of illness, Mary (Doreen) died January 5, 2003.

LINDA DANLY, born August 9, 1945 in Chicago, is a songwriter/composer and film music historian. Her television credits include music for the series, *Jim Henson's Mother Goose Stories*, and the Disneyland bicentennial theme song, *Now is the Time*. She has scored background music for several children's albums, including *The Little Prince*, narrated by Louis Jourdan.

After earning a degree in Radio, TV and Film at Northwestern University (1967), she did graduate work in musical composition and education. Her career as a composer began with an educational program, "Dash McTrash and the Pollution Solution," a one-hour film strip and cassette package featuring her own cartoon characters and six original songs. She also formed an audio-visual company with her two sisters, Maria and Anne, creating educational materials for various publishers in New York. In 1976, she moved to California to work for Walt Disney Productions, where she wrote and produced radio and television commercials for Disneyland.

She began her studies in film music composition with veteran film composer, Walter Scharf. While studying composition, she and Maria produced a recording of their songs called *Lullaby River*, a project Maria had begun for a creative writing class in high school. Featuring the voice of actor Richard Dysart as "Tucker the Turtle," this won a Notable Children's Recording Award and is distributed nationally along with a second original production, *Rockabye Bunny*, which received a Notable Children's Recording Award in 1988.

Danly lives in Sherman Oaks, California, where she continues to write music and lecture on film music at USC and other institutions. She has produced a video on the life of MGM film composer Herbert Stothart (1993), and written a book, *Hugo Friedhofer: The Best Years of His Life* (Scarecrow Press, 1999), on the life of prolific film composer **Hugo Friedhofer** (1901–81), who won the Academy Award for his score for the 1946 film *The Best Years of our Lives*, and was principal orchestrator for movie music immortals **Erich Wolfgang Korngold** (1987–1957) and **Max Steiner** (1888–1971).

Danly is on the board of trustees of the Film Music Society.

ANNE DUDLEY is a musician, composer, arranger and producer in both the classical and pop genres. She studied classical music for three years at London's RCM gaining a performer's diploma, and was awarded the BM prize for the highest marks in her year. She earned her master's degree the following year at Kings College. The pop side came after college, with a competitive career as a session musician. This began her professional—and continued—relationship with Trevor Horn. Her rich orchestral textures and unique keyboard style made classics of many hits, including "Lexicon of Love" and "Buffalo Gals" which she co-wrote with Malcolm McLaren.

She was a founder/member in 1983 of The Art Of Noise, an innovative "rock" band whose influence extends to music production of today, and which helped pioneer the art of *sampling*—capturing the tonal qualities of sound and reproducing them on a keyboard. Their most famous collaborations in the '80s were with Duane Eddy ("Peter Gunn"), Max Headroom ("Paranoimia") and Tom Jones ("Kiss"); while "Moments in Love," "Close to the Edit" and "Crusoe" provided a blueprint for the age of *remixology*—using snips of famous songs and taking the art of *variations* to a new extreme. In 1999, the group—with keyboards, Anne on piano, voice and her orchestral arrangements—re-invented itself for the millennium with the album "The Seduction of Claude Debussy," which goes back a hundred years to pay homage to the early definer of 20th century music.

On the "pop" side, Anne has also written with, and arranged for, artists from Elton John to the Spice Girls. She arranged the music to Michael Flatley's hugely successful show, "Lord of the Dance." In the classical realm, her critically acclaimed solo album, "Ancient & Modern" was released on Echo Records (1995). The concert piece *Music and Silence*, including the unusual instrument, glass harmonica, was premiered at the Royal Festival Hall, September 2002.

Her television music includes *Kavanagh Q.C.*, *Jeeves & Wooster*, *The Perfect Blue*, and the December 1999 BBC/S4C New Testament feature animated film *In My Father's House*, starring Ralph Fiennes as the voice of Jesus. Film music credits are *The Crying Game*, *Buster* (which won a Brit Award for Best Soundtrack), *Felidae*, *The Sadness of Sex*, *The Grotesque*, *Hollow Reed* and her Academy Award for "Best Original Score (Musical or Comedy)" for *The Full Monty*, one of the highest grossing films in the U.K. With its recording at triple platinum, the soundtrack from the film won another Brit Award. Tony Kaye's first feature for New Line Cinema, *American History X*, with Dudley's score, was released in the UK, March 1999. 2000 brought *Pushing Tin*, for Twentieth Century Fox.

Anne's long relationship with Trevor Horn has provided the music for many of his brilliant award winning commercials for Volvo, Reebok, Guinness, *et al.*

Cynthia Millar

CYNTHIA MILLAR was born in London, June 5, 1956. Her parents are celebrated art historians. Sir Oliver Millar was for many years surveyor to the royal art collection, and Delia Millar, in the course of her career, has catalogued all the watercolors in the collection of Queen Victoria. Her illustrious family of writers, artists and actors also includes cousin Dame Daphne du Maurier (1907–89), famed author of *Rebecca* (1938), *My Cousin Rachel* (1952) and other romantic novels; and great-great-grandfather George du Maurier (1834–96), creator of the sinister musician/hypnotist Svengali in the first ever bestseller, *Trilby* (1894).

Cynthia began piano at five and later added stringed instruments. At Oxford, where she received a degree in literature, she sang in the Schola Cantorum. All of which was good preparation for mastering the unique and ethereal *ondes martenot*, a modern variation of the *theremin*, she now plays with orchestras all over the world. (See Performers.) After her graduation she returned to music, working as an assistant to **Elmer Bernstein**, who asked her to research this unusual instrument for use in many of his films, including *Heavy Metal*, and for his Broadway show *Young Merlin*. She has gone on to play the ondes in *Ghostbusters*, *My Left Foot*, *The Age of Innocence*, *Buddy*, and *The Rainmaker*, all the while adding to her composing experience.

Although she did not think about becoming a composer until the late '80s, Millar's apprenticeship with Bernstein provided the inspiration and foundation of a burgeoning career. She now has to her credit *Crazy in Love* (1992), Martha Coolidge's *Three Wishes* (1995), Peter Yates' *The Run of the Country* (1995), *Digging in China* (1998), Arthur Penn's *The Portrait* (1993), starring Lauren Bacall and the late Gregory Peck, *Foreign Affairs*, *A Storm in Summer*, directed by Robert Wise (1999), *Confessions of an Ugly Step Sister* (2001), directed by Gavin Millar, and Jason Freeland's *Brown's Requiem*, featuring the *ondes martenot*, which premiered at the London Film Festival

(1998). Her television music includes *Voices from Within*, *Beyond Reason*, and the six hour documentary series, *Stephen Hawking's Universe* (WNET, New York, and BBC, 2003), and *Cecil B. DeMille: An American Epic* (2004) for which she was music producer.

Millar resides both in London and Los Angeles.

At age eighteen, **HÉLÈNE MUDDIMAN** was signed to EMI Records and EMI Music Publishing as a recording artist. EMI's music library then invited her to compose an album for film and television entitled *Quirky and Curious*, which proved so successful around the world that the sequel *Quirky and Curious II ½* soon followed. Subsequent film scores are *Candy* and *Jean* both from Elysian Films, directed by Tony Fabian. Her themes and incidental music for television dramas include *Jake's Progress* (Elvis Costello & Richard Harvey for Channel 4 UK), *Pride* (BBC London, directed by Edwina Vardey), *Four Walls* (BBC Scotland, directed by Caroline Roberts), *Edinburgh Nights*, *Tip Top Challenge*, and the series *Animal Zone* (BBC Bristol, directed by Sarah Ford). Two other series, *The Murder Game* and *Welcome to Britain*, were co-written with French composer **Sophia Morizet**. Hélène's music is also featured on talk shows, quiz shows and children's entertainment. She has achieved success with her production music titles, which have been used in a diverse selection of programs including *Mr Bean* and *Dream On* (for USA). Her composition and arrangement credits for commercials include Andrex, Sky TV Christmas promotion, *International Herald Tribune*, Wightlink, Jacobs Club, ESCOM and Talking Pages.

Muddiman owns her own studio, and performs live with her band.

Rachel Portman

One of the most successful film composers, **RACHEL PORTMAN** was born December 11, 1960, in Haslemere, Surrey, England. Her classical music background began as a child with piano studies at eight, violin at ten and organ at thirteen. She began composing at fifteen. She read (majored in) music at Worcester College, Oxford University, and while there began to write theater music for student productions. Through a lucky coincidence, a BBC-backed film, *Privileged* (1982), about the university, made by Oxford students and scored by Rachel, came to the attention of major British film director, Alan Parker. This led to her first professional assignment for David Putnam, *Experience Preferred . . . But Not Essential*. From there her career took off.

By 1988, she had won the British Film Institute's Young Composer of the Year award and was nominated for the BAFTA Award for Best Score for *Oranges Are Not the Only Fruit* and *The Woman in Black*. Besides the Carlton Television Award for "Creative Originality for Women in Film," she has been nominated for three other British awards, among them for *Where Angels Fear To Tread*. Her numerous BBC-TV scores include *Elizabeth R*, *Flea Bites*, and *Falklands War. Untold Story*, as well as *Monster Maker* and the eight-part *Storyteller. The Greek Myths* for the Henson Organization. With a goal to write music that "communicates," her melodies—gentle, joyful, funny, sad— are an integral part of the action and impact of each film she scores, and her filmography has reached extensive proportions. A partial list names: *The Joy Luck Club* (1993), *Ethan Frome*, *Used People*, *Adventures of Pinocchio*, *Marvin's Room*, *Addicted to Love*, *Home Fries*, *Emma* (1996)—for which Portman was the first female composer to win the Academy Award—Oprah Winfrey's *Beloved* (1998), British drama *Ratcatcher*, which won the Flanders International Film Festival Award (1999), *The Cider House Rules* (1999)—for which she received her second Oscar nomination for Best Original Score as well as nominations for a Grammy and the Ivor Novello Award—Robert Redford's golfing drama *The Legend of Bagger Vance* (2000), and the same year, *Chocolat*, for which she received another Academy Award nomination. 2002 featured *Hart's War*, *The Truth About Charlie*, *The Emperor's New Clothes* and *Nicholas Nickleby*. 2003 brought *The Mona Lisa Smile*, starring Julia Roberts, Kirsten Dunst, Maggie Gyllenhaal and Marcia Gay Harden, and a 2004 remake of *The Manchurian Candidate*, Jonathan Demme, director. Her children's fantasy opera, based on Antoine St. Expury's *The Little Prince*, directed by Francesca Zambello, was successfully staged by Houston Grand Opera, May 31–June 22, 2003. In 2004, it was produced in Milwaukee. A filmed version with young singers was broadcast on the BBC at Christmas.

Because of Winn Dixie, Wayne Wang, director, and Roman Polanski's version of *Oliver Twist* were released in 2005, showing a deeper side of Portman's style.

Rachel is married to film producer Uberto Pasolini of *The Full Monty* fame. Their children are Anna, born September 27, 1995, Giulia, March 20, 1998, and Niky, August 19, 1999. The family resides in London, working there, as well as New York and Los Angeles.

PATRICE RUSHEN, born 1954, in Los Angeles, attended USC where she received training as a classical and jazz pianist. She is the composer of an award-winning symphony and other classical works—commissioned assignments from major orchestras. Multi-talented, her success as a recording artist and musical director prompted a crossover to popular music, working with such notables as Sheena Easton, the late Lionel Hampton, and Michael and Janet Jackson, as music director for the latter's world tour, "janet."

A multi-talented musician, singer, songwriter, arranger and producer, she broke another barrier for black women when she entered the television and film music field. Rushen's impressive list of "firsts" include being the first woman in forty-three years to serve as head composer/music director for television's Emmy Awards, and first female music director for the NAACP Image Awards broadcast, an honor she has held for over a dozen consecutive years.

She has so far been the only woman music director/composer for the *People's Choice Awards*, HBO's *Comic Relief*, CBS' *The Midnight Hour* and the first American Achievement Awards broadcast on CBS from Kennedy Center, for which she composed and performed special tributes to Michael Landon, Ted Turner, Lucille Ball, Desi Arnaz, the Temptations, James Garner, and Leonard Bernstein among others. Her 1998 CD, *Signature*, received a Grammy nomination, an NAACP Image Award nomination, and landed in the top ten of the adult-contemporary jazz charts.

Her list of credits include Emmy-nominated television movies and series such as Showtime's *The Killing Yard*, starring Alan Alda; the Sundance Film Award-winning *Our America*; for BET Network's *Fire and Ice*; HBO's *America's Dream*, with Danny Glover and Wesley Snipes; the Wonderful World of Disney telefilm, *Ruby Bridges*; Masterpiece Theater's *Cora Unashamed*, with Regina Taylor and C.C.H. Pounder; *Brewster Place*, starring Oprah Winfrey; a PBS documentary, *A. Phillip Randolph*; and the hit sitcom series, *The Steve Harvey Show*.

Rushen's feature film credits include *Men in Black*, *Waiting to Exhale*, Sandra Bernhardt's *Without You I'm Nothing*, Robert Townsend's *Hollywood Shuffle*, the song "The Nearness of You" for the film *Indecent Proposal*, sung by Sheena Easton, which led to an album of jazz standards, and *No Strings*, which Patrice produced and MCA released in 1993. ASCAP honored her publishing company for *Men in Black* in the category of most Performed Song from a Motion Picture for the year 1997.

Rushen was composer-in-residence with the Detroit Symphony, 2000–01.

Shirley Walker

Composer, conductor, orchestrator, pianist, synthesist and producer **SHIRLEY WALKER** has the distinction of becoming the first woman to score, orchestrate and conduct the session for a major Hollywood motion picture. Born April 10, 1945, in Napa, California, she grew up in Pleasant Hill across the bridge from San Francisco. Music affected her deeply at an early age. She attended San Francisco State College on a piano scholarship, where she studied composition with Roger Nixon, and further piano studies with Harald Logan at Berkeley. While still in high school, she soloed with the San Francisco Symphony. In her late teens she played for ballet classes, jazz and art bands, and church choirs before discovering music's image-enhancing power by composing for industrial films beginning in 1965. Her stint as pianist with the Oakland Symphony Orchestra gave her inside knowledge of the workings of an orchestra and rehearsal techniques. She was also the Cabrillo Festival Orchestra pianist for two seasons.

After suspending her career to raise a family (Shirley married Don Walker in 1967, gave birth to Colin in 1970, who now plays guitar with a Brazilian group, and Ian in 1972, a bassist and studio player), she re-entered the scoring field as a house player for American Zoëtrope, assisting on the soundtrack for Francis Ford Coppola's *Apocalypse Now*, and graduating to co-composing. Her major orchestrating and conducting work has been on such films as *Cujo* (1980), *Anatomy of An Illness* (1982), *Black Rain* (1983), *Batman* (1984), *Children of a Lesser God* (1986), *National Lampoon's Christmas Vacation* (1988), *Scrooged* (1988), *Edward Scissorhands* (1989), *Arachnophobia* (1990), *Dick Tracy* (1990), *Radio Flyer* (1991), *The Butcher's Wife* (1991), *A League of Their Own* (1992), *True Lies* (1994), *Free Willy II* (1995), *Batman Forever* (1995), *Rasputin* (1996) and *Backdraft*. She also orchestrated a concert suite from Disney's *The Little Mermaid* (1990). Her television composition credits include the series *Spawn*, *Space: Above and Beyond*, *The Others*, *The Flash*, two episodes of *Cagney and Lacey*, eleven of *Falcon Crest*, three of *Lou Grant* and eight of *Viper*.

Walker was composer/supervising composer on the Warner Animation Series *The Animated Batman*, *Superman*, *Batman Beyond*, and *The Zeda Project*, for which she received two Daytime Emmys and seven Daytime Emmy nominations. Her feature work includes *Final Destination*, additional music for *Mystery Men*, *Turbulence*, *Escape From Los Angeles* and *Batman: Mask of the Phantasm*. She has scored the television movies *Disappearance*, *Asteroid*, *The Garbage Picking, Field Goal Kicking, Philadelphia Phenomenon*, *The Love Bug II* and *The Crying Child*. She is also orchestrator/conductor on most of the recordings of these soundtracks, including *The Black Stallion* (1979) which she co-composed.

June 7, 2000 saw the UC Santa Barbara Symphony Orchestra, led by Jeff Schindler, perform their first commissioned piece: Shirley Walker's *Oncogenic Quietude*, an orchestral tribute to her husband who overcame the horrifying diagnosis of lung cancer via a courageous complete change of lifestyle.

New Line Cinema's hit film, *Final Destination*, was released on DVD August 2000, featuring Shirley's commentary plus isolated score track. In May 2001 her team, including Kristopher Carter, Michael McCuistion and Lolita Ritmanis, received an Emmy Award in the category "Outstanding Achievement in Music Direction and Composition" for their collaborative effort on the score for the animated series *Batman Beyond*. This was her eighth Emmy nomination and her second win, the first was for the original *Batman* animated series. Other Emmy nominations include her scores for the *Superman* animated series, and a Primetime Emmy nomination for *Space: Above and Beyond*. Two new scores for 2003 include *Final Destination 2*, a sequel to the 2000 film, and *Willard*, a re-make of the 1971 cult classic horror film. 2006 brought *Final Destination 3*.

Her memberships include: Academy of Motion Picture Arts & Sciences (AMPAS), Broadcast Music Inc. (BMI), Recording Musicians Association (RMA), Academy of Television Arts & Sciences (ATAS), Society of Composers & Lyricists (SCL), American Society of Composers Authors & Publishers (ASCAP), National Academy of Recording Arts & Sciences (NARAS) and American Federation of Musicians.

As a record/CD producer, she has to her credit: Roland Vazquez *Further Dance*; the soundtrack of *Mask of the Phantasm* and *Memoirs of an Invisible Man*; the LA Jazz Ensemble's *Feel Your Dreams*; *Art Of The Balalaika* and *Art Of The Mandolin*; and the LA Vocal Arts Ensemble's *Liebeslieder* and *Sins Of My Old Age*. She was Sheffield Labs' producer on *The Irving Berlin Century*, editor on *Moscow Musical Summit*, and editor on harmonia mundi's *Swanne Alley* and *Senesino*.

Shirley Walker is in the happy position of doing what she wants to do and having the talent and skills to do it. She writes for film in a unique manner: her melodic music weaves brilliantly throughout the scenes.

DEBBIE WISEMAN, born in London, May 10, 1963, began piano at eight and learned percussion, all the while in love with Mozart, Beethoven, Debussy and Messiaen. After graduating from Guildhall, 1984, she was certain of wanting to be a film composer and sent showreels to directors and producers. Her first commission was on a drama documentary called *a Strike out of Time* for Channel 4, and went on to win the Silents to Satellite Award for *Shrinks* (1991).

Her BBC-TV scores and filmography are long enough to fill a whole chapter, including the TRIC (TV & Radio Industry Club) Award for *the Good Guys* (1993); 1994 nominations for

Debbie Wiseman

two Academy Awards, the Alexander Korda Award for Outstanding British Film, and BAFTA Awards for *Tom and Viv* (the story of T.S. Eliot and his wife Vivienne Haigh-Wood); *Death of Yugoslavia* got a 1995 Ivor Novello Award nomination and the1996 Royal Television Society Award; a 1997 Ivor Novello Award nomination was for *Wilde*, the story of iconoclast, scandal-ridden writer Oscar Wilde. She won an Emmy for *Deep In My Heart* (1999), and the Royal Television Society Award for *Warriors* (2000), which also garnered Winner of Best Drama-South Bank Show Awards and Best Drama Serial, BAFTA. *Stig of the Dump*, a children's tale, added a 2002 Emmy. Her over a dozen CDs include *Something Here*, featuring Wiseman's most popular scores with the composer conducting the Royal Philharmonic.

2004 brought an MBE (Member of the British Empire), from the Queen's Honours List.

In 1987, Debbie married Tony Wharmby who is, ideally, in the music preparation and copying field.

Putting Words to the Music

Dorothy Fields

A few women have made their names in the field of *lyrics*. **DOROTHY FIELDS** (1904–74) collaborated with **Jerome Kern** (1885–1945) on such immortal ballads as "Lovely to Look At" (1935), "A Fine Romance" (1936), and "The Way You Look Tonight" (1936) among the many which made their way from Broadway into the movies. She partnered with Jimmy McHugh for "I'm in the Mood for Love" (1935), "On the Sunny Side of the Street" (1930), and other hits. She also wrote film scenarios with her brother, Herbert. Some of the films bearing her name are *Annie Get Your Gun* (1946), music by **Irving Berlin** (1888–1989), *A Tree Grows in Brooklyn* (1951), starring Dorothy McGuire, and *Sweet Charity* (1966), with Shirley MacLaine.

Betty Comden

As early as 1944, **BETTY COMDEN,** born May 13, 1919, collaborated with her partner, **Adolf Green**, writing the libretto for Leonard Bernstein's *On the Town*. After many successful Broadway musicals, they came to Hollywood and wrote a slew of hits (words and music) in such movies as *The Barkleys of Broadway* (Fred Astaire and Ginger Rogers, 1949); *On the Town* (film version, 1949); the Academy Award winning *Singin' in the Rain* (Gene Kelly and Debbie Reynolds, 1953); *The Band Wagon* (Fred Astaire and Cyd Charisse, 1953); and *Bells Are Ringing* (Judy Holliday and Dean Martin, 1960).

Wonderful Town, starring Rosalind Russell, reunited them with Leonard Bernstein and opened on Broadway February 25, 1953. Based on the comedy *My Sister Eileen*, it was made into a movie in 1955, starring Janet Leigh and Jack Lemmon, using the original title. In December 2003, *Wonderful Town* hit Broadway once again in a sparkling successful revival at the Al Hirschfeld[54] Theatre.

1991 brought Kennedy Center Honors for the team. In 2001, they received the Screen Laurel Award. In May 2002, they were presented with a lifetime achievement award in theatrical writing from The Dramatists Guild—the third recipients after Arthur Miller and Edward Albee. September 2002 saw screenings across the country celebrating the fiftieth anniversary of *Singin' in the Rain*. A newly-remastered DVD was released September 24.

Comden worked with Green for almost sixty years until his death October 24, 2002, at eighty-seven. New York Mayor Bloomberg proclaimed Tuesday, December 3, 2002, Adolph Green Day in the city.

June 2003, Betty Comden received the Kaufmann Center's Creative Arts Award at a gala ceremony in New York City. She died Thanksgiving Day, November 23, 2006.

SYLVIA FINE (August 29, 1913–October 28, 1991), wife of popular singing comedian **Danny Kaye** (1913–87), was already an established songwriter before their marriage, January 3, 1940. Their daughter, Dena, was born December 17, 1946.

---

54. Named after the famed caricaturist (1903–2003).

Born in Brooklyn, Sylvia began piano lessons at six, and harmony and theory at ten. She went to Thomas Jefferson High School and Hunter College. Uncomfortable performing before large audiences, she instead developed her interests in writing and composing.

Fine wrote the distinctive material for her husband's unique talents, including incredibly fast speech and patter song delivery, in his major films: *Up in Arms* (1944), *Wonder Man* (1945), *The Kid From Brooklyn* (1946), *The Secret Life of Walter Mitty* (1947), *The Inspector General* (1949), *On the Riviera* (1951), *Knock on Wood* (1954), *The Court Jester* (1956), *The Five Pennies* (1959), and *On the Double* (1961). Her songs included "The Lobby Number," "Melody in 4F," "Bali Boogie," "Anatole of Paris," "A New Symphony for Unstrung Tongue," and "Pavlova" in *The Kid from Brooklyn*—first used in *The Straw Hat Revue* (1939). The tongue-twisting, lip-curdling lyrics for the memorable *chalice from the palace* routine were in *The Court Jester*. "Happy Times," for *The Inspector General*, was used after her death in the film *The Straight Story* (1999). She also wrote and produced her husband's television specials during the 1960s.

She gave a lecture series at USC and Yale which was incorporated into two television specials: Musical Comedy Tonight I and II, aired in 1979 and '81.

Singer **Dory Langdon Previn**, second wife of conductor/composer **André Previn**, contributed her talents in the field with many songs, both lyrics and music, for Broadway and the silver screen.

Marilyn Bergman

MARILYN BERGMAN represents half of one of the most respected song writing teams in music, and with her husband Alan Bergman, is one of the most prolific lyricists in the entertainment industry. A music major at New York's High School of Music and Art, she went on to study psychology and English at NYU. After college, she moved to Los Angeles and resumed the musical thread of her life. Although born in the same hospital and raised in the same area of New York, she met and later married Alan in Los Angeles while they were both working independently with the same composer. They have one daughter, an executive at Caravan Pictures.

In 1985, Bergman became the first woman to be elected to the board of directors of the American Society of Composers, Authors and Publishers (ASCAP), the world's foremost performing rights organization. In 1994, she became president, and in January 1995 her title was changed to chairman of the board. She is a member of the executive committee of the music branch of the Academy of Motion Picture Arts & Sciences, a member of the National Academy of Songwriters and the Nashville Songwriters Association. She was the only creator to serve on the advisory council to the National Information Infrastructure (NII).

Among her many honors was induction—with Alan—into the Songwriters Hall of Fame (1979) and receiving the Crystal Award from Women in Film (1986). She is on the board of directors of the National Academy of Songwriters; a founder of the Hollywood Women's Political Committee; member of the Women's Trusteeship and the National Women's Forum; and served on the board of directors of the Streisand Foundation.

The couple won Oscars in 1968, 1973 and 1984 for the songs *The Windmills of Your Mind*, *The Way We Were* and the score from Barbra Streisand's *Yentl*. In the '90s, the Bergmans had three TV theme songs on the air: *In the Heat of the Night*, *The Powers That Be* and the Golden Globe winning series, *Brooklyn Bridge*, for whose song they received an Emmy nomination. They wrote the opening ceremonies theme, "An American Reunion," for the Clinton Presidential Inauguration festivities at the Lincoln Memorial, aired live on HBO, January 17, 1993. In 1994, they scripted the legendary Barbra Streisand Concert Tour and HBO Special which received a Cable Ace Award nomination. They *did* receive the Cable Ace Award for the show's original song, *Ordinary Miracles*. Together, they wrote the acclaimed "One Voice" concert for Streisand, with Marilyn as co-executive producer. Marilyn was also executive producer of the PBS Special, "The Music Makers: An ASCAP Celebration of American Music at Wolf Trap."

Since their first Oscar nomination in 1968, their lyrics have received sixteen nominations for such songs as "What Are You Doing the Rest of Your Life?" from *The Happy Ending* (1969), "It Might Be You" (*Tootsie*, with

Dustin Hoffman, 1982) and, in 1996, nominations for both a Golden Globe and Academy Award for "Moonlight" from the film *Sabrina*, starring Julia Ormond and Harrison Ford. The same year marked the release of the CD, *America: The Dream Goes On*, a celebration of July 4th, written with Alan, music by John Williams. By 2001, Bergman's "score" was three Academy Awards, three Emmys, two Grammys, and one Cable Ace Award. She has appeared on numerous talk shows and panels, and hosted the PBS special, "Women in Song." In 2002, the Bergmans collaborated with Cy Coleman for an intermissionless concert: "Portraits in Jazz," which played at Kennedy Center in May. This was expanded into a "non-traditional musical," *Like Jazz*, which played at Los Angeles' Mark Taper Forum, December 4, 2003–January 25, 2004.

The Bergmans are recipients of honorary doctorates from the Berklee (Massachusetts) College of Music (1995). The same year, Marilyn received a National Academy of Songwriters Lifetime Achievement Award. 1996 brought France's cultural medal of honor, Commander of the Order of Arts and Letters, and 1997 the Johnny Mercer Award from the Songwriters Hall of Fame. The Cultural Medal of Honor from the Spanish performing rights organization SGAE, came in June 2001. In 2002, Marilyn became the first chairman of the Library of Congress National Sound Recording Preservation Board.

Wielding the Small Stick

A woman must be better than a man if she is to conduct prestigious groups, and I made it my career always to be 100 percent prepared and know all scores tremendously well.

—Frédérique Petrides

Eva Vale Anderson (1893–1985), Long Beach Women's Symphony

Ebba Sundstrom (1896–1963), Women's Symphony Orchestra of Chicago

D'Zama Murielle, Portland Women's Symphony

Emma Steiner (1852–1929), Operetta Conductor

Mabel Swint Ewer, Philadelphia Women's Symphony

Josephine Weinlich (1848-87), Vienna Ladies' Orchestra

Carmen Studer (1907–?), European Guest Conductor

Gertrude Herliczka (1902–?), U.S./European Guest Conductor

Elizabeth Kuyper (1877–1953), Women's Orchestra, Berlin

Alma Rosé (1906–1944), Wiener Mädeln Orkester

Jane Evrard (1893–1984), Women's Orchestra of Paris

Marie Wilson (1903–?), BBC Promenade Concert Orchestra

Caroline B. Nichols (1864–1939), Boston Fadette Ladies' Orchestra

Gena Branscombe (1881–1977), Branscombe Chorale

Ethel Leginska (1886–1970), Boston Women's Orchestra

Nadia Boulanger (1887–1979), Guest Conductor

Antonia Brico (1902–89), Denver Businessmen's Orchestra, Brico Symphony

Frédérique Petrides (1903–83), Orchestrette Classique

Ruth Thall Quinn (1920–), Columbus (Ohio) Miniature Symphony

Sarah Caldwell (1924-2006), Boston City Opera, Global Guest Conductor

Margaret Hillis (1921–1998), Chicago Symphony Chorus, Elgin (Illinois) Symphony

Judith Somogi (1937–1988), Frankfurt Opera

Iona Brown (1941–2004), Academy of St. Martin in the Fields, Norwegian Chamber Orchestra

The history of women conductors can be traced to the proliferation of all-women orchestras that were formed around the same time as the founding of three major American music schools. The Institute of Musical Art in New York came first, in 1905, in order to establish an academy to rival European conservatories. When wealthy textile merchant **Augustus D. Juilliard** died in 1919, his will contained the largest single bequest for the advancement of music at that time. Thus the Juilliard Graduate School came into being in 1924, merging with the Institute in 1926, to become the Juilliard School of Music. In 1921, the Eastman School of Music, Rochester (upstate New York), was founded by photography pioneer/philanthropist **George Eastman** (1854–1932). The Curtis Institute in Philadelphia followed in 1924, through the generosity of **Mary Louise Curtis Bok**. (See The Unforgotten.) As these institutions poured out accomplished women performers who literally had no place to go—all major orchestras being bastions of good old boys—they were left with only two choices: to teach or play in ensembles of their own gender.

Predating its sisters, the Los Angeles Women's Orchestra was founded in 1893. In the '20s and '30s, women musicians wanted career options other than teaching. This led to the establishing of female ensembles in Philadelphia, Chicago (two), Boston (three), New York (four), Long Beach (California), Portland (Oregon), Cleveland, Pittsburgh, Stockton (California), Baltimore, St. Louis, Mason City (Iowa), Minneapolis, and into the next decade with Montreal (Canada, 1940) and Detroit (1941). Besides opening opportunities to female instrumentalists and conductors, these aggregations sometimes featured works by women composers.

Pioneers of the Podium

Caroline Nichols

Among the first ladies to ascend the podium was **Caroline Nichols** (1864–1939), who founded the *Boston Fadette Women's Orchestra*. Beginning with six players in 1888, it grew to become the first professional all-woman orchestra. They played in parks, summer resorts, vaudeville, accompanied silent films, and toured the U.S. and Canada. By the time they disbanded in 1920, they had played over 6,000 concerts and gained much prestige. **Eva Vale Anderson** (1893–1985) conducted the Long Beach Women's Symphony, 1925–1952, which also began as a small group and grew to 120 members. Anderson's husband, Herbert Whitaker, their manager, was fond of pointing out that the orchestra's success was due in part to having *one source* of leadership—his wife—who had his full support. **Ebba Sundstrom** (1896–1963) led the Women's Symphony Orchestra of Chicago, founded in 1925. Numbering 100 musicians, they stood comparison to any major male orchestra. On occasion, they played to audiences of 20,000 at outdoor summer concerts at Grant Park. In 1928, the orchestra was briefly under the leadership of British pianist/composer/conductor **Ethel Leginska**. **D'Zama Murielle** founded the Portland (Oregon) Women's Symphony in 1934. **Emma Steiner** (1852–1929) directed over 6,000 performances of operas and operettas, including Gilbert and Sullivan—the first woman conductor in this field—leading major orchestras, among them the Metropolitan Opera. She was also a composer.

Men in the Harem

Some female groups had male conductors, like the Women's String Orchestra, under Carl V. Lachmund. Established in New York in 1896 with eighteen players, by 1900 there were thirty-eight. The Woman's Orchestra of Los Angeles was conducted by its 1893 founder Harley Hamilton (1861–1933), who was also the conductor of the Los Angeles Philharmonic. In the Women's Orchestra he was followed by an Italian, D. Cesar Cianfoni. J.W.F. Leman was director of the Philadelphia Women's Symphony Orchestra, which made its debut in January 1921. Their founder, **Mabel Swint Ewer**, played trumpet in the orchestra for eight years, and out of her own pocket enabled the organization to survive the stock market crash of 1929. It also helped that the great **Leopold Stokowski** (1882–1977), who had been leading the Philadelphia Orchestra since 1912, gave these women his personal recommendation. He was truly a pioneer supporter of "co-ed" orchestras. Meanwhile, **Nikolai Sokoloff** (1886–1965) set a precedent by hiring two women violinists and two violists for the Cleveland Orchestra as early as 1918.

The only sizeable women's orchestras still in existence in 21st century America are the **Cleveland Women's Orchestra**, founded in 1935 and conducted for fifty-six years by **Hyman Schandler**, and The Women's Philharmonic in San Francisco which, unfortunately, had to fold for financial reasons in 2004.

Rocking the Boat Across the Atlantic

Gertrude Herliczka

The Vienna Ladies' (Wiener Damen) Orchestra was the first of its kind seen in America when they began their tour in New York, September 1871, under the baton of its founder **Josephine Weinlich**, Austrian pianist, violinist, conductor, teacher and composer. Born in Vienna in 1848, she received her first lessons from her father, Francisco Weinlich, and then studied piano with **Clara Schumann**. But it was as a violinist that she gave recitals throughout Austria. With her daughter as a soloist in the orchestra, they toured Europe, specializing in the works of Johann Strauss. In January 1879, Weinlich went to Lisbon with her husband and became the conductor of an orchestra there. Subsequently, she turned to piano teaching. Some of her compositions were published in the journal *Gazette Musical*, owned by her husband. She died of tuberculosis at the young age of thirty-eight in Lisbon, January 9, 1887. **Carmen Studer** (1907–?) conducted several European orchestras before becoming the fifth wife, in 1932, of her conducting teacher, renowned maestro **Felix Weingartner** (1863–1942). In March 1935, however, she was sabotaged by the all-male[55] Vienna Philharmonic, who refused to play under a woman. The same month and year, Viennese **Gertrude Herliczka** received better treatment at the hands of the New York Philharmonic, conducting a much-praised concert at Town Hall. She also guest conducted throughout Europe with such orchestras as the Paris Opera Comique, sharing the podium with illustrious colleagues like **Bruno Walter**, **Wilhelm Furtwängler**, **Victor de Sabata** and **Bernadino Molinari**. Like **Frédérique Petrides**, Gertrude married a supportive husband, and had one child, a son, Peter. **Elizabeth Kuyper** (1877–1953) founded the sixty-five member Women's Orchestra in Berlin in 1910, of which most of the winds and all the brass section were made up of cooperative male musicians. She kept the orchestra going until her funds ran out, experiencing similar financial failure when she tried to start a women's orchestra in New York after WWI. **Alma Rosé** founded the *Weiner Waltzermädeln* (Viennese Waltzing Girls) in 1935—in today's terminology, "girls" being young women. (See Violinists.)

Although French composers **Augusta Holmès** and **Cécile Chaminade** had led orchestras non-professionally, while Herliczka and Studer had guest conducted in the capital, one of the last groups to be inaugurated—Spring 1930—was the Orchestre feminin de Paris (Women's Orchestra of Paris), under the baton of violinist **Jane Evrard** (1893–1984). At first considered somewhat of a joke, in 1933 when its twenty-three string players toured Spain, the critical raves got back to the French press making Paris proud and respectful of the ensemble. Evrard commissioned and premiered works of such contemporary composers as **Albert Roussel** and **Joaquín Rodrigo**, among others. Her circle included the artistic elite of Paris: writer **Colette**, dancer **Isadora Duncan**, actor/author **Sacha Guitry**, composers **Claude Debussy**, **Maurice Ravel**, **Reynaldo Hahn**, **Vincent d'Indy**, **Manuel de Falla**, violinist **Jacques Thibaud**, pianist **Alfred Cortot**. Circa 2002, the city of Paris honored Evrard with a plaque on the rue de Passy.

In 1935, violinist **Marie Wilson** (1903–?) became director of the prestigious BBC Promenade Concert Orchestra, out of whose ninety members eleven were women. She was with the orchestra from its inception in 1930 until 1944. The British Women's Symphony Orchestra flourished from 1920 until World War II.

Talkies Silence the Music

Two major causes for the extinction of smaller ensembles were the "talkies" and the Great Depression. The advent of talking pictures in 1928 gradually eliminated the theater musicians who had traditionally accompanied

---

55. As of 2004, the Vienna Philharmonic is still all male, except for one female harpist—they also have a male harpist. **Anna Lelkes** (b 1940) hung in there, 1987–2001, relegated to the edge of the stage. Bowing to threats of boycott from the IAWM and others prior to their U.S. tour in 1997, Lelkes was finally admitted as *a full member with voting privileges*, February 27, 1997. Her name *first appeared on the program*, March 1995, when the orchestra played at Carnegie Hall. twenty-one-year-old **Charlotte Balzereit** was hired in 2001 as her replacement. (See Orchestras.)

the action of silent movies. (See Conductors: Gillian Anderson.) The worldwide economic depression of the 1930s, brought about by the crash of the New York Stock Market, October 1929, was felt in the musical field when restaurants, hotels, resorts and other establishments employing live orchestras had to give up this luxury. President Franklin Delano Roosevelt's Works Progress Administration (WPA), set up to help the unemployed in areas that spanned from roadwork to building dams, infiltrated the music arena with thirty-six federally-funded orchestras. This provided some jobs for women, as did the twenty all-female orchestras in existence at the time. A few ladies were even able to storm all-male strongholds such as the Philadelphia Orchestra, which admitted cellist **Elsa Hilger** to its ranks in 1935, and violinist Lois Putlitz the following year. In 1937, French hornist **Ellen Stone** was accepted by the Pittsburgh Symphony, and two string players made it into the Los Angeles Philharmonic by 1938. 1938 was also the year the National Federation of Music Clubs requested that all auditions take place behind a screen to eliminate unjust discrimination. (Over sixty-five years later, this is still not a universally honored policy . . .)

World War II brought openings for female musicians as men were drafted into the military. Most female orchestras (thirty operated in the U.S. between 1908–'30s) were disbanded after the war with the exception of Detroit, which survived until 1971. Today, the Cleveland Women's Orchestra remains the sole survivor of the era. Founded in 1935 by Hyman Schandler, it was under his conductorship for fifty-six years until his death at age ninety in 1990, when his colleague, Robert L. Cronquist, took over the baton. Setting longevity records is member **Sabine Berman**, viola, who had been in the orchestra since its inception, retired from playing in 2006 at age ninety, her seventy-second year, but remained on the board and went to rehearsals. Other over fifty year stalwarts include Arlene Nehamkin, violinist, Esther Isenstadt, principal bass, Marge Roberto, bass, Fern Vogt, trombone and Marion Russell, principal flute, who retired in 2003 after fifty-six years. In 1991, three generations—a grandmother, mother and two daughters—were all members. In 1993, the orchestra participated in the 100th anniversary celebration of the 1893 Chicago Columbian Exposition—the first world's fair to officially recognize women's achievements. 1996 saw the orchestra as part of the city's bicentennial celebration, which included opening a time capsule left by women of 1886. Programs and photographs went into a new capsule to be opened in 2096. With diverse ethnic groups in the area, celebrations for their sixty-fifth season (1999–2000) included a Spring 2000 program of Czech music in historic Bohemian Hall. Their sixty-sixth season also honored Cleveland's Hungarian community with a concert celebrating the 1,000th anniversary of Christianity for Hungary. October 2001 again marked their all-Czech program. April 21, 2002 brought the annual fundraiser at Severance Hall for the orchestra's sixty-seventh year. (Their debut concert was November 17, 1936). Besides their many outreach and cultural events of each season, May 1, 2005 saw their seventieth anniversary concert. Keeping this all together is former president of the board, and current project manager, Joan Ferst, happily celebrating her eleventh year as Mrs. Cronquist in September 2006.

Other Podium Pioneers

Women conductors have achieved fame and recognition in various ways. Some have slipped in the "back door" through the cumulative reputation of their performances, others by the sheer force of their personality. Their common ground was, and continues to be, a superior talent impervious to denial by their male counterparts.

CAROLINE B. NICHOLS was born in 1864, in Dedham, Massachusetts. She was a student of **Julius Eichberg**, German-born director of the Boston Conservatory, who stood practically alone at the time in his encouragement of girls taking up the violin. In 1888, six women formed the nucleus of an orchestra uniquely called the **Fadettes**, after Fanchon Fadette, the do-good heroine of one of Caroline's favorite novels, *La petite fadette*, by George Sand (the mistress of Chopin). Nichols wanted an outlet for herself and other women musicians. By 1890, there were fifteen members, soon expanding to twenty: four first violins, two seconds, one viola, one cello, two double basses, one flute/piccolo, two French horns—said to be the only two women playing that instrument at the time in the whole country—two cornets, one trombone, one tympanist, a drummer and a harpist. In 1895 they incorporated, and became the first professional all-woman orchestra. With financial help from the conductor's brother-in-law, Geroge H. Chickering, president of the piano company bearing his name, the Fadettes gave their first recitals in Chickering Hall to enthusiastic reviews.

With a repertoire of 600 works, including symphonies, overtures, opera and salon music, by 1898 they were touring the country coast to coast, as well as Canada. They also played in parks and resorts and, until the Musicians' Union stepped in, had a short stint accompanying silent films at New York's Roxy Theater. In the summer of 1902, vaudeville impresario Benjamin Franklin Keith (1846–1914) gave the Fadettes a two week tryout in his Boston theater. They were so well received they were asked to finish the season. Thus, a women's orchestra made history by usurping the summer jobs of Boston Symphony male musicians! They also joined Keith's winter circuit.

In the course of her career, Nichols shared the podium with such greats as **John Philip Sousa** (1884–1932), **Walter Damrosch** (1862–1950) and **Victor Herbert** (1859–1924). She retired to Boston in 1920, but continued training new orchestra members until her death at seventy-five, August 16, 1939. It was said she had enabled more women to become professional, paid orchestra members than any other person. It was estimated that by the time the orchestra disbanded, they had racked up over 6,000 concerts and shared a payroll of half a million dollars— probably equivalent to half a billion today—among 600 women. In 1952, a fiftieth anniversary reunion was held by nine of the original Fadettes.

Gena Branscombe

GENA BRANSCOMBE, born November 4, 1881, in Ontario, Canada, was already accompanying her older brother in public by the age of six. At fifteen, she entered the Chicago Musical College, studying piano with its founder, **Florenz Ziegfeld**, father of the showman of Follies fame. Composition was with **Felix Borowski** (1872–1956). She received her BA in 1900. In 1903, she joined the college's piano faculty. Two years later she went to Berlin, where she studied for a year with the "original" (or real) **Engelbert Humperdinck** (1854–1921), composer of the classic children's opera, *Hansel and Gretel* (1893).

Returning to America, Branscombe took conducting lessons. She became a U.S. citizen in 1910 and married John Ferguson Tenney, October 5. Their four daughters were: Gena, born 1911, Vivian, 1913, Betty, 1916, and Beatrice, 1919.

In 1914, her *Festival Prelude* for orchestra was premiered at the MacDowell Colony, then in New York and later at the San Francisco Exposition. The oratorio *Pilgrims of Destiny*, for soloists, chorus and orchestra (1919), about the *Mayflower*, was appropriately performed in Plymouth, Massachusetts (1929). At the request of the Library of Congress, she submitted the manuscript and orchestral parts in 1960. The composer conducted the Chicago Woman's Symphony in the premiere of *Quebec*, a symphonic suite for tenor and orchestra, about the early settlers in 16th century Canada.

Serving the "Illumined Force"

In 1921, Branscombe turned her energies to conducting, studying with **Frank Damrosch** (1859–1937)—older brother of Walter—among others, at the Institute of Musical Art which later became Juilliard. In 1934, she organized the Branscombe Chorale, a women's chorus she directed for the next twenty years. She also guest conducted her own songs and choral works throughout America, Canada and England. During WWII, she led the first American Women's Voluntary Services Chorus, which sang in uniform.

In 1941, Branscombe was chosen to conduct a chorus of a thousand voices for the Golden Jubilee celebration of women's achievements in Atlantic City, New Jersey. Her favorite composition was *Coventry's Choir*, for soprano solo, four-part chorus and orchestra, a setting of a poem by Violet Alvarez about the bombing of that great English cathedral during WWII.

President of the Society of American Women Composers, Gena had lifelong friendships with conductor **Antonia Brico**, and composers **Amy Beach**, **Mary Howe**, **Marion Bauer** and **Mabel Daniels**, and programmed many works by women composers. Her last commission, in 1973, was to write an *Introit*, *Prayer Response* and *Amen* for a special service at New York's Riverside Church. Active and energetic throughout her long life, she was working on her autobiography when she died at age ninety-five, July 26, 1977. Her own music was used at her funeral. After her death her music seemed lost to history, but, since 2002, mezzo-soprano Kathleen Shimeta has presented a one-woman show on Branscombe, featuring her biography and song selections.

Branscombe's famous quote reflects a not so dated female philosophy, "Having a home, a husband and children to love and serve brings enrichment of life to a woman, but being part of the world's work in humbly serving and loving the illumined force which is music, brings fulfillment."

ETHEL LEGINSKA, born April 13, 1886, in Hull, in the north of England, showed a natural talent for music at an early age. Her piano debut was at six, and she had an extensive career until 1924, when she switched to conducting. (See Pianists.) She studied with **Sir Eugene Goossens** (1897–1988), one of England's greatest maestros; with Robert Hager (1886–1978) in Munich; and in Chicago with Italian-American Genaro Papi (1886–1941), conductor of the Met (1916–26) and Chicago Civic Opera (1925–32). She became one of the first women to direct major orchestras in Munich, Berlin, Paris and London, including grand opera. She also conducted Beethoven's 9th (Chorale) Symphony in Havana (Cuba), and Dallas (Texas). Her American debut, January 1925 with the New York Symphony, designated her the first woman to conduct in Carnegie Hall. This was followed in August by a triumphant Hollywood Bowl performance, despite some male harassment within the orchestra.

In 1926, Leginska organized and directed first the 100-man Boston Philharmonic Orchestra, then the sixty-five member Boston Women's Orchestra—with a **Radie Britain (**See Pen Women Composers) work on the program— taking them on tour to Washington, St. Louis, Cleveland, Chicago, Milwaukee and Buffalo. Between 1930–32, she composed her first opera, *The Rose and the Ring*, but it was not performed until 1957 in Los Angeles. She conducted the Montreal Opera during the 1932–33 season. Her next opera, *Gale*, was premiered in 1935 with the Chicago Civic Opera. **John Charles Thomas** sang the title role under her direction, yet three years later helped sabotage the career of **Antonia Brico** by refusing to sing under *her* at the Met.

As the "novelty" of her appearances tapered off, Leginska settled in Los Angeles in 1939, teaching piano into the 1950s. In 1943, she founded the *New Venture in Music*, a series of programs and recitals in which students were presented. Each season a different composer's music was featured. She also presented an annual series of orchestral concerts with soloists, featuring the Leginska Little Symphony Orchestra.

She remained active until her death at eighty-three, February 26, 1970.

A French Legend

Paris-born **NADIA BOULANGER** (1887–1979) left her immortal imprint on the world as a teacher, yet for almost thirty years she thought of herself as a performer, conductor and composer. As a performer, Boulanger was soloist with the New York Symphony Orchestra (1925) under **Walter Damrosch** (1862–1950), in Copland's Organ Symphony—a work whose composition she had nurtured while he was her student. She was the first woman to conduct a complete concert of the Royal Philharmonic Society (London, 1937), and regular subscription concerts of the Boston Symphony (1938), New York Philharmonic (February 11, 1939), and Hallé Orchestra (Manchester, 1963). Even the Paris Philharmonic was inspired by her genius. She conducted without a baton, and in the early years had to overcome initial unruliness of the all-male composition of these aggregations. Usually it only took a few words at rehearsals for the orchestra members to realize that she was a serious musician who knew what she was doing. Her plain black clothing, attitude and professionalism accomplished the rest.

She made her debut at a matinee outside Paris, April 17, 1912, with her Conservatoire mentor, **Raoul Pugno** (1852–1914), conducting excerpts from her own cantata, *La Sirène*, with an evening performance of her *Prière* and

Cantique, and directing Pugno in his *Concertstück*. January 17, 1913, she was featured in a concert of women's compositions in Berlin, again with Pugno as piano soloist, where she conducted the Blüthner Orchestra in the premiere of her *Rhapsodie variée* written for him. The same year, not permitted to conduct in Paris or Belgium, she directed her *Fantasie for Piano and Orchestra* in Nice with Pugno at a Gala Concert in the Grand Théâtre of the Municipal Casino. By 1933, in the course of her career, Boulanger had established herself as a conductor, both within her classes or at salons in private auditoriums such as that of the Princess de Polignac, one of her wealthiest sponsors. It took until February 1934 to lead the orchestra of the École Normale, where she was a member of the faculty. The critics praised the event as "memorable." December 18, 1934, marked her long-awaited debut on one of the great stages of Paris, the Théâtre des Champs-Elysées, conducting Heinrich Schütz' *St. Matthew Passion*. In 1935, she organized a concert of Polish Music at the École Normale, honoring her many Polish students. However, the critics did not like the modern dissonance.

In February 1938, on a three month tour of America, she became first woman to conduct the Boston Symphony. After initial rudeness by the all male members during rehearsal, she admonished them to concentrate on the music. The result was an inspiring rendition of the Fauré *Requiem*. After the performance, BSO director **Serge Koussevitzky** and each member of the orchestra lined up to shake her hand. In an unprecedented departure from her usual reserve, Nadia hugged and kissed each man on stage in front of the audience! In April, she put on a program of early music, directing from a harpsichord lent her by the New England Conservatory.

An admirer of Debussy and Ravel, and promoter of Igor Stravinsky from the outset of his career, in May 1938 she conducted the premiere of his *Dumbarton Oaks Concerto* at the mansion/estate of the same name near Washington, DC. (This was later the site of important WWII conferences, April–October 1944, to set up the United Nations.)

In 1937, leading the Orchestre Symphonique de Paris, Boulanger recorded the Piano Concerto of her student Jean Françaix (1912–97), with the twenty-five-year-old composer as soloist. In February 1938, she again performed this work with Françaix, this time with the New York Philharmonic. To avoid Ethel Leginska's ill-fated attempt to lead this all-male bastion, **Walter Damrosch** gave a special luncheon to introduce Nadia to the musicians. The concert was a gala event. The program also included directing her own choral ensemble in several selections, as well as the Mozart *Concerto for Two Pianos*, with her at the second instrument. The rapport between conductor and orchestra was electric, as was the admiration of the audience. In the second half, she stepped off the podium to play the organ for her sister Lili's *Pour les funérailles d'un soldat* with the orchestra's regular maestro, Britain's **John Barbirolli** at the helm. Her success continued March 6, conducting the Philadelphia Orchestra for the first half of two subscription concerts. Critic Brailsford Felder admitted, "The prejudice against women conductors, which lurks in the bosom of every orchestra player, breaks down instantly when it comes to Mademoiselle Boulanger."

Since March was the month she reserved each year for mourning her sister, her most ambitious undertaking was staging a commemorative Mass in memory of both Lili and her mother who had also died in March, calling it the Lili Boulanger Memorial Fund Concert. With members of the Boston Symphony, plus the Radcliffe and Harvard Glee Clubs, she further dazzled the society audience by wearing a white gown instead of the usual black. By the time she returned to France in June, she had an enormous following with many students going to Fontainebleau that last summer before Europe was engulfed in World War II, which was declared on September 3, 1939.

After months of pleading for her to get out of France, her friends prevailed, and she caught a ship from Lisbon, arriving in New York November 6, 1940, to stay until January 1946. (See International Musicologists for a description of her myriad activities during the war years in America.)

Always hounded with feminist questions from the press, her attitude towards her pioneer invasion of the male domain was summed up in her answer after she conducted in Boston. When asked how it felt to be both a woman and a conductor, she replied, "I've been a woman for a little over fifty years, and have gotten over my initial astonishment. As for conducting an orchestra, that's a job. I don't think sex plays much of a part."

ANTONIA BRICO, born June 26, 1902, in Rotterdam, Holland, was brought to California at age five, and graduated from UC Berkeley in 1923 with a degree in music. In 1925, she studied in New York with Polish pianist Sigismund Stojowski (1869–1946), then realized one of her dearest dreams, to visit the land of Beethoven. In Germany, Brico studied with renowned international conductor **Karl Muck** (1859–1940), and was the first American to graduate from the Berlin Hochschule für Musik. She played piano recitals in Europe, but her main interest was conducting. She conducted a special concert with the Berlin Philharmonic on January 10, 1930.

With Hitler and Nazism already a looming threat to foreigners, she returned in 1932 to an America at the height of the Depression. In 1934, with backers such as First Lady **Eleanor Roosevelt**, conductor **Bruno Walter** and Mayor **Fiorello LaGuardia**, Brico organized the New York Women's Symphony Orchestra. In 1938, she became the first American woman to conduct the New York Philharmonic, and went on to guest conduct in Buffalo, Detroit, Los Angeles and San Francisco. A jarring chord was struck when, after two performances with the Metropolitan Opera, she was dismissed because **John Charles Thomas** (1891–1960) refused to sing under a woman—an ironic turnabout since the baritone had sung the title role in Ethel Leginska's opera, *Gale*, under the composer's direction.

In 1937, Brico took up the challenge, which the music world was buzzing about at the time, regarding Spanish pianist **Jose Iturbi**'s statement that "women were incapable of greatness in either music or sports." Brico wanted a competition of women versus men playing in front of blindfolded judges. She was vociferous in her certainty that half those elected would be women and this would break the taboo on mixed orchestras. Iturbi quickly backed down, claiming to have been misquoted.

The two idols of Brico's life were the Finnish composer **Jean Sibelius** (1865–1957), and **Albert Schweitzer** (1875–1965), the humanitarian Renaissance man who combined the careers of theologian, philosopher, physician, organist/organ builder, and authority on Bach. She visited Dr. Schweitzer in his jungle hospital in Lamboréné, French West Equatorial Africa (now Gabon), and took lessons from him on Bach interpretation. After World War II, she went to Finland and met her other idol. In 1946, she conducted an all-Sibelius program with the Helsinki Symphony by special request of the composer.

Brico's career suffered a four decade "hiatus" due, in part, to the influence of the wealthy, powerful patroness of the arts, Minnie (Mrs. Charles S.) Guggenheimer, who, despite her dedication to bringing music to the people and providing opportunities for young artists—she ran summer concerts for over forty years at New York's outdoor Lewisohn Stadium—let it be known that she thought it a "disgrace" for a woman to conduct the New York Philharmonic! Despite such illustrious supporters as maestro **Bruno Walter**, pianist **Arthur Rubinstein** and composer **Jean Sibelius**, concert managers refused to hire Brico because they were afraid that she would antagonize women subscribers.

In 1942, she moved to Denver, directing the five annual concerts of the Denver Businessmen's Orchestra for the next thirty years. In 1969, the aggregation was renamed the Brico Symphony in her honor. She also established a reputation as a teacher of voice, piano and conducting, as well as lecturing and guest conducting abroad.

In 1974, her pupil, folksinger **Judy Collins**, co-produced the documentary film *Antonia: A Portrait of the Woman*, which pleaded the cause for women in music. Its impact brought Brico back to the podium at age seventy-two. In August 1975, Antonia Brico conducted the National Symphony of Washington, DC, and was honored at Kennedy Center. She died August 3, 1989, in Denver.

FRÉDÉRIQUE PETRIDES came into the world in Antwerp, Belgium, September 26, 1903, an auspicious year to be born! The Wright brothers flew their first airplane, a car made the first coast-to-coast trip across America, and **Marie Curie** won the Nobel Prize in Physics.

Frédérique began life in an ambiance of culture. Her mother, Seraphine Sebrechts Mayer, was a well-known pianist and composer and had taught at the Royal Conservatory in Antwerp.

Frederique Petrides

Her father, Joseph Mayer, owned two factories. "Riki" inherited the gift of perfect pitch possessed by three generations of her mother's family. At seven, she started violin, being already proficient at the piano. With her two older brothers, Jan and Gottfried, and her mother, they formed a family string quartet. Fortunately for posterity, Seraphine began experimenting in the infant medium of photography—even in color on glass plates, some poses of which were masterpieces—leaving us a pictorial history of her lovely daughter. Given the best musical education, the child was taken to concerts—during and after World War I—where she personally met contemporary artistic giants like violinist **Fritz Kreisler** (1875–1962), composer-pianist **Camille Saint-Saëns** (1835–1921), cellist **Pablo Casals** (1876–1973), classical guitarist **Andrés Segovia** (1893–1987), pianists **Alfred Cortot** (1877–1962) and **Alexander Brailowsky** (1896–1976), modern dance originator **Isadora Duncan** (1878–1927), and most of the famous actors and actresses of the time including **Sarah Bernhardt** (1844–1923). One of Riki's personal heroes was Austrian conductor **Felix Weingartner** (1863–1942).

This idyllic life ended in 1914 with the advent of World War I. Belgium was invaded by the Germans. Her father was put under house arrest because he was German-born, then given forty-eight hours to leave the country. The family made their way to Holland in a two-wheeled cart. As an adult, Petrides still remembered watching the bombardment of Antwerp fifteen miles across the border. To distract the children, Seraphine put Beethoven's Sixth Symphony on the player piano. (It was years before the conductor could bring herself to program that piece.) After the War the family returned to Belgium—this time to Brussels—and in 1921 moved to Darmstadt, Germany. In 1923, the year after her father's death, Riki, eighteen, tall, slim, blond and lovely, was sent for the summer to her godmother's brother's home in Connecticut. She never left America. She began studying violin in New York, did some teaching and gave recitals. She was invited by maestro **Dimitri Mitropoulos** (1896–1960) to watch rehearsals of the New York Philharmonic, which reinforced her conducting aspirations. When her brother, Jan, came to live in New York, she moved in with him, and enrolled in conducting class at NYU where her skills were found to be far beyond the rest of the male class.

She met handsome, cultured, Greek-born Peter Petrides, whom she married in 1931. Running into the sex barrier—no women conducted major orchestras in the '30s—Riki founded the Orchestrette Classique the same year, with her husband's complete support. She kept the orchestra to thirty players, learned the business side of music, and never needed a manager. With a dedication to excellence and careful programming, the group performed for the next twelve years with great success.

From 1935–40, Petrides published *Women in Music*, a free monthly newsletter containing current happenings in the field. The masthead slogan, "No Crusading. No Pleading," was strictly adhered to. The contents—authentically reproduced in the book *Evening the Score*[56]—provide priceless information on contemporary women conductors, and quote both disparaging and encouraging remarks by contemporary male "authorities" in music.

November 21, 1938, marked the birth of daughter Avra,[57] who inherited the family gift of perfect pitch. During the '30s and '40s, Petrides headed the string department at the exclusive Masters School in Dobbs Ferry on the Hudson River in upper New York State. Here, after the disbanding of the Orchestrette in 1943, she founded and spent seven seasons as director of the Hudson Valley Symphony Orchestra, a community ensemble of students and local musicians.

Back in Manhattan, Petrides organized and conducted a series of outdoor concerts on the East Side (1958–62), and West Side (1962–77). From the time she founded the Orchestrette, she was never without an orchestra. This included the Festival Symphony, which she formed in the '60s using Philharmonic men and forty members of the

56. *Evening the Score*, a great book on Petrides by **Jan Bell Groh**, with annotations on Petrides' Newsletters. (See Bibliography and Musicologists.)
57. In a pleasurable telephone conversation February 20, 2004, with Avra, who has enjoyed an acting and producing career, I learned that she was in the process of acquiring New York's Hamilton Theater which, after renovation, will become, according to her plans, the scene of the rebirth of vaudeville!

American Symphony. Harold Kohon, former concertmaster of the Baltimore Symphony, was her concertmaster for sixteen years.

In May 1979, **Julia Smith**, pianist, composer and charter member of the Orchestrette, as chairman of the National Federation of Music Clubs, presented the maestra their Merit Award in recognition of her contribution to the status of women musicians. (In 1962, a letter was sent to then First Lady Jacqueline Kennedy acquainting her with Petrides' dedication and role model for women in *all* professions.)

Besides her programming of new music, along with little-known classical compositions—in itself a truly unique contribution to the American concert scene—Frédérique Petrides devoted her life to the constant battle against discrimination of her sex. She died in New York, January 12, 1983.

The battle rages on . . . .

Margaret Hillis

MARGARET HILLIS, one of this country's most distinguished conductors for over forty years, was born October 1, 1921, in Kokomo, Indiana. She began piano at five, continuing on woodwinds and double bass. At age eight, she was taken to hear a concert by **John Philip Sousa** (1854–1932) and his band. From that moment she knew she wanted to be a conductor! Her first practical experience was as assistant leader of her high school orchestra. She entered the music program at Indiana University, but suspended her studies during World War II to become a civilian flight instructor for the U.S. Navy. After graduating with a BM in composition in 1947, she studied conducting at Juilliard with **Julius Herford** (1901–81), and **Robert Shaw** (1916–99), later becoming assistant conductor of Shaw's Collegiate Chorale.

It was at Juilliard that one of her teachers, recognizing her talent and knowing the obstacles facing women in the field, told her, "If you want a conducting career, forget symphonic and go into choral conducting." She took his advice and launched a career that would span almost four decades.

In the fall of 1950, Margaret Hillis organized the Tanglewood Alumni Chorus and presented a full series of concerts in New York. The ensemble became known as the American Concert Choir and Orchestra, and performed in a long series of concerts and recordings, constituting a brilliant chapter in the history of American choral singing. The U.S. Department of State invited the group to represent America at the Brussels World's Fair in 1958.

As assistant conductor of the City Center Opera of New York in the spring and fall of 1957, Hillis conducted **Beverly Sills** at the beginning of *her* illustrious career. Famed baritone **Sherrill Milnes** sang in Hillis' chorus for four years. In 1959, she launched his career by introducing him to opera producer **Boris Goldovsky** (1908–2001), who featured him as Don Giovanni in his touring opera company. She also recommended Milnes to a New York manager who snapped up this talent.

In 1957, at the request of **Fritz Reiner** (1888–1963), she founded the Chicago Symphony Chorus, which she directed until her retirement in 1994 when she was named conductor laureate. Under Hillis, the Chorus appeared with the orchestra nearly 600 times, recorded forty-five works, won nine Grammy awards, plus accompanying the CSO on domestic—including performances at Kennedy Center and Carnegie Hall—and foreign tours, with a 1989 European debut in London and Salzburg. It is considered America's finest choral ensemble.

Hillis was also founder and music director of the American Choral Foundation. For many years she was music director of the Elgin Symphony and Kenosha Civic Orchestra—both in Illinois—and director of choral activities for the San Francisco Symphony during the 1981–83 season. She was visiting professor of conducting at her alma mater, Indiana University, and was associated with Northwestern University as professor of conducting and director of choral organizations. She taught at Juilliard and Union Theological Seminary, served as choral conductor of the American Opera Society, choral director of the New York City Opera, and conductor and choral director of the Santa Fe Opera and the Cleveland Orchestra Chorus. She directed many workshops, including the Chorus America Conductors Workshop (Lake Saranac, New York), Master Schola Music Conference (Cape Cod, Massachusetts), Westminster Choir College and the Interlochen (Michigan) Music Festival.

She made her Chicago Symphony subscription-concert debut in 1972—substituting for **Rafael Kubelik**—directing the Orchestra and Chorus in performances of Handel's *Jeptha*. In 1977, she led the CSO and chorus in Mahler's Eighth Symphony at Carnegie Hall, replacing an ailing **Georg Solti**. The audience groaned at the announcement of Solti's cancellation, but cheered when Hillis was named as his replacement. The performance received a standing ovation and critical raves.

A sought-after guest conductor, Hillis led performances of many American orchestras and choruses. Besides being frequently called on to perform at civic functions in the Chicago area, in the spring of 1979 Miss Hillis and a select group of chorus members entertained President Carter, Vice President Mondale and distinguished dignitaries at the White House. Thousands enjoyed her talents at the annual "Do-It-Yourself *Messiah*" in Orchestra Hall, which she directed beginning 1976.

Her honors include the Leadership for Freedom Award from the Women's Scholarship Association of Roosevelt University, Alumni Achievement Award of Kappa Kappa Gamma (both 1978), three awards from the national music sorority Sigma Alpha Iota, the 1965 "Who's Who" Award for Women, and numerous honorary doctor of music degrees including Temple, Indiana and Notre Dame Universities. She was honored by the YWCA in Chicago for outstanding achievement in the arts, and received both the Steinway and the Friends of Literature awards for her contributions to the cultural life of the city. In 1978, she was named "Woman of the Year in Classical Music" by the *Ladies Home Journal*, and in 1981 was given a citation from the National Federation of Music Clubs for her outstanding service to music. She received the Governors' Award from the Chicago Chapter of the National Academy of Recording Arts and Sciences (NARAS). Appointed by President Reagan, she served for six years as a member of the National Council on the Arts.

In February 1978, Hillis earned her first Grammy Award when the RCA Red Seal release of Verdi's *Requiem*, conducted by Sir Georg Solti, was named Best Choral Performance (other than opera) by NARAS. She went on to win eight more Grammys: Beethoven's *Missa Solemnis*; Berlioz' *Damnation of Faust*[58]—also winner of the 1982 Grand Prix du Disque; Brahms' *A German Requiem* (James Levine/RCA); Haydn's *The Creation*;[59] Bach's *B-Minor Mass*;[60] Orff's *Carmina Burana* (Levine/Deutsche Grammophon) and Bartók's *Cantata Profana* (Boulez/DG). NARAS also awarded her a Certificate for Schoenberg's *Moses und Aron*.[61] In addition, she recorded for CBS Masterworks, Epic, Vox and Decca, and appeared as conductor of choral and orchestral programs on all three major television networks. In 1996, she conducted the premiere recording of Jerre Tanner's opera/oratorio *The Naupaka Floret*.

In my 1998 telephone interview with Miss Hillis, when asked what event stood out in her many wonderful memories, she replied, "the time in the fall of 1977, when I substituted on short notice for Sir George Solti and conducted the Chicago Symphony Orchestra and Chorus, soloists, and other choral forces in Mahler's Eighth in Carnegie Hall." (The critics called it "stunning!")

A heavy smoker, Miss Hillis passed away February 4, 1998, of lung cancer, after battling the disease for several years. Her collection of scores, instrumental parts bearing her personal markings, books, Grammys, photographs, papers and correspondence are housed in the Samuel and Marie-Louise Rosenthal Archives of the Chicago Symphony.

JUDITH SOMOGI, born May 13, 1937 in New York, studied violin, piano and organ at Juilliard. She became assistant to **Thomas Schippers** at the Spoleto Festival, and to **Leopold Stokowski** at the American Symphony Orchestra in New York. Joining the New York City Opera in 1966, she made her conducting debut there with *The Mikado* in 1974. Her European debut with Mozart's *The Abduction from the Seraglio* at the Saarbrucken (Germany) Opera was in 1979. She also appeared with the Louisville, Tulsa, San Francisco, San Diego, San Antonio and Pittsburgh opera companies and conducted the Los Angeles Philharmonic, Cincinnati, Milwaukee, Syracuse and other symphony orchestras.

58–61. All with Solti on London Records. (Sir Georg Solti was conductor of the CSO 1969–1992. He died on vacation in Antibes, France, September 5, 1997.)

In 1984, Somogi became the first woman to conduct at a major Italian opera house when she directed Gluck's *Orfeo ed Euridice* at Teatro La Fenice in Venice. After conducting *Madama Butterfly* at Frankfurt Opera in 1981, she was appointed their first woman principal conductor (1982–87). Her promising career was tragically cut short by her death from cancer on March 23, 1988, in New York.

Iona Brown

IONA BROWN was one of the few conductors who followed the original tradition of directing an orchestra from her chair as first violinist. Her instrument was the Booth Stradivari, dating from 1716. Born January 7, 1941, in Salisbury, England, into a highly musical family, her father was a pianist and organist and her mother a violinist in the Bournemouth Symphony, where Iona's sister, Sally, played viola from 1959–2004. Her brother Timothy is principal horn with the BBC Symphony Orchestra, and brother Ian is a sought after pianist and chamber musician.

Iona studied in Rome, Brussels and Vienna, and in Paris with **Henryk Szeryng** (1918–88). She played in the Philharmonia Orchestra of London (1963–66) and had a solo career before she turned to conducting. After a ten year association with the Academy of St. Martin-in-the-Fields, under Sir Neville Marriner, she was appointed its artistic director in 1974, inaugurating an acclaimed series of recordings, and touring as conductor/soloist. In 1981, she also became artistic and music director of the Norwegian Chamber Orchestra, making successful CDs and touring with them throughout Europe, Scandinavia and the UK, which included a spectacular 1991 Sir Henry Wood Promenade Concerts debut at the Royal Albert Hall, London. She had appeared at the Proms since 1964. From 1985–89, she guest conducted the City of Birmingham Symphony. She was music director of the Los Angeles Chamber Orchestra (1987–92). Under her direction they achieved tremendous success, including their Hollywood Bowl debut. Other concert venues in America included Kennedy Center, Carnegie Hall (1995) and guesting stints with the St. Louis, San Diego and National Symphonies and the St. Paul Chamber Orchestra. Worldwide, she directed chamber orchestras in Salzburg, Leipzig, Stuttgart, Stockholm and Amsterdam, among other venues.

Her numerous recordings with the Academy of St. Martin-in-the-Fields, as the violin soloist, include Vaughan Williams' *The Lark Ascending*, Beethoven's *Violin Concerto*, Vivaldi's *Four Seasons*, Handel's *Concerto Grosso* Op. 6, and the complete Mozart *Violin Concerti*. She also recorded Bartok's *Second Violin Concerto* with **Sir Simon Rattle** and the Philharmonia, and David Blake's *Violin Concerto*, written for and dedicated to her.

In the Queen's 1986 New Year's Honors List, Iona Brown was awarded the Order of the British Empire (OBE) for her services to music. She was also honored by King Harald, with an award of Knight of First Class Order of Merit, in recognition of her contribution to Norway's musical life. She was named "Instrumentalist of 1993" by the Royal Philharmonic Society.

After a valiant three-year battle with cancer, she passed away June 5, 2004, survived by her devoted husband, Bjørn Arnils.

RUTH Thall QUINN, a native of Columbus, Ohio, born May 6, 1920, was a conductor of short duration, but during an important time in Columbus' musical history. Her cousin, a pianist, worked at the local radio station, also accompanying young contestants on the station's talent show. Ruth says that her first attempt at singing was so bad, her cousin gave her her father's violin which she began studying at ten. Playing throughout high school, because she sat first chair, Ruth was often asked to conduct the school orchestra.

During the late 1930s, the Columbus Orchestra ceased to exist, and the only music was the Marion Civic Orchestra, conducted by Abram Ruvinsky, with whom Ruth studied. In 1939, to fill the music void, Ruth founded the Columbus Miniature Symphony, with players from her high school and the community. These were Depression years when people were fortunate just to have instruments. The Symphony collected dues, parents helped out, and local businesses contributed, which paid for renting performance venues and a piano if they had a soloist. Ruvinsky donated the music, but if there was a concerto soloist, music had to be rented from New York.

Ruth conducted her symphony from 1939 to 1942, marrying Leonard Quinn in 1941. George Hage, in a 1941 newspaper article said: "If Columbus can't have an adult orchestra . . . they may be on the way to having another Meremblum[62] children's orchestra."

April 27, 1941 was the debut concert by the Columbus Philharmonic, conducted by Ruvinsky. Its origin was in August 1940, when Philip Rabin, activities director at the Schonthal Community Center, Abram Ruvinsky, and Norman Nadel, trombonist and newspaper columnist, met in Ruth's home to discuss if an orchestra could succeed in Columbus. With Ruth's young people from her orchestra, and Ruvinsky's ability to recruit players, this became a reality. But the success of the Philharmonic was the end of the Miniature Symphony, since most of the players moved up. Quinn was part of the board of directors, and played in the first violin section. After the first season, the board hired Izler Solomon (1910–87), conductor of the Illinois Symphony and the Chicago Womens Symphony. He led the Columbus Philharmonic until 1949, moving to the Indianapolis Symphony (1956–75.)

Ruth stayed in the violin section until 1946. That year her son David was born, August 11, followed by Susan, November 2, 1948, and Gary, September 24, 1950. Motherhood brought an end to her music career, but as of 2006, at age eighty-six, she was still an active supporter of the Columbus Philharmonic.

SARAH CALDWELL was hailed as "opera's first lady" by *Newsweek*, "the best opera director in the U.S." by *Time* and "a national treasure" by *The New Yorker*. Equally esteemed as a symphonic conductor, she has led many major orchestras, including the Boston, Chicago, Montreal and National Symphonies, Cleveland and Philadelphia Orchestras, and the New York Philharmonic.

Born March 6, 1924, in Maryville, Missouri, her musical studies began with the violin and eventually took her to the New England Conservatory in Boston, where she fell in love with opera. Before the age of twenty she staged a performance of Vaughan Williams' *Riders to the Sea* at Tanglewood, after which **Serge Koussevitzky** invited her to join the faculty of the Tanglewood Opera. She was also an assistant to **Boris Goldovsky** (1908–2001) at the NEC, and shortly thereafter became head of the opera department at Boston University.

In 1957, with the help of a small group of Bostonians, she founded the Boston Opera Group, which became The Opera Company of Boston, specializing in American music, plus world premieres such as Schoenberg's *Moses and Aron*, Prokofiev's *War and Peace*, Berlioz' *The Trojans* (presented uncut), Nono's *Intolleranza*, Rameau's *Hippolyte et Aricie*, Tippett's *The Ice Break*, Sessions' *Montezuma*, Zimmermann's *Die Soldaten* and Davies' *Taverner*, besides the standard repertoire. In seventy-five operas, Caldwell was the impresaria, conductor for most, and stage director for all. Her innovative stagings are legendary, such as the witch flying over the audience in her production of *Hansel and Gretel*.

In 1960, Caldwell's production of Offenbach's uncompleted opera, *Voyage to the Moon*, was presented at the White House to an audience which included President John F. Kennedy, aviation pioneer Charles Lindbergh, and several American astronauts.

During the 1975–76 season, she debuted with the New York Philharmonic and became the first woman to conduct at the Metropolitan Opera, leading a production of *La traviata*. Her picture was on the cover of *TIME* (November 10, 1975), hailed as "Music's Wonder Woman." In February 1976, she conducted the Pittsburgh Symphony in the world premiere of John La Montaine's *Be Glad Then America*, which she also staged. In the fall of 1976, she staged and conducted *The Barber of Seville* at New York City Opera. During the 1977 season, she returned to the Met to conduct Donizetti's *L'elisir d'amore*. The following year she made her first recording, Donizetti's *Don Pasquale*, with a cast including luminaries **Beverly Sills**, Donald Gramm, Alan Titus and Alfredo Kraus.

---

62. Russian born violinist Peter Meremblum (1890–1966), who studied with Leopold Auer, was the founder/conductor of the California Junior Symphony in Los Angeles, 1936–66. Now called the Peter Meremblum Youth Orchestras, sponsored by the California Junior Symphony Association, they continue training young musicians for symphonic careers.

For two seasons Caldwell served as music director of the Wolf Trap Festival. In the summer of 1981, she conducted *La traviata* with China's Central Opera Theater in Beijing. During the 1980s, she developed a new opera company in the Philippines, which produced Mozart's *The Magic Flute*. In 1983, she became artistic director of the New Opera Company of Israel. In 1987, she was honored by the America-Israel Opera Foundation for her contributions to the development of a richer operatic life in that country. Also during the 1980s, she acquired the Keith Memorial Theater for the OCB. With a home, the company did not have to wander from venue to venue, however the legal, real-estate, property maintenance and tax issues were a financial drain. She sacrificed most of her personal property and assets to keep the theater alive. The last production was in 1990.

In 1988, she and Soviet composer **Rodion Shchedrin** (*b* 1932) initiated *Making Music Together*, a unique collaboration between the two countries. The first phase took place in Boston for three weeks under her direction, and featured Russian contemporary music and dance productions. In January 1991, the second phase began in Moscow and continued during the first six months of the year. Through the course of the festival, Caldwell conducted several Soviet orchestras in programs of American works, and staged and conducted Robert Di Domenica's opera, *The Balcony*, at the Bolshoi Theatre.

After appearing on the podia of the New York Philharmonic, Philadelphia Orchestra, Montreal Symphony, Washington, DC's National Symphony, Chicago's Grant Park Festival, Cape Town (South Africa) Symphony, and other venues, in October 1993 Caldwell became principal guest conductor of the Sverdlovsk Philharmonic Orchestra in Ekaterinburg,[63] where she served until 2001. This appointment followed her success with that orchestra in the first Russian presentation of Debussy's *Pelléas et Mélisande* in concert form.

In 1996, she received the National Medal of Arts from the NEA. In 1999, she sold her Boston home and joined the faculty at the University of Arkansas, Fayeteville, where she expanded the opera theater program and, with the support of the University, created the World Center for Ancient Asian and Mid-Eastern Music Preservation to bring to life music unheard by human ears for over 1,000 years, by transcribing, performing and preserving it for future generations. Her tenure there was marred by several long periods of illness. But in 2003, at seventy-nine and in improved health, she moved to Maine to be near friends and former colleagues.

In Boston, her company was succeeded by Boston Lyric Opera and the smaller Boston Academy of Music—now reorganized as Opera Boston. Through careful administration they sometimes reach the quality of her Caldwell's productions, but without the risk-taking she was famous for, they fall short of her international level.

Caldwell died of a heart attack at eighty-two, March 23, 2006, in Portland, Maine.

---

63. Site of the assassination of the Russian Royal Romanov family by the Bolsheviks in 1917.

On the Podia in the 21st Century

Marin Alsop, Colorado Orchestra (1993–03), Bournemouth (2002–) Baltimore (2006–)
Gillian Anderson, Silent Film Music Researcher/Arranger: Library of Congress
Nvart Andreassian, Armenian National Opera
Dalia Atlas, Technion Symphony Orchestra, Israel, Global Guest
Gisèle Ben-Dor, Santa Barbara (1994–2005), Annapolis, Boston Pro-Arte, Israel Chamber
Elke Mascha Blankenburg, Clara Schumann Orchestra, Germany
Victoria Bond, Roanoke Symphony Orchestra, Virginia
Carolyn Waters Broe, Four Seasons Orchestra of Scottsdale, Arizona
Lucinda Carver, Music Director/Conductor Los Angeles Mozart Orchestra
Mary Chun, International Guest Conductor
Catherine Comet, Grand Rapids Symphony (1987–97), Global Guest
Fiora Contino, Bowling Green, Indiana Symphony, Opera Illinois
Carol I. Crawford, Tulsa Opera
Joan Dornemann, Met Opera Coach, Rehearsal Conductor
Agnieszka Duczmal, Amadeus Orchestra, Poland
Sian Edwards, English National Opera (to November 1995)
JoAnn Falletta, Long Beach (1989–2000), Virginia Symphony, Buffalo Philharmonic, Honolulu
Deborah Freedman, St. Joseph (Missouri) Symphony
Jane Glover, English National Opera
Noreen Green, LA Jewish Symphony, Congregation Valley Beth Shalom,
Agnes Grossmann, Europe/Canada Guest Conductor, Vienna Choir Boys
Susan Haig, Windsor (Ontario) Symphony
Emmanuelle Haïm, Concert d'Astrée, France
Patricia Handy, Associate Conductor, Greenwich (Connecticut) Symphony
Apo Hsu, Former Women's Philharmonic
Monica Huggett, Portland Baroque Orchestra
Janna Hymes-Bianchi, Columbus Women's Orchestra
Sarah Ioannides, Assistant Conductor Cincinnati Symphony
Sara Jobin, San Francisco Opera
Karen Keltner, San Diego Opera
Tania León, Brooklyn Philharmonic Community Concert Series
J. Karla Lemon, Formerly Stanford University Symphony
Susanna Mälkki, Ensemble intercontemporain
Anne Manson, Kansas City (Missouri) Symphony (1998–2003)
Odaline De La Martinez, Lontano (London) Women's Orchestra
Amy Mills, National Women's Symphony, La Crosse Symphony, Wisconsin
Chean See Ooi, Malaysian Philharmonic
Eve Queler, Opera Orchestra of New York

Andrea Quinn, London Philharmonic, Youth Orchestra London, NYC Ballets, Norrland Symphony, Sweden

Teresa Rodríguez, Guest, Mexican Orchestras

Kay George Roberts, University of Massachusetts Orchestra

Madeline Schatz, Fairbanks Symphony, Hawaii (2001–)

Elizabeth Schulze, Baltimore, former Co-Associate National Symphony

Frances Steiner, Carson-Dominguez Hills Symphony, California

Anu Tali, Nordic Symphony, Estonia

Kate Tamarkin, Catholic University, formerly Monterey, East Texas

Beverly Taylor, Boston's Back Bay Chorale

Carmen Helena Téllez, U.S./Latin America Guest

Maria Tunicka, Space Coast Philharmonic (Florida)

Barbara Day Turner, San José Chamber Orchestra (to 2000)

Nan Washburn, West Hollywood Orchestra

Lara Webber, Assistant, Baltimore Symphony

Diane M. Wittry, Allentown (Pennsylvania), Norwalk (Connecticut)

Rachael Worby, Wheeling (West Virginia, 1986–2003), Pasadena Pops, California

Barbara Yahr, former Resident Staff Director: Pittsburgh Symphony

Simone Young, Paris Opera, Opera Australia, Global Guest Conductor

Zheng Xiaoying, Xiamen Philharmonic (China)

Xian Zhang, Associate Conductor, New York Philharmonic

WORTHY OF MENTION

Avlana Eisenberg, The Future?

Suzanne Acton, Michigan Opera Theater Chorus, Rackham Sym. Choir

Sebrina Maria Alfonso, Frederick (Maryland) Symphony

Nyela Basney, New York Ensembles

Marietta Cheng, Colgate University Chorus & Chamber Singers

Janet Canetty-Clarke, Ditchling Choral Society of Sussex (England)

Mary Culbert, Merion Concert Band, Pennsylvania

Margery Deutsch, University of Wisconsin Orchestras, Milwaukee Youth Symphony

Yvette Devereaux, Progressive Symphony (Los Angeles)

Morna Edmundson, World of Children's Choirs, Elektra Women's Choir, Canada

Susan Farrow, English National Ballet

Claire Gibault, international guest conductor

Mary Woodmansee Green, Phila Fest, Kennett Symphony, Hilton Head, Mary Green Singers

Sabina Haenebalcke, Flanders Symphony - Antwerp Music Festival, Belgium

Anne Harrigan, Baltimore Chamber Orchestra, Lafayette Symphony

Laura Hemenway, Antelope Valley Symphony, California

Sarah Hatsuko Hicks, associate conductor, Richmond Symphony

Monica Buckland Hofstetter, Guest - Bohuslav Martinu Philharmonia (Czech Republic)

Laura Jackson, assistant conductor, Atlanta Symphony

Doris Lang Kosloff, Connecticut Opera Association

Sharon Lavery, resident conductor, USC orchestras

Diane Loomer, Chor Leoni, Elektra Women's Choir, Canada

Ramona Luengen, Phoenix Chamber Choir, Vocal Collegium Musicum

Marsha Mabrey, Seattle Philharmonic

Marie-Louise Oschatz, Vienna Chamber Ensemble (1987–92)

Laura Rexroth, Bands & Wind Ensembles: College of William and Mary

Cornelia von Kerssenbrock, Guest - with Vancouver Chamber Choir

Dr. Antonia Joy Wilson, Mostly Mahler Orchestra & Chorus, Global Guest

Keri-Lynn Wilson, former Assistant, Dallas; International Guest Conductor

Angela Yeung, University of San Diego Orchestra, Chamber Music Ensemble

Marin Alsop

MARIN ALSOP is one of the major maestra of the 21st century, at one time directing three large orchestras on three continents with an incredible schedule. Her major post has been music director of the Colorado Orchestra (1993–2003).

Born October 16, 1956, in New York City, her father was concertmaster and her mother a cellist in the New York City Ballet Orchestra. At age seven, seeing **Leonard Bernstein** on the podium was her defining moment. She later became his protégée. After attending Yale, she received her MM from Juilliard.

Also an avid jazz violinist, in 1981 Marin founded an all-female fourteen piece swing band named "String Fever," which released the successful CD *Fever Pitch*. In 1984, she formed her own New York-based sixty piece chamber orchestra, Concordia, which combined classical repertoire with American jazz and 20th century works. She recorded *Blue Monday*, a CD (Angel) of music by George Gershwin, with them. 1988–89, as a conducting fellow at Tanglewood, she studied with **Leonard Bernstein** (1918–90), and **Seiji Ozawa**, conductor of the Boston Symphony from 1973–2002.

Alsop holds a singular record of "firsts." She was the first woman to be awarded the Koussevitzky Conducting Prize and win the Leopold Stokowski Conducting Competition (1989), sponsored by the American Symphony Orchestra. In 1990, she became the first woman to conduct the Boston Pops in its 107-year existence, and was immediately re-engaged. In 1991, she was the first woman to conduct subscription concerts with the Los Angeles Philharmonic. She made her Canadian debut, May 1993, with the Vancouver Symphony, and her European debuts the same year in Vienna, Rimini (Italy), and at the Schleswig-Holstein Festival (Germany), conducting the music of her mentor, Leonard Bernstein. Her UK debut came in February 1996 with the Royal Scottish National Orchestra.

In February 1995, she was appointed creative conductor chair with the St. Louis Symphony, a newly designated position where she continued to build on the orchestra's established artistic profile as well as experiment with non-traditional formats. She left St. Louis when the Colorado Symphony, of which she had been principal conductor since 1993, elevated her position to music director in recognition of her achievements and successes with the orchestra. Under her direction, they won two ASCAP awards for their programming (1996–97, 1999–2000).

Alsop has been music director of the Cabrillo Contemporary Music Festival in Santa Cruz, California, since 1992. In 2006, CMF was in its forty-third year. At the end of the 1995–96 season, she relinquished her long term directorships of the Long Island (NY) Philharmonic (since 1990), Eugene (Oregon) Symphony (since 1989), where she holds the title of conductor laureate, and Oregon's Festival of American Music, which she founded in 1992, to devote more time to her new positions. She has guest conducted major orchestras in the U.S. and Canada, including the National (DC), Atlanta, Cincinnati, Houston, Milwaukee, Florida and St. Louis Symphonies, New York, Los Angeles, Florida and Buffalo Philharmonics, and the Minnesota, Louisville and Philadelphia Orchestras. In 2000, she conducted her first production of *La traviata*. 2003 marked her debut with ENO directing *Rigoletto*.

Principal guest conductor of the City of London Sinfonia, and of the Royal Scottish National Orchestra since 1999, she had great success there with the first installments of her complete Barber orchestral cycle on Naxos, the first disc of which was nominated for Gramophone and Classical Brit Awards. Other recordings include works by Christopher Rouse with Concordia (Koch) and with the Colorado Symphony (RCA Red Seal), *Fanfares for the*

Uncommon Woman by **Joan Tower** (Koch), the first recording of Gershwin's early opera *Blue Monday* with Concordia, and the cover disc—Saint-Saëns' Organ Symphony and Second Piano Concerto with the BBC Philharmonic—of the BBC Music Magazine. Her schedules are, to put it in the vernacular, "unreal," zig-zagging across the globe from America to Europe to Australia and back again. Down under, she conducted in Sydney, Brisbane, Perth and Adelaide. Up over, along with Colorado, she directed in Minnesota, St. Louis, Atlanta, Toronto, and Montreal. Across the Atlantic, besides her London orchestras, she led the Hallé (Manchester), City of Birmingham and Liverpool orchestras. On the Continent, the Bavarian Radio Symphony had her share a concert with Lorin Maazel, while other German appearances included the Hamburg and German Chamber Philharmonics, Berlin, Frankfurt and Stuttgart Radio Symphonies, and Berlin Comic Opera. She has guested with the Helsinki Philharmonic, Swedish Radio Symphony, Netherlands Radio Chamber (filmed for Dutch television), Amsterdam Concertgebouw, Vienna Musikverein, Orchestre National du Capitol de Toulouse, Orchestre National de Lyon and Orchestre de Paris—all in addition to her annual summer stint at the Cabrillo Festival.

After being appointed in 2001, in the 2002–03 season Alsop became principal conductor for the Bournemouth (England) Symphony, with a contract for an initial four years, where she will perform up to twelve weeks per season, including national and international tours and recordings. Summer of 2004 found her at the Hollywood Bowl.

Celebrating a decade with the Colorado Orchestra, Alsop remained there as music conductor laureate until 2005. The same year she signed a three-year, fourteen weeks per season, contract to become the first woman to conduct a major American orchestra, the Baltimore Symphony, beginning 2007–08, with six weeks during 2006–07 as music director-designate. This makes her the twelfth music director in the orchestra's ninety-year history. Recording projects and a European tour, 2008–09, are also on the calendar.

GILLIAN ANDERSON occupies a unique place in the world of music. A conductor and musicologist, she was music librarian at the Library of Congress (1978–95), and is a board member of the Film Music Society and the Film Music Museum. Specializing in American and film music, she undertakes the highly delicate and painstaking task of restoration and reconstruction to give premiere performances of original orchestral scores written to accompany over thirty-four great silent films. She is also an international lecturer on her subject.

Born November 28, 1943, in Brookline, Massachusetts, she has a BA in Biology (Bryn Mawr, 1965), MM (U of Illinois, 1969), and MLS (U of Maryland, 1989). She studied choral conducting at Harvard (1963), and German at the University of Vienna (1965–66). In 1969, she married physicist Gordon Wood Anderson.

Anderson has conducted orchestras in synchronization with the projection of silents at film festivals, concert halls and universities all over the world. Her huge roster includes *La Bohème* (Vidor, 1926), shown at the Library of Congress, March 1998, *Carmen* (DeMille, 1915), *The Circus* (Chaplin, 1928), *The Covered Wagon* (Cruze, 1923), *Old Ironsides* (Cruze, 1926), *Orphans of the Storm* (Griffith, 1921), *Parsifal* (Edison, 1904), *Way Down East* (Griffith, 1920), *The Thief of Baghdad* (Fairbanks, 1924) with the Brabants Orkest (Holland), and *Wings* (Wellman, 1927) done with the Basque Country Orchestra at the San Sebastian (Spain) Film Festival. 1996 saw a full reorchestration of *Ben-Hur* (Niblo, 1926) at Malmö, Sweden, and a restoration of *Birth of a Nation* (Griffiths, 1915) in Portugal. *The White Sister* (Fleming, 1933) was shown at the National Gallery of Art, July 1997, and Cecil B. DeMille's *The Ten Commandments* (1923) at Hollywood's restored Egyptian Theater (December 1998).

Her numerous articles, manuals, books and performing editions include *Freedom's Voice in Poetry and Song*, chosen as the best reference book of 1978 by *Choice* Magazine. "Putting the Experience of the World at the Nation's Command; Music at the Library of Congress 1800–1917" was awarded the Music Library Association's Richard Hill Award for best article in 1989. *Film Music: Bibliography I* was published by the Society for Film Preservation in 1996. CDs include *Nosferatu* (BMG Classics) with the Brandenburg Philharmonic and Cecil B. De Mille's *Carmen* (1915) recorded with the London Philharmonic, January 1996.

In June 2001, Anderson was one of the moderators at a Music/Image in Film and Multi-Media Conference at NYU, analyzing the relationship between music and images in a variety of audiovisual products with the participation of academics and the composers, artists, filmmakers, animators, psychologists, computer specialists and industry representatives who present these products to the public.

The meticulous, far flung research involved—sometimes with nothing more to go on than a torn scrap of paper—in the restoration of these masterpieces is a continuing challenge for this dynamic musical Sherlock Holmes. Anderson's performances have been rightfully described as "brilliant," "extraordinary," and "an enormously involving experience."

(I experienced this magic at a performance of the 1926 film, *The Black Pirate*, starring Douglas Fairbanks, with Anderson conducting the San Diego Symphony, February 25, 2006.)

NVART ANDREASSIAN, born November 4, 1952 in Istanbul, Turkey, studied at the Moscow Conservatory, winning a first prize for conducting chorus and orchestra (1971). Nvart left the USSR in 1976 for conducting courses at the École Normale de Musique in Paris, where she was a winner in the International Competition of Young Conductors at Besançon. From 1971–72, she was assistant conductor of the Philharmonic Orchestra of Armenia. Since 1985, she has been artistic director of the Polychromie Association and permanent leader of the Polychromie Ensemble, specializing in contemporary music. In 1993, she was appointed musical director of the Armenian National Opera. She regularly guest conducts other European orchestras, and has broadcast and recorded on radio and television in Belgium, Holland, France, Germany, Italy, Romania and Moscow. In 1979, she was made laureate of the Concours de Besançon. In 1982, she won a Yehudi Menuhin Foundation award.

2004–2005 featured a China tour, performances with Armenian National Opera and the Armenian New Music Ensemble. 2005–06 brought a South American tour.

In her never-ending search for new talent, Andreassian constantly renews her repertoire with works by composers of all nationalities. She is the driving force behind many new pieces created at the Polychromie Festival, and for persuading many top performers and composers to take part in it. Her quest is to awaken new audiences to contemporary music.

Dalia Atlas

DALIA ATLAS, a graduate of the Rubin Academy of Music in Jerusalem, was born November 11, 1933, in Haifa. She always knew she was destined to become a conductor. Beginning her education in Israel in piano, composition, voice development, and teaching, with a scholarship from the American/Israeli Cultural Foundation she went on to study conducting with world-famous maestros: **Franco Ferrara** (1911–85), **Sergio Celibidache** (1912–96), **Hans Swarovsky** (1899–1975) and **Pierre Boulez** (*b* 1925), in Vienna, Italy, Switzerland and America.

A pioneer of women conductors, Atlas forged a career and reputation being the first woman to win numerous international conducting competitions, prizes and medals: In the U.S., the Dimitri Mitropoulos Competition, Leopold Stokowski Prize and the Philadelphia Orchestra's Eugene Ormandy Award; Internationally, the Villa-Lobos International Competition for Conductors (Brazil); Guido Cantelli Award, and "Personality of the Year" by Centro de Studi e Ricerche delle Nazioni (Italy); plus the Royal Liverpool Philharmonic Award (England).

Atlas is a professor of music at the Technion in Haifa, and founder, music director and principal conductor of several musical organizations in Israel: the Technion Symphony Orchestra and Choir, Pro-Musica Orchestra and the Atlas Camerata. Her recordings receive outstanding reviews. A video concert made by Israeli National TV is in worldwide distribution.

With a repertoire of some 700 scores, Dalia Atlas, who has conducted over sixty-nine major orchestras in twenty-eight countries throughout the world, was considered by the late **Lord Yehudi Menuhin** to be "one of the most effective and impressive conductors . . . " *Musical Opinion* named her "First Lady of the Baton." Her research on the life and works of the great Jewish composer Ernest Bloch (1880–1959) resulted in two CDs (London Philharmic, 1996), (Atlas Camerata, 1997) of his rare works. In 2000, she organized a symposium to commemorate the 120th anniversary of his birth. She also recorded Vaughan Williams' *The Lark Ascending* with violinist **Zina Schiff** and the Israel Philharmonic.

Gisele Ben-Dor

GISÈLE BEN-DOR ranks with JoAnn Falletta as one of America's top maestras. Born in Montevideo, Uruguay, to Polish parents, she began piano at four and has conducted since she was twelve, becoming music director of her school at fourteen. The family moved to Israel, where she studied conducting and piano at the Rubin Academy, Tel Aviv. She came to the U.S. in 1980, and earned a master's in conducting from Yale. Her sensational debut was in 1982, leading the Israel Philharmonic in Stravinsky's *The Rite of Spring*, taped by the BBC, London, and broadcast throughout Europe. Her American career began in 1984, when she was selected as a conducting fellow at the Los Angeles Philharmonic Institute and directed several performances at the Hollywood Bowl. A year later she became a conducting fellow at Tanglewood, where she and **Leonard Bernstein** shared a special concert celebrating Aaron Copland's eighty-fifth birthday. She was named a Leonard Bernstein Fellow and invited to conduct the Bavarian Radio Orchestra for the inauguration of the Schleswig-Holstein Festival.

In 1986, Ben-Dor won the Bartók Prize of the Hungarian Television International Conductors Competition, which led to directing at the Bartók Festival and other orchestras in Eastern Europe. From 1989–91, she was resident conductor of the Houston Symphony, which she led at the Kennedy Center, for the first President Bush inauguration. Chosen as one of the prominent "Young Artists of 1990" by *Musical America*, she made her Carnegie Hall debut, February 1991, during their 100th anniversary celebration. Also in 1991, she was appointed music director of the Annapolis Symphony and the Boston Pro-Arte Chamber Orchestra—retaining these posts until 1996 and 2000, respectively—plus the title conductor emerita in Boston. In September 1994, she was appointed music director of the Santa Barbara Symphony by unanimous request of audiences, orchestra members and the board of directors. She performed to sold-out houses in the historic Arlington Theater. At the same time she continued an unbelievable schedule of guest directing in North and South America, Switzerland, Italy, Israel, Finland, Great Britain, Denmark, Holland, France, Spain, and Australia, with orchestras such as the London Symphony, English Chamber, St. Paul Chamber, Orchestre de la Suisse Romande, Spanish Radio and Television, Ulster Orchestra, Helsinki and Israel Philharmonics, Jerusalem Symphony, Los Angeles Philharmonic, Israeli Opera, Boston Pops, and New World Symphony.

A Dazzling Debut of Supreme Irony—and a Well-Deserved Encore!

Of particular mention is the evening of December 7, 1993 when, with less than a day's notice, Ben-Dor made an impressive New York Philharmonic debut substituting for the indisposed **Kurt Masur**. Without rehearsal, she conducted a brilliant program featuring **Anne-Sophie Mutter** playing Brahms' Violin Concerto. The artists received a standing ovation. BUT by an ironic twist of fate, as this was not the first performance of the program, *not a single reviewer was present!* In July 1995, she scored a rousing success conducting the NYP in outdoor concerts in Central Park with audiences numbering 100,000. She has also led members of the orchestra in a three-hour concert marathon of contemporary British music. But it was in March 1999 that Ben-Dor returned to the NY Philharmonic podium once again in dramatic fashion, conducting without rehearsal or scores, as she substituted for Daniele Gatti in a program of Mahler and Beethoven. *This* time, however, there *were* critics in the house and the *New York Times* wrote "If Ms. Ben-Dor had merely survived in a work as complex as the Mahler under the circumstances, she would have done well; she did more, making the interpretation . . . her own."

Her CDs are stacking up: Béla Bartók with the Sofia Soloists (Centaur); American composer Ezra Syms with the Boston ProArte Chamber Orchestra (CRI); a landmark recording of Argentinian **Alberto Ginastera's** (1916–83) *Variaciones Concertantes* with the London Symphony, and his *Glosses on Themes of Pablo Casals* with the Israel Chamber Orchestra (Koch). 1996 brought *American Journeys*, music of John Adams and David Ott with the London Symphony. In April 1999, BMG/Conifer released a world premiere recording of Ginastera's complete Ballets *Estancia* (1952) and *Panambí* (1935) with the London Symphony. The final work of Mexican composer

Silvestre Revueltas (1899–1940), the ballet *La Coronela* (The Lady Colonel), was recorded on Koch with the Santa Barbara Symphony (1998). In September 2000, again with Santa Barbara Symphony and Chorus, was a world premiere of Heitor Villa-Lobos' Symphony #10, *Amerindia*. This event, plus her recordings of Ginastera and Revueltas, fulfilled Mark Swed's assertion in the *Los Angeles Times* that she is "just the conductor we have been waiting for to make a really persuasive case for Latin composers . . . a ferocious talent." Also in September, she conducted and recorded a new production and European premiere of Ginastera's last opera, *Beatrix Cenci*, at the Grand Théâtre de Génève (Geneva, Switzerland). November found her in Madrid, conducting Ginastera's *Turbae Ad Passionem Gregorianam*, a passion for orchestra, soloists, adult and children's choruses. In 2004–05, Delos released a world premiere recording of music by **Astor Piazzolla** and Academy Award winner Luis Bacalov on a CD entitled *The Soul of Tango*, and EMI's *Don Rodrigo*, music from Ginastera's first opera, with **Plácido Domingo**.

2002 added guest conducting with Florida's New World Symphony in a Latin American program, with only twenty-four hours' notice, which led to an immediate re-engagement. She also debuted with the London Philharmonic in a romantic program, and returned to the BBC orchestra—leading to a third re-engagement.

Putting the Latins into America

The Revueltas Music Festival she created in January 2000 cast national and international attention upon Santa Barbara and its orchestra, eliciting rave reviews for its imaginative approach and wide-ranging commitment to the cause of the composer. The *Tango and Malámbo*[64] Festival, Ben-Dor's next brainchild, in cooperation with the City of Santa Barbara, took place February 6–15, 2004, leading up to the symphony's subscription concerts. The Festival was a collaborative effort of the orchestra, State Street Ballet, Santa Barbara International Film Festival, UCSB "Arts and Lectures" and music department, Tango Santa Barbara, public library and local businesses, as well as the Ben-Dor Music Discovery Project: *Celebrating the Art/Music of Latin America*. The latter, founded in 2002 by the maestra, aims to promote awareness and achieve global recognition of serious classical Latin American composers, preserving their works and legacy. The Festival was, in Ben-Dor's words, " . . . an unprecedented, roaring sold-out success with record ticket sales for the Symphony and Ballet."

Debuts for 2005 were with Israeli Opera (*Rigoletto*), The Hague Philharmonic, Israel Symphony, Orchestre de Cannes, returns to the Israel Philharmonic, Jerusalem Camerata, and Orchestre de Piccardie (France) among others. The year also marked the conclusion of her highly successful decade as music director of the Santa Barbara Symphony, where she was the ninth director and first woman to hold the position. In those ten years, the symphony budget went from $1.15 to $1.65 million. She is credited with raising the artistic level of the orchestra and increasing its national prominence via their recordings. Her other accomplishments were the expansion of the symphony's youth concerts and widening the repertoire to include Latin American composers.

Ben-Dor was awarded the honorary title, conductor laureate, from the Santa Barbara Symphony.

A Narrow Escape!

After a decade of contending with today's complexity of cross-country commuting, perhaps what occurred September 2004, implemented the decision to leave. While driving at night from the Los Angeles airport to Santa Barbara, Ben-Dor was in an auto accident. (She credits her seat belt and airbag for surviving the car rolling over several times!) With injuries to her arm that made it impossible to conduct all but the last two spring concerts, Lawrence Leighton Smith filled in at the last moment, having to learn a complex score. This was actually hard-won poetic justice, as during the 1980s, when Ben-Dor was assistant conductor to Leighton

---

64. With African origins, the tango was popular in the bars and slums of Buenos Aires until exported to Paris after World War I, where it gained international respectability. The Malambo, formed in the early 17th century in the Pampas grasslands, is a tournament of gaucho skills danced solely by men. These two 20th century Latin musical art forms traverse the line between classical and popular.

Smith in Louisville, the orchestra was famous for performing obscure contemporary music. "He would give me the most difficult scores to learn with a few hours' notice before a concert."

The future looks bright with guest conducting in Europe, including 2006–07 debuts at the Rotterdam Philharmonic and Bern Symphony.

A U.S. citizen since 2000, Gisèle makes her home on the East Coast with engineer husband Eli, and their two sons, Roy, born 1983, an honor business and psychology graduate of Duke University and JP Morgan Fellow, and Gabriel, born 1991.

ELKE MASCHA BLANKENBURG, born in 1943, in Germany, studied church music, choir and orchestra conducting in Heidelberg and Cologne, and with Hans Swarowsky in Vienna. From 1970–90, she was choir director of Christ Church in Cologne-Dellbrück. There she founded the Cologne Kurrende (choir) with whom, since 1981, she has won many national and international choir competitions, including a silver medal at the Riva del Garda in Italy (1994).

In 1978, she founded the organization "Women and Music," beginning extensive research on the music of women composers "overlooked" by history. In 1986, she founded the Clara Schumann Orchestra. Funded by the Deutschen Bundesbank, they released their first CD, the *Clara Schumann Piano Concerto* (1991).

In 1989, Blankenburg was named "Musician of the Town" for the city of Unna, where she has established an International Library of Women Composers and organized two Women Composer Festivals. In 1990–91, she directed the research project "The Status of Women Musicians in Germany" under the auspices of the Ministry of Education and Science. She founded the Clara Schumann Orchestra of Rome in 1995, and continues guest conducting internationally.

VICTORIA BOND was the first woman to receive a conducting grant from the National Institute for Music Theater to work at the New York City Opera. She consequently became music director of the Empire State Youth Orchestra, where several of her compositions were premiered. In 1984, she guest conducted her commissioned fanfare overture, *Ringing*, with the Houston Symphony as part of the state's sesquicentennial celebration. Her major tenure was as music director of the Roanoke Symphony Orchestra beginning in 1986, and artistic director of Opera Roanoke from 1989. After eight highly successful seasons, she stepped down from the Roanoke podium in June 1995 to devote more time to composition, recording and international requests for guest conducting. In 1997, she was appointed artistic advisor and principal guest conductor of the Wuhan Symphony in China. She also guest conducts with Opera Carolina and is artistic director of the Harrisburg Opera in Pennsylvania. (See Contemporary American Composers.)

CAROLYN WATERS BROE, born July 6, 1957, in Santa Monica, California, began piano at six, violin at eight and viola at ten. By 1969, she was playing in a string quartet. She continued viola at UC Irvine, and with a presidential scholarship to Chapman University School of Music, completed her BM in Viola Performance (1979). While attending Cal. State Long Beach, where she received her master's in musicology and performance in 1984, she played with the Long Beach Symphony and attended master classes of **Leonard Bernstein** and **Herbert Blomstedt**, director of the San Francisco Symphony (1985–95).

Carolyn Broe

In 1980, Carolyn married Steve Broe, administrator of American Childcare, preschool providers. She became principal violist with the Capistrano Valley Symphony (1986–92), and was a member of the Orange County Philharmonic. She was also a founding member of the Opus Four String Quartet (1982), the Mozart Camerata, Capistrano Chamber Players (1985), and director of the Capistrano Chamber Music Series—all in California.

In 1991, Carolyn, her husband and their seven-year-old son Jean René, born July 19, 1987, moved to Scottsdale, Arizona. There, she became founder/director of the Four Seasons Orchestra of Scottsdale, and the Four Seasons String Quartet. The ensemble was nominated for a Grammy in the Best Small Ensemble and Composition for Small Ensemble categories, for "Overture to the Lonely Heart," a cut on the CD *Just Wishing on the Moon*. In 1993, she founded the Paradise Valley Community College Chamber Orchestra, conducting this and, until 1995, the Glendale Community College Chamber Orchestras (both in California). 1995 was also the summer that she was chosen to be an associate conductor at Tanglewood, working with Boston Symphony director **Seiji Ozawa**. On December 2 of that year, Jasmine Broe came into the world!

As a composer, Broe has written numerous miniatures for viola. Her husband's induction into the Zen priesthood inspired *Tokudo* (The Gate of Enlightenment) and other viola pieces reflecting her interest in oriental arts and transcendentalism. During the '70s when students were deluged with serial music, she foresaw the return to neo-romantic. Her style is based on tonality and pure melody. In 2001, she completed her doctorate on undiscovered composer **Louise Lincoln Kerr** at Arizona State University. (See 20th Century American Composers.)

Lucinda Carver

LUCINDA CARVER, music director/conductor of the Los Angeles Mozart Orchestra, has studied piano with such greats as **Gary Graffman** and **Murray Perahia**, and conducting with William Schaefer and Hans Beer. Born in Seal Beach, California, her BA from UC Santa Barbara (1979), MM from Manhattan School of Music (1981), and artist diploma from the Salzburg Mozarteum (1984), are in piano performance. Her DMA from USC (1989) covers piano, conducting, harpsichord and music history. She has been on the faculties of Occidental College and Cal. State, Fullerton.

Her performances, both as pianist and conductor, have been broadcast on NPR. As a Fulbright Fellow to Austria, she concertized throughout Europe. She has been the featured soloist with the L.A. Mozart Orchestra, Santa Barbara Chamber Orchestra, and Manhattan Philharmonia, among others, also appearing as recitalist at numerous festivals. Appointed to her present position in 1992, under her leadership the orchestra has been named to the California Arts Council Touring Roster as one of the city's "most valuable small ensembles." During the 1995–96 season, she led their first recordings for RCM: an all-Mozart CD of Symphonies Nos. 17, 29 and 34, and an all-Haydn CD of the rarely-recorded Symphony Nos. 43 (*Mercury*), and 48 (*Maria Theresa*), plus the overture to *Lo speziale*. During the 1996–97 season, LAMO made two national tours under the auspices of Columbia Artists, highlights of which were featured on *CBS Sunday Morning*.

Carver also guest conducts nationwide. The 1995–96 season saw her debut with Minnesota Opera, directing the St. Paul Chamber Orchestra in Mozart's *Don Giovanni*, leading the Brooklyn Philharmonic in the New York premiere of Richard Einhorn's live opera-oratorio for Carl Dreyer's 1927 silent film, *The Passion of Joan of Arc*, as well as the West Coast premiere at the John Anson Ford Amphitheater in Hollywood. Her Lincoln Center debut, conducting *Don Pasquale* for New York City Opera, came in the fall of 1997. In 1998, she made her debut appearance conducting the Pacific Symphony. Another first was leading the LAMO, soloists and chorus in a concert version of Mozart's *Abduction from the Seraglio*.

Since its founding in 1975 by David Keith, the LAMO has had no permanent home. Their 2000–2001 Silver Anniversary season found them in residence at the Colburn[65] School of Performing Arts, where they present ten concerts annually in the new 416-seat Zipper Concert Hall.

Carver fits her love of teaching into her performance schedule as a Lecturer at her *alma mater*, USC's Thornton School of Music.

Focusing on opera and new music, **MARY CHUN** conducted the Canadian and European premieres of John Adams' *I was Looking at the Ceiling and then I saw the Sky* at the Festival de Théâtre des Amériques, Montréal, the Festival d'Automne, Paris, and the Thalia Theatre, Hamburg, with the Finnish contemporary ensemble *AVANTI*. She conducted *Carmen* with the East Slovakian State Opera in a successful tour of Germany, Austria and Switzerland, and *Madama Butterfly* with the Pacific Repertory Opera, California. Back in the Slovak Republic, she

---

65. Named for philanthropist Richard D. Colburn.

gave the European premiere of the American composer Martin Kalmanoff's *Insect Comedy*. American stage director Peter Sellars and composer Tan Dun asked her musical assistance with the opera *Peony Pavilion*.

Chun has also been a member of the conducting staffs of opera companies in the U.S. and France, such as Opera Theater of St. Louis, Los Angeles Music Center Opera, San Francisco Opera, Opera Theater of St. Louis, Châtelet Theatre in Paris and Opéra de Lyon, where she was also the director of musical studies for maestro **Kent Nagano**.

Her recording credits include a CD of works by American composer Peter Allen, Disney commercials and independent film projects. She has been responsible for musical preparation and artistic supervision of more that 350 contemporary works, including many recordings of 20th century repertoire.

Catherine Comet

CATHERINE COMET, born December 6, 1944, in Fontainebleau, France, was taken to concerts early in life, and decided to become a conductor at the ripe age of four. Her "neighbor," famed pedagogue **Nadia Boulanger** (1887–1979), accepted her as a student at twelve. At fifteen, she already had her piano baccalaureate. She came to New York and earned her BM at Juilliard in two years (1962), and her master's in orchestral conducting in one year. Russian conductor/composer **Igor Markevitch** (1912–1983), French flutist/conductor **Jean Fournet** (*b* 1913), and **Pierre Boulez** (*b* 1925), founder of IRCAM, the Paris electronic music studio, were among her illustrious teachers.

Returning to France, she won conducting awards and began her career with the Ballet Company of the Paris Opera (1972–75). Offered a lifetime tenure in 1976, she opted for love instead, married American Michael Aiken, and moved to this country in 1976. They have one daughter, Caroline, also born in 1976. Michael became provost of the University of Pennsylvania. He is now Chancellor of the University of Illinois at Champaign-Urbana.

In 1978, Comet began directing the University of Wisconsin (Madison) Symphony and Chamber Orchestra. In 1981, she won an Exxon/Arts Endowment assistant conductorship with the St. Louis Symphony, where she made her first recording. Under her direction, in July 1983, the St. Louis Symphony Youth Orchestra won first prize at the Twelfth International Youth and Music Festival in Vienna. From 1984–86, she was associate conductor of the Baltimore Symphony. With options in the mainstream, she chose to answer the invitation of the Grand Rapids (Michigan) Symphony, to which orchestra she brought national recognition, winning such honors as the 1987 Governor's Arts Award, 1987 and 1988 ASCAP awards, and the 1990 YWCA Tribute Award for her contributions to music. As a recipient of the 1988 Seaver/NEA Conductors Award, designed to provide opportunities for travel and work with master conductors, the maestra generously committed the major portion of the grant toward the making of the Grand Rapids Symphony's first recording.

Concurrently, she was music director of the American Symphony Orchestra in New York (1989–1992). She retired from Grand Rapids in 1997, electing to guest conduct to allow more time for a home life—although her new schedule has taken her to Australia, New Zealand, Singapore, Japan, Germany, Spain, and the leading orchestras of North America, including San Diego, where we finally met.

FIORA CONTINO, daughter of baritone Ferruccio Corradetti, who sang with La Scala before coming to the U.S., began studies with her father in solfeggio, piano and violin. An Oberlin graduate, she studied conducting with **Nadia Boulanger**, returning to Indiana University for degrees in conducting (MM, PhD,1964). She was director of opera at Bowling Green, returning to Indiana in 1966 as principal conductor and chairman of the choral department. She has guest-conducted opera and orchestras throughout the U.S., and was a choral director at Aspen. Since 1988, she has been general director of Opera Illinois. In 1994, she founded Teatro Grattacielo, a concert opera company performing in Lincoln Center's Alice Tully Hall, which presents neglected turn-of-the-century Italian operas unlikely to be produced by major companies. She also maintains a studio in New York, coaching opera singers in Italian repertoire.

CAROL I. CRAWFORD, appointed artistic director of Tulsa Opera in September 1993, has a goal to present more 20th century American opera. The 1995 new production of Robert Ward's *The Crucible*, based on the Arthur Miller play, was critically acclaimed, as was her innovative pairing of the traditional and contemporary with *Cavalleria Rusticana* and Leonard Bernstein's *Trouble in Tahiti* during the 1995–96 season.

Born December 6, 1955, in Hackensack, New Jersey, Carol was brought up in Stamford, Connecticut, where her childhood inspiration was her musical grandmother, Isabelle—after whom she adopted her middle initial. She played trombone and other winds in the high school band. Undergraduate studies were at Juilliard, Manhattanville College and the Salzburg Mozarteum, in music education and piano performance with mentors like **Leonard Bernstein**, **Otto Werner-Mueller** and **Boris Goldovsky**, plus master classes with **Sir Georg Solti** in Chicago. First prize in the San Diego Opera Young American Opera Conductor's Competition led to her professional opera conducting debut with Verdi's *Nabucco* (1981). In 1982, she was selected for the inaugural conducting class of the Los Angeles Philharmonic Institute, appearing as a featured apprentice conductor in the 1984 television documentary, *Leonard Bernstein: Conductor, Teacher, Composer*. Bernstein had her assist in the 1984 La Scala premiere of his opera *A Quiet Place* in its revised version incorporating *Trouble in Tahiti*. She also assisted at Houston Grand Opera's 1989 world premiere of Sir Michael Tippett's *New Year*.

Crawford has held positions with opera companies in Memphis, San Francisco, Houston and Virginia, and guest conducted in St. Louis, North Carolina, New Jersey, Omaha, Chautauqua (NY), Delaware, Florida and Tulsa. She has also conducted many musicals, operettas, and cabarets with community theaters in the Northeast. In 1993, she served on the ASOL special task force examining the future of U.S. professional orchestras; and also conducted an Elvis Presley tribute concert in conjunction with the issue of his U.S. commemorative stamp. She has received many awards, and has been profiled in both the *New York Times* and *Opera Monthly* magazine (1993, 1996).

In 1996, she made her conducting debut with Minnesota Opera (*La Bohème*), and Portland (Oregon) Opera with *Jenůfa*. A tireless advocate of arts education, Crawford established the Tulsa Youth Opera in the spring of 1997 with a premiere production of Hans Krása's *Brundibar* (A children's opera written in the Theresienstadt concentration camp), featuring 140 "baby" opera singers. In 1998, Crawford directed a revival of David Carlson's *Dream-eepers* (premiered in Utah in 1996) as part of Tulsa's fiftieth anniversary. The 2000–01 season featured Verdi's *Il Trovatore* and *Rigoletto*, and Janacek's *The Cunning Little Vixen*. The 2004–05 season began with a special presentation of *The Sound of Music*, followed by *Madame Butterfly* with Ai-Lan Zhu, *Eugene Onegin*, and the "twins," *Cavalleria Rusticana* and *I Pagliacci* with Stephanie Blythe.

In 2000, Crawford was the speaker at the University of Tulsa's 105th commencement.

JOAN DORNEMANN—*Joan-in-the-Box*—is one of the most highly respected opera coaches in the world. In her position as assistant conductor of the Metropolitan Opera of New York, she prepared the most prominent international artists such as **Luciano Pavarotti**, **Plácido Domingo**, **Mirella Freni**, **José Carreras**, **Sherrill Milnes**, **Kiri Te Kanawa**, **Renata Scotto**, **Marilyn Horne**, **Alfredo Kraus** and **Montserrat Caballé** for their performances. She has also prompted[66] under the batons of renowned maestros **James Levine**, **James Conlon** and **Carlos Kleiber**, amongst many others. As a coach, she is the orchestra at the piano, conducting rehearsals.

Born in Boston and trained in piano from childhood, after graduating with a music degree from Hofstra College on Long Island, she studied at Juilliard and in Florence. Then, like **Ruth Schönthal**, she supported herself playing in cocktail lounges in her early days in New York. She became interested in opera when she accompanied her friend—a singer—to his rehearsals, and got a job accompanying at the class of the great Austrian actor-turned-drama-teacher **Ludwig Donath**. She also worked at NYCO.

---

66. An opera prompter sits in a hidden alcove, below center stage, and cues in each singer's entrances—actually *singing* the lyrics ahead of their opening their mouths—a fantastic feat considering the amount of movement onstage and the orchestra playing in the pit. Joan has built such a reputation of expertise that many singers refused to go on unless they knew she is in that box!

She met the famous diva **Montserrat Caballé** while working in Barcelona as a coach/accompanist. It was she who interested Joan in her first prompting assignment at the Gran Liceo. This led to engagements in Trieste, the Spoleto Festival, New York City Opera and, in 1974, at the Met. There she became the first person to combine the roles of prompter and coach. Caballé was very influential to Joan's career. Once when her New York management arranged for her to have a male accompanist at a recital, the soprano refused to appear unless she could have Dornemann accompany her. (She got her way).

A great supporter of young singers, Dornemann is director of the Israel Vocal Arts Institute and teaches master classes there and throughout the U.S., as well as Puerto Rico, Canada and New Zealand. She received an Emmy Award for her collaboration in the first *Live from the Met* telecast of *La Bohème* with **Luciano Pavarotti** and **Renata Scotto**. She has been featured in *People* Magazine, appeared on the *Tonight Show*, and was subject of a segment on *Sunday Morning with Charles Kuralt*, produced by **Eugenia Zukerman**. Dornemann is the author, with Maria Ciaccia, of *Complete Preparation: A Guide to Auditioning for the Met*, published in the U.S. and Europe.

AGNIESZKA DUCZMAL was born January 7, 1946, near Poznań, Poland, into a musical family. She graduated with distinction from the Poznań Academy of Music. In 1968, while still a student, she established a chamber group which, in 1977, became the Polish Radio Amadeus Chamber Orchestra (ACO). After graduation, she was employed as assistant conductor of the Poznań National Philharmonic and later as conductor of the Poznań Opera, for whom she prepared the Polish premiere of Benjamin Britten's *A Midsummer Night's Dream*.

In 1970, Duczmal won an award in the First National Conducting Competition in Katowice (Cracow). She earned a distinction in the Fourth International Herbert von Karajan Conducting Competition in West Berlin in 1975, and the following year won the Herbert von Karajan Silver Medal at the Youth Orchestras Conference in Berlin. In 1982, under the auspices of UNESCO and the Italian president, she received the *La Donna del Mondo* (Woman of the World) Award of the St. Vincent International Culture Centre in Rome, for outstanding achievements in the fields of culture, science and social activities.

She was the first female conductor at Teatro La Scala, Milan.

Under her direction the ACO has made strikingly superior recordings, and have been featured on Polish radio and television in the series "Agnieszka Duczmal's Guests in Stereo and in Color." These have been aired in Europe, North and South America, and Asia, where the orchestra toured with famous soloists. The ACO also collaborates with the broadcasting companies of other countries, including the BBC (London), CBC (Montreal), and Mexican Radio.

The clarity and rich, thrilling sound of the Amadeus Orchestra—most of whose members have matured with the ensemble since its inception as a youth orchestra over twenty years ago—has been heard all over Europe, Russia and America under their dynamic conductor.

SIAN EDWARDS, born August 27, 1959, in West Chiltington, Sussex, graduated from the Royal Northern College of Music, then studied with renowned conductors **Sir Charles Groves**, **Norman Del Mar** and **Neeme Järvi**. From 1983–85 she was at the Leningrad Conservatory. In May 1984, she won the first Leeds Conductors' Competition. Returning to Britain in 1985, she developed her symphonic and operatic repertoire, working with most of Britain's leading orchestras, including the London Philharmonic, Royal Philharmonic, Royal Scottish National and City of Birmingham Symphonies, and the Hallé Orchestra of Manchester. She made her operatic conducting debut in 1986 in a new production of Kurt Weill's *Mahagonny* for Scottish Opera, and returned for performances of *Carmen*. In summer 1987, she worked in the Glyndebourne Festival Opera with *La traviata* and Ravel's *L'Heure Espagnol*. Both productions were subsequently televised. She returned to Glyndebourne in 1988, again for *La Traviata*, and that autumn conducted Janáček's *Káta Kabanová* for their touring company. The same summer she gave the world premiere of Mark Anthony Turnage's *Greek* at the Munich Biennale, which was then brought to the 1988 Edinburgh Festival. The same year, she was the first woman conductor at the Royal Opera House, Covent Garden, in a new production of Sir Michael Tippett's *The Knot Garden*. This led to a three year contract with the company. During 1989–90 season, Edwards appeared for the first time with the Orchestre de Paris, St. Paul Chamber Orchestra in the U.S., and English National Opera (ENO), conducting Prokofiev's *The Gambler*. Other engagements that season included concerts with the San Francisco Symphony Orchestra, and a nationwide tour of Australia for their ABC network. In 1990–91, she conducted Tippett's *New Year* for the Glyndebourne Touring Opera. 1991–92 saw a highly successful debut with the Los Angeles Philharmonic. Other orchestral engagements included concerts in Paris, St. Petersburg, Brussels, Montpellier (France), Scotland and Birmingham. Operatic engagements for 1992–93 were *Madama Butterfly* (Covent Garden) and *The Queen of Spades* (ENO). '92–'93 orchestral engagements included extensive and enormously successful tours in Europe, America, and her Proms debut with the Docklands Sinfonietta. 1993–94, her first season as ENO music director, brought *La Bohème*, *Jenůfa*, *The Marriage of Figaro*, and a new **Judith Weir** commission, *Blond Eckbert*. 1994–95 marked returns to Vienna and Rotterdam Operas, and concerts with the National and Atlanta Symphonies, Philadelphia and Minnesota Orchestras, the Los Angeles Philharmonic, and a European tour with the Ensemble Moderne.

The 1995 season at ENO featured Edwards with an acclaimed production of Mussorgsky's *Khovanshchina*, the latest revival of *The Mikado*, and the new production of Declan Donellan's *The Rise and Fall of the City of Mahagonny*. In November 1995, she resigned her post at ENO.

In 1999, she conducted the Welsh National Orchestra and the young Welsh soprano **Charlotte Church** in her super selling first CD, *Voice of An Angel*. The end of the year found her back at Glyndebourne with *The Bartered Bride*. May 2000 brought *Eugene Onegin* with ENO (London).

2001 covered John Adams' *The Death of Klinghoffer*[67](February, Helsinki), *Peter Grimes* (June, Frankfurt), and *Don Giovanni* (October, Copenhagen). 2001 marked her debut with the Royal Danish Ballet in Copenhagen. *Peter Grimes* was reprised by Frankfurt Opera, April 2002.

The 2004–05 season put Edwards on the podium for the world premiere of Hans Gefors' *Clara* (Opéra Comique, Paris), *Cosí fan tutte* (Aspen), a return to ENO for *Eugene Onegin*, *Don Giovanni* (Copenhagen), *Damnation de Faust* (Helsinki) and *Peter Grimes* (Frankfurt). January 2005, she was in Birmingham (England) for a concert leading the CBSO.

Besides achieving world status as a conductor with major orchestras, Sian Edwards has made many acclaimed recordings, including the disk with Charlotte Church.

JoAnn Falletta

JOANN FALLETTA is in the top echelon of American women conductors. Born February 27, 1954, in New York to first generation Italian parents, she began music studies on guitar at age seven, adding piano a few years later. From age twelve she knew her vocation, and in her late teens entered the conducting program at the Mannes College of Music, continuing at Queens College.

Her first orchestral job came in 1978, directing seniors in a community ensemble. By 1989, she had built this group into a full-sized orchestra. Meanwhile, in 1982, she won the Bruno Walter Award and a full scholarship to Juilliard where, in the next five years, she earned her masters and doctorate in orchestral conducting. In 1983, she became musical director of the Denver Chamber Orchestra. In 1986, she was engaged as music director of The Women's Philharmonic in San Francisco, which promoted the music of women composers. Nine years later (1995), she stepped down from this position to, in her words, "open the opportunity for other women to gain experience on the podium." She continued her association with the orchestra as artistic advisor, and was co-founder of their Conductor Initiative program. Assuming the directorship of the Long Beach (California) Symphony in 1989 established Falletta as the first American-born woman to lead a regional orchestra. After ten years there, she left in June 2000 to lead the

---

67. *The Death of Klinghoffer* is based on the 1984 hijacking of the Italian cruise ship *Achille Lauro* by Palestinian terrorists and their murdering of one of the passengers, a retired, wheelchair-bound American Jew named Leon Klinghoffer.

Buffalo Philharmonic, a full-time orchestra with an annual budget of over $9 million. Since 1991, she has also led the Virginia Symphony Orchestra in Norfolk.

Her guest appearances have taken her throughout the U.S., including Hawaii, plus South America, Canada, Europe, South Africa, New Zealand and the Orient. She participates in major summer festivals throughout the world. Her 2000–2001 guest conducting season covered four continents, including concerts with the Singapore Symphony, National Symphony of China, Símon Bolívar Orchestra (Caracas, Venezuela) and Orquesta Filarmonica (Mexico), besides traversing America from Arizona to Louisiana. 2002 gave the author a reunion with hugs for the two of us when JoAnn directed the San Diego Symphony in February.

Falletta's honors include the prestigious Stokowski, and Toscanini Awards, as well as an Associate Conductorship with the Milwaukee Symphony under **Lukas Foss**—a position she held for three seasons. In April 1995, Falletta received the Claudette Sorel Award for Excellence in Music from the Center for Women in Music of NYU, and the Ditson Award in Conducting (1998). She was the recipient of the 2002 Seaver/NEA Conductors Award, given to exceptionally gifted directors heading for major careers. There has also been over a decade of ASCAP awards. As of 2004, the count was up to ten.

In 2003, she gave the premieres of two fanfares commissioned by The Women's Philharmonic, which unfortunately, for financial reasons, was forced to disband in 2004. In June of that year, the Buffalo Philharmonic returned to Carnegie Hall for its first performance there in more than fifteen years. The same month they were honored to receive an ASOL award for Adventurous Programming for the '03–'04 season, one of eight the maestra has received. Summer 2004 saw the inaugural JoAnn Falletta International Guitar Concerto Competition, presented by the BPO and station WNED. Ten musicians from nine different countries traveled to Buffalo to compete for the opportunity to perform with the orchestra.

Falletta's discography of over forty titles range with the Virginia, Long Beach, London, New Zealand and Czech National Symphonies, English Chamber Orchestra and Buffalo Philharmonic, among those under her baton. Her 2004 BPO Naxos recording of Charles Tomlinson Griffes' orchestral music was selected as an Editor's Choice Recording by *Gramophone* magazine. She was also a 2006 Grammy nominee for her recoding with the London Symphony (Naxos) of Kenneth Fuch's *Eventide*, a concerto for English horn, harp, percussion and string orchestra.

In 2004, she signed a new, three-year contract with Buffalo, taking her through the 2007–2008 season. The 2004–05 season began with an Opening Night Gala featuring violinist/violist **Pinchas Zukerman** plus the Philharmonic's first performance of Mahler's mammoth 7th Symphony with soprano **Dawn Upshaw**. Violinist **Gil Shaham** was programmed, as well as a fully staged production of Shakespeare's *A Midsummer Night's Dream* with Mendelssohn's music. During the 2005–06 season, Naxos issued two CDs with the BPO: recordings of Aaron Copland and Ottorino Respighi; and an '06–'07 release of music by John Corigliano.

Falletta continues as music director of the Virginia Symphony, opening the 2005 season in their new home, the Ferguson Center for the Arts in Newport News. She is also artistic advisor to the Honolulu Symphony. 2005–06 guest appearances were with the (DC) National Symphony and orchestras of Montreal, Philadelphia, San Francisco, Toronto, Detroit, Milwaukee, Honolulu and Omaha, where she conducted the opening of their new hall and the premiere of **Joan Tower**'s Viola Concerto, *Purple Rhapsody*, written for Paul Neubauer. Debuts with the Tokyo Metropolitan and Jerusalem Symphonies, plus return engagements all over Europe and America fill her calendar for years to come.

Hailed by the *New York Times* as " . . . one of the finest conductors of her generation," and having witnessed her in action several times, this author can heartily second that.

DEBORAH FREEDMAN has been music director of the St. Joseph (Missouri) Symphony Orchestra since 1988, a position that also involves administrative duties, fund-raising, public relations, and the musical life of the orchestra—subscription and children's concerts. As an

Deborah Freedman

associate professor of music at Missouri Western State College, she teaches French horn and conducts *their* community orchestra. Before joining SJSO, she held the same positions at Portland (Oregon) State. From 1977 to 1981, her career progressed from teaching and conducting high school orchestras in Bridgeport (Washington), Green Bay (Wisconsin) and Baltimore (Maryland), to assistant conductor, Annapolis Symphony (1983–86), founder/director, Maryland Women Composers Orchestra (1985–87), Phoenix Choir and Chrysalis Singers (1985–86)—all in Baltimore—and director of the St. Joseph Youth Symphony (1988–90).

In 1994, Dr. Freedman was musical co-coordinator of a unique outdoor event at Mattfield Green, Kansas, where she conducted the Symphony of the Prairie,[68] comprised of women from orchestras throughout the Heartland. It drew a crowd of over 4,000. Guest conducting stints with many regional orchestras include the Nebraska State Honor Orchestra and the International Women's Brass Conference, both in 1997. Trombonist **Abbie Conant** (See Brass) has soloed with the St. Joseph Symphony and her husband, William Osborne, had his children's opera, *Alice Through the Looking Glass*, receive its U.S. premiere there.

Born December 2, 1953, in Green Bay, Deborah's childhood included being part of a gymnastics troupe—good training for the stamina required of all maestros. (Try waving your arms in the air for two hours!) She began piano at age six. Her high school diploma is from the Interlochen Arts Academy (1972). Her B. Mus. Ed. is from the University of Minnesota (1977), where she conducted the University Brass Ensemble (1975–77). Her MM (1983) and DMA (1985) are from Peabody with a dissertation on **Thea Musgrave**'s opera, *Mary Queen of Scots*.

Deborah married Keith Rhodes in 1984. A former lawyer, he became a professor at Northwest Missouri State, then joined his wife at Missouri Western. Son Aaron was born November 17, 1990, and daughter Abbey, October 29, 1993. A career woman who puts her family first, she looked for a position and location where she could settle and raise her family. With her talents utilized to the fullest extent at home, in the Academe, and on the podium, this maestra has found her niche.

Jane Glover

JANE GLOVER was born May 13, 1949, in Helmsley, Yorkshire. After hearing her first *Messiah* at age nine, she knew she was going to be a musician. She met **Benjamin Britten** (1913–76) when she was sixteen. He arranged an internship for her at his Aldeburgh Festival between high school and university. She made her conducting debut in 1975, and received her PhD from Oxford (1978) on 17th century Venetian opera. Her eight year association with Glyndebourne Opera, under Dutch conductor **Bernard Haitink**, began in 1980, serving first as a *répétiteur*, then chorus master ('81–'85), and music director of the touring company, taking their production of *A Midsummer Night's Dream* to the Hong Kong Festival (1986). She has conducted a wide repertoire for Glyndebourne, as well as working with the Central Opera Company of Peking.

From 1984–91, Glover was artistic director of the London Mozart Players, expanding their repertoire beyond the great 18th century classics to contemporary works, and touring with them throughout Europe, Japan and the Far East, plus many Proms concerts. She began working with English National Opera (ENO) in their 1988–89 season, conducting *Don Giovanni*, the first of many productions for them. Her Royal Opera House, Covent Garden, debut was *The Abduction from the Seraglio* (1988).

International debuts include *Le Nozze di Figaro* for Canadian Opera, the Vienna Konzerthaus (1991), and Glimmerglass (Cooperstown, NY) Opera Festival (1994). She took part in the Lincoln Center symposium on *Performing Mozart's Music*—part of his Bicentennial celebrations. 1992 expanded her appearances to Scotland, Denmark, Spain, Netherlands, Belgium, Finland and New Zealand. 1994 brought her New York debut in a gala concert featuring **Jessye Norman** and the Orchestra of St. Luke's at Lincoln Center, televised throughout North America, the Center's *Mostly Mozart* Festival, a debut with the St. Paul Chamber Orchestra, and the China Philharmonic. 1996 marked her "down under" debut with *Alcina* for Australian Opera. 1997 saw her debut with

---

68. Philanthropist Jane Kolar underwrote and donated part of her 7,000 acre ranch at Hay Meadows for this event.

Opera de Nice (France), in Handel's *Giulio Cesare*. She made her New York City Opera debut in 1997, returning in 1999. Her 2000–01 season included appearances with the Indianapolis Symphony, Opera Theater of St. Louis, Chicago Opera Theater, Cleveland Opera, NYCO, and again St. Paul Chamber. During the 2002 season she conducted *Così Fan Tutte* (COT), *Agrippina* (NYCO), Monteverdi's *Orfeo* (Brooklyn Academy of Music), and *Marriage of Figaro* (Cincinnati Opera). 2003 brought *Don Pasquale* at Cleveland. Besides Music of the Baroque, Glover's engagements in 2003–04 included *Cenerentola* with Opera Australia, concerts with the New Jersey Symphony, Sydney Symphony, and Northern Sinfonia of England, her Carnegie Hall debut with the Orchestra of St. Luke's, *L'Incoronazione di Poppea* with Chicago Opera Theater, *The Secret Marriage* with Opera Theatre of St Louis, and her return to the BBC Proms. In 2004, the Royal Albert Hall was transformed into a fairytale setting with a superb performance of Humperdink's *Hansel and Gretel* at the BBC Proms with the BBC Concert Orchestra. Other venues have been the Royal Danish Opera, and Teatro La Fenice, and other repertoire includes all Mozart operas, Handel's *Tamerlano* and *Ariodante*, her own editions of the Monteverdi trilogy, Gluck's *Orfeo ed Euridice* and *Iphigenie en Tauride*, and many more early works. Other operas include *Fidelio*, *Barbiere di Siviglia*, *Albert Herring*, *A Midsummer Night's Dream*, *Turn of the Screw*, and Knussen's *Where the Wild Things Are*, based on the Maurice Sendak children's story.

Glover's many recordings feature a series of Mozart and Haydn symphonies for ASV, and arias with **Felicity Lott**, all with the London Mozart Players, plus Haydn, Mozart, Schubert, Britten and Walton with the London Philharmonic, Royal Philharmonic, and the BBC Singers. Her extensive BBC broadcasting covers the television series *Orchestra and Mozart*, and radio series *Opera House* and *Musical Dynasties*.

Glover's special affinity for great English choral works brings her before major choral societies. She records regularly with the BBC Singers, and is principal conductor of both the London and Huddersfield (Yorkshire) Choral Societies, one of the oldest in England, dating back over 175 years. Re-engagements are continuous, and there are many excellent recordings to her credit.

Jane Glover is also a musicologist, researcher and lecturer. Since 1979, she has been on the music faculty at Oxford, and from 1990, governor of the Central Music Advisory Committee and the RAM. She has received many awards and honorary doctorates and is a fellow of the Royal College of Music.

She was created a CBE in the Queen's 2003 New Year's Honors.

NOREEN GREEN received her MM in choral conducting from Cal. State, Northridge, where she was director of the Woman's Chorale (1985–92). 1991 brought her DMA in choral music from USC. Her nearly twenty years of conducting experience has been with synagogues, community and university ensembles, including music director at Temple Ramat Zion, Northridge, and the American Jewish Choral Society. Nationally recognized for her work in Jewish music, she has collaborated with peers in Israel, the Netherlands, Germany, Russia, Argentina and Ukraine. Her doctoral treatise on Russian synagogue composer David Nowakowsky led to her appointment as the West Coast music director of the David Nowakowsky Foundation. She studied conducting with **Lukas Foss**, Helmuth Rilling at the Oregon Bach Festival, and with her mentor, **Murry Sidlin**, at Aspen. She is the director of Congregation Valley Beth Shalom in Encino and artistic director and conductor of the Los Angeles Jewish Symphony.

Since founding the LAJS in 1994, the symphony has carved its identity as a bastion of Jewish music and Jewish music education, involving the community. Green prefaces each concert with insights on the composer, including his/her time and work, adding understanding and enjoyment of the music. On April 16, 2000, she premiered *Women of Valor*, an oratorio by **Andrea Clearfield**. (See Composers.) This brought to fulfillment Noreen's dream, which had its inception in 1994 when she met the composer at Aspen, to have an oratorio about Jewish women, written by a Jewish woman, performed by women and conducted by a woman. Also on the program was *Ouverture* by **Fanny Mendelssohn**, and *Strings-Bow and Arrow* by **Tsippi Fleischer**.

In May 2000, the LAJS traveled to Israel for concerts at the Rubin Academy in Tel Aviv. Green extended her stay to research contemporary Israeli composers in order to bring their music back to the U.S. for performance with the orchestra. January 2001 brought a program celebrating Jewish composers of film music, including Erich Wolfgang Korngold, Max Steiner, Miklos Rozsa, Franz Waxman and Alfred Newman, whose daughter, composer **Maria Newman**, guested as concertmaster.

As part of the celebration of National Women's History Month in March 2004, the LAJS celebrated its own tenth anniversary joining with other California orchestras in *Voices of Women*, a statewide salute to female composers and conductors, initiated by The Women's Philharmonic in partnership with the Association of California Symphony Orchestras. Green conducted a concert featuring the works of six contemporary female Jewish composers, Michelle Green Willner, **Maria Newman**, Meira Warshauer, **Andrea Clearfield**, Sheli Nan and Sharon Farber. In July, as part the John Anson Ford Amphitheatre Summer Series, the orchestra presented *Two Streams in the Desert-Celebrating Judeo-Español and Klezmer/Yiddish Jewish Music*. Thus the LAJS continues to make its unique contribution to the community.

AGNES GROSSMANN has made a name for herself in Canada. Born April 24, 1944, in Vienna, her first piano lessons were with her famous father, Austrian conductor/composer **Ferdinand Grossmann** (1887–1970), artistic director of the Vienna Boys Choir. Agnes continued her studies at the Vienna Academy of Music with Bruno Seidlhofer.[69] On a state scholarship from France, she took classes with Pièrre Sançan at the Paris Conservatory. In 1968, she received her piano diploma from the Wiener Hochschule für Musik. The following year she became assistant to her step-grandmother, world-famous pianist **Lili Kraus** (1903–86), at Texas Christian University (Fort Worth). Kraus was her true artistic mentor.

From 1969 on, Grossman played solo concerts all over Europe and Japan, and founded the Vienna Flute Trio (with Wolfgang Schulz, principal flute of the Vienna Philharmonic, and Heidi Litschauer, cello). In 1972, she received the Mozart Interpretation Prize in Vienna and toured the U.S. and Canada under the prestigious Columbia Artists Management agency. In 1973, she was forced to cancel all engagements due to injuring her right hand. (The same malady which incapacitated pianists Leon Fleischer and Gary Graffman.)

Changing career directions, from 1974–78 Grossmann returned to the Vienna Hochschule, this time to study orchestral and choral conducting with Karl Österreicher,[70] Günther Theuring and Hans Swarowsky.[71] In 1979, she was appointed professor of Solfège for conductors and composers at the Hochschule and assistant conductor of the Vienna Jeunesse (Youth) Choir. 1981–83 marked a leave of absence to become visiting professor at Ottawa University, where she directed their orchestra and choir. Concurrently, she made numerous guest appearances with Canadian orchestras, tours of Western Canada with the Canadian Chamber Ensemble, plus concerts with the Vienna Chamber Orchestra.

Back to her home town, from 1983–86 Grossmann was artistic director of the Vienna Singakademie, the first woman director of this renowned choir, which was founded in 1858 and numbers among its conductors **Johannes Brahms** (1863), and **Gustav Mahler** (1901).

1984 marked her appointment as Music Director of the Chamber Players of Toronto, with whom she performed until 1986, making a triumphant European tour in 1985. She combined appearances at the Singakademie with tours of Austria and Canada. From 1986–95, Grossmann was Artistic Director and Conductor of l'Orchestre Métroplitain de Montréal. In 1987, the city named her "Woman of the Year in the Arts." The same year, she made her debut with the Toronto Symphony. 1988 saw debuts with the National Arts Centre Orchestra, Ottawa, and the Orchestra of the Mozarteum, Salzburg. From 1989–95, she was music director at the Orford Arts Centre near Quebec. In 1992, she debuted with the Vancouver Symphony, touring Singapore and Japan. Her CD with the World Youth Orchestra in Quebec came out in 1993.

Grossmann was awarded an honorary doctor's degree from Mt. Saint Vincent University (Halifax, (1991) and the Austrian Government Silver Cross for outstanding artistic achievement (1992). In 1994, she received the Gold Medal of Merit from the City of Vienna. In 1997, following in her father's footsteps, she became artistic director of

---

69–71. The same teachers of a student named Raffi Armenian, whom she married many years later in 1984.

the Vienna Boys Choir—the first woman in this position in their 500-year history. In 1998, however, she resigned following a dispute with the school director over the principle that she felt the boys were too exploited commercially and that the responsibility for fund-raising should fall on benefactors and philanthropists. Meanwhile, she launched the Children's Opera Series of the Vienna State Opera, conducting Hans Krasa's *Brundibar*, which had last been performed in Theresienstadt concentration camp. (See **Alma Rosé**.) Her educational reforms for the Institution included acceptance of girls in the kindergarten, which created a worldwide positive echo. She also introduced a comprehensive educational program for the children.

In 1999, she resumed her international guest conducting career, including performances with ProCoro Canada (Edmonton), Arcadia Chamber Orchestra and Choir (Osaka, Japan), and a highly successful debut with the Montreal Symphony Orchestra, for whom she conducted the Mozart *Requiem* and Handel's *Messiah*. In October 1999, she was asked to resume the artistic directorship of the Orford Arts Center, a position that demands countless hours of administration, and numerous concerts to direct. In November 2000, she returned to the podium of the Osaka Arcadia Chamber Orchestra and Chorus for the Mozart *Requiem*, and made her debut with the Contemporary Chamber Orchestra and Choir of Taipei, Taiwan. The season also held guest conducting debuts with two Canadian orchestras: Orchestra London (Ontario), and Victoria Symphony Orchestra (B.C.). The summer was spent at the helm of the Orford Arts Center. She made her debut with the Kitchener-Waterloo Symphony Orchestra in April 2002. Grossman continues her numerous orchestra and choral concerts in Canada, as well as re-engagements to Europe and Japan.

On the faculty as conductor of the University of Toronto's Wind Ensemble, in June 2004, Agnes Grossman received an honorary doctorate from Rector Gilles Patry at the spring graduation ceremony.

SUSAN HAIG was artistic director and principal conductor of the Windsor Symphony (Ontario, Canada), 1991–2001, following three great seasons as resident staff conductor of the Calgary Philharmonic. Under her leadership, the Windsor Symphony has become recognized as one of the most successful and innovative professional orchestras in Canada.

Born April 19, 1954, in Summit, New Jersey, Susan received a BA from Princeton, and MM and DMA degrees in Orchestral Conducting from SUNY, Stony Brook. Her training includes conducting programs at San Diego Opera, and Aspen and Tanglewood Music Festivals.

Haig has served as a coaching/conducting fellow with Juilliard's American Opera Center and as assistant conductor with the New York City, Minnesota, Santa Fe, and Canadian Opera companies. She has conducted opera performances and concerts throughout Canada, and is heard on the CBC as a conductor, proponent of new works and arts advocate. She was honored with the 1992 Heinz Unger Conducting Award, and a Canada 125 citizenship medal. In 1999, she received the Mayor's Award of Excellence in the Performing Arts. Beginning with the 2001–2002 season, she divided her time between director of the Toronto Symphony Youth Orchestra and the South Dakota Symphony. With the 2003–2004 season, she left South Dakota and became associate conductor of the Florida Orchestra, as well as continuing her guest conducting engagements.

EMMANUELLE HAÏM is one of the leading conductors of baroque and early classical repertory. A *BBC Music Magazine* cover story calls her "Belle of the Baroque."

She began piano at four in a highly musical French family in Brittany. Her mother, a retired doctor, and her father, retired from an advertising career, are both pianists. Her aunt and her teacher, Yvonne Lefebure, made her practice Bach preludes and fugues. Emmanuelle was eight when she conducted a church chorale, and later, at school, she performed Bach concertos, directing from the keyboard. At the Paris Conservatoire, she was immersed in the organ when she discovered the harpsichord. This instrument placed her in productions with baroque specialists throughout Europe. From there, she coached singers in baroque style, including **Natalie Dessay**, with whom she worked on a Handel recording.

With an established expertise in early music, in 2001 the Glyndebourne Touring Opera invited her to conduct Handel's *Rodelinda*. Since then she has conducted in New York—five operas with William Christie at the Brooklyn

Academy of Music—London, Vienna, Chicago Opera Theater, the Orchestra of the Age of Enlightenment, City of Birmingham Symphony, and her own ensemble, Le Concert d'Astrée. Her several recordings, include Purcell's *Dido and Aeneas* with **Susan Graham** and Ian Bostridge (Virgin Classics), and Monteverdi's *L'Orfeo*.

Haïm's Concert d'Astrée, formed with like-minded musicians, has grown from four engagements per season since its inception, to sixty. She also conducts modern orchestras, but only in certain repertoire. Because she is so comfortable with her genre, she has a natural authority even without formal conducting studies. Of symphonic repertoire, she says, "I don't think I would have done it."

Meanwhile, she follows where the music takes her on her crowded calendar . . .

Patricia Handy

PATRICIA HANDY, born October 22, 1952, in Baltimore, holds degrees from Juilliard, Peabody, and Catholic University. Her principal teachers include world-famous conductors **Karl Richter** (1926–81), **Leon Barzin** (1900–1999), **Sixten Ehrling** (1918–2005), and **Gunther Schuller** (*b* 1925). While still at Peabody, she won a scholarship for the Hochschule für Musik in Munich, where she became a member of the Munich Bach Choir. Upon completion of her degrees, she concertized as an organist before turning to conducting.

She inaugurated a series of youth concerts praised by *Symphony Magazine* as one of the most exciting in the country. She also developed the Goliard Chamber Orchestra—of whom she is now conductor laureate—an assemblage of talented young vocal and instrumental artists, recognized for its innovative programming and special interest in 20th century repertoire. In 1979, the Greenwich (Connecticut) Symphony invited her to serve as the orchestra's associate conductor. She is also music director of the GSO Young People's Concerts series, and presents the popular pre-concert lectures. She guest conducts such aggregations as the Louisiana Philharmonic, the Colorado, Utah, Syracuse, Spokane, Eugene, and Colorado Springs Symphonies and the Kiel Philharmonic in Germany.

The recipient of numerous awards and grants, including a Lila Acheson Wallace Fellowship at Juilliard, and a Boston Symphony Orchestra Fellowship at Tanglewood, Handy has worked with **Seiji Ozawa** and **Leonard Bernstein**. She was a member of the choral faculty of Juilliard, as well as conductor of the Juilliard Pre-College Symphony, and chorus master of the Juilliard Opera Center. She was the first American woman to receive a conducting fellowship to the Tanglewood Music Center.

June 2004 found Handy conducting Greenwich POPS Orchestra (in its nineteenth year) under the stars along with the Greenwich Choral Society, conducted by Paul Mueller, before an audience of 5,000.

Apo Hsu

APO HSU, born October 7, 1956, is a native of Taiwan. She received her BA in piano performance from the National Taiwan Normal University in Taipei. Her MM in double bass performance, and artist diploma in Conducting, was earned from the Hartt School of Music (Connecticut). She then studied at the Pierre Monteaux Domaine School for Advanced Conductors, Conductors Institute in Columbia, South Carolina, and at the Aspen Music Festival. Her teachers include Charles Bruck, Harold Farberman, Murry Sidlin and Gary Karr.

She was conductor-in-residence for the Peter Britt Music Festival (Oregon, 1991), artistic director of the Oregon Mozart Players (1991–96), and assistant conductor with the Oregon Symphony (1991–94). As artistic director and conductor of The Women's Philharmonic in San Francisco (1997–2001), she received three consecutive adventuresome programming awards from ASCAP and the ASOL. In March 2000, she and TWP were filmed in a PBS documentary series called *Sing It, Tell It*, and in May in a film documentary, *Cool Women*, broadcast on cable TV. Their first CD together featured the music of African-American composer Florence Price, released on Koch International (2001).

Hsu has been music director/conductor of the Springfield (Missouri) Symphony since 1995, initiating the annual Paff and Hellam Young Artists Competitions in the strong belief that exposing children to music at an early age will beneficially affect the rest of their lives.

Guest appearances take Hsu all over the world. A highly successful interactive Youth Education Series with the National Symphony at Kennedy Center was followed by a seven-concert engagement with the National Symphony Orchestra in Taipei (Taiwan), conducting regular subscription concerts as well as a Youth Series. Other performances for youth have been with the St. Louis Symphony, a summer concert with the Minnesota Orchestra, appearances with the San Francisco Symphony, a residency with the Irkutsk Philharmonic (Russia), the Guam Symphony (Philippines) and a return concert tour in Taiwan, November-December 2002, part of ongoing engagements with this orchestra. 2004 brought a guest conducting stint with the Baltimore Chamber Orchestra in a concert entitled *A Journey of Sonic Wonder*.

MONICA HUGGETT, like the late **Iona Brown**, conducts from the first violin chair, and is one of the foremost baroque violinists of our time. Born May 16, 1953, in England, she was the fifth of seven children. Violin lessons began at six, graduating to studies with Manoug Parikian at the RAM. Introduced to the baroque violin in her teens, Monica felt it suited her personality and playing style more than the modern instrument. After playing both for several years, she decided to concentrate exclusively on the early violin. In her interpretation, the instrument becomes a human voice in sound and technique, while her repertoire covers the baroque, classical and romantic.

In 1980, Huggett co-founded the Amsterdam Baroque Orchestra with former Portland (Oregon) Baroque Orchestra Artistic Advisor **Ton Koopman**, leading them until 1987. As director of the Hanover Band (1981–86), she recorded Beethoven's Symphonies Nos. 1, 2 and 5, conducting from the violin. Her many other releases include Vivaldi's *La Stravaganza* with the Academy of Ancient Music directed by **Christopher Hogwood** on Decca; the Beethoven and Mendelssohn Violin Concertos with the Orchestra of the Age of Enlightenment under **Charles Mackerras** on EMI; the Mozart Violin Concertos with the same orchestra on Virgin Classics; numerous chamber works with her own ensemble, **Trio Sonnerie**, on Virgin, harmonium mundi, Teldec and ASV; *Hausmusik* on EMI; and her acclaimed two discs of the complete Bach unaccompanied Sonatas and Partitas (Virgin Classics, 1998).

After serving as professor of baroque and classical violin at the Hochschule für Künste in Bremen (Germany), she went on to become professor of baroque violin at the RAM, where she was made a fellow in 1994. In 1998, she toured the U.S. with flutist **James Galway** in a critically acclaimed program of Mozart orchestral works, performing on an 18th century violin. She makes regular guest appearances with the Orchestra of the Age of Enlightenment, Raglan Baroque Players, the European Union Baroque Orchestra, Amsterdam Baroque Orchestra, Hanover Band and many other early music ensembles.

Since 1995, Huggett has been the first artistic director of the Portland Baroque Orchestra. 2004–05 marked their twenty-first season.

She performs on a violin made in Cremona in 1618 by Hieronymus and Antonius Amati.

JANNA HYMES-BIANCHI, born November 3, 1958, in New York, is the youngest of three children. Her father was a lighting consultant for NBC, and her mother worked as the public relations director for American Ballet Theatre before going into Broadway production. Older brother Jeffrey is a sports producer, younger brother Tommy, a writer in Los Angeles. In this creative family, only Janna has a career in music. Prompted by her mother, she began piano at an early age and fell in love with music-making. Her years as a cellist at the High School of Music and Art changed direction when, one day, the teacher fell ill and Janna jumped on the podium to conduct a rehearsal. Amazed at the orchestra's positive response, she decided conducting was for her. After a BM from the University of Wisconsin, she went on to an MM at the Cincinnati College-Conservatory with a conducting fellowship. Summers were spent in master classes at Tanglewood, Aspen, Sandpoint and the Conductors' Guild Institute, where her teachers included **Leonard Bernstein**, **Gustav Meier**, **Otto Werner-Mueller** and **Gunther Schuller**. She also studied at Yale, Mannes and Juilliard.

Working her way up, from 1982–84 Hymes was music director of the Young People's Symphony in Stamford, Connecticut. 1987–88, she was director of Orchestral Studies at the Cincinnati School for Performing Arts, during which time she guest conducted the Philharmonia Orchestra of Cincinnati, Orquestra Sinfonica del Estado de Mexico, Spokane Symphony and Orchestre National de Lyon (France). The same year, she founded and directed the I Solisti Cincinnati Chamber Orchestra. 1988–89 found her as a Fulbright Scholar in Palermo (Sicily), as assistant conductor of the Teatro Massimo Opera House. In 1988, she was a prize winner at the Besançon (France) International Conducting Competition. From 1987–92, she was music director for the Cincinnati Composers' Guild. She was also assistant conductor of the Canton Symphony until 1993, and director of orchestras at the University of Akron until 1994. A specialist in electronic and computer music, she was a faculty member at the Worcester (Massachusetts) Polytechnic Institute, 1994–95. During this time she was appointed principal guest conductor of the Delta Ensemble in the Netherlands. Resident conductor of the Charlotte Symphony Orchestra in North Carolina since 1994, and music director of the Columbus Women's Orchestra, in October 1997 she was appointed associate conductor of the Indianapolis Symphony, the first woman on the conducting staff in the orchestra's sixty-eight year history. She retired from this position in 2000 to become music director of Maine Grand Opera, and concentrate on guest conducting, which included being the first woman to conduct the Costa Rica Symphony. In 2004, she became director of the Williamsburg (Virginia) Sinfonia. The same year she was invited to return to Costa Rica.

Janna has two sons, Evan, born February 19, 1993 and Oliver, April 17,1997.

SARAH IOANNIDES, born in 1972, in Canberra, Australia, grew up in the UK where she studied violin, piano and French horn, earning an MA in Music from Oxford. She received a conducting prize from London's Guildhall School of Music and, with a Fulbright Scholarship entered the Curtis Institute in Philadelphia. Her MM in Conducting was earned at Juilliard. During 2000, she was assistant conductor to composer Tan Dun, touring Japan, China, Hong Kong, Russia, France, Germany, Sweden and the UK. 2001 brought the JoAnn Falletta Award. In May 2002, she was appointed assistant conductor of the Cincinnati Symphony under **Parvo Järvi**, the first woman on the conducting staff in CSO history, where she was also director of the Cincinnati Youth Symphony, the tenth since its founding in 1963. In 2005, she became music director for both the Greater Spartanburg (South Carolina) Philharmonic and the El Paso (Texas) Symphony Orchestra.

Sara Jobin

SARA JOBIN was inspired to become a conductor while watching Leonard Bernstein in the summer of 1986, while a piano student at Tanglewood. Born October 26, 1970, she started playing the piano and singing in the church choir when she was eight. Throughout elementary and high school she dabbled in as many orchestral instruments as she could lay her hands on: viola, flute, French horn, and mallet percussion. After college, she added oboe and trumpet. Her love of languages has helped tremendously in the field of opera. She studied Spanish at school, and taught herself the Russian alphabet during French class. A quick learner, she started reading at four and spent a lot of time in school entertaining herself. She attended Radcliffe and Harvard at age sixteen and, upon graduation with highest honors, was awarded the John Knowles Paine Traveling Fellowship. She used this to study conducting for five summers with Charles Bruck at the Pierre Monteux School in Maine, and privately with him in Paris. Moving to San Francisco in 1992, she worked as assistant conductor with the Peninsula Symphony Orchestra in San Mateo, and the Palo Alto Philharmonic, before being asked in 1998 to direct an orchestra of her own, the Tassajara Symphony Orchestra in the San Ramon Valley—all in California. After her fourth season as assistant conductor with Opera San Jose, on May 28, 1999, she was named the winner of the JoAnn Falletta Conducting Award by The Women's Philharmonic. The award, named for TWP's music director (1986–96)—now conductor of the Buffalo Philharmonic—carries with it a cash award funded by Dr. Henry and Sandra Stein. The Steins, after being inspired by seeing Falletta conduct, initiated the scholarship in her honor.

2002 began with Jobin conducting the Tassajara Symphony in "The Genius of Beethoven." On May 5, she directed a thrilling "An Evening with Frederica von Stade," a Benefit Gala for Music in the Schools. (Released 2005 on the Chris Brubeck CD, *Convergence*). The summer featured the orchestra's first Pops Concerts.

Christmas 2003 brought performances of *The Nutcracker* for San Francisco Ballet. In addition to her conducting positions, Jobin was with San Francisco Opera graduating from prompter, rehearsal conductor to staff conductor. In 2004, she became the first woman to conduct main stage performances at SFO with *Tosca* in November and *The Flying Dutchman* in December. In November 2005, she conducted four performances of Bellini's *Norma*, as guest conductor. Now freelancing, a highlight of 2006 was the production of *Transformations*, an opera by Conrad Susa for the SFO Merola Center Program for Young Artists.

Sara earned her black belt in judo and has been an international medalist in kata competition.

Karen Keltner

KAREN KELTNER marked her twenty-fifth year as resident conductor for San Diego Opera in 2006. Born December 24, 1947, in South Bend, Indiana, she received her BM, MM and PhD from Indiana University School of Music, as well as earning degrees in French there and the Université de Strasbourg. While in France, she studied with **Nadia Boulanger** at Fontainebleau. From 1976–80, Keltner was assistant professor of music at the University of Central Florida and assistant conductor of the Brevard Symphony in Melbourne, Florida. She traveled to California in 1980 as one of the five participants—and the only woman—in San Diego Opera's first Young American Opera Conductors Program, and was promptly invited by **Tito Capobianco**, founder of the program, to conduct the San Diego Opera Institute's productions that fall. She later became the first recipient of a National Opera Institute conducting apprenticeship (1981–82), enabling her to remain in San Diego. She made her surprise debut when the maestro thrust her in the pit without rehearsal to conduct the final performance of Prokokiev's *The Love for Three Oranges* in 1981. At season's end, Keltner was offered her present position as San Diego Opera's associate conductor and music administrator. Two years later, when the position became open, she was made resident conductor. She also acts as collaborator and backup to a variety of illustrious guest conductors, amongst whom have been Richard Bonynge, Heinz Fricke, Christopher Keene, and Edoardo Müller.

In 1994, she won the "Women Who Mean Business" Award in Performing Arts, sponsored by the *San Diego Business Journal*.

Keltner spends summers guest conducting opera at such venues as Chatauqua and Glimmerglass (both in New York), Anchorage (Alaska), Orlando (Florida), Charlotte (North Carolina) and Sacramento (California). In 1993, she directed the premiere of *The Pearl Fishers* in San Diego, appeared with Utah and Seattle Operas, opened Opera Carolina's season, and that summer made a heralded debut with New York City Opera, conducting seven performances of *La Bohème* at the New York State Theater, Lincoln Center, and on tour at Wolf Trap. 1995 saw engagements in Charlotte with Opera Carolina (*Salomé*), Opera Company of Philadelphia (*Salomé*), Pittsburgh (*Lucia di Lammermoor*), Salt Lake City (*Abduction from the Seraglio*), Glimmerglass Opera (*Yeomen of the Guard*), a twin bill in Anchorage with *The Magic Flute*, and a celebration of the seventy-fifth anniversary of women's suffrage with *The Mother of Us All* at Eastman (Rochester, New York). 1996 featured *The Elixir of Love* and *La Cenerentola*, her seventeenth production at San Diego Opera, her debut at Cincinnati Opera with *Madama Butterfly*, and Pittsburgh Opera (*The Barber of Seville*). February 8, 1997, marked the San Diego premiere of *L'Italiana in Algieri*. March 1, she directed the stunning world premiere of *The Conquistador* by Myron Fink, a tour de force dealing with the *conversos*, Jews forced to become Catholics to escape persecution by the Spanish Inquisition which followed them to the New World, continuing its barbaric practices for centuries. *La Cenerentola* came in April at Opera Columbus (Ohio). (The preceding three operas all featured rising star mezzo **Vivica Genaux**.) The summer brought a revision of Frank Loesser's *Green Willow* at the Utah Festival in Logan, then *Tosca* with Opera Carolina in October. The *Barber of Seville*, and *Salomé*, featuring the **Ciesinski** sisters **Kristine** and **Katherine**, were directed by her in the 1998 San Diego season. In October, she opened Opera Carolina's thirtieth anniversary season with *Aida*. In 1999, she also opened Syracuse Opera's twenty-fifth anniversary season with *Aida*, followed by Piedmont (North Carolina) Opera with *La Bohème*, and Anchorage Opera with *Rigoletto*, where she returned in 2001 with *Lucia di Lammermoor*. 1999 in San Diego brought Maurice Sendak's production of *Hansel and Gretel* (with the lovely **Adria Firestone** as an unbelievably ugly witch!) and the San Diego premiere of Carlisle Floyd's *Of Mice and Men*. Summer 2000 found Keltner at Utah Festival Opera Company with *The Mikado*. After conducting the San Diego premiere performance of Andre Previn's *A Streetcar Named Desire* (2000), came *Cold Sassy Tree* (2001), which she directed at Opera Carolina in 2002. She opened the 2002–03 SDO season with *Rigoletto*, conducted the western premiere of Tobias Picker's opera *Thérèse Raquin* and closed the season with *The Flying Dutchman*. The summer found her at the Utah Festival Opera with *Nabucco*, and *La Bohème* at Anchorage Opera, where she has been principal guest conductor since 2002. Summer of that year, she opened the UFO with *Rigoletto*.

In February 2004, Keltner directed San Diego Opera's new production of Bizet's *The Pearl Fishers* with imaginative stage sets and costumes by flamboyant British designer **Zandra Rhodes**. The cast included the beautiful, young, fast-rising soprano **Isabel Bayrakdarian**. The critics used the word "superb" when describing the production and the conducting. A fiery *Carmen*, with **Marina Domashenko,** blazed into March 2006.

J. KARLA LEMON, born August 6, 1954, in Walnut Creek, California, has the gift of making community and student orchestras sound like professionals. She was already playing violin when, at age eight, she conducted her first concert using a baton that had come inside a Time-Life book on classical music. Her orchestra was on an LP. Admission was 5¢. At fifteen she was conducting fellow students. As a bassist, she majored in music at UC, Berkeley, conducting their orchestra (1979–85). Further studies were with **Maurice Abravanel** (1903–93), **Edo de Waart** (*b* 1941) and **Gunther Schuller**. Winning the Alfred Hertz Memorial Travelling Fellowship in 1979 got her to the Hochschule für Musik in Freiburg (Germany) for a master's in conducting. Returning to the West Coast, her teachers included Michael Senturia and Denis de Côteau. In 1988, she won recognition at the NEA Affiliate Artists' Conducting Competition.

Her posts have included founding conductor/music director of the Rohnert Park Symphony, near Santa Rosa (1989–94), which she built from a fledgling group into a paid professional ensemble; the experimental music ensemble EARPLAY (San Francisco, 1985–91); and the Alea II Ensemble for Contemporary Music. In 1993 she became the first woman conductor of the Stanford University Symphony since its inception in 1949. Under her guidance, in May 1994 they were named Orchestra of the Year in the Bay Area, citing Lemon for the West Coast premiere of Henryk Górecki's *Symphony of Sorrowful Songs*. She then led the orchestra on a critically acclaimed tour of China. Fall '97, she was promoted to associate professor. In June 2002, the Stanford Symphony appeared in Carnegie Hall, beginning a tour that included London, Oxford and Paris.

Lemon spoke on women composers at the 1994 National Conference of Conductors Guild in San Francisco. January 1995, she recorded **Elinor Armer's** *Open and Shut* (Koch International), Mark Winges' *Aural Colors* (Vienna Modern Masters, 1996), and in 2002, Eric Moe's *Sonnets to Orpheus*, with Christine Brandes, soprano (Koch).

In November 2003, she gave the world premiere of *Open Night*, composed by University of Pennsylvania's Jay Reise, the first work commissioned for Philadelphia's Kimmel Center Presents Fresh Ink, a new music series. The program also included *wissahickon poeTrees* (1998) by **Jennifer Higdon**, and **Chen Yi's** *Qi* (1997).

Lemon's guest conducting engagements include performances with the Henry Mancini Institute[72] in Hollywood, Santa Rosa Symphony, The Women's Philharmonic, Scotia Festival (Halifax, Canada), Oberlin Dance Collective, San Francisco Ballet, San Francisco Contemporary Music Players and the "Works and Process Series" at the Guggenheim Museum in New York.

TANIA LEÓN is a world class conductor born in Cuba. (See Composers.)

---

72. The Henry Mancini Institute (HMI) in Los Angeles is a non-profit organization founded in 1997 by composer/conductor Jack Elliott to honor one of the most successful composers in the history of television and film, a popular pianist and concert conductor. Its mission is to provide year round professional training, outreach programs and performances to nurture the future of music.

Finnish conductor **SUSANNA MÅLKKI** had a career as a cellist, rising to principal of Sweden's prestigious Gothenberg Symphony, 1995–98. At the Sibelius Academy, where she was the only woman in the final year, she studied with Jorma Panula, teacher of Osmo Vänskä—conductor of the Minnesota Orchestra. In 1999, she conducted the Nordic premiere in Helsinki, of Thomas Ades' *Powder Her Face* at the Musica Nova festival, and was then asked by the composer to conduct further performances at the Almeida Festival in London. Other opera commitments have been in Copenhagen and with the Finnish National Opera.

With a broad repertoire, she has conducted symphony and chamber orchestras, contemporary ensembles and opera, including the Birmingham Contemporary Music Group, ASKO Ensemble, Avanti! (Helsinki) and the prominent Ensemble intercontemporain, founded by Pierre Boulez, at the 2004 Lucerne Festival, which was the catalyst for her appointment as their music director. She was artistic director of the Stavanger Symphony (Norway) until 2005, when she took over the Ensemble intercontemporain.

Guest appearances have been with Rotterdam Philharmonic, WDR Cologne, Oslo Philharmonic, Finnish Radio Symphony, Danish National Symphony, Munich and Dresden Philharmonics, Berlin Symphony, City of Birmingham, Hallé and BBC Symphonies.

ANNE MANSON, born September 28, 1961, in Boston, is a Harvard music graduate who also trained at King's College, London, and the RCM, under **Norman Del Mar** (1919–94). She subsequently became a conducting fellow at the Royal Northern College of Music (RNCM) and won the top conducting prizes at both universities. A grant from the British government permitted her to work as **Claudio Abbado**'s assistant on the Salzburg Festival's new production of Janáček's *House of the Dead*. She made history in 1994 as the first woman to conduct at the Festival, when she led an all star cast in a performance of *Boris Godunov* with the Vienna Philharmonic, to public and critical acclaim.

As the founder and music director for eight years of the Mecklenburgh Opera in London—recipient of the 1991 Prudential Award for Opera—she initiated an adventurous repertory of 20th century works, including *The Emperor of Atlantis* (Viktor Ullmann),[73] *Die Weisse Rose* (Udo Zimmermann) and *Manekiny* (Zbigniew Rudzinski), as well as the traditional *Hansel and Gretel* by the original Engelbert Humperdinck, and Mozart's *Marriage of Figaro*, *Così fan Tutte* and *Magic Flute*. Other productions included first British performances of *Petrified*, a one-act opera by the Slovak composer Juraj Beneš (1992), and the London premiere of *Brundibar* by Hans Krasa[74] (1993), which formed part of the South Bank Centre's Czech Music Festival. In 1994, she conducted the world premiere of the newly commissioned *Craig's Progress*, by Martin Butler. Other operatic engagements included John Hawkins' *Echoes* for the Royal Opera House Garden Venture and performances of *Don Pasquale* and *Don Giovanni* with the English Touring Opera. In the 1992–93 season, she conducted the Endymion Ensemble in the premiere of **Nicola Lefanu**'s opera, *Blood Wedding*, mounted by the Women's Playhouse Trust, and made her debut at deSingel with *Il Combattimento*, in a triple bill of operas by Monteverdi and **Judith Weir**, which formed part of Antwerp's "Year of Culture," and was repeated at the Théâtre de la Monnaie, Brussels.

The 1994 season brought *Boris Godunov* with the Vienna Philharmonic, Washington Opera's production of Samuel Barber's *Vanessa* at Kennedy Center, plus guesting with the Iceland and Kansas City Symphonies and the London Mozart Players. 1995–96 saw debuts with the Residentie Orchestra (The Hague), Ensemble intercontemporain (Paris), Spanish National Radio, Orquestra de Madrid, a return to the Vienna Chamber Orchestra, and conducting the London Proms. In 1997, she returned to Washington Opera to conduct a new production of Conrad Susa's *Dangerous Liaisons*.

Present at the Iceland concert was **Henry Fogel**, then president of the Chicago Symphony who, on hearing the concert, recommended Manson to the search committee for the Kansas City (Missouri) Symphony. In October 1998, she made her debut as their music director—her first professional American orchestra—where she spent a successful five years. On leaving the KSO in 2003, she commented to the *Kansas City Star*, "The growth of the

---

73–74. Theresienstadt concentration camp composers who perished in Auschwitz.

orchestra has been incredible, and it has been incredible to be a part of that . . . but I have personal and professional goals, and I really want to spend more time conducting in Europe . . . particularly opera."

She plans to continue her American guest appearances, which have been with the Grant Park Festival (Chicago), Honolulu, Houston, Indianapolis, New Jersey and Utah Symphonies, as well as Saint Paul Chamber Orchestra and Los Angeles Philharmonic.

Citing anecdotes about women conductors, Anne's favorite is, "A concertmaster in Vienna told me my stick technique was excellent, but that . . . my career would go a lot further if I got a more glamorous hairdo."[75]

Odaline Martinez

ODALINE de La MARTINEZ, born October 31, 1949, in Matanzas, Cuba, emigrated to America in 1961, studied at Tulane University (New Orleans), and became a U.S. citizen in 1971. After studying at the RAM (1972–76), she made London her home, founding the chamber ensemble Lontano, which she conducts worldwide in programs of contemporary music. She is also founder-conductor of the London Chamber Symphony (1982), and was the first woman to conduct a BBC Promenade Concert (1984). In the Summer 1994 Proms, she directed a rare production of Dame **Ethel Smyth**'s opera, *The Wreckers*. This was released on a two-CD set by Conifer Records.

In 1988, the Brazilian government awarded de la Martinez the Villa-Lobos Medal in recognition of outstanding work promoting and conducting his music. In 1989, she directed the City of Birmingham Symphony, together with **Simon Rattle** (*b* 1955), in a work for two orchestras by **Toru Takemitsu** (1930–96). That summer she was co-director, with the late **Eduardo Mata**, of VIVA, a festival of Latin American music at London's South Bank Centre. Her New York debut was at Merkin Hall, January 1990. She was honored the same year as a Fellow of the RAM. In October 1990, she made her first return visit to Cuba, on tour with Lontano.

She formed Lorelt, Lontano Records Ltd. (1992), to concentrate on neglected music, as in "British Women Composers" Volumes 1 and 2, which included her own *Canciones* (1983). Her first opera, *Sister Aimée*—based on evangelist Aimée Semple McPherson, premiered in America in 1983. Her second opera is *Esperanza*. In 1992, she programmed and conducted a "fiesta" of Latin American music, *Lontano/Latino*, touring Australia and New Zealand where she took up residency as a special guest of the New Zealand Arts Council. In 1998, she was appointed principal guest conductor of the Mexico City based Camarata of the Americas. She has also performed in Colombia, Sweden and Canada. August 2004 marked the BBC presentation of de la Martinez and Daniel Asia directing Lontano in a concert of American works by Asia and Earle Brown. The same year, CDs were released featuring New Zealand women composers, and the Concerto for Violin, Horn and Orchestra with BBC Philharmonic.

De la Martinez champions music by women and the rich classical repertoire of Latin America. She commissions more British and international composers in a single season than many conductors in an entire career. As musical director of Lontano, the European Woman's Orchestra, and the London Chamber Symphony, she is a key figure in the city's musical life, and maintains a busy worldwide schedule of tours and lectures.

Born in Rome, **SILVIA MASARELLI** studied there and Paris, making her conducting debut with the Ensemble International de Paris (1991). She received a scholarship from the French government and the Nadia and Lili Boulanger Foundation to study conducting at the Paris Conservatoire. A year later she won the Grand Prix de Direction d'Orchestre at the Forty-third International Competition in Besançon, as well as the Special Press Prize at the International Prokofiev Competition in St. Petersburg. She has conducted many premier orchestras including the Vienna Chamber Orchestra, Orchestre du Capitol de Toulouse (France), and the New York Philharmonic. Her first CD by Phoenix Classics contains unpublished music for flute and chamber orchestra by C. P. E. Bach, Stamitz and Schwindel.

---

75. Are male maestros ever told to change their hairstyles? Author's query.

Amy Mills

AMY MILLS, founder and conductor of the National Women's Orchestra, was born September 26, 1955, in Milwaukee, Wisconsin. Interested in all instruments from early childhood, she started piano at age five, clarinet in fifth grade and guitar in sixth. She got a chance to conduct her high school band and realized that this was the perfect vocation to encompass all her musical skills and abilities, and enable her to shape and mold the entire texture of the music. She went to Northwestern University for her B. Mus. Ed. (1977) and MM in conducting (1978), then to Catholic University for her Conducting DMA (1987). She also studied privately with Gustav Meier and **Margaret Hillis**. Beginning her series of firsts, Amy was the first woman to conduct CU's marching band before 60,000 football fans. Upon graduation, she received an offer from the Air Force. Although she became the first woman to pass the conducting audition, she rejected the offered position, not yet ready to commit her life to the military. After gaining two valuable years of experience teaching and leading high school bands, she joined the Air Force in 1980, beginning a highly distinguished ten-year career accumulating more "firsts" as first woman to conduct the *Singing Sergeants* (1987), promotion to vice commander of the premier USAF Band (1989), and first female acting commander, during the Gulf War. She resigned from active duty in June 1991, having already founded the National Women's Symphony.

As its music director, with fifty-two union members of both genders, this professional orchestra is dedicated to filling the yawning programming gap by providing a showcase for the music of women composers, past and present. The orchestra has also collaborated with the Norwegian and Canadian embassies in presenting American premieres of women composers of their countries. Since its first concert, June 1992, the ensemble annually draws ever enlarging, enthusiastic audiences, who were treated to the first performance, May 23, 1999, of **Melinda Wagner**'s *Concerto for Flute, Strings and Percussion*, a work that was awarded the 1999 Pulitzer Prize just a few weeks before.

The La Crosse (Wisconsin) Symphony Orchestra, in 1995, chose Amy Mills as the first woman music director in its over one hundred year history. Since then, its concert schedule has doubled, and through her personal involvement in fund-raising, its budget has increased 78 percent, with musicians' pay risen to attract higher level players. Besides recording its first CD, Mills has initiated commercial radio broadcasts of concerts, and since 1998 co-hosted and co-produced a radio show prior to each concert on Wisconsin Public Radio. January 2005 marks the fifth annual Rising Stars Tri-State Concerto Competition for students fourteen through eighteen years of age.

Her guest conducting has taken her to the Houston Symphony for the 1988 presidential inauguration. She has led the Symphonies of New York City Centre, Arlington (Virginia), Springfield (Missouri), Acadiana (Louisiana) and Winona (Minnesota). She has served as cover conductor for the National Symphony Orchestra in Washington, DC. Her Russian debut was in 1997 conducting the Dubna Symphony. Her Polish debut came in March 2003. In the summer of 2002 she served on the faculty of the Conductors' Institute at Bard College.

Amy married Ley Mills, an accountant, in 1987.

CHEAN SEE OOI became resident conductor of the Malaysian Philharmonic Orchestra in 1997, which gave its inaugural concert in the capital, Kuala Lumpur, August 1998. Born in Malaysia, she studied piano as a child. By 1987, she was in Cologne studying conducting with Volker Wangenheim, graduating in 1991. The same year, she won first prize at the International Conductors Competition in both Halle and Hamm. She remained in Germany until 1994 as first conductor of the Classic Philharmonic of Bonn, subsequently guest conducting in Halle (birthplace of Handel), in the Beethovenhalle, Bonn (birthplace of Beethoven), Bremen, the Southwest German Chamber Orchestra, Czech Philharmonic, Bohemian Chamber and Czech Virtuosi. In collaboration with Dresden State Opera, she directed *Fidelio* and *The Magic Flute* in Salvador de Bahia (Brazil). She has led workshops in Germany, France, and with the Jeunesses Musicales World Orchestra in Manila (Philippines). In 2002, she was awarded the prestigious Eisenhower Fellowship, for which she came to the U.S. to be among the other recipients from around the world who have been rewarded for excellence in their profession and potential for advanced leadership.

Eve Queler

EVE QUELER founded the Opera Orchestra of New York (OONY) in 1967 to give young singers and instrumentalists performance experience without the expense of staging and scenery. Besides this accomplishment, she is a woman of many firsts: the first American woman to hold a full time conductorship; the first woman to conduct the symphony orchestras of Philadelphia, Cleveland, Toledo, Hartford, New Jersey, San Antonio, Jacksonville, Kansas City, Montreal and Edmonton (Canada) and Puerto Rico; the first woman to conduct a concert at Lincoln Center; the first American woman, for over thirty-five years, to have conducted major orchestras in Europe, including ORTF (Radio France), Rome Opera, Prague National Theater and the New Philharmonia of London.

Born in New York, January 11, 1936, she began formal piano lessons at five when she won a scholarship to the High School of Music and Art in the Bronx. Her studies with famed conductors included **Carl Bamberger** (1902–87) at New York's Mannes College of Music, **Walter Susskind** (1913–80) in St. Louis, plus **Igor Markevitch** (1912–83) and **Herbert Blomstedt** (*b* 1927) in Europe. From 1965–70, Queler served as assistant conductor and musical coach with the New York City Opera.

Her European opera debut was with Verdi's *I Vespri Siciliani* with Plácido Domingo and **Montserrat Caballé** in Barcelona. She conducted *Carmen* and *Rigoletto* at the Smetana Theater in Prague. With Czech origins in her family, it was Queler who introduced Czech opera *sung in its native language* beginning with Smetana's *Daliborin* in 1978, followed by Janáček's *Kát'a Kabanová* and *Jenůfa*. In 1987, she was the first person to conduct Dvořák's *Rusalka* in Czech in the U.S. She premiered Shostakovich's version of *Khovanshchina*, Smetana's *Libuse* and Respighi's *Belfagor*.

She regularly conducts opera and chamber concerts in Czechoslovakia. Her 1994 debuts included three performances each of *Don Pasquale* at Hamburg Opera and Janáček's *Jenůfa* in Bonn. In 1995, she returned to Bonn for *La traviata*, Canada for Rossini's *Barber of Seville* and South Africa for *Tales of Hoffmann*, plus symphonic concerts there. Performances of Massenet's *Hérodiade*, Rimsky-Korsakov's *The Tsar's Bride*, Bellini's *I Puritani* and *Norma*, and a gala duet concert with **Olga Borodina** and Dimitri Hvorastovsky in Carnegie Hall with the Opera Orchestra of New York.

Queler's extraordinary gift for communication through her music-making results in a rapport with the world's greatest singers, many of whom have appeared with her on numerous occasions. She is a pioneer in exploring repertoire never staged or recorded. Among her firsts in this genre are Verdi's *Arnoldo* with Caballé, Massenet's *Le Cid* (Domingo), Puccini's *Edgar* (Carlo Bergonzi, **Renata Scotto**), Donizetti's *Gemma di Vergy* (Caballé), Strauss' *Guntram*, Boito's *Nerone* and Janáček's *Jenůfa* (**Gabriela Beňačková**, **Leonie Rysanek**).

On the international scene, in 1996 she conducted *Fidelio* with Bonn Opera, and *Flying Dutchman* in Kassel, Germany. In 1997 it was *I Puritani* in Aarhus, Denmark, and Rossini's *Tancredi* with Frankfurt Opera. With OONY, in 1997, she did *Tristan und Isolde*, and Verdi's *Ernani*. In 1998 her season included Verdi's *Jérusalem* and Donizetti's *Poliuto*. March 2001, she presented Donizetti's *La Favorita*, nuancing the *bel canto* part with an orchestra and chorus three times the size any 19th century composer would have written for, followed in April with Meyerbeer's *Les Huguenots*, an opera not heard in New York since 1969, not because the style is out of fashion, but because it requires enormous forces and singers who can negotiate treacherous lines. May brought *Les Huguenots*, and *Maria Stuarda*, with **Ruth Ann Swenson** and **Lauren Flanigan** at Carnegie Hall.

Abroad, Queler has guested at Nice Opera (France), Teatro Liceu (Barcelona) presenting *I Vespri Siciliani* with Caballé and Domingo, Australian National Opera in Sydney (*Abduction from the Seraglio*), NYCO (*Marriage of Figaro* with Samuel Ramey), Las Palmas (*Elisir d'Amore*), *Mazeppa* at the Mariinsky Theater/Kirov Opera, St. Petersburg, *Jenůfa* at the National Theater Brno (Czech Republic), Hamburg Staatsoper (*Don Pasquale*), Kassel Opera (*Der fliegende Hollander*), Narodni Divaldo (National Theater), Prague (*Carmen*, *Rigoletto*) and at Bonn, *Jenůfa*, *La traviata* and *Fidelio*. She also conducted concert version performances at the Salle Pleyel in Paris, a gala performance of Bellini's *I Puritani* with Alfredo Kraus and the Philharmonic Orchestra at the Royal Festival Hall, London, and Giordano's *Fedora* for the French Radio ORTF in Paris. In South Africa she directed a production of *Tales of Hoffman* at the Pretoria Arts Center, as well as an opera gala for the South African TV, plus Orff's *Carmina Burana* and the Sibelius violin concerto. In Canada, she presented *Il Barbiere di Seviglia* with Opera Hamilton. Gala Verdi concerts in Mannheim and Wiesbaden, came in January 1996. In June the same year, she guested at the Las Palmas Opera Festival with *Fidelio*.

In symphonic repertory, Queler has worked with the Philadelphia, Cleveland, Montreal, Edmonton, San Antonio Orchestras, Rome Opera and many others.

Maestra Queler has been highly commended for having the courage to put on these works. Thanks to her, major companies have been enriched with new repertoire of operas in their native language. Monday, March 11, 1996, was proclaimed by New York Mayor Rudolph Giuliani as "Opera Orchestra of New York Day" in honor of Queler's twenty-fifth anniversary as founder/conductor. Greetings poured in from all over the world.

On November 3, 2003, Eve Queler received the insignia of the Chevalier of the Order of Arts and Letters from Jean-René Gehan, Cultural Counselor of the French Embassy.

Eve has been married to Stanley N. Queler since 1956, when she worked at a variety of musical jobs to help him get through law school. (Which he successfully did.)

Andrea Quinn

ANDREA QUINN, born in 1964 in England, studied conducting at the Royal Academy of Music graduating in 1989 with the Ernest Read and Ricordi Conducting Prizes. She then earned the National Association of Youth Orchestras Conductor's Bursary for study abroad, which took her to Hungary for the Bartók International Seminar. Next came a one year conducting fellowship at the Birmingham Conservatory. In 1992, she worked as an assistant conductor to Oliver Knussen on the Contemporary Performance and Composition course at Snape Maltings. She was music director of the London Philharmonic Youth Orchestra (1994–97), meanwhile making her debut with the London Philharmonic in November 1995, conducting the chamber ensemble in Britten's *War Requiem* at Royal Festival Hall.

In 1993, she won the *Conduct for Dance* competition, which led to guest conducting the Birmingham Royal Ballet for the 1993–94 season, and acted as music director for the Royal Ballet's 1996 spring tour of three newly-commissioned works. In 1995, she participated in the Oxford Contemporary Music Festival directing the Endymion Ensemble. She conducted the English National Ballet's *Nutcracker* at Royal Festival Hall and led the European Chamber Opera in a new production of *Don Giovanni* in 1996. Other guest appearances have been with the London Symphony, Royal Philharmonic, BBC National Orchestra of Wales, Scottish Symphony and the Hallé Orchestra. She made her BBC Proms debut in 2000. On the Continent, she was in Oslo (Norway), Germany and Italy. She has also been "down under" with the Adelaide and Melbourne Symphonies. Until December 1994, Quinn was music director of the Lloyd's Choir. In 1997, she accepted the post of music director of the Hertfordshire Chamber Orchestra, and made her debut at the Royal Opera House conducting the Royal Ballet's *Anastasia*, with whom she also did *Swan Lake* in Boston, as well as excerpts from ballets by Copland, Adams and Shostakovich for NYC Ballet at the Edinburgh Festival, and performances with the National Orchestra of Puerto Rico and Norrlands Opera. From 1998–2001, she was music director of the Royal Ballet in London.

For her 2001 EMI CD of Paul McCartney's *Tuesday* with the London Orchestra, she was nominated Female Artist of the Year, by the British Phonographic Industry's inaugural Classical Brit Awards.

In June 2001, for the first time in its history, the New York City Ballet had a woman in charge of its orchestra when Quinn became their music director, succeeding Gordon Boelzner who retired after forty-one years. In making the appointment, Ballet Master Peter Martins said, "With Andrea Quinn we have found the perfect person to ensure that the company's musical heritage will be fostered at the highest possible level . . . she has already earned the respect and affection of our musicians and dancers."

After five years she relinquished this position in June 2006, to return to London to live in Europe with her husband and children. Her new position is music director and chief conductor of the Norrlands Opera and Symphony Orchestra in Umea, Sweden.

Kay Roberts

KAY GEORGE ROBERTS, born September 16, 1950, in Nashville, Tennessee, grew up in a musical family close to Fisk University where her father, Dr. Shearly Oliver Roberts, was chair of the psychology department. Her mother was a pianist, but in the segregated schools of the '50s, black children had no opportunities to make music until Robert Holmes, a teacher, appealed to the Supervisor and was given permission to organize an all-black ensemble, the Cremona Strings, in which fourth grader Kay became an excellent violinist. Not until 1964, with the advent of Thor Johnson to the Nashville Symphony, was its Youth Symphony open to blacks. By her senior year in high school, she was playing professionally with the parent orchestra throughout her undergraduate years at Fisk.

In 1971, Arthur Fiedler, conductor of the Boston Pops (1930–79), organized the World Symphony Orchestra with participants from sixty countries, thirty-four states, and the District of Columbia. First violinist Roberts represented the Nashville Symphony, one of five blacks, three of whom were women.

She met **Leonard Bernstein**, during a violin fellowship at Tanglewood in her junior year, who convinced her to switch from math to music. She also attended master classes of world-famous maestros, **Seiji Ozawa**, **André Previn**, **Edo deWaart** and **John Eliot Gardiner**. With several scholarships, including the National Fellowship Fund for Black Americans, she was able to go to Yale Music School where her 1975 MMA degree denoted completion of pre-doctoral studies required for the doctor of musical arts degree—the latter conferred only after a candidate has demonstrated his or her qualifications through distinguished achievement in the profession. Her graduate conducting courses with **Otto Werner-Mueller** gave her the opportunity to lead rehearsals when she accompanied him on guest appearances. Her professional debut came in 1976, conducting her hometown Nashville Symphony. In 1978, she accepted the position of assistant professor of music and conductor of the orchestra of the University of Massachusetts at Lowell, concurrently serving as assistant conductor for several regional New England orchestras. Her administrative skills were in evidence as executive director, 1984–85, of Boston's Project STEP (String Training and Educational Program for Minority Students), sponsored by the Boston Symphony, Boston University, and the Greater Boston Youth Symphony Orchestra.

In 1986, she became the first woman to receive a DMA in orchestral conducting from Yale. That summer she was invited to Thailand, and became the first woman and first black, to conduct the Bangkok Symphony. She returned the following year for a concert honoring the King on his sixtieth birthday. The celebration was publicized as one of the most important cultural events of the year. July 1987, she made her New York conducting debut with the New York City Housing Authority Symphony, a professional orchestra founded in 1971, with sixty members from minority groups. She has directed them several times, including at Lincoln Center.

Roberts reached the big league when she conducted the Detroit Symphony, in 1989, in their "A Celebration of African-American Sacred Music" program. During the same year, she led a chamber ensemble in a performance of Gloria Coates' "Voices of Women in Wartime" as a part of the American Women Composers Fourth Annual Marathon in Watertown (Massachusetts.)

She took a sabbatical year (1989–90) in Germany, where she was appointed conductor of the Artemis Ensemble in Stuttgart, performing and recording works by women composers. She also received a grant from the German Academic Exchange Service for research on German women composers, and founded Ensemble Americana, a professional chamber group promoting contemporary American music in Germany. Composed of American and German professional musicians in the Stuttgart area, the group has an ongoing relationship with Roberts. In America, she directs the Black Music Repertory Ensemble of Chicago, a professional group with classical repertoire by African-American composers from the 1800s to the present.

A highlight of her career was her conducting the Cleveland Symphony's annual Martin Luther King, Jr. Concert, January 1993, which included singers of all races and creeds from sixty-two church choirs. Her success secured a return engagement the following year.

Roberts is a recipient of the 1991 Outstanding Woman in the Performing Arts from the League of Black Women, Chicago, the 1993 National Achievement Award from the National Black Music Caucus, and the Tenth Anniversary Celebration Award, 1999, from the Lowell (Massachusetts) Office of Cultural Affairs for her contribution to cultural development over the past decade.

She has also guest conducted with Dallas, Indianapolis, Jacksonville, Louisiana Philharmonic, Nashville, and National Symphony Orchestras, among others, with re-engagements during the 2000 season at the Blossom Festival in Cleveland, Shreveport, plus a highly acclaimed debut at the Lugano Festival with the Orchestra Svizzera Italiana.

Her goal is to have audiences experience the range of styles of American composers, and bring new insights to the classics, leading audiences to new and overlooked music. While the podium pecking order is still European men, American white men, minority men, white women, and finally, minority women, Kay George Roberts is, in her own words, unfazed by being "a minority within a minority," and seeks only to be known as a qualified conductor.

TERESA RODRÍGUEZ (García) was born in Saltillo, Coahuila, Mexico. Her family was not musical, although her grandmother had a piano in her house. Teresa's introduction to music was in the form of piano lessons in elementary school. She studied piano and orchestral conducting at the National Conservatory of Mexico, in the Olleen Yolizply School of Life and Movement and the Higher School of Music in Paris. She won a scholarship from the National Fund for Culture and Arts.

Her orchestral conducting debut was in the Teatro de la Ciudad in 1979. In New York she specialized in choral conducting. She also worked in the National Opera Company for five years, as well as the New Jersey Opera Company, and in workshops in North Carolina, Israel, Italy and Shanghai.

Among the operas Rodríguez has directed are *El niño y los Sortilegios* (The Child and the Enchantments), *Don Pasquale, Gianni Schicchi, Il Campanello, I Pagliacci, The Medium, Bastian and Bastienne, The Telephone, Amahl and the Night Visitors.* She has directed the orchestras of Guanajuato, Pachuca, Youth Symphony of Mexico, Coahuila Chamber, Madrigal Choir and the Carlos Chavez Symphony, with whom she gave the world premieres of *Ingesu* by Chapela and *Concerto for Piano and Orchestra* by **Georgina Derbez**. She was assistant conductor of the Youth Symphony of Toluca.

As the artistic director of the Artescenica Foundation, she receives support from FONCA via the Mexico en Escena (Mexico in Scene) Competition, and has organized opera summer workshops in Saltillo, Coahuila, from 2002–05. She is the director of the SIVAM opera workshop. A very personable maestra, most of her performances have been in Mexico.

Teresa has two children Gabriel and Andrea, from her former marriage to tenor Fernando de la Mora.

Madeline Schatz

MADELINE SCHATZ, born June 22, 1947, in New York, received her musical training in Los Angeles with some of the world's foremost virtuosi: **Josef Gingold** (1909–95), **Eudice Shapiro, Henryk Szeryng**, violin; **Willliam Primrose** (1903–82), viola; **Michael Tilson-Thomas** (*b* 1944) and **Daniel Lewis** (*b* 1925), conducting. Her MM (*summa cum laude*) is from Indiana University. Her DMA (*summa cum laude*) from USC was received as a Kent Fellow, sponsored by the Danforth Foundation of St. Louis—the first music major to have this honor.

A five-time grand prize winner in the International Coleman Chamber Music Competition, Schatz studied with the Juilliard, Netherlands and Amadeus Quartets. She has performed internationally as a concert artist on violin and viola, as well as a member of the Los Angeles and California Chamber Symphonies, playing under such conductors as **Zubin Mehta** and **Erich Leinsdorf**.

With extensive conducting experience at music festivals, regional orchestras and The Women's Philharmonic, Schatz was music director of the Fairbanks (Alaska) Symphony and Arctic Chamber Orchestra, as well as professor and head of the music department at the University of Fairbanks, 1990–2000. Her description at the time was most poetic: "Sitka is my favorite place in Alaska. I play in the music festival most summers. The performance hall has a glass wall in back and looks out on the bay with eagles soaring, while the music provides a gorgeous background for Mother Nature. It was in Sitka that I disembarked from my Princess cruise eleven years ago and declared to myself that I was going to move to this State. Synchronicity provided me with a job opening to apply for as soon as I returned home to Utah! The rest is history!"

She developed an in-school education program, between the Fairbanks Symphony Orchestra and the Fairbanks North Star Borough Public School, to interest young people in classical music. June 2000 marked the MMC-CD release of *Powell Canyons*, a work she commissioned from Henry Wolking, with her conducting the London Symphony at the Abbey Road Studios. In her words, "The work is fabulous, the recording is beautifully mastered, and I had the time of my life doing the recording in 1996."

She moved to Hawaii in 2001 and is teaching music and orchestra at the Hawaii Preparatory Academy in Kualema on the Big Island.

ELIZABETH SCHULZE became music director of the Maryland Symphony on July 1, 1999, after completing four years as associate conductor of the National Symphony Orchestra where she was appointed by Maestro **Leonard Slatkin**. She was the first woman to join the conducting staff of the NSO. Her subscription, educational and Pops programs at Kennedy Center and Wolf Trap were highly successful. Called on April 6, 1995, to step in at the last minute, she made an acclaimed Classical Subscription debut featuring Berlioz' *Symphonie fantastique* at Kennedy Center. (She had made her NSO debut appearance, Labor Day 1994, before an audience of over 50,000 in a critically acclaimed concert on the Capitol lawn, and appropriately conducted her last concert with them, Labor Day, 1998.)

Born October 2, 1957, in Waterloo, Iowa, Schulze comes from a long line of musicians. Her great great-uncle, Benno Eban, was an early conductor of the Cincinnati Symphony. His three sons were also musicians. Wilhelm, a concert cellist, played with **Victor Herbert**. In 1901, when President William McKinley was shot at the Buffalo Pan-American Exposition, the assassin, Leon Czolgosz, tried to hide in Wilhelm's cello case! (What history has not recorded, according to Uncle Wilhelm, was that although that new-fangled invention called an X-ray machine existed, it was *not* used on the president to locate the bullet, which the doctors could not find, and which killed him eight days later.)

Besides playing the violin since she was seven, Elizabeth liked to conduct any music she heard and was encouraged by her mother, a poet of Irish extraction. An honors graduate of the Interlochen Arts Academy and Bryn Mawr College (BA *cum laude*, philosophy), she holds graduate degrees in orchestral and choral conducting from SUNY, Stony Brook. She was the first doctoral fellow in orchestral conducting at Northwestern University (Illinois), working with Victor Yampolsky. She was also a conducting fellow at *L'École d'Arts Américaines* in France as well as at prestigious music festivals in America. At Aspen, she worked with **Murry Sidlin**, **Lawrence Foster** and **Sergiu Commissiona**. As a Tanglewood Fellow, she worked with **Seiji Ozawa**, Gustav Meier and **Leonard Bernstein**.

As music director of the Waterloo/Cedar Falls (Iowa) Symphony, 1994–97, her challenging programming brought that orchestra to new levels of achievement. Sponsored by the NEA, she served as assistant conductor of the Buffalo Philharmonic Orchestra, 1992–95. She also had seven seasons as music director of the Kenosha (Wisconsin) Symphony and was assistant conductor at the 1992 Aspen Music Festival, where she had won the first Aspen Music School Conducting Award (1991). Besides numerous guest appearances, her operatic conducting engagements include *Cavalleria Rusticana* (Colorado Opera Troupe) and *Hansel and Gretel* (Tulsa Opera).

In 1992, she guest conducted the Bastille Opera (Paris). 1996 saw her European debut leading the Mainz Chamber Orchestra for the opening concert of the Atlantic Festival in Kaiserslautern, Germany. She appeared in

Paris, London, Frankfurt, Amsterdam, and Vienna with the NSO during their 1997 European tour. The same year, she led the American Composer's Orchestra in educational and family concerts throughout the five boroughs of New York and in Carnegie Hall. For several years she conducted the Kennedy Center/NSO Summer Music Institute for gifted youth. Her interest in music education led to interactive broadcasts of concerts to classrooms throughout Iowa. She originated the acclaimed multimedia series "Sight, Sound and Symphony."

Besides her Maryland Symphony post, Schulze is a guest conductor with the University of Maryland Symphony and the Omaha Symphony. She returned for a third season at Denver to conduct the Colorado Opera Troupe's production of *La Bohème*. Most prestigious is her selection as conducting assistant and cover conductor for the New York Philharmonic.

An excerpt from a 2004 visiting Korean student's essay on attending a concert is quite illuminating:

> The orchestra began tuning and soon the lights were turned off. When a conductor walked out of the backstage, I was fairly stunned to see that the conductor was a woman, since it is very rare to find a female conductor in Korea.
>
> Elizabeth Schulze, led the orchestra with an enthusiasm and powerfulness that I had never seen before, even from male conductors. What was really interesting was that she explained some significant parts of the music so that the audience could easily appreciate the piece that was thought to be difficult to figure out.

> —Eun Young Hur

FRANCES STEINER, a native of Portland, Oregon, has many firsts in her field. In 1977, she was the first woman to direct a professional orchestra—the Glendale Symphony—at the Los Angeles Music Center, in the Dorothy Chandler Pavilion. In 1984, she was the first female conductor of the Maracaibo (Venezuela) Symphony, and the next year, first to conduct the National Symphony Orchestra of the Dominican Republic.

Born February 25, 1937, to a violinist mother and a cellist/conductor father, the child was surrounded by music and, like her older sister Diana who plays violin, Frances has perfect pitch. The family moved to Philadelphia in 1939 so that Diana could attend Curtis, whose faculty at the time included such luminaries as violinist **Efrem Zimbalist** (1889–1985), pianist **Josef Hofmann** (1876–1957) and cellist **Gregor Piatigorsky** (1903–76). Frances began her musical studies on the cello at age three, and at eight won a scholarship to study with the legendary **Gregor Piatigorsky** at Curtis. The same year, her composition *Country Dance* won a children's composition contest that was conducted in concert by **Eugene Ormandy**. She received her BS in education from Temple University (1956), and an MA, focusing on composition, from Harvard (1958). In the summer of 1957, she won a scholarship to the Fontainbleau School in France to study with **Nadia Boulanger**, who shortly after spent a month in Cambridge, Massachusetts, where Frances had the honor of performing with her.

1965 brought a move to Los Angeles, and four years later a DMA from USC. 1965 also marked Frances' marriage to lawyer, Mervyn Tarlow. She joined the faculty of Cal. State Dominguez Hills in 1967, where she formed a community/student orchestra which became the Carson-Dominguez Hills Symphony. Concurrently, she was principal cellist in the Glendale Symphony, conducted by **Carmen Dragon** (1914–84), whose ranks teemed with some of the best film studio players, and the assistant principal with the Los Angeles Chamber Orchestra. She was one of only four female conductors nationwide in 1974. In 1975, daughter Sarah arrived, who in her college years studied history at Oxford.

A former principal cellist with the New York Festival Orchestra at Lincoln Center, she was also an instructor in music theory, orchestra, counterpoint instrumentation, conducting, interpretation, baroque and classical history. She is a recipient of the Status of Women Elizabeth Mathias Award.

Steiner has been music director and conductor of the Chamber Orchestra of the South Bay since 1974, and the Carson-Dominguez Hills Symphony since 1977—both in Southern California. She has made guest appearances with the Long Beach and Oakland Symphonies, and orchestras of the Dominican Republic and Maracaibo, Venezuela. She won the Conductor's Guild Prize in the American Conductors Competition in 1978. In 1999, COSB played the world premiere of their commissioned Flute Concerto by **Augusta Read Thomas**, which received excellent reviews in the *Los Angeles Times*. In May 2004, their featured soloist was 2001 Van Cliburn winner, **Olga Kern**.

ANU TALI, with her twin sister Kadri—the practical businesswoman—founded the Nordic Symphony Orchestra of Estonia in 1997 for the celebrations of Finland's eightieth birthday. Striking blondes, locals belittled them as "glamour queens," but their debut was so promising they now perform annual concerts in the capital, Tallinn. The orchestra, composed of young musicians from fifteen countries, perform five times a year. Despite their youth—they were born in 1972—senior musicians are not alienated, as Kadri says: "as long as they think you are ambitious and trying to achieve something. They know how much work is involved in running an orchestra."

Anu began training as a pianist at the Tallinn Music High School, graduated in conducting from the Estonian Music Academy (1995), then studied at St. Petersburg Conservatory, and with Jorma Panula at the Sibelius Academy, Helsinki. She has appeared with the Estonian National Symphony and guest conducted in Finland, Latvia, Slovakia, Russia, Austria, Sweden and Germany. Since 2002, she has been the conductor of Vanemuine Opera of Estonia, and during 2004–05 led the Japan Philharmonic and the New Jersey Symphony.

The NSO has released two CDs with Warner Classics: *Swan Flight* (2002) and *Action Passion Illusion* (2005). At the Echo Klassic Awards (2003) in Germany, Anu was named Young Artist of the Year for *Swan Flight*, and received the Cultural Award of Estonia (2003), and Presidential Award of Estonia (2004) for her work introducing Estonian music to the world.

Kate Tamarkin

KATE TAMARKIN, born November 26, 1955, in Newport Beach, California, was brought up with music. Her mother, Dorothy, studied ballet and flamenco dancing, and participated in the USO entertaining troops during World War II. In high school, Kate taught herself French horn and earned a horn scholarship to Chapman College. She had no thought of becoming a conductor until she took the required course as part of her music teaching credential and was inspired. She received her MM from Northwestern and DMA from Peabody, becoming a conducting fellow at Aspen and a student at the Accademia Musicale Chigiana (Siena, Italy), where one of her teachers was famed maestro **Franco Ferrara** (1911–85).

Tamarkin's "apprentice" years included teaching a junior high school ensemble of ninety guitars, and thirty-two vocal classes from kindergarten through eighth grade. Her first music directorship was with the Fox Valley Community Orchestra in Appleton, Wisconsin (1982–90), while commuting to Baltimore to attend Peabody. In 1987, she was a winner in the Association of Professional Vocal Ensembles National Conducting Competition. As a conducting fellow at Tanglewood that same year, she studied with **Seiji Ozawa** and **Leonard Bernstein** (1918–90). In June 1988, she was one of three young conductors to work with Bernstein and the Chicago Symphony, and was chosen to conduct that orchestra in a performance of Strauss' *Don Juan* as part of the American Conductors Program. At the ASOL annual conference, she conducted in front of 2000 concert managers, which led to her appointment, beginning in the 1989–90 season, as associate conductor of the Dallas Symphony under the late **Eduardo Mata** (1942–95), who was tragically killed in a private plane crash. At the invitation of the city of Dallas, she had the honor of directing a command performance for Her Majesty Queen Elizabeth II of England during her American tour in 1991. Tamarkin won high praise for inaugurating the orchestra's first televised Christmas concert, viewed by half a million, followed by re-engagements for telecasts in 1993 and 1994. In summer 1994, she conducted the orchestra in a special concert at the American Guild of Organists annual convention. She left Dallas at the end of the season.

Winning the post over 400 applicants, she was music director of the Vermont Symphony Orchestra from 1991 until May 1999. While in this position, she took the orchestra to an unprecedented number of communities throughout the state, led a performance of Bernstein's *Chichester Psalms*, marking the debut of the Vermont Symphony Chorus under the direction of Robert De Cormier, and programmed works of major women composers. Charming hundreds of new classical music listeners through her innovative repertoire, she increased the concert season from thirty to forty-five concerts and the budget from $700,000 to $1.2 million and, as an advocate of education, initiated the "Side-by-Side" program with the Vermont Youth Orchestra. A fund has been established in her name to support the youth activities of the VSO.

She was music director of the East Texas (Tyler) Symphony 1992–2002, as well as pursuing a busy guest conducting schedule. Since 1997, she has served as visiting director of orchestra programs at the University of Minnesota. One of her guest appearances was with the Monterey (California) Symphony in November 1998, enthusiastically received by both orchestra and audience. In June 1999, she became—after their two year search—the first woman music director in the seventy-five member orchestra's fifty-four year history. Another 1999 accolade was being chosen by the National Women Conductors Initiative, conceived by The Women's Philharmonic in San Francisco, to serve on its fifteen-member steering committee, helping nurture and identify young women conductors. A personal $10,000 development grant accompanied this honor.

February 27, 2002, Tamarkin directed the Monterey Symphony in the world premiere of their commissioned work honoring the 100th birthday of John Steinbeck (1902–68). A Salinas native, and one of the world's most widely-read authors, his major fiction is set in Northern California's Monterey County. The thirty-minute piece, *And in the air these sounds*... "a monodrama for baritone and orchestra," was composed by Allen Shawn with original text by Jamaica Kincaid. Other engagements include the Edmonton Symphony (Canada), Carolina Chamber Symphony, a rousing return to the Vermont Symphony, and in May 2004, the Shanghai Symphony (China).

Filling the cup for Tamarkin was her marriage, October 1999, to physicist Clifford Arnold, thus instantly becoming the mother of a teenage son, Nathan. (As of 2007, a political science senior at the University of Wisconsin, Milwaukee.)

In 2003 Kate accepted a faculty position at the Benjamin T. Rome School of Music, Catholic University of America (Washington, DC). Their first, full-time conductor, she built up their orchestra and developed a graduate conducting program. Besides having to relocate from her Minnesota home, and because of the coast to coast commute, she decided not to renew her Monterey contract after the 2003–2004 season. A 2005 highlight was conducting *The Magic Flute* for Summer Opera Theatre. In June 2006, chosen from 100 applicants representing three continents, Tamarkin accepted the position of music director—the third in their history—of the Charlottesville and University Symphony Orchestra, as well as the New Music Ensemble. As a professor on the UVA faculty, she teaches courses in instrumental conducting and "Exploring the Orchestra." With extra perks like directing the Peabody Conservatory production of *Marriage of Figaro* November 2006, Kate feels that she has truly found her niche.

BEVERLY TAYLOR, born February 1, 1951, in Philadelphia, holds degrees from the University of Delaware and Boston University School for the Arts, studying with, among others, Gustav Meier, Herbert Blomstedt and choral directors **Robert Shaw** and **Margaret Hillis**. She was associate director of choral activities at Harvard (1981–95), conducting both the Harvard-Radcliffe Chorus and the international prize-winning Radcliffe Choral Society. She led the groups on frequent domestic and international tours, directed a number of premieres of American music and produced recordings on the AFKA label. From 1989–96, she was music director of the Back Bay Chorale of Boston, leading their concerts with the Pro Arte Chamber Orchestra. In 1995, she became assistant conductor of the Madison Symphony Orchestra, director for the Madison Symphony Chorus, and director of choral activities at the University of Wisconsin, conducting the concert choir, the 200-voice Choral Union, and heading the graduate choral conducting program. As a guest conductor, Taylor has led the Arthur Rubinstein Philharmonic of Poland, St. Louis Symphony Chorus, Vermont Symphony, Harvard Chamber Orchestra, Air Force Band and Orchestra and, working with John Williams, directed the Boston Pops Chorus in a July 4th concert.

A recipient of an advanced conducting fellowship with Chorus America, Taylor is a lecturer, competition adjudicator, and participates at festivals throughout the United States.

CARMEN HELENA TÉLLEZ, born September 25, 1955, in Caracas, Venezuela, studied piano and composition at the Caracas Conservatory, then came to America with a scholarship from the *Gran Mariscal de Ayacucho* Foundation to study at the Indiana University School of Music. There she received her DMA in choral conducting in 1988. Her *Musical Form and Dramatic Concept in Handel's Athalia* won the Julius Herford National Dissertation Award in 1991.

Since beginning her professional career in 1985, Téllez has conducted orchestras, choruses and opera in North and South America and Europe, giving special emphasis to the contemporary and Latin American repertoire and to genres which combine music with other arts. She is a regular guest conductor of major orchestras in her country, including the Venezuela and Maracaibo Symphonies, Municipal Orchestra of Caracas and the National Philharmonic. She has also been director of special projects and guest conductor of the Caracas Sinfonietta.

During the 1987–88 season, Téllez was the guest artistic director of the National Chorus of Spain. She conducted at the Casals International Festival of 1987, and the first national tour of the Tenerife (Canary Islands) Symphony to much acclaim. Her performances in Spain won her the special invitation to conduct for King Juan Carlos and Queen Sofia in January 1988.

From 1990–91, she was resident conductor of the Hopkins Center for the Arts and guest professor of conducting at Dartmouth College (New Hampshire), where she founded and co-directed the First Inter-American Music Festival. Before joining the faculty at Indiana, she was a guest lecturer and conducted Tchaikovsky's opera, *Eugene Onegin*, at the thirtieth anniversary gala concert of the Latin American Music Center. She assumed directorship of the Center and the Contemporary Vocal Ensemble July 1992, focusing on works by U.S. and Latin American composers. In March 1995, she commissioned, produced and conducted the *Suite de Santa Fe* for guitar, narrator and orchestra, for the Santa Fe Symphony. In April 1995, she premiered Mario Lavista's *Missa Brevis*, a work she commissioned with a grant from the U.S.-Mexico Fund for Culture. On February 16, 2002, she conducted the Pacifica String Quartet and Indiana University Contemporary Vocal Ensemble in *PRAISE*, an oratorio for bass-baritone, double chorus and chamber ensemble by **Ralph Shapey**, in celebration of his eightieth birthday, March 12, 2001. (He died June 13, 2002.) During 2001–2002 she became music director of the Contemporary Chamber Players of Chicago, and conducted a second performance, as well as the Midwest premiere, of Stephen Hartke's Pulitzer finalist work *Tituli*. In the 2002–2003 season she conducted the Midwest premiere of John Adams' *El Niño* in her own semi-staged production, plus the premiere of John Eaton's opera, *Antigone*.

She initiated a series of recordings with the center and the ensemble, as well as publications with IU Press. Besides being a consultant and co-sponsor of international projects in Latin American and contemporary music, she is artistic director of the biennial Inter-American Composition Workshops in Bloomington, and has contributed to the *Revised New Grove Dictionary of Music*.

Téllez is also one of the founders/directors of Aguavá New Music Studio, a creative group of artists dedicated to the promotion of contemporary composers. She has toured the U.S., Mexico, Colombia and Israel with the ensemble and produced their recordings. The first, *Itineraries of the Night*, was released in 2000. The second,

Maria Tunicka

Canticum Novum, in 2002, elicited rave reviews in the international press. The third, Cary Boyce's oratorio *Dreams within a Dream*, 2003, was produced in collaboration with the Bloomington Chamber Singers. The same year brought the commission and world premiere of Boyce's cantata *Ave Maris Stella* at the Festival Cervantino in Mexico City in October, and Juan Trigos's *Missa Cunctipotens Genitor* in November at IU. Meanwhile, her successful international guest conducting career continues in full swing.

MARIA TUNICKA and her twin sister Krystyna were born September 15, 1936, in Pinsk, Poland (Now Russia). The girls sang duets from early childhood. After World War II, the

Communists sent their physician father to a prison camp in Russia for having "collaborated" with the Germans. Actually, he was forced to treat their wounded under threat of having his wife and children killed. But this was the reason Maria was not permitted to study medicine. Instead, she went into music, becoming a member of the State Artistic Ensemble. Against tough odds, Maria won the right to enter the all-male conducting class at the Warsaw Academy of Music. One of the class requirements was conducting the Warsaw Philharmonic, which she did in a triumphant graduation concert in 1963—despite much opposition, both from the class and the orchestra, because of her gender. She earned her master's degree with distinction in conducting from the academy, then directed a series of concerts with the Warsaw National Philharmonic and the Polish Radio Orchestra. She went on to win the International Conductors' Competition in Venice (1963), the Radio Broadcasting Competition in Poland (1964), and engaged in further studies with **Paul Kletzki** (1900–73) in Poland, **Franco Ferrara** (1911–85) in Italy, and **Walter Susskind** (1913–80) in the U.S.

The notable exception to Tunicka's undergraduate discrimination was the encouragement and support of Aleksander Ciechanski (whom she married on Palm Sunday, 1963), principal cello of the Warsaw Philharmonic and artist-in-residence at the academy. In the late '60s the latter embarked on a U.S. tour with the Warsaw Quintet. A romance having begun, Maria asked and received permission from the Ministry of Culture to also come to New York—at her own expense—to participate in the Mitropoulos Conducting Competition. On her arrival, she was informed that she needed a letter from the Polish government certifying her as an official entrant. She sent a cable to Warsaw. The reply came. She was forbidden to participate! Later she learned that this was linked to the 1967 War in Israel, since the competition was sponsored by Hadassah, and the Polish government would not permit recognition of a Jewish organization. This was the last straw for Tunicka. She told Aleksander that she would not return. He could not abandon her—though it meant leaving a prestigious and secure position.

There was an initial struggle to survive, then with references from no less than the world's premier cellist **Pablo Casals** (1876–1973), and **Maxim Shostakovich** (*b* 1938), famed son of famed Russian composer **Dmitri Shostakovich** (1906–75), Aleksander was welcomed as a cellist in the St. Louis Symphony in 1969. (He retired in 1992.) Meanwhile, Maria served as music director of the Kankakee Symphony (1970–74), the Brevard (North Carolina) Symphony (1976–86), and associate conductor of the Florida Symphony (1975–78). With a vast repertoire from baroque to avant-garde, she has guest conducted the St. Louis Symphony, Chicago's Grant Park Orchestra and the World Youth Symphony at Interlochen, as well as orchestras in Europe and Asia. She was appointed artistic director and conductor of the Space Coast Philharmonic (Florida) in 1986, where she retired in 1995.

When she is not guest conducting in Europe, she can be found sailing solo on the seven seas on "Polonez," her thirty-five-foot Pearson yacht, or perched atop the mountains she loves to climb. She and Aleksander live on Merritt Island, Florida.

Barbara Turner

BARBARA DAY TURNER, born July 6, 1956, in Framingham, Massachusetts, was bent on becoming a brain surgeon. She began with a double major of pre-med and music at USC. When music turned out to be the harder subject, she chose that. From 1987–2000, she was resident conductor and artistic administrator of Opera San José, founder/music director of the San Jose Chamber Orchestra (1991) and conductor of the San Jose University Symphony (1990–98). In her repertoire of some fifty operas, including several world premieres, and countless musical theater productions, she has presented *Grand Hotel* for the San Jose Civic Light Opera; Opera in the Park with the San Jose Symphony; *Carmen, Don Giovanni, Romeo et Juliette, The Rake's Progress, Il Turco in Italia*, and the world premiere of *The Tale of The Nutcracker* for Opera San José; *Don Giovanni* for Opera Memphis; *Die Zauberflöte* for Nashville; *Elixir of Love* for El Paso and Taconic Opera (NY); *The Merry Widow* with Rogue Valley (Oregon); *Cenerentola* for the Rheinsberg Festival (Germany); *Sing it Yourself Messiah* in San Francisco's Davies Hall, *Das Rheingold* for the Wagner Society, and concerts with The Women's Philharmonic.

She has served the NEA Opera-Music Theater program as an on-site evaluator and new works program panelist, is an evaluator for the Villa Montalvo (California) Composer Residency program and the Massachusetts Cultural Council new works program, as well as an adjudicator for competitions, including the Metropolitan Opera Regional Auditions.

Besides guest appearances, Turner lectures on conducting and harpsichord. She studied the instrument with the late Fernando Valenti, and has soloed with many of the Bay Area orchestras.

An ardent advocate for contemporary composers, Turner has premiered numerous new works for harpsichord including Michael Touchi's *Concerto for Harpsichord and Strings*, *Pacific Concertante* by Philip Collins, Craig Bohmler's *Chiaroscuro and Pentimento* for harpsichord and strings, and Allen Strange's *Twitter: Velocity Study for Harpsichord and Computer-Driven Electronics*.

Nan Washburn

NAN WASHBURN, as of 2006 in her ninth season as the popular music director of the Plymouth (Michigan) Symphony and West Hollywood Orchestra, is the former director of the orchestra and wind ensemble of San Francisco State University, Camellia Orchestra (Sacramento, 1990–96), Oakland-based American Jazz Theater, Acalanes Chamber Orchestra and principal conductor for the Channel Islands (California) Symphony.

Born June 24, 1954, in Denver, Nan began her music education studying flute at the Music Academy of the West, received a BM with highest honors from UC, Santa Barbara, and her MM in Performance from the NEC, studying with **Lois Schaefer** of the Boston Symphony. She was a professional flutist in several California orchestras. She began her conducting studies in 1984, working with Denis de Coteau at CSU Hayward, continued with Harold Farberman at the Conductors Institute and the Aspen Music Festival. She also participated in conducting workshops sponsored by the ASOL, working with **Daniel Lewis** (*b* 1925), **Gustav Meier** (*b* 1929) and **Lawrence Leighton Smith** (*b* 1936).

Washburn came to prominence as a co-founder, artistic director and associate conductor of The Women's Philharmonic (San Francisco, 1980–90), where she also played principal flute. She was also founder/director of the National Women Composers Resources Center at TWP, and repertoire consultant to orchestras across the country. In addition to her unique programming, and research and editing of numerous historical scores by women composers, she developed projects such as the in-school children's concerts, New Music Reading Sessions, American composer commissioning projects, and was Music Producer for the first TWP CD, *Baroquen Treasures*.

Her guest engagements include, in California, the Stockton, Sacramento, Berkeley, Marin, and Napa Valley Symphonies, plus orchestras of Richmond (Virginia), Eugene (Oregon), Cheyenne (Wyoming), Dubuque (Iowa), Cumberland Valley Chamber Players (Pennsylvania), Oregon Mozart Players, Colorado and California All State Honor Orchestras and National Women's Music Festival Chorus and Orchestra. She served as cover conductor for the Colorado Orchestra, January 1997. In 2002, she was on the faculty at the Conductors Institute at Bard College (Annandale-on-Hudson, NY), founded in 1980 by Harold Farberman.

For her pioneering work, Washburn has been featured on NPR and in many publications such as *Symphony*, the magazine of the ASOL. She has worked with leading American composers Ned Rorem, **Libby Larsen**, **Ellen Zwilich**, John Corigliano, **Chen Yi**, Lou Harrison, Tobias Picker, **Jennifer Higdon**, **Joan Tower** and **Hilary Tann**. Her awards include the 1992 Distinguished Service Award from the New York Women Composers, 1998 *Sonoma County Independent* Indy Award, and, in what may be a record, by 2004 she had won fifteen ASCAP awards for Adventuresome Programming from the ASOL.

LARA WEBBER became assistant conductor of the Baltimore Symphony under Yuri Temirkanov in the 2000–2001 season after completing her tenure as associate conductor of the Charleston Symphony Orchestra, where she directed more than sixty concerts. Prior to that she served as music director/conductor of the Los Angeles Debut Orchestra, to which she was appointed after national auditions in June 1993. She was the first woman to hold this post following such illustrious names as **André Previn**, **Lawrence Foster** and **Michael Tilson Thomas**. During 1994–95, she shared the podium with Tilson Thomas for the Debut Orchestra's fortieth anniversary concert. As their conductor, she premiered the winner of the BMI Composer Competition each season. Her guest conducting includes performances with the symphony orchestras of Baltimore, Houston, Pittsburgh, San Antonio, Louisville and Colorado Springs. Lara was also conductor of the Orange County Philharmonic for their annual Concerts on Campus series (1994–95).

A recipient of a grant from the Geraldine and Emory Ford Foundation, Webber was assistant conductor of Mozart's *Abduction from the Seraglio* at Glimmerglass Opera (1999). The 2000–01 season included performances with the Baltimore, San Antonio, and Lubbock Symphony Orchestras and a return to Glimmerglass Opera as assistant conductor of their new production of *Salome*.

Strongly committed to arts education, she was one of the conductors of the Emmy-nominated Disney's Young Musicians Symphony Orchestra in television specials airing nationally on the Disney Channel. With the Debut Orchestra, she developed and performed several educational outreach concerts in Los Angeles area schools. As associate conductor of the Charleston Symphony Orchestra, she programmed and performed concerts for children of all ages in the area. She also served as the CSO's principal Pops conductor, leading two masterworks series performances and five chamber orchestra series performances during the 1999–2000 season. In June 2000, the Charleston Regional Business Journal honored Webber with the "forty under forty" award in recognition for her outstanding leadership in the Charleston business community.

A native of Seattle, Lara's musical interests started with piano and cello lessons at age nine. She started her conducting studies at Oberlin with Robert Spano, receiving a BM in Vocal Performance (1991). She continued her studies at the Sweelinck Conservatory in Amsterdam with Joop Van Zon. Her MM in Orchestral Conducting is from USC, where she studied with **Daniel Lewis**. She participated in the conducting seminars at Aspen and Tanglewood, mentored by such podium luminaries as **Simon Rattle**, **Seiji Ozawa**, **James DePreist** and **Leonard Slatkin**. In February 1996, she was one of nine nationally selected conductors invited to conduct the Kansas City Symphony in the American Symphony Orchestra League's prestigious National Conductor Preview. In May 1998, she was one of thirty internationally selected conductors invited to conduct the Danish Radio Orchestra in the Malko Competition for Young Conductors.

Webber is the recipient of several awards, including the YMF/BMI Foundation, Inc., Lionel Newman Conducting Study Grant, the Alfred Newman Scholarship and the Leonard Bernstein Music Award. Upon completion of her tenure with the Debut Orchestra in May 1996, in recognition for her outstanding service to the community, Lara was honored with a Los Angeles City Council Resolution. 2004 marked her fourth season with the Baltimore SO, as associate conductor.

DIANE M. WITTRY, born October 11, 1961 in Pasadena, is the daughter of a science professor, and one of five children—three of them boys. With their mother's encouragement, four of the siblings took violin. Playing in youth orchestras, Diane thought she would become a violinist. Not until she was in the inspirational conductor **Daniel Lewis'** (*b* 1925) select four-student class of Instrumental Conducting at USC, did she even consider this career—there not being a role model. Named outstanding graduate in her field, she received her MM in 1985. The following year she served as the conducting assistant for the Great Woods Summer Institute under **Michael Tilson Thomas** (*b* 1944), and in summer 1987 was a conducting fellow at Aspen with Paul Vermel. That fall she was one of twenty young conductors selected to study with the great **Erich Leinsdorf** (1912–93) at a symposium sponsored by the ASOL and the New York Philharmonic.

Diane Wittry

Out of 400 applicants in 1991, she won the position of music director/conductor of the Symphony of Southeast Texas, at Beaumont, even though at the time she thought she was just the token woman on the candidate list. During her tenure, the orchestra experienced artistic growth and financial prosperity which was used for educational purposes to reach over 10,000 students via regional concerts, an after school string program for elementary schools, plus youth and family holiday concerts. She has also initiated educational programming for adults. After completing a nine year tenure in 2001, she remains artistic advisor. While in Beaumont, she was on the Lamar University faculty until 1996. She has also taught at UCLA and USC.

In spring 1995, she became the first female, and only the third music director of the Allentown (Pennsylvania) Symphony, founded, in 1949, with **Donald Vorhees**, famed conductor of the "Bell Telephone Hour," over thirty years, 1951–1983.

Wittry has guest conducted numerous orchestras, including the Symphonies of Houston, Pasadena, Stockton, San Diego and Wichita Falls, as well as the Ojai Festival Chamber Orchestra, Southern California Sinfonia, and Los Angeles, Florida and Olympia (Washington) Philharmonics. In 1988, she was understudy conductor to **Sir Peter Maxwell Davies** (*b* 1934) for the American Tour of the Scottish Chamber Orchestra. In the area of education, she was featured as the guest conductor for the prestigious Utah All-State Orchestra (1992), and the Louisiana All-State Orchestra (1995–96). (There are all-state youth orchestras in most of the fifty states, who compete annually.) She also serves on the National Board for the Conductor's Guild.

In 1996, Diane won the prestigious Helen M. Thompson Award.[76] It was presented to her at the National Conference of the ASOL. In 1999, she conducted seven concerts with the Osaka Symphony, becoming the first American woman to conduct a professional orchestra in Japan. The same year, she was honored with the "Arts Ovation Award" from the City of Allentown, received the "Woman of Excellence" Award from the Beaumont YWCA, and became the June bride of commercial artist, Richard Peckham. This made her a stepmother to his son John, twenty, a graphic designer, and daughter Sarah, twenty-three, who made her a "grandmother" by giving birth to a daughter in 2001. The same year, Wittry won top prize in the conducting competition of the Florence Accademia del Artes.

2002 brought the prestigious "Fiorino D'Oro Award" from Vinci, the Italian sister city of Allentown. Wittry is only the third American, and first woman, to receive this honor. This was also the year she expanded her art, studying the Russian—quite different from the American—approach to conducting with Leonid Korchmar, conductor at the Kirov Opera and Ballet, and Associate with the St. Petersburg Conservatory. By 2002, she had made two trips guest conducting in Russia and Ukraine. In June of that year, she won the post of conductor of the Norwalk (Connecticut) Symphony. 2004 marked her ninth season with Allentown.

Diane Wittry's book, *Beyond the Baton*, covers aspects of conducting not taught in school, namely years ahead planning, various types of concert programming, subscription, pops, educational, etc., organizing rehearsals, giving speeches to the community, working within negotiated contracts, working with the board of directors and other responsibilities. For this she received a grant from the Swiss Thyll-Dürr Foundation to begin the work during a three week stay in a lovely villa on the Isle of Elba,[77] off the west coast of Italy.

Rachel Worby

RACHAEL WORBY, born April 21, 1949, in Nyack, New York, enjoyed a childhood filled with culture and music, including attending Leonard Bernstein's Young People's Concerts in Carnegie Hall. She remembers, "I didn't want to be *like* Leonard Bernstein. I wanted to *be* him!" And by 1984, she *was* on his podium, conducting around thirty concerts annually until 1996, reaching over 22,000 New York City school children.

She began her music studies on piano at age five, and after graduating from SUNY Potsdam, in piano performance, studied musicology and conducting at Indiana University, later earning a DMA in musicology at Brandeis. Formal conducting studies began in 1976 with Jacques-Louis Monod, and a 1982 Martha Baird Rockefeller grant permitted study with **Max Rudolf** and

---

76. The Helen Thompson Award was established in 1982 and named to honor the memory of the person who, more than any other, developed and promoted the cause of symphony orchestras in America. The $1,500 prize is given to young music directors and orchestra managers early in their careers. The qualifications are that the candidate be under thirty-five, the nominated orchestra have a budget of $1 million or less, and that the recipients have been in their position for at least two seasons.

77. Where Napoleon was exiled, 1814–15.

Otto Werner-Mueller. Her professional career began in 1982 as an Exxon/Arts Endowment conducting assistant with the Spokane Symphony. Since then she has led many major U.S. orchestras, and launched Houston Symphony's outreach series, "Sounds Like Fun," presented to those who had never heard a concert.

On television, Worby created, narrated and conducted the Pittsburgh Symphony in the "Disney's Young Persons' Guide to Music" series. In 1991, on the 100th anniversary of that venerable venue, she appeared on PBS' "Carnegie Hall at 100: A Place of Dreams."

Chosen in 1986 from more than 160 applicants, Worby became conductor of the Wheeling (West Virginia) Symphony, soon tripling ticket sales and the performance schedule. In 1989, she was introduced to the newly elected State Governor, Gaston Caperton. It was love at first sight. They were married May 25, 1990. As First Lady, she founded a Governor's School for the Arts, and brought together writers, musicians and artists with her West Virginia Artists Series. Each year she also hosted "a giant Seder"—probably the only Jewish Passover feast ever held in a governor's mansion.

1994 marked Worby's European conducting debut with concerts in Germany and Romania. President Clinton appointed her to the National Council on the Arts. She received an honorary doctorate from her alma mater in May, and in July was awarded the West Virginia Public Theatre's Lifetime Achievement Award. The conductor's podium was endowed in her honor in 1996. The same year brought the Spirit of Achievement Award from Albert Einstein College. Other honorary degrees are from Claremont (1995) and Marshall (1996) Universities.

January 1997 marked an end to the Governor's two terms. Caperton taught at Harvard that semester, while Worby carried on in Wheeling and conducted her first fully staged opera in Bucharest (Romania) in February. In 1998, she created an annual American Music Festival in Cluj, Romania, going on to guest conduct the Manchester (England) Camerata, National Symphony of Colombia, Brazilian Symphony, and leading a successful 1999 tour with the Irish Chamber Orchestra. The 2001–2002 season found her at California's Ojai Festival, and back in Cluj with the Transylvania Philharmonic, celebrating her Third Annual American Music Festival. April took her to England and the London Philharmonic for another all-American program, and May back to the U.S. and the Norwalk (Connecticut) Symphony. May 13–30, she was off on her first Australian tour, covering the Queensland and Adelaide Symphonies for enthusiastic audiences.

The Capertons divorced in 1998. In 1999, Worby was appointed music director of the Pasadena (California) Pops Orchestra. At the end of the 2002–2003 season, she concluded her seventeen-year tenure with Wheeling, leaving behind a remarkable record: revitalizing the seventy-five-year-old orchestra, having increased the yearly concerts from six to thirty-eight; bringing in top name guest artists; creating a sold-out Pops series; having successful touring programs; plus special projects like *Symphony on Ice* and concert productions of *Carmen*, *Fidelio*, *Candide* and *Porgy and Bess*. She drew over 20,000 to the symphony's annual outdoor *Music Under the Stars*—an ongoing fifty-year tradition—and launched two CDs, bringing national attention to the orchestra. In September 2002, Worby was named conductor laureate.

She continues guest conducting. May and November 2003 found her in Barcelona with concerts of film music. January 2004, it was back to the deeper classics, Mussorgsky, Dvořák, Beethoven and Shostakovich in the UK with the Hallé Orchestra of Manchester. March took her to Costa Rica.

Her innovative programming is already in evidence at the Pops with patriotic, space, movies, *Hot Latin Nights and Hot Summer Stars*, *Brush Up Your Shakespeare* and other enticing themes, including another orchestral presentation of *Carmen* with LA Opera singers. Much in demand as a speaker, Rachael Worby has become an integral part of the Pasadena music scene.

ZHENG XIAOYING was born in Yongding City, Fujian Province, September 1929. She graduated from China's Central Conservatory of Music, going on to study conducting at Moscow's Conservatory of Music.

She was principal conductor of China's Central Opera Theater and dean of the conducting department at the conservatory. She has conducted more than 1,000 opera and symphonic performances, and has been guest director/professor in Russia, Japan, Australia, Singapore, Hong Kong, Taiwan, Thailand, Macao, America, and throughout Europe, where she received the French Literature and Arts medal of honor. In the 1990s, she founded Ai Yue Nu, the Women's Philharmonic Chamber Orchestra, which expanded into the first women's symphony in China and performed at the United Nations' Fourth World Conference on Women.

In 1997, she was invited back to her hometown to found the Xiamen Philharmonic, the first orchestra funded by local enterprises. In her concerts she is both conductor and lecturer, introducing classical and modern music to her audiences.

Barbara Yahr

BARBARA YAHR was born April 20, 1958, in Scarsdale, New York. She first conducted at age twenty at the École Normale de Musique (1978–79) when she went to Paris in her junior year of college. In 1984, she studied at the **Pierre Monteux** School in Hancock, Maine, with Charles Bruck, a student of the great French maestro. An MM in Theory from the Manhattan School of Music (1985) was followed by studies with Max Rudolf at Curtis, whose conducting faculty she joined (1985–88).

In 1988, Yahr was a winner in the Affiliate Artist conducting competition, the video of which, seen by **Lorin Maazel**, inspired him to invite her to join the Pittsburgh Symphony as resident staff director (1990–94). In this capacity she conducted the Pops, Summer Casual, Saturday Morning Live family series, educational concerts and the Youth Symphony. Her 1993 subscription series debut marked the premiere of American composer **Conrad Susa**'s (*b* 1935) *Rhapsody for Flute and Orchestra*, and **Morton Gould**'s (1913–96) *The Jogger and the Dinosaur*. She accompanied Maestro Maazel as assistant conductor to Jerusalem and the Shira Festival in Eilat (Israel), December 1992—January 1993. Yahr learned well from Maazel, a meticulous musician who knows every detail of phrasing and tempo he wants from the orchestra. In October 1993, Barbara was called in to replace Sir Richard Hickox, who was recovering from surgery. It was the opening of the season and the program was challenging. One review read, "The real power of the evening was unleashed when Yahr conducted Sibelius' Symphony No. 2 that shall not soon be forgotten."

She was invited to become principal guest conductor with the Bavarian Radio Orchestra (Munich), and has directed major symphony orchestras throughout the U.S., Europe, the Middle East and Asia, including the National, Detroit, Columbus, Calgary, Chattanooga, Louisiana, New World, and Singapore Symphonies, Ohio and St. Paul Chamber Orchestras, and the Radio Orchestra of Frankfurt.

Yahr's other forte is conducting opera. Her repertoire includes *The Crucible*, *La Fille du Regiment*, *Abduction from the Seraglio*, *The Magic Flute*, and Vaughan Williams' *Sir John in Love*. She debuted with Tulsa Opera, April 2000, with what *Tulsa World* called a "superb" performance of *Tosca*, and made her German operatic debut with *Rigoletto* at the Giessen Stadtheater. Other opera performances include *La Cenerentola* (Minnesota), *Carmen* and *Samson and Delilah* (Cincinnati), and *Elisir d'Amore* (Opera Frankfurt). She has also performed with Pittsburgh Opera Theater, Fort Worth Opera, New Orleans Opera, Calgary, Stadtheater Hannover, Frankfurt Radio Orchestra, Deutsche Kammerphilharmonie, Saarbrücken, (all in Germany), Vienna, Janáček Philharmonic (Czech Republic), Orchestra Sinfonica Siciliana (Italy), NHK Symphony Orchestra (Japan), and the Singapore Symphony.

Barbara now resides in New York City with her husband, Dr. Alex Lerman. March 2002 brought the joyous occasion of the birth of their son Benjamin.

SIMONE YOUNG was born March 2, 1961 in Sydney, Australia. She studied piano, flute, guitar, and at the Sydney Conservatory, composition. Her first conducting jobs were with new-music ensembles. Drawn into vocal coaching, she obtained a job with Australian Opera. The proverbial substituting for a sick colleague with only a few hours' notice, made possible Simone Young's sensational 1985 debut at the Sydney Opera House. By 1987, she was named "Young Australian of the Year," winning a scholarship enabling her to study in Europe. Shortly thereafter, she was employed by Cologne Opera with a contract that included conducting. This led to an engagement as assistant to general music director **James Conlon**. She was also in the right place at the right time to assist **Daniel Barenboim** during his legendary production of Alban Berg's *Wozzeck* in Paris, and at the Bayreuth Festival for Wagner's *Ring* cycle.

In the autumn of 1992, important debuts followed one another. At Harry Kupfer's Comic Opera, Berlin, she was entrusted with the productions of *La Bohème* and the double bill, *Cavalleria rusticana* and *I Pagliacci*, as well as their Japan tour. The beginning of the 1993–94 season brought Kupfer's new production of Rimsky-Korsakov's *Tale of the Tsar Sultan*. Young's debut with the State Opera Unter den Linden (Berlin) with Mozart's *Abduction from the Seraglio*, plus several highly acclaimed performances of Beethoven's *Fidelio*, earned her appointment as *Kapellmeister* for the '93–'94 season. She continues as their guest conductor. Other operas under her baton in Berlin have been *Tosca, Madama Butterfly, Barber of Seville, Jenůfa*, Wagner's *Ring* and the ballet performance of Schoenberg's *Verklärte Nacht* on a twin bill with *The Miraculous Mandarin*. At the same time, her November 1993 debut at the Vienna Volksoper (Peoples' Opera) marked the first time a woman had ever conducted this "strictly men's society." Lavish praise came from critics, audience and the musicians. 1993–94 brought revivals here of Verdi's *Nabucco* and Tchaikovsky's *Eugene Onegin*. A new production for the *Festwochen* (Festival Weeks) was Ambroise Thomas' *Hamlet*. This breakthrough season continued with *Tales of Hoffman* at the triumphant opening of the Opera de Paris, Bastille. Her Covent Garden debut, with *Rigoletto*, marked the only European opera company where she was not the first woman director. Her colleagues **Jane Glover** and **Sian Edwards** had preceded her. After this, she moved from Berlin to Sussex, forty miles south of London, where she lives with her husband, Greg Condon, and their daughter Yvann.

April 1995 brought more enthusiastic acclaim for her first appearance at the Bavarian State Opera with Richard Strauss' *Elektra*. 1995–96 performances included *The Flying Dutchman, Tosca, Rigoletto, Peter Grimes*, and a revival of *Fidelio* with **Hildegarde Behrens**. April 10, 1996 marked the beginning of Young's association with the Met with a rousing performance of *La Bohème*. It was both her American debut and Met debut, being only the second woman to lead the company after **Sarah Caldwell** twenty years earlier. Young went on to conduct *Cavalleria / Pagliacci* on January 6, 1997, *Il Trovatore* and *Tales of Hoffman*, 1998. She also had contracts with Chicago and Houston Operas.

With all this, the concert field has not been neglected. May 1994 saw her Italian debut at the Maggio Musicale Fiorentino. She plans to return to Florence regularly. Other concerts were in Berlin, Vienna, Tokyo and the Bregenz Festival (Austria). In 1996, after many years, Simone returned to her native city to conduct a series of performances of *Aida* at the Sydney Opera House and a Wagner concert in Melbourne. Concerts with leading Australian orchestras followed. During 1999, she conducted concerts in Norway, Munich and Berlin, Vienna for *Eugene Onegin*. 2000 brought her once again to Sydney conducting the Symphony to critical acclaim in the Sydney Festival's production of *Elektra* and the opening ceremony of the 2000 Sydney Olympics.

Awards are gushing in, beginning with the *Chevalier des Arts et Lettres*, a high honor from France, and an honorary doctor of music from Australia's University of New South Wales, May 2000. February 2001, an *Opera* magazine article noted that she was the first woman to conduct Wagner's *Ring Cycle* at the Berlin State Opera, with the production directed by the illustrious Harry Kupfer.

Having made her debut with the Los Angeles Opera in 2002, and conducted a broad range of operatic and symphonic repertoire for major opera companies and orchestras around the world, Young was appointed Opera Australia's music director and artistic administrator in the new millennium, giving her a chance to return to her homeland. With her working repertory of over sixty scores, and fluency in Italian, German, French, and a passable Russian, Young has contracts with leading opera houses and orchestras. She may hold the record as the world's most sought after maestra.

XIAN ZHANG was born 1974 in Dandong, China. Piano lessons began at age four, majoring on that instrument at the conservatory's affiliated high school. She received her BM and MM degrees from the Central Conservatory of Music in Beijing, where she became conductor of the Jin Fan Symphony, and conductor-in-residence at the China Opera House.

In 2000, while completing her doctorate there, she was appointed assistant professor of conducting, and music director of the concert orchestra at Cincinnati College Conservatory. At twenty-six, she was their youngest faculty member. During the summer, she was music director of the Lucca Festival Orchestra and Opera Theater of Lucca, the Italian birthplace of Giacomo Puccini, and site of his home and a museum of his artifacts.

After winning the Maazel/Vilar conducting competition in 2002, which included mentorship with Maazel, Zhang was named cover conductor for the New York Philharmonic during the 2002–04 seasons. She became assistant conductor in 2004, and associate conductor in 2005, the first woman to hold an official title at the Philharmonic. During that year she conducted the orchestra's "Concerts in the Parks," which includes Central Park with its audiences of thousands, and one concert during their residency at the Bravo! Vail Valley Festival in Colorado. She has also made guest appearances with the London Symphony, New Zealand's Auckland Philharmonia, Cincinnati Opera and Symphony, Colorado Symphony and Minnesota Opera.

One to Watch Over . . .

Every once in a while one meets a young person whose obvious talent makes it possible to intuit those stars in her future. The precocious eight-year-old the author met a few moons ago has turned into a beautiful young woman, who excels in whatever she undertakes.

AVLANA EISENBERG, born November 3, 1976, in San Francisco, to a well-known doctor father, began violin studies at three with her mother, outstanding concert soloist **Zina Schiff**. After making her performance debut at seven with the Shreveport Symphony, Avlana continued studies with Erick Friedman, soloed with the Monroe, Palomar, and San Luis Obispo Symphonies, and was concertmaster of the Marin Youth Symphony and Interlochen Orchestra. She also studied conducting with **Murry Sidlin** and **David Zinman** at Aspen, and **Gunther Schuller** at the Festival at Sandpoint (Idaho). Selected as one of the Top Ten College Women of 1996, she was featured in *Glamour Magazine*—as was her mother some twenty years before her! (They appeared in the magazine together, October 2001.) Avlana began conducting at Yale (BA in humanities, 1997), where she studied with **Lawrence Leighton Smith** and Shinik Hahm, and was founder, music director and conductor of the Silliman Symphony. Among other honors at Yale, she was awarded the Irish Browne Prize for Excellence in the Performing Arts. During graduate conducting studies at the Moores School of Music (University of Houston) with Franz Anton Krager, she directed the orchestra in numerous concerts, as well as a production of Stephen Sondheim's *Into the Woods*. She was also assistant conductor of the Moores Opera Center and Chamber Orchestra.

From August 2000 to June 2001, a Fulbright fellowship took her to Paris to continue conducting studies at the École Normale. While there, she spent time at the Paris Opera working with a voice coach.

Eisenberg has guest conducted the New Symphony of Boston, Hot Springs Music Festival Orchestra, Peabody Symphony, University of Michigan Orchestra and the Young Musicians Foundation Orchestra in Los Angeles. In 2001, she served as music director at the Edinburgh Festival's world premiere musical production of Hawthorne's *The Scarlet Letter*, to critical acclaim. In November of that year, the author was in the audience when the slender, blue-eyed, golden-haired beauty made mother-daughter history conducting the orchestra, with Zina as soloist, in a concert given at Tifereth Israel, a major synagogue in San Diego, California. Avlana served as assistant conductor of the Stanford Symphony Orchestra (2003–2004) while completing her law degree at the University. Summer of 2005 found her in Bulgaria, where she conducted the New Symphony Orchestra in Sofia. The 2006–07 season brought graduate work in conducting at Peabody. She was assistant musical director for Baltimore Opera's production of Verdi's *Nabucco*. A bright future sparkles ahead.

Darts and Flowers

In past years, several lady daredevils have risked the mire and stigma of leaving hearth and home to brave the dizzying twelve-inch heights of a conductor's podium! The odds of a woman being appointed to lead one of the top ten orchestras in this country, let alone Europe or Asia, continue to be almost impossibly imbalanced.

Praises and insults have been hurled at ladies of the baton ever since British diarist Samuel Pepys commented in 1661 that he had gone to the Globe Theatre and seen "a woman with a rod in her hands keeping time to the musique while it plays, which is simple methinks." Considering how many centuries men have felt it their inherent right to dog (or hog) the daïs, some of them have been good sports about letting a daintier foot set metatarsal upon "their" domain.

In 1774, English critic, Dr. Charles Burney, heard Vivaldi's all-girl Orchestra of the Ospidale Mendicanti (Orphanage) in Venice, and was surprised "to see as well as hear every part of this excellent concert performed by females [playing] violins, tenors, basses and harpsichords . . . " In 1916, **Leopold Stokowski** declared that not hiring women was a waste of "splendid power," yet he did not hire a woman for the Philadelphia Orchestra until 1930—harpist **Edna Phillips**—and in 1936, cellist **Elsa Hilger**. **Serge Koussevitzky** felt that "[women's] presence in an orchestra conduces to good discipline in the ranks." But although he directed the Boston Symphony from 1924–49, its first woman, bassoonist Ann C. de Guichard, was not hired until 1945.

As early as 1880, the Poet Laureate of the South, **Sidney Lanier** (1842–81), coined the immortal phrase, "It is more than possible that . . . the superior daintiness of the female tissue might finally make a woman a more successful player than a man." On the other hand, Spanish pianist/conductor **Jose Iturbi** (1895–1980) stirred up a hornets' nest when an interviewer in the *Toronto Press*, February 3, 1937, quoted him as saying, "Women can never achieve greatness in music or sports." Of the outraged outcries, none was more voluble than that of **Antonia Brico**, who challenged him to a competition of male versus female musicians before blindfolded judges.[78] The *New York Times* declared "women can be anything they want to be." A Los Angeles newspaper pointed out that "women have been given no chance until recently to show whether they could produce a Bach or a Beethoven." Speaking of Iturbi's own instrument, the Chicago *Musical Leader* stated that, "Women may not have the power to punish the piano, but artistically their standard is no lower than that of the gallant sex to which Mr. Iturbi belongs."

In attempting to get both feet out of his mouth, Iturbi was quoted as saying he was *mis*-quoted and that he only said, "Women in some fields are inferior to men," and "Women are limited to their natural endowments . . . " —statements which not only worsened the situation, but were all the more amazing since Iturbi had often concertized with his own sister, Amparo.

Perhaps the best example of respect accorded a professional is this evaluation by Brailsford Felder in *Cue* magazine (New York, 1939). As a male, however, he could not refrain from the obligatory comparison to masculinity, "The prejudice against women conductors which lurks in the bosom of every orchestra player, breaks down instantly when it comes in contact with Mademoiselle [**Nadia**] **Boulanger**'s master touch. For she is one woman who knows her business. She can read a score as readily as the best of men conductors, and her vast knowledge and understanding of music has the virile intellectuality usually achieved by men."

It was **Frédérique Petrides**, conductor/founder of the Orchestrette Classique, who said, "A woman must be better than a man if she is to conduct prestigious groups." She left a marvelous record of what was going on in the world of women and music—especially conductors—in five years of priceless newsletters (1935–40), aptly titled *Women in Music*. There were thirty-five issues in all, sent free of charge to newspaper and magazine editors, libraries, music schools, and interested individuals—amounting to about 2,500 copies per issue. These have been beautifully reproduced by the University of Arkansas Press in **Jan Bell Groh**'s book, *Evening the Score*, and have added much to my knowledge. In fact in reading them, I got delightfully lost in the world of the '30s and the activities of so many famous names that it was a shock to come back to the present and realize these pioneers of the podium are no longer with us.

---

78. Jose never took Antonia up on her challenge.

Oompah! Pah!

Mention should be made of women band instructors in schools still fortunate enough to have the budget for a music program! The umbrella organization recognizing their accomplishments is *The Women Band Directors International*. The WBDI, officially chartered December 18, 1969 in Chicago as the Women Band Directors National Association, adopted its current name in December 1997, celebrating their thirtieth anniversary, December 1999, at the Chicago Midwest Clinic.

WBDI is an organization in which every woman band director is represented, regardless of the length of her experience or grade level of instruction. It is the only international organization for women band directors, and is intended to serve as an association which supports, promotes, and mentors women in the band field. Its highest award is given only when a qualifying participant is found. The International Golden Rose Award honors women of national and/or international reputation for outstanding achievement in instrumental music—recipients receive a gold medallion. Thus far, the list reads:

1972 - **Maria Tunicka**
1974 - **Nadia Boulanger**, France
1976 - Virginia McChesney
1979 - **Margaret Hillis**
1982 - Elizabeth Green
1983 - **Judith Somogi**
1986 - **Ida Gotkovsky**, France
1988 - Anne McGinty
1989 - Elizabeth Ludwig-Fennell
1990 - Gladys Stone Wright
1992 - Coby Lankester, Holland
1997 - Barbara Buehlman
2002 - Linda Moorhouse
2003 - Judith Grimes
2004 - Paula Crider

Apologia

For every name listed in this section there are so many others worthy of mention. The following list just scratches the surface of podium talent:

Suzanne Acton, chorus master and conductor for Michigan Opera Theater, with whom she made her debut in 1986. In 1996 she was appointed director of the Rackham Symphony Choir, established at the University of Michigan in 1949, and the official chorus of the Detroit Symphony since 1952. Sharing the podium with Steven Mercurio and John DeMain, she conducted the RSC and MOT Chorus at the historic opening of the Detroit Opera House in 1996, featuring fifteen international artists, including tenor **Luciano Pavarotti**.

Sebrina Maria Alfonso, second place winner of the 1994 Stokowski Conducting Competition, energized the entire community of her birth to bring into being the Key West (Florida) Symphony Orchestra in 1998, and is now involved in opening a new performing arts school. In 1991, she was chosen music director of the Frederick (Maryland) Symphony. She has guest conducted and recorded with the Prague Radio Symphony and the Czech Philharmonic, appeared with regional American orchestras and The Women's Philharmonic. The 1990 premiere of her composition, *Freedom Crossing, 1980*, marked the tenth anniversary of the *Mariel* escaping from Cuba to Key West, with thousands risking their lives to gain freedom.

Nyela Basney, after more than 500 performances as a violist and pianist, brings that experience to her conducting of ensembles in New York, including The Little Orchestra Society, and eighteen productions with New York Grand Opera. She also conducts orchestras in Texas and Virginia, and is associate conductor of the Shreveport (Louisiana) Symphony. A distinguished honors graduate of Eastman, she directed a gala benefit concert with the Rochester (NY) Philharmonic, starring **Renée Fleming**.

Marietta Cheng, a full professor at Colgate University, directed their Chorus and Chamber Singers (1976–93), and is conductor of the Orchestra of the Southern Finger Lakes. She led the Corning Philharmonic from 1986–95—all in upstate New York. She has conducted over twenty-six concerts for the Music Educators National Conferences. In the choral field, she has directed over thirty oratorios. She was chosen as one of the one hundred women in Lifetime Television's *National Summit on Women in the 21st Century*. As a pianist, she has appeared with the Boston Pops, Manhattan String Quartet, and at Colgate.

Janet Canetty-Clarke has led the Ditchling Choral Society of Sussex, England since 1965. Their eightieth year was in 2001. In 1984, she guest conducted the First All-Women Chamber Group of Austria. In 1992, she became an Associate of the RAM, in recognition of her services to music, and in 1999 was a finalist for European Woman of Achievement.

Mary Culbert, French hornist, has led the Merion (Pennsylvania) Concert Band since 1977.

Margery Deutsch is professor of conducting and director of orchestras of the University of Wisconsin and Milwaukee Youth Symphony since 1984. She has participated in the Edinburgh Festival and National Youth Orchestra Festival 2000 in Sarasota (Florida), and is on the board of the Youth Orchestra Division of the ASOL.

Yvette Devereux

Yvette Devereux, conductor and violinist, is the founder of the Progressive Symphony and Batonic Music Publishing Company. She was the first African-American woman in the conducting programs of Chapman University and Peabody, where she received her MM. A crossover artist, she has appeared as violinist with pop stars Natalie Cole, Vanessa Williams, Johnny Mathis and Barbra Streisand. Her movie and TV credits include *The Jackson Story*, *What's Love Got to Do With It: The Tina Turner Story*, *Little Mermaid* cartoon, and *60 Years of Disney*.

Morna Edmundson, Canadian choral director for over twenty years, was executive director of World of Children's Choirs-2001 Festival, which brought forty-seven international youth choirs to Vancouver. She is co-founder/co-director of the Elektra Women's Choir, and in 2000 was awarded the Willan Award for Outstanding Service to the British Columbia Choral Federation.

Susan Farrow is the British music director of the Dulwich Choral Society, Southgate Festival Chorus, Alleyn Chorale, St. Monica's Singers, Concordia, Mosaic, Janus Ensemble (choral/orchestral), North London Sinfonia and Saint Cecilia Chorus—all in or near London. 2002 marked her third season with the English National Ballet. She has appeared throughout the UK, Europe and the U.S.

Frenchwoman **Claire Gibault** has guest conducted opera at La Scala Milan, Covent Garden (London), Edinburgh, Glyndebourne, San Francisco and São Paolo (Brazil). She is the first woman to conduct the Berlin Philharmonic (April, 1997), and the first woman to win first prize for orchestra conducting at the Paris Conservatory, quite an achievement in 1969.

Mary Woodmansee Green is director of the Philadelphia Festival Orchestra, Kennett Symphony, Chester County Youth Orchestra—all in Pennsylvania—Hilton Head (South Carolina) Orchestra, and the Mary Green Singers, with whom she has toured in France and performed at the Vatican.

Belgian **Sabina Haenebalcke** conducted soloists, five Flemish choirs, and the Symphony Orchestra of Flanders in Antwerp at the Music in the City Festival. Her career is expanding to larger choirs.

Anne Harrigan was music director/founder (1983) of the Baltimore Chamber Orchestra, and conductor of the Lafayette (Indiana) Symphony (1994). Her interactive family concert, "Colors of the World," produced for Maryland Public Television, received an Emmy. Her community leadership contributed to Lafayette being named

"All American City." She has guest conducted in the Eastern U.S., and, as a conducting fellow of the Los Angeles Philharmonic Institute in 1988, was heard at Royce Hall and the Hollywood Bowl. She has performed with major artists such as cellists Janos Starker and Lynn Harrell, violinist **Chee-Yun** and pianist Leon Fleisher. With her husband accepting an important cancer research position in Grand Rapids, Michigan, in 2000, she now commutes to her conducting positions at the Lafayette Symphony Orchestra in Indiana and the Battle Creek Symphony Orchestra in Michigan. Having a daughter who was seven in 2005, she finds her hectic performance schedule easier than being a "Mom" . . .

Laura Hemenway is professor of music at Antelope Valley College (California) and has been conductor of the Antelope Valley Symphony for fifteen years.

Sarah Hatsuko Hicks, born January 14, 1971, in Tokyo, was raised in Honolulu. She studied piano at Juilliard, going on to Harvard for a BA *magna cum laude* in composition. There she was assistant to the conductor of the Harvard-Radcliffe Orchestra and music director of the Harvard Lowell House Opera. Next, she received an artist's degree in conducting from Curtis where she studied with Otto-Werner Mueller.

She was founder/music director of the Hawaii Summer Symphony in Honolulu (1991–96), guest conducted in the U.S. and abroad, including the Silesian Philharmonic (Poland), Tokyo Philharmonie, Chamber Orchestra of Philadelphia and Richmond (Virginia) Symphony. In February 2002, she guest conducted the New National Theatre, Tokyo, in a production of *The Magic Flute*. She also led Verdi's *Aida* with the East Slovak State Opera Theater and was a coach/conductor at the Moravian Theater (Oloumoc, Czech Republic), and was appointed resident conductor of the Florida Philharmonic (2002–03). A proponent of new music, Hicks has taken part in festivals such as Verbier (Switzerland) and Aspen. A member of the Curtis faculty, she is staff conductor of their orchestra.

In 2005, the Richmond Symphony selected Hicks as associate conductor and Youth Orchestra director.

British-Swiss **Monica Buckland Hofstetter** is permanent guest conductor of the Bohuslav Martinů Philharmonia Zlin (Czech Republic), and appears with many orchestras of Eastern Europe, as well as Switzerland, where she has conducted the famed Tonhalle Orchestra. She has premiered several works of contemporary composers, and won conducting prizes from the Swiss Musicians Association/Kufer Habltizel Foundation.

Laura Jackson was assistant conductor of the Atlanta Symphony via an American Symphony Orchestra League Conducting Fellowship beginning Fall 2005.

Doris Lang Kosloff, born March 14, 1947, in Brooklyn, New York, studied in the Preparatory Division at Juilliard (1955–61). She graduated Phi Beta Kappa from the Aaron Copland School of Music (Queens College CUNY, 1967) and received her MM from Boston University (1969). After a series of musical coaching and assistant directorships at Tanglewood, Boston Opera, Wolf Trap—for its 1971 opening—Washington Opera, and Connecticut Operas (1974–88), she served as artistic director of Connecticut Opera and as director of the Camarata Conservatory (1988–90). She taught at Hartford College for Women (1979–88), and wrote the libretto for the notable children's opera *Goldilocks and the Three Bears* (1985), composed by her sister, **Judith Zaimont**, with whom she played duo-piano professionally in her youth. She contributed the article "The Woman Opera Conductor: Personal Perspective," Volume I, *The Musical Woman: An International Perspective*. She guest conducts, lectures and gives workshops for various musical organizations. Married, Doris has two grown children.

Sharon Lavery (BM, Michigan State, 1991, MM, Clarinet Performance, 1993 NEC, MM Orchestral Conducting USC, 2000), is Professor of Conducting at USC, and Resident Conductor of their Thornton Symphony, Chamber Orchestra and Wind Ensemble, a position especially created for her in 2003. Her collaboration with world-renowned conductors and guest appearances, including Carnegie Hall, plus her talent for choral conducting, place her on the threshold of young conductors destined for a major career.

Diane Loomer, co-founder/conductor with **Morna Edmundson** of the Elektra Women's Choir, and founder/conductor of the all male Chor Leoni, is on the faculty of the University of British Columbia. Her choral works have been performed internationally. A frequent CBC commentator on the national arts in Canada, her awards include Vancouver's Woman of Distinction (YWCA, 1994), Distinguished Alumni Award (UBC, 1997), and the Order of Canada, the country's highest civilian honor, in recognition of her service to music.

Canadian conductor/composer **Ramona Luengen** is artistic director of the Phoenix Chamber Choir and Vocal Collegium Musicum Ensemble at her alma mater, the University of British Columbia. Her extensive choral compositions have been commissioned by the CBC and Canada's finest choirs, and performed all over the world. Her *Stabat Mater* (1995) was awarded "Outstanding Choral Work" and "Choral Event of the Year" by the Association of Canadian Choral Conductors.

Marsha Mabrey, music director of the Seattle Philharmonic since 1996, has led regional orchestras in Oregon, California, Michigan and Georgia. She has been a consultant on educational programs with the San Jose and Detroit Symphonies, Philadelphia Orchestra, and served on the faculty of the University of Oregon.

Chilean-German conductor **Marie-Louise Oschatz** led the Vienna Chamber Ensemble (1987–92), was music director of two productions for the annual Austrian opera festival (1994), and in 1995 founded *Helios 18* for the performance, on period instruments, of 18th century music, a genre in which she is gaining recognition throughout Europe.

Laura Rexroth is director of bands and wind ensembles of the College of William and Mary.

Cornelia von Kerssenbrock has conducted choirs and regional orchestras throughout Germany, as well as Romania, Bulgaria and Italy, and made a guest appearance with the Vancouver (Canada) Chamber Choir.

Dr. Antonia Joy Wilson, former director of the Maryland Women's Symphony and the Jefferson Symphony, Golden, Colorado, is founder and principal guest conductor of the Mostly Mahler Orchestra and Chorus, San Francisco. Her debut at twenty-one with the Colorado Symphony, designated her the youngest woman to lead a major orchestra. She has also guested in China, India, Romania, Bulgaria, Macedonia, Ireland and Argentina.

Canadian conductor **Keri-Lynn Wilson**, a native of Winnipeg, was a flute soloist when she took up conducting at Juilliard. An assistant to **Claudio Abbado** at the Salzburg Festival, she was hired as associate conductor at Dallas Symphony upon graduation. After five years there, she has taken her operatic and orchestral conducting career international. She is married to Peter Gelb, former president of Sony Classical, and General Manager of the Met as of 2006. They have two children.

Angela Yeung, associate professor at the University of San Diego and director of their orchestra and chamber music ensemble, has toured as cello soloist in Taiwan and guest directed in Hong Kong. She was on the Orvieto (Italy) Musica-2002 faculty with **Nyela Basney**, and trumpeter **Amy Gilreath**.

And the List Continues . . .

The American Symphony Orchestra League lists over 100 orchestras in the U.S. which have women conductors. These, plus all the dedicated directors of university and youth symphonies, community and small town orchestras, chamber groups and ensembles, carry the torch—possibly the *antidote*—to our socially turbulent and, in too many cases, economically-strapped venues of culture, as they and their players bring the gift of music to those who live too far away to take the subway to Lincoln Center or the freeway to the San Francisco Opera.

Future Tense?

Are the hurdles less daunting today for womankind to make the giant leap onto that small space, the conductor's podium? If we are talking of the top ten orchestras in America (forget Europe) this is still akin to climbing Mount Olympus. **Elizabeth Schulze** had her foot in the door at the National Symphony, **Kate Tamarkin** was close in Dallas, as was **Barbara Yahr** in Pittsburgh. **JoAnn Falletta** merited a few lines in *Time* magazine, and **Marin Alsop** accomplished the ascent to the mile-high city of Denver to lead the Colorado Symphony, then "graduated" to major British orchestras and the Baltimore Symphony. She was quoted in *Reader's Digest* regarding her retort when a European conductor commented, "Oh, you're fine in the lighter stuff, but you couldn't possibly do the heavy repertory!" To which she replied, "The baton weighs about an ounce; what do you *mean* I can't do heavy repertory?" **Gisèle Ben-Dor** almost had it made when she substituted for Kurt Masur and led the New York Philharmonic, December 7, 1993, *except there was no media coverage in the audience!* She was luckier March 9, 1999, when she again jumped in with no score or rehearsal and got a rave review in the *New York Times* for her Mahler interpretation.

At some point at the beginning of the 21st century the "score" stood at: JoAnn Falletta (Buffalo Philharmonic, Virginia Symphony, Honolulu Symphony), Gisèle Ben-Dor (Santa Barbara Symphony), Anne Manson (Kansas City Symphony), Keri-Lynn Wilson (Dallas Symphony), Anu Tali (Nordic Symphony Orchestra), Elizabeth Schulze (Maryland Symphony), Andrea Quinn (Royal Opera House Ballet, London, and New York City Ballet), Emmanuelle Haïm (Glyndebourne Festival Opera, Le Concert d'Astrée), Xian Zhang (China Opera House, associate conductor of New York Philharmonic), Sara Jobin (San Francisco Opera), Susanna Mälkki (Ensemble intercontemporain) and Zheng Xiaoying (Xiamen Philharmonic Orchestra, China).

Meanwhile, the podium peregrination will continue to be as interesting as the March of Time.

Women in Military Bands

The heyday for women in military bands was during World War II. Although women had long served in the U.S. military, mostly as nurses, the war demanded assistance from the half of the population which had been excluded from military service. As a result more than 350,000 women became a part of the armed forces. The Navy was the first, founding the WAVES (Women Accepted for Volunteer Emergency Service) in 1942. The following year the Marine Corps and Army formed units, joining the Army and Navy Nurse Corps. The Air Force had their WASPS (Women in Air Service Pilots), and the Coast Guard SPARS,[79] which stood for the Coast Guard motto, *Semper Paratus* (Always Ready). Since most of these women had clerical or stenographic experience, they took over bookkeeping, inventory and supply duties, releasing men to the war effort.

The SPAR recruiting motto was "Release a Man for Sea," and more than 13,000 women served during the war. Opened in 1943, their training station was the Biltmore Hotel in Palm Beach, Florida. By July the SPAR Band was created, beginning with seven women, directed by **Lt. Martha M. Reddick**. Women, most of whom had musical experience, began joining the Coast Guard because they could play in the band. Within a year there were thirty-five members. Their day began with the "Star Spangled Banner" at 8:00 A.M., followed by marching practice (always in skirts), concert band rehearsal, individual and sectional rehearsals, then preparation for concerts and other programs. In addition, each band member had two extra hours of duty which included desk jobs, file clerks, telephone operators, gate guards or duty drivers. The band cornetist, **Betty Frank**, was the ambulance driver, sometimes called out in the middle of the night.

Early in 1945, the Palm Beach facility closed and the band moved to Washington, DC. They continued the programs, dances at military bases, performed at schools, for wounded troops in hospitals, and gave concerts at the White House. The SPARS marched in President Roosevelt's funeral parade, and the VJ and VE Day parades. When the war ended the band was closed down, its members sent to various Coast Guard units. By the summer of 1946, the SPAR program had ended and the Coast Guard was once again all male—not to hire a woman again until almost thirty years later.

The Women's Army Corps - the WAC Band

In 1976, the Army ended the thirty-two-year tradition of an all-female band, and the unique career of the Fourteenth Army Band (WAC). The Fourteenth, activated on August 16, 1948, had begun its career in 1943 as the 400th Army Service Forces Band, one of the five WAC bands organized during World War II. The five bands, numbered 400 through 404, were at Daytona Beach, Fort Oglethorpe (South Post), Fort Oglethorpe (North Post), and Fort Des Moines, which also housed the 404th ASF Band with the designation (cld)*—standing for "colored," the * for WAC. All these bands were deactivated between 1945 and 1947.

On March 5, 1949, the Fourteenth Army Band (WAC) began with ten members and its warrant officer bandmaster, **Katherine V. Allen**, a Juilliard graduate. In the next three months, sixteen more bandwomen joined the

---

79. SPARS material courtesy of Joanna Ross Hersey, former MU1 U.S. Coast Guard.

unit, playing for parades, march-outs, graduations and dances. When the unit acquired its full complement of thirty-four women, Allen formed small groups—a dance band, Dixieland jazz combo, and a barbershop quartet—to provide a variety of entertainment. In 1951, the band began touring to assist the campaign to build WAC strength during the Korean War. It also played at the New York's World Fair in 1956, and marched in three presidential inaugural parades (1953–'57–'61). The tours between 1951–73 took the band through almost every state, including a 1972 trip to Puerto Rico.

When Allen completed her tour in 1952, she was replaced by 2nd Lt. (later Captain) **Alice V. Peters**, who remained until 1961. Several officers served until 1964, when Specialist 6th Class **Ramona J. Meltz**, a nine year veteran of the band, took over as director. Her leadership over the next ten years established an *esprit de corps* unparalleled among WAC units.

In 1966, a few women began attending the U.S. Naval School of Music (now the Armed Forces School of Music), but only as an exception to policy, and perhaps as a "test." The school was not open to women until after the "integration" of women into the other bands in the service. By 1968, the band had increased to sixty members. In 1967, they played at the White House when President Johnson signed the bill removing promotion restrictions for women officers. It was at the peak of its development when, in 1972, the Army ordered the unit integrated with male personnel. The WAC Commander moved to preserve the all-female status by requesting that it be designated a special band, but this was disapproved because Army staff could not spare the spaces required, and stated that "maintenance of the Fourteenth Army Band as a female-only unit appears to be in conflict with EEO (Equal Employment Opportunity) policies relating to discrimination based on sex." The next year, an Army-wide reduction in force trimmed the band from sixty-four to twenty-eight. The losses devastated morale, and members went to other bands or retired. They were permitted to play their final concert as an all-woman band on their thirty-second anniversary, May 1976. In August, with the accession of a chief warrant officer (CWO 4) male bandmaster, the acronym WAC was removed from the band's title, ending the concept of an enlisted director. On January 1, 1977, the band became fully integrated.

United States Marine Corps

In 1943, because of the war, Captain William F. Santelmann, director of the USMC Band, made history by organizing the only all-woman band in the annals of the Marine Corps. Under the baton of **Charlotte Plummer Owen**, for the two years of its existence until the end of the war, they gave over twenty-eight performances a month, including concerts, dance band performances, war bond tours, radio broadcasts and military reviews. Owen held the rank of Master Technical Sergeant and was in charge of the forty-five women who comprised the band. It was not until 1973 that the Marine Band in Washington, DC, again accepted a woman musician.

Charlotte Owen

Charlotte Owen, born January 31, 1918, in Minneapolis, by fourth grade had moved with her family to Portland, Oregon. Her mother taught piano, but saxophone and clarinet were Charlotte's school instruments. She concentrated her studies on the latter, graduating from the University of Oregon in 1939. She was directing high school bands in LaGrande, Oregon, when, in the middle of World War II, she learned that an all-women band was to be organized by the Marine Corps. She applied and was not only accepted, but became the first woman conductor of a military band. There were thirty charter members of what was officially known as the USMC Women's Reserve Band. This expanded to forty-three players and two reserves. They played concerts at the Naval Hospital, camp theaters, weekly dress parades, rallies for Marines being shipped overseas, and performed at stateside Marine camps throughout the duration of the war. Presidents Roosevelt and Truman were sometime members of their audience. A fifteen piece dance band, which Charlotte fronted with clarinet and saxophone, and sometimes conducted, kept a busy schedule both on and off base at Camp Lejeune, North Carolina.

Love Joins the Band

Of the three officers who had come from Washington to Camp Lejeune to set up the band, one of them, Technical Sgt. Charles Earl Owen, became Charlotte's husband, September 1945, at war's end. His peacetime career was principal percussionist of the Philadelphia Orchestra under **Eugene Ormandy**, while Charlotte raised their daughter, Susan, and played first clarinet with the Mainline Symphony in Philadelphia, becoming their first chairwoman of the board of directors. Summers were spent at the Aspen (Colorado) Music Festival, which now features a Charles Owen Percussion Scholarship. After his retirement from Philadelphia, Charles became head of the percussion department at the University of Michigan (1972–82). He passed away in 1984. At eighty-three (2001), Charlotte had had sixteen busy summers conducting the Ann Arbor Civic Band. She also taught clarinet and saxophone for over fifty-five years, until the last summer of her life. She lived happily near her daughter, Susan Owen-Bissiri, and her grandchildren, Matthew Bissiri and Julie Bissiri Patterson and *her* husband Dale.

Active in the Mu Phi Epsilon professional sorority for women musicians for over sixty years (now open to men), Charlotte was a member of Women Band Directors International, Association of Concert Bands, and a charter member of the Women Marines Association. In October 1997, when the Memorial to Women in Military Service was dedicated at Arlington National Cemetery, Owen was one of three invited to conduct the Alumni Band, made up of past and present women musicians from different branches of the service. She received the Distinguished Alumna Award from the University of Oregon School of Music, and on September 30, 2004 was honored with the DAR Woman of the Year Award.

A devout Christian Scientist, Charlotte learned of her heart condition only a few weeks before her peaceful passing, December 18, 2004.

This is the Army

The United States Military Academy Band at West Point is the oldest in continuous service, predating the Revolutionary War when fifers and drummers were attached to the Minutemen stationed across the Hudson River. In 1778, West Point was established as a permanent military post with fifty-five fifers and drummers and eight other instrumentalists. The Academy was founded in 1802, and by 1815 the band had a full range of instruments. They have played for historical events, such as the opening of the Erie Canal, the Chicago and New York World Fairs, and the funerals of Ulysses S. Grant and Franklin D. Roosevelt. The official title, "United States Military Academy Band," was bestowed in 1866.

Already qualified musicians before they audition, band members today receive basic army training and enter with the rank of Sergeant. Four components combine to form the marching band: the Concert Band, the Hellcats, the Jazz Knights and support staff. The Academy Band is one of thirty-eight active component bands. The others are fifty-four National Guard bands, and nineteen U.S. Army Reserve bands.

Women at West Point

Not until April 1973—with exception of those bands attached to combat divisions—were women authorized to be assigned to any U.S. Army Band. The first female assigned to the USMA Band, **Susanne Edick**, a bassoonist from Allentown, Pennsylvania, arrived in October 1975, nine months prior to the admission of the first female cadets to the academy. Since then, twenty-one women have been assigned to the band. These included four flutists, six clarinetists, one bassoonist, two euphonium players, one trombonist, one percussionist, two buglers with the Field Music Detachment—The Hellcats—two support staff members and two vocalists in the Jazz Knights.

A Lady Leads the Band!

From 1988–92, Lieutenant Colonel **VIRGINIA ALLEN** was deputy commander and associate conductor of the Band. She was the senior female musician in U.S. military bands. Her father, Colonel Eugene Allen, was a commander of the U.S. Army Bands, and part of "Pershing's Own" when he retired in 1992. "Ginny" studied French horn and conducting at the Catholic University of America in Washington, DC, where she earned a B.Mus.Ed. degree and an MM in performance. She also has a diploma in wind band conducting from the University of Calgary. Allen received a direct commission into the Army in 1977. Her first assignment took her to the Armed Forces School of Music in Norfolk, Virginia, where she served as student company commander, adjutant and training officer. When she assumed command of the U.S. Army Forces Command Band at Fort McPherson, Georgia, in 1979, she was the first woman to command and conduct an active duty military band since women were integrated into the program. Three years later, she was selected for assignment to the Army's premier touring band, the United States Army Field Band, at Fort Meade, Maryland. In addition to serving as associate conductor of the Concert Band and as the unit's public affairs officer, she directed the Soldiers' Chorus during the Field Band 1984 European tour. In 1985, she was assigned to the Pentagon as an officer in the Office of the Chief of Public Affairs, Department of the Army. The following year, she returned to Fort McPherson as the forces command staff bands officer. Her arrival at West Point marked the assignment of the first female officer to the band since its organization in 1815. From December 1992, until her retirement in 1997, Lieutenant Colonel Allen was the Department of the Army Staff Bands Officer at the U.S. Total Army Personnel Command in Alexandria, Virginia, supervising the 111 bands attached to the United States Army.

The Military Music Women

As an example of the caliber of musicians, these women comprised the female contingent of the West Point Band in 2000:

Lynn Nicole Cunningham—flute—whose father graduated from the Naval Academy, started flute at age seven and piano at ten. Her BM in applied flute is from the University of Wisconsin at Madison (1978), and MM in flute performance from Arizona State University (1980), after which, seeing a vacancy notice hanging on her teacher's door, she auditioned and was accepted to West Point. She is married to computer consultant William G. Ray. Their son, Kevin, was born June 26, 1985.

Julie Williams Hill—flute—began piano at five and flute at ten. Both parents being musicians influenced her to perform at local Nashville churches. She earned her BM from Vanderbilt (1990) and was accepted at USMA, January 1991. She is married to Kelvin C. Hill, a bassoonist.

Rachel Bose Grasso—Clarinet—learned the B-flat clarinet at ten, and E-flat clarinet ten years later. She holds a B. Mus.Ed. from the University of Houston (1985), and MM in clarinet performance from Indiana (1988). She is married to Carmine P. Grasso, also in the band. Their two children are Meaghan, born 1990, and Patrick, 1991. Grasso auditioned twice. She was accepted the first time, but declined the position in order to finish her graduate education. She re-auditioned after her master's, and accepted her placement.

Jennifer L. Tibbs—clarinet—from nearby Syracuse, saw her older brother play clarinet, and started on the same instrument at twelve. She received her BM from Cincinnati Conservatory and became part of the West Point Band, September 1993.

Diana Lynn Cassar—clarinet—started her instrument at nine. Growing up in the area, she had been attending the band's concerts since she was eleven She studied all woodwind and percussion instruments at Ithaca College, from which she graduated with a BM in music performance in 1995. She was accepted into the band during her senior year.

Lois Hicks—alto saxophone—having begun saxophone at eleven, studied at Interlochen Arts Academy, University of North Texas, and received her BM from Florida State. In 1996, her concert at Weill Recital Hall of Carnegie Hall, was her prize for winning the Artists International Presentations competition. The same year, she joined the band.

LeeAnne Newton—trumpet—started in sixth grade. Both parents were musicians and college music majors. LeeAnne's B.Mus.Ed (1980) is from the University of Regina, Saskatchewan, Canada. Advertisements for openings brought her into the West Point band that November. She is married to William R. Newton, whom she calls "a gifted and meticulous carpenter."

Lori D. Salimando—trombone—had a childhood filled with sounds of the harmonica and Italian accordion played by various relatives. She started trombone as a young girl, earned a BM from Eastman (1983), and MM from Catholic University of America (1987). She has played with both the U.S. Naval Academy Band and Marine Corps Music Program, but was always attracted to the military and musical tradition of the USMA Band, which she joined in January 1996.

Susan Davidson—French horn—came to the band in 1997, after playing in the Frankfurt and Heidelberg Army Bands in Germany. She received her BM from Ball State and MM from Ithaca College.

Joan Follis—euphonium—who helped gather these profiles, enjoyed hearing the two boys next door play trumpet and trombone in the high school marching band. She learned cornet at ten, baritone horn at thirteen and the euphonium at eighteen. Her B.Mus.Ed. is from Bowling Green State, Ohio (1975). She was accepted at West Point, February 1976, becoming the second woman ever assigned to the band. After twenty-one years of service, she retired in 1997.

United States Army Band

The United States Army Band at Fort Meyer, Virginia, is the official band for diplomatic and state functions in the nation's capital. Known as "Pershing's Own," it was founded in 1922 by the heroic Army Chief of Staff General John J. "Blackjack" Pershing (1860–1948), to emulate European military bands he heard during World War I. "Pershing's Own" led President Calvin Coolidge's inaugural parade in 1925, initiating a tradition that continues to the present. During World War II, the band was ordered overseas and performed throughout North Africa and Europe. After the war, the band expanded to keep pace with the demand for specialized assignments. Performing units added were the Ceremonial Band, Army Orchestra, Chorus and Herald Trumpets. The band's training and performance facility, Brucker Hall, was constructed in the mid-1970s, at which time the Army Blues jazz ensemble, Chorale and Brass Band were established as performing ensembles. The touring representative of the Army is the United States Army Field Band. It travels from its home station at Fort Meade, Maryland, presenting a variety of music in America and countries around the world. In November 1997, "Pershing's Own" celebrated its seventy-five year history with a grand concert at Carnegie Hall, New York.

Liesl Whitaker is lead trumpet with the *Army Blues Jazz Ensemble*. (See Brass.)

Beth Steele

Major Beth T.M. Steele was Commandant, U.S. Army Element, School of Music in Norfolk, Virginia, 2003–05. The first woman associate bandmaster of "Pershing's Own," as well as director of the ceremonial and brass bands, she was born August 8, 1966, in Ames, Iowa, growing up in a family with a pianist mother, vocalist sister and trumpet-playing brother. She began musical training on piano, later violin, and in junior high school switched to trumpet, which she played in bands and orchestras throughout the U.S. and Europe, and was a two-time national finalist in the Music Teachers National Association Collegiate Artist Competition. She holds a BM in trumpet performance and MM in conducting from Northwestern, where she attended on an ROTC scholarship. The Distinguished Military Graduate of her class, she also earned the basic parachutist's badge. She was commissioned in 1988, and is a member of Sigma Alpha Iota music fraternity and Phi Kappa Lambda National Music Honor Society. She served as executive officer and associate conductor of the Army Ground Forces Band in Atlanta, Georgia, and was the commander of Student Company, U.S. Army Element, School of Music. Of the twenty-one commissioned officers in the band system, she was the only woman until Spring 2005 when 2nd Lt. Shannon Leopold (trumpet) was hired. After a year's training, Leopold's assignment may be the School of Music or the Fort Monroe band.

As of July 2005, **Lieutenant Colonel** Beth Steele became deputy commander and associate conductor of the U.S. Army Field Band. Stationed at Fort Meade in the DC area, they work directly for the Chief of Army Public Affairs. Their mission is to travel around the country and tell the Army Story, which puts them on the road 100–120 days per year. Their four performing ensembles are the Concert Band and Soldiers Chorus (who travel together), the Jazz Ambassadors (Jazz Band), and the Volunteers (rock/pop ensemble).

Living History

Also at Fort Meyer is the *Old Guard Fife and Drum Corps* of the Third U.S. Infantry, which has provided historical music from the Colonial era for Washington functions. Wearing uniforms circa 1781, they recall the days of the American Revolution. The sixty-nine member Corps use eleven-hole fifes, handmade rope-tensioned drums, and single-valved bugles. There is no conductor, the musicians respond to silent commands from a spontoon[80] carried by the drum major. They average 500 performances annually, entertaining in parades, pageants and historical celebrations throughout the U.S. They also serve abroad as American goodwill ambassadors.

Jeanne Pace

Beginning August 1996, this unit was commanded by its first woman, Chief Warrant Officer **Jeanne Y. Pace**, daughter of Air Force Major (Ret) Edward L. Pace and former Women's Air Force member Faye J. Pace. She was born in Fukuoka, Japan, enlisted in the Army after high school graduation in 1972, and entered warrant officer ranks in 1985. Her previous commands were Army bands in Fort Hood, Texas, Fort Clayton, Panama, and Fort Leonard Wood, Missouri. Although she played clarinet and saxophone in high school bands, her BS is in liberal arts and her dual master's degrees from Webster University are in human resource development and management. Her military awards include Meritorious Service Medal (fifth award), Army Commendation Medal (fourth award), Army Achievement Medal (second award), and the Military Outstanding Volunteer Service Medal.

Pace made Chief Warrant Officer five in 2002. After eight years in command, she left the Old Guard Fife and Drum Corps, September 2004, receiving a Legion of Merit upon her departure. She went on to serve as the Army Bands Proponency Officer at the Adjutant General School, Soldier Support Institute, Fort Jackson, South Carolina. In this capacity, she advises the Chief of Army Bands on all technical matters pertaining to the 106 Army bands: Active Duty, Army National Guard and U.S. Army Reserves, providing expertise on the mission, function and utilization of bands.

She is the senior warrant officer/bandmaster on active duty and can claim the honor of being the last of the former members of the Women's Army Corps Band still on active duty. When she left the band, October 1977, the unit was about 50 percent men and 50 percent women. The number of women in the other Army bands at the time was between two and three. Within a few years, the Fourteenth Army Band demographics were much the same as other Army bands.

Tell It to the Marines

The United States Marine Corps Band was established on July 11, 1798, when President John Adams approved a bill that officially brought the Corps and the United States Marine Band into being. The band consisted of a drum

---

80. A short spike similar to a halberd—an 18th century weapon carried by infantry soldiers.

major, a fife major, and thirty-two drums and fifes. Their headquarters were in Philadelphia until the capital was moved to Washington. From Thomas Jefferson to the present, the Marine Band has played at every presidential inauguration and at the White House when called upon by the president. Jefferson is credited with giving the Marine Band the title of "The President's Own."

John Philip Sousa (1854–1932), while director from 1880–92, wrote many of the pieces that earned him the title of "The March King." He also organized the band's first concert tour in 1891. Since then, the fall tour has become an annual event, interrupted only by the Spanish-American War (1898), and the two World Wars (1917–18), (1941–45). Beginning in the 1890s, the Marine Band was one of the first ensembles to be transcribed on Thomas Edison's phonograph, recording dozens of cylinders of waltzes, polkas and Sousa marches. With the advent of radio, the band became even more familiar. Its broadcasts lasted to the mid-1950s.

Today, the Marine Band performs over 600 commitments annually, ranging from solo performances to the full concert band. Components include the concert and marching bands, the chamber orchestra, string ensembles, dance band and Dixieland band. In addition to the 143 musicians who make up "The President's Own," there is "The Commandant's Own," a seventy-nine piece drum and bugle corps. There are also twelve other Marine Corps bands located nationwide, and in Hawaii and Japan. Made up of fifty members each, they perform for concerts, ceremonies, and in jazz and reception combos.

All bands play for military ceremonies, visiting dignitaries, receptions, dances and educational programs. Overseas, they provide a morale link with home. Naval recruiting is also one of their prime functions. Keeping up with the times, there are jazz and rock units, as well as brass, saxophone, wind and string quartets, and specialty choirs and soloists. The 6th Fleet maintains two bands in Naples, which cover the major ports of Europe, the Black Sea and North Africa, fulfilling some 500 engagements before audiences numbering over 30 million. According to the Navy, the overall number of engagements of all the bands is over 7,500 per year.

(**Cherilee Wadsworth**, whose husband was also a Navy musician, was a fleet vocalist, composer/arranger with the CINCSOUTH Band in Italy. Some of the information in the preceding paragraph is excerpted from her article in the IAWM Journal, June 1997, based on a paper presented at the Society of Composers National Conference, March 1997.)

Roxanne Haskil

Chief warrant officer and conductor **Roxanne Marie Haskill** was head of the USMC Music Program, Washington, DC, 1997–2000, a position whose responsibilities include developing and revising all policies through and by which Marine Music organizations operate, including the military training courses at the School of Music. Born on Valentine's Day, 1954, from fourth grade through high school she played clarinet and saxophone, but always knew she wanted to be a conductor. As a college sophomore, she switched to French horn, graduating in 1977 with a double major in music and art history from the University of Massachusetts (Lowell). She taught high school marching bands, was principal horn of the Prince William Symphony Orchestra (Virginia), and the Plymouth Philharmonic (Massachusetts), at the same time being in the National Guard Reserves of the U.S. Air Force. In 1979, she enlisted in the Marine Corps and played horn in the Quantico, Virginia, band. It was here she met her husband, David Haskill, a bassoonist. After attaining the rank of sergeant, she took the advanced course at the Armed Forces School of Music. In 1985, assigned to Cherry Point, North Carolina, Haskill became the first female band conductor in the Marine Corps.

She and her husband served in Saudi Arabia during Desert Storm, where David sustained injuries that separated him from the Corps in 1991. As one of the three bands in Saudi Arabia, where members wore their rifles while playing, the band also served as the Security Unit for personnel assigned to Major General Moore and his battle staff.

(What distinguishes members of the Marine Band from other service bands is that the Corps considers them Marines first and musicians second—an opinion not always held by the players themselves . . .)

Returning to the U.S., Haskill took over the band at the El Toro (California) base, at the same time earning an MM in instrumental conducting from California State University (Long Beach), where she was a student of well-known band director, Larry Curtis. She received the Graduate Dean's List of University Scholars and Artists Award, was nominated into the national music honor society, Phi Kappa Lambda, and recruited by USC and UCLA as a doctoral candidate in conducting—a future endeavor.

Haskill's many military honors include the Navy Commendation Medal (second Award), Navy Achievement Medal (second Award), and the Colonel George S. Howard International Award for musical excellence as a conductor. Since her retirement, she is teaching at East Tennessee State University (Johnson City) and accepting numerous guest conducting invitations.

Music O'er the Seven Seas

The United States Naval Academy was founded in Annapolis, Maryland, 1845. Its band consisted of one fifer and one drummer. By 1852, the need for music prompted the Secretary of the Navy, John Pendleton Kennedy, to authorize one bandmaster and six musicians. In 1865, the band increased to twenty-eight musicians, all wearing Navy uniforms and subject to Navy discipline. In 1894, an order was issued prescribing Marine Corps uniforms for all Navy musicians. This lasted until 1925. Meanwhile, in 1910, Congress established the forty member band to be part of the regular Navy. This meant that bandsmen, who previously served as civilians, now could not hold outside employment.

Over the years the band grew to its present size of sixty-two enlisted musicians, of which eleven are women, with two commissioned officers as leaders. The music covers a wide range of styles from concert band to chamber music groups, which include a woodwind and brass quintet, a trombone, tuba, and saxophone quartet and a percussion ensemble. For community outreach, they perform demonstration concerts for elementary school children. Each year, a High School Festival Concert features student musicians performing with Academy Band members. Besides Tuesday evening summer concerts at the City Dock, the band has a fall and winter concert series on the Academy grounds, playing classic band repertoire, vocal and instrumental solos and popular music hits.

In 1972, the band enlisted its first female member, **Gayle Holmes**, who went on to become the lead singer in the band's rock music ensemble, the Electric Brigade. She retired from the Navy in 1992 to pursue a civilian music career. Currently, women comprise nearly 15 percent of the band's membership.

Anchorettes Away

The Navy itself employs approximately 700 musicians, who play in twelve fleet and regional bands stationed across the country and abroad, plus its two special bands, the U.S. Naval Academy and the premiere Navy Band at the Navy Yard in Washington, DC, comprised of four officers and 162 enlisted personnel, thirty-nine of them women. This band is used for presidential and government functions.

Senior Chief **Nancy Stanly**, a flutist, joined the Navy Band with her husband, Bruce, trumpet, in 1974. In 1979, her husband transferred to the Marine Band. For two years, Nancy was the only woman onstage other than a vocalist. After eighteen years of playing, she became the Band Librarian. In their twenty-five years of service, she reflects that, "My husband and I financed many a teen's college fund with our use of babysitters due to concerts and engagements at the White House." Their daughters pursued college degrees in piano and music education. Caroline is a missionary in Russia. Celeste teaches music in elementary school.

Nancy Stanly

The Stanlys retired in 2000. Nancy earned an MMus.Ed from George Mason in 2003 and teaches Early Music Education to two-to-five-year-olds, first and second grades, and band for fifth to eighth graders.

Gender Representation

Lorelei Conrad

Lieutenant Lorelei Conrad, in 1991, after twelve years of service, became the Navy's first female commissioned officer bandmaster. Born in Geneva, Illinois, July 26, 1955, to a doctor father and registered nurse mother, the family enjoyed music, and by age six Lorelei was studying piano. In her fourth grade year, she saw the movie *Stars and Stripes Forever*, depicting the life of John Philip Sousa. From then on she knew she wanted to play cornet. She also fantasized that if she could win the John Philip Sousa Award, she could assume the March King's identity. With cornet studies through junior and senior high, by graduation time she was president of the band and did indeed win the Sousa Award, there was, however, no miraculous transformation!

Conrad went on to study trumpet at Carthage College (Kenosha, Wisconsin) as a music education major, played principal trumpet with the Kenosha Symphony, and was the student conductor for Chapel Choir, football band, Wind Ensemble and Brass Ensemble. In 1976, she met **Dr. Antonia Brico** on a lecture/conducting tour and accepted a scholarship to study with her in Denver. A degree in trumpet performance was earned at Metropolitan State College (Denver), while acting as assistant conductor of the Brico Symphony, the Metropolitan State College Orchestra and the Jefferson Symphony in Golden, Colorado.

Conrad auditioned for the Naval Academy Band in 1979, and became their enlisted conductor, as well as playing trumpet and solo cornet in the wind ensemble, big band, concert, ceremonial, marching, chapel and German bands. She was accepted into the Limited Duty Officer program, and in 1991 attained her pioneer position. Her first assignment was the (now defunct) Navy Band San Francisco, on Treasure Island—the only all-male Navy stateside band.

After applying for the Navy Graduate Education program, Lorelei was accepted at Northwestern in the graduate conducting program, finishing with honors in 1993. Her next assignment was the Navy Band, Washington, DC, as associate conductor and administrative department head. She conducted programs at the White House, including the Inaugural Ball for President Clinton, full honors funerals at Arlington Cemetery, concerts at the Capitol Building, and was Captain "La Baton Rouge" for children's Lollipops Concerts at the Sylvan Theater, near the Washington Monument.

From April 1997–99, she was Seventh Fleet bandmaster in Yokosuka, Japan, the first woman assigned to a seagoing band. She also served as musical advisor to the Commander of the Seventh Fleet, now four-star Admiral Robert J. Natter, who appreciated what musical diplomacy could do for the Navy and the U.S. Conrad's travels with the band included port visits in Japan, Fiji, New Caledonia, Indonesia, Malaysia, Singapore, Russia, China, Hong Kong, Thailand, Australia, Saipan, and Guam. She also guest-conducted the Russian Navy Band in Vladivostok, the Chinese People's Liberation Army/Navy Band, and three performances with the Tokyo Symphony.

In May 1999, she became director of training at the School of Music at Little Creek, Virginia, where she was responsible for all basic, intermediate, and advanced courses, staff and students. She served as the primary conducting instructor for all Navy and Marine Corps Advanced Conducting students. For the first time she had an assignment only four hours' drive to home and husband in Annapolis. In July 2001, the now **Lieutenant Commander** Conrad reported for duty as fleet bandmaster, U.S. Atlantic Fleet. In July 2002, visiting her ailing mother in Arizona prompted the decision to retire there. Since fall 2003, with husband Ray playing trumpet, Lorelei plays in the Green Valley Stage Band and Bavarian Brass Band, and leads the Green Valley Concert Band, whose seventy-five members range in age from fifty to ninety-seven.

April 2005 found Conrad back in Norfolk, fulfilling the request of one her former students and band members: administering the oath of office to Ensign Diane Nicholls on her becoming assistant at the Naval Academy Band—the second woman in naval history to serve as a bandmaster. On May 1, 2006, her high school outside Chicago honored Lorelei Conrad by placing her in the Hall of Fame in their new Arts Center.

Ever seeking new challenges, Lorelei passed Arizona requirements for an accelerated nursing program and has been assigned to a local hospital.

The Armed Forces School of Music

The Armed Forces School of Music, located in Norfolk, Virginia, originated in the early 1900s as a school for Navy musicians. In June 1935, then called the Navy School of Music, they relocated to Washington, DC. The classes graduated as complete ensembles, transferring intact to serve aboard ships in the U.S. fleet. By 1951, the school began accepting Marine and Army personnel, outgrowing its space and resources. With the exception of the Air Force, all military musicians are now trained at the School. The new facilities in Norfolk rival those of most conservatories. There are more than 100 practice studios, nine rehearsal areas, a library of over 13,000 manuscripts and a repair facility to service the 3,000 instruments on inventory. The twenty-two-week basic course includes music theory, ear training, instrumental performance, and a trio of auditions over the course of instruction. The staff includes more than twenty instructors chosen from the top performers in the Army, Navy, and Marine Corps ensembles worldwide. Designed with the career musician in mind, the School offers courses in arranging, ceremonial conducting and musical unit leadership. In addition to the advanced training received, many musicians hold music degrees from civilian universities and conservatories. Graduates return to their individual units to become musical ambassadors throughout the U.S. and abroad.

The United States Coast Guard

The United States Coast Guard, originally known as the Revenue Cutter Service, was established in 1790 by Secretary of the Treasury Alexander Hamilton, on orders from President Washington, to enforce customs and tariffs on maritime commerce. The original ten vessels battled pirates, privateers and smugglers to safeguard the economy of the new nation.

In the 1800s, the Bureau of Navigation and Steamship Inspection Service and the Life-Saving Service were created. In 1915, the Life-Saving Service and the Revenue Cutter Service joined to form what was then named the U.S. Coast Guard. In 1939, the Lighthouse Service, and in 1942 the Bureau of Navigation and Steamship Inspection Service, were both absorbed into the USCG.

By the end of World War II, the Coast Guard was multi-mission, providing ice breaking service, protection of ports and waterways, maintaining navigational aids and providing ships and planes with navigation and weather information, as well as responding to over 70,000 search and rescue calls each year.

Anatomy of a USCG Band

The USCG Band was organized in 1925 with the assistance of Lt. Charles Benter, leader of the United States Navy Band, **Dr. Walter Damrosch**, conductor of the New York Philharmonic, and **John Philip Sousa**. In 1965, President Lyndon Johnson signed congressional legislation establishing the Coast Guard Band as one of the five premier service bands in the United States.

The Coast Guard did not enlist women as musicians until 1973, the exception being the SPAR band which existed two and a half years during World War II. Originally a small command band at the Coast Guard Academy, since 1965 it has toured nationally and worldwide, performed at presidential functions, and for the Secretary of Transportation and other cabinet officials on formal and other occasions. It was the first U.S. military band to perform in the Soviet Union, and gave nine performances in four days in southern England for events commemorating the fiftieth anniversary of VE-Day (Victory in Europe, May 8, 1945). They have also given performances in Carnegie Hall with the New York Pops.

In 2000, the Band consisted of forty-five men and twelve women:

Chief Musician **Cheryl L. Six** (piccolo) joined in 1977 after graduation from the University of Northern Colorado with a BM, *summa cum laude* in flute performance.

C M **Jill Maurer-Davis** (flute) came in 1980. With a BA and MA from the New England Conservatory, and diplomas from the Orff Institute and Mozarteum in Salzburg, she has performed with the Boston Symphony, and Pops, Hartford and Worcester Symphony Orchestras and Connecticut Opera, and served on the faculties of Brown, Clark, and Central Connecticut State and Hartford Universities, and Hartt School of Music.

Musician First Class **Barbara Devine** (flute) arrived in 1982, with a BM from Duquesne University and MM from Arizona State. She has presented master classes at Bowling Green State, and taught at the Community Music School, Centerbrook, Connecticut.

C M **Anne G. Megan** (oboe), joined 1980. She attended Eastman and received her BM from Boston University (1975). She has been principal oboist with the Eastern Connecticut Symphony since 1977, and teaches at Connecticut College.

C M **Judith L. Buttery** (bassoon) dates from 1979. Her BM is from Calvin College, Grand Rapids, Michigan, and MM from Michigan State. In 1978, she participated in the National Opera Orchestra Workshop, directed by **Eve Queler**. Buttery is adjunct instructor of Bassoon at Connecticut College and performs with the Wallingford (Connecticut) Symphony.

Musician First Class **Rebecca J. Noreen** (bassoonist), joined in 1985, with a BA from Western Washington State, and MM from Manhattan School of Music. She performs with the Hartford, New Haven, and Eastern Connecticut Symphonies, Orchestra New England, and Harmonie Hartford.

Musician First Class **Marjorie Virginia Sturm** entered the band in 1984 as principal horn. Her BM is from the University of Kentucky and MM from DePaul University (Chicago). She has performed with the Colorado Philharmonic, Civic Orchestra of Chicago, and Lexington (Kentucky) Philharmonic. Her teachers included **Gail Williams**, former co-principal horn of the Chicago Symphony.

Musician First Class **Joanna R. Hersey** won first place in the Vermont All-State Competition and a scholarship to the Vermont Mozart Festival in 1989. She attended Arizona State on a full music scholarship, and joined the band as a tubist in 1992. In 1999, she left the band to begin master's work in performance at NEC.

Senior Chief Musician **Constance I. Coghlan** joined the band's percussion section in 1973, the first woman to be accepted into the band. She has a BM from the University of Wisconsin (Madison) has performed with the New London Contemporary Ensemble, Hot Cross Brass, Eastern Connecticut Symphony, and taught at Central Connecticut State University.

Musician First Class **Tracy J. Thomas** is the band's vocalist. She has a BM from Indiana University School of Music and an MM in vocal performance from Cincinnati College-Conservatory, where she also completed her doctoral academic residency. In addition to singing many Mozart dramatic roles, she was lead soprano with the Cincinnati Philharmonic Orchestra in the world premiere of Schubert's opera *Der Graf von Gleichen* on the Centaur label.

(My thanks to trombonist/band manager Mark Weaver who kept in updating touch for over four years, and even lent his charming Connecticut cottage to my husband and me when we overnighted in his territory in 2000. On April 22, 2002, the Coast Guard Band gave a concert in San Diego, making for a happy reunion.)

The Blue Yonder

The United States Air Force has a total of twelve bands worldwide. Their two premier bands—larger than regional bands—have a national touring mission. They are the USAF Band at Bolling Air Force Base, Washington, DC, and the Band of the Rockies, formerly at the Academy, but now at Peterson AFB, Colorado Springs. The regional bands are in Hawaii; Anchorage, Alaska; Ramstein (Germany) and Tokyo. (There are NATO bands in Italy and Belgium which include USAF members.) The Air Force has an authorization for close to 1,000 personnel in their bands, of which approximately 20 percent are women. Like the Army WAC bands and the Women's Marine Band, the Air Force had a women's band, the 534th USAF Band (WAF) at Lackland (Texas) Air Force Base, from 1951–59. It was led by **Captain Mary Belle Nissly**, who had served with the 400th ASF Band (WAC) during World War II.

Women in the Air

In 1978, the U.S. Air Force, after having opened the career field for women, was actively seeking a qualified conductor. Newly graduated with a master's in music, **Amy Mills** (See Conductors) was the first woman to pass the audition and offered a position to lead one of the twenty bands, but turned it down because she was not yet ready to commit her life to the military. After spending two years teaching and leading high school bands, she joined the Air Force in 1980. Her first honor was becoming Distinguished Graduate of the Officers Training Corp at Lackland, January 1991.

Ten years' active duty saw Mills conducting at Colorado Springs, Shreveport, Louisiana, and Washington, DC. In 1987, she became the first woman to conduct the *Singing Sergeants*, a full time professional vocal choir. In 1989, she was promoted to Vice Commander of the USAF Band, the premier band of the service. In this capacity she supervised twenty-five staff persons, handled a $2.3 million budget and oversaw operations for 1,800 performances per year. Uniquely, when the Commander retired in November 1990, Mills substituted in the position during the three and a half month hiring process—which included the Persian Gulf War—making her the first woman in the world to be the commander of a premier military band! (However, as a captain, she could not retain the post which was reserved for the rank of Lieutenant Colonel and above.) She resigned from active duty in June 1991 to pursue a professional orchestra conducting career, and is now music director of the National Women's Symphony, Washington, DC, and the La Crosse (Wisconsin) Symphony Orchestra.

In 1972, when Senior Master Sergeant **Karen L. Ehrler** began her Air Force career, she was the first woman to play in any of the premier bands in Washington, DC. A graduate of the Catholic University of America, she earned her BM in clarinet performance and MM in musicology. After playing principal third clarinetist in the USAF Concert Band, she retired in 1997.

Chief Master Sergeant (E-9) **Glenda R. Shepela** is the first woman in the entire American military music field to obtain this highest enlisted rank. She is also the first woman to hold the title NCOIC (non-commissioned officer-in-charge) of a premier unit, the *Singing Sergeants*, a position she held 1988–95. She joined the Air Force in 1974, after graduating from Northern University with a B.Mus.Ed. Featured as a vocal soloist for her entire career, since 1995 she has been director of operations for the USAF Band at Bolling Air Force Base, Washington, DC.

C M Sgt **Donna Baldwin Abraira** is the NCOIC of the *Singing Sergeants*, the position held by CMS Shepela until her promotion. Abraira has a BM from Ithaca College, and began her Air Force career in 1979. A 1993 graduate of the Senior NCO Academy of the Air Force, she became director of personnel for the group in 1994, and in 1995 began her current duties.

Daisy Jackson

C M Sgt **Daisy Jackson**, director of public affairs was, since 1994, chief of marketing and media relations, as well as Talent Coordinator for the USAF Band. She began her career in 1982 as a soprano vocalist with the *Singing Sergeants*. A graduate of the University of West Florida with a B.Mus.Ed., in 1975 she completed her MM in vocal performance at Peabody and graduated from Curtis in 1979. Her vocal performance became the hallmark of the USAF Band. She has also performed as a recitalist and oratorio soloist, winning numerous awards including the regional Metropolitan Opera Auditions. She has the distinction of being the first minority (black) female to hold the rank of E-9 in American military bands. In April 2000, she was the recipient of the DAR Award for Distinguished Women in the Military. With her, also receiving the award, were Major General Jeanne M. Holm (Ret), author of the definitive history *Women in the Military: An*

Unfinished Revolution, and Brigadier General Wilma L. Vaught (Ret), President of Women in Military Service for America Memorial Foundation. A notable retirement ceremony honored Jackson May 1, 2002, with her official retirement being August 1. She moved to Los Angeles and, utilizing her vast experience, established Diva Daisy Consultancy, a West Coast representative for performing artists.

C M Sgt **Robin Forrester-Meadows** began her career in 1977, after earning undergraduate and graduate degrees from the University of Arizona. She played English Horn in the Tucson Symphony and Tucson Opera Company prior to becoming principal oboist with the USAF Academy Band. She was assigned to the band in Washington, DC, taking the position of chief of supply before returning to performing.

Master Sergeant **Laurel Schmitt McFayden** founded in 1991 and directed *High Flight*, the premier show group of the USAF Band. A graduate of Montclair State College (BMusEd) in clarinet performance, with courses in vocal performance at the Manhattan School of Music and vocal pedagogy at Columbia University, she began her military career as a clarinetist and vocalist with the West Point Academy Band, joining the USAF Band in 1981 as vocal soloist with the *Singing Sergeants*.

Top Brass

There are two women of note in the brass section of the Concert Band. Master Sergeant **Ann Baldwin Shrieves** began her career in 1988, and in 1991 became the first woman to play principal euphonium in an Air Force Band. She is a *summa cum laude* graduate of the University of Akron with a BM and MM from the University of Michigan. In 1984, she was third place winner at the International Brass Congress Solo Euphonium Competition, and in 1986 was winner of the International Solo Euphonium Competition at the University of Texas at Austin.

Senior Master Sergeant **Jan Z. Duga**, with the Band since 1983, is the first woman tuba player in a premier band. She has a BS from Ohio State University, and MM in solo tuba performance from Arizona State. She has performed with the USAF Symphony Orchestra, Ceremonial Brass, and Airmen of Note. She also freelances in the Washington area and teaches privately in the Northern Virginia school system.

Obviously, the academic credentials of these women adequately equal their counterparts in civilian orchestras. As of 2000, there were 880 musicians in the Air Force, 183 (21 percent) of them, women.

Allowing for normal turnover, many of the women profiled herein may have retired or moved on.

2005 Overview of Women Principals in American Orchestras

Atlanta Symphony   **Robert Spano**   *(31 women out of 96)*

Violin	Cecylia Arzewski	concertmaster
Viola	Amy Leventhal	assistant principal
Cello	Dona Vellek Klein	assistant principal
Bass	Gloria Jones	assistant principal
	Jane Little	assistant principal
Flute	Christina Smith	principal
Oboe	Yvonne Powers Peterson	assistant principal
Clarinet	Laura Arden	principal
Bassoon	Elizabeth Burkhardt	assistant principal
Horn	Susan Welty	assistant principal
Harp	Elisabeth Remy	principal

Baltimore Symphony   **Yuri Temirkanov**   *(31 women out of 96)*
(**Marin Alsop** 2006–)

Violin	Madeline Adkins	assistant concertmaster
	Melissa Zaraya	assistant principal second violins
Cello	Chang Wo Lee	assistant principal
Flute	Emily Skala	principal
Piccolo	Laurie Sokoloff	principal
Oboe	Jane Marvine	English horn

Bismark-Mardan Symphony   **Thomas Wellin**   *(45 women out of 67)*

Violin	Rosemary Person	principal second violin
Viola	Mary Hoberg	principal
Flute	Linda Schmidt	principal
Oboe	Deidre Fay	principal
Clarinet	Rhonda Gowen	principal
Bassoon	Sara Boyd	principal
Horn	Teri Fay Storhaug	principal
Timpani	Vicki Willman	principal
Harp	Louise Zuern	principal

Boston Symphony Orchestra   **James Levine**   *(24 women out of 98)*
Violin   Tamara Smirnova   associate concertmaster
                                 Elita Kang   assistant concertmaster
Viola   Cathy Basrak   assistant principal
Cello   Martha Babcock   assistant principal
Flute   Elizabeth Ostling   associate principal
Harp   Ann Hobson Pilot   principal

Buffalo Philharmonic   **JoAnn Falletta** (See Conductors) *(27 women out of 75)*
Violin   Amy Glidden   associate concertmaster
                                 Jacqueline Galluzzo   associate principal second violins
Viola   Valerie Heywood   principal
                                 Natalie Piskorsky   associate principal
Oboe   Carolyn Banham   English horn
Contra Bassoon   Martha Malkiewicz
Flute   Christine Lynn Bailey   principal
                                 Natalie Debikey   piccolo
Harp   Suzanne Thomas   principal

Chicago Symphony Orchestra   **Daniel Barenboim**   *(25 women out of 106)*
Violin   Yuan-Qing Yu   assistant concertmaster
Harp   Sarah Bullen   principal
Piano   Mary Sauer   principal

Cincinnati Symphony   **Paavo Järvi**   *(26 women out of 97)*
Violin   Rebecca Culnan   assistant concertmaster
                                 Sylvia Samis   assistant concertmaster
                                 Kathryn Woolley   second assistant concertmaster
                                 Catherine Lange-Jensen   associate principal second
Viola   Marna Street   principal
Harp   Gillian Benet Sella   principal
Flute   Joan Voorhees   piccolo

Cleveland Orchestra   **Franz Welser-Möst**   *(26 women out of 105)*
Violin   Yoko Moore   assistant concertmaster
                                 Ellen de Pasquale   associate concertmaster
Viola   Lynne Ramsey   assistant principal
Flute   Mary Kay Fink   piccolo
Clarinet   Linnea Nereim   bass clarinet
Harp   Lisa Wellbaum   principal
                                 Trina Struble   assistant principal
Piano   Joela Jones   principal

Colorado Symphony Orchestra   **Jeffrey Kahane**   *(28 women out of 79)*
Violin   Yumi Hwang-Williams   concertmaster
Viola   Catherine Beeson   assistant principal
Flute   Pamela Endsley   principal
                                     Catherine Lum Peterson   assistant principal
                                     Julie Duncan Thornton   piccolo
Oboe   Monica Hanulik   assistant principal
Horn   Carolyn Landis   assistant principal
                                     Kristin Jurkscheit   associate principal
Harp   Courtney Hershey Bress   principal

Dallas Symphony Orchestra   **Andrew Litton**   *(36 women out of 94)*
Violin   Alexandra Adkins   associate principal second violins
                                     Sho Mei Pelletier   associate principal second violins
Viola   Ellen Rose   principal
                                     Barbara Hustis   associate principal
                                     Ann Marie Hudson   associate principal
Flute   Jean Larson   principal
                                     Deborah Baron   assistant principal & piccolo
Oboe   Willa Henigman   assistant principal
Harp   Susan Dederich-Pejovich   principal

Detroit Symphony Orchestra   **Neeme Järve**   *(27 women out of 97)*
Violin   Emmanuelle Boisvert   concertmaster
                                     Laura Rowe   assistant concertmaster
Cello   Marcy Chanteaux   assistant principal
Harp   Patricia Masri-Fletcher   principal
Oboe   Treva Womble   English horn

Houston Symphony   **Hans Graf**   *(31 women out of 96)*
Violin   Ming Qi   assistant concertmaster
                                     Marina Brubaker   acting assistant concertmaster
                                     Jennifer Owen   principal second violins
Flute   Aralee Dorough   principal
                                     Cynthia Meyers   piccolo
Oboe   Anne Leek   principal
Harp   Paula Page

Indianapolis Symphony Orchestra **Mario Venzago**   *(33 women out of 86)*
Violin   Christal Phelps Steele   assistant concertmaster
                                     Mary Anne Dell'Aquila   assistant principal second violins
Viola   Theresa Langdon   associate principal
                                     Beverly Scott   assistant principal
Flute   Karen Moratz   principal
                                     Rebecca Price Arrensen   assistant principal & piccolo
Harp   Diane Evans   principal

Los Angeles Philharmonic — Esa-Pekka Salonen   (33 women out of 105)

Violin	Bing Wang	associate concertmaster
Viola	Dale Hikawa Silverman	associate principal
Flute	Anne Diener Zenter	principal
	Janet Ferguson	principal
	Sarah Jackson	piccolo
Oboe	Marion Arthur Kuszyk	associate principal
	Carolyn Hove	English horn
Clarinet	Michele Zukovsky	principal
	Monica Kaenzig	E flat clarinet
Bassoon	Patricia Kindel	contrabassoon
Keyboard	Joanne Martin Pearce	principal
Harp	Lou Anne Neill	principal

Metropolitan Opera Orchestra — James Levine   (46 women out of 130)

Despite the three to one ratio this roster shows the most women in principal positions:

			Since
Violin	Laura Hamilton	associate concertmaster	1986
	Nancy Wu	associate concertmaster	1988
	Shirien Taylor	principal second	1987
Viola	Caroline Levine	assistant principal	1983
	Marilyn Stroh	Member over forty years!	1960
Bass	Jacqui Danilow		1980
Flute	Trudy Kane	principal	1976
Oboe	Elaine Douvas	principal	1977
Bassoon	Patricia Rogers	co-principal	1976
Horn	Julie Landsman	principal (See Brass)	1985
Harp	Deborah Hoffman	principal (See Harpists)	1977
	Mariko Anraku	associate principal	1995

Milwaukee Symphony Orchestra — Andreas Delfs   (38 women out of 91)

Violin	Samantha George	associate concertmaster
	Karen Smith	assistant concertmaster
	Anne DeVroome Kamerling	associate concertmaster emeritus
	Jennifer Startt	assistant principal second violins
Flute	Jeani Foster	principal
	Glenda Greenhoe	assistant principal
	Judith Ormond	piccolo
Clarinet	Diana Haskell	assistant principal & E flat clarinet
Bassoon	Beth Giacobassi	contra bassoon
Harp	Danis Kelly	principal

Minnesota Orchestra	**Osmo Vänskä**	*(34 women out of 98)*
Violin	Jorja Fleezanis	concertmaster
	Sarah Kwak	first associate concertmaster
	Stephanie Arado	assistant concertmaster
	Julie Ayer	assistant principal second violin
Cello	Janet Horvath	associate principal
	Beth Rapier-Ross	assistant principal
Flute	Barbara Leibundguth	co-principal
	Roma Kansara Duncan	piccolo
Oboe	Marni Hougham	English horn
Harp	Kathy Kienzle	principal

Orchestre Symphonique de Montréal	**Kent Nagano**	*(33 women out of 97)*

The Montreal Orchestra was founded 1930. In 1934, some of its members formed Les Concerts Symphoniques, which, in 1954, became Orchestre Symphonique de Montréal.

Violin	Brigitte Rolland	first assistant second violins
	Katherine Palyga	second assistant second violins
Viola	Jean Forrin	first assistant
Oboe	Margaret Morse	associate principal
Flute	Virginia Spicer	piccolo
Bassoon	Stéphane Lévesque	principal
Harp	Jennifer Swartz	principal

National Symphony Orchestra	**Leonard Slatkin (1996–2007)**	*(34 women out of 98)*
Violin	Nurit Bar-Josef	concertmaster
	Elisabeth Adkins	co-concertmaster
	Marissa Regni	principal second violins
	Pamela Hentges	assistant principal second violins
Harp	Dotian Levalier	principal
Flute	Toshiko Kohno	principal
	Carole Bean	piccolo
Oboe	Carol Stephenson	assistant principal
	Kathryn Meany Wilson	English horn
Bassoon	Sue Heineman	principal
Horn	Laurel Bennert Ohlson	associate principal

New York Philharmonic	**Lorin Maazel**	*(35 women out of 107)*
Violin	**Sheryl Staples**	associate concertmaster
	Michelle Kim	assistant concertmaster
Viola	**Cynthia Phelps**	principal
	Rebecca Young	associate principal
	Irene Breslaw	assistant principal
Cello	Hai-ye Ni	associate principal
Flute	Sandra Church	associate principal

	Mindy Kaufman	piccolo
Oboe	Sherry Sylar	associate principal
Bassoon	Judith LeClair	principal
Harp	**Nancy Allen**	principal
Piano	Harriet Wingreen	principal

Oregon Symphony	**Carlos Kalmar**	*(44 women out of 93)*
Violin	Erin Furbee	assistant concertmaster
	Chien Tan	principal second violins
	Delores D'Aigle	assistant principal second violin
Cello	Nancy Ives	principal
Flute	Dawn Weiss	principal
	Martha Herby	acting principal
	Carla Wilson	piccolo
Trumpet	Sally Nelson Kuhns	assistant principal
Keyboard	Katherine George	principal
Harp	Jennifer Craig	principal

Pacific Symphony Orchestra	**Carl St. Clair**	*(35 women out of 88)*
Violin	Jeanne Evans	assistant concertmaster
Viola	Janet Lakatos	assistant principal
Flute	Louise DiTullio	principal
	Cynthia Ellis	piccolo
Oboe	Barbara Northcutt	principal
	Lelie Resnick	English horn
Percussion	Mindy Ball	principal
Keyboard	Sandra Matthews	principal

Philadelphia Orchestra	**Christoph Eschenbach**	*(23 women out of 112)*
Violin	Nancy Bean	assistant concertmaster
	Kimberly Fisher	principal second violins
Oboe	Elizabeth Starr Masoudnia	English horn
Bassoon	Holly Blake	contra bassoon
Horn	Jennifer Montone	principal
	Shelley Showers	assistant principal
Tuba	Carolyn Jantsch	principal
Piano	Kiyoko Takeuti	principal
Harp	Elizabeth Hainen De Peters	principal
	Margarita Csonka Montanaro	co-principal

Phoenix Symphony	**Michael Christie**	*(25 women out of 78)*
Violin	Magdalena Martinic-Jercic	associate concertmaster
	Dian D'Avanzo	assistant principal second violin
Viola	Annie Center	associate principal
Cello	Blythe Tretick	associate principal
Oboe	Marian Pendell	principal

	Paula Engerer	assistant principal & English horn
Bassoon	Bonnie Wolfgang	principal
	Marlene Mazzuca	assistant principal
Horn	Barbara Bingham	associate principal
	Nancy Diamond	assistant principal
Harp	Paula Provo	principal

Pittsburgh Symphony Orchestra	**Sir Andrew Davis**	*(30 women out of 97)*
	Yan Pascal Tortelier	
	Marek Janowski	
Violin	Jennifer Ross	principal second violin
Cello	Anne Martindale Williams	principal
	Lauren Scott Mallory	associate principal
Bass	Betsy Heston	assistant principal
Harp	Gretchen Van Hoesen	principal
Flute	Rhian Kenny	piccolo
Oboe	Cynthia DeAlmeida	principal
Bassoon	Nancy Goeres	principal
Trombone	Rebecca Cherian	co-principal
Keyboard	Patricia Prattis Jennings	principal

St. Joseph (Missouri) Symphony	**Deborah Freedman**	*(31 women out of 70)*
Violin	Margaret Kew	concertmaster
	Janet Kvam	principal second violin
Viola	Judith Koster	principal
Cello	Brenda Allen	principal
Flute	Cecelia Trabert	principal
Oboe	Meribeth Risebig	principal
Bassoon	Claudia Risebig	principal
Trombone	Stephanie Cox	principal

St. Louis Symphony Orchestra	**David Robertson**	*(41 women out of 98)*
Violin	Elisa Barston	associate concertmaster
	Heidi Harris	assistant concertmaster
	Allison Harney	principal second violins
Viola	Kathleen Mattis	associate principal
Cello	Catherine Lehr	assistant principal
Bass	Carolyn White	associate principal
Harp	Frances Tietov	principal
Flute	Jan Gippo	piccolo
Oboe	Barbara Herr Orland	assistant principal
Trumpet	Susan Slaughter	principal
Piano	Barbara Liberman	principal

St. Paul Chamber Orchestra   *(14 women out of 35)*
Violin   Leslie Shank   assistant concertmaster
                    Carolyn Gunkler   assistant principal second violin
Viola   Sabina Thatcher   principal
                    Evelina Chao   assistant principal
Flute   Julia Bogorad-Kogan   principal
Oboe   Katherine Greenbank   principal

San Diego Symphony Orchestra   **Jahja Ling**   *(39 women out of 86)*
Viola   Nancy Lochner   associate principal
Cello   Ru-Pei Yeh   principal
Bass   Susan Wulff   associate principal
Flute   Elizabeth Ashmead   piccolo
Clarinet   Sheryl Renk   principal
Contra Bassoon   Leyla Zamora
Horn   Tricia Skye   assistant principal
Harp   Sheila Sterling   principal
Percussion   Cynthia Yeh   principal
Piano   Mary Barranger   principal

San Francisco Symphony   **Michael Tilson Thomas**   *(32 women out of 106)*
Violin   Nadya Tichman   associate concertmaster
                    Darlene Gray   associate principal second violin
Viola   Geraldine Walther   principal
Flute   Robin McKee   principal
                    Catherine Payne   piccolo
Oboe   Julie Ann Giacobassi   English horn
Keyboard   Robin Sutherland   principal

Santa Barbara Symphony   **Gisèle Ben-Dor** (See Conductors)   *(48 women out of 90)*
Violin   Gloria Autry   principal second violin
Viola   Ann Tischer   principal
Flute   Francin Jacobs   principal
Oboe   Leann Becknell   principal
Bassoon   Elise Unruh   principal
Harp   Michell Temple   principal

Seattle Symphony Orchestra   **Gerard Schwarz**   *(32 women out of 90)*
Violin   Maria Larionoff   concertmaster
                    Janet Fisher Baunton   principal second violin
Viola   Susan Gulkis Assadi   principal
                    Dorothy Shapiro   assistant principal
Cello   Susan Williams   associate principal
                    Theresa Benshoof   assistant principal
Clarinet   Laura DeLuca   E-Flat clarinet

Harp	Valerie Muzzolini	principal
Keyboard	Victoria Bogdashevskaya	principal

Toronto Symphony   Peter Oundijian   *(21 women out of 87)*

Violin	Wendy Rose	assistant principal second violins
Viola	Susan Lipchak	principal
Flute	Nora Shulman	principal
	Julie Ranti	associate principal
	Camille Watts	piccolo
Bassoon	Kathleen McLean	associate principal
Keyboard	Patricia Krueger	principal

Utah Symphony   Keith Lockhart   *(28 women out of 87)*

Violin	Wen Yuan Gu	associate principal second violins
Viola	Roberta Shulman-Zalkind	associate principal
Flute	Lisa Byrnes	associate principal
Oboe	Holly Gornik	English horn
Harp	Louise Vickerman	principal

Wheeling (W. Virginia) **Symphony**   **André Raphel Smith**   *(33 women out of 71)*

Cello	Kathleen Melucci	principal
Flute	Barbara H O'Brien	principal
	Gail Looney	piccolo
Clarinet	Mary Beth Malek	principal

CHAPTER ELEVEN
PART E

Ladies of the Orchestra

For each soloist displaying her talent in front of the orchestra, there are at least twenty women providing harmonic support behind her in the ranks. Statistically, the more major the orchestra, the keener the competition when an opening arises. Women have secured these hard-won positions through education, training and superior musicianship. In 1996, 1999, 2000, 2003[81] surveys of major and regional orchestras, the average ratio of men to women has remained three to one. In this section, where available, biographical sketches are given of women principals, assistant and associate principals. Self-evident is the preponderance of women in strings and woodwinds. Female brass players continue making inroads, but there is still a paucity in percussion.

ATLANTA SYMPHONY (Robert Spano)

The Atlanta Symphony was formed in 1947 from the Atlanta Youth Orchestra, founded 1944. The orchestra became professional in 1967, under the direction of **Robert Shaw.**

On July 19, 1996, with the advent of the Centennial Olympic Games in Atlanta, the then ninety-six member Atlanta Symphony became the largest orchestra ever to perform in an opening ceremony. They also played six concerts during the Olympic Arts Festival with guest performances by soprano **Jessye Norman** and violinist **Itzhak Perlman.** The Orchestra has made two European tours (1988, 1991), won twenty-one Grammy Awards, was nominated "Best Orchestra of the Year" for the 1991–92 season by the first Annual International Music Awards, and received four ASCAP awards for "Adventuresome Programming of American Music."

Cecylia Arzewski

Cecylia Arzewski - concertmaster born in Krakow, Poland, began violin at age five. The family emigrated to Israel in 1957, where she attended the Tel Aviv Conservatory studying with **Odeon Partos** (1907–77). Coming to America, she attended Juilliard and the New England Conservatory, studying with **Joseph Silverstein**, then concertmaster of the Boston Symphony. From 1969–70, she played with the Buffalo Philharmonic, after which she spent seventeen years with the Boston Symphony, becoming assistant concertmaster in 1978. Her position as associate concertmaster for the Cleveland Orchestra lasted from 1987 to 1990 when she joined Atlanta as concertmaster. The first female concertmaster of a major U.S. orchestra, Cecylia has also performed with the Georgian Chamber Players throughout Europe, and with pianist Lois Shapiro in recitals in Boston and Atlanta.

Beth Newdome

Beth Newdome - associate concertmaster, born in Mansfield, Ohio, began violin studies with her mother at age three and a half. Her degree and performer's certificate are from the Eastman School of Music. She was assistant concertmaster of the Jacksonville (Florida) Symphony and a member of the Dallas and Columbus (Ohio) Symphonies before joining the orchestra in 1991 as assistant concertmaster. She took a leave of absence in 2002, joined the faculty of Florida State University and left the orchestra.

---

81. Allow for variances in numbers for retirements, moving on, etc. See 2005 Orchestra List.

Amy Leventhal - assistant principal viola is founder and artistic director of the Primrose Series of concerts at Emory University, where she is a member of the music faculty. She studied at Indiana University and Oberlin Conservatory, joining the Symphony in 1990. Her husband, Scott Douglas, is a percussionist in Atlanta.

Dona Vellek Klein - assistant principal cello grew up in a family of musicians. Her mother played oboe in the Chicago Symphony and Minneapolis Orchestra. Her sister is a violinist with Seattle. A graduate of the New School of Music (Philadelphia), Klein played in the Buffalo Philharmonic for three years before joining ASO in 1981. She is the founder/director of the Atlanta Quartet, composed of symphony string players, and the chamber group *Sempre Sonare*. Her husband is an Atlanta attorney. Their daughter, Andrea, shows singing talent.

Gloria Jones - assistant principal bass grew up in Greenville, South Carolina, where she studied piano and violin until age twelve when she took up the bass. She attended Interlochen for six summers and Aspen for two, studied at the University of Michigan, and joined ASO in 1984 at age twenty. Her husband is Ralph Jones, the orchestra's principal bass.

Jane Little - assistant principal bass in her sixty-second year in 2006, is the only original member of the Atlanta Youth Symphony, which she joined in 1944 at eighteen, who is still playing in what is now the Atlanta Symphony. She commuted to the city for concerts after classes at the University of Georgia, became a professional member as the organization matured, and made the shift to full-time when ASO upgraded from a part-time orchestra. Guest conductors under whom she has played include Pierre Monteux, Sir John Barbirolli, Leopold Stokowski and Igor Stravinsky.

Christina Smith - principal flute a native of Sonoma, California, began flute studies at age seven and was a soloist with the San Francisco Symphony at fifteen. She graduated from the Interlochen Arts Academy and Curtis Institute, joining the orchestra in 1991 as principal flute. She has performed at the Blossom, Tanglewood, and Marlboro festivals, and regularly appears in recitals, chamber music and master classes in the Southeast.

Yvonne Powers Peterson - associate principal oboe studied at Ohio University and the Cleveland Institute of Music. She came to ASO in 1992 from the Grand Rapids (Michigan) Symphony, where she was principal oboe from 1985. Her previous positions include the Canton and Evansville (Indiana) Symphonies, the Orquestra Sinfonica de Veracruz, Mexico, and the Cabrillo (California) Music Festival. Peterson teaches at Emory University and plays in the chamber group *Atlanta Winds*.

Laura Ardan - principal clarinet since 1982, attended Juilliard on scholarships from the school and the Naumberg Foundation. For four years prior to joining ASO, she was the resident clarinetist and teaching artist at the Lincoln Center Institute, and played in the Metropolitan Opera Orchestra for two seasons.

Elizabeth Burkhardt - assistant principal bassoon joined ASO in 1989, having played in the Richmond (Virginia) Symphony and the New Philharmonic Orchestra of Portugal. Her performer's certificate is from Eastman, with further studies at the Manhattan School. She is the founder of the *Atlanta Winds*.

Susan Welty - assistant principal horn a graduate of Northwestern University (Illinois), moved to Atlanta in 1984 teaching at Columbus College where she was a member of the *Southwind Woodwind Quintet*. She taught horn at Southeastern Music Center and, before joining ASO in 1988, played in the Atlanta Ballet and Atlanta Opera Orchestras.

Elisabeth Remy - principal harp since 1995, studied with **Ann Hobson Pilot** in Boston, spent summers at the Salzedo Summer Harp Colony, and graduated from Harvard with a double major in music and French. She recorded the demanding harp accompaniment to Britten's *Ceremony of Carols* on the Telarc recording of *A Robert Shaw Christmas: Angels on High*. She teaches privately at Emory and Kennesaw Universities, and Georgia State. She wed Livingston Johnson, June 11, 2005.

BALTIMORE SYMPHONY (Yuri Tamirkanov) (Marin Alsop 2006–) Founded 1914.

Madeline Adkins - assistant concertmaster a native of Denton, Texas, and graduate of University of North Texas, received her MM from the New England Conservatory (2000). Since 1989, she has performed baroque violin with the Handel & Haydn Society and Boston Baroque. She was the winner of the 1997 Stulberg International String Competition, the 1998 ASTA National Solo Competition, and second place winner of the 1999 Irving Kline International String Competition.

Chang Woo Lee - assistant principal cello a graduate of the Seoul (Korea) National University, in 1967 was offered a scholarship by Janos Starker to Indiana University where she received an artist's diploma. She played in Mexico and Canada before joining the BSO in 1978.

Emily Controulis Skala - principal flute received her BM from Eastman (1983). She joined Baltimore in 1988, after being a member of the Pittsburgh (1986–88), North Carolina (1984–86), and San Diego (1981–83) Symphonies. Soloist with Baltimore and the Filharmonia Sudecka in Walbrzych, Poland, she has also performed at music festivals in Edinburgh, Osaka, Hollywood Bowl, Great Woods, Wolf Trap and Aspen. She is solo flutist for the Baltimore Choral Arts Society, and has been on the Peabody faculty since 1989.

Elizabeth Rowe - assistant principal flute from Eugene, Oregon, has a BM from USC, and was principal flute with the Ft. Wayne Philharmonic before joining BSO in 2001.

Laurie Sokoloff, a graduate of Curtis, has played piccolo since 1969.

Jane Marvine - English horn holds a BM and MM from Northwestern University, is on the faculty at Peabody and has played with the orchestra since 1978.

Julie Gregorian - assistant principal bassoon

Eileen Mason - harp born in San Diego, California, she holds degrees from the University of Redlands, Cincinnati College Conservatory and University of Kentucky. She was principal harp with the Kansas City Philharmonic, Aspen Festival Orchestra, and Indianapolis Symphony. She retired in 2002.

BOSTON SYMPHONY ORCHESTRA (James Levine 2002–) (Seiji Ozawa 1973–2002)

Founded in 1881. In 1940, they formed the Tanglewood (formerly Berkshire, 1937) Music Festival and school for young musicians.

Tamara Smirnova - associate concertmaster born in Siberia, 1958, is a 1981 graduate of the Tchaikovsky Conservatory in Moscow, and was concertmaster of the Zagreb Philharmonic. A 1985 bronze medal winner at the Queen Elisabeth Competition in Brussels, she made her American debut in 1986, and was a 1989 BSO concerto soloist.

Elita Kang - assistant concertmaster attended Juilliard Pre-College Division before Curtis, where she received her BM in 1997. She studied with **Pamela Frank** and Louise Behrend, and substituted with the Philadelphia Orchestra before joining the BSO in the 1997–98 season. In 2001, she was appointed assistant concertmaster.

Sheila Fiekowsky has been a member of the BSO violin section since 1975. She first appeared as a soloist with the Detroit Symphony at age sixteen. A graduate of Curtis, with an MM from Yale where she studied with **Joseph Silverstein**, she is a regular performer in Symphony Hall Supper Concerts and Tanglewood Prelude Concerts. She has been heard in numerous chamber music and solo performances in the Boston area where she lives with her husband and two children.

Ikuko Mizuno joined BSO in 1969—the first woman member of the violin section. She attended Tokyo's Toho-Gakuen School of Music in her native Japan, and came to the U.S. as a winner of the Spaulding Award, which enabled her to study at Boston University where she earned her MM. She also holds diplomas from the Accademia Musicale Chigiana in Siena, Italy, and the Geneva Conservatory. Mizuno is on the faculties of Boston University School for Fine Arts and the BU Tanglewood Institute. She has been a guest professor at the Taho-Gakuen School. Since 1985 she also performs in the Chicago area, and returns to Japan for recitals and performances with orchestra. In 1984, she was invited as guest concertmistress for the inaugural concert of the Women's Orchestra of Japan. She maintains two homes, one in Boston, the other in Chicago with her husband, Dr. Jean-Paul Spire, a faculty member of the University of Chicago School of Medicine.

Cathy Basrak - assistant principal viola is a 2000 graduate of Curtis. Besides participating in the Marlboro and Norfolk Chamber Music Festivals, and Banff Center for the Arts, she has soloed with the orchestras of Chicago, Philadelphia, and Detroit. She is principal viola in the Boston Pops.

Martha Babcock - assistant principal cello and principal with the Pops Orchestra, joined BSO in 1973 and was appointed to her current position in 1982. She is a graduate of Radcliffe, and graduate school at BU's School for the Arts. After winning the Piatigorsky Prize while a fellow at Tanglewood in 1972, her professional career was launched at age nineteen as the youngest member of the Montreal Symphony Orchestra. She performs with the Boston Symphony Chamber Players and, with her husband, violinist Harvey Seigal, and pianist Robert Spano, former BSO assistant conductor, now director of Atlanta, plays chamber music as the Higginson Trio. She has made several recordings. Babcock plays the "ex-Feuermann" cello made by David Tecchler (1666–1748) in Rome, dated 1741.

Carol Procter

Carol Procter - cello and twin sister Lucille, were born to composer parents, Leland H. Procter and Alice McElroy, a 1940 Eastman PhD graduate. Carol also studied at Eastman and holds BM and MM degrees from the NEC. She was a member of the Springfield Symphony and Cambridge Festival Orchestra, and in 1965 turned down a Fulbright Scholarship to join the BSO. In 1969, she spent a year abroad as part of the BSO musicians exchange program with the Japanese Philharmonic. A member of the New England Harp Trio (1971–87) and Curtisville Consortium (1972–81), she performs chamber music frequently and has soloed with the Boston Pops. She retired in August 2003 after spending the summer at Tanglewood, and is now devoting her time to her vocations of energy healing and transformational breath work.

Elizabeth Ostling - associate principal flute a 1994 graduate of Curtis, joined the orchestra in 1994 as assistant principal and has been associate principal since the 1997–98 season. She also performs with the Boston Symphony Chamber Players and Boston Artists Ensemble.

Geralyn Coticone - piccolo graduated from Boston University, studied with **Doriot Anthony Dwyer** and joined the National Symphony in 1988. She has been with Boston since 1990.

Ann Hobson Pilot - principal harp joined the BSO in 1969 after being with the Pittsburgh Symphony (1965–66), and principal harp with the National Symphony (1966–69). In 1980, she was appointed to her current position. (See Harpists.)

CHICAGO SYMPHONY (Daniel Barenboim)

Founded 1891 by Theodore Thomas, the orchestra was named after him until 1906. Their summer concerts are held at the Ravinia Festival.

Yuan-Qing Yu - assistant concertmaster came to Chicago in 1995 from the Houston Symphony. A native of Shanghai, she began violin at age six, attended middle school affiliated with the Shanghai Conservatory, and was accepted at the conservatory in 1988. In 1989, she won the Chinese Nationwide Violin Competition and second prize in the Menuhin International Violin Competition. She received an artist's certificate and MM in violin performance from Southern Methodist University, Texas.

Sarah Bullen - principal harp was appointed to Chicago in 1997, after being principal with the New York Philharmonic (1987–97) and the Utah Symphony (1981–87). A native of Long Island, New York, she attended the Interlochen Arts Academy and holds BM and MM degrees from Juilliard. She has conducted master classes in Europe and the U.S., was chairperson of the harp department at the Manhattan School, and author of *Principal Harp: A Guidebook for the Orchestral Harpist*. She has appeared countless times as a soloist, and has served as a lecturer and judge for the AHS and the USA International Harp Competition. She is a professor of harp at Chicago Musical College of Roosevelt University.

Mary Sauer - principal keyboard has been with the CSO since 1959, when she joined at the invitation **Fritz Reiner** (1888–1963). On the faculty of DePaul University, she coordinates the keyboard program and is keyboard coach with the Civic Orchestra of Chicago. She received both her BM and MM degrees from the Chicago Musical College. Her commitment to chamber music involves many years' collaboration with the Chicago Symphony Chamber Music Series, Symphony Chamber Soloists of Chicago, Chicago Symphony String Quartet, and the Alistaire Trio. In demand as a soloist, recitalist, and chamber musician, she has performed as soloist with the Peninsula Music Festival in Wisconsin for over twenty seasons. She and husband Richard Hannenberg, have a daughter Kristin, who is a professor and director of the deaconess program at Concordia University.

CINCINNATI SYMPHONY (Paavo Järvi)

Founded 1895, since 1984 they have held their summer series at the River Bend Music Center. In 1967, they were the first American orchestra to go on a world tour. Jesús López-Cobos retired in 2001 after fifteen years, the longest tenure of any musical director at the CSO.

Rebecca Culnan - associate concertmaster joined in 1978 in her present position. Besides soloing with the orchestra, she has taught at the Cincinnati College-Conservatory and was assistant to the late **Dorothy DeLay** at Aspen. She is married to Daniel Culnan, associate principal cellist. They have two children, Elizabeth, born 1987 and John, 1989.

Sylvia Samis - assistant concertmaster a native of Munich, Germany, graduated from Temple University, Philadelphia, and was a member of Concerto Soloists of Philadelphia, New Orleans Philharmonic and Cincinnati Chamber Soloists. She joined Cincinnati in 1973 and also performs at music festivals and in the Area Artist Series.

Katherine Robertson - second aassistant concertmaster

Catherine Lange-Jensen - associate principal second violin joined the orchestra in 1984, attaining her current position in 1986. She graduated from Indiana University and was a member of the Florida Symphony before moving to Cincinnati, where she also performs with the Symphony Chamber Players and the Corbett Quartet.

Marna Street - principal viola is a graduate of Juilliard. She played in the Pittsburgh Symphony before her appointment to CSO in 1980. She is an active recitalist and enthusiastic participant in the orchestra's *Music For Children* program.

Gillian Benet Sella - principal harp came to Cincinnati in 1995 after being principal harp of the Kennedy Center Opera House Orchestra. A native of California, she won the National Competition of the AHS at age fifteen, studied at the Royal Conservatory of Toronto, and is a graduate of Harvard.

Joan Voorhees - piccolo a graduate of the University of Maryland, has played professionally since age fourteen. After a busy career as a freelance flutist in the Washington, DC area, where she played with the Kennedy Center Opera, National Symphony and Washington Ballet, she joined the CSO in 1991.

Robin Graham - former principal French horn, began her professional career when, as a twenty-year-old senior at Juilliard, she won the principal horn position with the Houston Symphony, becoming their youngest player and the first woman to hold a principal horn position in a major American orchestra. After six years as principal with the Los Angeles Chamber Orchestra, she joined Cincinnati in 1985. She has performed with the Guarneri String Quartet, American String Quartet, Academia String Quartet, Music from Marlboro and the Chamber Music Society of Lincoln Center, also touring throughout Europe. She has soloed with many orchestras, and served on the faculties of Rice University, California Institute of the Arts, UCLA, Aspen Festival. She and her husband are parents of Michael, born 1990, and Stephen, March, 1994.

CLEVELAND SYMPHONY (Franz Welser-Möst)

Founded 1918, since 1968 their summer series has beem at the Blossom Music Center.

Yoko Hiroe Moore - assistant concertmaster was born in Japan and attended the Toho School of Music. From 1972–75, she played with the New Japan Philharmonic directed by **Seiji Ozawa**, one of her former classmates at the Toho School. After moving to the U.S., she played in the first violin section of the Dallas Symphony, then concertmaster of the Tulsa Philharmonic, and joined Cleveland in 1982. She frequently performs in recitals and solo performances with Japanese orchestras. Her daughter is also a violinist.

Ellen dePasquale - associate concertmaster was appointed to the position in March 1999. She earned her BM from Curtis (1994), and was doing graduate work at Indiana University when she won the audition as concertmaster for the Florida Orchestra in 1996 at age twenty-two. For four years she attended both the Cleveland Institute's summer program, Encore School for Strings, and the Marlboro Music Festival. Previous women to hold this Cleveland chair were **Cecylia Arzewski** (1987–90), now concertmaster in Atlanta, and **Sheryl Staples** (1996–98), now principal associate concertmaster with the New York Philharmonic.

Lynne Ramsey - first assistant principal viola since 1989, received her BM and MM degrees from Juilliard (1976). Prior to joining Cleveland in 1988, she was principal viola with both the St. Paul Chamber Orchestra and Rochester Philharmonic, and a member of the Pittsburgh Symphony. She is married to Jeff Irvine, professor of viola at Oberlin, where she has taught viola and chamber music since 1985. She is part of the Amici String Trio with fellow orchestra members Takako Masame (violin) and Ralph Curry (cello).

Lisa Wellbaum - principal harp began studies on her instrument at age nine with her mother when both parents were members of the Cincinnati Symphony. She spent several summers studying at the Salzedo Harp Colony with **Alice Chalifoux**, then principal harpist with Cleveland. She subsequently studied with Chalifoux at the Cleveland Institute, where she earned her BM. Before joining Cleveland in 1974, she was principal with the New Orleans Philharmonic, Winnipeg Symphony and, for six seasons, the Santa Fe Opera. Wellbaum heads the harp department at Baldwin Wallace College, and performs as a recitalist and chamber musician. Her husband, Stephen Geber, is principal cellist with Cleveland. They have two daughters, Stephanie and Lauren.

Joela Jones - principal keyboard as a young child studied at Florida State University with **Edward Kilenyi** (1910–2000), and attended master classes of Hungarian pianist **Ernst von Dohnányi** (1877–1960). At twelve, she appeared as soloist with the Miami Symphony and the following year won a scholarship to Eastman. Her MM is from the Cleveland Institute. She has appeared as soloist with the orchestras of Boston, Chicago, Detroit, Houston, Philadelphia and San Francisco, and performs in chamber and solo recitals. A member of the orchestra since 1970, playing piano, harpsichord, organ and celesta, she is also principal accompanist for the Cleveland Orchestra Chorus and visiting singers. She has performed over fifty solo works with the orchestra. She is married to Richard Weiss, first assistant principal cellist. They are the parents of Justin Jordan.

The orchestra has three other married couples: violinists Stephen Rose and Jeanne Preucil Rose—sister of concertmaster William Preucil; violinist Keiko Furiyoshi and librarian Ronald Whitaker; and violinists Carolyn Gadiel Warner and Stephen Warner.

An interesting glimpse into history is this list of past and long-term women musicians in the Cleveland Symphony:

Marion Brown	viola	1953–55	
Sally Burnau	viola	1960–61	
Muriel Carmen	viola	1951–1994	(See Violists)
Alice Chalifoux	harp	1930–1973	(See Harpists)
Elizabeth Glendenning	first violin	1959–61, 1963–67	
Cathleen Dalschaert	first & second violin	1960–67	
Martha Dalton	harp	1947–51, 1952–80	(See Harpists)
Eugenie Fichtenova	first violin	1947–48	
Rosemary Goldsmith	viola	1967–81	
Margaret Hillis	Chorus Director	1969–71	(See conductors)
Audrey Meyer	second violin	1966–79	
Marie Setzer	first violin	1961–90	

Joan Siegel	second violin	1965–
Roberta Strawn	second violin	1962–84
Shirley Trepel	cello	1952–55
Halina Voldrich	first violin	1967–72

COLORADO SYMPHONY (Jeffrey Kahane)

Renamed in 1989 from the Denver Orchestra, formed in 1934, its last director was eminent French pianist and conductor Philippe Entrement.

MARIN ALSOP - conductor laureate. After six seasons as music director of the Long Island Philharmonic and the Eugene Symphony, she joined Colorado as principal conductor in 1993. In February 1995, the board changed her title to music director in recognition of her artistic achievements and successes with the orchestra. In 2002–03 she became principal conductor of the Bournemouth (England) Symphony, and in 2006, conductor of the Baltimore Symphony. (See Conductors.)

Yumi Hwang-Williams - concertmaster was born in Seoul, Korea, and immigrated to the U.S. in 1979. She attended the New School of Music at Temple University, and at fifteen soloed with the Philadelphia Orchestra. That same year she was accepted at Curtis, graduating in 1991. She played four seasons with the Philadelphia Orchestra, and was a member of the Concerto Soloists Chamber Orchestra. From 1995–99, she was principal second violin with the Cincinnati Symphony, and was one of the founding members of the Felix Quartet.

Catherine Beeson - assistant principal viola played freelance in New York before joining the orchestra in 1999. Her summers are spent in the Andirondack Mountains at the chamber music workshop Loon Lake Live!

Pamela Endsley - principal flute came to the orchestra in 1966, after playing in the Pittsburgh Symphony. She is coordinator of pre-concert entertainment. She and husband, Gerry, are the parents of Shane and Marguerite.

Catherine Lum Peterson - assistant principal flute has a BM from San Francisco Conservatory and MM from University of Michigan.

Monica Hanulik - assistant principal oboe

Carolyn Landis - assistant principal horn

Kristin Jurkscheit - associate principal horn studied at the NEC, receiving a grant for post-graduate study at Norway State Academy of Music in Oslo. She came to Colorado in 1992, after playing in New York's Concordia Chamber Orchestra, Jupiter Symphony, American Ballet Theatre Orchestra and the Boston Opera Company.

Courtney Hershey Bress - harp

DALLAS SYMPHONY (Andrew Litton)

Founded 1911, it became fully professional in 1945 under Antal Dorati.

Alexandra Shtarkman Adkins - associate principal second violin is a native of Russia who emigrated to the U.S. in 1979. She studied with **Dorothy DeLay** at the Cincinnati College Conservatory and with **Joseph Gingold** at Indiana University. She joined the symphony in 1988, after having played with the Columbus Symphony and the Ohio Chamber Orchestra.

Sho Mei Pelletier - associate principal second violin has been with the orchestra since graduating from Indiana University. She has also played with the Santa Fe Opera, Dallas Chamber Orchestra, Phoenix and Colorado.

Ellen Rose - principal viola since 1980, is a graduate of Juilliard. In recitals throughout the U.S., she has appeared in chamber music performances with **Itzhak Perlman**, **Pinchas Zukerman**, **Lynn Harrell**, and **Ralph Kirschbaum**. She is principal violist and faculty member of the Aspen Music Festival, viola professor at Southern Methodist University and teaches master classes at the Cleveland Institute, Oberlin and Juilliard. She was a guest artist at the 1995 International Viola Congress.

Ann Marie Hudson - associate principal viola joined Dallas in 1999. A 1996 winner of the Nakamichi Foundation Viola Concerto Competition, she is an honors graduate of Interlochen Arts Academy, received her BM from the Cleveland Institute and MM from Juilliard, where she was awarded the William Schuman Prize. She has also served on the faculties of Baylor and Interlochen.

Jeanie Larson - principal flute a native Texan and graduate of the University of Texas at Austin, studied in Europe with **Jean-Pierre Rampal**, and James Pappoutsakis at Tanglewood. Since joining the orchestra in 1971, she has played throughout the country as a soloist and chamber musician at the Mainly Mozart Festival in San Diego, Tanglewood Festival, and Music in the Mountains, a festival in Purgatory, Colorado. She is a member of the Dallas Woodwind Quintet, and serves on the faculty of Southern Methodist University. She and her husband, Lorin, principal horn with the Fort Worth Symphony, have a son, Glen.

Deborah Baron - assistant principal flute/piccolo who holds her BM and MM from Juilliard, has been with the orchestra since 1985. Before coming to Dallas, she performed with the Springfield (Massachusetts) Symphony, the Metropolitan Opera Orchestra, and the Grand Teton Festival Orchestra. Formerly on the faculties of Smith College and Wooster School, she now maintains a private studio, plays with the Dallas Bach Society and the ensemble Triptych. She and husband Winston Stone, a teacher in Dallas, have a son Zachary.

Willa Henigman - assistant principal oboe joined Dallas in 1996. After receiving her BM from Oberlin and MM from Juilliard, she performed with the festivals at Blossom, Tanglewood and Norfolk, and was principal oboist with the Wichita Symphony, 1990–96, during which time she was on the faculty at Wichita State University.

Susan Dederich-Pejovich - principal harp is a graduate of the Cleveland Institute of Music. She was principal harp with the Oklahoma Symphony, and New Orleans Symphony for three years, prior to joining the DSO in 1977. She has toured as soloist with the American Wind Symphony and the Oberlin Wind Ensemble. She is Adjunct Professor of harp at Southern Methodist University and music director of the school's Harp Ensemble. During the summer she is a regular member of "Music in the Mountains" in Purgatory, Colorado. Her husband, Steve Pejovich, is an economics professor at Texas A&M. They have a daughter, Mira.

DETROIT SYMPHONY (Neeme Järvi 1990–2005) (Antal Doráti 1997–81)

Founded 1914, the orchestra lapsed twice after 1940 and was reformed in 1951 under **Paul Paray**, its conductor 1951–1962.

Emmanuelle Boisvert

Emmanuelle Boisvert - concertmaster was, at twenty-five, the youngest woman to head the string section of a major American orchestra. Born in Canada, she began musical studies at three, entered the Conservatoire de Musique de Québec at six, continued her training at the Meadowmount School of Music, and graduated in 1984 from Curtis where she was a student of **Ivan Galamian**. Following graduation, she played for the Concerto Soloists Chamber Orchestra of Philadelphia and the Marlboro Festival. She is a member of the Detroit-based St. Clair Trio, an international chamber ensemble. She was with the Cleveland Orchestra before joining Detroit in 1988. She and her husband, television producer John Wyland, have three children, Manon, born 1994, Adrian, 1995, and Gabriel, 1997.

Laura Rowe - assistant concertmaster a University of Michigan graduate, studied chamber music with Michael Tilson Thomas and William Preucil. She played with the Aspen Festival Orchestra, Ann Arbor and Grant Park Symphonies and was concertmaster with the New World Symphony before joining Detroit as in 1995, after competing against 150 musicians in three audition sessions.

Patricia Masri-Fletcher - principal harp joined the orchestra in 1988 after having played with National Grand Opera in New York, and the Monterey and Santa Cruz County Symphonies in California. She studied with **Susann McDonald** at Juilliard. Her ensemble performances include the Spoleto "Festival of Two Worlds," the American Institute of Musical Studies Orchestra (Austria), San Jose Ballet Orchestra and Carmel Bach Festival—both in California. She is soloist with the Lyric Chamber Ensemble.

Long-term Members:

Beatriz Budinszky-Staples - violin - 1964 - born in Budapest, whose late husband, Gordon Staples, was former concertmaster of the DSO. Son Greg was a violinist in the Atlanta Symphony before returning to Detroit in the second violin section.

Linda Snedden Smith - violin - 1967 - entered the Cleveland Institute at age four, studied at Eastman and Juilliard, has soloed with the orchestra, plays in chamber groups and is married to DSO violinist Bruce Smith.

Barbara Hassan - cello - 1967 - owns three cellos: one, c1760, another, made for her in 1978 by third generation Hungarian violin maker Max Frirsz, is a copy of a Montagnana[82] cello and the third, a nearly perfectly preserved 1875 by François Louis Pique of Paris.

LeAnn Toth - violin - 1973 - joined the symphony after college graduation from the University of Missouri and further studies at New England Conservatory and University of Michigan.

Catherine Compton - viola - 1973 - is a graduate of the University of Michigan and Oberlin.

Treva Womble - English horn - 1975 - began playing oboe in the fourth grade, after four years of piano, and earned a BM in oboe performance from Eastman. She joined the Dallas Symphony in 1964, as second oboe, becoming assistant principal and principal English horn in 1969. She is married to DSO principal bassoonist Robert Williams. Their sons are Seton, a trumpet player, and Trevor, a pianist.

Debra Fayroian - cello - 1976 - was principal cellist for the Toledo Symphony. Her husband is DSO tuba player, Wesley Jacobs.

Lenore Sjoberg - second violin - 1980.

Ann Strubler - violin - 1980.

Carole Gatwood - cello - 1981.

Marguerite Denslippe-Dene - violin - 1982 - a Canadian, was concertmaster of the Windsor (Ontario) Symphony. Her husband, Dan Dene, is producer of DSO's national radio broadcasts, and recording engineer for the orchestra's recordings with Neeme Järvi. They have two sons, Mark born 1988 and Aaron, 1996.

Victoria King - bassoon - 1984.

Shelley Heron - oboe - 1985 - a graduate of the University of Toronto was principal oboe of Orchestra London (Ontario, Canada). Her husband, Ronald, is principal horn of Orchestra London.

HOUSTON SYMPHONY ORCHESTRA (Hans Graf)

Ming Qi - assistant concertmaster

Marina Brubaker - acting assistant concertmaster. A native of Tucson, she has a BM from Wichita University and graduate degree from Yale. She has been with the symphony since 1988. From a family of musicians, her mother played in the Tucson Symphony, brothers David and Steven are in the Minneapolis and Tucson Symphonies, and sister Catherine is a violist in the Chicago Symphony.

Jennifer Owen - principal second violin. A graduate of Canberra Institute of the Arts, her graduate work was at the University of North Texas and the Hartt School. She was principal violin with the Tasmanian Symphony (1995–99) before joining Houston. She plays a 1770 Nicolo Gagliano.

Aralee Dorough - principal flute graduated from Oberlin in 1983, continuing studies at Yale. She joined the orchestra in 1985 and was named principal in 1991. On the faculty at Rice University (1989–95), she teaches at the Festival Institute in Round Top, and presents master classes. She and her husband, Colin Gatwood, second oboe in Houston, have a son Corin, born in 1999.

Cynthia Meyers - piccolo

---

82. Domenico Montagnana (1690–1740) was one of Stradivarius' best pupils. He also made violins and violas. His instruments are extremely rare and valuable.

Anne Leek - principal oboe

Paula Page - harp. A graduate of the Cleveland Institute of Music, she was born in Texas and raised in Philadelphia. She was a member of the Oklahoma and Pittsburgh Symphonies before joining Houston in 1984. She has been on the faculties at University of Oklahoma, Temple, Carnegie-Mellon, Interlochen Arts Camp, and is associate professor of harp at the Shepherd School of Music at Rice University. During the summers, she is on the faculty of Texas Music Festival and the International Festival at Round Top, combining performance with teaching as did her mentors **Alice Chalifoux** and **Edna Phillips**.

Long-term Members:
Roberta Plesner - viola - 1960.
Christine Pastorek - violin - 1969.
Phyllis Herdliska - viola - 1971.
Margaret Bragg - violin - 1974.
Myung-Soon Lee - cello - 1976.
Martha Chapman - violin - 1980.
Mi-Hee Chung - violin - 1981.
Linda Goldstein - viola - 1981.
Nancy Goodearl - horn - 1981.
Fay Shapiro - viola - 1981.
Susan Valkovich - violin - 1981.
Ruth Zeger - violin - 1981.

INDIANAPOLIS SYMPHONY (Mario Venzago) Founded 1930. **(Raymond Leppard** 1987–2001**)**

Christal Phelps Steele - assistant concertmaster began her association with the ISO in 1973, after her graduation from the University of Indianapolis. She was on the Butler University faculty and is an active chamber player. She and her husband, Norman, have a son, Eric, who plays French horn, and was in the Purdue University Varsity Men's Glee Club, while daughter Emily majored in clarinet performance at Indiana University in preparation for a major symphony career.

Mary Anne Dell'Aquila - assistant principal second violin prior to this position was with the North Carolina Symphony, Canton Symphony String Quartet and concertmaster with the Canton Symphony.

Theresa Langdon - associate principal viola came to the ISO in 1979, after having played with the Aspen Festival Orchestra, New Haven Symphony, and Buffalo Philharmonic. She is a graduate of Indiana University and has a master's degree from Yale.

Beverly Scott - assistant principal viola

Karen Moratz - principal flute has a BM from Peabody, and MM from the Musikhochschule, Freiburg, Germany. She came to the ISO from the New World Symphony (Florida) in 1989, after having been with Harrisburg (Pennsylvania) Symphony. She participated in ensemble performances with Annapolis Symphony, Baltimore Chamber Orchestra and the Chamber Orchestra of Freiburg. Now on the faculty of Butler University, she was visiting professor of flute at Indiana University.

Rebecca Price Arrensen - assistant principal and piccolo

Diane Evans - principal harp a native of Cleveland, is a graduate of Oberlin. A former member of the Toledo and Omaha Symphonies, she has been principal with the ISO since 1981. She is also a soloist, chamber musician and teacher. In 1989, she was a featured soloist at the American Harp Society Convention. She is married to an attorney.

Marianne Williams Tobias is program annotator and music lecturer for the symphony. She holds a BA in European history from Harvard and an MFA and PhD from the University of Minnesota. A pianist as well as musicologist, she performs with the Tarkington Trio and makes chamber and recital appearances throughout the Midwest. She is on the faculty of the University of Minnesota.

LOS ANGELES PHILHARMONIC (Esa-Pekka Salonen)

The Los Angeles Symphony, founded 1897, had by 1919, developed union and financial problems. The intent of millionaire William A. Clark (1877–1934) was to build an orchestra without the social intrigues of the old symphony. Clark spent $3 million on the Philharmonic Orchestra of Los Angeles, as it was then known. It debuted on October 19, 1919. The old symphony lasted only one more year. The LA Phil held summer concerts at the Hollywood Bowl, starting in 1922. In 1991, the Hollywood Bowl Orchestra was formed, John Mauceri conductor. The Roger Wagner Chorale, founded 1948, was renamed the Los Angeles Master Chorale in 1965, and is the resident choir of the LAP.

Bing Wang joined LA in the 1994–95 season as **associate concertmaster**, coming from the Cincinnati Symphony which she joined in 1991, becoming principal second violin in 1993. A native of China, she studied violin at the Shanghai Conservatory. Her future teacher, Berl Senofsky, visited China and brought her to the U.S. on a four-year scholarship at Peabody (1985). This was followed by graduate studies at Manhattan School of Music where her teacher was **Glenn Dicterow**, concertmaster of the NY Philharmonic and former concertmaster of the LA Philharmonic.

Dale Hikawa Silverman - associate principal viola began violin at thirteen. Her BA is from Chicago Musical College (1974), MA from USC (1977), after which she played two years in the St. Louis Symphony. Maestro Carlo Maria Giulini hired her as a violinist for LA in 1979. She switched to viola, and in 1984 Giulini's successor, André Previn, appointed her to her present position.

Anne Diener Zentner became **principal flute** in 1971 after receiving her MM from Juilliard. She has made many solo appearances with the orchestra, with maestros Zubin Mehta, Carlo Maria Giulini, André Previn and Esa-Pekka Salonen. On the faculty of USC, she was appointed visiting professor of flute at Rice University (Houston) for the 1995–96 academic year. She is the featured flutist on the orchestra's Deutsche Grammophon recordings of the Bach Brandenburg Concertos under Pinchas Zukerman.

Janet Ferguson joined LA as **principal flute** in 1985, coming from the San Antonio Symphony where she had been principal since 1974. Her graduate degrees are from Eastman and Northwestern. She has been a recital soloist and guest artist throughout the country. In 1987, she premiered Maestro Esa-Pekka Salonen's *YTA 1* for alto flute. In February 1995, she and co-principal **Anne Diener** gave the world premiere performances of contemporary composer Steven Stucky's *Concerto for Two Flutes*, dedicated to the two soloists. She has performed at flute conventions, and with the Philharmonic Chamber Music Society and New Music Group. She and her husband are parents of daughter, Hope, born July 1992.

Marion Arthur Kuszyk - principal oboe joined LA in 1995 as associate principal. From Washington, DC, she received her BM from Oberlin and MM from Eastman. Her prior position was in the Kansas City Symphony for five years. She has made concerto appearances with several orchestras, including the National Symphony. She is married to Brent Kuszyk, percussionist with the Virginia Symphony.

Carolyn Hove - English horn joined LA in 1988. She was English horn and assistant oboe at the San Antonio Symphony (1986), English horn with the Colorado Music Festival Orchestra, and co-principal oboe with Colorado Philharmonic. After her 1980 Oberlin graduation, she played in Chicago and Texas. In 1993 she premiered Esa-Pekka Salonen's *Second Meeting* with pianist **Gloria Cheng**—the duo are featured on a CD of 20th century works. In April 1995, she was soloist for Maestro Salonen's *Mimo II* for oboe and orchestra. Hove is a guest lecturer at major universities.

Michele Zukovsky - principal clarinet joined the orchestra in 1961 while still a student at USC. She studied with her father, Kalman Bloch, former LA principal clarinet. Besides being on the faculty of USC, she has made guest appearances with the orchestra at the Hollywood Bowl and Los Angeles Music Center, toured with **Pinchas**

Zukerman in Australia, and gave the premiere of John Williams' Clarinet Concerto with the Boston Pops. She performs regularly in the Chamber Music Society Concerts of the Philharmonic.

Patricia Kindel - contrabassoon joined the orchestra in October 1981. A native of Los Angeles, she received her MM from USC. Active in film and TV recording studios, she was formerly principal associate with the Long Beach Symphony. She has taught at Pomona College, Cal State, Los Angeles, and is on the faculty at USC.

Lou Anne Neill - harp was appointed by Giulini in 1983. Before this she was with the American Ballet Theatre and a studio musician. She received her BM and MM degrees from UCLA, and was a member of the Young Musicians Foundation Debut Orchestra under Michael Tilson Thomas. She is co-author of *Writing for the Pedal Harp, A Standardized Manual for Composers and Harpists* (U of California Press, 1985). Besides solo appearances, she has recorded two albums and co-produced *TO HER GLORY, A Tribute to Mother Earth*, inspired by the music of Handel, shown at film festivals in Europe and America.

MILWAUKEE SYMPHONY ORCHESTRA (Andreas Delfs) Founded 1958.

Samantha George - acting concertmaster is a graduate of the Interlochen Arts Academy. Her BM, MM and performer's certificate are from Eastman, and her doctorate in violin performance and music theory is from the University of Connecticut. She studied chamber music with members of the Emerson, Muir, Fine Arts and Cleveland Quartets, and has attended the Grand Teton, Norfolk Chamber, and Heidelberg Castle (Germany) Music Festivals. She was concertmaster of the Hartford Symphony and the assistant concertmaster of Colorado before joining Milwaukee in 1999.

Karen Smith - assistant concertmaster

Anne DeVroome Kamerling - associate concertmaster emeritus

Jennifer Startt - assistant principal second violin

Jeani Muhonen Foster - principal flute has a BM from USC and an MM from the Manhattan School of Music. Her former positions were principal flute with Colorado Springs and Florida Gulf Coast Symphonies. She was Festival Artist and faculty member of the Colorado College Summer Conservatory, flute instructor at the Colorado College and Lecturer at the University of Denver. With guitarist Nicholas Goluses, she has given concerts in Europe and the U.S., and premiered Mark DiPalma's *Duo Concerto* (1992) and his *Sextet for Flute, Guitar, and String Quartet* (1997). She has performed with the Metropolitan and Santa Fe Opera Orchestras, and with the Colorado Symphony and Colorado Ballet.

Glenda Greenhoe - assistant principal flute received her BM from Cincinnati Conservatory in 1969. Since her graduation, she has been with the MSO with whom she has performed as a soloist. She has extensive experience as a chamber player, teacher, and clinician. She is married to MSO trombonist Gary Greenhoe. They have two children, Kirsten and Dylan.

Diana Haskell - principal clarinet came in 1990, after being principal clarinet with the Buffalo Philharmonic. She studied at Interlochen, Eastman and Juilliard (MM). She was a finalist in the Naumberg Competition, 1986, soloed at the International Clarinet Society, 1988, and in 1989 was soloist with the Savannah Symphony, where she was also principal. She is a regular participant at summer festivals.

Linda Raymond Siegel - principal percussionist graduated from the New England Conservatory and, before joining the MSO in 1970, played with the Boston Symphony and Pops, as well as that city's ballet and opera orchestras. In addition to private students, she has taught at the University of Wisconsin, Green Bay. She lives in Milwaukee with her husband and son.

Danis Kelly - harp attended high school at the Interlochen Arts Academy, and studied with **Carlos Salzedo** at the Salzedo Harp Colony. Her other teachers were **Marilyn Costello** and **Alice Chalifoux**. After graduation from the Cleveland Institute, Kelly became principal harpist of the Florida Symphony. She has been principal harpist with the Santa Fe Opera for over twenty seasons, and was on the faculty at the University of Wisconsin-Madison for thirteen years. She has been with Milwaukee since 1969.

Wilanna Kalkhof - principal piano is an MM graduate of the University of Louisville School of Music. Since 1977, she has been the pianist for the MSO and has appeared as a soloist in the orchestra's Classical Series, Youth Concerts, and tours. She is also the choir director and organist at Roundy Memorial Baptist Church. Her husband, Les Kalkhof, is an MSO violinist.

Judith Hagen - violin attended Manhattan School of Music and received a performer's certificate from the Hartt School. In 1962, she met a childhood friend and schoolmate, Janet Ruggeri, who had studied as a child with her parents. Janet, then MSO assistant principal violinist, informed Judy of orchestra auditions. She won a position and joined the orchestra that year, also becoming one of the original members of the Milwaukee Chamber Orchestra.

Shirley Rosin - violin grew up in Oak Park, Illinois, studying with her mother, then a violinist in the MSO. She joined the orchestra in 1964, at a time when several members of the orchestra, including her mother, commuted from Chicago. At the time, they were the only mother-daughter combination in the violin section. Shirley and her husband, Richard, have a son Chris, a computer scientist who plays piano and harpsichord, and a daughter Cindy, an artist and pianist.

Wendy Gannett - viola joined the MSO in 1968, after completing her studies at the University of Iowa. Much of her career has been in the study of small ensemble literature. Chamber music, she maintains, is as difficult as the solo repertoire, yet must be performed with a commitment to the unity of the ensemble.

MINNESOTA ORCHESTRA (Osmo Vänskä)

Founded 1903, it gained international reputation under Eugene Ormandy's tenure, 1931–36.

Jorja Fleezanis - concertmaster joined the orchestra in 1989 after nine years with the San Francisco Symphony, eight of which as associate concertmaster. Violin studies began at eight in the public schools of her native Detroit then went to Interlochen, the Cleveland Institute and Cincinnati Conservatory. At twenty-three, she joined the Chicago Symphony, but left that position to form the Trio d'Accordo, and become concertmaster of the Cincinnati Chamber Orchestra. Since 1984, she has played in a trio with pianist Garrick Ohlsson and Michael Grebanier, principal cello of the San Francisco Symphony. She has taught at the San Francisco Conservatory of Music, and is on the faculty of the University of Minnesota.

Sarah Kwak - associate concertmaster from Boston, is a graduate of the Curtis Institute. She joined the orchestra in 1988, and is first violinist with the Rosalyra Quartet.

Stephanie Arado - assistant concertmaster a native of Chicago, was a two-time winner of the Chicago Symphony Youth auditions, earning a debut with the CSO at age twelve. Her MM is from Juilliard, where she studied with **Dorothy DeLay**. She joined the orchestra in 1991, has soloed with several regional orchestras, and is a member of the Bakken Trio.

Julie Ayer - assistant principal second violins came from the Houston Orchestra in 1976. Her degrees are from the Universities of Washington and Indiana.

Janet Horvath - associate principal cello a native of Canada, has been with the orchestra since 1980. She soloed with the Milwaukee Symphony, Indianapolis Symphony, and has presented recitals in Chicago, Los Angeles, London, Paris, Rome and Canada. She gave the U.S. premiere of Paul Hindemith's Cello Concerto with Minnesota in 1987. She is a founding member of the Minneapolis Artists Ensemble and has played in the Marlboro Festival. A lecturer on the medical problems of musicians, she directs national conferences on the subject "Playing (Less) Hurt."

Beth Rapier-Ross - assistant principal cello in the orchestra since 1986, and in her current position since 1991, has appeared as soloist with the Louisville Orchestra and Colorado Philharmonic, and with her husband, Anthony Ross, principal cellist, performed Minnesota's premiere of David Ott's *Concerto for Two Cellos*. She has been a member of the Apple Hill Chamber Players at the University of New Hampshire, and is also a member of the Rosalyra String Quartet.

Barbara Leibundguth - co-principal flute is a Northwestern graduate (BM, 1976) from Chicago. She has been with the orchestra since 1987.

Marilyn Zupnik - co-principal oboe is from Cleveland and a graduate of Curtis. Formerly co-principal oboe of the Israel Philharmonic and principal oboe of Orchestra London in Canada, she joined Minnesota in 1980.

Kathy Kienzle - principal harp received her BM from Juilliard in 1972, and MM from the University of Arizona (1975). Her principal teachers were **Marcel Grandjany** and **Susann McDonald**. She joined the orchestra in 1993, and appears frequently with the St. Paul Chamber Orchestra. She gave the world premiere of Lowell Liebermann's *Concerto for Flute and Harp* with **James Galway** in the Minnesota subscription concerts.

NATIONAL SYMPHONY ORCHESTRA (Leonard Slatkin, 1996–2007)

Founded 1931, their summer concerts are held at Wolf Trap Farm Park. (See The Unforgotten.)

Nurit Bar-Josef - concertmaster attended the Juilliard School Pre-College (1988–92) as a pupil of **Dorothy DeLay**, and earned her BM from Curtis (1996). She was concertmaster in both school orchestras. A winner of the BSO Youth Concerto Competition in 1990, and a Tanglewood Music Center Fellow, 1993–94, she served as concertmaster at Tanglewood under **Seiji Ozawa**. She was assistant principal second violins in St. Louis, 1997–98, assistant concertmaster with Boston Symphony, 1998–2001, and made her solo debut in 2000 with the Boston Pops Orchestra. In 2001, at the age of twenty-six, she was hired by National.

Elisabeth Adkins - associate concertmaster the daughter of musicologists, began playing violin at four, becoming professional in her teens. Her seven siblings include four violinists, two cellists and a soprano. The Adkins String Ensemble debut in Dallas Symphony's Meyerson Hall was honored by the *Dallas Morning News* as one of its "Top Ten Concerts of 1994." She is a founding member of the American Chamber Players, has made several concerto appearances and plays in recital with her husband, pianist Edward Newman. As solo violinist of the 20th Century Consort, she is a noted interpreter of contemporary repertoire.

Marissa Regni - principal second violin is a graduate of Juilliard's pre-college division and holds a BM and MM from Eastman with performer's certificate in violin. She came to NSO in 1996, after being assistant principal second violins with the St. Louis Symphony. In addition to a performance schedule in the DC area, she is a member of the Manchester String Quartet.

Pamela Hentges - assistant principal second violin holds both BM and MM degrees from Catholic University of America. Before joining the NSO in 1997, she was with the Kennedy Center Opera House Orchestra, and principal second violin with the Richmond Symphony, 1983–97. While in Richmond, she was a member of the Richmond Symphony Quartet, the Richmond Chamber Players, and was a founding member of the Oberon String Quartet at St. Catherine's and St. Christopher's schools. The Oberon maintains a teaching schedule for eighty-five string students in grades two through twelve.

Dotian Levalier - principal harp is a graduate of Curtis. Before joining the symphony in 1969, she was principal harp with the Philadelphia Chamber Orchestra. She was also principal with the 20th Century Consort. She has appeared with the Chamber Music Society of Lincoln Center, Emerson String Quartet, Theater Chamber Players and the National Symphony at Lincoln Center, Kennedy Center and Wolf Trap.

Toshiko Kohno - principal flute is a native of Tokyo, who studied at Eastman with **Doriot Anthony Dwyer**, former principal flute of the Boston Symphony. She joined the symphony in 1978, after playing with the Buffalo Philharmonic, 1973–76, and as associate principal with the Montreal Symphony. She is a member of the National Symphony Orchestra Wind Soloists and has appeared as soloist with the National Symphony on several occasions.

Carol Stephenson - assistant principal oboe received her BM from the University of Wisconsin at Madison, and at the Aspen Music Festival studied with **Richard Woodhams** principal oboe of the Philadelphia Orchestra. Before coming to NSO in 1978, she performed with the New York String Orchestra, Chicago Symphony and Chicago Chamber Orchestra.

Sue Heineman - principal bassoon holds a BA from Rochester, BM from Eastman and MM from Juilliard, where she studied with **Judith LeClair**, principal bassoon with the New York Philharmonic. A Fulbright Scholarship allowed study at the Hochschule Mozarteum in Salzburg. Previous orchestras have been New Haven, Memphis, New Mexico and New Zealand.

Laurel Bennert Ohlson - associate principal horn a *magna cum laude* graduate of Boston University, has performed frequently with the Boston Symphony and Boston Opera prior to joining the NSO in 1980. She is also a member of National Musical Arts, Columbia Players, and Capitol Woodwind Quintet. She has appeared with the Handel Festival Orchestra and the Washington Bach Consort, and in 1985 was a guest artist at the seventeenth Annual Horn Convention in Baltimore.

NEW YORK PHILHARMONIC (Lorin Maazel)

Founded 1842, during the 1920s the aggregation absorbed several orchestras, including the New York Symphony Orchestra, and became the Philharmonic Symphony Society Orchestra.

Sheryl Staples - associate concertmaster was appointed in September 1998. A Los Angeles native, she was born into a musical family—her father was a seventeen year veteran trombonist in the Lawrence Welk Orchestra. She studied privately with **Robert Lipsett** from age nine; was a scholarship student at the Crossroads School for Arts and Sciences; and a W. M. Keck Scholar at the Colburn School for Performing Arts. She received her artist's diploma from USC in 1991—this, a specific performance degree attained through a rigorous audition process designed for high profile careers—while spending summers at the Cleveland Institute's Encore School for Strings. Her concertmaster positions in Southern California were with the Debut Orchestra under **Jung Ho Pak** from age seventeen to twenty-one, Santa Barbara Chamber Orchestra, Japan America Symphony in Los Angeles and Pacific Symphony, while holding faculty positions at the Colburn School and USC.

She was invited to audition for associate concertmaster in the Cleveland Orchestra, and in 1996, at age twenty-six, became the youngest person ever to hold this position. An active chamber musician, she has performed in the music festivals of Santa Fe, La Jolla SummerFest (California), Sarasota, Tucson and Seattle, where she has played with such illustrious artists as **Cho-Liang Lin**, **Lynn Harrell** and **James Buswell**. Her solo career includes appearances with over forty orchestras including Los Angeles, San Diego, Cleveland, Japan, Mexico and the New York Philharmonic.

Michelle Kim - assistant concertmaster is a graduate of the Thornton School of Music at USC and, since 1996, on the faculties of USC and the R.D. Colburn School in Los Angeles. She has appeared with orchestras in Fresno, Riverside, Los Angeles, New Jersey, and chamber orchestras in La Jolla, Palos Verdes, Santa Barbara and Santa Fe. She joined New York in 2001.

Kerry McDermott - violin became the youngest member of the New York Philharmonic at nineteen in 1981, and has appeared as their soloist, including the 1995 North American tour. At seventeen, she was the youngest winner in the history of Artists International Auditions, resulting in her debut at Carnegie Recital Hall. She has appeared in recital and chamber concerts throughout the U.S., Europe and Asia, garnering prizes and awards including the Montreal International Violin Competition and the International Tchaikovsky Competition in Moscow.

An alumna of the Manhattan School of Music and Yale, she studied with Raphael Bronstein and Vladimir Spivakov, and has worked with such noted artists as **Yehudi Menuhin**, **Erica Morini**, **Joseph Gingold** and **Henryk Szeryng**. She is a member of the **McDermott Trio** with sisters **Anne-Marie**, pianist, and **Maureen**, cellist, and has recorded for New World Records and Melodia. She has appeared on television, international radio and in the film, *Fame*.

Cynthia Phelps - principal viola joined the orchestra in 1992. A native of Los Angeles, her mother and four sisters all played instruments. She started viola at eleven, and has a BM and MM (1984) from the University of

Michigan. After a year in the San Diego Symphony with David Atherton, she joined the Minnesota Orchestra (1986–91) under **Edo du Waart**. Winning competitions since 1988 has earned her a place as a foremost recitalist and solo performer throughout the U.S. and abroad. She toured South America, Germany and Israel with the Zukerman and Friends ensemble. The orchestra has featured her during the regular season as soloist in Berlioz' *Harold in Italy* (1994), Bartók's Viola Concerto (1996), and Strauss' *Don Quixote* (1997). In April 1999, she and Rebecca Young were soloists in the world premiere of **Sofia Gubaidulina**'s *Two Paths (Dedication to Mary and Martha)*, a commission by Tomoko Masur, former violist and wife of Kurt Masur. In addition to many recordings, her solo CD, *New York Legends*, part of a twelve disc series featuring a recital program by a Philharmonic principal player, was released in 1996. With principal harpist **Nancy Allen** and flutist **Carol Wincenc**, they formed the flute trio *Les Amies*. She has two daughters, Christina, born in 1991 and Caitlin, 1997.

Rebecca Young - associate principal viola began her musical studies on violin and switched to viola at age sixteen. Four years later she became the youngest violist in the Philharmonic. She spent three summers at Tanglewood, and in 1993 was accepted as principal violist of the Boston Symphony. In 1994, she returned to her family in New York and resumed her position with the Philharmonic. She performs with prominent chamber groups in Boston and New York, and on the Sony Classical label can be heard in Schubert's *Trout* Quintet with **Yo-Yo Ma**, **Emanuel Ax**, **Pamela Frank**, and Edgar Meyer. She and husband Jack Schatz have two sons, Brian and Michael.

Hai-ye Ni - associate principal cello since 1999, was born in Shanghai in 1972, first studied with her mother, then at the Shanghai Conservatory. Later studies were with Irene Sharp at the San Francisco Conservatory, Joel Krosnick at Juilliard, and William Pleeth in London. She was a winner in the 1991 Naumberg International Competition, the 1996 Paulo Cello Competition in Finland, and second place in the 1997 Rostropovich Competition in France. In 2001, she was one of four Avery Fisher Career Grant recipients.

Orin Y O'Brien - double bass joined the Philharmonic in 1966, under **Leonard Bernstein**, as the first contracted female member in the orchestra's history. (See Bassists.)

Sandra Church - associate principal flute with BM and MM degrees from Juilliard, joined the Philharmonic, 1988, making her solo debut with the orchestra, 1990. She was formerly principal flute with the New Jersey, Chautauqua and Colonial Symphonies. In 1992, she joined the faculty of Manhattan School of Music. She is married to Lawrence Feldman, a saxophonist and studio musician.

Mindy Kaufman - piccolo has been with the orchestra since 1970. Her early studies were on piano, then flute and, while at Eastman, at age nineteen, won her first job as second flute with the Rochester Philharmonic. After graduation she toured with the Eastman Wind Ensemble, and the following year joined the Philharmonic. She remains active as a flutist and piccoloist in recitals and chamber music, and teaches at Columbia University and SUNY at Purchase.

Sherry Sylar - associate principal oboe holds a BM from Indiana University and an MM from Northwestern. She joined the Philharmonic in 1984, after having performed with the Louisville Orchestra and teaching at the University of Evansville, Indiana. She regularly performs chamber music and solo concerts, and was a featured soloist with the Philharmonic in Bach's Second Brandenburg Concerto.

Judith LeClair has been **principal bassoon** since 1981 at age twenty-three. Her professional debut was at fifteen with the Philadelphia Orchestra. She studied at that city's Settlement Music School and graduated from Eastman. Before joining New York, she was principal in the San Diego Symphony and San Diego Opera Orchestras. As recitalist and chamber musician she has played with the Guarneri Quartet on Great Performers Series at Lincoln Center. She is on the faculty at Juilliard, and lives in New Jersey with husband, pianist Jonathan Feldman. 1995 marked her solo appearance in the debut of *The Five Sacred Trees*, a concerto written for her by John Williams, commissioned by the Philharmonic as part of its 150th anniversary celebration.

Nancy Allen - principal harp has substituted in the orchestra for several years. She became a contracted member in 1999. With **Cynthia Phelps**, viola, and **Carol Wincenc**, flute, she plays in the *Les Amies* Trio. (See Harpists.)

Harriet Wingreen - principal piano is a graduate of Juilliard and on the faculty of the Manhattan School of Music. In addition to her position as pianist and celesta player, she assists conductors and soloists in rehearsal. As a chamber music performer she has performed with many luminaries, and toured the U.S., Europe, Canada, Mexico, South America and the Far East.

OREGON SYMPHONY (Carlos Kalmar)

Founded 1896 as the Portland Symphony Orchestra, it was renamed in 1967. This was the first orchestra in the Western U.S.

Erin Furbee - assistant concertmaster since 2001, is a graduate of Rice University and University of Minnesota as a graduate fellow. She was with the Colorado Symphony from 1992.

Chong-Chien Tan - principal second violins a graduate of the Cleveland Institute of Music, has been with the symphony since the 2000–2001 season.

Delores D'Aigle - assistant principal second violins is a graduate of Northwestern. She played with the San Antonio Symphony before joining Oregon in 1980.

Nancy Ives - principal cello has a DMA from Manhattan School of Music. She was with the Portland Opera Orchestra and Oregon Ballet Theatre before joining the orchestra in 2000.

Dawn Weiss - principal flute entered in 1977 as second flute, attaining principal position three years later. Her musical family background includes a mother who teaches piano, and two brothers, David Weiss, former principal oboe in the Los Angeles Philharmonic, and Abraham, principal bassoon in the Rochester Philharmonic. The three teamed up in an album, *The Weiss Family Woodwinds*. Dawn has taught at many of Portland's local colleges and soloed with various orchestras.

Martha Herby - second flute received her MM from Eastman, played with the Rochester and Chautauqua Symphonies before joining Oregon in 1981. She was principal flute with the West Coast Chamber Orchestra from 1980–90.

Carla Wilson - piccolo knew by seventh grade she wanted an orchestral career. She received her BM from Lewis & Clark College, and from school joined the orchestra in 1973. She earned an MM in flute performance from Northwestern, where she studied with Walfrid Kujala, piccoloist with the Chicago Symphony. She and her husband, Jerry, have three children, Christopher, Daniel and Jessica.

Sally Nelson Kuhns - assistant principal trumpet began her instrument at age nine, refusing to be discouraged by those who said "girls don't play trumpet." She earned her performance degree on full scholarship from the New School of Music. After hearing **Adolph Herseth**, former principal trumpet in Chicago, she immediately enrolled at nearby Northwestern, studying with him and earning an MM in performance. After playing with the Fort Wayne Philharmonic, Chicago Civic Orchestra and American Wind Symphony, she joined Oregon in 1977. She has played with the Peter Britt, Sunriver, and Oregon Coast Music Festivals, and is the founder of the brass quintet, *The Metropolitan Brass Company*. Her husband is architect Thomas Kuhns, whom she met while he was project manager on the renovation of the concert hall.

Katherine George - keyboard gave her first public performance at three, first solo recital at eight and grew up playing on the radio, television, and winning competitions. As soloist for the Portland Youth Philharmonic, she played at the Seattle World's Fair. She earned her BA and MA in music education from Portland State and a performance degree from the Royal College of Music in London. Well-known in the Portland area as recitalist, accompanist and orchestral pianist, she has been with the Oregon Symphony for over thirty years. She is on the faculty at Lewis and Clark College. She and her husband have twin daughters, Jennfier and Janet, both with musical careers.

Jennifer Craig - principal harp an Oregonian, began studying her instrument at seven, and at eleven was the youngest member of the Portland Junior Symphony. In 1970, she toured Europe as soloist with the group, and on her return substituted in with the Oregon Symphony. The next season she applied for and won the principal harp position at age nineteen. From 1980–90, she was also principal with the West Coast Chamber Orchestra. She has appeared as soloist with the Oregon Symphony, as well as numerous festivals and chamber concerts, including the Portland Chamber Orchestra, the Peter Britt Festival Orchestra, and the Oregon Bach Festival.

Her teachers include the upper echelon of harp pedagogues: American **Mildred Dilling** (1894–1982), who taught Harpo Marx; French genius **Marcel Grandjany** (1891–1975), who taught at Juilliard from 1938 until shortly before his death in 1975; and in France with **Catherine Michel**.

PHILADELPHIA ORCHESTRA (Christoph Eschenbach) (Eugene Ormandy 1938–80)

Founded in 1900, under Leopold Stokowski (1912–41) it became one of the world's leading orchestras known through recordings and tours. The musicians struck, September 15, 1996, forcing cancellation of the opening gala. Reason: they wanted their bonuses from radio appearances and recordings. But since there had been no appearances or recent recordings, they ended their walk-out on the sixty-fourth day, November 18, settling for some pay increases.

Nancy Bean - assistant concertmaster studied at Curtis. She has made solo appearances in regional orchestras and participated in chamber music festivals. She also performed with Concerto Soloists of Philadelphia and was assistant concertmaster of the Santa Fe Opera Orchestra. She joined Philadelphia in 1983, becoming assistant concertmaster in 1989. She is a member of several chamber groups.

Elizabeth Starr Masoudnia - English horn/oboe came to the orchestra in the 1995–96 season after having been acting English horn in the Minnesota Orchestra since 1988. She also served as substitute principal oboe of the St. Paul Chamber Orchestra (1990–91), principal oboe and concerto soloist on the Asian tours of the New York Symphonic Ensemble (1990, '91, '92), and participates in many chamber ensembles and summer festivals. Born in Philadelphia, she attended the Manhattan School of Music, received her BM at Curtis (1984), and studied with Louis Rosenblatt, whom she replaced upon his retirement after thirty-two years with the orchestra. She is an affiliated faculty member of the University of Minnesota and the College of St. Catherine in St. Paul.

Holly Blake - contrabassoon joined the orchestra in 1992. She graduated from Curtis and received her BM from Temple. She has performed with the Orquesta Filamonica de Caracas, soloed with chamber ensembles, was on the faculty of the University of Delaware and a member of their Del'Arte Woodwind Quartet. She is on the faculty of Trenton State College.

Elizabeth Hainen DePeters was selected **principal harp** in 1994 from auditions of forty-six candidates. She began harp at ten and earned two performance degrees from Indiana University, studying with **Susann McDonald**. Her father, a violinist with the Toledo Symphony, took her to hear the Philadelphia Orchestra at their annual spring music festivals in Ann Arbor, Michigan—the beginning of her dream of playing with them. Her previous position was principal harp with the Kennedy Center Opera House in Washington, DC. In 1989, she won a silver medal at the USA International Harp Competition and was guest artist at the 1989 Tokyo Soka International Harp Festival.

Margarita Csonka Montanaro - co-principal harp joined the Philharmonic in 1963 upon graduation from Curtis. She is a founder of the Philharmonic Chamber Ensemble and has played in the Marlboro Festival and the Philharmonic Orchestra Chamber Music Series. Beginning in the 1992–93 season, she served as acting principal harp after the retirement of the late **Marilyn Costello**, principal harp, 1945–92. Montanaro was appointed co-principal in 1994. In May of the same year she received the prestigious C. Hartman Kuhn Award given to "a musician who has shown both musical ability and enterprise of such character as to enhance the musical standards and reputation of the Philadelphia Orchestra."

Shelley Showers - horn a graduate of the Curtis Institute, began horn studies in fourth grade. Her first professional post was third horn of the New Jersey Symphony (1985–87), while also active in chamber music in New York City. During the 1987–88 season she was acting assistant principal horn with the Cincinnati Symphony, then returned to New Jersey for the 1988–89 season. In 1989, she became principal horn for the Utah Symphony, a position she held until her appointment to Cleveland in 1995. She has been with Philadelphia since 1998.

Carolyn Jantsch - tuba (See Brass.)

PHOENIX SYMPHONY (Michael Christie)

Magdalena Martinic-Jercic - associate concertmaster was born in Burlington, Vermont, and began violin at age six. Her father, a radiologist, played keyboard and cello. Her mother was a professional flutist. She has her BM and MM from the University of Michigan, and played with the Vera Cruz Symphony in Mexico before attending Eastman. In 1984, she married Borivoj Martinic-Jercic, the concertmaster of Phoenix, and in 1986 joined the orchestra. She also plays with the Orpheus Chamber Orchestra, and the couple plays with the Santa Fe Opera Orchestra. They have two daughters, Marija and Ivana.

Annie Center - associate principal viola began piano at age five and viola at ten. Since leaving her native Taiwan in 1984 to study in the U.S., she has been an soloist, chamber musician and orchestral player on both instruments. As a piano soloist, she debuted at age eighteen with the San Francisco Symphony, and in 1992 was a prize winner at the Irving Klein International Competition.

Blythe Tretick - associate principal cello made her debut with the Indianapolis Symphony in Lalo's Concerto for Cello. After receiving her BM from the Hartt School of Music, she was appointed to the St. Paul Chamber Orchestra. In 1978 she joined the faculty of Ball State University (Indiana), toured Italy with the North Carolina String Quartet, and was assistant principal in the Piedmont (North Carolina) Chamber Orchestra. Before joining Phoenix in 1984, she was principal with the Florida Orchestra and Grand Rapids Symphony.

Elizabeth Buck - principal flute since 1994, graduated from Juilliard with a BM and MM, studying with **Carol Wincenc**. Before joining Phoenix, she performed with the Houston Grand Opera and New York City Opera. She plays with the Manhattan Wind Quintet, and with them has given recitals, master classes, and workshops in chamber music throughout the New York area. 1996 saw the release of an album of contemporary American composers, *When Angels Speak*, on Albany.

Marian Pendell - principal oboe came to Phoenix in 1982, after being principal oboe for the Kansas City Philharmonic for five seasons. She has also been principal for the Mainly Mozart Festival of Phoenix and the Flagstaff Festival of the Arts. She and her husband, Carter, a violinist in the orchestra, have a daughter, Elizabeth.

Paula Engerer - principal English horn a graduate of the Indiana School of Music, performed with the Indianapolis Symphony, was principal oboe with the Indianapolis Chamber Orchestra, and a recording artist with studios in the Indianapolis area. As well as her position in Phoenix, she is solo oboe and English horn with the Nashville Chamber Orchestra.

Bonnie Wolfgang - principal bassoon studied at Oberlin and has her BM from Curtis. She debuted with the Philadelphia Orchestra in 1966. Her other orchestral performances include the National Orchestra of El Salvador, Pablo Casals International Festival Orchestra in Mexico City and the National Symphony Orchestra of Opera and Ballet in Mexico City. She was principal bassoonist for the Eastern Philharmonic Orchestra prior to joining Phoenix in 1976.

Marlene Mazzuca - assistant principal bassoon has her BM from the New England Conservatory and MM from Temple University. Before joining Phoenix in 1983, she was with the St. Paul Chamber Orchestra, Buffalo Philharmonic, and London (Ontario) Symphony. Seasonal engagements include a fourteen-year position with the Eastern Music Festival, where she performed in orchestra, chamber music, as well as teaching bassoon and coaching woodwind sectionals.

Barbara Bingham - associate principal horn received her BM from USC in 1977, then played with the Honolulu Symphony for nine years. There, she lectured on horn at the University of Hawaii and performed with the Honolulu Brass and Chamber Music Hawaii. She played with the San Francisco Symphony and Opera prior to joining Phoenix in 1986, and also performs as principal horn with the Flagstaff Festival of the Arts and the Mozart Festival. She and her husband, Kevin Deutscher, have a daughter, Jennifer.

PITTSBURGH SYMPHONY (Andrew Davis)

Founded 1926. The Mendelssohn Choir, founded in 1909, performs with the symphony. Its origins can be traced to the Pittsburgh Orchestra, founded in 1895, and disbanded in 1910 after playing almost 1,000 concerts.

Jennifer Ross - principal second violins a graduate of Curtis, began her career with the Honolulu Symphony. She spent five years with Cincinnati Symphony, performed with the Indianapolis and Detroit Symphonies and the l'Orchestre symphonique de Montreal. After three years as concertmaster of the Vermont Symphony, she joined Pittsburgh in 1998.

Jennifer Orchard - assistant principal second violins joined Pittsburgh in 2001. She is a graduate of Juilliard and Curtis.

Anne Williams

Anne Martindale Williams - principal cello began piano at six, and cello soon after, completing her professional training at Curtis. She joined the PSO as assistant principal in 1976, and became principal in 1979. She has taught and participated in many summer festivals. On the faculty of Carnegie Mellon University, she is also a member of their Trio. Her instrument is a 1701 cello made in Rome by David Tecchler (1666–1748). She is married to Joseph Williams, a trombonist in the Benedum Center Orchestra and a member of the Pittsburgh Brass Quintet.

Lauren Scott Mallory - associate principal cello began her cello studies growing up in Greensboro, North Carolina. After graduating from Indiana U. (BM, 1969) she joined the PSO, advancing to her present position in 1979. She was a founding member of the Pittsburgh Chamber soloists, and has performed as a soloist in Pittsburgh, New Hampshire Music Festival and Eastern Music Festival. Her teaching includes private students and a faculty position at the University of Pittsburgh. Her cello was made in 1991 by Peter and **Wendela Moes**. She and her husband, PSO cellist Hampton Mallory, have two children, Claire and Evan.

Betsy Heston - assistant principal bass is a native of Pittsburgh who played with the Pittsburgh Youth Symphony while studying with PSO bassist Tony Bianco. After graduating from the Cincinnati College Conservatory (BM, 1975), she was a member of the New Orleans Philharmonic, and an adjunct professor at Loyola University. She joined the PSO in 1990, teaches at Chatham University, and is married to Neal Tidwell, principal tuba of the River City Brass Band.

Gretchen van Hoesen

Gretchen van Hoesen - principal harp comes from a distinguished musical family. Her father was professor of bassoon at Eastman, her mother is a cellist and sister Catherine is a violinist in the San Francisco Symphony. A graduate of Eastman Preparatory Division, she was a student of **Eileen Malone**, and Juilliard (BM and MM) where she studied with **Marcel Grandjany** and **Susann McDonald**. She has been principal harp of the PSO since 1977, prior to which she was principal in the National Orchestral Association, Spoleto (Italy) Festival Orchestra, Jeunesses Musicales Orchestra (Germany), New York Lyric Opera, New York City Ballet and Virginia Opera. She gave the 1976 New York premiere of **Alberto Ginestera**'s Concerto for Harp, encoring it with the PSO in 1978. Performances with her husband, PSO oboist James Gorton, include the world premiere of **Witold Lutoslawski**'s *Double Concerto for Oboe, Harp and Chamber Orchestra* (1985), and in 1993 two pieces written for the duo, Robert Kelly's *Modal Variations*, and James Legg's *Suite for Oboe and Harp*.

An artist-lecturer throughout the country, van Hoesen is on the faculty of Carnegie Mellon and Duquesne Universities. She also has private students, gives master classes and serves as a judge in American Harp Society National Competitions.

Rhian Kenny

Rhian Kenny - principal piccolo was born in Libya and grew up in Calgary, Canada, where flute studies started at nine, continuing at McGill University in Montreal (BM). She joined the PSO in 1990 as principal. She is active in the orchestra's education and outreach programs, speaking to groups throughout the Pittsburgh region, and teaches both privately and at Duquesne University.

Cynthia Koledo DeAlmeida - principal oboe was born in Vermont, and studied at the University of Michigan (BM, 1981), and Temple University (MM, 1983) as a student of **Richard Woodhams**, principal oboe of the Philadelphia Orchestra. She became principal oboe in the PSO in 1991 after two years as associate principal in the Philadelphia Orchestra. Featured in festivals and chamber groups, she is on the faculty at Carnegie Mellon. She and her Brazilian-born husband, José, have two children, Veronica and Danny.

Nancy Goeres - principal bassoon was principal with the Cincinnati Symphony, Florida Symphony, Caracas Philharmonic and Florida Orchestra, before joining Pittsburgh in 1984. An avid chamber musician, she performs at Tanglewood, Marlboro, Aspen, La Jolla and Mainly Mozart (San Diego) and other festivals. In 1993, she premiered the **Ellen Zwilich** Bassoon Concerto, a work commissioned for her by the Pittsburgh Symphony Society. She performed the work again in 1996, at the International Double Reed Society Conference, where it was hailed as a major contribution to 20th century bassoon concerto repertoire. Her solo appearances with the PSO include John Williams' *Five Sacred Trees*, Concerto for Bassoon and Orchestra, and Mozart's Bassoon Concerto in B-flat Major in 1998. She is a faculty member at Carnegie Mellon and the Aspen Music Festival, and has given master classes in Buenos Aires, Caracas, Taipei and Seoul.

Rebecca Cherian - co-principal trombone with an MM (1981) from Yale, joined the orchestra in the 1989–90 season. Previous positions were principal trombone with the Springfield (Massachusetts) Symphony and the Rhode Island Philharmonic, and second trombone with the Vermont Symphony. She has been a trombone instructor at the University of Connecticut since 1982.

Patricia Jennings

Patricia Prattis Jennings - principal keyboard a native of Pittsburgh, first appeared with the orchestra at fourteen. With a BM and MM from Carnegie Mellon in piano performance, she also studied with **Natalie Hinderas**, and joined PSO in 1964. She has performed with the Baltimore and Houston Symphonies among others, and plays solo recital and chamber performances. In 1977, she was invited by **Benny Goodman** to perform Gershwin's *Rhapsody in Blue* at Avery Fisher Hall with a jazz band specifically assembled for the occasion, conducted by Morton Gould. From 1988–94, she was the editor/publisher of *SYMPHONIUM*, a newsletter for and about the professional African-American symphony musician. In 1988, she was voted Best Classical Instrumental Performer by *In Pittsburgh* magazine. She made her debut as narrator with the orchestra in *Peter and the Wolf* (1989), and has written the Christmas song, *Gifts of Love*.

Akiko Sakonju - violin began her studies at age eleven in her native Japan. In 1972, she came to the U.S. to study at Curtis, and upon graduating in 1977 joined the PSO.

Charlotta Klein Ross - cello holds a BS from Michigan State and an MFA from Carnegie Mellon. She was a member of the Dallas and North Carolina Symphonies before joining PSO in 1968. A founder of the Pittsburgh Quartet, she performs with her husband, Paul Ross, PSO violinist.

ST. JOSEPH (Missouri) **SYMPHONY** (Dr. Deborah Freedman)

Margaret Kew - concertmaster is also associate professor of music, and concertmaster of the Benedictine College-Atchison (Kansas) Symphony. She was concertmaster of the Des Moines Symphony (twenty-one years) and on the faculty of Drake University (sixteen years).

Elaine Brown - principal flute has been with the symphony since 1983, and principal since 1988. Her BM in education is from Emporia State University and MM in flute performance from the University of Missouri-Kansas City. In addition to teaching privately, she is the artist-instructor in flute and woodwind techniques at William Jewell College in Liberty, Missouri.

Meribeth Risebig - principal oboe since 1991, has played with the Wichita Symphony, Dallas Wind Symphony, and the Sunflower Music Festival. Besides St. Joseph, she is with the Kansas City Symphony and Kansas City Camarata.

Claudia Risebig - principal bassoon since 1990, has played with the Wichita and Topeka Symphonies, and is with the Kansas City Chamber Orchestra and Kansas City Camerata.

Stephanie Cox - principal trombone since 1989, is a graduate of the Conservatory of Music at the University of Missouri-Kansas City, and is the founder of the Brookside Brass Quintet, which performs for the Kansas City Chapter of Young Audiences. Besides freelancing, she also plays with the Kansas City Northland Symphony.

ST. LOUIS SYMPHONY (David Robertson) (Leonard Slatkin 1979–96)

Founded 1907. First European tour, 1968.

Elisa Barston - associate concertmaster holds a BM from USC and MM from Indiana. She was with the Cleveland Orchestra before joining St. Louis. Her husband, Jim Hsu, is a violinist and orthopedic surgeon.

Kristin Ahlstrom - associate concertmaster has both BM and MM degrees from Indiana University. She was with the Colorado Symphony (1995–96) before joining St. Louis.

Heidi Harris - assistant concertmaster joined the orchestra in 1992 after graduating from the New England Conservatory. She played three years with the Chicago Symphony, and returned to St. Louis in 1998. Her solo debut was with the Utah Symphony at age thirteen. While in school, she played with the Boston Philharmonic and Boston Symphony. She is married to principal bass Erik Harris. They have a son, Asher.

Alison Harney - principal second violins began violin studies at age seven, debuting with the Los Angeles Philharmonic at thirteen. She continued her studies at Eastman (BM, 1986), and the New England Conservatory (MM in Performance). Prior to joining the SLS she was a member of the Franciscan String Quartet, with whom she concertized internationally.

Beverly Schiebler - former associate principal second held the longest tenure of any woman in the orchestra! Her first season was 1957 when she was twenty. Her musical training included voice and violin. She had to make the choice between an operatic career or violinist. Her life has been a combination of musician, mother and home owner. Of her appointment she reminisces: "There were hardly any women [in 1957] . . . they had me in the back and asked me to put my hair up. I was told by the personnel manager to come in, do my job, and not bother anyone. And the conductor told me as long as I wore a skirt I'd never sit on the first stand." With two fingers injured in a lawnmower accident, she was forced to retire in 2005.

Kathleen Mattis - associate principal viola joined SLS in 1977 at the age of twenty-one, after graduating *magna cum laude* from USC. She is a founding member of Trio Cassatt, and tours with the Amabile Piano Quartet. She was principal violist and a faculty member with the Aspen Music Festival. She was also on the faculty of the St. Louis Conservatory and Washington University. In recognition of her commitment to bring classical music to the widest possible audience, she was selected by the Missouri Arts Council for their solo and recitalist touring program. She and her husband, former SLS bass trombonist Melvyn Jernigan, have a son, Tommy, and daughter, May.

Catherine Lehr - assistant principal cello (BM Eastman, MM Indiana University) joined SLS in 1975. She has been featured soloist with the Rochester Philharmonic and the State of Mexico Symphony Orchestra. She is also a founding member of Trio Cassatt, and performs with the Chamber Music St. Louis series. She has been an artist-in-residence at Washington University.

Frances Tietov - harp prior to joining the SLS in 1970, was harpist with the National Ballet Company, the Pennsylvania Ballet, and principal harpist with the American Symphony Orchestra. She studied with **Marcel Grandjany** at Juilliard, and received her BM from Curtis. She has also played with the Marlboro and Stratford (Canada) Festivals.

Janice Smith - assistant principal flute joined the SLS in 1969. She received her degree from Eastman where she studied with **Doriot Anthony Dwyer**. Before coming to St. Louis she was a member of the Quebec Symphony and the Birch Creek Music Center in Wisconsin. She performs in the Chamber Music St. Louis series, and is on the faculty of Washington University.

Barbara Herr Orland - assistant principal oboe studied at Oberlin and Temple University before joining St. Louis in 1976. She performs in Summerfest and Chamber Music St. Louis series.

Susan Slaughter - principal trumpet joined the SLS in 1969 and four years later became the first woman ever to be named principal trumpet of a major symphony orchestra. (See Brass.)

Jennifer Montone - principal horn, a graduate of Juilliard, studied with **Julie Landsman**. She has played with the New York Philharmonic, Met Opera, Orpheus Chamber and Chamber Music Society of Lincoln Center. She was third horn with the New Jersey Symphony and associate principal with Dallas (2000–03). She was awarded the Paxman Young Horn Player of the Year in 1996. In 2006 she became principal in the Philadelphia Orchestra.

Barbara Liberman - principal keyboard instruments (BM Juilliard, MM Washington University) first appeared with the SLS at seventeen when she was soloist for an educational concert. She started playing regularly with the orchestra in 1971, and four years later became the keyboard instrumentalist. In addition to being the accompanist for the St. Louis Symphony Chorus, she often appears as orchestral soloist.

ST. PAUL CHAMBER ORCHESTRA

Founded 1959, it performs many contemporary works and commissions.

Leslie Shank - assistant concertmaster has been in her current position since 1985. She was concertmaster of the National Orchestra of New York, and has appeared as soloist with the Concerto Soloists of Philadelphia, Seattle Symphony, National Orchestral Association, Racine Symphony and major summer festivals.

Carolyn Gunkler - assistant principal second violin joined the orchestra in 1968. Previous positions were with the symphonies of Springfield (Massachusetts), Portland (Maine) and the Cambridge Festival Orchestra. A graduate of the New England Conservatory, she has also studied and performed as a pianist. Her summers are spent in New Hampshire where she is principal second violin of the University of New Hampshire Festival Orchestra and a member of the Great Bay Chamber Players.

Sabrina Thatcher - principal viola joined SPCO in 1989. She is a member of the faculty at Aspen, and performs with the Rosalyra String Quartet.

Evelina Chao - assistant principal viola came to St. Paul in 1980 and performs frequently as a soloist. The daughter of Chinese immigrants, began studies at age eight and attended Juilliard where her mentor was **Dorothy DeLay**. Accomplished on the violin as well as viola, she has served as acting concertmaster of the Indianapolis Symphony and toured as first violinist with the Amici Quartet. She teaches at summer festivals throughout the country.

Julia Bogorad-Kogan - principal flute joined the orchestra at age twenty-two. She combines this career with recital and solo performances at Ravinia, Marlboro and Grand Teton Festivals, and has appeared at Tanglewood as acting principal flutist of the Boston Symphony. She is on the faculty of the University of Minnesota.

Katherine Greenbank - principal oboe has been with the orchestra over fifteen years. She has performed at the Rolandseck Festival in Germany (1984–85), Marlboro Festival (1988–) and Aspen, where she has been on the faculty since 1983. A 1982 graduate of Curtis, she has played with the Orpheus Chamber Ensemble (NY), and the Philadelphia Orchestra. She has been on the faculty of the University of Minnesota since 1989.

SAN DIEGO SYMPHONY (Jahja Ling 2003–**) (Yoav Talmi** 1989–96**) (Jung-Ho Pak** 1997–2002**)**
Founded 1914, for thirty years they were a summer orchestra in Balboa Park. They began a winter series in 1959. Their Symphony Hall was built in 1929 as the Fox movie theater, the third largest on the West Coast. It was renovated in 2002.

Nancy Lochner - **associate principal viola**.

Mary Oda Szanto - cello - Joined in 1977

Susan Wulff - Joined 1998, **associate principal bass** since 2003

Sarah Tuck

Sarah Tuck - flute is from Syracuse, New York, a graduate of Phillips Academy in Andover, Maine. Her BM and MM are from Indiana University. She was a student of **Jeanne Baxtresser** at Manhattan School of Music. She has been with the symphony since 1993, and was principal (1998–2004) as the orchestra reorganized from bankruptcy.

Elizabeth Ashmead - piccolo, flute - has been with the orchestra since 1975.

Sheryl Renk - principal clarinet is a former member of the San Francisco Symphony, and is the principal clarinetist of the San Francisco Ballet Orchestra. She completed her music education at San Francisco State University and the San Francisco Conservatory of Music, where she studied with Donald Carroll. She continued her clarinet studies with Rosario Mazzeo, formerly with the Boston Symphony Orchestra. She performs throughout the West Coast with various orchestras, opera orchestras, and chamber music groups, including the Santa Fe Chamber Music Festival, the Mainly Mozart Festival in San Diego, La Jolla SummerFest, Carmel Bach Festival, and Bear Valley Music Festival. In 1991, out of 120 applicants, she won the principal position with San Diego. Her husband, Frank, is second clarinet.

Sheila Sterling - Harp grew up in New York with a father who played oboe, clarinet, French horn, and saxophone. She toured with the Martha Graham Dance Company, the Ballet Russe, and subbed in the New York Philharmonic and NBC Symphony under **Arturo Toscanini**. She studied at Juilliard, with **Susann McDonald** in Pasadena, and Stanley Chaloupka, principal harp of the Los Angeles Philharmonic. Then a single mother with two small sons, she has been with San Diego since 1969. She is now married to symphony bassist, Alan Rickmeier.

Cynthia Yeh

Cynthia Yeh - principal percussion, born August 10, 1977, in Taipei, began piano at four. Her family moved to Vancouver when she was ten. Her high school orchestra gave her the opportunity to play xylophone and drums. At the University of British Columbia (BM, 1999), she switched to percussion in her junior year, determined to become an orchestral musician. She was the only woman at Temple University of the three students accepted by Alan Abel in his master's program (MM, 2001). She received the Canada Council Grant for the Arts, British Columbia Arts Council Grant, Sir Ernest MacMillan Memorial Scholarship, and Charles Owen Memorial Scholarship (See Charlotte Plummer Owen-Military.)

She freelanced and substituted in the orchestras of Chicago, Philadelphia, Delaware, Harrisburg, Springfield, Hartford and Vancouver. Joining the Battery Four Percussion Group, she married its founder, Matthew Strauss, percussionist with the Houston Symphony, in 2002. She came to San Diego in 2004.

Mary Barranger - keyboards was winner of the Pittsburgh Concert Society Youth Auditions in 1964. Her 1970 relocation to California to attend San Diego State led to dual roles as teacher and performer. She has been in-orchestra pianist for the San Diego Symphony since 1976, principal pianist for the San Diego Chamber Orchestra since 1988, and an accompanist for the San Diego Master Chorale (1976–87).

Eileen Wingard - violin. A pillar of the Symphony (1967–2004) as well as the San Diego Opera Orchestra, she conducted pre-concert lectures, student instrumental groups and initiated a violin program at Community Centers. She was the first teacher of her youngest sister, noted violinist **Zina Schiff**.

Long-term Members:

Anthony[83] **Swanson** - violin - 1956–2004
Pat Francis - violin - 1956 - since high school!
Lynn Feld - violin - 1969
Rebekah Campbell - viola - 1971
Dorothy Zeavin - viola - 1978
Marcia Bookstein - cello - 1978
Peggy Johnston - bass - 1975
Betsy Speer - oboe - 1975

NEW ADDITIONS
Sayuri Yamamoto - bass

SAN FRANCISCO SYMPHONY (Michael Tilson Thomas) (Herbert Blomstedt 1985–95)

Founded 1911, the orchestra was brought to international level under Pierre Monteux (1936–52), and has been on foreign tours since 1968. After the building of Louise Davies Hall in 1980, the orchestra became independent of the SF Opera and increased its activities. So secure are the personnel that the musicians actually went on strike from December 1996 to February 1997, and received a salary raise which elevated them to the ranks of the country's top five highest paid orchestras!

Nadya Tichman - associate concertmaster has been with the orchestra since 1980. Born in New York, the daughter of musicians, she began violin at ten. From 1972–76, she was a scholarship student at Juilliard studying with **Dorothy DeLay**. She received her BM from Curtis with such famed teachers as **Ivan Galamian** and **Jaime Laredo**. Before joining SFS she played in the Santa Fe Opera Orchestra, and numerous summer festivals. With assistant concertmaster Jeremy Constant, violist Nancy Severance and then assistant principal cellist Dianne Farrell, she founded the Donatello Quartet, which performed throughout the Bay Area, 1987–92. A regular participant in the symphony's pre-concert chamber series, Tichman has recorded on the New Albion label. She was a soloist in the 1991 concert honoring the seventy-fifth birthday of Lord Yehudi Menuhin.

Geraldine Walther - principal violist began violin in public school in Tampa, Florida. At age ten her father bought her a viola in a pawn shop. After playing in the Marlboro Music Festival in 1967, she studied with famed violist **Lillian Fuchs** (1903–95) at the Manhattan School, and with Michael Tree of the Guarneri String Quartet at Curtis. In 1976, after assistant principal positions with the Pittsburgh and Baltimore Symphonies, she joined SFS. She was first prize winner of the 1979 William Primrose International Viola Competition, and has played with chamber music ensembles throughout the Bay Area, Marlboro Festival and, for over a decade, at the Santa Fe Chamber Music Festival. Solo appearances with SFS include the viola concertos of William Walton, Thea Musgrave, Krzysztof Penderecki and Sir Michael Tippett's Triple Concerto. She can be heard on London Records with Herbert Blomstedt in Hindemith's *Trauermusik*, and *Der Schwanendreher*. She plays a Storioni viola made in 1784. One year after arriving in San Francisco she met her husband Tom. They have two daughters, Argenta and Julia.

Robin McKee - associate principal flute whose parents were orchestral musicians and educators, started her on piano, but after four years she switched to flute. She played in the Tulsa Youth Symphony and the Oklahoma All-State Orchestra before attending Oberlin, where she met her husband, Tim Day, also a flutist. They both played in the Baltimore Symphony before Robin joined SFS in 1984. They have two children, Britton and Ruby, who may one day play Robin's gold flute that she got from *her* grandfather.

---

83. Yes! That is her name!

Catherine Payne - piccolo is a graduate of Tufts and the New England Conservatory. She performed with the Boston Symphony, Boston Pops, Boston's Pro Arte Chamber Orchestra and the New Hampshire Symphony before joining SFS in 1996.

Julie Ann Giacobassi - English horn began clarinet at age ten and switched to oboe when her high school band director asked for a volunteer. Already accepted in the University of Michigan nursing school, she opted for music, and after graduating taught college in Louisiana and played principal oboe in the Shreveport Symphony. When she moved to Washington, DC, she played in the National Ballet Orchestra as a replacement for a sick oboist, which began a ten year freelance career for the opera and ballet at the Kennedy Center and Wolf Trap. In 1980, she won an audition for the SFS and has since converted her scientist husband into an avid concertgoer.

Long-term Members:

Nancy Ellis - viola - Both her parents were amateur musicians, and at age ten she became the second violinist in the family quartet. At twelve, she switched to viola because she preferred the sound. While attending Oberlin, she came to San Francisco to attend a five week chamber music seminar at the San Francisco Conservatory and never left. After graduating from Mills College in Oakland, she joined the SFS in 1975.

Kum Mo Kim - violin - a native of Seoul, Korea, has a BM from the University of Michigan, an MM from Juilliard, and also studied at the Mozarteum in Salzburg. She has been with SFS since 1975.

Margaret Tait - cello - both parents taught piano at the Shenandoah Conservatory. She studied piano until taking up cello at age eight. She graduated from USC, played with the orchestra in Birmingham, Alabama, then returned to USC for their master's program. She joined SFS in 1974, completing her MM at the San Francisco Conservatory. She is a founding member of the Aurora String Quartet.

Mariko Smiley - violin - Began studies with her father, David Smiley, violinist with the orchestra, 1962–73. She learned chamber music in her family quartet, her mother on cello, and brother Dan, a violinist now with the orchestra. At Juilliard she studied with **Dorothy DeLay**, and received BM and MM degrees. Returning to San Francisco, she freelanced until 1982 when she joined the orchestra. A long-time member of the Aurora String Quartet with SFS colleagues, she is a frequent participant in Chamber Music Sundaes.

SEATTLE SYMPHONY (Gerard Schwarz) Founded 1903.

Maria Larionoff - concertmaster is a graduate of Juilliard and a former member of the Los Angeles Philharmonic. Since her solo debut at age twelve, she has performed regularly in recital and with the San Francisco and Los Angeles Orchestras, and the New York Philharmonic. Her versatility as a violist as well as a violinist has led to appearances with the International Music Festival of Seattle, the Seattle Chamber Music Festival, and the Mostly Mozart Festival in New York and Japan. She is on the faculty of the University of Washington, and is the principal violin and viola coach of the Seattle Youth Symphony.

Janet Fisher Baunton - principal second violin won fellowships to the Aspen Music Festival and Oberlin Conservatory, and earned her BME at the University of Wichita. After several years of teaching in the Wichita public schools and the University of Wichita, she took a position with the Seattle Symphony in 1968.

Susan Gulkis - principal viola (BM, Curtis, 1988), before joining Seattle was principal viola in the San Francisco Opera Orchestra. As a chamber musician she has played with the Brandenburg Ensemble, Concerto Soloists of Philadelphia and the New American Chamber Orchestra. She participates regularly in such festivals as Taos, Tanglewood, Steamboat Springs and La Jolla SummerFest.

Dorothy Sapiro - assistant principal viola a native of the Pacific Northwest, is a graduate of the University of Washington where she studied both violin and viola. Her further studies on viola were in Europe with **Henryk Szeryng** (1918–88). She has been with Seattle since 1970, and is a regular performer on the Chamber Music Series in the area.

Susan Williams - associate principal cello is a graduate of the University of Illinois with both a BM and MM. She joined the Seattle Symphony in 1977, and was appointed to her present position in 1983. She has been a featured soloist in several Seattle Symphony series and is a frequent chamber performer with the Belle Arts Ensemble and the Seattle Art Museum concerts.

Zartouhi Dombourian-Eby - principal piccolo hails from New Orleans, where she received her BM and MM from Louisiana State University. Her doctor of music degree is from Northwestern. Prior to joining Seattle, she was a member of New Orleans Pops, Baton Rouge Symphony and the Colorado Philharmonic. She is an affiliate artist at Pacific Lutheran University, where she performs and records with the Camas Wind Quintet.

Victoria Bogdashevskaya - principal keyboard is a graduate of the Leningrad Conservatory (1968), where she also taught and performed, 1965–1978. During those years she toured extensively across the USSR. She joined the Seattle Symphony in 1979, less than a year after emigrating from Russia.

Long-term Members:

Norma Durst - viola - began her career with the Symphony in 1948! She studied under Alexander Schneider and Emanuel Zetlin. Her BA is from the University of Washington, Seattle. She retired July 2004 after 55 years with the orchestra.

Corinne Odegard - violin - studied at the University of Washington, then with Ivan Galamian and **Dorothy DeLay** at Juilliard. She joined the symphony in 1955, retiring in 1999—a record forty-four years!

Nadia Aronson - bass - has a BM and MM from UC Santa Barbara in Bass and Piano, and taught piano at Fresno State University before joining the orchestra in 1969. She retired in 1999.

TORONTO SYMPHONY (Peter Oundjian)

Founded 1906, disbanded 1914. In 1926, the new symphony acquired the charter of the original orchestra.

Wendy Rose - assistant principal second violins started violin at age six in Montreal, studied at Juilliard and graduated from the University of Toronto with her degree in music performance in 1978. She played in the Hamilton Philharmonic, Chamber Players at Toronto, and Canadian Opera Company Orchestra prior to joining the Toronto Symphony in 1981. She performs in chamber music recitals locally, and coaches both the National Youth Orchestra and Toronto Symphony Youth Orchestra. She also participates in the Toronto Symphony Education Program with cellist Marie Gelinas.

Susan Lipchak - principal viola (BM, DePauw, 1968; MM, University of Michigan, 1969) was assistant principal violist with the Toledo (Ohio) Symphony (1968–1970). She joined Toronto in 1970, and has been in her current position since 1972. In addition to her involvement with the Symphony's Community Education Program, she performs locally with chamber music ensembles and Toronto Symphony's Evening Overtures series.

Nora Shulman - principal flute

Julie Ranti - associate principal flute, her father was principal trumpet with the Montreal Symphony, her mother was a professional harpist, and her brother, Richard Ranti, is a bassoonist in the Boston Symphony. Her studies began in Montreal at age ten, and after graduating from Juilliard in 1982 became, at twenty-four, the youngest member of the Toronto Symphony. In addition to her symphony work, she is a faculty member at the Royal Conservatory of Music and performs with the Bach Consort.

Patricia Krueger - principal keyboard a native of Toronto, began her music studies at age three. A graduate of the Royal Conservatory of Music in Toronto, her BM is from the University of Toronto. After performing as soloist and recitalist in Canada and the U.S., she joined the orchestra in 1977 playing both keyboard and percussion. Interested in furthering music education, she has appeared as a guest lecturer for the Women's Committee, the Associates, the Maestro's Club of the Toronto Symphony and the Ontario Music Educators' Association.

UTAH SYMPHONY (Keith Lockhart)

Founded 1940 as the Utah State Symphony Orchestra, it was renamed and became fully professional in 1946. Conducted by **Maurice Abravanel** from 1947 to 1979, their new concert hall is named in his honor.

Wen Yuan Gu - associate principal second violins performed with the Houston Ballet and Opera, and the Grand Teton Music Festival before joining Utah in the 1998–99 season.

Roberta Zalkind - associate principal viola began piano at eight, and viola at sixteen when she entered the Music Academy of the West. After graduating from USC, she studied chamber music with the Tokyo String Quartet at the Yale School of Music. She joined Utah in 1981, assuming her current position in 1987. She also teaches and is a chamber musician in the Salt Lake City area. She is married to Larry Zalkind, principal trombone with the Symphony. They have two children.

Holly Gornik - oboe and English horn has been with the symphony since 1974. She has an MM from Northwestern, is an adjunct professor at the University of Utah and teaches at Weber State University and Westminster College. She is married to co-principal trumpet, Edward Gornik, and has two sons.

Louise Vickerman - harp, a native of Glasgow, graduated from the Royal Scottish Academy of Music and Drama and has an MM from Eastman. Before joining Utah in 1999, she was with the San Antonio Symphony, New World Symphony in Miami, Royal Scottish National Orchestra, Scottish Chamber Orchestra and BBC Scottish Symphony.

DEATH and LIFE of a SYMPHONY - The Saga of San Diego

In this era of so many kinds of "mod" music, the classical genre is practically extinct in some parts of this country. What happened in "America's Finest City," as San Diego, California, likes to call itself, is an example of culture losing out to the sports mentality.

Playing to a packed house on Saturday, January 13, 1996, Israeli Maestro Yoav Talmi waved his baton over the final concert of the San Diego Symphony—an orchestra which traces its origins to the turn of the century. Despite generous donations over the years by local philanthropists such as Sol Price (Price Club—now Costco), Joan and Irwin Jacobs (Qualcomm), newspaper publisher Helen Copley (*San Diego Union-Tribune* with a half million circulation), among many, many others, on July 9th the board was forced to declare bankruptcy.

A Dark Stage

Why was this tragedy allowed to happen? Was the ever-leaking cash flow brought on by chronic mismanagement? In the early '90s, Joan and Irwin Jacobs, president of Qualcomm, a company in the forefront of cell phone and telecommunications, underwrote half a million dollars for a successful acoustical onstage renovation. This, after having poured over $2 million into the orchestra over previous years. Ellen Revelle, widow of famed UCSD physicist, Roger Revelle, donated over a million for the musicians' payroll. Helen Copley, who took over San Diego's main newspaper after her husband's death, donated $2.5 million to retire the mortgage on the Concert Hall. Subscribers—like my husband and I—forfeited their money when the rest of the season was cancelled.

But the tap root of the demise should be blamed on the cultural malaise which blights the world's richest nation. When educational funding is short, *Music* in the elementary schools—when children are open and eager to learn— is usually the first program to be cut. Junior high, Middle and high school bands are practically an extinct species. Classical music stations are bought up by consortiums and switched to more lucrative rock or country music formats—which is what happened to San Diego's fifty-year-old KFSD-FM in February 1997. For a while Mount Wilson Broadcasters, which included KKGO in Los Angeles and KKHI in San Francisco, owned by the generous **Saul Levine**, erected a tower across the Mexican border in Tijuana, and from March 1997 to December 2000, good music returned to San Diego via X-BACH, followed by a fifteen month switch to jazz, and a return to classical until

March 2002. Absorbing a $3 million loss, KKHI expired December 1998. In March 2000, KKGO became KMZT (K-Mozart) and continues to thrive in Los Angeles. Meanwhile, XLNC1 hit the airwaves for San Diego from Tijuana at 90.7 FM on Valentine's Day 2000. For over two years listeners had to look up what was playing on the station's web page. By 2006 taped announcers named the titles in Spanish before, and English after, most selections. The Metropolitan Opera Radio Broadcast was a welcome addition to their programming.

San Diego is home to many wealthy families. At the time the Symphony was drowning for want of $6 million, the City Council issued revenue bonds in the amount of **$69** million for an addition to the sports stadium to benefit the San Diego Chargers football team. And somehow in the contract the city (read taxpayers) was responsible for reimbursing the *private owners* for *all empty seats* at games!!! The expansion continued despite voters' protest groups and a class action lawsuit. As if this were not enough, a later ballot measure managed to get enough votes to build a separate facility—PetCo Park—for the Padres baseball team, adding some $200 million more to the taxpayers' burden.

From the moment Copley Symphony Hall closed its doors, viable efforts to resurrect the orchestra were underway from various sources: the musicians who stayed in town, the Musicians Union, the citizens' group VOSA (Voice of the Symphony Orchestra), Advocates for Classical Music—scion of the Symphony's original Women's Auxiliary—to a $2 million pledge from businessman Larry Robinson to provide the foundation for what the orchestra has always lacked, an *endowment*. Meanwhile, several members found positions in the Oregon, Chicago, Pittsburgh, San Francisco and London Symphonies and the New York Philharmonic—proving the high caliber of musicianship and loss to San Diego.

The National Orchestral Scene

Between the late 1980s and early '90s, eight of the nation's 350 or so professional orchestras went out of business, but fortunately all managed a comeback. The picture continued in 2002–03 when again eight orchestras, including the Florida Philharmonic, San Antonio, Colorado Springs, New York Chamber, San Jose, Savannah and Washington Chamber Symphonies, plus the Tulsa Philharmonic, declared bankruptcy and went into reorganization proceedings. Milwaukee and Oregon musicians were taking pay cuts and even the great Chicago, Detroit, Pittsburgh and National Symphonies were facing financial challenges, along with Charleston (South Carolina) and Columbus (Ohio).

The Fantastic News

For San Diego, the tireless efforts of the Robinsons, the Jacobs, the John Moores, Theodore Graham, an attorney who donated his skills on behalf of the musicians, VOSA, cellist Richard Levine and violinist Eileen Wingard, who kept the remaining members united, Tom Lennon, CPA, who worked *gratis* for two years to retain assets like the extensive music library, and former San Diego Opera Guild President **Sandra Pay**, one of the city's most effective cultural leaders who moved from chairing San Diego's Commission for Arts & Culture to Mayor Susan Golding's Symphony Task Force, and an assembled new board of directors, all finally paid off! Under the direction of **Jung-Ho Pak**, former assistant conductor, the orchestra came back to life with a successful Summer Pops season, July-September 1998, and continued into their regular winter season. By 1999–2000, their future seemed brighter. By 2003 world-renowned maestro Jahja Ling was named the new director.

In January 2002, the Jacobs' announcement of *$100 million* for the New World Endowment Campaign plus *$20 million* for the operating budget brought national attention to the San Diego Symphony as the largest bequest ever given to an orchestra. (See **Joan Jacobs**, The Unforgotten.)

Around the World with a Few Women

The following is a 2000 survey of worldwide major orchestras who responded to my request for rosters in order to determine the ratio of men to women. The profiles of two American women who made it into European orchestras, **Abbie Conant** (former trombone, Munich Philharmonic), and **Julia Studebaker** (First Horn, Amsterdam Concertgebouw) are included in the Brass Section, as is Norwegian **Frøydis Ree Wekre** (former principal Horn, Oslo Philharmonic). Extra information is given when available. The numbers speak for themselves.

BBC Symphony (London)
Jiří Belohlávek ('06–)

Leonard Slatkin (2000–05)   *(33 women out of 91)*

David Robertson -principal guest ('05)

Violin	Anna Colman	principal second violins
	Dawn Nellor	co-principal second violins
Viola	Caroline Harrison	co-principal
Cello	Susan Monks	co-principal
Harp	Sioned Williams	principal
	Louise Martin	co-principal
Flute	Patricia Morris	piccolo
Bassoon	Rachel Gough	co-principal
	Clare Glenister	contra bassoon

Berlin Philharmonic   **Sir Simon Rattle**   *(13 women out of 117)*

This orchestra, founded in 1882, has had some of the foremost conductors in musical history: Hans von Bülow, Arthur Nikisch, and Wilhelm Furtwängler. After WWII, the orchestra and musical life in Berlin was rebuilt. Sergiu Celibidache conducted, then a return of Furtwängler, and in 1955, Herbert von Karajan became permanent conductor until April 1989, just four months before his death.

Other than a harpist, there are no principal chairs filled by women. **Sabine Meyer** was solo clarinet, but only for one year (1983–84). The first woman hired was Madeleine Carruzzo, in 1982, one hundred years after the founding of the orchestra. Of the eighteen women who have played since 1982, here are the ten current members.

Violin	Maja Avramovic	1994
	Susanne Calgéer	1988
	Madeleine Carruzzo	1982
	Kotowa Machida	1997
	Ursula Schoch	1998
	Eva-Maria Tomasi	1990
Viola	Tanja Schneider	1993
Harp	Marie-Pierre Langlamet	1993

Flute	Jelka Weber	1997
Contra Bassoon	Marion Reinhard	1999

City of Birmingham Symphony Orchestra	**Sakari Oramo**	*(28 women out of 90)*
Violin	Jacqueline Hartley	co-leader
	Anne Parkin	principal
	Briony Shaw	section leader second violins
	Louise Shackelton	co-section leader second violins
Bassoon	Margaret Cookhorn	principal contra bassoon
Horn	Claire Briggs	section leader

Long-term Members:

Violin	Sheila Clarke	1971
	Diane Youngman	1978
Viola	Carol Millward	1965
	Jennifer Whitelaw	1972
Cello	Elspeth Cox	1968
Percussion	Annie Oakley	1969

Cologne Philharmonic	**Markus Stenz**	*(25 women out of 127)*

German Opera Berlin	*(16 women out of 131)*

Finnish Radio Symphony	**Sakari Oramo**	*(28women out of 98)*

The first woman hired was a harpist, Pia Juvonen-Tallgren, in 1940

Women's Chamber Orchestra of Austria

The first women's Chamber Orchestra was founded by **Brigitte Ratz** in 1982, with the aim of offering top quality female musicians the opportunity to perform as an ensemble. Their repertoire includes works of all epochs with an emphasis on contemporary music and the music of women composers. With a membership of forty-five, they are making an important contribution to the cultural life of Vienna and all of Austria.

Gewandhaus Orchesta Leipzig	**Riccardo Chailly**	*(31 women out of 188)*

Helsinki Philharmonic	**Leif Segerstam**	*(23 women out of 98)*

Founded in 1882, it is the oldest professional symphony orchestra in Scandinavia. The first woman, Selma Kajanus, piano and harp, who happened to be the conductor's sister, was engaged in 1895. So much for the audition process of today's orchestras. The first female violinist hired was Anna Forsell (1908–11). Marja Kantola was with the orchestra for thirty-five years, 1963–98. Still playing are Hellevi Kari (second violin since 1966), Eija Hirvonen (viola since 1967), and Sinikka Leino (first violin since 1967). Women in principal positions are the associate concertmaster, flute and harp, and deputy principals in second violin, viola, clarinet and harp.

Helsinki University Orchestra

This is a student orchestra (non-professional) with approximately ninety members with fifty women. Since its founding 253 years ago, women have played in the orchestra. Claudine Borris, archivist for the Berlin Philharmonic, noted that "Not only did this orchestra exist for 250 years, and there have always been women in it, German women didn't even get access to universities that long ago."

Israel Philharmonic	**Zubin Mehta,** **principal guest conductor**	*(35 women out of 118)*
Viola	Miriam Hartman	acting principal
Cello	Shulamit Lorrain	assistant principal
	Alla Yampolsky	assistant principal
Harp	Judith Liber	principal
Horn	Dalit Gvirtzer	assistant principal
Keyboard	Milka Laks	co-principal

London Philharmonic	**Kurt Masur**	*(23 women out of 76)*

London Symphony	**Sir Colin Davis**	*(22 women out of 99)*
Violin	Janice Graham	assistant concertmaster
English Horn	Christine Pendrill	principal
Harp	Karen Vaughan	co-principal

Moscow State Radio Symphony Orchestra and Chorus	**Nikolai Alexeyev** Chorus	*(24 women out of 80)* *(32 women out of 64)*

This orchestra was created in 1978, to answer the need for symphonic repertoire of the 18th, 19th, and 20th centuries to be broadcast in Russia. Soviet Leader Leonid Brezhnev decided the broadcasts would be based on the BBC Symphony's radio series in England. In addition to radio and television work in Russia, they record for Russian, European, and American film productions and with the Chorus have toured throughout Europe, England, the United States, and the Far East.

New Zealand Symphony	**James Judd**	*(35 women out of 92)*

The National Symphony Orchestra of New Zealand was founded in October 1946. It consisted of sixty-five players, fifty men and fifteen women. Women players have always received equal pay with their male colleagues. The National Orchestra became the New Zealand Broadcasting Symphony Orchestra in 1964, and changed to its present name in 1975.

Violin	Wilma Smith	concertmaster
Flute	Bridget Douglas	principal
	Nancy Luther-Jara	piccolo
Oboe	Ellen Sherman	English horn
Clarinet	Marina Sturm	principal
	Rachel Vernon	bass clarinet
Bassoon	Sue Heineman	assistant principal
Harp	Carolyn Mills	principal

Long-term Members:

Violin	Julianna Radaich	twenty-four years
	Sharyn Evans	twenty-seven years
Cello	Vivien Chisholm	twenty-eight years
Cello	Vivienne Gordon	thirty-six years
Bass	Victoria Jones	twenty years
Flute	Nancy Luther-Jara	twenty-six years

Orquesta Filarmónica Nacional   **Pablo Castellanos**   *(18 women out of 80)*
Caracas, Venezula

Founded in 1987, women have never been discriminated against. Three women date from the orchestra's founding: Alba Acone (piano), Alba Quintanilla (harp and celesta), and Omaira Naranjo (cello).

Orchestra National de France   **Kurt Masur**   *(29 women out of 116)*

Violin	Liliane Béguin-Rossi	principal second violins
	Florence Binder	associate principal second violin
Viola	Sabine Toutain	principal
Cello	Muriel Pouzenc	assistant principal
Harp	Isabelle Perrin	assistant principal

Orchestre Philharmonique de   **Myung-Whun Chung**   *(51 women out of 138)*
Radio France

This orchestra, founded in 1976 after the dissolution of the ORTF (the French National Radio and Television corporation) and of the Radio France Foundation, was compiled from members of the Orchestre Lyrique, Orchestre de Chambre, and the Orchestre Philharmonique. The woman of longest tenure was France Dubois, 1962–99, who was with the Orchestre Lyrique.

Orchestre de la Suisse Romande   **Marek Janowski**   *(25 women out of 112)*
Founded in 1918, this orchestra has had women since 1926, when a harpist was hired.

Philharmonic State Orchestra   **Roger Epple**   *(34 women out of 104)*
of Halle (Germany)

Angelika Triemer Bülow was with this orchestra since 1960.

Radio Orchestra of Middle Germany   *(25 women out of 120)*

Royal Concertgebouw   **Mariss Jansons**   *(26 women out of 115)*
Orchestra (Amsterdam)

Founded in 1888, there have always been women in the orchestra since their harpist, Paula Fischer-Haeberman, was hired in 1904.

Flute	Emily Beynon	principal
English Horn	Ruth Visser	principal
Horn	**Julia Studebaker**	principal (See Brass)
Harp	Sarah O'Brien	principal

Royal Philharmonic Orchestra   **Daniele Gatti**   *(13 women out of 75)*
London

Under Sir Thomas Beecham, who was one of the first to allow women into a British orchestra, Tina Bonifaccio was hired in the late '50s as the "token" harpist. In 1967, four women violinists stepped in on tour as extras when male players dropped out in sympathy for a fired colleague. One of those was Gil White, still a member. In 1969, Sue Milan (flute) replaced James Galway. Prue Whittaker (clarinet) joined in 1973. Until the '70s, men were chosen over women because it was felt the lifestyle was not suitable for women.

Violin	Gaby Lester	associate concertmaster
	Ursula Gough	co-principal second violins
Cello	Christine Jackson	co-principal
Oboe	Jill Crowther	principal
Bassoon	Julie Price	principal

Royal Stockholm Philharmonic   **Mats Engström**   *(26 women out of 100)*

Violin	Anna Lindal	assistant concertmaster
	Amus Kerstin Andersson	assistant principal second violin
Viola	Kari Manum Lindgard	associate principal
Harp	Laura Stephenson	principal
Piano	Lucia Negro	principal

St. Petersburg Philharmonic   **Yuri Temirkanov**   *(16 women out of 111)*

Harp	Anna Makarova	principal
Flute	Marina Vorotsova	assistant principal

Sydney Symphony Orchestra   **Gianluigi Gelmetti**   *(37 women out of 100)*

This orchestra had its humble beginning in 1932 as a radio broadcasting ensemble of twenty-four musicians. They gave their first annual season in 1936, and in 1947 had its first chief conductor, world famous Eugene Goossens. He was followed by Sir Charles Mackerras, the late Stuart Challender, and Edo de Waart.

Violin	Kirsten Williams	associate concertmaster
	Marina Marsden	assistant concertmaster
	Fiona Ziegler	assistant concertmaster
	Susan Dobbie	associate principal second violins
	Emma West	assistant principal second violins
Viola	Esther van Stralen	principal
	Anne Louise Comerford	associate principal
	Yvette Breen	assistant principal
Cello	Catherine Hewgill	principal
Harp	Louise Johnson	principal
Flute	Janet Webb	principal
	Alison Mitchell	associate principal
	Rosamund Plummer	piccolo
Oboe	Diana Doherty	principal

Symphony Orchestra of Baden-Baden	Werner Stiefel	*(21 women out of 100)*

Symphony Orchestra of Stadt Münster	Will Humburg	*(15women out of 62)*

Thüringer Philharmonic	Jean-Paul Perrin	*(23 women out of 82)*

Tonhalle Orchestra Zürich	David Zinman	*(26 women out of 101)*

Their first woman was a harpist, Corinna Blaser, hired in 1918, who played until 1954.

Violin	Julia Becker	assistant concertmaster
	M.E. Alexander-Woodside	principal second violin
Harp	Eva Kauffungen	principal

Vienna Philharmonic	top guest conductors	*(1 women out of 155)*

With a 103-year history of prohibiting permanent membership to women, harpist **Anna Lelkes** (*b* 1940) survived from 1971–2000 at the side of the stage where, according to President Werner Resel, "she does not disturb the emotional unity of the orchestra." [!] Threats of boycott from the IAWM, and other organizations in California and New York, on their American tour may have helped her admission (finally) as a member with a vote, February 27, 1997. Her name first appeared on the program March 1995 when the orchestra played at Carnegie Hall.

In March 1999, the orchestra began a three-concert tour in New York and, despite its vote in 1997 to end the ban against women, the all-Mozart program didn't need a harp and no female was in sight. They did, however, play Mozart's "Maurerische Trauermusik" in memory of **Judith Arron**, the late executive director of Carnegie Hall, who brought the orchestra to the Hall for thirty-three concerts during her ten years in charge. She was notified of her award of the Vienna Philharmonic's coveted Franz Schalk Gold Medal (See The Unforgotten) in September 1998, before her death in December.

The Vienna State Opera Orchestra and the Vienna Philharmonic are the same orchestra, but musicians must complete a three-year tenure in the former before becoming members of the Philharmonic. In 2000, twenty-year-old **Charlotte Balzereit** was hired as Lelkes' replacement. She entered the Philharmonic in 2002. The orchestra also has a male harpist. Violist Ursula Plaichinger hired in 2002, would have completed her tenure and become a member by 2006, but took a leave of absence. Cellist Ursula Wex hired in 2003 is eligible for membership in 2007. In 2005, two violinists, French Isabelle Caillieret and Bulgarian Iva Nikolova won State Opera auditions, qualifying them for the Philharmonic, September 2008. Meanwhile, almost ten times as many men have been hired in the same period.

Warsaw Philharmonic	Antoni Wit	*(29 women out of 110)*
Violin	Ewa Marczyk	co-concertmaster
	Zofia Muszyńnska	principal second violins
Clarinet	Hanna Wollczedska	principal
Harp	Barbara Witkowska	principal
Piano	Maria Rzepecka	co-principal

Winnipeg Symphony Orchestra	**Andrey Boreyko**	*(25 women out of 66)*
Violin	Gwen Hoebig	concertmaster
	Ann Chow	principal second violins
	Kathryn Sigsworth	assistant principal second violins
Viola	Elsie Lavalléée	assistant principal
Cello	Julie Banton	assistant principal
Flute	Martha Durkin	piccolo

Ladies Take a Bow

VIOLINISTS

Wilma Norman-Neruda
  (1838–1911)
Camilla Urso (1842–1902)
Tersina Tua (1867–1955)
Nettie Carpenter (1865–?)
Geraldine Morgan (1868–1918)
Arma Senkrah (1864–1900)
Leonora Jackson (1879–1969)
Jeanne Franko (1855–1940)
Kathleen Parlow (1890–1963)
Gabrielle Wietrowitz (1866–1973)
Marie Soldat-Röger (1863–1955)
Irma Sänger-Sethe (1876–19?)
Marie Hall (1884–1956)
Maud Powell (1868–1920)
Erica Morini (1904–95)
Gioconda De Vito (1907–94)
Guila Bustabo (1916–2002)
Ginette Neveu (1919–1949)
Ida Haendel
Stephanie Chase
Kyung Wha Chung
Pamela Frank
Miriam Fried
Monica Huggett
Dylana Jenson
Ani Kavafian
Ida Kavafian
Viktoria Mullova
Anne-Sophie Mutter
Nadja Salerno-Sonnenberg
Zina Schiff
Kyoko Takezawa
Adele Anthony
Lidia Baich

Rachel Barton
Nicola Benedetti
Sarah Chang
Chee-Yun
Jennifer Frautschi
Karen Gomyo
Hilary Hahn
Leila Josefowicz
Juliette Kang
Tamaki Kawakubo
Jennifer Koh
Natasha Korsakova
Min Lee
Catherine Manoukian
Anne Akiko Meyers
Midori
Lara St John
Réka Szilvay
Baiba Skride
Livia Sohn
Akiko Suwanai
Elina Vähälä
Elizabeth Wallfisch
Carmit Zori

HONORABLE MENTION

Helen Armstrong
Maria Bachmann
Margaret Batjer
Emanuelle Boisvert
Catherine Cho
Pip Clarke
Mirijam Contzen
Christiane Edinger
Vesna Gruppman
Anna Helleur

Rebecca Hirsch
Latica Honda-Rosenburg
Judy Kang
Anastasia Khitruk
Elissa Lee Koljionen
Bojidara Kouzmanova
Ida Levin
Isabelle Lippi
Nicola Loud
Anat Malkin-Almani
Silvia Marcovici
Kerry McDermott
Priya Mitchell
Lydia Mordkovich
Nurit Pacht
Alyssa Park
Tricia Park
Sha
Ora Shiran
Sheryl Staples
Diana Steiner
Ruth Waterman
Antje Weithaas

ENSEMBLES

Ahn Trio
Eroica Trio
Jalina Trio
Colorado String Quartet
Da Vinci Quartet

LEGENDS

Dorothy DeLay (1917–2002)
Alma Rosé (1906–1944)

Since the dawn of recorded history—in the Bible, on Greek frescoes, urns and vases, in sketches of 12th and 13th century French female troubadours (*trobairitz*), in Renaissance paintings and the like—women are seen plucking stringed instruments. Lutes, lyres, kitharas, citterns, psalteries, harps *et al*, are depicted languishing on ladies' laps, the necks of their instruments impinging gently 'gainst well-endowed bosoms. But there is nary a violin to be found 'neath a dainty chin.

The violin as we know it reached its perfection in the 17th century via the Italian master craftsmen of Cremona—Amati, Guarneri, Stradivari—as well as in Germany, where Matthias Klotz (1656–1743) brought the art of the luthier to the small Alpine town of Mittenwald near the Austrian border. (His descendants and those of his apprentices continue the tradition to this day.) Along with the evolvement of bowed instruments—viola, cello, bass—came the male-dictated concept that sticking a fiddle under a maidenly chin and sawing away with a bow was not "ladylike." It took another century to break this barrier and women virtuosi gradually appeared on both sides of the Atlantic.

One of the first was Czech-born **WILMA NORMAN-NERUDA** (1838–1911), who came from a distinguished family of violinists. Taught by her father, **Josef Neruda** (1807–75), almost as soon as she could walk, the prodigy excited much attention in Vienna, and made her debut in London at age eleven. From 1848–52, she also played in a trio with her sister Amálie (piano) and brother Viktor (cello). By 1863, she was made chamber musician to the King of Sweden. The following year she married Swedish conductor-composer **Ludvig Norman** (1831–85) but, unlike most women artists of the time, continued her career. The Normans separated in 1869, after which she began concertizing each winter and spring with England's major orchestras. By 1877, she became musically associated with famed German-born British pianist-conductor **Sir Charles Hallé** (1819–95). They married in 1888, the year he was knighted, and toured Australia in 1890 and 1891. After Hallé's death[84] the Prince of Wales (Edward VII), in conjunction with the Kings of Sweden and Denmark—Viktor Neruda was conducting orchestras in both Scandinavian countries—arranged a public subscription in Lady Hallé's honor, 1896. She toured America in 1899, then settled in Berlin in 1900, where she taught at the Stern Conservatory. In 1901, after the long reign of Queen Victoria, with the ascension of Edward VII to the British throne, the title of Violinist to Queen Alexandra (his wife) was conferred upon Neruda.

A New Pioneer for America

The first American woman violinist of note was **CAMILLA URSO**, born in Nantes (France) June 13, 1842. Her mother was a Portuguese singer and her father, Salvatore Urso, a Sicilian flutist who played in the theater and the opera house. From age four the child begged for violin lessons, at first a cause for amusement, but her insistence resulted in being allowed to begin just before age six. When she appeared in public at a benefit concert a year later, her parents realized their daughter's gift and took her to Paris to try out for the Conservatoire. Since the minimum enrollment age was ten, and no girl had ever been admitted, it took nine months—during which time, in order to survive, her mother had to take in washing and sewing—before an audition was granted by the director, opera composer **Daniel François Auber** (1782–1871). Hearing her, he immediately admitted the eight-year-old. By the time she left at ten, she had won the coveted first prize in violin. She was also offered a three year tour of the U.S. at the princely sum of $20,000 per year, promised by an American businessman. When they arrived in New York, October 1852, the man pleaded bankruptcy, leaving the family stranded. Italian opera singer Marietta Alboni heard of their plight and featured Camilla in one of her own concerts. The rave reviews led to a Boston appearance sponsored by Jonas Chickering of piano building

Camilla Urso

---

84. The Hallé Orchestra of Manchester, founded by Sir Charles in 1858, is still going strong with some eighty global concerts per year.

fame. Her performance at the Harvard Music Association was hailed by influential male musicians with comments such as: "It is not enough to say it was a wonderful performance for a woman; it was a consummate rendering, which probably few men living could improve on." After this, Urso's career was assured and, apart from a self-imposed and never explained "retirement" from age thirteen to twenty (1855–62), she remained at the top.

Beginning in 1868, she spent summers in France and married Frenchman Frédéric Luer, who managed her Camilla Urso Concert Company. It was the custom of the times for small groups of instrumentalists, plus a singer, to tour together giving variety programs in small towns and rural areas to acquaint audiences with classical music. Urso felt that it was an artist's duty to educate the public, a tradition that would be more than fulfilled by the dynamic woman who followed in her footsteps, **Maud Powell**.

Urso's repertoire included all the classic violin concerti and bravura ("show-off") pieces. Moreover, unlike her contemporaries, with diligent practicing everything was memorized. Her schedule was international and hectic. It took a strong constitution to withstand the discomforts of travel and sub-standard food. In 1874 alone, the company played 200 concerts in the U.S. and Canada, then went on from California to New Zealand and Australia. Until her retirement in 1895 in New York, Urso had taught briefly in Boston, attracting students from all over North America.

The highest compliment paid to the virtuosa was by New York critic Henry E. Krehbiel, who said, "She belongs in the rank of the foremost of living artists. In her case the idea of sex which . . . modifies critical judgment . . . is never thought of . . . She does not play like a man or a woman, but like a noble, earnest and inspired musician."

Speaking at the Women's Musical Congress of the 1893 Chicago World's Fair, Urso pointed out the hardships of a solo career, decrying the fact that *this*, or teaching, were the only options open, since women were not permitted to join symphony or theater orchestras for which they would be so well suited. Short of money during her last years, she had to play in vaudeville. Yet the critics defended her "stooping down," by remarking that even in this medium she maintained her dignity and brought good music to the masses.

Camilla Urso died in New York, January 20, 1902.

First Fiddlers

Other prominent women violinists of the era were the Italian **TERSINA TUA** (1867–1955), whose accompanist and joint artist on one tour was none other than **Sergei Rachmaninoff**. She married a Count and, after being widowed, taught at the Accademia of Santa Cecilia before becoming a nun.

American **NETTIE CARPENTER**, born in 1865, played in London at age twelve, won first prize at the Paris Conservatory in 1884, and had a very successful career in Europe and America touring with such notables as pianists **Anton Rubinstein** and **Josef Hofmann**, and opera singers **Marcella Sembrich** and **Adelina Patti**. Her short-lived marriage in 1891 to English cellist Leo Stern brought about her apparently permanent retirement.

GERALDINE MORGAN (1868–1918), daughter of John Paul Morgan, founder of the Oberlin Conservatory of Music, was a lifelong friend of **Maud Powell**—they met as students of Joseph Joachim in Berlin. Morgan was the first American to win the Mendelssohn Prize, and gained fame playing the Bach *Concerto for Two Violins* with her illustrious teacher at the Crystal Palace Concerts in London. She made her U.S. debut in 1892, playing the Bruch Concerto on a Stradivarius lent her by Joachim. Later, she formed the Morgan String Quartet and, based at Carnegie Hall, established the Joseph Joachim School for Violin, which claimed to be the only such institution authorized to use his method. She married Benjamin Roeder in 1901 and had one son, born in 1906.

ARMA SENKRAH (her name, Harkness, spelled backwards) was born in 1864 in New York. At age nine, her mother took her to Germany, and three years later to Paris where she was admitted to the Conservatoire. She studied with violin "giants," **Henry Vieuxtemps** there, and with **Henry Wieniawski** at the Brussels Conservatory. Her promising career ended with her marriage, in 1888, to a German attorney. When her husband became infatuated with an actress, Arma committed suicide in 1900 by shooting herself.

Boston-born **LEONORA JACKSON** (1879–1969) was another of Joachim's students to win the Mendelssohn Prize (1897). After successful tours of Europe, she debuted with the New York Philharmonic in January 1900, and by 1902 had performed almost 200 concerts in the U.S. In 1903, she went to Prague to study with the renowned **Otakar Sevčik** (1852–1934), who still haunts today's violin students with his books of exercises. Although she continued to perform benefit recitals, her career ended with marriage in 1907, to Dr. W. Duncan McKim, a widower much older than she.

JEANNE FRANKO (1855–1940), born in New Orleans, had two violinist brothers. She studied with **Vieuxtemps** in Paris and concertized in New York from the 1880s to 1890s. In 1895, she formed a trio. After her marriage, she continued to teach and give occasional performances. (Her sister Thelma was the mother of famed bandleader Edwin Franko Goldman.)

Canadian-born **KATHLEEN PARLOW** (1890–1963), was a pupil of **Leopold Auer**, the teacher of Heifetz, Milstein, Zimbalist (Sr.) and Mischa Elman. He called her a "genius." Her performing career peaked from 1910–29, during which time she made five concert tours of Canada and the U.S., and a twenty-two-month tour of the Far East. In 1929, she performed a series of concerts in Mexico City, where she was praised as superior to even Heifetz. She taught at Mills College (California) from 1929–36, then at Juilliard, but with the outbreak of World War II she returned to Canada, teaching at the Royal Conservatory in Toronto. She formed the Canadian Trio with **Zara Nelsova** and Sir Ernest MacMillan, both from the Toronto Symphony, performing until 1944. The Parlow String Quartet debuted in April 1943, and performed for the next fifteen years throughout Western Canada. In 1959, she was appointed head of strings at the College of Music of the University of Western Ontario, where she taught until her death in 1963. She never married, believing that to be an outstanding violinist required complete dedication.

Among those who continued their careers after marriage were German-born **GABRIELLE WIETROWITZ** (1866–1937), who formed the first female string quartet which rivaled its male counterparts, and Austrian **MARIE SOLDAT-RÖGER** (1863–1955), a Mendelssohn Prize winner. Both were students of Joachim, who in the 1900s turned to chamber music and teaching.

Belgian **IRMA SÄNGER-SETHE**, born 1876, won first prize at the Brussels Conservatory in 1891.

MARIE HALL (1884–1956), born in Newcastle-on-Tyne, received her first lessons from her father, a harpist in the orchestra of the Carl Rosa Opera Company. When she was nine, world famous violinist **Émile Sauret** heard her and got her into the RAM. She also received instruction from **Edward Elgar** in 1894. In 1901, she went to Czech pedagogue **Sevčik**, whom she credited for her remarkable technique. Her first public performance was in Prague, November 1902, followed by Vienna, January 1903, and her London debut, February 16, 1903, all to great acclaim, which followed her on her American tour. In the course of her successful international career, she was considered England's foremost woman violinist.

Four of a (Unique) Kind

Mention should be made of German born **Julius Eichberg** (1824–93), who studied under famed violinist/composer **Charles de Bériot** (1802–70) at the Brussels Conservatory, emigrating to the U.S. in 1856. Moving to Boston two years later, by 1868 he was made director of the newly founded Boston Conservatory. A dynamic teacher, he actually encouraged girls to take up the violin, and they flocked to him from everywhere. He saw to it that his prize pupils appeared in concert, and founded the Eichberg Quartette, the first composed of women. The original members, Lillian Shattuck and Abbie Shepardson (violins), Lillian Chandler (viola), and Lettie Launder (cello), went on to become fine teachers, as did some of Eichberg's other students, like Edith Winn who also wrote articles on womens' rights, and **Caroline Nichols**, who formed the successful, long-lived (1888–1920) Boston Women Fadettes Orchestra, one of the first of its kind.

Maud Powell and the Crime of the Century!

After reading the superbly researched biography by Karen Shaffer, *Maud Powell, Pioneer American Violinist*, I questioned several violinists and was incredulous to find that the name of the first American-born, and highest-ranked violinist—not just *woman* violinist—for almost half a century, was virtually unknown to most. It is indeed a crime that this outstanding artist, whose character and career garnered consistently high praise from critics, and love and adulation from audiences worldwide, should be consigned to near oblivion!

Prodigy and Pioneer

Maud Powell

MAUD POWELL was a child prodigy who bloomed into a poised beautiful woman. A dazzling virtuoso, she was also a pioneer who took upon herself the mission to educate *all* of America—from the cultured eastern cities to the smallest towns in the farthest western wilderness—a mission she thoroughly accomplished, but at great personal cost. Throughout her life, she reigned on the same exalted footing as her illustrious male contemporaries: Belgian violinist **Eugène Ysaÿe** (1865–1918), Austrian **Fritz Kreisler** (1875–1962), Frenchman **Jacques Thibaud** (1880–1953) and Russian-American **Efrem Zimbalist** (1899–1985) among the select few.

Born in 1868, in Peru, Illinois, her father, Bramwell Powell, was a pioneer in educational methods, fighting against the prevalent and stifling rote learning. In his later position as Superintendent of Schools for Washington, DC, he constantly battled Congress for his reforms. Maud's uncle, John Wesley Powell, lost an arm in Civil War, and retains his fame by having made the first geological survey of the Grand Canyon. (Lake Powell is named after him.)

Maud showed her gifts early. Her mother Minnie, whose musical ambitions had been supplanted by marriage and motherhood, ignored society's dictum that violin-playing was unladylike and placed a baby violin in her daughter's hands. At age seven, Maud was taken to a concert featuring **Camilla Urso**, and immediately knew what she wanted to do with her life. She was fortunate that, from her first lessons with a local German-born teacher, she learned only excellent technique. By age eight, she was traveling each week to Chicago to study with **William Lewis**, who was also one of America's renowned violin makers. She learned piano as well. At thirteen, European training was called for, and mother, Maud and nine-year-old Billy made the long journey to Leipzig (1881–82), to study with renowned pedagogue **Henry Schradieck** (1848–1918), who had been a student of **Ferdinand David** (1810–73), a close friend of Mendelssohn.

Following this thorough grounding in the German School of violin playing, Maud went on to absorb the more lyrical French technique in the six months—October 25, 1882 to April 25, 1883—spent at the Paris Conservatory with **Charles Dancla** (1817–1907). After Paris came London where, by coincidence, the Prince of Wales (Edward VII) opened the Royal College of Music May 7, 1883, the week after Maud's arrival. Its first director was **Sir George Grove**, famous for his *Dictionary of Music and Musicians* (1879–89), whose subsequent editions are now printed in twenty-volume sets costing thousands. **Jenny Lind**, the "Swedish Nightingale," was on the RCM faculty. Queen Victoria was on the throne. Opera was thriving. Gilbert and Sullivan operettas were at the height of their popularity, and **Edward Elgar** was just becoming recognized. The fifteen-year-old prodigy concertized for appreciative audiences up and down the British Isles and began to accumulate the accolades that were to be hers for the rest of her life—and this in a country which was home to two of the finest women violinists, Marie Hall and Wilma Norman-Neruda, Lady Hallé. In February 1884, Maud got to hear the world's greatest living male violinist, **Joseph Joachim** (1831–1907), and female pianist, **Clara Schumann**. Through an introduction, Maud played for Joachim who declared her talent was of such high order that she must come to Berlin at once to study with him. For the next year she absorbed the cream of violin technique from a master who, as a boy of twelve, was already playing chamber music with Felix Mendelssohn, and for whom Brahms wrote his only Violin Concerto. In 1885, she concluded her studies with Joachim, culminating in her successful Berlin Philharmonic debut playing the Bruch Concerto with the composer present.

On July 30, 1885, Powell launched her American career in Chicago with the most respected maestro in the country, German-born **Theodore Thomas** (1835–1905), who forged a "Musical Highway" through the Midwest and was the first educator of classical music. Maud became his "musical grandchild." Later the same year, she made her debut with the New York Philharmonic under his baton—a rare honor—for which she won rave reviews. At the 1893 Chicago World's Fair, she performed with composer **Amy Beach** in her *Romance for Violin and Piano* (dedicated to Powell). In 1894, she formed the Maud Powell String Quartet, which lasted until 1898, and went on a worldwide tour. On one thirty-week American circuit she played two concerts a day. She would, at great physical expense, give more recitals in this country than any other native violinist. She presented the American premieres of concertos by composers such as **Bruch, Dvořák, Lalo, Sibelius** and **Tchaikovsky**, as well as introducing works of Amy Beach and **Marion Bauer**—most of whom she knew personally.

In 1909, the New York Philharmonic Society engaged Gustav Mahler to guest conduct. A representative of the orchestra went to Europe with the proposed concert schedule, which included Maud as the soloist for the Beethoven Violin Concerto. Mahler's reaction was, "What? I play Beethoven with a woman, and an American?" He crossed her out of the classic series and put her down for the Mendelssohn in the romantic series. After the first rehearsal, Mahler realized her talent and asked if she would play the Beethoven at Carnegie Hall, *in addition to* the Mendelssohn? She did. According to her husband, the memory of the Beethoven with Mahler remained a happy one to the end of her career.

She toured South Africa (1905–06), then alternated annual European and American tours for five more years, after which she remained in the U.S., trailblazing the West from Texas to Colorado to California—following her mission to bring music to those who could not ordinarily hear a top rank artist. With Texas-born Francis Moore (1886–1946) as her accompanist, in September 1913 she began a ten-week tour of thirty-eight communities in fifteen states. That kind of determination was further demonstrated by the next three tours. Winter-Spring 1914: twenty-one cities in twelve states; Fall 1914: twenty-three recitals in twelve states; and Winter-Spring 1915: twenty-two communities in eleven states. During WWI, she entertained troops at military camps and hospitals.

In her own extremely articulately-written articles, as well as in interviews, Powell was realistic about the hardships inherent to a concert career, having set the example with her own strict musicianship. She had stringent rules for practice, believed all violinists should play piano also, and felt that "the performer should serve the music, not their own virtuosity." The combination of her talent, intelligence and diligence resulted in unanimous praise from critics and audiences throughout her entire career. Although she supported the cause of women's rights—her mother had been a suffragette—she abhorred militancy, perhaps because from the start the men in her life supported her completely. Her father, in essence, sacrificed his own marriage with his wife away so many years chaperoning their daughter. Billy came back to be with his father when he was twelve. Her husband was her manager and shouldered all the business responsibilities of her career.

At age thirty-seven Maud married Godfrey Turner, called Sunny, because of his unfailingly pleasant disposition. An English concert manager who had arranged her two highly successful tours with the popular Sousa Band, he lovingly devoted his expertise for the rest of his life to his wife. There were no children—this being one of the sacrifices for her career.

A Powell Who's Who

It is a fact that Maud personally knew more composers and performers than any other artist before or since: **Franz Liszt, Johannes Brahms, Clara Schumann, Max Bruch, Antonin Dvořák, Jean Sibelius, Christian Sinding,** and the star-studded faculty of the Paris Conservatoire, **Léo Delibes, Gabriel Fauré, César Franck, Jules**

Massenet, **Camille Saint-Saëns**. The top violinists: Russian pedagogue **Leopold Auer** and his pupils, **Jascha Heifetz**, Mischa Elman, and **Efrem Zimbalist**, who married her friend, soprano **Alma Gluck**. The great pianists: **Fannie Bloomfield-Zeisler**, **Teresa Carreño**, **Ignace Paderwski**, **Vladimir de Pachmann**, **Moriz Rosenthal**, **Josef Hofmann**, **Feruccio Busoni** and **Leopold Godowsky**. Cellists: **May Mukle**—who was in Maud's Trio with her pianist sister **Anne Mukle Ford**—and **Pablo Casals**. In the operatic world she was acquainted with **Geraldine Farrar**, **Nellie Melba**, **Enrico Caruso**, **Ernestine Schumann-Heink** and **Luisa Tetrazzini**. It was also estimated that she had the largest repertoire of any violinist.

A Majestic Exit

Maud Powell wanted to play the violin up until her last minute of life, and just about got her wish. On Thanksgiving Day, 1919, in St. Louis, she played the Mendelssohn Concerto with her new piano accompanist, Axel Skjerne, then a Brahms Sonata, and managed to finish her transcription of the spiritual *Nobody Knows the Trouble I've Seen*. After the last note she stood for a moment in a daze, then, through sheer will-power, managed to walk to the piano and lay down her precious Guadagnini before she slid, unconscious, to the floor. It was 9:25 P.M. There were two doctors in the stunned audience. Maud was carried to her dressing room and laid on the floor for lack of a couch. After fifteen minutes, she regained consciousness long enough to stop one of the doctors from giving her a morphine injection. At the hospital she slipped back to semi-consciousness. Sunny was summoned from New York. Amazingly, she recovered from this heart attack and insisted on resuming her schedule, making two recordings in New York, December 29 and 30.

January 7, 1920 found her, Sunny and Axel in Uniontown, Pennsylvania. At 6:30 P.M., just before the concert, she collapsed at the hotel. Sunny was at the theater. The doctor ordered the performance cancelled. Maud spent a restless night with a frantic Sunny at her side. In the morning, she actually whispered to her husband that for the first time in her career she wanted to rest. Later, Sunny, who had gone to fetch medicine, managed to return before her spirit departed at 11:30 A.M. Her heart worn out, America lost its greatest violinist and patriot at age fifty-two.

In the early 1900s, Powell was the first instrumentalist chosen by RCA Victor to make phonograph recordings. (Until that time only vocalists had been recorded.) In the 1990s, some of her recordings, considered "jewels in the national treasury," were put on compact discs by Biddulph of London and the Maud Powell Foundation. In 2005, Naxos released four volumes: *Maud Powell, The Complete Recordings* (1904–17).

In the summer of 2005, director/violinist **Rachel Barton Pine** invited musicologist **Karen Shaffer**, who has done so much to promote Maud Powell, to lecture at the Musicorda Festival in South Hadley, Massachusetts. February 22, 2006 witnessed Rachel's tribute to Maud at Washington's National Museum of Women in the Arts. *American Virtuosa – A Tribute to Maud Powell* is Rachel's 2007 CD on Cedille.

John C. Freund, editor of *Musical America*, pointed out the great debt America owed Maud Powell, whom he called "the Grand Woman of American musical life . . . "

(It is this author's aspiration that this insert will help restore Powell to her rightful place in music history.)

From the Roaring Twenties to the Throttled Thirties

After the First World War, since positions in the male-dominated symphonies were still barred, there was a proliferation of women's orchestras. In the solo field, however, in the three decades between the wars, one prominent woman held the violin spotlight.

ERICA MORINI, born January 5, 1904, in Vienna, started violin at the age of three at her father's school of music. By eleven, she entered the Vienna Conservatory to study with **Otakar Sevčik**, making her debut with the Vienna Philharmonic the same year. This was followed in 1918 with her debut at the Leipzig Gewandhaus Orchestra under the great **Artur Nikisch**

Erica Morini

(1855–1922), who said of her, "She is not a wonder-child; she is a wonder and a child!" Her closest childhood friend was **Alma Rosé**.

Maud Powell's will bequeathed her beautiful Guadagnini "to the next great woman violinist." Thus, exactly one year after her death in 1920, it was loaned[85] to Erica on the occasion of her American debut at Carnegie Hall, January 1921—unfortunately, it proved to be too big for her hands. In 1925, in Paris, for the then truly enormous sum of $10,000, her father bought the great "Davidov" Stradivarius—named for the famed Russian cellist who once owned it. Its present day value is $3.5 million.

Before and after World War II, Morini played with almost all major American orchestras, as well as touring South America, Australia and the Orient. Critics raved over her flawless technique. She made impressive recordings of most concertos. After returning to Europe for a while, she settled in New York, becoming an American citizen in 1943. She married a Sicilian diamond broker, Felipe Siracusano, who died in 1985. There were no children, Morini being of the same mind as Powell, that it was not possible to combine a family and a career. During the '60s she devoted her time to teaching. In 1976, at seventy-two, with arthritis-plagued fingers, she gave a final recital in New York. It was hailed as "one of the most musically satisfying events of the season."

Morini, always resentful of being identified as "the greatest woman violinist" [of her time], when questioned in a February 1940 *New York Times* interview said, "What does it matter whether I am a man or a woman? . . . I am either a great violinist or I am not [!]"

For twenty years her 1727 Stradivarius was locked in a closet, taken out only when a fellow musician came to visit. On October 18, 1995, the ailing Morini was taken to the hospital by her caregivers. She asked anxiously about her treasure, which in her will was designated to be sold and the money given to the blind, the elderly, and handicapped children. Her friend checked in the closet to find it gone! There were no signs of forced entry . . .

Morini came home to die November 1st. She never knew her violin had been stolen. The FBI issued an international alert. The executor has offered a $100,000 reward. The violin is well known to dealers. "Fencing" it would be a risk. Out of the 1,200 violins made by Antonio Stradivari (1644–1737), there are approximately 635 violins surviving in the world. *Will, through criminal and self-serving greed, the magnificent voice of the Davidov-Morini be forever silenced?*

Shooting Stars

Three other women violinists flitted fleetingly across international footlights. **GIOCONDA DE VITO**, born Martina Franca, July 26, 1907, in Lecce, Italy, who, despite her name and birthplace, was considered an English violinist. She studied with Attilio Crepax and Remy Principe. In 1932, she won an international competition in Vienna, which led to concert appearances and her appointment as principal professor of violin at the Accademia di Santa Cecilia, Rome. In 1947, she went to London to make recordings, debuting there in 1948 with the London Philharmonia. She married in 1949, settled in England, and was heard on the BBC, sometimes under the direction of the famed **Wilhelm Furtwängler** (1886–1954). She formed a duo with pianist Tito Aprea, and also made recordings with Yehudi Menuhin and Edwin Fischer. Her finest interpretation was the Brahms Concerto, which she recorded twice. She retired at fifty-four in 1961, and died in Rome in 1994. Among the famous violins she owned were a 1762 Gagliano, plus two Stradivari, the "ex-Bazzini" (1715) and the "Tuscan" (1690).

GUILA BUSTABO, born February 25, 1916, in Manitowoc, Wisconsin, the daughter of an Italian-French father and a Bohemian mother, studied at Juilliard, and with **George Enescu** and **Jenō Hubay** in Europe. A true prodigy, she could read music by age three, and made her debut with the Chicago Symphony when she was four. At eleven,

---

85. There are conflicting opinions as to whether Powell's violin was ever in Mornini's hands. It was definitely played by French soloist Renée Chemet, but by 1925 it was sold by Sunny Turner and ended up in Henry Ford's collection in Dearborn, Michigan—which leads this author to add her voice to the communal artistic complaint: *Why must so many glorious instruments lie mute in the closets of the wealthy?*

Guila soloed with the New York Philharmonic, playing the Wieniawski First Violin Concerto. At the urging of **Toscanini**, she toured Europe when she was fourteen, playing under Willem Mengelberg with the Amsterdam Concertgebuow, and Herbert von Karajan in Berlin. In Finland, she performed the Sibelius Concerto for the composer. In Italy, **Ernano Wolf-Ferrari** dedicated his violin concerto[86] to her. She also toured Asia.

Bustabo's star was dimmed by the onset of World War II when she chose to stay in Italy, thus curtailing the best years of her career. After the war, she continued playing in Europe, despite having been arrested in Paris, accused of being a Nazi sympathizer because of her association with Mengelberg.[87] The accusation against her was eventually dropped. From 1964–70, she was professor of violin at the Innsbruck (Austria) Conservatory. She was still teaching in her eighties.

Despite her fame, her name rarely appears in anthologies. Her few recordings had all but disappeared when Tom Clear, of New York, generously underwrote the making of copies of her records from his private collection. She died in Jefferson (Alabama), April 27, 2002.

GINETTE NEVEU, born in Paris on August 11, 1919, is another name barely remembered. A grandniece of distinguished organist/composer/teacher **Charles-Marie Widor** (1844–1937), she studied with her mother and made her debut at age seven, brilliantly playing the Max Bruch Concerto #1 in G minor with the Colonne Orchestra in Paris, drawing such comments as, "the impact of a volcano" and adjectives like "powerful . . . intense . . . passionate." She entered the Paris Conservatory, and after winning first prize at age eleven, completed her training with **Carl Flesch** (1873–1944)—who also left a legacy of violin exercises—and foremost Rumanian composer, **George Enescu** (1881–1955). She graduated in eight months, tying the record made by Henryk Wieniawski fifty years before! At sixteen, Ginette won first prize in the 1935 Wieniawski Competition in Warsaw, with future virtuoso **David Oistrakh**, aged twenty-seven, coming in second. The same year she recorded the Sibelius in Berlin—only the second after Heifetz—and six months later, the Brahms under Russian maestro **Issay Dobrowen** (1891–1953), and other works with von Karajan. She toured Poland and Germany (1935), Russia (1936) and the U.S. and Canada (1937). In England she was a favorite with maestro Sir John Barbirolli. During World War II she, like many other artists, played very little, living reclusively during her country's occupation. After the end of the War she made her London debut in 1945. In 1947, she played in Boston, New York and South America to standing ovations. Tragically, on October 29, 1949, on her way to the United States again, her plane crashed over the Azores. It is documented that Neveu was clutching her precious Stradivarius as the plane plunged to earth. Thus three treasures—violinist, violin and her brother Jean-Paul, a talented pianist and her accompanist—were lost. Four years later, violinist Jacques Thibaud (1880–1953) was also killed in an airplane crash, causing some, like Yehudi Menuhin, to abandon air travel for some time until flights became safer. Neveu's few priceless recordings have been transferred to LPs and have now been issued on CD on the Dutton label.

Une Grande Dame du Violin

One of the world's most durable lady violinists is **IDA HAENDEL**, born in Chelm, Poland, December 15, in 1923, '24 or '28—the latter she vouchsafed to me personally. The discrepancy was apparently caused shortly before a concert in 1937, when her manager was told that no child under fourteen was allowed to work in England. To rescue her appearance, he said that Ida actually *was* fourteen, but for promotional reasons had been passed off as younger. Ida (pronounced Eeda) technically began violin at three and a half, when she took her sister's violin and played the song her mother was singing. Her artist father recognized her talent, and devoted himself to furthering her career. By five, she had already won the Hubermann Prize at the

Ida Haendel

---

86. Not too well-known, this piece was recorded in 1995 by **Zina Schiff**.
87. Mengelberg (1871–1951) directed the Concertgebouw Orchestra from 1895–1945, a record tenure for any conductor.

Warsaw Conservatory, and by seven, a gold medal. The same year, she was a finalist in the 1935 Wieniawski Competition, whose winners were Ginette Neveu, first, and David Oistrakh, second. After leaving Poland, she continued her studies with **Carl Flesch** in London (1935–39), and later with **George Enescu**.

Her professional career as a child prodigy began in 1937 at the Queen's Hall (London), under the baton of **Sir Henry Wood**, playing the Brahms Violin Concerto. During World War II, living in London, Ida became a British subject, giving many concerts for the troops. Her international career developed as soon as the War was over, with performances worldwide throughout Europe, Israel, North (1946) and South America, the Far East and Russia— then the USSR. A regular soloist with all major British orchestras, she has accompanied them on foreign tours, such as the London Philharmonic to the first Hong Kong Arts Festival (1973), and on their subsequent tour of China; the BBC Symphony to Germany, Australia and Hong Kong; and the English Chamber Orchestra to Mexico.

The list of eminent conductors and fellow artists with whom Haendel has collaborated reads like an honor roll. Amongst them, Bernhard Haitink, Sir Simon Rattle, Sir Adrian Boult, Sir Eugene Goossens, Vladimir Ashkenazy, Zubin Mehta and Rafael Kubelik, with whom in 1948–49, she recorded the Beethoven and the Bruch with the Philharmonia Orchestra.

In 1952, Ida relocated to Montreal. 1957 marked her premiering Luigi Dallapiccola's *Tartiniana Seconda*. 1970 saw the publication of her autobiography, *Woman With Violin*, written with Victor Gollancz. In 1979, she moved to Miami (Florida).

In September 1982, she was awarded the Sibelius Medal by the Sibelius Society of Finland on the twenty-fifth anniversary of the composer's death, in recognition of her distinguished performances of his violin concerto. In the 1991 New Year's honors list, she was made a Commander of the British Empire (CBE) for her outstanding services to music.

Haendel continues to makes regular appearances at major festivals, such as Edinburgh and the BBC Proms. 1993 found her with the Berlin Philharmonic. Her 1994 rendition of the Benjamin Britten Concerto, with Andrew Davis and the BBC Symphony, was hailed for its brilliant virtuosity.

Her career has been entwined with leading conductors and prominent orchestras around the world. Her performance of the Brahms Violin Concerto in Berlin (1997), with the Deutsches Symphonie Orchester conducted by Vladimir Ashkenazy, earned the plaudit, "This was violin playing that belonged to another Universe . . ." (*Die Welt* 15.09.97). In 1998, she took part in a tour to Japan with the City of Birmingham Symphony with Sir Simon Rattle. 1999 found her with the Florida Philharmonic Orchestra, Montreal Symphony, Rishion Lezion Orchestra (Israel), National Arts Centre Orchestra, Ottawa (Canada), playing the Dvořák Concerto with the Boston Symphony under Andrew Davis, and doing a concert in Kuala Lumpur. 2000 included a performance of the Brahms with the Budapest Festival Orchestra, and receiving an honorary doctorate from the Royal College of Music from the hands of Prince Charles.

Devoted to her vocation, Ida Haendel never married. She speaks seven languages, and is working on the second volume of her autobiography. A two-part television documentary about her life was aired on the CBC She has been seen on the BBC in the UK and PBS in the U.S.

She records for EMI and Decca. A 1996 release on the Testament label included Bach solo works. She admits to not having to practice long hours. This is talent! Her violins include a Guarneri and a 1696 Stradivarius.

The Second Half of the 20th Century

The post-World War II years saw the restrictions and discriminatory barriers for women instrumentalists begin their gradual—but still far from complete—consignment to history. With savvy concert managers and international agency networks, today's artists are marketed via television appearances, recordings "plugged" on classical music stations and a barrage of modern publicity. The ease of air travel has made it possible to hop all over the globe in a state of perpetual jet lag. An ever-increasing number of women virtuosos are scaling artistic heights formerly attained by very few of the "gentler sex"—and then at some personal cost. Today's artists marry, have children and still manage to get on with their careers. Of the multitude of talented female musicians who play in orchestras both great and small, and soloists with steady exposure, the following are a sample of those who have made it to the "big time."

Stephanie Chase

STEPHANIE CHASE, born in Evanston, Illinois, October 1, 1957, had her first recital at age two with her mother's students. Her two older sisters also played violin. As a child prodigy, concertizing began at age nine when she won the Chicago Symphony Youth Competition (1966), after which she toured nationwide. Among her celebrated teachers were **Josef Gingold** (1909–95) and **Arthur Grumiaux** (1921–86), who remained her mentor until his death, and chamber music coaches **Rudolf Serkin** (1903–91), **Felix Galimir** (1910–99), **Marcel Moyse** (1889–1984), and **Rudolf Firkusny** (1912–94) at the Marlboro Festival in Vermont.

In the course of an illustrious career, her 1986 tour of China as soloist with the Hong Kong Philharmonic set a precedent for other artists. Besides television appearances and radio broadcasts, her numerous recordings include Beethoven's *Violin Concerto* and *Romances*, with Roy Goodman and the Hanover Band, performed on period instruments, featuring her original cadenzas. Her research into the violin concerti of Beethoven, Mozart, Mendelssohn and Brahms has recreated an authentic text from autographed scores and other early sources. A guest performer at major summer festivals, Chase collaborates with ensembles, including the Boston Chamber Music Society. Besides adjudicating competitions, she was artist-in-residence at the Boston Conservatory (1982–89), on the adjunct faculty at MIT (1983–89) and has conducted master classes throughout the U.S. and Mexico. Her honors include "Outstanding Young Woman of America" (1983) and, following her win at the Tchaikovsky Competition in Moscow, a 1987 Avery Fisher Career Grant. She performs on the *ex-Paschell*, a 1742 Pietro Guarnerius violin which has been in her family for over fifty years, and her principal instrument since she was eleven. In 2002, she co-founded the Music of the Spheres Society, Inc., which promotes classical music through innovative programs of chamber music concerts, lectures and workshops. The programs are presented in New York City and on American tours.

Stephanie is married to Stewart Pollens, a conservator at the Metropolitan Museum of Art, and author of books on Stradivarius' design, an analysis of the early pianoforte (1400[?]-1761), the French bowmaker François Xavier Tourte, and a museum catalogue of archaic musical instruments.

Kyung Wha Chung

KYUNG-WHA CHUNG, born in March 26, 1948, into a musical family in Seoul, Korea, began studying violin at age six. Six years later she was touring in Korea and Japan, and in 1961 came to New York to study with **Ivan Galamian** (1903–81), winning a full scholarship to Juilliard where she studied for seven years. In 1967, she shared first prize in the Leventritt Competition with **Pinchas Zukerman**, a triumph which served as a springboard to internationally acclaimed debuts beginning in 1970 with the London Symphony, and continuing with recital and solo appearances with major orchestras throughout North America, Europe and the Far East. In 1972, the government of South Korea awarded her its highest honor, the medal of Civil Merit.

The 1993–94 season marked the beginning of her collaboration with recital pianist **Peter Frankl**, highlighted by a joint recital in Carnegie Hall and concerts in Europe and Tokyo. As the Chung Trio, with her brother, pianist **Myung Whun**, and sister, cellist **Myung Wha**, they have performed in Europe. In January 1995, they played Beethoven's Triple Concerto in Rome with the Santa Cecilia Orchestra. Their CDs include trios by Mendelssohn, Brahms, Tchaikovsky, Dvořák, Shostakovich and Beethoven.

The 1994–95 season included solo appearances at Carnegie Hall and two performances with the London Symphony in honor of Maestro Pierre Boulez' seventieth birthday, as well as concerts with the San Francisco, Philadelphia, London Philharmonic and Philharmonia orchestras. Chung's recording of the Richard Strauss and Respighi sonatas on Deutsche Grammophon won a Grammophon Award. She recorded the Dvořák Concerto with the Philadelphia Orchestra and Riccardo Muti, the Bruch Concerto No.1 with the London Philharmonic and Klaus Tennstedt, and the Beethoven Concerto with the Concertgebouw on Angel/EMI—the latter marking EMI's first orchestral video release. Another bestseller is the Bartók Concerto No. 2, and his two rhapsodies, with the City of Birmingham Orchestra under Simon Rattle. In 1998, EMI released the Brahms' violin sonatas, with Peter Frankl on piano; in 1999, *Souvenirs*, a violin and piano recital with Itamr Golan; and in 2001 Vivaldi's *The Four Seasons*, a recording made with St. Luke's Chamber Orchestra.

One of the highlights of Chung's career was being called on to replace **Nathan Milstein** as soloist for seven performances with the Israel Philharmonic, on only two days' notice.

After two decades of appearing in recitals and with all the major orchestras of North America, Europe and the Far East, her ambitious schedule of over 120 concerts a year has now been halved in order to spend more time with her two sons, Frederick and Eugene. During 1998–99, she performed with the Boston Symphony, Helsinki Philharmonic, Berlin Staatskapelle and Munich Philharmonic. 1999–2000 included concerts in Europe, Toronto and Philadelphia. In 2000–01, she toured Korea and Canada, and concertized in New York, Los Angeles, San Francisco, Chicago, Anchorage and Vancouver.

PAMELA FRANK has established an international reputation for her recitals, chamber music collaboration and solo appearances with major orchestras throughout the world. Born in New York City, June 30, 1967, she is the daughter of noted pianists **Claude Frank**—with whom she played in recitals— and **Lillian Kallir**. Violin lessons started at age five, and after eleven years with Shirley Givens, she continued her studies with **Szymon Goldberg**, and **Jaime Laredo**. Her professional debut in 1985 was with the New York String Orchestra at Carnegie Hall under **Alexander Schneider**. An Avery Fisher Career Grant recipient in 1988, she graduated the following year from Curtis, making her orchestral debut with Leonard Slatkin and the New York Philharmonic, performing the Dvořák Concerto. In May 1993, she was one of the performer-teachers assisting **Isaac Stern** in his chamber music master classes at Carnegie Hall. 1994–95 marked performances

Pamela Frank

with the orchestras of Philadelphia, Boston, Cleveland, Baltimore, Detroit, Milwaukee, Phoenix, Seattle, and her Carnegie Hall recital debut. Abroad, she played with the Vienna Chamber Orchestra, Orchestre de Paris, Israel Philharmonic, and toured Germany with the Cincinnati Symphony. At the Berlin Festival, she joined pianist **Peter Serkin** and cellist **Yo-Yo Ma** for a trio program and Beethoven's Triple Concerto. There were also recitals in London, Paris, Amsterdam and Vienna, and a return trip to Japan. Her summer festival appearances in Europe and the U.S. have included Tanglewood, Mostly Mozart at Lincoln Center, Grant Park and Ravinia in Illinois, Riverbend and Blossom in Ohio, as well as Aldeburgh (Scotland) and Prague. Her recital tours have included her partnership with her father, with whom she performed a Beethoven Sonata cycle at Wigmore Hall in December 1997. She performed regularly with pianist Peter Serkin, and other chamber music colleagues, including **Emanuel Ax** (cello), **Eugenia Zukerman** (flute), and **Paul Meyer** (clarinet). Critically acclaimed recordings include a Beethoven Sonata Cycle with her father at the piano, and the Chopin Piano Trio with Emanuel Ax and Yo-Yo Ma. On March 26, 1998, she premiered at Carnegie Hall, with the Orchestra of St. Luke's, Hugh Wolff conducting, the *Concerto for Violin and Orchestra*, which was written for her by **Ellen Zwilich**. In the summer of 1999, she made her second tour of Australia, and a German tour with the Academy of St. Martin-in-the-Fields. In 1999, with fellow violinists Sarah Chang and Nadja Salerno-Sonnenberg, she was awarded the Avery Fisher Prize, the first time in twenty-five years the prize has gone to a woman. This was also the happy year she married Alexander (Andy) Simionescu. During the 1999–2000 season, she appeared with the orchestras in Boston, Cleveland, Cincinnati, Philadelphia, St. Louis, Israel and Munich. Her recital tour with her father included Chicago, Los Angeles, New York, and in Japan and Europe. In the spring of 2000, she joined the Danish National Symphony, led by Yuri Temirkanov, as the soloist for their American tour, and concerts with the orchestras of Boston, Detroit, Tonhalle, and the Leipzig Gewandhaus. Sadly, her mother, world-famous pianist **Lillian Kallir** passed away October 25, 2004.

An arm injury in early 2001 suspended concertizing. During this time, Pam has found a new facet to her career on the faculties of Curtis, Peabody and SUNY, Stony Brook, where she has many students and teaches chamber music, as well as master classes in the U.S. and abroad. This was still her career status in 2006.

Miriam Fried

MIRIAM FRIED is on the full time faculty of the New England Conservatory, since 2006. Born in Romania, September 9, 1946, her family emigrated to Israel when she was two. While studying at the Rubin Academy in Tel Aviv, she played for such visiting luminaries as Isaac Stern, Nathan Milstein, Yehudi Menuhin, Henryk Szeryng, Zino Francescatti and **Erica Morini**. She came to the U.S. as a protégée of Stern, continuing her studies with two of the world's most renowned teachers, **Ivan Galamian** (Juilliard) and **Josef Gingold** (Indiana University). In 1968, she won first prize in Genoa's Paganini International Competition, and three years later became the *first woman* to win top honors in the Queen Elisabeth International Competition in Brussels. She has concertized with virtually every major orchestra in North America and in the cultural capitals of Europe, as well as Israel, Mexico, Japan and Russia. Her most frequent guest appearances have been with the orchestras of Boston, Chicago, Cleveland, New York Philadelphia, and Pittsburgh. Besides being a member of the Mendelssohn String Quartet (2001–), her chamber music collaborations have been with such distinguished artists as **Isaac Stern**, **Pinchas Zukerman**, **Garrick Ohlsson**, **Nathaniel Rosen** and her husband violinist/violist **Paul Biss**, son of cellist **Raya Garbousova**. Their sons are Daniel and Jonathan, a career pianist.

Fried has been artistic director of the Ravinia Institute since 1993, which involves regular performances at the festival, plus recitals and concerts with the Chicago Symphony. She was on the faculty of the Indiana University School of Music (1986–2006). In 1985, after three years of international performances, she gave recitals in New York of the complete Bach sonatas and partitas for solo violin. She recorded this music in France (Lyrinx, 1999). Heralded for her technical mastery, emotional depth and superb musicianship, her other prized recording is of the Sibelius Concerto, with the Helsinki Philharmonic under Okko Kamu, on the Finlandia label.

She plays a 1718 Stradivarius, favorite of its 18th century owner, German composer-conductor **Louis** (**Ludwig**) **Spohr** (1784–1859), previously owned by Regina Strinasacchi (1762–1839), who played Mozart's Sonata in B-flat major, written for her and accompanied by the composer, in a concert before the Emperor Joseph II.

Monica Huggett

MONICA HUGGETT is a conductor as well as a violinist. Born May 16, 1953, in England, the fifth of seven children, she began playing the violin at six, later studying with Manoug Parikian at the RAM. Introduced to the baroque violin when she was a student, she felt it suited her personality and playing style more than the modern instrument. After playing both for several years, she decided to concentrate exclusively on the early violin with an interpretation that gives the instrument a human voice in sound and technique, and a repertoire covering the baroque, classical and romantic.

In 1980, she co-founded the Amsterdam Baroque Orchestra with harpsichordist Ton Koopman, and was its leader until 1987. She is regarded as one of the foremost baroque violinist of our time, and has recorded the Beethoven and Mendelssohn violin concerti and all the Mozart violin concerti with the Orchestra of the Age of Enlightenment, and the unaccompanied violin sonatas and partitas by Bach, released in 1997 for Virgin Classics. As director of the Hanover Band, she recorded the Beethoven Symphonies and Vivaldi's *La Stravaganza* among many other releases. In recent years directing has taken a lager part of her time, guest conducting the Orchestra of the Age of Enlightenment, the European Union Baroque Orchestra and various groups in Europe. She is also the founder/director of the baroque Ensemble Sonnerie, who tour in Europe. Since 1995, Huggett has been the artistic director of the Portland (Oregon) Baroque Orchestra in the U.S. She was a professor of baroque and classical violin at the Academy Für Alte Musik in Bremen (Germany), and now holds a post at the Koninklijk Conservatorium in The Hague, Holland. In 1994, she was made a fellow of the Royal Academy of Music, London. (See Conductors.)

Dylana Jenson

DYLANA JENSON made her professional debut at age eight in California with the Long Beach Symphony, and for several years was the only child prodigy on the scene. Born in Los Angeles, May 14, 1961, the fifth of six talented children, she was surrounded by music. Her older brother, Kevan, wanted to play cello since he was two, but no one knew how to teach such a young child. After two years of "frustration," by the time he was four and Dylana was two, Dr. Shinichi Suzuki had come to town to demonstrate his phenomenal method. There not being any classes as yet, the children's mother, Ana, fascinated with the concept, bought a book and began teaching herself so she could tutor her children. As Dylana became far advanced, the family moved to Bloomington so she could study with **Josef Gingold** at Indiana University. From age twelve, she traveled to Zurich for four summers to take master classes with **Nathan Milstein**. Meanwhile, with the loan of a glorious Guarnerius del Gesù violin to augment her talent, her career took off with debuts at eleven with the Cincinnati Symphony playing the Tchaikovsky concerto, and at twelve with André Kostelanetz and the New York Philharmonic playing the Mendelssohn. The same year, she debuted with the National Symphony of Costa Rica. It was the first televised concert and the entire nation was watching. In 1976, her mother, who is of Costa Rican descent, was made the country's arts liaison at the United Nations, and Dylana became an honorary citizen. The next year marked her European debut with the Zurich Tonhalle Orchestra. Engagements followed with Philadelphia, Chicago, Cleveland, Minnesota, Los Angeles and San Francisco, plus tours to Latin America, Germany and the Soviet Union. At seventeen, Dylana was the youngest winner of a silver medal at the Tchaikovsky Competition in Moscow and the first American violinist to achieve such an honor. After her acclaimed Carnegie Hall debut at nineteen, she toured the U.S., Europe, Japan, Australia, Latin America and the [then] Soviet Union.

Losing Her "Voice"

With a major career in the making, the unbelievable happened! Love walked in and her precious violin walked out! In 1983, Dylana wed conductor/cellist/composer **David Lockington**, music director of the Grang Rapids Symphony.(They now have four children.) The terms of the contract—the violin was on loan until she became a professional—coincided with her marriage. The glorious instrument had to be returned to its owner, and her career practically went on hold.

The Search of the Decade

The impossible challenge was how to find something equal to the tone of the Guarnerius del Gesù Dylana was accustomed to, and the sound her audiences had come to expect. Using other violins brought less than ecstatic reviews, which prompted the artist to reject major dates and recording offers. She maintained her career with regional engagements. In the course of her instrument search, she played some twenty-three violins—probably more than any other soloist. Meanwhile, she adopted Mariana in 1984, gave birth to Eva in 1987 and adopted Devan in 1990.

It was her friend, cellist Yo-Yo Ma, who suggested Dylana visit the New York shop of Samuel Zygmuntowicz. When Isaac Stern loaned her his own Zygmuntowicz to familiarize herself with the power of these masterful violins, she immediately commissioned one in 1995 and was pleased with the result. Thus we can once again look for reviews like, "Uncompromising artistry!" "Unsurpassed since Heifetz!" "The sound rockets forth from her violin and fills the hall with irresistible Niagaran force!" Her 2001–02 appearances included a U.S. tour with the Polish Orchestra, and performances with the symphonies of Baltimore, New Mexico and Kansas City.

ANI KAVAFIAN is a soloist, chamber musician, and teacher who has performed with most major orchestras of the world. She is an artist-member of the Chamber Music Society of Lincoln

Ani Kavafian

Center. Part of the Walden Horn Trio with **Anne-Marie McDermott** and Robert Routch, she plays at chamber music festivals throughout the U.S. including Lincoln Center's Mostly Mozart Festival, often performing with her sister, Ida. She has also played with late pianist **Ruth Laredo**. Her numerous honors include the Avery Fisher Prize and three White House performances. From the late '90s, she has served as co-artistic director of "Mostly Music" chamber series in New Jersey with cellist Carter Brey.

Born in Istanbul, May 10, 1948, of Armenian descent, Ani began studying the piano at age three. After her family moved to America, she switched to the violin at nine. At sixteen, she won first prizes in both piano and violin competitions at Interlochen, and two years later began studies with **Ivan Galamian** at Juilliard, receiving her MM with top honors. She served on the faculties of McGill University (Montreal), the Manhattan School of Music and Mannes College of Music, and in 2002 joined the faculties of SUNY, Stony Brook and Yale.

Ani lives near New York City with her husband Bernard Mindich and their son, Matthew. Her violin is the 1736 Muir McKenzie Stradivarius.

Ida Kavafian

IDA KAVAFIAN, sister of Ani, was born in Istanbul, October 29, 1952. The family immigrated to America when she was three, and she began violin studies at age six. Her MM is from Juilliard, where she was a pupil of the renowned **Oscar Shumsky** (1917–2000). She was a recipient of the Avery Fisher Career Grant in 1988. She served on the faculty of Yale, and is now on the faculties at Hartt, Mannes and Curtis. A founding member of the group TASHI over twenty-five years ago, her chamber appearances include every major festival worldwide. She has toured and recorded with the Guarneri String Quartet and the Chamber Music Society of Lincoln Center, of which she is an Artist Member. Equally proficient on the viola, she often performs with her sister. They have appeared together on television and made many recordings. She founded, and for ten years guided, the festival *Bravo!* in Vail, Colorado, and since 1995 has served as artistic director of *Music from Angel Fire* in New Mexico, where she coordinates, programs and selects artists for over forty concerts each summer. For six years (1992–98), she was the violinist of the famed Beaux Arts Trio, considered the premiere ensemble of its kind and *Musical America*'s 1997 Ensemble of the Year. She is a co-founder of the piano quartet Opus One, with pianist **Anne-Marie McDermott**, violist Steven Tenenbom, and cellist Peter Wiley.

Ida Kavafian's solo appearances include the orchestras of Boston, Montreal, New York, Tokyo, Hong Kong, Buenos Aires, and London. Contemporary composer Toru Takemitsu (1930–96) wrote a concerto for her. She has also toured and recorded with jazz great, Chick Corea.

Ida has homes in Philadelphia and Connecticut with her husband Steven Tenenbom. They raise champion Hungarian Viszla dogs.

Her violin is a 1751 J.B Guadagnini crafted in Milan, her viola was made in 1987 by Peter and **Wendela Moes**. (See Luthiers.)

Viktoria Mullova

VIKTORIA MULLOVA, born in Moscow, November 27, 1959, studied at the Central Music School of Moscow, and the Moscow Conservatory with **Leonid Kogan** (1924–82). She won first prize in the 1980 Sibelius Competition in Helsinki, and the Gold Medal at the Tchaikovsky Competition in 1982, after which she defected from the Soviet Union—one of the last artists to do so—with her then fiancé, Vakhtang Jordania, who relinquished his position as conductor of the Kharkov Symphony to begin an international career. Viktoria left Vakhtang in New York three years later and moved to London, where she met Claudio Abbado at the London Symphony Orchestra. Although he was married, a strong attraction developed and she moved into the conductor's penthouse in Vienna. However, with the impending birth of Misha in 1991, the relationship fell apart and she returned to London. Abbado supports his son, but does not see him.

Mullova has performed with the Berlin, Israel, New York and Royal Philharmonics, and the orchestras of Boston, Chicago, Washington and Los Angeles. 1992 marked her Salzburg debut, with Sir Neville Marriner and the Academy of St. Martin-in-the-Fields. 1994–95 included concerts with the Leipzig Gewandhaus, Zurich Tonhalle, Vienna Symphony, Berlin, Florida and Los Angeles Philharmonics and the Pittsburgh Symphony. During this time her second child, Katia, resulted from a one-year relationship with Alan Brind, a player in the European Community Youth Orchestra.

The 1997–98 season saw concerts with the Leipzig Gewandhaus, the Orchestre de Paris, Royal Concertgebouw, Amsterdam, and the Philharmonia's Ligeti Project in Japan. The 1998–99 season featured recital tours in Europe, America, and Australia, and concerts with the Philharmonia, Amsterdam, and the Zurich Tonhalle. Her career has since expanded to cover Turkey and Asia.

An exclusive recording contract with Phillips has produced Vivaldi's *The Four Seasons*, solo works of Bartók, Bach, and Paganini, the Shostakovich Concerto No. 1 and the Prokofiev Concerto No. 2. with **André Previn**. The 1995 release of the Brahms B major Trio No.1 and Beethoven *Archduke Trio* features Previn as pianist and Heinrich Schiff, viola. Mullova has won the Grand Prix du Disque and the Diapason d'Or—both from France—a Japanese Record Academy Award, as well as the German Schallplattenkritik prize for the Brahms Violin Concerto, recorded live in Tokyo with Claudio Abbado and the Berlin Philharmonic. Her recording of the Bartók and Stravinsky concerti with the Los Angeles Philharmonic, under Esa-Pekka Salonen, came out in 1998. During the 2000–01 season, Phillips released her non-classical recording, *Through the Looking Glass*, a collection of arrangements of works by jazz greats Miles Davis and Duke Ellington, as well as the Beatles, Yousou N'Dour and Alanis Morissette.

Mullova explores the full potential of her instrument via authentic interpretations of baroque composers while maintaining the modern set-up of her 1723 "Julius Falk" Stradivarius. With a group of like-minded musicians, in 1994 she formed the Mullova Chamber Ensemble, which, after its inaugural tour of Italy, has since made tours of Germany and the Netherlands. During the 1999–2000 season, she performed with the Israel Philharmonic, Leipzig Gewandhaus, in America with the Philadelphia and Los Angeles orchestras and, for the first time, was soloist and director with the Orchestra of the Age of Enlightenment.

In 1996, she married British cellist Matthew Barley. It was he who introduced *and* induced "Vika," as she is called, to play jazz and other pop music. This, she says, has given her a new freedom of expression. Their daughter, Nadia, was born in 1999. With three children, Mullova insists that family is more important than music, promising each year to stay more at home.

Anne-Sophie Mutter

ANNE-SOPHIE MUTTER, has remained at the pinnacle of a dazzling career for over thirty years. Born in Rheinfelden, Baden (Germany), June 20, 1963, at age six she was the youngest first prize winner in the annals of the Young Musicians Competition. Playing at the Lucerne Festival at thirteen, she came to the notice of German maestro **Herbert von Karajan** (1908–89), who invited her to be soloist with the Berlin Philharmonic during the 1977 Salzburg Easter Festival. As his protégée, she recorded many violin concertos with him and the orchestra. Her American debut came in 1980 with the New York Philharmonic under Zubin Mehta, which led to concerts with every major U.S. orchestra, and popular summer festivals such as Ravinia, Tanglewood and New York's Mostly Mozart. In 1985 she was taken under the wing of Swiss conductor Paul Sacher, who saw to it that prominent contemporaries Witold Lutoslawski, Norbert Moret, Wolfgang Rihm, Krzysztof Penderecki and Sebastian Currier composed works for her. She gave the world premieres of Rihm's *Time Chant*, and Penderecki's Second Violin Concerto (1995). Her recording of the latter, with the London Symphony Orchestra conducted by the composer, received two Grammy awards in 1999. The Rihm and her recording of the Berg Violin Concerto netted her a 1994 Emmy. Her discs of traditional classics continue bestsellers. Her rendition of the complete Beethoven sonatas, recorded live during her 1998 worldwide recital tour with pianist Lambert Orkis, was awarded a Grammy in 2000. (It was Rihm who said, "Her playing is as radiant as the sun.")

Other awards include the Deutscher Schallplattenpreis (German Recording Prize) at age sixteen, Internationaler Schallplattenpreis, French Grand Prix du Disque and the U.S. Edison Award. As an honorary fellow and first holder of the international chair of violin studies (from 1986), she taught at the RAM. Her philanthropic pursuits established the Rudolf Eberle Endowment, a foundation she established in 1987 to support talented young string musicians throughout Europe. The endowment was later incorporated into the Munich-based Anne-Sophie Mutter Foundation and Friends Circle. She holds the Order of Merit (First Class) of the Federal Republic of Germany.

Mutter celebrated the Millennium year with a festival of 20th century violin music with pianist Lambert Orkis, entitled *Back to the Future*, plus three orchestral concerts with the New York Philharmonic under Kurt Masur, followed by a twelve-city recital tour of the U.S. She repeated the program with the London Symphony in London, Stuttgart, Frankfurt, and in Amsterdam with the Royal Concertgebouw. Her 2001 season highlights included performances with the Vienna Philharmonic, during which she performed all the Mozart concertos on two evenings, assuming overall musical direction. In a residency with the International Music Festival in Lucerne, she presented the first performance of André Previn's *Tango Song and Dance*. She restructured the 2001 Carl Flesch Violin Competition, held in Monte Carlo, in order to establish new requisites for violinists in its third millennium.

Anne-Sophie was widowed in 1995 from her seven year marriage to Detlef Wunderlich, von Karajan's lawyer and twenty-seven years her senior. They had two children, Arabella, born in 1991 and Richard,1994. On August 1, 2002, she became the fifth wife world-renowned U.S. conductor-composer Sir **André Previn**, seventy-three—knighted by Queen Elizabeth II in 1996. Mutter had premiered his Violin Concerto, written for her the previous March, and had also been part of the London Symphony Orchestra concerts he directed in June and July. Another common bond was their both having been born in Germany. Previn's Jewish family fled from Hitler before WWII and settled in Los Angeles.

The thirty-four year age difference apparently took its toll. Rumored to have separated in May, their quiet divorce in Munich was confirmed August 2006. In October of the same year she announced that she would retire "around her forty-fifth birthday" in 2008.

NADJA SALERNO-SONNENBERG, one of today's foremost violinists, was born in Rome, January 10, 1961, of Italian-Russian descent. Abandoned by both her father and stepfather, her mother, Josephine, brought her daughter to America in 1969. Josephine taught in the Philadelphia public school system, and as a pianist was strict about Nadja's practicing. She studied with the top violin pedagogues, **Jascha Brodsky** at Curtis until 1975, and **Dorothy DeLay** at Juilliard. She won the Naumberg International Violin Competition (1981) and an Avery Fisher Career Grant in 1983. Her 1989 children's book, *Nadja: On My Way*, tells of her experiences as a young musician.

Nadja Salerno-Sonnenberg

The Day that Changed Her Life

On Christmas Day, 1994, while slicing vegetables, the knife slipped almost severing the pinkie finger of her left hand. The surgeon's skill repaired the injury, but during the months of healing she trained herself to use only three fingers. The traumatic experience launched the rebirth of her career. After almost losing her ability to play, Nadja realized her *need* to play the violin and now does so with the dedication of one who has been given a second chance.

Numerous television performances, including Bravo's *Arts and Minds*, PBS' *Live from Lincoln Center* and *Backstage at Lincoln Center*, plus many appearances on the *Tonight Show* have made her instantly recognizable. With over fifteen CDs to her credit, her popular recordings include *Humoresque* (Nonesuch, 1998), featuring music from the 1947 movie of the same name, plus classical and pops classics; *Night and Day* and *Bella Italia* (Angel/EMI), a collection by various composers recorded at the Aspen Music Festival, and *It Ain't Necessarily So*, a medley of encore pieces. During the 1998–99 season she performed in Japan, and with the National, New Jersey, and Vancouver Symphonies, and a national tour with the St. Paul Chamber Orchestra. 1999 saw her with the symphonies of Colorado, Milwaukee, Baltimore, Toronto, Dallas, Seattle, and New Mexico. In May, New Mexico State University presented her with an honorary degree in appreciation for her many performances there—the first honorary degree the university ever awarded. (The institution holds a special place in her life as Dr. Marianna Gabbi, professor of music at NMSU for over twenty years, was Nadja's first violin teacher in Italy.) A documentary on Sonnenberg, *Speaking on Strings*, premiered at the 1999 Sundance Film Festival, becoming an Academy Award nominee in 2000. Also in 1999, she was named the winner of the Avery Fisher Prize, sharing the distinction with fellow violinists **Pamela Frank** and **Sarah Chang**—the first time the prize has gone to women.

Continuing a career to rave reviews in every major country in the world, Salerno-Sonnenberg collaborated with the Brazilian guitar duo Odair and Sergio Assad in a Nonesuch (2000) recording titled *Gypsy Airs*. This includes music based on traditional gypsy music drawn from Russia, Romania, Turkey and Spain, composed by Sergio. The recording was so well received that during her 2001 season, besides her performances nationwide, the trio made two recital tours. Following her 2002 summer schedule, which included performances with the Philadelphia Orchestra, Aspen Festival and her debut at the BBC Proms, she appeared in Baltimore, Calgary, Dallas, Minnesota and Oregon. In August, she performed with the Boston Pops in a world premiere of Christopher Brubeck's *Interplay of Three Violins and Orchestra* with jazz violinist **Regina Carter** and Irish country violinist **Eileen Ivers**. In 2005 she launched her own recording label, NSS Music, which is already a resounding success.

Zina Schiff

ZINA SCHIFF, a native of Los Angeles, is considered the world's foremost performer of Hebrew music, receiving rave notices wherever she performs. Since her Carnegie Hall debut, she has concertized in major North American and European cities, as well as Israel and Australia. Her highly acclaimed first CDs, *The Lark Ascending* and *Bach/Vivaldi* with the Israel Philharmonic Orchestra under **Dalia Atlas**, were followed by *King David's Lyre*, a selection of Jewish music, and *Here's One*, a recital of American music, both of which were selected "Critics' Choice, Best of 1997" by *American Record Guide*. She was seen on PBS-TV's *NOVA*, played the solo violin score for the MGM film *The Fixer*, by Academy Award winner Maurice Jarre, and has performed on NPR, WQXR (NY) and WGBH (Boston), which featured her recording of the Lee Hoiby Sonata on its "Art of the States" program broadcast in fifty countries.

Beginning lessons at age three with her sister, **Eileen Wingard**, a thirty-five-year member of the San Diego Symphony, Zina was a protégée of the great **Jascha Heifetz** (1901–87), and studied with **Ivan Galamian** at Curtis. Her honors include the Young Musicians' Foundation Debut Award, San Francisco Symphony Foundation Award, a Martha Baird Rockefeller Fund for Music grant and named "Outstanding Young Artist" by *Musical America*. She is the only violinist to have won both the Junior and Senior Auditions of the Philadelphia Orchestra. She also played to an audience of 12,000 in the Dome Arena with the Rochester Philharmonic under **André Kostelanetz** (1901–80). In 1975, as a senior at UC Berkeley, Zina was selected as one of the "Top Ten College Women" by *Glamour Magazine*. (Her daughter, Avlana Eisenberg, was chosen by the same magazine twenty years later!) In 1998, Zina received the Distinguished Alumni Award from Louisiana State University (Shreveport), where she had earned her master's degree in liberal arts.

Besides her enormous classical repertoire, Schiff champions the work of contemporary composers, with the world premiere of the Peter Jona Korn Concerto which she subsequently recorded on the Premiere label. The "Solo Sonata" by David Hush is the centerpiece of the CD *King David's Lyre*. In November 1998, Schiff played the New York premiere of Richard Nanes' *Rhapsody* with the Brooklyn Philharmonic in Manhattan's Cathedral of St. John the Divine, with return engagements in New York's largest church in the fall of 2000, '03, '05 and '06. May 1999 found her touring as soloist with the Israel Kibbutz Orchestra. March 2000 marked the West Coast premiere of the Nanes *Rhapsody* with the San Diego Symphony. In February 2001, she performed a recital at Texas A & M, honoring bio-chemist Dr. Joseph Nagyvary for his twenty-five years of violin research into the secrets of the

Cremona School. She demonstrated the sounds by switching violins for each piece. *The Stradivarius Puzzle*, is a CD of this unique presentation. On November 13, 2001, history was made at Tifereth Israel Synagogue, San Diego, when, in a mother-daughter appearance, Zina performed Jewish music under conductor Avlana! (See Conductors.)

In 2002, Schiff was soloist with the Shreveport Symphony in the rarely performed Bloch Violin Concerto in celebration of the 100th Anniversary of Agudath Achim Synagogue in that city. The same year brought the Naxos CD of the works of American composer Cecil Burleigh (1885–1980) on the American Classics Series, with pianist **Mary Barranger,** and Zina's younger daughter, Cherina Carmel, as both producer and other pianist. This received the American Record Guide Critics' Choice Award for 2002. *The Golden Dove*, featuring selections from the Jewish Folk Music Society (4–Tay Records), also produced by Cherina, who accompanied her mother in several selections. 2005 saw the release of *Elijah's Violin* (4-Tay), which contains the world premiere of *Sonata for Violin and Piano* by David Amram, in honor of his seventy-fifth birthday. Her recording of the Bloch Concerto No. 1 with the Scottish National Symphony is on a Naxos 2007 release.

On March 31, 2003, Schiff soloed at the Larry Lawrence Jewish Community Center in an homage to Jascha Heifetz, accompanying the traveling Heifetz Exhibit from Los Angeles. May 2006, at the same venue, she played "Music from Terezin," the only camp without gas chambers. Two survivors told their stories.

Why is this superb performer not as well-known as Mutter or Sonnenberg? Because twenty years ago agents could get away with discrimination against women who were also mothers. Concurrent with her career, she raised two fine musicians, aspiring conductor **Avlana Eisenberg**, and pianist/producer Cherina Carmel. Zina also needed to follow the career path of her husband, prominent radiologist/author Dr. Ronald Eisenberg. Today, this slim, youthful virtuosa continues on the road to the recognition she deserves—at the very top!

Kyoko Takezawa

KYOKO TAKEZAWA was born in Nagano, Japan on October 30, 1966, into a family of violinists. Presented with a violin on her third birthday, she started Suzuki group classes. She also had private lessons with a teacher who had been a student of Ivan Galamian. By seven, she was touring the U.S., Canada, and Switzerland as a member of the Suzuki Method Association. In 1982, she won first prize in the Fifty-first Annual Japan Music Competition, which brought solo appearances in Tokyo and Nagoya. At seventeen, she came to America to study with **Dorothy DeLay** at the Aspen Music School, and continued studies with her at Juilliard where she graduated in 1989. She won the Gold Medal at the 1986 Indianapolis International Violin Competition, whose judges included Ruggiero Ricci, Dorothy DeLay and Josef Gingold.

Her career blossomed with appearances in Germany, France and England. She also toured Europe with the Osaka Philharmonic. 1994–95 marked debuts with the Boston and San Francisco Symphonies, a tour of Japan with Sir Neville Marriner and the Academy of St. Martin-in-the-Fields, concerts at the Pacific Music Festival with Michael Tilson Thomas conducting the London Symphony, plus summer festivals at Aspen and Ravinia. 1995–96 saw her in France, Spain and Vienna. In her native country, she concertizes regularly with the New Japan Philharmonic and the NHK Symphony, with whom she toured Europe in April 1997. During the 1998–99 season, she performed with the London Symphony, BBC Philharmonic, the Royal Scottish National Orchestra, and with the Symphony Orchestra of Barcelona and the Tonhalle Orchestra. Recital appearances in 1999–2000 were throughout Europe and Japan, with a summer debut at the Mostly Mozart Festival in New York. She also appeared with orchestras in Honolulu, San Jose, Montreal, Hong Kong, Finland, Wales, the Academy of St. Martin-in-the-Fields and the London Symphony. Her 2001–02 season included appearances in the U.S., England, Scotland, Ireland, Germany, Mote Carlo, Japan, China, Hong Kong, Singapore and Malaysia. She toured the U.S. with the Moscow Philharmonic; Hong Kong, Singapore and Kuala Lumpur with the NHK Symphony; and England and Ireland with the Sapporo Symphony of Japan. During SummerFest La Jolla (California) 2001, **Dorothy DeLay** was scheduled to conduct the master classes, but cancelled due to ill health. (Her death came a few months later in March 2002.) Director **Cho-Liang** "Jimmy" **Lin** chose Kyoko and her string-mates at the festival, Mark Kaplan and

Michael Tree, to hold the classes. The 2002–03 season included appearances with the Montreal, San Francisco and Swedish Radio Symphonies, at the London Proms with the BBC (Wales) Symphony, plus the Royal Scottish National and Monte Carlo Orchestras, and the Malaysia Philharmonic. In December, she substituted for **Pamela Frank** as guest soloist with the New World Symphony of Miami in the Samuel Barber Violin Concerto. During 2003–04, she performed with the symphonies of Jacksonville (Florida), Spokane (Washington), the Hallé Orchestra of Manchester (UK), Bournemouth Symphony (UK), Rochester Philharmonic (NY), New York String Orchestra at Carnegie Hall, Vancouver and Singapore Symphonies. She toured Japan as guest soloist with the Berlin Radio Orchestra, and was heard with the Osaka Philharmonic, Kyushu Symphony, and Kanagawa Philharmony. In 2005 and 2006, she returned to SummerFest La Jolla.

Takezawa is co-director of the Suntory Festival in Tokyo, where she has performed chamber music twice yearly with such artists as **Yo-Yo Ma**, **Wolfgang Sawallisch**, **Josef Suk** and the late **Isaac Stern**. She also participates in the Grand Teton and Aspen Music Festivals. Under exclusive contract to RCA Victor Red Seal, her CD *French Violin Sonatas*—music of Debussy and Ravel—was chosen as one of the best recordings of 1995 by *Stereo Review*. This was followed by a CD and video of the Bartók Violin Concerto No. 2, featured in the internationally telecast series *Concerto!* hosted by Dudley Moore. Other releases include the concertos of Mendelssohn, Elgar, Brahms and Barber. In 1995 Kyoko Takezawa earned Japan's Idemitsu Award for her outstanding musicianship. Her violin is the Stradivarius "Composelice" (1710), provided by the Nippon Music Foundation.

The Prodigious Generation

"Talent is nature's way of being unfair," is the comment of British musicologist Antony Hopkins (not to be confused with actor Anthony H.). The 1970s and '80s gave us a nucleus of prodigies who have become the core of 21st century violinists. Despite the distractions of "rock" and "rap" deafening juvenile senses, and television sapping creative energies and stultifying the imagination of the young, these decades produced an elite côterie of young stars whose background, culture and upbringing made them impervious to peer pressure. Thus they were able to concentrate on classical music studies with those superior gifts which qualified them for the cognomen: *prodigy*. In the art of the violin, these ladies have followed through from that early precarious perch to varying pinnacles of success in their prime.

ADELE ANTHONY, born in Singapore October 1, 1970, was raised in Tasmania where she began violin at two-and-a-half, and pursued early studies with Beryl Kimber at the University of Adelaide (Australia). Her father, Alphonse Anthony, was a violist with the Adelaide Symphony.

She debuted with the Adelaide Symphony Orchestra in 1983, and was the youngest winner of the ABC Instrumental and Vocal Competition, performing the Sibelius Violin Concerto with the Queensland Symphony. She attended Juilliard (BM 1992), where she studied with **Dorothy DeLay**, **Felix Galimar**, and **Hyo Kang**. She won second prize at the 1993 Jacques Thibaud International Violin Competition in Paris and was a prizewinner at the 1994 Hanover International Violin Competition.

Since winning first prize in Denmark's Carl Nielsen International Violin Competition in 1996, she has debuted with the Buffalo Philharmonic, Iceland Symphony, Hong Kong Chamber Orchestra, and played return engagements with all six symphony orchestras of the Australian Broadcasting Corporation (Sydney, Melbourne, Queensland, West Australian, Tasmanian, Adelaide), as well as the Auckland Philharmonia and New Zealand Symphony Orchestra.

Chamber concerts have taken her to the Chamber Music Society of Lincoln Center, Japan's *Saga* and Bombay's *Sangat* Festivals. At La Jolla *SummerFest* 2001 and 2006, she appeared with her husband, famed violinist **Gil Shaham**, whom she met at Juilliard in 1988 and married November 24, 1998. They are seen together in recital tours both in the U.S. and Europe. The 2005 Aspen Festival witnessed a special treat, pianist **Orli Shaham** playing with her sister-in-law, Adele—they have known each other since their pre-teen years—and then in a trio with Gil. This gave the listeners the sound of two legendary Stradivari violins: Gil's made in 1699 and Adele's 1728.

Adele has recorded the Violin Concertos of Philip Glass (Naxos), Carl Nielsen (Centaur), and Arvo Pärt's *Tabula Rasa* (Deutche Grammophon).

On September 30, 2002, she and Gil secured the next generation of violinists with the birth of their son, Elijah!

In 1998, at 16, **LIDIA BAICH** won the European EBU Grand Prix as *Austrian Young Musician of the Year*. Born in St Petersburg (Russia) in 1982, into a musical family, by age two she could play and harmonize any melody on the piano, and at five received her own special sized violin and started lessons. Her first international competition success followed at age eight. She began studying at the Conservatorium of Vienna in 1990, under Boris Kushnir. She has concertized throughout Europe and performed at the Austrian *Wiener Festwochen* (Vienna Festival). 2000 brought a performance with the Bavarian Radio Orchestra, plus concerts with the Hong Kong Philharmonic, St. Petersburg Philharmonic, NHK Symphony, Radio Symphony of Vienna, and Vienna Chamber Orchestra, among others. She has several CD, Radio and Television recordings to her credit, and plays a 1723 Carlo Bergonzi violin, on loan to her from the Austrian National Bank.

Rachel Barton

A native of Chicago, **RACHEL BARTON PINE**, born in 1974, began violin at three, made her professional debut at seven with the Chicago String Ensemble, and gave performances at ten and fifteen with the Chicago Symphony as a student competition winner. During her early teens, she was concertmaster of the Civic Orchestra, training orchestra for the CSO, appeared at the Ravinia Festival's *Rising Star* series, and often substituted with the symphony. At this point she was the main breadwinner in her family. She won many regional and national competitions, appearing more than fifty times as soloist with American orchestras. She was the top American prize winner in international competitions: Montreal (1991), Szigeti (Budapest, 1992), Kreisler (Vienna, 1992), Paganini (Genoa, 1993), Queen Elisabeth (Brussels, 1993), and Gold Medalist at the Quadrennial J.S. Bach International (Leipzig, 1992).

Barton was home-schooled from age eight to accommodate her musical training at the Music Institute of Chicago with Almita and Roland Vamos. She played chamber music with younger sisters Sarah, cello, and Hannah, violin, and coached youth orchestras until her schedule became too busy. After performing the national anthem in a 1995 Chicago Bulls playoff game, she had people tell her they never knew violins were "so cool!" As one of a growing number of musicians bringing new listeners to classical music through creative programming, she goes on air at rock radio stations playing Metallica and Led Zeppelin, followed by Paganini and Bach. In 1996, she was part of the torchbearer relay for the Paralympics, which involves elite athletes with any disability (not to be confused with the Special Olympics for the mentally challenged). She later played with the Atlanta Symphony in the opening ceremonies.

Besides Chicago, Barton has appeared with the symphonies of St. Louis, Dallas, Montreal, Vienna and Budapest, Camarata Academica at the 2000 Salzburg Festival, and many others. By 2006 there were over twelve CDs to her credit, including *Scottish Fantasies*, Celtic themed works like Bruch's *Scottish Fantasy*, and a two-CD set with the Chicago Symphony of the concerti of Joachim and Brahms.

On June 9, 2002, she performed a Tribute Recital at the **Maud Powell** Music Festival, held in Peru, Illinois—birthplace of this American pioneer violinist.

The Rachel Elizabeth Barton Foundation's Instrument Loan Program was established in 2003 to promote the work of young artists and to assist in career development.

On June 5, 2004, Rachel and Gregory Pine, her long time devoted companion, were married in Chicago before 400 guests. "It was a large wedding by normal terms," she noted with a smile, "but a small audience by my standards." Present were the Chicago Childrens Choir, organist David Schrader and violinist/composer **Mark O'Connor**, who performed his *Appalachian Waltz*.

During 2005, Barton Pine was elected to the Chicago chapter board of directors of the National Academy of Recording Arts and Sciences (NARAS), and performed the Tchaikovsky Concerto and John Corigliano's "Red Violin" Chaconne (from the fabulous 1998 film) with the Illinois Symphony. The summer featured her second tribute recital to **Maud Powell** at the Women in Music Series of the National Museum of Women in the Arts in Washington, DC. In February 2006, she was a guest with the Iceland Symphony, and performed the entire Corigliano "Red Violin" Concerto with the Tallahassee (Florida) Symphony. In May, she chaired the Music Institute of Chicago's Seventy-fifth Anniversary Gala, "Go Where the Music Takes You," honoring violinist Midori's dedication to music education.

In April 2006, the Rachel Barton Pine Violin Chair, endowed through a generous gift from the Sage Foundation, was established to recongnize members of the Music Institute of Chicago's violin faculty. In June, Rachel performed a tour de force at St. James United Church in Montreal. Titled "A Date with the Devil!" she played all twenty-four Caprices of "fiendish" violinist-composer Niccolò Paganini (1782–1840) in a single concert—the zenith of violin virtuoso accomplishments! 2007 brought her Cedille CD, *American Virtuosa - a Tribute to Maud Powell.*

Rachel's 1742 Joseph Guarnerius del Gesù, the "ex-Soldat," is on loan from her patron.

NICOLA BENEDETTI born in Scotland in 1987, began violin lessons at age five. She entered the Yehudi Menuhin School in 1997, where she studied with Natasha Boyarskaya. She left there at the end of 2002 and has been studying privately with Maciej Rakowski, living in London and enjoying a busy schedule.

During the 2004–2005 season, Nicola made her solo recital debut at Wigmore Hall in October, and performed at Holyrood Palace, Windsor Castle, and for Her Majesty Queen Elizabeth II during the Opening Ceremony of the Scottish Parliament. Other appearances included the Royal Philharmonic Orchestra, Royal Scottish National Orchestra, Academy of St-Martin-in-the-Fields, City of London Sinfonia, London Mozart Players, European Union Chamber Orchestra and Scottish Ensemble. June 2005 found her in New York in a recital for the "Academy of Achievement Summit." Returning to the UK for a tour of schools in conjunction with the Sargent Cancer Care for Children Practice-a-thon, she encouraged pupils of all ages to pick up their instruments and enjoy classical music.

In September 2005, Nicola made her BBC Prom in the Park debut with the BBC Concert Orchestra in London's Hyde Park. The autumn brought her U.S. debut tour with a Merkin Hall recital, and orchestral performances in several states. Her 2006 schedule began with the Royal Liverpool Philharmonic Orchestra, BBC Symphony Orchestra and the Philharmonia Orchestra, London.

Since signing with Universal/Deutsche Grammophon in 2004, her debut album, with Daniel Harding and the London Symphony Orchestra, was released in May '05. It features Szymanowski's Violin Concerto No. 1, which she played with the BBC Scottish Symphony Orchestra, winning her the BBC Young Musician of the Year 2004 title. Nicola plays a 1751 Guarnerius violin.

Sarah Chang

When **Zubin Mehta** first heard **SARAH CHANG** play at age eight, he was so impressed he invited her to be a surprise guest soloist with the New York Philharmonic at Avery Fisher Hall two days later to play the Paganini Concerto No. 1. She was also immediately engaged by **Riccardo Muti** for the Philadelphia Orchestra's gala ninetieth anniversary concert in January 1991, and has since performed to rave reviews all over the world, including Hong Kong, Japan, Singapore and South Korea, with a host of famous conductors.

Born December 10, 1980, in Philadelphia to Korean parents, Sarah began her violin studies at age four. In 1987, her talent earned her the Starling Scholarship at Juilliard, where she studied with **Dorothy DeLay** and Hyo Kang. In May 1992, she was the youngest ever recipient of an Avery Fisher Career Grant. She has been profiled in the *New York Times, Washington Post, San Francisco Chronicle, Philadelphia Inquirer, Life, People, USA Today, The Times* (London), *Strad* (the violin magazine), *Le Figaro* (Italy), *Berliner Morgenpost, Stern,* and just about every newspaper in the world. Her television appearances include *Good Morning, America,* NBC's *Today* show, *CBS, This Morning, CBS, Sunday Morning,* a PBS special, "Gifted Children," and the BBC's *Blue Peter* and *Our Common Future*—telecast in more than 100 countries—as well as on French and German television. Her first appearance with John Williams and the Boston Pops was telecast on PBS' *Evening at the Pops.* Her London Symphony debut was the basis of a documentary on ITV's *The Young South Bank Show,* one of Britain's most acclaimed arts programs.

1994–95 was highlighted by two major concert broadcasts: Zubin Mehta and the Berlin Philharmonic from the Teatro Communale in Florence (Italy), and Kurt Masur and the New York Philharmonic for the PBS telecast "Live from Lincoln Center." Chang also made her Carnegie Hall debut with Charles Dutoit and the Montreal Symphony. 1995–96 featured concerts with the New York Philharmonic, Philadelphia Orchestra, Baltimore, Dallas and Detroit Symphonies as well as a Carnegie Hall appearance with the Metropolitan Opera Orchestra under **James Levine**. European engagements were with Zubin Mehta and the Israel Philharmonic in Paris, André Previn and the London Symphony, the Philharmonia of London, Simon Rattle and the City of Birmingham Symphony, David Zinman and the Tonehalle (Zurich) Orchestra, Herbert Blomstedt and the Bamberg Symphony, Wolfgang Sawallisch and the Hamburg Philharmonic and James de Preist and the Helsinki Philharmonic. There were also many U.S. and European recitals, including San Diego, Dublin, Reading (England), Hanover and Bologna. The 1997–98 season included recital debuts in Europe and at Carnegie Hall. The 1998–99 European season included appearances with the London Philharmonic, the London Symphony Orchestra and the Vienna Philharmonic. Also in 1999, she joined Charles Dutoit and the NHK (Japan) Symphony on their U.S. tour, with recital performances at the Aspen, Tanglewood, and the French St. Ricquier and Montpellier festivals. Her 2000–01 season was highlighted by return engagements with the Bavarian State Orchestra in Munich, Danish National Symphony Orchestra, Helsinki, Los Angeles, New York and Monte-Carlo Philharmonics, Montreal Symphony, Philadelphia and Philharmonia Orchestras, San Francisco and Toronto Symphonies. Her close association with the London Symphony Orchestra continued with several concerts in London as well as major tours of the U.S. and Spain. She also travelled to China for appearances at the Beijing Music Festival.

Her first CD, *Debut*, featuring virtuoso pieces by Sarasate, Paganini, Elgar and Prokofiev, was recorded when she was nine, using a quarter-size violin. It quickly reached *Billboard*'s chart of classical bestsellers. Subsequent releases are the Tchaikovsky, Paganini and Vieuxtemps' concerti, Lalo's *Symphonie espagnole*, Vaughan Williams' *The Lark Ascending*, plus works of Saint-Saëns.

Chang received a special award, "Young Artist of the Year" in 1993, from *Gramophone* (magazine), the German "Echo" Schallplattenpreis and the "Debut" award from Britain's Royal Society of Music. She played on the PBS "Great Performances" worldwide broadcast of "Concert for Planet Earth" at the Rio de Janeiro Earth Summit in 1992. In 1994, she was honored with the "Newcomer of the Year" prize at the International Classical Music Awards, and South Korea bestowed their country's highest musical honor, the "Nan Pa" award upon her. In February 1997, EMI Classics released *Simply Sarah*, a collection of shorter pieces for violin and piano, and in March 1998 the same label brought out her rendition of the Sibelius and Mendelssohn Violin Concertos with the Berlin Philharmonic under Mariss Jansons. Other releases include the Richard Strauss Violin Concerto with Wolfgang Sawallisch (1999), and Goldmark's Violin Concerto in A minor, plus his Overture from *Prometheus Bound* (2000). 2001 produced an album of popular short works for violin and orchestra, with Plácido Domingo conducting the Berlin Philharmonic, and 2002, a recording of chamber music for strings, Dvořák's *Sextet* and Tchaikovsky's *Souvenir de Florence*, with current and former members of the Berlin Philharmonic.

Besides globe-circling recitals and concert appearances with the world's top orchestras, Sarah Chang's prolific career was highlighted with the 1999 awarding of the Avery Fisher Prize, an honor she shared with fellow violinists **Pamela Frank** and **Nadja Salerno-Sonnenberg**—the first time in its (then) twenty-five year history that the award has gone to a female.

CHEE-YUN was born in Seoul, April 30, 1970. With music lessons an accepted part of Korean upbringing, of the four children in the family, her two older sisters were already playing instruments. (Her oldest sister Cheu-Yun is making a name for herself as a pianist.) Chee-Yun chose violin and made her first public performance at age eight, winning the Grand Prize of the *Korean Times* Competition. At age thirteen, she came to the U.S. and was invited to perform the Vieuxtemps Concerto No. 5 in a Young Peoples Concert with the New York

Chee Yun

Philharmonic. Although no one in her family spoke English, her parents left their successful importing business to support their daughter. Her father opened a liquor store in Manhattan.

In New York, Chee-Yun trained with **Dorothy DeLay** and Hyo Kang, and Felix Galimir for chamber music at Juilliard. She was a winner of the Young Concert Artists International Auditions (1989), recipient of the Avery Fisher Career Grant (1990), and nominated for Best Debut in the first annual Cannes Classical Awards at the MIDEM international music convention (1994). Highlights of her career include appearances at the Kennedy Center's "Salute to Slava" Gala honoring the retiring of Mstislav Rostropovich from the National Symphony, the first concert at the Danny Kaye Playhouse at New York's Hunter College, Lincoln Center's Mostly Mozart Festival, the Spoleto Festival in Charleston, North Carolina, and the Pacific Music Festival (Japan) with Michael Tilson Thomas, in a premiere of Lou Harrison's *Suite for Violin and String Orchestra*. In the 1994–95 season, she debuted with the New York Chamber and the Cincinnati Symphonies. 1995–96 included a debut tour of Israel for six concerts with the Haifa Symphony, return performances with the Royal Philharmonic, a tour of Germany, Japan (with the St. Petersburg Camerata) and concerts with the Bilbao (Portugal) Symphony, the Nagoya Philharmonic and the Aarhus Festival in Denmark. In 1998, she made her debut with the San Francisco Symphony and returned with them for their 2000 Charles Schwab National Tour with Michael Tilson Thomas. Her 1999–2000 season included debuts with the Oregon and Utah Symphonies, a return to Japan to tour with the NHK Symphony, and in August with La Jolla *SummerFest* 2000. During the 2000–01 season, she appeared throughout Europe, Asia, and North America, and performed with the Spoleto Festival USA chamber music tour, a project with which she has been associated since its inception. Her return appearance with the Hong Kong Philharmonic featured a performance of Krzystof Penderecki's Second Violin Concerto with the composer on the podium. 2002–03 found her performing throughout the U.S. in concert venues, and at the festivals of Spoleto, Bravo! Vail Valley and La Jolla *SummerFest*. Other performances were in Shanghai, Toronto, Korea, and Finland. She began 2003 with the Spoleto Festival USA tour, and a return engagement with the San Diego Symphony.

As a recitalist, Chee-Yun made her New York debut at the 92nd Street Y in the 1989 Young Concert Artists Series and has given numerous other recitals in music centers throughout the U.S. and abroad. Her acclaimed recordings—exclusively for Denon—include an album of virtuoso encore pieces, the violin sonatas of Debussy, Fauré and Saint-Saëns, and the concertos of Vieuxtemps and Mendelssohn, among a myriad of others. She has been heard frequently on NPR and KBS Television in Korea.

In 1993, Chee-Yun traveled to Korea and, like Sarah Chang, received the "Nan Pa" award, the country's highest musical honor. On her return to the U.S., she was further honored with an invitation to perform at the White House for President Clinton, Vice President Gore, Isaac Stern and Leontyne Price, in honor of the recipients of the National Medal of the Arts.

In 1997, she married pediatric surgeon Eugene Kim. They make their home in New York. If music is the universal language, then playing styles know no boundaries of time. Superb violinist **Michael Rabin** (1936–72) died tragically at thirty-five, yet when a little nine-year-old Korean girl heard his recordings she felt a personal link with his romantic renditions in the legacy of Mischa Elman and Fritz Kreisler. Now Chee-Yun perpetuates this tradition with her lush, sensual, and "old-fashioned" technique.

JENNIFER FRAUTSCHI, born in Pasadena, California, in 1973, began violin at age three, later taking formal studies at the Colburn School for the Performing Arts in Los Angeles with Robert Lipsett. Her college career covered the USC School of Music, Harvard and Juilliard, where she studied with Robert Mann and became a teaching assistant to the Juilliard String Quartet. In 1990, she was honored with a *United States Presidential Scholar in the Arts* scholarship. She made her debut with the Los Angeles Philharmonic at sixteen and has since concertized throughout the U.S., Europe and Mexico. As well as receiving the 1999 Avery Fisher Career Grant, Jennifer has won a range of prizes including the Washington International Competition, Irving Klein International String Competition, the 1998 Naumburg Violin Competition and, in 1997, the prestigious Queen Elisabeth of Belgium International Violin Competition, after which she gave a recital at the Monnaie Opera House in Brussels and played with the Royal Philharmonic Orchestra of Flanders, a critically acclaimed performance that was broadcast repeatedly on television throughout Northern Europe. Other concerts have been in Switzerland, at the San Miguel de Allende Music Festival, and with the Mexico City Philharmonic. Her Washington, DC, recital debut was at the Phillips Collection, in New York at Lincoln Center's Alice Tully Hall, the Dame Myra Hess Series in Chicago and the Gardner Museum in Boston. She has also appeared with her sister, violinist Laura Frautschi, who holds degrees from Juilliard and Harvard and is a member of New York's Sospespo Ensemble, a modern music chamber orchestra. For several seasons, Jennifer was a frequent performer on New York classical radio station WQXR's weekly show, "On-Air," which features a blend of live performance and discussions about music.

By 2002, she had performed on NPR, at the Santa Fe Chamber, New York's Mostly Mozart and Caramoor Festivals, the Spoleto Festival in Italy, and the Piccolo Spoleto Festival in South Carolina. The following year, she made her Chicago Symphony debut under the direction of Christoph Eschenbach at the Ravinia Festival, with the Seattle Symphony and Gerard Schwartz, and Los Angeles Philharmonic debut with Pierre Boulez, performing the Berg Violin Concerto.

She was selected to take part in Carnegie Hall's Rising Stars/Distinctive Debuts series. This series is a collaboration between Carnegie Hall and the European Concert Hall Organization (ECHO), designed to offer young artists a forum from which to launch their international careers. Her New York City recital debut was at Carnegie's Weill Hall, followed by performances in major European cities during the 2003–04 season. For her December 2005 concert with the San Diego Symphony, she performed Leonard Bernstein's challenging *Serenade*, for violin, string orchestra, harp and percussion, a "concerto" written for Isaac Stern in 1954.

Equally at home with classical and 21st century repertoire, Frautschi's Artek CDs include works of Stravinsky and Ravel, solo pieces by Bartok, Ysaÿe, Kreisler, Davidovsky and Harbison, released in 2002, and both Prokofiev's Concerti with Gerard Schwarz and the Seattle Symphony (2003). She can also be heard on the Naxos CD of Schoenberg's Concerto for String Quartet and Orchestra, and works of Webern, conducted by Robert Craft.

Jennifer performs on a 1722 Antonio Stradivarius violin known as the "ex-Cadiz," previously owned and performed upon for over forty years by the great American violinist Joseph Fuchs (1900–97).

KAREN GOMYO, born in Tokyo in 1982, moved to Montreal in 1984 and began playing in public at age five. At seven, she won a prize in the Musici de Montreal Competition, and at nine first prize in the Canadian Music Competition in Ottawa. After playing in a master class for **Dorothy DeLay**, she was invited to study with the renowned pedagogue at Juilliard, where she was awarded a full scholarship in the pre-college program. She continued her studies at the University of Indiana (Bloomington) and went on to become part of the studio of Donald Weilerstein at the New England Conservatory. In 1997, she won the YCA International Auditions. The following year, she appeared as soloist with the National Symphony conducted by Christopher Hogwood, gave recitals on a five-city tour of Japan, and November 1998 opened the Thirty-eighth Young Concert Artists Series with her debut at the 92nd Street Y—the youngest artist ever presented in the series. 1999–2000 season found her with Sweden's Norrköping Symphony Orchestra, the Minnesota Orchestra under Eiji Oue and Claus Peter Flor, a recital debut at the Louvre (Paris) and at the Ravinia *Rising Stars* of the Chicago Symphony. By 2001–02, she had appeared with the Houston, Baltimore Indianapolis, National, and San Antonio Symphonies, Cincinnati Chamber Orchestra and the Tokyo and Hiroshima Symphonies, as well as at the Aspen Music Festival. She has been heard in New York on WQXR and WNYC Radio, and throughout America on NPR's "Performance Today." Gomyo was featured with YCA alumnus cellist Carter Brey on A&E Television's "Breakfast with the Arts," in a segment celebrating the fortieth anniversary of Young Concert Artists.

Karen Gomyo is a recipient of support from the Jack Romann Special Artists Fund of YCA, and has been awarded grants from the Heckscher, Edward John Noble, Dorothy Richard Starling, Clarisse B. Kampel, Brady Dougan, and Cho Chang Tsung Foundations, the Salon de Virtuosi, plus continuing support from the Bagby

Foundation for the Musical Arts. She plays the rare "Ex Foulis" Stradivarius of 1714 on permanent loan to her from a private sponsor.

Hilary Hahn

HILARY HAHN was born November 27, 1979, in Lexington, Kentucky, but lived in Baltimore from age three. She began violin at four in the Suzuki program at the Peabody Conservatory near her home. From the age of five, she studied privately with Klara Berkovich until, at ten, was admitted at Curtis to study with **Jascha Brodsky**. For her audition she played the now rarely heard Viotti concerto—one of Maud Powell's *tours de force*. Having been home-schooled from fifth through eighth grade, Hilary finished her high school program at age twelve (at Curtis) and went on to get her BA there by fifteen. She has also been taught by **Jaime Laredo**, and studied chamber music with **Felix Galimir** and pianist **Gary Graffman**. Her orchestra debut was in 1991 with the Baltimore Symphony Orchestra under **David Zinman**. Next came performances with the New York Philharmonic, Philadelphia Orchestra, Cleveland Orchestra and Pittsburgh Symphony. In 1994, she appeared as a recitalist in Ravinia's "Rising Stars." 1995 saw her European debut with **Lorin Maazel** and the Bavarian Radio Symphony, playing the Beethoven Concerto, the Marlboro Music Festival in Vermont, and a performance of the Bach Double Concerto with Jaime Laredo and the New York Chamber Symphony. In May 1995, she received an Avery Fisher Career Grant. 1996–97 was a full season with concerts in La Jolla, California (where she met the author), Detroit, a fall European tour, again with Lorin Maazel and the Bavarian Radio Symphony which visited Amsterdam, Munich and Hanover. October brought recital debuts in Rotterdam, Paris, Hanover and Munich. November marked her Carnegie Hall debut playing the Saint-Saëns Concerto No. 3 under Christoph Eschenbach, and December, Bach's Six Branden-burg Concerti with the Lincoln Center Chamber Orchestra. 1998–99 saw her Paris debut with the Orchestre Philharmonique, a recital debut at Lincoln Center, and a return engagement at Carnegie Hall with the St. Louis Symphony and Hans Vonk. Other appearances were with the New York Philharmonic, Los Angeles Philharmonic, and National Symphony. The season concluded with a five-week tour of Australia.

In 1996, Sony Classical made her one of the youngest exclusive artists in that label's century-long history. Her first release was the Beethoven Violin Concerto and the Bernstein *Serenade* with the Baltimore Symphony and David Zinman, her mentor and colleague since she was ten. Her recording of the concertos of Samuel Barber and Edgar Meyer (the latter written for her in 1999) was released in April. 2001 brought her critically acclaimed recording of the Brahms and Stravinsky Violin Concertos, with Sir Neville Marriner conducting the Academy of St. Martin-in-the-Fields. A 2002 disc coupled Mendelssohn and Shostakovich (No.1) Violin Concertos with Hugh Wolff and Marek Janowski conducting the Oslo Philharmonic Orchestra.

The new century saw her debut with the Berlin Philharmonic, re-engagements with Cleveland, Los Angeles and the Bavarian Radio Symphony Orchestras, a fifteen-city recital tour in the U.S. and Europe and orchestral debuts in Dallas, San Francisco, Oslo, Copenhagen, Helsinki, Stockholm, Toronto, and a return to San Diego in 2001. Highlights of 2002–2003 included performances of the Meyer Violin Concerto in Frankfurt, a subsequent a tour of Germany and central Europe with the San Francisco Symphony Orchestra, as well as recitals in Carnegie Hall, Milwaukee, Honolulu, Los Angeles and Wilmington. The season also covered Montreal, Venice, Zurich, Munich, Istanbul, Lyon, Vienna and Dusseldorf, performances of the Bach violin concertos in Lucerne, Vienna and Salzburg, and Elgar with the Munich Philharmonic, and the Spohr Violin Concerto No. 8 in Lisbon and Copenhagen.

Leila Josefowicz

The reviews of **LEILA JOSEFOWICZ** read uncannily like those of Maud Powell. "All her energy is concentrated on the memorable sound she produces . . . incredibly alive and intense, with the vibrance and luminosity of Jascha Heifetz . . . the mastery one would expect from Perlman or Stern . . . glowing from within . . . her inner spirit [is] fully apparent . . . [she] had the house mesmerized . . . her performances have the depth and insight that show she has gone far beyond the printed notes . . . complete virtuosity . . ."

Born in Toronto, October 20, 1977, Leila began her studies at age three in the Suzuki program in Los Angeles. Discovered to have perfect pitch—as a child she even knew in what key the vacuum cleaner "played"—she went to **Robert Lipsett** at the Colburn School of Performing Arts. She also had private lessons with **Josef Gingold** at Indiana University. At age ten, her performance of Wieniawski's *Scherzo-Tarantelle* for the NBC television special, "America's Tribute to Bob Hope," brought her immediate national attention. Since then she has been featured on programs telecast in the U.S., UK and Canada, including *Evening at the Pops* with John Williams and the *Tonight Show* with Johnny Carson. She has appeared with every major orchestra in North America including Cleveland, Philadelphia, Chicago, St. Louis, Atlanta, National, Toronto, Montreal, Detroit, Houston, Cincinnati, San Diego and Vancouver.

In 1994, Leila was awarded an Avery Fisher Career Grant. The 1994–95 season saw her Carnegie Hall debut performing the Tchaikovsky Concerto with Sir Neville Marriner and the Academy of St. Martin-in-the-Fields, a tour of Japan performing to sold-out halls in Tokyo and Osaka, and concerts with the Los Angeles and London Philharmonics. The fall of 1995 marked her Boston Symphony debut with Seiiji Ozawa, and another concert at Carnegie Hall playing with the same aggregation. 1996 brought return engagements with Cleveland and Philadelphia. She returned to Asia in 1998, performing in Japan, China, Korea, Hong Kong, and in Australia and Tasmania. During the 2000–01 season, she continued her appearances with major American symphonies, made her Ravinia Festival debut, and performed with orchestras in Vienna, Berlin, Zurich and London.

Josefowicz' exclusive contract with Phillips has produced CDs of the Tchaikowsky and Sibelius concertos—which won the *Diapason d'Or* prize—plus the music of Bartók, Kreisler, Ysaÿe, Ernst and Paganini.

To give her the opportunity to study with famed **Jascha Brodsky** and **Jaime Laredo** at the Curtis Institute (graduated 1997), and chamber music with **Felix Galimir**, in the fall of 1991 her family—mother Wendy, a geneticist, father John, a physicist, and her younger brother Steven—moved from California to Philadelphia. On December 16, 1991, respected critic Robert C. Marsh, after hearing her play at the Rising Stars series in Ravinia, wrote in the *Chicago Sun-Times*, "If she is only thirteen, when did she study with **Leopold Auer** (1845–1930) the great mentor of the Russian violin school? She comes straight from the Auer tradition, the tradition of Jascha Heifetz, Nathan Milstein and Mischa Elman . . . "

Early in her career the young artist was lent a 1735 Guarneri del Gesù by the Chicago dealer Bein and Fushi. She now plays the 1708 "Ruby" Stradivarius on a long term loan from the Stradivarius Society of Chicago. She lives in Florida with her husband, conductor Kristjan Järvi, youngest son of Estonian maestro and former Detroit Symphony conductor, Neeme Järvi. Their son Lucas was born April 2000.

For a child who at six announced that practicing was *fun*, and "Hey, I'd like to be this when I grow up . . . going places and seeing the world!" it would appear that the dream of Leila Josefowicz has already been more than fulfilled.

Over ninety years ago, Maud Powell prescribed: "It seems superfluous to emphasize that one's program numbers must have been mastered in every detail. Only then can one defy nervousness, turning excess of emotion into inspiration." At fourteen Leila stated, "I know I have to work until I am ready, and then I'm not nervous . . . I just have to do everything I can to reach everybody in the audience."

JULIETTE KANG was born in Edmonton, Alberta (Canada) September 6, 1975. Seeing her two older sisters playing in Suzuki violin classes established her natural progression to joining them at age four. She made her concerto debut in Montreal at seven. At nine, she was accepted at Curtis to study with renowned teacher **Jascha Brodsky** (1906–97), and earned her BM in 1991. The same year she performed the Bach *Concerto for Two Violins in D Minor* with **Pinchas Zukerman** at Lincoln Center to commemorate the thirtieth anniversary of Young Concert Artists. Meanwhile, a 1987 tour of Belgium yielded an award from the Alex de Vries Foundation, and in 1989 she gained the distinction of being the youngest winner—at thirteen—of the Young Concert Artists (YCA) International auditions. She was first prize winner in the 1992 Yehudi Menuhin International Violin Competition in Paris. At Juilliard Graduate School, her teachers were the great **Dorothy Delay** and her assistant, Hyo Kang.

Julliette earned her master's in 1993, the same year she received the Sylva Gelber Award and the Canada Council Grant. In 1994, she won the Gold Medal at the Fourth Quadrennial International Violin Competition. Capturing more prizes than anyone in the competition's history, Kang was noted for her performance of *Subito*, the newly commissioned work by Polish composer Witold Lutoslawski.

In an upward-spiraling career, she has performed with the Montreal Symphony Orchestra, the Orchestre National de France (under Lord Yehudi Menuhin), the CBC Vancouver and Korean Broadcasting Symphonies, the Juilliard and New York String Orchestras, the Chicago Sinfonietta, and at Kennedy Center, plus chamber concerts at summer festivals. 1995 saw recitals in Boston, Buffalo and Seoul, and the premiere of the Khrennikov Second Violin Concerto with the American Symphony Orchestra in Lincoln Center's Avery Fisher Hall. There were also appearances with the Hong Kong Philharmonic, and concerts throughout Canada. 1996 brought tours that included France and Mexico City, and her Carnegie Hall recital debut in March. The following year she appeared at the Spoleto Festival.

Juliette Kang received the YCA Mortimer Levitt Career Development Award for Women Artists and a 1990 Jack Romann Special Artists Grant. She has also won prizes in the Hanover (Germany) and Beijing International competitions as well as many awards in her native Canada. In 2000, she was featured soloist on two CBC recordings: *Affairs of the Heart* and Schumann and Wienawski Concertos with the Vancouver Symphony Orchestra. She played these two concertos with the Greenwich (Connecticut) Symphony in November 2002. The same year she was featured on New York's classical radio station, WQXR.

She plays on a 1689 Baumgartner Strad, on loan from the Canada Arts Council under their Musical Instrument Bank program.

Tamaki Kawakubo

TAMAKI KAWAKUBO, born October 10, 1979, in Palos Verdes, California, grew up with classical music. Her three years older sister, Kaori, plays piano and her three years younger sister, Kozue, the cello. Tamaki started piano at four, but wanted to try the violin. She began studies at five in Los Angeles with **Robert Lipsett** at the Colburn School. In September 1995, her family, like so many others who change their lives to accommodate a gifted child, moved to the New York area for the convenience of Tamaki's career and the opportunity to study at Juilliard with **Dorothy DeLay** and Masao Kawasaki. An adjunct to her career were studies with Zakhar Bron at the Musik Hochschule in Cologne (Germany).

A veteran of the concert stage at fifteen, Tamaki has concertized with the San Francisco Symphony with both John Williams and Michael Tilson Thomas, the Detroit Symphony (Neemi Järvi), Houston Symphony, the New York Youth Symphony at Carnegie Hall, San Diego Symphony and Los Angeles Philharmonic. Her Summer 1994 appearance with the Boston Pops was televised nationwide. 1995–96 included return engagements with San Diego and Albany, Charles Dutoit and the Montreal Symphony, and a recital in Ozawa, Japan. In 1997, Tamaki was winner of the Avery Fisher Career Grant. In 1999, she performed with Christoph Eschenbach at Chicago's Ravinia Festival. Her 1999–2000 season included a return to San Francisco, plus concerts in Quebec and Naples (Florida). In 2000–01, she was heard with the Seattle, Pacific, Indianapolis and Fresno Symphonies. Her festival appearances include Germany's Schleswig-Holstein, Cleveland's Blossom Summer Festival, and New York's Mostly Mozart, including their tour of Japan. She was the 2001 winner of the Pablo Sarasate International Violin Competition. During 2001–02, she appeared with the New World Symphony and Michael Tilson-Thomas, plus orchestras in Toledo, Knoxville, and Rhode Island, St. Petersburg (Russia) Symphony with Yuri Temirkanov and with the EOS Orchestra in a performance of *Chaconne* from John Corigliano's soundtrack to the film *The Red Violin*. She also concertized throughout Japan with orchestras and in recital.

Kawakubo's television debut was on *Entertainment Tonight* as the soloist at the Command Performance Gala. She was featured on the "Hour of Power" broadcast from the Crystal Cathedral, near Los Angeles, to thirty-one countries. Other appearances were on the Emmy Award-winning "Musical Encounter," and in a cameo spot in the Twentieth Century Fox film, *For the Boys*.

She plays the 1707 "Cathedral" Stradivarius, on loan from the Mandell Collection of Southern California.

(After hearing and seeing Tamaki playing the difficult Dvořák Concerto with the San Diego Symphony under Yoav Talmi, November 25, 1995, I visited her backstage. Audiences and critics had already marveled at the maturity of her technique and depth of emotion. The word "exquisite" was frequently applied to her playing. During the performance we experienced an ageless virtuoso, but when the tumultuous applause erupted so did the smile of this unspoiled girl whose philosophy even then was, "It feels good to express music that connects to the audience's feelings.")

JENNIFER KOH was born in 1977 to Korean parents in Glen Ellyn, Illinois. She studied at the Music Institute of Chicago with Almita and Roland Vamos, teachers of fellow Chicagoans Rachael Barton Pine and Isabella Lippi. At thirteen she appeared with the Chicago Symphony, and at fifteen won first place in the Illinois Young Performers Competition. In 1994, she won the International Tchaikovsky Competition and in 1995 first prize in the Concert Artists Guild Competition and received the Avery Fisher Career Grant. She made her Carnegie Hall debut in 1999, and in 2000 was a participant in the Young Performers Support Initiative, sponsored by the Association of Performing Arts Presenters' Classical Connections program. She received her BA in English literature and performance diploma from Oberlin, and studied with Jaime Laredo and Felix Galimir at Curtis.

She has soloed with the symphonies of Chicago, Detroit, Cincinnati, San Diego, Tulsa, Houston, National Symphony, and abroad in Iceland, Helsinki and Moscow. As a recitalist, Koh has appeared at Kennedy Center, Wolf Trap, Marlboro, Mostly Mozart, Ravinia, Spoleto, Schleswig-Holstein (Germany), Vancouver, Santa Fe, and Bravo! Vail, Colorado, music festivals. One of her most important contributions is her outreach program, *Jennifer Koh's Music Messenger*, in the course of which she performs in classrooms around the country, introducing children to music and encouraging music-making as a means of self-expression. She is also a member of the board of directors of the National Foundation for the Advancement for the Arts, a scholarship program for high school students in the arts.

The 2002–03 season included appearances at New York City's Miller Theatre in a program entitled "New York Hardcore," part of the "Sounds of New York" series, and the September 12, 2003 much-awaited opening of Carnegie Hall's Zankel Hall, performing Lou Harrison's *Concerto in slendro*, conducted by Pulitzer Prize-winning composer John Adams. 2003–04 concerto performances were with the BBC National Orchestra of Wales, Czech Philharmonic, St. Louis Symphony and KBS Symphony of Seoul, Korea, Aalborg Symphony (Denmark) and the San Diego Symphony. 2005 featured concerto performances with the Bolshoi Opera Orchestra (Moscow), Singapore Symphony, a tour with New World Symphony (Florida), and recitals at Disney Hall, (Los Angeles), the Hollywood Bowl, Seoul, Metropolitan Museum of Art and 92nd Street Y (New York).

Her recordings include chaconnes by Bach, Barth, and Reger (Cedille Records), the violin concertos of Menotti (Chandos), Nielsen (Kontrapunkt), Klami (BIS), and fantasies by Schubert, Schumann, Schoenberg and Ornette Coleman (Cedille, 2004).

Her violin, on loan from a private patron, is the 1727 Ex Grumiaux Ex General DuPont Stradivarius.

Russo-Greek violinist **NATASHA KORSAKOVA** comes from a family of distinguished musicians. Her grandfather was concertmaster of the Moscow Radio Symphony Orchestra and her father was famous Russian violinist, Andrej Korsakov. Natasha began violin at five, studying at the Central Music School of the Moscow Tchaikovsky Conservatory under her father. After his death, she continued her studies in Germany under Ulf Klausenitzer and Saschko Gawriloff, and began winning international competitions at a young age. Among her awards are Russian "Artist of the Year" (1994); Grand Prix, European Radio Recordings Competition (1995); Silver Medal, Concours Henryk Szeryng, (Mexcio, 1997); "Artist of the Year," (Chile, 1998); third prize, Antonio Stradivari International Violin Competition (Cremona, Italy, 2001).

She made her debut in 1994 in Berlin with the Leipzig Gewandhaus Orchestra. The following year found her in Cologne for a concert commemorating German reunification, plus performances in England with the European Union Chamber Orchestra and recital at the Litchfield Festival. 1996 saw recitals at Wigmore Hall, London, the

Mecklenburg Vorpommern Festival, Germany, and Rome's Accademia di Santa Cecilia. After a concert at the Moscow Conservatory, well known bowmaker Rudolf Neudörfer presented Natasha with a bow made especially for her as a token of his admiration of her artistic merit. In 1997, she was invited to Paris by Mrs. Irina Shostakovich, widow of the composer, to perform in the concert for the opening of the Dimitri Shostakovich Association; she also toured all over Germany. 1998 brought invitations from **Mstislav Rostropovich** to play the Beethoven Violin Concerto, and **Gidon Kremer** to take part in his Lockenhaus (Austria) Festival. 1999 marked debuts with the Innsbruck Philharmonic and the Netherlands Radio Orchestra at the Concertgebouw. Her recital debut in Vienna came in 2000, along with chamber music performances in Germany and Holland, and an appearance in Odessa, performing the First Violin Concerto of Dmitri Shostakovitch at the opening concert on the occasion of ESTA (European String Teachers Association) Congress. In 2002, she was again invited to the Concertgebouw in Amsterdam, where Korsakova resides. Her busy career continues with recitals and performances in Europe, Japan, Mexico and South America.

Natasha's mentor is renowned Italian violin virtuoso **Salvatore Accardo**. Her violin was crafted by a Carlo Bergonzi student, Vincenzo Panormo (1770).

MIN LEE, born 1983, is known as Singapore's poster girl of classical music. She began studies at two, and has been performing since five. She enrolled in Yale's masters program at fourteen, studied with Erick Friedman (1939–2004), graduating in 2000. In a reversal of the normal order, she completed a BM from the University of Michigan, May 2005. She has performed with the Royal Philharmonic, Vienna and Prague Chamber Orchestras, Academy of St. Martin-in-the-Fields, and Adelaide (Australia) Symphony. With the Philharmonia Orchestra, under Vladimir Ashkenazy, she recorded for Universal Music, *Debut*, the concerti of Wieniawski, Tchaikovsky and Prokofiev. March 2006, she played the Tchaikovsky with the San Diego Symphony, a piece she learned at thirteen. She says her love of Russian music comes from her teacher, a student of Nathan Milstein and Jascha Heifetz. Her instrument is the Guarnerius del Gesu 1728 from the Rin collection. Her performances have raised over $5 million for charitable organizations, including the Hong Kong Red Cross, NAC Gifted Young Musicians, Nanyang Academy of Fine Arts, Singapore, and Children with Renal Failure in Shanghai.

Catherine Manoukian

First-prize winner of the 1994 Canadian Music Competition, in which she obtained the highest mark in all categories, was fourteen-year-old violinist **CATHERINE MANOUKIAN**. Born in Toronto, June 1981, into a musical family, her father was her first violin teacher. Her interest in music began to show at age three, and her first stage appearance followed the next year. She gave her Toronto debut recital in November 1993, at the St. Lawrence Centre for the Arts, and in March 1994, by the invitation of Fukoku Concert Management, made her Tokyo debut recital. In July 1994, she won first prize at the Provincial and then the National Finals of the Canadian Music Competition, which resulted her performing the Paganini Concerto No.1 with the Vancouver Symphony at a gala concert in the Orpheum Theatre. In a burgeoning career, she has toured in Canada, including Toronto's Ford Centre, and recorded on the CBC, played in Nevada and Los Angeles and had a successful New York debut at Carnegie Hall. The 1995–96 season included performances with the Kitchener-Waterloo (Ontario) Symphony and the Hitachi Symphony Orchestra in Japan.

Since then, Manoukian's career has included solo appearances with Canadian and international orchestras, recitals in New York, Boston, Los Angeles, Paris, Tokyo and Toronto, and music festivals, including Aspen and Newport. She also was a guest soloist at the ceremony honoring Seiji Ozawa for his twenty-five years with the Boston Symphony. Her radio and television performances and interviews have been aired on CBC, *Voice of America*, Boston's WGBH, and Bravo Television's *Artist of the Day*. In her 2001 season, she returned for a fifth tour of Japan, plus recitals in North America, and the premiere performance of American composer Ronald Royer's *Partita for Violin and Orchestra*. Her third CD, recorded with Jukka-Pekka Saraste and the Toronto Symphony, features Elgar's Violin Concerto in B minor.

When in New York, Catherine studied with **Dorothy DeLay**.

Anne Akiko Meyers

ANNE AKIKO MEYERS became well-known in the '90s. She was the only recipient of the Avery Fisher Career Grant in 1993. Born May 15, 1970, in San Diego, California, she began violin at age four, making her debut with orchestra at seven. She studied with **Alice Schoenfeld** at the R.D. Colburn School[88] in Los Angeles, and Josef Gingold at Indiana University. At fourteen, she moved to New York to study with **Dorothy DeLay**, Masao Kawasaki and Felix Galimir at Juilliard. Her brilliant career has taken her to the Australian Bicentennial in Sydney, where she was the only classical artist before an audience of 300,000. This was a national PBS telecast with John Williams and the Boston Pops. Her performance with the Japan Philharmonic was simulcast in Japan, Russia and the U.S. In 1995, she gave the televised opening gala concert at the Concertgebouw in Amsterdam, toured the Far East with **David Zinman** and the Baltimore Symphony and later in the year made her tenth recital tour to the Far East. 1996 saw return engagements to Carnegie Hall, the Hollywood Bowl, and concerts with the Concertgebouw and Swedish Radio Orchestras, as well as a landmark recording of Prokofiev's first and second violin concertos with the Frankfurt Radio Symphony. At this juncture in her career, Meyers has collaborated with just about every illustrious maestro and every major orchestra on four continents. Her 1999–2000 season included concerts in Tokyo and Dallas, and tours with the St. Paul Chamber Orchestra, and in the Netherlands with the Nieuw Sinfonietta. Festival appearances have included Ravinia, Tanglewood, Aspen, Vail, the Hollywood Bowl, and in July 2000, the Mainly Mozart Festival in San Diego, California, with David Atherton. For 2000–01, she appeared in California, Florida, and Texas, a recital and concert tour of the Far East, and in Germany and Austria with the Polish Radio Symphony. The 2002 season included the world premiere of Joseph Schwantner's violin concerto *Angelfire*, with **Marin Alsop** and the National Symphony at Kennedy Center, and concerts with the China and Hong Kong Philharmonics led by Kryzstof Penderecki.

Akiko Meyers' many recordings are always on the bestseller list and include the Barber and Bruch concertos, sonatas of Saint-Saëns and Fauré, Lalo's *Symphonie Espagnole*, and Bruch's *Scottish Fantasy*. Two recital discs include encore pieces entitled *Salut d'Amour*, and an album with pianist **André-Michel Schub** of works by Copland, Ives, Piston and David Baker. A 21st century release is with the Frankfurt Radio Symphony featuring both Prokofiev violin concertos. She performs on a 1718 Stradivarius.

Midori

MIDORI (Goto Mi Dori) was born in Osaka, Japan on October 25, 1971, and studied with her mother, Setsu Goto, until 1981 when they came to America. She continued her training with **Dorothy DeLay** at Juilliard, and attracted the attention of Zubin Mehta, who featured the ten-year-old as guest soloist with the New York Philharmonic and took her on their Asian tour of Hong-Kong, Korea, Singapore, Thailand and Japan. In 1986, during a Tanglewood concert with Leonard Bernstein, she broke two strings, switching violins twice without losing a beat, and made front-page news for her self-confidence. Her career launched, Midori has collaborated with the best artists around the globe, including **Claudio Abbado**, **Daniel Barenboim**, **Leonard Bernstein**, **Yo-Yo Ma**, **Kurt Masur**, **André Previn**, **Isaac Stern** and **Pinchas Zukerman**. In the U.S. and worldwide her performances are sell-outs, as are her wide and varied recordings for Sony Classical, beginning with her 1990 Carnegie Hall recital debut. Her recording with pianist Robert McDonald of the Elgar and Franck Violin Sonatas in 1997 was her first in three years, followed by a disc pairing the Tchaikovsky Concerto and Shostakovich's Violin Concerto No.1, recorded live with Claudio Abbado and the Berlin Philharmonic, plus an all-Mozart recording with Christoph Eschenbach and the NDR Symphony released in 2001. Numerous honors include the Los Angeles Music Center's Dorothy B. Chandler Performing Arts Award, Japan's Suntory Hall Award and, for her dedication to the community, awards from the City of New York, the Cathedral of St. John the Divine

88. This non-profit organization, named after its major contributor, philanthropist Richard D. Colburn (1911–2004), was originally part of USC beginning in 1950. It operates under Colburn's vision "to provide the best possible training . . . to as many youngsters as possible, starting as early in their lives as possible." From the vast Colburn collection, priceless violins are loaned to give a start to budding performance careers.

(1995), and National Arts Award (1998). Her television appearances include the 1992 Winter Olympic Games, *CBS Sunday Morning, Sesame Street,* the *Tonight Show* and Carnegie Hall's 100th anniversary concert which have made her a familiar personality.

In 1992, in a move extraordinary for someone her age, she founded Midori & Friends, a non-profit organization whose programs seek to inspire children by bringing music into their lives. To this end, she works to generate music awareness in schoolchildren by giving special concerts and other educational activities in schools and hospitals where children do not have the opportunity for direct involvement with the arts. She was very active in giving special concerts for these young audiences in both the United States and Japan. However, since 2001 the program's scope has been limited to New York City, and a second organization, Music Sharing, has been formed in Japan, which includes traditional Japanese music.

She also founded Partners in Performance (PiP), University Residencies Program (URP) and Orchestra Residencies Program (ORP). PiP supports presenting organizations with small budgets by providing high-profile recitals or chamber performances for fundraising and community-relations events. URP encourages collaboration across departments within universities, and ORP, bonding between adult and affiliated youth orchestras.

In 2001, Midori turned thirty, her foundation turned ten, she celebrated the twentieth anniversary of her debut, received the Avery Fisher Prize for achievement and excellence in music, and was named *Musical America's* Instrumentalist of the Year. Giving about ninety-five concerts a year, in 2002 she performed in the U.S., toured Japan, was at the Salzburg Festival, and in an unusual two-week residency with the Los Angeles Philharmonic in November, played both the Barber and Sibelius concertos and participated in educational and community outreach programs with the orchestra and conductor Esa-Pekka Salonen.

She lives in New York City, where she completed a BA in psychology at the Gallatin School of NYU. She also took graduate courses at Oxford in psychology and gender studies. Her violin is the 1734 Guarnerius del Gesù "ex-Huberman," on a lifetime loan from the Hayashibara Foundation. Despite a full touring schedule, she is on the faculties of the Manhattan School of Music and Thornton School of Music at USC, where she was appointed to the Jascha Heifetz Chair in 2004.

She was honored for her dedicated work in music education at the Music Institute of Chicago's Seventy-fifth Anniversary Gala, "Go Where the Music Takes You,"chaired by **Rachel Barton Pine**, May 8, 2006.

Midori is living proof that prodigies can go from childhood to mature artist, keeping their personalities and musical gifts intact.

Lara St John

LARA ST. JOHN was born 1971, in London, Ontario, and began playing at age two. She first soloed with an orchestra at five, and made her European debut with the Gulbenkian Orchestra in Lisbon at ten. After touring Spain, France, Portugal and Hungary at twelve and thirteen, she entered Curtis at fourteen, graduating at seventeen. She also spent two years in England at the Guildhall School, holds a certificate from the Mannes College, and an artist's diploma from the New England Conservatory. After winning the Sylva Gelber Prize in Canada, the Minnesota and Philadelphia Orchestra Competitions, and the Grand Prize of the Canadian Music Competition, she won the use of the 1702 "Lyall" Stradivarius from the Canada Council for the Arts under their Musical Instrument Bank program. She presently performs on the 1779 "Salabue" Guadagnini lent by an anonymous donor and Heinl & Co. of Toronto, saying that "the Guadagnini simply sounds better."

After being eliminated in the semi-final rounds of the 1995 Montreal International Music Competition, she realized that those who do not project much personality do not get the prizes. In 1996, Well Tempered Productions released BACH: *Works for Violin Solo*, a controversial CD in that the cover pictured her wearing little more than her violin. It has sold over 30,000 copies. Since then, she has gained as much notice—and notoriety—for her album covers as for her playing. She has not only the technical mastery, but her playing has passion and boundless joy that infuses everything she plays. From her home, now in New York, she travels throughout the world giving approximately seventy concerts each year. In a field awash in young violinists, she says it is her mission to persuade young audiences to share her love of music. To do so, she plays familiar standards, but also plays the 20th century repertoire. Her wish to play more of the modern repertoire is only limited by the conductors and orchestras able to devote the rehearsal time for these works. Her second CD, produced by WTP in 1997, is *GYPSY*, with selections by Waxman, Bartók, Kreisler, Sarasate and Ravel, with arrangements by her accompanist Ilan Rechtman. The cover photo is more conservative than the first, but the technical display, earthy tone and spontaneous feeling for phrasing and rhythm are what makes this violinist stand out.

Following the release of her third CD, *Bach: the concerto album*, on her own Ancalagon label in 2002, Sony Classical signed her to an exclusive contract to record both innovative and core classical projects. Her first release was unusual arrangements of the music of J.S. Bach, with English composer/producer Magnus Fiennes, the brother of film stars Ralph and Joseph.

The vulnerability of us all was demonstrated by an incident that happened to Lara on January 22, 2001. At a photo shoot in Toronto, she was given a glass of water that was by mistake a 35 percent solution of hydrogen peroxide. For four days she was in the hospital on IVs, with surgeons ready to operate to repair her stomach and esophagus. Miraculously, this proved unnecessary! Her life shortly went back to normal with a full performing schedule.

Born in Helsinki, April 16, 1972, into a Hungarian-Austrian family, **RÉKA SZILVAY** started violin at four with her father, Géza Szilvay, a professor at the Sibelius Academy, originator of the Colourstrings Method of teaching violin to children, and conductor of the Helsinki Strings. At twelve, she entered the Sibelius Academy, studying with Tuomas Haapanen. From 1992–98, she was at the University of Music in Vienna, participating in master classes with Sándor Végh, György Kurtág, Liana Issakadze and Max Rostal. In 1999 she earned her violin diploma from the Sibelius Academy.

As a child soloist, by age ten Réka performed with the Finnish Radio Symphony and appeared on Finnish television (YLE) over fifty times. Her outstanding interpretation of Sibelius' violin concerto at the Vienna Musikverein in 1999, with the Helsinki Philharmonic under the baton of Leif Segerstam, launched her international career. During 2001, she was chosen to appear at the prestigious *Distinctive Debuts* series in Carnegie Hall's Weill Recital Hall, and the *Rising Stars* series throughout Europe at Vienna's Konzerthaus, London's Wigmore Hall, Birmingham Symphony Hall, Concertgebouw, Amsterdam, Cité de la Musique, Paris, Palais des Beaux-Arts, Brussels and Megaron Concert Hall, Athens. Her mother, Lieslotte Jank-Szilvay, was her manager until 2002.

In addition to performing with major European orchestras under conductors such as Jukka-Pekka Saraste, Osmo Vänskä, Markus Stenz, Jin Wang, Eri Klas, Fabio Luisi, Adam Fischer, Wolf-Dieter Hauschild, Shuntaro Sato, Juha Kangas, János Fürst and Marc Tardue, Szilvay has also toured in Japan, China and Taiwan. During the 2000–2001 season, she returned to the Vienna Musikverein. She appeared at the fourth Tokyo International Music Festival Super World Orchestra "Evening of Tchaikovsky," July 4, 2002, at Suntory Hall, and the same year debuted with the Kirov Orchestra and Valery Gergiev, Birmingham Symphony with Sakari Oramo, and the London Philharmonic under Libor Pesek. She has guested at international festivals including Kuhmo Chamber Music, Helsinki; Opera Savonlinna, Turku; BHS Bratislava; Haydn Festspiele Eisenstadt; and Singapore Arts, as well as on Austrian (ORF) and Hungarian (MRT) television.

Réka plays a 1702 Stradivarius owned by the Sibelius Academy. Critical acclaim for her artistry is securing Szilvay's place among the violin world's stars.

All in the Family

BAIBA SKRIDE, first-prize winner at the 2001 Queen Elisabeth Competition in Brussels, was born February 19, 1981, into a musical Latvian family in Riga, beginning lessons at four. Her list of top prizes includes the International Competition for Violin at Kloster Schöntal (Germany, 1995), Jeunesse Musicales International

(Bucharest, 1997), and the Lipizer International Violin Competition in Gorizia (Italy, 2000). In 2001–02, she concertized with the Orchestre National de Belgique under Lorin Maazel, Helsinki Philharmonic, Het Residentie Orkest Den Haag (Holland), Orchestre Philharmonique de Liège (Belgium), Festival Strings Lucerne, and the St. Petersburg Camerata, as part of this Russian city's festival.

Her regular pianist is her award-winning sister, **Lauma Skride** (*b* 1982), who made her debut at age eleven. As a chamber musician, Baiba gives trio concerts with sister **Linda** (viola) and Lauma. She also plays with her mother, Liga, a celebrated accompanist and adjunct at Rostock Conservatory of Music and Theater.

Baiba's instrument is the Stradivarius "Huggins" violin (1708), on generous loan from the Nippon Music Foundation.

Livia Sohn

LIVIA SOHN was born in New York on January 30, 1976, to Korean parents. Her father is a urologist, and her mother a cellist, who studied with Bernard Greenhouse, a founding member of the Beaux Arts Trio. Her older sister, Clara, studied piano, cello, and clarinet, but not did pursue music professionally.

Livia studied at Juilliard, pre-college division and BM (1998). Her teacher was **Dorothy DeLay**. After winning first prize in the 1989 Yehudi Menuhin International Violin Competition, she limited her performances to twenty-five per season while completing her studies.

She played John Corigliano's Sonata as part of the opening ceremony of Harris Hall at the Aspen Music Festival (1994), was an artist-in-residence for NPR's "Performance Today" (1999), and soloed with Lukas Foss and the Brooklyn Philharmonic Orchestra at the "Eleventh Annual New Year's Eve Concert for Peace," at New York City's Cathedral Church of St. John the Divine.

Internationally, Sohn has performed with the Cologne Philharmonic, Czech National Symphony, City of London Sinfonia, conducted by Yehudi Menuhin, Iceland Symphony, Mexico City Philharmonic, Auckland Philharmonia, Asia Philharmonic, and Korea's Seoul and Pusan Philharmonics. A five-city tour in South Africa included the National Symphony and KwaZulu-Natal Philharmonic. Another tour saw her in concert and recitals in Nicosia (Cyprus), and Jerusalem, Tel Aviv and Haifa.

In the U.S., she has soloed with the symphonies of Cincinnati, Milwaukee, San Antonio, Louisville, Oregon, Phoenix, Aspen Chamber Orchestra, Chicago Sinfonietta and Boston Pops.

A frequent artist at the Newport Music Festival, Sohn has also been featured in festivals at Ravinia, Brevard, Aspen, Caramoor, New York City's Mostly Mozart, Hawaii's Prince Albert and Finland's Kuhmo Chamber Music Festivals.

2001–2002 season debuts were with the Budapest Philharmonic, and Holland's Limburg Symphonie Orkest, with Murry Sidlin. In 2002, she performed with Gerard Schwarz and the Seattle Symphony. For 2003, she premiered the Violin Sonata *Sink or Swim*, written for her by Jonathan Berger, at the National Gallery of Art in Washington, DC, plus performances with the Rochester Philharmonic, New York Chamber Symphony, Pittsburgh and Edmonton Symphonies. Her first appearance with the San Diego Chamber Orchestra was in 2003, with a return engagement March 2005, when we met.

Livia resides in Connecticut with her husband, Geoff Nuttall, first violinist of the St. Lawrence String Quartet. They met playing together at the Newport (Rhode Island) Music Festival, and were married June 11, 2000.

Livia plays a J.B. Guadagnini, crafted in 1774, on loan to her from the Kumho Group of Seoul, Korea.

AKIKO SUWANAI was the youngest first-prize winner in the history of the International Tchaikovsky Competition in 1990, and received the Best Bach Performer Award and the Best Tchaikovsky Performer Award. She was also the youngest entrant and winner in the thirty-fifth International Paganini Violin Competition, the fourth International Japan competition and the Queen Elisabeth of Belgium International Competition.

Akiko Suwanai

Born in Tokyo, February 7, 1972, she began violin lessons at the age of three and soon after entered the prestigious Toho Gakuen Music Class for Children. She won first prize in the grade school division of the All Japan Students' Music Competition in 1981, and first prize in the junior high school division in 1985. In 1987, she received first prize for the Japan National Music Competition, as well as the Matsushita Award, which guaranteed her delegation to international competition overseas. She graduated with honors from the Toho Gakuen School of Music College, and subsequently studied with **Dorothy DeLay** and **Cho-Liang Lin** at Juilliard and Columbia.

Her international career has taken her to the major cities of Asia, Europe, Russia, North and South America with such renowned conductors as Mstislav Rostropovich, Seiji Ozawa, Sir Neville Marriner, Yvgeny Svetlanov, and Lorin Maazel. She toured Japan with the National Symphony and Leonard Slatkin, and the Montreal Symphony with Charles Dutoit. During the 1999–2000 season, she again toured Japan and Asia performing the Penderecki Violin Concerto No. 2 under the baton of the composer, a collaboration they continued in Europe in 2001. During the 2000–01 season, again with Charles Dutoit, she debuted with the Berlin Philharmonic, made a European tour with the Orchestre National de France, and performed with the Montreal Symphony. She also played with the Orchestre National de Lyon, Budapest Festival Orchestra and Czech Philharmonic. March 2002 found her in a performance of the Bruch Concerto with the Japan Philharmonic under Neeme Järvi. Akiko makes her home in New York and Paris. Her violin is a 1727 Stradivari, loaned to her from Suntory Limited, Japan.

Finnish violinist **ELINA VÄHÄLÄ** was born in Iowa while her parents were students there, after which the family returned to Finland. Elina attended the Conservatory in Lahti, studying with Seppo Reinikainen and Pertti Sutinen. In 1999, she won first prize in the YCA International Auditions, as well as a Bärenreiter Prize for the Best Historical Performance for Strings, and the Mortimer Levitt Career Development Award for Women Artists. Later that year, she opened the thirty-ninth YCA Series with her New York debut at the 92nd Street Y. In 2001, she was again presented in the YCA Series at Carnegie's Weill Recital Hall, performing with her husband, pianist Ralf Gothóni.

Vähälä frequently plays with the English Chamber Orchestra, with whom she has appeared in London, Krakow and South Africa. Other concerts have been with Seattle's Northwest Chamber Orchestra, Danish Radio Sinfonietta, and Virtuosi di Kuhmo (Finland). Other Finnish orchestras include the Lahti Philharmonic, with concerts in Finland, Stockholm and St. Petersburg; Helsinki Philharmonic, Tapiola Sinfonietta, Kuopio Symphony, Pori Sinfonietta, Ostrobothnian Chamber Orchestra of St. Michael, Lappeenranta Orchestra, Vivo Symphony and Turku Philharmonic. Her many venues include festivals in the U.S., Kyoto (Japan), and the Forbidden City (Beijing, China); Sweden's Laplands Festival; Flanders Festival (Belgium); La Roque d'Antheron and Pablo Casals Festivals in France; Poznan (Poland); and the Helsinki, Kuhmo, Turku and Korsholm Festivals (Finland). 2003 brought her back to the U.S., and recitals in Egypt.

ELIZABETH WALLFISCH, born in Melbourne, January 28, 1952, made her concerto debut at age twelve, and appeared with the Melbourne Symphony State final of the ABC Concerto Competition before leaving Australia to study at the RAM. She won the first Franco Gulli Senior Prize for violin at the Accademia Chigiana in 1972, the same year winning joint first place at the Mozart Memorial Prize. In 1974, she won the Carl Flesch Violin Competition for her solo Bach performances. She is a recognized interpreter of early violin music from the 17th, 18th and 19th centuries. Besides concerto solo performances, often directing from the violin, she is a recitalist with the Locatelli Trio (now re-named Convivium), which she founded in 1989. She frequently leads the Orchestra of the Age of Enlightenment and the Raglan Baroque Players.

Wallfisch has recorded the complete violin concerti of Bach and Haydn (Virgin Classics), as well as a landmark first modern recording of Locatelli's *Violin Concertos Op 3, L'Arte del Violino* (Hyperion, 1994) with the Raglan Baroque Players, designated the "Best Recording: Solo with Orchestra" by the Cannes Classical Awards. While enjoying a reputation as a specialist in "early" violin repertoire, she also plays works from the later periods, including the Brahms' Double Concerto with her husband, cellist Raphael Wallfisch.[89] Since 1993, she has been a soloist and concertmaster at the annual Carmel Bach Festival (Northern California). Her teaching positions include the RAM, and professor of baroque violin at the Royal Conservatoire in The Hague. She regularly returns to Australia for tours and festivals.

Elizabeth is now based in London, where she and Raphael have two sons and a daughter, Joanna. Benjamin was born in 1979, studied at the Guildhall School of Music and followed the prestigious "Joint Course" of the Royal Northern College of Music in conjunction with Manchester University. By 2006, his composition and conducting career were in full gear, with works broadcast on BBC Radio, plus major festivals and venues. He was unanimously awarded first prize in the 2001 British Reserve Insurance Conducting Competition. In September 2002 he was appointed associate conductor of the English Chamber Orchestra. Simon, born in 1982, started playing the cello at five. He is also a singer and jazz pianist. He was a finalist in the Jewish Performer of the Year competition and received the Foundation Scholarship at the RCM, and a scholarship to Guildhall. After his 2003 operatic debut, he sang the role of Don Alfonso in a concert performance of *Così fan tutte* in June 2004.

Carmit Zori

By age thirteen, **CARMIT ZORI** was chosen by the America-Israel Cultural Foundation to perform on the international television special "Music from Jerusalem." Two years later, at the recommendation of Alexander Schneider and Isaac Stern, she came to the U.S. to study at Curtis with Ivan Galamian, Jaime Laredo and Arnold Steinhardt. She has by now performed with the New York and Rochester Philharmonics, the Philadelphia Orchestra, and toured in Latin America, Europe, Japan and Australia. Her recitals include the Chamber Music Society of Lincoln Center, Los Angeles County Museum of Art, Boston's Gardner Museum, the Dame Myra Hess Series, the Phillips Collection—a concert hall and art gallery—in Washington, DC, as well as in Chicago, Paris, Rome, Tel Aviv and Jerusalem. Winner of the Leventritt and Pro Musicus Foundation Awards, and Naumberg International Violin Competition, she has recorded on Arabesque, Koch International and Elektra-Nonesuch labels.

Honorable Mention

Many other fine violinists are pursuing careers in a field where competition is constant. Among them are:

HELEN ARMSTRONG who made her debut in Lincoln Center in 1976, has appeared with the Boston Pops, Indianapolis Symphony and Martha Graham Dance Company, among others. As a recitalist, she has toured North America, Europe and Asia. Her degrees are from Juilliard, studying with the renowned **Dorothy DeLay** and **Ivan Galamian**. Her honors include awards from the Society of American Musicians and the Musicians Club of America. She has recorded on Musical Heritage and CRS labels. In 1982 she founded the Amstrong Chamber Concerts to broaden the public interest in chamber music. Their concert series is from October to May in Greenwich and Washington, Connecticut, as well as New York City. She conducts music enrichment programs in schools throughout Connecticut. Her violin is a Guadagnini, dated 1760.

MARIA BACHMANN is a proponent of contemporary music, with American composers **George Rochberg**—with whom she also studied composition—and **Leon Kirchner** writing works for her. She holds degrees from Curtis, where she studied with **Szymon Goldberg** and **Ivan Galamian**. Of Hungarian descent, she is noted for her interpretations of Bela Bartók, and was invited by the Library of Congress to recreate the legendary Szigeti/Bartók recital of 1940 on a national broadcast. She has soloed with major orchestras throughout Europe, America and the Orient. Her many awards include first prizes in the Fritz Kreisler Competition in Vienna and the Concert Artists Guild International Competition in New York, Pro Musicis International Award

---

89. Raphael is the son of musicologist/pianist Peter Wallfisch, and cellist **Anita Lasker-Wallfisch**, who played in the concentration camp orchestra of **Alma Rosé**.

(1989), as well as laureate in the Tchaikovsky Competition in Moscow. She was named Outstanding Artist of the Year by *Musical America*. Besides being an exclusive BMG/RCA recording artist, she is an avid chamber musician, and in 1994 formed the Bachmann-Klibonoff-Fridman Trio with her long-time accompanist Jon Klibonoff and cellist Semyon Fridman. She also plays with the Lark Quartet and Trio Solisti, for whom she is the artistic director of their concert series at New York's Morgan Library. Besides being the director of the San Juan Islands Chamber Music Festival in Guemes, Washington, Bachmann is on the adjunct faculty of Adelphi University. Having played the magnificent 1708 "Ruby" Stradivarius, on loan from the Stradivari Society of Chicago, she now plays on a 1986 violin by American maker Sergio Peresson.

MARGARET BATJER, who made her debut with the Chicago Symphony at fifteen, is a graduate of Curtis, where she studied with Ivan Galamian and David Cerone. She has appeared with the symphonies in Philadelphia, St. Louis, Seattle, Dallas, return engagements with Chicago, the New York String Orchestra, and the Prague Chamber Orchestra, Chamber Orchestra of Europe, and Berlin Symphony. She performs regularly with festivals at Marlboro, Minnesota, Vancouver, and La Jolla (SummerFest 2001). Invited by Maurizio Pollini, she appeared with the Quartetto Accardo at the 1995 and 1996 Salzburg Festivals, and again in Pollini's Carnegie Hall *Perspectives* series in 2001. Since 1998, she has been concertmaster of the Los Angeles Chamber Orchestra.

EMANUELLE BOISVERT, a native of Quebec, is concertmaster of the Detroit Symphony. She joined the orchestra in October 1988, at age twenty-five, becoming the youngest woman to head the string section of a major American orchestra, and the first woman in the orchestra's history to win this prestigious post. Prior to this, she was a member of the Cleveland Orchestra. A successful chamber music collaborator, she is a member of the Detroit-based St. Clair Trio, which performs internationally. She is also on the staff of the Center for Creative Studies at the Institute of Music and Dance in Detroit. She began her musical studies at age three, and entered the Conservatoire de Musique de Québec at six. She graduated from Curtis (BM, 1984). (See Orchestras.)

Born in Ann Arbor, Michigan, **CATHERINE CHO** gave her first public performance at age four and made her official concert debut at eleven with the Tivoli Symphony in Copenhagen. A graduate of Juilliard, her teachers were Ruggiero Ricci, Franco Gulli, and Michael Avsharian. Awarded the 1995 Avery Fisher Career Grant, she has won top prizes in major international events, including the Hanover, Queen Elisabeth and Montreal International Violin Competitions. She received the Sony ES award for Musical Excellence and was named Presidential Scholar in the Arts. In the course of 2001, she appeared in Belgium, Holland and London. 2002 found her at the Skaneateles Festival in upstate New York, and the following year brought her to the National Art Centre Ottawa. She has given recital and chamber music performances at Kennedy Center, Ravinia, the Chamber Music Society of Lincoln Center, Casals Hall, Seoul Arts Center, and with Musicians from Marlboro (Vermont).

She plays a 1709 Stradivarius on loan from Marlboro Music.

PIP CLARKE, born in England on September 28, 1968, began studies at seven and made her debut at sixteen in London's South Bank Centre after graduating from the Guildhall School of Music (1989). Before emigrating to the U.S., she concertized all over England and appeared on television with renowned British maestro, Sir Michael Tippett. Her 1994 debut recording, *Romantic Violin Showpieces*, received two Grammy Award nominations. During the 1999–2000 season, she performed with U.S. orchestras, including Buffalo and Colorado. She appeared at the gala opening concert of the Hollywood Bowl in the summer of 1999, where she was heard by the director of the motion picture, *15 Minutes*, and was chosen as the featured soloist for the movie. Her 2000–01 season included sell-out concerts on tour with the Royal Scottish National and Honolulu Orchestras. For the 2001–02 season, she performed with the Syracuse and Utah Symphonies, toured in Southern California, and returned to San Jose and the Mission Chamber Orchestra for their continuing Mozart cycle. She has appeared at the Ravinia Festival, and returns to Europe for performances at leading international festivals. *But Beautiful* is a 2006 CD. 2007 featured a Carnegie Hall concert with the New York Pops.

In 1989, she married Christopher Ling, an associate of the RCM, founding director of Encore Concerts in the UK and, since 1992, president of CHL Artists [Agency] of Beverly Hills. They are the parents of Francesca Ruth Ling, born September 10, 1998, who already has a remarkable ear for music.

MIRIJAM CONTZEN, born in Munster, Germany, 1976, picked up the violin at age two and by her third birthday was taking lessons. Her formal schooling started at the Junior Music School in Detmold, continuing at the *Musikhochschule*. Beginning in 1988, she attended the *École des Cordes de Sion* (Switzerland) studying with Hungarian violinist Tibor Varga. With numerous prizes from the German *Jugend Musiziert* Competition, in 1991 she won the *Concertino Praga*, an international Czechoslovakian competition. 1996 brought further success with a win at the International Violin Competition, *Tibor Varga*, in Sion, Switzerland. Invitations to perform throughout Europe followed, launching a successful career.

Berlin-born **CHRISTIANE EDINGER** began violin lessons at age five, later continuing at the Berlin Hochschule für Musik with Vittorio Brero, and in Switzerland with Nathan Milstein. Her debut was with the Berlin Philharmonic at age nineteen, playing the Mendelssohn Concerto. She came to New York to study at Juilliard with **Joseph Fuchs**, making her Carnegie Hall debut in 1985 with the American Symphony. She has been a featured soloist with many major American orchestras, but the majority of her appearances are in her native Europe. Her 2002–03 season covered concerts throughout Germany, including Berlin and Hamburg, as well as Lucerne, Switzerland. She is also the first violinist in the Edinger Quartet, home based in Germany. In 2003 the quartet toured in Korea and North America.

Vesna Gruppman

VESNA Stefanovic **GRUPPMAN** started early as a six-time winner of Yugoslavia's National Violin Competition, before going on to Moscow's legendary Central Special Musical School and the Moscow Conservatory where she met her husband. A violin and viola soloist, Vesna has appeared with the Prague, Moscow, Ukraine, Florida and London Philharmonics, Munich Chamber Orchestra, Edmonton (Canada) Symphony, as well as recitals at London's Wigmore Hall and St. John's Smith Square, Kiev Philharmonic Hall and Mozart's Bemtraka in Prague—all to critical acclaim.

She regularly appears as a chamber musician with her husband, Igor,[90] in the Gruppman Duo (violin, violin/viola), and has collaborated with the Tokyo String Quartet, principal players of the Academy of St. Martin-in-the-Fields, violinists Pinchas Zukerman, Itzak Perlman, Jamie Laredo and cellist Lynn Harrell.

In 2003, Igor and Vesna founded the Gruppman International Violin Institute, created specifically to teach highly gifted violin students from all over the world commuting via the latest computer technology. Among their many recordings, the Malcolm Arnold Concerto for Two Violins and Orchestra, with the San Diego Chamber Orchestra under Donald Barra, won a 1994 Grammy for the Koch label.

Vesna and the author were happily reunited at the Gruppmans' appearance with the SDCO, February 2006. They are currently based in Rotterdam (Holland).

ANNA HELLEUR, born in England March 21, 1974, began lessons at age three, appearing in her first public concert the following year. At nine, she won a place in the famous Pro Corda course, with whom she concertized for the next four years. At twelve, she was awarded a full scholarship to a special music school for gifted children. Three years later she made her debut at South Bank Centre, and broadcast on National Television, performing for Sir Yehudi Menuhin and the Lord Mayor of London. In 1989, she won second prize in Britain's first national violin competition. As of 1990, she began touring the U.S., settling in Los Angeles. Her first CD, on the Classic Jewel label, was released in 1995.

---

90. Igor Gruppman was named conductor of the Orchestra at Temple Square—which also accompanies the Mormon Tabernacle Choir—in 2003. A violin soloist, conductor, concertmaster and chamber musician, he appears worldwide in these capacities.

After studying at the RCM, **REBECCA HIRSCH** was awarded a scholarship to Tanglewood. Her debut recording of Poul Ruders' First Violin Concerto with the Odense Symphony (1991) led to a second concerto written especially for her by the composer, which she premiered in Copenhagen with the Collegium Musicum. In the 1994–95 season, she gave the world premiere of Bent Sorensen's Violin Concerto "Sterbende Gärten" with the Danish National Radio Symphony to rave reviews.

German-born **LATICA HONDA-ROSENBURG** was brought up within a Croat-Japanese family of musicians. By nine she was being tutored by Tibor Varga at the Academy of Music in Detmold. Following three years study in Lubeck and Madrid, she graduated from the Escuela Superior de Musica Reina Sofia with special mention. In 1993, she received her concert degree, and moved on to further studies at Juilliard. She has concertized throughout Europe, America, Israel and Japan, performing with such aggregations as the German Symphony, the Beethovenhalle Orchestra, Prague, Stuttgart and Zurich chamber orchestras, as well as the Russian State Orchestra and Tokyo Symphony. Her U.S. debut came in 1999 with the Delaware Symphony. 2000 brought her first recording, an album of Ernest Bloch's Complete Violin Works on the Arte Nova label. Subsequent releases include the Shostakovich 1st and Tchaikovsky violin concertos. In October 2001, she appeared on the Franco-German TV channel, Arte.

Latica plays a Domenico Montagnana violin built in 1732. (Montagnana (c 1687–1750) was one of the violin makers closest to the Stradivari school.)

JUDY KANG was born in Toronto in 1979, and began violin at age four. At eleven, she was accepted on full scholarship to Curtis where she obtained her BM under the direction of Aaron Rosand. Her master's studies were at Juilliard with Robert Mann.

Her mounting awards include the Canadian Music Competition, first place in the Canadian National Shean Strings Competition and grand prize winner of the CBC Radio National Competition for Young Performers.

Since her solo debut at age four, she has received accolades for her numerous performances with the Toronto Symphony, National Arts Centre Orchestra, Edmonton Symphony and CBC Montreal Chamber Orchestra, among others. She is a frequent solo recitalist and chamber musician, with many of her performances broadcast on Canadian, U.S. and international radio and television. In March 2002, she was heard on CBC Ottawa.

Competitions for the loan of instruments from the Canada Council for the Arts Musical Instrument Bank are held as instruments become available, upon their acquisition, or at the end of a loan period. In 1997, Judy won a competition for the loan of the 1689 Baumgartner Stradivarius.

ANASTASIA KHITRUK comes from a musical and artistic family. She studied at Moscow's Central Music School and made her orchestral debut at age eight. Since then, she has appeared worldwide from Aspen to Adelaide, Australia, as well as Teatro Carlo Fenice (Venice), the Great Hall of the NDK in Sofia, the Conservatoire de Musique, Geneva, Boston, Los Angeles, New York, London, Paris and Moscow. She received dazzling reviews for a 2000 series commemorating the 250th anniversary of J.S. Bach's death. She is also an avid proponent for modern music.

Khitruk's commitment to developing young audiences is demonstrated by her work as president of the Manhattan Music Society, a non-profit foundation based in New York.

No Shortage of Instruments for Elissa

ELISSA LEE KOLJIONEN (or Kokkonen), a pupil of Aaron Rosand at Curtis from age eleven, was born in 1973 in Hong Kong of a Korean mother and Finnish father. She was co-winner of the Henryk Szeryng Award Competition (1992), where she used a Vuillaume violin. As a Colburn grant recipient, in March 1993 she was loaned a priceless Montagnana. At the Flanders Festival in September 1993, she was described "holding her 250-year-old Guadagnini high up." Reviewing her performance at the Zino Francescatti Festival in Aix-en-Provence (France), in the January 1994 *Strad* Magazine violin authority Henry Roth wrote: "[she] understands

Mozartian style as do precious few young violinists." The Sibelius concerto, which Roth calls " . . . a dark and complex portrait of human experience," claimed it "[had its] deep secrets unlocked by a twenty-three-year-old violinist with the flourish of a bow." In May 1994, in an Antibes (France) paper, critic Philippe Depetris wrote of her interpretation of the Beethoven Concerto at the Young Soloists Concert, "with her magnificent Guarnerius she was able to express her profound inner richness and surmount the technical difficulties of this score to express all her musical sensitivity." In April 1995, after a "stunning" performance of Bruch's *Scottish Fantasy*, critic Susan L. Peña went on to comment on the "silken, seductive sound from one of the world's great violins—a 1735 Guarneri del Gesù violin."

Koljonnen has played with orchestras on both sides of the Atlantic, as well as appeared in recitals with accompanist to the super-famous, pianist **Samuel Sanders**. It is obvious, whatever the instrument—and last heard it was the 1735 ex Mary Portman, ex Fritz Kreisler, Guarneri del Gesù, on extended loan from the Stradivari Society—the talent shines through. Critical acclaim marked her debut at Queen Elizabeth Hall with the London Mozart Players, and her appearance with the Orchestre Philharmonique de Monte Carlo in a concert celebrating the 700th anniversary of the Grimaldi Dynasty (1997). By 2002, she was in Scandinavia, Seoul, and in the U.S. in Oregon, Pittsburgh, and with the Philadelphia Orchestra and Chamber Orchestra. Her recitals have been heard throughout Europe and America. She also plays at many international summer festivals, and records for Dorian Records.

BOJIDARA KOUZMANOVA was born September 20, 1977, in Plovdiv, Bulgaria. After studying at the Music High School in Sofia, she went on to win numerous awards throughout Europe, including first prizes in both the Bela Bartok and National Violin Competition for German Music (1995). Her tours have thus far taken her to Spain, Greece, Austria, Slovakia, Germany, Italy, Portugal, France, Israel and America.

Ida Levin

IDA LEVIN, born in Santa Monica, California, January 29, 1963, began studies at three. Her professional debut was at ten with the Los Angeles Philharmonic. Her BM and MM are from Juilliard, and she participated in master classes of **Itzhak Perlman** and **Pinchas Zukerman**. The recipient of an 1983 Avery Fisher Career Grant, and a former Leventritt Artist, she appeared with Rudolf Serkin in a joint recital for President and Mrs. Reagan, broadcast on PBS as "In Performance at the White House." She performed with the American Symphony Orchestra at Carnegie Hall and Kennedy Center, and tours in the U.S., England, France, Germany, Italy, Switzerland and Israel. She is a member of the Boston Chamber Music Society, a senior artist at Marlboro Music, and a regular guest with the Chamber Music Society of Lincoln Center. In addition to giving master classes, Levin has been on the faculties of Harvard, the European Mozart Academy, and the Sándor Végh International Chamber Music Academy in Prague.

Her recordings are on Philips, EMI, Dynamic, Music Masters, Nonesuch, Stereophile and BCMS.

Chicago-born **ISABELLA LIPPI** came to prominence at age ten touring with the Haag Leviton Suzuki Performing Group. She studied with Almita and Roland Vamos, teachers of fellow Chicagoans **Rachel Barton Pine** and **Jennifer Koh**, Robert Lipsett at the Colburn School in Los Angeles, and **Dorothy DeLay** at Juilliard. At seventeen, she won first prize in the Illinois Young Performers Competition and appeared with the Chicago Symphony. She won the 1989 St. Louis Symphony Young Artists Competition and, for the first time in the fifty-five years of the competition, was invited to play for the subscription series with the orchestra under **Leonard Slatkin**. She has appeared with orchestras in the U.S., the Mexico City Philharmonic, Orchestra Sinfnice de Bilbao (Spain), and the Moscow Symphony. Her New York recital debut in 1993 was at the Tisch Center for the Arts. As a Presidential Scholar in the Arts, Lippi also played for the subscription series at Kennedy Center. She recorded the complete works for violin and piano, and solo works by Miklos Rosza for Koch International.

In 1990, at age fifteen, British violinist **NICOLA LOUD** became the BBC *Young Musician of the Year*. She took carefully chosen engagements while completing her schooling, spending four years at the RAM. After graduation, she moved to New York for further studies at Julliard, returning to Britain at twenty-four. She has since performed extensively in Britain and abroad, with the Royal Liverpool Philharmonic, the Hallé, Ulster, and BBC Concert orchestras and the Presidential Symphony of Turkey. The 2001–2002 season marked her debut with London's Philharmonia and Royal Philharmonic orchestras.

ANAT MALKIN-ALMANI, born September 19, 1976, in Hadera, Israel, began violin studies at age five with her father, famed Israeli pedagogue Isaac Malkin. By six, she was already soloing, and at ten, toured Norway, Mexico and California performing with orchestras. She made her Carnegie Hall debut at sixteen under the baton of **Alexander Schneider**. Her training included working with **Josef Gingold**, and studies at the Manhattan School of Music, where her father is on the faculty. She was a student of Cho-Liang Lin at Juilliard (BM, 1997), the Maastricht Conservatorium (Holland), with Boris Belkin (MM, 1999), plus additional studies with Belkin at the Accademia Chigiana, Italy. She also pursued graduate studies in Middle Eastern politics at Columbia. Concertizing with orchestra, and in recital, has taken her through-

Anat Malkin-Almani

out Holland, Israel, Italy, South Korea, the UK and the U.S. Winner of numerous competitions, she was a featured performer on the McGraw Hill Young Artists Showcase hosted by Robert Sherman and broadcast on WQXR New York. In 1993, she took part in a memorial tribute to Alexander Schneider, "Celebrating Sasha," at Carnegie Hall. The 2004–2005 season included a concert at Carnegie Hall's Weill Recital Hall.

An active chamber musician, Malkin-Almani performs regularly with her sister, violinist Bracha Malkin, as part of the Malkin Duo. In 1996, they made their debut at Weill Recital Hall as prizewinners of the Artist International Auditions. Other duo highlights include recitals in Israel and Italy, a return to Weill, the world premiere, in San Diego, of David Ward-Steinman's *Concerto for Two Violins*, and a recital at St. Paul's Chapel at Ground Zero as winners of the 2003 Trinity Concert Series Auditions. Malkin-Almani has also collaborated with other well-known artists including Peter Winograd.

A gifted teacher, she is a member of the violin faculty at the Manhattan School of Music, Preparatory Division, and an artist faculty member of the Academy of Music Festival in New Jersey. She has presented master classes in Siena, Italy and in Israel. (At age five, she and the author's son aged seven, were in her father's class!)

A Catastrophe and a Miracle!

In 1996, Anat was involved in a major car accident. She spent eight years in and out of surgery with twelve operations on her left hand and right shoulder. The doctors had to repair severed and torn nerves, ligaments and tendons, and remove glass and gravel. (Pieces of glass are still making their way out of her hand.) No one thought she would be able to play again! She has endured years of grueling physical therapy and rehabilitation. As far as is known, she is the only violinist in history to have resumed playing after such a major catastrophe!

(In his book, entitled *Violin Virtuosos from Paganini to the 21st Century*, Henry Roth named her as one of the "gifted young violinists who are among the vanguard leading the march of violin art into the 21st century.")

Anat married Yossi Almani on the beach at Tel Aviv, September 4, 2003. A lawyer, he was also a financial correspondent for Israel's largest newspaper. They now make their home in New York.

SILVIA MARCOVICI was born January 30, 1952, in Bacau (Romania), studying there and in Bucharest under Stefan Gheorghiu. She won the Marguerite Long/Jacques Thibaud Competition in Paris in 1969, and the George Enescu Competition in Bucharest in 1970. Her professional debut was at age fifteen, in The Hague. Her 1972 performance of the Glazunov concerto was for 90th birthday celebration of Leopold Stokowski with the London Symphony at London's Royal Festival Hall. She has appeared with many orchestras in North and South America, Japan, Israel and Europe. Her recordings include the ten Beethoven sonatas for violin and piano as well as many concertos. She is married to the violinist Diego Pagin. They have two children and live in Strasbourg. Her violin is a circa 1800 P. Albani.

PRIYA MITCHELL was born in 1971, and raised in Oxford. Her musical apprenticeship began with violin lessons at age four. At nine, she entered England's Yehudi Menuhin School under the tutelage of David Takeno.

During the 1997–1998 season, she was British Representative for the European Concert Halls Organization's (ECHO) *Rising Stars* series. This privileged role took her to Paris, Vienna, Frankfurt, Amsterdam, Brussels and New York for her U.S. debut at Carnegie Hall. She has performed Bach's *Double Concerto* with Nigel Kennedy and the English Chamber Orchestra, the Bruch Concerto with the Royal Liverpool Philharmonic, and Sibelius with the Royal Philharmonic. Her debut with the BBC Symphony included performances of the Mendelssohn Concerto, Vaughan William's *Lark Ascending* and a studio recording of Berlioz' *Reverie et Caprice*.

LYDIA MORDKOVICH, born in Saratov, Russia, 1950, attended the Odessa Conservatory and studied with **David Oistrakh**. In 1974, she moved to London and made her debut in 1979 with **Walter Susskind**, and her American debut with **Sir George Solti** and the Chicago Symphony (1982). She has played with the Hallé Orchestra, the Bournemouth Sinfonietta, Riccardo Muti and the Philadephia Orchestra, as well as in Rotterdam, The Hague, Scandinavia and other parts of Europe. In 1990, she won *Gramophone*'s Best Concert Award.

KERRY McDERMOTT became the youngest member of the New York Philharmonic at nineteen in 1981, and has many times appeared as their soloist, including the 1995 North American tour. At seventeen, she was the youngest winner in the history of Artists International Auditions, resulting in her debut at Carnegie Recital Hall. She has appeared in recital and chamber concerts throughout the U.S., Europe and Asia, garnering prizes and awards including the Montreal International Violin Competition and International Tchaikovsky Competition in Moscow.

An alumna of the Manhattan School of Music and Yale, she studied with Raphael Bronstein and Vladimir Spivakov, and has worked with **Yehudi Menuhin**, **Erica Morini**, **Joseph Gingold** and **Henryk Szeryng**. She is a member of the **McDermott Trio** with sisters **Anne-Marie**, pianist (a member of the Chamber Music Society of Lincoln Center), and **Maureen**, cellist. Kerry has appeared on television, international radio, and in the film *Fame*. She is married to violist Paul Neubauer, who joined the New York Philharmonic in 1984 at age twenty-one and was the youngest principal string player in its history. The couple reside in New York with their children, Oliver Patrick, born September 28, 1999 and Clara Bridget, 9/11/01 (!)

NURIT PACHT grew up in Texas, and made her first solo public appearance at age twelve, performing on National Television in a PBS Christmas Special. In 1990, at seventeen, she debuted with the Houston Symphony. She has since won prizes in international competitions in Europe and America, including the Tibor Varga Competition in Switzerland.

In the spring of 1996, immediately following the cease-fire, under the sponsorship of the United Nations and the European Mozart Foundation, she performed in six of the worst war-devastated cities of Bosnia. At the invitation of the European Commission, she also performed on the occasion of the inauguration of the European Monetary Union in Brussels. Among her other orchestral appearances in Europe were the Mecklenberg (Germany) Vorpommern Festival, Wroclaw (Poland) Chamber Orchestra, Georges Enesco Philharmonic (Romania), Moldavian Philharmonic, Brasov (Transylvania) Philharmonic and Filarmonica di Roma (Italy).

Pacht's travels have taken her to India, where she performed specially composed ragas with Pandit Ram Narayan, a sarangi virtuoso. She played with the Brooklyn Philharmonic and Santa Rosa (California) Symphony in 2001. Other career highlights have included the world premiere of *Relative Light*, a multi-media concert during which she performed solo works of J.S. Bach and John Cage. She also toured China as a soloist with the Young Israeli Philharmonic.

Nurit plays an instrument built by Nicola Amati in 1678.

ALYSSA PARK made her professional debut with the Cincinnati Chamber Orchestra at age eleven. She studied at the Cincinnati College-Conservatory, at Aspen, and with **Dorothy DeLay**. In 1990, at sixteen, she became the youngest prizewinner—with high distinctions—in the history of the International Tchaikovsky Violin Competition. She also won the Aspen Music Festival Concerto Competition. 1991 saw her acclaimed New York recital debut at Lincoln Center, which included the premiere of David Diamond's *Concert Piece*. Her European debut was with the Bavarian Radio Orchestra under Sir Colin Davis. In 1995, she performed with the Austrian

Radio Orchestra in a live radio/TV broadcast throughout Europe. 1996 marked performances in Hamburg, Barcelona, Japan, Singapore, Korea and a U.S. tour with the Czech Philharmonic. In 1995, she was the youngest faculty member of the Aspen Music Festival.

(So-Yun) **"TRICIA" PARK**, the daughter of Korean-born physicians, was born in 1977 in Ohio, but raised in Seattle since the age of two. She began violin studies at five, zipping through all ten Suzuki books in less than three years. In 1987, she won the Seattle Young Artists Competition. A judge at the competition, and colleague of **Dorothy DeLay**, arranged for the talented girl to study with the world's most celebrated violin teacher. Her mother and younger brother moved with her to New York to make this possible. Tricia started in Juilliard's pre-college division, and took her non-musical classes at the Professional Children's School. She made her solo orchestral debut with the Baltimore Symphony in 1989, playing the Paganini Concerto No. 1. In 1992, she made her debut with the Seattle Symphony. She performed with **Pinchas Zukerman**, her friend and special mentor, at the Aspen Music Festival in 1993, and again with the Dallas Symphony in 1994. This year also marked her Lincoln Center debut at Avery Fisher Hall in the Lincoln Center Mostly Mozart Festival, with **Hans Vonk** conducting. Her 1994–95 season included twenty-five recital and solo appearances including Canada and South America. 1995–96 took her to Montreal, Chicago for the Ravinia Rising Stars Festival, plus Aspen and Rio de Janeiro.

Prodigy-wise, Park's professional debut at fifteen was "late," but as she justifies, "The questions of youth and age can only be answered on the stage." Meanwhile, she has already been dubbed as having the Midas touch for her "golden-toned artistry," and Zukerman calls her "a jewel."

SHA, born in Shanghai, grew up with the musical role models of her father, Cao Peng, one of China's respected conductors, and her mother, Hui Ling, an opera singer and former director of opera at the Shanghai Conservatory. Sha took up the violin at age six, soon becoming known as a child prodigy and appearing on television and radio. At eleven, she began studies at Beijing Central Conservatory. In 1981, she was a prizewinner at the Chinese National Music Competition and took part in premiering the works of Shostakovich in China. European prizes came in 1982 when she was awarded the Menuhin Chairman Prize at the International String Quartet Competition in England. Soon afterwards, she became a faculty member at the Beijing Central Conservatory. In 1985, she came to California to study at USC with Dr. Edward Shmider. She made her American debut with the Florida Orchestra. Sha has now performed throughout the U.S., Portugal, China and Scandinavia. In 1998, she gave the American premiere of *W Zhou-Jun*, the sister composition to Chen Gang's concerto, *Butterfly Lovers*. She has made several recordings of Chinese violin concertos with the Russia Philharmonic.

Israeli born **ORA SHIRAN** studied at Julliard. Delving into chamber music, supported by a Ford Foundation Grant, she started a violin program with Itzhak Perlman at Brooklyn College. She returned to Israel in 1983 and taught at Tel-Aviv University. As a recitalist, she performs in the U.S., Canada and her native country. She tours Europe as a member of the Idan Piano Trio, and has been concertmistress and soloist with the Israel Chamber Orchestra, the Israel Philharmonic and the Haifa Symphony.

Sheryl Staples

SHERYL STAPLES was appointed associate concertmaster of the New York Philharmonic in September 1998. A Los Angeles native, she was born into a musical family—her father was a seventeen year veteran trombonist in the Lawrence Welk Orchestra. She studied privately with **Robert Lipsett** from age nine, was a scholarship student at the Crossroads School for Arts and Sciences, and a W.M. Keck Scholar at the Colburn School. She received her Artist's Diploma from USC in 1991—this is a specific performance degree attained through a rigorous audition process designed for high profile careers—while spending summers at the Cleveland Institute's Encore School for Strings. Her concertmaster positions in Southern California were with the Debut Orchestra under **Jung Ho Pak** from age seventeen to twenty-one, Santa Barbara Chamber Orchestra, Japan America Symphony in Los Angeles and Pacific Symphony, concurrently holding faculty positions at the Colburn School and USC. Invited to audition for associate concertmaster of the Cleveland Orchestra in

1996, at age twenty-six she became the youngest person to hold this position. An active chamber musician, Staples has participated in music festivals in Santa Fe, La Jolla SummerFest, Sarasota, Tucson, and Seattle, performing with such illustrious violinists as **Cho-Liang Lin** and **James Buswell**, and cellist **Lynn Harrell**, and has been a faculty artist at Aspen and Sarasota. Her solo career includes appearances with over forty orchestras, including Los Angeles, San Diego, Cleveland, orchestras in Japan and Mexico and the New York Philharmonic.

Staples is on the faculty at Manhattan School of Music.

DIANA STEINER holds the record as the youngest student ever accepted to Curtis in its seventy-two year history. She was five years old when she auditioned for the immortal pianist **Josef Hofmann** (1876–1957), then the director, and **Efrem Zimbalist, Sr.** (1889–1985) for piano and violin respectively—both accepted her immediately. The family moved from Portland (Oregon) to Philadelphia. She made more history when, at nine, she played the Mendelssohn Violin Concerto as soloist at the New York Philharmonic Young People's Concert, February 23, 1942. (This was a year younger than Yehudi Menuhin at his debut.) Her BM is from Curtis and MM from USC, where she studied with the "Grand Master," **Jascha Heifetz** (1899–1987).

Steiner has soloed with the New York and Los Angeles Philharmonics, Philadelphia Orchestra and Chicago Symphony, appeared at many festivals and broadcast on radio and television. Among her honors are the National first prize from the Friday Morning Music Club of Washington, DC, the Young Artist Award from the National Federation of Music Clubs and the New York Town Hall Debut Award from the Naumberg Foundation. A former member of the board of directors of Curtis, Steiner is a professor of violin at Cal. State, Dominguez Hills. She is on the board of the Debussy Trio Music Foundation, is a certified master teacher of the MTNA, and maintains a private studio in Los Angeles. She is a proponent and exponent of American contemporary music. She is also the mother of harpist **Marcia Dickstein**, and the sister of conductor **Frances Steiner**.

British born **RUTH WATERMAN** learned violin from her father and piano from her mother beginning at age five. After studies at the Royal Manchester College of Music, she went to Juilliard. When Yehudi Menuhin chose her to play at the Bath Festival, her immediate success blossomed into offers to perform at the BBC Promenade Concerts and in the Royal Festival Hall in the presence of Her Majesty the Queen. She came to American attention with the "International Artists Series" sponsored by the Carnegie Hall Corporation. In 1981, she set a precedent as the first violinist to perform the Bach Partitas with ornamentation. This resulted in appearances at the Madeira and Stuttgart Bach Festivals, the Bach Gesellschaft of New York, and the International Bach Society. Her interest in chamber music led to collaboration with Elly Ameling, Artur Balsam, Richard Goode and Peter Schreier. She lectures in universities worldwide, including a series on Bach for Oxford. Her teaching positions at NYU and the RAM provide continual development of knowledge and talent. In February 2002, with the Carmel Music Society (California), she gave her violin/lecture recital series "Music Talks!" Waterman has held a Professorship at the University of the Arts in Berlin since 1999.

ANTJE WEITHAAS, born in 1966 in what was East Germany, started her musical studies at age five, later studying at Berlin's Hans Eisler Hochschule für Musik. After the reunification of Germany in 1989, her career was launched with the winning of a first prize in the 1991 Joseph Joachim Competition. Her concert with the Deutsches Symphonie-Orchester (Berlin), under **Vladimir Ashkenazy**, resulted in tours to Italy and France, plus an appearance in a film with Ashkenazy and cellist Michael Sanderling. Her repertoire ranges from classics to contemporary. As a member of the *Ex Aequo Trio* chamber music ensemble, she has performed throughout Europe. While mainly appearing in Germany, her concerts and recitals have taken her to the U.S., Canada, Europe and Israel. Festival appearances include the BBC Proms, Bath, Schleswig-Holstein, Prague, Ravinia and Vancouver. During 2000, she toured South Africa, Great Britain, Japan, France, Italy and Canada.

And Then There Were Three . . . or Four . . . .or . . .

Ahn Trio

The **AHN TRIO** is composed of sisters Angella (violin), and twins Lucia (piano) and Maria (cello). Originally from Korea, they attended Juilliard, and gained public attention in 1987 when they were featured in *Time* magazine as, "Asian-American Whiz Kids." They tour the world with over 100 concerts a year, and conduct master classes and workshops for children and adults, including Lincoln Center Institute's program to promote music in the schools. In May 2000, they released their latest CD for EMI, *Ahnplugged*.

THE EROICA TRIO - *Classical Music Evangelists*

Eroica Trio

Their name is taken from Beethoven's "heroic" Third Symphony. Passionate and emotional, they are the vanguard of a new generation of artists changing the face of classical music. Their unique concert programming has done away with single composer or musical era recitals in favor of romping throughout the 300-year history of classical music, from baroque to classical to contemporary. An all-female chamber ensemble, they are helping break an age-old gender barrier.

As the 1997 official representatives for Carnegie Hall, their European tour included performances of **Ellen Zwillich**'s *Trio* for *Piano, Violin and Cello*. This was met with such success that three new triple concertos were written for them, and they received a recording contract with Angel/EMI Classics. Their first CD featured Ravel's *Piano Trio*, Benjamin Godard's *Berceuse*, an arrangement of three Gershwin Preludes and Paul Schoenfield's *Café Music*. Their second (1998) combines Dvořák, Shostakovich and Rachmaninoff. The third (1999), titled *Baroque*, has an arrangement of Bach's *Chaconne* by Academy Award winning film composer **Anne Dudley**. A 2000 release, *Passion*, included music of Turina and Villa-Lobos, and in 2002 they recorded Brahms' Piano Trios No. 1 and 2.

During the 1998–99 season they performed the Beethoven Triple Concerto more than any other trio in the world with orchestras all over America. 1999–2000 covered seventy-five concerts here and abroad. Adjunct to their concert and recording schedule are concerts and master classes at schools throughout the country, creating an open forum for discussion with students about their lifestyle as performing artists, their emotions as they play, and their relationship as a trio, all with the perspective of a young, female group endeavoring to fill the void in music education today.

Award-winning soloists who have performed around the world, there is now little time for solo activities when the trio gives up to eighty performances in a year.

Erika Nickrenz, piano, who made her concerto debut in New York's Town Hall at age eleven, was featured on the PBS series *Live from Lincoln Center*, and has had a solo career in Marlboro, Spoleto, and Tanglewood Festivals, and appearances Canada, Italy, Switzerland and Australia. The first of the trio to become a mother, Zachary Herman was born April 11, 2001. Erika was back at the keyboard two weeks later. Having been trained *in utero*, the baby immediately demonstrated his love for the instrument!

Adela Peña, violin, won first prize at the Washington International and Hudson Valley competitions, and has toured as a soloist in the U.S., Europe and South America. In addition to the Eroica Trio, she is a member of the New York Philomusica and Orpheus Chamber Ensembles. Her son, Neal Whitney, arrived June 5, 2001.

Sara Sant'Ambrogio, until age sixteen, received cello instruction from her father, who had studied under world-renowned **Leonard Rose**. Her next teacher was **David Soyer** at Curtis, cellist for the great Guarneri String Quartet. Three years later, Leonard Rose heard Sara play and invited her to Juilliard where, within weeks, she won the all-Juilliard Schumann Competition, resulting in her first performance at Lincoln Center. She also studied under the venerated **Felix Galimir**, who would later serve as a mentor to the Eroica Trio. She won a bronze medal at the 1986 International Tchaikovsky Cello Competition. Her career includes tours of the U.S., Canada, Europe and the Middle East. Her contribution to the future male Eroica Trio, Sebastian Jonathan, was welcomed by his happy parents, Sara and Alan Miller July 26, 2004.

At the Trio's appearance for The Women of the Mainly Mozart festival in San Diego, California, April 3, 2004, their encore selection of a tango by Piazzola was replaced, with Sara saying, "If we play the tango, Sebastian [then in utero] won't sleep and neither will I."

(This concert was another opportunity for the author to visit with these lovely ladies.)

Girls at Play

The women have a unique history, in that they have known each other since childhood. Erika and Adela began performing together at age nine. Erika and Sara studied piano and chamber music with Isabelle Sant'Ambrogio, Sara's grandmother. As a teenager, Adela coached chamber music with Sara's father, John Sant'Ambrogio, principal cellist of the St. Louis Symphony (1968–2006), who was her first teacher. Another early coach of the trio was Erika's father, violinist Scott Nickrenz, who heads the chamber music sections of Spoleto Festival, USA, Florida's New World Symphony, and is artistic director of the Gardner Museum series in Boston.

Since the trio signed with Angel/EMI, all their CDs have been produced by Erika's mother, concert pianist and three-time Grammy Award winning record producer, Joanna Nickrenz. The trio was founded in 1986 while its members were students at Juilliard. They won the Walter F. Naumberg Foundation's Chamber Music Competition in 1991, and since then have glamorized classical music with their adventure some programming and sleek wardrobes. Their reviews are as much about their playing as about what they wear, which becomes irrelevant when one hears these intelligent musicians demonstrating their love of the art of music and the craft of their combined talents.

Jalina Trio

THE JALINA TRIO features pianist Natsuki Fukasawa and sisters Line Fredens, violin, and Janne Fredens, cello. Founded in 1995 when the women met during their studies at the Academy of Music in Prague, they have also studied with Ferenc Rados (Liszt Academy, Budapest), the renowned Emerson Quartet, Robinson-Laredo-Kalichstein Trio, cellist Emmanuel Ax and pianists Leon Fleischer and Wu Han. They perform in Denmark, tour England, the Czech Republic, Hungary, Italy, Norway, Australia, America and ever expanding venues. They participated in the Isaac Stern Chamber Music Workshop at Carnegie Hall, and Music Encounters in Jerusalem, with the late Isaac Stern as their leading mentor. The trio's honors include top prizes in the Trapani International Chamber Music Competition, Trondheim International Chamber Music Competition, Radio Competition of Denmark, and "Best Chamber Music Recording of 2004," from the Danish Music Awards for their Mendelssohn/Brahms CD. Other CDs feature Danish composers.

Natsuki Fukasawa was born June 28, 1970, in Portland, Oregon, where her music-loving parents happened to be at the time, but grew up in Japan. She returned to America when she was fourteen. With a piano teacher mother, both music and the instrument came naturally to her. She gave her first public performance at eight, and has since performed throughout the U.S., Japan and Europe. A Fulbright Scholarship recipient, she has won awards in the Frinna Awerbuch International and Japanese-American Music Competitions. Her BM (1992) and MM (1995) are from Juilliard—where she met her future husband—plus studies at the Prague Academy (1994–97), which led to the formation of the trio. She married Richard Cionco in 1998 who, she says, is a "fantastic" pianist. He is an associate professor at Cal. State Sacramento, where the couple reside. Both play many solo recitals and concerts. Natsuki has been heard on NPR, WQXR, WNYC and other radio broadcasts.

Line Fredens, born June 11, 1972, in Aarhus, Denmark, began violin at age seven, sharing her father's violin until she got her own. With very supportive parents, she practiced every day with her mother as piano accompanist. After attending the Aarhus Conservatorium (1988–91), she graduated with a soloist diploma from the Royal Danish Conservatory (1992–97). Her honors include the Jacob Gade, Betty and Valdemar van Hauens, and Aennchen and Egil Herbys Foundation Awards. Her solo concert debut in Copenhagen in 1997 was followed by performances at Tivoli Hall (Copenhagen's equivalent of Carnegie) and the Malmö Concert Hall (Sweden). She lives in Copenhagen with her husband, Jacob Dam Fredens, *née* Nielsen (he changed *his* name upon marriage in a quite unique custom-reversal), a bassoonist with the Royal Danish Orchestra. Line is a principal violinist in the Malmö Symphony Orchestra, just a ferry ride from Denmark to Sweden across the Öresund, until the building of the Freedom Bridge, completed in 2000, cut the commute to fifteen minutes.

Janne Fredens was born August 9, 1974, in Aarhus, Denmark, played violin from ages three to eight, beginning cello at nine, and making her debut on that instrument at ten. Like her sister, her mother accompanied her on piano. She began playing in a chamber orchestra at age eleven. A graduate, at nineteen, of the Royal Danish Academy of Music in Aarhus, she won the Jacob Gade Legatet Prize (2000), received a full Danish Government Scholarship to study at the Prague Academy (1994–97), and one year at the Edsberg Chamber Music Institute in Stockholm. Her teachers included **Ralph Kirshbaum**, **Zara Nelsova** and **William Pleeth**—teacher of Jacqueline duPré. Besides her trio participation, Janne performs throughout Europe as a recitalist and soloist.

Janne (pronounced Yahnay), Line (Leenay) and Natsuki (Natski): the JA-LI-NA (Yah-Lee-Nah) Trio. (Clever, eh?)

The **COLORADO STRING QUARTET** began as an undergraduate foursome in residence at the University of Colorado at Boulder. They soon gained recognition by winning chamber music's two highest awards, the Naumberg Prize and Canada's Banff International String Quartet Competition. **Deborah Redding**, violin, who co-founded the group in 1976, was born in New York City of musician parents, but grew up in Colorado. She received her BM from the University of Colorado and MM from Juilliard, studying with Szymon Goldberg. She is the only remaining founding member of the quartet.

Julie Rosenfeld, violin, a native of Los Angeles, joined the quartet in 1982. She received her training at Curtis, USC and Yale. Her major teachers were Szymon Goldberg, Nathan Milstein and Yukiko Kamei. She has appeared as a recitalist and soloist with orchestras throughout the U.S. and Europe, and has recorded two albums of French chamber music with André Previn. She frequently performs with the Chamber Music Society of Lincoln Center, and at the Santa Fe and La Jolla Festivals. In 1992, she became the first female judge at the Banff International Quartet Competition.

Marka Gustavsson, viola, holds degrees from Indiana University, Mannes College of Music, and received her DMA from CUNY. She has studied with Mimi Zweig, Joseph Gingold, Felix Galimir, and Daniel Phillips. A guest artist with Da Capo Chamber Players, Sequitur, Lincoln Center Chamber Music Society's "Meet the Music," and on Robert Sherman's WQXR Young Artists' Programs, she has also performed internationally in chamber music events including the Festival Presence at Radio-France, and the Pundaquit Festival in the Philippines. She has served on the faculties of Hofstra University and the Kinhaven Music Festival.

Francesca Martin Silos, viola, also joined the quartet in 1982. Born in Los Angeles, she is a graduate of the California Institute of the Arts and studied with the great **William Primrose** (1903–82) among others. A dedicated teacher, she is a guest artist at major festivals such as the La Jolla SummerFest. On January 4, 2000 she gave birth to her second child, Christopher George Silos, and retired from the quartet. She was replaced by Marka Gustavsson.

Diane Chaplin, cello, also an Angeleno, joined the Quartet in 1988. She received her BM from the California Institute of the Arts. Her MM is from Juilliard, after training with Harvey Shapiro. She has concertized throughout the U.S., Canada and Europe, and is the winner of a special prize from the International Cello Competition in Viña del Mar, Chile, plus a Certificate from the International Tchaikovsky Competition in Moscow. Besides teaching privately, she is administrative director of the Soundfest Chamber Music Festival and the Institute of String Quartets, held for two weeks each June on beautiful Cape Cod, Massachusetts.

In September 2000, the Colorado Quartet began a long-term appointment as assistant professors at Bard College in New York State. The ensemble was quartet-in-residence for 1998–99 at Oberlin, and has also held artist residencies at the New School in Philadelphia, as well as Swarthmore, Skidmore, and Amherst Colleges. They have given master classes at Eastman, Northwestern University, The Banff Centre, Indiana University, University of Michigan at Ann Arbor and the University of Toronto.

The **Da VINCI QUARTET**, co-founded in 1980 by **Jerilyn Jorgensen**, violin and **Katharine Knight**, cello, was based at the University of Colorado (Colorado Springs) where, as artists-in-residence, they were sponsored by the College of Letters, Arts and Sciences. An NEA grant enabled the quartet to appear coast to coast and in Canada. Their repertoire ranged from Beethoven to Bartók and Berg. Their 1991 CD featured the never before recorded Fanny Mendelssohn-Hensel Quartet, paired with brother Felix's Quartet in E-flat. They also released the complete quartets of Arthur Foote, music of Loeffler, and the *Tango* among other discs. In March 1995, Da Vinci placed third in the prestigious Naumberg Quartet Competition.

Beginning with Jorgensen, **Joo-Mee Lee**, violin, **Margaret Miller**, viola, and Knight, over the years there were several changes in the second violin and viola positions, always a challenge to the cohesion of personalities and fabric of the tone. The last roster featured **Susan Jensen**, violin, and **Leslie Perna**, viola.

In July 2005, after twenty-five years of successfully championing women composers and musicians, the retirement of the quartet was announced. A record to be proud of!

Jerilyn Jorgensen, founding member of the DaVinci Quartet, successfully combines an active performing and teaching career with raising a family. In addition to her concert schedule, which has taken her across the U.S. and abroad, she joined the faculty of Colorado College in fall of 2000 as Instructor of Violin. She is married and has two children.

Her teachers included Joseph Fuchs, Leonard Sorkin, and Zvi Zeitlin. She holds a BM from Eastman, and MM (1979) from Juilliard. The Juilliard Quartet influenced her life and performing career, giving her an affinity for late Beethoven, early 20th century works of Bartók and the second Viennese School. She plays a violin of Italian origin, circa 1850, formerly in the possession of the great **Henri Temianka** (1906–92).

Growing up in a family of artists, actors and writers, **Katharine Knight** fell in love with the cello at age ten. A native of Baltimore, she attended Peabody studying with a succession of protégés of the great Russian cellist, Gregor Piatigorsky, principally Stephen Kates and Laurence Lesser, whom she followed to the New England Conservatory for graduate studies.

A co-founder of the DaVinci Quartet, Knight describes her involvement with the group as a matter of calling, part obsession, part act of devotion, part pure indulgence. She called their inter-relationships a "musical alchemy." She performs as a recitalist, and guest artist with other chamber ensembles, including Hot Celli, a duo with husband and fellow cellist, Richard Slavich.

Knight joined the faculty of Colorado College in the fall of 1999 as Instructor of Cello. Her instrument was made in 1997 by husband and wife team **Joseph Grubaugh** and **Sigrun Seifert**. (See Luthiers.)

Susan Jensen (violin), has a BM from the Cincinnati Conservatory, where she studied with **Dorothy DeLay**. She also studied with Eudice Shapiro at USC (MM) and the La Salle and Tokyo String Quartets. She was a member of the LA Opera orchestra under Kent Nagano and Plácido Domingo. In 1995, she performed three complete cycles of Beethoven's string quartets with the Southwest Chamber Music Society. In 1997, she toured southern China presenting master classes, performing chamber concerts, and appearing on TV. She has played with the Viklarbo Ensemble, Bach Camarata, and is a member of the contemporary ensemble Xtet. Her TV soundtrack credits include *Providence*, *The West Wing* and *American Dream*; and the films, *X Files*, *John Q*, and *Pollack*. Jensen is on the faculty of Lamont School of Music (University of Denver), and plays on a 1697 G. B. Rogeri violin.

Leslie Perna (viola), was in the quartet from 2003–05. With their disbanding, she joined the faculty at the University of Missouri. She now plays with the Esterhazy Quartet and the Concordia Trio.

Korean born **Joo-Mee Lee (violin)**, received her BA from the RAM (London), MM from the New England Conservatory, where she founded the string quartet "Tonos," and DMA from Boston University. She has given solo recitals and chamber music performances at the festivals in Aspen, Banff, and Sarasota.

Margaret Miller (viola), studied at Indiana University, and the University of Wisconsin-Milwaukee where she received a certificate in chamber music and MM. She toured Germany and Italy as a member of the Novello Quartet, and appeared on live radio broadcasts in Chicago with members of the Fine Arts Quartet before joining DaVinci in 1985. She is instructor of viola at Colorado College, and teaches privately.

There are, of course, a myriad of women who play in a multitude of chamber groups of single or mixed gender, and the many, *many* dedicated female orchestra musicians. The *Women in Orchestras* Section attempts to give an overview to this dedicated segment of WOMEN in Classical Music.

An American "Legend"

Dorothy Delay

While France can be justly proud of their legendary **Nadia Boulanger**, who was considered the teacher of the century by the music world and by her many notable students, America can name **DOROTHY DeLAY** as its own pedagogic icon—or, to put it simply, no discussion of violinists can be complete without the woman who taught the brightest stars in the Fiddlers' Firmament. The lustrous list includes Itzhak Perlman, Shlomo Mintz, Gil Shaham, Nigel Kennedy, Robert McDuffie, Mark Peskanov, Mark Kaplan, Cho-Liang Lin, Nadja Salerno-Sonnenberg, Kyoko Takezawa, Anne Akiko Meyers, Midori, Chee-Yun, Sarah Chang, Catherine Manoukian, and a host of others. Concertmasters of major orchestras, who were under DeLay's tutelage, are Erez Ofer (Israel Philharmonic), Jaap Van Zweeden (Amsterdam Concertgebouw) and Kolya Blacher (Berlin Philharmonic). Violinists from famous chamber music groups number the Juilliard String Quartet, Tokyo String Quartet, Cleveland Quartet, American String Quartet, Mendelssohn String Quartet and Takacs Quartet of Hungary. Many of her other students are now members of conservatory faculties around the world, including fourteen at Juilliard.

Miss DeLay was born in Medicine Lodge, Kansas, March 31, 1917. Her father, Glenn, was a cellist and her mother, Cecile, a pianist. Dorothy attended Oberlin College (1933–34), began violin studies with Michael Press at Michigan State (BA, 1937), then went to Juilliard Graduate School, where her teachers were **Louis Persinger** (1887–1966) a pupil of **Eugène Ysaÿe**, and Hans Letz. She received her diploma in 1941, and after working as an assistant to the equally legendary **Ivan Galamian** (1903–81), began her Juilliard teaching career in 1947. Other faculty positions were at Sarah Lawrence College (1948–87), Meadowmount School of Music (founded by Galamian) at Westport, New York (1948–70), Aspen School of Music (1971–2000), University of Cincinnati College-Conservatory (1974), Philadelphia College of the Performing Arts (1977–83) and the New England Conservatory (1978–87). She taught master classes in Europe, Korea, Israel, Japan, China and South Africa. At Juilliard, she held the Starling Chair. Summers were spent at Aspen. While her critics claimed she had no prescriptive method of teaching, and her success came from taking on only the cream of the crop, what she *did* was teach her students to think for themselves and gain confidence from their ability to do so.

Dorothy married writer Edward Newhouse in 1941. (They met on a train at St. Louis and he proposed by the time they got to Trenton, New Jersey!) He was the aide to Army-Air Force Commander H.H. Arnold in World War

II, and was present at the historic 1943 Teheran Conference of Roosevelt, Stalin and Churchill. From the late 1930s to the '70s Newhouse was a fiction writer for *The New Yorker* magazine. Their son Jeffrey (*b* 1942), is a radiology doctor-professor at Columbia University. Daughter Alison Dinsmore (*b* 1946), is married to a radiology doctor-professor at Harvard Medical School. Jeffrey added daughter Amy and another Edward (Ted) to the family, and Alison has contributed two daughters, Molly and Susie.

DeLay's numerous honors included the American Teacher Award of the American String Teachers Association, the King Solomon Award of the American-Israel Foundation, and honorary doctorates from Oberlin, Columbia, Michigan State, University of Colorado and Brown University. She was a Fellow of the Royal College of Music and the first teacher ever to receive the NEA's National Medal of the Arts, presented to her by President Clinton at a 1994 White House ceremony. In 1995, she received the National Music Council's annual Eagle Award. Yale University presented her its highest award in 1997, the Sanford Medal, for distinguished contributions to music. In 1999, the Order of Sacred Treasure was conferred upon her by Emperor Akihito of Japan. In 2000, Amadeus Press published her biography, *Teaching Genius—Dorothy DeLay and the Making of a Musician*, by Barbara Sand. *Musical America*, in their 2001 edition, presented to her its first-ever Educator of the Year award as a teacher who, for over fifty years, influenced hundreds of students.

The last year of Dorothy's life was, sadly, a battle with cancer. She was able to celebrate her sixty-first wedding anniversary, March 5, but passed away March 24, 2002, a week before her eighty-fifth birthday. She has a permanent place in the history of music.

Alma Rosé - A Life That Must Never Die

Alma Rose

ALMA ROSÉ is a name that should be known to all who love classical music, but until the 2000 publication of *Alma Rosé: From Vienna to Auschwitz*, by Richard Newman, the only acquaintance Americans may have had was through the 1980 HBO movie *Playing for Time*. Starring a shorn Vanessa Redgrave as French singer and concentration camp survivor Fania Fénelon, and Jane Alexander, who won a supporting actress Emmy for her portrayal of Alma, it was, unfortunately, a distorted and inaccurate characterization of this legendary woman! By good fortune I was led to this book, which has enabled me to include one of the most unique, talented, courageous women to grace these pages.

Alma was born into musical "royalty," November 3, 1906, when Vienna, the imperial city under the beloved Emperor Franz Joseph, was the hub of the music world. "Waltz King" Johann Strauss had died just seven years previously, but life was still literally a series of palatial balls, the dark clouds of World War One not yet a shadow on the horizon. Alma's father was **Arnold Rosé**, leader of the world famous *Rosé Quartet* and concertmaster of the greatest orchestra in the world, the Vienna Philharmonic, a position he had assumed by virtue of his phenomenal talent at the tender age of seventeen in 1881, under his original name Rosenblum. Her mother, Justine, was the younger sister of celebrated Austrian composer **Gustav Mahler** (1860–1911). The baby was the namesake of his wife, **Alma**.[91] Her four years older brother, Alfred, destined to be a professional musician, clarinetist, pianist, conductor and teacher, would be her lifelong friend and supporter. One of her closest childhood friends was **Erica Morini**, who would become one of the world's greatest women violinists. By age six, Alma knew she wanted to follow in her father's footsteps.

1914–18 were Europe's World War I years. During and after the war, the Rosé Quartet and the Vienna Philharmonic and Opera continued performing to audiences huddled in overcoats for lack of heating fuel. Teenagers Alma and Erica joined the crowds standing in grocery store lines. The next decade of lack of food, inflation and unemployment provided a ripe breeding ground for an obscure Austrian corporal named Adolf Hitler to rally a defeated Germany to a new cause and new hates.

91. See International Composers.

Meanwhile, at fifteen, Alma presented a well-received solo debut on July 29, 1922, at an elite summer resort; her father and brother were also on the program. Her formal Vienna debut, December 16, 1926, included playing Bach's Double Violin Concerto with her father. (A later performance of this concerto is the *only* recording of her playing.) Mixed reviews praised her technique, but her more deliberate "masculine" musicianship was less than favorably compared to the fiery style of Morini, who by this time was the toast of Europe and America. As one critic pointed out, Alma was carrying the burden of too many famous names. Nevertheless, over the next few years her career progressed.

In 1927, handsome, dashing twenty-seven-year-old Czech violin virtuoso **Vása Príhoda** entered Alma's life. They were married in 1930. Now, under the name Alma Rosé-Príhoda, she played several solo recitals, and sometimes toured with her husband. Too often, however, Vása left her behind since he was in great demand in Europe and the Middle East and even appeared in a few films, which led to gossip about his relationship with glamourous stars.

In 1932, Alma, already despondent over her failing marriage, had an inspiration which gave her a new lease on life. Following in the tradition of Viennese all-female salon orchestras she, with invaluable help from her father and other musicians, organized the *Weiner Waltzermädeln* (Viennese Waltzing Girls). Averaging from nine to fifteen members, they comprised two harpists, a pianist—sometimes two—a singer and strings. Alma, who usually played a solo at each concert, was a strict director, maintaining high artistic standards and insisting that all music be memorized. The ensemble's Vienna debut in 1933 immediately attracted a large following, but March of the same year found the group stranded in Munich. Their concert was canceled at curtain time due to anti-semitic demonstrations in the streets by gangs of brown-shirted thugs. Hitler had been in power since January, and his Third Reich policies were already in evidence. Vása sent money for the orchestra's fare back to Vienna, and Alma vowed never again to accept an engagement in Munich. Meanwhile, in the few remaining years of comparative artistic freedom, the *Weiner Waltzermädeln* successfully toured Budapest, Prague, Warsaw, Zurich, Geneva, The Hague, Copenhagen, Stockholm, Paris and Berlin. Although her husband sporadically appeared with the orchestra, by 1934 the programs bore only Alma's maiden name. In 1935, Príhoda filed for divorce, and although Alma agreed for his sake, she was devastated.

On the advice of influential friends, the Rosés were baptized Catholic, a procedure many Jews were adopting as a means of protection against the ever-mounting Nazi threat, but arrests were escalating, even for those who had converted. In November 1938, Alma flew to Amsterdam and London to seek avenues of escape for her father and herself. Her mother, whose health had declined, had died in August 1938 and was spared seeing her world collapse in ruins. Alfred and his wife, Maria, had been sponsored to America.

Alma met with conductors **Bruno Walter** in Amsterdam and **Adrian Boult** in London. She also lunched with one of her admirers, **Rudolf Bing**, then artistic director of England's Glyndebourne Opera. (He would become general manager of New York's Metropolitan Opera for over twenty years, 1950–72.) Everyone pledged support, and through Walter's connections, a residency and work permit for Arnold was obtained from the British Home Office. She returned early dawn of Christmas morning. While she was gone, the dark hours of November 9–10, 1938, would become known forever as *Kristallnacht*, the "Night of Shattered Glass," when the Nazis staged pogroms [demonstrations] throughout Germany and Austria, during which over 200 synagogues were burned, 10,000 home and shop windows smashed and 30,000 Jews transported to death camps. The damage was estimated at $23 million—for which the *Jews* were ordered to pay a billion marks! In Vienna, 15,000 were rounded up and severely beaten and twenty synagogues burned. The SS came to question Arnold about his son. If Alfred had remained in Vienna, he would have been arrested.

The Rosés arrived in London May 1, 1939. England declared war on Germany, September 3. Alma began an active musical life playing second violin in her father's string quartet, and private concerts, but lack of money and her innate ambition for a solo career prompted her to accept an offer to play at the Grand Hotel Central in The Hague, in still neutral Holland. Her successful tours there enabled her to send money to her father, but also delayed her return. In 1940 the Germans captured Holland, and Alma was trapped. Curfews and travel restrictions were enforced, and she was reduced to giving concerts in people's homes. To survive, Alma entered into an unconsummated marriage with the extremely eccentric scion of a well-established Dutch family, but she was still in danger of arrest. She refused offers to go into hiding, and finally attempted the last possible escape route to Switzerland. But she was captured in France and arrived at Auschwitz, the death camp in German-occupied Poland, on July 20, 1943. She was assigned to the "Experimental Block," where doctors performed sterilization and other grisly procedures, mostly under non-sterile conditions without anesthesia.

An enigma of the brutal Nazi character was their love of music. While the men's camp was entertained by the entire (all male) arrested Polish Radio Orchestra, the women had only a few amateur musicians. Like wildfire, the news swept the camp that a professional violinist had arrived, and Alma was whisked from the fate of a barbaric death to a new destiny. For the next nine months, she served as director of the women's orchestra. Working ten hours a day, Alma molded these amateurs—both Jews and Catholics—into a creditable performing group. Moreover, thanks to her, anyone sent to the "Music Block," even those who could not play an instrument and were conscripted for secretarial and music copying duties, was saved from the gas chamber.

Alma commanded such respect that she was the only inmate in the history of this Hell-on-Earth ever to be addressed by the courteous title, Frau (Madame). She had a tiny room to herself at the end of the cell block and received a little extra food, which she usually shared. On April 3, 1944, there was a birthday party among the block "commandos" (captains). Alma apparently ate some contaminated food, and became deathly ill with a high fever and chest pains. In the camp hospital, she received unprecedented care. Seven doctors—both Jewish and German—tried frantically to save her, but she went into a coma and died two days later. The musicians never recovered from Alma's death. After almost disbanding, a talented gypsy violinist, Lilly Mathé, led them, but only in light music. As **Anita Lasker**, the only cellist, was to say in her 1996 book, *Inherit the Truth*, which recounts her own survival, "Alma *was* the orchestra!"

As mentioned earlier, it was Fania Fénelon, a survivor from the "Music Block," who preserved the memory of Alma in her 1976 book, *Sursis pour l'orchestre* (in France), *Das Mädchenorchester in Auschwitz* (in German), and in English, *Playing for Time*. In the 1980 film, Fénelon, whose major contribution to the orchestra was her prodigious memory in making musical arrangements, gave herself a major role while portraying Alma as a harsh taskmistress who lived in fear of the Nazis and was a cold tyrant in her dealings with the musicians. This was *not* the Alma discovered by Richard Newman in his twenty-two years of research, or described by Anita Lasker who, on her arrival in Auschwitz, December 1943, was saved by Alma and put into the orchestra. Fénelon also caused much pain with her derogatory descriptions of some of the players. Surviving orchestra members reacted strongly to these distortions of the truth. The real Alma was a dedicated, highly talented professional who, through her gift of music, inspired these doomed women to shut out the unspeakable horrors that surrounded them, and by her example and courage, enabled many to survive.

In 1969, the City of Vienna at last recognized Alma as a martyr of the Nazi regime. Alma Rosé Gasse forms one side of a quiet little square in the tenth district—a living memorial to a legend whose flame will now glow forever . . .

One day I shall stroll there . . .

That "King-Size" Violin

Lillian Fuchs*

Virginia Majewski

Muriel Carmen

Rosemary Glyde

Rivka Golani

Nobuko Imai

Kim Kashkashian

Cynthia Phelps

Karen Elaine

Denyse Nadeau Buffum

Pamela Goldsmith

Donna Lively Clark

Patricia McCarty

Nokuthula Ngwenyama

Karen Phillips

Veronica Sallas

Karen Tuttle

*Jeanne Mallow (third generation)

As women violinists gained acceptance, and chamber music maintained its popularity, several women took up the viola, an even larger instrument to balance under the chin. With the dearth of solo repertoire, violists—mostly male—were usually in ensembles and orchestras. The picture has changed for the better on both counts: there are more compositions being written for viola solo, and there are more women orchestral musicians. Much credit is due to the efforts of Englishman **Lionel Tertis** (1876–1975) and Scottish-born **William Primrose** (1903–82), whose artistry and effort put the viola into prominence as a solo instrument. Primrose settled in America in 1937 and taught at Indiana University (1965–82). **Rebecca Clarke** (1886–1979)[92] joined the prestigious Queen's Hall Light Orchestra in 1912, becoming the first woman in a professional orchestra in London.

Lillian Fuchs

One of the first great women viola soloists, **LILLIAN FUCHS**, was born into a highly musical family in New York, November 18, 1903. In 1924, she graduated with the highest honors from the New York Institute of Musical Art (now Juilliard), where she studied composition with Percy Goetschius and violin with Louis Svecenski and **Franz Kneisel** (1865–1926), the German-born concertmaster of the Boston Symphony and founder of the famed Kneisel Quartet (1886–1917) which helped popularize chamber music in America. Lillian later played in his daughter Marianne's quartet. She made her debut as a violinist in 1926. Her switch to viola was encouraged by her participation in the Perolé String Quartet and her concert appearances with her famous brothers, violinist **Joseph** (1900–97), who gave a recital in Carnegie Hall in 1994 at *age ninety-four,* and **Harry** (cello). She also soloed with major orchestras, including the New York Philharmonic and Casals Festival Orchestra.

She was the first violist to perform and record the Six Bach Suites, originally for solo cello, and was an important teacher of viola and chamber performance at the Manhattan School of Music (1964–90), Aspen Music School (1971–93) and Juilliard, where she remained on the faculty as professor emeritus until her death in New Jersey, October 6, 1995. Her first pupil was "a boy from the West Coast" named **Isaac Stern** (1920–2001), who became one of this century's greatest violinists. She also taught **Pinchas Zukerman** (*b* 1948), encouraging him to learn viola as well as violin—thus making his mark as a virtuoso on both. Fuchs composed several important works for the viola, and made an arrangement of Mozart's Violin Concerto in G (K. 216) for her instrument. She was

---

92. See British Composers.

married to Ludwig Stein, who died in 1992. They had two daughters, Barbara Stein Mallow, a cellist, and Carol Stein Amado, a violinist. Granddaughter Jeanne Mallow has a rising violist career.

VIRGINIA MAJEWSKI, studied at Eastman and Curtis. She went to Hollywood in 1938 and became principal violist in the MGM, Universal and RKO studio orchestras. She was a member of the ancient instrument trio of the Pilgrimage Concerts, and played chamber music with the greatest vituosos of the time, violinist **Jascha Heifetz**, violist **William Primrose** and cellist **Gregor Piatigorsky**, as well as the American Art String Quartet. She recorded works with guitarist **Laurindo Almeida** (1917–95), playing both viola and viola d'amore, and was the featured soloist in the films *On Dangerous Ground* (1951) and *Atlantis* (1955). Principal violist of the Glendale (California) Symphony for many years, she died October 9, 1995, at the age of eighty-eight.

MURIEL CARMEN holds the longevity record for a woman in the Cleveland Orchestra. Hired by George Szell in 1941, when orchestra ranks were being depleted by men going off to World War II, he was looking for "a girl violist." Just a year earlier, she had run into prejudice when her successful audition at Pittsburgh was overridden in favor for a male. According to Carmen, as pioneers, women musicians had to outdo themselves to earn the respect of their male colleagues. When she came to Cleveland she was one of three women. When she retired at the age of seventy-one in 1994, there were nineteen out of 105. *(Great galloping progress! Author's comment.)*

ROSEMARY GLYDE was born in Auburn, Alabama, September 16, 1948, to Edgar, a violist on the faculty of Auburn University and Dorothy, a cellist. Her sisters, Wendy and Judy, played violin and cello and the family performed and sang together from Rosemary's infancy. A gifted soprano also, she chose to concentrate on the violin, studying with her father until she enrolled at Connecticut's Hartt College of Music. In 1970, she went to the Manhattan School of Music and Raphael Bronstein. She entered the masters program at Juilliard with **Dorothy DeLay**, but switched to viola and **Lillian Fuchs**, earning her DMA in 1973. Her dissertation was the discovery of the *Concerto pour l'Alto Principale* (*c* 1800), the Amon viola concerto, which she edited, published and performed. She also won the Juilliard Viola Competition, which led to her New York debut at Alice Tully Hall in Lincoln Center, playing the William Walton Viola Concerto. She subsequently performed this with the Dallas and Houston Orchestras. She was a founding member of the Manhattan String Quartet, with Eric and Roy Lewis and her sister, Judy.

In 1981, she took time out from her career to give birth to her only child, Allison. Always a devoted mother, Glyde did not resume concertizing until her 1984 debut in Merkin Hall, and concerts at Tully and Weill Recital Halls (1988), the latter featuring her transcription of the Six Bach cello suites, which she recorded, and three viola de gamba sonatas. Both concerts received great critical acclaim.

In January 1990, she married longtime friend, noted New York bowmaker **William Salchow**, who had been making and rehairing her bows since her Juilliard days. His supportiveness infused her career with new energy. Always a leader in viola performance and research, after serving as treasurer of the American Viola Society for six years from 1987, Glyde founded and was the first president, in 1992, of the New York Viola Society, was editor of their newsletter, *The New York Violist*, as well as contributing articles to *The Instrumentalist* and *The Journal of the American Viola Society*. The same year, she joined the faculty of the Mannes College of Music. Also in 1992, Bernard Hoffer wrote a viola sonata for Glyde which she featured in three recitals of the Kosciuszko Foundation. In 1993, he wrote a concerto for her which she performed with her own cadenza at the American Viola Society Congress in Evanston, Illinois. She composed a solo fantasy, *Whydah*, inspired by the pirate ship of the same name raised at Cape Cod, and commissioned and premiered several other works for her instrument, including Norman Cazlon's Viola Concerto and a series of compositions by Judith Shatin.

In June 1993, she was belatedly discovered to have a tumor, which, with treatment during the next six months, was considered to have been shrunk. That fall, she composed her *Suite for Four Violas*, commissioned by violist **Karen Ritscher** and the New York Viola Society. It was performed January 10, 1994, as Rosemary lay in a coma.

Besides her talent for contemporary music, Glyde's playing of romantic literature on her precious Benjamin Banks 1786 viola was described by *Strad Magazine* as "old fashioned in the best sense." Her untimely and sudden death, January 18, 1994, was a loss to music lovers everywhere.

William Salchow wrote of her: "She rejoiced in the beauty of the world and . . . reached out to those in sorrow and despair, lifting them with her indomitable high spirits. Her music reflected this . . . encompassing the entire range of human emotion. She wrote of Bach, that he was above all a man with feeling of passion and devotion, who loved life. This was equally true of Rosemary."

Contemporaries

Rivka Golani

RIVKA GOLANI is recognized as one of the major violists of our time. Her contributions to the advancement of viola technique have already given her a place in the history of the instrument and have been a source of inspiration to other players and contemporary composers. To date more than 200 compositions have been written for her, including thirty concertos.

Born in Israel (then Palestine), March 22, 1946, Rivka began on the violin at age seven. Besides being gifted musically, she also proved herself talented in mathematics and visual art. By the time she entered university she had already given several exhibitions of her paintings and drawings. It was not until her last year at the University of Tel Aviv, where she studied with Israeli composer/professor **Oedeon Partos** (1907–77), that she decided the viola was to be her career, and began playing with the Israel Philharmonic Orchestra.

In 1974, she moved to Canada with her first husband Otto Erdes, an innovative instrument maker who had built her distinctive viola—carved for optimum sound, "with a bite taken out of it." She was appointed professor of viola at the University of Toronto. On December 20, 1975, she gave birth to son Michael.

Known both as a unique interpreter of traditional repertoire and a champion of new music, she has soloed with some of the world's major orchestras, including the Boston Symphony, Royal Concertgebouw, Bern Symphony, Radio Symphony Orchestra of Berlin, Israel Philharmonic, ORP Radio Orchestra of Vienna, Tokyo Metropolitan Orchestra, Royal Philharmonic, BBC Symphony, BBC Philharmonic, Hallé Orchestra and the London Promenade Concerts. Her CDs of major works for viola include the Elgar Cello Concerto, arranged for viola by eminent English violist **Lionel Tertis**, *Phantasy* for viola and orchestra, by Sir Arnold Bax, Berlioz' *Harold in Italy* with the San Diego Symphony under Yoav Talmi, and concertos by Martinů, Yvasa, Bartók, Malcolm Arnold, Tibor Serly, Michael Colgrass and Edward Rubbsa, as well as the Brahms viola sonatas. An accomplished painter, Golani also works with composers as a visual artist, presenting multi-media performances of works for viola and orchestra. Exhibitions of her paintings have been held throughout Great Britain, Germany, Israel and North America. She lives in London, Ontario (Canada) with her second husband Jeremy Fox.

Nobuko Imai

NOBUKO IMAI, another world career artist, is the only violist ever to win the grand prize in both the Munich and Geneva International Competitions. Born March 18, 1943, in Tokyo, she attended the Toho School of Music there, then went on to Yale and Juilliard. She has performed with orchestras around the world, such as the Royal Concertgebouw of Amsterdam, Berlin and Vienna Philharmonics, Boston Symphony and all London orchestras, under the greatest conductors, Sir Michael Tippett, Leonard Slatkin, Seiji Ozawa, Kurt Masur, Charles Dutoit, Sir Colin Davis and Neeme Järvi. She is admired for her interpretations, especially the 1989 world premiere of Toru Takemitsu's *A String Around Autumn*, written for her. Her recordings include Tippett's *Triple Concerto*, Berlioz' *Harold in Italy*, and Mozart's *Sinfonia Concertante*.

Imai regularly appears in music festivals, including the London Promenade Concerts, Casals Festival, London's South Bank Summer Music, and collaborates in chamber music with the world's greatest cellist **Yo-Yo Ma**, violinists, **Gidon Kremer**, **Midori**, **Itzhak Perlman**, **Pinchas Zukerman**, and the late **Isaac Stern**, pianists **Andras Schiff** and **Martha Argerich**, and major ensembles, Guarneri Quartet, Tokyo Quartet and the New York Chamber Music Society of Lincoln Center. She now makes her home in Amsterdam (Holland).

Born of Armenian descent in Detroit, August 31, 1952, **KIM KASHKASHIAN** graduated from Peabody. A guest artist with the Chamber Music Society of Lincoln Center, she has performed with the Tokyo, Guarneri, and

Galimir Quartets, and toured with violinist **Gidon Kremer** and cellist **Yo-Yo Ma** among many others. Summer festival performances include Lucerne, Salzburg, Bergen (Norway), *Mostly Mozart* (New York) and Malboro (Vermont), and concertized in the world's major cities. A progressive musician, she has commissioned and premiered works by contemporary composers **Barbara Kolb, Sofia Guaidulina, Krzysztof Penderecki** (*b* 1933), and **Alfred Schnittke** (*b* 1934). Critical acclaim went to her American premiere of the Penderecki Concerto with **Stanislaw Skrowaczewski** conducting the Minnesota Orchestra. Penderecki himself conducted her Paris performance. She played Schnittke's Viola Concerto under conductor Dennis Russell Davies with Germany's Saarbrücken Radio Orchestra, and Kanceli's Viola Concerto with the Orchester der Beethovenhalle, Bonn (Germany). Her landmark recording of the complete Hindemith sonatas won a 1988 Grammy nomination, this was followed by Hindemith's *Trauermusik*.

While living in Germany, Kashkashian was professor of viola at the Freiburg Hochschule für Musik. In the new century, she divides her career between teaching viola at the New England Conservatory, performing concertos with European orchestras, and touring America playing chamber music.

Cynthia Phelps

CYNTHIA PHELPS is principal viola of the New York Philharmonic. Born June 16, 1960, in Los Angeles, she is one of five sisters all of whom play an instrument. With her mother on the violin, there was always music in the house. Cynthia chose viola at age eleven because she liked the sound, and by that age her hands were big enough to hold and finger it. For the next nine years she studied with Sven Reher, principal violist in the Walt Disney studio orchestra, who had been a pupil of the great Carl Flesch. In 1981, she took a two month summer master class with **William Primrose** on Vancouver Island. She got her BM and MM at the University of Michigan. In 1984, she won first prize at the Lionel Tertis Viola Competition on the Isle of Man (England). This led to a recital the same year at London's Wigmore Hall. She was again a first prize winner, this time at the International String Competition in Washington, DC—a singular honor since this contest covers *all* stringed instruments, and violins usually outnumber their brethren. Winning the 1988 Pro Musicis International Foundation Award guaranteed sponsorship in this country and abroad, and resulted in debuts in Paris, Rome, Los Angeles and New York's Carnegie Hall.

After a year in the San Diego Symphony with conductor David Atherton, Phelps joined the Minnesota Orchestra (1986–91) as principal viola under **Edo du Waart**, which included solo appearances. As a member of the Pinchas Zukerman and Friends Ensemble, she has performed chamber music throughout South America, Israel and Germany. Other performances have been with the Chamber Music Society of Lincoln Center, Bargemusic series, Boston Chamber Music Society, Chicago Chamber Musicians and New York Philharmonic Chamber Music Ensemble Series at Merkin Hall. She has also played with stellar violinists **Joseph Silverstein, Joseph Suk, Salvatore Accardo, Isaac Stern, Itzhak Perlman** and **Yefim Bronfman**, cellists **Yo-Yo Ma** and **Lynn Harrell**, and guested with the Guarneri, Brentano, American and Prague String Quartets, as well as the **Kalichstein-Laredo-Robinson** Trio.

Principal violist with the New York Philharmonic since 1992, Phelps has regularly appeared with them as a concerto soloist, including the 1999 premiere of **Sofia Gubaidulina**'s *Two Paths* (*Dedication to Mary and Martha*), commissioned by Tomoko Masur, former violist and wife of NYP director Kurt Masur (1991–2002).

In the media Phelps has been featured on the *MacNeil-Lehrer News Hour,* CBS *Sunday Morning*, St. Paul *Sunday Morning*, Radio France, RAI (Italy), and WQXR, New York. Her recordings are on the Marlboro, Polyvideo, Nuova Era, Covenant and Virgin Classics labels.

Somehow in her hectic schedule she found time to become the mother of Christina, born December 11, 1991, from her first marriage to baritone David Malis. She married cellist Ronald Thomas, September 1996. Caitlin arrived October 2, 1997. Thomas' daughter Lili has become Cynthia's "much-adored step-daughter."

Having heard Phelps in concert in 2001 with the San Diego Symphony, in the 2002 La Jolla SummerFest, and as part of the *Les Amies Trio*, with **Nancy Allen,** harp, and **Carol Wincenc,** flute, in The Women of Mainly Mozart Series in February 2004, the author can attest to the truth of the *Wall Street Journal* statement that the "deep richness of sound she conjures from the instrument is sensuously breathtaking."

In the Académe, and Other Violists of Note

Karen Elaine

San Jose-born **KAREN ELAINE** began her music studies on the violin at age ten, switching to viola the next year. She graduated in 1987 from Curtis. From 1988–90, she studied string pedagogy and viola performance. This began a career in 1989 as adjunct professor of viola at San Diego State University. Winning the 1988 Bruno Giuranna International Viola Competition in Brazil led to a recording session of the Bartók Viola Concerto. She has commissioned and premiered works by contemporary composers. Her recording with the City of London Sinfonia received a 1992 Grammy Award nomination. A tour of Australia during the 1993–94 season featured the world premiere of Gordon Kerry's Viola Concerto.

Her orchestral career includes acting principal viola, San Diego Symphony, 1987–90; soloist/acting principal San Diego Chamber Orchestra, 1987–90; Sun Valley (Idaho) Summer Symphony, 1991–1998; and the California Philharmonic (Arcadia) since 1998.

Residing in Venice, California, she is a busy freelance artist, global scuba diver/instructor and photographer.

DENYSE NADEAU BUFFUM, related by marriage to **Dorothy Chandler,** is a native of French Canada. She was admitted to the Conservatoire de Quèbec at age five. The youngest of four girls in a musical family, she began playing at the age of ten throughout Canada's Eastern provinces as a member of the "Nadeau Quartet." At twelve, she went to New York to study with Daniel Guilet (violinist with the original Beaux Arts Trio), then to the Manhattan School of Music to study with Raphael Bronstein and **Lillian Fuchs** on viola. Two years later, the Nadeau Quartet debuted at Carnegie Recital Hall, which led to a five-year contract with super agency Columbia Artists Management (CAMI) to concertize extensively in Canada and the U.S. with over fifty engagements per season, with Denyse performing on both violin and viola.

After graduating from Manhattan, she moved west. In 1972, with her violinist husband, Thomas, they formed a chamber group, the Buffum Ensemble, comprised of members of his family. They performed throughout Southern California. Buffum also played with the California Chamber Orchestra under noted violinist/conductor **Henri Temianka** (1906–92). She remains active playing for major motion picture film scores and recordings.

DONNA LIVELY CLARK, born in Indianapolis, January 19, 1948, received her exposure to music via the public schools. (Those were the days!) Although she wanted to play violin in fifth grade, the only instrument available was a viola. She took it, and by 1965 won a full scholarship to study with **William Primrose**—additional study and chamber coaching were with the Juilliard and Cleveland String Quartets. After getting her MM from Butler University, she joined their faculty in 1982. By 1993, she was full-time assistant professor of music building a strong viola program of master and orchestral repertoire classes, recitals, chamber music and music education. She founded the local chapter of the American Viola Society, of which she became secretary.

Clark has appeared with the Aspen and Bach Festival Orchestras, Indianapolis Symphony and Duo Piacere. She is principal viola and soloist with the Indianapolis Chamber Orchestra, the Lockerbie String Quartet and the American String Trio.

Recipient of an Indianapolis Arts Council award, she researched Argentine music, performing and recording new compositions using viola in combination with a tango band, bandoneon, folk drums and guitar. She formed *Duo Criollo* with guitarist-composer Sebastián Zambrana, touring South America and the U.S. Their Centaur CD, *Una Viola Porteña*, features unique adaptations of the Argentine tango.

Author of *The Viola Survival Handbook*, her articles are published in various string journals. Donna is the mother of Hillary, born 1980, and Adelle, born 1982.

PAMELA GOLDSMITH was born in Houston, Texas, December 2, 1941. During WWII, her father headed a top secret FBI division whose assignment was to keep German spies attempting to infiltrate across the Mexican border out of the United States. After the war she was raised in Los Angeles, where in school she fell in love with the sound of the viola and knew this was *her* instrument. She attended UCLA, Mannes College of Music (New York), and Stanford University where she received her DMA. Her teachers were **Paul Doktor** (1919–89), **William Kroll** (1901–80) and "the father of the viola," **William Primrose** (1903–82).

A member of the American Symphony Orchestra, under the fabled **Leopold Stokowski** (1882–1977), Casals Festival Orchestra, and Lincoln Center Chamber Orchestra, she was principal viola of the Cabrillo Music Festival in Santa Cruz, California. Her chamber music experience includes playing with the Group for Contemporary Music at Columbia, Camerata String Quartet, Stanford Chamber Players, and the Sitka (Alaska) Music Festival. She has participated in numerous premieres of contemporary music, and presented solo recitals across the country as well as playing on radio, television, recordings and film soundtracks. She has performed and lectured at the International Viola Society Congress, International Viola d'Amore Congress in Stuttgart and England, and International Master Courses in Kapaonik, Yugoslavia. Goldsmith's teaching positions include Stanford, the California State Universities at Fullerton and Northridge and USC, where she is on the faculty teaching Viola, Chamber Music and Pedagogy.

Pamela was vice president and secretary of the American Viola Society, and serves as secretary of the International Viola Society. Her articles on the application of scholarly research to performance style have appeared in many journals.

Since winning the first silver medal and radio prize in the Geneva International Competition at age eighteen, **PATRICIA McCARTY** has performed throughout the U.S., Europe and Japan, appearing as both soloist with orchestra, in recital, and as a chamber musician at many festivals including Sarasota, Aspen, Marlboro, and Tanglewood. Born in Wichita, Kansas, July 16, 1954, she attended a private school where music was an important part of the curriculum. Summers, from 1967–74, were spent at Interlochen, at the High School level in Michigan's famous summer music enrichment camp. She received her BM (1974) and MM (1976) from the University of Michigan. From 1977–79 she taught viola at Ithaca College (New York), with the Lenox Quartet in residence. In the fall of 1979, McCarty became assistant principal viola in the Boston Symphony, a position she held until she retired in 1993 to continue her solo career.

Besides her classical and avant-garde repertoire, she plays the music of modern American and women composers, jazz and country fiddle tunes. On the faculties of the Boston Conservatory and SUNY, Purchase, McCarty serves on the advisory board of the American Viola Society and is editor of the Viola Forum of the *American String Teacher*. Her awards include two NEA Solo Recitalist Grants, and the John Knowles Paine Award. She records on ECM.

In 1982, she married fellow BSO violist Ronald Wilkison.

Nokuthula Ngwenyama

NOKUTHULA NGWENYAMA (pronounced No-ko-too-la En-gwen-ya-ma)—her name is Zulu—inherited her exotic looks from a Zimbabwean father and a Japanese mother, but grew up in America. Born in Los Angeles, June 16, 1976, as a toddler she accompanied her big brother to his Santa Monica Youth Orchestra rehearsals and loved the music! She was also taken to concerts. She began piano at four and violin at six. From twelve to fourteen she played both violin and viola, after which she stayed with the viola, studying with Michael Tseitlin, Alan de Veritch and Donald McInnes. She received scholarships from the Young Musicians' Foundation, the Colburn School and Crossroads School in California. At age seventeen, she won the 1994 Young Concert Artists International Auditions—the first violist to win in fourteen years.

In 1992, Nokuthula was featured on PBS' nationally-televised *Sound of Strings* in the Musical Encounter Series. Winner of the first prize in the 1993 William Primrose Viola Competition at the twenty-first Viola Congress in Chicago, her other awards include second prize in the 1993 Los Angeles Philharmonic Bronislaw Kaper

Competition and Co-Grand Prize in the 1993 KCET Emerging Black Artist Competition in Los Angeles. She gave a stunning performance, May 1994, at a House Committee hearing in Washington, DC, as an advocate of continued funding for the NEA.

Her Washington debut opened the Sixteenth Young Concert Artists Series at Kennedy Center in January 1995, to rave reviews. In March came her New York debut in the YCA Series, sponsored by the Mortimer Levitt Career Development Award for Women Artists of YCA. In August, the NEA invited her to Washington again to perform and speak at a meeting of the National Council on the Arts. *CBS Sunday Morning* aired a segment about her in June. Summer 1996, marked her first appearance at the Davos Festival in Switzerland.

The 1997–1998 season included a re-engagement with the Baltimore Symphony Orchestra, conducted by Daniel Hege, as well as concertos with the Columbus, Tucson, Buffalo, Modesto, and San Luis Obispo symphonies, and the Chamber Orchestra of Albuquerque. Nokuthula made her debut concert tour of Japan that season, including a recital at Tokyo's Suntory Hall, and recitals at the Louvre in Paris, Merkin Concert Hall in New York, the Kravis Center in West Palm Beach, Florida, and the Classics in the Garden Series in the Virgin Islands. The 1998–1999 season saw Ngwenyama return for the third successive season to the Baltimore Symphony, performing the Walton Concerto which she also performed with the National Symphony and **Elizabeth Schulze**, the Madison Symphony Orchestra with **Catherine Comet**, the Lexington Philharmonic with George Zach, and the Fresno Philharmonic with Raymond Harvey. She was also soloist with the New Jersey, New Mexico, Elgin and Southwest Florida Symphonies. 1999–2000 featured recitals at the chamber music series of the Universities of Purdue, Georgia, Western Illinois, Bowling Green and Wisconsin. She has performed at the Ford Center for the Performing Arts in Toronto, Vancouver Recital Society, given recitals coordinated with educational residencies at universities, and is a regular performer at the Spoleto Festival USA, Marlboro, Banff and Vancouver Festivals, Bolzano Festival in Italy, and France's Festival de Radio-France at Montpellier.

As a soloist, Ngwenyama has appeared with regional orchestras, and in March 1996 debuted with the New York Chamber Symphony, conducted by Lawrence Leighton Smith, as a recipient of the Aaron and Irene Diamond Soloist Prize of the YCA.

She coached with **Karen Tuttle** at Curtis and earned a masters in theological studies from Harvard Divinity School in 2002.

KAREN PHILLIPS, born December 29, 1942 in Dallas, is a triple winner. She studied piano at Eastman, theory at Juilliard, took viola lessons, gave recitals on each instrument, made a name for herself as a violist, and has written four symphonies, a cello concerto, chamber and piano music.

Born December 31, 1949, in Santiago, Chile, **VERONICA SALAS** came to America in 1957. Settling in Santa Clara, California, her mother, Elba, had the challenge of raising two daughters alone, without knowledge of English. With hard work, both girls became successful musicians. Jacqueline is a Stanford PhD. Veronica studied with Albert Gillis at San Jose State, who suggested she switch to the viola. She continued her studies for seven years with **Lillian Fuchs** at Juilliard, where she earned her masters and doctorate. In 1975, she won the Aspen Music Festival Competition over a slew of other string instrumentalists.

Salas has been guest artist with the Group for Contemporary Music, New Music Consort, American Composers Orchestra, Rosewood Chamber Ensemble and Pro-Arte Chamber Orchestra of New York, as well as being principal violist in the Manhattan Philharmonic, Opera Orchestra of New York, Brooklyn Philharmonic and the American Symphony Orchestra. She has been on the faculties of Bennington, Pepperdine and Mount Holyoke, and given master classes at the Universities of Taiwan and the Philippines.

On the board of the New York Viola Society, she has edited some of the solo viola works of **Rosemary Glyde**.

So Many More![93]

Other fine violists who have carved careers in performance and teaching are **Sally Peck** (first woman principal viola in a major orchestra—the Utah Symphony under Maurice Abravanel); **Kirsten Docter** and **Lynne Ramsey** (Cleveland Institute); **Karen Dirks** principal, San Diego Symphony, who moved to the Chicago Symphony in 1997; **Martha Strongin Katz**, student of Galamian, Fuchs and Primrose, a founder-member of the Cleveland Quartet, who played for President Carter, and was on the faculties at Eastman and NYU; **Maria Newman**, daughter of film composer, Alfred Newman, who has played in studio orchestras and composes; **Geraldine Walther** (principal viola, San Francisco Symphony, 1997–2006) to begin a new career with the Takacs Quartet in 2005–06.

The Magistra of the Viola

Karen Tuttle

KAREN TUTTLE entered the world in Lewiston, Idaho, March 28, 1920, only because the hospital was there. Her family lived on a wheat ranch across the border in Washington state. When hailstorms decimated the crops they tried a cherry orchard, but that was for the birds—who ate most of the fruit. All her childhood she listened to her father's expert fiddling and the lovely cello playing of her sister. After eighth grade graduation, she refused further schooling. Her mother agreed, but only if Karen practiced her violin the equivalent number of hours she would spend in the classroom. She did! One day she heard **Willliam Primrose** in concert with the London String Quartet on tour in this country, and simply asked him to become her teacher. That got her to Curtis, and the viola. As his star rose, Primrose made her his assistant while he fulfilled his concert engagements. She succeeded him after he left.

In a peripatetic career spanning over fifty years, this master teacher has been on the faculties of Mannes, Manhattan School of Music, Peabody, Aspen, Banff, Juilliard (since 1987, and co-chair of the viola department, 1992–2002), and Curtis since 1950. From her 1959 debut in Carnegie Hall, she has played in the Little Orchestra Society of New York with **Thomas Scherman**, (1917–79), NBC Symphony under **Arturo Toscanini** (1867–1957), Saidenberg Chamber Orchestra, Academy Trio, Galimir, Gotham and Alexander Schneider String Quartets, as well as on television programs like Sid Caesar's *Show of Shows*. Tuttle has also performed at the Prades and Casals Festivals, the William Primrose Tribute at the seventh International Viola Congress in Provo, Utah (1979) and six Marlboro Festivals with **Rudolf Serkin** among countless other concerts.

Karen has one daughter, Robin, two grandchildren, and has been happily married since 1956 to Dr. Mortimer Herskowitz of Philadelphia—which is one of the main reasons she spent so many years commuting from her beloved New York.

The author met Karen, slim and petite, in 2004, in her lovely Philadelphia "trinity"—a traditional three-story row house, with long, steep staircases—where Dr. Herskowitz still practices in his ground floor office. She was still climbing those stairs when this book went to press in 2006.

---

93. See Ladies of the Orchestra.

'Cello and Bass – The Really Unladylike Instruments!

CELLO - BASS

Lisa Cristiani (1827–53)
Elsa Rügger (1881?–?)
May Mukle (1880–1963)
Guilhermina Suggia (1885–1950)
Beatrice Harrison (1892–1965)
Marie Roemaet-Rosanoff (1896–1967)
Margaret Avery Rowell (1900–1995)
Elsa Hilger (1904–2005)
Eva Heinitz (1907–2001)
Raya Garbousova (1909–97)
Eva Czako Janzer (1926–78)
Eleanor Aller (1917–1995)
Zara Nelsova (1918–2002)
Jacqueline DuPré (1945–87)
Han-Na Chang
Allison Eldredge
Pamela Frame
Nancy Green
Natalia Gutman
Bonnie Hampton
Ofra Harnoy
Natalia Khoma
Nina Kotova
Dorothy Lawson

Winfred Mayes
Shai-Ye Ni
Sharon Robinson
Shauna Rolston
Eleonore Schoenfeld
Irene Sharp
Tania Simoncelli
Frances-Marie Uitti
Christine Walewska
Anita Lasker-Wallfisch
Wendy Warner
Alisa Weilerstein

CELLO (Quartet):

Maria Kitsopoulos
Laura Koehl
Maureen McDermott
Caryl Paisner

DOUBLE BASS

Orin O'Brien
Rachel Calin
Jacqui Danilow
Marji Danilow
Deborah Dunham

The idea of a lady, young or otherwise, squatting on a chair with a huge fiddle between her legs has never presented an ethereal picture. Furthermore, the thickness of cello strings and the extra strength it takes to press them down, especially in *vibrato*—vibrating the finger on the string to produce a resonating tone—presents a daunting challenge to dainty digits. But hurdles exist to be overcome, and overcome them women did, even to playing this instrument whose lengthy original name, violoncello, has been shortened to *cello*.

First of the Foremost Few

One professional female cellist is known from the first half of the 19th century. **Lisa Cristiani** (or Christiani) had a short but brilliant career. Born in Paris in 1827, she made an acclaimed debut at eighteen, touring in Germany. Mendelssohn dedicated his *Song Without Words* Op. 109 to her. She died in Siberia in 1853 while attempting to recapitulate a tour of the remotest regions of the Russian Empire undertaken by Belgian cellist Adrien François Servais (1807–66). Her 1720 Stradivarius, now known as the "Cristiani," was owned by renowned cello teacher **Hugo Becker** (1864–1941). Well-known German-born violinist, **Julius Eichberg** (1824–93), who settled in Boston in 1859, gave opportunities within his Eichberg Quartet to cellists **Lettie Launder**, **Laura Webster** and **Georgia Pray Lasselle**, the latter going on to a solo career. The 1888 Mendelssohn Prize was shared at the Berlin Conservatory by **Lucy Müller-Campbell**, born in Louisiana but trained in Germany, the first cellist of either gender to receive this honor. Around the turn of the 20th century, Swiss **Elsa Rügger** (*b* 1881–?) made an extensive American tour—New York, Pittsburgh, Detroit, Cincinnati, Cleveland, St. Louis—soloing with orchestras and in recital. **Josephine Donat** (Viennese), **Agga Fritsche** (Danish), and **Cato van der Hoeven** (Dutch, 1874–?) all made names for themselves before disappearing into marriage. Belgian **Marie Roemaet-Rosanoff** (1896–1967) studied with W. Willeke, Lief Rosanoff (whom she married), and **Pablo Casals** (1876–1973). Teaching at Peabody and the Third Street Music School in New York, she brought the Casals style to the U.S., and edited the Bach *Suites for Unaccompanied Cello* according to his interpretation. She and her husband founded a summer music school at Blue Hill, Maine, and sent one of their students, Marta Montañez, to Prades, to then eighty-year-old Casals, inadvertently becoming matchmakers for one of the world's most famous "May-December marriages." Married August 3, 1957, the union lasted sixteen years until his death, October 22, 1973. Marta married pianist Eugene Istomin (1925–2003) in 1975. (See Women in the Business of Music.)

The Big Names

Englishwoman **MAY MUKLE** became well-known in America through her association with violinist **Maud Powell**. Born in London, May 14, 1880, of an English mother, her German father, Leopold, was an expert organ builder, and the inventor of a coin-operated music machine—the world's first juke box! May studied at the Royal Academy and was already earning a sizable income with concert performances by age eleven. Enhanced by her magnificent Montagnana cello, a gift from an anonymous donor from the Hill collection, critics spoke of her "beautifully controlled style," and "the considerable power of her singularly mellow tone." Her musicianship was recognized early as on a par with **Pablo Casals**—then the world's foremost cellist, and a close friend. Known for her hospitality, her London flat hosted such upcoming composers as **Ralph Vaughan Williams**, **John Ireland**, **Maurice Ravel**, and artists like Casals.

In May 1905, she toured with Powell in South Africa, playing forty-two concerts in seven weeks, accompanied by her pianist sister, **Anne Mukle Ford**. It was Sunny Turner, Maud Powell's husband-manager, who enticed Muckle to come to America. In 1908, Sunny had her booked from January to May—sometimes with Powell—with orchestras and in recitals in Montreal, Quebec, Chicago, Buffalo, Pittsburgh, Detroit, Oberlin (Ohio) and other midwestern cities. On New Year's Eve, 1907 (even then!), May was mugged in New York, and one of her eyes badly injured, but she still made her debut January 5, in Mendelssohn Hall, patched like a pirate. After this, she was called "the Maud Powell of the Cello." The same season, she and Maud were the first two women to play Brahms' *Double Concerto*. Anne was sent for from England, and they toured all over America as the *Maud Powell Trio*, playing to packed houses and consistent critical raves. Their repertoire included the *Trio in A minor* by the popular Frenchwoman, **Cécile Chaminade**. (See Composers.) On April 28, 1909, May and Anne sailed back to England leaving behind a multitude of fans. In 1920, May played the British premiere of Ernest Bloch's Rhapsody for Cello and Orchestra, *Schelomo*, under **Sir Henry Wood**.

In 1959, at seventy-nine, Mukle was in a car accident and suffered a broken wrist. She resumed performing as soon as she recovered. She had undertaken another recital tour in America in spring of that year with piano accompanist Pearl Sutherland. This was in the style of "barnstorming"—finding places to play, like churches, mimeographing their own programs and putting out a collection plate for contributions.

May Mukle enjoyed a long, successful career, covering most of the globe, including America, Canada, Australia, Hawaii, Japan, China, Burma, India and Africa. Much esteemed, she died in London, February 20, 1963, at the age of eighty-three.

The RAM awards an annual May Mukle Prize in her honor to a deserving student.

Beatrice Harrison

BEATRICE HARRISON was born in Roorkee, India, December 9, 1892, and taken to England as an infant. She entered the Royal College of Music in London, studied four years with **William Whitehouse** (1859–1935), becoming one of his most famous students. She won a prize at age ten, and was fourteen when she made her first public appearance as a soloist with a London orchestra, May 29, 1907, Henry Wood conducting. She crossed the Channel to study with **Hugo Becker** at the Berlin Hochschule für Musik, and became the first cellist and youngest competitor, to win the Mendelssohn Prize. She gave a debut performance at London's Bechstein Hall in 1910, and made many European tours, often with her sisters, violinist May, and pianist Margaret. She toured the U.S. in 1913 and 1932.

Frederick Delius wrote his double concerto for Beatrice and May after hearing them play the Brahms double. He also became a close family friend, and Beatrice gave the first performance of his cello sonata, with **Hamilton Harty**[94] in 1919. She also gave the British premiere of Delius' Cello Concerto, under **Eugene Goossens**,[95] as well as its first radio performance. Delius also dedicated his *Caprice* and *Elegy* to her.

Other British premieres were those of Ravel's *Sonata for Violin and Cello* (with her younger sister Margaret in 1923), and Kodály's unaccompanied sonata. While Whitehouse's other most famous student, Felix Salmond, premiered the Elgar Cello Concerto, Harrison gave its first radio performance, with the composer conducting, and *twice* recorded it with him. Her instrument was made by Peter Guarneri, and was culled from the Baron Johann Ludwig Knoop (1846–1918) collection.

She originated unique nightingale broadcasts—playing the cello in her garden to evoke the bird's singing. One such broadcast, May 21, 1931, was picked up as far as America and Australia!

Beatrice died in Smallfield, Surrey, March 10, 1965.

(Like many prominent women in music, Harrison received her share of snubs and jibes from the male contingent, but it was she who suffered one of the crudest sexist put-downs in musical history from that personification of male chauvinism, conductor **Sir Thomas Beecham**. Displeased with her playing at a rehearsal, he exclaimed: "Madam, you hold between your legs an instrument that could give pleasure to thousands, and all you do is sit there and scratch it!")

MARGARET AVERY ROWELL was born in Redlands, California, in 1900. She had moved to the San Francisco Bay area as a child of eight, and lived there all her life. She graduated from UC-Berkeley in 1923, and married UC philosophy professor Edward Rowell in 1936. She taught cello at the San Francisco Conservatory of Music, and served on the faculties of UC, Berkeley, Stanford, Mills College and San Francisco State University.

An excellent cellist and teacher, she was known as a teacher of teachers, her method concentrating on more than technique, involving the whole person. Her watchword was "I don't teach the cello, because the cello can't learn . . . I teach the human being!"

In the early 1950s, she organized the California Cello Club, which hosted many great cellists, including Casals, Piatigorsky, Rostropovich, Starker and Greenhouse. The cello club grew to encompass all Bay Area cello teachers and students.

Rowell traveled extensively in the U.S. and Europe with **Irene Sharp**, also of the San Francisco Conservatory, giving workshops for cellists and string teachers. She died April 21, 1995, in San Francisco.

EVA HEINITZ, well-known around the world as an inspirational teacher and performer, was professor emeritus of cello at the University of Washington (Seattle) where she had taught for twenty-eight years, beginning in

---

94–95. Both conductors were later knighted.

1948. She performed in solo and chamber concerts throughout Europe and North and South America, appearing as soloist with the Chicago, Pittsburgh, Seattle, and Vancouver symphonies.

Born in Berlin, February 2, 1907, she grew up in one of the great musical centers of the century. Music was a large part of her childhood. The concerts she was taken to featured legendary maestros **Erich Kleiber**, **Wilhelm Furtwängler**, **Otto Klemperer**, **Bruno Walter** and **George Szell** conducting the Berlin Philharmonic or the State Opera. Her father, a lawyer and amateur pianist who loved chamber music, sometimes hired violinists and cellists to perform at their elegant twelve-room apartment, with the large Steinweg (Steinway) piano.

From her earliest years, Eva knew she would become a musician, focusing on the cello. At fifteen, she was admitted to the Berlin State Academy of Music, where she studied with the renowned **Hugo Becker**. (She later admitted that she found many of Becker's cello techniques to be somewhat unnatural.) It was also in Berlin where she played chamber music with **Albert Einstein**, whom she considered a great man, though not a great violinist—an opinion seconded by Gregor Piatigorsky when asked by the genius scientist, himself. Still in her twenties, Heinitz was soloing with Europe's great orchestras until 1933 when Hitler and the Nazis came to power. Jews, loyal to their homeland, could not at first believe what was happening. With her mother's sudden death, and persecution beginning its destruction and ostracization, the half-Jewish Eva joined the exodus of hundreds of prominent Jews in the arts. She settled as a refugee in Paris, where she studied with Pablo Casals' teaching partner, **Diran Alexanian** (1881–1954).

Besides her cello, through her concerts she was helping the world rediscover the *viola da gamba*, an almost forgotten relative of the cello. Self-taught, she became so proficient that she was known as the "Wanda Landowska[96] of the Viola da Gamba." Having difficulty holding the instrument while performing in a silky concert gown, at the suggestion of German-born composer and violist Paul Hindemith she placed an *endpin* on her gamba. Considered a Bach authority, she concertized as solo gambist with Furtwängler and Klemperer, yet she said: "Who could be an authority on Bach? I know something about him, but nothing a reasonably intelligent and hard-working musician couldn't figure out."

When pianist **Artur Schnabel** invited Eva to play in the 1939 "New Friends of Music" series at Town Hall in New York, she moved to America, becoming a naturalized citizen five years later. She joined the Pittsburgh Symphony (1942–46), under **Fritz Reiner**, as assistant principal. Despite his affection for her, Reiner never allowed her to advance to principal because she was a woman, the reason she left the orchestra. Yet it was often she, and not the principal, who was chosen by him to play chamber music with such visiting greats as violinists Yehudi Menuhin, Nathan Milstein, Josef Szigeti, Isaac Stern and Jascha Heifetz, of whom she said, "He was a tremendous fiddler, of course, but a dreadful chamber player." She was also a close friend of famed cellist/pedagogue **Janos Starker**.

In 1948, with $2.50 in her purse, she went to Seattle to join a faculty quartet at the University of Washington and was immediately hired as faculty cellist. During her twenty-eight-year tenure she also became one of the founders of the early music revival, bringing a renewed interest in the music and instruments of the 17th and 18th centuries through her work with the UW's Collegium Musicum ensemble, as well as her courses and master classes from Berkeley to New York. She made recordings for the Delos, EMS, Amadeo/ Vanguard and Columbia labels, one of which was gamba and cello music called *Authentic Baroque Music Performed in a Non-Authentic Manner*. Her reasoning for the title was, "I don't believe in authenticity for the simple reason that nobody really knows how people played 200 years ago."

In 1991, the University of Indiana (Bloomington) Music School and their Eva Janzer Cello Center honored Heinitz with the Grande Dame du Violoncelle award.

---

96. Landowska (1879–1959) was a one-woman crusade bringing the harpsichord back to prominence. Eva did play with her while living in Paris. (See Harpsichordists)

In 1994, Eva donated her 1700 Matteo Gofriller cello to the University of Indiana. The sale of this instrument provided seed money for the Eva Heinitz Scholarship Fund, which annually gives significant help to many young cello students at the School of Music—site of the largest cello enrollment in the country.

In her last years, she raged against old age. "I'm too old," she grumbled at ninety, and would answer phone calls with, "I'm not dead yet!"

Greatly honored, Eva Heinitz passed away in Seattle, April 1, 2001, at ninety-four.

RAYA GARBOUSOVA was born in Tiflis (Russia), September 15, 1909. Her father was principal trumpet in the Tiflis Symphony and a conservatory professor. She began piano at four, but later changed to the cello. Her first teacher was Konstantin Miniar, a pupil of the legendary Karl Davidov (1838–89). Her Tiflis debut won immediate praise. At fifteen, Raya performed Tchaikovsky's *Rococo Variations* in Moscow and Leningrad, receiving comparison with the more mature **Emanuel Feuermann** (1902–42), who later became a close friend. She also played chamber music with violinist **Nathan Milstein** and pianist **Vladimir Horowitz.**

In 1925, she went to Leipzig, intending to study cello with **Julius Klengel** (1859–1933). He auditioned her for three hours, playing etudes and concertos, then proclaimed that she could not be his student because she already knew everything! Later, she studied with **Hugo Becker** and **Pablo Casals**, the latter urging her to study with **Diran Alexanian**, who became a tremendous influence in her cello technique and musicianship. Petite in stature, she proved that it was flexibility, not finger length which counted.

Garbousova knew all the great musicians and composers of the 20th century, and was responsible for many first performances, including the Martinů *Third Sonata*, and Prokofiev Sonata. She made her U.S. debut December 4, 1934, thereafter concertizing throughout the country. In 1946, with the Boston Symphony Orchestra under Serge Koussevitzky, she premiered Samuel Barber's *Cello Concerto*, which was commissioned and written for her. She also played chamber music with **Albert Einstein**, whom she liked very much but who, she claimed, always played a little out of tune. She was a protagonist for 20th century music such as Debussy, Stravinsky and Hindemith.

She married Dr. Kurt Biss, and settled in DeKalb, Illinois, where she lived and taught at the University of Northern Illinois (1979–91). Before that she was at the Hartt School of Music in Connecticut (1970–79) and on the faculties of the Cleveland Institute and Indiana University. Their son, Juilliard-trained **Paul Biss,** was a professor of violin at the IU School of Music (1979–2006).

In the course of the years she owned several marvelous cellos: a Seraphin, Matteo Gofriller, Nicolas Lupot, Stradivarius and G. B. Guadagnini.

Raya died at age eighty-eight, January 28, 1997. A memorial service was held on the IU campus on April 12. **Laszlo Varga**, former principal cellist of the NY Philharmonic, member of the Borodin Trio and then professor at University of Houston Moores School of Music, conducted an ensemble of twenty-two cellists. One of the works performed was *Hommage to Raya*, by American **Gunther Schuller**, which had been commissioned and premiered in Tempe, Arizona for the 1990 Cello Congress.

ELEANOR Catherine **WARREN**, cellist, teacher and broadcaster, was born in London, June 15, 1919. Her German born mother was an amateur cellist who gave her daughter an eighth-sized cello when she was five. Eleanor enrolled in the London Cello School, where she befriended **Zara Nelsova** who had come from Canada to London in 1927. In 1934, Warren was awarded the school's premier prize.

Foremost cellist of the time, **Gregor Piatigorsky** (1903–76), introduced Warren to his agent, Harold Holt, who in early 1936 promoted her in a pair of concerts at Wigmore Hall. More recitals followed, and in 1937 she joined the all-female Ebsworth String Quartet with the Ebsworth sisters (Eileen, first violin and Phyllis, viola) and Elizabeth Hunt (second violin), who were unique in contrast to the usual middle-aged, male ensembles. The Quartet played throughout WWII, boosting home front morale. Warren also took part in the November 27, 1938 farewell concert for famed Irish tenor John McCormack (1884–1945). She shared the artist list with pianists

Gerald Moore (1899–1987) and Betty Hamby, who married maestro Sir Thomas Beecham (1879–1961) in 1943. (She died in 1957.)

During the post-war years, Warren took part in renowned English pianist **Dame Myra Hess**' concert series at the National Gallery, and played with the English Chamber Orchestra. When the Ebsworth Quartet disbanded in the 1950s, Eleanor formed a trio with the violinist Yfrah Neaman and pianist Lamar Crowson, until a back injury forced her to abandon playing in 1964. Beginning the next important phase of her career, she joined the BBC Concurrently, she coached the cello section of the Essex Youth Orchestra, taught at Dartington and ran the chamber concerts when Queen Elizabeth Hall opened in 1967. In 1969, she started the St John's series of live broadcasts in a deconsecrated church in Smith Square, central London, until it moved to Wigmore Hall.

At the BBC, Warren initiated a series of young artists' recitals broadcast live, fostering a close relationship between these and the Leeds International Piano Competition, which in the early 1970s had winners such as Radu Lupu, Murray Perahia and Dmitri Alexeev, who went on to world fame. She was appointed head of radio music programs in 1975. In 1977, she left the BBC to join the Royal Northern College of Music as head of strings, remaining there for seven years. During the '80s and '90s, she was head of chamber music at the Guildhall School of Music and Drama, and played a key role in securing the Takacs Quartet's residency. She was also chamber music director at the Royal College of Music, and sat on various selection panels and adjudication boards, offering verdicts and words of encouragement and support. The Musicians Benevolent Fund, Pierre Fournier Award and BBC Young Musician of the Year all benefitted from her dedication and commitment. In her honor, the Royal Northern College of Music continues to offer an annual Eleanor Warren Prize for salon music.

When the Hungarian violin-piano duo Gyorgy Pauk and Peter Frankl were looking for a trio partner in 1972, Warren introduced them to Texan-born cellist, **Ralph Kirshbaum**, who created the triennial International Cello Festival at Royal Northern in 1988.

Eleanor married Czech-born conductor Walter Susskind (1913–80) in 1943, and had a son. Susskind conducted the Scottish National Orchestra from 1946 to 1952. They divorced in 1953.

Warren was appointed Member of the Order of the British Empire (MBE) in 1991. She died August 25, 2005. The same year, Ralph Kirshbaum dedicated his performance at the Edinburgh International Festival, with the Michelangelo String Quartet, to her memory.

EVA CZAKO JANZER was born in Calcutta (India) in 1926, and raised in Budapest where she studied cello at the Academy of Music, receiving a Diploma of Virtuosity, and winning third prize in the Geneva Competition in 1946. She married Georges Janzer, violist of the Vegh Quartet, and toured with them worldwide as the second cellist in Schubert and Brahms works. She taught at the Hanover (Germany) Music Academy, meanwhile forming a string trio with her husband and violinist **Arthur Grumiaux**, touring and recording, as well as appearing widely as a soloist. When the quartet dissolved, she came to Bloomington with her husband who took over the great William Primrose's position as viola professor in 1972. Eva first was an assistant to Janos Starker, then became an associate professor with a large class. Much loved and admired as a performer and teacher, she was taken from the world by cancer in 1978. Georges Janzer died seven years later. Their son, Robert, is a doctor/researcher in Lausanne, Switzerland.

The Eva Janzer Memorial Cello Center, a member of the American Cello Council, was established shortly after her death. The purposes of the center are: to celebrate the memory of a great artist by providing support for cello performance, teaching and research across the nation and throughout the world; to honor members of the cello community through the awarding of the "Chevalier du Violoncelle" or "Grande Dame du Violoncelle" titles; to provide scholarships for outstanding cello students; and to work closely with similar organizations, such as the American Cello Council and the American String Teachers Association.

Since 1979, honorées of the "Chevalier du Violoncelle" or "Grande Dame du Violoncelle Award" have included Pierre Fournier, Bernard Greenhouse, **Raya Garbousova**, **Margaret Rowell**, Aldo Parisot, Antonio Janigro, **Zara**

Nelsova, Samuel Mayes, **Eleanor Aller Slatkin**, Harvey Shapiro, Paul Tortelier, **Eva Heinitz**, Laszlo Varga, Daniel Saidenberg, David Soyer, **Eleonore Schoenfeld**, Takayori Atsumi, Jules Eskin, Martin Ormandy and Uzi Wiesel. The Janzer Conference is held each fall at the IU School of Music.

Another All in the Family

ELEANOR ALLER (Slatkin) was born May 20, 1917, in New York. Her mother was a pianist and her father, who played in the New York Symphony under the legendary **Walter Damrosch** (1862–1950), was her main teacher. When she was fifteen, the family moved to Hollywood. The older of her two brothers was pianist Victor Aller. She returned to New York to attend Juilliard, from which both her sons would also graduate: Leonard has a dozen honorary doctorates and Fred got his PhD there.

After graduation in 1937, Eleanor went back to Hollywood where a mutual friend introduced her to a young violinist who had moved out from St. Louis that year. **Felix Slatkin** (1915–63) came to the Allers' house to play quartets, then forged a permanent duo by marrying Eleanor in 1939. Their son Leonard,[97] who conducted the St. Louis Symphony for twenty years and assumed directorship of the National Symphony in 1996, arrived September 1, 1944. Fred[98] was born March 10, 1947. Discovering the original family name, Zlotkin, he adopted this at age thirty. He has been principal cello in the New York City Ballet Orchestra since 1971, soloist with St. Louis, Minnesota, National and other orchestras, often performs with the Chamber Music Society of Lincoln Center, and is a frequent substitute with the New York Philharmonic.

Eleanor was first cello in the Warner Brothers Studio Orchestra (1939–60), while Felix was concertmaster at Twentieth Century Fox until 1941. The war catapulted him into the role of conductor for the Army Air Force Tactical Command Orchestra, an offshoot of the Glenn Miller band, which boasted leading U.S. musicians, broadcasting and touring throughout the country, and raising over $100 million in war bonds. After the war, in 1945, he went back to Fox and also gained fame conducting at the Hollywood Bowl.

Meanwhile, Eleanor and Felix (first violin), co-founded the Hollywood String Quartet in 1941, reorganizing it after the war in 1947. Its wartime recordings were reissued on CD in the late '90s on the Testament label from London. Aller can be heard playing solo cello in the film *Deception* (1946),[99] in which Paul Henreid, in his role as a cellist, starred with Bette Davis and Claude Rains.

After her husband's death February 8, 1963, Aller taught at the DePaul School of Music in Chicago for a year, then came back to Los Angeles to play first cello in the Twentieth Century Fox Orchestra until 1985, when she retired. In 1988, she was honored with the Eva Janzer Memorial award, Grande Dame de Violoncelle. Two weeks after our friendly telephone interview, she passed away, October 12, 1995.

Her parents had emigrated from Russia to Winnipeg, where her sisters, Anna (violin) and Ida (piano), and her brother were born. **ZARA NELSOVA** came into the world as Sara Nelson, December 23, 1918. Their mother could speak only Yiddish, their father, broken English. Ambitious for his children to the point of being a tyrant, he would lock them in their rooms to practice for hours on end. An infant prodigy, Zara was nine when her penniless family moved to London from Canada, desperate for financial help and musical tuition. A committee was set up to help them. Zara's debut, with the London Symphony under Sir Malcolm Sargent, was at age twelve playing the Lalo *Symphonie espagnole*. A few years later, her parents returned to

Zara Nelsova

97. Leonard is married to singer **Linda Hohenfeld**. Their son Daniel was born in 1994.

98. Fred's wife Amanda—a music teacher to the very young—presented him with a son in 1991, who was given the name Felix; and a daughter, Madeleine, in 1996.

99. Playing his mother's Andreas Guarnerius cello, Fred was in a February 2003 BBC presentation of the Korngold Concerto featured in the film. Also on the program was Miklos Rózsa's *Sinfonia concertante*.

Canada leaving the children to fend for themselves. As the Canadian Trio, Zara concertized for a grueling eighteen months with her sisters, touring England, South Africa, Australia and the Far East. She escaped WWII by returning to Canada and becoming principal cellist of the Toronto Symphony (1940–43), despite never having played in an orchestra before. Concurrently, she played in another Canadian trio with violinist **Kathleen Parlow** and pianist Ernest MacMillan. Visiting conductors and soloists were so impressed with the quality of Zara's work, offers of solo engagements came pouring in from all over the U.S. 1942 saw her American debut in New York's Town Hall. During this time, she studied with cello greats **Gregor Piatigorsky** and **Emmanuel Feuerman**, who were weathering World War II in America.

After the war, she also spent a summer at Prades in the Pyrenees with Pablo Casals. She became an American citizen in 1953. In 1966, she made a triumphant Soviet Union appearance, the first ever by an American soloist. She was married from 1963–73 to American pianist **Grant Johannesen** with whom she toured.

Nelsova was a recipient of Canada's Centennial Medal of the Confederation, and the Jubilee Medal, "in recognition of valuable service to the nation." She was a fellow at the RAM, on the board of governors as professor of music at Rutgers, and graced the Juilliard faculty from 1962 to early 2002. Modern composers found her progressive style conducive to their own. She gave the American premieres of the Barber *Cello Concerto*, and Bloch's *Schelomo* under the composer's direction. An admirer, he also dedicated his solo cello suites to her. In England, she premiered Sir William Walton's *Cello Concerto* under his baton, and Hugh Wood's *Concerto* at London's Royal Albert Hall, then at Tanglewood with the Boston Symphony.

Confident of her destiny, she turned down offers of orchestral work to concentrate on her solo career at a time when cellists were not considered salable items by music managers, especially women. With no financial help, her determination and talent led to worldwide fame and appearances with virtually every major orchestra. She can be heard on London Decca, Vanguard, Vox and Golden Crest.

After an heroic battle with cancer, this "Grande Dame of the Cello" died in New York, October 10, 2002. Her cello was **Guilhermina Suggia**'s 1726 "Marquis de Corboron" Stradivarius.

A Most Unkind Destiny

Jacqueline Dupre

JACQUELINE DuPRÉ, born in Oxford, January 26, 1945, entered the London Cello School at age five. While still a child, she began studies with her principal teacher **William Pleeth** (1916–99). She also studied with the world's most eminent cellists: **Pablo Casals** in Zermatt (Switzerland); **Paul Tortelier** in Paris; and **Mstislav Rostropovich** in Moscow. Her first public appearance was on British television at twelve. Upon graduation from the Guildhall School of Music (1960), she received a gold medal and the Queen's Prize. Her formal debut was March 1, 1961, in Wigmore Hall. Her Carnegie Hall debut May 14, 1965, playing Elgar's Cello Concerto, was a triumph. On June 15, 1967, in Jerusalem, she married pianist-conductor **Daniel Barenboim** (music director of the Chicago Symphony since 1989). They concertized together until 1973, when she was diagnosed with multiple sclerosis and had to abandon her career. She continued to give master classes as her condition permitted. In 1976, she was made an Officer of the Order of the British Empire, and in 1979 received an honorary doctorate from the University of London. The Jacqueline DuPré Research Fund was established to help MS research.

Her life was the subject of a 1981 Broadway play, *Duet for One*, the book, *A Genius in the Family*[100] (1998), by her brother Piers and sister, flutist Hillary DuPré, as well as a film, *Hillary and Jackie* (1999), based on the book. Jackie died in London, October 19, 1987. Her legacy lives on in her instruments. **Lynn Harrell** has her Stradivarius

---

100. The book was renamed *Hillary and Jackie* after the film came out.

(1673), named by him, *the Jacqueline DuPré*; the *Davidoff* Stradivarius (1712) was left to **Yo-Yo Ma**, and a modern instrument, made by Sergio Peresson of Philadelphia, is now played by **Allison Eldredge**.

An Orchestra Pioneer

Elsa Hilger

Cellist **ELSA HILGER** was born April 13, 1904, in Trautenau, Austria, (later Trutnov, Czechoslovakia). She was the youngest of eighteen children—including four sets of twins—only four of whom survived due to lack of proper medical knowledge and accessibility to doctors. The family moved to Písek when Elsa was seven so that her older sister could study violin with **Otakar Sevčik** (1852–1934), noted Czech violinist and pedagogue. Watching Maria's lessons, the younger child rejected learning violin because she didn't like the standing. Sevčik suggested the cello, a decision that marked the beginning of a remarkable concert career. Elsa's other sister, Greta, began studying piano. The professor was so impressed with the girls' talent, he secured scholarships for all three at the Vienna Conservatory. The family moved to Vienna in 1912, and within a year Elsa, only nine, was playing first chair in the conservatory orchestra. At twelve, she soloed with the Vienna Philharmonic accompanied, she recalled, " . . . by a growling stomach. There was a war—and no food!" In the next two years she appeared half a dozen times with the Vienna Philharmonic. Renowned tenor **Leo Slezak** (1873–1946) thought she was a wonder, and the foremost cellist in the world, **Pablo Casals**, called her "a genius on the cello." The novelty of three sister prodigies created wide attention. The trio performed throughout Europe until 1920, when the family came to America.

Within the first year, Elsa gave three solo recitals in New York's Aeolian Hall. She met composer-cellist **Victor Herbert** (1859–1924), who asked her to play his *Cello Concerto* with maestro **Walter Damrosch** (1862–1950) and the New York Symphony. The promised concert never materialized, however, because Herbert died suddenly in 1924. During the Depression, Elsa and her sisters, chaperoned by their mother, began a series of coast-to-coast concert tours bumping an old Buick over rutted, barely paved highways. Elsa always drove because, "My sisters were too nervous." In March 1932, they played a concert honoring the eightieth birthday of their mentor, Sevčik, who was then in Boston. Touring continued until 1936, when an opening came up in the cello section of the Philadelphia Orchestra. Elsa, who had already soloed with them, was asked to audition by **Leopold Stokowski** (1882–1977), prompted by pianist Olga Samaroff, his wife (1911–23), who had heard Elsa and her sisters performing on tour. The maestro hired her, thus making her the first woman instrumentalist in a major orchestra—other than the occasional female harpist. (**Edna Phillips** had been principal harp in the same orchestra since 1930, and **Marjorie Tyre** became their second harp in 1932. Violinist Lois Putlitz came in 1936.)

On joining the orchestra, Elsa surprised the male members who were dubious as to whether this petite young woman could stand up to the physical demands of a touring schedule. "I was used to driving 200 to 300 miles a day *and* playing a concert in the evening!" she reminisced to me. "Not only could I stand it, I could stand it better than the men!"

Hilger began in the last chair of the section, was appointed second chair in 1945, and held this position until 1963 when she graduated to associate principal, never attaining first chair, although **Eugene Ormandy** (1899–1985), who led the orchestra from 1938–80, inferred that he would have invited her to fill that position "if she had worn longer pants." She actually did share the first chair *stand* until her retirement in 1969. It was the same chair occupied by her father-in-law, Dirk Hendrik Ezerman, in 1901.

With the exception of maternity leave, Elsa was proud of her record of missing only one performance in her thirty-four-year career. It was a Saturday night in her last year with the orchestra, and the entire cello section refused to fill her seat! She was very popular with her colleagues—becoming a mother confessor to all. In 1939, she married prominent dentist Willem Ezerman, part of a respected Philadelphia family. Their son, Robert, became a doctor, and *his* son, Alex, like his grandfather, is a professional cellist.

During her years with the orchestra, Elsa performed in solo appearances, recitals, and had a distinguished teaching career at the Philadelphia Conservatory, where her colleagues included **Edna Phillips**, **Olga Samaroff**, composer **Vincent Persichetti** (1915–87), and other well-known artists. When asked about teaching cello to women and the strict self-discipline required, she remarked: "True, then along comes a talent like **Jacqueline DuPré** [then twenty-four] whose extraordinary virtuosity makes you think the cello is a toy. But the instrument *is* large and clumsy, and playing it requires the strength of a football player."

In 1956, Hilger was awarded an honorary doctorate from Temple University and, in 1965, received the Philadelphia Orchestra's C. Hartman Kuhn award, presented annually to an orchestra member "whose character enhances the standard and reputation of the orchestra." In 1966, she won the Americanization Medal of the DAR. In addition to Temple, she held honorary degrees from Curry, Stonehill, and Saint Michael's Colleges. She retired to Vermont in 1969, where she received the Governor's Award for Excellence in the Arts.

Like her acquaintance, Maria von Trapp of *Sound of Music* fame, Elsa chose Vermont because it reminded her of Austria. She had spent forty summers on Lake Dunmore, where she indulged in her *other* passion, fishing, before making Middlebury her permanent home in 1979. It was then she met piano teacher/adjudicator **Catherine Baird** (MM, University of Michigan School of Music). Baird grew up listening to the Philadelphia Orchestra, admiring Elsa from a distance. Decades later, with both of them living in the same state, they began a twenty-year collaboration, playing on public radio and television, and giving recitals and concerts in the Eastern U.S. and Canada. There were also annual birthday recitals for Elsa at St. Lawrence University in Canton, New York, and Christmas concerts in Catherine's spacious home recital room, "South Bay Hall." When Elsa's husband died in 1990, she moved to Williston Woods to be near her son and family. In May 1999, Catherine Baird died suddenly. Elsa, forty years her senior, sadly played at her beloved accompanist's funeral.

Events such as these are often turning points in one's life. Elsa pondered many months about giving her cello to her grandson, Alex Ezerman, a 1998 PhD from SUNY, Stony Brook, and since 1999 on the cello faculty of Texas Tech. In August of that year, his grandmother parted with her beloved Gagliano so that Alex could carry on the legacy. He is first chair in the Lubbock Symphony. On August 10, 2002, he married one of his DMA students.

[Thanks to my friend, Vermont scenic photographer Betsy Melvin, I met Elsa in her new home, April 12, 2000, one day before her ninety-sixth birthday. Surrounded by mementoes and wall to wall photos of a great career, we spoke for over an hour. Small and slim, her eyes clear and mind sharp, we hit it off like old friends, and parted with warm hugs.]

Living in her own apartment, in an assisted care facility, and swimming almost daily, Elsa celebrated her ninety-eighth birthday, April 13, 2002, giving a brush-up lesson to Melissa Brown, a teacher and Vermont Symphony cellist since 1961 who, at age fifteen—over fifty years ago—had her first lessons with Elsa at the Philadelphia Conservatory. Elsa celebrated her ninety-ninth birthday among friends in 2003! In April 2004, her 100th birthday was celebrated with a concert played on her cello by grandson Alex, a huge cake and many guests.[101]

In the course of 2005, age took its toll. Elsa lived to celebrate her one hundred and first birthday, but by then the pain of severe arthritis forced her to give up her beloved swimming, and her memory was failing.

On Monday afternoon, May 16, 2005, Robert Ezerman visited his mother at her retirement home and found her comatose. He gently took her hands and spoke to her. When she did not respond, he put on a recording of her playing. As the room filled with the harmonious sound of her cello, Elsa opened her blue eyes and looked at her son. A whispered, "Hi," escaped her lips.

The music brought her back to consciousness.

"It's so beautiful, who is playing?"

"That's you, Mum!"

---

101. In April 2004, my husband and I drove across the country and were present at Elsa's 100th birthday. For the occasion I wrote a biographical booklet, *Celebrating Elsa Hilger*, with photographs of her illustrious career culled from her scrapbooks.

For a little while, her pain quieted by morphine, the power of music revived Elsa's life flow, transposing her face from waxen pallor into beatific serenity.

Lulled by the melodies, Elsa fell into a peaceful sleep.

At three the next morning she crossed over to take her place on stage in the eternal realm of heavenly music.

Contemporary Women Cellists

HAN-NA CHANG, born in Korea, 1983, began her musical studies at three on piano, then switched to cello. She participated on a full scholarship in the master classes of **Mischa Maisky** in Siena, and studied privately with both Maisky and **Mstislav Rostropovich**. In October 1994, she entered the Fifth Rostropovich International Cello Competition in Paris, winning first prize and the Contemporary Music Prize. She was unanimously chosen for both awards by Maestro Rostropovich and ten other jury members.

Her formal debut, March 1995, was in her native Seoul with **Giuseppe Sinopoli** conducting the Dresden Staatskapelle, this establishing a continuing collaboration. In 1996, she made her Carnegie Hall debut with Charles Dutoit and the Montreal Symphony, then went on to work with Rostropovich and the London Symphony, **Seiji Ozawa** and Boston—for its 1996–97 season opening gala concert with violinist **Isaac Stern**—**Charles Dutoit** and Philadelphia, **Leonard Slatkin** and Cleveland at the Blossom Festival, **Eiji Oue** and Minnesota, **Riccardo Muti** and La Scala, and **Yuri Temirkanov** and the Young Israel Philharmonic at the Verbier Festival (Switzerland).

During 1997–99, her appearances included **Mariss Jansons** with Pittsburgh, Jesús López-Cobos with Cincinnati, plus the Montreal and National Symphonies. Internationally, she performed in Germany with Munich's Bayerischer Rundfunk (Bavarian Radio) Orchestra, Tokyo's NHK Symphony, Rome's Santa Cecilia Orchestra, the Helsinki Philharmonic, Orchestre National de France and the Hong Kong Philharmonic. She also toured Japan with Giuseppe Sinopoli and the Dresden Staatskapelle and gave a concert in Seoul with **Zubin Mehta** and the Israel Philharmonic. In the 1999–2000 season, she debuted with the Berlin Philharmonic, Orchestre de Paris under **Lorin Maazel**, Monte Carlo Philharmonic (Sinopoli) and the San Francisco Symphony with **Herbert Blomstedt**. She made return engagements with Bavarian Radio led by Maazel, and Santa Cecilia with **Myung-Whun Chung**.

Summer 2000 saw her Australian debut with the Sydney Symphony led by **Leonard Slatkin** as part of the cultural celebrations during the Olympic Games, followed by a Japan tour in October, covering Nagoya and Tokyo, with Lorin Maazel and the Tokyo Symphony. December found her in Budapest, Gyor and Debrecen (Hungary), with the Orchestre Nationale de Lyon, performing Saint-Saëns Cello Concerto No. 1. Other performances in 2000–2001 included Cincinnati, New York, and a European tour with the Cincinnati Symphony.

Han-Na's first recording for EMI Classics (November 1995) was with Rostropovich and the London Symphony, featuring Tchaikovsky's *Rococo Variations*, Saint-Saëns' Cello Concerto No. 1, Fauré's *Elegie* and Bruch's *Kol Nidrei*. 1998 brought the two Haydn Cello Concertos with Sinopoli and the Dresden Staatskapelle. *The Swan*, plus selections by Bruch, Rachmaninoff, Fauré and Panufnik with Slatkin and the Philharmonia Orchestra, was released in 2000.

Chang's television appearances include the 1997 "Victoire de la Musique" awards, televised throughout Europe, the 1998 Easter Day concert from Munich (Maazel and Bavarian Radio), and Kennedy Center's Twenty-fifth Anniversary Gala with Slatkin and the International Chamber Orchestra. She was profiled by *CBS Sunday Morning* and CNN.

In 1997, she was honored with the *Young Artist of the Year* prize at the ECHO Classical Music Awards in Germany.

ALLISON ELDREDGE began her musical training at age three on piano with her mother, concert pianist Yoshie Akimoto. Her first public appearance came at six. By nine, she had switched to the cello, and played to a sold-out UCLA audience two years later. While rehearsing for a Kennedy Center performance the next year, she played for **Mstislav Rostropovich**, who recommended her for Juilliard. Her studies there led to a 1989 Avery Fisher

Career Grant, launching a career which has included performances with the New York Philharmonic (**Zubin Mehta**), Los Angeles Philharmonic (**André Previn**), St. Louis Symphony (**Leonard Slatkin**), Montreal Symphony (**Charles Dutoit**), San Diego Symphony (**Yoav Talmi**), plus orchestras all over the world. Her performance with **Daniel Barenboim** and the Chicago Symphony marked the Maestro's first collaboration with a cellist since the death of his wife, **Jacqueline du Pré**, nearly twenty years earlier. Eldredge's music has taken her on several tours of Japan; Israel, with the Haifa Symphony; England with the Academy of St. Martin-in-the-Fields; and America with the Warsaw Sinfonia, which included her 1995 Carnegie Hall debut. In her numerous summer festival appearances, she has shared the stage with **André Previn**, **Joshua Bell**, **Yo-Yo Ma** and **Gil Shaham**, among other notables in music. Recordings include concertos of Lalo and Saint-Saëns with the Royal Philharmonic; a recital disc with her mother; *Romantic Duet*, opera duets transcribed for violin, cello and orchestra; and on Denon, *If I Loved You*, arrangements of Broadway and film songs for cello and piano.

PAMELA FRAME is associate professor of cello at the Eastman School of Music. She first met Rostropovich at age eighteen, when he came to Eastman to play the Dvořák Concerto with the Rochester Philharmonic. He had to leave next day for Toronto, but said he would give her an audition. She drove to Toronto, found him, and played the Schumann Concerto for him. He told her she could have a lesson anytime she wanted. All she had to do was find ways of being in the right city at the right time for lessons—something she managed to do for the next seven years!

Frame has toured with the Orpheus Chamber Orchestra and appeared at the Marlboro, Skaneateles (New York) and Casals festivals. During summers, she has taught at Interlochen and with The Quartet Program.

A native of Boston, **NANCY GREEN** studied at Juilliard. After graduation, and following master classes with **Rostropovich**, she was awarded a Rockefeller Grant to study with **Jaqueline DuPré** in London and Johannes Goritzki in Düsseldorf, where she was recipient of the prestigious Schmolz-Bickenbach Prize. She made her concerto debut in New York playing the Dvořák at Lincoln Center, was named a "Young Artist of the Year" by *Musical America* and won prizes and awards including the Concert Artists Guild Award, which sponsored her first New York recital.

Nancy Green

Besides international radio and television, Green has performed as soloist in Boston's Symphony Hall, New York's Alice Tully Hall, Kennedy Center, Munich's Herculessaal, and London's Wigmore Hall as well as major venues in Shanghai, Taipei and Seoul. She has recorded for GM, JRI, Aton, and Biddulph, and was the first cellist to record the complete Hungarian Dances of Brahms arranged by Alfredo Piatti, and the complete cello works of Robert Fuchs and Mario Castelnuovo-Tedesco. Her CD of solo sonatas on JRI by Donald Francis Tovey and Zoltan Kodaly was among the top critics' choice of 2000 in *Fanfare* magazine. In addition to her concert and recording career, Green was a professor at London's Guildhall School of Music (1989–94). In 1995, she joined the faculty at the University of Arizona in Tucson where she lives with her son Jonathan, born in Essen (Germany), October 3, 1986.

Russian cellist **NATALIA GUTMAN** received her early musical training from her grandfather, Anisim Berlin, as well as Galina Kozolupova, **Mstislav Rostropovich**, with whom she studied at the Moscow Conservatory, pianist **Svjatoslav Richter** (1915–97), and her husband, violinist **Oleg Kagan**. After winning first prizes at the 1967 Tchaikovsky Competition, she received first prize in the Munich ARD Competition, launching an international career which has taken her around the world to Europe, Japan, North and South America, and Australia, with such orchestras as the London Symphony, Concertgebouw, Amsterdam, the Philharmonics of Vienna, Berlin, St. Petersburg, Munich, and countless others. She has been featured at the prestigious Salzburg Festival and at the Wiener (Vienna) Festwochen (Festival Weeks), and has performed with such legends of the podium as Claudio Abbado, Sergiu Celibidache, Bernhard Haitink, Kurt Masur, Riccardo Muti, Wolfgang Sawallisch, Yevgeny Svetlanov, Yuri Temirkanov and Rostropovich. Her recital performances have featured presentations of the complete Bach cello solo suites in Moscow, Berlin, Munich, Madrid and Barcelona.

An active chamber player, Gutman's regular partners have included pianists **Martha Argerich**, Elisso Virsaladze, Yuri Bashmet, Alexei Lubimov, Svjatoslav Richter and Kagan. She has premiered many contemporary works. **Alfred Schnittke** dedicated both a sonata and his challenging First Cello Concerto to her. With Kagan, she premiered Schnittke's Concerto Grosso No. 2 for Violin, Violoncello and Orchestra (1985) which the composer dedicated to wife and husband.

In the new century, Gutman's performances include soloing with the Seattle Symphony with Gerard Schwarz, the Eleventh Costa Rica Festival, August 2001, and a May 2002 concert in Avery Fisher Hall with the New York Philharmonic under Kurt Masur, performing the Schnittke.

Her recordings include the Shostakovich Concertos Nos. 1 and 2 with the Royal Philharmonic, the Dvořák Cello Concerto with the Philadelphia Orchestra, the Schumann Concerto coupled with the Schnittke No. 1 with the London Philharmonic, plus all Schumann's chamber music with partners such as Argerich and fellow cellist **Misha Maisky**. Since the early '90s, live performances of Natalia Gutman have been released on the Live Classics label. The company edited the *Natalia Gutman Portrait Series*, documenting the development of her art from its beginnings to the present.

Since 1991, Natalia has been teaching at the Hochschule für Musik in Stuttgart. With **Claudio Abbado**, she initiated "Berlin Encounters," giving young musicians an opportunity to play chamber music with "stars." Each July, she invites internationally renowned artists to the Bavarian Alps to participate in the International Musikfest am Tegernsee, which she founded in 1990 with her husband, and which now bears his name in dedication after his untimely death in 1990, at age forty-six.

BONNIE HAMPTON was born in Berkeley, California, into a musical family. Her mother, an amateur violinist and co-founder of a youth orchestra, took Bonnie to chamber concerts from age six. She began studying cello at eight. When she was fifteen, the Griller Quartet took up residence at UC Berkeley. She availed herself of their coaching and fell in love with chamber music. At sixteen, she had an opportunity to play for **Pablo Casals** in Prades in the French Pyrenees. At twenty, she studied with **Zara Nelsova**. The following year, she spent several months in Prades, the first of many extended periods of study with Casals. She said of him, "The most important thing I learned from him was that it is a lifetime task to find one's own direction, one's own voice, one's own connection with the music." He said of her, "I consider her one of the most outstanding talents of her generation. She possesses an extraordinary musical sense together with an accomplished technique."

At twenty-five, Bonnie made her debut with the San Francisco Symphony, then spent five summers at the Marlboro Festival in Vermont. In the mid '60s, she formed the Hampton-Schwartz duo with her husband, pianist Nathan Schwartz, and the Francesco Trio with violinist David Abel—replaced in 1987 by Miwako Watanabe. The Trio won the 1974 Naumberg Chamber Music Award, and can be heard on several CDs. Hampton has performed all the standard repertoire, and most of the 20th century cello concertos with orchestras nationally. Her involvement with new music has given her the opportunity to work with such composers as **Elliott Carter**, **Aaron Copland**, **Roy Harbison**, **Zoltan Kodaly** and **Darius Milhaud**. She participated for many years in the Casals, Marlboro, Ravinia and Santa Fe chamber music festivals, and has performed at Chamber Music West, Seattle. Her guest artist appearances have been with such prestigious ensembles as the Juilliard, Guarneri, Cleveland and Mendelssohn String Quartets.

Hampton taught at Mills, Grinnell, Stanford and UC Berkeley, and has been on the faculty of the San Francisco Conservatory of Music as professor of cello and chamber music since 1972. Summers are spent at the Yellow Barn (Putney, Vermont), and Tanglewood music centers. She served as president of Chamber Music America (1993–96), which is the promoter, mentor and advocate for all chamber music activities in the country. In 1998, she was the recipient of the Award for Excellence in Teaching from the San Francisco Conservatory. She relocated to New York in 2003 upon joining the Juilliard cello faculty.

Born in Israel, January 31, 1965, **OFRA HARNOY** was described by the *New York Times* as "born to the instrument." The family emigrated to Canada in 1972 and Ofra began studying with her father, making her solo debut at age ten. Her further education included training with **William Pleeth** in London, Vladimir Orloff in Toronto, and master classes with **Mstislav Rostropovich**, **Pierre Fournier** and **Jacqueline DuPré**. First prize winner of the Montreal Symphony (1978), and Canadian Music Competitions (1979), in 1982 she became the youngest first prize winner of the New York Concert Artists Guild, which led to her Carnegie Hall debut in 1983, the same year as her acclaimed premieres of the (then) recently discovered Offenbach *Cello Concerto in G*, the Viotti Cello Concerto in C and the Bliss Cello Concerto. Besides playing internationally, in 1991 Prince Charles invited her to join **Plácido Domingo** and **Jessye Norman** in a major fund raising gala with the English Chamber Orchestra for the restoration of Salisbury Cathedral. The performance was recorded on video and CD. Later that year, she again performed for the royal couple when they visited Canada. She has also played for the Japanese Emperor and the Imperial Family. Since 1988, she has contributed to the Japanese magazine, *Un Carillon*. A collection of her essays was published as a book in Japanese and English. She has performed for Canadian Prime Ministers Jean Chrétien, Brian Mulroney, and Pierre Elliott Trudeau, as well as U.S. President Bill Clinton.

In 1987, she joined the artists' roster of RCA Victor Red Seal, becoming the first Canadian since pianist **Glenn Gould** to gain an exclusive contract with a major record label. Her over forty recordings have garnered numerous awards, including five JUNOs for Instrumental Artist of the Year, the 1988 Grand Prix du Disque, three Critics' Choice, Best Records of the Year from *Gramophone*, as well as *High Fidelity*, *Ovation*, and *CD Review*, and the 1988 Prix Anik Award for her contribution to the film sound track of *Two Men*.

In 1995, Harnoy received the prestigious Order of Canada, from the country's governor-general.

Ofra is married to Robert S. Cash, who acts as her manager. They reside near Toronto.

Careers: Small, Medium and Large

As has been the format throughout this book, the author has endeavored to highlight not only media-acclaimed soloists for each instrument, but to also present performers whose careers, while less publicized, are equally viable, as well as women who contribute their talent within the academia.

Since winning the All-Ukrainian Competition in 1981, cellist **NATALIA KHOMA** has won top prizes at the Budapest Pablo Casals (1985), Markneukirchen (Germany, 1987), Tchaikovsky (Moscow, 1990), and first prize at the 1990 Belgrade (Yugoslavia) International Cello Competitions.

A native of Lviv, Ukraine, she studied at the Lviv Central Music School, the Lviv Conservatory, and from 1982–90 at the Moscow Conservatory with professor Natalia Shakhovskaya. She has since distinguished herself as a recitalist and soloist with orchestras throughout the former USSR, as well as America, Canada, Germany, Norway, Belgium, Italy, Spain, Hungary, Yugoslavia and Israel.

She has performed as a soloist with the Berlin Radio Orchestra, Belgrade Philharmonic and Budapest Philharmonic Orchestras, and the Franz Liszt Chamber Orchestra.

Nina Kotova

Russian born **NINA KOTOVA** spent her youth studying cello, piano and composition, and gave her first performance at age seven. She was accepted by the cello faculty at the Moscow Conservatory at seven, while a student at the School for Specially Gifted Children. In 1985, at age fifteen, she won first prize at the Prague International Competition, and completed her BA the following year. Her father, Ivan Kotova, a virtuoso bassist, had been exposed to the West and was deemed a political risk. When he fell ill, he was refused medical treatment and died at age thirty-five. This caused Nina's career to evaporate. When her cello teacher learned she was to visit friends in Germany, he advised her to get out of Russia, and gave her a letter of introduction to a colleague at the Cologne Conservatory, where she was accepted, graduating with honors in 1990. She returned to a more liberated Russia, but realized her future lay elsewhere. In 1992, she was offered a scholarship at Yale, and made her way to America, having to leave her state-owned cello at the Moscow Conservatory. She was at Yale only a short time before her savings ran out. She moved to New York looking for work. Fortuitously, in a matter of months during 1993, she became a success as a fashion model. After several years of modeling for Chanel, Armani, magazines and fashion shows, never having lost her direction, she was able to buy her own instrument. She moved to London to join her mother and stepfather, Robert Poole, and made her way back to music giving her July 22, 1996 recital debut in Wigmore Hall. The program included a premiere of her own composition *Sketches from the Catwalk*. (A catwalk being the ramp upon which models parade at a fashion show.)

Kotova has performed with the English Symphony Orchestra, the St. Louis Symphony, and on Chicago Symphony's Ravinia's *Rising Stars* Series. She made her Carnegie Hall debut October 16, 1999, with the Moscow Chamber Orchestra, followed by a tour including Brazil and Japan. She also toured with the Prague Radio Symphony Orchestra in Japan, and gave recitals in Taiwan, Hong Kong, Malaysia, Singapore and Korea.

Her eponymous debut album *Nina Kotova*, on Philips Classics, includes romantic encores by Tchaikovsky, Rachmaninoff, Rimsky-Korsakov, Fauré, and *Sketches from the Catwalk*. Kotova has also written piano preludes, a piano trio, a cello concerto she premiered with The Women's Philharmonic (2000), and a cello sonata she first played in 2001 at the Cerritos Center for the Arts in Los Angeles. In 2003, she performed with the Boston Symphony. In August of that year, she co-founded and served as artist director of the Tuscan Sun Festival in Cortona, Italy, which celebrates not only music, but literature, art and film, bringing together artists, musicians and writers from all over the world.

Barrett Wissman, chairman of IMG Artists, one of the largest classical music agencies, holds an MM from Southern Methodist University, and a doctorate. He set up a fund to loan fine instruments to deserving string players. One night at a concert in London, he was swept off his feet by the cello soloist. On June 30, 2001, he married Nina Kotova on his ranch in Red Lodge, Montana.

She now plays on the 1696 Guarneri "Bear" cello.

DOROTHY LAWSON was born in Toronto, May 18, 1958, to a piano teacher mother and a music-loving father, who was head of that city's planning department. In the third grade, Dorothy was offered the chance to play cello. (It should be noted, in contrast to American schools' dwindling music programs, that in her 1,000 student high school, 500 played instruments, were in the choir, orchestra or band.) Dorothy graduated from the University of Toronto (BM, 1979), which at the time had the best music department in Canada. She also attended summer classes at the Salzburg Mozarteum, given by famed Italian cellist **Antonio Janigro** (1918–89). Her next major teacher, and most important one for her, was Andre Navarra at Vienna's Hochschule für Musik (1979-82). Next came Juilliard (MM, 1984), with **Leonard Rose** (1918–84), and a DMA in 1990, after study with **Harvey Shapiro**, formerly of the NBC Symphony under **Arturo Toscanini**.

Lawson has appeared with the Toronto Symphony and Orpheus Chamber Orchestra among others, as well as specializing in chamber music. She is a founding member of the Andreas Trio, Lotus Trio, Rosetti Quartet, and cellist of the groundbreaking *Ethel* (formerly known as Hazardous Materials), a quartet which showcases the idiosyncratic styles of New York composers.

Her first solo CD (1999) contains the North American premiere of the Borodin Cello Sonata, unearthed by the late Russian violinist-musicologist Mikhail Goldstein (1927–89), who sent it to pianist **Nadia Reisenberg** in 1981. Very ill at the time, she stashed it into a filing cabinet, not to be rediscovered until after her death by her son, broadcaster-musicologist **Robert Sherman**. In 1994, Dorothy married performing arts and Carnegie Hall house photographer **Steve J. Sherman,** son of Robert, and thus "inherited" this treasure.

In January 1996, she toured Lithuania with the American Symphony to perform the Berthold Goldschmidt Concerto, as a preview for its Lincoln Center performance by **Yo-Yo Ma**. In March 1996, she played *L'Olmeneta*, the **Alessandro Ghedini** (1892–1965) concerto for two cellos, with **Carter Brey** at the Metropolitan Museum of Art.

On May 8, 1998, Dorothy and Steve had a baby girl, Fiona, a uniquely awaited event. (See Theremin: Clara Rockmore.) On May 30, 2002—this family likes May birthdays—son Jesse Sherman arrived!

WINIFRED MAYES (née Schaefer) was the first woman string player in the Boston Symphony. The older sister of piccolo player **Lois Schaefer**, she was born August 23, 1919, in Prescott, Washington. At age ten, she began study with a cellist who made regular trips from Seattle to the then small town of Yakima. In 1938, after high school, she auditioned and was accepted at Curtis. In her fourth year there she married cellist **Arthur Winograd**, who later became one of the founders of the Juilliard String Quartet. They had a son, Nicholas, a research chemist on the faculty of Pennsylvania State University. The marriage lasted nine years, and was followed by a position as principal cello in the Fort Wayne (Indiana) Philharmonic (1949–56).

When a cello opening occurred in Boston in 1956, Winifred won the audition. In 1962, she married principal cellist Sam Mayes. They remained in the orchestra until 1964, leaving at the same time as maestro **Charles Munch** (1891–1968). That year **Eugene Ormandy** offered the couple positions in the Philadelphia Orchestra, Sam as principal and Winifred as section player. In 1974 Sam, tired of the routine of orchestral playing, accepted a professorship at the University of Michigan. After three years of a long distance marriage, Winifred resigned her post and joined her husband in Ann Arbor (1977), quickly finding a teaching post in a local college. In 1985, they retired to Mesa, Arizona, until Sam's death in 1990. In 1995, the two sisters moved to Gilbert, Arizona, into a house specifically designed for them.

HAI-YE NI, born in Shanghai, in 1972, began cello studies with her mother, then went on to the Shanghai Conservatory of Music. She continued her musical education with **Irene Sharp** at the San Francisco Conservatory of Music, with Joel Krosnick at Juilliard, and with **William Pleeth**. She came into prominence via her New York debut at Alice Tully Hall in 1991, the result of capturing first prize at the Naumberg International Cello Competition—the youngest recipient of this distinguished award. In 1996, she was the unanimous choice for first prize in the International Paulo Cello Competition in Finland. Her performance with the Chicago Symphony, under the baton of **Christoph Eschenbach**, was a highlight of 1997, a year which also included winning second prize in the International Rostropovich Competition in France, as well as a fourteen-city tour of the U.S., introducing Bright Sheng's new cello concerto *Two Poems*, for which she was recommended by Yo-Yo Ma. This was aired on *CBS Sunday Morning*. During the 1998–99 season, she performed as a member of the Lincoln Center Chamber Music Society II. She also played in recital in London, at Harvard and at the Freer Gallery/Smithsonian Institute in Washington, DC, with Cho-Liang Lin. The 1999–2000 season saw her appointment as associate principal cellist for the New York Philharmonic. In 2001, she made her Kennedy Center debut, and received the coveted Avery Fisher Career Grant.

Ni's engagements have included the Vienna Chamber Orchestra, San Francisco, Vancouver, Houston, and Odense (Denmark) Symphonies; Marlboro, and international cello festivals in Brazil, Casals (Prades, France), as well as Kuhmo and Naantali (Finland). She has had return engagements with the Ravinia Festival, Finnish Radio Symphony, Spoleto (Italy), Santa Fe Chamber Music Festival, Hong Kong Philharmonic, Singapore Symphony, Korsholm (Finland), and the Peninsula Festival. She has performed with such artists as **Jean-Yves Thibaudet**, **Joshua Bell**, Emanuel Pahud, Leonidas Kavakos, Barry Douglas, **Ida Kavafian**, **Pinchas Zukerman**, **David Shifrin** and **Bobby McFerrin**.

Her performances have been broadcast throughout the U.S. on NPR. She was featured on the ABC television show *20/20* and the PBS documentary of the Tchaikovsky International Cello Competition in Moscow. She was the cover story in the May/June 1997 issue of *Strings* magazine and is featured along with Yo-Yo Ma in the book *Twenty-first Century Cellists*. Her first solo disc, on Naxos, was chosen "CD of the Week" by *Classic FM*, London.

Hai-Ye's awards include the 1995 SONY ES Career Award, and the best performance prize at the 1994 International Tchaikovsky competition in Moscow.

SHARON ROBINSON, born December 2, 1949, in Houston, Texas, comes from a musical family—her mother was a violinist, her father a bass player, and all her siblings are string players. She gave her first concert at age seven and made her orchestral debut at fourteen with the

Sharon Robinson

Houston Symphony. A Peabody graduate, she won the Avery Fisher Recital, Leventritt Foundation, and 1984 Gregor Piatigorsky Memorial Awards. As a soloist, she has enjoyed engagements with the Los Angeles Philharmonic, London, San Francisco, Houston, Pittsburgh, Dallas and other U.S. symphony orchestras, as well as tours and festivals in Europe, Australia, New Zealand and Japan. In 1977, with her husband, violinist **Jaime Laredo,** and pianist **Joseph Kalichstein,** they debuted as the **Kalischstein-Laredo-Robinson Trio** at the White House for President Carter's inauguration (1978). Since then, the trio has performed classic works and new repertoire around the world. Championing music by women, the trio's performances of **Rebecca Clarke**'s Piano Trio have been heard all over the world and in Carnegie Hall. Their commissions of **Ellen Zwillich**'s Double and Triple Concertos are on a Koch CD. 2003 featured a commission of a cello/piano work by **Katherine Hoover** for the Tucson Music Festival, and the world premiere of **Joan Tower**'s Piano Trio.

Performances in collaboration with **Isaac Stern, Yo-Yo Ma, Pinchas Zukerman, Emanuel Ax** and **Itzhak Perlman** have given Robinson distinction as a unique chamber musician. Her full performance schedule is due to the ability to move from solo, chamber, and orchestral repertoires. Close relationships with contemporary composers Ellen Zwilich, Ned Rorem, Leon Kirchner, and David Ott have led to numerous commissions for pieces of solo, duo and trio formats.

Sharon's solo recordings are on Vox, the Laredo/Robinson Duo on Arabesque, and the Trio on Arabesque and Chandos.

The Kalichstein-Laredo-Robinson Trio was selected as "Ensemble of the Year" by 2002 *Musical America*. 2005 marked the start of their thirtieth anniversary celebrations, which included performances of Beethoven cycles in the U.S. and Europe, a Carnegie Hall celebration, and the complete Brahms Trios at their spiritual birthplace, the Kaufmann Concert Hall of New York's 92nd St Y.

Sharon personally celebrated 2005 in August, beginning as a tenured professor of cello at Indiana University, Bloomington.

Shauna Rolston

SHAUNA ROLSTON was born in Edmonton, Alberta (Canada), January 31, 1967. Her parents, pianist Isobel Moore and violinist Thomas Rolston, were on the faculty of the University of Alberta. As professional musicians and prominent music educators, they started Shauna on cello when she was two. Her father had an instrument maker create a one-eighth size cello. The child's first instruction was with cellist Claude Kenneson, a trio member with her parents. Kenneson is the author of *Musical Prodigies: Perilous Journeys, Remarkable Lives* (Amadeus Press, 1999), an insight into the lives of forty-four musical prodigies, beginning with an intimate portrait of Shauna. At four, she began playing chamber music with her parents. They limited her public appearances and never marketed her as a prodigy. (Shauna is able to declare, "I never felt like a wind-up toy, I was, rather, a young person who liked to play music.")

By age eleven, she was playing on a full size cello, an 1824 French Chanot, which is still her instrument. The family moved to Banff when Shauna was twelve, her father having been appointed director of music and her mother assistant director at the Banff Arts Centre. Shauna attended the Banff Community High School, and while she had no regular music lessons, she played for famous artists such as Janos Starker, **Zara Nelsova** (1918–2002), and Aldo Parisot, who came to Banff to teach master classes. She also performed chamber music with renowned pianist **Menachem Pressler.** Famed cellist **Leonard Rose** heard her play when she was thirteen and invited her to study with him at Juilliard, but she was more attracted to the mountains of Banff than the canyons of New York. At fifteen, she was the youngest member, along with violin prodigy **Joshua Bell,** to attend the Geneva Conservatory, where she studied with **Pierre Fournier,** and then at the Britten-Pears School in Aldeburgh (Scotland), with the world's top cello pedagogues and **William Pleeth,** teacher of Jaqueline DuPré. At sixteen, she made her debut at New York's Town Hall, with her mother at the piano. With no immediate plans, having graduated from high school, and with so much excellent private instruction in all aspects of music, she did not feel compelled to go to a conservatory, so she spent the next two years concertizing. Then, wanting to study further with Aldo Parisot, she entered Yale where he was the cello professor, choosing to major in art history "for fun" while performing and studying. She stayed on as Parisot's teaching assistant after completing her BA, and received an MM (1992).

Having been named "Young Artist to Watch" by *Musical America* (1986), Rolston is considered the finest cellist Canada has thus far produced. She plays with intensity, although not nearly with the abandon of **Jacqueline du Pré**, with whom she is often compared. Her pristine technique vies with her musicality. Her large orchestral repertoire is enhanced by her commissioning an impressive number of new works. In the 1997–98 season, she premiered five concertos written for her, including works by fellow Canadians **Kelly-Marie Murphy** and **Heather Schmidt**. Other works have come from **Augusta Read Thomas** and **Karen Tanaka**. Two other Canadians, who introduced her to theory and analysis of music, and wrote for her are the late **Jean Coulthard** (1908–2000) and **Violet Archer** (1913–2000), her mentors since she was a toddler.

In chamber music she has performed and recorded with many artists and ensembles, including Menahem Pressler, the Gallois Quintet, founded by French flutist Patrick Gallois (to whom she was briefly married in 2000), and three European colleagues, Pavel Vernikov (violin), Pierre-Henri Xuereb (viola), Fabrice Pierre (harp) and Shauna on cello. With pianist/composer **Heather Schmidt**, Rolston has presented duo recitals at the Winnipeg New Music Festival (2002), in Finland and Iceland (2003), a tour of the Maritime Provinces (2004) and a North American tour (2005). Their collaboration led to the film *Synchronicity* for BRAVO.

Notwithstanding concert and recital appearances, in 1994 Rolston joined the music faculty of the University of Toronto where she is a professor and co-head of the string department. She is also a visiting artist for the music and sound programs at the Banff Center.

Internationally known **ELEONORE SCHOENFELD** is a professor of cello at the Thornton School of Music at USC. Her dancing career began at age two in her native Austria (now a part of Slovenia), and by eleven she was in the Berlin State Opera where she experienced great music. She studied piano and violin, then began cello with Karl Niedermeyer, a student of Hugo Becker. She progressed so quickly she entered Berlin's Hochschule für Musik at fourteen—the traditional age being eighteen. She studied with Adolph Steiner, receiving an artist diploma. Besides recitals and soloing with leading philharmonic and radio orchestras, she played on four continents as a duo with her concert violinist sister, Alice. The family came to Los Angeles in 1952. In 1959, she and Alice were invited to join the USC faculty, which at the time numbered world class artists Gregor Piatigorsky (cello) and Jascha Heifetz (violin) among its members.

A renowned pedagogue, Schoenfeld has presented master classes worldwide at such national and international music festivals as Schleswig-Holstein (Germany), Centre d'Arts Orford (Canada), Croatian String Teachers Association, Music Academy of the West (Santa Barbara, California), Bowdoin and Interlochen. She is also a teacher at the R.D. Colburn School in Los Angeles, and the Arts Academy in Idyllwild, California.

Her students have been top prize winners in prestigious competitions like the Tchaikovsky, Casals, European Broadcasting Union, Geneva, South Africa, Antonio Janigro, National American String Teachers' Association, Presidential Scholars, Coleman Chamber Music, Concert Artist Guild and Young Musicians Foundation, and have performed as soloists with major orchestras including the New York Philharmonic, Chicago Symphony, Los Angeles Philharmonic, Los Angeles Chamber Orchestra, Georgian Chamber Orchestra, Moscow Radio Orchestra and Bamberger Symphony under eminent conductors Zubin Mehta and Esa-Pekka Salonen among others. Many pursue successful solo and chamber music careers and are members of major orchestras and college faculties throughout the world.

Director of the International Gregor Piatigorsky Seminar for Cellists at USC since 1979, this important opportunity brings together distinguished artists and teachers and twelve chosen gifted young cellists to study and perform a varied repertoire and discuss artistic, technical and professional issues.

Schoenfeld has made numerous solo and chamber music recordings for major European radio stations, plus Everest and Orion Master labels. She has served as chairperson and juror in national and international solo and chamber music competitions, including ARD (Munich), Leonard Rose (U.S.), Antonio Janigro (Croatia), Caltanissetta (Italy), Karl Klingler (Germany) and Piatigorsky (New York). July 2003 found her at the fifth Adam International Cello Festival & Competition in Christchurch, New Zealand. In June 2005, she was at the Encore Music Festival sponsored by the Cleveland Institute of Music.

Her honors include the USC Ramo Music Faculty Award (1990), the Eva Janzer Memorial Award "Grande Dame du Violincelle" from Indiana University (1993), and ASTA National Distinguished Service Award (1996). In Spring 2005, Eleonore was named to the extremely prestigious Piatigorsky Chair in Cello at Thornton.

Concurrently, with their busy teaching careers, both sisters continue their performances. Summers usually find them on concert stages in Europe.

IRENE SHARP has been acclaimed internationally for her teaching. She has given master classes for the American String Teachers Association (ASTA), European String Teachers Association, Australian String Teachers Association, and the Suzuki Association of America. Although based in San Francisco, she has worked with students in New York, London, Salzburg, Hamburg, Sydney, Tokyo, and Taipei. Currently on the faculty of the Mannes College of Music, where she conducted the Irene Sharp Cello Seminar, she has also served on the faculty of the Meadowmount School for Strings, Bowdoin (Maine) Summer Music Festival, and Indiana University's String Academy. She is artistic director of California Summer Music, a festival for young string players, pianists, and composers ages twelve to twenty-three, held at Pebble Beach, California. She has been an invited speaker at the national meetings of the Music Teachers' National Association (MTNA), and the Music Educators' National Conference, and has given numerous teacher workshops worldwide. In 1992, she received an award for her teaching from the ASTA. She collaborated with the late **Margaret Rowell**, and performed in Pablo Casals' master class in Berkeley, California.

TANIA SIMONCELLI, born in Philadelphia, began playing piano at age six and cello at ten. She completed a BA in biology with a minor in music performance from Cornell (1993), where she studied with John Hsu. She was principal cellist of both the University Symphony and Chamber Orchestra. Moving to California in 1996, she studied with **Bonnie Hampton**, Millie Rosner, and **Irene Sharp**. While completing her MS in energy and resources, she was principal cellist of the UC Berkeley Symphony. In 1997, she was a winner of both the Mu Phi Epsilon Young Artist Competition and the UC Berkeley Concerto Competition.

An active orchestral and chamber music performer, recording artist and teacher in the San Francisco Bay Area, Tania frequently performs with the Sacramento Philharmonic, Monterey County and Berkeley Symphonies, and Festival Opera. She is the acting artistic director and teacher for the Martin Luther King Cello Program in Sacramento, a non-profit organization which provides group and private cello lessons to elementary school children. She performs and records regularly with the Kevin Keller Trio chamber group, and is a first call studio musician for the Stillwater Sound Recording Studio in San Francisco, where she has been featured on several CDs from modern, classical, to jazz and Celtic. (She even takes on fun gigs like cruise ships, which is where the author and her husband met her against a backdrop of Alaskan glaciers.)

Four Strings Are Not Enough!

FRANCES-MARIE UITTI, composer/performer, pioneered a revolutionary dimension to the cello by transforming it into a polyphonic instrument capable of sustained two, three, and four-part chords, and intricate multi-voiced writing. Using two bows in one hand, this invention permits contemporaneous cross accents, multiple timbres, contrasting four-voiced dynamics, simultaneous legato/articulated playing that was unattainable in her previous work with a curved bow. *Ricercar* (1987) played on a colo cello gives the sensation of an entire string quartet.

Composers of what came to be called "new" music in the 20th century used this technique in works dedicated to Uitti, among them Louis Andriessen, John Cage, Elliott Carter, Brian Ferneyhough, Luigi Nono, **Pauline Oliveros** and Iannis Xenakis.

Uitti has made several recordings and concertizes from New York City to Mongolia, as well as appearing at world festivals.

CHRISTINE WALEWSKA (or Walevska) was born in 1945, in Los Angeles, into a musical family. Her mother played the violin, and her father was an antique violin dealer. She began her first cello lessons at age eight on a small Bernadel with her father. By thirteen, she was studying with one of the world's greatest, **Gregor Piatigorsky**, and performed the Saint-Saëns Concerto with the National Symphony of Washington, DC. At sixteen, she joined Maurice Marechal's class at the Paris Conservatoire, where she became the first American to win first prize in both cello and chamber music. (Marechal's dictum was to surrender oneself to the music and play as intuition prompted.) Two years later, Walewska began a successful global career as a concert artist. In the 1970s, she recorded the standard European cello concerto literature on the Philips label, including *the first recording* of the Saint-Saëns D minor Concerto. She played the Brahms Double Concerto with famed violinist **Henryk Szeryng**. At eighteen, she toured South America and fell in love with Argentina. She married and settled in Buenos Aires, where she performed at the Téatro Colón, as well as all over South America. She was the first American artist to perform in Cuba under the Castro regime.

At the Prague Spring Festival in 1975, in both solo recital and with orchestra, critics compared her to **Emanuel Feuermann** and called her Piatigorsky's successor.

She also studied with Bolognini, whom both Feuermann and Casals called the world's greatest cellist. He composed a suite of six pieces, *Serenata del Gaucho*, in which the cello is played like a flamenco guitar, and dedicated it to Walewska on the condition that she never give the music to anyone else. Despite requests from Piatigorsky and others, she has honored the composer's wishes and regularly performs the piece as a breathtaking encore.

After living in Argentina for twelve years, in the '90s Christine and her husband moved to New York, where she still performs from time to time. Still at the height of her artistic powers in 1998, she gave a recital for the New York Cello Society.

A Cello - the Means to a Miraculous Survival

Anita Lasker-Wallfisch

ANITA LASKER-WALLFISCH arrived in the world July 17, 1925, in Breslau (now Wroclaw, Poland). One of three daughters born to her lawyer father and violinist mother, her sister Marianne (1921–52) played piano and Renate (*b* 1924) violin. Anita began cello as a child, and at thirteen was sent to Berlin for advanced studies. With the mounting discrimination against Jews, and the outbreak of WWII, September 3, 1939, she returned home and gave her first public appearance in 1941. In April 1942, her parents were deported to a concentration camp never to be seen or heard of again. Marianne had already escaped to England some years before. Now Anita and Renate were sent to an orphanage. They worked in a paper factory, where they helped forge papers for POWs. This, and their link with the French Resistance, caused their arrest in 1942. After months in filthy prisons where they were separated, Anita was transported to Auschwitz-Birkenau in late 1943. Here, her life was saved by becoming the only cellist in the camp orchestra of **Alma Rosé**. During this time, miraculously, Renate arrived, and out of the thousands of doomed souls was reunited with her sister. She became an orchestra messenger, which saved *her* life. Following Alma's death in April 1944, the orchestra became a shadow of its former self. As the Nazis tried to erase the evidence of their crimes before the oncoming Allied armies, stepping up the gassings, the sisters were again spared and transferred to Bergen-Belsen in October. Getting there involved one the "death marches" survived only by a small percentage. After the liberation of Belsen in April 1945, the girls, with no sponsors, remained there working for the British Army until December, when they managed to get to Brussels. Anita took up her lessons and played in the Brussels University Orchestra before she and Renate finally reached London in March 1946. There, Anita studied with William Pleeth, and in 1948 became a founding member of the English Chamber Orchestra, with whom she played for the next fifty years. She and her husband, pianist/musicologist Peter Wallfisch (1924–93), whom she married on January 19, 1952, were cele-brated, well-known figures on the British music scene. This legacy is now carried on by their cellist son, Raphael, his wife, Australian violinist **Elizabeth Wallfisch**, and their two sons. Benjamin, born in 1982, is a pianist, com-poser, and conductor who, in 1997, formed the Lasker Ensemble, conducts the University of Manchester Sinfonietta and has already had a work performed by the Hallé Orchestra (1999). Simon, who began cello at age five, is a singer and jazz pianist studying at the Guildhall School of Music and Drama. Anita also has a daughter Maya, whose children, Johanna and Abraham-Peter, as of 2005, were still in school.

Although no longer concertizing, this great lady lectures all over Europe so that the past—as so dramatically illustrated in her book, *Inherit the Truth: 1939–1945*, her memoir of the Holocaust and her own miraculous sur-vival—will not be forgotten by future generations.

Wendy Warner

WENDY WARNER began cello lessons at age six. She studied with the renowned **Mstislav Rostropovich**, and is a graduate of Curtis. In 1990, she won first prize in the Fourth International Rostropovich Competition in Paris. She was awarded a prestigious Avery Fisher Career grant. After her debut with the National Symphony (Washington, DC), October 1990, she soloed with them on a North American tour the following year. She has performed recitals and appeared as soloist with orchestras throughout the world, including a 1991 European tour with the Bamberg Symphony and an appearance with violinist **Anne-Sophie Mutter** in Paris. In 1993, she made her Carnegie Hall debut. 1995 saw the release of her recording of the Grieg and Rachmaninoff sonatas on Erato. In 1996, she toured Japan as soloist with NHK and the Japan Philharmonic, made appearances with the Dallas Symphony, and in New York's *Mostly Mozart* Music Festival at Avery Fischer Hall. Summer 1998 found her at the Grand Teton Music Festival in a performance of the Dvořák cello concerto with **Eiji Oue**. Her debut with the Montreal Symphony playing the Haydn C Major Concerto was January 1999. She also appeared with the Moscow Virtuosi, and Vladimir Spivakov in Toronto, Chicago and New York's Carnegie Hall. The same season brought her recital debut in Munich, followed by recitals and orchestral solo performances in Paris and in Los Angeles, as well as her debut with the European Soloists of Luxembourg at Frankfurt's Alte Oper (Old Opera), her solo debut with the Detroit Symphony (with Leslie Dunner), and performances with the Orchestre National Bordeaux Aquitaine (France).

Continuing with her dedication to America's youth in music, March 1999 marked a special concert at Boston's Symphony Hall with the Greater Boston Youth Symphony under the baton of David Commanday. The same year, her CDs were released with works for cello by Hindemith on Bridge Records and the Cecille label, and duos for cello and violin with **Rachel Barton**. 2000 found Warner all over North America concertizing with the Orchestre Symphonique de Québec, Calgary Philharmonic, Colorado Orchestra, and Hartford, Nashville, Delaware and Omaha Symphonies.

Subsequent seasons have expanded her career to appearances with the Chicago, Boston and San Francisco Symphonies, and Minnesota and Philadelphia Orchestras. In Europe and around the world, she has performed with the London Symphony (Barbican Center), Berlin Symphony (Philharmonie Hall), Hong Kong Philharmonic, French Radio Philharmonic Orchestra (Salle Pleyel, Paris), Iceland Symphony (Reykjavik), and L'Orchestre du Capitole de Toulouse (France). A performance of the Barber Concerto with the Royal Scottish National Orchestra under **Marin Alsop** and was recorded for Naxos.

Other highlights of Warner's international career have been her debut with the St. Petersburg Philharmonic under Yuri Falik, playing the Vivaldi Double Concerto with **Mstislav Rostropovich** in Rheims (France), and being part of the maestro's grand seventieth birthday celebration concert in Kronberg (Germany).

The 2003–2004 season saw performances with Gidon Kremer at New York's Carnegie Hall and Los Angeles' Walt Disney Hall, as well as with orchestras across the country. Her 2004–2005 season included a tour with the St. Paul Chamber Orchestra in Minnesota, and concerts with the Utah Symphony under Keith Lockhart.

A Nova in the Galaxy

Alisa Weilerstein

ALISA WEILERSTEIN, born in Cleveland, Ohio, April, 14, 1982, to professional musician parents, began her studies at four and a half, performed a public concert six months later, and made her Cleveland Orchestra debut at thirteen. By fifteen, she had already appeared at Japan's Suntory Hall and the Louvre in Paris. A graduate of the Young Artist Program at the Cleveland Institute, she went to Columbia University in 2000, the year she won the coveted Avery Fisher Career Grant, which she used for her four years at Columbia. In the summer, she appeared at the Blossom (Cleveland), Caramoor (New York), Santa Fe (New Mexico) and Verbier (Vevey, Switzerland) Festivals. In 2001, she was selected for membership in Lincoln Center's *Chamber Music Society II*, the young artist programs at Chicago Symphony's Ravinia *Rising Stars* recital series, and ECHO. The latter, European Concert Hall Organization, involves a tour of seven celebrated concert venues in Europe: Symphony Hall in Birmingham (England), Wigmore Hall (London), Athens Concert Hall (Greece), Cologne Philharmonic, (Germany), Konzerthaus (Vienna), Palais des Beaux Arts (Brussels) and the Concertgebouw (Amsterdam). She also debuted at Carnegie's Weill Recital Hall (New York), and performed with the orchestras of Baltimore, Florida, Hartford, Jacksonville, and New York Chamber and Colorado Symphonies. While in Europe, she soloed with the Barcelona Symphony. 2001–02 brought standing ovations for concerts with the Symphonies of San Francisco, National, Detroit, Houston, Kansas City, and Indianapolis; a national tour with the Chamber Music Society of Lincoln Center; and acclaimed concerts with the Melbourne and Adelaide (Australia) Symphonies in August. Among highlights of 2002–03 were raves for her performance of the *Elgar Cello Concerto* with the Colorado Symphony under **Marin Alsop** at the Vail Valley Music Festival, and the Saint-Saëns *Cello Concerto No.1* in two Central Park concerts in August with the New York Philharmonic under **Asher Fisch**, Israeli conductor of the new Tel Aviv Opera. One night's audience numbered 80,000. The 2003–2004 season included recital appearances in Atlanta (Spivey Hall), Baltimore (Shriver Hall), Cleveland (Museum of Art), San Francisco (Florence Gould Theater) and Portland (Oregon).

Alisa's recitals with her mother, Vivian Hornik, on piano, are taking the pair all over the globe. She also plays regularly with both parents—her father, Donald, is a long-time first violinist of the Cleveland Quartet—as the Weilerstein Trio.

Her first was CD was released (EMI Classics Debut series) when she was sixteen. The critics compared her to her heroine, **Jacqueline du Pré**. She despises the word "prodigy," but settles for "precocious." With tales of burnouts and breakdowns, the challenge was getting through the teenage years intact. Weilerstein communicates her joy of playing to each audience. "I'd love them to go away feeling . . . that they have touched beauty that is untouchable in any other way . . . "

Four of a Kind!

Cello

A quartet of cellists! All women, all glamorous! This unique entity was created in 1988 and simply named CELLO. Defying the traditional image of chamber music, they perform varied programs ranging from classical to jazz to Beatles' songs to original compositions, such as Peter Schickele's *Queen Anne's Lace Dance Suite for Four Cellos*. Their New York debut was at Weill Recital Hall in 1991. They have played many venues in the area, including Lincoln Center as part of the Great Performers series, the Philadelphia Museum of Art, and Kennedy Center, colleges throughout the country, and have been featured on NPR. In 1995, they were invited by the Rencontres Internationales d'Ensembles de Violoncelles to Beauvais, France, for a series of European debut performances. They returned to Beauvais to open the 2001 festival. In 2002, CELLO made a ten-concert tour of Taiwan, with an appearance at the National Theater in Taipei. They have also toured Europe. Their first CD (Pro-Arte, 1990) was entitled CELLO. The second, *Subliminal Blues and Greens*, came in 1996 (d'Note Classics).

In 2005, composer Andy Waggoner wrote a concerto for CELLO entitled *Stretched on the Beauty*.

Founding members of the Quartet were:

Caryl Paisner received her BM and MM from Yale, and MBA from Columbia (1993). She has performed and recorded with the Ron Carter Nonet and toured Japan with the American Symphony. Her Broadway orchestra show career includes *Phantom of the Opera, Miss Saigon, Kiss of the Spiderwoman* and *Beauty and the Beast*. Her recordings are on Angel, Blue Note, Koch, Elektra and Delos. She is married to artist Mikel Glass.

Maria Kitsopoulos made her Alice Tully Hall debut in 1987, and has appeared as soloist with the Phoenix Symphony and at the Graz (Austria) Festival. She is on the faculty of the Juilliard Advancement Program, and performs regularly with the Orpheus Chamber Orchestra, Continuum Ensemble, and Composers' Guild in New York City. She has played in the Broadway orchestras of *Tommy* and *The Secret Garden*, among others. She was part of CELLO from 1990–97. In 1996, she won the audition which placed her in the New York Philharmonic cello section.

Laura Koehl received her BM and MM from Juilliard. She has performed at Avery Fisher Hall with Quartet Tedesca as part of the Lincoln Center 1991 Mozart Bicentennial celebration. In 1992, she received a fellowship to the Aspen Music Festival as a member of the Aspen Contemporary Ensemble. She has also performed with the Jupiter Symphony. In 1995 she wed Tom Bontrager and now uses her married name.

Maureen McDermott, who graduated with honors from the Manhattan School of Music, made her New York debut in 1987 at Carnegie Recital Hall. Since then she has appeared at Carnegie Hall, the 92nd St. Y, Lincoln Center, Kennedy Center, concertized in Texas, Minnesota and California and participated in festivals at Ravinia, Newport, Bravo! Colorado, and Les Recontres International d'Ensembles de Violoncelles in France. She also plays with her sisters, Anne Marie (piano), and Kerry (violin), as the **McDermott Trio**, and records on Pro-Arte, Angel, Sony and BMG. She was on the faculty of the Third Street Settlement School. Married to Dan Crisan, their first son, Liam Thomas, was born October 23, 2000. Maureen resigned from CELLO in the Spring of 2005, in expectation of their second son in August 2005.

As of June 2005, the quartet was made up of **Julie Albers**, **Laura Bontrager** and **Caroline Stinson**.

Raised in Longmont, Colorado, **Julie Albers** began violin studies at two with her mother, switching to the cello at four. She moved to Cleveland during her junior year in high school to pursue studies through the Young Artist Program at the Cleveland Institute of Music. Her 1998 debut, at twenty-three, was with the Cleveland Orchestra, performing Dvořák's Cello Concerto. Her international career was launched the following season with concerts in Germany, France and New Zealand. Winner of numerous competitions, including the Johansen International String Competition (Washington, DC), Munich's International der ARD, and the Wilhelm Weichsler Prize of Osnabrück in 2001, in 2003 she won the Grand Prize of $25,000 (U.S.) at South Korea's Gyeongnam International Music Competition. Her current season includes return engagements with the Long Island Philharmonic, and Syracuse and Indianapolis Symphonies.

A native of Edmonton, Alberta, **Caroline Stinson** studied at Interlochen, the Cleveland Institute, and Cologne (Germany) Hochschule für Musik. As cellist of the Cassatt String Quartet from 2000–03, she was in residence at Syracuse University, the University of Pennsylvania, and SUNY Buffalo. She has performed with Lynn Harrell, Pinchas Zukerman, the Ying Quartet, and collaborated with composer **Joan Tower**. Her recordings are on Naxos, Koch Classics International, Albany and New World Records. Her performances have been broadcast on Radio France, CBC Radio, Canada, and WNYC and WQXR in New York. Stinson is on faculty with the New York Youth Symphony Chamber Music Program, and at Syracuse University, for which she coordinated a chamber music program in Strasbourg, France, for several years in conjunction with the Conservatoire Nationale de Région de Strasbourg.

CELLO leads a growing number of unusual ensembles who are pioneering the next wave of chamber music to make this genre accessible and fun!

An Unknown Legend Across the Atlantic

As the author of this tome, after a decade of research, I should cease to be amazed at discovering women whose names have been covered with the dust of centuries and neglect, but the following cellist, who passed away just a little over fifty years ago, and whose career for decades rivaled, paralleled and was personally *entwined* with the ubiquitous **Pablo Casals** (1876–1973) was a real find! Thanks to the website CelloHeaven which has a sub-category of "Women Cellists of the Past," plus information gleaned from an article by professor of humanities, Anita Mercier, PhD, in the online Juilliard Journal, XVII, No 6., March 2002, entitled "Queen of Cellists," who researched Portuguese authors and visited sources in Lisbon, we have a portrait of an unforgettable musician who *has been* forgotten—but is now being returned to her rightful place in posterity!

Guilhermina Suggia

GUILHERMINA Xavier de Menim SUGGIA was born in Porto, Portugal, June 27, 1885. She was one of the first women to have a professional career as a cellist at a time when this instrument was *definitely not* considered appropriate for young ladies. Her father, Augusto Jorge de Menim Suggia, a native of Lisbon, was of Spanish and Italian descent. A professional cellist, he had served on the faculty of the Lisbon Conservatory before taking a teaching position in Porto in the early 1880s. He started his daughter on her life's vocation when she was five. The benefits of playing with an endpin—a metal, rubber-tipped rod screwed into the bottom of the instrument and making contact with the floor—was a new innovation gaining importance for *all* cellists, but particularly for women, in that it permitted a more feminine posture, even a "side saddle" position. Augusto used an endpin, so this was included on the half-size cello he ordered from Paris.

Guilhermina's sister, Virginia, three years older, studied piano. The musical progress of both girls was so rapid that between 1892 and 1895 joint recitals of *las prodigiosas* made them celebrities in local salons. These brought recognition for Augusto, enhancing his reputation as a music teacher. His vision for his daughters' futures was most farsighted for the times and social strictures on women. The foundations for Guilhermina's development and ultimate success were laid by him. Augusto not only identified her talent, but would continue to support her ambitions all his life. By 1904, when she began to tour regularly in Europe, her father managed everything necessary for the launching of her career. Meanwhile, Porto violinist/conductor **Bernardo Valentim Moreira de Sá** (1853–1924) had created the Orpheon Portuense in 1882. Originally intended as a venue for choral works, the hall came to feature chamber music and symphony concerts. In its thirty years of existence it resounded with music of past masters, and contemporaries who were to become the masters of the next generation: Borodin, Debussy, Dvořák, Franck, d'Indy, Rachmaninoff, Saint-Saëns and Tchaikovsky. (Ravel's music was heard for the first time in Portugal when he was invited to the Orpheon in 1928 for a concert devoted entirely to his works.) Visiting artists of the time are now also legends of the past, such as pianists Harold Bauer, Ferrucio Busoni, Alfred Cortot, and Artur Schnabel; violinists Fritz Kreisler, Jacques Thibaud, Eugène Ysaÿe, composer/violinist Georges Enesco; and harpsichordist, **Wanda Landowska**.

In 1898, twenty-two-year-old **Pablo Casals** appeared on the scene, giving highly popular weekly solo recitals in Porto. When Augusto brought Guilhermina for an audition, the former prodigy immediately recognized the thirteen-year-old's potential, and gave her weekly lessons until he returned to Barcelona at the end of the summer. By this time, Guilhermina was already performing professionally as a soloist in concert and chamber groups, and as first cellist in the Orpheon orchestra, directed by Moreira de Sá.

Around 1901, Guilhermina and Virginia were invited to play at the Palácio das Necessidades in Lisbon for King Carlos, Queen Amelia, and members of the royal family. Afterwards, the young cellist was granted a government scholarship to study in Leipzig for three years, beginning in 1902. Her teacher, **Julius Klengel**, had a roster of the world's greatest cellists, now also legends. Among them: Emanuel Feuermann, Alfred Wallenstein, Joseph Schuster, Gregor Piatigorsky and William Pleeth—the latter with his own Milky Way of students, including **Jacqueline DuPré**.

On February 26, 1903, the eighteen-year-old Guilhermina debuted with the Gewandhaus Orchestra conducted by **Arthur Nikisch**, playing the challenging Robert Volkmann concerto. Between 1903–06, she journeyed regularly from Porto to perform in the music centers of Germany: Leipzig, Dresden, Frankfurt, Bayreuth, Berlin and Hamburg. She was also heard in Budapest, Brussels, Stockholm and London. In Prague, she met Dvořák's daughter, who told her that she was interpreting her father's music exactly as he would have wished.

After completing her studies at Leipzig Conservatory, the Suggia sisters toured Europe together and separately. Ultimately, Virginia chose love over music, marrying Parisian editor/bookseller Leon Pinchon, and abandoning her career, while Guilhermina spent her life committed to hers.

Since she had been independent, unconventional, and focused on her goals from an early age, Guilhermina was to have lovers, but refused commitments that detracted from her chosen path. One engagement netted her a Stradivarius. She broke the engagement, but kept the cello. Only when she reached forty-two would she agree to marry, but had no children.

They Meet Again - A Dynamic Combination!

In 1906, she landed in Paris where, besides performing, she did some teaching and once again met Casals. The next seven years were one of the most significant periods of her life. While no verification of a marriage exists, from 1908–13 concert programs listed her as "Guilhermina Suggia-Casals" or "Guilhermina Casals." If Pablo's touring schedule separated them for more than a few days, she traveled with him. They both performed in St. Petersburg in 1908. With Casals, Suggia was at the center of an international circle of the most famous literati, artists, and musicians of the day. Casals' trio partners were Cortot and Thibaud, or pianists Bauer, Busoni, Raoul Pugno and Mieczyslaw Horszowski; violinists Kreisler, Enesco and Ysaÿe; and violist **Pierre Monteux**, who would go on to make his name as one of the world's greatest conductors. Guilhermina's glamorous life with Casals was fraught with an undercurrent of unrest. Neither could stand being subordinate to the other, and each needed to be in control. She also felt stifled in her career. She could not be a dedicated cellist and a woman living in Casals' shadow. Thus, it was she who precipitated their breakup for the sake of her identity. Ironically, they both went to great lengths to conceal their romance. Letters were burned and newspaper stories buried. She and Casals never played together again.

Invading the Brits - A Glorious Victory

Suggia moved to England in early 1914, and began a new chapter of her life. She had visited England in 1905, as part of post-Leipzig touring, and played a concert at London's Bechstein Hall. She also accompanied Casals on one of his tours in England in 1912–13, but had played only at informal musical events. Now, within a decade, she became one of the most celebrated women in the country, with her pick of prestigious bookings. She was adored by critics and the general public, socialized with the rich and powerful, and acquired enough wealth to maintain residences in both England and Portugal.

Programs and reviews from 1922 to the eve of World War II document a full concert schedule in Great Britain, plus tours in Spain and Portugal. Suggia's well-earned success was based on supreme musicianship. The press recognized her as one of the two greatest living cellists, the other being Casals. She published articles in the British journal *Music and Letters* regarding the most valuable aspects of Casals' teaching.

In 1919, she had become engaged to wealthy aristocrat Edward Hudson, a director of the firm that published *Country Life* magazine which gave her a great deal of publicity throughout the '20s. But she eventually broke the commitment, foreseeing conflict with her career. This was the occasion where she kept her engagement gift of a 1717 Stradivarius cello. When Hudson died in 1937, he bequeathed £250 to Guilhermina in appreciation of her "valued friendship and glorious music."

A Portrait in Crimson

1920 marked the beginning of the three year time period it took to complete *La Suggia*, the famous portrait by English artist Augustus John (1878–1961). Seated in a glamorous red gown with her cello, the painting was exhibited at the Alpine Club, March 1923, and was the sensation of the season. It was bought for £5,000 by American William P. Clyde, Jr., owner of the Clyde Steamship Company, who flew in from Monte Carlo to make the purchase. Clyde generously loaned it for exhibition in museums in Philadelphia, Cleveland, Pittsburgh, Washington and Michigan, but English fans felt cheated by the loss of their new "national treasure." In 1925, wealthy art dealer Sir Joseph Duveen succeeded in convincing Clyde to sell it to him for an undisclosed amount. Duveen donated the painting to London's Tate Gallery.

Pride and Prejudice

Female soloists were still rare, and those who did make a name for themselves often suffered ill-disguised prejudice. Even her contemporary, noted cellist **Emanuel Feuermann** (1902–42), parroted the insistence that women lacked the physical strength to produce a big tone on the instrument, and dismissed Suggia as a "drawing-room player." Despite such barbs, she managed to win almost universal acclaim and respect with the combination of her personal magnetism and musical power, qualities that paved the way for female cellists who followed. In the 1930s, the London Symphony, London Philharmonic and Manchester's Hallé Orchestra were still all-male bastions. The more liberal BBC Orchestra employed some women, but specifically banned female cellists, who, with other instrumentalists of their gender, were forced into segregated ensembles like the British Women's Symphony.

In the 1930s, Suggia added more major works to her repertoire, including the Elgar Concerto and sonatas by Rachmaninoff, Mendelssohn, Franck and Debussy, whose sonata she performed late in her life in 1947. Her sister, Virginia, had been her most frequent accompanist before World War I, but after moving to London she began to collaborate with the pianists Gerald Moore and George Reeves, the latter accompanying her regularly until World War II.

In her long career, Guilhermina shared the stage with many celebrated musicians. In 1920, **Ethel Smyth** conducted the prelude to Act II of her opera, *The Wreckers*, after Suggia's rendition of the Schumann Concerto at the Queen's Hall. At a recital in 1926, and again in 1934, she collaborated with **Artur Rubinstein** (1887–1982), considered the world's greatest pianist in his time. A joint appearance with pianist **Wilhelm Backhaus** (1884–1969), in 1927, was described as "the perfect cooperation of genius." One of the highlights of Suggia's career was a performance before an audience of 10,000 at the Albert Hall marking Queen Mary's sixty-fifth birthday, May 26, 1932. (The reigning British monarch until 1936 was George V.) She also performed with the famous Hungarian **d'Aranyi** sisters, **Jelly** (1893–1966) and **Adila** (1886–1962), and violist **Rebecca Clarke**.

In addition to the Stradivarius given her by Edward Hudson, Suggia owned two cellos she purchased herself, another Stradivarius and a Montagnana, made in Cremona, c1700. She also possessed a Lockey Hill made in London at the end of the 18th century.

She never followed through on an invitation to tour the United States in the late 1920s, fearing to subject her instruments to a transatlantic voyage.

Suggia had little interest in making recordings, only producing three: a 1924 recording of pieces by Senaillé and Popper; a 1928 recording of the Haydn Concerto, the Sammartini sonata, the Bach Suite in C, Bruch's *Kol Nidrei*, and Fauré's *Elégie* with an unidentified orchestra conducted by the British **Sir John Barbirolli**; and in 1946, a recording of the Lalo Concerto with the London Symphony conducted by Spanish maestro **Pedro de Freitas Branco**.

On August 27, 1927, at forty-two, she married Dr. José Casimiro Carteado Mena, fifty-one, a wealthy radiologist in her native Porto, and head of the Pasteur Institute in Portugal. They had met in 1923 when he became her mother's physician. The benefits of this marriage, which began without passion but grew into tenderness, was a dependable helpmate and a home base. Despite the English "ways" she had acquired, Guilhermina was still extremely popular in Portugal. In 1923, the government made her an official of the Order of Santiago da Espada, an honor rarely bestowed upon a woman, and in 1937, she was promoted to full Commander of the Order. In 1938, she was awarded the gold medal of the City of Porto.

Throughout the 1930s, her full schedule continued in both countries. The outbreak of World War II, in 1939, kept Suggia in Porto until 1942. With little concertizing, she focused on teaching and volunteer efforts for British soldiers. This temporary retirement ended in 1943 when **Sir Malcolm Sargent** came to Lisbon to do a series of concerts with her and the Orquestra Sinfónica da Emissora Nacional, sponsored by the Círculo de Cultura Musical. Her return to the stage in her 60s, in England in 1946, introduced her to a new generation of British concertgoers. She had lost none of her magic, and an appearance at the Edinburgh Festival in the summer of 1949 was a triumph. In October of that year, she played at the Bournemouth Winter Gardens, which turned out to be her last performance in England.

In the spring of 1950 a long-anticipated American tour, planned with the help of **Sir Rudolph Bing** of the Metropolitan Opera, was canceled because of Suggia's declining health. Her last recital was in Aveiro, Portugal, May 31, 1950. In June, surgery at the London Clinic disclosed inoperable cancer in her liver, gall bladder and appendix. Although cheered by the attention of many friends, and a note and flowers from Queen Elizabeth,[102] she made arrangements for a final voyage to Porto, where she died at her home, July 30.

The Swathe of La Suggia

The status of women in classical music evolved enormously in the course of Suggia's lifetime. By 1950, professional female instrumentalists were no longer token exceptions. They played every instrument alongside men in major symphony orchestras, and many were celebrated soloists. Guilhermina contributed significantly to these changes as a concert artist, teacher, and mentor to the next generation of young cellists, which included **Raya Garbousova** and **Zara Nelsova** who played at her memorial concert in London with Sir Malcolm Sargent and the LSO.

Suggia dedicated a substantial portion of her estate to the support of young cellists. In her will, the Montagnana was bequeathed to the Porto Conservatory which loans it to members of the Porto Symphony, and awards the Guilhermina Suggia Prize annually to an outstanding cello student. The Lisbon Conservatory received the Lockey Hill in remembrance of her father. The Stradivarius and two bows went to the Royal Academy of Music, with the understanding that proceeds from their sale would be used to establish a scholarship for young cellists. The Suggia Trust, established with the £10,000 sterling that comprised her wealth in her adopted country, is administered by the Arts Council of Great Britain, awarding scholarships to international cello students under the age of twenty-one. The Stradivarius was sold by the London dealers W.E. Hill & Sons to Edmund Kurtz in 1951 for £8,000. The long-established firm declined to take a commission on the sale in order to maximize Suggia's bequest to the RAM. The latter's Suggia Prize also supports the careers of gifted young cellists. One of its most famous recipients was **Jacqueline du Pré** who, in 1955, at age ten, was awarded a scholarship that paid for six years of lessons with William Pleeth. Additional funding from the Suggia Trust enabled her take master classes with Casals at Zermatt in 1960, and go to Paris in 1962 to study with **Paul Tortelier**.

---

102. Elizabeth Bowes-Lyon (1900–2002), wife of George VI, a symbol of courage during WWII, and known to this generation as the "Queen Mum."

Although she never graced American stages, Guilhermina Suggia should be remembered worldwide for her power, personality and pioneering of the cello as a fitting and attainable instrument for women.

Really Low! - The Longest Strings

Only in the last few decades have women double bass players been appearing in orchestras. The huge instrument lends itself to few solo compositions, although Beethoven *did* write a concerto for bass for his friend, **Domenico Dragonetti** (1763–1846). Famed maestro **Serge Koussevitzky** (1874–1951) was a virtuoso bassist. There are many fine women players of this grandaddy of strings in many orchestras in the U.S.—and perhaps even a few in Europe where traditional barriers still rear their obstructions. The following artists provide a sample.

ORIN Y. O'BRIEN was born in Hollywood June 7, 1935. Her father, George O 'Brien, acted in seventy-five films in a four decade career spanning 1924–64. Her mother, Marguerite Churchill, came from the Broadway stage and also appeared in movies. Orin began piano at age six, studying for eleven years, but when the Beverly Hills High School Orchestra needed tall students to handle the bass, this became her instrument. Scholarships enabled her to attend the Music Academy of the West in Santa Barbara, UCLA, and Juilliard, where she studied with the New York Philharmonic assistant principal bass, Fred Zimmerman, graduating in 1957. She ushered at Carnegie Hall during those years. In the next decade she freelanced, becoming a member of the New York City Ballet Orchestra (1956–66), substituting at the Metropolitan and New York City Operas, playing and recording with the Saidenberg Little Symphony (1958–62) and meeting the exacting standards of **Leopold Stokowski** and his American Symphony (1961–65)—all of which contributed to a growing reputation. However, the letter arranging for her Philharmonic audition was addressed to *Mr.* Orin O'Brien. She joined them in 1966, under **Leonard Bernstein**, becoming the first female member of a section in the (then) 125-year history of the orchestra. At the time, *New York Times* music critic Donal Henahan wrote, "The New York Philharmonic is a complex city-state that is 88 percent married, 98 percent male, 99 percent white and 100 percent well-to-do and well-educated."

Participation in chamber music festivals led to O'Brien's premiering Gunther Schuller's *Quartet for 4 Double Basses*. Among many collaborations, she has performed at Vermont's Marlboro Music Festival and with the Guarnerius Quartet. She has been recorded on Columbia, Deutsche Grammophon, GM, Kapp, RCA and London.

O'Brien is on the faculties of Manhattan School of Music, Mannes College of Music and Juilliard, where she co-chaired the bass department from 1992 to 2002.

As of 2005, she is still going strong in all areas of her career.

Catch a Rising Star

An O'Brien student since she was eleven, **Eleonore Oppenheim** was in her second year at Juilliard in 2002, performing with their New Music Ensemble. According to her teacher, "Eleonore can play absolutely anything . . . including jazz!"

A Few Names from a Long List

Rachel Calin

RACHEL CALIN was born in Scranton (Pennsylvania) January 23, 1975. With non-musical parents, the child had to plead to enrol in the school string program where the only first year instrument was the violin. The second year provided a choice. Why the double bass? As Rachel explains it, "If you leave a nine-year-old alone in the toy store to choose one item, it will probably end up being the biggest store has!" Now she had to convince her skeptical parents not only to let her change instruments, but switch to one that would necessitate their buying a station wagon until she went to college. Eventually they agreed, and a career foundation was laid.

In 1994, she won the Juilliard Concerto Competition, making her Alice Tully Hall debut with the Juilliard Orchestra. She received her BM (1996) and MM (1998) from Juilliard. As a chamber musician, Calin has given numerous recitals and collaborated with top artists Itzhak Perlman, Ron Leonard and Myung-Wha Chung. She has served as solo bassist for the International Sejong Soloists, Ensemble America, the Metamorphosen Chamber Orchestra and the Camerata String Orchestra of Ramat Hasharon (Israel). As an orchestral musician, she has performed in both principal and assistant principal positions with the Aspen Chamber Symphony and the Prometheus Chamber Orchestra, as well as the New York Philharmonic *Live from Lincoln Center*, and the *Mostly Mozart* Festival. Since 1998, she has been on the faculty of the Perlman Music Program, which offers training for violin, viola, cello, bass, and piano students ages eleven to eighteen, with an intensive summer program, year-round mentoring and an international study/performance tour.

JACQUI DANILOW, born in Long Beach, New York, July 13, 1954, begged her older brother Peter to start teaching her the bass at age ten. After his tragic death at eighteen, "the instrument was just standing there . . ." so she began to study in earnest, first at the Juilliard Pre-College division, and later at the Manhattan School of Music. After graduating from MSM, she enrolled in Juilliard for her masters in performance, which she earned in 1977. Her career has included positions with the New Jersey and American Symphonies. She has been playing with the Metropolitan Opera Orchestra since 1980,[103] and is principal bass of the Stamford (Connecticut) Symphony.

In 1987, she helped organize the Art Farm, a music festival in Sonoma, California. Besides being a classical performer, she sits on the boards of organizations that represent recording musicians, and finds relaxation playing electric bass in a country rock band.

During the 1999–2000 season, she toured with the Met in Lisbon, Madrid, Hamburg, Baden-Baden, Vienna, Prague, Cologne and Geneva, played with the New York Philharmonic during its summer festival at Lincoln Center and Parks Concerts, and accompanied the Mostly Mozart ensemble on their tour to Tokyo.

Marji Danilow

MARJI DANILOW, sister of Jacqui, appeared on the scene April 21, 1948, and since her siblings were playing that huge instrument, it seemed the thing to do. She, too, studied at Juilliard with Homer Mensch and David Walter, graduating in 1980.

Her diverse career includes performing and touring with the conductorless Orpheus Chamber Orchestra, Smithsonian Chamber Players, with Annen Bysma and the L'archibudulli Mozzatiato, a woodwind sextet with double bass and original instruments, and the Metropolitan Opera Orchestra, often sharing a stand with her sister. She has recorded on Sony Classical and BMG, and the best-selling Vivaldi *Four Seasons* with violinist **Gil Shaham** on Deutsche Grammophon.

Danilow appears regularly with the New York Philharmonic, American Composers' Orchestra, Brooklyn Philharmonic, New York City Ballet and other area ensembles. Formerly principal bass with the New Jersey Symphony, and a member of the New York City Opera Orchestra, her virtuoso chamber performances have been heard at the festivals in Santa Fe, La Jolla SummerFest, Colorado, New England Bach Festival, Grand Teton Music Festival and Aston Magna. 2001 found her back at Santa Fe.

Born in Gary, Indiana, April, 15, 1956, into a music-loving family of Hungarian descent, **DEBORAH DUNHAM** grew up in the Pacific Northwest as one of five siblings encouraged to play an instrument. She began piano at seven, took up the double bass at twelve and was soon playing with community and youth orchestras. At eighteen, she became an army wife, a role that took her to Thailand where she started her associates arts degree at an extension campus of the University of Maryland; then on to Texas, where she subbed with the San Antonio Symphony and took classes at the University of Texas (San Antonio); and finally to Augsburg (Germany) and more liberal arts classes—again at a U of M campus. She also attended courses at the Leopold Mozart Konservatorium.

---

103. Jacqui prefers the flexibility of being a non-contracted player.

In between travels, Deborah gave birth to daughter Angela, September 1, 1976. By 1980, Deborah chose to conclude the marriage.

1982 found her in Seattle, where she earned her BFA from Cornish College of Arts, greatly inspired by faculty members composer Paul Dresher and tenor John Dykers. Concurrently, she was performing with the Seattle New Performance Group. Her MFA was earned in May 1984 from the California Institute of Arts (Valencia). During these years, Angela became best friends with a little girl named Nami, and in a life-simulates-the-movies scenario the children brought their single parents together. Deborah married violist James Dunham, August 25, 1984. In 1987, he joined the Cleveland Quartet and the faculty at University of Rochester's Eastman School of Music. After a partial contract, Deborah was hired full time by the Rochester Philharmonic, becoming one of four "core" bass players for the next ten years. She also served as artistic director for Rochester's Society for Chamber Music, and played with the Eastman Chamber Ensemble.

In December 1995 the Cleveland Quartet disbanded, and her husband transferred to the New England Conservatory. Taking a leave of absence, Deborah soon found herself busy coaching chamber music at NEC, directing Boston's South End Community Music Center Chamber Orchestra, and freelancing for the Boston Symphony and Pops Orchestras. She also became principal bassist with Boston Baroque, Boston Modern Orchestra Project, Emmanuel Music, Boston Musica Viva, Collage New Music and Bay Chamber Concerts. Her summers are at the chamber music festivals of Aspen, Tanglewood, Grand Teton, Portland and Rockport (Maine), plus annual appearances since 1993 at the Festival der Zukunft (Switzerland), and an appearance at the 1997 Hong Kong Musicarama. In recordings, she was among those who received a 1991 Grammy nomination for the Bridge CD *Jan DeGaetani Sings Berlioz and Mahler*. Besides a recording on Telarc with Boston Baroque, she has commissioned and performed works for her instrument released on the New Albion and Mode labels.

In 2001, with James invited to join the faculty of Rice University's Shepherd School of Music, they moved to Houston, and Deborah entered the doctoral program under Paul Ellison. She performs as an extra with the Houston Symphony, but returns to the rich and diverse performance environment of Boston whenever possible.

More Where These Came From . . .

A solid corps of excellent string players make their careers in orchestras. (See Ladies in the Orchestra.)

EMBRACING THE "TOO BIG FOR A WOMAN" INSTRUMENT

Women Bassists in U.S. Orchestras

Atlanta Symphony: Gloria Jones, Jane Little
Charlotte Symphony: Felicia Konczal
Colorado Symphony: Susan Cahill
Columbus Symphony: Jena Huebner
Dallas Symphony: Paula Fleming, Elizabeth Patterson
The Florida Orchestra: Dee Moses, Deborah Schmidt
Florida Philharmonic: Janet Clippard, Susan Dirgins-Friend, Martha Schimelpfenig
Fort Worth Symphony: Julie Vinsant
Indianapolis Symphony: Nami Akamatsu
Kansas City Orchestra: Nancy Newman
Louisville Orchestra: Patricia Docs
Metropolitan Opera: Jacqui Danilow

Milwaukee Symphony: Catherine McGinn, Laura Snyder
Nashville Symphony: Elizabeth Stewart
New Jersey Symphony: Norine Stewart
New York City Ballet Orchestra: Marji Danilow
New York City Opera Orchestra: Gail Kruvand
New York Philharmonic: Orin O'Brien, Michele Saxon
Pittsburgh Symphony: Betsy Heston
Saint Louis Symphony: Carolyn White
San Diego Symphony: Susan Wulff, Margaret Johnston, Sayuri Yamamoto
San Francisco Symphony: Lee Ann Crocker
Utah Symphony: Claudia Norton

The Art of the Luthier

Peg Baumgartel

Jennifer Becker Jurewicz

Lynn Armour Hannings

Andrea Hoffman Simmel

Sue Lipkins

Wendela Taylor Moes

Carrie Scoggins

Sigrun Seifert

Carla J. Shapreau

Margaret Shipman

Elizabeth van der Veershank

Marilyn Wallin

Rena Weisshaar

Isabelle Wilbaux

European Luthierès

Andrea Frandsen

Irene Loebner

Hutchins Consort

Carleen Maley Hutchins

"I'll Swap You a Neck Graft for a Broken Bridge!"

No, this is not a dialogue betwixt a surgeon and a dentist, but what goes on between Sigrun Seifert and Joseph Grubaugh, a husband and wife team in the violin making and repairing business. Yes! There are women stringed instrument builders and bow makers. Of the 150 or so by-invitation-only members of the American Federation of Violin and Bow Makers, Inc. (AFVBM), headquartered in New York, there are barely a dozen women, and at least four of those work in partnership with their husbands. Talented and committed, these ladies either inherited the genes or early in life felt "the call" of dedicating themselves to a craft dating back to the 16th century, which reached its zenith with the legendary artisans of 17th century Cremona. There was the **Amati** family, with **Andrea** (*c* 1505–*c* 1580), his sons, **Antonio** (*c* 1538–*c* 1595), and **Girolamo** (*c* 1561–1630) and *his* son, **Nicola** [or Niccolò] (1596–1684), and *his* son **Girolamo** (1649–1740) whose work was deemed inferior to that of his elders; the **Guarneri** family, who signed their violins with the Latin, *Guarnerius*, founded by **Andrea** (*c* 1625–98),[104] his sons **Pietro** (1655– ?), and **Giuseppe** Giovanni Battista (1666–*c* 1739), and the most celebrated, the nephew of Andrea, Giuseppe **Antonio** Guarneri (1687–1745), known as *del Gesù*, for signing his instruments "I.H.S." (Iesus Hominum Salvator—Jesus, Savior of Mankind); and most prominently, **Antonio Stradivari** (1644–1737),[105] who signed his work *Antonius Stradivarius Cremonensis*, and made his last instrument at the age of ninety-two.

Because most violin makers originally made lutes, and other ancient stringed instruments, they are still known as *luthiers*.

Take a Bow!

The first known bows appeared in India in the 5th or 6th century. Ancient art works depict arc shaped bows. In the sixteenth, seventeenth and first half of the 18th century, violin makers made bows as well as instruments. When musical demands from the composers and players required more individual attention be given to the making of instruments and bows, certain luthiers chose to solely concentrate on bows and became *"Maîtres Archetiers,"*

104–105. Both students of Nicola Amati.

French for bow makers. In the 18th century, the bow began evolving towards the shape of the modern bow. Centers of bow making were established in France, Germany and England. Although antique French bows are sought after by collectors, dealers and some players, the finest quality antique bows made in other countries should not be overlooked. Today, around the world, there are master bow makers whose work rivals the finest old French archetiers—some are even said to surpass them.

The Guilds

The concept of guilds dates back to the later Middle Ages and the Renaissance, when European artists and craftsmen were organized into guilds that looked after their economic interests and regulated trade procedures. In the luthier and bow making professions, today's associations serve to maintain high standards and recognition of excellence in the craft.

The American Federation of Violin and Bow Makers (AFVBM) was founded in 1980 to provide the musical community with a criteria of work and expertise upon which they could depend. Founding members include the most renowned names in the field: **Carlos Arcieri**, **René Morel**, **Hans J. Nebel** and **William Salchow** in the New York area; **Carl F. Becker**, Chicago; **Peter Prier**, Salt Lake City; the late **Frank Passa**, San Francisco; and **Paul Siefried**, Port Townsend, Washington. With strict requirements for qualification, its members include the finest makers, dealers, and restorers in the U.S., Canada and France. Besides submitting an example of work for review, a prospective member must have at least nine years of experience in the profession—including six years of formal apprenticeship and training in all aspects of the making, repair, and restoration of fine instruments and bows. The Federation also has a Missing Property Registration to aid in the identification of lost or stolen instruments. Over the years this has helped recover several missing items, including a Stradivari violin.[106] Its photographic archive—now on a computer database—is a compilation of the finest works of the masters of the craft. Exclusive membership in 2001 numbered 106 with six women and one woman associate.

Founded in 1974, the **Violin Society of America** (VSA) is a non-profit organization created for the purpose of promoting the art and science of making, repairing and preserving stringed musical instruments and their bows. Membership in the VSA is open to all sharing an interest in the violin family, its history, performers, technique, performance practice and repertoire. 2001 membership was about 1,800 with approximately 150 women. Although based in America, its biennial competitions are international, attracting hundreds of entrants from all over the world eager to win their Gold and Silver medals and other certificates of recognition. The VSA also sponsors the annual Oberlin Bow Making Workshops, which take place for two weeks each summer at the Oberlin College Conservatory in Ohio, and are attended by selected professional bow makers from around the world, some of whom act as pedagogues. The emphasis is on an open exchange of bow making techniques, ideas, and discussions. The event casts a deserved limelight on the fact that both makers and restorers should be as valued as their luthier counterparts . . . for what is a violin without a bow?

The Entente Internationale des Maîtres Luthiers et Archetiers d'Art is a world organization founded August 18, 1950, in Geneva, Switzerland. In order to apply for membership one must be at least thirty years of age, have completed an apprenticeship with a recognized master, or have a degree from an accredited school, have been active in the profession, after training, for a minimum of five years, own either a stringed instrument or bow making enterprise and be sponsored by two members. In 2001, membership was 179, including eleven women, plus three women *associate* members.

---

106. See Sigrun Seifert and Carla Shapreau.

Ingeborg Behnke, Germany

Edith Dittrich, Switzerland

Andrea Frandsen, France

Lynn Hannings, USA

Irene Loebner, Germany

Wendela T. Moes, USA, Germany

Cornélie Möller, Netherlands

Sigrun Seifert, USA

Margaret Shipman, USA

Rena Weisshaar, USA

Associate Members

Edda Bünnagel, Germany

Gertrud Reuter, Switzerland

Ute Wegerhoff, Great Britain

The following represent most of the American women members of this select profession—proving, once again, that women can excel in any field.

PEG BAUMGARTEL - *Bowing à la française*

Peg Baumgartel

Peg Baumgartel was born in Altoona, Pennsylvania, May 22, 1964, to parents who own a farm on Blueberry Hill! She started piano at four, violin at six and the double bass, which was to become her instrument, at ten. After high school, she headed west to Los Angeles. A very few weeks later, her life changed forever. The horse the eighteen-year-old was riding threw her headfirst. With great fortune, she escaped the fate of Christopher Reeve, but her right arm was completely smashed. It would take ten years for the nerves to fully heal. Her career was over before it had begun. So she worked odd jobs, and tried studying jazz in case her fingers would one day be strong enough to pluck the strings.

In 1987, she chanced to walk into the bow-repairing shop of Paul Siefried, who mentioned that he needed an apprentice. Peg immediately volunteered, but got the, *women don't do this!* response. Normally shy, she insisted he give her a chance. She got the job which entailed answering phones, taking orders and being at the counter so that the boss could concentrate on his craft. Although her training came in dribs and drabs, over the next seven years she learned her art and the appreciation of antique French bows from the 18th, 19th and 20th centuries, like priceless *Tourtes*[107] and *Peccattes*[108] made from the Brazilian *penambuco* wood. If Italy is the historic base for violins, France has that honor for bows.

When Siefried relocated in 1994, Peg bought the business and ran it until 1998 when she moved to a small town in New Jersey, exactly ninety miles from Manhattan and ninety from Philadelphia. By this time the excellence of her craft had garnered clientele from major violin shops in the U.S. and Europe, so she could work from anywhere. She also wrote articles and created technical illustrations, some of which have appeared in *Strings* magazine and the book *Discovering Bows for the Double Bass* by Christopher Brown (1997). She became a member of the AFVBM and VSA, and participated in the Oberlin Bow Making Workshops since 1995. She has won certificates of merit in several international bow making competitions.

In 2001, Baumgartel moved to Washington State to be with fellow bow maker Morgan Anderson, expanding her expertise to *making* as well as executing complex restorations of historical bows. In 2004–05 she created a special hybrid bow for a cellist with rheumatoid arthritis; designed a poster for the International Penambuco Conservation Intiative (see Hannings), and was mentioned in a 2004 *Smithsonian* article on the IPCI.

In her own words: "Without a bow, the best *Strad* or *del Gesù* can't make a sound! And the better the bow, the better the sound. If a student has to choose between getting a good instrument or a great bow, I'd recommend getting the great bow. *The bow reaches down into the soul oif the instrument and brings it forth.*"

JENNIFER BECKER JUREWICZ - *The Dynasty Continues*

Born in Chicago, August 14, 1955, Jennifer is the granddaughter of Carl G. Becker (1887–1975), who was known as "Dr. Violin." Grandson of pioneer American luthier Herman Macklett, Carl made his first violin at fourteen in 1901, and at eighteen repaired an Amati cello which had been smashed in a streetcar accident. He

---

107–108. Tourte, Peccatte and Voirin are the Stradivari of bows. Antique ones have fetched upward of $50,000.

also made a replica so perfect that experts were hard put to identify the original. His son, Carl F. Becker—Jennifer's father—began assisting him at age sixteen. Both were employed by William Lewis and Son, Chicago's largest violin dealer. In 1968, after years of valuable experience, they formed their own company, Carl Becker and Son. Summers were, and still are, spent in Wisconsin making new instruments. Winters are devoted to selling, repairing, restoring and appraisals. In this environment, Jennifer learned piano at five, cello at ten and began building her first violin at eleven, working in the summer months and completing it "in the white" at fifteen. It took another three years to finish varnishing it. Meanwhile, she joined the company full time at sixteen in June 1972. Her brother, Paul Carl, also became part of the company after making his first violin in 1974 at age fifteen. Her sister Marilyn, already twenty-one, became a piano teacher and an accountant. Carol, the eldest, besides being a piano and organ teacher, is a liturgist for a large Lutheran church in Virginia.

In 1978, Jennifer married Romuald Jurewicz, an electronic design engineer. They moved to Minneapolis, where she gave birth to Eric in 1982, Stephanie in 1985, and a new *Carl Becker & Son* shop in 1986. Their second daughter, Alya, born May 21, 1992, at age three already showed precocious musical talent and was playing with all those interesting toy-tools just like her mother. By 2001, at nine, she was carving roses and anxious to start on her first violin.

There have been many thrills along the way. In the late sixties, a wealthy Chicago collector ordered eighteen violins, six each from Carl G, Carl F and Jennifer. At the Violin Society Convention (VSA) in 1987, the late Lord Yehudi Menuhin, who had known Grandfather, bought a 1958 Becker from the AFVBM exhibit. Famed cellist Yo-Yo Ma had his bow rehaired in Minneapolis while Jennifer was within three weeks of giving birth to Alya. Years earlier, he had brought his Stradivarius cello in for maintenance.

After more than 800 violins, violas and cellos, created over nine decades among the family members, as of 2001 some of the traditional *Carl Becker & Son* instrument labels began to read: *Carl, Paul and Jennifer Becker*, and *Carl F. Becker and daughter*. Of the instruments, Jennifer says, "What's two years in the making when you're creating something to last for centuries?"

LYNN ARMOUR HANNINGS - *Archetier Extraordinaire*

Lynn Hannings

Lynn was born June 13, 1950, in New York City, and moved to Ridgewood, New Jersey, at age ten. Both parents were involved in the arts. She started the double bass at age fourteen, and by eighteen entered the New England Conservatory. In 1970, she began an apprenticeship in bowmaking with William Salchow in New York City. In 1989, she received a Fulbright Grant for advanced study with Bernard Millant in Paris, an authority in the French tradition. Her studies in physiology, anatomy, and occupational therapy enable her to make bows to meet the special needs of musicians with physical problems.

She was elected to the AFVBM in 1984. A resident of Maine, Hannings is an active double bassist in the New England area. In 2001, she was elected to membership in the Entente Internationale des Maîtres Luthiers et Archetiers d'Art (EILA), whose headquarters are in Geneva. To be invited into this prestigious organization of only 140 members worldwide, is an extremely high honor.

Since 2004 she has been president of the International Pernambuco Conservation Initiative (IPCI), working to conserve and develop a restoration for the primary wood used in bowmaking, She teaches the French tradition of repair and rehairing at the University of New Hampshire (Durham), and College of the Redwoods in Eureka, California. These Pernambuco-free classes are researching alternative species to save the dwindling Brazilian trees. She is also a competition bow judge and guest lecturer.

By 2006 Hannings' business had expanded to sell parts and supplies to bow restorers internationally. Her bows are used by musicians around the world.

ANDREA HOFFMAN SIMMEL - *In the Tradition of Mittenwald*

Andrea Hoffman Simmel was born May 22, 1941, in Konstanz (Germany) into a family of amateur musicians and singers. Violin began at seven. At age eleven, she became interested in woodworking and was enrolled in a

Andrea Simmel

crafts course. Bored with weaving place mats in the girls' division, she asked to be transferred to where the boys were handling saws, knives and gouges. She carved a set of small wooden figures, which became the centerpiece of the school's Christmas exhibit. When she was fifteen, her parents took her to the shop of Jürgen von Stietencron and bought her a violin made in Mittenwald around 1750. As she observed the making of a violin in the shop, Andrea realized that the combination of woodwork and music exactly suited her gifts. Stietencron, one of the best known master luthiers of Europe, encouraged the girl to start building a violin of her own. At her graduation from Gymnasium–equivalent of the first two years of college—she played the finished instrument.

During Andrea's girlhood, Konstanz had its own symphony, which she and her friends attended regularly. There were also summer festivals featuring internationally renowned chamber groups and orchestras. These concerts, held in a medieval building enhanced by wonderful acoustics, helped form Andrea's discrimination of sound. In the spring of 1960, Andrea was accepted at Mittenwald. In her four years there, she met and became friends with Rena and Michael Weisshaar. She also built a baryton—an instrument fashionable in the time of Haydn—with seven bowed strings and nine strings underneath the fingerboard which are plucked with the thumb. After graduation, she married fellow student, Steve McGhee, and moved with him to New York where their sons, Paul and Geoffrey, were born, respectively in 1965 and 1970.

For the next few years, Andrea repaired and restored instruments in the shop of Jacques Français, under René Morel, Carlos Arcieri, and later in her own shop. For the last thirty years, she has been making violins and violas of concert quality. Played by musicians around the world, they have been displayed in Germany, Italy, Japan and America, receiving awards for tone in international competitions, including Freiburg 1987, where she was the first woman luthier to win a violin making competition in Germany.

As of 2001, this dedicated artisan, and member of AFVBM, has made over forty violins and violas, and converted modern violins into baroque style. She likes to try out her new instruments in chamber music sessions. It was at one of these she met sociologist Arnold Simmel, whom she married.

Andrea spends summer and fall in the Berkshire Mountains of Massachusetts crafting instruments in serene surroundings. Winter and spring find her in New York, where her shop allows her to perform maintenance work, repairs, and the delicate art of sound adjustment.

SUE LIPKINS - *Bowing to BASSics*

Sue Lipkins was born in New York City, May 18, 1958. Assigned to the string orchestra in junior high (1972), she accidentally was chosen to play the double bass and ended up loving it. She went on to the famed High School of Music and Art and then Juilliard, where she received both a BM (1980) and MM (1981) in Performance on Double Bass. After graduation, she was offered a job in sales at William Salchow's bow making shop. She accepted on the proviso that she could apprentice. While there, Yung Chin was head of the workbench and key to her learning bow making and repairs. After leaving Salchow's, she studied briefly with François Malo, David Samuels, and Mitsuaki Sasano, both in their shops and at several Oberlin Bowmaking Workshops, and with Stephane Thomachot in Paris. In 2001, she was accepted by the AFVBM.

Her devotion to her instrument has made bass bows her natural specialty.

Sue's son, Akira Shimizu, born May 1, 1991, played baritone horn in the elementary school band and looks forward to switching to tuba when he grows big enough. Since Sue's brother, Lenny, went to Juilliard on tuba, this runs in the family.

WENDELA TAYLOR MOES - *A Keen Ear*

Born in Boston, August 8, 1949, the fourth child in a family of five, all of whom took music lessons, Wendela grew up in an academic household which, besides her mother's math and science background, had a strong interest in the arts and humanities. By age five, Wendy wanted to play the violin, but through a series of mishaps—in elementary school the instrument broke, in junior high she fell out of a tree and injured her arm—she didn't actually get lessons until she was fifteen. Visits to repair shops piqued her interest in violin making. Between classes at the University of Wisconsin, Madison, she learned bow rehairing from a local violin maker . . . after overcoming *his* bias that this was not "woman's work." Eighteen months of studies convinced her to give up on becoming a violinist. In New York, summer 1970, she managed to be a "guest" for two weeks at the prestigious Wurlitzer shop. She showed such talent for repairs, not just rehairing bows, that she impressed Fernando Sacconi and Hans Nebel—master Italian luthiers from the Cremona School—and shop owner Roth. He sent a recommendation to Germany getting Wendy accepted the following year to Mittenwald (1971), to join the (then) thirty-five students and seven master teachers.

After one semester, in spring 1972, she met Peter Albrecht Moes. They married December 22. Graduating together Spring 1975, they went to Los Angeles to work for noted violin maker **Hans Weisshaar**. In summer 1977, they returned to Europe to freelance for a year, then moved to London and into a partnership with Peter Biddulph. In October 1981, five weeks after the birth of Saskia, they moved to New York establishing their own shop, Moes & Moes. (Wendy worked full time, even after the birth of their second daughter, Phoebe, April 16, 1985.) She also specializes in sound adjustments, done by appointment at the home shop, or in the city. Like **Andrea Simmel,** Wendy possesses that exceptional talent—super aural retention—required for this singular procedure.

Their growing business took time from the workbench and family nurture. After ten years, they left New York in 1991 for Boston, but ended up in Stamford, Connecticut, enjoying country living and being close to their Manhattan clientele.

In summer 2004, the Moes moved back to Peter's homeland, buying and restoring a 450-year-old farmhouse in Peissenberg, with a view of the Austro-Italian alps! They make several trips a year to take care of their American clients. Daughter Saskia is a creative jewelry designer in America. Phoebe may be exporting/importing horses from Germany. Their new lifestyle is definitely rejuvenating their health.

CARRIE SCOGGINS was born in Walnut Creek, California, December 5, 1958. Her mother had played trumpet in school, and Carrie followed her lead playing violin in school. She earned her AA degree from Diablo Community College in Pleasant Hill, California (1978). Her journeyman's degree is from the Violin Making School, Salt Lake, City, Utah (1983). She occasionally plays both violin and viola in the Salt Lake Symphony, while her classical guitar, recorder and rebec are now seldom played.

She met her husband, Michael Gene Scoggins, at the Violin Making School, where Michael started in 1978 and Carrie in 1979. They were married in 1982 and worked for school owner Peter Prier who also has a luthier business. For four years Carrie taught varnish and set up for the school, while Michael was foreman of the repair shop before graduating to teaching woodworking—everything before varnish.

In 1988 they left Prier and opened their own shop, Scoggins & Scoggins, in Salt Lake City.

Although divorced in 2003, the partnership flourishes. Their children are Spencer, born December 5, 1988, Courtney Anne, June 16, 1990, and Douglas, May 7, 1992.

Carrie was awarded a Certificate of Merit for tone at the 2004 VSA violin making competition.

SIGRUN SEIFERT - *Part of Another Dynamic Duo*

Sigrun Seifert

Born September 20, 1955, into a large family in Bad Kreuznach near Mainz, in what was then West Germany, Sigrun's father and mother were both artists and teachers. When she was nine they moved to Simmern, a nearby small town. Always busy with wood, nails and glue, the child often accompanied her brother to get his violin out of the repair shop, and announced that she wanted to be a violin maker. She began violin at seven, cello at ten, continuing her studies through her twenties. She applied to Mittenwald at the beginning of 1972, only to find that enrollment was filled. An obedient daughter, she began training as an elementary school teacher when, in October, she got a call from Mittenwald giving her three days' notice to report.

A life changing decision for a seventeen-year-old! Despite her parents' initial skepticism, Sigrun stayed the seven semesters—in the course of which she met **Peter** and **Wendy Moes**—and graduated March 1976, with a journeyman degree. June found her in Los Angeles studying violin restoration with **Hans Weisshaar**. Here, she met fellow luthier, Joseph Grubaugh who, as an "Air Force brat," had spent much of his childhood abroad and developed a love for European traditions, among them violin making. In 1979, Sigrun moved to the Bay Area with Joe, buying a house the following year in Petaluma, across the Golden Gate Bridge, thirty-seven miles north of San Francisco, where they set up their atelier. They married in 1982. Their son, Sebastian, was born in 1983, and their daughter, Stephanie, in 1988. While Sigrun's parents were living in Germany (her mother died in March 2006), the family often traveled to Europe. By eighteen, Sebastian had developed a passion for Italy, and Stephanie was at home on both sides of the Atlantic.

Seminars at the Smithsonian's Analytical Laboratories in Washington, DC have enhanced Seifert's restoration skills to establish her as one of the best artisans in the country. She continues to enhance the field with her own additions to the art of violin making and restoration. Since 1982, she has won many awards from the VSA, including a gold medal for a viola in 1984. Starting in 1988, she has collaborated with her husband in making[109] and restoring instruments. Together, they have added four silver medals and four more gold medals to her honors, plus numerous certificates for workmanship and tone quality. In 1998, they were awarded the *Hors Concours* from the VSA, a most interesting honor that excludes the winners from further competition! It is awarded to makers who have achieved at least three gold medals in three different competitions. (A gold medal is awarded on instruments that have been unanimously voted on by three workmanship judges and three tone judges.) As of 2001, there were only about fifteen makers who have achieved this status, with Sigrun the only woman. Seifert and Grumbaugh are members of the AFVBM and the ELIA. In 2002, my husband and I spent five glorious hours in Sigrun's shop being shown the various stages of instrument creation.

Finding a Treasure

In the course of restoring instruments, whose conditions range from being run over by a car to being eaten by worms, in January 1994 a violin was brought into the shop whose identifying marks the couple recognized as the 1732 Stradivarius listed missing since 1967 from UCLA. The court case involved was handled by **Carla Shapreau**. (See next insert.)

One of the most heartwarming aspects of this particular duo, as became evident in interviews, is the pride and respect each has for the other. Sigrun gives Joe much credit by stating, "Behind every successful woman stands a loving and supportive partner!" (A delightful flip side to "the little woman" label . . .)

An Inside Glimpse of Changing Times

Life at Mittenwald in 1972 as described by Sigrun Seifert: One had to find a room to rent in a private house . . . not an easy task. Mittenwald is a tourist town in the Alps, therefore only places not rentable to tourists were available. That meant quite shabby conditions. One had to cook in their room when possible. My first landlady would not allow cooking in the room, except a little water heater, a cup and a breadboard to make sandwiches. I learned how to cook five-minute rice in a cup that way. Very soon you found out where the good rooms were and tried to line up a move as the current occupant graduated from school.

"*Women belong behind the kitchen stove and it is a waste of time to teach them as they won't stay in the profession.*" This was the comment to my face by the acting director. With only forty-plus students in the whole school, my group started with three women and three men. By the end of the first semester, the other two women had left. A year later, the whole situation started to change. About 50 percent of incoming students would be women who stayed the course, which shifted the make up of

---

109. One of their cellos was taken to an audition for the Boston Symphony. Although the performer was not chosen, the examining board was so impressed with the quality of the instrument they asked who the maker was!

the student body. With the exception of one teacher, I felt neither unequal treatment by other instructors or by my male schoolmates. I was twice voted student speaker. For the most part, the way you were respected and treated depended on personality; how you applied and stood up for yourself. It had nothing to do with gender.

CARLA J. SHAPREAU - *Luthier, Lawyer, Wife, Mother . . .*

Born in Los Angeles, July 7, 1952, to an inventor father and a teacher-designer mother, in her freshman year in college Carla heard a female student playing a violin on campus, and a sympathetic chord vibrated in her spirit. (Many years later an aunt informed Carla that her Russian immigrant grandfather had been a woodworker and had contributed to the wood carvings of Carnegie Hall!) At eighteen, she started her studies on violin and viola, but needed a violin. Browsing through the library, she came upon a book published by Popular Mechanics Press entitled, *You Can Make a Stradivarius, Too!* Set on making her own violin, one of her professors referred her to a violinmaker. After spending the summer studying violin making with Victor Gardener, Carla went on several maple and spruce tree cutting expeditions (with Forest Service permission) and since then has literally made her violins from scratch! Utterly entranced with the craft, she quit school and went to study in Massachusetts with renowned artisan Donald Warnock.

She studied violin making and restoration five more years with several craftsmen in San Francisco, including Boyd Poulsen at Cremona Musical Instruments, and Roland Feller, who had been trained at Mittenwald. By 1975, Carla entered her first violin in an Early Musical Instruments exhibit at UC, Berkeley. Since that time, her prize winning instruments have been in VSA and AFVBM competitions, where she was a finalist, and in Cremona (Italy). Her instruments are played by artists in Italy, Germany, Norway, Sweden and throughout America. Besides her first preference, making new violins, beginning in 1980 she became a restorer for the Salz Collection[110] at UC, Berkeley. A member of VSA and AFVBM, she has been self-employed since 1981.

Shapreau returned to college in 1983 to earn a degree in music and art from Humboldt State University. After five years, feeling the isolation of her work, she decided to add law to her list of accomplishments, graduating in 1988 with a JD degree from UC Hastings College of Law. As an attorney, she rose to partnership in a prominent San Francisco Bay area law firm where she specializes in intellectual property and art law litigation. Carla often provides pro bono services to professional organizations and individuals involved in the art and music fields. She has written many articles for legal, arts and violin publications, on such diverse topics as copyright law, art law, art theft (including violins), legal issues in the recovery of sunken treasure and disputes over title to artifacts and other cultural property. She frequently lectures on copyright and art law issues. *L.A. Times* magazine *West*, featured her work as their cover story, February 2006.

Wanted! "The Duke of Alcantara"[111]

It was *lawyer* Carla Shapreau who was hired to recover a 1732 Stradivarius that had been missing for twenty-seven years. The violin, valued at approximately $800,000, was either stolen from, or lost by, a violinist in the Feri Roth String Quartet, the resident quartet at UCLA in 1967. Devastated, he immediately reported it missing—which led to the violin's inclusion on the AFVBM's registry of missing violins. In January 1994, the violin teacher of Teresa Salvato brought her student's violin for repair to the Petaluma (Northern California) shop of **Sigrun Seifert** and her husband Joseph Grubaugh. The couple spotted identifying characteristics of the master violin maker, and identified it as the missing "Duke of Alcantara," built when Antonio Stradivari (1644–1737) was eighty-eight, and

---

110. The Salz Collection is a fine stringed instrument collection at UC, Berkeley, containing many Italian and French instruments including makers such as Stradivari and Amati.

111. Title of Shapreau's article which appeared in the Sept/Oct 1994 issue of *Strings* magazine. In 1997, she brought out a book on this unique case. She has also written several articles for two publications: *Art, Antiquity and Law* and *The International Journal of Cultural Property* (Oxford UP) regarding legal issues relating to the battle for title to sunken treasure (2001).

allegedly named after the original owner, a Spanish nobleman in the service of King Don Carlos in the 18th century. When confronted, Salvato refused to return the instrument, claiming that Duke of Alcantara, along with another violin in the Alcantara's double case, had been given to her ex-husband by his aunt on her deathbed in 1979. The aunt had claimed to have found the violins in a double case on the side of a freeway in Southern California. Teresa had received both instruments in the divorce settlement. Handling the complex legal issues applying to the recovery of stolen artwork and antiquities, in October 1994 Shapreau and the University of California's in-house counsel filed a complaint in Los Angeles County Superior Court asking that the violin be returned to the university. On December 1, 1995, Savato agreed to surrender the violins to UCLA for a settlement of $11,500.

In 1997, Shapreau co-authored, with Brian W. Harvey, the second edition of *Violin Fraud—Deception, Forgery, and Lawsuits in England and America*, published by Clarendon Press, Oxford (England). The only scholarly work of its type in the English language, this important work examines the many legal issues that arise in the world of violin commerce.

In addition to her law practice, Carla continues making and restoring violins and violas, and is a wife and mother. (Need we add, only a woman could manage all that?)

Margaret Shipman

MARGARET SHIPMAN - *In a Master's Hand Prints* . . .

Margaret was born in Denver, October 7, 1946. Her parents, who had lived through the Depression, made sure that all their six children had music lessons. (On her they rubbed off . . .) She got a BM in cello from Eastman (1968), and an MM from USC (1970).

In 1969, she took her cello for repair to the shop of Hans Weisshaar in Los Angeles. When she got it back, the sound was so much improved that her playing was "like a year's progress without practicing." More amazing was that when she expressed her interest in his skill, he invited her to come and work in the shop. This was the beginning of a twenty-one-year "apprenticeship"—learning violin making and restoration—until Weisshaar's death in June 1991. Since then, Shipman has been president of the corporation. Together, Hans and Margaret co-authored the book, *Violin Restoration: A Manual for Violin Makers*. Published in 1988, it has made its way around the world, and is known as "the standard bearer for the profession." Many Weisshaar-Shipman trainees have gone on to open their own shops and earn fine reputations.

In the 1978 international competition sponsored by the Violin Society of America, Shipman won a gold medal for craftsmanship, and a certificate of merit for sound for a viola. She has given lectures for VSA on the subject of color matching and varnishing—"everyone's biggest problem in repair."

Shipman has been a member of the AFVBM—of which Hans Weisshaar was a founder-president—since 1980, serving on its board of governors, 1985–87. 1987 also brought Margaret membership in the prestigious Entente Internationale des Maîtres Luthiers et Archetiers d'Art (EILA), for which her mentor had served as the American delegate, later becoming both their vice-president and president.

In 2004, after devoting thirty-six years to the craft, Shipman sold the firm to London-trained luthier Georg Ettinger. For the next two years she will phase out her work. In 2005 a branch of Weisshaar under Ettinger's proprietorship was opened in Berlin.

ELIZABETH Vander VEER SHAAK, born in Brooklyn, New York, November 11, 1954, took piano at six, and guitar at twelve, but was not exposed to classical music in her childhood. Instead, she heard the Beatles at their height, her mother's square dance records, and a two-year experience, when her family temporarily moved to Florida, of what she calls the best Cuban music—which has left her with a predilection for *Salsa*. In 1976, she graduated from Ithaca College (New York) with a double degree of a BA in fine arts and a BS in audiology, which she felt satisfied both sides of her brain as to arts and sciences. She also took graduate courses at Bryn Mawr (Pennsylvania). Between 1978–86, she traveled, and took up ethnographic music studies in Bulgaria where she came into contact with the *gadulka*, a three-stringed folk fiddle known in English as a *kemenche* or *rebec*, which is held upright and has no fingerboard, the strings being stopped in mid air. Back in the U.S., she formed a band that lasted three years, featuring a drum, a flutelike *kaval*, and a *tambura*, which looks like a mandolin, and is plucked.

Always wanting to do something with her hands, and something to do with music, she began her training in rehairing at William Salchow's shop in New York, 1986–87, and spent part of the time with Jean Gruneberger, Stefan Thomachot and Pierre Guillaume in Paris. In 1988, she went to Brazil to buy *penambuco*. Her contact left her stranded in a denuded area gazing at piles of the precious wood. She managed to find her way back, and the following year married attorney Richard Buchanan. With the birth of Juliana, July 17, 1991, and Gabriel, August 31, 1993, not to mention remodeling the house, her bow making, while not abandoned, took a back seat until 1995 when a visit from a bow maker re-inspired her. Since then, she has attended the Oberlin Workshops each year and watched her ratings go up in successive competitions. Her clientele even includes country fiddlers who can appreciate that a fine bow will make them sound better.

Besides being busy professionally and maternally—with a supportive husband—Elizabeth also sings in a professional Balkan choir, and is glad she ignored the "expert" in France who told her back in 1982 that women should stick to restoration.

MARILYN WALLIN - *Teacher & Creator*

Born in Lincoln, Nebraska, in 1954, she is the great-granddaughter of pioneer homesteaders. Her father had a career as a professional woodworker, and music education was highly valued in her family. She, her sister and brother each studied piano and one orchestral instrument, and went to concerts as a family, from opera to jazz bands.

Her love of music and woodworking came together as a career choice in a single instant when, at nineteen, she met a violinmaker for the first time. David Wiebe became her mentor. After earning a BM (1978) in viola performance from the University of Iowa with the renowned **William Preucil** (father of the present Cleveland Symphony concertmaster of the same name), she attended the Chicago School of Violin Making, completing the course in 1982 and returning to graduate in 1984. In the interim, she completed the training to be a violin restorer at the prestigious Chicago firm of Bein and Fushi Rare Violins, Inc.

For twelve years (1986–98), she was director and instructor of violin making at the North Bennet Street School in Boston, during which time thirty-five students completed 350 instruments and their training under her tutelage. She remains an advisor to the program. In 1998, she founded the Boston Violin Makers Cooperative in Waltham, Massachusetts. It is, thus far, the main workshop of seven professional violin makers, and a drop by place for many others. It was designed, and is fulfilling its potential, as a place for the continuing growth of professional violin makers.

The VSA has been helpful in the development of her career with the winning, thus far, of two silver medals and nine certificates of merit in international competitions between 1988 and 2000, to show for her expertise. Wallin has received recognition in both main categories, Tone and Workmanship, and is now a member of the board of directors of the VSA. As of 2001, her prodigious output totaled 125 instruments: forty-six violins, fifty-one violas and twenty-eight cellos.

Marilyn's devoted husband, John Bogert Emery (Harvard, 1973), is a professional violinist. Her older daughter, Hollie Elizabeth Emery, born June 24, 1984, has studied string bass since she was eleven years old with Pascale Delache-Feldman at the Rivers School of Music. She began making her first violin in 2001, and attends conferences on violin making with her mother. Younger daughter, Julia Dale Emery, was born July 11, 1990. By age eleven she was studying cello and piano very seriously, performing regularly and attending master classes.

So, not only is this luthier a credit to her art, but she and John have contributed their talents to the next generation! (Author's note: Discussing the fact that even in the late 19th century it was not considered "ladylike" for a woman to put a violin under her dainty chin . . . Marilyn commented, "And now I carve the things with my bare hands, and no one shuns me for such an act!" So ladies, despite the sparse numbers, at least in *this* field women have come a long way . . .)

Rena & Michael Weisshaar

RENA WEISSHAAR - *Sharing an Illustrious Name*

Born in Berlin, February 8, 1940, Rena left the bomb-riddled city with her mother, her new-born sister and her older brother when, in 1943, the orders came that all women and children were to be evacuated. Her father, a lawyer who did not wish to be involved in Nazism, got a job managing the pharmaceutical factory belonging to a wealthy Jew who had fled to Switzerland. Cough syrup and eye ointment were considered important enough to exempt him from army service. Thus, her mother was one of the few fortunate wives not to be left alone. The family lived in the Harz Mountains until 1950, when they moved to Munich. Her father became legal counsel for a film company until 1964, at which time Berliners were hoping for unification despite the Wall having been erected in August 1961. (The Wall did not come down until November 1989, and East and West Berlin once again became one city in October 1990.)

Rena started cello at age eleven with Liselotte Richter, a pupil of one of the Hindemith brothers, but although she continued her studies for twelve years and became quite accomplished, despite being left-handed, her teacher advised against a professional career. (Peter Moes was also one of Richter's students and had visited the violin shop for cello repairs.)

Playing in a community orchestra, whose musicians were given a boost by the inclusion of Munich Conservatory students, the group was invited to perform at Mittenwald for their 100th anniversary (1959). This, plus a visit to the annual Craft Show at Munich where Rena saw a Mittenwald violin maker at work, sparked a fascination with wood. After some pleading, her parents let her go to the centuries old school where, at the time, of forty students, five were girls. Although there was some prejudice, for the most part the crafts-men-teachers were gentlemanly. One of them kept a log, and noted that the girls had better statistics when it came to sticking to a craft. After almost four years, Rena passed the tough Journeyman's exam. (During one summer vacation, she went to Italy and, under the tutelage of an Italian master, built her own cello.)

Like **Wendela** and **Peter Moes**, Rena met her husband at the school. Michael, who had been sent to perfect his technique, was the son of noted Los Angeles violin maker Hans Weisshaar. She and Michael married in Spring 1964, and with her husband having to finish his course, went by herself to her father-in-law's shop in Hollywood. The couple were reunited by Christmas. Working for hard taskmaster Hans for the next nine years proved challenging. Meanwhile, Rena gave birth to Nina in 1966 and Daniel in 1967 and, under the circumstances, with her mother-in-law's help, could manage both the babies and the work. (Hans died in 1991.)

In July 1975, she and Michael started their own successful shop in Costa Mesa, fifty miles south of Los Angeles. In 1980, they received another blessing in the form of their second daughter, Marianne, who became a proficient violinist. Nina became a first class physical therapist, has a sports trainer license, plus an MA from Duke University. Married to a Coast Guard Lieutenant, she presented Rena with her first grandchildren, Jacob Adam, born June 1998, and Diana, who arrived December 1999.

After a degree from Pomona College in Classic Latin, Greek mythology, and a minor in music, Daniel studied violin-making in France, near Fontainebleau, with Bernard Camurat, who had spent ten years in Hans Weisshaar's shop, and in Chicago under Mittenwald-trained Michael Becker (no relation to the Carl Becker family). He joined his parents in October 1999, in their new, larger shop on Orange Avenue, where they had moved in April, a block away from their original place.

Like Wendela and Peter Moes and Sigrun Seifert and Joseph Grubaugh, Rena and Michael work well together. At 300 woman-hours per violin—allowing for variables in wood and varnish—plus all the repairs and other duties, Rena produces two to three instruments per year. Her customers are only too glad to wait for them, as was Haroutune Bedelian, a concert violinist and professor of violin at UC Irvine, whom the author was privileged to hear in recital. In June 1996, he had asked if Rena would craft a copy of his 1699 Giovanni Rogeri violin. (Rogeri, like Antonio Stradivari, apprenticed in the workshop of Niccolò Amati.) The work took until May 1997. Bedelian's reactions: "It feels just like my violin! and the tone, Excellent! . . . Great! . . . Bravo!"

When a violin leaves her shop she feels a vacuum, but there is always the satisfaction of what Hans would say, "It's good work."

In July 2000, the Weisshaars celebrated twenty-five years in Costa Mesa with a grand party. In April 2006, Rena shared the excellent viola she had made for her son at the Players Meet Makers event at the twenty-fifth anniversary of the AFVBM held at the Library of Congress. On July 5, my husband and I visited the store and were warmly welcomed by Rena, Michael and Dan.

ISABELLE WILBAUX - *Expertise with a French Accent*

Isabelle was born in Tournai, Belgium, in 1965. In 1988, she graduated from the International School of violin making in Cremona, where she was awarded the prize from the Walter Stauffers Foundation for the construction of a baroque violin. From 1989–90, she worked as a restorer in France and Spain. Since 1991, she has devoted herself mainly to the making of new instruments, participating in many international competitions in Paris, Prague, Cremona, Mittenwald, Poznan (Poland) and Salt Lake City. Her numerous prizes include: a tonal prize in Mittenwald (1993); three prizes in Cremona (1994); the S.F. Sacconi Best Craftsmanship in the viola category; and Best Woman Violinmaker. 1995 brought the Belgian Vocation Foundation Prize for the project of making a string quartet, and in 1998, a special prize for her quartet at the VSA competition in Salt Lake City.

In 1998, she and her French-Canadian husband **Martin Héroux**, whom she met when he was studying in Brussels, decided to establish a workshop together in Montreal. Martin has an international reputation for his great restoration abilities. Besides repairs, restorations and sales, they now share the skills learned in the best workshops of Europe and North America, combining their talents and experience to create instruments which they sign together.

EUROPEAN WOMEN LUTHIERS

Although the profession was traditionally a masculine one, even in Europe things have changed in the last twenty years, and now a good number of women are in this trade.

Female members of the Entente Internationale des Luthiers et Archetiers (EILA) in Europe include **Ingeborg Behnke** of Berlin, one of the first women in the field in Germany; **Edda Bünnagel**, an associate member who works with her husband Wolfgang in Cologne; **Edith Dittrich**, in Switzerland; **Andrea Frandsen** in Angers (France); **Irene Loebner** in Munich, who specializes in repairs and restorations; **Gertrud Reuter** in Basel (Switzerland), who works with the famed Roland Baumgartner; and **Cornélie Möller** in Amsterdam who, while not a luthier herself, oversees her late husband's workshop to carry on the name Berend Max Möller, which was in the third generation until his tragic death in 1989 at the hands of burglars. Their children are Yolande Marie, born 1977, a pharmacist, and Jan-Berend Max, 1979, a lawyer.

In France: **ANDREA FRANDSEN** was born in Stege, on the Isle of Møn, Denmark, September 17, 1957, into a farmer's family where music was rarely heard. Not until she was a teenager did she get into the music of the '70s and Scandinavian folk music. Her violin studies did not begin until she was twenty. She had already met her future husband, Patrick Robin, when, in 1981, she went to England to study music in Newark-on-Trent, a college which has one of the best violin-making courses in Europe. Patrick was in the Violin-Making School when Andrea, visiting workshops and meeting enthusiastic students, caught the spirit and joined the "lutherie" the following year, receiving her diploma, in 1985, with "distinction."

They are both members of EILA, and Andrea's awards include a gold medal in 1991 for a viola presented to the first "Concours International de la ville de Paris"; a VSA gold medal in 1994, for a violin entered in Oakland, California; and a VSA silver medal for a viola at Fort Michel, Kentucky, in 2000. Her violins, violas and cellos are played by soloists from l'Opéra de Paris, the Finnish Radio Orchestra, the Royal Chapel Orchestra in Denmark, the Bayerischer Rundfunk (Bavarian Radio), and by musicians from l'Orchestre de Paris, l'Orchestre National des Pays de Loire, l'Ensemble Jean Wiener, le Mahler Orchestra, the symphonic orchestra in Gunma, Japan, orchestra

"Liceu" of Barcelona, and many others. Meanwhile, the instruments of her numerous gold medal-winning husband can be heard in the Berlin Philharmonic, Vienna Chamber Orchestra, Vienna Folk Opera, Helsinki Philharmonic, Jean Sibelius Quartet, l'Orchestre de Paris, l'Opéra de Paris, l'Orchestre Philarmonique de Radio France, l'Ensemble Orchestral de France, etc.

Andrea, and French-born Patrick, married in 1983, and established their workshop in 1988 in Angers, France. Of their three daughters, the first two were born in Bremen (Germany), Nina, January 15, 1986, and Nicoline, June 27, 1987, when Patrick worked for the firm of Geigenbau Machold, specializing in the fine art of restoring instruments of the great classical schools. Elisa arrived in Angers, July 28, 1996.

As of 2001, Andrea was learning to play drums!

In Germany: **IRENE LOEBNER** has her workshop in Mühldorf, specializing in restoration and repair, and also works with the Wolfgang Zunterer Company in Munich. Born June 3, 1953, in Markt Schwaben, with her parents' encouragement she began violin at seven, and as an adult studied cello. Wanting to use both her brain and her hands, her love for music led her into violin making. She studied at Mittenwald (1974–77) and received a Gold Medal upon passing her master examination (1982). Besides her craft, she is the co-author of several publications, including *Violins and Bows of the Past*, and has lectured on violin labels, with focus on the Kloz family of Mittenwald.

Irene has two daughters, Veronica, born 1992, and Laura, 1990.

Further French Connections

L'Association des luthiers et archetiers pour le développement de la facture instrumentale (ADALFI), the Association of Violin and Bow Makers for the Development and Building of Instruments, was founded in 1982, in France, to improve and monitor the quality of instruments built in Europe, and offer competitions for excellence. ADALFI members have won many competitions all over the world, such as Cremona, Mittenwald, Kessel (Germany), Paris, Sofia (Bulgaria), Ottawa (Canada), and Portland (Oregon), home base for the AFVBM. In a roster of over seventy-five, these women are listed: **Florence Bigorgne**, **Martine Duboisson**, **Nicole Dumond**, **Christine Foundain**, **Maryse Fuhrmann**, **Katia Louis**, **Christine Morin**, **Andrea Panitz** (Switzerland), **Isabelle Perrin**, **Nelly Poidevin**, **Agnès Rosenstiel** and **Claire Ryder**.

Nicole Dumond was born in Nîmes (France) in 1952. After obtaining her degree in letters at Paul Valery University, Montpellier, she entered the Cremonese Violin Workshop in Italy, under the guidance of masters Alceste Bulfari and Giorgio Scolari. She completed her training with courses in advanced restoration with Gil Solomon, himself a product of Hill & Son of London, and bow-making with Giovanni Lucchi, receiving her luthier diploma in 1980.

While in Cremona, Nicole also studied lyrical singing at the Montiverdi School with Professor Ginevra. Returning to France, she entered the Music Conservatory of Montpellier in 1981, receiving a diploma in singing in 1985. She became the lead vocalist with a number of different jazz and rock groups around Montpellier. She also sang with a theater group, with which she staged a production at the Festival of Avignon.

She shares a workshop with Ghaleb Hassan, whom she met in Cremona in 1988, and who specializes in creating new violins and violas. He participates in the annual international violin makers' fairs MUSICORA in Paris and the Tokyo MUSIC FAIR.

Groupement des Luthiers er Archetiers d'Art de France (GLAAF), GLAAF is the other "guild" for these gifted artisans. Their handful of women members include **Dorian Bodart**, **Claudia Höbel**, **Verana LeCanu**, **Silvie Masson**, **Christine Morin** and **Silvie Sauret**.

Seeing the Trees for the Wood

The town of Mittenwald (literally meaning in the middle of the forest) is located in Bavaria (Germany) in the Alps near the Austrian border close to Innsbruck. An important trading center of the 14th and 15th centuries, it became famous for instrument-making by the 17th century. It was around 1672, at age twelve, that Mathias Kloz (pronounced Klotz), a tailor's son interested in music and instruments, was sent to Italy to study the art of violin making. He returned in 1683, a prosperous, skilled lute and violin maker and established his own workshop. With maple and spruce growing abundantly on the surrounding mountains, and the advantageous site on the trade route connecting Southern Germany and Italy, business flourished. Not only did Kloz train his own sons in five-year apprenticeships, but also those of fellow citizens in the town and surrounding villages. At his death in 1750, there were fifteen violin makers, the foundation of the *Geigenbauschule* (violin building school), which was officially established a century later, in 1858, under the rule of the intellectual, arts-supporting King Maximilian II (1811–64).

Originally, instruments were sold via peddlers to the surrounding monasteries and nearby towns. When this market became saturated, artisans left the trading to relatives, who were dealers and merchants with travel routes extending to Cologne, Frankfurt, Leipzig, and even Vienna, Budapest, Russia, Portugal and England. By 1807, over one third of Mittenwald's income was generated by approximately eighty luthiers and ten bow makers, who comprised over 30 percent of the male inhabitants.

Already an Alpine tourist town, in 1930 Mittenwald added a museum of violins and violin making to its attractions. This was moved to larger quarters in 1960, and the building was purchased outright by the town in 1980. 1983 was marked with big celebrations of the town's 300th anniversary and the 125th anniversary of the violin school.

Beginning with only German students, as the school's reputation gained fame others came from China, Japan, Sweden, Switzerland, USA, Mexico, France, Denmark, Belgium, Austria, Norway, Finland, etc. Many well known masters in all countries have graduated from Mittenwald. The curriculum, based on the old German and Italian traditions, spans seven semesters covering all phases of stringed instrument making, including the reconstruction of the historical *viola d'amore* and *viola da gamba*, as well as repairs. The rest is theory, technical drawings, music and art history, physics/acoustics, plus instrumental and orchestral playing. A department for plucked instruments was added in 1982. After three years, a graduating student is ready to take the journeymen's examination.

A model for violin making schools throughout the world, and much in demand for enrollment, Mittenwald, now under the Bavarian Ministry of Culture, enters its 4th century with descendants of Mathias Kloz still associated with the school.

No accounting of women luthiers would be complete without the inclusion of Carleen Hutchins.

Luthier-Acoustical Scientist Extraordinaire!

Carleen Hutchins

CARLEEN MALEY HUTCHINS, who was ninety-five, May 24, 2006, is the founder of, and driving force behind, the New Violin Family Association (1998); creator-in-chief of the Violin Octet family; co-founder of the Catgut Acoustical Society (1963); Fellow of the Acoustical Society of America (ASA); and trained luthier, who has been working at the interface of violin making and acoustical science for more than half a century.

Born in Springfield, Massachusetts, May 24, 1911, to musical parents, she grew up in Montclair, New Jersey, where she still lives. She blew the bugle for many years in her Girl Scout troop and soloed on trumpet in school bands, but when she got to Cornell it was entomology, then pre-med and biology, which became her fields. Accepted to Duke Medical School in 1933, the Depression and lack of money curtailed this pioneer opportunity, sending her instead to work at the Brooklyn Botanical Gardens Elementary Education Program (1933–34), and then to the progressive Woodward and Brearley Schools to teach science to *girls*. She even designed a progressive Science Room for the New York public schools.

During this time her friends, especially **Helen Rice** (1901–80), wanted her to play chamber music with them, so she learned the viola at age forty, after getting one for $75 from Wurlizter. Having worked in wood all her life—she built the house in New Hampshire where she still summers—and having an uncle whose hobby was making violins, she set about, with a little advice, a book, a blueprint, and proper wood from a luthier, to build her own instrument.

She also began studying violin making with two prominent luthiers: Carl Berger (1954–59) and Simon Fernando Sacconi (1959–62), at the Wurlizter Shop. 1943 saw her marriage to Morton A. Hutchins, a Harvard graduate and Dupont research chemist in the then pioneer field of plastics. Their son William Aldrich was born in 1947, and daughter Caroline (Cassie) in 1950. (She has three granddaughters and a grandson.)

It was Helen Rice—known as the "Great Lady of Chamber Music" and founder of the Amateur Chamber Music Players Association, whose original handful of members now number over 8,000 worldwide—who introduced Carleen to Professor Fred A. Saunders in 1947. Retired from Harvard since 1942, he had been experimenting with the acoustics of stringed instruments, but was not able to take the valuable ones apart. Hutchins made him some instruments for that very purpose, greatly aiding his research. Joined in the 1950s by John C. Schelleng, a fine cellist and research director at Bell Laboratories, their acoustical experiments were advanced when Robert E. Fryxell, a chemist and cellist, added his knowledge to their efforts. All being chamber music buddies, Schelleng now dubbed the four, the "Catgut Musical Society."

Carleen joined the American Acoustical Society in 1961. The 1962 publication of a joint Saunders and Hutchins paper, "Subharmonics and Tap Tones in Violin Acoustics" (the latter subject being her contribution), and her article, "The Physics of Violins" in *Scientific American* (1963), brought this unique research to wider attention. Through these years Hutchins began further acoustical research, going back to Felix Savart in 1819, Backhaus and Moinel in Germany, C.V. Ramad in India, and violin makers from Australia to Philadelphia. She scoured major national libraries and added to the reprints left her by Saunders upon his death in 1963.

The Catgut Acoustical Society

From 1963, Hutchins' energies centered on her **Catgut Acoustical Society**, pioneering the development of scientific insights and their application to the construction of new and conventional instruments of the violin family. She developed the innovation of tuning the free plates of an instrument *before* its assembly, methods now used by violin makers around the world. The initial CAS membership of twenty has grown to over a thousand in thirty different countries, bringing together researchers in musical acoustics, luthiers, composers, string players and lovers of the music they make. Their Library contains the most complete repository in the world of writings on the acoustics of stringed instruments. In 1992, the Stanford University Center for Computer Research in Music & Acoustics (CCRMA) was selected as the permanent home for these files.

The Violin Octet

The result of all the physics research, dating back to 1937, was the Violin Octet, a set (consort) of eight finely matched instruments in a series of sizes and tunings to cover the entire range of written music, starting at the bottom with the oversized large bass tuned as a double bass, and finishing at the top with the tiny, treble violin tuned one octave above the violin. Ten years of experiment and development in the dimensions, fittings, and resonances of a large number of instruments by Hutchins and Saunders made it possible, for the first time in string history since ancient viols, to create a whole family of acoustically matched instruments with violin tone qualities.

In 1976, Carolyn Field, wife, mother and chamber music player, wandered into Carleen's New Jersey shop to get her cello repaired. This led to her being a student of Hutchins, becoming a violin maker in her own right, her mentor's main assistant in the construction of Octet instruments, and a lifelong friendship.

The New Violin Family Association

The NVFA was formed in 2000, as a separate entity from CAS, to establish acceptance of these new instruments worldwide. It is developing an archive of the history and science behind their construction which, with an Octet set, is housed in the American Shrine to Music Museum in Vermillion, South Dakota, near Minneapolis.

Hutchins' many awards include: two Guggenheim Fellowships, four grants from the Martha Baird Rockefeller Fund for Music, Fellow of American Association for the Advancement of Science, four honorary doctorates (D. Eng., Stevens Institute, New Jersey; DFA, Hamilton College, New York; D. Sc, St. Andrews Presbyterian College, North Carolina; LLD, Concordia University, Montreal), the First Silver Medal from the Acoustical Society of America and, in 1998, an *honorary fellowship*—the Society's highest award—as yet bestowed only fourteen times, the first of which was to Thomas Alva Edison in 1929.

In addition to constructing over one hundred instruments for the Violin Octet[112] family since 1958, she has constructed eighty violins, 170 violas and fifteen cellos. By studying the acoustical properties of each instrument during construction and assembly (as related to its final tonal characteristics), her work has resulted in a test that violin makers worldwide are using to produce consistently fine sounding instruments. Hutchins has published over 100 technical papers, taught violin making to fifty-plus students, and given over 200 demonstration lectures with the Violin Octet. She has written the violin acoustics section for Grove's *Dictionary of Music and Musicians*, and edited two sets of volumes of Collected Papers in Violin Acoustics, covering the seminal work from 1800–1993. She continues construction of new instruments, research into the acoustical properties of stringed instruments, and serves as the executive director of the New Violin Family Association, Inc., which she founded in 1999, to educate the public about the New Octet Violins through writings, concerts, lectures and demonstrations. She encourages players to use the instruments in public performance and teaching, as well as stimulating composition, and instructs others in their construction. An archive containing documents and other material relating to these violins is being created.

In 1965, the great conductor **Leopold Stokowski** said of the Octet, "A major step has been taken toward renovating the strings for the first time in 200 years . . . Bravo!"

Kudos for Modern string instruments

Cellist **David Finckel**, husband of pianist **Wu Han**, who himself owns a modern instrument, made this erudite statement in *Strings* magazine (February-March, 2000): "I really believe in today's instrument makers. I think they are going to save us, as old instruments are being increasingly priced out of the range of performers . . . they are a wonderful group of dedicated, hard-working people whose lives are centered on timeless values: patience, craftsmanship, and beauty."

Further insight comes from a luthier: "It's *wood* that keeps you fascinated! Each time you start on a new instrument, the wood invites you to explore its unique qualities . . . and the excitement begins again . . . even after forty-two years!" —Rena Weisshaar, July 5, 2006

112. Six sets of Octets are presently located in the Stockholm (Sweden) Musik Museum; Museum of Edinburgh; Shrine to Music Museum, Vermillion, South Dakota; in Denver with Robert Miller, VP of the NVFA; the Hutchins Consort—named after Carleen—in Encinitas, California [fifteen minutes from my home]; and the Metropolitan Museum of Art, New York City. In 1997, the set in St. Petersburg (Russia) was transferred to the Iceland Symphony on loan.

Other Strings Attached

Liona Boyd
Annette Degenhardt
Alison Gould
Sharon Isbin
Eleftheria Kotzia

Virginia Luque
Wu Man
Anoushka Shankar
Myrna Sislen

The Guitar

Forerunners of the guitar—lute, lyre, and like instruments—were played by women before Greek and Roman times. The history of the guitar dates back 5,000 years, having been played in the time of Egyptian pharaohs. The conquering Romans brought it to Spain, where by 1500 it had become the national instrument under the name *vihuela*. The conquistadors brought it to Mexico. Early Spanish composer **Louis Milan** (1500–61) wrote a book with playing instructions and sixty-eight pieces for the guitar. The instrument became known in other European countries during the baroque period. It was adopted in the French Court of Louis XIV, and appeared in many famous paintings. In the 1920s, the guitar replaced the banjo in American jazz. Electric guitars became the mainstay of rock and roll beginning in the mid-1950s. It was **Andrés Segovia** (1893–1987) who brought the instrument into the concert hall with his transcriptions of Bach and other classicists. The unique **Romero Family**—Celedonio (1913–96) and his three sons, Celin, Pepe and Angel, and now the grandsons, Lito and Celino—have brought further popularity to the classical guitar, as did Brazilian **Laurindo Almeida** (1917–95). Flamenco artists **Carlos Montóya** (1903–93) and **Manitos de la Plata** graced the concert stage with another unique dimension of this instrument. There is still a scarcity of compositions for its classical role, especially as an orchestral instrument. Three of the most popular concertos written for guitar are by **Joaquín Turina** (1882–1949), **Mario Castel-Nuovo-Tedesco** (1895–1968), and **Joaquín Rodrigo** (1901–99).

In our century, two feminine names were unearthed in 1995 from old 78-rpm records. **Luise Walker**, born in Vienna, 1910, studied with Catalán guitarist **Miguel Llobet** (1878–1938) who was a pupil of the great Spanish composer **Francisco Tárrega** (1852–1909). French-Italian **Ida Presti** (1924–67) had a major career concertizing as duo-guitarists with her husband **Alexandre Lagoya**. The two women also performed together. Today, several women have made careers as both classical and crossover guitarists.

Composer/guitarist **LIONA BOYD** has developed a musical style encompassing classical, pop, jazz and Latin music. Born in London, her family moved to Canada when she was six. She asked her parents for a guitar when she was fourteen, and took private classes with some of the top artists in the world: **Andrés Segovia**, **Alírio Díaz**, **Narciso Yepes** and **Julian Bream**. After her bachelor's in music performance from the University of Toronto, she studied for two years in Paris with Alexandre Lagoya. Upon returning to North America, she recorded her first album and made her debut at Carnegie Hall.

She has performed with orchestras and participated in festivals around the world, from New Delhi to Istanbul to Edinburgh, Seoul and Tokyo. Breaking from classical tradition, she toured with Gordon Lightfoot and Tracy Chapman, and made numerous appearances on television, including the *Tonight Show*. As a soloist, she was the first performer to appear at the new Paris Opera House.

Her many recordings cover repertoire from baroque to Christmas albums to her new age/pop project featuring Eric Clapton and Yo-Yo Ma. The album, *Dancing on the Edge*, combines nouveau flamenco, jazz, and new age styles—similar to her near-platinum *Persona* album. Other disks have gone gold and platinum. She often performs her own music.

Boyd, who also plays for many fundraisers and charity concerts, has had the opportunity to perform in private concerts for many world leaders, including the British Royal Family, the King and Queen of Spain, the Chancellor of Germany, prime ministers of Canada and Great Britain, U.S. and Mexican presidents, Cuba's Fidel Castro, and at the New Year's gala at the Kremlin shortly before the demise of the Soviet Union. She has received several honorary degrees and Juno Awards for Instrumental Artist of the Year, was inducted into the "Gallery of Greats" of *Guitar Player Magazine* and presented the prestigious Order of Canada.

Annette Degenhardt

ANNETTE DEGENHARDT, born in Mainz (Germany), 1965, studied guitar at the College of Music and Art in Frankfurt am Main (1985–90). Her first recording (1986) of her own compositions for guitar is entitled *Nicht eingebracht, nicht wild erfühlt* (Not Taken in, Not Wildly Fulfilled), her second is *Zwischentöne* (Between Sounds, 1992), next came *Waltzing Guitar*, featuring twelve lilting waltzes of her own composition (1994), followed by *Umwege* (Detours, 1996), a set of thirteen waltzes on the theme of roaming. *Muse-Musette* was released in 1998, *Farewell* in 2000, and *Best of Andeg* (2001) represents a cross-section of her work within the last fifteen years. 2004 brought *The Land of My Childhood*, with Irish and Scottish songs, plus a composition for the harp by Turlough O'Carolan, which she arranged for the guitar.

Degenhardt continues to concertize throughout Europe.

Sharon Isbin

Considered one of the foremost guitarists, and first woman to reach the pinnacle of the solo guitar world, **SHARON ISBIN**, born August 7, 1956, studied with Jeffrey Van in her hometown, Minneapolis. Her father, a professor at the University of Minnesota, was on sabbatical in Italy when, at age nine, she began her studies with **Oscar Ghiglia**, and later Andrés Segovia, the great Spanish guitarist and pioneer of classical arrangements for guitar, responsible for elevating the instrument to the concert stage. At fourteen, Sharon won a competition and played with the Minnesota Orchestra, then went on to win first prizes in Toronto, Munich, and the 1979 Queen Sofia Competition in Madrid. Further studies were at the Banff Music Festival in 1972 with Alírio Díaz, the Aspen Music School (1971–75), and ten years with Bach specialist **Rosalyn Tureck**, who prepared her for the recording of the J.S. Bach: *Complete Lute Suites* (transcribed for guitar). She received her BM (1978) and MM (1979) from Yale. She has made annual tours of Europe since she was seventeen. In an international concert and recital career that includes over sixty concerts a year, she has been heard throughout North and South America, Japan, the Orient, New Zealand, Australia and Israel.

With over twenty CDs, her music spans from baroque, Spanish/Latin, contemporary, to crossover and jazz fusion, performing with New England jazz saxophonist Paul Winter, and Brazilian guitarist Thiago de Mello. Besides many solo and chamber works, she has commissioned some dozen guitar concerti over the years, with John Corigliano's *Troubadour*s (1993)—one of the most successful—and the ninth, *Concert de Gaudí*, by Christopher Rouse, premiered January 2000.

Isbin teaches at the Aspen Music Festival, and is director of the guitar department at Juilliard, which she founded in 1989. Since its inception, it has attracted female students from over fifteen countries. She has been profiled on television's *CBS Sunday Morning*.

ELEFTHERIA KOTZIA was born in Greece, and studied guitar at the conservatories of Athens and Paris, as well as London's Guildhall School of Music with support from the British Council and the Hellenic Foundation. She was twice chosen to participate in the master classes of Julian Bream (1977, 1984), was the first prize winner of the sixth International Guitar Competition in Milan (1977), and of the "Ville de Juvisy" (France, 1982). Since her London debut in 1985, she has toured regularly throughout Europe, Scandinavia, North Africa, Canada, America, Israel, Australia and the Far East. Her 1989 recording, *The Blue Guitar*, featuring the premiere of Sir Michael Tippett's *Sonata*, was selected by *Gramophone* magazine as a "Critic's Choice Recording of the Year." Many contemporary composers have dedicated works to her.

Now residing in London, Kotzia's popular programs include "La Guitarra Latina" and "Eleftheria and Friends." Her broad repertoire also features the music of many Greek composers.

The father of **VIRGINIA LUQUE** brought home a guitar for himself one Christmas, and told his three-year-old daughter not to touch it. Not only did she disobey, but played a carol, astounding family and friends. Born in Algeçiras, (Spain), by age six she was studying flamenco guitar and the next year started classical. At thirteen, she met the great Andrés Segovia, who encouraged her to go to the conservatory in Málaga, from which she graduated at seventeen with the prize of honor. She also received first prize at the Manuel de Falla International Competition for Classical Guitar. She met Segovia again in a master class in Granada. This time he suggested she apply to Juilliard, and that he would give her lessons whenever he was in New York. (These sometimes lasted five hours!) With her parents' support—and their life savings—the family came to America where Virginia won the Lincoln Center Scholarship and was able to complete her MM at Juilliard (1991) as a pupil of **Sharon Isbin**.

The talent of Virginia Luque matches her classic Spanish beauty. She has performed solo recitals in the U.S. and abroad, including appearances at Carnegie Hall, the Met, and in Spain and Germany. She was a professor of music and classical guitar at the Málaga Conservatory (1982–86) and at Adelphi University (1991–94).

From Ancient Times

Alison Gould

ALISON GOULD, born May 9, 1948, in Birmingham, England, studied ballet as a child and became a dance teacher. She subsequently trained and worked in London and Frankfurt mastering the lute under Lutz Kirchof. She also studied vocal technique from ancient to modern times. Her repertoire of authentic medieval and renaissance songs combines expert knowledge and high musical ability with an entertaining approach which has been heard all over Europe, including radio and television. Her performances in renaissance costume recreate the concept of *trobairitz*, the female troubadours of 12th century France. She also concertizes on the guitar.

An associate in early music at the RCM, London, Gould resides in Frankfurt.

Born, raised, and educated in Washington, DC, **MYRNA SISLEN**, a graduate of American University, plays the vihuela—the aforementioned Spanish renaissance forerunner of the classical guitar as we know it today. One of the few artists on this instrument in the Western world, this rare talent has provided a great deal of exposure for the artist. She has performed at Kennedy Center and Carnegie Hall. On the faculty at George Washington University, she oversees the Myrna Sislen Guitar Scholarship Fund, founded by a generous benefactor in 1983. She arranged and edited *First Classical Pieces for Guitar* (1984), which has become a basic text for students worldwide. A member of the Washington Guitar Quintet, she exercises her flexible repertoire of jazz, pop, Latin American and classical works with fellow group-member, jazz great Charlie Byrd.

Exotic Instruments

Wu Man

WU MAN was cited by the *Los Angeles Times* as "the artist most responsible for bringing the pipa to the Western world." The pipa is a plucked instrument in the lute family. She was trained in the Pudong School of playing, the classical style of Imperial China. She earned her MM in pipa performance from Beijing's Central Conservatory. Since coming to the U.S. in 1990, she has become a proponent of both traditional and contemporary repertory. Concertos and chamber works composed for her have come from **Chen Yi**, **Bun-Ching Lam**, Tan Dun, Zhou Long, and Bright Sheng. In 1999, she won the City of Toronto/Glenn Gould Protégé Prize.

She has since toured and recorded with Yo-Yo Ma as part of the his Silk Road Project, in concerts in Europe, Japan and the U.S., including SummerFest La Jolla, 2005. She has also performed with Cho-Liang Lin, the Kronos Quartet, Ensemble Modern, and the Los Angeles Philharmonic New Music Group. She gave the world premiere of Lou Harrison's pipa concerto with the Stuttgart Chamber Orchestra at Lincoln Center, 1997, and in 1998 Tan Dun's concerto for pipa and string orchestra with Gerard Schwartz and the Seattle Symphony.

Anoushka Shankar

The daughter of world famous sitarist, Ravi Shankar, **ANOUSHKA SHANKAR** was born in London, June 9, 1981. She grew up in both Southern California and India, where she spends part of every winter performing with her father and visiting her family. Completely trained by Ravi since she was nine, she began on a "baby" sitar built especially for her. At age thirteen, she made her debut in New Delhi. The same year, she entered a recording studio for the first time to play on her father's disc, *In Celebration*. In 1997, she assisted as conductor with her father and his friend and frequent colleague, Beatle, George Harrison, on the Angel release, *Chants of India*. An exclusive contract with Angel/EMI Classics brought out her first solo recording, *Anoushka*, in the fall of 1998. Her second album, *Anourag*, was released in August 2000, both to great acclaim.

She tours the world with her father's ensemble, performing in India, Europe, Asia and America. She also showcases her father's Concerto No. 1 for Sitar and Orchestra, which she first performed with Zubin Mehta and the London Philharmonic, March 1997. She premiered a new Ravi Shankar work for sitar and cello with Mstislav Rostropovich at the Evian Festival, July 1999. In February 2000, Anoushka became the first woman ever to perform at the Ramakrishna Centre in Calcutta.

In recognition of her artistry and musicianship, on July 17, 1998, the British Parliament presented Anoushka with a House of Commons Shield. She is the youngest, as well as the first female, recipient of this high honor.

During 2005, she accompanied her father on his eighty-fifth birthday tour. Despite Air France breaking their instruments, two sitars were brought in from India in time for their concert in July, in Arles (France).

In honor of his birthday tour, on August 2, Ravi and Anoushka performed in the BBC Proms at the Royal Albert Hall. It was the first time that either of them have appeared at the Proms, and the first time that the Proms has presented any music other than Western classical. Anoushka performed her father's Sitar Concerto with the BBC Symphony Orchestra, conducted by Jurjen Hempel, and then they played traditional Indian ragas.

Angelic Sounds — Harpists Past and Present

Stéphanie-Félicité de Genlis (1746–1830)
Sophia Dussek (1775–1828)
Dorette Spohr (1787–1834)
Ekaterina Walter-Kiune (1870–1931)
Henriette Renié (1875–1956)
Ksenia Erdeli (1878–1971)
Winifred Bambrick (1892–1969)
Lily Laskine (1893–1988)
Mildred Dilling (1894–1991)
Marie Goossens (1894–1991)
Maria Korchinska (1895–1988)
Lucile Rosenbloom (1898–1992)
Clelia Gatti-Aldrovandi (1901–1989)
Eileen Malone (1906–1999)
Edna Phillips (1907–2003)
Alice Chalifoux (1908–)
Vera Dulova (1909–2000)
Phia Berghout (1909–1986
Lucile Lawrence (1907–2004)
Inga Gråe (1910–1986)
Marjorie Tyre (1910–2003)
Emmy Hürlimann (1914–2001)
Ann Stockton (1916–2006)
Phyllis Schlomovitz (1917–2003)
Martha Dalton (1919–)
Anne Adams (1919–)
Acacia de Mello (1921–)
Dorothy Remsen (1921–)
Marilyn Costello (1924–1998)
Judy Loman (1936–retired)
Nancy Allen
Maria Casale
Marcia Dickstein
Sonja Gislinge
Catherine Gotthoffer

Ann Griffiths
Deborah Hoffman
Yolanda Kondonassis
Marie-Pierre Langlamet
Heidi Lehwalder
Susann McDonald
Carrol McLaughlin
Nora Mercz
Susanna Mildonian
Emily Mitchell
Marielle Nordmann
Ann Pilot
Olga Ortenberg Rakitchenkov
Marisa Robles
Sunita Staneslow
Joann Turovsky
Naoko Yosino
Laurie Buchanan
Amy Lynn Kanner
Christina Tourin
Mary O'Hara

A Newer Generation

Mariko Anraku
Charlotte Balzereit
Jana Boušková
Cristina Braga
Catrin Finch
Bridget Kibbey
Isabelle Perrin
Emma Ramsdale
Gwyneth Wentink
Patricia Wooster
Sylvia Hartman

Ancient Twangings

The harp in its many forms has been popular through the centuries, especially since it is so well suited to accompanying the voice. Women harpists can be traced back to ancient history via the usual Greek urns, paintings and friezes. Roman statuary and bas-reliefs depict carefree maidens twanging their *lyres*—small hand-held forerunners of the harp. The Irish harp—with differing sizes and number of strings—existed in the Middle Ages, and found its way to the European Continent by the 9th century. In epics like *Beowulf*, "harpers" are referred to as entertainers and chroniclers. The early English king, Alfred the Great (849–99), was said to have been an excellent player during the Age of Chivalry, which viewed facility on the small medieval harp as one of the social graces, along with jousting and combat. With the passing age of knights and troubadours, the harp was appropriated by the ladies of the court. From the 16th century onward, it was transferred from minstrels in feudal halls to the salons of high-born women.

The Harp Goes On Stage

Although piano and harpsichord, but not organ, were the only accepted instruments for refined young women until past the mid-19th century—because they could be played in a demure, seated position—amazingly, the harp was exempted from the stigma of "unladylike." It took until the last part of the 18th century, however, for the harp to be elevated to the status of an orchestral instrument. By 1720, the instrument had advanced to the single-action pedal harp, allowing selected strings to be raised one halftone. In 1810, **Sébastien Érard** (1752–1831), better known for making the first pianoforte in France, invented the ingenious double-action pedal system, which enabled the harp to play in all keys. He did for the harp what the luthiers of Cremona had done for the violin a century before.

Royalty continued to enjoy performances of accomplished harpists. One of the most notable was the mistress of France's Duke of Orleans. Other aristocratic women were musicians in their own right.

COMTESSE STÉPHANIE-FÉLICITÉ de GENLIS, born in Burgundy, January 25, 1746, is remembered as the harpist who tried to incorporate the fifth finger into technical usage. History records her as a member of royalty during the French Revolution, and her influential role as mistress of the Duc d'Orléans, "Philippe Égalité." At the peak of her beauty, she became the governess of his daughters. Her education standards were so innovative that the Duke dismissed his sons' tutors and sent his sons to her, making her the first woman in such a role. She was also the first woman to have a writing desk in her apartments. Under her guidance, Philippe became sensitive to the plight of the people, a political stance which saved his children from the guillotine. Her books, educational theories and political views were held in high respect both on the Continent and in England. When her life was imminently threatened by the French Revolution, she managed to escape to Switzerland *with her beloved harp!* She lived to see Philippe ascend the throne of France. She died at the advanced age of eighty-four on December 31, 1830.

SOPHIA GIUSTINA CORRI DUSSEK, born May 1, 1775, in Edinburgh, was trained by her father, Italian composer Domenico Corri, in voice and piano. Her first husband, Bohemian pianist and composer **Jan Ladislav Dussek** (1760–1812), taught her the harp. Under his guidance, she became as competent at this as she was a singer and pianist. In 1801, she gave birth to their daughter, Olivia, whom she trained and who also mastered the harp, piano, organ, as well as composing for these instruments and publishing songs. Dussek became a partner in his father-in-law's publishing firm in London, but since neither was much of a businessman, they ran into debt. Dussek fled the country, leaving Corri to be jailed for bankruptcy. After her second marriage in 1812 to violist **Johann Alvis Moralt**, a member of the famous German string quartet family, Sophia published her own compositions for harp and piano. She died c1828.

DORETTE SCHEIDLER SPOHR, born in 1787, had already established her career as a brilliant harpist before her 1806 marriage to German violinist/composer/conductor **Louis** (Ludwig) **Spohr** (1784–1859). He had been introduced by her mother, a singer at the court of the Duke of Gotha. He wrote compositions for harp and violin which the couple performed throughout Europe. Craving adulation, Louis needed to keep on the move. He used his wife's dowry for a special carriage to carry all their instruments. Tours and various court positions continued through the Napoleonic Wars (1799–1815). Dorette gave birth to their first child, Emilie, in 1807. One month after a concert for Napoleon, a second daughter, Ida, was born. A subsequent tour, which ended in Vienna, brought Spohr a post at the State Theater. Dorette played in the orchestra. Their son was born in Vienna in 1913, but died three months later. Tiring of the city, Spohr returned to Gotha where Sophie gave birth to their fourth child, Theresa, in 1818. Napoleon's armies conquering the German cities on their routes, and the constant stress, caused Dorette recurring bouts of fever. Nevertheless, in 1820 she mastered the demanding new Érard harp for their London performances. Tours, childbearing, raising three children, plus the difficulty of her last concert on the new harp took its toll. She gave up the harp—although for two more years she continued accompanying her husband at the keyboard—and retired from the concert stage. Worn out, she succumbed to one of her "nervous fevers" and died in Kassel, November 1834.

EKATERINA ADOLFOVNA WALTER-KIUNE, born in St. Petersburg, 1870, entered the conservatory there at age eleven to study harp and piano. She graduated in 1888. Her concerts, on both harp and piano, took place in the salons of aristocrats in Russia and abroad. She also made her own transcriptions on themes from popular operas. In 1891, she was instrumental in restoring harp classes into the curriculum of the Smolny Institute. In 1903, she became a member of the orchestra of the Maryinsky Theater, famous for the ballet performances of immortal ballerina **Anna Pavlova** (1881–1931), and from 1904–17 taught at the Smolny Institute and St. Petersburg Conservatory. Of her many pupils, the most famous was **Ksenia Erdeli**, whom she saved from an unwanted marriage. With the onset of the October 1917 Revolution, she left Russia for her husband's native Rostok, Mecklenburg, in Eastern Germany, where she died in 1931.

Henriette Renie

HENRIETTE RENIÉ, one of the world's greatest harp pedagogues, was born in Paris, September 18, 1875, and studied piano with her maternal grandmother until she was eight. She went on to **Alphonse Hasselmans** (1845–1912), considered the Father of the French School—or method—of the harp. (He and Renié are credited with maintaining the popularity of the double-action harp.) She became a regular student at the Paris Conservatoire at ten, and remarkably, at age eleven in 1886, won the Premier Prix. The first place winner the year before had been twenty-five years old, and the second place winner in 1886 was hired as professor of harp at the Brussels Conservatory.

Winning the Premier Prix was considered as being completely prepared for a career, thus the twelve-year-old girl was thrust into a male world to establish a name for herself on this "novelty," the pedal harp. She returned to the Conservatoire to finish her music education, including harmony and composition, and at fifteen gave her first solo recital in Paris. With her father's guidance, Henriette taught, concertized and played for royalty. By eighteen, having passed through the age when most girls were married, she decided against marriage over her career. In 1897, she was hired to represent the Érard Company at the Brussels World Fair. By 1901, she had written her *Concerto in C minor* and a solo work, *Légende*, a piece still used in competitions. This was the era when **Clara Schumann** was performing her late husband's works, and **Augusta Holmès** and **Cécile Chaminade** were making their names as the only two prominent French women composers.

Renié's success made Hasselmans jealous, so he only referred students to her who were destined for society or the convent, not those interested in careers. When she presented her most gifted student, **Marcel Grandjany**, aged eleven, to the Conservatoire in 1903, Hasselmans kept him on auditor status for the first year. Two years later the prodigy won the Premier Prix.

On Hasselmans' retirement, **Marcel Tournier** (1879–1951) was appointed professor of harp at the Conservatoire, a position many felt should have gone to Renié. Her teaching was now confined to her private studio. Internationally, her students were teaching her method throughout the world. By the end of World War I her fame reached America through the work of **Mildred Dilling**, whom she had met in 1914, and Marcel Grandjany, who went to teach in the U.S. Her niece, Solange Renié, taught in Japan and China. Even **Harpo Marx** came to Renié for training.

In May 1914, she inaugurated the first Henriette Renié International Harp Competition. When WWI caused the cessation of concerts, tours, recitals and money, she formed a special artists fund for musicians. Her own life was spared, although she often dared fate by performing secretly in rented theaters with the background accompaniment of German guns.

After World War II, **Mildred Dilling**, **Susann McDonald**, **Emily Hürlimann** and **Sally Maxwell**[113] were among American students who flocked back to her studio. Renié's work continued with transcriptions of the classics to bolster the meager harp repertoire. She taught and performed until her eightieth year. At her death, on March 1, 1956, an apt analogy proclaimed, "the harp owes to Renié what the guitar owes to Segovia."

Known as the "Leopold Auer[114] of harp teachers," in the course of Renié's long tenure at the Paris Conservatoire her most celebrated pupils were **Marcel Grandjany** (1891–1975) and **Carlos Salzedo** (1885–1961), each of whom went on to develop his own school (style) of harp playing which has been perpetuated through the next two generations of harpists.

KSENIA ALEXANDROVA ERDELI, born in Ukraine, February 20, 1878, was exposed to the arts by her father, who made his home a center for lovers of music, literature and theater. At eleven, she was sent to St. Petersburg to live and study at the Smolny Institute. Among visiting artists there were **Robert** and **Clara Schumann** and Ekaterina Kiune, who was trying to re-establish the harp department. Ksenia was entranced and became Kiune's student, using an ancient instrument until the Institute purchased an Érard in 1893. She even got to play for Czar Alexander III, whose wife was also a harpist. After her graduation it was Kiune, with her husband U. F. Walter, director of a fortepiano factory, who took the young woman into their home and directed her musical education for the next two years. This saved her from a marriage her mother was trying to force her into because her father had died and they needed money.

Erdeli was invited to join Moscow's Bolshoi Theater Orchestra where, after her probationary year, she became first harpist. One of the bassists was **Serge Koussevitsky**, who would become the renowned conductor of the Boston Symphony for a quarter of a century (1924–1949).

With her marriage in 1907 to N. N. Engelhardt, a descendant of Russian composer Mikhail Glinka, Ksenia had to return to St. Petersburg, but regretted leaving her best pupil, young **Maria Korchinska**. By 1908, she was assisting Kiune at the Smolny Institute, since the latter was raising three children and also playing at the Maryinsky Theater. Erdeli took over all the harp classes in 1911. In 1918, with the death of the Russian dean of harpists, **Aleksandr Slepushkin** (1870–1918), she was invited to take his position at the Moscow Conservatory. Her return to Moscow also allowed her to return to the Bolshoi where, since the Revolution, audiences had become quite coarse—also both musicians and dancers suffered in the unheated theater. Maria Korchinska, whom she had not seen for eleven years, was in the orchestra. In 1921, the brilliant eleven-year-old **Vera Dulova** became Erdeli's

---

113. After joining the faculty in 1974, since 1980 concert artist and competition adjudicator Sally Maxwell has been head of the harp department founded by her mother, Doris Calkins, at the University of Oregon at Eugene in 1934. A major force in the American Harp Society, Sally has worked on the biography of Renié, wrote the preface, and translated from the French, for Wenonah Milton Govea's definitive 1995 book, *19th and 20th Century Harpists* (see *Bibliography*), a rich source for some of the material in this chapter. Govea is professor emeritus, Cal State, Hayward.

114. Leopold Auer (1845–1930), a pupil of the legendary violinist Josef Joachim, was the teacher, at the St. Petersburg Conservatory, of some of the world's most famous violinists, including Jascha Heifetz, Efrem Zimbalist and Mischa Elman. Tchaikovsky originally dedicated his Violin Concerto to Auer.

pupil. In 1938, Ksenia resigned from the Bolshoi to teach at the conservatory and the Central Children's Music School founded by pianist Aleksandr Goldenweiser. She also helped **Rheinhold Glière** (1875–1956) write his Harp Concerto.

During WWII, she was in the group with Goldenweiser and Prokofiev evacuated to a "safer" part of Russia in the Caucasus. When the war came closer she was moved to Tblisi, Georgia, and then to Erevan, Armenia. In September 1943, she was allowed to return to Moscow to teach, play and compose. In the course of her long life, Erdeli performed at three celebrations in her honor: 1937 for thiry-five years of accomplishment, 1954 for her seventieth birthday, and 1962 for sixty-five years of artistic contributions. She wrote her memoirs at ninety and died in Moscow, May 27, 1971, at ninety-seven.

WINIFRED ESTELLA BAMBRICK, born in Ottawa, February 21, 1892, was one of the earliest Canadian harpists. Only four feet, eight inches tall, she was taken for a child prodigy when she made her New York debut in 1913 at age twenty-one. She was the first harpist to record on Edison Diamond Discs (1914). She toured with the **John Philip Sousa** band (1920–30). In 1934, she went to London to work with the BBC, then played at the Alhambra Theater for two years before joining a circus orchestra which toured Europe and India until 1939. That year, in Leipzig, she and her mother, who always traveled with her, were almost stranded with the outbreak of WWII. They managed to catch the last train for Holland, sail across the Channel to England, and get a passage across the U-boat infested North Atlantic back to Canada. Her narrow escapes were published in novel form, *Continental Review*, for which she received the 1946 Canadian Governor-General's Award for fiction. She retired in 1960 from a career covering over 1,000 concerts worldwide, and died in Montreal, April 11, 1969.

Lily Laskine

LILY AIMÉE LASKINE was born in Paris, August 31, 1893, to Russian parents who had settled there for her father's medical career. Devoted to music, mother and child played piano—her mother having studied in Russia with a pupil of Chopin. Lily's first instrument was piano, but at eight her mother managed to get her taken as a beginning harp student with **Alphonse Hasselmans**. Lily adored her father and really wanted to become a doctor, but he made her realize that such a choice was not an option for a girl at the turn of the century. At thirteen, she won the Premier Prix in harp, and was therefore considered a graduate and no longer eligible for lessons. This was the extent of her formal studies. By fourteen she was giving lessons and concertizing. Not wanting to be limited to a concert career, in 1909 she applied to the Paris Opera Orchestra. Because of her youth, she could only substitute until she reached the proper age. Nevertheless, she was the first female to be accepted in the history of the Paris Opera. She also became solo harpist with the Orchestre Lamoureux, Orchestre Straram, and Orchestre Koussevitzky. In 1930, she met violinist Roland Charmya, a member of the Lamoureux and professor at the conservatory. They married in 1938, and during WWII lived in Marseilles, where the Orchestra National—in which Roland also played—had relocated. After the war they returned to Paris, and in 1948 she became professor of harp at the conservatory as well as playing for almost fifty years with the Comédie Française at the Théâtre Français, where she recorded and accompanied such popular singers as **Edith Piaf** and **Maurice Chevalier**. She also recorded film scores. Known as the "Empress of the Harp," Lily Laskine died in Paris, January 4, 1988, at ninety-five.

Mildred Dilling

MILDRED DILLING, born February 23, 1894, in Marion, Indiana, began piano at six. On her twelfth birthday she was given a harp. She studied throughout high school in Indianapolis, after which she went to New York where one of her teachers was **Carlos Salzedo**. Chaperoned by her mother, she went to Paris where Salzedo introduced her to **Henriette Renié**, with whom she studied for many summers. For several years she and French singer **Yvette Guilbert** toured France, England and Germany. On her return, she began her long relationship with the Community Concert Series, and gained her own spotlight playing fifteen minutes of harp music before the New York Philharmonic concert broadcasts on NBC. After appearing on the Bing Crosby radio hour, she became known to many show people and introduced the harp to

Laurence Olivier, Deanna Durbin and Bob Hope. Her most famous student was Harpo Marx, who took lessons with her for thirty years. It was she who introduced Harpo to Henriette Renié.

Dilling played for five U.S. presidents in the course of her career. World War II halted her European tours, so she played at hospitals for wounded servicemen. In 1943, at age forty-nine, she married Clinton Parker, a banker who had also never been married. In 1961, the State Department sent her on a goodwill tour of the Orient, where she appeared in recital and on radio and television in Hong Kong, Indonesia, Japan, Malaya, Taiwan, Thailand and Singapore. So popular was the tour, she was sent around the world again (1963–64) to India, Israel, Lebanon, Philippines and Turkey. In 1966, the State Department sent her to Mexico, a trip she extended to Central America, South America and Cuba. In 1967, she joined her violinist sister, Charlene, for another tour of the Orient. In 1971, she appeared with the Iceland Symphony, sharing her last concert there at the U.S. Embassy with Charlene who died the following year. Mildred died in New York, December 30, 1982.

MARIE HENRIETTE GOOSSENS was born into a celebrated musical family in London, August 11, 1894, one of five children, all of whom started on the piano, progressed to their major instrument, and went on to successful musical careers. When Marie was eight, she was found to be suffering a nervous disorder for which the cause was never discovered. (She was unable to walk or speak for almost two years.) Her sister, Sidonie, had started harp lessons, and sharing these helped Marie's recovery. By sixteen, she had played at the Liverpool Philharmonic Hall. Next came the Royal College of Music, where she studied with Miriam Timothy, principal harpist of the London Symphony. She received her first contract in 1915. During WWI she played with Muriel Jack's Ladies Orchestra. After a few tours there were not enough gigs, so for the next two years she did government work. During this time her brother, Eugene, was conductor of the Rochester (New York) Philharmonic (1923–31), whose harpists were **Lucile Rosenbloom** and **Eileen Malone**.

Marie was called to play for the 1919 season of the Diaghilev Ballet. Known for her excellent sight reading, she was sought after by ballet, opera, musical theater and recording companies. Meanwhile, her sister became the harpist for the BBC, and by 1930 was their principal, a position she held for fifty years.

In 1926, Marie married Frederick Laurence, a widower with two children. He later became manager for one of the greatest English conductors, **Sir Thomas Beecham** (1879–1961). Two more children were born, Anthony, 1928, and Jean, 1930. After her second child, Marie became principal harp of the London Philharmonic under Beecham. One of their tours was to Germany in 1936, where Hitler was almost at the height of his power. The advent of WWII, in 1939, and the London Symphony bankruptcy, brought an end to concert and theater work. Her husband also lost his job and was reduced to becoming an air raid warden. Marie freelanced. Because of the Blitz (June 1940–April 1941)—Hitler's effort to reduce London to fiery ruins with nightmarish, ceaseless air raids raining bombs on homes and priceless monuments—she traveled by underground train, the last safe place in the beleaguered city.

Like most children, theirs were evacuated out into the country. This separation, a bomb hit on their house, shortage of food and the overall stress of the war caused Frederick's collapse and death in 1942. By 1943 the severity of the war lessened, the children returned, the London Symphony reorganized and Marie's career was revitalized, playing with the top English maestros, musical artists and film stars.

Marie Goossens was made a fellow of RCM—she retired from teaching at seventy—receiving the Order of the British Empire (OBE) in 1984 from Queen Elizabeth II. She retired from concertizing at eighty-seven. Even after her death, December 18, 1991, she continues her contribution to music with sales of her book, *Life on a Harp String*, whose proceeds fund the Marie Goossens Prize at the RCM.

MARIA KORCHINSKA was born in Moscow, February 17, 1895, to a Polish father and Moldavian mother. Her musical aptitude got her accepted into the very strict Moscow Conservatory. Piano was required of all students, and by eleven Maria was so advanced her instructor felt she was ready for a solo career. But with so many pianists, her father insisted the child study harp. She began with **Ksenia Erdeli** and then **Alexsandr Slepushkin**. At her graduation in 1911, Maria was the only student to win the Gold Medal in harp—in fact the only one to do so in her lifetime. She was immediately hired by the dynamic young Koussevitzky Orchestra, which drew its members from the Moscow Conservatory and the Bolshoi.

After the 1917 Revolution, Lenin nationalized the arts, conservatories, etc., making it possible for the common people to enjoy performances heretofore reserved for the upper classes. In 1918, with the death of Slepushkin, Korchinska took his position as head of the conservatory harp department. She also took Slepushkin's position as first harpist with the Bolshoi Theatre. Much of the development of the Soviet school of harp is to her credit. For several years she played cultural programs for the Red Army. Once she played in a prison from 7:00 in the morning until 10:00 that night. She played at Lenin's funeral. The harp became her lifeline—she was paid in food.

In 1922, she married Count Benckendorff, whose late father had been the last Imperial Russian ambassador to Great Britain. With the political situation even more precarious after Lenin's death, Maria feared for her husband's life. He had twice been arrested and was under suspicion by the Soviet authorities. With his diplomatic visa, he was able to leave and join his widowed mother in London. In 1924, Maria also managed a visa for a concert tour— from which she never returned. With two harps and her baby daughter, Natalia, she made it to England. In 1926 her son, Alexander, was born and, after five years' residence, the family became British subjects. Despite WWII and more hard times, Korchinska began to reestablish her career as a soloist, eking out a living with orchestral and film work. During the war years she entertained tirelessly, traveling from one end of England to the other. After the war she was active with the Wigmore Ensemble, touring with them in France and Spain. In 1960, she joined **Phia Berghout**, helping with the operation of Harp Week in the Netherlands. Korchinska was a judge for the Israeli International Harp Contests from 1959 until her death on April 17, 1979.

LUCILE JOHNSON ROSENBLOOM, born in New York, December 17, 1898, began piano lessons at six and harp at thirteen. At sixteen, she went to Massachusetts to study with the Viennese born Alfred Holy, principal harp of the Boston Symphony. With World War I making New York a mecca to European artists, Lucile moved there, studying with **Carlos Salzedo** for three years, and touring with his harp ensemble. Like **Lily Laskine**, she preferred orchestral work rather than having a solo career which limited her to the scanty harp repertoire of the time. After the war (November 1918), Paris regained its status as the world's artistic center. Lucile spent a year there studying with **Marcel Tournier**, to whom she returned every summer until the outbreak of World War II. In 1919, **George Eastman**, who founded the Kodak camera company in Rochester, New York, created a music conservatory there. When the harp department was established, Lucile was chosen to head it. She influenced many young harpists, notably **Eileen Malone**, who followed in her position. When Eastman sponsored the founding of the Rochester Philharmonic with Eugene Goossens—brother of Marie—conducting, Lucile was hired as principal harpist. She played there until guest conductor **Fritz Reiner** (1888–1963), taken with her talent, "stole" her for the Pittsburgh Symphony, which he directed from 1934–48. Here she met one of the orchestra founders, Charles J. Rosenbloom, who became her husband.

Lucile Rosenbloom was the only woman on the 1940 NBC Symphony South American tour with the legendary **Arturo Toscanini** (1867–1957). She was a judge at the First International Harp Competition in Israel in 1959. She helped establish the American Harp Society in 1962 to promote the appreciation of the harp and encourage the composition of music for the instrument and improve quality of performance. She attended the Netherlands Harp Week where she met the Czech harpist **Marcela Kozikova**, with whom she recorded, played duo recitals and produced a radio series, "Great Harpists of the World." She also played with Kozikova at the White House during the Jimmy Carter years. Recipient of many honors, Lucile died in Pittsburgh, September 25, 1992.

20th Century Pioneers

CLELIA GATTI-ALDROVANDI was born May 30, 1901, in Mantova, Italy. She studied with her pianist mother and organist grandfather, and debuted on piano at age nine. After courses at the Musical Lyceum in Turin, her first position was principal harp in the orchestra of the Teatro Regio. She played there for two years before deciding on a solo career, restricting her teaching to her best pupils to fit her performance schedule. She urged composers to enlarge the harp repertoire. After her marriage to musicologist Guido Maggiorino Gatti, their home became a meeting place for artists, musicians, writers, poets and academicians. With the birth of daughter Vanna, Clelia's concertizing cut back and her list of pupils grew. Active with the World Harp Congress, International Association of Harpists, and Friends of the Harp, she served on national/international harp competition juries. Hindemith's *Sonata for Harp* was dedicated to her.

She died in Rome, March 12, 1989.

Eileen Malone

EILEEN MALONE, born in New York, August 16, 1906, spent her career life at Eastman and in the Rochester Symphony. She began piano at eight, but when her father brought home an Irish harp, her choice was made. Living near Rochester, she studied with **Lucile Rosenbloom**, and after high school enrolled at Eastman, whose infant harp department numbered four students. Eileen's progress and dedication was such that Lucile arranged for her to study with *her* teacher, **Marcel Tournier**, in Paris. In five intense months of study, she never heard him play the harp—he demonstrated on the piano to avoid "cloning" his pupils. On her return, she took the second harp position in the Rochester Philharmonic, played local and national radio shows and taught preparatory harp courses at the conservatory. Her stature as a teacher and musician caused Eastman's director, prominent American composer **Howard Hanson** (1896–1981), to choose her as Rosenbloom's successor on *her* retirement, despite the fact Malone was unknown nationally. Under Hanson's guidance, Eastman gained national and international status. Malone's reputation also grew, but she turned down invitations to play elsewhere, preferring to stay in the Rochester Symphony and continue her teaching, radio and TV work.

Always eager to better herself, she studied with **Marcel Grandjany** when he joined the Juilliard faculty in the '30s. They became friends and he dedicated his *Erie Canal Fantasy* to her. After the 1959 Harp Competition in Israel, where she served as a judge, the idea for creating the American Harp Society was born. Malone and Grandjany were responsible for gathering the founding committee. In 1969, she hosted the sixth American National Harp Conference in Rochester. She received an honorary doctorate from Nazareth College and was named "1985 Musician of the Year" by the Rochester chapter of Mu Phi Epsilon.

In the tradition of Henriette Renié, Eileen Malone never married, believing it would take time and energy away from her devotion to the instrument and her teaching. She retired in 1989 after a fifty-nine year career. Many of her students moved on to major symphonies and universities in America and abroad.

Shortly before her death on June 1, 1999, at ninety-two, she donated her gold Lyon & Healy Harp to Eastman to give students the chance to perform on a high quality instrument.

Edna Phillips

EDNA PHILLIPS, born in Reading, Pennsylvania, January 7, 1907, started violin at eight, switched to piano after three years, but resisted the harp until she was eighteen. She first studied with **Florence Wightman**, who became principal harp in the fledgling Cleveland Orchestra in 1929. Later, Edna was accepted as a student of **Carlos Salzedo** at Curtis, who trained her for the second harp position in the Philadelphia Orchestra. At the audition, **Leopold Stokowski** (1882–1977) confounded both teacher and student by insisting that she become first harp. This was a musical milestone, making Phillips the first woman principal appointed to a major symphony orchestra in America—an amazing situation considering that, although she had studied piano all her life, she had only been playing harp for five years. Thus she began her career as a neophyte, with much to learn, not only musically, but of breaking the gender barrier in an exclusive and competitive profession.

In the early days, she tried to make herself as insignificant[115] as possible—not easy with the size and impact of her instrument, and the fact that she sat near the front. By 1932, she had soloed in Mozart's Flute and Harp

---

115. Both Stokowski and Ormandy were well-known womanizers. Edna was kept on her mettle to resist advances . . .

Concerto with principal flutist **William Kincaid** (1895–1967), and recorded Debussy's *Danses Sacrée et Profane* for Victor. (She played a modern concert grand harp when there were only three in existence in the country—the other two belonging to Salzedo and his wife.)

In 1933 Edna married Samuel R. Rosenbaum, an attorney and member of the board of directors of the Philadelphia Orchestra Association. He became the first trustee to administer the vital Recording Industries Musicians' Trust Fund.[116] When asked to appear as soloist with the orchestra, Edna was embarrassed by the sparsity of harp literature. Beginning in 1940, her husband underwrote new works for the harp. This began what came to be known as the Edna Phillips Commissions. Between 1940–56, there were twenty-three works in a perpetuating contribution from composers such as **Norman Dello Joio**, **Ernst Von Dohnányi**, **Ernst Krenek**, **Peggy Glanville-Hicks** and **Alberto Ginastera**. Mostly premiered by Phillips, many of these works are now established in the repertoire. The Ginastera Concerto was premiered by famed Spanish harpist **Nicanor Zabaleta** in 1956, as by that time Edna had set aside her performing career to devote herself to the Young Audiences programs.

Except for time off to have her babies—Joan was born in 1934, and David Hugh in 1938—Phillips spent almost sixteen years with Orchestra. When she retired in 1946, **Eugene Ormandy** (1899–1985), Stokowski's successor in 1938, called her "the greatest of orchestral harpists."

Her decision to retire was promulgated by the mindset of the times: "a mother was supposed to be home with her children." Although well cared-for, daughter and son chafed at their mother being gone so much. Her husband had always supported her career, but when Joan was eleven and David eight, Edna decided to give her home life top priority. But she did not stay away from music, and continued to appear in concert, recital and chamber performances in Cuba, North and South America, and also on television. Partly concurrent with her orchestral years, from 1932–62, she was head of the harp department of the Philadelphia Conservatory of Music (predecessor of the present Philadelphia Musical Academy). She taught many of the major harpists active today, including Boston Symphony principal **Ann Hobson Pilot**, who became her protégée and whom she helped overcome racial barriers.

Honors for Edna Phillips' accomplishments include the Mayor's Award (1955), for artistic preeminence as a citizen of Philadelphia, an honorary doctor of music degree from the Philadelphia Conservatory (1957), Pennsylvania's Mother of the Year (1960), a Distinguished Daughter of Pennsylvania (1961), and the Gimbel Philadelphia Award for public service (1962).

I interviewed Edna Phillips in 1996, at her retirement facility near the city—still sharp at eighty-nine—and kept in touch through 2001. Her daughter, Joan Solaun, is head of the Foreign Student Exchange Program at the University of Illinois, Urbana. Her granddaughter, Emma, born 1970, is an attorney in New York. Son David Hugh resides in London.

Edna spent her last years surrounded by treasured memories, not the least of which was her longtime friendship with **Alice Chalifoux**, and the echo of the words of the great maestro **Arturo Toscanini**, who described her as "an angel—with beauty of tone, of face and of soul."

She passed away December 2, 2003. The Philadelphia Harp Society honored her memory by performing several works she had commissioned in the course of her career. In January 2004, Edna Phillips Rosenbaum's personal collection of manuscripts, letters and memorabilia was donated to the Music Library of the University of Illinois by her daughter.

LUCILE LAWRENCE, born February 7, 1907, in New Orleans, saw her great-grandmother and her aunt playing their single action harps—one of the refined accomplishments for a Southern belle. Her mother, devoted to the development of her daughter's talents, chaperoned her travels to lessons and tours. Her aunt had studied harp with the legendary **Alphonse Hasselmans** (1845–1912) in France, and knew of the equally renowned **Carlos**

---

116. The RIMTF works with local musicians' unions allocating funds—through a percentage of record sales—to qualifying performers and/or organizations to present free concerts in the community.

Salzedo. When the latter came to New Orleans after WWI, she arranged for an audition. Impressed, Salzedo persuaded the family to let the eleven-year-old study with him for the summer in Seal Harbor, Maine. For the next eighteen years their lives were entwined. Lucile stayed with a great-aunt in New York, commuted to the city for lessons with Salzedo, spent summers in Maine and winters in New Orleans—a schedule which lasted until her high school graduation in 1922. In 1925, she toured Australia and New Zealand, but it was not until 1927 that she debuted at Curtis where she began teaching first year students for Salzedo's advanced instruction. Three of her students were **Edna Phillips**, **Alice Chalifoux** and **Marjorie Tyre**. Against her family's advice, Lucile and Salzedo, twenty-two years her senior and once divorced, were married in 1928. They collaborated in writing and performing, and moved the Salzedo School from Seal Harbor to New Jersey. Their marriage was tempestuous, and in 1936 they divorced but maintained a friendship and continued their artistic collaboration until his death. From 1932, Lawrence played principal harp at Radio City Music Hall and, like many artists during the Depression, turned to radio as a livelihood. There she met Paul Dahlstrom, whom she married in 1938. The following year their son, Larry, was born.

Though she played under many great conductors, and was invited to join many orchestras, it was never her ambition to become an orchestral musician. She was known for her teaching abilities, and at eighty-nine was still on the faculties of Boston University, Curtis, Manhattan School of Music, Mannes College, as well as heading harp seminars at Tanglewood during the summer. Her teaching schedule did not change for over thirty years. She commuted from her home in River Edge, New Jersey, to New York, and once a week arose at 3:00 A.M. for the 200-plus mile trek to Boston University.

Known to students and colleagues as "Miss Lawrence," Lucile is credited with helping to revolutionize harp technique. In collaboration with Salzedo, she wrote three highly influential method books: *Method for the Harp*, *The Art of Modulating*, and *Pathfinder to the Harp*. In addition to these, her editions of key harp pieces are used by harpists throughout the world.

On October 10, 2000, BU presented her with a ninety-third birthday tribute. Participants included faculty members, former students, flutist **Doriot Anthony Dwyer**, and former School of Fine Arts Dean **Phyllis Curtin**. The concert highlighted some of the most dramatic and difficult music ever composed for the harp, performed by colleagues, and former students who can be found soloing onstage or in orchestras throughout the world.

Only at ninety-five, in June 2002, did she "retire," remaining on Manhattan's staff and retaining a few students. We spoke on her niney-sixth birthday in 2003, at which time Lucile was busy editing the harp sections in new compositions sent her by New England composer **Gunther Schuller**. Active to the end, Miss Lawrence passed away July 8, 2004.

Alice Chalifoux

ALICE CHALIFOUX, born January 22, 1908, in Birmingham, Alabama, was not raised as a retiring Southern belle, but rather in a whirlwind of musical activity. Her mother was schooled in piano, violin and harp. Her father, trained at the Paris Conservatory, was a violinist until a broken wrist ended his promising career. At eleven, Alice entered a convent school in Birmingham where she had piano lessons, but many of her classmates studied harp. By fifteen she wanted to make the harp a career, even though the post WWI era had done nothing to change the expectation that a southern girl should marry and stay home. At eighteen she tried studying in Chicago, but was dissatisfied. Her mother had read of Salzedo's work at Curtis, and in 1926 Alice went to Philadelphia. After the four years at Curtis—where she became lifelong friends with **Edna Phillips**—she was given a contract as principal harpist with the Cleveland Orchestra. Like Phillips, with little orchestral experience, it was only the patient and generous guidance of Salzedo that got her through her first years in the orchestra. She also joined the faculties of the Cleveland Institute and Western Reserve University (now Case-Western).

In 1937, she married John Gordon Rideout, whose premature death occurred fourteen years later. Her daughter, Alyce Gordon Rideout Lelch, also plays harp, but has made a successful career in real estate.

During and after Chalifoux's phenomenal forty-three year career at Cleveland (1930–73)—performing with the world's most famous conductors, **Nikolai Sokoloff** (1918–33), **Artur Rodzinski** (1933–43), **Erich Leinsdorf** (1943–46), George Szell (1946–70), and Pierre Boulez (1970–72)—she also taught at Oberlin and Baldwin-Wallace Conservatories.

At his death in 1961, Salzedo willed Alice his house in Camden, Maine, where, for over four decades, she took over the responsibilities of the Salzedo Summer Harp Colony each year. Recipient of many awards, including the Cleveland Arts Prize in 1986, Chalifoux was still making the weekly hundred mile round trip teaching trek in the Blizzard of 1996, at age eighty-eight. In 1997, she moved to Virginia to be with her daughter and son-in-law. In 1998, the Alice Chalifoux Scholarship Fund was established to benefit future generations of harp students at CIM. As of 2001, she was teaching locally and spending her summers in Maine. In 2003, she sold the house and its furnishings to private owners. It marked the end of an era.

InAugust 2005, Alice told me she still had some students, but had stopped counting birthdays. I spoke with daughter Alyce, January 8, 2007, who told me students and fans around the world were poised to wish the great lady of the harp a happy ninety-ninth.

Chalifoux's list of students reads like a Who's Who in Orchestras. They include:

Susan Dederich, principal harp - Dallas Symphony

Lisa Wellbaum, principal harp - Cleveland Orchestra (Alice Chalifoux Chair)

Tina Struble, assistant principal - Cleveland Orchestra

Ann Hobson Pilot, principal harp - Boston Symphony

Sarah Schuster, assistant principal - Boston Symphony (1990–97)

Chai-Ho Lee, principal harp - Taiwan Symphony

Alice Giles, Concert Harpist Germany

VERA GEORGIYEVNA DULOVA came into the world in Moscow on January 27, 1909, with music in her genes. Her grandfather played the violin, her grandmother studied piano with **Nikolai Rubinstein**, founder of the Moscow Conservatory, and harmony with none other than **Tchaikovsky** (1840–93), who considered her the most brilliant virtuosa of her time. Vera's father was a professor of violin at the conservatory, her mother an international opera singer. A music career was ordained. At age nine, two years after the 1917 Revolution, Vera began harp studies with **Ksenia Erdeli** at the conservatory. She also studied with **Maria Korchinska**, who had taken over the studio of *her* teacher, **Alexandr Slepushkin**. In 1929, she graduated with a scholarship for further study which she took with Max Zaal in Berlin. After her return from Germany, she joined the Bolshoi Orchestra in 1934. The following year, she participated in the Second All Union Competition in Leningrad, where she and violinist **David Oistrakh** (1908–74) received the highest award. This launched her concertizing career throughout the USSR, covering vast areas—even in the mines of Siberia—greatly lifting morale everywhere she appeared. During the war years, Bolshoi artists were evacuated to "safety" in Kuybyshev to live under Spartan conditions. There, Dulova and her husband met **Dmitri Shostakovich** (1906–75), whose Seventh Symphony subsequently had its "premiere" on an old piano in their lodgings. With the end of WWII, the Bolshoi returned to Moscow.

The most important enduring contribution of her career was her research into harp literature. She explored the archives of each city she visited, and unearthed 17th and 18th century manuscripts in Berlin, a tattered Mozart *Variation for Harp* in Vienna, and numerous other treasures. She also worked on harp reconstruction.

Like violinist **Maud Powell** and pianist **Teresa Carreño**, she followed an Amazonian schedule. No village was too small, no area too far to trek. She toured from the Ural mountains to Siberia to the Russian Far East to Central Asia. She played underground for miners, and above for industrial workers. She even went to the North Pole in March 1955. After the concert, a group arrived who had been traveling since the night before to attend, so she and the other artists played the program over again. That trip alone covered 25,000 km (15,000 miles) using plane, tractor, sled, and Shank's mare (walking). In thirty-three days they presented forty-eight concerts, plus thirty meetings, lectures and workshops.

Vera Dulova became chair of the Russian Federation of Harpists, and a professor at the Tchaikovsky Conservatory, but despite all the touring, concertizing, teaching, competition judging and public work and her choice of the direction of her career, Vera never left her post in the Bolshoi Orchestra.

With but a glimpse into the 21st century, this great lady of the harp left us on January 5, 2000.

Phia Berghout

PHIA (Sophia Rosa) **BERGHOUT** was born in Amsterdam, December 14, 1909. Her father was a composer and director of church choirs, her mother, a pianist. Her two brothers played violin and cello. Phia began piano at five and violin at six, soon joining the family Sunday chamber concerts. Her interest in the harp got her into the Royal Conservatorium as a student of **Rosa Spier**, who had taught **Emmy Hürlimann**. Concurrently, Phia earned a living playing with the Fritz Hirsch Operette, a musical comedy group. At the end of her training she played with the Arnhem Orchestral Association until there was an opening in the Amsterdam Concertgebouw. Spier, then first harpist, insisted Berghout apply, and in 1933 she started as second harpist in the orchestra. After World War II, Spier became first harpist with the Radio Philharmonisch and Berghout was promoted to principal in the Concertgebouw, also taking over Spier's teaching position at the Conservatorium.

The new conductor of the Concertgebouw was one of Holland's most famous maestros, **Eduard van Beinum** (1900–59), who was sympathetic to Berghout's attempts to promote the status of the harp. In 1954, she initiated harp courses on a private estate where Dutch and foreign students met to promote contact between conductors and soloists. After the first International Harp Competition in Israel (1959), she was inspired to launch the first Harp Week in Holland in 1960 with the help of **Maria Korchinska**, who traveled from England, and **Inga Gråe** from Denmark.

Phia continued teaching at the Amsterdam and Maastricht Conservatories, but resigned from the Concertgebouw in 1961 to devote more time to her dream of expanding her project to include other than just harpists, and institute a Baroque Week. As news of her work spread, wind, brass, and string players came to participate in their particular weeks. The courses continued at various venues until 1963, when enough money was raised to purchase Queekhoven, a 17th century estate. Berghout presided over Queekhoven, drawing students from all over the world. But in 1975, when she reached retirement age, there was no one to carry on her work. She managed to continue Harp Week until 1983, which coincided with the first meeting of the World Harp Congress, begun by **Susann McDonald** and others, which met in Maastricht, Berghout's residence. The new organization would continue the work Phia had begun, but only for the harp. Her death, March 22, 1993, leaves the need for heirs to perpetuate her valuable legacy so that future talent on other instruments can experience equal opportunities. Phia Berghout's dream should not die with her.

INGA GRÅE was born March 4, 1910, on the Jutland Peninsula of Denmark. Although the harp had a history in the area dating back to pagan times, it was relegated to accompanying singers. Orchestras and opera companies imported harpists from France or Germany to fill the positions as needed. Gråe obtained a diploma in piano from the Royal Danish Academy of Music (RDAM), with accreditation on organ. She did not take up harp until she was a mature woman, when she studied with Henrik Boye, a student of Tournier, and later with **Janine Moreau**, who played in the Stockholm orchestra. (Danish conservatories did not even offer harp classes until 1955!) Inga freelanced until 1956 when Boye retired after one year at the RDAM, and she took over his position. She visited conservatories in Moscow, Paris, Vienna, and Brussels to learn how harp education was structured and, after years of neglect, built her harp department from scratch. When the academy was nationalized, her efforts received some government support. Her friendship with **Phia Berghout** was of great influence to Danish harpists. Gråe retired from the RDAM in 1980 at age seventy. Through her dedication, the harp became recognized as a career instrument in Scandinavia. She died in Copenhagen, June 2, 1986.

MARJORIE TYRE was born September 16, 1910, in Philadelphia, to architect Philip Scott Tyre, and Mabel Campbell Marcy, a nurse. Piano studies began at six and harp at twelve, studying with Blanche Hubbard. Noticed playing in a harp ensemble, **Carlos Salzedo** invited the sixteen-year-old to Curtis, but her father forbade her to go, believing scholarship schools were for poorer students. Instead, she went to the Leefson-Hille Conservatory, concentrating on piano and studying harp with **Marcel Granjany**. Several years later, when her father was ill from a stroke, Marjorie applied and was accepted to Curtis. On his recovery, her father was told of her action, and when he realized that Curtis scholarships were given only to students of highest musical promise regardless of income, he was delighted.

In 1932, while still at Curtis (BM, 1936) studying with **Lucile Lawrence** and Salzedo, Tyre was hired by Leopold Stokowski, becoming the second woman in the Philadelphia Orchestra, joining fellow harpist **Edna Phillips** who had been there since 1930. (Cellist **Elsa Hilger** arrived in 1935.) Marjorie was part of their first transcontinental tour (April 14–May 18, 1936) comprising 106 musicians on a ten-car train, covering 10,000 miles and twenty-eight cities. The following year the orchestra went coast-to-coast again, with **Eugene Ormandy** and **Jose Iturbi** as conductors. She also appeared as a soloist with the orchestra under Stokowski and Dimitri Mitropoulos at the Robin Hood Dell summer venue. In 1937, she married orchestra clarinetist Robert McGinnis, giving birth November 17, 1938, to daughter Barbara[117] who would give her three grandchildren.

When McGinnis left the Philadelphia Orchestra in 1945 to join the New York Philharmonic, Tyre became staff harpist with radio station WOR Symphony Orchestra (Mutual Broadcasting in New York), playing on *Mutual's Music Box*. In March 1948, the Union ban on "live" television music was lifted, and radio programming, in competition with television, began replacing music with script shows. Even though it was rather late in her career to have to audition, Marjorie did so, and entered the Metropolitan Opera Orchestra, its only woman member in 1952. During summers she played at the Lewisohn Stadium with the New York Philharmonic. Although her marriage to McGinnis had dissolved in 1957, he was playing with New York in 1959 under new musical director, **Leonard Bernstein**. A European tour was under way needing a second harpist—preferably the wife of an orchestra member. McGinnis asked, "How about an ex-wife?" She got the job, traveling to twenty-six countries in Europe and Russia. The following year, she toured with them to Hawaii, the Northwestern states and Berlin.

Meanwhile, she met the love of her life, Maltby Sykes, and married him in 1962. She resigned from the Met in 1964, moving with her husband to Auburn, Alabama. Sykes (1911–92), called Billy, born in Aberdeen, Mississippi, was a friend of the Chalifoux family of Birmingham. Marjorie first met him when she and **Alice Chalifoux** were students at Curtis, and on vacation together. Well known, he was professor of art and artist-in-residence at Auburn University. Marjorie became a member of Auburn's music faculty in 1967, founded the harp department there, and taught until both she and her husband retired in 1977. For the next fifteen years she was head of the harp department at Sewanee (Tennessee) Summer Music Center, founded the Tyre Harp Ensemble made up of her students, and concertized throughout the Southeast both as soloist and with the Ensemble.

In 1965, Marjorie founded the Auburn Chamber Music Society. Her first coup was bringing to Auburn the just formed Guarneri String Quartet. (The quartet celebrated their fortieth anniversary in 2004. Of the founding members, only violist Michael Tree is still with them.) She recognized the virtuosity and knew their reputation would skyrocket. She arranged their performance by knowing harpist Janet Putnam, wife of the Guarneri cellist. Janet had preceded Marjorie at the Met and followed her to WOR. Ten years after the Quartet played in Auburn, they played at the Birmingham (Alabama) Chamber Music Society, where a patron noted, "Of course you're way ahead of us down in Auburn—you have Marjorie Tyre!"

After Marjorie's death, August 8, 2003, the Auburn Chamber Music Society dedicated their fortieth anniversary season to her. Her harp, music, and career memorabilia were left to her long time student and assistant, Katherine Lake Newman,[118] who earned her harp BM (1971) and MM (1976) at Auburn, was a member of the Tyre Harp Ensemble and has been principal harpist with the Huntsville (Alabama) Symphony since the 1980s. Through the years Tyre had often brought Katherine in as second harp.

---

117. Daughter Barbara McGinnis Pritchard moved into her mother's house in Auburn to care for her in her last five years.
118. Much appreciation to Ms Newman who supplied priceless information, articles and photographs of her mentor.

(An excellent two-part biography on Marjorie Tyre by Mary Brigid Roman (Florida State, Tallahassee) is in the AHS *Harp Journal*, Summer 1994, and Winter 1995 editions.)

EMMY HÜRLIMANN, born in Richterswil, near Zürich, Switzerland, July 4, 1914, began harp at seventeen, after having studied piano and organ since childhood, and being part of her family's chamber group. In 1931, she began studies with Corinna Blaser-Potenti, first harpist with the Tonhalle Orchestra and Theater Orchestra of Zürich. During her conservatory years in that city (1932–36), she played second harp and substitute principal for Blaser. After graduation, she continued studies in Italy and Holland, and spent a year in London learning English to add to her knowledge of French and Italian. While there, she played with BBC harpists Jeanne Chevreau and **Sidonie Goossens**—sister of Marie. In 1938, she began studies with **Henriette Renié** in Paris, returning each summer until WWII closed the Continent, and continuing after the war (1946–56).

Neutral Switzerland was a haven for prominent musicians driven from their countries by Hitler. Many were in the Lucerne Orchestra where Hürlimann played, 1938–39, and 1943–59. In 1959, she founded the Zürich Harp Trio with Willy Urfer, flute, and Walter Gerhard, violist, both with the Radio Orchestra Beromünster. They played for twenty years in Switzerland and other countries. From 1954–76, Emmy was solo harpist with the Tonhalle Orchestra and the Zürich Opera and Ballet. From 1972–82, she was professor of harp at the Conservatory and Music School of Zürich, where she revitalized the curriculum of the department.

In 1983, Hürlimann was elected vice-president of the World Harp Congress, and in 1988 founded the Association Suisse del'Harpe. She acted as a competition judge for many years, continued her dedication to furthering the harp and its music, and played, although not in public, until she was eighty-five. She died in Zürich May 28, 2001.

ANN MASON STOCKTON, born October 30, 1916, in Santa Barbara, California, had harp and piano lessons at an early age. At nine, she began studying with Alfred Kastner, first harp of the Los Angeles Philharmonic. In her sophomore year in high school, she won the Theodore Presser Scholarship to attend Interlochen Music Camp, and was heard by **Carlos Salzedo** who offered her a scholarship to Curtis, but her family declined. After the Depression, during which time her harp studies were postponed, she again studied with Kastner, and finished her education at UCLA where she added composition classes with the avant-garde **Arnold Schoenberg**, who had fled Nazi Germany. At this time, May Cambern resigned as second harp with the LA Philharmonic and, with Kastner arranging the audition, Ann took her place, playing from 1935–42. Through Cambern, she also graduated to a career with movie studio orchestras. Her first studio recording was for *Gone With the Wind*, and over the next fifty years played for over 800 motion pictures, with radio and TV spots along the way. She retired in 1994, with the title Chair Emerita of the World Harp Congress. She passed away August 10, 2006.

PHYLLIS SCHLOMOVITZ was born in January 9, 1917. Her parents were actors Kate Holland and Goldwyn Patton, who had appeared with the Barrymores. Her brother, Phillip, was a Hollywood director and early television producer. Phyllis' teachers included **Mildred Dilling** and **Marcel Grandjany** and, in Paris, **Renée Benda** and **Henriette Renié**. A brief wartime marriage moved her to Milwaukee, where she became principal harpist with the Lindner Viennese Salon Orchestra (1944–51), the Milwaukee Symphony and Florentine Opera Company (1954–69). She was on the faculty of the Wisconsin College of Music for seventeen years. In May 1952, she wed Benjamin Schlomovitz, a cardiologist. Their daughter, Renée, was born January 4, 1957.

Widowed in 1969, Phyllis received an unexpected phone call from wealthy restauranteur John Rickey, who had heard one of her recordings. He paid the airfare for mother and daughter, and put them up in one of his motels. Thus Phyllis began a new chapter of life, moving to Palo Alto, California, and branching into the entertainment style of harp, played at Rickey's famous Dinah's Shack for twenty years. Concurrently, she was invited onto the faculties of the San Francisco Music and Arts Institute and UC Santa Cruz, and became adjunct harp professor at the universities of San Jose State and Santa Clara. In 1971, she met Kenneth Sorenson, an engineer, whom she married in 1972. Having ushered her daughter, Renée Quinn, into a career as a harpist, Phyllis retired from her university posts, and became director of her Schlomovitz-Quinn Harp Studio, employing a staff of four instructors, and sponsoring an annual international festival attracting visiting teachers and performers from all over the world. In 1998, Renée's husband's employment necessitated a move to Colorado.

As a soloist, Schlomovitz played with the Chamber Orchestras of San Francisco and Chicago, and performed recitals in New York, London, with the Concertgebouw (Amsterdam), the Salzburg Mozarteum, and in Australia, New Zealand, Japan, Korea and Israel. She also toured with the late pianist/composer **Claire Polin**, becoming her close friend. Phyllis was a soloist for the American Harp Society's National Conference in New York (1966), World Harp Congress in Vienna (1987), Copenhagen (1993), and for the Japan International Harp Festival at Soka Shi (1989, '91, '94, '96), plus Guest Artist at the Lyon & Healy International "Pop" Harp Festival in Monterey, California, June 1997. She can be heard on over a dozen recordings.

Beginning to experience declining health, Phyllis and Ken joined Renée in Colorado in 1999. She passed away, February 7, 2003. (I just happened to telephone for an update, February 8.)

Having played with a chamber orchestra in an elegant Milwaukee restaurant, plus her twenty years at Dinah's Shack, she loved to say, "They fed us really well. The best perk of being a professional musician was twenty-seven years of not having to cook!"

MARTHA DALTON, born February 25, 1919, in Hutchinson Kansas, began her musical training on the piano until a harp was delivered to her father's music store and her career began. She received her BM from Oberlin, later studying with **Carlos Salzedo** and **Alice Chalifoux**. After graduation, she taught harp and piano for two years at the University of Texas (Austin). She was accepted into the Cleveland Orchestra in 1947 as second harp. Apart from a hiatus, 1950–51, her career continued until 1981. She married George Dalton, one of the architects who designed the Blossom Music Center, the site of the Orchestra's summer concerts. They had three children, Anne, born 1945, Douglas, 1948, and Deborah, 1952. The girls studied piano and harp, and Douglas French horn and flute.

ANNE EVERINGHAM ADAMS was born April 6, 1919, in New York. Her mother, Phyllida Ashley, was an accomplished pianist who had studied with **Fanny Bloomfield-Zeisler** in Chicago, and in New York with Sigismund Stojowski, a student of Polish statesman/composer/pianist **Jan Ignatz Paderewski** (1860–1941). There she married Dr. Sumner Everingham, and after WWI returned to her hometown, San Francisco, establishing her career concertizing on the West Coast and playing on radio, while her husband practiced surgery. At six, Anne began studies with her mother and within three years was playing concerts on the radio. She was introduced to the harp at nine and studied with Annie Louise David,

Anne Adams

but by thirteen, like **Lily Laskine**, she wanted to follow her father's medical profession. He, too, discouraged her, pointing out the discrimination against women doctors—although it was thirty years later!

The summer after high school, Anne studied harp in New York where **Carlos Salzedo** heard her and invited her to Curtis, but the family objected, so she returned to the West Coast to UC Berkeley and UCLA. The threat of war prevented a trip to France to study with **Marcel Grandjany**, but fortuitously he came to California to teach a master class at Mills College (Oakland). Unable to go home because of WWII, he accepted a position at Juilliard and invited Anne to be a part of his first class. This time her parents acquiesced.

Burton Adams, a young surgeon interning with Dr. Everingham, met Anne when she came home for Christmas in 1940. Inseparable during her nine day visit, he arranged to be transferred to New York's challenging Bellevue Hospital just to be near her. Finishing at Juilliard in 1941, she heard of an opening for second harp in the San Francisco Symphony. She auditioned and won the spot, leaving so soon that fellow student, **Catherine Gotthoffer**, had to play Ravel's *Introduction and Allegro* at the graduate school concert with only two weeks' notice. Meanwhile, Adams had been called to active duty, but luckily was posted to Fort Ord, eighty miles south of San Francisco. Unbeknownst to him, this was just two days before his future father-in-law also reported to Fort Ord! The couple married February 22, 1942, and when Anne returned for symphony rehearsal conductor **Pierre Monteux** greeted her with the orchestra playing the *Wedding March* from Wagner's *Lohengrin*.

In 1943, Adams joined the faculty at Mills College and became friends with modern French composer **Darius Milhaud** who was teaching there. *Sonata for Harp*, his last major piece, was written for her.

In 1951, Adams took over as principal harp of the San Francisco Symphony, and in 1952 became principal in the Opera and Ballet orchestras. She kept up this schedule until 1981 when Davies Hall was built and the symphony moved to its new venue. She stayed with the opera until 1989, when she retired to have time for teaching, solo and chamber playing. In 1998, ill health forced her to give up teaching. In June 2001, she stopped playing, but was still enjoying car trips visiting her ten grandchildren. In the course of their married life, Anne and Burton traveled through every state, every Canadian province, every continent, over every ocean, to ninety-two countries and one hundred and sixteen islands—as tallied by math-minded Dr. Adams.

Of their four daughters, Carolyn is an office manager, Nancy has taken after her father and is an internist, and Valerie is a PhD professor of nursing. Patricia followed her mother into music, studying with **Susann McDonald** at the University of Arizona (MM), and has played harp with the Tucson (Arizona) Symphony and Opera since 1964. She and her mother recorded *Two Harps As One: Anne Adams & Patricia Harris* in 1995. (Dr. "Math" calculated that there are forty-three years of college, thirteen degrees earned and sixteen universities attended within the family.)

The Anne Adams Award, providing annual scholarships via competition to three young harpists, was instituted in 1989. The *American Harp Journal* named Anne as one of the forty-five most influential forces for the harp in the 20th century.

The author's late father-in-law, **Charles R. Bubb, Jr.**, principal trumpet in the San Francisco Symphony, 1945–60, told an anecdote of the two families sharing one summer vacation. He was practicing on a small cornet to "keep up his lip" while on holiday, and asked Anne what she did to retain the necessary calloused on her fingers—harps being bulky baggage. She explained, "I just push the mattress onto the floor and strum the bed springs." Anne's husband adds that later they travelled with an eighteen-inch harp, or a tennis racquet with purposely missing strings, or a wire cheese cutter to keep those fingers in shape! I last spoke with Dr. Adams in 2006.

ACACIA BRAZIL de MELLO, born May 24, 1921, in Rio de Janeiro, began harp at seven with the only teacher in the capital. Two years later, Lea Bach arrived in Rio from Spain, where she had studied with a pupil of Hasselmans, and brought his "French Method" to Brazil. Acacia studied with Bach at the Rio Instituto Nationale de Musica until she left, then with Jandyra Costa. With the latter's death, de Mello succeeded her as professor of harp. She inherited one student and an ancient school instrument. By the time she retired in 1991, there were twenty-five students and new harps. In 1973 and 1976, she was on the jury of the Isreli Harp Competition, in 1977 she founded the Rio de Janeiro chapter of the American Harp Society, and from 1983–90 was a director of the World Harp Congress, where she remained *emeritus*.

Despite her teaching and orchestral career, Acacia managed a happy marriage and raised three children—at a time when women, especially in her culture, were relegated to the home. In 1975, when her husband, Ernesto de Mello, was inaugurated as president of Rotary International, she was asked to play the harp. His speech reflected his supportiveness. "I am here, not as president of Rotary, but as the husband of the harpist." Honored at the 1st International Harp Festival, Rio de Janeiro, May 2006, but too ill to attend, she was represented by her granddaughter, Ingrid Vorsatz.

DOROTHY SPENCER REMSEN, born June 22, 1921, in New London, Connecticut, began her music studies on piano with her grandmother. At age eleven, she started harp and xylophone, which she considers an invaluable aid to playing contemporary music. Her professional career began at sixteen. After high school, she entered Eastman where she became the first harp graduate under **Eileen Malone**. After her marriage to Lester Remsen, whom she met at the conservatory, they spent the next six years in Washington, DC, during World War II, with Les playing in the Marine Corps Band and Dorothy performing with the National Symphony. After the war, Les auditioned for the LA Philharmonic and Dorothy played one year in the Minneapolis Symphony. By 1951, they were both in Los Angeles, where Les founded the LA Brass Society and was first trumpet in the LA Brass Quintet until his retirement, and Dorothy played in the LA Chamber and LA Opera Orchestras and the Hollywood Bowl. In 1952, she joined Disney Studios, where she played until her retirement in 1993.

A member of the American Harp Society since its formation, she was a charter member of the Los Angeles Chapter and member of the AHS board of directors for six years, serving as chapter president, Western regional director and national secretary. In 1974, she was appointed executive secretary, a one-woman office serving over 3,000 members, a position from which she retired in 2000.

Remsen was guest of honor at the 1970 and 1973 International Harp Contests in Jerusalem, and Queekhoven (Holland) in 1972. She was voted Most Valuable Harp Player, 1983 and 1984. She is the subject of several articles in harp journals and is featured in many recordings.

MARILYN COSTELLO was principal harpist of the Philadelphia Orchestra—succeeding **Edna Phillips**—from 1946 until her retirement in 1992. Born in Cleveland in 1924, she began her musical training at an early age and graduated from Curtis, where she studied with **Carlos Salzedo**. She succeeded him on the faculty upon his death in 1961.

Her illustrious career as soloist and recording artist covered America and Europe in recital and chamber concerts. She participated in the Yehudi Menuhin Festival in Gstaad, the Vevey Festival—both in Switzerland—and many U.S. festivals. Her recording of the Mozart *Flute and Harp Concerto*, with Menuhin conducting, was awarded the Phonographic Critics Award of Italy in 1965.

Among the many juries on which she served were the USA International Harp Competitions in Bloomington, Indiana (1989, 1992) and the International Harp Contest in Israel (1994).

One of the most respected harp pedagogues, Marilyn was professor of harp at Curtis and nearby Temple University. Her students are among the outstanding harpists in the world. The great lady passed away in Philadelphia, January 18, 1998.

Judy Loman

JUDY LOMAN, born November 3, 1936, in Goshen, Indiana, had a church organist father and a mother who studied voice for a stage career. The family had all been members of the Waltz Family Circus and were endowed with great physical stamina. Attracted to the harp, Judy began studies at five and added piano at nine—both instruments taught by a nun, Sister Trinitas, in the style of Carlos Salzedo. Thus, she was well prepared when she entered Curtis to study with the master. It was he who suggested her name change from Judith Ann Leatherman to Judy Loman.

In 1956, she became associate harpist to Salzedo in the Salzedo Concert Ensemble. Despite her love for the instrument, she was not sure she wanted to build a career on such sparse repertoire. In 1957, her husband, Joseph Umbrico, accepted the position of principal trumpet with the Toronto Symphony—where he is now principal emeritus. The move led to playing with the National Ballet, plus recording with the CBC Symphony and Canadian Opera. After three years of substituting with the Toronto Symphony, she was offered the principal position when the regular harpist retired in 1960. 1965 saw a tour to London and Paris, 1979 to Western Canada and the United States, 1987 Western Canada and the Northwest Territories.

Loman has soloed with major orchestras such as the BBC and Detroit Symphony, string quartets Orford and Allegri, many performances with Nexus and on the CBC radio and television, and been featured in films by Rhombus Media. She has been a soloist for the World Harp Society and World Harp Congress, for whom she has adjudicated competitions and was a board member. She has also been on the juries for the International Harp Contest (Israel), the Fukui Harp and Composition Competition (Japan). She has served on the faculty of the Universities of Toronto, Montreal, McGill (Montreal, 1993–96), and Curtis (1998).

In addition to raising her four children—one daughter is a violist—concertizing and recording, Loman finds her most meaningful experiences in discovering and performing new compositions for the harp.

In July 2000, she conducted master classes in the ornate Villa Medici-Giulini in Briosco, north of Milan. 2002 marked her forty-third and final season with the Toronto Symphony. To honor her retirement as principal harpist with the TSO, Marquis Records asked her to select her favorite recordings. The resulting album *Judy Loman: Favourites* was released in 2002.

Contemporary Glissandos

Nancy Allen

NANCY ALLEN, after freelancing since 1996, officially became principal harp of the New York Philharmonic in the 1999–2000 season. Born July 11, 1954, in Mineola, on New York's Long Island, she is the middle—between Jane and Barbara—of three harpist daughters. She began piano at five, continuing study until entering Juilliard. Her family moved north of New York City when she was twelve, and the three girls began harp lessons with Pearl Chertok. At fourteen, Nancy won first prize in the American Harp Society National Competition. In one of those last minute substitutions for a sick performer, Nancy got to play a performance of *The Nutcracker*, and its singular harp cadenza, with the Hudson Valley Philharmonic under **Claude Monteux** (son of Pierre), who was impressed enough to hire her and encourage her career. In the summer of 1971, Chertok sent the sisters to study with **Lily Laskine** in Paris. In 1972, Nancy entered Juilliard under the tutelage of **Marcel Grandjany**. After his death in 1975, she had one year with Jane Weidensaul[119] who replaced him, then **Susann McDonald**, to prepare for her Carnegie Hall debut. She graduated with an MM, and now serves as head of Juilliard's Harp Department. Of her sisters, Barbara is first harpist with the American Ballet Theater, and Jane is principal harpist with the Eugene (Oregon) Symphony.

A guest artist and faculty member of the Aspen Festival since 1978, Allen records extensively and concertizes throughout North America as orchestral soloist, recitalist and chamber musician. Her numerous collaborations include flutists **Jean Pierre Rampal** (1922–2000), **Eugenia Zukerman**, and **Carol Wincenc**, clarinetist **Richard Stoltzman**, and the chamber group TASHI. She was featured in 1990 with **Kathleen Battle** on PBS' *Great Performances*. In 2001, she toured with the NY Philharmonic to South America and Germany, premiering the Siegfried Matthus *Concerto for Flute and Harp* with Robert Langevin. In 2003, Allen became part of the trio Les Amies, with Wincenc and violist **Cynthia Phelps**, principal of the NYP. They made their debut in David Atherton's *Mostly Mozart Festival*, in San Diego, February 2004.

Allen records for EMI and has collaborated on numerous film soundtracks, performing for *The Cell*, released in 2000, *Score* in 2001, and the 2002 movies *Vulgar* and *The Lord of the Rings: Fellowship of the Ring*.

Light of her life, daughter Claire Marie, born 1992, is becoming proficient on piano and cello.

MARIA CASALE was born December 13, 1962, in Santa Monica, California, but spent her youth in Milwaukee, Oregon. She saw her first harp at age three, and loved the sound. Lessons began at age six with Sister Emerentia at Marylhurst College in Portland (Oregon). The nun introduced Maria to **Mildred Dilling** in 1975, and the next five summers were under the tutelage of "the Great Lady of the Harp." Dilling introduced her young pupil to **Susann McDonald** and, beginning September 1979, Maria traveled to Los Angeles every six weeks for a lesson. This continued through high school, after which she was accepted to Juilliard and earned her BM (1984) and MM (1985)—still with McDonald who, for several years, taught on both coasts. In 1989, Casale was the gold medal winner of the USA International Harp Competition in Paris, where she played with the orchestra of the Opera Comique. She was a finalist in the thirty-second International Music Competition in Munich, a first prize winner in the AHS Advanced Division, and twice received the Ruth Lorraine Close Award.

As a soloist, Casale has concertized in Europe, Israel, Mexico and Japan, playing with the Los Angeles and Israel Philharmonics and the Orquestra Sinfonica Nacional de Mexico, among others. Chamber music recitals and summer festivals round out a busy schedule. She was on the faculty of Pepperdine University in 1991, and continues her position as professor at Cal State, Northridge.

---

119. Harpist Jane Weidensaul, born June 30, 1935, in Philadelphia, was the teaching assistant and "adopted daughter" of Marcel Granjany. She was editor of the *Harp Journal* of the AHS for many years beginning in 1979.

Spring 1997 marked the premiere of the *Divertimento for Harp and Orchestra*, written for Casale by Sister Magdalen Fautsch of her alma mater, Marylhurst, where Sister Emerentia Berndorfer, still enjoying life at age ninety-nine, passed away, October 2, 1996.

MARCIA DICKSTEIN, born July 6, 1965, in Santa Monica, is the founder (1987) and artistic director of the Debussy Trio, which has established an important image of the harp, performing a variety of music of all eras. They have inspired composers to create a rich, varied body of new works, such as **Augusta Read Thomas**' *Triple Concerto for Flute, Viola and Harp*. Awards for commissions have come from the NEA, Aaron Copland Fund for Music, and the Los Angeles Cultural Affairs Department. The Trio was chosen "1990 Young Artist(s) of the Year" by *Musical America* and has performed in Copenhagen at the World Harp Congress, in Prague and Honolulu's Orvis Auditorium among many other venues. July 25, 2002, marked the premiere by the Debussy Trio of *Turn-out*, a triple concerto for harp, flute and viola with orchestra by American composer Vince Mendoza at Victoria Hall, Geneva.

Dickstein's own nationwide tours as soloist with orchestra and recitalist have included concerts at Kennedy Center, major universities and live radio broadcasts such as *St. Paul Sunday* and *Performance Today* aired over 200 NPR stations, as well as *Voice of America*. She has recorded on RCM, harmonia mundi, Klavier, Koch, First Edition and Sierra Classical labels. Her playing is heard in films such as *A Bug's Life*, *Toy Story* and *The Matrix*, and for television on the *Tonight Show* and *Star Trek*.

An adjunct professor of harp at Cal. State, Long Beach, and San Luis Obispo, she has a private studio in Los Angeles and holds master classes throughout the U.S. for students and composers. She composes, transcribes, and compiles scholarly editions, including an educational series of original solo and method books for harp students published by the Theodore Presser Company.

Marcia is the daughter of pianist **Diana Steiner** and the niece of conductor **Frances Steiner**. She married Fred Vogler in 1993, a sound engineer for the LA Philharmonic and Opera, who also records the LA Master Chorale. They have two daughters, Lena, born January 21, 1997 and Mattie, June 19, 2000.

SONJA GISLINGE was born November 28, 1939, into a farm family on the isolated island of Mors in the Bay of Lim in northwestern Jutland (Denmark). The sixth of eleven children—six boys and five girls—they all played instruments and sang to entertain themselves, but Sonja was to become the only professional musician. At fifteen, she entered the Jutland Music Academy as a pianist. When she was nineteen, the local symphony needed a harpist and she took the position while continuing piano studies. She began harp with **Inga Grae**, and after receiving her piano diploma, entered the RDAM as a harp major. In 1965 she became the first Danish graduate in harp. She played in the Tivoli (Copenhagen) Symphony, where she met her husband Frederik. The arrival of her three children, Katrine, 1969, Nicolai, 1970, and Christoffer, 1975, suspended her orchestral career, but she continued chamber playing and teaching at the Esbjerg Academy of Music. By 1979, the marriage had failed and she returned to the orchestra. Following the retirement of Inga Grae, Gislinje was named to her position at the RDAM as a concurrent career. In 1982, Sonja married Jens Nielsen, a violist, who gave up orchestral playing to become general manager of the Århus Symphony Orchestra in Denmark. Besides Grae, Phia Berghout and Susann McDonald have had the most influence on Gislinje's career.

CATHERINE JOHNK GOTTHOFFER, born April 12, 1923, in Kiowa, Kansas, moved to Los Angeles as a child. She started violin at five, and during her school years played violin and harp in the famed youth orchestra of **Peter Meremblum**, whose young players in later years included violinist **Zina Schiff** and conductor **Leonard Slatkin**. Catherine's harp teacher, Joseph Riley, manager of the Lyon & Healy Harp Salon, encouraged her to apply to Juilliard where she met her trumpeter husband, Bob. There, she studied with **Marcel Grandjany** and freelanced wherever she could.

While playing at New York's Roxy Theater, her legs suddenly became paralyzed. Diagnosed as multiple sclerosis, only sheer willpower over the next ten years gradually improved the impairment of both arms and legs. Her eyesight, however, suffered permanent damage.

After World War II, Catherine and Bob played in the Dallas Symphony until 1951. Through her husband's uncle, first violist in the Philadelphia Orchestra, who knew the violist in the MGM Orchestra, Catherine was introduced to film conductor/composer **Johnny Green**, then head of the studio music department. After a successful audition, she remained with MGM, appearing at thirteen Academy Award shows, numerous Grammy and Emmy Award productions, plus radio, TV and recording jobs.

Following the 1959 International Harp Competition in Israel, participants decided to return to their home countries and start Harp Societies. Marcel Grandjany called Catherine, and through her efforts founded the Los Angeles Chapter of the AHS.

ANN GRIFFITHS, born October 26, 1934, in Caerffili, Wales, began piano studies at five, but because of her petite size did not start on the harp until eleven. Since native harp players all speak the mother tongue, her BA is in Welsh. During her harp studies' she met her husband, Lloyd Davies, a doctor and amateur musician who studied with the same teacher. In 1955, she went to France to study with **Pierre Jamet** (1893–1991) at the Paris Conservatory, and in 1958 won the Premier Prix. A purist, she prefers to play on the harp for which the music was written, thus she owns many harps from different eras, including an Obermeyer, thought to be the oldest in existence. Her interest in antique harps led to a master's in musicology (Birmingham University, 1982), with a thesis on non-mechanized harps from 1546.

Griffiths' career began as solo harp at the Royal Opera House, Covent Garden, concerts at the Royal Festival Hall and living the life of a traveling artist with radio broadcasts, television appearances and commercial recordings. In 1971, she suffered a back injury from years of lifting harps, which severely curtailed her playing. She turned to teaching and writing, and joined the faculties of Cardiff University, London's Guildhall and other schools in Wales and England. The summer schools she directed and organized (1961–79) led a now established trend. Her written contributions include the entire harp section to *The New Grove Dictionary of Music and Musicians*, teaching manuals for adults and children, research into early harp music, arranging and composition—all enhanced by her fluency in Welsh, English, French, Spanish and German. She became editor-and-chief for Adlais, a Welsh music publisher. Ann performed on EMI's 1998 release of *Virtuoso Harp Classics for Pleasure*.

Griffiths is heartened that her small native country teaches harp beginning in the primary grades, thus ensuring the future of the instrument.

DEBORAH HOFFMAN was born in Vancouver, Canada, July 11, 1960, to a conductor father and concert violinist mother. Music was intrinsically a part of her life, and that of her three brothers. (Joel, a composer-pianist, is at the Cincinnati Teachers Conservatory, Gary, a cellist, lives in Paris, and Toby, is a violinist.) Deborah started on piano at age four, and added harp at ten. During her high school years she played in the school orchestra, and in the summers (1974–78) went to Europe, where she played in the Belgian Radio Orchestra. She received both her BM and MM (1983) from Juilliard, studying with **Susann McDonald**. Further studies were with **Susanna Mildonian** at the Brussels Royal Conservatory. In 1979, she won top prizes in both the Israeli and International Harp Competitions, in 1983 top prize in the Bavarian Radio Orchestra Competition, and in 1993 won the AHS Competition. She played second harp in the Pittsburgh Symphony (1983–86), and in 1986 won the principal chair—over 200 other applicants—in the Metropolitan Opera Orchestra. She is also solo harp with the Orchestra of St. Luke's (New York City). She has toured throughout Latin America as soloist with the national orchestras of Chile, Costa Rica and Colombia, and performed at the festivals of Aspen, Holland (Michigan), Spoleto (South Carolina), Caramoor (Katonah, upstate New York), Waterloo (Iowa), Sitka (Alaska) and Flagstaff (Arizona). In August 2001, she was part of the La Jolla (California) SummerFest.

As a family, the Hoffman Chamber Soloists toured throughout Canada and the U.S. before individual careers separated them—they still try to get together whenever possible.

YOLANDA KONDONASSIS was born in Norman, Oklahoma, November 29, 1963. Her father, Alex, is a Greek emigré who taught economics at University of Oklahoma, mother Patricia is a pianist, and her brother, seven years older, a cellist. Yolanda was already playing piano when her mother, in an effort to subdue her tomboyishness, took

Yolanda Kondonassis

her to a spectacular Lyon and Healy harp exhibit in Chicago and sealed her future. Lessons began at nine with **Susan Dederick**,[120] then principal harp with the Oklahoma City Symphony, who had studied with **Alice Chalifoux**. Yolanda attended the Interlochen Arts Academy, graduating from their high school in 1982 and winning the Young Artists Medal in a competition against *all* instruments—the first harpist ever to do so. She is also the first harpist to receive the Darius Milhaud Prize and **Ima Hogg**[121] Competition (1987). Her BM and MM in performance are from the Cleveland Institute. Summers were spent with Alice Chalifoux at the Salzedo Summer Colony in Camden, Maine. In 1988, she won the Naftzger Competition, the AHS Young Concert Artists Auditions and the **Maria Korchinska** International Competition in England. While director of the St. Louis Symphony, **Leonard Slatkin** was instrumental in arranging Kondonassis' debut, at eighteen, with the New York Philharmonic under **Zubin Mehta**.

As a soloist and recitalist, she has performed in major cities around the country, and as an orchestral harpist, recorded and toured with many major U.S. and international ensembles. A devoted chamber musician, she performs at many summer festivals, is the co-artistic director of the chamber ensemble *Myriad*, and maintains a concert schedule with flutist **Eugenia Zukerman** in the Kondonassis/Zukerman Duo. Much time is spent travelling, either with her 120-pound harp, or prepared to be her own technician on borrowed instruments.

An advocate of contemporary music, Kondonassis has premiered several works composed for her. She received a Solo Recitalists Grant from the NEA and, in 1993, presented the opening Gala Recital at the American Harp Conference. The same year she married Michael Sachs, principal trumpet in the Cleveland Symphony.

Since her 1993 debut album, *Scintilation* (Telarc), she has released *Music of Hovhaness, Sky Music, Pictures of the Floating World* and *Quietude*, created to evoke a mood of calmness. Following September 2001's tragic events, she contributed to a benefit CD, *We Stand . . . As One World*, to benefit families of the victims. *The Romantic Harp*, another Telarc project, was released in January 2003. In the tradition of Carlos Salzedo, as well known for his transcriptions as his original compositions, she has transcribed and recorded Vivaldi's *Four Seasons* with the Orchestra of Flanders (Belgium). In addition to her performing and recording schedule, Yolanda heads the harp departments at the Cleveland Institute and Oberlin.

2004–05 saw the publication of her books, *On Playing the Harp*, a comprehensive approach to the multifaceted art of playing the harp, and *The Yolanda Kondonassis Songbook*, over thirty of her popular transcriptions and arrangements for the harp.

MARIE-PIERRE LANGLAMET, born in France, 1967, studied at the Nice Conservatory, with Elizabeth Fontan, and took masterclasses with Jacqueline Borot and **Lily Laskine**. She came to the U.S. for two and a half years, continuing her training at Curtis. Her prizewinning began in 1983, with first and second at the International Contest on England's Isle of Man. 1984 brought first prize in the Louise Charpentier Contest, 1986 a first and second at Geneva, 1989 the "Concert Artists Guild" Award and 1992, first in International Harp Contest of Israel. She is also prize winner of Juventus (the Council of Europe). In 2003, she received the Simone Foundation and Cino del Duca Prize of the Academy of Beaux Arts.

Harp soloist with the Met Orchestra (1988–93), she has soloed with the all-male Berlin Philharmonic beginning 1993. Her solo and chamber career also covers the Israel Philharmonic, Swiss-Romande, Orchestre National de Lille and, in Paris, Théâtre de Ville, de Châtelet, Champs Elysées, plus many festivals. Her chamber music partners are Emmanuel Pahud (flute), Tabea Zimmermann (viola) and Jana Bouskova (harp).

Recordings include the Mozart *Concerto for Flute and Harp* with Pahud and the Philharmonic Orchestra of Berlin directed by Claudio Abbado (EMI) and the Ginastera Concerto with the Orchestra of Picardy under Edmon Colomer.

---

120. Susan Dederich-Pejovich has been principal harp of the Dallas Symphony since 1977. (See Orchestras.)
121. Philanthropist "Miss Ima." (See The Unforgotten.)

Langlamet regularly gives master classes at Juilliard.

HEIDI LEHWALDER, born 1950, in Seattle, was given a harp at age seven by her mother, a Seattle Symphony cellist. She took to the instrument and, other than in her teens, has performed only as a soloist, appearing with the Seattle Symphony over fifty times—the first at age nine under **Milton Katims** (1909-2006)—in the course of a career which by now has spanned four decades in appearances with over sixty-five orchestras, including the New York and Los Angeles Philharmonics, Atlanta, Seattle and Cleveland Symphonies, under the leadership of such renowned conductors as Leonard Bernstein, Claudio Abbado, Erich Leinsorf and Charles Dutoit. As a chamber musician, she has performed at such festivals as Spoleto, Caramoor, *Mostly Mozart*, Santa Fe, Korean International Chamber Music Festival and played with the Chamber Music Society of Lincoln Center from 1975 to 1992, including their Thirtieth Anniversary Gala in 1999.

It was at Rudolf Serkin's *Music from Marlboro* that she became friends with flutist **Paula Robison**, and violist Scott Nickrenz. In 1972, the three formed the popular Orpheus Trio, playing some forty concerts per season. Heidi toured with them for eight years. She has also performed extensively with flutist **Carol Wincenc**. Inspiration for numerous harp concerti, written for and dedicated to her, include José Serebrier's *Colores Magicos*, Robert Camano's *Concerto for Harp*, Michael Colgrass' *Auras*, and *From Darkness Emerging* for harp and string quartet by **Sheila Silver**.

Her prolific recordings include the Grammy nominated Nonesuch album of solo music of Carlos Salzedo, a CD featuring Ravel's *Introduction and Allegro* with James Galway, Richard Stoltzman and the Tokyo String Quartet on RCA Red Seal, and Vanguard Classic's 2001 release *French Music for Flute, Viola and Harp*. She has appeared on NBC's *Today* show and PBS. In July 1992, she became artistic director of Belle Arte Concerts in Seattle. She is also the founder (1988) and artistic director of the Fredericksburg (Virginia) Festival of the Arts, in its seventeenth year in 2005.

Lehwalder has the distinction of being the very first recipient of the Avery Fisher Career Grant (1976). Awarded to musicians of outstanding talent and marked professional success, this includes playing a concert with the New York Philharmonic. After that performance, conductor Peter Davis called her "an accomplished virtuoso."

Susann McDonald

SUSANN McDONALD, one of the world's foremost harpists, was born May 26, 1935, in Rock Island, Illinois. She began harp at five to please her grandfather, active in prison ministry, who needed a harpist to accompany his religious services and lead hymn singing. By age twelve, she was advanced enough to study with Marie Ludwig in Chicago. The following year she was invited to join the Tri-City Symphony Orchestra, thus at thirteen she was not only an orchestral harpist, but a member of the Musicians Union. At seventeen, Ludwig took Susann to **Mildred Dilling** who was so impressed she suggested **Henriette Renié**. So Susann's junior year of high school was spent in France, where she returned after graduation for more study with Renié. She also enrolled at the École Normale Supérieure de Musique to add a solid grounding in musicianship. After one year she was accepted by **Lily Laskine** into the harp program at the Paris Conservatory. The next year she won the *Premier Prix, Premier Nommé*, and was ready for a solo career.

In addition to concert appearances throughout the world, McDonald was artist-in-residence (1963–70) and associate professor (1970–81) at the University of Arizona, lecturer at USC (1966–81) and head of the harp department at Juilliard (1975–85). She is artistic director of the World Harp Congress, founder and music director of the USA International Harp Competition, and has served on the juries of major international harp competitions where her students have been among the top prize winners—many now holding positions with the New York and Berlin Philharmonics, Metropolitan Opera, Detroit and Seattle Symphonies. In 2002, she collaborated at a master class in Huémoz (Switzerland).

Established by Madeleine Wheeler in 1985, the Susann McDonald Harp Study Fund provides support to students studying harp under McDonald.

She holds the rank of distinguished professor of music at Indiana University, whose faculty she joined in 1981, chairing what has become the largest harp department in America. She has published numerous volumes of harp music, both original compositions and transcriptions. Her popular recordings feature most of the solo harp repertoire.

Carrol McLaughlin

CARROL McLAUGHLIN has toured internationally as a soloist, as well as appearing with major orchestras across America, her native Canada, Europe, Israel and South America. In Chile, she performed the Ginastera Harp Concerto with the Orchestra de Santiago and gave a recital in Punta Arenas, the southernmost city in the world. She is among a select few to have toured India, and the only western harpist to conduct master classes and recitals in both the Beijing and Shanghai Conservatories. In Shanghai, she gave a full recital playing a Chinese harp—a rarity among western performers. Her Hong Kong concert, featuring classics and jazz, was broadcast live. Ten solo tours of Japan included performances in Tokyo's Santori Hall, Soka City Harp Competition and Festival, Nippon Harp Festival, and Karuizawa Music Summer School and Festival.

Harpo Could Really Play the Harp!

Besides the great harp repertoire of Salzedo, Spohr, Albeniz, and Fauré, McLaughlin includes the contemporary—with cleverly arranged favorites such as *Take 5* and *12th Street Rag*. Chosen by the Marx estate to perpetuate the musical legacy of **Harpo Marx**, she presents his compositions and collaborates regularly with Harpo's son, Bill.

McLaughlin has been opening recitalist of the AHS National Conference, the 1993 World Harp Congress in Copenhagen, and a featured artist at the Maria Korchinska Memorial Competition and Festival on the Isle of Man (England). In 1994, Carrol was the featured artist at the Festival of the Caribbean, San Juan, Puerto Rico, and the Lily Laskine Harp Festival in Paris. She has been seen on *Entertainment Tonight*, and heard on *The Listening Room* with Robert Sherman (WQXR, New York), as well as numerous live recital broadcasts for the CBC, NHK (Japan), Radio Peru, Radio Hong Kong and BBC radio and television.

Works composed for her include Alan Rae's *Mirror of Galadriel*, inspired by J.R.R. Tolkien's *The Lord of the Rings*, premiered at Carnegie Hall; *Textures*, a London, Wigmore Hall premiere; *Dialogue for Two Harps* and *Concerto for Two Harps and Orchestra* by Bill Marx; and Canadian composer R. Murray Schafer's *The Crown of Adriadne*, which requires her to perform on the harp plus a battery of percussion instruments surrounding her on stage. Her albums include *A Celebration of Harp*, *Jazz Harp*, and *From Harpo with Love* with Bill Marx, featuring the music of Harpo. *Desert Reflections* is a unique CD featuring **Harpfusion**, an ensemble of fourteen of her students from the University of Arizona—the largest touring group of harpists in the world. Playing music written or arranged by their own members, they have concertized in each of their native countries: China, Taiwan, Japan, Croatia, UK, Australia, Canada, Puerto Rico and the U.S.

Born in Alberta, May 29, 1952, Carrol was principal harpist of the Calgary Philharmonic Orchestra at age fourteen. Her teachers include **Susann McDonald** at Juilliard (where she received her MM), and **Maria Korchinska**, with whom she studied in London. She created the ensemble HarpFusion in 1978 when she arrived at the University of Arizona to begin doctoral studies. Graduating in 1980, she holds one of the first harp performance doctorates ever awarded anywhere. In 1982, she was hired to head UA's harp department, which has become one of the largest in the U.S. In 1994, she received their most prestigious honor, the Five Star Teaching Award for educator excellence. She is the director of the Lyon & Healy International Jazz and Pop Harpfest, held biennially in the U.S., and in July 2000 performed at the First European Jazz & Pop Harpfest in Remagen (Germany). In 2003, McLaughlin and HarpFusion celebrated twenty-five years at the University of Arizona.

Carroll resides in Tucson, Arizona, with her husband and daughter, Kelly, born 1990, who has toured throughout Asia, Canada, America and Mexico performing with her mother.

NORA MERCZ was born in Budapest, April 1, 1942, before the Communists came into power. Her first interest was ballet, but a childhood illness curtailed that dream. At twelve she began piano. By the time she was ready for college, she was thinking of a career in psychology, law or art history when she recalled the harp of her early ballet classes, and began studying at the Béla Bartók Music School and the Academy of Music, graduating in 1967. One of her teachers was **Anna Molnar**, the first woman to get a harp degree and become a professional harpist in Hungary. By this time her country, which she calls "constantly harassed by history," was under Communist rule, and she received a scholarship to study in the Soviet Union (1970–1972). Returning home, she began teaching privately and in 1973 took a long term position with the Franz Liszt Academy of Music in Budapest and at the Béla Bartók School (1978–88). In 1981, she published a National Harp Curriculum for the Ministry of Education. In 1987, she married János Gyöngyösi, a physician who supports her teaching, solo and recital career and her commitment to the Hungarian Harp Center which, after the fall of Communism in 1989, she established in 1992. She also performs on radio and television, and records on the Naxos label.

SUSANNA MILDONIAN, born July 2, 1940, in Venice, was the first first prize winner of the First International Harp Competition held in Israel in 1959. Armenia, which has been the scene of "ethnic cleansing" throughout history, was undergoing yet another "holocaust" in 1915 when her father managed to escape to Italy. Susanna began piano at age five and harp at ten. She studied for nine years with Margherita Cicognari at the Benedetto Marsello Conservatory in Venice. Having no contact with other harpists, she had no real idea of her competence, thus the trip to Israel was more of a holiday for the family. Winning top honors *and* a brand new Lyon and Healy model 30 harp[122] was a complete surprise. After this, she studied with **Pierre Jamet** (1893–1991) in France and become principal harp with the Belgian National Symphony.

Other awards include first prize at the International Music Competition (Geneva), and first prize, Marcel Tournier International Competition (Paris), where she was also awarded the Grand Prix du Disque.

Mildonian, founder and music director of the U.S. International Harp Competition, has been head of harp departments at Juilliard, USC, University of Arizona and Cal State, Los Angeles. She is a professor at the Royal Conservatory of Music, Brussels, plays numerous concerts yearly, including those for the royal families of Belgium, Holland and Japan, and performed at the final concert of the Eighth World Harp Congress in Geneva in 2002. She has recorded most of the major solo harp repertoire and published numerous volumes of harp music, including original compositions and transcriptions.

Mother of Alice, born in 1966, Susanna is now married to Peter Steven Reis, an American attorney specializing in international law, who is instrumental in having works commissioned for his wife.

In the course of her career experiences, Mildonian is ready to write a horror story book on harps-lost-in-transit-and-getting-a-playable-harp-just-before-stepping-onstage.

EMILY MITCHELL has earned acclaim as a concert harpist and singer accompanying herself on the Celtic harp. Born in Fort Worth, Texas, May 4, 1953, she is a graduate of Eastman and London's RCM. Recipient of many awards, she became recognized after winning first prize in the seventh Israeli International Harp Competition— as of 2004, still the last American to do so since 1979. Since then she has performed all over the world, with appearances at the White House, Carnegie Hall, on Radio France, Wigmore Hall and Queen Elizabeth Hall in London, before Britain's Royal Family. She has collaborated with such prominent musicians as flutist **James Galway**, clarinetist **Richard Stolzman**, baritone **Hermann Prey**, conductors **Norman Del Mar** and **Julius Rudel**, and composer/arrangers Marvin Hamlisch, Johnny Mandel and Ennio Morricone.

As a crossover artist, she has worked with Michael Jackson, Aretha Franklin, Carly Simon, the late Ray Charles, and other stars in the popular music universe, and played in the historic 1995 Barbra Streisand tour. Television credits cover the *Today Show*, *Good Morning America*, CNN, BBC and DRS Swiss TV. She can also be heard on numerous film soundtracks and recordings.

---

122. She still plays this harp, as well as owning a Louis XV model #1689, considered to be the greatest concert harp in the world.

Mitchell is principal harpist of the EOS Ensemble, and an affiliate artist at SUNY, Purchase. Besides recording for RCA Victor and Red Seal, with *Irish Harp Songs* and *The Holly and the Ivy, Carols on the Celtic Harp, Flying Dreams* (1995) for both concert and Celtic harp with flutist **James Galway**, she recorded *Impromptu* (JMR, 2000), a solo recital album, featuring the works of Fauré, Hasselmans and Tournier.

Emily lives outside New York City with her husband, jazz trumpeter Lew Soloff, and their two daughters, Laura and Lena.

Marielle Nordmann

MARIELLE NORDMANN, born January 24, 1941, in Montpellier, France, began piano at six. Her grandmother introduced her to the harp, and at ten Marielle began studies with **Lily Laskine**. At the Paris Conservatory she won the Premier Prix in harp at sixteen, and the Premier Prix in chamber music at eighteen. She played duo-harp with Laskine for ten years, and in a flute, cello and harp trio for fifteen years. Besides performing with orchestras and chamber ensembles at music festivals throughout Europe, she maintained a long time partnership with world-famous flutist **Jean-Pierre Rampal** (1922–2000).

2002 brought the release of numerous albums featuring her work, including *Concert at Mrs Récamier* (Arion) and *The Trio Sonatas of Debussy* (Sapphire). Her concert schedule shows no let up with 2004 finding her all over France, including summer festivals, the 10th International Days of the Harp at Arles in October and several Trio Fontanarosa performances in November and December.

Marielle's miraculous survival from a 1984 car crash has given her a deeper perspective on life. Artistic director of the Lily Laskine Competition, she also founded a class for children aged nine to twelve. She is a motivating force in making the harp a popular member of chamber groups, and maintains her own ensemble consisting of string quartet, flute, clarinet and harp.

Married to violinist Patrice Fontanarosa, of the Trio Fontanarosa—consisting of his brother Renaud, cello, and sister Frédérique, piano—they have three children, born between 1969 and 1973. The two daughters are pianists and son Guillaume plays violin. The families are very close.

Ann Pilot

ANN HOBSON PILOT joined the Boston Symphony in 1969, and has been principal harp since 1980. Born in Philadelphia, November 6, 1943, she began lessons with her concert pianist mother at six. She started harp at fourteen in ninth grade, through the public schools, then studied with **Edna Phillips** and her successor, **Marilyn Costello**, at the Philadelphia Musical Academy, took summer courses at the Salzedo Harp Colony with **Alice Chalifoux**, and earned her BM, 1986, at the Cleveland Institute. From there she was appointed principal at the National Symphony (1966–69). She had been substitute second harp in Pittsburgh. She joined Boston in 1969, the same year she married Prentice Pilot, a bassist and (now retired) teacher in the Boston public schools. They formed the Boston Music Education Collaborative, and instituted a concert series on their favorite islands, St. Maarten and St. Croix. Ann also founded the New England Harp Trio.

In 1991, Pilot received the Distinguished Woman of the Year Award from Sigma Alpha Iota. Her honorary doctorate from Bridgewater State College was awarded 1988.

In addition to solo appearances with the BSO, the Boston Chamber Players and the Pops, Pilot has appeared as soloist with many American orchestras, performed at the Sarasota Music Festival with flutist **James Galway** and given master classes during the BSO's historic tour of China. She is a member of the contemporary music ensemble "Collage" and serves on the faculties of the New England Conservatory, Boston University, Tanglewood and since 2003, runs the BU Tanglewood Institute Harp Seminar for high schoolers. Besides her many BSO recordings, she can be heard on chamber music CDs, including the Mathias Harp Concerto[123] with the English Chamber Orchestra led by African-American conductor **Isaiah Jackson** (1993). Her 2001 release on the Denouement label

---

123. William Mathias (1934–93) was a foremost Welsh composer for the harp.

features music by Ravel and Debussy, accompanied by members of the BSO. The Harp Concerto she commissioned from American composer Kevin Kaska was recorded in London with the LSO.

After twenty-seven years with the BSO, Ann took a sabbatical September 1996–May 1997, accompanied by her husband, to research the origin of the harp, said to have its beginnings in Africa, where they toured in March 1997. This project is tied to the writing of her biography and workbooks, and is an ongoing collaborative between ten Boston public schools, the BSO, NEC and radio/TV station WGBH. All is captured in her 1998 video, *A Musical Journey.*

In 2003 Pilot joined the all African-American Ritz Chamber Players. In June 2004, she was featured at the AHS Convention at the University of Pennsylvania. She soloed with Sir James Galway in Mozart's *Flute and Harp Concerto* at Tanglewood, Summer 2005, and was soloist there Summer '06 in Joachim Turina's *Theme and Variations for Harp & Strings* with the BSO.

OLGA ORTENBERG RAKITCHENKOV was born in Moscow, October 15, 1949. Her mother played piano and her great-grand uncle was a member of the Budapest String Quartet. Olga started piano at six and harp at eleven. She attended Gnesin, a school for gifted children. (Now prominent pianist **Evgeny Kissin** was also a student there at the time.) In 1968, she was accepted to the Moscow (Tchaikovsky) Conservatory, where she studied for five years with **Vera Dulova**. In 1973, she won an audition for the Bolshoi Ballet and Opera Orchestra. In 1974, out of thirty-seven applicants, she won first prize at the Geneva International Harp Competition. Beginning in 1980, her family applied for papers to leave Russia, and for eight years languished in the ranks of "*refusniks*"—would-be emigrants whose requests were consistently denied.

Olga married Sergei Rakitchenkov, assistant principal viola in the orchestra, in 1975. Their daughter, Elizaveta, was born September 20, 1978. Although they toured Bulgaria, Rumania, Greece and France with the orchestra, the couple were never together, which eliminated any attempt to defect to the West.

Finally, in 1987, through a Jewish-sponsored organization, the whole family, Olga's mother, father, brother and his wife and children, were allowed to leave the country. But Olga was not permitted to take her lovely American Lyon and Healy, or French Érard harps out of Russia—a cause for temporary unhappiness. They arrived in Vienna in April. After a week they went on to Rome, where there was a ten-week delay before they could procure more documents. The family finally landed in Oakland, California, via New York, July 15, 1987. None could speak a word of English! In three weeks, Sergei had a position with the San Francisco Opera Orchestra. In 1989, Olga won an audition and became their principal harp. She has since been able to buy three beautiful Lyon and Healy harps, all of which get excellent use.

MARISA ROBLES [Maria Luisa Robles Bonilla] was born May 4, 1937, in Madrid, and at an early age studied with Luisa Menárgues, a student of both Alphonse Hasselmans (1845–1912) and Wilhelm Posse (1852–1925). She made her debut at age nine. Graduating from the Madrid Conservatory in 1953, she had her formal concerto debut in that city the following year, playing the Mozart Concerto for flute and harp with **Jean-Pierre Rampal**. Appointed professor of harp at the Madrid Conservatory in 1958, she left Spain after her marriage, and in 1960 became a British subject, living with her family in London since 1964.

Her London debut was at the Royal Festival Hall in 1963. She taught at the RCM 1971–93, having been made a fellow of the Royal College in 1983. A very successful series of television appearances highlighted her personality and talent, creating new audiences for harp music. She was artistic director of the First World Harp Festival (1991), and World Harp Festival II (1994), both in Cardiff (Wales).

From the early 1970s, Robles was involved in chamber music, often with her second husband, flutist Christopher Hyde-Smith. Many works were dedicated to her by composers such as William Alwyn, Stephen Dodgson, Alun Hoddinott, William Mathias, John Metcalf, Malcolm Williamson and Manuel Moreno-Buendia, whose concerto she had premiered with the Spanish National Orchestra in 1958. In 1994, he dedicated to her his *Concierto Neo-Clasico* for harp, marimba and strings. Other Spanish composers who wrote concertos for her include Joaquín Rodrigo, whose *Sones en la Giralda* she first performed in 1969 in Madrid.

Robles has worked with such celebrated conductors as Zubin Mehta, Kurt Masur, Rafael Frühbeck de Burgos, Mstislav Rostropovich, Yehudi Menuhin, artists James Galway and Isaac Stern, and performed with orchestras all over the world, touring Europe, America, Japan, Australia and, in 1988, China. In 1994, she took part in the TV series *CONCERTO!*, in which she appeared with the LSO, Dudley Moore, Michael Tilson Thomas and James Galway, and received the prestigious Emmy Award in New York.

Her discography includes more than two dozen recordings for ASV, Argo, BMG, Decca, RCA and Virgin Classics, featuring performances with the Academy of St. Martin-in-the-Fields and Iona Brown, and the Philharmonia with Charles Dutoit, plus an album of solo works, *The World of the Harp*, on Decca. Robles and James Galway have given more than 1,000 performances of the Mozart Flute and Harp Concerto, and made four recordings of the work: with the Chamber Orchestra of Europe, the London Symphony under Eduardo Mata and Michael Tilson Thomas respectively, and the Academy of St Martin-in-the-Fields with Sir Neville Marriner.

Sunita Stanislaw

SUNITA STANESLOW was born April 21, 1962, in Ithaca, New York, but raised in Minneapolis, where her father taught Hindi at the University of Minnesota, hence her Indian first name. She started piano lessons in first grade. Although she really wanted to play the flute, because her hands were too small, she began harp at eight. Her parents were a little reluctant, but finding an instrument and teacher were not difficult. She played piano until fifteen, and got to play the flute through high school. After her BA (Tufts, 1984) she spent two years in Israel, at which point, she realized, "Everything fell into place and I made the decision to become a professional harpist."

In 1986 she married Fred Shlomka, a Scotsman she met in Edinburgh, who had emigrated to Israel. She worked with Judith Liber, principal harp of the Israel Philharmonic, became active in the folk music community, was principal harpist for the Jerusalem Symphony, also playing with the Israel Philharmonic. Back to Europe, she studied with **Lily Laskine** in Paris, then returned to the U.S. to study with **Lucile Lawrence**, receiving an MM from Manhattan School of Music (1989).

When, in 1989, her husband gave her a Clarsach (Scottish folk harp), she began performing with folk musicians, especially Jewish and Celtic music. In her home territory, Stanislow became principal harp with Minnesota Opera (1995–98). Back in Israel, besides folk ensembles, Sunita performs with the Israel Chamber Orchestra and is principal harpist with the Ra'anana Symphonette. She received a 1998 McKnight Foundation Fellowship in recognition of her work with Jewish music, and is considered the premier Celtic harpist in her adopted country.

By 2006 she had written eleven books on harp music, including her own transcriptions, and recorded fourteen CDs of solo and chamber works. In addition to performing, her workshop tours take her to Europe and America. She has been featured at the World Harp Congress, Edinburgh International Harp Festival, and International Folk Harp conventions. She also provides therapeutic harp music, which is recognized as a musical art, in hospices, hospital ICUs, and neo-natal clinics. She trains and supervises others in this work, and is a founding member of NEVEL: Jerusalem Harp Network.

Sunitra lives in Kfar Saba, north of Tel-Aviv, with her husband and children Mikhael, born October 26, 1990, and Maya Ruth, March 30, 1993.

JoANN TUROVSKY took over as adjunct associate professor at USC when **Susann McDonald** left for Indiana in 1979. Born September 30, 1954, to a violinist father who guided her to the harp, she began lessons at seven. She studied with McDonald for ten years through high school and college. Her BM is from USC (1975), and MM from the University of Arizona (1977). Besides her teaching career, she has appeared with the Los Angeles Mozart Orchestra and is principal harpist with the Pasadena Symphony (1977–), the Long Beach Symphony (1977–), Los Angeles Chamber Orchestra (1988–), Joffrey Ballet Orchestra, and is a member of the contemporary music ensemble XTET. She has been chairman of the triennial American Harp Society Competition, Young Professional Division, since 1980. She helped organize the World Harp Congress, which met in America for the first time in

Tacoma, Washington, July 1996, showcasing up and coming harpists, and featuring a night each of concerts, chamber music and solo recitals.

Turovsky has won numerous awards for both her solo and chamber performances. These include first prize in the AHS National Competition, Young Professional Division, first prize in the Coleman Competition for Chamber Music, a winner at the Fifth International Harp Competition in Jerusalem, and many other honors.

Another facet of her career is playing for motion picture soundtracks. In 1999, she was featured on the soundtrack of *Angela's Ashes*, performing a solo piece composed for her by John Williams. Other film composers she has recorded with are Jerry Goldsmith, Randy Newman and David Newman. The latter's sister, composer **Maria Newman**, was commissioned to write a song cycle based on the poems of African-American conductor **James de Preist**, which was premiered by Turovsky at the 1996 World Harp Congress.

NAOKO YOSHINO was born in London, December 10, 1967, while her father, Shinji, was posted there in his banking business. When she was three, the family returned to Japan and she entered the Music Class for Children at the Toho Conservatory. Her mother, Atsuko, the first Japanese harpist to give a recital in her country, had studied with Josef Molnar, **Maria Korchinska** and **Susann McDonald**, and instilled the love of music in her daughter, who began piano at five. When her father was transferred to Los Angeles, Naoko began harp studies with **Susann McDonald**. Four years later the family again returned to Japan, and through her high school years Naoko studied with her mother and McDonald, to whom she went for a few weeks each summer and winter. She never attended a conservatory, but graduated from the International Christian University as a humanities major. In 1979, she won the Los Angeles Young Musicians Foundation audition; in 1981, second prize at the First International Harp Contest at the Santa Cecilia Academy in Rome and received the Mobil Music Award for Brilliant Young Musicians; in 1983, she played at the International Harp Week in Holland; and in 1985 won first prize at the International Harp Contest in Israel.

The 21st century has taken her to Vienna, Spain in concert with the Frühbeck de Burgos National Orchestra in commemoration of the 100th anniversary of Jaoquín Rodrigo, plus engagements with the North West German Philharmonic and with the Leipzig Gewandhaus Orchestra. Other career highlights include tours with Seiji Ozawa; the Mito Chamber (Europe) and Saito Kinen Orchestras (America); trio recitals throughout Japan; the Schleswig-Holstein and Lucerne Festivals with Veronika Hagen and Wolfgang Schulz; Salzburg Mozart Week; duo concerts in Japan with Berlin Philharmonic harpist Marie-Pierre Langlamet; and the world premiere of Toshio Hosokawa's Concerto for Harp. Her recordings are on Sony Classical and Philips Classics, plus a recording with the late Lord Yehudi Menuhin on Virgin Classics.

Miracles from Earthbound Angels

Harps have long been associated with angels, and it is said of San Antonio Symphony harpist **LAURIE BUCHANAN** that she plays divinely. But instead of flowing white robes and a halo, she wears a mask and hospital scrubs as part of a unique experiment exploring the healing powers of music. The ancient Greeks believed harp strings resounded in harmony with the nerves and muscles of the body, and plucked strings release tension through sympathetic resonance. Thus, when not in the orchestra pit, Buchanan can be found in the operating room, rippling heavenly glissandos with remarkable effects—like lowered blood pressure and the need for less anesthesia—on patients of all ages. Research has shown that the soothing tones penetrate the subconscious, proving the beneficial power of *good* music!

AMY LYNN KANNER, MD, combines her passion for music with a commitment to the well being of the sick, elderly and infirm. Following a childhood fascination with music and physiology, piano and theory studies began at age seven, violin at thirteen, followed by guitar and recorders, with a graduation from the Pennsylvania School of Medicine in 1982.

Inspired by an introduction to the Celtic Harp in 1990, she mastered the instrument and made an album in 1993. In 1997, she completed Christina Tourin's International Harp Therapy Program, and, accompanying herself on the instrument, now gives her presentation, "Music, Medicine and the Magic of the Harp" in retirement centers, hospitals, hospices and before groups of all ages throughout the country. Dr. Kanner continues to pursue her medical career in the San Diego area.

Teacher, composer, performer, **CHRISTINA TOURIN** is a second generation harpist who began her instrument at age four. With music and education degrees from the University of Vermont, and harp study at the Salzburg Mozarteum and McGill University (Montreal), she played in the Vermont and New Haven (Connecticut) Symphonies, off-Broadway productions, plus concertizing and recording internationally. She also performed at the Trapp Family Lodge in Stowe, Vermont, for many years. In 1982, she founded the Scottish Harp Society of America and, since the early 1970s, has been instrumental in the revival of the folk harp.

By 2002, she had begun an International Harp Therapy Program to train harpists to use their talent "for the bedside" in hospitals and hospices, as well as teaching workshops in Healing with Sound-Resonant Kinesthesiology. Moving to San Diego in 1999, she set up the national headquarters for the hospice division of her program, working with San Diego Hospice, one of the few such teaching facilities in America. The same year, a large grant was given to work at San Diego Children's Hospital—fifty-five beds of youngsters with severe disabilities. In the course of this vital work, Tina has witnessed such miracles as patients coming out of comas on hearing the harp.

Summers have been spent in Europe and England, with U.S. tours during the fall. The month of May has seen tours up and down the West Coast. September 2004 found her giving workshops and concerts at the huge Los Angeles City of Hope Medical Center, and the National Convergence of Therapeutic Musicians in Sedona, Arizona, among other venues. Her CD count is over fifteen. Her latest book is *Harp Therapy—A Cradle of Sound* (2006).

March 17, 2006, was celebrated with Tourin's gathering in San Diego of 125 harpists from around the world (World Harp Orchestra) in a benefit concert for Disaster Relief. She plans this to become a regular event, to be televised globally.

A Unique Career

MARY O'HARA was born in 1935, in Sligo, on the west coast of Ireland. She made her first national broadcast while still in school, singing and accompanying herself on the Celtic harp. Her reputation as a singer soon spread beyond her native country, helped by appearances at the Edinburgh Festival, the *Ed Sullivan Show* and BBC television, from which public response resulted in her own prime-time BBC television series and her first recording contract with Decca Records—all this happening in the mid-1950s. Music historian Karl Haas featured her each year on his St. Patrick's Day radio broadcast.

At age twenty-one, she married the young American poet Richard Selig, then a Rhodes Scholar at Oxford University. They moved to the U.S., but tragically, within fifteen months of their marriage, he died. After his death, the zest had gone out of life for Mary. Nevertheless, she spent the next four years traveling the globe giving concerts and appearing on radio and TV, including a highly successful 1959 tour of Australia and New Zealand. Critics everywhere were unanimous in their praise, but the greater her success the more she felt the call to withdraw from the world. In 1962, she entered an English Benedictine Monastery where she remained for twelve years.

In her "absence," her recordings continued to sell out. When her health began to give way under the rigors of monastic life, Mary decided to return to her career.

History repeated itself. After an appearance on the *Russell Harty TV Show*, her impact on the public had the channel switchboard swamped with requests for her reappearance. Shortly after came the first of many concert appearances at London's Royal Festival Hall, a resounding success that became a best-selling record.

Since 1977, Mary O'Hara has continued at the top of her career and appeared in most major venues, including London's Royal Albert Hall, Toronto's Roy Thompson Hall, Carnegie Hall and the Sydney Opera House, plus tours that have covered America, Canada, Australia, New Zealand, Great Britain, Ireland and Europe.

As of 2001, she had recorded twenty-three long-playing albums, and written three popular books. Her autobiography, *The Scent of the Roses*, has sold over a million copies!

And A Newer Generation . . .

In every field prodigious talent springs up, and when discovered is welcomed into the field as past generations pass away or retire after having given the world their gift of musical joy.

MARIKO ANRAKU has been associate principal harpist of the Metropolitan Opera Orchestra since 1995, and is also an active soloist and chamber musician. She studied oriental art history at Tokyo's Sophia University. The recipient of an artist's diploma from the Royal Conservatory of Music in Toronto, where she studied with **Judy Loman**, she went to Juilliard (BM, MM) where she was a student of **Nancy Allen**.

Since her debut with the Toronto Symphony, she has performed with the Vienna Chamber Orchestra, the New Japan Philharmonic and the Yomiuri Symphony among others. As a recitalist, she has been heard at Weill Recital Hall at Carnegie Hall, Jordan Hall in Boston, Bing Theater at the LA County Museum, the Opéra Comique in Paris, the Palazzo dell'Esposizioni in Rome and the Casals, Kioi and Oji Halls in Tokyo.

Her recording *Beau Soir*, with flutist Emmanuel Pahud, and a solo compilation are on the EMI Encore series. She contributes to community service projects by performing in hospitals, drug rehabilitation centers, prisons, schools for the blind, homes for the elderly and other similar facilities in the U.S., France, Italy and Japan.

Charlotte Balzereit

CHARLOTTE BALZEREIT began her tenure with the all-male Vienna Philharmonic in the 2001–2002 season, succeeding **Anna Lelkes**.[124] Born April 8, 1980, in Wiesbaden, Germany, her father, Reiner, is an engineer and her mother, Erika, a dentist. Charlotte started harp at age seven with her aunt, a professional harpist and teacher. At eleven, she went on to advanced studies at the Musikhochschule in Munich. From sixteen to nineteen, besides taking the standard curriculum, she reached the A levels in English and speaks the language fluently. She received her performance diploma in 1999, and was immediately hired by the Munich State Opera until 2000, when she went to Paris for one year, studying with Isabelle Moretti at the Paris Conservatory.

With the announced retirement, after thirty years, of Anna Lelkes—the first female member ever in the Vienna Philharmonic since its beginnings in 1842—the orchestra sent personal audition requests to twenty-five women throughout Europe. Charlotte was chosen. With the two year probation required of all members, her name did not appear on the program until September 2004.

JANA BOUŠKOVÁ, born in Prague, 1970, studied at the Prague Conservatory, Ostrava University with her mother, professor Libuse Vachalova, and, as a Fulbright scholar, pursued her education with **Susann McDonald** at Indiana University. In 1992, she won the U.S. International Harp Competition, receiving a Lyon & Healy harp she plays to this day. She placed second at the eleventh International Competition in Israel, 1998, was the winner of Concours International de Musique de Chambre (Paris), and earned the 1999 Harpa Award of Switzerland, for her exceptional achievement as a concert artist and her outstanding contribution to the advancement of the art of harp interpretation.

She has appeared both as a soloist and as a member of various chamber music ensembles in festivals in her home country and internationally (Alice Tully Hall; Gewandhaus in Leipzig; Théâtre de la Ville in Paris; Berlin

---

124. Lelkes' name did not appear in the program until 1995. She was denied membership voting privileges until 1997, after the orchestra was picketed for its discriminatory policies by the IAWM and NOW while on tour in California. Lelkes had been playing as an associate member since 1971. She was forced to retire in 2001, when twenty-one-year-old Balzereit took her place.

Philharmonic Hall; Suntory Hall in Tokyo; and Rudolfinum in Prague). As a soloist, she has performed with the Czech Philharmonic, Prague Philharmonia, Chicago Sinfonietta, Israel Philharmonic, the MDR Symphonie orchester Leipzig, and the Tokyo Chamber Orchestra.

Since 1993 she has been a professor at the Prague Conservatory and artistic director of Prague's Academy of Music. She was artistic director of the Seventh World Harp Congress (Prague, 1999), was a visiting professor at Indiana University in 2002, and has given masterclasses in San Francisco and Japan.

She has made over two dozen CDs for both Czech and international record labels in a wide-ranging repertoire of all periods and styles. In contemporary music, she has had many works written for her by composers in the Czech Republic and the rest of the world.

CRISTINA BRAGA studied at the School of Music of the State University of Rio De Janeiro, and with **Susann McDonald** in Indiana. In 1992, she won the Gold Medal contest, sponsored by her university (UFRJ), and became the first harpist of the Symphonic Orchestra of the Municipal Theater of Rio De Janeiro. Her professional debut was with the Brazilian Symphonic Orchestra and Symphonic Orchestra Pró-Música. From 1993–96, Braga was one of the directors of the World Harp Congress. She has recorded with the instrumental quintet Opus 5, and in 1997 became a member of the group Bamboo, with whom she recorded *Brazilian Native*, a disc of Christmas repertoire.

Welsh harpist **CATRIN FINCH**, born in 1980, began her studies at the age of six. At ten, she played at the World Harp Congress in Paris, and at eleven became the youngest member to perform at a BBC Promenade concert at the Royal Albert Hall, as principal harpist (1990–96) of the National Youth Orchestra of Great Britain. Her studies continued at the Purcell School of Music, and then with Skaila Kanga at the Royal Academy of Music.

She won first prize in the junior section of the 1991 World Harp Festival, and in 1994 the second prize in the senior competition at the age of fourteen. Her other awards include the Nansi Richards prize in 1997, the Blue Riband at Wales' National Eisteddfod in 1998, and the 1999 winner of the Marisa Robles Harp prize in the Royal Overseas League Competition. In September 1999, she won first prize at the Lily Laskine International Harp Competition in Paris. The Victor Salvi Foundation provided her with a new Salvi "Aurora" harp, and a generous sponsorship. In March 2000, she gave her London debut recital at Wigmore Hall.

She won the 2000 Young Concert Artists International Auditions, as well as the Princeton University Concerts and the Orchestra New England Soloist Prizes. The Young Concert Artists Series presented her at recital debuts at the 92nd Street Y in New York, the Isabella Stewart Gardner Museum in Boston, and a U.S. recital tour that continued into the 2003–04 season. Her UK appearances with orchestra include the Sinfonia Cymru in Dublin and Birmingham, English Chamber Orchestra, London's Academy Symphony Orchestra and National Polish Radio Symphony Orchestra.

The Prince of Wales, after hearing Catrin perform at his fiftieth birthday party in Buckingham Palace, revived the post Royal Harpist to HRH The Prince of Wales, last filled by Queen Victoria in 1871. Catrin performs at a number of events for Prince Charles, and he commissioned a double harp concerto for her which she premiered with the BBC National Orchestra of Wales.

Her CD *Crossing the Stone* was released on the Sony Classical label, and the Lutoslawski Concerto for Oboe and Harp and Debussy's *Danses*, recorded with the National Polish Radio Symphony Orchestra, is on Naxos.

BRIDGET KIBBEY holds both BM and MM degrees from Juilliard, where she studied with **Nancy Allen**. She won the 2001 Premier Prix at the International Chamber Music Competition of Arles, France, performed at the 2002 World Harp Congress in Geneva, Switzerland, and the Amadeus Concert Series of Washington, DC. She toured as soloist with the U.S. Army Orchestra in Arlington (Virginia), Chicago, and New York, and enjoys presenting performances to the Boroughs of New York City as an affiliate artist of the Carnegie Hall Neighborhood Concert Series.

She is a winner of the 2003 Astral Artistic Services National Auditions which, like YCA, presents career development and performance opportunities. Her honors include Juilliard's Peter Mennin Prize for musical leadership and excellence, Corpus Christi Harp Performance Award, AHS **Anne Adams** Award, Mustard Seed Foundation Harvey Fellowship, and a Borletti-Buitoni Trust International Award nomination.

Kibbey has appeared as featured soloist with the Juilliard Symphony, Israel Youth Philharmonic in Tel Aviv, Eastern Philharmonic Orchestra, New York Philharmonic, Boston Symphony and Orpheus Chamber Orchestra.

With an interest in new music, she was a featured soloist in New York's 2003 Music at the Anthology Festival, 2002 Sonic Boom Festival, Carnegie Hall's Elliot Carter Workshop, Juilliard FOCUS Festival, and performed on Carnegie Hall's "Meet the Composer" Series. She has also performed with Speculum Musicae, Ensemble Sospeso, Perspectives Ensemble, New York New Music Ensemble, and the Nouvelle Ensemble Moderne of Montreal. In September 2003, she joined a hand-selected group of young musicians in presenting the first concert in Carnegie Hall's Zankel Hall.

ISABELLE PERRIN, after completing her studies at the Conservatoire de Nice, France, gave her first recital at age seventeen at the Festival Méditerranée des Jeunes Solistes. Following this, she studied at Juilliard for three years before joining the San Francisco Symphony Orchestra. On her return to France, she gave recitals throughout the country for three years, introducing the harp to a wider public. She was then named co-principal harp of the Orchestre National de France.

She has toured in Europe, USA, Tunisia, South Africa, China and Japan. Following the world premiere in France with the Orchestre de Bretagne of Piérick Houdy's *Concerto Français* for harp and orchestra, written for her, she performed it with the Baton Rouge (Louisiana) Symphony. Also written for her is Bernard Andres' *Danses d'Erzulie* for harp, string orchestra and percussion, which she premiered with the Cincinnati Symphony, June 2000.

Her CDs include a recital of works by Bernard Andres; works of Arnold Bax for flute, viola and harp with the Turner Trio, of which she is the founding member; and a recording on a period instrument of the works of French opera composer François-Adrien Boieldieu (1775–1834), featuring his Harp Concerto (1800).

Perrin is the youngest French musician to obtain a degree to teach at the conservatory level. In September 2002, she joined the École Normale Supérieure de Paris. She also gives master classes all over the world, and was a guest teacher at Indiana University, Bloomington.

British **EMMA RAMSDALE** studied in her native London at the RAM with Daphne Boden and Skaila Kanga. She has soloed with major British orchestras throughout the UK, and abroad in Russia, Denmark, France, Greece and Norway. Closer to home, she has made a series of solo recordings for the BBC Radio 3's "Overture" series. She also performs with Catherine Harper, soprano, and as half of the *Habañera Duo* with flutist Rachel Jeffers.

Ramsdale was selected to participate in the South Bank's Young Musicians' 2001 Series. She plays in "Live Music Now," which brings music into all areas of the community from prisons to nursing homes, and has become a wedding specialist. Her harp was purchased though the philanthropy of the Countess of Munster Musical Trust, Abbado European Musicians Foundation and Musicians Benevolent loan fund.

At seventeen, Dutch harpist **GWYNETH WENTINK** won first prize in the 1999 Young Concert Artists International Auditions, the first solo harpist to win a place on the YCA roster. She was also awarded the Beracasa Foundation Prize for a performance at the Montpellier Radio-France Festival, and the Mortimer Levitt Award for Women Artists, which sponsored her 2000 New York debut in the YCA Series at the 92nd Street Y. Wentink debuted in Boston that year, at the Isabella Stewart Gardner Museum. During the 2000–2001 season, she gave her New York concerto debut for YCA at Alice Tully Hall with the New York Chamber Symphony, and played at the Morgan Library in New York with YCA alumna flutist **Eugenia Zukerman** in a special series celebrating the fortieth anniversary of Young Concert Artists. March 4, 2002, YCA presented her at Carnegie's Weill Recital Hall with YCA violinist **Ju-Young Baek**, another award-winning young woman.

The prodigy has won first prizes since age eleven. In 1998 it was the International Harp Competition in Israel, the Gulbenkian Prize for best performance of the new R. Murray Schafer Harp Concerto and first prize in the Torneo Internazionale di Musica in Rome. In 1996, she captured top prize in the International Harp Competition in Tokyo. In 2001, she was awarded the Netherland-America Foundation Prize.

Wentink's solo performances have been with *I Fiamminghi* in Brussels, with the Lille Philharmonia in France, Residentie Orkest in The Hague, the Nieuw Sinfonietta in Amsterdam, the Orquesta Sinfonica Gran Mariscal de Ayacucho (Caracas, Venezuela), and the San Diego (California) Chamber Orchestra, where the author met this lovely, modest, new talent and her equally gracious mother. She has given recitals at Wigmore Hall (London), the Concertgebouw (Amsterdam), as well as in Tel Aviv, Bucharest, Prague, Barcelona, Paris, Rome, Venice and Rotterdam.

Born in 1982, in Utrecht in the Netherlands, of Hungarian and Dutch musician parents, Gwyneth had her first lesson on a Celtic harp at the age of five. At eight, she played Mozart's *Concerto for Flute and Harp* with the Netherlands National Youth Orchestra in Rotterdam, and at ten performed for Queen Beatrix. She graduated *cum laude* from the Utrecht Conservatory (2001), where she was a student of Erika Waardenburg, and has performed in master classes for Maria Graf, **Susann McDonald**, Catherine Michel, Andrée Laurens-King and **Susanna Mildonian**. She performs on a harp provided by the Victor Salvi Foundation.

Her CDs receive top marks with Dutch critics.

PATRICIA McNULTY WOOSTER has served as principal harpist and soloist with orchestras on both West and East coasts. Since resigning as principal harp with the Tacoma Symphony, she has concertized with the Northwest Sinfonietta, and in both a harp duo and a harp/flute duo. Holding degrees in both music and education, she teaches harp at the University of Puget Sound and Pacific Lutheran University. She presents workshops, has performed at national conferences of ASTA and the AHS, and serves as a judge for their National Competition.

She was chairman of the Sixth World Harp Congress International Music Festival that brought more than 1,000 harpists from over thirty countries to Tacoma for an eight-day music festival in July 1996, and with her daughter, Elizabeth, presented a duo harp performance at the AHS National Conference in St. Paul, June 2002.

Wooster founded and directs the harp-training program for the Tacoma Youth Symphony Association, and in her private studio teaches some thirty-five harp and piano students, ranging from age eight to senior citizens. She is past president of the AHS and has been chairman of the board of the World Harp Congress.

And then there are . . .

. . . besides the many talented orchestra harpists, myriads of other talented ladies who play all styles of music adapted for harp, in hotels, clubs, luncheons, banquets, weddings and a host of other functions—even my book signings—lending the uniquely lilting sound of this singular instrument to the ambience of the occasion . . .

And there are . . . Multi -Talents

It has been the policy of this book to present not only the most prominent women in each musical discipline, but shed a little spotlight on the many talents who may never grace the stage of Carnegie Hall or the Hollywood Bowl, but who radiate a bright glow in there own sphere.

SYLVIA LORRAINE HARTMAN is one of these, *in spades*! One of six children, Sylvia was born in Northern Minnesota into a musical family. Her father, Roy Newcomb, was choir director at their church, with her mother, Virginia, lead soprano soloist. Sylvia began piano lessons at age five, later adding clarinet, oboe, string bass, harp and organ. Her studies included classical and sacred music, but she also developed a love of theater music. Always a singer with the family choir, at twelve she also became a church organist, and at sixteen won first place in the piano division of the Young Artist Competition of the Minnesota Music Teachers' Association. Her harp teacher was Francis Miller, ninety-two as of this writing (2006), and still teaching.

Hartman has become one of those rare, versatile musicians who can make good music in a multitude of ways. Since moving to San Diego, California, she has appeared in local theater stage roles, performed her piano lounge act at local hotels, is the choral accompanist and harpist for the San Diego Festival Chorus, Helix Charter High

School, and organist/choirmaster for Christ the King Church in Alpine, where she resides with her family. In addition to being a vocal coach and harp teacher, she is also the harpist, and doubles in the percussion section, with Tifereth Israel Community Orchestra. At their final concert of the 2005 season, she was the featured piano soloist in De Falla's *Nights in the Gardens of Spain*, and elevated the audience into a blissful state singing the soprano part with local supermezzo **Pat McAfee**, in the glorious *Flower Duet* from Delibes' *Lakmé*.

Hartman's special music gifts are already handed down. Her older daughter, Olivia, performs as a singer and actress, younger daughter, Melissa, plays flute and bassoon, and son, Matthew, piano and guitar. Husband Tom's role is an appreciative and supportive audience.

Did I mention that Sylvia has conducted a few local orchestras?

Women to the Winds

RECORDER
Michala Petri
Marion Verbruggen

FLUTE
Lois Schaefer
Jeanne Baxtresser
Leone Buyse
Doriot Anthony Dwyer
Susan Milan
Yoki Owada
Susan Palma
Marina Piccinini
Paula Robison
Er'ella Talmi
Carol Wincenc
Eugenia Zukerman

CLARINET
Thea King
Emma Johnson
Sabine Meyer
Orit Orbach

BASSET HORN
Georgina Dobrée

OBOE
Marsha Heller
Pamela Pecha

BASSOON
Julie Feves
Nancy Goeres
Judith LeClair

CONTRA BASSOON
Susan Nigro

SAXOPHONE
Cynthia Sikes
Karolina Strassmayer
Leigh Pilzer
Anat Cohen
Scheila Gonzalez
Lisa Parrott
Jane Ira Bloom

Tootling From the Beginning of Time

Wind instruments date from prehistory. Stemming from nature, they were made of animal horns, bones, wood, shell—even stone. It was man's ingenuity, however, to bore holes, join pipes together and add other accessories to enable the player to produce a range of tone and melody.

The position of women as priestesses in ancient civilizations, their contribution to music in the cloisters of the Middle Ages, as troubadours—*jongleuresses, trobairitz*—of 12th and 13th century Europe, and their presence in the courts of Renaissance nobility eventually led to the beginnings of public performance. This progression, dating back to depictions of Greek women playing the *aulos*—forerunner of the oboe—and other early winds such as the *recorder, cromone* (crumhorn), *shawm* (another ancestor of the oboe), *bass shawm* (early bassoon) and *chalumeau*—which led to the invention of the clarinet—indicates that women have long been making music on wind instruments. The *transverse flute*—played horizontally—came from Byzantium and Slavic countries, spreading to western Europe where, in the Middle Ages, it was primarily a military instrument. The vertical flute (flageolet), made of wood, was of Asian origin, and found its way west around the 11th century. The resurgence of the popularity of ancient music, beginning in the 1970s, has made these early instruments once again familiar.

As with other instruments, male standards imposed the connotation as to which were "suitable for ladies," a dictum that relegated women to the keyboard until the middle of the 19th century—although mention is made of the *Concerts Spirituel*, established in Paris in 1725, featuring women performing in public on the flute, horn, harp, fortepiano, harpsichord, organ and violin.

The Only Recourse

The entrance of women into conservatories, with graduates finding no outlet for their talents other than teaching, led to the proliferation of female orchestras at the turn of the 20th century, each embodying skilled instrumentalists in all sections. The Chicago Women's Symphony had among its organizers in 1925, Lillian Poenisch, a clarinetist, and Adeline Schmidt, a flutist. Conductor **Antonio Brico** spoke of **Lois Wann**, oboist in her New York Women's Symphony (1935), as "a phenomenal player." In today's "co-ed" orchestras[125] women, although still outnumbered, hold their own in the mastery of their instruments. While the majority of women can still be found in the string sections, woodwinds come a close second with flute, clarinet and oboe predominant, and a respectable number hold principal or associate principal positions. The following have made their mark as solo artists.

RECORDER - A Relic of Ancient Times

One of the oldest of the wind instruments, the recorder—Latin, *recordari*, to think over or to recall; Italian, *ricordo*, a souvenir or memento—is a member of the "fipple flute" family, those using a whistle-type mouthpiece. Called the "common flute" for many centuries, it was featured in most orchestras until around 1800. Used to create atmosphere for love scenes, depict pastoral settings, imitate bird songs, or describe other worldly beings such as angels, it was much written for by baroque composers such as **Henry Purcell** (c1659–95), **Johann Sebastian Bach** (1685–1750), **George Frideric Handel** (1675–1750) and **Georg Philipp Telemann** (1681–1767). It was also highly popular as an instrument for amateur musicians, and played at home in family ensembles. Henry VIII owned seventy-six recorders among his many other musical instruments.

As early as 1680 the "German" or *transverse* flute, a wooden flute with a conical bore, one key, and played horizontally, had already been perfected. Bach wrote for both types of flutes, but by 1800 the recorder was all but obsolete, its tone not strong enough for the larger orchestras and concert halls of the 19th century which had replaced chamber groups in the salons of the aristocracy. With the renaissance of early music in the 20th century, the recorder has had a rebirth, both in music of its original period and works of modern composers. Today there are four basic sizes: the descant or soprano, the treble or alto, the tenor, and the bass, which uses a metal crook or pipe similar to the bassoon to bring air to the top of the instrument.

Michala Petri

One of the major artists to put the instrument into a solo spotlight is **MICHALA PETRI**. Born in Copenhagen, July 7, 1958, she began playing recorder at age three, and was first heard on Danish radio when she was five. Her debut as a concert soloist took place at Copenhagen's Tivoli Concert Hall in 1969. She studied at the Hannover Hochschule für Musik (1970–76), after which she toured widely in a trio made up of her mother, a harpsichordist, and her cellist brother. Her U.S. debut was at the 92nd Street Y in 1982, and internationally in Japan, 1984. Since then she has performed extensively throughout Europe, North America, Israel, Australia and the Far East, with a repertoire ranging from early baroque to avant-garde, including contemporary compositions written especially for her.

---

125. See Orchestral Overview

On the 4th of July, 1992, Michala married Danish guitarist and lute player Lars Hannibal, forming a duo which has toured in Europe, America, Japan, Germany, England and Australia, and made many recordings. They have two daughters, Agneta, born 1994, and Amalie, born 1996.

In addition to a discography that exceeds thirty titles, in 1998 she released an album with Berliner Barock Solisten (Berlin Baroque Soloists), in 1999 an album of popular Scandinavian music with the London Philharmonic Orchestra, plus an album with percussionist **Evelyn Glennie**. In 2001, the duo released *Kreisler Favorites*, featuring familiar classics. For this, Petri used modern recorders, developed in cooperation with Joachim Paetzold, Nikolay Tarasov and the instrument-making firm of Conrad Mollenhauer. The new recorders have expanded tonal potential and dynamics, making it possible to play transcriptions of the Romantic repertoire.

Petri's awards include the Order of the Knight of Dannebrog, awarded her by the Queen of Denmark in 1995, and the 1997 "Deutscher Schallplattenpries" (German Recording Prize) for her collaboration with **Vladimir Spivakov** and the *Moscow Virtuosi*, performing Vivaldi flute concertos. In 1998, she received the Wilhelm Hansen Music Prize and the Hans Christian Lumbye[126] Prize for her achievement in bringing classic music to a wide audience.

2001–2002 marked further extensive touring and a return to America.

MARION VERBRUGGEN, born in Amsterdam, August 2, 1950, began playing the recorder at seven, and progressed so quickly that by sixteen was enrolled at the Amsterdam Conservatory. She went to the Royal Conservatory at The Hague in 1967, studying with the master Franz Brüggen. She received her diploma in 1971 and Solo Diploma *cum laude* in 1973. At her graduation, the twenty-two-year-old was offered a teaching position there. Besides her extensive baroque recorder repertoire, she won the 1973 Nicolai Prize for her performances of contemporary Dutch music. She combines her position on the faculty of Utrecht Conservatory with recitals and chamber music collaborations, such as the Amsterdam Baroque, Musica Antiqua (Cologne) and Tafelmusik (Toronto), which take her throughout Europe, North America, and Asia. She has recorded on EMI, Philips, Titanic, Hunaroton, Asv-London, L'oiseau Lyre, Monumenta Belgicae, and harmonia mundi. She has made many appearances on European television.

Her global master classes have taken her from Malmö (Sweden), Trondheim (Norway), Copenhagen and Jerusalem to the other end of the world to New York, Toronto, Montreal and Stanford University (California). 2000 found her as soloist in a St. Paul Sunday program in Minnesota.

A Dream and a PICCOLO

LOIS SCHAEFER had a dream to play in the Boston Symphony Orchestra. Born March, 10, 1924, in Yakima, Washington, she describes herself as part of a long line of women musicians in her family: "Grandma taught music in Iowa schools, Mother played piano, taught music in Washington schools and was a choral director. Sister Winnie, five years older, was already proficient on the piano, although cello became her instrument. (See **Winifred Mayes**.) Music floated through the house from the old Capehart radio-phonograph: the New York Philharmonic, the Firestone Hour, Toscanini and the NBC Symphony, and the Boston Symphony.

In sixth grade, the genuine equivalent of "professor" Harold Hill (*The Music Man*), arrived in Yakima, offering instruments. Lois chose a trumpet, which her mother promptly made her trade for a clarinet. But there were already too many clarinets, so she ended up with a flute. With few opportunities to study in the then small town, she had to take lessons with a violinist who knew a little about the flute. Once in a while a flutist from the Seattle Symphony came to town—very inspiring to the young girl. In high school, she continued her flute studies with a *piano* teacher. In her junior year, she saved enough money to go to Interlochen (Michigan) Music Camp, where she maintained her first chair status the entire summer despite competition from twenty-six others. Playing there

---

126. Hans Christian Lumbye (1810–74) was one of Denmark's greatest composers.

for American composer **Howard Hanson** (1896–1981) earned her a coveted scholarship to Eastman, which she declined in favor of five years at the New England Conservatory to study with Georges Laurent, principal flutist of the BSO. The fifth year marked the initiation of the Artists Diploma Program of which Lois was "the first guinea pig." She graduated in 1947, having also incorporated two summers at Tanglewood with BSO maestro **Serge Koussevitzky** (1874–1951) and his favorite student, **Leonard Bernstein** (1918–90), participating in *his* conducting the premiere of Benjamin Britten's *Peter Grimes*.

After freelancing in Boston, in 1952 she became assistant first flute in the Chicago Symphony under **Rafael Kubelik** (1914–96). When Kubelik and famed principal flutist **Julius Baker** left in 1953, Schaefer remained assistant for one year under **Fritz Reiner** (1888–1963) before leaving for New York.

The next decade of her career (1955–65) was spent at the New York City Opera Company as a piccolo player, working her way from second to principal. In 1965, the opportunity finally came to realize her dream, an opening in the BSO under **Erich Leinsdorf** (1912–93). She remained there until 1990—one quarter of a century. She stayed in the area and taught privately until sister Winnie became widowed and called in 1995 with an offer of joining her in Gilbert, Arizona, where Lois is enjoying her real retirement.

Silver and Gold - The Female and the FLUTE

Jeanne Baxtresser

JEANNE BAXTRESSER, from 1984 to 1997, was principal flute of the principal orchestra of the United States, the New York Philharmonic. Her musical background stems from her mother, concert pianist **Margaret Barthel Baxtresser**, who studied with **Olga Samaroff**. Jeanne made her debut with the Minnesota Orchestra at age fourteen. At Juilliard, she studied with the Dean of Flute, **Julius Baker**, then Philharmonic principal. Winning an audition right after graduation gave her the principal flute position with the Montreal Symphony (1969–78), where **Zubin Mehta** often guest conducted. In 1978, she joined the Toronto Symphony as principal until 1984, when she was hired by Mehta for New York. Meanwhile, in Montreal, in 1976, she married bassoonist David Carroll. He was accepted by the NYP six months before her, rising to associate principal. In 1992, Jeanne gave the New York premiere of **Ellen Zwilich**'s Flute Concerto. After a one-year leave of absence, she retired from the Philharmonic before the 1997–98 season.

Since her "retirement," Baxstresser has become a sought-after soloist for major orchestras and music festivals. Chamber concerts have taken her throughout the U.S. and Europe. Her Summit CD, *Orchestral Excerpts for Flute*, includes her commentary on major flute solos from orchestral literature. She is the author of *Orchestral Excerpts for Flute with Piano Accompaniment* (Theodore Presser, 1995), which has become a vital part of the flute pedagogy. Her philosophy has been that when a musician's career is secure, it is time to share the wealth of that experience with the next generation. As such, she is in demand as a teacher and competition adjudicator. Her students occupy principal and section positions in orchestras in the U.S., Canada and Europe. In addition to presenting master classes worldwide, she is on the faculty of Juilliard, and is the Heinz professor at Carnegie Mellon University (Pittsburgh).

Leone Buyse

LEONE BUYSE, born in Oneida, New York, February 7, 1947, attended concerts as a child with her mother, a piano major at Eastman. At summer camp, she took baton twirling and flute, as she says, "because I was attracted to cylindrical silver objects." After graduation with distinction from Eastman in 1968, she was awarded a Fulbright grant which allowed her to study in France with Michael Debost, Marcel Moyse, and **Jean-Pierre Rampal**. Also an accomplished pianist, she served for two years as accompanist at Rampal's summer master classes in Nice. In addition to a performance certificate from the Paris Conservatory, she has her MM from Emporia State, Kansas. While in Paris, she studied Dutch at the Sorbonne, and speaks Dutch, French, German, Spanish, and is mastering Japanese for her growing career in that country.

Buyse has been assistant principal flute with the San Francisco Symphony, played flute and piccolo with the Rochester Philharmonic, and at the New Hampshire Music Festival she was principal flute for ten years. In 1983, she was invited by Seiji Ozawa to join the Boston Symphony as assistant principal, and principal flute with the Boston Pops. She was acting principal flute with Boston from 1990–93 when she retired after twenty-two years as an orchestral musician to pursue a more active teaching and solo career.

Her teaching posts have been at the New England Conservatory, Boston University, Tanglewood, Eastman and, in 1999, served on the faculty at the Aspen Festival, Colorado. She has presented recitals and master classes in the U.S., Canada, Japan and New Zealand, and traveled as an adjudicator and clinician. Since 1997, Buyse has been on the faculty of Rice University's Shepherd School of Music as professor of flute and chamber music.

With her husband, clarinetist Michael Webster, also on the Shepherd faculty, she performs in the Buyse-Webster Duo, and with pianist Chizuko Sawa in the Webster Trio. Her CDs include: *The Sky's the Limit*, 20th century American music for flute; *Contrasts*, 20th century American music for flute and harp with **Ann Hobson Pilot**; *Tour de France*, music of Bizet, Debussy, Fauré, and Saint-Saëns, (Webster Trio); and *Sonata Cho-Cho-San*, music of Bizet, Mozart, and Puccini, arranged by Michael Webster (Webster Trio).

Leone met Michael at Eastman in 1964, as a guest at his first wedding. The pair became romantically involved in 1980 when she was in San Francisco. After a long term and long distance relationship, they married in September 1987. Her three stepsons, Phillip, Eric, and Brian are all computer scientists with a love of music.

Doriot Dwyer

Following in the tradition of her ancestor, Susan B. Anthony, **DORIOT ANTHONY DWYER** has also made history. In her case it was as the first woman to become a principal player in a major American orchestra. In 1952, world-famous maestro **Charles Munch** (1891–1968) promoted her from second to principal flute of the Boston Symphony, a position to which she brought recognition for the next thirty-eight years until her retirement in 1990. Born in Streator, Illinois, in 1922, her father was the inventor of the hydraulic hoist for trucks—opening his own manufacturing plants all over the world, much to the chagrin of Henry Ford who had initially wanted to buy the invention from him. Her mother was a fine flutist who gave Doriot her first lessons. Later she studied at Eastman.

As a recitalist, soloist, and chamber musician, Dwyer has appeared under such maestros as **Leonard Bernstein**, **Claudio Abbado**, **Michael Tilson Thomas** and **Seiji Ozawa**. During the 1956 BSO Russian tour, composer **Aram Khatchaturian** authorized her to arrange his violin concerto for flute. Of her many premieres and recordings, in 1992 she made a Grammy-nominated disc containing three of the many works written for her: a flute concerto by **Walter Piston**, **Leonard Bernstein**'s *Halil*, which she first played at Tanglewood, and **Ellen Zwilich**'s Flute Concerto, written to celebrate Dwyer's retirement concert.

Active as a music editor and pedagogue, Dwyer has been on the faculties of Boston University and the Boston Conservatory since 1973, as well as teaching privately. Her seminars have taken her all over the world. Through the Asian Youth Orchestra, she has given master classes in Hong Kong, Japan and Singapore. Part of each summer is spent at Tanglewood, where on July 2, 1995 she participated in a combined birthday salute to violinist **Itzhak Perlman**, cellist **Yo-Yo Ma**, and BSO music director **Seiji Ozawa**, before an audience of 15,000. Her many awards include election to the Women's Hall of Fame, and honorary doctorates from Harvard, Simmons and Regis Colleges, plus the prestigious Sanford Fellowship of Yale—the first orchestral musician to receive this honor.

Susan Milan

SUSAN MILAN, born in England in 1947, studied flute at the RCM and the Guildhall School of Music in London. She began her career as principal flute of the Bournemouth Sinfonietta, and in 1974 became principal flute, and the first woman member, of the Royal Philharmonic Orchestra. Since leaving the RPO, her career as a soloist soared internationally, performing with orchestras in Britain and Europe. Tours have covered Japan, America, Scandinavia, Hong Kong, Australia, New Zealand and the Far East. She performs at major

British festivals and records frequently for the BBC. Her commissions and premieres include works by contemporary composers Richard Rodney Bennett, Robert Saxton, Ole Schmidt, Carl Davis, and Robert Simpson, but her enormous repertoire encompasses all eras. Besides orchestral appearances, Milan has given duo recitals with pianist Ian Brown, formed the London Sonata Group with harpsichordist Ian Watson and cellist John Heley, and the Debussy Trio with Caryl Thomas, harp, and Graham Oppenheimer, viola. They are sometimes joined by Krzystof Smietana, violin, and Robert Bailey, cello, to form the Instrumental Quintet of London.

A distinguished teacher, Milan is a professor at the Royal College of Music, holds two annual summer master class courses at the Hindhead School of Music, and in 1991 was appointed chairman of the British Flute Society. Her home life is spent with husband William and two sons.

Yoki Owada

YOKO OWADA studied at the Toho Gakuen University of Music in Japan, and in 1977 entered the Paris Conservatory, receiving the first prize in flute upon graduation. Next came the soloist course at the Hochschule für Musik in Freiburg (Germany)—with teachers such as **Jean-Pierre Rampal**—where she again received top honors. While still a student, as a result of winning the East and West Artists Audition for Young Performers in New York (1980), she made her debut at Weil Recital Hall at Carnegie Hall. She has gone on to win many other competitions. Her homeland debut concert was in 1981 with the New Japan Philharmonic. She has since participated in music festivals across Europe and Asia. In 1990, she gave a concert at the Casals Hall in Tokyo. The same year marked her landmark performance at Suntory Hall, playing all three Mozart flute concerti in one recital, the first flutist ever to do so.

Owada now divides her time between performing, judging competitions, and teaching at the Ueno Academy of Music and Toho Gakuen University. Besides her mastery of Western music, she is a pioneer of contemporary Oriental music as heard on two CDs of Japanese new music, *Flute Message from Yoko I* and *Flute Message from Yoko II*. The brilliance of her playing and her mission of bringing the past and present together is summed up by a critic: "Her sound transcends the borders of time . . ."

SUSAN PALMA has been a member of the Orpheus Chamber Orchestra since 1980. Besides performing with them all over the world, she has made many recordings with them, including the Mozart *Flute Concerto* and the *Flute and Harp Concerto.* As a member of the Bach Chamber Soloists, she performs throughout the U.S. She has premiered and recorded numerous contemporary works with Speculum Musicae, featuring such composers as **Elliott Carter**, **Peter Maxwell** and **Milton Babbitt**, the first group recipient of the Naumberg Chamber Music Award. She is principal flute of the American Composers Orchestra and has been soloist and principal with the Madeira Bach Festival, the Stuttgart and Royal Ballet companies, the Martha Graham and Paul Taylor Dance companies and Santa Fe Opera. She made her Mostly Mozart Festival debut in Lincoln Center performing with the outstanding Swiss oboist, **Heinz Holliger**.

A native of Midland, Michigan, Palma received her musical training at the University of Michigan and Juilliard. She has served on the faculty of Columbia University. Her recordings, numbering more than fifty, are on Deutsche Grammophon, Columbia, New World, CRI, Bridge and Nonesuch.

Susan, who is also a painter, lives in New York with her husband, attorney and restauranteur Richard Nidel.

MARINA PICCININI, born in Canada, began flute with **Jeanne Baxtressor**. She is a BM and MM honor graduate of Juilliard, where she studied with **Julius Baker**, former principal flute of Chicago, Pittsburgh and New York. At twenty, she won first prize in the CBC Young Performers Competition and a year later first prize in New York's Concert Guild International Competition. She was named "Young Artist to Watch" in *Musical America* (1989), and in May 1991 became the first (and as of 2006 still the only) flutist to be awarded the Avery Fisher Career Grant. She also received grants from the Canada Council and the NEA. Her concertizing covers the U.S., Canada, Europe and Japan, appearing as soloist with such orchestras as Boston, St. Louis, Cincinnati, Toronto, Vancouver and Tokyo Symphonies, as well as the Minnesota Orchestra, St. Paul Chamber, and National Arts Center Orchestra. A devoted chamber musician, she has appeared with the Takacs and Miró String Quartets, Philharmonia Virtuosi and other ensembles, and been a frequent festival guest at Lincoln Center's *Mostly Mozart*, Marlboro, Santa Fe, Newport, La Jolla, Davos (Switzerland), Tivoli (Copenhagen), Kuhmo (Finland) and, at the invitation of Seiji Ozawa, the Saito Kinen (Japan) Festival. Her interest in new music has led to commissions and premieres, including John Harbison's Flute Concerto, and the flute and orchestra version of Lukas Foss' *Three American Pieces*, with the composer conducting, at the Metropolitan Museum of Art in New York. She has given master classes at Juilliard, Yale, the Cleveland Institute, Banff School of Fine Arts, and the Universities of British Columbia and Toronto. In September 2001, she joined the faculty of the Peabody Conservatory.

Her recordings are on the Connoisseur Society, CBC, and Sony labels. In 2000, CLAVES Records released her *Belle Epoque* to critical acclaim. 2001 brought her CD of 20th century flute and piano sonatas with pianist Ewa Kupiec. She has been resident artist for WQXR, the *New York Times* classical music station, has hosted her own series, and broadcast in Canada, Japan, Germany, and Switzerland.

On August 8, 1987, she married the talented Swiss pianist, **Andreas Haeflinger**.

Paula Robison

Internationally renowned **PAULA ROBISON** was first heard nationally when she played the flute solo in a New York Philharmonic's Young People's Concert, and on the recording with Leonard Bernstein's narration, of Saint-Saëns' *Carnival of the Animals*. In his introduction he predicted that "this is a young flutist who will be heard from!" He was right. Even with all the competition, she has been dubbed "First Lady of the Flute."

Born June 8, 1941, in Nashville, Tennessee, she was raised in Los Angeles where she first studied piano, but turned to flute at eleven. After attending USC, she went to Juilliard at nineteen to study with **Julius Baker**, graduating in 1963. She also studied with the celebrated French pedagogue **Marcel Moyse** (1889–1984) in Marlboro (Vermont) and New York, where she made her recital debut in 1961. She shared first prize in the Munich competition in 1964, and two years later became the first American to capture first prize for flute in the Geneva International Competition. It was then **Leonard Bernstein** invited her to be guest soloist with the New York Philharmonic. A member of Lincoln Center's Chamber Music Society since 1969, she was made co-artistic director of chamber music at the Spoleto Festival of Two Worlds in Italy and South Carolina (1977), and the Spoleto/Melbourne Festival of Three Worlds (1986). In 1987, she was awarded the Adelaide Ristori Prize for her contribution to Italian cultural life.

Besides touring in the Far East and Austria, she has performed with Claudio Scimone and *I Solisti Veneti* at Lincoln Center's Avery Fisher Hall, and played Bernstein's *Halil* with **Michael Tilson-Thomas** and the London Symphony, both in London and Vienna. She reprised the Bernstein in 1996–1997 with Tilson Thomas and the San Francisco Symphony, then guested at New York's "Mostly Mozart," Marlboro (Vermont) and Seattle International Music Festivals, plus recitals in London and Washington, DC. The same season included concerts with Florida's New World Symphony and the Oklahoma City Philharmonic; a German tour with guitarist Eliot Fisk (with whom she also appeared in recital at Curtis); and the continuation of her annual, usually sold-out, four concerts at New York's Metropolitan Museum of Art. These unique events, performed in the spectacular Temple of Dendur—a permanent exhibit—feature the music of Vivaldi and his contemporaries, performed on modern instruments in period-instrument style. Active as a teacher, Robison has commissioned and premiered many contemporary works. Her TV appearances include *CBS Sunday Morning*, *Live from Lincoln Center* and *Christmas at Kennedy Center*. She records exclusively for Arabesque.

The career of **ER'ELLA TALMI** has been inextricably linked with that of her husband, Yoav. She was born October 26, 1942, on an Israeli kibbutz where the music of her childhood was the sound of guns as Jordan and Iraq marched across their borders in their unsuccessful attempt to drive the new nation into the sea. Other harmony was provided by coyotes and hyenas howling in the snake-infested wilderness outside the compound fence. In the mandatory school music program, seven-year-old Er'ella showed such talent on the recorder that the one and only flute—an ancient wooden object—was given to her. This soon cracked, and she was given

Er'ella Talmi.

another of some inferior metal. Not until she was sixteen, when her friends took up a collection, did she own a good flute. In her high school years, she made the three hour journey to Tel Aviv in a hot dusty bus to study with Uri Shoham, first flutist of the Israel Philharmonic. During her compulsory two year army stint, she was accepted into the band where she met a euphonium player named **Yoav Talmi**. They were married in September 1964. Their son, Gil, born December 15, 1968, has become a successful Grammy-nominated composer for films and television.

Both Talmis won a grant from the America-Israel Cultural Foundation for study at Juilliard—Er'ella with **Julius Baker**. After graduation, in 1968, both were hired by the Louisville Symphony, then under Jorge Mester—Er'ella as flute/piccolo player, Yoav as assistant conductor. In 1971, she was appointed principal flute of the Israel Chamber Orchestra in Tel Aviv. Summer 1972 found the family in London, were Yoav studied conducting with large orchestras. Daughter Dana born there, August 18, 1973, is a graduate of the University of North Carolina, master of social work (MSW). She works for the American Jewish World Service (AJWS), is married and on May 20, 2005, presented the family with their first granddaughter, Yahli.

In 1974, Yoav became conductor of the Gelders Orchestra in Arnem (Holland). Er'ella often soloed with the orchestra, gave recitals and participated in chamber music. She made two recordings, one with the late, great pianist **Malcolm Frager** (1935–91). In 1982, these were transferred to compact disks. Since 1984, the Talmis have made their home near Tel Aviv while Yoav was director of the Israel Chamber Orchestra (1984–88), and the Israeli Opera (1985–88). From 1989–96, they made the long commute to California while Yoav was music director of the San Diego Symphony. In 1998 Yoav became director of the Quebec Symphony. Er'ella is the founder/music director of the chamber series "Sounds and Colors at the Museum." (Musée des Beaux Arts du Quebec, Canada.)

Er'ella's career takes her all over the world. She has made CDs with her husband at the piano, and several chamber group recordings. *Talmis Play Talmi* (Centaur, 2006) features Israeli songs and the music of Yoav and Gil.

CAROL WINCENC was born in Buffalo, New York, June 29, 1949. She studied at the Academia Chigiana in Siena (Italy) and the Academia Santa Cecilia in Rome. In the U.S., she attended Oberlin, the Manhattan School of Music (BM, 1971), and Juilliard (MM, 1972). She was principal flute with the National Orchestra Association in New York (1970–71), Aspen Festival Orchestra (1970–72), and the St. Paul (Minnesota) Chamber Orchestra (1972–77). After winning the Concert Artists Guild Award, she made her debut in Carnegie Hall (1972), and won the Walter W. Naumburg Solo Flute Competition (1978). She has soloed with many of the world's major orchestras, and appeared as a recitalist and chamber musician with such renowned ensembles as the Toyko, Guarneri, Emerson, and Cleveland String Quartets, and performed with soprano **Jessye Norman**, pianist Emanual Ax and cellist Yo-Yo Ma.

Wincenc founded the International Flute Festival in St. Paul (1985–87), and served on the faculty of the Manhattan School of Music (1980–86), Indiana University (1986–90), Juilliard (1988–), Rice University (1989–95) and SUNY Stony Brook (1998–).

Commissioned concertos from Peter Schickele, Lukas Foss, Roberto Sierra, **Jennifer Higdon**, **Joan Tower** and Henryk Gorecki enhance her repertoire, as do Paul Schoenfield's *Klezmer Rondos*, which she recorded for Decca, and Pulitzer Prize winner Christopher Rouse's Flute Concerto, premiered with the Detroit Symphony (1994), and recorded with the Houston Symphony (Telarc). This won France's Diapason d'Or prize. In collaboration with soprano **Barbara Hendricks**, Wincenc commissioned Tobias Picker's *The Rain in the Trees*, whose somber theme is extinction of the planet. This was premiered with the Pittsburgh Symphony, April 1996, and the Atlanta Symphony the next month. May also saw a performance of John Corigliano's Flute Concerto with the Eugene (Oregon) Symphony conducted by **Marin Alsop**, and with the American Ballet Theatre at the Met in 2001. She has recorded for Deutsche Grammophon, Nonsuch, Arabesque, D'Note, and for Naxos the Charles Tomlinson Griffes *Poem* for Flute and Orchestra with **JoAnn Falletta** and the Buffalo Philharmonic.

Carol was the featured flutist for La Jolla SummerFest 1990, '92, '94, 2000. She appears regularly with the New York Woodwind Quintet, in duo with harpist **Nancy Allen**, and in the trio *Les Amies*, with Allen and violist

Cynthia Phelps. The trio made their debut with David Atherton's festival, Mostly Mozart, in San Diego, February 2004.

Her son Nicola, born January 5, 1993, studies at the School of American Ballet, and at eleven was already a serious pianist.

(The first time we spoke, Nicola was celebrating his third birthday at the height of the Blizzard of 1996. We met at a concert in La Jolla, February 2000, and again, February 2004.)

Eugenia Zukerman

EUGENIA ZUKERMAN is a multi-media person. As a flutist, after winning the 1971 Young Artists Award and making her New York debut to rave reviews, for over twenty-five years she has performed in North America, Europe, Asia, and the Middle East, appearing with most major chamber groups and orchestras including the National Symphony, Colorado Orchestra, National Symphony of Mexico, Modesto Symphony, and Hong Kong Philharmonic, plus festivals throughout the U.S., Edinburgh, London, Italy, Germany, and Switzerland. She has played with such stars as cellist **Yo-Yo Ma**, pianist **Emmanuel Ax**, actress Claire Bloom, and harpist **Yolanda Kondonassis**. For over sixteen years, she has collaborated in a lecture/performance series at the New York Public Library with keyboardist Anthony Newman, a forerunner of the popular rush hour concerts performed by many orchestras today. Respected for her programming and performances, she became artistic director, in 1998, of Bravo! the Colorado Vail Valley Music Festival. She has recorded over twenty albums on CBS Masterworks, Pro Arte, Vox Cum Laude and Newport Classics. In 1996, Delos released *Music For a Sunday Morning* with the Shanghai Quartet, the unique *Heigh-Ho! Mozart*, favorite Disney Tunes in the style of great classical composers, and in 2000, a live recording with the Dallas Symphony of Lowell Liebermann's *Concerto for Flute and Orchestra*.

In the visual media, Zukerman has been arts commentator for *CBS Sunday Morning* since 1980, bringing over 300 artist profiles to national attention. She has also appeared on a variety of other TV programs. The new century is seeing more nationwide and international performances.

As an author, she has been published in many periodicals, has had three screenplays purchased by Twentieth Century Fox, MGM and Universal Pictures, respectively, and written two novels, *Deceptive Cadence* (Viking, 1981) and *Taking the Heat* (Simon & Schuster, 1991). For St. Martin's Press (1997), she co-authored with her pediatric nephrologist sister, Dr. Julie Ingelfinger, the non-fiction book *Coping with Prednisone*, which deals with her 1994 onset of eosinophilic pneumonitis, from which she thankfully recovered.

Born in Cambridge, Massachusetts, September 25, 1944, she began her training with Carl Bergner at the Hartford (Connecticut) Symphony. After two years at Barnard in New York, she transferred to Juilliard to study with the premier flute master, **Julius Baker**. While at Juilliard, in 1968, she met and married fellow student, violinist **Pinchas Zukerman**, with whom she had two daughters, Arianna and Natalia. After their marriage ended in 1983, she met director and screenwriter, David Seltzer. Married since 1988, they share an apartment on Manhattan's Upper West Side.

Eugenia can now be heard in recital with her soprano daughter, Arianna Zukerman.

Sweet Licorice - Women CLARINETISTS

Emma Johnson

EMMA JOHNSON, born in London in 1966, began her study of the clarinet at age nine. In 1984, she won the BBC "Young Musician of the Year" contest, establishing herself in tours throughout Europe, America, Japan, Australia, and South Africa. Her recordings include clarinet concertos from the baroque to the contemporary. Since her mid-twenties, she has had a full career, appearing as soloist with the Royal Philharmonic, London Symphony, English Chamber Orchestra, Hallé Orchestra, Netherlands Radio Symphony, New Japan Philharmonic and Polish Chamber Orchestra, and compiling a large discography.

Following her U.S. concert debut in 1989, she has returned for recital appearances in New York, Kennedy Center, and Los Angeles. A visiting professor of clarinet at Royal College of Music London, she was awarded an MBE in the Queen's Birthday Honours List in June 1996.

Thea King

THEA KING, born December 26, 1925, in Hitchin, Hertfordshire, England, is both a clarinetist and a pianist. She did not (literally) pick up the clarinet until she was seventeen—there happened to be one lying around when the BBC Symphony Orchestra was evacuated out of the danger of much-bombed WWII London to Bedford where she was living. She studied at the RCM (1943–47) with Frederick Thurston, whom she married in 1953 for one brief year of happiness. He died at fifty-two in 1954. As soloist with orchestra and as a recitalist, she has performed with most of the principal orchestras of England, including the Melos Ensemble of which she has been a member since 1973, the Robles Ensemble (from 1984), English National Opera Ballet—then known as Sadlers Wells—and the English Chamber Orchestra with whom she played most frequently. Her numerous recordings range from Mozart, Mendelssohn, Spohr, Bruch and Brahms to the 20th century Gerald Finzi and Sir Charles Villiers Stanford. She has even made a double broadcast playing both piano and clarinet.

King has arranged and "resuscitated" music of Bach, Schumann and Mendelssohn for clarinet solo and duets, which have been published by Boosey and Hawkes and Chester Music. Her tenure on the faculty of the RCM lasted from 1961 to 1987, and in 1988 she began at the Guildhall School of Music, receiving a Fellowship in 1992. In 1985, Thea was made an Officer of the Order of the British Empire (OBE) by Queen Elizabeth II.

German-born **SABINE MEYER** studied with Otto Hermann in Stuttgart and Hans Deinzer in Hanover. She became a member of the Bavarian Radio Symphony Orchestra in Munich, and then the Berlin Philharmonic as solo clarinetist—where she encountered such gender discrimination she left a year later. Her solo career escalated, and since 1983 she has performed internationally in Brazil, Israel, Canada, U.S., Japan and Africa. She also plays with the "Trio di Clarone" with her husband, Reiner Wehle, and brother **Wolfgang Meyer**. In 1993, the trio made a popular tour with Jazz clarinetist Eddie Daniels. The "Bläserensemble Sabine Meyer" (*bläser* means windblowing) was founded in 1988 with musicians brought together from different countries, performing worldwide. They have released several discs. Meyer received the "Artist of the Year" award in 1993 for her recording of the Stamitz concertos with the Academy of St. Martin-in-the-Fields, **Iona Brown** conducting.

In May 1998, she released a disc featuring Copland's Clarinet Concerto, Stravinsky's *Ebony Concerto* and a selection of Benny Goodman arrangements with Ingo Metzmacher and the Bamberg Symphony. 1999 was a prolific year of releases: *Night at the Opera*, a selection of transcriptions of operas by Mozart, Rossini, Weber and Verdi, with Franz Welser-Möst conducting the Zürich Opera Orchestra; an album with Brahms' *Clarinet Quintet* with the Alban Berg Quartet; a new recording of the Mozart Clarinet Concerto, and works by Takemitsu and Debussy with **Claudio Abbado**; and Beethoven's Octet, Op. 103, Rondino, and Septet Op. 20, with the Bläserensemble. 2000 brought Reger's *Clarinet Quintet* and the *String Sextet* with the Wiener Streichsextett, and *Modern works for Wind Ensemble*, which includes octets by Denisov, Obst and Catiglioni, and pieces by Raskatov and Hosokawa. 2001 added Mendelssohn, Weber and Baermann to Meyer's vast discography.

Summer Festival appearances in 2000 included Edinburgh, Rheingau, Lockenhaus and Lucerne, where she was artist-in-residence and performed "A Tribute to Benny Goodman," and the world premiere of Hosokawa's Clarinet Concerto with the Chamber Orchestra of Europe. The 2000–2001 season included concerts with the Gewandhaus Orchester Leipzig, Danish Radio Symphony Orchestra, Orchestre Philharmonique de Strasbourg (France), Orchestre de la Suisse Romande (Switzerland), as well as many recital and chamber music appearances.

Sabine Meyer has outdone herself to bring the clarinet to prominence as a solo instrument.

ORIT ORBACH was born in New York in 1968. Her family emigrated to Israel in 1970, where she started clarinet at seven. Two years later, she won top prize in the 1975 Youth Talent Competition, and twice won first prize at the Tel Aviv Rubin Academy, as well as many other competitions. A scholarship from the America-Israel

Foundation brought her to the New England Conservatory, from which she received her BM with academic honors in 1991. Her MM is from Northwestern (1992), the year she premiered Robert Starer's *Kli Zemer* with the Jerusalem Symphony. Since then she has participated in many music festivals in the U.S. and Israel, collaborating with artists **Shlomo Mintz**, **Schmuel Ashkenasi** and **Raphael Wallfisch**. She has appeared with most of Israel's leading orchestras, including the Israel Philharmonic under **Zubin Mehta**, and has held principal clarinet positions with the Israel Symphony, the Tel Aviv Chamber Orchestra and the Haifa Symphony.

When is a Horn Not a Horn?

The dictionary describes a basset horn as: "an 18th century type of clarinet, invented in 1770 with the same mouthpiece as a clarinet, but longer and with an upturned metal bell. It is now rarely used." The challenge of refuting the last statement was taken up by Georgina Dobrée.

GEORGINA DOBRÉE, born in London, January 8, 1930, plays both clarinet and basset horn—the latter actually an alto clarinet in the key of F, a whole tone higher than the regular E-flat alto clarinet. She attended the RAM (1946–49) and, with a scholarship from the French government, studied in Paris the following year. One of her teachers was the great English clarinetist **Reginald Kell** (1906–81). Her professional career as chamber musician and soloist began in 1951. In 1953, she was awarded the prize for performance of contemporary music at the Darmstadt (Germany) Festival. Interest in 20th century music has not precluded standard repertoire. She has performed a wide range of works for music societies throughout Great Britain, and for the BBC, as well as concerts and broadcasts on the Continent and tours in America and Canada, which have included lecture recitals and master classes. She was a professor at the RAM (1967–86).

Dobrée also developed an interest in early music from her research into performance practices of the mid-1700s, specifically the manuscripts of the Molter concerti which she recorded for His Master's Voice (HMV) Baroque Library Series in 1968. In 1975, she formed her own company, Chantry Recordings, specializing in ancient and modern music for clarinet, including commissioned works such as **Elisabeth Lutyens'** *This Green Tide*, Op. 103, for Basset Horn and Piano. Chantry Publications was established in 1988, through which Dobrée has edited such books as *19th Century Music for Clarinet and/or Basset Horn*. She has also served as editor for Oxford University Press and other publishers.

A dedicated chamber music artist, Dobrée has performed with many ensembles and in recital, playing a range of clarinet sizes, from the small E-flat to the large bass clarinet—including concertos written for the instruments in D and C as well as for the basset horn in F. She specializes in music for the basset horn, with repertoire from Mozart to the present day. A number of new works have been written for her, which she played in the Czech Republic, the U.S. and Belgium. Several of these received London premieres at Wigmore Hall.

Her honors include a First Fellowship of the Royal Academy bestowed upon her in 1982.

Tuning In - The OBOE

Cleveland-born **MARSHA HELLER** studied at Oberlin College, the Salzburg Mozarteum, and at Juilliard with Harold Gomberg, winning the Concert Artists Guild competition in 1970 and making her debut at Carnegie Hall the following season. In 1973, she became the principal oboist of the American Symphony Orchestra. She has subsequently performed with the Queens Symphony, Martha Graham Dance Company and New Baroque Soloists in New York. She is on the faculty of the School of Arts at Rutgers University. As a chamber musician, she is a member of the Trio Bell'Arte with **Elaine Comparone** and Daniel Waitzman. She toured Japan with the New York Pops Orchestra, and is featured in several chamber music recordings. Also an accomplished painter, Heller's first New York City exhibition—a collection of abstract landscapes—was at the Montserrat Gallery in Soho.

PAMELA PECHA holds the distinction of being the first woman oboist ever appointed to one of America's "Top Five" orchestras. She was assistant principal oboe of the Cleveland Orchestra (1978–1990). At the time, maestro

Pamela Pecha

Lorin Maazel commented, "We broke the Cleveland tradition, we hired a woman in the wind section . . . we chose her because she was the very best."

Born in Syracuse, New York, she was raised in Florida, beginning piano studies at seven. She was an active pianist and accompanist, and performed as a piano soloist with the Miami Philharmonic. Her first oboe teacher was her father, Emerich Pecha, who has held positions with the Pittsburgh and Houston Symphonies. At the Cleveland Institute of Music (1969–73), she won the **Marcel Tabuteau**[127] Memorial Scholarship. She attended the Eastern Music festival (1967–68) and returned there as a member of the faculty and principal oboist with their orchestra. A fellowship member at Tanglewood in 1972, she was awarded the C.D. Jackson Prize for outstanding oboe playing by **Seiji Ozawa**. She has been a member of the Akron, Canton, Cincinnati, San Antonio and Baltimore Orchestras, the Orchestra of the Americas (Mexico City), and participated in the Marcel Moyse Seminar and Cleveland's Blossom Music Festival in 1970 and 1971. Besides her orchestra appearances, she has joined the Audubon Quartet and other groups in recital.

Her 1994 CD of the oboe concertos of Handel, Haydn and Mozart was released by ProArte. In 1995, she premiered a new oboe concerto she commissioned from composer **Peter Schickele**, creator of Johann Sebastian's fabled fictitious son, "PDQ Bach." She made several recordings between 1999–2001.

BASSOON - Grandfather of Woodwinds

JULIE FEVES was born August 9, 1946 to a talented mother who was both sculptor and feminist. Music was part of family life. She has a brother who plays cello in the Amsterdam Radio Orchestra in Hilversum (Holland), the other plays bass in a community orchestra. In junior high school, Julie was immediately fascinated with the bassoon, but had to play clarinet until the bassoonist graduated. She then took up the instrument and played it all through high school. Her teachers urged her to apply for Juilliard, so she set out for the Big Apple, was accepted, and earned her BM (1968), and her MM (1969). Since then she has performed as soloist, chamber musician and orchestra principal, in music ranging from baroque to avant-garde. Her orchestral appearances include the Los Angeles Chamber Orchestra, Los Angeles Philharmonic, Sacramento, New Jersey and American Symphonies and Aspen Festival Orchestra. Besides performing baroque music on early bassoons, her contemporary music appearances have been with the New York Philharmonic Prospective Encounters Concerts, **Pierre Boulez** conductor, and the Chamber Music Society of Lincoln Center.

Her numerous recordings are on the Columbia, Nonesuch, Desto, Delos, harmonia mundi, Leonarda, and 1750 Arch Records labels. Feves has been principal bassoonist for the Long Beach Symphony since 1992. She also frequently performs for motion picture soundtrack recordings. Summers are spent at festivals such as Chamber Music Northwest (Portland, Oregon), Music From Angel Fire (New Mexico), Bravo! Colorado (Vail) and Aspen. In her teaching career, she has served on the faculties of Center for Chamber Music at Apple Hill (1971–77), Smith College (Massachusetts, 1974–75), Sonoma State (California, 1981–82), UC Santa Cruz (1980–83), Cal. State, Northridge (1988–89), and since 1987 as assistant dean and director of the performance programs at the California Institute of the Arts in Valencia.

She is the mother of son Loren, born Februay 3, 1983, who plays the cello.

Nancy Goeres

NANCY GOERES is principal bassoon of the Pittsburgh Symphony Orchestra, which she joined in 1984, and where she holds the W. & Mrs. William Genge and Mr. & Mrs. James E. Lee principal bassoon chair. Born in Lodi, Wisconsin, April 17, 1953, she started piano at seven. Her sister played clarinet and wanted Nancy to try the bassoon which, blessed with long fin-

---

127. From its founding in 1915, the Philadelphia Orchestra has only had three principal oboists: **Marcel Tabuteau** (1887–1966), who held the position 1915–1954; **John DeLancie** (1920–2003), who joined the orchestra in 1946, and was principal 1954–74; and **Richard Woodhams**, 1974–present.

gers, she was able to master at eleven. She received her BM (1975) from Boston University and earned positions as principal bassoonist with the Cincinnati and Florida Symphonies, Florida Orchestra and Caracas Philharmonic. An avid chamber musician, she performs at the Aspen, Marlboro, La Jolla SummerFest, and San Diego *Mainly Mozart* festivals, as well as New York's 92nd Street Y and other chamber series.

In 1993, she premiered and recorded the **Ellen Zwilich** *Bassoon Concerto* with **Lorin Maazel** conducting the PSO—a work commissioned by the Pittsburgh Symphony Society. Her other performances of the Zwilich were at the Aspen Music Festival and the 1996 conference of the International Double Reed Society, where it was hailed as a major contribution to 20th century bassoon concerto repertoire. Following performances in Martha's Vineyard and La Jolla SummerFest, the premiere recording of the André Previn *Sonata for Oboe, Bassoon and Piano* was recorded on Crystal Records with Goeres, Cynthia DeAlmeida, oboist, and the composer at the piano.

Goeres is on the faculties of Carnegie Mellon University and the Aspen Music School, lectures at major American music schools and conservatories, and has given master classes in Europe, Asia and South America. She is an active member of the International Double Reed Society and serves on its executive board.

JUDITH LeCLAIR is principal bassoon of the New York Philharmonic. She has held this position since 1981, then only twenty-three. Her professional debut was at fifteen with the Philadelphia Orchestra. She studied at that city's Settlement Music School, and graduated from Eastman. Before joining New York, she was principal in the San Diego Symphony, under David Atherton, and San Diego Opera Orchestras. As recitalist and chamber musician she has played with Guarneri Quartet on Great Performers Series at Lincoln Center. She is on faculty at Juilliard, and lives in New Jersey with husband, pianist Jonathan Feldman. 1995 marked her solo appearance in the debut of *The Five Sacred Trees*, a concerto written for her by **John Williams**, then director of the Boston Pops, which was commissioned by the NYP as part of its 150th anniversary celebration.

CONTRA BASSOON - The Great-Grandfather

Susan Nigro

Although her grandfather owned a music store, her father played amateur trumpet, and her mother the piano, there is an element of uniqueness about a female musician making a career of playing a fifteen lb. instrument made up of eighteen feet of tubing. Yet that is just what native Chicagoan **SUSAN NIGRO** does successfully. Through the schools, she started on the flute at twelve. In high school, she had the opportunity to play bassoon, added contrabassoon in her senior year, but did not get serious about it until she entered Northwestern University where she earned her BM and MM degrees, and an additional graduate degree from Roosevelt University. Her teachers were Burl Lane, Ferdinand Del Negro, Willard Elliot, Leonard Sharrow, Sherman Walt and Wilbur Simpson. She gained ensemble expertise in the Civic Orchestra of Chicago, and at the Tanglewood Music Center, where she was awarded the Henry B. Cabot Prize. She has since played many recitals and made numerous appearances with Midwest-area bands and orchestras, including the Chicago Symphony and the St. Paul Chamber Orchestra, premiering several new works. She has frequently been a featured artist in the annual Double Reed Society Conferences. She has also guested at the Rome Festival (Italy), Aspekte Festival of Salzburg, the Grand Teton (Wyoming) Music Festival, and was an artist-in-residence at the Third Annual Contrabassoon Festival (Utah).

She received an honorable mention prize in the Rome Festival 2000 Concerto Competition, won a Pro Musicis International Career Development Grant, and was a finalist in the Chicago Park District Talent Search. Her quest for contrabassoon solo literature includes many commissions. She has premiered more solo works for this instrument than any other bassoonist. Six of these commissions have been published as the "Susan L. Nigro Contrabassoon Recital Series." Her CDs include *The Big Bassoon* (1995), *Little Tunes for the Big Bassoon* (1997), both on Crystal, and *The Bass Nightingale* (2001, GM Recordings).

Nigro has been on the State Artists Rosters of eight states. She is a founding member of the Chicago Bassoon Quartet, and also of The Two Contras—with Burton Lane—probably the only contrabassoon duo in existence. Her artist biography is included in the archives of the International Music Museum in London, England. She is listed in the fourteenth edition (1994) of International Who's Who in Music, and holds memberships in Intertel and Mensa. In addition to her musical talents, she authored two books of "musician humor," *Laffs from the Bottom of the Pit* and *More Laughs from the Bottom of the Pit*. Until a challenger comes along, Susan Nigro reigns as the only contrabassoon soloist in America.

SAXOPHONE - Crossbreed and Crossover

Invented by Belgian clarinetist **Adolphe Sax** in 1846—he also invented the baritone horn, the tenor horn and perfected the tuba—the saxophone was quickly adopted in wind bands by the 1870s. It is a cross-breed, in that while made of brass, it has a mouthpiece and reed like a clarinet which classifies the instrument as a woodwind. *Crossover* refers to the fact that, although used in some classical compositions, it carved an indispensable niche in the jazz bands of the '20s and '30s and the swing bands of the '40s.

First of the Few

One of the first women saxophonists was a virtuosa named **Elise Hall**, usually listed in programs as Mrs. R.J. Hall. A pupil of Georges Longy, principal oboist of the Boston Symphony, she had studied at the Paris Conservatory. She was also manager of the Orchestral Club of Boston, founded in 1899, which Longy conducted. Hall was the first "amateur" to ever appear with the Boston Symphony, playing the long saxophone solo in Bizet's *L'arlesienne*, because no one else could be found to play it. Longy and **Vincent d'Indy** were among composers who wrote for her. By 1909, she had taken up the new double bass clarinet.

Nowadays, thanks to contemporary composers, the saxophone is receiving a new incarnation in classical music.

Casting Classical Roles for a Jazzy Performer

CYNTHIA SIKES is probably unique in her field. She has performed with the New York Philharmonic under **Zubin Mehta**, the Denver and New Orleans Symphonies, The Women's Philharmonic (San Francisco) and Israel Philharmonic, where she was the first saxophone soloist in that orchestra's history. As a chamber musician, she has appeared with the Chamber Music Society of Lincoln Center, Chicago Chamber Players, and Hunter College series, among others. As an educator, she is Woodwind and Jazz Coordinator of Children's Programs (ages four through eighteen) at CUNY's Aaron Copland School at Queen's College. She teaches saxophone, theory, music literature and music history. One of her students, Maya Levina, daughter of Russian immigrants, wrote a complete saxophone concerto at age twelve which was featured on television when Sikes appeared on *CBS Sunday Morning* in January 1996.

Born in Midland Texas, September 10, 1960, an only child, Cynthia began piano at eight, but really wanted to sound like "Boots" Randolph, famed for his "Yakity Sax" renditions. In ninth grade, she attended her first jazz concert and declared she wanted to be a jazz saxophonist, to which her father replied, "You are *not* going to end up in sleazy dives!" So Cynthia stayed on the classical track. When the family moved to Traverse City, Michigan, next door to Interlochen, she got her first taste of a real saxophone teacher, who taught at the University of Michigan. That clinched her attendance there, receiving her BM in 1982. After a two-year teaching stint at the University of East Texas, she joined her parents who had moved to New Orleans. In the process of earning her MFA at Tulane, she met faculty member **Deborah Drattell** who became her friend and the catalyst for staying in the music field. Drattell introduced her to the First Monday Contemporary Chamber Ensemble of which Sikes became manager.

She also taught at Xavier University, and appeared with the New Orleans Symphony until it disbanded in 1987. From 1987–88, she worked on her DMA at Eastman, then decided to go to New York in 1989. The very next day, out of 300 saxophonists in the union, she was chosen for the faculty opening at Queens College!

A strong advocate of contemporary music, Sikes has given premieres of works by **Ralph Shapey**, Deborah Drattell and **Victoria Bond**, borrowing from the latter's concerto, *Urban Bird*, to name her own trio, "Urban Birds" (saxophone, cello and piano). As one of the trio's founders, she has played a key role in commissioning over thirty works showcasing contemporary and Latin jazz, thus establishing a chamber music genre for the saxophone. Her international performing career is combined with her position as music director for the Inter-American Center for Arts and Architecture (INCA+A), through which she promotes and showcases music of the Americas in two festivals: Florence, Italy, and Buenos Aires, Argentina. In November 1996, her trio opened the Architectural Biennial, fulfilling Sikes' dreams of using music as an ambassadorial medium.

As is obvious, the saxophone found its forte in jazz. In order to spotlight a few of the many women who have a career playing sax, here are the five in the Big Band known as DIVA (or No Man's Band) led by drummer, **Sherrie Maricle**. (See Percussion.) As seen, most of them are also in touch with the classics.

Growing up in a tiny village in the heart of the Austrian Alps was a remote setting for a saxophonist career. However, listening to recordings of alto saxophone great Cannonball Adderley, **KAROLINA STRASSMAYER** was dazzled by the energy of the music and set out to learn all about jazz.

After obtaining her master's degree in jazz performance from the Musikhochschule in Graz, she was chosen Outstanding Musician of the Year and received a full scholarship to study at the Mannes/New School Jazz Program in New York. Upon graduation, Karolina was immediately recruited to work with DIVA as their lead alto saxophonist and featured soloist. When the quintet Five Play, comprised of DIVA members, recorded *On the Brink*, it was chosen Best Album of the Year by Jazz Times.

Strassmayer has been featured with the New York Pops at Carnegie Hall and Bobby Sanabria's Afro-Cuban Jazz Dream Big Band. *Live & in Clave* was nominated for a Grammy Award, and voted one of the Top Five Albums of the Year by the Annual Critics Poll in 2000 as well as Best Afro-Cuban Jazz Album of the Year by the Jazz Journalists Association. Other big band work includes the Duke Ellington Orchestra, and the jazz orchestras of Scott Whitfield, Chico O'Farrill's Afro-Cuban, Michael Mossman's Latin, and Lew Anderson's All-American Big Band.

Her valuable experience, plus her own voice as an improviser and composer, can be heard with her new, innovative group, KLARO! Lawrence Brazier, of *Jazz Now*, observed: "Karolina would frighten timid men with her wildly swinging solos. She plays the alto with a fierce attack. Sigmund Freud would have loved her."

LEIGH PILZER began her musical training on piano and cello, switching to saxophone at eighteen after discovering **Count Basie**. She attended the Berklee College of Music (Boston), where she majored in Jazz Composition and Arranging. After graduation, she returned to her native city of Washington, DC, and launched upon a freelancing career, working with such artists as Nancy Wilson, Natalie Cole, Mel Tormé, Steve Allen, Harry Connick, Jr., Rosemary Clooney, and Chuck Brown. In the classical field, she performs frequently with the National Symphony on their televised PBS specials, and at Kennedy Center, Wolf Trap and Carter Barron Amphitheater.

International engagements have been at Badenscher Hof, and Trane in Berlin, the NSO's 1997 European tour, and performances with DIVA (Alto 2) in Germany and England. In June 2003, Leigh was featured as soloist/arranger with UFRJazz in Rio de Janeiro.

Big band remains a special interest for Pilzer as a writer and performer. Many of the DC area military bands feature her arrangements, including the Navy Band Commodores, Army Field Band Jazz Ambassadors, and Army Blues Jazz Ensemble. She has played and/or recorded with many jazz bands, plus the Duke Ellington Orchestra, Air Force Airmen of Note, and the Navy Commodores.

Leigh holds a master's degree in jazz studies as well as a master's in saxophone performance, both from the University of Maryland in College Park, where she served as an adjunct member of the jazz studies faculty for the 2005–2006 academic year.

Originally from Tel Aviv, **ANAT COHEN** has performed around the world from Europe to Asia, the Middle East to South America. With her natural ability to absorb the music of different cultures, she is a major force on the global music and jazz scene with her extraordinary abilities on soprano and tenor saxes, clarinet and flute.

After performing extensively in Israel, Cohen spent two years as a saxophonist/clarinetist with the Israeli Air Force Big Band. A scholarship to the Berklee College of Music brought her to Boston, earning a BA in professional music and MA in 1996. She moved to New York City, performing with various bands as well as keeping a busy global touring schedule.

As of 2005, she has been with DIVA (Tenor 1) and Five Play, for six years, and is featured on their CD, *Sherrie Maricle & the DIVA Jazz Orchestra, Live in Concert*. She is also an integral part of the Choro Ensemble, the only New York-based group dedicated to the authentic instrumental choro tradition of Brazil. They have been featured at the Apollo Theater, with trumpeter Wynton Marsalis and the Lincoln Center Jazz Orchestra.

Cohen's new role as a bandleader in New York clubs was marked by the 2004 debut performance of her quartet at Sweet Rhythm, New York's premier jazz club in Greenwich Village. The same year, her project with pianist Alon Yavnai brought out the CD, *Duo*. Anat also appears together with her two brothers, Yuval and Avishai Cohen, on BMG's *Summa Cum Jazz*. The three Cohens' debut CD, *One*, was released February 2004.

She has been a member of Duduka Da Fonseca's NY Samba Jazz (Brazilian Jazz), Brazooca Band (Brazilian Pop Music), Argentinean pianist/composer Pablo Ablanedo's Octet, and Ecuadorian Bassist Alex Alvear's Mango Blue Band (Afro Latin). She has also recorded and toured with Colombian bassist/composer Juan Sebastian Monsalve. Classically, she has been a guest artist with the New York Pops, Binghamton Philharmonic, and others.

The winner of several prestigious awards, Anat manages to be an innovator while respecting the value of preserving traditional musical forms.

SCHEILA GONZALEZ was first introduced to music at age five by her mother. Since then, her talent has enabled her to perform and study with such jazz luminaries as Joe Williams, Diane Schuur, Diane Reeves, Ray Brown, **Clora Bryant**, Harry "Sweets" Edison, Nancy Wilson, James Moody, and Lionel Hampton.

Recipient of the Shelly Manne Memorial New Talent Award, she was selected to participate in the first Thelonious Monk Institute of Jazz Workshop at Aspen. She has also been recognized by the Los Angeles Jazz Society.

Scheila has performed throughout the U.S., Europe and Japan as a member of Ann Patterson's Maiden Voyage, Bobby Rodriguez' HMA Salsa Jazz Orchestra, and DIVA (Tenor 2).

LISA PARROTT was born in Australia, 100 miles north of Sydney, and started studying clarinet and piano from age six. As a teenager, she switched to saxophone when she moved to Sydney after high school and discovered jazz. She came to New York in 1993, after receiving two Australia Council for the Arts grants to study with saxophonists/composers Steve Coleman and Lee Konitz.

Her career has taken off here as a leader as well as sideperson, performing with such notables as Dave Brubeck, Nancy Wilson, Skitch Henderson, Gunther Schuller, Gregory Hines, and the Big Bands of Jason Linder, Kit McClure, Jimmy Heath, Jimmy Dorsey and DIVA (Baritone). She has toured with the best of Australia's ensembles: John Pochee's Ten Part Invention, Paul Grabowsky's Australia Art Orchestra, Lloyd Swanton's The Catholics, and James Morrison's Big Band.

Besides being featured numerous times on television, and in magazines like *Downbeat, CMJ Music, Billboard, Vogue* (Australia), *Australian Jazz and Blues*, her performance venues are Lincoln Center, Carnegie Hall, Kennedy Center, plus International Festivals (since 1987) in Canada, Australia, Germany, Austria, Jamaica, and Indonesia.

Something Different . . .

In the modern sphere, soprano saxophonist/composer **Jane Ira Bloom** has been developing her unique voice for over twenty-five years. A pioneer in the use of live electronics and movement in jazz, she has been termed by *Pulse* magazine as the possessor of "one of the most gorgeous tones and hauntingly lyrical ballad conceptions of any soprano saxophonist."

Winner of the 2003 Jazz Journalists Award for soprano sax of the year, the Downbeat International Critics Poll for soprano saxophone, and the Charlie Parker Fellowship for Jazz Innovation, she is the first musician ever commissioned by the NASA Art Program, and was honored to have an asteroid named for her by the International Astronomical Union, *asteroid 6083janeirabloom.*

Commissions include the Doris Duke New Works grant for her CD, *Chasing Paint*, a series of compositions inspired by painter Jackson Pollock, and the Philadelphia Music Project for the premiere of *Unexpected Light*, a new collaborative work for jazz quartet and lighting design at the Sedgwick Cultural Center in Philadelphia. Her last five albums are on Arabesque Jazz, and *Like Silver, Like Song* is on the innovative Artistshare label.

Bloom collaborates with top names in the field, and performs at such diverse venues as the Museum of Modern Art (MOMA), Kennedy Center, BAM, the Hayden Planetarium, the San Francisco and Willisau (Switzerland) Jazz Festivals, as well as regular engagements at Sweet Rhythm, and Tonic, a Toronto nightclub, with her current quartet. Her commitment is to "push the envelope" and follow her own vision in the music she creates.

And Many More . . .

For the profusion of other talented women wind players, see Orchestras and Military Bands.

Women Polish Their Brasses

FRENCH HORN

Sylvia Alimena
Michelle Baker
Barbara Bingham
Mary Bisson
Jill Boaz
Julie Bridge
Jennifer Burch
Susan Carroll
Nicole Cash
Elizabeth Cook-Shen
Nancy Dimond
Lisa Ford
Nancy Goodearl
Robin Graham
Mary Grant
Marian Hesse
Haley Hoops
Barbara Jöstlein
Kristin Jurkscheit
Vladimira Klánská
Carolyn Landis
Julie Landsman
Cathy Leach
Justine LeBaron
Lucinda Lewis
Andrea Menousek
Sharon Moe
Jennifer Montone
Diana Morgen
Kristy Morrell
Marie Neunecker
Laurel Ohlson

Rebecca Root
Anne Marie Scharer
Shelley Showers
Tricia Skye
Ellen Dinwiddie Smith
Susan Standley
Julia Studebaker
Denise Tryon
Elizabeth Vaughn
Carolyn Wahl
Joan Watson
Frøydis Wekre
Susan Welty
Lori Westin
Gail Williams

TRUMPET

Bibi Black
Linda Brown
Clora Bryant
Barabara Butler
Lauraine Carpenter
Lorelei Conrad
Karen Donnelly
Lynn Erickson
Amy Gilreath
Joyce Johnson-Hamilton
Sally Kuhns
Anne McAneney
Karen Muenzinger
Carole Dawn Reinhart
Susan Rider
Stacy Simpson

Susan Slaughter
Marie Speziale
Beth Steele
Liesl Whitaker

TROMBONE

Heather Buchman
Monique Buzzarté
Rebbecca Cherian
Abbie Conant
Betty Glover
Jeanie Lee
Patricia McHugh
Julia McIntyre
Donna Parkes
Debra Taylor

TUBA/EUPHONIUM

Stacy Baker
Kathy Brantigan
Velvet Brown
Mary Ann Craig
Jan Z. Duga
Joan Follis
Sharon Huff
Angie Hunter
Carolyn Jantsch
Laura Lineberger
Gail Robertson
Deanna Swoboda
Helen Tyler
Constance Weldon

Brass instruments have, for centuries, been associated with armies and *men*. They imply force, loudness and aggressiveness. These are *not* supposed to be feminine traits. Besides, and behind, these reasons is the absolute conviction that the exertion needed to toot a horn was too strenuous for delicate lady lung power. Over thirty years ago, however, **Carole Reinhart** proved that by being shown how to blow *properly*—in her case from age two—ability had nothing to do with strength. Nevertheless, the bastion of playing brass instruments has been one of the last to be stormed by women. After nearly 400 years, information regarding early women brass players is still virtually nonexistent. A few names and records have surfaced:

1594	Convent San Vito, Ferrara, a concert was noted featuring women on cornets and sacbutts.
c1600	Faustina Borghi, a nun at the convent of San Geminiano, played the cornetto.
1655	Johanna von Hoff was paid twenty florins for performing before Emperor Leopold I, and was the sole female listed in the Imperial Trumpet Guild.
1691	Records indicate there were trumpet-playing nuns in Nonnberg, a Benedictine convent in Salzburg, Austria, including Sister Maria Magdalena Carolina and Sister Maria Rosa Henrike, who were (respectively) the granddaughter and sister of noted violinist/composer **Heinrich Ignaz Franz von Biber** (1644–1704).
1771	Girls played brass—as well as all other instruments—at Venice's Music School of the Mendicanti (orphanage), and were praised by famed English critic, Charles Burney. The Pio Ospedale della Pietá, orphanage music school, was taught by prolific composer/priest **Antonio Vivaldi** (1678–1741).

(The Summer 2005 IWBC Newsletter featured a fascinating article by Dr. Ken Shifrin, principal trombone in the City of Birmingham Symphony Orchestra, on brass-playing Bohemian nuns going back to 1697.)

Turning the Century: Banded Women, Jazzy Types in Black & White, and the Classical Few

1800s	**Georgia Dean Spaulding** led the Ladies Cornet Band with her gold cornet.
1800s	**Ruth Reed**, first known black woman cornetist.
1880s	**Fannie Rice**, cornetist, advertised her services around Boston for "concerts and entertainments."
1885	**Eva Hewitt**, cornet, was hired "as a novelty" to play with the New Orleans Symphony.
1917	**Mabel Keith**, trumpet, known as "The Sousa Girl."
1920s	**Leora Meoux Henderson** (c1890–1958) was taught "hot trumpet" by **Louis Armstrong**. Negro Women's Orchestra, **Olivia Shipp**, leader, **Hilda Magingault**, trumpet.
1900–30s	**Gertude Harrison Howard**, cornet, Chicago Colored Women's Band.
1910	**George Bailey's Female Brass Band** of Indianapolis: **Nettie Lewis**, cornet, **Susie Stokes**, trombone, **Alda Low**, baritone horn, **Ella Clifford**, tuba.
1924	**Louise Hensel**, trumpet, played for silent movies, starting at fifteen with father and sisters.
1925	**Mabel Swint Ewer**, trumpet, founded the Women's Symphony of Philadelphia. **Shirley Harris Hagen** (*b* 1914), Juilliard graduate, played trumpet in New York City area.
1930s	**Bertha Fields**, one of the first woman trumpet teachers (Joliet University, Illinois).
1934	**Ina Rae Hutton's Melodears**: **Ruth McMurray**, trombone, **Elvira Rohl**, **Jane Sager**, **Kay Walsh**, trumpets, **Althea Conley**, **Alice Wills**, trombones.
1934	**Phil Spitalny and His All-Girl Orchestra**: **Frieda Gertsakov**, **Pat Harrington**, **Jennings McLean**, **Louise Smith**, trumpets.
1939	**International Sweethearts of Rhythm**: **Viola Allen**, cornet, **Floye Bray**, **Nancy Brown**, **Clora Bryant**, **Norma Carson**, **Ray Carter**, **Flo Dreyer**, **Nora Lee McGee**, **Jennie Lee Morse**, **Sadie Pankey**, **Augusta Perry**, **Johnnie Stansbury**, **Terry Texara**, trumpets, **Ina Bell Byrd**, **Ione Grisham**, **Julia Travick**, **Jean Travis**, trombones.
1940s	**Lois Ashford**, trumpet, **Ozzie Nelson's** Band.

1940s	**Laurie Frink**, toured world as lead trumpet with **Benny Goodman**'s Orchestra.
1940s-50s	**Billie Rogers** (*b* 1919), trumpet, **Woody Herman**'s Band.
1937	**Ellen Stone** (*b* 1917), principal Horn, Pittsburgh Symphony, hired by **Otto Klemperer**.
1945	**Melba Liston** (1926–99), trombonist, major jazz arranger/composer, associated with **Dizzy Gillespie**; toured with **Billie Holliday** in 1949; rejoined Gillespie for State Department funded tours of Europe, the Middle East, and Latin America (1956 and '57). 1973–79, was director of Afro-American Pop and Jazz, Jamaica School of Music, Kingston. Formed her own mixed band on return to U.S. A stroke left her partially paralyzed in 1985, but she continued arranging into the '90s.
1950–60	**Dorothy Zeigler** (c1925–c1985), principal trombone, St. Louis Symphony, professor at Illinois University, and University of Miami.

All-Female Bands and Brass Women Overview

The above ensembles, and no doubt many others, provided employment for the majority of competent women brass players of the era.

Ina Rae Hutton (real name Odessa Cowan, 1916–84), "the blonde bombshell" conductor-trumpeter, dressed in (the expected) glitzy costumes, led her professional *Melodears* for a decade in arrangements that could compare with any male band. They also appeared in a few movies.

Phil Spitalny (1889–1970), born in Russia, studied clarinet, violin and piano at the Odessa Conservatory, emigrated to America in 1905 and turned to popular music. He formed his famous *All Girl Orchestra* in 1934, which lasted, like many good things, until the advent of television.

The International Sweethearts of Rhythm, led by **Anna Mae Winburn** (*b* 1913), was a sixteen-piece black and white women's swing band which moved from a one-room Mississippi school and more than held its own alongside Phil Spitalny and Ina Rae Hutton. They toured throughout America 1940–45. After they disbanded, Winburn and her husband, Duke Pilgrim, formed *Anna Mae Winburn's Sweethearts of Rhythm* which continued into the 1950s. A documentary film was made in 1980 about the original group by Greta Schiller and Andrea Weiss.

Other names worth noting in the popular field are **Valaida Snow** (1909–56), known as the "Queen of the Trumpet," who also sang and danced. She first gained recognition in 1922 in Barron Wilkins' Harlem Cabaret. She played second trumpet to **Louis Armstrong** in Chicago, among many other band affiliations. Touring internationally, she was captured by the Nazis, made a prisoner of war and released—weighing sixty-eight pounds—in an exchange in 1942 at the height of WWII. Known in Europe as "Little Louis," after the war she received a gold trumpet from Queen Wilhelmina of the Netherlands.

Leona May Smith (1914–99) made her first radio broadcast at age nine (WNAC, Boston); at eleven she soloed with the **Edwin Franko Goldman** Band, and played her first professional gig at fourteen in the Boston Women's Symphony. She was the first woman trumpet soloist (1943–47) in New York's Radio City Music Hall Orchestra. She was also soloist with **Fred Waring and His Pennsylvanians** at the Arturo Toscanini concerts, and American and Canadian Music Festivals. She broadcast an educational series on NBC with critic **Olin Downes**, played principal trumpet under **Sir Thomas Beecham** when he conducted the Brooklyn Symphony, and was an extra in the Met Orchestra for seventeen years. A major part of her career was devoted to teaching. She and her husband, composer George W. Seuffert, founded a "Music for Youth" summer program in Vermont. After retirement, she worked on a beginner's method for trumpet. She was made "Musician of the Year" in New York, and in 1961 became a member of ASCAP. She was honored at the 1997 convention of the IWBC.

Jeannette Boulay Banoczi (*b* 1922) was first trumpet with Phil Spitalny's orchestra in the 1940s, and Ina Ray Hutton's orchestra in the 1950s. After many years as the owner of various radio stations, she settled in Palm Springs (California) and in 1992 founded and plays in the Coachella Valley Symphony. Her dedication to music, and the loss of music instruction in public schools, led her in 1995 to co-found the Buddy Rogers

Youth Symphony in Palm Desert. The CVS League honored her eighty-fifth birthday with a campaign for orchestra chair sponsors.

Jazz trumpeter and composer **Clora Bryant** (*b* 1929) was under age when she joined the *International Sweethearts of Rhythm* in 1940. Having been accepted at Oberlin, she chose Prairie View College in Texas, an historically black institution, because of its all-girl band, the *Prairie View Coeds*. In her illustrious career she performed with **Duke Ellington**, **Lionel Hampton**, **Count Basie** and **Stan Kenton**. Her mentor was jazz trumpeter **Dizzy Gillespie**. After the War, when musicians' unions pressured bands to hire returning veterans, she moved to Los Angeles. She performed throughout the 1980s, including a 1989 concert in Russia at the invitation of Mikhail Gorbachev.

Bryant received the 1993 Distinguished Achievement Award for her contributions to African-American Music from the University of Massachusetts at Amherst. In 2002, at seventy-three, recovering from heart surgery, she said, "I'm still kind of touring, it's in my blood."

Our era can also boast a successful all-women's "Big Band." DIVA, featuring fourteen musicians, was the brainchild of Stanley Kay, a former drummer for the Buddy Rich Big Band. In 1990, Kay was conducting a band featuring drummer **Sherrie Maricle**. Impressed, he wondered if there were other women with a similar caliber of musicianship. A nationwide audition of players produced a core of Diva musicians who performed their first concert in March 1993. Besides Maricle, **Noriko Ueda** (bass) and **Chihiro Yamanaka** (piano)—both from Japan—the rest of the women are brass players. There are five saxophonists, Austrian-born **Karolina Strassmayer** (lead alto), **Leigh Pilzer** (alto 2), Israeli-born **Anat Cohen** (tenor 1), **Scheila Gonzalez** (tenor 2), Australian **Lisa Parrott** (baritone); **Deborah Weisz** (trombone 1), **Jen Krupa** (trombone 2), **Leslie Havens** (bass trombone); **Liesl Whitaker** (lead trumpet),[128] **Barbara Laronga** (trumpet 2), **Tanya Darby** (trumpet 3) and **Jami Dauber** (trumpet 4) and manager.

In the Classical Vein

As women's orchestras sprang up to provide employment for the multitude of females flowing out of conservatories, which had finally opened (most) of their classes to them, women brass players became more visible. One of the most successful of these aggregations, the Boston-based **Fadettes**, incorporated in 1895, boasted of having the only two women French horn players in the country (at the time). They also had two cornets and one trombone. In 1937, **Otto Klemperer** hired twenty-one-year-old **Ellen Stone** as first horn for the Pittsburgh Symphony—a *real* first for a major orchestra.

The Cleveland Women's Orchestra, founded 1935 with eighty women from sixteen to sixty, has consistently had fine brass players. As of 2005, their roster included **Patricia Lawrence** and **Maria Farris**, trumpets; **Linda Hodges**, trombone; and **Ethel Epstein**, **Amanda Moskowitz**, **Marge MacNeal** and **Connie West**, French horn. (See Conductors.)

While the major portion of today's feminine classical brass talent lurks in the (orchestra) pits, in the past three decades a few women have managed to make a career out of soloing as well as being orchestral and military band musicians. **Lynn Anne Newton**, with a BME from the University of Regina (Saskatchewan, Canada) for example, joined the United States Military Academy Band at West Point as a trumpet player and bugler in November 1980, thus becoming the first female member of the *Hellcats*, the USMA Band's Field Music Group. (See Military Bands.)

FRENCH HORNS

SYLVIA ALIMENA joined the National Symphony in 1985. A native of Long Island, New York, she began playing horn at age nine. She completed her studies at Boston University, winning their Concert-Aria Competition in

---

128. See Trumpets

1981, the year she was awarded a fellowship at the Berkshire Music Festival (now Tanglewood). She played with the Boston Ballet, Lyric Opera, Boston Pops, and New Hampshire Symphony before going to Washington, DC. She has been music director and conductor of Eclipse Chamber Orchestra since 1992, and has guest conducted the Spokane and University of Maryland Symphonies, among others.

MICHELLE BAKER, a graduate of University of Houston and Juilliard, formerly with the New Jersey Symphony, is second horn with the Met Opera. She has toured with the Marlboro Music Festival.

BARBARA BINGHAM, associate principal horn with the Phoenix Symphony, received her BM from USC in 1977, after which she played with the Honolulu Symphony for nine years. She lectured on horn at the University of Hawaii and performed with the Honolulu Brass and Chamber Music Hawaii. She played with the San Francisco Symphony and Opera prior to joining Phoenix in 1986, and also performs as principal horn with the Flagstaff Festival of the Arts and the Mozart Festival. She and her husband, Kevin Deutscher, have a daughter Jennifer.

MARY BISSON, over twenty years as third horn in the Baltimore Symphony, began her career with the Orquestra Sinfonica de Maracaibo (Venezuela), then with the Louisville Orchestra and Chatauqua (NY) Symphony. She is on the faculty at Peabody.

JILL BOAZ is a member of the horn section in the Indianapolis Symphony and a faculty member at the University of Indianapolis Community Music Center.

JULIE BRIDGE plays with the Syracuse Symphony.

JENNIFER BURCH is with the Rochester Philharmonic.

SUSAN CARROLL is in the Seattle Symphony.

NICOLE CASH is in the Dallas Symphony horn section.

ELIZABETH COOK-SHEN is with the Los Angeles Philharmonic.

NANCY DIMOND is assistant principal horn in the Phoenix Symphony.

LISA FORD studied at Interlochen and the Norwegian State Academy of Music, where her teachers included **Frøydis Ree Wekre**. She has performed with the Florida Brass Quintet, Chicago Civic Orchestra and, since 1993, has been principal horn in the Gothenburg Symphony, the National Orchestra of Sweden.

NANCY GOODEARL is with Houston Symphony.

ROBIN GRAHAM, former principal French horn with Cincinnati, began her professional career as a twenty-year-old senior at Juilliard, when she won the principal horn position with the Houston Symphony, becoming their youngest player and the first woman to hold a principal horn position in a major American orchestra. Going on to principal with the Los Angeles Chamber Orchestra, after six years she joined Cincinnati in 1985. She has performed with the Guarneri, American and Academia String Quartets, Music from Marlboro and the Chamber Music Society of Lincoln Center, also touring throughout Europe. She has soloed with many orchestras, and served on the faculties of Rice University, California Institute of the Arts, UCLA and the Aspen Festival. She and her husband are parents of Michael, born 1990, and Stephen, born March 1994.

MARY GRANT is third horn with the Oregon Symphony. She performs frequently with the Minnesota Orchestra, with whom she recorded Stravinsky's *Rite of Spring*, Bruckner's Symphony No. 9, and Richard Strauss' *Die Frau Ohne Schatten*.

MARIAN HESSE holds an MM from Yale, where she was a recipient of the Kirchoff Tapp Award for her proficiency in chamber music. She plays horn as a member of the New Haven (Connecticut) Symphony and the Orchestra New England, and performs regularly with the Pennsylvania Ballet Orchestra and the Northeastern Philharmonic. She also plays with the Chestnut Brass Company, who perform over a hundred concerts a year in such locales as France, Germany, Italy, the Caribbean, America, Canada and Mexico. She can be heard on the soundtrack recording of *The Civil War*, a film by Ken Burns, released on Elektra.

HALEY HOOPS is with Dallas Symphony.

BARBARA JÖSTLEIN, former member of the Jerusalem Symphony and assistant horn with the Met for two years, was promoted to 4th horn. Her teachers included **Julie Landsman** and Nancy Fako.

KRISTIN JURKSCHEIT, associate principal horn in the Colorado Symphony, trained at the New England Conservatory, receiving a grant for postgraduate study at Norway State Academy of Music in Oslo. She joined Colorado in 1992 after playing in New York's Concordia Chamber Orchestra, Jupiter Symphony, American Ballet Theater Orchestra and the Boston Opera.

A student of the Czech musical school, horn player **VLADIMIRA KLÁNSKÁ** graduated from the Prague Conservatory and Academy of Music and Drama, and was a laureate of a competition of the Bavarian Radio. Her experience spans from orchestral player, chamber performer to concert soloist.

CAROLYN LANDIS is assistant principal horn in Colorado.

Julie Landsman

§ **JULIE LANDSMAN** has been, since 1985, principal horn of the Metropolitan Opera Orchestra. Prior to her appointment, she was co-principal of the Houston Symphony under **Sergiu Comissiona**, and principal of the St. Paul (Minnesota) Chamber Orchestra. She has been featured soloist with Houston and other symphonies. While a freelance musician in the greater New York area, she appeared regularly with the New York Philharmonic, Orpheus Chamber Orchestra and at many summer festivals.

Born in Brooklyn, New York, April 3, 1953, as a child she dabbled on piano, banjo and folk guitar. By sixth grade she set her sights on the high school band as English horn. They needed a *French* horn, however, and offered free lessons as a lure. Her mother could not resist such a bargain. Julie made the band and later won a Naumburg Scholarship to study at Juilliard with Howard Howard (yes!), principal French horn of the Met, famed brass pedagogue Carmine Caruso, and James Chambers, former principal horn of the New York Philharmonic. She earned a BM (1975), and joined the Juilliard faculty in 1989. She also taught at Houston and Rice Universities. Her recordings include performances with the New York Philharmonic and Orpheus. She is horn soloist in the Wagner Ring Cycle recordings with **James Levine** and the Metropolitan Opera Orchestra.

JUSTINE LeBARON is in the Florida Orchestra and has appeared as a guest soloist at the Festival International de Boyaca in Colombia.

LUCINDA LEWIS and **ANDREA MENOUSEK** are with the New Jersey Symphony.

SHARON MOE performs as principal horn for the Long Island Philharmonic, New York Chamber Soloists, Bronx Arts Ensemble, Colonial Symphony, and New York City Opera.

Jennifer Montone

In 2006, at twenty-nine, **JENNIFER MONTONE**, after three years as principal horn with the St. Louis Symphony won that position with the Philadelphia Orchestra, becoming the first woman principal in one of the "Big Five." Born in Fairfax, Virginia, she began horn at age ten. A graduate of Juilliard, studying with **Julie Landsman**, she was third horn with the New Jersey Symphony, going on to the Orpheus, Chamber Music Society of Lincoln Center, the Met and the New York Philharmonic, becoming associate principal horn with Dallas (2000–03). She has taught at Southern Methodist University, held master classes at Juilliard and Manhattan School of Music, and is a faculty member at the Aspen Music Festival and School. She was a featured soloist at the 1999 and 2005 International Horn Society workshops, the 2000 IWBC, and 2005 La Jolla SummerFest.

DIANA WADE MORGEN is with the Louisville (Kentucky) Orchestra.

KRISTY MORRELL, second horn with the Los Angeles Chamber Orchestra, holds a DMA from USC where she is on the faculty. She has performed with Los Angeles Philharmonic, Rochester and Utah Symphonies and Chamber Orchestra of Santa Fe. She is also a freelance performer and studio musician.

MARIE LUISE NEUNECKER studied the horn and musicology in Cologne, Germany. She has won many awards, including first prize at the International Competition of the Concert Artists' Guild in New York. She soloed

Marie Neunecker

in the Bamberg Symphony from 1979, and held the same position at the Hessian Radio Symphony Orchestra from 1981–89. She made her debut with the Vienna Philharmonic in 1989. She toured with the Frankfurt (Germany) Symphony as soloist in South America, 1991, and has appeared at numerous international festivals, as a well as performing with orchestras in the U.S., Europe and Japan.

Hailed for her talent on both modern and valveless horns, Neunecker is a frequent guest artist at Marlboro, Salzburg, Berlin and Schleswig-Holstein festivals, and participates in chamber music with such celebrated colleagues as cellist **Yo-Yo Ma**, pianists **Emanuel Ax** and **Martha Argerich**, and violinist Frank Peter Zimmerman.

Laurel Ohlson

LAUREL Bennert **OHLSON**, associate principal horn with the National Symphony, is a *magna cum laude* graduate of Boston University in horn performance and mathematics and has performed frequently with the Boston Symphony and Boston Opera prior to joining the NSO in 1980. She is also a member of National Musical Arts, Columbia Players, Capitol Woodwind Quintet, and Eclipse Chamber Orchestra. (See Sylvia Alimena.) She has appeared with the Handel Festival Orchestra, the Washington Bach Consort, and in 1985 was a guest artist at the Seventeenth Annual Horn Convention in Baltimore.

REBECCA ROOT was principal horn with the Rochester Philharmonic for twenty years and Chatauqua Symphony for thirty. She was also principal horn with the Aspen Chamber Orchestra and the New Orleans Philharmonic, as well as positions in other orchestras. She attended Eastman and the Interlochen Arts Academy. She has taught horn at Columbus College (Georgia), Nazareth College (Rochester) and the Chatauqua Festival (New York).

ANNE MARIE SCHARER, a graduate of Indiana, studied at Juilliard with **Julie Landsman**. She was associate principal horn with Columbus (Ohio) Symphony, and principal horn in Oviedo, Spain. Now third horn in the Met Orchestra, she also plays with St. Luke's Orchestra in New York.

Shelley Showers

§ SHELLEY SHOWERS has been assistant principal/utility horn of the Philadelphia Orchestra since 1997. A native of Pennsylvania, and graduate of Curtis, she began horn studies in the fourth grade. Her first professional post was third horn in the New Jersey Symphony (1985–87), while also active in chamber music in New York City. During the 1987–88 season, she was acting assistant principal horn with the Cincinnati Symphony, then returned to New Jersey for the 1988–89 season. In 1989, she became principal horn for the Utah Symphony, a position she held until her appointment to Cleveland, 1995–97. She has participated in the Aspen Festival School as principal horn and faculty member during 1997, 2000 and 2001. Shelley is on the faculty of the Temple University School of Music and the Philadelphia Biblical University.

TRICIA SKYE is assistant principal in San Diego Symphony.

ELLEN DINWIDDIE SMITH is third horn with Minnesota Orchestra.

SUSAN STANDLEY plays with the New Jersey Symphony.

§ JULIA STUDEBAKER is first horn in the Royal Concertgebouw Orchestra of Amsterdam. Born September 11, 1951, in East Chicago, Indiana, and raised in Elmhurst, Illinois, near the "real" Chicago, by the time she was nine she was playing her mother's cornet—thus the example of a woman playing a brass instrument had always been part of her life. The school orchestra needed a French hornist, so by age eleven she switched instruments and was soon in demand, including the Youth Orchestra of Greater Chicago, and the Chicago Civic Orchestra—training ground for the Chicago Symphony. She entered Northwestern in 1972, at the same time auditioning for the Chicago Lyric Opera Orchestra and the Grant Park Festival of the Chicago Symphony. She got to play as an extra in these aggregations without the fairness of *behind screen* auditions—men less qualified got the permanent posts. In January 1973, she went to Germany and was immediately appointed First Horn of the Berlin Radio

Symphony Orchestra. That summer she attended the prestigious Salzburg Mozarteum. One year later, she auditioned and won her present position. In her personal life, she married a Dutch industrialist, Oscar van Leer. Their daughter Madeleine was born in 1978. Of her professional experiences, she says, "Sometimes I felt pitted against German attitudes, but I never felt that people were picking on me because I was a woman."

DENISE TRYON is second horn with Baltimore Symphony.

ELISA VAUGHN, fourth horn with Dayton Philharmonic, received her BM from Capitol University (Columbus, Ohio), did course work at Eastman and received her MM from the University of Cincinnati. Her teachers included **Julie Landsman** and **Michelle Baker**.

CAROLYN WAHL is in the Florida Orchestra.

JOAN WATSON retired as associate principal in Toronto.

§ Born in Oslo, Norway, July 31, 1941, **FRØYDIS REE WEKRE** had an amateur violinist father and a piano teacher mother. Her four-year-old brother was having lessons and she demanded, at age three, to learn the notes. Both children had perfect pitch. By age six she switched to violin, but at seventeen wanted to learn horn. Her parents did not approve of her changing instruments again, so she paid for the horn lessons herself while continuing with the violin until she got her first job at nineteen—third horn in the Norwegian Opera Orchestra. She studied with Wilhelm Lanzky-Otto in Stockholm, and Vitaly Boujanovsky in Leningrad. In 1961, she began as third, then second horn in the Oslo Philharmonic, and by 1965 was promoted to co-principal, a position she held until 1991 when she left to become professor of horn and chamber music at the Norwegian State Academy of Music, where she had been teaching part-time since 1973. She has maintained an active career as a soloist with orchestras, and as a recitalist throughout Europe and the U.S. She remains a teacher, lecturer, and adjudicator in competitions, and is associated with festivals in Banff, Sarasota, Florida and Musica Riva in Italy.

In 1983, she married American-born Daniel Rauch, a horn maker whose business is near Oslo. Her interest in contemporary music has resulted in commissions from Scandinavian and women composers. Her recordings are on Crystal CD. Wekre's interpretations have been compared to the great English hornist **Dennis Brain** (1921–57).

Besides authoring the book *Thoughts on Playing the Horn Well*, Frøydis is the first woman to be an honorary member of the International Horn Society.

SUSAN WELTY, assistant principal horn with Atlanta Symphony, is a graduate of Northwestern University (Illinois). She moved to Atlanta in 1984 to join the faculty at Columbus College, where she was a member of the *Southwind Woodwind Quintet*. She taught horn at Southeastern Music Center and played in the Atlanta Ballet and Atlanta Opera Orchestras before joining the ASO in 1988.

LORI WESTIN, an Eastman graduate, played with Phoenix before joining the San Francisco Symphony horn section in 1979. Illness forced an early retirement in1999.

GAIL WILLIAMS joined the Chicago Symphony in 1979, becoming associate principal horn in 1984 until her retirement in 1998 to join the faculty of Northwestern, where she earned her MM, as associate professor of horn. She is a founding member of the Chicago Chamber Musicians and Summit Brass, and former principal horn with Lyric Opera of Chicago. She received an honorary doctorate of fine arts from Ithaca College.

She is married to Larry Combs, clarinetist in the Chicago Symphony, who also teaches his instrument at De Paul University. They have two children, Elizabeth and Michael.

Gail Williams

KIMBERLY WRIGHT, a graduate of Ouachita Baptist University (Arkansas), has her MM in performance from University of North Texas, Denton, and joined the San Francisco Symphony in 1999.

Trumpets

First Lady of the Trumpet

§ CAROLE DAWN REINHART has been considered one of the best trumpet players in the world. (Not "just" *women* trumpet players . . .) Born December 20, 1941, in Roselle, New Jersey, her mother, a teacher, played piano and trombone. The child's first lessons were from her, at age two and a half, on a small slide cornet. Thus blow-

Carole Reinhart

ing would always be as natural as breathing. By first grade she had advanced to a valve cornet, and she and her brother, Rolfe, six years her senior, began playing together, a duo that lasted through her high school years. Throughout her childhood, Carole was in school bands and orchestras as well as the Salvation Army Band, with whom she continued playing during college. At eleven, she won a scholarship to Juilliard (Preparatory Division). Her father had no musical training, but acted as her manager and mentor during her early career.

Finishing high school in 1959, like her brother Rolfe, she entered the University of Miami on an orchestra scholarship. (He went on to become a doctor.) She graduated in 1963, and won a Fulbright Scholarship to study with Helmut Wobisch at the Academy of Music in Vienna. When she received her diploma in June 1964, she was the first and only woman to do so on a brass instrument. (Most of the other women were woodwinds.) During her year in Vienna she met Manfred Stoppacher, an Austrian trumpet player.

She returned to New York in the fall of 1964 and entered Juilliard, again studying with Edward Treutal. In 1966, she received her BM and MS, was accepted into Leopold Stokowski's American Symphony, and also played with the Radio City Music Hall Orchestra. She continued her solo performances and concerts for the Salvation Army, making a USO tour in 1968. By 1971, she left Radio City and moved to Berlin for better career opportunities. She found some solo work and jobs like "back-ups" for pop singers and records, and was substitute First Trumpet for the German Opera in Berlin until the position was filled by a man. At this time she again met Stoppacher, now lead trumpet in the RIAS (Radio in the American Sector)[129] Dance Orchestra. They were married in December 1972. By 1975, Reinhart's career took off with eighty to one hundred concerts a year. During the '80s the demanding schedule continued, adding appearances at music festivals, including Salzburg (1985, '88). In March 1983, twenty years after setting the record as its first female brass graduate, Reinhart became professor of trumpet at what is now called Vienna's Universität für Musik und darstellende Kunst (University of Music and Performing Arts), the first woman to hold such a position.

In June 1995, she was asked to represent Austria at the Council of Europe's workshop on "Under-representation in European Higher Education," held in Cambridge, England. Her report showed that the Vienna Philharmonic still had no intention of allowing women into the orchestra, and that only 2½ percent of University and Hochschule professors in Austria are women.

On New Year's Day, 1996, at the magnificent Bayer Chemical Company facility[130] in Leverkusen, Germany, she played her last public concert. After three decades of a professional career, she is refocusing her priorities to pass on her priceless experience and technical knowledge to produce excellent players. She adjudicates solo competitions and gives master classes around the world.

In 1994, the Vienna University Press published the book *Carole Dawn REINHART—Aspects of a Career* (updated, 2002).

BIBI BLACK, a native of Decatur, Alabama, graduated from the Interlochen Arts Academy High School, then Curtis. While there, she performed as soloist with the orchestras of the Eastern Music Festival, Decatur Chamber

---

129. Until the fall of the Berlin Wall, November 1989, reuniting East and West Germany, West Berlin was an enclave in the Soviet zone, divided into three sectors—American, British and French.

130. Like many other major corporations in Europe and Japan, Bayer nurtures the cultural pursuits of its employees by underwriting a Philharmonic Orchestra, a ballet, a chorus, as well as a soccer team. When will America follow suit?

and the Curtis Institute. In 1985, she won the Graham Stahl Trumpet Competition, and in 1988 the Young Artists Competition which gave her the opportunity to solo with the Philadelphia Orchestra. Upon graduation from Curtis, she was appointed to the second trumpet chair with Philadelphia, a position she held for one year before leaving to begin her solo career.

In 1991, she toured Switzerland as soloist with the European Youth Orchestra under the direction of **James Judd**. In 1992, she toured Japan as soloist with the Camerata Musica Berlin. She returned to the Far East for performances in Taiwan, Japan, and with the Seoul Philharmonic, and played recitals in the U.S. and Europe.

As a clinician for Yamaha (manufacturer of brass instruments), she gave seminars in the U.S. and Japan and was a guest artist and instructor at the International Trumpet Seminar in Japan. Her recordings for EMI Records include a CD made with the Philharmonia Orchestra of London, with **Claudio Scimone**, and a CD recorded at the Fukashima City Concert Hall in Japan with organist Naomi Matsui. 1997 began a hiatus from her career in favor of marriage and motherhood.

LINDA BROWN, a native of Alberta, Canada, has been with the Calgary Philharmonic Orchestra for twenty years. Also on the faculty at Mount Royal College in Calgary, she has presented masterclasses from Eastman to the Conservatory of Music in Shanghai.

§ **BARBARA BUTLER**, born in Waterloo, Iowa, 1952, loved music "from the beginning." After trying piano in second grade, she took to the cornet in fourth. Her BM degree in performance is from Northwestern University, where she studied with Vincent Cichowicz and **Adolph Herseth**, who was principal trumpet of the Chicago Symphony from 1948–2001. Her master's work was interrupted by winning the position of co-principal trumpet in the Vancouver (Canada) Symphony (1976–80). Before that, she was principal trumpet in the Grant Park (Illinois) Symphony (1975–79) and was acting co-principal with the St. Louis Symphony. In 1980, she became professor of trumpet at Eastman where she enjoyed a spectacular eighteen year career, during the course of which she was awarded the prestigious Kilbourn professorship. In 1998 she joined the faculty of Northwestern University in Evanston, Illinois, near Chicago, also as Professor of trumpet. At her new location she is co-principal/soloist with *Music of the Baroque, Chicago Chamber Musicians*, and continues her summers as principal trumpet in the Grand Teton Music Festival Orchestra. She has been heard in recital on the CBC, and American NPR, and is featured on many recordings.

Barbara is married to Charles Geyer, former second trumpet with Chicago Symphony, former principal trumpet with Chicago Lyric Opera, as well as Grant Park and Houston Symphonies. He was also a professor at Eastman and is now at Northwestern. They have a daughter, Jorie Butler-Geyer, born 1994.

LAURAINE CARPENTER is principal trumpet with the Toledo Symphony Orchestra, professor of trumpet at the University of Toledo and principal trumpet of two Brass Quintets. She received her BME from Ithaca College and her MA from NYU. While living in New York, she performed with a wide variety of musical organizations, including the New York City Ballet, and a rock tour with Robert Palmer. After relocating to California, she won the second trumpet position with the San Jose Symphony (1991–98), principal trumpet with the Oakland East Bay Symphony, and performed regularly with the San Francisco Opera and Symphony, and the Cabrillo Festival in Santa Cruz (California). She accepted a one year position with the San Antonio Symphony as assistant principal trumpet, then returned to San Francisco for one year before moving to Ohio. During the summer season, she is a faculty member for the Eastern Music Festival in Greensboro, North Carolina.

LORELEI CONRAD is a retired Lieutenant Commander in the U.S. Navy. With a degree in trumpet performance from Metropolitan State College (Denver), she joined Naval Academy Band in 1979, and in 1991 attained her pioneer position as the Navy's first female commissioned officer bandmaster. In July 2001, she reported to the Atlantic Fleet Band for duty as Fleet Bandmaster. She retired in 2002. (See Military Bands.)

KAREN DONNELLY holds an MM from McGill University. She performed with the Montreal Symphony and Les Grands Ballets Canadiens Orchestra before her appointment as principal trumpet with the National Arts Centre Orchestra of Ottawa. She is also a member of the Riedau Lakes Brass Quintet, giving educational concerts and workshops in schools. In September 2002, Karen joined the faculty of the music department at the University of Ottawa.

LYNN ERICKSON has been second trumpet with the St. Paul Chamber Orchestra since 1991. She serves as an adjunct faculty member at Augsburg and Macalester Colleges in Minneapolis and Saint Paul.

Amy Gilreath

AMY GILREATH is principal trumpet with the Peoria and Illinois Symphonies and Opera Illinois. She has performed with the St. Louis Symphony, Monarch Brass and the Monarch Brass Quintet. She is professor of trumpet at Illinois State University, a member of their faculty Brass Quintet, and is the brass instructor for the Orvieto Musica Chamber Music Festival in Italy.

JOYCE JOHNSON-HAMILTON, BME and MM (University of Nebraska), has been principal trumpet of the Portland (Oregon), Oakland and San Jose (California) Symphonies. In 1968, in one of the first blind auditions held by a major orchestra, she won a position in the San Francisco Symphony as assistant principal trumpet. Her interest in early music instruments and conducting led to her Stanford DMA, where she became a trumpet instructor. She is also conductor of the Diablo Symphony in Walnut Creek, near Oakland, was director of the youth concerts for the San Jose Symphony, and founder of the Sinfonia of Northern California, specializing in 17th and 18th century music. Since 1983, she has also been conductor/arranger and trumpet soloist with the Seoul Philharmonic of South Korea, where she introduced symphonic pops.

SALLY NELSON KUHNS, assistant principal trumpet of the Oregon Symphony, began her instrument at age nine refusing to be discouraged by those who said, "girls don't play trumpet." She earned her performance degree on full scholarship from the New School of Music. After hearing **Adolph Herseth**, principal trumpet in Chicago, she immediately enrolled at nearby Northwestern, studying with him and earning an MM in performance. After playing with the Fort Wayne Philharmonic, Chicago Civic Orchestra and American Wind Symphony, she joined Oregon in 1977. She has played with the Peter Britt, Sunriver, and Oregon Coast Music Festivals, and is the founder of the brass quintet, *The Metropolitan Brass Company*. Her husband is architect Thomas Kuhns, whom she met while he was project manager on the renovation of the concert hall.

CATHY LEACH is principal trumpet and featured soloist of the Knoxville Symphony and Knoxville Chamber Orchestra, Indianapolis Chamber, and Orchestra of Santa Fe. She has been professor of trumpet at the University of Tennessee, Knoxville since 1981. In 1988, she became a clinician for the Bach/Selmer Corporation (manufacturers of brass instruments), and in that capacity performs with bands, orchestras and solo recitals throughout the Southeast. She can be heard on the Musical Heritage and Opus 1 labels. She is a member of the board of the International Trumpet Guild.

ANNE McANENEY's appointment as principal trumpet to the Orchestra of the Royal Ballet in 1985 made her the first woman to hold such a position in any British orchestra, an achievement that remains unique. She joined the famed *London Brass Ensemble* when it came into existence in 1986, after the disbanding of the *Philip Jones Brass Ensemble* (in 1951) by its founder and namesake. She took Philip Jones' place as a flugel horn specialist. Anne is also a freelance player with London's leading symphony and chamber orchestras and professor of trumpet at the Guildhall School of Music. In January 2002, she married BBC Symphony Orchestra trombonist Roger Harvey.

KAREN MUENZINGER, specializing in classical and Mexican folk music, has performed with the Apple Hill Chamber Players, Empire Brass Quintet, Granite State (New Hampshire) Symphony and other orchestras in the Boston area. She has appeared on WUNI-TV and WGBH radio. She holds an MM from Boston University School of the Arts, where she studied with Roger Voisin and Rolf Smedvig. She is on the faculty at Brookline Music School in Brookline, Massachusetts.

SUSAN RIDER is a member of the trumpet/cornet section of "The President's Own" United States Marine Band in Washington, DC, and teaches at the Shenandoah Conservatory in Winchester, Virginia. Her BM is

Susan Rider

from University of Northern Iowa, MM and DM from Indiana University. She has performed with orchestras in Iowa, Indiana, Kentucky, Texas, Florida and Pennsylvania. She is also co-editor of the IWBC newsletter.

STACY SIMPSON has played with the Cincinnati Symphony, Pops and Opera Orchestras, St. Louis Symphony, Cincinnati Ballet, Louisville Orchestra and Monarch Brass. An associate instructor at Indiana University, she holds degrees from Universities of Louisville, Indiana, and Cincinnati-College Conservatory, where her primary teacher was **Marie Speziale**. She is secretary for the IWBC.

Susan Slaughter

§ SUSAN SLAUGHTER, after joining the St. Louis Symphony in 1969, became principal trumpet in 1974—the first woman appointed to this position in a major orchestra. Born July 5, 1945, in McCordsville, Indiana, she started piano at age five, and was exposed to trumpet through church revival music. Her parents were farmers—although her mother had studied history at Indiana University. Susan chose the cornet in school, starting in the band when she was ten and playing through high school. A graduate of Indiana University, she received the coveted Performer's Certificate in recognition of outstanding musical performance. Before joining the SLS, she spent two years as principal trumpet of the Toledo (Ohio) Symphony. She has been on the faculty of the Grand Teton Orchestra Seminar for several years, and founded "Trumpet Lab," a week-long workshop for young musicians to study orchestral literature with professionals—a program that has become a model for similar workshops nationwide.

In 1992, Slaughter made musical history founding the **International Women's Brass Conference** (IWBC), held at Washington University in St. Louis. (See end of chapter.)

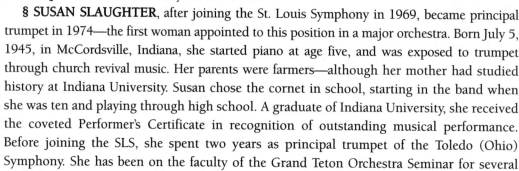

Marie Speziale

§ MARIE SPEZIALE was hired as associate principal trumpet for the Cincinnati Symphony in 1964 upon graduating from the University of Cincinnati College-Conservatory, becoming the first woman to play trumpet in a major American orchestra. She retired in 1996 with career highlights that included a solo appearance with Duke Ellington, performances on the *Tonight Show* and at Interlochen with Dave Brubeck, freelance jazz work, and being on the soundtrack for the TV series *Star Trek-Voyager*. In 1997, she received the "Leading Woman in the Arts" award from the Cincinnati Coalition of Women's Organizations. Summer 1999 found her in Italy, playing in the *Monarch Brass Ensemble* with other prominent brass women, **Susan Slaughter**, **Abbie Conant**, **Carol Dawn Rheinhardt** and **Frøydis Wekre**. She performed with the Summit Brass (1998–2000), and was featured guest artist at the International Trumpet Guild conferences of 1998, 1999 and 2001.

In addition to being an adjunct associate professor at Cincinnati College-Conservatory(1979–), on the board of directors of the Northern Kentucky Symphony, a member of the International Trumpet Guild, on the editorial committee of the MTNA Journal, president of the IWBC (1997), in 1999 Speziale became professor of trumpet at the Indiana University School of Music (Bloomington), the first woman ever on their brass faculty. Besides teaching trumpet, she subbed with the Cincinnati Symphony, Pops and Ballet orchestras, coached chamber brass ensembles and was responsible for developing a brass orchestral repertoire program. Her three pronged career involved a 150-mile commute. Two homes, two offices and four phone numbers put new meaning to the musicians' expression, "Have Trumpet—Will Travel."

In 2001, Marie stepped down as president of the IWBC, and the following year retired from her positions at Cincinnati and Indiana. July 2002 brought a new role as professor of trumpet and chair of the brass department at the Shepherd School of Music at Rice University, Houston. In 2003, she began subbing with the Houston Symphony, and became third trumpet with Houston Grand Opera in 2004. The same year, she was adjudicator of the Fischoff National Chamber Music Competition after having adjudicated the National Trumpet Competition (2001–04). She presents master classes and workshops throughout the U.S.

BETH STEELE, a lieutenant colonel in the Army, is Commandant of the U.S. Army Element, School of Music, and is also associated with the North American Brass Band Association (NABBA). (See Military Bands.)

Liesl Whitaker

§ **LIESL WHITAKER** was awarded the lead trumpet chair, March 2000, with the *Army Blues Jazz Ensemble* of their major band, "Pershing's Own," based at Fort Myer, Virginia. Born June 4, 1969, she began playing the horn in fourth grade and trumpet in eighth, which she first played with the wrong hand and wrong fingerings. After attending Appalachian State University and the Cincinnati Conservatory, she became a charter member (1992) and lead trumpet with the all woman big band DIVA, based in Manhattan and led by drummer **Sherrie Maricle**. Liesl has played cruise ships—where she met her husband Shaun—Broadway pit orchestras, concert halls and jazz festivals worldwide. Shaun and Liesl married September 2, 1994. September 28, 2001, marked the entrance into the world of their son, Shane Newton Whitaker.

Trombones

Blowing Away in Europe

Abbie Conant

§ **ABBIE CONANT** was born in Pryor, Oklahoma, March 14, 1955. Her introduction to the trombone came about at age fourteen when it was recommended as an instrument she could play in the band and thus get out of her eighth grade typing class. She was soon good enough to be awarded a scholarship to the famous Interlochen Arts Academy in Michigan, where she received a diploma in 1973. After her BM *cum laude* from Temple University, studying under Dee Stewart of the Philadelphia Orchestra, she received a scholarship to Juilliard where she studied with Per Brevig, solo trombonist of the Metropolitan Opera, earning her MM in 1979, the year she was also a finalist in the Young Artists Competition.

Her professional career began with a year as solo trombone at the Royal Opera House of Turin, Italy, at the same time studying with Vinko Globokar at L'Accademia di Chigiana in Siena. In 1980, she won the solo chair with the Munich Philharmonic. In 1984, she received a diploma from the master class of Branimir Slokar at the Staatliche Hochschule für Musik in Cologne. In 1992, after thirteen years with the Munich Philharmonic, she left the orchestra and took the position of professor of trombone at the State Conservatory of Music in Trossingen, Germany. With her composer/director husband William Osborne— whom she married in 1974—she is a founding member of "The Wasteland Company," developing the concept of music theater using the texts of Samuel Beckett.

She performs internationally as a concerto soloist, recitalist, and has appeared with the Hessische Rundfunk (Radio) Symphony, Munich Chamber, Lithuanian Chamber, Munich Philharmonic, St. Joseph (Missouri) Symphony, and the Hallé Orchestra of Manchester (England). Her work as a performance artist has taken her to most of the large state theaters in Germany. She plays solo concerts with organ, harp, guitar, and orchestra, and has recorded a CD under the "audite" label entitled *Posaune und Orgel* (Trombone and Organ) with Klemens Schnorr.

In 1992, Conant was elected to the board of directors of the International Trombone Association, and in both 1992 and 1995 was selected as featured soloist at the ITA Workshops in Detmold, Germany, and Las Vegas, Nevada.

A Case of Mistaken Identity and Its Incredible Aftermath!

While the above biography reads like that of any successful musician, it is the tip of an iceberg of gross discrimination. Her hiring in 1981, for the position of solo trombone in the Munich Orchestra, was as MR. Abbie Conant—no photograph had been required with the application. Conductor **Sergiu Celibidache** (1919–96) had also just been newly appointed, and did not want to ruin his image by creating a scene over this gender discovery. After completing her probationary year, however, Conant was demoted from her position when the now entrenched maestro told her, "You know the problem. We must have a *man* for principal trombone."

Thus began an eleven year legal battle with Abbie fighting for both her rightful position and a salary equivalent to her male colleagues, all those years having to live in the discomfiting atmosphere of being unwelcome. At the final court hearing, March 10, 1993, she recovered over $100,000, most of which was pay withheld during her thirteen year tenure. She was also offered a severance contract, enabling her to accept the prestigious position of full professor at the Trossingen Conservatory. Asked to comment on the court decision, Norbert Thomas, manager of the Philharmonic, would only say: "We are happy that Ms. Conant is no longer with us."

In the course of this eleven year legal "pilgrimage," Conant established a clear and detailed documentation of sexism in the Munich Philharmonic. This has become a well known case in Germany and internationally. Far from being considered a meddling foreigner, her actions have been embraced and applauded by millions of German people. Since her experiences were so astounding, a ninety minute documentary film about the saga was broadcast nationally on German television. Through the effects of the film, German politicians began examining the laws against discrimination and calling for sanctions to enforce the laws protecting all women in the work place.

And Now There Are None . . .

Abbie Conant was the only woman brass player in a principal position in a German orchestra. Now there are none, but she remains the first and only woman professor of trombone in the history of Germany. Since only 3 percent of the professors in Germany are women, her presence is a special source of encouragement to women students, especially to those wanting to study brass instruments.

Based on her experiences, Abbie has put together a one woman theater work entitled "Miriam," which she has performed throughout Germany and forty American cities. Of the many professionals who have been influenced by her work, **Sylvia Alimena**, conductor of the Eclipse Chamber Orchestra and a section horn player with the National Symphony (Washington, DC), observed: "You cannot imagine the power of this piece unless you were there in the room. All those professional women [were] just shaken to their cores by [it]. Of course it resonates particularly with other players, because—believe it—the kind of treatment Abbie went through in Munich is not, by any stretch of the imagination, unknown in the United States."

Although the past is behind the Osbornes, Malcolm Gladwell's 2005 bestseller, *Blink*, has brought the spotlight back, using Conant's case as a prime example of gender bias.

Besides teaching, Abbie and her husband enjoy a successful performing career on both sides of the Atlantic. In 2004, at the Roy and Edna Disney Cal Arts Theater, they premiered *Cybeline*, a multi-media music theater work for trombonist/performance artist, with libretto and cartoons by Abbie, and music, video and sound design by William, who has written many articles on women's rights, especially "Taking on the Vienna Philharmonic."

HEATHER BUCHMAN, (former) principal trombone with the San Diego Symphony (1988–96), is a graduate of Eastman (BM and performer's certificate in trombone) and winner in the 1984 New York Philharmonic Young Artists Concerto Competition. In 1989, she was the only American prizewinner—on any instrument—in the International Music Competition in Munich. In 1993, she premiered her commission of the David Ott *Concerto for Trombone*. She has given master classes in the U.S. and Europe. In September 1997, she moved to Ann Arbor to earn a master's in conducting and freelanced with ensembles in Detroit and Chicago. In 1999, she became part of Juilliard's prestigious Professional Studies Program in Conducting with Otto Werner Mueller. Upon completion in 2001, she joined Hamilton College (Clinton, New York) as assistant professor of 20th century music history and conductor of their orchestra and College Brass Ensemble. She also directs the chamber music program and teaches courses in 20th century music and conducting. Her solo performances cover San Francisco, Los Angeles, New York City, Minneapolis, St. Louis, Munich, Rome and Japan.

Monique Buzzarte

§ MONIQUE BUZZARTÉ, a freelance trombonist in New York, is an avid proponent of contemporary music, and has commissioned and premiered many works for solo and chamber ensembles. Born August 26, 1960, in San Pedro, California, there was no music in her family background, but she was enchanted by the trombone, and at age eleven firmly resisted being allocated a clarinet in public school music classes. Later, she studied with avant-garde trombonist Stuart Dempster, received her BM from the University of Washington (1982), and MM from the Manhattan School of Music (1993). For over a year she toured as the onstage trombonist with Joel Grey in the national production of *Cabaret*.

As an author and educator, she received an NEH grant for her research on the brass compositions of women composers published in *The Musical Woman*, Vol. III. (See Bibliography.) Her recordings include John Cage's *Five to the Third* with the Arditti Quartet and *Thirteen* with Essential Music. She is on the boards of the IWBC and IAWM, and played a key role in publicizing the Vienna Philharmonic's treatment of harpist **Anna Lelkes**, which may have helped their finally granting her full membership after twenty-seven years in the orchestra.

In 2002, she received an artist-in-residency at *Harvestworks Digital Media Arts* for the development of an interactive performance system for the trombone. Harvestworks Digital Media Arts Center, located in New York, is a not-for-profit organization founded in 1977 to cultivate artistic talent using electronic technologies. Their facility is designed so artists and students can gain an understanding of how to use digital tools as well as how to conceptualize a project.

Rebbecca Cherian

REBECCA CHERIAN, who received her MM from Yale in 1981, has been co-principal trombone of the Pittsburgh Symphony since 1989. Previous positions were principal trombone with the Springfield (Massachusetts) Symphony and Rhode Island Philharmonic, and second trombone with the Vermont Symphony. She was trombone instructor at the University of Connecticut from 1982, and since 1993 has been on the faculty of Carnegie Mellon. She was a founding member of the International Women's Brass Conference.

BETTY S. GLOVER retired in 1992 after forty years as a faculty member of the Cincinnati College-Conservatory. She had been conductor of their brass choir, 1969–1992. From 1952–85, she was bass trombone and tenor tuba in the Cincinnati Symphony and Opera, the first female bass trombonist in a major orchestra. From 1950–52, she was instructor of brass and conductor of the brass choir at Otterbein College in Westerville, Ohio. Previous to that, she served five years as principal trombone with both the Kansas City and Columbus (Ohio) Symphony Orchestras. She is spending her retirement years in France.

Jeanie Lee

JEANIE LEE holds a BM *summa cum laude* from Ohio State University, and MM and DMA with highest honors from the University of Michigan. She is assistant professor of trombone at Morehead State University in Kentucky, and a clinician for Edwards Instrument Co. Her previous positions were principal trombone with Midland-Odessa, Big Spring, and Anchorage Symphonies. She is a member of the Horizon Brass Quintet, Kentucky Jazz Repertory Orchestra, and DiMartino/Osland Jazz Orchestra. She is co-editor of the IWBC newsletter.

PATRICIA McHUGH joined the Louisville Orchestra in 1962 while still a student at the University, where she earned her BM and MM degrees. In 1966, she became principal trombone of the Louisville Orchestra, a position she held until her retirement in 2003. She has also played with the Santa Fe Opera Orchestra, Louisville Ballet, Louisville Opera and the Pittsburgh Wind Symphony.

JULIA (Bantin) McINTYRE at age twelve was studying trombone, voice and piano, and at fourteen began studies on the bass trombone with Murray Crewe, Doug Sparkes and Gordon Sweeney. In 1991, she attended the Interlochen Arts Camp in Michigan, and the following year went on to win the top brass trophy in the Kiwanis Music Festival of Toronto. A graduate of the University of Toronto (bachelor of music performance, 1996), during the summers of 1993 and 1994 she played and toured with the National Youth Orchestra of Canada, and in the summer of 1995 won the bass trombone position in the l'Orchestre Symphonique de Québec. She has performed with the Toronto and Montreal Symphony Orchestras, the Hamilton Philharmonic and the National Arts Centre Orchestra. She is a member of the Monarch Brass Ensemble, Aurora Trombone Quartet, and a board member of the IWBC. In May 2003, she won the audition for principal bass trombone in the Winnipeg Symphony.

Australian trombonist **DONNA PARKES** is with the Virginia Symphony Orchestra.

DEBRA TAYLOR was principal trombone with the Grant Park (Illinois) Symphony before becoming principal trombonist with the New Mexico Symphony, and trombone instructor at the University of New Mexico.

Blowing Low: Euphonium and Tuba

Stacy Baker

§ STACY BAKER is assistant professor of tuba and euphonium at Morehead State University, Kentucky. She holds MM and BM degrees from the University of Michigan, where she graduated *summa cum laude*, and earned her DMA in Performance and Literature, with highest honors, at the University of Illinois. She has performed with the Detroit, Warren, Allen Park, Illinois, Champaign/Urbana, and Danville Symphonies. She appeared as a featured soloist at the 2000 U.S. Army Band Tuba/Euphonium Conference, the 1999 Southeast Regional Tuba/Euphonium Conference, the 1998 International Tuba/Euphonium Conference, and the 1997 Second International Women's Brass Conference. She was honored in 1995 as a finalist for the Krannert Debut Award at the University of Illinois for her achievements as a solo performer. She is a member of Junction,[131] a tuba/euphonium quartet, formed to build a broad repertoire through the performance of new original works and arrangements. The other quartet members are Velvet Brown, Sharon Huff and Angie Hunter. Also with the Monarch Brass Ensemble, the Lexington Brass Band, the Athena Brass Band, and the Timbre Brass Quintet, she has performed throughout the U.S. and Europe. She is editor of the IWBC newsletter.

Kathy Brantigan

KATHY Aylsworth **BRANTIGAN** holds BM and MM degrees from the University of Michigan. She and her husband, Charles, are founders/directors of the *Denver Brass*, with whom she plays in addition to the *Aries Brass Quintet*. She is chair of the brass department and Instructor of Tuba at the University of Denver, Lamont School of Music. In February 2004, she received the Denver Mayor's Award for Excellence in the Arts. An active member of the ITEA, in 2006 she was their treasurer. In June of the same year she hosted the International Tuba-Euphonium Conference at the University of Denver.

Velvet Brown

VELVET BROWN was principal tuba with the New Hampshire Music Festival and Nashua Symphony. Formerly associate director of athletic bands at Boston University, she holds a BM from West Virginia University in performance/theory/composition, an MM in music performance and music education from Boston School of Music, and attended Indiana University for doctoral studies. Her teachers included Samuel Pilafian, a star student of **Constance Weldon**. As a member of the Chamber Brass of Boston, she was one of the founders of the *Boston Tuba Quartet*. She is an orchestral, solo, and chamber performer, having made appearances in Europe, Japan and the U.S. She was featured at the 1999 Swiss Brass Week, the Italian Wind Festival, the 1999 and 2000 Mid-Europe Conferences, and as soloist at the International Tuba and Euphonium Conferences. A past board member and vice-president of IWBC, Velvet is a member of the board of directors and is program editor for the Tubists Universal Brotherhood Association (TUBA), now ITEA. She is a founding and current member of the Monarch Brass Quintet and Brass Ensemble, and with Stacy Baker, Sharon Huff, and Angie Hunter, performs with Junction, a tuba/euphonium quartet. She has released a solo

---

131. Junction premiered Franz Cibulka's *Concerto for Tuba/Euphonium Quartet and Wind Band*, with the German Army Concert Band, at the Mid-Europe Festival in Schladming, on July 12, 2002, concluding their tour of Austria.

CD, *Velvet*, on the Crystal Records label and can also be heard on the Nicolai Music Label. She taught at Ball State University, was professor of tuba and euphonium at Bowling Green (Ohio) State University, and in the Fall 2003 became professor of tuba and euphonium at Pennsylvania State University. She enjoyed one year in Italy as the 1999–2000 winner of the Fulbright Fellowship-Vinciguerra Award.

Mary Ann Craig

§ **MARY ANN CRAIG** is the first female to hold the office of president (2003–05) in the thirty year history of the International Tuba-Euphonium Association (ITEA), formerly Tubists Universal Brotherhood Association (TUBA). For four years prior to her election, she served as secretary for the organization and was elected in 2001.

Born August 28, 1947, in Sandy Lake, Pennsylvania, Mary Ann was exposed to music at an early age. Her father, while not a musician, volunteered to drive the bus for the Sandy Lake Fireman's Band in the evenings for their parades in neighboring towns. One day he brought home a baritone horn for his daughter because he loved the counter melodies played by that instrument in marches. For Mary Ann, only seven years old, it was love at first sight. She began taking lessons immediately, and on entering third grade was the youngest player in the school band. By ninth grade, she won first chair in the Carnegie Mellon (then Carnegie Tech) Honors Band in Pittsburgh, and was again its youngest member. She was also selected for the School Band of America, drawn from the best young musicians in the country, which toured Europe.

Degrees came from Baldwin-Wallace College in Berea, Ohio, (B.Mus.Ed., 1969) and Indiana University (MM, 1970; DME, 1981), where she holds the distinction of being the first euphonium player to be awarded the coveted Performer's Certificate—this by obtaining the necessary seven out of nine votes from a faculty committee. (Two members of the committee did not consider the euphonium enough of a "high brow" instrument to merit such an award.)

As a performer and teacher, Craig has appeared throughout the U.S., Japan, Europe and Australia, where she taught at Goulburn College and Wollongong Conservatorium (1972–73). She has been a soloist at the International Tuba-Euphonium Conference and has toured Europe with the *Colonial Tuba Quartet*, of which she is the only woman member, as well as appearing in ensembles with Harvey Phillips in Carnegie Hall. Her first solo euphonium albums include *Euphonium . . . Out On a Limb* (1995), and *Mary Ann Craig, Euphonium* (1987). She has commissioned many works for solo euphonium, including *Erica and the Euphonium* for solo and orchestra, by Anthony Plog, which she premiered with the Arizona State Symphony Orchestra, her former teacher Henry Charles Smith III conducting. Along with the other members of the *Colonial Tuba Quartet*, she has also commissioned several works for tuba-euphonium ensemble. The quartet has recorded several of these works on their CD, *Spectraphonics*.

In 1996, Dr. Craig founded the Colonial Euphonium and Tuba Institute, an international week-long festival for low brass players. Participants attended from throughout America, Canada, Japan, Australia, England and Costa Rica. The second CETI was held at Indiana University of Pennsylvania, hosted by Dr. Gary Bird. In addition, she has served as the chair of the Society for Music Teacher Education-Eastern Division, state chair for research for the New York State School Music Association, and is on the board of the IWBC.

Craig was professor of music at The College of Saint Rose in Albany, New York, until 1996, when she accepted the position of director of bands at Montclair State University in Upper Montclair, New Jersey. Her commissions are now for band, with the MSU Band premiering many new works, some of which can be heard on their CD, *Live on Stage!* Concurrently, she is active as a guest conductor and adjudicator at band and ensemble festivals around the world.

She has also developed a close liaison with countries in Eastern Europe by conducting some of the most prestigious professional concert bands in Russia. In 2001, she conducted the top service band in Ukraine, and a World Honors Ensemble in Finland. Her Montclair State University Symphonic Band toured Russia in May 2002, and because of their outstanding performance at the Moscow Conservatory, they were invited to have a relationship with the conservatory. In March 2003, the university sent a contingency of administrators there to work out the details, and now Montclair is the only university in the U.S. that has a liaison with Moscow Conservatory, sending five students to Moscow to study for a semester. After being interviewed for radio and television broadcasts of the People's National Radio of Russia, Craig was awarded the title of honored professor of Moscow State University of Culture and Arts for the contributions she has made to the development of Wind Bands in Russia.

March 2004, she co-hosted, with Russian Anatoly Dudin, the first tuba-euphonium conference in Russia, where she brought in guest artists from New Zealand, Canada, Finland and the U.S. During the summer, she conducted the Hungarian Military Band in concert at the Franz Liszt Academy in Budapest.

January 2005 found Craig once again in St. Petersburg where she had the wonderful opportunity to give a master class at St. Petersburg Conservatory. Her hosts were the director of the Navy Band and the tubists of the Mariinsky Opera and St. Petersburg Symphony.

March 2006 brought a landmark as Mary Ann became the first woman to conduct the Pennsylvania Inter-Collegiate All-State Band in the fifty-nine year history of the festival.

Future plans involve creating an Arts component for the *Hands Across the Nile* volunteer program in Egypt. Plans are in progress for a trip there in 2007.

Jan Duga

§ JAN Z. DUGA, a senior master sergeant USAF, has been assistant principal tubist with the Air Force Concert Band at Bolling Air Force Base since 1983. She is the first woman tuba player in a premier band. Her BS in music education is from Ohio State University, and MM in solo tuba performance from Arizona State University. She also performs with the USAF Symphony Orchestra, Ceremonial Brass, *Airmen of Note*, freelances in the Washington area and teaches privately in the Northern Virginia school system. In addition, she serves on the board of directors and was a founding member of the IWBC.

JOAN FOLLIS enjoyed hearing the two boys next door play trumpet and trombone in the High School Marching Band. She learned cornet at ten, baritone horn at thirteen, and the euphonium at eighteen. Her BME is from the Bowling Green State University of Ohio (1975). She auditioned for the West Point Band in February 1976 and was accepted. Upon joining in May of that year, she became the second woman ever to be assigned to the band. After twenty-one years of service, she retired in 1997.

JOANNA R. HERSEY won first place in the Vermont All-State Competition and a scholarship to the Vermont Mozart Festival in 1989. She attended Arizona State University on a full music scholarship, and joined the U.S. Coast Guard band as a tubist in 1992. In 1999, she left the band and earned her MM in performance at the New England Conservatory. She is principal tubist with the New Hampshire Symphony and an instructor at the University of Hartford, Hartt School of Music.

Sharon Huff

§ SHARON HUFF earned her BME degree *summa cum laude* from Illinois State University, her MM and DMA degrees from the University of Illinois. She is on the faculty at Millikin University in Decatur, Illinois, where she teaches tuba and euphonium. Her previous positions were at Illinois State University and St. Norbert College in Pere, Wisconsin, teaching Low Brass Methods and Brass Pedagogy and Literature. Serving for her seventh year as conferences coordinator for ITEA (formerly TUBA), Dr. Huff is also the president and executive director of the International Women's Brass Conference (IWBC). In demand as a clinician, conductor, adjudicator, lecturer and euphonium soloist, she has performed and conducted across the Midwestern and Eastern U.S. as well as in Finland, Australia, New Zealand, Italy, Germany, and Austria. She is the founder and former member of Junction, a tuba/euphonium quartet which, when founded included Stacy Baker, Velvet Brown and Angie Hunter.

ANGIE HUNTER, originally from Greenwich, Ohio, studied the euphonium at Bowling Green State University (BM, 1983) and at the University of Illinois at Urbana-Champaign (MM, 1986), with classmates Stacy Baker and Sharon Huff, as well as trombone at the Conservatory of Music in Trossingen, Germany (Artist's Certificate, 1999).

She was the winner of the first Leonard Falcone International Euphonium/Baritone Horn Competition in 1986. Hunter appeared as a soloist at the International Tuba-Euphonium Conferences in Chicago and in Riva del Garda, Italy. She has performed at the International Women's Brass Conferences (IWBC) in St. Louis and Cincinnati. She has given recitals and workshops at several universities in the USA and completed a euphonium CD. Her teachers included Kenley Inglefield, Fritz Kaenzig, Brian Bowman and **Abbie Conant**. Since 1989, she has been on the music faculty of the German Bible Institute in Koenigsfeld, Germany. With Stacy Baker, Velvet Brown and Sharon Huff, she performs with the tuba/euphonium quartet Junction.

Laura Lineberger

LAURA LINEBERGER, librarian with the United States Army Band, was the first woman euphonium player in the history of "Pershing's Own." She has performed solo performances with the U.S. Army Brass Band, Concert Band, and Army Orchestra. At the 2002 North American Brass Band Association (NABBA) championships, held in Cincinnati, Ohio, she brought together ladies of the various bands and formed the Athena Brass Band, which made its debut at IWBC 2003. She is a board member of the IWBC.

Gail Robertson

From Pompano Beach, Florida, **GAIL ROBERTSON** began musical studies at the University of Central Florida, and as a full scholarship graduate assistant, received her MM and performance certificate in euphonium at Indiana University. She returned to Orlando, becoming a founding member of Walt Disney World's "Tubafours." An instructor of euphonium and tuba at her alma mater, she also tours with the New Sousa Band, Brass Band of Battle Creek, Athena Brass Band, the Brass Band of Central Florida, and performs with Florida orchestras. Her compositions and arrangements are published by the Tuba and Euphonium Press. A board member of the ITEA and IWBC, she was co-host of the IWBC 2006.

DEANNA SWOBODA is a tuba artist for C.G. Conn, on the adjunct faculty at UNLV, a member of the Dallas Brass, and tours the U.S. performing workshops for music students.

HELEN TYLER, British baritone player, began playing the euphonium at age ten with the Rotherham Schools Band before moving on to play with the National Youth Brass Band of Britain at sixteen. She switched to the baritone before being offered a place at the Royal Northern College of Music, where she continued her studies. In 2002, she became Solo Baritone for Foden's Brass Band. She performed at the 2002 International Euphonium and Tuba Conference in Lahti, Finland, and has been invited to perform in the U.S. on several occasions, including the 2003 IWBC.

Constance Weldon

§ **CONSTANCE J. WELDON**, born January 25, 1932, in Winter Haven, Florida, started music in the fourth grade as a drummer. Tiring of that, she turned to trumpet, then French horn, valve trombone, and finally, baritone horn—which looks like a small tuba. It was easier to carry, and she was relieved from having to be at the front of the marching band. About the time her mother was wishing Connie had taken up the flute, her father brought home a *tuba*! She blew one note and knew this was to be her life instrument. It was the best sound she had ever produced. Later, she found out the band director needed a tuba and hinted to her father something about "a scholarship to college."

After high school, she attended the University of Miami (BM, 1952; M.Mus.Ed.,1953). Having been a scholarship student at Tanglewood in 1951, playing under a young **Leonard Bernstein**, she returned there in 1954, was auditioned by **Arthur Fiedler**[132] for the Boston Pops Touring Orchestra, and played with them for the next two years. She also commuted to New York to take lessons with the great tuba pedagogue Bill Bell (1902–71), then with the NY Philharmonic.

---

132. The somewhat irascible Fiedler had just lost his tuba player, who was also his barber. He told Connie if he hired her she would have to do more than just play, so she became his "Girl Friday" secretary until she left.

In 1956, Connie married hornist Barth Bennitt. They were on the road seven years, mostly in the same orchestra. After one season with the North Carolina Symphony, in 1957 she won a Fulbright Scholarship to Amsterdam which gave her the opportunity to study with **Adrian Boorsma** of the Concertgebouw. She learned Dutch, played with the Netherlands Ballet Orchestra, and then took Boorsma's place in the Concertgebouw, but neither she nor her husband wanted to spend the rest of their lives in Europe. They left in 1958. After two years with the Kansas City Philharmonic, they returned to Florida and the Miami Philharmonic where Weldon remained from 1965–77. Meanwhile, in 1963 she got an amicable divorce—she and Barth are still good friends.

Having taught periodically at the University of Miami since 1951, she started full-time as associate director of the preparatory division in 1960, becoming assistant dean in 1972. She was active as a clinician and performer from 1960–91. One of her legacies is organizing a tuba ensemble with her students in 1960, which is still blowing strong—the first ever to get college credit for their performing.

At her send-off celebration, April 5, 1991—dubbed "Connie's Final Toot"—she was honored as the Distinguished Alumna for the University of Miami School of Music. On May 9, she was the keynote speaker at the School of Music graduation ceremony.

Spending her retirement years between Lake Placid, Florida, and Beech Mountain, North Carolina, Connie has literally set up shop in both residences to indulge another of her passions—woodworking. She helped her father build a shed when she was a young girl! She also took up organ playing to entertain her neighbors.

2001 was a celebratory year, finding her conducting many former students at the seventy-fifth anniversary of the Miami University School of Music and her own fiftieth anniversary of joining their faculty. May 2002 saw the International Tuba-Euphonium Association (ITEA), celebrate its forty-second year with a convention in Greensboro, North Carolina, with Weldon taking an active part.

The International Women's Brass Conference (IWBC)

An ingrained gender bias, *not* poor performance or lack of physical strength, has kept women brass players from being selected for many orchestra positions. "We need a man for the solo part" remains a constant challenge and frustration. The purpose of the IWBC is "To provide opportunities to educate, develop, support, employ and inspire women brass musicians who wish to pursue professional careers in music." It provides a forum for all brass players, women and men, professionals and students, to meet on common ground and provide role models for young female brass players. Through competitions, they showcase up and coming musicians and bring into the limelight outstanding (but mostly unrecognized) women brass players. An example being **Patricia McHugh**, principal trombone with the Louisville Symphony since the 1960s. A feature of the first conference was the compilation of historical documents, entitled *Women Brass Musicians: Past and Present*, researched by the Pioneer Committee headed by trumpeter **Ramona Galey**, which discovered women brass players dating back to 1594. Another benefit of the IWBC was the creation of the all-women *Monarch Brass Ensemble*, representing a group of the cream of American women solo and orchestral brass players who perform throughout the USA and Europe. Their first tour in 1996, conducted by **Marin Alsop**, then music director of the Colorado Symphony, took them to the Summer Wind Festival (Oklahoma City), Interlochen (Michigan), and Brass on the Bluestem at the Homestead Ranch (Matfield Green, Kansas), site of the 1994 "Symphony of the Prairie."[133]

A flexible group, in 1999 Susan Slaughter and Marie Speziale were joined by **Frøydis Wekre**, **Abbie Conant** and **Carol Dawn Rheinhardt** in their European jaunt through Italy.

The second successful IWBC was held June 26–29, 1997, as was the third in 1999. Beginning in 2000, subsequent conferences were held at the College Conservatory of the University of Cincinnati (Ohio). The June 2003

---

133. Inspired by her love for classical music, philanthropist Jane Kolar underwrote and donated the use of part of her 7,000 acre ranch at Hay Meadows for those events.

conference was held at Illinois State University, Normal, Illinois. The site of the 2006 conference was the University of North Florida in Jacksonville.

Stop the Presses!

Just as this book was going to press, a milestone occurred that had to be recorded!

The Opportunity of a Lifetime is Earned by a Woman!

With only one tuba in an orchestra, job openings usually occur once within a generation. In the prestigious Philadelphia Orchestra that opening came when tubist Paul Krzywicki retired after thirty years (1972–2005).

Carol Jantsch

CAROLYN JANTSCH, from Mt. Vernon, Ohio, began piano at six, euphonium at nine, and settled on tuba at twelve. She completed her BM at the University of Michigan (2006), studying with Fritz Kaenzig. As a sophomore she auditioned for the New York Philharmonic, making it to the semi-finals. She was a runner-up in 2005 in Milwaukee, and was chosen for the Ann Arbor Symphony in 2006. When the Philadelphia position opened, she submitted her résumé, but was rejected as too inexperienced. She sent a CD to Blair Bollinger, music director of Bar Harbor Brass, in an application for their summer workshop. Bollinger, bass trombone for Philadelphia, was also chair of their tuba search committee, who were equally impressed with the CD. Competing with 194 others, Carolyn won the coveted position, becoming the only female tuba player with a major American orchestra. With the new tubist aged just twenty, the next opening may not occur for another thirty . . . or forty years . . .

§ Major players and organizers of the IWBC.

CHAPTER TWELVE
PART I

Ladies Slowly Get to Bang the Drums!

Evelyn Glennie
Sherrie Maricle
Mutsuko Taneya

Looking at major orchestra rosters, one is hard put to find women in the percussion sections. Like brass, banging drums has a military and therefore traditionally male connotation. Once again, we must hark back to womens' orchestras, whose percussion sections were ably "manned" by ladies. Some of the last of that tradition being the Cleveland Women's Orchestra, and the "Big" band, DIVA, whose leader is drummer **Sherrie Maricle** who helped form the band in 1992.

Today, some women can be found in regional orchestras, but the number is still sparse in the majors. The Cleveland Women's Orchestra has **Donna Nycum** on Timpani and **Linda Allen** on keyboard and percussion. (See Women in Orchestras.)

There are three women, however, who have managed to emerge into a solo spotlight.

MUTSUKO TANEYA, one of Japan's most prominent and versatile marimbists, is equally at ease performing the music of Bach, the Romantics, or the contemporary. A native of Kochi, she is a graduate of the Osaka National University and *the first* to be awarded a bachelor's and master' degrees in the marimba department, designed especially for her. Her international career began with a tour of China, which served as an introduction of her instrument to that country. Her concerts there have been broadcast live on Peking Radio and televised in Tenjin. She was featured in recital in Melbourne and Sydney, Australia. In America, she performed at the 1988 Arcady Music Festival in Maine, and made a successful New York debut in 1989 at Weill Recital Hall at Carnegie Hall.

Taneya is a professor at the Osaka Shinai Women's College, a faculty member at both the Osaka National University of Education and Kobe Women's University, and a special member of the Japan Marimba Association and the Tokyo Bach Research Association.

Utterly and Universally Unique!

Evelyn Glennie

EVELYN GLENNIE stands alone in her field as the most successful percussion soloist—male or female—in the world. The xylophone started out as her main instrument, to which she added a thirty piece gamelan set, plus other instruments to total around 1,400—she averages sixty per performance—literally weighing a ton, and taking four hours to set up and two to dismantle. She also plays the bagpipes. Her debut at the BBC London Proms in 1989 marked the first solo percussion recital in history.

Born in Aberdeen, July 19, 1965, Evelyn was brought up on the family farm in North East Scotland. She began to lose her hearing at age eight, and by twelve was diagnosed as "profoundly" deaf. She had started piano and clarinet early, and now switched to timpani and percussion because "it looked like fun"—also she could feel the vibrations. Entering the RAM in 1982, she won the Shell/London Symphony Orchestra Scholarship in 1984, graduated in 1985, and won a Munster Trust Scholarship in 1986 for further studies in Japan. Tours of the Far East, Australia, New Zealand, India, Indonesia, Denmark, France, Turkey, Spain and America, playing with major orchestras, have cemented her reputation throughout the world.

Hailed as a unique cultural exchange between East and West, Glennie has concertized and conducted workshops with Indian music scholars in Bombay, Bangalore, Calcutta and New Delhi. In 1994, she made history in Indonesia performing with one of Jakharta's foremost Gamelan orchestras, and in Venezuela with concerts and a master class for over eighty-five nationally prominent musicians. The same year she performed on the Continent with the German Symphony Orchestra conducted by **Sian Edwards**.

To enlarge the repertoire of percussion works, she established the Evelyn Glennie Percussion Composition Award, and by the turn of the century had commissioned some 1,000 works. Solos have been written for her by James MacMillan, Dominic Muldowney, Richard Rodney Bennett, Dave Heath, Derek Bourgeois and **Thea Musgrave**.

Her autobiography, *Good Vibrations*, was published in 1990, and two documentaries of her life have been made by the BBC and Yorkshire Television. In September 1993, a second BBC series, *Sound Bites*, was aired with Glennie as both presenter and performer. In 1994, she made a musical travelogue of Korea for the BBC-TV series *Great Journeys*, which has been screened worldwide. She also writes music for television, film and documentaries. Her many acclaimed recordings include *Rebounds*, *Rhythm Song*, and *Light in Darkness*. The Bartók *Sonata for Two Pianos and Percussion*, which she performed with Sir Georg Solti, Murray Perahia, and David Corkhill, won the 1989 Grammy for Best Chamber Music Performance. Her 1994 release of James MacMillan's *Veni, Veni Emmanuel* received a "Classical CD" Award. *african sunrise/manhattan rave* was released in 2001, by which year she had thirteen CDs out and two more Grammy nominations.

Glennie's multitudinous honors include the Royal Philharmonic Society's "Soloist of the Year" award (1991), Fellow of the Royal College of Music (1991), Royal Academy of Music (1992), Welsh College of Music and Drama (1995), Royal Northern College of Music, plus honorary doctorates through 2000 from Aberdeen, Warwick, Loughborough, Bristol, Portsmouth, Exeter, Southampton, Durham, Essex, Leicester, Surrey, Dundee Universities and the Alexander Graham Bell Association. She was further honored with an Order of the British Empire (OBE), presented by Queen Elizabeth II in 1993. She has received other acclaim, such as Best studio percussionist, Best live percussionist, Belfast Drummie Award, *DRUM* Magazine Percussionist of the Year Award, and Rotary Foundation International Achievement Award. 2001 brought an honorary fellowship from the Guild of Musicians & Singers, and in 2002 her album, *Perpetual Motion*, received a Grammy award for best Classical Crossover Album. In 2003, she was chosen as "Instrumentalist of the Year" by *Musical America*.

Other claims to fame are that Evelyn was the first, and is still the only, full-time solo classical percussionist in the world, and the first classical musician to have her own website. She plays special teaching concerts for children, and established the Evelyn Glennie National Scholarship Award Program, administered through the Children's Hearing Institute, in New York, to encourage instrumental study among hearing-impaired children. She has performed in over forty different countries. Her globe-circling schedule includes four months of each year touring the USA.

Glennie is married to Greg Malcangi who acts as her music producer, sound reinforcement, and information technology manager.

No World of Silence!

Evelyn Glennie has lectured and written on the concept of deafness in an effort to remove the "handicapped" label from herself and myriads of others so branded. Much of the following is her own philosophy and experience.

"Deaf" used to be paired with "dumb," with the conception that people who were deaf could not understand the spoken word and were therefore stupid and unable to speak. Helen Keller proved otherwise.

To understand the nature of deafness, one first has to understand that hearing is basically a specialized form of touch. Sound is vibrating air picked up by the ear and converted to electrical signals, which are then interpreted by the brain. The sense of touch does the same. Deafness does not mean that one cannot hear, only that there is something wrong with the ears. Even someone who is completely deaf can still hear and feel some sounds.

Evelyn spent a lot of time as a child, with the help of Ron Forbes her percussion teacher, refining her ability to detect vibrations. With the sense of perfect pitch she possessed before losing her hearing, she managed to distinguish the rough pitch of notes by associating where on her body she felt the sound: low sounds mainly in her legs and feet and high sounds at particular places on her face, neck and chest.

She is *profoundly* deaf. Profound deafness covers a wide range of symptoms, but is commonly taken to mean that the quality of the sound heard is not sufficient to be able to understand the spoken word. With no other sound interfering, Evelyn can usually hear someone speaking, although she cannot understand them without the additional input of lip-reading. In her case, the amount of volume is reduced compared with normal hearing, i.e. the quality of the sound is very poor. For example, when the phone rings she hears a kind of crackle. This is, however, a distinctive type of crackle, thus she knows the phone is ringing.

In thinking of music only in terms of sounds, Glennie says, "My career, like that of Beethoven's and a number of others, is an impossibility." She goes on to explain: "I simply hear in a different way to most people, and point out that deaf people have to do a lot of work to train their voices or learn to lip-read, but after a while it becomes second nature. Their hearing impairment becomes no more a defining part of who they are than their hair color."

And so our respect goes to Evelyn Glennie, an UN-handicapped woman with a singular, vital and unique career.

DRUMBEAT

SHERRIE MARICLE is the leader and drummer of the all-woman DIVA Jazz Band, also known as "No Man's Band." Born in Buffalo, her family moved to the village of Endicott (New York). At age eleven, she was taken to a concert in Binghamton (NY) to hear Buddy Rich and his Killer Force Orchestra. It was a life-defining experience. She began studying snare drum in sixth grade, and jazz drums became her focus. While an undergraduate at SUNY Binghamton, she played professional gigs from jazz to symphony to Broadway. Earning her bachelor of arts, she moved to New York City, and completed an MA and PhD in Jazz performance at NYU.

Maricle's decision to found an all-woman jazz orchestra stems from fourth grade, when, having decided to play the trumpet, was told, "Girls don't play trumpets," and was handed a metal clarinet which she quickly abandoned for the cello. Fortunately, an opening came up in the school band for a bass drum player, and she managed to get it.

The original DIVA was the brainchild of Stanley Kay, a former drummer with artists such as Josephine Baker, Patty Page, Frankie Laine and Buddy Rich. In 1990, impressed by the caliber of musicianship of his drummer, Sherrie Maricle, he conducted a nationwide audition which produced a core of female players who performed their first concert in March 1993, with Sherrie as the leader. Kay's reputation gave him the edge to push DIVA to the forefront of the jazz field. By now the band has toured worldwide, performing in such venues as jazz festivals in Bern, Salzburg and Berlin, as well as Rome, Portugal, Finland, Japan and Korea, plus cruise ship tours. In the U.S., they have played at Carnegie Hall, Hollywood Bowl and at the twenty-fifth Anniversary of Kennedy Center.

Besides DIVA, Maricle founded the Quintet 5 PLAY. She is a busy freelancer, performing regularly with New Jersey Symphony, Concordia, Broadway shows, and with many jazz luminaries. Other musical credits include appearing on stage in the Broadway production of *Cabaret*, a feature with DIVA on *CBS Sunday Morning*, with the New York Pops on the PBS specials "Great Love Songs," and Skitch Henderson's Eightieth Birthday Gala.

She has often appeared with Skitch Henderson and the New York Pops. Their '05–'06 season ended May 8, with a gala concert for Henderson's eighty-eighth birthday. (He died November 2, 2005.) The Pops gave the world premiere of Maricle's orchestral piece, *Touch of the Earth*. *FanFare From the Street* was debuted by the Binghamton Philharmonic, March 27, 1999.

As a composer, performer and teacher, Maricle has The Kennedy Center Alliance Award for Outstanding Contributions and Achievements in the Arts, a grant from Meet the Composer and a doctoral fellowship from NYU. She is the past New York State president of the International Association of Jazz Educators, the New York Pops Education coordinator for the five boroughs of New York City, and a clinician for Yamaha Drums, Sabian Cymbals and Vic Firth Drumsticks, the world's largest manufacturer.

She is on the jazz and percussion faculty of New York University and the Hartwick College Summer Music Festival, in addition to running a private drum-set and percussion studio. She is also the creator of the Rhythm, Rhyme, and Rap Workshop for children.

Percussion Perks

As of 2005, five women graced the percussion sections of the following orchestras:

Charlotte:	tympani Carol Stumpf
Chicago:	percussion Patricia Dash
Ft. Worth:	tympani-percussion Deborah Mashburn
Milwaukee:	percussion Linda Raymond Siegel
San Diego:	percussion Cynthia Yeh
San Francisco Opera:	percussion Patricia Niemi

CHAPTER TWELVE
PART J

The Harpsichord Still Sings

Elizabeth Chojnazka
Elaine Comparone
Alice Ehlers
Wanda Landowska
Sylvia Marlowe

Jennifer Paul
Yella Pessel
Zuzana Růžičková
Lotta Van Buren

Developed in Europe in the 14th or 15th century, harpsichords were widely used from the 16th until early 19th century, when they was superseded by the stronger sounding piano. During the 18th century, harpsichords were built in France by the Blanchet family, in Germany by the Hass family, and in England by Jacob Kirkman. The outbreak of the French Revolution (1789) marked the end of harpsichord building in France. The Paris Conservatory gave its last harpsichord prize in 1798. The last known Kirkman instrument was built in England in 1809.

It was **Arnold Dolmetsch** (1858–1940) who laid the foundation for the reincarnation of the harpsichord. His life goal was the interpretation of the music of the past on authentic instruments. Born in France, after completing his musical studies in Brussels, 1883, he moved to London and attended the RCM. By 1894 he had built his own harpsichord, and began giving concerts of early music. In 1902, he came to the U.S. for a two-month concert tour. He returned in 1904 for a seven week tour, whose success kept it expanding with added engagements. Support was so great, he decided to make his home in America. He settled in Boston (1905–11), concertizing and working for the Chickering Piano Company building harpsichords. When the company fell victim to the 1910 economic depression, he returned to England, continued to make instruments, and in 1915 published a book on 17th and 18th century music—the groundwork for the resurgence of interest in early music. This bore fruit in the talented artists who made the harpsichord their instrument.

LOTTA VAN BUREN (1877–1960) benefitted from Dolmetsch's research. Her father was a nephew of the eighth president, Martin Van Buren. She studied piano, and in 1912 went to Germany to do research on Wagner. On her return, she spent time with Dolmetsch in England, learning how to repair the harpsichord she had purchased from him earlier. Beginning in 1922, she gave lectures on Wagner and his music, and also devised a series of lecture-recitals featuring 17th and 18th century harpsichord music. Her interest in the music and instruments expanded to restoration techniques, which became an important part of her subsequent career. She returned to England in the summers of 1923, '24, and '25, to again work with Dolmetsch. Back in the U.S., she restored instruments in the Morris Steinert Collection for Yale University, Cooper Union Collection, Joline Collection at Barnard College, and John D. Rockefeller's Colonial Williamsburg in Virginia. She continued touring with private concerts and lecture-recitals until her retirement in 1940. In 1955, five years before her death, she gave her collection of music and instruments to Brigham Young University in Salt Lake City, Utah.

Credit for the true revival of the harpsichord belongs to **WANDA LANDOWSKA**. Born in Warsaw, July 5, 1879, she studied piano at the Warsaw Conservatory, and in Berlin with **Moritz Moszkowski** (1854–1925). After experimentation, she realized that the music of her beloved Bach, Handel, Haydn and Mozart sounded better on the instrument for which it was written, the harpsichord. She moved to Paris in 1900, where she married Henri Lew, an ethnomusicologist, and with his help searched out instruments in museums and private collections. She traveled widely in Europe as a pianist and harpsichordist from 1903. In 1909, she toured Russia and played for Tolstoy, who showed interest in her ideas on classical music. In 1912, dissatisfied with the instruments in her collection, she commissioned the Pleyel firm to build a two-manual harpsichord. Introduced at the Breslau Bach Festival in 1912, it became the standard Landowska vehicle. In 1913, she was invited by director Herman Kretzschmar (1848–1924) to give a special course in harpsichord playing at the Berlin Hochschule für Musik. Thus, the outbreak of World War I, in 1914, found her in Germany where she was interned until the Armistice, November 11, 1918—the same year her husband was killed in an automobile accident in Berlin.

In 1919, she gave master classes in harpsichord and performed at Switzerland's Basel Conservatory. Returning to Paris in 1925, she bought a villa in St.-Leu-la-Fôret, near the city, assembled a large collection of harpsichords, and established a school for the study of early music which attracted students from all over the world. She also taught at the Fontainebleau Conservatory, all the while continuing to concertize in Paris.

Her American debut was November 20, 1923, with the Philadelphia Orchestra under **Leopold Stokowski** (1882–1977). She went on to play with the New York and Chicago Symphonies, Boston and Detroit Orchestras, and made her first recordings at the RCA Victor studios in Camden, New Jersey. As its most famous exponent, Landowska's concerts engendered new enthusiasm for the harpsichord, an excitement lacking since the departure of Dolmetsch twelve years earlier. She returned to America five times in subsequent years. In 1926, she premiered **Manuel de Falla**'s concerto for harpsichord and five solo instruments in Barcelona, with the composer conducting. In 1929, **Francis Poulenc** wrote his *Concert champêtre* for harpsichord and small orchestra for her. (The American premiere waited twenty years, with Stokowski and the New York Philharmonic performing it in 1949.)

When the Germans invaded France in 1940, Landowska fled to Switzerland, abandoning her villa, her library, and her instruments. She reached New York in 1941, and by 1942 had established herself in an apartment on Central Park West. She taught, concertized and made immortal recordings. By 1950, she had settled in Lakeville, Connecticut, teaching and recording[134] until 1954. She died there August 16, 1959, but continues as a legend—the greatest harpsichordist of our time.

In 1952, *Time* magazine referred to the virtuosa as " . . . [The] Pint-sized (four feet eight inches) unchallenged high priestess of the plunky, double-keyboard instrument."

Also renowned as a musicologist, Landowska's writings include *Bach and His Interpreters*, (Paris, 1906), and *Ancient Music*, (French, 1909, English, 1924). A collection of her articles was published posthumously under the title *Landowska on Music* (1964).

ALICE EHLERS was born April 16, 1887, in Vienna, where she started piano studies with the great **Theodor Leschetizky** (1830–1913). In 1913, when **Wanda Landowska** began teaching at the Berlin Hochschule as the first 20th century professor of harpsichord, Alice became her first student and the first member of a second generation of resurgent harpsichordists.

In the course of her five student years, she became an assistant to her teacher, taking over the instruction of beginning students. Although she had access to several Pleyel instruments belonging to Landowska, her own first

---

134. By this time she refused to go to the studios in New York, so RCA had to come to her. She didn't care about her walls and floors being ripped up for soundproofing—as long as it matched her decor . . .

harpsichord was the one Mahler had purchased for the Vienna State Opera. It was relegated to the basement after his tenure there. Upon graduation, Alice was co-recipient of the Mendelssohn Prize, and engaged to succeed Landowska. She retained her position until 1933. During those years, her concert career blossomed with trips throughout Europe, South America and Russia. She gave lecture classes at the Milan Conservatory and toured throughout Italy with **Paul Hindemith** (1895–1963), performing as a viola-harpsichord duo.

She left Nazi Berlin in 1933, settled in London, and in 1936 made her first visit to America, giving concerts in Boston and New York. In 1938, she taught a summer class at Juilliard, after which she traveled to Los Angeles to visit her daughter, then a film actress. During her visit, she met director William Wyler, and the following year she and her harpsichord made their film debut in his *Wuthering Heights*, starring Laurence Olivier and Merle Oberon. After appearing with Bing Crosby on his radio hour, Ehlers' American career flourished. She was offered a teaching position at USC and began a twenty-six year association with the University. Her popular class on baroque interpretation attracted conductors-to-be **Roger Wagner**, and **Michael Tilson Thomas** and singers **Marilyn Horne** and **Carol Neblett**.

In addition to her tenure at USC, she taught courses at Juilliard, UC Berkeley, and the Universities of Washington and Wisconsin. She became a prominent figure on the West Coast, appearing with the Los Angeles Philharmonic, and playing solo and chamber music concerts into her eighties. She died in Los Angeles on March 1, 1981.

Another prominent harpsichordist of the 1930s in the U.S. was (Gabriella) **YELLA PESSL** (Sobotka). Born in Vienna, 1906, she was educated at the Academy of Music, where she studied organ and harpsichord with Alexander Wunderer (1877–1955). After finishing her studies, she debuted in America in 1931 and decided to make her home in New York, where she co-founded the Bach Circle, a group of performers specializing in the lesser known works of JSB. In 1938, she accompanied the von Trapp Family in their Town Hall debut. An active performer for more than half a century, she had her own radio program on WQXR, playing ancient music. During nearly twenty years of concertizing on the East Coast, she was chosen three times by **Toscanini** to play on the air with the NBC Symphony. At the time, she used a Maendler-Schramm instrument built in Munich. She also taught interpretation courses at Eastman, but her long-term appointments were at Columbia University and its then all women's satellite, Barnard College, where she was on the faculty from 1938 until her retirement in 1952. After two years of researching Italian music in the Vatican Library, she returned in 1950 to live in Massachusetts, reducing her teaching and performing schedule. Her husband, Dr. Harry Sobotka, a biochemist at Mount Sinai Hospital, died in 1970. Pessl died at eighty-five, December 8, 1991, at her home in Northampton.

SYLVIA MARLOWE was born in Brooklyn, New York, September 26, 1908. She studied piano and organ, and at eighteen accepted an opportunity to spend four years with **Nadia Boulanger** at the École Normale de Musique in Paris, where she studied piano, organ, and composition. During that time she heard Landowska play in the Salle Pleyel—the first time she had ever heard a harpsichord. After her return home, she played piano recitals on the CBS radio network from November 1932 to May 1933. By 1936, she turned her attention to the harpsichord. She taught herself by listening to Landowska's recordings, and reading everything she could on the instrument. In 1939, she played the complete Bach *Well-Tempered Clavier* on the harpsichord in four concerts at Town Hall, the first American presentation on the instrument for which the work was intended.

Crossing over into popular music, she played on radio programs, including the Chamber Music Society of Lower Basin Street where she appeared with many jazz greats. She was given her own weekly radio program on NBC, which lasted for ten years, bringing the sound of the harpsichord to a new generation. In 1948, she married landscape painter Leonid Berman, and was appointed to the faculty at the Mannes School of Music.

Contemporary compositions dominated her programs. In 1952, she formed the Harpsichord Quartet with Claude Monteux, flute, Harry Shulman, oboe, and Bernard Greenhouse, cello. They commissioned Alan Hovhaness' *Quartet* (1951), Elliott Carter's *Sonata for Flute, Oboe, Cello and Harpsichord* (1952), and Ben

Weber's *Serenade*. In 1957, she formed the Harpsichord Society, which continues to commission works of contemporary composers.

In 1956 she toured the Orient with her husband, a two-manual harpsichord and a technician. In three months she gave twenty concerts, appearing in Tokyo, Surabaja, Bandung, and Singapore. Her programs included works of Bach, Scarlatti, and Couperin, and some contemporaries. Her harpsichord was made by the American John Challis (1907–1974), who had learned his art from Dolmetsch in England. (Challis also built a pedal harpsichord for the great organist, E. Power Biggs.)

Marlowe's recordings range from Couperin, Purcell, and Bach's *Goldberg Variations*, to pieces from piano literature, and new works she commissioned. Twenty years before her death, she predicted the end of the 20th century may well be remembered as another "Age of the Harpsichord." By the 1970s, many *consorts*—ensembles of ancient instruments—had been formed and have continued in popularity. Her prophecy confirmed, Sylvia Marlowe died in New York, December 11, 1981.

The Latest Generation

ELISABETH CHOJNAZKA, born in Warsaw, won first prize at the International Harpsichord Competition in Vercelli, Italy, 1968. She has performed throughout Europe, in the U.S., Japan and Mexico. Known primarily as a performer of contemporary music—although her repertoire ranges from the 16th to the 20th century—she has many acclaimed recordings. In 1983, she won the SACEM Prize for Contemporary Music. In commissioning numerous works, she has done a great service for harpsichordists worldwide.

Czech-born **ZUZANA RŮŽIČKOVÁ** studied at the Prague Academy of Music, winning the Munich International Competition in 1956. She co-founded the Prague Chamber Soloists with conductor **Vaclav Neumann** in 1962, and joined the academy faculty the same year. She married Viktor Kalabis in 1952, has appeared in recitals with **Josef Suk** beginning in 1963, and was named Artist of Merit in 1969.

Since her New York debut as a Concert Artists' Guild Award winner, **ELAINE COMPARONE** has maintained a career as soloist with orchestra, recitalist, chamber musician, recording artist, impresario, teacher, arranger, and collaborator with choreographers, poets and video artists. Born in Lawrence, Massachusetts, into a family of musicians, she began piano at age four with her mother. As a child, she played violin, flute (her father was her teacher) and pipe organ, but it was not until her student years at Brandeis University that she discovered the harpsichord. Her success with it resulted in a Fulbright Fellowship to study with Isolde Ahlgrimm at the Academy of Music in Vienna.

A recipient of Solo Recitalist and Recording Grants from the NEA, she has given solo recitals in Alice Tully Hall, Merkin Hall, Weill Recital Hall, the 92nd St. Y, Metropolitan Museum of Art, Dayton (Ohio) Art Institute, the Library of Congress, and guest appearances with Chamber Music Society of Lincoln Center, New York Virtuosi, Handel Society of New York and Washington, Pro Arte Chamber and Stuttgart Chamber Orchestras and popular festivals. In October 1993, she stepped in at the last minute for the harpsichordist of the Vivaldi Orchestra of Moscow—an all-woman string orchestra—for their first American tour and debut concert at Tully Hall. She was subsequently invited to perform at the May Festival in Moscow by Svetlana Bezrodnaya, the orchestra's founder and conductor.

As founder/director of **Harpsichord Unlimited** (1978), dedicated to expanding awareness of the harpsichord as a contemporary instrument, Comparone directs and performs in an annual series of chamber music concerts and recitals in New York, highlighting such composers as Mozart, CPE Bach and Johann Christian Bach. The series has won awards from the New York State Council on the Arts, while the *New York Times* hailed Comparone as "one of the foremost exponents of Carl Philipp Emanuel Bach's keyboard music in this country." In 1988, HU was the only New York City musical organization to commemorate the death of **Carl Philipp Emanuel Bach** (1714–88) with a concert of his works. In 1989, she founded *Bach with Pluck!* (harpsichord and guitar). *Trio Bell'Arte*, another

Comparone innovation, with Karla Moe on flute and Marsha Helleron on oboe, made its New York debut in 1991, and celebrated its twentieth anniversary in 2001.

In 1996, Comparone recreated the Queen's Chamber Band, a concept originated in 1762 by **Johann Christian Bach** (1735–82), youngest son of JS, who journeyed to London to accept a position with the King's Theatre. He was also appointed music master to Queen Charlotte Sophia (wife of "Mad" King George III) and the Royal Family. With eight close musical friends, the "London Bach" formed an ensemble to entertain Her Majesty in her private chambers.

In addition to her busy performing and recording career, Comparone serves as organist and choir director of the First Moravian Church in New York.

Among her recordings are Harpsichord Sonatas by Persichetti and Scarlatti (Laurel); *Bach With Pluck!*, Volumes I and II (ESSAY); *The Entertainer: Rags and Marches* by Scott Joplin; *The Bueckeburg Bach* (Premier); and Viva! Italia (4TAY). With Chilean video artist Juan Downey, she made an interactive video disc, "Bach's Fugue in B minor for Voyager." This award-winning documentary was broadcast on PBS-TV nationwide.

Elaine enjoys standing at the harpsichord to play. She cites Vermeer paintings as an inspiration for this. Under her direction, Hubbard Harpsichords designed and built the tall oak stand that elevates the instrument.

JENNIFER PAUL, born June 25, 1954, in Long Beach, is a third generation Californian who grew up seeing her father and brother playing piano. She started lessons at seven, and the following year began on drums, which, in junior high school, made her the only girl drummer in the band. The family moved to San Diego in 1974. She received her BM (1976) in piano performance from the New England Conservatory, studied conducting for six months in Denver with **Antonia Brico**, then realizing her true focus, returned to the NEC for her MM (1979) in harpsichord performance. After winning the Frank Huntington Beebe Scholarship, she continued her studies in Amsterdam (1982) with Dutch harpsichordist/conductor, **Ton Koopman** (*b* 1944), founder of the Amsterdam Baroque Orchestra. She lived in a converted warehouse dating from 1650. When Tjalling Terpstra, the tenant in the apartment below, came by one night to complain about the noise of her electric typewriter, Jennifer invited him in for a drink. They were married in San Diego, June 2, 1984. Just before that, Jennifer realized one of her other ambitions and, on Friday the 13th of April 1984, made her Carnegie Recital Hall debut. August 8, 1987 marked the birth of her son, Jurrian, who plays violin and shows an interest in the keyboard.

Paul's career covers international concert appearances in Great Britain, Hong Kong, Singapore, Sydney and Auckland. In 1996, she returned to New Zealand and Australia where she played in the Melbourne International Festival of Organ and Harpsichord. She has also performed at the Library of Congress (1994)—a concert broadcast over a 100 stations—playing the harpsichord music personally collected by Thomas Jefferson. She was a recipient of the 1990 NEA Solo Recitalists Grant, one of only twelve honored with this award. In 1997, she went to Boston to demonstrate the harpsichord at the Early Music Festival. From September to November, she toured Ireland as a duo with a hurdy-gurdy player in another of her unusual series, *HarpsiGurdy*. She took her own instrument and her partner took two of his 18th century instruments.

Jennifer Paul has managed her own career since 1984, sometimes scheduling sixteen concerts in eighteen days. Rather than follow the "early music circuit" of concert series, she prefers to venture to places where no one has ever heard or seen a harpsichord—like the cattle ranch in the middle of the Australian outback 600 miles from nowhere, because the owner had a harpsichord and wanted to hear it played properly. Her biggest reward is being approached after a concert and asked where a recording can be purchased, or where to find a harpsichord. An intrinsic interpreter of Bach, Scarlatti and the French school, she also runs the gamut to contemporary music, such as the Bohuslav Martinů and Frank Martin concertos for harpsichord. She makes her concerts even more interesting by giving her audience friendly, informative background, and the sometimes spicy "low-down" on the composers whose works she performs.

From 1992–2001, Jennifer has continuously been in the California Arts Council Touring/Presenting Roster. In 1994, she was honored as Alumna of the Year by the Bishops School in La Jolla, California, where the author met her, and where the author's sons went through seventh through twelfth grades. Lovely place!

Bringing the Past into the 21st Century

Through the performances of these and other artists, plus the proliferation of early music ensembles, Sylvia Marlowe's vision has come to pass—the Age of the Harpsichord is, and remains, with us.

A Mystery Solved

It is interesting to note that many harpsichords are decorated with paintings of trees. I found the reason for this on a harpsichord made by Alan Grove in 1993 in Warwickshire, England. Painted in gold letters inside the lid was the Latin:

DVM VIXI TACVI
MORTVA DVLCE CANO

which poignantly translates to:

In Life I was silent
In Death I sing . . . .

CHAPTER TWELVE
PART K

Ladies of the Keyboard

Clara Wieck Schumann (1819–1896)
Marie Pleyel (1811–1875)
Marie Leopoldine Blahetka (1811–1887)
Amy Fay (1844–1928)
Marie Jaëll (1846–1925)
Julie Rivé-King (1854–1937))
Teresa Carreño (1853–1917)
Fannie Bloomfield Zeisler (1863–1927)
Marguerite Long (1874–1966)
Rosina Lhévinne (1880–1976)
Olga Samaroff (1882–1948)
Ethel Leginska (1886–1970)
Irene Scharrer (1888–1971)
Dame Myra Hess (1890–1965)
Magda Tagliaferro (1893–1983)
Clara Haskil (1895–1960)
Guiomar Novães (1895–1979)
Harriet Cohen (1895–1967)
Ania Dorfmann (1899–1984)
Maria Yudina (1899–1970)
Lili Kraus (1903–1986)
Nadia Reisenberg (1904–1983)
Grete Sultan (1906–2005)
Eileen Joyce (1912–1991)
Gina Bachauer (1913–1976)
Rosalyn Tureck (1914–2003)
Dame Moura Lympany (1916–2005)
Marian McPartland (1918–)
Hephzibah Menuhin (1920–1981)
Constance Keene (1921–2005)
Tatyana Nikolayeva (1924–1993)
Natalie Hinderas (1927–1987)
Hazel Harrison (1883–1969)
Jessie (Ernestine) Covington Dent (1904–2001)
Margaret Bonds (1913–1972)
Lillian Kallir (1931–2004)
Philippa Schuyler, (1931–1967)
Claudette Sorel (1932–1999)
Ruth Laredo (1937–2005)

IN THE LIMELIGHT

Martha Argerich
Idil Biret
Imogen Cooper
Bella Davidovich
Cecilia Dunoyer
Margaret Fingerhut
Hélène Grimaud
Wu Han
Angela Hewitt
Olga Kern
Alicia de Larrocha (1924–retired)
Cecile Licad
Anne-Marie McDermott
Ursula Oppens
Cristina Ortiz
Cecile Ousset
Maria-Joao Pires
Carol Rosenberger
Ann Schein
Ruth Slenczynska (1925–retired 2006)
Maria Tipo
Mitsuko Uchida
Ilana Vered

THEIR OWN SPOTLIGHT

Liane Alitowski
Diana Ambache
Lydia Artymiw
Marta Aznavoorian
Mary Barranger
Margaret Baxtresser (1922–2005)
Judith Burganger
Katja Cerovsek
Angela Cheng
Gloria Cheng
Sally Christian
Jodie De Salvo
Virginia Eskin

Janina Fialkowska
Katie Gogoladze
Gila Goldstein
Babette Hierholzer
Edith Hirshtal
Veronica Jochum
Diana Kacso
Sylvia Kersenbaum
Elena Klionsky
Nina Kogan
Israela Margalit
Juliana Markova
Mina Miller
Ilana Mysior
Barbara Nissman
Gail Niwa
Sarina Ohno
Yumiko Okawa
Estela Olevsky
Edith Orloff
Rebecca Penneys
Julie Rivers
Heather Schmidt
Nadia Shpachenko
Jacquelyne Silver
Eleanor Sokoloff
Susan Starr
Dubravka Tomsic
Sylvia Traey
Althea Waites

Yu-Mei Wei
Emily White
Lilya Zilberstein

ACCOMPANISTS
Jean Barr
Janet Goodman Guggenheim
Sandra Rivers

DUO-PIANISTS
Mar Barrenechea and Clavel Cabeza
Claire and Antoinette Cann
Misha and Cipa Dichter
Katia and Marielle Labèque
Valentina Lisitsa and Alexei Kuznetsoff
Georgia and Louise Mangos
Virginia Morley and Livingston Gearhart
Güher and Süher Pekinel

THE NEW GENERATION
Edith Chen
Evelyn Chen
Naida Cole
Rossina Grieco
Emily Hsieh
Chu-Fang Huang
Helen Huang
Orli Shaham

KETZEL

The "Revolutionary" Instrument

Literally revolutionizing the musical scene, the piano made its appearance in 1709, invented by harpsichord-maker **Bartolomeo Cristofori** (1655–1731), music curator for the Medici family. He called it a *gravicembalo col piano e forte*—"a keyboard instrument with soft and loud"—its strings activated by hammer strokes instead of plucking (plectra) like the harpsichord. By 1725, German builders were taking over. One of the most important improvements came from **Johann Andreas Stein** (1728–92) who invented an *escapement*—making the hammer action capable of playing repetitive notes. This was the foundation of the "Viennese" piano praised by Mozart. In 1777, Stein's daughter, Anna Maria "**Nannette**" (1769–1833), was apprenticed to the shop, and later his son, Matthäus Andreas (1776–1842), also known as André. Nannette was very active in the business during her father's last years. He died in 1792, and at age twenty-three she and her brother, only sixteen, took over the business as *Geschwister* (Siblings) *Stein*.

Nannette Streicher: A Woman Builds Pianos

In 1794, two years after her father's death, Nannette married pianist **Johann Andreas** (coincidence!) **Streicher**, who went into the firm when she and her brother moved it to Vienna from Augsburg. In 1802, Andreas left the partnership to establish a rival company, André Stein, which was then carried on by *his* son, Carl Andreas (1797–1863), who was also a pianist and composer. Nannette's son, Johann Baptiste (1796–1871), who had been an apprentice, entered the firm in 1823. The name was now changed to Nanette Streicher, née Stein, and Son. J.B. took complete control after his parents died in 1833 within four months of each other—Nanette, January 13, Johann Andreas, May 25. Johann Baptiste completed the last piano underway: serial #2657, affixing his new nameplate, *J.B. Streicher*, although the soundboard still bore his mother's name. J.B. invented the action of the hammer striking from above. Like his mother, he was on friendly terms with **Ludwig van Beethoven**. In 1857, his son Emil (1836–1916) became a partner, and until 1870 the nameplates read J.B. Streicher and Son. The business was dissolved on Emil's retirement because *his* son, Theodor (1874–1940), pursued a (not very successful) composing career.

Famous Fingers Striking Streichers

Major names in the music world known to have used or owned Streicher pianos include Carl Maria von Weber, Ludwig van Beethoven, Clara Schumann, Ferdinand Lachner, Adolph Henselt and Johann Reichardt, father of **Luise**. (See Composers.) Johannes Brahms owned a piano made by J.B. Streicher from 1870 until his death in 1896.

Pianos, Pianos, Everywhere!

By the 1800s, piano factories were all over Europe. Bechstein,[135] Blüthner[136] and Steinweg[137] in Germany, translated to Steinway[138] in English speaking countries, Bösendorfer[139] in Austria, Érard[140] and Pleyel[141] in France, and Broadwood[142] in England—the latter building, in 1817, a six octave instrument able to do justice to Beethoven's forceful style. (The modern piano is seven octaves.) Interest in the harpsichord declined because the piano could be heard above the larger orchestras. In the 1820s, John Hawkins of Philadelphia replaced the wooden frame with one of cast iron, permitting more tension on thicker strings which gave the instrument the fuller, more brilliant sound we are accustomed to hearing today.

The Piano Girl

There not being the stigma of "unladylike" applied to keyboard instruments, pianos and their ancestors, harpsichords, virginals and clavichords, have always been available to women or, in earlier times, the *gentle*women of the upper classes. Not until the upright "parlor" piano became a fixture of every household in the mid-19th century did the middle classes have access to this form of entertainment, with every girl expected to take lessons. A succession of professional lady pianists literally set the stage of a new career for women. Before the turn of the 19th century, the lady church organist also emerged on the scene.

Prima Donnas of the Keyboard

MARIE PLEYEL was born Marie Moke in Paris, September 14, 1811, the same year as Franz Liszt. One of the most admired pianists of the mid-19th century, she was a prized pupil of eminent Czech-born composer, conductor, pianist and pedagogue **Ignatz Moscheles** (1794–1870). At fourteen, she made her debut in Brussels. The following year she created a sensation with her virtuosic tour of Belgium, Austria, Germany and Russia. From 1848 to 1872, she was a professor of piano at the Brussels Conservatory, although even a "star" of her caliber

---

135–142. All of the above are still thriving in business to this day!

was relegated to teaching only young ladies. **Franz Liszt** (1811–1886) admired her as much for her teaching as her playing, and was rumored to have added her to his list of conquests. French composer **Hector Berlioz**[143] (1803–69), also in love with her, on hearing she had been unfaithful, rushed back to Paris ready to shoot or poison her, then himself—fortunately, neither of which happened. Instead, Marie, in 1830, married **Camille Pleyel** (1788–1855), who had followed in the footsteps of his famous father as a piano manufacturer. Austrian-born Paris citizen **Ignaz Josef Pleyel** (1757–1831), the twenty-fourth of thirty-eight children, was also a music publisher, composer, pianist and, in his youth, a pupil of **Franz Josef Haydn** (1732–1809).

A friend of **Fanny Mendelssohn-Hensel** and other illustrious women, Marie became a powerful voice in music society. Throughout her lifetime, her playing consistently received extravagant reviews. She died in Brussels March 30, 1875.

(MARIE) **LEOPOLDINE BLAHETKA** was born November 15, 1811, near Vienna, of a journalist/teacher father and musician mother, who was her first teacher. She, too, studied with Moscheles, then went on to **Carl Czerny** (1791–1857)—whose finger exercises still plague today's pupils—and celebrated French pianist/pedagogue **Frédéric Kalkbrenner** (1785–1849). She also studied composition. After her debut in 1818, she became part of the elite music world of Vienna and of **Schubert**'s circle of friends. In 1829, she met **Chopin** during his visit to her city, and presented him with one of her compositions. Her successful performing career took her all over Europe. In 1840 she settled in Boulogne (France), and began concentrating on teaching and composing. Her over 70 works, mostly salon pieces for piano, and a romantic opera, *Der Räuber und Der Sänger* (The Robber and the Singer) were all published during her lifetime. She died in Boulogne, January 12, 1887.

The Greatest!

CLARA (WIECK) SCHUMANN, born in Leipzig, September 13, 1819, was considered the world's greatest woman pianist of the time. From age five, she was under the complete control and training of her father, **Friedrich Wieck**. She made her debut at the Leipzig Gewandhaus at nine. Her extensive tours began in 1830. Playing before the crowned heads of Europe, she was acclaimed as a child prodigy in every country, including Russia, and compared to Mozart. When struggling young composer **Robert Schumann** came to study with Wieck in 1833, he fell in love with Clara, then fifteen, and waited four years to get permission from her father. This was completely refused, and the couple had an ugly, public four year court battle against Wieck before they could marry in 1840.

Clara somehow managed to continue her career during and between ten pregnancies. After her husband's death of mental disease in 1856, she provided the sole livelihood of her brood. Her career continued in full gear, with a major portion of her repertoire promoting Robert's music at the expense of her own excellent compositions. During these years she had the support and friendship of **Johannes Brahms**. In 1878 she settled in Frankfurt, teaching at the Hochschule (Conservatory). Her last public appearance was in 1891. Her passing, May 20, 1896, was mourned throughout the music world. (See Composers.)

AMY FAY may be considered the first prominent American woman pianist. Born in Bayou Goula, Louisana, May 21, 1844, she was the fifth of nine children—six girls, three boys. Her mother, a self-taught pianist, was also a gifted singer and played violin, flute, harp, guitar and organ. The rich musical environment she created for her children was further enhanced by their father giving them a classical education. Amy learned to speak, read and write Latin, Greek, French and German. When her mother died, the eighteen-year-old went to live with her oldest sister, Zina, an ardent feminist, writer, lecturer and organizer, who provided a strong role model. Amy studied with the prominent mentor of the first recognized American composers known as the New England School of Music, **John Knowles Paine** (1839–1906). She then went to Germany, where she had to suffer the snobbish prejudice against American students until she went to Weimar, in 1873, to study with Europe's greatest pianist, **Franz Liszt**, whom

---

143. His other unrequited infatuation, Irish actress Harriet Smithson, was the basis of his *Symphonie fantastique*.

she idolized. During her stay, she got to hear Clara Schumann and violinist **Joseph Joachim** (1831–1907), among other virtuosos.

Returning home in 1875, Fay concertized in Boston for the next three years, after which she moved to Chicago where her brother, Norman, initiated the founding of the Chicago Symphony Orchestra. This was established in 1871 with **Theodore Thomas** (1835–1905) as music director. In 1890, her sister, Rose, became the second Mrs. Thomas, and used her position to organize what became the National Federation of Music Clubs—still a moving force—to champion women's full participation in performance and composition, and lay the foundation for the appreciation of classical music in America.

Rose and Amy, with **Maud Powell**, **Camilla Urso** and **Amy Beach**, were prominent voices in the Women's Musical Congress of the 1893 World's Columbian Exposition in Chicago. Moving to New York, Amy and Zina were active lecturing, writing and encouraging women to value their talent and intelligence. In 1899, Zina founded the Women's Philharmonic Society of New York, which supported women musicians in performance, music history, composition and theory. It also funded an all-woman orchestra and chorus which, besides monthly musicales, gave four large concerts in Carnegie Hall each season. Amy served as their president, 1903–14. During this time she wrote on women in music in the *Etude*, *Music* and *Musical Courier* periodicals. Her letters to Zina, containing her impressions of Europe and a personal profile of Liszt, became a book, *Music-Study in Germany* (1881), that went through twenty-five printings with French and German translations. It was said to have inspired over 2,000 Americans to study abroad before World War I.

In 1919, her health failing, Amy moved back to Cambridge to live with her brother Norman. She died February 28, 1928, in the same nursing home where Zina had passed away in 1923.

Amy Fay remains a significant voice in the history of women in music, as well as advancing the cause of a more prominent place for women in society.

In France, **MARIE** Trautmann **JAËLL** was born in Steinseltz, north of Strasbourg (Alsace), August 17, 1846. Her father, George Trautmann, was mayor of the village, and her mother, Christine Schopfer, appreciated the arts and encouraged her daughter's musical education. Marie was taken to Stuttgart for studies with Ignaz Moscheles. By nine she was a prodigy, giving concerts in Germany, Switzerland and France. Tutored by Heinrich Herz (1803–88) until she was old enough to register at the Paris Conservatory, at sixteen she won their prestigious Premiere Prix in piano.

In 1866, at twenty, she married pianist Alfred Jaëll (1832–82), fifteen years her senior. A student of Czerny, Alfred was an internationally recognized virtuoso who knew Chopin, Brahms, Nikolaï Rubinstein and Liszt. The couple toured Russia, France, Germany, Switzerland, Italy and England, performing solos, duets—two piano and four-handed pieces were very popular—their own compositions, and works by contemporary masters. With her husband's connections, in 1868 Marie was introduced to Liszt. He took her as his student. The Jaëlls' dream was to live in Leipzig, where Alfred would take Moscheles' position at the conservatory, and run the *Neue Zeitschrift für Musik* magazine founded by Schumann in 1842. But this was thwarted by the outbreak of the Franco-Prussian War in 1870.

Developing an interest in composition, Marie began studies with **César Franck** and **Camille Saint-Saëns**. In 1871 her first piano music was published, followed by some eighty compositions, including two piano concertos, more piano and vocal pieces, plus works for various other instrumental combinations. Her *Valses* Opus 8, for four hands, had the unique honor of being premiered in Bayreuth in 1878 by two of the world's greatest composer/pianists, Liszt and Saint-Saëns. Six of the thirteen *Valses* were recorded in 1979 by **Marielle** and **Katia Lebèque** for the Strasbourg Bibliothéque Nationale et Universitaire (National Library), where most of Jaëll's correspondence, compositions, books, and articles are located.

After fifteen years of marriage Alfred died, and during 1883–86 Jaëll spent a few months each year with her musical mentor Liszt at Weimar, where he had been appointed Kapellmeister in 1848. She performed at his musicales, did his secretarial work, and was privy to teaching sessions that included some of the finest pianists of the day. She also wrote the last lines of the third *Mephisto Waltz* and proofread his *Faust Symphony*. In 1887, proposed by Saint-Saëns and Gabriel Fauré, she became one of the first women admitted as a member of the Société des Compositeurs de Musique—a great honor for both sexes.

During the 1890s, Jaëll's immense performing repertoire included being the first pianist to play all Beethoven's piano sonatas in Paris, and all of Schumann's works (1901). Her concerts of Liszt's complete piano works caused the great Saint-Saëns to declare: "Only one person in the world knows how to play Liszt, it is Marie Jaëll!"

After 1895 she almost completely left the concert stage, and taught at the Paris Conservatory for many years. She became prone to bouts of painful tendonitis, resulting in some uncomplimentary reviews. To better understand her condition, she developed an interest in piano pedagogy, her principal goal being to communicate to posterity the physiological method of Franz Liszt. This resulted in eleven books on piano technique, emphasizing economy of movement, careful use of arm weight and hand posture, and practicing slowly but not at length. Her benefit was living in the industrial age, when the science of physiology was gaining acceptance as people studied the brain and nervous system.

Albert Schweitzer was a pupil of Jaëll. He translated her book, *The Touch* (1894), into German. In his book, *Ma vie et ma pensée* (My Life and Thought), he wrote: "How much do I owe to this woman of genius!"

Greatly respected, Marie Jaëll died in Paris at seventy-nine, February 4, 1925.

JULIE RIVÉ-KING was born in Cincinnati, October 30, 1854. Her early lessons were with her mother, after which she went to New York to William Mason, and Leipzig with Carl Reinecke, completing her studies with Liszt. She returned to America in 1875 and played Liszt's Piano Concerto #1 with the New York Philharmonic. This started a career in the course of which she gave over 4,000 solo recitals and made over 500 appearances with orchestra. Even though her repertoire seemed endless, and her industry inexhaustible, she was not considered as grand a virtuoso as Austrian born **Fannie Bloomfield Zeisler** who outshone her as an outstanding American woman pianist. Rivé-King died in Indianapolis, July 24, 1937.

The Lioness of the Keyboard

Teresa Carreno

The long, successful career of **TERESA CARREÑO** was to the piano what Maud Powell's was to the violin. Their personal lives, however, were quite different. A grandniece of Venezuelan hero Simon Bolivár, Teresa was born December 22, 1853, in Caracas. Her first teacher was her father, who was also the Finance Minister. In 1862, forced by a revolution to flee Venezuela, the family settled in New York, and the eight-year-old made her American debut, November 25. When famed American composer/pianist **Louis Moreau Gottschalk** (1829–69) heard her play, he offered to teach her whenever he was in the city. After five concerts, the prodigy embarked on twenty more in the Boston area. She made her Havana debut, April 1863. In the fall, she played for President Lincoln at the White House. (She would return fifty-five years later to play for Woodrow Wilson). Her tenth birthday was celebrated with another Boston concert, which included some of her own compositions.

A Dual Career

In 1866 the family went to Europe. May saw Teresa's debut at the Salle Érard, the Carnegie Hall of Paris. Here she met prominent composers **Giachino Rossini**, **Charles Gounod**, **François Auber**, **Hector Berlioz** and **Franz Liszt**, the latter offering to teach her gratis. (She never took him up on it, there being some personal "strings" attached.) Russian composer/pianist **Anton Rubinstein** also offered to teach her after hearing her play and became her mentor. Paris publisher Heugel began printing her works. Her acquaintance with soprano **Adelina Patti** influenced her, at fourteen, to begin voice study, thus developing her talents as both a singer and musician. The outbreak of the Franco-Prussian War (1870) stranded Teresa in England. An extensive tour was arranged, which included the Promenade Concerts, then under the baton of **Sir Arthur Sullivan** (of Gilbert and Sullivan fame). When, in 1872, the lead soprano fell ill, Carreño was suddenly called on to make her opera debut in Edinburgh as the Queen in Meyerbeer's *Les Huguenots*. She learned the difficult role in a few days.

A Teen-Age Marriage

In the fall of the same year, she returned to America to play in Canada, New York, Boston, and Charleston with Patti's sister Carlotta, and one of the leading violinists of the era, **Émile Sauret** (1852–1920). In 1873, at the age of nineteen, she married Sauret, settled in London and gave birth to Emilita, March 23, 1874. After joint concerts in England that spring, June found the young couple back in America for a coast to coast tour the end of which coincided with the end of the marriage. Sauret returned to England alone. The lady who had looked after Emilita in London had become so attached to her that Teresa agreed to let her adopt the baby. To recover emotionally, she went to Boston, concentrated on voice lessons, and made her debut as Zerlina in Mozart's *Don Giovanni*. Although reviews for this and subsequent other productions were favorable, she decided to return to the piano. The souvenir of her opera career was Giovanni Tagliapetra, the tenor playing the Don, who became Teresa's second husband. They took up residence in New Rochelle, outside New York City, and had three children: Lulu, born 1878, who died in her third year, Teresita, 1882, and Giovanni, 1885. Although Carreño would have liked to retire, continued concertizing was necessary between babies because her husband turned out to be a drinker, philanderer and compulsive gambler.

In the spring of 1883, Carreño premiered Grieg's Piano Concerto with **Leopold Damrosch** (1832–85), father of conductor Walter Damrosch, (1862–1950). She subsequently made the work famous throughout the country. In 1884, she premiered the *Suite Moderne* of her former pupil **Edward MacDowell**[144] (1860–1908), whose work she had encouraged and promoted and who became a much-loved American composer. He dedicated his Concerto in D minor to her. During the 1880s, she made many tours of North America and Canada with and without her husband.

On the Podium, Good-bye Giovanni, Hello Eugene

In 1885, Carreño returned to her native country for the Bolivar centenary celebration and was treated as a national heroine. She was also invited to form an opera company to open the next year. The organizational details she asked of her husband were evidently too much for him. The Teresa Carreño Opera Company would have been a disaster had she not taken the baton and conducted the first few performances herself. Giovanni's letting her down hastened the finale to her second marriage.

Carreño's stormy personal life did not diminish her popularity. She went to Germany in 1889, debuting with the Berlin Philharmonic November 18, playing the Grieg. She was an instant success, even winning praise from chauvinistic pianist/conductor **Hans von Bülow** (1830–94), who conceded she was the only woman who could play Beethoven. The next seven years were spent touring all over Europe. Like Maud Powell, her schedule was incredible. In May 1891 alone, she performed almost every night. Flamboyant and passionate, she was becoming known as "The Lioness of the Keyboard."

One of the major pianists of the time was Scottish-born **Eugene d'Albert**, who had been a student of Liszt. The two artists met in 1891. Love blossomed despite Eugene being eleven years younger, and smaller in stature than

---

144. Just before Edward's early death, his wife Marian (1867–1956) founded the MacDowell Colony in 1907, in a wooded area in Peterborough, New Hampshire, and devoted her remaining forty-eight years to expanding the acreage and guiding the colony. During her lifetime nearly 500 writers, 200 composers, and 170 painters used the colony as a working retreat. It is now controlled by the Edward MacDowell Association, Inc. [Do the math: Marian lived to be ninety-nine!]

Teresa. They moved to Dresden, marrying the next year in time for the arrival of daughter Eugenia in November. The other children had already joined them. Not satisfied with his success as a performer, d'Albert turned to composing, and although his wife performed his music, it was her playing, not his work which drew acclaim. Never easy to get along with, the wounded egoist accused Teresa of undermining him. Shortly after the birth of second daughter, Hertha, in September 1894, they were divorced.

Now, besides her strenuous schedule, Carreño developed exercises for teaching and wrote articles for music journals. Summers were spent with the children. January 1897 found her back in America, again thrilling audiences with both her classical and romantic interpretations. Now elevated to "The Goddess of the Piano," she championed contemporary American music. On her return to Germany, she introduced **Amy Beach's** Violin Sonata on October 28, 1899 in Berlin, with Carl Halir, violinist. The following year, Beach dedicated her Piano Concerto, Op.45, to Carreño.

Fourth Time Lucky

On June 30, 1902, she shocked the public again by taking a fourth husband, Arturo Tagliapetra, brother of the now deceased Giovanni. This was her happiest marriage. In her fifties and financially secure, Carreño continued concertizing, even undertaking the long journey to New Zealand and Australia (1906–07); 1908, across America again; 1909, a return to New Zealand and Australia, then off to South Africa, London (1913) then back to America (1914). She performed in Europe during World War I, but left Berlin in 1916 to settle in New York. (Both she and her husband were U.S. citizens.) That year she played seventy-two concerts. Her spring 1917 tour of Cuba was interrupted by illness. She returned to New York and died within a few weeks on June 17. Her funeral was attended by the renowned of the music world and she was eulogized everywhere as a great artist and a great woman. In 1938 her ashes were taken to Caracas, her final resting place.

FANNIE BLOOMFIELD ZEISLER was born in Austria, July 16, 1863, and came to Chicago when she was four. After her concert debut in Chicago in 1875, at age twelve, she went to Vienna where she studied with the renowned **Theodor Leschetizky** from 1878–83. For the next ten years she played annually in America, and in 1893 made a tour of Germany and Austria which established her reputation as one of the world's best women pianists. In October 1885, she married Chicago lawyer Sigmund Zeisler. Her European tours continued almost annually until 1914, when she returned to Chicago. Her farewell concert there was on February 25, 1925, marking her golden jubilee. She died August 20, 1927, at age ninety.

La Grande Dame de la Musique Française

One of France's most renowned pianists and master teachers, **MARGUERITE LONG**, was born in Nîmes, November 13, 1874. She studied at the Paris Conservatory where in only two years, at sixteen, she won the highest honors, including the Premier Prix. From 1891–98 she lived with a prominent family, taught their children, played in their salons and made intellectual and political connections which elevated her into important circles. Her reputation grew with recitals at Salle Pleyel and other important venues, and composers began writing pieces for her. Still wanting to perfect herself, she asked her conservatory teacher, **Antonin Marmontel** (1850–1907), for more lessons. He was soon sending her some of his students, and in 1906 saw to it that she was appointed as an instructor for teaching girls in the Classe Preparatoire at the Conservatoire, a position which lasted thirty-four years until 1940. It took almost twenty of those years before she was promoted from the regular class to the coveted "Classe Superiére," where she taught both sexes. In 1907, she married a handsome young army officer, Joseph, Marquis de Marliave, a cultured self-taught musicologist and writer, and friend of **Gabriel Fauré** (1845–1924). Tragically, Marliave was killed in 1914, in the first month of World War I. Marguerite never got over it and never remarried. In 1920, she founded her own music school, which lasted until 1960 and produced many fine pianists. In 1943, she collaborated with France's most famous violinist and established the *Concours*

Marguerite Long-Jacques Thibaud. This has become one of the major competitions in the world and was taken over by the French government in 1962 to assure its perpetuity.

The Embodiment of French Music

Long played a unique role in promoting French music and was without peer in her performances of Fauré, Debussy and Ravel, all of whom were her personal friends. She made Fauré's music known to the world. In 1932, she debuted Ravel's *Piano Concerto in G major*, dedicated to her, with the composer conducting. Debussy claimed that Long's interpretation of his music was closest to his own. She gave annual master classes featuring scintillating lectures and recitals by her students. Virtually every contemporary French composer wrote for her. She was influential in the lives of the younger generation of composers such as Darius Milhaud, Albert Roussel, Arthur Honegger, Jacques Ibert (1990–1962) and Francis Poulenc (1899–1963). She made several trips to Brazil, receiving many honors from that country. France bestowed its highest honors upon her. She was the first woman musician to receive the Cravate de Commandeur of the Légion d'Honneur (1938), and the first woman awarded the Grand Croix de l'Ordre du Mérite (1965), the country's highest insignia. Not beautiful, her charm and influence were inestimable.

After teaching thousands of young pianists for over sixty years, Long wanted to leave a written record of her methods, technique and philosophy. She published *Le Piano* in 1959, and *La Petite Méthode* in 1963, for which many prominent composers had written juvenile pieces. She also wrote a book on Gabriel Fauré.

Her ninetieth birthday was celebrated throughout Europe. She was given a Golden Book containing over 200 autographed messages from President Charles de Gaulle to every major public figure in the world, especially in music. Marguerite died peacefully in her home in Paris on February 13, 1966. In accordance with her wishes, the heavenly Fauré *Requiem* was performed at her funeral. She was greatly mourned.

(A definitive book on Marguerite Long was written in 1993 by **Cecilia Dunoyer**. See Musicologists.)

ROSINA LHÉVINNE, noted Russian pianist and pedagogue, was born in Kiev, March 28, 1880. After her graduation from the Moscow Conservatory in 1898, she appeared throughout Europe until after World War I. In 1919, she and her renowned pianist husband, **Josef Lhévinne** (1874–1944), came to America, opening a music studio for private lessons, as well as teaching at Juilliard from 1922. Her famed students include Van Cliburn, Misha Dichter, Garrick Ohlsson and Hiroko Nakamura. She died in Glendale, California, November 9, 1976, at ninety-six.

Olga Samaroff

OLGA SAMAROFF, born in San Antonio, Texas, August 8, 1882, started life with the name of Lucie Mary Olga Agnes Hickenlooper. Her manager, Henry Wolfsohn, suggested the more classy foreign sounding *nom d'artiste*. After studying with her mother and grandmother, herself a former concert pianist, at age twelve Olga was taken to Europe by her grandmother and became the first American girl admitted to the Paris Conservatory where she studied with Elie Delaborde. In 1900, she returned to the U.S. to study with Ernest Hutcheson, then went back to Europe to finish her studies with Ernst Jedliczka in Berlin. Her concert debut was in 1905 with the New York Symphony Society. She then appeared with orchestras in Europe and America, and gave joint recitals with **Fritz Kreisler**, **Efrem Zimbalist** and other famous violinists. She was married to conductor **Leopold Stokowski**, 1911–1923, with whom she had a daughter, Sonya. An injury to her arm compelled her to leave the concert stage, after which she became a music critic for the *New York Evening Post* (1927–29). She joined the faculties of both Juilliard and the Philadelphia Conservatory (1924–48), traveling between New York and Philadelphia, until her death. Her best known students were Eugene List, Alexis Weissenberg, William Kapell, **Rosalyn Tureck** and **Claudette Sorel**.

As a lecturer, she appeared at Yale, Harvard, Columbia, and major universities. Realizing the need of a music course for listeners, she wrote *The Layman's Music Book* (1935; revised 1947 as *The Listener's Music Book*). Her autobiography, *An American Musician's Story*, was published in 1939.

Olga died in her New York apartment after a brief illness, May 17, 1948.

Ethel Leginska

ETHEL LEGINSKA, was born into a poor family, April 13, 1886, in Hull, in the north of England, as Ethel Liggins. Showing a natural talent for music at an early age, she debuted at age six. Sponsored by a Hull shipping magnate, she studied piano at the Hoch Conservatory in Frankfurt (1896), then for three years with the great Polish virtuoso **Theodor Leschetizsky** (1830–1915), who taught her without charge. She changed her last name to the more important-sounding Leginska under the illusion that a Polish name would help her artistic career. At sixteen, she made her piano debut in London under **Sir Henry Wood** (1869–1944), after which she concertized on the Continent before coming to America in 1912, appearing annually in recitals in New York's Aeolian and Carnegie Halls until 1919. Her demanding programs and innovations, such as playing an entire Chopin program without intermission, drew raves from critics. She was called "the Paderewski of women pianists" after the great Polish statesman/pianist Jan Ignatz Paderewski (1860–1941).

In 1907, she married American composer Emerson Whithorne (1884–1958), who lived in London between 1907–15. He acted as her impresario in Germany until 1909. In their much publicized 1916 divorce, she lost custody of their six-year-old son.

In the summer of 1918, she studied with **Ernest Bloch** (1880–1959) and began to compose, writing three operas, songs, symphonic poems, piano, chamber music and a fantasy for piano and orchestra. In 1920, she won a prize in the Berkshire Chamber Music Festival Competition for *Four Poems for String Quartet After Tagore*. Most of her compositions were performed, including *Beyond the Fields We Know* (1922), *Six Nursery Rhymes* (1923), *Two Short Pieces for Orchestra* (1924)—first performed by Pierre Monteux and the Boston Symphony—and *Quatre sujets barbares* (1924). According to her biographer, Carol Neuls-Bates: "It is to her credit that Leginska was able to secure performances of her larger works at a time when women's compositions were rarely heard in public." In the midst of her career as a pianist, she developed an interest in conducting. (See Conductors.)

IRENE SCHARRER was born in London, February 2, 1888. She studied at the RAM with **Tobias Matthay** (1858–1945), known for his psychological and physiological approach to piano playing, and made her academy debut in 1904, after which she toured throughout England and Europe. She debuted in the U.S. in 1925, appearing as soloist, recitalist and chamber music artist. She also gave duo-piano recitals with her cousin, **Dame Myra Hess**, who was her partner at her farewell performance in London in 1958. She died there January 11, 1971.

Dame MYRA HESS, one of England's greatest pianists, was born in London, February 25, 1890. She studied at the RAM with Tobias Matthay and made her concert debut in London in 1907, performing Beethoven's G major concerto. Her outstanding career covered tours throughout Europe and America, with her U.S. debut in 1922. In 1939, she organized the National Gallery Concerts and courageously continued performing in them throughout World War II, even during the "Blitz" of 1940–41, when London was deluged with German air raids raining down incendiary bombs and destruction night after night. For her dedication and effort, Hess was made a Dame Commander of the Order of the British Empire (OBE) by King George VI in 1941.

In her earlier years, she cultivated an intimate chamber music technique. The later, more powerful style was heard in her performances of the concertos of Beethoven and Brahms, part of her huge repertoire. Her arrangement of the Bach chorale, *Jesu, Joy of Man's Desiring*, remains the definitive version for piano. Dame Myra died in London, much honored, November 25, 1965.

MAGDA TAGLIAFERRO was born in Petropolis, Brazil, January 19, 1893. After studying at the São Paulo Conservatory, she went to Paris where she graduated from the Conservatoire with a first prize in 1907. In 1929, she gave the premiere of *Momoprecoce* by Brazil's most famous composer, **Heitor Villa-Lobos** (1887–1959). Also a pedagogue, she taught at the Paris Conservatory, 1937–39. During World War II she was active in America, returning to France in 1949. Her international concert career spanned seventy-five years. Her last recital on this side of the Atlantic was in 1980. She played a concert in London three years later at the age of ninety. She died September 9, 1983 in Rio de Janeiro (Brazil).

CLARA HASKIL, one of Hungary's most renowned woman pianists, was born in Budapest, January 7, 1895. At age six, the Queen of Romania provided a scholarship to study in Vienna where the child gave her first recital at age eight. She entered the Paris Conservatory, studying with the great **Alfred Cortot** (1877–1962) and **Ferruccio Busoni**, graduating with the Premier Prix at age fourteen. A concert tour of Europe was interrupted in 1913 by an onset of scoliosis (lateral curvature of the spine). She did not resume concerts until 1918. During the 1940s and '50s she made her reputation as a brilliant Mozart interpreter, giving recitals and appearing as a soloist with orchestras all over Europe and America. Even though her physical problems impeded her career, she continued playing concerts during periods of remission of her ailment. Critics praised her interpretations of Classical and early Romantic works. After World War II, she settled in Switzerland. Her friend and neighbor in Switzerland, Charlie Chaplin, assessed her gift as intuitive, pure and poetic, feeling she was someone of true genius. She died in Brussels on December 7, 1960. A stirring eulogy for her by Cortot can be heard in French via the Internet.

The remarkable Brazilian pianist **GUIOMAR NOVÃES** was born in São João da Bôa Vista, February 28, 1895, the seventeenth of nineteen children. Her family moved to the capital, São Paulo, and at seven she started piano with Luigi Chiaffarelli, a pupil of the great Italian Ferruccio Busoni, who was responsible for the child's superb tone, a combination of flowing legato, dynamic left hand technique and ethereal sound of the sustained pedal. At thirteen, the gifted prodigy was called to the attention of the government and received a grant for four years of study in Europe. In Paris, she took first place among 389 candidates who auditioned to enter the Conservatoire. The jury included Debussy, Fauré and Moritz Moszkowski (1854–1925). She studied with Isidor Philipp (1863–1958), and on graduating in 1911 won the Conservatoire's first prize. Already known for her inner concentration, her teacher called her "a force of nature." Her official debut was with the Châtelet Orchestra under Gabriel Pierné (1863–1937). She then toured England, Italy, Switzerland and Germany.

The outbreak of World War I, August 1914, interrupted her European career, sending her back to Brazil. An invitation to America in 1915 saw her debut at Aeolian Hall, New York, after which she made frequent American tours for the next fifty-seven years. Critic James Huneker, referring to the great Polish statesman/pianist Jan Paderewski, called her "the Padereska of the Pampas."

Meanwhile, in Brazil in 1922, Guiomar married one of her greatest admirers, architect Octavio Pinto. They had two children, Ana Maria and Luiz Octavio. Pinto, was also a composer, whose piano suite *Scenas Infantis* (Scenes of Childhood) was published by G. Schirmer and recorded by his wife. She often played it as an encore in her recitals. In 1956, Novães received the Award of Merit from the Brazilian Government for being a Goodwill Ambassador to the United States. In 1967, she was invited by Elizabeth II to play at the opening of London's Queen Elizabeth Hall, April 30. Her last American recital was at Hunter College in 1972. Known for her interpretations of Beethoven, Schumann, Chopin and others of the Romantic era, she also introduced Brazilian composers to North America, especially Villa-Lobos. After a consistently successful career, Guiomar Novães died at her home in São Paulo, March 7, 1979.

HARRIET COHEN was born in London, December 2, 1895. She studied piano with her parents, then with Tobias Matthay (1858–1945), making her first public appearance as a soloist at age thirteen. She became a professor at Matthay's school in 1922, and represented England at the Salzburg Music Festivals for several years. She had a highly successful career as an orchestral soloist and chamber musician, with concert tours in the U.S., England and Europe, specializing in Bach and early keyboard music, as well as contemporary repertoire. In 1934 she accompanied Albert Einstein, who played violin at a benefit concert for German scientists seeking refuge from Nazi Germany. In 1938, she was made a Commander of the Order of the British Empire (CBE), also receiving honors from France, Italy, Spain, Belgium, Czechoslovakia, Finland and Brazil. She performed for British and

American soldiers during WWII, despite being hospitalized three times from injuries received in the incessant London air raids of 1941, known as The Blitz.

Among English composers who wrote specific works for her were Ralph Vaughan Williams and Sir Arnold Bax, who loved her and wrote most of his piano works for her. In 1948, she fell while carrying a tray of glasses, cutting the artery and nerves in her right hand. Despite her doctor's fears she would never play again, after two years of determined practice she played Bax's concerto for the left hand. Two more years, and she was able to return to the concert stage until 1960, when eye trouble, aggravated by practicing eight hours a day, forced her to retire. She never married, saying "My constant traveling would have been unfair to any husband."

She wrote a book on piano technique, *Music's Handmaid* (1936, second edition, 1950). Her memoirs, *A Bundle of Time* (1969), were published after her death in London, November 13, 1967.

Russian-American pianist and teacher **ANIA DORFMANN** was born in Odessa July 9, 1899. As a child in Russia, she performed with prodigy violinist **Jascha Heifetz** (1901–87) in duo recitals, then was accepted at age twelve at the Paris Conservatory where she studied with Isidor Philipp. She returned to Russia before the Revolution, but left in 1920 to concertize in Europe. She emigrated to the U.S. in 1936, giving her first American recital in New York on November 27 of that year. Among other prominent venues, she appeared as soloist with **Toscanini** and the NBC Symphony December 2, 1939. In later years she devoted herself to teaching and was on the faculty at Juilliard. She died in New York, April 22, 1984.

MARIA YUDINA, born near Vitebsk, September 9, 1899, enjoyed a very long concert career (1921–1969). She was educated at the Petrograd (St. Petersburg) Conservatory, and joined the piano faculty there (1921–30). From 1932–34 she was at Tiflis Conservatory, then 1936–51 at the Moscow Conservatory, where she also taught singing. Her last position was the Gnessin Institute (1944–60). An ardent champion of modern music, her programs included compositions of Prokofiev, Shostakovich and Stravinsky (with whom she maintained regular correspondence), as well as Schoenburg, Berg, Webern and Bartók, these at a time when their works were not acceptable in Russia.

Born Jewish, she converted to Christianity and wore a big cross over her dress. (A daring challenge in the Communist USSR!) A legend exists about Yudina, heard on a British documentary about musical life in the USSR, that in the latter 1940s she played a Mozart Piano Concerto on a late night radio broadcast. It so happened that chronic insomniac Josef Stalin listened to the broadcast and liked the performance. A few moments after the concert ended, a phone rang on the desk of the director of the radio station.

"Was the performance recorded?" asked the recognizable heavily Georgian-accented voice.

"Y-yes , Comrade Stalin," mumbled the director.

"Very good. Send me the disc in the morning."

The concert was, in fact, *not* recorded, so KGB cars were sent to pick up the musicians, conductor and Yudina. They recorded all night, and in the morning a single record was printed and sent to Stalin. It was accompanied by a note from Yudina: "I am glad that you liked my concert. The fact that you love music proves there is something human about you after all. I will pray for the salvation of your black soul."

In the atmosphere of suffocating fear that reigned in Stalinist Russia, it is remarkable that someone would even dare write such a letter. Even more amazing is the fact that nothing actually happened to Yudina as a result of such impertinence. The legend is perpetuated with the belief that the night Stalin died, March 5, 1953,[145] he was listening to this recording.

Yudina left her piano forever in Moscow, November 19, 1970.

LILI KRAUS was born in Budapest, March 4, 1903, to stonegrinder Victor Kraus and Irene Back Kraus, an excellent amateur singer from whom she inherited her musical gifts. After early training, at seventeen Lili was

---

145. It is interesting to note that, in order not to take away from the panoply of the Iron Dictator's demise, the news that foremost composer Sergei Prokofiev had died on the same date was kept from the public for several days!

accepted as a student by Hungary's two major contemporary composers, **Béla Bartók** (1881–1946) and **Zoltán Kodály** (1882–1967), at the Budapest Academy of Music. She went to the Vienna Conservatory and also took master classes in Berlin with the great **Artur Schnabel** (1882–1951). In a flourishing career, she concertized throughout Europe, South Africa, Australia and Japan. Besides being lauded for her Chopin and Mozart interpretations, she gained fame as a "true Beethovenian" in duo recitals with violinist **Szymon Goldberg**. In the late 1930s, Lili and her Jewish husband, philosopher Otto Mandl, famous for translating H.G. Wells into German, and their two children, moved to London. She became a British subject in 1948.

Precious Fingers in Filthy Sewers!

Meanwhile, in 1942 during the height of World War II, Kraus foolhardily undertook a Dutch East Indies tour, was captured by the Japanese, and interned for three years in a forced labor camp on the island of Java. Although one of the overseers—a Japanese conductor with whom she had performed in Tokyo—attempted to ease her lot, she still had to dip her precious fingers into foul gutters to unclog drains. Other women in the camp gladly offered to do the heavy labor to protect her hands. Despite this, she emerged from the ordeal with a loss of sensitivity in her fingers. A devout Catholic, she felt enriched by the experience, saying that she played music in her mind and learned that what counts is what one has within. After the war, as her fingers recovered, she resumed her career, appearing at leading music centers.

A New Country

During the 1966–67 season, Kraus decided to remain in the U.S. and lived on a 400-acre farm in North Carolina which she co-owned with Dr. Fergus Pope, the pediatrician husband of her daughter Ruth, with their three children, Zazi, Daniel and Vassi. Lili's son, Michael, a psychiatrist, had four children.

From 1967–83, Kraus was artist-in-residence at Texas Christian University, made recordings, toured, appeared on television and taught master classes. A victim of rheumatoid arthritis, her final concert was in 1982 at Swarthmore College. She died in Asheville, North Carolina, November 6, 1986, of complications from intestinal surgery. Of her many honors, the most outstanding came in 1978 with the awarding of the prestigious Austrian Cross of Honor for Science and Art.

The Russian Refugee

The renowned **NADIA REISENBERG** was born in Vilnius (Lithuania), then a part of Russia, July 14, 1904, to Aaron and Rachel Reisenberg. Her sister Anna (Newta) was born two years later, and Clara[146] in 1911. The three sisters were extremely close throughout their lives. When Nadia was six, a kind uncle sent the family a piano and the child immediately knew she would be at the keyboard for the rest of her life. Her talent demanded that the family move to St. Petersburg for study at the conservatory, where the director, famed Russian composer **Alexander Glazunov** (1868–1936), took a special interest in the gifted girl. By 1918, the aftermath of the Revolution, plus the hunger and danger from the lawless new regime, drove the family out of the country—first to relatives in Vilna (Poland). There she played her first orchestral concert in 1921 with the Warsaw Philharmonic under a young **Artur Rodzinski** (1892–1958) making his conducting debut. (Twenty-four years later they again performed together, this time in Aeolian Hall with the Philharmonic Symphony Orchestra of New York.) Clara also played many recitals with her sister to earn money.

Nadia Reisenberg

---

146. Clara Rockmore found fame mastering the *Theremin*, the world's first electronic instrument. She played a Theremin recital with Nadia at the piano in New York's Town Hall, February 1945. (See Unique Instruments.)

Flight to Freedom

The Reisenbergs continued traveling through Europe wherever they could get visas, often crossing borders illegally. By 1922 they were able to get visas to America, and after a long, terrible voyage in steerage with everyone seasick, landed at Ellis Island where a friend of a friend, Russian banker Isaac J. (Sasha) Sherman, eased their entry through Customs. He also arranged private concerts for Nadia in the homes of the wealthy at the then princely fee of $100. Meanwhile, she began studying with Alexander Lambert and **Josef Hofmann** (1876–1957), and made her debut, December 1922, in Carnegie Hall with the City Symphony, playing Paderewski's *Polish Fantasie* with the composer present and very pleased with the interpretation. From there her career took off. In 1924, she performed with the New York Symphony under **Walter Damrosch**, sharing the program with the great French harpist, **Marcel Grandjany**. She also played under **Serge Koussevitzky** and other maestros, often specializing in Russian concertos that had not been heard in the West, such as that of Rimsky-Korsakov. She made many tours of Europe and Russia before World War II.

Career and Family

On June 24, 1924, Nadia married Sasha Sherman. It was an ideal match. He was a completely supportive husband, respecting her career and assisting her with the business end. Their son, Alexander, was born in 1925, and Robert, who became a well-known broadcaster, critic, lecturer, commentator and author, arrived in 1932. The boys were brought up with an understanding of their mother's stature, and appreciated the time she managed to spend with them.

In 1940, Reisenberg embarked upon the *tour-de-force* of playing all of Mozart's Piano Concertos in sequence on twenty-nine weekly broadcasts on New York station WOR.[147] In the words of conductor **Alfred Wallenstein** (1898–1983), "Some of my happiest moments were the broadcasts with Nadia Reisenberg . . . [they] were live, without commercials, and splendid musicians were playing great music for millions of people." (Whatever happened to exposing the public to culture?)

The pianist loved playing chamber music, and frequently performed with cellist **Joseph Schuster**, violinist **Erick Friedman** (*b* 1939), clarinetist **Benny Goodman** (1909–86) and the celebrated Budapest String Quartet. Later, her fans multiplied through her performances on weekly radio broadcasts on WQXR (NY), hosted by her son, Robert Sherman. In 1950, Alex married a girl named Ruth. In 1956, Bob married another girl named Ruth. The same year Alex and his Ruth gave Nadia her first grandchild, David, born November 28. In August 1955, Sasha died suddenly, leaving Nadia devastated. She bravely continued fulfilling her engagements, eventually assuaging her grief with her music. In 1959, Bob and *his* Ruth presented her with another grandson, Steve, who became a photographer of classical artists and married cellist **Dorothy Lawson**. In 1964, his brother Peter was born. (Bob was divorced in 1978, and is now married to Veronica Bravo.)

Meanwhile, Nadia's recordings were receiving great reviews. By the 1950s she had given up most of her touring, and was focusing more on chamber recitals and teaching, saying: "I have never felt in any way that teaching is somehow a substitute for something I no longer do. I find it exciting, gratifying and rewarding, and it's always been that way." After three years on the faculty of Curtis she returned to New York, and from 1955 was a professor at the Mannes School of Music. She also taught at Juilliard and had private pupils. In 1960, she slipped into Israel to visit her sister Newta, who had lived there fifteen years while her husband, Meir Sherman, a nephew of Sasha, was minister of economics. Word got around, and master classes at the Rubin Academy in Jerusalem and recitals were quickly arranged to benefit from Nadia's presence. The acclaim was so great that she visited Israel every other year for the next twenty years, devoting twenty-five hours a week for six weeks teaching before some

---

147. In 2006, Robert was working on a CD, through the University of Maryland, of Nadia's historic feat. [Saint-Saëns (1835–1921) accomplished this Mozart marathon in Europe.]

150 spectators eager to hear both the students—who were often teachers themselves—and the maestra. Her last visit to Israel was in 1981, accompanied by son Bob who also taught a class. 1961 saw her return on stage in recital with violinist **William Kroll** (1901–80) in London's Wigmore Hall, as well as performances in Amsterdam and Germany. She again played with Kroll in New York in 1968. In June 1974, she received the first Tarbut (Culture) Medal from the America-Israel Cultural Foundation, presented to her at the Juilliard Theater in Lincoln Center.

Reisenberg celebrated her seventy-fifth birthday playing a recital at the Caramoor Festival in Katonah, New York. In 1979, she performed at Mannes and with violinist Erick Friedman in Carnegie Hall, still to critical raves. In 1980, she played with the Juilliard String Quartet at the Library of Congress, leading reviewer Joan Reinthaler to comment: "The years have in no way diminished her art. She plays with the same consummate musicianship that made her famous. Her fingers seem every bit as nimble, and her enormous experience shines through everything she does."

The great artist's last concert was October 3, 1981, at Carnegie Recital Hall. She passed away peacefully at her home, June 10, 1983, a Liszt Etude open on the piano. Charles Kaufman, then president of Mannes, phrased a fitting eulogy: "Hers was one of our century's richest and most giving lives in music."

In 2004, son Robert Sherman inaugurated the biennial Nadia Reisenberg Award Competition at Mannes—the prize a recital at Merkin Hall. The same year Bridge Records reissued her two piano Mozart Concerto rendition with Artur Balsam, and Ivory Classics brought out a 100th Anniversary Tribute.

Johanna Margarete **GRETE SULTAN** was born June 21, 1906, in Berlin. Her musical family included two aunts who had studied with **Clara Schumann**. The famed of the music world, composer **Richard Strauss**, and pianists **Artur Schnabel** and **Ferruccio Busoni** were regular visitors to her home. So was American pianist Richard Buhlig, who introduced her to **Henry Cowell** and the music of other contemporary composers.

She studied piano at the Hochschule für Musik in Berlin with Leonid Kreutzer, but her mentor was pianist/conductor **Edwin Fischer**, teacher of world class pianists **Alfred Brendel**, **Paul Badura-Skoda**, and **Daniel Barenboim**, to whom she gave private lessons after her graduation. Her concert career was curtailed by Hitler's rise to power, after which Jewish pianists could no longer play German music. In 1941, Buhlig helped Grete escape to America, where she arrived with one suitcase and the clothes on her back. Her mother joined her after WWII, in 1946.

Sultan began teaching at Vassar College and New York's 92nd Street Y, before taking a post in 1952 at the Masters' School in Dobbs Ferry on the Hudson River north of the city. She returned to New York in 1971 to teach privately. Buhlig introduced her to his former student **John Cage** (1912–92), to whom she became a mentor. Her roster also included composer **Lucia Dlugoszewski**, who moved to New York in 1948 to study Bach with her, which is how the nineteen-year-old met the love of her life, dancer/choreographer Erick Hawkins, whose studio was next door to Grete's.

Known for her interpretation of Bach's *Goldberg Variations*, before Glenn Gould's 1955 recording made the piece familiar, Sultan was also a proponent of the avant-garde, and performed in concerts throughout her life playing Schoenberg, Stravinsky and contemporary composers Earle Brown, Stefan Wolpe, Alan Hovhaness, Ben Weber, Jacob Feldman, Cage and Christoph Wolff. In 1996, shortly after her ninetieth birthday, she played the Goldberg Variations at Carnegie's Merkin Hall. The same year brought the release of the first of two retrospective CD sets that preserve the greatness of her performances and repertory.

After a week's illness, she died at St. Vincent's Hospital, in New York, June 25, 2005, exactly ninety-nine.

EILEEN JOYCE was born in Zeehan, Tasmania, November 21, 1912. She studied at the Leipzig Conservatory, and attended the master classes of famed pianist **Artur Schnabel**. She settled in London, and gained a reputation for playing with technical precision and clarity. Her success assured, for a time she restricted her repertory to popular works. She also developed theories that associated colors with composers, which led her to vary the color of her clothes according to the music she was playing. Her many recordings included the concertos of John Ireland and **Dmitri Shostakovich**. Equally skilled as a harpsichordist, she regularly took part with George Malcolm,

Thurston Dart and Denis Vaughn in concertos for three and four harpsichords. Her efforts in saving the London Philharmonic during World War II were rewarded with an honorary doctorate in 1971. Joyce appeared in several films. One of them, *Wherever She Goes*, told her own life story. Some of her recordings have been reissued on CD. She is also included on *Historic Interpretations of Grieg*, a CD which features some of the greatest, late (or early) pianists of all time: Edvard Grieg himself, Percy Grainger, Walter Gieseking, Wilhelm Bachaus, Josef Hofmann, Sergei Rachmaninoff and **Olga Samaroff**. Joyce died in Kent (England) March 25, 1991.

GINA BACHAUER was born of an Austrian father and an Italian mother in Athens (Greece), May 21, 1913. At eleven she entered the Athens Conservatory. In 1929, she went to Paris to study with **Alfred Cortot** at the École Normale de Musique. In 1933, she won the Medal of Honor at the International Contest for Pianists in Vienna. Between 1933–35, she studied occasionally with **Sergei Rachmaninoff**, and in 1935 debuted with the Athens Symphony Orchestra under the direction of **Dimitri Mitropoulos**. In 1937, she was a soloist in Paris under the direction of **Pierre Monteux**. During World War II she lived in Alexandria, Egypt, where she played many concerts for the Allied Forces in the Middle East. Her London debut was in 1946 under the direction of Alec Sherman, who became her second husband. Unknown in this country, her first concert in New York in 1950 was attended by only thirty-five people. The critics, however, raved (chauvinistically), "not since **Teresa Carreño** has there been a woman who played so like a man!" Her career was assured. A romantic with a virtuoso technique, her repertoire ranged from Mozart to Stravinsky. Her untimely death from a heart attack, August 22, 1976, came on the day she was to perform with the National Symphony at the Athens Festival in Washington, DC. Her devoted husband, Alec, saved all her personal effects and, on his passing in 1992, they were given to the Gina Bachauer Archive at Brigham Young University.

The Gina Bachauer International Piano Competition

One of the most prestigious contests for young artists—ages nineteen to thirty-two—in Salt Lake City, June has been designated "Gina Bachauer Piano Month" by decree of the governor. Auditions are held in cities throughout the world, and the finalists perform solo, in chamber groups and with orchestra in Symphony Hall. Selected by a jury of top international musicians, the winners receive generous cash awards, a grand piano and major concert engagements, including a New York recital. Founded in 1976 by Paul C. Pollei at BYU, the competition came under the sponsorship of the Utah Symphony in 1982, and has functioned as an independent arts organization in Salt Lake since 1986.

ROSALYN TURECK was internationally renowned as an interpreter of the music of Bach on the harpsichord, clavichord and piano. Born in Chicago, December 14, 1914, the granddaughter of a famous Kiev cantor, about whom her father told her of a carriage pulled by eight white horses, taking *his* father on tour for the high holy days. Her first public recital debut was in Chicago at age nine. At sixteen, she auditioned for Juilliard, surprising the panel by offering to play most of Bach's forty-eight preludes and fugues from memory. At ten, she met Leon Theremin. His electronic instrument made a huge impression on her. At Juilliard, she heard of a year-long scholarship available to a would-be student of the theremin. She auditioned and won the award. She would subsequently give a Carnegie Hall concert on the instrument, April 1932. (She continued championing electronic instruments by Robert Moog, who gave her one of his synthesizers, and Henry Beniof, with whom she worked for twenty years developing an electronic piano.) Harpsichord study was with Gavin Williamson, and piano with **Olga Samaroff**, graduating in 1935. She had experienced a strange episode in a Juilliard practice room. Working on a Bach fugue, she blacked out for a moment, coming to with a revelation that she needed to create a keyboard technique specific to the playing of Bach. For the rest of her life she never stopped perfecting this concept.

Her New York recital debut was in 1935. The same year, she gave her first all-Bach series. She would give annual all-Bach series in New York (1944–54, 1959 to the 1980s), London (from 1953), Copenhagen (from 1956) and Pasadena (California, 1960s–70s). Her first European tour came in 1947 after WWII. At twenty-two, she made her orchestral debut in New York with the Philadelphia Orchestra, under Eugene Ormandy at Carnegie Hall, playing Brahms' Second Piano Concerto—a large undertaking for small hands.

Her career included tours of South Africa, Israel and South America, garnering honors like the Officer's Cross of the Order of Merit from the German Federal Republic (1979) for her work on Bach, and five honorary doctorates—one of only four American women to receive a music PhD from Oxford. As a conductor, in 1958 Tureck directed the New York Philharmonic, leading Bach's keyboard concertos from the piano. She also formed her own orchestra, the Tureck Bach Players, active in Britain and America. To show the flexibility of Bach's keyboard technique, she played his music on the Moog Synthesizer in a 1971 concert, "Bach and Rock." Her *An Introduction to the Performance of Bach* (3 vols.) was published in London (1959), Japanese (1966) and Spanish (1972). Some of her 1940s performances were rereleased on VAI under the title *The Young Firebrand*.

In 1966 she founded the International Bach Institute, and in 1981 the Tureck Bach Institute, Inc. The Library for the Performing Arts at Lincoln Center permanently houses the Rosalyn Tureck Recorded Archives, which include lectures, recitals and events of her two societies, available for research. She lectured and taught at universities in England and America, including Oxford, Juilliard, Columbia, Philadelphia Conservatory and UC-San Diego (UCSD). Her continued involvement with contemporary music brought her, at eighty-five, to speak on Theremin at the Brussels 2000 Convention, in association with the Musée Instrumentale.

Rosalyn died at eighty-eight in New York, July 17, 2003.

Her immortal statement to premier harpsichordist **Wanda Landowska** will indeed live forever:

"You play it your way. I play it Bach's way!"

Moura Lympany

With a career spanning over six decades, **Dame MOURA LYMPANY**, born Mary Johnstone in Saltash, Cornwall (Southern England), August 18, 1916, was considered a legend in her own time. Her mother was her first piano teacher. Her father was an army officer during WWI. At six, already knowing French, she attended a convent school in Belgium, studied in Liège, then won a scholarship to the RAM. At age twelve, she debuted at Harrogate with conductor Basil Cameron (who would direct the San Francisco Symphony 1931–34), playing Mendelssohn's G minor Concerto. He considered her surname, Johnstone, too ordinary, and convinced Moura to use her mother's maiden name, Limpenny, with the more exotic spelling. At eighteen, the prodigy made her first appearance at London's famed Wigmore Hall. She studied with Paul Weingarten in Vienna, and in England with Mathilde Verne, who had taught the great British pianist, **Solomon** (Solomon Cutner), and had herself been a student of **Clara Schumann**. After Verne's death in 1936, Moura went to Tobias Matthay, teacher of **Harriet Cohen**, (Dame) **Myra Hess** and her cousin **Irene Scharrer**.

In 1938, Lympany took second place at the Brussels' Ysaÿe Competition, the winner that year, Emil Gilels (1916–85). One of the adjudicators was Arthur Rubinstein, who was so impressed by her, he induced his Parisian manager to take on the young artist. She then toured Italy, France, Holland, Belgium and South America, followed by performances in England at the Cambridge Theatre and National Gallery Concerts—founded by Myra Hess. Her repertoire included Brahms' Second and Rachmaninoff's Third concertos, which laid the foundation for an international career. In 1940, she gave the British premiere of Khachaturian's Concerto at the Queen's Hall, one of the pieces which became most closely associated with her, causing critics to say her performance was " . . . as agreeable to concertgoers in wartime London as a friendly firework in the black-out." First offered to Clifford Curzon (1907–82), he was too busy and recommended her saying, "Moura Lympany learns so quickly." She was given the concerto in manuscript form and learned it in one month. She was paid fifteen guineas[148a] for her performance. A

---

later highlight was playing the Khachaturian *Concerto-Rhapsody*, conducted by the composer, at the Royal Albert Hall (1955). She played in England during WWII, in the course of which she met and married Lt. Col. Colin DeFries. After the war, she collaborated with foremost maestro Sir Adrian Boult for concerts in Paris (1945), the first British artists to perform there after the liberation, and in 1946 appeared at the Prague Spring Festival, again with Sir Adrian. 1948 saw her American debut, where she met Bennet Korn, a radio-advertising executive. Already separated from DeFries, she divorced him and married Korn, moving to New York City. Two miscarriages and a son who died shortly after birth, plus the demands of her musical career, led to another divorce in 1961.

The first pianist to record the complete Rachmaninoff Preludes, Lympany also interpreted the works of Prokofiev and Saint-Saëns to equal acclaim. Over sixty appearances at London's Promenade Concerts, amongst a multitude of performances in Europe, America, Canada, Australia, New Zealand and India, led to a CBE in the January 1979 New Year's Honours List. In 1989, she celebrated her sixtieth jubilee with an all-Chopin recital at the Royal Festival Hall. In 1992, she was made a Dame Commander of the British Empire by Queen Elizabeth II, and received the medal of the Chevalier des Arts et Lettres from the French government. On August 17, 1995, Lympany was presented with Portugal's highest honor, the Medal and Cross of Prince Henry the Navigator. Meanwhile, during 1993, at age seventy-seven, besides the Proms, she gave recitals at the Royal Festival Hall, stepping in for **Tatyana Nikolayeva** who died while on tour in San Francisco.

Since 1982, Dame Moura lived in Monte Carlo and France, where she died on March 28, 2005. Her unique artistry lives on forever in recordings, especially the 1999 remastered *Dame Moura Lympany Tribute to a Legend* with Sir Malcolm Sargent from 1964 and 1967 on Ivory Classics.

Marian McPartland

MARIAN (Turner) **McPARTLAND** was born March 20, 1918, in Windsor, England. She started on violin, then at seventeen, studied classical music and piano at the Guildhall School of Music in London, but left three years later to pursue a career in jazz. During World War II, she joined ENSA, the British equivalent of the USO, and later, the USO, performing for the soldiers. In Belgium, she collaborated with cornetist Jimmy McPartland, later marrying him in Aachen, Germany. In 1946, she arrived in America with her husband, playing with his quintet in Chicago. She formed her own trio in 1950, making her debut at the Embers Club in New York. In 1952, a two-week engagement at New York's Hickory House turned into a long-running commitment for the Marian McPartland Trio, culminating in several recordings, including *Marian McPartland at the Hickory House*. This led to the establishment, in 1970, of *Halcyon*, Marian's own record company, thriving over the decades with over two dozen recordings. Besides her skill as a pianist, McPartland is a gifted composer. "In the Days of Our Love" was recorded by Peggy Lee and "Twilight World" by Tony Bennett. Her composition, *Ambiance*, was nominated for a Grammy, and her music for two educational film projects won awards at the Chicago Film Festival. She started a public radio show "Marian McPartland's Piano Jazz" to showcase jazz musicians, including Bobby Short, Mel Tormé, Herbie Hancock, Dizzy Gillespie, Dudley Moore, Wynton Marsalis, Tony Bennett and André Previn. Her book, *All in Good Time*, is a collection of priceless memories. Her television appearances and performances in the U.S. and Europe have been recognized with the Peabody Award, she received the Duke Ellington Fellowship Medal from Yale and honorary doctorates from Ithaca, Union and Bates Colleges.

Still going strong into the 21st century, the McPartland Trio was heard at UC Santa Barbara, May 2001. "Live at Shanghai Jazz" (Concord CD) was released in August 2002. I last spoke with this vibrant lady January 12, 2007.

HEPHZIBAH MENUHIN was born in San Francisco, May 20, 1920, making her debut there in 1928. She lived in France, Switzerland and Italy for eight years, studying under Marcel Ciampi and Rudolf Serkin. Although their father was against girls playing in public—younger sister Yaltah was a promising cellist—

Hephzibah started playing sonatas October 1934 with violinist brother Yehudi[148b] in Paris. In 1938 she married Lindsay Nicholas, an Australian sheep farmer from Victoria, settling there for nineteen years. They had a son, Kron. After the second World War, after giving a concert in Prague, Hephzibah visited the notorious Theresienstadt (Terezin) concentration camp. This affected her so deeply, she vowed that she could no longer lead a privileged life. Her marriage having disintegrated, she fell in love with Viennese sociologist, Richard Hauser. They settled in London in 1957 and set up The Centre for Human Rights and Responsibilities.

As a musician, Hephzibah had a wide repertoire, but Mozart was her favorite. Her recordings include Schubert's "Trout" Quintet with members of the Amadeus Quartet, Mozart concertos with her brother conducting, and trios with Yehudi and Maurice Gendron —a collaboration that lasted twenty-five years.

After her untimely death at sixty-one, from cancer, in London on New Year's Day, 1981, the Hephzibah Menuhin Memorial Scholarship Fund for young pianists was established in conjunction with the New South Wales (Australia) State Conservatorium of Music. A tribute documentary, "Hephzibah Menuhin," directed by Curtis Levy, was broadcast on Radio National later in 1981.

Marutha Mnuhin, as the original name was spelled, mother of Yehudi, Hephzibah and Yaltah, died November 15, 1996, after a short illness in Los Gatos, South of San Francisco, at 104. Lionel Rolfe, son of Yaltah, recalls his grandmother as "a very, very strong-willed woman."

CONSTANCE KEENE, pianist and master teacher, was born in Brooklyn, February 9, 1921. At thirteen she began studies with pianist/composer/writer **Abram Chasins** (1903–87), with whom she played as a duo, and married in 1949. During WWII, she toured with the USO. At one Army camp, she played eight concerts in three days for 65,000 soldiers!

She taught at Mannes, but was a major force on the faculty of the Manhattan School of Music since 1969—she joined their board of trustees in 1997—as well as conducting master classes in Europe, Asia and South Africa. Her pupils included Peter Nero and **Anne-Marie McDermott**. Besides acclaimed recitals, she performed with the New York Philharmonic, Philadelphia Orchestra and others, and toured with Benny Goodman as soloist in Gershwin's *Rhapsody in Blue.* Career highlights include Keene being the only woman ever to have substituted for the great **Vladimir Horowitz** (1903–89), before an audience of 4,000, and her concert with **Yehudi Menuhin** at his Gstaad (Switzerland) Festival (1977). He invited her back in 1981 to play in the memorial tribute for his sister, Hephzibah (1920–1981), with whom he concertized before she married and went to live in Australia.

Winner of the 1943 Naumberg Prize, Constance served on juries of the Van Cliburn, Concert Artists Guild, YCA, National Guild of Piano Teachers, and Pretoria, South Africa, International competitions. Her recordings include Bach, Handel, MacDowell, Schumann, Beethoven, Rachmaninoff and Chasins. Of her 1964 rendition of the Rachmaninoff Preludes, the great pianist **Arthur Rubinstein** (1887–1982), whose children she had taught, wrote, "I cannot imagine anyone, including Rachmaninoff himself, playing [them] more beautifully." Her recordings of Mendelssohn won the Critics Choice Award, and of Bach, the Special Merit Award. The celebrated **Josef Hofmann** called her technique, "superb."

In 1995, at seventy-one, she was invited to celebrate the Tenth Singapore Arts Festival and the Tenth Annual Festival in Hong Kong, giving master classes and performances at the American School of the Arts. In September, the same year, she served on the jury of the Scottish International Competition in Glasgow. In October, she opened the series for the Chopin Foundation Council of Greater New York at the Consulate General of the Republic of Poland. During 2001, she gave master classes and a recital at Greenwich House Music School, and the University of Iowa in conjunction with their Piano Festival.

148b. Yehudi, born in New York April 22, 1916, had a sparkling prodigy career, continuing as a foremost global violinist into his seventies when he switched to conducting. Making his home in England—he once lived in the London apartment beneath our family—he received an honorary knighthood from Queen Elizabeth II in 1965, the year he founded the Yehudi Menuhin School of Music in Stoke d'Abernon, Surrey. In 1985 he became an honorary British subject making him formally Sir Yehudi, an honor he retained until 1993 when the Queen created him a Life Peer as Lord Menuhin of Stoke d'Abernon. He died in Berlin, March 12, 1999.

Keene has written for *Keyboard Classics*, contributed to the book *Remembering Horowitz*, and is featured in Benjamin Saver's[149] *The Most Wanted Piano Teachers in the U.S.A.*

Survived by her second husband, Milton Kean, Constance passed away December 24, 2005.

TATYANA NIKOLAYEVA was born in Russia, May 4, 1924. She progressed from the Moscow Central Music School to the Moscow Conservatory, where she also studied composition, graduating in 1950. The same year she won first prize at the Leipzig Bach Festival, astounding the judges by asking them which of the forty-eight preludes and fugues from the *Well-Tempered Clavier* they wanted her to play. Present was **Dimitri Shostakovich** who, inspired, consulted with her and wrote his twenty-four preludes for her. After a successful career in Russia, she performed in Western Europe and America. She was a teacher (1959–65) and professor (from 1965) at the Moscow Conservatory. Among her compositions are several symphonies, two piano concertos, a violin concerto, a piano sonata, a piano quintet and many other piano works. She died dramatically, suffering a brain hemorrhage during a recital in San Francisco, November 22, 1993.

Crossing the Color Bar

NATALIE HINDERAS was born June 15, 1927, in Oberlin, Ohio. Her father was a jazz musician and her mother, Leota Palmer, a piano teacher who taught many years at the Cleveland Institute of Music. Natalie was considered a child prodigy, giving her first full-length recital at age eight. By twelve, she had performed the Grieg Concerto with the Cleveland Women's Symphony. She graduated from Oberlin with a BM at eighteen, the youngest graduate of the Conservatory, and continued her studies at Juilliard with **Olga Samaroff**, who convinced her to change her name from Henderson—as Samaroff had changed *her* name from Lucie Hickenlooper to the more exotic Russian pseudonym. Hinderas made her New York debut in 1954, and from then on appeared with orchestras throughout the country—most prominently in the '70s and '80s. There were also tours of Europe, Asia and Africa, with the U.S. State Department twice selecting her to travel abroad as a cultural ambassador.

Her history-making was not just concertizing. When, in 1971, she gave the American premiere of Brazilian composer Alberto Ginastera's Piano Concerto with the Philadelphia Orchestra, Eugene Ormandy conducting, she was the first black female soloist ever to play in subscription concerts with the orchestra. When she appeared with the Los Angeles Philharmonic at the Hollywood Bowl in 1972, it was a personal triumph. Decades earlier, a business manager, reflecting the then accepted prejudice, told her, "You know, Natalie, a little colored girl like you can't play in the Hollywood Bowl!"

Hinderas was also an inspiring educator, teaching at Philadelphia's Temple University School of Music and at the Settlement Music School, where she guided minority students in pursuit of musical careers. She served on NEA panels and judged many national and international competitions. Through her records, she helped popularize the music of African-American composers such as George Walker, Nathaniel Dett, **William Grant Still**, and Stephen Chamber.

When, at age sixty, Natalie learned she had terminal cancer, her devout faith was embodied in her statement, "God must need another pianist in heaven!" She died in Elkins Park, Pennsylvania, July 22, 1987.

The Missing Star . . . Redeemed!

South Broad Street in Philadelphia, where it is bordered by the Academy of Music, the Shubert Theater and the University of the Arts, is referred to as the "Avenue of the Stars." Here, embedded in the sidewalk, are over two dozen plaques honoring the city's most renowned performing artists. This *Walk of Fame*, to give it its real name, was dedicated in 1986. Each year new names from the classical and popular music world are added. It took until 1995—eight years after her death—for the name of Natalie Hinderas to be placed among the stars of her native city of "brotherly love."

---

149. Saver is founder/president of the annual World Pedagogy Conference.

Other Black Ladies of the Keyboard

Natalie was not the first black classical pianist. That distinction belongs to **HAZEL HARRISON**, born May 12, 1883, in La Porte, Indiana, who held the undisputed title "premiere black pianist" male or female, for almost four decades. In the tradition of most American musicians of the era, she went to Europe to study in her early twenties. There was also less discrimination and more opportunity on the Continent. For several years she studied with Ferruccio Busoni in Berlin, gave recitals, and appeared with the Berlin Philharmonic. Returning to the U.S., she performed in Chicago and was so popular that two women sponsored her return to Europe for more studies. She spent 1911–14 again with Busoni, this time launching a full-time career in Europe and the U.S. until 1931, when she began her teaching career as head of the piano department at the Tuskegee Institute in Alabama. In 1936, she transferred to Howard University in Washington, DC, where she taught until her retirement in 1955. (Both are all black institutions.) She balanced teaching with concertizing with orchestra, and in solo recitals throughout America. In 1958, she was lured out of retirement into joining the faculty of Alabama State A&M College and later, Jackson College. Harrison died April 29, 1969, in Washington, DC. A biography, *Born to Play: The Life and Career of Hazel Harrison*, by Jean E. Cazort and Constance T. Hobson, was brought out in 1983 by Greenwood Press.

Other black women classical concert pianists include **Jessie** (Ernestine) **Covington Dent** and Margaret Bonds. Dent was born May 19, 1904, in Houston, and studied with **James Friskin** and **Olga Samaroff** at Juilliard (1924–28). She toured nationally after graduation, and was then appointed to head the piano department at Bishop College in Dallas (1929–1931). After 1931, she lived in New Orleans where her husband, Albert W. Dent, was president of Dillard University (1941–69). She continued to teach privately and performed occasionally. Jessie died at age ninety-seven in New Orleans, March 10, 2001.

Margaret Bonds (1913–1972) studied piano and composition at Northwestern University and Juilliard. She was well-known as a pianist, composer and teacher in Chicago, New York and Los Angeles. (See Black Composers.)

Another black pianist, most worthy of recognition, was **Philippa Schuyler**. Only four years younger than Natalie Hinderas, she was born August 2, 1931, in New York. Also a child prodigy, she began performing in public at age four and winning numerous prizes while still young. In 1946, she made her debut performing the Saint-Saëns *Piano Concerto in G minor* with the New York Philharmonic. She toured worldwide, giving solo recitals and appearing with leading orchestras in Europe, South America, East Asia and Africa. Also a skilled composer, she wrote several large works as well as smaller compositions. Her manuscripts are in the Schaumberg Center for Research in Black Culture in New York. As an author, she published five books between 1960–62 related to her travels. Tragically, Schuyler died in a helicopter accident May 9, 1967, in Vietnam, where she was evacuating children from an orphanage. Three weeks before her death, she gave a concert on South Vietnamese television. She was working on a book about Vietnam. This was published posthumously as *Good Men Die*.

Lillian Kallir

LILLIAN KALLIR was born in Prague, May 6, 1931. Her family fled the Nazis to Switzerland, and arrived in America in 1940, where she studied with Isabelle Vengerova (1877–1956) at the Mannes College of Music. At sixteen she won the National Music League Award and the American Artists Award of the Brooklyn Institute of Arts and Sciences. Her solo debut with the New York Philharmonic the following year led to tours throughout North and South America, Europe and Israel. A major adjunct to her prominent solo career was her participation in chamber music, performing with many of the major string quartets of her time: Cleveland, Emerson, Guarneri, Juilliard and Tokyo; as well as with cellist Yo-Yo Ma and clarinetist Richard Stoltzman.

Lillian met pianist Claude Frank in 1947 at Tanglewood. They were married in 1959, and often performed duorecitals. She especially enjoyed playing Mozart's Two-Piano Concerto with her husband. On June 30, 1967, they became the parents of a baby girl who grew into the notable violinist **Pamela Frank**.

Kallir's last appearance was with the Boston Symphony in the Mozart Two-Piano Concerto at Tanglewood in 1990. Meanwhile, she had joined the Mannes faculty in 1975, coaching students into the 21st century.

Survived by Claude and Pamela, this great artist who loved life to the fullest, was taken by cancer in her Manhattan home, October 25, 2004.

CLAUDETTE SOREL was born in Paris, October 10, 1932. She studied in the U.S. with **Olga Samaroff** and **Rudolph Serkin**. At age ten she made her Town Hall debut, later graduating from Juilliard and Curtis and receiving a mathematics degree from Columbia. Her teaching positions were at Ohio State, University of Kansas, and as distinguished professor at SUNY, Fredonia. She authored *Compendium of Piano Technique*, and edited three nocturnes of Rachmaninoff and the Arensky etudes. She performed over 2000 recitals, and appeared with over 200 orchestras worldwide in the course of her career. She recorded for RCA Victor and the Musical Heritage Society, and adjudicated many competitions including the Van Cliburn International. She was a co-founder of the Women in Music Series at NYU, where we met in 1995. She passed away, August 6, 1999. An Award in her name has been established.

RUTH LAREDO (née Meckler), born in Detroit, November 20, 1937, started piano in early childhood. She studied at Curtis with **Rudolf Serkin** (BM 1960), and made her debut in 1962 with **Leopold Stokowski** and the American Symphony Orchestra at Carnegie Hall. In 1964, she married Bolivian-born violinist **Jaime Laredo** appearing in many recitals with him. (They divorced in 1974.)

Her New York Philharmonic debut was in 1974, and her solo-concert debut at Carnegie Hall was in 1982. In the 1970s, she made pioneer recordings of the entire fiendishly difficult piano solo repertoire of Sergei Rachmaninoff, and sonatas of Alexander Scriabin, bringing attention to this composer. Other career highlights include a European tour with Serkin and his son, Peter, appearances at Kennedy Center, Library of Congress, the White House, a 1993 U.S. tour with the Warsaw Philharmonic and concerts with top American and European orchestras.

A founding member of the Music from Marlboro (Vermont) Summer Festival, and collaborator with the Tokyo String Quartet, Laredo served as artistic director of a thirteen-hour Robert Schumann marathon at Symphony Space in New York. A tour of Russia and Ukraine was incorporated into the *CBS Sunday Morning* television program with the late Charles Kuralt. Her presentation at the Harvard/Radcliffe Women's Leadership Conference (1989) and performance/lecture series at New York's Metropolitan Museum of Art were to sell-out crowds.

She was nominated by *Ladies Home Journal* for "Woman of the Year." The *Ruth Laredo Becoming a Musician Book*, based on her personal experiences, is a guide for young musicians. In the 1990s she was known as "The First Lady of the Piano."

Ruth, assailed by ovarian cancer, died in her sleep May 25, 2005, in her New York apartment. She was the proud mother of Jennifer Laredo who, with her husband, cellist Paul Watkins, lives in London, and who gave her a granddaughter.

In the previous decade, Laredo concentrated on chamber music and recitals. Her last performance was May 6, 2005, at the Metropolitan Museum of Art, one of the popular "Concerts With Commentary" series she had been a part of for seventeen years.

Two days after the attack on the World Trade Center, she celebrated the twenty-fifth anniversary of her Alice Tully Hall debut with a recital there. It was the opening concert of the 2001 Lincoln Center season. Her memorable words to the audience were, "Great music gives us spiritual sustenance and gives us hope."

In the Limelight: the Second Half of the 20th Century

Argentine pianist **MARTHA ARGERICH**, one of the foremost pianists of our time, was born June 5, 1941, in Buenos Aires, where she made her orchestral debut in 1949. Between the ages of five and ten she studied with Vincenzo Scaramuzza. After four years of additional study with Francisco Amicarelli, Argentinian president Juan Perón appointed her diplomat parents to Vienna where Martha studied with Friedrich Gulda (1930–2000). She also received coaching from Madeleine Cantacuzene Lipatti, (wife of famed pianist Dinu Lipatti), Abbey Simon, and Nikita Magaloff, renowned for his interpretations of Chopin, who prepared her for the challenging Geneva and Busoni Competitions held only two weeks apart in 1957. As a result of winning both competitions, she was booked for several years of European concert engagements. Her debut recording for Deutsche Grammophon (1960) included the Liszt *6th Hungarian Rhapsody* and Prokofiev's *Toccata*, which critics compared to the classic Vladimir Horowitz versions and for which the great pianist himself expressed admiration.

Argerich gave up performing for some years, emerging from this hiatus in 1964 when she met Polish-born pianist Stefan Askenase (1896–1985) and his wife, who convinced her to return to the piano. She took first prize at the Warsaw Chopin Competition (1965), resumed her concert schedule, and in 1966 made her American recital debut in Philharmonic (now Avery Fisher) Hall. In 1980, she returned to Warsaw as a judge for the Chopin Competition. The next decade of her career was blemished by unpredictability, last-minute canceled concerts and, again, a two-year sabbatical from concertizing. She also quit playing solo recitals in favor of collaborations with friends and colleagues, including pianists Nelson Freire and Stephen Kovacevich, violinists Ruggiero Ricci and Gidon Kremer and cellists Mstislav Rostoprovich and Mischa Maisky.

Her artistry, that effortless technique and spontaneous, almost out-of control quality that enthralls audiences, can be heard on some fifty CDs. In November 1999, she performed Prokofiev's *Third Piano Concerto* at Carnegie Hall with the Philadelphia Orchestra conducted by her former husband **Charles Dutoit**. In May 2001, she played with the New York Philharmonic, again with Dutoit. September brought a tour with the San Francisco Symphony, playing the Schumann Concerto in Turin, Lucerne, Düsseldorf, Hanover and London's Royal Albert Hall, the latter telecast on the BBC She returned to San Francisco in the 2001–02 season.

Argerich was named "Musician of the Year 2001" by *Musical America*—a real honor!

Born in Ankara (Turkey), November 21, 1941, **IDIL BIRET** started her piano studies at age three. By eleven, she had played the Mozart concerto for two pianos with the great virtuoso **Wilhelm Kempff** (1895–1991). She studied at the Paris Conservatory with **Nadia Boulanger**, graduated at fifteen with three first prizes, highest honors, and continued studies with the elite in the piano field, **Alfred Cortot**, **Edwin Fischer**, and Wilhelm Kempff. Since age sixteen, she has performed all over the world with major orchestras. Her American debut was in 1962 with the Boston Symphony under **Erich Leinsdorf**. Her career covers more than eighty concerts in the former Soviet Union, sixty in Australia, and several tours of Japan which were recorded on Toshiba/EMI. She has appeared at most international festivals, including the Istanbul Festival in her homeland, where she performed Beethoven's sonatas with **Yehudi Menuhin**. She participated in the eighty-fifth birthday celebration of **Wilhelm Backhaus** (1884–1969), and the ninetieth of Wilhelm Kempff. In 1986, Biret made a landmark recording of the complete set of Beethoven's nine symphonies in the piano transcriptions by Liszt. From 1990–92, she completed a dazzling project for Naxos: thirty CDs, including the complete solo works and concertos of Brahms, Rachmaninoff, and Chopin—of whom she is a superb interpreter. The Chopin recording won a Grand Prix du Disque Chopin in Poland in 1995. Her numerous awards include the Lily Boulanger Memorial Fund (Boston, 1954, '64), Harriett Cohen-Dinu Lipatti Gold Medal (London, 1959), Polish Artistical Merit Prize (1974) and the Chevalier de l'Ordre National du Mèrite (1976). She has been a jury member in many competitions, including the Van Cliburn (USA), Queen Elisabeth (Belgium), Montreal (Canada), Busoni (Italy), and Liszt (Weimar, Germany).

London-born **IMOGEN COOPER** started her six years of training with **Jacques Février** and **Yvonne Lefébure** at the Paris Conservatoire at age twelve, winning the Premier Prix there in 1967. She studied with **Alfred Brendel**, **Paul Badura-Skoda** and **Jörg Demus** in Vienna, then won the Mozart Memorial Prize in 1969 back in London. She has appeared with all major British orchestras, and plays regularly with the London BBC Promenade concerts since her televised debut in 1973. She has made repeated visits to Japan, Australia, and America where she made her debut in 1984 with the Los Angeles Philharmonic. Her recordings include the complete solo piano works written in the last years of Schubert's life, and Mozart's Double and Triple Concertos with **Alfred Brendel** and the Academy of St. Martin-in-the-Fields under Sir Neville Marriner, with whom she collaborated on the soundtrack of the film *Amadeus*. A disc of Schubert Piano Trios, with Raphael Oleg and Sonia Wieder-Atherton for BMG France, was released in 1998. Her 2001–02 season included concerts and recitals in Italy, Germany, Netherlands, and England. Her programs were of Schubert, Mozart, Brahms and Schumann. Concerts in Wigmore Hall presented Robert and **Clara Schumann** Lieder. As a Lieder recitalist, she has partnered with Wolfgang Holzmair in Vienna, Paris, London and Frankfurt.

Bella Davidovich

BELLA DAVIDOVICH, one of the greatest pianists to come from Russia, was born in Baku (Azerbaidzhan), July 16, 1928. Her father was concertmaster of the Baku Opera, and her mother, a pianist. Bella began formal training at six. At nine, she played the Beethoven First Piano Concerto with the Baku Philharmonic. She studied at the Moscow Conservatory 1946–54, and was on their faculty 1962–78. Winning the Chopin Competition in Warsaw, 1949, launched her career in Russia and Eastern Europe. In 1967, she made her first appearance outside the Soviet Union in Amsterdam, but when her son, violinist Dmitri Sitkovetsky (*b* 1954) defected to the West in 1977 to study at Juilliard with **Ivan Galamian**, her concerts abroad were cancelled. The following year she emigrated to the U.S. where, at the age of fifty-one, made her Carnegie Hall debut. Since then she has performed in Japan, Israel, South America, Europe and the United States. She joined the Juilliard faculty in 1982, and became a U.S. citizen in 1984. She continues her illustrious international career, has collaborated with the Borodin, Guarneri and Tokyo String Quartets and is a frequent guest artist at music festivals such as La Roc d'Antherron, Schleswig-Holstein, Piano Festival Ruhr, Verbier and Sviatoslav Richter's December Evenings Festival. She also plays duo-recitals with her son. In the summer of 1999, she returned to Baku to give master classes to young musicians there. During the 2001–02 season she appeared in Belgium, England, Germany, Holland, Iceland, Italy, Lithuania, Norway, Portugal, Scotland, Spain, Sweden, Brazil and Japan. She has also served on the juries of the Queen Elisabeth and Chopin International Piano Competitions.

Born in Tripoli to a French father (a geophysicist drilling for oil in the Sahara) and an American mother (a pianist and Fulbright Scholar from Stanford), **CECILIA DUNOYER** grew up in Italy, Austria, Switzerland and France. Following studies in Paris, during a visit to the U.S. she received a scholarship to the University of Michigan, where she earned her BM and MM in piano, studying with György Sandor. 1990 brought her DMA from the University of Maryland. Her solo and chamber music performances in the U.S., Mexico and Europe have included French recitals in 1987, commemorating the fiftieth anniversary of Ravel's death, and 1995–96 season concerts celebrating the 150th anniversary of Fauré's birth. She is the author of *Marguerite Long, A Life in French Music*, published by Indiana University Press (1993). (See Musicologists.)

MARGARET FINGERHUT was named "Young Musician of the Year" by the Greater London Arts Association in 1981. Born in London, she studied with Cyril Smith and Angus Morrison at the RCM where she won many prizes. Scholarships enabled her to study with **Vlado Perlemutter** in Paris and **Leon Fleischer** in Baltimore. She was invited by Lord Yehudi Menuhin to participate in his "Live Music Now" series. She has played internationally, with most major British orchestras, and appeared on BBC television and radio. Her numerous recordings on Chandos have made her world-famous.

Helene Grimaud

With an ethnic mix of North African, Corsican, and Italian-Jewish roots, **HÉLÈNE GRIMAUD** was born and raised in Aix-en-Provence, France. At age nine, she began studies with a private tutor in Versailles. She later studied in Marseilles with Pierre Barbizet, and at thirteen entered the Paris Conservatory where, after taking first prize in Jacques Rouvier's class in 1985, she was in the master classes of **György Sander**, **Leon Fleisher** and **Jorge Bolet**, and participated in the Tchaikovsky Competition. It was her performance of Rachmaninoff's Second Sonata that gained the then fifteen-year-old international attention. Since her 1988 debut with the Orchestre de Paris under **Daniel Barenboim**, she has appeared throughout Europe and the U.S. She moved to America at age twenty-one. 1990 saw her recital debut at Kennedy Center and her orchestral debut with the Cleveland Orchestra. Since performing with the San Francisco Symphony as a Shenson Young Artist in 1993, she has appeared with most of the major orchestras in U.S. During the 1999 season, she appeared with the New York Philharmonic under **Kurt Masur**, performing the Beethoven Concerto #4, later released on Teldec. In 2000, she appeared with Boston, Philadelphia, Atlanta, Toronto and Vancouver Symphonies, recitals in Seattle, Mexico City and New York, and performed with the Chamber Music Society of Lincoln Center. She toured Germany and Austria with Neeme Järvi and the Göteborg Symphony (Sweden), and played with the San Francisco Symphony in Germany as part of their European tour. Her 2001–2002 season included her Carnegie Hall debut, concerts throughout the U.S., and a tour with the Orchestre de Paris and Christoph Eschenbach. Her recordings for Erato and Denon feature works of Rachmaninoff, Chopin, Liszt, Schumann, Ravel and Brahms. Now recording for Teldec, her 2001 release is of the Rachmaninoff Second Piano Concerto with the Philharmonia Orchestra under Vladimir Ashkenazy.

Taiwan native **WU HAN** began piano studies at age nine, and within a few years took first prizes in all major competitions. She was the pianist of choice for visiting chamber artists who encouraged her to perform in America. She came to the U.S. in 1981, when she was twenty-two, and studied with Raymond Hanson at the Hartt School (Connecticut), as well as Herbert Stessin, **Lilian Kallir** and **Menahem Pressler**. Winner of the 1994 Andrew Wolf Chamber Music Award, she performs as orchestral soloist, recitalist, chamber musician and has appeared in England, Germany, Austria, Spain, Denmark, Japan and Taiwan, with concert series in San Francisco, Los Angeles, Chicago, Philadelphia and Seattle. Her festival appearances have been at Caramoor, Ravinia, Aspen, Vail (Colorado), Santa Fe (New Mexico) and La Jolla (California). Duo concerts with her cellist husband, David Finckel,[150] have been throughout Europe and the U.S. For three seasons (1998–2000) the pair were the artistic directors of SummerFest La Jolla, receiving acclaim for innovative programming and bringing in world-class artists. In 2005, they became artistic directors of the Chamber Music Society of Lincoln Center. Together, they are members of the faculties of the Isaac Stern Chamber Music Encounters at Carnegie Hall and the Jerusalem Music Center. Their daughter, Lilian, born 1994, is already proficient in piano and frequently travels with her parents.

Angela Hewitt

First prize winner of the 1985 Toronto International Bach Piano Competition, Canadian **ANGELA HEWITT** has performed throughout North America, Mexico, Europe, Australia, Japan, China, and Russia. Born July 26, 1958, in Ottawa into a musical family, her mother, Marion, a pianist and girls' choir director, was her first piano teacher beginning at age three. Her father, Dr. Godfrey Hewitt, was organist and choirmaster at Christ Church Cathedral (Ottawa) for fifty years. In her formative years, Angela also trained in violin, recorder, singing and classical ballet. She studied at the Toronto Royal Conservatory (1964–73), then with Jean-Paul Sevilla at the University of Ottawa (BM 1976). As a child, she was an admirer of fellow Canadian pianist **Glenn Gould** (1932–82) and **Rosalyn Tureck**, but it was her father's organ playing that initiated her love of Bach. She placed First in Italy's Viotti Competition (1978) and was a top prize winner in the International Bach competitions of Leipzig and Washington, DC, as well as the Schumann Competition in Cleveland, and the Dino Ciani Competition at La Scala, Milan. In 1985, she was the winner of the Toronto International Bach Piano Competition, which highlighted her career as the Bach pianist of her generation.

Hewitt is equally adept with Romantic and Modern composers, and has many recordings to her credit, including Granados' *12 Spanish Dances* (CBC Records), the works of Oliver Messiaen on Hyperion, and in 2001, she began recording the complete solo works of Ravel. She performs chamber music, appearing with singers and instrumentalists in North America and Europe, as well as giving lecture-recitals and master classes on Bach. In 1986, she was named Artist of the Year by the Canadian Music Council. In 1995, she was awarded an honorary doctorate from the University of Ottawa, in 1997 received the Key to the City of Ottawa, and in 2002 was made an Officer of the Order of Canada.

---

150. David was a student of **Elsa Hilger** - see Cellists

In 1994, she embarked on a heralded ten-year project to record all the major keyboard works by Bach for Hyperion. Completed thus far are the *Inventions, French Suites, Partitas,* the complete *Well-Tempered Clavier,* and the *Goldberg Variations.* Both Book I and II of the *Well-Tempered Clavier* were chosen among the Top 50 CDs of 1999 by *BBC Music Magazine.* Book I received a Juno Award in Canada. In 1997, the *Sunday London Times* hailed her as "one of the outstanding Bach pianists of our time." In addition to North America and Europe, she has performed in Japan, Australia, China, Mexico and the former Soviet Union. In 1998, she toured New Zealand for the first time.

During 2000, the 250th anniversary of Bach's death, she gave complete performances of the forty-eight Preludes and Fugues in Canada, America, England and Germany, and in December performed and conducted all the Bach keyboard concertos with the New York Chamber Symphony in Alice Tully Hall. In 2001, following recital tours on both sides of the Atlantic, she made her debut with the Philadelphia Orchestra. Highlights of 2002–03 included appearances with the BBC Symphony Orchestra in a world premiere of a concerto by Dominic Muldowney; the Cleveland, Houston, Dallas, and Detroit Symphonies; her debut in Amsterdam's Concertgebouw; tours with the German Chamber Philharmonic of Bremen and the Australian Chamber Orchestra; and Schwetzingen, Cheltenham and Oslo Festivals.

Although known as a Bach specialist, Hewitt's repertoire includes Mozart, Schumann, Beethoven, Liszt and Fauré. When performing the works of different composers she says, "You must read the performance practices while studying the works, and inhabit the world of the composer while playing him."

With five other prominent Canadian pianists, **Angela Cheng**, **Janina Fialkowska**, **Marc-André Hamelin**, **Jon Kimura Parker** and **André Laplante**, she is a founding member of *Piano Six,* a project dedicated to keeping "live music" alive by taking their music to schools, small towns and rural communities in Canada to those who otherwise would not hear live music.

After having lived in France for seven years, since 1985 Angela makes her home in London, which provides her proximity for European performances, and puts her in the major center of early and period music.

OLGA KERN was born into a family of musicians. Her great-great-grandmother was a friend of Tchaikovsky, and her great-grandmother sang accompanied by Rachmaninoff. Olga began piano at five, and formal training with Evgeny Timakin at the Moscow Central School, continuing with Sergei Dorensky at the Moscow Tchaikovsky Conservatory, where she was also a postgraduate student. Other studies were with Boris Petrushansky at the Accademia Pianistica Incontri col Maestro in Imola, Italy. She is the recipient of an honorary scholarship from the president of Russia and a member of Russia's International Academy of Arts.

Winner of the first Rachmaninoff International Piano Competition when she was seventeen, Kern is a laureate of eleven international competitions. She has performed in the Great Hall of the Moscow Conservatory, the Bolshoi Theatre, Symphony Hall (Osaka), La Scala (Milan), Salle Cortôt (Paris), and Kennedy Center. She has appeared as soloist with the Moscow, Belgrade and La Scala Philharmonics, and the St. Petersburg, Russian National, China, Torino and Cape Town Symphonies.

In June 2001, Kern was awarded the Nancy Lee and Perry R. Bass Gold Medal at the Eleventh Van Cliburn International Piano Competition—the first woman to have achieved this distinction in more than thirty years. Captivating fans and critics, she was awarded international concert engagements and career management, plus a CD of her award-winning Cliburn Competition performances on the *harmonia mundi* label. As a result of her success at the competition, she made her Boston Pops debut during the summer, and performed at the Kennedy Center Honors with **Renée Fleming** in a tribute to Van Cliburn in December.

The 2001–2002 season saw her with the El Paso, San Antonio and Eugene (Oregon) Symphonies and recitals in Atlanta, Boulder, Chicago, Los Angeles, New Orleans and Portland (Oregon). International performances were in San Juan (Puerto Rico), France, Germany, Italy, Mexico, Portugal and Russia, with an extensive tour of South Africa, June 2002.

The 2002–2003 season began at the Ravinia Festival with the Chicago Symphony, led by Christoph Eschenbach, in Rachmaninoff's Piano Concerto No. 2, followed by engagements with the Columbus, Dallas, North Carolina, Syracuse, and Utah Symphony Orchestras, and the Kirov Orchestra, under Valery Gergiev. After giving recitals in Texas, California, Arizona, Kansas, as well as in Milan, Zermatt and Moscow, Olga was guest artist at the Klavier Ruhr and Kissinger Summer festivals in Germany, Radio-France Montpellier and Casadesus festivals in France, Ohrid Festival in Macedonia, and the Busoni Festival in Italy.

During 2004, she toured Austria with the Warsaw Philharmonic led by Antoni Wit, followed by a twenty-three-city tour of the U.S. She appeared with the Fort Worth, Houston, San Juan (Puerto Rico), San Diego,[151] and Tucson Symphonies, and made her New York recital debut at Carnegie Hall's new Zankel Hall in May. 2005 included a return to South Africa in February and March, and summer engagements at Ravinia and the Hollywood Bowl.

Kern was featured in *Playing on the Edge*, the Peabody Award-winning documentary about the Van Cliburn Competition, which aired on PBS stations across the United States. Her Competition performances with the Fort Worth Symphony were showcased in the PBS series *Concerto*. She recorded the Tchaikovsky Piano Concerto No. 1 with the Rochester Philharmonic, Christopher Seaman conducting, on *harmonia mundi usa* (2003), with a forthcoming CD of solo Liszt/Rachmaninoff transcriptions.

Olga lives in Moscow, devoting her free time to her young son, Vladislav.

ALICIA de LARROCHA was born in Barcelona, May 23, 1923. At age three she literally banged her head and cut it open against the locked piano. Her family gave in and let the child begin lessons. Her first public appearance was at six, and at eleven she was already playing with the Madrid Symphony. Pianist **Arthur Rubinstein** (1887–1982) predicted a great career for her. Her only teacher was Frank Marshall (1883–1959), who established the Marshall Piano Academy, founded in her native city in 1901 by Enrique Granados.[152] De Larrocha has served as the third president of the academy since 1959.

Alicia de Larrocha

Her first tour outside Spain was after WWII in 1947. Her British debut came in 1953, followed by her American debut in 1955 with the Los Angeles Philharmonic conducted by **Alfred Wallenstein** (1898–1983). She received the Paderewski Memorial Medal in London in 1961 and international honors for her early recordings. Her second appearance in the U.S., 1965, established her as one of the world's greatest classical pianists. During the 1995–96 season, she celebrated the thirtieth anniversary of her debut with the New York Philharmonic with an encore performance of Manuel de Falla's *Nights in the Gardens of Spain*.

While her interpretations of Spanish music are without peer, she once modestly said that she was not a specialist in the Spanish repertoire—it is just that her audience continuously demands her to play it. She is, however, legendary for the music of her native Spain and that of Mozart. How her feather-light touch coaxes her trademark voluminous sound from the percussive keyboard remains a mystery.

She has toured the U.S. each year since 1965, and plays regularly with the great orchestras, festivals, and recital series worldwide. Within her catalogue of recordings are four Grammy Awards for Albeniz' *Iberia* (1974), Ravel's two concerti (1975), a digital re-recording of *Iberia* (1989), and Granados' *Goyescas* (1991). Late '90s recordings include the Schumann *Piano Concerto*, Mozart *Double Concerto* and Beethoven *Piano Concerto #1*. The Beethoven is part of a video cassette series entitled "*Concerto*."

On the fiftieth anniversary of her debut, 1979, *Musical America* named de Larrocha "Musician of the Year." In 1982, the Spanish National Assembly awarded her its gold medal, "al merito en las bellas artes" bestowed upon her by King Juan Carlos. In 1994, she was awarded the Principe de Asturias Prize, given by a private foundation in Spain to honor her achievements in humanities, science and the arts. In 1998 a piano scholar-

---

151. Her February 7, 2004 performance in San Diego engendered an enthusiastic meeting between author and artist.

152. Enrique Granados (1867–1916), best known for his piano piece *Goyescas*, later used the music in the opera of the same name which premiered at the Met, January 28, 1916, with the composer present. On his return trip to Europe, he ran afoul of World War I. His ship was sunk by a German submarine.

ship fund was established in her name at California State University at Fullerton, as a tribute to one of the world's most admired pianists. In 1999, she was awarded the Premio Fundacion Guerrero de la Musica Española. In her 1999 appearance with the Los Angeles Philharmonic, **Jesus Lopez-Cobos** guest conductor, the reviews raved not only at her playing, but declared: "At seventy-six, she remains a wonder and pianistic treasure." Likewise, after her Seattle Symphony concert in October 2000, a review stated [she is] . . . " legendary among today's pianists." Legend is the right word for a modest lady who has been playing before the public for over three quarters of a century.

Cecile Licad

CECILE LICAD was born in Manila, May 11, 1961. Her surgeon father and pianist mother were so certain she would be a pianist they named her after Saint Cecilia, the patron saint of music. She began piano studies at three with her mother, later with Rosario Picazo, making her concert debut at age seven with the Philharmonic Orchestra of the Philippines. At age twelve she came to the U.S. to study at Curtis, where her teachers for the next five years were **Seymour Lipkin**, **Mieczyslaw Horszowski** and **Rudolf Serkin**. In 1979 she soloed with the Boston Symphony in Tanglewood, and in 1981 became one of the youngest musicians to win the Leventritt Gold Medal, launching an international career. Initially touted by the media as an icon of youthful glamour, she has proven herself a serious musician, regarded for her interpretations of Schumann, Brahms, Chopin and Rachmaninoff. In addition to her orchestral performances throughout the U.S., which in 2000 included Vancouver, Honolulu, and Phoenix, she appears in Europe, Asia with the Hong Kong Philharmonic, Tokyo's NHK Symphony and her native Philippine Philharmonic. As passionate a chamber musician as a recitalist and orchestral soloist, she has played with the New York Chamber Symphony, St. Paul Chamber Orchestra, Guarneri Quartet, Chamber Music Society of Lincoln Center and Music from Marlboro. Her festival appearances include Tanglewood, *Mostly Mozart* (both New York and Tokyo), International Music Festival of Seattle, Santa Fe, and La Jolla SummerFest, where she was featured in 2005, and where the author had the pleasure of meeting her.

CD releases include solo recordings of Ravel and Schumann, Chopin Etudes (Opus 25 and 10), a sonata album with violinist **Nadja Salerno-Sonnenberg**, the Rachmanioff Piano Concerto #2 and Rhapsody on a Theme of Paganini with the Chicago Symphony conducted by **Claudio Abbado**. Her rendition of the Chopin and Saint-Saëns Second Piano Concertos with André Previn conducting the London Philharmonic won the Grand Prix du Disque Frédéric Chopin. After years of living in Europe, she and her son, Otavio, returned to New York in 2000. During the 2001 season, she appeared in recital in Annapolis (MD), Rockford (IL), at the Gardner Museum in Boston, and Washington, DC's National Gallery, as well as performing Beethoven's Third Piano Concerto at Carnegie Hall with the New York Youth Symphony. She appeared with the Hong Kong and Philippine Philharmonic orchestras, and during the summer of 2002 was soloist on an extensive tour of the Far East with the Asian Youth Orchestra under the direction of Sergiu Comissiona, performing in Hong Kong, Kuala Lumpur, Manila, Singapore, Kyoto and Tokyo.

Anne-Marie McDermott

ANNE-MARIE McDERMOTT, who could be dubbed the "Concert Pianist Stand-In Artist," was born in New York, July 17, 1963, and began piano at five. Her mother, an Irish step-dancer, loved music and made sure her four children had lessons. By ten, Anne-Marie was "hooked" and never needed coaxing to practice. At twelve, she played with the National Orchestral Association in Carnegie Hall. As a scholarship student at the Manhattan School of Music, she studied with **Constance Keene** and **John Browning**, and participated in master classes with such luminaries as Leon Fleischer, Menahem Pressler, Misha Dichter, Abbey Simon, **Rosalyn Tureck**, Michael Tilson-Thomas and Mstislav Rostropovich. Her numerous recital appearances cover New York's 92nd Street Y, the New York Pops at Carnegie Hall, Lincoln Center, Kennedy Center, and soloing with many orchestras throughout the U.S., Europe and Japan. In 1991, she won the silver medal in the first Hamamatsu Piano Competition, playing with the Osaka Philharmonic.

Desperate for a Substitute? Call McDermott!

Through quirks of fate, Anne-Marie has gained a reputation for concert readiness at the drop of a telephone receiver. In 1990, she was standing by, gowned and in the wings, for **Alicia de Larocha** who was performing Mozart's 25th piano concerto in "Live at Lincoln Center"—the Spanish pianist, having been unaware that this was really a *live* performance, almost bowed out. In 1992, Mc Dermott stepped in at the last moment for the indisposed **Murray Perahia** to solo with the Atlanta Symphony. In 1993, she again saved the night, replacing at short notice Portuguese pianist **Maria-João Pires** with the Dallas Symphony under the late Eduardo Mata. In November of that year, when **Grant Johannesen** was taken ill, she had to play Beethoven's Second, which she had not touched in eight months, with the Florida Philharmonic under **James Judd**. Her plane sat three hours before take-off from New York, and she just made it just in time to walk on stage after intermission. It was a great performance and the audience never knew what it took to get the soloist there. July 1995 again found her in the wings ready to substitute for **Martha Argerich**, known for last-minute cancellations. (Ironically, Anne-Marie lives in New York, yet when needed *there*, many times she has had to fly in from some other part of the country!)

Chamber Music, Honors, and a Family Affair

As a chamber musician, McDermott has appeared at most important U.S. festivals, plus the Casals (Puerto Rico) and the Dubrovnik (Yugoslavia). Her honors include the 1983 Young Concert Artists Auditions, the 1987 Avery Fisher Career Development Award, Joseph Kalichstein Piano Prize, Paul A. Fish Memorial Prize, Bruce Hungerford Memorial Prize and the Mortimer Levitt Career Development Award for Women Artists. In 1995, she received the Andrew Wolf Memorial Chamber Music Award. She performs in the McDermott Trio, with her sisters, Kerry,[153] violin, and Maureen,[154] cellist, formed when they were teenagers. They have been playing publicly since 1983. (Sometimes they add their violist brother.) In September 1995, McDermott became an Artist Member of the Chamber Music Society of Lincoln Center, with whom she toured throughout the country in 1996. The same year witnessed her orchestral debuts in Germany and with the Hong Kong Philharmonic under **David Atherton**, who also conducted her in the San Diego *Mainly Mozart* Festival in June 1996. She has been a regular at this venue where we met (again) in June 2005. This time I was introduced to Michael Lubin, her husband as of New Year's Eve, 2003.

Born in New York, February 2, 1944, **URSULA OPPENS** studied piano with her mother, Edith, later receiving her MM from Juilliard, where she studied with **Felix Galimar** and **Rosina Lhévinne**. 1969 marked her Carnegie Hall debut, and first prize in the Busoni Competition in Italy. In 1971, she co-founded Spectrum Musicae, a chamber music ensemble specializing in contemporary works. In 1976, her winning the Avery Fisher Prize led to a performance with the New York Philharmonic. She has made many recordings from her vast repertoire of contemporary, classical and romantic music, receiving two Grammy nominations for her *American Piano Music of Our Time*, Volume I, and *The People United Will Never be Defeated* by Frederic Rzewski. She has played with the Los Angeles Philharmonic and the San Francisco Symphony among other prominent orchestras. Her debut with the Chicago Symphony Orchestra, under the late **Erich Leinsdorf**, featured an acclaimed rendition of the Lutoslawski Concerto. In June 1990, she was the first woman Chief Marshal at a Harvard Commencement, performing Rachmaninoff's *Rhapsody on a Theme of Paganini* with the Boston Pops as part of the graduation festivities. She was one of the first pianists to extend the borders of traditional concert programming by performing both classics and contemporary pieces.

In 2000, Oppens joined the faculty as the John Evans distinguished professor of music at Northwestern University in Evanston, Illinois.

---

153. Kerry McDermott has played in the first violin section of the New York Philharmonic since she was nineteen (1981).
154. Maureen McDermott is co-founder of the four women group, CELLO.

CRISTINA ORTIZ, one of today's most prominent classical pianists, was born in Brazil, April 17, 1950. She began her studies in Rio de Janeiro before moving to Paris to continue training with Brazilian-born pedagogue **Magda Tagliaferro** (1893–1986). After winning the Van Cliburn Competition in 1969, she made her recital debut in New York in 1971. Further studies with **Rudolf Serkin** at Curtis launched an international career by 1973. In 1994, she gave the world premiere of Lalo Schifrin's Piano Concerto No. 2, *The Americas*, with the National Symphony Orchestra, and performed the Shostakovich Piano Concerto No. 2 at the BBC Proms with the Royal Philharmonic. In 1995, she played with the Prague Chamber Orchestra, directing from the keyboard. The same year, she returned to her homeland appearing with the Brazilian Symphony Orchestra, and giving recitals as part of the South American International Piano Series. Her many recordings range from Mozart, Beethoven, Schumann, Chopin and Brahms, to the great exponents of French, Spanish, and Brazilian repertoire. A 1995 Decca release features all five Villa-Lobos Piano Concertos with the Royal Philharmonic Orchestra. Ortiz has appeared with virtually every principal orchestra in the world, touring the U.S., Australia, New Zealand, Japan, and the Far East.

CÉCILE OUSSET, one of the most successful of international pianists, was born in Tarbes (France) March 3, 1936. She gave her first recital at age five, then studied at the Paris Conservatory winning the first prize in Piano upon graduation at age fourteen. She has won many of the world's foremost competitions: Van Cliburn, Queen Elisabeth of Belgium, Busoni, and the Concours **Marguerite Long**-Jacques-Thibaud. She made her U.S. debut with the Los Angeles Philharmonic and Minnesota Orchestras in 1984, and returned there annually for engagements including concerts with the Boston Symphony and the National Symphony (Washington, DC). February 2000 saw her third return to the New York Philharmonic under Kurt Masur's tenure. February 1996 was her first tour after many years to South Africa, and during 1998 she revisited Hong Kong, Australia/New Zealand and Japan, where she performed with the NHK Symphony Orchestra. Throughout Europe and England, she regularly appears with the leading orchestras and at major festivals. BBC-TV has telecast many of her performances, plus a special profile of her on the program, *Omnibus*. Her recordings have won worldwide acclaim, including the Grand Prix du Disque for her Brahms 2nd Concerto with the Leipzig Gewandhaus Orchestra, conducted by Kurt Masur. Her relationship with EMI produced prize-winning recordings, including the Saint-Saëns Concerto No. 2, Liszt No. 1 and Rachmaninoff No. 2; Grieg and Mendelssohn 1st Concertos with the London Symphony Orchestra and Neville Marriner; recital recordings of Liszt, Chopin, Debussy and Ravel; Rachmaninoff's Concerto No. 3 with the Philharmonia Orchestra and Guenter Herbig; both Ravel concertos with the CBSO/Rattle; and the Tchaikovsky Concerto No.1 and Schumann Concerto with the London Philharmonic/Kurt Masur. She recorded Gershwin's *Rhapsody in Blue* and Piano Concerto in F with the Stuttgart Radio Orchestra under Neville Marriner for Capriccio, and BBC Music Worldwide released a CD of a Chopin/Ravel recital recorded live at the Wigmore Hall, March 1999. In 2001, after some years of serious back pain which led to her having to limit the repertoire she was able to perform, she decided to end her remarkable performing career. Based in Paris, one can only hope she continues her master classes in the beautiful medieval village of Puycelsi near Albi.

MARIA-JOÃO PIRES, born in Lisbon, Portugal, July 23, 1944, made her recital debut at age five, and soloed with orchestra at age seven playing a Mozart concerto. From 1953–60 she studied theory, composition and music history at the Lisbon Academy of Music, then went to the Munich Hochschule für Musik. In 1970, she won first prize in the Beethoven Competition in Brussels. Her North American debut was with the Montreal Symphony (1986). Her first U.S. tour was in 1988. She has concertized throughout Europe, Africa, Israel, Canada and Japan, and is known for her interpretations of Mozart, Beethoven, Schubert, Schumann and Chopin. Since 1997, with French violinist Augustin Dumay and Chinese cellist Jian Wang, she has appeared as a trio in concerts throughout France and Spain.

CAROL ROSENBERGER, born in Detroit, studied in the U.S. with Webster Aitken (1908–81), in Paris with **Nadia Boulanger** (1887–1979), and in Vienna with harpsichordist **Eta Harich-Schneider** (1897–1986), a pupil of the great **Wanda Landowska**. Her 1970 debut tour was delayed ten years due to an attack of polio at the outset of her career. She spent part of that time in Vienna perfecting her German, and studying harpsichord, theory, lieder, opera, instrumental music and literature. Rehabilitated, she concertized internationally. Settling in Santa Monica, she has been on the faculties of USC, Cal. State, Northridge, and Immaculate Heart College. She now accepts only a limited number of concerts, preferring to concentrate on recordings. Her many releases on the Delos label include Howard Hanson's *Variations on a Theme of Youth*, Gerard Schwarz conducting, which won a 1991 Grammy Nomination for Best Performance Soloist with Orchestra. In charge of Artists and Repertoire at Delos International, where she has been a vice president for over ten years, Rosenburger produces the Music for Young People Series.

Ann Schein

ANN SCHEIN has enjoyed a global career spanning six decades. Born in White Plains, New York, November 10, 1939, contrary to Ruth Slenczynska, she had, "the best parents one could ever have had." Her father was an attorney—raised by a violinist father who played nightly in Chicago opera and show orchestras and refused to allow any of his eight children to pursue the same career. Her mother was a violinist with a Chicago Musical College background. At three, Ann was at the piano imitating music from the radio. First lessons came at four, so she would learn to read music properly. The family moved to Washington, DC, in 1945 where her childhood was enriched with symphony and chamber concerts, recitals, plays and shows to implement cultural and artistic exposure. From age seven, she saw the Ballet Russes, English Prima Ballerinas Margot Fonteyn, and Moira Shearer in the 1948 film, *The Red Shoes*. At ten, Ann produced the full length ballet, **Swan Lake**, for her elementary school, creating the choreography, and painting scenery. She started cello in junior high, playing that instrument for five years. At eleven and thirteen she went to Interlochen. The second summer she became the youngest winner in the history of their concerto competition, performing the MacDowell D minor with orchestra. In 1953, she auditioned and was accepted at Peabody, studying with Mieczyslaw Munz (1900–76), whose students included Emanuel Ax and **Illana Vered**.

Schein's professional debut was in Mexico City (1957) with the Rachmaninoff Third. In 1961 and 1962 she studied with Arthur Rubinstein in Paris, and **Dame Myra Hess** in London. During the late 1950s and early '60s, her artistry was recorded on the Kapp label. After her Carnegie Hall debut, 1962, she performed with eminent maestros and orchestras in New York, Cleveland, Philadelphia, Los Angeles, Baltimore, the National Symphony, London Philharmonic and BBC Symphony, as well as Europe and South America. Throughout the 1980 season, she presented a complete Chopin cycle at Alice Tully Hall.

Frequent chamber music collaborations have included the American and Cleveland Quartets, American Brass Quintet, and as a duo with her husband, violinist Earl Carlyss, a twenty-year member of the Juilliard String Quartet (1966–'86). (They were married May 24, 1969.)

On the piano faculty of Peabody (1980–2000), she originally commuted from New York to Baltimore with her then two small daughters, Linnea born January 24, 1971 and Pauline, April 6, 1973. (A vocal major, Linnea is now a career mother to *her* two small daughters.)

Schein's three years as accompanist to soprano **Jessye Norman**, included a 1995 U.S. and Brazil tour. They recorded the Alben Berg Songs on Sony Classical. An artist-faculty member of the Aspen Music Festival since 1984, in the summer of 2005 Ann initiated a series of complete Beethoven sonatas performed by the piano faculty. In August 2005, Schein performed Beethoven's fourth and fifth concertos with the Santa Fe Symphony, Stephen Smith conducting, followed by chamber music performances, teaching and master classes at Cleveland's Blossom Music Festival.

The 1998 recording of her two memorable recital pieces, Schumann's *Davidsbündlertänze* and *Humoreske*, are on Ivory Classics, whose specialty is releasing remastered classic pianist recordings. November 2005 brought the CD release of the twenty-four Chopin preludes and his B minor sonata on the MSR Classics label.

Schein gives master classes, serves as a competition adjudicator and, for twenty years, was president of the People to People Music Committee, presenting music and instruments to schools in many countries. She has been selected to receive the Distinguished Teacher's Chair established by Victoria and Ronald Sims at the Aspen School of Music for the summers of 2006, 2007.

Ruth Slenczynska

One of America's most famous prodigies, **RUTH SLENCZYNSKA** was born in Sacramento, California, January 15, 1925. Her father, Josef Slenczynski, was a second-rate violinist obsessed with having a great musician in the family. At one and a half Ruth was already humming the tunes *in perfect pitch* that she heard from her father's piano students. By three he permitted her to go to the upright piano. She quickly mastered all major and minor scales. It was then he tried to put a quarter size violin into her hands. She burst into tears, flung it across the room and smashed it, declaring she only wanted the piano! He transferred his obsession of molding her into a famous violinist and began a regimen of what amounted to nine hours a day of piano practice beginning at 6:00 A.M., in her nightgown in a cold house. After three hours, which included a slap across the face for any slip she made, she was allowed to dress and have the first reward of the day, breakfast. Her mother taught her the alphabet and numbers and beginning reading. Her father always took a nap between two and three, after which it was back to the piano to practice *in her underwear* (so as not to ruin dresses with perspiration) until supper, after which came more practice with the metronome setting getting faster. He also had her write down theory and music. There was no bedtime until Father was satisfied. Since he was already making money in real estate, he gave up his pupils and concentrated on Ruth. But even he realized his limit and found local piano teachers for her—all of whom taught her without a fee—and to whom he never gave credit, claiming that he was his daughter's only teacher.

What must be realized is that Josef, coming from Poland, subscribed to the European attitude that a child was the possession of the father. He had suffered at the hands of *his* father. The term "child abuse" had not yet become a concept, even in America. When Ruth cried after being slapped, and her mother rushed in to try to stop her husband, she was told to see to the younger children, Helen and Gloria, and that Ruth was *his* "work!" The little girl, utterly under the power of wanting to please her father, made a valiant effort to stifle her sobs during subsequent rages—several of which showed a man completely out of control! She was also afraid he would take the piano away from her. (Her first taste of ice cream was at age six . . .)

Ruth's first public concert came at age four, May 11, 1929, at Mills College in Berkeley near the family's home. It was a sensation, despite her father's prediction that if she made a mistake rotten eggs and tomatoes would be thrown at her! Her name came to be known with current violin prodigies Ruggiero Ricci, Isaac Stern, Yehudi Menuhin and his sister, Hephzibah, a piano star at six. World-famed pianist **Josef Hofmann** heard the child and declared he wanted to teach her at Curtis. Father and daughter moved to Philadelphia after her "farewell recital" in San Francisco, March 16, 1930. But because of Hofmann's concert schedule, her primary teacher was the venerated Isabelle Vengerova (1877–1956). This was not good enough for Slenczynski. After a few months he returned to California where his finagling managed to procure a meeting with his idol, violinist Mischa Elman, who made the dream come true of getting wealthy San Francisco backers to pay for three years' European study, which included transporting the family to Berlin. The monies raised were pocketed by Josef as remuneration for his efforts. Lessons from **Arthur Schnabel**, **Alfred Cortot**, **Alexander Glazunov**, **Georges Enesco**, **Nadia Boulanger**, **Egon Petri** and **Sergei Rachmaninoff** were free of charge. Although repulsed by the ill-mannered father, the great masters were charmed by the child. Even Bechstein in Berlin and Pleyel in Paris saw to it that a beautiful piano from each of their famous showrooms was installed in their hotel room.

At age six, Ruth gave a concert in Berlin, and the cabled report to the *New York Times* declared her to be "the most astounding of all prodigies heard in recent years on either side of the ocean." After the concert, German critics mounted the stage to examine the full-size grand piano—with shortened legs and pedal adjustments—for hidden mechanisms to account for sounds produced by an undersized six-year-old.

On November 13, 1933, the eight-year-old gave a recital at New York's Town Hall, performing works of Bach, Beethoven, Mendelssohn and Chopin. The *New York Times* said the playing was "an electrifying experience, full of the excitement and wonder of hearing what nature had produced in one of her most bounteous moods." Her story was serialized in eighteen daily chapters syndicated to 500 American newspapers. At nine, the girl filled in the cancelled tour of **Ignacy Paderewski**. Her career was in top gear, including a Paris concert in 1936—where she was heralded as the first true child prodigy since Mozart. At age twelve, there, she finally asserted herself enough to stop having to sleep in a bed in her parents' room and was allowed to sleep on a couch in her sisters' room. Her mother offered to return to California, but still Ruth would not leave her music. The strain was becoming unbearable when World War II broke out. People were rushing to get out of Europe. Fortunately, a fan was the wife of the president of a steamship company and the five Slenczynskis were packed into a stateroom designed for two. They were even able to procure a cabin for Mr. and Mrs. Fritz Kreisler, who had stood in endless lines of desperate passengers with them. Ruth was having fun with her sisters and other girls aboard ship when her father reached out and slapped her in front of everyone. She realized that she had escaped Adolf Hitler, but not Josef Slenczynski.

Back in Berkeley, they moved to a bigger house. Ruth was beginning to see her father as the arrogant sadist he was, not the god she worshipped and the beatings she resigned herself to as punishments deserved for her errors. From now on he was someone to be eluded. A Concert for Polish Relief proved to be a turning point. All these years Josef bought expensive clothes for himself, but expected his wife to wear the same old dresses. Ruth got clothes too big for her so they could be handed down. On this occasion, with the help of a friend, women and girls went to San Francisco and were outfitted in new gowns.

After years of adulation playing all over Europe and America, by age fourteen, critics were pointing out that her playing had not matured. The irony of this was that the pianist knew exactly what was wrong. She was not being allowed to follow the valuable lessons of her renowned mentors. Her father had so instilled in her that she was nothing without him, that she obeyed his insistence on playing the music *his* way. Each negative review brought ever more violent thrashings. A Town Hall concert in November 1940 was the breaking point. A recurring pain in her side was ignored. The concert was a failure. Her father disowned her, she had disgraced him. Is this what he had sacrificed his life for, he threw at her. The girl was in misery physically and emotionally. Five days after their return to Berkeley she was in the hospital having her appendix out. The doctors said that in another half hour she could have died.

After a taunt from her father, Ruth passed the UC Berkeley entrance exam, and for the first time tasted the "normality" of college life. She even found a job as librarian in the music department to be able to buy a few clothes. She returned to the piano, accompanying classes. Her father had instilled in her that she was fat and ugly and would never marry. But she met fellow student, George Born, who loved music. The two eloped after a short engagement in 1944. This time without physical abuse, she once again became the puppet of a man who insisted that she return to the stage despite the fact that she loved her teaching position at the Convent of Our Lady of Mercy, a young ladies' school in Burlingame, near San Francisco. The marriage ended in divorce in 1953.

In 1954, after earning a BA in psychology, she resumed her concert career on her own terms, using the feminine name ending Slenczynska instead of her father's Slenczynski, once again gaining critical plaudits. She toured with Arthur Fiedler and the Boston Pops for three years, and in 1956 performed Chopin's F minor concerto with Dimitri Mitropoulos and the New York Philharmonic. He had conducted her Minneapolis Orchestra concert when she was twelve, and considered this performance "the discovery of a brilliant new artist on the threshold of a great career ahead." It was also the year she appeared on Ralph Edward's *This is your Life* recalling her stranger-than-fiction real life story.

In 1958, Ruth returned to Town Hall to celebrate her Silver Jubilee. She performed across the country, and in 1961 played the Khachaturian Concerto with the San Francisco Symphony, under a twenty-five-year-old guest conductor named Seiji Ozawa, who would return as principal conductor 1970–77.

In 1964, she accepted a full-time position at Southern Illinois University at Edwardsville as artist-in-residence. In 1967, Slenczynska married Dr. James Kerr, a professor of political science at SIUE. She published a book of memoirs, *Forbidden Childhood* (1957), describing her life as a child prodigy, and *Music at Your Fingertips: Aspects of Pianoforte Technique* (1961). The Ivory Classics label has released two live recordings: *Ruth Slenczynska in Concert* (1984) and *Ruth Slenczynska: Schumann* (1999), and a remastered version of *Historic Performances* from the 1950s (1998).

Slenczynska's last major tour was in 1985 when she played in Korea, Singapore, Thailand, Taiwan, Malaysia, China and New Zealand, giving 115 concerts. After her husband's death in 2001, she moved to New York, but spent several months in Taiwan teaching and concertizing to help recover from her loss. The month of January 2006 found her in Taipei and Japan for eight recordings and forty concerts, the highlight of which was an invitation from Her Majesty Michiko, Empress of Japan, to play at the Imperial Palace—a very unique experience. The Empress, a piano aficionado, takes lessons from Madame Shuku Iwasaki, one of Japan's greatest teachers.

Ruth called me when she returned, reasonably sure that she *really* was going to retire . . .

MARIA TIPO, born in Naples, December 23, 1931, gave her first public recital at age four. Her mother and first teacher, Ersilia Cavallo, also a fine pianist, had been a student of the great **Ferruccio Busoni** (1866–1924). At seventeen, Maria won second prize at the Geneva International Piano Competition. (There was no first that year—she won first the next year.) In 1952, she came in third in the Queen Elisabeth of Belgium Competition, after which she established a successful concert career playing with the foremost conductors and orchestras of the world. An exponent of Italian music, her disc of twelve Scarlatti Sonatas won the *Diapason d'Or* and was hailed as "the most spectacular record of the year." She also made an historic first recording of the sixty-three complete Clementi sonatas. A member of the Academy of Santa Cecilia in Rome, she taught at the Conservatories of Bolzano and Florence for over twenty years, at the Music School of Fiesole, near Florence, and held the chair for virtuosity classes at the Geneva Conservatory for over a decade.

MITSUKO UCHIDA, born in Tokyo, December 20, 1948, began her studies in her native city. Her parents, who were diplomats, moved to Austria when she was twelve, and she enrolled at the Vienna Academy of Music. In 1968, she won second prize in the Beethoven Competition and in 1970, second prize in the Chopin Competition. Dissatisfied with her playing, she retired from the competition circuit. 1982 brought recognition in London and Tokyo for her performances of the complete sonatas of Mozart. In 1985–86, she appeared as soloist and conductor of the English Chamber Orchestra, playing all the piano concerti of Mozart. On February 15, 1987, she made her New York recital debut. Her Philips label disks of the Mozart Concerti and Sonatas won a 1989 Gramophone Award and became a part of the legendary "Mozart Edition" brought out in his bicentenary year (1991). During the 1990s, she won particular notice for her Debussy and Schubert solo piano recordings and her Beethoven concerti, and has been a champion of the music of Schoenberg, Bartók and Berg. Her recitals and orchestral concerts cover most of the major cities in Europe and the U.S. though, like Martha Argerich, to whom she is sometimes compared, she does not record or concertize prolifically. She toured Japan with the Cleveland Orchestra in 1994, and played the acclaimed U.S. premiere of Birtwistle's piano concerto, *Antiphonies*, with the Los Angeles Philharmonic. In 2001–02, she and pianist Richard Goode were appointed artistic directors for Musicians from Marlboro, the touring extension of the Vermont festival which presents the most outstanding young musicians in partnership with leading senior concert artists.

ILANA VERED was born December 6, 1939, near Tel Aviv, to a pianist mother and violinist father who owned a music school. To get attention, the two-year-old started playing the piano. By three it was obvious she was a prodigy, and at age five her parents adapted their lives to her career. After playing with major orchestras in the new state of Israel (1948), at twelve she won a government grant to study at the Paris Conservatory. Her teacher was **Vlado Perlemutter**, who had been a student of Maurice Ravel. At seventeen a tour of Brazil was arranged, and the following year Ilana was back in Israel where a young American medical student fell in love with her. She has been married to neurologist Dr. Peter Herman for many years. Coming to America, she debuted in Carnegie Hall and studied at Juilliard with **Nadia Reisenberg** and **Rosina Lhévinne**. One of the first winners of the Young Artists International Competition, in 1969 she received a Martha Baird Rockefeller Grant for a

European tour. In 1970, with her children in their early teens, she tried to give up playing to devote time to the "ordinary" life she had never experienced. Several years and bouts of depression later, she returned to her "life's blood" and resumed her career.

Vered's many cultural contributions include founding and directing Summerfest Series at the 92nd Street Y, the Hamptons in Long Island, and at Rutgers University. Her *Artists to End Hunger* has sponsored concerts at Avery Fisher Hall and Carnegie Hall and raised over a million dollars. In April 1993 she produced *In Praise of Women*, celebrating the achievements of women in music, featuring performers like **Anne-Marie McDermott, Sharon Robinson, Eugenia Zukerman, Beverly Hoch** and the **Anonymous 4**, with works by **Katherine Hoover** and **Deborah Drattell.** Two years later, in collaboration with composer **Laura Kaminsky,** she conceived *Ladyfingers*, a marathon of women pianists and pianist/composers performing all styles and genres. A second production was mounted in March 1996. Besides television and radio, Vered's recordings of major piano works include the five Beethoven concerti (Pro Arte, 1993) and the complete Chopin and Moszkowski etudes. Acclaimed versions of the concertos of Mozart, Chopin, Tchaikovsky, Brahms and Rachmaninoff are on the London label

Apart from visiting her grown children in the New York area, in recent years Ilana spent time painting in Italy and revisited Israel, where she was living in 2006.

Their Own Spotlight

Fame is an uncertain mistress. Much depends on being at the right place at the right time—both for artist and agent—plus publicity, recording contracts, distribution, media coverage and a thousand *et ceteras*. The following accomplished, but perhaps not so well-known, pianists are pursuing their own spotlight.

LIANE ALITOWSKI, born in New York City December 27, 1961, began piano at age seven with her mother, Sarita, then at Westchester Conservatory and continued at Indiana University (BM, MM), studying with **Menahem Pressler.** She has performed at the Banff Festival of the Arts, and throughout the U.S., Canada, South America, England and Japan. From 1988–92, she was the orchestral pianist with **Michael Tilson Thomas'** *New World Symphony,* collaborating with **Joshua Bell, Sharon Robinson, Jean-Yves Thibaudet,** and members of the Lincoln Center Chamber Music Society. Following her orchestral tenure, she moved to Israel where she was on the faculty at the Israel Conservatory in Tel Aviv. With her return to the U.S., she was on the faculty of Queens College School of Music. Several summers have been spent in the delightful avocation of being a featured soloist aboard cruise ships such as the *QE2, SS Rotterdam, Universe Explorer,* Royal Princess and World Cruise Lines.

In May 2001, she married Evyatar Marienberg, a professor of Jewish Studies at McGill University. They lived in Montreal from January 2001–June 2002. During this time she completed her doctorate from SUNY, Stony Brook, and learned a great deal of French! She also participated in a Leonard Bernstein Festival, performing with the faculty of Concordia College (Montreal). August 2002 through August 2003 was spent in Stockholm, where Alitowski taught a year long course on the History of Jewish Music at the Paideia Institute, as well as performing several solo and chamber music recitals there and in Paris at the American Church with soprano **Patricia Prunty.** In 2003, the couple's next exciting chapter was relocating to a safe (we hope) area of Israel, where Liane was involved in duo-piano recitals and more CD production.

(The author met Liane on the *Universe Explorer* cruise to Alaska, August 2000. She had just become engaged and was floating higher than the ship . . .)

DIANA AMBACHE has the distinction of being one of the first women in Britain to found and direct her own chamber orchestra. She has performed in over thirty countries, including Korea, Hong Kong, Australia and the Middle East, specializing in the music of women composers and performing works by Clara Schumann, Germaine Tailleferre, Maria Hester Park, Julie Candeille, and Wilhelmine von Bayreuth, as well as chamber music by Louise Farrenc and Princess Anna Amalia. She also produces successful programs on words and music with leading actors. Her work has earned a grant from the Arts Council of England. She is the artistic director of *Women of Note,* the first major London concert series with much of the music composed by women. June 6, 2001 featured a concert at St John's Smith Square as part of her series, *Not Your Eine Kleine*, which presents lesser known works of Mozart, plus a piano concerto for her to solo.

Beginning piano at four, **LYDIA ARTYMIW** made her professional debut four years later with the Philadelphia Orchestra, while studying at Curtis. After winning prizes in the 1976 Leventritt and 1978 Leeds International Competitions, she graduated from Philadelphia's University of the Arts, won an Avery Fisher Career Grant in 1987, the Andrew Wolf Chamber Music Prize in 1989, and embarked upon an international career playing with over one hundred orchestras worldwide, including the Boston and San Francisco Symphonies, New York and Los Angeles Philharmonics, and orchestras in London, Berlin, Rome, Milan, Paris, Korea, Taiwan, New Zealand and Singapore. Her chamber collaborators include Richard Stoltzman, Yo-Yo Ma, Michael Tree, the Guarneri, Vermeer, American and Shanghai Quartets. She participated in the first BBC International Radio Broadcast from North America, performing a solo recital broadcast to a worldwide audience. In 1995, she appeared with the Philadelphia Chamber Music Society. With her musicologist husband, David Grayson, she is on the faculty of the University of Minnesota, Minneapolis, where in 2000 she received the "Dean's Medal" for outstanding professor, and in May 2001 was awarded the Distinguished McKnight Professorship, making her the first performer ever to receive this prestigious award. In the 2000–01 season, Artymiw launched a piano trio with violinist Arnold Steinhardt of the Guarneri Quartet and cellist Jules Eskin, principal of the Boston Symphony. She performed in the 2002 Montreal Chamber Music Festival.

MARTA AZNAVOORIAN began piano at five. At twelve, she won the Stock-Sudler Medal to solo in a series of concerts with the Chicago Symphony. She was the first prize recipient of both the 1985 International Stravinsky Competition and the 1989 Union League Civic and Arts Foundation Young Adult Music Scholarship, and won the American Opera Society Music Scholarship. In her senior year of high school (1991), she performed at Kennedy Center as a Presidential Scholar in the Arts. She has played concerts with her Juilliard-trained sister, cellist **Ani Aznavoorian**. She is on the faculty of the Community Music School at DePaul University and the Music Institute of Chicago in Winnetka.

MARY BARRANGER was the winner of the Pittsburgh Concert Society Youth Auditions in 1964. Her 1970 relocation to California to attend San Diego State University led to dual roles as teacher and a performer. She has been in-orchestra pianist for the San Diego Symphony since 1976, principal pianist for the San Diego Chamber Orchestra since 1988, and an accompanist for the San Diego Master Chorale (1976–87). She has soloed in the San Diego Summer Pops and with the San Diego Opera Orchestra in their educational touring group and ensemble. Besides solo recitals, she has appeared in concert with violinist **Zina Schiff** on many occasions, with whom she recorded *The Stradivarius Puzzle*. She has performed solo piano music for Compton New Media Encyclopedia software, and records for Koch and Pro-Arte. On staff teaching piano at San Diego Mesa College, she is an active member of the chamber ensemble *Camarada*. Her CD with Zina Schiff of the music of Cecil Burleigh was released on Naxos in 2002.

MARGARET BAXTRESSER, a pianist of international reputation, was born in Deford, Michigan, June 10, 1922, began studies at five, gave her first recital at eight, and appeared as soloist with the Detroit Symphony at thirteen. In 1950, she won the Naumberg Award—a singular achievement at the time—when the competition was open to every category: voice, piano, strings, etc. She soloed with the Cleveland, Chicago, and Detroit Symphonies and the St. Paul Chamber Orchestra, and in Europe at Wigmore Hall, London, the Concertgebouw in Amsterdam and the Hochschule für Musik, Berlin. In the Far East she has played in India, Sri Lanka and Japan. Her 1994 concert tour included Hong Kong, Malaysia and Vietnam, and master classes at the University of Seoul (Korea). The first American to perform in Hanoi since Washington lifted its quarter century trade embargo, she performed Schumann's Piano Concerto with the Vietnamese National Symphony. The conservatory had broken windows and no heat. Her hosts asked to borrow her score so that they could copy it by hand. By her third visit, she officially bequeathed her entire music library to them, and was honored as a cultural representative of the U.S. A decade later, the government had built a new conservatory, and had a scholarship named for Baxtresser in recognition of her support.

A retired professor of music at Kent State University, Baxtresser was known for innovative recital programming. Her "Debussy and the Impressionists" presentation had music accompanied with slides of Monet, Degas and Renoir. This program was given at colleges and art museums. In September 2001, Western Michigan University (Kalamazoo) presented Baxtresser in a multi-sensory experience of sound, sight and imagination. Her granddaughter Amy, then an undergraduate horn player, was in the audience.

Vital to the end, on Monday morning, June 6, 2005, Margaret suffered a stroke in her physical therapy class, and died at Akron General Medical Center the evening of Tuesday, the 7th.

As Akron's official music ambassador, she helped shape the town's classical music community for the last forty years. Margaret was the mother of two sons and two daughters, including **Jeanne Baxtresser**, principal flute of the New York Philharmonic (1984–97).

Judith Burganger

JUDITH BURGANGER is the first American to win first prize at the Munich International Piano Competition, among other honors. She performs with distinguished orchestras in North America, Europe, and Japan, and is the artistic director and founder of the FAU Chamber Soloists and Brahms Festival Concerts. She has been on the faculties of the Cleveland Institute, Texas Tech, Carnegie-Mellon, and is now at Florida Atlantic University, as director of the Conservatory of Music. An international duo with husband, Leonid Treer, they are featured in duo-piano recitals.

KATJA CEROVSEK, born in Vienna, October 1, 1969, was raised in Vancouver. She began studies at six, and at seven began taking RCM exams, graduating at thirteen with a diploma in piano performance, the gold medal, the *highest grade* in Canada. She is a six-time national finalist and first place winner in the Canadian Music Competition. In 1984, she entered Indiana University (BM 1988, MM '89, both with highest distinction), was studio accompanist for famed cellist **Janos Starker**, completed her DMA and was appointed associate instructor of piano.

Since her debut with the Calgary Philharmonic at age ten, she has appeared all over Canada. Her U.S. debut was with the Indianapolis Symphony (1985). She has since concertized in Boston, San Francisco, at Kennedy and Lincoln Centers, London, Italy, Istanbul, Taiwan and Tokyo, sometimes appearing in recital with her brother, international violinist Corey Cerovsek. When last heard from she had married, moved to La Jolla, California, teaches privately and continues her successful career.

Angela Cheng

ANGELA CHENG, born in Hong Kong, now a Canadian citizen, received her BM (1992) from Juilliard and MM (1994) from Indiana University, where she was a student of **Menahem Pressler**. Hailed by critics for her technique and musicianship, she is one of Canada's most distinguished and respected pianists. She was the 1986 gold medal winner at the Arthur Rubinstein International Piano Masters Competition, and the first Canadian to win the Montreal International Piano Competition (1988). In the same year, the Canada Council awarded her a Career Development Grant. She also received the Sir James Lougheed Award of Distinction from the Alberta government. For her interpretations of Mozart, she received the Medal of Excellence at the Mozarteum in Salzburg, 1991. In the U.S. she has made solo appearances with Boston, St. Louis, Houston, Indianapolis, Utah, Syracuse, Colorado, New Orleans, Grand Rapids and Honolulu orchestras. She has also appeared with the Israel Philharmonic and major orchestras in Canada. As a recitalist and chamber musician, she has played in New York, Washington, St. Louis, Los Angeles, Pittsburgh, London, Salzburg, Toronto, Vancouver and Montreal. Her CDs include two Mozart concerti with the Vancouver Orchestra, Clara Schumann's Concerto in A Minor with **JoAnn Falletta** and The Women's Philharmonic (Koch), selected works of Clara and Robert Schumann (CBC Records), and four Spanish concerti with Hans Graf and the

Calgary Philharmonic. She was on the faculty of University of Colorado, Boulder, and since 1999 has been on the piano faculty of Oberlin College and Conservatory of Music, where her husband Alvin Chow is also a professor.

GLORIA CHENG, born November 15, 1954, in New Jersey, holds an economics degree from Stanford, and graduate degrees in music from UCLA and USC. In 1987, she was one of three finalists at the international competition for the Paris-based Ensemble intercontemporain, under **Pierre Boulez**. That led to her engagement for the 1989, 1992 and 1996 Ojai Festivals as a featured soloist at the request of music director Boulez. Her solo, chamber, and orchestral appearances have established her as an able executant of contemporary music, and has made her a favorite guest artist with the Los Angeles Philharmonic and its New Music Group. She was a member of the California E.A.R. Unit and Xtet, and appears annually on the *Piano Spheres* concert series in Pasadena, California. She won performer competitions of the ISCM (1992), and first prize in the National Association of Composers USA (1993). Her CD on Koch International featured music by Olivier Messiaen (1995), followed by a Telarc release of piano works by John Adams and Terry Riley, including the world premiere recording of his *The Heaven Ladder, Book 7* (1998). Cheng is a member of the Southwest Chamber Music Society, and is on the board of directors of the American Music Center, a national service and information center for new American music.

SALLY CHRISTIAN has appeared with the Orpheus Chamber Orchestra and other ensembles. A champion of contemporary music, she is also a polished interpreter of Spanish music and has performed as soloist with famed flamenco dancer Jose Greco and his company, as well as touring throughout Mexico with the Xalapa Symphony. Her recitals include well-received Carnegie Hall appearances.

One of the artists on the California Arts Council Touring Roster, she appeared frequently as a guest artist for the nationally syndicated television series *The Best Is Yet To Be*. Her all Ravel CD, released in 1994 on Classical West Records, was followed by a double CD of the complete *Iberia* by Isaac Albeniz (1995). Christian earned her MA from Cal. State, Fresno, after receiving the Amparo Iturbi[155] Scholarship. She also studied at Stanford, and privately with renowned Chilian-American pianist **Claudio Arrau** (1903–91).

JODIE GELBOGIS De SALVO, a graduate of the Manhattan School of Music, made her New York debut at Weill Recital Hall (1988). A 1976 European debut with the Greater Hartford Youth Orchestra led to performances in Germany, Poland, Hungary, Ireland, Wales, and Italy. She has been heard in recital at many universities and summer festivals, and is a guest artist on Indiana's Touring Artist Program.

VIRGINIA ESKIN performs as soloist throughout the U.S., Europe and Israel. A teacher at Northeastern University, she has also lectured at Harvard, Georgia State and the University of Washington. In 1994, she was awarded an honorary Doctorate of Humane Letters by Keene State College (New Hampshire). Her popular symphony appearances include San Francisco, Boston Pops, Boston Classical and the Israel Sinfonietta. She performs at many music festivals, has appeared as guest soloist with the New York City Ballet at Lincoln Center and is a featured artist at the *Art of Music* concert series in the Boston area. Her twenty recordings feature works by American composers Arthur Foote and George Chadwick; with the Hawthorne Quartet, *Chamber Music from Theresienstadt*[156] (Channel Classics); of Afro-British composer *Music of Samuel Coleridge Taylor* (Koch), and *Silenced Voices* (Northeastern); with the Portland String Quartet, Dvořák's Piano Quintet (Arabesque). She is widely known for her ragtime project, which includes *Fluffy Ruffle Girls: Women of Ragtime* (Koch, 1999), featuring compositions by **Judith Zaimont** and **Libby Larsen** among others; *American Beauties: The Rags of Joseph Lamb* (Koch, 2000 re-release); and *Spring Beauties* (Koch, 1998), featuring works of contemporary composers. Other releases are *Mrs. H.H.A. Beach* (Koch), works of **Marion Bauer** and **Ruth Crawford** (Albany, 1998) and with Irina Muresann, violin, and Deborah Boldin, flute, previously unrecorded works of Marion Bauer (Albany,

---

155. Sister of pianist Jose Iturbi. (See Conductors.)
156. Theresienstadt or Terezin, was one of the few concentration camps without gas chambers. Here flourished an inmate orchestra, several composers and performers. The CD also features music of Czech composer **Vitaslava Kapralova**, who died in Paris on the way to being shipped out to Terezin. Mention should be made here of Nurse Ilse Weber who wrote down the songs composed by camp children with touching accompanying drawings. These have been preserved at the Yad Vashem Museum in Israel.

2001). In 2000, her research unearthed more compositions by **Louise Henritte Viardot**, daughter of **Pauline Viardot**. (See Romantic Composers.)

Summers are spent as a soloist and chamber player at Monadnock Music (New Hampshire). She was a featured soloist at the Aaron Copland Centennial program held in 2000 at Northeastern University, a Chopin recital, November 2002, at St. Anselm's College in the Salon of Georges Sand, named after the composer's great love, and in March 2003, a concert of Women Composers at Wellesley College.

Eskin's *First Ladies of Music* Series for radio, consisting of thirteen one-hour shows, began March 2006, airing on many major stations including Detroit, Pittsburgh, WGBH, Boston, and ten New Zealand affiliates. The broadcasts helped to change public perception of women composers.

JANINA FIALKOWSKA was born in Montreal to a Polish father and Canadian mother, who started her on piano at age five. She studied at the École de Musique Vincent d'Indy and received BM and MM degrees from the University of Montreal (1968) when she was seventeen. In 1969, she won first prize in the Radio Canada National Talent Festival, and went to Paris to study with Yvonne Lefebure. The following year she entered Juilliard, studied with Sascha Gorodnitzi, and became his assistant for five years. In 1974, she won Arthur Rubinstein's inaugural Master Piano Competition in Israel.

Her annual European tours include Amsterdam, Germany, London, Poland and France. She has also performed in Israel and Hong Kong. In North America her appearances included the Symphony Orchestras of Chicago, Cleveland, Los Angeles, Philadelphia and Pittsburgh, and in Canada with Montreal, Toronto, Ottawa, Calgary and Vancouver. Her repertoire covers the Classical and Romantic. She is a recognized interpreter of Chopin and Liszt, and is also a champion of 20th century Polish composers.

Her world premieres include a newly discovered concerto by Franz Liszt with the Chicago Symphony (1990) and **Libby Larsen**'s Piano Concerto with the Minnesota Orchestra (1991). Other concerto premieres are by Sir Andrzej Panufnik with the Colorado Symphony (1992), and Marjan Mozetich with the Kingston Orchestra (2000).

Fialkowska is a founding member, with Canadian colleagues Marc-André Hamelin, André Laplante, Jon Kimura Parker, **Angela Cheng** and **Angela Hewitt**, of *Piano Six*. They donate ten days each season at a fraction of their fees, to perform in schools, churches and concert halls throughout rural Canada, bringing music to those who would otherwise not be able to attend concerts.

KATIE GOGOLADZE was born in Tbilisi, Georgia (Russia) in 1969. Via listening to her mother's students, she was picking out Bach preludes on the piano. Her mother, a promising pianist, sacrificed her career for that of her daughter, but later became a professor at the Tbilisi State Conservatory, where Katie studied. Her first public appearance was at age nine with the Georgia Symphony playing a Bach concerto. Two years later she performed Beethoven's Concerto No. 2 and, in 1982, the Rachmaninoff Concerto No.1 with the same orchestra. Selected "Student of the Year," she was the youngest participant of the "Symphony Series." After winning many competitions and appearing in concerts, television and radio appearances in Europe, she was chosen in 1992 to study at Indiana University (MM). She then studied in New York with **Ilana Vered**, meanwhile giving recitals, including the French Music Gala at Lincoln Center's Alice Tully Hall.

GILA GOLDSTEIN, born in Israel, received a BM in piano performance from the Rubin Academy of Music at Tel-Aviv University. Her MM is from the Manhattan School of Music, and now resides in New York.

A board member of the American Liszt Society, since 1992, she has been the founder and president of its New York Chapter. On the faculty of the Choir Academy of Harlem, she has toured with the Boys Choir of Harlem, including the 1999 Israel Festival.

Goldstein made her New York recital debut at Merkin Hall, and UK debut at the 10th London International Jewish Music Festival. Internationally, she has played in Mexico City, Canada, Paris, Tel-Aviv and Jerusalem, and in the U.S. in St. Louis, Chicago and California. Her festival appearances include Ravinia, the Gardner Museum in Boston, Sala Casals, Puerto Rico, and Musée de Louvre, Paris.

Her CD, *Piano Works of Paul Ben-Haim*, is on Centaur (2001).

A native of Freiburg, Germany, now living in New York, **BABETTE HIERHOLZER** began her piano studies at age five in Berlin, making her professional debut at age eleven in Philharmonic Hall with Mozart's Concerto K. 488. She studied with Herbert Stessin at Juilliard, Paul Badura-Skoda in Vienna, and **Maria Tipo** in Florence, which led to extensive concertizing in the U.S., Europe, South America and Africa. Her 1978 debut with the Berlin Philharmonic was followed by many performances with that orchestra. Her 1986 American debut was with the Pittsburgh Symphony, performing Liszt's Concerto No. 1. She later played the same piece with the Orquesta Sinfonica de Chile in 1993 and the Staatskapelle in Berlin. In 1994, she performed the Clara Schumann Piano Concerto with the St. Louis Symphony and made her Canadian debut. Her recordings with MARUS/EMI include works by Couperin, Debussy, Mozart, Scarlatti, and a rare Schumann piece, *Exercises*, variations on a theme of Beethoven. She appeared as a stand-in for actress Nastassja Kinski (who played Clara Wieck) and performed the soundtrack for the movie *Spring Symphony* (1983), chronicling the life of Robert Schumann.

EDITH HIRSHTAL studied with **Leon Fleisher** at Peabody. She has served on the faculties of Temple University, Bryn Mawr Conservatory, and the Downeast Summer Chamber Institute, and is now a professor of piano at Cal. State, Long Beach, where she became founder/director of the Long Beach Chamber Players. Her recitals and concert venues include Lincoln Center, Metropolitan Opera Company, Philadelphia Opera Company and the Sequoia Quartet. Winner of numerous awards, including the Galica Prize and the 1978 University of Maryland International Piano Competition, she has been heard on KUSC's "Sundays at Four," highlighting skilled musicians, and is the soloist on the soundtrack for the 1990 film, *Impromptu*, based on the life of Chopin.

The daughter of conductor Eugene Jochum, German pianist **VERONICA JOCHUM** was destined for a career in music. After graduating from the Hochschule für Musik in Munich, she attended master classes with **Edwin Fischer**, and came to the U.S. to study with **Rudolph Serkin**. She has performed worldwide with such orchestras as the Boston Symphony, London, Berlin and Munich Philharmonics, Orchestre National de France, and Vienna Symphony. Her New York debut was in 1981 with the 92nd Street Y Chamber Orchestra. With a repertoire from Mozart to modern—she commissioned Gunther Schuller's second Piano Concerto, premiering it at the Sandpoint Festival—she has become known for her "commentary concerts." Her pioneer recordings include Ferruccio Busoni and Clara Schumann, as well as standard classical composers. She received the Cross of the Order of Merit of the Federal Republic of Germany (1994), and was made a Fellow of the Bunting Institute of Harvard University (1996–97).

When not performing, she teaches in Munich and at the New England Conservatory.

A native of Rio de Janeiro, **DIANA KACSO** has soloed with the Israel Philharmonic, London Mozart Players, and the Baltimore and Utah Symphonies, among others. She began her studies at the Brazilian Conservatory of Music, completing her education with a scholarship to Juilliard, studying with the late Sascha Gorodnitzki (1904–86). She performed in a trio with cellist **Nancy Green** and the late violist **Rosemary Glyde**. Her recitals have been heard in most major American cities. Her performance of the twelve Liszt Transcendental Etudes at the University of Southampton (England) was recorded by the BBC She won the Chopin Competition in 1975, and second prize in the 1977 Arthur Rubinstein International Competition. She is on the roster of Steinway Artists.

SYLVIA KERSENBAUM was born December 27, 1941, in Buenos Aires, Argentina, and began musical training with her mother before earning degrees in Performance, Pedagogy and Composition from the National Conservatory in her home city, as well as artists' diplomas from the Italian academies of Chigiana in Siena and Santa Cecilia in Rome. Her recital and solo career covers Europe, North and South America and the Far East with noted orchestras and conductors. Well-received Angel-EMI recordings include the complete Chopin etudes and sonatas, Liszt transcriptions, Paganini-Brahms and Handel-Brahms Variations, and the Tchaikovsky Piano Concerto No. 2. Her version of the Tchaikovsky Concerto, under Jean Martinon, was reissued on CD (EMI Europe) and the Liszt *Hexameron* was included in their series *100 Virtuosi of the Twentieth Century.*

She was guest artist of the American Liszt Society in 1986 for the 150th anniversary of the composer's death, and in 1990 was awarded an honorary membership in the American Beethoven Society. She was one of five award recipients of the distinguished Konex Award for "outstanding performer" for the last decade of the 20th century in Argentina.

Professor of piano at Western Kentucky University (Bowling Green) since 1976, she received the 1990 Award for Creative Research. Under the pen name of Simon Papett,[157] she wrote the music for Edgar Allen Poe's *Mask of the Red Death*, premiered as a ballet in October 2001, at WKU.

Kersenbaum's ever-busy schedule projects to 2005 with performances of the entire cycle of Beethoven's 32 Piano Sonatas at WKU and in Argentina. She previously presented this cycle to much critical acclaim in Montevideo (Uruguay). A duo-piano recital with her sister, **Estela Kersenbaum Olevsky**, for the Argentine-Israeli Cultural Association (AMIA) was held August 2003, in their home town of Buenos Aires.

ELENA KLIONSKY, born in St. Petersburg, Russia, April 19, 1964, began playing the piano at age five, giving her first public performance at six. All through elementary school she was ostracized—often beaten up—because she was Jewish. (There were three Jews out of forty children.) Her father, a celebrated artist whose paintings of the Holocaust carried with them the threat of being exiled to Siberia, was able to take advantage of the 1973 Nixon pact signed with Brezhnev. This involved an exchange of a certain amount of Russian people for American wheat. With an allowance of $90 per person, the family emigrated to America in 1974. They also managed to send for their piano from St. Petersburg and—miraculously—have it arrive safely in New York! From age fifteen to nineteen, Elena studied with **Nadia Reisenberg**. Concurrently, she was in the Pre-College Division of Juilliard, making her debut at Lincoln Center while in high school. She earned her BM (1987) and MM (1988) at Juilliard, receiving the prestigious Petschek Scholarship while a master's candidate. Her mentor was Robert Harris, a protégé of Vladimir Horowitz, and the first African-American to graduate from Juilliard.

Solo recitals, orchestral appearances, television and radio performances have taken Klionsky across the U.S., Canada, Mexico, Western Europe and Russia. A sold-out audience attended her debut in Carnegie Hall's Weill Recital Hall (1990), the same year she married Roman Pipko, an international investment lawyer. Their daughter Elizabeth Tatiana (E.T.) was born June 26, 1995. From 1992–94 the couple lived in London. Six months of 1994 were spent in Moscow where, at the time, Elena needed a bodyguard, there being so much danger in the streets.

Klionsky's benefit appearances include Elizabeth Taylor's Concert for AIDS in Helsinki, and Isaac Stern's seventieth birthday celebration at the Ben Gurion University. In 1997, she expanded her horizons with a tour of Taiwan, Singapore, Malaysia and Korea. November 2001, she was in New Orleans for a program of Brahms, Persichetti and Beethoven with Klauspeter Seibel conducting the Louisiana Philharmonic.

She now makes her home in New York, where she is on the Board of the American Russian Young Artists Orchestra (ARYO), founded in 1990 by then First Ladies Hilary Clinton and Naina Yeltsin as a diplomatic initiative to bring the two nations together through youth and music. Today, after nine world tours with concerts in nearly fifty cities and over 500 musicians in the ranks of its alumni, ARYO has gained international recognition as a musical ambassadorship and a world-class orchestra. Leon Botstein, president of Bard College and music director of the American Symphony Orchestra, serves as music director. The first ladies of both countries served as ARYO's honorary chairmen since its inception.

Daughter of famous violinists **Leonid Kogan** (1924–1982), and **Elisabeth Gilels** (Kogan) (*b*1919), sister of celebrated pianist **Emil Gilels**, **NINA KOGAN** has music in her genes. Her violinist brother, Pavel, won the 1970 Sibelius contest in Finland and is now conducting. After early training and a doctorate from Moscow State Conservatory, she was appointed assistant professor there. Her many awards include participation in the Aram Khachaturian and Marguerite Long-Jacques Thibaud International Competitions. She has appeared as a recital and concert soloist in major cities on every continent, including the Hong Kong Arts Centre with the Moscow State

---

157. As a cat lover, Sylvia chose the names of two of her own pets for her pseudonym as a composer.

Symphony. Her recordings include chamber and solo music, as well as clarinet and piano repertoire with her husband, clarinetist Julian Milkis.

She began concertizing at the age of twelve, and at thirteen started performing with her father—it grew into a unique collaboration that lasted almost sixteen years until his untimely death in 1982. During these years she was the only pianist he ever performed with.

Nina has played with the Orchestra of the Bolshoi Theater, Moscow Philharmonic, Moscow Radio Symphony Orchestra, Moscow State Symphony Orchestra, Moscow Chamber orchestra, St. Petersburg Philharmonic Orchestra, Orchestre National de Paris, Antverpen Philharmonic, Zagreb Philharmonic, Dresden Philharmonic, Stockholm Symphony, Lugano Orchestra and in the U.S. with the symphonies in Chicago, Boston, Philadelphia, Los Angeles, San Francisco, Detroit and Washington, DC.

She has recorded for Deutche Grammophon, EMI, Sony, Philips, Chant du Monde, Melodya and Video-Kultur. She performs a vast variety of chamber music, and gives master classes all over the world. 2002 found her again on the faculty of the Niagara International Chamber Music Festival.

Israela Margalit

After a Munich debut, **ISRAELA MARGALIT** concertized throughout Europe, North and South America and Israel. In 1975, she took a six-year leave of absence to bring up her two children. Returning to the concert stage, she added the roles of producer/writer/presenter of TV music programs. She created *Beethoven*, a one hour program for A&E (1983), and wrote and performed *The Well-Tempered Bach*, with Peter Ustinov for PBS Great Performances (1985), which received an Emmy nomination. The response was so great, she enlisted Ustinov for *The Immortal Beethoven* (1987), followed by *Mozart Mystique*, for which she won an NEA Award for excellence in broadcasting. Also in 1987, she founded *Music and More*, Inc., presenting innovative programs of performance and commentary with herself and guest artists in an annual series of concerts in New York, and special programs for schoolchildren.

In 1992 she debuted in Russia, and 1993 in China at the Beijing International Music Festival. Her Brahms First Piano Concerto was hailed as one of the greatest recordings of that piece, and her Saint-Saëns No. 2 was compared to the renowned Arthur Rubinstein's interpretation.

JULIANA MARKOVA was born in Sofia, Bulgaria, July 8, 1945. She studied at the conservatory there, then at the Verdi Conservatory in Milan, where she graduated with highest honors in 1969. Meanwhile, she won the Georges Enesco Competition in Bucharest (1964) and the Marguerite Long-Jacques Thibaud Competition in Paris (1965). Known for her interpretations of Romantic piano literature, she originally began her music career to complement her ballet study, but switched paths. Besides recitals, she has soloed with leading orchestras in Europe and America, and appeared on RAI Milan, and German television. Her American debut with Allied Arts in 1973 led to a Three by Three series at Carnegie Hall the next year. Markova settled in London, married British pianist (of Viennese parents) Michael Roll, and continues her successful career. Their son Maximilian was born in 1982.

New York City native, **MINA MILLER** enjoys international recognition for her interpretation and knowledge of the music of Danish composer **Carl Nielsen** (1865–1931). Her Hyperion double CD features his complete piano music. She studied piano at the Manhattan School of Music, took master classes at the Accademia Musicale Chigiana (Siena, Italy), and at the Mozarteum (Salzburg), and has a PhD from NYU. She made her 1987 European solo debut at London's Wigmore Hall and her orchestral debut in 1992 with the Prague Chamber Orchestra. Under the sponsorship of the Danish Government and Cultural Institute, she presented over sixty concerts in Denmark (1987–88).

Miller is a professor of music at the University of Kentucky, editor of the critical edition of Nielson's complete piano music (Copenhagen: Edition Wilhelm Hansen), *A Nielson Companion* (London: Faber & Faber), and author of *Carl Nielson: A Guide to Research* (New York: Garland Press). A guest lecturer-recitalist at universities and conservatories in Europe and America, her performances have been heard on NPR, the BBC, Radio France and Danish and Norwegian National Radio. In 1998, Mina founded Music of Remembrance, a Seattle-based organization dedicated to advancing the preservation, understanding and performance of music related to the Holocaust, its origins and aftermath. She serves as the organization's president and artistic director. By 2002 they had, according to Melida Bargreen in the *Seattle Times*, "amassed an impressive record of performances with some of the region's finest musicians and repertoire." Their board of directors includes such notables as John Corigliano, Kurt Masur, Murray Perahia, Gerard Schwarz, David Shifrin and Pinchas Zukerman.

ILANA MYSIOR, born July 25, 1938, in Tel Aviv, came to New York with her family when she was one. Her first teacher was her pianist mother. At nine, she began studies with Ruth and Artur Balsam. Moving to California, she won all the Los Angeles City College Music Awards, the first Young Musician's Foundation competition (1950), and the Coleman Chamber Music Competition. At UCLA (BM, 1959), she trained with **Jan Popper** in the Opera Workshop and **Roger Wagner**, and was the first student to receive an MM in accompanying (1960).

She founded and directed the accompanying department at the Tel Aviv Conservatory (1960–63). Her accompanying and vocal coaching positions include Radio America/Israel Cultural Foundation Concerts, Symphonic Chorale, Casals International Competition, the newly formed San Diego Opera Company (1964–66), San Diego Symphony (1965–66), and San Diego Chamber Music Workshop (1977–2000). As professor of music at the University of San Diego (1966–91), she created their opera workshop and instrumental ensemble classes. Her continuous chamber music career covers a Carnegie Hall debut with the ERA Trio (1982), to the founding the same year of the Gennaro Trio—with Ronald Goldman, violin, and Mary Lindblom, cello, with whom she has broadcast and toured in Central and North America. She was voted Outstanding Musician of the Year by the Jewish Community Centers of San Diego (1986). The ensemble was voted "Best Piano Trio of 1999" in the area.

In 1991, Mysior was diagnosed with Marfan Syndrome, a degenerative connective tissue disorder that appears to attack very tall people, causing enlargement of the aorta and possible instant death. She underwent a metallic aortic valve replacement and had the vulnerable artery "wrapped" in a surgery, May 1991. While she continues to teach piano and coach singers, Ilana now plays benefit concerts for, and lectures on, the rarely publicized killer Marfan (which has more victims than MS) coast to coast from Stanford University in Palo Alto, California, to the Peabody Conservatory in Baltimore, Maryland.

BARBARA NISSMAN, born in Philadelphia, December 31, 1944, received her doctorate in music from the University of Michigan, where her principal mentor was **György Sandor**. Her international career took off after her debut in 1971 with the Philadelphia Orchestra, when she undertook a highly successful tour of Europe sponsored by conductor Eugene Ormandy. She has subsequently appeared with orchestras in North and South America, Europe and the Far East.

Nissman is also a noted Prokofiev scholar, and was one of the first artists to begin recording his cycle of complete piano sonatas in the late 1980s. In 1989, she made history by becoming the first pianist to perform all his piano sonatas in a series of recitals in both London and New York. This monumental feat, spanning three volumes, was released on the Newport Classics label, becoming the finest complete Prokofiev piano sonata cycle in the last twenty years. She was invited to Moscow to collaborate with leading Soviet musicians in a detailed study of Prokofiev manuscripts kept at the Central State Archives. In commemoration of his 100th birthday, Nissman performed the complete sonatas throughout the U.S. and Europe during the 1991–1992 season. She was invited back to the Moscow Conservatory in 1998 to give concerts and teach master classes on Prokofiev. During this trip, she also taught at the St. Petersburg Conservatory. For the fiftieth anniversary of his death, in 2003, she recorded and performed all five Piano Concertos throughout Europe and the Far East.

Her other specialty is contemporary repertoire, especially the music of Brazilian **Alberto Ginastera** (1916–83), who dedicated his third piano sonata to her. Nissman's two-volume set of Ginastera's complete piano solo and chamber works won Record of the Year nominations from both *Gramophone* magazine and *American Record Guide* in 1989. During 2002, in addition to her American concerts, she appeared in Spain, Holland, England and Mexico, and in 2003 returned to Australia and New Zealand. Nissman lives on a farm in the Allegheny Mountains of West Virginia.

GAIL NIWA is the first woman to capture the top prize—the gold medal—as well as the Audience and Chamber Music Prizes at the 1991 Gina Bachauer International Piano Competition in Utah. This led to a New York recital debut in Alice Tully Hall. Her Kennedy Center debut in 1987 was the result of winning the Washington International Competition. She has also won top prizes in the International Chopin Competition, the YCA Association Competition and the Mae Whitaker Competition.

Born in Chicago of musical parents (her mother Eloise was her first teacher, her father was a violinist in the Chicago Symphony), Gail made her Chicago Symphony debut at age eight and received a scholarship to Juilliard, where she earned her BM and MM as a student of Adele Markus. She has given recitals in the U.S. and Europe and toured Scandinavia and the Far East. Also an outstanding ensemble player, in 1986 she won the Best Accompanist Award at the Moscow Tchaikowsky Competition for violinists. She has performed with several chamber orchestras and recorded with violinist David Kim. Columbia University opened their 2002–03 season with Niwa as soloist.

SARINA OHNO, born March 20, 1970, in Tokyo, was raised in Germany where she began piano studies with her mother. She received a BM from the Hochschule für Musik in Stuttgart, an artist diploma from Indiana University, and DMA from Queens College, New York, (1998). She has performed as a recitalist and chamber musician throughout Germany, Switzerland, Japan and America. A founding member of the Pacific Ensemble, she was in residence at the Institute of Chamber Music at the University of Wisconsin, Milwaukee, playing with members of the Fine Arts Quartet. She is on the faculty of the Bloomingdale School of Music in New York.

Born in Chiba, Japan, **YUMIKO OKAWA** began piano at age three. Later, she studied at the Hochschule für Musik in Munich, graduating with a master class diploma. In 1987, Okawa received the Luis Coleman Award for performers of Spanish music. She lives in Japan, performing in concert and recital there as well as in Europe. Her two outstanding CDs of Isaac Albeniz piano music on Pro Arte Musicae—*Cantos de España* (1990) and *Recuerdos de Viaje* (1991)—have received deserved rave reviews.

Estela Olevsky

ESTELA (Kersenbaum) **OLEVSKY** was born August 13, 1943, in Buenos Aires. Her Austrian father, Oscar, had left Berlin in 1935 and met and married Italian Teresa Sacchero, who was playing violin in a ladies orchestra in Buenos Aires. Estela made her debut there at age eight, and at sixteen was the youngest graduate to receive the Diploma Artistico de Piano from the Conservatorio Nacional de Musica. She also earned a conducting diploma from the Instituto Superior del Teatro Colón, and studied composition with Alberto Ginastera. She has toured all over the world—Europe, North and South America, New Zealand, and the Far East—to unanimous acclaim. She has performed with numerous distinguished soloists, such as sopranos **Phyllis Curtin** and **Paulina Stark**; violinists Leon Spierer, Julian Olevsky, Henryk Szeryng and Charles Treger; cellists Paul Olefsky and Matt Haimovitz; and flutist **Carol Wincenc**.

Her recording credits include the complete piano trios of Brahms, with the Olewsky Trio[158] for the Musical Heritage Society, and the complete Mozart violin and piano sonatas with her late husband, Julian Olevsky (1926–85). Both of the above collections have recently been re-released on the Amatius Classics label. Recordings with European orchestras include Richard Strauss *Burleske* for piano and orchestra (Opus) and the Ravel Piano Concerto in G Major (Stradivari Classics). Solo CDs are: *Piano Solos of Latin America* (Centaur, 1994); and *Frédéric Chopin (1810–1849)*, featuring the Mazurka in E minor Op. 41, the 24 Preludes Op. 28, and Sonata in B minor Op. 58 (Amatius Classics, 2000).

Olevsky joined the faculty of the University of Massachusetts at Amherst in 1968, where she was head of applied piano studies until her retirement from full-time teaching in June 2002. She was honored with the title professor emeritus. She was also visiting professor of piano at the Hartt School of Music, Mount Holyoke College,

---

158. The trio used the family name, while cousins Paul (cello) and Julian (violin) anglicized their names differently.

Amherst College, Brazil's Universidad Federal de Rio de Janeiro and the National Conservatory of Buenos Aires. She is listed in *Who's Who in Music*.

In December 2001, she appeared at Kennedy Center with jazz pianist Billy Taylor in an innovative program entitled "It's All Music," presented as part of the Center's Educational Program Series, which alternates virtuoso piano solos from both the classical and jazz idiom. Her 2002–03 schedule included the Chopin First Piano Concerto with long-time friend, conductor Melvin Strauss, and the Wenatchee Valley Symphony (Washington), duo recitals with soprano Paulina Stark at Florida Atlantic University, Boca Raton, Florida (January 2003), soloist with Asheville (North Carolina) Symphony Orchestra (March), recitals at University of Massachusetts and a duo piano recital with her sister, **Sylvia Kersenbaum**, for the Argentine-Israeli Cultural Association (AMIA) series in Buenos Aires (August).

Estela came to America in July 1965 to marry violinist Julian, whom she had met while concertizing in Latin America. They were wed in 1966. Their daughter, Diane Olevsky Gluck, born October 26, 1970, is beauty director of *Marie Claire* magazine in New York.

A graduate of the California Institute of the Arts, where she worked with Jerome Lowenthal and Reginald Stewart, **EDITH ORLOFF** received further training at the Music Academy of the West and in the '70s participated in master classes at USC with **Rosina Lhévinne**. She also studied in Houston and Italy, performing in Verona as a member of the American Academy of the Arts. Besides her solo work in recital, with orchestra and at summer festivals, she has accompanied renowned instrumentalists. She is concert coordinator of the summer chamber music program at Idyllwild Arts in Southern California, where she has served on the faculty since 1976. In 1980, she became a founding member of the Los Angeles-based Pacific Trio, which serves as trio-in-residence for Idyllwild Arts, and annually tours the U.S. and Europe. 1998 saw a successful solo recital debut in Germany, where she is a regular guest artist with the *Ensemble Con Brio* in Bruchsal. She performs frequently with the Houston Symphony Chamber Players. Her husband, David Peck, is principal clarinetist of the Houston Symphony.

The 2002–2003 season included a European tour, recordings, and solo and chamber recitals in Houston and throughout California. Summer festival appearances, often with her husband, have been at La Jolla SummerFest, San Luis Obispo, Grand Tetons, Ventura, and Musique-at-the-Moulin, in Andé, France.

Born in Los Angeles, **REBECCA PENNEYS** made her debut at age nine. Her New York debut was in 1972 at Alice Tully Hall. Teachers such as **Rosina Lhévinne** and **Menachem Pressler** insured an international career which has taken her to Asia, New Zealand, Australia, Europe, Israel, and throughout America. In chamber music, she has collaborated with such greats as cellist **Janós Starker**, violinist **Ruggiero Ricci**, pianist **Paul Badura-Skoda**, flutist **Carol Wincenc**, as well as prominent string quartets. As pianist-founder of the New Arts Trio, she has twice won the Naumburg Award for Chamber Music. She has been on the faculties of North Carolina School of the Arts, International Institute of Music at Santander (Spain), head of the music department at the University of Wisconsin, at Eastman since 1980, and chair of the piano department at the Chautauqua Institution, where she has been a resident artist for over twenty seasons.

Penneys has gained recognition in both pedagogical and medical fields as the creator of a revolutionary keyboard technique which enables pianists to achieve maximum emotional expression with minimum movement, thus preventing painful and crippling neurological and muscular injuries assailing many musicians. For this extraordinary work, she was invited to serve as guest editor for the 1989 issue of the medical journal, *Seminars in Neurology*, focusing on the medical problems of performing artists. Her "Motion and Emotion" seminars at Eastman are attended by performers, teachers and students—the latter only too happy to follow her credo: "Finger exercises are not music, and practicing them endlessly amounts to waging war against what the action [of the piano] already does to the pianist." By the time musicians have finished her course they are delighted to find that they "feel better, practice less, and accomplish more." She was featured in the October 2001 issue of the piano magazine *Clavier*.

Louisiana-born **JULIE RIVERS**, daughter of a Swedish immigrant, began playing the piano at age two. She studied with Austrian virtuoso **Stefan Bardas**, and made her debut with the Dallas Symphony. At the University of North Texas, from which she graduated with high honors, she won all awards offered to pianists by the School of Music. She was also "Top Coed on Campus." She was twice honored in the publication "Outstanding Young Women in America." In 1992, she was part of a competition/performance honoring women composers sponsored by the National League of American Pen Women at their 36th Biennial Composition Competition in Washington, DC. She was a winner in that competition again in 1998 for music from *One Starry Night*. It was through this historical organization she met and teamed up with composer **Eugènie Rocherolle**. The pair played an acclaimed duo-concert at the 2006 NLAPW Biennial.

Founding her own company, *Earth Star Recordings* (Julie is also an astronomer), her first CD was a collaboration with Rocherolle on an outstanding multi-track disc performing Eugènie's works in the delightful 1995 recording *Spinning Gold*. Their second effort was *Tidings of Joy*, with Rocherolle's version of Christmas music. This was followed by *Christmastide*, featuring Rivers' arrangements and soloed by her. February 1999 saw the world premiere of *The Kiss of the Sun*, celebrating the dazzling romance of day—the much-anticipated sequel to *One Starry Night*. Radio Kansas selected both disks for their popular New Age program, "Nightcrossings." The two albums were listed simultaneously on the Hastings Books Music and Video "Top Ten."

Rivers was recognized by the Kansas Arts Commission with a state Fellowship Awards for composition and has received two ASCAP awards. She has been called a "treasured Kansas artist" by State First Lady Linda Graves, and is listed in the 1998/1999 *Who's Who in Entertainment*.

As part of a teaching career spanning from the University of North Texas to Interlochen, she is the founder of Topeka's "Put Piano in Your Summer," whose classes in composition, duets and ensembles use her original workbooks. For almost three decades she has appeared as an orchestral soloist and recitalist, concertizes with her *Starry Night Trio*, and in duo concerts with her former husband, James Rivers. They have two sons, David Aaron, born 1968, and James Arthur, born 1971.

HEATHER SCHMIDT, from Calgary, Alberta, Canada, is both pianist and composer. Her recognition comes through performances, broadcasts, commissions and awards in Canada, America, France, Germany, Switzerland, Poland, the Czech Republic, England, Finland, Iceland, Mexico and Brazil.

She began piano lessons at age four, composing at five, and made her first public appearance at six. Her studies were at the University of Calgary with composer Allan Bell, then Indiana State where she received BM and MM degrees with double majors in composition and piano performance. In 1996, at age twenty-one, she became the youngest student to receive a music doctorate there. She then completed two years of studies at Juilliard: composition with Milton Babbitt, and piano with Yoheved Kaplinsky.

Her awards include first prize in the 1992 Austrian-Canadian Mozart Competition, 1992 Gold Medal at the Kiwanis Music Festival, first place at the 2000 Canadian Concerto Competition and first prize in the 2001 Eckhardt-Gramatté National Music Competition for the Performance of Canadian Music. Her 2002–03 season included recitals in New York City, Chicago, Toronto, Ottawa, Calgary and Dallas, with concerto engagements throughout Canada and with the Aguascalientes Symphony Orchestra (Mexico).

As a chamber musician, Heather has performed with many renowned artists, including cellist **Shauna Rolston**. Their collaboration began with a successful duo recital at the 2002 Winnipeg New Music Festival, and continued in Finland and Iceland (2003), a tour of the Maritime Provinces (2004), a North American tour (2005), and the film *Synchronicity* for BRAVO television.

Schmidt has written four piano concertos, as well as concertos for flute, voice, viola and cello. Her first symphony was premiered by the Hamilton Philharmonic (May 2005). Her Cello Concerto (1998), featuring Shauna Rolston with the CBC Vancouver Orchestra under Mario Bernardi, was released by CBC Records (2001). *Transcendence*, for two pianos, was premiered with **Angela Cheng** at the Vancouver Chamber Festival (July 2005).

Heather was composer-in-residence for the Hamilton Philharmonic Orchestra in Ontario (2002–05), as well as serving short-term residencies at festivals throughout Canada.

Nadia Shpachenko

NADIA SHPACHENKO, born February 24, 1977, in Kharkov, Ukraine, was influenced by her mother, Sima Shwartz, a pianist and teacher, and began studying piano and cello at age five. At thirteen she was recognized as a composer and pianist, performing with the Kharkov Philharmonic, and placing second in the All-Ukrainian Young Composers Competition. She was a founding member of the Ukrainian Folk Hebrew Orchestra, performing as cellist, before emigrating to Israel where her studies continued. She also played at the annual Tel-Hai International Summer Festival. A scholarship enabled study at the Longy School of Music in Boston where she earned her BM in 1997. She moved to California, completing her MM (1999) and DMA (2004) from the University of Southern California (USC). A gold medal winner of the California International Young Artists Piano Competition, bronze medal at the Wideman International Piano Competition, a first prize winner of the MTNA Collegiate Artist Piano Competition, Culver City-Westchester Symphony Concerto Competition, and Redlands Bowl Young Artists Competition, she has played at the Music Academy of the West, Aspen, van Cliburn, Sarasota, Manchester (Vermont) and Saluzzo (Italy) International Music Festivals.

Her appearances in the U.S. and Europe, in recital and with orchestra, include the Los Angeles County Museum of Art, Concertgebouw, Amsterdam, Château de Modave in Belgium, the Phillips Collection in Washington, DC, and Carnegie Hall. Her performances have been featured on classical radio—KMZT, Los Angeles, WQXR, New York, and television. Her CDs include *Life, Death and Rain*, with selections by Chopin, Debussy and Kirchner, plus an all Beethoven disc with the Piano Concerto in G major and the Sonata in C major (Waldstein).

Nadia is married to Barry Werger, a robotics research engineer at NASA.

The St. Louis roots of **JACQUELYNE SILVER** are rich with the sounds of the ragtime and jazz gleaned from her musician father. After pursuing traditional studies at Juilliard and Fordham University (New York), she appeared on "The Great Performers" series at Avery Fisher Hall with **Marilyn Horne**, and helped **Leonard Bernstein** direct his "Songfest" with the New York Philharmonic and the National Symphony in Washington, DC. She has served as musical director for regional New York Opera Companies, and conducted several performances of *Tosca* and *Madama Butterfly* for the American Trial Lawyers Association. She is an authority on Scott Joplin and ragtime. Her film credits include a documentary on the life of Bèla Bartók. She composed, directed and conducted Lincoln Center's *A Child's Christmas in Wales*, by Dylan Thomas, and has produced performances of operas for children by the Little Orchestra Society of New York. As a lecturer, Silver is in demand for her entertaining and knowledgeable pre-concert presentations and music appreciation seminars.

ELEANOR (Blum) **SOKOLOFF** came to the Curtis Institute in 1931 as a piano student, with early training at the Cleveland Institute. In 1936, still a student, she began teaching as a "temporary" substitute for a faculty member on leave. Asked to remain on staff after graduation (piano, 1938), she continued teaching for sixty-five years. She was married to Vladimir Sokoloff (1913–97), her piano partner and classmate, who himself made a mark at Curtis as a mentor and musician. Over seventy-five of her students have performed with the Philadelphia Orchestra. On May 5, 2001, she was honored with a Curtis Alumni Award. Her daughters have continued the family's musical legacy. Laurie (Curtis alumna) plays piccolo with the Baltimore Symphony, and Kathy is director of development at the Settlement Music School. At 94 in 2006 Eleanore was still teaching...

SUSAN STARR's Philadelphia Orchestra debut at age six distinguished her as the youngest soloist to ever appear with a major orchestra. After her 1961 Curtis graduation, she auditioned for a top agent who reflected the times when he frankly told her, "If you were a man, I'd sign you in a minute." Only after winning the prestigious bronze medal at the First International Mitropoulos Competition (New York) and second prize in the Tchaikowsky Competition (Moscow, 1962), did she obtain management. Since then, she has performed with major orchestras all over the world: Europe, Russia, South America, the Far East and Hong Kong. In 1977, she played at the White

House at the request of President Jimmy Carter. She has made over fifty appearances with the Philadelphia Orchestra, and played with the New York Philharmonic, Chicago and National Symphonies and at many festivals. She has served on the faculties of Curtis, Florida International University and the Philadelphia College of Performing Arts. In 1994, she returned to the Tchaikovsky Competition as a judge.

DUBRAVKA TOMSIC, born in Dubrovnik, Slovenia, 1940, gave her first public recital at age five. In 1952, after playing for **Claudio Arrau** in London, she moved to New York where her professor father was studying under a Rockefeller Fellowship. Here she attended Juilliard, made her debut with the New York Philharmonic, and presented a Carnegie Hall recital in 1957 which captured the attention of the then greatest pianist in the world, **Arthur Rubinstein**, who became her teacher until she returned home to Slovenia in 1959. Her career soared in Europe, Australia and Asia, with appearances at world festivals. Her prizes include the Brussels Mozart Festival International Competition (1967), Zupancic Prize (1970), Golden Lyre (1970), and the Gold Medal with "Ordre de Saint Fortunat" (1987). After a twenty year absence, she was welcomed back to the U.S. with an opening night recital at the Newport Festival, and went on to acclaimed concerts in Chicago, San Francisco, Atlanta and Boston. Her rendition of Beethoven's Concerto No.5 with the Boston Symphony (1994) led to a return engagement, as well as another appearance in Carnegie Hall in 2001. With over forty recordings to her credit, encompassing the music of Brahms, Beethoven, Chopin, Grieg, Liszt, Mozart, Debussy and Schumann, Tomsic continues her performance career while maintaining a teaching position at the Ljubljana (now Serbia) Academy of Music. She has served as juror for many international piano competitions, including the 10th Van Cliburn International Piano Competition in May 1997, Leeds International Piano Competition in September 2000, and Beethoven International Piano Competition in Vienna in June 2001. She makes her home in Ljubljana.

SYLVIA TRAEY was born in 1950, in Antwerp, Belgium. At sixteen, she began to study piano with her father, Eugène Traey, at the Royal Flemish Conservatory of Music. Three years later she gave her first piano recitals at home and abroad. From 1976–77, she completed her studies at Curtis under **Leon Fleischer**. Her many awards include the Tenuto Competition Brussels (1971), Queen Elisabeth of Belgium Competition (1978) and the Johannes Brahms Competition (1990). Besides her performing career, she teaches piano at the Conservatory of Music in Ghent (Belgium).

ALTHEA WAITES, born in New Orleans, January 29, 1939, holds degrees from Xavier University (Louisiana) and Yale School of Music. Her mentor, the late Alice Shapiro, guided her into a career distinguished by performances of women composers, especially those of African, Latin, and Asian backgrounds. Equally noted are her interpretations of Liszt, Chopin, and Scriabin—acclaimed on her Russian tour. A 1988 tour of Germany was sponsored by the International Congress of Women in Music. In 1990, she concertized in Denmark and Japan, and in 1991 participated in the Artes de Mexico, a festival presented by the Mexican government, the U.S. and the city of Los Angeles, to celebrate Mexican cultural heritage. *Black Diamonds* is her 1991 CD of African-American music. The same year she was the recipient of the National Association of Composers USA Award. The summer of 1996 was spent concertizing in Bali. She is active throughout California as a soloist and chamber musician, has been on the Performance Faculty of Cal. State, Long Beach, and teaches at the Los Angeles County High School of the Performing Arts.

YU-MEI WEI, one of the foremost pianists of Taiwan, has won numerous honors, including first place in the Kingsville International Young Artists, the 1990 Taipei Competition, Corpus Christi International Young Artists, Joseph Fisch International, and San Diego Musical Merit. Born in Taipei, May 22, 1969, she began piano lessons at six, and took up the flute at nine. She came to the U.S. earning her BM in piano performance at Indiana University (1991) and her MM from USC (1993). Her teachers included **Ilana Mysior** and **Menachem Pressler**. She has performed with orchestras and played solo recitals in the U.S., Europe and Asia. She is a member of the Taipei Fine Arts Trio and on the faculty of several Taiwan universities.

EMILY WHITE, born December 15, 1962, in Miami, Florida, is a 1983 graduate of the University of Maryland. She moved to New York and completed her MM at Juilliard in 1985. In 1986, the London Symphony Orchestra awarded her a foundation grant to continue her studies at the RAM where she remained on fellowship for four years, taking a recital diploma in 1987. She has a performance degree from the Manhattan School of Music, and is a faculty member of the Juilliard Evening Division and the Brooklyn College Preparatory Center for the Performing Arts.

LILYA ZILBERSTEIN, born in Moscow, 1965, started piano at five. From 1971–83, she studied at Moscow's Gnessin School in Moscow, graduating with a gold medal. Training at the Gnessin Pedagogical Institute continued until 1988. In 1985, she won first prizes in both the USSR and the Pan-Soviet Competition in Riga, Latvia. International success came in 1987 with her first prize in the Busoni Competition, Bolzano, Italy. May 1988 marked her first tour of the West, starting at the Maggio Musicale Festival in Florence and covering Austria, France and Germany—including her debut at the Schleswig-Holstein Festival. Since then, she has concertized throughout Europe—Amsterdam Concertgebouw, Berlin Philharmonic, Lucerne Festival with the Chicago Symphony, and in Japan. She has also given recitals with violinist **Gil Shaham** and cellist **Matt Haimovitz**. Her Deutsche Grammophon recordings run the gamut from Rachmaninoff—Concerto Nos. 2 and 3 with Claudio Abbado and the Berlin Philharmonic—Taneyev, Mussorgsky and Shostakovich to Schubert, Liszt, Brahms, Debussy and Ravel. In 1993, she recorded Grieg's Piano Concerto with **Neeme Järvi** and the Gothenburg Symphony as part of the anniversary edition celebrating the composer's 150th birthday. For many years she performed as a duo with **Martha Argerich**, concertizing in Norway and on the Continent. Their CD of Brahms' *Sonata for Two Pianos* is on EMI.

She was the 1998 Prizewinner of the Accademia Musicale Chigiana.

Lilya moved to Hamburg in 1990, where she lives with her trombonist husband and two sons.

The Special Talent of Accompanists

JEAN BARR was the first keyboard artist to be awarded a *doctoral* degree in accompanying. Born July 1, 1942, in Waukesha, Wisconsin, her mother, Gertrude, was a church organist for fifty-five years, eighteen of them as organist/choir director of All Saints Episcopal Cathedral, Milwaukee. She was also head of organ music at the Wisconsin Conservatory. Seeing and hearing her mother's pupils from her playpen, Jean soon showed her own talent. She played her first public concert at six. Her BM is from Northwestern, her MM and milestone DMA are from USC, where the degree was developed for her, and where she studied with **Gwendolyn Koldofsky**, who had created the accompanying department—the first in any university—in 1947. During her years at USC, Jean was chosen to be the accompanist for the master classes of three of the world's greatest soloists, cellist **Gregor Piatigorsky**, violist **William Primrose** and violinist **Jascha Heifetz**.

Barr has made numerous chamber appearances throughout the U.S., Europe, Asia, including China, and Australia, collaborating with such distinguished artists as **Pierre Fournier**, **Daniel Heifetz** (no relation to Jascha), **Mstislav Rostropovich** and **Zvi Zeitlin**. In the academia, she has been on the faculties of Southeastern Louisiana University (1965–69), Arizona State (1972–76), Music Academy of the West (summers: 1974–82, 1985, 1987), University of Texas at Austin (1976–80) and USC (1980–88), where she was coordinator of the Accompanying Department of the School of Music. Since 1988 she has been at Eastman, where she established new graduate degrees in accompanying and chamber music. In 2004 she received the Susan B. Anthony Lifetime Achievement Award. 2006 marked seventeen years on the faculty.

JANET GOODMAN GUGGENHEIM is one of the world's leading accompanists. Born in Spokane, Washington, August 24, 1938, her first instructor was her father, a pianist, teacher and music store owner. Early musical impressions were the thrill of hearing monumental artists such as pianists **Arthur Rubinstein**, **Rudolf Firkusny**, **Shura Cherkassky**; violinists **Bronislaw Huberman**, **Nathan Milstein**; singers **Jan Peerce**, **Robert Merrill**, and other greats lured to Spokane by her parents, Roy and Elizabeth, pioneers in the 1950s in bringing chamber music to the Northwest as part of the Roy Goodman Greater Artist Series. Janet still plays the piano which bears the autographs of these luminaries, many from the 1940s when they would practice at the house. As a child she would sit on the staircase, long past her bedtime, absorbing the conversations of the musicians who gathered in the Goodman home after their concerts. Her father was a great admirer of the late renowned pianist **Josef Lhévinne** (1874–1944). In 1949, at age eleven, Janet had the opportunity to audition for his wife, the legendary teacher **Rosina Lhévinne** (1880–1976), who taught during the summer at the Los Angeles Conservatory. After hearing Janet play a movement from a Mozart concerto, she stated, "I do not accept children, but I will make an exception." Thus, nearly every summer, Janet studied with Madame Lhévinne in Los Angeles, and later at Aspen. In high school, she played in the dance band and accompanied the chorus.

While a music major at UC Berkeley, one of the world's greatest cellists, **Pablo Casals** (1876–1973), honored Janet by selecting her as pianist for his master classes which were recorded on national public television and later released on video. After graduating with honors, she entered Juilliard, continuing her studies with Lhévinne. She was awarded the Josef Lhévinne Scholarship and won the concerto competition playing a Mozart Concerto with the Juilliard Orchestra under the direction of **Jean Morel** (1903–75). Her interest in chamber music sparked in this environment and resulted in her becoming accompanist in the studios of super-famous teachers like cellist **Leonard Rose** (1918–84), violinist **Josef Fuchs** (1900–97) and mega-pedagogues **Ivan Galamian** (1903–81), and **Dorothy DeLay** (1917–2002). It was an exhilarating experience to be present at the lessons of talented violinists and cellists who later went on to grand careers.

After her MM from Julliard, Guggenheim received a Hertz Fellowship from the University of California, giving her the opportunity to be coached by England's premier lady pianist, **Dame Myra Hess** (1890–1965), in London. She also got a Martha Baird Rockefeller Foundation Grant for performances in Europe. One of her great inspirations was having Dame Myra in the audience at her London recital.

In 1964 Janet married Dr. Ray Guggenheim. Their attorney son was born in 1966. Their daughter, a special education teacher of the hearing impaired, in 1968. Fortunate in being able to continue performing in the San Francisco Bay Area while the children were young, she played in many chamber groups. She was a founding member of the Chamber Soloists of San Francisco and performed frequently with members of the San Francisco Symphony.

In 1971, she had the opportunity to accompany a young violinist named **Itzhak Perlman** (*b* 1945) whom she had met at Juilliard. Since that time she has performed with this now premier world artist—and successor to **Jascha Heifetz** (1901–87)—throughout the world, and appeared on NBC's *Tonight Show*. Her other collaborations have been with violinists **Young Uck Kim**, **Nadja Salerno-Sonnenberg**, **Pinchas Zukerman**, **Zina Schiff**, **Christiane Edinger** and cellists **Pierre Fournier** and **Matt Haimovitz**, as well as the American String Quartet.

Guggenheim's awards include the San Francisco Symphony Foundation, National Federation of Music Clubs and the San Francisco Critics' Circle, presented to her in concert with the San Francisco Symphony under Boston Pops legend **Arthur Fiedler**.

In 1989, Guggenheim joined the music faculty at her alma mater UC Berkeley until she and her husband moved to Oregon in the summer of 1995, where she has appeared with the Oregon Symphony under conductors James du Preist and Murry Sidlin.

Her CD releases include *Perlman Live in Russia* (EMI), the Prokofiev Cello Sonata, and Rachmaninoff cello and piano works, both with Michael Grebanier on Naxos.

On January 9, 2005, the author was able to meet Janet when she accompanied Perlman at a fantastic recital in San Diego. The concert should have been billed Perlman-Guggenheim. The pair whizzed through Mozart and Beethoven sonatas and other bravura pieces, proving once and for all that a soloist must have an accompanist of equal stature!

SANDRA RIVERS, a native of New York, attended New York's Professional Children's School before going to Juilliard (MM, 1972). At the Tchaikovsky Competition in 1978, she was the winner of the Best Accompanist award. Since that time she has accumulated impressive credentials as a chamber musician and accompanist, collaborating with soprano **Kathleen Battle**, and violinists **Itzhak Perlman**, **Nadja Salerno-Sonnenberg**, Cho

Liang Lin and **Sarah Chang**. As a soloist, she has appeared with the Dallas Symphony and the Louisiana Philharmonic, among others. Since 1986, she has been a professor of accompanying at the Cincinnati College-Conservatory of Music.

Double the Pleasure - The Rich Sound of Duo-Pianists

BARRENECHEA and **CABEZA** is the duo of Mar Barrenechea, born September 28, 1962, in Torreón, Mexico, and Clavel Cabeza Peñalba, born August 6, 1964, in Burgos, Spain. Both are graduates of the Royal Conservatory, Madrid—Clavel with further studies in Paris, and Mar studying at Indiana School of Music. They each have many solo piano awards. As a duo they have played throughout Spain and Mexico, winning in 2000 Mexico's statuette Xochipilli, (goddess of music) in recognition for their talent and dedication to music.

Twin sisters **CLAIRE** and **ANTOINETTE CANN** studied together at London's RCM. Their busy career has taken them throughout their native England, especially their highly acclaimed concert series at the Royal Festival Hall, as well as Europe, America, Canada, New Zealand and the Far East. They premiered Max Bruch's Duo Concerto at the South Bank Centre, Timothy Blinko's *Gemini*, Martin Butler's *Spells and Chants*, and *Fiesta* by Lionel Sainsbury. By invitation of the Queen Mother, they entertained the Royal Family at the Royal Lodge in Windsor. They have released many popular titles, including *Rhapsody*, and *La Danse*, which was selected "Best of 1993" by *Gramophone* magazine.

Cipa Dichter

MISHA and **CIPA DICHTER** first performed together at the Hollywood Bowl in 1972. Since then they have performed many neglected works for two-piano and piano-four-hands, including the world premiere of Robert Starer's *Concerto for Two Pianos* with the Seattle Symphony in 1996. Misha, born 1945 in Shanghai, where his Polish parents had fled World War II, grew up in Los Angeles. Cipa was born in Rio de Janeiro of Polish-Russian parents. They met at Juilliard where they both studied with **Rosina Lhevinne** (1880–1976), and married in 1968. While he had a solo career, she raised their two children, Gabriel and Alexander. Now that the boys are grown, their parents enjoy recital and concert engagements in the U.S. and Canada and all the leading summer festivals. They have an apartment in Manhattan and a home in Westchester County.

Katia and Marielle Labèque

KATIA and **MARIELLE LABÈQUE**, one of the top duo-piano teams in the world, were born in Hendaye, on the Basque coast of France near the Spanish border, March 3, 1950, and March 6, 1952, respectively. Their father, Pierre, was a pediatrician, their mother, Ada, a piano teacher and student of **Marguerite Long**. Even as a baby Katia would improvise on the piano, and at age three demanded to be taught. Not until Katia gave her first concert in Paris, at age seven, did Marielle also show interest. While one girl had her music lesson, the other was taught math by her father. In the afternoons they had private tutors. They made their formal debut in Bayonne in 1961. Having learned all their mother could teach them, they entered the Paris Conservatory, studying with **Jean-Bernard Pommier**. During this time they lived closer to Paris with their old Spanish nanny, and had to make a one and a half hour journey each day into the capital. In their final year, 1968, out of seventy-five students, five—including the Labèques—graduated with distinction. Although they had had separate classes, they now made the decision to play together. Concentrating on contemporary music, they immediately embarked upon a highly successful career which took them all over Europe, the Middle and Far East and North America. Besides their strikingly brilliant duo-piano recitals, they have appeared with most of the world's leading orchestras. They participated in the Piano Grand! TV-Gala in Washington, DC, celebrating the 300th anniversary of the piano, which was broadcast in the U.S. (PBS), Europe (BBC) and in Asia (NHK, Japan). Their extraordinarily extensive repertoire ranges from the classics to contemporary to jazz, and includes more than twenty recordings. Champions of Gershwin, among their prize-winning recordings is their Philips label two-piano version of *Rhapsody in Blue*—sales have topped 600,000—*Piano Concerto in F* and *An American in Paris*, for which they won a Gold Disque. They have also released Mozart's Double and Triple Concertos, Concertos for Two Pianos by Poulenc, Bartók, Bruch and Mendelssohn, *Symphonic Dances* from Leonard Bernstein's *West Side Story*, *España* featuring Spanish music, *Tchaikovsky Fantasy*, Stravinsky's *Los Noces* and a video disc, "The Loves of Emma Bardac" on SONY Classical, and Luciano Berio's *Concerto for Two Pianos* under the direction of the composer.

The Labèques have appeared on television in the UK, Germany, Japan and the U.S. A biographical BBC-TV documentary was aired in October 1992. Katia, who likes jazz, sometimes plays alone in that field, and has recorded with Chick Corea, Herbie Hancock, Joe Zawinul, Michael Camilo, and with Gonzalo Rubalcaba on the album *Little Girl Blue* for the jazz label Dreyfus. In the autumn of 1995, *both* sisters included some jazz in their duo-recitals in Britain.

Personally, there is no rivalry between the two. Their reviews garner as much commentary on how they look (always fabulous—never basic black) as how they sound. Both slender, their stage costume is usually pants and a designer highwayman's jacket. Katia is more outgoing, while Marielle has a mysterious quality about her. She speaks only after her sister has finished speaking—a habit of long standing since the older has always looked after the younger. They live in London.

It is very difficult to play two pianos together. The sisters have a unique awareness of each other, almost breathing in synchronization, which is part of the secret why they receive consistent raves for the seamless coordination and synergy of their performances. Vital as are their interpretations of Brahms, Schubert, Debussy, and their specialty, Mozart, audiences get extra enthusiastic with Bernstein's *America* from West Side Story, Poulenc's Double Concerto or Gershwin's *Rhapsody in Blue*, in arrangements for two pianos and orchestra fashioned by them.

Their grueling schedule has been "reduced" to sixteen concerts in three weeks—it used to be more! (Katia carries all the dates in her head.) Their interest in 18th century music led them to participate in the Bach Centennial in 2000 with Musica Antiqua Köln and also Il Giardino Armonico. These tours took them to Germany, Spain and Austria. Their fame now insures that—at least most of the time—they get to play on *two* good pianos.

Lisitsa & Kuznetsoff

Ukrainian husband and wife duo Valentina **LISITSA** and Alexei **KUZNETSOFF** exploded on the American scene with their 1991 win at the International Murry Dranoff Two Piano Competition in Miami, where one juror reacted with, "the greatest romantic duo-piano team in history."

When they met at the Kiev Conservatory (she was born 1970, he 1967), they were both winners of solo and chamber music competitions. Faced with economic problems and dismal career prospects in the Soviet Union, they gave up solo careers to form the duo. Since their Miami triumph they have lived in Indiana. In 1995, they debuted in New York with the *Mostly Mozart* Festival, and appeared at the Van Cliburn Recital Series in Fort Worth.

During the last decade seasons they toured as soloists with the Orchestre National de France, under Charles Dutoit, and made a twenty-nine-city recital tour. Valentina has released two solo CDs, and two as a duo, Lisitsa & Kuznetsoff, Vols. 1 and 2.

GEORGIA and **LOUISE MANGOS** earned their BM degrees at the New England Conservatory. Georgia got her master's from Boston University, and Louise from the University of Wisconsin. They were coached as a two-piano team by Adele Marcus at Juilliard and Dr. Bela Nagy of the Catholic University of America.

They have participated in International Chamber Music Festivals and performed in Europe for the International Chopin Society. They studied at the Munich Hochschule, earning the coveted Performance Certificate and were presented in master classes by celebrated pianists **Jörg Demus** and **Paul Badura-Skoda**.

In March 1986, the sisters were awarded the S.T.A.R. grant of the Illinois Arts Council. The following year they were selected as one of twelve teams out of 129 contestants from all over the world to compete in the Murray

Dranoff International Duo-Piano Competition. Here they premiered Morton Gould's *Two Pianos* which had been commissioned for the event.

Faculty members of Elmhurst College, Illinois, Georgia serves as director of piano pedagogy, Louise is artist-in-residence with the Bellezza Wind Ensemble. They perform extensively in the Chicago area. Their recordings include the Lizst Symphonic Poems.

Virginia Morley

MORLEY and **GEARHART** were a dynamic pair of duo-pianists who held the spotlight from 1940 to 1954, touring the U.S. and Canada twenty-six times, performing from Carnegie Hall to the Hollywood Bowl, accompanied by their two nine-foot Steinway concert-grands in a custom van.

Virginia Clotfelter (she adopted the more euphonic name) was born in Dinuba, California, October 18, 1915, and Livingston Gearhart in Buffalo, New York, December 31, 1916. They met in Paris, 1937, where they were students of Robert Casadesus (piano) and **Nadia Boulanger** (composition). They fled Paris in 1939 to escape WWII, and were married in New York, February 28, 1940. Their concerts, in which many of the two piano arrangements were by Gearhart, brought them to the attention of Fred Waring, director of the *Pennsylvanians*—a choral group and orchestra that reigned on radio and early television for sixty years. The pianists appeared with them between tours.

Although a son, Paul, was born, the marriage ended in divorce in 1954 due to Gearhart's increasing mood swings. Virginia, her career over, returned to California to recover. Most surprised when Waring declared his love, they married December 2. Son Malcolm was born March 7, 1957.

During Fred's final illness, Virginia directed the Pennsylvanians on a thirteen-week tour, and remained their artistic director until 1991. After her husband's death in 1985, at eighty-five, she became chairman of the board of his various enterprises, including Shawnee Music Press, and his inventions—the Waring Blender and an instant steam iron. In 1997, she wrote the book *Fred Waring and His Pennsylvanians*. In 2002 she published *Letters from Fontainebleau*, her girlhood correspondence with her family from 1937–39. Retired to Rancho Mirage, California, she continued her involvement in civic and professional activities. January 2006 marked the inauguration of the Virginia Waring International Piano Competition dedicated in her honor.

GÜHER and **SÜHER PEKINEL**—their names mean "gemstone" and "waterfall"—are, so far, the world's only *twin* duo-pianists, as well as being one of the top teams in this exclusive league. Of mixed Turkish/Spanish parentage, they were born in Istanbul, March 29, 1951. (They also have a brother.) As toddlers, they fought over who could get to the piano first. Lessons from their mother—almost a professional herself—began at age five. By six they gave their first public concert. Their first orchestral concert, with the Ankara Philharmonic, came three years later before President Ismet Inönü and the public. This was broadcast throughout the country. When they were twelve, they went to Paris to study at the Conservatoire with **Yvonne Loriod**, wife of experimental composer Olivier Messiaen. In 1965, the twins moved to Frankfurt for high school and studies at the Musikhochschule with **August Leopolder**, a student of the renowned **Egon Petri** who had been a pupil of **Teresa Carreño** and the great **Ferrucccio Busoni**. Here, the Peckinels also attended Goethe University, where Süher obtained a degree in Philosophy, and Güher in Psychology. In 1978, the sisters represented West Germany at the UNESCO World Music Week in Bratislava, and came away with the first prize. This was only one of the many competitions in which they captured the top prizes, both as soloists and in tandem. After winning the radio competition in Hanover, they immediately had bookings for sixty concerts!

An invitation from **Rudolf Serkin**, then director of the Curtis Institute, brought them to Philadelphia (1970–72). There they played "in-house" with the Guarneri Quartet and the Budapest Quartet. Serkin's lessons were as soloists, wanting each to develop their individuality. Their duo playing continued under **Mieczyslaw**

Horszowski[159] (1892–1993), who literally taught them how to "breathe in unison." For their master's, the sisters switched to Juilliard and Adele Marcus. In Süher's words, "At Curtis the only reality is to make music. At Juilliard the impetus is on virtuosity—and both are very important!" At this point they were also under the aegis of Young Concert Artists, after which they were snapped up by Sheldon Gold, president of ICM, who catapulted their career to the stars.

The twins have played with an impressive list of world-famous orchestras, including the Philharmonics of Berlin, Israel, Los Angeles and New York, as well as the Cleveland and Concertgebouw (Amsterdam) Orchestras, and worked with soloists like pianists **Leon Fleischer** and **Claudio Arrau**. Their tours have touched all the major music centers of the U.S., Europe and Japan, and festivals such as Salzburg (Austria) and *Mostly Mozart* (New York). They have recorded for Deutsche Grammophon, Berlin Classics, Teldec and CBS.

Often appearing on radio and television, the Peckinels' musical life was the subject of a sixty-minute documentary aired in Europe during the 1995–96 season, which also includes their tours of Italy and Germany. Wherever they play, the sisters fascinate audiences with their special aura which transports the listeners to a musical world where tones, sounds and expression intertwine in unforgettable vitality.

The Next Generation

Grand prize winner of the first Ivo Pogorelich International Solo Piano Competitions (December 1993), **EDITH CHEN** has launched an international career with concerts from North America to Europe to the Far East. Born in Taiwan in 1972, she began studying piano at age six. In 1980, she emigrated to California with her family, attending the Los Angeles High School for the Performing Arts. She earned her MM at Juilliard, studying privately with the great **Byron Janis**. Still in her twenties, she twice won the Gina Bachauer Scholarship Competition, and has been awarded prizes in the Richner and the Stravinsky International Piano Competitions, as well as the UCLA and Tchaikovsky Competitions. She has performed with the Taipei Symphony, and the Bergen (Norway), Leningrad and Moscow Philharmonics. In North America, she has soloed with the Oregon Symphony, Los Angeles Philharmonic and at the Aspen Festival. She was chosen for the gala debut of the new Colorado Orchestra, playing the Tchaikovsky Piano Concerto No.1 before a crowd of 15,000. Her numerous recitals include debuts at the National Concert Hall in Taipei and, in April 1992, Carnegie's Weill Recital Hall.

April 1994 marked a triumphant recital debut in Munich, with further appearances at the Ivo Pogorelich Summer Festival in Bad-Wershofen (Germany), the Russian National Orchestra in Moscow, and solo performances in Zagreb (Yugoslavia), Spain and Germany, plus more tours throughout North America. She has subsequently played with the Hong Kong Philharmonic, under David Atherton (with whom she appeared in Los Angeles), Costa Mesa, Santa Barbara, San Francisco and Vancouver. She was featured soloist on the U.S. and Mexico tour of the Moscow Radio Symphony Orchestra conducted by Vladimir Fedosayev.

Born in Taiwan on September 15, 1967, **EVELYN CHEN** came to America when she was twelve. Her mother told her that as a baby she would stop crying when she heard music, and could hum along to songs in pitch and rhythm when she was only one year old. Her sister, Wen, studied piano and cello, her brother, Johnny, violin and piano. As children, they played trios, but only Evelyn has pursued a professional career. Like so many dedicated Asians, her parents moved to America to further their talented child's training and career opportunities, which enabled her to receive a BA in composition from Harvard, an MM from the New England Conservatory, and a DMA from Juilliard, May 1998.

---

159. It should be noted about **Mieczyslaw Horszowski** that, besides numbering among his pupils **Peter Serkin**, son of Rudolf, and **Cécile Licad**, this revered performer/pedagogue "rushed" into his first marriage at age eighty-nine, and played an impeccable recital in Los Angeles, January 31, 1990, at age ninety-eight. He passed away May 22, 1993, in Philadelphia.

First prize winnings began in 1981 at the Bach International Competition in Washington, DC, the 1984 Piano Guild International Recording Competition, 1993 Mieczyslaw Munz International Competition, 1994 International Gina Bachauer Scholarship Competition and the 1995 Petschek Recital Award.

Chen has played with orchestras in Taiwan, Hong Kong, Mexico, Vienna, Moscow, and throughout the U.S. She recorded Rachmaninoff's Piano Concerto No. 2 with Leonard Slatkin and the Philharmonia Orchestra in London (BMG), and Miklós Rózsa's Piano Concerto with James Sedares and the New Zealand Symphony (Koch). On the same recording is Rózsa's Cello Concerto played by Brinton Smith, formerly with the San Diego Symphony and now principal cellist of the Fort Worth (Texas) Symphony. The pair met at Juilliard in 1992, and after years of a long-distance relationship, were married October 2000. In addition to her regular concertizing, in May 2001 Helen performed the Beethoven Triple Concerto in Oregon with her husband and violinist **Adele Anthony**, wife of Gil Shaham.

Friday the 13th of July 2001 marked their most important production so far, the birth of Calista Ro-Jei Smith.

Born in 1974 in Toronto, **NAIDA COLE**, who has perfect pitch, began piano at four. In 1979 her family (she has an older brother) moved to Saudi Arabia for three years, where her father practiced medicine. With no piano teacher available, she started flute, an instrument she continued to study. Returning to North America, she studied piano with **Leon Fleisher** at Peabody, Marc Durand at the Université de Montréal, and Marina Geringas at the Royal Conservatory of Music (Toronto), where she became one of the youngest graduates of the associate diploma program in piano—second only to Glenn Gould. She was also the highest-placed Canadian in the prestigious Van Cliburn International Piano Competition (1997), and the only Canadian to appear on the Deutsche Grammophon CD celebrating its 100th anniversary in 1999.

With a repertoire ranging from contemporary to romantic, Cole has soloed with major Canadian orchestras, plus the Copenhagen Philharmonic and NHK Symphony, with recitals in Europe, Korea, Japan, London's Wigmore Hall, and Washington's Kennedy Center.

As a chamber musician she has appeared in the Ravinia, Spoleto (USA) and Ottawa chamber music festivals. A frequent guest at Gidon Kremer's Lockenhaus (Austria) Festival, she has toured with his ensemble Kremerata Baltica in Europe and America, performing in Carnegie Hall, Severance Hall (Cleveland), and the Dorothy Chandler Pavilion, Los Angeles.

A Decca recording artist, Cole's first CD with music by Fauré, Chabrier, Satie and Ravel was nominated for a Juno Award in Canada. Her second, *Reflections* (2003), includes Ravel's *Miroirs*, Bartók's *Improvisations* and Liszt's *Sonata*. She is also on the Grammy award winning Gidon Kremer Nonesuch CD, *After Mozart*.

Her 2004–05 season included recitals in the U.S., Germany and Japan, performances with the Vancouver, Calgary and San Diego Symphonies, a tour of Germany with the Nordhausen Orchestra/Max-Bruch Philharmonie and appearances at the Lanaudière (Quebec), and Highlands (North Carolina) festivals.

EMILY HSIEH (Pronounced "Shay") began her performing career at age nine, soloing with orchestras throughout the U.S. and in Moscow. She won top prizes at the 1989 Young Keyboard Artists Competition in Los Angeles, 1990 Steinway Piano Concerto Competition, 1991 Friday Music Club Competition in New York, and first prize at the 1992 International Tchaikovsky Competition for Young Musicians in Moscow.

Born in Ohio to Taiwanese parents, Emily began piano at age six in Denver, and also studied at the Salzburg, Mozarteum and in London. A student of Yohoved Kaplinsky at Juilliard, she took academic classes at the Professional Children's School.

Her recital debut in Denver was followed by appearances in Brazil, Salzburg, Canada, Germany, Russia, and the U.S. She has performed in Taiwan at the Presidential Hall in Taipei before the president, and received a special achievement award for her exclusive recording contract with the ChiMei Cultural Foundation. Her radio and television performances include a live telecast in Moscow, and an interview on WQXR's Young Artist Showcase with Robert Sherman.

CHU-FANG HUANG, born in China, 1983, began piano studies at age seven, and at twelve was the youngest student at the Shenyang Conservatory. After winning first prize at the 1997 Southeastern Asia Competition, she moved to the U.S. in 1998, making a recital debut on the Prodigy Series of the La Jolla (California) Music Society. She studied with Claude Frank while earning a BM at Curtis (2004), and in 2006 was pursuing an MM at Juilliard. She has performed in China, at the Ruhr Piano Festival (Germany), Concertgebouw (Amsterdam), Sydney Australia Weill Recital Hall, New York, and with U.S. orchestras in Charleston, and Fort Worth. 2004 brought prizes at the Beijing and Sydney International Competitions. She was a finalist in the 2005 Van Cliburn Competition, and winner of the Cleveland International Competition, which earns the highest cash prize world-wide. Her recordings are with Alpine, Camus and Naxos. She returned to La Jolla in March 2006 for a masterful performance of the Beethoven Concerto No. 4 with the San Diego Chamber Orchestra.

Helen Huang

HELEN HUANG was born in Japan, of Chinese parents, October 1982. The family moved to America in 1985, where Helen began piano lessons at five. She won her first competition within a year, and debuted with the Philadelphia Orchestra just after her eighth birthday, having won their student concerto competition. Living in Cherry Hill, New Jersey, she attended the preparatory division of the Manhattan School of Music, winning its concerto competition in 1992, and became a student of Yoheved Kaplinsky at Juilliard. In 1994, she was selected by the New York Philharmonic to receive Lincoln Center's Martin E. Segal Award for promising young artists. In May 1995, she became one of the youngest recipients of the prestigious Avery Fisher Career Grant, and in the same year made two appearances with Kurt Masur and the New York Philharmonic. She has appeared with them each season since, including their 1999 Asian tour and their 2000 North American tour. She has also debuted with other North American orchestras, including the National and St. Louis Symphonies—touring the Far East with the latter. Her national television debut was with the Boston Pops Orchestra for PBS "Evening at the Pops." Summer engagements have included the Casals Festival in Puerto Rico and concerts in Paris. More European appearances have followed, including a concert with the London Symphony at the Barbican Centre, celebrating the fiftieth anniversary of the United Nations. Her live performances of the Beethoven Concerto No. 1 and the Mozart Concerto No. 23, with Kurt Masur and the New York Philharmonic, have been released on the Teldec label, followed by the Mendelssohn No. 1 and the Mozart No. 21 concertos. During the 1998–99 season, she made her first recital appearance in Beijing, followed by European and U.S. recitals, and her debut with the Hong Kong Philharmonic at the seventeenth Asian Arts Festival. She also participated in a gala concert with Yo-Yo Ma and Isaac Stern in Seoul (Korea). 1999 saw return engagements with Cincinnati, and the Pittsburgh Symphony, both in Pittsburgh and on their West Coast tour, and joined NYPO on its first Asian tour. Helen was a featured performer at SummerFest La Jolla 2001, where we met.

Orli Shaham

ORLI SHAHAM, born in Israel, November 5, 1975, as a toddler watched her two brothers playing piano and begged her mother for lessons at the age of three. At five, she attended a concert in Jerusalem and sat so rapt in the music that a teacher noticing the child offered to teach her free. That same year she was awarded her first scholarship for musical study from the America-Israel Cultural Foundation. At that time she was a student of Luisa Yoffe at the Rubin Academy of Music in Jerusalem. When her father accepted a position to teach astrophysics at Columbia University, the family emigrated to New York. At seven, Orli began studies with Nancy Stessin. A year later she was accepted as a scholarship student at Juilliard by Herbert Stessin. She holds the record for the length of time she spent as a pre-college student there—ten years! She is a graduate of the Horace Mann School in Riverdale, New York, and, having taken all possible music courses, she majored in history at Columbia University—"for fun!" In what she calls her "spare time," she worked on a master's in musicology. In 1995, she was a winner of the Gilmore Young Artist Award, and in 1997 a recipient of the Avery Fisher Career Grant.

Orli's career has already taken her around the world, with festivals at Aspen, Ravinia, Caramoor, Spoleto, Verbier, Davos Chamber Music—the latter two in Switzerland—returning annually to Aspen and Spoleto, plus appearances in San Diego, Chicago, Munich, Frankfurt, and the home of the Israeli Ambassador in Washington. 1994, '97, and '98 saw tours of Japan. Debuts during 1997–98 were with the Cleveland and Philadelphia Orchestras. In the 1998–99 season she joined the Jerusalem Symphony as soloist on its American tour, as well as making her debut with St. Louis, where she met her soulmate in their new director David Robertson. They wed January 3, 2003. The summer of 2000 took her to Lincoln Center and the Mostly Mozart Festival, Gerard Schwarz conducting. In addition to soloing, she and her brother, world-famous violinist **Gil Shaham**, have appeared in recital together. Their first CD was *Dvořák for Two*, (Deutsche Grammophon, 1997). In 2001, they performed together on a two-month tour in Europe and the U.S. In October 2002, Orli was Performance Today's young artist-in-residence for a week of live performances and conversation on NPR.

The 2004–05 season included engagements with the Los Angeles Philharmonic, Chicago, San Francisco, Atlanta and Dallas Symphonies. In January 2005, she appeared with her husband and the St. Louis Symphony, performing with the orchestra again at Carnegie Hall in April. Passionate about chamber music, Orli joined her brother for a seven-city U.S. tour that culminated at Carnegie Hall's Isaac Stern Auditorium. An all-Prokofiev CD was released on Canary Classics (distributed by Vanguard) in conjunction with this tour. The 2005 Aspen Festival witnessed a special treat, Orli playing with her sister-in-law, violinist **Adele Anthony**—they have known each other since their pre-teen years—and then in a trio with Gil joining the ladies. This gave the listeners the sound of two Stradivari violins: Gil's made in 1699 and Adele's 1728.

Unlike **Hephzibah Menuhin** (1920–81), an excellent pianist who lived in the shadow of her famous violinist brother, Yehudi Menuhin (1916–99), Orli Shaham maintains her own solo career with some seventy concert and recital appearances a year.

A Special Twist of Fate For an Ascending Star!

Rossina Grieco

ROSSINA GRIECO was born October 15, 1994, in San Diego, California, with an outsize gift of musical talent. By age four, her clarinetist mother, Molly Chen, had trained her in the fundamentals of piano, after which "Sina" became the student of Luba Tzvibel Ugorski.

The best possible teacher, Ugorski was a 1980 graduate of the St. Peterburg Conservatory who spent the next twenty years in their Children's School of Special Music—a training ground for prodigies. Leaving Russia in 1990 with flutist husband Valéri, she pursued a solo and orchestral career, and became the mother of Eugene Ugorski, an international violinist in his teens!

Sina, as Grieco is known, began public performance at six as winner of the San Diego Symphony Young Artists Competition in 2001. She was the youngest winner of the SDSO "Hot Shots" competition (2003), the youngest soloist to perform with the San Diego Symphony Summer Pops, and the La Jolla Chamber Music Society Discovery Series. 2004 found her on the national radio show *From the Top*, which spotlights pre-college age musicians from all over the country. 2006 brought the prestigious Bronislau Kaper Award with the Los Angeles Philharmonic, named after the Polish film composer (1902–83), as well as winning the California International Competition.

With her Shanghai-born mother, Sina visits China frequently, performing with the Shanghai and Guangzhou Symphonies, Shanghai Oriental Symphonietta, Xiamen Philharmonica, the China Philharmonic, and at the 9th International Beijing Music Festival.

Our audience was mesmerized as this child's nimble fingers flew over the keys presenting us with a flawless Mozart Rondo, brilliant von Weber Konzertstück, and heartwarming Liszt *Romance*. (It was January 23, 2007. My manuscript had been completed that morning. It was sent to the printer the next day. This fantastic talent just *had* to be included in the book!)

To All the "Piano Girls"!

The author wishes to make a most respectful bow of recognition to *all* the women who ply keyboards for church choirs, ballet schools, opera rehearsals, school programs, and the myriad ways a multitude of competent pianists use their talent to brighten our lives.

Plus a special kudo to mothers who don't give up on getting their children to practice those scales. Out of those little fingers will come our next generation of concert pianists to keep all that wondrous treasure chest of piano music overflowing!

The Tail End

Ketzel

Morris Cotel, a Juilliard graduate and former chair of the composition department at Peabody Conservatory, begins each day at the keyboard with a Bach prelude and fugue: "My daily vitamin B," he calls it. One morning his cat, **KETZEL**, decided to join in, and slowly walked down the keyboard. Instead of shooing her away, Morris copied down the impromptu notes, all eleven bars of them. Three months later, he happened to read a notice of a competition for piano works lasting sixty seconds or less, sponsored by the *Paris New Music Review*. Neither he nor his students have ever written anything that short, but then he remembered Ketzel. He sent in the piece with an explanation of how it had come about.

Returning from an out-of-town trip, he found a large white envelope containing a certificate of special mention from the organizers of the competition. On the phone, Cotel told the publisher of the *Paris New Music Review* how delighted he was the judges had enough sense of humor to consider such a piece. He was told the judges were just shown the music, only afterward did they find out it was composed by a cat! The *Review* even asked for Ketzel's picture to post on their website. The *New York Times* picked up the story, as did National Public Radio (NPR).

On January 21, 1998, "Piece for Piano, Four Paws" received its world premiere at Friedberg Concert Hall, performed by Shruti Kumar, a Peabody Preparatory student. The program also featured works by Cotel and fellow faculty members **Chen Yi** (see Composers), and **Robert Sirota**—husband of **Victoria Sirota**. (See Musicologists.)

Two months later, the work received its European premiere, March 28, in Amsterdam, under the auspices of the *Paris New Music Review*, with partial sponsorship by the Galianos Foundation—a real credit to her "father" who had won second prize in the 1975 Schoenberg Competition sponsored by the Galianos Foundation, also in Amsterdam.

"Who would have thought that my cat would be following in my footsteps with a premiere in the same town twenty-five years later?" was the delighted declaration of her proud owner, who began a new career as a Rabbi in New York City, but still travels with his enlightening musical presentation, "Chronicles: A Jewish Life at the Classical Piano."

Ketzel's "Compawsition," as Jane Rubinsky categorized it in the March 1998 *Juilliard Journal*, has had several airings since its premiere. It was heard at Thanksgiving, 2000, and featured on NPR Weekend Show, Memorial Day, 2002, among other pussyfootings.

This feline-loving author is happy to include this entry to enable a unique female composer to place her paw-print into posterity.

PART L

Mastering the King of Instruments

Sophia Hewitt (1799–1845)
Elfrida Andrée (1871–1929)
Roberta Bitgood (1908–retired
Lady Susi Jeans (1911–1993)
Claire Coci (1912–78)
Catharine Crozier (1914–2002)
Jeanne Marie Madeleine Demessieux (1921–68)
Marie-Madeleine Duruflé (1921–99)

21ST CENTURY
Marie-Claire Alain
Diane Meredith Belcher
Diane Bish
Beth Chenault
Lynne Louise Davis
Carla Edwards
Janette Fishell
Roberta Gary
Nancy Granert
Judith Hancock
Yanka Hékima
Wilma Jensen
Joyce Jones
Marilyn Keiser

Margaret McElwain Kemper
Kei Koito
Susan Landale
Joan Lippincott
Karen McFarlane
Marilyn Mason
Dorothy Papadakos
Jane Parker-Smith
Mary Preston
Christa Radich
Cherry Rhodes
Victoria Sirota
Ann Elise Smoot
Sandra Soderlund
Phyllis J. Stringham
Carole Terry
Marianne Webb
Dame Gillian Weir
Carol Williams
Anne Wilson

THE FUTURE
Chelsea Chen

Dating back two thousand years, the organ has been associated with Roman gladiators, medieval monarchs, the church, and in theater design, accompanying silent movies, radio plays, television "soap operas," plus enjoying popularity in concert recitals spanning the 1920s to the '50s. In the 12th century, players carried portative organs—looking like accordions—with a strap. Small reed organs similar to harmoniums graced wealthy 16th century homes. The peak of organ music was the baroque period from the early 1600s to the middle 1700s. Called "the king of instruments" because it can imitate an entire orchestra, it was the means of livelihood and inspiration for early baroque and classical composers like Dietrich Buxtehude and J.S. Bach (Germany), George Frideric Handel (England), Jan Sweelinck (Holland), Giralmo Frescobaldi, Domenico Gabrieli and Tomaso Albinoni (Italy), François Couperin, Jean Titelouze, Nicolas de Brigny and Louis Marchand (France), and Juan Bautista Cabanilles (Spain), who freed it from church service exclusivity and gave it new dimensions in the recital sphere—albeit that concerts still had to be performed in churches.

These innovators were followed a century later by Charles Widor, Cesar Franck, Camille Saint-Saëns and other (mostly) French composers. The organ's multiplicity evolved musical forms such as the *fugue*, *toccata*, *partita*, *chorale-prelude*, and the core of organ playing, *improvisation*, with the development of *theme and variations*. The organ was also the first instrument—as early as 1868—to be powered by electricity and, in its modern form, one of the first to become electronic when, beginning in 1934, electrical circuits and amplifiers replaced bulky pipes, making it possible to manufacture home models. Modern solid state circuitry has tremendously simplified *programming* (setting the stops), or "orchestrating" the organ for the sound needed. Being a keyboard instrument put it within the sanctioned stratum of the feminine gender.

Overcoming Puritanism in the Colonies

Because of the Puritan prejudice against instruments used in worship services, organs did not appear in American churches until after 1800. In 1820, the prestigious Handel and Haydn Society of Boston engaged organist/accompanist **Sophia Hewitt**, born in New York, June 13, 1799, a child piano prodigy and organist's daughter. She remained there for a decade, sometimes playing in Boston's two principal churches, Chauncey Place and the Catholic Cathedral. She married and gave birth to a daughter, all without losing her job. (She died in Portland, Maine, September 3, 1845.) With the turn of the century, as more churches acquired organs, the number of women organists increased on both sides of the Atlantic, but few made it to the concert hall.

In 1917, the world's largest organ—232 stops and 18,000 pipes—was installed in the Wanamaker department store in Philadelphia. Fifteen years later, the 1,233 stops and 32,000 pipes of the organ at the Convention Hall in Atlantic City claimed that title. During the early 1920s, motion picture theaters installed organs to provide accompaniment for silent movies. With the advent of sound films these gradually vanished, but there are still theater organ societies and able players to prevent their complete extinction. Modern church organs combine the best features of the baroque with the newest techniques and materials. While home instruments benefit from the latest technology, their sales and popularity are up against the competition of electronic keyboards, which can make an even greater variety of sounds for one tenth the price and have complete portability.

By 1925 the Boston Organ Players Club had been formed. The American Guild of Organists (AGO), founded in 1896 with only four women out of 145 members had, by 1925, 250 women to 536 men. It would take another fifty years before a woman was elected president of the Guild, **Roberta Bitgood** (1971–75). Maggie Kemper (1994–98) has been the only other woman president to date. The 2001 roster showed over 21,000 members, of whom almost 50 percent are women.

From the hundreds of women in Western countries employed as church organists, a cadre of the most talented have become well-known soloists, able to combine two careers via today's easier means of travel and the publicity of recordings. Herewith, an overview of prominent ladies who have ascended the throne of the king of instruments:

ELFRIDA ANDRÉE was the first woman organist in Sweden, the first to compose chamber and orchestral music, and the first to conduct a symphony orchestra. Born in Visby, February 19, 1841, she and her sister, Fredrika Stenhammer, who became a famous opera singer, were initially taught music by their father. In 1855, Elfrida went to Stockholm where, two years later, she passed the examination as an organist. Between 1860–70, she studied composition and used her influence to bring about the revision of a discriminatory law, thus enabling women to hold the post of organist. In 1861, she got her first position in Stockholm. In 1879, she was appointed as a member of the prestigious Swedish Royal Academy of Music. She moved to Göteborg in 1867, where she was organist in that famous cathedral until her death on January 11, 1929.

Influenced by the style of contemporary Scandinavian composers like Grieg and Niels Gade, as well as Mendelssohn and Schumann, Andrée composed over 100 works. During the 1980s new interest in her music arose. Her chamber works are now widely performed in Scandinavia and her Organ Symphony is in the repertoire of most organists. Many of her works have been resurrected, edited and annotated by musicologist **Susan Pickett** and published by Hildegard Publishing Company.

Roberta Bitgood

ROBERTA BITGOOD, who enjoyed a celebrated five-decade career, was born in New London, Connecticut, January 15, 1908, into a line of strong-minded women. Her grandmother had marched in suffragette parades and her mother traveled all over the U.S. as a speaker for the Methodist Missionary Society. "Bertie" began piano at seven, and played violin in the school orchestra at the Williams Memorial Institute (WMI), which her mother and aunt had attended. She would continue playing this instrument in community orchestras, but became fascinated by the organ at church and took lessons with amateur organist Howard Pierce, who had had polio and could not use his right foot. Thus, Roberta became a "left-footed" player. She continued playing violin at the Connecticut College for Women, but switched to organ with J. Lawrence Erb who forced her to play with *both* feet. He was also an excellent theory teacher. After earning a BA in math and science (1928), a scholarship enabled her to attend the Guilmant Organ School run by William C. Carl, and named after the great French organist **Alexandre Guilmant** (1837–1911). She then earned her master's in sacred music from Union Theological Seminary (1935). During this time she played at the First Moravian Church in New York, discovering many interesting facts about this religion, including that it was the first denomination to break away from the Catholic Church. Further research into Moravian music provided the subject for her master's thesis. Her first position after graduation was at the Westminster Presbyterian Church in Bloomfield, New Jersey (1932–47). Meanwhile, on May 18, 1939, she married J. Gijsbert Wiersma (Bert) who had been one of the lodgers in her grandparents' large rooming house. "Bert" discovered his niche as an occupational therapist and had no trouble getting jobs as Roberta moved around the country to different locations. (This was an early case of the husband following the wife's calling . . .) Their daughter, Grace, born October 4, 1942, is a librarian at MIT. (She earned her PhD in China.)

1947–52 found the family in Buffalo (near Niagara Falls) with Roberta at Holy Trinity Lutheran. 1952–60 brought a position at Calvary Presbyterian in Riverside, California, where she worked with five choirs, including children. The next fifteen years began with a migration to Michigan: Detroit's Redford Presbyterian (1960–62), Bay City First Presbyterian (1963–69) and the Battle Creek First Congregational (1969–75). It was during this time that Bitgood became the first woman president of the AGO (1975–81), having joined the Guild in the early '30s. She traveled thousands of miles in that capacity. After being honored on her eighty-fifth and ninetieth birthdays, she received the Guild's prestigious President's Award at the 1998 national convention in Denver.

Leaving Michigan marked Bitgood's first "retirement," and the return to her roots in Quaker Hill, Connecticut, and "Best View," the property on which the house of her childhood had stood. Soon she was back on the organ bench, first at St. Mark's in Mystic until 1984—shortly before her husband's death—and then in Harkness Chapel on the campus of her *alma mater* Connecticut College, where the Waterford (later renamed Crossroads) Presbyterian Church was meeting until they moved to their own property in 1989, and for whom Bitgood was "instrumental" in acquiring a pipe organ for which she had personally outlined the specifications with the builder. (She had also helped two other churches acquire large Moller organs in the course of her career.) In 1999, she "retired" once again, but continued entertaining at "old folks" homes well into her own nineties!

Bitgood wrote close to 100, mostly choral, published works: anthems, hymns, Christmas and Easter music, Responses, three Cantatas and Sacred Organ Solos—most of which receive consistent performance. The carol *Rosa Mystica* (1935) was one of her earliest successes. *The Roberta Bitgood Organ Album* (Belwyn, 1991) is still in print, and an anthology of her compositions was issued in 1980. Some of her work is featured on a '92 CD on **Barbara Harbach**'s Hester Park label. Her biography, *Swell to Great: A Backward Look From My Organ Loft* (Bayberry Press, 2000), was co-written with her former student, Julia Goodfellow, an organist, music director and educator in Flint, Michigan.

The Roberta Bitgood Archive, an extensive collection of papers and meticulously kept scrapbooks documenting her career, is at the Shain Library of Connecticut College, which also houses many other distinguished folios, including that of environmentalist Rachel Carson.

In an interview in February 2003, at ninety-five, Roberta was still keeping up with music events around her. In 2006, she enjoyed her ninety-eighth birthday with good friends and her daughter.

(Lady) **SUSI JEANS** was born in Vienna on January 25, 1911. An organist, keyboard player and musicologist, she studied at the Vienna Music Academy, the Institute of Church Music in Leipzig, and with Charles-Marie Widor (1844–1937) in Paris. As a recitalist on tour in England, she met and married, in 1935, Sir James Jeans (1877–1946), a scientist and amateur organist whose book *Science and Music* (1937) was dedicated to her. They had two sons and a daughter. She became a naturalized British subject, and after WWII gave the first performance of Joseph Haydn's organ concerto in C major at a Promenade concert in London (1947), and later at the Salzburg Festival.

After her husband's death, Lady Jeans resumed her career as a soloist and attained a prominent position in the British organ world. In 1952, she played and lectured at the International Congress of Church Music in Bern (Switzerland). In 1954, she played in one of the opening recitals of the new organ at the Royal Festival Hall, and in 1956 was one of the adjudicators at the International Improvisation Councours in Haarlem (Holland). She gave numerous lecture recitals and master classes in Britain, the Continent, and the U.S., performing on the organ, pedal harpsichord, clavichord and virginal. In her busy year of 1965, she toured the U.S. for two months, and later in the year played on the Compenius organ at Fredericksborg Castle at the Royal Danish Ballet and Music Festival, joining eminent musicologist/keyboardist **Thurston Dart** (1921–71) in a harpsichord duet concert at Liege (Belgium). She also played in Holland and Austria, and gave joint recitals in Czechoslovakia with her daughter Katharine, on recorder. That autumn she led a party of forty-eight organists through Holland to see and hear famous old organs. In January 1966, she was awarded an honorary fellowship to the Royal College of Organists. In January 1967, she spent a semester in America as visiting organist professor at the University of Colorado, Boulder.

Specializing in pre-Romantic and early English organ music, Lady Jeans was a crusader for the restoration of old organs, and researched obscure musical instruments like the pedal-clavichord and water-organ. There were three such priceless organs at her home, Cleveland Lodge in Dorking (Surrey): a two-manual neo-baroque organ, a one-manual English organ *circa* 1820 and a three-manual organ by Hill, Norman & Beard, built to Sir James' specifications and played by him. There were also two clavichords, a pedal harpsichord and a water-organ. She broadcast frequently from Cleveland Lodge.

A contributor to Grove's Dictionary (Supplement), her writings on performance practice of early organ and keyboard music are archived at the Lady Susi Jeans Center for Organ Historiography at the University of Reading (England). Lady Susi Jeans died at her home, January 7, 1993.

CLAIRE COCI had a brilliant career combining her talent, personality and stage presence. She was born March 15, 1912, in New Orleans, began piano at five, organ at ten, and at fourteen was already organist of the city's Church of the Immaculate Conception. Her first public organ recital was at Christ Church in 1933. After early training with William C. Webb, she spent the summers of 1935 and '36, and the academic semesters in '37–'38, studying with Palmer Christian at the University of Michigan. The summer of 1937, she went to Charles Courboin in New York, and 1938 to Paris and the legendary **Marcel Dupré**. Her New York debut was in 1938 at Calvary Church.

In 1939, she made history by being the first woman to give an organ recital in the Cadet Chapel at West Point Military Academy, where she later made a recording. Besides extensive concert tours, she taught at Hartwick College (Oneonta, upstate New York), Oberlin College (Ohio, 1942),Westminster Choir College (Princeton, New Jersey), and in the '50s in New York City at the Dalcroze and the Mannes Schools of Music, and School of Sacred Music (Union Theological Seminary).

Between 1952–55, Coci was the first woman to become the official organist of the New York Philharmonic. In 1958, she founded the American Academy of Music and Art near her home in Tenafly, New Jersey. Still at the height of her career, she was tragically killed in a car accident near her home, September 30, 1978.

Catharine Crozier

CATHARINE CROZIER, born in Hobart, Oklahoma, January 18, 1914, became one of the most distinguished organists of the times. Awarded a scholarship to Eastman, she studied with **Harold Gleason** (1892–1980)—whom she later married—and graduated with a BM and MM in music literature. She was a member of the Eastman faculty (1938–55), replacing her husband as head of their organ department in 1953 when he retired. The couple moved to the warmer climes of Florida, and Catharine became organist of the Knowles Memorial Chapel at Rollins College, Winter Park, for fourteen years (1955–1969), and was also on the faculty. Concurrently, she made orchestra appearances and gave recitals throughout the U.S., Canada and Europe. In 1962, she had the great honor to be chosen, along with **Virgil Fox** (1912–80) and **E. Power Biggs** (1906–77)—the most distinguished American organists of the time—to play the inaugural recital at Philharmonic Hall in Lincoln Center. In 1975, she performed a concerto with orchestra at the inauguration of the organ at Lincoln Center's Alice Tully Hall.

Crozier served on juries at the International Organ Competitions at Bruges, St. Albans and Chartres. She received honorary degrees from Smith College, University of Southern Colorado and Baldwin-Wallace College. In 1976, she earned the Eastman Alumni Achievement Award, and in 1979 was International Performer of the Year for the New York City chapter of the AGO.

After a long and successful career, in 2001 at eighty-seven, she still held the position of artist-in-residence at Trinity Cathedral, Portland (Oregon). She passed away September 19, 2002.

JEANNE Marie Madeleine DEMESSIEUX was born in Montpellier (France), February 14, 1921. A pupil of Magda Tagliaferro, Jean and Noel Gallon, and **Marcel Dupré** (1886–1971) at the Paris Conservatory, she won the Premier Prix in Harmony (1937), Piano (1938), Fugue and Counterpoint (1940) and Organ (1941). Meanwhile, she had been organist of the Saint Esprit Church in Paris since 1933, and after thirty years, in 1962, moved to the famous Sainte Marie Madeleine. Her first public recital was after WWII at the Salle Pleyel (1946). The following year she concertized in England, becoming the first woman to play in Westminster Cathedral (Roman Catholic) and Westminster Abbey (Anglican). In 1952, she was organ professor at the Liège Conservatory. 1953, '55, and '58 marked tours in America, and in 1967 she played at the dedication of the Liverpool Metropolitan Cathedral. Her untimely death struck November 11, 1968.

Besides being a brilliant improvisationist, Demessieux was also a composer. Her few published compositions reflect her virtuoso technique. They include six Etudes (1946), *Sept Méditations sur le Saint Esprit* (1947), *Triptyque*, Op. 7 (1949), *Poème for Orgue et Orchestre*, Op. 9 (1949), Twelve Chorale Preludes on Gregorian Themes, Op. 8 (1954), *Te Deum*, Op. 11 (1965), *Prelude and Fugue in C*, Op. 12 (1965) and posthumously, *Répons pour le temps Pâques* (1968).

MARIE-MADELEINE DURUFLÉ, born in Marseilles, May 8, 1921, was appointed titular organist of the Cathedral of St. Veran de Cavaillon when she was eleven, and entered the Conservatory of Avignon at age twelve. In 1946, she began studies with **Marcel Dupré** at the Paris Conservatory and was awarded the Grand Prix International-Charles Marie Widor for organ and improvisation in 1953. Her husband, **Maurice Duruflé**, organist at the Grand Organ of St. Etienne-du-Mont (Paris) since 1930, shared many performances with her. In 1953, they began playing together at St. Etienne and also toured worldwide. Highly acclaimed in both the former USSR and Europe, the couple were warmly received during their 1964 American debut at the AGO National Convention. After this initial triumph, they returned to the U.S. four more times in performances of Maurice's *Requiem*, which had been conceived in the aftermath of WWI. Tragedy struck the pair in 1975 when a horrible automobile accident ended Maurice's career as a performer and severely injured Marie. After much surgery, she regained enough strength to continue playing Sunday Mass at St. Etienne. Maurice died in 1986. Three years later, Marie-Madeleine performed a complete retrospective of his music in New York. In 1990, another U.S. tour included two recitals for the AGO National Convention in Boston. From January to June 1992, she served as artist-in-residence at North Texas State University. In the fall of 1996, she returned to America for a fifteen city recital tour.

Mme. Duruflé died in Paris, October 5, 1999.

Women Organists in the 21st Century

Marie-Claire Alain

MARIE-CLAIRE ALAIN was born into a musical family in Saint-Germain-en-Laye near Paris, August 10, 1926. Of her brothers, Jehan (1911–40, killed in WWII) was an organist and composer, and Olivier (1918–94) a pianist, musicologist and composer. She studied music at the Paris Conservatory with **Maurice Duruflé** (1902–86) and **Marcel Dupré**, winning four first prizes. Since her 1950 Paris debut, she has performed all over the world, giving over 2,000 concerts! A faculty member at the Conservatoire National de Region de Rueil-Malmaison, outside Paris, she is in demand for her specialization in organ literature and early music. After teaching sixteen summers (1956–72) in Haarlem (Netherlands), she presided over a work-shop in Romainmotier, Switzerland.

Her extensive recordings, numbering over 250, include the complete works of Bach, Pachelbel, Brahms, Böhm and Guilain. In 1984, she was named "International Performer of the Year" by the New York City chapter of the AGO. As an outgrowth of her interest in the baroque pipe organs of her own country, she served on commission of the French Government for the promotion and construction of new pipe organs.

Following a recital on April 9, 2002 at Royal Festival Hall, Professor Curtis Price, head of the RAM, presented Alain with an honorary membership of the Royal Academy, their highest honor.

On March 18, 2002, my husband and I attended a fantastic recital and met this ageless lady at San Diego's All Souls Episcopal Church, which boasts a beautiful replica baroque organ built in 1985. In 2004 Alain played in Colorado, Maryland, Virginia and Texas. Among her eightieth birthday celebrations (2006), was a recital at the College of the Holy Cross, Worcester, Massachusetts, November 2005.

Diane Belcher

DIANE MEREDITH BELCHER is a graduate of Curtis and Eastman. In 1987, she became an associate of the AGO, for whom she has been a featured artist at conventions through 2005. A prize-winner at both the St. Alban's International Organ Competition (England) and Grand Prix de Chartres (France),she has soloed with numerous orchestras, led many workshops and master classes, and adjudicated national and international competitions. An active church musician for over thirty years, she served as organist/choir director at several churches, including Christ Episcopal, Memphis (Tennessee), during which time she also taught music theory at the University of Memphis and was founding director of the Memphis Concert Chorale.

Belcher was named "Outstanding Keyboard Soloist of 1998" by the *Arkansas Times*. Besides teaching and performing, her CD—on which she plays the celebrated Glatter-Götz/Rosales organ in Claremont, California— received the Golden Ear Award in 2000. She was appointed co-organist/choirmaster of Saint Mark's Church, Philadelphia, July 2005.

DIANE BISH is a concert and recording artist, composer, and international television personality. Growing up in Wichita, Kansas, she won a Fulbright grant to study in Amsterdam, and in Paris with **Nadia Boulanger**. In 1989, she won the National Citation of the National Federation of Music Clubs of America, for "distinguished service to the musical, artistic, and cultural life of the nation." (Other recipients of this award were Leonard Bernstein, Irving Berlin and Van Cliburn.) She was the first American woman to record on the four organs of Germany's Freiburg Cathedral, and has performed on organs played by Bach, Handel, Mozart and other immortals. Her compositions include major works for organ with orchestra, choir and narrator, which are included in over thirty recordings. Her international television series, *The Joy of Music*, brings together the music of the organ with world famous soloists, ensembles and orchestras. She combines the performances with informative narrative. The show is taped at sites around the globe and broadcast to over 300 million people each week.

As a church musician, Bish served as senior organist and artist-in-residence at the Coral Ridge Presbyterian Church in Fort Lauderdale, Florida, for over twenty years, and designed their 117-rank Ruffatti organ, considered one of the great organs in America. The Diane Bish Signature Series by Allen, a line of digital organs, is her latest creation.

BETH CHENAULT performs with her husband, Raymond, throughout the U.S. and Europe, making significant contributions to the organ duet literature through their commissions and recordings. Their duet career began in 1979, when Arthur Wills of England's Ely Cathedral composed *Toccata for Two* for them. This was followed by John Rutter's *Variations on An Easter Theme*. Other commissions have come from over forty composers, providing the Chenaults with a busy schedule. They have been featured artists at conferences and conventions of the AGO, American Society for 18th Century Studies, Association of Anglican Musicians, and the Spoleto Festival, Charleston, South Carolina. Recitals at such locations as the Crystal Cathedral (Garden Grove, California), Washington National Cathedral, and in England at St. Paul's Cathedral, York Minster, and the Birmingham Town Hall have highlighted their career.

Natives of Virginia, the couple completed music degrees at Virginia Commonwealth University (1972), having studied with Wayne Fisher at Cincinnati Conservatory. After Raymond received his MM, he became a Fellow in Church Music at Washington Cathedral. Since 1975, the Chenaults have been organists and choir directors at All Saints' Episcopal Church in Atlanta, and since 1976 have taught choral music at the Lovett School, where Raymond is director of fine arts and choral director of the Upper School, and Elizabeth is director of the Middle School. Their choirs have won many national competitions and performed at the American Choral Directors' Convention at Carnegie Hall, Avery Fischer Hall, Washington Cathedral and New York's Cathedral of St. John the Divine. The duo's recitals have been featured on NPR's "Pipedreams" and "Performance Today."

Named "Organists of the Year" by Sacred Music USA, they record for Gothic Records. Their commissioned works are published by Warner Brothers/Belwin Mills as *The Chenault Organ Duet Library*.

"Organ, four hands, four feet" has become virtually synonymous with the Chenaults.

LYNNE Louise **DAVIS** became the "American in Paris" when she never returned home, except to concertize, instead marrying French organist Pierre Firmin-Didot[160] in 1981, and having a daughter Caroline, April 25, 1983. Pierre was president/founder of the prestigious Chartres International Organ Competition, and as a couple they were a major part of the French organ music scene.

Lynne was born August 25, 1949, in St. Johns, Michigan, to a violinist and artist mother and a father with a great voice. The church attended by the family had five choirs and a fine organ, and by thirteen she was taking lessons from the organist/choir director. After graduating with honors from the University of Michigan, where she studied with Robert Clark, in 1971 she went to Paris to continue with **Marie-Claire Alain**. There, she earned diplomas under Jean Langlais at the Schola Cantorum, and École César Franck under Edouard Souberbielle. Her career was launched by taking first prize at the prestigious St. Albans International Organ Competition in England (1975). Further studies with **Maurice** and **Marie-Madeleine Duruflé**, as well as other European master organists, were concurrent to her duties as Titular Organist at the Church of St. Peter and St. Paul in Clamart, near Paris.

A member of many international competition juries, and professor of organ at the Conservatoire de Musique in Clamart, Davis is the first American ever to earn the coveted French teaching diploma "Certificat d'Aptitude de Professeur d'Orgue" (1994). By 1995, she was appointed titular organist of the Church of St. Pierre in Dreux.

Lynne played an important role in the organization of the 1992 exhibition "The Organs of Paris," and served as artistic coordinator for the recordings made by Erato of twenty instruments in the French capital. This series

---

160. Founder of the "Chartres, Sanctuary of the World" Association, Pierre Firmin-Didot (1921–2000) had for several decades, devoted his time to the preservation of the 800-year-old cathedral. With his efforts, and the support of then Minister of Culture André Malraux, the renovation of the great organs was completed in 1971, after five years of fundraising which drew thousands of donors. Pierre had been a choirboy at Chartres.

won the President of the Republic Prize from the Charles Cros Academy. Her CDs include *Musique pour Cathédrales* (1998), and other releases on the Chartres organ, discs of the Schulze organ at Armley (England), and broadcast recordings for the BBC, Bavarian Radio, France Musique and Radio Classique.

Davis is active as a lecturer, especially on French organ literature and history. She was appointed professor of organ at the French National Regional Conservatory in Caen in 1997. She performs to critical acclaim both in Europe and in North America where she was featured soloist at the AGO Centennial Convention in 1996. She is a member of the Sigma Alpha Iota International Music Fraternity for Women. In April 2000, she served on the jury of the Second Dallas International Organ Competition. She also participated in the 2002, 2004 AGO conventions.

CARLA EDWARDS, a native of Kansas City, Missouri, holds a BM *with highest distinction* from the University of Kansas, MM from University of Alabama, and DMA in organ performance from Indiana University (1996). Her many awards include winning the Region V AGO Competitions (1985), finalist in 1986 and winner of the nineteenth Annual Fort Wayne National Organ Playing Competition (1988). She has played extensively in America and England, and was a featured artist at the AGO Conventions in Dallas (1994), Evansville (1997) and Fort Wayne, Indiana (2001). In August 1990, she performed twelve concerts in Finland. Her performances have been broadcast on "Pipedreams." Her CDs are on the Calcante label and include *Carla Edwards and Friends and Twentieth Century Organ Music from the Auditorium* (Latter Day Saints Auditorium in Independence, Missouri).

Professor of organ, harpsichord and theory, and University Organist at DePauw (Indiana), she has held positions at Christ Episcopal, Tuscaloosa, St. Mary's Episcopal, Birmingham—both in Alabama—and was visiting lecturer at the University of Illinois, Urbana (1994–95). Edwards was honored by DePauw with the Distinguished Professor Award (2003) and as Cassel Grubb Professor of Music (2004).

JANETTE FISHELL is director of degree programs in organ performance and sacred music at Northwestern University, where she received her DMus (with highest honors) following a BM and MM from Indiana University. She has been a solo recitalist throughout the U.S., including recitals and lectures at six regional and national AGO conventions, and abroad at music festivals, universities, concert series, and the Prague Spring Festival. She has made multiple concert tours of Asia, Australia and New Zealand, South Africa, Europe and South America.

Recognized as an authority on music of Czech composer Petr Eben, she has premiered several of his solo organ works, and published numerous articles in *The American Organist*, *The Diapason*, *Het Orgel* and the British Dvořák Society's *Eben festschrift*. Her recordings include Eben, J.S. Bach, Marcel Dupré, as well as duet literature with Colin Andrews. Active as a choral conductor, clinician and adjudicator, Fishell is past chair of the AGO National Committee on Women and Careers, and sits on the National Young Artist Competition in Organ Performance Committee.

On the faculty since 1967, **ROBERTA GARY** is head of the division of keyboard studies and professor of organ at the College-Conservatory of Music of the University of Cincinnati, where she teaches organ, organ pedagogy, and a graduate seminar in organ literature. Her degrees are from the University of Cincinnati (BM, piano; MM, organ) and Eastman (DMA and Performer's Certificate in Organ). As a soloist and workshop clinician, Gary has presented numerous concerts, master classes, lectures and workshops in America and Canada, covering Bach, Messiaen, French classic literature, 19th century romantic literature, early performance practice and pedagogy. She has been a member of the faculty of Capital University (Ohio), conducted the Choate Organ-Harpsichord Seminars in Connecticut, Bach Week at Columbia College (South Carolina), and Scranton (Pennsylvania) Summer Organ Week. She was a featured recitalist for the 1976 and 1990 AGO National Conventions, and has served as a member of the AGO National Committee on Professional Education for many years. Her recording of Liszt and Reubke was released in 2001 on the Arsis label.

Her husband, Thomas Miles, is organist at Christ Church Cathedral, and the Isaac M. Wise Temple. He maintains a private Suzuki piano studio through the Cincinnati Music Academy, and conducts European study tours, as well as accompanying the Christ Church Cathedral Choir and Cincinnati Christian Chorale on their trips to Europe. Their book, *What Every Pianist Needs to Know about the Body* (2004) has an important section on organists.

NANCY GRANERT has been organist for major churches in New England. Born in Evanston, Illinois, January 2, 1952, she was brought up in nearby Glenview. She began piano at seven and organ at thirteen. Since her mother played jazz, the lessons were her introduction to classical music. She continued piano through Oberlin, from which she graduated with a BM in 1974. She also took private organ lessons. A journey to Barcelona gained her study with eminent organ pedagogue **Monserrat Torrent**. She earned her MM from the New England Conservatory in 1976 and got her first position at Boston Unitarian (1976–79). From there she spent 1980–81 at the Church of the Advent as assistant to choir director Edith Ho. Next came seventeen dedicated years at Harvard Memorial Church (1981–98).

1998 saw *Choral Music for a New Millennium* on a Pro Organo CD with Granert at the organ and the Harvard Choir. The same year she moved to Boston's Emmanuel Church, where she was still serving as organist in 2006. She is also organist for Temple Sinai in Brookline, and a teaching assistant at Boston University.

Judith Hancock

JUDITH HANCOCK, born October 18, 1934, in Milwaukee, is a graduate of Syracuse University, where she studied organ with Arthur Poister before going to Union Theological Seminary, where she met husband, Gerre, and earned her MSM. She also studied at Eastman. As associate organist of St. Thomas Church, Fifth Avenue, one of New York's largest, she assisted Gerre in conducting the choir for more than thirty years. Other past venues have been organist/music director at St. James, Madison Avenue, St. James the Less, Scarsdale, New York, Episcopal Church of the Redeemer, Cincinnati, and churches in Bronxville, New York, and Durham, North Carolina.

A leading interpreter of Romantic organ repertoire, in 1983 Judith established an ongoing series of solo organ recitals at St. Thomas, and in 1985 celebrated the 300th birthday of J.S. by playing four all-Bach recitals. In 1987, she was the soloist during the St. Thomas Choir's performance at King's College Chapel and St. John's College, Cambridge (England). She also performed with the choir at King's Lynn and Aldeburgh Festivals, and Westminster Abbey, where the choir had the honor of a one week residence, singing the daily services. Besides countless AGO conventions, Hancock appeared with the St. Thomas Choir on concert tours of Italy and Austria, where her masterful talent was heard in the cathedrals of Venice, Trieste, Vienna and Salzburg.

She performs many duo recitals with her husband who serves on a visiting basis on the faculties of Juilliard, Eastman, and Yale Institute of Sacred Music. Their CDs are on Decca/Argo, Koch International, Priory and Gothic Records.

In May 2004, St. Thomas Church honored the couple who had been part of their music program since 1971. In August 2004, the Hancocks joined the faculty of the University of Texas at Austin as senior lecturers in organ and sacred music, to build a Graduate Sacred Music Studies Program. They finished the year with a holiday organ concert.

Their two daughters are Deborah, an interior designer in New York, and Lisa, a photographer in Los Angeles.

Born in Sofia, Bulgaria, **YANKA HÉKIMOVA** began her career as a pianist and at an early age performed recitals and orchestra concerts in her native city. She finished her studies in both piano and organ at the Tchaikovsky Conservatory in Moscow, then settled in Paris devoting herself to her career as an international artist, performing in concerts and festivals around the world.

In addition to an extensive repertoire, she has written transcriptions for organ of orchestra and piano works by Vivaldi, Handel, Mozart, Liszt, Wagner, Saint-Säens, Tchaikovsky and Ravel.

In 1998, in collaboration with the City of Paris, ARGOS and sponsorship from the Hippcrène Foundation, Hékimova conceived and performed a series of concerts for children that were so well received they have become an annual event.

She has recorded several CDs, two featuring the organ of Saint Eustache (Paris), which include original works and her transcription of Mozart's "Jupiter" Symphony, plus a live recording of *Symphonic Dances* by Rachmaninoff, performed by Hékimova and Jean Guillou (who wrote the transcription for two organists). A 2000 release of the 6 Sonatas by J.S. Bach on two CDs, was recorded at the Tonhalle in Zürich.

WILMA Hoyle **JENSEN**, known as the "Dean of American Organists," began piano with her mother, and at age eleven became the regular organist in the church where her father was minister. Studying organ with Catharine Crozier and Harold Gleason, she received BM and MM degrees from Eastman with a performers certificate in organ, supporting herself during her studies by holding positions in Rochester churches. After graduation, she began her recital career throughout the U.S., and tours of Norway, Sweden, Denmark, England, (then) West Germany, France and Poland. This was followed by fourteen years on the adjunct faculty of Oklahoma University while playing full time at the First Presbyterian Church. She was also on the faculty of Indiana University (1978–81), and professor of organ and church music at Scarritt Graduate School, as well as professor of organ on the adjunct faculty of Blair School of Music at Vanderbilt University (1981–88), both in Nashville. A dedicated church musician, she was choirmaster/organist at St. George's Episcopal Church in Nashville until her retirement in May 2002, after nineteen years. She is now professor emerita.

Her CDs are *Mors et Resurrectio* on the Arkay label, and *Sketches and Improvisations in the French Tradition* (Pro Organo). Both recorded at St. George's, 1998.

On May 5, 2002, several of Jensen's former organ students and choir members gathered from across the country at St. George's to play and sing in a special tribute concert, recorded on CD.

JOYCE JONES is the Joyce Oliver Bowden professor of music and organist-in-residence at Baylor University (Waco, Texas). Born February 13, 1933, she received her BM *summa cum laude*, and MM and DMA from the University of Texas at Austin. Her masters in sacred music (MSM) is from Southwestern Baptist Theological Seminary.

She made her professional debut with the Dallas Symphony as winner of the G.B. Dealey Award. Known for her superb musicianship and phenomenal technique, Jones has given concerts throughout the U.S., including four return engagements with the San Francisco Symphony, and international tours of Canada, Mexico, Japan and Europe. A Fellow of the AGO, she is author/editor of instructional methods, including *The King of Instruments*, and collections of organ music.

In 1997, she received the National Federation of Music Clubs' highest award, a National Citation "in recognition and sincere appreciation of her unselfish devotion and dedicated service to music as a concert organist, inspiring teacher and composer." She also received a Baylor University Award for Outstanding Creative Artist.

Marilyn Keiser

MARILYN KEISER, born July 12, 1941, in Alton, Illinois, received her BSM from Illinois Wesleyan University, where she studied with Lillian McCord, and her MSM *summa cum laude* from Union Theological Seminary (1965), studying with Alex Wyton. Following her graduation, she became assistant organist of the Riverside Church in Manhattan, and a year later was appointed associate organist/choirmaster at New York's largest Protestant church, the Cathedral of St. John the Divine, a position she held until 1970. From 1970–83, she was organist and director of music at All Souls Parish, Asheville, North Carolina, and music consultant for the Episcopal Diocese of Western North Carolina. Concurrently, she earned her DSM from UTS in 1977.

A Chancellor's Professor of Music at Indiana University, Bloomington, Keiser teaches courses in sacred music and applied organ. She is past president of the Association of Anglican Musicians, a contributing editor to the hymnal *Ecumenical Praise*, and was a consultant to the music committee for the *Episcopal Hymnal 1982*. Her recordings are on Lyrichord and Wicks Organ Company labels. In 1995, she was awarded a doctorate of humane letters from the Virginia Theological Seminary in Alexandria. 1997 brought the Unitas Citation from UTS, and the following year received a Teaching Excellence Recognition Award from Indiana University School of Music.

She has been a member of the AGO National Council, served as national registrar and member of the national nominating committee, and Dean of the Western North Carolina Chapter. Her Associate, Choirmaster and Fellowship degrees are from the Guild. In constant demand for recitals and workshops, she has appeared throughout the country sponsored by churches, colleges, AGO chapters, and conventions, for which she played at Kennedy Center, and with the Detroit Symphony. She was featured artist for the International Congress of Organists in Cambridge, the Southern Cathedrals Festival in Winchester (England), and at London's Royal Victoria Hall with the Singapore Symphony, as well as the American Cathedral in Paris, and the Universidade Federal do Rio Grande do Sul (Brazil).

Her performances on radio have been heard on stations in New York and NPR. Recordings include *Music of Paris in the 1920s and 1930s* (Loft), *The People Respond-Amen, Spiritual Pairs, Studies in Relief and In Praise of the Organ: Latin Choral* and *Organ Music of Zoltan Kodaly* (Pro Organo). 2004 CDs are *Seasons of Festivity* at Fairmount Presbyterian Cleveland Heights, Ohio, and *Centennial Flourish* at St. James, Hendersonville, North Carolina.

MARGARET McELWAIN KEMPER, although an organ major, did not decide to go into church music until the end of her sophomore year. It was a choice which gave her a career she grew to love.

Born December 12, 1938, in Kenosha, Wisconsin, her mother, an excellent piano teacher, was a major influence, starting her daughter at seven. Violin came in junior high and organ in high school, although as a regular churchgoer Maggie was drawn to the organ early in life. After graduating from DePauw University as a student of Arthur Carkeek (1960) with a BM in organ performance, she went to Paris as a Fulbright scholar to study with André Marchal (1960–62). Returning to Evanston to study with Barrett Spach, she received a master's in organ from Northwestern University (1963), which institution would present her with an alumni service award in 1980. A few years later, she traveled to Haarlem (Netherlands) for study with **Marie-Claire Alain** and Anton Heiller at the Summer Academy for Organists.

Like many organists, Kemper has three part time jobs as a church musician and teacher. She was organist at Glencoe Union Church (1978–2001), where she played a two-manual twenty-seven rank Casavant organ built in 1980. In December 1994, she was appointed director of music and organist at Presbyterian Homes, a retirement community in Evanston, Illinois, with 650 residents. Their newly renovated chapel is home to a new Dobson tracker, two-manual, twenty-six rank instrument, which she plays at Wednesday and Sunday afternoon services, also directing a staff choir, administering a series of recitals, with artists from England, Germany, Italy, Hungary, Ukraine, Russia, Belgium and South Africa.

Her previous positions in Illinois include the First Presbyterian Church of Oak Park, First Presbyterian Church of Evanston, and North Shore Congregation Israel in Glencoe for ten years. For nineteen years she was the summer substitute organist/choral director at the Fourth Presbyterian Church in Chicago. Her third position is associate professor and coordinator of organ and church music studies at Northwestern University. In addition to her private organ studio, she teaches organ pedagogy, organ literature, a course in professional concerns for the church musician, and the sacred music colloquium in cooperation with Garrett Evangelical Theological and Seabury-Western Theological Seminaries.

Kemper's AGO affiliations are membership in the North Shore Chapter since 1963, service as dean, subdean, secretary and board member; Illinois district convener (1978–81); Region V councillor and convener of Regional Councillors on the national council (1981–86); and national secretary (1988–94). As national president (1994–98), she was only the second woman in that position. In August 1998, she was leader for an organists delegation to the Czech Republic, Poland and Hungary, sponsored by the People to People Citizen Ambassador Program.

October 2001 found her in recital at Moscow's Glinka Museum and presenting a master class at the Tchaikovsky State Conservatory. These appearances are a result of the friendship with Tatiana Zenaishvili, who performed at Presbyterian Homes during her Spring 2000 Northwestern residency as a Fulbright Scholar.

September 1, 2001 marked Kemper's latest position as organist of the Kenilworth Union Church. Living in Northfield, a suburb of Chicago, Maggie is happily married to John Scribner Kemper, a telecommunications expert. Their daughter, Katherine, was born in 1969 and son Scott in 1973. Kathy, and son-in-law Don, presented her with granddaughter Sophia Schubert Featherstone on June 23, 2000. In 2004 she gave a recital at her alma-mater, De Pauw University.

KEI KOITO, born in Japan, January 4, 1950, into a family of artists, is a gifted performer of Bach's organ works. She began studying music at an early age with lessons in voice, piano, cello and organ. At the Tokyo University of Fine Arts, she received first prize for organ while simultaneously pursuing philosophy, psychology and musical aesthetics—all with highest distinction. She was also unanimously awarded first prize with distinction at the Geneva Conservatory. Her teachers were Pierre Segond (Geneva), Luigi-Ferdinando Tagliavini (Freiburg), Xavier Darasse (Toulouse), Anton Heiller (Austria), and Reinhard Goebel (Cologne).

Besides Bach, she also excels in the repertoire of the Romantic and modern eras. Since 1978, she has performed over 100 contemporary works, more than half as world premieres dedicated to her. With scholarly research and knowledge of historical treatises, she worked on a series of recordings of the complete organ works of J.S. Bach, including *The Art of the Fugue*, for Harmonic Records (France). Her recordings of the C.P.E. Bach sonatas for organ have been chosen as a reference for the "Guide des musiques à l'ancienne," (Repertoire/France, June 1994).

Koito's international career began in 1980 with the success of her recital at the Maurice Ravel Auditorium, Lyon, and Victoria Hall, Geneva. She has soloed with symphonic and baroque orchestras, and performed as a recitalist in many prestigious venues around the world. She has composed instrumental and choral music, and pieces for chamber ensemble.

The artist resides in Switzerland, where she is professor of organ at the Lausanne Conservatory of Music. In 1997, she founded and is director of the Lausanne Bach Festival and International Bach Competition. She is also the founder/director of "Organ Week," involving research through conferences, seminars and concerts centering around the unique collection of historic and symphonic instruments in Swiss Romande, begun in 1998. She performs each season throughout Europe and is in demand abroad as both performer and adjudicator for international organ competitions. She increasingly tours North America beginning in 2002.

Susan Landale

SUSAN LANDALE, born in Edinburgh, July 18, 1935, graduated with a BM from Edinburgh University, and resides in Paris where she is a concert organist, teacher and organist for the church of Saint-Louis des Invalides. As professor of organ at the National Regional Conservatory in Rueil-Malmaison, near Paris (1977–2000), her classes have produced many prize-winning students. She is in demand for juries, master classes and seminars, and has adjudicated in Chartres, St. Albans, Calgary, Prague, Odense, Lübeck and Warsaw. In 1984, she joined the staff of St. Louis des Invalides, and was appointed titular organist of St. George's Anglican Church (Paris), a post she held for eighteen years. Author of articles on contemporary music, her study of the organ music of Petr Eben, and *The Musical Language of Olivier Messiaen in his Organ Works*, have been published in several languages.

Winner of the first International Organ Playing Competition at the St. Albans' International Festival, England, she has soloed with leading orchestras in Paris, London, Prague, Hamburg, Heidelberg and other European cities and was guest artist at festivals as far flung as Melbourne (Australia), Reykjavik (Iceland), Calgary (Canada), and Edinburgh. Her numerous CDs of the works of Petr Eben, Olivier Messiaen, Louis Vierne, Charles Tournemire and others have received the highest acclaim from French critics. In 2004 she was appointed a professor of organ at the RAM. She was part of the 2005 AGO convention in the U.S.

Joan Lippincott

JOAN LIPPINCOTT, born Christmas Day, 1935, in East Orange, New Jersey, studied piano with the great **Robert Casadesus** (1899–1972), and began organ at thirteen on entering high school. She graduated from Princeton's Westminster Choir College with a BM, a student of

Alexander McCurdy, and Curtis with an artist's diploma. Additional graduate work was at Union Theological Seminary. She has been on the faculty of Westminster Choir College since 1960, becoming head in 1967, thus chairing the largest organ department in the world. Her participation on summer faculties has been at the New England Conservatory, University of Wisconsin and at many music conferences. In 1993, she was appointed principal organist at Princeton, where she recorded on the renovated Mander Organ. She left that post in June 2000 to devote more time for recitals and recordings which, besides 20th century music, include Bach, Mendelssohn, Widor and other classics on major American organs.

In 1969, she instituted a European Organ Study Tour to provide students with the opportunity to hear and play the most important historic and contemporary organs in Holland, Denmark, Sweden, Germany, Austria, Switzerland and France. She is sought as a consultant by churches purchasing new instruments.

As a featured recitalist at Regional and National Conventions of the AGO, including 2005, she has premiered contemporary organ works such as Malcolm Williamson's *Organ Symphony* at Washington Cathedral, Iain Hamilton's *Paraphrase for Organ* at Riverside Church, New York, and the world premiere of *Epiphanies* by Daniel Pinkham at House of Hope Presbyterian Church, St. Paul, Minnesota.

Lippincott has been a soloist in Arizona, Massachusetts, Michigan, New York, Ohio, Oregon, Spoleto USA Festival, (South Carolina) and at conventions of the AGO and Organ Historical Society, as well as Yale, Harvard, Duke and Princeton Universities on the most prominent organs in America. She is an honorary member of Sigma Alpha Iota and has received both the Alumni Merit Award and Distinguished Merit Award from Westminster Choir College.

Karen McFarlane

KAREN McFARLANE took piano lessons from an early age, had good public school music classes, and sang in a high school choir, leading to her interest in choral music. She began organ study in her sophomore year in college, and graduated from Lindenwood College in Missouri (BMusEd, 1964). As a church musician, she spent six years as assistant to **Frederick Swann** at New York's Riverside Church, eight years as director of music/organist at Park Avenue Church, New York City, and since 1986 has been associate choirmaster at the Church of the Covenant in Cleveland, where she works with music director and organist Todd Wilson. She conducted half the anthems recorded on the choir's CD *American Music*, and co-directed three "Pipe Organ Encounters" for young people interested in learning about the instrument. She is co-author with Stephen Smith of *Presenting Concerts in Your Church and Community* (published by the AGO).

Listed in *Who's Who in America*, *Who's Who in Entertainment* and *The World Who's Who of Women*, Karen has been involved with the guild on local and national levels, from chapter Dean to serving on national committees, as well as working with the biennial winners of the National Young Artists Competition of the AGO, assisting them in establishing performance careers. For her "outstanding musical contributions" she received the 1993 Avis H. Blewett Award from the St. Louis chapter, and the first Edward A. Hansen Leadership Award of the AGO (July 2000) for her eighteen years of volunteer work with national competition winners of the guild. November 2000 brought a Certificate of Appreciation by the Cleveland chapter. From 1976–2000, she ran her successful Karen McFarlane Artists, Inc. (See Agents.)

MARILYN MASON, born June 29, 1925, studied at Oklahoma State and the University of Michigan, as well as with **Arnold Schoenberg**, **Nadia Boulanger** and **Maurice Duruflé**. She began teaching at the University of Michigan in 1946, was made chairman of the organ department in 1962, and full professor in 1965.

In 1987, Mason was awarded an honorary doctor of music by the University of Nebraska. In 1988, she was chosen as Performer of the Year by the New York Chapter of the AGO. She has served as adjudicator at almost every major organ competition in the world. Her discography, on Columbia and Musical Heritage Society labels, includes Bach, Handel, the complete organ works of Pachelbel, as well as contemporary composers.

She has made more than twenty research tours focused on historic organs all over Europe. During the course of one year, recital and concert invitations found her on five continents: America, Europe, Africa, South America and Australia. In August 2001, she led a tour of forty organ enthusiasts through Germany, Austria and the Czech Republic. She was the first American woman organist to perform in Westminster Abbey, the first woman organist to play in Latin America, and the first American organist to perform in Egypt (1970, 1995). Her over seventy-five contemporary commissions came from such prominent composers as Henry Cowell, Ross Lee Finney, Ulysses Kay, Ernst Krenek, Arnold Schoenberg and Virgil Thomson. In 2004, she coordinated and participated in the Ann Arbor Summer Festival which takes place on the University of Michigan campus.

In tribute to Mason's outstanding career, she was presented with the Distinguished Faculty Award, and the installation of the Marilyn Mason Organ in a specifically built recital hall. This instrument, created by C. B. Fisk, is a replica of those of 18th century organ builder Gottfried Silbermann, whose instruments were familiar to Bach.

Marilyn was married for thirty-seven years to Richard K. Brown, professor of electrical engineering at the University of Michigan. He died July 23, 1991. Their two sons are Merritt Christian Brown, an associate professor at Harvard University Medical School, and Edward A. Brown, a freelance photographer in Reseda, California. Her second husband is William R. Steinhoff, professor emeritus of English literature, University of Michigan.

DOROTHY PAPADAKOS was, for thirteen years (1990–2003), the second woman organist of the Cathedral of St. John the Divine in New York City. She was born October 22, 1960, to actress mother Dorothy Johnson, who had been a regular on the 1950s *Bob Cummings Show*, had appeared in movies with Pat Boone and Frank Sinatra, as well as being first runner-up to Miss America (1956). [In 1994, her daughter would be one of the judges in the pageant.] Dorothy's father, Peter Papadakos, had fallen in love with his future wife after seeing her on the Groucho Marx TV Show, *You Bet Your Life*. Founder/president of Gyrodyne Helicopter Company (1954), he holds a place in aviation history as the only American helicopter pioneer to see his coaxial design (Drone Anti-Submarine Helicopter) put into mass production for the Navy, with over 800 built, many of which are still flying.

After divorcing Peter, her mother moved to Reno where Liberace, with whom she had done publicity, frequently had both "girls" at his show. His style greatly influenced Dorothy's improvisation technique. She began piano at age nine with Loren McNabb, a Reno nightclub pianist. She taught herself guitar at thirteen. From ages eleven to seventeen, she played jazz gigs around Reno. It was only after she began studying with Trinity Church organist James Poulton that she was exposed to classical music. She began playing for the 9:00 A.M. Sunday service, combining her classical and folk music interests. After Poulton's death, when she was sixteen, she took over the main service at 11:00 A.M. On weekdays, her prowess in piano, guitar and synthesizers added a teenage career of teaching folk guitar and having her own band at the church, playing folk music and being lead vocal and lead guitar. Her composing began at this time, with popular songs and settings to the mass. Jazz piano study continued with renowned pianist/arranger Don Rae until age eighteen when, in 1979, she drove cross country to live with her father on Long Island.

In New York, she attended SUNY Stony Brook (1979–80) followed by Barnard, formerly the women's adjunct of Columbia, earning a BA in music (1982), and MM from Juilliard (1986). Her teachers included conductor Dennis Keene and Jon Gillock, organ, the latter specializing in Messiaen; Gerre Hancock, organ improvisation; and Lyle Mays, jazz pianist with the Pat Metheny Group. Experience with "World Music" came in 1984 from her association with the Paul Winter Consort, one of the earliest (1967) exponents of the genre, which combines elements from African, Asian, and South American cultures with jazz, incorporating the growing interest in the natural world and voices of the animal kingdom while exploring a richer texture of sound.

During this period (1980–85), Papadakos was organist at St. Mark's Episcopal Church, Islip, Long Island. Hearing the improvisations of Paul Halley on his brilliant solo recording, *Nightwatch*, changed her life forever. She wrote asking to study with him, but as organist of the Cathedral of St. John the Divine (1978–1989), he answered that he didn't take students, but would listen to her. She played for him and, to her utter amazement, he accepted her in 1983 as his only organ improvisation student. The same year she won first prize in the New York City AGO Competition. Never charging for lessons, Halley trained Papadakos to become cathedral organ scholar in 1985, and assistant organist in 1987. While Halley was on sabbatical in 1989, Dorothy was interim head organist. (From 1980–89 she had been "nightwatch organist," playing for teens and retreat guests on weekends, doing "midnight blowouts.") She was officially appointed to the head position as cathedral organist in 1990, when her mentor left to pursue other career goals. This designated her as the first woman *worldwide* to ever hold this position in a cardinal cathedral.

During her tenure, she was the founder/director of the Great Organ Restoration Fund, an effort to acquire $2 million to restore all five pipe organs at the Cathedral. Her "Adopt-A-Pipe" Program raised a substantial amount of money for the Great Organ. Another Papadakos original was heard every Sunday evening after Vespers, when she initiated the Vespers Organ Improvisation Series, showcasing artists talented in that specialty from around the world.

At the end of 2001, a catastrophe rocked the cathedral. The structure, begun in 1892, was actually never finished, with work on the north transept having ceased after the attack on Pearl Harbor, December 7, 1941. (The south transept was never begun. Fifty feet of the proposed tower was built in the 1980s in a program that temporarily brought master masons from England to teach young apprentices in the area.)

Another Tragedy of 2001

As if the destruction of the World Trade Center Towers, September 11, was not enough for one year, December 18, 2001 saw a fire—caused by faulty wiring—which gutted the north transept, destroying the gift shop, whose $1.5 million income contributed to one fourth of an annual budget of $4 million. The debacle left six inches of water welled around the central altar. A smoky haze filmed over the rose window, the largest in the country. Besides scrubbing soot from everywhere, clean up involved finally dismantling the ninety-five-foot-high steel scaffolding from 1941! The most serious damage was to several tapestries, which were sent to the laboratory on the cathedral grounds to be cleaned and, hopefully, rewoven. The cathedral did manage to hold its Christmas Eve service that year, but by 2005 restoration had barely begun. In 2006, the pipe organ was still being cleaned and restored, not to be returned until December 2008, after the renovation is completed and the air clear of dust. Meanwhile, an electronic instrument was being used.

Romance on the High Plateaux!

Dorothy's interests, inherited from her father, in the arts, entomology, horticulture and the healing arts, have made her a world traveler from Vietnam and Laos to Russia, Indonesia, Europe, and the Galapagos Islands—wherever there are tropics and high elevation. She speaks many languages in varying degrees of fluency— French, Greek, Spanish, German, a little Russian, less Mandarin Chinese. It was through one of these equatorial adventures that, in 1999, she met Tracy McCullen, president/founder of *Landscapes Unique*, in Wilmington, North Carolina. They were wed May, 20, 2000. (For two years she commuted to New York, where she had an apartment on the cathedral grounds along with bishops, canons and staff members.)

Departure for a New Career

Papadakos is celebrated for her organ improvisations in every style, avant-garde recordings with ethnic instruments and organ, as well as infusing jazz into the liturgical language. She has concertized in recitals, and soloed with orchestras such as St. Luke's Chamber, Brooklyn Philharmonic and Little Orchestra Society of New York. Her international tours have included Japan and Singapore with the Paul Winter Consort, and the Three Choirs Festival in Worcester (England, 2004). A featured guest on NPR's *Weekend Edition*, *The Today Show*, CNN's *Headline News*, Japan's Fuji TV *News Hour*, and radio broadcasts, she has been the subject of articles in *Smithsonian Magazine*, *New York Times*, *NY Daily News*, *Keyboard Magazine* and numerous other newspapers and journals. Her compositions include *1990 Overture & Variation in E flat* for Woodwind Quintet, the ballet *Triantafilia*, performed in Carnegie Hall with dancers from the New York City Ballet (1992), as well as choral, organ and instrumental works and music for independent films. Her CDs on the Pro Organo Label are: *Dorothy Over the Rainbow* (1996), *I Do! Me Too!* (1998), *Shades of Green* (1999), *Christmas Traveler* (1999) and *Cafe St. John* (2001). Her 1999 TV score for Discovery Channel's *The Science of Whales* was a New York Film Festival finalist. She also wrote the under score for the Off-Broadway production of *Mona 7.*

After leaving St. John, she again took up her career writing for musical theater, completing the book, lyrics and music—the first woman to accomplish all three facets—for *Pompeii, the Musical,* a tale of *carpe diem* and passion from the point of view of Bacchus, the God of Wine, who enjoyed quite a few parties in his favorite city in the course of 1,000 years. *Pompeii's* highly successful world premiere came November 2005, in Wilmington, North Carolina, with paths opening for the production to reach Broadway and London. Dorothy plays yet another role with her own company, World Premiere Theatrical Productions, and is ready to produce other musicals waiting in the wings.

Jane Parker-Smith

JANE PARKER-SMITH, born in Northampton, England, 1950, studied at the RCM (London) were she won the Walford Davies Prize for organ performance. After further work with concert organist Nicolas Kynaston, a French Government Scholarship enabled her to complete her studies in Paris with legendary blind organist Jean Langlais, perfecting her technique of 20th century French organ music for which she is internationally renowned. She made her London debut at Westminster Cathedral at age twenty, and two years later her first solo appearance with the BBC Promenade Concerts in the Albert Hall, followed by a Royal Festival Hall debut in 1975. The success of this resulted in being invited to perform regularly in the International Organ Series. Besides numerous radio and television programs on the BBC, German and Swiss television, her concert career includes performances throughout the UK, Finland, Sweden, Hong Kong, Canada, France, Argentina, Switzerland, Japan, Greece, Korea, and Severance Hall, Cleveland. In 1996, she gave solo concerts at the AGO National Centennial Convention in New York City, and was a featured artist for the 2002 AGO National Convention in Philadelphia. She has recorded a wide range of solo repertoire, and collaborated with the renowned **Maurice André** in a duo recording of music for trumpet and organ.

Parker-Smith is an honorary fellow of both the Guild of Musicians and Singers, and the North and Midlands School of Music, as well as music director/organist of the German Christ Church in Knightsbridge, London.

MARY PRESTON graduated with honors, receiving her MM from the University of North Texas with post-graduate study at Eastman. Her early training in San Francisco was followed by Oberlin, San Jose State and Southern Methodist University. She has coached and played in masterclasses with Jean Guillou, **Marie-Claire Alain**, Pierre Cochereau and Michael Radulescu.

Her North American performances include San Francisco, Chicago, Dallas, Salt Lake City, Cleveland, Pittsburgh, Ottawa, Los Angeles and New York's Riverside Church. She appeared at Nôtre Dame de Paris by special invitation of the late Pierre Cochereau (1924–84). In the summer of 1994 her European recital tour took her to the Merseburg Cathedral, Berlin, St. Nikolai Church, Leipzig, the Lichtenstein Palace, Prague, and Oliwa Cathedral, Poland.

Preston is curator of the Lay Family Concert Organ in Meyerson Symphony Hall. Her first recording on this instrument, built by C. B. Fisk, Inc., was music of Widor and Duruflé, on Gothic (1996). Resident organist of the Dallas Symphony, with whom she has performed numerous recitals, she also serves as organist/director of music and worship at King of Glory Lutheran Church.

Her appearances as featured artist with AGO include the national conventions in Houston (1988), Denver (1998), and Los Angeles (2004).

CHRISTA RAKICH, born in Waterbury, Connecticut, November 11, 1952, sat in the organ loft when her mother sang in the church choir. She received degrees in organ and German from Oberlin, and took second prize at the 1975 Bruges International Organ Competition. As a Fulbright Scholar, she studied two years with Austrian organist Anton Heiller (1923–79) at the Vienna Hochschule für Musik. After receiving her MM from the New England Conservatory (1979), she served on their faculty for the next ten years. Other positions include associate professor of organ and harpsichord at Westminster Choir College, Princeton, and director of music at the Jesuit Urban Center, Church of the Immaculate Conception in Boston. She has also served on the faculty of the University of Connecticut, as assistant university organist at Harvard, and artist-in-residence at the University of Pennsylvania. She was featured soloist, performing on the famous Flentrop organ at St. Mark's Cathedral, at the 2000 National AGO convention in Seattle. She returned to the NEC in 2002 as titular chair of the organ department.

As fortepianist and harpsichordist, Rakich is a founding member of Ensemble Duemila. Her recordings include J.S. Bach's *Clavierübung III* (Titanic), *Christa Rakich in Recital at St. Mark's Cathedral* (ReZound), *Deferred Voices: Organ Music by Women Composers* and *Transcriptions from St. Justin's* (AFKA).

Cherry Rhodes

CHERRY RHODES, the first American to win an international organ competition (Munich, 1966), was born in Brooklyn, New York, June 28, 1943. Brought up in Westport, Connecticut, Boston and Gloucester, Massachusetts, she began piano at four, and by seven her stepfather, Frank Hanson, teacher of Steinway rebuilding at the NEC plus long time head piano technician for Boston Symphony Hall and Tanglewood, had the child daily practicing an hour of technique, which she loved! He was a powerful influence on her taking up the organ at eleven. Her first teacher was Berj Zamkochian. The household resounded with classical music, while their mother, Edo Rhodes, who painted, sculpted and played piano, had Cherry, her brother, Warren, and sister, Jocelyn, doing improvisational dancing. They were also taken to concerts, theater and museums. (The kind of fun and exposure to culture rarely enjoyed by today's glued-to-the-computer-or-TV younger generation.)

Entering Curtis at fifteen, Cherry graduated with a BM in 1964 after four years of piano with **Vladimir Sokoloff** (1913–97), and six years of organ with Alexander McCurdy. She received Fulbright and German government grants to study in Munich for three years with Karl Richter (1926–81), and Rockefeller and Alliance Française de New York grants for two years in Paris with **Marie-Claire Alain** and Jean Guillou (*b* 1930), for whom she was assistant at St. Eustache. Winning the international organ competition in Munich was followed by another top prize in Bologna in 1969. She played recitals at the Cathedral of Notre Dame in Paris, at international organ festivals in Bratislava and Presov (Czechoslovakia), Freiburg, Munich, Nuremberg, St. Albans, Vienna, Luxembourg and Poland. Besides International Bach Festivals in Paris and Marburg, she has given Bach recitals throughout the U.S. and performed at numerous AGO conventions. She has also been a soloist with the South German Radio Orchestra, the Chamber Orchestra of the French National Radio, Pasadena Chamber Orchestra, Los Angeles Philharmonic, Phoenix Symphony, and the Philadelphia Orchestra, with whom she made her debut at age seventeen. Many of her performances have been broadcast throughout the U.S., Canada and abroad.

From 1972–1975, Rhodes taught organ at Peabody and was concurrently artist-in-residence at All Souls Church, Unitarian, in Washington, DC. Other venues include Royal Festival Hall (London), Lincoln Center, Orchestra Hall (Chicago), Meyerson Symphony Center (Dallas), Performing Arts Center (Milwaukee), and the opening recital of the new organ at Kennedy Center.

She edited **Joan Tower's** organ work *Ascent*, and co-edited *Prelude and Variations on "Old Hundredth"* by Calvin Hampton. She has recorded with Eugene Ormandy and the Philadelphia Orchestra, is featured on the CD *Pipedreams Live!* (Minnesota Public Radio), *Comes Summertime* (JAV Recordings), *Everyone Dance* (Pro Organo) *Cherry Rhodes in Concert* (Delos International) her acclaimed solo recording. Many composers have written and dedicated works to her.

Rhodes is Adjunct Professor of Organ at USC (Los Angeles) Thornton School of Music. Her students have won awards, grants, and top prizes in competitions in the U.S. and Europe. She has served as a national and international adjudicator for competitions. The Royal College of Organists invited her to give a master class and recital in Manchester Cathedral, and serve on an international jury which selected the International Performer of the Year 2000—she was the only American to serve in these capacities. She serves on the board of directors of the Ruth and Clarence Mader Memorial Scholarship Fund, is a member of the AGO and MTNA, and is listed in *International Who's Who in Music.*

In April 2005, she performed at Walt Disney Hall in what she termed "the organ concerto of all times: *Symphonie Concertante* by Joseph Jongen in an impressionistic style [it] is lush, playful, full of fire!" She played the first full length recital on the new Dobson organ at Kimmel Center for the Performing Arts (Philadelphia, 2006).

In 1977, Cherry married internationally well-known organist Dr. Ladd Thomas, professor of music and chair of the USC organ department.

Victoria Sirota

VICTORIA R. SIROTA was born July 5, 1949, in Oceanside, New York, to a minister father who provided piano lessons when she was four with his church organist. She started organ in sixth grade, at the same time playing piano at her parochial school services and Christmas programs. At Oberlin in 1967, she met her husband-to-be Robert Sirota. They married in 1969. After Victoria graduated with a BM in theory and organ (1971), they spent the next year abroad, where Robert studied with **Nadia Boulanger** in Paris and Victoria with two renowned organ pedegogues, **André Marchal** (1894–1980), also in Paris, and Gustav Leonhardt in Amsterdam. She earned her degrees in organ performance from Boston University (MM, 1975, DMA, 1981).

She taught organ at Boston (1983–1991), and has given recitals in France, Germany and America, including concerts at Harvard, Yale and Dartmouth. She has premiered many of her husband's compositions, and performed his organ concerti at Oberlin, Boston, Yale, Peabody and Lincoln, Nebraska. She was the coordinator for the 1990 AGO Convention in Boston and the National Consultant for the 1996 AGO convention in New York. She became their chaplain in 1998, and from 2000–2002 was a regular columnist in their magazine, *The American Organist.* An organ recital is slated for the 2007 AGO Region VI Convention. Her CDs include: *Christmas Antphonies* (organ continuo for Praetorius and Pinkham), with the John Oliver Chorale (Northeastern Records, 1986); *Fanny Mendelssohn Hensel: Rediscovered* (producer, organist and annotator) listed in the *Boston Globe* Top Ten Records; and Robert Sirota: *Easter Canticles for Cello and Organ* (Gasparo, 2000).

Reverend Sirota became an assistant minister and consultant for liturgical ministry at New York's Cathedral Church of St. John the Divine (2006). She continues concertizing and lecturing. (See Musicologists.)

Ann Smoot

British born **ANN ELISE SMOOT**, after completing two honors degrees at Yale, studied organ and harpsichord at the Royal Academy of Music, and with **Dame Gillian Weir**. She launched her international career winning third prize in St. Albans (1997) and first prize in the AGO National Young Artists Competition (1998).

She performs regularly throughout the UK, U.S. and Europe, with a repertoire ranging from the 14th century to contemporary. Passionate about bringing organ music to a wider audience, Smoot co-founded the London Organ Summer Course, which takes place every July and attracts students from all over the UK, Ireland and the U.S.; and the London Organ forum, to encourage organists to consider their repertoire in a wider musical context.

Director of the St. Giles Junior Organ Conservatory, a program for teenage organists, she has taught and performed at the Oundle International Festival for young organists, and has tutored several Royal School of Church Music courses. She is in demand for master classes throughout the UK and North America. In 2000, Smoot made three U.S. tours, giving recitals in over a dozen cities.

A 2004 JAV CD recorded at Washington, DC, National Cathedral, features French music and her own transcription of Ravel's *Tombeau de Couperin.* She is scheduled for the 2007 AGO Convention in NYC.

SANDRA SODERLUND teaches harpsichord and organ at Mills College in Oakland, California, and is the organist at Unitarian Universalist Church of Berkeley. She received her BM at Bethany College, Kansas, MM from USC, DMA from Stanford, and has served on the faculties of San Francisco State University, Sam Houston State University, Simpson College and the University of Colorado. In addition to her many recitals and workshops throughout the U.S., Holland, Germany and Korea, including those for AGO, she also performs on harpsichord and both modern and early piano.

On the editorial board of the *Early Keyboard Journal*, she is the author of articles on performance practices, and the editor of editions of keyboard works, including the Two-Part Inventions and Four Duets of J. S. Bach and the *Livre d'Orgue* of L.N. Clérambault. Her two books are *A Young Person's Guide to the Pipe Organ* and *Organ Technique: An Historical Approach*, a standard text since its publication in 1980. As of 2005 she was expanding the book to be "A History of Keyboard Technique" and, as part of her research, spent six weeks in England studying early keyboard instruments. Soderlund has recorded for Arkay and Albany Records.

PHYLLIS J. STRINGHAM, a native of Grand Rapids, born January 30, 1931, was guided to music by her parents, beginning piano at age seven and organ at seventeen. Her BA is from Calvin College, Grand Rapids, and MM from the University of Michigan, where she studied with **Marilyn Mason**. Later studies were with **Nadia Boulanger** and organist André Marchal (1894–1980), both in Paris, and **Marie-Claire Alain** at the Summer Academy for Organists at Haarlem, Holland. A past dean of the Milwaukee Chapter, and Wisconsin State chairman for the AGO, Stringham is on the faculty of Carroll College, Waukesha, Wisconsin, where she is college organist and professor of music. In addition to teaching and concertizing, she runs Phyllis Stringham Concert Management to assist other organists in their performance careers.

CAROLE TERRY has performed extensively as a soloist and chamber musician on both organ and harpsichord, and maintains a busy recital, master class and adjudication schedule since coming to the University of Washington. Her appearances throughout the U.S. include Stanford, Harvard, Berkeley, UCLA and Cornell Universities, and such notable churches as Grace Cathedral, San Francisco, and National Cathedral, Washington, DC, as well as at the world's largest outdoor organ, the Spreckels in San Diego's Balboa Park. She has been a lecturer and panelist for the *American Institute of Organ Builders*, *Historical Organs in America* and *The Organist in the 21st Century*, held at Stanford. European tours have covered Germany, Austria, Switzerland and Spain. Her 1999 concert tour of Japan took her to Tokyo, Gifu and Hiroshima. She has performed at several AGO conventions and was a featured artist at the national convention, summer 2000, in Seattle.

Terry is a graduate of Stanford, where she received her DMA in early music performance practice. While there, she specialized in early keyboard music, studying organ with Herbert Nanney, harpsichord with Margaret Fabrizio, and fortepiano and clavichord with Joan Benson. She earned her BM at Southern Methodist University and MM from Eastman. Her teachers included Robert Anderson and David Craighead, organ, and Larry Palmer and Erich Schwandt, harpsichord.

She has recorded the complete organ works of Johannes Brahms and *Brombaugh Organs of the Northwest* for the Musical Heritage Society, as well as the harpsichord works of Albright, Cowell, Persichetti and Rorem for the CRI label, and baroque chamber works on Crystal Records.

Professor of organ and harpsichord at the University of Washington School of Music, she directs their Baroque Chamber Ensemble. In addition to organ and harpsichord instruction, she presents courses in performance practice, keyboard harmony and transposition, organ repertoire, pedagogy and baroque dance. She has served as resident organist of the Seattle Symphony.

MARIANNE WEBB has been professor of Music and University Organist at Southern Illinois University (Carbondale) since 1965, before which she was on the faculties of Iowa State and James Madison University (Harrisonburg, Virginia). Born August 4, 1936, in Topeka, Kansas, she received her early training from Richard M. Gayhart. She continued as a pupil of Jerald Hamilton at Washburn University, where she earned a BM *summa cum laude*. A scholarship to the University of Michigan enabled study with **Marilyn Mason**, under whom she earned her MM. A Fulbright took her to Paris, where she perfected her technique with the celebrated blind organist/pedagogue **André Marchal** (1894–1980). Further graduate study was with Arthur Poister at Syracuse University, and Russell Saunders at Eastman.

Her concerts in America and Europe, performing at colleges, universities, cathedrals and churches, continue in conjunction with an active schedule of workshops, master classes, and seminars for church music conferences. A dedicated member of the AGO, she has served in various chapter offices and performed at numerous national and regional conventions.

In the year 2000, Marianne completed thirty-five years of continual service on the faculty of SIU. In recognition of this milestone, she recorded her first CD on the Reuter Organ at Shryock Auditorium, with a program of works from the traditional, classical repertoire to one selection by contemporary American composer, William Bolcom. Titled *Celebration*, it is the first commercially-released recording on this fifty-three-stop, three–manual concert organ.

On April 10, 2001, at a ceremony in Shryock Hall, the instrument was named the Marianne Webb Pipe Organ, while the honorée received the title of *Distinguished* university organist and music professor. This was officially Webb's "retirement." Nevertheless, she accepted a fantastic post-retirement position created just for her, in which she continues to teach all the organ students and head the organ department, but is relieved of two sections of five days a week freshman Music Theory and sixty papers to grade every night! A fitting denouement to an illustrious career.

Gillian Weir

British organist **Dame GILLIAN WEIR** was born January 17, 1941. Winner of the St. Alban's International Organ Competition, she made her debut at the Royal Festival Hall and appeared at the Royal Albert Hall Proms on opening night. Her world tours, television appearances, master classes, and research have won new audiences and stimulated a new generation of performers in England. In 1989, her six-part BBC-sponsored television series entitled "The King of Instruments," featured her as both presenter and performer for a survey of famous organs from six countries. She was awarded a CBE (Commander of the British Empire) at the Queen's Birthday Honors in 1989. Her achievements as virtuoso, teacher and scholar have been rewarded with many honors, the greatest being named Dame Commander—the female equivalent of knighthood—of the British Empire in 1996. On January 17, 2001, a great celebration attended her sixtieth birthday in the Royal Festival Hall where she played a solo recital to a packed house. That same year, she performed in the Rededication Series of the E.M. Skinner organ at Severance Hall in Cleveland, Ohio. 2005 found this indefatigable talent globe hopping with appearances in Germany, UK, Ireland, Norway, Russia, Singapore, America and Canada. She was also featured at the AGO convention in June. Dame Gillian's first recording on the newly refurbished monumental organ at the Royal Albert Hall, was released in 2006.

Her honorary doctorates are from the universities of Birmingham, Leicester and Aberdeen.

Appointed October 2001, **CAROL WILLIAMS** is the first woman and seventh person to become San Diego (California) civic organist and artistic director of the Spreckels Organ Society.[161] Actually, she is the first female civic organist appointed anywhere in America. Her instrument, the largest outdoor organ in the world, was a gift of entrepreneur John D. Spreckels (1853–1926), a leader in bringing culture to the fledgling city. The instrument was unveiled December 31, 1914, for the Panama-California Exposition of 1915. It has four keyboards, seventy-three ranks and 4,518 pipes.

Williams participates in the summer International Organ Festival, Sunday afternoon concerts, and educational outreach projects which attract over 11,000 students each year. Performances attract some 100,000 people a year.

---

161. The 2,000 member non-profit Spreckels Organ Society was founded in 1988 to preserve, program and promote the instrument as a world treasure with some 100 concerts a year.

Born in Wokingham, Hampshire, England, February 3, 1962, of Welsh parents, Carol Williams' father's mother was a talented church organist, her father, Tudor, a civil engineer, played the theater organ, her mother, Jean, the piano. Carol grew up hearing classical and popular music. She began piano at five, progressing so rapidly that she could read music before words. At age twelve, she fell in love with the organ, and her supportive parents found her a Hammond home instrument. She began formal organ lessons at seventeen. Her teacher, Gilbert Moore, was organist at Surrey's Guildford Cathedral. Heaven for Carol when she was permitted to practice on the glorious cathedral organ.

The next five years were spent at London's Royal Academy of Music as a student of David Sanger. She earned the Academy's prestigious Recital Diploma together with an organ and piano Licentiate (LRAM), and won all major prizes for organ performance. She also became a Fellow of the Royal College of Organists (FRCO), and Trinity College, London (FTCL), as well as being elected an associate of both the RAM and RCM. Later titles were Honorary Fellow of the North and Midlands School of Music (HonFNMSM) and Fellow in Performance of the Australian Society of Musicology and Composition (FPerfASMC)—all in recognition of her tremendous contribution to music. She also studied in Paris with Daniel Roth, organist of St. Sulpice.

1994 marked an American concert tour. The following year, Williams returned to the U.S. for postgraduate work at Yale under Thomas Murray. While there, she was appointed University Chapel Organist and earned an artist diploma, plus the Charles Ives Prize for outstanding achievement. Moving to New York, she became the associate organist at the Cathedral of the Incarnation in Garden City (Long Island), and studied with Professor McNeil Robinson at the Manhattan School of Music, receiving the Helen Cohn Award with her DMA degree.[162]

Touring throughout America, Europe and Asia, Williams has performed at Notre Dame and St. Sulpice, in Paris; Westminster Abbey; St. Paul's Cathedral; King's College, Cambridge; Queen's College, Oxford; Blenheim Palace,[163] (England); Roskilde Cathedral, Denmark; Woolsey Hall, Yale; Harvard Memorial Chapel; Washington National Cathedral and, in New York, St. Patrick's Cathedral, St. Ignatius Loyola and Riverside Church. She has also given concerts in Poland, Czechoslovakia, Sweden, Finland, Estonia, Holland and Germany. In Singapore, with London's BBC Concert Orchestra, and the Beijing Symphony, she played the inaugural concerts on a newly-installed Austin organ in the Forbidden City Concert Hall. Her video, "Carol Williams: A Musical Tour of Blenheim Palace," and CD, "Music from Blenheim Palace," earned high praise from critics and public, as have other CDs, including popular music on Wurlitzer theater organs.

Interviewed on radio, Carol expounds her profound love of the organ. In the video "Pulling Out All the Stops," she was filmed in concert at St. Thomas' Church on New York's Fifth Avenue. She was amongst the foremost artists taking part in the Virgil Fox Memorial Concert at the Riverside Church in the fall of 2000. A recording of that notable event was released as a double-CD by Gothic Records.

The same year, Carol married Alfred Buttler, the New York representative for Austin Organs, which built the original Spreckels Organ. The couple have homes in New York and San Diego, and adopted a friendly Airedale who came with the prepossessing name of Ambush Rattletrap.[164]

Balboa Park's outdoor seating area holds 2,400 listeners, for free, year-round concerts. Audiences are made up of those who come to hear the music, and passers-by. Williams says of the location, "I'm bringing the king of instruments to a wide public. That's something I feel I was born to do."

---

162. Williams' doctoral dissertation covers concert organs and organists of 19th century England, the heyday of municipal organ construction, which in America was 1890–1920. Cities vied with each other to build the biggest and best instruments, with the result that organs represented the cutting edge of musical technology, capable of sound effects from brass to percussion to an entire orchestra.

163. Blenheim Palace, residence of the Dukes of Marlborough, dates from 1705. Its present fame rests upon it being the birthplace of Winston Churchill (1874–1965).

164. Carol asks, "Is calling *Ambush! Ambush!* in a public park in the same category as yelling *Fire!* in a crowded theater?

ANNE WILSON was born May 22, 1964, in Patuxet River, Maryland. Her mother played trumpet, her father, a Naval officer, the clarinet. Each morning the children were awakened with strains of Brahms, Beethoven or Wagner on the phonograph. Anne began piano at six and, with strong maternal support, a Hammond electronic organ. With a good teacher, she began organ lessons at seventeen. She liked the instrument immediately and went to Cincinnati College-Conservatory earning her B.Mus.Ed in Organ (1976), and MM (1978). Her church career began in Toledo, Ohio (1979–80), after which she moved to Garden City, Long Island, New York, to spend the next ten years at the Cathedral of the Incarnation as assistant organist to her husband, Todd. Daughter Rachel was born November 25, 1985. There were further moves to Cincinnati, West Chester (Pennsylvania) and finally Cleveland, two weeks after second daughter Clara arrived, August 27, 1989. Anne is now well situated in a solo career as organist and director of four choirs and a concert series at Forest Hills (Ohio) Presbyterian Church, as well as teaching at the Laurel Independent School for Girls where, besides classes, she is director of their orchestra, choirs and guitar ensemble. In 2002, she founded the Greater Cleveland Classical Guitar Society. Also a composer, her works have been performed at such venues as the Chautauqua Institution (New York), Museum of Women in the Arts (Washington, DC) and the Aspen Music Festival.

Todd and Anne combine their talents to present innovative programs of music for two players, and as a duo have won seventeen organ competitions, among them the French Grand Prix de Chartres. The Fort Wayne National Organ Competition was won by Todd; the Fuller International Competition in the French tradition and Diane Bish International Organ Competition were won by Anne. Both are active members of the AGO.

A Glimpse into the 21st Century

On April 22, 2001, my husband and I chanced to hear a piano and organ recital by an eighteen-year-old young lady about to graduate from La Jolla High. Switching between the two keyboards in the course of the program, her expertise on each instrument was breathtaking. Born December 30, 1983, to a physician father from Taiwan and violinist mother from Oklahoma, **CHELSEA CHEN** has played the piano since age four, and in 1997 won the San Diego Concerto Competition. She began studying organ in 1999, with scholarships from the Pacific Council of Organ Clubs and the San Diego Chapter of the AGO, winning AGO regional competitions in 2001. She had just received the news of her acceptance at Juilliard as an organ student of Dr. John Weaver.

Forward Flash: She now has her Juilliard BM (2005) and MM (2006) in organ performance, won their John Erskine Prize for scholastic and artistic distinction, and was a leader of their Christian fellowship. She ran the 2003 NYC Marathon, and that summer premiered her "Taiwanese Suite" at San Diego's outdoor Spreckels Organ. She won first prizes in the 2003 Region IX of the AGO RCYO (American Guild of Organists Regional Competitions for young artists under twenty-three), 2005 Augustana/Reuter national undergraduate organ and 2005 Musical Merit Foundation competitions–the latter earning her a 2006 summer at Aspen. Since 2003, Chelsea has been organist at Emmanuel Presbyterian Church in Manhattan.

Her debut CD and DVD was recorded on the Heinz Chapel organ at the 2005 Convention of the American Institute of Organbuilders. She was featured at the July 2006 AGO Convention in Chicago.

Winning a Fulbright gave her nine months (2006–07) in Taiwan to make organ adaptations of Chinese folk music.

After hearing Chelsea in recital at the organ of San Diego's St. Paul's Episcopal Cathedral, July 22, 2006, I can repeat the words I wrote five years ago: *Nurturing talent such as this gives one faith that the future of the "King of Instruments" is in good hands.*

Another "insurance" for the future is Pipe Organ Encounters (POE), begun by the AGO, which are annual regional workshops to introduce students to the instrument. For a vital week churches open their doors and teachers volunteer their experience to recruit the next generation of organists and save a 400 year tradition.

Sitting on the Bench

In 1909, an organist writing on bias against women remarked that men can get away with indifferent ability, but women must play *doubly well* in order for it to be said, "she plays as well as a man!" Has anything changed? Yes. While there continues to be a legion of underpaid church organists, many of whom double as choir directors, women are more prominent and accepted–many outclassing their male counterparts—while salaries have become more equable. (Church jobs are not sought for getting wealthy.)

Musically, ministers trying to entice the younger generation into church are requesting organists to play "happy, clappy" music. Classically trained organists often have to compromise with rock bands at an earlier service.

Many seminaries are no longer teaching church music, and too often young ministers come to their positions rarely knowing the classics or what standard of music is appropriate for the calling. There is also the challenge of pianists with day jobs, hiring on part time at churches for sub-standard pay and without real knowledge of the organ, taking work away from trained musicians.

To quote **Dorothy Papadakos:** "I've always believed an organist's job is primarily . . . to provide music which lifts and inspires . . . it's about bringing people closer to their innermost selves and connecting to that Higher Being and place. "

CHAPTER TWELVE
Part M

Instruments of Mystery

Clara Rockmore
Cynthia Millar

There are two instruments which do not fit into the traditional orchestral "families," but were forerunners of the sophisticated electronic synthesizers and keyboards of today.

The THEREMIN

The history of this singular instrument begins with **Lev Sergeivitch Termen**, born in St. Petersburg, August 15, 1896. At the University, he studied physics, astronomy, cello, and music theory. Working on a radio in 1919, the physicist became interested in the strange sounds he was receiving. This provided the beginnings of his unique invention. His theremin is *the* original electronic instrument. It is unique in that it is played without being touched. Two antennae protrude from it, one controlling pitch, and the other volume, each surrounded by high frequency, electro-magnetic fields. As the performer's hands move towards and away from the antennae, they alter the fields. As a hand approaches the vertical antenna, the pitch gets higher. Nearing the horizontal makes the volume softer. Because there is no physical contact with the instrument, playing it requires precise skill and perfect pitch.

By 1920, he had invented a prototype he called the *thereminovox*, and changed his name to **Leon Theremin**. He gave a demonstration for Communist dictator Lenin (1870–1924), who wanted to bring electricity to Russia, but Lenin was among the foremost instigators of the bloody 1917 revolution, in the course of which the entire Royal Family of Romanovs were assassinated.

In 1927, Theremin went to Germany, France and America where, in 1928, he obtained a patent for his instrument. From this, RCA Victor built approximately 500 theremins, manufactured by General Electric and Westinghouse. On April 29, 1930, Leon presented a concert at Carnegie Hall with an ensemble of ten theremins in conjunction with what was probably the world's first color and light show. On April 1, 1932, also at Carnegie, he introduced the first electrical symphony orchestra, including theremins and keyboards. He established an acoustical laboratory in New York and invented the *rhythmicon*—forerunner of the electronic keyboard—for playing different rhythms simultaneously. Amongst many scientists, **Albert Einstein** was most interested in Theremin's work, while Maestro **Leopold Stokowski** experimented with the theremin in the Philadelphia Orchestra.

Out of this World!

Predating the electric guitar and electric organ, the theremin is the precursor of the first synthesizer. Its ethereal sound has been used in many movie soundtracks to provide an eerie, other-worldly atmosphere. **Miklos Rózsa** used the theremin in his music for two films: *Spellbound* (1940), the psychological thriller with Ingrid Bergman and Gregory Peck, and the Oscar winning *The Lost Weekend* (1945), the first film ever to depict the nightmarish hallucinations of an alcoholic, played by Ray Milland. Dr. Samuel Hoffman demonstrated the instrument on a 1956 Mickey Mouse Club television show. In one scene of *The Delicate Delinquent* (1956), comedian Jerry Lewis actually tries to play a theremin. The instrument was also used in the landmark 1961 film, *The Day the Earth Stood Still*, about a flying saucer landing in Washington. On the "pop" scene, the theremin appeared in such hits as "Good Vibrations" (Beach Boys) and "Whole Lotta Love" (Led Zeppelin).

Today, this magical instrument is once again in the musical spotlight. There are several websites providing building kits and availability to purchase new and used models. Until his death in 2005, Robert Moog continued active in the field building modern transistorized versions.

Clara Rockmore—Exponent Extraordinaire

Clara Rockmore

CLARA ROCKMORE holds a unique place in music history as the star performer of the theremin. Born in Russia, March 9, 1911, she was one of three musically gifted girls. Her oldest sister, **Nadia Reisenberg**, became a world famous concert pianist. (See Pianists.)

Clara inherited the family trait of perfect pitch and could pick out melodies on the piano at age two. At four, she was accepted as an exceptional student at the St. Petersburg Imperial Conservatory to study violin, and became a prized student of **Leopold Auer** (1845–1930). Clara and Nadia received permission to leave Russia and concertize in Western Europe. As living conditions deteriorated after the Russian Revolution, the Jewish Reisenbergs managed to get a visa to Poland to stay with relatives. The girls' playing provided an income. The family emigrated to America in 1922, settling in New York.

At age seventeen, Clara injured her bow arm, cutting short a brilliant violin career. The following year, at the height of her beauty, she met Theremin and after concentrated studies with him, became the greatest exponent of his invention. Although the inventor courted Clara, she married attorney Robert Rockmore. Later, Theremin wed Lavinia Williams, principal ballerina of the first American Negro Ballet Company.

Clara gave her debut solo theremin concert in 1934, and for the next twenty years performed as soloist with major symphony orchestras in the course of three coast-to-coast tours. 1977 marked the release of the first commercial recording of her playing, *The Art of the Theremin*. In 1987 it was released on CD. In the '90s she was still performing at private recitals. In 1997, she fought off several incapacitating strokes, determined to live to see the birth of her grand niece, the baby of celebrity photographer Steve Sherman[165] and his wife, cellist **Dorothy Lawson**. Fiona Sherman arrived May 8, 1998. Clara passed away in her Manhattan apartment, two days later.

In 2006 Rockmore's nephew Robert put together a CD featuring many never before released performances by his aunt, including a Glinka song with violin obbligato by Erick Friedman.

Disappearing Act

In 1938, Leon Theremin was kidnapped from his Manhattan studio by the NKVD (forerunner of the KGB) and sent to a Siberian labor camp. By 1945, rumors of Theremin's death reached the West. In reality, the Soviets were using his expertise by putting him to work in a military prison to create secret electronic apparatuses. He invented the "bug"—the first electronic eavesdropping device—and methods for cleaning up noisy audio recordings. He was forced to help supervise the bugging of the American Embassy and Stalin's personal apartment—with the dictator's knowledge. For this he received the Stalin Prize, one of the USSR's highest honors. From 1964, Theremin taught at the Moscow Conservatory of Music, and continued experimenting and building his instruments, but was *not* allowed to pursue modern electronic music. He was told that *electricity should not be used for music, but for the execution of traitors*. In the late 1980s, a *New York Times* correspondent visited the conservatory, recognized the

---

165. Steve is her sister Nadia's grandson from *her* son Robert Sherman, longtime classical WQXR broadcaster.

inventor, and wrote an article about him. This got Theremin fired and his irreplaceable instruments destroyed with an axe. In 1991, film maker Steven M. Martin, long fascinated by the instrument, embarked upon the documentary, *Theremin—An Electronic Odyssey*. He traveled to Moscow, found Leon, then aged ninety-five, and reunited him with Clara Rockmore in New York. (She had for years been trying to use her influence to find Leon behind the Iron Curtain.) The movie chronicles the history of the instrument, the life of Leon Theremin, and his close relationship with Clara. In the finale we see the frail inventor making his way up the corridor to Rockmore's apartment. She opens the door and they embrace.

Leon Theremin died November 1993, the day after the film opened in London. He has left the world the legacy of synthesized music which dominates much of modern culture. Until her death, Clara Rockmore basically remained the only exponent of the historic instrument, but had been teaching the daughter of her friend, Ruti Warshaw, who had been a student of **Nadia Reisenberg**. That daughter is pianist/composer **Dalit Warshaw**. (See American Contemporary Composers.)

Son of Theremin - the Moog Synthesizer

As a teenager, **Robert Moog** (1934–2005) fell in love with the theremin and started building them from schematic diagrams in a hobby magazine. Combining this with his knowledge of electronics and music, he developed the first modern music synthesizer. Among its champions were the Beatles and the Beach Boys. The landmark release of artist Walter[166] Carlos' *Switched on Bach* on the Moog Synthesizer brought together electronic music and rock. The 1968 LP recording sold over a million copies, won three Grammys and established the synthesizer as a musical instrument. In 1992, Wendy[167] Carlos used the latest computer technology in the CD boxed set *Switched-on Bach 2000*, which outsold the original.

The Ondes-Martenot

Ondes-Martenot

Maurice Martenot, born in Paris, 1898, was a cellist, and radio operator in World War I. He became fascinated by the purity of the sine wave and wanted to reproduce that sound. He met Theremin in 1923, and between 1928–37 built a series of instruments he named *ondes-martenot—ondes* meaning *waves* in French. On the same principle as the theremin, this early electronic instrument also manipulates radio waves made by oscillators and makes sounds of swooping and soaring glissandos, but it is far more versatile and controllable, with an immense dynamic range from a whisper to a (musical) roar. Its greatest feature is its amazing emulation of the human voice—a voice of superhuman strength and power with a seven octave range that can soar effortlessly over a huge orchestra.

Shaped like a spinet piano, it has a six octave keyboard. Above the keyboard, is a ribbon device (*ruban*), attached to the player's finger by means of a metal ring which is slided laterally and can produce vibrato like a string player. Thus the right hand prepares the *pitch* while the left produces the *sound* by pressing the raised white "lozenge" or *touche* in the drawer on the left of the instrument—the more pressure, the greater the volume. Sound colors can be combined and amplified through three speakers, one of which, the *Metallique*, is an orchestral gong with a drive mechanism which turns it into a speaker diaphragm capable of mysterious soft trills.

By 1948, Martenot was a professor at the Paris Conservatory, and the instrument was quite well-known in France where avant-gardists such as **Arthur Honegger** (1892–1955) and **Edgard Varése** (1883–1965) incorporated it into some of their compositions. But it was **Olivier Messiaen** (1908–92), who wrote the seventy-five minute symphony *Turangalila* (1948) featuring a battery of percussionists, that allowed the ondes-martenot to be

---

166–67. Walter, at age thirty-two, switched to Wendy in a much publicized gender change procedure. (See American Contemporary Composers.)

heard in its full range. In 1974, tubes were replaced by transistors and the speakers added. Martenot continued to revise the instrument until his death in a street accident in 1980.

A Composer and Lady Ondiste

CYNTHIA MILLAR was born in London, June 5, 1956, and comes from an illustrious family including two great novelists, cousin Dame Daphne du Maurier and great-great-grandfather George du Maurier, and her art historian parents.

Introduced to the *ondes-martenot* in 1981 through her research with composer **Elmer Bernstein** (1922–2004), she had originally heard it at age thirteen on a radio performance of Messiaen's *Trois Petites Liturgies*, and was fascinated by the sound of this uniquely haunting and human-sounding electric instrument.

Her quest took her to John Morton, who became her first teacher. Although she was only supposed to learn enough to show another musician how it worked, the difficulty of mastering the *ondes* became her own challenge, and she ended up in the orchestra pit of a Broadway show, becoming quite accomplished.

She also studied with **Jeanne Loriod** (1928–2001), who with her half brother, Olivier Messiaen, did much to bring the instrument to a wider public. Since Cynthia first performed Messiaen's *Turangalila Symphonie* at the BBC Promenade Concerts in London with Mark Elder and the National Youth Orchestra of Great Britain, she has given more than seventy performances of this work with such orchestras as the Sydney Symphony, Maggio Musicale (Florence), London Symphony, National Orchestra of Wales, Swedish Radio Orchestra, and played a European tour with director Mark Wigglesworth. In April 2001, she gave three performances of the Messiaen symphony at Kennedy Center with Leonard Slatkin and the National Symphony, and later in the year with the BBC Philharmonic. As a concert artist she has soloed with noted maestros Sir Simon Rattle, Sir Andrew Davis, André Previn, Esa Pekka Salonen, Edo de Waart, Yan Pascal Tortelier, David Robertson, Kent Nagano and Franz Welser-Möst.

Performing engagements during the 2001–02 season included *Turangalila* with the Cleveland Orchestra and Franz Welser-Möst, San Francisco Symphony, Orchestre National de Lyon, the Edinburgh Festival with David Robertson, and London Philharmonic Orchestra with Kent Nagano. 2003 included performances of Messiaen's *Trois petites liturgies* with the Cleveland Orchestra, and *Turangalila* with the New Zealand Symphony and Mattias Bammert. In summer 2004 she was the soloist in a European tour with the Cleveland Orchestra.

Millar has been featured on the soundtrack of over one hundred feature and television films, including *A Passage to India* (music by Maurice Jarre) and *Enchanted April* (music by Richard Rodney Bennett); on over thirty sound-track albums and CDs, such as *Monster Movie Themes* by Henry Mancini, *Spellbound* and *Lost Weekend*, music of **Miklós Rózsa**, three Michael Crawford[168] albums, two with the London Symphony, one with the Royal Philharmonic; and the Puccini/Verdi disk, *The Academy Goes to the Opera* with **Sir Neville Marriner** and the Academy of St. Martin in the Fields. To celebrate her mentor's eightieth birthday, she gave the world premiere of Elmer Benstein's *Ondine at the Cinema* in a special concert with the Royal Philharmonic Orchestra at the Royal Albert Hall, London. (For Millar's own compositions see Film Composers.)

Another name in the field worthy of mention is **Christine Ott** whose biography tells us only that she was born in Arizona, has ten brothers and sisters and three children. She appears to have settled in France, where she teaches the instrument at the National Conscructory of Strasbourg. Besides classical and opera, she is forging new experimental frontiers in contemporary music, jazz, improvisations, theater, dance and the French chanson.

In 2002 she won first prize in the François Competition at the Roubaix World Festival in Antibes.

There are also a select few male *ondists* in Europe.

---

168. Michael Crawford was the original Phantom in the London production of Andrew Lloyd Webber's *Phantom of the Opera* (1986).

Immortal Divas—Breaking the Chains of Silence

Julie Candeille (1767–1836)

Anna Milder-Hauptmann (1785–1838)

Maria Malibrán (1808–1836)

Jenny Lind (1820–1887)

Pauline Viardot-Garcia (1821–1910)

Adelina Patti (1843–1919)

Lillian Nordica (1857–1914)

Marcella Sembrich (1858–1935)

Nellie Melba (1861–1931)

Ernestine Schumann-Heink (1861–1936)

Luisa Tetrazzini (1871–1940)

Clara Butt (1872–1935)

Mary Garden (1874–1967)

Emmy Destinn (1878–1930)

Geraldine Farrar (1882–1967)

Amelita Galli-Curci (1882–1963)

Maria Jeritza (1887–1996)

Lucrezia Bori (1887–1960)

Lotte Lehmann (1888–1976)

Maggie Teyte (1888–1976)

Kirsten Flagstad (1895–1962)

Conchita Supervia (1895–1936)

Rosa Ponselle (1897–1981)

Lily Pons (1898–1976)

Lotte Lenya (1898–1981)

Grace Moore (1898–1947)

Helen Traubel (1899–1972)

Marian Anderson (1899–1993)

When the Roman Emperor Constantine legalized Christianity at the beginning of the 3rd century, it marked the end of women being allowed to take an active part in church ceremonies, including participation in choirs or any form of music. It was under his ægis that our present version of the Bible was written and passages honoring women—including Mary Magdalene's true role in Jesus' life—were conveniently eradicated. Using St. Paul's injunction to the Corinthians, "Let your women keep silence in the churches . . ." (I Cor. 14:34), the male hierarchy took off on fifteen centuries' worth of female subjugation which determined not only the course of music, but of the entire scope of Western civilization.

To keep these embers banked, two subsequent Popes: Innocent XI, in 1686, and Clement XI in 1703, issued edicts to the effect that women should not even *learn* music lest this keep them from their "proper occupations," namely childbearing and waiting on their husbands. During the Dark and Middle Ages, after the fall of the Roman Empire in the 5th century, culture was put into hibernation for almost five hundred years, yet the church survived, albeit fragmented into isolated monasteries and nearby convents. Within their cloisters, nuns made music, composing and raising their voices to God. (It should be remembered that this life of abnegation and chastity was only open to daughters of the aristocracy.) A large body of compositions of the great mystic Abbess **Hildegard von Bingen** (1098–1179) has not only survived, but was recorded on several CDs in the early 1990s. (See Chapter One.)

In the secular field, the 13th and 14th centuries witnessed women minstrels and domestic musicians of the lower classes, and revealed the legacy of the poetry and music of some two dozen lady troubadours (*trobairitz*) of noble families. By the 15th and 16th centuries, invading warrior chiefs had evolved into the ruling nobility. Secure in their castles and palaces, they could turn their attention from war to finer aspirations. The courts of Italy became renowned for their patronage of music, with women like **Isabella d'Este** (1474–1539) of Mantua, and **Margherita Gonzaga** of Ferrara, herself an accomplished musician and singer who, with her husband Duke Alfonso II d'Este, employed a highly talented female group of singer/musicians, the *concerto delle donne*—**Laura Peverara, Anna**

Guarini, **Livia d'Arco** and **Tarquinia Molza**—which set the example for the other Italian courts. Mention should also be made of the convent of San Vito in Ferrara which, besides a choir, had an orchestra with members playing instruments unheard of for women such as cornets, trombones and bagpipes.

An exclusive opportunity for some women was the good fortune to be born into a family of professional musicians. This applied to **Francesca Caccini** (1587–*c* 1640) whose father, singer-composer **Giulio Caccini**, was part of the Medici court in Florence. She was the first woman to write an opera, *La Liberazione di Ruggiero* (1625), commissioned by Maria and Christina de Medici who were joint regents of the city. Caccini's younger sister, Settimia, was also a fine singer. Another singer/composer in the category of being part of a musical clan was **Barbara Strozzi** (1619–64), daughter of Venetian composer **Giulio Strozzi**, who founded a music academy—literally a private showcase—for her reputedly glorious voice. She also composed madrigals.

The French court of Louis XIV gave opportunities to women such as **Antonia Bembo** (*c*1643–*c*1715) and **Elisabeth Claude Jacquet de la Guerre** (1666–1729) who both wrote operas. In Vienna, **Marianne von Martinez** (1744–1812) studied with the celebrated Italian opera singer **Nicola Porpora** (1686–1768), but is only recorded as performing when she was a child. She later founded a music school which produced many fine women vocalists.

Until the end of the 18th century, with opera now performed not only at court but in public theaters, female singers had to overcome the stigma of being women of loose morals if they appeared on the stage, as well as contending with their rivals, men who impersonated them. These were the *castrati*, boys who had been castrated before puberty in order to keep their high voices. It was the church who first employed these *musici*, as they were also called. They were needed to fill in parts in the church liturgy from which women were forbidden. That there was a church law proscribing a death sentence for anyone performing this operation, was "overlooked."

High Voices Without the High Price

With opera performances becoming the most popular cultural events of the 18th century, *castrati* were sought to make the crossover from church to theater, and many became idols for the public. Gradually, women infiltrated the arena. Considering the competition, they had to be supremely talented to succeed, plus gain respect for their profession. Some of the earliest to do so were **Corona Schröter** (1751–1802) at Weimar (Germany), **Julie Candeille** (1767–1836) in Paris, and **Maria Malibran** (1808–36) and her sister, **Pauline Viardot-Garcia** (1821–1910), who as daughters of professional singers were already performing as children with the family troupe.

The French Revolution and other enlightenments changed the structure of, and in many countries eliminated, the ruling classes. Castrati became symbols of despotism and fell from favor, although the last known, **Alessandro Moreschi** (1858–1922), did not leave the Sistine Chapel choir until 1913. (His is the only castrato voice preserved on recordings made in 1902–03.)

With the proliferation of voice teachers by this time, many well-trained women singers were ready to step out of the wings. Opera composers, meanwhile, had become more sophisticated in their delineation of female characters—they were also able to write higher notes for real women's voices. Now it was the turn of the *prima donna* to dominate the limelight and be idolized.

The following section gives biographical sketches of the most famous bygone divas, with subsequent tracing of succeeding generations of singers who followed their immortal imprints. The term *prima donna*, literally translated as "first lady," has come to mean a combination of arrogance and imperiousness, which many divas resorted to.

Today's market, however, features fierce competition between agents for their many clients. Major venues are eagerly sought, but managers are now in command, and the cost of mounting a production precludes allowances for temperament. Furthermore, another form of competition is the lure of multitudinous forms of other entertainment claiming the attention of that irreplaceable commodity, the audience. Therefore, even the top contemporary opera singers—with very few exceptions—can no longer afford to act like "prima donnas."

There were (and are) many gracious ladies within this elite côterie, dedicated to their music and their public, and very careful to preserve what Lily Pons called, "the silver flute in my throat . . . entrusted to me by God."

EARLY IMMORTALS OF OPERA

AMÉLIE-JULIE CANDEILLE had a most colorful career. Born in Paris, July 31, 1767, to composer/singer father Pierre Candeille, he was her principal teacher, grooming her for the operatic stage—the most lucrative form of musical entertainment at the time. Julie also became accomplished at piano and harp, and was a successful actress, composer, librettist and author.

At fourteen, she was already singing with the Opéra, and one year later appeared in the title role of Gluck's *Iphigénie en Aulide*. In 1783, she made her fortepiano debut in a concerto by Muzio Clementi, and began performing her own concerto. She composed throughout her life, mostly salon music: sonatas, duets for two pianos, and songs with French text.

When she took up acting, her first five years were with the Comédie Française. In 1792, she joined the Théâtre Française, where she was the star performer, playwright and composer. A major highlight of her career was acting in 154 performances of her comic opera *Catherine, ou La belle fermière*, accompanying herself on piano and harp. *Opéra comique* was a well established genre in the 1790s, providing relief during Napoleon's "Reign of Terror."

In 1794, Candeille produced *Le commissionnaire* at the Théâtre de l'Egalité. In 1795, *La bayadère* opened under her own name at the Théâtre de la République. Her most ambitious stage work was a two-act opéra comique, *Ida, ou L'orpheline de Berlin*, which opened in 1807, based on the life of her sister, Stéphanie de Genlis, harpist/writer and influential mistress of Philippe, Duc d'Orléans, who later ascended the throne.

After being the mistress of two prominent revolutionaries who ended under the guillotine, in 1794 Candeille married military doctor Louis-Nicolas Delaroche, divorced him in 1797, and in 1798 married wealthy Belgian coach builder, Jean Simons. They separated in 1802. She returned to Paris, gave piano lessons, and published music, essays, memoirs and several historical novels. During Napoleon's last "Hundred Days" [March-June, 1815], she sought asylum in England where she gave a series of concerts.

When Napoleon went into final exile, and the monarchy was re-established, Candeille returned to Paris in 1816, having been granted a pension of 2000 francs by Louis XVIII. In 1822, she married the painter Hilaire-Henri Périé de Senovert. They lived in Nîmes until his death in 1833, when she returned to Paris. She died of apoplexy, February 4, 1834.

ANNA MILDER-HAUPTMANN an Austrian soprano admired by Mozart, Schubert and Beethoven, was born in Constantinople, December 13, 1785. She studied with **Antonio Salieri** (1750–1825), and made her debut in 1803 as Juno in **Franz Süssmayr's** *Der Spiegel von Arkadien* at the Theater an der Wien. She was the first to sing Leonore in all three versions of Beethoven's *Fidelio* (1805, 1806, 1814), and created the title role in **Luigi Cherubini's** *Faniska* (1806). She also performed the Vienna premiere of his *Medée* (Medea, 1814). Moving to Berlin, she made her debut as Emmeline in Joseph Weigl's *Der Schweitzerfamilie* (1816), then sang at the Hofoper (Court Opera), whose music director was the bombastic Italian **Gaspare Spontini** (1774–1851). She was Statira in the Berlin premiere of his opera *Olimpie*, and stayed with the house until 1829 when she quarreled with Spontini—who was dismissed in 1842—and returned to Vienna. She sang there until her retirement in 1836, her powerful voice magnificently interpreting Gluck's heroines. She died in Vienna in 1838.

One of the most famous mezzos of her time, **MARIA MALIBRÁN** was born March 24, 1808, in Paris, to Spanish tenor **Manuel García** (1775–1832) and soprano Joaquina García. (Her younger sister was composer **Pauline Viardot-García** (1821–1910).) Maria's first public appearance was in Naples at age five. At fifteen she began voice lessons with her father, and made her debut at seventeen as Rosina in *The Barber of Seville* at the King's

Theatre, London (1825). In the same role, she went to New York's Park Theatre as part of the Garcia Opera Company, which included other members of her family. She became a popular favorite singing established repertoire, plus the two operas written for her by her father, *L'Amante astuto* and *La Figlia dell'aria*. The extraordinary power and flexibility of her voice was such that both Donizetti and Bellini adapted parts for her. Bellini's *La sonnambula* has a lower-keyed version called the Malibran edition.[169]

While in New York, she married a French merchant, François Eugène Malibran—an attempt to escape the domination of her father. When Malibran went bankrupt, Maria returned to Europe without him in 1827. From then on she alternated appearances between Paris and London, as well as making her La Scala (Milan) debut in 1834. Meanwhile, beginning in 1829, she lived with celebrated violinist **Charles de Bériot** (1802–1870). They were wed in 1836, after her first marriage was annulled. Tragically, the same year while pregnant, she suffered serious injuries when thrown from her horse, developed complications and died September 23. Besides her successful vocal career, Malibran, was also a fine pianist and composed nocturnes, romances and chansonettes which were published in an album.

In 1996, Venice's Teatro La Fenice, built in 1792, was ravaged by fire. The orchestra and opera company took up temporary residence in the restored 900-seat Teatro Malibran, which had opened in 1678 as Teatro di San Giovanni Crisostomo and was renamed after Maria sang two benefits for the theater in 1835. It was Venice's premiere house before the opening of La Fenice.

JENNY LIND was born October 6, 1820, in Stockholm, making her first professional appearance there at age ten, and entering the Royal Opera School the same year. Her operatic debut as Agathe in von Weber's *Der Freischütz* at the Royal Opera in 1838 led to her appointment as Court Singer of the Royal Swedish Academy of Music in 1840. After a brief sojourn to study in Paris, she returned to Stockholm in 1842, singing major operatic roles there as well as in Germany and Denmark. Meyerbeer wrote the character of Vielka in his opera *Ein Feldlager in Schlesien* for her. Her London debut as Alice in *Robert le Diable* (1847) was well-received, as was her creation of Amalia in Verdi's *I masnadieri* later that year. She made farewell appearances in Stockholm as Norma (1848) and London as Alice (1849), then embarked on her New York debut, September 11, 1850, under the auspices of circus impresario P.T. Barnum. Crowds were drawn by lavish advertisements, but after that her voice and personality sold itself and she became the idolized "Swedish Nightingale," touring throughout America in sold-out concerts. In 1852, her marriage to her accompanist, Otto Goldschmidt, made equally blazing headlines. Returning to England in 1858, she continued giving recitals until her retirement in 1883, when she became a faculty member of London's Royal College of Music. Lind died in her adopted country, November 2, 1887. Among her most famous admirers were Felix Mendelssohn, Robert and Clara Schumann, the critic Eduard Hanslick and Queen Victoria's Prince Albert.

Mezzo **PAULINE VIARDOT-GARCIA** was born in Paris July 18, 1821, the daughter of Spanish tenor Manuel del Popolo García (1775–1832) and singer Joaquina Sitches García. Although of Spanish heritage, she is considered French because of her birth and death in that country. Her vocal training was with her mother, piano with **Franz Liszt**, and composition with Antoine Reicha. She was eleven and her father's studio accompanist at the time of his death.

Her concert debuts were in Brussels (1837) and Paris (1838). Her stage debut at age seventeen was as Desdemona (*Otello*), London, May 9, 1839, and Paris in October. This was the same age her sister **Maria Malibran** (1808–36) made *her* debut. Pauline's marriage in 1840 was to Louis Viardot (1800–83), twenty-one years her senior, a writer and manager of the Théâtre-Italien. Their home became a center for writers, musicians and artists. As her manager, Louis accompanied his wife on tours throughout Europe. In 1843 she toured Russia, singing both Italian and Russian music *in Russian*, the first foreigner to do so. She was the principal singer to bring Russian music to the West.

---

169. The Metropolitan Opera produced this edition in the 2002–03 season with **Natalie Dessay**.

The Viardots had four children: Louise Héritte (1841–1918), a contralto who devoted herself to teaching in St. Petersburg, Frankfurt, Berlin and Heidelberg; Claudie (1852–1914) married printer Georges Chamerot; Marianne (1854–?) was engaged to Gabriel Fauré, but married the French pianist/composer Victor-Alphonse Duvernoy (1842–1907); and Paul (1857–1941), a violinist, composer, and conductor at the Paris Opera.

Pauline helped launch the careers of Gounod, Massenet and Fauré. Robert Schumann's op. 24, Fauré's opp. 4 and 7 and Saint-Saëns' opera *Samson and Dalila*, are dedicated to her. In 1849, she created the role of Fidès in Meyerbeer's *Le Prophète* at Paris Opera, and the title role in Gounod's *Sapho* (1851). Following a succession of tours, in 1859 she sang Orpheus in Berlioz's French version of Gluck's *Orfeo ed Euridice*. The Second Act of *Tristan und Isolde* was first heard in her salon (February 1860) with Viardot as Isolde.

Considered the summit of her singing career, she sang some 150 performances over the next three years, with witnesses like Charles Dickens confirming that she reached tragic heights rarely seen on stage.

She retired in 1863 and left France, moving with her family to Baden-Baden (Germany) until 1870 when, because of the Franco-Prussian War, they went to London for a year. From 1871, back in Paris, she devoted herself to teaching and composition. She died in the capital May 18, 1910. (See Romantic Composers.)

ADELINA PATTI was born in Madrid, February 19, 1843. Her two elder sisters, Amalia (1831–1915) and Carlotta (1836–89) were also singers. Her father was Italian tenor Salvatore Patti, who later became an opera manager in New York, and her mother was soprano Caterina Chiesa Barilli-Patti. Taken to New York in 1844, Adelina began studies with her half brother, Ettore Barilli, and made her first public appearance in a charity concert at age seven. She toured the U.S. as a child prodigy with her brother-in-law Maurice Strakosch and the famous Norwegian violinist **Ole Bull**, and later (1857) with American composer **Louis Moreau Gottschalk** (1829–69). Nicknamed the "little Florinda," her formal debut was in New York, November 24, 1859, as Lucia. Her European debut followed at London's Covent Garden as Amina in *La sonnambula*, May 16, 1861. She returned there each season for the next twenty-five years. Concurrently, she sang in Berlin, Vienna, Brussels, Amsterdam, The Hague and Paris. Her first tour of Italy was 1865–66. She was hailed as the true successor of **Giulia Grisi** (1811–69), the Italian soprano who had had a phenomenally successful career in Europe for almost three decades.

Patti made her first appearance at La Scala as Violetta (*La traviata*), November 3, 1877. She returned to the U.S. for a concert tour in 1881–82, then sang opera there during the next three seasons, earning an unheard of $5,000 per performance. In 1886–87, she again toured America, this time making her Metropolitan Opera debut in the spring of 1887, with return engagements in 1890 and 1892. Her last appearance at Covent Garden was in 1895. Her operatic farewell took place in Nice (France) in 1897, a final American tour was in 1903 and her official retirement concert at London's Albert Hall was December 1, 1906. Her last public appearance was at the same site, October 20, 1914, in a benefit concert for the Red Cross during WWI.

Patti's first marriage, to the Marquis de Caux in Paris, lasted from 1868 until their divorce in 1885. Next, she married the French tenor, Nicolini, and one year after his death in 1898, wed Swedish nobleman Baron Rolf Cederstrom. Her jewels, with which she always traveled, necessitated her having bodyguards. One of the greatest coloraturas of the 19th century, she was renowned for such roles as Lucia, Zerlina, Rosina, Norina, Elvira, Martha, Adina, Gilda, Aida and Gounod's Marguerite. She died at Craig-y-Nos Castle, near Brecon, Wales, Sept. 27, 1919.

Lillian Nordica

LILLIAN NORDICA, known as the "Yankee Diva," was one of the first American sopranos to make a name for herself internationally. Born in Farmington, Maine, December 4, 1857, she studied at the New England Conservatory for four years, graduating in 1876. For the next year and a half she toured the U.S. with Patrick Gilmore's Band, and in the spring of 1878 went with them to Europe, accompanied by her mother. Throughout the nineteenth and into the early 20th century, American singers, of both sexes, had to train in Europe, not only to become fluent in the languages of opera, but because there were so few venues in their native country.

With the final payment of her salary in Paris, she and her mother managed to subsist on a shoestring for the next five years while Lillian studied in the French capital and then at the Milan Conservatory, where her teacher, Antonio Sangiovanni, "italianized" her name from Norton. She made her debut at the Teatro Manzoni in Milan, March 10, 1879, as Donna Elvira in *Don Giovanni*, then toured other Italian cities, all to great acclaim. In 1881, she sang for Czar Alexander II in St. Petersburg, one week before he was assassinated. After touring in Germany, she made her successful Paris debut at the Opéra, July 22, 1883, as Marguerite in Gounod's *Faust*.

Having married Frederick Gower, January 22, 1883, she returned with him to America, repeating the role of Marguerite for Mapleson's Opera Company at the New York Academy of Music in November. The following year she began divorce proceedings, but Gower disappeared while crossing the English Channel in a balloon.

Nordica's Covent Garden debut in London was March 12, 1884, as Violetta in *La traviata*. She sang there again in 1898, '99, and 1902. Her Met debut came December 18, 1891, in Meyerbeer's *Les Huguenots*. In 1895, she returned as Isolde and was such a triumph that she sang mostly Wagnerian roles from then on. She was the first American soprano to sing in Bayreuth (Elsa, 1894), where she was coached by Wagner's widow, Cosima. Her last appearance at the Met was in 1909, after which she began international concert tours. Meanwhile, she had married Hungarian tenor Zoltan Doeme in 1896, to divorce him eight years later. Her third husband (1909) was London banker George W. Young. Her final performance was in Melbourne, Australia, November 25, 1913, after which she suffered a breakdown. Still ill, she sailed for further Asian destinations, but relapsed and died in Batavia, Java, May 10, 1914.

Her book, *Hints to Singers*, is full of suggestions about study, personal appearance, travel and launching a career. The Nordica Memorial Homestead Museum in Farmington, Maine, is a repository of the diva's memorabilia, including costumes, opera scores with her annotations, concert gowns and jewelry.

Outstanding Polish-American soprano **MARCELLA SEMBRICH** was born Prakseda Marcelina Kochaska (Sembrich was her mother's maiden name) in Wisniewczyk, Galicia, February 15, 1858. After receiving early musical training on piano and violin, she entered the Lemberg (Lvov) Conservatory where her principal teacher was Wilhelm Stengel, whom she subsequently married in 1877. In 1874 she played and sang for **Liszt**, who urged her to train her voice. She studied in Vienna and Milan, and made her operatic debut in Athens, 1877, as Elvira in *I Puritani*. With training in the German repertory, she sang Lucia di Lammermoor at the Dresden Court Opera in 1878, where she stayed until 1880, the year she debuted at Covent Garden as Lucia, remaining with this company for five seasons. She was Lucia again for her Met debut in 1883. Thereafter, she sang at the principal houses of Germany, Austria, France, Spain, Scandinavia and Russia until 1898, then became a regular member of the Met, 1898–1909. In later years, she remained active as a lieder singer until her retirement in 1917. She taught at both Curtis and the Institute of Musical Art in New York, where she died January 11, 1935. Besides Lucia, her repertoire consisted of over forty roles, including Susanna, Zerlina, Gilda, Rosina, Violetta, Queen of the Night, Eva (*Die Meistersinger*) and Elsa (*Lohengrin*).

Australian soprano **Dame NELLIE MELBA**, born May 19, 1861 in Melbourne, first sang in public in that city's Town Hall when she was six, but her father did not approve of a stage career and refused to provide voice lessons. Instead, she was permitted to study piano, violin and harp. Not until her 1882 marriage to Captain Charles Armstrong could she realize her ambition, and after training with a local teacher made her official debut at a benefit concert in Melbourne in 1884. Two months after her son was born, she left her husband and accompanied her father in order to study in Paris when he was transferred to London. She gave her first concert in London in 1886. Her operatic debut was as Gilda at the Théâtre Royal de la Monnaie in Brussels, 1887. There she caught the eye of British impresario Augustus Harris, who signed her for Covent Garden. Her first real success, however, was at the Paris Opera in 1888, after which she appeared all over Europe to continuously mounting popularity. Bemberg wrote *Elaine* (1892) and Saint-Saëns wrote *Hélène* (1904) for her. She sang all the classic soprano roles, but her one try at

Wagner was a disaster. She began a teaching career in 1915, but returned to Europe a few times before retiring from the stage to her native Australia in 1926, after a farewell performance at Covent Garden.

For over forty years, she reigned as opera's greatest diva. Once asked by a duchess if she would rather be a duchess or herself, Nellie replied, "There are lots of duchesses, but only one Melba." She was created a Dame Commander of the Order of the British Empire in 1918.

Born Helen Porter Mitchell, she took her stage name from her birthplace. It is a name that lives on in her honor in the dessert, Peach Melba, and the thin, dry Melba Toast.

Nellie died in Sydney, February 23, 1931, the result of an infection following a facelift operation.

A 1953 film, *Melba*, was made about her life starring diva **Patrice Munsel**.

Austrian contralto/mezzo **ERNESTINE SCHUMANN-HEINK** was born June 15, 1861 near Prague. Her talent was inherited from her Italian mother, who had been a singer. After being a member of the Ursuline Convent choir, she made her operatic debut at the Dresden Court Opera in 1878. She was a member of the Hamburg Opera 1883–97, during which time the company made a guest appearance at London's Covent Garden (1892). Her 1898 American debut in Chicago as Ortrud (*Lohengrin*) was followed by a Met career from 1899 to 1903. Her powerful voice encompassed a repertoire of 150 roles and was well-suited to Wagner. She participated in the Bayreuth Festivals from 1898 to 1914, where she became friends with the composer's widow, **Cosima Wagner** (1837–1930).

She took her names from her first husband, Ernst Heink, whom she married in 1882 and divorced in 1893, and her second from actor Paul Schumann, whom she wed in 1893 and who died in 1904. She became a U.S. citizen in 1908, after marrying Chicago lawyer William Rapp, Jr., in 1905. She divorced him in 1914. She spent her last years as a teacher, and died in Hollywood, November 17, 1936.

Italian soprano **LUISA TETRAZZINI**, born in Florence, June 29, 1871, studied at the Instituto Musicale there. She made her debut in Florence at nineteen, 1890, toured Italy and spent five seasons in South America before appearances in Warsaw, St. Petersburg, Madrid and San Francisco. She arrived in London virtually unknown, but her Covent Garden debut, November 1907, as Violetta, caused a sensation. She was engaged by Oscar Hammerstein I for his Manhattan Opera, where she repeated her London triumph in the same role, January 15, 1908. For three seasons she sang with Manhattan as Gilda, Violetta and Lucia, and also with Philadelphia, Baltimore, Boston and San Francisco. When the Met bought out Hammerstein for $1.2 million in 1911, Giulio Gatti-Casazza added Tetrazzini to his roster. On December 27, 1911, she sang Lucia, then joined **Enrico Caruso** in *Rigoletto*, but did not return to the Met because of her enormous fees for recitals and concerts. She returned to the U.S. after World War I, continuing her recital and concert tours. Her farewell appearance was in 1932. Known to have a Falstaffian appetite, she gained the girth to match, until she could only sing seated on a chair. Her final tour of England was in 1934, her tonal beauty and technical polish just as it was twenty-six years before at Covent Garden. As she left Colston Hall, trussed and corseted, her accompanist said, "Madame, that was wonderful." She replied, "It was not wonderful, it was a miracle!" She died in Milan, April 28, 1940.

Luisa wrote two books, *My Life of Song* (London, 1921) and *How to Sing* (New York, 1923) which was reprinted as *The Art of Singing* (New York, 1975).

English contralto[170] **Dame CLARA BUTT** was born in Steyning, Sussex, February 1, 1872, the second child of Clara Hook and Henry Butt, captain of a small ship. Music was always present, both parents having good voices. Clara's three sisters also developed fine voices, eventually singing professionally as Pauline, Ethel and Hazel Hook.

Originally thought a soprano, when her headmistress heard Clara practicing she thought it was a boy singing. The girl studied with Daniel Rootham in Bristol, who told her, "You have gold in your throat my child." She sang in local choirs and, because of her unusual range, was entered for an open scholarship to the RCM. The judges were impressed not only by her voice, but by her physical stature of six feet two. She was placed in 1890 to study voice with J. Henry Blower, and piano with Marmaduke Barton (1865–1938).

---

170. Contralto voices, with a rich lower register, are rarely heard in opera or on the concert platform today. (Exception, see Ewa Podlés.)

While still a student, she was accepted by Sir Joseph Barnby to sing contralto solos in the oratorios *Israel in Egypt* (Handel) and *Elijah* (Mendelssohn) with the Royal Choral Society. Her Royal Albert Hall debut was in the *Golden Legend*, December 7, 1892. Three days later, she sang Orpheus in an RCM production of Gluck's *Orpheus and Eurydice* at the Lyceum Theater in a special command performance for the Prince of Wales. From then on Butt's success was assured, although entirely on the concert stage. Her only other operatic appearance was to repeat Orpheus in 1920 with Sir Thomas Beecham at Covent Garden.[171]

Clara consequently received a command from Queen Victoria, conveyed by **Sir Arthur Sullivan**, to appear at a State concert in Buckingham Palace. This became a series of command performances. For her fourth year of study, she was sent to Paris under the Queen's patronage to work with Henry Louis Charles Duvernoy (1820–1906). Her return to England was followed by her first solo recital in London's Queen's Hall, and appearances in the Hanley and Bristol Music Festivals with the Royal Choral Society.

In 1894, Butt appeared in her first Handel Festival, and later in the year was again commanded to appear before royalty, this time at Balmoral Castle, Scotland, together with the soprano Dame Emma Albani (1847–1930). After further concert appearances, she returned to France in 1896 to study with the baritone Jacques Bouhy (1848–1929), where she met Camille Saint-Saëns who wanted her for his *Samson et Dalila* in London. However, the Lord Chamberlain's Office decreed that a fully staged performance was not permissible because of the biblical subject. Saint-Saëns felt that the world had lost a perfect Delilah.

Despite her growing reputation, Butt engaged in further studies with Hungarian soprano Etelka Gerster (1855–1920) in Berlin, where she was introduced to the German Royal Family. She became their favorite singer and enjoyed their patronage for a series of concerts in Vienna, Paris, Budapest and Prague.

In 1899, she introduced Sir Edward Elgar's dramatically beautiful song cycle *Sea Pictures* at the Norwich Festival, after which she sailed to America where she was acclaimed "the greatest contralto of the generation . . . without parallel" and, "the noblest voice before the public." Following her Carnegie Hall concert, she gave a recital at the Waldorf-Astoria Hotel with pianist Albert Morris Bagby (1859–1941), whose fifty years of "Musical Mornings" at that location began in 1891 and featured Nellie Melba, Lillian Nordica, and other great voices from the Metropolitan Opera. (Bagby was a student of Franz Liszt, 1882–84.)

During 1898–99, Butt sang with English baritone Kennerley Rumford (1870–1957), and a romance developed. Their marriage in Bristol Cathedral, June 26, 1900, was a civic occasion attended by leading figures from the music world. A special anthem composed by Sir Arthur Sullivan was sung by Dame Albani in the couple's honor.

After Queen Victoria's death in 1901, Clara continued giving performances for King Edward VII and Queen Alexandra, in company with other outstanding artists of the time.

Following the birth of her three children, Clara made no overseas trips until 1907, when she was able to travel with her family. She accepted an invitation to sing in Australia. Discussing her programs with Dame **Nellie Melba**, she was famously told, "sing 'em muck . . . it's all they understand." Instead, to their audiences' delight, Clara and Rumford sang classical lieder, ballads, operatic and oratorio solos. Extra concerts had to be arranged. Her growing reputation initiated a similar tour to South Africa in 1911, and a 1912 worldwide tour covering Canada, America, New Zealand, again Australia and Tasmania, plus recitals in Honolulu and New York on the way home.

In England, 1914, Clara raised money for charities, even donating her fees to help the needy during WWI. She took part in the "Empire Pageant for Fair Women," written by Louis N. Parker, in which she was featured as Britannia; helped produce a run of Elgar's oratorio, *The Dream of Gerontius*; and participated in a Red Cross concert at the Albert Hall with a choir of 250 voices with every famous singer of the day. (Even Dame Albani come out of retirement at Clara's request.) With her husband appearing in khaki, having obtained leave from the Front,

---

171. Gluck's original Italian version called for title role to be sung by an alto castrato. In France this was sung by a tenor. The French considered the castrato an object of ridicule.

Butt helped to raise over £100,000. In recognition of her work, she was made a Dame of the British Empire by Edward VII.

The following years were filled with concerts in Britain and overseas. Sadly, her eldest son, Roy, died of meningitis in 1923, and in 1931 Clara began to suffer from back pain following an accident, serious enough to confine her to a wheelchair. She continued recording until 1933, and even attempted another tour of Australia and New Zealand in 1934 during which she became unwell and was rushed back to England for treatment. While in the hospital, news reached England from Rhodesia that her second son, Victor, had lost his life in a farming accident, although his mother was not told for some time. In 1935, Clara went to Germany for further treatment, but what turned out to be cancer of the spine was too far gone. She died at her home in North Stoke, Oxfordshire, January 23, 1936.

Mary Garden

Scottish soprano **MARY GARDEN** was born February 20, 1874, in Aberdeen. As a child, she moved to America to study violin and piano. She began voice lessons in Chicago in 1893, continuing in Paris in 1895. Her operatic debut was unexpected—in 1900 she took over the role of Charpentier's *Louise* when the prima donna became ill. She created Diane in *La Fille de Tabarin* in 1901 at the Opéra-Comique, and her landmark role of Mélisande[172] in the premiere of Debussy's opera in 1902. Her American debut was Thaïs at Oscar Hammerstein I's Manhattan Opera Company (1907), then performed the U.S. premiere of *Pelléas et Mélisande* in 1908. Manhattan Opera managed to compete with the Met by producing contemporary and French repertoire which were Garden's specialties. With the demise of Manhattan in 1910 (their assets were sold to the Met for $1.2 million), she joined Chicago Grand Opera, making French opera her calling card, singing almost all her roles in French.

Garden was a modern-music singer, and all but four of her thirty-five roles were in operas composed in her lifetime. By January 1921, CGO's general director had died, the music director resigned, and Garden became "directa"—her own title. In January 1922, $1 million in debt, a new company was organized known as Chicago Civic Opera. Garden resigned in April saying, "I am an artist, and I have decided my place is with the artists, not over them." She remained with the company until her last performance—in Boston, February 6, 1931. (The company collapsed in 1932.) After 1930, she made few appearances. In 1935, she gave master classes at the Chicago Musical College and acted as technical advisor to opera sequences in Hollywood films. She returned to Scotland in 1939, with one more American visit for a lecture tour in 1947. Her memoirs, *Mary Garden's Story*, written with Louis Biancolli, were released 1951. She died in Inverurie, Scotland, January 3, 1967.

Czechoslovakian soprano **EMMY (Kittl) DESTINN** was born in Prague, February 26, 1878. Her first musical studies were on violin and piano, her vocal abilities being discovered at age fourteen by Madame Loewe-Destinn, whose name she adopted as a token of appreciation. She made her debut with the Kroll Opera in Berlin, July 19, 1898, in the role of Santuzza (*Cavalleria Rusticana*), then joined the Berlin Royal Opera until 1908. She specialized in Wagnerian operas, and became a protégée of **Cosima Wagner**. She was the Bayreuth Festival's first Senta (*The Flying Dutchman*) in 1901. Because of her reputation for singing difficult roles, **Richard Strauss** (1864–1949) selected her for the title role in both the Berlin and Paris premieres of *Salome*. She made her Covent Garden debut in 1904 as Donna Anna, sharing the stage for the first time with her most famous partner, **Enrico Caruso** (1873–1921). Her success was such she continued to sing in England until the outbreak of World War I. Meanwhile, she made her American debut at the Met in 1908, as Aida, with **Arturo Toscanini** (1867–1957) conducting. She sang their first Minnie at the 1910 premiere of *La fanciulla del west*, remaining at the Met until 1914 when her career was interrupted by the war. She returned in 1919 to again

---

172. After hearing Mary Garden as his Mélisande, Debussy is said to have declared, "That was indeed the gentle voice I heard in my innermost soul!"

sing Aida. Although she retired from the opera stage in 1926, she continued to make concert appearances until shortly before her death January 28, 1930.

GERALDINE FARRAR, born February 28, 1882, in Melrose, Massachusetts, studied music in Boston, New York, Paris and Berlin. Her 1901 operatic debut as Marguerite in *Faust*, with the Berlin Opera, was well received and she went on to sing at Monte Carlo Opera from 1903–06. Her American debut at the Met in 1906, as Juliette, began a sixteen year membership on their roster, which ended with Leoncavallo's *Zaza*, (1922). Her last public performance in 1931 at Carnegie Hall was followed by retirement in Connecticut, where she died in Ridgefield, March 11, 1967. Her greatest success was Madama Butterfly—she performed the role more than 100 times—and gave its American premiere at the Met, February 11, 1907, with **Enrico Caruso**. She was also a great Carmen, and appeared in a 1915 film version which launched a mini-film career for her that lasted until 1921. In 1916, she married actor Lou Tellegen, a leading man of Sarah Bernhardt, but they were subsequently divorced. Tremendously popular with the public, Farrar wrote an autobiography, *Such Sweet Compulsion*, in 1938. It was reprinted in 1970. Personal artifacts, and the fan she used in *Madama Butterfly*, reside in the permanent collection at the Library of Congress in Washington, DC.

AMELITA GALLI-CURCI was born November 18, 1882, in Milan. At fifteen, she had graduated from the conservatory there having won every prize including first prize for piano. It was in this career that she first made a living. It became known that she was also gifted vocally. At a dinner party, where she both played and sang, one of the guests, opera composer **Pietro Mascagni** (1863–1945), was amazed to learn that she had never had a voice lesson. His words, "I would recognize your voice twenty years from now . . . Remember, there are many gifted pianists, but not singers . . . " were prophetic. She looked at her small hands and made the switch, still without training, singing Gilda in the little town of Tranie. Her success there gave her the nerve to go to Rome and demand an audition with the director of the Teatro Costanzi. Intrigued by her audacity, he agreed, and was most surprised when she ably accompanied herself on the piano. He hired her for a series of *Rigolettos*. Gilda was to become her good luck role. Other major roles were Rosina, Lucia, Violetta, Amina and Elvira. Success followed her to Spain, Russia and South America, until the advent of World War I when she went to America and made a sensational 1916 debut at Chicago Opera as Gilda. Meanwhile, she had married painter Luigi Curci in 1910, but was divorced in 1920. (She later married her accompanist, Homer Samuels.) It was at this time that the Victor Company signed her to a long contract. Her first record with them, the Bell Song from *Lakmé*, outsold Caruso's recordings. Her first appearance at the Met was as Violetta in 1921—Caruso had died suddenly that summer, and manager Gatti-Casazza needed a star. Her name was enough to sell out the house. She reigned as queen there until 1930 when, unfortunately, she developed a goiter condition. Although successfully operated upon, her voice never recovered its flexibility. After a disastrous comeback as Mimi at Chicago Opera in 1936, she confined herself to concert recitals, eventually retiring to La Jolla, California, where she died November 26, 1963.

Moravian soprano **MARIA JERITZA**, born October 6, 1887 in Brno, studied there and in Prague. Her debut as Elsa in *Lohengrin* in 1910 led to membership in the Vienna Volksoper (Folks or People's Opera Company), and later at the Vienna Court Opera in 1912, after Emperor Franz Josef heard her sing. **Richard Strauss** chose her to create the title role in *Ariadne auf Naxos* (1912) and the role of Empress in his *Die Frau ohne Schatten* (1919). Her Met debut in 1912 was in the first American production of Erich Wolgang Korngold's *Die tote Stadt* (The Dead City), and successive roles such as Tosca—which she also sang at Covent Garden in 1926—Turandot and Salome kept her on the Met roster until 1932. She became an American citizen in 1943. Always maintaining her love for Vienna, she performed there in recital and concert before and after WWII. Following the tradition of the glamorous *prima donna assoluta*, she went through three marriages, numerous affairs, and legendary fights with her peers. Her autobiography, *Sunlight and Song*, was published in 1924. At age sixty-four, she appeared as Rosalinda at a Met benefit performance of *Die Fledermaus* (1951). She died in Orange, New Jersey, July 10, 1982.

Lucrezia Bori

LUCREZIA BORI, whose original family name was Borja, was born in Valencia, December 24, 1887, supposedly of the Spanish branch of the original Borgia dynasty. First educated in a convent, she later studied at the Valencia Conservatory, made her debut in Rome, October 31, 1908, as Micaëla, then sang in Milan and Naples. By a stroke of fortune, when the Metropolitan Opera Company was in Paris on its 1910 European tour, their Manon Lescaut, Lina Cavalieri, had to cancel. The great Italian music publisher **Tito Ricordi** recommended Bori, who auditioned before no less than **Puccini** (1858–1924), **Toscanini** (1867–1957), and Met director, from 1908–35, **Giulio Gatti-Casazza** (1868–1940). She received unanimous approval and with **Caruso** as her partner and Toscanini in the pit, was an unabashed triumph. In 1911, she sang at La Scala, made her Met debut in New York, November 11, 1912, again as Manon Lescaut, remaining there until the end of the 1914–15 season. She created Fiora in *L'amore dei tre re* by Montemezzi, with Toscanini in 1914. After a period of retirement, due to the nightmare of all opera singers, nodes on the vocal cords, she reappeared in 1919 at Monte Carlo as Mimi (*La bohème*), returning to the Met in 1921 in the same role. In 1925, she also succeeded as Mélisande, even though the original interpreter, Mary Garden, was still singing the role in Europe. Bori also brought Puccini's *La rondine* to the Met repertoire in 1928.

Unlike her buxom contemporaries, slim and feminine Bori, famous for tact and diplomacy—she refused to criticize anyone—continued singing at the Met with increasing popularity through the 1935–36 season. Of the twenty-nine roles she had sung there, Mimi was first with seventy-five performances, *La traviata* with sixty-one and Nedda (*I Pagliacci*) with forty-four. Her retirement did not cease her fund raising efforts to preserve her beloved Met. It is said that no singer has ever shown more loyalty to the house. She became indispensable to her close friend, tenor **Edward Johnson** (1878–1959), who became general manager in 1935 and guided the Met through the financially rocky war years and until his retirement in 1950. She was also president of the Bagby Music Lovers Foundation, which gave anonymous help to retired artists. She never married. When she died in New York, May 14, 1960, the opera world mourned the passing of "La Grande Mademoiselle."

The great German-American, Wagnerian soprano **LOTTE LEHMANN** was born February 27, 1888, in Perleberg, studied in Berlin and made her debut in 1910 in *Die Zauberflöte* at Hamburg Opera, remaining there five seasons. But it was the Vienna State Opera she called home from 1914. There, **Richard Strauss** chose her to sing the Composer role in the premiere of his *Ariadne auf Naxos* (1916). A lifelong champion of Strauss' works, she sang Octavian and the Marschallin roles in his *Der Rosenkavalier*—the latter one of her signature pieces—and created Christine in *Intermezzo* and the Dyer's Wife in *Die Frau ohne Schatten*. Another highlight of her career was singing Leonore in *Fidelio*, as well as Wagnerian roles at the Salzburg Festival (1927–37), many times with Toscanini. Meanwhile, she appeared in South America (1922) and Covent Garden (1924), continuing to sing there until 1935, with one more pre-WWII performance in 1938.

Lotte's Austrian husband, Otto Krause, a former cavalry officer whom she married in 1926, gave up his job as an insurance salesman to manage her career. He proved indispensable, and never missed one of his wife's performances until his death from tuberculosis at age fifty-six, January 22, 1939, in Saranac, New York.

Lehmann took a courageous stand against the Hitler regime from the outset of the Nazi rise to power. Hermann Göring, Hitler's second-in-command and a great opera buff, wired her to come to Berlin where he offered her the title of National Singer—the highest honor—and a fabulous contract with the Berlin State Opera which, however, included the proviso that she never sing outside Germany. When she refused, he shouted that she would never sing in the fatherland again. With the Anschluss—the forced "unification" of the two countries—German troops occupied Austria on March 12, 1938, and Lotte and her husband had to flee their home and the beloved Vienna State Opera. She spent World War II in America, becoming a citizen in 1945. The Vienna Opera House received a direct hit in an Allied bombing raid just eight weeks before the end of the war—March 12, 1945! Productions were moved to the Theater an der Wien, sharing space with the Volksoper. The house was rebuilt and reopened November 5, 1955, but Lehmann never returned there.

Her U.S. debut as Sieglinde with the Chicago Opera had been October 28, 1930. She repeated the same role for her 1934 Met debut. Here she built up a loyal following in the course of seventy-three performances, making her farewell as the Marschallin in 1945, when she was featured as the cover story of *Time* magazine. After a final Marschallin at San Francisco Opera in 1946, she devoted herself to concertizing, teaching—mainly at the Music Academy of the West[173] in Santa Barbara—and publishing several books, including her autobiography, *Anfang und Aufsteig.* (Beginning and Ascent.)

In 1955, Lotte received the highest recognition from the Vienna Opera in the form of a specially made ring. Wanting to ensure being remembered, she left a letter in a sealed envelope to be opened after her death, directing the artists' union of the opera to decide who should inherit the ring. Meanwhile, when asked in 1957 who she thought was the foremost upcoming young soprano, she named **Leonie Rysanek**.

Lehmann gave her last recital in Santa Barbara in 1951. She died there August 26, 1976. A large woman, she was the traditional prima donna, a law unto herself. After her death, no one ever disputed that Lehmann was one of the century's greatest lieder singers. As for the ring,[174] it was indeed Rysanek who was chosen to receive it!

English soprano **Dame MAGGIE TEYTE** was born April 17, 1888, in Wolverhampton. She studied in London before travelling to Paris in 1903, making her debut at the Mozart Festival in France under her original last name, Tate. (She later changed the spelling to make sure the French would pronounce it properly.) Her 1907 operatic debut in Monaco as Tyrcis in Offenbach's *Myriame et Daphné* was highly successful. She often appeared with **Debussy** at the piano, having been chosen by the composer in 1908 to be the successor of **Mary Garden** as Mélisande. She sang at opera houses worldwide—Opéra-Comique, Paris (1908–10), Chicago (1911–14), Boston (1914–17), Covent Garden, London (1922–23, 1930, 1936–38), in such roles as Nedda, Mimi and Madama Butterfly. She created the Princess in Holst's *The Perfect Fool*, then went on to operetta and musical comedies in London, later giving French song recitals which have been preserved on priceless recordings. Her farewell appearance in opera was as Purcell's Belinda in 1951. Her last concert was in 1955.

Recipient of numerous awards and honors, Teyte was made a Chevalier of the French Légion d'honneur in 1957 and a Dame Commander of the Order of the British Empire in 1958. She had two husbands and two famous lovers, Sir Thomas Beecham in London and Georges Enesco in Paris. Her book of memoirs, *Star on the Door*, was published in London in 1956. She died in London, May 26, 1976.

One of the world's greatest Wagnerian sopranos, **KIRSTEN FLAGSTAD** was born July 12, 1895, in Hamar, Norway. Gifted with a naturally well-placed voice, she studied first with her mother (her father was a conductor) and with Ellen Schytte-Jacobsen, before making her debut in Christiania (Oslo) in 1913. For the next twenty years, she sang throughout Scandinavia and was thinking about retiring when she was called to Bayreuth in 1934 and scored a major success as Sieglinde (*Die Walküre*). The following year—virtually unknown this side of the Atlantic—her triumphant Met debut in the same role, and as Brünnhilde, not only established her as the foremost Wagner interpreter of her time, but her sold out performances rescued the opera house from near bankruptcy. Apart from her Covent Garden debut in 1936 as Isolde, to more rave reviews, she continued to perform in America for the rest of the 1930s—at Chicago and San Francisco Operas and with major orchestras—returning to her native country in 1941 to be with her husband, despite Norway being occupied by the Germans. (She later had to overcome unfounded allegations of being a Nazi sympathizer, although during the war she sang only in neutral Switzerland.) Her husband died in 1946, and to support herself Flagstad once again had to give up any thought of retiring. After WWII, she returned to Covent Garden and then to the Met in 1951 where, her golden tones undi-

---

173. Founded in 1947 by Lehmann, Lawrence Tibbett, Ernest Bloch, and music director for twenty-five years, Maurice Abravanel, its mission is the preparation of young musicians for professional careers. The concept of the masterclass was begun here by Lehmann, where she directed the voice program until 1962. Successive directors include Marni Nixon (1980–96) and Marilyn Horne (1997–). The academy is on nine acres of the John Percival Jefferson estate in Montecito, a gift from Helen Marso, Jefferson's personal secretary of thirty-six years.
174. When Leonie Rysanek died in 1998, the Lotte Lehmann Memorial Ring was passed to Hildegard Behrens.

minished after a ten-year absence, she once again had audiences at her feet. She made her New York farewell as *Alceste* in 1952, but continued her beloved lieder recitals. On May 2, 1950, in London, she sang the premiere of Strauss' *Four Last Songs*, the final compositions of the composer who had died just a few months before. It was an unforgettable performance.

Finally retiring in 1954, she served as director of the Norwegian Opera in Oslo from 1958–60. Never realizing her dream to live quietly by the North Sea, she died in the capital, December 7, 1962. Her autobiography, *The Flagstad Manuscript*, written with Louis Biancolli, was published in 1965.

Kirsten Flagstad will remain one of the greatest prima donnas of all time. Known for her complete absence of ego—she never employed a dresser, and always did her own make-up—an example of her innate modesty was her delight in having a rose named after her at a Detroit flower show. "After I have left this world and my voice is forgotten, my name will be remembered because of this rose . . . "

(But thanks to recordings, her voice will always be with us. The complete *Tristan und Isolde*, conducted by Leon Furtwängler, offers the finest memorial to her art.)

Spanish mezzo-soprano **CONCHITA SUPERVIA** was born, according to her British passport, in Barcelona, December 9, 1889, or 1895 when she had something to say about it. Little is known about her early training, except that she studied at the Colegio de las Damas Negras in her native city and made her debut with a visiting opera company at the Teatro Colón in Buenos Aires, October 1, 1910. She sang Octavian, the trouser role, in the Italian premiere of *Der Rosenkavalier* in Rome, 1911—the opera was booed, but she was applauded. Next came *Carmen* in Bologna, 1912, and a year with the Chicago Opera (1915–16). In 1918, she became pregnant by lawyer Francesco Santamaria. Her mother, a controlling influence, persuaded her to go to South America to have the baby. (As an adult, her son, Giorgio, called himself George Supervia.) Returning to Italy in 1924, Conchita appeared frequently at La Scala and other music centers. Contrary to legend, although she endeared herself to the Italian public by carrying on the popularity of Rossini operas, she did not "reclaim" those roles for the mezzo range. The tradition was never lost, but carried on by mezzos **Fanny Anitua** (1887–1968) and **Gabriella Besanzoni** (1888–1962) in *Il Barbiere di Siviglia* and *La Cenerentola*, **Guerrina Fabbri** (1866–1946) in *L'Italiana in Aligeri*, and later by **Teresa Berganza**, **Marilyn Horne**, **Joan Sutherland**, **Frederica von Stade** and **Cecilia Bartoli**.

In 1931, Supervia married British industrialist Sir Ben Rubenstein, a match disapproved of by his family. To make the marriage work, she learned English, converted to Judaism and scaled her career to the concert hall, except for a Covent Garden stint, 1934–35. Although warned of the danger, she conceived Ben's child in an effort to save the marriage. The baby died at birth, and Conchita followed a few days later, March 30, 1936. She was buried in the Jewish cemetery in the northwest London suburb of Golders Green. Her modest savings and property were pounced upon by her voracious in-laws.

Hers was not a powerful voice, but her overt sexuality came through in all her roles, as is vividly apparent in the small part she played in her only film, *Evensong* (1934). There also exists a priceless two-disc Nimbus CD set, featuring songs and arias, remastered from some of her early recordings.

ROSA PONSELLE was born Rosa Ponzillo, January 22, 1897, in Meriden, Connecticut. With no vocal training, at eighteen she followed older sister **Carmela** (1888–1977) to New York, where they enjoyed a lucrative vaudeville career. After only five months of opera coaching with William Thorner, he introduced Rosa to **Enrico Caruso**. Impressed, the world's greatest tenor arranged an audition with Met manager Gatti-Casazza who, without any publicity, put the unknown onstage as Leonora in *La forza del destino* opposite Caruso, November 15, 1918. She was an overnight star, going on to sing 411 performances with the Met, the last as Carmen in 1937. Her Covent Garden appearances were from 1929–1931. She sang at the inaugural of the Maggio Musicale Fiorentino (Florence) in 1933. In 1936, she married a former Baltimore mayor's son, Carl Jackson, who built her a villa in Green Spring Valley, Maryland. They were divorced in 1950, but the villa remained a haven for her and was the site of her lavish eightieth birthday (1977) party. She died there, May 25, 1981.

1997, the 100th anniversary of Ponselle's birth, was marked with worldwide celebrations and a memorial stamp.

Loved by everyone who came in contact with her, petite French coloratura soprano **LILY PONS** was born April 12, 1898, in Draguignan near Cannes, to an engineer father and a mother of Italian descent. She first studied piano, her accomplished technique even meriting praise from composer Darius Milhaud. Toward the end of WWI, she took vocal lessons from Alberti di Gorostiaga, who made the most of her small voice, and appeared in ingenue roles on the Paris stage. She debuted in *Lakmé* (1927), which was to become a signature role, touring throughout France. (Her recording of the Bell Song is a cherished classic.)

At the Met, Gatti-Casazza was desperate. His major star, **Amelita Galli-Curci**, had been forced to bow out due to her advanced goiter condition, and other prominent divas of the time were past their prime. When agents imported the petite, unknown Pons—she kept her 104 pound figure all her life—for his inspection, the manager decided to take a chance. With no pre-publicity, he launched her in a January 3, 1931 matinee of *Lucia di Lammermoor* with a strong supporting cast of two world famous Italians, tenor **Beniamino Gigli** as Edgardo, and basso **Ezio Pinza** as Raimondo. The public went wild over the new "French Nightingale." Despite the Depression, they lined up at the box office. Her timing was also right for Hollywood. The movies had just found sound, and studios needed singers. RKO hyped her as their answer to Columbia's **Grace Moore**. Her films, *I Dream Too Much* (1935), *That Girl from Paris* (1936) and *Hitting a New High* (1937), set no records for plot-lines, but her personality shone through giving us a permanent visual keepsake. *Carnegie Hall* (1947), called by James Agee "The thickest and sourest mess of musical mulligatawny I have yet had to sit down to," nevertheless preserves a showcase of the foremost artists of the time, including mezzo **Risë Stevens**, basso **Ezio Pinza**, tenor **Jan Peerce**, violinist **Jascha Heifetz**, pianist **Artur Rubinstein**, big band trumpeter **Harry James**, and the New York Philharmonic with **Bruno Walter** and **Leopold Stokowski**.

In 1941, Pons became an American citizen. She continued to dazzle Met audiences until 1944, with return engagements between 1945–58, never appearing more than ten times each season. Concurrently, she sang for twenty-seven years with San Francisco Opera, since their season started in early fall. Her major roles were Rosina, Gilda, Lucia, Lakmé, and Marie from *The Daughter of the Regiment*, a long-neglected Donizetti opera which she convinced Edward Johnson to stage. Performed December 28, 1940, it was a smash hit, and later a great vehicle for **Joan Sutherland** and **Beverly Sills**. Although her official retirement was in 1962, Lily made an unexpected appearance in Lincoln Center's Philharmonic Hall in 1972, under the baton of her then ex-husband. She sang six arias and brought down the house. This concert was used as part of the television documentary dedicated to her.

Her twenty-year marriage (1938–58) to **André Kostelanetz** (1901–1980), if not a love match, was a lucrative artistic arrangement. Conductor of his own orchestra, they concertized and recorded extensively—this apart from her solo recitals. During WWII, always wearing elegant evening gowns, she braved the jungles of Burma and the stifling heat of India and China to entertain troops. Her sojourn in India gave her a deeper understanding of the accursed caste system, after which there was a new dimension to her portrayal of the Hindu princess, Lakmé.

Pons spent her time between her house in Palm Springs, California, an apartment in Cannes—she visited France for two months each year—and an apartment in Dallas, where she died quite suddenly, February 13, 1976, barely a month after the dire diagnosis of pancreatic cancer. Her popularity was such that the state of Maryland named the town of Lilypons after her.

Austrian-American **LOTTE LENYA** was born Karoline Wilhelmine Charlotte Blamauer in Vienna, October 18, 1898. She began her career in Zurich in the theater and as a dancer. As a singer, her first role was the hairdresser's assistant in *Der Rosenkavalier*, under the baton of the composer, Richard Strauss. Relocating to Berlin in 1921, she met composer **Kurt Weill** (1900–50) and married him in 1926. With an idiosyncratic, yet highly expressive voice suited to the half-sung, half-spoken style of Weill's operas, her operatic debut came in 1927 at Baden-Baden in Weill's *The Rise and Fall of the City of Mahagonny*. Devoted to her husband's music, she created roles in several of his works, including Miriam in *The Eternal Road*, the Duchess in *The Firebrand of Florence* and, the most famous, Jenny in the Brecht-Weill *Die Dreigroschen-oper* (The Threepenny Opera) in Berlin, 1928. Weill said of her: "She is a miserable housewife, but a very good actress. She can't read music, but when she sings, people listen. (For that matter, I pity any composer whose wife can read music)." Lenya looked at it differently: "I never took a singing lesson. Any Viennese can sing, really, it's in their blood!" Fleeing from Hitler's Germany in 1933, the pair settled first in Paris, then London and finally New York, where Weill experienced success before his death in 1950.

In 1951, Lotte married George Davis who encouraged her to perform again. He convinced her to appear in Marc Blitzstein's English adaptation of *The Three Penny Opera*. It ran off-Broadway from 1955 to 1961, and won Lenya a Tony Award. There were numerous popular music and even jazz versions of the opera's most famous song, "Mack the Knife," including one by Louis Armstrong who improvised her name into the lyrics. Davis died in 1957, but by then he had guided Lenya to an international career.

She spent the remainder of her life keeping Weill's works fresh on the American scene. Best remembered by the 007 generation is her movie appearance as Rosa Klebb in the James Bond film, *From Russia With Love* (1963). She died in New York, November 27, 1981. In 1956, critic Harold Schonberg said in the *New York Times*, "She has a rasping voice that could sandpaper sandpaper." Late in her life the singer cited another description of her voice, "an octave below laryngitis."

American soprano **GRACE MOORE** was born in Nough, Tennessee, December 5, 1898. She studied in Maryland and New York and sang in a few well-forgotten musical comedies such as *Hitchy-Koo* (1920), *Up in the Clouds* (1922) and *Music Box Review* (1923, 1924), the latter featuring Irving Berlin's immortal "What'll I Do?" and "All Alone." She then went to Antibes (France) to study with Richard Berthélmy. Returning to America in 1928, she made her operatic debut as Mimi at the Met, singing there intermittently until 1946 in such signature roles such as Tosca, Manon and Louise. For the latter, she went to Paris to study with its composer, establishing a special rapport with the aged **Gustave Charpentier** (1860–1956). She also sang at the Paris Opéra-Comique (1928), and London's Covent Garden (1935) and other European houses, as well as at Chicago Opera (1937). Meanwhile, she continued her Broadway career with *DuBarry* (1934) before being lured to Hollywood, where she earned more popularity with *A Lady's Morals*, *New Moon* (music by **Sigmund Romberg**) both in 1930, *One Night of Love* (1934), for which she was an Oscar nominee, *Love Me Forever* (1935), *The King Steps Out* (1936), *When You're in Love* (1937) and *I'll Take Romance* (1937). Her voice and personality did much to popularize opera. She made a fortune from these films, and her recitals sold out everywhere within a few hours. At Covent Garden, Lady Cunard (of the shipping line) and Sir Thomas Beecham resigned from the board when they found out that Moore was being paid double the fee of other artists.

During the war, Moore spoke out against mixing art and politics, particularly when it came to boycotting certain works because of their national origin. She thought it "uncivilized" for *Butterfly* to be banned when those who created her were not responsible for the present hostilities. Scheduled to sing in Seattle at this time, she wanted to fly there, but her husband, Valentine Parera,[175] begged her not to. The plane she would have taken exploded over Wyoming, but Grace Moore was not to cheat destiny a second time. The light of this warm, vibrant star was extinguished January 26, 1947 when, on her way to Stockholm to begin a world concert tour, her plane cracked up at the Copenhagen airport.

Her autobiography, *You're Only Human Once*, was published in 1944. A 1953 film, *So This is Love*, starring Kathryn Grayson, was based on her life. A second biography, *Grace Moore and Her Many Worlds* by Rowena Rutherford Farrar, came out in 1982.

MARIAN ANDERSON (1899–1993). (See Black Heritage.)

---

175. An actor, he was known as the "Spanish Ronald Colman" after the debonair British-born (1891–1958) American screen idol of the '30s and '40s.

HELEN TRAUBEL was born in St. Louis, June 20, 1899. Raised in a German-speaking home, her mother, Clara Stuhr, had been a professional lieder singer. Helen studied with Lulu Vetta-Karst, making her concert debut with that city's Symphony in 1923, and concertized until her Met debut in 1937 as Mary Rutledge in *The Man Without a Country*, by conductor **Walter Damrosch** (1862–1950). Her first major role, Sieglinde in *Die Walküre*, was the foundation of her becoming America's leading Wagnerian interpreter. On October 6, 1938, she married William Bass, an investment broker who became her business manager. Over the next two years, she sang with Arturo Toscanini and the NBC Symphony, Leopold Stokowski at Philadelphia, and Pierre Monteux at Ravinia. On December 6, 1941, she sang her first Brünnhilde. The next day, America was at war. **Kirsten Flagstad** stayed in Norway, **Marjorie Lawrence** was stricken with polio, and Traubel became America's leading soprano of the 1940s, singing week after week, year after year, when Wagner operas were the core repertory at the Met. She became a national symbol, singing recitals and concerts, appearing in San Francisco, Chicago, Mexico and South America, and singing for the troops. The war years prevented her from appearing in Europe during her prime, which accounted for her not receiving international acclaim. Her long career at the Met came to an abrupt close in 1953 when manager **Rudolf Bing** (1902–97) objected to her nightclub "moonlighting." A multi-talented performer, she appeared on Broadway in Rodgers' and Hammerstein's *Pipe Dream* (1955); in the films *Deep in My Heart* (1954), Hollywood's version of the life of Sigmund Romburg, and *Gunn* (1967), based on the Peter Gunn TV series; and television, The Jimmy Durante Show (1952), and as Katisha in *The Mikado* (1960), a Bell Telephone Hour presentation. She also authored two mystery novels, *The Ptomaine Canary* and *The Metropolitan Opera Murders* (1951), as well as her 1959 autobiography, *St. Louis Woman*.

After his daughter's singing was negatively criticized by a reviewer, President Harry Truman had Traubel coach Margaret from February 1949 to June 1950. In October 1950, Helen became part owner of the St. Louis baseball team—for whom she had rooted since childhood. She appeared on the cabaret circuit with such entertainers as Red Skelton, Groucho Marx, Jerry Lewis and Jimmy Durante, with whom she performed at Lake Tahoe (California) in 1964. She died of a heart attack in her home in Santa Monica, California, July 28, 1972, and was survived by her husband.

Of course there are many other "immortals" which space prohibits from including, but it is safe to say the singers listed here comprise the cream of the crop who were as idolized as movie stars before there were movies, and who attracted full houses before radio brought concerts into homes with the turn of a dial, and television beamed entire operas into our living rooms.

Into the 20th Century

1900 to 1929

Jennie Tourel (1900–73)
Erna Berger (1900–90)
Gladys Swarthout (1900–69)
Bidú Sayão (1902–99)
Jeanette MacDonald (1903–65)
Zinka Milanov (1906–89)
Elena Nikolaidi (1906–2002)
Marjorie Lawrence (1907–79)
Jarmila Novotná (1907–94)
Rose Bampton (1908–)
Licia Albanese (1909–)
Dorothy Kirsten (1910–92)
Magda Olivero (1910–)
Kathleen Ferrier (1912–53)
Ljuba Welitsch (1913–96)
Risë Stevens (1913–)
Eleanor Steber (1914–90)
Janine Micheau (1914–76)
Elisabeth Schwarzkopf (1915–2006)
Hilde Güden (1917–88)
Birgit Nilsson (1918–2005)
Mado Robin (1918–60)

Blanche Thebom (1918–)
Frances Bible (1919–2001)
Lisa Della Casa (1919–)
Eileen Farrell (1920–2002)
Nan Merriman (1920–)
Phyllis Curtin (1921–)
Renata Tebaldi (1922–2004)
Regina Resnik (1922–)
Victoria de Los Angeles (1923–2005)
Mimi Benzell (1922–70)
Maria Callas (1923–77)
Nell Rankin (1923–2005)
Christa Ludwig (1924–)
Patrice Munsel (1925–)
Leonie Rysanek (1926–98)
Joan Sutherland (1926–)
Galina Vishnevskaya (1926–)
Régine Crespin (1927–)
Pilar Lorengar (1928–96)
Rosalind Elias (1929–)
Beverly Sills (1929–)
Gabriella Tucci (1929–)

Of those born in the two decades before the World War II, most retired from their stage careers before the turn of the 21st century. Some have gone into teaching, some, like **Beverly Sills** until 2005, into directing or other administrative work within the field, while others rest on their well-earned laurels.

Those Who Have Left Us

MIMI BENZELL, born April 6, 1922, in Bridgeport, Connecticut, was exposed to music early in life. Her grandfather, who emigrated from Russia, was a Jewish folk singer. After studies at New York's Mannes College of Music, she made her professional debut at a Mozart festival in Mexico City under the baton of **Sir Thomas Beecham**. Her Met debut was January 5, 1945, as the Queen of the Night in *The Magic Flute*, and in the course of the next five years sang eighteen roles in ninety-seven performances there, including Gilda and Musetta. In 1949, she switched careers and appeared in nightclubs and Broadway shows, including *Milk and Honey* (1961). Her last project was an interview show on WNBC radio. Survived by her husband, concert manager Walter Gould, and a son, she died far too young, of cancer, in Manhasset, Long Island, New York, December 23, 1970.

ERNA BERGER, born near Dresden, October 19, 1900, studied voice there and made her debut with the Dresden State Opera in 1925, with whom she sang until 1928. She was at the Berlin State Opera from 1929–33, concurrently spending the summers at Bayreuth and Covent Garden, 1934–47. On November 21, 1949, she appeared at the Met as Sophie in *Der Rosenkavalier*, returning there, 1953–54. Some of her other major roles were Constanze, the Queen of the Night, Rosina and Gilda. She retired in 1955, settling in Hamburg as a voice teacher. She gave her last solo recital—still in fine voice—in Munich on February 15, 1968, at the age of sixty-seven. Her autobiography *Auf Flügeln des Gesanges* (On Wings of Song) was published in Zurich, 1988. She died in Essen, June 14, 1990.

FRANCES BIBLE was born in Sackets Harbor, New York, January 26, 1919, not 1927 as many biographies claim. After studying at Juilliard with Belle Julie Soudant and Queena Mario, she made her 1948 debut at NYCO as the Shepherd Boy in *Tosca*, remaining with the company until 1977. With a mellow mezzo, an attractive stage presence, and genuine theatrical flair, her technique allowed her to sing *bel canto* in Verdian drama. She was with NYCO when it lacked glamour, and though her colleague **Beverly Sills** moved upward, Bible's competition at the Met was Risë Stevens and Blanche Thebom. Her best years also overlapped with the great voices of Teresa Berganza, Christa Ludwig, Fedora Barbieri, and Giuletta Simionato.

Known for her trouser roles, where no one really surpassed her, she created the role of Elizabeth Procter in Robert Ward's *The Crucible*, and so owned the role of Augusta Tabor in *The Ballad of Baby Doe* many thought she had created it. She sang in Glyndebourne, San Francisco, Dublin and most second-tier houses throughout America. She sang concerts everywhere, and will always be remembered for the 1959 recording of *Baby Doe* made with Beverly Sills and Walter Cassel (1910–2000), released by PolyGram in 1999. After retiring from NYCO, Bible taught at Rice University in Houston, and spent her last years living in Hemet, California, near San Diego, where she died January 29, 2001.

One of the most venerated and controversial opera divas of the 20th century was American-born, December 3, 1923, in New York, **MARIA CALLAS**, who went to Greece in the 1930s when her family returned to their homeland. She studied voice at Athens Royal Academy of Music with the Spanish soprano Elvira de Hidalgo, and made her professional debut at sixteen in a minor role in *Boccaccio*, at the Royal Opera, Athens. Her first major role there was Tosca in 1942. After WWII, she returned to New York, auditioned and was accepted by the Met, but then decided to go to Italy where she sang the title role in *La Gioconda* (1947). Celebrated Italian conductor **Tullio Serafin** (1878–1968) became her mentor and contracted her to sing Aida and Isolde at various venues in his country. She became a member of La Scala in 1951, and after overcoming her weight problem—she slimmed from 210 lbs to 135—with her classic Greek features, whatever she lacked in voice was made up for by her dramatic abilities. As Medea, she mesmerized audiences with her passion. In 1949, she married Italian businessman Giovanni Meneghini, who became her manager. She separated from him a decade later, and maintained a famous liaison with shipping tycoon Aristotle Onassis, until his marriage to Jacqueline Kennedy in 1968—he only gave Maria twenty-four hours' notice of the event, instigating a bitter rivalry between the two women.

Callas made her American debut as Norma at the fledgling Chicago Lyric Opera, at the personal request of **Carol Fox**, in 1956. She left La Scala in 1958, but returned 1960, '62. She was with Covent Garden 1952–59. At the peak of her success, she finally debuted at the Met, October 29, 1956. She, too, ran afoul of the management— Rudolf Bing fired her because there were fist-fights over her. Since everyone loved Tebaldi, he went with *her*.

Callas returned to the Met in 1958, after an uneasy truce, to sing Violetta. Since she was still feuding with Bing, she joined friend Lawrence Kelly, founder of Dallas Opera, and sang *Lucia*, *Traviata* and *Medea* there. Her presence brought other name singers to Dallas, and regional opera was changed forever. She did not appear in New York again until 1965, when she sang Tosca. She retired from opera the same year.

By her own wishes, she appeared in some operas very few times. At the other end of the scale she sang her favorite roles, Aida and Medea, thirty-one times each, Lucia, forty-three, Tosca, fifty-two, Violetta, fifty-eight, and Norma eighty-four times. Yet it was Medea for which she was renowned. The role brought out her temperament in all its fury and permitted her superior acting abilities to cover any vocal deficiencies.

Her mania to sing everything possibly contributed to the breakdown of her voice—Norma being one of the most taxing roles in the repertoire. She turned to other forms of her beloved music. Her master classes[176] at Juilliard during 1971 were enthusiastically attended. She gave recitals, but her 1974 tour with tenor **Giuseppe di Stefano** was a disaster, when both singers were past their vocal prime.

Callas personified the imperious prima donna of a bygone era, demanding things be done her way. She was known to walk off the stage during a performance, or cancel at the last minute, or not show up at all. (To her credit, she was always musically prepared.) Scandals, fits of temper, a sharp tongue, people falling in or out of favor with her—nothing detracted from the loyalty of the legions of fans who idolized her. Returning to Paris in 1977, on September 16, Maria Callas died in her apartment of a sudden heart attack. To the end she symbolized the tragic Greek heroine.

Spanish (Catalán) soprano **VICTORIA de LOS ANGELES** was born in Barcelona, November 1, 1923, into a musical family. She spent her early years at the Liceo Conservatory in Barcelona, singing her first Mimi there in 1941. Her official debut was with the Teatro Lírico as Mozart's Countess Almaviva in *The Marriage of Figaro* (1944). In 1947, she won the Geneva International Singing Competition, prompting the BBC to invite her to sing Salud in a studio broadcast of de Falla's *La vida breve*. Her Covent Garden debut came in 1950. Her American debut was in the form of a Carnegie Hall recital, October 24, 1950. Her Met debut followed, March 17, 1951, as Marguerite in *Faust*. Her association with New York lasted ten years. Meanwhile, her highly successful international career took her to Paris, Vienna, Milan, Bayreuth, Scandinavia, Buenos Aires, South Africa and Australia, with repertoire ranging from Wagner to Puccini. She performed mainly in French and Italian and occasionally in German, but remained quintessentially Spanish. She formally retired in 1969, but continued to concertize, excelling in French and Spanish songs, of which there are priceless recordings, plus twenty-one operas and more than twenty-five recitals.

de Los Angeles sang at the closing ceremonies of the 1992 Olympics in Barcelona, but retired from the stage in 1998 after the death of one of her sons. Admitted to the hospital in Barcelona on December 31, suffering from bronchitis, she died January 15, 2005.

(I was in the audience of her recital at the Palace of Music in her native Barcelona, May 1993—the house was packed with adoring fans. At age seventy, she could still hit a respectable number of high notes!)

EILEEN FARRELL was born February 13, 1920, in Willimantic, Connecticut, to vaudevillian parents. Her mother, a contralto, recognized her daughter's natural soprano voice. Serious music studies in New York began after high school. By 1941, she had her own radio show, *Eileen Farrell Sings*, which lasted six years. She also appeared on The Prudential Family Hour, The American Family Hour and others, in those wonderful years when the American radio listener was exposed to classical music. She toured North and South America 1947–49. Her 1950 song recital in New York brought further recognition, and was followed by appearances with the NBC Symphony Orchestra under **Arturo Toscanini**, and concerts with other famed conductors like **Pierre Monteux**, **Leopold Stokowski** and **Dmitri Mitropoulos**. Later, she had a special relationship with **Leonard Bernstein** and the New York Philharmonic. Her operatic debut as Santuzza in Mascagni's *Cavalleria rusticana* with San Carlo Opera (Tampa, Florida, 1956), was followed by performances with Chicago Lyric Opera (1957) and San Francisco (1958). Her Met debut in 1960 was in Gluck's *Alcestis*. She remained on their roster until 1964, returning '65–'66, the last season at the old location. After retiring from the stage, Farrell became a Distinguished Professor of Music at Indiana University (1971–80), then held the same title at the University of Maine, from 1984.

---

176. In 1995, the play *Master Class*, based on Callas' life, opened on Broadway to fairly good reviews. I saw it there in 1996.

In 1946 she married to Robert V. Reagan, a New York City policeman. The marriage lasted forty years and produced to a son and a daughter. She died in her home in New Jersey, March 23, 2002.

Kathleen Ferrier

Contralto **KATHLEEN FERRIER**, born April 22, 1912, in Lancashire (England), studied piano and voice. Before winning first prize for piano and voice at the Carlisle Competition, she had worked as a telephone operator. The award steered her into serious vocal studies in London. The original crossover artist before the term was coined, her glorious voice shimmered a ray of sunlight on the BBC during the bleak days of the 1940 London Blitz in World War II, when the German Luftwaffe bombed the British capital night after night. Featured in such programs as *Housewives' Choice, Forces' Favourites* and singing popular and folk songs on the Light Programme, she was equally inspiring in the classics and opera. She soloed in *Messiah* at Westminster Abbey in 1943, and was chosen by Benjamin Britten to originate the title role in his *Rape of Lucretia* at Glyndebourne (1946), and *Abraham and Isaac*, both of which he wrote for her. She had the stoic German Herbert von Karajan in tears when he conducted her in Bach's *St. Matthew Passion*. Her Covent Garden debut led to an American triumph with the New York Philharmonic under **Bruno Walter**, singing Mahler's *Das Lied von der Erde* (1948). Her fame spread throughout Europe, at the Salzburg Festival, Paris, Amsterdam and Scandinavia. **Wieland Wagner** (Richard's grandson) wanted to book her for the Bayreuth Festival, but her legendary career was sadly cut short. Just after the double honors of being made a Commander of the Order of the British Empire and receiving the Gold Medal of the Royal Philharmonic Society, she died of breast cancer, in London, October 8, 1953.

Fifty years after her death, during October 2003, she was commemorated in her home town, Blackburn, and in London. Decca released a two-CD set, *Kathleen Ferrier: A Tribute*.

Popular Austrian singer-actress **HILDE GÜDEN** was born in Vienna, September 15, 1917. She studied at the conservatory there, making her operetta debut at the age of sixteen. Her opera debut was as Cherubino, 1939, in Zurich, where she sang until 1941. She continued her career during WWII, appearing in Munich (1941–42), Rome (1942–46), and sang at the Salzburg Festival after the war in 1946, after which she became a leading member of the Vienna State Opera until 1973. Her first performance at Covent Garden was in 1947, and her Met debut as Gilda came in 1951. She continued to sing there until 1960. Her repertoire ranged from Mozart to contemporary composers such as Blacher and Britten. She also excelled in operetta. Her other strong roles included Despina, Sophie, Zerbinetta and Anne Trulove. She died in Klosterneuberg, September 17, 1988.

Blonde lyric soprano **DOROTHY KIRSTEN** was born July 6, 1910,[177] in Montclair, New Jersey, into a musical family. Her mother was an organist, and her aunt, Catherine Hayes, had been an opera singer. Her father was a builder. Her grandfather was a conductor and one-time president of his local branch of the musicians' union. To earn money for singing lessons, which she took at night in New York, she worked for the New Jersey Telephone Company and for Singer Sewing Machine, eventually becoming secretary and maid for her teacher, Louis Darnier, who had been the coach of famed Italian tenor **Beniamino Gigli** (1890–1957). Her first singing jobs were with dance orchestras, and in 1937 with the Kate Smith Singers on radio. She was heard by the great soprano **Grace Moore**, who became her mentor and benefactress. She arranged for Dorothy to study with Astolfo Pescia in Rome, but after one year the outbreak of WWII in 1939 forced her return to America. Thus, Kirsten was one of the few divas almost completely American trained. She sang at the 1939 New York World's Fair, and on the recommendation of Moore was admitted into Chicago Grand Opera, 1940, making her professional debut as Pousette in *Manon*, plus fifteen other minor roles until she sang Musetta to Moore's Mimi the same year. As Violetta in NYCO's first *La traviata*, she was so well received it consolidated the company's reputation as well as her own, and she received contracts the following year for San Francisco and the Met.

---

177. Kirsten's birth year had been given out as 1915 until her death.

She sang at the Met for 281 performances over thirty seasons, two-thirds of which were in Puccini roles. Her final opera performance was Tosca in 1979. Among her finest roles were Butterfly, Manon Lescaut, Nedda (*I Pagliacci*), Marguerite (*Faust*), and Louise—for which she was coached by its composer, **Gustave Charpentier**. Although this opera had a great reputation in Europe—Toscanini considered it a work of art—Kirsten could not get Rudolf Bing to mount it at the Met. He did, however, ask her to sing Marie (*Wozzeck*), which she declined after she saw the score and shuddered at the thought of exposing her voice to, as she put it, "screaming that cruel, dissonant music!" Constantly tied up with American contracts—there were many performances in San Francisco—and although she had many offers, the timing was never right and she missed out on international exposure.

Kirsten also sang on radio, television, recordings, operetta, musical comedy, and had a great recital career—the latter always a source of greater income and less stress for every opera singer. Another prima donna to hit Hollywood, she appeared in numerous films, including *The Great Caruso* (1950) with Mario Lanza, and *Mr. Music* with Bing Crosby (1950). Her autobiography, *A Time to Sing*, was published in 1982.

In 1955, she married Dr. John Douglas French, head of the Brain Research Institute of the University of California Medical Center at Los Angeles. When she retired, she devoted the rest of her working life as chairman of the French Foundation for Alzheimer Research, an organization she founded to combat the illness that had victimized her husband. After a wonderful life and robust health, it was in that hospital she died November 18, 1992, of complications following a stroke, November 5.

Australian soprano **MARJORIE LAWRENCE** was born in Dean's Marsh, Victoria, February 17, 1907. She first studied in Melbourne, then Paris (1929–32), and made her debut as Elisabeth in *Tannhäuser* at Monte Carlo, 1932, after which she sang with the Paris Opéra, 1933–36. At the end of 1933 she was offered a Met contract for the 1935–36 season, but it required that she prepare the three Brünnhildes, Isolde, Kundry, Elsa and Ortrud, all in German. With her commitment to Paris Opéra, she felt it would be too much to learn the roles and declined. She eventually made her American debut with the Met in 1935, as Brünnhilde in *Die Walküre*, remaining there until 1941 when she premiered Gluck's *Alceste*. Concurrent guest appearances were with the opera companies of San Francisco, Chicago, St. Louis and Cincinnati. While in Mexico in 1941, she contracted polio which devastated her career. Although never again able to walk unaided, she made recital and radio appearances, and sang eleven performances of *Tannhäuser* and two of *Tristan und Isolde* at the Met. She retired in 1952, and devoted herself to teaching, first at Tulane (Louisiana, 1956–60), and as director of the opera workshop at Southern Illinois University from 1960. Her autobiography, *Interrupted Melody, The Story of My Life*, was published in 1949, and made into a film in 1955, starring Eleanor Parker[178] and Glenn Ford. Lawrence died in Little Rock, Arkansas, January 13, 1979.

Spanish soprano **PILAR LORENGAR**, born Pilar Lorenza Garcia, January 16, 1928, in Saragossa, began singing in her convent school choir, and in the 1940s moved to Madrid where she studied with Angeles Ottein and sang in a zarzuela company (the Spanish form of operetta with spoken dialogue) for several years. She made her opera debut as Cherubino in *The Marriage of Figaro* at Aix-en-Provence, 1951, and the same year debuted in the U.S. with the Little Orchestra Society of New York in Granados' *Goyescas*. Her Covent Garden debut came in 1955. She also sang at Glyndebourne Festivals, 1956–60. Meanwhile, 1958 marked her first appearance with the Berlin Deutsche Oper. Her American opera debut as Liù in *Turandot* with San Francisco was the beginning of a twenty-five year association. She made her Met debut in 1966 as Donna Elvira, singing there often until her last appearance, as Fiordiligi, in 1982. Although best known for her portrayals of Mozart heroines, she was also featured as Elsa (*Lohengrin*), Eva (*Die Meistersinger*), and the title roles in *Manon Lescaut*, *Madama Butterfly*, *Tosca*, *La traviata* and Desdemona in *Otello*.

---

178. Parker's vocals in the film were dubbed by **Eileen Farrell**.

Lorengar sang all over the world, but resided in Berlin and considered her artistic home the German Opera, where she sang for more than thirty years. She received the prestigious title Kammersängerin of the Deutsche Oper in 1963, and in 1984 was made a lifetime member of the company on the occasion of her twenty-fifth anniversary. She died of breast cancer in Berlin, June 2, 1996.

A unique singing career was that of glamorous **JEANETTE MACDONALD**, born in Philadelphia June 18, 1903. She began as a chorus girl and model in New York, and after winning praise for her soprano role in the 1923 musical *The Magic Ring*, reached stardom in operettas and musicals. Recommended to Paramount Studios, they signed her immediately. Her first films were opposite **Maurice Chevalier**, after which she went on to gain international recognition as a singing actress in twenty-nine films, especially the eight in which she was paired with baritone **Nelson Eddy** (1901–67) beginning 1933. Although each was happily married to someone else—she, since 1937, to actor Gene Raymond—the pair were known as "America's Sweethearts," and their movies grossed millions on both sides of the Atlantic.

World War II destroyed the innocence of the movie-going public, and musical films fell from popularity. MacDonald retired from the screen into the concert hall, made an operatic debut in Montreal in 1944, as Juliette, and also sang in Chicago, but her voice, so beautiful in films, was too small to meet the demands of large opera houses. She died January 14, 1965 in Houston, Texas.

Lovely **JANINE MICHEAU** was born in Toulouse, April 17, 1914, and studied there as well as at the Paris Conservatoire. She made her debut in a minor role in Charpentier's *Louise* at the Opéra Comique in 1933. By 1935, she was singing the title role of Mélisande in Amsterdam, which she subsequently reprised elsewhere in Europe and in San Francisco. Her Covent Garden debut was in 1937 as Micaëla, a role she also sang in Chicago, 1946. She remained with Opéra Comique until 1956, concurrently singing at the Paris Opéra, 1940–56. While specializing in French roles, she also established precedents as the first French Zerbinetta (1943) in Strauss' *Ariadne auf Naxos*, written in 1912, and the first French Anne Trulove (1953) in Igor Stravinsky's *The Rake's Progress*, written in 1951. Her other roles included Juliette, Gilda, Violetta, Pamina and Sophie. She created the roles in two of Darius Milhaud's operas, Creusa (*Medée*) and Manuela (*Bolivar*, 1950). Admired for her wide vocal range, flexibility and even production, she retired from her successful career in 1968, and died in Paris, October 18, 1976.

Another in the line of imperious grande-dame divas with a forty year career to her credit was Croatian-American soprano **ZINKA MILANOV** born May 17, 1906, in Zagreb. She studied at the Academy of Music with the legendary Wagnerian **Milka Ternina** (1863–1941), who had been the first Tosca at the Met and Covent Garden. As Zinka Kunc (pronounced Koonch), her family name, she made her debut in *Il trovatore* as Leonora, in Ljubljana, 1927, and became a principal soprano of the Zagreb Opera (1928–35). She also appeared at Prague's German Theatre. Called to Vienna to substitute for an ailing singer, she got to sing Aida with the great **Bruno Walter** (1876–1962) in the pit. He arranged an audition with **Toscanini**, who was looking for a soloist for the Verdi *Requiem* he was conducting at the 1936 Salzburg Festival. While in Vienna, Milanov was also a great success as a guest Tosca. She almost missed her chance for a Met tryout. Director Edward Johnson and Maestro Artur Bodansky were in Prague while she was singing out of town. On her return, as they were about to leave, they were persuaded to grant her a special audition, which resulted in a contract.[179] She made her Met debut in 1937 as Leonora, and sang mainly Verdi—including seventy-eight performances of *Aida*—until 1947, when she married General Lubomir Ilic, Ambassador to Scandinavia, Switzerland and Mexico for Yugoslav ruler, Tito. (She was married to Predrag Milanov from 1937–46.)

A broadcast of the last act of *Rigoletto* made her a household name. (Those were the days with plenty of classical offerings on radio.) She returned to the Met when **Rudolf Bing** took charge in 1950, and gave her April 16,

---

179. Since Zinka sang her roles in Croatian and German, the contract stipulated they had to be relearned in Italian for the Met. They were also relieved that she used her married name. It is interesting to note that Milanov started at a salary of $75 a week, and ten years later was only getting $300—which is why singers prefer concerts and recitals.

1966, farewell performance as Maddalena in *Andrea Chénier*, the night the old Met building at Broadway and 39th also saw its final opera. Having preserved her voice with a careful selection of roles, Milanov did not really want to retire, but Bing "suggested" it was time to give the next generation a chance. She turned to teaching, not because she enjoyed it but, as she said, "Because [there is] the hope that some of my knowledge can survive . . . me." She died in New York, May 30, 1989.

ELENA NIKOLAIDI was born in Izmir, Turkey, June 29, 1906. She trained at the Greek National Conservatory, and made her first appearances at Athens Lyric Theatre. In 1936 the contralto began a twelve year residence with the Wiener Staatsoper, while also appearing at Salzburg, Covent Garden, La Scala and Prague. She came to the U.S. in 1949, sang with Dmitri Mitropoulos and the New York Philharmonic in Carnegie Hall, and made her San Francisco debut in 1950 as Amneris. She had seventeen appearances at the Met before joining the voice faculty of Florida State University in 1960. In 1977, Carlisle Floyd invited her to teach at the Houston Opera Studio, where her students included **Denyce Graves**. She retired in 1994, and died in Santa Fe, New Mexico, November 14, 2002.

One of the greatest Wagnerian sopranos of the century, **BIRGIT NILSSON** was born on a Swedish farm in Västra Karups, May 17, 1918. Her vocal talents were discovered at a young age and she was one of two candidates chosen for acceptance into the Royal Academy of Music at Stockholm. She made her debut at Stockholm's Royal Opera House in 1946 as Agathe in *Der Freischütz*, later Lady Macbeth, Sieglinde, Donna Anna, Venus, Senta, Aida, and Tosca, which led to major roles in Wagner, Verdi, Puccini and Strauss operas, and international performances at La Scala, Covent Garden, Paris Opera, Munich Opera, Copenhagen Opera, Teatro Colón, Lyric Opera of Chicago and San Francisco. Her long-awaited Met debut came in December 1959 in her signature role, Isolde, and led to a lifelong affiliation. She sang 222 times at the Met in sixteen roles, making her finale at the October 1983 centennial gala. Her other long-term association was with the Vienna State Opera, where she sang 232 times. She also toured Japan and South Africa.

Her full-length recordings include *Tristan and Isolde*, *Die Walküre*, *Turandot* and as Brünnhilde in the definitive 1960s recording of the *Ring Cycle* with Sir Georg Solti and the Vienna Philharmonic. She was awarded Denmark's prestigious Leonie Sonning Prize for her contribution to the Arts, an honor also bestowed upon Leonard Bernstein and Laurence Olivier. Her own country conferred its highest title upon her, *Hovsangerska* (Swedish Court singer). She published *Mina minnesbilder* in Sweden (1977), with an English translation, *My Memoirs in Pictures* (1981). She retired in 1984, with her last magnificent public appearance, April 27, 1996, at the Metropolitan Opera Gala celebrating the twenty-fifth anniversary of maestro James Levine.

During her Met career, she had no Wagnerian rivals. She was a phenomenon, with a huge soprano range, and reveled in the high climaxes that tortured many who sang Brünnhilde and Isolde. Electra was perhaps her finest role, but the sheer power of her voice made her an ideal Turandot. Her reputation in opera lore came on December 28, 1959, when she sang *Tristan und Isolde* opposite three tenors. Her co-star, Karl Liebel, was ill as were his two covers, Ramon Vinay and Albert DaCosta. Rudolf Bing persuaded each to sing one act so the performance wouldn't have to be cancelled.

Her sense of humor among colleagues was recounted in Johanna Fiedler's book about the Met, *Molto Agitato*. Nilsson was unhappy with the gloomy lighting Herbert von Karajan wanted for his production of the *Ring*. To show her displeasure, she appeared for a 1967 rehearsal wearing a coal miner's helmet with searchlight and wings.

May 16, 1998, the Royal Opera of Stockholm mounted a concert in honor of her eightieth birthday where the title of professor was added to her many awards, in recognition for her contribution to the education of young singers via her Birgit Nilsson Scholarship.

She married Swedish restaurateur Bertil Niklasson in 1949.

With her death on Christmas Day 2005, King Carl XVI Gustaf said, "With Birgit Nilsson's passing, Sweden has lost one of its greatest artists.

The Metropolitan Opera Guild staged a Memorial Tribute, May 23, 2006, at Alice Tully Hall, with anecdotes by friends and colleagues, as well as photos and TV and film clips from her thirty-five year career.

JARMILA NOVOTNÁ was born in Prague, September 23, 1907, where, beginning in her teens, she studied with celebrated Czech soprano **Emmy Destinn**. At just eighteen, she made her debut at Prague Opera as Maenka in *The Bartered Bride* (1925). Six days later, she was *La traviata*, followed by the Queen of the Night, Rosina, and other roles in the course of her two year stay there. Her international exposure began in Verona, where she had her first confrontation with "the claque"—the notorious segment in Italian audiences who demand payment in order *not to boo* the leading singers. She had no money to give them, but her singing was so superb they applauded instead. From 1928, she sang in Berlin's Kroll Opera in the days of the grand maestros, **Alexander Zemlinsky** (1871–1942) and **Otto Klemperer** (1885–1973). 1931 was a banner year. She married Baron George Daubek, scion of one of Bohemia's most distinguished families, and gave an unforgettable performance as Helen of Troy in Offenbach's *La Belle Hélène*, with **Erich Wolfgang Korngold** (1897–1957) as conductor, and renowned Austrian director/producer **Max Reinhardt** (1873–1940), who had staged the premieres of *Der Rosenkavalier* and *Ariadne auf Naxos*.

Tall, slim and beautiful, she had already made one film in Prague in 1925. Now in Berlin, six months pregnant with her daughter, Jarmilina, her condition disguised with a bouffant peasant costume, she played Marie (Maenka) in a film version of *The Bartered Bride* (1933). She made several other pictures there, plus two in Vienna, another in Prague, and *The Last Waltz* in Paris. Movie mogul Louis B. Mayer offered her a five year contract at a thousand dollars a week, which she turned down. She was not about to give up her singing career. Ten years would elapse before she made her next screen appearance, this time in Hollywood with Montgomery Clift in *The Search* (1948), in which she gave a poignant performance in the non-singing part of a mother seeking her lost child in post-war Europe. Her last movie was *The Great Caruso* (1950) with Mario Lanza.

As a member of the Vienna State Opera (1933–38), Novotná was honored with the title Kammersängerin, and often partnered with divine tenor **Richard Tauber** (1892–1948). She gained distinction in what was to become one of her finest roles, Octavian. In 1934, operetta king **Franz Lehar** (1870–1948) wrote his first opera, *Giuditta*, for her. A great hit, it was repeated many times until 1938 when war clouds began to gather. In the course of her career, Novotná and **Toscanini** became great friends, performing together at the last Salzburg Festival before WWII. She was singing Tatyana in *Eugene Onegin* at the Vienna State Opera when, on the night of March 12, 1938, the Germans overran Austria in a matter of hours! With a valid excuse to leave—she was expecting again—she got out of Vienna and hied back to her country place, the castle of Liten in Bohemia. (Her husband, a gentleman farmer, and a great connoisseur of music, never interfered with his wife's career.) Fortunately, they decided to give birth in England, where George, Jr. was born in 1938.

Toscanini had invited Novotná to sing at the opera season he was conducting at the New York World's Fair, the site of which was outside the city in Flushing Meadows, right next to La Guardia airport. She arrived in New York, March 15, 1939, to be greeted by the news that Czechoslovakia, too, had been gobbled up by Hitler!

Honoring her contract, she was rehearsing *La traviata* while frantic with worry as to the whereabouts of her husband and children. Thankfully, Toscanini canceled the production because he simply could not conduct in a theater with planes constantly overhead. To make up for dragging Jarmila across the Atlantic, he swallowed his pride and personally took her to meet Edward Johnson at the Met, from which house he had parted on less than friendly terms back in 1915. Johnson signed her immediately, with a debut date of January 1940. She returned to Europe and was singing *The Marriage of Figaro* in Scheveningen under **Bruno Walter**, September 3, 1939, the day war was declared. Her husband, children, and their nanny were with her in Holland, and the Baron managed to book the last six ship passages to America, arriving at the end of September without a cent.

Because contracted Italian singers had had their passports confiscated in Europe, Jarmila was rushed to San Francisco where she made her American debut as Madama Butterfly (October 18, 1939), a role she would never sing at the Met because, after the Japanese bombing of Pearl Harbor, December 7, 1941, the opera was taken out of the repertory since the heroine was Japanese. (This was "intellectually" akin to Hitler not allowing any music of Jewish composers to be played in Germany.)

As scheduled, Novotná debuted at the Met as Mimi, January 5, 1940, with the handsome Swedish tenor **Jussi Björling** (1911–1960). (Actually, New Yorkers heard her for the first time in Carnegie Hall, December 2, 1939, with Toscanini and the NBC Symphony, as a soloist in Beethoven's Ninth.)

Soon, critical raves pinnacled Jarmila as the greatest singing actress of the period. Not on comfortable terms with Rudolf Bing after his 1950 accession as director, she remained on the Met roster only until 1951, but did return 1952 -1956. In her seventeen seasons, besides roles in Czech operas, she was noted for Pamina, Donna Elvira, Violetta and Mélisande, yet most frequently called on to sing the trouser roles of Octavian, Cherubino and Count Orlofsky. A superior linguist, she had also sung at La Scala and Teatro Colón, Buenos Aires.

The moment the war ended in Europe, May 1945, the Daubeks rushed back to Czechoslovakia to rebuild and refurnish their castle, which had been devastated by Russian troops. Adding to all the charity work she had done for Czech exiles in the U.S., finding them homes, jobs, etc., she sang a recital for the Red Cross in her own country in the presence of the new post-war President Eduard Beneš and his wife. When the Communists came into power in 1948, they also took over all private property. Once again, the 3,700 acre estate, the castle, all the businesses and properties, were confiscated. Jarmila could not even get her photograph albums returned to her!

Settling in New York, she took a respite from opera, appearing on Broadway in the part of a concert singer in *Sherlock Holmes* (1953) with Basil Rathbone, who was to immortalize *that* role in films, and *Helen Goes to Troy*, adapted by Korngold, who had gained fame as a film composer.

Amazingly, Novotná managed to keep her private life separate from her professional. Many socialites did not realize that the Baroness Daubek was the opera star Jarmila Novotná. Like Lucrezia Bori, she was the soul of tact, and never criticized her colleagues. In fact there were times she kept a production together by pouring her special brand of oil on troubled waters. In 1957, she and her husband moved to Vienna where the Volksoper saw her final stage performances. After the Baron's death in 1981, she moved back to New York to be near her children and became, once again, part of Metropolitan Opera functions. Close to eighty-seven, and still remarkably beautiful, she died in her Manhattan apartment, February 9, 1994.

Her wartime tape, *Songs of Lidice*, has been transferred to a CD. Ably accompanied at the piano by **Jan Masaryk** (1886–1948), diplomat/statesman and son of Czechoslovakia's first president,[180] the recording is a deeply moving tribute to a village ruthlessly destroyed by the Nazis in 1942. It embodies the lovely voice of a lovely person who loved her country.

Mezzo-soprano **NELL RANKIN** was born in Montgomery, Alabama, January 3, 1923. She began singing on radio at age four, studied voice with Jeanne Severin, a former European opera star living in Birmingham, and spent her summers teaching the children of Montgomery to swim to pay her way through the Birmingham Conservatory of Music.

In 1943, Helen Traubel came to Montgomery, and Nell went backstage to audition for Traubel's accompanist, Coenraad V. Bos (1875–1955), also the accompanist for Ernestine Schumann-Heink and Geraldine Farrar, and who taught at Juilliard 1934–52. His verdict was that her voice was good but not yet good enough, and offered further coaching if she came to New York. Her studies continued, also with Karin Branzell (1891–1974), and in 1947 she made her debut at New York's Town Hall.

No contract was offered from the Met, where conductor Max Rudolf said: "At your age, the Met is not for you. They would grind you up. Go to Europe!" She continued to study and to sing until 1948, when she went to Switzerland where the Zurich Opera Company was recruiting young singers. She auditioned for general director Hans Zimmermann, singing in perfect German. Her debut with them in 1949 was Ortrud in *Lohengrin*. She sang 126 performances in fifteen operas in her first season.

---

180. Tomáš Masaryk (1850–1937), who served from 1918–35, was called the architect of his country. He championed the young soprano, placing her likeness on a 100 koruna coin as a symbol of the fledgling republic. His son, Jan Masaryk, became an ambassador-in-exile, returning to his country after the war. In March 1948, one month after the Communists seized power, he purportedly "threw himself to his death" out of his office window . . .

In 1950, Rankin became the first American to win the Concours de Musique in Geneva. (Four years later Victoria de los Angeles would win, beginning *her* career.) A successful career followed, singing with the Basel Opera, Vienna Staatsoper, and La Scala, which engaged her as its leading mezzo for the 1951 season. The same year, she won the Metropolitan Opera Auditions of the Air and made her debut on November 22, as Amneris. She appeared regularly with them over the next twenty-four years, singing more leading roles than any other mezzo in the history of the Met, especially Amneris (thirty-nine times), Ortrud, Gutrune, Ulrica and Azucena.

In 1953, she gave a solo recital for the coronation of Queen Elizabeth II, and sang Carmen for her debut at Covent Garden. She debuted in the same role for San Francisco (1955), and appeared at the Teatro Colón, Buenos Aires, plus opera houses in Mexico, Naples and Vienna. She sang Carmen only twice at the Met, the role being "the property" of Risë Stevens.

The State of Alabama honored her in 1957 for her victory in the Concours de Musique and recognized her as the first "cultural ambassador of the state." In 1972, the board of the newly created American Arts Hall of Fame voted to make Rankin a member of its first class, inducting her into the Alabama Academy of Honor in 1976. That year she retired, teaching at the Academy of Vocal Arts in Philadelphia and running a private studio at Carnegie Hall, but soon realized her marriage was more important.

Nell died after a long illness—polycythemia vera, a rare bone marrow disease—in New York, January 13, 2005. She is survived by her husband, Dr. Hugh Davidson, an internist, she married in 1951.

French soprano **MADO ROBIN** was born near Tours, December 29, 1918, studied voice with Giuseppe Podestà, and made her operatic debut as Gilda at the Paris Opera in 1945. Besides the Opera Comique, she appeared in Belgium, San Francisco and Russia. She is best known for her Lakmé and Lucia. She also found appreciative audiences as a recitalist. Some memorable recordings preserve the memory of her clear high range. She died in Paris, December 10, 1960.

LEONIE RYSANEK, born in Vienna, November 14, 1926, studied at the Vienna Academy, making her debut in Innsbruck in 1949 as Agathe in *Der Freischütz*, later singing at Saarbrücken where her roles included Arabella, Donna Anna, and Senta. After a triumphant debut at the 1951 Bayreuth Festival, she joined the Staatsoper in Munich. There, she performed the title roles of *Der Liebe der Danaë*, *Die ägyptische Helena*, *Salome*, *Lady Macbeth*, *Turandot*, *Tosca*, *Santuzza* and *Medea*. Her 1953 Covent Garden debut was as Danaë, her American debut followed in San Francisco (1956) and Met audiences first heard her in 1959 as Lady Macbeth, when she replaced **Maria Callas**. In 1986, she celebrated the thirtieth anniversary of her American debut by singing Kostelnicka at San Francisco and Ortrud at the Met. She sang Kabanicha (*Kát'a Kabanová*) in Los Angeles (1988), Herodias (*Salome*) at Stuttgart (1989), and Klytemnestra at Geneva (1990). She retired in 1996 with a performance of Tchaikovsky's *Queen of Spades* at the Met, January 2—for which she received an unprecedented forty-minute ovation—and again, Klytemnestra in Richard Strauss' *Elektra* in Salzburg in August, a fitting climax to a brilliant career spanning forty-seven years!

Three years after the death of Lotte Lehmann, the Vienna State Opera chose Rysanek in 1979 to be the second recipient of the cherished ring, as the best soprano singing German repertoire at VSO. In later life, Leonie began the tradition of naming her own ring successor. She chose her dear friend and colleague, **Hildegard Behrens**.

Rysanek died in Vienna, March 1998.

Brazilian soprano **BIDÚ SAYÃO** (Balduina de Oliveira Sayão) was born May 11, 1902, in Rio de Janeiro. Her brother was sixteen years older, and her father died when she was four. Since her mother would not hear of her becoming an actress, she decided on a singing career. Only the best teacher would do, who happened to be Rumanian soprano Elena Teodorini who had retired to Rio. After three years, Madame decided to return to her homeland, and Bidu followed her. In Bucharest, she got to sing before Queen Marie for the visit of Japan's Crown Prince Hirohito. The Queen, a great patroness of music, sent Sayão to Vichy where she was accepted by **Jean de Reszke** (1850–1925), one of the greatest tenors of all time, whose sister Josephine was a magnificent soprano, and brother Edouard, an outstanding basso. Bidu studied every day with him for the last two years of his life. After a successful start on the concert stage, her mother permitted her to pursue an operatic career. She studied in Rome with Emma Carelli, who had been married to opera manager Walter Mocchi, who later became Bidú's husband from 1927–1934.

Her 1926 operatic debut as Rosina in *The Barber of Seville* was at the Teatro Municipal in Rio. Carelli died in a tragic car accident in 1928, but by that time Sayão's career was launched. Rome had become her home base. She was chosen to sing at the January 1930 marriage for Crown Prince Umberto and Princess Marie José, daughter of the King of the Belgians.

Italian baritone **Giuseppi Danise** (1883–1963), with whom she had often sung in South America, had retired in 1935 and become a sought-after teacher. He took Bidu in hand and was responsible for her American career, bringing her to New York in 1936 just as Toscanini was looking for the right voice to sing Debussy's cantata *La demoiselle élue*. Winning the audition, she made her debut at Carnegie Hall. Lucrezia Bori had retired, and the Met was looking for someone to take over her roles. Sayo's debut there in February 1937, as Manon, led to a happy association that lasted until 1952. On her retirement, a month before her fiftieth birthday, she said, "I am proud, and I did not wait until I was asked to leave." In all, she sang more than 200 performances of twelve different roles at the Met. Her crystal clear voice cut like a diamond across the orchestra in her unmatched interpretations of Juliette, Mélisande, Violetta, Gilda, Mimi, Adina, Rosina, Norina, Zerlina, Susanna, Mimi, Violetta and Lakmé. She was equally at home at San Francisco Opera, where her last performance was, appropriately, *La demoiselle élue*, this time with **André Cluytens** (1905–1967) conducting. Counting concerts and recitals, at her 1958 retirement her entire career had spanned thirty years.

Recipient of many honors from European royalty, Sayão was presented the Palmes Académiques by the French government and, in 1972, was made a Commandante by the Brazilian government. She married Danise in 1947. He died in 1963 at the age of eighty. Her mother died three years later. After her husband's death she divided her time between the Salisbury Hotel in Manhattan and her home in Lincolnville, Maine, both filled with wonderful and unique memories. She died on March 12, 1999, in a hospital in Rockport, Maine.

German soprano **ELISABETH SCHWARZKOPF**, born in Jarotschin, near Posen, Germany, December 9, 1915, studied at the Berlin Hochschule für Musik, making her debut as a Flower Maiden in *Parsifal* in 1938 at the Berlin State Opera, then appearing in more important roles by 1941. Her debut as a lieder artist came in Vienna in 1942. The same year, she debuted at the State Opera, and remained there until the Nazis closed the house in 1944. Having registered as a member of the Nazi party in 1940, after the war she had to be cleared by the Allies before she was permitted to rejoin the VSO in 1946 and tour with them to London to appear at Covent Garden. She subsequently sang there until 1951, when she began her international career.

In 1946, she auditioned for Walter Legge, a recording executive, who signed her to an exclusive contract with EMI. They began a close partnership, with Legge acting as her manager. They were married, October 19, 1953, the year she became a naturalized British subject.

Her first Salzburg Festival was 1947, singing there until 1964. She was a regular at La Scala, 1948–63. **Wilhelm Furtwängler** (1886–1954) invited her to sing his performance of Beethoven's 9th at the reopening of Bayreuth in 1951, the same year she created the role of Anne Trulove in Stravinsky's *The Rake's Progress* in Venice. 1953 marked her first recital at Carnegie Hall. Her American operatic debut was as the Marschallin (her most famous role), in 1955 at SFO, where she sang until 1964. Her Met debut in the same role did not come until 1964. She continued with the Met until 1966. Her successful Mozart and Strauss roles included Donna Elvira, the Countess (*Marriage of Figaro*), the Marschallin, Fiordiligi, and Countess Madeline (*Capriccio*). She also excelled in Viennese operetta and was incomparable as a lieder interpreter.

Her last operatic performance was as the Marschallin, December 31, 1971, in Brussels, with a final U.S. tour in 1975. Her husband died March 20, 1979, and she edited his memoir, *On and Off the Record* (1982). In retirement in Zurich, Schwarzkopf taught and gave masterclasses. On New Year's Day, 1992, she was created a Dame

Commander of the Most Excellent Order of the British Empire (DBE) by Queen Elizabeth II. She died peacefully at her home in Schruns, Austria, July 27, 2006, at age ninety.

ELEANOR STEBER, born July 17, 1914, in Wheeling, West Virginia, began voice studies with her mother, and then at the New England Conservatory where she received her BM (1938). In 1940, she won the Metropolitan Opera Auditions of the Air and made her debut as Sophie in *Der Rosenkavalier* that December, remaining with the Met until 1962 for 286 performances in New York and 118 times on tour. Her best known roles include Donna Anna, Pamina, the Countess (*The Marriage of Figaro*), Violetta, Desdemona, Marguerite, Manon, Mimi, and Tosca. She also sang Wagner, Marie in Berg's *Wozzeck*, the title role in the premiere of Samuel Barber's *Vanessa* (1958), and appeared at most major summer festivals including Edinburgh, Bayreuth and Vienna. After she left the stage, Steber taught at the Cleveland Institute of Music (1963–71), Juilliard and the New England Conservatory, both from 1971, and the American Institute of Music Studies in Graz, Austria (1978–80, 1988). She established the Eleanor Steber Musical Foundation in 1975 to help young singers. Much mourned, she died in Langhorne, Pennsylvania, October 3, 1990.

Like Dorothy Kirsten, mezzo **GLADYS SWARTHOUT** was an American who performed only in her own country. She came into the world on Christmas Day, 1900, in Deepwater, Missouri. After singing in a church choir from age twelve, she studied at the Bush Conservatory in Chicago, debuted in a minor part with Chicago Civic Opera in 1924, then made regular appearances with the Ravinia Opera Company. November 15, 1929 marked her Met debut as *La Cieca*. She continued performing there until 1945. Her finest roles were Carmen, Norma, Lakmé and Mignon. Small and slim, she also inherited the traditional trouser parts. In 1932, she married singer Frank Chapman. His own career going nowhere, he took over the management of his wife's and, including her recitals, made her one of the highest paid singers in America. As beautiful as she was talented, Paramount brought her to Hollywood in the 1930s to provide competition to Columbia's **Grace Moore** and MGM's **Jeanette MacDonald**. She made five films: *Rose of the Rancho, Give Us This Night* (1936); *Champagne Waltz* (1937); *Romance in the Dark* (1938); and *Ambush* (1939). This exposure elicited offers from abroad, but she preferred to stay home. Plagued with a heart condition throughout her life from having had rheumatic fever as a child, by limiting her appearances and taking four months' rest each year—she bought a villa in Italy in 1954—Swarthout managed to sustain a thirty year career. She belonged to the operatic elite of the era, Lucrezia Bori, Lawrence Tibbett, Grace Moore, Lily Pons and Jarmila Novotná, who came later.

When her husband died in 1969, Swarthout was lost. He had molded her life completely. In an interview at the time, she stated simply that life without him no longer held any meaning, and that the best was all behind her. In a classic case of a broken heart (now coldly and clinically called "co-dependence"), she succumbed a few months later on July 7, at her villa near Florence. Her autobiography, *Come Soon, Tomorrow* was published in New York, 1945.

Celebrated Italian soprano **RENATA TEBALDI** was born February 1, 1922, in Pesaro, Rossini's home town. She began lessons on piano, and when her teacher recognized vocal potential she enrolled at the Arrigo Boito Conservatory in Parma. The following year she returned to Pesaro for study at the Rossini Conservatory. She made her operatic debut in Rovigo as Elena in *Mefistofele* in 1944. During the next few years, war-torn Italy was not fertile ground for the arts. In 1946, after appearing in Trieste, word got around that a wonderful new voice had appeared, and she was chosen by **Toscanini** for the reopening concert of La Scala, restored from bomb damage during WWII. She continued to be associated with the house, 1949–55, and 1959–60. In 1950, she sang Desdemona at Covent Garden with the La Scala touring company, debuting as Aida in San Francisco, September 26 the same year. She was at SFO for only four seasons, where she sang her first Amelia in *Simon Boccanegra* in 1965, and her first Countess in *Le Nozze di Figaro*—the only time she sang a Mozart role in the U.S. She went on to perform in Naples, London, Paris, Rome, Vienna, Buenos Aires, Chicago and New York.

In 1955, she made her Met debut as Desdemona, beginning a relationship with the house that lasted until 1973, with 267 performances devoted to fourteen operas. Returning to San Francisco for *Tosca* in 1955, Tebaldi created an SFO legend by doing something no other singer had done in the history of the company: she gave in to public demand and repeated an aria in the middle of the performance—a custom common in the 19th century.

Her repertoire was mostly Italian, with Violetta, Tosca, Mimi and Butterfly her notable roles. There was also some Wagner: Elisabeth (*Tannhäuser*), Elsa (*Lohengrin*), and Eva (*Meistersinger*), sung only in Italian at Italian theaters. All attempts to get her to sing Wagner in the U.S. failed. Although loyal fans fostered a rivalry between her and **Maria Callas**, she wanted no part of it, and refused to sing *Norma* because she felt the role belonged to the dramatic soprano.

She recorded most major Verdi and Puccini works, among many others.

Renata retired from opera in 1973, but continued concertizing three more years. In May 1974, she returned to Milan for the first time in fourteen years with a concert in fine voice at Piccola Scala. There were also two Russian tours, 1975 and 1976.

Looking back on a brilliant career, she was still shocked by the death onstage, March 4, 1960, of renowned baritone **Leonard Warren** during their performance of *Don Carlo*.

Much honored, Tebaldi died in San Marino, December 19, 2004.

Mezzo-soprano **JENNIE TOUREL**, born in Vitebsk, Russia, June 22, 1900, studied flute and piano before beginning her formal voice training with **Anna El-Tour**. She changed her own name, Davidovich, to an inverted version of her teacher's. After her debut in Paris at the Opera Russe in 1931, she was at the Opéra-Comique 1933–39, and sang Mignon at the Met in 1937. She managed to get out of France to Portugal in 1940 before the Germans invaded, and eventually emigrated to America during World War II. She was on the Met roster between 1943 and 1947, and became a U.S. citizen in 1946. Besides roles such as Cherubino, Rosina and Carmen, in 1951, in Venice, she created the role of Baba the Turk in Stravinsky's *The Rake's Progress*. In later years she gave concerts and recitals, utilizing her excellent French repertoire. She also taught at Juilliard and Aspen. She died in New York, November 23, 1973.

Austrian soprano of Bulgarian birth, **LJUBA WELITSCH** was born July 10, 1913, studied violin as a child and attended the Sofia Conservatory and University of Sofia. She studied voice in Vienna, making her debut at the Sofia Opera (1936). She sang in Graz (1937–40), Hamburg (1942–43), and Munich (1943–46) before joining the Vienna State Opera. She had sung there in 1944, for the eightieth birthday celebration of Richard Strauss, as Salome, which became her signature role.[181] With the Vienna SO, she debuted in London as Donna Anna (1947) and repeated the role at the Glyndebourne Festival (1948). Her Met debut as Salome was in 1949, staying with the company until 1952. Her other roles were Aida, Musetta, Minnie, Rosalinde, Jenůfa and Tosca. Ill health and improper care of her voice cut her career short, but she did appear in character parts in Vienna. She died there, September 2, 1996.

Living Legends

LICIA ALBANESE, born July 22, 1909, in Bari, Italy, studied in Milan and made a dramatic debut at the Teatro Lirico there in 1934 as Cio-Cio-San in *Madama Butterfly*, stepping in for a soprano who had been taken ill in the first act. Her 1935 official operatic debut, in the same role, in Parma, was such a success she was snapped up by La Scala and subsequently performed worldwide, 115 times in twenty-seven roles including Mimi, Marguerite, Violetta, Desdemona and Tosca. Her Met debut came February 9, 1940, in her favorite, Cio-Cio-San, a role she would sing seventy-two times. In her twenty-six years of association with the house, she was in 286 performances.

Licia married Italian-American businessman Joseph Gimma in 1945. Her final Met performance was April 16, 1966. Her last public appearances were an aria recital at Carnegie Hall, February 22, 1970, and at a benefit for the

---

181. She considered Catherine Malfitano her successor in the role.

Puccini Foundation at Town Hall, February 5, 1975. Reflecting her stature were the many honors she received, including Italy's Order of Merit, and the Lady Grand Cross of the Equestrian Order of the Holy Sepulchre awarded her by Pope Pius XI.

ROSE BAMPTON, born November 28, 1908, in Lakewood, near Cleveland, Ohio, studied at Curtis, taking her traditional academics at Drake University in Iowa, where she graduated with a Doctor of Fine Arts degree. Singing with the Philadelphia Orchestra from 1929–32, she began as a contralto, became a mezzo, then added the soprano range, making her one of the few divas to have sung both Amneris (Covent Garden, 1937) and Aida. Her Met debut in 1932, in *La Gioconda* as Laura, began regular appearances there, including Wagner roles, until 1945. From 1942–48, she performed annually at Buenos Aires' Teatro Colón, returning to the Met 1947–50. She was married in 1937 to Canadian conductor Wilfred Pelletier (1896–1982), who founded the Metropolitan Opera Auditions of the Air in 1936.

RÉGINE CRESPIN, born February 23, 1927, in Marseilles, began studying pharmacology before she switched to voice in Paris. Her 1950 debut as Elsa at the Mulhouse Festival led to appearances at Paris Opera and the building of a strong Wagnerian repertoire. For the next six years her career was advanced in the provinces, singing German and Italian roles in French. At the request of producer/designer **Wieland Wagner** (1917–66), the composer's grandson, she sang Kundry in *Parsifal* at Bayreuth from 1958–60. Conductor **Herbert von Karajan** (1908–89) had her sing Brünnhilde at the 1967 Easter Festival in Salzburg, a role she repeated nine times—three at the Met. First as a soprano, later a mezzo, Crespin performed at La Scala, Covent Garden and other great European houses, as well as Boston, San Francisco and South America. Her Met debut in 1962, in the role of the Marschallin, was directed by no less than **Lotte Lehmann**! Crespin remained with the Met until her 1987 retirement. Beginning in 1975, she sang mezzo roles, slimming down thirty pounds to become a sultry, voluptuous, very Parisian Carmen. Her last role was Madame De Croissy in *Dialogues of the Carmelites*, a fitting climax to an illustrious career since she created the role of the New Prioress at the opera's Paris premiere, June 21, 1957.

Her best recordings are Berlioz' *Les Nuits d'Été*, Ravel's *Shéhérazade*, a two-disc set of French works, *Prima Donna in Paris*, and a 1968 Decca recording, with George Solti conducting, as the Marschallin. In the mid-1990s, she was *not* offered the directorship of the Paris Opéra School, which caused her to write in her autobiography *La Vie et l'Amour d'une Femme* (published in the U.S. as *On Stage, Off Stage*), "I have arrived at the disappointing conclusion that, in my country, my name doesn't mean very much." At the turn of the 21st century, living in Paris, she was still active, giving master classes and teaching sessions, including a long association with SFO's Merola program. She was a recipient of the first Opera News Award For Distinguished Service, November 20, 2005.

PHYLLIS CURTIN was born in Clarksburg, West Virginia, December 3, 1921. She studied violin and sang in the school glee club. At Wellesley College (BA, International Relations, 1943), she took singing lessons in addition to her overloaded class schedule. After graduation she stayed in Boston, singing new music and studying with Boris Goldovsky at the New England Conservatory and Tanglewood.

She debuted with the New England Opera Theater in Boston (1946) as Lisa in *The Queen of Spades*. Her recital debut was at New York's Town Hall, 1950, and at NYCO, 1953, in Gottfried von Einem's *The Trial*. She stayed with the company until 1960. Other appearances were at Teatro Colón, Buenos Aires (1959), Glyndebourne Festival (1959), Vienna State Opera (1960–61), and La Scala (1962). Her Met debut was as Fiordiligi (1961), returning for the 1966–70 and 1972–73 seasons. Her concert and recital career included worldwide appearances until her retirement in 1984.

Her most rewarding and enduring relationship was with Carlisle Floyd, for whom she sang the world premieres of *Wuthering Heights*, *The Passion of Jonathan Wade*, *The Flower and the Hawk*, and the classic opera, *Susannah*, which she and Mack Harrell premiered in Tallahassee, 1955. At NYCO, Norman Treigle sang Olin Blitch, becoming the definitive performer of the role.

Curtis taught at Aspen, Tanglewood, Yale (1974–83), and Boston University (1983–), where she retired as Dean of the School of Arts in 1992, but continued to teach.

Known for her Mozart and Richard Strauss roles, **LISA DELLA CASA**, born February 2, 1919, in Burgdorf, Switzerland, began vocal studies at the age of fifteen in Zurich and made her opera debut in 1941 as Cio-Cio-San. From 1943–50, she was a member of the Zurich City Theater. 1947 marked her Salzburg Festival debut as Zdenka, followed by the Countess in *The Marriage of Figaro* at the 1951 Glyndebourne Festival. She also sang at Covent Garden in 1953 and 1965, performing her signature role as Richard Strauss' Arabella. While a leading member of the Vienna State Opera (1952–74), she made her Met debut as the Countess in 1953, remaining a regular there until 1968. She sang the Marschallin at the 1960 opening of the new Salzburg Festival House. Culminating a prominent international career, which included many fine recordings, she retired in 1974.

Mezzo **ROSALIND ELIAS**, born March 13, 1929, in Lowell, Massachusetts, studied at the New England Conservatory and Accademia di Santa Cecilia in Rome. After attending the Berkshire Music Center (Tanglewood), she spent four years with the New England Opera Company (1948–52). Her Met debut was in 1954 as one of the Valkyries. Her record ended with thirty seasons, forty-nine roles and 640 performances—316 at the original opera house, which (*incredibly*) was torn down instead of being preserved—158 at Lincoln Center and 166 elsewhere with the company. She sang Fenena in the Met premiere of *Nabucco*, October 24, 1960, and created roles in two Barber operas—Erika in *Vanessa* (1958) and Charmian in *Antony and Cleopatra*, which marked the 1966 opening of Lincoln Center. Following a debut with the Scottish Opera singing Rossini's *Cenerentola* in 1970, she turned to directing several operas in the U.S. in the 1980s, including *Carmen*. She remained active as a singer and stage director. Her recordings include *La Gioconda, La Forza del destino, Il trovatore, Falstaff, Madama Butterfly, Rigoletto* and *The Flying Dutchman*.

Christa Ludwig

Named 1994 "Musician of the Year" by *Musical America*, after celebrating her retirement the year before, mezzo soprano **CHRISTA LUDWIG**, born March 16, 1924, in Berlin, remains one of opera's most charismatic personalities. Her father, tenor Anton Ludwig, who also managed the opera house in Aachen, and her mother, mezzo-soprano Eugenie Besalla, one of **Herbert von Karajan**'s principal dramatic sopranos, avidly supported their daughter's career. Christa studied with her mother, who remained her teacher and artistic counselor for her entire career, and Felice Hüni-Mihaczek before attending the Hochschule für Musik in Frankfurt, where she made her debut in 1946 as Orlofsky in *Die Fledermaus*. She remained in Frankfurt until 1952, then widened her horizons debuting in 1954 at Salzburg as Cherubino, where she sang until 1981. She joined the Vienna Staatsoper in 1955, remaining there over thirty years. Her American debut came in 1959 as Dorabella in Chicago, followed by her Met debut as Cherubino. She sang with the latter until 1990, with impressive performances of Wagner and Strauss, as well as fine interpretations of Italian operas. She went on to Covent Garden, La Scala, Paris, San Francisco, Hamburg and Munich. Though born a mezzo, many of her great successes were in soprano roles.

Three conductors acted as mentors and friends: **Karl Böhm**, whom she credits with teaching her to be truthful to note-timing; **Herbert von Karajan**, for the beauty of phrasing; and **Leonard Bernstein**, for the depth of meaning of the music. With their careful guidance, her forty-five-year career on the great stages of the world was extremely successful, with critics extolling not only her operatic roles, but the excellence of her lieder concerts. With both Bernstein and von Karajan, she re-recorded Mahler's *Das Lied von der Erde*, first recorded when she was only 26 with **Otto Klemperer** and the Austrian tenor **Fritz Wunderlich** (1930–66). She was married from 1957 to 1970 to Austrian baritone **Walter Berry** (1929–2000) with whom she has a son, Wolfgang Marc Berry. They often sang together even after their divorce. She later married Paul-Émile Deiber, a leading actor with the Comédie-Française, who was the director of her 1971 *Werther* performance in New York.

Since Ludwig's retirement, they now live in Nice. In her enormous cache of honors and awards are Kammersängerin of Austria (1962), the Cross of Merit, First Class of the Republic of Austria (1969), the Golden

Ring (1988), honorary member of the Vienna State Opera (1981), the Silver Rose from that all-male bastion, the Vienna Philharmonic, France's two top awards, Chevalier du Legion d'Honneur and L'Ordre des Arts et des Lettres—both in 1989—and the Medaille de Ville Paris in 1993, the same year Japan presented her with the Shibuya Prize. 1994 brought the Echo Recording Prize, the Berlin Bär, the von Karajan Prize, and the Ehrenmitglied (honorary fellow) of the Vienna Philharmonic in 1995. Her year of farewell appearances began in Paris, February 19, 1993, followed by a March Carnegie Hall recital, a Met finale as Fricka in *Die Walküre* in April, and recitals in Vienna, her adoptive home. In the fall of 1999, she was in New York to promote her autobiography, *In My Own Voice*, published in the U.S., an impressive documentary of the hard times growing up in war-torn Germany, and the high times of a worldwide career.

Nan Merriman

Mezzo-soprano **NAN** (Katherine-Ann) **MERRIMAN**, born April 28, 1920 in Pittsburgh, studied in Los Angeles with **Lotte Lehmann**. In 1940, Merriman took part in a tour together with Laurence Olivier and Vivien Leigh: during set changes of *Romeo and Juliet*, she sang Palestrina and Purcell arias. She had been making regular concert appearances for five years before she made her operatic debut as La Cieca (*La Gioconda*) at Cincinnati Summer Opera in 1942. In 1943, she "won" fifteen minutes of NBC air time—first prize in the National Federation of Music Clubs. Arturo Toscanini heard the broadcast and invited her to sing with him and the NBC Symphony on the radio and make several recordings.

Soon after World War II, Merriman went to Europe where much of her career was to be centered. She was an admired Dorabella (*Cosi fan tutte*) at Aix-en-Provence in 1953, '55 and '59, the Piccola Scala (1955–56) and Glyndebourne (1956). She appeared as Baba the Turk in the British premiere of Stravinsky's *The Rake's Progress*, Edinburgh (1953) and Laura in Dargomizhsky's *The Stone Guest* (1958). Throughout the 1950s she also appeared at many of the leading European opera houses, including Vienna, Milan, Rome and Paris. Other notable roles were Maddalena (*Rigoletto*), Emilia (*Othello*), and Meg (*Falstaff*). She was not engaged at the Met—light voices had no chance there. She was much admired in the Netherlands, where she became a particular favorite singer in recitals and on the concert platform.

Nan married and retired completely from the stage in April 1965. Her husband was an accomplished oratorio singer, who sang the tenor part in the *St. Matthew Passion* under Anthon van der Horst. His talents were discovered relatively late and he took lessons at the Maastricht Conservatory. He was widowed in the early sixties and father of ten children. She decided to give up her career in order to be with him and take care of his family. Unfortunately, her husband died of a stroke in 1966. She stayed in the Netherlands taking responsibility for the children. When they reached adulthood, she moved to Los Angeles in 1973 and never returned to Europe.

PATRICE MUNSEL, born May 14, 1925 in Spokane, Washington, studied in New York and won a Met audition, making a successful debut there—their youngest singer at the time—December 4, 1943, as Philine in Ambrose Thomas' *Mignon*. She remained on their roster until 1958, also making European tours. Her best roles were Lucia, Violetta, Gilda, Rosina and Lakmé. She played Nellie Melba in the 1953 bio-film, *Melba*, and was popular in operetta and Broadway musicals.

Italian soprano **MAGDA OLIVERO** was born March 25, 1912, in Saluzzo, near Turin. She studied at Turin Conservatory and made her debut in *Gianni Schicchi* in that city in 1933, after which she sang throughout Italy. [At the time of her debut, the majority of the forty-four composers whose operas she sang over her fifty-year career were still alive.] In 1938, she sang with Beniamino Gigli in Francesco Cilea's *Adriana Lecouvreur*, having been coached by the composer for the part. It was to become her signature role. She married in 1941 and retired from the stage until 1951, when Cilea asked her to sing Adriana Lecouvreur. Her career took off again, appearing at La Scala, Paris and London, and made her U.S. debut (1967) at Dallas in Cherubini's *Medea*. In 1975, at age sixty-three, she made her Met debut as Tosca. Two years later she appeared in recital at Carnegie Hall. Her last stage appearance was in Verona, 1981. Her dynamic characterizations were internationally acclaimed in roles such as Violetta, Fedora, Liù, Suor Angelica and Minnie. She has been called "the last *verismo* (realism) soprano."

Throughout her career, her voice exhibited the *verismo* qualities of the fragile young girl with a slender shining tone, and the tempestuous mature woman with a large dark voice.

Her final recording of Adriana, at age eighty-three, was for the Italian label Bongiovanni (1993). She called it "her last will and testament."

LEONTYNE PRICE was born in Laurel, Mississippi, February 10, 1927. (See Black Heritage.)

REGINA RESNIK, born in New York, August 30, 1922, started out as a soprano, beginning her professional career in 1942. In 1944, she won the Metropolitan Opera audition contest and made her debut as Leonora in *Il trovatore*, December 6 of that year, replacing **Zinka Milanov**. Within the next ten days she sang Santuzza, Aida, and a Sunday Night Concert, all for an $86–dollar-a-week contract. She continued there, while participating in Bayreuth Summer Festivals, until 1954, when she took a leave of absence for further study, returning in 1955 as a mezzo. She enjoyed diva status in her European career during the '50s and '60s, but remained at the Met, which she considered her artistic home, until 1971, performing such roles as Carmen, Lucretia, Mistress Quickly and Klytemnestra. Also associated with NYCO, she sang her first Carmen there in 1948, and in 1990 was Madame Armfelt in *A Little Night Music*. Her Covent Garden debut in 1957, as Carmen, began a fifteen-year relationship with that house. In 1971, she made a career shift to opera producer, with *Carmen* in Hamburg, *Elektra* in Venice and *Falstaff* in Warsaw among her credits. She returned to the Met in 1983 to sing in a gala performance.

Living in Venice, in 2004 she celebrated the sixtieth anniversary of her Met debut.

German soprano **ANNELIESE ROTHENBERGER**, born June 19, 1924 in Mannheim, made her debut in Koblenz, 1943. A member of the Hamburg State Opera at two different periods, 1946–57 and 1958–73, she joined the Vienna State Opera in 1958, meanwhile singing in Europe's major houses. Her Met debut was in 1960 as Zdenka in Richard Strauss' *Arabella*. A versatile singer, she was as equally skilled at interpreting the works of Mozart and Verdi as the challenging Marie in Alban Berg's avant-garde *Wozzeck*, and the even more demanding title role in his *Lulu*. She published her autobiography, *Melodie meines Lebens* (The Melody of My Life) in Munich, 1972.

Beverly Sills

At the height of her operatic career, **BEVERLY SILLS** was universally acclaimed not only for her wonderful voice and brilliant virtuosity—a November 1971 *TIME* magazine feature hailed her "America's Queen of Opera"—but also for her intellectualism, which in her fifties, sixties and seventies was channeled into her considerable administrative gifts, first as general director of New York City Opera, 1980–90, which she rescued from the brink of bankruptcy, then as the first woman chair of Lincoln Center, July 1994–May 2002. At age seventy-three, in 2003, she became chairwoman of the Metropolitan Opera, where circumstances did not see her upon their stage until she was forty-five.

The road to her present lofty position began in Brooklyn, New York, May 25, 1929, as Belle Miriam Silverman. Her father was from Romania and sold insurance. Her mother was from Russia and loved music. Three years later the little girl won a radio prize as "Bubbles"—which has remained her nickname. At four, she was part of a children's Saturday morning program. At seven, she sang in a movie and started formal studies with soprano/pedagogue **Estelle Liebling** (1880–1970), with whom she remained associated for the rest of that lady's life. Meanwhile, she appeared on early television. Her operatic debut in 1947, as Frasquita in *Carmen* with Philadelphia Civic Opera, was followed by touring with other companies, including an appearance with SFO (1953). For years she had tried to get into New York City Opera. Finally, in 1955, she was hired and soon became one of its most valuable members. She made her debut, October 29, 1955, as Rosalinde in Johann Strauss' *Die Fledermaus*, drawing raves from the critics. In 1958, singing the title role in the premiere of *The Ballad of Baby Doe*, fully established her as a leading soprano. The Met beckoned with a first performance as Donna Anna at the outdoor Lewisohn Stadium in a 1966 summer production of *Don Giovanni*. Meanwhile, with her legendary success in the coloratura role of Cleopatra in Handel's *Gulio Cesare*—also in 1966—she began to explore *bel canto* in depth and expanded her repertoire to more than seventy operas, including *Louise, Manon, Roberto Devereux, Anna Bolena,*

Maria Stuarda, La traviata, I Puritani, Lucia de Lammermoor, Abduction from the Seraglio, Don Pasquale, Thaïs, Il barbiere di Siviglia, Le coq d'or and *Baby Doe*. Offers from Europe led to the challenging role of the Queen of the Night (*Magic Flute*) in Vienna (1967), Pamira (*The Siege of Corinth*) at La Scala (1969), Covent Garden with Lucia (1970), and back to the U.S. at Boston (1971). The formal treading of Met boards at Lincoln Center came in 1975 as Pamira—Rossini roles having become one of her fortes—followed by more than 100 performances until her 1979 retirement from the stage.

After appearing in virtually all the world's leading opera houses, including La Scala, Covent Garden, Berlin Opera, Vienna State Opera, La Fenice, Teatro Colón and San Carlo in Naples, plus all notable American venues, Sills formally retired from singing in 1980 when she accepted the position as general director of the New York City Opera.

During her ten-year tenure as general director of NYCO, she promoted American singers and widened the operatic repertoire. Under her leadership, many young singers were discovered and went on to international careers. The most difficult moments were telling former colleagues they would not be re-engaged because their voices were past their prime.

Sills launched City Opera's first summer season, and introduced American audiences to the use of *surtitles*—singer synchronized English translations on a screen above the stage—for all foreign language productions, an innovation now taken for granted at just about all major houses. From 1989–90, she served as president of the NYCO Board. She also produced TV shows dealing with opera and concert singing on her weekly "Lifestyles" show for NBC-TV, *Live from Lincoln Center, Gala of Stars, In Performance at the White House*, CBS-TV's *Young Peoples Concerts* and the PBS series, *Skyline with Beverly Sills*. She authored three best-selling autobiographies, *Bubbles: A Self-Portrait* (1976), *Bubbles—An Encore* (1982) and *Beverly—An Autobiography* (1987), with Lawrence Linderman. A prolific recording artist, Sills has eighteen full-length operas and many solo recital discs to her credit.

When San Francisco Opera staged Walter Moore's *The Ballad of Baby Doe* in 2000, it brought memories of the 1958 premiere at City Opera. After 102 sopranos had been rejected for the elfin heroine, Beverly, then a staff soprano at City Opera, felt she would be reject #103 given her height and voluptuous figure. But, after hearing her, Moore awarded her the role on the spot. A recording, made in June 1959, with Sills, Walter Cassel, and **Frances Bible** was finally released by PolyGram in 1999, giving opera lovers the opportunity to marvel at Beverly in her prime. Donizetti's *The Three Queens*, a 2001 Deutsche Grammophon (DG) release, is a seven-disc set which includes *Anna Bolena, Maria Stuarda* and *Roberto Devereux* with her in each title role.

Sills' honors include the Presidential Medal of Freedom, Heinz Award in the Arts and Humanities, New York City Handel Medallion and Kennedy Center Honors, plus honorary doctorates from Harvard, NYU and the California Institute of the Arts. She has served on the boards of the Met Association, Lincoln Center Theater, Time Warner Inc., American Express, and in the medical field, Human Genome Sciences, Multiple Sclerosis Society and Hospital for Special Surgery. She is the retired national chairman of the March of Dimes Birth Defects Foundation for which, from 1971, she helped raise over $70,000,000.

Beverly wed Peter Buckley Greenough, whose grandfather founded the *Cleveland Plain Dealer*, on November 17, 1956. Upon her marriage, she "inherited" a twenty-five room French chateau on Lake Erie and three small daughters—one mentally handicapped—from her husband's previous marriage. She took a hiatus from her career to spend time with the children, returning in January 1964 to sing the Queen of the Night. Two children were born to them. Meredith, called Muffy, in 1959, who at age two was discovered to be profoundly deaf, and Peter Jr., called Bucky, in 1961, who was found to be deaf, epileptic, severely mentally handicapped and autistic. At age eight he was placed in a special school, where he remains and for which his mother has also engaged in considerable fundraising. Muffy, who was able to be taught to speak and read and lead a normal life, has a position in charge of the hiring of the disabled for the New York Telephone System.

In her many lectures and fund raisers for the cause of Birth Defects, Sills advises parents to focus on the child and not give up nurturing his/her potential. In her words: "Having a handicapped child is a tragedy, but on the other hand, the triumphs you have with them just can't be compared with the triumphs you have with normal children. When a deaf child says her first word, you feel like you've conquered the moon."

Of her marriage, Mrs. Greenough comments, "Balancing an illustrious career and a complicated motherhood has been easier because I made a sensational choice in my husband." (Which was a great outcome from coming home almost fifty years before and telling her mother, Shirley, that she had just met the man she was going to marry, and that he was a married man with a missing wife, three daughters and he was not Jewish!)

It was daughter and husband who convinced Beverly that six months of "smelling the roses" was enough retirement from Lincoln Center and that she should accept the chair of the Metropolitan. She did so in 2002, staying until January 26, 2005. With her sudden resignation, she ended a sixty-year career in the arts as a reigning diva, an opera manager, Lincoln Center overseer, and fundraiser. Her decision, she said, was based on two events: suffering her third fracture in a year—this time, her knee—and the necessity of having to place her ailing husband in a nursing home.

To honor her, the Met established the Beverly Sills Artist Award. The $50,000 prize is funded from an endowment gift from Agnes Varis, managing director on The Met board, and her husband, Karl Leichtman. Candidates will be between twenty-five and forty years old, and must have appeared in a solo role with the Met. The award is specifically designated to aid recipients in career enhancement. The first annual award was made in the 2006–07 season.

Her departure was followed in 2006 by the retirement of Met General Manager **Joseph Volpe**, who had started at the opera as a carpenter thirty years before, and whose replacement is former president and Met CEO, **Peter Gelb**, whose experience working with Volpe made him the perfect candidate for his new position. Beverly's successor is **Christine F. Hunter**. (See Business.)

Risë Stevens

Famed mezzo-soprano **RISË STEVENS** [Steenberg] was born in New York, June 11, 1913. After appearing in small roles with the New York Opera-Comique, she worked as a dress model until offered free lessons at Juilliard from **Anna Schoen-René** (1864–1942), who had been a pupil of **Pauline Viardot-Garcia**. Stevens then studied at the Salzburg Mozarteum. **George Szell** engaged her as a contralto for the Prague Opera (1936) as Mignon, after which she went on tour to Cairo with Vienna Opera, and Buenos Aires. Her American debut was with the Met on tour in Philadelphia, November 22, 1938, as Octavian, appearing one month later in New York as Mignon, remaining with them until 1961, where she sang only sixteen roles. The following year she married Czech actor Walter Surovy, who became her business manager. She appeared at major opera houses worldwide, but among traditional roles, including Delilah and Gluck's Orpheus, became best known for her *Carmen* which, beginning in 1945, she performed 124 times at the Met, followed by seventy-four Octavians and thirty-two Delilahs. Like other glamorous prima donnas, she was lured to the movies. In 1941, she appeared in *The Chocolate Soldier* with Nelson Eddy, and in 1944 sang the Habañera from *Carmen* in the Bing Crosby vehicle, *Going My Way*. She retired in 1964, then served as General Manager of the Metropolitan Opera Touring Company until 1966, joined the Juilliard faculty in 1975 and served as president of the Mannes College of Music (1975–78). She is still a board member of the Met Opera Guild.

In 1990 she was a Kennedy Center honoree for bringing opera to the American public her entire career, and saving the Met in 1961. The company had cancelled performances because of labor negotiations, but a call to President Kennedy resulted in his ordering the secretary of labor to arbitrate, and the season was saved.

On January 9, 2006, the Metropolitan Opera Guild and *Opera News Magazine* honored her at Rose Hall at Lincoln Center with a retrospective of her opera, film and television performances. Hosted by Van Cliburn and Jennifer Larmore, tributes and reminiscences came from Licia Albanese, Denise Graves, Kitty Carlisle Hart, Anna Moffo and Patrice Munsel. The evening ended with Cliburn's story of when Rudolf Bing asked Walter Surovy if Risë would sing Amneris in *Aida*. He agreed, but the Met would have to change the name of the opera because his wife only sang title roles.

Joan Sutherland

One of the greatest sopranos of the 20th century, **Dame JOAN SUTHERLAND** was born in Sydney, Australia, November 7, 1926. She first studied with her mother, making her concert debut in Sydney, 1947, as Dido in *Dido and Aeneas*. She continued her training in London at the Royal College of Music, making her Covent Garden debut in *The Magic Flute* in 1952, subsequently attracting attention when she created the role of Jenifer in *The Midsummer Marriage* (1955) by British composer **Sir Michael Tippett** (1905–98). She sang Gilda there in 1957, and Lucia in 1959. Meanwhile, in 1954, she married conductor **Richard Bonynge**, who coached her in the *bel canto* repertoire that became her forte. The pair traveled internationally as Sutherland triumphed, performing the operas of Mozart, Rossini, Bellini, Donizetti, Verdi and Massenet. Massenet's *Esclarmonde* was all but forgotten when San Francisco produced it for Sutherland in 1974. She reprised the opera role at the Met in 1976 and Covent Garden, 1983. Her North American debut was in Vancouver (*Don Giovanni*, 1958) as Donna Anna, followed by her 1960 U.S. debut in Dallas in the title role of Handel's *Alcina*. The following year marked her first triumphant appearance at the Met as Lucia. She continued to sing in major houses on both sides of the Atlantic, took her own company to Australia in 1965, returning in 1974, and made many acclaimed appearances during her husband's directorship of the Australian Opera (1976–86).

In 1961, she was made Commander of the Order of the British Empire and in 1979 named Dame Commander—the feminine equivalent of knighthood—of the Order of the British Empire. She established *The Merry Widow* as one of her late career roles, with the operetta giving her a chance to indulge her hearty sense of humor. She gave several performances in Australia, San Francisco, 1981, and Dallas, 1989. After a career spanning over forty years, singing hundreds of brilliant Lucias, Normas and Amnias, Dame Joan's final appearance on the operatic stage was October 2, 1990, in *Les Huguenots*, in her native Sydney. During her career, cancellation was an anathema. She sang through fevers, pneumonia, and excruciating back pain, maintaining the opera stage was no place for sissies. Since her retirement, she has sat on distinguished juries of international music competitions, appeared in an Australian film in the major role of Mother Rudd, and given master classes with her husband. In 1998, her classes included those presented by the Marilyn Horne Foundation and Juilliard. Her authorized biography, written by Norma Major, wife of Britain's former prime minister, came out in the U.S. in 1994. Her autobiography is titled *A Prima Donna's Progress*. During 1996–97, her seventieth birthday was marked with gala celebrations throughout the world. December 2004 brought official Kennedy Center Honors, the American equivalent of Britain's Command Performance.

Mezzo-soprano **BLANCHE THEBOM**, born September 19, 1918 in Monessen, Pennsylvania, made her operatic debut at the Metropolitan as Fricka in 1944, remaining there for the next fourteen years, and returning from 1960–67. She also had great successes in London, Paris, Brussels, Milan, and was the first American to sing at Moscow's Bolshoi. Her repertoire included, amongst much Wagner, Ortrud (*Lohengrin*), Azucena (*Il trovatore*), Laura (*La Gioconda*), Amneris (*Aida*) and the trouser role, Orlofsky (*Der Rosenkavalier*). There are videos of her appearances on "The Voice of Firestone" TV program (1950, 1966), featuring popular arias, and songs from *My Fair Lady*. After her appointment as head of the Southern Regional Opera in Atlanta, Georgia (1967–68), she became director of the opera workshop at San Francisco State University for several years beginning in 1980. In the course of her career, Thebom was married to banker Richard Metz for ten years.

I spoke to her in July 2005, at which time some fortunate students were still under her tutelage. She confided, "I *love* teaching!" She also recalled her 1957 London Covent Garden debut as Dido in the first major production of Berlioz' *Les Troyens* (The Trojans), staged by Sir John Gielgud and conducted by Rafael Kubelik. She remembered the two segment performance taking four hours, with a dinner break between.

I shall always treasure that marvelous moment, speaking in person to one of opera's immortal divas!

GABRIELLA TUCCI was born in Rome, August 4, 1929, studied at the Accademia di Santa Cecilia, and with Leonardo Filoni whom she later married. After winning the international singing competition in Spoleto, 1951, she sang in provincial Italian opera houses, made an Australian debut in 1955, and her La Scala debut in 1959. The same year saw her American debut as Madeleine in *Andrea Chénier* with SFO, where she sang until 1969. Her Met debut, October 1960, was as Cio-Cio-San. She continued her successes there until 1973. Her European career was equally renowned, with leading roles at Covent Garden, San Carlo, Naples, Vienna State Opera, Berlin Deutsche Oper, Bavarian State Opera (Munich), Bolshoi (Moscow), as well as in Buenos Aires and Japan. From 1983–86, she taught at the Indiana University School of Music.

GALINA Pavlova VISHNEVSKAYA was born in Leningrad, October 25, 1926. After vocal studies with Vera Garina, she appeared in operetta with Leningrad Light Opera Company, 1944–48. She sang with the Leningrad Philharmonic Society 1948–52, the year she joined the operatic staff of the Bolshoi Theater. There, her more than twenty roles included Violetta, Tosca, Madame Butterfly, and the repertoire of soprano parts in Russian operas. She reigned as their prima donna for almost twenty years. In 1955, she married world-famous cellist **Mstislav Rostropovich**, with whom she has two daughters. She has frequently appeared with him in concert. Her 1960 American tour with the Moscow Philharmonic, launched her recital career in this country. Her Met debut came in 1961 as Aida and Cio-Cio-San. She also performed at La Scala, Vienna State Opera, and in England at Festival Hall, Covent Garden, and the Aldeburgh, Edinburgh and Rostropovich Festivals, but because of Russian politics and the Cold War, she mostly remained at home. With the differences between Rostropovich and the cultural authorities of the Soviet Union—he openly protested the treatment of dissident writer Alexander Solzhenitsyn—Galina's career came to an end. They emigrated to the U.S. in 1974, when her husband was appointed musical director of the National Symphony (1977–96). They made a triumphant return visit to Russia in 1990 after the disintegration of the Communist regime, too late for Galina to resume a career. They live in Paris, and she makes occasional trips to New York to see her children and grandchildren. She also spends time in Moscow, working with singers at the Galina Vishneskaya Opera Center. In 1991, she was a member of the jury for the Cardiff Singer of the World competition. In 1984, she published her autobiography *Galina: A Russian Story*.

As with the "Immortals," this era of sublime singers handed the torch to the generation of Godgiven talent born in the '30s and '40s who made *their* mark in opera houses around the world, and paved the way for the next crop of Living Legends.

The Next Generation

1930–1949

Marni Nixon (1930)

Roberta Peters (1930)

Shirley Verrett (1931)

Anna Moffo (1932–2006)

Janet Baker (1933)

Montserrat Caballé (1933)

Renata Scotto (1933)

Elly Ameling (1934)

Marilyn Horne (1934)

Martina Arroyo (1935)

Teresa Berganza (1935)

Mirella Freni (1935)

Dame Gwyneth Jones (1936)

Grace Bumbry (1937)

Hildegarde Behrens (1937)

Elena Obraztsova (1937)

Teresa Stratas (1938)

Adriana Maliponte (1938)

Tatiana Troyanos (1938–93)

Brigitte Fassbänder (1939)

Arleen Augér (1940–93)

Shirley Love (1940)

Eva Marton (1943)

Anna Tomowa-Sintow (1943)

Gabriela Beňačková (1944)

Kiri Te Kanawa (1944)

Jessye Norman (1945)

Frederica Von Stade (1945)

Barbara Daniels (1946)

Carol Neblett (1946)

Katia Ricciarelli (1946)

Lucia Valentini Terrani (1946)

Felicity Lott (1947)

Rosalind Plowright (1947)

Kathleen Battle (1948)

Catherine Malfitano (1948)

Barbara Dever (1949)

Ann Murray (1949)

The generation born in the decades before and after World War II was as equally star-studded as those who came before.

Stilled Voices

ARLEEN AUGÉR, born in Los Angeles September 13, 1939, studied piano and violin and received a BA in education from California State, Long Beach, 1963. She studied voice from 1965 to 1967, the year she won the Viktor Fuchs Vocal Competition. The prize included airfare to Vienna, where she was signed by, and made her debut at, the Vienna State Opera. In the course of a twenty-four year career, she appeared in over fifty European and American music festivals, and made thirteen worldwide recital tours. Her discography, ranging from Bach to Schoenberg, numbers over 170 recordings on more than ten labels with dozens of awards. Her last recording was *Sonnets from the Portuguese*, by **Libby Larsen**, at the Ordway Music Theater in November 1991. Tragically, she died of a brain tumor June 10, 1993.

ANNA MOFFO, American soprano of Italian descent, was born in Wayne, Pennsylvania, June 27, 1932. She studied voice at Curtis, later going on a Fulbright fellowship to the Accademia di Santa Cecilia in Rome. She made her debut at Spoleto in 1955 as Norina in *Don Pasquale*, and subsequently sang at La Scala, Vienna State Opera and in Paris before making her 1956 American debut as Cio-Cio-San in a televised *Madama Butterfly*, directed by future husband Mario Lanfranchi. She sang Mimi at Lyric Opera of Chicago (1957). November 1959 marked her Met debut as Violetta. She continued performing major roles—Zerlina, Violetta, Gilda, Lucia, Manon, Marguerite, Juliette, Mélisande, Liù and Mimi—at the Met and other major U.S. and European houses, as well as television appearances on *The Bell Telephone Hour*. Having being pushed too fast in her career, a vocal breakdown occurred in 1974. After working with Beverly Johnson, she resumed her career in 1976, making her last Met appearance as Violetta in March. She sang Thaïs in Seattle, and Adriana Lecouvreur at Parma (1978). Although her voice never really recovered, she did return to the Met to sing with Robert Merrill at their centennial gala, October 1983.

Moffo appeared in two films: *Austerlitz* (1960) and *The Adventurers* (1970). Her recordings include *La bohème*, *Carmen*, *Lucia di Lammermoor*, *Madama Butterfly*, *Carmen*, *Hansel and Gretel* and *Luisa Miller*. She received Grammy nominations for *A Verdi Collaboration* (1962) and *Songs of Debussy* (1970).

After divorcing Lanfranchi, in 1974 she married Robert Sarnoff, head of NBC television in the 1950s and '60s, and later a recording executive with RCA. He died in 1997, and Anna retired from the public stage. She died in New York, March 10, 2006. The MET gave her a star-studded memorial tribute September 20.

Mezzo **TATIANA TROYANOS** was born in New York, September 12, 1938, to a Greek father and a German mother, both with good voices, but who apparently did not provide a very stable home for her. At age seven, she was sent to the Brooklyn Home for Children, a welfare-supported institution. It was there that she started to study the piano with Louis Petrini, first bassoonist in the Metropolitan Opera Orchestra for twenty-five years. He arranged for a scholarship to the Brooklyn Music School. She left Brooklyn to live on East 19th Street at the Girls Service League. Always drawn to music, she loved Mario Lanza and Jane Powell in the movies and heard **Risē Stevens** and **Maria Callas** on the radio. While working as a secretary, someone got her into Juilliard Preparatory School and her first voice teacher. From there she went to New York City Opera, and made her debut as Hippolyta in *A Midsummer Night's Dream* in 1963. In 1964, she turned down an offer of small roles and covers at the Met and left for an audition tour to Hamburg, Frankfurt and Zurich. She was a member of the Hamburg State Opera, 1965–75, during which time she sang at Covent Garden (1969), and Paris Opera (1971). The same year she appeared as Ariodante in the first operatic production at Kennedy Center. In 1975, she was sensational at her San Francisco debut in the title role of *L'Incoronazione di Poppea*. In 1976, Troyanos finally made her Met debut as Octavian, and went on to become one of the company's leading members, singing for ten seasons and 167 performances. Outstanding roles included Dorabella, Cherubino, Adalgisa, Kundry, Poppea, Charlotte, Carmen and the Composer—she was very believable in trouser roles.

Always striving to better herself, and secretive about her personal life, her death from liver cancer August 23, 1993 was a shock to everyone.

Relinquishing the Limelight

As both Shakespeare and Andy Warhol observed, we strut our finite lifetimes upon a stage—but most of us are unknown to the rest of the world. Those, however, who have been warmed in the spotlight of fame and nourished by adulation and applause need extra courage to relinquish the cornucopia of privileges and, in many cases, great wealth, earned by their talent and hard work. Artists in all fields born in the 1930s and '40s have for some years been facing the inevitability of age dictating gracious retirements and seeing younger generations take their turn upon that stage.

It is a comfort that this generation of talent is able to leave us a legacy of recordings, videos and other immortal memories. Singers who turn to teaching give the extra gift of passing their training and experience to future talented singers to continue bringing the fantasy world of opera to life for the rest of us.

The following are in this generational category. Many have retired to rest upon their deserved laurels, a few continue with recital careers, while others have become teachers, or gone into administration. The most outstanding example of the latter being the remarkable second and third careers of **Beverly Sills**.

Dutch soprano **ELLY AMELING**, born February 8, 1934, in Rotterdam, studied there and The Hague before completing her training in Paris. After numerous concert appearances and the winning of several competitions, she made her London debut in 1966, and her New York debut in 1968. Her first actual operatic appearance, as Ilia in *Idomeneo* with the Netherlands Opera, was not until 1973. Finding her concert and recital career more sustaining, she has continued to perform worldwide. To commemorate her winning of the Hertogenbosch Competition in 1956, she initiated the Elly Ameling Lied Prize to be awarded at this competition. She was honored by the Dutch government in 1971, receiving the title Knight of the Order of Oranje Nassau. Her repertoire, lieder as well as works with orchestra, ranges from Monteverdi and Bach through Mozart, Schubert, Schumann, Wolf and Debussy, to composers of the later 20th century such as Britten, Menotti, Poulenc and Gershwin. Many of her more than 150 recordings have been awarded the Edison Prize (four times), France's Grand Prix du Disque, and Germany's Schallplattenpreis, among others.

Ameling has received three honorary degrees from the USA and Canada.

MARTINA ARROYO was born February 2, 1936, in New York. (See Black Heritage.)

One of the most outstanding mezzos England has produced, **Dame JANET BAKER**, born August 21, 1933, in Hatfield, Yorkshire, grew up in a music-loving family. Despite the distance from the North of England, she made the journey to London for singing lessons and also participated in a master class of **Lotte Lehmann**. In 1956, she won a scholarship to attend classes at the Salzburg Mozarteum. The same year she made her debut with the Oxford Opera Club in Smetana's *The Secret* and sang in the chorus of that summer's Glyndebourne Festival. After appearing in many Handel and other baroque opera productions, she gained attention as the soloist in Mahler's Resurrection Symphony at the 1961 Edinburgh Festival. The next year she joined the English Opera Group, formed by **Benjamin Britten** in 1947. This raised her career to a higher plane with such premieres as Britten's *Owen Wingrave*, 1971, which was televised, and *Phaedra*, 1976. Meanwhile, she made her first American appearance in 1966 with SFO, singing Mahler's *Das Lied von der Erde*, and sang a New York solo recital that December. Both performances received excellent reviews.

Janet Baker

Besides stints with Scottish Opera and ENO, Baker has performed all over the world. Although she sang some Strauss and Berlioz, her concentration was in the lyrical works by Monteverdi, Purcell, Gluck, Mozart, Walton and Britten. In 1970, she was made a Commander of the Order of the British Empire (CBE), and in 1976 Queen Elizabeth II named her a Dame Commander (DBE). Other honors include doctorates from the Universities of Birmingham, Leicester, Hull, Lancaster, York, Cambridge, Oxford and London. She was also presented with the Gold Medal from the Royal Philharmonic Society. In 1991, she was appointed Chancellor of the University of York, and Trustee for the Foundation of Sports and Arts.

Dame Janet retired from opera in 1982 after singing Gluck's *Orpheus and Eurydice* in Glyndebourne, and *Alceste* at Covent Garden. Respected as an intellectual artist, her brilliant concert career—so satisfying and polished as to make opera irrelevant—with its impressive repertoire of German lieder, French and English songs, particularly those of Schubert, Schumann, Brahms, Mahler, Elgar (Heavenly! "The Land Where Corals Lie," *Elgar's Sea Songs*), and Britten, came to a close with a performance of *Orpheus* in Carnegie Hall (1989). Her wonderful recordings on major labels fill a library section. Her final operatic season is recounted in her 1983 book, *Full Circle*.

HILDEGARD BEHRENS, born February 9, 1937, in Oldenburg, Germany, graduated with a law degree from the University of Freiburg before switching careers and going to the Freiburg Academy of Music. She became a member of the German Opera in Düsseldorf, 1972, where she was discovered by **Herbert von Karajan** who helped establish her brilliant career. Her 1976 debut at Covent Garden was as Leonore (*Fidelio*) and the same year Giorgetta (*Il tabarro*) at the Met—where she completed over two decades on their roster. She is considered one of the greatest Salomes—with her Salzburg Festival debut in 1977. Other notable roles are Fiordiligi, Agathe, Marie (*Wozzeck*), Rusalka, Emilia Marty (*The Makropulos Affair*), and the Wagner hero-

Hildegard Behrens

ines. Her Berlin performance of Brünnhilde in the '94–'95 season marked the sixth production of the complete *Ring* which she has sung all over the world since her first Bayreuth Festival in 1983. This proved to be a significant role. On April 28, 1990, near the end of a six-hour *Götterdämmerung* at the Met, a piece of scenery—a wooden beam wrapped in styrofoam and canvas—fell too soon, injuring some vertebrae. The accident cost three years of her career, changed her life, compelled her to give up alcohol, become a vegetarian and start a strict fitness regimen. Elektra, which she first sang in 1986 at Paris Opera, marked her 1994 recovery triumph at the Met, with a subsequent 1996 European *Ring* tour bringing further raves, especially at her homecoming to Salzburg. 1996–97 also saw her in *Tristan und Isolde* at the Inaugural Performance for Munich's newly rebuilt Prinzregenten Theatre, and once again as Brünnhilde in the complete *Ring* cycle in Vienna, as well as appearances in Berlin, Houston and Carnegie Hall with pianist **Christoph Eschenbach**.

Behrens' popular performances with the world's greatest orchestras, led by the most celebrated conductors, continued into her sixties, and opera appearances in Bayreuth, London, Paris and Salzburg remained an instant draw. Referred to as the greatest living Brünnhilde, she earned equal acclaim for her other signature role, Elektra. The 1998–99 season included *Ring* productions in Vienna, London and Berlin, plus performances of *Fidelio* in Vienna, and *Wozzeck* in San Francisco. In 2000, she sang Kundry in *Parsifal*, her debut in Cherubini's *Medea*, and in 2001, her debut as Kostelnicka in Janáček's *Jenůfa*.

Her discography on major labels contains many of her acclaimed performances, including recitals and over twelve complete operas. In May 1995, the Republic of Austria bestowed upon her its highest honor, the title *Österreichische Kammersängerin* (Austrian Chamber Singer) of the Vienna State Opera, followed in 1998 with Denmark's "Léonie Sonnings Music Prize." After the death in 1998 of **Leonie Rysanek**, the previous holder of the Lotte Lehmann Memorial Ring, the treasured award passed to Behrens, May 25, 1999.

Hildegard lives with her husband, Seth Schneidmann, outside Washington, DC. She is the mother of Sara, born 1982, and Philip, born 1970, whose wife presented her with granddaughter, Maria, in 1995.

"Retirement," she says, "is not remotely in the picture, but when leading roles are no longer possible I see myself doing the old-lady parts—certainly not giving up the stage."

GABRIELA BEŇAČKOVÁ was born March 25, 1944, in Bratislava, Czechoslovakia, where she studied voice at the conservatory, won the 1962 Janáček and 1963 Dvořák Competitions, and made her debut in 1970 at the National Theatre, Prague, as Natasha in Prokofiev's *War and Peace*. In 1975, her Prague performance as Jenůfa became a signature role which she has sung in major opera houses worldwide. She is equally well-known for other Czech roles: Janáček's *Kát'a Kabanová*, Amsterdam (1976) and Carnegie Hall (1979), and for her Met debut, 1991. 1979 brought her London Covent Garden debut as Tatyana in *Eugene Onegin*. She returned there in 1992 for *Fidelio*.

Her vocal versatility encompasses Wagner heroines (*Lohengrin*, *Tannhäuser*, *The Flying Dutchman*), plus Strauss, Verdi and Puccini. Besides operatic appearances, Beňačková regularly appears in lieder recitals, concerts with renowned orchestras and maestros, TV broadcasts, videos and CDs. She was nominated for a 1994 Grammy Award by the National Academy of Performing Arts and honored as a Czech National Artist in 1985.

Spanish singer **TERESA BERGANZA**, born in Madrid, March 16, 1935, studied in her native city with Lola Rodriguez Aragon, a pupil of **Elisabeth Schumann-Heink**, making her debut in 1957 as Dorabella in *Così fan tutte* at Aix-en-Provence. Her American debut in Dallas, 1958, as Isabella in *L'italiana in Algieri*, was followed by her first Covent Garden appearance in 1960 as Rosina. In the course of mastering Rossini, she developed the heavier tone which she later adopted to sing *Carmen* at Edinburgh (1977–78), Hamburg (1980), San Francisco (1981), and Paris (1989). She appeared as Zerlina in the Joseph Losey film, *Don Giovanni* (1979). Her memoirs, *Flor de soledad y silencio: meditaciones de una cantante* (Flower of Solitude: Meditations of a Singer) were published in 1984.

She was still going strong in 2005 as featured in a Paris *Match* article, February 20.

GRACE BUMBRY was born January 4, 1937, in St. Louis. (See Black Heritage.)

MONTSERRAT CABALLÉ, born April 12, 1933, in Barcelona, was accepted at the Conservatory at age eight where she studied for twelve years and won a Liceo Gold Medal in 1954. Joining the Basel Opera in 1956, she sang standard roles—Mimi, Pamina, Tosca, Aida—as well as the more modern, challenging Strauss heroines Arabella, Chrysothemis and Salome. After appearing at several European opera houses, and the Glyndebourne Festival, her career went into high gear April 20, 1965, when she substituted for **Marilyn Horne** in a Carnegie Hall performance of *Lucrezia Borgia*. The critics were ecstatic and continued to be so for her other American appearances, especially her Met debut, December 15, 1965, as Marguerite in *Faust*. She continued singing with them in traditional roles, as well as worldwide appearances which added Rossini, Bellini and Donizetti *bel canto* operas to her repertoire. Her 1972 Covent Garden debut was as Norma, and in subsequent years there she sang Leonora (*Il trovatore*), Amelia (*Ballo in maschera*) and Aida. Regarded by many as Maria Callas' successor, Caballé is acclaimed for her mastery of Verdi and Donizetti.

On September 24, 1989, she created the role of Queen Isabella in Leonardo Balada's *Cristóbal Colón* in Barcelona. In 1992, she sang Madame Cortese in Rossini's *Il viaggio a Reims*. Meanwhile, during the 1980s and '90s, she branched out to a successful recital career, gathering renown as an exponent of Spanish songs. Her recordings include *Lucrezia Borgia*, *La traviata*, *Aida* and *Salome*. Among her honors is the Cross of Isabella the Catholic.

Caballé has been married to Spanish tenor Bernabé Marti since 1964. They have one son.

BARBARA DANIELS, born in Grenville, Ohio, May 7, 1946, studied at the Cincinnati College-Conservatory (BM, 1969; MM, 1971), making her debut with the West Palm Beach Opera in 1973 as Mozart's Susanna. 1974 saw her at Innsbruck (Austria), as Fiordiligi and Violetta. She made her Covent Garden debut as Rosalinde (*Die Fledermaus*, 1978), sang Norina (*Don Pasquale*) at Kennedy Center (1979), Zdenka (*Arabella*) with San Francisco (1980), and Musetta at the Met (1983). She has also sung in Cologne, Zurich, Vienna, Paris, Chicago and returned to the Met as Minnie in *La Fanciulla del West* (1991), and Alice in *Falstaff* (1995–96).

BARBARA DEVER was born Christmas Day, 1949, in Carlisle, Pennsylvania. At age twelve, she began taking piano and voice lessons from Klara Kase Bowman, teacher of **Nelson Eddy**. As a student, she had leading roles in *The Sound of Music* and *Carousel*, then became a folk musician. By 1980, she had settled down with her husband and two children in Pittman, New Jersey. As music director at her church, she rekindled her love for song, and took more voice lessons. Her teacher urged her to audition for the Met, and by 1994 she was sharing the stage with **Luciano Pavarotti** in *Great Performances at Lincoln Center*. With sparkling reviews, she made her Met debut the next evening as Amneris in *Aida*. Her career is now international, but she remains at Sacred Heart.

Noted German mezzo **BRIGITTE FASSBÄNDER**, born July 3, 1939, in Berlin, studied with her father, Willi Domgraf-Fassbänder at the Nuremberg Conservatory and made her debut at the State Opera in Munich, 1961 as Nicklaus in *The Tales of Hoffmann*. Her 1964 Clarice in *La pietra del paragone* (The Touchstone), was a highlight of her career. Her debuts at Covent Garden (1971) and the Met (1974) were as Octavian. In 1976, she introduced the role of Lady Milford in Von Einem's *Kabale und Liebe* in Vienna. In 1986, she returned to the Met as Fricka. She also sang at Bayreuth (1983–84), Salzburg (1989) and Glyndebourne (1990).

After reigning as one of the world's leading mezzos, as well as being a consummate concert artist and recitalist, Fassbänder turned producer. In 1989, she staged *Der Rosenkavalier* at Munich. Other productions include *La Cenerentola* (1990) and *The Magic Flute* (1993) at Coburg, *Hansel and Gretel* at Augsburg, *Der ferne Klang* (The Distant Sound) for Opera North (England), both in 1992, *A Midsummer Night's Dream* (1993) in Amsterdam. She also gives master classes at international symposia. Since 1964, she has made over 100 recordings.

MIRELLA FRENI, born February 27, 1935, in Modena, Italy, is known for her portrayals of Mimi, Susanna, Desdemona, Micaëla, and Marguerite (*Faust*). Her colorful and exciting career was almost predestined when she and **Luciano Pavarotti** shared the same wet nurse. (His mother and hers worked at the same tobacco factory.) She sang for the legendary **Benianimo Gigli** when she was twelve. As a teenager, she used to wait in line all day for standing room tickets, one of the reasons she never turns visitors away after a performance, no matter how tired she is. She made her debut, February 3, 1955, in Modena as Micaëla. Beginning as a light soprano, her voice matured into heavier roles. Early in her career, after a performance of *La bohème* at La Scalla, Charlie Chaplin came backstage to congratulate her, saying: "You are incredible, fantastic, but not only with the voice. You are a great artist." She was married to Leone Magiera, a friend of Pavarotti and conductor of many of his concerts. In 1977, she married her second husband, basso **Nicolai Ghiaurov**, who died in 2004.

1989–90, the thirty-fifth season of her career, was marked by Italian President Francesco Siga awarding her the title "Cavalier of the Great Cross" to celebrate her contributions to music and to Italy. Her Met debut was September 29, 1965—in the old house—as Mimi. She opened her twenty-fifth Met season (1990–91) in the same role, as well as sharing a gala with tenor **Alfredo Kraus** and **Ghiaurov**—all celebrating their twenty-fifth anniversaries. She sang thirteen roles in her Met career. Freni has captivated audiences around the world, made numerous television appearances, and more than fifty recordings with other celebrated singers. In a 1997 profile in *Opera News*, playwright Albert Innaurato called her "the last prima donna."

Freni was Joan of Arc in Washington National Opera's *The Maid of Orleans* (March 2005), and on May 15 the Met honored her with a gala concert marking the fiftieth anniversary of her professional debut and fortieth of her first performance at the Met. The concert included her singing selections from *Manon*, *Adriana Lecouvrer*, *The Maid of Orleans* and *Eugene Onegin*, with colleagues **Frederica von Stade**, James Morris, Marcello Giordani, Dmitri Hvorostovsky, and Salvatore Licitra.

Marilyn Horne

MARILYN HORNE made her public debut at age four, singing at an FDR political rally in Bradford, Pennsylvania, where she was born January 16, 1934. Her father, a fine amateur singer, coached her as a child and impressed upon her the importance of proper training. She and her older sister, Gloria, sang in bond rallies, church choirs and band concerts. The family moved to Long Beach, California, in 1945 for better music education opportunities. While attending USC, "Jackie," as she has been permanently nicknamed from birth by her brother, sang with the newly formed Roger Wagner Chorale, often as part of the background chorus in movies. At the right place at the right time, she was chosen to dub the singing for Dorothy Dandridge in the 1954 film *Carmen Jones*, Oscar Hammerstein's modernized version of *Carmen*, with an all-black cast featuring Harry Belafonte as Joe (Don José). The same year she met **Igor Stravinsky**, who would dedicate his orchestrations of two Hugo Wolf songs to her shortly before his death.

From 1956–60, she was engaged by the Gelsenkirchen (Germany) Opera, which gave her a thorough grounding in traditional soprano roles. Her last appearance there, May 22, 1960, was in the demanding part of Marie in *Wozzeck*. There being only five divas in the world at that time who could sing this role, word of Horne's rave reviews rippled all the way to the West Coast, kindling the interest of **Kurt Herbert Adler** (1905–88), director of San Francisco Opera. Everything happened that July 4th weekend in 1960. She flew from Germany to Los Angeles, married her long time friend, African American conductor **Henry Lewis** (1932–96), and winged to San Francisco (on Cloud Nine) to render a thrilling audition. The *Wozzeck* premiere, October 4, 1960, put her into orbit on this side of the Atlantic. Meanwhile, husband Henry was making a name for himself with his Los Angeles Chamber Orchestra, and guest conducting the Los Angeles Philharmonic—a black conductor being a *cause célèbre* in those days. Daughter Angela was born June 14, 1965. Although the Lewises later divorced, they remained friends and often worked together until Henry's death January 28, 1996.

In 1968, after alternating soprano and mezzo roles, Horne declared herself a true coloratura mezzo/contralto. From her 1970 debut as Adalgisa in *Norma*, she was one of the Met's principal stars, making her mark as Delilah, Rosina, Isabella, Orfeo, Fides (*Le Prophète*), Princess Eboli (*Don Carlo*), Amneris and Carmen—the latter becoming a signature role. Significantly, she became the next link in the chain of *bel canto* singers. Forgotten masterpieces of Rossini, Donizetti and Bellini had been revived by **Maria Callas** beginning 1952. This vital contribution was continued by **Joan Sutherland** with Marilyn as her mezzo counterpart—a duo of heavenly vocal blending that thrilled thousands. Noted for her mastery of Rossini, Horne is credited with reviving both his authentic style and the true sound of the coloratura contralto. With her performances of *Tancredi*, and Arsace in *Semiramide*, she ascended to super-stardom, receiving the Abbiati Prize for Best Dramatic Interpretation of the Year at the Rossini Festival in Pesaro and, in 1982, created especially for her, Italy's *Premio-d'Oro-Rossini*, honoring her as the greatest female singer in the world.

In January 1984, with a production of Handel's *Rinaldo*, the Met celebrated its 100th anniversary, and Marilyn both her fiftieth birthday and her thirtieth year with the company. In 1992, she starred in the 200th birthday gala for Rossini at Avery Fisher Hall. Her last opera performance was as Isabella in *L'Italiana in Algieri* at Covent Garden (1993). Since then, she continues to sing other roles, including Mistress Quickly (*Falstaff*) Geneviève (*Pelléas et Mélisande*), and stole the show at the 1992 premiere of the Met commissioned John Corigliano opera, *The Ghosts of Versailles*, as Samira, the Turkish diva—a role written for her.

Horne's recitals—over 1,300 of them—with Martin Katz, her accompanist of over thirty years, are sold out far in advance. In addition to her busy performance schedule, on her sixtieth birthday, January 16, 1994, she launched the Marilyn Horne Foundation, whose mission is to support, promote and preserve the vocal recital through presentations and education programs, with a concert at Carnegie Hall. Joining her were Brigitte Fassbänder, Helen Donath, Montserrat Caballé, Ruth Ann Swenson, Renée Fleming, Warren Jones and James Levine. By its third year, the Foundation had gone from two recitals per season to sixteen. In January 1997, the foundation and the Juilliard School of Music collaborated in a special project, *The Art of Vocal Recital*, a two-day event with seminars and master classes taught by **Christa Ludwig** and Marilyn, culminating in *The Song Continues*, the Fourth Annual MHF New York Recital, featuring some of America's most promising young singers. In January 2001, the master classes at MHF were taught by **Shirley Verrett** and Marilyn.

Horne's vocal gifts are forever preserved on marvelous recordings of *bel canto*, including *Orlando Furioso*, a Vivaldi work that had not been performed for 200 years, plus other operas, a *Rossini Birthday Celebration*, choral works, and *Men in My Life*, her first crossover album. Her many awards include twelve honorary doctorates, Commander of the Order of Arts and Letters of the French Ministry of Culture, Commandatore al Merito della Republica Italiana, the National Medal of Arts, presented at the White House by President George H. Bush, being chosen to sing the national anthem and other songs at the 1993 Inauguration of President Bill Clinton, and the Kennedy Center Honors, awarded December 1995, at the Center, and also at the White House.

Her frank and entertaining autobiography, *Marilyn Horne: My Life*, written in collaboration with her friend, Professor Jane Scovell, was published in 1983. An updated version, Baskerville Press (2004), includes her work at Music Academy of the West and the tenth anniversary of her Marilyn Horne Foundation. Their 2006 concert guest starred **Frederica Von Stade.**

Her seventieth birthday celebration, benefitting the foundation, was held in Carnegie Hall, February 1, 2004, with an array of opera stars including Isabel Bayrakdarian, Stephanie Blythe, Olga Borodina, Barbara Cook, David Daniels, Denyce Graves, Ben Heppner, Audra McDonald, Thomas Quasthoff and Frederica von Stade lending their talents to the occasion. Horne joined in two duets, her tone still clear and pure after a four-decade career. Further honors came September 26, when *Gramophone* Magazine, in association with WQXR—the radio station of the *New York Times*—presented her with the Gramophone 2005 Lifetime Achievement Award.

Dame GWYNETH JONES, born November 7, 1936, in Wales, made her debut at the Zurich Opera in 1962 as a mezzo-soprano in *Der Rosenkavalier*, and in 1963 as a soprano in *Un ballo in maschera*. Major debuts include *Fidelio* at Covent Garden, 1964, and *Il trovatore* with La Scala, 1967. Becoming the principal dramatic soprano in 1963 with Covent Garden was followed by the same title at the Deutsche Oper, Berlin, Vienna State Opera, and the Bavarian State Opera—the last two awarded in 1967. Among her numerous recordings are *Fidelio*, *Der Rosenkavalier*, *Otello* and several Wagner operas. Given the prestigious title of Dame Commander, Order of the British Empire in 1986, Jones also received the Commandeur de l'Ordre des Arts et des Lettres (France) in 1992, and holds an honorary doctorate of music from the University of Wales.

English soprano **Dame FELICITY LOTT**, known as "Flott," was born in Cheltenham, May 8, 1947. Music was an important influence early in her life with piano lessons beginning at age five and her first singing lesson at twelve. As a student at the University of London's Royal Holloway College, she majored in French and Latin with a view to becoming an interpreter, but during a stay in France she continued to take singing lessons at the Conservatory of Grenoble. By 1969, her love of music propelled her back to London and the RAM, from which she left in 1973 with an LRAM graduation certificate and the Principal's Prize.

In 1975, Flott made her debut at ENO as Pamina in Mozart's *Magic Flute* and the following year was in the premiere of Henze's *We Come To The River* at Covent Garden. She began her long association with Glyndebourne who, while rejecting her for the Chorus, gave her the role of the Countess in *Capriccio* on their tour. In 1977, she appeared at the Festival for the first time as Anne Trulove in Stravinsky's *The Rake's Progress*. Since then her circuit has been through the major opera houses of the world: Vienna, Milan, Paris, Brussels, Munich, Hamburg, Dresden, Berlin, New York and Chicago with roles such as Strauss Marschallin (*Rosenkavalier*), Countess Madeleine (*Capriccio*), *Arabella*, Christine (*Intermezzo*), Mozart's Countess Almaviva (*Le Nozze Di Figaro*) Fiordiligi (*Cosi fan Tutte*), Donna Elvira (*Don Giovanni*), Britten's Ellen Orford (*Peter Grimes*), The Governess (*The Turn Of The Screw*), Lady Billows (*Albert Herring*), Charpentier's *Louise*, Poulenc's Blanche (*Les Dialogues des Carmelites*) and Elle (*La Voix humaine*).

Operetta has also become a favorite. In 1993, Lott sang the title role in Lehar's *Merry Widow* with Glyndebourne Festival Opera on an EMI recording. (She had sung the role on stage in Nancy and Paris in the 1980s.) In 1999, she sang Rosalinde (*Fledermaus)* in Chicago, and Offenbach's *La Belle Hélène* at the Châtelet in Paris, all to great acclaim.

As a concert artist, Dame Felicity has performed with major orchestras and festivals under Carlos Kleiber, Sir Georg Solti, Bernard Haitink, James Levine, André Previn, Neeme Järvi, Klaus Tennstedt, Andrew Davis, Kurt Masur, Franz Welser-Möst and many more. She also excels with the songs of English and French masters, and the lieder of Strauss, Schubert, Schumann and Brahms. She is a founder/member of the *Songmakers' Almanac*, a group of singers founded in 1976 by the pianist Graham Johnson, her accompanist since student days. Their quest is discovering and performing less well-known songs and ensembles. Lott's duet recitals with her friend, Irish mezzo-soprano **Ann Murray**, have become legendary.

Her honorary doctorates are from the Universities of Sussex, Loughborough, London, Leicester, Oxford and the Royal Scottish Academy of Music and Drama, Glasgow. The French Government awarded her the titles of Officier dans l'Ordre des Arts et des Lettres (1990) and Chevalier dans la Legion d'Honneur (2001). In 1990, Felicity Lott was also made a CBE, and in 1996 she was created a Dame Commander of the British Empire, the feminine equivalent of a knighthood. In 2003, Dame Felicity was awarded the highest German music title, Bayerische Kammersängerin (Chamber Singer of Bavaria).

The lovely lady is married to actor Gabriel Woolf. They live in Sussex with their daughter Emily, born 1984.

Shirley Love

Mezzo **SHIRLEY LOVE**, born in Detroit, January 6, 1940, has sung forty-five roles—of her repertoire of 100—in 729 performances in forty different operas in her twenty seasons at the Met since her 1963 debut in *The Magic Flute*. Born January 6, 1940, in Detroit, she is a graduate of Wayne State University. As a recitalist, she has sung major choral works throughout the U.S. and Europe. In 1976, for her artistic achievements, she received a Proclamation and Key to the City of Detroit. In 1990, she was awarded the Achievement in the Arts Award. On the faculty of the Music Academy of Westchester (NY), she spends her summers at the International Academy of Music in Lucca (Italy).

Versatile dramatic soprano **CATHERINE MALFITANO** was born April 18, 1948, in New York to a violinist father and dancer/actress mother. Her father, a former member of the Met orchestra, was her first teacher, after which she went to the High School of Music and Art and the Manhattan School of Music. Her roles range from Monteverdi's Poppea, Beethoven's Leonore, to Mozart's ladies, Verdi and Puccini heroines, to Salome, Lulu and many untraditional roles. She has a repertoire of over sixty roles performed at the world's major opera houses. As a proponent of new operas, she has premiered works written especially for her: Conrad Susa's

Transformations (1973), *Bilby's Doll* by Carlisle Floyd (Houston, 1976), Thomas Pasatieri's *Washington Square*, (Michigan, 1976), William Bolcom's *McTeague* (1992); and sung revivals of Samuel Barber's *Antony and Cleopatra* (Chicago Lyric) and Vienna State Opera's *Der Ferne Klang* (The Distant Sound) by Franz Schrecker. She also performs the traditional Mimi, Violetta, Manon, Carmen and Cio-Cio-San. After being on the NYCO roster (1974–79), she made her Met debut in 1979 as Gretel, returning there after a long hiatus of other commitments—La Scala, Covent Garden, Paris Opera, Netherlands, etc.—to sing Butterfly (1994) and her signature role, Salome (1996), which she recorded with director **Christoph von Dohnányi**. The late Austrian soprano **Ljuba Welitsch** (1913–96), one of the greatest Salomes of the past, considered Malfitano her successor.

One billion people saw her as Tosca in a 1993 world telecast from Rome, which earned her an Emmy for best performance by a classical artist. The 1995–96 season began in Salzburg for *Don Giovanni* and her debut with San Francisco Opera in *Madama Butterfly*. 1997–98 returned her to the Met as Emilia Marty in *The Makropulos Case*, followed by *Kát'a Kabanová* (1998–99). 2000 brought her first Wagnerian part as Kundry in *Parsifal*, in San Francisco, followed by Senta in *The Flying Dutchman* at Lyric Opera of Chicago, *The Makropulos Case*, again for the Met, and *Tosca* for Covent Garden. Her Met roles for 2001–02 included *Butterfly* and *Tosca*. In June 2003, Malfitano was soloist for Cincinnati Opera's triple bill of Poulenc's *La Voix Humaine*, Weill's *Die Sieben Todsünden*, and William Bolcom's *Medusa*, written especially for her. Her recordings, including a disc with her father, *Music for Voice and Violin*, are on the EMI, CBS, and Decca/London labels. In 2005 she directed *Madama Butterfly* at Central City Opea in Colorado.

Versatile Italian soprano **ADRIANA MALIPONTE** was born in Brescia, December 26, 1938. After studying in Italy and Germany, she made her debut, 1958, at the Teatro Novo in Milan in *La bohème*, and in 1960 won the Geneva International Competition. Her Paris Opéra debut as Musetta came in March 1962. The following year, she attracted international attention when she created Sardula in Menotti's *Le dernier sauvage* at the Opéra-Comique. Her first appearance at La Scala was in 1970 as Mimi. She made her Met debut as Gretel on December 24, 1979, remaining on their roster until 1985, taking part in 113 performances in roles such as Eurydice, Pamina, Juliette, Luisa Miller, and Micaëla in the posthumously re-created production of *Carmen* conceived by **Grab Genteel** (1917–72), who died tragically in an automobile accident in Sardinia, July 18, after having begun his tenure as Met manager in New York the month before.

Maliponte's first appearance at Covent Garden was as Nedda in 1976. She performed several times with San Diego Opera, including the title role in the West Coast premiere of *Giovanna d'Arco* (June 1980). Back in Italy, she was Gemma di Virgy in Donizetti's opera at Bergamo (1987), and Luisa Miller in Turin (1990).

EVA MARTON, born in Budapest June 18, 1943, studied at the Franz Liszt Academy there. She made her operatic debut at the Hungarian State Opera in 1968, where she remained until joining the Frankfurt Opera, 1971. She became a member of the Hamburg State Opera in 1977. In 1975, she made her U.S. debut in New York in the world premiere of Alan Hovhaness' oratorio *The Way of Jesus*, and in 1976 her Met debut as Eva in *Die Meistersinger*. After singing at the Bayreuth Festival in 1977 and La Scala in 1978, she returned to the Met as the Empress in *Die Frau ohne Schatten* (1981), becoming one of its most important artists and singing there through 1988. After her Covent Garden debut as Turandot, she returned there in 1990 as Elektra. The early '90s found her singing at San Francisco, Budapest, Barcelona, and Salzburg. She has made TV films—*Turandot*, *Tosca*, *Tannhäuser*,

Ann Murray

Trovatore, *Andrea Chenier*, *La Gioconda*—and recorded Wagner and Puccini arias, Strauss songs, scenes from Salome and Elektra, and Brunhilde, among others.

Mezzo **ANN MURRAY**, born in Dublin, Ireland, August 27, 1949, studied voice at the Royal Manchester College and the London Opera Centre. Well-known in Europe, she won acclaim for her *Alceste* with Scottish Opera, and performs regularly at the Salzburg Festival. Her Covent Garden debut in 1976 was as Cherubino, with subsequent appearances there as Siebel (*Faust*), Ascanio, Tebaldo (*I Capuleti ei Montecchi*), the Child in Ravel's *L'enfant et les sortilèges*, the Composer (*Ariadne auf Naxos*), Octavian (1989), Sifare in *Mitridate* for the 1991 Mozart

Bicentennial, and Handel's *Alcina*, 1993. Meanwhile, Sextus and Annio in *La Clemenza di Tito* were her Met debut roles in 1984. She has appeared in concert at the London Proms, and recorded several operas and much sacred music. She can be seen on video in *Xerxes* and *Mitridate*. Married to English tenor Philip Langridge, she was made DBE in 2002.

CAROL NEBLETT, born February 1, 1946, in Modesto, California, studied with **Lotte Lehmann** and **Pierre Bernac** at USC. She toured with the Roger Wagner Chorale from 1965 and, in 1969, made her stage debut as Musetta with the New York City Opera, returning there to sing in *Die Tote Stadt*, *Poppea* and Boito's *Mefistofele*. In 1973, she gained great "exposure" when, as Thaïs at New Orleans Opera, she chose to disrobe at the end of the first act. Subsequent debuts were with Chicago Lyric as Chrysothemis (*Elektra*, 1975), Dallas Civic (*The Tales of Hoffman*, 1975) and as Minnie (*The Girl of the Golden West*), Vienna State Opera (1976) and Covent Garden (1977).

Her Met debut came in 1979 as Senta in *The Flying Dutchman*. She returned there as Tosca, Amelia, Manon Lescaut and Alice Ford in *Falstaff*. She has since appeared in opera houses and festivals all over the world in traditional as well as modern roles. In 1990, she was Madame Lidoine in San Diego Opera's West Coast premiere of *Dialogues of the Carmelites*. Besides a thriving concert and recital career, she has made several recordings.

Carol's son, Stefan, born 1974, is from her former marriage to conductor Kenneth Schermerhorn. In 1981 she married Dr. Philip Akre. Two daughters were born to them. Marianne, 1982, who was tragically killed in an auto accident in 2001, and Adrienne, 1985.

MARNI NIXON, born February 22, 1930, in Altadena, California, played violin as a youngster. She studied with **Carl Ebert** (1887–1980), co-founder of the Glyndebourne Opera (1934) and director of the USC opera department (1948–56). **Jan Popper** was her teacher at Stanford, and **Boris Goldowsky** and **Sarah Caldwell** at the Berkshire Music Center. Her debut in Mozart's *Requiem*, for the Los Angeles Philharmonic when she was just seventeen, led to a multifaceted career as an orchestral soloist with appearances in major American cities, London and Israel, various opera roles in the U.S., and a career in the film industry for which *Time* magazine named her "Ghostess with the Mostess" for dubbing the voices of Deborah Kerr in *The King and I*, Audrey Hepburn in *My Fair Lady* and Natalie Wood in *West Side Story*. She sang Eliza Doolittle in *My Fair Lady* on Broadway and had her own children's television program, which earned her four Emmy Awards. Nixon served as director for the vocal department of the California Institute of the Arts (1969–71) and at the Music Academy of the West (1980–96). Among her many recordings are the *Complete Works of Anton Webern*.

JESSYE NORMAN - (see Black Heritage)

Russian mezzo **ELENA OBRAZTSOVA** was born in Leningrad (now back to St. Petersburg), July 7, 1937. As a child, she lived through Leningrad's blockade by the Germans. After the war, she studied at the Musical School in Rostov, the Leningrad Conservatory, and won a gold medal at the Helsinki Festival in 1962. Upon graduation, she made her debut at the Bolshoi Opera as Marina in *Boris Godunov*. That first season, while on tour with the Bolshoi, she made her La Scala debut (1964) as Maria in *War and Peace*, and the Governess in *Pique Dame*. She went on to perform in France, Italy, Spain, Germany, Austria and Japan. Her American debut was at SFO as Azucena in *Il trovatore* (1975) with **Luciano Pavarotti** and **Joan Sutherland**. The following year, she thrilled audiences at her Met debut as Amneris in *Aida*. In 1977, she returned to SFO in *Adriana Lecouvreur* with **Renata Scotto**, and as Delilah at the Met. In 1978, also at the Met, she sang Charlotte (*Werther*) and Carmen, followed by a Covent Garden debut as Azucena, and at La Scala in *A Masked Ball* and *Don Carlos*. She has worked with such maestros as **Claudio Abbado**, **Herbert von Karajan** and **Daniel Barenboim**, and has made many recordings. In 1973, she was named national artist in her own country, and in 1975 received the Lenin Prize. In 1987, she appeared in recital in New York, and returned to the Met after an almost ten-year absence.

Known for her fantastic *tessitura* (range of strongest notes) brilliant in all registers, she has sung the entire Russian opera repertoire as well as Norma, Delilah, Eboli and Carmen.

She began 2001 touring North America with Moscow's Viktyuk Theater in *Antonio for Elba*. She subsequently appeared at the Met in *The Gambler*, then came concerts in Barcelona, Madrid and Majorca, followed by concerts and master classes in Portugal, Valencia and Tokyo. In 2002, she was at the Met for *War and Peace*.

In addition to her appearances around the world, she coaches other members of the Bolshoi. In 1999, she established the *Elena Obraztsova Competition* for young singers, with **Valery Gergijev**, director of the Mariinsky Theater, as honorary president.

Her first marriage, 1966, was to Vyacheslav Markarov. In 1983, she married Bolshoi conductor Algis Ziuraitis.

Roberta Peters

ROBERTA PETERS, born May 4, 1930, in New York, showed such natural talent that at thirteen she attracted the attention of celebrated tenor **Jan Peerce**, who recommended proper training. By nineteen, she was auditioned by impresario **Sol Hurok**, who immediately presented her to Met manager **Rudolf Bing** who was equally impressed. Before she could sing her scheduled role of the Queen of the Night, she stepped in for an ill soprano and, completely unknown, made her debut, November 17, 1950, as Zerlina, after which her star was borne on wings of success. She remained on the Met roster until 1985, celebrating her thirty-fifth anniversary—an unrivaled record. Her other longevity records include twenty-five appearances on the "Voice of Firestone" and sixty-five on the *Ed Sullivan Show*. She also sang at San Francisco, Chicago, Vienna, Covent Garden, Leningrad, Moscow, the Salzburg Festival, and toured extensively in China, Japan, the Far East and Israel, where she established the Roberta Peters Scholarship Fund of the Hebrew University in Tel Aviv.

One of the leading coloratura sopranos of her generation, she has been a favorite performer at the White House since John F. Kennedy. She represented her country in the Soviet Union and became the first American artist to receive the Bolshoi Medal. She has also sung in operetta, *The Merry Widow*, and musicals, *The King and I*, *West Side Story*, Noel Coward's *Bittersweet*, and made many recordings. Besides her still active concert and recital schedule, she has been on the boards of the National Cystic Fibrosis Foundation, the Met Guild and the Carnegie Hall Corporation. She was appointed by President Bush to the National Council for the Arts, a post she retained until 1996. In April 2001, Peters was the keynote speaker for "Kaleidoscope 2001: An Aria for Everyone's Life" at Michigan State's annual alumni event, which included a vocal performance and profile of her fifty year career.

In 2000, over fifty years after her Met debut, Peters gave a recital in Alice Tully Hall, as she put it, "to begin the next fifty years." Her program was one many sopranos, let alone those still singing at age seventy, would find daunting. Throughout, she demonstrated the vocal beauty, discipline, and musical intelligence that has made her famous. At evening's end, she and accompanist Warren Jones performed the appropriate "I'll See You Again" by Noel Coward.

In private life, after a brief marriage in 1952 to the late Robert Merrill, Peters became the wife of prominent real estate investor Bertram Fields, and the mother of Paul and Bruce, one of whom gave her a lovely granddaughter.

ROSALIND PLOWRIGHT, born May 21, 1949, in Worksop, England, studied at the Royal Northern College of Music in Manchester. She made her ENO debut in 1975 as Miss Jessell in Benjamin Britten's *The Turn of the Screw*, subsequently appearing there as Desdemona, Elisabeth in *Maria Stuarda*, Tosca, and many other roles. Her Covent Garden debut came in 1980 as Orlinde in *Die Walküre*, after which she performed at the Bern, Frankfurt and Munich Operas (1980–81) and covered most of Europe in major roles through the next two decades. U.S. debuts were with the Philadelphia Orchestra under **Muti**, and San Diego Opera in Verdi's *Il Corsaro*. She is also heard in concert and recital, was featured artist in *Opera* Magazine, 1992, and has won many honors.

Katia Ricciarelli

KATIA RICCIARELLI, born January 18, 1946, in Rovigo, Italy, studied at the Benedetto Marcello Conservatory in Venice, making her debut in Mantua, 1969, as Mimi. She sang throughout Italy before making her American debut in 1972 at Chicago Lyric. A reprise of Mimi followed at Covent Garden in 1974, the same role she sang for her Met debut in 1975. Subsequent Met performances have been Micaëla, Desdemona, Luisa Miller and Amelia.

Internationally known for her leading Verdi interpretations—*La Traviata, Luisa Miller, Don Carlo, Il trovatore, Simon Boccanegra, Aida* and *Otello*—she starred in the 1985 Franco Zeffirelli film/video version of the latter with **Plácido Domingo**. Other significant roles include *Anna Bolena, Suor Angelica, Semiramide,* and *Lucrezia Borgia*. Besides appearing at the world's major opera houses with the most celebrated maestros, she also devotes time to her music academy in Mantua, and the voice competition which bears her name.

RENATA SCOTTO, born February 24, 1933, in Savona, Italy, studied at the Giuseppe Verdi Conservatory in Milan, where she made her 1953 debut as Violetta at the Teatro Novo. She joined La Scala, singing secondary roles until she stepped in for **Maria Callas** as Amina in *La sonnambula* during the company's visit to the Edinburgh Festival. This brought her into the limelight. During the 1950s, she built up her repertoire with such roles as Mimi, Adina, Violetta and Donna Elvira. She made her American debut at Chicago Lyric as Mimi in 1960, her Covent Garden debut as Butterfly in 1962, and was Mimi again in her 1965 Met debut. She was a sensation in the same role in the Met's telecast, "Live from Lincoln Center" (March 15, 1977), which catapulted her to the top tier. In the course of her long, brilliant association with the Met—until 1987—she took on heavier roles such as Leonora, Amelia, Desdemona, Giorgetta, Anna Bolena and Lucia. Besides many recordings, her autobiography, *More Than a Diva*, was published in New York (1984).

Having sung the Marschallin at the Spoleto Festival, USA, a few years earlier, in November 2000, Baltimore Opera celebrated its 50th season with *Elektra*, in a production with Scotto's first portrayal of Klytämnestra. As well as singing, she directed **Debra Voigt** in *Tosca* for Florida Grand Opera, March 2001.

TERESA STRATAS was born May 26, 1938, in Toronto, in modest circumstances to a family of Greek origin, and grew up in her family's restaurant business with an ambition to sing. A childhood case of tuberculosis, which left her with a scarred lung, made her chosen career a strenuous one. From age twelve, she began singing in night-clubs in order to save the money necessary to support her education. She won a scholarship to study under Irene Jessner at the University of Toronto. She came to the Met in 1959, a winner of the National Council Auditions, and debuted as Poussette in *Manon*. Her Met portrayal of Liù in *Turandot*, with **Birgit Nilsson** and **Franco Corelli**, propelled her entry into the international arena where she continued to thrive, and became known for her dramatic and thoroughly musical performances. Her collaboration with Franco Zeffirelli for the Metropolitan's production of *La bohème* led to the filming of *La traviata*, again with Zeffirelli. Her recordings, a very short list, include the non-operatic *Show Boat*, and two albums of songs by Kurt Weill, for which she was coached by Weill's widow, **Lotte Lenya**. Other career highlights included two long runs at the Met in *The Ghosts of Versailles*, her portrayal of Berg's *Lulu*, and Weill's Jenny in *Mahagonny*, January 1995, the last of her 385 Met performances. Notorious for canceling, she said that having been ill as a girl, anything that upset her constricted her throat and she couldn't sing. Her self-imposed exile has given her the status of opera's Garbo.

Stratas has also received appreciation for her charity work, which included a sabbatical in India to care for leper victims, under the guidance of the late Mother Teresa.

New Zealand soprano **Dame KIRI Te KANAWA** was born in Gisborne, Auckland, March 6, 1944, to a Maori father and an Irish mother. By the age of twenty she had won all major vocal prizes available in New Zealand and Australia, and received a grant for study at the London Opera Centre with Vera Rozsa. Her operatic debut was in the Camden Festival, 1969, in Rossini's *La Donna del Lago*. She caught the attention of Sir Colin Davis and gained legendary status almost overnight with her debut as the Countess in *Marriage of Figaro* at Covent Garden, 1971, reprising the role the same year in her American debut at Santa Fe Opera. On February 9, 1974, she was called on a few hours notice to substitute for **Teresa Stratas** as Desdemona in the Met's *Otello*. Her performance won unanimous praise, and moved her into the front rank of international opera where she became the most famous soprano of the 20th century, in both lyric Mozart roles and Verdi dramatic characters. Her opera appearances have been at every major house worldwide, with concerts throughout Europe, America and Australia, including the desert outback. Her recordings feature the most famous of her opera roles, and outside the opera field the successful *Songs of the Auvergne, Blue Skies* with Nelson Riddle and his orchestra, song albums of George Gershwin, Cole Porter and Jerome Kern, three classics of the musical stage, *My Fair Lady*, *South Pacific* and *West Side Story*, and the world premiere of Beatle Paul McCartney's *Liverpool Oratorio*.

In 1981, as a soloist at the wedding of Prince Charles and Princess Diana, she sang before the largest telecast audience (estimated at over 600 million) of any singer in history. In 1982, she was made a Dame Commander of the British Empire. For her fiftieth birthday celebration, she gave a spectacular concert at the Royal Albert Hall. In the 1995 Queen's Birthday Honours List, she was awarded the Order of New Zealand. Te Kanawa made her last Met appearance January 1998, but continues as a sought-after recitalist. For the opening of the New York Philharmonic season, September 20, 2000, she joined the orchestra and Kurt Masur for arias of Mozart and Strauss. February 2001 saw her in Barber's *Vanessa* with Opera Monte Carlo, June brought a concert with the Israel Symphony, and August a recital at Tanglewood. After singing *Vanessa* for Washington Opera in 2002, she repeated the role at Los Angeles Opera, November 2004. 2006 marked duo recitals with **Frederica Von Stade**.

Since her 1997 painful divorce from Desmond Park, ending a thirty year marriage, she lives in East Sussex, England. Their adopted children, Antonia and Tom, are both adults. Her singing, Kiri says, "will continue for the moment, because I want to keep a bit of profile for the foundation," referring to her foundation devoted entirely to New Zealand singers and musicians.

LUCIA VALENTINI TERRANI, born in Padua, Italy, August 28, 1946, made her debut at the Teatro Grande in Brescia, in *La Cenerentola*, a signature role she performed at La Scala, Vienna State Opera, Teatro Colón (Buenos Aires), Aix-en-Provence Festival, Bolshoi Theatre, Covent Garden, Chicago Lyric Opera and Kennedy Center. She annually participates in the Rossini Opera Festival in Pesaro. Winner of the Italian critics' Abbiati Award as the top female interpreter in 1981, she sang the title role of *L'Italiana in Algieri* at the Met, 1974, and at La Scala, 1973, with whom she toured the Far East. Her repertoire also includes *Werther*, *Mignon*, *Falstaff* and *Boris Godunov*. She has made numerous successful recordings.

ANNA TOMOWA-SINTOW, born September 22, 1943, in Stara Zagora, studied at the Bulgarian State Conservatory in Sofia, and made her operatic debut as Tatyana (*Eugene Onegin*) in 1965. She joined the Leipzig Opera in 1967, became a member of the Berlin Opera Company (1972–76), and won the International Singers Competition in Rio de Janeiro (1971). In 1973, **Herbert von Karajan** chose her for the world premiere of Orff's *De temporum fine comedia* at the Salzburg Festival. She has performed in Munich, San Francisco, Chicago, Florence, Covent Garden, Vienna, Paris, and made her Met debut in 1978 as Donna Anna. Among her other roles are Elsa, Aida, the Marschallin, Amelia Boccanegra, Elisabeth (*Tannhäuser*), Yaroslavna (*Prince Igor*), and the Countess Almaviva. She has many recordings to her credit, including several Mozart works and choral performances with the late, great Herbert von Karajan.

SHIRLEY VERRETT was born May 31, 1931, in New Orleans. (See Black Heritage.)

FREDERICA VON STADE, or Flicka, as she is affectionately known to her fans, is one of the world's most beloved mezzos. Her mastery of *bel canto* operas receives continual worldwide acclaim. Born June 1, 1945, in Somerville, New Jersey, she was educated at the Norton Academy in Connecticut, apprenticed at the Long Wharf Theatre, New Haven, and studied at Mannes College of Music in New York. After reaching the semi-finals of the Met auditions in 1969, she attracted the attention of **Sir Rudolf Bing**[182] who arranged her 1970 debut at the Met as a Genie in *The Magic Flute*. In 1973, she sang Cherubino in Paris, Nina in the 1974 premiere of Pasatieri's *The Seagull* in Houston, and Rosina in '75 at Covent Garden. There followed extraordinary success in lyric mezzo roles. Her mentor, and then husband, Peter Elkus, guided her through an expanding repertory and worldwide schedule. He is the father of her two daughters, Jenny and Lisa,

Frederica Von Stade

---

182. Vienna-born Sir Rudolf Bing (1902–97) was Met manager from 1950–72, an eventful and turbulent period legendary for his run-ins with prima donnas. Knighted in 1971 by Queen Elizabeth II, he wrote two autobiographies, *5000 Nights at the Opera* (1972) and *A Knight at the Opera* (1981).

but after twelve years their marriage broke up. In 1990, she married businessman Michael Gorman, and lives in Northern California.

During the 1976 Bicentennial, she was the only American to appear with the visiting La Scala and Paris Opera companies in *La Cenerentola* and *The Marriage of Figaro*, respectively. Winner of numerous awards, von Stade holds honorary doctorates from Yale, Georgetown School of Medicine and Mannes College. In 1983, her contributions to the art world were recognized by an achievement award given by the late President Ronald Reagan, and in 1998 she was awarded France's highest honor in the arts when she was appointed as an officer of *L'Ordre des Arts et des Lettres*. From Strauss' Octavian to Mozart's Cherubino, her slender build has been ideal in having become the world's favorite interpreter of the great trouser roles. As a singing actress, she has portrayed the wonderful works in operetta and musical theater, especially *The Merry Widow* and *A Little Night Music*. During the '94–'95 season, she sang Marguerite in *La Damnation de Faust* at La Scala, and Rosina in *Il Barbiere di Siviglia* at Lyric Opera of Chicago. Her recordings are universal bestsellers. She has also starred in several PBS-TV specials.

Singing the title role in *Pelléas et Mélisande* in the 1994–95 season marked the twenty-fifth anniversary of her Met debut. She was also among the star-studded cast who sang for James Levine's Twenty-fifth Anniversary Gala, April 27, 1996. In 1998, American composer Richard Danielpour helped her realize a personal dream when he wrote *Elegies*. The work is a tribute to her father, Charles von Stade, who was killed in World War II. The text is based on the letters he sent her mother during the war, through which his daughter came to know him.

Her repertoire continually expands with the works of contemporary composers. For Dallas Opera, she created the role of Tina in Argento's *The Aspern Papers*, based on the Henry James book, and premiered Madame de Merteuil in Conrad Susa's *Dangerous Liaisons* at San Francisco. When Jake Heggie wrote *Dead Man Walking*, he offered Flicka the leading role. She realistically told him this needed a younger woman, and saw to it that **Susan Graham** got the role. The opera premiered in January 2001, in San Francisco. This concern for younger singers illustrates her selflessness, making her a unique and important role model in the competitive world of opera. In March 2000, in celebration of her thirtieth anniversary at the Met, their first-ever production of *The Merry Widow* was staged with von Stade in the leading role. At fifty-four, she said, "I'm so grateful for *The Merry Widow!* At last I'm singing someone my own age." She sang for the Met Gala, January 21, 2001, celebrating Plácido Domingo's sixtieth birthday. September 2005, she was in Los Angeles for Offenbach's operetta *La Grande-Duchesse de Gérolstein*, followed in December with a recital at the Kennedy Center Terrace Theater, with Richard Stillwell.

A busy 2006 included the International Summer Festival in Montreal, and unique duo recitals with Dame **Kiri Te Kanawa** beginning September at UC Berkeley, Urbana, Illinois, Columbus, Georgia and on to Europe covering Helsinki, London, Birmingham and Paris! Then back to Los Angeles Opera in November for *L'incoronazione di Poppea*.

21st Century Prima Donnas

June Anderson
Aïnhoa Arteta
Christine Barbaux
Cecilia Bartoli
Isabel Bayrakdarian
Stephanie Blythe
Barbara Bonney
Olga Borodina
Jane Bunnell
Sally Burgess
Zheng Cao
Katherine Ciesinski
Kristine Ciesinski
Rebecca Copley
Marianne Cornetti
Michele Crider
Yun Deng
Natalie Dessay
Jane Eaglen
Maria Ewing
Adria Firestone
Lauren Flanigan
Renée Fleming
Barbara Frittoli
Elizabeth Futral
Inessa Galante
Lesley Garrett
Viveca Genaux
Angela Gheorghiu
Angela Gilbert
Christine Goerke

Galina Gorchakova
Susan Graham
Denyce Graves
Maria Guleghina
Anja Harteros
Hei-Kyung Hong
Sumi Jo
Rosemary Joshua
Solveig Kringelborn
Jennifer Larmore
Lorraine Lieberson (1954–2006)
Margquita Lister
Karita Mattila
Sylvia McNair
Waltraud Meier
Susanne Mentzer
Aprile Millo
Erie Mills
Nelly Miricioiu
Heidi Grant Murphy
Noemi Nadelmann
Anna Netrebko
Mzia Nioradze
Anne Sofie von Otter
Ewa Podleś
Emily Pulley
Ashley Putnam
Patricia Racette
Sondra Radvanovsky
Deborah Riedel
Jean Rigby

Andrea Rost
Martile Rowland
Gabriele Schnault
Diana Soviero
Cheryl Studer
Sharon Sweet
Ruth Ann Swenson
Dawn Upshaw
Carol Vaness
Veronica Villaroel
Deborah Voigt
Yoko Watanabe (1956–2004)
Jennifer Welch-Babidge
Janet Williams
Karen Williams
Dolora Zajick
Elena Zaremba
Elena Zelenskaya
Ai-Lan Zhu
Delores Ziegler

Rising to the Top
Diana Damrau
Mary Dunleavy
Cristina Gallardo-Domas
Lisa Milne
Dorothea Röschmann
Ekaterina Kiurina
Krassimira Stoyanova
Violeta Urmana

June Anderson

Although some of the singers here profiled are over fifty, with today's accent on health and diet, it would be safe to turn the clock back at least ten years to compare the vitality of these women—and their careers—with forty-year-olds of previous decades. It should be kept in mind that the average female lifespan in 1900 was around forty-seven! (To sink into the vernacular: Do the Math!)

JUNE ANDERSON, born in Boston, December 30, 1952, first gained acclaim at seventeen as the youngest finalist in the Metropolitan Opera National Auditions. After graduating from

Yale, she made her debut October 26, 1978, as the Queen of the Night in *The Magic Flute* at New York City Opera, where she remained until 1981. Her European debut was in 1982 as Semiramide in Rome. In the course of her highly successful career, she continues to appear at the world's major opera houses in roles such as Desdemona, Lucia, Violetta, Donna Elvira, Gilda, and Isabella (*Robert le Diable*). Some career highlights have been appearing in a docudrama of the life of Adelina Patti, singing in concert at the 1989 opening of the Bastille Opera, Paris, the same year she made her Met debut as Gilda (*Rigoletto*). She was part of the Pavarotti Thirtieth Anniversary Gala in 1991, and has made several TV appearances and recordings. She also performed at the Twenty-Fifth Anniversary Gala of Met conductor James Levine,[183] April 27, 1996. In 1998 she was Leonora in *Il trovatore* at the Met, and the following year *La traviata* in Buenos Aires, and *Norma* in Geneva. Her voice, both strong and flexible, is ideally suited to the *bel canto* repertoire. Called upon by family friend Mark Weinstein, general director of Pittsburgh Opera, she opened their season in a role debut of *Anna Bolena*. For the 2001–02 season at the Met she returned for *La traviata*, a role she reprised at Palm Beach Opera in 2003. The same year she was in *Die Fledermaus* at Washington Opera.

Aïnhoa Arteta

AÏNHOA ARTETA, born September 24, 1964, in Tolosa, in the Basque region of Spain, came to international attention in 1993 when she won both the Met National Council Auditions and the Concours de Voix d'Opéra, Plácido Domingo. Beginning in 1990, Domingo picked her to accompany him in a series of recitals throughout Spain, followed by joint concerts in Berlin, Leipzig, Munich, Paris, Istanbul and Rio de Janeiro. 1993–94 brought Violetta and Oscar (*Un ballo in maschera*) in Graz (Austria), San Sebastian (Spain), Gilda in Madrid, Gilda and Marguerite (*Faust*) in Mexico and Micaëla (*Carmen*) at Scottish National Opera. The following season she made debuts as Mimi and Violetta at the Met, Marguerite at Seattle, plus more concerts in Spain. In 1995–96, she made her Italian debut at Naples' Teatro San Carlo as Mimi, and her Netherlands debut in the same role. She also sang Magda (*La Rondine*) in Bonn, directed by the tenor's wife, **Marta Domingo**, and performed in Portugal, Barcelona, Brazil, Mexico, Michigan and in a gala concert with the Washington Opera celebrating Plácido Domingo's appointment as artistic director.

1996–97 marked a return to the Met as Violetta, and Olga (*Fedora*), debuts at Washington Opera as Violetta, the Grand Théâtre Municipal de Bordeaux as Leïla (*The Pearl Fishers*), an acclaimed concert with Domingo in San Diego, and the summer Met-in-the-Park performances as Micaëla. For the 1999–2000 season she debuted with San Francisco Opera as Musetta (*La bohème*), repeating the role at the Met. The remainder of the season included over a dozen recitals in her native Spain, and productions of *La traviata* in Las Palmas, *The Barber of Seville* in Valladolid, and *Figaro* with LA Opera. During the 2001–02 season at the Met she was in *Parade*, An Evening of French Music Theatre, and Poulenc's *Les Mamelles de Tirésias*.

A Sony release features Arteta performing in concert with Domingo. This artist has certainly fulfilled her early promise.

French soprano **CHRISTINE BARBAUX**, born in 1955 in Saint-Mande, studied at the Paris Conservatory, and made her debut in 1977 at Strasbourg as Despina (*Così fan tutti*). By 1978 she was singing in Paris, as well as Vienna and Salzburg under **Herbert von Karajan**. She has since performed in major centers throughout Europe in such roles as Ophelia in Ambroise Thomas' *Hamlet*, Blanche Force (*Dialogues of the Carmelites*), Alice Ford (*Falstaff*) and Gilda. Her recordings include *Werther*, *Pelléas et Mélisande*, and Fauré's *Pénélope*.

As the daughter of two opera singers, **CECILIA BARTOLI**, born in Rome, June 4, 1966, made an early operatic debut singing the Shepherd in *Tosca* at the Rome Opera when she was just nine years old. After a brief adolescent foray into flamenco dancing, at seventeen she realized where her real future lay and began serious study with her mother, Silvana Bazzoni, who remains her only voice teacher, aside from classes at the Academy of Santa

---

183. James Levine (*b* 1943) has been the popular Met conductor since 1971, maintaining its reputation of world standing. He also guest conducts worldwide, and in 2003 assumed the directorship of the Boston Symphony.

Cecilia in Rome. At nineteen, she sang at the memorial concert for **Maria Callas**. Her career was launched in a special television appearance, singing the Barcarolle duet from *The Tales of Hoffmann* with **Katia Ricciarelli**, and the duet from *The Barber of Seville* with Leo Nucci. Her rendition of the final aria from *La Cenerentola* at a Paris Opera gala so impressed **Daniel Barenboim** that he engaged her for an orchestral concert at the Salle Pleyel in Paris, conducting her in two Rossini and Mozart arias—her *forte*. After three amazing sell-outs at Lincoln Center's Avery Fisher Hall, her future was secured. *Time* magazine voted her the "1992 Top Recording Artist" in both the classical and popular categories, which included three Rossini albums and two Mozart albums for Decca/London. Chandos released a DVD titled *Cecilia and Bryn* at Glyndebourne, a 1999 recital with Welsh baritone **Bryn Terfel**, featuring music of Handel, Mozart, Rossini, Haydn and Donizetti. September 15, 1995 brought her to San Diego with a recital and a friendly meeting with the author.

Her eagerly-awaited Metropolitan Opera debut came February 8, 1996, as Despina in *Così fan tutte*. Her Met appearances, tarnished by cancellations, have not been as frequent as her fans would like. She was to have opened the 2001–02 season in *La sonnambula* with Mexican tenor **Ramón Vargas**, but when he cancelled, and the Met could not promise her a tenor she knew, she likewise cancelled. It was to have been sung in the lower-keyed Malibran edition written by Bellini for mezzo **Maria Malibran** (1808–36).

Cecilia has said of herself, "I am *Cancilia*—the false star who never shows up." Many years before, it was **Teresa Stratas** who had become known in opera circles as the "Canceller of the Exchequer." (The Met can fill the house with the popular *Bohème*, *Carmen*, *Tosca*, and *Aida*, no matter who is singing, so it no longer relies on stars as in the past.)

In March 2000, in Zurich, where the acoustics are perfect for Bartoli, she sang Fiordiligi, making her perhaps the first to have performed all three female roles in *Così fan tutte*. Though most of her performances are in Europe, she gave a Carnegie Hall recital February 2001, drawn from her Decca *Vivaldi Album*, a triumph of magically acute passage work and ornamentation—evidence of her dedicated training. Multiple standing ovations were rewarded with four encores. The following day the album, whose music was unearthed by Bartoli and her companion, musicologist Claudio Osele, was awarded a Grammy.

A disc of French songs presents Bartoli in a more modern vein with well-known Ravel songs, not so well known songs of Bizet and completely unknown songs by **Pauline Viardot Garcia**, whom Bartoli regards as an extraordinary singer and composer. Continuing work in the period has resulted in albums of Gluck and Antonio Salieri who, despite the untrue legend he poisoned Mozart, wrote extraordinary music. Her CD *Opera Probita* (2005), with Les Musiciens du Louvrearias, has arias by Handel, Scarlatti and Caldara.

On May 28, 2003, Bartoli was presented with the "Outstanding Contribution to Music" award at the Classical Brits awards in London's Royal Albert Hall, where she gave a spellbinding performance of Vivaldi repertoire—televised on UK ITV1.

Cecilia divides her performance time of about seven months of the year into one third opera, one third concerts and one third recitals. Although she has recorded others, on stage she concentrates on five main roles: Despina, Cherubino, Zerlina, Rosina and Cenerentola, with a sixth, Haydn's *Euridice*, already recorded with Christopher Hogwood. Another opera added to her repertoire is Paisiello's *Nina, O sia la pazza per amore*.

ISABEL BAYRAKDARIAN was born in Lebanon of Armenian parents and raised in Canada from age fourteen. A biomedical engineering honors graduate from the University of Toronto, she also began voice studies at the Royal Conservatory to improve her church singing. With degrees in both fields, it was her singing career that took off. She had sung recitals in Canada, and won the 1997 Met's National Council Auditions. The following year, she studied at **Marilyn Horne's** Academy of the West in Santa Barbara (California). Horne invited her to perform at her January 2000 sixty-fourth birthday celebration in Carnegie Hall, with **Renée Fleming**, **Dolora Zajick**, and Bryn Terfel. Also in 2000, Isabel won the Operalia Vocal Competition. Her Weill Recital Hall debut came in 2001.

In 1999, she sang Catherine in the world premiere in Chicago of William Bolcom's *View from the Bridge*, then made her Met debut in the same role, December 2002. November 2001 brought *Orfeo ed Euridice* in Ann Arbor, with **Ewa Podleś**, and Valencienne in *The Merry Widow* for San Francisco in December. She again teamed up with Podleś in Handel's *Giulio Cesare* with the Canadian Opera Company (Toronto, 2002). 2003 saw Susanna (*The Marriage of Figaro*) for Chicago, and Teresa in *Benvenuto Cellini* at the Met in December. During 2004 she was Leila in *The Pearl Fishers* for San Diego,[184] reprised Susanna for Los Angeles and Pittsburgh, and Zerlina (*Don Giovanni*) at Chicago, a role she sang at the Met in 2005. The same year brought her back to Chicago for Marzelline in *Fidelio*. She sang in the gala performance at the Met (September 2005), honoring retiring director Joseph Volpe.

Concert appearances have been at Carnegie Hall, and recitals with Minnesota and San Francisco Symphonies, and Canada in Victoria, Vancouver, Montreal, Edmonton and Toronto. She has also given recitals in Spain, where she and her concert pianist husband, Serovj Kradjian, have a home.

Her recital disks include *Joyous Light* (CBC Records, 2002), a celebration of Armenian sacred music that marked the 1,700th anniversary of Christianity as Armenia's state religion. So successful, it led to an offer to record "Evenstar" for the soundtrack of *Lord of the Rings: The Two Towers*. This was followed by *Azulão*, featuring the sensuous songs of Granados, Rodrigo, De Falla, and Villa-Lobos' *Bachianas Brasileiras # 5* for soprano and eight cellos. This won Best Classical Album of the Year at the 2004 Juno Awards. In 2004 she recorded *Cleopatra*, selected arias from operas by German baroque composers. Her fourth CD, *Pauline Viardot-Garcia* (Analekta, 2005), contains the music of this singer/composer (1821–1910), sister of famed mezzo, **Maria Malibran** (1808–36). (See Immortal Singers.)

A small-town girl born in Mongaup Valley, in New York's Catskill Mountains, 1970, mezzo **STEPHANIE BLYTHE** entered SUNY Potsdam's Crane School of Music intending to be a music teacher. Instead, she came out of the Met's Lindemann Young Artist Development program as an accomplished singer with a voice and personality adaptable to a wide range of characters and musical styles. After graduation (1993), she received a two-year Tanglewood summer fellowship. She made her Met debut at twenty-five as the Voice in *Parsifal* (1995). The same year she received the Richard F. Gold Career Grant, Opera Index award and, in 1999, the distinguished Richard Tucker Foundation award.

1999–2000 brought *La Grande-Duchesse de Gérolstein* in France, *The Italian Girl in Algiers* in Philadelphia, a striking Carmen in Tulsa, Fricka in Stephen Wadsworth's Seattle production of *Das Rheingold* and *Die Walküre*, returning for the complete *Ring* in August 2001, and *Giulio Cesare* at the Met—where she stole the show—followed in 2001–02 by *Falstaff* and *Hänsel und Gretel*.

Blythe has also made her mark as a recitalist, appearing January 21, 2001, at the 92nd Street Y in an all-American program that included Alan Smith's song cycle *Vignettes: Ellis Island*, written especially for her. As an American, she believes an all-American program is called for. "Not all the time," she allows, "but we have all this great material of our own, so why do recitals of lieder and chansons?" (It has already been observed that she could be a great cabaret singer.)

Her star continues to rise. The Met heard her as Jocasta in Stravinsky's opera-oratorio *Oedipus Rex*, February 2004, and Eduige in Handel's *Rodelinda*, January 1, 2005. During 2005–06, she was in *Falstaff*.

Barbara Bonney

BARBARA BONNEY, born April 14, 1956, in Montclair, New Jersey, is renowned for her roles in Mozart and Strauss operas. She spent two years at the University of New Hampshire as a music and German major before enrolling at the University of Salzburg for further German studies. Accepted into the vocal program at the Mozarteum in Salzburg (1979), she subsequently joined Darmstadt Opera as Anna in *The Merry Wives of Windsor*. After appearing at Munich, Frankfurt, Hamburg, Vienna, Geneva and Zürich, she made her London Covent Garden debut in 1984. Her interpretations of Sophie in *Der Rosenkavalier* under Sir **Georg Solti** (1912–97) and **Carlos Kleiber** have both been released on video, as has her La Scala perform-

---

184. So alluring were the publicity photos of Bayrakdarian for San Diego Opera's *Pearl Fishers*, NYCO used the same theater poster advertising their production of the opera despite the fact she was not in it.

ance of Pamina (*Die Zauberflöte*). A regular at the Met, where she debuted in 1989 as Najade in *Ariadne auf Naxos*, in November 1999 she was in San Francisco for *Idomeneo*, then back to the Met for the 1999–2000 season in *The Marriage of Figaro*, and Richard Strauss' *Arabella* (2001–02). Other Met appearances were *Falstaff* and *L'elisir d'amore*, and *Figaro* and *Der Rosenevalier* at the Bastille in Paris. She toured Japan with **Seiji Osawa**, and had a major European tour with the Oslo Philharmonic and **Mariss Jansons**. One of the finest lieder singers of her generation, Bonney's concert appearances include the Vienna Philharmonic under Ozawa and **Riccardo Muti**, and the Berlin Philharmonic with **Claudio Abbado**. In her summer Tanglewood residency, she appeared with the Boston Symphony Orchestra.

Her CDs include *lieder* by Richard Strauss, Hugo Wolf, Mendelssohn and Schubert, plus complete recordings of Mozart's *Marriage of Figaro*, *Don Giovanni*, *Magic Flute*, *La clemenza di Tito* and Humperdinck's *Hansel and Gretel*. Recent releases include for Decca, *Exultate jubilate* with Trevor Pinnock, and *Carmina Burana* with André Previn (DGG). Purcell's complete songs with Robert King and the King's Consort are on Hyperion.

Barbara was married to Swedish baritone, **Håkan Hagegard**. They have two children. She withdrew from performing at the end of the 2006 season.

Mezzo **OLGA BORODINA**, known for her Delilah, Carmen, Amneris and Eboli, was born July 29, 1953, in Minsk, Russia. As a star of Kirov Opera, she appeared in live television broadcasts of Mussorgsky and Prokofiev operas, and performed all over the world. She made her Paris debut in 1992 at Opera Bastille in *Boris Godunov*, a role she reprised in 2002. Her London debut was at Covent Garden with **Plácido Domingo** in *Samson et Dalila*, where she was invited back for *La Cenerentola* and as Marguérite in *La damnation de Faust* with Sir Colin Davis. She came to the Met with the Kirov Opera, with whom she has toured in Spain, Germany, Italy and Japan. In 1989, she won the Barcelona Competition and first prize in the Rosa Ponselle International Vocal Competition. 1997 marked her Salzburg Festival debut in *Boris Godunov*, with returns in 1999 and 2001 for Eboli (*Don Carlo*). La Scala heard her as the Principessa in *Adriana Lecouvreur* (1999), Delilah with Domingo in 2002, and Carmen in 2004.

Borodina's American debut was in 1995 in San Francisco with *Cenerentola*, returning there for her first Carmen in 1996, *The Tsar's Bride* came in 2000 and *Samson and Delilah* in 2001. Her long awaited Metropolitan Opera debut came in 1997 with *Boris Godunov*. She returned to the Met for opening night (1998–99) in *Samson and Delilah*, again with Domingo. Subsequent Met engagements have included *Pique Dame*, *Aida*, *Carmen* and more *Samson and Delilah*. 2003 saw her as Dido (*Les Troyens*), and Isabella in *L'Italiana in Algieri* in 2004. After a September 2005 appearance at San Francisco for *The Italian Girl in Algiers*, she was back at the Met in October for *La Cenerentola* and began 2006 as Amneris, and in *Samson et Dalila*.

After her 1985 debut with the New York City Opera, **JANE BUNNELL**, born December 19, 1952, in Madison, New Jersey, has performed extensively in the U.S. and Europe with a repertoire of favorite roles, including Suzuki (*Madama Butterfly*) and Natalie (*The Merry Widow*). At the Met she is known for Dorabella (*Così fan tutte*), Cherubino (*Le Nozze di Figaro*), Rosina (*Il barbiere di Siviglia*), and the pants role, Nicklausse (*Les Contes d'Hoffmann*). She has been a frequent guest at Lincoln Center's Mostly Mozart Festival, and has performed with the New York Chamber Orchestra, Israel Philharmonic, Baltimore Symphony, Atlanta Symphony and the St. Paul Chamber Orchestra. Among the major vocal competitions she has won are the Metropolitan Opera National Council Auditions. New York City Opera presented her its Stanley Tausend Memorial Award and the coveted Diva Award.

Bunnell is an adjunct instructor at the University of Indiana Department of Music and Performing Arts Professions School.

Mezzo **SALLY BURGESS**, born October 9, 1953, in Durban, South Africa, has an extensive repertory. She has sung Carmen at the Met, Opèra National de Paris, Bavarian State Opera, (Munich), Bregenz Festival (Austria) and in Zurich, Berlin and New Zealand. A regular with England's Opera North, she has performed in *Aida*, *Orfeo*, *The Trojans*, *Carmen* and *Il trovatore*. At English National Opera, she won raves for her debut in David Pountney's production of *Carmen*. 1996 saw her at the Met as Isabella in *The Voyage* by Philip Glass. Other roles include Kabanicha (*Kat'a Kabanová*); Fricka (*The Ring*) in Geneva and for Scottish Opera; Ottavia in David Alden's production of *L'Incoronazione di Poppea* for Welsh National Opera, also recorded for BBC TV; Dalila (Nantes Opera); Orfeo for Opera North; Judith (*Bluebeard's Castle*) and Dulcinèe (*Don Quixote*) for ENO, where she also enjoyed success as Widow Begbick (*The Rise and Fall of the City of Mahagonny*); Herodias (*Salome*) and Mère Marie (*Dialogues des Carmelites*) for WNO.

She sang in the world premiere of Paul McCartney's *Liverpool Oratorio* at the American premiere at Carnegie Hall and on the subsequent EMI recording. In the popular field, she was nominated for "Best Actress in a Musical" at the Olivier Awards for her performance in the RSC/Opera North co-production of *Showboat* in London's West End, a musical she also recorded for TER Records, as well as *West Side Story* and *The King and I*. Her songs range from the classics of Gershwin, Cole Porter and Jerome Kern to works by contemporaries Sondheim and Bernstein. A CD of this music was released in 2003. She presented her one-woman show, *Sally Burgess' Women*, written especially for her, at the Lyric Theatre, Hammersmith (London), and sang in a Gershwin Centenary Gala at Barbican Hall. For the 2003–04 Met season she sang *The Merry Widow*.

ZHENG CAO, a native of Shanghai, holds degrees from both the Shanghai Conservatory and, after coming to the U.S. in 1988, an MM from Curtis. A former Adler Fellow, she made her SFO debut in the trouser role Siébel (*Faust*, 1995). Other SFO stagings have been *Die Walküre*, *Rusalka*, *Salome*, *Electra*, *The Marriage of Figaro* (Cherubino, 1998) and Idamante (*Idomeneo*, 1999). Her *Madama Butterfly* performances have been in Geneva, San Diego (as Suzuki), Opéra de Lyon, and NYCO. Other appearances were in *The Marriage of Figaro* in Ghent, *The Barber of Seville* in Washington and Michigan, Zerlina in *Don Giovanni* with Los Angeles Opera, and Siébel in *Faust*, San Diego. She has concertized in Europe, the U.S. and, in 1998, was one of the soloists for the opening ceremony at the Winter Olympics. After more than half a dozen performances in Europe and the U.S., she retired Suzuki from her repertoire for three years so as not to be permanently typecast, but in 2002 reprised the role for SFO, which she calls home. Besides the usual mezzo roles, she sings Monteverdi and Jake Heggie, who dedicated the three-song cycle *Before the Storm* to her in 1998. Now a U.S. citizen, Zheng credits her adaptation to America to Troy Donahue, with whom she has been for over ten years. They met when she was singing shipboard concerts on a cruise line.

Mezzo **KATHERINE CIESINSKI** has been lovingly described by her sister Kristine as a musical genius with perfect pitch and a photographic memory. Her non-musical family had no idea of this until Grandma's piano was moved to their house, and Katherine was picking out tunes by the time she was four. She has memorized and performed an entire operatic score on forty-eight hours' notice—a feat often repeated with symphonic and chamber works.

Born in Delaware, October 13, 1950, she was valedictorian of her high school class and one of Temple University's "Most Distinguished Woman Graduates" (BM, 1972; MM, 1973). One of the youngest students to be accepted into the Curtis opera program, after graduation (1976) she won the Geneva International Competition—the first woman to win first prize in twelve

Katherine Ciesinski

years. The following year a *unanimous* jury placed her first in the Paris International Vocal Competition. Her association with American opera began with Erika in Samuel Barber's *Vanessa*, at the 1978 Spoleto Festival, telecast on PBS. Since then, she has given the world premieres of *The Aspern Papers* (1988) and *The Dream of Valentino* (Dominick Argento), both at Dallas, *Resurrection* (Tod Machover), and *Little Women*, by NYCO composer-in-residence Mark Adamo (*b* 1962)—these at Houston. Her successful international career covers the Met, Covent Garden, Paris Opera and every major house on both sides of the Atlantic, as Carmen, Waltraute, Judith (*Bluebeard's Castle*), Laura (*La Gioconda*), Octavian (*Der Rosenkavalier*), Mère Marie (*Dialogues of the Carmelites*), Nicklausse (*Tales of Hoffmann*), Octavia (*Coronation of Poppea*), Hansel, Xerxes, Cassandre (*Les Troyens*), Adalgisa (*Norma*), Dulcinée (*Don Quichotte*), Cornelia (*Giulio Cesare*), Countess Geschwitz (*Lulu*), and countless others, as well as performing with the world's leading orchestras, and in solo and duet recitals with her sister. In 1997, she sang her first Herodias in Santa Fe Opera's production of *Salome*, reprised the role for Houston and, in February 1998, in San Diego, where, also for the first time, she sang opposite her sister Kristine's Salome. In 1998 she was Adelaide in Richard Strauss' *Arabella* with **Renée Fleming** at HGO.

Ciesinski's mounting discography on Decca, Columbia, CRI, BMG, and Erato includes the world premiere of Brian Ferneybough's *On Stellar Magnitudes*, the title role of Mark Blitzstein's *Regina*, a Grammy nomination for *Pique Dame* with **Mirella Freni**, conducted by **Seiji Ozawa**, and a Grand Prix du Disque for her recording of Dukas' *Arriane et Barbe Bleue*. In 2000, EMI released the American premiere of Kurt Weill's *Die Bürgschaft*, which she had sung at the Spoleto Festival. The same year she sang Ma Moss in *The Tender Land* for Copland's centennial celebration at HGO, and Barber's *Vanessa*, this time as the Baroness, at Moores Opera Center. In 2001, she was in Colorado, home of Central City Opera—the house is an historic landmark, built by Welsh gold miners in 1878—for further performances as the Aunt in *Little Women*. In 2002, she was Larina (*Eugene Onegin*) at HGO, Kostelnička (*Jenůfa*), Long Beach (California) Opera, and Geneviève (*Pelléas et Mélisande*) for the Round Top Festival in Texas. Opening the 2002–2003 season at the Met, she sang the Countess of Coigny (*Andrea Chenier*) with **Plácido Domingo**. 2004 brought the world premiere of *The End of the Affair* by Jake Heggie with Houston Grand Opera.

In September 1994, Ciesinski joined the faculty of the University of Houston where, as chair of voice studies at the Moores School of Music, she became a fully-tenured professor in 2002.

Kristine Ciesinski

KRISTINE CIESINSKI was born in Wilmington, Delaware, July 5, 1952. With her sister as a role model, music was immediately part of her life. After graduating from Boston University (BFA, 1974), she studied with Todd Duncan, Gershwin's original *Porgy*, in Washington, DC (1977), and made three big wins: a scholarship to study at the Mozarteum, the annual Salzburg Opera Competition and first prize in the Geneva International Competition—won by her sister the previous year. She was then engaged by Salzburg Opera for three seasons, during which she mastered a basic repertoire. As her career flourished in Europe, she met and married William Henry, concertmaster of the San Diego Symphony until his tragic death from cancer in 1984. She then settled in New York and began appearing in opera and concert performances throughout the country, shifting from lyric to more dramatic roles, including *Tosca*, *Salome*, *Così fan tutte*. Back to Europe in 1985, she was the leading soprano at the Bremen State Opera, and became known all over the Continent as her singing ability, combined with athleticism and youthful looks, made her a favorite choice of directors looking for a believable Salome, Ariadne, Elisabeth (*Tannhäuser*), Leonora, Chrysothemis, the Foreign Princess in Rusalka, Medea, La Wally and Lady Macbeth. In 1986, she made her debut as Donna Anna with Scottish National Opera, followed by Senta (*The Flying Dutchman*) and Cassandra (*The Trojans*) at Opera North, a role she also sang at Welsh National Opera. In 1989, she made her London debut with ENO (where she has given 100-plus performances) as Anna Maurrant in Kurt Weill's *Street Scene*.

The '90s saw her at La Scala, Opera Bastille, Basel, Leipzig and the European houses where most of her appearances are. Her signature roles are mostly "crazy ladies"—Salome, Lady Macbeth of Mtsensk, Verdi's Lady Macbeth, and Marie (*Wozzeck*). Equal acclaim greets Kristine's recital and concert appearances in the music capitals of the world.

Both sisters appeared in San Diego Opera's *Salome* (February 1998), where her collection of body stockings was used for the famous Dance of the Seven Veils. She does not strip for this and never intends to. "I think it makes the audience nervous and tittery, as opposed to the presentation being erotic or mysterious." (The author, in the audience, can vouch for that.)

In January 1992, Kristine starred with her second husband, British Wagnerian bass-baritone Norman Bailey, in a BBC drama-documentary film, *The Secret Life of Alban Berg*. The couple met in Cincinnati in a production of *Die Meistersinger*, 1985, with Bailey as Hans Sachs and Kristine singing her first Eva. 2003 found her in Amersterdam for *The Makropolos Case.* 2005 brought *The Bassarids* (followers of Bacchus) by Hans Werder Henze in the same city, and *Wozzeck* in Hamburg.

In 2002, Kristine became a licensed pilot. She owns her own plane and teaches gliding.

Rebecca Copley

REBECCA COPLEY received her training at Bethany College in her native Lindsborg, Kansas, and continues to reside in this unique Swedish community. Her notable roles have been Desdemona with **James McCracken** in *Otello* (1987), plus title roles in *Turandot* for NYCO (1991), *Aida* with Arizona Opera (1994) and performances with San Diego Opera (1995). Her Met debut in 1992 was Amelia in *Un ballo in maschera.* She returned there for *The Magic Flute* ('93–'94), and Donna Anna in *Don Giovanni* ('94–'95, '95–'96). Other Met appearances have been *Don Giovanni* and *Il trovatore* in their New York City Parks concerts and East Asian tour. During the 1998–99 season, she debuted in Bilbao (Spain) in the title role of the Basque opera *Amaya*, opened the Fort Worth season with *Turandot*, and sang *Norma* with Baltimore Opera. The Prague Festival opener came September 1999, and a performance with the Bach Festival Society in an all-Wagner program was in April 2000. Another Turandot was with Minnesota Opera, 2000–01. 2002–2003 found Copley at Avery Fisher Hall for Verdi's *Requiem*, participating in Opera Montreal's Seventh Gala, joining the Columbus (Ohio) Symphony for Haydn's *Lord Nelson Mass*, and performing several regional recitals and master classes. Her season opener for 2003–2004 was with Opera Carolina, singing Abigaille opposite Mark DeLavan's *Nabucco*, after which the Met welcomed her back in the same role, and later as the Foreign Princess in Dvořák's *Rusalka.*

Copley also continues as featured soloist with major symphonies throughout the U.S. and Europe.

Mezzo **MARIANNE CORNETTI**, born in Butler, Pennsylvania, November 4, 1964, sang her first Aida in 1996 with Hawaii Opera, and subsequently at Arena di Verona, Minnesota Opera, Opera Carolina and Opera Omaha. She has sung at the Met, Pittsburgh, Washington and Wolf Trap Opera, as Dorabella (*Così fan tutte*), Charlotte (*Werther*), Emilia (*Otello*), Rosina (*Barber of Seville*), and First Maid (*Elektra*). She debuted at Catania's Teatro Bellini as Azucena (*Il trovatore*), reprising the role with Pittsburgh Opera. During the 2000–01 season, she sang Amneris (*Aida*) in Vienna, debuted at La Scala as Azucena, and again at Rome Opera, then Eboli (*Don Carlo*) in Genoa. After her San Diego debut as Amneris, she repeated the role for Baltimore and Vienna. Her 2002–03 season included *Samson et Dalila* for the Teatro Carlo Felice in Genoa, Azucena with the Teatro Giuseppe Verdi in Trieste, and Amneris at the Met.

MICHELE CRIDER (See Black Heritage.)

YUN DENG has earned widespread recognition as a mezzo since her Met debut in 1985 as Olga in *Eugene Onegin*, returning there for productions of *Madama Butterfly, Manon Lescaut, Rigoletto, Salome, I Puritani, L'Enfant et les sortileges* and *Parsifal.* Born in Canton, China, she came to the U.S. to study at Juilliard, where she joined the American Opera Center. Suzuki has become a signature role which she has performed in Dallas, Philadelphia, San Diego, Washington, Baltimore, San Antonio, Miami, Montreal, Spain, in Japan under **Seiji Ozawa** (1995–96) and Hawaii (2000). She has also appeared at the Spoleto Festival (Italy) and in Taipei and Hong Kong in *Il trovatore* and *Norma*, among other worldwide performances, orchestral engagements and recordings with the Cologne and West Berlin Radio.

French soprano **NATALIE DESSAY**, born 1965, grew up in Bordeaux, and at thirteen gave up ballet for acting. When an acting role required singing, she found that not only could she sing in tune, but she had a naturally high voice. In 1990, she won the Mozart Competition in Vienna, and after international engagements joined the Vienna State Opera. Her Met debut was in 1994 as Arabella, with a 1997–98 return as Zerbinetta in *Ariadne auf Naxos* with **Deborah Voigt**, and a flawless coloratura Olympia in *Tales of Hoffmann*, even to a high G at the end, sung while she was pregnant with her second child. In the fall of 1999, she sang Handel's Alcina at the Bastille and Lyric Opera of Chicago. She was to repeat Zerbinetta with Voigt, April 2001, but had to cancel when her doctor put her on three months' vocal rest. The "rest" ended in surgery and being sidelined for nearly two years.

After a decade of singing light coloratura roles, working on Italian technique with her teacher Jean-Pierre Blivet and British pianist-coach Gerald Martin-Moore, La Scala invited her to do Amina in Bellini's *La sonnambula*, where **Maria Callas** had sung the role in 1955, followed in later years by distinguished *bel cantos* **Joan Sutherland**, **Renata Scotto** and **June Anderson**. The Met, which rarely stages *bel canto* works, was planning *La sonnambula* with Cecilia Bartoli in the lower-keyed Malibran (mezzo) edition, but when Bartoli cancelled, they kept it for Dessay in the 2002–03 season. She has studied with Renata Scotto, who drove herself to become a dramatic soprano, but Dessay says her voice won't let her go that far. She did sing *Lucia di Lammermoor* in January 2004 at Lyric Opera of Chicago, and Violetta later in the year. For the Met 2005–06 season she sang in *Roméo et Juliette*.

Natalie is married to baritone Laurent Naouri. They both maintain their careers, and take turns staying home with their two children.

MARINA DOMASHENKO was born in Kemerovo, Siberia, in 1971, spending her childhood and early teens as a pianist. Her two and a half years younger triplet sisters are respectively, a violinist, cellist and pianist. She graduated from the Kemerovo Arts Institute as a pianist and orchestral conductor, and also began to study singing. She continued vocal training at the Ekaterinburg Conservatory under the distinguished Svetlana Zaliznyak, graduating in 1998. Experience in all three fields has made a solid foundation for her operatic approach. She quickly became in demand at major opera houses and in concert series around the world.

First prize winner in the Dvořák International Vocal Competition in 1997, Domashenko made her European debut in 1998 with the Prague State Theatre, singing Olga (*Eugene Onegin*). She went on to sing Pauline (*Queen of Spades*), Dorabella (*Così fan tutte*), and Carmen at the Prague National Theatre and on their 1999 Japan tour. Also in 1999, she won first prize in Italy's Concorso Internazionale.

In 2000 she made her American debut at San Francisco Opera, singing Delilah at a gala concert with Plácido Domingo. During the 1999–2000 season she was Orlovsky (*Die Fledermaus*) and Paul (*Queen of Spades*) at Opera Bastille. In July, 2000 she was a soloist in Rossini's *Stabat Mater* at France's Montpelier Festival, where she returned July 2001, singing Russian romances with the Moscow Chamber Orchestra. The same month she appeared with Domingo in a gala concert in Moscow's Cathedral Square of the Kremlin. *Nabucco* (Vienna State Opera, Berlin Opera); concert appearances at Lincoln Center and London's Barbican Theatre, both with Sir Colin Davis and the London Symphony Orchestra were included in the season. 2002 reprised Pauline at Teatro Communale (Bologna, Italy), Puccini's *Suor Angelica* (Concertgebouw, Amsterdam), Olga (*Eugene Onegin* Moscow New Opera), and *Alexander Nevsky* (Athens and Venice).

In March 2006, she was a fiery, sultry Carmen in a flapper-style, excitingly staged production for San Diego Opera with **Karen Keltner** conducting.

Marina lives with her husband, Yuri Yakovlev, in Prague.

JANE EAGLEN was born April 4, 1960, in the small working-class town of Lincoln in Northern England, where her mother still lives. Her father died when she was ten. She studied at the Royal Northern College of Music, took master classes with **Elisabeth Schwarzkopf** and **Tito Gobbi**, and made her 1984 debut at ENO as Lady Ella in Gilbert and Sullivan's *Patience*. For the next seven years she sang various parts, *Madama Butterfly* with the Lyric Opera of Queensland (Australia), Mimi in *La bohème*, and in 1990 Donna Anna (*Don Giovanni*) with Scottish National Opera. Since then she has built up her repertory and her voice. In 1995, she sang in a concert performance of *Norma* with OONY, and word quickly spread **Eve Queler** had snared an up-and-coming sensation. This was a few weeks before Eaglen's Met debut in *Don Giovanni*, after which she was Turandot in Seattle, at the Met, and San Diego (1997). 1998–99 brought Norma in Paris, Isolde in Seattle and Brünnhilde in San Francisco. January 2000 saw her back in Chicago as Isolde, in the same production as Seattle. To this Englishwoman, Chicago is a second home, the site of her first *Ring*, first *Siegfried* and *Götterdämmerung*, and *La Gioconda*. In November it was back to the Met for Turandot, and in 2001 she was Norma. August brought a return to Seattle for their *Ring* cycle.

The fact that Eaglen has this broad range of roles is a testament to her versatility and courage. Since the retirement of **Birgit Nilsson**, there have been numerous contenders for the title, "world's great Wagnerian soprano." Jane, who is full-figured and virtually immobile onstage, acts with her voice, and has moved from contender to sole survivor. Married to Brian Lyson, whom she met in Seattle during the '96 *Turandot*, she says after years of touring on her own, she now has someone at her side helping with her schedule and business.

Her highly praised Norma was recorded with **Riccardo Muti**, on EMI. Other recordings include several discs for SONY: Strauss' *Four Last Songs*, Wagner's *Wiesendonck Lieder*, Berg's *Seven Early Songs*; *Jane Eaglen Sings Mozart and Strauss* with Zubin Mehta and the Israel Philharmonic; *Jane Eaglen: Bellini & Wagner Arias*; and for Chandos, Puccini's *Tosca* (in English).

2003 found her back at the Met for *Tristan und Isolde*, the first time in four years the house had put on this production, and in April 2004 she was Brünnhilde in three of the four *Ring* operas: *Die Walküre*, *Siegfried* and *Götterdämmerung*. This was followed by *Fidelio* at Seattle, and Senta at San Francisco Symphony's June festival in a semistaged *Flying Dutchman*.

Soprano turned mezzo, **MARIA EWING** was born in Detroit, March 27, 1950, to a Dutch mother and a Sioux Indian father, a talented pianist who filled the home with music. She started piano until one day at age thirteen, while accompanying her sister's singing, her mother realized that her younger daughter also had vocal talent, and lessons began. Maria made her debut in 1968 at the Meadow Brook Festival with **James Levine**, and studied at the Cleveland Institute with the famed **Eleanor Steber** (1914–90). During her two years there, Maria established an important friendship and collaboration with Levine, who became Met music director in 1971. Further training was in New York with diva **Jennie Tourel** (1900–73).

In 1973, Ewing debuted at the Ravinia Festival with the Chicago Symphony, her mentor James Levine conducting. The next few years she sang in Washington, DC, Boston, Santa Fe, Houston, San Francisco and Cincinnati. Her 1976 Met debut as Cherubino was followed by Mélisande at La Scala the same year. Back at the Met, she sang Rosina, Dorabella and Carmen. In 1978, she made her debut at Glyndebourne as Dorabella, becoming a regular there. From 1982–90 she was married to Sir Peter Hall, artistic director of Glyndebourne Festival Opera. They continue to work together. *Salome* marked both her 1988 Covent Garden and Chicago debuts, both to critical acclaim.

Considered a most dramatic stage personality, Ewing's repertoire includes *bel canto* and traditional roles, which she has sung all over the world including Japan and Australia. After a five year absence, she returned to the Met in 1993, as Dido in *Les Troyens*. In 1995, she toured with a Covent Garden production of *Carmen* in Israel, then returned to the Met as Katerina Ismailova in Shostakovich's *Lady Macbeth of Mtsensk*. In concert and recitals she has worked with **Sir Simon Rattle** and the City of Birmingham Symphony, the Royal Concertgebouw of Amsterdam and the London Symphony Orchestra. Maria makes her home in East Sussex, England, with her daughter Rebecca.

Adria Firestone

Best known for her portrayal of Bizet's *Carmen*—since her first performance in 1980 she has sung the role more than 100 times around the world—born in Los Angeles and raised in Miami, mezzo **ADRIA FIRESTONE** is of Spanish-Italian heritage. She studied with Sara Sforni-Corti at the Giuseppe Verdi Conservatory in Milan, and in New York. Since her debut, she has sung to sold out houses throughout the U.S., Mexico, Australia, New Zealand, Singapore and South America. Her other roles include Maddalena (*Rigoletto*), Candelas (*El amor brujo*), Abuela (*La vida breve*), Dalila (*Samson et Dalila*), Prince Orlovsky (*Die Fledermaus*), *Der Rosenkavalier* and Madame Flora in Gian Carlo-Menotti's *The Medium*. In 1997, she returned to San Diego as Carmen to the Don Jose of **Richard Leech**, and later in the season sang Doña Francisca in the San Diego world premiere of Myron Fink's *The Conquistador*. In 1999, in a major departure from her usual roles, she sang the Witch in SDO's production of Humperdinck's *Hansel and Gretal*, wearing adorably ugly make-up and an outlandish costume. Her distinguished recital career has taken her throughout the Far and Middle East, including a performance for U.S. troops in the Persian Gulf during Desert Storm. Her talent crosses over into musical theater, with more than 250 performances in such favorites as *Show Boat*, *West Side Story*, *Kismet*, *The Threepenny Opera* and *Man of La Mancha*. She is featured on many recordings, including a CD of John Cage works.

American soprano **LAUREN FLANIGAN** debuted with NYCO in 1991 as Musetta (*La bohème*) and the following year at the Met's world premiere of John Corigliano's *The Ghosts of Versailles*. She sang opposite Luciano Pavarotti in *I Lombardi*, as Curley's Wife in *Of Mice and Men*, and in the world premieres of **Judith Weir**'s *Vanishing Bridegroom* and Hugo Weisgall's *Esther*. In 1999, she made her debut with SFO in the final scene of *Salome*, returning in 2000 with the orchestra in the American Mavericks Festival. She is a frequent guest at Glimmerglass, the summer opera festival in upstate New York, where she received raves for her performance in the Deborah Drattell/Wendy Wasserman's *Central Park*, the center one act opera in the trilogy, *Festival of Regrets* (1999). At NYCO she was in Virgil Thompson's *The Mother of Us All*, *Roberto Devereux*, and in the April 2001 revival of their 1975 production of Korngold's *Die Tote Stadt* (The Dead City). During the 2001–02 season she appeared in *Nabucco* with ENO, *Maria Stuarda* with OONY, and Ernani at Teatro Colón, Buenos Aires. In 2003, she performed her first Norma for Cincinnati Opera. With composer **Deborah Drattell**, she founded and co-produced the concert series "Under the influence of . . . " in New York, and "The Stray Dogs" for the Greenwich House of Music.

Renée Fleming

RENÉE FLEMING, the daughter of two music teachers, was born on Valentine's Day, 1959, in Indiana, Pennsylvania, and grew up in Rochester, New York. She received her music education degree at SUNY Potsdam, and studied with Patricia Misslin. To combat her shyness, she started singing jazz. After getting her masters at Eastman she went to Juilliard, where she supported her tuition working as a secretary. The winner of a Fulbright Grant in 1984, she went to Germany, studying with **Arleen Augér** (1939–93) and **Elisabeth Schwarzkopf** (1915-2006). She returned home, spent two seasons with Virginia Opera, won the 1988 Met Opera Auditions, and the Richard Tucker Award in 1989. Over the next seven years, she built a solid reputation with good reviews and a wise choice of repertory with roles such as *Rusalka*, acclaimed in Washington, Seattle and Houston, and Mozart's Countess in *The Marriage of Figaro* at Covent Garden, Vienna State and Paris Operas, and at her Met debut in 1991. She returned to New York as Pamina, Tatyana (*Eugene Onegin*) and Rosina in the 1991 premiere of John Corigliano's *The Ghosts of Versailles*. Other roles include Donna Elvira, her La Scala debut, Madame de Tourvel in Conrad Susa's *The Dangerous Liaisons* at SFO, Dirce in Cherubini's *Medée* at Covent Garden and the title role in Carlisle Floyd's *Susannah*—her Chicago Lyric Opera debut.

In 1994, she opened the new theater in Glyndebourne in *Figaro*, after having sung *Così fan tutti* for the last performance in the old house, and inaugurated the Bath and Wessex Opera as Mimi. The same season she sang Tatyana for her debuts with Dallas and San Diego. '95–'96 it was back to San Diego for Rusalka, and the Met opposite **Plácido Domingo** in *Otello* for a televised opening of their season. The same year she came under the wing of the late **Sir Georg Solti**, who fell in love with her voice, and was instrumental in persuading his record company, Decca, to sign her to a contract. From that point she went from useful lyric soprano to superstar. '98–'99 found her all over the world: Chicago, Houston, Munich, Milan and Paris. In September 1998, she was in the SFO world premiere of *A Streetcar Named Desire*, written specially for her by **André Previn**. Back at the Met, January 2000, she was the Marschallin (*Der Rosenkavalier*), and a special Valentine's Day appearance as Lucrezia Borgia with OONY. Then on to London, recitals in Paris and Brussels, *Louise* in Toulouse and Donna Anna at the Salzburg Festival in August. In October, at Avery Fisher Hall, she kicked off Lincoln Center's Great Performance series in a concert with baritone Dmitri Hvorostovsky.

Of her over thirty recordings, the best known are *Divas' in Song* with **Marilyn Horne**, the 1998 recording of *Rusalka* with Sir Charles Mackerras and the Czech Philharmonic—the first recording of this opera in fifteen years, which won the Belgian Music Critics Award—the 1999 Grammy Award for the glorious CD, *The Beautiful Voice*, the 2000 recording of *Thaïs* with Thomas Hampson, Yves Abel conducting the Bordeaux Opera Orchestra, and in 2005, *Haunted Heart*, a foray into "pop" music. Rusalka has been her signature role, especially the beautiful aria

"O Silver Moon" which she has made her own. The reason for her affinity for this role is that her great-grandparents were born in Prague and she heard the language spoken as a child.

Fleming ends all her recitals with songs by Duke Ellington, and hopes one day to record an album in the real jazz idiom rather than the less demanding cabaret style most classical singers use for their crossover recordings. She has been seen on national television with **Luciano Pavarotti** on "Live from Lincoln Center-Pavarotti Plus," James Levine's Twenty-fifth Anniversary Gala, April 27, 1996, at the Met, the 1997 PBS "Live from Lincoln Center," New York Philharmonic Season Opening Gala, the 1998 SFO world premiere of *A Streetcar Named Desire*, Carlisle Floyd's *Susanna* at the Met (1999), and *Star Crossed Lovers* Gala with Plácido Domingo and the Chicago Symphony.

In 2001 Fleming was booked solid through 2006, including Met performances of the Marschallin, *Don Giovanni* and *Arabella*. In the 2002–03 season she was in *Il Pirata*, *Rusalka*, sang the title role in Massenet's *Thaïs*, and her first Violetta (*La traviata*), February 2004. She was at the Met, January 2005, as Handel's *Rodelinda*, and in September as *Manon*. April and May 2006 again was *Manon* and *Rodelinda*.

Her album "Bel Canto" was released in 2002, winning the Grammy for best solo performance in 2003. Viking-Penguin editor Richard Kot signed her for a book on music interpretation, singing and performing, published late 2004.

Despite stardom in a viciously competitive profession, her natural girl-next-door approach prompted the staff at CBS' *60 Minutes* in their televised interview to call her *The Diva Next Door*. The appellation is based on the fact that despite her prima donna status, after the break-up of her marriage to Richard Ross, Renée considers herself a single working mother with two daughters to support and raise.

BARBARA FRITTOLI, born in Milan, 1970, studied at the Giuseppe Verdi Conservatory. She made her operatic debut in the 1991–92 season as Mimi in *La bohème* at the Teatro San Carlo (Naples) and appeared at the Rossini Opera Festival in *Pesaro* under **Claudio Abbado**. Her American debut came in 1992–93 as Micaëla (*Carmen*) in Philadelphia. She was Micaëla and Mimi at Vienna State Opera, and Antonia in *Les Contes d'Hoffmann* opposite **Plácido Domingo**, a role she reprised the following year at Berlin State Opera. Other debuts have been at the Théâtre de la Monnaie (Brussels), Covent Garden, Teatro Comunale (Florence), Teatro Regio (Turin), as Desdemona, and Donna Elvira (*Don Giovanni*), among others. Her 1995–96 Met debut was as Micaëla. She was Desdemona to Domingo's *Otello* at the Salzburg Easter Festival with Claudio Abbado and the Berlin Philharmonic. 1996–97 marked a new production of *Marriage of Figaro* at La Scala, Mimi at the Met and Fiordiligi at Glyndebourne. During the 1999–2000 Met season, she sang in *Otello*. 2001–2002 included *Otello* and *Don Giovanni* at Bastille Opera, Vienna State Opera, *Luisa Miller* at Covent Garden, and an appearance at the Salzburg Festival. The summer of 2001 found her at concerts in Ravenna and Istanbul. She was part of a 2002 commemorative concert at Ground Zero in New York, site of the terrorist destruction of the World Trade Center skyscrapers. At the Met in 2005 she was in *Don Carlo* and *Così fan tutte*, and began 2006 in *Lusia Miller*.

Her recordings include *Le Triptique* (Decca), *Il Viaggio a Reims* (Sony), *Il Barbiere de Sevilla* (Teldec). Frittoli is now signed with Erato Disques.

American soprano **ELIZABETH FUTRAL** made her San Francisco debut in the world premiere of André Previn's *A Streetcar Named Desire*, creating the role of Stella. San Diego audiences were treated to this performance, April 2000.

Born in 1965 in Smithfield, North Carolina, to a minister father and musical mother who played piano and flute, the family moved to Covington, Louisiana, when Elizabeth was quite young. Growing up, she loved classical music. Singing in school and church brought her talent early recognition, but she had no voice lessons until she attended Samford University (Birmingham, Alabama), where she studied with Virginia Zeani, earning an MM (1988), after which she was selected for the Lyric Opera Center for American Artists in Illinois. Her 1991 winning of the Met National Council Auditions provided the launch for her career. Other awards were the MacAllister Competition, Opera Index and Richard Tucker Music Foundation Grants.

Between 1993–97 Florida Grand Opera featured Futral in *The Magic Flute, Romeo and Juliette, Ariadne auf Naxos* and *Lucia di Lammermoor*. At Lyric Opera of Chicago, 1994–2000, she sang in *Candide, Xerxes, Ghosts of Versailles, Götterdammerung, Das Rheingold, Siegfried, Marriage of Figaro, Romeo and Juliette* and *Elixir of Love*. 1999 brought *Lucia di Lammermoor* at Minnesota Opera. The same year came the long awaited Met debut in the same role, which she reprised in Vancouver, and New Orleans (2000)—where she collaborated with her husband, conductor Steven White—and Dallas (2001). Los Angeles had not seen *Giulio Cesare* for thirty-five years when Futral sang it in February 2001, exhibiting the vocal agility necessary to interpret Handel. April 2001 found her at NYCO for their production of *The Ballad of Baby Doe*, the role which launched the career of an unknown **Beverly Sills**. Hero (*Beatrice and Benedict*) and Zerbinetta (*Ariadne auf Naxos*) both at Santa Fe Opera, *Lakmé* at New Orleans Opera and Susanna (*Le nozze di Figaro*) Lyric Opera of Chicago completed the season.

Internationally, Futral has sung at the Brussels' Theatre de la Monnaie, Teatro Comunale di Firenze, Covent Garden, Barbican Hall, Dublin, Barvarian State and Edmonton (Canada) Operas. She has also appeared at the Pesaro (Italy) Rossini Opera Festival, and England's Wexford Festival.

Besides opera, Futral performs in concert with such celebrated conductors as Sir Colin Davis, Zubin Mehta, Leonard Slatkin, Herbert Blomstedt, Bruno Bartoletti, Daniel Barenboim and Raymond Leppard.

Her vast discography includes live recordings of Meyerbeer's *L'Etoile du Nord* (Marco Polo), Rossini's *Matilde di Shabran* and Richard Strauss' *Deutsche Motette* (both for RCA/BMG), Ravel's *L'Enfant et les Sortilèges* (DG), Philip Glass' *Hydrogen Jukebox* (Euphorbia), Hugo Weisgall's *Six Characters in Search of an Author*, from the play by Luigi Pirandello (New World), and scenes from Kurt Weill's *The Firebrand of Florence* with Thomas Hampson (EMI).

The 2003–04 season found Futral at the Met as Princess Eudoxie in Jacques Halévy's (1799–1862) *La Juive* (The Jewess), their first performance of this opera since the 1935–36 season. During 2005–06 Met season she was again *Lucia di Lammermoor*.

INESSA GALANTE, born in Riga, entered the Latvian Music Academy in 1977. Her career began while still a student, with performances at the Riga Opera House and in other former eastern bloc countries, including the Kirov Opera, St. Petersburg. Despite the Communist divide that segregated Europe at this time, Galante was able to visit America and Canada, performing with a Latvian ensemble. However, not until the disintegration of the Soviet Union in 1992 was she able to take her career to Western Europe and beyond. In 1992, she signed a debut contract with Mannheim Opera (Germany), and appeared as Pamina in Mozart's *The Magic Flute*. 1994 saw a return to Riga and her first CD, *Début* (Campion), which has sold 200,000 copies worldwide. She moved to the Oper am Rhein in Düsseldorf in 1996, with roles such as Leonora, Mimi and Donna Elvira. The same year brought debut performances in Britain with the Royal Scottish National Orchestra. Appearances at the Evian Festival in France followed in 1997. In 1999, she ended her German opera contracts in order to step onto a wider stage.

Since 2000, Galante has been performing throughout the world, beginning with an appearance at London's Albert Hall, then traveling to Korea, Australia, The Hague and Rotterdam. During 1999–2000, she sang *La bohème* in Detroit, Florida and Baltimore. 2001 brought a world premiere recording of Mozart's *Mass in C* with Douglas Bostock. 2002 marked her return to the Bolshoi in Moscow for a production of *Adriana Lecouvreur*.

LESLEY GARRETT, born April 10, 1955, in Doncaster, Yorkshire, England, was principal soprano with the English National Opera. Her wide repertoire includes most Mozart roles, as well as Euridyce, Mimi, Oscar (*A Masked Ball*), Adele (*Die Fledermaus*), Alisi in the European premiere of Philip Glass' *The Making of the Representative for Planet 8* (1988), Rose in Kurt Weill's *Street Scene*, Yum-Yum (*The Mikado*), as well as acclaimed recordings and videos. She was the recipient of the Decca-Kathleen Ferrier Prize (1979) and the prestigious Countess of Munster Award. She studied at the RAM and National Opera Studio. Touring with ENO, her engagements have taken her around the world, including Russia's Bolshoi and Kiev Operas.

In November 2003, BBC-TV aired Garrett in "The Singer," inspired by the lyrics of Michael Head. Lesley represents the magical character in the song. As she sings, she takes a journey, passing through people's lives, touching on themes of travel, love and loss. The repertoire ranges from small, simple folk songs to epic, cinematic scale music. The audience saw an exciting new aspect of Garrett as she presented her voice in its purest form, ethereally blending the mysticism and lyricism of the beautiful Devon landscapes in the unfolding stories.

Viveca Genaux

Coloratura mezzo **VIVICA GENAUX** was born July 10, 1969, in Fairbanks, Alaska. Although she played violin for nine years, she began singing in the eighth grade when she found out the Fairbanks Fine Arts Summer Camp was doing *My Fair Lady*. She studied with Dorothy Dow in Galveston, Texas, and learned not only the songs from *My Fair Lady*, but also operatic arias. After two years at the University of Rochester as a genetics major, she transferred to Indiana University School of Music, where she earned her degree in vocal performance. She also studied with **Claudia Pinza**, the lyric soprano daughter of famed Italian basso Ezio Pinza (1892–1957), at Duquesne University, Pennsylvania. In 1995, she debuted with Dallas Opera in *La Cenerentola* with **Cecilia Bartoli**, and has since sung with Florentine Opera, Cincinnati Opera and Opera Columbus, as well as crossing over into musical theater, appearing in *Hello Dolly*, *My Fair Lady*, *Oklahoma*, *South Pacific*, and with the Cincinnati Pops Orchestra under **Erich Kunzel** in an evening of Bernstein. A winner of many competitions, she is a participant in the Ezio Pinza Council for American Singers of Opera program.

1996 marked her New York debut with Eve Queler and OONY as Smeton in *Anna Bolena*, with L'Opéra de Montréal, and her European debut at the Semper Opera in Dresden. In 1997, she made two San Diego Opera debuts, the title role of Rossini's *The Italian Girl in Algiers*, and Isabel de Martos in the world premiere of Myron Fink's *The Conquistador*. She sang the title role in *La Cenerentola* for Opera Colorado and participated in New York's Caramoor Festival in July before going to Italy for a recital concert with Mariella Devia in Ravello. 1997–98 included a recital and singing Rosina (*The Barber of Seville*), both in San Diego, returning there in 2002 for *Ariodante*, and in 2006 as Sextus in *Julius Caesar in Egypt*.

Genaux has gone from unknown novice to sought-after singer by remaining focused on the baroque and *bel canto*, and has become regarded for her Rosina, her debut role at the Met in 1997, which she has performed more than seventy times around the world. She affirms the renaissance of interest in *bel canto* has been a boon, garnering the title role in Handel's *Ariodante* at Dallas Opera (1998), and 2002 in San Diego. At Minnesota Opera, January 2001, she performed the trouser role[185] of Romeo in Bellini's *I Capuleti e i Montecchi*, and in April she made her Paris debut in Hesse's *Marco Antonio e Cleopatra*. Baroque music was written at 415 and today's orchestras play at 440. She says her voice is more comfortable at the baroque pitch, and would like to try singing with a period orchestra.

Genaux was nominated for a 2003 Grammy for her "Arias by Farinelli."[186]

Lyric soprano in the French and Italian repertory, **ANGELA GHEORGHIU** was born in Adjud, Romania, 1966, and able to take full advantage of the free but strict training given to true talent—one of the few pluses of communism. Separated from her family at fourteen, her graduation from the Bucharest Music Academy in 1990 timed perfectly with the 1989 downfall of dictator Nicolae Ceausescu's regime. In 1992, she made her international debut as Mimi at Covent Garden, returning there as Liù (*Turandot*), Micaëla (*Carmen*), a role she gives depth of character to, Zerlina (*Don Giovanni*) and Violetta (*La traviata*), conducted by **Sir George Solti** (1994). Her brilliance in this role caused the BBC and Decca/London to clear their agendas in order to immediately televise and record the next performance. Also in 1992, she made her Vienna State Opera debut as Adina (*L'elisir d'amore*), returning there for *La bohème*, *Falstaff*, and *La traviata*. Her 1993 Met debut as Mimi has led to her becoming one of their most popular guests. Other appearances have taken her across Europe and to Japan. Her '96–'97 season included *La traviata* at Teatro La Fenice; another Liù, plus *L'elisir d'amore* at Covent Garden; Liù, Micaëla, Violetta and Juliette

---

185. Trouser roles, or *travesti*, are male characters traditionally sung by women. (See Opera Glossary.)
186. An 18th century castrato known for his extraordinary vocal range.

at the Met, and her brilliant debut with French-born Sicilian tenor **Roberto Alagna** in *La bohème*. Romance blossomed and the pair were wed April 1996.

1998 marked another Juliette at Chicago Lyric and Violetta at the Bastille. In 2000, she and her husband were part of the San Francisco Symphony Gala to open the last season of the century, followed by a return to the Met for *L'elisir d'amore*, then back to Covent Garden for *Roméo et Juliette* and *Les Contes d'Hoffmann*, *La bohème* in Naples, *La traviata* in Rome, and the Verdi *Requiem* with **Claudio Abbado** and the Berlin Philharmonic. *Turandot* and *La bohème* graced the 2001–02 Met season.

In September 2005, she sang *Pagliacci* in Los Angeles. Both Gheorghiu and Alagna were booked at the Met through 2006, when she sang *La traviata* in February. Angela's MI disc of *Arias and Duets* with Roberto was followed by their recording of *Roméo et Juliette*, released after their Met 1998 appearance in the opera. The couple live in Switzerland with Alagna's daughter Ornella, from his first marriage, which ended tragically when his first wife died of a brain tumor. Further tragedy struck in July 2001, when Angela's sister Eleni was killed in a car crash. Angela and Alberto adopted Eleni's orphaned daughter, Ioana. As of 2006 the girls were fifteen and sixteen years old.

Taking her cue from past mistakes of many divas, Gheorghiu chooses roles intelligently, careful to preserve her voice.

ANGELA GILBERT, born in Cape Town, South Africa, February 25, 1974, studied at the South African College of Music there. Following the end of apartheid, the new government slashed arts funding, forcing Cape Town Opera to let many of their soloists go. Her professor—also the opera director, said, "Have I got a job for you!" She walked into the opera and, as she said, "Sang leads because I was stupid and cheap." Her roles included Lauretta (*Gianni Schicchi*), Susanna (*Le nozze di Figaro*), Antonia/Olympia and Giulietta (*Les Contes d'Hoffmann*), Norina (*Don Pasquale*), Sandrina (*La finta giardiniera*), title roles in *Lucia di Lammermoor*, *The Merry Widow* and *La traviata*, and Micaëla in Peter Brook's staging of *La Tragédie de Carmen* (a reduction of the original), which toured South Africa and Namibia. Concert engagements have been with the Cape Town and Natal Philharmonics.

In Germany, Gilbert sang Morgana in *Alcina* at the Handel Festival, and performed a series of opera concerts at the Hanover Festival. In the 2000–2001 season, she joined the Lindemann Young Artist Development Program at the Met, appearing in Young Artist Gala Concerts, and as the Unborn Child (*Die Frau ohne Schatten*), Dew Fairy (*Hänsel und Gretel*), Peasant *(Marriage of Figaro)* and Shepherdess (*L'Enfant et les Sortilèges*).

With **Eve Queler**'s OONY, she sang the title role in *Adelia*, Inez in *La Favorite* (both by Donizetti) and Elena in Rossini's *La Donna del Lago*. At Wolf Trap Opera, she was Madame Hertz in Mozart's *The Impressario*, Norina, and a solo recital with pianist Steven Blier. She appeared again with Blier at the New York Festival of Song.

In 2003, Gilbert was chosen to represent South Africa at the Cardiff Singer of the World Competition in Wales. A videotape of her performance so impressed Ian Campbell, he scheduled her for San Diego Opera's *Lucia di Lammermoor* (February 2006) with Richard Leech, conducted by Richard Bonynge. Bonynge's wife, Dame **Joan Sutherland**, is Gilbert's heroine, and responsible for reviving Donizetti's *bel canto* repertory. The same year found Angela at the Klein Karoo Festival, South Africa, and Konstanze (*Abduction from the Seraglio*) for Icelandic Opera. Campbell has engaged her for the title role in San Diego's *Maria Stuarda*, 2008.

CHRISTINE GOERKE is heralded as a dramatic soprano of the future. Voice studies were at SUNY Stony Brook, not far from where she grew up in Medford, Long Island. After one semester of clarinet, during a sight-singing test for instrumentalists the chorus master suggested she audition for the voice program. Feeling that singing must be easier than the clarinet, eighteen languages later she was not so sure. While at SUNY she was also in **Robert Shaw**'s choral workshop, which got her, at age twenty-four, singing in Britten's *War Requiem* at Carnegie Hall (1994). She sang with Shaw again in a concert of the Rachmaninoff *Vespers* at New York's Cathedral of St. John the Divine, a performance he rehearsed, but was unable to conduct. (He died in 1999.)

In 1992, Goerke began training in the Met's Lindemann Young Artist Development Program, and in 1994 received a Richard Tucker Music Foundation Study Grant. 1997 brought a Career Grant, and 2001 the Richard

Tucker Award. The same year she was a hit in the title role of Gluck's *Iphigénie en Tauride* for Glimmerglass and NYCO, which was followed by a Telarc recording of the opera with Martin Pearlman and the Boston Baroque, featuring a period-instrument ensemble. In the Spring of 2000, she was the Third Norn in the Met's *Götterdämmerung* after which she had the lyric part of Armida in Handel's *Rinaldo* at NYCO. June through August 2001, she was Vitellia in *La clemenza di Tito* in Paris, Donna Elvira at Teatro Colón, Fiordiligi in Japan with Seiji Ozawa, back to Glimmerglass for *The Rape of Lucrecia*, finishing the summer at Lincoln Center's *Mostly Mozart* Festival. For the 2002–03 season, she sang Donna Elvira for Pittsburgh, Opera Pacific and Covent Garden. March 2004 brought Donna Elvira at the Met—an incredible schedule highlighting a burgeoning career.

GALINA GORCHAKOVA, born March 1, 1962, in Novokuznetsk, Siberia, also got to take advantage of the socialist system to study at the Novosibirsk Academy and Conservatory—the only cultural center for thousands of miles. Here she met her husband Nikolai Mikhalski. Her operatic appearances in Russia began in 1988 as Tatyana, Butterfly, Liù, Leonora (*Il trovatore*), Yaroslava (*Prince Igor*), Katerina (*Lady Macbeth of Mtsensk*) and Lisa (*Pique Dame*). She was a prizewinner in the Mussorgsky and Glinka Competitions.

Moscow was the cultural capital during the Soviet regime, and through the Bolshoi some artists managed to be seen in the West. Now St. Petersburg has emerged as the hub, with its Kirov Opera the great stepping stone. Thus, after the Soviet Union disbanded in 1990, Gorchkova's career took off when she was invited to join the Kirov, touring with them to Covent Garden, Bastille, La Scala, Vienna and the Met (1992), where audiences loved her. In 1995, she made her own Met debut as Cio-Cio-San (*Butterfly*), returning in 1997 as Tatyana and Tosca. In the 1998 season, she made her debut with the Vienna State Opera in *Eugene Onegin*, *Madama Butterfly* and *Tosca*, a return to the Met for *Butterfly*, and a Munich Opera debut as Tosca. During the 2000 season, she reprised Tosca for Washington and Munich, appeared in recital for San Diego, sang Tatyana in Florence, and Lisa (*Pique Dame*) at Salzburg. In 2002, she was Tosca in San Diego, returning in 2003, as Norma. The same year brought out a CD of operatic favorites with the Philharmonia of Russia, under the baton of its founding director, Russian-American conductor Constantine Orbelian.

Susan Graham

With heavy, dramatic roles as her forte, Gorchakova has been compared to the great **Galina Vishnevskaya** (*b* 1926), wife of maestro/cellist **Mstislav Rostropovich**.

Mezzo **SUSAN GRAHAM**, born July 23, 1960, in Roswell, New Mexico, moved to Midland, Texas at thirteen. During college at Texas Tech, she went to Santa Fe in the summers for standing room at the opera. In the 1980s, after her first year at the Manhattan School of Music, she auditioned for an apprenticeship at Santa Fe, thinking this would be a shoe-in since John Crosby ran Santa Fe and was Manhattan's president. She didn't get past the preliminary round!

After graduation from Manhattan, Susan was winner of the Metropolitan Opera National Council Auditions, the Schwabacher Award of San Francisco Opera's Merola Program, and recipient of a career grant from the Richard Tucker Foundation. She returned to Santa Fe in 1989 as Flora (*La traviata*) and covered **Frederica von Stade** as Massenet's Chérubin, the result of having sung that role at Manhattan, which was its American stage premiere. Her advice is, "Don't ever be put off by an initial rejection . . . it happens to all of us. I couldn't buy my way into this place as an apprentice, and then I came back as a principal artist!"

Graham was with Santa Fe (1989–91). In 1990, she sang Dorabella and her first Composer (*Ariadne auf Naxos*). In 1991, she was Cherubino (*Marriage of Figaro*) with Bryn Terfel's first Figaro and Heidi Grant Murphy's first Susanna. She returned in 1998 for *Beatrice et Benedict*.

A frequent guest at the Metropolitan Opera since her 1991 debut, she premiered John Harbison's *The Great Gatsby*, was Cherubino, Octavian (*Rosenkavalier*) and in Massenet's *Werther*. Her 1999–2000 season included *La Damnation de Faust* with Seiji Ozawa at Japan's Saito Kinen Festival, Mahler's *Des Knaben Wunderhorn* with the Berlin Opera Orchestra, *Ariadne auf Naxos* in Munich and *Der Rosenkavalier* at Covent Garden. A favorite artist at the Salzburg Festival (*Le nozze di Figaro, La clemenza di Tito, Falstaff, L'Orfeo* and Mozart's *Lucio Silla*), she returned in 2000 to sing the title role in a new production of Gluck's *Iphigénie en Tauride*. In September 2000, she created the role of Sister Helen Prejean[187] in SFO's world premiere of Jake Heggie's *Dead Man Walking*, with **Frederica von Stade**.

In September 2001, Graham celebrated the tenth anniversary of her Met debut with performances of *Idomeneo* opposite Plácido Domingo. During 2002, Graham toured Paris, Berlin, London, Lisbon and Amsterdam in recital, reprised Idamante (*Idomeneo*) at the Palais Garnier (Paris Opera House) and appeared in one of her signature roles, Marguerite, in *La Damnation de Faust*, at the Théâtre de la Monnaie (Brussels).

After appearing in *Ariodante* and *The Merry Widow* in Houston in early 2003, Graham went to Santa Fe where, "I bought an old house out in the middle of nowhere, halfway between the town and the opera." After three days of appearances at California's Ojai Music Festival in June, she spent the summer in the title role of Offenbach's *La Belle Hélène*. During Hélène's twelve performance July-August run, she squeezed in concerts (July 25) at the Ravinia Festival and Manhattan's *Mostly Mozart* Festival (August 8–9). After Santa Fe, Graham flew to Paris for her role as Didon in *Les Troyens* at the Châtelet. She also recorded Purcell's *Dido and Aeneas* for EMI at the end of 2003.

After the Met's 2003–04 season revival of *The Merry Widow*, she went Toulouse in April for *Werther* and, following a European recital tour, in June was the Composer (*Ariadne*) at Covent Garden. September 2004 marked her first Donna Elvira to open Lyric Opera of Chicago's fiftieth anniversary season. For 2005, she was back in trousers at Houston's *Idomeneo*, Octavian at the Met in April, Santa Fe in July for *Lucio Silla*, the new Met season for *Ariadne auf Naxos* in September, and the December world premiere of Tobias Picker's *An American Tragedy*,[188] based on the Theodore Dreiser adaptation of a true story, with an all-star cast that included Graham, Patricia Racette, Jennifer Larmore and Dolora Zajick.

Graham's discography features over twenty titles, including Ned Rorem's songs (2000), *C'est ça la vie, c'est ça l'amour. French Operetta Arias* (Erato)—named one of the best classical music albums of 2002 by *Entertainment Weekly*, it won the Editor's Choice awards from *Gramophone* and *Opera News*—Purcell's Dido conducted by **Emmanuelle Haïm**, and an album of Charles Ives songs that won a Grammy for Best Classical Vocal Performance (2005). Drawn to the French music of Berlioz, Debussy and Fauré, with the wealth of song and orchestral music, her concert work has grown to match her opera career. Her Carnegie Hall recital, April 2003, was released as *Susan Graham at Carnegie Hall* (Warner Classics).

Major recognition in 2004 was being named "Vocalist of the Year" by *Musical America*. On January 12, 2004, she and composer Ned Rorem received decorations as Chevaliers in the Order of Arts and Letters at the French Embassy in New York. November 2005, she received the *Opera News* Award for Distinguished Achievement.

DENYCE GRAVES (See Black Heritage.)

Born in Odessa in August 1959, **MARIA GULEGHINA** studied at the conservatory there. After her marriage to Mark Guleghin, she sang small roles at the State Opera in Minsk until she won the Glinka Competition in 1984. Shortly after the birth of her daughter, Natalya, she made her La Scala debut with **Luciano Pavarotti** in 1986. A number of Italian and Russian roles followed. Suffering the strictures placed on Soviet artists, in September 1990 she, her husband and daughter, acting like tourists, escaped to the West. Her Met debut came in 1990 as Maddalena in Tommaso Giordano's *Andrea Chenier*, returning later that season for the premiere of *Tosca* conducted by **Plácido Domingo**.

---

187. Author of 1993 Pulitzer Prize nominated book of the same name by prison ministry nun Prejean (*b* 1939), on her firsthand experiences of the Louisiana execution process. It was made into 1996 film—nominated for four Oscars—starring Susan Sarandon as Sister Prejean. When Heggie wrote the opera, he offered Flicka the leading role. She realistically told him this needed a younger woman, and saw to it that Graham got the role.

188. It was also made into the 1951 film, *A Place in the Sun*, starring Elizabeth Taylor and Montgomery Clift.

She has appeared in leading theaters around the world. Identified with Tosca, she has sung the role for her debuts in Vienna ('92–'93), Chicago Lyric ('94–'95), San Francisco ('94–'95), Bastille (1995), Berlin, Hamburg and La Scala. Her repertoire also includes Aida, Rosina, Elisabeth de Valois and Tatyana (*Eugene Onegin*). 1996 saw her return to the Met as Lisa in *The Queen of Spades* and another Met tour of Japan with **James Levine**. Her first Norma was in Seville (Spain) in 2000, six weeks after her son was born. She was Abigaille in *Nabucco* for the Met's February 2005 production, followed in April as Tosca, and in September at Washington National Opera in *I Vespri Siciliani*.

Guleghina makes her home in Luxembourg.

ANJA HARTEROS, born 1972 in Bergneustadt, Germany, started her musical training with violin, sang in choirs and appeared in school musicals. At age thirteen, her performance as Zerlina in a school production of *Don Giovanni* prompted her teacher to encourage Anja's talent. After studying with Lieselotte Hammes at Cologne Conservatory, at twenty-three she joined the roster of Gelsenkirchen Opera, where she sang many roles, including operetta. After two years she moved to Opera Bonn, and two years later broke away from the German ensemble system.

In 1999, she won the Cardiff Singer of the World competition in Wales, then appeared at the Salzburg Festival and Frankfurt Opera. She debuted in Munich as Agathe in *Der Freischütz*, and Vienna as Mimì (*La bohème*) and Eva (*Die Meistersinger*). Her 2003 Met debut as the countess in *The Marriage of Figaro* was followed by Donna Anna (*Don Giovanni*) in 2004. Her impressive performances gained her a cover story in the March 2004 *Opera News*, the prestigious magazine put out by the Metropolitan Opera. The same year she sang a magnificent Violetta in *La traviata* in San Diego. So well received, she returned to San Diego in March 2005 as Amelia in *Simon Boccanegra*.

Harteros credits her success in expanding her roles to conductors Zubin Mehta and James Levine. Director Ian

Campbell has given her the chance to try new roles and gain experience at San Diego Opera, as he did in the early careers of Richard Leech, **Vivica Genaux**, Rodney Gilfry, Ramon Vargas and **Renée Fleming**.

Lyric soprano **HEI-KYUNG HONG**, born July 19, 1958, in Seoul, Korea, is a graduate of Juilliard, where she participated in the master classes of **Elizabeth Schwarzkopf**, Tito Gobbi, Walter Legge and Gerard Souzay. She was one of four young American singers invited to attend **Herbert von Karajan**'s opera classes at the 1983 Salzburg Festival. Winner of the 1982 Met Auditions, she made her 1984 debut as Servilia in *La Clemenza de Tito*, and since

Hei-Kyung Hong

then has returned to the Met every season for over 150 performances of eighteen different roles including Mimi, Despina, Susanna, Adina, Lauretta (*Gianni Schicchi*), Gilda and, during the 1991 Mozart Bicentennial, Ilia (*Idomeneo*) and Pamina. '94–'95 brought Ilia opposite **Plácido Domingo**, Zerlina, and Rosina in *The Ghosts of Versailles*. Hong has sung in the great houses all over the world—Vienna, Paris, Nice, Netherlands Opera—as well as soloed in orchestral and choral works, including appearances at Lincoln Center's *Mostly Mozart* Festival. In '95–'96, she traveled to Korea for a series of recitals and concerts—including two with Domingo—celebrating the fiftieth anniversary of Korea's independence, and returned to the Met as Mimi, Zerlina and Juliette. She sang at James Levine's twenty-fifth Anniversary Gala, April 27, 1996, and in the March 1997 Met production of *Das Rheingold*.

In the 1999–2000 Met season she repeated *Le nozze di Figaro*, *Das Rheingold*, *La bohème*, and returned to her native Korea in May 2000 for duet concerts with **Jennifer Larmore**. Her 2000–01 season included *Fidelio*, *Don Giovanni*, and Liù in *Turandot*. *Idomeneo* came in 2001–02. At the Met, she sang in *The Marriage of Figaro* (December 2003) and as Zerlina in *Don Giovanni* (March 2004), and for 2005–06 season was in *La bohème*, *The Marriage of Figaro*, and *La traviata*.

Hei-Kyung lives in New York with her husband and three children.

Sumi Jo

Coloratura soprano **SUMI JO** was born November 22, 1962, in South Korea, studying in her native country before enrolling at Santa Cecilia in Rome (1983), from which she graduated with honors in 1986. The same year she won first prize in the Carlo Capelli International Competition in Verona—open only to *first prize* winners in other competitions. She has appeared on Italian radio and TV. Her operatic debut was in Seoul as Susanna in *Le Nozze di Figaro.* After singing in Lyon, Nice and Marseilles (1987–88), she was discovered by **Herbert von Karajan** who asked her to sing Barbarina (*Marriage of Figaro*) in the 1988 Salzburg Festival. Since then she has sung in Japan, the U.S. and all over Europe. Met audiences heard her Lucia and Gilda (1988, 1990). She was the Queen of the Night at Chicago Lyric's 1990 production of *Magic Flute* among many other appearances. Her recordings on London Decca, Deutsche Grammophon and Philips are with **Sir Georg Solti**, and Herbert von Karajan in Mahler's 8th, Rossini's *Messe di Gloria*, and operatic arias. Her popular recording, *Only Love*, sold an astonishing 750,000 copies. Her 1998–99 season included *Lucia di Lammermoor* with Los Angeles Opera, and 2000 brought *Rigoletto* at the Met, *Daughter of the Regiment* in Strasbourg, and *Carmina Burana* with the Cincinnati Symphony. After a new production of *Tales of Hoffmann* at the Paris Bastille, Sumi Jo and **Vivica Genaux** appeared in the Minnesota Opera's January 2001 production of Bellini's *I Capuleti e i Montecchi.*

Sumi Jo makes her home in Rome.

Welsh soprano **ROSEMARY JOSHUA**, born in 1965, has made her mark in England's opera houses, debuting at Glyndebourne Festival in 1997. As she says, "The Welsh are exposed to Music from the word go—it is just our culture. There's no escaping it . . . think of the Eisteddfod."[189]

After her 1992 debut at the Aix-en-Provence Festival in a Handel oratorio, European performances followed, with a further performance in New York. One of Britain's finest baroque sopranos, she is best known for Handel roles. She sang Angelica in *Orlando* at the Aix-en-Provence Festival, plus *Semele* there and at Innsbruck, Flanders, Cologne and English National Opera (ENO). Next came Poppea in *Agrippina* in Cologne, Brussels and Paris, and Cleopatra in *Giulio Cesare* in Florida.

After San Diego Opera director Ian Campbell first heard Joshua at Covent Garden in 1994, he brought her to SDO for *Romeo and Juliet* in 1998, her first full opera in America. Glyndebourne asked her back in 2000 as Anne Trulove in *The Rake's Progress*, and she returned to San Diego in 2002 as Ginevra in *Ariodante.* For the 2002–03 season, she made her debut at the Met as Adele in *Die Fledermaus*, at La Scala in the title role of *The Cunning Little Vixen*, Bavarian State Opera singing Euridice (*Orfeo et Euridice*), and as Sophie in *Der Rosenkavalier* at ENO. In 2005, she returned to the Glyndebourne Festival as Cleopatra in *Giulio Cesare.*

Her concert appearances have been with the Philharmonia, Royal Scottish National and Freiburg baroque orchestras, Akademie für Alte Musik, Berlin, Les Musiciens du Louvre, Bach's *B Minor Mass* with the London Philharmonic Orchestra under Mark Elder, and Beethoven's 9th and Mahler's 8th Symphonies with Sir Simon Rattle. Recordings include *Venus and Adonis, Dido et Aeneas* (harmonia mundi), and Sophie in *Der Rosenkavalier* (Chandos).

Rosemary is married to French baritone Oliver Lalouette. Their son, Louis, was born October 12, 1997 and daughter Lily, January 20, 2001. The children are always with her wherever opera beckons on both sides of the Atlantic.

Norwegian soprano **SOLVEIG KRINGELBORN** was born in 1964. Her parents told her she sang very well from when she was two years old. She joined a choir at six, gave performances accompanying herself on guitar when she was eight, and started singing lessons at twelve.

It was theater that attracted her to opera. "For me, it's just as important to be a good actress as to have a good voice," she says. "I ended up doing opera because I loved theater." Her studies at the Royal Academy of Opera in Stockholm included a year spent working only on acting. "You don't do opera productions, you do theater productions."

---

189. Eisteddfod - annual Welsh Music Festival and Competition.

She made her debut as Papagena with Royal Swedish Opera in 1987, sang many light roles in Sweden and Norway, and won a Norwegian Critics' Award for her performance of Mimi in 1990, a role she first sang in 1988. She sang easy soubrette roles, but says, "when I had children, my voice changed. It grew and got darker, fuller and richer. With each child, it has changed a little."

A contemporary song cycle launched Kringelborn on her international career. She had performed in Warsaw with composer **Witold Lutoslawski** (1913–94) in the audience. He asked her to sing the world premiere of his *Chantefleurs et Chantefables* at the BBC Proms in 1991. Previously unknown outside Scandinavia, Klingelborn found herself invited to perform this work with other orchestras in Europe. A recording was made with Daniel Harding and the Norwegian Chamber Orchestra (Virgin Classics, 1996). After the French premiere of the work at the Bastille, she was invited to sing at Paris Opera.

Klingelborn sang *Jenůfa* when she was twenty-seven. At thirty-eight (2002) she expanded her career to a repertoire ranging from Mozart's Fiordiligi, Countess and Donna Elvira (her debut role at the Met in 2000 with **Bryn Terfel**, **Renée Fleming** and **Hei-Kyung Hong**) to *The Queen of Spades* (Pique Dame) in Barcelona in 2002, Eva and Elisabeth in *Tannhäuser*, which she sang for the first time in Hamburg, January 2002, to Marie in *Wozzeck*, which she sang at the Aix-en-Provence Festival in 2003, followed by *Lady Macbeth of Mtsensk* for San Francisco the same year.

In 2002, her husband, Bjørnar, and their three sons (then aged nine, seven and two-and-a-half), came from their home in Oslo to spend a few weeks with Solveig in New York when she was singing Tatyana (*Eugene Onegin*) and preparing for her first Eva in *Die Meistersinger* (2003), a role James Levine asked her to sing when she auditioned for Donna Elvira. So in between performances of Onegin, she was working on Eva with John Fisher, Met coach and director of music administration. She sang Rosalinde (*Die Fledermaus*) and *Don Giovanni* at the Met in 2004.

Solveig's Song, a new recording of music by Grieg, was released in Scandinavia and she recorded Sibelius brief opera *The Maiden in the Tower*. Her recital disk *Black Roses* (Virgin Classics), with pianist Malcolm Martineau, won a Norwegian Grammy Award.

American mezzo **JENNIFER LARMORE** was born June 21, 1958, in Atlanta, Georgia. Her father, an amateur opera singer, played Saturday afternoon Met broadcasts on the radio for his four children, which they hated, she says, but obviously rubbed off. She went to Westminster Choir College in Princeton, New Jersey, where she perfected her natural voice and learned to blend with other voices. When she was nineteen the Westminster Choir went to the Spoleto Festival, and she met the founder, Italian-American composer **Gian Carlo Menotti**, and sang the Beggar Woman in his *The Egg*. She also met bass-baritone William Powers, whom she married two years later.

After three years' private study with John Bullock, she travelled to New York where, in one day, she auditioned for opera companies in Georgia, Syracuse, New York and Nice, France. France offered her contracts and there she went. After establishing a career in Europe, she returned to the U.S., won the 1994 Richard Tucker Award, and debuted at the Met in 1995 as Rosina in *The Barber of Seville*, a role she had already sung over 250 times in Europe. Her career has blossomed with international performances of *L'Italiana in Algieri*, *Così fan tutte*, *Le Comte Ory*, *L'enfant et les sortilèges*, *La Cenerentola*, *Giulio Cesare* and *I Capuletti e i Montecchi*. An equally acclaimed concert career features choral masterpieces, Mahler works and solo recitals. She can be heard on recordings of *L'incoronazione di Poppea*, *Julius Cæsar*, *The Barber of Seville*, *Hansel and Gretel*, *Lucia di Lammermoor*, *Semiramide*, *La Cenerentola*, *Il Signor Bruschino*, *Carmen* and Rossini songs.

Larmore has returned to the Met each season, with concurrent appearances in Los Angeles, San Francisco, Chicago and Dallas. In 2000, she was in Los Angeles *and* at the Met for *La Cenerentola* and *Giulio Cesare*, returning to New York in 2001 for *The Italian Girl in Algiers*, and *Hänsel und Gretel* in 2002. Her European schedule remains full at all the major houses including Vienna, Geneva, La Scala, Paris and Edinburgh. For the Met's

2005–06 season she was in the world premiere of Tobias Picker's *An American Tragedy*, with an all-star cast that included Patricia Racette, Susan Graham, and Dolora Zajick.

2003 saw the release of the Teldec CD of French arias *L'étoile* (The Star), with the Vienna Radio Symphony under Bertrand de Billy. In 2002, the French government honored her talent with a Chevalier des Arts et des Lettres—their Medal of Honor for the Arts.

Lorraine Lieberson

Mezzo **LORRAINE HUNT LIEBERSON**, born in San Francisco, March 1, 1954, began her musical studies on piano and violin, and embarked upon a career as a violist in the San Francisco Bay area, despite having begun the opera program at San Jose State. Following a summer at Tanglewood, she went to Boston becoming active on the new music freelance circuit, and resumed vocal study at the Boston Conservatory. In 1985, the Handel tricentenary year, she sang in a Peter Sellars' production of *Julius Caesar* in Purchase, New York, followed in '87 as Donna Elvira. Opera buffs were taking an interest in this new voice. Sellars had the instinct to work with her and focus her power and energy.

Hunt's first recording was with **Seiji Ozawa** and the Boston Symphony in Fauré's incidental music from *Pelléas et Mélisande*. This brought her voice to international audiences. In 1997, she sang the premiere of Peter Lieberson's opera *Ashoka's Dream* in Santa Fe, and a year later married the composer. (After his divorce. He has three daughters.)

Hunt performed the songs of John Harbison in Weill Hall in 1998, made her Met debut, December 1999, in Harbison's *The Great Gatsby*, sang her husband's songs at the Santa Fe Chamber Music Festival, July 2001, followed by August concert performances at the Edinburgh Festival and the October Romaeuropa Festival in Italy. Subsequent concerts featured Mahler's Symphony No. 3 with the Boston Symphony and **James Levine**; Berg's *Seven Early Songs* with the Berlin Philharmonic under **Kent Nagano**; Mahler's *Songs of a Wayfarer* with the Los Angeles Philharmonic and **Esa-Pekka Salonen**; Didon in concert performances of *Les Troyens* at the Edinburgh Festival with **Donald Runnicles**; Berlioz' *Les Nuits d'été* (Summer Nights) in Paris with **Roger Norrington,** and also in the San Francisco Area with the Philharmonia Baroque under Nicholas McGegan. Berlioz' *L'enfance du Christ* was performed at Carnegie Hall with the Orchestra of St. Luke's under **Sir Charles Mackerras**. Recital appearances at Lincoln Center, Wigmore Hall, the Concertgebouw, Amsterdam, and Boston's Jordan Hall were among the many venues graced by this singer.

Her discography covers *Idomeneo* (EMI), and Britten's *Phaedra* with the Hallé Orchestra (Erato), nominated for a Grammy Award. Also on Erato are *Hippolyte et Aricie* and *Médée*, with Les Arts Florissants. harmonia mundi has recorded Handel's *Ariodante, Susanna, Theodora, Messiah, Clori, Tirsi e Fileno, Arias for Durastanti* and Purcell's *Dido and Aeneas*. The BBC released a recital disc of Handel, Mahler and Peter Lieberson. Schumann songs are on Koch, and music of Harbison is on Archetype. Lieberson was seen on international television broadcasts and video releases of Peter Sellars' productions of *Don Giovanni* (Donna Elvira), *Giulio Cesare* (Sesto), and *Theodora* (Irene).

2001 Musical America named her "Vocalist of the Year," with the comment, " . . . a holy fire . . . glows in every kind of music this extraordinary artist sings."

March 2006 witnessed cancellations of her very full '06–'07 calendar. On July 3, 2006, at fifty-two, Lorraine succumbed to breast cancer at her home in Santa Fe, New Mexico.

MARQUITA LISTER is enjoying a thriving career. (See Black Heritage.)

KARITA MATTILA, born in Somero, Finland, September 5, 1960, studied in Helsinki, then moved to London in 1984 for further training after being chosen as the first-ever "Cardiff Singer of the World" in 1983. The title launched her into such roles as the Countess (*Le Nozze di Figaro*), Musetta (*La bohème*) and Chrysothemis (*Elektra*). She went on to sing in Chicago, Vienna, San Francisco, Madrid and tour Japan. Her Covent Garden debut was in 1986 as Fiordiligi, with many return engagements. She is a popular Proms artist. At the Met, she has sung Eva and Elvira (1990), and again Eva in a new production of *Die Meistersinger* (1993). The 1996–97 season began with Elsa in San Francisco, and at the Bastille and Covent Garden. 1997–98 featured *The Merry Widow* at the Bastille, and *Lohengrin* at the Met. As a recitalist, she has appeared in Barcelona, Paris, Berlin, Istanbul and throughout Finland. Her first Carnegie Hall recital was February 1999, in October she was *Manon Lescaut*. In October 2000, she sang the taxing role of Leonora in *Fidelio* at the Met, which she has also sung in Helsinki and Paris. For the 2001–02 season, she was in the Met production of *Meistersinger*, in Paris for *Otello*, and Covent Garden for Lisa in Tchaikovsky's *Queen of Spades*, which she sang in New York (1995) and Paris (1999).

Mattila's recordings include opera and concert works on the Philips, Sony, EMI, and Deutsche Grammophon labels. Although she and her husband, Tapio Kuneinen, make their home in London, she maintains an apartment in Turku, near the Finnish countryside where she grew up on a farm with three brothers. Her operatic life is in London, Paris, New York and Salzburg, but she returns to Finland's Tampere Hall to try out new roles. For her fortieth birthday, she threw a party for 11,000 guests at Helsinki Hall, backed by **Jukka-Pekka Saraste** and the Finnish Radio Symphony. The party recital, recorded by Ondine and titled *Karita Live*, features opera aria favorites to *Diamonds are a Girl's Best Friend*, and Gershwin's *Summertime*. If this were the 1930s, Karita would be snapped up by Hollywood studios as were **Grace Moore** (1901–47) and **Lily Pons** (1898–1976), because Mattila, besides a superb singer, is a consummate actress.

Following performances in *Jenůfa* and *Fidelio*, she took on the title role in *Salome*, which opened at the Met, March 2004, and ended the season in December in *Kát'a Kabanová*. During 2005, April brought *Die Meistersinger*, and October at Chicago Lyric in *Manon Lescaut*. 2006 at the Met was *Lohengrin* and *Fidelio*.

Musical America 2005 named her Musician of the Year, observing, "She was more than a dozen years into a successful international career before people stopped describing her as 'promising'."

SYLVIA McNAIR, born into a musical family in Mansfield, Ohio, June 23, 1956, studied violin until her sophomore year in Wheaton College when she decided to take voice lessons. She earned a master's in performance from Indiana University, and after winning the 1982 National Metropolitan Opera Auditions made her London debut on the American Artists' Series. She is a premier recitalist with major orchestras in the United States, Europe and Japan. Her roles range from Mozart to Anne Trulove in *The Rake's Progress*, in such venues as Chicago Lyric, San Francisco, Covent Garden, L'Opéra Bastille, Vienna State Opera, the Blossom, Glyndebourne and Salzburg Festivals and Hollywood Bowl.

In 1990, she was the first recipient of the Marian Anderson Award. She won a 1996 Grammy for Best Classical Performance on the CD, *The Echoing Air: The Music of Henry Purcell*. Her over seventy other recordings include *Come Rain or Come Shine: The Harold Arlen Songbook*, a Jerome Kern Songbook disc, *Sure Thing*, with André Previn, a CD of Handel and Mozart arias, Euridice in Gluck's *Orfeo ad Euridice*, Mozart's *Mass in C minor*, *Requiem* and *Il re pastore* (all on Philips Classics) and Susanna on Deutsche Grammophon's *Marriage of Figaro*.

Most of McNair's time was spent on the opera stages of Europe, so U.S. audiences knew her only from concerts and recitals, but the 1996–97 season saw her as Tytania in *A Midsummer Night's Dream* at the Met for the first time since her 1992 *Fidelio*, recitals at Carnegie Hall and appearances with the New York Philharmonic, the Philadelphia Orchestra and the Boston Symphony at Kennedy Center.

The 1998–99 season included return engagements with the orchestras of Cleveland, Chicago, Philadelphia, and the New York Philharmonic celebration of George Gershwin's 100th birthday. She was Cleopatra in the 1999–2000 Met production of Handel's *Giulio Cesare*, and sang a recital at the Supreme Court accompanied by her husband, Hal France, conductor, pianist and artistic director of Opera Omaha. During the 2000–01 season she sang with orchestras throughout the U.S. and the Hollywood Bowl in August, and in Paris, Berlin, Amsterdam, Vienna, the Met production of *The Magic Flute*, and her Carnegie Hall debut recital, March 15. She returned to the Met in 2001–02 for *A Midsummer Night's Dream*.

In 2003, McNair announced that she was leaving behind classical music and opera in favor of popular music, musical theater and cabaret.

WALTRAUD MEIER, born in Würzburg, Germany, January 9, 1956, brings dynamism to everything she sings. A language and education student, she did not begin vocal lessons until her late teens. By 1978, she had moved to Mannheim Opera adding Carmen and Wagnerian roles to her repertoire. She has appeared as Siegliende (*Die Walküre*) at the Met, La Scala, Vienna and Munich. Her breakthrough came at the 1983 Bayreuth Festival, where she electrified audiences as Kundry in *Parsifal*. She has been a permanent guest there ever since. Her Met debut in 1987 was Fricka in *Das Rheingold*. Return appearances include Santuzza, *Cavalleria Rusticana*, 1993, and a most innovative, untragic Carmen in March 1997. As a dramatic mezzo-soprano, she specializes not only in Wagnerian roles, but explores Verdi, *verismo*, modern—Marie in *Wozzeck*—and French repertory as Dalila for the Met, 1998. In the Met 2005–06 season, she was in *Parsifal*. Half her career is devoted to international concerts and recitals. She has appeared in videos of *Götterdämmerung* and *Tannhäuser*, and multitudinous other operatic and symphonic recordings. In February 1996, she was awarded the prestigious title, Bayerische Kammersängerin (Bavarian Chamber Singer) in Munich.

Mezzo **SUSANNE MENTZER**, born in Philadelphia, January 21, 1957, was a sophomore at University of the Pacific, spending a summer at Aspen in 1976, when she sang her first Nicklausse in *The Tales of Hoffmann*. She finished her musical training with BM and MM degrees at Juilliard. After being a member of the Houston Opera Studio, and appearing with other American opera companies in the early '80s, she made her Covent Garden debut in 1985 as Rosina, returning there in 1988 as Giovanna Seymour (*Anna Bolena*), and 1989 as Dorabella. In San Diego, she was Rosina in 1987 and Octavian in *Der Rosenkavalier* in 1992. In 1989 she made her Met debut as Cherubino, reprising the role in 1991, along with *Idomeneo*, and singing the Composer in *Ariadne auf Naxos*, 1993. The 1995–96 season saw her as Zerlina in *Don Giovanni* with Lyric Opera of Chicago and Norma with HGO, the company with whom she launched her career.

While building her reputation for trouser roles, which have been a staple of her international career, such as Octavian (*Der Rosenkavalier*), Nicklausse (*Tales of Hoffman*) and Annius (*La clemenza de Tito*), she also excels in the traditional female roles, Rosina, Zerlina, Marguerite, Cendrillon (*Cinderella*) and the very feminine Mélisande, which she sang at the Met in 2000–01, along with *Ariadne auf Naxos*. She returned to the Met in 2001–02 for *Falstaff*. She is comfortable in all musical styles from Handel to contemporary, but enjoys the lieder and chamber-music repertoire which has taken up a larger part of her schedule in recent years. Her recordings, which include *Anna Bolena*, opposite **Dame Joan Sutherland**, *Il barbiere di Siviglia*, *Idomeneo*, Mozart masses and the Bruckner *Te Deum*, have been released on the Philips, Angel/EMI, and Decca labels. Koch released *The Eternal Feminine*, with her long-time collaborator, pianist Craig Rutenberg. She often appears with guitarist **Sharon Isbin**, with whom she recorded *Wayfaring Strangers*. Summers feature appearances at many festivals, including Ravinia, Tanglewood, and Rossini Festival (Pesaro, Italy). Besides teaching at Aspen, in 2003 she sang the music of Hector Berlioz as part of his bicentennial. She also made concert appearances in *Romeo et Juliette* with the New York Philharmonic, and *Les Nuits d'été* with the Pittsburgh and Indianapolis Symphonies.

For the 2003–04 season, she made her fourteenth consecutive season appearance at the Met in *The Barber of Seville*, then made orchestral appearances with Pittsburgh, Indianapolis, Boston, and Ravel's *Shéhérazade*, San Diego (January 2004).

Aprile Millo

Mentzer is a visiting professor of voice at DePaul University School of Music in Chicago.

APRILE MILLO was born in New York, April 14, 1958, to a tenor father and soprano mother. After living in Europe, the family moved to Los Angeles when she was eleven. She studied with her parents until 1983 when she met Rita Patane, wife of conductor Giuseppe (1932–89), with whom she made her first recording. In 1977, she won first place in the San Diego Opera competition, received the Geraldine Farrar Award, sang a small role in Aida and stayed with the company through 1980. In 1979, she won first prize in the Concorso Internazionale di Voci Verdiane in Busseto, Italy, and received the Montserrat Caballé Award in Barcelona. By 1980 she had sung *Aida* with Salt Lake City, followed by Elvira in Verdi's *Ernani* at La Scala in 1982. Her Met debut came in 1984 as Amelia in *Simon Boccanegra*, substituting for the ailing Bulgarian soprano **Anna Tomowa-Sintow**, and has since made it her artistic signature singing the Verdi roles which are her specialty. After winning the Richard Tucker Award (1985) and the Maria Callas Foundation Award (1986), she performed at Carnegie Hall (1987), the Baths of Caracalla (Rome) Festival (1988–90), and in major houses on both sides of the Atlantic. She recorded Verdi's *Don Carlo* and *Luisa Miller*, conducted by James Levine, and appeared in videos of Met productions of *Aida*. During the 1999–2000 season she sang Elena in *Mefistofele* for the Met, and Tosca in Oslo. At the twenty-fifth Richard Tucker Foundation gala at Avery Fisher Hall, February 4, 2001, she teamed up with **Dolora Zajick** giving the audience true Italianate singing. After some challenging years in the '90s, Millo is back in fine voice, as proved by her Tosca for Connecticut Grand Opera. Celebrating her twentieth year at the Met in 2004, in the Spring of 2005 she sang Amelia in *Ballo* and Tosca, returning in May 2006 for another Tosca.

ERIE MILLS, born in Granite, Illinois, June 22, 1953, studied at Interlochen (Michigan) Music Camp, and received her BM from the College of Wooster, Ohio, and MM from the University of Illinois. She made her professional debut in 1979 as Ninette in Prokofiev's *Love for Three Oranges* at the Chicago Lyric Theater. Her first role with NYCO was Cunegonde in *Candide*, after which she sang there regularly. In 1984, she received a Richard Tucker Career Grant. Her 1987 Met debut was as Blondchen in Mozart's *Abduction from the Seraglio*. Guest appearances at Cincinnati, Cleveland, San Francisco, Minnesota, Washington, DC, New Orleans, Houston and Montreal Operas were followed by debuts in La Scala, Vienna and Hamburg. Known for her singular coloratura sound, her other roles include Rosina (*The Barber of Seville*), Zerbinetta (*Ariadne auf Naxos*), Olympia (*Tales of Hoffmann*), Marie (*La fille du régiment*) and the title role in *Romeo and Juliet*. She has also concertized extensively throughout the world and appeared on television.

2002 saw the release of her CD *Always It's Spring*, a recital of songs by American composers.

Mills is a member of the voice faculty of San Jose State University and resides in the San Francisco Bay area with her husband, Dr. Thomas Rescigno.

Born in Adjud, Romania, **NELLY MIRICIOIU** studied in Bucharest, making her debut as the Queen of the Night in *Die Zauberflöte* in Iasi, Romania. After completing vocal studies in Italy, she sang with Brasov Opera from 1975–78. Beginning with her debut at Scottish Opera in 1981 as Violetta and Tosca, she made international debuts, including Covent Garden (*Pagliacci*) 1982, Paris Opera (*Les Contes D'Hoffmann*), La Scala (*Lucia di Lammermoor*) 1983, Vienna State Opera as Manon Lescaut, 1986, and her Met debut in 1989 as Mimi (*La bohème*). In 1986, she began a series of Vara Matinee Concerts at the Amsterdam Concertgebouw, which over the years expanded her repertoire of *bel canto* heroines. She appeared as Tosca in San Diego—where I drove her around in the rain!—and Berlin, 1996, and has recorded this opera on Naxos. Her other complete opera recordings are Donizetti's *Rosamonda D'Inghilterra* and *Maria de Rudenz*, Mercadante's *Orazi e Curiazi*, Rossini's *Ricciardo e Zoraide*, Pacini's *Maria d'Inghilterra*, Mascagni's *Cavalleria Rusticana*, and Respighi's *La Fiamma*. Her solo CDs include *Nelly Miricioiu—A Rossini Gala*, and *Nelly Miricioiu—Bel Canto Portrait*. Opera Rara has, for twenty-five years, recorded the Bel Canto masters. In 2002, they released the recording of *Roberto Devereux* she sang in at Covent Garden.

Her performances in roles such as Violetta, Nedda, Maria Stuarda, Lucrezia Borgia, Semiramide, Mimi and Butterfly take her around the world, including a 1996 appearance with Australian Opera in *Lucrezia Borgia*. 1997 performances of *Luisa Miller* in Amsterdam and *Don Carlos* in Brussels, Rome Opera's opening 1998 season of Respighi's *La Fiamma* was followed by Butterfly in Hamburg and a concert with the Concertgebouw in Amsterdam. For the 2000–01 season she appeared as Norma at Covent Garden, Rome and Greece, *Adriana Lecouvreur* at La Scala, and Isabella in *Robert Le Diable* at the Deutsche Staatsoper (German State Opera). In 2001–02, she was Tosca in Geneva and Paris Bastille, in *Roberto Devereux* at Covent Garden and Santiago (Chile), *Vespri Siciliani* in Vienna and more concerts in Amsterdam, plus concert versions of Bellini's *Il Pirata* at Washington Opera and Queen Elizabeth Hall, London.

Nelly lives in England with husband Barry Kirk and their son Daniel, born 1991.

HEIDI GRANT MURPHY, born in 1968, grew up in Bellingham, Washington (state) and attended Western Washington and Indiana Universities. In 1988, she won the Metropolitan Opera Competition and was selected by music director James Levine for the Met Young Artist Program, a three year course of intensive vocal study. She sang onstage in minor roles beginning in 1989, graduating to Oscar (*Un ballo en maschera*), Nannetta (*Falstaff*), Sister Constance (*Dialogues of the Carmelites*), Sophie (*Der Rosenkavalier*) and Pamina (*The Magic Flute*). Her now successful operatic and concert career takes her worldwide with the finest opera companies and orchestras. She has sung in Carnegie Hall and London's Barbican Centre. Her recordings on Telarc and Deutsche Grammophon include Barbarina (*Marriage of Figaro*) with the Metropolitan Opera Orchestra and Ilia (*Idomeneo*) with **Plácido Domingo** and **Cecilia Bartoli**. One of her most significant appearances was special soloist on the live telecast from St. Patrick's Cathedral for the 1996 Christmas Eve Mass. She was back at the Met for the 1999–2000 *Der Rosenkavalier* and sang Constance in *Dialogues of the Carmelites* (2002–03). The same season saw her in **Kaija Saariaho's** *Cinq Reflects* from *L'amour de loin* at the Ravinia Festival, and three new CDs: *Times Like This*, featuring Broadway show tunes; Mahler's 4th Symphony with Dallas; and *Clearings in the Sky*, works by **Lili Boulanger** and Rachmaninoff.

2003–04 brought Sophie (*Der Rosenkavalier*) for Netherlands Opera, Gretel in a concert version of *Hansel and Gretel* with the Milwaukee Symphony, Mozart's *Requiem* with Houston, *Carmina Burana* (Dallas), Mahler's 4th (Detroit), and Mostly Mozart Festival's fully staged opera *Il re pastore*. Murphy was also named visiting distinguished professor at East Carolina University for the 2003–04 academic year. She was Servilia in the Met's May 2005 *La Clemenza di Tito* and September in *Falstaff*.

Heidi is married to Kevin Murphy, an assistant Met conductor. They reside in New York with their son Christopher.

Swiss soprano **NOËMI NADELMANN** was born in Zurich, March 6, 1962. Her father, Leo Nadelmann (1913–89) was a concert pianist whose career ended that year when, like Robert Schumann, an injury to his hand prevented further playing. Her mother, Rachel Ritter, an actress from Odessa whose signature role was Anne Frank which, with her youthful looks, she played into her 30s, settled for the role of motherhood when Noëmi was born. Piano lessons with her father began at age four, and voice at seventeen with Carol Smith in Switzerland. When her teacher moved to Indiana University, Bloomington, Noëmi followed and studied with her for two more years (1984–86). Returning to Switzerland, she made her debut at La Fenice (Venice) as Musetta in *La bohème* to the Mimi of **Renata Scotto**.

During the 1990s, Nadelmann appeared at the three major houses in Berlin: State Opera, Berlin Opera, and the Comic Opera run by the great Harry Kupfer. By 1999, she had appeared at Cologne as Donna Anna, Munich as Zerbinetta, and her signature roles in *The Merry Widow* at Zurich, Bastille (Paris), and Vienna; Musetta at Berlin Comic Opera, Amsterdam, Paris, Vienna, Lyric Opera of Chicago, and the Met (her 2000 debut); *Die Fledermaus* in Zurich, Vienna, Cologne, and San Diego (debut in 2005); and *La Traviata* in Hamburg, Zurich and Bern where she also sang Lucia in *Lucia di Lammermoor*.

Added to her CD of Gershwin and Cole Porter, her 2003 disk with the Budapest Symphony, *Noëmi Nadelmann sings Operetta*, contains the jewels of Johann Strauss, Franz Lehár and Emmerich Kálmán.

ANNA NETREBKO, born September 18, 1971, in Krasnodar, in the Caucasus, was guided by the focus on the arts in Russian culture. Her interests progressed from gymnastics to ballet to singing, with vocal training at St. Petersburg Conservatory. After winning first prize in Moscow's 1993 National Glinka Competition, she was invited by mezzo-soprano Irina Arkhipova to take part in a concert at the Bolshoi Opera. She began her career in 1994 with the Kirov Opera as Susanna and continues to appear with them both at the Mariinsky Theatre and on tour. As of 2003, she was still studying with **Renata Scotto**.

Anna became an overnight sensation in 1995 with her triumphant debut at San Francisco Opera as Lyudmila in Glinka's *Ruslan and Lyudmila*, after which she was seen as Zerlina, Musetta, Ilia, Adina (*L'elisir d'amore*), Nannetta (*Falstaff*), Louisa (*Betrothal in a Monastery*), and Marfa in Rimsky-Korsakov's *The Tsar's Bride*. 1998 marked her first appearance at the Metropolitan Opera in performances with the Kirov Opera as Lyudmila and Louisa. During the 1999–2000 season, she appeared at Covent Garden as Natasha (*War and Peace*), the same role for her first appearances at La Scala and Madrid's Teatro Real. Her 2002 Met debut was as Natasha, in performances led by Russian maestro, **Valery Gergiev**. Because of the resemblance, a New York critic called her "Audrey Hepburn with a voice."

She was at the Salzburg Festival as Donna Anna in the season-opening new production of *Don Giovanni*, under **Nikolaus Harnoncourt**; at Covent Garden (*La clemenza di Tito*), and Washington Opera (*Rigoletto, Le nozze di Figaro, Idomeneo*). Also in 2002, she appeared at the inaugural performances of the Moscow Easter Festival, again led by Gergiev, and debuted at the Verbier Festival as soloist in Mahler's *Fourth Symphony* directed by James Levine, returning the following season for performances of Pergolesi's *Stabat Mater*. Viennese audiences saw her for the first time as Violetta at the State Opera, the same role she sang for her debut with Bavarian State Opera, July 2003.

In 2003–04, Netrebko made her concert debut at the Salzburg Festival in a program of Mozart concert arias with the Dresden Staatskapelle Orchestra, led by Daniel Harding, and in September appeared as Donna Anna in *Don Giovanni* for the opening night of the new season at Covent Garden. She was Mozart's Susanna with the Teatro Communale di Firenze, under the direction of Zubin Mehta, before she traveled to Los Angeles Opera for her debut in the title role of *Lucia di Lammermoor*, November 2003. She remained on the West Coast for a recital at the Herbst Theatre in San Francisco, and a performance of Handel's *Messiah* with the San Francisco Symphony conducted by Donald Runnicles. Following her debut at the Saito Kinen Festival, in performances as Musetta led by Seiji Ozawa, she repeated that role at San Francisco Opera in June and July 2004. Fall 2005, she was at the Salzburg Festival in *La traviata*, and at the Met in December for *Rigoletto*, followed in March with *Don Pasquale*.

Georgian mezzo **MZIA NIORADZE** was born in Tbilisi, Georgia (Russia), graduated from the Tbilisi Conservatory in 1992, and continued her training at the Music Academy in Ozimo, Italy. She was a prizewinner at the Julio Gayari International Vocal Competition (Spain, 1994); at the Elena Obraztsova International Vocal Competition (St Petersburg, 1999); and received awards at the Rimsky-Korsakov Vocal Competitions in St. Petersburg, and the International Hans Gabor-Belvedere Competition in Vienna.

During the 1991–92 season, she became a Soloist of Paliashvili Opera and Ballet Theatre (Tbilisi), where her repertoire included Princess Eboli (*Don Carlo*), Azucena (*Il trovatore*), Maddalena (*Rigoletto*), and Natella (*Absalom and Eteri*).

She joined the Mariinsky Theatre in 1996, where she made her debut in the title role of *Carmen*. Her other roles there include Suzuki (*Madama Butterfly*), Cherubino (*Le nozze di Figaro*), Teresa (*La sonnambula*), Preziosilla (*La forza del destino*), Maddalena (*Rigoletto*), Konchakovna (*Prince Igor*), Flosshilde (*Das Rheingold*), and Dalila (*Samson et Dalila*). She took part in international tours with the Mariinsky and was featured in a new staging of *War and Peace* at the Opéra National de Paris with the company in 2000.

She was seen as Konchakovna in Francesca Zambello's new production of *Prince Igor* at Houston Grand Opera, *Rusalka* in Lyon, made her San Francisco Opera debut as Paransema in the world premiere of *Arshak II*, and was in *Boris Godunov* at the Met in 2003–04.

Swedish mezzo **ANNE SOFIE von OTTER**, born May 9, 1955, studied at the Royal Conservatory in her native Stockholm, then with Erik Werba in Vienna and, in 1981, at London's Guildhall School of Music with Vera Rozsa, considered a "patron saint" by British and Scandinavian singers. In 1982 she joined the Basel Opera as a principal, singing Cherubino, Dorabella and Sesto (*La Clemenza di Tito*). In 1984, she performed at the Aix-en-Provence Festival in France. Her Covent Garden debut in 1985 was as Cherubino, the same year she made her U.S. debut with the Chicago Symphony as a soloist in Mozart's *C minor Mass*. Appearances at La Scala, Milan, and the Bavarian State Opera, Munich, came in 1987. While she has appeared in most major European opera houses performing such roles as Romeo (*I Capuleti*), Octavian (*Der Rosenkavalier*) and Idamante (*Idomeneo*), it is her recordings which have cemented the reputation of her talent as a linguist and the clarity and range of her voice. In early music, conductor **John Eliot Gardiner** adopted her as soloist of choice for his recordings of Bach's *Christmas Oratorio* and Monteverdi's *Orfeo* (1987), Gluck's *Orphée et Eurydice* (1989), *Iphigénie en Aulide* (1990), Mozart's *Idomeneo* (1991), and *La clemenza di Tito* (1992). Her Deutsche Grammophon CD of twenty-five rarely heard Grieg songs with Bengt Forsberg, her pianist and music collaborator since 1980, was selected as

Grammophon magazine's 1993 Record of the Year. Recordings are a key element of von Otter's musical life, but she is also an onstage star who has the advantage of rejecting more offers than she accepts. Opera performances are time away from home in Stockholm and her two sons born 1989 and 1991.

Making up for her rare American appearances, she debuted at the Met in 1988 as Cherubino, was Octavian in the 1989 Lyric Opera of Chicago's *Der Rosenkavalier* productions and returned to the Met (1995–96) as Idamante, followed by the April '96 James Levine Gala. The same month, she made her New York recital debut at Lincoln Center. In 1994, she was named by the *Oakland Tribune* "the most prominent international singer never to have appeared in the Bay Area." She made up for that, also in 1996, when she sang with the San Francisco Symphony. *Musical America* 1996 named her "Vocalist of the Year."

Von Otter's return to the Met was in the 2001–02 production of *Idomeneo*. Released in 2001 were three recordings, two with the Brodsky Quartet in *Quartets by Peter Sculthorpe* and *Quartets by Respighi*, and *For the Stars*, in songs by Elvis Costello. January 2004 brought a San Diego recital. In February 2005 she was Mélisande at the Met, followed in May as Sesto in *La Clemenza di Tito*.

Ewa Podleś

EWA PODLEŚ possesses that rare, lowest range of the female voice and is considered the world's leading *contralto*. Born in Warsaw April 26, 1952, Ewa (pronounced Eh-vah) began her onstage opera career at age three as the baby son of Madame Butterfly. She studied at the Warsaw Academy with Polish soprano, Alina Bolechowska (1924–2002), and credits her success both to her teacher and her husband, Jerzy Marchwinski, a pianist and conservatory professor. After winning prizes at competitions in Moscow, Toulouse, Barcelona and Rio de Janeiro, she was engaged by Warsaw's Wielki Theatre, with roles ranging from Cenerentola to Konchakovna (*Prince Igor*). In 1984, she sang Rosina at Aix-en-Provence and made her Metropolitan debut as Handel's Rinaldo, a trouser role. During 1985–89, she sang Cornelia in Handel's *Giulio Cesare* (Rome), Malcolm in Rossini's *La Donna del lago* (Trieste) and Adalgisa—a second soprano role—in Bellini's *Norma* (Vancouver). Her Covent Garden debut came in 1990 as Hedwige in Rossini's *Guillaume Tell* and her La Scala debut as Ragonde in Rossini's *Le Comte Ory* (1991), the year she also sang Delilah at Opéra Bastille (Paris) and Arsace in *Semiramide* at La Fenice (Venice). Her flexible, rich-toned voice, with its very individual timbre, is ideal for Rossini coloratura contralto roles, notably Tancredi, which she sang at La Scala (1993) and recorded to acclaim. In 1997, she performed and recorded the title role of Handel's *Ariodante* with Les Musiciens du Louvre. An Alice Tully Hall recital in November 2001, in a program of Slavic art songs, was with pianist **Garrick Ohlsson**, winner of the 1970 International Chopin Competition in Warsaw. The pair also recorded *Live: Songs by Chopin, Mussorgsky, Rachmaninoff* from a concert in Warsaw, December 8, 2002.

Her 2003 season included Adalgisa for Seattle Opera in March, where she brought the audience to their feet. A scheduled—sold out months in advance—May recital for San Diego Opera was postponed due to an automobile accident in Albuquerque. After a recovery at home in Poland, in October she "stole the show" as Ulrica at Michigan Opera Theater's *Un Ballo in Maschera*—an amazing accomplishment since she only sings in one scene. She sang the postponed San Diego recital in November, where this author was part of the audience who had clung to their tickets for seven months. It was an event worth waiting for.

Her 2004 season included Eboli at Opera Company of Philadelphia, Ulrica in a concert performance at Carnegie Hall, and Azucena at Milwaukee's Florentine Opera. October 2005, she was in Barcelona for *La Gioconda* with Deborah Voigt. She gave a recital at Avery Fisher Hall, February 2006, in Rossini's cantata *Joan of Arc* and Mussorgsky's *Songs and Dances of Death*, with Moscow Chamber Orchestra. That was followed in April with *Giulio Cesare* in San Diego.

With her mezzo-contralto range, Podleś is singing more opera, but made her reputation as a concert singer. An accomplished recitalist singing the coloratura pieces of Handel and Vivaldi, made popular through their revival by **Marilyn Horne**, she is also admired for her orchestral appearances in Verdi's *Requiem*, Mahler's *Das Lied von der Erde* and other symphonic works.

In a rather unique opera career, soprano **EMILY PULLEY** has been on the roster of the Met since 1994, after winning the Met Auditions in 1993. She has steadily worked her way up from performing small comprimario roles to consistently understudying and singing leads, in addition to her numerous regional and international engagements.

Born April 14, 1967, Emily was raised in College Station, Texas, in a home where music meant Glenn Miller and Tommy Dorsey. She played flute and piccolo and was drum major in her high school band. She also played bass guitar in the jazz band. Although she was very active in choral activities, and was twice selected for the Texas All-State Choir, a career in opera was the furthest thing from her mind. She credits her voice teacher at West Texas State University for gradually and almost surreptitiously transforming her into a classical singer. After graduating *summa cum laude*, Emily continued her studies at the University of North Texas, completing her master's degree requirements while already employed by the Met.

In 1999, one of her first starring roles was Rosalinda in an uproarious *Die Fledermaus* at Colorado's historic Central City Opera. 2000–2001 featured her in *Carmina Burana*, and as Nedda (*I Pagliacci*) at Minnesota Opera; Alice Ford (*Falstaff*), Opera Omaha; *Elijah* and Gretel (*Hansel und Gretel*) with the National Symphony Orchestra of Taiwan; and her debut with Los Angeles Opera as the Countess (*Le nozze di Figaro*). At the Met she was First Lady (*Magic Flute*), while the Summer of 2001 included a Verdi and Puccini concert at the Ravinia Festival, and gala concerts with Berkshire Opera.

2001–2002 saw her debut as Mimi at the Royal Opera House, Covent Garden, her first Tatyana (*Eugene Onegin*) with Opera Colorado, Violetta (*Traviata*) at Toledo (Ohio) Opera, and at the Met, Gretel, Thérèse (Poulenc's *Les mamelles de Tirésias*), and Musetta.

In 2002–2003, Pulley added three new roles to her Met repertoire: Blanche (*Les dialogues des Carmelites*), Marguerite (*Faust*), and Anne Trulove (*The Rake's Progress*). After performing all summer with Central City Opera as Nedda and Rosario (*Goyescas*), she returned to the Met for the 2003–04 season to understudy **Renée Fleming** as Violetta (*La Traviata*) and **Elizabeth Futral** as Rachel in Jacques Halévy's (*La Juive*), as well as reprising Musetta (*La bohème*), and Valencienne (*Merry Widow*). The season also saw her New York City Opera debut as Lavinia in Richard Strauss' *Mourning Becomes Electra*, and her Glimmerglass Opera debut as Minnie in *Fanciulla del West* (Puccini's *Girl of the Golden West*). She returned to the Met in 2005–06 for *La bohème*.

ASHLEY PUTNAM, born August 10, 1952, in New York, first studied flute at the University of Michigan before switching to voice. She received her BM, 1974, and MM, 1975, apprenticing with the Santa Fe Opera right after graduation. In 1976, she made her debut in the title role of *Lucia di Lammermoor* with the (Norfolk) Virginia Opera Association. The same year she won first prize in the Metropolitan Opera Auditions. Her European debut was Musetta at the 1978 Glyndebourne Festival, where she returned in 1984 for Arabella. On September 15, 1978, she won accolades as Musetta in her NYCO debut. Covent Garden first heard her in 1986 as Janáček's Janůfa, and the Met was treated to Donna Elvira in 1990. She returned there for Marguerite in *Faust*. January 1992, she was in San Diego as the Marschallin in *Der Rosendavalier*.

She has appeared throughout the U.S., Europe and South America in many other major roles, such as Kát'a Kabanová, Ellen Orford (*Peter Grimes*), Vitellia, Fiordiligi, Donna Anna and the Marschallin. Her concert career features engagements with the Los Angeles and New York Philharmonics, the Concertgebouw Orchestra, Amsterdam, and regular appearances at Carnegie Hall. She has recorded *The Mother of Us All*, *Mary Queen of Scots* and Musetta (*La bohème*).

Patricia Racette

Putnam has been on the faculties of DePaul (1999–2000), Eastman (2001–2002), Manhattan (MSM, 2001–), and maintains a private voice studio since 1996.

PATRICIA RACETTE, born January 29, 1967, in San Francisco, received her training as a member of the Merola[190] Opera Program. A 1989–90 Adler Fellow with numerous Opera Center credits, she made her 1989 SFO debut as Alice Ford (*Falstaff*). As a resident artist, she toured Japan, Guam and Saipan in *Butterfly*, and sang the other roles of Rosalinde (*Die Fledermaus*), Freia (*Das Rheingold*) and Helmwige (*Die Walküre*). In 1992, she won the Richard Tucker Foundation Career Grant. The same year, she appeared as Micaëla and participated in the Rossini Festival with SFO. 1992 also marked her debut with the Vienna State Opera as Mimi, and with NYCO as Musetta, a role she repeated the following year at the Lisbon Festival as well as Geneva and Wales. Other debuts in the '92–'93 season were at the Netherlands Opera, St. Louis, Vancouver, and concerts at the Ravinia Festival and with the Chicago Symphony. 1994 marked her Met debut as Musetta, the year she won the Marian Anderson Award. 1995 brought her San Diego Opera debut as Mimi, plus concert appearances with the Boston and San Francisco Symphonies. She also returned to SFO as Margherita (*Mefistofele*), Vancouver as Ellen Orford (*Peter Grimes*),Violetta in Minnesota, and a gala concert for the twenty-fifth anniversary of the Opera Theatre of St. Louis.

The '95–'96 season saw debuts at Covent Garden and Opéra Bastille as Musetta. Her Santa Fe Opera debut, 1996, was in the title role of *Emmeline*, a world premiere by American composer Tobias Picker (*b* 1954). SFO reprises included Mimi ('95–'96), Antonia and Micaëla ('96–'97). Two role debuts were Fiordiligi with the Opera Company of Philadelphia and Marguerite at Vancouver. '97–'98, found her back at the Bastille as Violetta, and to the Met as Liù with **Pavarotti**, plus Mimi, Musetta, Antonia (*Tales of Hoffman*) and her La Scala debut as Ellen Orford. Her HGO debut as Violetta was in 1998, the year she won the prestigious Richard Tucker Award. In 2001, five years after her San Diego debut, she returned to sing Love Simpson in Carlisle Floyd's *Cold Sassy Tree*, the role she created the previous year for its world premiere at Houston. She then returned to San Francisco for *Luisa Miller*, and a role in which she is becoming one of the world's leading interpreters, Violetta (*La traviata*). 2001–02 again found her in Houston as Elisabetta in *Don Carlo*, *Eugene Onegin* in Santa Fe, and to the Met for *La bohème*. April 2004, she was Kát'a Kabanová in San Diego, and at the end of the year was Cio-Cio-San at Houston, *Jenůfa* for Dallas, and Antonia in *Hoffman* at the Met. She reprised her Musetta at the Met in February 2005, was Nedda (*Pagliacci*) in March, and at year's end was in Falstaff and the world premiere of Tobias Picker's *An American Tragedy*, with an all-star cast that included Jennifer Larmore, Susan Graham, and Dolora Zajick.

Sondra Radvanovsky

SONDRA RADVANOVSKY, born April 11, 1969, in Berwyn, Illinois, grew up in Richmond, Indiana, and is considered the classic small town girl. Her parents listened to classical music. Her first voice lesson was at age eleven, soloing in her church choir, the same year. After seeing Plácido Domingo in *Tosca* on television she knew that opera was for her.

First training as a mezzo at USC, she was later classified as a dramatic soprano. Other studies were at Cincinnati, Tanglewood with Ruth Falcon, and the Music Academy of the West with Martial Singher (1904–90), who told her: "I have good news and bad news for you. The good news is you're going to have a career. The bad news is you have no idea how hard it's going to be."

Her operatic debut was at twenty-one in the supporting role of Flora in *La traviata*. After winning the 1995 Met Opera National Auditions and the Loren L. Zachary Society Competition first prize, she joined the Met's Lindemann Young Artist Development Program where James Levine wanted her to sing Mozart and Handel for one year. Thinking herself a Verdi singer, she was devastated, but the three year Met program transformed her. In 1997, she won the George London Foundation Competition.

---

190. Italian born Gaetano Merola (1881–1953) was SFO director 1923–53, raising this company to rank only second to the New York Met.

Summer 1998, at the Met Opera Parks Concerts, her Leonora was so well received that by Spring 1999 she was on the Met's main stage as the High Priestess (*Aida*), and Micaela (*Carmen*). After being in Japan's Saito Kinen Festival's *Dialogues of the Carmelites*, she debuted in Dallas as Freia (*Das Rheingold*), Houston as Elena (*Mefistofele*), and an October Leonora (*Il trovatore*) with Pittsburgh. February 2000 she was Leonora at San Diego and Gutrune (*Die Götterdämmerung*) at the Met in March. October 2002 brought the title role in Carlisle Floyd's *Susannah*—a character she feels kinship to—at Lyric Opera Chicago.

June 2003 found her at Paris Opera for Hélène in *Les Vêpres Siciliennes*, followed in August by the Verdi *Requiem* with the Boston Symphony at Tanglewood, and Beethoven's Ninth—her previous singing this symphony was in 1992, in the chorus. She returned to Met in November for Leonora, and Donna Anna (*Don Giovanni*) in January 2004. March brought *Don Carlo* in San Diego, then to Europe for *Il trovatore* in Florence, Paris, and Deutsche Oper Berlin. She was back at the Met in December, again as Hélène in *Les Vêpres Siciliennes*. At the end of 2005, she was in Bilbao for *Rusalka*. January 2006, the Met had her in *Die Fledermaus* and *Cyrano de Bérgérac* with Plácido Domingo, broadcast on radio.

Sondra married Duncan Lear in 2002. They live in Toronto.

Australian soprano **DEBORAH RIEDEL**, born July 31, 1958, in Sydney, studied at the New South Wales Conservatorium and in London. She began her career as a mezzo, but changed to soprano in 1988 from which time she sang major roles with Australian Opera and Victoria State Opera, as well as appearing with the Australian Pops in Melbourne. Her Covent Garden debut, 1991, was Freia (*Das Rheingold*), Mimi and Donna Elvira. 1993–94 saw her back in Australia on tour with **José Carreras**. Besides the major houses of Europe, she has leapt across the globe to San Diego in 1994 for *La sonnambula*, 1996 as Adina (*L'elisir d'amore*), 1997 as Violetta, 1999 as Alice Ford, and 2000 in *Don Giovanni*. Her San Francisco, Vienna and Munich debuts were as Donna Anna. She sang Mimi in Victoria State Opera's "Puccini Spectacular" in Sydney and Melbourne, and with the Haifa (Israel) Symphony. Among numerous appearances with Australian Opera and Maestro **Richard Bonynge**, she sang the four female roles in *The Tales of Hoffmann*. 1997 marked her Met debut as Donna Anna. 1998 highlighted Ellen Orford in San Francisco and Marguerite for Lyric Opera Queensland (Australia). Her many concert and recital engagements have also taken her around the world. Her recordings include the Mozart Bicentennial Concert, Lehar's *Giuditta* and *Paganini* with tenor **Jerry Hadley**, and videos of *The Gypsy Princess* and *Dialogues of the Carmelites*.

Riedel is the recipient of many honors in her native country.

JEAN RIGBY, born December 22, 1954, in Fleetwood, Lancashire, England, enjoyed a reign as one of Britain's top mezzos. After initial music studies at the Birmingham School of Music she went to the RAM and later to the National Opera Studio. Joining the ENO led to such roles as Amastris in *Xerxes*, Marika in *Boris Godunov*, Octavian in *Der Rosenkavalier*, Dorabella in *Così fan tutte* and the title role in *The Rape of Lucretia*. Her 1983 Covent Garden debut in *Don Carlo* won rave reviews, as did appearances at the Scottish National Opera and the celebrated Glyndebourne Festival Opera, from 1985. In the U.S., she has been heard in San Diego as Charlotte in Massenet's *Werther* (1993).

One of Britain's leading concert artists, Rigby sings at the London Proms, and in such masterworks as Mahler's 2nd and 8th Symphonies, the Verdi *Requiem* and other major choral works. 1997 engagements included Charlotte for Seattle Opera, Mahler's 2nd in Boston and London, and concerts with Leonard Slatkin at the Istanbul Festival. 1998–99 she was at Glyndebourne, where she sang Geneviève (*Pelleas and Melisande*). She is featured on video with ENO's *Rigoletto*, and the Glyndebourne production of Benjamin Britten's *Albert Herring*. She has received many honors in the UK.

ANDREA ROST, born 1965, in Hungary, studied voice at the Budapest Conservatory, and in 1986 was a prize winner at the Hertzogenbosch Competition. The following year she was a finalist at the Maria Callas Competition, and also won the Mirjam Helin Competition in Helsinki. In 1987, she appeared in concert in Mozart's *Mass in C-minor*, and in 1989 became a member of the Hungarian State Opera, making her debut in the title role in *Romeo et Juliette*. Since 1991, she has been a member of the Vienna State Opera, performing there annually. Her Salzburg Festival debut in 1992 led to many return engagements. After her success there, **Riccardo Muti** invited her to make her La Scala debut in 1994 in *Rigoletto*. At the 1995 Salzburg Festival she sang the title role in *La traviata*. The same year she made her Covent Garden debut as Susanna (*Figaro*), going back later in the season to reprise Violetta, as well as appearing in Vienna and Paris Bastille as Lucia. 1996 marked her debut at Chicago Lyric Opera as Zerlina, and her Met debut in the autumn as Adina in *L'elisir d'amore*. 1997–98 included Gilda for her San Francisco Opera debut, *La traviata* in Chicago, and *Rigoletto* at the Met, where she appeared in their 1999–2000 production of *Lucia di Lammermoor*, 2001–02 *Marriage of Figaro*, January 2004 *Rigoletto*, February 2005 *Marriage of Figaro*, and April 2006 *Marriage of Figaro*. Returns to Vienna, Paris Bastille and La Scala continue on her busy schedule.

Her discography features Mahler's 8th with **Cheryl Studer**, **Sylvia McNair** and **Sophie von Otter**, Claudio Abbado, conducting; *Marriage of Figaro* with Studer, McNair, Bartoli and Abbado; and *Rigoletto* with tenor Roberto Alagna, Riccardo Muti, conducting.

American soprano **MARTILE ROWLAND** went from understudy to star status when, in 1991, on three hours notice, she substituted for an ailing colleague at Carnegie Hall to sing Elisabetta in *Roberto Devereux* and was catapulted to international success. In the 1990–91 season she made her Met debut as Elvira in *I Puritani*, then reprised her role of Elisabetta in Mexico City, sang Vitellia (*La clemenza di Tito*) in Bielefeld, Germany, and the Queen of the Night in her debut with Opera de Nice (France). She also was the soloist in the Verdi *Requiem* with the Denver Symphony and the Teatro Colón in Buenos Aires. She returned to Carnegie Hall for the **Richard Tauber**[191] Centennial Gala, then on to Miami and Atlanta Operas to sing Lucia. The 1992–93 season marked her European debut at Frankfurt as Violetta and Musetta. 1993–94, she returned to the Met for Lucia, and Miami as Violetta. She also made her first appearance in the Netherlands in a KRO Radio concert, and was back in Mexico City for her first *Anna Bolena*. She sang Norma, a new role, in her Spanish debut in Málaga, Lucia in San Diego (1995), Donna Anna at Michigan Opera, and Odabella (*Attila*) at Stuttgart. 1997 found her as Norma in Rio de Janiero, artist-in-residence at Colorado College in February, followed by Donna Anna for NYCO, and a summer stint as stage director for Colorado Opera Festival's *Carmen*. In 2000 she returned to Atlanta Opera as Turandot.

Artistic director of the Vocal Arts Symposium at Colorado College, in 2001 she founded Opera Theatre of the Rockies, drawing singers from the region for a production of *The Merry Widow*. 2003 saw the ambitious undertaking of staging The *Ballad of Baby Doe* with a fifty-four-member cast. 2006 marked her eighth year as Director of Vocal Arts Symposium, an intensive three-week training and performance program for singers from the U.S. to as far away as China, Korea and Greece.

Born in Mannheim in 1953, **GABRIELE SCHNAUT** studied in Frankfurt and Berlin, making her debut in 1976 at Stuttgart State Opera as a mezzo and proceeding from there to Darmstadt, Mannheim, Opera on the Rhine, and Düsseldorf. In 1985, she switched to soprano roles and has freelanced since 1991, when she made her American debut at San Francisco as Isolde. She went on to build an international career with performances at La Scala as Elektra and Brünnhilde, the Bayreuth Festival with the *Ring der Nibelungen* (Brünnhilde), *Lohengrin* (Ortrud), *Tannhäuser* (Venus), *Die Walküre* (Sieglinde) and at the Vienna State Opera's Ring as Brünnhilde, Isolde, Kundry (*Parsifal*), Turandot, Elektra, and the Dyer's Wife in *Die Frau ohne Schatten*. She repeated many of these roles at Hamburg State Opera, Covent Garden and Tokyo. The Met has heard her Brünnhilde, Elektra, and the Dyer's Wife. Berlin and Munich have also featured this repertoire. Her interest in modern opera put her in the role of Ophelia in the premiere of Wolfgang Rihm's *Hamletmaschine* and the rarely performed operas *Cardillac* by Paul Hindemith and *Der Schatzgräber* by Franz Schrecker. 2001–02 found her back at the Met for *Die Frau ohne Schatten*, in Zurich for Brünnhilde, and at the Munich and Salzburg Summer Festivals—the latter televised. 2003–04 Met appearances were in *Die Walküre* and *Götterdämmerung*.

---

191. Richard Tauber (1892–1948), beloved Austrian born tenor, was especially popular in Lehar operettas. He fled to England during WWII.

Her song repertory from Beethoven, Schubert, Brahms and Mussorgsky to Berg, Strauss and Wolf, has featured her with noted maestros Christian Thielemann, James Levine, Peter Schneider, Zubin Mehta, Franz Welser-Möst, Marcello Viotti, Fabio Luisi, Simon Rattle, Bernard Haitink and Giuseppe Sinopoli. Recordings include her showpieces: excerpts from *Die Walküre* and *Lohengrin*.

Lauded for her dramatic singing and acting ability, in 1995 Gabriele was appointed Kammersängerin at the Hamburg State Opera. In 1998, *Opera World* Magazine voted her "Singer of the Year."

DIANA SOVIERO, called one of the last of the *verismo* sopranos, was born 1952, in Jersey City, New Jersey. Her career began at NYCO as Leila in Bizet's *Les Pêcheurs de Perles*. After singing with many companies, including Miami, San Francisco and Chicago, her Met debut came as Juliette. In 1988, she sang in Geneva and San Diego, and in 1989 made her Covent Garden debut. 1991 brought the acclaimed portrayal of *Manon Lescaut* at the Bastille Opera in Paris. Between 1993 and 1995, she appeared at the Met, Berlin State Opera, Covent Garden and Miami as Tosca, Carmen, Butterfly and Musetta. She has subsequently sung in the leading North American and European opera houses and in Sydney. A highlight of the 1994–95 season was her triple appearance at the Met in *Pagliacci*, *Butterfly* and *La bohème*. The 1995–96 season marked her debut at the Bavarian State Opera as Cio-Cio-San (*Butterfly*), with a return to the Met to reprise the role. The 1996–97 season included her debut in Bilbao, Spain, and two Met performances, Manon Lescaut and Nedda. Soviero has served on the faculty of the Israel Vocal Arts Institute (IVAI).

Her popular CD is Telarc's *Divine Sopranos*, in which she shares honors with Elly Ameling, Kathleen Battle, Arleen Auger, Barbara Hendricks, Sylvia McNair and Dawn Upshaw.

CHERYL STUDER began musical studies on piano and viola in Midland, Michigan, where she was born, October 24, 1955. Her vocal training began at twelve with encouragement from her mother, who presented her with a stack of Maria Callas recordings. After graduating from Interlochen, she was awarded full scholarships from **Leonard Bernstein** to attend the Tanglewood-Berkshire Music Center (1975–77), where she caught the attention of **Seiji Ozawa** who engaged her for concerts with the Boston Symphony in 1979. She completed her formal education at the Hochschule für Music in Vienna. In 1980, she became a member of the Bavarian State Opera, debuting as Helmwige in *Die Walküre*. In the early 1980s she toured worldwide as a member of this company, as well as the State Theatre of Darmstadt, and Deutsche Oper (German Opera) of Berlin. Her American debut, as Micaëla, was with **Plácido Domingo** at Chicago Lyric in 1984.

After Studer's arrival on the American scene, she made many recordings of Mozart, Verdi, Rossini and Donizetti. A last minute request to sing Elisabeth in *Tannhäuser* launched a highly successful 1985 Bayreuth Festival debut, opening the way to sing the heavy Wagner and Strauss roles and a comparison with German soprano **Lilli Lehmann** (1848–1929). 1987 marked Studer's debuts at La Scala in Verdi's *Requiem*, and Covent Garden reprising Elisabeth. Her performances in that role from 1985–89, and as Elsa, 1988–90, were televised Bayreuth productions. Also televised and recorded were her appearances as the Empress in Richard Strauss' *Die Frau ohne Schatten* (The Woman Without a Shadow), in the 1992 Salzburg Easter and Summer Festivals. She sang Micaëla in her 1988 Met debut and has returned there many times. April 1996 saw her performance of Strauss' *Four Last Songs* with the Dresden Staatskapelle under **Giuseppe Sinopoli**, and 1997 marked an Asian recital tour.

Besides her many CDs, Studer won France's Grand Prix du Disque, 1989, Edison Award, 1992, for her recording of *Salome*, and is the first recipient of the International Classical Music Award for "Best Female Singer of the Year" in 1992. 1994 *Musical America* honored her as "Vocalist of the Year." Her title role in Carlisle Floyd's *Susannah* for Virgin Records received the 1995 Grammy.

After a six year absence, Studer made her return to the Met, November 2000, for *Der Rosenkavalier*. Her 2001 season took her to Dresden, Vienna and Munich in *Die Frau ohne Schatten*, *Ariadne auf Naxos*, *Lohengrin* and *Der Rosenkavalier*. 2002 appearances were also in Vienna, Dresden and Munich with *The Flying Dutchman*, *Der Rosenkavalier*, *Die Walküre* and *Arabella*. 2003 found her at Hamburg Opera, Munich National Theater, Teatro

Colón, Buenos Aires, Knoxville Opera for a "From Bel Canto to Broadway" concert, Athens for a Maria Callas Commemorative Concert, plus performances in São Paulo (Brazil) and Antwerp (Belgium).

Happily married to her second husband, Ewald Schwarz, they had their first child in 1995. Cheryl also has a child from her former marriage.

SHARON SWEET, born Abel, in Gloversville, New York, August 16, 1951, started piano at five. An automobile accident at sixteen damaged the nerves of her spine, ending her concert pianist dreams. She entered Roberts Wesleyan College, hoping to become a professional accompanist. This course of study also required voice lessons, and her potential was discovered. After earning her BS, she went for her MM at Ithaca College. It was then she tried out for her first Metropolitan Opera audition in Toronto, placed first in the district, but not the regionals. However, a judge recommended her to the faculty at Curtis, and she moved to Philadelphia to study with Margaret Harshaw. When Harshaw went to Indiana University, Sweet auditioned for the renowned Marinka Gurewich in New York, who accepted her in 1977. She shaped the young singer's technique, perfecting her high notes, and transformed the not so sure mezzo into a sparkling soprano. (Sharon remained with Gurewich until her death at eighty-eight, December 23, 1990.)

Coinciding with these developments was her marriage to Philadelphia minister John Sweet and the arrival of three children: Joshua, 1986, and twins Sarah and Zachary, 1988. Thus, she commuted to New York twice a week. Highly musical, her husband supported her 100 percent, saying that he had fallen in love with her voice first and truly believed God wanted her to sing. So she was able to survive 1980–85, a time of 150 auditions without a single hiring. When Helen Kupfer, her coach for German diction, invited Sharon to sing at a small party in her home, one of the guests sent a supportive letter with a check to cover an audition tour of Germany. In Munich, Sweet was hired as a last-minute replacement in a concert version of *Aida*. On her return home, she got a call from a German agent who had seen the performance. Ilse Zellermayer coaxed her back to audition for Wolfgang Sawallisch in Munich, Rolf Liebermann in Hamburg, and at Dortmund and Düsseldorf Operas. Dortmund offered a contract for three performances as Elisabeth in *Tannhäuser* the following spring, launching her European stage debut.

Her good review in the important German magazine, *Opernwelt* (Opera World), prompted the touring Berlin State Opera to hire her as Elisabeth for their *Tannhäuser* opener in Zurich, and give her a contract for 1986–87 to replace Cheryl Studer, who had decided to freelance. John determined that after seven years it was his wife's turn to have a career and gave notice to his church. That summer they sold everything they owned and arrived in Germany, August 4, with three children and twenty pieces of luggage and no home. In the ensuing years, Sharon's star rose rapidly, while her husband worked on his PhD in philosophy and theology, and the children went to a bilingual German school.

Politically, Sweet lucked out with state-supported theaters just before the reunification of Germany would dry up those funds. The rest of her success is history. She gained recognition for her Leonora (*Il trovatore*) and Elisabeth (*Tannhäuser*). Her Paris Opera debut in 1987 was Elisabetta di Valois in *Don Carlo*. Her Met debut in 1990, as Leonora, established her mastery of Verdi and Wagner. In 1993–94, she performed *Aida*, *Trovatore*, *Otello* and *Falstaff* all over the world, and sang the Met premiere of Verdi's *Stiffelio*. Her first Norma was at the Théâtre Royale de la Monnaie, Brussels, and her first Italian appearance was Aida at the Arena di Verona. These became signature roles. She has been Norma in Rome, Barcelona, Lisbon and Bilbao. Aida introduced her to American audiences in San Francisco in 1989. 1999–2000 took her to Paris for Norma, Aida in Munich and Turandot in Barcelona.

She has sung with such celebrated maestri as Claudio Abbado, Carlo Maria Giulini, Sir Colin Davis and Zubin Mehta, and was part of the James Levine Twenty-fifth Anniversary celebration at the Met, April 1996. Her significant discography includes complete recordings of *Don Giovanni* under Sir Neville Marriner (Philips); *Falstaff* and *Lohengrin* under Sir Colin Davis (BMG); *Der Freischutz* with Janowski (Erato); the Verdi *Requiem* under Giulini and Schoenberg's *Gurrelieder* with Abbado (DGG); *Turandot* was with Gaylord Pretre, and *Il Trovatore* with the London

Symphony (Chandos); Strauss' *Four Last Songs* with Frübeck de Burgos (Collins Classics); and Mahler's Symphony No. 8 with Maazel for Sony and Sir Colin Davis for BMG.

In 1999, she joined the faculty of Westminster Choir College of Rider University in Princeton, New Jersey, as assistant professor of voice. In 2000 she became full-time. The same year brought a Chandos release of *Il Trovatore*—proof of her proclamation that she is *not* retiring from singing!

After a childhood influenced by two operatic parents, **RUTH ANN SWENSON**, born 1958, in Bronxville, just outside New York, naturally made singing her career. Training at the Hartt College of Music, Connecticut, and Philadelphia's Academy of Vocal Arts, at twenty-one she made it to the semi-finals of the Met Opera Auditions, but was too young for the finals. Instead, she joined the Merola Program at SFO, making her debut as Despina in the 1983 production of *Così fan tutte*. Since her 1991 Met debut as Zerlina in *Don Giovanni*, she has been heard there in many subsequent seasons. She has also appeared in major opera houses in the U.S. and Europe, with a Covent Garden debut in 1996 as Handel's *Semele*. In October 2000, she sang in the SFO production of *The Ballad of Baby Doe*, and *Semele* in November. Her other 2000–01 season appearances included *Traviata* and *Manon* at the Met, Norina in *Don Pasquale* in Los Angeles, and Donizetti's *Maria Stuarda* with OONY. In June 2001, she was Gilda in *Rigoletto* for the Met's Japan tour. 2001–02, she returned to the Met for *The Barber of Seville*, *Rigoletto* and *L'Enfant et les Sortilèges*, and Gilda and Rosina in 2003–04. During 2005–06, she was Mimi in *La bohéme*, Carmen, *L'eisir d'amore*, and *Marriage of Figaro*.

Swenson has recorded *Roméo et Juliette*, *La bohème*, a recital disc with **Placido Domingo** and **Thomas Hampson**, and four solo albums, *Con Amore*, *I Carry Your Heart*, *Positively Golden* and *Endless Pleasure*. She resides in San Francisco with her husband, vocal instructor David Burnakus.

Dawn Upshaw

DAWN UPSHAW, born July 17, 1960, Nashville, Tennessee, grew up in a suburb of Chicago in a family where her schoolteacher mother played piano and her minister father played guitar. At five, she began singing folk songs with them and her older sister in the Upshaw Family Singers. After graduating in 1982 with a BA from Illinois Wesleyan University, she studied with David Nott, who was to become her future father-in-law. She went to the Manhattan School of Music, then won entrance to the Met's Young Artist Development Program and Young Concert Artists. Beginning with small roles, artistic director **James Levine** was enthusiastic about her as a fresh new Mozartian. In 1988, she made a storybook Met debut as the last-minute replacement for **Kathleen Battle** in *L'elisir d'amore*, and since then enjoys a sparkling operatic career. Instead of following the well-beaten path of soubrette roles, however, she has established herself in the recording arena with Samuel Barber's *Knoxville: Summer of 1915*, plus compositions by Menotti and Harbison, whose *Mirabai* Songs were part of a Nonsuch disc released in 1989, and *The Girl with Orange Lips*, a collection of unusual contemporary pieces. Both discs won Grammys. The purity of her voice carries convincingly in both popular and classical music. Upshaw's fantastic third recording, as soloist in Polish composer Henryk Gorecki's Symphony No. 3 (The Symphony of Sorrowful Songs), became an unexpected classical crossover hit on the British pop charts in 1993. These were followed in 1994 with *I Wish It Were So*, unfamiliar theater songs of Kurt Weill. In her recordings of Rodgers and Hammerstein, Marc Blitzstein, Leonard Bernstein, Stephen Sondheim and Vernon Duke, Upshaw has turned their music into genuine American art songs. She has recorded over fifty albums and won three Grammys. In 1994, she was Susanna to the Figaro of Welsh baritone **Bryn Terfel** in his highly publicized Met debut. After Peter Sellars' Salzburg production of *Saint François d'Assise*, and her Theodora in a staging of Handel's oratorio with **Lorraine Hunt Lieberson** in 1996, plus recitals of Bach cantatas, she went to the modern end of the repertory with the 1997 Salzburg Festival production of *Pelléas et Mélisande*, and the Met's *Rake's Progress*. She was among the stars at the James Levine 1996 Gala.

The choice of new music writers, Philip Glass wrote the soprano part of his Symphony # 5 (Choral) for her, and John Harbison chose her as Daisy in the Met world premiere of his *The Great Gatsby*, December 1999. *Musical America* named her "2000 Vocalist of the Year," after which she was in the Met's 2000–01 season in *Pelléas et*

Mélisande and *Così fan Tutte*, and in 2001–02 a return of *The Great Gatsby, Hänsel und Gretel* and *Idomeneo*. At Tanglewood's Summer Festival in 2003, she was Margarita Xirgu in Osvaldo Golijov's new opera *Ainadamar*, a far cry from the soubrette stardom predicted when she started at the Met twenty years ago. April 2004 marked a San Diego concert with the Australian Chamber Orchestra.

Dawn lives in New York with husband Michael Nott, a musicologist, and their two children, daughter Sadie born in 1990 and son Gabriel, 1994.

CAROL VANESS, born July 27, 1952, in San Diego, California, took piano lessons through her college years, concentrating on voice at Cal State Northridge, where she earned a master's in 1976, the year she won the San Francisco Opera Auditions. She made her debut with the NYCO as Vitellia (*La clemenza di Tito*) in 1979, and stayed on their roster until 1983. Her Glyndebourne Festival engagements as Donna Anna became a favorite with European audiences. Her Met debut was in 1984 as Armida in Handel's *Rinaldo*. Since then, she continues her successful career with appearances throughout the world in such roles as Elektra, Fiordiligi, Rosina, Violetta and Mimi. In 1997, she opened the SFO season as Tosca. Her recordings, on prominent labels, include *Don Giovanni, Così fan tutte*, Masses by Haydn, Rossini's *Stabat Mater* and Beethoven's 9th Symphony.

She sang Tosca, January 2001, at the Met, then for Seattle Opera. While preparing for the June 2001 San Francisco production of *Simon Boccanegra*, Vaness was also conducting master classes at SFO's Merola Opera Program. She returned to the Met in October 2001 for *Idomeneo*, and in March 2004 as Tosca. She came "home" to San Diego for *Idomeneo* in 2001 and Samuel Barber's *Vanessa*, April 2005. In October, she was appointed to the voice faculty at Indiana University. The part-time position will not cut back on singing, with the Marschallin scheduled at Seattle Opera, and Maddalena in *Andrea Chénier* in Berlin.

A native of Santiago, Chile, born in 1962, **VERONICA VILLARROEL** never aspired to a music career. Her father's severe heart attack in 1984 forced her to join the chorus of the local Zarzuela company to support her family. After seeing an advertisement for auditions for the Teatro Municipal, she took a chance and was accepted without knowing a single aria. In her second year, she was chosen to perform Musetta in *La bohème*, which put her on stage with **Renata Scotto** as Mimi. Impressed with Veronica's talent, Scotto arranged for a scholarship to Juilliard. After a stunning 1990 debut at the Liceo in Barcelona, performing Fiordiligi (*Così fan tutte*), Villarroel has since sung at the Met, 1991, 1996, and 2004 in *Madama Butterfly*, as well as La Scala and other major houses in the U.S., Europe and South America. She also sings many concerts, and has recorded with **Plácido Domingo** as Cecilia in Gomes' *Il Guarany* and Solea in the zarzuela *El Gato Montes*.

2003 marked the DVD release of Verdi's little-known *Jerusalem* starring Villarroel.

Deborah Voigt

DEBORAH VOIGT was born August 4, 1960, in Wheeling, outside Chicago. She began piano at nine, but after four years her heart had gone into singing. As a child, she said, "My image of an opera singer was forged by television viewings of two films, *Going My Way* and *Chocolate Soldier*, both with **Risë Stevens**. (Voigt plays well enough to accompany herself for dressing-room warm-ups.) After junior high, her family moved to Los Angeles. She attended Chapman College as a choral-conducting major, then participated in SFO's Merola Program, with fellow apprentice **Dolora Zajick**. She was a winner in the Met Opera Auditions, Pavarotti International Competition (Philadelphia, 1989), Verdi Competition (Busseto, Italy, 1990), Tchaikovsky International Competition (Moscow, Gold Medal), and named the Opera Debut of the Year (1991) by the *New York Times*. She debuted at the Met in 1991 as Amelia in *Un ballo en maschera*, and in 1992 was awarded the Richard Tucker Award. She also sang at the Vienna State Opera in Wagner's *Der fliegende Hollander* and Strauss' *Ariadne auf Naxos*. Her Covent Garden debut in 1995 reprised Amelia. The same year, she made a solo recital tour across America, which included her debut in Lincoln Center's Alice Tully Hall. In 1996, she recorded one of her signature roles, Chrysothemis (*Elektra*), for Deutsche Grammophon under **Giuseppe Sinopoli**. The same season she sang in three operas at the Met, and in the televised gala celebration of James Levine's Twenty-fifth Anniversary. She has been lauded for her Straussian voice and the range of her repertoire—from Verdi to Wagner. Her recitals take her around the globe. During the 1998–99 season, she was in productions of three of her most famous roles, the Kaiserin in *Die Frau ohne Schatten* in Berlin, *Ariadne auf Naxos* with Lyric Opera of Chicago, and Elsa in *Lohengrin* at the Met. The 1999–2000 season at the Met included *Aida* and *Die Walküre*, a return to Opéra Bastille for *The Flying Dutchman*, *Die Frau ohne Schatten* in Vienna and *Die Walküre* in San Francisco. She opened the 2000–01 season at Los Angeles Opera with *Aida*, under the baton of Plácido Domingo. Her first Tosca was sung at Florida Grand Opera, March 2001, under the direction of **Renata Scotto**, followed by Vienna where she was Aida, and both Venus and Elisabeth in *Tannhäuser*. During the 2003–04 season, she was in the Met's Ring cycle and *Die Frau ohne Schatten*, and the most anticipated performance of the year, Isolde at Vienna State Opera, where curtain calls went on for twenty minutes.

Considered one of the leading dramatic sopranos singing in the first decade of the 21st century, her big voice came in a big body. In Spring 2004, Covent Garden paid her contract, but let her go because the director deemed her too large for "the Little Black Dress" of his staging concept. After long consideration, and having struggled with her weight since adolescence, on June 7, 2004, she underwent gastric bypass surgery. Considered extremely dangerous, since weight loss has been known to cause a singer to lose vocal luster as well—Maria Callas being the notable example—Voigt took the risk. Since her surgery, she says she has made adjustments to her singing, especially concentrating on her technique. Her Elisabeth at the Met, December 2004, received great acclaim.

A March 2005 *New York Times* article showed her 100 pounds lighter. In a CBS' *60 Minutes* interview, aired January 29, 2006, she said she had gone from a size-30 dress to size-14. Also interviewed was James Conlon, conductor of the Cincinnati Symphony with Voigt and Ben Hepner in a concert version of the second act of *Tristan und Isolde*, who said he thinks Deborah is in better voice now. Her new body is benefitting her career. "I'm doing many more Toscas than I ever thought I would," she said. Also, her dream of singing Salome, a role she has done only in concert—joking that on stage she would need seventy-seven veils—came true October 2006 at Chicago Lyric Opera. (She was able to make do with seven.)

Signed with Angel/EMI Records, her debut album was a Wagner-Strauss program recorded in Munich, September 2003. It was released April 2004, the same month as her Carnegie Hall recital debut, partnered with James Levine. 2005 brought *All My Heart*, a CD tribute to American composers Charles Ives, **Amy Beach**, Leonard Bernstein, and Charles Tomlinson Griffes. April 2005 brought her back to the Met as Amelia in *Un Ballo en Maschera*, and October took her to Barcelona for Ponchielli's only opera in the repertoire, *La Gioconda*, with **Ewa**

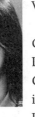

Podleś. Beginning 2006 at the Met was *La Forza del Destino* and *Tosca*. And for a happy ending, Voigt has been rehired by the Covent Garden for Ariadne in 2007–2008.

Considered the pre-eminent interpreter of *Madama Butterfly*, **YOKO WATANABE** sang Cio-Cio-San in her 1986 Met debut and 1995 San Francisco debut, as well as in San Diego, Chicago Lyric Opera, Los Angeles, Buenos Aires, London's Covent Garden, Berlin, Munich, Monte Carlo, Tokyo and Vienna. Born July 12, 1953, in Fukuoka, Japan, piano and dance studies were initial passions, but judged too tall for a dancer she studied voice and piano at Tokyo National University of Fine Arts and Music (1976). She entered the Scuola di Perfezionamento at La Scala, Milan, then began her professional career in Treviso as Nedda in *Pagliacci*. She sang lyric-soprano repertoire in Europe for several seasons, then, in 1982, debuted as Cio-Cio-San in Strasbourg, which became her signature role. In 1985, she sang Liù in *Turandot* for La Scala, a role she also sang worldwide. Her repertoire also included *Manon Lescaut*, *Adriana Lecouvreur*, *Faust* and *Tosca*. In 1998 she was Cio-Cio-San in San Diego.

Yoko Watanabe

Watanabe sadly retired from the stage in 2000 upon being diagnosed with cancer. She died in Milan, July 15, 2004, survived by her husband, Italian tenor Renato Grimaldi.

Recipient of a 2001 ARIA Award and a 2001 Richard Tucker Career Grant, soprano **JENNIFER WELCH-BABIDGE**, born in 1972 in Aulander, North Carolina, is a graduate of the North Carolina School of the Arts (MM vocal performance). Winner of the Metropolitan Opera's National Council Auditions in the spring of 1997, she was in their Lindemann Young Artist Development Program in the 1997–98 season. In the summer of 1998, she joined Wolf Trap Opera as Blondchen in Mozart's *Die Entführung aus dem Serail* and Despina in *Così fan tutte*, returning the next summer as Anne Trulove in *The Rake's Progress* and Papagena in *Die Zauberflöte*. She made her Met debut during 1998–99 in *Le nozze di Figaro*.

She was in the Met revivals (1999–2000) of *Le nozze di Figaro* and *Moses und Aron*, and sang Gilda in *Rigoletto* for the Met in the Parks concerts. She also performed Berg's *Lulu Suite* with the Met Orchestra at Carnegie Hall with James Levine, and made her Boston debut in Handel's *Messiah* with Boston Baroque. She was in *Les pêcheurs de perles* with the Washington Concert Opera, made her European debut at the Schleswig-Holstein Festival in concerts of arias, and her Salzburg Festival debut in Mozart's *Waisenhausmesse*.

During the 2000–01 season she appeared at the Met as Marzelline in *Fidelio*, Valencienne in *The Merry Widow*, and Kristina in *The Makropulos Case*. She also made her debut with the Opera Company of Philadelphia as Sophie in *Werther*.

For the 2001–02 season, she returned to the Met as the Guardian of the Threshold in *Die Frau ohne Schatten* and the Celestial Voice in *Don Carlo*. She performed Mahler's *Symphony No. 2* with the Santa Barbara Symphony and the Mozart *Mass in C minor* with the Winston-Salem Symphony. During the summer, she performed the title role in *Lucia di Lammermoor* with the Opera Theatre of Saint Louis, followed by performances with the San Francisco Symphony as Cunegonde in *Candide*, and the Met Opera Orchestra tour with James Levine, in Berg's *Lulu Suite*, and a Flower Maiden in *Parsifal* at the Salzburg Festival.

In 2002–03, she made her SFO debut as Blondchen, sang Zerbinetta (*Ariadne auf Naxos*) with the Opera Company of Philadelphia, returned to Opera Theatre of St. Louis as Constanze (*The Abduction*) and was Adele in *Die Fledermaus* with Seiji Ozawa at the Saito Kinen Summer Festival (Japan).

In 2004, she was Gilda in *Rigoletto* with Opera Colorado, Violetta at Opera Pacific, and at the Met, Olympia in *Contes d'Hoffman*, Frasquita in *Carmen*, and Freia in *Das Rheingold*.

In 2005–06, she was Leila in *The Pearl Fishers* at Opera Carolina, Norina in *Don Pasquale* at Houston, and Marzelline in *Fidelio* for the Met.

Married to baritone Darrell Babidge since July 2000, they have two sons, John Chandler and Joseph. The second made operatic history with his debut *in utero*, when his mother made her NYCO debut, September 2003, as Lucia and director James Robinson decided to incorporate her then six month pregnancy into the scenario *visually*—making it obvious that the lovers had been intimate—without changing a word of the libretto.

Dolora Zajick

JANET WILLIAMS, KAREN WILLIAMS, see Black Heritage.

Verdi dramatic-mezzo **DOLORA ZAJICK**, although born into a music-loving family in Salem, Oregon, 1952, originally aspired to a career in medicine as a student at the University of Nevada in Reno, where she had lived since age nine. Voice lessons from Ted Puffer, artistic director of the Nevada Opera, proved her fine alto range and led instead to earning her BM (1976) and MM (1978) in music, while singing small roles with Nevada Opera, after which she trained at the Manhattan School of Music with Helen Vanni (1979–82). Supporting herself by singing in the First Presbyterian Church Choir, the congregation collected the funds necessary for her to compete in the Seventh International Tchaikovsky Competition in Moscow (1982). There, she took honors with a bronze medal—the only non-Soviet winner—and the first American in twelve years to place in that event. On her return, she was accepted into the prestigious Merola Program of SFO, and became an Adler[192] fellow. (Her fellow apprentice was **Deborah Voigt**.) In 1986, Zajick won the Richard Tucker Music Foundation Award in New York, and opened the SFO summer season with a brilliant Azucena. Since then she had few rivals in Verdi's great mezzo roles of Eboli and Amneris, singing these in Germany, Paris, Geneva, Italy and

192. Kurt Herbert Adler (1905–1988) first associated with SFO in 1943, succeeded Merola in 1953, doubled their season by 1972 and expanded the repertoire and importance of the company.

Spain. She has long been a favorite at the Met, even though they choose her primarily for Azucena and Amneris. Despite her formidable voice, she also sings the *bel canto* role of Adalgisa in *Norma*, a role she debuted in 1995 in Barcelona.

Zajick performs worldwide, and has shared the stage with such luminaries as **Plácido Domingo** (*Aida*) and **Luciano Pavarotti** (*Il trovatore*). Her maestros include Zubin Mehta, James Levine and Riccardo Muti. During the 1994–95 season, she sang her first *Herodiade* and reprised Azucena with SFO, and Amneris for Chicago's Lyric Opera. During the 1999–2000 season at the Met, she sang in *Aida, Il trovatore*, and *Cavalleria rusticana*, returning in 2001 for *Norma*, and as Jezibaba in *Rusalka*, April 2004. During 2005–06, she was Aida, and in the world premiere of Tobias Picker's *An American Tragedy*, with an all-star cast that included Jennifer Larmore, Susan Graham and Patricia Racette. November 2005, she received the *Opera News* Award for Distinguished Achievement.

ELENA ZAREMBA was born July 10, 1957 in Moscow, to parents who were both opera singers (soprano and bass). At her birth, the doctor prophesied, "Here is another singer!" After her parents' divorce, her mother's career travelling dictated that the child live with her grandmother, a teacher. Although they were poor and could not afford records, the TV and radio broadcast much classical music in Communist Russia. Elena started out as a rock singer—a rebellion against years of having to sing Communist songs extolling Lenin and the regime—but by eighteen, she had discovered classical music and decided that this was where her future lay. However, after four years of study at Gnessin Music School in Moscow, she found her vocal range had narrowed and her technique was deteriorating, so she found a private teacher who repaired the damage. In 1984, a friend urged her to audition for the great Bolshoi Theater, a presumptuous idea since she was still just a student. Although sick on the day of the audition, she went through with it and, to her own amazement, was accepted. Her debut at the Theater was as Laura in Dargomyzhsky's *The Stone Guest*.

Zaremba made her first appearance in the West in 1989 as part of a Bolshoi tour, singing Vanja in Glinka's *A Life for the Tsar* at La Scala. Since her 1991 San Francisco Opera debut in *War and Peace*, she has appeared with that company as Ratmir (*Ruslan and Lyudmila*, 1995), Konchakovna (*Prince Igor*, 1996), Maddalena (*Rigoletto*, 1997), Carmen (1998)—a role she has performed at major houses worldwide—Erda, Fricka and the First Norn in the 1999 *Ring* Festival, and Ulrica (*Un ballo in maschera*). Acclaim for these performances has led to engagements with Vienna State Opera, Paris Bastille, La Scala, plus Salzburg, Bregenz and Edinburgh Festivals, and concerts with the Berlin Philharmonic, London Symphony and Cleveland Orchestra, among others. Her Met debut was as Azucena (*Il trovatore*) with a return in 2000–01 for *A Masked Ball*. Other career highlights include *Pique Dame, War and Peace* and *Rigoletto* at the Bastille; *Un ballo in maschera* at Bregenz; and concerts in Rome, Krakow and Tokyo. *Carmen* reprises were in Lisbon, Munich, Berlin and Hamburg; *War and Peace* in Paris; *The Queen of Spades* in Munich; as well as concerts and recordings such as Beethoven's *Missa Solemnis* in Bonn, *Masked Ball, Prince Igor, A Life for the Tsar, Lady Macbeth of Mtsensk, Boris Godunov, Das Rheingold*, Rimsky-Korsakov's *Christmas Eve*, Mussorgsky's cantata *Joshua*, and a Shostakovich song cycle.

Taking realism too far, at the 1995 Munich performance of *Carmen*, with tenor Neil Shicoff, the props included a real knife for the last act when Don Jose stabs Carmen to death. The stars became so caught up in the action that Shicoff wielded the knife too realistically. Elena sensed his intensity and tried to catch his hand, causing her arm to be sliced open. Not realizing what had happened, she stood up for the curtain call and felt something was pouring down her arm. Fortunately, her husband, Sergei, is a physician. Sitting in the audience, he saw both stars looking very pale for the curtain call. He went backstage, took one look at his wife's wound and got her to a hospital where they sewed her up and put the arm in a splint. An operatic career can be dangerous!

Zaremba returned to the Met in 2004 for Tchaikovsky's *Queen of Spades* on Valentine's Day, and the *Ring* cycle as Erda (*Das Rheingold*) in March and *Siegfried* in April.

Russian soprano **ELENA ZELENSKAYA**, a leading soprano at the Bolshoi Theatre Opera, won first prize in the Rimsky-Korsakov International Voice Competition, and second in the Glinka National Competition. Her full calendar of tours in Russia and abroad includes Gorislava in Glinka's *Ruslan and Lyudmila* in Italy and at Lincoln

Center. Munich and Paris saw her as Queen Elizabeth in Donizetti's *Maria Stuarda*. She was featured in a Gala Concert at Carnegie Hall (1994), and as a soloist with the Vienna Chamber Opera, performing Donna Elvira (*Don Giovanni*), and the Countess (*Marriage of Figaro*) at the Mozart Festival in Schönbrunn Palace.

One of Zelenskaya's major roles is Verdi's Lady Macbeth, with which she made a successful debut at the Lucerne State Theater, Minnesota Opera and Tel Aviv Opera. At the Wexford Festival, she sang Stefana (*Siberia*) by Giordano. She is the first Russian Wally (*La Wally* by Catalani). Other definitive roles are Leonora (*Forza del destino*) and Aida, which she sang at the International Opera Festival in Savonlinna (Finland), Royal Danish Opera, Copenhagen, and the Cæsarea Festival, held in this ancient Israeli town built at the time of Cæsar. Her Aida was also heard at Deutsche Oper Berlin and Deutsche Oper am Rhein. Tosca graced the Royal Opera in La Monnaie (Brussels). Being soprano soloist in Verdi's *Requiem* took her to the Lubliana (Slovenia) International Festival, while Britten's *War Requiem* was heard with the Los Angeles Philharmonic. Her successful Mimi (*La bohème*) was at Barcelona Grand Opera, and Amelia (*Ballo in maschera*) at Mannheim, and the Met where she sang with **Plácido Domingo**. She also participated in the new production of *Andrea Chenier* with the New Israeli Opera, and in Prokofiev's *Maddalena* at the Concertgebouw (Amsterdam). She sang Gorislava in *Ruslan and Lyudmila* with the Moscow New Opera at Carnegie Hall during that company's American tour. After singing Lady Macbeth in Tel Aviv in December, she was Aida for San Diego Opera, May 2001, followed by their Verdi *Requiem*. She then made her Met debut in *A Masked Ball*, and went back to Israel as Leonora at Caesarea. A reprise of *La forza del destino* was at the Met, March 2006—a very busy career.

Soprano **AI-LAN ZHU**, born in Nanking, China, 1957, began her studies at the Beijing Conservatory and has made several recordings with the Central People's Broadcasting Station. She came to the U.S., appeared with Texas Opera, making her debut as Mimi on a 1987 tour, and made her Met debut as the Rheinmaiden Woglinde in *Das Rheingold*. 1989 saw her as Zerlina in Peter Sellars' production of *Don Giovanni*, filmed in Vienna and staged in Paris. She has performed throughout the U.S. in major roles in *La traviata*, *Rigoletto*, *Carmen*, *Turandot* and *Madama Butterfly*. She has also appeared in Scotland and returned to China for concert performances. She was Liù in San Diego in 1997 and 2004.

American mezzo **DELORES ZIEGLER**, born December 4, 1951, in Atlanta, Georgia, studied at the University of Tennessee. Beginning with a concert career, she made her stage debut as Flora in *La traviata* at Knoxville, 1978. From 1978–1979, she was a member of the Santa Fe Opera apprenticeship program. In 1978, she appeared as Verdi's Maddalena in St. Louis. By 1981, she was in Europe singing Emilia (*Otello*), Dorabella (*Così fan tutte*), and Octavian at Bonn Opera. She reprised the latter role, plus Cherubino and Orlofsky, as a member of the Cologne Opera from 1982. In 1984, she appeared as Dorabella at her Glyndebourne debut, and as Bellini's Romeo at her La Scala debut where she spent 1984–87, and then had the distinct honor of being the first singer in the Romeo role at Moscow's Bolshoi Opera. She was chosen by **Beverly Sills** as the recipient of the 1983 Debut Artist Award from NYCO.

Appearances have been at Lyric Opera of Chicago, San Francisco, San Diego, Toronto, Vienna, Munich, Hamburg, Oslo, plus Glyndebourne, Aix-en-Provence, Salzburg, Athens and Florence May Festivals, as well as Maggio Musicale, Florence.

Her Met performances, 1989–91, included the trouser roles of Siébel and Octavian. Other leading roles have been in *Ariadne auf Naxos*, *Idomeneo*, *Le nozze di Figaro*, *Der Rosenkavalier*, *I Capuleti e i Montecchi*, *Orfeo*, *Faust*, *La clemenza di Tito*, *La damnation de Faust* and *Falstaff*.

Besides many excellent choral and operatic recordings under the distinguished batons of Riccardo Muti, Nikolaus Harnoncourt, Bernard Haitink, James Levine, Robert Shaw, James Conlon, Claudio Schimone *et al*, Ziegler, as Dorabella, was featured in the last film of director Jean-Pierre Ponnelle, which was on European television. With a repertoire from *bel canto* to *verismo*, Ziegler is the most recorded Dorabella in operatic history. Other disks include Sara (*Roberto Devereux*), Giovanna Seymour (*Anna Bolena*), and Ned Rorem's song cycle *Evidence of things not seen*.

An appropriate concluding quote to the dazzling array of vocal talent presented in these pages comes from **Cecilia Bartoli**:

"The voice is a gift of God . . . it's the personality behind the voice which makes the artist."

New Voices in the Upper Stratosphere

As this book finally goes into print after eleven years of love's labors giving birth, yet another bevy of new names make their appearance at New York's Metropolitan Opera House, signaling a well-earned high point in the careers of the following:

German soprano **DIANA DAMRAU**, born 1972, made her European opera debut in 2002, where she has sung the Queen of the Night, Europa in Salieri's *Europa Riconosciuta* at the reopening of La Scala, December 2004, and Gilda. Her Met debut as Zerbinetta in *Ariadne auf Naxos* was September 2005, a role she sang the following year at Lyric Opera of Chicago. For the Met's 2006–07 season she was in *The Barber of Seville*, and Aithra in March 2007—part of the Met's first staging since 1928, of Strauss' *Die Ägyptische Helena* (The Egyptian Helen.)

MARY DUNLEAVY, born in Connecticut and raised in New Jersey, received her undergraduate degree from Northwestern and MM from the University of Texas, Austin, where she gives master classes.

Her 2004–05 season featured Gilda at Chile's Teatro Municipal de Santiago; *La traviata*, San Francisco Opera; Giunia in Mozart's *Lucio Silla* at De Nederlandse Opera, Amsterdam; her Naples debut as Adina (*L'elisir d'amore*); Léïla (*The Pearl Fishers*) NYCO) and Amina (*La Sonnambula*) Bilbao, Spain. A concert performance of *La traviata* at Amsterdam's Concertgebouw, and a duo-concert with mezzo **Jennifer Larmore** at Québec's Festival International de Lanaudière are also stars in her crown.

The 2005–06 season marked her Dallas Opera debut singing all four heroines in Offenbach's *Tales of Hoffmann*. The audiences rewarded those performances by voting Mary the winner of DOC's Maria Callas Debut Artist of the Year Award, which recognizes the singer "who has made the biggest impact in his (or her) debut." Presented since 1992, it is named for Callas who gave a concert to inaugurate the company in 1957. Previous winners include tenor Jerry Hadley, **Cecilia Bartoli** and **Denyce Graves**.

Dunleavy joined the St. Louis Symphony for *Messiah*, conducted by David Robertson in his inaugural season as music director. With the MET, her artistic home since 1993, she sang Pamina (*Magic Flute*) and her most celebrated role, Violetta (*La traviata*). At the Opera Company of Philadelphia, she added the Countess (*Marriage of Figaro*) to her gallery of Mozart heroines. Other triumphs have been at the Cincinnati May Festival and Hollywood Bowl with Leonard Slatkin and the Los Angeles Philharmonic.

CRISTINA GALLARDO-DOMÂS was born in Santiago, Chile, where she studied music at the Escuela Moderna de Musica, with postgraduate work at Juilliard. Her 1990 debut in Santiago was Cio-Cio-San in *Madama Butterfly*. In 1993 she made European debuts at the Spoletto Festival as *Suor Angelica*, and *La Rondine* at La Scala. Since then she has sung at Vienna, Paris, Covent Garden, Munich, Berlin, Amsterdam, Buenos Aires, Florence, Tokyo, Zurich, and the Ravinia and Salzburg Festivals in leading roles of Contes d'Hoffman, Faust, Manon, Turandot, Traviata, Bohème, Pagliacci, Simon Boccanegra, Mefistofele and Otello.

In 2003 and 2005 she sang *Butterfly* at Covent Garden, and won the Laurence Olivier Award for Outstanding Achievement in Opera. Her 2006–07 season included *Madama Butterfly* for the September opening night at the Met, and later in the season *La bohème*; *Don Giovanni* (Festival de Musica de Canarias), *The Consul* (Turin), *Don Carlo* (Geneva), *Il Trovatore* (Zurich) and *Manon Lescaut* (Los Angeles).

Her recordings include an aria recital *Bel Sogno* (Teldec); *Aida* (Teldec); *Suor Angelica* (EMI); *Verdi Sacred Pieces* and *La bohème* (TDK).

She is recognized as one of the today's top lyric sopranos.

LISA MILNE, born in Aberdeen, studied at the Royal Scottish Academy of Music and Drama, winning the 1993 Maggie Teyte Prize and the 1996 John Christie Award. Her professional debut came as Gianetta in Scottish National Opera's *L'elisir d'amore*, and from 1994–97 took a three-season principal contract with the company. In 1998, she made her Wigmore Hall and Edinburgh Festival debuts. She has sung with the Gabrieli Consort, National Youth Orchestra of Scotland, Scottish Chamber Orchestra, Royal Philharmonic, London Philharmonic and Royal Liverpool Philharmonic. Her recordings on Hyperion include Händel and Vivaldi cantatas with the King's Consort, a solo album of Marjory Kennedy-Fraser's *Songs of the Hebrides* and John Ireland songs. Other engagements include Ilia (*Idomeneo*) for Royal Danish Opera, Copenhagen; her first Sophie and Despina for Scottish Opera; *Rodelinda* at Glyndebourne; and her Met debut in *Orfeo ed Euridice* with **Heidi Grant Murphy**, 2006–07.

DOROTHEA RÖSCHMANN, born in Flensburg, Germany, 1967, at seven sang in the Flensburg Bach choir, beginning vocal studies at twelve. Her training includes the Hochschule für Musik, Hamburg, Akademie für Alte Musik, Bremen, Natalie Zimonick, Los Angeles, Thomas LoMonaco, New York, and since 1992, Vera Rosza, London. Initially identified as an interpreter of early music, she sang at the early music festivals in Innsbruck and Göttingen. From 1994, her contract at the Berlin Staatsoper, has broadened her repertoire.

Since 1986 her concert schedule has covered Europe, Canada and America, including Carnegie Hall. Between 1992–95, she has sung at the Händelfestpiele, Halle, Göttinger Händel Festival and Salzburg Festival, where she returns annually in a line-up of Mozart heroines, and with the Haifa Symphony, Israel. In 2003, she made her Royal Opera London debut as Pamina, and Anne Trulove (*The Rake's Progress*), in Munich. Her Met debut was '06–'07 in *Julius Cæsar*.

Soprano **EKATERINA SIURINA**, a native of Sverdlovsk, Russia, studied choral directing before vocal studies with Aleksandr Titel at the Russian Academy of Performing Arts. In 2000 she was a prize winner of the **Elena Obraztsova** Competition in Moscow and the Rimsky-Korsakov Competition in St. Petersburg. Her first stage experiences were as a member of the Moscow State Theater and the Novaja Opera. She sang Gilda with the Royal Opera, Covent Garden and the Savonlinna Festival, and Najade (*Ariadne auf Naxos*) with Berlin's Lindenoper. Her Vienna Staatoper debut was Olympia, and Bastille Opera as Servilia. Gilda was her 2006 Met debut role. February brought her La Scala debut as Susanna, and in April she was Adina at the Hamburg Staatsoper.

Bulgarian soprano **KRASSIMIRA STOYANOVA** began her career as a soloist with the Sofia National Opera in 1995. Since then she has been a regular at the Vienna Staatsoper and made her 2001 Met debut as Violetta, and has sung Anna Bolena to **Jennifer Larmore's** Jane Seymour, Liù in *Turandot*, with **Andrea Gruber** and Nedda in *Pagliacci*.

Born in Lithuania, **VIOLETA URMANA** was first a mezzo and well known for her Kundry in *Parsifal* and Eboli in *Don Carlo*. After a debut as Sieglinde in *Die Walküre* at the Bayreuth Festival, her real soprano debut, December 2002, was in *Iphigénie en Aulide* for the season opening of La Scala. Also in 2002, she received the Royal Philharmonic Society Award for singers in London. Further successful debuts were Maddalena (*Andrea Chénier*) Vienna, Lady Macbeth, Seville, Isolde, Rome, *La Gioconda*, and Leonora (*La Forza del Destino*) London. In 2005 she was Tosca in Florence and Los Angeles, Ariadne at the Met, La Wally at the Vienna Konzerthaus and Norma in Dresden.

Her 2006–07 season included Elisabetta (*Don Carlo*) Turin, Aida at La Scala, Amelia (*Masked Ball*) Florence, *La Forza*, Munich, Florence and Vienna, *Parsifal* in Munich, *La Gioconda* at the Met with **Olga Borodina**, *Cavalleria rusticana*, Madrid, *Andrea Chénier* and *Tosca* in Vienna, London and Chicago, *Don Carlo*, Naples, and *Macbeth*, Paris.

Both a concert and recital singer, her recordings include *La Gioconda*, excepts from *Tristan und Isolde* and *Götterdämmerung*, *Il Trovatore*, Verdi's *Oberto*, Beethoven's Ninth "Choral" Symphony, whose last movement features soloists and choir, Zemlinsky's *Maetterlinck-Lieder*, Stravinsky's *Le Rossignol* (The Nightingale), Mahler's Second Symphony and *Das Lied von der Erde* (The Song of the Earth). She is Kundry in Tony Palmer's film *The Search for the Holy Grail*.

The Legacy of Black Singers— A Courageous Heritage

Elizabeth Taylor Greenfield (*c.* 1820–76)
Sissieretta Jones (1869–1933)
Marian Anderson (1899–1993)
Dorothy Maynor (1910–96)
Roberta Alexander
Martina Arroyo
Kathleen Battle
Grace Bumbry
Michele Crider
Mattiwilda Dobbs
Denyce Graves
Reri Grist

Cynthia Haymon
Barbara Hendricks
Ruby Hinds
Marquita Lister
Leona Mitchell
Jessye Norman
Leontyne Price
Shirley Verrett
Camilla Williams
Janet Williams
Karen Williams

The post-Civil War era (1865–) was not a conducive time for the flowering of black talent, therefore it was a miracle that one woman, with only superior talent and courage to aid her, managed to make a career in classical singing *before* the great conflict—albeit, she was considered a curiosity.

ELIZABETH TAYLOR GREENFIELD was born a slave, in Natchez, Mississippi, in the 1820s, to an African father and a Seminole Indian mother, both of whom were the property of wealthy landowner, Elizabeth Greenfield. Self-taught, since no white voice teacher dared take her as a pupil, the soprano began performing in public in her twenties. By 1851, she had acquired a manager and toured the Northeast, singing excerpts from opera. Her concerts, which sometimes needed police protection in the halls, were barred from blacks. She was not beautiful. It was the raw power of her voice, spanning three and a half octaves—from low G in the bass to E above high C— and her flawless pitch that had critics comparing her with **Jenny Lind**, even claiming that she surpassed the "Swedish Nightingale" and calling her the *Black Swan*. Comments were consistent about her untrained voice, yet even when she could offer double the going rate, no teacher would accept her. Despite this, along with criticism of her dress and poise, she set an audience record at her New York debut at Metropolitan Hall, March 31, 1853, drawing a crowd of 4,000 whites. To placate the barred, angry blacks, she repeated the concert for them at the Broadway Tabernacle.

A tour in England rid her of the shackles of American prejudice. Not only was she well-received, she even acquired patrons among the aristocracy and the friendship of **Harriet Beecher Stowe**, author of *Uncle Tom's Cabin*. She also finally acquired formal tutelage. After her return to America in 1854, she gave concerts and set up a studio in Philadelphia. By the time she died in 1876, Greenfield left a legacy for black singers of both sexes, not only as a role model but, in the words of Rosalyn M. Story in her 1990 book about black sopranos, *And So I Sing*, had "etched an impression on the cultural consciousness of her era."

The next major black voice to rise to stardom was that of **SISSIERETTA JONES**, born January 5, 1869, who managed to get training at the New England Conservatory. After her New York debut at Steinway Hall, April 5, 1888, she toured with the Jubilee Singers, the Patrick Gilmore Band and other groups. Her solo recitals included appearances at the White House for four presidents—Benjamin Harrison, Grover Cleveland, William McKinley and Theodore Roosevelt—in London for the Prince of Wales, and tours in South America and the West Indies with the Tennessee Star Concert Company. In 1894, famed Bohemian composer Antonín Dvořák, then director of the National Conservatory in New York, having just written his New World Symphony partly inspired by black folk melodies, conducted a concert of black students from the conservatory, and invited Jones to be a soloist.

The reigning diva at the turn of the century was Italian-American prima donna **Adelina Patti**, and Jones became known as the "Black Patti." The Met even considered her for the African roles in *Aida* and *L'Africaine*, but bowed to racial attitudes. Thus, although restricted from performing in a complete opera, Jones was a *diva* in every other sense of the word. Attractive, of medium height and build, she was described as elegant and majestic, and captivated her audiences. Her voice spanned two and a half octaves, with a lower register the depth of a contralto. From 1896 to 1916, she toured with a vaudeville troupe known as the *Black Patti Troubadours*, singing opera excerpts and classical songs. The popularity of minstrel shows waned in the years before and during World War I as audiences and performers became more sophisticated. The group gave their final performance at New York's Gibson Theater in 1916. Jones returned to her home in Providence, Rhode Island, to care for her ailing mother. She never sang professionally again, and poverty forced her to sell what property she had accumulated. When funds ran out, she went on relief, dying penniless, of cancer, at the Rhode Island Hospital, June 24, 1933.

Throughout her career, Jones was never given credit for the gifted singer she was, but viewed as an imitation of a white ideal. While critics acknowledged her beauty, their highest praise was often condescending. Her contribution to the music of black women in America, however, is immeasurable, as she obliged whites to see her race as dignified, talented and capable.

MARIAN ANDERSON, dubbed as "the voice of the century," the granddaughter of former slaves, was born in Philadelphia, February 17, 1899, into a poor family. Her father sold ice and coal, her mother took in laundry. Her public singing began at the Union Baptist family church. Roland Hayes, a successful black tenor and graduate of Fisk and Harvard Universities, took an active interest in her voice, becoming an advisor and mentor. In her mid-teenage years, realizing her need for formal training, Marian approached a music school in Philadelphia to be informed, "We don't take colored." She began private studies with a local soprano, and later funds were raised so she could coach with tenor Giuseppe Boghetti—a student-teacher relationship that lasted for twenty years, until his death in 1941. In 1923, she won a vocal competition to sing with the Philadelphia Orchestra, and in 1925 a first prize to sing with the New York Philharmonic at the outdoor Lewisohn Stadium. Slowly, her career gathered momentum. In 1929, she gave a recital at Carnegie Hall, and the following year, beginning in London, embarked upon a path of continuous successes throughout Europe with concerts in Denmark, Norway, Sweden and Finland (1933–34). In 1935, she toured Poland, Russia, Latvia, Switzerland, Belgium, Austria, Italy and Spain. It was at the Salzburg summer music festival that her impressive concert evoked Toscanini's now legendary plaudit, "Yours is a voice one hears once in a hundred years!"

News of this triumph reached the U.S., causing the mogul of impresarios, **Sol Hurok**, to arrange for a proper homecoming with a Town Hall concert, December 30, 1935. The critics were now so enamored of the voice, as well as the persona, that Anderson's performances were sold out for the rest of her long career. By 1939, she was one of the highest-paid concert artists in the country, topped only by **Lily Pons**.

A Long Overdue Retraction

For almost seven decades, the Daughters of the American Revolution have been maligned for their refusal to let Anderson sing in their Constitution Hall, in Washington, DC, in 1939—an anti-black policy supposedly adopted in 1932. First Lady Eleanor Roosevelt, long a fan—she had invited Marian to sing at the White House—without checking the facts, wrote that the hall had been denied the singer because of her color, and resigned from the DAR. Records show, however, that Roland Hayes had sung there on January 31, 1931, and the black choir from the Hampton Institute of Virginia performed there March 31 of that year. There were other factors, including the prevalent bias of those years which was not confined to the DAR. Also, a black jazz group had performed in the hall, whose audience had wreaked major damage to the ancient building. By 1946, policies were changing and the Tuskegee Choir sang a benefit concert for the United Negro College Fund. Anderson herself performed there in 1953, 1954, 1955, 1956, 1958 and 1960. What really happened in 1939 was that the hall was already booked by the National Symphony.

Early in her career, Anderson had also been denied admittance to other venues. Hurok solved this particular problem by sending his press agent, along with NAACP president Walter White, to Harold Ickes, Secretary of the Interior. Ickes granted permission for a concert on Easter Sunday, April 9, 1939, on the steps on the Lincoln Memorial. Before an audience of 75,000, her performance became an *event*—making the soprano the reluctant forerunner of the equal rights movement. Even in her 1956 autobiography, *My Lord, What a Morning*, she shied away from the controversy, remaining mute on the subject. Not until 1949, in her column, "My Day," did Mrs. Roosevelt admit, "I do not think one can hold the DAR alone responsible."

Bing Pulled the Strings at the Met . . .

Despite her popularity, it took until 1954 for Anderson to sing in a complete production. The Metropolitan Opera board had long maintained an unstated policy not to hire blacks. In 1950, the evanescent **Rudolf Bing** (1902–97) became general manager, invoking a new philosophy. Overriding all objections, he hired Anderson to sing Ulrica, in Verdi's *Un ballo in maschera*, making her the first black to sing with the Met. Although Bing could have given the honor to someone younger, like **Mattiwilda Dobbs** who had already sung at La Scala, the gesture was a tribute to the older star's rank and achievement as an artist of international fame. Anderson continued to sing at the Met until 1956, when her voice, showing the wear of travel and brutal scheduling, was no longer suited to opera. Bing's gesture was significant in symbolizing the progress of black artists. Her concert career lasted until 1965 when, after thirty years before the public, she announced her retirement at a farewell concert in Carnegie Hall, April 18. In June of that year, she sang one last time at Robin Hood Dell, the summer venue of the Philadelphia Orchestra, where 35,000 fans packed in to hear her under the direction of her nephew **James DePreist** (*b* 1936), then assistant conductor of the New York Philharmonic. She retired to her Connecticut farm with her husband of twenty-three years, architect Orpheus Fisher.

Among her many honors, Anderson was chosen by President Eisenhower to be a delegate to the General Assembly of the United Nations, 1958, sang at the inaugural ball for President Kennedy, 1961, and was given the Presidential Medal of Freedom by President Johnson, 1963. In 1978, Congress struck a gold medal in her honor, and in 1986 she was awarded the National Medal of Arts. She died in Portland, Oregon, April 8, 1993.

In 1997, her 100th birthday was celebrated with a three month exhibition at the Rose Museum of Carnegie Hall, and a gala concert featuring **Denyce Graves**, **Sylvia McNair**, **Jessye Norman**, violinist Isaac Stern and James DePreist, among others. The same year, black mezzo **Ruby Hinds** gave the first performance of her biographical tribute to the diva, "See There in the Distance." In 2000, Scribner published *Marian Anderson: A Singer's Journey*, by Allan Keiler, a fine reference of one of the greatest artists America has produced.

On October 19, 2005, the Metropolitan Opera Guild presented the program *Marian Anderson: The Artist And Her Legacy* at Alice Tully Hall, with **Leontyne Price** as honorary chair and **Martina Arroyo** as host. The same year the U.S. Postal Service issued a stamp in Anderson's honor.

DOROTHY MAYNOR, born in Norfolk, Virginia, September 3, 1910, was sent at fourteen to the Hampton Institute in Hampton, Virginia, a preparatory school and college founded in 1868 for freed slaves. Preparing for a teaching career, she studied home economics and sang in the school choir. The chorus director recognized her talent, and for the next four years prepared her for a singing career. She won a scholarship to the Westminster Choir College, Princeton, New Jersey, and in 1936 began studies in New York. In 1939, at the Berkshire Music Festival in Tanglewood, she had an informal audition before **Serge Koussevitsky** (1874–1951), who was so impressed he proclaimed her "a musical revelation." With such publicity, her New York Town Hall debut, November 19, 1939, was the musical event of the season. In a soaring career, she sang with leading orchestras, including New York, Boston and Philadelphia. One of the biggest box office attractions of the day, Maynor recorded with RCA and sang on radio with "The Firestone Hour" and "The Ford Sunday Evening Hour." (Those were the days when radio provided some form of higher culture.) Her countless concerts, world tours, and recordings had kept her away from her husband, Presbyterian minister Shelby Rooks, and in 1963 when he suffered a heart attack, she retired to be with him. It was then she realized her dream of a music school for young black students, and founded the Harlem School of the Arts for underprivileged children, serving as its director until her retirement in 1979 when her protegée, **Betty Allen**, took over. Maynor's voice lives on in the new generations of talent graduating from her school. She died in West Chester, Pennsylvania, February 19, 1996.

20th Century Progress

ROBERTA ALEXANDER was born in Lynchburg, Virginia, March 3, 1949. Raised in Yellow Springs, Ohio, she attended the University of Michigan at Ann Arbor, graduating with a BM in 1971. She appeared at Houston Grand Opera, Santa Fe Opera and in Zurich. Following a European tour, she debuted at the Met in 1983, and in 1985 alternated with **Grace Bumbry** singing Bess in Gershwin's *Porgy and Bess*. She has taken up residence in Amsterdam, and appears with major houses in Europe.

MARTINA ARROYO, born February 2, 1936, studied at Hunter High School and Hunter College, at whose Opera Workshop she was introduced to **Thea Dispeker** (See Agents), her future manager, and Marinka Gurewich, who became her voice teacher for the next thirty years. After graduation, Arroyo taught public school in the Bronx, then became a social worker for the welfare department. In 1958, she shared the top honors at the Met auditions with **Grace Bumbry**, but her roles were mostly Rhine maidens. In 1963, she toured Europe and made appearances with the Vienna State Opera, Berlin State Opera and Zurich Opera. Back in America, she soloed with the New York Philharmonic and other orchestras. She arrived at the top when she filled in for an ailing **Birgit Nilsson** at the Met in 1965. Her Aida was recognized

Martina Arroyo

as one of the best. She became a favorite in the 1970s and held the record for season-opening performances. She married Italian violist Emilio Poggioni in the early 1960s, becoming a jet-age diva, shuttling between New York and Zurich. Health problems curtailed her singing from 1978 to 1983, but with the Met's 100th anniversary "Gala of the Stars" and a Carnegie Hall recital in 1983 she regained the momentum of her earlier career. She then eased her schedule and divided her time between performances and teaching at Louisiana State University. She retired at age fifty in 1986. Arroyo was honored, along with several dozen Verdi singers, at the Met's sixty-sixth annual luncheon, April 20, 2001, commemorating the 100th anniversary of Verdi's death. She now imparts her wisdom to young singers at Indiana University and privately in New York.

On October 19, 2005, the Metropolitan Opera Guild presented the program *Marian Anderson: The Artist And Her Legacy* at Alice Tully Hall, hosted by Arroyo, with Leontyne Price as honorary chair.

KATHLEEN BATTLE, born in Portsmouth, Ohio, August 13, 1948, the youngest of seven children, was grounded in the gospel music of the African Methodist Episcopal Church. She studied voice with Franklin Bens at Cincinnati College Conservatory, where she received her BM and MM (1971). She began a teaching career, meanwhile making her debut at the Spoleto Festival in 1972 in the Brahms *Requiem*. She subsequently sang with the New York Philharmonic, Cleveland Orchestra, Los Angeles Philharmonic, and other leading U.S. orchestras.

Her Met debut came in 1978, and at Covent Garden in 1985. Excelling in light, lyric soprano repertoire, her domain is Mozart, Rossini and Strauss. **Herbert von Karajan** chose her as his soloist for the prestigious Vienna New Year's Day Concert in 1987.

On February 21, 1994, manager Joseph Volpe fired her during a rehearsal of the Met's production of *La Fille du Régiment*—this after a mounting history of being late, displaying temper tantrums and generally unprofessional behavior. Battle denied the charges, and continues her career with concert and recital appearances, but has never set foot again on the stage of the Met or any other opera company.

There were splendid reviews from recitals in Seattle in 2003; Bergen, New Jersey in 2004; and a concert with the Grand Rapids Symphony, celebrating their seventy-fifth anniversary in 2004; but at a recital in Albuquerque, October 2004, the reviewer wrote: "No one has ever doubted that Kathleen Battle has the voice of an angel. It's just a pity she hasn't the personality to match."

(I was present at her San Diego Summer Pops 1995 concert. Living up to her *diva assoluta* reputation, after the last note she rushed into her limo and was gone while the audience was still applauding, waiting for her encore of "Summertime" which she and the orchestra had rehearsed at great length. Even the orchestra was disappointed.)

GRACE BUMBRY, born in St. Louis January 4, 1937, began piano at seven with her mother, herself a talented singer, before coming to a professional teacher. At seventeen, Grace sang for her idol, **Marian Anderson**, who was impressed enough to report the find to **Sol Hurok**, who in later years recruited the young singer into his stable of performing artists. An appearance on Arthur Godfrey's "Talent Scouts" resulted in scholarship offers from major schools. She chose Northwestern (1955), attending master classes of **Lotte Lehmann**, who would shape her career and profoundly affect her life. Lehmann had retired to Santa Barbara, California, where she taught at the Music Academy of the West. Taken with her talent, Lehmann arranged for Grace to spend a summer under her tutelage. The three-month stay lasted three-and-a-half years. During that time she also studied voice with Armand Tokatyan, who saw her as a dramatic soprano, not the mezzo Lehmann envisioned. When Tokatyan died in 1960, the dispute was over. Bumbry the mezzo began her rise to recognition. She won the Kimber Foundation Award in San Francisco, Marian Anderson Award and Metropolitan Opera Auditions of the Air. She used the prize money for her first trip abroad to study French art song with baritone Pierre Bernac. In 1960, she made her operatic debut as Amneris in *Aida*. In 1961, just months after Leontyne Price's Met debut, **Wieland Wagner** chose Bumbry to be Venus in *Tannhäuser* at the Bayreuth Festival, the first black to be featured as the goddess. She repeated the role in 1963 at Chicago Lyric Opera and in Lyon (France). In 1962, First Lady Jacqueline Kennedy invited her to sing at White House. Her 1965 Met debut, as Princess Eboli in Verdi's *Don Carlo*, was followed by the title role in *Carmen* at the Salzburg Festival and again at the Met in 1967. A classic recording from the Met broadcast series, *Aida* with **Leontyne Price** from February 25, 1967, was re-broadcast January 22, 2005. In 1970, she sang *Salome* at Covent Garden, and at the Met in 1973. In 1985, with Simon Estes, a noted African-American bass-baritone, she premiered *Porgy and Bess* at the Met. With her adaptability to sing either mezzo or soprano roles, Bumbry has been seen as both Amneris and Aida, and Venus and Elisabeth in *Tannhäuser*. In 1990, she sang Cassandra in *Prise de Troie* at the opening of the Bastille Opera in Paris, conducted by **Simone Young**. As one of opera's more tempestuous divas, not everyone loved her. The fact that she alternated between soprano and mezzo caused comments around the Met, such as, "The greatest voice anybody ever ruined." When Bumbry left the stage at age sixty, this rumor persisted.

Then, in February 2000, some time after her unannounced last performance as Klytämnestra to Eva Marton's Elektra in the Roman amphitheater for Opéra National de Lyon, she arranged a private concert in the hall of SRI in Zurich for her New York manager, Jack Mastoianni, to show him what she could do. Also there was Albert Innaurato, who wrote for *Opera News*: " . . . we expected Bumbry to be a solid professional with voice left, but the burnished abundance of tone and breath, the well-centered pitches, the sense of immense power in reserve were stunning."

After appearing with the Brooklyn Philharmonic February 15 and 16, 2002, she paid tribute to her mentor, Lotte Lehmann, with a recital at Alice Tully Hall, February 21. Reviewer Ira Siff said of her still-beautiful and sizable voice, "When did you last attend a lieder recital at which the piano lid was completely raised?"

Michéle Crider

MICHÉLE CRIDER, born April 22, 1959, in Quincy, Illinois, studied voice at the University of Iowa. A two time winner in the District Met Opera Auditions, in 1987 she was chosen to sing for the governor's Homecoming Benefit in Des Moines with bass-baritone **Simon Estes**, who made a personal recommendation for her to join the Zurich Opera Studio. After making her home in Switzerland, she won the rarely awarded International Grand Prize of the Geneva International Music Competition (1989), singing Leonora in *Il trovatore*. Since then, she has sung the role in many productions throughout Europe. As a specialist in Verdi, she has performed at the Deutsche Oper Berlin, Hamburg Staatsoper, Vienna Staatsoper, Covent Garden and La Scala. On the concert stage she has soloed in Verdi's *Requiem* at the Theater Basel, Rossini's *Stabat Mater* in Stuttgart, Tippett's *A Child of Our Time* with the London Symphony, and Mahler's Eighth Symphony at the 1995 Lisbon Festival. She made her American debut in April 1996, in San Diego, singing the title role in *Aida*, repeating the role in two new productions in Hamburg and Florence. Her Met debut was in 1997 as Cio-Cio-San in *Madame Butterfly*. For her 2000–01 season she sang Aida in San Francisco (her debut role with the company in 1997), *Trovatore* and *A Masked Ball* at the Met. Her recordings include *Un ballo in maschera* with tenor **Richard Leech**, and the Verdi *Requiem* with the London Symphony Orchestra. In April 2004, she sang Amelia in *A Masked Ball* at Carnegie Hall with the Collegiate Chorale and **Ewa Podleś** as Ulrica. Considered one of the top five Aidas, during the 2004–05 season Crider sang the role in Berlin, Brussels, Dresden, made her Los Angeles debut February 2005, eight months pregnant (she had Melinda on March 12), and at the Met in October. Older daughter Melissa was born December 16, 1997. Michéle has been living in Switzerland since 1987.

Mattiwilda Dobbs

MATTIWILDA DOBBS, born in Atlanta, Georgia, July 11, 1925, studied piano from age seven, and sang in her church choir. She began formal voice studies at Spelman College (BA, 1946), and earned her MA at Columbia (1948), the same year she won the Marian Anderson Award. She studied with **Lotte Lehmann** (1946–50), and won scholarships to the Opera Workshop at the Berkshire Music Center and Mannes College of Music. A John Hay Whitney Fellowship enabled her to study in Paris with Pierre Bernac (1950–52). Winning first prize at the Geneva Competition (1951) launched her European career with Netherlands Opera, plus recitals and orchestral concerts in France, Sweden, Holland and Luxembourg. In 1953, she debuted at La Scala in *The Italian Girl in Algiers*, the first black artist to sing in that house. That performance was followed by appearances at England's Glyndebourne Festival and Covent Garden. Returning to the U.S., she made headlines with her San Francisco Opera debut in 1955, a Town Hall recital debut the following year, and Met debut as Gilda in *Rigoletto*, November 9, 1956. Dobbs became a regular at the Met and San Francisco, singing the most difficult coloratura roles. A recording of the Met broadcast of *Tales of Hoffmann*, February 7, 1959, in which she sang Olympia, was re-broadcast on January 15, 2005. In the '60s she lived in Stockholm, where she was married to a Swedish newspaper man, continuing as a recitalist and singer in the Stockholm, Oslo and Helsinki operas. She also toured in Australia, New Zealand and Israel. In the 1970s, she returned to the U.S., and was a visiting professor at the universities of Texas (1973–74), Illinois (1975–76), Georgia (1976–77), and Howard (Washington, DC) from 1977 until her retirement, May 31, 1991. She still spends several months a year living in Sweden.

Denyce Graves

Mezzo-soprano **DENYCE GRAVES** was born in 1964, in Washington, DC. After her parents separated, her mother worked as a laundress and typist, barely making enough to support her three children, but she instilled in them that they could be whatever they wanted to be. At age nine, a music teacher recognized Denyce's talent and arranged for an audition at the Duke

Ellington School of Performing Arts. Seeing a dress rehearsal of *Fidelio* at Kennedy Center made her determined to become an opera star, and perform at the Met! She was accepted by Oberlin at sixteen. To survive, she cleaned dorms, washed dishes and delivered pizzas. When her teacher, Helen Hodam, moved to the New England Conservatory, she followed. By twenty-three, Graves' voice had become a rich mezzo, but she began to feel pain in her throat. A national finalist in the Met Auditions, March 1988, she was forced to withdraw. The doctor ordered her to stop singing, but specialists could not find the cause of the problem. She took a secretarial job and shut down her dreams. Later that spring, a doctor diagnosed a treatable thyroid condition. Her voice returned stronger than ever. By summer, an offer came from Houston Grand Opera to enter their young artists program where her teacher was **Elena Nikolaidi**. In 1991, she got to sing at their Twentieth Anniversary Gala Concert with world famous tenor **Plácido Domingo**. In 1992, he asked Denyce to sing Delilah opposite his Samson at Chicago's summer Ravinia Festival. Her success there was the entré to the great opera houses of Europe, including La Scala. On October 7, 1995, she fulfilled her dream, singing Carmen for her Met debut. The critics called her "sultry, sexy, sinuous, with a smoky voice and feline physicality"—which made her the Carmen of the '90s. With her signature roles, Carmen and Delila, she has performed at the major houses in Europe and the U.S. Her other operas include *Werther*, *Tales of Hoffmann*, *Così fan tutte*, *Aida* (as Amneris), and for the Met 2001–02 season, *Luisa Miller* and *Rigoletto*. She was Marguerite in *The Damnation of Faust* at Los Angeles Opera, September 2003. Her recital performances feature German lieder, French and English art songs, and melodies from Broadway, jazz, and American spirituals.

Graves' recordings include five full-length opera performances with James Levine and the Metropolitan Opera, *Denyce Graves: A Cathedral Christmas* (also a PBS video filmed at Washington National Cathedral), *Angels Watching Over Me*, *Denyce Graves sings French Heroines*, and a 2003 RCA release *The Lost Days*, a crossover recording of South American/jazz fusion songs, many of which were written for her. She has won such honors as the Grand Prix du Concours International de Chant de Paris (1990), first prize, Eleanor Steber Music Award, and the Marian Anderson Award, presented to her by Miss Anderson herself. In 1998, Oberlin awarded her with an honorary doctorate. On April 12, 2000, she was presented with the Distinguished Washington Award in Literature and Arts from the University Club of Washington, DC., whose president, Scott E. Beck, cited her for achievements on the opera stage and encouraging others to pursue musical excellence. Long-time admirer Supreme Court Justice Ruth Bader Ginsburg spoke at the event.

Following the September 11 terrorist attacks, which brought down the World Trade Center towers and damaged a portion of the Pentagon, it was Denyce who sang *God Bless America* at Washington National Cathedral, at "Ground Zero,"[193] and the *Star Spangled Banner* at the fourth game of the 2001 World Series in New York, October 31, delayed because of the attack.

In 2000, Graves' vocal cords began bleeding, requiring surgery in the summer of 2001. It temporarily ended her career, caused four years of depression and the end of her fifteen year marriage to classical guitarist David Perry. In 2004, in Paris, with her health, voice and career back, she began a relationship with French composer Vincent Thomas. Their daughter Ella, named after Ella Fitzgerald, was born in June. Back in March however, although visibly six months pregnant, she sang Delila at Covent Garden.[194] October brought Azucena (*Il trovatore*) for Washington National Opera—the name change from Washington Opera came in February 2004.

While singing Delilah at the Met in February 2005, she sang for Gala VII at CUNY, Stony Brook, appearing on the same program with pianist **Navah Perlman**, the thirty-four-year-old daughter of violinist **Itzhak Perlman**. In April, she was at Michigan Opera with **Jessye Norman** in *Margaret Garner*, by Richard Danielpour and Toni Morrison. September brought Carmen at Lyric Opera of Chicago, following in the same role at the Met in October.

Although Denyce made her home in Leesburg, Virginia, she has now bought a house west of Paris.

---

193. The then debris-laden site of the collapsed towers.
194. This is the opera company which dismissed Deborah Voigt because she could not fit into "the little black dress."

RERI GRIST was born in New York, February 29, 1932. While studying, she was in theater, not singing until 1956 when she was Cindy Lou in Carmen Jones at New York City Center. Her real breakthrough was part of the first cast in *West Side Story* (1957)—as Consuelo, one of the Shark girls. She told Leonard Bernstein she could sing music other than *West Side Story*, which led to engagements with the New York Philharmonic with him, and singing the Fauré Requiem with **Nadia Boulanger**. She made her opera debut as Blonde at Santa Fe (1959), then was with Zurich (1961–64) where she first sang Zerbinetta *(Ariadne auf Naxos)*, a role in which she excelled and also recorded. She sang at Covent Garden as Queen of Shemakha, Olympia, Gilda, Susanna and Oscar, another famous role. She was with San Francisco (1963–69), making a Salzburg debut in 1965 as Blonde (there is a DVD from the Salzburg Festival of 1965), returning as Despina in 1972. She made her Met debut in 1966 as Rosina, where over the next twelve years she sang Sophie, Norina and Adina. With an ebullient personality and silvery voice, she excelled in the Mozart soubrette roles. In 1981, in San Francico, she sang Manon with moderate success. Her last performance, 1991, was in Morton Feldman's *Neither* in Amsterdam.

Reri makes her home now in Hamburg with her husband, musicologist Ulf Thomson. She has taught at the Munich *Hochschule*, but spends most of her time giving master classes in San Francisco, Ravinia, Bloomington, and Zürich.

A graduate of Northwestern University, **CYNTHIA HAYMON**, born September 6, 1958, in Jacksonville, Florida, has made debuts at Covent Garden, Glyndebourne, Hamburg and Munich. Her 1985 debut, as Thea Musgrave's *Harriet, A Woman Called Moses*, led to her appearance at Covent Garden in *Porgy and Bess*. Her San Francisco Opera debut was as Micaëla in *Carmen*. She is the winner of a 1990 Grammy Award for her recording of *Porgy and Bess*. For Portland Opera, she was Leila in *The Pearl Fishers*, November 2001, and Liu in *Turandot* in the 2002–03 season. August 2003 found her with Andrew Litton and the Minnesota Orchestra's Summerfest, performing in his version of *Porgy and Bess*. For James Conlon's 2003 May Festival with the Cincinnati Symphony, she sang Mendelssohn's *Elijah*, and Handel's *Messiah* for their twenty-fifth anniversary season. March 2005 took her to England for the centenary celebration of Sir Michael Tippett (1905–98), singing his oratorio *A Child of Our Time* with the Northern Sinfonia.

Haymon is an assistant professor of voice at the University of Illinois, Champaign-Urbana.

BARBARA HENDRICKS, daughter of a Methodist minister and schoolteacher mother, was born in Stephens, Arkansas, November 20, 1948. A graduate of the University of Nebraska, she majored in mathematics and chemistry. She began singing in church, and was introduced to classical music through her school chorus. She earned her way singing with a jazz band, and began formal vocal training with mezzo **Jennie Tourel** at Aspen (1968), continuing under her guidance at Juilliard, from which she graduated in 1971. Summers were spent touring Europe with Tourel, who was teaching masterclasses. In 1971, Hendricks won the Geneva International Competition, and the following year first prize in the International Concours de Paris. Opera debuts began with the Glyndebourne Festival, and San Francisco in *L'Incornonazione di Poppea*

Barbara Hendricks

(1974). In 1978, she appeared as Susanna in *The Marriage of Figaro* in Berlin under **Daniel Barenboim**.

In January 1977, Swedish-born Martin Engstrom, her European manager and friend since 1973, proposed marriage. She accepted him after a two-day courtship, and by April they had made Paris their home, and France was happy to adopt her. Her Paris Opera debut in *Romeo et Juliette* was 1982.

Of her more than twenty roles, Susanna became Hendricks' signature, which she has sung throughout Europe. One of her other popular roles is Nanetta in *Falstaff*. She has toured Japan, the Far East, and the former Soviet Union. Her Met debut came in 1986, as Strauss' Sophie. In 1988, she sang at the seventieth birthday celebration for Leonard Bernstein at Tanglewood. Since most of her U.S. appearances were as a recitalist, other than Boston and Santa Fe Operas, when she appeared in 1990 on NBC's "Christmas in Washington" and the PBS "Boston's Christmas at Pops," many Americans wondered who she was.

She sang Liu in the premiere performance of *Turandot*, given in Beijing in 1998, with Zubin Mehta conducting. In November 2004, she was the Angel in the world premiere of Peter Eötvös' *Angels in America* at the Châtelet in Paris. In addition to her operatic career, she has won distinction as a recitalist with her vast repertoire of German lieder, as well as being a leading interpreter of French, American and Scandinavian music. Her recordings (EMI) of opera, orchestral, chamber music and solo number eighty plus.

With her appointment, in 1987, as a Goodwill Ambassador for the United Nations High Commission for Refugees, Hendricks has worked eighteen hour days in primitive countries like Namibia, Malaysia and Cambodia, receiving many awards for her work. In 1991 and 1993, she gave concerts in Dubrovnik and Sarajevo (former Yugoslavia). In 1998, she founded the Barbara Hendricks Foundation for Peace and Reconciliation in her struggle for the prevention of conflicts in the world.

In 1986, the French Government made her "Commandeur des Arts et des Lettres," the same year she received a French Grammy for best French performer of classical music, and in 1992 elected her Chevalier de la Légion d'Honneur. Spain awarded her The Prince of Asturias Foundation Award (2000) for her advocacy for human rights and the contribution of her artistic work to mankind's cultural heritage.

By virtue of marriage, Hendricks is a Swedish citizen and has been a member of the Swedish Academy of Music since 1990. She and her husband live in Switzerland with their two children, Jennie, named after Barbara's mentor, and Sebastian.

Mezzo **RUBY HINDS** was born in the West Indies in 1953. The family moved to Brooklyn when she was very small. She studied at the Hartt School of Music in Hartford, Connecticut where, for the visit of the great **Marian Anderson**, 1974, Ruby was chosen to sing a spiritual and was complimented by the great diva. This encounter forever made an impact on Ruby's life. She made her debut in 1984 at Rome Opera in *The Civil Wars* by Robert Wilson and Philip Glass, and had the distinction of singing her first Wagnerian role, Ortrud (*Lohengrin*), for the New Bulgarian Opera in its premier season. She sang Eboli (*Don Carlo*) for Nice Opera. Her debut performance of Venus in Wagner's *Tannhäuser* was for Hawaii Opera. Her first Adalgisa was in Kentucky Opera's production of Bellini's *Norma* (1990–91). The same season she was in Prokofiev's *Alexander Nevsky*. She was described as an "imperious and sensuous" Carmen for Canada's Opera Ebony. In 1992, she sang the title role in the ballet/opera the *Mother of Three Sons* by Leroy Jenkins with librettist Anne T. Greene and choreographer Bill T. Jones, for the Munich Biennnale Festival. The success of these performances led to engagements with Aachen (Germany), Houston and New York City Operas. 1993 brought Robert Greenleaf's *Under the Arbor*, an opera depicting African-American traditions of the deep South.

Hinds has performed at Kennedy Center, Lincoln Center, and made her Carnegie Hall debut as Orsini in *Lucrezia Borgia* with Opera Orchestra of New York. Other appearances include choral works with the New York Philharmonic under **Zubin Mehta**, and the Los Angeles Philharmonic with **Michael Tilson Thomas**. She also performed with her two sisters, Esther and Grace, as the Hinds Trio. (Esther had a successful solo career in the U.S. and abroad.)

Hinds' latest project is playing and singing the part of Marian Anderson in a one-woman show, "See There in the Distance," which had its first performance in California in 1997, the year celebrating the centenary of Anderson's birth. The official premiere at the Orange County Performing Arts Center was May 2001. This tribute was developed out of the realization that Anderson's legend was fading, and many were forgetting, or did not know of the first black woman to sing at the Met. The script, written by older sister Esther, while necessarily having to show the prejudice and restrictions against "coloreds" throughout the first half of Anderson's career, attempts to do so without antagonizing the present day audience—the positive aspect being Marian's success in Europe. The greatest incident of Anderson's life—despite her character being the furthest from a political activist—is, of course, the supposed refusal[195] of the DAR to permit the renting of their Constitution Hall, at the time Washington, DC's

---

195. See Marian Anderson in this chapter.

largest concert venue, for Anderson's 1939 Easter Concert—and the much publicized in protest resignation from the DAR of First Lady Eleanor Roosevelt—with the U.S. Department of the Interior arranging for the Lincoln Memorial as an alternate venue, which enabled 75,000 to attend the performance, and millions more to hear it live on radio.

The setting of the bio-drama is in Anderson's dressing room as she is about to make her 1957 Met debut, and has her life portrayed in a series of flashbacks. The title, explains Hinds, " . . . is that she was seeing her entire career—her success off in the distance, and she ultimately gained that."

Touring with this show is planned for students and audiences throughout the country.

Marquita Lister

Forging a respectable niche for herself is slim, attractive **MARQUITA LISTER**, who began her operatic career as Clara in the 1986 Tulsa Opera production of *Porgy and Bess*. Born in Washington, DC, April 24, 1961, where she makes her home, she earned her BM at the New England Conservatory and MM at Oklahoma City University. Since her professional debut, she has sung Mimi, Fiordiligi (*Così fan tutte*), Micaëla (*Carmen*), and her first Vitellia in Houston Grand Opera's Mozart anniversary production of *La Clemenza di Tito*. She made an acclaimed debut as Aida in Mexico City during the 1991–92 season. Her first Nedda (*I Pagliacci*) was received with equal enthusiasm. The same season she appeared with **Plácido Domingo** at the gala concert at Houston. The 1992–93 season began with Liù in Baltimore Opera's *Turandot*, and a reprise of Aida at the Festival Cultural Sinaloa (Mexico) and in Houston, plus the title role in *Porgy and Bess*. The following season she added Elisabetta (*Don Carlo*) at Portland and Musetta in Verona (Italy). 1995–96 she was in *Porgy and Bess* in San Diego (where we met) and Aida with Pittsburgh Opera, a performance so successful she was voted Pittsburgh Opera's Female Artist of the Year. She toured with Houston Grand Opera's production of *Porgy and Bess* in America, Japan, at La Scala, and the Bastille, then on a European tour with the Leipzig Radio Symphony as soloist in the Requiems of Verdi and Andrew Lloyd-Webber. Her 1996–97 season started with the SFO production of *Aida*. Released in 1999, by Telarc, is her recording with the Cincinnati Pops and Erich Kunzel of Gershwin's *Blue Monday*, a one-act jazz opera written for George White's *Scandals of 1922*, plus selections from *Porgy and Bess*. Her 2000 season included *Aida* in Calgary and Dresden, *Porgy and Bess* for NYCO, *Tosca* for Connecticut Opera, where she also sang *Il Tabarro* and *I Pagliacci*. Her first Madame Butterfly was in Austin, and after *Aida* in Berlin, she returned to Boston for *Salome*. In August, she was chosen as the representing artist for the Negro Spiritual Scholarship Foundation Gala Concert in Orlando, Florida, where African-American composers write or arrange an existing spiritual for competition. The 2002 season brought *Porgy and Bess* for New Orleans Opera, and a return to NYCO for *Don Giovanni*. For the 2003–04 season, she sang Tosca for Boston Lyric and Connecticut Operas. In 2005, celebrating the twenty-fifth anniversary of Connecticut Opera, she sang the final scene of *Salome*.

Leona Mitchell

LEONA MITCHELL, born in Enid, Oklahoma, October 13, 1948, was one of fifteen children in a musical and religious family. Her father was a minister, her mother an amateur pianist. Gospel music figured heavily in their lives. She sang in church choirs throughout her school years, and was encouraged toward opera by her high school chorus teacher. She received her BM from Oklahoma City University (1971), where Inez Silberg groomed her for a professional music career. After graduate studies at Juilliard, she attended San Francisco's Merola Program, and debuted with San Francisco Opera in 1972 as Micaëla in *Carmen*. A $10,000 Opera America Grant enabled her to study with Ernest St. John Metz in Los Angeles. A recording of *Porgy and Bess* with Lorin Maazel and the Cleveland Orchestra catapulted her to international recognition, and SFO director **Kurt Herbert Adler** (1905–88) paved the way for her Met debut in 1975, where she became one of the most reliable and regular exponents of Puccini and Verdi heroines for over eighteen seasons. She also performed with Rome Opera, Sydney Opera and Covent Garden, continuing her career both in the U.S. and abroad. In 1999–2000, she was in *Turandot* for Australian Opera and *Don Carlo* in Melbourne. In 2001, she was inducted into the Oklahoma Music Hall of Fame. January 2003 took her to London for *Aida*. She sang for a Tulsa Opera benefit in February 2004, the year she was named Cultural Ambassador of Oklahoma by Governor Brad Henry.

Leona is married to Elmer Bush, who taught in Los Angeles before becoming her manager. They have a son, Elmer Bush IV.

Jessye Norman

JESSYE NORMAN, born in Augusta, Georgia, September 15, 1945, sang in church and learned piano from her mother, as did all five children in the family. At sixteen, she entered the Marian Anderson Award contest in Philadelphia, where, despite lack of training, she received encouraging words from the judges. On her way home, she sang for Carolyn Grant at Howard University who recommended her for a full scholarship. After graduation, she studied at Peabody with Alice Duschak, and then at the University of Michigan with Pierre Bernac. She won the Munich Competition (1968) and settled into the European lifestyle of a young diva. She made opera and recital appearances with every major house, including Berlin Deutsche Opera, La Scala and Covent Garden. She abandoned opera temporarily to build a respectable career as a recitalist until her Met debut in 1983, which led to other Met productions. Her last Met appearance was as Emilia Marty in the ill-fated opening performance of the Czech opera *The Makropulos Case* (February 5, 1996), when sixty-four-year-old tenor **Richard Versalle** suffered a heart attack in the first act and fell to his death from a twenty-foot ladder.

But it is in recital singing with the music of Poulenc, Satie, Brahms, Schubert, and Strauss that Norman continues to gather worldwide acclaim in Paris, London, Jerusalem and other corners of the earth. She premiered the song cycle *woman.life.song* by **Judith Weir**, with texts by Toni Morrison, Maya Angelou and Clarissa Pinkola Estes, commissioned for her by Carnegie Hall. Her numerous recording awards include the Paris "Grand Prix National du Disque," Gramophone Award in London, Edison Prize in Amsterdam, and Grammy Awards in the U.S. In 1997, she was the youngest recipient of the Kennedy Center Honors, the same year she sang in Ottawa for the National Arts Centre Gala, with Pincus Zukerman.

Norman has received some thirty honorary doctorates from colleges and universities, decorations and distinctions from governments around the world, and was appointed as an honorary UN ambassador in 1990.

In 2000, she released her first jazz CD, *I Was Born in Love With You: Jessye Norman Sings Michel Legrand*.

For three evenings at Carnegie Hall (February 24, March 1 and 6, 2001), she and pianist/maestro **James Levine** presented a "Songbook Series" of everything from Beethoven to Berg, showcasing Norman's great artistry. In October 2002, the Châtelet (Paris) opened its season with Schoenberg's *Erwartung* and Poulenc's *La Voix humaine*—two showpieces for her voice. The audience rewarded her with a prolonged standing ovation.

Her 2005 recital schedule covered (Florida), Germany, Austria, Poland and Lithuania. In April, she was at Michigan Opera with **Denyce Graves** in *Margaret Garner*,[196] based on a true story, by Richard Danielpour and 1993 Nobelist Toni Morrison, librettist.

Overlooking the Savannah River in her hometown, Augusta, Georgia, the amphitheater and plaza are named for Jessye Norman.

(Mary Violet) **LEONTYNE PRICE**, born in Laurel, Mississippi, February 10, 1927, began piano lessons at three, and sang throughout her school years. She studied voice at the College of Education and Industrial Arts in Wilberforce, Ohio, graduating in 1948. With the help of celebrated black basso **Paul Robeson** (1898–1976), whom she met in 1948, she was awarded a scholarship to Juilliard where she studied with Florence Page Kimball. **Virgil Thompson** (1896–1989) heard her and invited her to sing in the revival of his opera *4 Saints*

---

196. Fleeing Kentucky's Maplewood Farm in 1856 to Ohio, Margaret Garner made the horrific decision to sacrifice her own children when facing recapture, rather than see them returned to the bonds of slavery. Her trial became the subject of intense national debate, addressing crucial issues in constitutional law and posing key questions at the core of the rift in the Union.

in 3 Acts with an all black cast (1952). She then sang opposite famous black baritone **William Warfield** (1920–2002) in *Porgy and Bess*, which toured the U.S. (1952–54) and Europe (1955). They married in 1952, separated in 1959, but were not divorced until 1973. In 1955, the year **Marian Anderson** made her Met debut, NBC hired Price for a televised version of *Tosca*. Her performance created a sensation both as an artist and as a member of her race taking the role of an Italian diva. Although some conservative stations refused to air the interracial performance, her voice and presence were so great she was retained for TV performances of *The Magic Flute* and *Don Giovanni*. In 1957, she made her debut with San Francisco in the American premiere of *Dialogues of the Carmelites*, then sang *Aida*, which became her signature role, with encores in 1958 in Vienna with **Herbert Von Karajan**, in London at Covent Garden and at La Scala (1959), where she was the second black, after **Mattiwilda Dobbs**, to sing with that "exclusive" opera company.

Her Met debut on January 27, 1961, in *Il trovatore*, was one of opera's historic events, proving her a star of the first rank. There followed a series of highly successful appearances, with the premiere and her creation of Barber's *Antony and Cleopatra* opening the new Met in Lincoln Center, September 16, 1966. Her classic recording from the Met broadcast series, *Aida*, with Grace Bumbry from February 25, 1967, was re-broadcast on January 22, 2005. Not only a famous singer, Price was a national heroine, singing Mozart in Salzburg, performing at Kennedy's inauguration, and touring the segregated South with the Met. **Rudolf Bing** made his policy clear, the company boycotted any post-performance parties where the singer was not welcome.

Price was more than favorably compared with other top divas of the time, and survived while the vocally wounded like Maria Callas, Renata Tebaldi, Elisabeth Schwarzkopf, Leonie Rysanek and Victoria De Los Angeles, who had been the era's giants, began to fade. In the 1970s, she sang more opera for the recording studios than the theater, and performed recitals in small cities whose audiences had few chances to see opera. Her farewell performance was a televised production of *Aida* in a "Live from the Metropolitan Opera" program on PBS, January 3, 1985. In the latter part of her career she became an American troubadour, popularizing opera and song.

Opera News magazine, in the mid-1980s, proclaimed, "No native born singer of her era has been so honored as Leontyne Price." She received the Presidential Medal of Freedom from President Lyndon Johnson (1965), Italy's Order of Merit, and the National Medal of Arts, presented by President Ronald Reagan (1985). For her considerable discography, she earned eighteen Grammy awards, receiving Grammy's Lifetime Achievement Award in 1989. In 1996, RCA released an eleven CD collection *The Essential Leontyne Price*, spanning twenty-five years of her career. Maria Callas once said, "You must be a lion to sing Verdi." Price was a lion. In May 1996, at the age of sixty-nine, she gave a recital in Newark.

Following the 9/11/01 attack on the World Trade Center, James Levine and the Met Chamber Ensemble gave a memorial concert at Carnegie Hall. It brought Price out of retirement and, at age seventy-four, she showed her still substantial technique, power and unbeatable charisma. Her fans took heart in her defiant artistry.

On September 23, 2003, she received *Gramophone* magazine's Lifetime Achievement Award. On October 19, 2005, the Metropolitan Opera Guild presented the program *Marian Anderson: The Artist And Her Legacy* at Alice Tully Hall. Price was honorary chair with Martina Arroyo as host.

Shirley Verrett

SHIRLEY VERRETT was born in New Orleans, May 31, 1931. Her father, Leon, a choirmaster at the Seventh Day Adventist church, gave her basic singing instruction. To get away from the racially prejudiced South, the family moved to Oxnard, California, while she was still in elementary school. She attended the Los Angeles Union Academy and Ventura Junior College. Tenor **John Charles Thomas** (1891–1960) heard the seventeen-year-old voice, and was so impressed he offered to pay for her studies with **Lotte Lehmann** at the Academy of the West. Shirley refused, saying she was too young, instead studying real estate law, sidelining her music while she sold property in Southern California during the early fifties.

She returned to her music studies, and in 1955 won an audition for the Arthur Godfrey Show, where she was heard by Marian Szekely-Freschl who invited her to Juilliard. She entered their opera department, which gave her a new direction. A summer at Tanglewood with famed coach **Boris Goldovsky** (1908–2001) prepared her for her 1957 debut with the New York City Opera. She graduated from Juilliard in 1961, but turned down Met offers for small roles still thinking of a recital career. She sang concerts throughout the South, mostly at small black colleges. By the late '60s, she married Italian-American artist Louis LoMonaco, and her career blossomed. She sang in England, the Spoleto Festival, Italy (1962), Bolshoi Opera (1963), New York City Opera (1964), and La Scala (1966). In 1968, she finally accepted the Met offer to sing *Carmen*.

Her desire was to sing soprano roles and, like **Grace Bumbry**, she was criticized for the idea. But in 1973, at the Met opening night, she made musical history singing Berlioz's *Les Troyens* as both Cassandra and Dido. She also sang Lady Macbeth at La Scala (1975), plus Norma and Delilah. In her extended range, it was difficult to tell where the mezzo ended and the soprano began.

Verrett lived in Paris with her husband and daughter in the 1980s, then in New York. She ended her Met career as Delilah in 1990, before making her home in Ann Arbor, teaching voice at the University of Michigan where her husband is a professor. She teaches with the same passion she had for singing, following her father's advice: "Never retire. Find something you can do with passion, and when that's done find another passion until you're not here any more." Failing health forced her abrupt exit from the world of music. Yet in 1994, Nicholas Hytner lured her to Broadway as Nettie Fowler in *Carousel*.

Written with Christopher Brooks, professor of African-American studies at Virginia Commonwealth University, is her memoir *I Never Walked Alone: The Autobiography of an American Singer* (John Wiley & Sons, 2003).

Like Bumbry and Price, Verrett was part of the bridge between Anderson and the next generation.

CAMILLA WILLIAMS was born October 18, 1922, in Danville, Virginia, into humble beginnings. Her father was the chauffeur of Lady Astor's niece. Both parents sang in their church. Camilla attended Virginia State College, whose Alumni Association subsequently raised funds for her to study in Philadelphia with **Marian Szekely-Freschl**. To support herself, she worked as a theater usher. By 1943, her career advanced with the winning of the $750 Marian Anderson Award. In the mid-1940s, her voice had attracted recording contracts (RCA) and a major manager, Arthur Judson (1881–1975), who had been Anderson's first manager, and whose agency later became the powerful Columbia Artists Management Inc. Retired soprano **Geraldine Farrar** became a supporter. The diva was also present at the New York City Opera, May 15, 1946, for Camilla's debut as the first black Butterfly. Made up as a geisha, the petite, attractive soprano proved that a black lead could fit into a white cast. She also became the first black artist to receive a full season contract with a major American opera company, and remained on NYCO's roster until 1954. This led to other firsts: the first black Aida at New York City Center, 1948; first New York performance of Mozart's *Idomineo*, with the Little Orchestra Society, 1950; first tour of Alaska, 1950; first European tour, 1954; first Viennese performance of Menotti's *The Saint of Bleecker Street*, 1955; first African tour for U.S. State Department (14 countries), 1958–59; first tour of Israel, 1959.

Williams was the guest of President Eisenhower in a concert for the Crown Prince of Japan, 1960; toured the Pacific and the Far East, New Zealand and Australia, 1962; and made her first tour of Poland, 1974. Besides appearing with many orchestras here and abroad, in the early '70s she joined the faculties of Brooklyn, Bronx and Queens Colleges (New York), before becoming the first black professor of voice at Indiana University (1978–98). In 1984, she served as a guest lecturer at the University of Beijing.

Janet Williams

JANET WILLIAMS, born in Detroit, September 24, 1959, received an MM from Indiana University, where she studied with **Camilla Williams**, who remained her teacher for many years. She began her professional career as an Adler Fellow at San Francisco Opera, then made her European debut in Lyon, France, in Strauss' *Ariadne auf Naxos*. 1990 saw her open Berlin State Opera's season as Pamina in *Die Zauberflöte* under **Daniel Barenboim**, followed by appearances in 1991 at Nice, Bastille Opera, and the Wexford Festival (England). She participated with the Theatre Royal de Monnaie in a series of Mozart concert arias in Brussels, Avignon, Seville, Amsterdam, Antwerp and Paris. In the course of the last decade, she returned to the Berlin

Staatsoper as Pamina, sang *Semele* at the Handel Festival in Halle (his birthplace), made her Chicago Symphony debut in *Carmina Burana*, her Carnegie Hall debut in Mahler's 2nd Symphony with the Israel Philharmonic, sang with the Mostly Mozart Festival under Gerard Schwarz in New York, and toured with them in Japan. 1995–96 saw her Met debut as Adele in *Die Fledermaus*, and a Washington Opera debut as Sophie in *Der Rosenkavalier*, a role she repeated at Berlin. She also appeared in concert for the Marilyn Horne Foundation and the Mostly Mozart Festival in New York, Frankfurt's Hessische Symphony Orchestra, and soloist in Mahler's 2nd Symphony at the Spoleto Festival in Italy. Other performances include *Semele*, *The Magic Flute*, *Der Rosenkavalier* and *The Barber of Seville*—all in Berlin—and appearances with Michigan Opera Theatre in *The Marriage of Figaro*, and *Messiah* in Ann Arbor. Her recordings include the Brahms *Requiem* (Chicago Symphony), *Messiah* (Philharmonia Baroque), and Graun's *Cleopatra e Cesare* (Concerto Köln).

KAREN WILLIAMS, born in Brooklyn, August 22, 1952, was one of ten American singers chosen to study with famed tenor **Carlo Bergonzi** at the Bel Canto Seminar in Busseto, Italy. Her Metropolitan Opera debut as Serena in *Porgy and Bess* drew highly favorable reviews, as have her many solo performances in church music and orchestral works. In 1985, she co-created the title role of Harriet in **Thea Musgrave**'s *Harriet, the Woman Called Moses* with Virginia Opera. She has appeared as Amelia with **Luciano Pavarotti** in the Opera Company of Philadelphia's production of Verdi's *Un ballo in maschera*. She continues with a thriving international career.

From slave beginnings, African-American singers have forged their way through centuries of prejudice and obstacles. It is fairly evident as we turn another century that, at least in opera, equal opportunities are becoming more available for those with talent and the hard work and dedication required to be a prima donna.

Other Fine Voices

Evelyn Buehler Snow
Christine Akre
Patricia Bardon
Efrat Ben-Nun
Ann Benson
Cathy Berberian
Jill Blalock
Dinah Bryant
Elisabeth Canis
Patricia Chiti
Cynthia Clayton
Priscilla Gale
Isabelle Ganz
Veronique Gens
Suzanna Guzman
Constance Hauman
Pamela Hinchman
Elizabeth Holleque
Catherine Ireland
Heulwen Jones
Liuba Kazarnovskaya

Joan LaBarbara
Patricia McAfee
Diana Montague
Rosemary Museleno
Carol Plantamura
Laura Portune
Patricia Prunty
Georgetta Psaros
Adrien Raynier
Teresa Ringholz
Amanda Roocroft
Pamela Sanabria
Kathleen Shimeta
Paulina Stark
Virginia Sublett
Elzbieta Szmytka
Jeanine Thames
Melissa Thorburn
Awilda Verdejo
Elisabeth von Trapp
Sylvia Wen

Jan Wilson
Patricia Wise
Sheila Wormer

START OF A CAREER
Priti Ghandi
Montsarrat Verdugo

UNUSUAL VOICES
Cynthia Karp
Joan Morris
Linda Hohenfeld
Lakshmi Shankar
Umm Kulthum
Yma Sumac

Just as smaller cities boast competent orchestras, so there are many fine vocalists—it is impossible to list them all—who grace opera companies other than the Met, Covent Garden or La Scala. They pursue viable careers off the main circuits, or sing comprimaria roles—secondary characters—or solo in church services. Some of the following may also be on their way to the "majors" . . .

A Voice From the Past

Evelyn Snow

Evelyn Buehler Snow was, for several years around 1913, a contralto soloist with the Tabernacle Choir under Welsh director Evan Stephens (1890–1916), and organist Alexander Shreiner. Born in Manti, Utah, May 23, 1892, her parents were very strict Mormons. She grew up with seven brothers and sisters. At age twenty-two she left for New York—a daring move for a woman in those days. There she studied at the Parnassus Club with **Lotte Lehman**, who offered her a scholarship to study in Germany. This she declined in favor of marriage to a handsome lad named Chauncey E. Snow. They had met while he was attending law school at Columbia University.

The couple moved to Hollywood where Snow set up his law practice. Chauncey played the cello and sometimes accompanied his wife. Both loved the opera and had a huge collection of scores. Evelyn kept her maiden name, Buehler, and was part of a radio trio with Fritz Kreisler, and Claire Mellanino. This was a first for female vocalists—taking place around 1929. Becoming quite a popular soloist, she sang many times with the Hollywood Bowl, John Steven McGroarty conducting. For three years, twice a week, Evelyn sang the role of Señora Yorba in the long running mission play at the Mission San Gabriel

Four children—Lynn, Hugh John, Patricia and Portia (twins)—shifted her career to motherhood. She died in 1976 at eighty-four, still entertaining friends with her warm and beautiful voice.

After graduating from the University of Illinois, **CHRISTINE AKRE** performed in such roles as Musetta, Fiordiligi and Alice Ford. Among her awards is winning the 1992 Luciano Pavarotti Voice Competition. She also plays the Japanese koto and participates in Kabuki dance rituals.

Irish-born **PATRICIA BARDON** first gained acclaim winning the 1983 Cardiff Singer of the World Competition. Known for her role as Maddalena in *Rigoletto* at the London Coliseum, Norway's Bergen Festival, Opera North, Covent Garden and ENO, she has also performed the title role in *Orlando*, as well as Suzuki at the Theatre des Champs Elysées and England's Opera North.

EFRAT BEN-NUN began singing at the age of three in her native Kibbutz Ma'agan Michael in Israel. Her classical career started with admittance into the Rubin Academy of Art as a flutist, 1990. Studying under the celebrated Natanya Dovrat, she discovered her voice talent and spent postgraduate years in Germany, where she was accepted by **Daniel Barenboim**, then musical director of Berlin State Opera, singing roles such as Pamina (*Magic Flute*) and the flower girl in *Parsifal*. She performs regularly in her homeland with the New Israeli Opera. Her tours of South America and Australia have received acclaim and her recordings of Brahms' *German Requiem* and Mendelssohn's *Elijah* foretell a promising career.

ANN BENSON holds a DMA from the University of South Carolina, plus degrees from Columbia and Indiana Universities. She has been guest soloist throughout the U.S., performing the title roles in *Tosca* and *Madama Butterfly*, among others, and has worked internationally with such conductors as Eduardo Muller, Nello Santi and Jeffrey Tate.

CATHY BERBERIAN was born July 4, 1925. With an incredible three-octave range voice, although she sang traditional classical music, her ability to evoke squeals, grunts, clucks, screeches and other animal noises, plus sub- and superhuman sounds, made her the darling of avant-garde composers to perform some of their otherwise unperformable vocal experiments. She also composed works for her unique abilities. She died in Rome, March 6, 1983. (See Composers.)

JILL BLALOCK, a recipient of the Hewitt Scholarship, completed a degree in Vocal Performance at Texas Tech University. She has performed internationally, notably as a member of the Musica Europa 2001 tour, during which she traveled to France and Spain as Violetta in *La traviata*. Other roles include Gretel, Despina and Lucia. Besides her operatic repertoire, she has also participated in musical theater in Japan.

DINAH BRYANT has performed extensively as a *lieder* recitalist in the U.S. and Europe, with a notable benefit appearance at a Red Cross Gala in Botswana. Her opera roles have included Mimi, Donna Anna, and Lauretta in *Gianni Schicchi*. Her Latin American debut in 1990 was most successful. She has also played the title role of *Salome* at her Met Opera debut in 1996.

Mezzo **ELISABETH CANIS** first came to international attention when she represented Argentina in the Cardiff Singer of the World Competition. She has since been engaged by companies in her native country as well as France, the Netherlands and Germany. She made her operatic debut in 1993 at the Teatro Colón (Buenos Aires) as the winner of the *Nuevas Voces Liricas Argentinas* Competition. Her North American debut was as Suzuki at the Met, where she also appeared as Magdalena in *Die Meistersinger*. This was followed by Olga in *Eugene Onegin* at SFO, Suzuki again at Tulsa, and Vera Boronel in Menotti's *The Consul* at Berkshire Opera, a performance recorded for the Newport Classics label. Other roles include the Third Lady in *The Magic Flute*, her debut with Florida

Grand Opera, and the Verdi *Requiem* with the Alabama Symphony. A graduate of the Instituto Superior de Arte of the Teatro Colón, Canis has coached with Heather Harper, Benita Valente and Marlena Malas.

British born mezzo **PATRICIA CHITI** has forged a singular career in Italy with the founding of *Donne in Musica*, a pioneer television series featuring women musicians, past and present. This has now been expanded into a book of the same name, published in several languages. She has performed throughout Europe. (See Musicologists.)

American soprano **CYNTHIA CLAYTON** spent four years as artist-in-residence with San Jose Opera before making appearances with Cleveland, Arizona and Fort Worth Operas. She has sung both Musetta and Mimi in *La bohème*, Cho-Cho-San in *Madame Butterfly*, and Countess Almaviva in *The Marriage of Figaro* for NYCO. In San Diego, she was Micaëla (*Carmen*, 1997), Musetta (*La bohème*, 2000), and Mary Willis Tweedy in *Cold Sassy Tree* (2001).

Cynthia Clayton

After completing studies at Juilliard and the Cleveland Institute, **PRISCILLA GALE** continued voice study in Rome and the American Institute of Musical Studies in Graz, Austria, where she was a finalist in Die Meistersinger Competition, receiving a recording contract with the Swiss-Italian Radio Orchestra in Lugano. Twice a finalist in the Met New England Regional Auditions, her performances on the concert and operatic stage include appearances throughout the East Coast, including the Boston Lyric Opera, Connecticut Concert Opera, Annapolis Chamber Orchestra, and Arizona Opera. Her Rosalinda (*Die Fledermaus*) and Violetta (*La traviata*) were well received. Her unique CD, *Dream Faces* (Centaur, 1999), is a collection of turn of the century Irish songs not published since 1896. This was followed by a Master Musicians Collective (MMC) recording, with the Seattle Symphony under **Gerard Schwarz**, of original works written for her by William Thomas McKinley. She also has a 2000 MMC release with the Moravian Philharmonic.

Gale is a popular performer with chorale and orchestral organizations and a member of the voice faculty at Wesleyan University in Middletown, Connecticut.

New Delhi (India) born **PRITI GANDHI**, a graduate of the University of California, San Diego, began her career in 1996 with the San Diego Opera Chorus. (See *A Budding Career* near the end of this section.)

ISABEL GANZ began her professional career at ten as piano soloist with the New York Philharmonic. She holds a DMA in voice and music literature from Eastman. She has taught at the American Institute of Musical Studies in Graz, the University of St. Thomas, and Houston Community College. Her *Go Away Tango* won first prize in the 1989 Lind Solo Song Award competition, sponsored by Cornell. She was the recipient of a Solo Recitalist grant from the NEA (1992–93).

A vocal soloist with numerous orchestras, chamber ensembles and music festivals throughout the U.S., Europe and Israel, Ganz is a champion of contemporary music, having premiered and recorded many works, including John Cage's *Ryoanji for Voice and Percussion* written for her. Her ensemble, *Alhambra*, specializing in the research and performance of Sephardic music, has toured Spain, England, Lithuania, Turkey, South America and New York. She also officiates as a guest cantor in synagogues during the High Holy Days of the Jewish calendar.

In 1966, Isabel married Dutchman Abbie Lipschutz—between them they have five children. She made her home in Holland from 1995–98, after which she returned to America and became artist-in-residence at the University of Houston, Moores School of Music, 2001–05.

French soprano **VÉRONIQUE GENS**, a first prize winner at the Paris Conservatory, was born in Orléans, April 19, 1966. Since her debut in 1986 with Les Arts Florissants, she has become a well-known name in baroque singing, with CDs of Pergolesi, Purcell, Lully, Couperin, Rameau and Handel prominent in her fifty-plus discography, which also includes Mozart, Berlioz, Brahms and Debussy. On stage she has appeared in numerous Mozart operas, notably as Donna Elvira (*Don Giovanni*), and Fiordiligi, and has soloed in his *Requiem* and Bach's *B minor Mass*. She tours all over Europe, records on harmonia mundi, Erato and Virgin Classics.

Mezzo **SUZANNA GUZMÁN** has been an associate artist of Los Angeles Opera since 1987, and has performed in San Diego Opera productions since 1985, including Eunice Hubbell in their 2000 production of *A*

Streetcar Named Desire, 2001 *Magic Flute* and 2002 *Rigoletto*. Other leading roles have been at the Met, Washington, Dallas, Hawaii, Madison, Columbus, Geneva and Dresden. Her Carnegie Hall debut was in 1997 with Dennis Russell Davis' American Symphony Orchestra. On the Board of UCLA's outreach group, Design for Sharing, which brings music to inner-city communities, she received the 1997 Plácido Domingo Award for Achievement in the Arts, and was featured in the 2000 edition of *PEOPLE* magazine en Español. She is the host of the radio program Sunday Opera Classics, and co-host with Rich Caparella of Los Angeles Opera Notes, both on KMZT (K-Mozart) in Los Angeles.

CONSTANCE HAUMAN, a graduate of Northwestern University, trained in dance and musical theater. She has performed in the U.S. and Europe in such diverse roles as Cunegonde in Leonard Bernstein's *Candide*, the title role of *Lucia di Lammermoor*, Tytania in Benjamin Britten's *A Midsummer Night's Dream* and Ariel in Lee Hoiby's *The Tempest*.

PAMELA HINCHMAN, known for her title role in Menotti's *The Bride from Pluto*, has also sung Zerlina in *Don Giovanni* in Pittsburgh and New Orleans. Other roles include Norina (*Don Pasquale*) in Kentucky and Chattanooga, Josephine in *HMS Pinafore* with Kentucky Opera and Mabel in Mississippi Opera's *Pirates of Penzance*. She has performed *Carmina Burana* many times, most notably in Miami with the late **Eduardo Mata**.

After winning the 1983 Metropolitan Opera National Council Auditions, **ELIZABETH HOLLEQUE** amassed a repertoire of roles that culminated in her 1992 Covent Garden debut in the title role of *Tosca* with **Luciano Pavarotti** as Cavaradossi, **Zubin Mehta** conducting. She has performed the role extensively at opera houses in America, Canada and Europe. Other roles include Elena (*Mefistofele*), Cio-Cio-San (*Madama Butterfly*) and the title role in *Vanessa*. Her Carnegie Hall debut with **Pinchas Zukerman** featured Mozart's *Exultate Jubilate*. She has twice (1987, 1988) received New York City Opera's Diva Award. She reprised Tosca in the Met's 1999–2000 season.

Australian soprano **CATHERINE IRELAND** has been a resident artist with Los Angeles Opera and San Diego Opera Ensemble [She was Susanna in *The Marriage of Figaro* in 1998] and received the prestigious Royal Opera House Covent Garden/Shell scholarship to study at the National Opera Studio, London. Her roles with LA include Frasquita in *Carmen* opposite Jennifer Larmore and Plácido Domingo, the Dew Fairy in *Hansel and Gretel*, and Annina, in *La traviata*. Her North American debut was Musetta (*La bohème*), and her European debut as Micaëla (*Carmen*) with the Welsh National Opera. While attending the Sydney Conservatorium of Music, she performed the title role in Massenet's *Cendrillon*, Purcell's *Dido and Aneas* and Monteverdi's *Coronation of Poppea*. Other performances include Gianetta (*L'elisir d'amore*), Yvette in *La Rondine* and, in Australia, the title role in Fauré's *Penelope*. In summer 2004, she appeared in "Opera on the Vine, from Mozart to Sondheim" at Murphys Creek Theatre in Northern California. Concert engagements have included featured artist with the San Diego Chamber Orchestra and the Sydney Symphony Orchestra in such repertoire as the *Messiah*, *Carmina Burana*, Beethoven's Ninth Symphony and the Fauré *Requiem*.

Ireland's voice can be heard behind the national television commercials for Skytel Pagers and Volvo automobiles. She was a national finalist in the Loren L. Zachary Competition, and a regional finalist in the Metropolitan Opera National Council Auditions. Now married, her newest role is mother to a baby daughter.

Mezzo **HEULWEN JONES** was born December 4, 1975, in Cardiff, Wales, to a musical Welsh father[197] and Trinidadian mother. The family moved to Canada where Heulwen began piano early, adding recorder and violin at school. An excellent sight reader, both vocally and instrumentally, she also has perfect pitch. She played violin in the Winnipeg Youth Orchestra, and received the highest grade in the Piano exam of the Toronto Royal

---

197. Heulwen's father is Keith Davies Jones, MD, vice president of the St. David's Society of Winnipeg, an organization devoted to perpetuating the language, history, culture and heritage of Wales. He heads the Radiation Oncology Department at the University of Manitoba Medical Center, is an administrative member of the St. David's Singers of Winnipeg, and the official ambassador to Canada of the Welsh Music Guild. Her mother, Gwyneth, is an endo-crinologist/radio-immunologist, PhD, who discovered an important hormone towards the cure of cancer.

Conservatory of Music. Jones' BMA is from the Canadian Mennonite University in Winnipeg, where she was a voice major and student of Henriette Schellenberg. She also studied at the Orford Centre for the Arts in Québec. She won the Royal Conservatory of Music Silver Medal, Edith Motley Vocal Award, several first and second place awards in the Winnipeg Music Competition Festival, and first place in the Eisteddfod held at the Welsh National Gymanfa Ganu in Ottawa, September 1, 2000.

Aspiring towards the operatic stage, she sings in the Manitoba Opera Chorus and with Nuova Opera in Edmonton. She also performs in recital, especially the music of **Morfydd Owen**, **Margaret Bonds**, Canadian composer Patricia Blomfield Holt, and her favorite, **Pauline Viardot-Garcia**.

Heulwen married a fellow musician, December 2003.

Beginning her musical studies at the Moscow Conservatory, **LIUBA KAZARNOVSKAYA** made her debut as Tatyana in *Eugene Onegin* with Bolshoi Opera. Following this, she was Leonora in *La Forza del Destino* with Kirov Opera in 1986, joining the Mariinsky Theatre in St. Petersburg as principal soprano. After singing the Verdi *Requiem* at Salzburg under **Riccardo Muti**, she was engaged by **Herbert von Karajan** as the Countess in *Le Nozze di Figaro*. Her 1992 Met debut as Tatyana was well received, and her Nedda in the 1994–95 Met season's *Pagliacci* with **Luciano Pavarotti**, led to solo and recital engagements worldwide.

Mezzo **JOAN La BARBARA**,[198] composer, vocal performer and sound artist, like musicologist/performer **Deborah Kavasch** (See Musicologists) and the late **Cathy Berberian**,[199] has developed extended vocal techniques and uses her voice as a multi-faceted instrument.

Known primarily for her interpretation of Mozart and Gluck, mezzo **DIANA MONTAGUE** won acclaim for her Ascanio in *Benvenuto Cellini* with Opera Bastille and Rome Opera. Other impressive appearances were Idamente (*Idomeneo*) and Sesto (*La Clemenza di Tito*). Her collaborations include **James Levine**, **Riccardo Muti**, **George Solti**, **Jeffrey Tate** and **John Eliot Gardiner**, with whom she recorded the award-winning *Le Comte Ory* and *Iphigènie en Tauride*, which have garnered positive reviews in Europe.

Soprano **PATRICIA McAFEE** was part of the SFO Merola program, a three-time regional finalist in Metropolitan Opera auditions, and received the Richard F. Gold Career Grant. Her Arizona Opera debut was as Gutrune in *Götterdämmerung* (1995) and returned as Gutrune, Freia and Ortlinde in their *Ring* cycles in 1996, 1998. She appeared in Portland Opera's *Eugene Onegin*, Pittsburgh's *Otello*, Opera San Jose as Mrs. Grose in *The Turn of the Screw* and, for Opera Pacific, Waltraute (*Die Walküre*), Marthe (*Faust*) and Inez (*Il Trovatore*). She began her appearances with San Diego Opera in 1994 in *The Tales of Hoffmann* and as Teresa in *La sonnambula*. Return engagements have been *Macbeth* (1995), Annina (*La traviata*), 1997, a slave in *Salome*, 1998, and Inez (*Il trovatore*) in 2000. Her orchestral solos include Rossini's *Stabat Mater*, Beethoven's Ninth Symphony, Handel's *Messiah*, Mahler's *Songs of a Wayfarer*, Haydn's *Mass in Time of War*, and John Rutter's *Magnificat*, heard in December 2004.

ROSEMARY MUSELENO, born in Northeastern Pennsylvania, is opera's "coal-miner's daughter." American/Italian ancestry provided her with a background of opera since childhood. In high school she played clarinet and crooned standards with regional big bands. In 1980, at age eighteen, she was selected by the State Department as vocal soloist for a big band tour through Romania. Encouraged by family and friends, she auditioned and was accepted on scholarship in the vocal program at Juilliard. Selected as the only student from this program to make her debut with the Opera de Lyon (France), she began her professional career as Servilia in *La clemenza di Tito* while still a fourth year student. Her performance was so successful the company offered her thirty-five appearances in five productions in a Mozart cycle that included Susanna and Despina. In 1994, she was awarded the $15,000 prize in the vocal competition of the Pope Foundation for the Arts in New York. She won international accolades for her first recording, the difficult and beautiful soprano part of Temperantia in the world premiere of Haydn's hitherto unknown secular oratorio, *Applausus*. Subsequent roles have been Mimi (San

Antonio Symphony), Liù (Colorado Opera Festival's *Turandot*), Brahms' *Requiem* (Lugano, Switzerland) and Musetta (San Diego Opera).

CAROL PLANTAMURA, a native of Los Angeles, is a graduate of Occidental College, with further studies in the opera department at USC, Rhine Music School, Cologne, and an MFA from SUNY, Buffalo. She is an original member of the Rockefeller-funded Creative Associates under the direction of composer **Lukas Foss**.

In the course of her twelve year residence in Italy, Platamura performed at major concert venues in Europe as well as in Australia, New Zealand, Japan and America, with a focus on 17th and 20th century vocal music, much of which is on CD, including 17th century music by Italian women composers on the Leonarda label. She founded and performed fourteen years with *The Five Centuries Ensemble*, a group specializing in these periods. Her collaborations with leading composers include **Pierre Boulez**, **John Cage**, **Luciano Berio**, **Pauline Oliveros**, **Betsy Jolas**, **Lukas Foss** and **Bernard Rands**. She is the author of a unique coloring book, *Women Composers* (Bellerophon Books, 1983), and *The Opera Lover's Guide to Europe* (Citadel Press, 1996). She is head of the voice department at UC San Diego, where she began teaching in 1978.

Soprano **LAURA PORTUNE**, born in Dayton, Ohio, March 28, 1976, started flute and saxophone in fifth grade, and French Horn and singing musical theater through high school. Her grandfather loved opera from his service in Italy during WWII. Notre Dame offered only opera for singers thus, while earning her BA (1998), Laura got into the field by default. Besides roles like Poppea, Zerlina, Despina and Serpina, she soloed in *Messiah*, was the official cantor to the president of the University, and the only female to have sung with the Glee Club.

While earning her MM (2000) from Ohio State, her rendition of Carlisle Floyd's *Susannah* earned her the Margaret Speaks Vocal Scholarship. She also worked with John Corigliano on her role of Marie Antoinette in a university production of his *Ghosts of Versailles*.

She participated in Young Artist Programs at Opera Theatre of Lucca (Italy), American Institute of Musical Studies, Graz (Austria, 1999), Des Moines Metro Opera (2000–01), San Diego Opera Ensemble (2000–02), where she created and recorded the role of Juliet Mouse in Myron Fink's *Animal Opera*, and Lake George Opera (2003). She was a finalist in competitions at Opera Columbus, Met Opera (San Diego), and Chicago Lyric Opera. Her Language Fluency Certificate (Universita per Stranieri, Perugia) and French program (Nice), complement her passions for travel and learning languages.

In her "second home," San Diego Opera, she was Kate Pinkerton in *Madama Butterfly* (2003), and Thibault in *Don Carlo* (2004). With Lyric Opera San Diego, she sang leading roles in *Barber of Seville*, *Pirates of Penzance*, *Merry Widow*, *Gondoliers* and *Countess Maritza* (October 2005).

After recitals in Perugia (2003) and Chianti (2004), March 2005 saw Portune in a world premiere with the North Czech Philharmonic, of New York composer Gary Papach's *The Last Leaf*, based on an O. Henry short story. Hugely acclaimed, it was recorded on CD and DVD. A blossoming career.

PATRICIA PRUNTY sang with Los Angeles Opera (1990–93), making her debut in 1992 as Cissy in *Albert Herring*, a role she sang the year before with San Diego Opera. She has also performed with the operas of Long Beach, San Jose, Santa Fe, Santa Barbara and Opera Pacific. Her concert appearances include the American Chamber Symphony of Los Angeles, Carmel Bach Festival, and being part of *The Glory of Easter* at the Crystal Cathedral. Following her New York recital debut, she appeared with the San Diego Symphony in Barber's *Knoxville: Summer of 1915*, and Mahler's *Fourth Symphony*. She is also a popular artist on cruise ships.

Mezzo **GEORGETTA PSAROS** has performed at Covent Garden, ENO, Opera Geneva, Carnegie Hall, and in London at the Royal Albert, Royal Festival, Victoria, and Queen Elizabeth Halls under such conductors as Sir Charles MacKerras, Sir Roger Norrington, Carlo Maria Giulini, Pierre Boulez and André Previn, with orchestras including the New York and Los Angeles Philharmonics and Swiss Romande. She is the winner of an Ebe Stignani Gold Medal, has recorded on EMI, Toshiba and Classic Digital, Prestige Artists (1998), and the 1999 RCA Victor Red Seal re-release, *Young Domingo*, in which she joins the famed tenor. Soloing with the Roger Wagner Choral for ten years gave rise to the Maestro's quote, "Who needs the Met when we have Georgette!"

Someone has to sing the small roles, or be part of an opera chorus. Mezzo **ADRIEN RAYNIER** is representative of this support corps, and has built a fine and interesting career in this special niche. Residing one mile from where she was born in Pasadena, California, she began singing in school. Throughout her college years at Chapman University, she sang in chamber groups, large chorales and with Los Angeles Opera. She met her husband, tenor Franz Brightbill, in college. The two have been professional singers ever since. Besides their individual careers, they perform duet recitals featuring lieder, opera and classical folk songs. Their son Lorien, age thirty-six (in 2006), is a string bass player married to **Christie Lawrence**, a lyric soprano with LA Opera.

TERESA RINGHOLZ attended Eastman in her native Rochester, New York, receiving two degrees in vocal performance. At age twenty-two, after stints in New York and North Carolina, she became a member of the SFO touring company, singing Gilda to audiences across the U.S. She began her European career with a debut in Strasbourg as Zerbinetta in *Ariadne auf Naxos* (1985). This led to her appointment as a solo soprano member of the State Opera of Cologne. She also performs regularly in Berlin, Stuttgart, Leipzig, Prague, Paris, Zurich as well as America. Well known for her role in Alfred Schnittke's *Life with An Idiot*, she recorded this on Sony.

AMANDA ROOCROFT, after training at the Royal Northern College of Music, made her debut in 1990 as Sophie in *Der Rosenkavalier*. This won her the Royal Philharmonic Society/Charles Heidsieck Debut Award. Her Covent Garden debut came in 1991, as Fiordiligi in *Così fan tutte*. In addition to her success in the UK, she has been lauded in Holland, Lisbon and Paris. Her television appearances include the 1991 documentary, *A Girl from Coppull*. In 1999–2000, she was in the Met's *Marriage of Figaro*.

PAMELA SANABRIA made her mark as Carlotta in the Hamburg premiere production of *Das Phantom der Oper*. She has also performed Violetta, Mimi and Sonia (*The Merry Widow*). A Chicago native, she earned her MM from Northwestern University and was the winner of the Marcella Sembrich Award from the Kosciuszko Foundation.

Kathleen Shimeta

Mezzo **KATHLEEN SHIMETA** is an interpreter of art songs, chamber music, oratorio and opera. She has a BM from St. Cloud University in Minnesota and MM from the University of Cincinnati College-Conservatory of Music. She has given concerts in Amsterdam, London, Devonshire, Berlin, and recitals in New York, Florida, and Maine, where she has performed in consecutive seasons at the Bar Harbor Music Festival. Besides Charlotte Opera and North Carolina Opera, she has sung the great oratorios of Handel, Bach, Mozart, Verdi, Brahms and Purcell. Contemporary works include George Rothberg's *Songs in Praise of Krishna*. Since 2002, she has presented a one-woman show of biography and songs of composter/conductor **Gena Branscombe** (1881–1977), and recorded a CD of her songs: *Ah Love, I Shall Find Thee*.

Paulina Stark

PAULINA STARK has performed internationally in concert, opera and recital, collaborating with such celebrated conductors as **Sergiu Comissiona**, **Lawrence Foster**, **Lukas Foss**, and the late **Margaret Hillis**, **Eduardo Mata** and **Sir John Barbirolli**. Specializing in crossover and ethnic repertoire, her CDs include *Unmined Cole: Unpublished Gems of Cole Porter* (Centaur,1998); *A Lullaby Journey: Sing Me to Sleep* (Gasparo Gallante, 2001), a reissue of a Spectrum LP, produced for UNICEF; *American-Jewish Art Songs* (Centaur, 1988); *I Have Taken an Oath to Remember: Art Songs of the Holocaust* (Transcontinental Music Publications, 2002); and *Darkness and Light* Vol. 4. *Terezin* (Albany Records, 2002). The latter three, plus concerts around the country, have brought Stark recognition as one of the foremost interpreters of classical American-Jewish vocal music. She has also recorded with pianist **Estela Olevsky**.

Serving on the faculty of the University of Massachusetts at Amherst (1985–2003), her award-winning voice students have performed in the SFO Merola program as well as Connecticut, Cincinnati and other opera companies. Several have placed in Met competitions.

Stark retired from full time teaching, January 1, 2004, to divide her time between private studio advanced students, and seniors and graduates from her university studio, preparing them for their Spring recitals.

VIRGINIA SUBLETT made her NYCO debut in 1987 as the Queen of the Night in *The Magic Flute*, drawing rave reviews. A native of Kansas City, Kansas, she received her BM from Louisiana State and MM from UCSD, with a concentration on 20th century French vocal music. She is also an accomplished pianist and harpsichordist and performs much church music.

Polish-born **ELZBIETA SZMYTKA** attended the College of Music in Cracow. Her extensive European performances include Susanna and Despina as part of her standing repertoire. In 1983, she captivated audiences as Blondchen (*Abduction from the Seraglio*) with the Breslau National Opera tour in Germany and Luxembourg.

JEANINE THAMES, a native of Beaumont, Texas, holds an MM from Juilliard. She has made a specialty of the Queen of the Night in *The Magic Flute* and has sung this role with the Opéra National de Paris, Berlin State Opera, Bavarian State Opera and De Vlaamse Opera, Antwerp. After her 1990 European debut with the Frankfurt Radio Orchestra, she spent the next two years in Bremen (Germany). During the 1991–93 seasons, she made American appearances with Cleveland and San Diego Operas. 1993–94 included *Parsifal*, with L'Opera de Nice, and *Carmina Burana* with the Illinois and Columbus (Ohio) Symphonies. No stranger to modern music, she premiered Alexander Goehr's *Behold the Sun* with the Brooklyn Philharmonic and later with the Los Angeles Symphony. Highlights of 1999–2000 included the title role in *Lucia di Lammermoor* with Fort Worth and several roles with the Deutsche Oper am Rhein in Düsseldorf, including Gilda (*Rigoletto*), Serpetta (*La finta giardiniera*), Marzelline (*Fidelio*), Queen of the Night, plus title roles in new productions of *La Fille du régiment* and *Hansel and Gretel*. Her other roles include Clorinda (*La Cenerentola*) with Dallas Opera, Despina (*Così fan tutte*) with Fort Worth, Blondchen in Bilbao (Spain), Zerbinetta (*Ariadne auf Naxos*) with the Pfalztheater, Kaiserslautern (Germany), and with the Sinfonia da Camera in Champaign-Urbana, Illinois.

American born mezzo **MELISSA THORBURN** began her career as a pianist, graduating from Louisiana State University. She studied voice with **Yvonne Lefébure** (1898–1986) in Paris, later completing her MM in voice at the New England Conservatory, and also studying with **Phyllis Curtin** (*b* 1921). She won the Met New England Regional Auditions and has performed with the Philadelphia Orchestra on a regular basis. She appeared in *Romeo et Juliette* with Sacramento Opera, *Don Giovanni* with the opera companies of Knoxville, Sarasota, and Kansas City, and *Marriage of Figaro* with Sarasota Opera. Thorburn also specializes as a sacred music soloist.

AWILDA VERDEJO, a native of Puerto Rico, is recognized in Europe for her *Tosca* in Vienna, Salzburg and Munich, and *Aida* in Hamburg, Munich, Frankfurt, Rome, Verona and Cairo. She is also well known for her solo work, especially the Verdi *Requiem*, which she has performed in Puerto Rico, Paris, Hamburg, Frankfurt, Cologne and Turin among other cities. In the U.S., she has sung Cio-Cio-San for New York City Opera and Kennedy Center.

ELISABETH von TRAPP is the next generation of the family of performers made famous by the stage and film versions of *The Sound of Music*, by Richard Rodgers and Oscar Hammerstein II, with the role of Maria played on Broadway by Mary Martin, and on film with Julie Andrews. Based on Maria von Trapp's book, *The Story of the Trapp Family Singers*, published in 1949, the musical ends in 1938, but that is when the real life story began.

The von Trapps arrived in America in 1938 and spent the next eighteen years performing on the road. In 1942 they settled in Stowe, Vermont, whose scenery is reminiscent of Austria, in a farmhouse on 600 acres. While touring, they rented their home to skiers, which began the von Trapp hotel business. In 1957, The Trapp Family Singers' twenty year career came to an end. Captain von Trapp had died May 30, 1947, which marked the beginning of the family's rebellion against living their life on the road. Maria ran the Lodge until her death in 1987. Of the ten children, six are still alive (as of 2005), with son Johannes the president of the Trapp Family Lodge, Inc.

Elisabeth, daughter of Werner, grew up on her family's farm in Waitsfield, Vermont. Inspired by her father's guitar playing and singing, she began piano and by sixteen was playing guitar and singing throughout New England. With a clear, ethereal voice, nurtured in classical, folk and pop music, she has also become identified as an art song interpreter with her original compositions.

Her albums included *Wishful Thinking* (1994), *One Heart, One Mind* (1996), and *Christmas Song* (1999) until in 2001 she received permission from Robert Frost's publisher, Henry Holt & Co., to set some of his poems to her original music. Her fourth album, *Poetic License*, was released in 2004. *Love Never Ends* came out in 2006.

Von Trapp has been heard throughout the U.S., Austria and Russia, and featured on NPR, BBC Radio and Television, Japanese National Radio and CNN Spanish Radio. Her TV appearances include CBS *Eye on People* and ABC's *Good Morning America*. She is married to Ed Hall who acts as her manager.

Chinese-American **SYLVIA WEN**, a well known performer on the West Coast, has sung such roles as Papagena, Micaëla and Lisa (*La sonnambula*). Her solo work includes Beethoven's *9th* with the San Diego Symphony, the lead in many operettas with San Diego Lyric Opera, comprimaria roles with San Diego Opera, and Bernstein's *Chichester Palms* with the Santa Barbara Symphony. A 1991 and 1992 winner of the Zachary Society National Auditions, she has also performed at the National Opera House in Beijing, and is much in demand as a sacred music soloist.

Mezzo **JAN WILSON** has the distinction of *not* wanting to be an opera singer! Her lovely singing voice well qualifies her for the grand stage, but soloing in large choral works is her chosen milieu. Born May 22, 1958, in Altoona, Pennsylvania, she grew up in the historic town of Hollidaysburg, began piano at six and never abandoned that instrument. She "found" her voice in high school where her mother, an organist, was her choral teacher. She received her B.Mus.Ed. from Westminster Choir College, and MM in voice performance from Penn State, where she was the winner of the Young Artists Competition. A Rotary Foundation Fellowship got her to the RCM where she received the certificate of achievement, and concertized with Sir David Willcocks and the Mayfield Festival in Sussex (England). Returning from London, she taught at both Penn State and Westminster, engaged in two years of competitions and, as a regional finalist at the Met auditions, presented her debut recital at Weill Hall in 1994. With teaching requiring so much use of voice, she switched to the business world, becoming executive director of the Altoona (Pennsylvania) Symphony, while maintaining her solo and choral career.

Jan now lives in New York City, working as manager of the Information Resource Center at the American Symphony Orchestra League. She is a frequent soloist at St. Patrick's Cathedral, as well as an ensemble singer with professional choruses under the direction of Kurt Masur, Pierre Boulez, Oliver Knussen, and **Jane Glover**. She has performed with Sherrill Milnes in Mendelssohn's *Elijah*, and during the 1999–2000 in Beethoven's 9th Symphony, the Verdi *Requiem*, Vivaldi *Gloria*, Rutter *Magnificat* and Prokofiev's *Alexander Nevsky*. The following years have included Mahler's 2nd Symphony and *Lieder eines fahrenden Gesellen* (Songs of the Wayfarer), as well as Brahms' *Alto Rhapsody*, among other glorious vocal masterpieces.

Kansas-born soprano **PATRICIA WISE** did not see her first opera until she was nineteen. After a year of training, she performed Susanna (*Marriage of Figaro*) in Kansas City. Her New York Opera debut as Rosina (*Barber of Seville*) led to her European debut in London's Covent Garden. In 1976, she became a guest artist at the Vienna Staatsoper, concentrating mainly on Strauss and Mozart roles. Her longtime affiliation with the State Opera was honored with the title of Kammersinger by the Austrian Government in 1989. She has been lauded for her portrayal of Berg's vocally challenging *Lulu*.

SHEILA WORMER, together with her husband Thomas Chambers, is part of the La Stella Duo, one of whose highlights is the nostalgic *A Salute to Mario Lanza*. Trained as a dancer, she is one of the few sopranos in the world who has sung Nedda (*I Pagliacci*) and Olympia (*Tales of Hoffman*) *en pointe*. Besides traditional roles, she makes the crossover to musicals and plays.

The Blossoming of an Operatic Career

PRITI GANDHI is, as of 2006, well on her way to a successful operatic career. Born December 4, 1972, in Mumbai, (Bombay is returning to the use of its original name) her parents left India when she was a baby. She grew up in San Diego, and considers herself a California native, although there are frequent family trips back to India.

Priti Gandhi

Indians love their own music and practice their own culture wherever they emigrate. As a result, Priti grew up knowing absolutely nothing about opera, but had an inborn love of music. Her piano studies from ages six to seventeen initiated a love for Western classical music.

She graduated from UCSD in 1994 with a BA in communications and theater. During her junior year, she began voice lessons with **Laurie Romero**, mother of Celino, the third generation of the famed Romero Guitar Family. Before this, Priti had only sung in community and church choirs, and the UCSD Concert Choir.

Romero discovered an operatic voice in her pupil and assigned arias. This opened a career possibility Gandhi had never considered. Working full time at a local radio station and aspiring to be an opera singer were not compatible, so she quit her job and moved back home. Her parents agreed to support her for a two year probation to confirm that she was serious about such a commitment. As of 2006, she had put in over a dozen years of dedication and her family is 100 percent behind her.

By going to Ian Campbell, general director of San Diego Opera, and asking him what it took to have an opera career, Priti was taken under the wing of SDO, becoming part of the Chorus and Outreach into the School and Community program for five years, with Campbell as her mentor.

Gandhi has now performed with San Diego Lyric Opera and the Mainly Mozart Festival. In 1999, she made her mainstage debut with Cleveland Lyric Opera as Thisbe in *La Cenerentola*. She was the Mexican Woman in SDO's *A Streetcar Named Desire* (2000), and Second Lady in *The Magic Flute* (2001). Her European debut was as Donna Elvira in *Don Giovanni* (Prague, 2001). The same year she appeared in *Rusalka* with Seattle. 2003–2004 brought Emilia in SDO's *Otello* and Varvara in *Kat'a Kabanová*, plus further roles with Seattle Opera. She made her Met debut in 2005, and was Cinderella for Lyric Opera San Diego in 2006. Stay tuned!

MONTSERRAT VERDUGO, born in Tijuana, Mexico, December 31, 1980, is the daughter of an insurance agent and an Art History teacher. She was first introduced to music through piano lessons at fifteen, although at the time she was devoting much effort training as a competitive swimmer. In 2004, she received her undergraduate degree from San Diego State University, followed in 2005 with an international business degree from CETYS University, Tijuana.

Meanwhile, in 2001, she got her first serious taste of music in her school choir. While this did not last long, she was able to get into another choir devoted to Sacred Music. Their first performance was Handel's *Messiah*, next came Mozart's *Requiem*, Bach choral works and Vivaldi's *Gloria*—a great start to classical immersion.

She joined the Tijuana Opera Chorus in 2004 during the Primero Festival de Opera en la Calle (First Festival of Opera on the Streets). The same year, she performed in *Don Pasquale*. In 2005, she was again in the chorus for *Romeo and Juliette*, under the direction of **Teresa Rodríguez.** (See Conductors.) Verdugo was also artistic coordinator for Tijuana Opera in this production, working with Maria Teresa Rique, a strong cultural promoter of opera in this border city with San Diego.

As of this writing, Montserrat continues studying vocal technique with renowned tenor José Medina, a good foundation for a blossoming career.

Unusual Voices, Singular Careers

A Gift from the Angels

Until the year 2000, **CYNTHIA LEIGH KARP** was a forty-year-old homemaker, wife of financial consultant Peter, mother of Brandon, born 1990, and Emma, 1994, and for seventeen years engaged in a vital vocation as a registered nurse specializing in oncology, in charge of a large staff, dealing daily with death and the dying. But a new destiny beckoned this woman based on two unique blessings, a voice with high notes that can transcend from a whisper to a shimmering cascade of ethereal elation, and a husband utterly devoted to her and the idea that she should become an opera star! With singular dedication, Peter Karp has taken charge of his wife's new career as a managing partner and founder of EMBRA Artists Management, LTD, an agency managing opera talent.

Born in Patterson, California, April 10, 1958, the oldest of three sisters, Cynthia developed an early interest in singing and dancing, and participating in musical theater from schooldays to community and professional companies, until 1998 when her opera training began.

Her list of coaches is impressive: Charles Riecker, who retired in 1997 after a four decade career at the Met; William Hicks, assistant Met conductor (1995–2001); Gregory Buchalter, Met chorus master; William Vendice, chorus master for Los Angeles Opera; **Georgetta Psaros** in San Diego; and **Rose Baum Senerchia-Kingsley**, one of this country's leading voice teachers, founder/director of the Opera Institute of California (San Jose). She was the only ballet dancer to perform with the Met and then return to its stage as a singer!

In five years, Cynthia's performances have included Frasquita (*Carmen*, October 2002, Monterrey Opera), recital with Georgette Psaros at Sherwood Hall (La Jolla, California, March 2003), soloist, Verdi *Requiem* (April 2003, Los Angeles), recital with baritone Gregorio Gonzalez—protégé of Plácido Domingo—(Center for the Performing Arts, Escondido, California, October, 2003), Queen of the Night (Cabrillo Opera, Santa Cruz, California, April 2004), Rosario in Granados' *Goyescas*, (Lyric Opera LA, October 2004), Laodice in Offenbach's *Les Pont des Soupirs*, (Pocket Opera, San Francisco, May 2005), Ilia in *Idomeneo* (California Music Festival, Walnut Creek, August 2005), Manon (Lyric Opera LA, January 2006), and the title role in *Lucia Di Lammermoor* (Capitol Opera Sacramento, February 2006).

Audience and patron recognition are gathering momentum, and national and international auditions are on the calendar for this exciting new voice.

Songstress of the Classical Popular

Joan Morris & William Bolcom

Away from opera, certain genres of what was once considered popular music have now become "classics." This covers hundreds of turn of the 20th century ballads like *Good Bye, My Lady Love* (1904) and *Love's Old Sweet Song* (1884), tunes of the '20s and '30s, Tin Pan Alley, Ziegfeld *Follies*, George White's *Scandals*, *Gaieties* and other variety shows, plus songs of better known composers such as **Vincent Youmans** (1898–1946), **Sigmund Romberg** (1887–1951), **Victor Herbert** (1851–1924), **Jerome Kern** (1885–1945), originator of the first show with a plot—based on Edna Ferber's novel, *Showboat* (1929), **Cole Porter** (1891–1964), to the early revues of **Richard Rodgers** (1902–79) and **Lorenz Hart** (1895–43), as well as countless musical films. Singing these favorites in a sweet strong voice, which has been compared to torch singer **Ruth Etting** (1896–1978), and clarity of diction reminiscent of Julie Andrews, is mezzo-soprano **JOAN MORRIS**.

Born February 2, 1943, in Portland, Oregon, Joan attended Gonzaga University in Spokane, Washington, before her scholarship studies at the American Academy of Dramatic Arts in New York. With her 1988 Pulitzer Prize winning composer/pianist husband **William Bolcom*** (*b* 1938), who has contributed his own cabaret songs with lyricist Arnold Weinstein, Joan has, for the last thirty years, brought a treasure trove of this uniquely American music to audiences around the world. This musical heritage is preserved on over two dozen recordings.

The couple's international engagements have thus far extended to London, Moscow, Lisbon, Cairo, Istanbul and Florence. Having performed at Tanglewood, Spoleto (USA) and Ravinia, among many festivals, their appearance at the 2003 La Jolla SummerFest, where Bolcom was composer-in-residence, brought a memorably nostalgic concert to yet another delighted audience—which included this author and her husband.

Bolcom and Morris reside in Ann Arbor, Michigan, where Bill has been on the faculty of the University of Michigan School of Music since 1973, and Joan since 1981. Literally brought together by a friend acting as a matchmaker, Bill and Joan were introduced to each other in 1972, while she was singing in the Waldorf Astoria's

Peacock Alley. Bill, who, along with his composing, was playing ragtime gigs, wrote a song for Joan. Before long he became her accompanist and the rest is history. Their thirtieth wedding anniversary fell November 28, 2005.

The 2006 Grammy for best classical recording (a Naxos three-disk set) was awarded to Bolcom's *Songs of Innocence and of Experience*, (A Musical Illumination of the Poems of William Blake). Joan is featured as one of the soloists. *Bolcom was named Composer of the Year by *Musical America*, 2007.

A Voice of Her Own

Linda Hohenfeld

Many women through the ages have had to live in the shadow of a prominent husband, but a few have attained their own place in the sun. Soprano **LINDA HOHENFELD** who consistently receives reviews praising the clarity of her voice, its crystalline tonality, exquisite delicacy and floating high notes, has managed to forge such a niche, despite being wed to one of the world's major maestros, Leonard Slatkin, whose tenures include the St. Louis Symphony (1979–96), and National Symphony (1996–2007).

Born in Cleveland to unmusical parents, between her grandmother's piano and the radio, she developed a love for classical music. Teaching herself violin, she was in her junior and senior high school orchestras. She received a double degree in music performance and education from Kent State (Ohio), and after summer stock in her home town, made her way to the Big Apple in 1978. Supporting herself by working in a music store and giving guitar and piano lessons, she gradually won singing roles. It was through the Kennedy Center run of the musical *Barnum* she met her future husband.

Continuing her career, Hohenfeld debuted with the Cleveland Orchestra at the 1990 Blossom Festival, returning there July 2002 to sing selections from Leonard Bernstein's *Wonderful Town*. With the National Symphony, under Zdeněk Mácal, she sang in Carl Orff's *Carmina Burana* at Wolf Trap. She appeared with the NSO at Carnegie Hall and, following 9/11, Kennedy Center's televised "Concert for America," September 24, 2001, singing the 5th movement of Mahler's 2nd Symphony with **Frederica von Stade**. Other engagements have been with the Minnesota, Philadelphia, San Francisco, St. Louis, Pittsburgh, and New York Philharmonic orchestras; in Europe with the BBC Symphony, City of Birmingham and Philharmonia (London) orchestras, where she soloed in Vaughan Williams' *Sinfonia Antartica*; as well as in Paris, Berlin, Hamburg and Vienna. At the National Museum of Women in the Arts,[200] March 2002, she appeared with five NSO women principals —concert mistress Nurit Bar-Josef, violinist Carol Tafoya, violist Mahoko Eguchi, cellist Yvonne Caruthers, flutist Toshiko Kohno and pianist James Tocco, singing works of Saint-Saëns, Roussel, Fauré and Ravel's exotic "Chansons Madecasses," sung in impeccable French. The program closed with a Broadway style rendition of Jerome Kern songs.

Her festival appearances include Cabrillo, Marlboro, Blossom, Aspen, Great Lakes Chamber Music where she sang the challenging Samuel Barber's *Hermit Songs*, and Copenhagen's Tivoli. In Japan, she has appeared in several televised concerts with the NHK Symphony.

Among her recordings are Vaughan Williams' Symphonies 1, 3 and 7; Bernstein's *Songfest*, Barber's *Knoxville: Summer of 1915*. She was a soloist on the 2006 Grammy Award winning *Songs of Innocence and of Experience*, by William Bolcom, the University of Michigan Symphony conducted by Leonard Slatkin,

Married to Leonard since March 29, 1986, son Daniel was born May 16, 1994. 2006 marked their twentieth anniversary!

A Pioneer of India

LAKSHMI (LAKSHMINARAYANA) **SHANKAR**, one of the foremost and well-known vocalists of India, was born in 1950, in Madras. Her initial training in the North Indian tradition was from Ustad Abdul Rehman Khan

---

200. Linda is co-artistic director with Gilan Tocco Corn, of the Shenson Chamber Music Concerts at the National Museum of Women in the Arts.

of the Patiala Gharana style. Later studies were with such masters as Professor B.R. Deodhar and sitar maestro **Pandit Ravi Shankar**, whom she assisted in many of his projects for ballets, films, concerts and festivals.

Her rich, melodious voice has been called "heavenly, sweet and clear," imbuing a sense of proportion and emotional qualities that have kept her in the forefront of popular vocalists for over fifty years.

Lakshmi is the first Indian classical vocalist considered a pioneer in popularizing her country's vocal music in the West. With numerous recordings to her credit—a praised Delos album is "Evening Concert"—she has lent her voice to many films, including the 1982 Academy Award-winning *Gandhi*, directed by Sir Richard Attenborough, starring Ben Kingsley and a top British and Indian cast.

Shankar is a recipient of the U.S. Durfee Foundation Award to teach Indian music to American students.

Music of Mohammed

UMM KULTHUM (sometimes spelled Omm Kalthum), is known as the "Star of the East" and "Empress of Arab tunes." Born in the Egyptian village of Tamayet-el-Zahayra in 1908, with a remarkable voice range, her career began dressed as a boy because virtuous maidens did not sing in public. In 1924, she moved to Cairo, where her concerts developed a cult following which has not diminished to this day. She rejected modern singing for Arab classical melodies that celebrated the Muslim faith. At a time when there was little worldwide focus on the religion, she kept alive the Islamic heritage and poetry of the desert. Her lyrics held such a sway over her people that during World War II both the Allies and the Axis (Germany, Italy, Japan) broadcast programs to the Middle East utilizing her records.

When Gamal Abdel Nasser (1918–70) became president of Egypt in 1956, he established a close relationship with Kulthum. Her voice became as important as his speeches. Important news items were broadcast before her concerts, and she became a national symbol of Egypt.

During the 1950s and '60s, she was the toast of Cairo, a national heroine, and was named "Ambassadress of Arabic Arts." She appeared in many films. She also became spokeswoman for various causes, advocated government support of Arabic music and musicians, endowed charitable foundations and donated proceeds from her concerts to the Egyptian government. Although she died in 1975, her voice continues to stir hearts in the Arab world and her records outsell every other Arabic female vocalist.

A film documentary of her life, *Umm Kulthum, A Voice Like Egypt*, narrated by Omar Sharif, was produced by Michal Goldman, based on the book *The Voice of Egypt: Umm Kulthum, Arabic Song, and Egyptian Society in the Twentieth Century* by Virginia Louise Danielson (University of Chicago Press, 1997).

Utterly Unique!

Yma Sumac

YMA SUMAC, given name Zoila Augusta Emperatriz Chavarri del Castillo, was born September 10, 1927 in Ichocán, Peru. Rumors are still circulated that she was an Inca princess, a direct descendant of Atahualpa, the last emperor of the Incas, a Golden Virgin of the Sun God, worshipped by the Quechua Indians. A self-taught voice of phenomenal range (reported to be five octaves), she toured South America in the early 1940s, then settled in the U.S. where she became a naturalized citizen in 1955. She married Moises Vivanco in 1947. They had one son, Charles, born in 1949. She performed with Vivanco's combo, Conjunto Folklorica Peruano, until she was contracted by Capitol Records in 1950, launching a flamboyant international career.

With her extraordinary voice conveying the gamut of emotions and tonal color, her Capitol recordings singing exotic "Hollywoodized" versions of Incan and South American folk songs made her an icon of the '50s. In 1951, she was featured in the Broadway musical *Flahooley*, followed by two films: *Secret of the Incas* (1954) and *Omar Khayyam* (1957). She divorced Moises in 1957, but remarried him for their six-month Russian tour in 1961 as the

"Inca Taki Trio," with his cousin Cholita Rivero as back-up vocalist and Vivanco on guitar. (Two years later they divorced again, but continued to collaborate.) Concertizing and recording went on through the early '70s, after which she returned to Peru to compose many of the songs used in later performances. In the 1980s, she came back to Los Angeles, giving concerts through that decade. In March 1990, she appeared as Heidi in Stephen Sondheim's *Follies* in Long Beach, California. Last confirmed appearances were several concerts in 1996 in San Francisco, and in 1997 at the Montreal (Canada) International Jazz Festival.

Yma Sumac claimed to be inspired from childhood by birdsongs. Five of her many immortal recordings have been reissued on Capitol CDs. The most famous titles are: *Voice of Xtabay, Legend of the Sun Virgin, Mambo, Legend of the Jivaro* and *Fuego Del Andes.*

Women Cantors

Vicki Axe

Roslyn Barak

Deborah Bard

Arlene Bernstein

Lori Corrsin

Marin Cosman

Rebecca Garfein

Kay Greenwald

Gail Hirschenfang

Sharon Kohn

Martha Novick

Barbara Ostfield

Alisa Pomerantz-Boro

Helene Reps

Sue Roemer

Judith Kahan Rowland

Sarah Sager

Benji Ellen Schiller

As women were gradually able to raise their voices in the churches or convents, it took more centuries for them to be heard in synagogues. The last twenty-five years has seen an explosion of women clergy in Protestant denominations, while as early as 1846, in a convention in Breslau (Germany), the Jewish Reform movement voted more equality for women. There appeared to be no rush to follow up on this new freedom, and whereas it may be assumed that after this many women sang from pulpits, it was without training, let alone ordination. The first woman rabbi, **Regina Jonas**, was ordained in Berlin in 1935, but perished in Auschwitz. As of 2001, a Swiss woman rabbi, Bea Weiler, who had studied in the U.S., was traced to Oldenburg, Germany. There are also a few women rabbis in France and several in England. An 1855 article pointed out that men and women singing in choirs together was sure to have "immoral consequences." One hundred and two years later, in 1957, when a woman appeared on the Ed Sullivan Show singing sacred songs in celebration of Jewish Music Month, there was great protest from the Executive Council of the Cantors Assembly.

Music plays a large role in Jewish religious services. The cantor (*hazzan*) leads the congregation in prayer. Professional cantors are ordained clergy, who perform many pastoral duties once confined to rabbis, such as conducting weddings, funerals and boy and girl confirmations (*Bar* and *Bat Mitzahs*), visiting the sick and teaching youth and adult education classes. Larger synagogues hire professional cantors, with both musical skills and training as a religious leader and educator. In Reform Judaism, in the U.S., **Barbara Ostfeld** of New York was the first woman invested as a cantor. That was 1975. Until her first cantorate at Temple Beth-El, in the affluent Long Island suburb of Great Neck, New York (1976–1988), no seminary-trained woman had stepped into a cantorial pulpit. The conservative movement waited another ten years to ordain a woman rabbi (1985) and a cantor in 1987. According to Mark Slobin, in his book *Chosen Voices*, Orthodox men still subscribe to the mindset of women as "sirens," but predictions in both Judeo and Christian religions, other than Roman Catholic or Jewish Orthodox, point to a 50 percent female clergy in the not too distant future.

The women here are a sampling of cantors across the country, many of them introduced to the author by San Francisco-based **Roslyn Barak**.

VICKI AXE was the first woman cantor elected president of the American Conference of Cantors (ACC), and the only person to serve two successive terms (1991–95). She was cantor and music director of the Greenwich (Connecticut) Reform Synagogue 1997–2003.

Born August 17, 1948, in Newton, Massachusetts, into a very musical family, the youngest of three daughters, she cannot remember when she didn't sing. Harmonizing with her sisters and choral singing were her first loves, which led her to a music teaching career. Religion being an important part of her life, it was when she was twenty-nine and pregnant with her first child that she realized that the cantorate combined all her talents, skills and loves—teaching, performing, caring for people, as well as Jewish learning and practice.

She received her B. Mus. Ed. from Temple University (Philadelphia, 1965) and MA in music education from Ohio State University (Columbus, 1971). She held subsequent teaching positions in Ohio, Massachusetts, Israel and New York. Her Sacred Music degree and investiture as a cantor came in 1983 from Hebrew Union College-Jewish Institute of Religion School of Sacred Music (HUC-JIR, SSM), where she is now a member of the advisory council and served on the faculty, 1986–88.

After her marriage to allergist Dr. Harold Axe, 1971, they spent two years in Israel, arriving October 8, 1973, just two days after the "Yom Kippur War" began. While there, Axe studied Hebrew, taught English as a second language to Israeli children, music at the American International School and sang in the Israeli National Opera.

As a conductor and teacher, Axe is on the faculty of the North American Jewish Choral Festival, and directed a 100-voice children's choir for the 1999 Council of Churches and Synagogues Celebration of Choirs. She was co-founding director of a community choir in Columbus, Ohio, where she served as cantor and music director of Temple Israel, 1988–97. She has presented workshops on Jewish choral music to public school music teachers, conducted regional and national choirs at UAHC conventions and conferences, and been composer-in-residence in many congregations across the U.S. She also taught at the Academy for Jewish Religion in New York City, 2000–2001.

Performing in Israel, Canada and America, she was guest soloist with the Connecticut Chamber Orchestra and the Columbus Symphony, performing with Marvin Hamlisch, and was soprano soloist with Dave Brubeck in a performance of his cantata, *The Gates of Justice*, which she also produced.

The recipient of many awards, Cantor Axe served for many years on the National Commission on Synagogue Music, as well as the Executive Committee of the Union of American Hebrew Congregations (UAHC). Besides her presidencies of the ACC, she is also a past president of the School of Sacred Music Cantonal Alumni Association, and as of 1995 has been on the National Commission on Religious Living and an officer of the Greenwich Fellowship of Clergy.

In 2003, she became the founding spiritual leader of Congregation Shir Ami in Stamford (Connecticut), where she officiates at services and life-cycle events, directs and teaches in the religious school and provides pastoral care.

Vicki lives in Stamford with her husband. They have four sons, Judah, born September 1, 1978, Noah, July 5, 1981, Gabriel, June 13, 1984, and Daniel, May 30, 1987.

Roslyn Barak

ROSLYN BARAK has served Congregation Emanu-El of San Francisco since 1987, one year after her graduation and investiture from Hebrew Union College.

Born March 2, 1950, in Forest Hills, Long Island (New York), Roslyn was a shy child with a lovely voice. She started piano early, sang in school choirs, including the enriching High School of Music and Art, now located in Lincoln Center, where she took up the violin, and from which she graduated in 1967 with a solid repertoire of Italian art songs, lieder and French chansons, plus operatic arias and ensemble singing, helped by a natural proficiency for languages. In the course of earning her BM at the Manhattan School of Music (1972), she had summer apprenticeships at Santa Fe Opera (New Mexico), and won the Minna Kaufman Ruud Foundation and Liederkranz Awards, as well as a Katherine Long scholarship to the Met Opera Studio. Her coaches included Otto Guth and William Taussig. She also made her Carnegie Hall debut with the Youth Symphony of New York, having won their competition for soprano soloist. After a year of freelancing in concerts and opera productions in New York, she was offered a contract to the Israel National Opera. During her three years in Israel, she became a known concert artist. She also married and gave birth to a son, Danny, born October 31, 1975. Her return to New York marked more performances, and for the first time she sang in the choir of a synagogue, Sha'aray Tefila, a Reform congregation on the Upper East Side. The experience convinced Roslyn that she wanted to become a cantor. Despite financial hardships, and already in her mid-thirties, she became a full-time student at HUC, graduating in 1986 with an all-woman class of eight. Her student "pulpit"—the term for a cantorial position—began in 1983, at Temple Isaiah in Forest Hills. She remained there a year after her investiture. San Francisco's Temple Emanu-El had been searching for a cantor for over two years. Barak was last in the pool, but her audition easily won her the position. She returned to school in 1994 to pursue a degree in psychology, and received her MA in clinical psychology in 1996.

Aside from her numerous cantorial duties, Barak appears regularly in concerts around the country and in Europe and Israel. She performed with the Sinfonia of San Francisco in 1990 in celebration of Kurt Weill's ninetieth birthday, and toured Germany in conjunction with the 1995 release of her much-lauded CD, *The Jewish Soul*. Sought after as a lecturer and scholar-in-residence, Barak has taught master classes at the North American Jewish Choral Festival, the Cantors Assembly Western Region conference, at Boston Hebrew College, as well as seminars at HUC. She served as chairperson of the ACC Publications Committee, and their representative to the Commission on Synagogue Music of the UAHC. As of 2000, she is on the Commission on Cantorial-Congregational Relations of the ACC/UAHC.

To celebrate Temple Emanu-El's 140th anniversary, 1990, Barak commissioned Canadian composer Ben Steinberg to create the first Sabbath morning service for female voice. *Avodat Hakodesh* (Sacred Service), features choir, organ and wind instruments, and also celebrates the lovely soprano register of this cantor's voice. In 1994, she commissioned a set of choral works, *The Consolations of Isaiah*, from composer Ami Aloni, who also wrote a magnificent version of the Alvin Fine text, *Birth is a Beginning*, for cello, organ and choir in celebration of Rabbi Fine's eightieth birthday. Barak considers these and future commissions to be some of her most vital contributions. In 2005 Barak was honored on her fifteenth anniversary at Congregation Emanu-El with the release of two CDs of her singing with the temple choirs.

DEBORAH BARD joined KAM Isaiah Israel, in the Hyde Park section of Chicago, in 1996, returning after many years on both coasts to the city where she was born October 2, 1954, into a musical family. When she was ten, the family moved to Long Beach, California. Her mother, Anita Jordan, a Juilliard graduate, had been a professional singer, performing with such greats as Serge Koussevitzky and Leonard Bernstein. As of 2002, she still had a voice studio in Long Beach.

A graduate of Berkeley (BA, Humanities, 1977), Bard embarked upon a career of religious teaching, meanwhile working towards graduate degrees from San Francisco State University in vocal performance (1977–78), and NYU towards an MA in creative arts education (1980 and '84). In June 1985, she received her BS in sacred music from HUC and was invested as a cantor.

Her student cantor years were spent in New Brunswick, New Jersey, and the North Country Reform Temple in Glen Cove, Long Island. 1985–90 marked her first pulpit at Community Synagogue in Rye, New York. From 1990–91, she was director of children's music and b'nai mitzvah studies at Riverdale Temple in the Bronx, then onto the West Coast to Congregation Beth Israel, San Diego, 1992–95, where she was succeeded by **Arlene Bernstein**, and moved on to her present position at KAM Isaiah Israel.

Bard has sung with the Berkeley Chamber Singers, Oakland Symphony Chorus, Los Angeles Master Chorale, San Francisco Symphony Chorus and *Sine Nomine Singers* in New York. Her soloist career includes Esther in the contemporary opera *Isaac Levi* by Raymond Smolover, and productions such as *Israel in Song*, *Shtetl to Broadway*, and *Kol Esha: The Woman's Voice in Jewish Music*, as well as numerous performances in temples and benefit programs like those for Hadassah Brandeis Women. Several CDs and videos attest to her talent. The 1992 release *of Holiday Songs Kids Love to Sing* continues as a bestselling recording.

Cantor Deborah married Rabbi Michael Sternfield of the Chicago Sinai Congregation in 1995. She has a daughter Rachelpenina, "RP" Whitmore-Bard, born February 9, 1988.

A celebration was held May 25, 2005, on her tenth anniversary with KAMII.

Arlene Bernstein

ARLENE BERNSTEIN is a native of Washington, DC. A graduate of the New England Conservatory, she has performed with the Ra'anana Symphony and the Jerusalem Symphony, and was principal bassoon with the Kibbutz Chamber Orchestra of Israel. She was a member of the faculty of the All Newton Music School, where she taught bassoon and was chair of the woodwind department, and the New England Conservatory Preparatory School. She has also been part of a Klezmer[201] band. In May 1993, she received her master's in sacred music from the HUC and was invested as a cantor. Her first position was at the Suburban Temple in Wantagh, Long Island, New York (1993–97).

Bernstein has given recitals in Washington, DC, New York, Toronto, and Jerusalem. A specialist in Sephardic music, she was a featured guest of renowned Israeli musicologist Dr. Edwin Seroussi, at a lecture series in Merkin Recital Hall, New York City. Since 1998, she has served as cantor of Congregation Beth Israel in San Diego, California.

LORI CORRSIN came into the world, November 16, 1954, in Detroit, Michigan, in a family that included professional musicians. She began piano at six, went on to the violin and flute and, after hearing her first charla concert at age ten, began to study voice. She received a BM in choral music (U. of Michigan, Ann Arbor, 1975), then moved to New York City where she established a career as a classical concert pianist. Concurrently, earning her master's degree from HUC (1992), she was invested as a cantor and served Larchmont Temple in New York for seven years. Moving back to Michigan, she served at Temple Israel in West Bloomfield as co-cantor with Harold Orbach. Corrsin's concert appearances have included Detroit, Princeton, New York City, Chicago, Albany, Baltimore, Dallas and Los Angeles. She was honored to be chosen to chant from the Torah at the Biennial Convention of UAHC and to be the officiating cantor at the HUC Founder's Day ceremonies. Her composition, *Shehecheyanu* (He Who Revives Us), was published by Transcontinental Music Publications. She is featured on the CD *Nashir B'Yachad B'nei mitzvah* (Let's Sing Together). In May 2004, she joined Temple Emanu-El, New York.

Married to Stephen D. Corrsin, PhD, they have a daughter, Alexandra, born May 1992.

Marin Cosman

MARIN COSMAN is the only entry in this section who is not an official cantor. Born in New York, October 24, 1961, of a prominent medical law professor/medievalist author mother, Madeleine (1937–2006), and surgeon father (1931–83), as a child she was constantly singing. This got her into the Preparatory Division at Manhattan School of Music from age eight to sixteen. She performed throughout her school years. A BA in Judaic studies from Yale (1984) was followed with a masters in voice and opera performance from the Manhattan School (1988). Her career took off as a soloist with opera companies and orchestras coast to coast, including Chautauqua, New York; Santa Fe, New Mexico, Opera Ensemble; Yale Bach Society; Tanglewood Chamber Orchestra; and recitals in San Diego, California. Her performances have benefitted Brandeis University, Hadassah, the Jewish Womens' Social Service Organization, and Agency for Jewish Education. Opting for a more traditional vocation, Marin became a practicing attorney after obtaining a law degree from the University of Chicago (1995), where she performed for several fund raisers and the Law School Centennial. She continued to sing at charitable functions, and for three years was cantorial soloist at Congregation Beth El in La Jolla, California.

---

201. Klezmer - music of East European Jews - with violin, clarinet, bass, drums, and assorted instruments, depending on the size of the band.

Love and marriage relocated Marin to New York City, where she performs concerts of Jewish music, crossover opera-cabaret concerts, plus lecture-recitals on opera, popular music, and Jewish liturgical music.

A native of Tallahassee, Florida, **REBECCA GARFEIN** is since 1999 senior cantor of Congregation Rodeph Sholom in New York City, the first female to hold this position. She graduated cum laude from Rice University's Shepherd School of Music. In 1993, she received her master's in sacred music and cantorial investiture from HUC. The first woman invited to participate in the Jewish Cultural Festival in Berlin (1997), the recording *Sacred Chants of the Contemporary Synagogue*, was made of the concert. The following year, Garfein again became the first female cantor to preside in a German synagogue. She has appeared in numerous recitals throughout the U.S., Israel and Europe. 2005 featured a Weill Recital (Carnegie) Hall concert, "Golden Chants in America," commemorating 350 years of Jewish music (1654–2004), from Spanish-Portuguese, to synagogue, Yiddish and Broadway theater—preserved on CD.

KAY GREENWALD was born in Clearfield, Pennsylvania, March 23, 1958. Her father, who emigrated from Germany with his sister and parents in 1939 when he was fourteen, played violin, mandolin and accordion. He had a lovely voice, sang folk songs, and loved opera and symphonic music. There was always a record playing. Kay used to sit on her father's lap and sing along. She picked up the guitar at age seven, to accompany her own singing as her father had done with his mandolin. She studied guitar until the middle of high school, then gave it up and started voice lessons.

She grew up in Claremont, California, attended Pomona College, receiving a BA in classical studies in 1981, after which she entered Eastman. She earned an MM in voice performance and went to Europe where she became a member of the Opera Studio at Vienna State Opera (1984–85), then stayed on appearing on Austrian radio and television, as well as in opera houses and concert halls throughout the country. Back in the U.S. by 1986, while still continuing her opera career, Greenwald chose to combine her love of Judaism and Hebrew with her love of music.

After two years at Graz College, Philadelphia, during which time she honored remaining performance contracts in California and Florida, she transferred to the School of Sacred Music at Hebrew Union College and earned a master of sacred music degree. She was invested as a cantor in 1992.

Moving to Northern California, she became assistant cantor at Congregation Beth Am in Los Altos Hills, south of San Francisco. After four years, she was promoted to associate cantor. In 1998, the senior cantor became emeritus and Greenwald became cantor.

She has been honored by the ACC by being asked to sing at their conventions in Jerusalem (1998), Beverly Hills (2000) and Washington, DC (2001). There, she also recorded a CD of the José Bowen Klezmer Shabbat Service with five other cantors.

Kay married Leland M. Greenwald, MD, May 1987. They have a son, William Walter, born May 16, 1993.

GAIL P. HIRSCHENFANG is cantor and education director of Congregation Shir Chadash in Poughkeepsie, New York. Invested in 1981 from the Hebrew Union College School of Sacred Music, her master's came in 1988. She also holds a BS in mathematics. A finalist in the 1985 Metropolitan Opera auditions, she has performed in the U.S. and Canada. She was the first reform cantor to give a concert at the newly opened Jewish Cultural Center in Moscow (1989). On the board of directors of the ACC, she is now their chair of endowment. She was also national cantorial chair for the UAHC Commission on Synagogue Music (2000–3). Her 1999 article, "Jewish Music—Setting the Course," is in the centennial publication of the ACC and Guild of Temple Musicians.

Gail is married to Rabbi Daniel F. Polish. They are the parents of Leah Yonina.

SHARON KOHN was born March 23, 1957, in Bloomington, Illinois. Love of music, the arts and all things Jewish were instilled by her parents. A good singing voice, and the desire to make a difference in people's lives, led to the cantorate—especially when she was *encouraged* by her rabbi who told her that the world had enough sopranos, but needed more cantors! She earned

Sharon Kohn

her BM in voice performance at Illinois State, Normal, 1980, and was invested in May 1985. Her master's of sacred music was awarded May 1989 from HUC, New York.

While in New York, she sang the title role in *The Ballad of Ruth*, a one-act opera; was featured in *The Last Judgment*, a cantata based on the story of fictional character Bonche Zweig, by Lazar Weiner; and was a soloist in Handel's *Judas Maccabæus*. Houston premieres included Samuel Adler's *Stars in the Dust*, written for the fiftieth anniversary of *Kristallnacht*,[202] and *Shema: 5 Poems of Primo Levi*, composed by Simon Sargon of Temple Emanu-El of Dallas.

Following investiture, she began serving Congregation Emanu-El in Houston, and was responsible for its music program. Her favorite duties were *Tot Shabbats* (worship experiences for toddlers and their families), the adult volunteer choir, conducting services, working with children—particularly *bar/bat mitzvah* age thirteen—and participating in interfaith ministries. In the fall of 1990, she began serving congregations in Louisiana and Texas. A music specialist for the Irvin M. Shlenker School of Congregation Beth Israel since 1995, she was also active with the Houston Cantorial Association, singing in their annual Cantors' Concert, as well as community-wide gatherings.

Kohn came to Cincinnati's Wise Temple, July 1997, on a part-time basis with a position at the Cincinnati HUC, guiding students in worship and Jewish music. In 2003, a full-time cantorate opened for her at the Temple Congregation B'nai Jehuda in Overland Park, Kansas.

Sharon married financial consultant Rick Simon, December 1989, and became stepmother to his three children, Carra, born 1975, Jason, born 1977, and Joel, born 1980. She now has two granddaughters.

MARTHA NOVICK has been cantor at Temple Emanu-El in Westfield, New Jersey, since 1986. She also teaches music workshops at Hebrew Union College and the Jewish Theological Seminary in Manhattan. Born May 1, 1952, in Orange, New Jersey, her childhood was filled with music, playing second violin in the family quartet with sister Emily on cello, mother at the piano and father as first violin. (At eighty-two in 2001, he was still conducting the South Orange Symphony Orchestra.)

Martha began piano at six, violin at nine, French horn at eleven and voice lessons at fifteen. She received her BS (1975), and MA (1977) from NYU, both in music performance. Motivated by her love of both music and Judaism, she enrolled in the five-year program at Hebrew Union College, getting her bachelor's in sacred music (BSM), and cantorial diploma in 1983. Her first pulpit was at Temple Emanu-El in Edison, New Jersey. Besides her present long time position at the temple of the same name in Westfield, she concertizes throughout the U.S. and has been heard in Toronto, Munich and Israel. She is the mother of Abby, born 1986, also possessed of a beautiful voice, and Seth, born 1989, who thus far has taken piano, trumpet, euphonium, trombone, bassoon, and is still trying to decide on his favorite instrument. One thing is sure. Juilliard is the school for him!

Barbara Ostfeld

BARBARA OSTFELD is history's first woman cantor. She was invested by the Hebrew Union College-Jewish Institute of Religion's School of Sacred Music in June 1975. Her first cantorate was at Temple Beth-El of Great Neck, Long Island, New York (1976–1988). She has served Temple Beth Am of Buffalo, New York, since 1990.

As a little girl, she sang in the temple youth choir. The choraleers had to wear one particular round-collared blouse and one particular black pleated skirt. She remembers her self-consciousness:

---

202. Krystallnacht NIGHT OF BROKEN GLASS, so called from the litter of broken glass left in the aftermath of a night of violence, November 9–10, 1938, against Jewish persons and property in Berlin, was carried out by the Nazis under the guise of "spontaneous demonstrations." The night's toll was ninety-one Jews killed, hundreds injured, thousands terrorized. Some 7,500 Jewish businesses were gutted and 177 synagogues burned or demolished. Police were ordered not to interfere. *Kristallnacht* triggered a major escalation in the Nazi program of Jewish persecution.

I didn't look like the other girls. For one thing my mother cut my hair herself. It was short, very short and unruly. Not the adorable, curly sort of unruly, either. Also I was plump and never so plump as when lined up with two-dozen other rail-thin girls in identical outfits. (I am trying not to remember the brown, gold-flecked, overly optimistic glasses I had to wear.) But I could sing. It didn't transform me by any means; but I could sing better than anyone. As a result I got lots of solos and compliments . . . Also my mother cried every time I sang, which I had learned was a good thing.

Soon the music and the ambience of the synagogue became more important to me.

Synagogues smelled of lemon polish. People were always soft-spoken and dressed up. Beautiful words were read aloud. There was both a rhyme and a reason. When we stood for the ark to be opened, I felt a surge of something. So there it was, I was going to be a cantor when I grew up . . . The decision was made, if not finalized, when I was eight.

Her tolerant parents smiled.

When, as a high school senior, she confided in her cantor and asked where he had gone to cantorial school, he laughed. Nevertheless, she requested an application form for the School of Sacred Music of the Hebrew Union College. The registrar told her over the phone that they had never before had such a request from a woman. That was the first time she realized she was a first.

After auditioning in a small classroom, when she tried to leave she could not get the door open. On the other side were several dozen enthusiastic and supportive rabbinic and cantorial male students who had been straining to listen to her singing.

Five and a half years later, June 1975, she was invested as the first woman cantor by the Hebrew Union College.

Ostfeld has served the American Conference of Cantors as secretary, vice president and Northeast regional representative. She has been a president of the HUC-SSM Student Organization (1974–75) and of the Cantorial Alumni Organization. For two years, she edited an early CAA newsletter called *Shalshelet: The Chain*. A specialist in Early Music with an interest in Judeo-Spanish *romanceros*, she enjoys writing poetry on religious themes.

She has appeared in concerts throughout the U.S. and Israel, can be heard on her own recording, "Hashmiini et Koleich," and was featured on the NBC special "Jerusalem: City of Peace," with Ed Asner.

Barbara married Todd Joseph in 1998. She has two daughters from a previous marriage, Jordana Horowitz, born 1983, and Aleza Horowitz, born 1986.

In 2000, Ostfeld was awarded an honorary doctorate in Sacred Music from Hebrew Union College on the occasion of her twenty-fifth anniversary as a cantor.

ALISA POMERANTZ-BORO grew up on Mercer Island, Washington, in a rabbinic home which instilled a love of Judaism and music. From an early age, she knew she would continue the long family line of rabbis and cantors. Her BA in Near Eastern Studies and Music is from the University of Washington.

She was invested as a *hazzan* (cantor) and earned a degree in sacred Jewish music from the Cantors Institute of the Jewish Theological Seminary of America in New York, where she was awarded the Jacobson Memorial Prize in *Hazzanut*—the art of cantorial singing. While in cantorial school, she held the position of assistant cantor at New York's prestigious Park Avenue Synagogue, where she was mentored by the renowned Cantor David Lefkowitz. Since her investiture, Pomerantz-Boro served as the *hazzan* at Tifereth Israel Synagogue in San Diego. Under her direction, the Tifereth Israel Youth Chorale performed all over California.

In May 1991, she was among the first fourteen women to be inducted into the Cantors Assembly, the professional organization of Conservative cantors. As of 2000, she became co-chair and convention chair of the Western Region. Additionally, she was on the National Executive Council and National Standards Committee of the Cantors Assembly.

Known for her moving renditions of liturgical music, Pomerantz-Boro's vast repertoire ranges from the classics to Broadway songs. She concertizes throughout the country, and was featured in the nationally televised

ABC special, "An Evening I Seek You," and the Showtime documentary, "An American Tapestry." March 2000 saw her debut with the San Diego Symphony in a Jewish Musical Heritage concert, which featured two other local cantors, **Marin Cosman** and **Arlene Bernstein**.

Alisa left Tifereth in the summer of 2004 for a position at Temple Beth El, Cherry Hills, New Jersey.

She is married to Stephen Boro, whom she considers one of the miracles in her life. The others are her daughter, Rebecca, born December 1995 and son Joshua, born (yes!) December 2001.

Upon her retirement from Temple Israel of New Rochelle, New York, **HELENE REPS** became the first woman *cantor emerita* in the U.S.—and perhaps in the world.

She was surrounded by music from her birth, September 27, 1934, in Pittsburgh, through her father, whose brother had been at the Moscow Conservatory. She began piano at age five, and was encouraged in all the arts.

A legacy from the late 19th and early 20th centuries, settlement houses served neighborhoods, much as the "Y" does today, socially and educationally. They helped educate and integrate the masses of immigrants into the American way of life. In Helene's case, the Irene Kaufman Settlement House, run by the Federation of Jewish Philanthropies, was her Sesame Street. Brilliant musicians, refugees from Hitler's Germany who should have been teaching in conservatories, gave their Sundays to the children. Helene learned clarinet, theory, dance, elocution and was immersed in the arts.

Since her mother's family owned a grocery store in Oakdale, outside Pittsburgh, the child was brought up in an irreplaceable small town atmosphere all but lost today. Neighbors went back three generations, knew each other and cared for each other. A crowning memory is of the 100th Anniversary celebrations of Oakdale in 1992, when her mother—ninety-three and still active in 2001—was carried around like a pageant queen.

Helene's charmed childhood continued in the 1940s and '50s, with summer music camp at Saranac Lake in New York's Adirondack Mountains as, from ages nine to twenty, she worked her way up from camper to counselor. Her college career began as a piano major at Carnegie-Mellon, then known as the Carnegie Institute of Technology. After two years, her solfeggio teacher persuaded her to change to voice. She won the student auditions and was alto soloist in the *Requiem* at a Mozart Festival with the Pittsburgh Symphony under William Sternberg. When she graduated in 1957, her voice was fully developed. A summer at Aspen had famed opera star **Jennie Tourel** (1900–73) urging her to pursue a singing career, but at this time in her life romance came first. On August 10, 1958, she married David Reps, who in 1980 became an economics professor at Pace College, in Pleasantville, New York. They had four children. Tamara, born July 11, 1959, Aaron, December 20, 1960, and twins, Steven and Jennifer, August 29, 1964. Her grandchildren score was up to seven in 2001.

Moving to Westchester County outside New York City in 1967, Reps sang in many concerts of renaissance and baroque music. She also began teaching in her local Reform Temple in White Plains. It was in 1974 that a friend suggested she go to cantorial school. Helene followed Barbara Ostfeld's ground breaking, and was invested from HUC in 1979. At that time, graduates did not have to go to Israel—later a first year requirement. Her student pulpit had been near her home in Rye. By 1980, she was accepted by Temple Israel in New Rochelle in her own neighborhood. She served for seventeen and a half years, retiring in 1997 to "make room in her own life," catching up with her grandchildren, where on many occasions her duties had necessitated her absence from her own children's birthday parties and such. She still teaches twice a week at a neighboring temple, and is rewarded for all her years of service when loyal congregants seek *her* to officiate at bar/bat mitzvahs and weddings.

SUE ROEMER has been a part of the Temple Beth Ami of Rockville (Maryland) staff since 1976. She began teaching music and prayer in the religious school and eventually combined her musical and teaching talents by becoming the cantor and director of music. Active in the Jewish community locally and nationally, she conducts workshops which include Jewish prayer, spirituality and music, as well as singing Jewish music in senior facilities.

Besides being one of the founders of CAJE (Conference on Alternatives in Jewish Education) and the Women Cantors Network, she started a JCC community chorus in 1971, which she has continuously directed since that time.

Roemer was the first woman to participate in conducting services at the national Rabbinic Assembly convention, which helped to pave the way for women to be accepted as cantors in the conservative movement. For several years, she has been part of an ecumenical group of clergy involved in educating the public regarding cults. She has taken part in many interfaith services, including those involving "issues for women's rights."

Sue is part of the Fabrangen Fiddlers, a group of five musicians whose music is known around the world.

JUDITH KAHAN ROWLAND was born March 3, 1956, in Lima, Ohio. Her childhood was filled with religious music as her father, a Reform rabbi, served several congregations. Her paternal grandfather was a cantor in Russia and, after immigrating to the U.S. in 1923, served in Omaha, Cleveland and Brooklyn. Judi began piano lessons at age five . . . "thanks to my mother but, I am told, I showed significant musical skills in pre-school, always getting to play the drum at 'instrument time' because I could keep a beat." Throughout her schooldays, she sang in her synagogue's Junior Choir and school choruses. Her older sister, Sylvia Kahan, a professional pianist, often accompanied her. Judi started studying voice in her senior year of high school (1973–74). After majoring in music and Judaic studies at SUNY, Binghamton (1974–76), she transferred to the Hebrew Union College- Jewish Institute of Religion, School of Sacred Music in Manhattan. Her teachers included Marlena Malas, Judith Oas, Susan Ormont in New York, and Ruth Drucker in Baltimore. She was invested as cantor in 1981, joining the ranks of only eleven women in the reform cantorate at that time.

She began her cantorate at Baltimore Hebrew Congregation in 1996, after having served Long Island (New York) congregations in Forest Hills, Oceanside and Spring Valley. In Baltimore, she oversees coordination of all worship services, administration of a *b'nei mitzvah* (preparing for confirmation) program of over 100 students, conducts adult and youth choirs, teaches in the day and religious schools and offers pastoral, spiritual and educational guidance within congregational life.

After serving as secretary (1992–93) and vice president (1993–95) of the American Conference of Cantors, she was elected president (1995–1998), and interim president (2000–2001). The ACC is the national body representing the North American professional Reform cantorate. Rowland's leadership role has had a major impact on the growth and recognition of the profession. She has also served on several national committees, including the Commission on Synagogue Music and the Joint Cantorial Placement Commission. As of 2000, she is on the UAHC Joint Commission on Religious Living and the HUC-JIR School of Sacred Music Advisory Council. She was featured in the cover article on the cantorate in the summer 1999 issue of *Reform Judaism Magazine*.

A highly sought after speaker and performer, Rowland has concertized extensively throughout the U.S. Spring 2001 saw her as a featured soloist with the Handel Choir and Baltimore Symphony in their premiere performance of *Israel in Egypt*.

A product of the Reform Movement and its camps, she began her career as a songleader for her National Federation of Temple Youth (NFTY) Region on Long Island and in several UAHC camps. She met her Londoner husband, Michael Rowland, an advertising executive at Eisner Communications in Baltimore, at the UAHC Eisner Camp in Great Barrington, Massachusets. They were married December 23, 1978. Their two children are Rachel, a New Year's Day baby, born 1983, and Benjamin, born February 27, 1986. She celebrated her fiftieth birthday in 2006 surrounded by the love of her family and congregation.

Sarah Sager

SARAH SAGER was born August 28, 1949, in Chicago, into a Conservative Jewish home. She says she became a cantor by accident!

I was actually pursuing both opera and the cantorate for a time. I didn't really take the cantorate seriously at first —I thought of it as a "gig" whereby I could support myself. I learned fairly quickly, however, that it was a wonderful feeling to be able to serve my people, to help to strengthen my faith and to be appreciated for what I was doing, all at the same time. It provided me with a very different experience from the highs and lows of pursuing an opera career. In a relatively short time, I abandoned my operatic aspirations in favor of the challenge, fulfillment and total involvement of the cantorate.

A Phi Beta Kappa and *magna cum laude* graduate of Brown University (Rhode Island), she holds a MM from the New England Conservatory and was invested by the Hebrew Union College-Jewish Institute of Religion, School of Sacred Music in New York in 1978, following shortly after pioneer woman cantor **Barbara Ostfeld**.

In addition to her pulpit responsibilities, Sager has sung for the Jewish community in Cleveland as well as Chicago, Boston and New York. She has performed with the prestigious performing group, *Cantica Hebraica*, both here and abroad, and made television and radio appearances. Besides the leading role in the New York premiere of Lazar Weiner's opera *The Golem*, she has, in her many concerts, demonstrated her versatility in liturgical, folk and classical music, Hebrew and Yiddish art songs, as well as musical comedy.

Sought after as a speaker on the topic of Judaism & Feminism, relating to the images of women in Jewish tradition, at the 1993 Biennial Convention of the Women of Reform Judaism in San Francisco her keynote address, *Sarah's Hidden Voice: Recovering and Discovering Women's Spirituality*, was a major contribution. This resulted in a vote by the Women of Reform Judaism to undertake the project of a transformative commentary on the Torah that would include feminist interpretation and scholarship to uncover and recover women's voices from past tradition and enable women to interact freely with sacred texts in the future.

Sager has received many honors for her spiritual leadership, contributions to the Jewish community and the Commission for Women's Equality of the American Jewish Congress. She serves on the board of the American Conference of Cantors and is the ACC representative to the Central Conference of American Rabbis' Committee on Liturgy. She is on the editorial committee of a new clergy manual for the Reform Movement. This marks the first time that the Central Conference of American Rabbis and American Conference of Cantors are undertaking a joint project in this historic committee.

Sarah is married to attorney William R. Joseph, and is the proud mother of Jennifer, born July 14, 1982, and Jonathan, born November 20, 1986.

In 2005, Cantor Sager celebrated her twenty-fifth anniversary with Anshe Chesed Fairmount Temple, (Beachwood, Ohio). The milestone was marked with a year-long celebration of concerts, lectures and a formal gala. She has been awarded a life contract with her congregation.

Benjie Schiller

BENJIE ELLEN SCHILLER is a professor of cantorial arts at Hebrew Union College-Jewish Institute of Religion, School of Sacred Music, in New York, where she trains cantorial students to forge the bridge between performance and spiritual leadership. She was invested as a cantor and received her HUC master's in 1997.

She was born April 14, 1958, in New York, to *non*-musical parents, yet grew up with her brother, Steve, considering music like breathing. One of the neighbors had a piano, which opened up a whole new world when she was five. She followed her musical calling and received her BM in composition from Boston University (1981). Her works include: *V'ye'etayu*; *Grace*; *Life-Song Cycle*, a series of pieces for Jewish life passage ceremonies; *Halleluhu*, a multi-rhythmic setting of Psalm 150; and various commissioned works for synagogues, choirs and interfaith liturgical groups. *World Fulfilled*, a solo recording of her compositions, was released in December 2001.

As a classical soprano soloist, Schiller has appeared with the John Oliver Chorale, Boston Zamir Chorale, Rottenberg Chorale, *Sine Nomine* (NY) and Tanglewood. She has served as cantor in several congregations. A national fellow of the Synagogue 2000 project, she toured the U.S. as a "cantor in residence," sharing new musical approaches to prayer and celebration.

Since 1989, Schiller has served as High Holy Day cantor with her husband, Rabbi Lester Bronstein, at Bet Am Shalom Synagogue of White Plains, New York. They also sing together in *Beged Kefet*, a philanthropic Jewish music ensemble. The ensemble's recordings feature Schiller's arrangements and compositions. She and her husband have recorded cassettes for the home prayer book, Shirim Uv'rachot, of the Kol Haneshamah Reconstructionist movement, as well as the UAHC's *Come Let Us Welcome the Sabbath*. She is a featured cantor in *Yamim Noraim*, a 1995 CD recording of High Holy Day music (Transcontinental) and in *A Taste of Eternity* with the Western Wind ensemble.

Benjie Ellen and Lester have three children, Liba, born January 21, 1987, Yonatan, April 14, 1991, and Avraham, September 24, 1992.

As of 2001, of the 270 ordained Reform cantors in the world, 145 are women.

CHAPTER FOURTEEN
PART A

American Musicologists

Sophie Drinker (1888–1967)

Diane Jezic (1942–89)

Carolyn Abbate

Christine Ammer

Linda Austern

Elaine Barkin

Jane Bernstein

Pamela Blevins

Adrienne Fried Block

Edith Borroff

Jane Bowers

Kristine Burns

Marcia Citron

Eileen Cline

Susan Cook

Suzanne Cusick

Marietta Dean

Cecilia Dunoyer

Nancy Fierro

Metche Franke

Bea Friedland

Halina Goldberg

Jane Gottlieb

Bonnie Grice

Beverly Grigsby

Jan Bell Groh

Lydia Hamessley

Deborah Hayes

Elizabeth Hinkle-Turner

Barbara Jackson

Barbara Jepson

Deborah Kavasch

Rosemary Killam

Ellen Koskoff

Laura Kuhn

Jane Weiner LePage

Kimberley Marshall

Susan McClary

Eve Meyer

Carol Neuls-Bates

Carol Oja

Karin Pendle

Joan Peyser

Marianne Richert Pfau

Susan Pickett

Carol Plantamura

Jeannie Pool

Deon Nielsen Price

Nancy Reich

Sally Reid

Ellen Rosand

Judith Rosen

Léonie Rosenstiel

Julie Anne Sadie

Karen Shaffer

Victoria Sirota

Catherine Smith

Ruth Solie

Carmen Téllez

Judith Tick

Judy Tsou

Mary Jeanne van Appledorn

Heidi von Gunden

Helen Walker-Hill

Gretchen Wheelock

Wanda Wilk

Elizabeth Wood

Judith Lang Zaimont

Alicia Zizzo

Musicologists represent a very special classification of women in music. Most are professors in conservatories and universities who, besides teaching, publish books and scholarly articles on myriad subjects relating to music. Internet websites, *Who's Who in Music* and other source books give only the barest details about these dedicated pedagogues. The majority manage a home life with husbands and children, while contributing a wealth of information and devoting themselves to their field. (Many, like this author, spend years of research to bring out one book!)

Whereas the traditional definition of *musicologist* has been "a musical historian," with the world becoming a global village there are now new perspectives in this diverse field. *Ethnomusicologists*, in particular, concentrate on non-Western and other multi-cultural aspects of music. Given the ever-increasing freedom of sexual expression, there has been a spate of literature propounding original thinking pertaining to gender and sexuality, which attempts to shed light on the anthropological, biological, social and sexual reasons why women (and men) wrote and write music as they do.

Traditional musicological history, sometimes facetiously referred to as "the music of dead, white males," left women in the margins. They cropped up now and then, in convents, in the courts of Renaissance Italy, and eventually on opera and concert stages. In our time, in the course of over half a century of female vocality, women musicologists have also been asserting themselves, as evidenced by the deluge of insightful papers, articles, essays and books on every conceivable element of feminism.

Pioneers to an Unknown Frontier

There were women forging their way through the discipline of musicology as early as **Sappho**, 7th century BC, and **Hildegard of Bingen** in the 12th century. In the late 19th century, Frenchwoman **Marie Bobillier** found it more expedient to write under the male *nom de plume*, **Michel Brenet**. It was not until the 1940s that the "discipline" of musicology was imported from Europe and infused into American university curricula. This led to a multitude of newly-written texts. Of these, a singular book was published in 1948 which, because of its uncredentialed author, was ignored by the academia, but favorably received by critics, and captured the imagination of the public—especially women involved in nurturing the first buds of feminism. *Music and Women*, by **Sophie Drinker**, is now recognized as a radical, insightful, trailblazer.

A Frontrunner in the Forties

Music and Women was written by a sixty-year-old housewife named **SOPHIE DRINKER**. Her music-loving, lawyer husband, Henry, a socially prominent Philadelphian, wrote music and compiled the Drinker Choral Library of sheet music, which he generously loaned to colleges and universities. In 1928, the Drinkers built a new house with a large music room in which they held (mostly amateur) performances. Looking for music for the women's chorus which met in her home, all Sophie could find was childish, sentimental drivel. So this lady, educated in private schools, accepted to Bryn Mawr—although never enrolled—embarked upon a twenty year research foray to find out why there was little or no music available written by women. Her social contacts enabled her to reach authorities all over the world, obtaining translations and gathering a vast amount of unique material. The result was a most unusual work: a combination of folklore, anthropology, sociology, archeology, plus a personal kind of musicology.

Drinker unearthed histories of ancient tribes honoring women's important roles in religious ceremonies, and the freedom and independence of women in civilizations like Lesbos—specifically **Sappho**—who were allowed to own property, travel as they pleased, and divorce their husbands. The author propounded the "spiritual catastrophe" of the Judeo-Christian theory of a male God—minus a mate—which excoriated the concepts of Mother Earth, ancient goddesses and homage to women as lifegivers. Although Jesus respected women, by the 3rd century AD, Christian doctrines had been manipulated to view females as "unclean," especially to be shunned during menstruation and after childbirth. Female musicians were considered temptresses. Early history corroborates that women who made a name for themselves in music were either in a convent, or relegated to the class of courtesan. It took until the 19th century and Clara Schumann and her fellow artists, to regain respectability status for public performance or composition.

Born in 1888, also of a "main line" Philadelphia family, the Hutchinsons, Sophie had the genteel Victorian upbringing of her class. Early in life she complained of her limitations as a woman, but went on to marry in 1911 and have five children. It was her *hysterectomy* at age forty-three in 1931 that, in her own words, "started her brain working." Freed from further childbearing and various female ailments she had suffered until then, she gradually became a full-fledged feminist, absorbing her ideas from the onrush of literature emerging in the '30s. To counteract any hint of radicalism, her original publishers,[203] Coward McCann of New York, covered themselves by

---

203. A Reprint of *Music and Women* was brought out by Zenger Publishers (1976), and an official 2nd Edition, October 1995, by The Feminist Press at the City University of New York (CUNY), with a *Preface* prepared by **Elizabeth Wood**, and a detailed biographical *Afterword* by **Ruth A. Solie**.

insisting, on the jacket flaps, that: "Though the book has a specific importance for musicians and a special interest for women, it is full of stimulating and challenging ideas about men and for men."

Also, their brief author biography appears to offer vindication of any hint of feminism: "Mrs. Drinker, as the mother of five and the wife of the distinguished musicologist, Henry S. Drinker, writes out of the fullness of a *normal* woman's experience." (Author's italics.)

How "normal" her experience was can be debated. She was certainly no ordinary housewife! Even during the war, her wealthy household supported five live-in servants, making it doubtful whether she ever had to change a diaper or shop at a supermarket. The Drinkers' personal lifestyle, as noted in Sophie's diary, insulated her further in that the family did not accept invitations to parties, go to musical comedies, attend church, or even own a radio—and only read the classics.

After the success of her book, Drinker continued writing the remaining nineteen years of her life. She died of cancer in the summer of 1967, leaving us a document recording the importance of women in prehistoric and bygone eras, when music was part of daily living and ritual, to their gradual and almost complete subjugation as music became consigned to professional performance before a non-participating audience. Her legacy is her consistent theme: *that our patriarchal society ignores women's needs and crushes their creativity.*

A Path Cut Short

DIANE PEACOCK JEZIC, author, professor, pianist, and her twin brother, Arthur Kenneth, were born January 31, 1942, in Philadelphia into a musical family. Her mother, Mary O'Kelly Peacock, wrote popular and semi-classic songs, piano pieces and musical plays, which inspired her daughter's article, *Women Performers in the Golden Age of Radio*, given as a paper at a CMS Conference. Mary Peacock continued to give piano recitals, directed a senior citizen chorus, and wrote musical plays for her retirement home in Cherry Hill, New Jersey, until her passing in 2002. Her ninetieth birthday, 1995, was celebrated with a show for the entire community with singing by elder daughter, Marilyn.

Diane received her BM from the College of Wooster (Ohio, 1963), MM from Northwestern (Illinois, 1965) and DMA from Peabody (Baltimore, 1974). Her dissertation on Austrian-born composer **Ernst Toch** (1887–1964) led to her book *The Musical Migration and Ernst Toch* (Iowa State U. Press), on emigré composers who came to this country during the European exodus in the '30s impelled by Hitler's rise to power.

On November 5, 1966, Diane married Dragan V. Jezic, a physician from Croatia, then finishing his training in Philadelphia. They moved to Baltimore in 1968, where he eventually became chair of the radiology department of Greater Baltimore Medical Center until his retirement in 1993. Their son Andrew, born in 1967, is an assistant district attorney in Maryland. Daughter Tamara, born in 1970, is a '98 graduate of Harvard Law School, who worked as a human rights attorney in Ecuador (1998–2000).

Diane taught music literature at Towson State University near Baltimore (1972–88), performed piano solo and chamber music recitals, and made three recordings on the EDUCO label. She was a member of the CMS, AMS, Sonneck Society for American Music, National Women's Study Association and the Pi Kappa Lambda National Music Honor Society. She wrote articles and reviews on her two areas of special interest, women composers and 20th century American music, in such publications as *Signs—The Journal of Women in Culture and Society*, *Music Educators' Journal*, *The American Music Teacher*, *Canadian Music Journal* and *Journal of the International Congress of Women in Music*. The first edition of her pioneer book, *Women Composers: The Lost Tradition Found* (Feminist Press of CUNY, 1988), the outgrowth of many years of research, covered twenty-five composers from **Hildegard von Bingen** to **Judith Zaimont**. Published November 1989, Jezic received a review copy on August 12. She died the next day.

The second edition, prepared by **Elizabeth Wood**, came out in 1993. Tamara Lee Jezic wrote the dedication:

Dr. Diane Peacock Jezic died August 13, 1989, after a ten year battle with cancer. As a pianist, music professor, author, and community volunteer, as a beloved mother, wife, daughter, sister and dear friend, Dr. Jezic seized each moment to share her love, joy, peace and artistry with all who surrounded her. In early 1986, unsure if she would live until Christmas, Jezic resolved to write one page a day, the stories . . . collected in *Women Composers: The Lost Tradition Found*.

Diane Jezic was inspired by her own mother, Mary O'Kelly Peacock, an accomplished composer and pianist, who continues to write and perform today at the [then] age of eighty-eight. May these stories inspire us to creatively and courageously bring the artist in each of us to its fullest expression.

In March 1990, Jezic posthumously received the 1989 Pauline Alderman Prize of the International Congress of Women in Music for her "outstanding contributions in the fields of music and women's studies." 1994 marked the world premiere, by the Baltimore Symphony under David Zinman, of Gordon Cyr's 2nd Symphony dedicated to Diane Jezic's memory. (Cyr was a colleague of Jezic at Towson.)

A Vocal Legacy

In 2003, director Margie T. Farmer renamed her Chestnut Ridge Women's Choir, formed in 1998, *The Jezic Ensemble*. Their inaugural performance, March 3, 2003, was titled the First Annual Diane Peacock Jezic Memorial Concert: Celebrating Women Composers. Pursuing their new mission of bringing the tradition of women in music to mainsteam audiences, the ensemble presented a concert of choral literature for women's voices, composed exclusively by women, to honor the life and work of their new namesake. Compositions by Libby Larson, Ysaye Barnwell, Lili Boulanger and Joan Szymko were featured. Their Third Annual Diane Peacock Jezic Memorial Concert, March 6, 2005, successfully incorporated emerging women composers by including a competition for choral works by contemporary women. The first winner (2004) was **Joelle Wallach** for "Why the Caged Bird Sings." The ensemble's cultural outreach covers schools, community centers, hospitals and retirement homes.

An Outpouring of Feminist Research

CAROLYN ABBATE is a foremost authority on opera. Her 1984 Princeton PhD dissertation is *The Parisian Tannhäuser*, after which she joined their faculty as an assistant professor. Her BA is from Yale (1977). She also studied at the University of Munich, 1979–80. As a full professor of music, her teaching includes interdisciplinary courses in the German department, Programs of European Cultural Studies, and Media and Modernity. With Roger Parker, she co-edited *Analyzing Opera: Verdi and Wagner* (1988), and is the author of *Unsung Voices* (1991), *In Search of Opera* (2001) and co-author of the comprehensive *Penguin History of Opera* (2005). A competent translator of French scholarly works, Vladimir Jankélévitch's *La Musique et L'Ineffable* (1960) was published in 2003 as *Music and the Ineffable*. Her own writings have been translated into French, Italian and Hebrew.

A frequent lecturer at the Met, she is often one of the panelists on the Met Opera Quiz live broadcasts, and contributed to publications of Covent Garden and the Berlin Staatsoper. She has written for the *New York Times, Times Literary Supplement, Stagebill* and *Opera News*, and presented public lectures at Cornell, Cambridge, Stanford, and the University of Chicago, among others.

Effective September 1, 2005, Abbate became professor of music on Harvard's Faculty of Arts and Sciences. She was also named the first Radcliffe alumnae professor at Harvard's Radcliffe Institute for Advanced Study, a post that allows her to spend four semesters at the Radcliffe Institute during the first five years in her new position.

CHRISTINE AMMER, born May 25, 1931, in Vienna, came to this country with her parents in 1938 and settled in Forest Hills, New York. She received her BA in English from Swarthmore College (1952). A writer and lexicographer, Ammer is the author of over twenty books in various fields. In music, her titles include the landmark, *Unsung, A History of Women in American Music* (Greenwood, 1980), the first original research of this kind. As a lexicographer, among the many monumental works she has compiled are: *A to Z of Foreign Musical Terms* (E. C. Schirmer, 1989), the *Harper Collins Dictionary of Music* (1971, third edition, 1995), articles for the *Norton Grove Dictionary of Women in Music*, *American National Biography*, *American Heritage Dictionary of Idioms* (Houghton Mifflin, 1997), *FIGHTING WORDS from War, Rebellion and Other Combative Capers* (NTC Contemporary Books, 1999), *COOL CATS, TOP DOGS and other beastly expressions* (Houghton Mifflin, 1999), *The New A to Z of Women's Health*, 4th edition (Facts on File, 2000), and numerous smaller books on linguistics.

Ammer has been a contract advisor for the National Writers Union since 1986, and a member of the American Dialect Society, Dictionary Society of North America, and International Alliance for Women in Music. She was on the Educational Advisory Board of the Maud Powell Journal, *Signature*, founded in 1995 and named after the American woman virtuoso violinist who lived from 1868 to 1920. In March 2001, Amadeus (Timber) Press brought out the second completely revised, updated and enlarged edition of *Unsung*.

Married to the late Dean Ammer, an economist, Christine has three grown children, a daughter and two sons.

LINDA PHYLLIS AUSTERN, born February 10, 1957, in Pittsburgh, has early childhood memories of being enchanted with live and taped music in the ballet studios where her mother taught, danced and studied. Begging for music lessons, at age seven her parents bought her a plastic soprano recorder and sent her off to a class. Within a few weeks, she was playing everything she heard around her by ear, and sight-reading bits of the baroque solo repertory. Her teacher suggested private lessons. Linda also began violin, and later viola da gamba and other Renaissance wind instruments.

When Linda was eleven, her father, a professor of physics, took his family on a sabbatical to Sydney, Australia, where she discovered 16th and 17th century English music in a school whose choir and madrigal group sang Morley, Byrd and Purcell. On her return, in addition to playing and singing in Western art-music chamber groups, she spent a number of years playing several instruments for Israeli dance groups and English country dance bands. As an undergraduate and graduate student, she composed music for several professional theatrical companies in Pittsburgh and Chicago, writing renaissance-style music for Shakespearean productions or avant-garde music for experimental plays.

Her BA is in early music performance (University of Pittsburgh, 1977) and PhD in musicology (University of Chicago, 1984). Her doctoral dissertation is "Music in English Children's Drama, 1597–1613." After being on the faculty of Notre Dame (1989), where she attained tenure, and visiting associate professor of musicology at the University of Iowa, she became an associate professor of musicology at Northwestern University, and member of the faculty of the interdisciplinary PhD in theater. She was a Bunting Fellow at Radcliffe (1988–89) and visiting professor at other American colleges, having won fellowships from the American Council of Learned Societies, Folger Shakespeare Library, British Academy, and National Endowment for Humanities (NEH). She is a member of the AMS, IMS, Renaissance Society of America, Royal Musical Association, Society for 17th Century Music, and Society for the Study of Early Modern Women.

Austern is a specialist in Renaissance and Baroque musical-cultural relations, as well as gender and feminist theory, music as related to the early history of science, music in 16th, 17th and 18th century England, plus European intellectual history and musical aesthetics. Author of *Music in English Children's Drama of the Later Renaissance* and *Music in English Life and Thought 1550–1650* (1992), she has written numerous articles and reviews for the *AMS Journal*, *Modern Philology*, *Music and Letters*, and *Renaissance Quarterly*. Her compilation, *Music, Sensation and Sensuality*, was published by Routledge (2002), and *Music and the Sirens* by Indiana University Press (2004).

Linda is married to a mathematician.

Composer/writer/teacher **ELAINE BARKIN** was born in New York, December 15, 1932. After receiving her BA Queens College, New York (1954), she studied composition with **Irving Fine** (1914–62), **Harold Shapero** (*b*

1920), and **Arthur Berger** (1912–2003) at Brandeis University where she received an MFA in composition (1956) and PhD in composition and theory (1971). She also studied with Boris Blacher (1903–75) at the Berlin Hochschule für Musik (composition and piano certificate, 1957).

Beginning in 1964, she taught at Queens College, Sarah Lawrence College, the University of Michigan, and Princeton. She was professor of composition and theory at UCLA (1974–97, now professor emerita), where she was actively involved in their Balinese (and Javanese) Gamelan. She spent 1994 on a faculty exchange at Victoria University, Wellington, New Zealand, and in 1996 taught a semester at sea and journeyed around the world on a ship. She was associated with *Perspectives of New Music* (1963–85) in an editorial capacity, as well as writing extensively on 20th century music for other journals. Since 1990, she, Benjamin Boretz, and Jim Randall have been co-producers of the *Open Space* series of CDs, scores, and books. She co-edited, with **Lydia Hamessley**, *Audible Traces: Gender, Identity and Music* (Carciofoli Verlagshaus, Zurich, 1999).

Around 1978, Barkin evolved from twelve-note and serial techniques to explore interactive performance, improvisation and tape collages. Her compositions include String Quartet (1969), *Plus ça change* for string orchestra and percussion (1972), *Sound Play* for violin (1974), *The Supple Suitor*, song cycle for soprano and chamber ensemble, with texts by Emily Dickinson (1978), *De Amore*, a chamber opera (1980), *At the Piano* (1981), five tape collages (1984), *3 Rhapsodies* for flutes and clarinet (1986), *Legong Dreams* for oboe (1990), *For My Friends' Pleasure* for soprano and harp (1995), *Poem* for Symphonic Wind Ensemble (1999), and *Song for Sarah*, solo violin (2001).

Since 1987, after six study trips to Bali, she has written for and performed in *Gamelan*, the classical Indonesian orchestra. Her works in this genre include *Encore for Javanese Gamelan Ensemble* (1988), *Gamélange* for harp and mixed gamelan band (1992), and *touching all bases/di mana-mana* for Balinese gamelan, electronic contrabass and midi percussion, collaboratively composed with I Nyoman Wenten.

Her awards include a Fulbright Award (1957) NEA Awards (1975, 1979), Rockefeller Foundation (Bellagio, 1980), and Meet the Composer (1994).

JANE A. BERNSTEIN has published widely in the fields of Renaissance and 19th century music including *Music Printing in Renaissance Venice: The Scotto Press (1539–1572)* (Oxford University Press, 1998), for which she won the distinguished Otto Kinkeldey Award from the American Musicological Society for the best book in musicology (1999). She has also edited a thirty volume edition of 16th century French Chanson (Garland, 1987–95), and *Philip Van Wilder, The Complete Works* (Broude, 1991). Her work in women's studies includes the introduction to the 1980 Da Capo Press edition of Ethel Smyth's *Mass in D*, and the essay, "'Shout, Shout Up Your Song!' Dame Ethyl Smyth and the Changing Role of the British Woman Composer" in *Women Making Music* (eds. Jane Bowers & Judith Tick, U. of Illinois Press, 1987). In 2001, Oxford University Press brought out her *Print Culture and Music in Sixteenth-Century Venice*. She has received several honors and fellowships from the Guggenheim Foundation, NEH, Delmas Foundation, American Council of Learned Societies (ACLS), and American Philosophical Society.

Born in New York, March 23, 1947, Bernstein went to the High School of Music and Art, where she majored in voice. She received her BA in music at City College of New York (1967), MM from the University of Massachusetts (1968), and PhD from UC Berkeley (1974). Her teaching career began at Vassar College in 1974. Two years later she joined the faculty at Tufts University, where she is the Austin Fletcher professor and former chair of the department of music. Married to James Ladewig, also a musicologist, they have a daughter, Lily, born in 1981.

PAMELA BLEVINS, born April 10, 1945, in Everett, Massachusetts, into a musical family, grew up listening to records in her home—big band, swing, blues, and popular music of the late '40s and early '50s. At age twelve she saw *Rhapsody in Blue*, the 1945 film version of George Gershwin's life, which launched her discovery of "serious" music. Fortunate to have attended public schools in Braintree, Massachusetts, where music appreciation was a required part of the junior high curriculum, by the time she reached high school she was able to take a full credit course in music appreciation developed by a visionary teacher, Mae Lindsay, who explored the musical roots of America, interweaving history, literature and geography. (Lindsey lived a long creative life. Born 1903, she died peacefully March 5, 2005, at age one hundred and one.)

Although Blevins became a journalist, photographer and later a public relations consultant, she continued to pursue her musical interests. In 1978, she created the lecture series "Silent Destiny: The Woman Composer." She served as managing editor of *The Maud Powell Signature: Women in Classical Music* (1995–1997)—an erudite, highly readable magazine which sadly had to fold its pages due to lack of funding.

In addition to her work on women composers, Pam is an authority on 20th century British music, penning several articles on composer-poet Ivor Gurney (1890–1937) and English musicologist-critic Marion M. Scott (1877–1953)—see International Musicologists—as well as being founder/president in 1983 of the Finzi Society of America, showcasing British composer Gerald Finzi (1901–56). She is also on the board of directors of the Elinor Remick Warren Society, which celebrates the life and works of this American composer who lived from 1900–1990, and whose centenary was celebrated in 2000 in Washington, DC.

Blevins' periodical publications include: "Ivor Gurney's Friends: Ethel Voynich—'E.L.V.' Revolutionary, Novelist, Translator, Composer"; "Ruth Gipps and Sir Arthur Bliss"; "Women, War and Words"; "Marion Scott: The Writer"; "Marion Scott: Critic and Champion of Contemporary Music and Women"; "Elinor Remick Warren: American Composer." 2006 works in progress were: *The Selected Writings of Marion Scott*, and a biography of Scott and Gurney.

ADRIENNE FRIED BLOCK earned a PhD in musicology from CUNY (1989). She has served on the faculty of the College of Staten Island, as well as Hunter and Brooklyn Colleges—all part of the City University of New York (CUNY)—as well as at Pace University, Marymount Manhattan College and the Dalcroze School of Music. She was a senior fellow/visiting professor at the Institute for Studies in American Music, Brooklyn College (1990), and is co-director of the Project for the Study of Women in Music, Graduate Center, CUNY. A specialist in both French 16th century music and music by American women composers, Block was co-editor and compiler of *Women in American Music: A Bibliography of Music and Literature* (Greenwood Press, 1979). Her two-volume study, *The Early French Parody Noel*, was issued by UMI Research Press (Ann Arbor), and "Timbre, texte, et air" has appeared in *Revue de Musicologie*. She has also written an introduction to *Amy Beach, Quartet for Strings in One Movement, Op. 89*, published as Vol. 3 of "Music in the United States of America" by the American Musicological Society, Fall 1994, revised edition, 2000.

In May 1995, Block introduced and was consultant for the milestone concert, "An Evening With Amy Beach," which featured the premiere of Beach's one-act opera, *Cabildo*, for voices and string trio, whose plot evokes the ghost of the pirate Pierre Lafitte. Also on the program were piano works whose dynamism was masterfully brought out by the artistry of Christopher O'Riley, and program songs by the equally brilliant **Lauren Flanigan**, soprano, and Paul Grove, tenor.

Fried Block's articles and essays on Beach's life and music have appeared in *American Music*, *Musical Quarterly*, and *Festschrifts* for H. Wiley Hitchcock and Eileen Southern, part of a monograph on seven women composers in the German publisher Furore's catalogue. Beach entries in reference books include the *New Grove Dictionary of Music and Musicians* (6th and 7th editions), *New Grove Dictionary of Women Composers*, *New Grove Dictionary of Opera*, *MGG* (*Die Musik im Geschichte und Gegenwart*—a German encyclopedia) and *American National Biography*, the American Council of Learned Societies. 1997–99 brought lectures as a speaker for the New York Council for the Humanities. She has also written liner notes for many recordings of Beach's music. After twelve years of research under an NEA fellowship, Block brought out *Amy Beach: Passionate Victorian: The Life and Works of an American Composer, 1868–1944* (Oxford U. Press, 1998; paperback, 2000). The book won the 2000 ASCAP-Deems Taylor Award and "Best Book of the Year" with the Irving Lowens Award from the Society for American Music (SAM), who also awarded Block with a Lifetime Achievement Award in 2004. 2006 brought the Distinguished Alumni Award from the PhD Association of the Graduate School, CUNY.

Block is a member of the AMS Publication Committee, was on its council, and has served in several capacities for the CMS, including organizing and chairing the Committee on the Status of Women. She organized and chaired two conferences on Beach (1998, '99), and was the main speaker at a third, at Murray State University (Kentucky) 2001.

December 2000, she spoke on "Music in the Empire City, 1860–80" at the CUNY Graduate Center, the first lecture of a series, "The Orchestra and its Audience," focusing on music in New York.[204] Since 2001 she has been co-director, with John Graziano of "Music in Gotham: The New York Scene 1862–1875," a project funded by the NEH, supplemented by the Baisley Powell Elebash Endowment. This study of performance and reception chronicles an era rich in music including opera, symphony, band, choral and chamber concerts, musical theater, minstrel shows, recitals of art and popular music. The project completes the first volume of a history of music in New York City, 1862–69, backed up by a searchable database of some 30,000 musical events. Already planned is a second volume covering 1869–75.

Adrienne married educator Arthur Block in 1970, inheriting two stepdaughters. Her two daughters from her first marriage to George Fried, are Linda, a Johns Hopkins Medical School director of the gerontology division, and Barbara, a Stanford law professor. Happily married, each has given her mother two grandsons.

Edith Borroff

EDITH BORROFF was born into an illustrious family, August 2, 1925, and brought up in New York City. Her grandfather, Albert Borroff, was, for thirty-six years, the only Christian cantor in the Chicago Temple.

Her mother, composer **Marie Bergersen** (1894–1989), was "apprenticed" to her piano teacher from age three, with lessons every day except her birthday and Christmas. By seventeen, she was established as a pianist and composer. Her best known work is *Theme and Variations* (1912) for piano. In 1913, she entered the Imperial Conservatory in Vienna, but World War I interrupted her studies and she returned home. She married Ramon Borroff in 1918, concertizing 1923–31, when she retired to raise her two daughters, Marie and Edith. In the 1940s she was organist and composer for NBC, writing piano works and background music for radio shows like "Jack Armstrong—All American Boy" and "Sky King." She also accompanied violinist **Maud Powell**. Retiring from NBC in 1951, she continued teaching and performing. Her last concert, 1989, was in Spain for the Duke of Santiago de Compostela who, hearing of Marie's arrival, commandeered a concert hall in order to get her to perform. She was complimented by Rachmaninoff as being "the best sight-reader in America." She lived to age ninety-five.

Following in the footsteps of her famous mother, Edith was also apprenticed to a piano teacher and gave her first public performance—a Mozart sonata—at age four, and last at sixteen, when she played the Beethoven Concerto #3 with the Chicago Symphony. More interested in composing, she began a long apprenticeship with composer **Irwin Fischer** (1903–77) in Chicago, which culminated in bachelor's (1946) and master's (1948) degrees in composition from the American Conservatory. From 1950, Borroff worked in the university system, earning a PhD in music history (University of Michigan, 1958). Besides guest lecturing at major colleges, she taught at the Universities of Wisconsin and Eastern Michigan and, from 1973 until her retirement in 1992, at SUNY, Binghamton.

As a scholar, she concentrated on French music, writing the very first book about a woman composer, *An Introduction to Elisabeth Jacquet de La Guerre* (Institute of Medieval Music, New York, 1966). Her other definitive books include *The Music of the Baroque* (1978), and *Three American Composers—Irwin Fischer, Ross Lee Finney and George Crumb* (1986). Her interest in the sweep of history and music history is chronicled in *Music in Europe and the United States* (1990); *American Opera: A Checklist* (second edition, 1992), identifying over 4000 works by over 2000 composers; *William Grant Still* (1991), about the first black symphonic composer (1895–1978); *Music*

---

204. The New York Philharmonic had already been established in 1842 as the Symphony Society of New York.

Melting Round: A History of Music in the United States (1995); and *Broadway, You're the Top!* (1996). In the 21st century, she brought out a book on her other facet of fascination, *Early Thought Patterns: A Prehistoric Esthetic of Numbers.*

Borroff's articles have appeared in many musical journals, plus contributions covering Lully and Josquin des Prés in the *Encyclopedia Americana*, and thirteen entries, including those on her "Three American Composers," in the *New Grove Dictionary of Music and Musicians* and *American Grove*. She, herself, is featured in the *New Grove*, *The International Cyclopedia of Women Musicians*, *Baker's Biographical Dictionary of Women Musicians* and *International Who's Who of Musicians*. She has written a myriad of papers on a variety of musical subjects, from sacred music under Louis XV to *Savages, Shakespeare and Schoenberg.*

With the burgeoning interest in music by women, Borroff the composer came into her own. Recipient of over eighty commissions, her œuvre contains song cycles, choral music—including *Light in Dark Places: Slavery and Freedom in Nineteenth-Century America* (1988), based on poignant texts by 19th century black women—music for piano and harpsichord, some thirty-five works for chamber music, and a significant number of organ works. Her style is lively, idiomatic, and rhythmically vital—three major virtues of music intrinsic to the apprenticeship system in which she was trained. She is the subject of a 1993 doctoral dissertation by Janet Regier (University of Oklahoma). The same year, all her papers were transferred into an archive at the Newberry Library in Chicago.

JANE BOWERS was born in Minneapolis September 17, 1936, taken to concerts at an early age, and began piano at four. At five, she and her sister Janet were appearing as duo-pianists on a local radio show. She started flute in seventh grade, which led to many recitals over the years. She received her MA in music history (1962) and PhD (1971) from UC Berkeley. She studied modern flute, baroque flute, and recorder at the Royal Conservatory in The Hague (Holland). By 1968, she was teaching at the University of North Carolina and by 1972 at Eastman. The history of the flute and flute music, especially of 18th century France, became one of her primary interests, producing a multitude of articles and an important study of the flute method of **François Devienne** (1759–1803), titled *François Devienne's Nouvelle Méthode Théorique et Pratique pour la Flute*: Facsimile of the original edition with an introduction, annotated catalogue of later editions, and translation by Jane Bowers, plus commentary on the original edition by Thomas Boehm (Ashgate Publishing Ltd.,1999).

Professor of Music History and Literature at the University of Wisconsin-Milwaukee since 1981, Bowers has been researching women in music for over thirty years. Utilizing one of her specialities, Italian women composers of the late 16th and 17th centuries, she co-edited, with **Judith Tick**, the Deems Taylor-ASCAP award-winning book *Women Making Music: The Western Art Tradition, 1150–1950*. (U. of Illinois Press, 1986, second ed. 1995). Author of many articles, one of her particular interests is the cross-cultural traditional role of womens' music-making with emphasis on the rituals of birth, puberty, marriage and death.

In 2000, *Frauen und Männerbilder in der Musik: Festschrift für Eva Rieger zu 60 Geburtstag* (a celebration of the sixtieth birthday of Eva Rieger), edited by Freida Hoffmann, Jane Bowers, and Ruth Heckmann, was published by the University of Oldenburg (Germany) Library and Information System. Bowers continues her years of research for a biography and repertoire study of Chicago blues singer/composer Estelle "Mama" Yancey.

In addition to concertizing on baroque flute with many musicians around the country, Jane performs with Milwaukee's Ensemble *Musical Offering.*

KRISTINE H. BURNS was born in Westwood, New Jersey, February 5, 1966, but grew up in West Chester, Ohio. With their mother singing in church and community groups, Kris and her younger brother sang in the school choir and played in the band. She began piano in third grade and added flute in fifth. Encouraged by her band director, she prevailed over her parents' wishes that she become a mathematician and majored in music. She received her BM in music education (Miami University, Ohio, 1988). Realizing that the high school band directing position she wanted was unattainable in a male dominated field, she returned to school for an MA in music theory and composition (U. of Denver 1990). Now interested in composition, and with a proficiency in computers, she never looked back, instead earning a PhD in music composition and theory, with a minor in musicology and music technology (Ball State University, Indiana, 1994). Her first appointment was assistant professor of electronic and computer music at Oberlin (1993–96), followed by assistant professor of music at Dartmouth (1996–97), and professor of music and director of the Electronic Music Studio at Florida International University (1997–).

Since 1993, when **Deborah Kavásch** and **Beverly Grigsby** introduced her to women in technology and multimedia, Burns has become an authority on women's activities in that field, creating and editing the educational web site, WOW/EM, Women On the Web/ElectronMedia. In January of that year, she was also an assistant to **Joan La Barbara** and her husband Morton Subotnick at the Atlantic Center for the Arts in New Smyrna, Florida.

Her multimedia compositions, including *Underwear* (contrabass, video, and stereo tape, 1988), a commission from Bertram Turetzky, and *Heavy Metal*, for video and stereo tape (2000), released on video by the Electronic Music Foundation, 2001, have been performed in the U.S. and Europe. She edited *Women and Music in America Since 1900: An Encyclopedia*, published by Greenwood Press, 2002, which, besides classical, covers folk, jazz, soul, rockand rap.

Burns is a member of CMS, International Computer Music Association, the Society of Composers, Inc., secretary for SEAMUS, and president of the IAWM (2001–03). She is married to composer Colby Leider.

MARCIA J. CITRON specializes in research on women composers and their music. Born in Brooklyn, New York, 1945, she received her BA from Brooklyn College (1966), MA (1968), and PhD (1971) in musicology, from the University of North Carolina. She has taught at Roosevelt University, Virginia Commonwealth University, Brooklyn College and, since 1976, at Rice University (Texas), where she is the Lovett Distinguished Service professor and chair of the musicology department.

Her many articles have appeared in major scholarly journals and collections. She has been awarded several grants. Her books include the prizewinning *Letters of Fanny Hensel to Felix Mendelssohn* (Pendragon Press, 1987), *Cécile Chaminade: A Bio-Bibliography* (Greenwood Press, 1988), and *Gender and the Musical Canon* (Cambridge University Press, 1993), (Reprinted: University of Illinois Press, 2000), for which she won the Pauline Alderman Award from the IAWM. The book is a landmark study examining the practices and attitudes which have prevailed throughout history to exclude women from the accepted canon of performance repertoire. Its publication evoked a spate of musicological treatises exploring gender as a factor in composition and the *still continuing* dearth of women's works from orchestral libraries.

Citron's article on Franco Zeffirelli's *Otello* (Musical Quarterly, 1994) served as a basis for a larger study on visually recorded treatments of opera, which includes her book *Opera on Screen, Television, and Video: Explorations in Medium and Meaning* (Yale University Press, 2000).

The extensive interview of Citron in the revised edition of *Women in Music: An Anthology of Source Readings from the Middle Ages to the Present 1995*, (ed. Carol Neuls-Bates) attests to her status as a leader in the field of feminist musicology.

EILEEN TATE CLINE, born June 25, 1935, grew up in Chicago, where her uncle was an arranger for the African-American Earl "Fatha" Hines' band of the '20s and '30s. Educated at the University of Chicago, she also earned degrees in piano performance and music education at Oberlin, and an MM in piano performance from the University of Colorado. During her twenty years there, she taught piano, founded and directed the Boulder Children's Choir, was involved in civic and professional organizations and international folk-dance teaching and performance, raised two children, and became an avid skier and mountaineer.

Widowed in 1978, she went on as a Danforth Fellow to add a doctorate "with highest distinction" from Indiana University, then became executive director of the Neighborhood Music School in New Haven, Connecticut. For three decades, she held teaching and administrative positions in the university and school systems in Indiana, Colorado, and Connecticut. In 1982, she was appointed associate dean for academic affairs at Johns Hopkins University's Peabody Conservatory, becoming dean of this distinguished music school in 1983. In 1995, she became Johns Hopkins' first University Fellow in Arts Policy. In 1999, her retirement from the institution was marked by a gathering of distinguished panelists and musicians for a symposium entitled "The Arts in America: Lifeblood of a Nation and its Citizenry—Past, Present and Future."

Cline's professional activities have included service as a music panelist for the NEA, trustee of Oberlin College, board member of the American Symphony Orchestra League, Kenan Institute for the Arts, Marlboro Music Festival and School, Berkshire Institute for Theology and the Arts, North American Folk Music and Dance Alliance, and being on the advisory board for the Van Cliburn International Piano Competition, where she was a juror in 2001. Her commentary, *Anyone can Win . . . Unless There Happens to Be a Second Entry*, relevant to the music teaching profession, was named the 1990 American Music Teacher "Article of the Year."

Susan Cook

SUSAN C. COOK, born May 4, 1955, Fort Leonard Wood, Missouri, became a feminist at age five when her grandparents gave her brother a plate, bowl and cup marked "David Cook," while her set merely said "Susan," implying that she would not always be Susan *Cook*. "I will, too!" she vowed, and has. Encouraged by her English professor father to follow in his footsteps, she was always interested in music. Piano lessons began when she was in second grade, although she wanted dancing lessons. (She still loves to dance, especially contra dances, the ancestors of square dancing.) By the time Susan reached high school she was grateful for the choice, which expanded into useful harpsichord technique by graduate school. Her BA in religious music studies is from Beloit College (Wisconsin), MA and PhD in musicology from the University of Michigan (1985). Her dissertation on German Opera during the 1920s was subsequently published as *Opera for a New Republic: The Zeitopern of Ernst Krenek, Paul Hindemith, and Kurt Weill* (1988).

Director of graduate studies and professor in the musicology area, Cook taught six years at Middlebury College (Vermont) before her appointment to the University of Wisconsin, Madison in 1991. Her teaching and research focus on the 20th century, American music, women's history and feminist philosophies. She holds a joint governance position in the University's internationally recognized women's studies program. She has also held elected offices in the AMS, Sonneck Society for American Music, International League (now Alliance) of Women Composers, and International Society for the Study of Popular Music.

Her work has appeared in journals, encyclopedias and books. She is co-editor with **Judy S. Tsou** of *Cecilia Reclaimed: Feminist Perspectives on Gender and Music* (University of Illinois Press, 1994); and a collection of essays, bringing together musical research and feminist methodology with her depictions of womankind in American folk ballads, *Cursed Was She: Gender and Power in American Balladry*. Other projects include American musical theater and historical popular music; a biography of social dancer Irene Castle, which examines the cultural meaning of dance, dance music and fashion; a study of gender and race in the life of jazz singer Billie Holiday; and a book on Ragtime dance and American culture before World War I, including her essay, "Watching Our Step: Embodying Research, Telling Stories," which won the Gertrude Lippincott Award from the Society of Dance History Scholars.

SUZANNE G. CUSICK, after a decade at the University of Virginia, joined the faculty at NYU. She has taught music and women's studies at Wells College, SUNY (Oswego, New York) and Oberlin (Ohio). Her PhD in music history is from the University of North Carolina, Chapel Hill. Her publications include: *Valerio Dorico: Music Printer in Sixteenth-Century Rome* (UMI, 1981); *Of Women, Music, and Power: A Model from Seicento Florence*, based on her 1975 dissertation (University of California 1993); "Gendering Modern Music: Thoughts on the Monteverdi-Artusi Controversy" (*AMS Journal*, 1993); "Thinking from Women's Lives: Francesca Caccini after 1627" (*Musical Quarterly*, 1993); "Feminist Theory, Music Theory, and the Mind-Body Problem" (*Perspectives of New Music*, 1993); "'And not one lady failed to shed a tear': Arianna's Lament and the Construction of Modern Womanhood" (*Early Music*, 1994). Cusick's research areas cover feminist criticism, cultural history of 16th and 17th century European music, early opera and 19th century American popular music.

MARIETTA DEAN, professor of music in voice at Western Illinois University since 1967, performs 20th century repertoire as well as standard works from the baroque and romantic. With BM and MM degrees from Cincinnati Conservatory, her postgraduate studies were in Italy, France, Germany and the Salzburg (Austria) Mozarteum. She has given recitals of American art songs abroad under the auspices of the U.S. Department of State. In Europe, she has concertized in Greece, Germany, Italy, Finland and the former Yugoslavia. For seven years she was a member of the Cincinnati Summer Opera, and made solo appearances with the Chicago and St. Louis Symphonies. In addition to new music festivals, orchestral concerts, opera and chamber music events, Dean presents recitals of works by women composers in the U.S., Central America, Australia and Europe.

Cecilia Dunoyer

CECILIA DUNOYER has made an everlasting contribution to the literature with her book *Marguerite Long, A Life in French Music* (Indiana University Press, 1993—simultaneous French publication, Éditions Findakly, Paris). Emanating from her DMA dissertation, and helped by a grant from the French Embassy, her research in Paris on the life of celebrated pianist **Marguerite Long** resulted in a highly readable, unique insight into the musical world of France during the first three decades of the 20th century. Long was both friend and premier interpreter of the music of **Fauré**, **Debussy** and **Ravel**, among other illustrious composers of the era, as well as a highly respected professor at the Paris Conservatory. The book and interviews with Dunoyer have been featured on National Public Radio (NPR).

Born November 6, 1957 in Tripoli (Libya), Cecilia started moving at three to Milan, at six to Vienna, where she was taken to operas and concerts, and finally settled in France from ages eight to nineteen. She grew up with music and three younger brothers, all of whom played instruments. Her own piano practice was a consistent two hours daily. Sixteen found her in Versailles (the place—not the palace), commuting to studies with Pierre Sancan at the Paris Conservatory. In the summer of 1976, she and her brother Louis—with whom she had sung Mozart opera since they were toddlers—made one of their first trips to America to the Interlochen (Michigan) Summer Music Camp. Her accompanist job there led to an audition and a scholarship to the University of Michigan, where she subsequently earned both bachelor's (1980) and master's (1981) degrees in piano performance with high distinction, studying with Hungarian pianist Gyorgy Sandor. In 1982, she married fellow student Taylor Greer. When he went to Yale for his PhD in theory, she went to the University of Maryland and earned her DMA, May 1990, a month after the birth of her first child. In 1987, her husband accepted a position of professor of music theory at Pennsylvania State University. Since 1991, after completing her book, Cecilia joined the piano faculty there as well, having been music advisor and education director at the Center for the Performing Arts (1991–93).

Recipient of numerous awards and prizes for her solo and chamber music performances, Dunoyer has concertized extensively in the U.S., Mexico and Europe. Her popular lecture-recitals and master classes related to piano music continue to take her to libraries, museums and university campuses throughout the country. In 1995, she was the guest for a series of ten radio shows for Radio-Canada (CBC, Montreal) entitled "Pour le Clavier." An associate fellow of Silliman College, Yale, since 1984, she pursues many scholarly projects, and has been published in the *American Music Teacher*, *Notes*, and *Piano*, a French publication.

In November 1997, *New York Times* critic Harris Goldsmith praised her debut performance at Carnegie Recital Hall, entitled "Paris-St. Petersburg," playing Fauré, Debussy and Mussorgsky's *Pictures at an Exhibition*. In May 1998, the *Times* again featured her performance of Debussy and Messiaen at Merkin Hall. Her lecture-recital on French Chamber Music at Washington, DC's Smithsonian Institute, November 1999, was such a success that she was asked to return and expand this into an eight-week course with live chamber music performances, April, May, June 2001. This too received a tremendous reception, was taped, and elicited immediate re-engagement plans for the autumn of 2002 on her return from her and the family's thirteen-month stay in France, July 2001–August 2002, a tremendous experience for the whole family. The Smithsonian presentations continued in Spring 2003 and '04. (She took a break in 2005.)

Home continues to be the town of State College, Pennsylvania,[205] with her husband and their three musical children, François, born 1990 (piano), Émile, 1993 (clarinet), and Juliette, 1998 (violin). Life has been good to Cecilia Dunoyer, who came to America for just twelve months, over thirty years ago . . .

NANCY FIERRO is a noted concert pianist, recording artist, scholar, lecturer and teacher who, in addition to her mastery of the traditional repertoire, is considered an authority on music by women composers, and specialist in the work of **Hildegard von Bingen**. She holds a DMA in Piano Performance from USC and a Certificate in Piano, Theory and Analysis for postgraduate work at the American School of Fine Arts in France, where the legendary **Nadia Boulanger** praised her as a "real pianistic talent with deep musical understanding,"and invited her to perform at the Conservatoire Américain. Other international appearances include recitals in Canada, Mexico and Germany. Her performances in the U.S. have been aired on NPR. When the Women's Movement began in the '70s, she was among the first to give lecture-recitals of works by women. In 1973, she brought out *Premiere Recorded Performances of Keyboard Works by Women* (Avant), one of the first compilations of women's music. This was followed by *The Romance of Women's Music* (Pelican), and *Rags and Riches* (Dorchester, 1995). She has given premieres of works by women, notably the Piano Sonata No. 2 by the Polish composer **Grazyna Bacewicz**. Fierro has also published numerous articles on women's music, including a unique monograph (Sheed & Ward) and an audio cassette (Sounds True Audio) on 12th century composer, scientist and theologian, Hildegard of Bingen.

The Third International Congress of Women in Music presented Fierro with a Certificate of Honor for her outstanding contributions to musical life. She received the Sigma Alpha Iota Radio-Television award for her production of "Nine Centuries of Women in Music," and was selected by the California Council of the Arts as a touring artist-lecturer 1992–1998.

2000 saw the release of her new lecture tape on Hildegard, published by Credence Communications. Entitled "Awakening to God's Love," it presents the Abbess's life by unfolding the mythical elements of her biography. It also discusses her music, medicine, illuminations and spirituality. In demand as a speaker, Fierro lectures at universities, is a frequent presenter for local and state meetings of the Music Teachers National Association, and regularly gives pre-concert lectures for the Los Angeles Philharmonic, Pasadena and Pacific Symphonies, Los Angeles Master Chorale and the Da Camera Society. She is on the music faculty at Mount St. Mary's College in Los Angeles and maintains a private piano studio.

2004–'05–'06 opened a promising new facet of her career, composition. However, a few years down the road is the vision of writing what Nancy calls a "reflective book" on the music of Hildegard von Bingen.

METCHE FARIS FRANKE, born November 8, 1935, in Falfurrias, Texas, earned her BM from Sul Ross University (Alpine, Texas, 1967), MM (1971) , and PhD in musicology (1978) from the University of North Texas, Denton. For over twenty years, beginning in 1975, she was on the faculty of Cal. State, Fullerton, where she taught subjects ranging from jazz history, women in music—especially Amy Beach—ethnic music to music theory, band arranging and counterpoint. She was a soloist and accompanist with several orchestras and choirs, and a member of the CSUF Speaker's Bureau. Her publications include a monograph, *Herstory: Investigations into the Music of Women* (1992), and co-editing theory, singing and piano method books, and articles. An NDEA Fellowship in Musicology from the University of North Texas, and an Academic Senate Faculty Enhancement Grant for Women in Music Instructional Materials (1992), are among her awards.

BEA FRIEDLAND wrote a definitive PhD dissertation (NYU, 1975) on **Louise Farrenc**, 1804–1875: *Composer, Performer, Scholar* (Univ. of Michigan, 1980, 1988). She was editor-in-chief for over thirty titles in the Da Capo Press *Women Composers Series*, whose scores each feature an introductory essay by a noted musicologist. She selected and edited *Critical Questions on Music and Letters, Culture and Biography, 1940–1980*, by Jacques Barzun (U.of Chicago Press, 1982), and wrote the foreword to the score "Le Treasor des Pianistes" (Farrenc's masterwork), reprinted by Da Capo Press, New York, 1977.

---

205. Where, in 2004, the author and her husband had a delicious home-cooked dinner with the Greers and three of the most well-behaved children we have encountered in this country! Which is why I recommend that classical music should be played for children, starting in utero!

HALINA GOLDBERG, MA, Queens College (1989), PhD, musicology (CUNY Graduate Center, 1997), is an assistant professor at Indiana University, and was assistant professor at the University of Alabama (2000–01). Her dissertation, *Musical Life in Warsaw During Chopin's Youth, 1810–1830*, was the basis for her book *Music in Chopin's Warsaw* (Oxford University Press). Her articles include "Chopin in Literary Salons," and "Warsaw's Romantic Awakening," published in the *Polish Review*, plus contributions on "Chopin-biography," "Chopin-works," and "19th-Century Ornamentation" to *Reader's Guide to Music: History, Theory and Criticism*.

Her papers have been heard at national meetings of the AMS, and the Polish Institute of Arts and Sciences of America. Other presentations have been on "Salon Arrangements of Chopin's Works with Orchestra" at the Second Chopin Congress in Warsaw, and "The Prophetic Voice in Chopin's Music" at Mannes College of Music. Radio interviews include WETA in Washington, DC, and Warsaw Two in Poland. She was a speaker at the 1998 International Conference on "Polish/Jewish/Music!" held at the Polish Music Research Center of the USC School of Music, and served as the organizer of "The Age of Chopin: A Sesquicentennial Chopin Symposium"—a series of interdisciplinary symposia and period concerts held at the University of Indiana, Bloomington, September 1999. Her paper, "Chopin in Warsaw Salons," published in the *Polish Music Journal*, was awarded the 1998 **Wanda Wilk** Prize for Research in Polish Music.

Goldberg has lectured at the Polish Chopin Academy (Warsaw); Jagiellonian University (Krakow) and the Smithsonian Institution, Washington, DC, among many other venues. She is on the editorial board for *Polish Music Journal* and editor of *The Age of Chopin: Interdisiplinary Inquiries* (Indiana University Press, 2004).

JANE GOTTLIEB has been head librarian, graduate studies, at the Juilliard School since 1986. Born in Brooklyn, December 8, 1954, she learned flute as a child. She holds a BA from SUNY, Binghamton, and an MS in library science from Columbia. Her previous affiliations include librarian, American Music Center (1978–82); reference librarian, General Library of the Performing Arts, Lincoln Center (1982–83); and head librarian, Mannes College of Music (1983–86). She was president of the American Library Association (1995–97). In the musicology field, she was associate editor of *The Musical Woman: An International Perspective* (Greenwood Press, 1983–1991, 3 vols.); editor, *Collection Assessment in Music Libraries* (Music Library Association, 1994); co-compiler, *Knowing the Score: Preserving Collections of Music* (Music Library Association 1994); co-editor, *A Basic Music Library: Essential Scores and Sound Recordings*, third edition (American Library Association, 1997); author of the "Awards" article in *The New Grove Dictionary of American Music* (1986); and contributor of biographical entries for the *Dictionary of American Biography* and *Scribner Encyclopedia of American Lives*. Her writings cover book and music reviews in *Notes: Quarterly Journal of the Music Library Association*, as well as articles in *The Journal of the American Liszt Society*, *Fontes Artis Musicae* and *The Reference Librarian*. She has presented papers at meetings of the International Association of Music Libraries, ALA, MLA and International Congress on Women in Music.

In 2005, Gottlieb's title at Juilliard became vice president for library and information resources.

BONNIE GRICE has done much research on women in music. As a broadcaster, she brought instant auditory information to the public about many of the subjects covered in books, recordings and other sources. She began studying flute at eight, then voice for four years. She graduated from Miami University in Ohio with a bachelor's in English, a minor in music, and a master's in mass communications, after which she worked for the NPR affiliate WKSU in Kent, Ohio. While there, in 1987, she wrote the libretto of the a two-act chamber opera, *Mrs. Dalloway*, based on Virginia Woolf's novel of the same name. With music by **Libby Larsen**, the opera, the first by two American women, was premiered by Lyric Opera Cleveland at the Cleveland Institute, July 1993. It is sanctioned by the Virginia Woolf Estate for future performances.

Grice accompanied the Cleveland Orchestra during its 1987 Far East tour and 1989 European tour as their reporter. Moving to Long Beach, California, she worked with KUSC-FM, flagship station of the University of Southern California, with network stations in Santa Barbara, Ventura County and Palm Springs. She was host and producer of the station's *WAKE UP L.A.* program, featuring music and live interviews. For several months in 1996 she conceived, produced and hosted *Live on Hope Street with Bonnie Grice*, a half-hour program encompassing the arts spectrum.

As a champion of keeping classical music accessible to children, she has been instrumental in drawing attention to the plight of public schools' cutbacks on musical education, with visits to Los Angeles area schools giving presentations, and emceeing children's concerts. Grice received the Los Angeles City Elementary School Music Association "Honorary Life Membership Award" in recognition of her work.

Based on her research of Western composers past and contemporary, jazz, blues, New Wave, and Broadway music, she compiled a CD guide, *From Z to A: The Classical Music Lovers Alternative*. Winner of the 1992 Susan B. Anthony Award from the Hollywood chapter of the Business and Professional Women, Grice is on the advisory board of the Hildegard Publishing Company.

BEVERLY GRIGSBY, a computer music pioneer on the West Coast, was born in Chicago, January 11, 1928. The family moved to Los Angeles in 1941. She started college as pre-med, but when her father became ill during her undergraduate years, and she correctly diagnosed his condition, the doctors ignored her evaluation and her father died soon after. The tragedy caused Beverly to quit all thought of a medical career.

She switched to music, studying with famed Austrian composer **Ernst Krenek** (1900–91), who had been married to **Alma Mahler**, and like many came to America to escape Hitler. He introduced Beverly to modern music giants **Igor Stravinsky**, **Arnold Schoenberg** and *electronic music*. Somewhere in this period she married, had two children, and earned a BA (1961) and MA (1963) from Cal State-Northridge. Her DMA came later, (USC, 1986). She explored computer music at Stanford's Center of Artificial Intelligence (CCRMA) and MIT (1975–76), and sought out pioneer builders like David Buchla in San Francisco and Dartmouth (New Hampshire) Professor Jon Appleton, key developer of the Synclavier. In 1981, she bought her first Fairlight system: an integrated computer music system which featured notation software, digital audio, sampling, and sequencing.

At the other end of the spectrum, she studied medieval music at London's RCM, and Solemnes, France. This was recognized when she was made a Carnegie-Mellon Fellow in technology (1987), and a Getty Museum Research Scholar with special interests in medieval and renaissance periods (1997).

Professor emerita at Northridge, where she taught theory, composition and musicology for thirty years (1963–93), her enthusiasm for computers and synthesizers, despite opposition from many colleagues,[206] led her to develop the school's Electronic Music Studio—by this time she was divorced and trying to make it on her own—and serve as director of the Computer Music Studio she established in 1976. By 1980, she had co-founded the State of California Consortium for Computer Assisted Instruction in Music. Students poured through the doors of the facilities. Graduates in industry would return and teach.

As a composer, Grigsby received an NEA grant for her opera, *Moses*. She is credited with composing the first computerized score for an opera, *The Mask of Eleanor* (1984). *The Vision of Saint Joan* followed in 1987. Other electronic compositions include a score for the film *Ayamonn the Terrible* (1964), *Preludes on Poems of T. S. Eliot* (1968), *A Little Background Music* (1976), and *Morning At Seven* (1981–82).

A Shaky Awakening

On January 17, 1994, Northridge was the epicenter of a 6.7 earthquake—so far the most expensive in California's history. Virtually every building at the campus (about 100 structures) suffered damage, requiring more than $400 million in repairs. The renovations were completed in 2001. The Women in Music Collection, housed in the Oviatt Library, had been compiled in 1992 with the transfer of the contents of the Library of the International Institute for the Study of Women in Music founded by Grigsby and **Jeanne Pool**. This includes the *International Encyclopedia of Women Composers* (1981, second ed. 1987) by Aaron I. Cohen—the first such major

---

206. Ironically, in all the years she worked with analog synthesizers and then the digital systems, not one of the people who were upset about her work ever came into the studio to learn anything about the equipment!

compilation—a gift to the University, containing files on over 6,000 women composers, plus 469 catalogued vinyl phonograph recordings and 388 catalogued books, scores and pamphlets.

Since her retirement, Grigsby continues to explore new technology in composition, travel, teach and produce her music in Europe, the U.S. and Canada. In 1999, she chaired the Eleventh International Congress of Women in Music for the IAWM in London.

Getting computers into the university was a tough road all the way, with Beverly having to dig into her own pocket many times. She has established a trust fund to keep new equipment coming into the studio. Having helped educate several generations of students, Grigsby serves as a role model to young women in arts technology.

JAN BELL GROH was born in El Dorado, Kansas, August 26, 1936. Her early role models were her grandmothers, one a church pianist, the other a singer, who filled her farm kitchen with music, hymn singing and folk songs. Her father died when Jan was three, leaving her mother the sole breadwinner. Despite the Depression, and her meager salary as a secretary—one of the few professional jobs open to women at the time—purchasing a piano for her daughter was a top priority. Jan began lessons at six. She finished her pre-college years with a summer at Interlochen. This, plus a summer at Aspen while she was in college, were formative experiences. She received her BME from Wichita State University (1958), where she met her husband-to-be, Jack Groh. They began a professional duet-singing career while still undergraduates. Upon graduation in 1958, they married and moved to California where both taught music in the Long Beach public schools. They also auditioned for the Hollywood Artists and Lecture Bureau, and signed their first management contract in 1960. Their son, Sean, was born in 1963. (In 1996, he and his wife presented Jan with a grandson, Jess.)

The Grohs continued singing professionally until they moved to the University of Arkansas, Fayetteville, in 1966. What was to be a two year assignment lasted until Jan's retirement in 1998. She taught music education and voice for a number of years before becoming assistant to the dean of the College of Education. Her husband was coordinator of vocal studies and director of choral activities in the music department until his retirement in 1997.

Jan Bell Groh's enlightening book, *Evening the Score: Women in Music and the Legacy of Frédérique Petrides*, was published by the University of Arkansas Press (1991). In 1992, the Gustavus Myers Center for the Study of Human Rights in the U.S. named it "Outstanding Book on the Subject of Human Rights in the U.S." In 1993, Groh received the Outstanding Research Award from her college. She has also been the recipient of a number of grants and is the author of many articles on women in music.

LYDIA HAMESSLEY joined the faculty at Hamilton College in Clinton, New York, in 1991, where she is an associate professor in medieval and renaissance music history, world music, women in music, and opera. Prior to this, as a lecturer, she taught jazz history and the music and art of Renaissance Italy at the University of Minnesota, where she began as a teaching assistant (1981–84). She received her BMusEd from Texas Lutheran College, *magna cum laude*, and an MA (1983), and PhD in musicology (1989) from the University of Minnesota. Her dissertation, "The Reception of the Italian Madrigal in England: A Repertorial Study of Manuscript Anthologies, *ca.* 1580–1620," traces the importation of Italian music into England.

Hamessley has served as reviewer for major books: *Musicology and Difference: Gender and Sexuality in Music Scholarship*, ed. Ruth A. Solie; *Women and Music*, ed. Karin Pendle; and many articles including "Signs: Journal of Woman in Culture and Society" and "American Ethnologist." She is the author of several articles on music in the Middle Ages and has presented many scholarly papers on a variety of topics including "Teaching Gender in the Music Curriculum," "Lost Honor and Torn Veils: A Depiction of Rape in the 17th Century Dramatic Song," "Teaching Courses on Women in Music: Sources, Methodologies and Approaches," as well as an edition of essays dealing with gender, sexuality and music, co-edited with **Elaine Barkin**.

Hamessley was coordinator for the conference "Feminist Theory and Music: Toward a Common Language," Minneapolis, 1991. In *Music & Letters*, she published "Queering The Pitch: The New Gay and Lesbian Musicology," and "Menacing Virgins: Images of Virginity in the Middle Ages and Renaissance." She is co-editor, with Elaine Barkin, of *Audible Traces: Gender, Identity, and Music* (Carciofoli Verlagshaus, Zurich, 1999).

Her continued research focuses on women in old-time and bluegrass music, and the music of Southern Appalachia. Lydia is an avid player of the clawhammer banjo, and a quilter—which is not an instrument, but a bedspread.

DEBORAH HAYES was born December 13, 1939, in Miami, Florida, but attended grades kindergarten through twelve in Piedmont, Northern California. From her mother, she learned to read music and play the piano, and took violin lessons at school. Given the advantage of attending small schools with strong music programs, she was asked to learn flute for the junior high band, and oboe and clarinet in senior high. She also sang in choirs, learned organ and was a substitute church organist. She pursued an interest in music history and theory through further academic study. Her BA is from Oberlin (1960), MA (1961) and PhD (1968) are from Stanford. In 1968, she joined the musicology faculty of the University of Colorado at Boulder, ascending the academic ladder from instructor (1968–70), assistant professor (1970–78), associate professor of musicology (1978–95), full professor (1995–2000) to associate dean of graduate studies of the College of Music (1994–99) and acting chair of the musicology faculty (1998–99), teaching courses in music history, especially the 18th, 19th and 20th centuries, and designed and taught courses on the history of women in music, until her retirement in May 2000 to concentrate on her writing.

Hayes is the author of bio-bibliographies on **Peggy-Glanville Hicks** (Greenwood Press, 1990) and Peter Sculthorpe (1993). Her other publications include translations of the theoretical writings of Jean-Philippe Rameau, an edition of *Keyboard Sonatas of Marie-Emmanuelle Bayon and Francesca LeBrun*, plus articles and reviews on European and American composers, 18th century to the present, which have appeared in the *New Grove Dictionary of Music and Musicians*, *Current Musicology*, *College Music Symposium*, and the Music Library Association journal, *Notes*. She is a member of the Sonneck Society for American Music, IAWM, CMS and AMS, where she was a committee member on the status of women (1991–94).

ELIZABETH HINKLE-TURNER, born in Norristown, Pennsylvania, May 25, 1964, into a cultured, musical family, was taken to concerts at an early age. She started piano at eight and violin at ten. Her BA (*summa cum laude*) in composition with applied studies in piano and violin, is from Trinity University (San Antonio, Texas, 1986), plus an MM in composition (1988), and DMA (1991) from the University of Illinois at Urbana. Her dissertation focused on the life, work and music of **Daria Semegen**. Besides receiving a Jory Copy Fellowship from the American Music Center (1992), she was a visiting composer at the Studios für electronische Musik of the Westdeutscher Rundfunk, Cologne (1989), visiting assistant professor at Oberlin (1991–93), visiting director of the Experimental Music Studios at the University of Iowa (1993–94), assistant professor in the cooperative extension program of the UIU School of Music (1995–96), visiting professor in the Music Technology Center at Florida International University (1996–97), and since 1998, at the University of North Texas (Denton), where she is an adjunct professor at the College of Music, and manager of the student services at the Computing Center. Her extensive computer knowledge (she is a Microsoft Certified Professional) is the basis for her teaching and composing.

Hinkle-Turner's publications have appeared in the *IAWM Journal*, *New Grove Dictionary of Women Composers*, *New Grove Dictionary of Music and Musicians*, *Leonardo Journal of Art and Technology*, and her book, *Crossing the Line: Women Composers and Music Technology in the United States* (Ashgate Press, London), is the history of women composers of electronic and computer music, and multi-media works. She has served as a reviewer for W.C. Brown Communications and Oxford University Press.

Her awards include the L'Institut International de Musique Electroacoustique de Bourges, ASCAP, Mu Phi Epsilon, Meet the Composer, and the American Music Center. She was treasurer (1996) of the Society for Electro–Acoustic Music in the United States (SEAMUS) and their secretary through 2005. She is Webmaster for the IAWM.

Her own works are in multimedia, electroacoustic, instruments and electronics, and have been recorded at the UIU Experimental Music Studios, performed throughout the U.S. and South America and broadcast in Europe.

She successfully branched out into video and software production with the 1996 issue of her CD-ROM, *An Introduction to Electro-Acoustic Music*, which has been followed by the CD-ROM *Full Circle*. She is the owner of WAVELIST, a website devoted to the discussion and study of gender issues in music technology; and creator and editor of the Selected Discography of Women's Electroacoustic Music, a catalog of women's electroacoustic music available on CD, updated quarterly. *A Stitch in Time*, an interactive video and sound work, was premiered at the SEAMUS 2000 conference.

BARBARA GARVEY JACKSON, born September 27, 1927, in Normal, Illinois, received her BM from the University of Illinois at Urbana (1950), MM (Eastman, 1952) and PhD in musicology (Stanford, 1959). In her thirty-seven years of teaching, of which thirty-two were at the University of Arkansas, her subjects included theory, music history and analysis, performance practice, plus graduate courses in the medieval through classical eras. She organized early music concerts and was director of the chamber group, Collegium Musicum. Besides chamber music participation, she was a violinist for many years in the North Arkansas Symphony Orchestra, and principal viola with the Little Rock Symphony. In recent years, her interests shifted from modern to baroque violin, viola da gamba and fortepiano.

Awarded the Master Teaching Award by Fulbright College of the University of Arkansas in 1988, she is an honorary member of Sigma Alpha Iota, Delta Phi Alpha and Pi Kappa Lambda. She served on the National Council of the AMS, on the board of the Midwest Historical Keyboard Society, and as a past president of the South Central Society for 18th Century Studies. She is co-author with Bruce Benward of *Practical Beginning Theory* (1963), now in its seventh edition and one of the leading texts used for music courses. She and Wesley Thomas, formerly of the UA German department, co-authored two books on the German *minnesong*, and is co-author with Joel Berman (U. of Maryland) of *The A.S.T.A. Dictionary of Bowing Terms* for the American String Teachers' Association. She has published articles in journals and encyclopedias on 20th century black composers **Florence Price** and **Margaret Bonds**, and 18th century composer **Camilla de Rossi**. She wrote the chapter on 17th and 18th century women in *Women in Music: A History* (Indiana U. Press, 1991), and contributed entries in the *New Grove Dictionary of Women Composers* (1994), plus reviews for *American String Teacher* and *Journal of the Viola da Gamba Society of America*.

Her publishing company, ClarNan Editions (named for **Clara Schumann**, **Nannerl Mozart** and piano builder **Nannette Stein Streicher**), specializes in historical music by women composers. Their catalogue features over two dozen performance publications of sheet music by women composers through the ages, with the catalogue growing continuously.

Jackson's other monumental contribution to music, the result of more than a decade of research, is *Say Can You Deny Me: A Guide to Surviving Music by Women from the 16th through the 18th Centuries* (U. of Arkansas Press, 1994), pinpointing locations in over 400 libraries in Europe, America, Canada, Latin America, New Zealand and Australia. A treasure trove for scholars and performers!

Barbara was made professor emeritus upon her retirement, May 1991.

BARBARA JEPSON writes regularly on classical music for the *Wall Street Journal* and the *New York Times*. Her articles have appeared in publications ranging from the *American Record Guide*, *Keynote*,[207] *Ovation*,[208] *Stagebill* and *Connoisseur*,[209] to *Town and Country* and *Smithsonian*.

Born January 2, 1946, in Teaneck, New Jersey, Barbara's earliest exposure to music came from her father, a self-taught guitarist, pianist and harmonica player, and her opera-loving mother. Piano lessons began at age nine. With music, art history and European history as areas of specialization, Jepson graduated *summa cum laude* with a BA in liberal arts from Marymount Manhattan College (1974). Additional studies in piano, music theory and music history followed at Mannes. A stint as associate editor of the *Feminist Art Journal*[210] (1975–77), spiked her interest in women's studies.

207–210. No longer published.

As a freelance journalist since 1976, Jepson is particularly interested in contemporary music. Her many articles on women in classical music encompass composers, conductors, performers and music industry executives. She wrote chapters in Volumes I (1983) and III (1990) of *The Musical Woman* (ed. **Judith Lang Zaimont**, Greenwood Press, NY, 1990) on women music critics and women in the recording industry. She has also contributed entries to the *New Grove Dictionary of American Music* (1986) and the *Norton/Grove Dictionary of Women Composers* (1995).

Her professional affiliations include membership in the Music Critics Association, where she served as a board member from 1998–2001, the American Society of Journalists and Authors, and the Authors Guild. In 1985, Jepson won the Deems Taylor Award for Music Journalism. In 1994, as the result of an article she had written in 1993 on pianist John Browning for the *New York Times Arts and Leisure* section, she was interviewed for a profile of the artist by *CBS Sunday Morning*. She has also composed several worship songs.

The titles of some of the articles convey the scope of Jepson's genre: "Who's That Man With Marilyn Horne?" a look at the unsung talents of accompanists (*New York Times Magazine*, April 16, 1989); "Managing Musical Superstars," a profile of **Lee Lamont**, chairman, ICM Artists (*NYT Magazine*, September 24, 1989); "A Woman's Place is on the Podium," featuring conductor **Marin Alsop** (*Wall Street Journal, Leisure and the Arts*, December 18, 1991); "For an Uncommon Woman, Fanfare Comes Full Circle,"on composer **Joan Tower**, (*NYT Arts and Leisure*, January 2, 1994); "A Prodigy Still, but Uneasily Older," about **Midori**, discussing the pros and cons of promoting young virtuosos (*NYT*, January 22, 1995); "Pioneer Composer and Folkie," reviews of a Deutsche Grammophon recording of the music of **Ruth Crawford Seeger**, and the biography of Seeger by musicologist **Judith Tick** (*WSJ, Weekend*, March 27, 1998); and "Viola Sisters Triumph in New Concerto," a review/discussion of a new work by **Sofia Gubaidulina**, premiered by the New York Philharmonic (*WSJ*, May 4, 1999).

With the new century, Jepson addressed many contemporary facets of classical music with such articles as "In Philadelphia, A Beautiful Hall With Mixed Acoustics," which evaluated the Kimmel Center (*Wall Street Journal*, December 20, 2001); and "Where Gehry Pulled Out All the Stops," a report on architect Frank Gehry and the opening of the new Walt Disney Concert Hall (*WSJ*, October 13, 2004). New conductors on the scene included "Sonic Boom: An Orchestra Moves Ahead," featuring Yuri Temirkanov and Baltimore (*WSJ*, April 23, 2003); and "Minn. + Finn = A Promising Combination," on the first season of Finnish Osmo Vänskä and the Minnesota Orchestra (*WSJ*, February 5, 2004).

Articles on performers featured **Martha Argerich** and Lang Lang in "Two Pianists, an Introvert and an Extrovert" (*WSJ*, May 29, 2002); "That's 'Pianist' Please, Not 'Conductor,'" about Japanese pianist **Mitsuko Uchida**, who also happens to be artistic director of Marlboro Music Festival (*WSJ*, May 8, 2003); and "The Orchestra's Tightrope Walker" a look at New York Philharmonic concertmaster Glenn Dicterow (*WSJ*, March 25, 2003). Jepson also continues authoring many articles in the *New York Times* and *Opera News*. A memorable excerpt from the latter's December 2001 issue covering her evaluation of fifteen years of opera supertitles—text translations projected above the proscenium—gives an example of the occasional mishap 'twixt text and technology. In the final act of *La bohème* at Washington Opera, Mimi, failing rapidly, clutched Rodolfo's arm and pleaded, "You won't leave me?" A laptop pressed into last-minute service flashed this unexpected rejoinder: "Your battery is failing and your screen has been dimmed to conserve power."

Barbara is married to investment advisor, Hans G. Jepson.

DEBORAH KAVÁSCH, born July 15, 1949, in Washington, DC, is the daughter of a minister. Her first childhood memories involved music. She would sing along with her "golden" records for hours, go across the street on Saturdays to play the piano in the church school, and sit in the front pew on Sunday mornings to marvel at beautiful sound of the choir. She started piano at eight and violin at nine.

In 1969, she spent a year studying German at the University of Salzburg, plus music theory and violin at the Mozarteum. From 1967–73, she attended Bowling Green State, Ohio (BA in German; BM, MM in theory and composition) and PhD (UCSD, 1978). Since 1979, Kavásch has been professor of music at Cal State Stanislaus, Central California.

Like **Joan LaBarbara**, she is noted for her pioneering work in modern vocal music, particularly in "extended vocal techniques"—sounds discovered through study of the music of other cultures that extend beyond traditional *bel canto*. As a Fulbright Senior Scholar, Kavásch further researched this field at the invitation of the Commission for Artistic Development at the State Academy of Music in Stockholm.

A founding member of the Extended Vocal Techniques Ensemble of UCSD, she continues to develop an ensemble and solo repertoire in the genre. With grants and residencies in composition and performance from the NEA, the Djerassi Foundation, California Arts Council and Meet the Composer, her works have been commissioned and performed in North America and Europe. She has appeared in concert in major international music centers and festivals. She uses her extensive range and unique vocal capabilities to evaluate traditional repertoire as well as the highly demanding vocal acrobatics of the contemporary scene.

Her many choral compositions include *The Bells*, *I Will Lift Up Mine Eyes*, *The Owl and the Pussycat*, *Beauty and the Beast*, *The Crow and the Pitcher*, *The Tortoise and the Hare* and *Requiem*. *Built on a Rock*, *Hallowed Be Thy Name*, *Rock of Ages*, *We All Believe in One True God* are for Women's Chorus. Instrumental works feature *Aviary Suite* (5 movements for solo clarinet), *Celestial Dreamscape* (2 movements for solo clarinet), *Kaleidoscope* (5 movements for solo tuba), *Nocturne* (2 movements for solo clarinet), *Trio for Violin, Clarinet, Piano* (8 movements) and *Evolutions*. *Desert Storm 1991* is for orchestra, *Inaugural Fanfare 1995* for brass and percussion, *Fanfare for Those Who Served 1999*, *Celebration 2000* for Band/Wind Ensemble, and *O Captain! My Captain!* for baritone, alto saxophone, percussion (2001). 2002 brought *Nocturne* (piano) and *Dragonslayer* (solo horn). *The Fox and the Grapes* (soprano, English horn), *Lacrimosa* (trilogy for soprano, baritone, piano), and *Feather on God's Breath* (mixed chorus, a capella) were among the 2003 output. *The Elements*, an arrangement of *The Star Spangled Banner* for SSAA, and *Songs of the Prairie*, performed by the composer to favorable reviews, were written in 2004.

Among her recordings are *The Dark Side of the Muse: Music of Deborah Kavásch* (Cambria, 1999) and *Fables & Fantasies: Music of Deborah Kavásch, composer/soprano* (TNC Classical, 2001). She is the featured soprano soloist on *Music of Beverly Grigsby*, containing *The Mask of Eleanor*, *The Vision of St. Joan*, and *Shakti II*. She has many articles to her credit.

2005 was an eventful year with her *Trio for Violin, Clarinet and Piano* (8 movements), revised in 2002, a winner of the Chamber Music Competition of the 2005 Athena Festival with the Murray State University Band/Wind Ensemble. Later in the year was the premiere of *Songs of the Swan Maiden* (English horn, harp and soprano) with performances on two of the San Francisco Symphony Series, Chamber Music Sundaes in Berkeley, and the Chamber Music Series at Davies Hall—which marked her singing debut at that venue.

Deborah is married to John Marvin, formerly oboe/English horn with the Kennedy Center Opera Orchestra, now retired and a fulltime composer.

ROSEMARY N. KILLAM is an organist and pianist with a BM from Eastman (1960), where she was a National Merit Scholar, an MM from George Washington University (1969), and DMA from Stanford (1976). After teaching at Stanford and San Francisco State University, she moved to Texas in 1977, where she has been on the faculty of the University of North Texas as professor of music theory. An authority on computer assisted instruction, her many presentations, papers, publications and books have been related to CAI and the use of Apple Computers in music notation. She serves on the board of the Missouri Folklore Society, and in 1990 was on leave as an invited scholar at the Stanford Institute for Research on Women and Gender. Since 1994, she has been a co-leader there in Women's Studies: An Interdisciplinary Survey. Her research centers on relationships of aural perception, folk music and music theory pedagogy within a context of feminist theories. Her work has been published in the *Journal of Music Theory*, *Music Theory Spectrum*, *Journal of Music Theory Pedagogy* and *Perspectives of New Music*.

ELLEN KOSKOFF, an ethnomusicologist and professor of musicology at Eastman, has been a visiting professor in the fine arts department at Syracuse University, NYU and UCLA. She is the editor of *Women and Music in Cross-Cultural Perspective* (Greenwood Press, 1987), *The Garland Encyclopedia of Music, Vol. 3, "The United States and Canada"* and author of *Music in Lubavitcher Life* (U. of Illinois Press, 2000). Her published articles include "Thoughts on Universals in Music" in *World of Music* (1984), plus others on gender and music, womens' roles in ritual and performance, and Hasidic music. She has also contributed to such journals as *Selected Reports in Ethnomusicology, World of Music* and *Ethnomusicology*, where she served as book review editor.

Koskoff was born in Pittsburgh, 1943, graduated from Boston University (1965), Columbia (1967), and received her PhD in musicology from the University of Pittsburgh (1976). She comes from a musical family which includes composer Henry F. Gilbert, and Hollywood composers/arrangers, Alfred, Lionel, and Randy Newman. She enjoys playing in Eastman's Balinese Gamelan and being host of a local NPR radio program, "What in the World is Music?" She was elected president of the Society for Ethnomusicology in 2000, and chosen in 2002 as an ASCAP-Deems Taylor Award winner.

Ellen lives in Rochester, New York, with her husband, composer and music theorist, Robert Morris. They have a son, David.

LAURA KUHN is a musicologist, writer, teacher and musician. Born January 19, 1953, in San Francisco, she inherited her love of music from her pianist father, her amateur opera-singing grandmother, and her grandfather, a professional pianist, one of whose pupils was **José Iturbi**. Her BA in music from Dominican College covers a double major of musicology and voice. Her master's and PhD in systematic musicology are from UCLA. From 1986–92, she worked extensively with **John Cage** (1912–92) on his Charles Eliot Norton lectures for Harvard (I-IV, 1989) and his *Europas 1 & 2* for Frankfurt Opera—the subject of her doctoral dissertation. As music advisor to the estate of John Cage, Kuhn collaborated with a team of eminent American and European scholars to complete an inventory of the Cage music manuscript collection, later placed in the New York Public Library of the Performing Arts. In early 1993, she worked with long-time Cage associate Merce Cunningham to establish a John Cage Trust, of which she is the director.

Kuhn's writings on subjects ranging from music and dance to visual arts and interdisciplinarity have appeared in *Perspectives of New Music, High Performance Magazine, The Musical Quarterly*, and both the *New York* and *Los Angeles Times*. Essays include "John Cage in the Social Realm: Blurring Distinctions/Seeing Wholeness" for the touring edition catalogue of the Los Angeles Museum of Contemporary Art; "Rolywholyover: A Circus," and "Technology, Environment and Art: Dynamics of Synergy in Cage's *Europas 1 & 2*," which appeared in Tokyo's *Music Today Quarterly* (May 1993) and *The Musical Quarterly* (Spring 1994).

An award winning teacher, Kuhn retired from her position as assistant professor of cultural history in the Interdisciplinary Arts and Performance program at Arizona State University West in 1996. She has given workshops and lectures in South America, England and throughout Europe. "Cage and Zen" was presented at the Days of Silence Conference (Warsaw, 1993). The symposium Art and Science Looking Into the Third Millenium (Lisbon 1994), featured her poetic *On the Ocean*, also given later that year at an international art and dance festival in Brussels. 1995 speaking engagements included "Interart Perspectives" in Lund, Sweden, and John Cage conferences in Berlin and at Mills College (Oakland). The same year, she was appointed secretary and executive committee member of the board of directors of the American Music Center, New York. She seeks to find bridges between people and the arts, as well as within and among the arts.

A major project for Kuhn was giving vital editorial assistance, along with researcher Dennis McIntire, to famed Russian-born American lexicographer **Nicholas Slonimsky** (1894–1995) for successive editions of his *Baker's Biographical Dictionary of Musicians* and *Music Since 1900*. She inherited the co-editorship—with McIntyre—of these tomes, as well as the additions to these founts of information, including *Baker's Biographical Dictionary of Contemporary Musicians* (Schirmer Books, 2001), which was issued in 6 volumes. (And cost $2,000!)

JANE WEINER LEPAGE is the author of an original trilogy of books, *Women Composers, Conductors and Musicians of the Twentieth Century* (University Press of America, Vol I, 1980; II, 1983; III, 1988), whose ten years of research took her and husband, William, from their home in Massachusetts across America to Europe and Australia to personally interview all fifty-two entries comprising the work. This oeuvre served as a foundation for many other studies to come, illuminating the contributions and accomplishments of gifted women musicians of the 20th century.

Born Jane Elizabeth Allen, May 7, 1931, in Montague, Massachusetts, she received her BM with a minor in trombone from Boston University (1956), and MS from the University of Massachusetts (1957). She was the recipient of fellowships from the Learned Societies of America and the Ford Foundation. In 1950, she married music teacher Benjamin Weiner, who also played trombone. They had four children[211] before she was left a widow in 1960. She has been married to William LePage for over forty years. Their one daughter. Renay, presented them with triplet granddaughters. An August 2006 phone call confirmed she now has seventeen grandchildren.

LePage was professor of music and chair of the music department of North Adams State College from 1967 until her retirement in 1990. She was selected a National Arts Associate in 1984 and has received numerous awards, including the Senior Faculty Award in 1989 for noteworthy scholarly contributions, which have bestowed honor on the college. Praised by the academic community for their independence, organization, focus and clarity, are national journal articles such as "Are We Discriminating Against Women Colleagues?" "Creative Musicians," "How Are Grants Determined by Major Orchestras?" "Reach Out and Create" and "The Author Speaks."

She has been a guest speaker at national and international conferences on the accomplishments of women in music. Her philosophy can be found in the preface of one of her books: *Ideally there should be no need to separate the sexes; merit should be based solely on artistic ability.*

Kimberly Marshall

KIMBERLY MARSHALL was born May 8, 1959, in Winston-Salem, North Carolina. She joined the faculty of Arizona State University as an associate professor of organ in 1998, where she heads the program of organ studies. As dean of postgraduate studies at London's Royal Academy of Music (1993–96), she created a new master's program in performance in conjunction with King's College, London. Her previous position was at Stanford as university organist and assistant professor of music (1986–93).

She began organ studies at the North Carolina School of the Arts. Her early interest in French music took her to France where she worked with L. Robilliard and Xavier Darasse, winning the Médaille d'Or in organ performance from the Lyon Conservatory, before returning to the University of North Carolina at Chapel Hill to complete her undergraduate degree in French. She received her PhD in music from University College, Oxford, where her dissertation was *Iconographical Evidence for the Late-Medieval Organ in French, Flemish, and English Manuscripts* (Garland, 1989). She has lectured on the performance practice of late-medieval organ music at meetings of the American Musicological Society, the Berkeley Organ Conference, and the organ course in Romainmotier, Switzerland. In recognition of her work, Marshall was awarded a Fulbright Scholarship to continue research and teaching at the Sydney Conservatorium (Australia, 1991). Winner of the St. Albans Competition in 1985, she has played in London's Royal Festival Hall, King's College, Cambridge, Chartres Cathedral (France), Uppsala Cathedral (Sweden), and the Dormition Abbey in Jerusalem. She has also performed on historic instruments such as the Couperin organ at Saint-Gérvais, Paris, the Gothic organ in Sion, Switzerland, the Cahmann organ in Leufstabruk, Sweden, and recorded for Radio-France, the BBC and ABC (Australia). Her CDs feature music of the Italian and Spanish renaissance, French classical and romantic periods, Bach, and organ works by women, including **Fanny Hensel**, **Ethyl Smyth** and

---

211. In her books, LePage credits daughters Jane Weiner Sumner and Renay LePage Colpoys with research and interview help, and daughter-in-law Susan Weiner for research in Canada, plus acknowledging the support of her sons, Bruce and Buddy.

Elfrida Andrée (1841–1929), the first woman organist of Sweden. She is a project leader for Göteborg Organ Research Center (GOArt) at the University of Gothenburg (Göteborg), Sweden.

Editor of *Rediscovering the Muses* (Northeastern U. Press, 1993), on female traditions of music-making, with contributions by well-known musicologists such as Suzanne G. Cusick, Paula Higgins and Marshall herself, this significant book traces important roles played by women in music from Non-Western as well as Western cultures. Her two-volume anthology, *The Origins of Keyboard Music: Surviving Repertoire before 1550, Vol I: Late Medieval Music* (2000) and *Vol. II: Renaissance Music*, were published by Wayne Leupold Editions (2004).

In December 2004, Marshall and her family embarked upon an Italian sabbatical near Florence in the town of Pistoia,[212] which has a great tradition in organ building. She performed on four historical organs there, including the famed instrument made in the second half of the 17th century by Flemish organ maker Willem Hermans, in the Chiesa del Spirito Santo (Church of the Holy Spirit). Other concerts on this tour included a May appearance in Naumberg (Germany) concertizing on, in her words, "a stunning Bach organ!"

In August 2005, the family returned to Phoenix where this talented woman holds the endowed Patricia and Leonard Goldman Professorship in Organ at Arizona State University, and leads a very balanced career between performance and teaching. Kimberly lives with her teacher husband Adam Zweiback and their three sons, Jacob, born in London, 1994, Noah, Berkeley, 1997, and Aaron, Phoenix, 1999.

Susan McClary

SUSAN McCLARY is a professor of musicology at UCLA. Born October 2, 1946, in St. Louis, Missouri, she received her BM (1968) in piano from Southern Illinois University, an MA (1971) and a PhD (1976) in musicology from Harvard. She taught at the University of Minnesota (1977–91), McGill University (1991–94), and as a visiting professor at several universities in North America and abroad. In 1999–2000, she served as a Phi Beta Kappa Visiting Scholar. Her pioneer work, *Feminine Endings: Music, Gender, and Sexuality* (U.of Minnesota Press, 1991; second ed. 2002), examines cultural constructions of gender and sexuality, in various musical repertories, ranging from early 17th century opera to the songs of Madonna. Her research interests range from cultural and feminist music criticism, 16th century to popular, and new music. She is also author of *Conventional Wisdom: The Content of Musical Form*, based on her Bloch Lectures at Berkeley (University of California Press, 2001); *Georges Bizet: Carmen* (Cambridge University Press, 1992); co-editor with Richard Leppert of *Music and Society: The Politics of Composition, Performance and Reception* (Cambridge 1987); and contributed columns on popular music to *The Village Voice*. Her compositions include *Hildegard*, a collaborative music-theater piece on cosmology, music and illuminations of **Hildegard von Bingen**, and *Susanna Does the Elders: Confessions of a Tanna Leaf Smoker*, a full-length music-theater piece.

McClary has been acting director, Center for Humanistic Studies, University of Minnesota (1984–85); co-editor of Music/Culture Series, Wesleyan University Press (1992–); and has been on the editorial boards of University of California Press (1995–2001), *Signs* (1990–), *Perspectives of New Music* (1993–), and the *Journal of the American Musicological Society* (1992–95). She says, "I believe my work sheds light on how music affects us and why it is so influential."

In 1995, she was the delighted winner of the exciting and generous MacArthur Prize.[213]

EVE R. MEYER, longtime editor of the IAWM Journal, was born in Philadelphia and began piano studies at age five. She received her BM and MM at Temple University, and PhD from the University of Pennsylvania. Rather

---

212. From the 1700s to the early 1900s the Tronci and Agati families built about a hundred instruments that are in the most important churches and the largest concert halls all over the world. Since 1975, Pistoia has been the seat of the Italian Music Academy for Organs.

213. This wonderful surprise is bestowed upon the recipient without prior notice. The foundation, which began in 1978 after the death of Chicago philanthropist John D. MacArthur, is a talent search for significant contributions by American citizens. Names are proposed by over one hundred designated nominators serving anonymously for one year. Their nominations are reviewed by a twelve member committee which meets eight times a year. There is no annual quota, no strings attached, and recipients are free to use the money any way they wish. Grants range from $150,000 to $375,000.

Eve Meyer

than embark upon a performing career, she decided in favor of marriage and a position as an educator and musicologist. She received her appointment to Temple, where she was professor of music history and chair of the department. In the course of this vocation, she won the coveted Lindback Foundation Award for Distinguished Teaching, and the Temple University *Great Teacher Award.* She has distinguished herself as a lecturer and scholar, specializing in European and American music of the 18th century. A leading authority on the Turks in European performing arts, she was the only musicologist to present a paper on the subject, "The Age of Suleyman the Magnificent," at the international conference held at Princeton (1987). She is also a leading expert on music in Philadelphia from colonial times to the present. As author and sole performer, in 1962 she appeared on six of the programs of the educational television series *University of the Air: The World of Music,* taped and syndicated throughout the U.S. She was on the editorial board of the College Music Symposium (1980–87), and on the National Executive Council (1974–77) of the AMS. Her books include *The Secular and Sacred Songs of Benjamin Carr, Benjamin Carr's Musical Miscellany,* and *Selected Divertimenti . . . of Florian Leopold Gassmann.* Since her retirement from Temple, June 1996, she has been editor-in-chief of the *International Alliance for Women in Music Journal.* She is a senior editor, and contributor of essays and editions of music to *Women Composers: Music Through the Ages,* and has written book chapters and articles for professional journals, the *New Grove* dictionaries, and the German *Die Musik in Geschichte und Gegenwart.* Meyer is also a consultant for major publishers such as Random House, Prentice-Hall, Schirmer, Macmillan, and the Educational Testing Service at Princeton.

CAROL NEULS-BATES received her BA *cum laude* from Wellesley (1961) and PhD in musicology from Yale (1970). Sponsored by the NEH in 1979, she participated in the Careers in Business Program at NYU's Graduate Program of Business Administration. From 1972–75, she was the managing editor of Repertoire Internationale Literature Musicale (RILM) Abstracts of Music Literature at the NYU Graduate Center, while concurrently serving as associate editor, 1973–75, of the *College Music Symposium Journal.* 1975–76 was spent as assistant to the curator of the Toscanini Memorial Archives at the New York Public Library. From 1976–79, she was co-principal investigator and project director for *Women in American Music: A Bibliography of Music and Literature,* funded by the NEH and the Ford Foundation. After four years as assistant professor at Brooklyn College (CUNY, 1978–82), Neuls-Bates entered the business world rising from account executive to, as of 1986, vice president of the John O'Donnell Company, a financial development and public relations firm for non-profit organizations.

It was in 1973, after being involved for three years in the women's movement on contemporary issues, that Neuls-Bates consulted the card catalogue of the music division of the New York Public Library and was amazed to find a sizeable category of references for women in music, dating from the turn of the 19th century. This discovery led first to her essay "Women's Orchestras in the United States, 1925–45" in *Women Making Music* (eds. Jane Bowers and Judith Tick, U. of Illinois Press, 1986), German edition (Furore Verlag, 1996). She also edited the *Women in American Music* bibliography, and *Women in Music: An Anthology of Source Readings from the Middle Ages to the Present* (Harper & Row, 1982), and its revised edition (Northeastern University Press, 1995).

Neuls-Bates is the author of numerous articles in *The New Grove Dictionary of American Music* (1986), *The New Grove Dictionary of Opera* (1992), and *The Norton/Grove Dictionary of Women Composers* (1995). In addition to Brooklyn College, she also has taught at the University of Connecticut, Yale and Hunter College (CUNY).

Carol Oja

CAROL J. OJA, born March 18, 1953, received her BA from St. Olaf College (Minnesota, 1974), M.Phil, (1980) and PhD (1985) from the Graduate School of CUNY. In her teaching career at Brooklyn College, Conservatory of Music, she went from assistant professor (1985–89) to associate (1989–94—tenured in 1990), to full professor (1995). In 1993, she became director for the Institute for Studies in American Music. She has been on the faculty of the PhD music program of CUNY's graduate school, and is the Margaret and David Bottoms professor of music, and professor of American studies at the College of William and Mary.

Oja's honors and awards include a Martha Baird Rockefeller Dissertation Research Grant (1982), NEH grants and fellowships, and a National Humanities Center Fellowship (1995–96). She compiled a discography of 20th century American composers, listing over 13,000 recordings, which received the American Library Association's "Best Reference Book of 1982" award. Her numerous writings encompass books on Stravinsky and modern American composers. She won the 1983 ASCAP/Deems Taylor Book Award.

In 2001, Oja was awarded the Irving Lowens Memorial Award for best book with her publication of *Making Music Modern: New York in the 1920s*. Her article "Women Patrons and Crusaders for Modernist Music in New York: the 1920s," appears in *Women Activists in American Music*, (U. of California Press, Berkeley; eds. Ralph Locke and Cyrilla Barr). Of her many reviews, *Women in Music* (ed. **Karin Pendle**) appeared in the *College Music Symposium*.

A member of the AMS, Oja has been on their Publication of American Music (1991–), and the 1995 New York Meeting Program Committees, as well as the 1995 panel for the first Herb Alpert/Cal Arts Award. One of her important projects as co-chair/founder of the AMS Committee on Cultural Diversity (1992–) is the development of an "Alliance for Minority Participation in Musicology"—a consortium of graduate programs recruiting minority students and funding their graduate work.

KARIN PENDLE was born in Minneapolis, October 1, 1939. As a child, participating in choral ensembles in school and church, she realized her singing talent, but did not receive formal voice instruction until college. She earned her BA in music from the University of Minnesota (1961). Soloist with many groups, including the London (Ontario) Symphony, Minnesota Orchestra, Cincinnati Symphony and May Festival Chorus, despite her many scholarships and academic honors she received more encouragement as a singer than a music historian. With fellowships and assistantships for graduate study at the University of Illinois, she received her MM (1963) and PhD (1970). Her teaching career spans Oberlin College (1964–69), the University of Western Ontario (1970–76), and the University of Cincinnati (1976–2004), where she was the only music person on the faculty of the Center for Women's Studies, held the rank of professor of musicology, and is now professor emerita. She has been an officer of UC's Association for Women Faculty, and the American Association of University Professors. She is a member of the Society for American Music, and the AMS—for which she was president of the Midwest Chapter and member of the National Council.

Many of her numerous publications reflect valuable in-depth research on French opera (1760–1860), with such books as *Eugène Scribe and French Opera of the Nineteenth Century* (UMI Research Press, 1979), *Opera in Context: Essays on Historical Staging from the Seventeenth Century to the Early Twentieth Century* (Amadeus Press 1996), and essays including "Opéra-Comique in Paris, 1762–1789," in *L'opéra-comique en France des origines à 1789*, "Opéra-comique as Literature: The Spread of French Styles in Europe circa 1760 to the Revolution," in *Grétry at l'Europe de l'opéra-comique*—both published by Pierre Mardaga, 1992—and "Paradise Found: The Salle Le Peletier and French Grand Opera" with co-author Stephen Wilkins. She edited and wrote the introduction, plus a chapter covering the years 1450–1600, in the definitive *Women and Music: A History* (Indiana U. Press, 1991). In the second edition (2000), she added her own chapter on contemporary music in Europe, Israel, Australia and New Zealand, along with an introductory chapter and a chapter dealing with women's music in the Early Modern Period. Of her many articles, "Thea Musgrave: The Singer and the Song" appeared in the *Journal of the National Association of Teachers of Singing* (Nov-Dec. 1986), and "Lost Voices" in July 1992 *Opera News*, featuring **Louise Talma**, **Miriam Gideon**, **Dorothy Rudd Moore**, **Julia Perry** and **Libby Larson**.

In a 1995 special issue of *Contemporary Music Review*, dealing with living American women composers, Pendle served as general editor, interviewed **Augusta Read Thomas**, and wrote the introduction and an article on women composers of music for the stage. She presented a paper on black women composers for the Conference on *Music, Gender, and Pedagogy* at Sweden's Göteborg University, April 1996, organized by

Margaret Myers. She also contributed information and music by Cincinnati composer Ethel Glenn Hier to the multi-volume set *Women Composers: Music through the Ages* (eds. S. Glickman and M. Schleiffer). In 2005, as part of the Routledge series, she brought out *Women in Music: A Resource and Information Guide* covering ethnomusicology of composers and performers all the way to jazz and rock.

Karin has been married to American historian Frank Pendle since 1966.

JOAN PEYSER was born in New York City, June 12, 1931. Her mother, an excellent amateur pianist, guided the girl to the right teachers. At five, she studied with Henrietta Michaelson at Juilliard. At thirteen, she played in Town Hall. Her undergraduate work was at Smith Collage and Barnard (BA, 1951), followed by an MA in musicology from Columbia (1956). During graduate school she began submitting articles to music magazines, which led to her first book contract and writing for the music page of the *New York Times*. A musicologist, writer and biographer, Joan was the editor of *Musical Quarterly* (1977–83), and script writer for "The World of Music" television series.

Her books, psychoanalytical biographies of musical figures, focus on the people of music rather than the music itself. They include: *The New Music: The Sense Behind the Sound* (1971), reprinted as *Twentieth Century Music: The Sense Behind the Sound* (1980); *Boulez: Composer, Conductor, Enigma* (1976); *Bernstein: A Biography* (1987), revised and updated (1998); *The Memory of All That: The Life of George Gershwin* (1993); *To Boulez and Beyond: Music in Europe since "The Rite of Spring"* (1999); and *The Music of Our Time: Collected Essays and Articles* (1993). Peyser was editor of *The Orchestra: Origins and Transformations* (1986), revised and updated (2000). Her honors include citations from the Association of American Publishers, Humanities Category (1986), National Federation of Music Clubs (1995), and ASCAP/Deems Taylor Awards (1968, '70, '82, '84, 2000).

Joan's twenty-five year marriage to psychiatrist Herbert Peyser ended in divorce. Their children are: Dr. Karen Seligman, a pediatric cardiologist; Tony Peyser, a financial manager; and Monica Parks, program editor of the New York Philharmonic. Since 1989, Joan has found happiness with Frank Driggs, a jazz historian and archivist.

MARIANNE RICHERT PFAU began her career as an associate professor coordinating the music program and teaching music history and literature at the University of San Diego. She was chair of the music department, 1993–96. Specializing in medieval musicology, her publications include the complete sheet music edition of all seventy-one *Sinfonia* chants of **Hildegard von Bingen** (1998), and a three-CD set of the first complete recording, in 1997, of the *Isorhythmic Motets of Machaut and Dufay*, which have been favorably received in the U.S. and abroad. As a performer of historical wind instruments (baroque oboe and recorder), she has toured Germany, England, France and America. She regularly performs and records with the Los Angeles Baroque Orchestra, the San Francisco Bach Society, Portland Baroque Orchestra and many others. She is in the *World Who's Who of Women*, and in 1993 was proclaimed "International Woman of the Year" for her contribution to the fine arts.

Born in Germany March 31, 1955, Marianne was trained from childhood in music (recorder, historical wind instruments, piano, violin), and was a repeat winner of the German youth competitions *Jugend Musiziert*. She received diplomas in Historical Performance Practices and Pedagogy from the Musikhochschule Hamburg (1979), is a licentiate of music therapy from the Guildhall School of Music and Drama in London (1981), holds masters degrees in performance and music history from Southern Illinois University (1983) and SUNY, Stony Brook (1985), as well as a doctorate in musicology from Stony Brook (1990), where she was the research assistant of renowned medieval musicologist **Leo Treitler**. Her dissertation "Hildegard von Bingen's Symphonia Armonie Celestium Revelatium" is an analysis of Music Process, Modality and Text Music Relations.

Marianne came to this country when her then fiancé Michael R. Pfau was offered a teaching position at Southern Illinois University (1982–83). She also got a position there, teaching German. Intrigued with the American University mode of PhD study, the pair decided to get their respective doctorates in this country. Pfau was assistant professor of musicology at Vanderbilt University (1988–89), and came to USD in 1989 with her husband, an associate professor who headed the political science department until 2003, after which he continued his classroom teaching.

Made a full professor in 2003, she balances her life teaching at USD and as an international lecturer and performer on baroque oboe. Her latest work (in German), *Hildegard von Bingen: Der Klang des Himmels* (The Sound of Heaven) co-authored with Stefan Morent, is part of Vol. 1: *European Women Composers,* and was published by Boehlau Verlag Cologne and Vienna (2004).

Susan Pickett

SUSAN PICKETT is concertmaster, and has been an often featured soloist, of the Walla Walla (Washington State) Symphony since 1987. She joined the faculty of Whitman College in 1981, and in 1996 was appointed the Catherine Gould Chism professor of music, an endowed chair. In 1990, through the Library of Congress and the New York Library for the Performing Arts, she began researching the dearth of compositions by women. By 2005, she has discovered over a thousand works by several hundred women from the 17th through 21st centuries, almost all of which were unknown to the contemporary performer and audience. Comprising over 20,000 pages of music, she has published thirty editions by classical and romantic-era women (Hildegard Publishing and Simon & Schuster). In addition, she has completed an exhaustive study of the career and many works of one of the first well-known American women composers, **Marion Bauer** (1882–1955), a Walla Walla native, with material going back to the composer's parents, early Northwest pioneers.

Photocopying previously unpublished manuscripts, usually with falling apart pages, Pickett recreates publishable editions via computer software using the original instrumentation. In the late '90s, she brought out many works of pioneer Swedish organist **Elfrida Andrée** (1841–1929), including the first edition of her 1861 string quartet. Working with microfilm of the manuscript score and parts acquired from Stockholm, Pickett's knowledge of theory and style enabled her to correct the composer's mistakes and insert accidentals, dynamics, bowings, etc. This information is featured in her editorial notes included with each published reproduction. Andrée's *Concert-Ouverture*, a work reconstructed from manuscript, was performed in 1998 by the Walla Walla Symphony, and by the Swedish Broadcast Orchestra for Swedish television the following year. Challengingly, the research indicates that of the Western world's 6,000 known female composers over the last four centuries, *not one composition by a woman is consistently in the repertoire of a major ensemble!*

Born August 15, 1952, in Los Angeles, Susan began studying violin at age ten. During high school and undergraduate years at Occidental College, from which she graduated *magna cum laude* and Phi Beta Kappa, she frequently appeared as a recitalist and soloist. Her MM from Indiana University in violin performance with minors in theory and musicology, was awarded with high honors. After teaching at the college level for a year, Pickett earned her PhD in fine arts at Texas Tech University, then joined the faculty of Whitman. Besides her active performance schedule, she also composes in collaboration with her husband, Robert A. Johnson, a cardiologist and poet. Their work *Glasses*, for speaker, soprano, violin, and viola, was premiered in New York in 1992, and *Polynominal*, for chorus and string orchestra, whose text contains the names of seventy-eight mathematicians, in 1994.

Pickett formed the group *Donne e Doni* (Women and Gifts) with pianist Debra Richter and soprano Sonja Gourley, who play recitals of the recovered works. Their CDs feature compositions by **Isabella Leonarda**, **Princess Anna Amalie**, **Clara Schumann**, **Amy Beach**, **Marion Bauer**, and contemporary **Gwyneth Walker** who composed *An American Concerto* for Pickett, which premiered with the Walla Walla Symphony, October 1996.

The ever growing amount of modern editions of "rescued" works include two piano quintets, an overture, a viola transcription and a reprint of a Cello Sonata by **Louise Farrenc**; a piano quartet by **Louise Heritte-Viardot**; the Emilie Mayer cello sonata; a Piano Quintet, Piano Trio, two sonatas for violin and piano, and a string quartet by **Elfrida Andrée**; three pieces for violin and piano by **Luise Adolpha LeBeau**; four songs by **Marion Bauer**; and a song, *Se Viver Non Posso* (If I Can't Live) for voice violin and piano, *c* 1770, by 18th century Italian, **Caterina Allessandra**. The sheet music (except for Bauer) is published by the Hildegard Publishing Company which, under founder **Sylvia Glickman**, greatly contributes to the mounting international interest in women's music.

Susan Pickett's work has been featured by the Associated Press, Chronicle of Higher Education, Voice of America, numerous NPR stations and *Good Morning America*. With constant inquiries throughout the western world, her editions continue to be widely disseminated and performed.

Carol Plantamura

CAROL PLANTAMURA, born in Los Angeles, graduated from Occidental College and earned her MFA at SUNY, Buffalo, where she was an original member of the Rockefeller-funded Creative Associates under the direction of composer **Lukas Foss**. She began her professional career as a soprano singing with famed French conductor **Pierre Boulez** at the Monday Evening Concerts. Other prominent collaborations include John Cage, Luciano Berio, **Pauline Oliveros**, **Betsy Jolas** and Bernard Rands. Her twelve years in Italy found her performing with *Nuova Consonanza* in Rome, and *Ensemble intercontemporain* in Paris, plus many opera houses and with symphonies in Europe, Australia, New Zealand, Japan and America.

Plantamura was a founding member of *Musica Elettronica Viva* and *Teatro Musica*, Rome, and *2e-2m*, Paris. For fourteen years she was associated with *The Five Centuries Ensemble*, a group she founded to specialize in 17th and 20th century music.

In addition to Wergo and DGG, she has recorded several discs of contemporary American music for CRI, 17th century Italian music for "Italia" Fonit/Cetra, and 17th century Italian music by Italian Women Composers for **Leonarda**.

In 1978, Plantamura joined the faculty at University of California, San Diego (UCSD), teaching music and opera appreciation, and stimulating renewed interest in live performances of western art music. She performs with SONOR, a contemporary music ensemble at the University. From 1990–92, she was chairman of the music department. She is also a preview lecturer for San Diego Opera, discussing historical background, musical information, and stories about the composers and their operas. Author of *The Opera Lover's Guide to Europe* (Citadel, 1996), reflecting her years of living and performing there, she has also authored *The Children's Guide to Italian Opera*, as well as collaborating on the unique coloring book, *Women Composers* (Bellerophon, 1991).

JEANNIE POOL, born in Paris, Illinois, November 6, 1951, grew up in Springfield, Ohio, with two younger brothers, Dale and Marshall. She began clarinet at seven, sang in a girls glee club, and performed with local community groups and churches. She attended Ohio University as a journalism major, then became a reporter in Martin's Ferry-Wheeling, West Virginia. In 1971, she moved to Connecticut, studying flute at Hartford Conservatory while working in an insurance company. In 1973, she moved to New York, continued flute with Met Orchestra flutist Harold Bennett and, at Hunter College, studied with **Louise Talma**, **Ruth Anderson** and **Annea Lockwood**, **Myron Fink**, Louis Martin and L. Michael Griffel—who encouraged her to go into musicology at Columbia, where she worked with early electronic music experimenter **Otto Luening** (1900–96) on his memoirs, *Odyssey of An American Composer* (Charles Scribner's Sons, 1981). Also at Columbia, Pool began lecturing on women in music. In March 1980, she organized a conference/workshop focusing on 20th century string quartets by women composers, funded by BMI, ASCAP and other grants, with performances aired on NPR. The following year she founded the National Congress on Women in Music, sponsored by NYU's Music Department. With thirty-one countries represented, she was attaining her dream of becoming international.

In 1981, she moved to Los Angeles. Two years later she married Kevin Barker, had Amelia, born 1983, and Elliott, 1987. (They later divorced.) Between 1981–97, she produced the KPFK radio show "Music of the Americas," devoted to contemporary composers and musicians, and became a fellow in the Program for the Study of Women and Men in Society at USC.

Asked to organize another international congress, this time on the West Coast, during April 1–4, 1982, 150 people from twenty-nine countries were represented. Pool was elected president of the International Congress of Women in Music, with goals set to promote and recognize these women, provide information and make governments, educational institutions, foundations and the music business aware of women's contributions. The first issue of the ICWM newsletter came out January 1983. It became a comprehensive, valuable resource journal. For a few years there was both a ICWM newsletter and ICWM journal.

In 1985, Pool inaugurated the ICWM Pauline Alderman Prize for new scholarship on women in music. This was named in honor of her mentor, a musicology professor at USC, and pioneer in the study of women's work, who died in 1983.

Subsequent congresses took place in Mexico City (March 1984), Paris (October 1984) San Francisco (March 1985), and Atlanta (1986). In New York, 1990, Pool announced the merger of the ICWM with the International League of Women Composers (ILWC), founded by **Nancy Van de Vate**. At the 1993 music-ALASKAwomen festival, Jeannie gave the keynote address urging all women's music organizations to unite. The ICWM also became affiliated with the International Institute for the Study of Women in Music, developed by **Beverly Grigsby** at Cal State, Northridge, where Pool taught research methodology for graduate students and became director of the Faculty Materials Center.

In 1995, Pool's vision was realized with the establishment of the International Alliance for Women in Music (IAWM), uniting the American Women Composers AWC, ICWM and ILWC. Without receiving personal monetary compensation, she had put together a remarkable institution, bringing the attention of the music world to the importance of women's contributions in composition, performance, musicology and related genres. The same year, she received the National Association of Composers, USA (NACUSA) Award for her work as an advocate for American music and composers.

From 1988–90, she was a producer for the California Institute of the Arts School of Music, and in 1990 became executive director of the Film Music Society in Los Angeles (formerly the Society for the Preservation of Film Music), where she worked with famed music composer David Raksin (1912–2004). She serves as an advisor to the IAWM. As a composer she has had many of her orchestral, choral and chamber works performed in the U.S., Europe and Canada. She is a member of ASCAP. As of 2005, she was producing a series of concerts by contemporary composers at several venues, including the Church of the Lighted Window in La Cañada, near Los Angeles.

DEON NIELSEN PRICE is a prize-winning composer, pianist, educator and author. Her BA with Gold Medal Piano Award is from BYU, MM in piano and composition from the University of Michigan, and a DMA with honors in accompanying from USC. She has served on the music faculties of USC, UCSB, Cal State, Northridge, and is retired from the piano/theory faculty at El Camino College in Torrance, California. She sits on the executive boards of the National Association of Composers, USA, where she was elected president in January 2004, and the IAWM where she was president (1996–99), and re-elected to the board in 2004. She represents the IAWM at meetings of the American Alliance of Composers Organization.

Among her many awards and commissions are a Certificate of Honor for Outstanding Contributions to Musical Life (1990) from the former ICWM; grants from Meet the Composer/California (1987–1990); Musicians Union, Local 47; Performance Trust Fund (1981–1991); and ASCAP. In 1997, she received a Meet the Composer Grant, which supported her artist/composer residency at the University of Northern Iowa. She lectures on women in music and the work of IAWM at universities and national and international women's organizations.

Culver Crest Publications publishes her music and books, including *Accompanying Skills for Pianists*, and *SightPlay with Skillful Eyes*. Cambria Master Recordings has released four CDs of her music: *SunRays: Music of Deon Nielson Price*, *SunRays II: City Views*, *A Century of Clarinet Gems* (2000), featuring the Price Duo with music by Price and other composers on the same label, and *Clariphonia: Music of the 20th Century on Clarinet* (2001). In 2004, Tantara released *Mormoniana*.

Price performs on piano and harpsichord, conducts orchestras and choirs in musicals, cantatas, and oratorio performances, coaches chamber ensembles and vocalists, teaches theory, composition, piano and piano accompanying, and serves as an adjudicator on competition juries. She is also music editor for the film "My Confession," and executive composer for the film trilogy, "The Light," which includes her compositions *Love Theme*, *Healing, Light*, *Rise Up!* and *Miriam and Elisheva Duet*.

She concertizes throughout the U.S. and Europe as the *Price Duo* with her son, Dr. Berkeley A. Price, clarinetist, who received his DMA from Eastman and is on the faculty of West Virginia Wesleyan College. During 1999–2000, they gave sixteen performances at universities in California, Utah, Texas, Louisiana, and West Virginia. A performance devoted entirely to her works was featured at the July 1999 Eleventh IAWM Congress in London.

During the *Price Duo* tour in China, June 2–7, 2001, Deon pronounced that "Detente is alive and well among musicians in China and the U.S." They played to enthusiastic audiences at the Shanghai Conservatory, Beijing Central Conservatory and Beijing Concert Hall, among other venues. Added to their regular program were two contemporary works written especially for them: *Scherzo* by Dr. Yao Henglu, professor of composition at Beijing Central Conservatory; and *Zhaxi Island Rhapsody* by **Li Yiding**,[214] composer for Chinese Central Television. (Li Yiding, a co-founder of the Chinese Association of Women Composers, is on the board of directors and China liaison for IAWM. It was she who arranged the tour after meeting Dr. Price at the 1999 IAWM Conference in London. She has produced annual IAWM concerts since then.)

In June 2002, the *Price Duo* performed at the IAWM Annual Chamber Music Concert at the National Museum of Women in the Arts (Washington, DC), playing music by Price and IAWM composers Li Yiding and **Alex Shapiro**. In March 2003, Deon performed music by women composers at the Hildegard Festival at California State University, Stanislaus. In April, with a grant from Arts International, she performed *Three Faces of Kim, the Napalm Girl* with Korean violinist Wharim Kim, at the International Festival of Women Composers in Seoul. Produced by the Korean Women Composers Association and IAWM, it included a week of performances with 300 participants from many countries. This was followed in October with concerts in Ohio celebrating the ninety-fifth birthday of African-American composer **Zenobia Powell Perry** (1908–2004), performing and recording her music.

Celebrating Deon's seventieth birthday, May 2004 brought a Los Angeles concert from her Sacred Choral Collection. August found the *Price Duo* at the Festival of the Arts at Revival of the Ancient Games in Nemea, Greece. Among many engagements in 2005, June took them on a one-week concert tour in Panama City, and in July, San Diego heard the premiere of Price's *America Themes*, performed by the Tifereth Israel Orchestra, David Amos conducting.[215]

Deon Nielsen Price is married to Kendall Owen Price, PhD, and is the mother of five children and grandmother of thirteen.

NANCY B. REICH is a major Clara Schumann scholar. A native New Yorker, BA, Queens College, MA, Teachers College, Columbia, PhD, NYU, she studied violin with Rachmael Weinstock. She was married to the late Haskell A. Reich, an IBM research physicist who encouraged her early articles on computers and music. She has a son, Matthew, a daughter, Susanna, and three grandchildren. Her teaching career spans NYU, Lehman (Hunter), Manhattanville, Bard and Williams Colleges. She was an assistant professor at the Rubin Academy of Music, Jerusalem (Summer, 1976), and a visiting scholar at the Stanford University Center for Research on Women (1982). She is a member of AMS, IMS, Robert-Schumann-Gesellschaft, and American Brahms Society, among others. Her honors include an NEH Fellowship (1982), the Pauline Alderman Prize for New Scholarship on Women in Music (1986), the Deems Taylor-ASCAP Award (1986) and the Robert-Schumann-Prize of the City of Zwickau (1996).

A musicologist with a special interest in the 19th century, Reich has written about Brahms, **Rebecca Clarke**, **Fanny Hensel**, Felix Mendelssohn, Franz Liszt, Johann Friedrich Reichardt, **Louise Reichardt**, Robert and Clara Schumann. Articles on Juliane Reichardt (vol. 3), Louise Reichardt (vol. 4), and the Vocal Music of Clara

---

214. See Asian Composers.
215. With the author's son, Adrian, as assistant concertmaster, and where author and composer met again—the first time being the 1995 Vienna Conference.

Schumann (vol. 7) have been published in *Women Composers: Music Through the Ages*, (G.K. Hall, 1996). One of Reich's major contributions is the definitive book *Clara Schumann: The Artist and the Woman* (Cornell University Press, 1985; Revised 2001), which has been translated into Japanese, Chinese and German. Other publications include articles in the *New Grove Dictionary of Women Composers* (1994) and the *Revised New Grove Dictionary of Music and Musicians* (2001). "Robert Schumann's Music in New York City, 1848–1898"[216] was published in *Schumanniana Nova* (2002), as part of the Festschrift [tribute volume] for the sixtieth birthday of Gerd Nauhaus, former director of the Robert Schumann House in Zwickau, with whom, as co-editor, Reich prepared *Clara Schumann, Jugendtagebücher 1827–1840*, to be published in German and English by Olms Verlag. These are the diaries kept by Clara Wieck and her father between 1827–40, that close on the day of her marriage.

A sought-after international lecturer, Nancy Reich has made presentations at the 1995 centennial of the Faculty of Music, University of Melbourne (Australia) and in 1996, during the centennial of the death of Clara Schumann, in Vienna, Zwickau,[217] Bonn, Heidelberg, Frankfurt and Dusseldorf. In November of that year, she participated in a Conference on Women Song Composers of the 19th century in Victoria, Canada, with a paper on Louise Reichardt. She was a member of a panel on Musical Biography at the International Musicological Society in London, 1997, and continues to give papers and participate in symposia at universities, music conservatories and international music festivals.

Sally Reid

SALLY REID is a professor of music, digital audio, advanced theory and oboe at Abilene Christian University (Texas), where she served as department chair (1978–90), and was director of their electronic studio. She took a leave of absence from 2000 until the fall of 2004, when she returned to ACU continuing a career that began in 1970.

Born in East Liverpool, Ohio, 1948, her B.Mus.Ed. with performance in oboe is from ACU (1969), MM in theory and composition from Hardin-Simmons University in Abilene (1971), and PhD in music theory from the University of Texas at Austin (1980). Her numerous journal articles are oriented toward women in music. She was an early expert on computers and their utilization in writing web-pages, archives, and music notation for orchestral work. It was she who set up the website for the IAWM.

She has received annual ASCAP awards since 1987 for her compositions, is a member of the American Composer's Forum, and SEAMUS. Her five songs for mezzo-soprano and clarinet, *On the Edge of Great Quiet: Songs from Alaska*, was brought out by Hildegard Publishing (1998), and her saxophone quintet, *Fiuggi Fanfare*, first prize winner at the Fifth International Festival of Women Composers, was published by Musicale Sonzogno, Milan (2001).

She was president of the IAWM (1999–2001) and administrator for their website, after being editor of the Journal of the ILWC (1991–94) and serving as first vice president of the newly merged International Alliance for Women in Music (1995).

Premieres of her music include: *Fiuggi Fanfare* (concert band version) during the second international symposium "Donne in Musica: Gli Incontri al Borgo"(1996), a commisssion from the City of Fiuggi and the Fundazione Adkins Chiti: Donne in Musica; *April* (clarinet and mezzo), from *On the Edge of Great Quiet*, during the Region VI Society of Composers conference at the University of Texas (Arlington,1998); *Elegy* (clarinet and piano) by the Price Duo at ACU (1999), with additional performances throughout the U.S. and Europe in the summer; *Midnight Sun* (clarinet and mezzo) from *On the Edge of Great Quiet*, performed by **Isabelle Ganz** and Richard Nunemaker on the Houston Composer's Alliance Composer's Now Series; *Sorrow's Moment: a rhapsody for orchestra and digital*

216. A 2006 revised version, edited by John Graziano, *European Musicians in New York City 1840–1900*—a collection of articles on "Music in New York City in the 19th Century"—was published by the University of Rochester Press.

217. May 16–19, 1996, Zwickau (Germany), birthplace of Robert Schumann, saw a three-day music festival honoring Clara Schumann on the 100th anniversary of her death. It was held at the Robert Schumann House. Besides concerts of her music, the events included Reich giving the opening address and being awarded the prestigious Robert Schumann Prize.

sounds, by the Abilene Collegiate Symphony; *Let it Take Years*, three songs for soprano, violin and piano, by Sonya Baker, at James Madison University in Harrisonburg, Virginia (March 2000).

Sally, a former member, sometimes substitutes with the Abilene Philharmonic Orchestra playing oboe and English horn. She is married to attorney/professor Brad Reid. They have two daughters, Sarah, born 1982, and Julia, 1985, and a son, William, 1988.

ELLEN ROSAND was born in New York City, February 28, 1940. With a BA (Vassar, 1961), MA (Harvard, 1964) and PhD (NYU, 1971), her teaching career began at Rutgers as assistant professor (1977–80), associate to full professor (1980–91), then professor Yale Music Department (1991), becoming chair in 1995. A member of the Renaissance Society and AMS, she was president of the society (1991–93) and editor of their journal (JAMS) to which she contributed several articles, including *Barbara Strozzi, The Composer's Voice* (1978). Her research in baroque and Venetian music, and history of Italian opera, resulted in "Music and the Myth of Venice" (*Renaissance Quarterly*, 1977), "The Descending Tetrachord: an Emblem of Lament" (*Musical Quarterly*, 1979), "In Defense of the Venetian Libretto" (*Studi Musicali*, 1980) and *L'Orfeo by Sartorio & Aureli* (Ricordi, 1983). She edited a volume of cantatas by **Barbara Strozzi** in a series on the *Italian Cantata in the Seventeenth Century* (Garland Press), and wrote *Opera in Seicento Venice: The Creation of a Genre* (UC Berkeley Press, 1991).

JUDITH ROSEN, born May 20, 1933, in San Francisco, received her BA from UCLA (1955). A researcher, lecturer and consultant on women composers and 20th century music, she has, since 1971, participated in numerous radio broadcasts, coordinated music festivals featuring womens' works and written articles for leading publications, including *High Fidelity*, *Musical America*, *The Musical Women* (Vols. I and II,) and *The New Grove Dictionary of American Music*. She is founding president of the board of the Arnold Schoenberg Institute at USC, has served on the executive board of the San Francisco-based Women's Philharmonic and was liaison/advisor to the National Women Composers Resource Center. On the advisory board of the Los Angeles Chamber Orchestra and a patron of the Los Angeles Music Center Opera Company, she is involved in the Los Angeles new music community and has presented a series of musicales in her home featuring local and internationally-known visiting composers and musicians. Rosen is listed in *Who's Who in American Music* and the *International Who's Who in Music*.

For her award-winning book on the noted Polish composer *Grazyna Bacewicz: Her Life and Works* (1984), Judith Rosen received the Amicus Poloniae badge of Poland.

Léonie Rosenstiel

LÉONIE ROSENSTIEL was born December 28, 1947, in New York City. Her father, Raymond, was an investor, and her mother, Annette, an anthropologist. Léonie's education included a music certificate from Juilliard (1964), a BA from Barnard (1968), the women's college attached to Columbia, from which she received her MA (1970) and PhD in music (1974). She also earned a diploma from the Mexican National Institute of Fine Arts (1975). Her memberships include the International Musicological Society, Authors Guild, Authors League of America, American Musicological Society, Music Library Association, Sonneck Society, and Columbia University Graduate Faculty Alumni Association. She was founder/director of the Barnard-Columbia Chamber Music Society (1965–67), associate editor (1969–71), and special projects editor, (1971–73) of *Current Musicology*, music instructor at a Manhasset adult school and founder/director of the Manhasset Chamber Ensemble (New York, 1974–76), and beginning 1980, president of Research Associates International, and vice president of Authors Aid Associates—both in New York. Other positions have been consulting editor of Da Capo Press (1976), and other publishers. She has received grants from the American Council of Learned Societies (1978), Rockefeller Foundation (1978–79), and the American Philosophical Society, plus several Latin American institutions.

Besides many articles, Rosenstiel's major contribution to music literature are her biographies of Lili Boulanger (1978)[218] and Nadia Boulanger (1982). Painstaking research and access to letters and papers from the hands of Nadia herself, interviewed in the final years of her life, permit us to share incisive portraits of both sisters: Lili the younger, whose promising career as a composer was cut short by her death at twenty-five in 1918, and Nadia, who became a legendary pedagogue from before World War I until well after World War II (she died in 1979) to young men and women who emerged as some of the 20th century's most well-known composers.

JULIE ANNE McCORNACK SADIE was born January 26, 1948 in Eugene, Oregon. As a child, she learned piano, and later cello and viola da gamba. Her BA and BM degrees are from the University of Oregon, and her MA and PhD in musicology from Cornell. She also earned an MA in museum and gallery management from City University, London. In 1978, she married writer and music lexicographer **Stanley Sadie**, noted editor-in-chief of the twenty-volume *New Grove Dictionary of Music and Musicians* (1980)—an eleven-year feat—and its twenty-nine volume revised edition (2001), plus *The New Grove Dictionary of Opera* (1992), and forty years' contribution to *the* music magazine, *The Gramophone*, among many others.

Julie Anne is the author of *The Bass Viol in French Baroque Chamber Music* (UMI Research Press, 1980), and *Companion to Baroque Music* (J.M. Dent & Sons, Ltd., 1990; Schirmer Books, 1991; Librairie Arthème Fayard, 1996), as well as numerous articles and reviews. She taught at Eastman, 1974–76, the first female musicologist on their staff. In September 1976, she went to Paris to complete the research and writing of her dissertation for Cornell. It was while in Paris she met Stanley, and her life took a new turn.

With her husband influential in saving the house where Handel once lived, Julie was director of London's Handel House Museum from 1995–98, which opened to the public in 2001.

As a musicologist, lecturer and music critic, one of Julie Anne Sadie's major contributions to gender musicology is her co-editing, with **Rhian Samuel**, *The Norton/Grove Dictionary of Women Composers* (Macmillan, 1995), which contains priceless information on just about every woman who ever put quill to parchment or pressed a key to activate the music writing program on her computer.

In the '90s, the Sadies moved to Somerset, in the lovely Southwest of England. Of their two musical offspring, Celia, born 1979, completed her doctorate in clinical psychology in 2005 and began a hospital position in December. Matthew, born 1983, got his BA in history, June 2005, but is engaged in full-time work experience in the recording industry.

Leaving a large gap in the musicological universe, Stanley, born October 30, 1930, passed away March 21, 2005 after a recent diagnosis of Lou Gehrig's disease. Julie organized a memorial concert to her husband November 1, at the Royal Academy of Music. The occasion was attended by the elite of the music world.

KAREN SHAFFER was born October 12, 1947, in Dayton, Ohio. Her earliest memories are of her mother playing Beethoven's *Moonlight Sonata* on the piano while she took her afternoon nap. She began piano at seven, clarinet at ten, guitar at fourteen, all the while singing in choirs. A keen reader, she predicted she would write a book someday—a great biography. Her first encounter with a violin in the school orchestra drew her irresistibly to this instrument. As a shy college freshman, she borrowed a violin from the music department and started taking lessons with Neva Greenwood who, in the 1970s, had begun gathering material on the life of American violinist **Maud Powell** (1867–1920). Drawn into the project, Shaffer began to supplement her teacher's research, and realized that this was the biography she was destined to write.

Extensive studies of literature, American history, music, violin, and women's history all came into play in reconstructing from original sources the story of Maud Powell's pioneering role in American classical music annals. Shaffer's degrees in international relations (1969) and Law (1972) from the American University, plus

---

218. In late 2004, the author found one extant copy of *The Life and Works of Lili Boulanger* in a London bookshop off Charing Cross Road! (See Bibliography.)

her subsequent law career, had honed her research and organizational skills—perfect preparation for this assignment. Neva Greenwood (1905–1986) lived to see the final manuscript completed, but passed away shortly after.

Karen founded The Maud Powell Foundation in 1986 (now The Maud Powell Society for Music and Education), in memory of her teacher and as an outgrowth of their work on this country's most famous and most neglected female violinist. It is dedicated to music in education and offers seminars, lectures and programs geared for parents, teachers, and students at all levels, and maintains the Maud Powell Archive, a resource for scholars, in Brevard, North Carolina. *Maud Powell: Pioneer American Violinist* was published in 1988, and the foundation reissued her prized recordings on three CDs in 1989. The biography is the first in the Women in Music series of biographies for children published by the foundation.

In 1994, the foundation sponsored the Maud Powell Exhibit at the Indianapolis Children's Museum during the International Violin Competition in that city, and the $5,000 Maud Powell Prize awarded at the competition. With Pamela Blevins, Karen co-founded *Maud Powell Signature - Women in Music*, a quarterly journal devoted to women in classical music, past and present. Five excellent issues appeared (1995–97), before publication was suspended due to lack of funds. Plans are being made to publish it online.

Inspired by Shaffer's accomplishments, the citizens of Peru, Illinois, the city of Powell's birth, commissioned an eight-foot tall bronze statue of the violinist, which may well be the first to honor a woman musician in the United States. She has also guided the formation of the annual Maud Powell Festival in Peru beginning in 1995. The Peru Public Library's exhibit of Maud Powell artifacts and memorabilia, loaned by Shaffer and the Maud Powell Society, includes Nicholas Brewer's oil portrait of the great violinist. The Aurora Fine Arts Recognition Committee in Aurora, Illinois, sponsored a Tribute to Maud Powell, September 2001. The concert included Andrea Swan, piano, and Kelly Barr, violin, a native of Aurora and member of the Boston Symphony Orchestra. On June 9, 2002, **Rachel Barton Pine** performed a Tribute Recital at the Festival in Peru. In 2005 Barton, who is the violinist/founder of Musicorda—the Summer Music Festival in South Hadley, Massachusetts—invited Shaffer to give a talk on Powell at the Festival. On February 22, 2006, at the National Museum of Women in the Arts (Washington, DC), the Maud Powell Society presented Rachel Barton Pine in a concert of rarely-heard works dedicated to Powell, as well as some of Powell's transcriptions.

Shaffer compiled, "Maud Powell's Favorites," a sheet music collection of her transcriptions and music dedicated to her, published in three volumes by Naxos (2006–2007). Her earlier collaboration with Naxos resulted in the reissue of Powell's recordings by the Victor Company, plus two never released. "Maud Powell, The Complete Recordings Volumes 1–4 (1904–1917)," are part of Naxos' Historical Series of Great Violinists (2001–04). This is one talent that shall not be buried in the sands of time!

VICTORIA R. SIROTA with degrees in organ performance from Boston University (MM, 1975, DMA, 1981), is primarily an organist, lecturer and theologian. Her dissertation, "The Life and Works of Fanny Mendelssohn Hensel," evolved from painstaking original research at the source in the Berlin Library, copying the precious material in longhand. Meanwhile, her husband, Robert Sirota, had become director of Boston University School of Music, having earned his PhD at Harvard (1979). Victoria followed the calling and obtained a master of divinity degree from Harvard University Divinity School (1992). Her senior thesis was "Clanging Cymbals: Development of a music curriculum for a University Divinity School." She was immediately hired by Yale Divinity School and the Institute of Sacred Music, Worship and the Arts, as assistant professor of church music, and director of music in the Marquand Chapel (1992–95).

On September 17, 1994—the Feast Day of Hildegard von Bingen, with whom she feels a mystical bond—she was ordained to the priesthood of the Episcopal Diocese of Massachusetts. The summer of 1995 necessitated a move, as Robert retired from his position of chairman of the music department and music professions at NYU, to become director of the Peabody Institute of Johns Hopkins University, which comprises the Peabody Preparatory School, Peabody Conservatory and Peabody Elder Hostel. Victoria, having already resigned her teaching position to follow her own calling, began her service as vicar of the Church of the Holy Nativity, an Episcopal urban mission. From 1997–2002 she was Adjunct Professor of Sacred Music at the Ecumenical Institute of Theology, St. Mary's Seminary and University, Baltimore.

As a consultant and authority on the subjects, Sirota has lectured on "Refusing to be Silenced: The Compositional Voice of Fanny Mendelssohn Hensel," and "Nadia Boulanger: Composer, Conductor, Teacher and Spiritual Guide to the Twentieth Century"—the latter in the Colloquium Series at Yale.

Victoria Sirota, priest, daughter of a Lutheran minister, and her supportive spouse have two children. Jonah, born 1976, earned his degrees in viola at the Rice University's Shepherd School of Music (BM, 1998), and Juilliard (MM, 2000, Artist's Diploma, 2005). *The Chiara String Quartet*, of which he is a founding member, was in the Rural Residency Program of Chamber Music America in Grand Forks, North Dakota (2001), at Juilliard (2003–2005), working with the Juilliard Quartet, and at the University of Nebraska (Lincoln). They have won numerous awards, and concertize all over the U.S. and Europe, specializing in commissioned pieces such as the string quartet *Triptych*, by Robert Sirota, a powerful 9/11 tribute which is also their first CD (2005). Nadia, born 1982, graduated from Baltimore School for the Arts and entered Juilliard, 2000, also majoring in viola. She received her BM (2004), and MM (2006), winning the viola concerto competition February 14, 2005, playing Hindemith's *Der Schwanendreher* (The Swanherder) with the Juilliard Orchestra, **Marin Alsop** conducting. As the new music coordinator, Nadia instituted the program *Juilliard Plays Juilliard*, which has students playing and being coached by Juilliard composers. She specializes in new music, and commissions composers to add music to the viola repertoire. How wonderful for parents to see their legacy perpetuated!

In November 2005, Bob Sirota, after ten years as Peabody's director, began his presidency of the Manhattan School of Music following the retirement, after twenty-two years, of **Marta Istomin**. Victoria served ten years as vicar of the Church of the Holy Nativity in Baltimore, and in 2006 became an assistant minister and consultant for liturgical ministry at New York's Cathedral Church of St. John the Divine. She continues to lecture widely on issues of music, spirituality and religious institutions. Her successful book, *Preaching to the Choir: The Role of Sacred Musician*, came out in Spring 2006 (Church Publishing). (See Organists.)

CATHERINE PARSONS SMITH, professor emerita of music history at the University of Nevada at Reno, since her retirement in 2000, was born November 4, 1933, in Rochester, New York. After earning a preparatory diploma from Eastman, she graduated *magna cum laude* from Smith College with a BA in history (1954). Her MM is from Northwestern and DMA from Stanford (1969), with a dissertation on *Characteristics of Transverse Flute Performance in Selected Flute Methods from the Early 18th Century to 1828*. As an expert in 18th century performance practice, she translated and wrote the Introduction to *On Playing Oboe, Recorder and Flageolet by Jean Pierre Freillon Ponçein* (Indiana U. Press, Bloomington, 1992). She was principal flute in the Reno Philharmonic from its founding in 1969 until 1999. She is the flutist on the 1987 Cambria CD *Elinor Remick Warren Art Songs*.

Smith's interests have been gender and race in the formation of American concert life. With Cynthia S. Richardson, she co-authored *Mary Carr Moore, American Composer* (University of Michigan Press, 1987). Her most prominent feminist essays include a chapter entitled "A Distinguishing Virility: Feminism and Modernism in American Art Music," in *Cecilia Reclaimed* (eds. **Susan C. Cook** and **Judy Tsou**, U. of Illinois Press, Urbana, 1994), and "Athena at the Music Club: Reflections on John Cage and Mary Carr Moore" (*Musical Quarterly* Vol. 79 #2, Fall 1995). She has also authored a series of essays on the formation of concert life in Southern California in *American Music, Nineteenth Century Music*, and *Selected Reports in Ethnomusicology*. *William Grant Still: A Study in Contradictions*, the first book on this prominent Afro-American composer (1895–1978), from outside his family, was published by the University of California Press (2000).

RUTH AMES SOLIE is the Sophia Smith professor of music and in the women's studies program at Smith College, whose faculty she joined in 1974, and where her discipline, historical musicology, includes feminist scholarship. She is an associate editor of *19th Century Music*, co-editor with Eugene Narmour of *Explorations in Music, the Arts and Ideas: Essays in Honor of Leonard B. Meyer* (Pendragon Press, Stuyvesant, 1988), editor of *Musicology and Difference: Gender and Sexuality in Music Scholarship* (UC Berkeley Press, 1993), and *The Nineteenth Century*, volume 6 of Strunk's *Source Readings in Music History* (1998). An authority on **Sophie Drinker**, she wrote the Afterword for the 1995 edition of the 1948 book, *Women and Music*.

Solie's writing includes both explicitly feminist essays and others in which the feminist perspective is integrated, including Victorian gender roles. She is an historian and author of articles on 19th century Europe and America, its intellectual and cultural history from a feminist perspective. Her BA is from Smith College, and MA and PhD from the University of Chicago, where her 1977 dissertation covered "Metaphor and Model in the Analysis of Melody."

Her 2004 book, *Music in Other Words: Victorian Conversations*, illustrates how Victorian-era people, English and other, experienced music and what they understood to be its power and its purposes, including the moral force that was attached to music in the public mind and the strongly gendered nature of musical practice and sensibility—suggesting the complex links between the history of music and the history of ideas.

Solie states that her latest project has to do with girls and piano lessons: "Why do so many girls take piano lessons? Did they want to? What did their parents (and society in general) think those lessons were going to do for them? What I've learned so far has very interesting implications for the ideology of family life, for the construction of Victorian gender roles, and for understanding some of the less obvious reasons that people in the 19th century took music seriously."

CARMEN HELENA TÉLLEZ is associate professor of music at Indiana University, director of the Latin American Music Center and Contemporary Vocal Ensemble. (See Conductors.)

JUDITH TICK is professor of music at Northeastern University in Boston. She earned her BA (1964) from Smith College, MA (1967) from UC Berkeley and PhD in music (1979) from CUNY. She has taught at Brooklyn College (1975–86), was a visiting research associate at Wellesley College Center for the Study of Women (1985–86), and a tutor at Harvard in the Women's Studies Degree Program (1990–92).

Her publications include *American Women Composers before 1870* (1983). She is the editor of *Selected Songs of Josephine Lang* (Da Capo Press, 1982), and prepared an edition of Ruth Crawford Seeger's *Five Songs on Poems by Carl Sandburg* for C.F. Peters, Publishers. She contributed the article "Women and Music" to the *New Grove Dictionary of American Music*. She is associate editor for the "American Music" section of the *Musical Quarterly*. From 1990–93, she was chair of the Committee on the Status of Women for the AMS. 1994–96 marked her term on the AMS board of directors. In 1994, she received an honorary award for contributions to women in music from the New York Society of Women Composers. Her editing collaboration with **Jane Bowers**, *Women Making Music: The Western Art Tradition, 1150–1950* (U. of Illinois Press, 1986, second ed., 1995), is a landmark book with contributions by major musicologists. In 1997, Oxford University Press published Tick's long-awaited book, the culmination of ten years' work, *Ruth Crawford Seeger, A Composer's Search for American Music*. It won the Irving Lowens Prize for best book of the year from the Society for American Music.

2000 was a busy year. Tick wrote the entry on "women and music" in the *Revised New Grove Dictionary of Music*; co-authored *Aaron Copland. A Cultural Perspective* with Gail Levin, and received a distinguished alumna medal from Smith College.

Polish-born **MAJA TROCHIMCZYK** was a professor of music history and literature at the Thornton School of Music, University of Southern California, and director of the Polish Music Center there from 1996–2004. (See International Musicologists.)

JUDY S. TSOU, assistant head and archivist of the Music Library at UC Berkeley, is now a lecturer at the University of Washington and head of the Music Library. She has contributed articles to the Norton/Grove *Dictionary of Women Composers* and catalogued the Women's Music Collection at the University of Michigan Music Library. In 1988 she co-wrote, with **Susan C. Cook**, the introduction to *Score Anthology of Songs: Pauline Duchambre et. al.* (Da Capo Press), and co-edited with Susan Cook—Foreword by Susan McClary—the notable *Cecilia Reclaimed: Feminist Perspectives on Gender in Music* (U. of Illinois Press, 1994).

MARY JEANNE VAN APPLEDORN holds the Paul Whitfield Horn professorship in music composition at Texas Tech. (See Contemporary American Composers.)

HEIDI VON GUNDEN is an associate professor at the School of Music, University of Illinois, Urbana. She was born in San Diego, California, on April 13, 1940. Her grandmother, Natalie Villar, a professional singer, was her first teacher, starting Heidi on piano at age five. She began her studies of theory and organ in eighth grade, and performed as an organ soloist with the San Diego Youth Symphony at seventeen. After graduating with a BM in Organ Performance and Music Theory from Mount St. Mary's College in Los Angeles (1963), she taught piano and organ, and was choir director in the diocese of Los Angeles until 1969. She returned to Mt. St. Mary's to teach until 1971, the year she received her MA in organ performance from Cal. State, Los Angeles, where she studied with **Ladd Thomas**. From 1971–75, she was a part-time instructor at Academy of Our Lady of Peace, San Diego, organist at St. Joseph's Cathedral, and teaching assistant to **Pauline Oliveros** at UCSD, where she received an MA (1974) and PhD (1977) in theory and composition. After an assistant professorship at Southern Illinois University, Carbondale, 1979 marked the beginning of her long career with UIU.

Von Gunden's works appear in many musical publications, including the *IAWM Journal* and the *New Grove Dictionary of Music*. Her four books, all published by Scarecrow Press, are: *The Music of Pauline Oliveros* (1983); *The Music of Ben Johnston* (1986), a composer on the UIU faculty from 1951–83; *The Music of Lou Harrison* (1995), an inventive composer and early proponent of the music of Ives, Ruggles, Varése and Cowell; and *The Music of Vivian Fine* (1999), winner of the 2000 ASCAP-Deems Taylor Award.

Both a performer and composer, she has written numerous works for piano, organ, chorus, chamber ensemble, and instrumentalists.

HELEN WALKER-HILL, pianist, pedagogue, writer and musicologist, was born in Winnipeg (Manitoba, Canada) May 26, 1936, received her early musical training from her piano teacher mother, Margaret Siemens, then continued piano studies with Emma Endres Kountz in Toledo. Her BA is from the University of Toledo (1957). A 1957 Fulbright Scholarship sent her to Paris to study with **Nadia Boulanger** at the École Normale de Musique (1959). She earned her MA from Smith College (1968) and DMA from the University of Colorado (Boulder, 1981), where she was an instructor on the piano faculty (1977–1981) and assistant professor adjunct (1983–1990). She also served as a visiting assistant professor at Muhlenberg College, Pennsylvania (1993–1994), and at the University of Wyoming (1993–1998).

Walker-Hill has been engaged in research and performance of music by black women since 1987. Her work has been featured on NPR's "Morning Edition" and "Horizons" programs. Her major publications include *Piano Music by Black Women Composers: A Catalog of Solo and Ensemble Music* (Greenwood Press, 1992), an anthology, *Music by Black Women Composers: A Century of Piano Music 1893–1990* (Hildegard Publishing Company, 1998), *From Spirituals to Symphonies: African-American Women Composers and Their Music* (Greenwood Press, March 2002), and a CD, *Kaleidoscope: Music by African-American Women* (Leonarda Records, 1995). She edited the Vivace Press series, *Music by African American-Women*. Her monograph, *Music by Black Women Composers: A Bibliography of Available Scores* (1995), was published by the Center for Black Music Research, Columbia College, Chicago.

Her numerous awards and honors feature a 1993 NEA recording grant; the Aaron Diamond Fellowship, Schomburg Center for Research in Black Culture, New York (1995–1996); Rockefeller Fellowship, Center for Black Music Research, Chicago (1998); Wyoming Council for the Arts grant (1998); and Thanks Be To Grandmother Winifred Foundation grant (1999).

Helen has two sons, Gregory Walker, a violinist/composer, born October 19, 1961, and Ian Walker, an actor/playwright, born February 13, 1964. She and Gregory have comprised the Walker Duo since 1983.

GRETCHEN A. WHEELOCK, who holds a BA from Wellesley, MA and PhD from Yale, with piano study with Bruce Symonds and Donald Currier, is professor of musicology at Eastman. Her research interests include Haydn, Mozart, 18th century aesthetics, reception history, and

Gretchen Wheelock

performance practice. She specializes in the Classical Period, focusing on the transition from private to public patronage in the late 18th century. She has written *Haydn's Ingenious Jesting with Art: Contexts of Musical Wit and Humor* (Schirmer, 1992) based on her 1979 dissertation, "Wit, Humor and the Instrumental Music of Joseph Haydn."

WANDA (Harasimowicz) **WILK** was born in 1921 of Polish-American parents in Hamtramck, Michigan. She graduated from Wayne University (Detroit), 1943, with a BM specializing in music education. In 1952, she married Dr. Stefan Wilk, and in 1955 resigned her teaching position to become a full-time wife, mother and homemaker.

When her daughter Diane enrolled at USC School of Architecture, Wanda returned to USC for her MM. Her thesis was to be the compilation of a bibliography on Polish music, but she discovered a complete lack of material in libraries throughout the U.S., and enrolled in a summer session at the Jagiellonian University, Krakow. In 1976 she completed her MM, and one year later was elected program chairperson of the International Committee of the Los Angeles Philharmonic, a position she held for three years. In 1980, she received the Mayor's Certificate of Appreciation for her participation in the Polish Cultural Exhibit at the California Museum of Science and Industry (Los Angeles), for which she organized the music section and presented seventeen musical programs.

In 1981, she secured the sponsorship of the USC School of Music for a Centennial Celebration honoring the Polish composer Karol Szymanowski (1882–1937). She established the USC Friends of Polish Music and helped organize a series of symphonic concerts, recitals and lectures, with the participation of artists, musicologists and students from England, Poland and America. Between 1983–84, she prepared a travelling exhibit on Szymanowski, which was shown in twenty-four university libraries throughout the North America, for which she received the Perspectives' Award from *Perspectives Magazine* in Washington, DC, and the Director's Award from the USC School of Music.

In 1985, Wilk established the Polish Music Reference Center (PMRC) at USC with a joint endowment gift from her husband and herself, and was appointed its director. She gave lectures at local universities and Polish-American associations. In 1988, she and her husband were awarded the Polonia Award from the Southern California chapter of the Polish American Congress, and a gold medal from the Polish Composers' Union (ZKP), of which she is an honorary member. In 1992, she received the Torchbearers' Award from USC.

With her husband, she established a new foundation, Ars Musica Poloniae, and under its label produced a compact disc entitled *Riches and Rags* (1992), which featured the music of Polish women composers **Grazyna Bacewicz** and **Maria Szymanowska**, performed by pianist **Nancy Fierro**.

Wilk wrote the first monograph in the Polish Music History Series (Karol Szymanowski, 1982) and became editor of this series. She is also the author of articles on Polish women composers and subjects pertaining to the history of Polish music. In 1994, Wilk initiated the creation of a website devoted to Polish music.

She retired in 1996 as director of the PMRC, becoming the center's honorary director, continuing as the president of the Friends of Polish Music, devoting her time championing the cause of Polish music, nationally and internationally. On May 28, 1996, the Polish Minister of Foreign Affairs, Dr. Robert Mroziewicz, presented her with the Cavalier's Cross, Order of Polonia Restituta, a medal and certificate signed by the then president of Poland, Lech Walesa.

2000 brought the Wilk Book Prize for Research in Polish Music, a scholarly competition for the best book on Polish music.

ELIZABETH WOOD was born in New South Wales, Australia, and educated at the University of Adelaide (BA with honors) and a PhD (1979). Her dissertation was on Australian opera from 1842–1970. She also studied piano and conducting. She helped pioneer Australian music studies in the 1970s, feminist studies of women in music, '70s–'80s, and lesbian studies in music theory, history and criticism in the '90s. Her teaching positions include the University of Adelaide, and in New York: Barnard, Sarah Lawrence, Queens and Hunter Colleges, plus Rutgers University (New Jersey). She has presented scholarly papers on women composers at colleges and conferences, and is a regular contributor on women in music to *Ms. Magazine*. Her publications include an article on the music of **Grazyna Bacewicz** (*The Musical Woman*, Volume I); an autobiographical essay, "Music Into Words," in *Between Women* (Beacon Press, 1984); a study of American women in the contemporary musical avant-garde (June 1983); studies on historiography and feminist biography for the Sixth Berkshire Conference of Women Historians (June 1984); *Lesbian Fugue: Ethel Smyth's Contrapuntal Arts*, her contribution to *Musicology and Difference* (University of California Press, ed. **Ruth A. Solie,** 1993); editing the second edition of the late **Diane Jezic's** *Women Composers: The Lost Tradition Found* (The Feminist Press of CUNY, 1993); *Queering the Pitch: The New Gay and Lesbian Musicology* (Routledge, 1994); *En Travesti: Women, Gender, Subversion, and Opera* (Columbia U. Press, 1995); *New Feminist Essays on Women's Suffrage* (Manchester U. Press, 1996); *Feminist Music Criticism* and many other essays, articles and book reviews. Her definitive book on **Ethyl Smyth**—a labor of many years—was brought out in London by Bloomsbury Publishers (1998).

Wood is the recipient of many awards, grants and fellowships. They include Fulbright Scholar; Commonwealth Postgraduate Research Grant; Visiting Fellow, Humanities Research Center, Australian National University; Distinguished Visiting Scholar, University of Adelaide; Senior Scholar, Carleton University, Ottawa; NEH Fellow.

She lives in New York, has one son, three daughters and two grandchildren.

JUDITH LANG ZAIMONT, as well as being a prize-winning composer and educator, is editor-in-chief of the award winning trilogy, *The Musical Woman: An International Perspective*, Volume I (1983), Volume II (1984–1985), Volume III (1986–1990), with contributions from many of the musicologists in this chapter. The books cover a wide range of topics: music education, genre surveys, national surveys, critical appraisals of featured musicians, music profession overviews and festivals, concert series and conferences. For the last twenty-five years, her main focus has been composition. (See Contemporary American Composers.)

Alicia Zizzo

ALICIA ZIZZO merits equal space in the performers' section. She is a pianist with a talent recognized by the legendary **Dimitri Mitropolous** after her Carnegie Hall recital at age eleven. Her teacher, Dr. Carlos Buhler, followed the tradition of *his* mentors, master pianists **Alfred Cortot** and **Ferruccio Busoni**. Like many women through the ages, Alicia gave up her career to raise her children, Peter, born 1967 and Claudia, 1968—in this case "suspended" is more the operating word. But she never stopped practicing the piano. When both were in college, she found an agent and within a matter of weeks was back onstage at London's Barbican Center, Amsterdam's Concertgebouw, Vienna's Musikverein, Budapest with the Budapest Symphony, Warsaw's Ostrowsky Palace for the Chopin Society, Glasgow, Edinburgh, Germany and New York—all to standing ovations. This, while suffering through the throes of her husband's fatal brain tumor (1977–87).

As a musicologist, Zizzo has made unprecedented contributions to the literature. It began when she was invited by the Polish government to play something American. Like most of the former Iron Curtain countries, one of the few American composers they knew and loved was **George Gershwin** (1898–1937). It was 1989 and Alicia's first exposure to George. The *Concerto in F* was a rousing success in Warsaw and Budapest. It was also the first time a woman had played this composition. At the close of a performance of it in New York, 1990, a gentleman emerged from the audience. He was the noted Gershwin scholar, Edward Jablonski (1922–2004). He wanted to produce a CD of her playing the *Concerto*, and the *Rhapsody in Blue*. Alicia had always felt something was missing in the latter work. She went to the Library of Congress, studied the original manuscript on microfilm and found over sixty deletions! She also discovered errors in the *Concerto*, noted them, and came to the conclusion that the publishers, in 1924, had altered the piece to accommodate the public's ear for the classical "Romantic," not yet being attuned to Gershwin's jazzy style. Not allowed to remove anything from the files, she painstakingly copied the original by hand. She then found a fragment of *Lullaby*, a haunting piece written in 1919 as a study in impressionism, and later rearranged for string quartet. She reconstructed this as a piano solo.

Zizzo recorded the three works in their original form on a landmark Pro-Arte Fanfare (London) CD—the first recording of a woman playing the concerto—and immediately heard from Warner Brothers Publishers who wanted her manuscripts for publication as sheet music. The *Lullaby* was published in 1992. Further requests led to her unearthing a twenty minute one-act opera, *Blue Monday*, set in Harlem and written for *George White's Scandals* of 1922. This proved to be the "embryo" for *Rhapsody in Blue, American in Paris*, the *Preludes* and *Porgy and Bess*.

By this time Alicia was acquainted with the Gershwin family, especially Frances, George's sister, with whom she consulted until the latter's death, January 18, 1999, at age ninety-two. Married to Leonard—son of famed Austrian pianist Leopold Goldowsky—in the '20s, it was "Frankie" who supported her brothers with her dance career bringing in $40 a week. It was she who sang George's songs for him first, but after *Rhapsody in Blue* catapulted her brother to fame and fortune, *he* was the king of the household. (Frances was to become a successful painter in her seventies.)

Permission was now granted by the Library of Congress to photostat copies. Zizzo created a solo piano suite out of the sketchy material of *Blue Monday*—a dream Ira, George's brother, did not live long enough to see fulfilled. Warner published this, and then asked for a new edition of the three piano preludes. Out of the blue, Jablonski made *another* three "lost" preludes available to her. One had been set aside for a song, the other two were published in an arrangement for violin and piano and considerably altered. Zizzo prepared all six and the fragment of a seventh for Warner. The new editions are the first Gershwin publications in over seventy years! Carlton Classics Records (London) brought out a CD of these in 1995. The next Herculean task was reconstructing the original *Rhapsody in Blue* manuscripts. Completed in 1995, it is now five minutes longer than the previous edition. This version was published in 1997 and given its world premiere by the Boston Pops.

1998 saw the second CD, *Gershwin Rediscovered, Vol II*; her edition of the *Preludes* and *Rhapsody in Blue* performed by the Budapest Symphony; and an honorary doctorate from Hofstra University (Long Island, New York). In March, the Library of Congress celebrated the sixtieth anniversary of Gershwin's death with four days of seminars and one concert for the invited VIP participants, with Alicia Zizzo as the only classical piano soloist on stage. The event was hailed in over a hundred newspapers across the world.

October 2000 brought another first, the release of *Piano Suite*, based on the never-before recorded Gershwin *background music* of the 1937 Fred Astaire-Ginger Rogers film, *Shall We Dance?* The score, arranged by Zizzo, is published by Warner Brothers. The CD, *Rhythm and Hues*, can be subtitled *Gershwin Meets Chopin*, since it features the latter's twenty-four preludes—a task Gershwin set himself, but did not have time to complete during his short lifetime.

I've Got Rhythm Variations is the first arrangement for piano solo. It was released on a Koch CD in 2001, and the sheet music by Warner Publications—Zizzo-Gershwin Editions.

Alicia Zizzo also conducts lectures and recitals to bring new material before the public and fellow scholars in order to entrench the concept of Gershwin as a serious classical composer. As of 2005, she continues her major project of converting hundreds of his unpublished songs into piano solos.

(Author's Note: I can hardly wait to collaborate with her on the book she wants to write chronicling these discoveries.)

International Musicologists

Nadia Boulanger (1887–1979) France
Antoinette Bobillier (1858–1918) France
Madeleine Milhaud (1902–) France
Marion Scott (1877–1953) England
Ethel Voynich (1864–1960) England
Eva Badura-Skoda, Europe - U.S.
Margaret Bent, UK
Claudia Böttcher, Germany
June Boyce-Tillman, UK
Patricia Adkins Chiti, Italy
Rhian Davies, Wales
Sophie Fuller, UK
Lucy Green, UK
Katrijn Kuypers, Netherlands
Rosamond McGuinness, UK
Vivienne Olive, Germany
Antje Olivier, Germany
Elena Ostleitner, Austria
Eva Rieger, Germany
Rhian Samuel, UK
Roswitha Sperber, Germany
Maja Trochimczyk, U.S. - Poland
Margaret Lucy Wilkins, UK
Angela Willes, UK

BELGRADE

Sonja Marinković
Tatjana Marković
Marija Masnikosa
Vesna Mikic
Roksanda Pejović
Ivana Perković
Tijana Popović Madjenovic
Sanja Radinović
Dragana Stojanović-Novicic
Mirjana Veselinović-Hofman
Mirjana Vukicevic-Zakic

RUSSIA

Yevgenia Lineva
Varvara Pavlovna Dernova
Elena Mikhailovna Orlova
Vera Andreevna Vasin-Grossman
Valentina Dzhozefovna Konen
Ol'ga Yevgen'evna Levasheva
Valentina Nikolaevna Kholopova

FINLAND

Riitta Valkeila

GREAT BRITAIN

Caroline Collingridge

IRELAND

Eibhlis Farrell

ISRAEL

Tsippi Fleischer

JAPAN

Kobayashi Midori

NETHERLANDS

Tera de Marez Oyens

ROMANIA

Valentina Sandu-Dediu

SWEDEN

Margaret Myers

SLOVAKIA

Iris Szeghy
Larisa Vrhunc

SPAIN
Mercedes Zavala

SOUTH KOREA
Hae-Sung Lee

VIENNA CONFERENCE
Marietta Dean
Annette Degenhardt

Alison Gould
Lily Hood Gunn
Deborah Kavasch
Mary Ellen Kitchens
Edda Kraenzmer
Kristin Norderval
Deon Nielsen Price
Sally Reid
Regina Himmelbauer

The Princess of Music

Nadia Boulanger

NADIA BOULANGER, while not a musicologist in the written word—in that she never published any articles or a book and, in fact, forbade publication of her mesmerizing lectures—was nevertheless, a legend unto herself as one of the greatest music teachers in history.

Born in Paris on her father's seventy-second birthday, September 16, 1887, both he, Ernest (1815–1900), and her grandfather, Frédéric Boulanger, were teachers at the Paris Conservatoire. Her Russian mother, Raïssa Mychetskaya, who claimed to be princess, came to Paris to study voice. She enrolled in Ernest's course, marrying her sixty-two-year-old professor when she was only nineteen. She gave Nadia her first music lessons and would continue to be a major force in her daughter's life until her death in 1936, when Nadia was forty-nine.

At her Conservatoire graduation, sixteen-year-old Nadia won first prize in each of her subjects: organ, piano accompaniment and composition—an unheard-of feat. She continued studies with organ genius **Charles-Marie Widor** (1844–1937), and famed French composer **Gabriel Fauré** (1845–1924), director of the Conservatoire 1905–20. In her 1908 initial try for the Prix de Rome, she won the second grand prize for her cantata, *La Sirène*. She made one other attempt for the Premier Prix the following year, but misogynist politics were against her.

Boulanger wrote several songs, solo organ, piano and cello pieces, two cantatas, a *Fantasie for Piano and Orchestra*, and collaborated on two operas with her Conservatoire mentor **Raoul Pugno** (1852–1914), another major figure in French music. Contrary to popular belief that she felt unable to compare with her sister Lili, who won the Prix de Rome on her first try at age nineteen and had success with her compositions before her life was cut short at twenty-five, according to **Léonie Rosensteil**'s definitive biography, Nadia consistently promoted her own and her sister's compositions.

Boulanger began teaching privately at seventeen, and was hired to teach elementary piano and accompaniment at the Conservatoire Femina Musica in 1907. Under the aegis of Pugno, she also performed with him, and several times conducted him as piano soloist in her compositions.

France was the most beleaguered European country during WWI, with the Germans entrenched on her soil on the stale-mated Western Front. There were severe food shortages and other supplies, lack of house heat and many casualties until U.S. "doughboys" arrived in 1917. Their very numbers helped turn the tide of the war to an Allied victory in 1918, after which Americans were heroes of the French.

In 1919, Nadia was invited to the faculty of the newly-opened École Normale de Musique—a more liberal rival to the Conservatoire National. Her subjects were harmony, counterpoint, piano accompaniment, music history and, for the first time entrusted to a woman, *composition*! By 1921 a group of influential American patrons, led by German-American conductor **Walter Damrosch**, established the Conservatoire Américain, a summer school for music and art at the Fontainebleau Palace outside Paris. Boulanger was part of the faculty from the outset. She became its director in 1949, a position she held for thirty years until her death. In the years between the two world wars, although an accomplished organist and pianist, it was as a teacher she established near legendary status. Her private classes gained the unique international reputation of instructing *three* generations of musicians—many American—including **Aaron Copland** (1900–90), **Roy Harris** (1898–1979), **Virgil Thomson** (1896–1989), **Elliott Carter** (*b* 1908), **Walter Piston** (1894–1976), **David Diamond** (*b* 1915), and of the women composers in this book, **Elinor Remick Warren**, **Grażyna Bacewicz**, **Marion Bauer**, **Louise Talma**, **Dana Suesse**, **Thea Musgrave**, **Eugènie Rocherolle**, **Erica Muhl**, **Marta Ptaszynska**, and conductors **Frances Steiner**, **Catherine Comet** and **Karen Keltner**.

During her much publicized first American tour, February–April 1938, Boulanger lectured to full classes at the then "all-girl" Ivy League colleges of Radcliffe and Wellesley, broadcast French choral music with her own singers over New York's WEAF, and became the first woman to conduct the Boston Symphony in a stirring performance of Fauré's *Requiem* with the Bach Cantata Club, whose New England accents she had to retrain into passable Latin. Among the many functions in her honor, she and **Amy Beach** were the lauded luncheon guests at the Musical Guild of Boston. **Frédérique Petrides** devoted her March 1938 newsletter, *Women in Music*, to Nadia. Another U.S. trip, beginning January 1939, took her from coast to coast giving 102 lectures in 118 days, and ending with a recital at the San Francisco Fair. (Also called the Golden Gate Exposition, in celebration of the opening of that bridge.)

A little over a year later she was back on American soil. At her friends' urging, Boulanger, who also begged Igor Stravinsky to leave, spent World War II in the U.S., arriving November 1940, with a three-year contract at the Longy School of Music in Cambridge, near Boston. Commuting from there to New York, Washington and Baltimore (teaching at Peabody), during the next five years she crammed in a superhuman schedule of teaching, concerts, recitals and lectures, which took her to both coasts as well as the Midwest. Highlights of her stay included a testimonial concert for Polish statesman/musician **Jan Paderewski** at Carnegie Hall, April 5, 1941, honoring the fiftieth anniversary of his first appearance there, with Nadia conducting forty-five members of the New York Philharmonic; a joint recital with Stravinsky at Mills College (Oakland, California) October 1944, and a November 1945 Gabriel Fauré Festival she fostered in Boston to celebrate the centenary of his birth.

With the liberation of Paris in 1944, Nadia rallied her wealthy American patrons to send packages of food and toiletries to her war-ravaged country. She herself filled forty trunks of supplies for what became her triumphant return, January 1946. At last her longtime dream was fulfilled, she was made professor of accompaniment at the Conservatoire National—a title she held until 1957 when, at seventy, she was forced to retire. Also, as director of the Conservatoire Américain at Fontainebleau, studying with her there became a much sought after badge of honor.

One of Nadia's most illustrious connections was with the royal family of Monaco, beginning with young Prince Pierre, a scion of one of her long-standing supporters, the Princess de Polignac. On ascending the throne after WWII, he made Boulanger his chapelmaster. Thus she helped organize the festivities marking the 1949 coronation of Prince Rainier when his father abdicated and, in 1956, arranged the music for his wedding to Grace Kelly. She gave their children their first piano lessons. It was at the palace that her eightieth birthday was celebrated with a gala dinner and fireworks. And it was Rainier who literally dragged her to his doctor for a cataract operation in 1973 when she was almost blind. However, she did not follow orders to rest, so her respite from blindness was only temporary. In her last years, her overall health began failing.

In an unparalleled career lasting almost seven decades, the "tender tyrant," as Nadia was affectionately dubbed by her illustrious pupils, celebrated her ninetieth birthday in 1977 with tributes from all over the world. The week before, she was upgraded from Chevalier to Grand Officier of the Légion d'honneur, one of the few women to attain this rank. In the course of her lifetime, other honors included the Gold Medal from the Académie des Beaux Arts, the Holland Medal from Yale, honorary degrees from Harvard and Washington College of Music, the Order of Polonia Restituta, for her work with many Polish pupils, and the Most Excellent Order of the British Empire from the hands of Queen Elizabeth II.

Nadia died in Paris, October 22, 1979. Her funeral was attended by the greats of the music world.

She spoke immortal words when she said of herself, "God made me a woman, but he also made me a musician, and of the two acts, the second is of much greater importance."

Mention must be made of **Annette Dieudonné** (1896–1991), Nadia's pupil since 1920 who, after the death of her fiancé on the WWI battlefield, became assistant and companion to the end of her teacher's life. During WWII, Annette stayed in Nadia's apartment and also became librarian at the Conservatoire. With the imminent invasion of Paris, she took valuable manuscripts to the country and buried them for safekeeping. Her actions were rewarded with the Croix de Guerre, one of France's highest wartime awards. As executor of her will, she divided Boulanger's priceless memorabilia among the Lili and Nadia Boulanger Foundation, Harvard Library, Polish Library of Paris, French Museum of Music, Lyon National Academy of Music Library, and the French National Library.

Annette truly lived up to the translation of her name, *God-given*!

ANTOINETTE CHRISTINE MARIE BOBILLIER (MICHEL BRENET) was born April 12, 1858, in Lunéville, France. An only child, she lived in Strasbourg, Metz and other cities due to her father's military career. In 1871, she settled in Paris. An attack of scarlet fever made her an invalid, and focused her intellectual energies on research. One of the earliest and most prolific musicologists, Marie Bobillier, under the pseudonym, Michel Brenet, gathered a huge amount of reliable information which she processed in an organized manner. She had access to primary sources, and gained a highly respected reputation as a music historian who opened avenues for further investigation. Her numerous writings include: *The History of the Symphony Orchestra Since its Origins up to Beethoven* (1882); *Grétry, His Life and Works* (1884); *Two Pages from the Life of Berlioz* (1889); *Jean d'Okeghem* (1893); *Processional Music* (1896); *Sébastien de Brossard* (1896); *Music of the Convents* (1898); *French Concerts Under the Ancient Régime* (1900); *Rameau's Younger Years* (1903); *Palestrina* (1906; third ed., 1910); *Haydn* (1909; in English, 1926); *Handel* (1912); *Military Music* (1917); *Dictionary of the History of Music* (posthumous; completed by A. Gastoué, Paris, 1926).

Although her interests were international, she showcased French composers to their advantage. After her sudden death, November 4, 1918, in Paris, her papers were donated to the National Library there.

Polish and Powerful!

ANNA MARIA KLECHNIOWSKA was a composer, pianist and teacher. Born to a noble family, April 15, 1888, in Borowka in the eastern borderlands of Poland, she studied until 1905 at the Warsaw Conservatory with K. Jaczynowska (piano) and M. Biernakci and G. Roguski (harmony); and 1905–06 at the Lwow Conservatory with Michal Soltys (piano and composition) and Stanislaw Niewiadomski (harmony). 1906 and 1908 took her to the Leipzig Conservatory for piano with J. Pembaur, and composition with S. Krehl. In 1908 she returned to Krakow, resuming piano studies until 1911, after which she was at Vienna's Academy of Music until 1917 with Heuberger and Schmidt. By 1918, she had written her first book on piano pedagogy and started her teaching career. 1918–1939 saw her own music courses for beginners in Warsaw. At the same time, she studied conducting at the Higher School of Music.

 In 1939, she left for Paris for studies with **Nadia Boulanger**. She returned after WWII to become director of the music division in the Department of Culture and Arts in Lodz, and was professor of piano performance at the music school there. In 1947 she settled in Warsaw, continued teaching and was director of music for children at the Polish Composers' Union. She received numerous awards for her works for children.

During her youth, Klechniowska had been a member of the Young Poland movement and a friend and colleague of Szymanowski. She was inspired by the turn-of-the-20th century aesthetic ideals. Her music was part impressionistic (inspired more by Ravel than Debussy), and part post-Wagnerian. The range of her research topics included Polish history and legends, and mythology of Greek antiquity. She wrote six works for orchestra, including the symphonic poem *Wawel* (1917), based on the legend of the founding of Krakow, the historical capital of Poland, and *The Seasons*, a symphonic overture (1953); six vocal-instrumental works, including cantatas for children and a symphonic cantata based on *Ode To Youth* by Adam Mickiewicz (1954); four ballets: *Blilitis*, based on Greek antiquity (1930), *Juria*, from a Belarus story (1939), *Bazyliszek* and *Fantasma* (1964), whose librettos describe intoxication and hallucinations induced by drugs—an area which also held the composer's interest.

Anna Maria Klechniowska died August 26, 1973 in Warsaw.

ZOFIA LISSA was born October 18, 1908, in Lwow, where she studied piano at the conservatory, and philosophy with Kazimerz Twardowski and musicology with Adolf Chybinski at the Jan Kazimierz University. In 1930, she received her doctorate with a dissertation on "The Harmony of Alexander Scriabin." She taught at Lwow schools and colleges, and worked for Lwow Radio. Of Jewish descent, she escaped from German-occupied Poland to the Soviet Union, and during 1941–42 taught music in Uzbekistan. In 1945 she was a cultural attaché of Poland in Moscow. A staunch member of the Communist party, she was the founder of Marxist approach to musicology. In 1947 she became vice director of the department of music at the Ministry of Arts and Culture and, until 1960, was one of the chief ideologues of socialist realism in art and a proponent of music analysis based on Marxist ideals. From 1948, she worked at the Warsaw University Institute of Musicology, and was its director 1958–75.

Lissa's broad scholarly interests emphasized aesthetics and philosophy of music. She was extremely active as a music historian, and internationally influential through UNESCO and the World Music Council. She organized the first international Chopin Congress (1960), and initiated yearly conferences for the study of early music in Eastern Europe, thus redefining the concepts of medieval and renaissance culture in Europe. As one of the earliest scholars interested in reception history[219] and popular music studies, she was a notable predecessor of all scholars active in these fields. Her approach to seeking reflection of social relationships and ideals in the music of a given time is echoed in the writings of **Susan McClary** and musicologists of this interest. Lissa was the first scholar to write a full theory and history of film music, comprising over twenty books and 200 articles.

She was also interested in *avant-garde* music, as well as other styles and periods. She wrote on Russian-Polish connections, and the composers Chopin, Lutoslawski, Szymanowski, and Beethoven—finding Polish themes in *his* music. Her polemics with Roman Ingarden (1893–1970), about the nature of musical works, still inspires music philosophers worldwide. Her textbooks include an introduction to musicology and edited volumes of the history of Polish music. The range of topics included defining musical culture, music in the context of culture, the definition of music in general, and social forces shaping musical culture and patronage. Fluent in German, Russian, French and Latin, her writings have been particularly influential in Germany, inspiring the interests of well known scholars Carl Dahlhaus and Hans Heinrich Eggebrecht, as well as their younger colleagues.

During her lifetime, Zofia Lissa was the most powerful person in the field of music in Poland, even *feared*—especially during the period of enforcement of Stalinist ideals in musicology (1948–1957). A brilliant teacher, she was an incisive, dedicated scholar, directing a range of her students, including **Zofia Helman**, **Slawomira Zeranska-Kominek** and **Maja Trochimczyk**, to distinguished musicological careers.

Lissa died March 26, 1980, in Warsaw.

MADELEINE MILHAUD, born March 22, 1902, in Paris, married composer Darius Milhaud (1892–1974) in 1925, and had a son, Daniel. After studies in Paris, she acted in several companies from 1933–39, during which time she was also professor of dramatic art at the Schola Cantorum. She appeared on French radio and in recitals under Stravinsky, Manuel Rosenthal, and her husband. She wrote booklets on, and helped produce, her husband's operas in America, and lectured at UC Berkeley and Mills College in Oakland, California, where the couple were in residence during World War II.

---

219. The history of the reception of music, i.e., contemporaneous criticism, literary reflections, audience sizes, and reactions based on newspaper clippings, journals and other written sources.

The Darius Milhaud Society, in cooperation with the Cleveland Institute of Music, Cleveland Museum of Art and Case Western Reserve University, honored Madame Milhaud with a gala in March 1995, featuring a screening of the film *Madame Bovary*, for which her husband wrote the music. She conducted a master class at the event. Still active on her 100th birthday (2002), as of this writing (2006), she is considered a *national treasure*—the last living person who knew everyone significant in the arts during the 20th century.

Two Women of Many Talents

MARION (Margaret) **SCOTT** was born in London, July 16, 1877, the eldest of three girls. From an interesting family on her mother's side, her aunt through marriage many generations back was one of the first women arrested—by John Hathorne, Nathaniel Hawthorne's grandfather—in the Salem (Massachusetts) witch hunts. In her fifties and ill, she died chained to an oak post in a Boston jail before they could hang her. Her great great great grandfather, George Prince, was a sea captain, ship owner, merchant, slave trader and adventurer—a prominent figure in Salem's "Golden Age of Sail." Her grandfather was a highly successful partner in a family import-export business in St. Petersburg (Russia). At twenty-one, he was managing a fleet of supercargo ships that sailed the world. Her father was a musician and, at twenty-one, London's youngest solicitor. At his death, aged eighty-six, he was the oldest attorney.

Her liberal parents encouraged their daughters to explore, challenge and follow their own direction in life. Sydney and Annie Prince Scott were social activists who used their wealth and influence to give support to such causes as the temperance and women's suffrage movements. From an early age, Marion was exposed to the inequities of society, particularly those affecting women. She would find the cruel indifference to those less fortunate intolerable and worked throughout her life to change public attitudes towards women, not just in music, but in society at large.

As a child, after years of dull piano lessons, she discovered the violin and by age fifteen was performing in public with her father as accompanist. She was so good that he bought her a Guadagnini violin. In 1896, she entered the RCM to study violin with Enrique Fernandez Arbos (1863–1939), piano with Marmaduke Barton (1865–1938), composition with Walford Davies (1869–1941), and later with Sir Charles Villiers Stanford (1852–1942). She was one of only two women named in a listing of Stanford's pupils, the other was **Rebecca Clarke**. Even as a student, Scott was in demand as a performer. In 1901, she achieved her childhood dream of performing at the Crystal Palace,[220] participating in a chamber concert. She was also a regular performer on the London recital circuit, often featuring music so new that the players had to work from the composer's manuscript. In 1906, Scott was one of the founders of the RCM Student Union—of which she became secretary—marking the beginning of her continued association with the college after her graduation in 1900. (In 1936, she became the editor of the RCM magazine, a post she held until 1944.)

In 1911, composition student Ivor Gurney (1890–1937) entered the RCM. The same year, Marion became a co-founder of the Society of Women Musicians whose aim was to promote cooperation among women in different fields of music, provide performance opportunities, as well as advice on business aspects of their profession. She was SWM president, 1915–16.

Scott's wide-ranging creativity included a book of poems, *Violin Verses* (1905), a body of compositions, and becoming a knowledgeable music critic, entrepreneur and writer/lecturer. As a freelance musician, she was an associate of violinist Joseph Joachim, formed her own string quartet (1908), organized concerts of British chamber music (1900–1920), and was for a time concertmistress of the Morley College orchestra under **Gustav Holst**. Her articles in London area newspapers covered topics such as salaries for women music teachers and music

---

220. The Crystal Palace, featuring over a million feet of glass, was erected for The Great Exhibition of 1851, celebrating England's Industrial leadership. Concerts were held in the huge arched Centre Transept, which also contained the world's largest organ. It burned down in 1936.

as a profession for women. By 1910 she had developed a lecture series on music history and performance, and taught workshops on composition, harmony, orchestration and technical aspects of music which she offered to organizations throughout London. In 1919, she began a full-time career as a critic for the *Christian Science Monitor*, an international daily based in Boston, for whom she would write until 1933. Besides contributing to a myriad of music magazines, she was also featured in two major English newspapers, *The Daily Telegraph* and *The Observer*.

In her personal life, she and sister Stella were acting as surrogate mothers for their toddler niece, Audrey Lovibond, whose mother Freda, the youngest of the Scott sisters, had died two weeks after giving birth in 1908. (In 1945, Stella suffered a devastating stroke and her care fell to Marion, almost seventy, and to Stella's husband, who was also ailing.)

Scott kept up correspondence with Gurney at the Front during WWI and in 1917—by which time she was in love with him—helped in the publication of his first volume of poetry, *Severn and Somme*, plus arranging performances of his music, an undertaking to which she devoted the rest of her life. Her relationship with Ivor—he suffered from severe bi-polar illness—was difficult and complex, especially after he was institutionalized in 1922. (He died in 1937.) Yet, until her own rich career was unearthed in the 1980s by musicologist **Pamela Blevins**, to whom I am indebted for much of this material, Marion has been mainly known through the "love connection," and her only other notoriety was through very public castigation by composer **Gerald Finzi** (1901–56), who was incensed because she refused to relinquish her personal collection of Gurney manuscripts.

In her fifties, Scott turned to musical scholarship with a distinctive style that also appeared in her occasional program notes. Her only full length book was on Beethoven (1934, revised 1974), a masterly biographical and critical study, exploring the spiritual forces in his music. It was reprinted a dozen times.

Victim of intermittent bouts of ill health, in summer 1953 she was diagnosed with colon cancer. With her published articles on Haydn[221] of documentary importance, although weak, she continued working on her monumental complete catalogue of his compositions. When she became too ill to finish, she dictated the material to her friend and assistant Kathleen Dale.

Psychically, Marion tried to hold onto life until December 26, the day Ivor died, but death snatched her two days before, in London, Christmas Eve, December 24, 1953.

ETHEL Lilian (Boole) **VOYNICH**, novelist, composer, translator, revolutionary, was born May 11, 1864, in County Cork, Ireland. She was the fifth daughter of mathematician George Boole (Boolean Theory) and Mary Everest Boole, a writer on scientific topics, whose uncle, George Everest, was the explorer who gave his name to the famous mountain. Ethel's father died six months after her birth, and the family soon became destitute. Mrs. Boole returned to her native England with the girls, living off a small government pension until she got the post of librarian at Queen's College, London. At age eight, Ethel contracted erysipelas, a bacterial infection called "the filth disease." Deciding that a change would help, her mother sent her to live in Lancashire with *her* brother, a religious fanatic and sadist who beat his own children and forced Ethel to play piano for him for hours. When the ten-year-old returned to London, she suffered a nervous breakdown. She dressed in black and called herself Lily. At eighteen, she received a small legacy that enabled her to study piano and composition at the Hochschule für Musik (1882–85).

In her teens she had read about Italian revolutionary Giuseppe Mazzini (1805–72), which marked the beginning of her political activism. In Berlin, her interest increased in the revolutionary causes of Russia and Central Europe. Back in London, she met the militant Sergei Kravchinski, known as Stepniak, and learned Russian from him. His revelations on the plight of his countrymen propelled her to St. Petersburg in 1887. En route, in Warsaw, she stood before the Citadel prison. One of the inmates, Polish nationalist Mikhail Babdank-Woynicz (1865–1930), saw her.

---

221. Her Haydn biography, based on more than twenty years of research, was left with only three completed chapters. Her collection of Haydn scores and pictures was bequeathed to the Cambridge University Library.

Ethel supported herself in St. Petersburg working as a tutor and governess, teaching English and music. She stayed with Stepniak's sister-in-law, Dr. Preskovia Karauloff, whose husband was in jail for his political activities. Ethel began bringing him food, witnessing firsthand the deplorable conditions and inhumane treatment of prisoners. Associating with dissidents, she grew more determined to help. Her first summer in Russia was spent helping Preskovia bring medical aid to peasants living in the Pskov Lake District.

The fledgling revolutionary returned to England and, with Stepniak, organized the Society of Friends of Russian Freedom. Meanwhile, the Polish prisoner had been exiled to Siberia, escaped, and made his way to London and connected with Stepniak. He changed his name to Wilfred Michael Voynich, became an antiquarian book dealer, and met Ethel Boole. By 1895, they were living together. They married in 1902. She became known as E.L.V. Both continued their activism, but ceased after Stepniak assassinated the chief of the Czarist secret police.

Voynich published her first novel, *The Gadfly*, in 1897. The controversial work, whose title character was based on Mazzini, was considered a combination of Nathaniel Hawthorne's *The Scarlet Letter* (1850) and Baroness Emma Orczy's *The Scarlet Pimpernel* (1905). It went through eight printings in its first four years. It remains a bestseller, and has become a classic in Russia, with millions of copies sold. Adapted for the stage in 1898 by George Bernard Shaw, it inspired three operas and two films, one with a score by Dmitri Shostakovich. Voynich's less well-known novels include *Jack Raymond* (1901), *Olive Latham* (1904) and *An Interrupted Friendship* (1911). She also wrote several translations of major Russian works, the most important of which is Chopin's letters (1931), for which she also provided a preface and editorial notes. It is the most complete edition of the composer's correspondence to appear in English and remains in print.

Ethel began to compose around 1910. She was a member of the Society of Women Musicians during World War I, and a social worker for the anti-war Quakers in London's East End. In 1914, shortly before the outbreak the war, Wilfred began to transfer his book business to New York, although he continued to visit his offices in London, Paris and Florence. Ethel followed him to New York in 1920, turning her full attention to composition with instrumental music and arrangements of shorter sacred works, cantatas and oratorios, including *Babylon*, *Jerusalem*, *Epitaph in Ballad Form* and *The Submerged City* for performance at the Pius X School of Liturgical Music, Manhattanville College of the Sacred Heart, where she taught music 1933–43. She also embarked on an intensive analytical study of music of all eras and from all countries and kept voluminous research notes.

She published her last novel, *Put off thy Shoes* in 1945, a lengthy, multi-generational chronicle set in the 18th century. The plot focuses on the Gadfly's British grandparents and great-grandparents.

Not until nearly sixty years after the publication of *The Gadfly* did she learn, in 1955, that she was a celebrity in the USSR. A Russian working at the UN discovered she was living in New York and went to visit her. He told her that her novel was regarded as a masterpiece, had been translated into the eighteen languages of what was then the Soviet Union, and that the critics ranked her with Mark Twain, Theodore Dreiser and Charles Dickens, and that she was as admired as Shakespeare! She was, in fact, "a second God" to the Russian people, and so highly regarded that the official Soviet newspaper, *Pravda*, upon learning that she was alive, blazed the headline "Voynich is Living in New York!" over a three column story. In 1956, Adlai Stevenson visited the Soviet Union to arrange for the payment of long overdue royalties for millions of copies.

Voynich's music was rarely performed during her lifetime and the bulk of it remained untouched at the Library of Congress where it was discovered in 2004 by **Pam Blevins**, who did the research for this entry.

Ethel Boole Vyonich died in New York City, July 28, 1960, at the age of ninety-six.

In Our Times

EVA (Halfar) **BADURA-SKODA**, born January 15, 1929, in Munich, spent her childhood in Vienna where she attended the University of Music, as well as studying musicology, philosophy and art history at the Universities of Heidelberg, Vienna and Innsbruck, receiving her PhD from the latter. In September 1951, she married world-renowned Austrian pianist, music editor, pedagogue, **Paul Badura-Skoda** (*b* 1927). They collaborated on many publications, including "Interpreting Mozart on the Keyboard," (Vienna, 1957; New York, St. Martin's Press, 1962). In 1964, she was the Brittingham guest professor at the University of Wisconsin (Madison). In 1966, she joined their faculty as professor of musicology until 1974, when she resigned to devote more time for research. During her tenure, her husband was artist-in-residence (1966–71).

A visiting professor and guest lecturer at universities in the U.S., Italy, Switzerland, Holland, Denmark, Germany, Austria, Canada, Hungary, Japan, Spain, South Korea, and at the Conservatories of Music in Moscow and Leningrad, she resides in America and Vienna. An active member of music conferences and symposia, she participated at the eighth, ninth, tenth, fourteenth and fifteenth congresses of the *International Musicological Society*. In 1986, she was decorated with the *Ehrenkreuz für Kunst und Wissenschaft* (Honorary Cross for Arts and Science) by the Austrian government.

Her numerous scholarly articles have been published in musicological journals and books. She edited three of Mozart's Piano Concertos in collaboration with her husband. Her scholarly contributions include articles for MGG (a music encyclopedia), the *New Grove Dictionary of Music* and *The Encyclopedia of the Piano*. She contributed a chapter on Schubert to *Piano Music in the Nineteenth Century*, and the chapter "Aspects of Performance Practice" for *Keyboard Music in the Eighteenth Century*—both by Schirmer Books (with later editions by Routledge). She edited "Schubert Studies" for Cambridge University Press, arranged and edited reports of the *International Haydn Congress Vienna 1982* and of the Conference "Schubert and His Friends." From 1984–90, she worked with her husband on the book, *Bach Interpretation*, which appeared in German (1990), and English (Oxford U. Press, 1992). From 1988–90, she wrote the scripts and managed the production of a three-part documentary film on the *History of the Hammerklavier* for Austrian Public Television. Her *History of the Pianoforte* became a 1999 video (available from Indiana University Press), in which virtuosi perform on more than 30 instruments housed in museums and private collections, featuring works from the time the instruments were built.

She helped discover the fourth extant Beethoven piano, made by Conrad Graf, which the composer used during his 1823 stay in Baden bei Wien where he took the waters. When he returned to Vienna that November, the piano remained in Baden and was stored in a basement which was flooded May 1824. Rescued at the end of the century by historian Dr. Carl Glossy, archivist/director of the Vienna City Library, and his wife, pianist Marie Glossy, the family had it in their home for nearly one hundred years. Dr. Badura-Skoda reconstructed the complex history of the instrument and, based on available facts, succeeded in establishing its authenticity.

(Her article can be read in Vol. 4 of the *Bonner Beethoven Studien*, Bonn 2005.)

In England, **MARGARET BENT** is a senior research fellow at All Souls College, Oxford University. Her research emphasis is on the 14th and 15th centuries.

Her publications include "Initial Letters in the Old Hall Manuscript," *Music and Letters* 47 (1966); "A Lost English Choirbook of the 15th Century," *International Musicological Society: Report of the Eleventh Congress* (Copenhagen, 1972); "The late-medieval motet," *Companion to Medieval and Renaissance Music* (1992); "Editing early music: the dilemma of translation," *Early Music* (August 1994); and "Accidentals, counterpoint and notation in Aaron's *Aggiunta* to the *Toscanello in Musica*," *The Journal of Musicology* (XII/1994). In 1996, a team of professors and students from Peabody Conservatory and Johns Hopkins University collaborated with her in the production of a CD-ROM based multimedia learning environment for the study of medieval and renaissance music. A 1998 medievalist text was the *Fauvel Studies: Allegory, Chronicle, Music, and Image in Paris* (Bibliothèque Nationale de France), edited by Margaret Bent & Andrew Wathey, presenting a wealth of new material on the politics, society and culture of the French royal court of the 14th century.

She is the first woman in music to become a fellow of the British Academy. She is also a fellow of the American Academy of Arts and Science, and has been chairman of the music departments at Brandeis and Princeton Universities, and president of the American Musicological Society (AMS). Bent received an honorary doctorate from the University of Glasgow in 1997.

CLAUDIA BÖTTCHER, born December 8, 1964, in Frankfurt-am-Main, Germany, studied at the Cologne Conservatory, receiving master's degrees in music education, opera singing, pedagogy and romance languages—besides her native German, she speaks English, French and Italian. Since 1987, she has performed with the opera companies of Düsseldorf, Hanover and Berlin, in international concerts, radio and television, and recorded Brahms' Requiem and the music of Jean Françaix. She has won important vocal prizes in her own country, and is a laureate of the International Association Yehudi Menuhin (Paris). Besides private voice and piano lessons, she organizes concerts, gives master classes throughout Europe, and teaches at the Municipal Music School of Frechen, preparing students for competitions. Her 1995 book, *Das Vokal und Orgelwerk von Jean Françaix*, covers the vocal and organ works of Jean Françaix (1912–97).

Claudia is married to physicist Dr. Jochen Schmidt. Their daughter, Morna, was born February 8, 1996.

JUNE BOYCE-TILLMAN's earliest memories of music are sitting on the end of a double piano stool while her grandfather played military two-steps and Mendelssohn's *War March of the Priests*. He was the dance band pianist at Ashurst, a village in the New Forest of Southern England, and wanted June to be a classical pianist. As a child, her forte was singing and dancing, but she had to give up dance lessons at seven because her family could not afford both. She studied music at Oxford, and completed a PhD at the London University Institute of Education. Her dissertation, *Towards a Model of the Musical Development of Children* has been translated into Dutch, Japanese, Italian, Portuguese and Polish.

She has taught in the London schools, and pioneered introducing composition activities into the classroom. In her lectures she encourages the promotion of music by women, holding international workshops for women in composing, ranging as far as Australia. Her interest in music and religious education has led to articles and workshops linking these areas together.

Her religious music and hymns have been performed in the cathedrals of St. Paul's, Southwark and Westminster. In 1991, Boyce-Tillman was warden of the music in the education section of the Incorporated Society of Musicians. Supervising research students from all over the world, she has developed a project in the area of music and ritual, specializing in the work of **Hildegard of Bingen**. She formed the Hildegard Network during the international conference *Hildegard von Bingen A Woman For Our Time*, held at King Alfred's College, Winchester, April 1996, whose participants from many countries and cultures reflected the eclectic and holistic inspiration displayed by Hildegard herself, 900 years ago, in her belief in the power of music to connect us with God and all creation.

Patricia Chiti

PATRICIA ADKINS CHITI has a multi-media career as performer, musicologist, television programmer and author. Born in England, Patricia started singing publicly at three. She made her debut in operetta as a teenager, receiving professional training at London's Guildhall School of Music and Drama, and master classes in London, Stuttgart and Rome. Following a period of study at Rome's Teatro dell'Opera with Luigi Ricci, she made her Italian debut, 1972, in an opera by Gian-Carlo Menotti, the youngest mezzo to appear at the Teatro Communiale in Bologna.

Internationally recognized for her performances of contemporary Russian music, especially the works of **Dmitri Shostakovich**, **Elena Firsova** and **Sofia Gubaidulina**, Chiti sang the 1996 world premiere of the latter's *Galgenlieder*, written for her. She has sung in major European opera houses and orchestras in Europe, Latin America, South Africa and the Orient, under such renowned conductors as **Maxim Shostakovich** (son of Dmitri), **Mstislav Rostropovich** and **Sir Yehudi Menuhin**. Her recordings include over 500 works for many European radio networks, ranging from Italian baroque to contemporary works composed especially for her voice by **Tsippi Fleischer**, **Myriam Marbé**, **Thea Musgrave** and **Marta Ptaszynska**, whose *Liquid Light* premiered November 1996.

As a musicologist, Chiti is a pioneer in the research of women composers. In 1978, she founded the first international festival of women's music in Fiuggi, Italy, "Donne in Musica," which continues to take place annually in

Rome. Her 1982 Italian book of the same title has been translated into Spanish, *Mujeres en Musica* (Alianza, Madrid, 1995) and *Women in Music* (Amadeus Press, 1998). Her second book, *Una voce poco fa . . .* (a voice a while ago), contains biographies of the prima donnas of **Gioachino Rossini** (1792–1868) plus selections of music they sang and/or composed. She has also written articles and monthly columns in prominent Italian journals, and contributed to *Women Composers: An Historical Anthology* (Editor-in-Chief, Sylvia Glickman, for G.K. Hall, Macmillan Publishers, 1995), *The International Encyclopedia of Women Composers* (ed. Aaron Cohen—the first such work), *The Musical Woman* (ed. Judith Zaimont, Greenwood Press, 1985), and *An International Perspective on Funding for the Arts* (Greenwood Press, 1996). *The Music of the Mythical Garcias* (Alfred Publishing, 1997) is about composer/father **Manuel Garcia**, and his famous singer daughters, **Maria Malibran** and **Pauline Viardot Garcia**, containing their music and biographies.

Representing the culmination of Chiti's research—rediscovery and reevaluation of the role of women in the history of music—she wrote and narrated her landmark program, also called "Donne in Musica," produced by the RAI (Italian television). Distributed in video, they reach homes and educational centers. The thirty installments feature soloists, ensembles and, in some segments, rare footage of divas of yesteryear. Together, they present an outline of the history of women musicians, composers and conductors, traced from the Sumerian civilization to the present day. A German magazine dubbed her the "Primadonna Detective!"

In 1993, Chiti became a member of the Italian National Commission for Scientific Research. In 1994, she was appointed to the State Commission for the Performing Arts, responsible directly to the president of the Republic. 1995 marked her membership in the Permanent Committee for the Empowerment and Representation of Women, under the National Council for Economy and Labor.

In December 1994, by permanent decree, the City Council of Fiuggi set up a fund for *Fondazione Adkins Chiti: Donne in Musica* (The Adkins Chiti: Women in Music Foundation). Created with her own music collection, and other gifts, it now has a library of over 15,000 volumes. The foundation encompasses forty-five Women in Music associations on five continents, and over 1,000 women composers in ninety-two countries. Since its birth, the Foundation has run yearly festivals and programmed hundreds of concerts featuring music of women composers. In 1996, this became directly affiliated with the International Music Council of UNESCO. The first International Symposium and Festival, commissioning six new works by women, including two for orchestra and two choreographies, was held September 17–22, 1996, in Fiuggi outside Rome. Patricia resides in Rome with her husband, composer Gian Paolo Chiti.

RHIAN DAVIES should be noted for her research on Welsh composer **Morfydd Owen** with her 1994 book, *Never so Pure a Sight, Morfydd Owen (1891–1918): A Life in Pictures*, and her University of Wales dissertation, *A Beautiful and Refined Talent: Morfydd Owen (1891–1918)*.

SOPHIE FULLER, born in England, August 26, 1961, is the author of many published books and articles. She holds a BA degree in Russian Language and Literature from the School of Slavonic and East European Studies, University of London (1984), and has studied in Russia and taught classes on the History of Russian Music. Her BA (1988) and MM (1989) are from King's College, London. Her PhD dissertation covers "Late Victorian and Edwardian British Women Songwriters." As a flutist, Fuller has given private instruction and performed with the London Veena Music Group. In 1987, she became a founder of Women in Music, a highly successful national membership support organization, which celebrates and raises public awareness of women's work in all types of music.

Television and radio interviews range in topics from St. Cecilia to Ethel Smyth, to contemporary composers, for which Fuller has written articles for accompanying booklets. Numerous important publications include "Dead white men in wigs: women and classical music today" in Girls! Girls! Girls!; "Essays on Women and Music," ed. Sarah Cooper (London: Cassell, 1995), and an essay on "Music and Feminism" (1996). A major contributor, Fuller has fifteen entries in *The Norton Grove Dictionary of Women Composers* (1995) and has contributed entries on women composers to *The Rough Guide to Classical Music* (1994; revised 1998), *The New Grove Dictionary of Music and Musicians* second edition (2001) and *The Revised Dictionary of National Biography*.

One of Fuller's most valuable adjuncts to music history is the definitive volume, *The Pandora Guide to Women Composers-Britain and the United States, 1629–present* (1994), containing excellent, readable coverage of its subject matter. She is contributor, and co-editor (with Lloyd Whitesell), of *Queer Episodes: Music and Modern Identity* (University of Illinois Press, 2002) and (with Nicky Losseff) of *The Idea of Music in Victorian Fiction* (Ashgate, 2003). Her research covers music and literature, Russian music and popular song, as well as different aspects of gender and sexuality in music, particularly on the role gender played in the musical life of late nineteenth and early 20th century Britain and the lives and works of Victorian and Edwardian women composers. Fuller is a professor at the University of Reading (UK).

Born 1957, in Calcutta, and raised in India until the age of ten, **LUCY GREEN** had little exposure to music, there being no radio or television available and no music in school. All she ever heard were Beatles songs sung by her friends who had been in boarding school in England. After her family returned to England, she received a degree in music education from Homerton College, Cambridge, with MM and PhD from Sussex University. After teaching private lessons in piano, and music in the schools, she now lectures in the sociology and aesthetics of music and music education at London University's Institute of Education. Her books include *Music on Deaf Ears: Musical Meaning, Ideology and Education* (1988); *The Sexual Politics of Music: Discourse, Musical Meaning and Education; How Popular Musicians Learn: A Way Ahead for Music Education* (Ashgate, 2001); *Issues in Music Education* (Routledge, 2001); *Aspects of Teaching Secondary Music: Perspectives on Practice* (Routledge, 2002); and articles on music education, including "From the Western Classics to the World: Secondary Music Teachers' Changing Perceptions of Musical Styles, 1982–1998" (British Journal of Music Education, Vol. 19, no. 1.).

Katrijn Kuypers

KATRIJN KUYPERS was born April 6, 1963, in Antwerp. She studied musicology at the University of Utrecht, where she joined a group of female students who were attempting to get more attention for women in music, and get such a course into the curriculum. This was the forerunner of *Stichting Vrouw en Muziek* (Foundation for Women in Music), for which she was the secretary (1986–1997).

Kuypers has produced expositions of Women Composers, the first in Breda (North Netherlands, 1985), on Nelly van der Linden van Snelrewaard-Boudewijns. Twelve Dutch women were the subject of the 1987 Groningen exposition, "100 Years of Dutch Women Composers," which featured their string quartets. Her book, *Dat komt enkel van een bad . . . Nelly van der Linden van Snelrewaard 1869–1926*, was published in 1992. Kuypers also writes for music journals. Since 2000 she has concentrated on working for amateur musicians, producing programs for the radio station, De Concertzender, covering choirs, folk music and brass bands. In this position, she is able to promote women's music. In 2003, she became a music consultant for the Province of Utrecht, which involves advising musicians on the organization of choirs, ensembles, etc., plus fundraising and other supporting activities.

Since 1993, Kuypers has been organizing choral concerts for the St. Peter's Church Concert Series. She is a member of several choirs, including a group which sings Gregorian Chants from 10th century manuscripts. She also dances baroque, renaissance and flamenco, and would like to see the introduction of such a discipline as "danceology."

Closely associated with the late **Tera de Marez Oyens**, Kuypers served as her assistant, collating her manuscripts, now housed in The Hague Municipal Museum.

ROSAMOND "CORKY" McGUINNESS was head of the music department at Royal Holloway College, University of London until her retirement in 1995, and chairman of the board of studies in music.

Born in Bridgeport, Connecticut, she graduated from Vassar (B Mus. History, 1951), continuing studies at Columbia, Smith, Princeton and Harvard. She began her doctorate in music history at Cornell in 1956, but left for Britain in 1957 where she was married—until 1969—to English philosopher and Oxford don, Brian McGuinness, with whom she had Catherine, Sara, Patrick and Lucy. From 1970–82 she was wed to Don Biddlecombe. Their union produced Elizabeth. After seven years' work and bearing four children, in 1964 McGuinness was awarded her Doctorate from St. Anne's College, Oxford University.

From 1992–95, McGuinness was an auditor for the Higher Education Quality Council and assessor for the Higher Education Funding Council for England. From 1995–98, she was undergraduate external examiner at the RCM, and the MA program in music for City University. She was one of the three external examiners (1996–99) for the undergraduate program at Guildhall, after which she became chief external examiner. She represented the UK in the four-year European Science Foundation Project (1998–2002) in musicology. She participated in many academic conferences in the U.S., UK and Holland. Her research has been published in journals and books, including *Economics of Art and Culture* (ed. V.A. Ginsburgh. Invited Papers at the Twelfth International Conference of the Association of Cultural Economics International), *Concert Life in Eighteenth-Century Britain* (eds. Susan Wollenberg and Simon McVeigh) and *The Circulation of Music in Europe. 1600–1750: A Sample of Case and Other Studies*, (ed. Rudolf Rasch).

McGuinness' other positions include the academic board, validation and review of music and drama courses at London University, admissions tutor for the music department, Special Entrance Committee of the University, chairman of examiners for the music degree in the Colleges of Education, doctorate examiner at Reading, Oxford and London Universities, and president of the British Society for 18th Century Studies. She is most noted for her work, begun in 1975, on the Register of Musical Data in London Newspapers, 1660–1800. This large-scale, long-term project, begun in 1986, has attained a solid foundation with award grants of nearly £130,000, much due to the Leverhulme Foundation. The register offers a varied body of "hard fact" to provoke new insights into the place and study of music, leading to a more precise understanding of the music itself. An adjunct to this is a complete list of extant London newspapers. Both complement the British Library's 18th Century Short Title Catalogue. This was close to completion by 2004. The same year, the author's non-academic book, *Move Still*, a personal memoir about the power of art as a life-changing force, was being prepared for publication.

Born September 5, 1924, in Lwow,[222] **KRYSTYNA MOSZUMAŃSKA-NAZAR** settled in Krakow after the second World War, studying piano with Jan Hoffman and composition with Stanislaw Wiechowicz, and earning diplomas in both areas in 1955 at the city's State Higher School of Music (now the Academy of Music). Her early prizes are from the Polish Composer's Union (1954) for *Oberek* from the *Suite of the Polish Dance*; from the International Competition for Women Composers, Mannheim, for *Hexaedre* and *Exodus* (1961, 1966); first prize and a gold medal at the International Competition for Women Composers for *Music for Strings* (Buenos Aires, 1962); third prize at the Artur Malawski Composition Competition for *Concertante Variations* (Krakow, 1966) and second prize at the Karol Szymanowski Composition Competition for *Polish Madonnas* (1974).

In 1963 she began her career at the Krakow Academy, lecturing on composition, instrumentation, fugue and contemporary compositional techniques. She was head of the composition department (1974–75), dean of faculty for composition, conducting and theory of music (1975–79), vice-rector and rector (1987–93). Meanwhile, she was chairman of the Krakow Branch of the Polish Composers' Union (1964–71), and active on the board of the Polish Composers' Union (1971–73), as well as sitting on juries of many Polish and foreign composition competitions. From 1993–99, she served on the Council for Higher Artistic Schools while continuing to give lectures in Poland and abroad on her works, contemporary music and new notation.

Honored five times by the Ministry of Culture and Art, she received the Prime Minister's Prize for her work for children and young people. She has also been decorated with the Gold Cross of Merit and the Chevalier's Cross, Commander's Cross and Officer's Cross of the Order of the Restoration of Poland. She is the recipient of the honorary title and medal "For Contributions to National Culture." In 1994, a television film entitled *Krystyna*

---

222. Now Lviv, Ukraine. On August 16, 1945, the USSR and Poland signed a treaty which shifted Poland's borders. It lost 69,860 square miles in the East and gained 38,986 square miles in the West.

Moszumańska-Nazar was made as part of the cycle *Albums of Krakow Music*. In 2003, she received an award from the Polish Culture Foundation, presented at the Museum of Krakow.

NORIKO OHTAKE, born in Wakayama, Japan, June 8, 1963, was guided to music by her parents and friends. "It was very popular at the time in Japan for girls to take piano lessons, so I started at five."

She came to America in 1978, and earned her BM (1985) and MM (1986) from Juilliard, and a DMA (1990) from the University of Maryland.

She has been a lecturer at Sagami Women's University, in Sagamihara City near Tokyo since 1997, teaching music and art appreciation and piano repertoire study. She also gives concerts and lecture-concerts.

Her books include *Creative Sources for the Music of Toru Takemitsu* (1993, Scholar Press, London), a major Japanese composer (1930–96), and co-author with Kikuko Nakamura, of *The Dictionary of Piano Composers and Their Compositions* (Yamaha, 2003).

Noriko's honors include first place, Enrico Fermi Foundation Competition (1981), first place, Brooklyn Arts and Culture Association Competition (1982), and the Homer Ulrich Award, University of Maryland (1987).

She is married to composer Yoshihiro Kanno. Their son, Shunsuke, was born August 9, 1993.

VIVIENNE OLIVE, although born in London, May 31, 1950, has made a name for herself in Germany, where she lives in Nuremberg. She studied organ and harpsichord at Trinity College, London (1966–68) earning a diploma in theory, and composition with Bernard Rands at York University, where she received her BA (1971) and doctorate (1975). Postdoctoral studies were with Klaus Huber and Brian Ferneyhough at the Musihochschule Freiberg, and further postgraduate harpsichord studies with Stanislav Heller (1976–78). She received the Stuttgart Prize for composition in her final year in Freiberg. She also studied in Milan and Vienna with Franco Donatoni and Roman Haubenstock-Ramati. In 1973, she was appointed music theory lecturer at the Fachakademie für Musik in Nuremberg and in 1979, theory professor at the Meistersinger-konservatorium there. She has been a visiting guest lecturer in Canada and Australia. Her awards in Germany are from the Bach Academy in Stuttgart for her *Stabat Mater*, the Stuttgart Composition Prize for *Tomba di Bruno*, and from Hamelin for *An English Suite*. Many of her works are commissions from soloists, chamber ensembles and radio on both sides of the English Channel.

Olive is the author of publications in the field of music theory, including "A Functional Approach to Harmony Style and Analysis" (Notable Arts, Australia), and a contributor to music journals including *Viva Voce*. A major focus of her research is the analysis of women's music. She has been a member of the board of the International Arbeitskreis Women and Music since 1995, and co-founder and joint artistic director of the Nuremberg New Music Festival and "Contempofest."

ANTJE OLIVIER, born January 16, 1944, in Alsfeld, Germany, studied languages and music. She has been a journalist since 1973, working for newspapers all over Europe. In 1981, she began establishing the European Archive of Women in Music, and after her seven year Herculean task became the founder of the *Europäsches Frauenmusikarchiv* (European Women's Music Archive) based in Düsseldorf. The same year saw the publication of *Komponistinnen von A-Z*, an anthology of international women composers. In 1990, she authored *Komponistinnen - eine Bestandsaufname*, Volume I, a compilation of more than 300 names of women composers past and present, their music, publishers and discography. 1994 brought Volume II. In 1996, she published, together with S. Braun, *Komponistinnen aus 800 Jahren* (Women Composers Through 800 Years). The collection gathers the works of European women composers over the course of eight centuries. The same year marked her biography of Fanny Mendelssohn, and in 1997 an edition of *Letters to Nadia Boulanger*. Olivier is the founder of Tokkata-Verlag and Edition Donna, two publishing companies, and since 1992 has been the manager of the International Woman Composers Library in Unna (Germany).

ELENA OSTLEITNER was born June 15, 1947, in Caracas, Venezuela. She studied at the Hochschule für Musik in Vienna, which included piano, and majored in sociology at the University of Vienna. In 1974, she gave birth to a son. In 1975, she became an instructor at the Hochschule and by 1982 was a professor and part of the Institute for Music Sociology (IMS). In 1992, she joined the University of Vienna faculty as a lecturer. In 1995, she was appointed vice president of the Austrian Latin American Institute. In recognition of her musicological expertise, she was appointed advisor on Music, Education and Women's Projects in both the Vienna and the Austrian Ministries of Culture. She lectures at universities and conferences throughout Europe, and is co-author of *Carole Dawn Reinhart: Aspects of a Career*, the biography of an American virtuoso trumpet player who teaches in Vienna. (See Brass.) Ostleitner's main areas of focus are woman and music, Latin American music, and functional music. In 1997, she became a strong voice in publicizing the gender discrimination of the Vienna Philharmonic, a policy she has been fighting against for over twenty years.

EVA RIEGER was the first musicologist in Germany to publish feminist work on women in music. After attending summer sessions for women in 1976, '77 at the Free University of Berlin—the first organized German conferences in which feminist issues were debated on a scholarly basis—she was encouraged to begin scrutinizing music archives in search of women composers. She became, in her own words, "stuck on the subject."

Born November 21, 1940, on the Isle of Man (England), when her father was minister of a German congregation in London, the family moved to Berlin in 1953, where Eva studied musicology, music education and English literature at the Hochschule für Musik, and at the Technical Institute, from which she received her PhD in 1976. Between 1973–91, her teaching career included positions at the Hochschule and Universities of Göttingen and Hildesheim. In 1991, she received a professorship for musicology and music pedagogy at the University of Bremen.

Her numerous publications cover the editing of *Frühe Texte: Frau und Musik* (Early Texts: Women and Music; Frankfurt, 1980; second ed. Kassel, 1989), *Frau, Musik und Männerherrschaft* (Women, Music and Male Domination; Berlin, 1981; second ed Kassel, 1989) with a Japanese translation. Recognition from English-speaking feminists came through her essays on women in music featured in *Feminine Æsthetics* (Gisela Ecker, ed., Boston, 1986); Volume 7 of "Source Reading in Music History" (Eds. Oliver Strunk and Leo Treitler, London, 1996); and the German translation for Furore Publishers of "Women's Orchestras in the United States, 1925–45" by **Carol Neuls-Bates**, which appeared in *Women Making Music* (Jane Bowers & Judith Tick, Eds. UIP, 1986). Eva's unique study of the musical description of gender roles in the films of Alfred Hitchcock was published by Pfaffenweiler (1996).

One of the main sources on the life of Mozart's sister is Rieger's biography *Nannerl Mozart: Leben eine Künstlerin im 18 Jahrhundert* (Nannerl Mozart: The Life of an Artist in the 18th Century, Frankfurt, 1991), which has a Swedish translation. This was followed by *Women and Music: Bibliography 1970–1996* (Hildesheim, 1999).

Her sixtieth birthday in 2000 was celebrated at the University of Oldenburg. She was presented with a "Festschrift" (compilation), published by the University, which includes articles by her colleagues Jane Bowers, Marcia Citron, Susan McClary, M. Michele Edwards, Judith Tick and Elizabeth Wood.

Since her retirement, Rieger resides in Vaduz (Lichtenstein) and Zurich. Her 21st century output covers: *Frauenstimmen, Frauenrollen in der Oper und Frauen-Selbstzeugnisse* (Women's Voices, Opera Roles and Autobiographies; co-edited with Gabriele Busch-Salmen, Centaurus, Herbolzheim, 2000); *Göttliche Stimmen: Lebensberichte berühmter Sängerinn von Elisabeth Mara bis Maria Callas* (Heavenly Voices: Women Singers tell of their lives from Elisabeth Mara [1749–1833] to Maria Callas; co-edited with M. Steegmann, Insel, Frankfurt, 2002); "Desire is Consuming Me: The Life Partnership between Eugenie Schumann and Marie Fillunger" in *Secret Passages* (Eds. Sophie Fuller and Lloyd Whitesell, Indiana University Press, 2002); "I married Eva: Gender Construction and Meistersinger" in *A Companion to Richard Wagner's Die Meistersinger von Nürnberg* (ed. Nicholas Vazsonyi, Camden House, 2002); the editor of *"Mit tausend Küssen Deine Fillu." Briefe der Sängerin Marie Fillunger an Eugenie Schumann 1875–93* ("A Thousand Kisses from Fillu." Letters from the Singer Marie Fillunger to Eugenie Schumann 1875–93 (Dittrich, Cologne, 2002); and *Minna und Richard Wagner: Stationen einer Ehe* (Minna and Richard Wagner: A Marriage Story; Arteis & Winkler, Düsseldorf 2003), which brings new insight on Wagner's first wife whom history has hitherto depicted as a long-suffering simple woman. In reality, Minna Planer was a successful actress who gave up her career to marry a young, unknown, unemployed composer. It was her love for him that enabled the couple to survive the many debt-ridden years and political exile.

In 2004 Rieger was working on the third edition of her Nannerl Mozart biography, a 2005 Insel publication for the 250th anniversary of Mozart's birth 2006.

JULIE ANNE McCORNACK SADIE. Married to the late Stanley Sadie (1930–2005), a foremost British music historian and writer, she collaborated with **Rhian Samuel** in the *Norton/Grove Dictionary of Women Composers*. (See American Musicologists.)

RHIAN SAMUEL was born in Aberdare, Wales, February 3, 1944. She received her BA (1966) and BM (1967) from the University of Reading (England). Her graduate studies were at Washington University, St. Louis, Missouri, (MA, 1970; PhD, 1978). Her dissertation: *Tonality, Modality and Musica Ficta in the Sixteenth Century Chanson*. Samuel taught at the St. Louis Conservatory (1977–83), after which she returned to the University of Reading as a lecturer (1984), head of the music department (1993) and reader (1994). In 1995, she began teaching at City University, London.

Her compositions date from 1978. By 1983 she had garnered an ASCAP/Nissim Award for *La belle dame sans merci* for chorus and orchestra, based on Keats' poem. *Before Dawn* for mezzo and orchestra was performed at the first concert of the New Music Project in New York (1989). She has received commissions from the St. Louis Symphony (*Elegy Symphony*), the BBC National Orchestra of Wales, and the Ensemble Bartòk of Santiago, Chile, among others. Her talent for the vocal medium is evident in her works for voice and orchestra, choral compositions, many to settings of poetry: *Intimations of Immortality* (Wordsworth, 1978), *The White Amaryllis* (May Sarton, 1988–91), *Lovesongs and Observations* (Emily Dickinson, 1989) and *Clytemnestra* (after Æschylus, 1994). Her *Scenes from an Aria* was premiered August 1996, at the Presteigne Festival. She is equally at home with instrumental technique, as evidenced in the *Elegy Symphony* and many chamber works.

As a musicologist, Samuel's writings include articles on new music, women composers, feminist musicology, contemporary musical techniques and composers—particularly **Judith Weir** and **Sir Harrison Birtwistle** (*b* 1934)—and text-music relations from the 16th century to the present day. She is co-editor, with **Julie Anne Sadie**, of the ground-breaking *Norton/Grove Dictionary of Women Composers* (1995), British Edition, Macmillan/Norton, 1994.

ROSWITHA SPERBER wears the triple crown of artistic director of the Cultural Institute for Women Composers, the International Festival of New Music (until 2000), and the Fall Conference of Women in Music (Gegenwelten), held each year since 1985 in Heidelberg. (After the 2004 festival, she turned the Directorship over to Professor Rudolf Meister, son of woman composer Siegrid Ernst. Meister is rector–president of the Mannheim University of Music and Performing Arts which has been funding the festival since 2003.)

Born July 16, 1937, in Ludwigshaven am Rhein, Roswitha grew up in a musical household. Her father, Dr. Hans Beck, a pioneer scientist in plastics, played the classics on the piano each evening. Her mother also played piano and had a beautiful voice. During WWII the family, after being bombed out of two houses, moved to the country and lived with a farmer. Later, Roswitha went to the Musik Hochschule in Mannheim, where she studied piano, music theory and voice. After completing her final exams with distinction, she taught voice there from 1982–88.

As a singer, Sperber has performed throughout Europe, concentrating on New Music, with numerous premieres, radio broadcasts and recordings. Many works have been commissioned and written for her. She is a member of Women in Culture and Media of the German Cultural Advisory Board, advisor to the Baden-Wurtemberg Society of Musicians, and the State Youth Competitions. She has contributed to the *New Grove Dictionary of Music and Musicians*, and is editor of the brochure, *Women Composers in Germany*. In 1986, she assumed her present positions and founded the Heidelberg Festival Ensemble, which specializes in new music and commissions works by women composers throughout the world in cooperation with the Baden-Wurtemberg Ministry of Arts. Since 1996, Sperber has been the guardian/board member of the cultural foundation Rhein-Neckar-Kreis, which offers scholarships for young composers and artists in the Dilsberg-Neckargemün region of Germany where she lives.

1996 marked the tenth anniversary of each of Sperber's foundations and the 100th anniversary of the death of **Clara Schumann**, celebrated throughout Germany with concerts, symposia, exhibits, papers and books, as well as the reunion of the prizewinning Cultural Institute honorées of past years.

In 2000, with the endorsement of the prime minister of Baden-Wurtemberg, Roswitha Sperber received the Order of Merit of the Federal Republic of Germany from Prime Minister Johannes Rau.

She is married to a retired surgeon and has two grown sons.

GEGENWELTEN FESTIVAL WINNERS

1987 - **Myriam Marbe** (Bucharest)
1990 - **Adriana Hölsky** (Stuttgart)
1991 - **Sofia Gubaidulina** (Moscow)
1992 - **Galina Ustvolskaya** (St. Petersburg)
1993 - **Ivana Loudova** (Prague)
1994 - **Ruth Schönthal** (New York)
1995 - **Younghi Pagh Paan** (Bremen)
1996 - **Ruth Zechlin** (Berlin)
1997 - **Babette Koblenz** (Hamburg)
1998 - **Christina Kubisch** (Berlin)
1999 - **Annette Schlünz** (Dresden - Strasbourg)
2000 - **Elzbieta Sikora** (Paris - Ulm) [In collaboration with Francia of the Institute of Women Composers in Heidelberg.]
2001 - No Festival this year [Due to lack of funding]
2002 - **Olga Magidenko** (Moscow - Heidelberg)
2003 - **Carolyn Breuer** (Munich) [Jazz composer/Saxophonist]
2004 - No prize given
2005 - **Roswitha Sperber** (Heidelberg) [This year marks the Festival's twentieth anniversary!]

From 1987–2000 the prize was known as the Heidelberg Women Artists Prize and presented by the Institute of Culture of Women Composers at Heidelberg, of which Sperber was the founder. This was in co-operation with the government Baden-Württemberg (1987–89), the German federal government (1990), and the town of Heidelberg (1991–2000). Since 2003, the name of the prize is Künstlerinnenpreis,[223] Rhein-Neckar Kreis (Women Composers Prize of the Rhein-Neckar Foundation of Culture) and is given by the Mannheim University of Music and Performing Arts in cooperation with the Foundation.

MAJA TROCHIMCZYK was a professor of music history and literature at the Thornton School of Music, University of Southern California, and director of the Polish Music Center there from 1996–2004.

Born December 30, 1957, in Warsaw, her undergraduate studies included music theory and history, and a Diploma in viola. Her MA in musicology is from the University of Warsaw (1986), and an MA in Sound Engineering from that city's Chopin Academy of Music (1987). After working for the Polish section of the International Society of Contemporary Music in Warsaw, she emigrated to Canada in 1988 where she earned her PhD in musicology from McGill University (1994), with a dissertation on space in contemporary music (written under the name Maria Anna Harley, with Bo Alphonce and Susan McClary as advisors). She held a Canadian government post-doctoral fellowship ('95–'96), and completed two research projects on contemporary Polish music prior to joining USC. In 2001–02, she was a recipient of a post-doctoral fellowship from the American Council of

---

223. The word Künstlerinnen means women artists—in this application, women *composers*.

Learned Societies. Dedicated to the study and promotion of Polish music, Dr. Trochimczyk organized several conferences and festivals in Montreal and Los Angeles, focusing on the music of Henryk Górecki and Polish Jews, among other subjects.

In addition to numerous articles and book chapters published in English, Polish and German, she has written two books, *After Chopin: Essays in Polish Music* (Los Angeles: Polish Music Center, USC, 2000), *The Music of Louis Andriessen* (New York: Routledge, 2002), plus "Henryk Górecki Studies," a collection of essays, interviews and the composer's lectures.

After fulfilling both teaching and directorship contracts, in May 2004 Trochimczyk left USC. Since then she has worked her way through a range of research and publication projects, including a book on *Polish Folk Dance in Southern California* (East European Monographs, 2005); a study of *Sound Constructions: Image and Space in Polish Music after 1945* (sponsored by ACLS); and two monographs of living composers Henry Brant and **Hanna Kulenty**. She edited *A Romantic Century in Polish Music*, PIASA Books (New York, 2006), for which she wrote the chapters: "From Mrs. Szymanowska to Mr. Poldowski: Polish Women Composers in the 19th and Early 20th Centuries," and "Paderewski's Mystique and Reception in North America."

Maja has three children, Marcin, born 1979, Anna 1989, and Ian 1993.

Margaret Wilkins

MARGARET LUCY WILKINS was born November 13, 1939, in Kingston-upon-Thames, Surrey. She was taught piano by her mother, and began composing when she was twelve. She studied piano and cello at Trinity College of Music, London, and Nottingham University (1957–60), followed by one year at the Institute of Education in London, where she received a postgraduate teaching diploma. While teaching in Nottingham, she married in 1962, and with her husband spent two years in Newfoundland before moving to Scotland in 1964. The next few years involved raising two children and giving private piano lessons. From 1969–76, she performed with the Scottish Early Music Consort. In 1970, her burgeoning career included the London performance of the *Concerto Grosso* and the vocal piece *Dieux Est*, which was broadcast on the BBC. *The Silver Casket* for soprano, harp and string trio, was performed and broadcast (1971), winning the Cappiani Prize from the Society of Women Musicians during its Diamond Jubilee year. In 1976, Wilkins was appointed senior lecturer in music at the University of Huddersfield, and in 1989 became director of the contemporary music group Polyphonia. She was a Maud Clarke visiting professor to the Queen's University in Belfast in 1995.

Her interest in medieval culture has inspired much of her music. Her orchestral works include *Hymn to Creation* (1973), *Revelations of the Seven Angels* (1988), *Symphony 1989* and *Musica Angelorum* (1991). Chamber works include *Struwwelpeter* (1973), *Etude: Burnt Sienna* (1974), *Ave Maria* (1975), *Gitanjali* (1981), *Rêve, Rêve, Révelation, Réverbérations* (1988). The multimedia work *Kanal* (1990) was performed at the 1992 International Society of Contemporary Music "World Music Days" in Poland. Her piano solos, *Study in Black & White Nos. 1 & 2* (1992), were performed and recorded by Ananda Sukarlan in 1994. *L'Attente* premiered in 1995.

As principal lecturer at Huddersfield, she initiated a new module, Women in Music, and as head of composition, teaches that subject from the first year through final year of PhD, using the contemporary music of women composers to illustrate styles and techniques. For the final year in composers' analysis work, she assigns a list of works by women composers (as she notes, "Possibly this represents an unequal opportunity . . . ") so that the analyses and the Women in Music seminars are presented together. Sharing the conducting with two colleagues of the University's *New Music Ensemble*, her programs always include works by women composers. In the last several years she has developed concerts for International Women's Day, which have included the other student performance groups, *Early Music Ensemble* and *Kaleidoscope*. For several years, the Kirklees International Women's Day Festival has given the University a small grant to mount concerts including, in 2001, a group external to the University, *Arioso*, a baroque ensemble performing 16th and 17th century music by women composers. Also in 2001, the department of music celebrated Wilkins' sixtieth birthday with a concert devoted to her own music.

There are many music festivals worldwide with different themes and foci. **ANGELA WILLES**, founder and organizer of the first Festival of Women in Music in Chard (Somerset, England), set a precedent, the Chard Festival being the only one of its kind in England. As the town clerk, she had attended a two-day workshop and with little experience brought her dream to life. In November 1988, she set the wheels in motion. Eventually, the biennial concerts led to her appointment as artistic director of the festival in 1994. Seeking to promote music of all kinds by women composers, and also provide an outlet for women to exercise their creativity, the festival aims, like Hildegard Publishing and Leonarda Records, to unearth works that have been overlooked or lost through the ages and present them in an innovative fashion.

Featured British performers have included the Wessex Women, with Somerset traditional and original songs; Eddie Upton, who presented a workshop on Somerset traditional songs collected from women by folklorist Cecil Sharp; Sammy Hurden, whose workshop ranged through music from Africa and Bulgaria into gospel and soul; jazz guitarist Deirdre Cartwright; a full concert by the Bournemouth Sinfonietta that featured music by composers **Priti Paintal**, **Grace Williams** and **Eleanor Alberga**; a workshop of traditional music by Frankie Armstrong; an eclectic program by the trio *Hysteria*; violist P.O. Lindburg and pianist Helen Vicary playing music by **Minna Keal** and **Rebecca Clarke**; *Black Voices*, a five-person a cappella group performing gospel, blues, and reggae; and the Scottish groups The Poozies and the Well Oiled Sisters singing Gaelic and Celtic tunes. The festival was still going strong in 2006.

WOMEN MUSICOLOGISTS and ETHNOMUSICOLOGISTS AT BELGRADE (YUGOSLAVIA) UNIVERSITY

SONJA MARINKOVIĆ, PhD, besides teaching music history, is a member of the editorial board of *New Sound* international magazine for music, and is engaged in research work on the national history of music in the first half of the 20th century. She has contributed to music magazines and is the author of high school textbooks.

TATJANA MARKOVIĆ, PhD, assistant professor, teaches general history of music and contributes to collections of papers and magazines. She participates in domestic and international scientific conferences and symposia.

MARIJA MASNIKOSA, MM, assistant lecturer, teaches the national history of music, particularly ancient Serbian music. Her research concerns problems of contemporary music. She contributes to music publications.

VESNA MIKIĆ, PhD, assistant professor, teaches general and national history of music, as well as Neoclassicism. She is the deputy editor in chief of *New Sound* international magazine for music. She was a member of the organization committee of the International Review of Composers.

ROKSANDA PEJOVIĆ, PhD, a retired full-time professor, is a mentor for lecturing and research work in the field of national history of the 19th century and first half of the 20th. She conducted a scientific research project entitled *Serbian Artistic Music - Development and Creations*. Author of several textbooks on Yugoslav music, she has contributed to encyclopedias, including *The New Grove Dictionary of Opera*.

IVANA PERKOVIĆ, MM, is an assistant lecturer on the national history of music. Like most of the women at the university, she participates in domestic and international scientific conferences and symposia.

TIJANA POPOVIĆ-MADJENOVIĆ, MM, assistant lecturer, teaches the national history of music and contributes to contemporary music publications.

SANJA RADINOVIĆ, MM, assistant lecturer, teaches musical folklore. Her research is on Serbian vocal folklore tradition, particularly rite songs. Like her colleagues, she participates in scientific conferences.

DRAGANA STOJANOVIĆ-NOVICIĆ, PhD, assistant professor, teaches national history of music of the 20th century. She has participated at symposia in Negotin, Belgrade, Sarajevo, among others, and published a monograph on the famous Belgrade children's choir "Kolibri." She is also a pianist, performing 20th century music. As of 2005, she was head of the department for musicology and ethnomusicology on the Belgrade Faculty of Music.

MIRJANA VESELINOVIĆ-HOFMAN, PhD, teaches 20th century music and history of music on the Faculty of Music in Belgrade and the Academy of Arts in Novi Sad. Her research is predominantly focused on contemporary creative trends in Serbian and European music. She is the editor in chief of *New Sound*, an international magazine for music.

MIRJANA VUKICEVIĆ-ZAKIĆ, MM, assistant lecturer, teaches musical folklore. Her research is primarily dedicated to instrumental folk music.

Most of these musicologists participate in domestic and international scientific conferences and symposia.

RUSSIAN MUSICOLOGISTS[224]

Musicologists in the former Soviet Union, as in the U.S., taught in universities and researched and wrote about their special interest. In Russia, music schools teach musicology before college age level and it is the conservatories which provide degrees in musicology.

The Original Patronesses

The Empresses Anna (1730–40), Elizabeth (1741–62), and Catherine (1762–96), are considered Russia's first music patrons. During the 18th century, they continued the cultural tradition and importation of Western music begun by Peter the Great.

The Original Women Musicologists

The earliest Russian women musicologists were usually related by family or marriage to men in that field, as in the case of Glinka's sister, **Liudmila Ivanovna Shestakova** (1816–1906) and wife of music critic Aleksandr Serov; and **Valentina Semyonovna Serova** (1846–1924), who co-published a music journal with her husband. The founding of conservatories by Anton Rubinstein in St. Petersburg (1862), under the patronage of the Grand Duchess Elena Pavlovna, and Moscow (1865), plus the rising tide of nationalism as demonstrated by composers such as the Russian Five: Balakierev, Borodin, Cui, Moussorgsky and Rimsky-Korsakov, added to the practice of collecting folk music and formed the beginnings of *ethnomusicology*.

Early Ethnomusicology

By the latter part of the 19th century, women such as **Ol'ga Agreneva-Slavianskaia** (1847–1920) and composer-pianist **Ella Adaevskaia** (1846–1926) collected and wrote about Russian folk music—the latter was the first woman graduate of the St. Petersburg Conservatory. Other women attending there were **Adelaida Spasskaia**, **Lidia Turygina** and **Anna Charnova**. Since women were not permitted to become professors, they founded their own music schools.

The most prominent scholar of her time was **Yevgenia Lineva** (1853–1919), who ushered ethnomusicology into the 20th century via the phonograph, making expeditions and recording folk songs. These were published in two volumes (1904, 1909). She was also a professional singer, debuting in Vienna in 1873, and appearing in Paris, London, Budapest and Moscow's Bolshoi Opera. Lineva's collection of folk songs was the most complete and accurate up to that time. She also helped found the Moscow Folk Conservatory (1905).

---

224. These names are taken from the essay by Ellon D. Carpenter in Volume III, p 456, of *The Musical Woman*, edited by Judith Zaimont. With permission. (See Bibliography.)

Into the 1920s

During the 1920s, more women became prominent as musicologists. The following are the most well-known.

VARVARA PAVLOVNA DERNOVA (1906–89) a graduate of the Leningrad Conservatory in 1930 in history pedagogy, continued her graduate studies while teaching at the Alma-Ata Conservatory. She received a candidate's degree in 1961, with a dissertation on Khazan folk music. Her recognition as a theorist came from her work on the music of **Alexander Scriabin** (1872–1915). Her book, *Harmony of Skriabin*, written in 1948, was not published until 1968 because of the inhospitable climate for such a work in Russia. Since its publication, it has received much attention from Western theorists.

ELENA MIKHAILOVNA ORLOVA (1908–85) graduated from the Leningrad Conservatory (1939) with degrees in history and theory. Her graduate studies in music history earned her a candidate of arts degree (1946) and a PhD in 1968. She taught at the Moscow, Leningrad and Ural Conservatories. Her three main interests were the music of Tchaikovsky, the theories of musicologist Boris Asafiev (1884–1949), and music pedagogy, on which she wrote many works for her conservatory students, including *Methodological Notes on the Teaching of Music History in the Conservatories* (1983). She also wrote *Pyotr Il'ich Chaikovskii* [alternate spelling of Tchaikovsky] (Moscow, 1980), and a work on the intonational theory of Asafiev (1984).

TAMARA NIKOLAEVNA LIVANOVA's (1909–86) contributions are in the areas of biography, history and bibliography, both Russian and Western. She graduated from the Moscow Conservatory in theory and composition (1932), receiving her DMA in 1940. She taught there and the Gnesin Institute, and in 1944 became a research assistant at the Institute of the History of the Arts. Her works on West European music include *The Musical Classics of the 18th Century* and a collection of articles, *The Russian Book about Bach*. During the 1950s, she concentrated on Russian music, including a biography of Glinka. Her most important research text, *Musical Bibliography of the Russian Periodical Press of the 19th Century*, covers all aspects of music and musical life in 19th century Russia.

VERA ANDREEVNA VASIN-GROSSMAN (1908–90), a graduate of the Moscow Conservatory in history and theory, taught there until 1957. She received a candidate of arts degree in 1941 and doctor of arts degree, 1954. Her research concentrated on vocal music with the published works: *The Romantic Song of the 19th Century*, *Masters of the Soviet Romance*, and *Music and the Poetic Word*. She covered all the major Russian composers of the 19th century from Glinka to Rachmaninoff. Her own favorite work was her two-volume book *Music and the Poetic Word*.

VALENTINA DZHOZEFOVNA KONEN (1910–91) lived in America during her youth, studying at both NYU and Juilliard, graduating in piano (1929). She returned to the Soviet Union and earned degrees in history and theory from the Moscow Conservatory (1938). She received a candidate's degree (1940) and DMA (1946) for her work on the history of American music culture. She taught at the Moscow and Ural Conservatories and the Gnesin Institute, and was a research associate of the Institute of the History of the Arts from 1960, as well as a music critic and radio commentator.

OL'GA YEVGEN'EVNA LEVASHEVA (*b* 1912), a graduate of the Moscow Conservatory (1943) in Theory and Composition, began teaching music history there in 1946. She was also a senior research assistant at the Institute of the History of the Arts, receiving her DMA (1963). Her major works include a Soviet biography of Edvard Grieg (1957) and a two-volume study of Glinka (1988). She was also the only woman to sit on the editorial board of the *Musical Encyclopedia*, and the ten-volume *History of Russian Music*. (She was still living in 2004.)

VALENTINA NIKOLAEVNA KHOLOPOVA (*b* 1935) was a 1959 graduate of the Moscow Conservatory, with a candidate's degree and DMA in composition and theory. Her writings include a study of rhythm in 20th century music, and two books, co-written with her brother, on Prokofiev's piano sonatas and the works of Anton Webern. Her 1983 book on Russian rhythm is a study on earliest chants through 20th century opera, in which she concluded that the Russian theory of musical rhythm has much in common with Western musical rhythm.

WOMEN IN MUSICOLOGY AROUND THE WORLD

A "Time Capsule" - Updated

I attended the Ninth International Congress of Women in Music in Vienna, April 27–30, 1995. These are edited excerpts from the information contributed by musicologists and composers. A decade later, the author traced several of these women and made updates reflecting both changes and stagnation.

FINLAND (Riitta Valkeila)

The history of Finnish music dates back only to the 18th century. The first professional orchestras and music schools began in the 1880s. Twenty years ago orchestras had jobs for about 450 musicians—a number now doubled. From twenty music schools in the 1960s there are now 140, plus eleven conservatories and the Sibelius Academy, a music high school/university. Two-thirds of music students are female, but most of the jobs open to them require little creativity. Men become conductors and composers. Out of 360 composers, seventeen are women. Women musicians make up 33 percent of Finland's orchestras. Between 1932–82, the Helsinki Philharmonic averaged 10 percent female players. They received 80 percent of the salary allotted to men. [By 2004, earnings reached equality.]

Like most of the world's performer history, the first female musicians were harpists. Next came string players. Since the 1980s, there has been a proliferation in woodwinds, double bass and brass. (Brass became more available to women in the next decade when training on those instruments was transferred from military bands into schools.)

The Turku City Orchestra pioneered the first female concertmaster, **Kerttu Wanne** (1927–28).

RIITTA VALKEILA, born 1954, studied musicology and æsthetic education in Jyväskylä University (Finland), continuing at the University of Hamburg. After graduation, she worked in the department of musicology at Jyvälskylä. She has been teaching in Helsinki's Sibelius Academy since 1985.

Other Finnish women musicologists are **Anne Sivuoja-Gunaratnam**, a professor at Turku University (Finland), and **Pirkko Moisala**, a professor at Åbo Academy (Sweden).

By the 21st century, the psychological climate of the patriarchal past was easing. Five women received diplomas from the conducting class of Sibelius Academy: Marjatta Meritähti, Jaana Haanterä, Johanna Almark, Eva Ollikainen, and **Susanna Mälkki**, conductor of the French Ensemble intercontemporain. In 2004, Aila Sauramo was General Manager of the Association of Finnish Symphony Orchestras. (See Women in the Business of Music.)

GREAT BRITAIN (Caroline Collingridge)

English women in music are benefitting from Alexandra Ankrah, head of Women in Arts, and Kathryn McDowell, the first female musical director at the Arts Council of England, the country's major funding and advocacy institution. There are ten regional arts boards, plus many trusts and foundations sympathetic to women's projects. A major undertaking of value to universities in Europe is "Women Composers—12th to 21st Centuries" initiated and run by **Margaret Lucy Wilkins** at Huddersfield University, comprising a database for the up-to-date catalogue of everything by and about women composers, including books, scores and videos.

CAROLINE COLLINGRIDGE studied flute, singing and composition, earning her certificate of music education and ARCM in flute. She continued flute studies at Guildhall and Goldsmiths College of the University of London, where she received her BM. She has combined professional solo, chamber and orchestra playing in both classical and jazz, with teaching and continued studies for a M. Ed. in creative arts therapy and reflexology. She is an advisor to the South East Arts Board and a national advisor for music to the Arts Council of England. She represented Britain's "Women in Music" organization at the seventh and eighth International Congresses (Utrecht, Bilbao) and at the "musicALASKAwomen" (1993). She coordinated a Romanian Music/Arts Tour of the Southeast Region in 1994.

IRELAND (Eibhlis Farrell)

There are more women than men in Ireland's music schools and colleges, with the majority, as in days of yore, only able to find jobs as teachers and performers. Upper education posts continue to be male dominated and there are few females in senior positions. Women faculty members teach performance rather than musicology or theory. Women are under-represented both in composing and conducting, although the establishment of the Contemporary Music Centre in Dublin, with a female director, has provided new support. The contemporary music ensemble *Concorde* has also been influential in bringing recognition to female composers. (See Jane O'Leary, International Composers.)

ISRAEL (Tsippi Fleischer)

As was the case twenty years ago, main positions are in choral conducting—especially children's choruses, which flourish under the batons of directors such as Eva Pitlik and Maya Shavit. Musicologist **Bathia Churgin** includes women composers in her lectures at Bar-Ilan University of Tel-Aviv. **Hagar Kadima**, **Rachel Galinne**, **Betty Olivero**, **Hilat Ben-Kennaz**, **Nurit Jugend** and **Elena Sokolovski** are successful contemporary composers. The older generation of European immigrants is represented by the late **Verdina Shlonsky** (1905–90), who strived to create a new Jewish cultural style. **Yardena Alotin** (1930–94) represented the second generation inspired by the first. **Tsippi Fleischer** is the established composer of the third generation whose main concept is blending avant-garde techniques with folk styles of both Israeli and Arab tradition. (See International Composers.)

JAPAN (Kobayashi Midori and Kurimoto Yuko)

Women represent about 17 percent of Japanese composers. In the Japan Federation of Composers, they number ninety-two out of five hundred and forty-six. In the Japan Federation of Modern Music, the ratio is forty-three out of two hundred and seventy-one. Western music was imported from Europe, and has not always been popular. Composers of both genders meet discrimination regarding contemporary music. Very few women can make a living composing, most have other jobs, usually teaching in school or at home.

Noted women composers in the operatic field include Kana Kikuko (1911–1986), who adapted the folklore of Okinawa and Hara Kazuko, who has experienced success in getting her work published. Masumoto Kikuko, Takashima Midori and Kinoshita Makiko are known for choral works. In the orchestral genre, in 1994, **Fujiih Keiko** was the first woman to win the Otaka Prize. Miyake Haruna composes, performs and has recorded her work on CD.

Musicologist **KOBAYASHI MIDORI** is a pioneer in Japan for her study of the issues of women in music. In February 1993, she and her colleagues established the Forum for the Study of Feminism in Music with a membership of fifteen, drawn from teachers at music colleges, librarians, performers and other musicologists. She was one of the first Japanese to study unknown women composers in Western music, with research done by her students at Kunitachui College of Music. October 1994 saw the country's first concert featuring the compositions of Western women from **Barbara Strozzi** to black modern composer **Valerie Capers**. This led to the establishment of Dr. Midori's seminar "Music and Women" at the college.

The NETHERLANDS (Tera de Marez Oyens)[225]

There was very little information on Women in Music until in 1985 Dutch musicologist **Helen Metzelaar** with pianist **Ro von Hessen**, one of the first lecturers on women composers, collaborated to collect data. The result was the 1986 publication of an Information Guide on Dutch women composers, plus an international list of books and articles. This was done with the cooperation of the newly formed *Stichting Vrouw en Muziek* (Women in Music

---

225. Tera left us too soon, on August 29, 1996. (See International Composers.)

Foundation), which has become an information research center, and organizes numerous concerts, lectures, projects and exhibitions, including the successful 1991 International Congress on Women in Music in Utrecht.

The period after World War II was still a time when women were expected to stay home and take care of the family. The late 1960s saw the feminist wave reach the Netherlands, paving the way for the women composers of today who, while they have to overcome the same obstacles as their male counterparts, are still not properly represented when it comes to concert performance. Neither do the texts used in conservatories mention women composers. (This did not hinder Tera [See West Euro. composers], whose role model was Beethoven.) The last three decades have brought little improvement in the balance of women's works performed or studied.

The road is easier for performers who are accepted into orchestras based on merit. If a woman wants to direct, however, what **Margaret Hillis** was told back in the '50s still applies: go for *choral conducting*. A female conductor in front of an orchestra is still an unusual sight in Holland.

ROMANIA (Valentina Sandu-Dediu)

Romania's talent was all but stifled during the Iron Curtain years (1948–89). Native born singers had successful careers abroad. One of the earliest women composers was Didia Saint-Georges (1888–1979). Maria Tanase (1913–63) carried on the tradition of folk music. The next generation to become well-known internationally includes **Miriam Marbe** (1931–96), **Irina Odagescu** (*b* 1937), **Cornelia Tăutu** (*b* 1938), **Liana Alexandra** (*b* 1947), **Marina Vlad** (*b* 1949), and **Doina Rotaru** (*b* 1951). Romanian composers who settled in other countries with successful careers are **Violeta Dinescu** (*b* 1953) and **Adriana Hölszky** (*b* 1953) in Germany, and Maya Badian (*b* 1945) in Canada. Most of these women are also conservatory teachers.

Romanian women who have made names for themselves in music education date back to pre-WWII with Florica Musicescu (1887–1969), whose most famous pupil was pianist Dinu Lipatti (1917–50), Cella Delavrancea (1887–1991), Constanta Erbiceanu (1874–1961), Aurelia Cionca (1888–1962) and **Clara Haskil** (1895–1960), one of the world's most gifted pianists.

At present, women graduating from music schools are in the majority, with degrees in theory, musicology and ethnomusicology. They are building careers on research, writing, and in radio and television production. There appears to be a future for women here.

SLOVAKIA (Iris Szeghy)

In 1995 there was no feminist movement in the Slovak Republic, then Czechoslovakia. There were two composers, **Iris Szeghy** and **Larisa Vrhunc**, no orchestra conductors, three choir directors, a few musicologists and no musicians on "male" instruments: brass, double bass, etc. There were, however, two women's organizations who saw their main role as motherhood. Strengthening communication with the West has helped improve the situation.

IRIS SZEGHY,[226] born 1956 in Prešov (Slovakia), studied composition and piano at the Košice Conservatory, and Composition at the Academy of Music and Drama, Bratislava.

LARISA VRHUNC,[227] born 1967 in Ljubljana, is a graduate of the Music Academy there, and a composer.

SOUTH KOREA (Hae-Sung Lee)

The situation in South Korea is subject to even more patriarchal contempt than that endured by European women. Nevertheless, the generation between ages thirty and forty can take pride of their progress and achievements towards independence and self-criticism. Today, Korean women are represented in the main areas of music: composers, instrumentalists, teachers, professors and university lecturers. 1981 saw the founding of the Korean

---

226–227. See Central and East European Composers.

Society of Women Composers, which organizes joint presentations of new works by women and arranges training seminars. In 1995, Kyung-Sun Suh was elected president.

The struggle continues for independence and equal rights, but the strength, discipline and determination of the organization looks to make improvements not just for women composers, but for social restructuring as a whole.

HAE-SUNG LEE was born in Seoul in 1961. She began piano at five. Her composition studies were with Byung-dong Park at the Ewha University in Seoul (1979–83) and Erich Urbanner at the Hochschule für Musik in Vienna (1984–90). Among several prizes, she received the Alban Berg and Wagner Scholarships. A member of Perspective Composers' Group, the Korean Society of Women Composers and the Contemporary Music Society in Seoul, Lee has been teaching at Ewha and Kyungwon Universities in the Korean capital since 1990.

SPAIN (Mercedes Zavala)

Musical education is taught at primary, secondary and academic levels. At the primary level, 50 percent of the teachers are women. Percentages decrease dramatically the higher the studies. It is still an exception for women to be part of collegiate faculties. Female instrument training remains archaic, with the piano the most popular, followed by strings—with the exception of the bass—guitar, harp, flute, clarinet and oboe, and almost no brass or drums. Musicology is an exception, with women gradually being incorporated into compositional and conducting studies, but only with male teachers.

Like Finland, Spain needs an organization to unify, collect and organize materials and activities to unite women, rather than diffuse them in competition with each other.

Mercedes Zavala

MERCEDES ZAVALA, born in Madrid, 1963, graduated with honors in Piano and Composition from the Madrid Conservatory, concentrating on performance of 20th century piano music, teaching and composition. Further studies in England were with Malcom Singer at the Yehudi Menuhin School and the Guildhall School in London. In addition to performances of her works throughout Spain, her compositions have been premiered in Vienna and performed in the U.S.

A member since 2000 of the Institute of Feminist Research at the University of Madrid, she dedicates much time to researching historical repetoire of the women composers. Zavala has assisted in programming of the Festivals of Music of the 20th Century (Bilbao 1999), International Electro-acoustic Music (Madrid 2001), Contemporary Music (Málaga, 2001), and in 2003: "Music Today": The New Generation, Autumn Festival (both in Madrid), Fifty-Second Festival of International Music and Dance (Granada). She is professor of harmony at the Conservatorio Superior de Madrid.

SWEDEN (Margaret Myers)

While there are no formal obstacles for women in the music professions in Sweden, the underlying problem is lack of awareness that women composers exist! (They constitute 5 percent of the Composers' Union, and less than 1 percent of concert programming.) Neither is the absence of women composers questioned in university and conservatory texts. At the Göteborg Conservatory, 91 percent of higher posts are held by men, with a similar ratio in related fields, concert halls, mass media, recording companies and other music distributors. Although women comprise a fair proportion of conservatory students, few reach the top. In the 1994 Young Soloist Competition, only two out of the eight winners were female. Symphony orchestras—low on the general pay scale—employ few women conductors, concertmasters or solo players despite behind-screen auditions.

While some progress is being made by individuals, until there is a united effort or organization in this country, only token representation will continue.

MARGARET MYERS, born in East London, South Africa, 1947, received her BA with honors in musicology at Southampton University (1968), MM from King's College, London University (1972), and PhD at Göteborg,

Sweden (1993), with a dissertation entitled *Blowing Her Own Trumpet: European Ladies' Orchestras and Other Women Musicians, 1870–1950*.

She has conducted community choirs and orchestras in Göteborg, and since 1993 has been a lecturer in music history at the department of musicology at Göteborg University. Her special project is the inclusion of women composers and musicians into the curriculum.

Myers is a founder/member and vice-chair of Swedish Women in Music "Euterpe." May 1995 marked the release of her CD of women composers. In April 1996, she organized a Conference on *Music, Gender and Pedagogy* at Göteborg, with speakers from all over the world.

Others Present and Accounted For

Other composers and performers at the conference represented a cross section of the scenario of women's musical activities.

MARIETTA DEAN, professor of music in voice at Western Illinois University, performs 20th century repertoire and standard works from the baroque and romantic. (See American Musicologists.)

ANNETTE DEGENHARDT, born in 1965 in Mainz (Germany), studied guitar at the College of Music and Art in Frankfurt am Main. She concertizes throughout Europe. (See Guitarists.)

ALISON GOULD, born May 9, 1948, in Birmingham, England, is an accomplished lutenist and singer. Her repertoire of authentic medieval and renaissance songs, in the style of the *trobairitz*, combines high musical ability with an entertaining approach, wearing a costume appropriate to the program. Her performances are throughout Europe, and on radio and television. (See Guitarists.)

LILY HOOD GUNN (BM, UCLA; MA, composition, SDSU; DMA, composition, theory, conducting, University of Maryland) was co-recipient of the first collaborative grant given by Pandora, an organization formed to foster multimedia creation between women in the various arts. Other honors include grants from the Rockefeller Foundation, NEA and Meet the Composer. As a conductor, she has championed her colleagues, performing the music of American women in the U.S. and Europe. An assistant professor of music at the University of San Diego (California),where she taught music theory and composition until 1995, she founded the San Diego Contemporary Music Ensemble, specializing in music of the 20th century, especially American composers. She also presented contemporary music through the Society of Composers, Inc., Pandora and the ICWM (now part of IAWM). As a member of the advisory council for composition in the CMS, she hosted a symposium in 1991 to celebrate the fortieth year of electronic music, featuring honored pioneer **Otto Luening** (1900–96).

Her own work includes the multimedia *Winter Solstice* for two pianos and piano interior with percussion and slides; pieces for voice and piano, and voice and chamber ensemble (*Illusions, Freefall, Compline*), an opera, *Owl of the Desert*, plus instrumental, electronic and computer works. In 1995, after years of "commuting," she joined her admiral husband in Washington, DC. He retired August 22, 2000.

DEBORAH KAVÁSCH is noted for her pioneering work in modern vocal music, particularly "extended vocal techniques"—sounds discovered through study of the music of other cultures that go beyond traditional *bel canto*. She is a professor of music at Cal State, Stanislaus (Central California). (See American Musicologists.)

MARY ELLEN KITCHENS, born in Houston, Texas, 1959, studied musicology at Yale, the Sorbonne, École Normale de Musique—both in Paris, and the Ludwig Maximilian University in Munich. Her conducting classes were with Pierre Dervaux and Sergiu Celibidache. From 1984–1991, she was artistic director of the Haydn Orchestra in Munich where, since 1986, she has been the director of the German-American Choir. She was also the conductor of the Kempten/Allgäu Orchestra, and has been working in the music documentation department of Bavarian Radio since 1991. She became head of this department in 2004.

Kitchens is a member of the executive committee of *Musica femina, München*, the women's music organization of Munich.

EDDA KRAENZMER, born in Germany in 1940, has been living in Sweden since 1970. Her compositions encompass classical entertainment music, Viennese waltzes, organ and choral works. A member of the Svenska musikerföbundet (Swedish Music Organization) and Svenski konstnärs-föbundet (Swedish Artists Organization), Edda is the author of choral and song texts, as well as a ceramic artist and nature photographer.

KRISTIN NORDERVAAL, Norwegian-American soprano, has appeared as a guest artist at many festivals in Europe and the U.S., including the Bergen International (Norway), Bang on a Can (New York), *New and Unusual Music* series (San Francisco), and *music-ALASKAwomen* (Fairbanks). Her venues include Santa Fe and Sarasota Operas, San Francisco Symphony, Stuttgart Philharmonic, the German Broadcasting Orchestra (Baden-Baden), and the Alkesund Symphony, Norway. In 1994, she created programs for the Guggenheim Museum's *Rolywholyover*, and *A Circus*—a celebration of the life and work **John Cage**. The same year, she developed a one-woman show for the Nordisk Forum Cultural Festival in Åbo-Turku, Finland, featuring diary entries of women artists. 1995 marked her performance of Erik Satie's monumental *Socrate: Drame Symphonique* with the Oslo Sinfonietta.

DEON NIELSEN PRICE (See American Musicologists.)

SALLY REID (See American Musicologists.)

Who Put it All Together?

Co-organizer, with journalist/political publicist **Ulrike Sladek**, of this Ninth International Congress of Women in Music, was **REGINA HIMMELBAUER**, who studied musicology and instrumental music education at the Vienna College of Music and Performing Arts, where she was the women's representative for the student body. She received her diploma with honors, and wrote her master's thesis on the *trobairitz*, the women troubadors found mainly in France in the 12th and 13th centuries. Based on research from French authors, it is entitled "Without a Picture, the Mirror Breaks." She is also an expert on the recorder.

From 1989–1991, Himmelbauer was editor of the feminist monthly *An Schläge*. From 1991–93, she was editor of the music magazine *Tritonus*. Since November 1993, she has been a teacher at the Conservatory of Eisenstadt, near Vienna, giving lectures on music history and culture studies, and education seminars. She has been published in Austrian and foreign magazines. Her book contributions include *Autonomy in Motion* (Vienna, 1991) and *Murderesses in Film* (Berlin, 1992). She has participated and lectured in many conference in Europe and America.

Eighteenth Asian Composers League Conference and Festival
Manila, the Philippines, January 19–26, 1997

Since the Vienna Conference, two years made gradual progress in some countries . . . as reported by several panelists:

NEW ZEALAND - Dr. Eve de Castro-Robinson, composer/secretary, Composers Association

This was the first country to grant women's suffrage. Their rights have been fairly equal. There have been several women-in-music festivals. Women composers have not been discriminated against.

KOREA - Professor Chan-Hae Lee, composer/secretary-general, Korean National Committee-ACL

There are five organizations for women composers, and opportunities are equal. Forums are held twice yearly to perform, record and publish their works with funding coming from membership and government grants. There is also a 5,000-year history of Shamanism, the Shaman being a female spiritual leader conducting rituals for the village. During the Yi Dynasty (17th–19th centuries), this role was diminished—which still impacts social life today.

PHILIPPINES - Professor Korazon Dioquino, musicologist

No discrimination. Women dominate music education, including universities at dean level. Early research bears out the continuing importance of women in tribal music-making.

JAPAN - Professor Reiko Irino, director of Japanese Music Life Seminar, Yoshiro Ino Institute of Music

There are numerous opportunities for women, e.g. professors, but not at the leadership level, deans, presidents or directors. Although there are several western style symphony orchestras, concertmasters are men. Until recently, traditional theater: *bunraki*, *kabuki* and *noh* allowed only male performers. The 20th century *takarazuka* was for females.

INDONESIA - Dr. Edi Sedyawati, director general for Culture, Department of Education and Culture.

Western music is fairly new to the culture. Traditionally, women danced, men composed and played. Gradually women became instrumentalists also, especially in the formation of gamelan ensembles, the first being in Jakarta.

CHINA - Chan Wing Wah, composer/music department and chairman, Chinese University of Hong-Kong

The only male panelist at the Conference, he pointed out that the chief secretary of Hong Kong was then a woman. Since ancient times there have been famous women composers, poets and musicians. Until the late 1950s, however, only men were allowed to perform at the Beijing Opera.

(Hong-Kong reverted to the Chinese Government, July 1, 1997, after having been under British rule since 1841. It is still a free port—this status to remain unchanged for fifty years. China became a country under two systems—the mainland continuing under Communism. In 2003, half a million Hong Kong residents demonstrated against proposed anti-subversion laws, curtailing civil rights. Chief Executive Tung Chee Wha scrapped the proposals!)

CANADA - Janet Danielson, composer/associate artistic director, Vancouver New Music

Of the large number of women composers, many are of Asian descent. While there is no discrimination, there is still a lack of interest from the general public.

AUSTRALIA - Eve Duncan, composer/chairman, Melbourne Composers League

Although the 1920s and '30s saw women's works being performed by major orchestras, there are very few contemporary women composers. (By the 21st century the situation was improving. Many musicologists and educators are women.)

This section has been excerpted from an article in the IAWM Journal, June 1997, by **Jin Hi Kim**, Asian Liaison at the conference for the IAWM. She is a composer and virtuoso performer on the Korean *komungo*—a 14th century fretted zither. Known for her bicultural series of compositions, *Living Tones*, she has received awards and commissions from the Rockefeller Foundation, Lincoln Center for the Performing Arts, Kronos Quartet, Mary Flagler Cary Charitable Trust, Meet the Composer/Readers' Digest Commission, Asian Cultural Council, NEA, Korea and Japan Societies.

Exploring Beyond

The obvious should be noted: Women musicologists do not limit themselves to writing about women, but explore topics as original, diverse and universal as do their male counterparts. Now it is up to the reader to explore beyond the confines of this overview to the vast library of music information waiting to be tapped.

CHAPTER FIFTEEN
PART A
Women in the Business of Music

Jane Aspnes	Arctic Chamber Orchestra	Former Manager
Deborah Borda	Los Angeles Philharmonic	Executive Director
Deborah Rutter Card	Seattle Symphony	Executive Director
NancyBell Coe	Cleveland Orchestra	Manager
Aurelie Desmarais	Houston Symphony	Artistic Administrator
Mary Ann Feldman	Minnesota Symphony	Public Relations
Judith Frankfurt	Philadelphia Orchestra	Former VP - General Manager
Martha Gilmer	Chicago Symphony	Former Artistic Administrator
Maryellen Gleason	Phoenix Symphony	President and CEO
Ruthanne Greeley	Santa Fe Chamber Music Festival	Director of Marketing
Cindi Hubbard	National Symphony & Women's Philharmonic	Former Artistic Director
Carla Ann Johnson	St. Louis Symphony	Orchestra Manager
Marianna Kankare-Loikkanen	Helsinki (Finland) Symphony	Public Relations Manager
Ann Kennedy	Houston Symphony	Executive Dir and CEO
Sandra Kimberling	L.A. Music Center	Former CEO
Ann Koonsman	Ft. Worth Symphony	Executive Director
Eleanor Long	Vermont Symphony	Administration
Susan Lundberg	Bismarck/Mandan Symphony	Executive Director.
Patricia Mitchell	Los Angeles Philharmonic	COO LA Philharmonic, Hollywood Bowl
Jane Moss	Lincoln Center	Vice President of Programming
Vanessa Moss	Chicago Symphony	VP Orchestra & Building Operations
Anne Parsons	Hollywood Bowl	Former General Manager
Aila Sauramo	Finland	Festivals/Orchestras
Rita Shapiro	National Symphony	Executive Director
Beverly Sills	Lincoln Center	Chairman (1994–2002)
Joan Squires	Phoenix Symphony	President/CEO
Jacqueline Taylor	Chamber Music Society Lincoln Center	Former Executive Director
Allison Vulgamore	Atlanta Symphony	President
Miryam Yardumian	Baltimore Symphony	Artistic Administrator

ASOL

Catherine French	American Symphony Orchestra League	Executive Director (1980–96)

ARCHIVISTS

JoAnne Barry	Philadelphia Orchestra (1990–2004)
Bridget Carr	Boston Symphony Orchestra
Barbara Haws	New York Philharmonic
Carol Jacobs	Cleveland Orchestra
Judith Johnson	Lincoln Center
Brenda Nelson Strauss	Chicago Symphony Orchestra

Symphony Positions

Music is *Big Business!* **Recording** companies bring the music into our homes. **Publishing** companies are the communication medium of the universal language of music. Soloists and orchestras must be seen and heard, therefore **Agents** and publicists exist to "sell" their artists to the world.

Orchestras and opera companies are not kept alive by the sheer beauty of their performances. Ticket sales cover barely 50 percent of the outlay required to put on each program. Unlike the policies—and pride—of most European countries in subsidizing their orchestras and opera houses, American musical aggregations can survive only in proportion to endowments, funding, and donations from fairy godparents. For this they need **managers, executive directors, artistic administrators, fund raisers,** *et al.*, a field abounding with an amazing number of talented women. A feasible explanation of this phenomenon comes from **Alison Ames**, former vice president at Angel/EMI Records, who suggests that women are more willing than men to cope with these often underpaid "dogsbody" positions requiring "hideous hours," and demanding everything from executive decisions to getting coffee.

There are also women in unique places, like the American Society of Composers, Authors and Publishers (ASCAP) which, as of 1994, elected **Marilyn Bergman** its first woman president and chairman of the board. Other women in music administration who should be noted are the late **Judith Arron** (see The Unforgotten), who revitalized Carnegie Hall from her accession as executive director in 1986, until her untimely death in 1998; **Anne Parsons**, who ran the Hollywood Bowl until 1998; and **Deborah Borda**, who served eight years as executive director of the New York Philharmonic before becoming executive vice president of the Los Angeles Philharmonic in January 2000. Opera companies such as San Francisco, Los Angeles, Chicago, Boston and New York's Metropolitan Opera, each have their behind-the-scenery lady "phantoms" in management and direction. **Beverly Sills** spent 1994–2002 as chair of Lincoln Center and, after a few months, decided she wasn't ready to retire at seventy-four, so in 2003 plunged into the offered chairmanship of the Metropolitan Opera, a company which had spurned her during the (1950–72) "reign" of manager **Rudolf Bing**, but was welcomed by general manager **Joseph Volpe** (1990–2006). She really did retire in 2005. Reaching a worldwide audience of 130 million, until her retirement in 2001, after twenty years, was the ingenuity of music director of *Voice of America*, **Judy Massa**. It is in the many facets of this business sphere that women have enjoyed a remarkable amount of success, and a penetrable ceiling of unusual equality.

Since it would require a separate volume to name all those on the executive staff of every symphony and opera company, as well as pinpoint every female agent who works diligently to place her "stable" on the most prominent—and profitable—concert stages of the world, consider the following a significant sampling of women who help thread together the intricate tapestry of the *business* of music.

Out of the (Orchestra) Pits

MARY LOU ALESKIE—*From East to West to East*, Mary Lou Aleskie is a graduate of Saint Peter's College, Jersey City, New Jersey. She began her career as a consultant with accounting firm Deloite & Touche, working with the

American Symphony Orchestra and NBC. She went on to become producer of the Saratoga International Theater Institute, an international festival based in New York City and Saratoga, upstate New York, as well as Togamura, Japan. She was artist manager with Helen Merrill, Ltd., an agency representing playwrights, authors, directors and designers. After five years as general manager/manager director of the Alley Theatre, Houston, one of the nation's largest and oldest professional theater companies, she became executive director of Da Camera of Houston, a chamber and jazz producer/presenter offering performances in Texas as well as touring to Lincoln and Kennedy Centers, and London's Barbican Centre, among others. At Da Camera, she was also responsible for commissioning and producing new works in collaboration with composers, poets, stage directors, designers, film makers, choreographers and other creative artists.

In 2002, Aleskie became president/CEO of La Jolla Music Society, responsible for leading and programming one of the largest presenting organizations in the Western United States, including orchestras, chamber ensembles and dance companies, during the autumn through spring months each year. She developed and supervised education and outreach programs, artist residencies, concerts in schools and neighborhoods, and an after-school music program for 300 inner city youth. Each August, LJMS produces the nationally-recognized La Jolla SummerFest, under artistic director (since 2001) violinist Cho-Liang Lin, who brings top artists from all over the world.

During the 2003–04 season, the organization changed its name from La Jolla Chamber Music Society to La Jolla Music Society as a reflection of its growing role as a major regional multi-disciplinary presenter. In September 2005, Aleskie accepted the position of executive director of the International Festival of Arts and Ideas in New Haven, Connecticut which, since its founding in 1996, has presented more than 8,000 artists and lecturers in nearly 2,800 events, celebrations, explorations, forums, exhibitions, debates and presentations in more than two dozen venues in and around New Haven. More than seventy countries have been represented in the festival since its inception.

Mary Lou is married to stage director Peter Webster, who has been affiliated with the Old Globe Theatre in San Diego, Houston Grand Opera Studio and NYU's Tisch School of the Arts. Their daughter, Rosemarie, was born in 2000.

Aleskie is a member of Chamber Music America, the Association of Performing Arts Presenters, and International Society for the Performing Arts.

JANE ASPNES—*Music Under the Aurora Borealis;* Jane Aspnes was manager of the Arctic Chamber Orchestra in Fairbanks, Alaska, 1978–97. Born in Waterloo, Iowa, January 2, 1942, into a not particularly musical family, her hometown was like "River City," the fictional community in Meredith Willson's 1957 hit show *The Music Man,* and the area in real life, true to the plot, had a proliferation of school bands. Jane began trumpet and cornet in second grade, playing in beginner bands. In those days, once a week the young musicians would be taken out of class in groups of four and given a concentrated music lesson. They were tested regularly and earned points and letters of achievement. Jane switched to French horn in junior high school. In 1964, she received her BM from Indiana University School of Music, and was immediately hired to play horn in the Quebec Symphony. In 1966, she went back to school at the University of Wisconsin, earning her MM in literature and performance. The same year, she married John Aspnes, a violin and tuba player.

1966–67 found the couple in Washington, DC, with Jane in the National Ballet Orchestra. In 1967, she joined the Portland (New Hampshire) Symphony, where she organized a brass quintet and became involved in promotion. In 1974, while her husband was getting his PhD there, she taught at Montana State University in Bozeman. In 1976, they went back to New Hampshire where Jane began her business degree, writing a thesis on the most efficient methods of running an orchestra. By 1978, she had a masters in resource administration and management. Meanwhile, she taught at the University of New Hampshire, as well as Keene and Plymouth State Universities, and played in many ensembles, including the American Wind Symphony, Concord Chamber Orchestra, Cambridge Brass Quintet, New Hampshire Brass Ensemble and Tri-City (Iowa) Symphony.

In 1978 they heard from Gordon Wright, founder (1970) of the Arctic Chamber Orchestra[228] in Fairbanks, Alaska. It was he who had inadvertently introduced the pair when, as students in Indiana, they had both accidentally come to his music shop an hour before it opened and whiled away the time getting to know each other. Wright had an opening for John as an electrical engineer at the University, and also found a position for Jane. Since they both loved nature, before they answered the call of the wilderness, they donated part of their 281 New Hampshire acres to the Forest Service to preserve the land for open space. One year after they arrived in Alaska, Jane became Manager of both the Arctic Chamber and Fairbanks Symphony Orchestras, and since 1980 has been a Lecturer and Horn instructor at the University of Alaska.

When the orchestra had to travel over vast stretches of snow-covered terrain, it was Jane who arranged for the nine five-passenger Cessnas, *or* fishing boats, *or* dog-sleds, or whatever other imaginative transportation was called for—probably a unique task in the annals of Orchestra Managerial duties. (Mush!)

Since 1992, Jane has played horn in the Fairbanks Symphony and *Borealis Trio*,[229] with John Harbaugh, trumpet (replaced by Rachel Epley) and James Bicigo, trombone, a group formed to promote brass chamber music and commission works. They were part of the Vatican Jubilee, *Women in Music 2000*, which included compositions by **Emma Lou Diemer** and **Mary Jeanne Van Appledorn**, and commissions by Ann Callaway, Adriana Figueroa Manas (Argentina) and Erika and Elizabeth Raum.

The Aspneses are also involved in PAWS (Personnel Available for Wilderness Search). Trained in search techniques, one of Jane's partners was her Bouvier des Flandres, Maya, while John had a Beauçeron named Inca. They and their four-legged children have assisted in many rescues of hunters, hikers, and even victims of foul play.

DEBORAH BORDA—*The Borda's Touch*; Deborah Borda, president and CEO of the Los Angeles Philharmonic Association, began her tenure in January 2000. One of her first projects was establishing a strong management and artistic team, focusing on the long-range planning for the Philharmonic's future home, the Frank Gehry designed Walt Disney Concert Hall. She was directly involved in the development of the hall's programming and operations in preparation for the 2003 inaugural season. (The official opening—with much pomp and fanfare—was October 20.) The world famous Hollywood Bowl also comes under Borda's aegis along with COO Patricia Mitchell, both active in the planning the construction of a new shell which inaugurated the Summer 2004 season.

Borda joined Los Angeles after eight seasons as executive director of the New York Philharmonic which, under her leadership, experienced an era of artistic growth and financial stability. During her tenure, the orchestra set a national precedent in negotiating a long-term agreement with its musicians; founded its own highly acclaimed record label; planned and implemented the Philharmonic's 150th Anniversary celebration; led an active international touring program; and returned the Orchestra to live radio after an absence of nearly a decade. Borda also introduced many successful new programs, including Rush Hour and Casual Saturday concerts; Conductor Debut week; Composer Festivals; Philharmonic "Celebrations;" and Children's Promenades.

Deborah has held positions at some of the country's most prestigious orchestras, including general manager and artistic administrator of the San Francisco Symphony, the Minnesota Orchestra's first female president, 1990–91, president and managing director of the Saint Paul Chamber Orchestra, and executive director of the Detroit Symphony, where she raised the funding necessary to rebuild Orchestra Hall, changed the corporate infrastructure, and led the music director search that culminated in the appointment of renowned Estonian-born music

---

228. The forty-member chamber group has toured the state for over twenty-five years, performing hundreds of concerts in 100 northern communities, bringing the only opportunity to hear live music. Repertoire is often exchanged as Eskimos and Indians play for the orchestra. The orchestra made their European debut in 1985 with concerts in Scandinavia and Switzerland. In 1987, they played a six-city tour in China—a challenge for the Manager to untangle the red tape involved in such an enterprise. 1989 marked a nineteen-city tour of Spain. Their concerts have been broadcast in the U.S. and Europe, and their many awards include a commendation from the Governor and the Alaskan Legislature, as well as 1982, '86, and '87 ASCAP "Adventurous Programming" Awards. In 1992, they received an NEA Challenge Grant for the purpose of building an endowment to ensure future touring within Alaska. 2004–05 marked their forty-seventh season.
229. The Fairbanks Symphony, Arctic Chamber Orchestra and Borealis Trio are all affiliated with the University of Alaska, Fairbanks.

director **Neeme Järvi** (*b* 1937). Her example gave corporate and government sponsors the impetus to contribute over $8 million to ensure security of the symphony's financial future.

Active internationally as a lecturer and consultant in the field of artistic and orchestral management, she has served as a member of the Board of the American Symphony Orchestra League and was on the faculty of the first *Leadership Seminar in Artistic Excellence* in Aspen, Colorado, sponsored by the Orchestra Leadership Academy. She was chairman of the Music Panel at the NEA as well as for a number of major managers' groups. She is on the Executive Council of the Seaver/NEA Conductors Award, the Avery Fisher Awards, and the Board of the Colburn School of the Arts. In 2003, she participated in the prestigious Salzburg Seminar, working with international leaders in the classical performing arts to address critical issues applicable to the field.

Born July 15, 1949, in New York City, Deborah studied violin and piano from the age of six and has been interested in music as long as she can remember. She began playing viola in her teens. An accomplished violist, she received her training at the New England Conservatory of Music, Bennington College, and London's Royal College of Music.

In 2001, she was featured in *Working Woman* magazine, as well as being on the cover of the Calendar section of the *Los Angeles Times* entitled, "She's All That." She was also named one of "The Most Powerful People in Music" in the *BBC Music Magazine*'s November 2000 issue. It is obvious that wherever she goes, everyone benefits from the "Borda's Touch."[230]

DEBORAH RUTTER CARD—*The "Other" Deborah;* Deborah Rutter Card was executive director of the Seattle Symphony (1992–2003), one of only two women administering more than a $5 million budget—the other being **Deborah Borda**, president/CEO of the LA Philharmonic. Beginning September 2003, she made an even bigger hole through the "glass ceiling" with her acceptance—voted unanimously by the trustees—of the presidency of the Chicago Symphony Orchestra, of the "Big Five." With an initial four-year tenure, she replaces **Henry Fogel** who, after eighteen years (1995–2003), moved on to be president/CEO of the American Symphony Orchestra League. (The other four major U.S. orchestras are New York, Philadelphia, Cleveland and Boston. The author votes for the "Big SEVEN"—with Los Angeles and San Francisco.)

Born September 30, 1956, in Pottstown, Pennsylvania, Deborah moved to Los Angeles as a child when her father accepted a position in a prominent law firm. Initiated into classical music by Deborah's mother, her father, Marshall Rutter, became president of Chorus America (1993–95), the organization which oversees all professional, independent and symphony choruses in the country. He was also chairman and president of the Los Angeles Master Chorale.

Deborah grew up in the harmony of her parents' amateur musicianship. She began piano and violin at an early age, majored in music at Stanford—she spent her junior year at the Vienna Hochschule—and graduated with a BM in 1978. Her MBA was earned in the course of five years (1980–85) while she was learning her job as orchestra manager for the Los Angeles Philharmonic (1978–86). This prestigious position—unheard of for a twenty-one-year-old, fresh out of college—came about through her internship during two summers in the education department of the Hollywood Bowl. It was the late Ralph Black of the ASOL who encouraged Rutter to consider orchestra management as a career, and referred her to the dean of American orchestra managers, executive vice president and managing director (1969–1998) of the LA Philharmonic, **Ernest Fleischmann**, who promised her a job after graduation. He delivered, and the graduate found herself in the music major leagues without even having had sandlot practice. She learned fast, justifying Fleischmann's "instinct" in one so young. In October 1986, she moved to the Los Angeles Chamber Orchestra. Here, during her six-year tenure, she tripled income and doubled contributions.

When Rutter arrived at Seattle, November 1992, like many U.S. orchestras it was fighting for its financial life. She made great strides to turn this around. Seattle Symphony Conductor **Gerard Schwarz**, who had the greatest

---

230. Author's nomenclature and compliment.

confidence in his executive director, called her "extremely qualified" and affirmed that she was *his* first choice for the job—"After all, she has worked with the legendary Fleischmann, one of the most respected (and feared) administrators in the arts . . . "

The idea for the creation of a new concert hall first glimmered in 1986, but it was not until 1993 that the philanthropic Benaroya family generously gifted $15 million towards the project and a matching fund raising campaign could be launched. Deborah (now) Card was in charge of every facet, at the same time, pregnant. Gillian Margaret arrived March 24, 1998. Benaroya Hall had its grand opening September 12. She was married to computer expert Peter Card, 1993–2002.

Rutter has served as board member (director emeritus) and president (1988–91) of the Association of California Symphony Orchestras (ACSO), was on the policy committee of the managers of American orchestras for the ASOL, and sat on numerous panels for the NEA, California Arts Council and the State/ Local Partnership. She served on the board of Chamber Music/LA, she was a member of the board of International Music Festival, and Rotary.

Facing a deficit of $6.1 million on a $60 million budget, she set to work, eliminating unnecessary staff positions, mediating musicians' pensions, negotiating that they start contributing to their own health insurance, putting her talents to work in programming and "re-energizing" the audience with after-work concerts and the like, plus educational and community outreach. By 2004–05 the deficit was down to $1.3 million with hopes for a balance by 2007. As Deborah herself put it: "We have to remember that every dollar we spend is a dollar that someone gives us in the belief we're going to do something good with it."

Her position makes Deborah Rutter Card one of the most prominent women in the music world!

NANCYBELL COE—*Hitting the Peak;* NancyBell Coe has been artistic administrator of the Aspen (Colorado) Music Festival and School since February 1999. Before that she was manager, then general manager of the Cleveland Orchestra (1990–98). That position involved overseeing the Orchestra and Musical Arts Association concerts, tours, broadcasting, recording and other media activities, educational programs and ancillary groups such as the Cleveland Orchestra Chorus, Children's and Youth Choruses and Youth Orchestra, as well as activities at Cleveland's summer home, the Blossom Music Center.

Coe came to Cleveland from the Los Angeles Philharmonic, where from 1986–90 she served successively as administrator of the Los Angeles Philharmonic Institute (a professional training program), orchestra manager and general manager. While there, she was a founding member of the music advisory committee of the Pasadena Arts Commission.

Before Los Angeles, she lived in Spokane, Washington, where she was a staff member of the Spokane Symphony, 1978–86, after having served as production stage manager from 1976. She also held the positions of audience development director, development director, assistant to the executive director, interim manager, was responsible for the orchestra's educational programs, and wrote and directed the orchestra's grants and special programs, two of which won national educational awards.

A writer and editor, Coe was lead author for the first edition of the handbook "How to Select a Music Director," published by the ASOL, June 1985. Other activities in the orchestral field include service on several national committees and task forces for the ASOL, plus presentations and workshops in operations and concert production for their professional training seminars.

Born September 27, 1948, in Beverly, Massachusetts, NancyBell was raised on Long Island, New York. In 1970, she graduated with a BA in music from Wellesley College (Massachusetts), where she was elected to Phi Beta Kappa. Before starting work in the orchestral field in 1976, she had experience in various areas, including working as a research assistant in an immunology laboratory; editing and publishing *Futures Conditional,* a small, independent magazine with 2,000 subscribers internationally, and designing and implementing citizen participation programs.

At Aspen she worked with a team, headed by music director David Zinman, on artists and programs for the nine-week Aspen Music Festival and the Winter Music concerts and, since 2000, on the American Academy of Conducting at Aspen. In 2003, she was appointed president of the Summer Music School and Festival.

In July 2004, Coe brought the wealth of her experience to her new position as president of The Music Academy of the West (Santa Barbara, California).

AURELIE DESMARAIS—*Deep in the Art of Texas;* Senior director of artistic planning of the Houston Symphony, French Canadian Aurelie was born December 13, 1959, in Wynyard, Saskatchewan, the third of four girls. Her interest in classical music developed via piano, starting at age ten—for which she had been begging since age five—and voice lessons at thirteen. She performed during her years at the University of Calgary, from which she holds a BM in music theory. Her MM in musicology is from the University of Toronto (1984). From 1984–86, she was with CentreStage Music, a presenter of chamber music and recitals in Toronto. Next came production assistant, then manager, for the Toronto Symphony (1986–91), followed by artistic administrator for the National Arts Centre Orchestra in Ottawa (1991–96). During this time she was a guest host on CBC's classical music program "Mostly Music." She married computer consultant Ed Struzynski, July 23, 1993.

In 1996, she was appointed artistic administrator with Houston, working with music director **Christoph Eschenbach** on programming and artists and guest conductors engagements for the orchestra's concerts. She is also a member of the Houston Symphony Chorus.

On June 9, 2001, Tropical Storm Alison swept through Houston costing the city $5 billion and the Symphony $10 million. The entire basement of the Jones Theater was flooded, ruining files, three grand pianos, a 1692 Testori double bass valued at $100,000 and an 1800 Justin Maucote bass valued at $30,000. Also "totaled" was most of the music library. Despite the turmoil, performances went on. It took one year to get back to normal. Many documents were saved via freezing, then vacuum tube drying. Insurance and donations helped replace some items. Fortunately, computer data back-ups were at a different site. Mother Nature can be really inharmonious!

MARY ANN FELDMAN—*A True Twin Citizen;* Mary Ann Feldman, born April 20, 1933, in St. Paul, Minnesota, heard her first orchestra concert at the old St. Paul Auditorium where the renowned Minneapolis Symphony, under the legendary **Dimitri Mitropoulos** (1896–1960), regularly performed youth concerts. It was then, at age eight, that she became a listener and concertgoer even before her first music lessons. In 1966, she was named program annotator for the MSO, which two years later changed its name to the Minnesota Orchestra. En route to that career, she earned a *summa cum laude* degree from the University of Minnesota, and MA in musicology from Columbia University, where she was both a Woodrow Wilson Fellow and Clarence Barker Scholar in Music. After receiving a fellowship from the Newberry Library in Chicago, where she collected the writings of 19th century music critic George P. Upton, she received a PhD in musicology from the University of Minnesota. Before joining the Minnesota Orchestra, she taught in the humanities department of her alma mater, and wrote music criticism for the *Minneapolis Star.*

In the course of the last forty years she has had a multi-faceted career with the orchestra, which has included editorship of *Showcase,* the MSO magazine, music advisor, commentator and charter member of the staff which developed the Orchestra's Viennese Sommerfest, held annually downtown. For the last nine seasons of its forty-four-year existence (to 1986), she served as vice president of the Metropolitan Opera in the Upper Midwest, coordinating this festival week co-sponsored by the Minnesota Orchestra Association and the University of Minnesota. A well-known lecturer, she introduced pre-concert talks from the stage at Orchestra Hall in its inaugural season of 1974. In 1999, she was named orchestra historian. In 2000, she toured Europe with the orchestra, writing the vignettes, *Tales of the Travelling Instruments,* from the point of view of the instruments! She contributed to the Minnesota Orchestra Centennial Book, *Minnesota Orchestra at One Hundred: a Collection of Essays and Images 2002–03.* Her numerous articles include "Chicago Pioneers: Women in Key Roles at the Minnesota Orchestra" (2002). She has long served as corresponding critic for *Opera News* magazine, and is the author of several entries in the *Grove Dictionary of Music and Musicians* and *The American Grove.* As the Minnesota

Orchestra's annotator, she has written over three million words of program notes![231] With a span of thirty-three years, Mary Ann can lay claim to the longest annotatorship[232] in the history of American orchestras!

Since 1995, Feldman has spent summers writing program notes and presenting talks for the Grand Teton Music Festival in Jackson, Wyoming.

In 2000, the MSO created a May Ann Feldman Fund for Education in her honor.

Mary Ann, a long time resident of Minneapolis, is married to Hal Feldman, a computer whizz.

JUDITH FRANKFURT—*Working in the Majors*; Born in New York City, Judith studied piano from age five, and voice (soprano) from fourteen. Advanced piano continued at the Longy School of Music, advanced vocal studies at the Boston Conservatory and Cleveland Institute of Music. Besides music, she studied archeology at the Hebrew University of Jerusalem. Her BA is from Harvard, where her interest in arts administration began with her appointment as manager of the Harvard-Radcliffe *Collegium Musicum*. A freelance professional performer throughout the years, Judith began her career in the music business working for the Boston Symphony at its summer home, Tanglewood. After college, she went to the St. Louis Symphony Orchestra as assistant manager, overseeing the orchestra's touring, operations and state-wide arts lobby. In 1980, she joined the Cleveland Orchestra as artistic administrator, and was subsequently promoted to artistic operations manager in 1983, and orchestra manager in 1987. From 1990–97, she was vice president and general manager of the Philadelphia Orchestra, which involved her directing all aspects of managing one of the country's oldest major orchestras.

Following her years in Philadelphia, she returned to Manhattan as a consultant to the Museum of Modern Art, the Brooklyn Philharmonic, and the ASOL, among others. In 1999, she joined the Brooklyn Museum of Art as deputy director for administration, where her responsibilities include the operational, financial, and administrative aspects of the country's second-largest art museum. She was still in this position in 2005.

Judith is married to James Oestreich, classical music editor/writer with the *New York Times*.

MARTHA GILMER—*The Complete Woman!* Martha Gilmer was appointed artistic administrator of the Chicago Symphony Orchestra, June 1985, and became vice president for artistic programming in 1996. Born in Burlington, Wisconsin, June 10, 1956, she began studying piano at age four and a half, and by junior high school was inspired by the band director to continue music studies. She attended Northwestern University, beginning as a piano major, but during her sophomore year chose to design an *ad hoc* major in arts administration, and was among the first graduates in this area of study. Part of her self-designed major included serving internships with the Chicago Symphony and Northwestern's Pick-Staiger Concert Hall, where she became assistant concert manager and house manager after her graduation.

The Chicago Symphony has been Martha's professional "home" since her 1976 student internship. In 1979, she was hired as assistant to the artistic administrator, Peter Jonas. In 1985, upon his accepting the post of director of English National Opera, she assumed the position of artistic administrator. During the ensuing years, Gilmer has been consistently stimulated by the variety of her duties: planning programs, scheduling concerts, engaging guest artists and conductors, formulating artistic plans with orchestra president **Henry Fogel** until his retirement in 2003,[233] and working closely with such luminaries as the orchestra's music director, **Daniel Barenboim** (*b* 1942), principal guest conductor, **Pierre Boulez** (*b* 1925) and the late music director Laureate, **Sir Georg Solti** (1912–97), conductor of the Chicago Symphony for twenty-two years (1969–92), all of whom she designates as, "Vivid, committed people with tremendous energy."

In addition to planning the CSO subscription concerts, Gilmer oversees the Chicago Symphony Chorus—the largest professional symphony chorus in the U.S., founded by the late **Margaret Hillis** (1921–98) (See Conductors), now directed by her successor, **Duain Wolfe**. The orchestra also has an extensive presenting program of forty-five concerts annually by visiting orchestras, recitalists and jazz ensembles, the Civic Orchestra for

---

231–232. From an in-person August 2004 telephone interview.
233. Deborah Rutter Card took the reins in 2003. (See Card.)

pre-professional training, and a far-reaching education and community concert program, all of which are supervised by Gilmer and her staff. Of the orchestra, she says, "The dedication of the musicians is one of the greatest inspirations for working here!"

Martha Gilmer, like so many women, manages a major career, is married, and a mother. David was born 1987, Matthew, 1990, and Jonathan, 1994.

MARYELLEN H. GLEASON—*A New Flight for the Phoenix;* Maryellen Gleason began her tenure as president and CEO of the Phoenix Symphony, December 2002, following the departure of **Joan Squires** to the Omaha Performing Arts Society. Moving to Arizona in 1984, Gleason engaged in an eighteen-year telecommunications and sales career. A Harvard graduate (BA *cum laude*, Liberal Arts, 1984), she worked for Harvard Student Agencies and played viola in the Harvard-Radcliffe Orchestra—the oldest ensemble in America—also serving as development director for the Pierian Sodality, the original Harvard social club founded in 1808, which 150 years later would become a serious orchestra. She led a successful $184,000 campaign for the HRO's 1984 tour of Europe and the former Soviet Union. In 2001, she earned her MBA from the Northwestern University's Kellogg Graduate School of Management Executive Masters Program. Besides being president of the Harvard Club of Phoenix, Gleason's membership on non profit boards and other community services are of great benefit to the outreach of the PSO. After some experiments with sexy, youth-oriented advertising in the previous season, under Gleason's aegis the orchestra returned to the more conventional. Her philosophy being, "The core audience just wants to know what's what."

Born in Boston, June 25, 1959, into a strong family tradition of music study, Maryellen began trombone at age eight, switched to viola at twenty and continued studies on that instrument for over twenty years. "Appropriately," in 1986, Maryellen married Kim Ohlemeyer, principal trombonist with the Phoenix Symphony. Their son, Eliot, born 1994, inherited the music genes and studies violin and piano, as well as being a member of the Phoenix Boys Choir. Jacob, born 1997, started cello before entering kindergarten.

RUTHANNE GREELEY—*Combining Chamber Music and Capricious Capers;* director of marketing and public relations for the Santa Fe Chamber Music Festival, which celebrated its thirty-fifth season in 2007, Ruthanne Greeley has a background in radio, television and journalism. Born June 29, 1957, in Kansas City, Missouri, she played clarinet in fourth and fifth grade, until the acquisition of braces forced her to stop. At twelve, she began piano lessons for several years from her aunt, a nun and music teacher in Kansas City. Her mother loved playing the piano, and her favorite recording was a boxed set of Mozart piano concertos. Not surprisingly, at twenty-two, Ruthanne's first adult subscription purchase was to the *Mostly Mozart* music festival series in Kansas City. Her 1979 BS in journalism and public relations is from the University of Kansas, which included the summer of 1978 at the Sorbonne in Paris. She worked for San Diego's public radio station KPBS, writing news releases, acting as assistant coordinator of their fundraising, and planned all special events. While working for the *San Diego Union-Tribune*, in 1993 she received the "Local Hero" award from the San Diego local of the Newspaper Guild for her work during a contentious labor battle with that newspaper. In 1998, she began as a marketing and public relations associate, and the following year became director, extending her responsibilities to include media relations, advertising campaigns and the budget.

When not at her "real job," beginning in 1996, former city girl Ruthanne has gone to the goats! Fourteen of them: seven does (females) and seven wethers (neutered males). Besides making a delicious French-style chèvre goat cheese, she has learned how to deliver a baby goat, give shots, run an IV to a kid (a baby goat—not a child!) with pneumonia—in a pinch, the dining room chandelier makes an excellent IV bag hanger—and other exciting veterinary skills. Her conclusion: "They are smart, funny, affectionate, and give me the greatest joy."

CINDI HUBBARD—*Coast to Coast and Back Again!* In April 2000, Cindi Hubbard became artistic administrator of The Women's Philharmonic in San Francisco, after an exciting period in the nation's capital as AA for the National Symphony. With music director **Leonard Slatkin**, she managed program development for classical, pops, family, education, outreach, and Wolf Trap summer series. As with many of her contemporaries in the field, she comes from a musical background. Her BA is from Montclair State University, New Jersey, and MA in music education from Columbia. A trained pianist, she taught for five years in Montclair, both in the school system and privately, before becoming executive assistant to the general manager of the San Francisco Symphony. When she left San Francisco after six years, she not only was orchestra personnel administrator, but had developed the symphony's first annual chamber music and pre-concert chamber music series. In 1995, when the Indianapolis Symphony needed an artistic administrator, Hubbard answered the call. Three years later she was back on the East Coast with the NSO. In 2000, the lure of love proved strong enough to follow her man and return to the West Coast and assume her new position, which lasted until May 2001, when The Women's Philharmonic once again had to embark on a restructuring phase to meet financial challenges. (TWP was forced to disband in 2004.) Meanwhile, Cindi became happily married.

May 2003 found Hubbard as consultant and artistic advisor to the Pacific Symphony in California's Orange County, which led to a full-time consulting practice. By 2004, she added the Memphis Symphony to her client list. Wearing another hat, she also works with a San Francisco company specializing in executive searches for non-profit arts and environmental organizations. In her own words, "As always, I continue to look for the next interesting project."

CARLA JOHNSON—*Heading East* . . . A graduate of the University of Michigan, Johnson received her MFA in arts administration from CUNY, Brooklyn. Starting with the Seattle Symphony in 1981, after thirteen years and positions including operations coordinator, orchestra manager and artistic administrator, she moved to the St. Louis Symphony. Beginning as the director of artistic administration, from 1997 she was the orchestra manager, working with music director **Hans Vonk**, (1996–2002) and his successor David Robertson in the programming and planning of concerts and tours of this internationally esteemed orchestra. She left St. Louis in June 2004 to become executive director of the Virginia Symphony (**JoAnn Falletta**, conductor) in their eighty-fifth season.

MARIANNA KANKARE-LOIKKANEN—*A Glimpse Across the Ocean*; Born in Helsinki, May 31, 1950, Marianna was a piano student at the Helsinki Conservatory for twelve years, receiving her BM and MA (1980) from Helsinki University in musicology and Russian literature. Her thesis on Shostakovich initiated her Russian studies. She is also fluent in Swedish—Finland's official second language—as well as German and English. The latter learned after spending 1978–79 in Massachusetts while her husband was completing his PhD at MIT. In the course of finishing her thesis, she studied in Leningrad which led, after graduation, to a four-year position as a tour guide in Russia. "An exciting period, especially from today's point of view, since that Soviet world doesn't exist any more." This was part of a ten-year tourism career which included the ancillary fields of public relations, media and publication as a freelance journalist, focusing on the Soviet musical culture. The experience was responsible for her being chosen over sixteen other candidates to fill the new post of publicity manager at the Helsinki Philharmonic. Since 1989, she has created this position and built up the publicity framework and image of the orchestra, and is chief editor of the Filharmonia newsletter.

Married in 1973, she and her husband, a professor of urban economics, have two sons, Lauri and Pekka. Lauri lives apart, but in the same apartment building as his parents in the heart of Helsinki. This is after living in the suburbs when the children were young, which involved a daily two hour commute downtown to work.

Marianna's working day at Finlandia Hall covers the necessary PR of putting on concerts: program printing, advertising, media releases and post-concert receptions. An example of how things can go wrong is a Thursday concert which included Alexander Zemlinsky's *Lyrical Symphony* (1922) for soprano and baritone. On Monday, the soprano canceled. Since this is a seldom produced work, substitutes are not easily to come by. But in London they found **Anne Evans**, who had sung the part eight months previously. By Tuesday, she was in Helsinki to rehearse, and the concert was a success.

Concerts in Finland are held on Wednesday and Thursday, since labor union agreements require double-time payment for playing Saturday and Sunday. Quite a change from the expectations of American audiences.

ANN KENNEDY—*Poised on International Recognition;* In February 2001, Ann Kennedy became executive director/CEO of the Houston Symphony, one of few women in such a major orchestral position. Her academic, management and marketing credentials span over two decades in the commercial field. She had already spent ten years on the symphony's board of directors, co-chaired an annual fund drive and headed committees on marketing, education and public policy, as well as serving on the boards of numerous Houston arts organizations, including the Cultural Arts Council of Houston/Harris County.

In the first three months of her tenure, Tropical Storm Allison wreaked chaos on the concert hall. With opening day of the new season approaching, Kennedy managed to secure office space at Enron, and opened on schedule in September. (See Aurelie Desmarais.)

Born in Omaha, Nebraska, June 13, 1952, Ann's parents guided her to classical music. She began piano at nine. After her BA in literature from Yale (1970), she moved to Houston in 1975 for further studies and immediately became a symphony subscriber. She married Geoffrey Walker, a corporate securities attorney, in 1978, earned a Harvard MBA in 1982, and had two children, Lucy born April 7, 1984 and Alec, October 7, 1985.

SANDRA A. KIMBERLING—*Lady of the Los Angeles Music Center;* Elected president of the Music Center Operating Company in April 1987, and then as COO, Sandie Kimberling was responsible for the overall management and operation of the Music Center of Los Angeles County. She came to the three theater complex as a department supervisor, subsequently working in the areas of insurance, accounting and administration before leaving in 1975 to join Technicolor. She returned to the operating company in 1978, advancing to assistant administrator under the leadership of William Severns. In 1984, she was named general manager.

Kimberling has also represented the operating company of the Los Angeles Area Chamber of Commerce and the Los Angeles Convention and Visitors Bureau. She was the principal member of the International Association of Auditorium Managers and the National Association of Performing Arts Center Executives. Her other affiliations include the Ad Hoc Arts Leaders of Los Angeles, the Convention and Visitors Bureau's Cultural Tourism Advisory Committee, the Blue Ribbon, and president of the board of directors of the Downtown's Women's Center.

She and her husband, Lawrence A. Michaels, a partner at the law firm of Mitchell, Silberberg & Knupp, are members of the board of trustees of the Autry Museum of Western Heritage and support many other community organizations. After an illustrious career, Sandie retired from her position in June 2000, "to enjoy just being a lawyer's wife . . . "

D. ANN KOONSMAN—*Two Decades of Harmony in the Heart of Texas;* D. Ann Koonsman served as executive director of the Fort Worth Symphony Orchestra Association 1980–2003. During her tenure, the association was recognized for both artistic excellence and financial stability. She was responsible for the management of both the Fort Worth Chamber Orchestra and the Fort Worth Symphony, along with supervision of the staff. FWSO ranks among the highest in the nation of orchestras with comparable budgets. Hallmarks of Koonsman's administration included three international tours, several acclaimed recordings, steadily increasing salaries and benefits for the musicians, and consistently balanced budgets. In 1994, the orchestra gained further international recognition as the American host orchestra for the Tokyo International Conducting Competition. 1999 marked the sesquicentennial of Fort Worth, with the symphony joining in the celebrations.

Koonsman has served on the Music Advisory Panel of the NEA and both Music and Touring Panels for the Texas Commission on the Arts. She is active in the ASOL, and in 1995 held national office as secretary of the Group Two Orchestras Executive Director meeting group. She was named "1988 Woman of the Year" by the Fort Worth Zonta Club chapter, an organization of women in business. She was chair of the artistic planning committee for the new Fort Worth Performing Arts Center, and is involved in numerous other community organizations and activities.

Born July 9, 1943, in Great Falls, Montana, music has always been part of her life. The family moved to Texas where she began violin in third grade as part of the Fort Worth public school string program (those were the days!), later adding piano. Her BM was earned at Texas Christian University (1968), and MM from Texas Tech (1974), with further graduate study at Texas Woman's University and New York's Mannes College of Music. In 1965, she married Ronald L. Koonsman, owner/CEO of Telephone Warehouse. Their son, Brandon, is a graduate of the University of Texas at Arlington.

The budget for 2001–02 was $9.9 million. An endowment campaign at the time raised $17 million within twenty-two months, bringing the fund to $23 million. Ann played an important role in this vital undertaking, which will serve this deserving orchestra in perpetuity.

In June 2003, Koonsman announced her retirement. She declared: "It has been my pleasure and honor to serve this wonderful symphony for more than two decades . . . And now it's time for me to spend more time with my family, travel and pursue new interests. Of course, I look forward to continuing to support the symphony and enjoying its concerts."

As a violinist, teacher, and orchestra administrator, D. Ann has devoted a major portion of her life to bringing the joy of music to others.

ELEANOR LONG—*Embodiment of the Vermont Symphony*; For over twenty-five years, Eleanor Long has performed a multitude of administrative jobs from overseeing auditioning to contracting and managing players, to being the librarian responsible for procuring and distributing music to performers, to proofreading programs, scripts and schedules, and co-ordinating school concerts the VSO hosts across the state. Before putting away her oboe to work behind the scenes, Eleanor sat in the woodwind section of the orchestra, performing with the VSO for sixteen years. In 2002, the symphony honored their faithful colleague by announcing the endowment of an orchestral chair in her name.

Elly grew up in South Burlington (Vermont) within a large music-loving family. At fourteen, when her high school needed an oboist, she took up the instrument. She graduated as valedictorian, going to Brown University as an English major and performed in their orchestra and various chamber music groups.

She auditioned for the VSO during her senior year, winning the second oboe seat. Concurrently, she took music classes at the University of Vermont before embarking upon a two-year leave of absence to study Music at the University of Iowa. There, she performed with the Tri-City Symphony in Davenport, and other ensembles. In 1979, she reclaimed her VSO seat. When the personnel manager and the librarian left, Eleanor assumed both jobs and juggled three careers. She took a year off from performing, but never returned to the stage, feeling satisfied with working in the wings. Despite offers from other national orchestras, Long remains faithful to the VSO.

(It runs in the family. Eleanor's mother, Carolyn, has been volunteer manager of the Vermont Youth Orchestra since 1968. In 2003, the VYO named their new building *The Elley-Long Music Center at Saint Michael's College*, in honor of Carolyn Long and *her* father, Dr Harold W. Elley, after whom Eleanor is named—a fitting tribute to Carolyn Long's service with the VYO and the substantial donation she bestowed on the Youth Orchestra.)

Susan Lundberg

SUSAN O. LUNDBERG—*At Home on the Prairie*; As executive director of the Bismarck-Mandan Symphony since 1992, Susan Lundberg represents the opportunities for women in regional orchestras. A native of Bismarck, North Dakota, she studied piano and voice, graduating from Stephens College, Columbia (Missouri), with majors in history and music. A master's in library science from Western Michigan University, for which she received a U.S. Office of Education scholarship, was followed by a master's in public administration from Cal State, Fullerton.

Her positions at the Bismarck Public Library, assistant professor/librarian at the University of Tennessee (Knoxville), and Coordinator of Children's Services for the twenty-five branches of the Orange County (California) Public Library, ran concurrently with vocal performances in operas, choruses and musicals. She chose to return to Bismarck to raise her daughter Melissa—now in theater administration in Minneapolis—and dedicate her experience for community service. Lundberg also performs as soloist with the Bismarck-Mandan Civic Chorus, Bismarck-Mandan Symphony Orchestra and Great Plains Jazz Society.

Their love of music inspired the family to create the Sleepy Hollow Summer Theatre in 1990, a venue providing opportunities in the arts for young people ages six to twenty via educational classes and the staging of a Broadway musical each season. (Melissa was their director, 1998–2003.) Celebrating its fifteenth year in 2004, the presentation of *Annie Get Your Gun*, July 21–August 1, with a cast and orchestra of 100, drew thousands of people. The only outdoor theater in central North Dakota, it has attracted over 100,000 people in a state whose total population numbers 642,000. For their philanthropic participation, the Lundberg family—mother Evelyn, sister, designer Stephanie Delmore, daughter Melissa, and Susan's late attorney father, Robert—received the Bismarck Art and Galleries Citation Award (1990) and the Light 4 Youth Award (2001).

Founder and chair of *Friends of The Belle*, Lundberg was a major force in bringing about the $2.6 million renovation of the **Belle Mehus**[234] City Auditorium, the new home of the symphony. An acoustically perfect concert hall, which first opened its doors January 19, 1914, and over the next half century hosted performances by such great names of the past as violinists **Fritz Kreisler**, **Joseph Szigeti** and **Isaac Stern**, pianist **Joseph Lhevinne**, opera divas **Ernestine Schumann-Heink**, **Marian Anderson** and **Beverly Sills**, tenor **Jan Peerce** and baritones **Leonard Warren** and **Nelson Eddy**. Even humorist **Will Rogers** twirled his lasso and expounded his wry philosophy upon its wooden stage. After WWII and the advent of television, use of *The Belle* declined. By the '90s it was in seedy disrepair. Concerned citizens saved the hall from being razed by getting it placed on the Register of Historic Places, and fund raising and renovation began. For this and her extensive other community services, Lundberg was recognized by the *Bismarck Tribune* with their Award for Accomplishment. On the centenary year of Mehus' birth, "The Belle," with its original superb acoustics intact, reopened its doors, October 11, 1996.

Also an oil and watercolor artist, with her mother, sister and daughter, Susan created a three generation art exhibit, "Scandinavian Threads of Inheritance," attracting over 30,000 to the Sheila Schafer Gallery in Medora, North Dakota.

Lundberg was chair of the Small Budget Orchestras—approximately 400 of them—for the ASOL, 2000–2002.

With the nation celebrating the bicentennial of the Lewis and Clark expedition's departure from the St. Louis area to explore the Louisiana Territory and seek a Northwest Passage to the Pacific Ocean, the Bismarck-Mandan region, where the forty member party spent two winters of their twenty-eight month, 8,000 mile journey, presented the opera, *Sakakawea*,[235] October 2004, with two Met sopranos.

At a concert, April 24, 2004, Susan was the most surprised recipient of a well-deserved honor. With an audience of 800 in on the secret, including Mayor John Warford and former Governor Ed Schafer—with whom Susan had gone to high school—and his wife, she was honored with a portrait of her to be hung permanently in the Belle Mehus City Auditorium. It is an absolute first in any of North Dakota's public buildings! (It turned out that a committee had been working on this idea for *three years*.) (On stage, Melissa presented her mother with a bouquet of roses.)

Whether acting as a performer, creator, producer or fundraiser, Lundberg's artistic and organizational abilities stem from her belief in the power and connection of the humanities, especially music. Susan's credo is, "Music is a lifelong pursuit of excellence that always offers new challenges . . . one can never learn enough . . . and I truly believe the Bismarck-Mandan Symphony is the most active orchestra of our size in the country!"

PATRICIA MITCHELL—*Always at the Top*; Patricia Mitchell has been chief operating officer of the Los Angeles Philharmonic Orchestra and the Hollywood Bowl since 2000. Before this she was executive director of Los Angeles

---

234. Belle Mehus (1896–1988) was the Grande Dame of Music in Bismarck, whose conservatory became the 834-seat home of the orchestra. In her later years, when the elderly lady needed a companion, Susan traveled with Belle throughout the U.S. and Mexico—an added impetus for Lundberg to have spearheaded the campaign to save this historic landmark from the demolition ball. (See The Unforgotten.)
235. Sakakawea was a Shoshone Indian girl, captured at age twelve, in 1800, by a war party of Hidatsas. As was customary, she was given a name by her captors, *Tsakakawias*, meaning Bird Woman. The spelling Sacajawea is Shoshone for *Boat Launcher*, and has nothing to do with her real name, Sakakawea (alternate spelling). It is a matter of state pride to North Dakotans that the form of her name should be as nearly as possible like the original.

Opera (1995–2000) where, during her administration, the annual budget doubled, the subscriber base tripled, and contributions increased more than 150 percent. In both prestigious positions, her responsibilities included marketing, public relations, development, educational and community outreach.

Born August 11, 1947, in the City of the Angels, her music-loving family stretches back a generation to when her mother played cello in a trio with *her* sisters on flute and piano. Pat's BA in theater (1969) from Occidental College led to a stint at the Guthrie Theater in Minneapolis. Here, she became a partner in Arts Development Associates, Inc., a national consulting firm, with a branch in New York, providing services in research, planning, program development, public relations and marketing for artists, art agencies and cultural institutions.

Mitchell previously served as executive director of the San Francisco Opera (1979–87), in which capacity she was responsible for all financial and administrative aspects of its management. After leaving there, she used her in-depth experience in union-labor negotiations to co-author *Autopsy of an Orchestra*, a major and much-read study on the bankruptcy of the Oakland Symphony, which serves as an example/warning for orchestras in trouble.

In October 1988, she accepted the position of deputy general director of the Los Angeles Opera. In February 1995, she became their executive director. In 2000, she resigned to become second in command (COO) to the executive vice president and managing director **Deborah Borda**. (Their friendship dates back to San Francisco Symphony days).

As one can deduce, the Los Angeles Philharmonic is in good hands.

JANE S. MOSS—*A Rock for Lincoln Center*, vice president for programming at Lincoln Center since 1992, Jane Moss became a force for innovation from the outset of her new career, importing famous musicians to New York, and exporting original stage productions of musical works to highlight the caliber of the facility. One of her greatest breakthroughs has been resurrecting an almost moribund *Mostly Mozart* which, founded in 1966, was America's first indoor summer music festival. By the time it reached its twenty-fifth anniversary in 1991, the bicentenary of Mozart's death, overexposure had set in. While her initial attempts were met with a barrage of criticism, she prevailed, cutting the schedule from seven to four weeks, bringing in a greater variety of guest artists and repertoire, and expanding venues from Avery Fisher Hall to Allice Tully Hall and the outdoor Damrosch Park, among others. 2002 marked the last of seventeen seasons under conductor Gerard Schwarz. 2003–04—the festival's thirty-eighth year—brought dynamic young French conductor Louis Langrée.

Born in Lancaster, Pennsylvania, 1953, her father taught geology at Franklin and Marshall College, and her mother worked for United Way. Both were music lovers, with Metropolitan Opera broadcasts an integral part of her childhood. The fifth of six children—all "achievers" according to Jane—she earned a philosophy degree at Franklin and Marshall and, with options for law or business school, instead chose theatrical administration, starting as an intern. By the mid-1970s, she was director of marketing at Baltimore's Center Stage, graduating to business manager. She became executive director of Playwrights Horizons in New York (1977), and of the Alliance of Resident Theaters New York (in 1981). Opportunities in the music field appeared, and from 1987–90 she was executive director of Meet the Composer, a national service organization, interacting with orchestras and concert presenters. She was working as a consultant for several arts organizations, including Lincoln Center, when the opening for director of programming became available.

Other presentations Moss is improving upon are *Great Performers at Lincoln Center* (which she would like to rename), a series of performances of classical and modern pieces by premier musical artists; *Midsummer Night Swing*, the Lincoln Center Festival she inaugurated in 1996; and *Lincoln Center Out of Doors*, its largest and longest-running community outreach program. In its thirty-sixth summer, August 2006, this New York tradition of *free* music, dance and literary events, representing cultures from around the world, draws tens of thousands of people each year.

Her special project, *New Visions*, was launched in 1999 with the goal to splice classical music, drama and dance, to expand concertgoing into a theatrical experience—literally creating a new genre. Thus far, programming has included a bardic recitation of the *Beowulf* epic in its original Anglo-Saxon, a dramatization of Gustav Mahler's *Kindertotenlieder* song cycle, and *Moondrunk*, a concert-meets-dream ballet fantasia with whirling dancers giving expression to Arnold Schoenberg's ethereal vocal work *Pierrot lunaire*.

Moss also initiates spontaneous festivals, such as the April-May 2003 "John Adams: An American Master," which opened with the New York premiere of his nativity oratorio, *El Niño*, led by Esa-Pekka Salonen with the Los Angeles Philharmonic and soprano Dawn Upshaw. It tells Christ's story from the viewpoint of female mystics and poets, many of them Hispanic, including, Sor Juana Ines de la Cruz, Rosario Castellanos, Gabriela Mistral and Hildegard von Bingen. The work is sung alternatively in English, Latin and Spanish.

Trying to figure out how to better promote contemporary music is the idea for a festival featuring major works written since 1945, "Music That Changed the World," with major international ensembles performing large single pieces or programs of single composers. She also hopes to develop a conservatory utilizing the presence of international artists who come to perform. Her innovations are enriched with lectures, symposiums and concerts guiding audiences towards what she calls "the art of listening."

The dedication and caliber of Jane Moss is revealed in the poignant speech she gave at a January 24, 2002 press conference on the effect of 9/11 on classical music: " . . . classical music, far from being just a soothing musical surround at the end of a busy day at the office, [is] filling an essential and communal human need."

And the call to teamwork and foresight: " . . . none of us individually can achieve what is our collective responsibility—namely to insure that the music and [its] creators . . . that were passed on to us, century by century, work by work, for our safekeeping and solace, move forward into a secure future."

VANESSA MOSS—*Part of the Chicago Team;* Vanessa Moss was appointed manager of the Chicago Symphony Orchestra in August 1986, and has been vice president for orchestra and building operations since October 1995. One of eight chosen from a field of over 300 applicants, she was a participant in the 1984–85 ASOL Orchestra Management Fellowship Program under which she received on-the-job training in the administrations of the San Francisco Symphony, Rochester Philharmonic and Canton (Ohio) Symphony.

In her present position, she is responsible for the day-to-day operations of the Chicago Symphony Orchestra and Symphony Center. This includes the scheduling and production of performances, radio and television broadcasts, recordings and tours, as well as the negotiation of musician, stagehand, and electronic media contracts.

A music major, with a minor in economics, Moss graduated from Wellesley College in 1984, having spent her junior year at New Hall College, Cambridge (England). She was valedictorian of the 1995 class in the executive master's program at Northwestern University's Kellogg Graduate School of Management.

ANNE PARSONS—*From a Bowl of Cherries . . . to the Pointe . . . to Motown!* Anne H. Parsons was born November 4, 1957, in Schenectady, New York, but spent most of her childhood in Bedford, Westchester County, outside the Big Apple. As is the "norm" for children who grew up to make careers in music, she was surrounded by it in her youth, taken to the theater and concerts by her parents—her father a jazz enthusiast, her mother, an amateur pianist. Anne began playing flute in elementary school, and later added saxophone in order to join her high school jazz band. At Smith College—where she continued flute studies and earned a BA in English (1980)—Anne helped to organize concerts for their orchestra, doing the duties of a manager, unaware that *that* was what she was actually being! Her life was set on its course with the visit of **Catherine French**, then president/CEO of the ASOL, who came to recruit candidates for the first Fellowship Management Program of the organization. Parsons applied, was chosen, and following her graduation, began the year's residency with three month internships in the Minnesota Orchestra, Phoenix and San Francisco Symphonies. In the course of this, she met and became close friends with **Allison Vulgamore** who was in the same group. On completion of the program, Anne was first hired by **Henry Fogel**, who had just accepted the post of executive director of the National Symphony (Washington, DC). Within one year of her 1981–83 term, Parsons was promoted from administrative assistant to orchestra manager.

An opening for the same position in the Boston Symphony came almost too soon. From the fall of 1983 until March 1991, Parsons supported the business end of one of the most prestigious orchestras in the country, managing issues of personnel, scheduling and all operations involving the BSO under **Seiji Osawa**, the Boston Pops and the Boston Esplanade Orchestras—both with **John Williams**—in Symphony Hall, Tanglewood, and on their regular tours throughout the U.S., Europe and Japan.

In 1991 Hollywood called, and in April of that year Parsons became general manager of the Hollywood Bowl and helped to organize the Hollywood Bowl Orchestra. This was the brainchild of executive vice president and managing director of the Los Angeles Philharmonic Association, the much-respected **Ernest Fleischmann** (*b* 1924), whose distinguished career included conducting appearances and general managership of the London Symphony (1959–67) before assuming his position in 1969. Working in harmony with **John Mauceri** (*b* 1945), former conductor of the Washington (DC) Opera (1980–82), the American Symphony of New York (1984–87) and Scottish Opera (1987–), Parsons was responsible for organizing up to seventy concerts per year at the Bowl, presenting programs of jazz and pop, as well as providing the summer home for concerts by the LA Philharmonic and the Hollywood Bowl Orchestra. In addition to the summer schedule, her work with the latter led to a stack of successful CDs, and three Japan tours.

On September 12, 1987, Anne married photographer Donald Dietz beside a lovely lake in the Adirondack Mountains of New York. Formerly their family consisted of Appin and Maia, two Saluki-Middle Eastern hunting dogs, whose breed dates back to 3600 BC, but that changed on August 4, 1997 when daughter Cara Alexandra was born.

Shortly after Fleischmann retired in 1998, Parsons, in a new career move, became general manager of the New York City Ballet—with a $44 million budget—a position she held until the 2005–06 season, when she accepted the executive directorship of the Detroit Symphony Orchestra, which also includes the title, president.

AILA SAURAMO—*Managing Finnish Orchestras and Festivals;* Aila Manninen Sauramo was born May 23, 1956, in Tampere, Finland's third largest city 100 miles north of Helsinki. While in secondary school, she sang in choirs and was interested in jazz. Her interest in classical music came later. After graduation with a master's degree from Tampere University (political science, 1982), she worked as a research assistant at the university.

Active in the Jazz Break Society, in 1984 she was asked to work for them as a manager and arrange concerts, as well as for the Tampere Jazz Happening festival, founded in 1982. Between 1984–98, Saraumo administered three very different festivals: the Contemporary Finnish Music Festival, the Tampere Biennale (founded 1986), and the Tampere International Choir Festival (founded in 1975).

1997–98 was spent in New York finishing her studies for the arts management professional diploma, which she received from the Sibelius Academy (1998). That year she moved to Helsinki, working as the executive director of Chamber Orchestra Avanti! (founded in 1983 by Esa-Pekka Salonen, Magnus Lindberg, Jukka-Pekka Saraste, and **Kaija Saariaho**). While with Avanti!, she was also a member of the board of the Association of Finnish Symphony Orchestras[236] of which, in 2001, she became executive director. The association was founded in 1965 by Anna-Maija Poussa, who served 1965–1989, and was followed by Ros-Mari Djupsund (1993–95).

Aila is married to Pekka Sauramo, PhD, a senior economist in macroeconomics and economic policy. In their free time they enjoy tour cycling, often in Latin America. Their daughter, Jenny Turunen, was born in 1980, and a granddaughter, Taika Turunen, arrived in 2003.

RITA SHAPIRO—*Another Break Through the Glass Ceiling;* Graduate of the College of Fine Arts School of Music (BM, 1976; MM, 1978, Voice), Shapiro served as operations manager for the Cleveland Orchestra, plan-

---

236. The Association of Finnish Symphony Orchestras has twenty-nine member orchestras. According to Aila, in 2003 there were 311, or 33 percent, female musicians in the orchestras. She points out: "The younger the orchestra the higher percentage of female musicians. In the Tapiola Sinfonietta, the average age is thirty-five years and 50 percent female membership. In the Kuopio City Orchestra, the average age is forty-seven years with 17 percent women. The trend is that new vacancies are often filled by talented young women."

ning and managing more than thirty tours throughout the U.S., Europe and Asia. In 1999, she became general manager of the National Symphony, heading its reorganization following September 11, 2001. This included the South Dakota residency program and Third National Conducting Institute, plus working with all aspects of Kennedy Center, supporting the artistic vision of the music director **Leonard Slatkin**. In August 2002, Shapiro was promoted to NSO executive director.

BEVERLY SILLS—*At the Pinnacle of the Arts*! As chairwoman of Lincoln Center from 1994 to May 2002, Sills, who enjoyed a forty-seven year career as a singer beginning at age three, oversaw the entire complex of this Center for the Performing Arts. This encompasses the New York Philharmonic, Metropolitan Opera, Chamber Music Society, Juilliard School of Music, New York Ballet, Mostly Mozart Festival, New York Public Library for the Performing Arts and a myriad of other arts associations. New York City Opera, of which Sills was general director, 1980–1990, as of 2006 was considering relocating the Lincoln Center to the proposed Cultural Complex to be built at Ground Zero.

When she left Lincoln Center, after a few months decided she wasn't ready to retire at seventy-four, so in 2003 plunged into the offered chairmanship of the Metropolitan Opera. She really did retire in 2005. (See 20th Century Singers.)

JOAN H. SQUIRES—*Riding into Western Sunsets* . . . As CEO and president of the Phoenix Symphony (1994–2002), Joan oversaw a budget of over $5.2 million. She worked with music directors James Sedares (1990–2000) and Hermann Michael (2000–) on all artistic planning; labor negotiations with the musicians; and directed financial, operational and human resource policies while enhancing the Symphony's programs and acting as chief spokesperson to the public and media. She also served as liaison to the community, including the board of directors, artistic personnel, administrative staff, plus corporate and cultural leaders and donors. Under her leadership, the Phoenix Symphony received a 2001 DREAMR Award, which recognizes individuals and organizations who have demonstrated a strong commitment to the Phoenix area, specifically revitalizing downtown.

This invaluable experience well qualified her for the position of president of the Omaha Performing Arts Society, which she assumed in September 2002. A non-profit corporation, OPAS is committed to enriching the cultural scene through the presentation of quality local, national and international artistic performances.

Born March 10, 1957, in Shippensburg, Pennsylvania, Joan's parents played instruments, and she was exposed to music in school. She started piano lessons at seven and organ at twelve, but did not attend a professional concert until she was eighteen—Eugene Ormandy and the Philadelphia Orchestra. In 1979, she earned her BS from Lebanon Valley College (Pennsylvania). Her MM and MBA were from the University of Michigan (1985). During her graduate student years she was running the Michigan Youth Symphony, including taking them on tour. Prior to graduate school, she taught music in elementary and high schools.

In 1985, Squires was accepted into the ASOL Orchestra Management Fellowship Program. (Now a member of the League, its Fellowship Task Force and Media Committees, Squires has served as a panelist at their National Conference.) Her residencies took her to the Cleveland Orchestra at the beginning of **Christoph Dohnanyi**'s tenure, the Florida Orchestra (Tampa) under **Irwin Hoffman**, and Houston Symphony during the transition from **Sergio Commissiona** to **Christoph Eschenbach**. She remained in Houston for three years, first as assistant to the executive director, then as assistant manager. 1988 found her as orchestra manager for the Utah Symphony under **Joseph Silverstein**. By 1990, she was at Milwaukee Symphony, progressing from general manager to acting executive director to executive director by March 1993. During this time she was responsible for several appointments, including **Stanislaw Skrowaczewski** as artistic advisor, and **Doc Severinsen** as Milwaukee's first principal Pops conductor. She also launched new education and outreach initiatives, as well as free concerts at community centers and area hospitals.

The call to Phoenix came literally out of the blue. She and her husband, Thomas Fay—they were married in 1991—had always wanted to live in the Southwest. He became director of development for the College of Fine Arts at Arizona State University. They resided in Scottsdale enjoying those sunsets.

In summer 2002, OPAS invested $10 million to renovate the Orpheum Theater. Built in 1927, this 2,500 seat venue is home to the Omaha Symphony, Opera Omaha, touring Broadway productions and other events.

With Joan Squires at the helm, ground was broken in April 2003 for the new $90 million Omaha Performing Arts Center. The hall was opened on November 5, 2005, with **JoAnn Falletta** guest conducting the Omaha Symphony in the premiere of **Joan Tower**'s Viola Concerto, *Purple Rhapsody*.

Joan Squires will be utilizing her impressive organizational skills for years to come, and enjoying more sunsets with her husband.

JACQUELINE M. TAYLOR—*Châtelaine of the Chamber*, Jacqueline Taylor began her business career as a booking manager for the instrumental division of Thea Dispeker Artists Management. Her degrees are from NYU and Juilliard, where she managed the pre-college orchestra for two years (1983–85). After Thea Dispeker, her next position was as managing director of the 92nd Street Y's Tisch Center for the Arts (1990–94). She was responsible for planning and budgeting all classical music programming, including concerts, recital and chamber music series, and educational outreach. Some of her presentations included the New York Chamber Symphony and the New York premiere of Shostakovich's complete preludes and fugues.

From 1994–2000, Taylor served as executive director of the Chamber Music Society of Lincoln Center, working with the board of directors to implement policies, developing programming with the artistic director, and overseeing all touring, marketing, fund raising, public relations and educational outreach. During her tenure, the Society saw the addition of new programs, including a family concert series, workshops for amateur musicians, outreach programs with schools and a healthy increase in contributed income and subscriptions.

She left the CMSLC in July 2000 to pursue graduate studies at NYU, focusing on the social history of the performing arts in the United States. She is also on the board of the Fan Fox and Leslie R. Samuels Foundation, a major supporter of the arts, especially Lincoln Center.

Taylor was succeeded in her position by **Norma Hurlburt**, who left the conductorless Orpheus Chamber Orchestra in 1998 and worked on special projects for organizations and arranging chamber concerts until coming to Lincoln Center. (Artistic directors for CMS are David Finkel and **Wu Han**.)

ALLISON VULGAMORE—*Going With the Wind*, Allison Vulgamore is president and managing director of the Atlanta Symphony Orchestra. Born in Boston, January 28, 1958, her home state is Ohio where she was raised in a musical environment—her mother played folk music on the dulcimer and autoharp. Her father, a Methodist circuit preacher, became president of Albion College, Michigan. His career also called for travel abroad, thus Allison's fifth grade year was spent in Germany, eighth grade in Lebanon, and voice study in Graz (Austria) when she was sixteen—all of which gave her fluency in German, French and Italian. Returning to the U.S., she was a voice major at Oberlin College Conservatory, graduating in 1980 with a BA in voice performance. (She now serves on their board of trustees). Like her friend, **Anne Parsons**, former General Manager of the Hollywood Bowl, Allison was one of the original eight Fellows in the first class (1980–81) of the Orchestra Management Fellowship Program of the ASOL. Her three residencies were with the Philadelphia Orchestra, where she experienced the joy of working with the late **Eugene Ormandy** (1899–1985) before his retirement in 1980, the Fort Wayne (Indiana) Symphony and the St. Louis Symphony under **Leonard Slatkin**. Back at the Philadelphia Orchestra (1981–82), as assistant to the executive director, she worked with **Riccardo Muti** (*b* 1941) who was beginning his twelve-year term as music director (1980–92).

1987 saw Vulgamore using her language skills with the National Symphony under **Mstislav Rostropovich** (*b* 1927) in the position of artistic administrator and general manager. One of her production highlights here was the 1987 gala honoring the sixtieth birthday of the cellist/maestro. Another jewel in her coronet was arranging the

Erato recording and video of *Boris Godunov*, starring *Mrs.* Rostropovich, soprano **Galina Vishnevskaya**. Summers were spent at the Casals Festival in San Juan, Puerto Rico, founded and named after another of the world's greatest cellists, **Pablo Casals** (1876–1973).

As orchestra manager of the New York Philharmonic (1987–93), Vulgamore worked closely with Maestro **Zubin Mehta** (*b* 1936). A highlight of this collaboration was her 1989 production of an outdoor concert for 200,000 in Singapore. After the NYP's transition to music director **Kurt Masur** (*b* 1927) in 1992, she collaborated on the orchestra's year-long 150th anniversary celebrations (1992–93). She supervised the building of the Carlos Moseley Music Pavilion—the state-of-the-art outdoor facility which is transported to the Central Park concerts in five semi trucks—and also oversaw the remodeling of Avery Fisher Hall by noted accoustician Russell Johnson.

The 1991 Gulf War (like the 9/11 terrorist attack ten years later) made its inroads on the arts with travel and other security restrictions, causing cancellations of bookings that had been made two to three years in advance. The major challenge was having to postpone the New York Philharmonic tour to Europe.

In September 1993, Allison accepted the call to join the Atlanta Symphony where she worked with Yoel Levi until the end of his twelve year tenure in 2000, principal guest conductor Donald Runnicles and subsequent director Robert Spano. On their fiftieth anniversary, she arranged two national television shows and an open house which accommodated 6,000 visitors. The 1996 Olympics in Atlanta were the occasion to establish a Cultural Olympiad with the Atlanta Symphony as its cornerstone, playing at the opening ceremonies before 4 billion television viewers. Further festivities included six concerts, two with soprano **Jessye Norman** in a performance of Mahler's 2nd Symphony, in collaboration with Atlanta Opera, which features soprano, contralto and chorus. The fifth concert was devoted to young operatic talent, and a grand finale starring violin virtuoso **Itzhak Perlman**.

In 1980, Allison married Peter Manton Marshall, harpsichordist, organist, chairman (1982–93) of the organ department at Catholic University of America (Washington, DC), and a very supportive husband.

Vulgamore's millennium project is the building of a $300 million Symphony Center on 14th Street in midtown Atlanta. The property was purchased by the ASO parent corporation, Woodruff Arts Center, March 2000. The unique 21st century design accentuates acoustical excellence and a feeling of community with the audience. Besides serving as the orchestra's performance and rehearsal venue, it will house the administrative offices and feature an office tower with retail space, as well as incorporating a large exterior public plaza with green areas. The scheduled opening is Autumn, 2008. Allison pinpoints an intrinsic, but not often recognized reality: "Orchestras are civic leaders. They always have been. Atlanta doesn't have an historic legacy of the arts. We're building one in real time."

Miryam Yardumian

MIRYAM YARDUMIAN—*Pride of a Baker's Dozen;* Miryam Yardumian has been the Music Administrator of the Baltimore Symphony under **David Zinman** (1985–98) and **Yuri Temirkanov** (1999–2006). The third of thirteen children—nine girls and four boys—of composer Richard Yardumian (1917–85), she was born at home in Bryn Athyn, north of Philadelphia. Amazingly, her mother, Ruth, still found time to help her husband and write fiction. At age five, Miryam, who "always played the piano," wrote *The Happy Man and His Dump Truck*, a children's story published by Golden Books and translated into five languages. (To this day it is the second of the three most popular Golden Books!) She was taken to Philadelphia Orchestra concerts as soon as she was able to sit still, and met her father's friends, such as conductor Eugene Ormandy, pianist Rudolf Firkusny and many other celebrities. She was a Performance major at the University of Colorado, studying for a year with Storm Bull, a nephew of famed Norwegian violinist Ole Bull. The following year at Northwestern, she worked as an assistant to the music librarian. She took piano there, then went to Western Illinois University as a piano performance major.

In 1966, she was offered a job as secretary to conductor **Anshel Brusilow** (*b* 1928), which marked the beginning of her career in orchestra management. In the fall of 1967, she worked briefly at Carnegie Hall then entered the intensive weeklong ASOL seminar in management by **Helen Thompson**. (See The Unforgotten.) From

1971–73, Yardumian was general manager of the Cape Cod Symphony, then became public relations director of the New Orleans Symphony (1973–75), and assistant manager (1975–80). July 1980 saw Yardumian as artistic administrator of the Minnesota Orchestra under **Sir Neville Marriner**, a position she held until 1986.

Erasing the Memories

In 1985, Miryam began to have headaches, blurred vision and severe pains in the neck. A Cat-scan revealed the necessity for surgery. Although successful, the procedure resulted in complete loss of memory. Her friends and the orchestra's continuous support speeded her recovery. She went from taking fifteen minutes just to cross the street, with no vocabulary, through six months of watching TV, then using a word or hearing a piece of music and retaining and regaining it. She came back to the office and gradually increased her workday hour by hour. By 1986, she was education and orchestra production administrator.

Back on the Job

David Zinman, while guest conducting the Minnesota Orchestra, encouraged Miryam to interview for the post of Music Administrator of the Baltimore Symphony. She did so in March 1989, and started there in June of the same year, filling a position she has successfully maintained ever since, working with him during his tenure (1985–98) and then with his successor, **Yuri Temirkanov**.

The American Symphony Orchestra League - the Well-Spring

The American Symphony Orchestra League provides leadership and services enhancing the artistic and financial strength of American orchestras. Founded in 1942, and chartered by Congress in 1962, it promotes the quality, tradition and value of symphonic music. The League serves close to 1,000 member symphony, chamber, youth and university orchestras, supporting a network of thousands of musicians, conductors, managers, governing and service volunteers, staff, and business partners.

CATHERINE FRENCH—*Forging New Frontiers;* From October 1980, until her retirement, December 31, 1996, Catherine French was chief executive officer of the ASOL. She joined the organization as assistant director in 1974, and subsequently served as vice president for public affairs, chief operating officer, and executive vice president. In 1992, she was named president.

Born November 13, 1946, in Bergenfield, New Jersey, her childhood was filled with singing, in her family and school. During sixth grade, Catherine joined a church choir and was inspired by the director who taught her to read Gregorian Chant, an interest she maintained throughout high school and college. At Manhattanville College (Purchase, New York), she wanted to be a sacred music major, but focused instead on music history. Meanwhile, she worked at the Pius X School of Liturgical Music, a center for the study of chant—then attached to the college. This was a time of change for Catholicism, with Latin texts being translated into English. Because of her knowledge of Gregorian Chant, Catherine was assigned to adapting English texts into chant format, and finding appropriate music and composers for the liturgy. In her freshman year, she was asked to be the business manager of the Glee Club, and in this role produced concerts in New York with symphony orchestras. Glee Club director, Ralph Hunter, was dedicated to finding music written specifically for womens' voices, and sought out repertoire from the **Ospidale of Venice** where orphan girls from Vivaldi's time were tutored in music.

After graduation (1968), Catherine was offered a fellowship at NYU to study musicology, concentrating on the Renaissance era. This never bore fruit, because during that summer an advertisement in the *New York Times* caught her eye: "Wanted: Girl Friday to work in symphony office." And thus it was that three weeks out of college, she landed a job with the American Symphony Orchestra under the great **Leopold Stokowski** (1882–1977) who, with board president Samuel Rubin, ran the show. By 1970, the maestro had promoted Cathy to executive director, causing the *New York Times* to run a headline, "Girl to Manage American Symphony!" Stokowski left in 1972, and French accepted the position of manager of the New Jersey Symphony, headquartered in Newark. In the course of these positions, she attended ASOL conferences and was known to the league's leadership. In November 1974, she was invited to join them as assistant director. As CEO, she led significant expansions of programs for the league's 900 member orchestras, adding services for artistic personnel, volunteers and trustees, while further developing management and information assistance and strengthening the advocacy role.

Past president of the National Music Council, French has been a member of its board of directors as well as those of the American Arts Alliance, National Cultural Alliance, and the New York Pops. She is an executive committee member of the National Coalition for Education in the Arts and on the editorial advisory board of the Mandel Center for Non-Profit Organizations, Case Western Reserve University. She has also served on the board of trustees of her *alma mater*, Manhattanville College. She was selected by The Women's Philharmonic in San Francisco to be a part of their National Women Conductors Initiative, a program to assist women currently working as conductors.

After a lifetime of service, Catherine French has earned the right to say: "I have friends who talk about making money early in their careers so that when they turn fifty they can retire from business and do good works. It's occurred to me that I have spent a good portion of the last forty-nine years doing good works."[237] Her career, with all its contributions, has indeed been one that anyone can be proud of!

Since leaving the ASOL, she has formed the Catherine French Group, an independent consulting firm that specializes in recruiting chief executive and senior staff leadership for orchestras, opera companies, music presenters, festivals and schools of music.

As of 2004, she was also serving as chairman of board of the Washington Chorus, vice chairman of the board of overseers of the Curtis Institute of Music, and a member of the board of the New York Pops.

Preserving the Past and Safeguarding the Future - The Archivists

The history of an orchestra is in the legacy of printed material—concert programs, records, files of administrators and trustees, photographs—plus sound recordings, film, videos, etc., of the maestros and artists who have performed with it. In many cases these treasures have lain around for years moldering in a basement or storeroom. There is a pattern of sporadic attempts by volunteers, and/or a temporarily hired professional, to make order out of the accumulated chaos. It has only been in the last fifteen years that the top six American orchestras have acquired as part of their staff a qualified archivist to undertake what can be a lifetime occupation of properly cataloging the memories. By coincidence, five of the six major symphony archivists are women.

JOANNE BARRY was appointed the **Philadelphia Orchestra** (founded 1900) Association's first professional archivist in 1990, and in that capacity was responsible for the historical collections of both the Philadelphia Orchestra and the Academy of Music. She remained with them until the archives department closed in May 2004. While in Philadelphia, she was also active as a church organist.

Born January 21, 1953, in Alexandria, Virginia, after early training in piano and organ she earned her BA in organ from James Madison University (Harrisonburg, Virginia), and graduate study in musicology at Radford University, also in Virginia. Her archival training was from the University of Maryland (College Park), where she earned a master of library science. During this time, she served as a project archivist in the International Piano Archives at Maryland and Special Collections of Music.

In 1990, she married Kenneth Boulton, a Seattle native with a BA from Washington State, and MM and PhD degrees in piano performance from the University of Maryland. His teaching positions were at Shippensburg

---

237. From her statement at the annual meeting of the league's membership, June 14, 1996, Cincinnati, Ohio.

and West Chester Universities in Pennsylvania, and head of the piano department at the Wilmington Music School in Delaware.

Coinciding with the archives closing, her husband became music professor at Southeastern Louisiana University, and director of the Community Music School. Building on their fourteen years as a duet team, with concert appearances in the U.S. and Europe, JoAnne now appears regularly in recitals and lectures of music for piano-four hands with Kenneth. (Their new home narrowly missed the path of Hurricane Katrina in August 2005.)

BRIDGET CARR, archivist of the **Boston Symphony Orchestra** since 1991, trained in the library science program at Simmons College, earning an MLS in 1985. Before coming to the BSO, she held positions at the Massachusetts State Archives, MIT Archives, and the Houghton Library at Harvard University. Hired under a one-year grant that provided funds to start up an archives and records management program, the position became permanent at the end of that period.

As archivist, it is her job to ensure the materials that document the history of the BSO (founded 1881), including the Boston Pops, Tanglewood and Symphony Hall, are collected, preserved and made available for scholarly use.

On March 14, 2004, she and Robert Miller, a six year archival volunteer, presented an overview of the archive and a review of the extensive materials maintained for the BSO, Boston Pops, Symphony Hall and Tanglewood. They discussed the extensive broadcasting tape archive, going back to the 1950s, and the restoration processes for the more than 7,000 reel-to-reel tapes.

BARBARA HAWS was born September 14, 1954, in Beatrice, Nebraska. In 1983, she was awarded her MA in history from New York University, with a certificate in archival management. In 1984, she became the archivist/historian of America's oldest symphony, the **New York Philharmonic**, founded in 1834. She also acts as a consultant to the Chicago Symphony, the Los Angeles Philharmonic, and the Leonard Bernstein Collection. She has been the project archivist for the Papers of Jackie Robinson, the Papers of William Livingston, Governor of New Jersey during the American Revolution, and Trinity Church on Wall Street, which miraculously withstood the nearby collapse of the World Trade Center Towers, September 11, 2001.

Barbara is married to attorney William Josephson. They have a son, Eliot, born in 1987.

(Her able assistant historian, and my fount of information for many years, has been **Richard Wandel**.)

(To celebrate the twentieth anniversary of the Philharmonic Archives, a campaign was established whereby for a gift of $250 or more, one's name would be inscribed on a commemorative archival document that would become part of the Philharmonic's permanent history. Leadership gifts of $1,000 or more earned a private tour of the archives with Barbara.)

CAROL JACOBS has been the archivist at Severance Hall for the **Cleveland Orchestra** (founded 1918) since July 1990. In this position, she is responsible for reference services for researchers, preservation of material, assembly of exhibits, coordinating tours of the hall, and managing the oral history program.

Born January 16, 1947, in Minneapolis, to musical parents, she took piano and cello, but received her BA in history from the University of Minnesota, a master of library science from Kent State (Ohio), and archival training at Oberlin College.

The Cleveland Orchestra has the oldest formally organized archive (1982) of the Big Five American orchestras, including such treasures as a parchment with the signatures of the entire orchestra from the 1930s, and a rare photo of Elisabeth Severance, to whom the hall was dedicated by her husband, and who died in 1929 before the groundbreaking. (See The Unforgotten.)

Upon assuming the post in 1990, Jacobs was faced with a collection that had been neglected since 1986 when the prior archivist left. She gives frequent tours of Severance Hall, sharing her discoveries and making the archives more visible. 2000 saw the publication of *The Cleveland Orchestra Story: Second to None*, a book by local music critic Donald Rosenberg, written with invaluable assistance from the Archives, which was given full credit.

Jacobs is married to William, a corporate lawyer. They have three daughters: Amanda, born October 20, 1974, a counselor at Pace University and graduate student at Columbia (2002); Christina, who arrived December 3, 1977, and is an accountant with Ernst & Young; and Gwen, born April 30, 1981, who majored in economics at Ohio State. They are all classical music lovers—a good omen for our future audiences.

JUDITH JOHNSON, although not on the staff of an orchestra, deserves mention as director of information resources (archivist) of Lincoln Center. Born in March 1953, and although she heard little of it at home, had an inbred love of classical music. After receiving her bachelor's in psychology from Miami University of Ohio, she moved to New York in 1978, where she earned her master's in library science from Columbia in 1980. She has been in her present position since 1989.

BRENDA NELSON-STRAUSS, former archivist of the **Chicago Symphony Orchestra**, was born in Aberdeen, Washington, April 10, 1957. She began piano studies at age five and flute at twelve. She continued both instruments through college, and in 1980 received her degree in flute performance from Western Washington University. Although she continued with the flute at Indiana University, she chose a more demanding career, a master's in library science with music specialization, which she received in 1985. She also engaged in folklore/ethnomusicology course work toward an MA. She began her career at IU as archivist for traditional music, a position she held until 1989, when she became the first archivist for the Chicago Symphony.

Building on her IU experience, where she was librarian, sound recording archivist, and assistant director for library services, she took on the daunting task of planning, organizing, directing and promoting activities of the archives of the Chicago Orchestral Association. She established an archive program, and directed the move into a new facility, which housed a sound/video studio, reading room and climate-controlled vault. She developed the system for the arrangement and description of materials in the archives, and established a records management program.

Beginning in 1991, she gave presentations for the Society of American Archivists and the ASOL on Preservation Priorities for Audio-Visual Media and the Utilization of Orchestra Archives. She has numerous publications to her credit involving the history of the Chicago Symphony (founded 1891). Some of her most important contributions have been as co-project manager for the publication of recordings of the CSO. CDs released from the archives include: *Great Soloists with the Chicago Symphony Orchestra*, *The Reiner Era*, *A Tribute to Carlo Maria Giulini* and *A Tribute to Rafael Kubelik*.

When her husband, Konrad, was offered the position of head of the recording engineering faculty, Nelson-Strauss left the CSO Rosenthal[238] Archives August 2002 to return to her alma mater and become head of collections at the Archives of African American Music and Culture at IU (Bloomington). Her areas of specialization: performing arts archives and recorded sound collections. In 2004, having served as first vice president, she was elected president of the Association for Recorded Sound Collection (ARSC).

Upon Brenda's departure, her assistant, and *my* cooperative helper, **Frank Villella**, became sole archivist.

The only other major orchestra with an archivist on its staff is the Los Angeles Philharmonic, which had the knowledgeable **Orrin Howard** from 1993–2000. **Steven Lacoste** came on board in 1991, becoming chief archivist on Howard's retirement.

For future generations, the worth of an orchestra will be measured in the history preserved by these—and the many other—dedicated archivists.

---

238. The Rosenthal Archives were so officially named in January 1998. Samuel R. (1899–1994) and Marie Louise (1907–2003) Rosenthal first established a generous endowment for archival preservation in 1988, which was instrumental in founding the archives during the orchestra's centennial in 1990. In 1997, Mrs. Rosenthal made an additional contribution to the Capital Campaign, ensuring the future of the orchestra's archival collections. Through her generosity, the Rosenthal Archives was expanded into a full-service preservation and research resource, one of the most extensive facilities of its kind for an American performing arts organization.

Lady Phantoms of the Opera

OPERA COMPANIES

Sarah Billinghurst	MET	Assistant Manager
Janet Bookspan	—	Stage Director
Mary Brinegar	Dallas	Former Associate General Director
Ann Campbell	San Diego	Director of Strategic Planning
Joan Dornemann	MET	Coach/Prompter
Marianne Flettner	San Diego	Artistic Administrator
Carole Fox/Ardis Krainik	Chicago Lyric	Founder/Director
Christine Hunter	MET	Chairman (2005–)
Margaret Juntwait	MET	Announcer/Commentator
Elizabeth Kennedy	Los Angeles	Director of Administration
Koraljka Lockhart	San Francisco	PR & Data (1970–74, 1983–2004)
Janice Mancini Del Sesto	Boston Lyric	General Director
Patricia Mitchell	Los Angeles	Executive Director (1995-2000)
Eve Queler	Opera Orchestra of New York	Founder/Executive Director
Pamela Rosenberg	San Francisco	General Director (2001–05)
Christine Scheppelmann	San Francisco	Artistic Administrator (1994–2001)
" "	Washington National	" " (2002–)
Marilyn Shapiro	MET	PR, Assistant Mgr., Exec. Dir. (1975-2000)
Beverly Sills	MET	Chairman (2003–05)
Kim Witman	Wolf Trap	Coach (1985–), General Dir. (1997–)

STAGING AND DIRECTING

Jeannette Aster

Gigi Capobianco

Marta Domingo

Sonja Frisell

Rhoda Levine

Karen Stone

Julie Taymor

Francesca Zambello

Rarely seen onstage, women in opera companies throughout the world work alongside men in infinite capacities of artistic direction and production to put together the spectacular extravaganzas that involve us in fantastic plots peopled with larger-than-life characters inhabiting imaginary kingdoms—all a part of what may be cultured society's most ostentatious and expensive, but passionately soul-stirring art form. The following ladies are but a few among the many, in the Business of Opera.

SARAH BILLINGHURST—*From Kiwi Fruit and Orange Groves to the Big Apple*; when she became assistant manager of the Metropolitan Opera in August 1994, Sarah Billinghurst brought with her twenty-two years of experience at San Francisco Opera under three administrations. She joined SFO in 1972 as assistant to artistic administrator **Kurt Herbert Adler** (1905–88), graduating to assistant manager by 1982, producing all concerts, recitals and special presentations, including the annual free Opera in the Park concert. Her very special projects included co-productions with the Bolshoi Ballet (1987), Kirov Ballet (1989, 1992) and Kirov Opera's new production of *Russlan and Ludmila* (1995). Advisor to the SFO Center in its training and touring programs, she served on the San Francisco State Local Advisory Task Force for the Arts, charged with creating an arts policy plan for the city. She was also a member of the Professional Companies Panel of the Opera/Music Theater program (1991,'92,'93).

At the Met she reports directly to Met general manager **Joseph Volpe** (1996–2006), **David Gelb** (2006–) and artistic director **James Levine**, who began his "reign" in 1971. As at SFO, she is responsible for the artistic departments, presentations, media, park concerts, recordings and tours to Japan, the Met Orchestra in Europe, in the U.S., and the season at Carnegie Hall. She organized the Kirov Festivals which presented the Kirov Opera and the Kirov Ballet. Special events included the James Levine Twenty-fifth Anniversary Gala, anniversaries of Pavarotti and Domingo and New Year's Eve celebrations.

A native of Wanganui, New Zealand, Billinghurst graduated from Wellington's Victoria University with a degree in political science. She is the mother of two adult children, Alexander and Rebecca.

JANET BOOKSPAN—*Hats and Coats of Many Talents*; wife of noted music critic, administrator, broadcaster, commentator and author **Martin Bookspan**, Janet combines multiple musical careers of stage director of opera and music theater, drama coach, actress, musician and educator. She has directed over forty productions for opera companies in America, Europe and Mexico. Known for re-creating neglected works, as well as standard repertoire, her venues include the Caramoor (New York) Festival, Lyric Opera of Chicago, Delaware, Columbus and Connecticut Grand Operas, plus the American premiere of Auber's *Manon Lescaut* in New York, Los Angeles, and the Cervantino International Music Festival (Mexico). She was drama coach and dialogue director for the Harold Prince production of Kurt Weill's *Silver Lake* for the New York City Opera, and stage director/drama coach for several Met Opera Finalists concerts.

As a performer/narrator, Bookspan has appeared with major orchestras, including the Boston, Dallas, Indianapolis and Phoenix Symphonies, Philadelphia Orchestra and New York Philharmonic. She has participated in the Great Performers series and Live From Lincoln Center national telecasts.

Her recordings span from William Walton's *Façade*, based on poems of Edith Sitwell, to *The Story of Babar-The King of the Elephants*, with music by Francis Poulenc; the world premiere of David and Anne Lepstein's *Night Voices*, with the Boston Symphony; and the complete *Nutcracker*, co-narrated with her husband. *Voices from the Gallery*, by Stephen Paulus, libretto by Joan Vail Thorne, is a tour de force eleven-section monodrama, depicting known paintings or statues. Since its 1991 world premiere in New York's Merkin Concert Hall, she has performed this work throughout the country. It is on a 1995 CD. *The 6 Senses*, also by Paulus and Thorne, commissioned by the Boston Modern Opera Project, was premiered in 2002.

Born in Worcester, Massachusetts, as a young child Janet was shy and stuttered. Her mother took her to a special education teacher who discovered her talent and developed a fifteen-minute radio show, "Baby Jan and Her Friends," in which, as the central character, Janet sang and recited monologues. She became a local celebrity. She stopped stuttering and kept on singing, which blossomed into a career encompassing opera, music theater, movies, television, cabarets/night clubs, and narration in symphonic orchestra concerts.

With her MA in theater and speech from Boston's Emerson College, and in 1984 their Alumni Award for Achievement in Communication, Bookspan has served on the faculties of Juilliard, Curtis, Carnegie Mellon, Eastman, Manhattan School of Music, Baylor and North Carolina School of the Arts. She was past head of the opera department at SUNY, Purchase. Her "Dramatic Perspectives of 20 Roles and Arias for Soprano" is in *Singer's Edition*, published by PST Press.

Formerly artistic director of "Opera at Noon" at New York's historic St. Paul's Church, she is much in demand as a performance coach and has served in that capacity for Affiliate Artists, Inc., and the Concert Artists Guild. Her master teacher classes and residencies have been held in the U.S., Europe, Mexico, Canada and Israel. She is the performance and communications consultant to Florida's New World Symphony, and Michael Tilson Thomas' Academy Orchestra in Miami Beach. In spring 2000, she directed Stephen Sondheim's *Passion* for the twentieth anniversary of *Pro Musica Columbus* (Ohio).

Janet met Martin on a blind date in Boston, arranged by a friend who wanted Janet to interest the gentleman in *her*. This obviously did not happen. Janet and Martin have been happily married enough years for their three children, Rachel, David and Deborah, to present them with six lovely grandchildren—two apiece.

In whichever of her multiple roles Janet Bookspan can be found, she wears all her "hats" very well.

MARY BRINEGAR—*Fundraiser Supreme*; there are women with a special ability to get others to contribute to a worthy cause. Mary Brinegar, associate general director of the Dallas Opera 1987–97, is one of these. Although no longer in this position, her efforts over that decade are worthy of note. Born in Dallas, October 11, 1947, she was raised in a music loving home and taken to concerts and operas throughout her childhood. Her parents also set the example for community service. After her 1969 elementary education BA from Southern Methodist University, she launched her fund raising career in as associate director of development for KERA-TV where, from 1978 to 1986 she managed the Channel 13 Auction, the station's largest fund raiser each year. As vice president of marketing and development for the Science Place Museum, she coordinated raising $11 million in a two-year period, setting new records for membership growth and operating income. She promoted the exhibit "China - 7,000 Years of Discovery," acting as the gracious liaison to the Chinese artisan delegation.

In 1987, Dallas Opera general director, Plato Karayanis, recruited Brinegar to take charge of their fundraising. After her restructuring of operations in marketing, development and public relations, all previous season and single ticket sales skyrocketed. Board member and patron contributions rose dramatically, corporate donations doubled, total contributors increased 176 percent, and matching contributions nearly tripled.

Brinegar's awards and recognition include the 1981 *Extra Mile Award*, annually sponsored by the Business and Professional Women's Club of Dallas and given to one working woman who has distinguished herself by outstanding community service. In 1982, she was selected to be part of the *Leadership Dallas* class of fifty, a one-year course designed to train future leaders of the city. In 1985, she was chosen by the Texas Foundation of Women's Resources to be one of fifty in *Leadership Texas*, a year course for women to train future leaders of the state. In 1989, she was among the 100 participants from twenty-seven states for *Leadership America*, a program of the combined Foundations of Women's Resources. In 1984, she was honored as the *Fundraising Executive of the Year* by the Dallas chapter of the National Society for Fund-raising Executives. She is also in several *Who's Who* and Halls of Fame.

By 1995, Mary Brinegar's campaigns had raised $55 million. She left Dallas Opera in 1997 to take the position of president and general manager of the Dallas Arboretum.

ANN CAMPBELL—*A Unique Wife and Husband Team*; the director of strategic planning and special projects at San Diego Opera, Ann Spira was the third of four children born into a cultured Milwaukee family. With a fine mezzo range, she was a voice performance major at Indiana University, but decided against an operatic career. Both her parents were successful in business, which led her to a BA in communications (1978) from the University of Wisconsin, Madison, where she also pursued graduate studies. From working for United Way's $18 million annual campaign to Festivals Inc.'s sponsorship director of ChicagoFest, then the country's largest music festival, to development director of the Milwaukee Symphony, where she oversaw the orchestra's $20 million endowment drive, Ann was ready, in 1983, for the same position at San Diego Opera, in which capacity she served for sixteen years. In 1997, she was promoted to her present position, overseeing the Endowment Campaign and $7.5 million Annual Fund to make possible a schedule of fifty-five events, featuring five major operas from January through May, two solo recitals and other functions. Meanwhile, in 1985 she married the man who had interviewed her, general director **Ian Campbell**.

Their union has become one of the most enduring and creative partnerships in American opera. With a mutual support system, community relations and fund raising skills, they have placed SDO into America's top ten opera companies—deficit-free since 1985—after the ambitious, but financially-challenged, regime of **Tito Capobianco**, 1975–83.

She served on such varied boards as the World Trade Center of San Diego, Congregation Beth Israel, Scripps Memorial Hospital and the San Diego Youth Symphony, Ann also manages to find time for lecturing on fundraising at the ASOL, Opera America and the Association for Fund Raising Professionals, among others. In 2003, she joined the faculty of the University of San Diego, teaching the Resource Development Course for the master's degree of Not for Profit Management Program.

The Campbells' own ongoing challenge is to spend quality time with their two sons, Benjamin, born 1987, and David, 1989, whose interest in music has already led to piano, clarinet, trombone and guitar lessons. Besides attending rehearsals, the boys have appeared as extras in some of the operas directed by their father—Benjamin in *The Elixir of Love* (1996), and both in *Falstaff* (1999). As of 2007 Ben is a pre-med major in college, and David a high school senior.

CAROL I. CRAWFORD—General manager, Tulsa (Oklahoma) Opera. (See Conductors.)

JOAN DORNEMANN—Metropolitan Opera coach. (See Conductors.)

MARIANNE FLETTNER—*Met Talent Heads West*, Marianne Flettner is the artistic administrator of the San Diego Opera, headed by general director, Australian-born **Ian Campbell**.

Born August 9, 1933, in Frankfurt am Main (Germany), Marianne received piano lessons early in life, and was taken to student opera performances in her high school years. She earned a diploma from the Hessel Business College in Frankfurt (1953) and came to America in 1958 to learn English. After varied employment in other fields, she interviewed and got her first position at the Met in 1963 as the special assistant to legendary general manager **Rudolf Bing** (1902–97). From 1975–79, she was assistant company manager, supervising rehearsals, and for five years joined the company on their annual spring tour throughout the country, the most strenuous and rewarding part of her job.

In 1979, equally legendary producer Tito Capobianco persuaded Flettner to relinquish her position and join him at San Diego Opera as executive artistic assistant. It was a major decision, but helped by the fact that Marianne had a brother, sister, nephews and nieces in California. When Campbell became general director of SDO in July 1983, Marianne assumed her present role and has been a mainstay of San Diego Opera ever since.

CAROLE FOX and **ARDIS KRAINIK**—*Important Voices at Chicago Lyric Opera* (See The Unforgotten.)

CHRISTINE F. HUNTER—*Sitting in Beverly's Chair*, On February 10, 2005, Hunter was elected unanimously as chairman of the Metropolitan Opera after the unexpected resignation of Beverly Sills. On the Met's board of managing directors since 1983, she was elected to the executive committee in 1987, and became its chairman in May 2003. Besides her long association with the Met, she had served at Washington National Opera as president, chairman of the board, and chairman of the executive committee, successively, from 1974 to 2004. In that period, WNO's budget grew from $600,000 to $35 million. In the 1980s, she worked for several years on the Opera/Musical Theater Panel at the NEA.

Christine's family has long been affiliated with opera. She is chairman of the Gramma Fisher Foundation founded by her father, J. William Fisher in 1957, and named after his mother, Edna. He was a managing director of the Met for twenty-seven years, and a vice president when he died in 1990. The foundation has granted millions to the Met and other American opera companies and arts groups.

Hunter commented: "Following in the footsteps of Beverly Sills is an unenviable task. She brought a unique history and experience to our company . . . I am honored to be chosen for this position and look forward to serving the Metropolitan Opera in this new capacity."

ELIZABETH J. KENNEDY—*Voices from the City of the Angels*; The director of administration at Los Angeles Opera, Elizabeth was born in New York City, November 8, 1952, her parents having met at a piano competition in grade school. Growing up surrounded by music, her father, as she delightfully puts it, "avocationally but relentlessly played his entire life." Elizabeth began studies at seven. After receiving her BA in philosophy (SUNY, Purchase, 1974) and her master's in public administration (University of Missouri, 1979), she worked with the Arts Council in Kansas City. In 1986, the first season of Los Angeles Opera,[239] she was hired by them to implement outreach programs. She then worked in development, where she oversaw fund raising campaigns, including the prestigious "Angels" campaign—an elite group of twelve donors giving $1 million or more—and organized those fun opening night galas, which require an enormous amount of work behind the scenes. In 1994, she became manager of Individual Giving and, in 1999, associate director of development. After a brief foray in the private sector, she returned to LA Opera, October 2001, to assume her administrative position, whose duties include all business aspects of the company, including finance, development, marketing, human resources and public relations. She reports directly to general director Plácido Domingo.

Elizabeth and her husband, Frederick Roberts, an aerospace engineer, have three children, Matthew, born 1983, Emily, 1985, and Annis, 1992.

KORALJKA LOCKHART—*Sites of the San Francisco Opera*; Koraljka was born in Dubrovnik, Yugoslavia, attended high school and, simultaneously, music school. She never missed a performance of concerts, theater or opera, particularly during the renowned Dubrovnik Summer Festival. While studying English at the University of Zagreb, she was offered a job with the USIS Library, then attached to the American Consulate, and spent several years in the arts and reference section there. She returned to Dubrovnik, worked for a travel agency, and by 1963 managed to leave the country and work for American Express in Rome. After obtaining a stateless passport in Italy, she immigrated to the U.S. with the help of the United Nations' International Rescue Committee. Making her way to San Francisco, she became librarian and programmer for the top-rated classical music station KKHI (now unfortunately defunct). In 1970, San Francisco Opera famed general director **Kurt Herbert Adler** employed Kori as assistant in the public relations department, having hired her after a late-evening "pop quiz," writing a publicity "spot."

Her position was advanced to press representative and lasted until 1974 when, upon receiving one dose too many of her Austrian boss' fiery temper, she walked out. For the next four years, she worked as director of promotion for the Committee for Arts and Lectures (now Cal Performances) at UC Berkeley. Trying to get out of public relations work, she freelanced for a year, then accepted the position of acting public relations director for the San Francisco Symphony. Amazingly, Adler lured her back in 1980 to become publicity and publications director for SF Opera.

Tiring of the publicity facet, Lockhart stayed on for the next twenty years as publications editor, publishing the opera's elegant performance magazines until her semi-retirement, June 2001. In 1995, she pioneered the launching of the opera's website, writing most of its content for the next five years. Working from home between 2001–04, she completed an in-depth database, cataloging every performance, singer, role, chorister, orchestra member, board member and sponsor in the history of the opera and its subsidiaries since 1923—a gargantuan undertaking!

JANICE MANCINI DEL SESTO—*Singing on the Other Side of the Footlights*; as general director of Boston Lyric Opera, Janice Mancini Del Sesto combines musical training with organizational management and fundraising talents that have earned her a highly respected reputation for turning cultural institutions around. From 1982–88, she was the director of development and communications for the New England Foundation for the Arts, which she transformed from an organization reliant solely on government support to having a fund base

Janice Mancini Del Sesto

239. Los Angeles Grand Opera Association was founded in 1924 with Gaetano Merola, who had organized San Francisco Opera the year before, as general director. The association operated for ten years until the Depression. Visits by San Francisco Opera (1937–65) and NYCO (1967–82) brought the only opera productions to Los Angeles until, under the leadership of founding general director Peter Hemmings, Los Angeles Opera made its debut with Plácido Domingo in Verdi's *Otello*, October 1986.

from corporate and foundation sources. Following this, Del Sesto became president of Sponsorship Consultants of Boston which identified, evaluated, and managed a wide range of arts patronage.

Born December 13, 1949, in Providence, Rhode Island, Janice has music in her genes. Her grandfather had been a conductor in Italy, also teaching violin, piano and voice. At five, the child was playing piano by ear, and at six started formal lessons. From first grade on she sang in children's choruses. By high school, at age sixteen, she was a professional singer on a weekly radio church music broadcast, and commuted for private voice lessons.

Del Sesto has performed in opera, oratorio, recitals, concerts and festivals throughout the country, taught voice and theory, and conducted the Harvard-Radcliffe Chorus and the New England Conservatory's Preparatory Division's Youth Chorus, which performs and records with the Boston Symphony. She has been a visiting faculty member and lecturer at the Radcliffe Seminar Program at Harvard, Northeastern University, Emmanuel College and Rhode Island College.

By 1982, feeling the need for a career change and using the business skills honed in the many concerts she had produced, Janice established her own arts consulting company. In 1992 a national search brought her to Boston Lyric Opera, whose budget during her administration has soared from $1.2 to over $6.3 million, with donors multiplying from fewer than 400 to above 1,500, and subscribers increasing from 1,500 to more than 7,000. In the last decade, the company's budget has grown from sixty-fourth in size to fifteenth out of 115 U.S. opera companies.

Her big challenge was to find a new facility to replace the 850 seat baroque Emerson Majestic Theatre. In 1998, she announced the company's move to the renovated 1,500 seat Shubert Theatre. The inaugural season (1998–99) was sold out for all nine performances of three productions. This is now expanded to twenty-eight performances of four opera productions. In addition, Opera New England, BLO's education and community programs division, annually produces an opera for children seen by thousands of students and families across the area.

The largest professional opera company in New England, BLO is recognized for its commitment to debuts featuring some of the world's most exciting young singers, directors, designers and conductors, and launching the careers of many prominent stars, including Deborah Voigt, Lorraine Hunt Lieberson and Patricia Racette. BLO's strategic plan, "The Balanced Scorecard," is taught as a best practice case study at Harvard Business School.

Named in *Boston Magazine*'s 1993 "People to Watch" issue as a person "making a difference," by May 2003 the publication included Del Sesto in its list of the city's "100 Most Powerful Women." She has been featured in articles and symposia on women and management, sits on vocal competition juries and has chaired NEA panels. A former member of the Board of Trustees of the NEC, and an overseer of its alumni association, in 1995 she was given an outstanding Alumni Award in recognition of her achievements and distinction in the arts. In 2003, she received an honorary doctor of arts from Curry College.

In the fall of 2002, BLO made history with the first ever fully staged opera performances on the Boston Common that attracted 140,000 people over one weekend. Under Del Sesto's leadership, Boston Lyric Opera has been recognized by OPERA America, the service organization of opera companies, as the fastest-growing opera company in North America. Which is all very amazing, because ever since she could remember she wanted to become a doctor . . .

In 1973, Janice married her high school sweetheart, high-tech consultant Gregory Del Sesto.

PATRICIA MITCHELL—was executive director of the Los Angeles Opera from 1995 to 2000. (See Business Symphony Section.)

EVE QUELER—*A Premiere Woman;* Eve Queler is founder of the Opera Orchestra of New York, which gives young singers and instrumentalists performance experience without the expense of staging and scenery. (See Conductors.)

Pamela Rosenberg

PAMELA ROSENBERG—*Woman of the Golden West*; with the retirement of San Francisco Opera's renowned general director **Lotfi Mansouri**, part of the company since 1963 and in the top position since 1988, his successor, Pamela Henry Rosenberg, took over the reins August 2001, just one month before disaster hit America.

Born in Los Angeles, April 24, 1945, during her four years at UC, Berkeley Pamela attended every SFO production. This experience inspired her to follow a career in the arts. After graduating in 1966 with a degree in history and a music minor, her studies continued in Europe at the Guildhall School of Music and Drama, London Opera Centre, the Bayreuth Festival, and an apprenticeship at England's Glyndebourne Festival Opera.

By 1968, she had met and married musicologist/journalist Wolf Rosenberg, a guest professor at the University of Illinois (1968–70). Here, Pamela became administrative coordinator, assistant producer and stage manager for the opera workshop of Ludwig Zirner, and teaching assistant for History of Opera courses. When the couple moved to Ohio State, she earned a master's in Russian history. She also gave birth to twins Paolo and Alexander (Sascha), January 17, 1970.

The family returned to Germany in 1971, which led to positions as production manager at ZDF Television, assistant producer at Munich Chamber Opera, artistic administrator and member of the Direktorium for Frankfurt Opera during the legendary Michael Gielen era through 1987, manager of artistic affairs of the Netherlands Opera (1988–90), and director of operations at Hamburg's famed Deutsches Schauspielhaus (1987–88). Joint general director and director of operations for Stuttgart Opera came 1991–2000, whose seasons produce some 170 performances of twenty-two operas and eighty ballets. A consortium of fifty European journalists surveyed in *Opernwelt* (Opera World) magazine judged Stuttgart to be Europe's "Best Opera Company of the Year" for 1994, 1998, 1999 and 2000—all during Rosenberg's tenure.

Widowed in 1996, and with her sons established in business in Germany, Pamela returned alone to her native state to begin a new era in her life and tackle the artistic challenges at SFO.

At her first press conference at the War Memorial Opera House, January 9, 2001, she announced the contract extension of music director Donald Runnicles to 2006, and presented her ambitious four year plan of over twenty-five operas under the headings, **Animating Opera**: **Seminal Works of Modern Times**, featuring 20th century operas; **The Faust Project**, with three traditional and one to be commissioned work on the trading one's soul with the Devil theme; **Composer Portrait**, featuring works of Janáček and Berlioz; **Women Outside of Society**, with portrayals of *Turandot*, *Madama Butterfly*, *Kát'a Kabanová*, *Alcina* and *Lady Macbeth of Mtsensk*; **Metamorphoses**: **From Fairy Tales to Nightmares** includes *Hansel and Gretel*, *Cinderella* and *The Cunning Little Vixen*; **Utopia in the Age of Enlightenment** covers *Abduction from the Sergalio*, *Fidelio*, *The Magic Flute*, *Don Giovanni*, *Così fan tutte* and *The Marriage of Figaro*, and **Outsiders or Pioneers**: **The Nature of the Human Condition** as defined in *Billy Budd*, *The Flying Dutchman* and *Macbeth*.

The levelling of New York's World Trade Center buildings, one month into her directorship, put SFO, like most of the country, into the temporary economic downturn, and Rosenberg was forced to cut programming from twelve operas/eighty-five performances, to six operas/sixty-five performances, cancel ancillary concerts, disband the Western Touring Opera and reduce staff. Despite this, she managed in the next three years to overcome daunting deficits and keep the company on track.

In June 2004, Rosenberg announced that she would not be renewing her contract in 2006, but would go ahead with the 2005 premiere of John Adams' *Doctor Atomic*, commissioned by SFO, about nuclear physicist J. Robert Oppenheimer, as well as a new production of Berlioz' five-hour epic *Les Troyens*, originally scheduled for 2005, but postponed to 2008. She will also plan the 2006–07 season.

Comments from her colleagues attest to Rosenberg's success. From Seattle Opera's Speight Jenkins: "Pamela is a brilliant opera director who has handled a difficult economic problem as well as anyone I have ever known in opera . . . and brought exciting repertoire to San Francisco [changing] the expectations of . . . audiences in a way that one would not have thought possible."

David Gockley, general director of the Houston Grand Opera, concurred. "She wasn't able to implement her vision completely, but what she has done has set a terrific example for American companies."

Careerwise, Rosenberg maintains she wants to concentrate more on overseeing new operatic productions. Personally, she wants to be closer to her sons and two grandchildren who all live in Germany.

In July 2005, the Berlin Philharmonic named her as *Intendantin* (administrative director), the first woman, and first American to hold the post. Orchestra director Sir Simon Rattle welcomed the board's decision, commenting, "I look forward to a long and close collaboration."

Rosenberg was succeeded at SFO by David Gockley, who accepted the career change after having been with HGO since 1972, thirty-two years which transformed that company into one of the nation's most consistently successful organizations.

CHRISTINA SCHEPPELMANN—*From East to West and Back Again*; Washington Opera has a new artistic administrator as of January 2002. This is the second major post for Germany's Christina Scheppelmann, coming from the same position she held at San Francisco Opera from June 1994 to August 2001, where she was the youngest and first woman artistic administrator in their history.

Born in Hamburg, November 21, 1965, Christina's love of music began at an early age when she studied violin and voice at the Youth Conservatory of Hamburg, and for five years sang in the Children's Chorus of Hamburg State Opera, later spending three years in the Hamburg Philharmonic Choir. Surviving the most complex apprenticeship in Germany, a two year program netted a Banking /Economics Diploma (1988). She worked in a bank for only two months when she was offered a job with Walter Beloch Artists Management in Milan. Although she did not speak Italian or have a work permit, she managed to get there, and for the next four years learned all the responsibilities of being an agent: initiating auditions, selling the right artist for the right role, checking out theaters, organizing performance calendars, making travel arrangements, seeing to reservations, visas, tickets, doing follow-ups—even making sure the artist had his/her music. Accompanying Beloch to auditions and performances across Europe, she met singers and agents from all over the world and, for fun, while in Milan, she joined the Complesso Internazionale Cameristico (International Chamber Chorus) and also sang as a *supernumerary*—an opera "extra."

After four years, an offer came which realized her long-held dreams to work *in* opera, and in Spain where her father was born and raised, the son of a German father and Spanish mother. The Scheppelmanns had often vacationed there. Her father always spoke to the family in Spanish, while Christina spoke German to everyone else. (She is fluent in German, Spanish, Italian, French and English.) In 1992, Christina became assistant to artistic director Dr. Albin Hänseroth at the Gran Teatre del Liceu in Barcelona. She also worked briefly at the Teatro La Fenice in Venice. Her agenting experience enhanced the new, more complex tasks like casting, auditions, negotiating artists' contracts and supervising rehearsals.

The call to America in 1994 was immediately enticing—San Francisco Opera being one of the most respected houses in the world. Her strong music background and international experience with most of the world's leading opera stars, plus scheduling to the end of the century, proved Scheppelmann a worthy successor to the indefatigable **Sarah Billinghurst** who, after twenty-two years, left SFO to become assistant manager of the Met.

After seven successful years in the Golden West, Christina headed back East to give the benefit of her experience to opera lovers at Kennedy Center as artistic administrator at Washington Opera. She works very closely with the general director, Plácido Domingo, whom she met during her SFO years, and who personally invited her to Washington. Her duties cover putting the schedule together, hiring singers—and understudies—conductors, directors, the chorus, and the design team. She attends rehearsals to see that all is going smoothly. She is the problem-solver, handles union negotiations, deals with the budget and hires staff for the artistic department, the orchestra manager, and music librarian.

Add to this the fact that Domingo is always on the lookout for new and exciting voices,[240] Christina also judges vocal competitions and holds master classes, teaching young performers how to audition, how to present themselves and what this business is all about.

The 2004–05 season represented a new set of challenges with *Andrea Chénier*, Domingo conducting, *Billy Budd*, *Il trovatore*, a new production of the zarzuela *Luisa Fernanda*, a WNO premiere with Domingo singing,[241] *The Maid of Orleans* by Tchaikovsky, *Die Zauberflöte*, *Tosca*, *Samson et Dalila* and the world premiere of Scott Wheeler's *Democracy: An American Comedy*—all with English surtitles.

Even if Plácido gets all the glory, Christina has found her very important niche!

MARILYN SHAPIRO—*Financial Wizardry*, named the executive director for external affairs for New York's Metropolitan Opera in August 1990, Marilyn Shapiro was, for fifteen years, responsible for the development and marketing programs of this prestigious pillar of American culture. Born September 10, 1941, in Brooklyn, New York, and weaned on opera, one of her fondest childhood memories was listening to the Texaco Metropolitan Opera broadcasts with her grandmother. Piano lessons began at six, and she was taken to concerts and many operas. A Wellesley graduate in political science (1962), she was elected to Phi Beta Kappa in her junior year. Her master's in law and government is from Columbia (1965), where she was a Woodrow Wilson Fellow and a National Defense Education Act Fellow. She completed all the requirements for a PhD except her dissertation.

Her series of interesting careers began as a staff member of the Rockefeller Brothers Fund Special Studies Project on the Performing Arts. She was assistant to New York City Mayor John V. Lindsay, 1967–70. In 1972, she became a research consultant with *Future Shock* author Alvin Toffler. After three years, she went on to serve as administrative assistant to Representative Elizabeth Holtzman (D-New York), with whom she traveled to Washington.

Shapiro's Met career began in the fall of 1975, when she joined the staff as public affairs officer. By June 1977, she was directing the opera's development programs. Under her management, revenues increased from $12.6 million in 1978 to an estimated $42 million by 1991. In January 1981, she was named assistant manager of the Metropolitan Opera. In the spring of 1986, she assumed responsibility for the association's marketing programs. In the 1994–95 season, the Met box office was 93 percent subscriptions—the highest in a decade. She directed the $100 million Centennial Fund campaign, which created the first significant endowment in the Met's history. She also directed the Silver Anniversary Fund to raise $25 million for capital improvements to the facility in connection with the twenty-fifth anniversary of the Opera House at Lincoln Center, September 1991. In August 1990, Marilyn became executive director of external affairs. After an enviable track record, she retired August 31, 2000, but continues her affiliation with the MET as a consultant.

BEVERLY SILLS—*A Triumphant Return*, after an impasse of many years with Metropolitan Opera general director (1950–72) **Rudolf Bing** who, despite public clamor for Sills' appearance, somehow managed to either offer her roles in which she was not interested, or was unable to coincide with an open date in her schedule. The "Queen of Opera" as she was known during her amazing ten year career at NYCO, finally made her debut at the Met in 1975, at age forty-five, singing some one hundred roles until her retirement from the stage in 1979. (See 20th Century Prima Donnas.)

In October 2003, at age seventy-three, she became chairman of the Met, an unpaid position like her chairmanship of Lincoln Center (1994–2002). She had been on the opera board since 1991. With their budget at $200 million, of which $75 million comes from benefactors, Sills' talent as a fundraiser was ready to meet the challenge. She worked closely with **Joseph Volpe**, director of the Met from 1990, who started *his* career there as a carpenter in 1966! (Forty years later he would retire, August 2006, with David Gelb, CEO of SONY, assuming the position.)

---

240. Domingo's interest in helping young singers has led to his annual international competition *Operalia*, with prizes close to $200,000. Since 1993 its sites have been: Paris (twice), Mexico City, Madrid, Bordeaux, Tokyo, Hamburg, Puerto Rico, Los Angeles, Washington and Bregenz—a coalition of Switzerland (St. Gallen), Austria (Bregenz) and Germany (Friedrichshafen). In September 2004, the competition returned to Los Angeles. Winners receive international recognition, and Domingo follows through in furthering their careers.
241. Both Domingo's parents, Pepita and Plácido Sr., sang in *zarzuelas*, a form of Spanish operetta.

For "Bubbles," as Beverly has been affectionately known since childhood, whose retirement from singing in 1980 "to smell the roses" just gave her an "allergy" to sitting around the house, the new job presented new fields to conquer, and a new role to play. On January 25, 2005, however, she made an overnight decision to resign her position, effective immediately, citing health reasons—she had experienced three fractures within a year, the most recent on her knee—and the necessity of placing her husband, Peter Greenough, for whom she had been caring the last eight years, in a nursing home. She leaves a large vacuum.

Her successor is **Christine F. Hunter**.

KIM PENSINGER WITMAN—*Springing from Wolf Trap*; general director of the Wolf Trap Opera Company, Kim Pensinger Witman is part of a foundation/not-for-profit corporation which administers programs at the internationally acclaimed Wolf Trap Farm Park, Filene Center,[242] an outdoor amphitheater seating 7,000, and the Barns of Wolf Trap, an intimate 350-seat venue. One of the largest presenting arts organizations in America, with a yearly operating budget in excess of $25 million, the facility presents over 300 performances annually, serving an audience base of over 500,000 patrons.

Witman was born in Hagerstown, Maryland, June 21, 1957. Although not from a musical family, her parents supported her interest in music with piano lessons at age six, followed by clarinet at nine and organ at twelve. She received her BS from Elizabethtown College (Pennsylvania, 1978), and MM in Piano from Catholic University (Washington, DC, 1983). She became interested in opera during graduate school, working as a teaching assistant in the opera program. At Wolf Trap, she began as an opera coach in 1985, moving on to principal coach, chorus master, music administrator and, since 1997, general director, a position in which she supervises national auditions, repertoire selection, production development and education programs via the Wolf Trap Institute for Early Learning, as well as staging three operas each year.

In addition to being an active performer in the Washington, DC area, she was a coach at Washington Opera (1986–95), music administrator (1988–92), and assistant conductor for Washington Concert Opera. She has been on the adjunct faculties at University of Maryland Opera Studio and Peabody Conservatory. She serves as a judge for vocal competitions, including the Metropolitan Opera National Council Auditions.

Married to music educator Don Witman, they have two children, Alexandra, born January 23, 1986, and Benjamin, May 1, 1990.

La forza dietra del scena

Women are not only behind the scenes in the *business* of opera, but have made their mark *staging* and *directing* opera.

JEANETTE ASTER—*The World is Her Stages!*; a native of Canada, Aster studied production at London Opera Centre. In 1974, she joined Netherlands Opera and was resident director there (1976–80). She made her Canadian debut as stage director in 1977 at the National Arts Centre in Ottawa with Mozart's *The Magic Flute*, the first live opera telecast by the CBC. She has staged numerous productions for Canadian Opera Company, including *La Cenerentola*, *The Barber of Seville*, *La traviata* and *Lucia di Lammermoor*. At the Ontario Stratford Festival she co-directed *Twelfth Night*, later adapting this production for a U.S. tour and CBC telecast. In Europe, Aster has directed at the Hamburg, Zurich and Berlin Operas, among others. She was responsible for mounting LA Opera's productions of *Salome* at Convent Garden and *Tristan und Isolde* at the Maggio Musicale, Florence.

She first joined Los Angeles in its inaugural season as associate director for *Otello* and *Salome*. She worked with Götz Friedrich on *Kát'a Kabanová*, then directed the revival of *Otello*. In 1990, she directed Verdi's *Falstaff* for L.A. and was artistic director of Opera Lyra, Ottawa (Canada), for whom she staged *La bohème* and *Carmen*. The next season's credits included Sir Michael Tippett's *New Year* at Glyndebourne and assistant director for a new production of *Samson and Delilah* at Vienna State Opera. 1996 brought *Salome* at Detroit's Michigan Opera Theatre. In

---

242. See The Unforgotten: Catherine Filene Shouse.

November 2000, she directed *Madama Butterfly* for the International Donau (Danube) Opera, a touring company headquartered in Rousse, Bulgaria and, in October 2002, restaged *La bohème* for Opera Ontario.

GIGI ELENA DENDA CAPOBIANCO—*An Operatic Husband and Wife Team*; called a child prodigy at age eight, Gigi was accepted at the National Conservatory of Dance in Buenos Aires. At thirteen, she became the youngest licensed instructor, and at seventeen was an acclaimed prima ballerina. Despite a secure future ahead in the world of dance, at twenty she decided to marry and have a family. While this marked the end of her career as a prima ballerina, it opened another avenue in the arts. She became the right hand of her husband, the flamboyant and charismatic opera director **Tito Capobianco**, born in Argentina, 1931.

In the course of their forty-plus years of marriage, Gigi has been responsible for creating the choreography, make up and lighting which breathes life on stage for such operatic greats as **Beverly Sills**, **Plácido Domingo** and **Luciano Pavarotti**.

In 1984, she made her Pittsburgh Opera directorial debut with *Manon*, followed in 1985 by her direction of *Tosca*. Her international credits as director, choreographer and lighting designer include performances in Hamburg, Berlin, Paris, Sydney, Buenos Aires, New York and San Diego.

The famous couple and their two sons have traveled throughout the world, bringing grand opera to thousands.

MARTA DOMINGO—*The Diva of Opera's Dynamic Duo*; Marta Ornales, born into an artistic family in Veracruz (Mexico), was studying piano and composition by age eight. Surrounded by books and music, she was taken to opera and theater and, as a teen, entered the National Conservatory in Mexico City to study singing. She was already established in that city's Opera Belles Artes—her numerous soprano roles included Marguerite, Mimì, Rosina and Donna Elvira, with Mexican critics naming Marta as the country's best Mozart singer for her performance as Susanna in *The Marriage of Figaro*—when twenty-year-old Plácido Domingo joined the company in 1961.

After a thirteen-month courtship, the young couple married and worked at their respective careers, initially moving to Tel Aviv for three years as apprentices of the Opera Company of Israel, singing an average of ten performances a month. Marta was pregnant when, in late 1965, they came to New York where Plácido had his first big triumph. After their sons were born, Plácido, Jr., October 21, 1965, and Alvaro, October 11, 1968, Marta willingly switched to full-time mothering. In 1991 a mutual friend, director Guillermo Martinez, was overcommitted and asked Marta to utilize her operatic talents and experience. With her husband's full support, she made her directorial debut with *Samson et Dalila* at Teatro de la Opera in San Juan, Puerto Rico. Next came *Tosca* in Seville's La Maestranza Theater (1992), with Plácido and **Maria Ewing**, *Rigoletto* at Los Angeles Opera with Plácido, and *Il barbiere di Siviglia*, again in Puerto Rico. These successes were followed by *La traviata* in Caracas (Venezuela), *Fedora* with Lyric Opera of Chicago, and a well-researched new interpretation of Puccini's *La Rondine* in Berlin. April 2001 saw the premiere of *The Tales of Hoffmann* at the Mariinsky Theatre in St. Petersburg (Russia), which she restaged for Kennedy Center and LA Opera. 2002 marked a return to the Met with Plácido in the title role of *Sly*, by Ermanno Wolf-Ferrari, with **Maria Guleghina**, based on the *Introduction to Shakespeare's Taming of the Shrew*, which Marta had resurrected and restaged for Washington Opera in 1999. May 2004 brought *La traviata* to DC.

For over thirty-five years, Madame Domingo has been her husband's unofficial coach and critic. He listens to her first. Of their sons, one is a composer and the other a film producer. Placido Jr., has already given them two granddaughters, Victoria, born 1995, and Paloma, 1997. In her sixties, when she was working, Marta was still putting in a twelve-hour day on her feet. But she does not consider this "work." She calls it *pleasure*, and "the logical development of my life."

In her own opinion, Marta Domingo has not had to live in her husband's shadow, and there have been no sacrifices, even during his terms as artistic director of Washington (1996–2000) and Los Angeles Operas (2000–04).[243] This woman has succeeded in all her roles: a fine singer, a supportive wife, a good mother, and an innovative director.

---

243. By 2006, Placido was going strong as general director in Washington, and Los Angeles—apparently with extensions to both contracts.

SONJA FRISELL—*A Woman Pioneer in an Alien Field*; born August 8, 1937, in Richmond, Surrey (England), Sonja studied piano and acting at Guildhall, and began her career in 1958 at a time when opera did not have women working in directorial positions, thus making it difficult to gain the respect of the singers, musicians and agents. Her main influences were famed French director **Jean-Pierre Ponelle** (1932–88), and the celebrated Italian **Franco Zefferelli** (*b* 1923), known for his innovative staging.

Frisell was associated with La Scala (Milan) for fifteen years, becoming staff producer there in 1972, and director of production, 1974–79. She made her American debut with Lyric Opera of Chicago, staging Mussorgsky's *Khovanshchina* in 1969, and has returned to this company for *Lucia di Lammermoor*, *La bohème*, *Simon Boccanegra*, *Un ballo in maschera*, *Il trovatore*, and *La traviata* (October 2001). Her Los Angeles Opera debut was in April 1990, directing Verdi's *Don Carlo*. A frequent guest at San Francisco Opera, her productions there have included a new staging of *The Marriage of Figaro*, *Khovanshchina*, *A Masked Ball* and Rossini's *Maometto II*.

Her work has been seen in La Fenice (Venice), Teatro Colón (Buenos Aires), as well as the opera companies of Rio de Janeiro, Paris, Rome, Edmonton (Alberta, Canada), Dallas, Miami, Philadelphia and San Diego. Other career highlights are *L'Italiana in Algieri* (Covent Garden), *Ballo in maschera* (Bologna), *La forza del destino* (Washington, DC), which has also seen her *Otello* (2000), *La cenerentola*, and *Don Carlo* (2001) at Kennedy Center—the latter a part of the centenary celebrations of Verdi's death.

Frisell's Met debut in 1989, with a new *Aida*, opened the season and was telecast on PBS' "Live from the Met" series. She returned there with the same opera October 1998, and January 2001. July 2001 found her back at La Scala with *La cenerentola*, followed by *L'Italiana in Algieri* in 2002. Her *Otello* again strode across the boards in 2003, this time at San Diego Opera. 2004 found her in Helsinki, Manitoba, Calgary, Arizona and Kentucky. So the momentum continues.

With over forty years' experience in the most important opera houses of the world, while Frisell's work is now highly respected, there remain those insidious shreds of resistance from female singers who cannot get used to being "commanded" by a woman.

RHODA LEVINE—*A Prolific Producer!* Rhoda Levine is a director and choreographer, college professor and author, with a BA from Bard College. She has directed productions at Chicago Opera, Houston Grand, San Francisco, Seattle and Utah. European venues include the Netherlands, Belgium and Scottish Operas. She directed the South African premiere of *Porgy and Bess* and the world premiere of *The Kaiser from Atlantis*. Her NYC Opera productions include the world premiere of *X, The Life and Times of Malcolm X* (September 1986), *The Ballad of Baby Doe* (October 1988), *House of the Dead* (August 1990), *Die Soldaten* (October 1991), *Mathis der Mahler* (September 1995), *Of Mice and Men* (November 1998) and *Lizzie Borden* (March 1999).

Regional opera productions include Kentucky's *Susannah* (1999), *Figaro* (2002) for the seventieth anniversary of Milwaukee's Florentine Opera, and *Of Mice and Men* celebrating Steinbeck's 100th birthday (March 2003), *Slip Knot*, Northwestern University (April 2003), *Little Women*, NYU (April 2003), *The Good Soldier Schweik*, Glimmerglass (New York, July/August 2003) and *Of Mice and Men*, New York State Theater (October 2003), and Opera Omaha (2004).

Levine teaches at NYU, Mannes, Manhattan School of Music, Curtis and Northwestern, where she has been visiting director of opera since 1996. She was previously on the faculties of Juilliard and Banff Center for the Arts. She is also the founding director of *Play It by Ear*, the improvisational opera group at American Opera Projects, as well as being creative consultant to composer Philip Glass and others. As an author, Levine has written eight children's books and provided libretti for Stanley Hollingsworth and Luciano Berio. She is a recipient of the National Institute for Music Theater Award.

KAREN STONE—*The British Invade Germany and America . . . again!* Newly appointed general director of Dallas Opera in 2003, Karen Stone rejoins music director Graeme Jenkins. The two worked together at Germany's prestigious Cologne Opera (1995–2000).

Born in Horsforth, Yorkshire (England) in 1952, Karen studied piano and voice at the RAM, where she was the recipient of the Isobel Jay Memorial Prize (1970–73), and at Rome's Conservatorio di Santa Cecilia (1973–76). After beginning her career in Germany as a singer, she went behind the scenes, becoming assistant director at the Freiburg State Theater. Her 1985 directing at English National Opera and the Royal Opera House, Covent Garden, opened doors to positions around the world. Among the many operas she has staged are *Un ballo in maschera* for the Brighton Festival (England) and Opéra de Monte Carlo, *Manon Lescaut* (Munich), *Tosca* (Houston Grand Opera), *The Flying Dutchman* (Auckland, New Zealand), *Rigoletto* and *Lucia di Lammermoor* (Santa Fe de Bogotá, Colombia), plus *Così fan tutte* and *Don Pasquale* (Cologne). One of her historic productions was working with Jonathan Miller on *Don Giovanni* at the Maggio Musicale Fiorentino (Florence), which she re-staged for Los Angeles Opera in 1999.

Settling once again in Germany in 1995, Stone became deputy director of opera and director of the opera Studio at Cologne's State Theater. In 1998, she was promoted to the top: general director of Cologne Opera (1998). In the two years previous to her appointment in Dallas, she was the general manager of the Theaters of Graz (Austria), where she handled programming and casting of nine operas, eleven plays and ten children's productions.

JULIE TAYMOR—*Out of the Volcano*; with her background of method acting, mime, film making, dance and puppetry, Taymor's work ranges from extravaganzas of ingenious staging to the sparsest of scenery. Born December 15, 1952, in Boston, to gynecologist Melvin Lester and political science teacher Elizabeth, she began working with masks when studying at L'École de Mime in Paris. Back in the U.S., she attended Oberlin College, refined her acting style at the Herbert Berghof School and studied anthropology at Columbia University.

With a Watson Fellowship (1975–79) to research theater and puppetry in Eastern Europe and Asia, in Indonesia she studied Javanese shadow puppetry and formed a mask/dance company, Teatr Loh, producing plays with masked dancers and life-size puppets, which performed in Java, Sumatra and Bali. Returning to New York, she began designing productions, progressing to directing in 1984, producing plays off Broadway. She directed and designed productions of Shakespeare's *The Tempest* (1986), *The Taming of the Shrew* (1988) and *Titus Andronicus* (1994), all lauded for their originality.

Taymor entered the opera scene when Maestro **Seiji Ozawa** asked her to stage *Œdipus Rex*, starring **Jessye Norman**, for the first annual Saito Kinen Festival in Japan in 1992. Her film of the opera won the Jury Award at the Montreal Festival of Films on Art, a 1993 Emmy Award and 1994 International Classical Music Award. In 1993, she directed *The Magic Flute* for Maggio Musicale in Florence, with Zubin Mehta, and in 1995, *Salome* for Kirov Opera, St. Petersburg (Russia), Germany and Israel, and *The Flying Dutchman* for Los Angeles Opera in a co-production with Houston Grand Opera. It was restaged in Los Angeles, April 2003.

Her musical-theater work, *Juan Darién: A Carnical Mass*, co-written with longtime collaborator, composer Elliot Goldenthal, received two OBIES and five Tony Award nominations, including best director. In 1998, she won a Tony Award for direction of a musical for *The Lion King*, which had opened in 1997 at the New Amsterdam Theater (New York). Her feature film directing debut was in 1999 with *Titus*, starring Anthony Hopkins and Jessica Lange, based on Shakespeare's *Titus Andronicus*. Other directing credits came with *The Haggadah*, a Jewish "Passion" play, *Transposed Heads*, based on the novella by Thomas Mann, and *Liberty's Taken*, a musical co-created with David Suehsdorf and Elliot Goldenthal. Carlo Gozzi's *The Green Bird*, first staged at the La Jolla Playhouse (San Diego) in 1996, was presented on Broadway in 2000. Further awards include the 1990 Brandeis Creative Arts Award and, in 1991, the coveted MacArthur Genius Fellowship and Guggenheim Fellowship. Taymor also won the first Dorothy Chandler Performing Arts Award in Theater. In 2002, she directed *Frida*, the biography of Mexican artist Frida Kahlo, wife of muralist Diego Rivera. Starring Salma Hayak and Antonio Banderas, the film was rated as one of the Top Ten by the American Film Institute.

An illustrated book on her career, *Julie Taymor: Playing with Fire - Theater, Opera, Film*, was written by Eileen Blumenthal (Abrams, 1995; updated, 1999), and her own book, *The Lion King: Pride Rock on Broadway*, was published by Hyperion (1997). A retrospective of twenty-five years of her work opened in the fall of 1999 at the Wexner Center for the Arts in Ohio, toured the National Museum of Women in the Arts (Washington, DC) and the Field Museum (Chicago).

A new production of *The Magic Flute* for the Met came in October 2004. Another project with Goldenthal is an original opera, *Grendel*, based on John Garner's retelling of the *Beowulf* legend, into which Taymor incorporates puppets and a revolving stage. Premiered at Los Angeles Opera, June 2006, it was subsequently staged for the tenth anniversary of the Lincoln Center Festival in July—all to great acclaim.

It has been said that in all facets of her work, Julie Taymor manages to "recapture the primitive energy once possessed by art." The reviews of *Grendel* certainly corroborated that!

FRANCESCA ZAMBELLO—*The Who's Who and What's What of Grand Opera!* Born in New York, August 24, 1956, and raised in Europe, Francesca's first opera was *Madame Butterfly* at Covent Garden when she was five, with a first impression of "a very large person making a very large sound." Fluent in French, Italian, German and Russian, she attended Moscow University in 1976 and graduated *cum laude* from Colgate University (New York State) in 1978. She began her career as assistant director to Jean-Pierre Ponnelle (1932–88). Returning to the U.S., she was co-artistic director, with Stephen Wadsworth, at Starlight Opera Theater (Milwaukee) for eight years. Her 1984 American debut was at Houston Grand Opera with *Fidelio*. Her European debut came in 1987 at Teatro la Fenice (Venice) with *Beatrice di Tenda*. Not afraid to be innovative, her productions reflect realism and sensuality. In August 1998, she directed *Tristan and Isolde* at Seattle Opera with all singers in debut roles, promulgating that company's claim as North America's pre-eminent Wagner producer.

Zambello's best known new operas are Daniel Catán's *Florencia en las Amazonas* (Houston, 1996), Tobias Picker's *Emmeline* (premiered Santa Fe and NYCO, 1998), Carlisle Floyd's *Of Mice and Men* (Bergenz [Austria] Festival, 2001; Washington Opera, 2001; Houston, 2002), and Picker's third opera, *Thérèse Raquin* (Dallas, 2001; L'Opéra de Montréal, 2002; and San Diego, 2003).

Zambello also promotes new music, theater works and opera for larger audiences worldwide. She prefers to work on each production a year ahead. In attempting to recreate each composer's intentions, she imbues new life into the standard repertory, filling opera houses to capacity.

Two Decades in the Life of An Opera Director

Because Francesca Zambello's body of work is SO impressive and extensive, the author bends her overview rules in this instance to give the reader an idea of the abilities and scope of one woman in this specialized field:

1984: *Fidelio*, Houston Grand Opera, (HGO-American debut); *L'Enfant et les Sortilèges*, Wolf Trap; *Albert Herring*, Savonlinna Opera Festival, Finland; *The Maropolous Case*, Skylight Opera Theater (Milwaukee); *La traviata*, Student Cast, SFO.

1985: *Rossini double bill*, Wolf Trap, Washington, DC; *Don Pasquale*, Skylight Opera Theater; *Tosca*, National Opera of Puerto Rico; *The Mikado*, National Opera of Iceland.

1986: *Cavalleria rusticana/Pagliacci*, Miami Opera; *Faust*, HGO; *Barber of Seville*, National Opera of Iceland; *Carmen*, Texas Opera Theater; *Tosca* Puerto Rico Opera with **Plácido Domingo**.

1987: *La cenerentola*, Opera Theater of St. Louis; *Bianca e Falliero*, American premiere, Miami; *Beatrice di Tenda* with **June Anderson**, Teatro La Fenice (European debut); *Faust*, SFO.

1988: *La bohème*, SFO (Video/Telecast with **Luciano Pavarotti**); *Don Giovanni*, New Israeli Opera, Tel Aviv; *Salome*, HGO; *The Devil and Kate*, Wexford Festival (Video/Telecast UK, Ireland); *Faust*, Seattle, San Diego; *Carmen*, Skylight Opera Theater; *L'elisir d'amore*, Teatro Regio, Parma (Italy).

1990: *La traviata*, Skylight Opera Theater (rewritten with Dumas text); *Ariadne auf Naxos*, Rome Opera; *War and Peace*, Seattle Goodwill Festival (Telecast Japan, England, France); *Xerxes*, Young Arts Program, Antwerp, Belgium.

1991: *Lucia di Lammermoor*, Dublin Grand Opera; *L'Assedio di Calais*, 20th Century Premiere, Wexford Festival; Berlioz' *Les Troyens*, American premiere of complete work, Los Angeles Opera; *Tosca*, Earls Court Arena, London, eight performances with 12,000 seating capacity, plus live relay; *La bohème*, Teatro Regio, Parma; *Oedipus*, American Premiere, Sante Fe Opera Festival.

1992: *Lucia di Lammermoor*, the Met; *Il Pirata*, Swiss Premiere, Zurich Opera House; *The Sorrows of Young Werther*, American Premiere, Santa Fe Opera Festival; *L'elisir d'amore*, Teatro Regio, Parma; *Benvenuto Cellini*, Swiss Premiere, Grand Theatre De Geneve; *L'Occasione Fa Il Ladro*, Teatro Massimo, Palermo, Sicily.

1993: *Jenůfa*, Dallas Opera; *Orphée*, world premiere, American Repertory Theater, Harvard, Brooklyn Academy of Music; *Cherevichki*, Wexford Festival (premiere of work outside Russia); *The Midsummer Marriage*, premiere, NYCCO; *La traviata*, Orange Festival, France (telecast); *Falstaff*, Göteborg Opera, Sweden; *Il Pirata*, Luzanne (Switzerland); *Romulus Hunt*, world premiere, the Met (recorded, EMI); *The Honey Spike*, world premiere, Abbey Theatre, Dublin.

1994: *Street Scene*, HGO; *Billy Budd*, Grand Theatre de Genève (Swiss telecast for Europe); *La Rondine*, English premiere, Opera North, Leeds; *The Barber of Seville, Blond Eckbert* (American premiere, Sante Fe Opera Festival; *Khovanshchina*, English National Opera (ENO), London, (Olivier Award for Best Opera Production).

1995: *Billy Budd*, Royal Opera House, Covent Garden, conductor **Robert Spano** (Olivier Award for Best Opera Production); *Street Scene*, Theater Des Westens (Berlin Premiere Telecast. Best Opera Video of the Year Prize for Europe from Global Video Arts); *Tannhäuser*, Royal Danish Opera, Copenhagen; *Modern Painters*, world premiere, Sante Fe Opera Festival; *Arianna*, world premiere, Royal Opera House, Covent Garden; *The Demons*, world premiere, American Repertory Theater, Loeb Center, Harvard University.

1996: *Billy Budd*, Opéra Bastille, Paris; *The Tales of Hoffmann*, State Theater, Essen (Germany); *Prince Igor*, SFO; *Die Meistersinger von Nurnberg*, Royal Danish Opera, Copenhagen; *Florencia en el Amazonas*, HGO, Los Angeles and Seattle Operas, Cervantes Festival, Opera Bogotá.

1997: *Lady in the Dark*, Royal National Theatre, London; *La traviata*, Opera de Bordeaux; *Iphigénie en Tauride*, Glimmerglass, NYCO; *Turandot*, Opéra Bastille, Paris; *Paul Bunyan*, Royal Opera House, Covent Garden at the Aldeburgh Festival.

1998: *Madama Butterfly*, HGO, San Diego, Grand Théâtre de Genève; *Flying Dutchman*, Opera de Bordeaux; *Emmeline*, Sante Fe, NYCO; *Salammbo*, Opéra Bastille, Paris; *Tristan and Isolde*, Seattle Opera (Production of the Year award, *USA Today*); *Dialogues of the Carmelites*, Saito Kinen Festival, Japan (telecast for Japan and Asia in co-production with Opéra de Paris); *Boris Godunov*, ENO (nomination for Best Opera Production, Olivier Awards, *Evening Standard* Award for Best Performance); *The Bartered Bride*, Royal Opera, Covent Garden, re-opening of Sadler's Wells Theater (BBC live telecast).

1999: *Paul Bunyon*, Royal Opera, Covent Garden; *Otello*, Bavarian State Opera (Munich); *Dialogues of the Carmelites*, Santa Fe Opera, Opéra de Paris, Palais Garnier (joint production with Saito Kinen Festival, Japan); *Turandot*, Opéra Bastille, Paris; *Aida*, Grand Theatre de Geneve.

2000: *War & Peace* (Critics' Circle Grand Prix, DVD, 2001); *Luisa Miller, Napoleon*, Shaftsbury Theatre, London; *Peter Grimes*, Netherlands Opera.

2001: *Florencia en el Amazonas*, HGO; *The Queen of Spades*, Royal Opera House, London; *Of Mice And Men*, Bregenz Festival (Austria); *ARSHAK II*, SFO; *Billy Budd*, Opéra de Paris, BBC 1 Musical Gala; *Of Mice And Men*, Washington Opera; *The Bartered Bride*, Royal Opera House, London; *Jenůfa*, SFO; *Thérèse Raquin* (world premiere), Dallas Opera.

2002: *Don Giovanni*, Royal Opera House, Covent Garden; *Of Mice And Men*, HGO; *Flying Dutchman*, Bordeaux Opera; *Madama Butterfly*, Pittsburgh Opera; *La Vestale*, ENO; *Boris Godunov*, Canadian Opera, Toronto; *Lady Macbeth of Mtzensk*, Australian Opera, Sydney.

2003: *The Trojans*, the Met; *William Tell*, Opéra National de Paris; *Pique Dame*, Grand Theatre de Geneve; *Thérèse Raquin* and *Madama Butterfly*, San Diego; *Fidelio* and *Die Walkyrie*, Washington Opera; *The Little Prince*, HGO; *West Side Story*, Bregenz; *Alcina*, New York Opera; *Don Giovanni*, Royal Opera House; *Il Travatore*, Opéra National de Paris; *The Little Prince*, Sante Fe Opera.

2004: *Tibet Through the Red Box*, Seattle Children's Theater; *La bohème*, Royal Albert Hall; *The Little Prince*, Skylight Music Theater, Milwaukee; *Peter Grimes*, Amsterdam Music Theater; *Fiery Angel*, Bolshoi Theater, Moscow; *West Side Story*, Bregenz; *Billy Budd*, Washington Opera; *Madama Butterfly*, HGO; *Dialogues des Carmelites*, Paris Bastille Opera; *Elektra*, Tokyo New Opera; *Jenůfa*, Dallas Opera; *The Little Prince*, Houston.

2005: *Luisa Miller*, Dallas; *War and Peace*, Bastille Opera.

As is evident, the world of opera provides many opportunities for women to hone their myriad managerial, organizational and directorial talents. It can be observed that, at least in this arena, there appears to be a wider opening in the glass ceiling.

Publishers — Music Between the Sheets

Stephanie Challener	Musical America	Publisher
Susan Feder	Schirmer	Vice President/Director of Promotion
Sylvia Glickman (1932–2006)	Hildegard Publishing	Founder/President
Linda Golding	Boosey & Hawke	President
Elaine Gorzelski	Harmonie Park Press	President
Barbara Harbach	Vivace Press	President
Florence Howe	Feminist Press	Owner
Mary Lou Humphrey	Schirmer	Senior Manager
Judith Ilika	Presser	Director of Performance Promotion
Renate Matthei	Furore	President

Fulfilling the vital need of printing the music used by performers, bringing out books on the subject, and all the other adjuncts thereto, are music publishers. Some have been in business, literally, for centuries. In Europe, **Breitkopf and Härtel** were established in Leipzig, 1719, also in Germany, **Schott** began in 1774 and **Peters** in 1814. Italy's oldest company is **Ricordi** (1808), France has **Durand** (1869), in England, **Novello** opened its doors in 1811 and Thomas **Boosey** was negotiating with Beethoven after entering the business in 1816. The latter's New York office was opened in 1892. The firm merged with **Hawkes** in 1930, now owning valuable editions spanning over a century, and opening branches in most major cities in the world. Another big name in the United States is **G. Schirmer**, which dates from 1861, although the company started in Germany almost a century earlier. Other U.S. music publishers are **Theodore Presser** of Bryn Mawr, Pennsylvania, where British born **Judith Ilika** heads the promotions department. This company publishes a great deal of music by women. (See Glickman.)

STEPHANIE CHALLENER—*Publisher of the Music Industry "Bible."* Musical America, an annual eight-by-ten, 800-plus glossy-paged book, is classical music's "Who's Who," listing just about every artist, manager, music festival, orchestra, opera and ballet company in the world. Stephanie Challener has been the associate publisher of this ambitious undertaking since 1999.

Born to music-loving parents, August 31, 1961, in New York City, she received her BA in international relations from Wooster College (Ohio, 1983). Her MM, 1990, is from Westminster Choir College, Princeton. She joined *Musical America* as administrative assistant in June 1993, progressing to advertising assistant (1994), advertising editorial assistant (1995), and advertising representative (1996). In December 2001, at the *Musical America* Annual Awards Reception, Challener received the well-earned promotion to *publisher*!

SUSAN FEDER—*A Feather in the Cap of Schirmer,* violin studies from age seven, school orchestras, music camps and playing chamber music through college and beyond, prepared Susan Feder for her lofty perch with the biggest classical music publisher in America. She is vice president of G. Schirmer, Inc., whose family history dates back to the mid-19th century. Prior to this position, Feder was editorial coordinator of *The New Grove Dictionary* *of American Music* (1981–86) and program editor of the San Francisco Symphony (1979–81). A writer on music, she has been program annotator for the American Composers Orchestra (1981–91), for which she won an ASCAP-Deems Taylor Award in 1986. She has written program notes, liner notes and music criticism for a number of organizations, and served on the Symphonic and Concert Committee at ASCAP, the Artistic Affairs Committee of the ASOL, the advisory board of the ACO, and on the boards of the American Music Center, Music Publishers Association, and the Charles Ives Society.

Feder holds a master's in history and literature of music from Berkeley (1979) and a BA from Princeton (1976), for whom she is a member of the Alumni Schools Committee and the Music Department Advisory Council. She is married to attorney and legal publisher Todd Gordon. They have a son, Sam, born in 1989 and a daughter, Basia, born 1991.

Sylvia Glickman

SYLVIA Foodim **GLICKMAN**—*Hildegard Lives On!* Rediscovering and sharing the works of women composers continues being the mission of Hildegard Publishing Company. Named after 12th century nun-composer **Hildegard von Bingen** (1098–1179), the firm was founded 1988 by Glickman in Bryn Mawr, Pennsylvania, to help redress the centuries of neglect of historic women composers by research and the publishing of first contemporary editions, as well as assisting contemporary composers.

Glickman, born November 8,1932 in New York, received BM (1954) and MM (1955) degrees in performance from Juilliard, where she won the Morris Loeb Prize and, as a Fulbright scholar, a Licentiate degree from the RAM (London, 1956), where she earned the Hecht Prize in composition. (Romance entered Sylvia's life as she crossed the Atlantic on the liner, *Queen Elizabeth*. Political science student Harvey Glickman was also heading for England and his Fulbright year. On their return, they were married September 2, 1956.)

Sylvia held positions at the New England Conservatory, Rubin Academy, Jerusalem, and was for nineteen years director of Chamber Music and pianist-in-residence at Haverford College, Pennsylvania, where her husband was on the faculty. While doing research at the Library of Congress for the twelve programs she performed on Philadelphia public radio during the 1976 Bicentennial celebration, she came upon long-lost 18th–19th century works ranging from a keyboard sonata by Marianna D'Auenbrugg to Eliza Pattianiís *Grand National Medley*, and made the decision to dedicate herself to bringing recognition to the works of women composers. She recruited several prominent female composers and musicologists to edit and transcribe earlier works, and in 1991 founded the Hildegard Chamber Players to bring this music to live audiences. After ten years of public concerts, the Hildegard Institute began funding recordings of music by women for wider promotion.

As a pianist, Sylvia had performed to critical acclaim since age eight, touring the U.S., Europe, Israel and Africa. In May 1986, she was honored by Women's Way of Philadelphia for her "exceptional talent as a musician and teacher, and for her unique contributions to women's music history." In 1995, New York Women Composers, Inc. presented her with their annual Award for Distinguished Service to Music Composed by Women.

Glickman's own compositions cover songs based on Emily Dickinson poems; choral music, including *The Seven Deadly Sins* (1987), and two complete Sabbath services; piano works such as *Dances and Entertainments* (1990); and chamber music, *Sound Elements for Trio* (1994), and a string quartet (2000).

Further commissions were *Carved in Courage*, for chamber orchestra, and *Am I a Murderer?* for basso and eight instruments. These holocaust remembrance works were released by Albany (2000) under the title, *The Walls Are Quiet Now*. The actual composition of that title, originally for chamber orchestra (1993), was inspired by a memorial built at the Grünewald railway station in Berlin—the point of deportation of Jews to concentration camps. *Walls* was later revised for large orchestra.

As a researcher, Glickman's anthologies include *Amy Beach: Virtuoso Piano Music*, and *Anthology of American Piano Music* (1865–1909), Volume IV for keyboard, of the multi-volume *Three Centuries of American Piano Music* (G.K. Hall/Macmillan, 1989–1992), which introduced her to editor Martha Furman Schleifer, a member of the music history faculty at Temple University. *From Convent to Concert Hall: A Guide to Women Composers* (Greenwood Press, 2003) was edited by Glickman with Schleifer, whom she invited to be a senior editor at Hildegard Publishing. Composed of scholarly contributions by various musicologists, its six chapters progress from the Middle Ages to the 20th century, with emphasis on styles and genres.

In 1995 Glickman, again with Schleifer as co-editor, embarked upon her most ambitious project: *Women Composers: Music Through the Ages*, in twelve volumes each covering a century, beginning *circa* 810–to the 20th century, with a format of scholarly articles, lists of works, bibliographies, discographies and extant music—also for G.K. Hall. Volume Eight ending in 1899 was completed ten days before Sylvia died of lung cancer, January 16, 2006.

The distribution of the complete Hildegard Publishing Catalogue (over 500 works by women from the 9th through 21st centuries) was taken over by the Theodore Presser Company in 2002.

Besides her husband, she is survived by daughters Lisa, born 1958, Nina, 1960, and son Peter, 1965. With Hildegard under Harvey's leadership, Sylvia's legacy is carried on.

LINDA S. GOLDING—*Pioneer President*; Linda Golding became the first female president of Boosey & Hawkes, Inc., January 1995, at the tender age of thirty-seven. One of the foremost music publishers in the world, Boosey & Hawkes originated from the merger in 1930 of two British companies, Boosey & Company (founded in the 1760s) and Hawkes & Son (founded in 1865). The company's promotional strength was demonstrated in the two-year planning campaign for composer Elliott Carter's ninetieth birthday celebrations, which took place around the world in 1999. The firm brought together record companies, performers, ensembles and administrators to pay tribute to Carter, an icon who had personally witnessed 90 percent of the 20th century. The following year, Golding coordinated Copland 2000, a multi-year initiative to bring all of Copland's works to international attention celebrating the centenary of his birth, and encourage new collaborations and new audiences for his music. This initiative was the first of its kind and has been used as a template for many subsequent projects.

Golding was responsible for signing long term exclusive publishing agreements with top contemporary composers John Adams, Steve Reich, Steven Mackey, Christopher Rouse and **Elena Kats Chernin**. On the marketing initiative, it was at her direction that B & H developed methods to promote music and teach about copyright to dance companies, creating a CD Dance Sampler and copyright brochure. These, too, became the templates for many other projects both at B & H and with other publishers.

Born in New York, April 26, 1957, Linda's childhood was filled with music, beginning with the recorder in first grade, followed by modern and ballet dancing, piano and cello lessons, theater, dance and music performances. She graduated from the prestigious Brearley School, going to Smith College to earn a BA in music (1979). After interning with the Springfield (Massachusetts) Symphony, she worked briefly at the ASOL, then went straight into New York City Opera shortly after **Beverly Sills** became general director, where Linda benefitted greatly from Sills' mentoring and work ethic. Working with such artists as Samuel Ramey, Sheryl Woods, Jerry Hadley, Diane Curry, Michael Tilson Thomas, Christopher Keene, Hugh Wolf, Frank Corsaro and Harold Prince, in the course of nine years Golding rose to associate music administrator and director of production coordination.

She came to Boosey & Hawkes in 1991 as general manager, becoming vice president in 1992, joining the publishing executive board in 1993 and attaining the presidency in 1995. Taking an active role in the industry, she served on the board of directors of the Music Publishers' Association. She also worked to raise the visibility of contemporary music of all genres through affiliations with OPERA America, American Opera Projects, ASCAP Symphony and Concert Committee, ASCAP Adventurous Programming Awards, ASOL and Chamber Music America.

She was on the faculty of the Arts Administration Certificate Program at NYU School of Continuing Education, held music publishing seminars at Juilliard, gave music rights and career planning panels for Dance USA, and composer marketing and visibility workshops with the American Composers Forum. She has served on the Boards of OPERA America and **Meredith Monk's** House Foundation for the Arts.

In 2001, Golding left B & H to found *The Reservoir*, in order to mentor, coach and guide performing arts professionals to identify and remove obstacles to developing, clarifying and implementing their creative ideas and objectives. The company also provides mediation and facilitation services for small organizations and non-profit boards.

ELAINE GORZELSKI—*Harmony in the Presses*; Elaine Gorzelski is president of Harmonie Park Press, a publishing company in Warren, Michigan, specializing in musical bibliography, musicology and monographs.[244]

Born in Detroit, March 19, 1941, Elaine modestly affirms that she was simply in the right place at the right time when, just out of school, she got a job in the Detroit Public Library Publication Department. This experience led to a position in 1967 with **Florence Kretschmar**, founder of *Music Index*, the most important basic guide to music periodicals and literature. (It has also brought out a monthly publication since 1949.) After Kretschmar's death in 1986, the business was sold to her three executive employees, and again modesty marks Gorzelski's statement, "I got to be president because no one else wanted the position."

Married in 1960 to a retired chief engineer at General Motors, Elaine is the mother of three grown sons and a daughter who, between them, have made her a grandmother four times.

BARBARA HARBACH is the owner of Vivace Press. (See American Contemporary Composers.)

FLORENCE HOWE—*An Original Feminist*; Florence Howe, founder and president of The Feminist Press, became closely involved with the women's movement after active participation in the civil rights movement during the 1960s. Through her teaching, writing, lecturing and association with the company, she has been a major contributor to changes in higher education over the past three decades, during which time she has served as the "record keeper" of women's studies programs in the United States and abroad, and historian of the movement.

Her academic career began as a teaching assistant at the University of Wisconsin and an instructor at Hofstra College in the '50s. Later, she was appointed to faculties at Goucher College and SUNY, College at Old Westbury. She was professor of English at City College and the Graduate School. She began teaching "women studies" courses before they were even given that cognomen, and was editor-in-chief of *Women's Studies Quarterly*, the first national journal to focus on feminist teaching (1972–82).

The tenure of Florence Howe at The Feminist Press saw a dramatic growth in both the books published and the outreach to readers, as well as an international scope of editorial direction. The company received Publishers Weekly Carey Thomas Award for creativity in publishing due, in large part, to Howe's successful efforts in bringing back into print and critical awareness, many outstanding but previously "lost" or "neglected" women writers. She has received four honorary degrees and many other awards, including "The Center for Women Policy Studies Jessie Bernard Wise Woman Award" (1990).

Howe has written or edited more than a dozen books and published more than 70 essays for the general and scholarly press in *The Nation*, PMLA, *Soundings*, *The New York Review of Books* and *The Women's Review of Books*. In 1993, Harper Collins Publishers brought out a new edition of *NO MORE MASKS! An Anthology of Twentieth-Century American Women Poets* edited by Howe, and considered a classic. In 1993, she published the second edition of the 1988 ground-breaking *Women Composers: The Lost Tradition Found* by the late **Diane Jezic**. (See American Composers.)

Howe retired in January 2001, but continues her involvement with the Press as co-director of **Women Writing Africa**. The board of directors appointed Jean Casella as the new publisher/director. More than a quarter century after its modest beginnings, The Feminist Press continues as a pioneer in restoring the lost culture and history of women, worldwide.

MARY LOU HUMPHREY—*Filling a Large Bill!* Director of international promotion at G. Schirmer, Mary Lou Humphrey represents the music of today's top classical composers. As a small child she listened to Gregorian

---

244. This book owes much of the excellent information on composer **Amy Beach** and pianist **Amy Fay** to two Harmonie Park Press books by Walter S. Jenkins and Sister Margaret McCarthy, respectively—see *Bibliography*.

chants, borrowed LPs of Wagner operas and Stravinsky's *Rite of Spring*. She also made "sonic explorations" on various stringed instruments. Her formal musical training began at age eight, playing violin, clarinet and guitar. As the daughter of non-musical parents, she was not exposed to the traditional classics—Mozart and Beethoven—until she was a teenager. A love of history and diverse music styles led her into musicology. She completed her PhD studies in contemporary music and opera history at the Graduate Center of CUNY.

Humphrey began her career in 1979 in the opera business, working first as an artists' manager then as an administrator for Beverly Sills at New York City Opera, for whom she has been program annotator since 1985. She has also written program notes for many organizations, including Lincoln Center, Chicago Lyric Opera, the BBC, Chamber Music Society of Lincoln Center, Seattle Symphony, and liner notes for Sony, EMI/Virgin, Nonesuch and Koch, among others. She writes music journalism for *Stagebill* and *Playbill* magazines, is a contributor to both New Grove Dictionaries on Opera and Music, and has published extensively on the music of contemporary composers, including Stephen Albert, John Corigliano, Aaron Kernis and Tan Dun. Since 1986, she has taught opera history at NYU's School of Continuing Education, delivered pre-concert lectures on contemporary music for the New York Philharmonic and the New York Chamber Symphony, and moderated pre-concert discussions for the Chamber Music Society of Lincoln Center and their Great Performers Series.

A passionate advocate for contemporary classical music and composers, Humphrey is a consultant to leading performers, music festivals, recording and film companies, and government arts organizations such as the NEA, Opera America, New York State Council for the Arts, and the Massachusetts Cultural Council. She is a founding board member of Re:Soundings, a production company for avant-garde arts, has been a jurist in many competitions, and serves as dramaturg for operas in development.

One of her specialties is "New Wave" Chinese music, about which she wrote a book with composer Tan Dun. In 1995, she was guest lecturer at China's three leading universities, Beijing, Shanghai and Sichuan, where she introduced contemporary American music to Chinese composers and musicologists.

To help maintain balance in her life, Humphrey is an oblate[245] of Holy Trinity Monastery in Arizona. She also enjoys trekking through the jungles of Latin America and Africa, collects art photography, and has been known to skydive.

JUDITH ILIKA—*A World Career*, Judith Ilika, director of performance promotion at Theodore Presser, one of America's oldest and most prominent music publishers, was born in Rotherham, Yorkshire (England), April 9, 1950. Music was a normal part of everyday life, with both her parents playing piano and her older brother, violin. He also sang in choirs and started an extensive record collection at age eleven, which gave Judith a great musical education. Her study of piano continued throughout her school years. At eleven, she took up the oboe which she played in the school orchestra until eighteen. She also took violin for a while and taught herself guitar. Feeling that she was not up to a concert pianist career, she followed her interest in languages, earning a BA from Hull University (Yorkshire), with a major in French language and literature and a minor in Italian language and literature. Following a post-graduate certificate in education, Judith began her world wanderings, teaching English as a foreign language at the University in Vientiane, Laos (1973–76), followed by English to foreign post-graduate students in Britain and Australia (1976–78), and teaching at the British Council Institute in Maracaibo, Venezuela (1978–84). She came to America as director of education at the Korean Community Center in Philadelphia (1984–90), after which she joined Presser.

This premier company was started in 1883 by **Theodore Presser** (1848–1925), co-founder of the Music Teachers' National Association in 1876. With a background of study at both the New England and Leipzig Conservatories, and $250 to his name, he began publication of *The Etude*, a pioneer music magazine providing teachers with music, guidance, and information about the international music world. This was such a success that he expanded into publishing music. Income enabled him, in 1906, to establish the Presser Home for Retired Music

---

245. A lay person affiliated with a specific religious community who has pledged to live the Benedictine monastic rule.

Teachers outside Philadelphia. In 1916 he formed the Presser Foundation, which continues to award scholarships, grants and funds to further the cause of music education. In the 1930s, Presser acquired the John Church and Oliver Ditson Companies, the latter a music publisher in Boston since 1783. In 1972, Presser acquired Elkan-Vogel and its agencies, making the company the most important distributer of French music in the U.S. In addition to their own catalogues, Presser now represents more than eighty American and foreign publishers.

In 1990, Ilika was hired by Presser as promotions assistant in the performance promotion department, and apart from a few months in the wholesale department, has remained in the PPD where she attained her present status in 1995. She is the primary contact for living composers with large concert works in the Presser rental catalogue, which are promoted to performing organizations and individual artists. Her department also disseminates information and fields all enquiries related to programming suggestions.

RENATE MATTHEI—*Exclusively for the Enduring Gender,* Renate Matthei is the president of Furore Verlag, based in Kassel (Germany), which publishes sheet music of women composers past and present, biographical and musicological books, produces CDs as well as postcards with pictures of composers, including sketches of those predating the camera. The company, founded in 1986, was the first publishing house to concentrate on printing music by, and books about, women composers. A large percentage of the publications are first printings of musical compositions, with works from all over the world and from different historical eras. Their 21st century output includes a string quartet by Augusta Le Beau; a new volume of "Duets," the facsimile of the 1841 piano cycle *Das Jahr,* and the piano vocal scores of *Oratorio* and *Lobgesang,* all by Fanny Mendelssohn Hensel; the Oratorio *Isacco* by Marianne Martines; piano pieces of **Pauline Viardot-Garcia**; a piano quartet of **Elfrida Andrée**; *Festspiel* and *Trio,* op. 45 of **Louise Farrenc**; *Concerto in G* for harpsichord and string orchestra, composed in 1735 by Wilhelmine von Bayreuth; and a new volume of solo sonatas by **Elizabeth Jacquet de La Guerre**. By 2002, Furore's catalogue comprised over 600 works by women composers, past and present.

Born in Kassel, March 4, 1954, Renate learned piano and flute in her youth, and received a bachelor of commerce degree. Besides her company, she works in many facets of the field of women in music, including being a member of the board of directors of Women in Music Germany, and music organizations such as the Stiftung (foundation) Maecenia, Landesarbeitsgemeinschaft Hessen für Frauen in Kunst und Kultur (Alliance for Women in Arts and Culture in Hessen—a German state), Kasseler Bücherherbst (an annual book convention in Kassel) and the Kasseler Kultursalon.

Honorable mention must be made of Renate's right hand woman, **Sabine Kemna** who, with a background of working in music publishing houses such as Zimmermann/Lienau, joined Furore in 1992 as the indispensable sales department manager.

The Recording Industry - Pinnacles of the Platters

Alison Ames	Deutsche Grammophon	Former Vice President Artists/Repertoire
Susan Napodano DelGiorno	Koch International	General Manager
Marnie Hall	Leonarda	Founder and President
Barbara Harbach	Hester Park Records	Owner
Amelia Haygood	Delos	Founder and president
Lynne Hoffman-Engel	Telarc	Vice President of Sales
Elaine Martone	Telarc	Vice President
Karen Moody	PolyGram	Former Vice President Development
Melanie Mueller	Avie	President - Music Company (London) Ltd.
Jane Welton	Protone	President (1971–2000)
Robina Young	harmonia mundi	Vice President, Producer/Artistic Director
Nancy Zannini	PolyGram	Former Vice President of Soundtracks

Several women have made it to the top in international recording companies, others run their own companies, while still others have artists subsidize their own recordings. Some names have been included even though they are no longer in their positions, to illustrate the variety and scope of this field.

ALISON AMES—*From Disc Spinner to Luthier to PR*... in September 1995, Alison Ames became a vice president at Angel/EMI Records, after having been with Deutche Grammophon since 1973, and serving as vice president of Artists and Repertoire for DG.

She began life January 4, 1945, in Bryn Mawr, Pennsylvania, and was exposed to New York Philharmonic broadcasts on Sundays, piano and flute lessons, and being taken to concerts—all the "normal" childhood pastimes which are rarely part of children's lives in our electronic age. With a BA in English from Hollins College (Roanoke, Virginia, 1966), Alison went into the world, and by 1973 was a secretary at the New York office of DG, working her way up to publicist. In 1977 she went to Germany, doing English translations for DG markets in Western Europe, North America and Japan. When DG and the Dutch recording company Philips joined with London Decca in 1980, under the Polygram Classics label, Ames returned to New York and, as vice president, ran DG until 1989. (History was made that decade with three women in major positions at the major labels: Nancy Zannini, Philips, Lynn Hoffman Engel, London/Decca, and Liz Ostrow, head of Artists and Recordings at New World Records.)

Helping to implement significant changes with artists, repertoire, and the way records were being made, Ames, as executive producer, dealt with such notables as **Leonard Bernstein**, the Orpheus Chamber Orchestra, Emerson String Quartet, **André Previn** and **Gil Shaham**, plus taking care of the logistics of orchestras recording under maestros like Pierre Boulez and James Levine. Metropolitan Opera recordings are conducted in the Manhattan Center, the last large scale studio extant in New York. Other recording sessions are held in the depths of the American Academy of Arts and Letters building on 155th Street, where it was not beneath a producer's dignity to fetch lunches. Her duties were: "to get all the people required to make a recording to show up at the same time, the same place, to do the same piece of music."

Between 1998–2001, Ames temporarily embarked upon a new career as a luthier, learning violin making at Boston's North Bennet Street School. By 2002, however, she was back in the classical music business freelancing in promotion and public relations. In 2003 she joined 21C Media Group, an independent publicity and marketing company for classical music, musicians and record companies, founded in 1999 by Albert Imperato, Glenn Petry and Jessica Lustig.

Utilizing yet another field of expertise, Alison has several times been heard as a quiz panelist on the Metropolitan Opera broadcasts.

SUSAN NAPODANO DelGIORNO—*Turning the World*; In a unique situation, KOCH International Classics, the third largest independent music company in the world, has been the only employer Susan DelGiorno ever worked for! While taking her music degree at Hofstra University (Long Island, New York, 1992), she began as an intern in Koch's publicity department. She became production manager (1992–97), and is now general manager. Her position allows her to explore her musical interests as they relate to the marketplace, where she acts as record producer, covering art direction, editing, business affairs and artist relations. Her major interests are in contemporary American composers and early music. A newer exploration is Latino music.

Susan was born in Brooklyn, New York, June 8, 1970. Her musical studies began with recorder at age five, guitar at seven, viola at nine, violin at ten, and clarinet at eleven—the instrument she still actively plays. While her love of music, instruments and performance was thus implemented early in life, she remembers that her mother never really enjoyed any recital piece written after 1850, and when she began practicing viola, her father came home from work wearing industrial ear protection. To make up for this, she has consoled herself with the conviction that, "Somewhere in my Italian roots I'd like to think there's a musical prodigy that inspired me to this career, and that my grandmother would have been proud and appreciative of my contributions."

In 1995, Susan married her college sweetheart, George DelGiorno, who was in the graphics department at KOCH until starting his own business in 2001. He still contributes design packages for the label, allowing husband and wife a close working relationship. On November 17, 2002, the DelGiornos welcomed their daughter, Joy, into their lives.

(Based in New York, KOCH Entertainment was founded, May 1999, with Michael Koch, president, as the new umbrella company for KOCH's North American record labels. It was nominated Medium Entertainment Supplier of the Year 2002 by the National Association of Recording Merchandisers (NARM).)

MARNIE HALL—*For the Record*; Beginning her career as a violinist with a MM in performance from the Manhattan School of Music, Marnie was playing in a women's quartet in the mid '70s when several inquiries about women composers' works for string quartet set her on the path to research this then sparse repertoire. Finding other compositions by women prompted her decision to start her own recording company in order to publicize this neglected treasure trove. Her first effort was a double LP entitled *Woman's Work* (1975). From this evolved the non-profit organization Leonarda Productions, Inc., named after **Isabella Leonarda** (1620–1704), an Italian nun who composed sacred music. Between 1979–85, the company brought out twenty-four LPs of women composers, past and present. Hall initially produced tapes—now CDs—to accompany the late **Dianne Jezic**'s book, *Women Composers: The Lost Tradition Found*. Digital recording—and its accompanying escalation of costs—slowed production down somewhat until 1992 when Hall was able to purchase her own recording and post-production equipment, gaining independence as a recording engineer and producer. By 2004, *Leonarda* had over two dozen CD releases of both male and female composers, with a continually growing list, including *Composers of the Holocaust*. Their catalogue, audio samples, composer and performer biographies can be found on their website.

BARBARA HARBACH is the owner of Hester Park Records. (See American Contemporary Composers.)

Amelia Haygood

AMELIA S. HAYGOOD—*The Lady from Delos*; Amelia Da Costa Stone Haygood was born in Gainesville. Her mother's side of the family goes back to the original Spanish settlers of Florida. With her family listening to opera broadcasts and recordings of "Golden Age" singers, Amelia grew up with an intense love for music, especially opera and art songs.

Her interest in languages and international relations took her to Paris, at sixteen, for studies at the Sorbonne. Back in the U.S., after majoring in history and international law, she went to Washington, DC, to work for the State Department Interdepartmental Committee for Cultural and Scientific Cooperation.

She married J. Douglas Haygood, a clinical psychologist, took courses, and joined him in his practice after they moved from Cleveland to Beverly Hills. She also worked in the Veterans' Administration, contributing to research and publication in the fields of spinal cord injury and neurosurgery. After the death of her husband, Haygood left private practice to become psychological consultant to the Los Angeles County Probation Department, developing a successful pilot treatment for juvenile offenders and their families, and conducting workshops for professionals in the field of family treatment.

In the early 1970s, Haygood reached a crossroads after seeing a close friend through a long terminal illness. Her lifelong passion for music, her interest in musicians and recordings, as well as her graduate study of psychoacoustics and the physics of music, merged in a new direction. As a friend to several American concert artists, Amelia wanted to provide them with a quality showcase for their talents. 1973 saw the birth of Delos and a whole new life for Amelia.

As executive producer of all recording projects, plus artistic and quality control of all stages of production, Haygood's intense interest in and vast experience with people from all cultural backgrounds has given Delos a unique perspective and direction, and a leading-edge on domestic and international sales. She is responsible for the company's Great American Composers Series, featuring the mid-20th century generation of American symphonists—Howard Hanson, Walter Piston, David Diamond, Aaron Copland, Samuel Barber and Alan Hovhaness—and has produced the Young People Series, combining great classical music with narrated stories in an attempt to counteract the lack of exposure to fine music experienced by today's children.

In the arts community, Amelia Haygood has been a member of the NEA Awards Committee and the National Association for Recording Arts and Sciences (NARAS) Screening Committee for over a decade.

LYNNE HOFFMAN-ENGEL—*From the Big Apple to Georgia Peaches*; a native of Elmhurst, Illinois, Lynne began piano at eight and voice at sixteen. Her mother was a teacher, and her father, an engineer, leader of the church choir, and an audiophile, filling the house with taped music. Her public school education included music programs where she sang in the choir, and was piano accompanist for many singers entering state contests. After a BA in music education from Saint Olaf College (1974), singing in their famed choir and touring Europe with them, she earned an MM in voice performance from the New England Conservatory (1976), also studying with Met stars **Eleanor Steber** (1916–90) and **Phyllis Curtin** (*b* 1921).

From 1984–96, Lynne was with Polygram, marketing all recordings for young violinist Joshua Bell—now world-famous—renowned pianists Vladimir Ashkenazy and Alicia de Larrocha, conductors Sir Georg Solti and Charles Dutoit, singers **Jessye Norman**, **Cecilia Bartoli** and Luciano Pavarotti. She also worked on *The Three Tenors*[246] audio and video project, including its release through PBS Television. Her last three years at Polygram were as senior vice president in sales and marketing for Deutsche Grammophon, London, Philips and Verve Records.

Leaving in 1996 to expand her experience in more musical genres, she joined the independent music company Platinum Entertainment, in Chicago. By 1999, she was relocated to Alpharetta, Georgia, rising to executive vice

---

246. Three of the world's greatest tenors, José Carreras, Plácido Domingo and Luciano Pavarotti, made history when, in 1990, they sang together for the first time at an outdoor concert in Rome, under the direction of Zubin Mehta. The performance was viewed by over 2 billion people.

president of Labels. In 2001, she became director of sales at Crossover Media, her answer to finding music opportunities outside the record companies. After her many years in the Big Apple, Hoffman-Engel enjoyed life in the Peach State, where in 2001 she was named Female Entertainment Executive of the Year, and Outstanding Georgia Citizen. She also returned to singing with the Michael O'Neal Chamber Singers, and as the soloist with the Glenn Chancel Choir at Emory University. In another career move, September 2003, she joined Telarc International in Cleveland as VP of sales.

Lynne is married to Robert Engel. They have a son, Marc, born 1987.

ELAINE MARTONE—*A Partnership Made on Earth;* vice president of production and artist relations, Elaine Martone began working at Telarc in 1980 when the company was in its infancy. Born in Rochester, New York, and raised on Long Island, she graduated with honors from Ithaca College, near her birthplace, with a BM in Oboe Performance (1979). She moved to Cleveland to study oboe, with aspirations of playing in the Cleveland Orchestra. Instead, she played in the Canton (Ohio) Symphony for seven years while working at Telarc, where she learned the basics from founders Robert Woods and Jack Renner. She started in quality control, moved to production manager within a year, became director of production by 1984, and vice president in 1990. An accomplished editor, she produced her first recording in 1988. Since then she has served as producer of both classical and jazz releases, including recordings of the Empire Brass, Atlanta Symphony, and jazz greats, McCoy Tyner, Ray Brown and Oscar Peterson.

Besides her own Grammy nominations, Telarc International[247] Corporation, now based in Cleveland, has won over forty Grammy Awards for performance, production and engineering, and was nominated for more than a dozen Grammys by NARAS for 2004 releases that included Elaine's productions of the Berlioz *Requiem* with Robert Spano and the Atlanta Symphony Orchestra and Chorus, and Mahler's Third Symphony with Benjamin Zander and the Philharmonia of London. Telarc has also won the French *Grand Prix du Disque* and *Diapason d' Or*, Japan's *Record of the Year*, and Germany's *Audiophile CD of the Year*.

Martone directs a staff of over fifty, oversees the recording and art departments, assists artists and repertoire selection, schedules releases, is artist liaison and travels to recording sites.

Romantically, Elaine married the boss—Telarc President Robert Woods—September 1992, and helped raise his two children, Melissa, born August 1983, and Jonathan, June 1986.

KAREN MOODY—*Platters from Polygram;* until January 1996, Karen Moody was vice president of development for PolyGram Classics and Jazz, then a division of PolyGram Deutsche Grammophon, London, Philips and Verve labels.

Born July 24, 1946, in Chicago, she studied ballet and piano as a child. With three musical sisters and her mother, there was always singing in the house. She received her BA in French from Northern Illinois University (1968) and her MA, also in French, from Penn State (1978). She taught high school French before returning to graduate school. She lived in Paris from 1973–78, working first as a bilingual secretary in an American law firm, and then for CBS Records—now Sony International. It became increasingly clear that, as an expatriate, a career path in France was impossible, so she returned to Chicago and found a position as a French-language specialist in the city's convention and tourism bureau.

The city's worst winter (1978), with sixteen consecutive days of below zero weather, drove Moody out of Chicago to New York and a position in the personnel department of CBS Records International. In 1980, she made another career move to PolyGram Classics, where she assisted then president, Gunther Hensler. For further creative stimulation, Karen enrolled in classes in music history in the Mannes College of Music.

When the publicist left DG, Moody won the position, whose responsibilities included handling the media, arranging recording sessions in the U.S. and working with such illustrious artists as pianists Vladimir Horowitz,

---

247. Telarc, a top independent recording company was, and continues to be, a pioneer in digital sound recording technique.

Maurizio Pollini; conductors Herbert von Karajan, Leonard Bernstein, Claudio Abbado and James Levine; violinists Anne Sophie Mutter and Gil Shaham; and singers Kathleen Battle and Plácido Domingo.

In 1989, Moody became DG's label vice president, a post she held until 1995 when she made a career change to work for a business magazine.

MELANNE MUELLER—*Staying in the Groove*; now settled in England, Melanne was born September 8, 1966, in Grinnell, Iowa. Her parents being amateur musicians, she began piano at age three and continued on this instrument for twelve years, meanwhile taking up oboe at age nine. She received her BM and MM degrees from the Manhattan School of Music, studying with Joseph Robinson, principal oboist of the New York Philharmonic. She performed with the New York Philharmonic, Manhattan Chamber Orchestra, Chamber Symphony of Princeton, and Newton Chamber Orchestra. She played John Corigliano's Oboe Concerto with the Manhattan Symphony and premiered Brian Kershner's *Pastorale* and *Scherzino for Oboe and Strings*, commissioned by the New Brunswick Chamber Orchestra. She also served on the faculty of the Brooklyn Conservatory of Music.

In 1993, she gave up concertizing to become media relations manager for recording giant BMG Classics, and moved to London in 1997 to take the newly created position of head of international for BMG Conifer Classics, an "alternative" repertoire source for BMG Classics. In 1999, the Conifer label was dissolved and Mueller took on the responsibility for international marketing and repertoire development for all of BMG Classics, Europe. This position included a diverse artist roster, and extensive travel throughout the Continent.

She left BMG in July 2000, and founded Music Company (London) Ltd. in August. By 2001, she had fourteen artists to manage, and over a dozen clients for whom she handled marketing and publicity. With partner Simon Foster, they have thirty-five years of experience between them, she started a new record label, *Avie*, which works in a unique business plan based on artists' ownership and copyright of their recordings, with the company assisting the performer from studio to manufacturing to distribution. Their first releases, 2002, included the San Francisco Symphony and Michael Tilson Thomas playing Mahler, the Strasbourg Philharmonic, violinist **Lara St. John** and composer **Errollyn Wallen**, and the Dufay Collective, an early music group, with Jeff Khaner, principal flutist of the Philadelphia Orchestra. By 2004, with the downsizing of the majors, many artists were no longer able to obtain new recording contracts or replace lost ones. *Avie* filled in this gap, enabling musicians to gain control over the recording aspect of their careers, which represents a large emotional investment. In 2005, *Avie* joined MicMacMusic, becoming part of a major British independent classical mail order and MP3 download catalogue.

Living in Wimbledon outside London, Melanne reports, "I'm thoroughly enjoying life over here, with wonderful holidays in France, Italy and Spain, and skiing in the Alps."

(Author's comment: Well, *someone* has to do it . . .)

JANE COURTLAND WELTON—*Transformation Artist*; owner and director of Protone Records, child prodigy Jane Courtland was born in Chicago to a composer/conductor father who taught at the American Conservatory and subbed as a bass player in the Chicago Symphony, with whom she made her piano debut at the age of ten. Her mother was a singer. The family moved to New York for Jane to attend Juilliard, where she studied with Carl Friedberg (1872–1955) whose pupils included Percy Grainger and **Ethel Leginska**. Summers were spent in Baden-Baden (Germany). After winning the school's Liszt Prize, Jane went to Hungary, living in Budapest and studying with the country's most prominent composers, Zoltan Kodály and Bela Bartók. When she returned to New York, she had her own live radio show playing solo and chamber music, and concertized in the New York area. In 1943, she married physician Philip Bond, who also sang bass in the New York City Opera. In 1945, their daughter Victoria[248] was born. After a move to Los Angeles in 1961, Courtland performed with the Chamber Arts Quartet. In 1971, she inherited the Protone recording company from her second husband, James Welton, transforming it

---

248. On July 13, 2003, the author was privileged to be invited by **Victoria Bond** (See Composers) to attend her mother's ninetieth birthday party in Bel Air, California. It was lovely to see both ladies again, the last occasion having been the 1993 premiere of Victoria's *Urban Bird* Saxophone Concerto in San Francisco.

from jazz and pop into a successful and respected chamber music label, which she ran until her retirement in 2000. Jane died in Los Angeles, May 24, 2005.

ROBINA Grace **YOUNG**—*Starting From Scratch*; Robina Young, vice president and artistic director of **harmonia mundi usa** (yes! they use only lower case letters), was trained as a classical musician. Born in Yorkshire, England, she worked as a pianist and accompanist before becoming fascinated by early music performance practice and studying harpsichord in Amsterdam. After moving to France in the late 1970s, she helped run the famous Dollar Academy and organized Kenneth Gilbert harpsichord master classes, which attracted an international student body. She became staff producer for **harmonia mundi france**, producing over fifty recordings. In 1982, she came to the USA to help found **harmonia mundi usa** and, starting from scratch, has carefully built an artist roster of international star quality, including the *a capella* group, **Anonymous 4**,[249] conductor Nicholas McGegan, The King's Noyse, Paul O'Dette, Paul Hillier, Romanesca, Frederic Chiu, Andrew Manze, Paul Goodwin and **Marion Verbruggen**—all specialists in early music, and most of whom record exclusively for this company.

Robina Young

By 2004, recordings numbered over 400, many having garnered prestigious awards in Europe and America, including Robina's sixth Grammy nomination for Classical Producer of the Year. Passionate about both music and sound quality, she still produces many of the recordings personally despite a hectic schedule.

NANCY ZANNINI—*On the Soundtrack*; until 1998, Nancy Zannini was vice president of soundtracks for PolyGram Classics and Jazz. This involves either putting on disk music already written for a film, or advising directors on a choice of music appropriate for their production, even suggesting a suitable composer.

Born in Chicago, Nancy was surrounded by music with her mother an amateur singer and her father an amateur pianist. She began piano lessons at six. After graduating from Rosemont College in Bryn Mawr, Pennsylvania, with a degree in English literature, in 1975 she joined Polygram as artists and repertoire coordinator for what was then Polymusic. The following year, she became director of publicity for their Philips label. By 1980, Zannini was vice president of Philips until 1992, when she was named vice president of soundtracks for PolyGram. Among the films she dealt with were Robert Altman's *Kansas City*; *Get Shorty* with Danny De Vito, John Travolta and Gene Hackman; *Little Odessa* with Vanessa Redgrave and Tim Roth; and Mel Gibson's *Braveheart*.

In 1999, she wed Chris Roberts, president of Universal Classics and Jazz, and went into independent consulting on soundtracks. Beginning in the summer of 2001, she embarked upon a new career of teaching reading and music in an afterschool program in New York City.

Into the 21st century, following the Global Village trend of business mergers, recording labels have also become glued together. (Whatever happened to anti-trust laws?) In 2004, BMG (Bertelsmann Music Group, Germany) merged with Sony Classics, part of the Sony conglomerate. Also in 2004, Warner and EMI are hanging in there, but rumors of a merger were strong. Koch is holding its own as an independent, as are Telarc and harmonia mundi, but Polygram and Deutsche Grammophon, London, Decca and Philips are now all part of Universal Vivendi, the biggest name in the business.

---

249. Sensational medieval chant singers, established 1986 who, by mutual consent, retired in 2004.

Different Drummers

Gloria Ackerman	World Piano Competition	Director since 1956
Betty Allen	Harlem School of the Arts	Executive Director Emeritus
Ella Baff	Jacob's Pillow Dance Center	Executive Director
Marilyn Bergman	ASCAP	Chairman of the Board
Ruth Felt	San Francisco Performances	President
Bonnie Hampton	Chamber Music America	Former President
Marta Istomen	Mannes School of Music	President (1992–2005)
Margaret Juntwait	The New Voice of the MET	Radio Announcer/Commentator
Judy Massa	Voice of America	Music Director (1962–2001)
Toby Mayman	The Colburn School	President/Executive Dir. (1980–2000)
Ann McKee	Wolftrap	Vice President Education
Margaret Mercer	WQXR Classical Music Radio NY	Program Director
Wende Person	WQXR	Website Manager
Estelle Popkin	*CBS Sunday Morning*	Producer

Many women hold, or have held, uniquely prominent positions which fitted only in their own category in the business of music. A sampling:

GLORIA ACKERMAN—*The World Piano Competition of Cincinnati;* a graduate of Toronto's Royal Conservatory of Music, Gloria came to Cincinnati in 1956 to continue studies at the College of Music and start a piano studio. After a year of teaching, she felt there should be some method of monitoring students' progress as they do in Canada. Knowing the examination idea alone would not be popular in the U.S., she offered a monetary prize. This was the beginning of the Cincinnati Music Scholarship Association. In 1965 **Claudette Sorel** (1932–99), then teaching at Ohio State, was a judge. She suggested the group's activities be expanded to include other cities. That year, the organization changed its name to the Ohio Music Scholarship Association. In 1972 André Watts was a judge and announced, "I've been looking for a competition to become involved with. This is the one!" It was his idea that in addition to a cash prize, master classes with leading pianists be included in the award. Thus the American Music Scholarship (AMSA), and its subsidiary, the World Piano Competition, came into being. By then, Gloria had spent twelve years creating *Repertoire and Musicianship Requirement Guides* and *Teachers Piano Syllabus* (Belwin Mills, publisher) to structure the AMSA program.

In 2006, celebrating their fiftieth anniversary, the first place prize was a $5,000 study grant. The master classes, which have been given by such notables as Artur Rubenstein, Malcolm Frager, Leon Fleisher, **Gina Bachauer** (1913–76), Lorin Hollander, Garrick Ohlsson, Claude Frank, André Watts, Jorge Bolet and **Rosalyn Tureck** (1914–2003), set this competition apart from many others. As Ackerman says: "Since all of the semi-finalists are invited to the master classes . . . *all* the contestants are winners!"

After fifty years of running this show, the septuagenarian shows no signs of slowing down as is evidenced by her statement, "It's my whole life, I love it. I get the greatest reward in the world from knowing that AMSA touches lives and helps young people."

BETTY ALLEN—*The Voice of Harlem*; mezzo-soprano Betty Allen, now president emeritus, was executive director of the Harlem School of the Arts and chair of the voice department after the retirement of its founder, African-American soprano **Dorothy Maynor** (1910–96) in 1979, until her own retirement in 1992. The school offers instruction in music, dance, drama and the visual arts to over 1,300 black students.

Born in Campbell, Ohio, March 17, 1930, Betty heard opera music coming from the houses in her Sicilian and Greek neighborhood. She also listened to the Met on the radio, attended local concerts and was a member of the school choir. She went to Central State University in Wilberforce, Ohio, and received a certificate from the Hartford School of Music. Her career included appearances as soloist with symphony orchestras, especially well-known for performances in Virgil Thomson's opera *Four Saints in Three Acts*, in which she appeared in 1952, and ANTA Theatre's 1973 mini-Met presentation of this and other major productions until 1982. As a recitalist, after her Town Hall debut in 1958, she toured North and South America, Canada, Europe, North Africa, the Caribbean and the Far East. In 1964, she made her formal opera debut at the Teatro Colón in Buenos Aires. Her North American debut was with San Francisco Opera, 1966, Canadian Opera and Bellas Artes in Mexico City, 1971, New York City Opera, 1973, and Metropolitan Opera's Mini-Met, 1974. Her festival appearances have graced Marlboro, Casals, Santa Fe Chamber Music, Ravinia, Saratoga, Tanglewood, Caramoor and the Cincinnati May Festival.

Allen's teaching talent has illumined the faculties of the Manhattan School of Music, Curtis, and the North Carolina School of the Arts (1978–1987). She has sat on vocal competition juries of the Met, Concert Artists Guild, International Vocal (Holland), Young Concert Artists, Plácido Domingo International, and the Oratorio Society.

She has served on the boards of Carnegie Hall, National Foundation for Advancement in the Arts, American Arts Alliance, and is a trustee of Manhattan School of Music, Chamber Music Society of Lincoln Center and Symphony Orchestra of the New York City Housing Authority. She served as co-chair of the Harlem Arts Advocacy Coalition, and as a member of the Schaumburg Commission, the New York City Advisory Committee for Cultural Affairs.

Her honorary doctorates have come from Wittenberg University (1971), Union College (1981), New School for Social Research (1994), University of Connecticut (1995), Adelphi (1990), Brooklyn College (1992), and Clark (1993). In 1988, she received the Exceptional Achievement Award from the Women's Project and Productions, and the American Eagle Award from the National Music Council; and in 1989, was named Philadelphia National Bank distinguished Artist of the Year, and presented with the Laurel Leaf Award from the American Composers' Alliance in recognition of "Distinguished achievement in fostering and encouraging American music."

Betty Allen married social worker R. Edward Lee, October 17, 1953, at which time they moved to New York. Their son, Anthony Edward, was born in 1966, and daughter, Juliana Catherine, 1969. They have three grandchildren, Brittany, Anthony, and Aaron Lee.

ELLA BAFF—*No Sleeping on This Pillow!* Ella Baff has been executive administrator of the Jacob's Pillow Dance Festival in Becket, Massachusetts, since 1998. Prior to that she was program director, artistic administrator and administrator of education and Outreach of Cal Performances, an international performing arts presenting program at UC Berkeley.

Born in New York, January 22, 1954, her first training was in violin, harp and piano. This was followed by ballet and modern dance study in New York, New Mexico and California. After graduating with honors from UC Berkeley, 1976, for several years she developed dance and theater programs in juvenile prisons, during which time she co-wrote, produced and directed *The Baddest*, a play by juvenile offenders, which they performed while serving time. She was also an artist-in-residence on the Aleutian Islands. She celebrated July 4, 1983, by marrying John Badanes, who sparked her interest in Indonesian music.

Her next position was project director for WNET/13 TV in New York for *America Dancing*, a national outreach project in conjunction with *DANCING*, a public television series on world dance, which aired nationally 1993–94.

Baff has been a consultant for foundations, arts organizations and government agencies, including the Wallace Funds, Zellerbach Family Fund, Packard Foundation and the NEA, for which she chaired the Dance Panel. She also served on task forces, panels and boards of Meet the Composer, National Dance Project, Asia Society, Arts International, *Vive Les Arts* Foundation/French Embassy, Boston, and the National Task Force on Touring and Presenting. As of 2004, she was on the boards of the Berkshire Visitors Bureau, Society of Performing Arts Presenters (ISPA), and MoCA (Massachusetts Museum of Contemporary Art) in North Adams, at this time, the largest contemporary art museum in America. She has participated in international cultural programs in Russia, Greece, Turkey, Portugal, Japan and Israel.

Her position as executive director of Jacob's Pillow entails responsibility for a professional school, archives, year-round education and community programs, and the International Dance Festival—the oldest dance festival in America. Her many accomplishments include the establishment of an endowment for the Pillow, creation of an internship program, expansion of public access to the growing collection of archives, improvements to the physical plant and the development of a program of free events. Under her aegis, for its contribution to cultural life in America, Jacob's Pillow was named in 2001 to the National Register of Historic Places, the only dance center so designated.

Located in Becket, Massachusetts, Jacob's Pillow was originally a family farm and a station on the "Underground Railroad," the route for smuggling slaves to freedom in the 1800s. In 1930, modern dance pioneer Ted Shawn bought the farm as a retreat. At that time, Shawn and his wife, Ruth St. Denis, were America's leading couple of the dance. In 1933, brawny Ted founded the dance center and a troupe of men to dissipate the male dancer sissy image. He succeeded. The public, press, and educators were accepting the dance as a honorable profession for men. In May 1940, the Men Dancers disbanded and joined the armed forces for WWII. On July 9, 1942, the Ted Shawn Theatre opened its doors, the first in this country designed specifically for dance.

MARILYN BERGMAN—*Emmys and Oscars and ASCAP - Oh, My!* In 1985, Marilyn Bergman, who has won three Academy Awards with her husband, Alan, for Best Song and Film Score—*The Windmills of Your Mind* (1968), *The Way We Were* (1973), *Yentl* (1984)—became the first woman to be elected to the board of directors of ASCAP, the world's foremost performing arts rights organization. In 1994, she succeeded American composer Morton Gould (1913–96), who had been president since 1986, and in January 1995, her title was changed to chairman of the board. (See Film Composers.)

RUTH A. FELT—*A Present to San Francisco*, Ruth Felt is the founder, president and executive director of San Francisco Performances, a non-profit organization established in 1979. Arriving in the city in 1971, she joined the staff of the opera, working until '79 with its internationally renowned General Director **Kurt Herbert Adler** (1905–88). Even with the existence of the SF Symphony, Ballet and American Conservatory Theater, Felt saw the need for a presenting organization to bring internationally acclaimed and emerging touring artists in the areas of classical chamber music, jazz in concert and contemporary dance to San Francisco. With a carefully chosen board, 300 subscribers, a budget of $100,000 and a five-year plan, the first SFP season (1980–81) presented six events—André Watts donated his fee for the premiere concert and joined the board.

Born April 8, 1939, in Willmar, Minnesota, after her father's death her mother relocated to Los Angeles when Ruth was in fifth grade. Reaping the benefits from the then excellent Music in the Schools program which included a festival of selected choirs to sing in the Hollywood Bowl, her devotion to the performing arts became ingrained with her participation in this event. Graduating from UCLA, 1961, the time was not yet ripe for women in arts administration, so she worked for a lawyer, then as assistant in speech writing for Vice President Hubert Humphrey. 1966–71 found her back at UCLA, serving as assistant concert manager for the department of fine arts productions.

With hard work and determination, Ruth has nurtured San Francisco Performances for over two decades, with the result that the 2001–02 season featured over fifty main-stage performances and 130 arts education programs in schools and community centers. With 2000 subscribers and a budget of $3 million, their honors include the first Harold Shaw (Recital) Award (1985), SF Chamber of Commerce major contribution award (1986), named in the NEA publication of exemplary presenters—one of twenty-one outstanding non-profit organizations (1988)—and a 1994 tribute from then California Governor Pete Wilson for educational outreach. In 1993, Ruth was honored by the San Francisco Community Music Center for her "exceptional commitment," and in 1997 received the Charles and Eleanor de Limur Award for "Distinguished Contributions to the Arts in San Francisco." In the 1990s, grants came pouring in from foundations such as Lila Wallace *Reader's Digest*, Doris Duke and the James Irvine Cornerstone Arts Program—all cognizant of the great contribution made by SFP via its dedicated founder.

2004–05 celebrated their twenty-fifth anniversary season.

BONNIE HAMPTON—*The Joy of Chamber Music*; cellist Bonnie Hampton was president of Chamber Music America from 1993–96. This organization acts as promoter, mentor and advocate for all chamber music activities in the country. Their Ensemble Residency Program assists groups in establishing long term residencies with host institutions like universities, thus enriching the cultural life of the community. The Commissioning Program funds the creation of new chamber music and supports multiple performances of the new repertoire. The Consulting Services Program provides technical assistance, funds to hire consultants, and sponsors an annual conference featuring workshops, panel discussions and social events. Educational programs offer seminars and awards for excellence in chamber music teaching, which are given to individuals in charge of students aged six to eighteen. The coveted CMA/ASCAP (cash) Awards for Adventuresome Programming acknowledges ensembles and presenters who demonstrate an outstanding commitment to contemporary music. The Distinguished Service Awards honor persons who have demonstrated extraordinary commitment to chamber music in their community. CMA is the advocate for the field's needs to funders, government agencies and the arts community. Their publications include *Chamber Music*, a bi-monthly magazine featuring articles, activities and projects; a membership directory and other organizational and educational newsletters and bulletins. Initially centered in the Northeast, the CMA has now established residencies throughout the country. Bonnie Hampton pioneered further decentralization to benefit young groups. (See Cellists.)

MARTA ISTOMIN—*The Innovator*; born in November 2, 1936, in Puerto Rico, Marta Montañez first demonstrated her gifts for music at the age of five as a violinist and cellist. Serious studies began at nine. By thirteen she came to New York to study at Mannes, which took her through high school. In 1954, she went to Prades (France) to study with the "Grand Master of the Cello," Pablo Casals (1876–1973). On August 3, 1957, she became the third wife of the eighty-year-old legend, and for the first few years concertized with him before giving up her performing career. Casals made his permanent residence in Puerto Rico in 1956 and, during their sixteen-year marriage, Marta became a major force for the development of fine music there, helping the maestro establish the Puerto Rico Symphony, the Conservatory of Music and his annual world famous Casals Festival. For three years after his death in 1973, Marta was co-chairman of the board and music director of the Casals Festival Organization, and instrumental in creating many programs. She taught cello at the Conservatory of Music in the capital, San Juan, concurrently teaching at Curtis in Philadelphia.

On February 15, 1975, Marta married another celebrated artist, American pianist **Eugene Istomin**. They had two weddings, one in New York for his family, one in Puerto Rico for hers. Now her energy and organizing skills thrust into new directions. She became artistic director of Kennedy Center (1980–90); general director of France's Evian Festival (1990–97); and president/artistic director of the Manhattan School of Music (1992–2005). All these positions were avenues of dedication to advancing the careers of young musicians.

At Kennedy Center, she scheduled American and international artists and companies for music, opera and dance. She founded the Center's Terrace Concerts, with a variety of recitals, vocal music, small ensembles and chamber orchestras for the series. She also included evenings devoted to the music of living American composers. Under her direction, the Center presented the largest ballet series in the country, featuring London's Royal Ballet, the Bolshoi, Kirov, Paris Opera Ballet and Royal Danish Ballet, and developed a strong contemporary dance series. 1989 saw a co-commissioning project in which six major American ballet companies received funding for new ballets premiered at the Center, giving opportunities to promising artists. In June 1989, she secured the exclusive American engagement of the Berlin Opera to present Wagner's *Ring*.

Istomin served on the board of directors of publishers Harcourt, Brace, Jovanovich, was a trustee of the Marlboro School of Music (Vermont) and the Marymount School (New York), a director of the World University of Puerto Rico, and co-founder/vice president of the Pablo Casals Foundation in Barcelona. She was appointed to the National Arts Council in 1990 by the first President Bush. Her presidency of the Manhattan School of Music brought thirteen years of inspired leadership, which resulted in attaining the highest level as a conservatory of international eminence, including the addition of a twenty-two story building that doubled the size of the campus.

Fluent in English, French, Spanish and Catalán, plus knowledge of Italian and German, Istomin has participated in international festivals and competitions and represented the U.S. in various countries. She gave the keynote address in Budapest at the "America Now" Exhibition, was a member of the first American cultural delegation to the People's Republic of China, and served as a consultant for the U.S. delegation to the UNESCO Conference on World Culture in Mexico City. The governments of Spain, France and Germany have decorated her with highest civilian honors for her achievements in the arts. She is also the recipient of several honorary doctorates and distinguished American awards.

On October 10, 2003, after twenty-eight years of marriage, Eugene Istomin passed away at age seventy-eight. In September 2004, Marta Casals Istomin announced that she would be retiring in the spring of 2005.

Robert Sirota, (Harvard, PhD, 1979) music chair at NYU (1990–95), president of the Peabody Conservatory (1995–2005) and husband of musicologist, the **Reverend Victoria Sirota**, was chosen to become the new president—a more than well-qualified candidate to follow in Marta's formidable footprints.

Margaret Juntwait

MARGARET JUNTWAIT—*The New Voice of the Met*; born March 18, 1957, in Ridgewood, New Jersey, Margaret began singing in high school. Although she took piano lessons, voice became her instrument of choice. Her first teacher was her choral conductor, who insisted on a performance level of the highest caliber.

She earned a BM at Manhattan School of Music (1980), involved herself in community theater yet, when she realized an opera career was not for her, turned instead to radio. She loved to listen to classical music on WQXR, and by the time she was an adult she was hooked on New York's Public Radio, WNYC. She wrote a letter to John Schaefer, whose program "New Sounds" was a favorite of hers, and asked if he needed an assistant. She found herself with a job as production assistant, "Barely scraping by, but as happy as anyone could be."

When Schafer learned to type his own playlists, Margaret learned the radio business and went on the air as the midday music host. Now the host of WNYC's *Evening Music with Margaret Juntwait*, and a weekday talk/music program, *Soundcheck*, she has also been heard nationally on Classic FM, BBC radio specials, and lent her voice to films and museum tours. She hosted the radio broadcast of the opening concert at Carnegie's Zankel Hall with the Emerson String Quartet and Emanuel Ax; New Year's Eve with the New York Philharmonic; the Philharmonic's broadcast of *Candide*; and the 2003 summer opening of Mostly Mozart from Avery Fisher Hall. She also co-hosted the BBC/WNYC *Music Party*, two programs that included conversation and performances by the Ritz Chamber Ensemble and the Orion String Quartet.

In September 2004, when the Metropolitan Opera announced the continuation of their seventy-three-year history of Saturday afternoon broadcasts, Margaret Juntwait was named the new announcer. On December 11, 2004, she was the third "Voice of the Met," following Milton Cross (1931–75) and Peter Allen, who took over January

1975 after Cross' sudden death. At age eighty-four, after twenty-nine years on the air, Allen announced his retirement April 24, 2004.

Although Texaco sponsored the broadcasts from 1940, after Chevron's buyout of Texaco in 2000 financing was withdrawn. Several foundations raised $7 million for the current year's broadcasts, and the opera began a "Save the Met Broadcasts" appeal with Beverly Stills, to raise $150 million over the next five years for the broadcasts' survival. With a radio audience of more than 10 million, the Saturday performances, carried by 360 stations in the U.S. and other countries, is the longest running cultural program in American broadcast history. Juntwait considers this position to be the high point in her career.

She is no stranger to the Met, having been the announcer for "The Met Celebrates Verdi," the 2004 Metropolitan Opera National Council Grand Finals Concert, and served as a standby announcer for Peter Allen for the last four years. When she learned she had been chosen to host the broadcasts, she said: "I always thought if I got the call I'd give out a whoop, but all I could muster was an awestruck, whispered 'oh, wow.' I'd always enjoyed bringing live performances to my New York audience on WNYC, now I was about to do it on the grandest scale ever. I was quite humbled."

Although there is uncertainty as to how long the broadcasts will receive needed funding, Juntwait's contract was renewed for the 2005–06, 2006–07 seasons. She is counting her blessings.

She is married to *Vibe* magazine editor James C. Katz. The ceremony took place on September 30, 2001, two weeks after 9/11. James' father is Dick Katz, noted jazz pianist, and his brother, Frank, is a fusion drummer. Her children are Gregory, born July 1982, who teaches English in Grenoble (France), and twins Bart and Steven, born December 1983, graduates of Drew University.

Judy Massa

JUDY MASSA—*The Voice of America*; her father and mother were civilian employees of the Canal Zone Government and U.S. Army, respectively, when Judy was born March 23, 1941, in the port city of Colón, Republic of Panama. Not only did she grow up in a family where music was performed and appreciated, but she lived at the "Crossroads of the World" where ships from around the globe gathered to transit the canal. It was an ambiance which provided her with a knowledge and interest in world cultures.

After being named "Outstanding Girl Graduate" of Balboa High School (Canal Zone), she went to DePauw University (Indiana), where she earned a BA *cum laude*. During her last two years, she served as vice president of the campus radio station WGRE. In the summer of her senior year she was selected, out of 110 applicants, one of the ten interns for the Voice of America. This led, upon graduation, to full-time employment at the prestigious international radio station.

Her first position was studio director for broadcasts to Latin America in Spanish and Portuguese. As a result of her outstanding programming of music for that region of the world, Judy was selected as the Popular Music Specialist of Voice of America. In 1984, she became host of VOA's program "Country Music USA," and was named the first VOA music director. In that role, she oversaw and coordinated the coverage of every genre: classical, jazz, pop, country, folk, etc., for all forty-seven VOA language services. She was also the primary music information resource for the entire Voice of America, providing information, guidance and instruction and, acting as a reporter, provided taped and live on-air coverage of noteworthy music events. In addition, she supplied technical broadcast support and served as liaison with artists' management, event management, recording company executives, and national and international media. She handled special assignments, including emceeing overseas entertainment tours, public appearances and PR. Her position required ongoing and extensive contact with radio listeners worldwide.

Massa has served as jurist at international festivals, including the Voice of Asia International Music Contest in Almaty, Kazakhstan, and the Golden Orpheus Pop Festival in Sunny Beach, Bulgaria. Her world travels encompassed a three-week visit to four cities in China in 1993 to conduct audio-visual presentations of American popular music, with emphasis on folk and country styles. She has covered artists' tours in Russia,

Japan and throughout Europe. In 1995, she went to India, Bangladesh, Thailand and Vietnam to promote VOA music broadcasts to South Asia.

Judy conceived, organized and co-hosted the acclaimed *Voice of America Fiftieth Anniversary Gift of Song Concert*, to which she invited guests representing many different styles of music to perform live for VOA's 130 million listeners worldwide.

After twenty years, her last broadcast was January 29, 2001, which evoked an e-mail barrage of "we will miss you!" from all over the world. She still plans to freelance at the studio.

With all this, she was happily married to Roland Sr., who also worked at the Voice of America until his passing in 2002. Of their sons, Roland Jr., born in 1973, is a financial planner, and Justin, born 1981, is in the biology field.

TOBY MAYMAN—*From Warehouse to Conservatory.* Dynamic arts administrator **Toby Mayman** was president and executive director of the Colburn School of Music in Los Angeles from 1980 to 2000. In 1980 she made possible the move from an abandoned cramped corner on the USC campus into a roomy warehouse in downtown Los Angeles. After devoting twenty years of her life to transforming the facility into a nationally acclaimed institute of over 1,500 students—the school accepts children as young as two and a half—it was she who persuaded philanthropist Richard Colburn to permit his name to be used.

Mayman also helped further the dream of the school's reaching conservatory status. In 2004 ground was broken for an adjoining building which provides another 384,000 square feet within thirteen stories to accommodate the expansion, offering advanced degrees for careers in music and dance—Colburn's vision of a "Curtis Institute" on the West Coast.

True to Colburn's prediction, "Toby will be a pillar of power to this school until her dying day . . ." although Mayman retired October 2000, she continues promoting the school part time as vice chair of the board of directors, where she is influential in expanding the board and developing closer relationships with other art institutions.

There can be no more fitting tribute to Mrs. Mayman than Richard Colburn's words at her retirement: "The school as it stands today is a living testimony to all that Toby has done." Mayman Hall has been named in her honor. (All is now in the capable hands of Executive Director Joseph Thayer who has been second-in-command since 1983.)

ANN McKEE—*Over Twenty-five Years on the Farm!* A graduate of Trinity University, Ann McPherson McKee has been a designer, technical director and producer for Michigan Opera Theatre and Houston's Wonderland Theatre, and was one of the founders and co-owners of the San Antonio Theatre Club and San Antonio's original Melodrama Theatre.

She has been a part of Wolf Trap since 1975, and is senior vice president of performing arts and education for the Wolf Trap Foundation.[250] She holds divisional responsibility for the scheduling, booking, budgeting and technical requirements of all productions at the Filene Center and the Barns of Wolf Trap, supervises the education department, Wolf Trap Opera Company, and serves as lead negotiator with all affiliated unions.

A member of design and construction management teams during the rebuilding of the Filene Center, 2003 saw the opening of the new $10 million Educational Center, providing space not only for Wolf Trap's Institute for Early Learning Through the Arts, but also for the renowned Wolf Trap Opera Company.

MARGARET MERCER—*Transmitting the World's Greatest Music;* Margaret Mercer has been program director of New York's WQXR[251] since 1998. She joined the station in 1984 as program coordinator. For six years before,

---

250. See Catherine Filene Shouse -The Unforgotten

251. WQXR, America's first classical music station, was founded in 1936 by John Vincent Hogan, a radio innovator and inventor of "single dial control," and advertising/publishing writer Elliott Sanger. Its mission to create a self-supporting station for the best in music began with transmitting a few hours a day from Long Island City via a homemade antenna attached to the roof of Hogan's laboratory. It became the first AM, and FM (1939) station in New York.

she was assistant music director for WNCN, and involved in the award-winning series on pianist Vladimir Horowitz, plus special programs on keyboard luminaries Claudio Arrau, Alfred Brendel, and composer/pianist Morton Gould. She edited the record, *The Piano in America.*

Margaret lives in Manhattan with her husband, Bill Mooney, a professor at the Fashion Institute of Technology, and their son, Will.

WENDE PERSON—*A Hit at the Website!* Wende Person was born in Buffalo, New York, November 24, 1952. Her next door neighbors, whom she calls her surrogate grandparents, began teaching her piano at six. Her great-uncle, Zee Person (one of the original trustees of Vermont's Marlboro Festival), gave her a piano when she was ten. But it was church music and singing in choirs all her life that led to her music studies in college. Her BA in music education is from SUNY, Fredonia, and master's in English education from University of Rochester (1978). While working her way through college there, she was placed at Eastman because she knew music. When she began working in their concert office, she realized she could do something other than perform or teach . . . she could organize and promote musicians! After graduation, she worked at the Wolf Trap Festival, then Pittsburgh Opera as the public relations/marketing director. She was the librettist for the opera *Patience & Sarah*, which had its premiere at Lincoln Center Festival in July 1998. She was producer and program director for WQED-FM, then spent ten years in the marketing and product management division for Deutsche Grammophon in New York City before leaving to manage the website of WQXR, the classical station of the *New York Times*. In 2002, she was named WQXR's executive director of programming.

ESTELLE POPKIN—*Always on Sunday;* one of the most dedicated and tireless on staff in the network, Estelle Popkin has been associated with *CBS Sunday Morning* since 1979, becoming a producer in 1982.

Born November 17, 1945, in Brooklyn, New York, she had no musical background other than taking piano lessons for one year at age eleven. She graduated from Barnard College (1966) with a degree in economics, after which she pursued post graduate studies at the London School of Economics. She arrived at CBS in 1967, starting as an economist for the first six years, going on to news division financial analyst in 1973. By 1975, she was production manager of *Magazine*, a position she subsequently held on *CBS Reports*. She was also part of the religious unit under Britisher Pamela Ilott, one of the first women executive producers in the business. They aired two shows, *Lamp Unto My Feet* and *Look Up and Live!* On January 29, 1979, these gave way to *CBS Sunday Morning*, a weekly hour featuring segments on current events and the arts with anchor Charles Kuralt, until his retirement in March 1994. (He died July 1997.) Charles Osgood became the new anchor. Initially, twice a month, the cultural spotlight focused on classical music personalities with arts correspondent flutist/writer **Eugenia Zukerman**, who has been with the program over twenty years. Lately, classical music segments have become rarer.

CBS Sunday Morning and Estelle Popkin were among the nominees in the twenty-fifth annual News and Documentary Emmy Awards—the ceremony was telecast September 25, 2004.

CHAPTER SIXTEEN

Agents — The Starmakers

AGENTS

The Grand Salon - Misia
Grace Denton (1890–1989)
Cecelia Schultz (1878–1971)
Ann Colbert (1906–2001)
Thea Dispeker (1902–2000)
Agnes Eisenberger (1923–2002)
CAMI Nelly Walter (1901–2001)
Mariedi Anders
Elizabeth Crittenden
Elizabeth Dworkin
Shirley Kirshbaum
Lee Lamont - ICMA
Edna Landau
Blanche Lewis
Karen McFarlane
Joanne Rile
Del Rosenfield

Charlotte Schroeder
Nancy Shear
Susan Wadsworth

PR

Mary Lou Falcone
Josephine Hemsing

EUROPEAN AGENTS

Gerhild Baron
Patrizia Garrasi
Mirjana Mitrovic
Judith Salpeter
Beatrice Vesper
Karin Wylach

IAMA

Virginia Braden

In Europe, the cradle of culture, the artists management business began with *impresarios*, the original "business" managers for the nobles who owned the first public opera houses. By the 17h century, in Venice, an impresario could even collect taxes for a term of years and pay the state a certain percentage. In turn, he was responsible for finding a concert hall, an opera, scenery, costumes and singers. Concerts with paid admission began in London in 1664, where by the 18th century there were numerous concert organizations, including one run by **Johann Christian**, the son of **Bach**, who made his home in England. During the Golden Era of Romantic Music, many wealthy women, while not making a business of it, nevertheless promoted the musicians of their day in their own homes. These concerts, known as *salons*, were prevalent throughout Europe, especially in Paris, Vienna and major cities in Germany, such as Leipzig, where the Mendelssohn family held sway. In the 20th century, perhaps the last man to hold the title *impresario* was **Sol Hurok** (1888–1974). Born in Russia, he emigrated to America in 1906, and for sixty years imported Russian talent such as ballerina **Anna Pavlova**, basso **Feodor Chaliapin**, pianist **Artur Rubinstein**, violinist **Mischa Elman**, cellist **Gregor Piatigorsky**, the Bolshoi Ballet, Moiseyev Dance Company and a multitude of other great international artists. There was, however, an American woman who quietly equaled the accomplishments of Hurok and his predecessors.

Madame Impresario

GRACE DENTON was born near Cleveland in 1890. She studied at Oberlin College Conservatory, graduating at eighteen with a public schools teaching certificate which included piano and voice. After a few years in this arena, and on the faculty of Otterbein University in Westerville, Ohio, in 1911 she went to Puerto Rico. On board the tossing ship she met Maurice H. Esser, a violinist and Phi Beta Kappa from Colgate University. They taught at the same government school until he was made principal of another and Grace was promoted to Supervisor of Music for the whole island. When World War I began raging in Europe, teachers were shipped back to the mainland. A scientist and linguist, Maurice became involved in the field of metallurgy, often working with Franklin D. Roosevelt when the latter was governor of New York.

In 1918, Grace worked in New York at Schirmer's Music Publishing Company, then at the *Musical Courier* magazine, which enabled her to see concerts every night of the week and twice on Saturdays and Sundays. She drank in this unique era before radio, when people flocked in droves to every kind of entertainment. The world's finest conductors were in their prime. Rachmaninoff, Dvořák, Tchaikovsky and other great composers visited America, performing their own music. The Met glittered with **Enrico Caruso**, **Geraldine Farrar**, **Mary Garden** and a host of other immortal stars.

After a few years of this heady existence, one of her college friends asked Grace to come to Toledo, Ohio, to help him in his artists' management business. After two years of gathering this new experience, she struck out on her own, renting a movie theater—without a dime to her name—but on the strength that she could hire the fabled Irish tenor **John McCormack** (1884–1945). Beginning in 1923, she engaged stars like Austrian diva **Ernestine Schumann-Heink**, prima ballerina **Anna Pavlova**, violist **Lionel Tertis**, and the entire Cleveland Symphony with **Nicolai Sokoloff** (1886–1965), its first director. This was just the beginning of a star-studded line-up that was to stretch for almost a quarter of a century. She expanded her territory to include Detroit, starting with a concert in the Masonic Auditorium which seated 4,600. She also presented a series of plays with the foremost actors of the day. **George Gershwin** played for her. Lawyer **Clarence Darrow** lectured to an overflow house. She presented a young **Jascha Heifetz** and an even younger **Yehudi Menuhin**, prodigies who were dazzling the world with their violin virtuosity, and managed the first Detroit appearance of **Andres Segovia**, pioneer of the classical guitar in the concert hall. She procured the superb pianist **Jan Ignatz Paderewski**, who at the time was also prime minister of Poland. In 1931, she even arranged a lecture appearance for **Winston Churchill**. She treated audiences to their first hearing of the fabulous voice of black soprano **Marian Anderson**.

Denton worked for the love of music. Her ticket sales were in the hundreds of thousands, but costs kept pace. She was always operating on a shoestring—all this and she was still only in her thirties.

The stock market crash of 1929 impacted the entertainment industry in that many wealthy patrons lost their funds. But not all. Denton went to Chicago in 1931 and, with help from the right sources, brought opera to that city, putting on *Tosca* with the glamorous Austrian **Maria Jeritza**, and presenting a recital by mesmerizing Russian basso, **Feodor Chaliapin**. She got Sol Hurok to bring the Ballet Russe to the Windy City—this for $32,000 and a fifty-fifty split with him. She was one of the signers for reopening Ravinia Park for Chicago Symphony summer concerts. In 1935, she was asked to be the manager of the new Chicago Opera, but the managers of the Chicago Auditorium, her original venue, "bought" her back. Yet, after staging the highly successful Auditorium Series in conjunction with Northwestern University, internal politics and lack of a written contract edged her out. Her philosophy was always, "Ah, well . . . time to move on!"

In 1938 Denton headed for California, ending up in Santa Barbara where she helped found the Music Academy of the West, which opened its doors in 1947 with such names on the faculty as **Lotte Lehmann**, **Ernest Bloch** and **Maurice Abravanel**. The '50s saw a stint at Aspen Music School and Festival, then three years as assistant manager of the Dallas Symphony. Invited to Palm Springs, Grace fell in love with the desert, but got sidetracked for another three years as manager of the Orange County Symphony. She returned to Palm Springs to work on the staff of an art gallery from 1964–68. She had come the full circle: music, theater, dance and the graphic arts.

Although she had said no to his first proposal, and later he married someone else, after his wife's death the faded romance re-bloomed, and on November 22, 1968, Grace finally married Maurice Esser. Although he died only eight months afterward, Grace was quoted as saying she had no regrets about not marrying earlier. "Music was so much a part of me . . . it grew and grew . . . and I was completely involved in my career." She died in Huntington Beach, California, June 13, 1989, at age ninety-eight, with few in the world knowing of her illustrious career.

CECELIA AUGSBERGER SCHULTZ—*The Grace Denton of the Northwest*; Cecelia Schultz was a promoter of theater and opera who managed the Seattle Symphony and the Moore Theater, bringing much music to the city. When she moved to Seattle in 1915, in her mid-thirties, she brought her love of music and organizational skills which led her to become the best musical promoter in the city's history. She was the only woman of her time to run her own theater after she took over management of the Moore in 1935. She earned the title "Seattle's Grand Dame Impresario."

Born 1878, in Trenton, Ohio, she learned piano at age five and graduated from Illinois Wesleyan College of Music at seventeen. In 1922, she married local businessman Gustav Schultz. In the early years, her natural talent for organization blossomed as she presented a series of "afternoon musicales" at the new Olympic Bowl's Spanish Ballroom. She broke into concert promotion on a large scale in 1933 when she booked the huge Civic Auditorium for "An Evening of Song with Lawrence Tibbett," drawing a sellout crowd of 6,300 music lovers. The same year, she presented the touring Salzburg Opera Guild. Such was her confidence that she committed $100,000—an enormous sum at the time—for a season of big name entertainers.

After taking over the management of the Moore Theater, she created a Great Artists Series that brought entertainment luminaries of the day to the Northwest. During the following decade she brought several operas to Seattle, and in the 1950s built the Community Concert Association into the largest organized concert series in the country. This served as a model for many other cities.

It was **Milton Katims** (1909–2006), coming from his position as co-principal viola and associate conductor (1943–54) of **Arturo Toscanini's** NBC Symphony to direct the Seattle Symphony (1954–76), who dubbed Cecelia Schultz, "the Sol Hurok of the Northwest." (And who told me about her in 2002 . . .)

The Grand Lady died in 1971 at the age of ninety-two. (Milton passed away at ninety-seven.)

Farewell Impresario . . . Hello, Ms Agent!
Pioneers Who Forged the Way

ANN COLBERT—*The Name Lives On*; Ann Colbert was born in Berlin February 8, 1906. She moved to America in 1936 and started Colbert Artists Management, Inc., with her husband, Henry Colbert, in 1948. Her star-studded roster included singers **Joan Sutherland, Elizabeth Schwarzkopf, Christa Ludwig,** Dietrich Fischer-Dieskau, José van Dam; conductors Sir Georg Solti, Christoph von Dohnanyi, Richard Bonynge; pianists Alfred Brendel and Mieczyslaw Horszowski (1892–1993); cellist Janoš Starker; oboist Heinz Holliger; the Juilliard String Quartet; as well as the late great flutist/conductor Jean-Pierre Rampal (1922–2000).

Colbert retired in 1991, leaving her company in the capable hands of **Agnes Eisenberger** (see below) who had been with the agency since the 1960s. Ann passed away February 25, 2001, at age ninety-five, survived by her daughter, Vera, two grandchildren and two great grandchildren.

THEA DISPEKER—*Forever Young*; her earliest dream was to join the circus. She almost succeeded when, as a small girl, she jumped from the balcony of a Bavarian peasant house into a passing circus cart. Only the swiftly pursuing feet of her nursemaid kept Thea from achieving this early goal. The disconsolate child could not know that a far more exciting future awaited her, that she would spend her life in an even more enchanted world of brilliant artists performing feats of vocal derring-do on the great stages of the world, and for more than half a century she would be a powerful and moving force in that world.

Born in Munich, September 28, 1902, into a highly cultured family who recognized and encouraged her musical gifts, Thea majored in musicology at the University of Munich, where she earned a PhD and graduated *magna cum laude*. On a post-graduation holiday in Italy she contracted polio and, while in Berlin, where she had gone to consult medical specialists, she worked with the renowned musicologist and critic Alfred Einstein on his "Musiklexicon." She also continued her piano studies in Munich with Professor Walter Lampe, who had been a student of **Clara Schumann**.

An opportunity came which enabled Thea to combine her musical gifts with her affection for children. Joining the Central Institute of Education, part of the Ministry of Culture, she developed several new concepts for early education in music from kindergarten through high school. She also devised and produced two long-running radio programs on music by and for children, which were broadcast nationally. The rise of Nazism, and the growing uncertainties of life in Germany, caused her family to leave in 1938. Since her father had been born in the U.S. and retained dual citizenship, his family were automatically American citizens. They made their home in New York. Thea immediately began working with the noted music critic **Olin Downes**, who was in charge of all musical productions at the 1939 World's Fair, and raising money for a children's music building. But funding was insufficient to develop Downes' cultural plans for the World's Fair at large, or Dispeker's dreams for the Children's Village to be realized. At this time she presented six concerts in three years at the home of Mrs. John Henry Hammond, which housed a 200-seat concert hall. Recruiting elite audiences of children from New York's private schools, she selected music instructive and pleasurable for young ears, and invited well-known artists to perform.

In 1942, she joined the W. Colston Leigh Lecture Bureau, building their concert division to a level where she managed some of the greatest artists of the time, such as soprano **Grace Moore**, Danish-born tenor **Lauritz Melchior** (1890–1973), and beloved American baritone **Lawrence Tibbett** (1896–1960). A few years later, she moved to the William Morris Agency to manage their Radio Division. In 1947, she formed her own agency. The same year she co-founded the Little Orchestra Society of New York, with **Thomas Scherman** as artistic director. She persuaded him to conduct children's concerts in the city and suburbs, and brought many artists famous in Europe—but still unknown in America—as soloists with the orchestra, such as singers **Kathleen Ferrier** and **Pilar Loringer**.

In subsequent years, Dispeker's activities included being administrative director of the 1959 New York City Handel Festival, for which she received the Handel Medallion—the city's highest arts award. The same year she received the Service Cross, Germany's most distinguished arts award, from Chancellor Konrad Adenauer. She also founded and produced the NYU Chamber Series, served as executive secretary for the prestigious Leventritt Foundation, and for four years was managing director of the Casals Festival—named for one of the world's greatest cellists, Spaniard **Pablo Casals** (1876–1973).

In November 1998, after half a century, she turned over the operation of Thea Dispeker, Inc. to Laurence Wasserman, whom she hired in 1960, and who, since 1980, was vice president and director of the vocal division. A graduate of NYU, with a double major in music and English, he is a pianist in the trio "Three for the Show," known for their repertoire of excerpts from opera and Broadway musicals.

Dispeker entered her ninth decade still at her desk, but in her home office where, as *Concertopera - Thea Greig, Consultant*, she represented a few select new artists. (Thea was married to banker Lawrence Greig from 1950 until his death in 1986.)

Eternal rest came quietly July 17, 2000, at age ninety-eight. Mourned throughout the music world, to the very end Thea retained the curiosity, enthusiasm and passion of that little girl whose first love was the circus. It is worthy of her memory that her name will live on in an agency illumined by stars of a special firmament.

AGNES EISENBERGER—*The Idealist*; Agnes to only close friends, Miss Eisenberger was one of the music industry's great ladies. President and owner of Colbert Artists Management, she died of cancer, December 26, 2002, in New York City. Her successor is **Charlotte Schroeder**, her friend and colleague of over thirty years with the company.

Born in Vienna, February 22, 1923, Agnes' father, concert pianist Severin Eisenberger (1879–1945), was a professor at Krakow Conservatory from 1914–21, and lived in Vienna for several years before the family moved to

America. He continued his recital career and was a soloist with the Cleveland Orchestra. His daughter graduated from Adelphi University, where she became immersed in great literature and poetry, an interest she carried with her throughout her life.

As an agent, she displayed unfailing belief in her artists. The career of Austrian born pianist **Alfred Brendel** (*b* 1931) is an example of this confidence. Coming to America in 1963 after a successful European career, she promoted him and established an equally loyal audience on this side of the Atlantic, beginning with a concert series at Carnegie Hall in 1972—where he played annually for many years.

Eisenberger joined Colbert Artists in the early 1960s, via her marriage to Austrian violist Paul Doktor (1919–89), and became executive assistant to Ann and Henry Colbert, who had founded the company in 1948. While her marriage ended in divorce, she continued following her passion for chamber music and, with the Colberts, managed over a dozen ensembles, including the **Juilliard String Quartet**. Until his death, she supervised the career of **Sir Georg Solti** (1912–97), Chicago Symphony director (1969–92), and helped arrange their American tours. She coordinated **Christoph von Dohnanyi's** directorship of the Cleveland Orchestra (1984–2002), and the popularization of the flutist/conductor **Jean-Pierre Rampal**. She did not approve of child prodigies, feeling it was asking too much too soon.

Miss E. was also part of the Colberts' introduction of singers **Joan Sutherland** at Town Hall, **Dietrich Fischer-Dieskau** at Carnegie, and **Christa Ludwig** at the Met. With her understanding of artists' temperaments, Agnes helped each to fulfillment. When Ann Colbert retired in 1991 (see above), Agnes assumed the ownership and presidency of Colbert Artists Management.

She completed her translation of *Brahms' Notebooks* (published in German in 1909), and with her Annotations and Introduction, the collection of 645 poems and passages admired by Brahms was brought out by Pendragon Press (2003).

Eisenberger maintained homes in New York City and Pawling (upstate New York) with her long-time companion James N. Ravlin, who pre-deceased her in 1997.

CAMI - The Friendly Giant

The world's largest agency, with its head office in New York and branches in Los Angeles and Berlin, harboring the biggest chunk of top talent in the classical music field, is Columbia Artists Management Inc., known in the trade by its acronym, CAMI. It was formed in 1930 when **Arthur Judson**, founder of CBS, merged seven concert managers to pool their musical, commercial and booking knowledge. Within the conglomerate are eighteen divisions, each run by a different manager. The 2005–06 season marked their seventy-fifth anniversary. A name which is an integral part of that history is **Nelly Walter**.

NELLY WALTER—*The Doyenne of CAMI*; like her compatriot **Thea Dispeker**, Nelly Walter was born in Germany just after the turn of the century, January 13, 1901, and was still at her desk every day at an age when most of humanity has left the Earth. (She did not retire until 1997.) Growing up in Dresden, Nelly, at ten, began attending the famous opera there. She studied at the conservatory while working in the program department of the State Theater. After receiving her teaching degree, she was working as an accompanist when she learned that Norbert Salter, the leading international opera manager, needed a secretary who knew opera and spoke several languages. She got the job and went to Berlin, launching her career in management. After a few seasons with Salter, she switched to the Otto Mertens Agency—his son, André, would later become her boss at Columbia Artists. Meanwhile, Walter began to develop her own network of clients in Europe and South America. Leading American managers came to Europe to engage clients from her. She met top names of the era, and remembers violinist Yehudi Menuhin as a boy in short pants. She traveled all over Europe, but especially loved Vienna, the birthplace of her parents.

The political upheaval beginning in 1930 changed her life. The Mertens Agency was closed when Otto died of a heart attack. By 1933, Nelly and her mother had to leave Germany for their safety because they were Jewish. Nelly went to Prague, where her friend, famed conductor **George Szell**, was music director of the opera. She was soon in danger again as the Nazi tide swept toward Czechoslovakia. She joined her mother who had gone to *her* family in Vienna, and continued her work there until Hitler invaded Austria in March 1938. Mother and daughter managed to get to Paris, where she met French modernist composer **Francis Poulenc**, American composer **Virgil Thomson** and other prominent musical figures. She attended the Paris Opera whenever she could, and even arranged a Scandinavian tour for the production of *Pelléas et Mélisande*. When the Germans marched into Paris, June 1940, she and her mother escaped and went into hiding in Marseilles. One morning, while on the daily search for food, she was picked up by soldiers and thrown into a French concentration camp in the Pyrenees mountains where she was put to work. (There were no gas chambers in the French camps.) Fortunately, she was freed by Maquis resistance fighters and returned to Marseilles and her mother. When the American Army liberated Europe, Nelly worked for them as a purchasing agent in the Quartermaster Corps—the only foreigner and the only female. Her efficiency was eventually rewarded with a visa to America.

Mother and daughter arrived in New York, June 11, 1946. Nelly started at Columbia Artists a few days later. Arthur Judson, founder of the conglomerate, was president, and Nelly became invaluable, shepherding foreign artists around. André Mertens came to CAMI to head a division, and Nelly became his right hand woman. After his death in 1963, she was promoted to a vice presidency. She signed up such potential stars as the young **Leontyne Price**, **Cesare Siepi** and her discovery, **Renata Tebaldi**.

Nelly Walters' seventy-plus year career put her in touch with the most famous talent in the world for over half a century. She loved her work, but was very firm about staying out of the spotlight.

Her health began to decline after her ninety-seventh year, and by ninety-nine she was bedridden. She rallied to celebrate her 100th birthday, January 13, 2001, when flowers, gifts and cards arrived from celebrities all over the world. Cared for in her last years by her lifelong friend and cousin, Alice Straschil,[252] Nelly passed away peacefully in New Jersey, October 25, 2001.

Musical America—The Agents' "Bible"

These days, for any artist, an agent is the indispensable medium between the esthetics of his or her talent and the realities of being marketed as a profitable commodity. *Musical America* (See Publishers) is the bible for modern impresarios to advertise their wares, and concert managers to make their selections. Indexes abound, listing every agent, orchestra, singer, instrumentalist, music festival, etc., in the world. In print since 1907, the publication began as a trade newsletter. In 1920 it appeared as an annual booking guide, separate from the monthly magazine of the same name—the latter published until 1992. By 1960, *Musical America* began to assume the daunting proportions it features today—800 pages, and by 2006 a cost of $120.00. Among the jewels in this treasury are enlightening articles on the music scene, and M.A.'s much coveted annual choices of "Composer of the Year," "Conductor of the Year," "Instrumentalist of the Year," "Ensemble of the Year" and the Grand Honorée, "Musician of the Year," who graces the front cover. 1994 featured soprano **Christa Ludwig**; 1995, mezzo **Marilyn Horne**; 2001, pianist **Margaret Argerich**; and 2005, soprano **Karrita Mattila**. Over the years, other women so honored were **Leontyne Price**, 1961, **Birgit Nilsson**, 1968–69, (one issue spanned both years), **Beverly Sills**, 1970, **Sarah Caldwell**, 1974, **Alicia de Larrocha**, 1978, and **Jessye Norman**, 1982.

Following is a montage of the many first rate agencies headed by women, as found in the pages of *Musical America* . . . .

---

252. Alice and the author have stayed in touch and met in May 2004.

MARIEDI ANDERS—*Opening That Golden Gate!* Mariedi Anders was born in Vienna into a music-loving family whose friends included many prominent musicians. The family moved to San Francisco in 1938, as many European artists also fled Europe (and Hitler) just before World War II. On the West Coast, they performed with the San Francisco Symphony and Opera, and once again they congregated at the Anders' home. When Czech conductor **Jan Popper** (1908–79) directed Domenico Cimarosa's (1749–1801) opera, *The Secret Marriage*, in Berkeley, Mariedi asked about seeing a performance in San Francisco. Popper confessed he did not know how to go about arranging this.

"I'll do it for you!" proclaimed Mariedi.

"Are you an impresario?" asked Popper.

"As of now!" she replied confidently.

Six weeks later, after finding her way in completely unknown territory, two weekends of performances played to full houses and Mariedi Anders Artists Management was launched.

Despite admonishments that the only way for an agency to succeed was to be located in New York, after over four decades in the business with an illustrious roster, Anders has proven that there *is* life in the West—and success—in the city by the Golden Gate.

Her stars include: Conductors **Barbara Yahr**, Hans Graf, and Nikolaus Harnoncourt; violinist **Silvia Marcovici**; tenor **Peter Schreier**; and many chamber ensembles including the Altenberg Trio and Borodin Quartet. (Anders also handled the late famed flamenco guitarist **Narciso Yepes** until his death in 1997.)

ELIZABETH CRITTENDEN—*Filling the Opera Houses*; Betsy was born into music. Her mother, a pianist with BM and MM degrees from Smith College, filled their home with harmonies. Television introduced Elizabeth to her first opera, *Amahl and the Night Visitors*. Piano studies began at age five. She sang in church choirs and school choruses, meanwhile earning a BM in music education (University of North Carolina, Greensboro), where she also completed a year of master's study in music history. Private voice studies in Manhattan with Adele Addison, classes at Juilliard, plus private Italian study in New York with Robert Cowart rounded out a background which has enabled her to give master classes on career advice to aspiring professional singers in schools and opera programs throughout the U.S. Crittenden started her business career acting as a tour guide at Lincoln Center (1969–73). In 1973, she became secretary/assistant in the New York office for Gian Carlo Menotti's Festival of Two Worlds in Spoleto, Italy, rising to their artistic administrator (1974–76). In the fall of 1976 she was hired as regional sales person at Kazuko Hillyer International, creating their vocal division in 1977. She remained as Vocal Manager until March 1981, when she joined CAMI as division head. She became vice president in 1983, and since the 2000–2001 season has served as head of their opera/vocal division.

Attesting to the stimulating and career-friendly environment of CAMI, other longtime women managers are (as of 2004): **Judie Janowski**, over thirty-five years; **Mary Jo Connealy**, twenty-five years; and **Michaela Kurz**, twenty-three years. A unique career change was that of **Joyce Arbib** who, after celebrating her twenty-fifth anniversary with the company, February 7, 1996, retired in 1998 to enter a convent.

ELIZABETH DWORKIN—*Triple Crown: Musician - Manager - Agent*; Elizabeth Dworkin is president of *dworkin eliason pARTners*, with Barbara Eliason, a Northern New Jersey concert management, public relations and consulting firm established 1991. Their roster ranges from composer Richard Danielpour to performers **Jennifer Frautschi**, violin, and violist **Cynthia Phelps**.

Born in New Jersey, and originally trained as a violinist, Dworkin earned a BM at the Manhattan School of Music. After teaching music in the schools, she began her arts administration career as personnel manager of the North Jersey Symphony and Manhattan Chamber Orchestra, also working at the Waterloo Music Festival. During her tenure as production manager of the Pro Arte Chorale, they performed with Zubin Mehta and the New York Philharmonic at Lincoln Center. As managing director of the Philharmonic-on-the-Hudson, she arranged their Carnegie Hall debut. She subsequently became the director of marketing, PR and subscriptions for the Chamber

Music Society of Lincoln Center. Her work for Juilliard, SONY, the National Guild of Community Schools of the Arts and other organizations supporting young musicians, reflects Dworkin's dedication to cultural education and its relevance to the future of the arts in the 21st century.

SHIRLEY KIRSHBAUM—*Small Roster - Tall Names*, celebrating over twenty years as founder/director of Shirely Kirshbaum & Associates, she took her long time associate Susan Barker Demler as a director and partner to become Kirshbaum Demler & Associates, Inc. in 1999. Born in Tyler, Texas, into a musical family, Shirley's late father, Joseph (1911–96), was a violinist and conductor of the East Texas Symphony, her mother was a harpist, and her brother Ralph is an internationally known cellist. Shirley was playing harp and violin by age five, and at seven took up piano, which she continued studying through her college years at the University of Texas, graduating with honors with a BM in piano performance and piano pedagogy.

Moving to London, 1974–77, she worked as an editorial assistant for the sixth edition of the *Grove Dictionary of Music and Musicians*, edited by the late Stanley Sadie. (See **Julie Anne Sadie**.) She also worked for two noted British artist management firms, Harold Holt, and Ingpen and Williams. On her return to New York, she was employed by ICM Artists, Ltd. during the agency's first two and a half years of formation. Her next valuable experience was as private secretary to two major musical personalities, violinist **Pinchas Zukerman** and baritone **Sherill Milnes**. In 1980, she put her unique background into the foreground and founded Kirshbaum and Associates. Her exclusive roster includes pianist/conductor Andras Schiff; violinist/violist/conductor Pinchas Zukerman; Orion String Quartet; cellist Ralph Kirshbaum; and soprano **Heidi Grant Murphy**. Kirshbaum also managed the late, great conductor Eduardo Mata, whose brilliant career was tragically cut short with the crash of his private plane in January 1995.

On the home front, Shirley is married to a neuropsychologist. They have two grown children.

Lee Lamont

LEE LAMONT—*The Chairman of the Board*, a native New Yorker, Lamont began her professional life in 1955 as a secretary, and worked her way to the very top. After an education concentrated in fine arts, she was hired to assist Sheldon Gold, a sales representative of the late impresario Sol Hurok. With the exception of one year (1957) with CAMI, she remained with the Hurok organization for ten years, rising to executive assistant to Vice President George Perper. Leaving Hurok in 1967, she worked directly with touring attractions, including Sarah Caldwell's American Opera Company. In 1968, **Isaac Stern** hired her to assist him with his many recording and touring duties, a position she held until 1976 when Gold, now president of the newly established ICM Artists, Ltd., asked for her help with developing the firm. Two years later, she became vice president. Upon Gold's death in 1985, she was appointed to the office of president. In 1995, she became chairman when David Foster was brought in as president and CEO of ICMA

With headquarters in New York and offices in Los Angeles and London, ICMA has seen a global expansion with the addition of a lecture division and a major increase in its holdings of top quality talent, especially in the Chamber and Instrumental divisions. Lamont's negotiations led to the signing of the first tours of Soviet attractions since the renewal of the Cultural Agreement between the U.S. State Department and the then USSR in 1985, plus the first Cultural Exchange Tours between the United States and China, resulting in tours of several of each country's greatest orchestras and performers. Scheduling foreign talent from Israel, Russia, Egypt, Hungary, Spain, Holland, etc., as well as great American talent, keeps her company growing. Her flair for marketing has given ICMA a solid reputation.

Wed at nineteen—a marriage that would last forty-nine years until the untimely death of her husband in a January 1998 car accident—Lee is the proud mother of daughter Leslie, a medical software administrator for a pharmaceutical company in Colorado.

On October 31, 2002, after a highly successful forty-seven year career, Lee Lamont retired to an advisory capacity with the title, chairman emeritus. Fortuitously, the house backing onto Leslie's was for sale. There are no fences between their back gardens . . . as my husband and I found out on a delightful visit in May 2004, and again in 2006.

EDNA LANDAU—*Sitting on Top of the Music World;* Like many of her colleagues, Edna Landau has had a thorough education in the field with a BA in music from New York's City College, and a master's in musicology from CUNY. She taught music history, voice, piano and theory at the High School of Music and Art (1968–73) before moving into "the business."

Her first job (1973–78) was with **Susan Wadsworth**, director of Young Concert Artists—considered the only non-profit agency in the world. She then joined forces with Charles Hamlen to form Hamlen/Landau Management, working under that name until 1984 when the agency was acquired by International Management Group (IMG), the largest sports representation and marketing company in the world.

At the inception of IMG Artists, Hamlen and Landau represented promising talent like violinist Joshua Bell, and pianist Jeffrey Kahane. Later added to the list were violinists Itzhak Perlman and **Hilary Hahn**, flutist James Galway, pianists Murray Perahia, Evgeny Kissin, and Leif Ove Andnes, cellist Lynn Harrell, guitarist Christopher Parkening, **Michala Petri**, recorder, the Emerson String Quartet, Canadian Brass, conductor Riccardo Chailly, and sopranos **Kiri Te Kanawa**, **June Anderson**, **Barbara Hendricks** and **Dawn Upshaw**. After Charles Hamlen left IMG in 1992, Landau became Senior International vice president and managing director. To bring great performers to all corners of the globe, she works in close collaboration with her colleagues at IMG offices in London, Paris, Italy, Kuala Lumpur and Singapore.

BLANCHE ARTIS LEWIS—*Management in the Midwest;* founder and president of Ovation! Management, Blanche Artis Lewis studied voice at Chicago Musical College, plus opera and lieder at the Salzburg Mozarteum. Besides performing in opera, concert, and oratorio, she was a leading contralto for the American *Savoyards* in 556 Gilbert and Sullivan operetta performances in New York. She also spent four years in recital nationwide on the Community Concert circuit. A new career began as assistant professor of voice and opera at the University of Tulsa, where she founded their Miniopera, which performed at elementary and high schools throughout the state. She has also taught at Bowling Green (Ohio), College of Lake County (Illinois), Bloomingdale School of Music (New York), and was only the second woman to be hired by Notre Dame (South Bend, Indiana).

In 1983 Lewis returned to Chicago, where she opened a private vocal studio. She formed the Opera Factory, then the only company in the world—now in its third decade—presenting *zarzuela*, a uniquely Spanish form of operetta, in Spanish and English. With orchestra and original designed costumes, they utilize the talents of Hispanic and other artists. Their performance of de Falla's *La vida breve* received accolades in the December 1995 issue of *Opera News* magazine.

In 1989, utilizing her years of experience, she opened her Chicago-based Ovation! Management agency with her husband Alex Boas. They are now well established with a gifted roster.

Among Lewis' honors, besides vocal scholarships and competitions, have been the Misericordia Humanitarian Award and Citizen of the Month award from the Chicago Lerner newspapers. A sought after adjudicator, she also serves as a panelist for grants from Chicago Community Assistance, Chicago Fine Arts and Detroit Chorale.

KAREN McFARLANE—*The Found Chord;* ran Karen McFarlane Artists, Inc. in Cleveland from 1976–2000, representing the world's finest concert organists, plus great Anglican cathedral and collegiate choirs. The firm, begun by Bernard LaBerge in New York, 1921, has an over eighty-year roster history of world-famous musicians, among them **Maurice Ravel** and **Arthur Honegger**. At LaBerge's death in 1952, his secretary, Lilian Murtagh, continued to handle the organ division for what was by then Colbert-LaBerge Concert Management. In 1962, she purchased the organ division and worked from her home in Canaan, Connecticut, touring, among others, **Marie-Madeleine** and Maurice Duruflé, Anton Heiller, Jean Langlais and Flor Peeters, until her death in 1976. She left Karen the management in her will.

In 1982, McFarlane established a program for the career growth of young organists. Three years later, she added major choirs to the roster, arranging North American tours for the choirs of King's College and St. John's College (Cambridge), the Cambridge Singers (John Rutter, director), Canterbury, Winchester, and Salisbury Cathedrals, Westminster Abbey, and St. Thomas Church (New York City).

With her retirement in 2000, booking director John McElliott took over direction, keeping the agency's name. Until 2005, Karen continued working with choir tours, as well as having a special interest in the competition winners represented by the management. (See Organists.)

JOANNE RILE—*Cutting a Slice Away from the Big Apple* . . . with degrees in painting and art history from the University of Pennsylvania, after graduation Joanne worked as a continuity director for the classical music station WFIN. She married graphic designer John Rile and, while raising three daughters and a son, developed both the artists' management and advertising companies. During this time, she won three awards for creative direction and copywriting from the Women in Advertising Club. Since 1972, Joanne Rile Artists Management, Inc., in Jenkintown, Pennsylvania, has grown into an internationally known agency, developing the careers of African-Americans, Hispanics, Asians and Europeans in the classical field, as well as actors, dance companies, jazz, folk and pop musicians. In 1982, her husband joined the firm as an active partner. Their clients include violinists **Monica Huggett** and **Dylana Jensen**; soprano **Mattiwilda Dobbs**; Israeli conductor **Dalia Atlas**; the **Ahn Trio** and **Colorado Quartet**. Rile sits on many cultural boards, and was a member of the NEA Music Panel. In 2000, she received the "Award for Excellence" from the National Association of Performing Arts Managers and Agents.

DEL ROSENFIELD—*Another Renaissance Woman!* The president of Del Rosenfield Associates grew up in Bangor, Maine, attending the city's symphony concerts. Early piano and flute lessons gained Del entry into the Pierian Sodality of 1808. No, that is not a misprint, but the original name of the Harvard-Radcliffe Orchestra in the days before the respective ivied halls were opened to co-education. College meant Boston Symphony concerts, singing in a group led by composer **Irving Fine** (1914–62), and reveling in the excitement of the early days of **Leonard Bernstein** (1918–90), **Lukas Foss** (*b* 1922), and **Igor Stravinsky** (1882–1971).

Her best friend, Mary Briggs Sadovnikoff, accidentally launched Del's career as an agent. Having purchased a fortepiano—the late 18th/early 19th century predecessor of the pianoforte—Mary, busy teaching at Wellesley and Brown, asked Del to find her playing engagements. A 1978 phone call to Robert Sherman's long running show "The Listening Room," on New York's classical music station WQXR, was the first coup. Next, she got an engagement at the 92nd Street Y for young Brazilian pianist Diana Kacso, who lived with Del's family while she attended Juilliard. Word got out and the roster gradually expanded from six to thirty-six, including dynamic conductor **Gisèle Ben-Dor**, who was with her for many years. Del attended booking conferences—where much of the manager-presenter networking goes on—such as Chamber Music America, the Association of Performing Arts Presenters (APAP), American Symphony Orchestra League (ASOL), Western Alliance of Arts Administrators (WAAA), and the National Association of Performing Arts Managers and Agents (NAPAMA), an advocacy organization for the profession which plays an active role in rallying support for the NEA.

During the early years of her marriage, while raising two sons and a daughter, Del taught nursery school, elementary school and children with learning disabilities, all the while working on her master's degree at Bank Street College—appropriate training grounds to manage that special class of artists with different instruments, repertoire, needs and interests.

Del's husband, Zachary, a retired architect and discriminating music lover, has always been supportive of her career. ("We're a great team!") They celebrated their golden anniversary in 1998.

After phasing down her company at the beginning of 1999, until October 2001 Rosenfield was manager of New World Classics, an agency specializing in touring international orchestras such as the *Mozarteum* of Salzburg, *I Musici* from Rome, and the Estonian Philharmonic Chamber Orchestra. As of 2003, she still continued as personal representative in North America for pianist **Babette Hierholzer**, Coull String Quartet (University of Warwick, England), and the New York Ragtime Orchestra.

CHARLOTTE SCHROEDER—*Continuing a tradition of dedication;* the third president of Colbert Artists Management since its inception by Ann and Henry Colbert in 1948, Charlotte Schroeder follows the steadfast footsteps of Ann Colbert and Agnes Eisenberger.

Born in Oklahoma City, her innate love of music was enhanced by inspirational teachers and attending live performances. She studied piano from grade school through University, and played flute in junior and senior high school marching and concert bands. This culminated in a BM in music performance from Oklahoma City University (1970).

Making her way to the Big Apple, she "kicked around for a year," then found a position with Colbert starting "in the mail room" and worked her way to the top. She also serves on the board of Chamber Music America.

A mark of the integrity of her company is Schroeder's own quote: "I was privileged to work for two strong, completely dedicated and uncompromising women who considered the artists' welfare first and foremost. My colleague, Christina Putnam, and our wonderful staff have continued that philosophy, and at the same time updated our systems and adjusted to the challenges of this modern world."

Charlotte's companion of many years is recording engineer Malcolm Addey. They had two kittens in 2004 which, I am sure, are cats by the time your read this.

NANCY SHEAR—*A Unique Agency;* Nancy Shear, born July 1, 1946, in Philadelphia, was brought up in the arts by a music loving mother. She studied cello with **Elsa Hilger**, received her BM from Temple University and attended the Philadelphia College for the Performing Arts.

Informally trained in the library of the Philadelphia Orchestra for five years, she was a library assistant working on scores and parts, meeting in rehearsal the greatest conductors and soloists. As an orchestra librarian (Philadelphia Orchestra, Curtis Institute, International Festival of Youth Orchestras), she worked with both **Leopold Stokowski** and **Eugene Ormandy** for over twenty years, as well as collaborating with recording companies and music publishers in their editorial and performance departments. From 1965, concurrent with her other occupation, Shear became private musical assistant to Stokowski until his death in 1977.

In addition to her articles, book liner notes, and authoring of *The Philadelphia Orchestra Story,* she was host/writer of the New Jersey Symphony's broadcasts on WNYC and NPR, as well as a New York Philharmonic pre-concert lecturer for eleven years.

Having worked with **Mstislav Rostropovich** on many musical projects, in 1978, when she had to turn him down because of other commitments, he suggested she open her own business. Thus was born the Nancy Shear Arts Services, a full public relations, publicity, marketing, advertising event production agency.

After co-hosting, with **André Previn**, the gala at the Caramoor Music Festival in Spring 2003, she produced and hosted NYU's Lillian Vernon Department of Foreign Affairs series "Music out of Conflict," featuring performances and discussions on the Holocaust, the Middle East situation and the Soviet regime.

Her ongoing and single-project clients include Arabesque Recordings, pianist/composer Lera Auerbach, Opus 118's Fiddlefest, the Guarneri String Quartet, **Anne-Marie McDermott**, the piano trio Sequenza, clarinetist Richard Stoltzman, and the Honens International Piano Competition.

SUSAN WADSWORTH—*Giving Them the Break of a Lifetime!* As founder and director of Young Concert Artists Inc., a non-profit organization, Susan Wadsworth, with Artist Managers Monica Felkel and Vicki Margulies, provides a unique service discovering and launching the careers of gifted young musicians. Her first series was presented in 1961 in a loft-restaurant in Greenwich Village with a litter of kittens running between the folding chairs. Since that time, her auditions have graduated to the grander Halls of Carnegie, Town, and Alice Tully, sans cats.

YCA differs from commercial management in that competition winners join YCA's roster until chosen by commercial management. During that time—two to seven years—they are presented in recital and concerto debut, and receive all management services without cost. Some of the talent who showed their first sparks of brilliance at the competitive auditions were flutists **Paula Robison** ('61) and **Eugenie Zukerman** ('70); pianists **Ilana Vered** ('61), Murray Perahia ('65), **Ursula Oppens** ('68), Emanuel Ax ('73), Steven de Groote ('77), Christopher O'Riley, Jean-Yves Thibaudet (both '81) and **Anne-Marie McDermott** ('83); violinists Pinchas Zukerman ('66)—fondly remembered as a very nervous teenager—**Ani** ('73), and **Ida** ('78) **Kavafian** and **Chee-Yun** ('89); violist **Nobuko**

Imai ('67); the Tokyo String Quartet ('70); trumpeter—and conductor of the Seattle Symphony since 1985—**Gerard Schwarz** ('71); and sopranos **Beverly Hoch** ('79) and **Dawn Upshaw** ('84). With its high artistic standards, YCA has over 400 applicants annually vying to get on the roster, which has so many times proven a springboard to fame and fortune. Celebrating their fortieth anniversary, New York's Pierpont Morgan Library presented a series featuring musicians who started their careers with YCA performing with newcomers of 2001.

Born in New York City, Susan studied violin and piano at an early age, and attended the Fontainebleau Conservatory (1954), where she studied piano with **Jean Casadesus** (1927–72) and theory with **Nadia Boulanger**. After her BA in English literature (Vassar, 1958), she went to the Mannes College of Music.

Wadsworth serves on numerous music competition juries and advisory committees: the Institute of International Education, Avery Fisher Prize Program, Van Cliburn Competition and Young Audiences. She is an NEA consultant, and an honorary board member of the Young Concert Artists Trust in London, which she helped found based on her own YCA concept. She gives seminars at conservatories and universities, and has participated on conference panels including the Aspen Institute and the ASOL.

Susan is married to Charles Wadsworth, pianist and founder/artistic director of the chamber music concerts at the Spoleto Festivals in Italy and Charleston, South Carolina and, for over twenty years, of the Chamber Music Society of Lincoln Center. They have a daughter, Rebecca.

Honorable Mention

There are, of course, many other women in the agency business and it would take a separate book to catalogue all of them and their accomplishments. I have dealt with several in the course of gathering material for this book, and they have, for the most part, gone out of their way to send me prompt responses for biographies, photographs and other information. A few have deluged me with pin-ups of their whole "stable," but one cannot blame them for trying. I mention a few more names with the strict understanding that there are many more with whom I am not acquainted.

Lynda L Ciolek runs Steorra Enterprises, in its third decade of specializing in publicity and promotion, as well as consultants to artists, groups, and facilities. **Jane Colwell** (Colwell Arts Management in Ontario, Canada) has established a reputation for singers of distinction, and represented cellist **Shauna Rolston** and pianist Bernadene Blaha, who performed as a duo. Blaha now appears with cellist Elizabeth Dolin. **Mary Ella Collins** has over ten years with operatic artists and conductors from her office in Dallas, Texas. **Pamela Curzon**, of Curzon & Associates, has over twenty seasons of bringing leading and emerging artists onto international stages, as well as working in television and radio productions. Formerly Curzon & Kedersha, **Julie Kedersha** moved to Medici Classics. **Susan Endrizzi** and David Osborne's California Arts Management in San Francisco handles classical music ensembles, performance theater and modern dance. **Laurelle Favreau** and Don Verdery combine thirty-five years of experience with their 1990 merger forming Gami/Simonds, Inc., covering a variety of artists from their Connecticut office. **Pat Feuchtenberger** has over twenty years in the business representing performers, also giving support to presenters to ensure concert success. **Marilyn Gilbert** Artists Management of Toronto has put in over two decades. **Judith Liegner**, besides lead singers, represents many artists sought after for vital secondary (comprimario) operatic roles. **Patricia Minton** has taken over Classical Performing Artists, headquartered in San Diego, with soprano **Patricia McAfee** and some of the bright stars at Lyric Opera San Diego. **Tittica Roberts Mitchell**, president of TRM, enjoyed forty-five years of representing conductors, instrumentalists, singers and actors. **Michal Schmidt**, in her eleventh year, 2006, includes in her representation **Patricia Handy**, conductor; **Angela Cheng** and **Lilya Zilberstein**, pianists; violinist **Stephanie Chase**; and cellist **Sharon Robinson**. **Jean Seidel**, in association with John Such Artists' Management, is dedicated to the promotion of young vocalists on both sides of the Atlantic. **Amy Sperling**, formerly with CAMI and ICM Artists, provides managerial services and public relations. **Beverly Wright & Associates**, since 1980, represents established as well emerging artists. She tours her artists throughout the world, and includes the all women Cassatt String Quartet, featuring Muneko Otani, Jennifer Leshnower, Tawnya Popoff and Nicole Johnson. Her services include career development for young artists, public relations and marketing for composers, and consulting for non-profit arts organizations. **Isabel Wolf**, a professional cellist who studied with **Janoš Starker** and has a BA in cello performance from Indiana University, created Wolf Concert Artists in Minneapolis (1988), relocated to Cambridge, Massachusetts (1989) and, at the request of her clients, moved to New York, August 1995, to be in the hub of the arts. In 1999, Prima International Artists Management of Italy merged with the agency to become Wolf Artists International. In January 2006 Intermezzo, a not-for-profit organization supporting young singers, directors and conductors through programs and competitions, acquired Wolf Artists from Isabel, who moved to Brussels July 2006, as managing director representing talent throughout Europe.

PR

There are also agencies dealing solely with *public relations* for their clients. Among these are **Mary Lou Falcone** and **Josephine Hemsing**.

Mary Lou Falcone

MARY LOU FALCONE, born August 5, 1945, in Orange, New Jersey, began piano at eight and voice at fourteen. After receiving her artist diploma from Curtis (1966), she sang professionally for eight years with WNET Opera Theater, St. Paul Opera, soloed with orchestras, in oratorios and recitals.

In 1974, drawn to communications and combining her musical experience, with encouragement from St. Paul Opera, she became their national/international representative. Word traveled, and she created M.L. Falcone, Public Relations. After thirty years, her "roster" includes: Carnegie Hall, Avery Fisher Artist Program, Juilliard School Centennial (2005–06), Vienna Philharmonic, Lucerne Festival, the orchestras of Chicago, Los Angeles, St. Louis, and Fort Worth Opera; Dennis Russell Davies, **Renée Fleming**, David Robertson, Russell Sherman, **Nadja Salerno-Sonnenberg**, Jean-Yves Thiboudet and **Eugenia Zukerman**.

Mary Lou lives in Manhattan with her husband, Nicholas Zann, is on the faculty of Juilliard, a board member of the Marilyn Horne Foundation, and sits on the Curtis Institute Music Board of Overseers.

HEMSING ASSOCIATES was founded by Josephine Hemsing in 1989. The first agency to handle publicity throughout Europe, they now have a branch in Paris. They coordinate with embassies and consulates to promote international cultural events.

European Agents

Gerhild Baron

GERHILD BARON owns one of the biggest agencies in Vienna, handling some of the world's major talent. Born in Vienna, October 6, 1940, she started piano lessons at six. From age fourteen she wanted to be a singer, but her parents insisted on a general education. After high school in Linz, she spent the next two years (1958–60) at the University of International Studies in Vienna, at the same time studying voice privately. Next came the Vienna Music Academy (1961–67), concurrently working in the overseas department of a travel agency, and making summer trips to study English, French, Italian and Spanish in those countries. In 1964, she met the celebrated pianist Paul Badura-Skoda, and began working part-time, taking care of his travel schedules, programs, etc. Thus she became acquainted with the world of music management, and got to know music managers, promoters and others in the business. Shortly after, she began her career as a singer, but due to health problems which affected her voice, she was forced to make the decision to pursue another track. Using her experience and knowledge of languages, organization, economics and music, she opened her agency in 1973 and has risen to the top by her own efforts. Her successful goals include personal, long lasting relationships with her artists, based on commitment and integrity. Besides discovering new talent, Baron represents top stars in general as well as local management. Artists on her impressive roster have included soprano **Grace Bumbry**, bass Ruggero Raimondi, cellists Boris Pergamen-Schikow and Mischa Maisky, pianists **Bella Davidovich** and (of course) Paul Badura-Skoda,[253] conductors Sergiu Comissiona and Jerzy Semkow, flutists James Galway (and the late Jean-Pierre Rampal), and trumpeter Maurice André[254] as well as bassoon player Milan Turkovic. She also arranges tours for chamber groups and symphony orchestras, including the Moscow State Symphony, Royal Scottish National Orchestra, the Peking Radio Symphony, RTL Symphony Luxembourg, German Symphony Orchestra Berlin, Royal Liverpool Philharmonic and the Vienna Symphony. In 1997, Gerhild Baron Management brought the Warsaw Chamber Opera for a very special project to Vienna: they performed all the Mozart Operas in seventeen days at the famous Theater an der Wien.

Baron was a member of the board of the European Association of Artists Managers for six years and is on the board of the Henryk Szeryng Foundation in Monaco. In 1986, she received the Order of Cultural Merit from the Polish Culture Ministry.

In 2001 she added a partner, Benedikt N. Weingartner, to the agency, which further enlarged their roster and engagements. Her New York contact is DeeAnne Hunstein of Hunstein Artists.

PATRIZIA GARRASI never studied music as a child, but got into the business through her passion for travel and archeology. In 1966, after a long journey in Syria and Egypt looking for a vocation, she began working for the Ada Finzi Concert Agency, the most important in Italy at that time, managing artists such as conductor Claudio Abbado, pianists Maurizio Pollini and Emil Gilels, and violinist Salvatore Accardo. In 1972 Garrasi opened her own agency, now called RESIA, which translates from the Italian to Representatives of International Artists. Her roster carries some of the most celebrated soloists and ensembles in the world, including pianists Alfred Brendel, Krystian Zimerman, violinist Gidon Kremer, and the Alban Berg, Guarneri, Emerson and Juilliard String Quartets.

Patrizia was born near Naples, August 30, 1941. She married Vittore Garrasi in 1968. Her son, Maurizio, born 1969, is an architect, who made her a grandmother to Bianca, born 1999, and Mattia, who arrived in March 2001. Daughter Donata, born 1971, earned degrees in political science and international relations, and has worked several years in Africa for UNICEF.

In the course of her thirty-five year career in the music business, Garrasi has taken a relevant part in many Italian and international events, such as the first tours of both the European Community Youth Orchestras and the Chamber Orchestra of Europe with Claudio Abbado, as well as the creation of the Orchestra Filarmonica della Scala and the International Chamber Music Festival of Naples—this, the very first chamber music festival founded more than twenty-five years ago by Salvatore Accardo. In 1994, together with Maurizio Pollini, Bruno Canino and the late Luciano Berio, Garrasi organized the First International Piano Competition Umberto Micheli, which immediately became one of the most important in the world.

2004 found Italy under its fifty-ninth government since World War II, featuring continued reduction of funds for culture and, according to Garrasi, women's social roles far too little advanced.

MIRJANA MITROVIC was born in Banja Luka, in what was then Bosnia, June 9, 1961, while her father, a test pilot, was stationed there. She grew up in Belgrade (Yugoslavia), beginning violin at ten, and studied at the University of Philosophy in the capital where she met one of the country's foremost pianists, **Ivan Tasovac**, a champion of Yugoslav music. Through him, she got to know the technical and business aspect of putting an artist on a stage. Big state-run agencies dictated the rules, and many times entertainers were obliged to cooperate under less than humane conditions. (Government-controlled culture blossomed under Tito and the Communist regime. As in the USSR, talent in state run music schools earned equal opportunity regardless of gender.)

---

253. At age seventy-five, in 2003, Paul Badura-Skoda made his fiftieth anniversary U.S. tour.
254. Maurice André gave his farewell concert November 5, 2003, aged seventy, in his native France.

When, in 1992, Tasovac cancelled a solo concert as a stand against adverse conditions, Mitrovic decided to go into the business in an effort to change the monopolistic conditions. After organizing several successful concerts, it was evident that audiences were eager for more.

Mirjana married Ivan on July 16, 1994. In his role as creative director of their agency, BEO-KONCEPT, his contacts provide the opening channels. The rest was his wife's work. In 1994, Mitrovic received the necessary official permits to operate the business, which rode the wave of new confidence in personal contacts pervading the commercial climate. In her words: "Living conditions—hyper-inflation, scarcity of food, medicine, fuel—in the last few years have deprived and degraded men as well as women. Yet the natural regenerative nature of the people is slowly taking hold. In 1993, women's studies programs came into being in major schools . . . and while some of these have developed into a struggle for sexual liberty, the overall influence should be far-reaching for the whole female population." At least the cultural barometer shows concerts get quickly sold out and tickets at a premium.

(Author's Note: I have not been able to contact Mirjana in some time, so all this may be history . . . but worth recording.)

JUDITH SALPETER was the CAMI representative in London until it closed its doors in December 2004. Born September 7, 1943, in London, she was surrounded by music. Her father, Max, was concertmaster of the prestigious Philharmonia of London (1949–56) and other London orchestras. He also led the Æolian String Quartet and formed and led the Prometheus Ensemble. Judy began cello lessons at eight, but had an abiding interest in ballet. She began her career working for newspapers and magazines before joining the London Symphony (1976–83) as concerts assistant, later becoming concerts manager—which she loved. From 1983–85, she worked for one of the UK's major agencies, Harrison/Parrott, as well as the City of London Festival, and Chamber Orchestra of Europe. She left these positions to join conductor Sir Colin Davis as his assistant in 1986. This involved working with his manager, CAMI President Ronald Wilford. In 1989, she started the UK office of Columbia Artists Management, Ltd., where she managed conductors and instrumentalists, and organized British tours of Amsterdam's Concertgebouw and the Vienna Philharmonic Series at the Royal Festival Hall, comprising three visits per season. The natural progression of the business now has many orchestras booking their own concerts.

By 2005 Judith was running her own exclusive agency, Salpeter Artists Management.

BEATRICE VESPER was artist manager for CAMI in Lucerne, Switzerland, until the office was closed, December 2004. Born in Germany, she grew up with music. Grandmother had a lovely voice and Grandfather accompanied her on the piano. Aunts and uncles sang in choirs and played instruments. Mother loved piano music. At five, Beatrice enchanted everyone with her own singing. At seven, she started piano. Dreams of a conservatory, however, were dashed at age twelve when her sister had an accident that involved expensive treatments. Instead, Beatrice went to a business college and learned foreign languages. After graduation, she began work as a translator in Düsseldorf going to many concerts, while drinking in the ambiance of Robert and Clara Schumann's city. After receiving a degree in English from night school, she went to Brussels to work as a business analyst for an American oil company. Here, she picked up a degree in black and white photography, and saw just about every performance of the exciting new ballet company, BEJART. Her next stop was Berlin, where she spent nine "breathtaking" years taking in Philharmonic concerts, ballet, opera and theater, featuring the world's top artists and getting drenched at one open air concert where Alexis Weissenberg gamely played through the downpour on his soaked Steinway.

During her first four years in the city Vesper absorbed diplomatic and organizational skills, working for the president of the Berlin-Wilhmersdorf City Assembly. The next five years were spent as translator, coordinator and co-organizer of special events in the Berlin Tourist Office. Next stop: France, Cannes and the Côte d'Azur (Riviera), to improve her French, then on to Monte Carlo to the job which would change her life.

Through an advertisement in the paper, she joined the agency of a great impresario, later becoming his office manager. The three years spent with him taught her everything she needed to know about the concert management business. There she met music's elite, conductors Lorin Maazel and Sir Georg Solti, cellist Mstislav

Rostropovich, violinists **Anne-Sophie Mutter** and Isaac Stern, and pianist Ivo Pogorelich—several of whom came onto her roster. She got to travel in Italy and Spain, and by the time she left had become chief of administration and organization, and was personally looking after artists, selling concerts and organizing their tours. Then she met **Karin Wylach** in Monte Carlo, who asked if she would like to work for Columbia Artists in Lucerne. Beatrice had always wanted to go to Switzerland! Thus, her birthday, April 21, 1991, marked the beginning of the newest chapter in her never-a-dull-moment existence.

While the Swiss CAMI office primarily concentrated on the local market, Vesper's experience and contacts enabled her to do business all over Europe, working with major artists and orchestras such as the Dresden Staatskapelle, Bavarian Radio Symphony and Philharmonia of London. She was the first to go to Belgrade and organize a concert there while war was still raging in the former Yugoslavia. "It was the most wonderful and most impressive experience I have had in this business, meeting incredible people who, with their belief in the importance of music in a country, filled a hall seating 2,500, where no cultural events had taken place since the war and the embargo. I shall always remember the warmth and generosity of these people in a forgotten country."

In June 1996, she traveled with one of her favorite discoveries, the Italian baroque ensemble "Il Giardino Armonico," whose local management she transformed from four concerts in Switzerland to over seventy appearances per year, worldwide. Accompanying them in 1997, Vesper made her first business trip to the United States[255] and Canada.

With the 1998 opening of a new concert hall on Lake Lucerne, designed by French star architect Jean Nouvel, the picturesque city of Lucerne has become a major music center, hosting three prestigious international festivals where, in the summer of 2001, Vesper represented violinist **Anne-Sophie Mutter** as "Artiste Etoile" (Star Artist) in a series of five concerts.

What will Vesper do next? Where will she go? That, again, is up to the winds of chance . . .

KARIN WYLACH inherited her father's thriving forty-five-year-old artists' agency in Wuppertal, Germany, when she was in her twenties. (One of his earliest clients was the Vienna Philharmonic.) She was already experienced from accompanying artists on trips since she was a student. Born May 23, 1954, in Wuppertal, she started piano at age five, and has been immersed in music ever since. She moved to Munich in 1985 and started her own agency, PERSONA MUSICA. She ran both offices, with Wuppertal mainly for representation and Munich for touring. From 1992–2000, she was also managing director of CAMI in Lucerne. Like so many professional women, Karin Wylach fits the superwoman profile. The mother of Benjamin, born 1993, she continued the tradition of her family agency for thirty years until she closed it in 2005 and embarked upon a new venture embodying 21st century electronic technology, Worldwide Ticket.

The IAMA - an Umbrella Over Europe

VIRGINIA BRADEN—*Over the Top from Down Under*

From January 1, 2000 to December 2002, Virginia Braden was the first woman (and non-English born) to be chairman of the International Artist Managers' Association (IAMA), based in London. The association was founded in 1954 as the British Association of Concert Agents, changing their name and status to an international association in 1996, with membership open to any professional artist management company. Its purpose is to maintain good business practices within the classical music industry, assisting its members with legal issues, taxation, management development, media and recording rights. From 1989 to 1998, IAMA published an annual *Directory of Artists* listing members and artists. Since 1999, this has become *Classical Music Artists—Who Represents Whom*, a joint directory replacing both the *Directory of Artists* and *Music in Europe*, a publication of the Association Europénne des Agents Artistiques.

---

255. At the 1997 performance in Berkeley, California, the author was able to meet Beatrice in person—one of the hundreds of disembodied voices she had been interviewing by phone in the course of ten years of writing this book.

Born in Ottawa (Canada[256]), January 4, 1945, Braden's musical parents encouraged their children to play instruments. Virginia, like her mother, played the piano. With her father in the diplomatic service, the family lived all over the world, including Washington and New York, and were exposed to a great variety of musical performances. Virginia was educated at the International School in Geneva, and Lauriston in Melbourne (Australia). Her BA in Oriental studies is from the Australian National University, Canberra, while she studied piano and ballet privately.

Braden has worked in the arts since 1976, co-ordinating the Sydney International Piano Competitions in 1977 and 1981. She was concert manager of the Sydney Conservatorium of Music, and assistant director of the Australian Music Center until she established her own firm, Arts Management Pty. Limited, in 1979, which, for a quarter century, has undertaken personal management for over 100 Australian and international conductors, instrumentalists, singers, directors, choreographers, and stage, costume, and lighting designers. In addition to artist management, the firm has managed Arts projects including the Australia Council, Musica Viva, the Cladan Cultural Exchange Institute, Sydney Opera House Trust, Bicentennial Authority, and the Department of Foreign Affairs.

Braden is a member of the Melbourne Symphony Council, External Advisory Council of the Sydney Conservatorium of Music, and Australian Classical Music Managers Association. With this illustrious background it is no wonder that she was picked for such a responsible position as chairman of the IAMA.

Virginia has been married since 1980 to architect and classical music enthusiast Ken Woolley, from whom she acquired three stepchildren and five grandchildren.

The dedication required of the agenting branch of the music business goes far beyond raking in commissions. These women become second mothers, confidantes, support systems and lifelines for their clients. Discovering markets, placing artists in the right venues, negotiating fees, and arranging programs is all part of the exciting world of dealing with that intangible, life-enhancing commodity, the Joy of Music!

In the words of Beatrice Vesper, "*Working in artists management is not a job, it is a passion!*"

A Final and Unique Glimpse Back Into History . . .

The Grand Salon

As mentioned in the introduction of this segment, wealthy women in Europe wielded great influence in art by means of their salons, to which they invited writers, poets, philosophers and artists, as well as composers and musicians, to perform for their elite audiences. In Leipzig, **Fanny Mendelssohn** entertained in her parents' home and then in her own after she married court painter Wilhelm Hensel. (She only played one concert in public.) In Paris, writer **Georges Sand** (Madame Aurore Dudevant), mistress and mentor of **Frederic Chopin**, was one of the many women to present the virtuosity of "the Poet of the Piano." The best PR of the time was for a musician to concertize in these elegant homes.

The Mystical Misia

One of the most powerful forces in the arts spanning the *fin de ciècle* (end of the 19th century) was **Maria Gobedska**, born in St. Petersburg, March 30, 1870, and known as **Misia**. Her father, Cyprien, was a sculptor, and her maternal grandfather, Adrien-François Servais, was one of the most celebrated cellists of his time. Her mother died in childbirth, and Misia was brought to the luxurious home of her maternal grandmother in Brussels where,

---

256. Children of diplomatic parents automatically take the father's nationality, Australian in this case, no matter where they are born.

to everyone's delight, the child was discovered to be a prodigy at the piano. She once played Beethoven while seated on the lap of a guest named **Franz Liszt**. Her happy life was shattered when she was sent with her brothers to live with her father and a stepmother, who had no love for either of them. She packed the girl off to a convent school to endure eight years of hardship. Allowed home once a month, Misia caught a glimpse of her stepmother's *salon* whose guests included writer **Alfonse Daudet** and composer **Gabriel Fauré**, to whom she was sent for piano lessons once a week. He imbued her with a lifelong love of music.

Misia married three times, at twenty-one to Thadée Natanson, the son of her stepmother, and editor of his own cultural magazine, *La Revue Blanche*. Their house was continuously open to writers, poets, composers and contemporary painters who would become world-famous. Misia was the subject of many early works—which later became priceless—by painters **Edouard Vuillard**, **Toulouse-Lautrec** and **Renoir**. **Claude Debussy** was a good friend, and Fauré brought his young pupil, **Maurice Ravel**, who would later compose *Ma Mère L'Oye* (Mother Goose) for Misia's niece and nephew. On a delayed honeymoon in 1894, the Natansons travelled to Norway and met playwright **Henrik Ibsen** and composer **Edvard Grieg**, whose music to Ibsen's *Peer Gynt* was being played in every parlor in Europe. Misia got to play this as a duet with the composer.

In a strange twist of fate, the richest man in Paris fell in love with Misia. The year was 1900. The Paris Exposition was in full swing. Electricity was "in." **Sarah Bernhardt** was a living legend. Alfred Edwards, half-English, half-French, owned the newspaper *Le Matin*, the Théâtre de Paris and its adjoining casino, plus other lucrative enterprises. Thadée had been borrowing to keep his magazine afloat when Edwards offered him the directorship of coal mines in Hungary, "an opportunity to make millions." But somehow this got him deeper into debt. In his absence, even Edwards' wife was pressuring Misia to become her husband's mistress! (*Vive la vie bohème!*) But she resisted that offer. Between Edwards' promise to save Thadée from bankruptcy, and the jewels showered upon her by the obsessed man, Misia was persuaded to go through the unorthodox arrangement. It took five years. Both divorces were final in 1904, and on February 24, 1905, she married Edwards. She could now wield the power of the very rich. Their châteaux and yacht, *L'Aimée*, were scenes of lavish parties at which the cream of society mingled with the known and unknown of the artistic world. When Ravel, after four years of trying to win the Prix de Rome, could not get the jury of the Conservatoire to even accept his application, in 1905 Misia got Edwards to publicize the situation in *Le Matin*. Given the young composer's popularity, the exposé of "in-house" favoritism caused the fustian Theodore Dubois to resign and the forward-looking Fauré to take his place as director of the Paris Conservatory.

In 1906, Edwards, then over fifty, fell in love with a young actress, Geneviève Lantelme. On February 24, 1909, he divorced Misia and married the ingenue five months later. During the night of July 25, 1911, aged twenty-four, Geneviève drowned in the Rhine, after mysteriously falling off the *L'Aimée*. On March 10, 1914, Edwards died of influenza. His will left no provision for Misia.

In 1908, wealthy Spanish painter **Jose-Maria Sert** was introduced to Misia by the famous novelist **Colette**. Now it was Misia's turn to fall in love. They were together for twelve years before they married, August 2, 1920. During that time she became a patron and lifelong friend of ballet impresario **Serge Diaghilev** who, thanks to her generosity and influence, was able to exploit his genius and change the world of dance forever. His greatest musical discovery was **Igor Stravinsky**, whose three ballet scores, *The Firebird*, *Petrushka* and *The Rite of Spring*, produced between 1910 and 1913, secured the young Russian composer's reputation. Misia also sent generous checks to the always financially-strapped Igor and his family, and for years acted as buffer and liaison between the two fiery-tempered Russians. *The Rite of Spring*, with its wild, pulsating themes and erotic choreography, caused a riot at its 1913 Paris premiere, conducted by **Pierre Monteux** (1875–1964). A year earlier, Misia had succeeded in interesting Diaghilev in the work of French artist **Jean Cocteau**, and composers Ravel and Debussy. Now he produced another revolution with the latter's *Prelude to the Afternoon of a Faun*. Dancer-choreographer **Vaslav Nijinsky** created such an intimate and suggestive characterization in the ballet even Parisian audiences were shocked, including Debussy himself. (The work has survived, especially since audiences have become less shockable.) **Pablo Picasso** was among other major talent commandeered by Diaghilev, and painted the sets of several of his ballet productions.

Misia's own career as a pianist had long since been put on hold, although she kept up her practicing, and as late as 1933, at age sixty-three, she played a benefit concert performing the Poulenc two-piano concerto with Marcelle Meyer, after which offers came pouring in. Her main talent was being far ahead of the public in recognizing masterpieces of modern music. The piano in her salon was the setting for the first hearing of many new compositions. Besides Stravinsky, **Erik Satie**, **Darius Milhaud**, and **Francis Poulenc** all benefitted from her approval and sponsorship.

One of Misia's greatest gifts to society was her sponsorship of a petite, unknown milliner named **Coco Chanel** into the world of *haute couture* and later, the perfume business. They became lifelong friends in a continuous love-hate, power struggle relationship. It was Chanel whose sleek fashions after World War I released women from cumbersome corsets, breathtaking stays, voluminous petticoats, frills, ruffles and long hair.

Around 1924, a nineteen-year-old Russian girl, Roussadana Mdivani, wandered into Sert's studio in Montparnasse engendering a strange relationship. The painter fell in love with her. But so did Misia!

"Roussy" could claim an aristocratic background, and Misia loved her like the daughter she never had, even though she realized she was losing her husband to the girl. On December 28, 1927, despite Sert's Catholic background, he contrived a divorce via civil arrangements in Holland—a Protestant country. Later, he even managed to get an annulment from the Catholic Church on the grounds that Misia could not bear children. This devastated her. When Diaghilev, who had been ill for some time, died in Venice, August 18, 1929, she was at his bedside. Then Roussy died of advanced tuberculosis in a Swiss clinic, December 16, 1938, aged thirty-two.

Coco Chanel was now her only confidante. Misia, who had gone to Lourdes seeking a miracle to save Roussy, came back from there instead with diminished eyesight, having been struck suddenly with stabbing head pains. She and Sert drifted back together again, but maintained separate domiciles. The artist plunged himself into his commissions from all over the world, including the decorations on New York's Rockefeller Center.

World War II arrived September 3, 1939, and Paris was occupied by the Nazis. Somehow Sert always managed to have plenty, and generously shared with friends short of food. After the Liberation, May 1945, he, who had always dismissed illness, was diagnosed with jaundice. Ignoring the doctors' advice, he went on working, enjoying his morphine, and eating and drinking what he pleased. Almost to the last day, he was climbing ladders, putting the final strokes on his murals at the Cathedral of Vich, near Barcelona, a commission from King Alfonso XIII, who had been the cornerstone of Sert's life for almost forty years. He died November 27, 1945. Misia, on her way to see him, was too late. "With him [gone]" she wrote, "disappeared all my reasons to exist." He left her his apartment in Paris with all its valuable furniture, library and *objêts d'art*.

Now addicted to morphine—as was Chanel—Misia spent most of her last years in Paris, dictating her memoirs to Boulos Ristelhueber, who had been Sert's secretary and was her last loving friend. In September 1950, after another trip to Switzerland with Coco to buy drugs, she took to her bed. On October 15, her mind clear, she was given last rites. (She had willed everything to Boulos.) In the afternoon, she stopped speaking. Late in the night, she stopped breathing. Coco, who was with her, dressed her in white, put on her jewels and make-up. Even in death, Misia was beautiful. As the last *doyennne* of the *Belle Epôque*, no one has ever taken her place.

CHAPTER SEVENTEEN

The Unforgotten

This final section of the book truly illustrates the power of women—especially when combined with wealth! Beginning with royal patronesses from the time of the renaissance, women have always been behind the scenes supporting artists, orchestras, opera companies, chamber groups, etc. The wealthy have donated money—even part of their estates—to the cause of the arts. The foundation of many orchestras, conservatories and other vital threads have been woven into the grand tapestry of music by these philanthropists—for which we are forever grateful.

In modern times, along with their less affluent sisters, they have given thousands of volunteer hours in ladies' auxiliaries, arranging luncheons, receptions, stuffing envelopes and organizing fund raisers. Professionally, women have transcended to the administrative arena with astounding accomplishments. Each entry here is a revelation of what can be achieved with a determined woman at the helm. Most of the following have left us, but should never be forgotten.

Leonore Annenberg	Philadelphia Orchestra & others	Philanthropy Extraordinaire
Judith Arron	Carnegie Hall	Executive & Artistic Director (1986–98)
Helen Black	Denver Symphony	Manager
Eleanor Caldwell	Wheeling Symphony	Benefactress
Artie Mason Carter	Hollywood Bowl	Founder/Executive Director
Dorothy Chandler	Los Angeles Music Center	Founder/Newspaperwoman/Philanthropist
Elizabeth Sprague Coolidge	Wolf Trap	Philanthropist
Helen Copley	San Diego Symphony Hall	Philanthropist
Marie Louise Curtis	Curtis Institute of Music	Founder
Louise Davies	Davies Symphony Hall	Philanthropist
Carol Fox	Chicago Lyric Opera	Founder/Director (1952–81)
Sybil Harrington	Metropolitan Opera, etc.	Largest Donor
Carol Colburn Høgel	Richard D. Colburn Foundation	Other Philanthropies
Ima Hogg	Houston Symphony	Founder/Philanthropist
Adella Prentiss Hughes	Cleveland Orchestra	Manager (1918–32+)
Christine Fisher Hunter	MET/Gramma Fisher Foundation	Pro Bono Chair
Florence Irish	Hollywood Bowl	Philanthropist/Executive Director
Joan and Irwin Jacobs	San Diego Symphony	Endowment Donor/Fund Manager
Louise Lincoln Kerr	Phoenix Symphony, *et. al.*	Philanthropist/Founder
Ardis Krainik	Chicago Lyric Opera	General Director (1981–97)
Belle Mehus	Bismarck, North Dakota	Music Lady of the Prairie
Marjorie Merriweather Post	National Symphony	Philanthropist
Elisabeth Severance	Severance Hall, Cleveland	In Memoriam

Catherine Filene Shouse	Wolf Trap	Endowment
Beverly Sills	Lincoln Center/MET	Pro Bono Chair/Fundraiser
Rosalie Stern	Stern Grove, San Francisco	Philanthropist
Alice Taylor	Los Angeles Philharmonic	Manager (1951–62)
Helen Thompson	Amer. Sym. Orch. League VP	Los Angeles Philharmonic Manager
Alice Tully	Alice Tully Hall-Lincoln Center	Philanthropist
Bea Vradenburg	Colorado Springs Symphony	Manager (1955–90)
Katherine Gladney Wells	St. Louis Symphony	Benefactor/Composer/Author

LEONORE ANNENBERG—*New Heights of Generosity*! Leonore Cohn Rosenstiel Annenberg was born, 1918, in New York. The daughter of Maxwell Cohn who, with his brother Harry, founded Columbia Pictures, she grew up in Los Angeles. After graduating from Stanford University (Palo Alto, California), in 1946 she married Lewis Rosenstiel, founder of Schenley (Whiskey) Industries. Two daughters were born to them, but the marriage ended in divorce. In 1951, she married Walter H. Annenberg (1908–2002), her perfect partner and soul mate. Walter ran Triangle Publications from 1942, when he inherited it from his father Moses, until 1988 when it was sold to media baron Rupert Murdoch. The company published the *Philadelphia Inquirer* newspaper, plus *Seventeen*, *TV Guide* and *American Bandstand* magazines. In 1969, Walter was appointed President Richard Nixon's Ambassador to England. He became the only U.S. envoy to receive honorary knighthood from Queen Elizabeth (1978). In 1986, Ronald Reagan presented him with the Presidential Medal of Freedom. Five years earlier, this president named Leonore as Chief of Protocol for the State. Her vast experience hosting royalty (including Queen Elizabeth II) and world celebrities both abroad and at the Annenberg homes near Philadelphia and their 220-acre estate, Sunnylands, near Palm Springs, California, made her a perfect choice for the position. She quipped that this was her first "paying job."

Leonore, and her late husband, have had a long association with the Philadelphia Orchestra, whose Philadelphia Orchestra Award they received in 1971 in recognition of more than thirty years of commitment and support. Mrs. Annenberg served as a member of the Orchestra's West Philadelphia Volunteer Committee since 1953 and was on its board of directors 1968–80 and 1981–86. She has also served on the boards of the Pennsylvania Academy of Fine Arts, Metropolitan Opera Associates, and the Academy of Music and Performing Arts Council of the Los Angeles Music Center.

Among the Annenberg Foundation's numerous donations has been $120 million, in 1971, to establish the Annenberg School for Communication at the University of Southern California (USC). (They had founded the Annenberg School for Communication at the University of Pennsylvania in 1958.) In 2001, $20 million went to New York's Metropolitan Museum of Art: $10 million for immediate use and $10 million for an endowment fund. Since her husband's passing, October 1, 2002, at age ninety-four, Leonore has been an active president of the Annenberg Foundation. In February 2004, she bestowed a gift of $15 million (to be paid over three years) to the Academy of Music, the Broad Street landmark owned by the Philadelphia Orchestra. This is for their endowment and to generate income for capital improvements to the 147-year-old building. Just four months previously, she had given a $50 million gift to the orchestra. This brings to both institutions bequests totaling almost $90 million—joining in philanthropic generosity the $120 million given to the San Diego (California) Symphony by Mr. and Mrs. Irwin Jacobs. (See Joan Jacobs.)

Judith Arron

JUDITH ARRON—*and the Renaissance of Carnegie Hall*. Judith Arron was general manager, artistic director (1986) and executive director (1988), as well as a member of the board of trustees, of Carnegie Hall from 1986 until her untimely death December 18, 1998. Prior to this position she was manager of the Cincinnati Symphony and Cincinnati May Festival. Beginning in 1969, she developed their outreach program which became the model for outstanding regional and educational programming in the country.

Born in Seattle, December 8, 1942, Judith was surrounded by a musical family which molded her tastes early in life. She graduated from the University of Puget Sound with a performance degree in cello and piano, and began her professional career on the staff of the American Symphony Orchestra League where she was associate editor of *Symphony* magazine, as well as coordinator of management courses and the orchestral studies programs. She also served as an orchestral research specialist for the U.S. Office of Education Study of Youth Concerts throughout America. 1966–69 found her in the service in Washington, DC, as part of the Army Strings. She played several performances at the White House.

In 1968, she married Ronald D. Arron, a violist in the Metropolitan Opera Orchestra. Their two sons are Joseph, born 1974, a '96 Princeton graduate who received his PhD at Rockefeller University and MD degree (May 2003) from Cornell Medical School; and Edward, born 1976, a '98 Juilliard cello graduate who often performs with cellist Yo-Yo Ma, tours worldwide with the Concertante Chamber Players and is artistic administrator for New York's classical station WQXR's "On A-I-R" series.

Beginning in 1986, Judith supervised the revitalization and renovation of Carnegie Hall, and organized its 1990–91 season-long Centennial celebration. With the Hall's then president, violinist **Isaac Stern** (1920–2001), and its chairman, Sanford Weill, Arron began an endowment campaign in 1995 which reached $87 million by 1999.

By invitation, she became the only American member of the European Concert Halls Organization (ECHO), an exclusive body comprised of the heads of the top venues in Europe: Amsterdam's Concertgebouw, Vienna's Musikverein, Paris' Cité de la Musique, Die Alte Oper of Frankfurt, the Cologne Philharmonie, London's Barbican Centre, Birmingham Concert Hall and the Stockholm Concerthusset. She had also been on the board of the International Society of Performing Arts Administrators and the ASOL. She served on advisory committees for Music for Life AIDS Benefits in New York, Seaver Conducting Awards, School for Strings, Brooke Russell Astor Awards for the New York Public Library and the Knight Foundation Symphony Orchestra Advisory Committee. She received the Arts Administrator of the Year Award in 1992, and is listed in *Who's Who in America*. Outside the music field, Judith was chair of the National Advisory Board for the Bone Marrow Transplant Program at the University of Colorado Health Sciences Center in Denver. (It was here she succumbed to her valiant eight-year battle with breast cancer.)

Her association with the Vienna Philharmonic, over a period of ten years, included thirty-three guest concerts at Carnegie Hall. In March 1999, her widower received the unique Franz Schalk[257] Medal from the Orchestra. Fortuitously, Judith had been given notice of this impending honor of honors in September 1998. The medal, established 1963, is the highest recognition given to an individual who has rendered outstanding service to the Vienna Philharmonic. Needless to say, Judith Arron was its first female recipient.

Near the end of her life, she was initiating an effort to turn the old Carnegie Hall Cinema—part of the building—into another performance venue to add to the Isaac Stern Auditorium and Joan and Sanford I. Weill Recital Hall. Now known as Judy and Arthur Zankel Hall, its 640-seat auditorium is named for Judith Arron.

The January 2, 1999 concert of the New York Philharmonic was dedicated to Judith's memory by maestro Kurt Masur. The January 19, 1999 Judith Arron Celebration held at Carnegie Hall was attended by many of the most important people in the music world, all expressing their love and admiration for this dedicated, warm and inspiring woman.

---

257. Franz Schalk (1863–1931) was conductor of the Vienna Hofoper (Court Opera)—whose members constitute the Vienna Philharmonic—in 1900, while it was still under the directorship of Gustav Mahler. Schalk became director of the Staatsoper (State Opera—as the Court Opera was renamed) in 1918 until 1929. He also conducted London's Covent Garden Opera (1898, 1907, 1911), New York's Metropolitan Opera (1898), and was a regular conductor of the Vienna Philharmonic until his death. He and his brother Josef (1857–1900), as students and champions of Anton Bruckner (1824–96), presented unauthorized versions of his symphonies—joining the many well-meaning "friends" who had a hand in chopping up and rearranging the works of this master. During and after World War I, Schalk took special care of the musicians in those lean economic times. "Wachet mir auf meine Philharmoniker"—Look after my Philharmonic—was the dying declaration of this dedicated director, and is the inscription on the medal created 100 years after his birth.

HELEN MARIE BLACK—*The Grand Dame of the Arts*; Helen Black was born in Washington, DC, June 2, 1896. She spent her childhood in New York, Chicago and Salt Lake City. She moved to Denver as a teenager, and following high school graduation was hired as one of the first female reporters for the *Rocky Mountain News*. Later, she became society editor for the *Denver Post*, eventually elevated to the music and drama critic—a fitting niche for a spirit who felt that the arts were essential to life.

Black was one of the forces in founding the Center City Opera (the house is an historic landmark, built by Welsh gold miners in 1878), and establishing the Denver Symphony (now the Colorado Orchestra), serving tirelessly for thirty years as its business and publicity manager. To implement her interest in bringing music to schools and educating and inspiring young people, she originated the Denver Symphony Youth Concerts. She also promoted Special Care Concerts for disabled children, and helped develop and send young artists on the road to success—two of them becoming the world-famous pianists Van Cliburn and John Browning.

In 1983, the Denver Women's Press Club, with the co-sponsorship of the *Rocky Mountain News*, inaugurated the Helen Black Arts and Letters Award to honor its longtime member for her many accomplishments and their lasting effects on the city. That year, the first was awarded to Black herself by violinist Isaac Stern. Many outstanding Coloradans have been recipients since. After her death in 1988, the award committee and Colorado Symphony Orchestra joined to establish the Helen Marie Black Education Fund as a lasting tribute to the person who had long been called "The Grand Dame of the Arts," and whose credo was, "God speaks to us through the arts."

Eleanor Caldwell

ELEANOR CALDWELL—*Small City in the Big Leagues*; born in 1887, Eleanor Davenport Glass Caldwell, founder of the Wheeling (West Virginia) Symphony, not only supported music, but devoted great organizational energy to perpetuate and promote the playing of classical music in Wheeling and its environs.

Her love of music was nurtured in her early education in Wheeling schools, at the Henry C. DeMille School in Pompton, New Jersey, the Ogostz School near Philadelphia, and Paris, where she was trained in advanced techniques of the classics. Her technical knowledge of music was exceeded only by her love for it.

A chamber music group organized by Caldwell in the early '20s had by 1929 grown into the Wheeling Symphony Society, which sponsors the Wheeling Symphony Orchestra. Caldwell played piano, drums, xylophone and cello in the orchestra, acted as the organization's librarian and served in any other capacity that was needed.

She and other music devotees founded the Thursday Music Club in 1942, in which she was chairman for education. This resulted in her meeting with state music educators and supervisors to devise a system whereby music would become a recognized high school course. Appointed to the state committee, she helped draw up the guidelines that were adopted as official state policy, providing a potential source of musicians and audiences for the symphony. She promoted the Symphony Auxiliary to lend continued financial support, established annual Young People's Concerts, the Youth Orchestra and Tri-State Music Association.

Her love for classical music helped maintain her longevity. Eleanor Caldwell died at ninety-two, in 1979. Thanks to her, Wheeling is the smallest city in the U.S. to support a metropolitan class symphony orchestra with an annual budget of more than $1 million.

ARTIE MASON CARTER—*Mother of the Hollywood Bowl*; born in Salisbury, Missouri, petite Artie Mason exhibited her passion for music and promotion when, at fourteen, she rented the town theater, performed as piano soloist, and induced a group of musicians to put on a program of classical music. Soon after her college graduation, she married medical student Joseph J. Carter. They moved to Vienna and, while he was finishing his studies, Artie took lessons with renowned pianist **Theodor Leschetizky** (1830–1915), all the while absorbing the centuries-old culture of her surroundings. When *Dr.* and Mrs. Carter returned to America they settled in Hollywood, where Artie threw herself into the civic and cultural life of the budding community. By 1919, she was president of the Hollywood Community Sing and organized the very first outdoor Easter Sunrise Service. Its success led to planning for the next year. She and her friend Aline Barnsdall, heiress to one of the early estates remaining from the original Spanish land grants, conceived the idea of having the second service on her beautiful hill of olive trees—aptly named Olive Hill—now Barnsdall Park. Artie convinced both the president, William Andrews Clark, and conductor, William Henry Rothwell—a one-time assistant to Gustav Mahler—of the young Los Angeles Philharmonic to play, and her chorus to sing. The service was an even greater success.

The following year, the event was planned in Daisy Dell in Bolton Canyon. It was Hugo Kirchhofer, when conducting the Community Sing on the site, who commented, "It looks just like a *bowl*!" The name stuck. In the pre-dawn darkness of March 27, 1921, two thousand people flocked on foot, bicycle and horseback to the place which then still resembled the Garden of Gethsemane, and spread their blankets on the ground, watching in reverent silence as the pink banners of dawn unfurled in the cool breeze. The softest notes of the Grail Scene from Wagner's *Parsifal* were audible in the natural acoustics of the "bowl."

After this triumph, Carter gave birth to her next brainchild, "Symphonies Under the Stars" for 1922—an original, far-reaching idea to keep orchestras working in summer. The saga that unfolded in the course of raising money to construct a shell, stage, seats and other necessities, including footlights which were donated by Hollywood High School at the last moment—for which they were granted the right to have their graduation exercises in the Bowl forever after—has filled books.[258] The coarse brush was cleared with picks and shovels and back-breaking human effort. The money dribbled in with donations, fundraising shows, dinners, ticket selling contests—25¢ each, $10 for a book of forty—and "Penny-a-Day" banks, conceived by a retired businessman who saw that his little yellow boxes were placed in every conceivable spot: stores, markets, banks, newsstands, movie theaters, etc. They alone raised over $10,000!

With Artie Carter at the helm, readying the Bowl has been described as "the most frenzied activity any community group has ever undertaken." Right down to the wire, she and fellow volunteers were planting hundreds of red geraniums to cover dusty, bare patches of terrain. After all that, the conductors they were counting on had other summer commitments and left town. Fate smiled in the person of Alfred Hertz, conductor of the San Francisco Symphony (1915–30), who stepped in and became a popular favorite with all. He conducted over 100 concerts there, becoming known as the "Father of the Hollywood Bowl."

The first season—sixty concerts over ten weeks—was a great success. Aline Barnsdall helped fund both the 1923 season and retire the debt on the Bowl. Mrs. Carter went onstage and ceremoniously burnt the mortgage papers. Gradually, the friendship between the two women cooled. Aline shocked the conservative Artie by having a child out of wedlock. She did, however, use her fortune in many other constructive ways, one of which was fostering the career of a young architect named Frank Lloyd Wright.

Meanwhile, Artie was getting edged off the board by the outspoken **Florence Irish**. The conflict between these two women came to a head in 1926 with the issue over expanding the seating area, which Artie wanted to keep intimate. She walked out, but kept her box at the Bowl until her death, September 15, 1967.

Artie Mason Carter's contribution will never be forgotten, neither will her prophetic words after the successful first season: "[This is] just the beginning . . . of a permanent [musical] achievement . . . of national credit to Los Angeles."

Still going strong, the Bowl has a new shell, replacing the one built in 1929. The architectural style has been preserved, but with vastly improved acoustics, new lighting and theatrical elements, all completed for the Summer 2004 concerts.

DOROTHY BUFFUM CHANDLER—*Miracle Worker of the Los Angeles Music Center*, it is quite possible that there might not be such a fabulous complex as the Los Angeles Music Center without a decade of fundraising effort (1954–64, to the tune of $20 million) on the part of this dynamic woman! Neither would we still have that his-

---

258. In 1996, a new history on the Hollywood Bowl, in the form of a handsomely illustrated coffee table book, was written to commemorate its seventy-fifth anniversary.

toric landmark, the Hollywood Bowl. She spearheaded the 1951 "Save the Bowl" crusade. It was her first major civic accomplishment, and she, more than anyone, bridged the gap between the two worlds of Los Angeles at that time—the old monied families and the influx of new post-war arrivals in Southern California.

Born Dorothy Buffum, in her first year, 1902, her family moved from Lafayette, Illinois, to Long Beach, California, opening a department store which grew into the successful Buffums chain. "Buffy" attended Stanford University, where she met Norman Chandler whose family owned the *Los Angeles Times*. They married August 30, 1922 and had two children, Camilla, born 1926, and Otis, 1928.

After Motherhood, a Second Career

From 1944, Dorothy and her husband shared power as publishers of the *Los Angeles Times* and *Times Mirror* enterprises. She chaired the Times Mirror Square Building Committee, which was responsible for erecting the corporate headquarters in Los Angeles. The dedication was 1973, the year Norman Chandler died at age seventy-four. His widow retired from the committee in 1976.

The reality of what this enterprising woman accomplished goes back to 1945, from which time all bond issues for an improved symphonic hall had failed to pass. After the death, 1959, of Dutch-born LA Philharmonic conductor **Eduard van Beinum**, the orchestra relied on guest conductors and played in the old auditorium or the Hollywood Bowl. After chairing the "Save the Bowl" committee in 1951, in March 1955 Chandler started the Music Center Building Fund. The fund grew slowly until 1959 when the former Brooklyn Dodgers, who had become the Los Angeles Dodgers in 1958, won the World Series. Civic pride blossomed—one of the rare occasions when sports and classical music had an effect on each other. When, by 1960, the fund stood at $4 million, the County of Los Angeles gave Chandler a site and assigned architect Weldon Becket. That year the publishing responsibilities were handed to son Otis, allowing his mother to devote full attention to the project. In July, Becket presented his plans for the Music Pavilion. Vacationing in London, Dorothy enjoyed the theaters there so much she felt that two theaters should join the Music Pavilion to have drama as well as music. Eight months later, she and Becket presented a new set of plans to the County Board of Supervisors, assuring them that she would raise $7 million more to augment the cost of the Music Center. So great was her track record that board chairman Ernest Debs said, "If Mrs. Chandler pledges it, the money is practically in the bank." By November, all the plans were approved. Construction began March 12, 1962.

In 1961, Dorothy Chandler was president of the Hollywood Bowl Association, executive vice president of the Southern California Symphony Association, a guarantor of the Los Angeles Civic Light Opera, a regent of the University of California and chairman of the Music Center Building Fund. Her goal was a permanent home and a music director for the LA Philharmonic. "Permanent" conductor **Sir Georg Solti** was available only twelve weeks out of the year, so she got a young guest conductor named **Zubin Mehta** to agree to fill in the rest of the time. Because Solti felt that he had not been consulted he quit, and Mehta became music director in 1962.

Many Titles, Hats and Honors

The Dorothy Chandler Pavilion opened December 6, 1964, the first public edifice in California named in honor of a person still living. Chandler immediately organized the Performing Arts Council to foster performances at the Music Center. In 1968, annual fund raising came under the Music Center Unified Fund, and Dorothy formed the Amazing Blue Ribbon 400, a group of women who contributed a substantial amount towards each year's campaign goal. Hollywood composer/conductor **John**(ny) **Green** called her "The greatest fund raiser since Al Capone."

After seventeen years, in 1981, Mrs. Chandler stepped down as chairman of the board of governors of the council, and was promptly elected to the newly created position of founder chairman of the board, a position held in perpetuity. She was also honorary life chairman of the Los Angeles Philharmonic Association and founding chairman of the Blue Ribbon 400.

Appointed by Governor Goodwin Knight, Chandler served as a regent of the University of California (1954–1968), was on the Trustees Board of Occidental College (1952–67), and honorary life trustee of the California Institute of Technology. She was the first woman to receive the *Herbert Hoover Medal for Distinguished Service* from the Stanford Alumni Organization. Variety Clubs International presented her with the 1974 Humanitarian Award. Honorary doctoral degrees were conferred upon her by the Universities of California, Redlands, Occidental, Pepperdine, Judaism, Portland, Loyola Marymount, USC, Mount St. Mary's College and the Otis Art Institute.

"Buffy" left us July 6, 1997, at age ninety-six, in Los Angeles, and was eulogized in print throughout the country. A true feminist in pioneer territory, Dorothy Chandler used her position and money in the cause of culture and showed a city what a woman could accomplish. If not for her, it is doubtful whether Los Angeles today could boast either the Music Center or the world renowned Los Angeles Philharmonic. On the cover of *Time* magazine (December 18, 1964), after the opening of the Music Center, her accomplishments were described as "the most impressive display of virtuoso money-raising and civic citizenship in the history of U.S. womanhood."

For years there had been dreams of creating a permanent downtown home for the LA Philharmonic. The Chandler Pavilion, a multi-purpose facility with a proscenium stage, was shared by the Philharmonic, LA Opera and the LA Master Chorale. For years, musicians had complained the acoustics were ill-suited to symphonic music and that the orchestra sounded better on the road!

In 1987, Walt Disney's widow, Lillian (1899–1997), made a $50 million gift to build a new concert hall at the Music Center. Executive Director (1969–98) Ernest Fleischmann mounted plans. After sixteen years and $272 million, including $25 million from the Walt Disney Company (not the family), the architecturally modernistic Walt Disney Concert Hall opened with great fanfare October 20, 2003. It is the fourth venue of the Music Center and permanent home for the LA Philharmonic and Los Angeles Master Chorale. Dorothy Chandler lives on!

ELIZABETH SPRAGUE COOLIDGE—*Windfall from the Windy City*, one of America's major benefactresses was born in Chicago, 1864, into the Sprague family, whose fortune was made in the wholesale grocery business. Educated privately, at eleven Elizabeth began piano, giving her first recital at eighteen. She travelled with her parents to Europe, Russia and Egypt, attending concerts and absorbing culture. As part of one of the prominent families responsible for founding the Chicago Art Institute (1879) and the Chicago Symphony (1890), she was well prepared for her leadership role in the arts.

Elizabeth Coolidge

At twenty-seven, Elizabeth married Frederic Coolidge, an orthopedic surgeon. They spent their first year of marriage in Vienna, where she continued her piano studies. Back in Chicago, the Coolidges gave musicales in their home. In 1893, she played the Schumann Piano Concerto at the Columbia Exposition, and performed with the Chicago Symphony under Theodore Thomas (1835–1905). She also composed songs. Her position in society, however, forbade these accomplishments to be considered anything but pastimes. In 1894, she gave birth to her son Albert.

An infection contracted while performing surgery forced Dr. Coolidge to relocate to Pittsfield, Massachusetts, where his health declined further with the onset of tuberculosis. Devoid of social life at this time, Elizabeth played music with her son who became a fine amateur violist and oboist. Tragedy struck threefold when her father died January 1915, her husband in May of the same year, and her mother in March 1916. Free and wealthy, Elizabeth began spreading her wings establishing memorials: Sprague Memorial Hall, housing Yale's music department ($200,000), for her father; a pension fund for the Chicago Symphony in memory of both her parents; and $100,000 to the Anti-Tuberculosis Association in Pittsfield for her husband. Close to her younger cousin, she contributed $50,000 a year to Lucy's Bureau of Educational Experiments, which became the Bank Street College of Education. Her next project was underwriting a quartet, with binding agreements that they perform in her summer home in Pittsfield—hence the name, Berkshire Quartet, after the surrounding mountains—and that she play with them on occasion. She was stimulated by the rehearsals held in her home. The quartet began with successful performances in the 1917–18 season, including two concerts in New York.

Coolidge's next project involved building the facilities for what was to become the Berkshire Festival of Chamber Music, the first held September 1918, with many famous musicians playing five concerts of classical and contemporary repertoire within a three day period. As a soloist, she received good reviews. One of the festival highlights was a composition competition which received nearly 100 entries. Participants came from all over the world, able through music to ignore the political schisms of the still raging World War I. Between 1918–1925, Coolidge herself presided over the festivals. Her commissions resulted in works by such greats as Barber (U.S.), Bartók (Hungarian), Bloch (Swiss-American), Britten (British), Honneger (French), Martinů (Czech), Ravel (French), Respighi (Italian), Schoenberg (Austrian), Stravinsky (Russian) and Webern (Austrian).

It was in 1925 that she founded the famous Elizabeth Sprague Coolidge Foundation at the Library of Congress. It was her way of obtaining official recognition from the government. Now aged sixty, she was able through the foundation to shift the responsibilities of her philanthropies to Washington. Through the Depression of the '30s, she helped underwrite radio broadcasts of "good" music, and concerts at educational institutions. She also underwrote festivals in Europe.

Elizabeth Sprague Coolidge continued her activities up to her last days. She died in 1953, aged ninety-one. Always modest about her philanthropy, she made the understatement of the century by saying that it gave her life "significance."

Helen Copley

HELEN K. COPLEY—*From Secretary to First Savior of the San Diego Symphony*, in 1987, despite years of philanthropic support, the San Diego Symphony faced bankruptcy. Copley gave the largest contribution in the orchestra's then sixty-two-year history, and one of the largest individual contributions to any local performing arts organization: $2.5 million to help retire the debt on their concert hall, the former Fox Theatre, built in the palatial decor of movie houses of the late 1920s, to which a highrise office building and major hotel had been added. Her example induced several local banks, and philanthropists Judson and Rachel Grosvenor who held mortgage notes, to also forgive over $2 million in debts. At first Helen wanted to be anonymous, but relented and designated the gift—from personal funds—as "a family contribution" on behalf of her son, her late husband and his father, Colonel Ira C. Copley. (She gave another half million five years later.) In June 1990, the large gold lettering on the wall in the lobby above the box office was changed to "**Copley** Symphony Hall."

Born Margaret Helen Kinney, November 28, 1922, in Cedar Rapids, Iowa, she attended Hunter College in New York. After a brief tour of duty in the WAVES during the 1940s, plus a short-lived marriage, she moved to San Diego with her mother in 1951, where her son David was born the following January. In 1953, she answered an ad and began working as a secretary for James Copley, who had become CEO in 1947 after the death of his father, the founder of Copley Press in Illinois (1905). In 1965, Helen married her boss, who adopted her boy.

After her husband's death from brain cancer, October 1973, at age fifty-seven Helen surprised the community by taking over the reins as chairman/CEO of the company which publishes nine other newspapers in California, Illinois and Ohio. By 1992, she merged the sagging morning and evening editions into the *San Diego Union-Tribune*. It became the third largest in California, twenty-fourth in the nation, and won two Pulitzers. She succeeded in her goal of keeping the company in the family by turning everything over to her son when she retired in her eightieth year, 2001.

Her able administration also covered civic dedication: she was the first woman elected to the board of directors of the California Chamber of Commerce (1974–77); President Gerald Ford appointed her to the executive committee of the National Commission on the Observance of International Women's Year (1975–76); California Governor Jerry Brown placed her on the Commission of Government Reform (June 1978). She was one of eight trustees selected in 1984 to oversee the Howard Hughes Medical Institute, which established a research and education center involving the University of California at San Diego (UCSD) and the Salk Institute.

Besides the Symphony, Helen's philanthropies extended to the San Diego Museum of Contemporary Art ($1.5 million) and, after reading of its deplorable condition, $2 million added to her friend[259] Joan Kroc's $2 million, to rebuild the city's Animal Shelter. In 1986, she helped launch the San Diego Council on Literacy, and underwrote the library at the University of San Diego (USD). Her many honors ranged from Humane Letters degrees from Coe College (1977), and the University of San Diego (1982), to Doctor of Laws from Pepperdine University (1979).

After some months of ill health, Mrs. Copley died in her home in La Jolla, August 25, 2004. She was listed in 2003 by *Forbes* magazine as 279th among the nation's richest Americans, with assets estimated at $960 million.

MARY LOUISE CURTIS (Bok)—*An Institution!* One of the greatest influences on the Philadelphia music scene was born August 6, 1876, the only child of Cyrus H.K. Curtis and Louisa Knapp, a musical couple who had met singing in a church choir. Originally from Portland, Maine, and later Boston, they moved to Philadelphia the year Mary was born. With Louisa as the first editor, they founded the Curtis Publishing Company, home of *The Saturday Evening Post* and *Ladies Home Journal.* Mary studied both organ and piano, and at twenty married Edward W. Bok, a Dutch journalist who succeeded Louisa as editor of the *Journal.* They had two sons, Curtis, born in 1897 and Cary, 1905.

Mary's music background led to her involvement in the Settlement Music School, which was founded in 1908 by Blanche Wolf Kohn and Jeanette Selig Frank to introduce the neighborhood's culturally and financially deprived children to classical music. With money from the estate of her mother, who died in 1910, Mary organized a conservatory division at the school, but soon realized that many talented, advanced students were unable to continue their careers because they could not afford private training. In 1924, she created the Curtis Institute of Music "to train exceptionally gifted young musicians for careers as performing artists on the highest professional level."

Two men were instrumental in helping Bok's vision of a conservatory, **Leopold Stokowski** (1882–1977), conductor of the Philadelphia Orchestra from 1912–36, and **Josef Hofmann** (1876–1924), the world-famous Polish-born pianist and frequent house guest of the Boks, who joined the piano faculty in 1924 and was director from 1926–38. In 1928, at his request, the institute began a merit-based full scholarship policy for *all* students. Today, Curtis remains the only major conservatory with such funding.

Proof of the Institute's caliber of students and instruction was that by 1930, twenty-seven graduates had qualified as members of the Philadelphia Orchestra, including harpist **Edna Phillips** who became the orchestra's first woman member. In addition to working as president of Curtis until 1969, when she turned the position over to her son, Cary, Mrs. Bok was on the board of directors of the Philadelphia Orchestra, as well as chair of the board and principal supporter of Philadelphia Grand Opera, which became affiliated with the institute.

Widowed in 1930, in 1943 Mary Louise Curtis Bok married Russian-born violinist Efrem Zimbalist (1889–1985). [Father of actor Efrem Zimbalist, Jr.] He had joined the Curtis faculty in 1928, and was its director, 1941–68.

Greatly mourned, Mary Louise Curtis died in Philadelphia in 1970 at age ninety-three. Her immortal words to Curtis students live on: "Music, beginning where speech leaves off, tells more of things human and divine, of nature, life and love, than we can stammer in words, and tells it in a language that is universal and understandable to every human heart."

LOUISE M. DAVIES—*The Musical Soul of San Francisco*, Louise M. Davies was born in May 1900, in Quincy, California. Convent-educated and raised in Oakland, her first job, at eighteen, was as a stenographer to the secretary of the secretary of the mayor of Oakland. One of her friends, Earl Warren, would become governor of California (1942–46, '46–'53), and chief justice of the Supreme Court (1953–69). She would later hobnob with presidents and other world figures. On a July 4th outing in 1924, she met Ralph K. Davies who had begun his

---

259. Joan Kroc, widow of MacDonald's founder, Ray Kroc, was also a super philanthropist.

career as an office boy at Standard Oil of California and, at thirty-three, was the youngest member of the board of directors in the firm's history. They were married in 1925. Ralph went on to also become chairman of the board of Natomas Corporation, of American President Lines, and Deputy Petroleum Administrator for War under FDR.

Having lived in the San Francisco Bay area since 1932, Louise's love of old houses, including her century-old Quincy family home, motivated her to rescue and restore a Russian Hill firehouse—earning the gratitude of many San Franciscans. It is now a museum assigned to the National Trust. Davies became an honorary fire chief, and a member of the Phoenix Society which aids fire victims. Other beneficiaries of her largesse are the Catholic Church, Notre Dame University, Catholic Youth Organization, San Francisco Opera, and Stanford University, on whose campus her family had lived. A trustee of the University of San Francisco, she sat on boards of the Exploratorium, Conservatory of Music, and Governors of the Symphony. In 1978, she was made a Dame of Malta.

Davies' involvement with the San Francisco Symphony dates back to 1934, from which year she held a season ticket. Before her husband died in 1971, she revealed that he told her it was better to do one big thing than a thousand little ones. Besides creating the Ralph K. Davies Medical Center in his memory, when asked to donate to the building of a new symphony hall her gift of over $5 million towards the total cost of $27.5 million for the hall was reason enough for the city to name the edifice Davies Symphony Hall.

Opening in 1980, the symphony gave three free performances: a "shakedown" concert for the construction workers; a gala inaugural; and an "All San Francisco Premiere." In the course of construction there was criticism as to this being an "elitist endeavor" benefitting only the rich. History has shown the hall's clean architectural lines enable people to feel comfortable in everyday clothes. Those who had been intimidated by the feeling of unattainable luxury in the old, ostentatious Opera House now come and discover symphonic music.

Louise Davies passed away at age ninety-eight, June 22, 1998. Maintaining that she and her husband loved music "because it lifts the heart," her generosity has, in the words of the *San Francisco Chronicle* obituary of June 24, 1998, " . . . lifted the hearts, minds, souls and well-being of countless people because of her extraordinary altruism."

CAROL FOX—*The Lyric Voice;* as the principal founder, and director of Chicago's Lyric Opera until 1981, Carol Fox built an opera house which transcended many obstacles to become one of the world's best. Born in Chicago, June 15, 1926, the only child of wealthy parents, Carol enjoyed a privileged upbringing, able to indulge her love of singing, piano, ballet, opera, languages and other fine arts with weekly classes. As a young thespian at the prestigious Girl's Latin School, Fox played the lead in many school productions. Although she took the Vassar entrance exam to please her father, she followed her own ambition and went to the Pasadena Playhouse in California to study acting. Later, she took voice lessons in Chicago and New York. There, she was coached in operatic repertory by the great **Fausto Cleva** (1902–71), then chorus master of the Met (1935–42), who would become its conductor (1951–71). Continuing her training for two years in Italy with celebrated tenor Giovanni Martinelli (1885–1969), Carol achieved a moderate degree of success.

Her return to Chicago in 1950 prompted a business alliance with promoter Lawrence V. Kelly and conductor Nicola Rescigno to revive the Chicago Opera. In 1952, with money from her father, Fox formed with them the Lyric Theatre of Chicago, using the empty Civic Opera House building. Two performances of *Don Giovanni* were produced in February 1954 to varied reviews. Nevertheless, she was encouraged to visit Europe on a talent search for major artists. Her persuasion brought La Scala's leading baritone **Tito Gobbi** (1913–84), tenor **Giuseppe di Stefano** (1921–2004), and mezzo **Giulietta Simionato** (1910–) to Chicago. Her largest accomplishment that year was convincing **Maria Callas** (1923–77) to make her American debut there in Bellini's *Norma*, ensuring that Chicago Lyric became a recognized and respected opera company worldwide. In the following season Lyric signed both Callas and her rival, soprano **Renata Tebaldi** (1922–2004), to the roster, sending ticket sales soaring. With the newfound success of the organization, a power struggle developed between Kelly, Rescigno and Fox, ending with Fox as the undisputed head of the re-named Lyric Opera, and the departure of the other two. The years that followed brought an emphasis on Italian works, earning Lyric the nickname "La Scala[260] West."

From fundraising to casting, Fox was an able administrator. Financial problems in the late '70s were caused less by her development skills than unforeseen circumstances, such as the delayed completion of Krzysztof Penderecki's *Paradise Lost*. She also began to have medical problems, which purportedly were the reason she was forced to resign her post, January 1981. She died July 21, 1981 of a heart attack at her home, some say of a *broken* heart . . .

Sybil Harrington

SYBIL HARRINGTON—*Liked Her Opera Grand*! Sybil Buckingham, born in Amarillo, October 13, 1908, was the granddaughter of Texas pioneers. As a child, she loved music and dance, ordered ballet shoes from a catalogue and persuaded her mother to take her to Fort Worth for classes. She also studied piano and organ. Listening to the first radio broadcasts of the Met inspired her love for the art form and the opera company.

In 1935, Sybil married Donald D. Harrington, a legend in the booming Texas oil and gas industry. She used her great wealth to support medical, educational and arts charities, becoming the largest individual donor in the Met's history. Grand opera was her passion. She once told an interviewer from *Town and Country* magazine: "It's all there—beautiful sets, great costumes, great music. What more could you want?"

After her husband's death in 1974, she became president of the Don and Sybil Harrington Foundation, making grants to organizations throughout the Texas Panhandle: $17.5 million to establish the Harrington Regional Medical Center; $1.2 million in scholarships for West Texas A&M; $4.35 million in oil and gas properties to the University of Texas; and the establishment of the Sybil B. Harrington Scholarship Fund of the Amarillo College Foundation. In the arts, she also supported the Amarillo Symphony, Lone Star Ballet, and Juilliard.

Harrington's favorite operas were the standards of Verdi, Puccini, Wagner and Mozart. She made possible some of the Met's most lavish and popular productions, like Franco Zeffirelli's *Bohème, Tosca* and *Turandot*, and Otto Schenk's *Meistersinger*. Altogether, she financed sixteen new productions. Her first gift resulted in John Dexter's staging of *Don Carlo* (1978–79). Other underwritings, which are still in use by the company, include *Manon Lescaut, Die Fledermaus, Das Rheingold* and *Don Giovanni*. One of her last gifts brought Elijah Moshinsky's production of *Otello* (1993–94). She also supported thirteen *Metropolitan Opera Presents* television broadcasts, and provided the funding for the company's computerized lighting board.

She became a member of the Metropolitan Opera Association in 1968, and a director of the Met's Managing Board in 1980. That year, she gave $20 million to the first endowment fund campaign.

Marilyn Shapiro, then executive director for external affairs, estimated that Mrs. Harrington's total donations came to over $30 million. In acknowledgment of her generosity, the Met's auditorium is named after her.

Sybil Harrington died at her summer home in Phoenix, September 17, 1998, four weeks shy of her 100th birthday. Of her far-reaching philanthropy she modestly commented, "Giving money away is hard work. But I got a kick out of it. I felt important for once in my life."

CAROL COLBURN HØGEL—*An Awesome Legacy*! Because of his unparalleled generosity, one *gentleman* must be profiled in this book about women! Ernest Fleischmann, managing director (1969–97) of the Los Angeles Philharmonic, said of **RICHARD D. COLBURN**, "He probably put more money into classical music than any other [individual]." He was also a supporter of Los Angeles Opera, and a co-founder of the Los Angeles Chamber Orchestra among *numerous* other music causes. Since his passing, his daughter Carol sits on the board of this unique institution.

Extremely private, Richard had to be coaxed to put his name on the Colburn School of Performing Arts, his

---

260. La Scala, Milan (Italy) is one of the world's greatest opera houses.

pride and joy. Founded in 1950 and originally located on the USC Campus, the university's preparatory music and arts school faced imminent closure by the 1970s. **Dr. Herbert Zipper** (1904–97), a Holocaust concentration camp survivor and international music educator, appealed to Colburn to save the facility. It proved a perfect outlet for the benefactor, and Zipper became its music director in 1980. (Named in his honor, Zipper Hall, built within the school in 1998 is a state of the art performance venue.)

Born June 24, 1911, in Carpentersville, Illinois, Richard grew up on a San Diego farm. His childhood love of music brought viola lessons, but all his life he rued that he had been badly trained. Nevertheless, he could hold his own, playing chamber music with cellist Yo Yo Ma, violinist Isaac Stern, flutist James Galway and countless other prominent musicians who were invited to his palatial home. Flying to New York or London or Salzburg for an opera or a concert was a regular part of his life.

Colburn kept the source of his largesse a secret. In his early twenties he became an accountant, then an investment banker, going on to wholesaling construction equipment. Living in an almost hidden estate in Beverly Hills, the lavishly tapestried music room—larger than many concert halls—housed a huge collection of priceless instruments, many of which would be loaned to budding artists—his philosophy, like mine, being, "Stradivari didn't make that violin or cello to be locked up in a cabinet." (The author and Mr. Colburn enjoyed many phone conversations during the writing of this book. In November 1999, attending a Dame Kiri Te Kanawa recital in Los Angeles, afforded my husband and me the opportunity to visit him and glory in those luxurious surroundings!)

The great philanthropist left us suddenly, but peacefully, in his own home, June 3, 2004, at age ninety-two. He had been married ten times to nine women, fathered eight children, and had seven grandchildren and three great-grandchildren. His daughter, **Carol Colburn Høgel**, a major international arts patron in her own right, carries on her father's legacy. A musician herself, University of Indiana (BM, piano, 1966), Yale School of Music (MMA, 1969) she received a Distinguished Service Award at the 2001 Yale Music Convocation. Residing mostly in the UK where she sponsors many artistic charities, in 2005 Ms. Høgel was made an honorary Commander of the British Empire (CBE).

Ima Hogg

IMA HOGG—*A generous luminary in the Lone Star State*; patron of the arts, Ima Hogg, among her other philanthropies, played a major role in founding the Houston Symphony. Named for the heroine of a Civil War poem written by her uncle, Miss Ima, as she was respectfully known, daughter of Sarah Ann (Stinson) and James Stephen Hogg, was born in Mineola, Texas, July 10, 1882. Much of her early life was spent in Austin with her three brothers, William Clifford, born 1875; Michael, 1885; and Thomas Elisha, 1887. Her mother died of tuberculosis in 1895. In 1899, Ima entered the University of Texas. Her father was elected governor when she was eight. In 1901, having played piano since age three, she went to New York to study music. After her father's death in 1906, Ima continued music studies in Berlin and Vienna, 1907–09, after which she came back to Houston and gave piano lessons to a select group of pupils. She helped found the Houston Symphony—which played its first concert, June 1913—serving as first vice president of the Houston Symphony Society and becoming president in 1917.

In late 1919 she suffered a breakdown, and for the next two years lived in Philadelphia under the care of a specialist in mental and nervous disorders. She returned to Houston in 1923.

Meanwhile, oil had been discovered on the Hogg property near West Columbia, Texas. With this newfound wealth, Miss Ima embarked upon several philanthropic projects, including her founding, in 1929, of the Houston Child Guidance Center, to provide therapy and counseling for disturbed children and their families. In 1940, with a bequest from her brother Will, who had died in 1930, she established the Hogg Foundation for Mental Hygiene, later called the Hogg Foundation for Mental Health, at the University of Texas. A lifelong Democrat, in 1943 she was elected to the Houston School Board where she worked to get equal pay for teachers regardless of sex or race, and deployed her interest in the arts to set up a painting-to-music program in the public schools and establish student symphony concerts. In 1946, she again accepted the presidency of the Houston Symphony Society, a post she held until 1956. In 1948, she became the first woman president of the Philosophical Society of Texas.

In the 1950s, she restored the family home near West Columbia and presented it in 1958 to the State of Texas as the Varner-Hogg Plantation State Historical Park. In the 1960s, she restored the Winedale Inn, a 19th century stagecoach stop at Round Top, Texas, which she gave to the University of Texas. The Winedale Historical Center now serves as a site for the study of Texas history, and is also the location of an annual fine arts festival. She also restored her parents' home at Quitman, Texas. The town, in turn, established the Ima Hogg Museum in her honor in 1969.

In 1953, Governor Allan Shivers appointed Miss Ima to the Texas State Historical Survey Committee (later the Texas Historical Commission), and in 1967 that body gave her an award for "meritorious service in historic preservation." In 1960, she served on a committee appointed by President Dwight D. Eisenhower for the planning of the National Cultural Center (now Kennedy Center) in Washington, DC. In 1962, at the request of Jacqueline Kennedy, Hogg assisted on an advisory panel to aid in the search for historic furniture for the White House. She was also honored by the Garden Club of America (1959), the National Trust for Historic Preservation (1966) and the American Association for State and Local History (1969).

In 1966, she presented her collection, begun in the 1920s, of early American art and antiques, to the Museum of Fine Arts in Houston—this along with *Bayou Bend*, the River Oaks mansion she and her brothers had built in 1927. The Bayou Bend Collection, recognized as one of the finest of its kind, draws thousands of visitors each year.

In 1968, Ima Hogg was the first recipient of the Santa Rita Award, given by the University of Texas system to recognize contributions to the university and to higher education. In 1969, Ima Hogg, Oveta Culp Hobby and Lady Bird Johnson became the first three women members of the Academy of Texas, an organization founded to honor persons who "enrich, enlarge, or enlighten" knowledge in any field. In 1971, Southwestern University presented Miss Hogg with an honorary doctorate in fine arts, and in 1972 the National Society of Interior Designers gave her its Thomas Jefferson Award for outstanding contributions to America's cultural heritage.

On August 19, 1975, at the age of ninety-three, Ima Hogg died of complications from a traffic accident while vacationing in London. Her funeral was held at *Bayou Bend*. She was buried August 23 in the Hogg family plot in Oakwood Cemetery, Austin. The major benefactor in her will was the Ima Hogg Foundation, a charitable non-profit organization she established in 1964.

The Ima Hogg Young Artists Competition of the Houston Symphony, created in 1976, rewards $5,000 as its first prize, $2,500, second and $1,000, third. Past winners include pianist Katioa Skanavi (1998), violinist **Pip Clarke** (1992), harpist **Yolanda Kondonassis** (1987) and violinist **Stephanie Chase** (1978).

Adella Hughes

ADELLA PRENTISS HUGHES—*Mother of the Cleveland Orchestra*; at a time when upper class women did not work for a living, Adella Prentiss Hughes became the first woman in America to manage a symphony orchestra. Born in Cleveland, November 29, 1869, into a prominent family, her maternal grandmother was descended from Oliver Cromwell. At Vassar College, Adella's music activities included being piano accompanist of the Glee Club, arranging tours for them and organizing a banjo club—all good experience for a future impresario. After her Phi Beta Kappa graduation in 1890, she and her mother took the grand tour of Europe—a tradition of the well-to-do. While on board ship, she served on the concert program committee. During their six months in Berlin, she attended Philharmonic concerts, studied piano and even met Kaiser Wilhelm. When she returned to Cleveland in 1891, she was prepared to become a professional accompanist. Her first production was in 1898, when she brought four New York vocalists to town for an opera recital, *In a Persian Garden*, with her as accompanist. The program was so successful that she organized a short tour. Her first stint as a concert manager came in 1901, when she brought the Pittsburgh Symphony for a three concert series at the Fortnightly Musical Club. Formed in 1894 to further the interests of music in Cleveland, she was a charter member of this prestigious women's club.

To expand the visiting orchestra series concept to the public, she appealed to wealthy Cleveland industrialists who, by 1915, had formed the Musical Arts Association. For the next twenty years, "Adella Prentiss Hughes Presents" became the symbol of musical events of the highest caliber. She arranged performances by the Metropolitan Opera, the Diaghilev Ballet Russe and the orchestras of London, New York, Chicago and Boston. Her roster of visiting maestros glittered with such names as **Arturo Toscanini**, **Gustav Mahler**, **Karl Muck** and **Ernest Ansermet**. **Victor Herbert**, who guest conducted the Pittsburgh Orchestra in Cleveland in the early 1900s, was quoted as saying: "She knows more about the business of music than anyone I ever knew. I would rather have her for my manager than any man in the world."

Attending the Ohio Teachers Music Convention in 1918 made Adella realize the importance of music in education. Having seen **Nicolai Sokoloff** (1886–1965) guest conduct the Cincinnati Symphony in a concert that included the participation of school children, she was determined Cleveland would have its own orchestra and Sokoloff would be the conductor. She appealed to the board of education and her wealthy contacts. John L. Severance guaranteed the maestro's first year salary, and by December 11, 1918 the Cleveland Orchestra made its debut with Sokoloff at the helm of fifty-four serious musicians from the community. Hughes was the unanimous choice for orchestra manager. A decade later she was the power behind getting a home built for the orchestra. She got Dudley Blossom[261] and other trustees to persuade Severance to pledge the first million for the hall that would bear his name. She also sought donations from other prominent donors, including John D. Rockefeller, Jr. who wrote her he would give $250,000 "as a tribute to what you have done in building up the musical values of the City." Severance Hall was dedicated in 1931.

When Adella married singer Felix Hughes in 1904, the marriage license listed her occupation as "none," despite the fact that she was already an impresario. Felix, who preferred the neon lights of Broadway to the high-brows in his wife's circle, left for New York in 1921 to open a voice studio. Two years later, his wife filed for divorce—the one discord in her harmonious life.

In 1932, Sokoloff left the orchestra and Hughes stepped down as manager, but stayed on the board as vice-president and participated in the Musical Arts Association until 1945. In 1947, she published her autobiography, *Music is My Life*. Childless, she enjoyed the title given her by the press, "Mother of the Cleveland Orchestra." She died August 23, 1950, at her home. When the Orchestra, under **George Szell** (1897–1970), opened the season on October 5, they performed Mozart's Masonic Funeral Music as a tribute to their departed colleague.

FLORENCE BEHM IRISH—*Lining the Bowl*; "A large, imposing inexhaustible fountain of energy" was the description of Florence Irish, who worked with Artie Mason Carter and succeeded her in 1926 as a pillar of the Hollywood Bowl. Born in Los Angeles, Florence was a third generation Californian whose great-grandfather had come out west in 1846. Her girlhood was spent on the 120-acre ranch of her grandparents—a Spanish land grant. In 1922, she added the Hollywood Bowl to other civic, political, cultural and philanthropic organizations to which she belonged, which included the Women's Committee of the Los Angeles Philharmonic. She also became one of the founders of the Southern California Symphony Association and vice president of both the Philharmonic and Hollywood Bowl Associations.

It was Irish who organized the gargantuan campaign to remodel the Bowl in the spring of 1926. The frenzy was equal to the initial preparation of barren land for the first concert in 1922, with fundraising seeking $150,000 toward the projected million dollar Permanent Improvement Plan. The grand opening revealed an acoustic disaster: three acres of seats set in steel and concrete to hold 20,000; the new shell, set on a steel and concrete stage 135 feet wide and 90 feet deep, was ugly, over-decorated and projected sound out only about 150 feet, causing many

---

261. The $8 million Blossom Music Center, twenty-five miles south of Cleveland, is the summer home of the Cleveland Orchestra. Built 1966–68, on 800 acres of rolling hills adjacent to the Cuyahoga Valley National Recreation Area within the city limits of Cuyahoga Falls, it honors the Dudley S. Blossom family, major supporters of the orchestra throughout its history. George Szell conducted the opening concert, July 19, 1968.

dead areas; the 5,000 feet of four-inch thick concrete walls which divided the seat sections created echoes. The natural resonance of the hills had been destroyed. More money was poured in to rectify some of these distortions. Nevertheless, the premiere was a success with the spectacle of twenty-four pianos on a moveable stage on rollers, appearing on as the orchestra rolled off. The Lions Club had their night with lions in cages around the perimeter of the stage, shocking austere British guest conductor **Sir Henry Wood** (1869–1944), who did not realize they were stuffed. At the intermission, when the spotlight remained on the beasts leaving him in utter darkness to take his bow, he stalked off to his Rolls-Royce, leaving the concertmaster to conduct the rest of the evening. Saving the reputation of the Brits was **Sir Eugene Goossens** (1867–1958), who also introduced the "new" music of Stravinsky, Ravel, Delius, Respighi and Percy Grainger to Western ears.

320,000 attended that year, sitting in the more comfortable seats, paying 25¢ to $1.00, first come, first served. In spite of lavish programming, high priced conductors, and other expenses, the 1926 season ended with a balance of $3,000, a princely sum in those days.

Irish had proven herself a worthy successor to Mrs. Carter. For fifteen years, longer than any of the other important women associated with the Bowl, she was its guiding light: counseling artists, bringing in major conductors from both sides of the Atlantic and creating a mecca for the world's finest singers and musicians. Even after she left, among all her philanthropic activities the Bowl continued to be her favorite, and she served it almost to the day of her death, April 13, 1971.

JOAN and IRWIN JACOBS—*An Unprecedented Gift*! Like many orchestras, the San Diego Symphony has had its share of financial ups and downs. Between May 1996–June 1998 it was on the brink of bankruptcy, saved only by the court's approval to reorganize under Chapter 11 proceedings. By October 1998, musicians and staff were back in the re-furbished surroundings of Copley Symphony Hall, operating with a $6.2 million budget culled from pledges and other donations.

Joan and Irwin Jacobs, who in the past had provided $500,000 for the orchestra's acoustical shell, donated more funds in October of 2001, enabling the management to sign a five-year contract with the musicians. In January 2002, their announcement of *$100 million* for the New World Endowment Campaign plus *$20 million* for the operating budget brought national attention to them as well as to the orchestra.

Born Joan Klein, in New York into a music-loving family, she received a BS degree from Cornell in Ithaca (upstate New York), and was trained as a dietitian. In 1954, she married Irwin Mark Jacobs, an electrical engineering and computer science professor at MIT. Their four sons are Gary, born 1957, Hal, 1960, Paul, 1963 and Jeff, 1966, the year Irwin joined the faculty of the University of California, San Diego, where he taught until 1972. In 1985 he co-founded Qualcomm, the San Diego-based pioneer of digital wireless technology, including cell phones and home satellite dishes. (Considered one of the richest men in the world, Dr. Jacobs officially retired at seventy-one in June 2005.)

As of 2006, all four sons are married and living in the area, with a total of ten grandchildren among them. Gary Jacobs has been a San Diego Symphony board member for several years and represents the next generation of orchestral involvement by the family. After serving as executive vice president, Paul is group president of QUAL-COMM Wireless & Internet Group. Responsible for several patents, he received his PhD in electrical engineering from UC Berkeley in 1989.

Modestly living in the same house they have owned for over thirty-five years, the philanthropy of this un-pretentious, loving couple extends to the UCSD Irwin and Joan Jacobs School of Engineering, the Joan and Irwin Jacobs Radio Broadcast Center at San Diego State University, and the Museum of Photographic Arts' Joan and Irwin Jacobs Theater in Balboa Park—San Diego's historic 1,200 acres adjoining the world famous zoo—which houses eighty-five museums, the Old Globe Theatre, and other cultural sites. In the Arts, the Jacobs also support San Diego Opera, La Jolla Music Society and the La Jolla Playhouse. (La Jolla [La Hoya] is a tony suburb of San Diego.)

Joan Jacobs heads the new San Diego Symphony Foundation which manages the orchestra's endowment, whose distribution is $50 million over the next ten years, of which only the interest may be spent; $20 million over the next ten years to be used directly for operating expenses; and the final $50 million remaining in the Jacobs' will during their lifetime.

The donation, the largest given at one time to an orchestra in the United States, ushered in a new era for Fine Arts in San Diego.

Louise Lincoln Kerr

LOUISE LINCOLN KERR—*An Oasis in the Desert*, Louise Lincoln Kerr maintained her studio in Scottsdale as a haven for chamber music, and developed an artists' colony there. Born April 24, 1892, into a wealthy family in Cleveland (her father invented the arc welder), she had advantages such as being able to study composition at Barnard (the female adjunct of Columbia) as early as 1910, and hobnobbing with the likes of Gershwin in her production job at New York's Aeolian Music Company, where he worked as a song plugger. In 1913, she became one of the youngest and the first ever woman violinist hired by the Cleveland Symphony, courtesy of **Leopold Stokowski**. Somehow she managed to squeeze marriage and eight children into her life, ending up in Arizona due to the health of one of her brood.

Widowed in 1939, she again took up her career as an orchestra musician, meanwhile composing over 100 works, for violin, viola, piano, chamber combinations and a violin concerto. In the late '40s and '50s, through inestimable contributions of money and land, she helped found the Phoenix Chamber Music Society, Phoenix Symphony, Scottsdale Center for the Arts, National Society of Arts and Letters, Monday Morning Musicals, Bach and Madrigal Society, Young Audiences, Musicians Club and the Phoenix (now Arizona) Cello Society.

Kerr was also extremely generous with her time and money to music and musicians in the "Valley of the Sun." Her donations to the School of Music at Arizona State established the Kerr Memorial Scholarship Fund, and her extensive music library is now part of the Arizona State Music Library. Her Scottsdale home and studio—now the Kerr Cultural Center—also went to ASU to be used as a chamber music venue. A most important donation was her over 100 manuscripts, now protected by the Department of Archives and Manuscripts, to the Arizona Collection of the Haydn Library. (See 20th Century American Composers.)

(I am indebted to Carolyn Waters Broe for "introducing" me to Louise Kerr and providing much material. See Conductors.)

Ardis Krainik

ARDIS KRAINIK—*A Worthy Successor for Chicago Lyric*, Ardis Krainik began her Chicago Lyric Opera career as a secretary in 1954, also singing minor mezzo roles until 1960 when her administrative skills earned her promotion to assistant manager, and in 1975 artistic administrator. She became general director and successor to **Carol Fox** in 1981. She also inherited an endowment that had shrunk from $3 million to $6,000. Cutting to the bare essentials, she managed to turn around the huge deficit. Ticket sales jumped from $4 million to more than $15 million, yearly attendance soared to 274,000 from 162,765, and donors increased over 50 percent. Her many achievements include her "Toward the 21st Century" series of American opera premieres, the best known of which was American composer William Bolcom's *McTeague* (1992), seven productions each season, and a complete Wagner *Ring Cycle* (1993–96).

A native of Manitowoc, Wisconsin, Krainik graduated from Northwestern in 1951 with a BA in Speech. Named as 1990 *Crain's Business Journal* "Executive of the Year," she had the distinction of being the first woman and first director of a non-profit corporation to win this coveted prize. She was also a Trustee on the board at Northwestern and its Kellogg School of Management, and had numerous corporate, professional and community affiliations. Her seventeen honorary doctorates and many awards include the *Commendatore della Republica Italiana*, Order of Lincoln of the State of Illinois, Grand Decoration of Honor in Silver for Services to the Republic of Austria (1994) and the European Friendship Award (1995).

Krainik made international headlines in 1989 by "firing" Luciano Pavarotti after he dropped out of a *Tosca* production on three weeks' notice. This was the last straw after he had let her down twenty-six out of his scheduled forty-six appearances over the years.

A strong Christian Scientist, Ardis was an active member of her community church. She was planning to retire in April 1997, but fell ill, November 1996, and died January 20, 1997, aged sixty-seven. She was succeeded in her post by William Mason.

Belle Mehus

BELLE MEHUS—*A Large House on the Prairie*; named after a native daughter, the Belle Mehus City Auditorium, an historic landmark completed in 1914, is the home of the Bismarck-Mandan Symphony. Born February 12, 1896, in Brinsmade, North Dakota, Belle's parents, Mikkel and Anne Myking Mehus, were from Norway. The young woman studied music at the Dakota Conservatory in Fargo, and piano at the American Conservatory in Chicago, as well as in Berlin with **Adele Aus der Ohe**,[262] who had been a pupil of **Franz Liszt**. She also studied with famed pianists **Rosina** and **Joseph Lhevinne**. After being on the faculties of McMurry College (Jacksonville, Illinois), Augsburg College and MacPhail School of Music, both in Minneapolis, she came to Bismarck. Her public career covered four years in the 1920s, traveling throughout the West as pianist for the Chatauqua Circuit concerts, as well as accompanying leading opera singers and string musicians in Minneapolis, and appearing in Twin Cities concerts herself.

After her mother's death in the 1918 influenza epidemic, Belle saw to it that her younger sister, Alma, received professional training, which led to a highly successful concert career until she married. Belle concentrated on teaching. In 1928, she opened a piano studio in Bismarck, which later became the Mehus Conservatory of Music. (The Conservatory building became the first home of the Bismark-Mandan Symphony.) She sent many qualified students on to major music schools, including Juilliard, Eastman and the Manhattan School of Music. During the '30s, she presented a series of weekly radio programs produced by the faculty and students of her Conservatory. An avid supporter of the Met's opera season in Minneapolis, she was one of three persons who attended *every one* of the 243 performances of this Midwest extension of the Met, which existed from 1944 to 1985.

A member of Sigma Alpha Iota National Music Fraternity, North Dakota and National Music Teachers' Association, Midwest Metropolitan Opera, Bismarck Arts Association and Chamber of Commerce, among many others, Bismarck's "Great Lady of Music," as she came to be called, died January 5, 1988, survived by her sister Alma Méhus Studness. In the course of the years, Alma, her daughter Anne Marit, and Belle each received the North Dakota Governor's Award in the Arts from three different governors—the only family to have such a distinction! [My thanks to **Susan Lundberg**, president of the Bismarck-Mandan Symphony, for this material.]

Marjorie Post

MARJORIE MERRIWEATHER POST—*American Royalty*; daughter of breakfast cereal magnate Charles William Post, Marjorie was born March 15, 1887, in Springfield, Illinois. A small town girl, she helped glue cereal boxes in her father's barn. As CW grew wealthy, he saw to it that his only child had the best education befitting a millionaire's daughter. His suicide in 1914 catapulted Marjorie, already married with two young daughters, into becoming sole heir of the Postum Cereal Company. Her lawyer husband, Ed Close, from an old moneyed family, did not prove adequate to the role of a director in the company—this being long before the days of a woman stepping in, no matter how well trained she was.

Under her second husband, broker E. F. Hutton, the company, renamed General Foods, was greatly expanded, helped by Marjorie's urging to buy Birdseye's Frosted Foods. Unfortunately, this marriage also ended in divorce when Marjorie discovered E.F.'s adultery. In 1935 she married diplomat Joe Davies, a friend of FDR, who made him ambassador to the Soviet Union, where he importantly helped cement the Soviet-U.S. alliance against Hitler. While living in Russia, January 1937–July 1938, Marjorie was shocked by the police-state way of

---

262. Adele Aus der Ohe began study at age three. She culminated her career premiering Tchaikovsky's First Piano Concerto, under the composer's baton, at Carnegie Hall in 1893.

life of which she wrote to Eleanor Roosevelt. The upside was finding women in government positions, and her being able to buy fabulous jewels, icons, china, Fabergé items and paintings—trappings of the former aristocracy the Communists were only too glad to be rid of. Back in the U.S., Marjorie was now able to take a more active and personal role in her company, while Davies, no longer in the post World War II diplomatic limelight, became increasingly cantankerous and suffocatingly possessive. Despite nineteen years of marriage, a third divorce was inevitable. Marjorie's next husband, businessman Herbert May, whom she wed in 1958, was discovered to be homosexual. She remained single for the rest of her life.

A great beauty, throughout her flamboyant lifestyle with palatial residences in Manhattan, Long Island, the Adirondacks, Washington, DC, and Palm Beach, Florida, where she threw parties fit for royalty—the Duke and Duchess of Windsor were among her friends—she never forgot the less fortunate. During World War I, in 1917, she outfitted an entire field hospital set up near the French trenches. In the Depression, she funded soup kitchens for women and children. Often anonymously, she supported the Red Cross, Boy Scouts and many other organizations and individuals. Like her father, she always saw to it that her company workers received fair wages and job security.

In 1950, she saved the National Symphony with a donation of $90,000 which wiped out the debt of the bankrupt orchestra, and became involved in the financial and artistic stability of the musicians. In 1955, after conductor Howard Mitchell mentioned that some 500,000 teenagers annually visited the capital on school tours, she decided to treat high school students to free concerts, underwriting "Music for Young America" with an initial donation of $100,000—the equivalent of a million dollars today. The first concert, April 1956, was attended by 1,300. By the end of the year the total was 50,000, with requests for tickets pouring in for following seasons. The series also gave the musicians five extra weeks of income. For a couple of years the Marjorie Merriweather Post Musical Competition earned the winner a scholarship to Juilliard. This was disbanded because the musicians were also the judges—an impossible situation, since they were accompanying the candidates. In 1958, Mrs Post—she reverted to her maiden name—anonymously donated $100,000 to build a National Cultural Center for the Performing Arts, later known as Kennedy Center.

The grande dame left us September 17, 1973, bringing to an end an era of opulence never duplicated. Her generosity was accompanied by modesty. Many recipients never realized the fount of their windfall. Her estates have become museums, allowing the public to share her fabulous art, china, Native American artifacts, Russian treasures and other collections. She was truly, in the words of biographer Nancy Rubin, an "American Empress."

Elisabeth Severence

ELISABETH SEVERANCE—*The Taj Mahal of Cleveland*; born Elisabeth Huntington DeWitt, 1865, she married John Long Severance, November 3, 1881. Her husband was president of the Colonial Salt Company, director of numerous banks and corporations and formerly associated with John D. Rockefeller's Standard Oil Company. The couple were generous patrons of the arts and other charities. In 1928, they pledged one million dollars towards the building of a permanent home for the then ten-year-old Cleveland Orchestra, which had been sharing its venue at Gray's Armory with poultry shows and circuses.

When Elisabeth died suddenly on January 25, 1929, after a short illness, John funded most of the cost of the building—three times the initial pledge—as a memorial to her. Severance Hall opened February 5, 1931, with a concert by the Cleveland Orchestra, under the baton of its founding director (1918–33), **Nikolai Sokoloff** (1886–1965), a festive, if sober note (Prohibition), in the second year of the Great Depression. The hall is a fitting tribute to a beneficent lady.

Catherine Shouse

CATHERINE FILENE SHOUSE—*A Woman for All Reasons*; an amazing lady who amassed fourteen honorary doctorates in humanities, humane letters and music from just about every major East Coast university, Catherine Filene was born June 9, 1896, the newest member of the prominent Boston department store family. In days when girls barely finished high school, she attended Vassar (1913–14) and went on to earn a BA in 1918 from Wheaton College (Norton, Massachusetts). While an undergraduate, she organized conferences to help promote jobs for women with higher education. In 1923, she was the first woman to receive a master's in education from Harvard. She also went to the University of Colorado in 1928.

In 1919, Catherine became the first woman appointed to the National Democratic Committee representing her state, founding the Women's National Democratic Club in 1925. Her book, *Careers for Women*, was published by Houghton Mifflin (1920; re-edited, 1932). She was the first woman appointed—by President Calvin Coolidge—as chairman of the first Federal Prison for Women, instituting a job training and rehabilitation program. In 1930, she divorced Alvin E. Dodd after eleven years of marriage and one daughter, Joan, who gave her four grandchildren, ten great-grandchildren and three great-great-grandchildren. In 1932, she wed the flamboyant former Senator from Kansas, Jouett Shouse. Although the marriage lasted only five years, she kept his name. He died in 1968.

From 1935–42, she organized the first chamber concerts performed in a Washington Museum. Known as the Phillips Collection, these are still going strong in a lovely old house on whose walls hang priceless French Impressionist paintings collected over the centuries. Shouse was vice president of the National Symphony Association (1951–68). In 1956, at the request of former President Herbert Hoover, she organized the Hungarian Relief Fund, raising half a million dollars in one month. President Eisenhower appointed her chairman of the President's Music Committee, People-to-People Program (1957–63), and in 1958 placed her on the first board of trustees of the National Cultural Center, which became the John F. Kennedy Center for the Performing Arts. She was re-appointed in 1962, and in 1970 by President Nixon for a ten-year term, after which she was made an Honorary Trustee. From 1965–72, she was on the board of the Washington Opera Society.

In 1961, Shouse donated forty acres of her land at her Wolf Trap Farm in Vienna, Virginia—where she bred champion hunting dogs—for the headquarters of the American Symphony Orchestra League. In 1966, she gave 100 acres to the government for a National Park for the Performing Arts, and donated the Filene Center Amphitheater. The formal opening was July 1, 1971, with First Lady Pat Nixon attending. In 1981, she donated and renovated two early 18th century barns for the foundation. The "Barns of Wolf Trap" were rebuilt on twenty-six acres adjacent to Wolf Trap National Park for the Performing Arts. 1980 donations included two houses, a garage and a swimming pool.

Among Shouse's numerous honors are the Presidential Medal of Freedom, the highest U.S. civilian award, bestowed by President Gerald R. Ford. Queen Elizabeth II made her a Dame Commander of the British Empire. The Government of France named her Officier dans l'Ordre des Arts et des Lettres. She was the first woman to receive the Commander's Cross of Merit from the German Federal Republic.

The great lady died on December 14, 1994.

ROSALIE MEYER STERN—*The Legacy of Levi Strauss*; Rosalie, arriving April 20, 1869, was one of eight children born to Eugene and Harriet Newmark Meyer in Los Angeles, where Eugene had settled after leaving his native Strasbourg (France). He worked for Lazard Frères, a French import firm in San Francisco and Los Angeles. In 1883, he took a position at the San Francisco branch of the London, Paris & American Bank.

In 1892, while in Paris with her mother, Rosalie met Sigmund Stern, a nephew of Levi Strauss who, in 1850, began the company that created the riveted denim work pants for gold prospectors. Levi never married, but his five nephews were like sons to him. Sigmund became president of the Levi Strauss Company.

Rosalie, twenty-three, and Sigmund, thirty-four, were married in San Francisco on October 3, 1892. In 1893, their daughter Elise was born in their palatial home on Pacific at Octavia Streets.

Levi had established scholarships at UC Berkeley, his *alma mater*, and was on the board of Associated Charities which, when he left that position in 1906, Rosalie took over. Although there had been orchestral events in San Francisco since 1881, the 1906 earthquake and fire destroyed half the city and most of its cultural life. In 1909, with the formation of the Musical Association of San Francisco to establish a symphony orchestra, Strauss contributed both his time and money. He was on the original board of governors of the San Francisco Symphony, inaugurated in 1911 under the baton of Henry Hadley.

After the marriage of Elise to Walter Haas in 1914, Rosalie devoted the next five years to the Boards of the Pioneer Kindergarten Society, San Francisco Playground Committee, the Children's Agency, as well as being field director of military relief for the American Red Cross, and a founding member of the San Francisco Opera Board (1923) under general director **Gaetano Merola** (1881–1953).

Through her thirty-seven years as respectively a playground commissioner, recreation commissioner, and recreation and park commissioner, her interest in providing parkland for San Francisco inspired her to purchase twenty-five acres, which she subsequently donated to the City as a memorial to her husband who died, April 24, 1928. The original outdoor amphitheater was constructed at her own expense, with the surrounding grounds, approaches and walkways developed as a WPA[263] project. Part of its funding now comes from the San Francisco Hotel Tax, and the Musicians Union Recording Trust Funds.[264] The first concert in Stern Grove was presented June 19, 1932.

Rosalie died February 8, 1956. Her family follows her tradition of civic responsibility and community service. In the early '30s, Elise Stern Haas initiated children's concerts by the San Francisco Symphony, of which she remained a board member emeritus. She studied sculpture, was an art collector and associated with such celebrated artists as Henry Matisse, composer Darius Milhaud, and numerous musicians and maestros. Her daughter, Rhoda, married Richard N. Goldman in 1946 and continued the legacy of philanthropy, funding geriatric day care centers, participating in environmental causes, and heading the committee for the Holocaust Memorial. After her mother stepped down from the chairmanship in 1968, she chaired the Stern Grove Festival Association. Rhoda passed away in February 1996 at the age of seventy-one.

Through women like this, the music flows on—in this case via over sixty years of free midsummer concerts in Sigmund Stern Grove, known as "Nature's Music Box."

ALICE TAYLOR—*Phantom of the Los Angeles Philharmonic*; I refer to Alice Taylor as a "phantom" because there appears to be *nothing* in the archives about this woman who, from 1951–62, was manager of one of the country's most prominent orchestras! What I gleaned was through an interview with **Bill Severns**—in his eighties, at the time—who started out as an usher at the Hollywood Bowl in 1933, and twenty years later became its manager. By 1969, he was an administrator of the Los Angeles Music Center. According to him, Alice began her career as a piano accompanist for singers, went on to help promote a campaign to bring the Metropolitan Opera to the West Coast, and became manager of the LA Philharmonic in 1951. Benefactress **Dorothy Chandler**, who saved the Hollywood Bowl from being torn down, worked with Taylor, 1954–64, during the time she [Chandler] was raising $20 million to build the Music Center.

Alice was admired for being one of the few who could handle temperamental guest maestro Edward van Beinum (1900–59). She left Los Angeles around 1962, went to San Francisco, and subsequently crossed the Pacific to manage the Honolulu Symphony for three or four years, but since then, no further information was available.

HELEN THOMPSON—*Trailblazer of the American Symphony Orchestra League*; although the organization was begun by Mrs. Leta Snow in 1942, who had founded the Kalamazoo Symphony (1921), it was Helen M. Thompson who developed the League from a group of smaller orchestras to becoming the protective umbrella of all major American symphonies.

---

263. Work Projects Administration: one of President Franklin D. Roosevelt's programs to help the country out of the Depression of the early 1930s.
264. Managed by Sam Rosenbaum—see harpist **Edna Phillips**.

Helen Mulford, born 1908, grew up in a musical atmosphere in Greenville, Illinois, and, as a student violinist, participated in various community musical activities before she entered the University of Illinois where she earned a BA in a triple major of psychology, sociology and philosophy (1932). Her private violin studies spanned from 1914 to 1940. After her graduation, she married Carl G. Thompson, a research chemist, had a son, Charles, did social work and eventually settled in Charleston, West Virginia, where she joined the local symphony as a second violinist and became their volunteer manager. By 1944, she had become active on the executive committee of the young League.

The League managed to survive the lean post-war years, meeting in Chicago (1944), Cincinnati (1946) and Charleston (1948). Managers, conductors, musicians and board members attended these meetings. After subsisting on $1,000 a year, at the 1950 Wichita meeting a businessman offered to contribute $2,000, providing that Helen Thompson was made executive secretary and he remain anonymous. The conditions were accepted and the Thompson home became League headquarters. (Her efforts in developing foundation funds have multiplied into a present day budget of over $1 million.)

During the next decade under her leadership, the League grew in size and importance, with most League activities originated by Helen. A significant success was her campaign to get the federal admission (ticket) tax removed for non-profit organizations. Also, by 1950, the League, which had represented only small civic orchestras, invited the "majors" as non-voting members. Boston and New York were the first to join. She also placed high priority on community interaction with concerts, education and leadership of cultural programs. Spokesperson for the League in government councils, foundations, and other sources of funding, Thompson, having written a booklet on the subject, gave presentations to local groups on organizing their orchestras. By hiring professional musicians, many orchestras outgrew their "civic" status, and had to learn how to utilize their city's financial resources. Non-professionals continue to find a venue for their talents in college-community orchestras comprised of students, faculty and other proficient musicians.

Training of conductors and managers came under Thompson's aegis. She originated music critic workshops, leading to the formation of the Music Critics Association. Her national conferences of arts councils resulted in the Associated Councils on the Arts, Inc., with help from the Rockefeller Foundation, for which she became a consultant. She gave great support to the many women's symphony auxiliary groups.

The concept of the League as a service organization extended to the publication of a newsletter, which became *Symphony* magazine in 1971. Thanks to its detailed reporting system, there is more information on symphony orchestras than any other branch of the arts.

In 1961, the League was offered a new home by **Catherine Shouse** on part of her Wolf Trap Farm estate. While League presidents were volunteers, Thompson was a top paid executive. In 1968, she received the title vice president. By now the League covered all major orchestras, and under her leadership created its organizational framework, making a profound impact on the symphonic scene. Thompson left in 1970 to assume the position of manager of the New York Philharmonic until 1973 when she moved to Carmel, California, to work as a private arts consultant. On June 25, 1974, in the process of organizing the annual meeting of the Association of California Orchestras, she died suddenly of a heart attack at age sixty-six.

Her many honors list the American Composers Alliance Laurel Leaf Award for Distinguished Achievements in American Music; Award of Merit from the National Association of American Conductors; Community Arts Councils Award for Distinguished Service; plus honorary doctorates from Cincinnati Conservatory (1961), and Marshall University, Huntington, West Virginia (1967). Presented with a Golden Baton upon leaving the League in 1970, the citation read: "To Helen Thompson for her leadership and guidance of the American Symphony Orchestra League from a small organization to the most representative professional group in the performing arts field in the United States."

Alice Tully

ALICE TULLY—*An Immortal Part of Lincoln Center*, Alice Bigelow Tully was born on September 11, 1902, in Corning, New York. Her father, William J. Tully, was a two-term New York State senator and general counsel for the Metropolitan Life Insurance Company. Her mother, Clara Houghton Tully, was the daughter of Amory Houghton, founder of Corning Glass Works. Alice began her devotion to music at age fifteen, when she heard a piano recital by one of the world's greatest pianists, **Josef Hofmann** (1876–1957). Although piano studies were a part of her schooling, her true love was singing. After studying voice for three years in New York, she went to Paris in 1922, training for seven years with Jean Périer, Miguel Fontecha, and Thérèse Leschetizsky. Her piano debut came in 1927 with the Pasdeloup Orchestra in Paris. Six years later she made her operatic debut at the Hippodrome in New York, singing Santuzza in *Cavalleria Rusticana*. She sang the title role in *Carmen* at the Manhattan Opera House, 1935, and throughout the 1930s performed as a recitalist in Europe and America.

At the beginning of World War II, Tully settled permanently in New York, suspending her career to support the war effort as a Red Cross nurse's aide at the French Hospital in Manhattan. She stopped singing in 1950 when she felt her voice was losing its flexibility.

In 1958, with the death of her mother, Tully inherited a substantial estate and began her philanthropic career. When her cousin, Arthur Houghton, Jr., one of the founders of Lincoln Center, asked for a concert hall contribution, she agreed and took an active role in its design, from seating capacity to interior decoration. Through her European research, she selected the Theodore Kuhn Company to build the hall's organ. On September 11, 1969, Alice Tully Hall opened with a program by the Chamber Music Society of Lincoln Center, the ensemble she created and on whose board she was chairwoman for many years. She also served on the boards of the New York Philharmonic, Metropolitan Opera and Juilliard. She contributed to the Metropolitan Museum of Art, Museum of Modern Art, Frick Collection, Morgan Library, as well as dance, art and humanitarian organizations.

Tully's many awards include the Handel Medallion, New York's top cultural award (1970), the Gallatin Medal from NYU for contributions of lasting significance to society (1976), National Medal of Arts (1985) and the American Red Cross Humanitarian Award (1988). A devoted Francophile, she received recognition from the French Government and was made an Officer in the French Legion of Honor. Much honored, she died in Manhattan, December 10, 1993.

BEATRICE VRADENBURG—*Another Peak in Colorado*, Bee Vradenburg gave close to four decades of her life to the Colorado Springs Symphony. Born November 1, 1922, in Manhattan, Kansas, she spent her childhood in Washington, DC, in a not particularly musical family, but did get to hear the great **Hans Kindler** (1892–1949), founder/conductor of the National Symphony—a source of great inspiration. When she was fourteen, her father became a professor at Rutgers University (New Jersey). She was studying art history at Oberlin College when she met and married a marine, George A. Vradenburg, Jr., in 1942, and gave birth to George III in 1943. After the war they moved to Colorado Springs, where George started a real estate business. (Her granddaughter, Alyssa, and grandson, Tyler, are in the film industry.)

Although busy in her housewife role, Bee started the Colorado Springs Symphony Guild in 1954. Beginning in 1955, for the first ten years, she *volunteered* her services as manager of the symphony. During her thirty-seven year administration, she saw the budget expand from $15,000 to $2.5 million. In 1968, she was among the founders of the Colorado Council on Arts and Humanities, remaining a member until 1974. She was on the board of directors of the ASOL (1977–78), a board member of arts and educational councils, NEA Orchestra Panel, business groups, banks and the Chamber of Commerce. She was also on the Advisory Boards of the University of Colorado, Opera Theatre of the Rockies and many charitable institutions.

Bee Vradenburg retired from her successful career in 1992. (The symphony directors discovered it was not an easy task to find a replacement.) She continued as a member of the Colorado Women's Foundation, an honorary trustee of the Colorado Springs Symphony, and for years enjoyed the thrill of housing guest conductors and artists. She passed away September 7, 2000. A memorial fund bearing her name was established in April 2001.

KATHERINE GLADNEY WELLS—*Bulwark of the St. Louis Symphony*, known by her nickname, Katch, she was one of the great women of the arts in St. Louis. Born suffering from influenza during the pandemic of 1918, she managed to survive. Her parents were Frank Y. Gladney, a founder of the Seven-Up Company, and Katherine Graves Gladney. From grades seven through twelve, Katherine attended the prestigious John Burroughs School, founded in 1923. It was there she met her husband, Ben H. Wells, who had been one of her teachers. He was to become chief executive officer of Seven-Up, as well as a civic and cultural leader.

Katch was a woman of multi talents and interests which ran from adopting stray dogs, raising parakeets and repairing clocks to writing music, poetry, articles and the definitive book, *Symphony and Song, The St. Louis Symphony Orchestra: The First Hundred Years 1880–1980.*

In 1969, Wells was named "A Woman of Achievement" in the creative category by the *St. Louis Globe-Democrat.* In 1972, the Aspen Musicians Guild awarded her "Best Program by an American Woman Composer." She was chairman of the board of the St. Louis Conservatory and Schools for the Arts (CASA), from whom she received an honorary degree in 1982. She was a joint recipient with her husband of the "Lifetime Achievement in the Arts Award" from the St. Louis Arts and Education Council in 1994, a year before his death.

In the course of decades of devotion to and support for the orchestra, Katch was made an honorary member and conducted it in special concerts of her own compositions, which included string quartets, art songs, musical shows and orchestral works. She endowed the principal cello *Frank Y. and Katherine G. Gladney Chair* in honor of her parents. (This position has been occupied since 1968 by John Sant'Ambrogio, father and first teacher of cellist **Sara Sant'Ambrogio** of the Eroica Trio.)

Wells was also an honorary member of Local 2197 of the American Federation of Musicians. Her compositions have been played by other orchestras, notably the Syracuse Symphony, under Daniel Hege, which performed her *Minor Reflection* for strings, written in the late '80s, in March 2002.

Katch Wells died at her home in St. Louis, December 24, 2003, at age eighty-five, after a long struggle with emphysema. She is survived by her daughter, Katherine Wells Wheeler, and son, Benjamin Gladney Wells, four grandchildren and five great-grandchildren.

These and countless women, known and unknown, past and present, are the continuous backbone and core of organizations keeping the finer arts alive in a world sadly polluted by crime, drugs, moral disintegration, obscenity of language, unchecked pornography, diseases of biblical plague proportions and species of "music" that research has proven to be most detrimental to one's physical and emotional health.

Most of these ladies lived in a kinder, more genteel time. May they never be forgotten and may all those following in their footsteps continue to elevate our hearts and spirits as their efforts preserve and secure the future for classical music and a better future for our planet!

Afterword

As can be seen throughout the pages of this book the history of women, after being accorded their rightful respect as caregivers and lifebringers in very early societies, settled into a consistent saga of subjugation based on the obvious: that most men are physically stronger than [most] women. As civilization progressed beyond clubbing and hair-pulling, humanity's built-in awe of unseen powers and fear of death evolved into the formidable domination of the Catholic Church with its dictates and indulgences. The process of female subjugation reached an epitome with the brand of Christianity Jesus never had in mind: *chastity* or *chattel*. Very few women had a choice. Only daughters of the upper classes could enter a convent, and many unwanted or unmarriageable girls of noble families were thrown into cloisters, or served as a tithe. The virtues of unrealistic celibacy, long hours, menial work and self-denial were the trade-off for the independence of not being a man's physical property. In the secular aristocratic world, marriages were arranged for advantageous political alliances and heir breeding. Women lived by rules laid down by men as to what was "ladylike" and, for the most part, had little option but to believe in modesty, humility and the inferiority of their sex.

Since tyranny usually breeds rebellion, and as the Renaissance unleashed emotions, women strained at their leashes despite their gender brainwashing—which lingers even into the 21st century. Strong wives intellectually overcame weak husbands and managed to wield influence within the confines of the bonds of matrimony. Money equals power, and many wealthy women used theirs to the benefit of the arts. The Industrial Revolution (1760–1830), the rising middle class, and women entering the work force were all factors in fostering fledgling forms of female independence. It has, of course, taken centuries to get to the serious business of "Women's Liberation," begun in America in the 1960s. The process was far from unanimous, with the majority of women reluctant to leave their main "comfort zone" of those times, the traditional housewife-mother roles. However, as more women ventured into the workplace, that second income which once provided luxuries has unfortunately, in today's economy, become a necessity—to the detriment of "latchkey" children who come home from school to empty houses. Over four decades later, "emancipated" women are still fighting for equal pay for equal work or, with the erosion of moral values, struggling as single mothers to bring up children without a second breadwinner or father figure. Their challenges are chronicled in the mounting statistics of drug abuse, AIDS, and juvenile crime, amongst other pandemic societal decay.

This book, being about music, has obviously focused on women who have made their mark in this field. Music, however, like all the arts, is a telling reflection in the social mirror, and cannot be separated from the course of history. Music is its own magnetic force affecting entire civilizations and generations. Divided in the past into church, secular or folk music, it has evolved into classical or "popular." Popular, in turn, has branched from ragtime to jazz and blues, to big band, romantic croon tunes, to country western, rock and rap, the latter proliferating into degenerate "heavy metal" and "gangsta rap," whose foulmouthed lyrics complete a vicious cycle of denigrating women.

Meanwhile, classical music is engaged in a continuous survival contest—witness the *one* classical station on the radio dial (in fortunate areas) versus the profusion of other blarings. Signs of the times are the attrition of symphony orchestras and the graying of concert audiences—not so much in Europe—versus the staggering salaries of rock "stars" and stadiums filled to capacity for live rock concerts. There remains, however, a loyal nucleus dedicated to the durability of "great" music. In performance, prodigies continue to appear and amaze, with many of Asian descent setting their work ethic example for the younger generation of other ethnic groups. In composition, just as the 1920s began "shocking" audiences with the strange sounds of the twelve-tone scale, atonalism, minimalism and serialism, the '70s opened the era of electronic and other experimental dissonance. Inevitably, the purse of the audience tends to dictate what remains popular in every artistic field.

Now, in the 21st century, the trend appears to be settling for something vaguely blanketed as *Neo-Romantic*, which covers anything short of the out and out bizarre. What is bizarre is also relative. Beethoven was "bizarre" as he forged out of the Classical into the Romantic Period. Stravinsky's *Rite of Spring* outraged Parisians of 1913, who threw vegetables *et al* at the musicians. Many beloved operas, symphonies and concerti received negative criticism at their premieres. Only time will show which newer cream will rise to the top and stay there.

The flip side, however, is the issue of how much *women's* music is actually performed. Today, this still needs to become part of major orchestra repertoire,[265] and should be played with regularity on classical stations to create listener familiarity, and therefore a demand for CDs and live performances. This has yet to happen.

A common cliché has been that, ideally, one should not be able to tell if a piece of music has been written or performed—on a recording—by a man or a woman. Yet a whole new line of musicology has sprung forth detailing *gender*, or *why* a woman writes as she does *because* of her gender. Women have always had the responsibility of perpetuating tradition. It is their challenge to remold the past into a future that holds justice and enlightenment for their sex.

While there are more opportunities for women in all fields of music today, it is evident that they are far from equal, especially on the podium, where the physical aspect of a woman wielding a stick over a group of (still) mostly male musicians is something society—and the male musicians—are as yet having trouble getting used to, especially in Europe, the prime example being the 97 percent all-male Vienna Philharmonic who for *twenty-seven years* denied full membership to their one female harpist. It is in the music industry, women have truly found their niche, dealing with performers, whether in the role of agent, orchestra/opera company manager, or in the recording or publishing business, etc.

The closest to equality is in the teaching field—long a women's domain. Musicologists have won major prizes and produced significant books and articles on all aspects of music, with an ever-growing vital concentration on feminine subject matter. The pioneer books, *The Musical Woman* (3 Vols. 1983–90, eds., **Judith Zaimont, Jane Gottlieb** &c), *Women Making Music* (1987 eds., **Jane Bowers** and **Judith Tick**), *Women and Music* (1991 ed. **Karin Pendle**), *Women in Music* (1996 ed. **Carol Neuls-Bates**), each contain ground-breaking essays of great enlightenment on their subjects. The much-awaited *Norton-Grove Dictionary of Women Composers* edited by **Julie Anne Sadie** and **Rhian Samuel** (1995), is a fine research resource. *Music and Women* (**1948!**) by **Sophie Drinker** was the real forerunner of books written by a single author. Over thirty years later came *Unsung* (1980, revised 2001), by **Christine Ammer**, *Women Composers, Conductors and Musicians of the 20th Century* (3 Vols. 1980-88) by **Jane Weiner LePage**, *Women Composers: The Lost Tradition Found* (1988), by the late **Diane Peacock Jezic**, *The Pandora Guide to Women in Music* (1994) by **Sophie Fuller**, *Women and Music in America Since 1900*, a two volume encyclopedia covering all styles of music, edited by Kristine Burns (2002), and *From Convent to Concert Hall—A Guide to Women Composers* (2003), written in formal scholastic style, edited by Sylvia Glickman and Martha Furman Schleifer.

My research for the two comprehensive chapters on women composers and conductors in my first book, *The Popular Guide to Classical Music* (1993), was my eye opener on the accomplishments of women in these genres, and provided the seed ground for *The WORLD of WOMEN in Classical Music*. This book attempts to

---

265. The 2006 statistic was still a pitiful 2 percent!

put a spotlight not just on the "stars," but the multitude of women who conduct regional or community orchestras, sing in opera choruses, churches and synagogues, play their instruments in other than Carnegie Hall, and whose compositions reach select audiences in smaller venues. They and the musicologists who pass on their knowledge in the academia and in print, plus those involved in the "business" of music, as well as the patronesses, fundraisers and countless volunteers who stuff envelopes in symphony offices, and usher in the concert hall, form the vast network of women who, along with their male counterparts, help keep classical music alive and thriving in its own worldwide sphere.

Despite the still bleak lot of women in the few primitive societies left on our shrinking planet, who endure tortures such as declitorization and other atrocities in Africa and India, where women are routinely murdered when their husbands tire of them, as well as the gross plunge backwards enforced by Muslim nations who have once again veiled and thrust women into medieval bondage, irrevocable seeds have been sown to forge a future which will shed and shred the *man*made rules and roles that have shackled women to traditions of the past.

The real resolution is that unique feminine characteristics should *complement* rather than *compete* with the best of masculine traits. The true ideal is that women be recognized, respected and equally compensated for their talent and ability in *every* field of endeavor!

Anne Gray, PhD
Christmas, 2006

Opera Glossary

ROLE	OPERA	COMPOSER
Abigaille	Nabucco	Guiseppe Verdi (1813–1901)
Adalgisa	Norma	Vincenzo Bellini (1801–35)
Adele	Die Fledermaus (The Bat)	Johann Strauss (1825–99)
Adina	L'Elisir d'amore (The Elixir of Love)	Gaetano Donizetti (1797–1848)
Adriana	Adriana Lecouvreur	Francesco Cilea (1866–1950)
Agathe	Der Freischütz	Carl Maria von Weber (1786–1826)
Agrippina	Agrippina	George Frederick Handel (1685–1759)
Aida	Aida	Verdi
Alcina	Alcina	Handel
Alice Ford	Falstaff	Verdi
Alminera	Rinaldo	Handel
Amelia	Amelia Goes to the Ball	Gian Carlo Menotti (1911–2007)
Amelia	Simon Boccanegra	Verdi
Amelia	Un ballo in maschera (A Masked Ball)	Verdi
Amina	La sonnambula	Bellini
Amneris	Aida	Verdi
Amor	Orfeo ed Euridice	Christoph W. Gluck (1714–87)
Anna Bolena	Anna Bolena	Donizetti
Ännchen	Der Freischütz	Weber
Annina	La traviata	Verdi
Anne Trulove	The Rake's Progress	Igor Stravinsky (1882–1971)
Antonia	Les Contes d'Hoffmann	Jacques Offenbach (1819–80)
Arabella	Arabella	Richard Strauss (1864–1949)
Ariadne	Ariadne auf Naxos	R. Strauss
Arminta	Il re pastore	Wolfgang A. Mozart (1756–91)
Azucena	Il trovatore	Verdi
Barbarina	Le Nozze di Figaro	Mozart
Blanche	Dialogues of the Carmelites	Francis Poulenc (1899–1963)
Blanche	A Streetcar Named Desire	André Previn (1929–)
Blonde	Die Entführung aus dem Serail	Mozart
Brünnhilde	Die Walküre, Siegfried, Götterdämmerung	Richard Wagner (1813–83)
Butterfly	Madame Butterfly	Giacomo Puccini (1858–1924)
Carmen	Carmen	Georges Bizet (1838–75)
Celia	Lucio Silla	Mozart
Charlotte	Werther	Jules Massenet (1842–1912)
Chrysothemis	Elektra	R. Strauss
Cinderella	La Cenerentola	Giaochino Rossini (1792–1868)

Cio Cio San	Madama Butterfly	Puccini
Cissy	Albert Herring	Benjamin Britten (1913–76)
Cleopatra	Giulio Cesare	Handel
Cleopatra	Antony and Cleopatra	Samuel Barber (1910–81)
Costanze	Die Entführung aus dem Serail	Mozart
Countess Almaviva	The Marriage of Figaro	Mozart
Dalila (Delilah)	Samson et Dalila	Camille Saint-Saëns (1835–1921)
Desdemona	Otello	Verdi
Despina	Così fan tutte	Mozart
Dido	Dido and Anæus	Gluck
Donna Anna	Don Giovanni	Mozart
Dorabella	Così fan tutte	Mozart
Dulcinea	Don Quixote	Massenet
Eboli	Don Carlo	Verdi
Elektra	Elektra	R. Strauss
Elena	Mefistofele	Arrigo Boito (1842–1918)
Elisa	Il re Pastore	Mozart
Elisabetta	Don Carlos	Verdi
Elisabeth	Tannhäuser	Wagner
Ellen	Peter Grimes	Britten
Elsa	Lohengrin	Wagner
Elvira (Donna)	Don Giovanni	Mozart
Elvira	Ernani	Verdi
Elvira	I Puritani	Bellini
Emilia	Otello	Verdi
Euridice	Orfeo ed Euridice	Gluck
Eva	Die Meistersinger	Wagner
Fenena	Nabucco	Verdi
Fiordiligi	Così fan tutte	Mozart
Fricka	Das Rheingold	Wagner
Friea	Das Rheingold	Wagner
Gilda	Rigoletto	Verdi
Gioconda	La Gioconda	Amilcaré Ponchielli (1834–86)
Gutrune	Götterdämmerung	Wagner
Hanna Glawari	Die Lustige Witwe (The Merry Widow)	Franz Lehár (1870–1948)
Helmwige	Die Walküre	Wagner
Herodias	Salome	R. Strauss
Ilia	Idomeneo	Mozart
Inez	Il Trovatore	Verdi
Isabella	L'Italiana in Algieri	Rossini
Isolde	Tristan und Isolde	Wagner
Juliette	Roméo et Juliette	Charles Gounod (1818–93)
Kabanicha	Kát'a Kabanová	Leoš Janáček
Klytämnestra	Elektra	R. Strauss
Konstanze	Die Entführung aus dem Serail	Mozart

Kundry	Parsifal	Wagner
Lady Macbeth	Macbeth	Verdi
Lakmé	Lakmé	Léo Delibes (1836–91)
Laura	La Gioconda	Ponchielli
Lauretta	Gianni Schicchi	Puccini
Leila	Les Pêcheurs de Perles (The Pearl Fishers)	Bizet
Leonore	Fidelio	Ludwig van Beethoven (1770–1827)
Leonora	Il trovatore	Verdi
Leonora	La forza del destino	Verdi
Lisa	La Sonnambula	Bellini
Liù	Turandot	Puccini
Louise	Louise	Gustave Charpentier (1860–1956)
Lucia	Lucia di Lammermoor	Donizetti
Lucrezia	Lucrezia Borgia	Donizetti
Luisa	Luisa Miller	Verdi
Maddalena	Rigoletto	Verdi
Madeleine	Andréa Chénier	Umberto Giordano (1867–1948)
Manon	Manon	Massenet
Manon	Manon Lescaut	Puccini
Margherita	Mefistofele	Boito
Marguerite	Faust	Gounod
Marguerite	Dammnation of Faust	Berlioz
Marie	The Daughter of the Regiment	Donizetti
(The) Marschallin	Der Rosenkavalier	R. Strauss
Martha	Martha	Friedrich von Flotow (1812–96)
Marzellina	Fidelio	Beethoven
Mathilde	Guillaume Tell	Rossini
Mélisande	Pélleas et Mélisande	Claude Debussy (1862–1918)
Micaëla	Carmen	Bizet
Mignon	Mignon	Ambrose Thomas (1811–96)
Mimi	La Bohème	Puccini
Minnie	La fanciulla del West	Puccini
Musetta	La Bohème	Puccini
Nannetta	Falstaff	Verdi
Nedda	I Pagliacci	Ruggero Leoncavallo (1857–1919)
Norina	Don Pasquale	Donizetti
Norma	Norma	Bellini
Norns (Three Norns)	Götterdämmerung	Wagner
Olga	Eugene Onegin	Pyotr Ilyitch Tchaikovsky (1840–93)
Olympia	Tales of Hoffmann	Offenbach
Ophélie	Hamlet	Thomas
Ortrud	Lohengrin	Wagner
Oscar	Un ballo in maschera (A Masked Ball)	Verdi
Pamina	Die Zauberflöte (The Magic Flute)	Mozart
Papagena	The Magic Flute	Mozart
Philine	Mignon	Thomas

Queen of the Night	The Magic Flute	Mozart
Mistress Quickly	Falstaff	Verdi
Rosalinde	Die Fledermaus	J. Strauss
Rosina	Barber of Seville	Rossini
Rusalka	Rusalka	Antonín Dvořák (1841–1904)
Salome	Salome	R. Strauss
Santuzza	Cavalleria Rusticana	Pietro Mascagni (1863–1945)
Senta	The Flying Dutchman	Wagner
Serpetta	La finta giardiniera	Mozart
Servilia	La clemenza di Tito	Mozart
Sieglinde	Die Walküre	Wagner
Sophie	Der Rosenkavalier	R. Strauss
Sophie	Werther	Massenet
Stella	A Streetcar Named Desire	Previn
Susanna	The Marriage of Figaro	Mozart
Susannah	Susannah	Carlisle Floyd (1926–)
Suzuki	Madama Butterfly	Puccini
Sylviane	The Merry Widow	Lehár
Tamyris	Il re pastore	Mozart
Tatiana	Eugene Onegin	Tchaikovsky
Thérèse	Thérèse Raquin	Tobias Picker (1954–)
Thaïs	Thaïs	Massenet
Tosca	Tosca	Puccini
Turandot	Turandot	Puccini
Ulrica	Un ballo in maschera (A Masked Ball)	Verdi
Valencienne	The Merry Widow	Lehár
Vanessa	Vanessa	Barber
Violetta	La traviata	Verdi
Vitellia	La clemenza di Tito	Mozart
Wally	La Wally	Alfredo Catalani (1854–93)
Waltraute	Götterdämmerung	Wagner
Wellgunde	Das Rhinegold	Wagner
Woglinde	Das Rhinegold	Wagner
Zdenka	Arabella	R. Strauss
Zerbinetta	Ariadne auf Naxos	R. Strauss
Zerlina	Don Giovanni	Mozart

TROUSER ROLES [*Travesti*] (Male Characters traditionally sung by Women)

Adriano	Rienzi	Wagner
Annius	La clemenza de Tito	Mozart
Ascanio	Benvenuto Cellini	Berlioz
Cherubino	Marriage of Figaro	Mozart
The Composer	Ariadne auf Naxos	R. Strauss
Feodor	Boris Godunov	Modest Mussorgsky (1839–81)
Goffredo	Rinaldo	Handel
Hansel	Hansel and Gretel	Humperdinck

Idamante	Idomeneo	Mozart
Julius Caesar	Giulio Cesare	Handel
Nicklausse	The Tales of Hoffmann	Offenbach
Octavian	Der Rosenkavalier	R. Strauss
Orlovsky	Die Fledermaus	J. Strauss
Oscar	Un ballo in maschera	Verdi
Romeo	I Capuleti e i Montecchi	Bellini
Sesto	La clemenza di Tito	Mozart
Siebel	Faust	Gounod
Ptolemy	Giulio Cesare	Handel

OPERA COMPANY ABBREVIATIONS

ENO	English National Opera
HGO	Houston Grand Opera
LOC	Lyric Opera of Chicago
MET	Metropolitan Opera of New York
NYCO	New York City Opera
OONY	Opera Orchestra of New York
SFO	San Francisco Opera

OPERA HOUSE LOCATIONS

Bastille	Paris
Bavarian State Opera	Munich
Bolshoi Theatre	Moscow
Covent Garden	London
La Scala	Milan (Italy)
Liceo	Barcelona
Maggio Musicale Fiorentino	Florence
Teatro San Carlo	Naples
Teatro Carlo Felice	Genoa
Teatro Colón	Buenos Aires (Argentina)
Teatro Comunale	Florence
Teatro Giuseppe Verdi	Trieste
Teatro La Fenice	Venice
Teatro Lirico	Spoleto (Italy)
Teatro Regio	Turin

Abbreviations

AAUW	American Association of University Women
ABC	Australian Broadcasting Commission
ACL	Asian Composers League
ACLS	American Council of Learned Societies
ACSO	Association of California Symphony Orchestras
ACUM	Society of Authors, Composers and Music Publishers in Israel (similar to ASCAP)
AGO	American Guild of Organists
AGO-RCYO	Regional Competitions for Young Artists (under twenty-three)
AHS	American Harp Society
AMS	American Musicological Society
AMSA	American Music Scholarship Association
ASCAP	American Society of Composers, Authors and Publishers
ASOL	American Symphony Orchestra League
BA	Bachelor of Arts
BAFTA	British Academy of Film and Television Arts
BBC	British Broadcasting Corporation
BM	Bachelor of Music
B M Ed	Bachelor of Music Education
Cal State	California State University System
CBC	Canadian Broadcasting Company
CBE*	Commander of the British Empire - Award at annual January 1st Queen's Honours List
CCM	Cincinnati College-Conservatory
CENIDEM	Centro Nacional de Investigación, Documentación e Información Musical (Mexico)
CMS	College Music Society
CUNY	City University of New York
Curtis	The Curtis Institute of Music (Philadelphia)
DAAD	German Academic Exchange Service
DBE*	Or KBE Dame Commander of the British Empire (female knighthood).
DG	Deutsche Grammophon (Recording Company)
DMA	Doctor of Musical Arts
Eastman	Eastman School of Music (University of Rochester, New York)
ECHO	European Concert Halls Organization
GBE*	Knight or Dame Grand Cross - High British Honour
GEDOK	German Visual and Musical Arts Organization.
Hartt	Hartt College of Music (Hartford, Connecticut)
IAWM	International Alliance of Women in Music
ILWC	International League of Women Composers (merged with IAWM)
IMS	International Musicological Society

IWBC	International Women's Brass Conference
Interlochen	Interlochen Music School and Summer Festival (Michigan)
IRCAM	Institut de Recherché et de Coordination Acoustique Musique
ISCM	International Society of Contemporary Music
IU	Indiana University - School of Music
JAMS	Journal of the American Musicological Society
Juilliard	The Juilliard School of Music (New York)
MA	Master of Arts
Mannes	Mannes College of Music (New York)
MBE*	Member of the British Empire - junior order of chivalry
Met	Metropolitan Opera (New York)
MGG	German Encyclopedia: *Die Musik in Geschichte und Gegenwart* - 20 volumes
MLS	Master of Library Science
MM	Master of Music
MSM	Manhattan School of Music
MSM	Master of Sacred Music
MTNA	Music Teachers National Association
NACUSA	National Association of Composers, USA
NARAS	National Academy for Recording Arts and Sciences
NATO	North Atlantic Treaty Organization (1948): made up of Allied countries vs threat of Communists
NEA	National Endowment for the Arts
NEH	National Endowment for the Humanities
NLAPW	National League of American Pen Women
NPR	National Public Radio
NYCO	New York City Opera Company
NYT	New York Times
NYU	New York University
OBE*	Officer of the British Empire - a prestigious honor medal
Oberlin	Oberlin College-Conservatory (Ohio)
ORTF	Office de Radio-Télévision Français
Peabody	The Peabody Conservatory - Johns Hopkins University (Baltimore, Maryland)
Proms	Promenade Concerts played during the summer months in the UK.
RAI	Radiotelevisione Italiana
RAM	Royal Academy of Music (London)
RCM	Royal College of Music (London)
RILM	Repertoire Internationale Literature Musicale - world's largest music database
Rundfunk	Radio (German)
SACEM	Society of Authors, Composers and Editors of Music (France)
SAM	Society for American Music, formerly the Sonneck Society
SDSU	San Diego State University
SEAMUS	Society of Electro-Acoustic Music in the United States
SUNY	State University of New York (State System)
Tanglewood	Tanglewood Music Center (aka Berkshire Music Center - Massachusetts)
TWP	The Women's Philharmonic (San Francisco)

UC	University of California (State System)
UCLA	University of California at Los Angeles
UCSD	University of California at San Diego
UI	University of Indiana
USC	University of Southern California (Los Angeles)
USD	University of San Diego
WWI	World War One (1914-18, Europe), (1917-18, US entry)
WWII	World War Two (1939-45, Europe). (1941-45, US entry)
Wolf Trap	Wolf Trap Farm Park for the Performing Arts (Vienna, Virginia, near Washington, DC)
YCA	Young Concert Artists

*The Most Excellent Order of the British Empire - an order of chivalry established June 1917 by King George V. Has five classes in civil and military divisions.

Bibliography

Ammer, Christine. *Unsung: A History of Women in American Music* (Westport: Connecticut: Greenwood Press, 1980, 2nd Edition, 2000)

Barr, Cyrilla. *Elizabeth Sprague Coolidge: American Patron of Music* (New York: Schirmer Books, 1998)

Bernstein, Jane A., ed. *Women's Voices Across Musical Worlds* (Boston: Northeastern University Press, 2004)

Block, Adrienne Fried. *Amy Beach, Passionate Victorian; the Life and Work of an American Composer 1867–1944* (New York & Oxford: Oxford University Press, 1998)

Bitgood, Roberta with Julia Goodfellow. *Swell to Great - A Backward Look from My Organ Loft* (Salem, Connecticut, The Bayberry Design Co., 2000)

Bogin, Meg. *The Women Troubadours* (New York, London: W.W. Norton, 1976)

Bookspan, Martin and Yockey, Ross. *Zubin: The Zubin Mehta Story* (New York: Harper & Row, 1978)

Borroff, Edith. *American Operas: A Checklist* ed. J. Bunker Clark (Warren, Michigan: Harmonie Park Press, 1992)

Borroff, Edith. *An Introduction to Elisabeth-Claude Jacquet de la Guerre* (Brooklyn, New York: Institute of Medieval Music, Ltd., 1966)

Bortin, Virginia. *Elinor Remick Warren: Her Life and Music* (Metuchen, New Jersey: Scarecrow Press, 1987)

Bowers, Jane and Judith Tick, eds. *Women Making Music: The Western Art Tradition, 1150–1950* (Urbana: University of Illinois Press, 1986)

Briscoe, James, ed. *Historical Anthology of Music by Women* (Bloomington: Indiana University Press, 1991) with accompanying tapes.

Britain, Radie. *Ridin' Herd to Writing Symphonies: An Autobiography* (Lanham, Maryland: Scarecrow Press, Inc., 1996)

Brody, Seymour. *Jewish Heroes and Heroines of America* (Hollywood, Florida: Lifetime Books, Inc., 1996)

Buelow, George J., ed. *The Late Baroque Era* (Englewood Cliffs, New Jersey: Prentice Hall, 1994)

Burns, Kristine, ed. *Women and Music in America Since 1900* (Westport, Connecticut: Greenwood Press, 2002)

Christiansen, Rupert. *Prima Donna: A History* (New York: Viking Penguin Inc., 1985)

Citron, Marcia J. *Gender and the Musical Canon* (UK: Cambridge University Press, 1993)

Citron, Marcia J. *The Letters of Fanny Hensel to Felix Mendelssohn* (New York: Pendragon Press, 1987)

Cosman, Madeleine Pelner. *Women at Work in Medieval Europe* (New York: Facts on File, 2000)

Crofton, Ian and Fraser, Donald. *A Dictionary of Musical Quotations* (New York: Schirmer Books, 1985)

Cross, Donna Woolfolk. *Pope Joan* (New York: Ballantine Books, 1996)

Cross, Milton J. *Milton Cross' Complete Stories of the Great Operas* (New York: Doubleday & Co. Inc., 1948)

Davies, Rhian. *Never So Pure a Sight - Morfydd Owen (1891–1918): A Life in Pictures* (Llandysul, Dyfed, Wales: Gomer Press, 1994)

DeLong, Thomas. *The Mighty Music Box: The Golden Age of Radio* (New York: Hastings House, 1980)

Denton, Grace. *Madame Impresario* (Yucca Valley, California: Manzanita Press, 1974)

Diamant, Anita. *The Red Tent* (New York, St. Martin's Press, 1997)

Dickerson, James. *Go, Girl, Go!: The Women's Revolution in Music* (New York: Schirmer Trade Books, 2005)

Dickson, Harry Ellis. *Arthur Fiedler and the Boston Pops* (Boston: Houghton Mifflin Co., 1981)

Drinker, Sophie. *Music and Women: The Story of Women in Their Relation to Music* New York: Coward-McCann, Inc., 1948), (3rd ed. New York: The Feminist Press, 1995)

Dubal, David. *Reflections from the Keyboard* (New York: Summit Books, 1984)

Dunoyer, Cecilia. *Marguerite Long: A Life in French Music* (Bloomington: Indiana University Press, 1993)

Edwards, Anne. *Maria Callas: An Intimate Biography* (New York: St. Martin's Press, 2001)

Emerson, Isabelle Putnam. *Five Centuries of Women Singers* (Westport, Connecticut: Praeger, 2005)

Fierro, Sr. Nancy. *Hildegard of Bingen and Her Vision of the Feminine* (Los Angeles: Carondelet Productions, 1994)

Frasier, Jane. *Women Composers: A Discography* (Detroit, Michigan: Information Coordinators, 1983)

Franke, Metche. *Investigations into the Music of Women* (Dubuque, Iowa: Brown and Benchmark, 1994)

Friedland, Bea. *Louise Farrenc (1804–1875): Composer, Performer, Scholar* (Ann Arbor: University of Michigan Press, 1980)

Gill, Dominic, ed. *The Book of the Violin* (New York: Rizzoli International Publications, 1984)

Glackens, Ira. *Yankee Diva: Lillian Nordica and the Golden Days of Opera* (New York: Coleridge Press, 1972)

Glickman, Sylvia and Martha Furman Schleifer, eds. *From Convent to Concert Hall - A Guide to Women Composers* (Westport, Connecticut: Greenwood Press, 2003)

Gold, Arthur and Fizdale, Robert. *Misia: The Life of Misia Sert* (New York: Morrow Quill, 1981)

Govea, Wenonah Milton. *Nineteenth and Twentieth Century Harpists* (Westport, Connecticut & London: Greenwood Press, 1995)

Gray, Anne. *The Popular Guide to Classical Music* (New York: Birch Lane Press,1993), (London: Robert Hale, Ltd., 1994), (Spanish ed: Buenos Aires, Madrid, JavierVergara, 1995), (Taiwan: Jack Lui, 1995)

Green, Mildred Denby. *Black Women Composers: A Genesis* (Boston: Twayne Publishers, 1983)

Groh, Jan Bell. *Evening the Score: Women in Music and the Legacy of Frèdèrique Petrides* (Fayetteville: University of Arkansas Press, 1991)

Guignebert, Charles. *The Jewish World in the Time of Jesus* (New Hyde Park, NY: University Books, 1959)

Handy, D. Antoinette. *Black Women in American Bands and Orchestras* (Metuchen, New Jersey: The Scarecrow Press, 1981)

Harrison, Conrad B. *5,000 Concerts: A Commemorative History of the Utah Symphony* (Salt Lake City: Utah Symphony Society, 1986)

Harvey, Brian W. and Shapreau, Carla J. *Violin Fraud Deception, Forgery, and Lawsuits in England and America* (Oxford: Clarendon Press, 1997)

Horne, Marilyn with Jane Scovell. *Marilyn Horne: My Life* (New York: Atheneum, 1983)

Jenkins, Walter S. *The Remarkable Mrs. Beach, American Composer* (Michigan: Harmonie Park Press, 1995)

Jezic, Diane Peacock. *Women Composers: The Lost Tradition Found* (New York: The Feminist Press at the City University of New York, 1988), (2nd Ed., 1994)

Johnson, Barbara Urner. *Catherine Urner and Charles Koechlin A Musical Affaire* (England: Ashgate, 2003)

Karas, Joža. *Music at Terez'n: 1941–1945* (New York, Beauford Books Publishers in association with Pendragon Press, 1985)

Karlin, Fred. *Listening to Movies* (New York: Schirmer Books, 1994)

Kellogg, Clara Louise. *Memoirs of an American Prima Donna* (New York: Da Capo Press, 1913 reprint)

Kenneson, Claude. *Music Prodigies: Perilous Journeys and Remarkable Lives* (Portland, Oregon: Amadeus Press, 1999)

Knighton, Tess and David Fallows, eds. *Companion to Medieval and Renaissance Music* (New York: Schirmer Books, 1992)

Lebrecht, Norman. *The Maestro Myth* (New York: Birch Lane Press, 1991)

Leeds, Joshua. *The Power of Sound: How to Manage Your Personal Soundscape for a Vital Productive and Healthy Life* (Rochester, Vermont: Healing Arts Press, 2001)

LePage, Jane Weiner. *Women Composers, Conductors, and Musicians of the Twentieth Century*, 3 vols. (Metuchen, New Jersey & London: Scarecrow Press, 1980, 1983, 1988)

Machlis, Joseph. *The Enjoyment of Music* (New York: W.W. Norton & Company Inc., 1963)

Marshall, Kimberly, ed. *Rediscovering the Muses: Women's Musical Traditions* (Boston: Northeastern University Press, 1993)

McArthur, Edwin. *Flagstad: A Personal Memoir* (New York: Alfred A. Knopf, 1965)

McCarthy, Margaret William. *Amy Fay: America's Notable Woman of Music* (Michigan: Harmonie Park Press, 1995)

McClary, Susan. *Feminine Endings: Music, Gender, and Sexuality* (Minnesota: University of Minnesota Press, 1991)

McPartland, Marian. *All in Good Time* (New York & Oxford: Oxford University Press, 1987)

Meckna, Michael. *Twentieth Century Brass Soloists* (Westport, Connecticut, Greenwood Press, 1994)

Meylan, Raymond. *The Flute* (Portland, Oregon: Amadeus Press, 1988)

Monsaingeon, Bruno. *Mademoiselle: Conversations with Nadia Boulanger* (Boston: Northeastern University Press, 1988)

Monteux, Doris G. *It's All in the Music* (New York: Farrar, Straus and Giroux, 1965)

Mordden, Ethan. *Opera Anecdotes* (New York: Oxford University Press, 1985)

Neuls-Bates, Carol, ed. *Women in Music* (Boston: Northeastern University Press, 1996)

Newman, Richard. *Alma Rosé: Vienna to Auschwitz* (Portland Oregon, Amadeus Press, 2000)

Nichols, Janet. *Women Music Makers: An Introduction to Women Composers* (New York: Walken and Co., 1992)

Ohanneson, Joan. *Scarlet Music: Hildegard of Bingen* (New York: Crossroads Publishing Co. 1998)

Palmer, Larry. *Harpsichord in America: A Twentieth-Century Revival* (Bloomington: Indiana University Press, 1989)

Pendle, Karin, ed. *Women and Music: A History* (Bloomington: Indiana University Press, 1991)

Pendle, Karin. *Women in music: A Research and Information Guide* (New York: Routledge, 2005)

Peyser, Joan. *The Memory of All That: The Life of George Gershwin* (New York: Simon & Schuster, 1993)

Plantamura, Carol. *Woman Composers* (Santa Barbara, California: Bellerophon Books, 1991)

Ranke-Heinemann, Uta. *Eunuchs for the Kingdom of Heaven: Women, Sexuality and the Catholic Church* (New York: Doubleday, 1990)

Rasponi, Lanfranco. *The Last Prima Donnas* (New York: Limelight Editions, 1994)

Reich, Nancy B. *Clara Schumann: The Artist and the Woman* (New York: Cornell University Press, 1985, Revised edition, 2001)

Rendina, Claudio. (Translated Paul D. McCusker) *The Popes: Histories and Secrets* (Santa Ana, California: Seven Locks Press, 2002)

Rosen, Judith. *Grazyna Bacewicz: Her Life and Works* (Los Angeles: Polish Music History Series, 1984)

Rosenbaum, Fred. *Visions of Reform: Congregation Emanu-El and the Jews of San Francisco 1849–1999* (Berkeley, California: Judah L. Magnes Museum, 2000)

Rosenstiel, Léonie. *Nadia Boulanger: A Life in Music* (New York: W. W. Norton & Co., Inc., 1982)

Rosenstiel, Léonie. *The Life and Works of Lili Boulanger* (New Jersey: Associated University Press, 1978)

Rubin, Nancy. *American Empress: The Life and Times of Marjorie Merriweather Post* (New York: Villard Books, 1995)

Sadie, Julie Anne, ed. *Companion to Baroque Music* (New York: Schirmer Books, 1990)

Schneider, David. *The San Francisco Symphony* (Novato, California: Presidio Press, 1983)

Schonberg, Harold C. *The Great Pianists* (New York: Simon and Schuster, 1987)

Schuller, Gunther. *The Swing Era* (New York & Oxford: Oxford University Press, 1989)

Schwartz, Elliott and Daniel Godfrey. *Music Since 1945: Issues, Materials, and Literature* (New York: Schirmer Books, 1993)

Shaffer, Karen A. and Greenwood, Neva Garner. *Maud Powell: American Pioneer Violinist* (Ames, Iowa: Iowa University Press, 1988)

Sherman, Robert and Alexander. *Nadia Reisenberg: A Musician's Scrapbook* (College Park, Maryland: The International Piano Archives, University of Maryland, 1986)

Sills, Beverly. *Bubbles: A Self-Portrait* (New York: Bobbs-Merrill, 1976)

Sirota, Victoria. *Preaching to the Choir: The Role of Sacred Musician* (New York: Church Publishing, Inc., 2006)

Slenczynska, Ruth and Brancolli, Louis. *Forbidden Childhood* (Garden City, New York: Doubleday & Co., Inc., 1957)

Slobin, Mark. *Chosen Voices: The Story of the American Cantorate* (Urbana: University of Chicago Press, 1989)

Smith, Catherine Parsons and Richardson, Cynthia S. *Mary Carr Moore, American Composer* (Ann Arbor: University of Michigan Press, 1987)

Solie, Ruth A., ed. *Musicology and Difference: Gender and Sexuality in Music Scholarship* (Berkeley: University of California Press, 1993)

Stolba, K. Marie. *The Development of Western Music: A History* (Dubuque, Iowa: Brown & Bench-Mark, 1994)

Story, Rosalyn M. *And So I Sing: African American Divas of Opera and Concert* (New York: Amistad Press, Inc., 1993)

Thomas, Adrian. *Grazyna Bacewicz* (Los Angeles: University of Southern California, 1985)

Tick, Judith. *American Women Composers Before 1870* (Ann Arbor: UMI Research Press, 1983)

Tick, Judith. *Ruth Crawford Seeger: A Composer's Search for American Music* (Oxford University Press, 1997, Paperback Edition, 2000)

Tucker, Sherrie. *Swing Shift* (Durham, North Carolina: Duke University Press, 2001)

von Gunden, Heidi. *The Music of Pauline Oliveros* (Metuchen, New Jersey: Scarecrow Press, 1983)

von Gunden, Heidi. *The Music of Vivian Fine* (Baltimore, Maryland: Scarecrow Press, 2000)

Walker-Hill, Helen. *From Spirituals to Symphonies* (Westport, Connecticut: Greenwood Press, 2002)

Waring, Virginia. *Letters from Fontainebleau* (Palm Desert, California: H.S. Publishing, 2002)

Willener, Alfred. *When Will the Walls Come Tumbling Down: An Essay on Women Playing Trumpet and Other Brass Instruments* (Portland, Oregon: Best Press, 1994)

Wilson, David Fenwick. *Music of the Middle Ages: Style and Structure* (New York: Schirmer Books, 1990)

Woodruff, Warren L. *First Lady of the Organ: Diane Bish* (Peoria, Illinois: Versa Press, Inc., 1994)

Zaimont, Judith Lang, ed. *The Musical Woman: An International Perspective*, 3 vols. (Westport, Connecticut: Greenwood Press, 1984, 1987, 1992)

Reference Books

Annals of the Metropolitan Opera, eds. Gerald Fitzgerald, Jean Seward Uppman (Boston: Metropolitan Opera Guild, G.K. Hall, Inc., 1989)

Baker's Biographical Dictionary of Musicians, 8th edition, ed. Nicolas Slonimsky (New York: Schirmer Books, 1992)

Concise Oxford Dictionary of Music, 4th edition, ed. Michael Kennedy (London: Oxford University Press, 1991)

A Dictionary of Musical Quotations, ed. Ian Crofton and Donald Fraser (New York: Schirmer Books, 1985)

The Encyclopedia of the Violin (New York: Da Capo Press. 1966)

Ewen, David. *The New Encyclopedia of the Opera* (New York: Hill and Wang, 1971)

Fuller, Sophie. *The Pandora Guide to Women Composers: Britain and the United States, 1629 – Present* (London: Pandora, 1994)

The Harper-Collins Dictionary of Music, ed. Christine Ammer (New York: Harper Perennial, 1995)

The Harper Dictionary of Opera and Operetta, ed. James Anderson (New York: Harper-Collins, 1989)

International Dictionary of Black Composers, ed. Samuel A. Floyd, Jr. (Chicago: Fitzroy Dearborn Publishers, 1999)

International Encyclopedia of Women Composers, 2nd edition, ed. Aaron Cohen (New York: Books and Music, Inc., 1987)

International Who's Who in Music, 15th edition, 1996–97, ed. David M. Cummings (Cambridge, England: Melrose Press Ltd., 1996)

Jackson, Barbara Garvey. *"Say Can You Deny Me" A Guide to Surviving Music by Women from the 16th through the 18th Centuries* (Fayetteville: University of Arkansas Press, 1994)

Katz, Ephraim. *The Film Encyclopedia* (New York: Harper & Row, 1990)

Musical America: International Directory of the Performing Arts, ed. Sedgwick Clark (East Windsor, New Jersey: Commonwealth Business Media, Inc., 1993 through 2006)

Riley, Maurice W. *The History of the Viola* (Ann Arbor, Michigan: Braun-Brumfield, Vol I, 1980, 1993, Vol. II, 1991)

The New Grove Dictionary of Music and Musicians, ed. Stanley Sadie (London: Macmillan, 1993)

The New Grove Dictionary of Opera, ed. Stanley Sadie (London: Macmillan, 4 Vols. 1997)

The Norton/Grove Concise Encyclopedia of Music, ed. Stanley Sadie with Alison Latham (New York: Norton, 1988)

The Norton/Grove Encyclopedia of Women Composers, eds. Julie Anne Sadie and Rhian Samuel (New York and London: Macmillan, 1994)

Oxford Companion to Popular Music, Peter Gammond (Oxford & New York: Oxford University Press, 1991)

Oxford Dictionary of Opera, John Warrack and Ewan West (New York and Oxford: Oxford University Press,1992)

Who's Who in British Opera, ed. Nicky Adam (Aldershot, Hants, England: Scolar Press, 1993; Brookfield, Vermont: Ashgate Publishing, 1993)

Women Composers: Music Through the Ages, eds. Sylvia Glickman & Martha F. Schleifer.

    Vol. 1 Composers Born Before 1599: (New York: G.K. Hall & Co. 1996)

    Vol. 2 Composers Born 1600–1699: (1996)

    Vol. 3 Composers Born 1700–1799: Keyboard Music (1998)

    Vol. 4 Composers Born 1700–1799: Vocal Music (1998)

    Vol. 5 Composers Born 1700–1799: Large & Small Instrumental Ensembles (1998)

    Vol. 6 Composers Born 1800–1899: Keyboard Music (1999)

    Vol. 7 Composers Born 1800–1899: Vocal Music (2003) This volume contains complete examples and discussions of vocal music by forty woman composers born in the 19th century, including Fanny Hensel, Johanna Kinkel, Clara Schumann, Rebecca Clarke and Nadia Boulanger. Intro. & Index.

    Vol. 8 Composers Born 1800–1899: Large & Small Instrumental Ensembles (2006)

Women in Music: Anthology of Source Readings from the Middle Ages to the Present, ed. Carol Neuls-Bates (New York: Harper and Row, 1982); 2nd ed. (Boston: Northeastern Univ. Press, 1996)

Unpublished Materials

Jobin, Sara. "MAESTRA: Five Female Orchestral Conductors in the United States." Master's Thesis, Harvard University, Boston, 1992.

Pfau Marianne R. "Hildegard von Bingen's ëSinfonia Armonie,' Celestium Revelationum: An Analysis of Musical Process, Tonal Modality, and Text Music Relationship." PhD Dissertation, State University New York, Stony Brook, 1990.

Sirota, Victoria Ressmeyer. "The Life and Works of Fanny Mendelssohn Hensel." D.M.A. Dissertation, Boston University School for the Arts, 1981.

Selected Discography*

Adams, Anne, Patricia Harris. *Two Harps As One*, Anne Adams, 1995.

Agudelo, Graciela. *Musica de Camara, Recompilacion*, Music Unlimited.

Agudelo, Graciela. *Cantos Desde el Confin*, Euram Records, 2001.

Alitowski, Liane. *Liane Alitowski Plays Haydn, Chopin and Ravel*, Klavierhaus Records, 1997.

Ameling, Elly. *Belioz - Les Nuits D'été Fauré, Pelléas et Mélisande*, Atlanta Symphony Orchestra, Robert Shaw, Telarc, 1985.

Anonymous 4, Portrait, Harmonia Mundi, 1997.

Arteta, Ainhoa. *Ainhoa Arteta and Dwayne Croft En Concierto*, Orquesta Sinfonica de Castilla y Leon, RTVE Musica, 2000.

Augér, Arleen. *The Art of Arleen Augér*, Koch International Classics, 1993.

Baker, Dame Janet and Jacqueline Du Pré. *Sir Edward Elgar*, (1857-1934), London Symphony Orchestra conducted by Sir John Barbirolli, EMI, 1965.

Barak, Rosalyn. *The Jewish Soul*, Balance, 1996.

Barton, Rachel, violin, Patrick Sinozich, piano. *Instrument of the Devil*, Cedille Records, 1998.

Beach, Amy. *Grand Mass in E Flat Major, The Michael May Festival Chorus*, Newport Classic, 1989.

Beach, Amy. *Symphony in E minor (Gaelic)*, Chandos, 1991.

Ben-Dor, Gisèle. *Bartok For Children, Romanian Folk Dances*, The Sofia Soloists, Centaur Records, 1995.

Ben-Dor, Gisèle. *Alberta Ginastera, Variaciones Concertantes*, London Symphony Orchestra and Israel Chamber Orchestra, Koch International Classics, 1995.

Boehm, Mary-Louise. *Mrs. H.H.A. Beach Concerto for Piano and Orchestra, Op. 45; Piano Quintet in F- Sharp minor, Op.67*, Westphalian Symphony Orchestra, Vox/Turnabout, 1991.

Bond, Victoria. *Yes: Molly ManyBloom; A Modest Proposal*, Albany Records, 2003.

Boulanger, Lili. *Clairières dans le ciel, Les sirènes, Renouveau, Hymne au soleil, Soir sur la plaine, Pour les funérailles d'un soldat*, The New London Chamber Choir, Martyn Hill and Andrew Ball, Hyperion, 1994.

Boulanger, Lili. *Du Fond de l'abîme, Psaumes 24 et 129*, Orchestra de l'Association des Concerts Lamoureux, Yehudi Menuhin, Clifford Curzon, EMI Classics, 1992.

Boulanger, Nadia, Augusta Holmès, Pauline Viardot-Garcia, Maria Malibran, Jane Vieu, Cécile Chaminade, Carol Robinson, Mary Howe, Juliana Hall, Felicia Donceanu, *From A Woman's Perspective*, Vienna Modern Masters, 1993.

Callas, Maria. *The Very Best of Maria Callas*, EMI, 2002.

Canat de Chizy, Édith. *Exultet, Siloël, Moïra*, Timpani/MFA/Arsenal, 1999.

Canepa, Louise. *Napa Valley Serenity*, Louise Canepa, 2002.

Carlos, Wendy. *Switched on Bach 2000*, Telarc, 1992.

Chase, Stephanie, Roy Goodman and the Hanover Band, *Beethoven*, Cala Records, 1992.

Chee-Yun. *Vocalise, Violin Show Pieces*, Denon Records, 1993.

Clarke, Pip. *Romantic Violin Showpieces*, Classic Jewel, 1993.

Clarke, Rebecca. *Viola Sonata*, Gamut Classics, 1992.

Conant, Abbie. *Trombone and Organ*, Audite Records, 1987.

Craig, Mary-Ann with James Staples and the Faculty Brass Quintet, Indiana University of Pennsylvania, *Euphonium…Out on a Limb*, Ark, 1995.

Davidovich, Bella. *Saint-Saëns Piano Concerto No.2 and Rachmaninoff, Rhapsody on a Theme of Paganini*, Concertgebouw Orchestra Amsterdam, Philips Digital Classics, 1981.

Degenhardt, Annette. *The Best of Andeg 1-6*, Andeg, 2001.

Degenhardt, Annette. *Farewell*, Andeg, 2000.

Degenhardt, Annette. *Muse, Guitar Solos*, Andeg, 1998.

Degenhardt, Annette. *Nicht eingebracht, nicht wild erfuhlt*, Andeg, 1994.

Degenhardt, Annette. *Umwege*, Andeg, 1996

Degenhardt, Annette. *Wåltzing Guitar*, Andeg, 1994.

Degenhardt, Annette. *Zwischentöne*, Andeg, 1994.

De Kenessey, Stefania, Beth Anderson, Nancy Bloomer Deussen. *Two by Three*, North/South, 1998.

Diemer, Emma, Lou. *Max Lifchitz Plays American Piano Music*, Vienna Modern Masters, 1991.

Diemer, Emma Lou, Alexandre Rudajev, Marilyn Ziffrin, Allen Brings and Richard Toensings, *Music at the Crossroads, New American Chamber Music*, North/South Recordings, 1994.

Dinescu, Violeta. *Portrait*, Gutingi, 2000.

Dinescu, Violeta. *Tautropfen*, GEMA, 1994.

Du Pré, Jacqueline, Baker, Dame Janet. *Sir Edward Elgar*, (1857-1934), London Symphony Orchestra conducted by Sir John Barbirolli, EMI, 1965.

Eiríksdóttir, Karólína. *Portait*, STEF, 1991.

Eiríksdóttir, Karólína. *Spil*, Saga, 1998.

Falletta, JoAnn. *Baroquen Treasures*, The Women's Philharmonic, Newport Classic, 1990.

Falletta, JoAnn. *The Women's Philharmonic*, Music of Boulanger, Tailleferre, Clara Schumann, Fanny Mendelssohn, Koch International Classics, 1992.

Fierro, Nancy. *Riches and Rags, A Wealth of Piano Music by Women*, ARS Musica Poloniæ,1993.

Fleischer, Tsippi. *Arabische Texturen, Art Music Settings of Arabic Poetry*, Koch International Classics, 1993.

Fleischer, Tsippi. *Around the World with Tsippi Fleischer*, Vienna Modern Masters, 1997.

Fleischer, Tsippi. *Cain and Abel*, ACUM, 2002.

Fleischer, Tsippi. *Israel at 50*, Opus One, 1998.

Fleming, Renée and Jean-Yves Thibaudet, *Night Songs*, Decca, 2001.

Fleming, Renée. *Renée Fleming*, Decca, 2000.

Fleming, Renée. *The Beautiful Voice*, English Chamber Orchestra, Jeffrey Tate, Decca, 1998.

Galante, Inessa. *Debut*, Latvian National Symphony Orchestra, Campion, 1995.

Galante, Inessa. *Arietta*, London Musici, World Wilson Editions, 1999.

Gale, Priscilla, Andrej Mentschukoff, *Dreamfaces*, Centaur, 1997.

Genaux, Vivica. *An Evening of Arias and Songs by Gioacchino Rossini*, Epcaso, 1999.

Gentile, Ada. *Paesaggi Della Mente*, Dischi Ricordi, 1994.

Gentile, Ada. *Criptografia, Shading*, Uniqum, 1988.

Golani, Rivka. Judy Loman, *Music for Viola and Harp*, Marquis Classics, 1994.

Green, Nancy. *Nancy Green, Cello, Frederick Moyer, Piano*, JRI Recordings, 1999.

Grimaud, Hélène. *Sergei Rachmaninov*, Philharmonia Orchestra, Vladimir Ashkenazy, Teldec, 2001.

Hammil, Joanne. *The World's Gonna Listen!*, JHO Music, 1994.

Hammil, Joanne. *Pizza Boogie*, JHO Music, 1987.

Han, Wu (piano), David Finckel (cello), *Grieg, Schumann and Chopin*, Artistled, 1997.

Harnoy, Ofra. *Salut d'Amour*, BMG Classics, 1990.

Hewitt, Angela. *Bach French Overture, Italian Concerto, Four Duets, Two Capriccios*, Hyperion, 2001.

Higdon, Jennifer. *Rapid Fire*, I Virtuoso Records, 1995.

Hidgon, Jennifer. *The Works of Jennifer Higdon*, Jennifer Higdon.

Hirschtal, Edith. *Despite The Odds*, Edith Hirschtal, 1994.

Hoover, Katherine. *KOKOPELI: Katherine Hoover Plays*, Parnassus, 2001.

Hoover, Katherine. *Night Skies: Orchestral Music of Katherine Hoover*, Slovac Radio Symphony, Parnassus.

Horne, Marilyn. *Just for the Record: The Golden Voice*, Decca, 2003.

Horstmann, Anne. *Neue Flötentöne*, GEMA, 2001.

Hutchins, Dr. Carleen M. *The New Violin Family*, The St. Petersburg Hutchins Violin Octet, Catgut Acoustical Society, Inc., 1998.

Harbach, Barbara. *Summershimmer, Women Composers for Organ*, Hester Park, 1996.

Isbin, Sharon. *American Landscapes*, Virgin Classics/Angel Records, 1995.

Isbin, Sharon. *Nightshade Rounds*, Virgin Classics, 1994.

Jalina Trio. *Mendelsohn & Brahms*, Classico, 2003.

Jalina Trio. *NOW! Denmark*, Piano Trios of Holmboe, Koppel, Nordentoft, Nørgård and Nyvang, Classico, 2003.

Jalina Trio, *Kaleidoscope*, Danish Piano Trios after 1945, Dacapo, 2005.

Kanner, Amy Lynn. *Garden of Delights*, Palmusic, 1993.

Larsen, Libby. *Eleanor Roosevelt*, New World Records, 1997.

Larsen, Libby. *Sound Encounters*, GMR.

Larrocha, Alicia de, *Spanish Serenade, Falla, Montsalvatge*, BMG Classics, 1994.

Lawrence, Lucile, *A Harp Recital by Lucile Lawrence*, Lucile Lawrence, 1997.

Leginska, Ethel. *The Complete Columbia Masters (1926-1928)*, Ivory Classics, 2001.

Ludwig, Christa. *Songs Of a Wayfarer*, EMI, 1988.

Luque, Virginia. *Rumores de España*, Virginia Luque, 1993.

Lympany, Dame Moura. *Tribute to a Piano Legend*, Ivory Classics, 1999.

Manoukian, Catherine. *Chopin of Violin*, Marquis Classics, 1999.

Marcovicci, Andrea. *Love Songs of World War II*, Marcovicci Enterprises, 1991.

Marcovicci, Andrea. *New Words, A Celebration of Contemporary Songwriting*, Cabaret Records, 1995.

Marez-Oyens, Tera de. *Composer's Voice*, Donemus Amsterdam, 1988.

Marez-Oyens, Tera de. *Tera de Marez-Oyens*, BVHaast Records, 1991.

Martinez, Odaline de la. *British Women Composers Part 1*, Music of Wallen, Cooper, Machonchy, Lefanu Lontano Records, 1992.

Martinez, Odaline de la. *A Life in Reverse, The Music of Minna Keal*, Lontano Records, 1996.

Marton, Eva, Renata Scotto, Kiri Te Kanawa, *Favorite Puccini Arias by the World's Favorite Sopranos*, Sony Masterworks, 1991.

Mattila, Karita. *Villa-Lobos, Bachianas Brasileiras, No 5*, Philips Digital Classics, 1987.

Mautner, Sophie. *Chopin*, Sony Masterworks, 1995.

The Macalester Trio. *Chamber Works by Women Composers*, VoxBox, 1991.

McDermott, Anne-Marie. *Schumann-Romance: Works for viola and piano*, Image Recordings, 2005.

McLaughlin, Carrol. *A Celebration of Harp*, Carrol McLaughlin, 1995.

McLaughlin, Carrol. *Desert Reflections*, The University of Arizona Board of Regents, 1995.

McNair, Sylvia, André Previn. *Sure Thing, The Jerome Kern Songbook*, Philips Classics Productions, 1994.

McPartland, Marian, George Shearing. *Alone Together*, Concord Records, 1981.

McPartland, Marian. *Marian McPartland Plays the Music of Mary Lou Williams*, Concord Records, 1994.

Mentzer, Susanne. *Women at an Exposition, Music composed by women and performed at the 1893 World's Fair in Chicago*, Koch International Classics, 1991.

Meyers, Anne Akiko, Sandra Rivers, piano. *Salut d'Amour*, BMG Classics, 1994.

Meyers, Anne Akiko. *Lalo Symphonie Espagnole, Bruch Scottish Fantasy*, BMG Classics, 1992.

Miller, Bette PhD, Sister Merita Dekat, S.S.S. *Classical Inspirations*, Windstar, 1999.

Monarch Brass, The Women's International Brass Conference, IWBC 2000.

Morley, Virginia and Gearhart, Livingston. *Morley and Gearhart Rediscovered*, Ivory Classics, 2001.

Morris, Joan, mezzo-soprano; and William Bolcom, piano. *Moonlight Bay–Songs As Is And Songs As Was*, Albany Records, 1998.

Nigro, Susan. *The Big Bassoon*, Crystal Records, 1995.

O'Hara, Mary. *Down by the Glenside: Songs of Ireland*, Tradition, 1997.

O'Hara, Mary. *Irish Traditional Folk Songs*, Legacy International.

Okawa, Yumiko. *Recuerdos de Viaje*, Pro Arte Musicæ, 1991.

Okawa, Yumiko. *Cantos de España*, Pro Arte Musicae, 1990.

Olevsky, Estela. *Piano Solos of Latin America*, Centaur, 1994.

Oppens, Ursula. *American Piano Music of Our Time*, Music & Arts Programs of America Inc., 1995.

Paul, Jennifer. *The Music of Armand-Louis Couperin*, Klavier Records International, 1993.

Pekinel, Güher & Süher. *Encores for Two Pianos*, Berlin Classics, 1995.

Pickett, Susan. *Donne e Doni*, Susan Pickett, 1994.

Pilot, Ann Hobson. *Ann Hobson Pilot*, Boston Records, 1991.

Podleś, Ewa. *Ewa Podleś, Garrick Ohlsson Live*, DUX, 2003.

Portman, Rachel. Soundtrack from *Marvin's Room*, Miramax, 1996.

Powell, Maud. *Maud Powell*, Biddulph, 1994.

Powell, Maud. *The Complete Recordings 1904-1917*, 4 volumes, Karen Shaffer, Naxos, 2001.

Price, Florence. *Florence Price*, The Women's Philharmonic, Apo Hsu, Koch International Classics, 2001.

Psaros, Georgetta, *Georgetta Psaros*, PA Digital, 1997.

Ptaszynska, Marta. *Marta Ptaszynska*, Polish Chamber Orchestra, Polskie Nagrania, 1991.

Reisenberg, Nadia. *Nadia Reisenberg: 100th Anniversary Tribute*, Ivory Classics, 2004.

Reisenberg, Nadia. *The Acclaimed Haydn Recordings*, Ivory Classics.

Richter, Marga. *Snow Mountain: A Spiritual Trilogy*, Leonarda, 1994.

Rivers, Julie. *Christmastide*, Earth Star Recordings.

Rivers, Julie. *Kiss of the Sun*, Earth Star Recordings, 1998.

Rivers, Julie. *One Starry Night*, Earth Star Recordings, 1996.

Rivers, Julie. *Romancing the Piano, The Music of Eugénie Rocherolle*, Aureus Recordings, 1998.

Rivers, Julie, *Spinning Gold, The Piano Music of Eugénie Rocherolle*, Aureus Recordings, 1995.

Rockmore, Clara. *The Art of the Theremin*, Delos International Inc, 1987.

Rolston, Shauna. *Elgar and Saint-Saëns Cello Concertos*, CBC Records, 1995.

Rolston, Shauna, Bernadene Blaha, piano. *Strauss, Debussy and Barber*, CBC Records, 1998.

Rosenberger, Carol. *Water Music of the Impressionists*, Delos International Inc, 1983.

Salerno-Sonnenberg, Nadja. *It Ain't Necessarily So*, EMI Classics/Angel Records, 1992.

Schein, Ann. *Schumann*, Ivory Classics, 2000.

Schiff, Zina. *Bach and Vivaldi*, Israel Philharmonic, Dalia Atlas, Jerusalem Records, 1989.

Schiff, Zina. *The Lark Ascending*, Israel Philharmonic, Dalia Atlas, Jerusalem Records, 1989.

Schiff, Zina, Mary Barranger, piano, *Cecil Burleigh, Music for Violin and Piano*, Naxos, 2002.

Schiff, Zina, Cameron Grant, piano. *Here's One*, 4 Tay Records, 1997.

Schiff, Zina, Cameron Grant, piano. *King David's Lyre*, 4 Tay Records, 1995.

Schiff, Zina, Cameron Grant, piano. *The Golden Dove, Masterpieces from the Jewish Folk Music Society*, 4 Tay Inc, 2002.

Schlomovitz, Phyllis, harp. *Ancient Ayres and Dances*, O.M. Records, 1988.

Schpachenko, Nadia. *Life, Death and Rain*, Ullanta, 2003.

Shapiro, Alex. *Recent Chamber Music*, Alex Shapiro, 2003.

Singer, Jeanne. *Of Times Past*, MMC Recordings, 1999.

Singer, Jeanne. *To Stir A Dream, American Poets in Song*, Cambria Records, 1990.

Slenczynska, Ruth. *Ruth Slenczynska: Historic Performances of Bach, Liszt and Chopin*, Ivory Classics, 1998.

Slenczynska, Ruth. *Ruth Slenczynska in Concert*, Ivory Classics, 1999.

Slenczynska, Ruth. *Schumann*, Ivory Classics, 2000.

Slenczynska, Ruth. *The Art of Ruth Slenczynska Last Chopin Recital 2005*, Okayama. Liu MAER, 2005.

Smyth, Ethel. *Mass in D, Mrs Water's Aria, The March of the Women*, Virgin Classics, 1991.

Smyth, Ethel. *The Wreckers*, BBC Philharmonic, Odaline de la Martinez, Conifer Records, 1994.

Sorel, Claudette. *Claudette Sorel Plays Edward MacDowell, Joachim Raff, Moritz Moskowski, Frédéric Chopin, Paul Creston, Sergei Rachmaninoff*, Claudette Sorel, 1992.

Spiegel, Laurie. *Unseen Worlds*, Laurie Spiegel Publishing, 1987-94.

Stark, Paulina, soprano, Judy Brown, Piano. *Unmined Cole: Unpublished Gems of Cole Porter*, Centaur Records, 1998.

Stark, Paulina, soprano, Nadine Shank, piano. *I Have Taken An Oath To Remember: art songs of the Holocaust*, Transcontinental Music Publication, 2002.

St. John, Lara, violin. Ilan Rechtman, piano. *Gypsy*, Well-Tempered Productions, 1997.

Sumac, Yma. *The Spell of Yma Sumac*, Pair, from Capitol Records, 1987.

Takezawa, Kyoko. *Mendelssohn Violin Concertos*, Bamberger Symphoniker, BMG Classics, 1994.

Talmi, Er'ella, Yoav Talmi, piano. *Flute Album*, CDI, 1988.

Talmi, Er'ella, Yoav Talmi, piano. *Sonatas and Sonatinas For Flute and Piano*, CDI, 1994.

Talmi, Er'ella, Yoav Talmi, piano. *Virtuoso Flute*, CDI, 1988.

Te Kanawa, Kiri. *Canteloube, Chants D'Auvergne*, English Chamber Orchestra, Decca, 1983.

Te Kanawa, Kiri. *Puccini, La Bohème*, London Symphony, Erato Disques, 1995.

Te Kanawa, Kiri. *Blue Skies* Nelson Riddle and Orchestra, Decca, 1985.

Te Kanawa, Kiri. *Kiri Sings Gershwin*, EMI/Angel Records, 1987.

Te Kanawa, Kiri. *Kiri Sings Kern*, The London Sinfonietta, Angel Records, 1993.

Te Kanawa, Kiri *Verdi & Puccini* London Philharmonic, John Pritchard, CBS Records, 1983.

Tourin, Christina. *Echoes of Angels*, Emerald Harp Productions, 1997.

Tsepkolenko, Karmella. *Chamber Music*, Karmella Tsepkolenko, 1994.

Tsepkolenko, Karmella. *Chamber Music*, Karmella Tsepkolenko, 1995.

United States Coast Guard Band, *Americana*, US Coast Guard Band, 1991.

Von Bingen, Hildegard. *Canticles of Ecstasy*, BMG Classics, 1994.

Von Bingen, Hildegard. *A Feather on the Breath of God, Sequences and Hymns by Abbess Hildegard of Bingen*, Hyperion Records, 1986.

Von Bingen, Hildegard. *Lieder und Antiphonen*, Christophorus, 1993.

Von Bingen, Hildegard. *Monk and the Abbess, Music of Hildegard Von Bingen and Meredith Monk*, BMG Classics, 1996.

Von Bingen, Hildegard. *Ordo Virtutum*, BMG Classics, 1990.

Von Bingen, Hildegard. *Vision, The Music of Hildegard Von Bingen*, Angel Records, 1994.

Von Trapp, Elisabeth. *Wishful Thinking*, von Trapp Music, 1994.

Von Trapp, Elisabeth. *One Heart - One Mind*, von Trapp Music, 1996.

Waites, Althea. *Black Diamonds, Althea Waites Plays Music By African-American Composers*, Cambria Master Recordings, 1993.

Wallen, Errollyn, *Meet Me at Harold Moores*, E.Wallen, 1998.

Warren, Elinor Remick. *Art Songs by Elinor Remick Warren*, Cambria Records, 1987.

Warren, Elinor Remick., *Good Morning America*, Cambria Records, 1989.

Warren, Elinor Remick. *The Legend of King Arthur, A Choral Symphony*, Cambria Records, 1990.

Wekre, Frøydis Ree. *Frøydis Ree Wekre, Horn*, Crystal Records, 1996.

Wentink, Gwyneth. *Gwyneth Wentink* (Harp), Egan Records.

Williams, Carol. *Music from Blenheim Palace*: Carol Williams Plays the Historic Father Willis Organ OS Digital Recordings, 1999.

Yi, Chen. *Sparkle*, Composer's Recordings Inc, 1999.

Zaidel-Rudolph, Jeanne. *Music of the Spheres*, Nedbank, 1994.

Zizzo, Alicia. *Virtuoso Piano Fantasies*, Mastersound Maximus Series, 1991.

Zukerman, Eugenia, flute, Anthony Newman, piano. *Time Pieces*, Newport Classics, 1989.

Zwillich, Ellen Taaffe. *Concerto for Flute and Orchestra*, Doriot Anthony Dwyer, flute. London Symphony Orchestra, Koch International Classics, 1992.

Compilation Works

Treasures of the Heart, Keepsakes from the Harp, International Harp Therapy Program, IHTP 1999.

Women Composers, The Lost Tradition Found, Leonarda, 1988.

* This Discography mainly represents artists and composers not found in leading record catalogues. Cambria, Hester Park, Hildegard, Leonarda, Presser and Vienna Modern Masters are among the recording companies who specialize in women's music. For top well-known performers with extensive discographies, the reader is directed to the Schwann Catalogue and other major listings for labels such as harmonia mundi, Telarc, RCA, Polygram, etc.

Most artists/composers have their own websites. These provide further detailed discographies and composition descriptions.

Photo Credits

Composers

Graciela Agudela	Courtesy Graciela Agudela
Franghiz Ali-Zadeh	Courtesy TVNET Muzika
Lettie Alston	Courtesy Helen Walker-Hill
Beth Anderson	Courtesy Beth Anderson
Violet Archer	*Edmonton Journal*, Courtesy Norma McCord
Leticia Armijo	Courtesy Leticia Armijo
Svitlana Azarova	Courtesy Svitlana Azarova
Grazyna Bacewicz	Courtesy Judith Rosen
Amy Beach	published drawing
Betty Beath	Courtesy Australian Composers
Elizabeth Bell	Paul Drake
Hilat Ben-Kennaz	Courtesy Hilat Ben-Kennaz
Marilyn Bergman	Courtesy ASCAP
Sonia Bo	Courtesy Ricordi
Sylvie Bodorova	Courtesy Radio Archive - CZ
Natasha Bogojevich	Courtesy Natasha Bogojevich
Victoria Bond	Courtesy Roanoke Symphony Society
Margaret Bonds	Courtesy Helen Walker-Hill
Lili Boulanger	M. Tamvico
Margaret Brandman	Courtesy Margaret Brandman
Francesca Caccini	published drawing
Ann Carr-Boyd	Courtesy Australian Composers
Teresa Catalán	Courtesy Diariodenavarra
Cécile Chaminade	Furore
Rebecca Clarke	published drawing
Betty Comden	IDBD
Jean Coulthard	With Permission
Tansy Davies	Malcolm Crowthers
Violeta Dinescu	Nicolae Manolache
Lesia Dychko	Courtesy Lesia Dychko
Karólína Eiríksdóttir	Courtesy Karólína Eiríksdóttir
Dilys Elwyn-Edwards	Welsh Music Vol. IX, Summer 1997
Pozzi Escot	Courtesy Dr. Escot
Evelyn Ficarra	Courtesy of Elise Ficarra
Dorothy Fields	Courtesy Broadway to Vegas
Vivian Fine	Alex Brown
Graciane Finzi	Patricia Dietzi
Tsippi Fleischer	Courtesy Tsippi Fleischer
Jacqueline Fontyn	Courtesy Baroness Fontyn
Tania French	Courtesy Tania French
Rachel Galinne	Jacob Aviram

Ada Gentile	Courtesy Ada Gentile
Ruth Gipps	Courtesy Ruth Gipps
Peggy Glanville-Hicks	With Permission
Julia Gomeloskaya	Courtesy Julia Gomeloskaya
Maria Granillo	Courtesy Maria Granillo
Sophia Gubaidulina	Jörg Morgener
Elisabeth de la Guerre	Furore
Hanna Havraylets	Courtesy Hanna Havraylets
Alice Ho	Courtesy Beauty in Music
Dulcie Holland	Courtesy Royal School of Church Music (RSCM)
Augusta Holmès	Furore
Imogene Holst	Nigel Luckhurst
Katherine Hoover	Georgianna Kellaway
Joan Huang	Courtesy Joan Huang
Miriam Hyde	Geoff Aitken
Jean Ivey	Nancy Shear Music Services
Adina Izarra	Courtesy Simon Bolivar University
Betsy Jolas	Theodore Presser Co.
Nurit Jugend	Courtesy Nurit Jugend
Hagar Kadima	Courtesy Hagar Kadima
Vítezslava Kaprálová	Courtesy Kaprálová Society
Elena Kats-Chernin	Courtesy Ruhrtriennale
Minna Keal	Courtesy Minna Keal
Betty King	Courtesy Helen Walker-Hill
Barbara Kolb	Jean Luce Huré
Hanna Kulenty	Courtesy Maja Trochimczyk
Bun-Ching Lam	Veiga Jardim
Ana Lara	Lorena Alcaraz
Libby Larsen	Courtesy Libby Larsen
Nicola LeFanu	Courtesy Dr. Lefanu
Tanya León	Michael Provost (courtesy Tanya León)
Annea Lockwood	Nicole Tavenner
Elisabeth Lutyens	Courtesy Wagner-Tuba
Elizabeth Maconchy	Suzie Madear, Courtesy Maconchy
Ursula Mamlok	Courtesy Ursula Mamlok
Ljubica Marić	Courtesy Klassika
Marianne Martinez	Furore Edition 842
Lena McLin	Courtesy Helen Walker-Hill
Fanny Mendelssohn	published drawing
Cynthia Millar	Courtesy Beauty in Music
Mary Carr Moore	Courtesy Sugar Pine Aviators
Undine Smith Moore	Courtesy Helen Walker-Hill
Erica Muhl	Courtesy Erica Muhl
Kelly-Marie Murphy	Courtesy Canadian Music Centre
Thea Musgrave	Courtesy Thea Musgrave
Katharine Norman	Courtesy Katharine Norman
Alejandra Odgers	Courtesy Alejandra Odgers
Nkeiru Okoye	Courtesy Helen Walker-Hill
Jane O'Leary	With Permission
Morfydd Owen	Welsh Music Vol. IX, Winter 1991

Tera de Marez Oyens	Courtesy Tera de Marez Oyens
Younghi Pagh-Paan	Courtesy University of Iowa
Barbara Pentland	With Permission
Julia Perry	Courtesy Helen Walker-Hill
Zenobia Perry	Courtesy Helen Walker-Hill
Victoria Poleva	Courtesy Victoria Poleva
Rachel Portman	Jofre Masceno
Florence Price	Courtesy Helen Walker-Hill
Alwynne Pritchard	Rick Koster
Marta Ptaszynska	Courtesy Marta Ptaszynska
Priaulx Rainier	Courtesy Klassiekemuziekgids
Shulamit Ran	John Reilly
Marga Richter	Alan Skelly
Julie Rivers	Nathan Ham
Eugénie Rocherolle	Andrew DiCambio
Marcela Rodriguez	Courtesy La Porta Classica
Kaja Saariaho	Maarit Kytoharju
Alex Shapiro	Courtesy Alex Shapiro
Ruth Schönthal	Paul Seckel
Corona Schroter	Furorre
Clara Schumann	Furore
Ruth Crawford Seeger	Courtesy Seeger Family
Alice Shields	Courtesy Alice Shields
Roberta Silvestrini	Courtesy Rassegnagigli
Netty Simons	Courtesy Shaw
Ethel Smyth	Furore
Barbara Strozzi	Furore
Germaine Tailleferre	published drawing
Louise Talma	Carol Bullard
Karen Tanaka	Courtesy Ballade
Hilary Tann	Martin Benjamin
Veronica Tapia	Courtesy Veronica Tapia
Alicia Terzian	Courtesy Alicia Terzian
Augusta Read Thomas	Courtesy Chicago Symphony Orchestra
Aljona Tomljonova	Courtesy Aljona Tomljonova
Joan Tower	Steve J. Sherman
Karmella Tsepkolenko	Courtesy Karmella Tsepkolenko
Catherine Urner	Courtesy Catherine Urner
Galina Ustvolskaya	Courtesy Archive International Sikorski
Nancy Van de Vate	With Permission
Diana Voda-Nuteanu	Courtesy Diana Voda-Nuteanu
Sláva Vorlová	Courtesy Kaprálová Society
Melinda Wagner	Steve Singer
Gwyneth Walker	Courtesy Gwyneth Walker
Shirley Walker	With Permission
Errolyn Wallen	Shaun Roberts
Elinor Remick Warren	Courtesy Elinor Remick Warren
Dalit Hadass Warshaw	Ned Harris
Judith Weir	Suzanne Jansen

Gillian Whitehead	Courtesy Victoria University of Wellington
Grace Williams	Welsh Music Vol. 8, Spring 1987
Debbie Wiseman	Doug McKenzie
Chen Yi	Jim Hair
Li Yiding	Courtesy Li Yiding
Iraida Yusupova	Courtesy Iraida Yusupova
Alla Zagaykevich	Courtesy Alla Zagaykevich
Jeanne Zaidel-Rudolph	Courtesy Jeanne Zaidel Rudolph
Judith Lang Zaimont	Courtesy Zaimont, photo by Leni
Ruth Zechlin	Courtesy RSCM
Ellen Taaffe Zwillich	New York Times/Andrew Sacks

Pen Women

Carrie Jacobs Bond	Courtesy NLAPW
Minuetta Kessler	Courtesy Minuetta Kessler
Mary Carr Moore	Courtesy NLAPW
Jeanne Singer	Courtesy Jeanne Singer
Marjorie Tayloe	Courtesy Marjorie Tayloe

Conductors

Marin Alsop	Cliff Coles Photographic Services
Dalia Atlas	Jakepglz Kellcop
Gisèle Ben-Dor	*Los Angeles Times*
Gena Branscombe	Courtesy Kathleen Shimeta
Carolyn Broe	Courtesy Carolyn Broe
Iona Brown	Morten Krogvold
Lucinda Carver	Courtesy University of Southern California
Catherine Comet	Steven J. Sherman
Yvette Devereaux	Courtesy Beauty in Music
JoAnn Falletta	Courtesy Genevieve Spielberg, Inc.
Deborah Freedman	Courtesy St. Joseph Symphony
Jane Glover	John Batten
Patricia Handy	Courtesy Michal Schmidt Artists International, Inc.
Gertrude Herliczka	Courtesy Jan Bell Groh
Margaret Hillis	Courtesy Chicago Symphony Orchestra
Apo Hsu	Courtesy The Women's Philharmonic
Sara Jobin	Courtesy Sara Jobin
Karen Keltner	Courtesy San Diego Opera
Odaline de la Martinez	Courtesy Odaline de la Martinez
Amy Mills	Courtesy Conductor's Cooperative Management
Caroline Nichols	Courtesy Jan Bell Groh
Frédérique Petrides	Courtesy Jan Bell Groh
Eve Queler	Steven J. Sherman
Andrea Quinn	Courtesy Clarion Seven Muses
Kay George Roberts	Jack Van Antwerp
Madeline Schatz	Courtesy Madeline Schatz
Kate Tamarkin	Jack Mitchell
Maria Tunicka	Courtesy Maria Tunicka
Barbara Day Turner	Courtesy San Jose Opera
Nan Washburn	Courtesy Nan Washburn

Diane Wittry	Courtesy Diane Wittry
Rachael Worby	Vidal
Barbara Yahr	Christian Steiner

Military

Lorelei Conrad	Courtesy of Conrad, photo by Sr. Chief Jim Richards
Roxanne Haskill	Sisson Studios
Daisy Jackson	Courtesy Daisy Jackson
Charlotte Owen	Courtesy Charlotte Plummer Owen
Jeanne Pace	Courtesy Jeanne Pace
Nancy Stanly	Courtesy Nancy Stanly
Beth Steele	Courtesy of Steele, Army Field Band

Orchestras

Cecylia Arzewski	Courtesy Atlanta Symphony
Emmanuelle Boisvert	Glenn Triest
Patricia Prattis Jennings	Courtesy Patricia Prattis Jennings
Rhian Kenny	Ben Spiegel
Beth Newdome	Courtesy Atlanta Symphony Orchestra
Carol Procter	Courtesy Carol Procter
Sarah Tuck	Victor Avila
Gretchen Van Hoesen	Courtesy Gretchen Van Hoesen
Anne Williams	Ben Spiegel
Cynthia Yeh	Courtesy of Yeh, photo by Mike Kehr

Violin

Ahn Trio	Courtesy Joanne Rile Artists
Anat Malkin-Almani	Henry Grossman
Rachel Barton	Cheri Eisenberg
Sarah Chang	Christian Steiner
Stephanie Chase	Lisa Kohler
Kyung-Wha Chung	Vivian Purdom
Dorothy DeLay	Christian Steiner
Eroica Trio	Andrew Eccles
Pamela Frank	Tania Maria
Miriam Fried	Courtesy Indiana University
Vesna Gruppman	Courtesy Vesna Gruppman
Ida Haendel	Georg Bongartz
Hilary Hahn	Janusz Kawa
Monica Huggett	Suzie Maeder
Jalina Trio	Tivoli Artist Management
Dylana Jenson	Joanne Rile Management
Lara St. John	Off Broadway Photography
Leila Josefowicz	Nick Briggs/ Philips Classics
Ani Kavafian	Courtesy American String Project
Ida Kavafian	Courtesy Musical Masterworks
Tamaki Kawakubo	Don Hunstein
Ida Levin	Murrae Haynes
Catherine Manoukian	Ivan Otis
Anne Akiko Meyers	Jun-ichi Takahashi

Midori — Satoru Ishikawa Courtesy The Midori Foundation
Erica Morini — Courtesy Doremi
Viktoria Mullova — Massimo Barbaglia
Anne Sophie Mutter — Courtesy Lugano Festival
Maud Powell — Courtesy Simon Jones
Alma Rosé — Richard Newman
Nadja Salerno-Sonnenberg — Christian Steiner
Zina Schiff — Joe Butts of San Diego
Livia Sohn — Courtesy Livia Sohn
Sheryl Staples — Diane Alancraig
Akiko Suwanai — Shintaro Shiratori
Kyoko Takezawa — J. Henry Fair
Camilla Urso — With Permission
Chee Yun — Courtesy ICM Artists Management
Carmit Zori — Steven Speliotis

Viola

Karen Elaine — Alexandra of La Jolla
Lillian Fuchs — Courtesy Sound Information
Rivka Golani — Courtesy Golani
Nobuko Imai — Courtesy Nobuko Imai
Cynthia Phelps — Courtesy Cedar Rapids Symphony
Karen Tuttle — Courtesy Karen Tuttle
Nokuthula Ngwenyama — Courtesy of Nokuthula Ngwenyama

Cello

CELLO — Beth Kelly
Jacqueline DuPré — Courtesy Beauty in Music
Nancy Green — Courtesy Nancy Green
Beatrice Harrison — Courtesy Elgar Society
Elsa Hilger — Betsy Melvin
Nina Kotova — Courtesy Island University
Zara Nelsova — Courtesy Guilhermina Suggia Association
Sharon Robinson — Steven Speliotis
Shauna Rolston — Taffi Rosen
Guilhermina Suggia — Courtesy Guilhermina Suggia Association
Anita Laker-Wallfisch — Courtesy EKG-Essen
Wendy Warner — Courtesy Classically Hip
Alisa Weilerstein — ICM Artists, J. Henry Fair

Bass

Rachel Calin — Courtesy Rachel Calin
Marji Danilow — Courtesy Concordia Players

Luthiers

Peg Baumgartel — Courtesy Peg Baumgartel
Lynn Hannings — Courtesy Lynn Hannings
Carleen Hutchins — Courtesy Carleen Hutchins
Sigrun Seifert — Courtesy Sigrun Seifert
Margaret Shipman — Genichi Sato
Andrea Simmel — Geoff McGhee, courtesy Simmel
Rena Weisshaar — Richard Carr

Guitar

Annette Degenhardt	Jora Henkel
Sharon Isbin	Courtesy of Columbia Artists

Lute

Alison Gould	Courtesy Alison Gould

Sitar

Anouschka Shankar	Dorothy Low

Pipa

Wu Man	Courtesy Wu Man

Harp

Anne E. Adams	Bruno of Hollywood
Nancy Allen	Christian Steiner
Charlotte Balzereit	Elke A. Jung Wolff
Phia Berghout	Courtesy Phia Berghout
Alice Chalifoux	Courtesy *American Harp Journal*
Mildred Dilling	Courtesy *American Harp Journal*
Yolanda Kondonassis	Tania Mara
Lily Laskine	Courtesy *American Harp Journal*
Judy Loman	Courtesy Judy Loman
Eileen Malone	Courtesy *American Harp Journal*
Susann McDonald	Courtesy Susann McDonald
Carrol McLaughlin	Courtesy Columbia Artists Festivals
Marielle Nordmann	Courtesy Nordmann
Edna Phillips	Gene Wieland, Jr.
Ann Hobson Pilot	Susan Wilson
Henriette Renié	Courtesy Sally Maxwell
Sunita Stanislaw	Courtesy Sunita Stanislaw

Woodwinds

Jeanne Baxtresser	Courtesy Jeanne Baxtresser
Leone Buyse	Courtesy Leone Buyse
Doriot Anthony Dwyer	Courtesy Gurtman and Murtha Associates
Nancy Goeres	Courtesy Nancy Goeres
Emma Johnson	Courtesy Emma Johnson
Thea King	Suzie Maeder
Susan Milan	Courtesy Musicians Gallery
Susan Nigro	Courtesy Universitat Mozarteum
Yoko Owada	Courtesy Yoko Owada
Pamela Pecha	Joanne Rile Artists Management
Michala Petri	Courtesy IMG Artists/ Suzie E. Maeder
Paula Robison	Christian Steiner
Er'ella Talmi	Courtesy Heinrich Klug
Eugenia Zukerman	Vidal

Brass

Stacey Baker	Courtesy IWBC
Kathy Brantigan	Courtesy Jason Ladd
Monique Buzzarte	Kaia Means. Courtesy Buzzarte

Velvet Brown	Courtesy University of Oregon
Rebecca Cherian	Courtesy IWBC
Abbie Conant	David Beyda. Courtesy William Osborne
Mary Ann Craig	Courtesy Music Finland
Jan Duga	Courtesy USAF Band
Amy Gilreath	Courtesy IWBC
Sharon Huff	Courtesy IWBC
Carol Jantsch	Courtesy Falcone Festival
Julie Landsman	Courtesy Great Gorge Chamber Music
Jeanie Lee	Courtesy IWBC
Laura Lineberger	Courtesy IWBC
Jennifer Montone	Courtesy Kendall Betts Harp Camp
Marie Luise Neunecker	Courtesy Michal Schmidt Artists International Inc.
Laurel Ohlson	Courtesy IWBC
Carole Reinhart	Courtesy Trumpet Guild
Susan Rider	Courtesy IWBC
Gail Robertson	Courtesy IWBC
Shelley Showers	Bubath Photography
Susan Slaughter	Courtesy Susan Slaughter
Marie Speziale	Courtesy IWBC
Constance Weldon	Courtesy Constance Weldon
Liesl Whitaker	Courtesy IWBC
Gail Williams	Courtesy Mid Texas Symphony

Percussion

Evelyn Glennie	Courtesy Amici Musica

Piano

Judith Burganger	Courtesy Judith Burganger
Teresa Carreño	Furore
Angela Cheng	Lisa Kohler
Bella Davidovich	Christian Steiner
Misha and Cipa Dichter	J. Henry Fair
Grieco, Rossina	Lynn Granbou
Hélène Grimaud	J. Henry Fair
Angela Hewitt	Courtesy Angela Hewitt
Helen Huang	J. Henry Fair
Lisitsa & Kuznetsoff	Iran Issa-Khan
Lilian Kallir	Courtesy Columbia Artists Management
Ketzel	Sivan Cotel
Alicia de Larrocha	Christian Steiner
Katia and Marielle Labèque	Brigitte Lacombe
Cecile Licad	J. Henry Fair
Ethel Leginska	Courtesy Michael Davis, Ivory Classics
Moura Lympany	Courtesy Ivory Classics
Israela Margalit	Robert Milazzo
Anne-Marie McDermott	Courtesy Anne-Marie McDermott
Marian McPartland	Courtesy Marian McPartland
Virginia Morley	Courtesy Ivory Classics
Estela Olevsky	Courtesy Estela Olevsky

Nadia Reisenberg	Courtesy Robert Sherman
Olga Samaroff	Courtesy Ivory Classics
Ann Schein	Courtesy Ivory Classics
Ruth Slenczynska	Courtesy Ivory Classics
Orli Shaham	J. Henry Fair
Nadia Shpachenko	Dr. Anne Gray

Organists

Marie-Claire Alain	Courtesy Orgues Chartres
Diane Meredith Belcher	Courtesy Karen McFarlane Artists Inc.
Roberta Bitgood	Grace Wiersma
Catherine Crozier	Courtesy Worldwide Pablo
Judith Hancock	Courtesy Reverend Bruce Parker
Marilyn Keiser	Courtesy Karen McFarlane Artists Inc.
Susan Landale	Courtesy Karen McFarlane Artists Inc.
Joan Lippincott	Courtesy Karen McFarlane Artists Inc.
Jane Parker-Smith	Courtesy Karen McFarlane Artists Inc.
Ann Elise Smoot	Courtesy Karen McFarlane Artists Inc.
Cherry Rhodes	Charis Photography
Dame Gillian Weir	Courtesy Karen McFarlane Artists Inc.

Theremin

Clara Rockmore	Courtesy Robert Sherman

Opera Singers

June Anderson	Courtesy Columbia Artists Management
Martina Arroyo	Courtesy Thea Dispeker, Inc.
Aïnhoa Arteta	Christian Steiner
Janet Baker	Bach-Cantata
Hildegard Behrens	Christian Steiner
Barbara Bonney	Decca/Jean-Pierre Mascle
Lucrezia Bori	Cantabile-Subito
Katherine Ciesinski	Courtesy Anglo-Swiss Artists Management
Kristine Ciesinski	Tino Tebaldi
Cynthia Clayton	Lisa Kohler
Rebecca Copley	Tania Maria
Michele Crider	Courtesy of San Diego Opera
Mattiwilda Dobbs	Courtesy Mattiwilda Dobbs
Kathleen Ferrier	Cantabile-Subito
Adria Firestone	J. Henry Fair
Renée Fleming	Decca/John Swannell
Vivica Genaux	Courtesy Robert Lombard Associates
Priti Gandhi	Courtesy Priti Gandhi
Mary Garden	Cantabile-Subito
Susan Graham	Courtesy Klassik in Berlin
Denyce Graves	J. Henry Fair
Barbara Hendricks	Courtesy Barbara Hendricks
Linda Hohenfeld	Courtesy of Hohenfeld, photo by Christian Steiner
Hei-Kyung Hong	Lisa Kohler
Marilyn Horne	Courtesy Columbia Artists Presents
Sumi Jo	Simon Fowler

Lorraine Lieberson	J. Henry Fair
Marquita Lister	Courtesy Marquita Lister
Shirley Love	Aryeh Oron. Courtesy Voice Teachers
Christa Ludwig	Courtesy Colbert Artists Management, Inc.
Nan Merriman	Bach-Cantata
Aprile Millo	Columbia Artists Management, Inc.
Leona Mitchell	Courtesy Columbia Artists Management, Inc.
Joan Morris	Peter Yates
Ann Murray	Courtesy Colbert Artists Management, Inc.
Lillian Nordica	Cantabile-Subito
Jessye Norman	Christian Steiner
Roberta Peters	Courtesy ICM Artists, Ltd.
Ewa Podleś	Courtesy La Scena Musicale
Patricia Racette	Courtesy The Living Room
Sondra Radvanovsky	J. Henry Fair
Katia Ricciarelli	Stan Fellerman
Kathleen Shimeta	Peter Schaaf
Beverly Sills	Don Purdue. Courtesy Doris O'Connell, Lincoln Center
Evelyn Buehler Snow	Melbourne Spurr
Paulina Stark	Courtesy Paulina Stark
Yma Sumac	Sonic
Dame Joan Sutherland	With Permission
Dawn Upshaw	Hollister Dru Breslin
Shirley Verrett	Christian Steiner
Deborah Voigt	Courtesy Deborah Voigt
Frederica Von Stade	Marcia Lieberman
Yoko Watanabe	Courtesy ICM Artists, Ltd.
Janet Williams	Columbia Artists Management, Inc. photo by Kranich
Dolora Zajick	Courtesy Dolora Zajick

Cantors

Rosalyn Barak	Carol de Nola
Arlene Bernstein	Courtesy Arlene Bernstein
Marin Cosman	Courtesy Marin Cosman
Sharon Kohn	Courtesy B'nai Jehudah Temple
Barbara Ostfeld	Courtesy American Conference of Cantors
Sarah Sager	Texler Photographers
Benjie-Ellen Schiller	Courtesy Synagogue 3000

Musicologists

Edith Borroff	Courtesy Edith Borroff
Nadia Boulanger	Courtesy Virginia Waring
Patricia Chiti	Courtesy Patricia Chiti
Susan Cook	Courtesy University of Wisconsin-Madison
Cecilia Dunoyer	Courtesy Talyor Greer
Katrijn Kuypers	Courtesy Katrijn Kuypers
Kimberly Marshall	Courtesy Kimberly Marshall
Susan McClary	Courtesy UCLA
Eve Meyer	With Permission
Carol Oja	With Permission

Susan Pickett	Courtesy Susan Pickett
Carol Plantamura	Courtesy Carol Plantamura
Sally Reid	With Permission
Léonie Rosenstiel	M. Warman
Gretchen Wheelock	Courtesy Eastman School of Music
Margaret Lucy Wilkins	Andrew Catchpool, Courtesy *Huddersfield Daily Examiner*
Mercedes Zavala	Courtesy Classical Composers
Alicia Zizzo	Claudia Zizzo

Women in the Business of Music

Gerhild Baron	Courtesy Gerhild Baron
Janice Del Sesto	Courtesy Boston Lyric Opera
Mary Lou Falcone	Harry Heleotis
Sylvia Glickman	Joan Fairman Kanes
Amelia Haygood	Courtesy Delos
Margaret Juntwait	Courtesy WNYC
Lee Lamont	Courtesy ICM Artists Management, Inc.
Susan Lundberg	Courtesy Susan Lundberg
Judy Massa	Courtesy Voice of America
Pamela Rosenberg	Courtesy San Francisco Opera
Miriam Yardumian	Courtesy Baltimore Symphony and Miriam Yardumian
Robina Young	Michael Putland

The Unforgotten

Judith Arron	Josef Astor
Eleanor Caldwell	Courtesy Wheeling Civic Center
Elizabeth Coolidge	John Singer Sargent
Helen Copley	Courtesy Life in Legacy
Sybil Harrington	Courtesy Texas Woman's University
Ima Hogg	Courtesy Main Street Houston History
Adella Prentiss Hughes	Courtesy Lake View Cemetery
Louise Lincoln Kerr	Courtesy Arizona Women's Hall of Fame
Ardis Krainik	Courtesy "2 Manitowoc"
Belle Mehus	Courtesy Susan Lundberg
Marjorie Post	Courtesy Wikipedia
Elisabeth Severance	Courtesy Western Reserve Historical Society
Catherine Shouse	Courtesy Hood College
Alice Tully	Courtesy The Town Hall Foundation

Author's Biography

Anne Gray hails from London, England, with degrees in music, speech and drama, a master's in English and a doctorate in human behavior. A professor of music history, keyboard, choral arts, speech and drama, her book, *The Popular Guide to Classical Music*, has been translated into several languages and can be found in all major Spanish-speaking countries. Her landmark 1,000-page definitive, *The WORLD of WOMEN in Classical Music*, hit the world in 2007.

Her other books include the highly effective motivationals, *Where Have You Been All Your Life?* and *How to Hang Onto Your Husband*. Juvenile works include two editions of the historical *The Wonderful World of San Diego*. She has contributed to the Grolier Encyclopedia plus numerous magazine and newspaper articles on a variety of topics, including the *IAWM Journal, Women of Note, American Harp Journal, The Pen Woman* Magazine and *San Diego Union-Tribune*. Her *Life as a Wife* columns, rivaling humorist Erma Bombeck, ran for several years in the *San Diego Woman* journal. In the performance field she was piano accompanist to her violinist son, Adrian, from his ages eleven to twenty-two. The duo performed as part of cheering programs for seniors.

Winner of numerous literary, music, public speaking and writing awards, Dr. Gray is president of WordWorld Literary Associates, a research and editing company. Its former subsidiary, Effective Speaking Image (ESI), trained speakers in elocution and stage presence, and provided original speech writing for maximum goal attainment. She is past president (1998–2002) of both the National League of American Pen Women, La Jolla Branch, and California South State Association; past president of Toastmasters of La Jolla; member of the International Platform Speakers Association, American Association of University Women (AAUW), College Music Society (CMS), American Musicological Society (AMS), International Alliance of Women in Music (IAWM), National Museum of Women in the Arts, and Music Fraternity, *Phi Mu Epsilon*. She is listed in the *Dictionary of International Biography, Baker's Biographical Dictionary of 20th Century Musicians* and *Who's Who in Music*. She has been married to the same man for an amazing number of years. They have two handsome sons.

Index